Social Workers' Desk Reference

Social Workers' Desk Reference

FOURTH EDITION

Edited by

Lisa Rapp-McCall
Co-Editor-in-Chief

Kevin Corcoran
Co-Editor-in-Chief

Albert R. Roberts
Founding Editor-in-Chief

OXFORD
UNIVERSITY PRESS

Oxford University Press is a department of the University of Oxford. It furthers
the University's objective of excellence in research, scholarship, and education
by publishing worldwide. Oxford is a registered trade mark of Oxford University
Press in the UK and certain other countries.

Published in the United States of America by Oxford University Press
198 Madison Avenue, New York, NY 10016, United States of America.

Library of Congress Cataloging-in-Publication Data
Names: Rapp-McCall, Lisa, editor. | Corcoran, Kevin, editor.| Roberts, Albert R., editor.
Title: Social workers' desk reference / [edited by] Lisa Rapp-McCall, Kevin Corcoran and
Albert R. Roberts Description: 4th edition. | New York, NY : Oxford University Press, [2022] |
Includes bibliographical references and index. Identifiers: LCCN 2021033408 (print) |
LCCN 2021033409 (ebook) | ISBN 9780190095543 (hardback) | ISBN 9780190095567 (epub)
Subjects: LCSH: Social service—Handbooks, manuals, etc.
Classification: LCC HV40 .S6464 2022 (print) | LCC HV40 (ebook) | DDC 361.3/2—dc23
LC record available at https://lccn.loc.gov/2021033408
LC ebook record available at https://lccn.loc.gov/2021033409

This material is not intended to be, and should not be considered, a substitute for medical or other professional advice.
Treatment for the conditions described in this material is highly dependent on the individual circumstances. And, while
this material is designed to offer accurate information with respect to the subject matter covered and to be current as
of the time it was written, research and knowledge about medical and health issues is constantly evolving and dose
schedules for medications are being revised continually, with new side effects recognized and accounted for regularly.
Readers must therefore always check the product information and clinical procedures with the most up-to-date
published product information and data sheets provided by the manufacturers and the most recent codes of conduct and
safety regulation. The publisher and the authors make no representations or warranties to readers, express or implied, as
to the accuracy or completeness of this material. Without limiting the foregoing, the publisher and the authors make no
representations or warranties as to the accuracy or efficacy of the drug dosages mentioned in the material. The authors
and the publisher do not accept, and expressly disclaim, any responsibility for any liability, loss, or risk that may be
claimed or incurred as a consequence of the use and/or application of any of the contents of this material.

9 8 7 6 5 4 3 2 1

Printed by Sheridan Books, Inc., United States of America

Gratefully dedicated to John. It's a privilege to share my love, friendship,
and life with you.
Lisa Rapp-McCall

Once again, it's all for Vikki. It is a quarter to three in Cambria!
Kevin Corcoran

Contents

Foreword

The fourth edition of the *Social Worker's Desk Reference* (SWD4), edited by Kevin Corcoran and Lisa Rapp-McCall, is an enormous contribution to the literature of social work. It is enormous for two reasons: (1) its size and extensive coverage and (2) the soundness and depth of chapters.

First, size. This book is, quite simply, huge. It contains 15 sections and a total of some 163 chapters! I know what some might say: "Ooooo; intimidating. It's too much for me." But anyone who says that would be wrong. The size of this book is a primary strength. You have just about anything you want to know about social work practice and issues in one place. This is not exactly a book to sit down with and read through all the chapters from beginning to end. Instead, it is a book that you use to find answers to just about any practice or professional question you might have. You just look up any chapter in which you are interested and savor, as I did, the depth of the coverage and the detailed knowledge presented therein.

Second, soundness and depth. Although size is important, if the material itself is lousy—that is, not accurate, not helpful, out-of-date, written by unaccomplished authors—then the size of a publication is meaningless. And here is where SWDR4 is magnificent. The authors selected to contribute to this masterpiece truly are the experts in their fields, truly the cream of the crop. Therefore, the chapters they wrote for SWD4 are top-notch: authoritative; up-to-date; and rich with detailed ideas and instructions about how to carry out changes, interventions, and assessments and to do those things in accord with practice evaluation and in the context of work with clients from different ethnicities and cultures. "Seek and ye shall receive." In other words, look at the Contents, organized by issues, and you will find what you need. Well, that's what I did, and I was richly rewarded.

I am retired now, but I wish this magnificent book had been available when I was teaching. It is truly a gift to the rest of us from two outstanding social work educators.

Aloha.

Joel Fischer

Professor (Ret.)

University of Hawai`i School of Social Work

Honolulu, HI

Acknowledgments

Building on the success of the first three editions of the *Social Workers' Desk Reference*, we assembled a revered group of associate editors, many of whom worked on the previous editions. In addition, new associate editors were included to add diversity, youthful energy, and talent. Succession is everything for our field, as knowledge continues to grow and we must grow and adapt with it. And what a year to talk about adaptation, as a pandemic, economic recession, and racial injustices sparked numerous stressors and called for incredible fortitude and coping. Our associate editors and contributors worked through all of these with determination and unwavering focus and still managed to meet their timelines. We are grateful to all the associate editors and contributors for the seriousness with which they addressed their tasks and for their dedication to producing excellent sections and, in total, a phenomenal fourth edition.

We are extremely grateful to all the staff at Oxford University Press, in particular Dana Bliss, Executive Editor, and the support staff. They have been terrific, and this book would be the lesser without them.

We are indebted to all our frontline social workers for their enduring work for our vulnerable clients. We hope this knowledge is helpful.

Lisa Rapp-McCall
December 2020

Contributors

Emily Reeder Abili, PhD, MSW
Mitigation Specialist
Clark County
Las Vegas, NV, USA

Mary C. Acri, PhD
Research Associate Professor
Department of Child and Adolescent
    Psychiatry
NYU Langone School of Medicine
New York, NY, USA

Monique C. Aguirre, BS, BSW
Research Associate
Department of Psychology
University of Utah
Salt Lake City, UT, USA

Travis J. Albritton, PhD, MSW, MDiv
Associate Dean of Diversity, Equity and
    Inclusion
School of Social Work
University of North Carolina at Chapel Hill
Chapel Hill, NC, USA

Wafa Alhajri, MSW
Adjunct Faculty
School of Social Work
Indiana University
Indianapolis, IN, USA

David K. Androff, PhD, MSW
Associate Professor
School of Social Work
Arizona State University
Tucson, AZ, USA

Victoria A. Anyikwa, PhD, MSW
Associate Professor
College of Education and Social Sciences,
    Graduate Social Work
Saint Leo University
Saint Leo, FL, USA

Valerie Arendt, MSW, MPP
Executive Director
North Carolina Chapter
National Association of Social Workers
Raleigh, NC, USA

Tyler M. Argüello, PhD, DCSW, LCSW
Associate Professor and Graduate Program
    Director
Department of Social Work
California State University, Sacramento
Sacramento, CA, USA

Lenore Arlee, MSW, LCSW, LADC
Associate Faculty
Department of Psychiatry and Behavioral
　Sciences
University of Oklahoma Health
　Sciences Center
Oklahoma City, OK, USA

Michael H. Baca-Atlas, MD
Assistant Professor
Department of Family Medicine
University of North Carolina at Chapel Hill
Chapel Hill, NC, USA

Stefani N. Baca-Atlas, MSW
Doctoral Student
School of Social Work
University of North Carolina at Chapel Hill
Chapel Hill, NC, USA

Heather Baker, LCSW
Instructor
Department of Psychiatry and Behavioral
　Sciences
University of Oklahoma Health
　Sciences Center
Oklahoma City, OK, USA

Carenlee Barkdull, PhD, LMSW
Professor
Department of Social Work
University of North Dakota
Grand Forks, ND, USA

Shant A. Barmak, EdD, PsyD
Clinical Psychologist
Licensed Psychologist and Adjunct Faculty
School of Human Development
San Diego, CA, USA

Kathryn K. Basham, PhD, LICSW
Professor
School of Social Work
Smith College
Northampton, MA, USA

Katherine J. W. Baucom, PhD
Assistant Professor
Department of Psychology
University of Utah
Salt Lake City, UT, USA

Jody Bechtold, MSW
CEO and Clinician
The Better Institute
Pittsburgh, PA, USA

Annette L. Becklund, MSW, LCSW, NBCCH
Owner/Director
Clinical Social Worker
Spring Hill, FL, USA

Sara Beeler-Stinn, LCSW, MPA, PhD
Assistant Professor
Jane Addams College of Social Work
University of Illinois Chicago
Chicago, MO, USA

Kia J. Bentley, PhD, MSSW
Professor
School of Social Work
Virginia Commonwealth University
Richmond, VA, USA

Autumn Asher Blackdeer, MSW, PhD
Professor
Brown School of Social Work
Washington University in St. Louis
St. Louis, MO, USA

Joan M. Blakey, PhD, MSW, LMSW
Associate Professor
School of Social Work
Tulane University
New Orleans, LA, USA

Tara Bohley, LMFT, MPA
Clinical Associate Professor
School of Social Work
University of North Carolina at Chapel Hill
Chapel Hill, NC, USA

Elisa Borah, PhD, MSW
Research Associate Professor
Steve Hicks School of Social Work
University of Texas at Austin
Austin, TX, USA

William Borden, PhD
Senior Lecturer Emeritus
Crown Family School of Social Work, Policy,
    and Practice and Department of Psychiatry
University of Chicago
Chicago, IL, USA

Natasha K. Bowen, PhD, MSW
Professor
College of Social Work
Ohio State University
Columbus, OH, USA

Stephanie Boys, PhD, MSW, JD
Associate Professor
School of Social Work
Indiana University
Indianapolis, IN, USA

Natasha Wine Miller Bragg, MSW
Adjunct Professor of Social Work and
    Doctoral Candidate
Department of Social Work
Indiana University School of Social Work
Indianapolis, IN, USA

Richard A. Brandon-Friedman, PhD,
LCSW, LCAC
Assistant Professor
School of Social Work
Indiana University
Indianapolis, IN, USA

Keith Bredemeier, PhD
Assistant Professor
Department of Psychiatry
University of Pennsylvania
Philadelphia, PA, USA

David L. Bringhurst, PhD, MSW
Clinical Associate Professor
Adult Mental Health and Wellness
University of Southern California Suzanne
    Dworak-Peck School of Social Work
Los Angeles, CA, USA

Denise E. Bronson, MSW, PhD
Associate Professor Emeritus
College of Social Work
The Ohio State University
Columbus, OH, USA

Leopoldo J. Cabassa, PhD, MSW
Professor
The Brown School of Social Work and the
    Center for Mental Health Services Research
Washington University in St. Louis
St. Louis, MO, USA

Daphne S. Cain, PhD, LCSW
Professor and Associate Dean of
    Administrative Services
Department of Social Work
University of Alabama
Tuscaloosa, AL, USA

Jayson Caines, MA
Human Services Supervisor
Hillsborough County Children's Services
Tampa, FL, USA

Khalilah L. Caines, MSW
MSW Field Director & Instructor
Graduate Social Work
Saint Leo University
Saint Leo, FL, USA

Michael Campbell, PhD, LCSW
Associate Professor and Associate Director
Graduate Social Work
Saint Leo University and College of Education
    and Social Services
Saint Leo, FL, USA

Lakeya Cherry, DSW, MSSW
Chief Executive Officer
The Network for Social Work Management
San Diego, CA, USA

Andrew Christensen, PhD
Distinguished Research Professor
Department of Psychology
UCLA—Semi-retired; Self-employed
Los Angeles, CA, USA

Paul G. Clark, PhD
Associate Professor and MSW Program
   Director
Department of Sociology, Anthropology, and
   Social Work
University of North Florida
Jacksonville, FL, USA

Carol Cleaveland, PhD
Associate Professor
Department of Social Work
George Mason University
Fairfax, VA, USA

Jacqueline Corcoran, MSSW, PhD
Professor and Faculty DSW Director
Department of Social Policy and Practice
University of Pennsylvania
Philadelphia, PA, USA

Kevin Corcoran, PhD, JD
Professor
School of Social Work
University of Alabama
Tuscaloosa, AL, USA

John A. Cosgrove, PhD
Research Data Analytics Manager
School of Social Work
University of Maryland
Baltimore, MD, USA

Lisa E. Cox, PhD, MSW, LCSW
Professor of Social Work & Gerontology
School of Social & Behavioral Sciences, Social
   Work Department
Stockton University
Galloway, NJ, USA

Pam Criss, LCSW, PhD
Full Professor (Retired, June 2020); Adjunct
   Professor (9/20—Current)
Department of Social Work (Within College of
   Behavioral and Social Sciences)
Southeastern University
Lakeland, FL, USA

Matthew J. Cuellar, PhD
Assistant Professor
School of Social Work
University of Alaska Anchorage
Anchorage, AK, USA

Claire A. Cunningham, LMSW
Therapist
The Dorm
New York City, NY, USA

Schuyler C. Cunningham, LICSW, LCSW,
LCSW-C, BCD
Director
The Washington DC Center for
   Neurocognitive Excellence LLC
Washington, DC, USA

Danielle L. DeMailo, MSW, LCSW
Clinical Social Worker, Community Advisory
   Board Member
School of Social Work, Tucson Campus
Arizona State University
Tuscon, AZ, USA

Alan J. Dettlaff, PhD, MSW
Dean and Maconda Brown O'Connor
   Endowed Dean's Chair
Graduate College of Social Work
University of Houston
Houston, TX, USA

Stephanie Diez, PhD, LCSW, MCAP, IGDC
Assistant Professor
Department of Social Work
Edinboro University of Pennsylvania
Edinboro, PA, USA

Xiao Ding, MSSA, LMSW
PhD Student
Department of Social Work
Steve Hicks School of Social Work
University of Texas
Austin, TX, USA

Eileen A. Dombo, PhD
Associate Professor
The National Catholic School of Social Service
The Catholic University of America
Washington, DC, USA

James Drisko, MSW, PhD
Professor
School of Social Work
Smith College
Northampton, MA, USA

Ray Eads, MSSW, LISW
Graduate Research Associate
College of Social Work
The Ohio State University
Columbus, OH, USA

Theresa J. Early, PhD, MSW
Associate Professor
College of Social Work
The Ohio State University
Columbus, OH, USA

Yvonne Eaton-Stull, DSW, MSW, LCSW
Associate Professor of Social Work and MSW
    Program Director
Department of Public Health & Social Work
Slippery Rock University of Pennsylvania
Slippery Rock, PA, USA

Tonya Edmund, PhD
Professor and Associate Dean for Social work
George Warren Brown School of Social Work
Washington University in St. Louis
St. Louis, MO, USA

M. Elizabeth Vonk, MSW, PhD, LCSW
Professor Emerita
School of Social Work
University of Georgia

Athens, GA, USA

Colita Nichols Fairfax, PhD
Professor
Ethelyn R. Strong School of Social Work
Norfolk State University
Norfolk, VA, USA

Aniko Felix, PhD
Executive Director
Goldziher Ignac Institute for Jewish History
    and Culture
Budapest, Hungary

Noelle L. Fields, PhD, LCSW
Associate Professor
School of Social Work
University of Texas at Arlington
Arlington, TX, USA

Kari L. Fletcher, MSW, PhD, LICSW
Professor and MSW Program Director
School of Social Work, Morrison Family
    College of Health
University of St. Thomas
Saint Paul, MN, USA

Edna B. Foa, PhD
Professor and Director of the Center for the
    Treatment and Study of Anxiety
Department of Psychiatry
University of Pennsylvania Perelman SOM
Philadelphia, PA, USA

Anne E. Fortune, PhD, MSW
Professor
Department of Social Welfare
University at Albany State University of
    New York
Albany, NY, USA

Cynthia Franklin, PhD, LCSW-S
Stiernberg/Spencer Family Professor in
    Mental Health
Steve Hicks School of Social Work
University of Texas at Austin
Austin, TX, USA

Eileen Gambrill, PhD
Professor of the Graduate School
Department of Social Welfare
University of California
Berkeley, CA, USA

Renée Bradford Garcia, LCSW
Psychotherapist
G2 Solutions
Round Rock, TX, USA

Daniel S. Gardner, PhD, MSW
Associate Professor
Silberman School of Social Work
Hunter College
New York, NY, USA

Felicia De La Garza-Mercer, PhD
Licensed Psychologist in Private Practice
Austin, TX, USA

Zvi D. Gellis, PhD
Professor and Director
School of Social Policy and Practice, Center
    for Mental Health & Aging Research
University of Pennsylvania
Philadelphia, PA, USA

Alex Gitterman, EdD, MSW
Professor of Social Work
Department of Social Work
University of Connecticut
Hartford, CT, USA

Richard S. Glaesser, PhD, MSW
Director of Professional Development
Professional Development and Training
Sunrise Community
Miami, FL, USA

Joanna Glover, LMSW
University of Arlington
Arlington, TX, USA

Rob Gordon, BA (Hons), PhD
Consultant Clinical Psychologist
Victorian Department of Families, Fairness
    and Housing
Government of Victoria
Melbourne, Victoria, Australia

Melissa D. Grady, PhD, MSW, LICSW, LCSW
Associate Professor
National Catholic School of Social Service
The Catholic University of America
Washington, DC, USA

Erlene Grise-Owens, EdD, LCSW, MSW, MRE
Partner
The Wellness Group, ETC
Louisville, KY, USA

William J. Hall, PhD, MSW
Assistant Professor
School of Social Work
University of North Carolina at Chapel Hill
Chapel Hill, NC, USA

Alice Schmidt Hanbidge, MSW, PhD, RSW
Associate Professor
School of Social Work
Renison University College, Affiliated with
    University of Waterloo
Waterloo, ON, Canada

Stacey D. Hardy-Chandler, PhD, JD, LCSW
CEO, Leadership Excellence & Adaptive
    Development Solutions, LLC and Director,
    Center for Children and Families (City of
    Alexandria DCHS)
Fairfax (LEADS); Alexandria (DCHS),
    VA, USA

Jean Paul Hare, LCSW, BCD
Research Associate
Steve Hicks School of Social Work
University of Texas at Austin
Austin, TX, USA

Mark R. Hawes, MSW
Social Work Doctoral Student
Brown School of Social Work
Washington University
Saint Louis, MO, USA

Carolyn Hilarski, MSW, PhD, LCSW-P
Professor Emerita
Department of Social Work
SUNY Buffalo State
Buffalo, NY, USA

Kathleen A. Hill, MSW
Associate Solution Specialist
Stratascale
St. Petersburg, FL, USA

David R. Hodge, PhD
Professor
School of Social Work
Arizona State University
Phoenix, AZ, USA

Laura M. Hopson, PhD, LMSW
Associate Professor
School of Social Work
University of Alabama
Tuscaloosa, AL, USA

Altaf Husain, PhD, MSSA
Associate Professor & Chair
Department of Community, Administration &
    Policy Practice Concentration
Howard University School of Social Work
Washington, DC, USA

Katie Ishizuka, MSW
Lecturer
University of California, San Diego
La Jolla, CA, USA

Andre Ivanoff, PhD
Professor and Director, Dialectical Behavior
    Therapy Training Program
School of Social Work
Columbia University
New York, NY, USA

Kathleen Leilani Ja Sook Bergquist, LCSW,
JD, PhD
Associate Professor
School of Social Work
University of Nevada, Las Vegas
Las Vegas, NV, USA

Bryan W. Jackson, MA
Founder and CEO
Attach Consulting, LLC
Washington, DC, USA

Shannon Johnson, PhD, MSW, MPP
Assistant Professor
School of Public Affairs
The University of Colorado Colorado Springs
Colorado Springs, CO, USA

Michelle Johnson-Motoyama, PhD, MSW
Associate Professor
College of Social Work
The Ohio State University
Columbus, OH, USA

Catheleen Jordan, PhD
Professor
Department of Social Work
University of Texas at Arlington
Arlington, TX, USA

Shawnmari Kaiser, MSW, LCSW, LISW
Assistant Adjunct Professor
USC School of Social Work
University of Southern California
Los Angeles, CA, USA

Isaac Karikari, PhD, MSW
Assistant Professor and MSW Program
    Director
Department of Social Work
University of North Dakota
Grand Forks, ND, USA

Kristen Kavanaugh, MSW
Executive Director
Military Acceptance Project
San Diego, CA, USA

Michael S. Kelly, PhD, MSW (deceased)
Lucian & Carol Welch Endowed Professor
School of Social Work
Loyola University Chicago
Chicago, IL, USA

Bonnie Kenaley, PhD, LMSW
Associate Professor
Department of Social Work
Boise State University
Boise, ID, USA

Stephanie Kennedy, PhD
Director of Research Dissemination
Florida State University Institute for Justice
    Research and Development
Tallahassee, FL, USA

Khadija Khaja, PhD, MSW
Associate Professor
School of Social Work
Indiana University
Indianapolis, IN, USA

Michael O. Killian, PhD, MSW
Assistant Professor
College of Social Work
Florida State University
Tallahassee, FL, USA

Johnny S. Kim, PhD
Professor
Graduate School of Social Work
University of Denver
Denver, CO, USA

L. B. Klein, PhD, MSW, MPA
Anna Julia Cooper Post-Doctoral Fellow &
    Incoming Assistant Professor
Sandra Rosenbaum School of Social Work
University of Wisconsin-Madison
Madison, WI, USA

Carolyn Knight, MSW, PhD
Professor Emeritus of Social Work
School of Social Work
University of Maryland Baltimore County
Baltimore, MD, USA

Karen S. Knox, MSSW, PhD
Professor Emerita
School of Social Work
Texas State University
San Marcos, TX, USA

David C. Kondrat, PhD
Associate Professor
Department of Social Work
Indiana University
Indianapolis, IN, USA

Shelley Cohen Konrad, PhD, LCSW, FNAP
Director and Professor, School of Social Work
Director, Center for Excellence in
    Collaborative Education
University of New England
Portland, ME, USA

Derrick Kranke, PhD
Health Science Specialist and Adjunct Lecturer
Veterans Emergency Management
    Evaluation Center
US Department of Veterans Affairs
North Hills, CA, USA

Stacy E. Kratz, PhD, MSW, BSW, BA
Clinical Associate Professor
Suzanne Dworak-Peck School of Social Work
University of Southern California
Los Angeles, CA, USA

Alan Kunz-Lomelin, LMSW, PhD (Student)
Social Worker and Graduate Research
    Assistant
School of Social Work
University of Texas at Arlington
Arlington, TX, USA

Sarah F. Kurker, MSW, LICSW
Faculty Instructor
School of Social Work
Arizona State University
Tuscan, AZ, USA

Eric Kyere, PhD
Assistant Professor
School of Social Work
Indiana University
Indianapolis, IN, USA

Craig Winston LeCroy, PhD
Professor
Department of Social Work
Arizona State University-Tucson Campus
Tucson, AZ, USA

Skyler Milligan LeCroy, BS
Special Projects Manager
LeCroy & Milligan Associates
Tuscon, AZ, USA

Jessica Euna Lee, PhD, LSW
Assistant Professor
School of Social Work
Indiana University
Indianapolis, IN, USA

Mo Yee Lee, PhD
Professor
College of Social Work
The Ohio State University
Columbus, OH, USA

Cynthia A. Lietz, PhD, LCSW
President's Professor
School of Social Work
Arizona State University
Phoenix, AZ, USA

Jan Ligon, PhD, LCSW
Associate Professor
School of Social Work
Georgia State University
Atlanta, GA, USA

Chris Lim, MBA
Human Trafficking Task Force Coordinator
Alabama Attorney General's Office
University of Alabama
Tuscaloosa, AL, USA

Brenda Lindsey, EdD, MSW
Teaching Professor
School of Social Work
University of Illinois at Urbana-Champaign
Urbana, IL, USA

Robert Lucio, PhD, LCSW
Associate Professor
Graduate Social Work
Saint Leo University
Saint Leo, FL, USA

Mark J. Macgowan, PhD, LCSW
Professor of Social Work and Associate Dean,
   Robert Stempel College of Public Health &
   Social Work
School of Social Work
Florida International University
Miami, FL, USA

Randy Magen, PhD
Professor
School of Social Work
Boise State University
Boise, ID, USA

Erica Magier, MSW, LSW
PhD Candidate
College of Social Work
The Ohio State University
Columbus, OH, USA

Susana E. Mariscal, PhD, MSW
Associate Professor
School of Social Work
Indiana University
Indianapolis, IN, USA

Leslie Martin, MSW, LCSW
Retired Director of PTSD Outpatient Services
   Team at West Los Angeles Veterans
   Administration
Social Work
University of Southern California
Los Angeles, CA, USA

Susan McCarter, PhD, MS, MSW
Associate Professor
School of Social Work
The University of North Carolina, Charlotte
Charlotte, NC, USA

Deidre McDaniel, MSW
PhD Student
Department of Social Work
Morgan State University
Baltimore, MD, USA

Monica McGoldrick, MSW, PhC (h.c.)
Clinical Social Work/Therapist
Multicultural Family Institute
Highland Park, NJ, USA

Michael E. McGuire, MSW
Director Substance Use & Addictions
    Specialist Program
Department of Social Work
UNC School of Social Work
Chapel Hill, NC, USA

Mary M. McKay, PhD, MSW
Neidorff Family and Cenetene Corporation Dean
Professor and Dean
Department of Brown School
Washington University in St. Louis
St. Louis, MO, USA

John L. McKnight, BS (Ret.)
Founder and Co-Director
ABCD Institute at DePaul University
Chicago, IL, USA

Molly M. McLay, MSW, LCSW
Doctoral Student and Therapist
George Warren Brown School
Washington University in St. Louis
Saint Louis, MO, USA

Kimberly H. McManama O'Brien, PhD, LICSW
Clinical Social Worker; Research Scientist
Division of Sports Medicine; Department of
    Psychiatry
Boston Children's Hospital; Harvard
    Medical School
Boston, MA, USA

Marcela Sarmiento Mellinger, MSW, PhD
Associate Professor
Department of Social Work
University of Maryland, Baltimore
    Country (UMBC)
Baltimore, MD, USA

Helen Hauser Midouhas, PhD
FFT Implementation Specialist
Functional Family Therapy, LLC
Seattle, WA, USA

Justin "Jay" Miller, PhD, MSW, CSW
Dean
College of Social Work
University of Kentucky
Lexington, KY, USA

Laura Miller, LMSW
Staff Therapist
Behavioral Psych Studio
New York, NY, USA

Terry Mizrahi, PhD, MSW
Professor Emeritus
Department of Social Work
Silberman School of Social Work at Hunter
    College of City University of New York
New York, NY, USA

Olga Molina, DSW, LCSW
Associate Professor
Department of Social Work
University of Central Florida
Orlando, FL, USA

Vitina L. P. Monacello, MSW
Live Support Specialist
School of Social Work
Columbia University
New York, NY, USA

Dorinda N. Noble, PhD, LCSW-S
Professor and Director, Retired
School of Social Work
Texas State University
San Marcos, TX, USA

Tim Norman, LCSW, MEd
CEO and Clinical Director
The ATTN Center
New York, NY, USA

Randall O'Toole, MSW
Clinical Assistant Professor
National Catholic School of Social Service
The Catholic University of America
Washington, DC, USA

Mary L. Ohmer, PhD, MSW, MPIA
Associate Professor and Chair, Community,
  Organization, and Social Action
  Specialization
Department of Social Work
University of Pittsburgh
Pittsburgh, PA, USA

Danielle E. Parrish, PhD, MSW
Professor and Editor-in-Chief Journal of
  Social Work Education
Diana R. Garland School of Social Work
Baylor University
Houston, TX, USA

David A. Patterson Silver Wolf, PhD (deceased)
Associate Professor
Brown School
Washington University
St. Louis, MO, USA

Elizabeth Perryman, PhD, LCSW, BCD
Family Medicine Residency Faculty
Department of Behavioral Medicine
Morgan State University
Baltimore, MD, USA

Carrie Pettus-Davis, PhD, MSW
Founder and Executive Director; Associate
  Professor
Institute for Justice Research and Development
  College of Social Work
Florida State University
Tallahassee, FL, USA

Betty Pfefferbaum, MD, JD
George Lynn Cross Research Professor
  Emeritus
Department of Psychiatry and Behavioral
  Sciences
College of Medicine, University of Oklahoma
  Health Sciences Center
Oklahoma City, OK, USA

Elizabeth S. Phillips, PhD, MSW
Associate Professor, Field Education
USC Suzanne Dworak-Peck School of
  Social Work
University of Southern California
Los Angeles, CA, USA

Barb Pierce, PhD
Associate Professor of Social Work
Department of Social Work
Indiana University
Indianapolis, IN, USA

Margaret E. Pittman, EdD
Assistant Professor
School of Social Work-MSW
Morgan State University
Baltimore, MD, USA

Elizabeth C. Pomeroy, PhD, LSCW
Bert Kruger Smith Centennial Professor in
  Social Work and Co-Director for Institute
  for Collaborative Health Research and
  Practice
Steve Hicks School of Social Work
University of Texas at Austin
Austin, TX, USA

Jeremy F. Price, PhD
Assistant Professor of Technology, Innovation,
  and Pedagogy in Urban Education
Department of Urban Teacher Education
Indiana University School of Education-
  Indianapolis at IUPUI
Indianapolis, IN, USA

James C. Raines, PhD
Professor of Social Work
Department of Health, Human Services, and
    Public Policy
California State University Monterey Bay
Seaside, CA, USA

Blanca Ramos, PhD
Associate Professor
School of Social Welfare
University at Albany
Albany, NY, USA

Estelli Ramos, MSW, MDiv
Instructor
School of Social Work and Department of
    Criminal Justice
University of Central Florida
Orlando, FL, USA

Lisa Rapp-McCall, PhD, MSW
Professor
Graduate Social Work
Saint Leo University
Saint Leo, FL, USA

Frederic G. Reamer, PhD
Professor
School of Social Work
Rhode Island College
Providence, RI, USA

William J. Reid, DSW (deceased)
Distinguished Professor and Chair, PhD
    Program
School of Social Welfare
University at Albany
Albany, NY, USA

Roberta Restaino, MSW
Adjunct Professor/Medical Social Worker
Graduate Social Work Program
Saint Leo University
Saint Leo, FL, USA

Melanie Reyes, PhD, MSW
Associate Director for Student Services and
    Programs
School of Social Work
Arizona State University
Phoenix, AZ, USA

Susan P. Robbins, PhD, LCSW
Professor and Associate Dean for Doctoral
    Education
Graduate College of Social Work
University of Houston
Houston, TX, USA

Aaron Rooney, LMSW
Clinical Director
Department of Aging Services
Stanley M. Isaacs Neighborhood Center
New York, NY, USA

Stephanie E. Rosado, MSW
PhD Student and Research Assistant
College of Behavioral and Community
    Sciences—School of Social Work
University of South Florida
Tampa, FL, USA

Julie M. Rosenzweig, PhD
Emerita Professor
Department of Social Work
Portland State University
Portland, OR, USA

Allen Rubin, PhD
Professor
Graduate College of Social Work
University of Houston
Houston, TX, USA

Robert T. Rubin, MD, PhD
Distinguished Professor Emeritus
Department of Psychiatry and Biobehavioral
    Sciences
David Geffen School of Medicine at UCLA
Los Angeles, CA, USA

Elizabeth Ruegg, MSW
Instructor
Graduate Social Work Program
Saint Leo University
Saint Leo, FL, USA

Cormac Russell, BaccPhil
Managing Director of Nurture Development;
    Co-Director of the Community Renewal
    Centre; Faculty Member of the Asset-Based
    Community Development Institute at
    DePaul University
Stean Centre
DePaul University, Chicago
Chicago, IL, USA

Christine Anlauf Sabatino, PhD
Professor and Assistant Dean
National Catholic School of Social Service
The Catholic University of America
Washington, DC, USA

Melanie Sage, PhD, LCSW
Assistant Professor
School of Social Work
University of Buffalo
Buffalo, NY, USA

Alison Salloum, PhD, LCSW
Professor
School of Social Work
University of South Florida
Tampa, FL, USA

Katherine Sanchez, PhD, LCSW
Associate Professor and Associate Dean of
    Research
School of Social Work
University of Texas at Arlington
Arlington, TX, USA

Diane Scotland-Coogan, MSW, PhD
Assistant Professor
Masters of Social Work
Saint Leo University
Saint Leo, FL, USA

Elizabeth A. Segal, PhD
Professor
School of Social Work
Arizona State University
Phoenix, AZ, USA

Patricia Senger, PhD
Associate Professor
Graduate Social Work
Saint Leo University
Saint Leo, FL, USA

Randy Shaw, JD
Executive Director, Tenderloin Housing Clinic
Tenderloin Housing Clinic
San Francisco, CA, USA

Emily Shayman, PhD, MSW, LSW
Assistant Professor
Department of Social Work
Lewis University
Romeoville, IL, USA

Lawrence Shulman, MSW, EdD
Dean and Professor Emeritus
School of Social Work
University at Buffalo
Buffalo, NY, USA

Jonathan B. Singer, PhD, LCSW
Associate Professor
School of Social Work
Loyola University Chicago
Chicago, IL, USA

Mark Smith, PhD
Associate Professor
Department of Social Work
Barry University
Miami, FL, USA

Leticia Villarreal Sosa, PhD, LCSW, PEL
school social work, CADC
Professor
School of Social Work
Dominican University
River Forest, IL, USA

Cheryl Waites Spellman, EdD, MSW
Professor, Social Work
School of Social Work
UNC Charlotte
Charlotte, NC, USA

David W. Springer, PhD, MSW
Distinguished Teaching Professor and Director
LBJ School of Public Affairs
The University of Texas at Austin
Austin, TX, USA

Shoba Sreenivasan, PhD
Psychologist
Forensic Services Division
Department of State Hospitals
Sacramento, CA, USA

Julie A. Steen, PhD, MSW
Associate Professor
School of Social Work
University of Central Florida
Orlando, FL, USA

Kirk von Sternberg, PhD
Associate Professor and Associate Director
Steve Hicks School of Social Work
University of Texas at Austin
Austin, TX, USA

Chris Stewart, PhD
Associate Professor
Department of Criminal Justice
University of Central Florida
Orlando, FL, USA

Fred P. Stone, PhD, MSSW
Clinical Associate Professor
Department of Social Work
University of Southern California
Fort Collins, CO, USA

Kimberly Strom, PhD
Smith P. Theimann Distinguished Professor of
    Ethics and Professional Practice
School of Social Work
University of North Carolina
Chapel Hill, NC, USA

Stephanie A. Sundborg, PhD
Director of Research and Evaluation
Trauma Informed Oregon
Portland State University
Portland, OR, USA

Hannah Szlyk, PhD, LCSW
Assistant Professor
School of Social Work
Rutgers University
New Brunswick, NJ, USA

Suhad Tabahi, PhD
Associate Professor
School of Social Work
Dominican University
River Forest, IL, USA

Paul- René Tamburro, PhD, MSW
Indigenous Consultant and Artist
Sunrise Drum, Inc. and Wijokadoak
Hobart, IN, USA

Andrea G. Tamburro, EdD, MSW
Interim Senior BSW Program Director
School of Social Work
Indiana University
South Bend, IN, USA

Kevin Tan, PhD, MSW
Assistant Professor
School of Social Work
University of Illinois at Urbana-Champaign
Urbana, IL, USA

M. Taqi Tirmazi, PhD, MSW
Associate Professor
School of Social Work
Morgan State University
Baltimore, MD, USA

Reginald Tarr, BSSW
Executive Director
United African Community
Grand Forks, ND, USA

Melissa A. Thompson, LCSW
Clinical Instructor
Online MSW Field Coordinator
School of Social Work
University of South Florida
Tampa, FL, USA

Hannah M. Thomson, MSW, LCSW
Private Practice
Clinical Social Work
Acacia Counseling and Wellness
Burbank, CA, USA

Bruce A. Thyer, MSW, PhD, LCSW, BCBA-D
Distinguished Research Professor
College of Social Work
Florida State University
Tallahassee, FL, USA

Stephen J. Tripodi, PhD
Associate Professor; Doctoral Program Director
College of Social Work
Florida State University
Tallahassee, FL, USA

Susan B. Trout, MSW, LCSW, MSPH, NCTTP
Associate Director—UNC Tobacco Treatment
    Program
Family Medicine Center
University of North Carolina at Chapel Hill
Chapel Hill, NC, USA

Valerie Trull, MS
Adjunct Professor and Researcher
School of Social Work
University of Alabama
Tuscaloosa, AL, USA

Francis J. Turner, DSW, LCSW
Associate Professor
School of Social Work
Marywood University
Scranton, PA, USA

Kielty Turner, DSW, LCSW
Associate Professor
School of Social Work
Marywood University
Scranton, PA, USA

Barbara Van Noppen, PhD
Vice Chair for Faculty Development
Department of Psychiatry and the Behavioral
    Sciences
University of Southern California
Los Angeles, CA, USA

Viola Vaughan-Eden, PhD, MSW, MJ
Associate Professor and PhD Program
    Director
Ethelyn R. Strong School of Social Work
Norfolk State University
Norfolk, VA, USA

Mary M. Velasquez, PhD
Centennial Professor in Leadership for
    Community, Professional and Corporate
    Excellence and Director, Health Behavior
    Research and Training Institute
Steve Hicks School of Social Work
University of Texas at Austin
Austin, TX, USA

Marisol Vargas Vilugron, LCSW
Clinical Social Worker
Lifeworks Counseling Center
Dallas, TX, USA

Froma Walsh, MSW, PhD
Professor Emerita
Crown Famly School of Social Work, Policy,
    and Practice
University of Chicago
Chicago, IL, USA

Joseph Walsh, PhD, LCSW
Professor Emeritus
School of Social Work
Virginia Commonwealth University
Richmond, VA, USA

Steven Warner, PhD, BCN, QEEG-D
Licensed Psychologist
Clinical Director, Stress Therapy Solutions
Chief Science Officer, Xtreme
    Performance Lab
Cape Canaveral, FL, USA

Nancy Boyd Webb, DSW
Distinguished Professor of Social Work Emerita
Department of Social Work
Fordham University
New York, NY, USA

Bret Weber, PhD, MSW
Department Chair/Professor
Department of Social Work
University of North Dakota
Grand Forks, ND, USA

Kathryn Conley Wehrmann, PhD, LCSW
Associate Professor Emerita, Immediate Past
    President of NASW (2017–2020)
School of Social Work
Illinois State University
Normal, IL, USA

Leslie Weisman, LCSW
Consultant and Trainer
Weisman Consulting & Training, LLC
Falls Church, VA, USA

Eugenia L. Weiss, PhD, PsyD, MSW/LCSW, MA
Associate Professor, MSW Director
School of Social Work
University of Nevada
Reno, NV, USA

Grace L. Whaley, LMSW
Associate Faculty
Department of Psychiatry and Behavioral
    Sciences
University of Oklahoma Health Sciences Center
Oklahoma City, OK, USA

Courtney Wiest, EdD, MSW
Assistant Professor and Director of Graduate
    Social Work
Graduate Social Work
Saint Leo University
Tampa, FL, USA

Javonda Williams, PhD
Associate Dean for Educational Programs
    and Student Services
Associate Professor
School of Social Work
University of Alabama
Tuscaloosa, AL, USA

Alyssa N. Wilson, PhD, BCBA-D
Associate Professor and Department Chair
Applied Behavior Analysis Department
The Chicago School of Professional
    Psychology Social Campus
Los Angeles, CA, USA

Kristen Zaleski, PhD, LCSW
Clinical Associate Professor
Suzanne Dworak-Peck School of
    Social Work
University of Southern California
Los Angeles, CA, USA

Anao Zhang, PhD, LCSW, ACSW, ACBT
Assistant Professor
School of Social Work
University of Michigan
Ann Arbor, MI, USA

PART I

The Professional Social Worker and Overarching Themes for the Profession

Overview of the Social Work Profession

Lisa E. Cox

What makes the profession of social work distinctive and exciting? How do social workers differ from sociologists, psychologists, and other counselors, advocates, and helping professionals? Which degrees, licenses, and credentials can social workers obtain? And in what kinds of work, or fields of practice, can social workers specialize? All these questions are worth considering when one feels led to become a professional social worker.

This chapter aims to provide an overview of the social work profession. Naturally, this general overview begins with a definition of social work and clarification of its mission. The Code of Ethics that guides social workers across practice levels is highlighted because social workers trained as either generalists or advanced specialists must adhere to high standards, including ethical practice and the personification of excellent values. Because social workers are professionals, a scaffolding of educational and licensure requirements are necessary and therefore discussed. Social workers often work on the front lines of injustice, trauma, stress, malfunction, and loss. They see and experience raw life—up close and personal—and serve as change agents. Because

social work advocacy and practice can be challenging work, social workers must be constantly aware of the need to stay healthy and practice self-care. Social workers use themselves and the term "conscious use of self" to convey the notion that when they engage and help clients and systems, their present and own "self" is required. A social worker's "self" is the most important tool in their armamentarium. Because social workers are also guided by theories, this overview chapter also entertains theories and perspectives that inform social workers. For example, the chapter highlights the importance of maintaining a strengths perspective; practicing with cultural humility; assessing person-in-environment; applying advocacy, empowerment, and systems theories; and employing the planned change process.

Defining Social Work's Mission and Requirements

The *Social Work Dictionary* defines social work as an applied science of helping people achieve an effective level of psychosocial functioning and effective societal changes to enhance the well-being of all people (Barker, 2014, p. 402). In slightly different wording, the National Association of Social Workers (NASW) professional organization defines social work as "the professional activity of helping individuals, groups, or communities enhance or restore" people's capacity for social functioning and "creating societal conditions favorable to this goal" (NASW, 2020). Social work may be viewed as a science and an art. "Social work is the only helping profession that explicitly embraces social change and the promotion of social justice along with its helping roles" (Anastas, 2014, p. 571).

At least three dimensions of social work exist: (1) therapeutic change efforts and support, (2) a solution-focused approach to help people resolve challenges and promote interpersonal and social harmony, and (3) social development and social change promotion (Adams et al., 2009, p. 2). Social workers engage, assess, plan and counsel, implement interventions, and evaluate efforts designed to support clients/systems. Solution-focused ideas are used by professional social workers to help clients/client systems problem solve and be harmonious. In addition, social workers involve themselves in social development and efforts to promote social change.

In the United States, and internationally, social workers help people increase their capacities to find solutions and cope well. Social workers also help people and systems obtain needed resources; facilitate interactions between individuals and between people and their environments; make organizations responsible to people; and influence social policies. Social workers may work directly with clients to address micro and mezzo issues, work at a systems level on regulations and policy development, and work as administrators and planners of large social service systems (Tice et al., 2020).

The mission or purpose of social work is to help individuals, groups, and communities enhance their well-being, meet basic human needs, and create societal conditions to support these goals, with special attention to the needs of disenfranchised, oppressed, and vulnerable individuals and groups. These goals are achieved as social workers pursue a mission of economic and social justice and pursue social change that targets poverty, unemployment, discrimination, and other types of injustice (Newhill et al., 2020, p. 4). The following are essential skills in social work practice:

1. Listen to others with purpose and understanding.
2. Elicit information and assemble relevant facts to prepare a social history, assessment, and report.
3. Create and maintain professional helping relationships.
4. Observe and interpret nonverbal and verbal cues and behavior and use knowledge of personality theory and diagnostic methods.
5. Engage clients (including individuals, families, groups, and communities) in efforts to resolve their own problems and to gain trust.
6. Discuss sensitive, emotional subjects supportively and without being threatening.
7. Create innovative solutions to address clients' needs.
8. Determine the need to terminate the therapeutic relationship.
9. Conduct research or interpret the findings of research and professional literature.
10. Mediate and negotiate between conflicting parties.
11. Provide interorganizational liaison services.
12. Interpret and communicate social needs to funding sources, the public, or legislators.

More recently, because social workers engage with systems of all sizes, other essential social work skills across practice levels have been identified. Multiple skills have been noted by social workers (Cox et al., 2019; Gasker, 2019), as illustrated in Table 1.1.

Values that social workers possess are illustrated in NASW's Code of Ethics, devised to help social workers operate and navigate as ethical practitioners and advocates. Essentially, this code is divided into four sections (Preamble, Purpose, Ethical Principles, and Ethical Standards) and aims to fulfill six purposes: (1) identify core values, (2) summarize general ethical standards, (3) identify professional duties amid conflict, (4) maintain accountability, (5) orient new practitioners to social work's mission, values, and ethical principles, and (6) define ethical misconduct. The underpinning core values of social work include the following: competence, honoring people's worth and dignity, human relationships, integrity, service, and social justice (Barker, 2014, pp. 398–399).

Ethical decision-making requires a continual process of examination. When social workers grapple with complicated situations or ethical dilemmas, the Code of Ethics can help guide their actions. In addition to the NASW Code of Ethics, many states operate social work licensure or ethics boards to protect consumers and "promote, monitor, and reinforce ethical social work practice" (Cox et al., 2019, p. 10). Indeed, social workers are professionals who possess a professional identity and continually work to enhance their self-awareness and "conscious use of self." Each level of degree attainment offers social workers increased levels of self-awareness, skill, and education.

Educational requirements (generalists/advanced generalists/specialists) vary for people who choose to major in social work. Accredited social work education is provided at undergraduate and graduate levels. Graduates of schools/departments/programs of social work (with bachelor's, master's, or doctoral degrees) can use their knowledge to provide social services for clients (e.g., individuals, families, groups, communities, organizations, or society), help people increase their capacities for problem solving and coping, and help people obtain needed resources. Social work graduates facilitate interactions between individuals and between people and their environments, make organizations responsible to people, and influence social policies.

The Bachelor of Social Work (BSW) degree is the entry level for social work professionals. This degree prepares generalists to work in multiple nonclinical settings across

TABLE 1.1 Essential Professional Social Work Skills Across Practice Levels

Active listening	Direct eye contact	Indirect eye contact	Pointing out strengths	Self-disclosure
Accurate empathy	Embodied mirroring	Labeling feelings	Preparatory empathy	Self-reflection
Clarification	Engaging smile	Managing door knob comments	Probing	Setting boundaries
Confrontation	Exploring taboo topics	Open-ended questions	Professional identity	Sympathy
Containment	Firm handshake (pre-COVID-19)	Opening statement	Professional presentation	Validation
Cultural humility	Getting informed consent	Pacing the interview	Professional use of self	Ventilation
Cultural responsiveness	Genuineness	Physical placement	Professional use of silence	Working through

multiple fields of practice. To garner third-party reimbursement for services, or work in settings such as hospice, schools, or U.S. Department of Veterans Affairs (VA) hospitals, social workers must obtain a graduate degree [Master of Social Work (MSW)]. Nationwide, social work schools vary in the advanced generalist or specialty tracks they offer those desiring a graduate degree. For the MSW degree, educational programs typically require courses in four core areas: social work practice, social policy, research methods, and human behavior in the social environment. Dual-degree programs and certificates are often available at the graduate level. Although an MSW is considered a "terminal degree" to teach in university settings and is enough to have a rewarding career, a small percentage of people decide to pursue either a Doctorate of Philosophy in Social Work (PhD) or a Doctorate of Social Work (DSW). The former degree prepares graduates to teach or carry out research or specialize in clinical practice. The latter degree assists graduates for advanced practice and administrative-type positions or other leadership roles in social work (Cox et al., 2019, p. 13).

Field education is considered the "signature pedagogy" of social work. At the BSW and MSW levels, students must document a required number of hours practicing in an assigned internship or fieldwork setting. As social work interns gain lived experience, they are evaluated on selected articulated measurable competencies and practice behaviors, set forth by the Council on Social Work Education in the form of Educational Policy and Accreditation Standards (EPAS).

In addition to EPAS, and according to the *Standards for the Classification of Social Work Practice* (NASW, 1981), social work requires knowledge in the areas of case management (casework), group work, community organization (resources and services), state

and federal social services programs, development of health and welfare services, basic economic and political theory, diversity intersections, evidence-based research (methods and techniques), practice concepts and techniques, social planning, and theories and concepts related to supervision. In addition, social workers are expected to understand theories and concepts related to social welfare administration, social and environmental factors affecting client systems, theories and methods of biopsychosocial assessment and intervention, and theories and methods of differential diagnosis (graduate level). Generalists, advanced generalists, and specialist social workers need knowledge about theory and behavior of organizational and social systems and of methods to encourage change. They also need to study community organization theory and techniques; advocacy theory and techniques; ethical standards and practices of professional social work; teaching and instructional theories and techniques; social welfare trends and policies; and local, state, and federal laws and regulations that affect health and social services (Barker, 2014).

Social work licensing involves protecting the public by ensuring that social work professionals have the proper education and training to provide competent and ethical services. Because social work is a regulated profession, licensure is common practice throughout the United States. Because licenses are granted to social workers by each state's regulatory board, criteria for licensure and levels of licensure vary by state. Depending on the state, you may be required to pay for a social work license if you want to call yourself a social worker or provide social work services. In other states, licensure is not required but often is preferred for typical social work positions. Job descriptions play an important role in obtaining licensure at the clinical level. Each time a new position is started, social workers ought to keep a copy of their job description.

Fields of Practice

Fields of practice and jobs that involve or require social workers range across levels of practice—micro, mezzo, and macro. Social work practice involves the use of social work knowledge and skills to implement society's mandate to provide social services in ways that are consistent with social work values. Practice may include remediation, restoration (rehabilitating those whose social functioning has been impaired), and prevention. Some of the most important social work practice roles are advocate, administrator, broker, caregiver, case manager, clinician, communicator, consultant, data manager, evaluator, mobilizer, community outreacher, planner, protector, researcher, socializer, supervisor, teacher, and upholder of equitable social values.

Multiple social work fields of practice exist. For example, social workers might choose to work in child welfare, family-centered practice, school social work, addiction treatment, mental health, developmental/disability practice, gerontology, forensic social work, or even veterinary social work. Other emerging fields of practice, ripe for social work professionals, include military social work, international social work, service to immigrant and Indigenous populations, and policy issues concerning diversity intersections (Dulmus & Sowers, 2012). Indeed, social work practice may occur in, between, and among micro practice, mezzo practice, and macro practice. Often, social workers work across practice levels and fields of practice simultaneously.

As Figure 1.1 illustrates, social workers may practice on the micro level when they are direct service workers (e.g., intake and permanency) in family and child welfare agencies; in group homes or centers for people who are challenged physically, developmentally, or cognitively; in substance use treatment centers; or in VA hospital settings. Mezzo-level social work practice often accompanies micro-level

work, especially when working with clients hospitalized or treated outpatient for health or mental health concerns or older adult clients who are cared for in long-term care settings or are trying to successfully age in place at home. Health, mental health, and clinical gerontological social workers often must advocate for policy and systems changes at the micro, mezzo, and macro levels. Macro-level social work especially occurs when helping professionals are involved in international social work, environmental justice issues, and changing workplace issues (e.g., need for telehealth as affected by the COVID-19 pandemic). Social work across levels of practice is quite evident in addressing societal issues of poverty, criminal justice, and safe and affordable housing.

Issues, Problems, and Opportunities

Social workers are involved in resolving issues and problems related to individuals, couples, families, groups, organizations, communities, and society. At the *micro* level, a social worker might find employment at a Division of Child and Family Services as an intake or permanency worker who assesses child maltreatment and family neglect and abuse issues. BSW-level social workers might work in group homes or agencies for people who are developmentally disabled, whereas MSW-degreed social workers might bill for counseling services they render in a substance use treatment center or VA hospital clinic setting. At the *mezzo* level, social work professionals may be responsible for discharge planning in hospitals or rehabilitation centers or for licensed clinical counseling at mental health centers for the chronically mentally ill or divorced couples, chronically ill older adults, or parents of an adolescent who died by suicide. At the *macro* level, social workers might take on the cause of poverty and inequality, advocate for smart

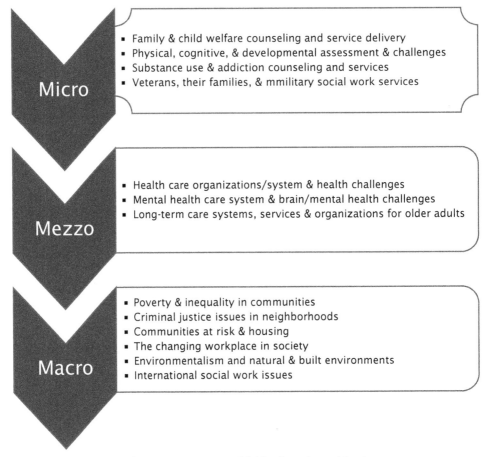

Micro
- Family & child welfare counseling and service delivery
- Physical, cognitive, & developmental assessment & challenges
- Substance use & addiction counseling and services
- Veterans, their families, & mmilitary social work services

Mezzo
- Health care organizations/system & health challenges
- Mental health care system & brain/mental health challenges
- Long-term care systems, services & organizations for older adults

Macro
- Poverty & inequality in communities
- Criminal justice issues in neighborhoods
- Communities at risk & housing
- The changing workplace in society
- Environmentalism and natural & built environments
- International social work issues

FIGURE 1.1 Examples of professional social workers' fields of practice and levels.

decarceration and safe housing, or be involved with conflict resolution in workplaces. In addition, macro social workers might be involved with economic, environmental, and social justice issues at both domestic and international levels (Tice et al., 2020).

Theories and Perspectives

Generalist or advanced social work professionals find their direct or indirect practice work easier if they draw upon ideas and assumptions derived from an assortment of social or psychological theories or social work theoretical frameworks or perspectives. Social work is often critiqued for not developing "theories of their own" that are testable and valid over time and with multiple populations and systems. However, social workers do rely on concepts and ideas from select psychological and sociological theories. For example, *systems theory* informs social workers about the importance of understanding people's interactions from multiple perspectives and in several settings and contexts. A client system might be a person, family, team members at work, a congregation, a social service organization, or a community. The *person-in-environment perspective* teaches social workers to consider people as constantly interacting with their environment(s) and assess how people or systems are influenced positively or negatively by their surroundings. Social workers try to help systems adapt to new ideas and experiences.

Empowerment theory provides social workers with notions about how to enhance possibilities for change. As a strategy for social work practice, "empowerment necessitates collaboration with informal groups, such as family and neighbors, and formal networks, such as agencies and organizations" (Cox et al., 2019, p. 45). The *strengths perspective* leads social workers to realize how every person or system has strengths to call upon to help resolve situations, dilemmas, and challenges.

A model for dynamic advocacy has been developed for social workers' use across micro, mezzo, and macro settings (Cox et al., 2019; Tice et al., 2020). Specifically, the *advocacy practice and policy model* (APPM) draws upon the theoretical foundations of systems theory, empowerment theory, the strengths perspective and person-in-environment (also referred to as ecological theory). This dynamic advocacy practice and policy model is built on the assessment and consideration of four interlocking components or tenets: (1) economic and social justice, (2) supportive environment, (3) human needs and rights, and (4) political access. Social workers who may choose to assess, advocate, and assist clients and systems, through applying the APPM, may increase their understanding about how to intervene and evaluate change efforts across micro, mezzo, and macro practice levels.

Social workers endeavor to carry out *evidence-based practice* (EBP) especially amid decision-making processes. When social workers adopt EBP and draw upon current research findings, they uphold professional and ethical practice standards.

Social workers' interventions often occur through direct services, such as the provision of information and referral. At other times, social workers deliver indirect services, which often involve advocacy and planning. Evidence-based intervention skills used by social workers often use problem-solving or solution-focused approaches, psychoeducational approaches, and multisystemic intervention approaches. Case or care management is an intervention that social workers frequently use. Multiple functions of case management exist. Roberts-DeGennaro (2008) identified the following functions of case management: (1) develop a resource network, (2) assess client's needs and strengths, (3) develop a care plan, (4) establish a contract, (5) implement the care plan, (6) monitor services, (7) evaluate, (8) close the case, and (9) follow-up. Woodside and McClam (2018) simplified complex case management tasks as (1) providing a broad range of services, (2) referring out, (3) coordinating providers, and (4) evaluating services.

To most effectively implement relevant and ethical case or care management functions, a social worker should endeavor to do the following: (1) provide direct support; (2) engage in crisis management; (3) provide short-term treatment; (4) broker or facilitate access to services; (5) enable, teach, or mediate situations; (6) advocate for the client; (7) coordinate services; and (8) track implementation (Frankel & Gelman, 2012).

Social workers use the *planned change process* when deciding on how to intervene. Typical steps or phases of the planned change process include the following: (1) engagement, (2) assessment, (3) planning, (4) implementation, and (5) evaluation. Experienced social workers know that the social worker–client relationship is key to effecting change. Therefore, social workers show empathy, warmth, and genuineness to clients to engage their trust so work can occur that is desired.

Overarching Issues for the Social Work Profession

As the social work profession continues to evolve, multiple overarching issues will require attention. For example, renewed attention must

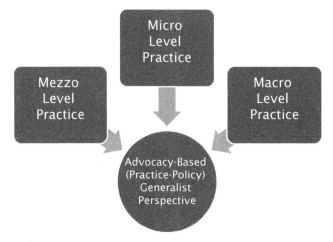

FIGURE 1.2 Evolution of modern social work.

be paid to self-care and social work safety; technology and telehealth; suicide; lesbian, gay, bisexual, transgender, and queer affirming practice; violence; social justice/oppression; emerging fields; and leadership.

Importance of Cohesion and Generalist Practice

Social work is a dynamic, full-fledged profession. Continually, practitioners work to manage diversity intersections; realize how policies affect practice; follow EBP; and make ethical decisions that consider the well-being of individuals, families, groups, communities, and society (Gasker, 2019). As Figure 1.2 illustrates, social work has evolved.

Professionals appreciate how social work does not exist in the silos of micro-, mezzo-, and macro-level practice. Instead, the field has embraced a blended model the APPM (Cox et al., 2020), which is appropriately generalist in its focus.

Helpful Resources

Bureau of Labor Statistics (www.bls.gov/ooh/ Community-and-Social-Service/Social-workers.

htm#tab-2w): Categorizes social work jobs by sponsorship and by the type of populations that social workers help.

Council on Social Work Education (http://cswe.org): The sole accrediting agency for social work education in the United States that advocates for social work education and research.

National Association of Social Workers chapters (https://www.socialworkers.org/About/Chapters): All chapters are listed by state.

References

Adams, R., Dominelli, L., & Payne, M. (Eds.). (2009). *Practising social work in a complex world.* Macmillan International Higher Education.

Anastas, J. W. (2014). The science of social work and its relationship to social work practice. *Research on Social Work Practice, 24*(5), 571–580. doi:10.1177/1049731513511335

Barker, R. L. (2014). *The social work dictionary* (6th ed.). NASW Press.

Cox, L. E., Tice, C. J., & Long, D. D. (2019). *Introduction to social work: An advocacy-based profession* (2nd ed.). Sage.

Dulmus, C. N., & Sowers, K. M. (2012). *Social work fields of practice: Historical trends, professional issues, and future opportunities.* https://ebookcentral-proquest-com.ezproxy.stockton.edu

Frankel, A., & Gelman, S. (2012). *Case management: An introduction to concepts and skills.* Lyceum.

Gasker, J. (2019). *Generalist social work practice.* Sage.

National Association of Social Workers. (1981). *NASW standards for the classification of social work practice.*

National Association of Social Workers. (2020). *Code of ethics*. Retrieved June 26, 2020, from https://www.socialworkers.org/About/Ethics/Code-of-Ethics

Newhill, C. E., Mulvaney, E. A., & Simmons, B. F. (2020). *Skill development for generalist practice: Exercises for real-world application*. Sage.

Roberts-DeGennaro, M. (2008). Case management. In T. Mizrahi & L. E. Davis (Eds.), *Encyclopedia of social work* (20th ed., pp. 222–227). NASW Press.

Tice, C. J., Long, D., & Cox, L. E. (2020). *Macro social work: Advocacy for change*. Sage.

Woodside, M., & McClam, T. (2018). *Generalist case management: A method of human service delivery* (5th ed.). Cengage.

Professionalism in the Field of Social Work

Patricia Senger and Courtney Wiest

Social work educators recognize that there are multiple dimensions in the process of becoming a professional social worker (Madden, 2000, p. 135). In addition to the requisite social work degree, professional social workers are encouraged to develop not only the skills but also the values, behaviors, and professional identity aligned with the profession. The development of a professional identity is a process that occurs over time, as professional social workers transition from behaviors aligned with a personal point of view to a professional point of view. Involved in this process is the development of a high degree of self-reflection [Council on Social Work Education (CSWE), 2015], which in turn helps modify behaviors into an alignment with a professional sense of self and serves to create a professional identity. The process of developing a professional identity includes adopting the values and norms of the social work profession (Adams et al., 2006). This is surely not a onetime process but, rather, occurs over time through formal and informal means, including, but not limited to, supervision, modeling workplace behaviors, and

continuing education. This chapter discusses the key components to developing one's professional identity.

Social Work Professional Culture

As a social worker, you are expected to be highly educated and knowledgeable regarding culture. A social worker should be conscious of the clients' culture and abreast of the cultural impact on the clients' situation. Social workers invest a significant amount of time and energy becoming informed and competent regarding intersectionality. However, before one can be an expert on the cultural impact of their clients, they must understand and embrace the professional culture of social work. Brown (2008) defined culture as "a shared, acquired pattern of values, attitudes, beliefs, and schemata that consciously and non-consciously shapes peoples' identities and behaviors" (p. 153). As professional social workers, there are shared beliefs, values, and skills that guide practice. This section examines the mission, values, and skills of the social work profession, which frame the profession.

Social Work Mission

The mission of a social worker is to help others. Professional social workers are change agents directing skills to assist humans in enhancing their overall well-being. Social workers ensure people's basic needs are met and continually advocate for oppressed, vulnerable, and marginalized populations. Furthermore, social workers promote change at all levels to enhance the well-being of individuals locally, nationally, and globally (CSWE, 2015). To achieve this mission, one must have high standards, values, and skills.

Social Work Values

As we examine the mission of professional social work, a review of the core values of the profession is crucial. To accomplish the mission of the profession, specific values and traits are necessary. The profession has identified the following core values [National Association of Social Workers (NASW), 2017]:

> *Service*: The primary mission and goal of the profession is to help others. Service to the client is above any self-interest the social worker may have. Client self-determination is an essential factor to consider in service implementation. Clients have the ability to make decisions about their needs, and it is the social worker's duty to assist the client in meeting those needs.
>
> *Dignity and worth of the person*: As a professional social worker, bias and personal judgments are set aside to respect the clients we serve. Social workers look beyond cultural differences, beliefs, and values to treat all clients with integrity and worth.
>
> *Social justice*: To be effective change agents and promote equality of basic

needs, social workers continually improve social justice at all levels. Social workers are expected to advocate for change, which promotes equality, opportunity, and protection for all.

> *Integrity*: Professional social workers are held and bound by the NASW's Code of Ethics to engage in honest, trustworthy, and ethical behavior.
>
> *Value of human relationships*: The social work profession is persistently striving to help people strengthen relationships, attain basic needs, and pursue self-actualization.
>
> *Competence*: Professional social workers are expected to practice within the scope of knowledge. Furthermore, social workers are expected to continually pursue and seek professional development to expand and refine their scope of expertise.

Social workers are expected to maintain healthy personal and professional boundaries outlined in the Code of Ethics. The NASW core values not only structure and guide our professional career but also, more important, guide our daily interactions with all individuals. As social workers, the values of the profession are encompassed and infused through all exchanges. The culture of the profession becomes the guiding principle of a social worker's life.

Social Work Skills and Knowledge

The social work professional is educated and trained in a vast number of skills. The skills and knowledge obtained with the degree are transferable across populations and settings. Social workers are armed with the skills and knowledge to be systematic helpers and problem solvers with any population. The generalist curriculum and competencies identified by the CSWE (2015) warrant that all social work graduates are competent in a core set of skills to assist clients and communities in need. These core skills and knowledge are separated into three sectors: practice, policy, and research skills knowledge. Along with the skills and knowledge, social workers are trained to systematically join with clients to problem solve and be effective change agents. In this process, the professional social worker is expected to effectively employ the following skills (Gasker, 2019):

- *Effective communication*: Social workers must be able to express their thoughts and treatment plan interventions to a wide variety of individuals. An essential skill for social workers is clear, concise written and verbal communication.
- *Highly organized*: In the profession, social workers are required to multitask client needs and priorities. In order to serve those in need, the worker must prioritize and organize the tasks to ensure everything is accomplished to benefit the client.
- *High engagement skills*: In order to join with clients in need, professional social workers must have high engagement skills. These skills are used to build a strong therapeutic alliance, which is 70% of the change process.
- *Active listening*: Social workers need to actively listen to their clients to effectively join, assess, and intervene according to the clients' desires and determination.
- *Critical thinking*: In the profession, social workers are expected to absorb significant amounts of knowledge and deploy interventions in the change process.

Along with these skills and knowledge, social workers are expected to be highly functional,

competent individuals. Covey (2004) identified seven habits of effective people: being proactive, being goal-oriented, developing prioritization skills, having a win-win mindset, seeking to understand others first, synergizing, and continually self-developing. In the profession, social workers need to apply skills, knowledge, values, and habits to work with clients at all levels to initiate change successfully.

Communication and Workplace Behavior
Use of Self in Relational Development

In the field of social work, the relational aspects between the professional social worker and client are of primary importance. This is true whether the type of practice is at the micro social work level working with individuals or families or at the mezzo social work level working with groups in communities and schools, in religious centers, and in local communities. This is also true even at the macro level when professional social workers are involved in significant research or advocacy on a large scale, such as in organizations at the state level or the national level. This relationship aspect is called the "use of self" and is utilized across all of these domains, specifically because professional social workers act as "change agents."

What is a "change agent"? The term *change agent* was first developed for interventions aimed at facilitating changes in business organizations (Lippitt et al., 1958). The term was then subsequently used in behavioral sciences, including social work. As a change agent in social work, the professional social worker is called upon to help cope with the problems of change and also to be a catalyst in bringing about changes in order to ensure greater justice and equality (Sanders, 1974). The use of self therefore is essentially an interpersonal process between the professional social worker and those with whom they engage. The professional social worker skill set is not simply limited to relationships with clients but, rather, involves all interactions, including relationships with colleagues, relationships with your supervisor, relationships with interdisciplinary team members, and the manner in which you engage others as you advance your career.

Essentially, everything you say and everything you do is a reflection of your professional self. This is effectively aligned with the CSWE Educational Policy 2.1.1, which states that when one identifies as a professional social worker, one must conduct oneself accordingly. Social workers serve as representatives of the profession, its mission, and its core values. Social workers practice personal reflection and self-correction to ensure continual development and attend to professional roles and boundaries and demonstrate professional demeanor in behavior, appearance, and communication (CSWE, 2015).

Use of Self to Advance Your Career and Lead Teams

Sometimes professional social workers may not fully realize the value of a Master of Social Work (MSW) degree. An MSW degree assists in the development of your own profound personal change, in terms of how you related to others before your degree and how you relate to others now. This is because the social work educational process serves to shape competent professionals aimed at being able to exercise leadership within the professional community (CSWE, 2015).

Consequently, the skill set of professional social workers is an ideal match for leading teams as you advance your career. As a result, professional social workers are often called to lead teams and facilitate organizational change. It would be wrong of professional social workers to think that they may not have the necessary skill set for leading teams and

promoting organizational change; as noted previously, it is the very nature of graduate social work programs to develop skills in students to be change agents. Clearly, then, leading teams to reach organizational goals is an integration of social work educational development aimed at developing social change agents and is the avenue to advancing your career.

Professional social workers need to uphold six values: service, social justice, dignity and worth of a person, the importance of human relationships, integrity, and competence (NASW, 2017). Effective team leaders possess qualities such as respect for others, integrity, clear communication, ability to negotiate, good facilitation skills, strong organizational skills, consistently being fair and kind, and the ability to influence others (Scott, 2019). Here, we see then that the very same core values that professional social workers uphold have high value in leadership positions.

Use of Self in Interdisciplinary Teams

The qualities of an effective interdisciplinary team member will inspire the trust and respect of a team. As a result, professional social workers are found on interdisciplinary teams in health care, education, government entities, and national and multinational corporations. Due to the complexity of challenges that organizations face today, professional social workers are identified as having the skill set required to communicate and negotiate what is required to help teams work together to collectively meet organizational goals.

The interventional skills that professional social workers use with individuals and families are not dissimilar to the skills used within the workplace to effect needed changes. Interdisciplinary teams are often composed of members from different departments with their own unique perspectives. Thus, the ability of the professional social worker to facilitate dialogue among the interdisciplinary team, explore perspectives, viewpoints, and needs, and then move that dialogue forward is the same process used in clinical social work interventions. Intervening in large systems utilizes the same process as intervening in individual or group work. Therefore, in interdisciplinary teams, the professional social worker is able to evidence their value as a transformational change agent because the focus of this work is on the interactions of an organization.

Professionalism

The interaction between professional social workers and their constituents requires emotional management. Managing emotions is a part of a professional social worker's everyday performance. This means that professional social workers must be cognizant of how all levels of their communication, both verbal and non-verbal, and all means of communication are construed by others. This is a significant challenge for the profession, particularly for those recently entering the field of professional social work, because both what is said and how it is said require a high degree of self-monitoring. However, this is of paramount importance, as can be seen throughout documents on the websites of the CSWE and the NASW, in which the words "profession" and "professional" are repeated numerous times. This is because professional social workers have a code of ethics, practice behaviors, and competencies that guide their practice.

Professional Comportment

The term *comportment* stems from the French words "comporter," which means "to carry," and "se comporter," which means "to behave." This is an accurate reflection of what is expected of professional social workers, who are required to *carry themselves* and to *behave* within the parameters of professional social work guidelines. These guidelines are named "competencies" and state that professional

social workers are to "demonstrate professional demeanor in behavior; appearance; and oral and written and electronic communication and use reflection and self-regulation to manage personal values and maintain professionalism" (CSWE, 2015).

How you manage your professional self is of paramount importance. One can say that this can "make or break" your career if left unregulated. Expectations for managing behavior include, but are not limited to, the following:

- Appropriate attire
- Respectful demeanor, communication, and interactions
- High level of integrity
- Appropriate boundaries
- Emotional self-regulation
- Effective collaboration with supervisors and colleagues
- Evidencing a high degree of self-reflection

Professional Use of Technology

With emerging technological advancements, the social work professional must be aware and educated on the best practices online. One of the core competencies for the professional social worker is the ability to demonstrate professional demeanor in behavior, appearance, and oral, written, and electronic communication (CSWE, 2015). Although this seems straightforward and aligns with the Code of Ethics, special attention and consideration are needed to address the best practices for online communication. Why is online communication an essential skill in the 21st century? The social work mission is to meet the client where they are at in the change process. Current trends suggest that more than 72% of the population utilize online communication, such as social media, for daily communication. This is a 65% increase over the past 10 years (Pew Research Center, n.d.). It is evident that clients are online and increasing their online use daily. Social workers need to have the competence, skills, and knowledge to engage and communicate with clients in the online environment. This section examines the best practices of online communication.

Online Communication Skills

Whether you are operating a private practice, working in community-based care, or a discharge planner in a hospital, as a social worker, you will engage in online communication to better serve your clients in need. Online communication has permanently changed avenues for communication across all populations and disciplines (Grobman, 2003). As you communicate online, it is essential to maintain a professional attitude. The best practices discussed next will provide you the required knowledge to achieve professional online communication with clients.

Email Communication Practices

One of the primary forms of online communication is emailing. In order to maintain professionalism in your email communication, Grobman (2003) outlined the following practices:

1. Utilize a professional email address. This may seem like common sense; however, you would be surprised at the inappropriate and unprofessional email addresses. Keep the email address simple. Do not attempt to make it cute or catchy.
2. Make sure your email box does not become full. This gives the perception that you are disorganized and have a time management problem.
3. As you would in professional documentation, make sure you are using proper grammar and do not have typos. This can be a challenge with smartphones and autocorrect; however, utilizing apps to double-check your communications is critical.
4. Make sure you are clear and specific in your communication. Provide deliverable dates and timelines so everyone is on the same page and aware of your expectations.
5. Utilize an appropriate, warm greeting to set the tone of the email—for example, "I hope this email finds you well" or "I hope you are well." Much like verbal communication, you want to engage the recipient first.
6. Stay away from cute emojis and graphics in professional emails; however, you can use softer language to ensure your email is conveying the message you intended.
7. Have a professional signature line. The signature line should include your professional social media information for networking purposes.
8. Be timely in your follow-up communications. You should respond within 72 hours.

Social Media Professional Communication

Like email communication, social media usage has increased drastically during the past 10 years. Social media forums, such as Facebook, LinkedIn, and Twitter, provide an equal voice for everyone. If utilized appropriately, social media can benefit the professional field of social work for advocacy, information sharing, service obtainment for specific populations, and relationship development (Duncan-Daston et al., 2013). However, along with the positive benefits, there are significant risks if not used with care. The following are some best practices of social media interaction:

Privacy: It is essential to recognize that online communication is never 100% private. Platforms such as Facebook, Twitter, LinkedIn, and other social networking sites have certain privacy settings; however, the information is generated for public information sharing (Duncan-Daston et al., 2013). Protecting your personal information becomes essential if you have an active presence on social media. Consider what information you share online, even with the most restrictive privacy settings. Last, align your social media interaction with the Code of Ethics regarding dual relationships and confidentially (Voshel & Wesala, 2015). Consider which platforms are for professional networking versus personal socialization. Be sure to maintain appropriate boundaries regarding connections on these platforms (NASW, 2017).

Communication with minors: Because social networking sites provide equal access across populations, remember that there are children and adolescents online. It is important to follow local and federal laws along with agency protocols regarding private communication with minors. A best practice guideline is not to have contact with anyone younger than age 18 years in a professional role online (Kimball & Kim, 2013). However, with increasing online service implementation, agencies and workers need to have detailed policies and procedures for online service delivery and communication with minors online (P. Nelson, personal communication, March 2020).

Social networking literacy: Educate yourself on the various guidelines and rules for the different social media platforms. If you plan to utilize social media for private or professional use, it is crucial to review the specific guidelines, rules, and net etiquette for each platform (Duncan-Daston et al., 2013).

Technology and various networking tools are powerful for professional social workers. These platforms provide increased communication, equal access, and relationship-building opportunities. However, before you dive into the online communication pool as a professional, it is essential to review and educate yourself on best practices. Furthermore, with the constant changes in the online arena, ongoing education and training are crucial (Duncan-Daston et al., 2013).

Professional Development

Professional development is a competency introduced to social work students at the start of the educational journey. One of the CSWE competencies outlined in the *2015 Educational Policy and Accreditation Standards* is "to engage in practice-informed research and research inform practice" (CSWE, 2015). In addition, professional development is an ethical standard for all social workers in the field. The MSW degree is a generalist degree. MSW graduates have a set of core foundation knowledge and skills; however, it is the social worker's duty to continue to develop that knowledge after graduation to better assist those in need. Professional development cascades into three domains: professional attitude, professional knowledge, and professional skills (Holman, 2009). In the profession, the social worker's expertise and skills are the tools deployed to promote change. To keep these tools in pristine working condition, social workers must pursue new knowledge throughout their career to stay current in the specialized field of work and attend to evolving trends in the profession to develop robust knowledge regarding the community served.

As for professional development in the field of practice or specialization, it is vital to remain informed and educated on emerging trends and interventions. The worker should identify the core population they are serving and acquire the knowledge, skills, and informed research to intervene with the population effectively (Kimball & Kim, 2013). The worker is continuously developing and refining their conceptual knowledge for assessment, intervention, and evaluation (Holman, 2009). Whereas the generalist skills are transferrable across populations, the evidence-based practices and interventions are specific to certain groups. Identifying and developing evidence-based practices are crucial as the professional social work engages with a core population.

Along with remaining current regarding the best practices with specific populations, the professional social work needs to stay informed and abreast of the growing trends locally, nationally, and globally that impact oppressed and discriminated groups. What are the current policies or laws that create barriers to service? What groups are being marginalized and impacted by inequality? It is the professional social worker's obligation to stay informed on these trends and to advocate for change at all levels.

Conclusion

The development of a professional social worker is not a onetime event but, rather, an ongoing process that involves continuing education. At each juncture of their careers, professional social workers are ethically required to stay current with research and information to serve their clients and constituents (NASW, 2020). Your decision to read this chapter and take advantage of the accompanying online resources serves as a personal investment in your own professional development.

Helpful Resources

Association of Social Work Boards: https://www.aswb.org
Council on Social Work Education: https://www.cswe.org

Hootsuite. *14 social media best practices you should follow in 2020.* https://blog.hootsuite.com/social-media-best-practices/amp
National Association of Social Workers: https://www.socialworkers.org

Professional Social Worker Career Development Resources
National Association of Social Workers. *Career center.* https://www.socialworkers.org/Careers/Career-Center
National Association of Social Workers. *Continuing education (CE).* https://www.socialworkers.org/Careers/Continuing-Education

References

Adams, K., Hean, S., Sturgis, P., & Clark, J. M. (2006). Investigating the factors influencing professional identity of first-year health and social care students. *Learning in Health & Social Care, 5*(2), 55–68. https://doi-org.saintleo.idm.oclc.org/10.1111/j.1473-6861.2006.00119.x

Brown, L. (2008). *Cultural competence in trauma therapy: Beyond the flashback.* American Psychological Association.

Council on Social Work Education. (2015). *2015 educational policy and accreditation standards.* https://cswe.org/Accreditation/Standards-and-Policies/2015-EPAS

Covey, S. R. (2004). *The 7 habits of highly effective people: Restoring the character ethic* (Rev. ed.). Free Press.

Duncan-Daston, R., Hunter-Sloan, M., & Fullmer, E. (2013). Considering the ethical implications of social media in social work education. *Ethics & Information Technology, 15*(1), 35–43. doi:10.1007/s10676-013-9312-7

Gasker, J. (2019). *Generalist social work practice.* Sage.

Grobman, L. (2003, Summer). Communicating online—professionally! *The New Social Worker, 10*(3). https://www.socialworker.com/feature-articles/practice/Communicating_Online-Professionally%21

Holman, S. (2009). *Guideline on professional development for continuing competence in social work practice: Practice Standard Committee.* National Association of Social Workers Colorado Chapter.

Kimball, E., & Kim, J. R. (2013). Virtual boundaries: Ethical considerations for use of social media in social work. *Social Work, 58*(2), 185–188. doi:10.1093/sw/swt005

Lippitt, R., Watson, J., & Westley, B. (1958). *The dynamics of planned change—A comparative study of principles and techniques.* Harcourt, Brace & World.

Madden, R. G. (2000). Gatekeeping in BSW programs. In P. Gibbs & E. H. Blakeley (Eds.), *Creating a bridging environment: The screening-in process in BSW programs* (p. 135). Columbia University Press.

National Association of Social Workers. (2017). *Read the code of ethics.* https://www.socialworkers.org/about/ethics/code-of-ethics/code-of-ethics-english

National Association of Social Workers. (2020). *Careers.* https://www.socialworkers.org/careers

Pew Research. (n.d.). *Social media trends.* https://www.pewresearch.org/fact-tank/2017/10/04/key-trends-in-social-and-digital-news-media/

Sanders, D. (1974). Educating social workers for the role of effective change agents in a multicultural, pluralistic society. *Journal of Education for Social Work, 10*(2), 86–91. www.jstor.org/stable/23038402

Scott, S. (2019). *The 10 effective qualities of a team leader.* https://smallbusiness.chron.com/10-effective-qualities-team-leader-23281.html

Voshel, E. H., & Wesala, A. (2015). Social media & social work ethics: Determining best practices in an ambiguous reality. *Journal of Social Work Values & Ethics, 12*(1), 67–76.

Established Fields of Social Work Practice

Valerie Arendt

The social work profession is as diverse as the individuals, families, and communities served. Social workers can specialize in serving a particular population or choose their field of practice based on the work environment that utilizes their professional strengths. Social workers are found in every community setting, including schools, hospitals, mental health clinics, senior centers, elected offices, private practices, prisons, the military, corporations, and public and private agencies [National Association of Social Workers (NASW), n.d. c].

Social workers in the United States are required to have a bachelor's or master's degree accredited by the Council on Social Work Education (CSWE) to enter the field. Depending on the state and the position, they also may need a state-issued license or certification. The purpose of licensing and certification in social work is to assist the public through identification of standards for the safe professional practice of social work. Each jurisdiction defines by law what is required for each category of social work licensure [Association of Social Work Boards (ASWB), n.d.].

Individuals with a degree in social work are guided by the profession's mission "to enhance human well-being and help meet the basic human needs of all people, with particular attention to the needs and empowerment of people who are vulnerable, oppressed, and living in poverty" (NASW, 2017). What sets the social work profession apart from other helping professions is social work's unique emphasis on promoting "social justice and social change with and on behalf of clients" (NASW, 2017). All fields of practice incorporate the mission and ethics of the social work profession.

In each field of practice, social workers can work at the micro level to directly assist individuals and families; at the mezzo level to serve in leadership roles or work with groups to promote small-scale cultural and institutional change; and at the macro level to intervene and advocate on a large scale, such as introducing legislation or advancing public awareness around social justice issues.

Although the social work profession is always advancing and new areas of practice emerge as populations and economic circumstances evolve or regress, this chapter focuses on introducing the roles, functions, and settings of nine of the more established fields of social work. Within each of these fields, social workers also serve in various roles in administration and leadership, community organizing, evaluation, education, research, and policy.

Aging

It is estimated that in 2034 in the United States, there will be 77 million people aged 65 years or older compared to 76.5 million younger than age 18 years (U.S. Census Bureau, 2018). In other words, the aging population will outnumber children for the first time in the country's history—a demographic shift that poses a unique set of public health challenges.

As this population expands rapidly, social workers have a significant role to play in helping older adults address their social, environmental, and personal needs. The aging population may disproportionately experience elder abuse and neglect, economic insecurity, and chronic health problems. Although life expectancy and overall health have improved in recent years for most Americans, not all older adults are benefitting equally because of factors such as economic status, race, and gender (Centers for Disease Control and Prevention, 2017). Indeed, social workers' education and training allow them to understand that an individual's identities will also impact their aging experiences.

Social workers link older adults with services that help them live independently and with dignity, thereby maximizing their quality of life and participation in society. Social work with older adults focuses on the physical, psychological, social, and economic aspects of daily living. This can be accomplished through counseling older adults and their families and caregivers, health and mental health support, and case and care management.

Common work settings for social workers working with aging adults include adult protective services, health care settings, adult day health programs, hospices, long-term care and nursing homes, residential care facilities, senior assistance programs, and hospitals.

Child Welfare/Family Services

A qualified and stable child welfare workforce is the foundation of child welfare service delivery. Social workers play a critical role in child welfare systems nationwide by protecting the well-being of children and supporting families in need. In 2018, an estimated 678,000 children in the United States were reported and found to have experienced abuse or neglect, with children younger than age 1 year being the most likely to have been maltreated (U.S. Department of Health & Human Services, 2018a). The national number of children who received a child protective services investigation response or alternative response increased 8.4% from 2014 (3,261,000) to 2018 (3,534,000). A total of 437,283 children and youth were in foster care in fiscal year 2018 (U.S. Department of Health & Human Services, 2018b).

Social workers know that working with a child means working with the whole family and with other environmental factors in a culturally competent way. Child welfare social workers specialize in building upon the strengths within a family and the family's community to help provide a safe environment for their children but also intervene to protect children from harm when necessary (NASW, n.d. a).

Degreed social workers trained in child welfare understand the multiple challenges facing families, such as poverty, limited resources, and lack of social supports. Social work education in child welfare teaches the application of a strengths-based approach to case management, human development, work in interdisciplinary teams, community-based services, and the importance of trauma-informed practice.

Social worker intervention includes a combination of therapeutic strategies and case management support. Child welfare social workers provide referrals and connect families with services they need, such as legal services, government benefits, employment assistance, and housing support. Social workers serve in state and county child protective services, family preservation support services, foster care and adoption, and clinical and case management services.

Clinical Social Work

Clinical social workers are the nation's largest group of mental health services providers, with an estimated 250,000 practitioners serving millions of clients and consumers (Congressional Research Service, 2018). Clinical social work is a health care profession based on theories and methods of prevention and treatment in providing mental health services with a focus on behavioral and biopsychosocial problems and disorders. Clinical social workers utilize the person-in-environment perspective, as well as emphasize clients' right to self-determination throughout their treatment plans.

In all U.S. jurisdictions, social workers who provide clinical mental health services must hold a Master of Social Work degree from a CSWE-accredited program and a clinical social work license in the state in which they practice or where the client resides if conducting telehealth services. Social work licensing and telehealth laws vary by jurisdiction. The ASWB reports there were approximately 440,000 state social work licenses in 2016, calculated by adding all individual state counts of active licensees. However, some social workers have licenses in more than one state (The George Washington University Health Workforce Institute, 2017).

The knowledge base of clinical social work includes theories of biological, psychological, and social development; diversity and cultural competency; interpersonal relationships; family and group dynamics; mental disorders; addictions; impacts of illness, trauma, and injury; and the effects of the physical, social, and cultural environment (American Board of Examiners in Clinical Social Work, n.d.).

Client consumers—individuals, couples, families, and groups—benefit from a variety of direct services from clinical social workers, including assessment, diagnosis, treatment planning, intervention and treatment, evaluation of outcomes, and case management.

Clinical social workers are employed in many settings, including, but not limited to, private practice, hospitals, community mental health, primary health care, schools, uniformed services, Veterans Affairs, and other nonprofit organizations and for-profit corporations.

Health Care

Social workers in health care settings provide services to patients with conditions spanning the entire health care continuum, including individuals with intellectual, developmental, or physical disabilities; people with mental illnesses; and those with a cancer diagnosis or other medical condition (NASW, n.d. b).

Health care social workers are trained to link patients with community and home-based services, address medical and psychosocial needs, as well as understand and identify the social determinants of the health of each patient. Social workers focus on incorporating both the patients' and caregivers' needs along with the needs of institutions or social services to provide an optimal care plan (Fabbre et al., 2011).

The role of a health care social worker will vary depending on the population they serve and whether or not they are in a clinical setting. Health care social workers can explain diagnosis and treatment options to patients and provide care coordination and case management. Some work in crisis response services or as grief counselors. Social workers arrange for discharge services such as hospice, assisted living, home health care, and referrals for additional emotional or psychological support. Social workers in health care settings can also support and connect with patients who have been abused, neglected, assaulted, or have experienced other forms of trauma.

In addition to clinical and case management roles, social workers are employed in hospital and facility leadership roles and may serve as mangers or administrators for specific hospital programs, such as mental health, aging, or community outreach (NASW Center for Workforce Studies and Social Work Practice, 2011).

Settings for health care social workers include hospitals, prisons, outpatient clinics, community health agencies, skilled nursing facilities, long-term care facilities, primary care offices, group homes, and palliative and end-of-life care.

Forensic Social Work

Forensic social workers work within the legal system and apply social work practice to issues relating to the law and the legal system. Forensic social workers can be involved in both criminal and civil cases, including those related to child welfare issues, termination of parental rights, child custody, guardianship, juvenile and adult justice services, elder abuse, corrections, drug courts, and mandated treatment (National Organization of Forensic Social Work, n.d.). Forensic social workers work with both victims and justice-involved individuals to ensure their voice is heard.

Many individuals entering the legal systems have significant mental health, substance use, and other related problems. People with mental illnesses are overrepresented in criminal justice settings in the United States, including jails, prisons, probation, and parole (Prins, 2014). Social workers have expertise in assessing and understanding client social history, and the social history of a criminal defendant is typically complex and can include trauma and mental illness. Diverting individuals with mental health and substance use conditions away from jails and prisons and to appropriate and culturally competent community-based mental health care is an essential role of social workers to help eliminate unnecessary involvement in the juvenile and criminal justice systems. Some forensic social workers provide support in death penalty mitigation investigations as a member of a capital defense team.

Forensic social workers provide diagnosis, counseling, and recommendations about mental health; serve as expert witnesses; provide consultation, education, or training to criminal justice and correctional systems, lawmakers, law enforcement personnel, attorneys, and members of the public; perform court-ordered evaluations of mental capacities; perform social and psychosocial investigations; and provide treatment, crisis intervention service, case management, and mediation (National Organization of Forensic Social Work, n.d.).

Forensic social workers can work in the court systems, public defender offices, psychiatric hospitals, correctional facilities, and for legal advocacy groups. In order to successfully practice forensic social work, qualified individuals must possess advanced knowledge and expertise in the law and its intersection with social work.

Military Social Work

Social workers, both active duty and civilian, have an extensive history of providing support and interventions to military personnel, veterans, and their families. Active and former military personnel can face unique psychological, emotional, and physical challenges because of the nature of their profession. Social workers can be embedded within every branch of active military units, civilian settings with off-duty military personnel and veterans, and on military bases.

Social workers' roles working with the military and veterans might include services such as medical social work with those being treated for traumatic brain injury; treatment and prevention of sexual abuse, assault, and domestic violence; treatment and prevention of substance misuse; posttraumatic stress disorder treatment; educating families and communities about available services; housing support for veterans experiencing homelessness or housing instability; reintegration post-deployment and post-discharge; and marriage and family support (Rubin & Daley, 2015).

The U.S. Department of Veterans Affairs (VA) is the largest employer of master's-level social workers in the country (VA, n.d.). Social workers hold vast roles within 62 program areas throughout the entire VA system, including mental health—inpatient and outpatient, recovery, patient advocacy, suicide prevention, veterans justice outreach, and a women veterans program. Social workers are key members of multidisciplinary treatment teams and work to ensure veterans return to a safe, supportive environment to facilitate readjustment in the community.

Both Military and VA culture are complex and rule bound; therefore, military social workers must understand the individual's role within military and veteran cultures and take the complex responsibilities of military personnel into account when making assessments. Social workers are required to be licensed or certified by a state to independently practice social work at the master's degree level for both military and VA positions.

Political Social Work

Political social work as a field of practice is social work practice, research, and theory that focus on policy and politics to create social change. It embodies an ethical responsibility for social workers (NASW, 2017):

> Social workers should engage in social and political action that seeks to ensure that all people have equal access to the resources, employment, services, and opportunities they require to meet their basic human needs and to develop fully. Social workers should be aware of the impact of the political arena on practice and should advocate for changes in policy and legislation to improve social conditions in order to meet basic human needs and promote social justice. (Standard 6.04)

All degreed social workers are trained to have an understanding of how social problems and policies impact the lives of those they serve on a micro, mezzo, and macro level; practice skills for advocating to policymakers; and are trained how to empower clients to become politically engaged. Social workers are ethically obligated to "facilitate informed participation by the public in shaping social policies and institutions" (NASW, 2017, Standard 6.02).

Social workers specializing in the political arena work more directly in a variety of political settings that include influencing elected officials and their agendas, working on election and public awareness campaigns, expanding political participation, working in full-time political positions, and holding elected and appointed offices (Pritzker & Lane, 2013).

Social workers can use their skills as campaign managers and volunteer coordinators; political directors; lobbyists; state and federal legislators; school board members; county commissioners; and secretaries of state Health and Human Services departments. Social workers also serve in legislative roles in which they shape policy and help constituents by working with federal, state, and local agencies to get individuals appropriate assistance.

School Social Work

School social workers serve in a critical role in educational systems tackling the social, emotional, behavioral, and mental health needs of school-age children that are proven barriers to student learning. School social worker services improve academic and behavioral outcomes, promote a positive school climate, and provide effective and vital student support services by maximizing school-based and community resources (NASW New York State Chapter, 2015).

Students who experience housing instability or homelessness, food insecurity, and other factors associated with childhood poverty or such issues as family conflict, social pressures and bullying, physical or mental illness, developmental disability, and abuse or neglect that affect children of all socioeconomic statuses are at risk for academic difficulties. Such issues are beyond the scope of teachers; this is where school social workers come in and are best equipped to address the social and psychological issues that can block academic progress by working closely with the student and the student's family or guardians.

Through individual and group counseling and crisis intervention and prevention programs, school social workers help young people overcome the difficulties in their lives and, as a result, give them a better chance at succeeding in school. School social workers are trained to think of solutions to complex problems, and their interventions often make a major difference for young people at risk for academic failure.

School social workers work with teachers, administrators, parents, and other educators to provide coordinated interventions designed to keep students in school and help families access the resources needed to promote student success (School Social Work Association of America, n.d.). Some states require a school social work license or certificate for employment in this field.

Substance Use and Addictions Social Work

Problematic tobacco, drug, and alcohol use and addiction pose a challenge to communities as a significant public health issue linked to poverty, violence, family stress, and a host of behavioral and physical health complications. Substance use disorders (SUDs) are often exhibited with co-occurring disorders—the use of more than one substance and/or one or more psychiatric disorders simultaneously.

Social work practice is in a unique position to influence the delivery of services to address the acute and chronic needs of clients with SUDs. Evidence-informed approaches to service delivery require that social workers be knowledgeable about the processes and dynamics of substance use, including misuse, dependency, and recovery. Social workers also need to have the knowledge and ability to work with clients to develop effective treatment plans using existing and emerging resources, including evidence-informed practices (NASW, 2013).

Social workers who work in the field of SUDs do so in the full spectrum of addiction care: prevention, intervention, treatment, recovery, and harm reduction. Social workers educate stakeholders on evidence-based prevention strategies that aim to reduce drinking and substance use among youths younger than age 21 years. Intervention includes assessment and diagnosis, referrals to treatment programs and counseling, and detoxification programs. Substance abuse treatment can incorporate outpatient services, intensive outpatient and partial hospitalization services, residential/inpatient services, and medically managed intensive inpatient services.

Recovery support services are nonclinical services that assist individuals and families working toward recovery from substance use conditions. Social workers connect clients with social supports and services such as child care, employment services, housing, peer coaching, and drug-free social activities.

Harm reduction is consistent with the social work value of self-determination and "meeting the client where the client is" (NASW, 2013). Social workers using the harm reduction perspective develop interventions that reduce drug-related harm without necessarily promoting abstinence as the only solution. These approaches recognize that for many drug users, total abstinence from harmful substances is not a feasible option in the short term (World Health Organization, n.d.). Social work in harm reduction programs includes work in needle exchange programs and medically supervised treatment of individuals with opioid dependency.

Substance use and addiction social workers can work in a variety of settings, including hospitals, residential treatment centers, outpatient clinics, schools, nonprofits and local advocacy organizations, courts, and police departments. Some social workers go into private practice providing psychotherapy and counseling related to substance use.

Conclusion

In many ways, social workers help people of every age and background throughout the world. The purpose of the social work profession remains solid—to enhance human well-being and meet the human needs of all people, to seek social justice and positive social change, and to practice ethically. As long as there is a need in each of these and the dozens of other social work fields of practice, social workers will continue to serve.

References

American Board of Examiners in Clinical Social Work. (n.d.). *Clinical social work described.* https://abecsw.org/clinical-social-work/clinical-social-work-described

Association of Social Work Boards. (n.d.). https://www.aswb.org/licenses/about-licensing-and-regulation. *Licenses* https://www.aswb.org/licenses/

Centers for Disease Control and Prevention. (2017). *Health disparities.* https://www.cdc.gov/aging/disparities

Congressional Research Service. (2018). *The mental health workforce: A primer.* https://crsreports.congress.gov/product/pdf/R/R43255

Fabbre, V., Buffington, A., Altfeld, S., Shier, G., & Golden, R. (2011). Social work and transitions of care: Observations from an intervention for older adults. *Journal of Gerontological Social Work, 54*(6), 615–626.

National Association of Social Workers. (n.d. a). *Child welfare.* https://www.socialworkers.org/Practice/Child-Welfare

National Association of Social Workers. (n.d. b). *Health.* https://www.socialworkers.org/Practice/Health

National Association of Social Workers. (n.d. c). *Types of social work.* Retrieved from https://www.socialworkers.org/news/facts/types-of-social-work

National Association of Social Workers. (2013). *NASW standards for social work practice with clients with substance use disorders.* https://www.socialworkers.org/LinkClick.aspx?fileticket=ICxAggMy9CU=&portalid=0

National Association of Social Workers. (2017). *Code of ethics.* https://www.socialworkers.org/about/ethics/code-of-ethics

National Association of Social Workers Center for Workforce Studies and Social Work Practice. (2011). *Social workers in hospitals and medical centers: Occupational profile.* https://www.socialworkers.org/LinkClick.aspx?fileticket=o7o0IXW1R2w%3D&portalid=0

National Association of Social Workers New York State Chapter. (2015). *NYS school social worker survival kit.* https://www.naswnys.org/wp-content/uploads/2015/06/SSWToolkitJune2015FINAL.pdf

National Organization of Forensic Social Work. (n.d.). *Home.* https://www.nofsw.org

Prins, S. (2014). The prevalence of mental illnesses in U.S. state prisons: A systemic review. *Psychiatric*

Services, 65(7), 862–872. https://www.ncbi.nlm.nih.gov/pmc/articles/PMC4182175

Pritzker, S., & Lane, S. (2013). Political social work. In Encyclopedia of *social work.* https://oxfordre.com/socialwork

Rubin, A., & Daley, J. (2015). Military social work. In K. Corcoran & A. R. Roberts (Eds.), Social *workers' desk reference* (3rd ed., pp. 113–117). Oxford University Press.

School Social Work Association of America. (n.d.). *School social workers' role in addressing students' mental health needs and increasing academic achievement.* https://www.sswaa.org/copy-of-about-school-social-work

The George Washington University Health Workforce Institute. (2017). *Profile of the social work workforce.* https://www.cswe.org/Centers-Initiatives/Initiatives/National-Workforce-Initiative/SW-Workforce-Book-FINAL-11-08-2017.aspx

U.S. Census Bureau. (2018). *National populations projections.* https://www.census.gov/newsroom/press-releases/2018/cb18-41-population-projections.html

U.S. Department of Health & Human Services, Administration for Children and Families, Administration on Children, Youth and Families, & Children's Bureau. (2018a). *Child maltreatment 2018.* https://www.acf.hhs.gov/cb/resource/child-maltreatment-2018

U.S. Department of Health & Human Services, Administration for Children and Families, Administration on Children, Youth and Families & Children's Bureau. (2018b). *The AFCARS report.* https://www.acf.hhs.gov/sites/default/files/cb/afcarsreport22.pdf, https://www.acf.hhs.gov/cb/report/afcars-report-25

U.S. Department of Veterans Affairs. (n.d.). *VHA social work.* https://www.socialwork.va.gov

World Health Organization. (n.d.). *Harm reduction.* https://www.euro.who.int/en/health-topics/communicable-diseases/hivaids/policy/policy-guidance-for-areas-of-intervention/harm-reduction

Self-Care for Social Workers

Erlene Grise-Owens and Justin "Jay" Miller

The profession of social work is dedicated to the overarching aims of human rights and well-being for all. As such, social work is a demanding, meaningful, and complex profession that requires myriad professional competencies. These encompassing aims require sustained, serious, and socially just attention to the well-being of the practitioners enacting the profession's mission. Social work's overarching aims also apply to social workers, whose well-being matters!

Self-care is a core practice competency that promotes the well-being of practitioners. This practice competency underlies the effectiveness of practice and, by extension, the viability of the profession (Miller & Grise-Owens, 2020; Newell & Nelson-Gardell, 2014; Sherr, 2019). This chapter provides the fundamental why, what, how, when, who, and where of this critical practice competency. After briefly outlining a rationale for self-care, the chapter defines holistic self-care, describes components for practicing effective self-care, offers critical considerations for the role of practice settings and macro-accountability for practitioner well-being, and concludes by underscoring the importance of attention to self-care in sustaining the profession.

Why Is Self-Care Essential for Social Work Practice?

Although the profession of social work has valiant aims, meaningful engagement, and significant impact, the work brings extreme stressors (Barsky, 2014; Cox & Steiner, 2013; Maclean, 2011; Miller et al., 2020). Practitioners experience an array of problematic employment conditions. These conditions occur in a macro context of increasing demands, decreasing resources, growing complexity of social problems, frustrating bureaucratic barriers, and compounding organizational management limitations.

The consequences for practitioners employed in these contexts can be debilitating. In alarming rates, social workers experience secondary traumatic stress, vicarious traumatization, moral injury, compassion fatigue, and burnout, among other phenomena (Haight et al., 2016; Mathieu, 2012; Van Dernoot Lipsky,

2009). These phenomena, both singularly and in combination, can negatively impact every facet of a practitioner's life. Unaddressed, these conditions lead to "professional depletion" (Greville, 2015, p. 14).

These consequences have significant systemic implications. Practitioners' well-being affects employee morale, staff turnover, absenteeism rates, and risk management. In turn, these factors impact organizational effectiveness and community capacity (Kanter & Sherman, 2017). Ultimately, practitioner well-being, or lack thereof, determines the quality of services proffered by practitioners, specifically, and the sustainability and viability of the profession, more broadly (Miller & Grise-Owens, 2020).

Increasingly, self-care is understood as necessary for assuaging these problematic phenomena (Bloomquist et al., 2015; Skovholt & Trotter-Mathison, 2011; Smith, 2017). As well, self-care can positively impact workplace culture (Cox & Steiner, 2013; Kanter & Sherman, 2017). In addition to research that emphasizes the importance of self-care, several professional membership organizations have affirmed that self-care is necessary for adept social work practice. For example, the National Association of Social Workers (NASW; 2009) policy statement titled "Professional Self-Care and Social Work" crystallized this important understanding. This crucial document laid out the rationale for self-care as "an essential underpinning to best practice in the profession of social work . . . [and] is critical to the survival and growth of the profession" (p. 268). Similarly, the International Federation of Social Workers/International Association of Schools of Social Work's (2004) "Ethics in Social Work, Statement of Principles" states that social workers "have a duty to take necessary steps to care for themselves professionally and personally in the workplace and society" (Article 5, Professional Conduct, No. 6). Clearly, engaging in self-care is necessary for responsible, ethical, and effective social work practice.

What Is Self-Care?

Despite growing attention to self-care among helping professions, in general, and in social work, specifically, self-care can be difficult to define. These difficulties, in part, stem from myriad myths and misperceptions. Notably, many conceptions of self-care are overly simplistic and framed as one-dimensional. Typically, that dimension portrays self-care as a solely physical act, such as jogging or going to the gym. Or, self-care is viewed through a consumerist lens, whereby self-care is promoted as an activity or product to be purchased, such as spa days and vacations. Simplistic self-care is framed as "extra"—something to be done after work to recover from work. These consumeristic, simplistic views reinforce misperceptions that self-care is a selfish or privileged activity. These limiting frameworks neglect the complex nature of self-care, leading to dismissive interpretations and diminished effects.

Emerging conceptualizations engage holistic views of self-care. These views assert that comprehensive approaches to self-care address every aspect of human-ness (Butler et al., 2019; Grise-Owens, Miller, & Eaves, 2016; Obuchowicz, 2019; Pyles, 2018; Smullens, 2015). That is, self-care is much more than merely a simplistic response. Rather, self-care is an integral way of how work is done. Indeed, self-care is a lifestyle—a way of *being* in the world.

As such, holistic conceptualizations of self-care entail multiple domains. Lee et al. (2020) described two overarching self-care domains: personal and professional. Others explicate multidimensional definitions of self-care (Bloomquist et al., 2015; Butler et al., 2019; Grise-Owens, Miller, & Eaves, 2016). Typical dimensions of self-care include physical, social, psychological, and spiritual domains. The common thread in all comprehensive self-care definitions is integrated attention to multiple domains associated with overall human well-being.

When Should One Engage in Self-Care?

Unquestionably, the social work practice landscape is evolving. Generational variations in the workforce, ever-changing regulatory dynamics, and emerging education and training models, among others, impact practice foundations. Couple these dynamics with contemporary challenges, such as the COVID-19 pandemic, and social workers—regardless of practice context and role—are experiencing unprecedented levels of complexity. Consequently, social workers are at increasing risk for inimical professional stressors and employment consequences.

The immediate and pressing concerns facing helping professionals have been recognized in significant ways. For instance, the 11th revision of the *International Classification of Diseases*, published by the World Health Organization (WHO, n.d.), recently recognized burnout as a syndrome linked to professional occupations; WHO warned of a pandemic of burnout without significant intervention. This information is especially troubling because burnout is particularly prevalent in helping professions, such as social work (Regehr, 2018; Smullens, 2015).

In this larger context, self-care is even more crucial. Practitioners often succumb to the myth that self-care will somehow happen or be easier to implement in the future. They envision a time when professional stress is reduced and life circumstances change. However, self-care is not an ideal future vision; self-care is an urgent *now* commitment. A common metaphor for self-care is the "emergency mask" put on during a plane crash. Although having some application, this metaphor is limiting. Instead of merely a mask, self-care is akin to breath (Grise-Owens, n.d. a). As such, self-care is not an emergency response for urgent situations. It is an essential aspect of daily life and integrated element of ethical practice.

How Does One Practice Self-Care?

Although essential, self-care does not just happen. Like other practice skills—for example, assessment, advocacy, and the like—self-care must be fostered and developed. This development requires intentionality. A competency-based approach is ideal for actualizing this intention.

According to the Council on Social Work Education (CSWE, 2015), competency involves interrelated facets of knowledge, skills, and values, as well as cognitive and affective processes. Competency entails an ability to carry out a task, or practice, effectively and efficiently. Improving competency increases the likelihood that an individual will engage in a practice. Competency in self-care involves acquiring knowledge about and skills for practicing self-care, considering affective and cognitive dimensions, and internalizing the values that undergird that practice.

Research about social workers in the United States (e.g., Miller et al., 2020) and globally (e.g., Miller et al., 2021) consistently concludes that a lack of knowledge is an impediment to engaging in adequate self-care practice skills. Likewise, much more attention to promoting the value of self-care is needed. In a professional ethos that promotes "selflessness" as the epitome, self-care is antithetical. In that dominant narrative, self-care is explicitly eschewed or implicitly ignored. Building self-care competence involves challenging those dominant narratives and promoting social work as a profession that is

TABLE 4.1 Common Self-Care Domains

Domain	Description
Physical	Movement/exercise; rest/sleep; nutrition/diet
Social	Connections; community; relationships with family and other spheres
Spiritual	Meaning-making; connecting to nature; exploring life purpose; engaging in rituals and practices to promote positive coping
Psychological	Mental and emotional aspects of well-being, such as mental health and emotional experiences; intellectual, recreational/leisure, and creative pursuits; and reflection, self-awareness, and growth
Professional/academic	Job or student role functioning, such as supervision/mentoring; professional development; healthy habits, positive coping strategies, and productive approaches
Practical	Daily routines, habits, functions, and tasks, such as homemaking; health maintenance; personal/familial/communal commitments

"self-full." Self*less*ness results in exhaustion and emptiness—leading to depletion. Instead, competency in holistic self-care promotes practicing out of fullness, abundance, and well-being (Grise-Owens, n.d. b).

Building competency requires critically (re)conceptualizing self-care, proactively planning, continuously implementing, and constructively evaluating. Through iterative attention, comprehensive self-care competency is developed and sustained.

Conceptualizing

When conceptualizing practices, it is imperative to emphasize that holistic self-care is not monolithic. The very term *self* connotes subjectivity. A one-size-fits-all approach to self-care does not exist. Effective self-care takes into account individual values, preferences, interests, goals, and life circumstances. Trying to implement someone else's self-care plan is a setup for failure and frustration.

Concomitantly, some domains are somewhat universal in actualizing holistic self-care. Table 4.1 delineates common domains with brief descriptions.

Additional domains may be included or modified, as pertinent to individual circumstances and preferences. Some domains may be divided into subsections, such as distinguishing mental and emotional dimensions of

the psychological domain. Religious practices can be designated a specific category. Spiritual can be subsumed/integrated in other domains. Specific considerations, such as financial self-care, may be designated as a specific category or subsumed under practical self-care. Political activism, community-building, or other spheres that interface with individual values and lifestyle may be explicitly included.

Planning

Intentional, integrated, and individualized self-care requires a structured plan. NASW (2009) advises every social worker enact a self-care plan. This plan should incorporate foundational domains and other pertinent areas consistent with a holistic approach to self-care.

Grise-Owens, Miller, and Eaves (2016) promote setting SMART self-care goals/objectives: *s*pecific, *m*easurable, *a*ttainable, *r*ealistic/*r*elevant, and *t*ime-limited. Commonly used in setting goals/objectives in professional roles, the SMART approach is readily transferable for self-care. Also, accountability measures are key in supporting self-care efforts. Accountability can take many forms, such as designated persons or groups, in personal and/or professional spheres. Formally or informally, practitioners can include self-care in professional development plans and gain support through

TABLE 4.2 Self-Care Plan

Care Domain	Specific Goals/Objectives (SMART)	Accountability Measure
Physical		
Social		
Spiritual		
Psychological		
Professional/academic		
Practical		
Other individualized domains		

SMART, specific, measurable, attainable, realistic/relevant, and time-limited.
Adapted from Grise-Owens, E., Miller, J., & Eaves, M. (2016). *The A-to-Z self-care handbook for social workers and other helping professionals.* New Social Worker Press.

individual and/or team supervision. Putting self-care commitments on the calendar/schedule is an important accountability step. Tools such as apps, journals, and daily tracking charts can provide accountability.

Table 4.2 provides a modified example self-care plan form, which can be readily expanded and adapted for individualized use.

Implementing and Evaluating

Typically, the initial plan should be piloted to test any unanticipated considerations. Usually, piloting reveals the need to refine the goals through additional SMART screening. For instance, objectives may need to be more specific or have more realistic time frames. Also, the SMART objectives should be monitored on a daily or regular basis. For example, a tracking form, calendar notations, journal, or other methods can be part of monitoring and accountability.

Implementing a self-care plan requires sustained effort and ongoing assessment. In an iterative fashion, self-care is continuously evolving. Thus, the self-care plan is an organic document. With deepening self-awareness and informed adaptations, the plan will become more nuanced and effective. As such, practitioners should actively engage in professional development opportunities associated with developing self-care competency.

Who Is Responsible for Self-Care?

Who is responsible for practitioner well-being and where does the onus lie? Here is a common response in promoting self-care: "Isn't self-care 'blaming the victim?' Isn't it the organization's responsibility to ensure a healthy work environment and staff wellness?" This misperception poses a counterproductive, false dichotomy.

Undeniably, if organizations functioned better, employees would have less need for self-care. But, self-care can boost one's ability to deal with dysfunction and even toxicity (Cox & Steiner, 2013; Wang et al., 2020). Self-care is definitively *not* blaming the individual or discounting an organization's responsibility. Promoting organizational wellness is imperative. And, self-care is essential. It is not an either/or (Grise-Owens, Miller, Escobar-Ratliff, et al., 2016).

A hallmark of social work is a multisystems approach (Newell, 2020), which represents the relationship between practitioner self-care and other organizational and societal facets. Figure 4.1 depicts a systemic understanding of self-care.

Because self-care and other aspects of organizational wellness have reciprocal effects, self-care can mitigate organizational dysfunction. A change in one part of the system affects

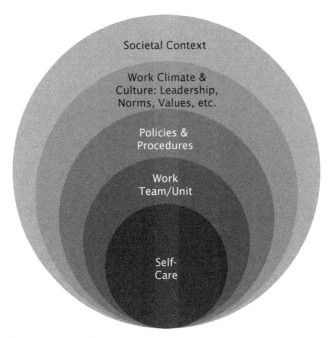

FIGURE 4.1 Systemic structure of self-care and organizations.

other parts of the system. Through activated self-care, practitioners can change responses and interactions with the organization and other stressors. Holistic self-care can modulate negative impacts and maximize positive strategies. Self-care develops and engages buffers to the negative aspects of an organizational context and job role. Self-care builds coping resources, personal resilience, and protective factors—that is, attributes and strategies that help in dealing more effectively with stress (Grise-Owens, Miller, & Eaves, 2016; Newell, 2020).

Organizations are composed of individuals. In practicing effective self-care, individuals have the competency for contributing to healthy organizational cultures. Through collaborative relationships, authentic advocacy, and leadership roles, individual self-care competencies can positively affect other parts of the system—that is, team dynamics, policies and procedures, and organizational climate and culture. Systemically, organizational (dys) function impacts the individual. Likewise, individual well-being influences organizational

change. The sphere in which individuals have the most influence is "self." The competency of self-care is foundational to other competencies necessary for effective practice in complex systems.

Notably, a systems understanding acknowledges that social work functions in a broader societal context. In the broader society, holistic self-care is counterculture to the myths and misperceptions elucidated in the previous discussion. Through radical dedication to self-care, practitioners can better manage stressors. Thus, practitioners can more constructively navigate and positively impact larger systems, such as organizations, communities, and even meta-global systems (Brown, 2020; Powers & Engstrom, 2020; Wang et al., 2020).

Critical Considerations of the Role of Self-Care

In addition to functioning in organizational broader societal contexts, social workers practice within a professional context. Socialization into the profession is a crucial process, which transmits what it means to be a professional social worker—such as core values, knowledge, and skills (S. Miller, 2013). Foundational socialization occurs in professional preparation, primarily educational programs. Schools of social work promulgate the competencies necessary to be a social worker; accrediting bodies, such as the CSWE, designate required competencies and curricular content (CSWE, 2015).

Increasingly, schools of social work are giving explicit attention to self-care as a professional practice essential. Faculty infuse self-care practices into their courses (Warren & Deckert, 2020); programs implement curricular self-care initiatives (Grise-Owens et al., 2018; Lewis & King, 2019). Schools give attention to field supervisors as key professional role models, including continuing education trainings (Martin et al., 2020; Miller, Grise-Owens, & Pachner, 2019). Much more attention is needed in this arena, however. For example, some language in the CSWE standards implicitly encourages development of self-care (e.g., "reflection and self-regulation" and "use supervision and consultation"; CSWE, 2015). However, to date, self-care is *not* explicitly designated a specific competency requirement for curricula.

In addition, it is pertinent that professional membership groups more explicitly address self-care. Some countries, such as Finland, have clear statements related to self-care in their professional ethical codes (Talentia Union of Professional Social Workers, 2019). In the United States, NASW's (2009) policy statement serves as a stellar example of explicit attention to self-care. However, the recommendations made in that pivotal statement have not been fully implemented by the profession (Miller & Grise-Owens, 2020). For instance, these recommendations have not yet been incorporated into NASW's Code of Ethics (COE). Integration of self-care into the COE would be both symbolic and substantive. The inclusion would underscore the validity of self-care

as essential to ethical practice and convey that self-care is a core practice competency.

Conclusion

This chapter provides foundational information for engaging self-care as an essential practice competency. This engagement will contribute to a social work practice culture in which burnout is rare and practitioner well-being is normative. Certainly, actualizing this culture requires ongoing development of "pragmatic models, useful frameworks, tested best practices, informed critiques, expansive research, and practice reflections on self-care" (Miller & Grise-Owens, 2020, p. 8). Sustaining the profession of social work and achieving the aims of well-being and human rights for *all* requires sustained investment in self-care.

Helpful Resources

The New Social Worker magazine provides professional development resources, including the Self-Care A–Z blog. https://www.socialworker.com and https://www.socialworker.com/topics/self-care-a-z

University at Buffalo School of Social Work's Self-Care Starter Kit has tools and resources for assessment and planning self-care. http://socialwork.buffalo.edu/resources/self-care-starter-kit.html

University of Kentucky College of Social Work's Self-Care Lab is the first lab established to study self-care in the helping professions. https://socialwork.uky.edu/centers-labs/self-care-lab

References

Barsky, A. (2014). Being conscientious: Ethics of impairment and self-care. *The New Social Worker, 22*(1), 4–5.

Bloomquist, K. P., Wood, L., Friedmeyer-Trainer, K., & Him, H. (2015). Self-care and professional quality of life: Predictive factors among MSW practitioners. *Advances in Social Work, 16*(2), 292–311.

Brown, M. (2020). Hazards of our helping profession: A practical self-care model for community practice. *Social Work, 65*(1), 38–44.

Butler, L. D., Mercer, K. A., McClain-Meeder, K., Horne, D., & Dudley, M. (2019). Six domains of self-care: Attending to the whole person. *Journal of Human Behavior in the Social Environment, 29*(1), 107–204.

Council on Social Work Education. (2015). *2015 educational* policy and accreditation standards. https://www.cswe.org/getattachment/Accreditation/Accreditation-Process/2015EPAS_Web_FINAL-(1).pdf.aspx

Cox, K., & Steiner, S. (2013). *Self-care in social work: A guide for practitioners, supervisors, and administrators.* NASW Press.

Greville, L. (2015). Self-care solutions: Facing the challenge of asking for help. *Social Work Today, 15*(3), 14–15.

Grise-Owens, E. (n.d. a). Self-care A–Z: Self-care is much more than a mask. The New Social Worker. https://www.socialworker.com/feature-articles/self-care/self-care-a-z-self-care-is-much-more-than-a-mask

Grise-Owens, E. (n.d. b). Self-care A–Z: Moving from self-less to self-FULL: The journey of self-care. The New Social Worker. https://www.socialworker.com/feature-articles/self-care/moving-self-less-to-self-full

Grise-Owens, E., Miller, J., & Eaves, M. (2016). *The A-to-Z self-care handbook for social workers and other helping professionals.* New Social Worker Press.

Grise-Owens, E., Miller, J., Escobar-Ratliff, L., Addison, D., Marshall, M., & Trabue, D. (2016). A field practicum experience in designing and developing a wellness initiative: An agency and university partnership. *Field Educator, 6*(2), 1–19.

Grise-Owens, E., Miller, J., Escobar-Ratliff, L., & George, N. (2018). Teaching self-care/wellness as a professional practice skill: A curricular case example. *Journal of Social Work Education, 54*(1), 180–186.

Haight, W., Sugrue, E., Calhoun, M., & Black, J. (2016). A scoping study of moral injury: Identifying directions for social work research. *Children and Youth Services Review, 70,* 190–200.

International Federation of Social Workers/International Association of Schools of Social Work. (2004, October). *Ethics in social work, statement of principles.* https://www.iassw-aiets.org/wp-content/uploads/2015/10/Ethics-in-Social-Work-Statement-IFSW-IASSW-2004.pdf

Kanter, B., & Sherman, A. (2017). *The happy, healthy nonprofit: Strategies for impact without burnout.* Wiley.

Lee, J. J., Miller, S. E., & Bride, B. E. (2020). Development and initial validation of the Self-Care Practices Scale. *Social Work, 65*(1), 21–28.

Lewis, M. L., & King, D. M. (2019). Teaching self-care: The utilization of self-care in social work practicum to prevent compassion fatigue, burnout, and vicarious trauma. *Journal of Human Behavior in the Social Environment, 29*(1), 96–106.

Maclean, S. (2011). *The social work pocket guide to . . . stress and burnout.* Kirwin Maclean Associates.

Martin, E. M., Meyers, K., & Brickman, K. (2020). Self-preservation in the workplace: The importance of well-being for social work practitioners and field supervisors. *Social Work, 65*(1), 74–81.

Mathieu, F. (2012). *The compassion fatigue workbook: Creative tools for transforming compassion fatigue and vicarious traumatization.* Routledge.

Miller, J., & Grise-Owens, E. (2020). Self-care: An imperative. *Social Work, 65*(1), 5–9.

Miller, J., Grise-Owens, E., Owens, L. W., Shalash, N., & Bode, M. (2020). Self-care practices of self-identified social workers: Findings from a national study. *Social Work, 65*(1), 55–64.

Miller, J., Grise-Owens, E., & Pachner, T. M. (2019). Self-care among field practicum supervisors: Assessing The Self-Care Wellshop. *Field Educator, 9*(2). https://fieldeducator.simmons.edu/article/self-care-among-field-practicum-supervisors-assessing-the-self-care-wellshop

Miller, J., Lianekhammy, J., & Grise-Owens, E. (2018). Examining social worker self-care practices: Implications for practice. *Advances in Social Work, 18*(4), 1250–1266.

Miller, J., Poklembova, Z., Podkowinsak, M., Grise-Owens, E., Balogova, B., & Pachner, T. M. (2021). Exploring self-care practices of social workers in Poland. *European Journal of Social Work, 24*(1), 84–93. doi:10.1080/13691457.2019.1653828

Miller, S. E. (2013). Professional socialization: A bridge between the explicit and implicit curricula. *Journal of Social Work Education, 49*(3), 368–386.

National Association of Social Workers. (2009). Professional self-care and social work. In *Social work speaks: National Association of Social Workers policy statement 2009–2012* (pp. 268–272). NASW Press.

Newell, J. M. (2020). An ecological systems framework for professional resilience in social work practice. *Social Work, 65*(1), 65–73.

Newell, J. M., & Nelson-Gardell, D. (2014). A competency-based approach to teaching professional self-care: An ethical consideration for social work educators. *Journal of Social Work Education, 50,* 427–439.

Obuchowicz, G. (2019). *Selfcarefully.* Thick Press.

Powers, C. F., & Engstrom, S. (2020). Radical self-care for social workers in a global climate crisis. *Social Work, 65*(1), 29–37.

Pyles, L. (2018). *Healing injustice: Holistic self-care for change makers.* Oxford University Press.

Regehr, C. (2018). *Stress, trauma, and decision-making for social workers.* Columbia University Press.

Sherr, M. (2019). Introduction to the JHBSW special issue. *Journal of Human Behavior in the Social Environment, 29*(1), 1.

Skovholt, T. M., & Trotter-Mathison, M. (2011). *The resilient practitioner—Burnout prevention and self-care strategies for counselors, therapists, teachers, and health professionals.* Routledge.

Smith, K. L. (2017). Self-care practices and the professional self. *Journal of Social Work Disability & Rehabilitation, 16*(3–4), 186–203.

Smullens, S. (2015). *Burnout and self-care in social work: A guidebook for students and those in mental health and related professions.* NASW Press.

Talentia Union of Professional Social Workers. (2019). *Work, values and ethics: Ethical guidelines for social welfare professionals.*

Van Dernoot Lipsky, L. (with Burk, C.). (2009). *Trauma stewardship: An everyday guide for caring for self while caring for others.* Berrett-Koehler.

Wang, Y., Zhang, H., & Yang, Y. (2020). The moderating effect of professional self-care training on novice practitioners' organizational citizenship behavior in China. *Social Work, 65*(1), 45–64.

Warren, S., & Deckert, J. C. (2020). Contemplative practices for self-care in the social work classroom. *Social Work, 65*(1), 11–20.

World Health Organization. (n.d.). *Burnout.* https://www.who.int/standards/classifications/classification-of-diseases

Safety for Social Workers
Responding to Workplace Violence

Pam Criss

A field coordinator met with a Bachelor of Social Work field class 4 weeks into the students' internships. One student began to recount going on a home visit with her supervisor to see a male client who was enrolled in the mental health program. They were invited into the home, but once inside, the client showed a gun and threatened to shoot them if they came any closer. They were able to deescalate the client, and nobody was harmed physically. When they told colleagues about this, everyone laughed. This scenario demonstrates that social workers feel uncomfortable acknowledging that violence has occurred in the workplace, perhaps concerned that they will be blamed and/or viewed as incompetent workers. This chapter addresses causes and effects of client violence, as well as safety measures that should be implemented by social workers.

Prevalence of Client Violence Toward Social Workers

Client violence occurs often in social work agencies. In 2009, the National Association of Social Workers (NASW) Center for Workforce Studies published a study of licensed social workers' assessment of the work environment. Forty-one percent of the respondents reported that they had experienced violence perpetrated by a client, and 25% reported that safety concerns were not adequately addressed by their agencies. In 2016, the Occupational Safety and Health Administration (OSHA) published a report stating that social service workers face significant risks for job-related violence. A previous study found that the national prevalence rate for social workers' exposure to client violence some time in their career was 86% (Ringstad, 2005). In addition, a national study of violence toward social work students found that almost half of the students experienced client violence during their internships (Criss, 2009).

Social workers may experience client violence indirectly, by seeing and/or hearing about violence toward coworkers. Dupree et al. (2014) found that social workers experienced significantly more vicarious violence than direct violence. Vicarious exposure to violence is associated with perceived risk of direct and vicarious aggression in the future. This negatively affected organizational attachment, as well as psychological and physical well-being.

Studies have found that there is a tendency to underreport violence toward social workers. Zelnick et al. (2013) cited several reasons for underreporting: being stressed about the time it might take to file the appropriate paperwork, fear of being blamed for incidents, fear of being viewed as an incompetent social worker, and ignoring violence as a part of the job. When violence goes unreported, workers suffer in silence.

Risk Factors for Workplace Violence

Personal factors may increase risk for experiencing client violence. Male social workers have been found to be exposed to more severe types of aggression, such as property damage and physical harm (Enosh & Tzafrir, 2015). In addition, younger workers have been found to be at greater risk of physical threat, threat of lawsuit, verbal abuse, and sexual harassment (Ringstad, 2005). Other risk factors include working with a client with a history of violence, gang membership, or abuse of drugs/alcohol (OSHA, 2016).

Organization factors may also contribute to client violence. Transporting clients or working alone in facilities or patients' homes, especially during evening hours, may increase risks of client violence (OSHA, 2016). Studies indicate that violence may be more likely to occur during home visits than in offices. One sample of home visiting social workers found that 93% had experienced client violence, and none of them felt completely safe (Vergara, 2006). In a study of social work students, those who made more home visits were found to experience more physical and verbal violence (Criss, 2009). Other organizational factors might include clients having long waits

for services, which may cause agitation and a sense of being undervalued. In addition, there may be inadequate staffing in agencies, causing higher social worker-to-client ratios, which may result in being isolated within the agency. Social workers may also be involved in court-ordered cases in which the client's behavior and progress must be documented, potentially affecting the client's ability to act independently.

OSHA (2016) states that organizational risk factors include poor environmental design of workplaces that may block vision or interfere with escape, poorly lit rooms and parking lots, lack of access to emergency communication, and visits required in neighborhoods with high crime rates. Risks may also include lack of agency safety policies for addressing client violence and inadequate security to protect workers. When these hazards exist, "the unspoken messages may be that violence is tolerated" (OSHA, 2016, p. 5).

Agencies may unintentionally invite aggression when they do not adequately address violent circumstances. Social work agencies should pay more attention to employees' workload (Enosh & Tzafrir, 2015). Overloading workers may cause stress, raising the prospect of failing to have regular contact with clients and/or inadequately addressing client needs. Worker overload may lead to issues with the way employees behave toward each other and toward clients.

In some types of agencies, workers may experience proportionally more violence. For example, verbal/psychological violence against child protection workers (CPWs) has been found to be commonplace. Residential CPWs may be assaulted and/or threatened frequently. Winstanley and Hales (2008) found that more than half of residential staff members had been assaulted, and the majority had been threatened by clients.

It is possible that violence toward CPWs may occur more frequently and intensively because parents have often lost the right to care for their children, which is threatening to parents. This might be applicable to other types of social work in which clients have lost their rights, such as court-ordered treatment in the following areas: criminal justice, substance abuse, domestic violence, and mental health. In these cases, social workers may encounter more challenges to their authority and perhaps blatant violent reactions.

Effects of Client Violence

When social workers are victims of client violence, they may initially experience effects of trauma that include becoming withdrawn, frightened, and nervous. Defraia (2015) stated that after workers are exposed to a work-related critical incident, symptoms may include "restlessness, insomnia, anxiety, detachment, intrusive images, poor concentration, social withdrawal and hypervigilance" (p. 168). Longer term effects of experiencing client violence may include symptoms such as re-experiencing the trauma, avoiding anything related to the trauma, numbing of responsiveness, and negative effects on health. At least 15% of workers' symptoms will be severe and of a duration that diagnosis of posttraumatic stress disorder may be warranted (Defraia, 2015).

Additional consequences of client violence may include loss of motivation on the job, intentions to leave the agency, calling in sick more frequently, or feeling detached from clients (Lamothe et al., 2018). Workers who experience client violence may lose objectivity. When assigned new cases, they may have preconceived notions about the client situations. Workers may tend to avoid contact with troublesome clients, and work priorities may be governed by fear of further violence. According to Shier et al. (2018), when workers experience interference, physical violence, verbal threats,

or yelling from clients, they may experience symptoms of depersonalization, intention to leave the agency, or increased emotional exhaustion. Violent incidents may also lead to workers being less positive in their work with clients. They may avoid anything that may make a client angry. There may be a tendency for workers to gravitate towards jobs that minimize direct practice with clients.

An unsafe environment at the organizational level is associated with lower organization commitment (Kim & Hopkins, 2015). The negative relationship between an unsafe environment and organizational commitment is more apparent for workers who have lower quality leader–member exchange. Social workers may perceive that when working with hostile clients, they receive insufficient support from supervisors. Hunt et al. (2016) found that workers had experienced death threats; threats with firearms, knives, and bombs; as well as physical assaults and being held captive in clients' homes. Yet, workers were uncertain where to seek support and how to cope with these situations. They believed that they were not allowed enough time to debrief and learn from difficult situations. Supervisors told workers that they had to accept violent, intimidating behaviors by clients. These workers wanted more proactive supervision, support, and acknowledgment of the emotional impact of working with violent clients. Supervisors' support may strengthen workers individually and may also strengthen workers' resolve to remain in the agency.

Positive Organizational Response

Studies have demonstrated the effects of positive organizational response to violence. Some victims of client violence have reported that they were able to cope positively by reaching out to colleagues and supervisors (Lamothe et al., 2018). Affected workers made reports of the violence, took part in aggression management training, and received help from employee assistance programs (EAPs). Kim and Hopkins (2015) found that even if workers perceive a negative safety climate in their organization, they may still demonstrate high organizational commitment if they have high-quality interactions with their supervisors. This can occur through open/constructive exchanges between workers and administrators, understanding needs and concerns of workers, and active problem solving with workers, thus helping reduce risks and improve safety. Strong social support may promote improved stress regulation for employees (Sipple et al., 2015). This increases worker self-confidence and feelings of belonging at an agency. It is particularly valuable when social workers believe that they may be at fault for some part of the violence.

Safety Measures

Agencies should require preliminary safety training before workers begin seeing clients. When agencies have commonly occurring critical incidents, prevention training is imperative (DeFraia, 2015). This includes training on resiliency, including "relative risks of various types of incidents, common stress responses, appropriate self-care measures, signs of traumatic stress, and availability of resources for assistance" (Defraia, 2015, p. 158). Risk assessments of clients and communities should be completed to more accurately predict probability of violence occurring and under what circumstances.

An agency safety team can provide ongoing evaluation of safety needs within the agency. NASW (2013) recommends that social workers participate in safety training at least once per year to help maintain workers' ability to practice safely. Nonviolent self-defense is a recommended part of training. In addition, workers are advised to revise

self-care plans in order to effectively manage exposure to primary and secondary trauma. Revised plans should include agency/home visit exit strategies, verbal de-escalation techniques, and alert systems activated from mobile devices. Also, whether in the office or on home visits, workers should have access to silent panic buttons linked to police stations or emergency rooms.

Understanding the origins of client violence helps workers address the needs of clients and de-escalate potential violent situations. Violence may occur when clients perceive a threat, are frustrated that their needs are not being met, or are unable to make decisions for self and/or family. Attempting to understand the cause of a client's hurts, fears, and/or frustrations may increase the social worker's ability to de-escalate a violent situation.

Some mental health disorders predispose clients to possible violent reactions. Thus, it is imperative to know the client's and family members' mental health history, as well as history of violence. Preemptively, when a worker is meeting with a client who is known to be potentially violent, arrangements should be made for an additional worker to attend the meeting.

Supervisor support is critical for workers, whether they have experienced violence or they are afraid of experiencing violence. Coping strategies should be discussed with all staff, with regular checkups to ensure that the coping strategies are helpful. Social workers must be assured that harm to agency workers is not acceptable.

The social worker's workspace should be arranged to optimize safety. Workers' chairs should be nearest to the door in the event that a quick exit is necessary. Workers need clear access to building exits. Security alarms should be conveniently accessible to every worker in the event of an immediate need. It is recommended that workers' offices not be in isolated areas. Within the office, it is recommended that workers remove any items that could be used as projectiles. Agencies must ensure that safe employee parking areas are supplied for workers.

Protocols should be in place to ensure social workers' safety during home visits. Cell phones should be supplied by the agency. Phones should be charged, and emergency contacts should be programmed. It is strongly suggested that visits be scheduled during the daytime. It is imperative that workers notify their office of the client's address and the time frame for the planned visit. Workers should sign out and sign back in when returning to the office. Before leaving the office, the worker must understand directions to the destination. The worker should be aware of who will be at the home when they arrive. Workers should place jewelry and valuables out of sight or leave at home. As the worker approaches the destination, they should be alert for any possible safety issues.

Once in the home, the worker needs to sit near an exit. If the worker does not feel safe prior to or during the visit, they can leave and/or make plans for an alternative visit location and time. If there is any reason to fear a client, other people in the home, or vicious animals, the worker can arrange to have the meeting at the office or in a public place.

When meeting with a client, the worker must have visible agency identification. The social worker's apparel should be chosen with discretion and not be revealing or distracting. Comfortable shoes are recommended during home visits.

It is essential that agencies have protocols for reporting incidents of client violence. This includes acts of physical or verbal violence, client threats of violence, damage to property, and threat of lawsuit.

When Client Violence Has Occurred

Even the best safety plans can be disrupted. Client violence may occur despite appropriate agency and social worker interventions. When violence does occur, it is essential that responsive recovery plans be put into place in a timely manner. Recovery plans should include strategies to reduce emotional and psychological effects from workplace violence (Defraia, 2015). These might include time off for the social worker, accessing mental health treatment to address the potential traumatic effects, and deliberate affirmation from supervisors and/or administrators. To address client violence, all safety breaches must be reported to administration to ensure that the needs of the client, worker, and organization are met. It is essential that supervisors are available to debrief workers. Harmed workers must be assured that they are not incompetent. If mental health symptoms are present, particularly indications of acute stress or post-traumatic stress disorder, workers should be referred to a mental health provider or EAP. The harmed worker may need more frequent supervision immediately after a critical incident. In addition, the worker may temporarily benefit from having another worker accompany/assist with client sessions, whether in the office or on home visits. Supervisors should be alert to workers' detachment from clients, frequent illnesses, or loss of motivation. When large numbers of workers in an agency have encountered violence, it is essential that this be processed in order to remind workers that client violence is unacceptable. Organizationally, reports of safety breaches allow the agency administration to identify possible patterns among clients at the agency and more broadly address problematic issues.

NASW, State, and Federal Safety Guidelines

In 2013, NASW published "Guidelines for Social Worker Safety in the Workplace," a concise booklet that contains 11 standards to manage workplace violence. This booklet covers the most significant safety factors that should be discussed with new workers and reviewed with veteran workers on a regular basis. It is strongly recommended that all agencies that employ social workers have a copy of these guidelines and that these guidelines be discussed in-depth during mandatory training of social workers and social work students.

OSHA (2016) has recommended the following requirements for violence prevention:

1. Commitment of management, employee participation.
2. Worksite analysis and hazard identification: Should include records review, review of procedures, employee surveys, and workplace security analysis. Recorded analyses should include patterns of violence and "near misses" (p. 9).
3. Hazard prevention/control: Preferably find ways to eliminate hazards or substitute a safer work practice (i.e., use of guards, door locks, metal detectors, panic buttons, better lighting, and more accessible exits).
4. Safety and health training: Should be a separate training component that is thoroughly discussed with new workers before they begin their jobs. Every worker should know that "violence should be expected, but can be avoided" (p. 25).
5. Record keeping/program evaluation: Helps evaluate the effectiveness of violence prevention. OSHA requires reports for specific incidents of violence.

It is strongly recommended that all workers and administrators become familiar with the entire OSHA document, including the Workplace Violence Program Checklists that can be adapted to fit the needs of specific agencies.

In recent years, violence toward social workers has begun to be recognized by the public in response to social workers' deaths while on the job. In some states, there are now laws to address client violence toward social workers. There have also been several efforts to introduce federal legislation addressing violence toward social workers. In February 2019, the Workplace Violence Prevention for Health Care and Social Service Act was introduced in the U.S. House of Representatives, and NASW's chief executive officer, Angelo McClain, urged its passage in testimony before the House's Committee on Education and Labor Subcommittee on Workforce Protections. It would require employers within the health care and social service industries to develop and implement a comprehensive workplace violence prevention plan. The bill was passed in the House and referred to the U.S. Senate. However, the bill was not passed in the Senate prior to the session ending and is currently still pending.

Social workers must continue to unite and advocate for policies that will help ensure social work safety and standardize appropriate safety responses for the benefit of social workers and clients. The profession must continue its mission to assist clients in moving toward safer, more productive lives while at the same time guarding the health of fellow social workers.

References

Criss, P. (2009). *Prevalence of client violence against social work students and its effects on fear of future violence, occupational commitment, and career withdrawal intentions.* Unpublished doctoral dissertation, University of South Florida, Tampa.

Defraia, G. (2015). Psychological trauma in the workplace: Variation of incident severity among industry settings and between recurring versus isolated incidents. *International Journal of Occupational & Environmental Medicine,* 6(3), 155–168. doi:10.15171/ijoem.2016.746.

Dupre, K. E., Dawe, K.-A., & Barling, J. (2014). Harm to those who serve: Effects of direct and vicarious customer-initiated workplace aggression. *Journal* of *Interpersonal Violence, 29*(13), 2355–2377. doi:10.1177/0886260513518841

Enosh, G., & Tzafrir, S. (2015). The scope of client aggression towards social workers in Israel. *Journal of Aggression, Maltreatment, & Trauma, 24*(9), 971–985. doi:10:1080/10926771.2015.1070233

Hunt, S., Goddard, C., Cooper, J., Littlechild, B., & Wild, J. (2016). "If I feel like this, how does the child feel?" Child protection workers, supervision, management, and organizational responses to parental violence. *Journal of Social Work, 30*(1), 5–24. http://dx.doi.org/10.1080/02650533.2015.1073145

Kim, H., & Hopkins, K. (2015). Child welfare workers' personal safety concerns and organizational commitment: The moderating role of social support. *Human Services Organizations: Management, Leadership, & Governance, 39,* 101–115. doi:10.1080/23303131.2014.987413

Lamothe, J., Couvrette, A., Lebrun, G., Yale-Souliere, G., Roy, C., Guay, S., & Geoffrion, S. (2018). Violence against child protection workers: A study of workers' experiences, attributions, and coping strategies. *Child Abuse & Neglect, 81,* 308–321. doi.org/10.1016/j.chiabu.2018.04.027

National Association of Social Workers. (2009). *The results are in: What social workers say about social work.* NASW Press.

National Association of Social Workers. (2013). *Guidelines for social worker safety in the workplace* [Brochure].

Occupational Safety and Health Administration, U.S. Department of Labor. (2016). *Guidelines for preventing workplace violence for healthcare and social service workers* (OSHA 3248-04R). Retrieved November 2019 from https://alertgps.com/wp-content/uploads/2018/02/Workplace-Violence-osha3148.pdf

Ringstad, R. (2005). Conflict in the workplace: Social workers as victims and perpetrators. *Social Work, 50,* 305–313. doi:1010932w/50.4.305

Shier, M., Graham, J., & Nicholas, D. (2018). Interpersonal interactions, workplace violence, and occupational health outcomes among social workers. *Journal of Social Work, 18*(5), 525–547. doi:10:1177/1468017316656089

Sipple, L., Pietrzak, R., Charney, D., Mayes, L., & Southwick, S. (2015). How does social support enhance resiliency in the trauma-exposed individual? *Ecology and Society, 20*(4), 136–145. http://dx.doi.org/10.5751/ES-07832

Winstanley, S., & Hales, L. (2008). Prevalence of aggression towards residential social workers: Do qualifications and experience make a difference? *Child Youth Care Forum, 37*(2), 103–110. doi:10.1007/s10566-008-9051-9

Zelnick, J. R., Slayter, E., Flanzbaum, B., Ginty Butler, N., Domingo, B., Perlstein, J., & Trust, C. (2013). Part of the job? Workplace violence in Massachusetts social service agencies. *Health and Social Work, 38*(2), 75–85. doi:10.1093/hsw/hlt007

Technology and Social Work Practice

Micro, Mezzo, and Macro Applications

Melanie Sage and Jonathan B. Singer

Developments in internet and computer technologies (ICTs) such as social networks, webcams, texting, virtual reality, and smartphone apps, combined with emerging social issues, have significantly changed the way we communicate with one another and our environment (Mishna et al., 2017). For instance, the demand for telehealth services increased significantly in 2020 during the COVID-19 pandemic (Hong et al., 2020), forcing legislators, insurers, providers, and consumers alike to consider the use of technology-mediated services. These shifts have caused a natural evolution toward new ways of providing social work services.

Social Work Responds

In the 6 years since the previous edition of this chapter was published (Singer & Sage, 2015), national organizations, educators, researchers, and practitioners have responded to the growing impact of technology on our field:

- The National Association of Social Workers (NASW) added 19 clauses to the 2018 Code of Ethics, mostly addressing technology (2017a), and updated the NASW technology standards for social workers (2017b) for practice and teaching.
- *Harness technology for social good* was identified as one of the 13 Grand Challenges for Social Work (Berzin et al., 2015).
- Educators have used technology to address gaps in training and education, such as the creation of the first online bilingual Master of Social Work program (https://www.luc.edu/socialwork/academics/graduate/maestriabilingueentrabajosocialenlinea/), improving access to students in rural and semirural areas and African American students (Council on Social Work Education, 2019), and clinical innovations such as online client simulation (Washburn & Zhou, 2018). These innovations are mirrored in social work scholarship addressing best practices for teaching with technology (Goldkind et al., 2018; Hitchcock et al.,

2019) and also how to train social workers to use technology in their future practice (Beaumont et al., 2017; Jivanjee et al., 2015; Jones et al., 2019).

- Researchers are harnessing technology to increase the reach of their scholarship (Singer, 2019) and exploring the ethical use of big data for decision-making (Rodriguez et al., 2019).
- Social workers acknowledge the ways in which technology can serve or harm vulnerable populations (Craig et al., 2015; Fitch, 2012) and its potential to improve social work interventions (Chan & Holosko, 2016).

Uses, Benefits, and Limitations of Technology in Service Delivery

Online Mental Health

Although some social workers were engaging in online mental health practice prior to the COVID-19 pandemic in the United States, spring 2020 was the first time that all U.S. mental health services were provided online. Legislative and insurance restrictions to online service delivery were temporarily lifted, in part because comprehensive reviews in counseling fields suggest that online mental health services are effective in treating mental health disorders (Kemp et al., 2020). This body of research has found few significant differences in outcomes between synchronous (e.g., live webcam) and asynchronous (e.g., email) therapy. Research comparing face-to-face (F2F) therapies to online therapies has consistently found that client outcomes with online therapy are as good and in some cases better than those with F2F therapies (Carlbring et al., 2018; Sweeney et al., 2019). Although it is possible that online environments are better suited for certain problem areas (e.g., virtual reality for treating post-traumatic stress disorder or phobias and

text-based reminders for medication compliance), that remains a question for empirical investigation (Pallavicini et al., 2013).

Types of Online Mental Health Services

Barak and Grohol (2011) suggest four distinct categories for online mental health services: (1) online counseling and psychotherapy; (2) online support groups and blogs; (3) interactive, self-guided interventions; and (4) psychoeducational websites. These categories vary in function, evidence base, and degree of interpersonal interaction.

Online Counseling and Psychotherapy

Online counseling and psychotherapy, also referred to as telemental health, is the provision of services by a mental health professional via technology in real time (synchronously) using a webcam or other technology or in delayed time (asynchronously) using email, texting, or video. Consumers of telemental health report that they use it for cost savings, convenience, and ease of use (Almathami et al., 2020). For providers, it minimizes travel time and overhead costs. Online therapy can reduce barriers to treatment, such as transportation and access to providers, but leaves out people who do not know how to access telemental health or do not have the technology or data plans to make use of it (Figueroa & Aguilera, 2020). Social workers who practice online therapy should be trained in best practices, from managing privacy to the best placement of a camera during synchronous sessions.

Online Support Groups and Blogs

Online support groups are peer-facilitated groups in which members meet online using ICTs such as chat, in virtual reality environments such as Oculus, or in webcam-mediated F2F settings using programs such as Google

Meet. Some research has found online support to be as helpful as psychoeducational websites and self-guided treatments (Fortuna et al., 2020; Griffiths et al., 2012). The benefit of participation increases with interaction (Yalom, 2005). However, the absence of a professional means that group members can share potentially dangerous misinformation. Unique in the online environment are groups that explicitly encourage self-harm, such as "pro-suicide" and "pro-anorexia" groups.

Blogs are written by consumers or providers of mental health services. Bloggers gain social benefits through feedback from people who follow the blog and leave comments. For consumers, this online community can counteract feelings of isolation, shame, or stigma associated with a mental illness. The act of writing a blog can itself be therapeutic (Hu, 2019; Murphy et al., 2020). Therapist blogs can offer resources similar to psychoeducation sites for consumers. NASW's (2017b) Technology Standards provide guidance to social workers about their online presence and technology-mediated communications.

Interactive, Self-Guided Interventions

These are self-directed web or mobile app interventions that can be used alone or as adjunct to other mental health services (Carper et al., 2011). The best-researched self-guided programs are computerized cognitive–behavioral therapy programs (Griffiths et al., 2010; Lintvedt et al., 2013). Unlike F2F therapy, self-guided computer-based programs are often free or cost very little, and they are easily scaled so that one person or 1 million people could use the program. Although they have high dropout rates, some have argued that the completion rates for self-guided therapy are no lower than those for F2F therapy (Andrews et al., 2010). Researchers have consistently shown that self-guided programs are as effective as F2F therapy at reducing depression

and anxiety symptoms for people who complete the program (Cuijpers et al., 2010). For youth, however, outcomes with self-guided interventions were only comparable when they received substantial support (Garrido et al., 2019), pointing to the developmental challenges of eliminating adult involvement when trying to reduce depressive and anxiety symptoms in youth.

Interactive and self-guided interventions are increasingly delivered over smartphone apps (Wang et al., 2018). The delivery of mental health services using mobile devices, called mHealth, has advantages: They travel with the client and they can be programmed to send alerts to take medication, call for an appointment, take a deep breath, or record an emotion or thought. GPS-enabled mobile devices can track exercise or sound an alert when a person is in a pre-established "no-go zone" such as a bar or casino. Despite their promise, the most capable app developers are not usually content experts, which means that most apps that bill themselves as mental health solutions are not evidence-based (Marshall et al., 2019). Therefore, social workers should inquire about the types of self-help technologies that clients are using and help educate them about apps or other self-paced treatments that are evidence-supported.

Psychoeducational Websites

Psychoeducational websites are online sources of information. Examples include the National Institute of Mental Health (http://www.nimh.nih.gov), the Substance Abuse and Mental Health Services Administration (http://www.samhsa.gov), and WebMD (http://www.webmd.com). However, psychoeducational websites are only as good as the information they provide. Providers and consumers should evaluate web resources based on the *authority*, *accuracy*, and *objectivity*; the comprehensiveness of the *coverage*; and how *current* the information is. Health-related websites have become a source of self-education and self-advocacy, where patients can come together around shared experiences. This means that patients are sometimes armed with more information about their health than practitioners, and it is important to not discount their knowledge and to help them assess the credibility of resources they have found.

Summary

Online mental health resources have a growing evidence base. Advances in self-directed interventions and mHealth point to a future in which social workers no longer provide some functions. Yet, the benefits of online therapy cannot be realized by those who lack access to technology, the technical skills to participate in therapy online, or the financial resources to pay for services. These barriers are social justice issues. Therefore, social workers have a professional responsibility to address the mezzo- and macro-level barriers to accessing and using ICT-based services.

Community Organizing

Social work's community organizing roots emerged in the late 19th century, in part as a response to social problems that developed out of technological advances brought on by the Industrial Revolution. For much of the 20th century, social workers struggled with the ways in which marginalized groups were adversely affected by technology (Hick & McNutt, 2002). In the 21st century, some problems, such as bullying and sex trafficking, shifted from occurring primarily on-ground to online. For some, lack of access to technology has itself become a social problem (McNutt, 2018). For instance, those with access to ICTs have advantages related to information access and are better able to find and apply for jobs online than people without internet access (Araque

et al., 2013). Although more Americans have internet access than ever before, lower income Americans increasingly rely on mobile phones rather than broadband service to connect to the internet (Araque et al., 2013). Digital organizing efforts that do not acknowledge or address this digital literacy divide may exclude the very groups that would most benefit from participation. And paradoxically, ICTs in the 21st century have also made it possible for some people who previously were marginalized because of geographical distance, physical or economic limitations, or social stigma to communicate and organize through virtual communities.

Social media technologies offer inexpensive ways to communicate with and mobilize stakeholders. #BlackLivesMatter and #MeToo are examples of social movements that used Twitter and Facebook for advocacy. Although online tools hold promise for organizing, they are underutilized by nonprofits (Young, 2018). Organizers should have a clear goal when adopting a new technology; for instance, social media can be harnessed for reputation management, connection with donors, advocacy, and collective action (Namisango et al., 2019).

Other technologies, such as geographic information systems (GIS), can be used to analyze information about specific geographical regions, such as neighborhoods, cities, or counties. For instance, GIS can be used by consumer rights advocates to identify areas that lack grocery stores that sell fresh food. Email lists and social networks are low-cost ways of distributing action alerts (e.g., "Call your representative!"), and targeted social media campaigns can be designed specifically to recruit certain disenfranchised groups (Russomanno et al., 2019). High-speed internet and free video conferencing (via Zoom or Google Meet) allow synchronous webcam-mediated gatherings, bringing together stakeholders virtually in real time for organizing.

Macro Issues

Licensing and Regulation of Online Therapy

As with other professions such as law, medicine, and nursing, licensing and regulation of social work occur at the state level. Online therapy has no geographic boundaries and thus creates complex regulatory issues. Social workers do not need a license to provide services that are not regulated, such as community organizing and some case management and service coordination. Some states allow social workers from other states to provide regulated services during a declared state of emergency. For all other regulated and covered services, social workers need to be licensed in the state in which they reside *and* in which their client resides. For example, if a client resides in Idaho and a clinical social worker works in Georgia, the social worker may need to be licensed in both states. Groups such as the American Telemedicine Association (http://www.americantelemed.org) are working toward best practices for telemedicine, and the Association of Social Work Boards has model legislation for how to include electronic social work in state licensing statutes.

Algorithms in Social Work

One future promise of technology in mental health is the ability to improve customized treatments using algorithms, which is currently an unregulated practice. Algorithms draw on past data sources to find a match for a future event. They are currently being tested to discover mental health diagnoses by finding similar patterns in past patients (Cho et al., 2019). They could similarly be used to find a treatment match for a patient. However, social workers should be aware that algorithms are already being implicated in perpetuating existing inequities. For example, in some states, for people who are convicted of crimes, algorithms are used to determine jail sentencing

using risk scores based on historical data or other people who were incarcerated. These algorithms have been shown to embed racial and sexist bias (Hamilton, 2019a, 2019b). Similar algorithms are used in child welfare to determine risk profiles for children and families, which is a controversial practice (Chouldechova et al., 2018; Gillingham, 2019; Saxena et al., 2020). As society relies more on these tools, social workers should lend their voice to promote social justice. Current efforts in algorithmic decision-making include work to make the systems more fair and to include affected participants in the design of the algorithms to improve accountability (Cech, 2020; Lee et al., 2019). Although computer scientists are the primary developers in these efforts, this is an excellent place for social workers to collaborate (Patton, 2020) so as to support innovations that empower communities and embed social work values.

Conclusion

Advances in ICTs have changed the way social workers think about and provide mental health services. Technology will continue to displace some social work roles and demand social work presence in new roles. In the coming decades, it is likely that some social work services will be entirely computer-based and that social workers will be increasingly called upon to provide digital services or address social justice issues related to new uses of technology. In an effort to address these needs, social workers should continue to develop their competency and comfort with technology.

Helpful Resources

Grand Challenges for Social Work. *Harness technology for social good.* https://grandchallengesforsocialwork.org/harness-technology-for-social-good
National Association of Social Workers. *Standards for technology and social work practice.* https://

www.socialworkers.org/Practice/Practice-Standards-Guidelines

The Social Work Podcast. http://socialworkpodcast.com

References

Almathami, H. K. Y., Win, K. T., & Vlahu-Gjorgievska, E. (2020). Barriers and facilitators that influence telemedicine-based, real-time, online consultation at patients' homes: Systematic literature review. *Journal of Medical Internet Research, 22*(2), e16407. https://doi.org/10.2196/16407

Araque, J. C., Maiden, R. P., Bravo, N., Estrada, I., Evans, R., Hubchik, K., . . . & Reddy, M. (2013). Computer usage and access in low-income urban communities. *Computers in Human Behavior, 29*(4), 1393–1401.

Barak, A., & Grohol, J. M. (2011). Current and future trends in internet-supported mental health interventions. *Journal of Technology in Human Services, 29*(3), 155–196.

Beaumont, E., Chester, P., & Rideout, H. (2017). Navigating ethical challenges in social media: Social work student and practitioner perspectives. *Australian Social Work, 70*(2), 221–228.

Berzin, S. C., Singer, J., & Chan, C. (2015). Practice innovation through technology in the digital age: A grand challenge for social work. Grand Challenges for Social Work Initiative Working Paper No. 12. American Academy of Social Work and Social Welfare.

Carlbring, P., Andersson, G., Cuijpers, P., Riper, H., & Hedman-Lagerlöf, E. (2018). Internet-based vs. face-to-face cognitive behavior therapy for psychiatric and somatic disorders: An updated systematic review and meta-analysis. *Cognitive Behaviour Therapy, 47*(1), 1–18. https://doi.org/10.1080/16506073.2017.1401115

Carper, M. M., McHugh, R. K., & Barlow, D. H. (2013). The dissemination of computer-based psychological treatment: a preliminary analysis of patient and clinician perceptions. *Administration and Policy in Mental Health and Mental Health Services Research, 40*(2), 87–95.

Cech, F. (2020). Beyond transparency: Exploring algorithmic accountability. In Companion of the 2020 ACM International Conference on Supporting Group Work (pp. 11–14). Association for Computing Machinery.

Chan, C., & Holosko, M. J. (2016). A review of information and communication technology enhanced social work interventions. *Research on Social Work Practice, 26*(1), 88–100.

Cho, G., Yim, J., Choi, Y., Ko, J., & Lee, S.-H. (2019). Review of machine learning algorithms for diagnosing mental illness. *Psychiatry Investigation, 16*(4), 262–269. https://doi.org/10.30773/pi.2018.12.21.2

Chouldechova, A., Putnam-Hornstein, E., Benavides-Prado, D., Fialko, O., & Vaithianathan, R. (2018). A case study of algorithm-assisted decision making in child maltreatment hotline screening decisions. *Proceedings of Machine Learning Research, 81*, 1–15. http://proceedings.mlr.press/v81/chouldechova18a/chouldechova18a.pdf

Council on Social Work Education. (2019). *From social work education to social work practice: Results of the survey of 2018 social work graduates.* Council on Social Work Education and National Workforce Initiative Steering Committee. https://www.cswe.org/CSWE/media/Workforce-Study/2018-Social-Work-Workforce-Report-Final.pdf

Craig, S. L., McInroy, L. B., McCready, L. T., Di Cesare, D. M., & Pettaway, L. D. (2015). Connecting without fear: Clinical implications of the consumption of information and communication technologies by sexual minority youth and young adults. *Clinical Social Work Journal, 43*(2), 159–168. https://doi.org/10.1007/s10615-014-0505-2

Cuijpers, P., Donker, T., van Straten, A., Li, J., & Andersson, G. (2010). Is guided self-help as effective as face-to-face psychotherapy for depression and anxiety disorders? A systematic review and meta-analysis of comparative outcome studies. *Psychological Medicine, 40*(12), 1943–1957. https://doi.org/10.1017/S0033291710000772

Figueroa, C. A., & Aguilera, A. (2020, June 3). The need for a mental health technology revolution in the COVID-19 pandemic. *Frontiers in Psychiatry, 11*. https://doi.org/10.3389/fpsyt.2020.00523

Fitch, D. (2012). Youth in foster care and social media: A framework for developing privacy guidelines. *Journal of Technology in Human Services, 30*(2), 94–108. https://doi.org/10.1080/15228835.2012.700854

Fortuna, K. L., Naslund, J. A., LaCroix, J. M., Bianco, C. L., Brooks, J. M., Zisman-Ilani, Y., Muralidharan, A., & Deegan, P. (2020). Digital peer support mental health interventions for people with a lived experience of a serious mental illness: Systematic review. *JMIR Mental Health, 7*(4). https://doi.org/10.2196/16460

Garrido, S., Millington, C., Cheers, D., Boydell, K., Schubert, E., Meade, T., & Nguyen, Q. V. (2019). What works and what doesn't work? A systematic review of digital mental health interventions for depression and anxiety in young people. *Frontiers in Psychiatry, 10*, 759. https://doi.org/10.3389/fpsyt.2019.00759

Gillingham, P. (2019). Can predictive algorithms assist decision-making in social work with children and families? *Child Abuse Review, 28*(2), 114–126.s

Goldkind, L., Wolf, L., & Freddolino, P. P. (2018). *Digital social work: Tools for practice with individuals, organizations, and communities.* Oxford University Press.

Griffiths, F., Cave, J., Boardman, F., Ren, J., Pawlikowska, T., Ball, R., . . . & Cohen, A. (2012). Social networks–The future for health care delivery. *Social Science & Medicine, 75*(12), 2233–2241.

Griffiths, K. M., Farrer, L., & Christensen, H. (2010). The efficacy of internet interventions for depression and anxiety disorders: a review of randomised controlled trials. *Medical Journal of Australia, 192,* S4–S11.

Hamilton, M. (2019a). The biased algorithm: Evidence of disparate impact on Hispanics. *American Criminal Law Review, 56,* 1553.

Hamilton, M. (2019b). The sexist algorithm. *Behavioral Sciences & the Law, 37*(2), 145–157.

Hitchcock, L. I., Sage, M., & Smyth, N. J. (2019). *Teaching social work with digital technology.* CSWE Press.

Hong, Y.-R., Lawrence, J., Williams, D., Jr., & Mainous, A. M., III. (2020). Population-level interest and telehealth capacity of US hospitals in response to COVID-19: Cross-sectional analysis of Google search and national hospital survey data. *JMIR Public Health and Surveillance, 6*(2), e18961. https://doi.org/10.2196/18961

Hu, Y. (2019). Helping is healing: Examining relationships between social support, intended audiences, and perceived benefits of mental health blogging. *Journal of Communication in Healthcare, 12*(2), 112–120.

Jivanjee, P., Pendell, K. D., Nissen, L., & Goodluck, C. (2015, Fall). Lifelong learning in social work: A qualitative exploration with social work practitioners, students, and field instructors. Advances in Social Work, 16(2).

Jones, N. P., Sage, M., & Hitchcock, L. (2019). Infographics as an assignment to build digital skills in the social work classroom. *Journal of Technology in Human Services, 37*(2–3), 203–225.

Kemp, J., Zhang, T., Inglis, F., Wiljer, D., Sockalingam, S., Crawford, A., Lo, B., Charow, R., Munnery, M., Takhar, S. S., & Strudwick, G. (2020). Delivery of compassionate mental health care in a digital technology–driven age: Scoping review. *Journal of Medical Internet Research, 22*(3), e16263. https://doi.org/10.2196/16263

Lee, M. K., Kusbit, D., Kahng, A., Kim, J. T., Yuan, X., Chan, A., See, D., Noothigattu, R., Lee, S., & Psomas, A. (2019, November). WeBuildAI: Participatory framework for algorithmic governance. *Proceedings of the ACM on Human–Computer Interaction, 3*(CSCW), 1–35.

Marshall, J. M., Dunstan, D. A., & Bartik, W. (2019, November 15). The digital psychiatrist: In search of evidence-based apps for anxiety and depression. *Frontiers in Psychiatry, 10.*

McNutt, J. G. (2018). *Technology, activism, and social justice in a digital age.* Oxford University Press.

Mishna, F., Fantus, S., & McInroy, L. B. (2017). Informal use of information and communication technology: Adjunct to traditional face-to-face social work practice. *Clinical Social Work Journal, 45*(1), 49–55.

Murphy, E., Donohue, G., & McCann, E. (2020). Exploring mental health issues through the use of blogs: A scoping review of the research evidence. *Issues in Mental Health Nursing, 41*(4), 296–305. https://doi.org/10.1080/01612840.2019.1666326

Namisango, F., Kang, K., & Rehman, J. (2019). What do we know about social media in nonprofits? A review. *PACIS 2019 Proceedings,* 16.

National Association of Social Workers. (2017a). *Code of ethics of the National Association of Social Workers.* NASW Press. https://www.socialworkers.org

National Association of Social Workers. (2017b). *NASW, ASWB, CSWE, & CSWA standards for technology in social work practice.* https://www.socialworkers.org/includes/newIncludes/homepage/PRA-BRO-33617.TechStandards_FINAL_POSTING.pdf

Pallavicini, F., Cipresso, P., Raspelli, S., Grassi, A., Serino, S., Vigna, C., . . . & Riva, G. (2013). Is virtual reality always an effective stressors for exposure treatments? Some insights from a controlled trial. *BMC Psychiatry, 13*(1), 1–10.

Patton, D. U. (2020). Social work thinking for UX and AI design. *Interactions, 27*(2), 86–89.

Rodriguez, M. Y., DePanfilis, D., & Lanier, P. (2019). Bridging the gap: Social work insights for ethical algorithmic decision-making in human services. *IBM Journal of Research and Development, 63*(4/5), 8:1–8:8. https://doi.org/10.1147/JRD.2019.2934047

Russomanno, J., Patterson, J. G., & Tree, J. M. J. (2019). Social media recruitment of marginalized, hard-to-reach populations: Development of recruitment and monitoring guidelines. *JMIR Public Health and Surveillance, 5*(4), e14886.

Saxena, D., Badillo-Urquiola, K., Wisniewski, P. J., & Guha, S. (2020). A human-centered review of algorithms used within the US child welfare system. *Proceedings of the 2020 CHI Conference on Human Factors in Computing Systems,* 1–15.

Singer, J. B. (2019). Podcasting as social scholarship: A tool to increase the public impact of scholarship and research. *Journal of the Society for Social Work and Research, 10*(4), 571–590. https://doi.org/10.1086/706600

Singer, J. B., & Sage, M. (2015). Technology and social work practice: Micro, mezzo, and macro applications. In K. Corcoran & A. R. Roberts (Eds.), *Social workers' desk reference* (3rd ed., pp. 179–188). Oxford University Press.

Sweeney, G. M., Donovan, C. L., March, S., & Forbes, Y. (2019). Logging into therapy: Adolescent perceptions of online therapies for mental health problems. *Internet Interventions, 15,* 93–99. https://doi.org/10.1016/j.invent.2016.12.001

Yalom, I. D. with Leszcz, M. (2005). *The Theory and Practice of Group Psychotherapy.* NY Basic Books.

Wang, K., Varma, D. S., & Prosperi, M. (2018). A systematic review of the effectiveness of mobile apps for monitoring and management of mental health symptoms or disorders. *Journal of Psychiatric Research, 107,* 73–78. https://doi.org/10.1016/j.jpsychires.2018.10.006

Washburn, M., & Zhou, S. (2018). Teaching note—Technology-enhanced clinical simulations: Tools for practicing clinical skills in online social work programs. *Journal of Social Work Education, 54*(3), 554–560. https://doi.org/10.1080/10437797.2017.1404519

Young, J. A. (2018). Equipping future nonprofit professionals with digital literacies for the 21st century. *Journal of Nonprofit Education and Leadership, 8*(1), 4–15.

Leadership in Social Work
A New Direction

Lakeya Cherry

Leadership development is a lucrative industry that continues to grow as companies realize the value of and prioritize investment in their talent (Beer et al., 2016; Gottfredson & Reina, 2020; Westfall, 2019). In 2000, Rank and Hutchison analyzed leadership in the field of social work and found that leadership development had not been a priority of social work education or its association, the National Association of Social Workers (NASW). Despite this oversight, leadership is synonymous with social work, and the profession as a collective must prioritize the training and development of its leaders. In doing this, it must also acknowledge that it can no longer remain in the background because the social worker's role as a leader is more paramount today than it has ever been.

Leadership

Scholars have attempted to define what leadership is and the role of leaders since the 1900s (Northouse, 2016; Woolever & Kelly, 2014). Leadership expert Peter Northouse (2016) defines leadership as "a process whereby an individual influences a group of individuals to achieve a common goal" (p. 6). His definition describes a leader as an influencer of others who through a "process" can accomplish goals. Brene' Brown (2018) defines the individual leader as "anyone who takes responsibility for finding the potential in people and processes, and who has the courage to help develop that potential" (p. 4). Courage is important to note because although many may be aware of the potential in people and things, they might not prioritize or be brave enough to develop this potential. This is what distinguishes those who are leaders from those who are not. To choose to be a leader is an act of courage. It involves a certain degree of risk and a willingness to practice and sometimes stumble.

Leadership can be learned, which means that anyone, regardless of their background or characteristics, can be a leader (Araque & Weiss, 2019; Northouse, 2016; Woolever & Kelly, 2014). It is the intentional development of self that contributes to one being ready and equipped with the skills needed to lead others. In an organizational context, those who are charged with the responsibility to see the potential in their employees and to develop these areas further are typically considered executive or "formal" leaders (Araque & Weiss, 2019). In the past, one might only attribute leaders and leadership with titles or positions. However, recent literature indicates that not only can anyone become a leader and lead others but also leadership is often situational.

Social Work Leadership

What does this mean for social work? Rank and Hutchison (2000) define leadership as "a process of advocacy and planning whereby an individual practices ethical and humanistic behavior to motivate others (clients and colleagues) to achieve common goals articulated by a shared vision" (p. 499). The authors describe social work leadership as "the communication of vision, guided by the NASW Code of Ethics, to create proactive processes that empower individuals, families, groups, organizations, and communities" (p. 499). When social workers can effectively communicate ideas in line with their code of ethics and empower those with whom they work through "process," they are behaving as leaders.

Social work as a profession has a rich history of leaders who have made significant contributions to the public sector. However, in choosing not to prioritize the development of its leaders, the profession has lost much of its power and competitive advantage in comparison to other professions (Brilliant, 1986; Holosko, 2009; Sullivan, 2016). Although many social workers behave as leaders, most are not developed to their full capacity as leaders, do not recognize their leadership potential, and thus have been unwilling to step into leadership roles (Rank & Hutchison, 2000). The NASW Code of Ethics (2017) indicates that social workers have an ethical responsibility to be competent:

Value: Competence
Ethical principle: Social workers practice within their areas of competence and develop and enhance their professional expertise.

This competence should include an understanding of leadership, how to become a leader, and how to effectively lead as a leader. A commitment to leadership by social workers will benefit the individual social worker and contribute significantly to their practice (i.e., employees, clients, organization, and partners) and the profession overall.

The Role of the Leader
Leading Others

Prentice (2004) describes leadership as "the accomplishment of a goal through the direction of human assistants" (p. 1). Leaders are expected to relate, inspire, motivate, encourage, and develop those who work with and for them. They must take the time to get to know their followers, what motivates them, and how to use that knowledge to inspire action. Leaders who take the time to understand the unique characteristics and interests of those with whom they work and are responsive to that will be most successful. Leaders who oversimplify their role and take for granted the unique characteristics and contributions of those with whom they work are not as successful as those who prioritize relationship building with their followers (Prentice, 2004). Social workers have unique backgrounds and experiences in addition to varying motivations. Leaders of all disciplines must acknowledge this about their followers or team members and learn how to use this information to identify and create roles and functions unique to those on their team. The best leaders are those who know each team member's strengths and can position the team to maximize these strengths (Buckingham, 2005; Mor Barak, 2017). Social workers use strength-based approaches with their clients, so social work leaders should adopt similar approaches for use with their team members.

Goleman (2013) encourages leaders to focus their attention on themselves, others, and the wider world. To do this, Goleman suggests that leaders should utilize an empathy triad:

- *Cognitive empathy*—the ability to understand another person's perspective
- *Emotional empathy*—the ability to feel what someone else feels
- *Empathic concern*—the ability to sense what another person needs from you

Leaders who can empathize with their followers in these ways are seen as more influential and persuasive. Social workers utilize similar methods and tools to establish rapport with their clients. In an organizational context, social work leaders can modify their clinical approaches to coincide with building relationships among team members. Leaders who invest in their team members, as they do their clients, will ultimately experience better outcomes and garner more respect from their team. The culture of the organization will benefit, and this increased morale will translate to better work with clients.

Inclusive Leadership and Racial Equity

Leaders must create an inclusive work environment. They should be aware of their biases and strive to build a race equity culture in their organizations. Social workers are familiar with the terms cultural competence and cultural humility. Social work leaders should leverage this knowledge in practice with their teams and organizations. Organizations in which employees feel included are more innovative and productive (Bourke & Espedido, 2020; Mor Barak, 2017). The field of social work has a code of ethics that indicates that social workers not only should be competent as it pertains to

diversity and cultural issues but also should not "practice, condone, facilitate, or collaborate with any form of discrimination on the basis of race" (NASW, 2017, p. 27). However, nonprofit organizations are not known for having racially diverse leadership (Kunreuther & Thomas-Breitfeld, 2017).

This commitment to social justice should be visible inside and outside the workplace. Social work practitioners and leaders alike have a responsibility to ensure their own competence and commitment to these values in addition to that of their employees and organizations through intentional, deliberate behaviors. This commitment to building a racial equity culture will positively impact their workplace culture and clients, and it is beneficial to society.

What Leaders Do

After a review of decades' worth of literature, Askenas and Manville (2018) determined that the best leaders

- unite people around an exciting, aspirational vision;
- build a strategy for achieving the vision by making choices about what to do and what not to do;
- attract and develop the best possible talent to implement the strategy;
- relentlessly focus on results in the context of strategy;
- create ongoing innovation that will help reinvent the vision and strategy; and
- "lead yourself"—know and grow oneself so that one can most effectively lead others and carry out these practices.

Kotter (2001) describes leadership as "coping with change" (p. 4). To do this, leaders must have a vision and strategy as Askenas and Manville (2018) described. Successful leaders motivate, unite, and align their teams around this vision. Leaders most successful at this invest the requisite time to build trust and strong relationships with their teams. Without trust, leaders are less credible to their team members or followers (Frei & Morriss, 2020; Kotter, 2001). Leaders must also strive to include their team members in decision-making. Leaders cannot assume they know all of the answers. They must create a culture of innovation, in which every person within the organization has a voice and space to problem solve and innovate. Last, but most important, leaders must be willing to further their development.

Managing Oneself

To effectively lead and manage others, social workers must know how to manage themselves. They are often trained to focus on the needs of their clients, which often results in them not focusing on their own development and competence. Although client-centered leadership is important, the competence of the individual leader is just as important and valuable to meet the needs of the client (Sullivan, 2016). This oversight is likely due to the limited focus on leadership development in social work education. Drucker (2005) encourages leaders to "manage themselves," which requires that one learn who they are, their strengths, their values, and the type of environment most conducive to who they are and how they work. Part of this work also includes learning to prioritize one's own self-care and well-being because this impacts overall competence. Brown (2018) uses the phrase, "Who we are is how we lead" (p. 11). To be an effective leader, social workers must know themselves, their biases, and their blind spots. They must not only be aware of these but also commit to further development.

Leadership Skills and Characteristics

Goleman (2004) identified five skills that leaders should possess to separate themselves from other leaders. An ability to be emotionally intelligent benefits the leader's performance and that of their team or followers. The following are emotional intelligence skills:

1. *Self-awareness*: Knowing one's strengths, weaknesses, drives, values, and impact on others
2. *Self-regulation*: Controlling or redirecting disruptive impulses and moods
3. *Motivation*: Relishing achievement for its own sake
4. *Empathy*: Understanding other people's emotional makeup
5. *Social skill*: Building rapport with others to move them in desired directions

Similar to the concept of leadership, these five skills can be learned and strengthened through professional development. Businesses with emotionally intelligent leaders tend to have better results (Goleman, 2004).

Many researchers have tried to answer the question, What makes an effective leader? Giles (2016) queried 195 leaders throughout the world to find the answer to this question. They were asked to select the top 15 of 74 leadership competencies. Their responses resulted in the following five themes: strong ethics and safety, self-organizing, efficient learning, connection, and belonging. Leaders who focus on themselves first are more apt to improve the performance of their teams.

Tropman and Wooten (2013) established the 7C approach as a method for organizing the key qualities of executive leaders across research studies. In this approach, the 7C's of executive leadership are characteristics, crucibles, collaborations, competencies, conditions, context, and change. Similarly, this approach starts with leaders focusing on themselves before their teams or organizations. Regardless of approach or theorist, social workers by the nature of their training are already equipped with many competencies that would lend to their being effective leaders.

Social Work Management Competencies

In 1997, The Network for Social Work Management (NSWM) introduced social work management competencies (Wimpfheimer, 2004). These competencies were created by social work leaders who recognized the need for standards to guide social workers working in management. Although leadership is different from management, both are crucial to the successful functioning of an organization. Without the other (i.e., leadership or management, respectively), an organization will never be able to operate at its full potential (Kotter, 2001). The 21 competencies are divided into four domains: executive leadership, strategic management, resource management, and community collaboration. NSWM (2018) identified the following 11 core competencies specific to an executive leader:

1. Establishes the vision, philosophy, goals, objectives, and values of the organization
2. Possesses interpersonal skills that support the viability and positive functioning of the organization
3. Possesses analytical and critical thinking skills that promote organizational growth
4. Models appropriate professional behavior and encourages other staff members to act in a professional manner
5. Manages diversity and cross-cultural understanding
6. Develops and manages both internal and external stakeholder relationships
7. Initiates and facilitates innovative change processes
8. Advocates for public policy change and social justice at national, state, and local levels
9. Demonstrates effective interpersonal and communication skills
10. Encourages active involvement of all staff and stakeholders in decision-making processes
11. Plans, promotes, and models lifelong learning practices

Social work leaders should strive to develop and strengthen these competencies to effectively manage health and human service organizations. Rank and Hutchison (2000) recommend that 21st-century social work leaders be able to (1) build community; (2) communicate well verbally and in writing; and (3) critically analyze social, political, and cultural trends. Although some of what NSWM (2018) and Rank and Hutchison (2000) recommend has been the focus of social work education and training, the vast majority of social work education prepares social workers for micro practice. This focus does not adequately prepare social workers to address the challenges internal and external to their organizations (Fisher, 2009; Sullivan, 2016; Woolever & Kelly, 2014). The social work profession must prioritize leadership development in its curriculum and the development of the social worker as a leader in practice if it intends to maximize its full potential to impact change in our complex world.

Social Work Leadership Development

Mindset is important for leadership (Gottfredson & Reina, 2020). Social workers should always assess their current level of competence to determine where they need improvement. This requires a growth and learning mindset. It is not enough to read literature and studies about leadership. This information must translate to practice. A belief in change and motivation to change is critical for leadership development. Dreyfus and Dreyfus (1986) created a model that describes levels of competence with the acquisition of skills. These levels are novice, beginner, journeyperson, expert, master, and maestro. This model allows one to self-identify their level of competence in a particular area. The NSWM's *Human Services Management Competencies* (2018) provides a similar tool specific to social work and human services professionals. This tool allows one to self-assess where they "stack up" or align with identified competencies. It also provides space for others, including supervisors, to assess one's readiness for leadership. Tools such as these help social workers and other professionals identify where to start with their development.

Training

Once social workers have identified areas for continued development, they must seek out opportunities to acquire these skills. These skills can be learned on the job through shadowing, direct practice, or training. Some organizations may not prioritize talent development. In these circumstances, social workers must take responsibility for securing and in some cases paying for the training they need. Development should not end once an individual completes a field placement and graduates with a social work degree. To become clinically licensed, social workers have to obtain a required number of clinical hours. Then once licensed, they must continue to satisfy continuing education requirements. In our ever-changing world, we must always strive for continued growth and development. Social workers must also commit to learning new skills and technologies outside of their typical area of practice. Social work is a business, and as the world changes, the profession and those in it must adapt to it. This will require agility and innovation, but social workers have what it takes to meet this challenge.

Mentoring

Every professional needs a mentor—someone who can serve as a guide personally, professionally, or both. Mentors can teach and recommend courses of action for their mentees based on their own experience. People who have mentors tend to perform better and advance more quickly in their careers (Gill & Roulet, 2019; Horoszowski, 2020). Mentors are useful at all stages of life and career, and

they can also provide support to help navigate transitions and organizational challenges (Gallo, 2011). Although most people would benefit from having a mentor, many people do not understand the value of mentorship or know the mechanics for finding a mentor. The NSWM created mentoring programs to help address this need within the profession. These programs identify qualified social work leaders and match them to aspiring social work leaders. However, any social worker can and should secure a mentor by first identifying goals, determining what they desire from a mentor, and crafting a plan to secure a mentor. The most productive mentor–mentee relationships are ones in which rapport has been established, there is an identified goal or goals, and the communication is routine and structured. Mentoring relationships in which there is mutual benefit or reciprocity tend to be most successful. Similar to work with clients, mentoring can be short or long term, and it is acceptable to have more than one mentor. Social workers are encouraged to assemble a personal board of advisors. This will allow them to learn from a variety of leaders with different experiences and perspectives.

Networking

Emotionally intelligent leaders must have social skills (Goleman, 1998). Leaders who can establish relationships with others are more persuasive and influential. They have greater networks and are more likely to accomplish goals. Networks provide access to information, skills, and power (Uzzi & Dunlap, 2005). Building a strong network is critical for leaders of all disciplines, including social work. These networks are useful for brainstorming, resource sharing, and the forming of coalitions (Cherry, 2019). Social workers are well versed in relationship building and establishing rapport with their clients. They should use these social skills to establish and build relationships with their colleagues internal and external to their organizations. They should also strive to have networks that are racially diverse and interdisciplinary. All professionals should take the time to assess their networks; identify opportunities for growth; and then, based on their awareness of self and interests, develop a networking plan. This might include identifying potential contacts and connecting with these contacts online through email and social media or in person at a training or conference. Attendance at professional conferences such as those held by NSWM or NASW is an excellent starting place for social workers to expand their networks.

Conclusion

Social workers are leaders. The profession was started by leaders and has sustained itself through social work leadership. However, leadership development is still not a priority for social work education, and social workers who are in leadership roles or leading in other capacities are not as visible. This must change. Social work has been slow to change and adapt to our volatile, uncertain, complex, and ambiguous environment, existing in the background while being the backbone that sustains and supports many of the most vulnerable in society. With their beliefs, values, knowledge, and training, social workers are uniquely positioned to improve society.

Although many researchers have considered what the future of social work looks like, the COVID-19 global pandemic made this inquiry a reality. Social workers had to quickly adapt, manage, innovate, and lead. This quick thinking and ingenuity coupled with an awareness of people, systems, and processes when strengthened would be a powerful force for change.

Social workers can no longer be resistant to change but, rather, must be a force for change. Current and future social workers must invest in and manage themselves.

Knowing the complexities of our world and the challenges our most vulnerable face, social work leadership is needed. Social work leaders must mentor and help develop the next generation of leaders. Those who do not identify as leaders must be bold and courageous and step up to the challenge. This investment in leadership development is an investment in social work's ability to respond effectively to the challenges of the future. It is an investment in racial equity and social justice. It is an investment in social work.

References

Araque, J. C., & Weiss, E. L. (2019). *Leadership with impact: Preparing health and human service professionals in the age of innovation and diversity.* Oxford University Press.

Askenas, R., & Manville, B. (2018, November 7). The fundamentals of leadership still haven't changed. *Harvard Business Review.* https://hbr.org/2018/11/the-fundamentals-of-leadership-still-havent-changed

Beer, M., Finnstrom, M., & Schrader, D. (2016, October). Why leadership training fails—and what to do about it. *Harvard Business Review.* https://hbr.org/2016/10/why-leadership-training-fails-and-what-to-do-about-it

Bourke, J., & Espedido, A. (2020, March 6). The key to inclusive leadership. *Harvard Business Review.* https://hbr.org/2020/03/the-key-to-inclusive-leadership

Brilliant, E. (1986). Social work leadership: A missing ingredient? *Social Work, 31*(5), 325–331. https://www.jstor.org/stable/23713967

Brown, B. (2018). *Dare to lead.* Random House.

Buckingham, M. (2005, March). What great managers do. *Harvard Business Review.* https://hbr.org/2005/03/what-great-managers-do

Cherry, L. (2019). Networking, community partnerships, and social media. In J. C. Araque & E. L. Weiss (Eds.), *Leadership with impact: Preparing health and human service professionals in the age of innovation and diversity* (pp. 138–158). Oxford University Press.

Drucker, P. (2005, January). Managing oneself. *Harvard Business Review.* https://hbr.org/2005/01/managing-oneself

Dreyfus, H., & Dreyfus, S. (1986). *Mind over machine.* The Free Press.

Fisher, E. (2009). Motivation and leadership in social work management: A review of theories and related studies. *Administration in Social Work, 33*(4), 347–367. https://doi.org/10.1080/03643100902769160

Frei, F., & Morriss, A. (2020, May–June). Begin with trust: The first step to becoming a genuinely empowering leader. *Harvard Business Review.* https://hbr.org/2020/05/begin-with-trust

Gallo, A. (2011, February 11). Demystifying mentoring. *Harvard Business Review.* https://hbr.org/2011/02/demystifying-mentoring

Giles, S. (2016, March 15). The most important leadership competencies, according to leaders around the world. *Harvard Business Review.* https://hbr.org/2016/03/the-most-important-leadership-competencies-according-to-leaders-around-the-world

Gill, M., & Roulet, T. (2019, March 1). Stressed at work? Mentoring a colleague could help. *Harvard Business Review.* https://hbr.org/2019/03/stressed-at-work-mentoring-a-colleague-could-help

Goleman, D. (2004, January). What makes a leader? *Harvard Business Review.* https://hbr.org/2004/01/what-makes-a-leader

Goleman, D. (2013, December). The focused leader. *Harvard Business Review.* https://hbr.org/2013/12/the-focused-leader

Gottfredson, R., & Reina, C. (2020, January 17). To be a great leader, you need the right mindset. *Harvard Business Review.* https://hbr.org/2020/01/to-be-a-great-leader-you-need-the-right-mindset

Holosko, M. (2009). Social work leadership: Identifying core attributes. *Journal of Human Behavior in the Social Environment, 19*(4), 448–459.

Horoszowski, M. (2020, January 21). How to build a great relationship with a mentor. *Harvard Business Review.* https://hbr.org/2020/01/how-to-build-a-great-relationship-with-a-mentor?referral=03759&cm_vc=rr_item_page.bottom

Kotter, J. (2001, December). What leaders really do. *Harvard Business Review.* https://hbr.org/2001/12/what-leaders-really-do

Kunreuther, F., & Thomas-Breitfeld, S. (2017). Race to lead: Confronting the nonprofit racial leadership gap. https://buildingmovement.org/reports/race-to-lead-confronting-the-nonprofit-racial-leadership-gap/

Mor Barak, M. E. (2017). Inclusive leadership: Unlocking the diversity potential. In M. E. Mor Barak (Ed.), *Managing diversity: Toward a globally inclusive workplace* (pp. 1–21). Sage.

National Association of Social Workers. (2017). *Read the code of ethics.* https://www.socialworkers.org/About/Ethics/Code-of-Ethics/Code-of-Ethics-English

Northouse, P. (2016). *Leadership: Theory and practice* (7th ed.). Sage.

Prentice, W. C. H. (2004, January). Understanding leadership. *Harvard Business Review.* https://hbr.org/2004/01/understanding-leadership

Rank, M., & Hutchison, W. S. (2000). An analysis of leadership within the social work profession. *Journal of Social Work Education, 36*(3), 487–502. https://doi.org/10.1080/10437797.2000.10779024

Sullivan, W. P. (2016). Leadership in social work: Where are we? *Journal of Social Work Education, 52* (1) S51-S61. https://doi.org/10.1080/10437797.2016.1174644

The Network for Social Work Management. (2018). Human services management competencies. https://socialworkmanager.org/wp-content/uploads/2018/12/HSMC-Guidebook-December-2018.pdf

Tropman, J., & Wooten, L. (2013). The 7C approach to conceptualizing administration: Executive leadership in the 21st century. *Administration in Social Work, 37*(4), 325–328. https://doi.org/10.1080/03643107.2013.831714

Uzzi, B., & Dunlap, S. (2005). How to build your network. *Harvard Business Review.* https://hbr.org/2005/12/how-to-build-your-network

Westfall, C. (2019, June 20). Leadership development is a $366 billion industry: Here's why most programs don't work. *Forbes.* https://www.forbes.com/sites/chriswestfall/2019/06/20/leadership-development-why-most-programs-dont-work/#31fae40361de

Wimpfheimer, S. (2004). Leadership and management competencies defined by practicing social work managers: An overview of standards developed by the national network for social work managers. *Administration in Social Work, 28*(1), 45–56. https://doi.org/10.1300/J147v28n01_04

Woolever, J., & Kelly, J. (2014). Leadership and leadership development. In *Encyclopedia of social work.* NASW Press/Oxford University Press.

Disasters in Times of Sheltering in Place

Social Work and the COVID-19 Pandemic

Daphne S. Cain

The COVID-19 Pandemic

The COVID-19 (coronavirus) pandemic was first identified in Wuhan, China, in December 2019 (Huang et al., 2020). The World Health Organization (WHO) declared COVID-19 a public health emergency of international concern on January 30, 2020, and a pandemic on March 11 (WHO, 2020a). As of mid-June 2021, more than 175 million cases of COVID-19 had been reported worldwide, resulting in more than 3.8 million deaths (WHO, 2020b).

The virus is primarily spread between people during close contact via small virulent droplets produced by coughing, sneezing, and talking, with less common infection spread by touching a contaminated surface and then touching one's face (WHO, 2020b). The COVID-19 virus can be spread by people who do not show active symptoms, as well as by symptomatic carriers (WHO, 2020b). Common symptoms of the virus include fever, cough, fatigue, shortness of breath, and a loss of sense of smell and taste (WHO, 2020b). Disease complications can include pneumonia and acute respiratory distress [Centers for Disease Control and Prevention (CDC), 2020a]. The time from exposure to onset of symptoms ranges from 2 to 14 days, with an average onset of 5 days (Velavan & Meyer, 2020). To date, there are 15 different vaccines being administered around the world (WHO, 2020b).

Preventive measures include handwashing, covering one's mouth when coughing, maintaining 6 feet of distance between people, wearing a facial mask in public settings, and monitoring for symptoms and self-isolating if symptoms arise or exposure to the virus is confirmed (WHO, 2020b). Nationally, authorities have employed the following measures in response to the pandemic: quarantine and shelter-in-place orders, travel restrictions, the temporary closing of nonessential businesses, implementation of restrictive policies governing essential businesses (including required facial mask wearing, social distancing, and temperature checks), increasing COVID-19 testing of symptomatic and asymptomatic individuals, tracing contacts among infected persons, and launching coronavirus vaccine trials. The pandemic has caused global social and economic disruption, including the largest U.S.

global recession since the Great Depression (Horsley, 2020).

The coronavirus pandemic has also disrupted the provision of social work services ranging from child welfare and school social work to clinical and psychiatric social work. The CDC (2020b) warns that the fear and anxiety associated with a novel disease can be overwhelming and cause strong emotions in both adults and children, and it encourages individuals to monitor their stress and anxiety and to seek mental health services when needed.

COVID-19 and Vulnerable and Marginalized Populations

Wilson (2020) notes, "The primary mission of the social work profession is to enhance human well-being and help meet the basic human needs of all people, with particular attention to the needs and empowerment of people who are vulnerable, oppressed, and living in poverty" (p. 1). Based on this core mission, social work professionals are concerned for the most vulnerable and marginalized members of society who may be disproportionately impacted by the COVID-19 pandemic.

Prior research suggests that members of vulnerable populations are less prepared for disaster such as a pandemic (Baker et al., 2012). These vulnerable groups include children (Brymer et al., 2006; Hayashi & Tomita, 2012), individuals who are medically frail and older (Barusch, 2011; Torgusen & Kosberg, 2006), individuals with serious mental illness and disabilities (Fox et al., 2010), pregnant women and mothers with young children, and individuals with substance use disorders (Amaratunga & O'Sullivan, 2006; Brymer et al., 2006). In addition, economically disadvantaged and minority communities are at greater

risk due in part to a lack of resources (Elliott & Pais, 2006; Zakour & Harrell, 2003).

In particular, older adults—those aged 60 years or older—appear to be at greater risk for coronavirus infection, especially those residing in nursing homes and long-term care facilities (CDC, 2020c). The Centers for Medicare and Medicaid Services (CMS) announced that nursing homes, skilled nursing facilities, and assisted living facilities should discourage visits and screen visitors for COVID-19 symptoms (Wilson, 2020). These requirements may reduce COVID-19 exposure; however, they may also lead to further medical complications associated with mental decline. Social isolation measures place limits on a family's ability to monitor elder care, and according to the American Association of Retired Persons, social isolation and loneliness are serious health issues among older adults (Tan, 2020).

Due to orders for schools to close to in-person instruction, low-income children are at risk of missing daily nutritious meals provided through free and reduced-price meals programs. Long-term school closures could lead to widespread food insecurity for impoverished school-aged children (Wilson, 2020). Children and families involved with the foster care system are also at risk. The foster care system is built on frequent in-person case worker investigations, supervision, service referral, and regular family visitation. Child welfare workers may be anxious about completing investigations and providing in-person services due to the fear of the spread of the virus. Potential foster families may decline to accept new children into their homes due to fear of family infection. Family courts throughout the country have suspended hearings regarding abuse and neglect adjudications and court-ordered child removal, leaving children in potential danger for longer and with less family monitoring and leaving children and families in limbo with regard to reunification (Kramer, 2020). Alternative services, including video conferencing between foster homes, group homes, and parents, have been recommended during the shelter-in-place orders; however, the availability of technology to meet these needs varies widely (Kramer, 2020).

In addition, although the federal government has not issued a mandatory stay-at-home order, 42 states, the District of Colombia, and Puerto Rico urged people to stay at home, accounting for 95% of the population (Mervosh et al., 2020). These stay-at-home orders have helped contain the spread of the coronavirus (Terry, 2020), but the national lockdown has also cost the nation in the form of massive unemployment. As of late May 2020, 38.6 million American workers had filed for unemployment benefits, rivaling the economic crisis of the Great Depression (Romm et al., 2020), and low-wage, hourly employees were disproportionately impacted. The COVID-19 pandemic has exposed the gaps in our national safety net with regard to low-income Americans and the inadequacy of state unemployment insurance systems.

COVID-19 will have a significant effect on the economic stability of low-income families, especially hourly wage earners who may lack health insurance and annual and sick leave (Wilson, 2020). In the United States, access to health insurance is tied to employment; therefore, the rise in unemployment rates has also triggered a corresponding rise in uninsured Americans, including both workers and their family members (Wilson, 2020). With this loss in employer-sponsored insurance, Medicaid enrollments have also increased (Moran, 2020). Thus, with the projected increases in unemployment caused by the pandemic, low-income Americans may face an even greater economic crisis.

Marginalized individuals residing in congregate living institutions such as jails, prisons, and immigrant detention centers are highly vulnerable to COVID-19 because these confined environments are incubators for infectious disease (Wilson, 2020). Immigrant families are also at greater risk because of their reluctance to seek medical attention due to fear of detention and/or deportation. The homeless population is also at risk. Many individuals experiencing homelessness live in congregate settings, including shelters, halfway houses, abandoned buildings, and encampments (Wilson, 2020). These living situations make regular hygiene difficult and heightened COVID-19 hygiene practices nearly impossible, leaving them at greater risk for virus transmission.

Data also show that African Americans are more likely to die from COVID-19 (Nania, 2020), suggesting that the social determinants of health, including health disparities such as inequalities in access to medical care, increase the risks of COVID-19 infection and complications leading to death (Wilson, 2020). Understanding and addressing the social determinants of health, including removing barriers to access to health care and providing testing and treatment for individuals without health insurance, are essential for reducing the morbidity and mortality rates in communities of color (Wilson, 2020). Outbreaks in rural communities with fewer health care resources have also resulted in higher coronavirus death rates (Galvin, 2020). To provide greater service availability, telehealth has become an important intervention for responding to COVID-19 (Wilson, 2020).

Telehealth

CMS has issued guidance on expanding the use of telehealth to cope with the COVID-19 public health emergency [National Association of Social Workers (NASW), 2020a]. Telehealth is "the use of telecommunications technologies to deliver health-related services and information that support patient care, administrative activities, and health education" (American Academy of Pediatrics,

2020, p. 1). An integral component of the future of health care, telehealth has the potential to provide health-related benefits, including greater access to care—especially in underserved areas—at a reduced cost. Under the CMS COVID-19 guidelines, licensed clinical social workers can be reimbursed at the same rate as that for in-person services for telehealth using communication technology, allowing real-time, two-way interactive communication including smartphones with video chat, Apple FaceTime, Skype, and video conferencing (NASW, 2020a).

Although the use of telemedicine and teletherapy is in its infancy, the COVID-19 pandemic and associated shelter-in-place mandates have shone a spotlight on the potential benefits of their use for social work practice, especially with vulnerable and underserved communities. Investment in educational opportunities to improve telehealth and teletherapy services is needed. Improving telecommunications nationally is also imperative. The pandemic introduced many social workers to telehealth, and this new and innovative practice paradigm seems essential for social work services in the future.

The U.S. 2020 Presidential Election, 2020 Census, and Social Work

The situation surrounding the novel coronavirus is further complicated by important intersecting events, including the 2020 presidential election and the 2020 Census, that may further negatively impact marginalized and vulnerable groups important to social work in unique ways. For the first time since the Spanish Flu pandemic of 1918, a U.S. presidential election may be jeopardized by the coronavirus pandemic. Social distancing policies designed to slow the spread of the virus will make in-person campaign rallies, nominating conventions, and in-person voting more difficult (Allen & Scott, 2017; Krimmer et al., 2020). The Brennan Center has recommended a number of ways to ensure the 2020 election will be free, fair, accessible, and secure. The Brennan Center recommends expanding early voting, universal vote-by-mail options, voter registration modifications including expanded online registration, and widespread voter education (Weiser & Feldman, 2020). Furthermore, the national 2020 Census coincides with the coronavirus pandemic. The potential disruptions in the U.S. Census Bureau's population count could impact data used to determine congressional representation; the number of Electoral College votes each state gets for the next 10 years; factors determining the redrawing of voting districts; and the share of federal funding for public services important to social work, including health care, schools, and community infrastructure that is sent to states (Homeland Security Today, 2020; Wilson, 2020).

Social Work Safety and Health During the COVID-19 Pandemic

NASW (2020b) has issued guidelines for safe social work practice during the COVID-19 pandemic. Following CDC (2020d) recommendations, NASW (2020b) and Berkowitz (2020) recommend the following to avoid the spread of COVID-19 in social work settings:

- Stay home when sick with flu-like illness.
- Wash hands frequently with soap and water for 20 seconds, or use an alcohol-based hand sanitizer.
- Avoid touching nose, mouth, and eyes, and cover coughs and sneezes.

- Keep frequently touched common surfaces, including telephones and computer equipment, clean.
- Do not use other workers' phones, desks, offices, or other work tools or equipment unless first cleaned with a disinfectant.
- Increase physical distancing between people to 6 feet.
- Protective face coverings should be required.

For private or group social work practices, NASW (2020b) recommends the following:

- Follow all CDC guidelines on cleaning and hygiene protocols for the workplace (CDC, 2020e).
- Through multiple channels, inform clients that you are implementing COVID-19 safety measures, including cleaning, arrangement of furniture, and flexible cancellation policies to reduce exposures from ill or potentially ill clients.
- Consider offering clients teletherapy options that meet their needs.
- Review malpractice insurance policies regarding provisions around telemedicine and teletherapy.

As a social work professional, you may want to engage in the national and community responses to the COVID-19 pandemic and the emerging public health crisis. NASW (2020b) recommends the following:

- Engage in national or local health care policy discussions and development.
- Engage in advocacy efforts on behalf of marginalized and vulnerable COVID–19 patients.
- Send letters to congressional leaders seeking COVID-19 relief for social workers and underserved communities.
- Implement evidence-informed COVID-19 policies and practices.

- Share community-based resources with clients and colleagues.

Guidelines for Reopening Social Work Practices After Sheltering in Place

During the COVID-19 emergency, states and localities issued emergency stay-at-home orders requiring the temporary closure of non-essential businesses, including some private social work practices. Following the stay-at-home orders and recommendations, many clinical social work practitioners began providing services virtually. With stay-at-home orders being lifted throughout the country, NASW (2020c) has provided guidelines on resuming in-person services for solo and group social work practitioners.

NASW (2000c) suggests that the decision to resume in-person social work service be based on local ordinances, laws, and recommendations. Furthermore, the context of regional and local circumstances, and professional and personal considerations, must also be considered. For example, NASW (2000c) recommends the following be considered:

- The age and medical condition(s) of the practitioner(s), and the age and underlying medical condition(s) of those in the practitioner's household
- Client demographics (including health status, risk factors and behaviors, and age)
- Physical characteristics of the office setting, including the size of therapy rooms, size of waiting areas, ventilation system(s), use of shared office spaces, and public access to restrooms
- Practitioner and client interest in and ability to provide effective virtual services, taking into consideration the client's access

to technology and their ability to utilize telehealth/teletherapy services

Furthermore, practitioners should develop pre-opening plans that include the following (NASW, 2020c):

- A soft-reopening plan to include a smaller volume of in-person clients—retaining some continued virtual clients until social distancing is no longer recommended.
- The provision of personal protective equipment (PPE) for the practitioner and other employees—maintain some PPE for clients who may not have protective equipment.
- Plans for potential COVID-19 exposure in the work environment, including alternative staffing needs and deep cleaning of work areas.
- Plans for how long employees will be asked to quarantine after exposure to COVID-19, and a plan for medical clearances prior to returning to work with periodic COVID-19 testing.
- Bringing employees back to in-person work spaces in phases, or working on alternating days, or different times during the day, to reduce contact and achieve social distancing.
- Allow only clients and those who participate in treatment with the client into the office for scheduled appointments.
- Schedule repair and maintenance work outside of normal work hours to minimize in-person contact.
- Rearrange waiting areas, receptionist areas, and shared spaces to increase distance between individuals.
- Remove items from the work area that are commonly touched and shared, such as coffee pots, reusable dishware and utensils (replace with disposable items), and vending machines.
- Post signs on entrance doors and in offices to direct flow of movement (entrance or exit only doors, one-way direction in hallways).

- Make hand sanitizer and tissue available in all offices.
- Disinfect all doorknobs, desks, chairs, telephones, and other commonly touched items after every session.
- Increase ventilation of office spaces as much as possible with open doors and windows.

Providers may want to update their policies and procedural manuals to alert clients and staff of COVID-19–specific changes, such as new office hours, cancellation policies (e.g., allowing for last-minute cancellations due to potential virus exposure and/or infection), the mandatory use of PPE, new waiting area rules, changes to informed consent forms, and how coworkers and clients will be informed if they come into contact with an employee or client who tests positive for COVID-19 (NASW, 2020c). Providers will want to post the new policies in common areas and have clients and staff sign the new policy agreement(s), and practitioners will want to reiterate new policies to clients during scheduled visits (NASW, 2020c). Prior to returning to in-person practice, practitioners may also want to contact their medical malpractice and general liability insurance providers to discuss current coverage and whether additional insurance may be warranted (NASW, 2020c).

Conclusion

As the world recovers from the COVID-19 pandemic, social work practice will adjust to the needs of our client groups. Our most vulnerable and marginalized populations will experience greater impacts on their health; welfare; economic stability; and access to medical care, education, and technology. Social work will have a valuable role to play in the amelioration of negative impacts that are devastating the United States and the world. The infusion of telemedicine and teletherapy in social work practice seems inevitable, and it is hoped that these will provide an efficient and effective new social work practice modality.

References

Allen, P. D., & Scott, J. L. (2017). Disaster after disaster: Unexpected thousand-year floods and presidential elections. *Reflections: Narratives of Professional Helping, 23*(2), 53–59.

Amaratunga, C. A., & O'Sullivan, T. L. (2006). In the path of disasters: Psychosocial issues for preparedness, response, and recovery. *Prehospital and Disaster Medicine, 21*(3), 149–155.

American Academy of Pediatrics. (2020). *What is telehealth?* https://www.aap.org/en-us/professional-resources/practice-transformation/telehealth/Pages/What-is-Telehealth.aspx

Baker, M. D., Baker, L. R., & Flagg, L. A. (2012). Preparing families of children with special health care needs for disasters: An education intervention. *Social Work in Health Care, 51*, 417–429.

Barusch, A. S. (2011). Disaster, vulnerability, and older adults: Toward a social work response. *Journal of Gerontological Social Work, 54*, 347–350.

Berkowitz, D. (2020). *Worker safety and health during COVID-19 pandemic: Rights and resources.* National Employment Law Project. https://www.nelp.org/publication/worker-safety-health-during-covid-19-pandemic-rights-resources/

Brymer, M., Jacobs, A., Layne, C., Pynoos, R., Ruzek, J., Steinberg, A., Vernberg, E., & Watson, P. (2006). Psychological first aid: Field operations guide (2nd ed.). National Child Traumatic Stress Network. http://www.nctsn.org/content/psychological-first-aid

Centers for Disease Control and Prevention. (2020a). *Interim clinical guidance for management of patients with confirmed coronavirus disease (COVID-19).* https://www.cdc.gov/coronavirus/2019-ncov/hcp/clinical-guidance-management-patients.html

Centers for Disease Control and Prevention. (2020b). *COVID–19: Coping with stress.* https://www.cdc.gov/coronavirus/2019-ncov/daily-life-coping/managing-stress-anxiety.html

Centers for Disease Control and Prevention. (2020c). *Responding to COVID-19 in nursing homes.* https://www.cdc.gov/coronavirus/2019-ncov/hcp/long-term-care.html

Centers for Disease Control and Prevention. (2020d). *Social workers.* https://npin.cdc.gov/audiences/social-workers

Centers for Disease Control and Prevention. (2020e). *Reopening guidance for cleaning and disinfecting public spaces, workplaces, businesses, schools, and homes.* https://www.cdc.gov/coronavirus/2019-ncov/community/reopen-guidance.html

Elliott, J. R., & Pais, J. (2006). Race, class, and Hurricane Katrina: Social differences in human responses to disaster. *Social Science Research, 35*, 295–321.

Fox, M. H., White, G. W., Rooney, C., & Cahill, A. (2010). The psychosocial impact of Hurricane Katrina on persons with disabilities and independent living center staff living on the American Gulf Coast. *Rehabilitation Psychology, 55*(3), 231–240.

Galvin, G. (2020, April 30). Rural counties seeing faster growth in COVID-19 cases, deaths. *U.S. News.* https://www.usnews.com/news/healthiest-communities/articles/2020-04-30/coronavirus-cases-deaths-growing-at-faster-rates-in-rural-areas

Hayashi, K., & Tomita, N. (2012). Lessons learned from the Great East Japan Earthquake: Impact on child and adolescent health. *Asia-Pacific Journal of Public Health, 24*(4), 681–688.

Homeland Security Today. (2020). *COVID-19 presents delays and risks to census count.* https://www.hstoday.us/subject-matter-areas/infrastructure-security/covid-19-presents-delays-and-risks-to-census-count

Horsley, S. (2020). *IMF warns of steepest recession since the Great Depression.* NPR. https://www.npr.org/sections/coronavirus-live-updates/2020/04/14/833995714/imf-warns-of-steepest-downturn-since-the-great-depression

Huang, C., Wang, Y., Li, X., Ren, L., Zhao, J., Hu, Y., Zhang, L., Fan, G., Xu, J., Gu, X., Cheng, Z., Yu, T., Xia, J., Wei, Y., Wu, W., Xie, X., Yin, W., Li, H., Liu, M., . . . Cao, B. (2020). Clinical features of patients infected with 2019 novel coronavirus in Wuhan, China. *Lancet, 395*(10223), 497–506. https://www.sciencedirect.com/science/article/pii/S0140673620301835

Kramer, A. (2020). *Covid-19 paused family reunification cases: They're resuming, but at what pace?* The New School Center for New York City Affairs. https://www.centernyc.org/reports-briefs/2020/4/20/covid-19-paused-family-reunification-cases-theyre-resuming-but-at-what-pace?rq=Covid%2019%20paused%20Family%20reunification%20cases

Krimmer, R., Duenas-Cid, D., & Krivonosova, J. (2020, May 22). Debate: Safeguarding democracy during pandemics. Social distancing, postal, or internet voting—the good, the bad or the ugly? Public Money & Management, 41, 8–10. https://www.tandfonline.com/doi/pdf/10.1080/09540962.2020.1766222?needAccess=true

Mervosh, S., Lu, D., & Swales, V. (2020). See which states and cities have told residents to stay at home. The

New York Times. https://www.nytimes.com/interactive/2020/us/coronavirus-stay-at-home-order.html

Moran, L. (2020, May 22). *Rising Medicaid rolls: COVID-19's impact on Medicaid enrollment and state budgets*. Center for Health Care Strategies. https://www.chcs.org/news/rising-medicaid-rolls-the-impact-of-covid-19-on-medicaid-enrollment-and-state-budgets

Nania, R. (2020, June 3). *Studies show heavy toll of COVID-19 on African Americans*. American Association of Retired Persons. https://www.aarp.org/health/conditions-treatments/info-2020/covid-burden-minorities.html

National Association of Social Workers. (2020a). Telehealth. https://www.socialworkers.org/Practice/Infectious-Diseases/Coronavirus/Telehealth

National Association of Social Workers. (2020b). Social work safety. https://www.socialworkers.org/Practice/Infectious-Diseases/Coronavirus/Social-Work-Safety

National Association of Social Workers. (2020c, May). COVID-19: Practice guidelines for reopening social work practices. https://www.socialworkers.org/LinkClick.aspx?fileticket=akHuTIoFNPM%3d&portalid=0

Romm, T., Stein, J., & Werner, E. (2020). 2.4 million Americans filed jobless claims last week, bringing nine-week total to 38.6 million. *The Washington Post*. https://www.washingtonpost.com/business/2020/05/21/unemployment-claims-coronavirus

Tan, E. (2020, March 16). *How to fight the social isolation of coronavirus*. American Association of Retired Persons. https://www.aarp.org/health/conditions-treatments/info-2020/coronavirus-social-isolation-loneliness.html

Terry, K. (2020, May 15). *Stay-at-home orders correlated with slower COVID-19 spread*. Medscape. https://www.medscape.com/viewarticle/930614

Torgusen, B., & Kosberg, J. I. (2006). Assisting older victims of disasters: Roles and responsibilities for social workers. *Journal of Gerontological Social Work, 47*(1–2), 27–44.

Velavan, T. P., & Meyer, C. G. (2020). The COVID-19 epidemic. *Tropical Medicine & International Health, 25*(3), 278–280.

Weiser, W. R., & Feldman, M. (2020, March 16). *How to protect the 2020 vote from the coronavirus*. Brennan Center for Justice. https://www.brennancenter.org/our-work/policy-solutions/how-protect-2020-vote-coronavirus

Wilson, M. (2020). *Social justice brief: Implications of Coronavirus (COVID-19) for America's vulnerable and marginalized populations*. National Association of Social Workers. https://www.socialworkers.org/LinkClick.aspx?fileticket=U7tEKlRldOU%3d&portalid=0

World Health Organization. (2020a, April 27). *WHO timeline–COVID-19*. https://www.who.int/news-room/detail/27-04-2020-who-timeline---covid-19

World Health Organization. (2020b). *Q & A on coronaviruses (COVID-19)*. http://www.emro.who.int/health-topics/corona-virus/questions-and-answers.html

Zakour, M. J., & Harrell, E. B. (2003). Access to disaster services: Social work interventions for vulnerable populations. *Journal of Social Service Research, 30*(2), 27–54.

Suicide

An Overview

Jonathan B. Singer

Scope of the Problem

In the 20 minutes it takes you to read this chapter, two people will die by suicide in the United States and another 28 will die by suicide in the rest of the world (Centers for Disease Control and Prevention, 2021; World Health Organization, 2021). In 2018, the most recent year for death statistics in the United States, more than 48,000 Americans died by suicide and more than 800,000 people died worldwide. These suicide deaths are tragic, in part because they were people who thought that the world would be better off without them and in part because of the grief and loss experienced by those left behind. Research by social work professor and past president of the American Association of Suicidology, Julie Cerel, found that for every person who died by suicide in the United States, 135 people were affected, totaling nearly 5.5 million U.S. residents every year who lose someone to suicide (Cerel et al., 2019).

One life lost to suicide is one life too many. The tragedy of suicide is particularly acute in Native/Indigenous communities, LGTBQIA+ communities, and increasingly in Latinx and African American communities.

Research by social work professors Michael Lindsey and Sean Joe found that African American youth were the only racial or ethnic group that evidenced a significant increase in suicide ideation and attempt in the 25 years between 1991 and 2017 (Lindsey et al., 2019). Among elementary-aged youth, African American youth are twice as likely to die by suicide as White youth (Bridge et al., 2018). Although beyond the scope of this chapter to explore, it is essential for all social workers to understand that one of the solutions to the problem of rising rates of youth suicide risk is addressing the racial and economic injustice in the United States. If we want a world in which people feel as if their lives are worth living, we cannot have a society that says that some lives are worth more than others.

Terminology
Preferred and Problematic Terms

Serious Versus Nonserious Attempts

This construct is problematic because framing any suicide attempt as nonserious diminishes the pain that the person who made the attempt is experiencing. Dese'Rae Stage (2020), suicide attempt survivor and founder of the Live Through This Project, describes it as follows:

> There is a lot of harm done by this hierarchy, wherein people who have made "less serious" attempts don't feel their pain is validated by folks they encounter, from their support systems, to law enforcement, to medical professionals. I cannot tell you the number of people who have said to me, "I don't know if you want to hear my story. My attempt wasn't particularly violent/serious." The fact that anyone feels or thinks that breaks my heart.

The preferred terminology describes the injury of the attempt. Although imperfect, a suicide attempt results in no injury or a nonfatal injury that significantly impairs one's life. This is described in more detail later.

Failed Suicide Attempt/ Successful Suicide

Any construct in which living is framed as failure and death is framed as a success is problematic. The preferred terminology eliminates the words failed and successful.

Committed Suicide

Feedback from suicide attempt survivors and loss survivors suggested that the term "committed" had negative connotations, such as committed murder or committed rape. The preferred term is "died by suicide" or "killed themselves." To read a case study about how preferred and problematic terms can affect clinical documentation, see Singer and Erreger (2015).

Key Terms and Challenges in Defining Suicide Risk

1. *Suicidal ideation* is thoughts about ending one's own life. Suicidal ideation is distinct from nonsuicidal morbid ideation, which is thoughts about one's death but not self-inflicted. The following example distinguishes the two: "When I was younger, I thought about dying a lot. I thought about the roof collapsing, or a car smashing into our car, or getting hit by a stray bullet and dying [*nonsuicidal morbid ideation*]. When I was 14, I remember getting into the car and thinking, 'when I'm old enough to drive, I'm going to kill myself but make it look like an accident so you, my parents, aren't doubly sad' [*suicidal ideation*]."

2. *Suicide attempt* is any action that someone takes to end their life. The attempt can result in no injury or a nonfatal injury. This might seem like an esoteric distinction, but it has important practical implications. Imagine someone has thoughts of suicide and wants to die. They reach for a bottle of pills with the intention of killing themselves by overdosing. Do they have to take any pills for it to count as a suicide attempt? No. The important part is the intention behind their action—to end their life. Injury is ancillary. Reaching for the bottle with the intention of ending one's life, regardless of whether it results in injury, qualifies as a suicide attempt. If they stop themselves, it is called an *aborted* attempt. If someone else stops them, it is called an *interrupted* attempt.

3. *Suicide* is an intentional self-inflicted fatal injury. Like suicide attempt, the concept of suicide seems straightforward. In practice, however, there are many factors that complicate making the determination that a death was self-inflicted and intentional. The person who can confirm intention is

dead. If someone said to you on Monday, "I'm going to kill myself by stepping in front of a bus," and on Wednesday they were hit by a bus and died, how confident would you be that they stepped in front of a bus with the intention of dying?

Why Do People Die by Suicide?

Counter to popular opinion, most people do not die by suicide because of a mental illness. A 2018 report found that 54% of suicide decedents were not known to have mental health conditions. Distinguishing suicidal thoughts and behaviors from diagnoses can help us avoid the trap of thinking that someone was suicidal because of underlying pathology. There are many reasons why people die by suicide.

Sociologist Emil Durkheim was the first person to conduct an empirical study of suicide (Durkheim, 1952/1897). His study suggested that people killed themselves because they felt that they did not belong (egoistic), they were unimportant in society (altruistic), they were morally adrift because of societal upheaval or lack of structure (anomic), or they were overburdened by societal restrictions (fatalistic). Although Durkheim's theory was proposed in 1897, many of his ideas inform current thinking about suicide (for an update of Durkheim's theory, see Mueller & Abrutyn, 2016).

Ideation-to-Action Frameworks

Since 2005, four theories, collectively known as ideation-to-action frameworks, have emerged that try to explain how people move from having thoughts of suicide to nonfatal or fatal suicide attempts. Klonsky, Saffer, and Bryan (2018) suggested that these frameworks view the processes involved in developing suicidal desire and suicidal behaviors as different.

The frameworks include: the interpersonal-psychological theory of suicide, the integrated motivational-volitional model, the three step theory, and the fluid vulnerability theory. Although space limitations prevent a thorough review of each theory, a brief review of the most well-researched framework, the interpersonal theory of suicide (IPTS; Van Orden et al., 2010), is instructive.

Interpersonal Theory of Suicide

The IPTS suggests that there are three conditions that have to be present for someone to die by suicide: thwarted belonging (i.e., loneliness), perceived burdensomeness (i.e., being a burden to others or society), and acquired capacity to kill oneself (i.e., given the means, the suicidal person could go through with it). When someone is lonely and views themself as a burden, they can develop the desire to kill themself. It is only once the third condition is met, the capacity to die, that fatal or not-fatal suicide attempts occur.

The IPTS has several implications for social workers. First, social connectedness is important because it give people a sense of belonging. The counter, social isolation (which Durkheim called egoistic), is one of the Social Work Grand Challenges and is frequently reported in suicide cases. Second, burdensomeness (which Durkheim called anomic) can occur because someone is unemployed, incarcerated, or is putting their family's health at risk (e.g., underpaid and underprotected essential workers during the COVID-19 pandemic), among other reasons. The counter is having a sense of purpose. Finally, acquiring the capacity occurs over time and is the construct with the weakest empirical support. However, there is evidence that adults who as youth engaged in nonsuicidal self-injury repeatedly, especially when they were feeling bad about themselves, are more likely to report suicidal thoughts and attempts. Helping youth find alternatives to nonsuicidal self-injury might reduce suicide risk in adulthood.

Suicide Risk Assessment

The following are purposes of suicide risk assessment:

- Understand the story of how and why someone became suicidal (Freedenthal, 2017)
- Identify points of prevention rather than prediction (Pisani et al., 2016). After the suicide risk assessment, the social worker, client, and family or friends should know what stressors or conditions might exacerbate the current suicide risk and have a plan to prevent those from happening. This contrasts with the traditional view of the suicide risk assessment as a tool for predicting the near future.
- Provide an experience of being seen, heard, and validated

For more details on suicide assessment, see Part XII on youth suicide.

Safety Planning

Safety planning is an empirically supported intervention shown to reduce suicide risk in youth and adults (Stanley & Brown, 2012; Stanley et al., 2018). Although it has been described as an update to the "no suicide contract" popular in the mid-1980s and mid-1990s, it shares only the signature line in common (Bryan et al., 2017). One of the reasons why safety planning appears to be effective when "no suicide contracts" were dangerous is because it is a conversation between the clinician, the client, and the client's family and friends. The safety plan is like a recovery plan or service plan in that it identifies specific action your client will take in order to achieve a goal. In this case, the goal is to be distracted from suicidal thoughts to temporarily reduce distress and experience

temporary relief. It also serves the function of connecting the suicidal person to friends and loved ones at a time when the person often feels disconnected from social supports.

Developing a safety plan is intended to be a collaborative process. Most people will be able to identify all of the action items on their own; others will need support from the social worker to brainstorm ideas; and in some cases the person will not be able to think of anything, leaving the social worker to make recommendations. Although the latter is generally discouraged in clinical relationships, when someone is in a suicidal crisis and experiencing cognitive constriction or is ruminating in the emotional brain, accessing the problem-solving functions of the prefrontal cortex can be challenging. The safety plan serves as a proxy to the functions of the prefrontal cortex during a time when people are most in need of problem-solving.

There are seven main sections in safety planning, each of which draws on client and community strengths and resources. The following is written as if you are speaking to the client:

1. Red flags: These are things that let you know you are not doing well. Write down a couple of things that let you know and let others know that you are moving into the suicide zone. These can be the same things or different.
2. Things I can do by myself: Imagine you are alone on a desert island with very good Wi-Fi. What can you do to temporarily distract yourself from your suicidal thoughts and feelings? What do you do that makes you feel good, at least temporarily?
3. Places I can go: Sometimes getting a change of scenery is distracting. Assuming there is no shelter-in-place order, what are some places you like to go?
4. People I can count on: Who can you reach out to for distraction and temporary relief?

These are not professionals such as therapists, doctors, or clergy. These are friends and family members whom you can call or chat who will support you unconditionally. You do not have to talk with these folks about your suicidal thoughts, nor should you say that everything is fine.

5. My list: Now we are going to rank order the items from 2, 3, and 4. The next time you need to be distracted, what is the first thing you want to do from your list? It could be something you do on your own, a place, or another person.

6. Professionals: After you have gone through everything on your list, if you are still having suicidal thoughts or feelings, are still distressed, or just want to talk with someone who has professional training and experience in this, write down the names and phone numbers of the professionals you would call. This could include mental health and medical professionals, crisis lines, clergy, among others.

7. Making your environment safe: If you have thought of how you would end your life, now is the time to make a promise to your current and future self that you will stay alive. One way you can keep that promise is by removing any lethal methods until you are out of this current suicidal crisis. This could mean having a neighbor hold on to your firearms and bullets, having someone take sharp objects, pills, and so forth.

Means Restriction

The academic way of saying "making your environment safe" is *means restriction*. For nearly 100 years, the first recommendation for reducing suicide risk has been to reduce access to lethal means. Mintz (1966) noted that "in 1931 Fairbank reported on a careful study, undertaken at the suggestion of Dr. Adolph Meyer, of 100 suicide attempts. Her conclusions regarding prevention include the following: '. . . I would suggest the restriction of the loose handling of firearms, poisons and sedatives'" (p. 898).

Means restriction has been shown to be an effective micro and macro suicide prevention strategy (Anestis et al., 2017; Sale et al., 2018). At the micro level, means restriction is a conversation between you and your client and their family/friends about how they will temporarily remove and limit access to the person's method(s) of choice (see the Suicide Prevention Resource Center's website at http://sprc.org for a free online training called "Counseling on Access to Lethal Means"). At the macro level, state legislation that restricts access to firearms through waiting periods and background checks has resulted in significantly fewer suicide deaths (Anestis et al., 2017). Means restriction at a macro level is not limited to firearms. In 2004, after Great Britain required acetaminophen/paracetamol to be sold in bubble packs, suicide deaths decreased significantly and remained low in the long term (Hawton et al., 2013).

The process of going through the previously described seven steps can take between 10 and 30 minutes. After talking through means restriction, I like to end with some questions commonly used in solution-focused therapy and motivational interviewing. I ask, "How likely is it that you will use this list the next time you're having suicidal thoughts?" and "How much do you think these actions will provide some relief?" When talking with youth, I find that approximately one-third of the time, they answer "not likely" to both questions. This honest answer gives me the opportunity to understand why they do not view this plan as something that will be helpful. The following is a statement I like to use:

I'm curious why you wouldn't use something that you came up with, that lists things that you like to do, places you like to go, and people you like to hang out with. I'm not telling you what to do. This is all you. Can you help me understand?

It is beyond the scope of this chapter to explore all the possible permutations of this conversation. Resources for clinical interviewing with suicidal people are included in the Helpful Resources section.

Psychosocial Interventions

Although the title of this chapter is "Suicide," social work students and practitioners are far more likely to work with people with suicidal thoughts and suicide attempts than people who will go on to die by suicide. Ninety percent of people who make a suicide attempt will die by a reason other than suicide. Because suicide is a low base-rate behavior, most intervention studies examine the effect of the intervention on suicidal ideation and attempt. A 2016 systematic review on psychosocial interventions for self-harm found that cognitive–behavioral therapy (CBT), and to a lesser extent dialectical behavioral therapy, was effective at reducing suicidal ideation and attempt (Hawton et al., 2016). In contrast, a 2018 meta-analysis of suicide found that CBT was not effective in reducing suicide deaths (Riblet et al., 2017). What is the difference? As mentioned previously, the processes for developing suicidal thoughts and behaviors are different from each other and from death by suicide.

Cognitive–Behavioral Therapy for Suicide Prevention

The psychosocial intervention with the most empirical support for reducing suicide risk in adults, and for which there is emerging evidence with adolescents, is cognitive–behavioral therapy for suicide prevention (CBT-SP)

(Brown et al., 2005; Rudd et al., 2015; Stanley et al., 2009). CBT-SP is organized in three sequential phases (Bryan, 2019):

- Phase 1 includes risk assessment, treatment, or recovery plan development; safety planning; and crisis stabilization.
- Phase 2 focuses on identifying and challenging the client's maladaptive beliefs and self-statements that contribute to suicidal behavior such as hopelessness, perceived burdensomeness, and feeling trapped.
- Phase 3 focuses on relapse prevention. Although it has a cognitive foundation, this phase uses concepts from motivational interviewing and behavioral skills training to reinforce new behaviors and skills for managing future distress.

For a comprehensive case study using CBT-SP, see Singer and Chaffee (2020).

Conclusion

There are only two kinds of social workers—those who have worked with suicidal people and those who have not yet worked with suicidal people. If you are concerned someone might be having thoughts of suicide, ask. Asking people if they are suicidal will not make them suicidal (DeCou & Schumann, 2018; Gould et al., 2005). Effective and professional work with suicidal people requires training in suicide risk assessment, safety planning, means counseling, and service coordination.

Helpful Resources

Freedenthal, S. (2017). *Helping the suicidal person: Tips and techniques for professionals.* Routledge.

Jobes, D. A. (2016). *Managing suicidal risk: A collaborative approach* (2nd ed.). Guilford.

Shea, S. C. (2002). *The practical art of suicide assessment: A guide for mental health professionals and substance abuse counselors.* Mental Health Presses.

Apps
NotOk: https://www.notokapp.com
Virtual Hope Box: https://www.my-therappy.co.uk/app/virtual-hope-box

Website
Live Through This (photos and stories of suicide attempt survivors): https://livethroughthis.org

References

Anestis, M. D., Anestis, J. C., & Butterworth, S. E. (2017). Handgun legislation and changes in statewide overall suicide rates. *American Journal of Public Health, 107*(4), 579–581. https://doi.org/10.2105/AJPH.2016.303650

Bridge, J. A., Horowitz, L. M., Fontanella, C. A., Sheftall, A. H., Greenhouse, J., Kelleher, K. J., & Campo, J. V. (2018). Age-related racial disparity in suicide rates among US youths from 2001 through 2015. *JAMA Pediatrics, 172*(7), 697–699. https://doi.org/10.1001/jamapediatrics.2018.0399

Brown, G. K., Ten Have, T., Henriques, G. R., Xie, S. X., Hollander, J. E., & Beck, A. T. (2005). Cognitive therapy for the prevention of suicide attempts: A randomized controlled trial. *JAMA, 294*(5), 563–570. https://doi.org/10.1001/jama.294.5.563

Bryan, C. J. (2019). Cognitive behavioral therapy for suicide prevention (CBT-SP): Implications for meeting standard of care expectations with suicidal patients. *Behavioral Sciences & the Law, 37*(3), 247–258. https://doi.org/10.1002/bsl.2411

Bryan, C. J., Mintz, J., Clemans, T. A., Leeson, B., Burch, T. S., Williams, S. R., Maney, E., & Rudd, M. D. (2017). Effect of crisis response planning vs. contracts for safety on suicide risk in U.S. Army Soldiers: A randomized clinical trial. *Journal of Affective Disorders, 212*, 64–72. https://doi.org/10.1016/j.jad.2017.01.028

Centers for Disease Control and Prevention (2021, June 18). *Suicide and Self-Harm Injury.* https://www.cdc.gov/nchs/fastats/suicide.htm

Cerel, J., Brown, M. M., Maple, M., Singleton, M., Venne, J., Moore, M., & Flaherty, C. (2019). How many people are exposed to suicide? Not six. *Suicide and Life-Threatening Behavior, 49*(2), 529–534. https://doi.org/10.1111/sltb.12450

DeCou, C. R., & Schumann, M. E. (2018). On the iatrogenic risk of assessing suicidality: A meta-analysis. Suicide and Life-Threatening *Behavior, 48*(5), 531–543. https://doi.org/10.1111/sltb.12368

Durkheim, E. (1952). *Suicide: A study in sociology.* Routledge & Kegan Paul. (Original work published 1897)

Freedenthal, S. (2017). *Helping the suicidal person: Tips and techniques for professionals.* Routledge.

Gould, M. S., Marrocco, F. A., Kleinman, M., Thomas, J. G., Mostkoff, K., Cote, J., & Davies, M. (2005). Evaluating iatrogenic risk of youth suicide screening programs: A randomized controlled trial. *JAMA, 293*(13), 1635–1643. https://doi.org/10.1001/jama.293.13.1635

Hawton, K., Bergen, H., Simkin, S., Dodd, S., Pocock, P., Bernal, W., Gunnell, D., & Kapur, N. (2013). Long term effect of reduced pack sizes of paracetamol on poisoning deaths and liver transplant activity in England and Wales: Interrupted time series analyses. *BMJ, 346*, f403. https://doi.org/10.1136/bmj.f403

Hawton, K., Witt, K. G., Salisbury, T. L. T., Arensman, E., Gunnell, D., Hazell, P., Townsend, E., & van Heeringen, K. (2016). Psychosocial interventions following self-harm in adults: A systematic review and meta-analysis. *Lancet Psychiatry, 3*(8), 740–750. https://doi.org/10.1016/S2215-0366(16)30070-0

Klonsky, E. D., Saffer, B. Y., & Bryan, C. J. (2018). Ideation-to-action theories of suicide: A conceptual and empirical update. *Current Opinion in Psychology, 22*, 38–43. https://doi.org/10.1016/j.copsyc.2017.07.020

Lindsey, M. A., Sheftall, A. H., Xiao, Y., & Joe, S. (2019). Trends of suicidal behaviors among high school students in the United States: 1991–2017. *Pediatrics, 144*(5), e20191187. https://doi.org/10.1542/peds.2019-1187

Mintz, R. S. (1966). Some practical procedures in the management of suicidal persons. *American Journal of Orthopsychiatry, 36*(5), 896–903. https://doi.org/10.1111/j.1939-0025.1966.tb02418.x

Mueller, A. S., & Abrutyn, S. (2016). Adolescents under pressure: A new Durkheimian framework for understanding adolescent suicide in a cohesive community. *American Sociological Review, 81*(5), 877–899. https://doi.org/10.1177/0003122416663464

Pisani, A. R., Murrie, D. C., & Silverman, M. M. (2016). Reformulating suicide risk formulation: From prediction to prevention. *Academic Psychiatry, 40*(4), 623–629. https://doi.org/10.1007/s40596-015-0434-6

Riblet, N. B. V., Shiner, B., Young-Xu, Y., & Watts, B. V. (2017). Strategies to prevent death by suicide: Meta-analysis of randomised controlled trials. *British Journal of Psychiatry, 210*(6), 396–402. https://doi.org/10.1192/bjp.bp.116.187799

Rudd, M. D., Bryan, C. J., Wertenberger, E. G., Peterson, A. L., Young-McCaughan, S., Mintz, J., Williams, S. R., Arne, K. A., Breitbach, J., Delano, K., Wilkinson, E., & Bruce, T. O. (2015). Brief cognitive–behavioral therapy effects on post-treatment suicide attempts in a military sample: Results of a randomized clinical trial with 2-year follow-up. *American Journal of Psychiatry, 172*(5), 441–449. https://doi.org/10.1176/appi.ajp.2014.14070843

Sale, E., Hendricks, M., Weil, V., Miller, C., Perkins, S., & McCudden, S. (2018). Counseling on Access to Lethal Means (CALM): An evaluation of a suicide prevention means restriction training program for mental health providers. *Community Mental Health Journal, 54*(3), 293–301. https://doi.org/10.1007/s10597-017-0190-z

Singer, J. B., & Chaffee, J. (2020). Clinical social work with suicidal youth and adults. In J. R. Brandell (Ed.), *Theory and practice in clinical social work* (3rd ed., pp. 610–635). Cognella Academic.

Singer, J. B., & Erreger, S. (2015, Fall). Let's talk about suicide: #LanguageMatters. *New Social Worker*, 18–19.

Stage, D. L. (2020, September 5). *On the suicide hierarchy: Serious attempts versus non-serious attempts* [Facebook]. Live Through This Facebook Group. https://www.facebook.com/livethroughthisproject/posts/3202215199897799

Stanley, B., Brown, G., Brent, D. A., Wells, K., Poling, K., Curry, J., Kennard, B. D., Wagner, A., Cwik, M. F., Klomek, A. B., Goldstein, T., Vitiello, B., Barnett, S., Daniel, S., & Hughes, J. (2009). Cognitive–behavioral therapy for suicide prevention (CBT-SP): Treatment model, feasibility, and acceptability. *Journal of the American Academy of Child and Adolescent Psychiatry, 48*(10), 1005–1013. https://doi.org/10.1097/CHI.0b013e3181b5dbfe

Stanley, B., & Brown, G. K. (2012). Safety planning intervention: A brief intervention to mitigate suicide risk. *Cognitive and Behavioral Practice, 19*(2), 256–264. https://doi.org/10.1016/j.cbpra.2011.01.001

Stanley, B., Brown, G. K., Brenner, L. A., Galfalvy, H. C., Currier, G. W., Knox, K. L., Chaudhury, S. R., Bush, A. L., & Green, K. L. (2018). Comparison of the safety planning intervention with follow-up vs usual care of suicidal patients treated in the emergency department. *JAMA Psychiatry, 75*(9), 894–900. https://doi.org/10.1001/jamapsychiatry.2018.1776

Van Orden, K. A., Witte, T. K., Cukrowicz, K. C., Braithwaite, S. R., Selby, E. A., & Joiner, T. E. (2010). The interpersonal theory of suicide. *Psychological Review, 117*(2), 575–600. https://doi.org/10.1037/a0018697

World Health Organization (2021, June 18) *Suicide Data*. https://www.who.int/teams/mental-health-and-substance-use/suicide-data

LGBTQ + Affirmative Practice in Social Work

Tyler M. Argüello

One of the great resiliencies of LGBTQ+[1] people and cultures is their critical relationship with language and communication.[2] LGBTQ+ people can be understood as *counterpublics* (Warner, 2002), marginalized people whose lived experiences involve shuttling between an oppressive world and their ground-up practices of reclamation and resistance. From that perspective, queer identities serve a strategic function: They mediate between one's marginalized lived experience and the larger culture of invalidation and injustice. Key to this is the language created and contorted by queer people to describe themselves and their lives. As such, the experiences of queer folks become inscribed into their communicative practices that articulate their found, claimed, and performative identities. These articulations effectively give life to queer people—and more critically describe what has too often been unavailable and nullified because of the impotency of normative language to fully appreciate sexualities and genders. Normative language and normative ideologies are insufficient to provide meaning to sexualities and genders, and typically they inadequately afford the operative space to explore them and the intersections therein. In this sense, LGBTQ+ identities are not simply nouns that start to cohere experiences. They also function as verbs—that is, a way of active questioning, a continual process of becoming and breathing life into queer possibilities.

In the grandest sense, tending to queer identities and making manifest these lived realities is a world-making project. This is where social work steps in. Social workers can support, advocate for, and intervene. Our technologies of confronting injustice, amplifying change initiatives, and leveraging hope provide

---

1. LGBTQ+ is an acronym for people who are lesbian, gay, bisexual, transgender, queer, questioning, intersex, Two-Spirit, or asexual. Queer is used interchangeably for economical reasons; however, Queer is a term deriving from critical theories on language and culture that targets normativities, especially in relation to sexualities and genders.

2. This chapter is adapted from *Queer Social Work*, by Tyler M. Argüello, ed. Copyright © 2019 Columbia University Press. Used with permission of Columbia University Press.

the space for differences to exist, to find footing in the world, and ultimately to thrive. In particular, social work programs are mandated to provide an educational culture that is inclusive and affirmative of LGBTQ+ people and cultures [Council on Social Work Education (CSWE), 2015]. The profession is committed to supporting diversity, promoting social justice, and challenging oppression [National Association of Social Workers (NASW), 2017]. Despite this commitment, a queer affirmative approach can be elusive in social work practice.

Social Work and LGBTQ+ Communities

As social workers, we attend to integration across fieldwork, courses, and competencies. But this integration can be poorly sustained or even absent when it comes to LGBTQ+ communities and their inequities. Still today, in social work education, it is common to inadequately or noncritically address queer communities and their disparities. In addition, it is more common to either not cover LGBTQ+ affirmative practice or to rely on panels of queer people, which fosters exoticization and places the burden on queer people to speak for their communities as well as onerously and inappropriately (have to) educate non-LGBTQ+ people.

Social work is catching up. In recent years, much original research has been published that illuminates the strengths, deficiencies, and perceived biases in LGBTQ+ content in social work programs (Craig et al., 2015; Craig, Dentato, et al., 2016; Dentato et al., 2014, 2016; Gezinski, 2009; Hicks & Jeyasingham, 2016; Martin et al., 2009; McPhail, 2004; Papadaki, 2016). This archive speaks to a paucity of LGBTQ+ material in social work courses, a dissatisfaction with training and preparation for practice, a failure to assess student competency around LGBTQ+ issues, a

tepid classroom culture, too few LGBTQ+ field placements, and an expressed need for cultural responsiveness and critical self-interrogation around queer issues by social work students and faculty. There is a body of literature that interrogates the interpersonal relationships among social work students and LGBTQ+ faculty and *between* heterosexual and LGBTQ+ faculty, including investigating forms of discrimination, microaggressions, and nullification. This body of literature shows chronic invalidations, systemic heteronormativity, disruption of the learning environment, erasure of LGBTQ+ content in social work history, hostility toward queer faculty, abject phobia, and damage to overall well-being (Dentato et al., 2016; Johnson, 2014; Messenger, 2009; Turner et al., 2018).

Finally, there are both research and practice by social work scholars that respond and work to redress these trends. In particular, the Council on Sexual Orientation and Gender Identity and Expression, a diversity council of the CSWE, has produced LGBTQ+ affirmative best practice standards for accredited social work programs. The recent *Rainbow Papers* translate both the implicit and explicit curriculum for social work programs to craft a comprehensive queer affirmative environment for learning (Austin et al., 2016; Craig, Alessi, et al., 2016). In addition, recent edited volumes on social work practice with LGBTQ+ communities (Dentato, 2017; Hillcock & Mulé, 2017; Mallon, 2017) provide a wide-ranging review of literature and best practices, steeped in affirmative approaches.

LGBTQ+ Affirmative Practice

One way to begin to conceptualize queer affirmative practice is that it is, in the style of Trinh T. Minh-ha (as cited in Chen, 1992), a "speaking nearby" that approximates queer clients and communities as well as brings the practitioner to a point of departure, not one of certainty. Affirmative practice facilitates an opening up of possibilities, for producing a space that allows queerness to exist. This requires both an immersion into new knowledge archives and a deep dive into the hard work of self-reflection.

Working as an ally (typically as an outsider) with a marginalized community is a hallmark of social work. Social workers' training and their ongoing practice must be geared toward cultural competence and social justice for LGBTQ+ communities, as well as other marginalized groups (CSWE, 2015; NASW, 2017). At face value and pragmatically, cultural competence means building relationships and trust with client systems, consciously tending to the ways in which knowledge is developed, using dynamic assessments, and deploying interventions consistent with the client system's worldview. Cultural competence is not voyeurism, fetishizing the (queer) Other, nor is it simply an intellectual endeavor. Rather, it involves active engagement with one's self and the environment in which one lives, as well as cultivating knowledge, awareness, and exposure. That is, cultural competence is experiential and unending, appreciating the person-in-environment (Adams & Bell, 2016; Adams et al., 2018).

A culturally competent approach involves understanding how oppression, power, and privilege affect, operate through, and become reproduced by individuals, groups, and structures. It takes into account how vulnerable populations lack power and privilege and how, in turn, they are marginalized, disenfranchised, and subject to inequities. This process requires that social workers increase insight into their own stigmas, biases, complicity, and participation in oppressive behaviors and structures—and it calls for engagement in allied behaviors working for social justice, equity, and empowerment. In addition, the

burden of culturally competent work is not for the Other (e.g., LGBTQ+ person or community) to educate the social work student or professional. It is the ethical imperative, moral mandate, and professional obligation of social workers to continually train themselves in service of increasing cultural competence and responsiveness.

The task does not end with cultural competence. Competence around queer matters and communities must be partnered with an affirmative standpoint and practice. [To be clear, both CSWE and NASW have published documents that oppose and condemn conversion and reparative therapies or sexual orientation change efforts (CSWE, 2016; NASW, 2015; NASW National Committee on Lesbian, Gay, and Bisexual Issues, 2000).] Generally, LGBTQ+ affirmative interventions involve an explicit validation of queer identities, inclusive of an appreciation for the diversity of identities along the spectrum of sexualities and genders (Alessi, 2014; Craig et al., 2013; Crisp & McCave, 2007; Pachankis, 2014); the starting point for this undoubtedly begins in the social work classroom setting and curriculum (Wagaman et al., 2018). LGBTQ+ affirmative care recognizes that queer people live with chronic stress and experience the social and health inequities that result from existing in an oppressive, discriminatory, and phobic society. So interventions with queer people and communities must tend to these domains, and social workers must be accountable to their clients. They must continually assess their own attitudes and beliefs and commit themselves to action to reduce stigma and discrimination.

We know that heterosexist attitudes among practitioners can reduce their empathy for LGBTQ+ people and even harm them (Love et al., 2015). Like the general population, social workers can and do often have both subtle and active phobias and practices toward queer people that are left unexamined and therefore appear in their practice. These prejudices, coupled with low knowledge and self-awareness, create poor service delivery, misdiagnosis, pathologizing, and deprecation (Love et al., 2015). In turn, queer people's experience of this sort of *non*-affirmative practice can result in dissatisfaction with services, avoiding care, or omitting critical information.

Vital to this queer affirmative work is formulating the case from a competent and critical standpoint. Case formulation, in general, is an essential part of any clinical work; this core skill is typically the bridge between assessment and intervention (Eells, 2015). Sexualities, gender identities, and gender expressions are not simply demographic variables to validate, affirm, and embed within the assessment nor quote in haphazard footnotes on treatment plans. Rather, they can be and must be starting points and the *leitmotif* of clinical work. In this vein, a more effective approach to working with LGBTQ+ people is a case formulation that is integrative, transdisciplinary, intersectional— and one that begins with matters of sexualities and genders. It is one that is both theoretically driven, often with a critical and constructionist edge, and evidence-based driven by knowledge about LGBTQ+ social and health inequities (Bostwick et al., 2014; Institute of Medicine, 2011; U.S. Department of Health and Human Services, 2013).

The Practical Work

All this said, the perennial question arises for students, supervisees, and practitioners alike: "Yes, but what does LGBTQ+ affirmative practice actually look like? How do you do *that*?" As I often tell my students, there is no way through the fire except *through* the fire. To do the work requires that you do the work. LGBTQ+ affirmative work is distinct from merely saying that you are an ally to queer people. As a response to this question and the larger matter of *doing* queer affirmative work, I convened LGBTQ+ social workers

and cases of them doing work with LGBTQ+ clients (Argüello, 2019). Overall, this edited volume aimed to bridge the divide between social workers and the queer people they serve (Brown, 1995). And, it sought to offer concrete, comparative case formulations that manifest contemporary, culturally responsive LGBTQ+ practice.

Related, I have written elsewhere about strategies to resist reproducing health and mental health inequities of LGBTQ+ people and communities (Argüello, 2020). In this, I have operationalized the ethos for queer affirmative work into practical, everyday strategies any social worker can harness. At baseline, affirmative work starts with an explicit validation of and appreciation for the wide spectrum of LGBTQ+ identities and expressions therein. In addition, it builds off an understanding of minority stress and a model for stress and coping (Alessi, 2014; Meyer, 2003; Pachankis, 2014). This explanatory model accounts for the multilevel oppressive experiences of the queer individual as well as the health and mental health inequities they suffer. And, minority stress accounts for the ways in which the queer person has internalized negative, phobic, and oppressive belief systems.

As such, an affirmative approach is a three-part process that can be overlaid onto any modality that a practitioner uses (Argüello, 2018, 2020). The first part is to adequately assess the client's experience of queer stress, accounting for histories with stigmas, phobias (external and internal), chronic stress (both individual and community level), and both disclosure and concealment of identities. The second part is to assess for resiliencies and coping, understanding abilities and skills for emotion regulation, social and interpersonal functioning, cognitive schemas, and for sexual and intimate relationships. The third part is to formulate the case within a queer affirmative perspective parallel to the clinical modality that the practitioner uses. Along with the traditional interventions conducted with the client, queer affirmative action needs to be taken. This would include consistent attention to the therapeutic alliance, cultural competence, strengths, and a person-in-environment understanding of health and mental health. In addition, the interventions offered must tend to issues of stigma, disclosure, stress and coping, and intersectional identities. This is all in service of cultivating well-being, a positive sense of self, and increased connections with communities. Finally, the work is multilevel just as chronic minority stress is multilevel; therefore, interventions need to address forces that impinge on or facilitate the client's health and mental health, whether micro, mezzo, or macro in nature.

In reality, it can be illusive in practice to see blatant examples of queer affirmative work. Practitioners may sidestep such an approach to formulating and intervening with cases for a variety of reasons, one of which may be lack of training and education (Argüello, 2020). This is when consultation, supervision, as well as thorough and ongoing conversations with clients can be helpful (O'Brien et al., 2018). For example, it can be helpful for organizations to have an LGBTQ+ client advocate on care teams when staffing clients or to appoint lead clinicians who are obligated to ensure that the advocacy and care for LGBTQ+ clients are responsive and affirmative.

Another place to start is considering the lines of inquiry utilized in clinical assessment interviews and initial encounters (Argüello, 2020). A persistent problem and effect of cisheteronormative systems is the encouragement toward an uncritical use of identity categories, an insistence on minority sexualities and genders as deviant or problematic, as well as an individual focus at the expense of an appreciation for the client's experiences interacting with prejudiced systems. Equally, providers at times focus too much or too little on the client's sexuality or gender identity, either overassociating or undercorrelating it with health and mental health issues. Accordingly, a queer affirmative approach would encourage a conversation with clients about how they square their sexuality and gender with the situation or problems at hand. This can be achieved through more narrative-oriented lines of inquiry (Semp, 2011), such as the following:

> How do you describe or think about your sexuality and/or gender to yourself?
> Is your sexuality or gender important to how you see yourself; if so, in what ways?
> Are there any other important areas of your identity?
> Have you had concerns about your sexuality or gender?
> How does your sexuality or gender figure into your health and mental health?

From there, it is important for clinicians and staff to consider how this information is documented, recorded, and then used to inform treatment and care.

Note that a queer affirmative framework is not limited to LGBTQ+ clients. A queer affirmative framework is generative and, dare I say, emancipatory for non-LGBTQ+ client systems. The specialty of a queer approach is to ardently interrogate normative structures and practices, and that applies to everyone. In the end, I recommend that social workers practice "speaking nearby" as well as *standing* nearby," by which I mean bearing witness to queer stories of pain, resilience, survival, and pride. This "nearby" sensibility gives us a point of departure, an opening up of possibility—and, perhaps most critically, it creates space in the world for LGBTQ+ people to exist.

References

Adams, M., & Bell, L. A. (Eds.). (2016). *Teaching for diversity and social justice* (3rd ed.). Routledge.

Adams, M., Blumenfeld, W. J., Chase, D., Catalano, J., DeJong, K. S., Hackman, H. W., Hopkins, L. E., Love, B. J., Peters, M. L., Shlasko, D., & Zúñiga, X. (2018). *Readings for diversity and social justice* (4th ed.). Routledge.

Alessi, E. J. (2014). A framework for incorporating minority stress theory into treatment with sexual minority clients. *Journal of Gay & Lesbian Mental Health, 18*(1), 47–66.

Argüello, T. M. (2018). HIV stress exchange: HIV trauma, intergenerational stress, and queer men. Paper presented at the 13th International Conference on Interdisciplinary Social Studies, Granada, Spain, July 25–27.

Argüello, T. M. (Ed.). (2019). *Queer social work: Cases for LGBTQ+ affirmative practice.* Columbia University Press.

Argüello, T. M. (2020). Decriminalizing LGBTQ+: Reproducing and resisting mental health inequities. *CNS Spectrums, 25*(5), 667–686. doi:10.1017/S1092852920001170

Austin, A., Craig, S. L., Alessi, E. J., Wagaman, M. A., Paceley, M. S., Dziengel, L., & Balestrery, J. E. (2016). *Guidelines for transgender and gender nonconforming (TGNC) affirmative education: Enhancing the climate for TGNC students, staff and faculty in social work education.* Council on Social Work Education.

Bostwick, W. B., Boyd, C. J., Hughes, T. L., & West, B. (2014). Discrimination and mental health among lesbian, gay, and bisexual adults in the United States. *American Journal of Orthopsychiatry, 84*(1), 35–45.

Brown, M. (1995). Ironies of distance: An ongoing critique of the geographies of AIDS. *Environment and Planning D: Society and Space, 13*(2), 159–183.

Chen, N. N. (1992). Speaking nearby: A conversation with Trinh T. Minh-ha. *Visual Anthropology Review, 8*(1), 82–91.

Council on Social Work Education. (2015). *Educational policy and accreditation standards for baccalaureate and master's social work programs.*

Council on Social Work Education. (2016). *Position statement on conversion/reparative therapy.* https://www.cswe.org/getattachment/Centers-Initiatives/Centers/Center-for-Diversity/About/Stakeholders/Commission-for-Diversity-and-Social-and-Economic-J/Council-on-Sexual-Orientation-and-Gender-Identity/CSOGIE-Resources/CSWEPositionStatementonConversion-ReparativeTherapy(003).pdf.aspx

Craig, S. L., Alessi, E. J., Fisher-Borne, M., Dentato, M. P., Austin, A., Paceley, M., Wagaman, A., Arguello, T., Lewis, T., Balestrery, J. E., & Van Der Horn, R. (2016). *Guidelines for affirmative social work education: Enhancing the climate for LGBQQ students,* staff, and faculty in social work education. Council on Social Work Education.

Craig, S. L., Austin, A., & Alessi, E. (2013). Gay affirmative cognitive behavioral therapy for sexual minority youth: Clinical adaptations and approaches. *Clinical Social Work Journal, 41*(3), 258–266.

Craig, S. L., Dentato, M. P., Messinger, L., & McInroy, L. (2016). Educational determinants of readiness to practice with LGBTQ clients: Social work students speak out. *British Journal of Social Work, 46*(1), 115–134.

Craig, S. L., McInroy, L. B., Dentato, M. P., Austin, A., & Messinger, L. (2015). *Social work students speak out! The experiences of lesbian, gay, bisexual, transgender, and queer students in social work programs: A study report from the CSWE Council on Sexual Orientation and Gender Identity and Expression.* Council on Social Work Education.

Crisp, C., & McCave, E. L. (2007). Gay affirmative practice: A model for social work practice with gay, lesbian, and bisexual youth. *Child and Adolescent Social Work Journal, 24*(4), 403–421.

Dentato, M. (Ed.). (2017). *Social work practice with the LGBTQ community: The intersection of history, health, mental health, and politics.* Oxford University Press.

Dentato, M. P., Craig, S. L., Lloyd, M. R., Kelly, B. L., Wright, C., & Austin, A. (2016). Homophobia within schools of social work: The critical need for affirming classroom settings and effective preparation for service with the LGBTQ community. *Social Work Education, 35*(6), 672–692.

Dentato, M. P., Craig, S. L., Messinger, L., Lloyd, M., & McInroy, L. B. (2014). Outness among LGBTQ social work students in North America: The contribution of environmental supports and perceptions of comfort. *Social Work Education, 33*(4), 485–501.

Eells, T. D. (2015). *Psychotherapy case formulation.* American Psychological Association.

Gezinski, L. (2009). Addressing sexual minority issues in social work education: A curriculum framework. *Advances in Social Work, 10*(1), 103–113.

Hicks, S., & Jeyasingham, D. (2016). Social work, queer theory and after: A genealogy of sexuality theory in neo-liberal times. *British Journal of Social Work, 46*(8), 2357–2373.

Hillcock, S., & Mulé, N. J. (Eds.). (2017). *Queering social work education.* UBC Press.

Institute of Medicine. (2011). *The health of lesbian, gay, bisexual, and transgender people: Building a foundation for a better understanding.* National Academies Press.

Johnson, L. M. (2014). Teaching note—Heterosexism as experienced by LGBT social work educators. *Journal of Social Work Education, 50*(4), 748–751.

Love, M. M., Smith, A. E., Lyall, S. E., Mullins, J. L., & Cohn, T. J. (2015). Exploring the relationship between gay affirmative practice and empathy among mental health professionals. *Journal of Multicultural Counseling & Development, 43*(2), 83–96.

Mallon, G. P. (Ed.). (2017). *Social work practice with lesbian, gay, bisexual, and transgender people* (3rd ed.). Routledge.

Martin, J., Messinger, L., Kull, R., Holmes, J., Bermudez, F., & Sommer, S. (2009). *Sexual orientation and gender expression in social work education: Results from a national survey—Executive summary.* Council on Social Work Education.

McPhail, B. (2004). Questioning gender and sexuality binaries: What queer theorists, transgendered individuals, and sex researchers can teach social work. *Journal of Gay & Lesbian Social Services, 17*(1), 3–21.

Messenger, L. (2009, September–October). Creating LGBTQ-friendly campuses. *Academe, 95*(5), 39–42.

Meyer, I. H. (2003). Prejudice, social stress, and mental health in lesbian, gay, and bisexual populations: Conceptual issues and research evidence. *Psychology Bulletin, 129*, 674–697.

NASW National Committee on Lesbian, Gay, and Bisexual Issues. (2000). *Position statement: Reparative or conversion therapies for lesbians and gay men.* NASW Press.

National Association of Social Workers. (2015). *Sexual orientation change efforts (SOCE) and conversion therapy with lesbians, gay men, bisexuals and transgender persons.*

National Association of Social Workers. (2017). *Code of ethics.*

O'Brien, R. P., Walker, P. M., Poteet, S. L., McAllister-Wallner, A., & Taylor, M. (2018). *Mapping the road to equity: The annual state of LGBTQ communities.* #Out4MentalHealth Project.

Pachankis, J. E. (2014). Uncovering clinical principles and techniques to address minority stress, mental health, and related health risks among gay and bisexual men. *Clinical Psychology: Science & Practice, 21*(4), 313–330.

Papadaki, V. (2016). Invisible students: Experiences of lesbian and gay students in social work education in Greece. *Social Work Education, 35*(1), 65–77.

Semp, D. (2011). Questioning heteronormativity: Using queer theory to inform research and practice within public mental health services. *Psychology & Sexuality, 2*(1), 69–86.

Turner, G. W., Pelts, M., & Thompson, M. (2018). Between the academy and Queerness: Microaggression in social work education. *Affilia, 33*(1), 98–111.

U.S. Department of Health and Human Services. (2013). *2020 topics & objectives: Lesbian, gay, bisexual, and transgender health.* https://www.healthypeople.gov/2020/topics-objectives/topic/lesbian-gay-bisexual-and-transgender-health

Wagaman, A., Shelton, J., & Carter, R. (2018). Queering the social work classroom: Strategies for increasing the inclusion of LGBTQ persons and experiences. *Journal of Teaching in Social Work, 38*(2), 166–182.

Warner, M. (2002). *Publics and counterpublics.* Zone Books.

Social Justice in Social Work

A Foundational Understanding

Natasha Wine Miller Bragg

Social justice is an inextricable component of social work. Supported by both the
International Federation of Social Workers
(IFSW) and the International Association of
Schools of Social Work (IASSW), the Global
Social Work Statement of Ethical Principles
positions social justice as a defining and essential objective to ethical social work practice worldwide (IASSW, 2018; IFSW, 2018).
Strategies such as "challenging discrimination
and institutional oppression" (IASSW, 2018,
p. 4) are central to social justice praxis within
the profession. As the principal social work
professional organization in the United States,
the National Association of Social Workers
(NASW) distinguishes social justice as one of
six core values and ethical principles within its
Code of Ethics (NASW, 2017a). Such values
and principles constitute the keystone for social work's fundamental mission, purpose, and
ethical code of conduct, which is an unwavering obligation to individual and social pros-
perity (Reamer, 2018). Although the code did
not use the term "social justice" until its 1980
amendment, its principles were evident within
the original code through themes expressing
equality of human rights and dignity (NASW,
1960, 1967, 1979).

Conceptualizations of Social Justice

Although the most recent adaptation of the
NASW Code of Ethics explicitly integrates
social justice within its framework, such as
by calling social workers to "challenge social injustice" and "pursue social change"
(NASW, 2017a, p. 5), it does not provide a
cohesive explanation of what social justice is.
Ultimately, the code operationalizes social
justice relationally as the antithesis of social
diseases such as discrimination and oppression. Oppression is defined by Gil (2013) as "a
mode of human relations involving domination and exploitation—economic, social, and
psychological—among individuals, among
social groups and classes within and beyond
societies, and globally, among entire societies"
(p. 12). Oppression theory provides a framework for understanding the suppression of
marginalized social groups—such as women,

non-White racial groups, and lower economic classes—and the intersectional associations between such groups (Gil, 2013; Robbins, 2011). Social justice can therefore be understood within the framework of oppression theory as both the purpose and the process of building awareness and dismantling social power imbalances at structural and individual levels. Social justice work is therefore anti-oppressive, recognizing the inherent power imbalances and exploitation of nondominant social groups and working toward their eradication (Danso, 2009; Gil, 2013; Payne, 2014; Vanderwood, 2016).

Still, what is social justice? Social workers across specializations appear to similarly conceptualize social justice, comparing it with ideas of "fairness, equal rights and opportunity, social responsibility, resource distribution, and decent standards of living" and also "empowerment [and] advocacy" (Olson et al., 2013, p. 38). McLaughlin (2011) incorporates these ideas by explaining social justice as "multidimensional, with a broad family of related issues: distribution of resources, rights, fairness, respect, and maximizing individual potential. Those inspired and committed to social justice may in fact be committed to different but related issues" (p. 248). Heller (1987, as cited in Mullaly, 2002) interprets social justice beyond the gauge of equality in societal resource distribution but as a social circumstance in which civic participation is promoted and facilitated among all people, despite their social ranking or memberships. In this way, through embracing human difference and openly exchanging ideas, all members of society are effective and cooperative partners in the creation of equitable social processes and institutions. This conceptualization of social justice—in which rules, policies, and social mores are made collaboratively—promotes self-determination and the fulfillment of human need.

Although social justice might not have a single, determinative definition, its fundamental principles are indivisibly part of the larger human rights narrative. First drafted in 1948 by the United Nations (UN) General Assembly, the Universal Declaration of Human Rights lists 30 articles demarcating a series of absolute rights invested within all people, everywhere. Examples include the rights to "life, liberty and security of person" (UN, 1948, Article 3) and "a standard of living adequate for the health and well-being of himself and his family, including food, clothing, housing, and medical care and necessary social services" (Article 25). Although not legally binding, member nations are encouraged to abide them as such. The coherency and universality of human rights as defined by the UN position them as a useful cornerstone for social justice within the context of global social work practice as they build upon our profession's own articulation of key values and ethical principles (Reichert, 2007). The IASSW (2018) includes human rights as one of its global ethical standards. In all, using human rights as a common language for social justice promotes cross-cultural, transglobal conversations on social justice issues such as identifying problems and needs and developing viable goals.

Social Justice in Social Work

From professional education to practice contexts, social justice is a coalescing value across all areas and varieties of social work (Nicotera, 2019). Although clinical social workers have accrued criticism for devaluing the importance of social justice work within their direct practice approaches (Specht & Courtney, 1994), it is of greater importance to focus on how social justice perspectives can and are applied in both community and clinical fields of practice. Furthermore, all professional social workers, despite their practice focus, are educated on advancing human rights and social justice as mandated by the Council on Social Work Education (CSWE, 2015; Harrison et al., 2016). Across clinical and community work, social workers must collaborate with clients in determining their relationship with social justice ideals and how those ideals should and can be incorporated into practice goals (Jeyapal, 2017; McLaughlin, 2011; Mullaly, 2002; Pyles, 2014; Solas, 2008).

Community Practice

Social workers skilled in "macro" areas of practice such as community organization, policy development, and activism are usually working toward client goals directly tied to social change (Allen et al., 2018; Kim, 2017; McBeath, 2016; Pyles, 2014; Reisch, 2016). Enacting social change occurs by challenging and directly disrupting oppressive status quos and exploitative conditions. Macro-oriented social workers must therefore build cooperative and trusting relationships with their constituents, groups, and/or communities in order to best assist their clients in identifying unjust systems and processes, brainstorming ideal outcomes, and developing practicable goals. Common strategies and abilities of community ("macro") social work practitioners include "resource development, mobilization, and management"; "advocacy, lobbying, public education, and coalition building"; "cultivating and exercising leadership"; and "facilitating the empowerment of clients and constituents and the groups they belong to" (Austin & Lowe, 1994, as cited in Reisch, 2016, p. 261). Refer to Pyles (2014) for in-depth descriptions and analyses of the multiple ideologies, perspectives, and methods of social work community practice.

Clinical Practice

Many social work clinicians embrace social justice as indispensable to their professional practice with individuals, groups, and families (Marsh, 2005; Marsh & Bunn, 2018; Maschi et al., 2011; McLaughlin, 2011; McLaughlin et al., 2015; Morgaine, 2014). Therapeutic approaches and assessments both identify clients' intrapersonal and external resources and reveal the ways they experience social injustice in their individual lives (Berzoff, 2011; Marsh & Bunn, 2018). Clinicians consistently use such client strengths and revelations toward goal development and achievement, which in turn empower clients' sense of self-determination and self-respect (Wakefield, 1988a, 1988b). Self-determination is not only related to social justice through social work standards but also an essential component of social justice as interpreted through the aforementioned human rights framework.

Clinical and direct-practice social workers can furthermore assist clients in achieving socially just outcomes through locating and applying for resources and services (McLaughlin, 2011). Accessing social services can be a difficult and frustrating process, especially if a client is lacking the technology, skill, or credentials needed to access or navigate often complex, web-based tools. Actively experiencing crisis can add further complication. Direct-practice social workers can help clients successfully steer through these processes, and many social workers value these interactions as social justice work (McLaughlin, 2011).

The Social Environment

Social work values and ethics cannot be interpreted apart from the society and culture they operate within, and thus social workers' attunement to present-day social, cultural, political, economic, and health issues at local, national, and transglobal levels is an ultimate necessity. Although social justice has been an instrumental unifying value within past eras of social work practice, it holds particular relevance in the cultural and political contexts of the present time (Bent-Goodley, 2017; Deepak et al., 2015; Estreet et al., 2017; Knight, 2017). Today, social work is challenged to confront interconnected threats to social justice within divisive sociopolitical atmospheres at the international level (Baron & McLaughlin, 2017). At the time of this writing in 2020, these expansive threats operate globally and are fueled by racism, xenophobia, ethnocentrism, misogyny, heterosexism, and political and economic oppression directly impacting the realities of individuals, families, communities, and societies. War-induced food insecurity and starvation in Yemen (Bibbo, 2018), the persecution of the Rohingya in Myanmar (Ahsan, 2018), and the plight of Syrian refugees amidst civil war (Fisseha, 2017) are but a few of many examples illustrating the extent of social justice violations worldwide. In the United States, crises of poverty and income inequality (Fontenot et al., 2018; Rank, 2005), mass incarceration (Kelley, 2019), homelessness (Baker et al., 2016; Desmond, 2016; Henry et al., 2018), hardline immigration policing (Golash-Boza, 2017; NASW, 2017b), police brutality, and institutionalized racism (CSWE, 2020; Society for Social Work Research, 2020) continue to afflict individuals and communities nationwide as systematic human rights violations. One's identity based on race, gender, ability, sexual orientation, age, citizenship, health, socioeconomic status, etc. affects peoples' experiences and interactions with such injustices. Examples include the disproportionately high degree of incarcerated Black people (Alexander, 2012; Martensen, 2012) and the above-average rate of homelessness in LGBTQ former foster youth (Capous-Desyllas & Mountz, 2019; Forge et al., 2018).

Social workers' response to unjust sociocultural conditions can also be from the stance of a unified professional body, as has been the recent case of social workers in the United States. Following the 2016 U.S. presidential election of Donald J. Trump, NASW (2017c) published a "transition document" specifically addressed to the upcoming executive administration. The document explained how social workers could help the United States move forward after experiencing a deluge of intensified racism, misogyny, and ideological divide (among other socially discriminatory proclivities) as a consequence of the recent election. This document clarified various ways social workers could assist the new presidential and congressional leadership in addressing present-day social concerns such as access to health care, reducing poverty levels, and supporting vulnerable populations such as foster youth and older adults. In defining this colossal task, NASW's transition document pressed the newly elected executive and legislative authorities to acknowledge historic and institutionalized oppression, demanding greater social inclusivity by means of changing socially unjust laws. Presenting such a manifesto to the highest levels of democratic representation is undeniable evidence that social workers prioritize social justice principles within contexts of modern sociopolitical environments.

Conclusion

In closing, let us remember that as dedicated present or future social work practitioners, social justice is realized through social change. Social workers have an ethical obligation to take an active position toward social justice and engage in social change efforts, from macro issues such as federal policy to state and community concerns. Moreover, many difficulties faced by individual clients are indicators of larger social problems, and "by responding to individuals, families, and groups to address needs and problems resulting from large-scale inequalities, social workers engage in justice work" (Marsh & Bunn, 2018, p. 652). Social justice work must also not forget the complexity and nuance of historical and political contexts that shape present realities, trends, and problems (Reisch, 2019).

Whether working with individuals, groups, or communities, all forms of social justice practice should emphasize client self-determination and empowerment, including the development of client-defined goals. Within the spirit of our discipline's values and ethics, the lived experiences and knowledge of the client should always take precedence in defining both client need and the desired outcomes of the client–social worker relationship. Collaboration is key, and it is expressly required for all variations of community and clinical practice. Furthermore, our professional efforts should be based within empirical research, the context of our clients' cultural worlds, and the intersectional ways in which they may endure the destructive consequences of social injustices—in all its forms and manipulations. Last, whether or not your pursuit to better understand social justice started with this chapter, I do hope that your exploration of this vastly complex subject does not end here. There exists a wealth of information worth studying from innumerable sources not limited to the social work discipline. As a starting point, I encourage you to mine through the references cited within these pages.

References

Ahsan, S. B. (2018). The Rohingya crisis: Why the world must act decisively. *Asian Affairs, 49*(4), 571–581. https://doi.org/10.1080/03068374.2018.1528791

Alexander, M. (2012). *The new Jim Crow: Mass incarceration in the age of colorblindness.* The New Press.

Allen, H., Garfinkel, I., & Waldfogel, J. (2018). Social policy research in social work in the twenty-first century: The state of scholarship and the profession; what is promising, and what needs to be done. *Social Service Review, 92*(4), 504–547. https://doi.org/10.1086/701198

Baker, L. A., Elliott, J., Mitchell, J. W., & Thiele, M. (2016). Many paths, one destination: New directions and opportunities for ending homelessness: Part one of a two-part series. *Journal of Housing and Community Development, 73*(2), 6–15.

Baron, S., & McLaughlin, H. (2017). Grand challenges: A way forward for social work? *Social Work Education, 36*(1), 1–5. doi:10.1080/02615479.2017.1283729

Bent-Goodley, T. B. (2017). Readying the profession for changing times. *Social Work, 62*(2), 101–103. https://doi.org/10.1093/sw/swx014

Berzoff, J. (2011). Why we need a biopsychosocial perspective with vulnerable, oppressed, and at-risk clients. *Smith College Studies in Social Work, 81*(2–3), 132–166. doi:10.1080/00377317.2011.590768

Bibbo, B. (2018, December 4). Yemen to face worst humanitarian crisis of 2019: UN. *Aljazeera.* https://www.aljazeera.com/news/2018/12/yemen-face-worst-humanitarian-crisis-2019-181204105615554.html

Capous-Desyllas, M., & Mountz, S. (2019). Using photovoice methodology to illuminate the experiences of LGBTQ former foster youth. *Child & Youth Services, 40*(3), 267–307. https://doi.org/10.1080/0145935X.2019.1583099

Council on Social Work Education. (2015). *Educational policy and accreditation standards for baccalaureate and master's social work programs.* https://www.cswe.org/getattachment/Accreditation/Accreditation-Process/2015-EPAS/2015EPAS_Web_FINAL.pdf.aspx

Council on Social Work Education. (2020, June 2). CSWE statement on social justice [Press release]. https://cswe.org/News/Press-Room/CSWE-Statement-on-Social-Justice

Danso, R. (2009). Emancipating and empowering de-valued skilled immigrants: What hope does anti-oppressive social work practice offer? *British Journal of Social Work, 39*, 539–555. https://doi.org/10.1093/bjsw/bcm126

Deepak, A. C., Rountree, M. A., & Scott, J. (2015). Delivering diversity and social justice in social work education: The power of context. *Journal of Progressive Human Services, 26*(2), 107–125. https://doi.org/10.1080/10428232.2015.1017909

Desmond, M. (2016). *Evicted: Poverty and profit in the American city.* Broadway Books.

Estreet, A. T., Jones, K., & Freeman, J. T. (2017). HBCUs respond: Social justice and social work education in a Trump era. *Reflections: Narratives of Professional Helping, 23*(2), 23–45. https://reflectionsnarrativesofprofessionalhelping.org/index.php/Reflections/article/view/1546/1481

Fisseha, M. (2017). Syrian refugee crisis, from Turkey to European Union—Methods and challenges. *Journal of Community Positive Practices, 17*(3), 34–57.

Fontenot, K., Semega, J., & Kollar, M. (2018, September). *Income and poverty in the United States: 2017* (Report no. P60-263). U.S. Census Bureau, U.S. Department of Commerce. https://www.census.gov/content/dam/Census/library/publications/2018/demo/p60-263.pdf

Forge, N., Hartinger-Saunders, R., Wright, E., & Ruel, E. (2018). Out of the system and onto the streets: LGBTQ-identified youth experiencing homelessness with past child welfare system involvement. *Child Welfare, 96*(2), 47–74.

Gil, D. G. (2013). *Confronting injustice and oppression: Concepts and strategies for social workers.* Columbia University Press.

Golash Boza, T. (2017). Structural racism, criminalization, and pathways to deportation for Dominican and Jamaican men in the United States. *Social Justice, 44*(2–3), 137–161.

Harrison, J., VanDeusen, K., & Way, I. (2016). Embedding social justice within micro social work curricula. *Smith College Studies in Social Work, 86*(3), 258–273. https://doi.org/10.1080/00377317.2016.1191802

Henry, M., Bishop, K., de Sousa, T., Shivji, A., & Watt, R. (2018, October). Part 2: Estimates of homelessness in the United States: The 2017 annual homeless assessment report (AHAR) to congress. U.S. Department of Housing and Urban Development. https://www.hudexchange.info

International Association of Schools of Social Work. (2018, April). *Global social work statement of ethical principles.* https://www.iassw-aiets.org/wp-content/uploads/2018/04/Global-Social-Work-Statement-of-Ethical-Principles-IASSW-27-April-2018-1.pdf

International Federation of Social Workers. (2018, July). *Global social work statement of ethical principles.* https://www.ifsw.org/global-social-work-statement-of-ethical-principles

Jeyapal, D. (2017). The evolving politics of race and social work activism: A call across borders. *Social Work, 62*(1), 45–52. https://doi.org/10.1093/sw/sww069

Kelley, S. (2019). Mass incarceration. *Human Ecology, 47*(1), 15. https://search.proquest.com/openview/5e41a383ceee7bad02e867fe790be1a6/1?pq-origsite=gscholar&cbl=27297

Kim, H. C. (2017). A challenge to the social work profession? The rise of socially engaged art and a call to radical social work. *Social Work, 62*(4), 305–311. https://doi.org/10.1093/sw/swx045

Knight, C. (2017). BSW and MSW students' opinions about and responses to the death of Freddie Gray and the ensuing riots: Implications for the social justice emphasis in social work education. *Journal of Teaching in Social Work, 37*(1), 3–19. https://doi.org/10.1080/08841233.2016.1273293

Marsh, J. C. (2005). Social justice: Social work's organizing value. *Social Work, 50*(4), 293–294. https://doi.org/10.1093/sw/50.4.293

Marsh, J. C., & Bunn, M. (2018). Social work's contribution to direct practice with individuals, families, and groups: An institutionalist perspective. *Social Service Review, 92*(4), 647–692. https://doi.org/10.1086/701639

Martensen, K. (2012). The price that US minority communities pay: Mass incarceration and the ideologies that fuel them. *Contemporary Justice Review, 15*(2), 211–222. https://doi.org/10.1080/10282580.2012.681165

Maschi, T., Baer, J., & Turner, S. G. (2011). The psychological goods on clinical social work: A content analysis of the clinical social work and social justice literature. *Journal of Social Work Practice, 25*(2), 233–253. https://doi.org/10.1080/02650533.2010.544847

McLaughlin, A. M. (2011). Exploring social justice for clinical social work practice. *Smith College Studies in Social Work, 81*(2–3), 234–251. https://doi.org/10.1080/00377317.2011.588551

McLaughlin, A. M., Gray, E., & Wilson, M. (2015). Child welfare workers and social justice: Mending the disconnect. *Children and Youth Services Review, 59,* 177–183. https://doi.org/10.1016/j.childyouth.2015.11.006

Morgaine, K. (2014). Conceptualizing social justice in social work: Are social workers "too bogged down in the trees?" *Journal of Social Justice, 4,* 1–18. http://transformativestudies.org/wp-content/uploads/Conceptualizing-Social-Justice-in-Social-Work.pdf

Mullaly, B. (2002). *Challenging oppression: A critical social work approach.* Oxford University Press.

National Association of Social Workers. (1960). *The original NASW code of ethics.* https://www.socialworkers.org/About/Ethics/Code-of-Ethics/g/LinkClick.aspx?fileticket=lPpjxmAsCTs%3d&portalid=0

National Association of Social Workers. (1967). *First revision of the NASW code of ethics.* https://www.socialworkers.org/LinkClick.aspx?fileticket=9PxSwiQrItA%3d&portalid=0

National Association of Social Workers. (1979). *Code of ethics of the National Association of Social Workers.* https://www.socialworkers.org/LinkClick.aspx?fileticket=eKQXR46sasc%3d&portalid=0

National Association of Social Workers. (2017a). *Read the code of ethics.* https://www.socialworkers.org/About/Ethics/Code-of-Ethics/Code-of-Ethics-English

National Association of Social Workers. (2017b). Social justice brief: Intersection of sanctuary cities, national immigration policies, and child welfare policies and practices in the Trump era. http://www.socialworkblog.org/wp-content/uploads/Social-Justice-Brief.pdf

National Association of Social Workers. (2017c). Transition document to the Trump administration: Advancing the American agenda: How the social work profession will help. https://www.socialworkers.org/LinkClick.aspx?fileticket=KdViBtJaxtw%3d&portalid=

Nicotera, A. (2019). Social justice and social work, a fierce urgency: Recommendations for social work social justice pedagogy. *Journal of Social Work Education, 55*(3), 460–475. https://doi.org/10.1080/10437797.2019.1600443

Olson, C. J., Reid, C., Threadgill-Goldson, N., Riffe, H. A., & Ryan, P. A. (2013). Voices from the field: Social workers define and apply social justice. *Journal of Progressive Human Services, 24*(1), 23–42. https://doi.org/10.1080/10428232.2013.740407

Pyles, L. (2014). *Progressive community organizing: Reflective practice in a globalizing world* (2nd ed.). Routledge.

Rank, M. (2005). *One nation, underprivileged: Why American poverty affects us all.* Oxford University Press.

Reamer, F. G. (2018). *Social work values and ethics* (5th ed.). Columbia University Press.

Reichert, E. (2007). Human rights in the twenty-first century: Creating a new paradigm for social work. In E. Reichert (Ed.), *Challenges in human rights: A social work perspective* (pp. 1–15). Columbia University Press.

Reisch, M. (2016). Why macro practice matters. *Journal of Social Work Education, 52*(3), 258–268. https://doi.org/10.1080/10437797.2016.1174652

Reisch, M. (2019). Lessons from social work's history for a tumultuous era. *Social Service Review, 93*(4), 581–607. https://doi.org/10.1086/706741

Robbins, S. P. (2011). Oppression theory and social work treatment. In F. J. Turner (Ed.), *Social work treatment: Interlocking theoretical approaches* (5th ed., pp. 343–353). Oxford University Press.

Society for Social Work Research. (2020, June). SSWR call and commitment to ending police brutality, racial injustice, and white supremacy [Press release]. https://secure.sswr.org/sswr-call-and-commitment-to-ending-police-brutality-racial-injustice-and-white-supremacy

Solas, J. (2008). What kind of social justice does social work seek? *International Social Work, 51*(6), 813–822. https://doi.org/10.1177/0020872808095252

Specht, H., & Courtney, M. E. (1994). *Unfaithful angels: How social work has abandoned its mission.* The Free Press.

United Nations. (1948, December 10). General assembly resolution 217 A: Universal declaration of human rights. https://www.un.org/en/about-us/universal-declaration-of-human-rights

Vanderwood, J. R. (2016). The promise and perils of anti-oppressive practice for Christians in social work education. *Social Work & Christianity, 43*(2), 153–188.

Wakefield, J. C. (1988a). Psychotherapy, distributive justice, and social work. Part 1: Distributive justice as a conceptual framework for social work. *Social Service Review, 62*(2), 187–210. https://www.jstor.org/stable/30011962?refreqid=excelsior%3A2705fbbd05eab9a7c733e358b2d5c90e

Wakefield, J. C. (1988b). Psychotherapy, distributive justice, and social work. Part 2: Psychotherapy and the pursuit of justice. *Social Service Review, 62*(3), 353–382. https://www.jstor.org/stable/30011976

Violence and Social Work

Lisa Rapp-McCall

Violence is defined by the World Health Organization's (2020) Violence Prevention Alliance as

> the intentional use of physical force or power, threatened or actual, against oneself, another person, or against a group or community, that either results in or has a high likelihood of resulting in injury, death, psychological harm, maldevelopment, or deprivation.

Violence in the United States was designated a serious public health problem by the U.S. Surgeon General in 1979 due to its high prevalence rate and serious consequences in its aftermath [Centers for Disease Control and Prevention (CDC), n.d.]. Violence causes injuries, death, trauma, biopsychosocial deterioration; limits achievement and opportunity; and exacerbates inequalities (Slutkin et al., 2018). Numerous studies during the past few decades have indicated a high prevalence rate of violence in America. According to the National Violent Death Reporting System, approximately seven people per hour die a violent death, and medical care and lost work due to violence, cost the U.S. economy almost $90 billion annually (CDC, n.d.).

The latest data on youth violence reveal that 9.2 children out of every 1,000 were victims of child abuse and neglect in the United States in 2018 (U.S. Department of Health and Human Services, 2018). The rate of violent victimization for students at school was approximately 38.1 per 1,000 (National Center for Education Statistics, 2018); 20% of students reported victimization by bullying and 16% of high school students admitted to carrying a weapon at school (Musu et al., 2019).

Regarding adults, 1 in 4 women and nearly 1 in 10 men have experienced sexual violence, physical violence, and/or stalking by an intimate partner during their lifetime (CDC, 2019). Four in 10 households have one or more firearms. Both firearm-involved murders and firearm-involved suicides have increased in recent years, with approximately 4.6 gun murders and 6.9 gun suicides in 2017 (Gramlich, 2019). The National Council on Aging (2020) notes that 1 in 10 elders (Americans older than age 60 years) has been a victim of elder abuse.

These are but a few illustrations of the level of violence that impacts citizens throughout the life span. This level of incidence suggests that professional social workers are unlikely to currently work with any client who has not been a victim/survivor, perpetrator, or witness of violence. Social workers need to be knowledgeable about the contagion of violence, the interrelationships between various forms of violence, and risk factors of violence, so they are prepared to accurately assess and provide evidence-supported treatment. This chapter addresses these issues and reviews violence through a holistic, public health lens versus a silo approach.

Contagion of Violence

Studies have found that violence is contagious [Institute of Medicine (IOM) and National Research Center (NRC), 2013]; in other words, violence begets violence. Huesmann (2011) found one violent family member increases the risk of violence by other family members. Violence by peers increases the chance of violence by other peers. Likewise, neighborhoods and communities breed violence, as do nations. An individual can be a direct victim of violence or a witness to it. Studies have found that direct victimization or exposure to violence increases the risk of future violent behavior 30-fold (Spano et al., 2010). Studies have indicated that it is rare to have experienced only one form of violence. In fact, *polyvictimization* is more common and leads to numerous deleterious consequences across the life span (White & Geffner, 2020). The contagion effect can be transmitted and received beyond space and time (Huesmann, 2011); for instance, someone watching violent events on the news can then be infected and susceptible to becoming violent. This phenomenon suggests that violence is a higher potential contagion than most other infectious diseases.

By studying violence carefully, researchers and practitioners note how it can cluster, spread/mutate, and grow. This is important for assessment and to identify points for prevention and intervention. For example, three children witness interpersonal violence between their parents. As they age, they can reproduce and continue that violence by becoming a repeated victim or perpetrator. Now there is a *cluster* of violence in the extended family and a cluster in the community. This also *grows* that type of violence by 75% (if each child becomes a victim and/or perpetrator). The violence can also *spread/mutate* as each child may engage in other types of violence (not only interpersonal violence) as they develop; perhaps one is a bully to other children at school, or another stalks a romantic partner or is abusive to an animal. Self-directed violence or suicide has also been shown to have a contagion effect within families and among peer groups and communities (IOM and NRC, 2013).

Interrelationship of All Violence

One reason for the contagion effect is that many types of violence occur in almost every social milieu. There is violence in the media, online, in communities, in schools, in parks, on roads, in movie theaters, in workplaces, and in homes; and there is violence against elders, adults, youth, and animals. In addition, all types of violence are related to at least one other type (Taillieu et al., 2020). For instance, child abuse is related to bullying, school violence, juvenile violence, animal abuse, domestic/dating violence, community violence, human trafficking, sexual assault, and elder abuse. Human trafficking is related to child abuse, bullying, dating/domestic violence, and sexual assault. Community violence is related to child abuse, bullying, school violence, animal abuse, human trafficking, domestic/dating violence, etc. (IOM and NRC, 2013; Taillieu et al., 2020). This means that one type may be a risk factor for another type or the consequence of another type, or the two types simply co-occur due to sharing the same risk factors.

Not everyone who has been exposed to violence will be a repeat victim or a perpetrator; however, some individuals will continue the contagion, especially if they have documented risk factors. As with other diseases, risk factors make an individual more susceptible to contagion and acting on that contagion. These risk factors are the same for all types and locations of violence. Several risk factors have been identified that increase the likelihood that individuals who are victims or witnesses of violence may experience further victimizations or may commit perpetrations themselves.

Main Risk Factors for Violence

Proximity to violence is a key risk factor. Studies have indicated that direct victimization by violence is often more serious than observation or exposure to violence. The interpersonal nature and physical and psychological injuries that result from this type of victimization make direct victimization more serious than witnessing or exposure to violence (IOM and NRC, 2013). Yet observing violence is also a risk factor, especially if the violence was directed toward someone the victim knows. Witnessing violence toward a family member or friend has been shown to be more traumatic than witnessing a stranger being victimized (Lambert et al., 2012).

The *dose* of violence, including the severity of violence (firearm violence vs. a slap), type of exposure, and frequency of exposure, drastically affects the risk of consequences and acting aggressively. The more violence to which one is exposed, and the more severe and frequent that violence, the more likely an individual is to act violently and/or be repetitively victimized. This is especially true of youth. A large body of research suggests that adverse childhood experiences (ACEs) have a significant effect on future victimization and violence (Taillieu et al., 2020). ACEs include all forms

of serious violence as well as other traumas, which studies have found impair brain development, damage neurocognitive processing, and lead to behavioral dysregulation and poor psychological coping strategies (Sheffler et al., 2020). Consequently, an accumulative effect of serious violence exposure, especially before age 18 years when the brain is developing, means a large dose or high risk for future offending or victimization. Bandoli et al. (2017) found that the accumulation of trauma makes an individual more sensitive to stress and further traumas. In other words, polyvictimization has a magnifying effect.

Proximity to and dosage level of violence create trauma that further perpetuates violence, but it can also create "social norms" that encourage or normalize aggression and violence (IOM and NRC, 2013). According to the CDC (n.d.), social norms include values, attitudes, and behaviors, and they can originate from and be reinforced by family, peers, neighborhood, community, and/or media. The longer a person is exposed to these norms, the more difficult it is to change those beliefs and behaviors. In addition, children and youth who are inculcated with aggressive/violent norms tend to be highly receptive to violent influences and more intractable in their aggressive behaviors (Lambert et al., 2012).

Social norms not only refer to a "normalization of violence" but also refer to normalization of inequality. At its roots, violence is based on unequal rights and a differential of power. In order for violence to occur, an individual or a group has to have power (physical, social, economic, psychological, and/or legal) over another person or group. This is found in all forms of violence. Prejudice and stereotypes drive inequality and are found at the roots of most types of violence. For example, violence toward women is rooted in patriarchy or sexist beliefs; both elder and child abuse are based on ageist attitudes that children and the elderly are not as valuable as young and middle-aged adults; and bullying highlights perceived inequalities based on race, athleticism, intelligence, attractiveness, alignment with social groups, etc.

Escalators of Violence

In addition to risk factors, which encourage violence, there are also *escalators* of violence. Escalators increase the magnitude (scale), lethality (strength), and/or facilitation of aggression or violence that is already present. Studies have found firearms and alcohol to be substantially related to escalation of violence (Branas et al., 2016; McGinty & Webster, 2017).

Firearms

Firearms are not the cause of violence, but they can potentially enhance its lethality. What may have begun and ended with a fist fight can instead result in serious injury or death. According to the Pew Research Center (Gramlich, 2019), three-fourths of all U.S. murders in 2017—14,542 out of 19,510—involved a firearm. Approximately half (51%) of all suicides that year—23,854 out of 47,173—involved a gun. When a firearm is stored in the home, the possibility of homicide increases by 170% and the risk of suicide increases by 460% (Miller et al., 2016). One of the reasons for these high statistics is that many adults admit that they store guns unlocked, loaded, or both (Crifasi et al., 2018). Research has found that males engage in more violence than females and that they purchase, use, and misuse firearms more often (Cukier et al., 2017). Individuals with a trauma history often struggle with behavioral dysregulation or the inability to contain impulsive thoughts and behaviors. Access to a weapon can increase lethality, and it facilitates acting on angry impulses that might have otherwise passed (Sheffler et al., 2020). This connection between firearms and violence provides social workers with instructional information on the connection between firearms, violent victimization, and perpetration of violence.

Alcohol

Alcohol and violence have been linked through decades of research. Approximately 50% of violent incidents involve alcohol consumption by perpetrators and victims (Pernanen, 1991). Interpersonal violence is especially affected by alcohol, as studies have noted that violent incidents are nearly three times higher for couples who drink heavily (Parrott & Eckhardt, 2017). Alcohol intoxication reliably increases aggression and violent responses. There are multiple theories explaining the link (which is beyond the scope of this chapter), but the main findings conclude that alcohol directly impairs areas of the brain responsible for inhibiting socially inappropriate behavior such as aggression. In addition, alcohol causes physiological arousal and impairment of cognitive functioning (Parrott & Eckhardt, 2017). For those who have a history of trauma, these responses occur in the same regions of the brain and body that may already have impairment, so traumatized individuals using alcohol may significantly escalate aggression and violence.

Assessment for Violence

Based on the frequency, consequences, and seriousness of violence to individuals, families, groups, and communities, all clients should be screened for a history of violence—as victim, witness, and/or offender. A comprehensive assessment can be used for three purposes: (1) to understand the client's future risk of further victimization and offending, (2) as a point of intervention regarding their trauma history and violent behavior, and (3) to prevent further violence exposure and/or violent behavior. The previous discussion provides guidance on the content and context of a holistic biopsychosocial violence assessment, and the following list outlines the kind of information that should be obtained:

> *Violence across the life span*: Type of violence, age when occurred, role (victim, witness known to victim, and/or perpetrator of violence), dosage (including frequency and severity), proximity
>
> *Interrelationship between violence*: Probe for other types of violence across the life span.
>
> *ACEs*: Trauma occurring before age 18 years, ACEs score (see Helpful Resources), and types of trauma (especially related to abuse and violence)
>
> *Firearms*: Access to guns, types of guns, storage of guns, storage of ammunition, carrying guns, firearms training
>
> *Alcohol*: Alcohol consumption levels, consumption frequency, others' consumption of alcohol in home
>
> *Diet of violence*: Consumption of violence from television, movies, social media, video games, music, books, direct observation (home, school, community)
>
> *Social norms toward violence*: Attitudes, beliefs, and behaviors that exhibit acceptance, appreciation, enjoyment of violence, and/or endorsement of power/control or inequality

After a biopsychosocial assessment is completed, specific standardized measures for practice should be utilized. Numerous standardized measurements are available on specific types of violence. Once the social worker better understands what the client has been a victim/observer/perpetrator of, specialty measurements can then be leveraged to obtain detailed information of that particular type of violence. A list of these measurements is provided in the Helpful Resources section.

Prevention and Intervention

Utilizing a public health philosophy toward violence allows us to consider violence akin to a contagious disease. Violence is, after all, contagious and affected by dosage and proximity; it clusters, grows, and spreads; and it is interrelated. Therefore, a combined strategy of prevention and intervention tactics must be a part of any effective method to eradicate it.

Prevention and intervention programs for specific types of violence are helpful, but in being too specific, other forms of violence are missed, the interrelationship of violence is overlooked, and outcomes are minimal. For instance, how could a youth attend prevention programs for all potential types of violence they may encounter through the life span (child abuse, bullying, human trafficking, school violence, family violence, dating violence, elder abuse, etc.)? Prevention of violence needs to occur through a universal lens that incorporates the interrelatedness and contagion of violence and its similarities to a contagious disease. Thus far, researchers, policymakers, and service providers have been working in specialty silos. Journals, organizations, and grassroots groups do the same. With poor communication and limited sharing between experts, services have been fragmented and advances regarding violence reduction have been minimal. In order to significantly reduce violence in the United States, several changes need to occur.

Heighten Awareness to Change Americans' Views on Violence and Challenge Social Norms

Violence prevention, like any prevention, should be started early and done throughout the life span. Awareness does not always change behavior, but it can be the first step in the change process. We need to educate the general public as well as clients about ACEs and the numerous, deleterious effects of violence. In addition, we can make individuals cognizant of the interrelated nature of violence, increase awareness about the contagion of violence, and analyze its relationship to our consumption of violence. The media needs to be aware that repeatedly showing violence inflames anger and violence and strengthens the social norm for violence as a legitimate way of behaving and solving problems (Anderson et al., 2017).

Messaging and awareness about the deleterious effects of violence and its persistence in our culture should take place in all institutions, including hospitals, schools, community centers, and places of employment, and should be conveyed to all adults, parents, youth, and children. Awareness of how inequality cultivates and perpetuates violence should also be underscored. Only with universal, continuous, and consistent messaging can a legitimate and constructive change in social norms toward violence occur.

Prevent ACEs

Children who are victims of abuse and/or violence prior to age 18 years are prone to having serious physical and behavioral problems, including an increased risk of being a victim, witness, or perpetrator of violence. Preventing ACEs would significantly reduce violence in the United States. Parents need to be aware of this and given support and training in effective parenting skills. The following parent education programs have been found to be effective: Nurse–Family Partnership, Parent Corps, Generation PMTO, Communities That Care, Family Foundations, Triple P System, Child First, and Incredible Years (see Blueprints for Healthy Youth Development in the Helpful Resources section). These programs teach effective parenting skills; improve family relationships; deter trauma; and should be offered to all parents free of charge in pediatrician's offices, schools, preschools, and community

centers. In addition to acquiring these skills, parents should also be encouraged to monitor and reduce their youths' consumption of violence, especially via social media, television, movies, and video games.

Provide Evidence-Supported Interventions for Each Type of Violence—Targeted at Micro, Mezzo, and Macro Levels

Trauma-informed and evidence-supported treatment is essential for victims and perpetrators of violence. Without it, many individuals and families will replicate victimization, exposure, and/or aggression. Treatment should address the risk factors for violence as a whole as well as the particulars of the type of violence of focus. Effective treatment should also address trauma bonding or dysfunctional attachments as well as ACEs. In addition, it should educate the client and family about the interrelatedness of different types of violence, the contagion, and the client's consumption of violence. See the Helpful Resources section for a list of evidence-supported programs.

One new mezzo-level intervention showing effectiveness is the *epidemic control approach*. It has been used to interpose other contagious diseases in the community such as HIV and tuberculosis. It works by hiring, training, supervising, and supporting outreach workers in targeted communities. These workers map out places with high levels of violence (hot spots), connect with individuals who frequently engage in violence (hot people), provide focused interventions for the specific form of violence being exhibited, detect others who are impacted by those individuals, and provide services to them with an overall objective to intervene and prevent further violence (Slutkin et al., 2018). These methods interfere with doses and frequency of violence to reduce transmission and therefore inhibit spread, clustering, and growth of violence. Over time, harmful social norms and behaviors are replaced with new ones. Numerous evaluations have found statistically significant reductions in violence across multiple sites, including a 70% reduction in shootings and killings in Chicago, Illinois (Skogan et al., 2012), and a 56% decrease in homicides in Baltimore, Maryland (Webster et al., 2012). The program is cost-effective because it is focused on a small area and specific individuals engaging in the most violence.

Reduce Firearm Availability to High-Risk Individuals and Educate All About Firearm Storage

If violence is contagious and interrelated and fueled by firearms, then we need to advocate and intervene on a macro level to reduce firearm purchase and possession for any individual who has engaged in any type of aggression or violence. This is a difficult political agenda and a cultural conflict, but it must be addressed. Canada and other countries have found success with education, screening, licensing, safe storage, and restrictions on access for high-risk individuals (Cukier et al., 2017). Although the cultural contexts are different, these successes could inform U.S. social workers on best practices.

Messaging regarding firearm safety is crucial for all citizens. Education will need to be thoughtful, clear, and well-planned. The intent should not be to reduce rights but, rather, to ensure safety for children, youth, and adults, especially for those who have histories of anger, violence, suicide attempts, impulsivity, and/or live in homes with violent individuals.

Collaborate with Alcohol Abuse Experts to Screen and Heighten Awareness of the Link Between Alcohol and Violence

In order to reduce violence, we need to collaborate with alcohol abuse experts. These specialists can assist in violence reduction by educating clients about the nexus between alcohol and violence; assessing for a history of victimization, exposure, and/or perpetration of violence; and screening for firearm access and use. This is an often forgotten avenue in reducing violence, but it is worth pursuing.

Social Workers Need to Be Outspoken Experts and Spokespersons to Reduce and Eradicate Violence

Finally, violence is a public health concern that needs to be addressed holistically to break down unnecessary practice, research, and policy silos that hinder advancement and ultimately prevention. Social workers interface with individuals who often have a history of violence. Thorough assessment of trauma and safety education for clients are critical. In addition, comprehensive interventions that address polyvictimization and contagion are needed.

On a larger scale, social workers are trained to connect groups, empower networks, and drive change. We should be advocates who speak for victims and demand action from our governmental agencies, as well as spokespeople for eliminating violence from American social norms. Self-effacement and suggestions are ineffective. It is time to think bigger and act swiftly and courageously.

Helpful Resources

Assessment

ACE's screening: https://www.acesaware.org/screen/screening-for-adverse-childhood-experiences

Assessment Tools for Children's Exposure to Violence: http://promising.futureswithoutviolence.org/files/2012/01/Assessment-Tools-for-Childrens-Exposure-to-Violence-2016.pdf

Fischer, J., Corcoran, K., & Springer, D. (Eds.). (2020). *Measures for clinical practice and research: A sourcebook* (6th ed., Vols. 1 and 2). Oxford University Press.

Life Events Checklist for DSM-5, standard and extended versions—screens for traumatic events including abuse and violence: https://www.ptsd.va.gov/professional/assessment/te-measures/life_events_checklist.asp

Stressful Life Events Screening Questionnaire: https://georgetown.app.box.com/s/nzprmm2bn5pwzdw1l62w

The National Child Traumatic Stress Network, Screening and Assessment: https://www.nctsn.org/treatments-and-practices/screening-and-assessment

Trauma History Questionnaire: http://ctc.georgetown.edu/toolkit

University of Miami, School of Nursing and Health Studies, Center of Excellence for Health Disparities, Violence Measures: https://elcentro.sonhs.miami.edu/research/measures-library/violence-construct/index.html

Vulnerability to Abuse Screening Scale: https://medicine.uiowa.edu/familymedicine/sites/medicine.uiowa.edu.familymedicine/files/wysiwyg_uploads/VASS.pdf

Prevention and Intervention Programs

Blueprints for Healthy Youth Development: https://www.blueprintsprograms.org/program-search

California Evidence-Based Clearinghouse: https://www.cebc4cw.org

CrimeSolutions: https://www.crimesolutions.gov

Cure Violence: https://cvg.org

Substance Abuse and Mental Health Services Administration, National Registry of Evidence-Based Programs and Practices: https://www.samhsa.gov/ebp-resource-center

The National Child Traumatic Stress Network, Trauma Treatments: https://www.nctsn.org/treatments-and-practices/trauma-treatments

Veto Violence: https://vetoviolence.cdc.gov/apps/main/home

References

Anderson, C. A., Suzuki, K., Swing, E. L., Groves, C. L., Gentile, D. A., Prot, S., Lam, C. P., Sakamoto, A., Horiuchi, Y., Krahe, B., Jelic, M., Liuging, W., Toma, R., Warburton, W. A., Zhang, X.-M., Tajima, S., Qing, F., & Petrescu, P. (2017). Media violence and other aggression risk factors in seven nations. *Personality and Social Psychology Bulletin, 43*(7), 986–998. https://doi.org/10.1177/0146167217703064

Bandoli, G., Campbell-Sills, L., Kessler, R., Heeringa, S., Nock, M., Rosellini, A., Sampson, N., Schoenbaum, M., Ursano, R., & Stein, M. (2017). Childhood adversity, adult stress, and the risk of major depression or generalized anxiety disorder in US soldiers: A test of the stress sensitization hypothesis. *Psychological Medicine, 47*(13), 2379–2392.

Branas, C. C., Han, S., & Wiebe, D. J. (2016). Alcohol use and firearm violence. *Epidemiologic Reviews, 38*(1), 32–45.

Centers for Disease Control and Prevention. (2019). Preventing intimate partner violence factsheet, 2019. Retrieved April 24, 2020, from https://www.cdc.gov/violenceprevention/pdf/ipv-factsheet508.pdf

Centers for Disease Control and Prevention. (n.d.). *Social norms.* Retrieved June 17, 2020, from https://vetoviolence.cdc.gov/apps/main/prevention-information/35

Crifasi, C. K., Doucette, M. L., McGinty, E. E., Webster, D. W., & Barry, C. L. (2018). Storage practices of US gun owners in 2016. *American Journal of Public Health, 108*(4), 532–537.

Cukier, W., Eagen, S., & Decat, G. (2017). Gun violence. In B. Bushman (Ed.), *Aggression and violence: A social psychological perspective* (pp. 169–183). Routledge.

Gramlich, J. (2019). *What the data says about gun deaths in the U.S.* Fact Tank, Pew Research Center. Retrieved April 24, 2020, from https://pewrsr.ch/2KPjZii

Huesmann, L. (2011, April 29). The contagion of violence: The extent, the processes, and the outcomes [Conference session]. National Academies of Sciences' Institute of Medicine's Global Forum on Violence, Washington, DC.

Institute of Medicine and National Research Center. (2013). *Contagion of violence: Workshop summary.* National Academies Press.

Lambert, S. F., Boyd, R. C., Cammack, N. L., & Ialongo, N. S. (2012). Relationship proximity to victims of witnessed community violence: Associations with adolescent internalizing and externalizing behaviors. *American Journal of Orthopsychiatry, 82*(1), 1–9.

McGinty, E. E., & Webster, D. W. (2017). The roles of alcohol and drugs in firearm violence. *JAMA Internal Medicine, 177*(3), 324–325.

Miller, M., Swanson S., & Azrael, D. (2016). Are we missing something pertinent? A bias analysis of unmeasured confounding in the firearm-suicide literature. *Epidemiologic Reviews, 38*(1), 62–69.

Musu, L., Zhang, A., Wang, K., Zhang, J., & Oudekerk, B. A. (2019). *Indicators of school crime and safety: 2018.* National Center for Education Statistics, U.S. Department of Education, and Bureau of

Justice Statistics, Office of Justice Programs, U.S. Department of Justice.

National Center for Education Statistics. (2018). *Indicators of school crime and safety: 2018*. Retrieved April 24, 2020, from https://nces.ed.gov/pubsearch/pubsinfo.asp?pubid=2020054

National Council on Aging. (2020). *Elder abuse facts*. Retrieved April 24, 2020, from https://www.ncoa.org/article/get-the-facts-on-elder-abuse

Parrott, D., & Eckhardt, C. (2017). Effects of alcohol and other drugs on human aggression. In B. Bushman (Ed.), *Aggression and violence: A social psychological perspective* (pp. 199–222). Routledge.

Pernanen, K. (1991). *Alcohol in human violence*. Guilford.

Sheffler, J. L., Stanley, I., & Sachs-Ericsson, N. (2020). ACEs and mental health outcomes. In G. Asmundson & T. Afifi (Eds.), *Adverse childhood experiences* (pp. 47–69). Academic Press.

Skogan, D. W. G., Hartnett, S. M., Bump, N., & Dubois, J. (2012). *Evaluation of CeaseFire–Chicago*. BiblioGov.

Slutkin, G., Ransford, C., & Zvetina, D. (2018). How the health sector can reduce violence by treating it as a contagion. *AMA Journal of Ethics, 20*(1), 47–55.

Spano, R., Rivera, C., & Bolland, J. M. (2010). Are chronic exposure to violence and chronic violent behavior closely related developmental processes during adolescence? *Criminal Justice and Behavior, 37*(10), 1160–1179.

Taillieu, T. L., Davila, I. G., & Struck, S. (2020). ACEs and violence in adulthood. In G. Asmundson & T. Afifi (Eds.), *Adverse childhood experiences* (pp. 119–142). Academic Press.

U.S. Department of Health and Human Services, Administration for Children and Families, Administration on Children, Youth and Families, Children's Bureau. (2020). Child maltreatment 2018. Retrieved April 24, 2020, from https://www.acf.hhs.gov/cb/report/child-maltreatment-2018

Webster, D. W., Whitehill, J. M., Vernick, J. S., & Parker, E. M. (2012). *Evaluation of Baltimore's Safe Streets program: Effects on attitudes, participants' experiences, and gun violence*. Johns Hopkins Bloomberg School of Public Health.

White, J., & Geffner, R. (2020). Fundamentals of understanding interpersonal violence and abuse. In R. Geffner, J. White, L. Hamberger, A. Rosenbaum, V. Vaughan-Eden, & V. Vieth (Eds.), *Handbook of interpersonal violence across the lifespan* (pp. 1–24). Springer. https://doi.org/10.1007/978-3-319-62122-7

World Health Organization. (2020). Violence prevention alliance. Retrieved April 24, 2020, from https://www.who.int/violenceprevention/approach/definition/en

Emerging Fields of Practice in American Social Work

Kathryn Conley Wehrmann

Since its beginnings, American social work has evolved in response to social injustices and human needs confronting our society. Social workers have assisted immigrants in resettlement and developed policy for financial assistance and alleviation of poverty for millions of Americans. They engaged in the fight for civil rights; worked to combat stigma; and gained services for many disenfranchised groups, including those afflicted with HIV, the mentally ill, the addicted, the homeless, and survivors of violence. As Kahn (1973) said, "Social work practice answers the call of its time" (p. vii). Today, social workers continue to respond to the call and lead the profession to new places. With the Code of Ethics and ethical training, our ability to reach people in respectful, compassionate, nonstigmatizing ways, our person-in-environment lens, and our professional knowledge and skill, we continue to be well-positioned to help people in need at both micro and macro levels.

We urgently need to consider the social work response in the face of a pandemic that has starkly highlighted the plight of the most vulnerable in our society who are disproportionately affected by COVID-19. The pandemic's devastating effects underscore social work's obligation to advocate for needed structural changes. As we confront COVID-19's lasting impact on society, we will learn how well we fit into many established and emerging practice contexts and how to improve that fit.

At the same time the United States is confronting COVID-19, systemic racism has been brought into sharp focus by the brutal murder of George Floyd at the hands of a Minneapolis police officer. Floyd's death was a galvanizing moment for the Black Lives Matter movement that has sought accountability for a long history of racist policing in America and the loss of many lives. Once again, social work is called to continue the fight for social and economic justice. We are called now to expand community-based services for mental health, health, substance use disorders, homelessness, and family violence— all areas of social work expertise—as alternatives to police intervention.

Envisioning Future Practice

From a workforce development perspective, two reports (2018 and 2019) and articles from a national symposium (2019) are especially helpful in thinking about what lies ahead for social work. To do our best work and contribute most to our society, social workers must envision future practices and the spaces in which social work can offer leadership. As a way of doing this kind of visioning and "imagineering," the Council on Social Work Education (CSWE) created the Futures Task Force, which published its findings in April 2018. The task force report acknowledged that the United States was facing increasing income inequality, an unfavorable political environment resulting in funding cuts and further fraying of the social safety net. One of the key ideas underpinning the work of the task force was to "develop greater clarity about the future of the profession of social work" (p. 2) before moving forward with strategic planning to set the direction of social work education. CSWE selected a scenario planning process that produced four "alternative futures for the social work profession" (p. 3). Creating the scenarios involved an environmental scan that included exploration of trends affecting the future, interviews with social work "thought leaders" and representatives of other professions, a survey sent to all CSWE-accredited schools and individual members, and a review of existing reports related to the workforce. The result of the analysis was the creation of four alternative scenarios: embracing technology to enhance practice, building on our successes, social workers as leaders everywhere, and social work leadership for a high-tech world. Each scenario described potential social work roles and the degree to which technology would be used and leadership taken. Certainly, our recent experience in ongoing efforts to respond to COVID-19 has proven the need for social workers to virtualize practice and expand possibilities for the future.

Three months earlier, in January 2018, the *Social Service Review* commemorated the 100th anniversary of the first meeting of the National Conference of Social Work with a symposium titled Whither American Social Work in Its Second Century? The event featured social work scholars who reflected "on the state of scholarship, and the profession itself, the core areas of social welfare policy development and analysis; administration of social services; community organization; and direct practice with individuals, families and groups" (Courtney, 2018, p. 488). Key points and messages from the symposium presentations formed the basis for articles published in a special issue of *Social Service Review*.

The discussion of community practice indicated that social work will be working on expanding economic, educational, and other opportunities that, according to Gutierrez and Gant (2018), will most likely require change in major social structures. Community practitioners will be focused on "working to build community assets that will necessitate challenging existing political and economic arrangements" (p. 637) and will be more involved in bringing multicultural and multiracial communities together. It is also likely that community-based practice will be responsive to calls for change in how public safety is conceptualized and carried out.

According to Austin (2018), preparation of future social work managers will need to incorporate new approaches such as dual-degree programs or an expansion of content from disciplines such as public health and public administration. Austin calls for CSWE to consider where management fits into the social work curriculum. As the premier professional association, the National Association of Social Workers (NASW) will likely need to provide additional professional development opportunities to prepare social work managers and administrators among the existing workforce.

For direct practice, Marsh and Bunn (2018) underscored social work's distinction in recognizing social context as a "powerful determinant of client problems" (p. 678). This distinction supports social work's efforts in the community to meet individuals where they are in situations involving police, or in the public library, or in integrated behavioral health care settings. Other emerging areas of practice for social work, according to Marsh and Bunn, include "LGBT communities, work with the incarcerated and formerly incarcerated, trauma focused social work and international social work" (p. 683).

The 2019 National Academies of Sciences, Engineering, and Medicine (NASEM) study report titled *Integrating Social Care Into the Delivery of Health Care: Moving Upstream to Improve the Nation's Health* presents an expansive view of what might be possible for health care outcomes in the United States if care is expanded to include the social determinants of health (SDOH). The study was commissioned and funded by 60 schools of social work, CSWE, NASW, and the Society for Social Work in Health Care. It presents the "strongest evidentiary case for moving beyond the medical model in health care into a model that addresses the person in his or her environment" (Allen et al., 2018, p. 533). This report has great significance for social work advocacy with policymakers and for the increasing numbers of social workers entering the health care sector.

NASEM's (2019) report found "consistent and compelling evidence" of how the SDOH shape health and that improvement in overall health metrics is needed. The report also noted that a shift in the health sector to value-based payments (as opposed to fee-for-service) has incentivized prevention and improved health and health care outcomes for persons and populations. The emphasis is on addressing health-related factors "upstream" before a visit with a health care provider is needed. Risk factors affecting improved health outcomes include access to housing, access to nutritious food, and access to reliable transportation. Social workers are already well positioned as members of interprofessional teams in health care and community-based settings to respond to the risk factors that impact physical and mental health status.

Caring in the Community

Increasingly, social workers are moving into spaces where they can provide help and support more readily and with less stigma than more traditional practice settings have afforded. Notable spaces include community-based settings such as police departments and public libraries. Other spaces include integrated health care settings in which behavioral health care is seamlessly provided alongside primary health care and provides a more holistic approach by recognizing connections between physical and emotional health. Social workers also are increasingly offering services within veterinary clinics as companion animals take on "family member" status and the health care decisions for them become more complex. And although social workers have long been involved in disasters as first responders, the COVID-19 pandemic is a strong impetus for the profession to reconceptualize the practice of social work in the face of a health crisis that requires a multidimensional response to needed social care.

The following descriptions of four emerging and evolving fields of social work practice are not intended to be exhaustive but, rather, to present exemplars of newer spaces that social workers are occupying.

Social Work in Integrated Behavioral Healthcare Settings

Health care in the United States can be described as very fragmented, a reality that the Affordable Care Act of 2010 (ACA) sought to change in addition to improving access to needed health care for more citizens. ACA also sought to make changes in health care delivery, with a focus on providing more comprehensive care that featured the integration of health care and behavioral care. Integrated behavioral health care is defined as follows (Integration Academy, 2019):

> The care a patient experiences as a result of a team of primary care and behavioral health clinicians, working together with patients and families, using a systematic and cost-effective approach to provide patient-centered care for a defined population. This care may address mental health and substance abuse conditions, health behaviors (including their contribution to chronic medical illnesses), life stressors and crises, stress-related physical symptoms, and ineffective patterns of health care utilization. (p. 2)

Increasingly, social workers are practicing in integrated health care settings because their education and training in both mental health and substance use disorders make them well-suited to these practice settings. Competencies for professional practice in integrated health care identified by the U.S. Agency for Healthcare Research and Quality (AHRQ, 2020) include the ability to identify and assess behavioral health needs, the ability to work as a member of an interprofessional team, the ability to use brief treatment modalities, and knowledge of common chronic illnesses and co-occurring behavioral problems.

Integrative health care as a model is important for several compelling reasons. According to the National Institute of Mental Health (NIMH, 2020), primary care settings, such as a doctor's office, provide approximately half of all mental health care for common psychiatric disorders in the United States. Another compelling reason for co-locating primary and mental health care is that adults with serious

mental illness and substance use disorders also have been shown to have higher rates of chronic physical illnesses and die earlier than the general population. In addition, people with common physical health conditions also have higher rates of mental health issues.

Blending the expertise of social workers with mental health and substance use disorders expertise and that of primary care clinicians, along with feedback from patients and their caregivers, creates a team-based approach that can produce better health outcomes and more cost-effective care. Coordinating primary care and mental health care in this way can better address both the physical health problems of people with serious mental illnesses and the mental health problems of physically ill people by providing access to more timely treatment.

Treating the "whole person" with respect to physical and behavioral health is essential for positive health outcomes and cost-effective care. Many people do not have access to mental health care or may prefer to visit their primary health care provider to receive help. Although most primary care providers can treat mental disorders, often through medication, it may not be enough for some patients. It has been difficult for primary care providers to offer effective, high-quality mental health care given both the economic and time demands they face (NIMH, 2020). In addition, primary care providers likely do not have the expertise needed to effectively treat mental health issues. Combining mental health services and expertise with primary care can reduce costs, increase the quality of care, and, ultimately, save lives.

Social Work and Public Safety

At the time of this writing, the United States is experiencing protests against policing that has disproportionately resulted in the deaths of Black Americans. A catalyzing moment occurred when thousands of Americans witnessed

George Floyd's death on television and social media. Protests that followed included calls to defund the police. These calls have been met with a variety of responses, including involvement of social workers in an approach to public safety that differentiates between the need for a police response to actual crime and responses to calls that relate to social issues such as mental health, drug use, homelessness, and minor theft. Although social workers have long partnered with police, many believe that greater involvement by social workers in changing the nation's approach to public safety is needed (Terry Mizrahi, personal communication, June 29, 2020). Others are concerned that the social work profession may be aligning itself with the criminal justice system or might be co-opted by law enforcement. Most agree that social workers have valuable knowledge and skills to bring to bear, along with a structural approach to eliminating racial bias and violence in policing (Dettlaff, 2020; Sharraden, 2020; T. Mizrahi, D. Bailey, S. Burghardt, & C. Lewis, Jr., personal communication, June 29, 2020).

Social work has a history of collaboration with police departments. Some schools of social work incorporate field opportunities with police departments. For example, a field education initiative at the University of Southern California Suzanne Dworak-Peck School of Social Work places practicum students within units of the Los Angeles Police Department in communities in which they work with officers to address a variety of social issues. The social work interns bring a holistic approach to work with at-risk youth and their families and apply the person-in-environment lens to help officers see beyond the crimes committed to better understand the contribution of other factors (MSW@USC Staff, 2018).

As the debate about the need to restructure the role of police continues in the United States, it is likely that more educational opportunities for social work involvement in public safety will be needed.

Library Social Work

Public libraries have been referred to as "the first social justice initiative of Western society" (Blank, 2014, p. 2). An increasing number of public libraries throughout the country have further operationalized this initiative by including professional social workers in their operations. Since the first known "library social worker," Leah Esguerra, LMFT, was hired by the San Francisco Public Library in 2009, many degreed social workers have been hired by large public libraries (Blank, 2014).

For many homeless individuals, the public library serves as a place of refuge and assistance in meeting basic needs. The social worker can link homeless individuals with community resources, including free shelters; places to eat, shower, store possessions, obtain free clothing, and apply for public benefits; and health care resources. In addition to linking people with resources for basic needs, library social workers also provide visitors with information about other resources that could be helpful to them, including eviction prevention information, access to low-income housing, free legal assistance, free bus tickets to support family reunification, support groups, and treatment for substance use issues.

The Brookings Institute identifies the public library as a "third space" institution in our society, meaning that it is not home (first space) and not work (second space) but an informal space that strengthens communities. It provides a place where people can meet in planned and unplanned ways and develop relationships, and where everyone is served regardless of income (Cabello & Butler, 2017, p. 1). The "community living room" is also a term used to describe public libraries as places where people can feel welcome regardless of circumstance (Kiger, 2019). Public libraries in general, and particularly those with social workers, serve as a protective factor for people because help may be found there. In some cases, library social workers have opportunities to advocate for additional resources in their communities.

Veterinary Social Work

Social workers who work in veterinary practices have two clients, and by serving one, they help serve the other (The University of Tennessee, Knoxville, 2020). Veterinarians serve "patients" who do not have long lives, and they are confronted on a daily basis with having to share difficult news with a companion animal's owner about diagnoses and the costs and effectiveness of treatments (Neumann, 2019). This means frequent conversations with anxious owners about options such as palliative care or euthanasia depending on the diagnosis and the owners' ability to pay for the treatment. Compassion fatigue along with additional factors, including demands of practice, work overload, practice management responsibilities, an ever-increasing educational debt-to-income ratio, and access to medications used for euthanizing animals, present genuine risks for veterinarians, as evidenced by a higher than average suicide rate (Centers for Disease Control and Prevention, 2018).

The veterinary social worker oath states, "Specializing in veterinary social work, I pledge my service to society by tending to the human needs that arise in the relationship between humans and animals" (The University of Tennessee, Knoxville, 2020). Veterinary social workers take on activities and interventions to help both owners and veterinarians manage the communication and decision-making processes that accompany serious animal health care situations. The social worker may also be key to helping pet owners make decisions about treatment and advising them how to best talk with children about a pet's illness and what may happen, including natural death or euthanasia. Social workers can help owners assess their animal's quality of life, and they can support owners in making critical decisions about pursuing treatment. They can also support owners in the grieving process through support groups and referrals to other community resources.

Influence of the COVID-19 Pandemic

As this chapter is being written, the world is continuing to manage the impact of COVID-19. We have only begun to glimpse the impact it will have on social work practice in the future. However, we know from history that pandemics bring both devastation and opportunity for change. Although not necessarily an emerging field of practice, as a consequence of the ravages of the pandemic and the sharp focus it has brought to structural issues that disproportionately affect so many in the United States and throughout the world; we may see a professional renaissance that invigorates efforts in the social work profession to create communities in which the emphasis is truly on developing systems that are more equitable and conducive to realizing human potential. One specific area of focus will be eliminating systemic racism in our communities and organizations.

On the micro level, social workers who are skilled in trauma-based work will also find their skills and expertise in greater demand as many first responders, health care providers, and families who experienced the loss of loved ones will require mental health services. Given extended quarantine periods in a variety of states and the anxiety many are experiencing, it is likely there will also be greater need for substance use treatment. Social workers skilled in working with children and families may also find their expertise in great demand as parents struggle to help children manage their pandemic-related anxiety. Spikes in intimate partner, child, and elder abuse have also been reported in the media.

Given the tremendous influence COVID-19 has had, along with the work of Black Lives Matter and the turbulent political landscape, it will be advisable to look to key social work organizations for additional clues about how practice will evolve in the future. Social work "futurists" also offer insight into ways social work will evolve. Laura Nissen, Director of the National Social Work Education Futures Lab, is leading an effort to explore a variety of trends to assess their impact on social work practice (Social Work Futures, 2020). Based on the NASEM study report, we might look forward to social workers taking on leadership roles in the health care arena. Because of social work's ability to adapt and respond to the call of its time, more social workers will likely move into the realms of innovation and entrepreneurism. As social workers become increasingly involved, perhaps human-centered design will become a more dominant approach in the profession as new interventions are developed for work with individuals, groups, and communities. As the development of the Grand Challenges by the American Academy of Social Work and Social Welfare (AASWSW) indicates, social work researchers and practitioners are vitally needed to identify micro- and macro-level interventions to address major societal problems in ways that are measurable and powered by science (AASWSW, n.d.). Keeping this in mind, social workers and researchers can contribute greatly to achieving results on a macro scale, such as housing for homeless people, reintegration of veterans, health care for all, employment opportunities for the unemployed, and eliminating institutional racism.

In 2020, with the occurrence of COVID-19, social workers in virtually every practice setting have had to rethink how to best serve their clients. For example, many social workers were called upon to quickly incorporate technology into their work. It is unlikely that the profession will return to "normal" in this regard. Opportunities for social work leadership in the elimination of institutionalized racism in policing and other major institutions in society will be plentiful. The 2020 presidential election has already had a great influence on the kind of political landscape the profession faces in its advocacy efforts. Innovation will be required. What will not change will be the profession's investment in antiracism efforts.

References

Agency for Healthcare Research and Quality. (2013). Lexicon for behavioral health and primary care integration. Rockville, MD. https://integrationacademy.ahrq.gov/sites/default/files/2020-06/Lexicon.pdf

Allen, H., Garfinkel, I., & Waldfogel, J. (2018). Social policy research in social work in the twenty-first century: The state of scholarship and the profession: What is promising, and what needs to be done. *Social Service Review, 92*(4), 504–547.

American Academy of Social Work and Social Welfare. (n.d.). *Grand challenges for social work*. https://grandchallengesforsocialwork.org

Austin, M. J. (2018). Social work management practice, 1917–2017: A history to inform the future. *Social Service Review, 92*(4), 487–503.

Blank, B. T. (2014). Public libraries add social workers and social programs. *The New Social Worker, 21*(4), 12–14.

Cabello, M., & Butler, S.M. (2017, March 30). *How public libraries help build healthy communities*. https://www.brookings.edu/blog/up-front/2017/03/30/how-public-libraries-help-build-healthy-communities

Centers for Disease Control and Prevention. (2018, December 20). New study finds higher than expected number of suicide deaths among U.S. veterinarians. https://www.cdc.gov/media/releases/2018/p1220-veterinarians-suicide.html

Courtney, M. E. (2018). Whither American social work in its second century? *Social Service Review, 92*(4), 487–503.

Council on Social Work Education. (2018, April). *Envisioning the future of social work: Report of the CSWE Futures Task Force* (pp. 1–22).

Dettlaff, A. J. (2020, June 18). An open letter to NASW and allied organizations on social work's relationship with law enforcement. *Medium.* https://medium.com/@alandettlaff/

an-open-letter-to-nasw-and-allied-organizations-on-social-works-relationship-with-law-enforcement-1a1926c71b28

Gutierrez, L. M., & Gant, L. M. (2018). Community practice in social work: Reflections on its first century and directions for the future. *Social Service Review, 92*(4), 617–647.

Integration Academy, Agency for Healthcare Research and Quality. (2019, April 30). What is integrated behavioral healthcare (IBHC). https://integrationacademy.ahrq.gov/products/behavioral-health-measures-atlas/what-is-ibhc

Kahn, A. J. (1973). *Shaping the new social work.* Columbia University Press.

Kiger, P. (2019, May 28). Library social work: Separating fact from fiction. Social Work SmartBrief. https://www.smartbrief.com/original/2019/05/library-social-work-separating-fact-fiction

Marsh, J. C., & Bunn, M. (2018). Social work's contribution to direct practice with individuals, families and groups: An institutionalist perspective. *Social Service Review, 92*(4), 647–692.

MSW@USC Staff. (2018, August 14). *How social workers improve relationships between police and communities.* https://msw.usc.edu/mswusc-blog/police-community-relations-social-work

National Academies of Sciences, Engineering, and Medicine. (2019, September). Integrating social care into the delivery of health care: Moving upstream to improve the nation's health care. https://www.nap.edu/resource/25467/09252019Social_Care_highlights.pdf

National Institute of Mental Health. (n.d.). *Primary care research program.* https://www.nimh.nih.gov/about/organization/dsir/services-research-and-epidemiology-branch/primary-care-research-program

Neumann, J. (2019, September 16). Need to make tough decisions about your pet? A veterinary social worker can help. *The Washington Post.* https://www.washingtonpost.com/lifestyle/wellness/need-to-make-tough-decisions-about-your-pet-a-veterinary-social-worker-can-help/2019/09/13/ce8090c8-d4c4-11e9-86ac-0f250cc91758_story.html

The University of Tennessee, Knoxville. (n.d.). *Attending to human needs at the intersection of veterinary and social work practice.* https://vetsocialwork.utk.edu

PART II

Social Work Values, Ethics, and Licensing Standards

Ethical Issues in Social Work

Frederic G. Reamer

Social workers encounter a wide range of ethical issues. Most such issues in the profession are routine and relatively straightforward. For example, social workers know that ordinarily they must obtain clients' consent before releasing confidential information, respect clients' right to self-determination, and obey the law. Sometimes, however, such common duties conflict with one another; when faced with these ethical dilemmas, social workers must decide which of their conflicting obligations should take precedence (Banks, 2012; Barsky, 2019; Dolgoff et al., 2012; Reamer, 2018a; Strom-Gottfried, 2007). For example, social workers' obligation to respect clients' right to self-determination may conflict with social workers' duty to protect third parties from harm. Or, social workers' duty to obey the law may conflict with their duty to challenge unjust legal policies and regulations.

Ethical Dilemmas

Ethical dilemmas in social work take many forms. Some involve direct or clinical practice—that is, the delivery of services to individuals, families, couples, and small groups. Others involve community practice, administration, advocacy, social action, social policy, research and evaluation, relationships with colleagues, and professional education (Reamer, 2001, 2012a, 2018c). The most common dilemmas involve actual or potential conflicts among social workers' duties; these are discussed next.

Client Confidentiality and Privileged Communication

Social workers must be clear about the nature of their obligation to respect clients' right to confidentiality and exceptions to this obligation. Ethical dilemmas occur when social workers must decide whether to disclose confidential information without client consent or against a client's wishes (Dickson, 1998; Reamer, 2015, 2018a). This can occur, for example, when a client threatens to seriously harm a third party, seriously injure themself, or abuses or neglects a child or older adult. Ethical dilemmas involving privileged communication occur when social workers are asked to disclose confidential information in the context of legal proceedings (e.g., when a client's estranged spouse requests confidential clinical records as part of a child custody dispute).

The emergence of digital and other electronic technology has created new confidentiality challenges for social workers (Reamer, 2012b, 2013). Practitioners must ensure that their digital, online, and other electronic communications with clients (e.g., email, video conferencing, and text messaging communications) protect client confidentiality and adhere to strict ethical and legal standards.

Client Self-Determination and Professional Paternalism

It is widely accepted among social workers that clients ordinarily have a fundamental right to self-determination. However, ethical dilemmas arise in exceptional circumstances when, in social workers' professional judgment, clients' actions or potential actions pose a serious, foreseeable, and imminent risk to themselves or others. In these instances, social workers must decide whether to limit clients' right to self-determination.

Limiting clients' right to self-determination to protect them from harm is called *paternalism*. Paternalism involves interfering with clients' rights for their own good; it can occur in several forms, such as withholding information from clients, misleading or lying to clients, or coercing clients. Whether paternalism is morally justifiable in any given situation—for example, misleading a client about their grim medical prognosis or placing a person who struggles with mental illness and homelessness in a psychiatric hospital against their wishes—is often controversial.

Laws, Policies, and Regulations

Ordinarily, social workers should uphold relevant laws, policies, and regulations. Such compliance is important to the smooth functioning of human service organizations and the broader society. Circumstances may arise, however, when ethical obligations and social workers' values conflict with laws, policies, and regulations. In such cases, social workers must take assertive steps to resolve such conflicts,

perhaps through consultation, mediation, lobbying, and other forms of advocacy and social action. Occasionally, social workers may be faced with difficult decisions of conscience concerning the obligation to comply with what they believe to be unjust laws, policies, and regulations.

Conflicts of Interest and Boundary Issues

Conflicts of interest occur when a social worker's services to or relationship with a client is compromised or might be compromised because of decisions or actions in relation to another client, a colleague, themself, or some other third party. Many conflicts of interest involve boundary issues or dual or multiple relationships. Boundary issues occur when social workers establish and maintain more than one relationship with clients (e.g., when a social worker socializes with a client, discloses personal information to clients online, or enters into a business partnership with a client). Dual or multiple relationships can occur simultaneously or consecutively (Reamer, 2012a).

Some dual and multiple relationships are patently unethical—for example, if a social worker maintains a sexual relationship with a client or borrows money from a client. Other dual and multiple relationships are more ambiguous and require careful analysis and consultation. Examples include social workers in rural communities who cannot avoid contact with clients in social settings, social workers who are invited by clients to attend an important life event, social workers' relationships with former clients, and social workers' unanticipated encounters with clients at an Alcoholics Anonymous meeting when both parties are in recovery. Social workers' and clients' use of digital social networking sites such as Facebook and Twitter has created new boundary-related challenges. Social workers must ensure that their online relationships with clients adhere to strict ethical standards with regard to unprofessional contact and practitioner self-disclosure (Reamer, 2012b, 2013).

Nontraditional and Unorthodox Services and Interventions

Ethical dilemmas sometimes arise when social workers consider providing nontraditional and unorthodox services and interventions that are not part of customary social work practice. On the one hand, services and interventions that are not grounded in sound theory or for which there is little or no empirical evidence of effectiveness can pose significant risks to clients. On the other hand, it is important for social workers to be receptive to innovative forms of practice.

The advent of online, remote, and distance counseling has created new ethical challenges. Some social workers now provide digital and online services to clients they never meet in person. These services expand clients' opportunities to receive help, especially when clients live in remote locations or find travel to an office difficult because of a disability. At the same time, these novel services pose significant risks related to quality control, protection of client confidentiality, and informed consent (Reamer, 2012b, 2018a).

Professional and Personal Values

Social workers sometimes find that their personal values clash with traditional social work values or the official positions of employers or other organizations with which they are affiliated professionally. This can occur, for example, when practitioners object to their employers' political views or positions on important public policy issues, such as reproductive rights, immigration rights, or welfare reform. Social workers may also find that their personal values conflict with those of their clients. This can occur when clients engage in illegal activity or behavior that seems immoral

(e.g., engaging in an extramarital affair or drug dealing). Reconciling these values-related conflicts can be difficult.

Scarce and Limited Resources

Social workers often are responsible for distributing resources, such as administrative funds, shelter beds, client stipends, and mental health services. In many instances, they struggle to locate and obtain sufficient resources and must make difficult decisions about how best to allocate available resources. When making these decisions, social workers must choose which allocation criteria to use (e.g., whether to distribute resources equally among eligible parties; based on first-come, first-served; or based on demonstrated need or affirmative action guidelines).

Managed Care

The pervasive influence of managed care—policies designed to enhance fiscal responsibility and cost containment in health care and human services—has created many difficult ethical dilemmas for social workers. Strict funding guidelines, reimbursement policies, and utilization review have forced social workers to make difficult ethical judgments about serving clients whose insurance benefits have run out, providing inadequate services to clients with complex problems, and exposing clients to privacy and confidentiality risks as a result of sharing information with managed care staffers.

Whistle-Blowing

There are times when social workers may be obligated to alert people or organizations in positions of authority to colleagues' unethical behavior or impairment (Jayaratne et al., 1997). Decisions about whether to blow the whistle on a colleague are very difficult (Reamer, 2019). Social workers generally understand that their obligation to protect clients and the public from unethical or impaired colleagues may require such action, but they also understand that whistle-blowing can have serious, harmful repercussions for colleagues whose behavior is reported to state licensing boards, the National Association of Social Workers (NASW), employers, or the media. Whistle-blowing can also pose some risk to the individuals who report collegial misconduct or impairment; this is also a relevant consideration.

Evaluation and Research

Many social service agencies involve clients in evaluation or research activities (e.g., clinical research, needs assessments, and program evaluations). Ethical issues can arise when, for example, social work researchers decide whether to withhold potentially valuable services from clients who have been assigned to a control group as opposed to an experimental (intervention) group, whether to disclose confidential information revealed in a research interview that suggests the respondent has harmed a third party, whether to interview a respondent who is vulnerable emotionally and whose capacity to sign an informed consent form is questionable, and whether any form of deception is justifiable in social work evaluation and research (e.g., concealing the true purpose of a study to avoid influencing respondents and contaminating the results). The advent of institutional review boards (IRBs) to protect research participants has helped social workers and others address these difficult questions, although simple answers are not always possible.

Ethical Decision-Making

In the 1970s, social workers began to explore the ways practitioners make ethical decisions and attempt to resolve ethical dilemmas. This development also occurred in many other professions during this period. Although discussions of ethics and values have taken place since the profession's formal beginning in the late 19th century, deliberate, systematic discussion of ethical decision-making strategies is more recent.

Social work, like most professions, has developed protocols to help practitioners make difficult ethical decisions when they encounter ethical dilemmas (Barsky, 2019; Dolgoff et al., 2012; Reamer, 2018a, 2018b; Strom-Gottfried, 2007). Most of these protocols include an outline of steps that practitioners can follow to approach ethical dilemmas systematically, drawing especially on ethical theory; relevant professional literature; codes of ethics; statutes, regulations, public policies, and agency policies; social work practice standards; and consultation. For example, one such model entails the following seven steps (Reamer, 2018a; also see Barsky, 2019; Dolgoff et al., 2012):

1. Identify the ethical issues, including the social work values and duties that conflict.
2. Identify the individuals, groups, and organizations that are likely to be affected by the ethical decision.
3. Tentatively identify all possible courses of action and the participants involved in each, along with possible benefits and risks for each.
4. Thoroughly examine the reasons in favor of and opposed to each possible course of action, considering relevant ethical theories, principles, and guidelines; social work practice standards; codes of ethics and legal principles; social work practice theory, principles, and standards; and personal values (including religious, cultural, and ethnic values and political ideology), particularly those that conflict with one's own.
5. Consult with colleagues and appropriate experts (e.g., agency staff, supervisors, agency administrators, ethics scholars, ethics committees, and, if there are pertinent legal issues, attorneys).

6. Make the decision and document the decision-making process.
7. Monitor, evaluate, and document the decision.

Some of the elements of this process require specialized knowledge and skill. For example, social workers should be familiar with ethical theories, principles, and guidelines related to professional practice. Most discussions of ethical theory in the profession's literature focus on what are commonly known as theories of normative ethics. Theories of normative ethics are typically divided into two main schools of thought: *deontological* and *teleological* (including *consequentialist* and *utilitarian* theories). Deontological theories (from the Greek *deontos*, "of the obligatory") claim that certain actions are inherently right or wrong as a matter of fundamental principle. From a strict deontological perspective, for example, social workers should always obey the law and regulations, even when they think that violating a law or regulation is in a client's best interest. From this point of view, social workers should always tell the truth and should always keep their promises to their clients, no matter how harmful the consequences may be.

In contrast, teleological (from the Greek *teleios*, "brought to its end or purpose") or consequentialist theories assert that ethical decisions should be based on social workers' assessment of which action will produce the most favorable outcome or consequences. According to the most popular teleological perspective, utilitarianism, ethical choices should be based on thorough assessments of what will produce the greatest good for the greatest number (positive utilitarianism) or the least harm (negative utilitarianism).

More recently, social workers and other professionals have broadened their application of ethical theory to include so-called virtue ethics and the ethics of care. According

to virtue ethics, professionals' ethical judgments should be guided by certain core virtues, such as kindness, generosity, courage, integrity, respectfulness, justice, prudence, and compassion (Beauchamp & Childress, 2019; MacIntyre, 2007). The ethics of care, which is related to virtue ethics, was developed mainly by feminist writers (Held, 2007). According to this view, men tend to think in masculine terms, such as justice and autonomy, whereas women think in feminine terms, such as caring. Proponents of the ethics of care argue that professionals should change how they view morality and the virtues, placing more emphasis on virtues exemplified by women, such as taking care of others, patience, the ability to nurture, and self-sacrifice.

These diverse philosophical perspectives are commonly used to analyze ethical dilemmas from different conceptual viewpoints. Thus, a deontologist might argue that social workers should always comply with child abuse and neglect reporting laws—because "the law is the law"—whereas a teleologically oriented practitioner might argue that social workers' compliance with these mandatory reporting laws should be based on their assessment of the likely consequences—that is, whether complying with the law will produce the greatest good or minimize harm to the greatest possible extent. A social worker who embraces virtue theory would be guided by their interpretation of the relevance of core virtues, such as autonomy, beneficence, compassion for clients, respect for human dignity, and justice (Beauchamp & Childress, 2019).

Social workers and others disagree about the strengths and limitations of these different philosophical perspectives. Nonetheless, there is general agreement that it is helpful for practitioners to examine ethical dilemmas using these different vantage points to identify, grapple with, and critically assess all pertinent dimensions of the ethical dilemmas they encounter.

Social workers also need to be familiar with updated and increasingly sophisticated professional codes of ethics, especially the current NASW Code of Ethics (NASW, 2017; Reamer, 2018b). The first section of the code, the preamble, summarizes the mission and core values of social work. The association has adopted and published in the code a formally sanctioned mission statement and an explicit summary of the profession's core values. These help distinguish social work from other helping professions, particularly with respect to social work's enduring commitment to enhancing human well-being and helping meet basic human needs, empowering clients, serving people who are vulnerable and oppressed, addressing individual well-being in a social context, promoting social justice and social change, and strengthening sensitivity to cultural and ethnic diversity.

The second section, "Purpose of the NASW Code of Ethics," provides an overview of the code's main functions, including identifying the core values, summarizing broad ethical principles that reflect these values, and specific ethical standards for the profession, helping social workers identify ethical issues and dilemmas, providing the public with ethical standards it can use to hold the profession accountable, orienting new practitioners, and articulating guidelines that the profession can use to enforce ethical standards among its members. This section also highlights resources social workers can use when they face ethical issues and decisions.

The third section, "Ethical Principles," presents six broad principles that inform social work practice, one for each of the six core values cited in the preamble (service, social justice, dignity and worth of the person, importance of human relationships, integrity, and competence).

The final and most detailed section, "Ethical Standards," includes specific ethical standards to guide social workers' conduct

and provide a basis for adjudication of ethics complaints filed against social workers. (The code, or portions of it, is also used by many state licensing boards charged with reviewing complaints filed against licensed social workers and by courts of law that oversee litigation involving alleged social worker negligence or misconduct.) The standards are grouped into six categories concerning ethical responsibilities to clients, to colleagues, in practice settings, as professionals, to the profession, and to the broader society. The code addresses many topics and issues that were not mentioned in the NASW's first two codes (1960 and 1979), including limitations of clients' right to self-determination (e.g., when clients threaten harm to themselves or others); confidentiality issues involving use of electronic media to transmit information; conducting online searches for information about clients without their knowledge or consent; storage and disposal of client records; case recording and documentation; sexual contact with former clients; sexual relationships with clients' relatives and close personal acquaintances; counseling of former sexual partners; physical contact with clients; dual and multiple relationships with supervisees; sexual harassment; use of derogatory language; bartering arrangements with clients; cultural awareness; labor–management disputes; and evaluation of practice. Although codes of ethics cannot provide simple, unequivocal solutions to all complex ethical dilemmas, they often provide sound conceptual guidance about important issues to consider when making difficult ethical judgments.

In addition to consulting the code, social workers can access professional ethics consultants, institutional ethics committees, and IRBs. Ethics consultation is now very common in health care settings and is increasingly available in other settings. Typically, ethics consultants are formally educated ethicists (usually moral philosophers who have experience working with professionals or professionals who have obtained formal ethics education) who provide advice on specific ethical issues that arise in practice settings. These consultants can help social workers and other staff identify pertinent ethical issues; assess ethical dilemmas; acquaint staff with relevant ethics concepts, literature, and other resources (e.g., codes of ethics, policies, statutes, and regulations); and make difficult ethical choices.

Institutional ethics committees formally emerged in 1976, when the New Jersey Supreme Court ruled that Karen Ann Quinlan's family and physicians should consult an ethics committee in deciding whether to remove her from life-support technology (a number of hospitals have had panels resembling ethics committees since at least the 1920s). Ethics committees often include social workers as members, along with representatives from various disciplines found in health care and human service settings, such as nurses, physicians, clergy, allied health professionals, and administrators. Some committees include a lawyer, although the lawyer might not be an employee of the agency to avoid a conflict of interest (Aulisio et al., 2003).

Most ethics committees focus on providing case consultation in the form of nonbinding advice. These committees make themselves available to agency staff, clients, and sometimes family members for consultation about challenging ethical issues. Many ethics committees also take steps to examine, draft, and critique ethics-related policies that affect agencies and their employees and clients. In addition, these committees may sponsor ethics-related educational events, such as in-service training, symposia, workshops, conferences, and what have become known as "ethics grand rounds" (Reamer, 2018a).

Social workers employed in settings that conduct research may be involved in IRBs. IRBs (sometimes known as a research ethics board or committee on the use of human participants in research) became popular in the 1970s as a result of increasing national interest in research and evaluation and concern about exploitation of research participants. All organizations and agencies that receive federal funds for research are required to have an IRB review the ethical aspects of proposals for research involving human participants.

Social workers' understanding of ethical issues has matured greatly. Literature on the subject, professional education, and in-service training have burgeoned. To practice competently, contemporary professionals must have a firm grasp of pertinent issues related to ethical dilemmas and ethical decision-making. This knowledge enhances social workers' ability to protect clients and fulfill social work's critically important, values-based mission.

References

Aulisio, M., Arnold, R., & Youngner, S. (Eds.). (2003). *Ethics consultation: From theory to practice.* Johns Hopkins University Press.

Banks, S. (2012). *Ethics and values in social work* (4th ed.). Palgrave Macmillan.

Barsky, A. (2019). *Ethics and values in social work* (2nd ed.). Oxford University Press.

Beauchamp, T., & Childress, J. (2019). *Principles of biomedical ethics* (8th ed.). Oxford University Press.

Dickson, D. T. (1998). *Confidentiality and privacy in social work.* Free Press.

Dolgoff, R., Loewenberg, F., & Harrington, D. (2012). *Ethical decisions for social work practice* (9th ed.). Brooks/Cole.

Held, V. (2007). *The ethics of care: Personal, political, global.* Oxford University Press.

Jayaratne, S., Croxton, D., & Mattison, D. (1997). Social work professional standards: An exploratory study. *Social Work, 42*(2), 187–199.

MacIntyre, A. (2007). *After virtue: A study in moral theory* (3rd ed.). University of Notre Dame Press.

National Association of Social Workers. (2017). *Code of ethics of the National Association of Social Workers.* NASW Press.

Reamer, F. G. (2001). *The social work ethics audit: A risk management tool.* NASW Press.

Reamer, F. G. (2012a). *Boundary issues and dual relationships in the human services.* Columbia University Press.

Reamer, F. G. (2012b). The digital and electronic revolution in social work: Rethinking the meaning of ethical practice. *Ethics and Social Welfare, 7,* 2–19. http://www.tandfonline.com/doi/abs/10.1080/17496535.2012.738694

Reamer, F. G. (2013). Social work in a digital age: Ethical and risk-management challenges. *Social Work, 58,* 163–172.

Reamer, F. G. (2015). 18 Ethical Issues in Social Work. *Social workers' desk reference,* 143.

Reamer, F. G. (2018a). *Social work values and ethics* (5th ed.). Columbia University Press.

Reamer, F. G. (2018b). *Ethical standards in social work: A review of the NASW code of ethics* (3rd ed.). NASW Press.

Reamer, F. G. (2018c). *The social work ethics casebook: Cases and commentary* (2nd ed.). NASW Press.

Reamer, F. G. (2019). The ethics of whistle blowing. *Journal of Ethics in Mental Health, 10,* 1–19.

Strom-Gottfried, K. (2007). *Straight talk about professional ethics.* Lyceum.

Regulating Social Work for the Public Good and for Professional Integrity

Dorinda N. Noble

How Licensure Developed

To protect the public, many countries regulate professions, such as medicine, nursing, social work, psychology, accountancy, and law. People can be harmed when practitioners in these professions practice illegally, unethically, or incompetently. Professionals are regulated through licensure, a term derived from the Latin word *licere*, meaning "permission to act" (Cody, 2014). The U.S. Constitution gives states the right to protect their citizenry's welfare, a process upheld by the U.S. Supreme Court decision *Dent v. West Virginia* (1889) [Association of Social Work Boards (ASWB), 2019f]. There is no U.S. federal licensure law. Canada regulates by registration of social workers in each province.

Social work regulation began in the United States in 1934; Canada launched social work regulation in 1969 (ASWB, 2019f). In 1979, what is now called the ASWB was incorporated to develop a standardized licensing examination to establish minimum competence (ASWB, 2020d). In 2019, ASWB administered licensing examinations to more than 50,000 social workers in North America (ASWB, 2020b, 2020d).

Practice Mobility

All licensed professions are aiming to make it easier for licensees/registrants to cross jurisdictional lines to do disaster work, deliver specialized services, and offer services remotely using online and digital technology. Canada enacted the 2017 Canadian Free Trade Agreement to reduce mobility barriers (Internal Trade Secretariat, 2020). In 2013, ASWB member boards in the United States identified practice mobility as a strategic objective (ASWB, 2013), working to achieve more consistency in license category names and in requirements to obtain and maintain licensure. These outcomes necessitate state boards working with each other to increase licensure by endorsement. Licensure by endorsement allows a state or provincial licensing board to recognize a social worker's existing license in issuing a new one. This reduces the burden on the social worker to provide supporting documentation and expedites licensing (ASWB, 2020a).

Protection of Public Health and Safety

Lori, a licensed social worker, provided counseling services to Ralph 3 years ago. Lori lives in a small, rural community and owns a home with a unique tiled roof in need of repair. Ralph is the only roofer in town who has the skills to fix Lori's roof. Because they had terminated their social work relationship a few years ago, Lori concluded it was appropriate to hire Ralph for the roofing job. He appeared at the job site to provide an estimate, accompanied by his new fiancé and her young children. Lori was distressed, remembering that in counseling Ralph had revealed that he had sexual fantasies about prepubescent children, although he claimed that he had never acted on them. Lori believed she may be obligated to warn this young mother that her children could be in danger. Lori knew that she could not report Ralph to child welfare authorities because she did not have evidence that he acted on his fantasies or planned to do so. Ultimately, Lori acted on her emotional instincts, tracked down Ralph's fiancé, and told her that Ralph had disclosed to her his sexual fantasies about young children. The fiancé dumped Ralph, and Ralph filed a complaint with the social work licensing board alleging that Lori breached his confidentiality rights. The board sanctioned Lori by suspending her license and placing her on probation for 1 year. During the probationary period, Lori was permitted to practice in an agency under supervision; she could not practice independently. Lori was also required to inform her clients that she was on probation. The board also required that she receive supervision and continuing education on confidentiality issues.

Social workers address many issues that affect people's physical, mental, social, and emotional health. Licensure provides checks and balances to ensure ethical and competent practice, as reflected in Lori's case. A social worker's unethical or incompetent practice has the capacity to harm members of the public.

Title Protection

Pat was a social work licensee with an independent clinical practice. As part of "treatment," she cast out demons from her clients. A client undergoing Pat's treatment attempted suicide. The client's family reported Pat to the social work licensing board. After investigation, the board found Pat's behavior violated regulations, including operating outside her scope of practice. (Casting out demons is not part of social work education or expectations.) The board concluded that Pat was a danger to the public and revoked her license. Pat then reopened her practice as a "theological counselor," a profession not regulated by the jurisdiction.

Regulation in many jurisdictions protects the title of "social worker." Title protection means that only individuals who are licensed may call themselves social workers. Individuals who refer to themselves as social workers without being formally licensed are violating the law. In such cases, the board may issue cease and desist orders to these individuals or ask the state to impose financial penalties. The public needs to know the qualifications and competencies of the professional.

Fitness for Practice

One night, Jim, an honors college student, drank alcohol excessively at a party and, while driving home under the influence, tragically hit another car, killing two people. He was charged by the police, found guilty of vehicular manslaughter, and sentenced to prison. Because he was a stellar prisoner and completed substance use disorder counseling, Jim was released on parole. Jim began working in a peer recovery program and applied to a local Master of Social Work (MSW) program. He was accepted into the program and, following graduation, applied for licensure. The licensing board required Jim to explain how he planned to avoid his previous problems. Jim was candid about his crime and provided evidence of ongoing treatment. The board was impressed that Jim accepted responsibility for his situation but explained that his felony history would likely prohibit employment in numerous social service areas. The board allowed him to take the examination, which he passed. Jim became a licensed social worker specializing in substance use disorders treatment.

Government jurisdictions must ensure that only qualified persons are permitted to practice social work as defined by law, meaning that licensees are fit to practice their profession competently, legally, and ethically. Social work regulation has several key features:

- Regulation is closely linked to social work values and seeks to protect consumers.
- Regulation establishes standards of competence for different categories of licensure and scopes of practice that define the services a professional can perform under the license.
- Regulation sets standards for who is qualified to pursue licensure. Standards address *education* (graduation from a social work education program accredited by or in candidacy with the U.S. Council on Social Work Education or the Canadian Association of Social Work Education), *experience* (as defined in the regulation for each category of licensure), and *examination* (to demonstrate entry-level competence).
- Most jurisdictions require evidence of good moral character, reflecting *ethical standards*. Many licensing laws allow boards to assess character by checking applicants' criminal history, credit history, prior applications for

licensure, or civil complaints and judgments (Atkinson, 2019). Many U.S. jurisdictions have expanded their right to revoke professional licenses to people who have not paid court-ordered child support or who have defaulted on student loan repayment. Such actions often lead to due process challenges (Cody, 2014).

Continuing Competence

Phil, a social work licensee, was raised in an ethnic community that valued herbal medicines. In his work at a medical clinic, Phil gave some of his clients herbal remedies. One diabetic, pregnant client accepted the herbal mixture. The next day, she was hospitalized and lost the baby. Her mother learned about the herbal remedies and filed a complaint with the board. The board conducted a hearing and ruled that Phil acted outside the scope of practice and acted incompetently. The state board of medicine also brought a complaint against Phil for practicing medicine without a license. Phil claimed he was trying to help his client by using age-old "native" remedies that are accepted in his culture. The board suspended Phil's license, placed him on probation for 2 years, and required that he complete continuing education in ethics.

Regulation ensures entry-level competency. It requires licensees to renew their license at regular intervals (e.g., every 2 years) and to engage in ongoing continuing education to maintain competence, enhance their skills, and expand their knowledge. Some social work boards require that practitioners complete continuing education on specific subjects (e.g., professional ethics, cultural competence, and substance use disorders). Regulatory boards also require licensees to maintain accurate records and communicate with the board about address changes, arrests, and other factors outlined in the rules.

Safe and Ethical Practice

A licensed social worker, Mary, worked with a college student to help her overcome a lack of confidence. The two became sexually involved. Twenty years later, while addressing this trauma with a new therapist, the client complained to the board about this boundary violation. Typically, the board would not investigate a report this old, but complaints alleging sexual misconduct are exempted from time limits, according to this state's regulations. At the hearing, Mary listened and cried as the client shared love letters the two exchanged during the intimate relationship. The client told the board that the affair has tormented her for many years. Mary admitted to the affair, but testified that she did not think about it much after the relationship ended. She told the board she was stunned to learn that her former client felt harmed by the affair. The board found that Mary violated regulations, suspended her license for 1 year, and required that she obtain ethics consultation and complete continuing education on boundary crossings before applying for reinstatement.

Regulation ensures that members of the public can bring concerns about social workers' services to the board for investigation. This process helps protect the public from unethical or unsafe practice that may be intentional, as in the case of Medicaid fraud, or unintentional, such as when a social worker inadvertently violates a client's confidentiality when responding to a subpoena of clinical records.

Enforcement

Ann, a social work licensee, was CEO of a domestic violence prevention program. She developed strategies to involve clients in working with other clients, which she considered progressive. Several employees, however, believed this strategy crossed boundaries and placed clients at risk. They filed a complaint with the board. Ann took advantage of her right to legal counsel and arranged for some state legislators she knew personally to plead her cause. Ultimately, the board found that Ann had not violated the regulations. However, they issued a letter of advisement, which encouraged her to formulate clearer policies about how to protect clients from harmful boundary crossings in a peer support program.

Social work boards use formal protocols to investigate complaints. If the board finds that a violation of law or rules occurred, it will address the issue with the licensee, often through a formal hearing. Some cases are resolved without a formal hearing when the social worker and the board enter into a consent order; in these instances, the social worker agrees to certain facts and sanctions without proceeding to a formal hearing.

The licensee may retain legal counsel and is guaranteed due process, meaning that the licensee has the right to know the nature of the complaint, who submitted it, and to respond to the complaint. These proceedings are a matter of public record, although clients' confidentiality rights are protected. Regulatory proceedings are civil—not criminal—matters; some cases may be addressed in both civil arenas and criminal courts (e.g., if a social worker is charged in criminal court with financial fraud).

When a board investigates a complaint and determines that the licensee did not violate regulations and is competent to practice, the matter is closed. When a board finds that the licensee violated regulations, the board may

- issue a letter to advise the licensee about expected behavior or a cease and desist letter to stop the unprofessional behavior;
- impose sanctions, such as a period of supervision; continuing education on specific topics; mental health/substance use disorder treatment; or probation, fees, and fines; or
- revoke the license.

Integrity of the Profession

Perry, a social work licensee, advertised himself as a sex therapist with a doctorate from a "university of sex therapy." Although this "university" exists online, it is not accredited by any recognized accrediting body. The state prohibited licensees from citing, as part of their professional education, a degree from an unaccredited school. A former colleague of Perry's filed a licensing board complaint against him after learning about the services and credentials Perry advertised. The board found that Perry violated the social work regulations that require honesty and accuracy when advertising one's field of practice, scope of practice, and qualifications. The board issued a cease and desist order and imposed a fine for as long as his advertisement ran on social media and other outlets.

A key purpose of regulation, with its emphasis on practice standards, is to promote the profession's integrity and encourage the public (as well as third-party payors) to recognize social work as a reputable profession. Licensure means that professionals are accountable to an authority that oversees their work and ensures protection of the public.

Regulatory Categories

In the United States, regulated social workers are recognized in different states by a number of licensure categories and titles. An Arkansas Licensed Certified Social Worker, for example, is comparable to a Texas Licensed Clinical Social Worker (D. Hyman, personal correspondence, 2017). This variety of license categories and titles can confuse both professionals and the public. ASWB aims to help jurisdictions develop more consistency in the license category names (ASWB, 2019b).

The major regulatory categories are clinical, master's, and bachelor's. Applicants for all of these categories must meet rigorous ethical standards. They must hold the appropriate social work degree from a program accredited by the Council on Social Work Education (United States) or the Canadian Council on Social Work Education. For the clinical category and the master's category, applicants must have earned an MSW from an accredited program. Clinical candidates also must have successfully worked in a supervised clinical setting for a specific number of hours. Applicants applying for the bachelor's category must have earned a Bachelor of Social Work (BSW) degree from an accredited program. Applicants must also pass the appropriate ASWB test. Those seeking clinical licensure take the clinical test, whereas aspiring master's candidates take the master's test. People aiming for the bachelor's license take the bachelor's test.

All U.S. jurisdictions and three Canadian provinces regulate at the clinical level. Forty-nine U.S. jurisdictions and all Canadian provinces regulate at the MSW level, and 43 U.S. jurisdictions and all Canadian provinces regulate at the BSW level (ASWB, 2019g). Jurisdictional laws and policies change over time, reflecting jurisdictional needs. ASWB (2019h) provides specific, timely jurisdiction regulation information.

Testing for Entry-Level Competence

Regulatory bodies partner with ASWB to administer the social work licensing examinations (ASWB, 2019b). Every 5–7 years, ASWB conducts an extensive practice analysis, surveying thousands of social workers to identify and rank the tasks they need to know on the first day on the job. This information provides a blueprint for the examinations, which are carefully created by licensed social workers and monitored by psychometricians. ASWB recruits and trains experienced social workers from diverse backgrounds and fields of practice in the United States and Canada to write test items, which reflect contemporary social work practice and are linked to current social work literature. All items are reviewed by the ASWB Examination Committee and select item consultants who are professionals with expertise in representative content areas (ASWB, 2020b).

ASWB has rigorous requirements to ensure that its examinations are fair and sensitive to cultural and ethnic diversity, following guidelines established by the American Psychological Association, Joint Commission on Standards for Educational and Psychological Testing, American Educational Research Association, National Council on Measurement in Education, and Equal Employment Opportunity Commission (ASWB, 2019a). Items are evaluated for bias and difficulty for various demographic groups (ASWB, 2019b).

Before taking the social work licensing examinations, candidates must (1) be approved by the regulatory board in the jurisdiction where they wish to be licensed and pay any licensing fees, (2) register with ASWB and pay the required examination fee, and (3) schedule their examination with test administrator Pearson VUE (ASWB, 2019c). Applicants take the examinations by appointment at Pearson Professional Centers worldwide (ASWB, 2020c). Candidates have 4 hours to complete the pass–fail examination on a computer (ASWB, 2019b).

The Future of Regulation

With more than half a million social workers licensed in North America, regulation is vitally important. It is not without challenges, however. Some lawmakers believe that regulation is anticompetitive and constitutes government overreach (ASWB, 2019e). For

some, strict regulation is a barrier to entering a profession and interferes with economic development (Shanor, 2016). Current research, however, indicates that licensure does not limit competition and instead enhances entry into professions, particularly for historically underrepresented groups (Redbird, 2017).

Some jurisdictions exempt government service providers from licensure, such as child welfare workers. Exemptions, which include 164 instances in 40 states, may confuse the public about social workers' qualifications and hinder public protection (ASWB, 2019d). In 2018, ASWB developed a strategic plan to "advance knowledge and acceptance of social work as a licensed profession," setting as the first objective to "decrease the number of licensure exemptions in social work regulation."

Social workers should inform themselves about licensure and social work regulations and get involved in the rule-making process. Statutory law authorizing social work regulation is usually worded broadly and typically lacks detail; implementing the law through rule-making and regulation is where "the rubber hits the road." Social workers have the opportunity to comment on proposed rules, and boards rely on the input of professionals.

Regulatory boards, which act as the conscience of the community, are subject to jurisdictional sunrise and sunset reviews. These reviews aim to make the board's work more transparent and accountable. Such reviews, however, may yield inconsistent assessments from year to year, and they may be influenced by political considerations (ASWB, 2019e).

Boards benefit greatly by having diverse membership that reflects the community. Many board members are gubernatorial appointments, so political affiliation and support can influence who serves. Many boards have public members—non-social workers who represent consumers of services. In reality, although professional members are also members of the public, their professional interests potentially threaten the public protection mission of the boards on which they serve. The U.S. Supreme Court decision in *North Carolina State Board of Dental Examiners v. FTC* (2015) reflects such concern. In this precedent-setting case, the North Carolina Dental Board, populated by practicing dentists, created a rule that teeth-whitening kiosks in a shopping mall constituted the practice of dentistry and therefore violated the law. The Court ruled that the members of the board likely created this rule to limit competition and that boards controlled by professionals must be actively supervised by another state entity to avoid putting professional interests above public interests (ASWB, 2019f). As a result of this ruling, numerous jurisdictional boards have added public members to promote fairness. Canada has "fairness commissioners" to assist regulatory bodies (ASWB, 2019f).

Ideally, licensing boards provide important checks and balances, ensuring entry-level competence of social workers through initial licensure and continuing competence through license renewals. Boards offer safe havens for consumers and do the difficult work of investigating and sanctioning licensees, when warranted. Regulatory boards protect public health and safety, as well as the integrity of the profession.

Helpful Resources

Association of Social Work Boards. (2013). *2014–2018 strategy map.* Author. Culpeper, Virginia.

Association of Social Work Boards. (2018). *2019–2021 strategic framework.* https://www.aswb.org/wp-content/uploads/2018/11/strategic-framework.pdf

Association of Social Work Boards. (2019a). *ASWB guide to the social work exams,* 2nd edition. Author. Culpeper, Virginia.

Association of Social Work Boards. (2019b). *Common exam concerns.* Author: Culpeper, Virginia.

Association of Social Work Boards. (2019c). *Steps for taking the ASWB exams* [Video]. https://aswb.org/exam-candidates

Association of Social Work Boards. (2019d, May). *Elimination of exemptions* [Information sheet]. https://members.aswb.org/wp-content/uploads/2019/05/Elimination-of-social-work-licensing-exemptions.pdf

Association of Social Work Boards. (2019e). Meeting regulatory challenges with information [D. Benton session of 2019 education meeting]. *Association News* Volume 29, Issue 3. https://www.aswb.org/news/volume-29/v29-issue-3/meeting-regulatory-challenges-with-information. Accessed March 15, 2020.

Association of Social Work Boards. (2019f). Regulatory trends and regulators' responses [Atkinson & Maciura session of 2019 education meeting]. *Association News,* Volume *29,* Issue 3. https://www.aswb.org/news/volume-29/v29-issue-3/regulatory-trends-and-regulators-responses. Accessed March 12, 2020.

Association of Social Work Boards. (2019g, June 11). U.S. social work license requirements [Research paper]. Author. Culpeper, Virginia.

Association of Social Work Boards. (2019h, November). *Compare license requirements for all jurisdictions* [Database report]. http://aswbsocialworkregulations.org/jurisdiction LevelsReportBuilder.jsp.

Association of Social Work Boards. (2020a). *What next after a new law is passed?* [Member exchange]. *Association News.* Volume *30,* Issue 1. https://www.aswb.org/news/volume-30/v30-issue-1. Accessed March 15, 2020.

Association of Social Work Boards. (2020b, April 9). About the exams. https://aswb.org/exam-candidates/about-the-exams/

Association of Social Work Boards. (2020c, April 9). Registered candidates. https://aswb.org/exam-candidates/registered-candidates

Association of Social Work Boards. (2020d, April 20). History of ASWB. https://www.aswb.org/about/history

Association of Social Work Boards. (2020e, April 17). *COVID-19 updates.* https://aswb.org/covid-19

References

Association of Social Work Boards. (2013). *2014–2018 strategy map.*

Association of Social Work Boards. (2018). 2019–2021 strategic framework. https://www.aswb.org/wp-content/uploads/2018/11/strategic-framework.pdf

Association of Social Work Boards. (2019a). *ASWB guide to the social work exams* (2nd ed.).

Association of Social Work Boards. (2019b). *Common exam concerns.*

Association of Social Work Boards. (2019c). Steps for taking the ASWB exams [Video]. https://aswb.org/exam-candidates

Association of Social Work Boards. (2019d, May). Elimination of exemptions [Information sheet]. https://mn.gov/boards/assets/ASWB%20Elimination%20of%20Exemptions%20Info%20Sheet_tcm21-410474.pdf

Association of Social Work Boards. (2019e). Meeting regulatory challenges with information [D. Benton session of 2019 education meeting]. *Association News,* 29(3). Retrieved March 15, 2020, from https://www.aswb.org/news/volume-29/v29-issue-3/meeting-regulatory-challenges-with-information

Association of Social Work Boards. (2019f). Regulatory trends and regulators' responses [Atkinson & Maciura session of 2019 education meeting]. *Association News,* 29(3). Retrieved March 12, 2020, from https://www.aswb.org/regulatory-trends-and-regulators-responses/

Association of Social Work Boards. (2019g, June 11). U.S. social work license requirements [Research paper].

Association of Social Work Boards. (2020a). What next after a new law is passed? [Member exchange]. *Association News,* 30(1). Retrieved March 15, 2020, from https://www.aswb.org/whats-next-after-a-new-law-is-passed-2/

Association of Social Work Boards. (2020b, April 9). About the exams. https://www.aswb.org/exam/

Association of Social Work Boards. (2020c, April 9). Registered candidates. https://aswb.org/exam-candidates/registered-candidates

Association of Social Work Boards. (2020d, April 20). History of ASWB. https://www.aswb.org/about/history

Atkinson, D. (2019). Related or not? Good moral character [Counsel's column]. *Association News,* 29(6). https://www.aswb.org/related-or-not-good-moral-character/

Cody, C. R. (2014). Professional licenses and substantive due process: Can states compel physicians to provide their services? *William and Mary Bill of Rights Journal, 22*(3). Retrieved March 12, 2020, from scholarship.law.wm.edu/wmborj/vol22/iss3/7

Internal Trade Secretariat. (2020, April). *Canadian Free Trade Agreement/Accord de Libre-Échange Canadien.* Canadian Internal Trade Secretariat. https://www.cfta-alec.ca

Redbird, B. (2017). The new closed shop: The economic and structural effects of occupational licensure. *American Sociological Review, 82*(3), 600–624. doi:10.1177/0003122417706463. https://journals.sagepub.com/doi/10.1177/0003122417706463

Shanor, A. (2016, December 5). Business licensing and constitutional liberty. *Yale Law Journal, 126,* 2016–2017. Retrieved March 12, 2020, from http://yalelawjournal.org/forum/business-licensing-and-constitutional-liberty

Navigating Complex Boundary Challenges

Kimberly Strom

Professional boundaries refer to "invisible demarcations between the client and the social worker that determine appropriate roles and behaviors between them" (Barsky, 2019, p. 126). Boundaries help ensure that actions or expressions by the worker are made in the client's interest and for the benefit of the services being provided, not for the worker's social, financial, or sexual needs. Boundaries can be exceedingly complex, with variations in norms across cultures, geographic regions, practice settings, and populations served. Depending on their setting, clientele, and individual disposition, professionals may maintain "thick" or "thin" boundaries (Hartmann, 1997). In either instance, the client–worker distinction exists, but the concept acknowledges that some workers and situations call for greater discretion and distance separating work and personal matters. Boundaries do not imply that clients are inferior to professionals; rather, they ensure that the helping relationship is sacrosanct, and clients' needs are accorded the utmost importance.

"Boundary crossings" indicate deviations from standard practices that are typically innocuous, done in the client's interests and without adverse effects, and are therefore not inherently unethical (Reamer, 2018). For example, professionals in small communities commonly see people they serve at school, church, and civic events, even at private occasions such as weddings and funerals. As a result, they create norms and processes to manage the interactions. In the wrong context or with the wrong client, however, even simple boundary crossings may represent problematic conflicts of interest or create the first step in a "slippery slope" toward client exploitation (Epstein & Simon, 1990). Boundary violations, such as dual or sexual relationships, are among the most common areas of ethical impropriety in social work and other professions, often resulting in lawsuits, ethics complaints, and licensure board sanctions (Boland-Prom, 2009; Daley & Doughty, 2006; Strom-Gottfried, 1999). Although these egregious and exploitive acts are valid areas for attention, subtle conflicts of interest are far more common and have less clear-cut solutions:

- If a professional in the field of disabilities also has a child receiving services in the same settings, how should they relate to parents who are simultaneously peers and clients?

- A social worker activist in the lesbian, gay, bisexual, and transgender community is often sought for services by members of that community. When do overlapping acquaintances become dual relationships?
- How should a social worker respond when a former client sends a request to connect via LinkedIn, Facebook, or another online networking site?
- A patient with a life-threatening illness asks the members of the treatment team to join her Caring Bridge site. Members of the team disagree about the propriety of accepting the invitation.
- Social workers who do home-based care must commonly consider offers of food, managing the presence of neighbors or extended family, and observations of distressing or illegal conditions. What choices keep the helping relationship in focus and which blur professionalism and purpose?

Conflicts of Interest

Boundary considerations are inherently linked to conflicts of interest. As suggested in the previous examples, conflicts of interest can arise when the needs of the worker threaten to take precedence over those of the client. This can occur when roles are blurred between friendships and working relationships, when a worker's financial interests lead them to file fraudulent claims or inflated bills for service, or when the need for power leads to abuse or sexual exploitation. Client–worker relationships are not the only source of boundary challenges. These tensions can also occur in teaching or administrative relationships: Consider supervisors whose need to be liked keeps them from holding workers accountable or professors who inflate class grades due to the fear of poor course evaluations.

A further variant on conflicts of interest occurs when workers have divided loyalties that keep them from objectively carrying out their roles. This may occur in conjoint or family treatment, when the worker's partiality for one member affects their ability to properly serve the other client–family members. In order to avoid similar favoritism in the workplace, rules against nepotism forbid employing people who are related. Nevertheless, online or personal social relationships with some staff members may compromise a supervisor's judgment and fairness to all members of the team.

The National Association of Social Workers (NASW) Code of Ethics (2017a) cautions practitioners to avoid or address potential conflicts of interest by taking "reasonable steps to resolve the issue in a manner that makes the clients' interests primary and protects clients' interests to the greatest extent possible" (standard 1.06a). Certain conflicts of interest, such as sexual relationships with clients, former clients, supervisees, students, and others, are expressly prohibited, and social workers are further cautioned to avoid business, professional, or social relationships with clients and former clients due to the risk of harm or exploitation. Ultimately, the social worker bears the responsibility for "setting clear, appropriate and culturally sensitive boundaries" (standard 1.06c).

Intersecting Standards

Detecting conflicts of interest and effectively setting boundaries require attention to other ethical standards, such as confidentiality, informed consent, professionalism, and competence. However, the connections between the standards and boundary setting are often implied rather than explicit. As such, social workers must be familiar with both the substance and intent of the standards.

Privacy is the foundation of the helping relationship. Social workers risk significant sanctions for the failure to protect sensitive information or for sharing client information for other than professional purposes. These professional pledges of confidentiality are challenging, particularly when workers learn information about a client (e.g., past criminal activity) that is distressing to the worker but is not reportable (Walfish et al., 2010). Ethics standards caution against soliciting information for or about clients (including via electronic search engines) unless for "compelling professional reasons" (NASW, 2017a, standard 1.07a). Obtaining informed consent at the outset of services alerts clients to typical limits of privacy, such as mandatory reporting or protections from harm, or limits related to the particular terms of service, such as disclosure of information to a court that referred the client for counseling or information required by the client's insurer. Informed consent processes should also alert clients to practitioner policies about access outside traditional business hours, contact via social media, and policies regarding contact after the working relationship has formally ended (Reamer, 2015).

Confidentiality also is challenged when personal and professional relationships overlap. Blurred personal and professional boundaries can reveal new or troubling information about the social worker, and in doing so they may affect working relationships with clients and colleagues. Consider, for example, the following:

- A social worker who is also a parenting peer support group member is frequently tearful and angry in group sessions. Simultaneously serving as a caseworker for group members is a perilous conflict of interest. The clients may feel protective of the worker or apprehensive about the worker's capacity to help them. And the worker may feel she cannot truly be herself in the support group because other members view her in her professional role, not as a parent with the same challenges they have.

- Outraged online posts about political events may alienate the social worker's clients, supervisees, or employer. Frivolous party photos that identify or "tag" the worker may come to the attention of clients or administrators who arc disturbed to see this side of the professional (Reamer, 2015). When medical students posed with pathology cadavers and an obstetrician lamented a patient's tardiness and mused about arriving late for the delivery, the posts and derisive responses went viral (Beck, 2013; Heyboer, 2010).

- The global COVID-19 pandemic and related stay-at-home orders forced many previously in-person services online. As such, it gave rise to conflict of interest dilemmas balancing policies, health protection, and client needs amid the cessation or change of services. Challenges to privacy and confidentiality have emerged for both clients and social workers as a result of video access to each other's homes and the shared distress of the pandemic experience (Banks et al., 2020a, 2020b).

Whether messages are sent verbally or in writing, passively or intentionally, in person or electronically, the meaning is made by the recipient. Seemingly innocuous statements made informally by a professional can easily become volatile, frivolous, or callous when heard by clients or colleagues. As such, a family photo of a happy beach vacation posted on social media or placed on the worker's desk may bring fond memories, but it will carry different connotations for the clients, staff, and colleagues who view it. Mindful of the effects that these reactions can have on therapeutic relationships, workers with thick boundaries may avoid displaying personal items such as photos or diplomas. In all cases, social workers are expected to demonstrate discretion and professionalism in their personal and electronic interactions with colleagues and clients. Even when social workers selectively use self-disclosure to reveal information about themselves in the course of their practice, they must consider how the information will be heard and used, possible consequences if the client discloses it to others, and the availability of other facilitative techniques that do not involve personal sharing (Farber, 2006). Robust search engines such as Google make it difficult to control information sharing. Clients, supervisors, community members, and social workers themselves can secure a wide array of others' sensitive or personal information, such as school history, home addresses, criminal records, family members, or news accounts. Although social workers are constrained from engaging in such searches except for compelling professional reasons, the availability of this information can create an uncomfortable level of exposure for professionals whose lives become "an open book."

To maintain boundaries around competence and self-disclosure, the NASW Code of Ethics stipulates that social workers should not

- "allow their own personal problems, psychosocial distress, legal problems, substance abuse, or mental health difficulties to interfere with their professional judgment and performance or to jeopardize the best interests of people for whom they have a professional responsibility" (NASW, 2017a, standard 4.05a); or
- "permit their private conduct to interfere with their ability to fulfill their professional responsibilities" (NASW, 2017a, standard 4.03).

Because the balance of overlapping relationships and interests is often highly contextual, familiarity with the NASW Code of Ethics is necessary but not sufficient in order to effectively set boundaries. Social workers must anticipate boundary challenges and use consultation, restraint, and risk assessment to navigate compelling competing goods.

Navigating Complex Boundary Challenges

Professionals have an array of resources at their disposal to address complex boundary challenges. Each dilemma requires the worker to anticipate the effects of the boundary crossing; consult with ethical standards and other resources, such as agency policies, licensing board regulations, and national practice standards; seek supervisory guidance; demonstrate self-restraint; and weigh the risks of prospective choices.

Anticipation

Based on practice setting, intake information, and the community served, social workers can often foresee an overlapping relationship and broach the topic with the others involved. For example, "We will probably run into each other at school and other events in the community, but I won't initiate conversations with you in public and I want to assure you that I don't reveal information from work with my family." Professionals who are likely to interact with clients or former clients in more than perfunctory ways (by being service recipients themselves, having friends or family in common, or participating in close-knit groups such as faith communities) must take responsibility for broaching the boundary conversation. For instance, to a new supervisee who previously received services at the agency, one might state,

> I suspect this may be awkward at first, but I want to acknowledge our past work together and let you know I'm glad you've been hired here. If apprehensions or issues arise for either of us, I hope

we'll be able to talk about them, or reach out to HR if we want help with that.

Although social workers routinely practice in clients' homes, the experience may be a novel one for the service recipient. Anticipation in these situations requires the worker to learn what they can about the client's local and related hazards or safety concerns. If possible, the worker should also prepare the client prior to the visit with information about the purpose and length of the meeting, the family members who will be expected to attend, and any questions the client may need to have addressed (Strom-Gottfried, 2009).

The prevalence of online activity demands that professionals routinely anticipate requests for electronic communications or networking (NASW, 2017b). The worker's policy should be based on ethical standards and addressed in writing and verbally at the outset of service (Reamer, 2011). For example, "Text and email messages may be used for scheduling concerns, but we should discuss *in person*, any other information involving your case"; "I do not use social networks"; "Our ethics code prohibits social networking with clients"; and "It is my policy not to 'friend' or otherwise connect with my students or supervisees online."

Professionals who are active on platforms such as Twitter, social networks, blogs, or photo sharing should be alert to the messages they are sending and the ways those messages will be received by various constituents. Restricting one's privacy settings, discretion, and disclaimers ("This blog represents my personal views, not those of my employer or profession.") will help put the worker's posts in context and provide nominal protection, but they are far from perfect. When in doubt, professionals are advised to exercise discretion, imagining how a new client, employer, or member of the public might interpret the post.

Consultation and Supervision

Codes of ethics, such as those promulgated by employer policies, state or provincial regulatory boards, or professional associations such as NASW, offer the first line of guidance around boundary dilemmas. Unfortunately, the utility of these documents is often limited by the use of contextual, vague, or unrealistic provisions (e.g., "Set appropriate boundaries"; "Disclose only in compelling circumstances"; "Assure that your personal conduct does not reflect negatively on the agency"; and "Never accept gifts from clients"). In addition, published standards lag behind rapid evolutions in service delivery, such as integrated health care, telemental health, and online therapy. For these reasons, social workers must actively and critically operationalize the guidance for their particular practice settings. Continuing education programs, information alerts from funders and insurers, FAQs, news articles, and staff meetings all provide opportunities to interpret standards and develop the accompanying practice norms.

Supervisors and peers can help colleagues understand policies and standards, think through the advantages and disadvantages of various boundary crossings, prepare for difficult conversations involved in setting boundaries, and evaluate the effects of overlapping relationships on the helping process. Competence, integrity, and professionalism require workers to take responsibility for cultivating and using these resources. Reluctance to seek feedback about an issue should be examined because it is a red flag about either the lack of trust in the supervisory relationship or the wisdom of the worker's intentions. The "principle of publicity" serves as a test of judgment and the advisability of certain actions (Kidder, 1995). If the clinician is apprehensive about seeking advice or sharing information with colleagues about an action or decision, it is likely that the action is unsound.

Self-Regulation

Cautious practice and ethical standards recommend that professionals assess whether a dual relationship is avoidable (Doyle, 1997) and "if the relationship is avoidable, avoid it" (Erickson, 2001, p. 303). What is avoidable? Generally, it is accepting as a client those with whom the social worker has had significant past or current involvement. Self-regulation may also include avoiding roles that lead to problematic boundary compromises—for example, declining nomination to a committee whose chair is a client or abandoning online discussion forums frequented by past or current patients. A professional in recovery may not be able to avoid attending 12-step meetings with clients but may forego roles (e.g., serving as a sponsor) that compromise their needs and those of the client. This may be even more challenging in smaller, rural communities, but if boundaries must be crossed, it should be done with self-awareness and respect (Silberstein & Boone, 2017). Some may say, "Why should I pass up opportunities just because of the possible complications?" Perhaps some prospects are so rare or special that they cannot be avoided. But for those that can be, or those that can be deferred to another time, the advantages are numerous. First, it is the clinician's fundamental obligation "to place the interests of those who are served above his own" (Kitchener, 1988, p. 217). The inability or unwillingness to do so should be cause for some self-examination. And, on a more pragmatic level, the client and the social worker are freed from the level of vigilance required to manage the conflicts and confidences that arise in overlapping relationships; both may take more pleasure and benefit from the activity without the other's presence in it.

Even when the clinician is confident that their judgment and handling of the working relationship will not be impaired by blurred boundaries, the appearance of a conflict may still make the arrangement unwise.

For example, a client who gives her worker a Christmas present may expect nothing in return, but the transaction may lead others to believe that gifts are required or that they will lose favor if they fail to do the same. A job applicant whose friend is on the search committee may not expect special treatment or inside information to help his prospects for being hired, but other applicants and committee members might well be suspicious if the friend does not recuse from the process.

Weighing the Risks of Complex Boundaries

In addition to anticipation, consultation, reflection, and restraint, social workers can employ decision-making models to weigh the risks and benefits of ambiguous boundary relationships (Erickson, 2001). One model evaluates, from the consumer's perspective, where the relationship falls on the dimensions of power, duration, and clarity of termination. Thus, it asks, "How great is the power differential? How long has the relationship lasted? And has it clearly ended?" (Gottlieb, 1993, p. 45). A traditional psychotherapeutic relationship would rate high on each measure and thus would pose a higher risk if combined with another relationship. If it is not as high on these measures (e.g., the social worker was responsible only for discharge planning following a brief hospital stay), then further consideration could be given to the additional relationship. The same dimensions are considered for the new relationship: "Would it involve great power over a long time with uncertain termination?" (Gottlieb, 1993, pp. 45–46). Thus, accepting a former client as an employee would rate high on these dimensions, whereas serving together as classroom parents for the elementary school would not.

Kitchener (1988) borrows from role theory in offering three additional factors on which to evaluate the risk of harm in a dual relationship. Risk is increased when the expectations between roles are incompatible, when obligations diverge, and when there are greater differences in prestige and power. For example, serving as a client's therapist and employer reflects high risk on all variables; the demands of the roles are incompatible, the obligations of the roles may well lead to divided loyalties or decreased objectivity, and the power differential in both roles is quite vast. Contrast this with the development of a social relationship with a former student or employee in which the power differential and role conflicts are minimal, in part because the dual relationships are not concurrent, but also because the differences in power, role expectations, and responsibilities are not as great.

Ebert (1997) offers another, more fully explicated model and suggests attention to additional factors, including where the secondary role relationship occurs (i.e., How public is it?), the purpose of the activity, the extent of contact, the presence of overt or subtle coercion, the likelihood that the behavior will create confusion, how the relationship appears to others, the context in which the conduct takes place, the danger of inhibiting future therapy, threats to clinician objectivity, and the strength of the client. Each of these questions helps the worker evaluate the potential for conflicts of interest or therapeutic complications and thus determine the relative risk of engaging in the secondary relationship. Buying groceries from a store owned by a client might be construed as lower risk than buying a car at a client's dealership because the former is a more common, less individualized transaction and one in which the prices are fixed and the threat of coercion in negotiating price is not an issue. Attending a cookout to celebrate a youth soccer team's season, when both the worker's and client's children are part of the team, may not raise significant, ongoing discomfort or become intrusive in the helping process, but repeatedly seeing clients at the local health club locker room might (Schank & Skovholt, 1997).

A home visit with an old acquaintance is more private, and thus more hazardous, than seeing the patient in an office setting.

Conclusion

Many situations and settings create complex boundary questions that invoke ethical considerations about conflicts of interest, privacy, and professionalism. Boundary issues are as old as the profession and as novel as the latest evolution in electronic technology. Social workers must engage in astute self-evaluation to determine when personal and professional activities can be reconciled and the client's interests upheld. Professional standards, personal policies, and dialogue with colleagues will prepare workers to set boundaries and navigate novel challenges.

Helpful Resources

Articles, research, and resources in psychology (Kenneth S. Pope, PhD, ABPP): http://www.kspope.com

Clinical Social Work Association: https://www.clinicalsocialworkassociation.org/CSWA-Ethics

International Federation of Social Workers. *Global social work statement of ethical principles.* http://ifsw.org/policies/statement-of-ethical-principles

National Association of Social Workers. *Code of ethics.* https://www.socialworkers.org/about/ethics/code-of-ethics/code-of-ethics-english

The New Social Worker: https://www.socialworker.com

Virtual Mentor (*American Medical Association Journal of Ethics*): https://journalofethics.ama-assn.org/home

References

Banks, S., Cai, T., de Jonge, E., Shears, J., Shum, M., Sobočan, A. M., Strom, K., Truell, R., Uriz, M. J., & Weinberg, M. (2020a). Practicing ethically during COVID-19: Social work challenges and responses. *International Social Work, 63*(5), 569–583.

Banks, S., Cai, T., de Jonge, E., Shears, J., Shum, M., Sobočan, A. M., Strom, K., Truell, R., Uriz, M. J., & Weinberg, M. (2020b). *Ethical challenges for* social workers during Covid-19: A global perspective. International Federation of Social Workers.

Barsky, A. E. (2019). *Ethics and values in social work: An integrated approach for a comprehensive curriculum* (2nd ed.). Oxford University Press.

Beck, L. (2013, February 5). *Uh-oh: OB-GYN complains about patient on Facebook* [Blog post]. http://jezebel.com/5981691/she-made-a-huge-mistake-ob+gyn-complains-about-patient-on-facebook

Boland-Prom, K. W. (2009). Results from a national study of social workers sanctioned by state licensing boards. *Social Work, 54*(4), 351–360.

Daley, M. R., & Doughty, M. O. (2006). Ethics complaints in social work practice: A rural–urban comparison. *Journal of Social Work Values and Ethics, 3*(1). https://jswve.org/download/2006-1/JSWVE-Spring-2006-Complete.pdf

Doyle, K. (1997). Substance abuse counselors in recovery: Implications for the ethical issue of dual relationships. *Journal of Counseling and Development, 75*, 428–432.

Ebert, B. W. (1997). Dual-relationship prohibitions: A concept whose time never should have come. *Applied and Preventative Psychology, 6*, 137–156.

Epstein, R. S., & Simon, R. I. (1990). The exploitation index: An early warning indicator of boundary violations in psychotherapy. *Bulletin of the Menninger Clinic, 54*(4), 450–465.

Erickson, S. H. (2001). Multiple relationships in rural counseling. *Family Journal, 9*(3), 302–304.

Farber, B. A. (2006). *Self-disclosure in psychotherapy.* Guilford.

Gottlieb, M. C. (1993). Avoiding exploitive dual relationships: A decision-making model. *Psychotherapy, 30*(1), 41–48.

Hartmann, E. (1997). The concept of boundaries in counselling and psychotherapy. *British Journal of Guidance & Counselling, 25*(2), 147–162.

Heyboer, K. (2010, March 26). Medical students' cadaver photos gets scrutiny after images show up online. *NJ.com.* http://www.nj.com/news/index.ssf/2010/03/medical_schools_examine_ethics.html

Kidder, R. M. (1995). *How good people make tough choices: Resolving the dilemmas of ethical living.* Simon & Schuster.

Kitchener, K. S. (1988). Dual relationships: What makes them so problematic? *Journal of Counseling and Development, 67*, 217–221.

National Association of Social Workers. (2017a). *Code of ethics.*

National Association of Social Workers. (2017b). NASW, ASWB, CSWE, & CSWA standards for technology in social work practice. https://www.socialworkers.org/LinkClick.aspx?fileticket=lcTcdsHUcng=&portalid=0

Reamer, F. G. (2011). Eye on ethics. *Social Work Today.* https://www.socialworktoday.com/news/eoe_070111.shtml

Reamer, F. G. (2015). Clinical social work in a digital environment: Ethical and risk-management challenges. *Clinical Social Work Journal, 43*(2), 120–132. doi:10.1007/s10615-014-0495-0

Reamer, F. G. (2018). Ethical issues in integrated health care: Implications for social workers. *Health & Social Work, 43*(2), 118–124.

Schank, J. A., & Skovholt, T. M. (1997). Dual relationship dilemmas of rural and small-community psychologists. *Professional Psychology, 28*(1), 44–49.

Silberstein, A., & Boone, L. (2017). Multiple relationships in recovery communities. In O. Zur (Ed.), *Multiple relationships in psychotherapy and counseling: Unavoidable, common and mandatory dual relations in therapy* (pp. 130–140). Routledge.

Strom-Gottfried, K. J. (1999). Professional boundaries: An analysis of violations by social workers. *Families in Society, 80*(5), 439–449.

Strom-Gottfried, K. J. (2009). Ethical issues and guidelines. In S. Allen & E. Tracy (Eds.), *Delivering home-based services: A social work perspective* (pp. 14–33). Columbia University Press.

Walfish, S., Barnett, J. E., Marlyere, K., & Zielke, R. (2010). "Doc, there's something I have to tell you": Patient disclosure to their psychotherapist of unprosecuted murder and other violence. *Ethics & Behavior, 20*(5), 311–323.

Privacy, Confidentiality, and Privileged Communication

Frederic G. Reamer

Social workers understand that confidentiality is an essential element of a trusting relationship between practitioner and client. Clients' right to confidentiality is not absolute. Social workers must be familiar with exceptions to clients' right to confidentiality as set forth in ethical standards and the law. To fully appreciate this complexity, social workers must understand the related concepts of privacy and privileged communication.

Privacy

Clients have a right to privacy. Privacy refers to the right to noninterference in individuals' thoughts, knowledge, acts, associations, and property. Once clients decide to share otherwise private information with social workers, practitioners must then apply relevant confidentiality standards. According to the National Association of Social Workers (NASW, 2017) Code of Ethics,

> Social workers should respect clients' right to privacy. Social workers should not solicit private information from clients unless it is essential to providing services or conducting social work evaluation or research. Once private information is shared, standards of confidentiality apply. (standard 1.07[a])

In clinical work especially, the trust between social worker and client, so essential to effective help, typically depends on the worker's assurance of privacy. Clients' willingness to disclose intimate, deeply personal details about their lives is understandably a function of their belief that their social worker will not share this information with others without consent.

Privacy is also relevant in other social work domains. Social work administrators need to understand their obligation to protect clients' and employees' private information. This may pertain to personnel matters or sharing of information with colleagues in other agencies and organizations (e.g., insurance companies, accrediting bodies, utilization review representatives, human services departments, and court and law enforcement officials).

Furthermore, protective service workers need to avoid excessive invasion of privacy while investigating reports of child or elder abuse and neglect. Social workers involved in community organizing need to appreciate the nature of privacy when they meet with local residents who air grievances about public officials. Social workers in social policy positions need to understand the tension between privacy rights and local open-meeting statutes, which may allow the public and media to attend sensitive high-level meetings.

Confidentiality

Once clients decide to share otherwise private information with social workers, practitioners must then apply relevant confidentiality standards (Dickson, 1998; Fisher, 2013; Reamer, 2015, 2018a). According to the NASW (2017) Code of Ethics,

> Social workers should protect the confidentiality of all information obtained in the course of professional service, except for compelling professional reasons. The general expectation that social workers will keep information confidential does not apply when disclosure is necessary to prevent serious, foreseeable, and imminent harm to a client or others. In all instances, social workers should disclose the least amount of confidential information necessary to achieve the desired purpose; only information that is directly relevant to the purpose for which the disclosure is made should be revealed. (standard 1.07[c])

Contemporary social workers recognize that confidentiality cannot be absolute; there are many exceptions to clients' confidentiality rights (Saltzman et al., 2016). Widely accepted exceptions related to protection of third parties (e.g., mandatory reporting of child or elder

abuse or neglect) and clients' threats to harm themselves sometimes require disclosure of confidential information. Hence, clients have a right to relative (vs. absolute) confidentiality.

The current Code of Ethics (NASW, 2017) includes many specific standards pertaining to confidentiality (standards 1.07[a–w]), addressing

- clients' right to privacy;
- informed consent required for disclosure;
- protection of third parties from harm;
- notification of clients when social workers expect to disclose confidential information;
- limitations of clients' right to confidentiality;
- confidentiality issues in the delivery of services to families, couples, and small groups;
- disclosure of confidential information to third-party payers, the media, and during legal proceedings;
- protection of the confidentiality of written and electronic records and information transmitted to other parties through the use of electronic devices;
- gathering and searching for information about clients electronically;
- proper transfer and disposal of confidential records;
- protection of confidential information during teaching, training, and consultation; and
- protection of the confidentiality of deceased clients (Reamer, 2018b).

Social workers' increasing use of digital technology to communicate with clients, deliver services, and store confidential information electronically has introduced a number of novel and challenging ethical issues. The 2017 update to the NASW Code of Ethics added a number of new standards that directly address these issues. According to the code, to respect clients' privacy and protect client confidentiality, social workers should do the following:

- Discuss with clients policies concerning use of technology in the provision of professional services. Clients should have a clear understanding of the ways in which social workers use technology to deliver services, communicate with clients, search for information about clients online, and store sensitive information about clients.

- Obtain client consent to the use of technology at the beginning of the professional–client relationship.
- Verify the identity and location of clients they serve remotely (especially in case there is an emergency and to enable social workers to comply with laws in the client's jurisdiction).
- Obtain client consent before conducting an online search for information about clients, as a way to respect clients' privacy (unless there are emergency circumstances).
- Be aware that clients may discover personal information about them based on their personal affiliations and use of social media.
- Take reasonable steps (e.g., use of encryption, firewalls, and secure passwords) to protect the confidentiality of electronic communications, including information provided to clients or third parties.
- Develop and disclose policies and procedures for notifying clients of any breach of confidential information in a timely manner.
- Inform clients of unauthorized access to the social worker's electronic communication or storage systems (e.g., cloud storage).
- Develop and inform clients about their policies on the use of electronic technology to gather information about clients.
- Avoid posting any identifying or confidential information about clients on professional websites or other forms of social media.

Privileged Communication

Privileged communication is a narrower concept. Privilege refers to the disclosure of confidential information in court or during other legal proceedings; these might include legal proceedings related to child custody, divorce, termination of parental rights, workers' compensation, and criminal prosecution.

Courts commonly cite the following four conditions that must be satisfied for information to be considered privileged:

1. The parties involved in the conversation assumed that it was confidential.
2. Confidentiality is an important element in the relationship.
3. The broader community recognizes the importance of this relationship.
4. The harm caused by disclosure of the confidential information would outweigh the benefits of disclosure during legal proceedings.

In various rulings, courts have identified numerous exceptions to the client's right of privileged communication. A number of these exceptions pertain to judicial proceedings, such as when a client introduces information in court that they received counseling for emotional problems resulting from a workplace accident that has led to a lawsuit for damages, or when a social worker's testimony about a client is required so that the social worker can defend themself against a lawsuit filed by the client.

Disclosure of privileged information may also be permissible when a client threatens to commit suicide, shares information in the presence of a third party, is a minor and the subject of a custody dispute, is involved in criminal activity, has been abused or neglected, is impaired and may pose a threat to the public (e.g., when a client is an impaired bus driver or airline pilot), has not paid their fees and a collection agency is retained, or threatens to injure a third party. Whether a social worker must disclose privileged information without a client's consent is often a matter of dispute and subject to relevant statutes, regulations, and judicial opinion.

If social workers practice in a state granting the right of privileged communication to their clients, avoiding compliance with a subpoena may be easier because the legislature has acknowledged the importance of the privilege. Also, a legitimate response to a subpoena is to argue that the requested information should not be disclosed or can be obtained from some other source. A subpoena itself does not require a social worker to disclose information. Instead, a subpoena is essentially a request for information, and it may be without merit.

Resisting disclosure of privileged information is appropriate. As the NASW (2017) Code of Ethics states,

> Social workers should protect the confidentiality of clients during legal proceedings to the extent permitted by law. When a court of law or other legally authorized body orders social workers to disclose confidential or privileged information without a client's consent and such disclosure could cause harm to the client, social workers should request that the court withdraw the order or limit the order as narrowly as possible or maintain the records under seal, unavailable for public inspection. (standard 1.07[j])

Social workers can use several strategies to protect clients' confidentiality during legal proceedings. If social workers believe a subpoena is unwarranted or without merit, they can arrange for a lawyer—often the client's lawyer—to file a motion (known as a motion to quash) asking the court to rule that the request is inappropriate. In addition, social workers, perhaps through a lawyer, may request that a judge review clinical notes and records in chambers to protect confidentiality and then

rule on whether the information should be revealed in open court and made a matter of public record. A judge may issue a protective order explicitly limiting the disclosure of specific privileged information to certain portions of a social worker's clinical notes or certain aspects of their interpersonal communications.

Social workers should acquaint themselves with relevant federal and state statutes and regulations, agency policies, and practice principles related to each of these situations. They should pay particular attention to federal guidelines related to the confidentiality of substance use disorder records, school records, and electronically stored and transmitted communications. Key guidelines pertain to the release of confidential information relating to alcohol and substance abuse treatment ["Confidentiality of Substance Use Disorder Patient Records," 42 C.F.R. 2.1 (2017)]. These strict regulations broadly protect the identity, diagnosis, prognosis, or treatment of any client in records maintained in connection with the performance of any program or activity relating to substance abuse education, prevention, training, treatment, rehabilitation, or research that is conducted, regulated, or directly or indirectly assisted by any federal department or agency. Disclosures are permitted (1) with the written informed consent of the client; (2) to medical personnel in emergencies; (3) for research, evaluation, and audits; and (4) by court order for good cause.

Social workers employed in educational settings should know the ins and outs of the Family Educational Rights and Privacy Act (FERPA) regulations. FERPA [also known as the Buckley–Pell Amendment, 20 U.S.C. § 1232g (2011)] specifies the conditions for student and parent access to educational records; the procedures for challenging and correcting inaccurate educational records; and the requirements for the release of educational records or identifying information to other individuals, agencies, or organizations. This law covers public or private educational institutions and agencies that receive federal funds. It spells out when educational records may be released without written consent of a parent or guardian, for example, to school officials and teachers who have a legitimate educational interest; for financial aid, audit, and research purposes; and in emergencies if disclosure of information in the record is necessary to protect the health or safety of students or other people.

Social workers must also be fluent in the provisions of the Health Insurance Portability and Accountability Act (HIPAA). Congress enacted HIPAA in 1996 in response to increasing costs associated with transmitting health records lacking standardized formatting across providers, institutions, localities, and states. HIPAA has three components: privacy standards for the use and disclosure of individually identifiable private health information, transaction standards for the electronic exchange of health information, and security standards to protect the creation and maintenance of private health information (Fisher, 2013; Hartley & Jones, 2014).

The well-known *Tarasoff* case and various other "duty to protect" cases that have been litigated since then have helped clarify the delicate balance between social workers' obligation to respect clients' right to confidentiality and their simultaneous duty to protect third parties from harm. It is important to note that some states' laws permit social workers to disclose confidential information to protect third parties from harm, whereas other states' laws require disclosure. Social workers should consult their respective states' laws to understand their unique legal obligations.

Although some court decisions in these cases are contradictory and inconsistent with one another, in general four conditions should be met to justify disclosure of confidential information to protect third parties from harm:

- The social worker should have evidence that the client poses a threat of violence to a third party. Although court decisions have not provided precise definitions of violence, the term ordinarily implies the use of force—such as with a gun, knife, or other deadly weapon—to inflict injury.

- The social worker should have evidence that the violent act is foreseeable. The social worker should be able to present evidence that suggests significant risk that the violent act will occur. Although courts recognize that social workers and other human service professionals cannot always predict violence accurately, social workers should expect to have to demonstrate that they had good reasons for believing that their client was likely to act violently.

- The social worker should have evidence that the violent act is imminent. The social worker should be able to present evidence that the act was impending or likely to occur relatively soon. *Imminence* may be defined differently by different social workers in different circumstances; some social workers think imminence implies a violent incident within minutes, whereas others think in terms of hours or days. In light of this difference of professional opinion, it is important for social workers to be able to explain their definition and interpretation of "imminence," should they have to defend their decision regarding the disclosure of confidential information.

- Some, but not all, court decisions imply that a practitioner must be able to identify the probable victim. A number of courts have ruled that practitioners should have specific information about the parties involved, including the potential victim's identity, to justify disclosure of confidential information against the client's wishes. The NASW Code of Ethics does not require social workers to be able to identify a potential victim (consistent with some states' laws).

It is extremely important for social workers to inform clients at the beginning of their working relationship about the limits of confidentiality. According to the 2017 NASW Code of Ethics,

> Social workers should discuss with clients and other interested parties the nature of confidentiality and limitations of clients' right to confidentiality. Social workers should review with clients' circumstances where confidential information may be requested and where disclosure of confidential information may be legally required. This discussion should occur as soon as possible in the social worker–client relationship and as needed throughout the course of the relationship. (standard 1.07[e])

That is, clients have the right to know what information they share with a social worker might have to be disclosed to others against clients' wishes (e.g., evidence of child abuse or neglect, or of a client's threat to harm a third party).

Social workers can take a number of steps to protect clients' privacy and confidentiality (Reamer, 2015). Social workers should be sure to provide training for all agency staff members, including all professional staff and nonprofessional staff (e.g., secretaries, clerical workers, custodians, and cooks in residential programs), on the concept of confidentiality, the need to protect confidentiality, and common ways that confidentiality can be violated. Training should cover the need to protect confidential information contained in electronic and written records and documents from inappropriate access by parties outside the agency (e.g., other human service professionals, law enforcement officials, insurance companies, clients' family members, and

guardians) and by other staff members within the agency who have no need to know the confidential information. All agencies should have clear policies governing access to confidential information by third parties and clients.

Staff should also receive training on inappropriate release of confidential information through verbal communication. Social workers and other staff members in social service agencies need to be careful about what they say in hallways and waiting rooms, in elevators, in restaurants and other public facilities, in voice mail messages, in email and text messages, and over the telephone to other social service professionals, clients' family members and friends, and representatives of the news media. According to the 2017 NASW Code of Ethics, "Social workers should not discuss confidential information, electronically or in person, in any setting unless privacy can be ensured. Social workers should not discuss confidential information in public or semipublic areas such as hallways, waiting rooms, elevators, and restaurants" (standard 1.07[i]).

In addition, social workers should prepare clear written explanations of their agency's confidentiality guidelines. These should be shared with every client (many agencies ask clients to sign a copy acknowledging that the guidelines were shared with them and that they understand the guidelines).

In this digital age, social workers should be especially careful with what is known as electronically stored information (ESI). ESI is generally defined as all information stored in computers and other electronic or digital devices. This includes email, voice mail, instant and text messages, databases, metadata, and any other digital images and files. During legal proceedings, attorneys typically seek to discover this information, usually through subpoenas and court orders. In fact, there is now a subspecialty known in legal circles as *e-discovery*, which refers to any process in which electronic data are sought, located, secured, and searched with the intent of using them as evidence in a civil or criminal legal case. For example, the Federal Rules of Civil Procedure, which, since 1938, have governed court procedure for civil cases in federal courts, have been amended to include guidelines pertaining to discovery of ESI. The rules now state that a party in a civil matter may formally request that another party

> produce and permit the requesting party or its representative to inspect, copy, test, or sample the following items in the responding party's possession, custody, or control . . . any designated documents or electronically stored information—including writings, drawings, graphs, charts, photographs, sound recordings, images, and other data or data compilations—stored in any medium from which information can be obtained either directly or, if necessary, after translation by the responding party into a reasonably usable form. (Rule 34)

To protect clients (and themselves), social workers should apply time-honored ethical standards when managing ESI, especially when doing so is associated with client privacy, confidentiality, informed consent, documentation, boundaries, and management of records. Social workers should be especially mindful of emerging ethical standards pertaining to protection and encryption of clients' sensitive information, disclosures of ESI in response to subpoenas and court orders, retention and destruction of electronic records, and clients' right to access their electronic records through online portals.

Social workers face special challenges in integrated service delivery settings. These are organizations that provide clients with centralized access to health and behavioral health (mental health) services. There is significant support among social workers for the underlying concept of integrated health care and implementation of carefully coordinated, comprehensive services (Horevitz & Manoleas, 2013; Nover, 2013). As social workers and other health care professionals have discovered, however, integrating health care and behavioral health services has produced a number of complex ethical challenges, especially regarding protection of clients' confidential information. Social workers and their colleagues need to establish strict guidelines that set forth which personnel have access to clients' confidential information. Common guidelines are based on the concept of "need to know"—that is, only staffers who have a compelling need to know sensitive details about clients should have access to those details.

Privacy and confidentiality are cornerstone values in social work. It is essential that social workers appreciate the complex ethical and legal standards that govern protection and disclosure of sensitive information about clients and third parties. Skillful management of clients' privacy and confidentiality rights is an essential component of sound social work practice.

References

Dickson, D. T. (1998). *Confidentiality and privacy in social work*. Free Press.

Fisher, M. A. (2013). *The ethics of conditional confidentiality: A practice model for mental health professionals*. Oxford University Press.

Hartley, C., & Jones, E. (2014). *HIPAA plain and simple: After the final rule* (3rd ed.). Chicago: American Medical Association.

Horevitz, E., & Manoleas, P. (2013). Professional competencies and training needs of professional social workers in integrated behavioral health in primary care. *Social Work in Health Care, 52*, 752–787.

National Association of Social Workers. (2017). *Code of ethics*.

Nover, C. H. (2013). Mental health in primary care: Perceptions of augmented care for individuals with serious mental illness. *Social Work in Health Care, 52,* 656–668.

Reamer, F. G. (2015). *Risk management in social work: Preventing professional malpractice, liability, and disciplinary action.* Columbia University Press.

Reamer, F. G. (2018a). *Social work values and ethics* (5th ed.). Columbia University Press.

Reamer, F. G. (2018b). *Ethical standards in social work: A review of the NASW Code of Ethics* (3rd ed.). NASW Press.

Saltzman, A., Furman, D. M., & Ohman, K. (2016). *Law in social work practice* (3rd ed.). Cengage.

Risk Management in Social Work

Frederic G. Reamer

To protect clients, third parties, and themselves, social workers need to be informed about prevailing standards to prevent ethics complaints and ethics-related lawsuits. Ethics complaints—filed with social work licensing boards or with professional organizations, such as the National Association of Social Workers (NASW)—typically allege that social workers violated widely accepted ethical standards in their relationships with clients, colleagues, employers, or other parties. Ethics-related lawsuits typically claim that social workers were negligent, in the strict legal sense, by virtue of their mishandling of some ethics-related phenomenon, such as processing confidential information or informed consent, maintenance of professional boundaries, conflicts of interest, use of controversial treatment techniques, use of technology to deliver services, or termination of services (Reamer, 2012a, 2015, 2018a).

The Nature of Risk Management

Social workers expose themselves to risk when they practice in a manner that is inconsistent with prevailing professional standards (Reamer, 2015; Strom-Gottfried, 2000, 2003). Some ethics complaints arise out of mistakes and oversights. Examples include social workers who forget to document important clinical information in a client's case record, inadvertently disclose sensitive personal information to a client in a text message or Facebook posting, or fail to protect confidential information disclosed to law enforcement officials. Other complaints and lawsuits arise from social workers' deliberate ethical decisions—for example, when social workers attempt to manage complex boundaries in their relationships with clients in rural communities, provide clinical services to clients remotely using technology, disclose confidential information without clients' consent to protect third parties, or terminate services to a noncompliant client. In addition, some complaints and lawsuits are the result of practitioners' ethical misconduct, such as sexual relationships with clients or fraudulent billing for services.

Social workers can be held accountable for negligence and ethical violations in several ways. In addition to filing lawsuits, parties can file ethics complaints with NASW or with state licensing boards. In some instances, social workers are also subject to review by other professional organizations to which they belong. In exceptional circumstances, criminal charges may be filed (e.g., based on allegations of sexual misconduct or fraudulent billing of an insurance company or state funding agency).

Ethics complaints filed against NASW members are processed using a peer review model. Recommendations may include sanctions or various forms of corrective action, such as suspension from NASW, mandated supervision or consultation, censure, or instructions to send the complainant a letter of apology. NASW also offers mediation in some cases in an effort to avoid formal adjudication, particularly when matters do not involve allegations of extreme misconduct.

State legislatures also empower social work licensing boards to process ethics complaints filed against social workers who hold a license (in some states, the boards are interdisciplinary, including social work and allied helping professions). Ordinarily, these boards appoint a panel to review the complaint and, when warranted, conduct a formal investigation and hearing (some state boards include public members in addition to professional colleagues).

Negligence claims or lawsuits filed against social workers typically allege that they engaged in malpractice in that they failed to adhere to specific standards of care. The standard of care is based on what "reasonable" and prudent practitioners with the same or similar training would have done under the same or similar circumstances. Departures from the profession's standards of care may result from a social worker's acts of commission or acts of omission. Acts of commission can occur as a result of misfeasance (the commission of a proper act in a wrongful or injurious manner or the improper performance of an act that might have been performed lawfully) or malfeasance (the commission of a wrongful or unlawful act). An example of misfeasance is disclosing confidential information

inadvertently on a practitioner's Facebook site; an example of malfeasance is sexual involvement with a client. An act of omission, or nonfeasance, occurs when a social worker fails to perform certain duties that should have been performed. An example of nonfeasance is failure to inform clients of exceptions to their confidentiality rights or failure to report suspected child abuse of a client.

Lawsuits and liability claims that allege malpractice are civil suits, in contrast to criminal proceedings. Ordinarily, civil suits are based on tort or contract law, with plaintiffs (the party bringing the lawsuit) seeking some sort of compensation for injuries they claim to have incurred as a result of the practitioner's negligence. These injuries may be economic (e.g., lost wages or medical expenses), physical (e.g., following a sexual relationship between a practitioner and client), or emotional (e.g., depression suffered by a client who did not receive competent care from a practitioner).

As in criminal trials, defendants in civil lawsuits are presumed innocent until proven otherwise. In ordinary civil suits, defendants will be found liable for their actions based on the legal standard of preponderance of the evidence, as opposed to the stricter standard of proof beyond a reasonable doubt used in criminal trials.

In general, malpractice occurs when evidence exists that (1) at the time of the alleged malpractice, a legal duty existed between the social worker and the client; (2) the social worker was derelict in that duty or breached the duty (i.e., the conduct fell below the profession's standard of care), either by commission or by omission; (3) the client suffered some harm or injury; and (4) the harm or injury was directly and proximately caused by the social worker's dereliction or breach of duty.

In some cases, prevailing standards of care are relatively easy to establish through citations of the profession's literature and practice standards, expert testimony, statutory or regulatory language, or relevant practice and codes of ethics standards. Examples include standards concerning sexual relationships with current clients, disclosing confidential information to protect children who may have been abused or neglected, fraudulent billing, use of technology, or falsified clinical records. In other cases, however, social workers disagree about standards of care. This may occur in cases involving controversial treatment methods or ambiguous clinical or administrative circumstances (Reamer, 2015, 2018b).

Key Risks in Social Work

Social workers' prevention efforts should focus on a number of risk areas (Reamer, 2001, 2015), which are discussed next.

Client Rights

Especially since the 1960s, social workers have developed a keen understanding of a wide range of clients' rights, many of which were established by legislation or court ruling. These include rights related to confidentiality and privacy, release of information, informed consent, access to services, use of the least restrictive alternative, refusal of treatment, options for alternative services, access to records, use of technology, termination of services, and grievance procedures.

Confidentiality, Privileged Communication, and Privacy

Social workers must understand the nature of clients' right to confidentiality and exceptions to these rights. Specifically, social workers should have sound policies and procedures in place related to

- solicitation of private information from clients;
- disclosure of confidential information to protect clients from self-harm and protect third parties from harm inflicted by clients;

- release of confidential information pertaining to substance use disorder assessment or treatment;
- disclosure of information about deceased clients;
- release of information to parents and guardians of minor clients;
- sharing of confidential information among participants in family, couples, and group counseling;
- disclosure of confidential information to media representatives, law enforcement officials, protective service agencies, other social service organizations, and collection agencies;
- protection of confidential written and electronic records—information transmitted to other parties through the use of computer and other digital technology;
- transfer or disposal of clients' records;
- protection of client confidentiality in the event of a social worker's death, disability, or employment termination;
- precautions to prevent discussion of confidential information in public or semipublic areas;
- disclosure of confidential information to third-party payers;
- disclosure of confidential information to consultants;
- disclosure of confidential information for teaching or training purposes; and
- protection of confidential and privileged information during legal proceedings (e.g., divorce proceedings, custody disputes, workers' compensation claims, paternity cases, criminal trials, and negligence lawsuits).

To protect clients and minimize risk, social workers should discuss with clients and other interested parties the nature of confidentiality and limitations of clients' right to confidentiality (Fisher, 2013). Depending on the setting, these topics can include

- the importance of confidentiality in the social worker–client relationship (a brief statement of why the social worker treats the subject of confidentiality so seriously);
- laws, ethical standards, and regulations pertaining to confidentiality (relevant federal, state, and local laws and regulations; ethical standards in social work);
- measures the social worker will take to protect clients' confidentiality (storing paper and electronic records in a secure location and limiting colleagues' and outside parties' access to records);
- circumstances in which the social worker would be obligated to disclose confidential information (e.g., to comply with mandatory reporting laws or a court order and to protect a third party from harm or the client from self-injury);
- procedures that will be used to obtain clients' informed consent for the release of confidential information and any exceptions to this (a summary of the purpose and importance of and the steps involved in informed consent);
- the procedures for sharing information with colleagues for consultation, supervision, and coordination of services (a summary of the roles of consultation and supervision, and coordination of services and why confidential information might be shared);
- access that third-party payers (insurers) or employers will have to clients' records (policy for sharing information with managed care organizations, insurance companies, insurance company representatives, utilization review personnel, employers, and staff of employee assistance programs);
- disclosure of confidential information by phone, computer, fax machine, email, text message, and the internet;
- access to agency facilities and clients by outside parties (e.g., people who come to the agency to attend meetings or participate in a tour); and
- audiotaping and videotaping of clients.

Informed Consent

Informed consent is required in a variety of circumstances, including release of confidential information, program admission, service delivery and treatment, videotaping, audiotaping, and use of technology to communicate with clients and deliver services remotely (Miller & Wertheimer, 2010). Although various courts, state legislatures, and agencies have somewhat different interpretations and applications of informed consent standards, there is considerable agreement about the key elements that social workers and agencies should incorporate into consent procedures (e.g., that clients should be given specific details about the purposes of the consent, a verbal explanation, information about their rights to refuse consent and withdraw consent, information about alternative treatment options, and an opportunity to ask questions about the consent process).

Service Delivery

Social workers must provide services and represent themselves as competent only within the boundaries of their education, training, license, certification, consultation received, supervised experience, or other relevant professional experience. They should provide services in substantive areas and use practice approaches and techniques that are new to them only after engaging in appropriate study, training, consultation, and supervision from people who are already competent in those practice approaches, interventions, and techniques. Social workers who use practice approaches and interventions for which there are no generally recognized standards should obtain appropriate education, training, consultation, and supervision.

Digital and Online Technology

Digital, online, and other electronic technology has transformed the nature of social work practice. Contemporary social workers can provide services to clients using online counseling, telephone counseling, video counseling, cybertherapy (avatar therapy), self-guided Web-based interventions, online social networks, email, and text messages. The introduction of diverse digital, online, and other forms of electronic social services has created a wide range of complex ethical and related risk management issues involving the delivery of services, communications with clients, and storage of sensitive information. Compelling ethical issues pertain to practitioner competence, client privacy and confidentiality, informed consent, conflicts of interest, boundaries and dual relationships, consultation and client referral, termination and interruption of services, and documentation (NASW et al., 2017; Reamer, 2012b, 2018c).

Boundary Issues, Dual Relationships, and Conflicts of Interest

Social workers should establish clear policies, practices, and procedures to ensure proper boundaries related to the following (Reamer, 2001, 2012a):

- Sexual relationships with current and former clients
- Counseling former sexual partners
- Sexual relationships with clients' relatives or acquaintances
- Sexual relationships with supervisees, trainees, students, and colleagues
- Physical contact with clients
- Friendships with current and former clients
- Encounters with clients in public settings
- Attending clients' social, religious, or life cycle events
- Gifts to and from clients
- Performing favors for clients
- The delivery of services in clients' homes
- Use of online and other technology to communicate with clients
- Financial conflicts of interest

- Delivery of services to two or more people who have a relationship with each other (e.g., couples and family members)
- Bartering with clients for goods and services
- Managing relationships in small or rural communities
- Self-disclosure to clients
- Becoming colleagues with a former client

Documentation

Careful documentation and comprehensive records are necessary to assess clients' circumstances; plan and deliver services appropriately; facilitate supervision; provide proper accountability to clients, other service providers, funding agencies, insurers, utilization review staff, and the courts; evaluate services provided; and ensure continuity in the delivery of future services (Kagle & Kopels, 2008; Reamer, 2005; Sidell, 2011; Wiger, 2009). Thorough documentation also helps ensure quality care if a client's primary social worker becomes unavailable because of illness, incapacitation, vacation, or employment termination. In addition, thorough documentation can help social workers who are named in ethics complaints or lawsuits (e.g., when evidence is needed to demonstrate that a social worker obtained a client's informed consent before releasing confidential information, assessed for suicide risk properly, consulted with knowledgeable experts about a client's clinical issues, consulted the NASW Code of Ethics to make a difficult ethical decision, or referred a client to other service providers when services were terminated).

Social workers should maintain and store records for the number of years required by state statutes or relevant contracts. Practitioners should make special provisions for proper access to their records in the event of their disability, incapacitation, termination of practice, or death. This may include entering into agreements with colleagues who would be willing to assume responsibility for social workers' records if they are unavailable for any reason.

Defamation of Character

Social workers should ensure that their written and oral communications about clients are not defamatory. Libel is the written form of defamation of character; slander is the oral form. Defamation occurs when a social worker says or writes something about a client or another party that is untrue, the social worker knew or should have known that the statement was untrue, and the communication caused some injury to the client or third party (e.g., the client was terminated from a treatment program or lost custody of a child, or a colleague was disciplined by an agency administrator).

Supervision

In principle, social workers can be named in ethics complaints and lawsuits alleging ethical breaches or negligence by those under their supervision. Social work supervisors should ensure that they meet with supervisees regularly, address appropriate issues (e.g., treatment and intervention plans, case recording, correction of errors in all phases of client contact, dual relationships, and protection of third parties), and document the supervision provided.

Consultation and Referral

Social workers should be clear about when consultation with colleagues is appropriate and necessary and also about the procedures they should use to locate competent consultants. Similarly, social workers have a responsibility to refer clients to colleagues when they do not have the expertise or time to assist clients in need. Practitioners should know when to refer clients to other professionals and how to locate competent colleagues.

Fraud

Social workers should have strict procedures in place to prevent fraud related to, for example, documentation in case records, billing, and employment applications.

Termination of Services

Social workers expose themselves to risk when they terminate services improperly—for example, when a social worker leaves an agency suddenly without adequately referring a vulnerable client to another practitioner or when a social worker terminates services to a very vulnerable client who has missed appointments or has not paid an outstanding bill. Practitioners should develop thorough and comprehensive termination protocols to prevent client abandonment.

Practitioner Impairment, Misconduct, and Incompetence

A significant percentage of ethics complaints and negligence claims are filed against social workers who meet the definition of impaired professional (impairment that may be due to factors such as substance abuse, mental illness, extraordinary personal stress, or legal difficulties). Social workers should understand the nature of professional impairment and possible causes; be alert to warning signs; and have procedures in place to prevent, identify, and respond appropriately to impairment in their own lives or colleagues' lives (Reamer, 2015; Strom-Gottfried, 2000, 2003).

In addition, social workers sometimes encounter colleagues who have engaged in ethical misconduct or are incompetent. Examples include social workers who learn that a colleague is falsifying insurance claims or client records or is providing services outside their areas of expertise.

In some instances, social workers can address these situations satisfactorily by approaching the colleague, raising the concerns, and helping the colleague devise an earnest, constructive, and comprehensive plan to stop the unethical behavior, minimize harm to affected parties, seek appropriate supervision and consultation, and develop any necessary competencies. When these measures fail or are not feasible—perhaps because of the serious-ness of the ethical misconduct, impairment, or incompetence—one must consider blowing the whistle on the colleague (Reamer, 2019). Whistle-blowing entails taking action through appropriate channels—such as notifying ad-ministrators, supervisors, professional organ-izations, and licensing boards—in an effort to address the problem.

Before deciding to blow the whistle, so-cial workers should carefully consider the se-verity of the harm and misconduct involved; the quality of the evidence of wrongdoing (one should avoid blowing the whistle without clear and convincing evidence); the effect of the decision on colleagues and one's agency; the whistle-blower's motives (i.e., whether the whistle-blowing is motivated primarily by a wish for revenge); and the viability of alterna-tive, intermediate courses of action (whether other, less drastic means might address the problem). Social work administrators need to formulate and enforce agency policies and pro-cedures that support and protect staffers who disclose impairment, misconduct, and incom-petence conscientiously and in good faith.

Management Practices

Periodically, social work administrators should assess the appropriateness or adequacy of the agency's government licenses, the agency's papers of incorporation and bylaws, the state licenses and current registrations of all profes-sional staff, protocols for emergency action, insurance policies, staff evaluation procedures, and financial management practices.

Implementing a Comprehensive Risk Management Strategy

Social workers can prevent ethics complaints and ethics-related lawsuits by conducting a comprehensive ethics audit (Reamer, 2001,

2015). An ethics audit entails thorough ex-amination of major risks associated with one's practice setting (whether independent or agency-based practice). The audit involves sev-eral steps designed to identify ethics-related risks and minimize harm to clients, social workers, and social service agencies:

1. Appoint a committee or task force of con-cerned and informed staff or colleagues.
2. Gather the information necessary to assess the level of risk associated with each ethics-related phenomenon (i.e., clients' rights; confidentiality and privacy; informed con-sent; service delivery; digital and online technology; boundary issues and conflicts of interest; documentation; defamation of character; supervision; staff development and training; consultation; client referral; fraud; termination of services; practitioner impairment, misconduct, or incompe-tence; and management practices) from such sources as agency documents, data gathered from interviews with agency staff, and national accreditation standards.
3. Review all available information.
4. Determine whether there is no risk, min-imal risk, moderate risk, or high risk for each risk area.
5. Prepare an action plan to address each risk area that warrants attention, paying par-ticular attention to the steps required to reduce risk, the resources required, the per-sonnel who will oversee implementation of the action plan, the timetable for comple-tion of the plan, the indicators of progress toward reducing risk, and plans to monitor implementation of the action plan.

In recent years, social workers have paid increased attention to the risk of lawsuits and ethics complaints filed against practitioners and agencies. To minimize these risks, and especially to protect clients, social workers need to under-stand the nature of professional standards of care, malpractice, and negligence. They also need to be familiar with major risk areas and practical steps they can take to prevent complaints.

References

Fisher, M. A. (2013). *The ethics of conditional confidentiality: A practical model for mental health professionals.* Oxford University Press.

Kagle, J. D., & Kopels, S. (2008). *Social work records* (3rd ed.). Waveland.

Miller, F. G., & Wertheimer, A. (Eds.). (2010). *The ethics of consent: Theory and practice.* Oxford University Press.

National Association of Social Workers, Association of Social Work Boards, Council on Social Work Education, & Clinical Social Work Association. (2017). *NASW, ASWB, CSWE, & CSWA standards for technology in social work practice.* NASW Press.

Reamer, F. G. (2001). *The social work ethics audit: A risk management tool.* NASW Press.

Reamer, F. G. (2005). Documentation in social work: Evolving ethical and risk-management standards. *Social Work, 50*(4), 325–334.

Reamer, F. G. (2012a). *Boundary issues and dual relationships in the human services.* Columbia University Press.

Reamer, F. G. (2012b). The digital and electronic revolution in social work: Rethinking the meaning of ethical practice. *Ethics and Social Welfare, 7*(1), 2–19.

Reamer, F. G. (2015). *Risk management in social work: Preventing professional malpractice, liability, and disciplinary action.* Columbia University Press.

Reamer, F. G. (2018a). *Ethical standards in social work: A review of the NASW Code of Ethics* (2nd ed.). NASW Press.

Reamer, F. G. (2018b). *Social work values and ethics* (5th ed.). Columbia University Press.

Reamer, F. G. (2018c). Ethical standards for social workers' use of technology: Emerging consensus. *Journal of Social Work Values and Ethics, 15*(2), 71–80.

Reamer, F. G. (2019). The ethics of whistle blowing. *Journal of Ethics in Mental Health, 10,* 1–19.

Sidell, N. L. (2011). *Social work documentation: A guide to strengthening your case recording.* NASW Press.

Strom-Gottfried, K. (2000). Ensuring ethical practice: An examination of NASW code violations. *Social Work, 45*(3), 251–261.

Strom-Gottfried, K. (2003). Understanding adjudication: Origins, targets, and outcomes of ethics complaints. *Social Work, 48*(1), 85–94.

Wiger, D. (2009). *The clinical documentation sourcebook: The complete paperwork resource for your mental health practice* (4th ed.). Wiley.

Social Work and Digital Technology

Ethical Issues

Frederic G. Reamer

In recent years, increasing numbers of social workers have begun to use technology extensively to deliver services, administer programs, communicate with and gather information about clients and colleagues, and educate students and practitioners. Some clinical social workers provide counseling services to clients they never meet in person, communicating with them only by video, email, telephone, text messages, and online avatar groups (Kanani & Regehr, 2003; Reamer, 2013a, 2018). Similarly, some social work supervisors are overseeing the work of supervisees they never meet in person. Some social work educators are teaching students without ever sharing a physical classroom with them, and some agency administrators conduct meetings primarily online. Other social workers are using technology to supplement face-to-face contact.

Many social workers recognize potential benefits associated with their use of technology, including making services available to clients who live in remote locations, have difficulty traveling due to disability, or whose work schedules do not lend themselves to office-based visits. However, some clinical social workers worry that the expanding use of distance counseling options dilutes the meaning of therapeutic relationship and alliance and compromises social workers' ability to comply with core ethical values and standards related to informed consent, privacy, confidentiality, professional boundaries, competent practice, and termination of services, among others (Finn & Barak, 2010; Lee, 2010; Menon & Miller-Cribbs, 2002; Santhiveeran, 2009; Zur, 2012). Clinicians who offer distance counseling services may find it difficult to maintain clear boundaries in their relationships with clients, in part because of ambiguity surrounding the temporal limits of their interactions that are no longer limited to office-based visits during normal working hours (Chester & Glass, 2006; LaMendola, 2010; Mattison, 2012; Reamer, 2012, 2015a, 2015b, 2018; Zur, 2012).

There is also some debate among social work educators (Casey, 2008; Reamer, 2013b, 2019; Rumble, 2008; Sawrikar et al., 2015).

Some applaud the use of distance education technology to expand social work education programs' reach, especially to remote and rural locations. Others decry the advent of degree programs that are entirely or primarily online, arguing that in-person contact between teacher and students is an essential component of quality education and gatekeeping.

These dramatic changes in the ways that social work services, supervision, administration, and education are provided have led to major efforts to develop pertinent ethical standards in social work. These efforts have occurred in three distinct, albeit related, domains: (1) practice standards, (2) regulatory and licensing standards, and (3) code of ethics standards. It is essential that today's social workers be thoroughly familiar with these significant developments to ensure that their practice complies with prevailing ethical standards.

In 2017, following unprecedented collaboration among key social work organizations in the United States—the National Association of Social Workers (NASW), the Association of Social Work Boards (ASWB), the Council on Social Work Education (CSWE), and the Clinical Social Work Association (CSWA)—the profession formally adopted new, comprehensive practice standards, including extensive ethics guidelines that focused on social workers' and social work educators' use of technology (NASW et al., 2017). Approved by these respective organizations' boards of directors, these transformational, comprehensive standards address a wide range of compelling ethical issues related to social workers' use of technology to provide information to the public; design and deliver services; gather, manage, and store information; and educate social workers.

Recognizing the profound impact that technology is having on social work practice, in 2013 the ASWB board of directors appointed an international task force to develop model regulatory standards for technology and social work practice. ASWB embarked on development of new ethics-related standards in response to demand from regulatory bodies throughout the world for guidance concerning social workers' evolving use of technology. The task force developed model standards, including extensive ethics guidelines, addressing seven key ethics-related concepts: practitioner competence; informed consent; privacy and confidentiality; boundaries, dual relationships, and conflicts of interest; records and documentation; collegial relationships; and social work practice across jurisdictional boundaries. These model standards, formally adopted in 2015, are now influencing the development of licensing and regulatory laws throughout the world.

In 2015, NASW appointed a task force to determine whether changes were needed in its Code of Ethics to address concerns related to the use of technology. The last major revision of the code was approved in 1996. Since 1996, there has been significant growth in the use of technology in various aspects of social work practice. In fact, many of the technologies currently used by social workers and clients did not exist in 1996. In 2017, NASW adopted a revised code that includes extensive technology-related additions pertaining to informed consent, competent practice, conflicts of interest, privacy and confidentiality, sexual relationships, sexual harassment, interruption of services, unethical conduct of colleagues, supervision and consultation, education and training, client records, and evaluation and research.

Emerging Best Practices

Emerging ethical standards pertaining to social workers' use of technology that are embedded in model regulatory laws promulgated by the ASWB, the revised NASW Code of Ethics, and standards of practice developed jointly by NASW, ASWB, CSWE, and CSWA highlight a number of common core concepts and themes: provision of information to the public; designing and delivering services; gathering, managing, and storing information; collegial relationships; and educating students and practitioners. This cross-cutting pattern reflects emerging consensus thinking across key national social work organizations about current "best practices" related to social work ethics when practitioners use technology (Reamer, 2021).

Provision of Information to the Public

Many social workers maintain websites that provide information to the public. Current ethical standards emphasize that when communicating with the public using websites, blogs, social media, or other forms of electronic communication, practitioners should take reasonable steps to ensure the accuracy and validity of the information they disseminate (Recupero, 2006). Social workers should post information only from trustworthy sources, having ensured the accuracy and appropriateness of the material. They should advertise only those electronic services they are licensed or certified and trained to provide in their areas of competence. Practitioners should periodically review information posted online by themselves or other parties to ensure that their professional credentials and other information are accurately portrayed; they should make reasonable effort to correct inaccuracies.

Designing and Delivering Services

Social workers who use technology to provide services should ensure that they have sufficient competence. This includes the ability to assess the relative benefits and risks of providing clinical services using technology; reasonably ensure that electronic services can be kept confidential; reasonably ensure that they

maintain clear professional boundaries; confirm the identity of people to whom services are provided electronically; and assess individuals' familiarity and comfort with technology, access to the internet, language translation software, and the use of technology to meet the needs of diverse populations, such as people with differing physical, cognitive, and other abilities.

Most jurisdictions have adopted the position that electronic practice takes place in both the jurisdiction in which the client is receiving such services (irrespective of the location of the practitioner) and the jurisdiction in which the social worker is licensed and located at the time of providing such electronic services (irrespective of the location of the client). If the client and practitioner are in different jurisdictions, social workers must be aware of and comply with the laws in both the jurisdiction in which the practitioner is located and that in which the client is located (NASW, 2017).

When providing social work services using technology, practitioners should inform the client of relevant benefits and risks (Barsky, 2019; Reamer, 2015a). Practitioners should consider clients' possible reluctance to use technology; difficulty affording technology; limited computer knowledge or fluency with technology; and the risk of cyberbullying, electronic identity theft, and compulsive behaviors regarding the use of technology (NASW et al., 2017). Practitioners must also assess their own competence in the use of technology to deliver social work services. They should continuously learn about changes in technology used to provide these services (NASW, 2017).

Technological innovations have introduced novel boundary-related challenges in social work. Current standards remind social workers to maintain clear professional boundaries in their electronic communications with clients (NASW, 2017; NASW et al., 2017). Practitioners who use technology to provide clinical services should take reasonable steps to prevent client access to social workers' personal social networking sites and, to avoid boundary confusion and inappropriate dual relationships, should not post personal information on professional websites, blogs, or other forms of social media (Gabbard et al., 2011; MacDonald et al., 2010).

Social workers who provide electronic clinical services may have clients who encounter emergencies or crisis situations. Some crisis services may be provided remotely, but others may require in-person communication or intervention. Practitioners should take reasonable steps to identify the location of the client and emergency services in the jurisdiction. If the social worker believes that a client may be at risk (e.g., having suicidal thoughts), the practitioner should mobilize resources to defuse the risks and restore safety. Practitioners should develop policies on emergency situations that include an authorized contact person whom the clinician has permission to contact (ASWB, 2015; NASW, 2017; NASW et al., 2017).

Gathering, Managing, and Storing Information

A number of current ethics standards require that social workers, as part of the informed consent process, explain to clients whether and how they intend to use electronic devices or communication technologies to gather, manage, and store protected health and other sensitive information (ASWB, 2015; NASW, 2017; NASW et al., 2017). According to current standards (NASW, 2017), social workers should obtain client consent before conducting an electronic search on the client. Exceptions may arise when the search is for purposes of protecting the client or other people from serious, foreseeable, and imminent harm or for other compelling professional reasons.

Practitioners should also explain the potential benefits and risks of using the particular electronic methods for gathering, managing,

and storing information. Practitioners should periodically review the types of precautions they use to ensure that these are appropriate given recent changes and identified risks in the use of technology (i.e., new forms of viruses, cyberattacks, or other potential problems). Social workers who gather, manage, and store information electronically should take reasonable steps to ensure the privacy and confidentiality of information pertaining to clients.

Social workers should be aware that statutes and legal regulations may dictate how electronic records are to be stored, and practitioners are responsible for being aware of and adhering to them. Organizations in various practice settings may have additional policies regarding the storage of electronic communications. Also, social workers should ensure that their means of electronic data gathering adhere to the privacy and security standards of applicable laws. These laws may address electronic transactions, client rights, and allowable disclosure (ASWB, 2015).

Collegial Relationships

Social workers increasingly use technology to communicate with and about colleagues, in addition to using technology to serve clients. Practitioners may need to gather information about professional colleagues for a variety of reasons—for instance, to find contact information to facilitate client referrals, determine client eligibility for services, determine the credentials and experience of colleagues, identify colleagues' policies and practices, and gather information in relation to a potential complaint or lawsuit concerning a colleague.

Current ethical standards suggest that when searching for information about a colleague online, social workers should take reasonable steps to verify the accuracy of the information before relying on it. To verify information, it may be appropriate to contact the original source of the information that is posted or speak directly with the professional colleague. It may also be appropriate to confirm the accuracy of the information by checking other sources (ASWB, 2015; NASW, 2017; NASW et al., 2017).

Practitioners should be aware of the laws and regulations in their jurisdiction about mandated reporting of colleagues if a practitioner discovers online information about a colleague that violates ethical standards. In such a situation, the social worker may have a legal obligation to report the colleague.

Social workers should think carefully about whether to use technology to search for personal information about colleagues. Current standards implore social workers to avoid using technology to pry into colleagues' personal lives (NASW et al., 2017). Practitioners should respect the privacy of professional colleagues in relation to personal activities and electronically accessible information that is not relevant to their professional services.

Also, practitioners should adhere to strict ethical standards when they communicate with and about colleagues using electronic tools, draw on colleagues' professional work, and review electronic information posted by colleagues. Social workers should avoid cyberbullying, harassment, or making derogatory or defamatory comments; avoid disclosing private, confidential, or sensitive information about the work or personal life of any colleague without consent, including messages, photographs, videos, or any other material that could invade or compromise a colleague's privacy; take reasonable steps to correct or remove any inaccurate or offensive information they have posted or transmitted about a colleague using technology; acknowledge the work of and the contributions made by others; avoid using technology to present the work of others as their own; and take appropriate action if they believe that a colleague who provides electronic services is behaving unethically, not using appropriate safeguards,

or allowing unauthorized access to electronically stored information (ASWB, 2015; NASW, 2017; NASW et al., 2017). Such action may include discussing their concerns with the colleague when feasible and when such discussion is likely to produce a resolution. If there is no resolution, social workers may need to report their concerns through appropriate formal channels established by employers, professional organizations, and governmental regulatory bodies. Also, they should take steps to discourage, prevent, expose, and correct any efforts by colleagues who knowingly produce, possess, download, or transmit illicit or illegal content or images in electronic format.

Educating Students and Practitioners

Many technology-related ethics standards focus explicitly on social work education, including undergraduate and graduate education, staff development, supervision, and continuing education (NASW et al., 2017). The standards focus on core issues related to competencies in the use of technology for educational purposes, academic standards and integrity, training social workers in the use of technology to serve clients, and social work supervision (practice-based supervision and field education). Current standards indicate that social workers who use technology to design and deliver education, training, and supervision must develop competence in the ethical use of the technology through appropriate study and training (Fange et al., 2014; Sawrikar et al., 2015). They must examine the extent to which education provided using technology enables students to master core professional skills and engage in appropriate education, study, training, consultation, and supervision with professionals who are competent in the use of technology-mediated tools for educational purposes (Siebert et al., 2006).

Social work educators who use technology should anticipate the possibility that some students will have special needs that require use of technology-based adaptive devices that enhance access. Social work educators who teach online courses must take these factors into account and, to the extent feasible, incorporate reasonable accommodations (Duncan-Daston et al., 2013; Fange et al., 2014; Goldingay & Boddy, 2017; Sawrikar et al., 2015).

Conclusion

Social workers are making increased use of technology to deliver services to clients, communicate with clients, gather information about clients, communicate with and about colleagues, administer programs, and educate and supervise students and practitioners. The advent of technology—including internet, text (SMS), email, video, and other forms of communication—has introduced novel and unprecedented ethical issues. It behooves social workers to be thoroughly familiar with emerging ethical standards. Essential knowledge in this digital age includes standards that are being added to licensing and regulatory statutes and regulations; professional codes of ethics; and practice guidelines. Technology-related developments in social work are both unpredictable and fast-paced. Thus, social workers should be vigilant in their efforts to monitor noteworthy adjustments in pertinent ethical standards.

References

Association of Social Work Boards. (2015). *Model regulatory standards for technology and social work practice*. Retrieved March 9, 2020, from https://www.aswb.org/wp-content/uploads/2015/03/ASWB-Model-Regulatory-Standards-for-Technology-and-Social-Work-Practice.pdf

Barsky, A. F. (2019). *Ethics and values in social work: An integrated approach for a comprehensive curriculum* (2nd ed.). Oxford University Press.

Casey, D. M. (2008). A journey to legitimacy: The historical development of distance education through technology. *TechTrends, 52*, 45–51.

Chester, A., & Glass, C. A. (2006). Online counseling: A descriptive analysis of therapy services on the internet. *British Journal of Guidance and Counseling, 34*, 145–160.

Duncan-Daston, R., Hunter-Sloan, M., & Fullmer, E. (2013). Considering the ethical implications of social media in social work education. *Ethics and Information Technology, 15*, 35–43.

Fange, L., Mishna, F., Zhang, V. F., Van Wert, M., & Bogo, M. (2014). Social media and social work education: Understanding and dealing with the new digital world. *Social Work in Health Care, 53*, 800–814.

Finn, J., & Barak, A. (2010). A descriptive study of e-counsellor attitudes, ethics, and practice. *Counselling and Psychotherapy Review, 24*, 268–277.

Gabbard, G. O., Kassaw, K. A., & Perez-Garcia, G. (2011). Professional boundaries in the era of the internet. *Academic Psychiatry, 35*, 168–174.

Goldingay, S., & Boddy, J. (2017). Preparing social work graduates for digital practice: Ethical pedagogies for effective learning. *Australian Social Work, 70*, 209–220.

Kanani, K., & Regehr, C. (2003). Clinical, ethical, and legal issues in e-therapy. *Families in Society, 84*, 155–162.

LaMendola, W. (2010). Social work and social presence in an online world. *Journal of Technology in Human Services, 28*, 108–119.

Lee, S. (2010). Contemporary issues of ethical e-therapy. *Frontline Perspectives, 5*, 1–5.

MacDonald, J., Sohn, S., & Ellis, P. (2010). Privacy, professionalism and Facebook: A dilemma for young doctors. *Medical Education, 44*, 805–813.

Mattison, M. (2012). Social work practice in the digital age: Therapeutic e-mail as a direct practice methodology. *Social Work, 57*, 249-258.

Menon, G. M., & Miller-Cribbs, J. (2002). Online social work practice: Issues and guidelines for the profession. *Advances in Social Work, 3*, 104–116.

National Association of Social Workers. (2017). *Code of ethics*.

National Association of Social Workers, Association of Social Work Boards, Council on Social Work Education, & Clinical Social Work Association. (2017). NASW, ASWB, CSWE and CSWA standards for technology in social work practice. NASW Press. Retrieved March 9, 2020, from https://www.socialworkers.org/includes/newIncludes/homepage/PRA-BRO-33617.TechStandards_FINAL_POSTING.pdf

Reamer, F. G. (2012). The digital and electronic revolution in social work: Rethinking the meaning of ethical practice. *Ethics and Social Welfare, 7*, 2–19.

Reamer, F. G. (2013a). Social work in a digital age: Ethical and risk management challenges. *Social Work, 58*, 163–172.

Reamer, F. G. (2013b). Distance and online social work education: Novel ethical challenges. *Journal of Teaching in Social Work, 33*, 369–384.

Reamer, F. G. (2015a). *Risk management in social work: Preventing professional malpractice, liability, and disciplinary action.* Columbia University Press.

Reamer, F. G. (2015b). Clinical social work in a digital environment: Ethical and risk-management challenges. *Clinical Social Work Journal, 43*, 120–132.

Reamer, F. G. (2018). Ethical standards for social workers' use of technology: Emerging consensus. *Journal of Social Work Values and Ethics, 15*, 71–80.

Reamer, F. G. (2019). Social work education in a digital world: Technology standards for education and practice. *Journal of Social Work Education, 55*, 420–432.

Reamer, F. G. (2021). *Ethics and risk management in online and distance social work.* Cognella.

Recupero, P. R. (2006). Legal concerns for psychiatrists who maintain websites. *Psychiatric Services, 57*, 450–452.

Rumble, G. (2008). Social justice, economics, and distance education. *Open Learning, 22*, 167–176.

Santhiveeran, J. (2009). Compliance of social work e-therapy websites to the NASW Code of Ethics. *Social Work in Health Care, 48*, 1–13.

Sawrikar, P., Lenette, C., McDonald, D., & Fowler, J. (2015). Don't silence the dinosaurs: Keeping caution alive with regard to social work distance education. *Journal of Teaching in Social Work, 35*, 343–364.

Siebert, D. C., Siebert, C. F., & Spaulding-Givens, J. (2006). Teaching clinical social work skills primarily online: An evaluation. *Journal of Social Work Education, 42*, 325–336.

Zur, O. (2012). TelePsychology or TeleMentalHealth in the digital age: The future is here. *The California Psychologist, 45*, 13–15.

PART III

Theoretical Foundations and Treatment Approaches in Clinical Social Work

Theoretical Pluralism and Integrative Perspectives in Social Work Practice

William Borden

Although most social workers come to characterize their clinical approach as eclectic, there is surprisingly little consideration of the ways in which practitioners engage differing theoretical perspectives, empirical findings, and technical procedures over the course of intervention. This chapter reviews comparative approaches to clinical theory and shows how mastery of the foundational schools of thought strengthens efforts to carry out integrative forms of psychosocial intervention. The first section describes four lines of inquiry that have shaped integrative approaches to practice, broadly characterized as technical eclecticism, common factors perspectives, theoretical integration, and assimilative integration. The second section introduces pluralist approaches to clinical theory and outlines core domains of concern in comparative analysis of explanatory systems. The third section presents a case report and shows how a pluralist orientation informs use of different perspectives over the course of intervention, broadening the range of theoretical concepts, empirical research,

and technical procedures applied in the clinical situation.

Integrative Perspectives in Contemporary Practice

As a starting point, it is important to acknowledge the growing emphasis on integrative approaches in contemporary psychotherapy and psychosocial intervention. Over the years, clinical scholars have increasingly realized the strengths and limits of different theoretical perspectives, and practitioners have drawn on psychodynamic, cognitive, behavioral, humanistic, and ecological perspectives in fashioning integrative models of practice, seeking to engage a wider range of clients, broaden the scope of intervention, and improve outcomes (Borden 2010, 2013, 2021).

Four lines of inquiry have shaped efforts to link theory, empirical data, and technical procedures in integrative formulations of therapeutic practice during the past quarter century, broadly characterized as technical eclecticism, common factors approaches, conceptual synthesis or theoretical integration, and assimilative integration (Goldfried & Norcross, 1995; Stricker, 2010). The perspectives emphasize differing elements and strategies in their attempts to enlarge the frame of psychosocial intervention and improve therapeutic outcomes.

Technical Eclecticism

According to conceptions of technical eclecticism, practitioners apply procedures pragmatically on the basis of clinical efficacy (Safran & Messer, 1997). The goal is to match specific techniques with circumscribed problems in functioning in light of empirical evidence and clinical expertise. For example, empirical findings and clinical experience support the use of cognitive and behavioral techniques for treatment of a range of problems in functioning associated with post-traumatic stress disorders and borderline personality organization. Procedures are frequently outlined in manuals that guide application in the clinical situation.

The foundation is empirical rather than theoretical, and practitioners assume that therapeutic methods can be applied independently of the theories from which they originate. Technical procedures are drawn from a variety of sources without necessarily endorsing—or even understanding—the supporting conceptual frameworks (Arkowitz, 1992; Goldfried & Norcross, 1995). In this sense, it is the most technically oriented approach to integration. The practitioner could, for example, combine procedures from cognitive, behavioral, experiential, and family systems perspectives in the course of an individual treatment. Representative examples include Arnold Lazarus' (2002) multimodal perspective and Larry Beutler's (2004) prescriptive model of intervention, specifying strategies

and techniques for treatment of circumscribed problems in functioning.

Common Factors Approaches

In his classic work, *Persuasion and Healing*, published in 1961, Jerome Frank explored the ways in which all forms of psychological healing share common elements, emphasizing the functions of the therapeutic relationship, the healing setting, conceptual schemes that provide plausible explanations of what is the matter and what carries the potential to help, and the core activities of psychosocial intervention that foster change and growth (Frank & Frank, 1991). More than half a century of psychotherapy research has documented the comparable effectiveness of a range of approaches, and there is growing agreement that all of the major systems of psychotherapy—psychodynamic, cognitive, behavioral, humanistic, and ecological—share common elements that account for their relative effectiveness (Stricker, 2010; Wampold & Imel, 2015).

The common factors approach is based on the assumption that all therapeutic systems exert their effects largely through the same underlying principles and processes. Clinicians reason that common factors are more important than the specific procedures that distinguish the particular schools of thought, and they argue that shared elements can serve as the basis for development of more effective approaches to practice.

Accordingly, practitioners focus on the core conditions and basic elements shared by the major schools of thought encompassed in the broader field of psychotherapy. In doing so, they consider (1) client factors, such as motivation and expectations of change; (2) practitioner characteristics, such as warmth, empathic attunement, and authenticity; (3) the provision of a rationale for problems in functioning and a coherent conceptual framework for interventions; and (4) strategic processes, such as experiential learning through interpersonal interaction; interpretive procedures that enlarge understandings of self, relationships, and life experience; and the role of reinforcement, exposure, modeling, and identification in change and growth (Arkowitz, 1992; Borden, 2010, 2021).

Practitioners attempt to identify which elements would appear to be most useful in the treatment of a particular individual on the basis of assessment data and experiential learning in the clinical situation. Some clients, for example, find it useful to explore earlier life events or process their experience of the helping relationship; others, however, make more effective use of task-centered, action-oriented, educational modes of intervention. Garfield's (2000) integrative model of intervention, emphasizing experiential learning, insight, hope, and the sustaining functions of the helping relationship, exemplifies the common factors perspective.

Theoretical Integration

A third approach emerged out of efforts to develop unifying frameworks that bridge theories of personality, problems in living, and methods of intervention; the aim is conceptual synthesis, beyond a blend of common factors and technical procedures (Goldfried & Norcross, 1995). Although the intervention strategies of the integrative system may encompass the procedures used in technical eclecticism, there are crucial differences in the assumptions and conceptualizations that inform decision-making and use of particular strategies (Stricker, 2010). Such frameworks broaden the range of psychological and social phenomena that potentially serve as the focus of treatment and offer varying points of entry. The enlarged conceptual perspective allows clinicians to expand the range of technical procedures used over the course of intervention (Borden, 2010, 2021).

By way of example, Paul Wachtel has developed a psychodynamic approach that encompasses behavioral, cognitive, humanistic, systemic, and ecological perspectives, extending his earlier integration of psychoanalytic theory and behavioral concepts (Wachtel, 2011). In the field of social work, Sharon Berlin has developed an integrative cognitive perspective that links neuroscience and cognitive psychology, the major schools of psychotherapy, and framing perspectives in the social work tradition (Berlin, 2010).

Assimilative Integration

A fourth approach, conceptualized as assimilative integration, encompasses elements of technical eclecticism and theoretical integration (Messer, 2001). In working from this point of view, the clinician establishes a "home base" in a theoretical paradigm and draws on ideas and techniques from other schools of thought in light of the particular needs and circumstances of the clinical situation. The concepts and techniques are blended within the conceptual framework of the central theoretical perspective. The approach potentially encompasses ideas and methods that would be viewed incompatible in more pure conceptions of the helping process.

The Role of Theory in Practice

The foregoing lines of inquiry deepen our understanding of common factors that operate across the schools of thought and the range of technical strategies employed in eclectic modes of treatment, offering pragmatic frameworks for psychosocial intervention. If clinicians are to carry out integrative forms of practice effectively, however, they must develop an understanding of the foundational theories of the field. In the absence of theoretical knowledge, practitioners do not have conceptual frames of reference to understand the dynamics of change processes or the technical elements they are trying to integrate in individualized approaches to intervention. Procedures are deprived of context, and clinicians run the risk of carrying out reductive, mechanized approaches to practice, lacking theoretical rationales for strategies and methods of intervention (Borden, 2010, 2021).

Pluralism as Comparative Perspective

Clinical scholars have drawn on philosophical conceptions of pluralism in their efforts to develop pragmatic frameworks for critical thinking and decision-making in comparative approaches to clinical theory (Borden, 2010, 2013, 2021). Although a review of this work is beyond the scope of the chapter, it is important to identify the defining features of pluralism and its implications for pragmatic use of theoretical concepts, empirical findings, and technical procedures in the clinical situation.

Pluralist points of view emphasize the limits of human understanding and assume that no single framework captures the variety and complexity of actual experience in the real world. Thinkers and practitioners approach concerns from multiple, independent perspectives, realizing that there are mutually exclusive descriptions of the world and equally valid points of view that inevitably contradict one another. In this respect, pluralist perspectives challenge notions of grand theory, which presume to assert universal truths, and take the more realistic position that theoretical formulations and empirical findings *at best* provide partial, incomplete understandings of experience. William James emphasizes the importance of immediate experience, practical consequences, and implications for action in his conceptions of pluralism and pragmatism (Borden, 2013).

From a pluralist point of view, then, theories serve a range of functions, providing tools for critical thinking and decision-making as practitioners carry out their work. Every theoretical system is distinguished by its particular concerns, purposes, methods, strengths, and limits, and no single approach—however encompassing it may seem—can possibly meet all needs over the course of intervention.

Despite the diversity of theoretical perspectives that inform psychosocial intervention, clinical scholars have identified core domains of concern that facilitate efforts to carry out comparative study, encompassing the following areas:

- Historical origins of the theoretical perspective; intellectual traditions, worldviews, and social, cultural, political, and economic conditions that have influenced the development of guiding assumptions and basic concepts; the types of clients, problems in living, and settings that have shaped clinical approaches
- Conceptions of personality, self, person in context, and development across life course; empirical support for basic propositions; congruence of concepts with core social work values
- Conceptions of resilience, health, well-being, and the common good
- Conceptions of vulnerability, problems in living, and psychopathology; the extent to which theorists encompass social, cultural, political, or economic contexts of understanding in formulations of vulnerability, need, and problems in functioning
- Conceptions of intervention: core assumptions, change processes, and curative factors; structure and process of intervention; range of application; empirical support for efficacy and effectiveness of approach; implications for emerging models of evidence-based practice (for comparative reviews of classical and contemporary therapeutic systems, see Messer & Kaslow, 2020; Wampold, 2010)

In comparative approaches to theory, practitioners master the foundational schools of thought and engage a range of ideas as they carry out their practice, without committing themselves to any single school or tradition. Pluralist perspectives attempt to foster dialogue across the divergent perspectives that shape contemporary practice, enlarging ways of seeing, understanding, and acting as clinicians work to understand what is the matter and what carries the potential to help. The practitioner engages different points of view and critically evaluates possible approaches, concepts, and methods in light of the particular circumstances of the clinical situation, assessing choices and potential courses of action as intervention proceeds. The validity of any theoretical concept or method is determined by its *practical outcome* in the context of the particular case (Borden, 2010, 2013).

Clinical Application

The following case illustrates the ways in which a pluralist frame of reference guides use of concepts and methods from divergent perspectives over the course of intervention.

Case Report

The client, age 63 years, developed diffuse anxiety, signs of depression, and dissociative states 8 months after he was injured in an automobile accident. He had completed a course of rehabilitation in an extended care facility, following recovery from life-threatening injuries, and had recently returned to his home. He described fluctuating periods of numbing detachment and intrusive recollections of the events surrounding the accident, and he reported a growing sense of dread—the feeling that "something bad is about to happen."

The client related a range of symptoms that met diagnostic criteria for post-traumatic stress disorder. Further sources of vulnerability emerged in his developmental history. His mother had died soon after his birth, and he described ongoing disruptions in caretaking arrangements through childhood and adolescence. He reported ongoing difficulties in establishing relationships in adulthood and described limited contact with extended family or friends; his experience of dependency and isolation following the accident had intensified longings for closeness and connection with others.

Although the focus of intervention centered on problems in functioning precipitated by the traumatic event, the practitioner realized that the client's history of early loss, disruptions in caretaking, and subsequent modes of attachment potentially limited his capacity to establish a collaborative relationship and negotiate the interactive experience of the therapeutic process.

In light of the crucial role of the therapeutic relationship in efforts to bring about change and growth, the practitioner attended carefully to the development of the working alliance, seeking to create conditions that would foster the client's engagement in the therapeutic process. The clinician's attunement and responsiveness facilitated the client's experience of acceptance, understanding, and support. The practitioner's use of self and relational provisions was informed by person-centered conceptions, the helping relationship, psychodynamic formulations of the therapeutic alliance and the holding environment, and developmental research on the ways in which early loss and disruption in caretaking influence modes of attachment and interpersonal functioning. The clinician reviewed conceptions of post-traumatic stress disorder, providing a heuristic that would deepen the client's understanding of the dynamics of his problems in functioning and the core activities of the therapeutic process.

In the first phase of intervention, the client related the course of events following the accident in a detached, impersonal manner, sometimes speaking in the third person. He showed an absence of emotional responsiveness, consistent with the denial phase of post-traumatic stress reactions, and appeared indifferent as he described events: "I don't know what good it does to talk about any of this . . . we can't change what has happened . . . I should be able to get beyond this and carry out my life." Relational concepts from self-psychology and person-centered perspectives guided the clinician's reflection and validation of the client's underlying feelings of fear, helplessness, and hopelessness. The worker's attunement and empathic processing of his reactions appeared to strengthen the alliance and constancy of care in the holding environment, creating conditions for more active, focused exploration of traumatic events.

The client's experience of numbing detachment fluctuated with periods of diffuse anxiety as he continued to process traumatic states in the middle phase of intervention. The clinician drew on cognitive and behavioral approaches in efforts to help the client manage intrusive recollection of events and disrupt vicious circles of thought, feeling, and behavior that perpetuated problems in functioning. He had come to view the world as a "dangerous place," restricting patterns of activity, and viewed people as unsupportive and unreliable, avoiding opportunities to resume contact with extended family and friends despite longings for connection.

The clinician used a range of cognitive procedures in efforts to help the client challenge and revise maladaptive schemata ("My life is over"), working assumptions ("Nobody really wants to see me"), and automatic thoughts ("I am broken") that perpetuated his experience of fear, demoralization, and avoidance of activities. The practitioner drew on behavioral methods of exposure in efforts to help the client engage feared aspects of inner experience (memories, images, and thoughts related to the accident) and feared activities in the outer world (interaction with others and activities of everyday life). The client and clinician worked collaboratively to identify tasks that provided occasions to expand patterns of activity and carry out social interaction. Such active modes of intervention provided opportunities for mastery and development of coping strategies and social skills, strengthening the client's morale, self-esteem, and sense of possibility.

The client made considerable progress in efforts to recognize and accept the experience of trauma, manage fluctuations in internal states, and engage relational life. In the final phase of intervention, the clinician drew on humanistic and existential perspectives as the client explored the meaning of the accident and the implications of the event, working to clarify core values and essential concerns that would shape his life plan.

The practitioner's mastery of psychodynamic, cognitive, behavioral, humanistic, and existential perspectives provided the theoretical underpinnings for use of differing concepts, empirical findings, and technical procedures over the course of intervention. Movement from one orientation to another was guided by the nature of specific problems in functioning, the focal concerns of intervention, and the client's capacities to make use of differing strategies. The clinician emphasized the following approaches and procedures in efforts to facilitate change and growth: (1) processing of interactive experience in the therapeutic situation to deepen understanding of modes of attachment and interpersonal behavior; (2) cognitive restructuring; (3) exposure to inner and outer domains of feared experience; (4) development of behavioral skills through modeling and experiential learning; and (5) interpretive procedures to enlarge assumptive world and deepen understanding of self, others, and life experience.

Conclusion

In the pluralist approach to theory described in this chapter, the foundational schools of thought provide contexts of understanding for use of differing concepts, empirical findings, and technical operations over the course of intervention. The clinician

- learns multiple theories, therapeutic languages, and modes of intervention;
- draws on concepts from a variety of perspectives in light of the specifics of the clinical situation; and
- judges the validity of theoretical concepts on the basis of practical outcomes in the context of the particular case.

Comparative perspectives make the multiplicity of competing approaches a defining feature of psychosocial intervention. The practitioner aims to establish an ongoing dialogue among representatives of the major schools of thought that sponsors clarification of differing points of view and theoretically informed integration of concepts, empirical findings, and techniques in individualized approaches to intervention.

Helpful Resource

Society for the Exploration of Psychotherapy Integration: http://www.sepiweb.org

References

Arkowitz, H. (1992). Integrative theories of therapy. In D. K. Freedheim (Ed.), *History of psychotherapy: A century of change* (pp. 261–303). American Psychological Association.

Berlin, S. (2010). Why cognitive therapy needs social work. In W. Borden (Ed.), *Reshaping theory in contemporary social work* (pp. 31–50). Columbia University Press.

Beutler, L. (2004). *Prescriptive psychotherapy.* Oxford University Press.

Borden, W. (2010). Taking multiplicity seriously: Pluralism, pragmatism, and integrative perspectives in social work practice. In W. Borden (Ed.), *Reshaping theory in contemporary social work* (pp. 3–27). Columbia University Press.

Borden, W. (2013). Experiments in adapting to need: Pragmatism as orienting perspective in clinical social work. *Journal of Social Work Practice, 27*(3), 259–271.

Borden, W. (2021). *Neuroscience, psychotherapy, and clinical pragmatism: Reflective practice and therapeutic action.* Routledge.

Frank, J., & Frank, J. (1991). *Persuasion and healing.* Johns Hopkins University Press.

Garfield, S. L. (2000). Eclecticism and integration: A personal retrospective view. *Journal of Psychotherapy Integration, 10,* 341–356.

Goldfried, M., & Norcross, J. (1995). Integrative and eclectic therapies in historical perspective. In B. Bonger & L. Beutler (Eds.), *Comprehensive textbook of psychotherapy* (pp. 254–273). Oxford University Press.

Lazarus, A. (2002). The multimodal assessment treatment method. In J. Lebow (Ed.), *Comprehensive handbook of psychotherapy. Vol. 4: Integrative-eclectic* (pp. 241–254). Wiley.

Messer, S. (2001). Applying the visions of reality to a case of brief psychotherapy. *Journal of Psychotherapy Integration, 10,* 55–70.

Messer, S., & Kaslow, N. (2020). Current issues in contemporary theory, practice, and research. In S. Messer & N. Kaslow (Eds.), *Essential psychotherapies* (pp. 3–32). Guilford.

Safran, J., & Messer, S. (1997). Psychotherapy integration: A postmodern critique. *Clinical Psychology, 4,* 140–152.

Stricker, G. (2010). *Psychotherapy integration.* American Psychological Association.

Wachtel, P. L. (2011). *Therapeutic communication.* Guilford.

Wampold, B. E. (2010). *The basics of psychotherapy.* American Psychological Association.

Wampold, B. E., & Imel, E. (2015). *The great psychotherapy debate: The evidence for what makes psychotherapy work.* Routledge.

The Life Model of Social Work Practice

An Overview

Alex Gitterman and Carolyn Knight

When Carel Germain and the first author began their collaboration in 1974, they envisioned a practice model that emphasized common methods and skills for working with client groups of all sizes. The authors developed an approach to social work practice that integrated traditional casework, group work, family work, policy practice, and community organization modalities (Germain & Gitterman, 1980, 1996; Gitterman & Germain, 2008). Germain and Gitterman realized that social workers also needed to appreciate the distinctive knowledge and employ skills uniquely tailored to form groups, work with families, and influence communities, organizations, and legislative processes. The effort to capture the integrative as well as the distinctive methods is evident in all previous editions of the life model and greatly expanded upon in the most recent edition (Gitterman et al., 2021).

The life model integrates the two traditions that have historically created tension within the profession between *cause* (social change in pursuit of social justice) and *function*

(treatment in pursuit of improved social functioning) (Addams, 1910; Lee, 1929; Richmond, 1917). Melding the profession's cause with its function remains an essential and defining aspect of the life model and reflects its origins in the principles of ecology.

Ecological Perspective

Humans exist within a social environment that includes family; friends; social networks such as work colleagues and neighbors; the community; and economic, legal, and social structures. Individuals also exist within a physical environment that includes the natural and human-made/built worlds. Finally, individuals exist within a cultural environment and its associated norms, values, traditions, and beliefs.

The ecological perspective emphasizes the interdependence of living organisms and their environment. It provides the theoretical underpinning for the life model's simultaneous focus on helping clients with life stressors and influencing their social and physical environments to be more responsive to their needs. The following 10 concepts drawn from ecology guide the life model's approach to social work practice:

1. *Reciprocity* of human beings' interactions with their social, physical, and cultural environments.
2. *Perceived level of fit* between humans and their environment may be *adaptive* and promote growth and development or *maladaptive* and undermine human growth and potential.
3. *Life course* is the unique, nonpredictable pathways of development that humans take within diverse environments and cultures, from conception and birth to old age.
4. *Life transitions* are ongoing and occur and reoccur throughout the life course.
5. Human beings exist within a *habitat* composed of physical, natural, and social settings and embedded in a cultural context.
6. Individuals, families, groups, and communities occupy a particular *niche*, or status, in their social environment.
7. *Coercive or exploitive abuse of power* results in the marginalization of vulnerable populations.
8. *Adaptation is ongoing* as humans continually interact with their environment, seeking to improve the level of fit.
9. *External life stressors* reflect maladaptive person–environment transactions and lead to *internal stress* due to human beings' inability to manage or cope with the life stressor.
10. *Risk and protective factors* include intra- and interpersonal variables as well as environmental ones that either promote or undermine humans' *resilience* and *adversarial growth*.

When applied to social work, the concept of *deep ecology* highlights the interconnectedness of human beings and their social and physical environments. Human activity has profoundly and negatively impacted the environment, leading to climate change and toxic and polluted waters and air, among others. This environmental degradation disproportionately affects disadvantaged and marginalized populations. Life-modeled social workers recognize that promoting social sustainability is yet another form of promoting social justice.

Purpose and Characteristics of Life-Modeled Practice

Life-modeled practice seeks to improve the perceived level of fit between individuals, families, groups, and communities and their environments. Over their life course, clients will confront life stressors in three interrelated aspects of living: (1) difficult life transitions and traumatic events, (2) environmental pressures, and (3) maladaptive interpersonal processes in families and groups and between workers and clients. The social worker helps individuals, families, groups, and communities mobilize intra- and interpersonal resources to deal with life stressors they encounter and recognizes the need to improve the responsiveness of social and environmental resources. This includes influencing organizations to develop responsive policies and services and local, state, and federal legislation and regulations to support social justice.

Ethical Practice

Life-modeled practice is grounded in the profession's code of ethics. The social work relationship is a fiduciary one, providing clients with certain protections such as informed consent, confidentiality, and privileged communication. An *ethics screen* (Dolgoff et al., 2012) provides practitioners with the means of resolving ethical dilemmas in ways that are consistent with their ethical and legal responsibilities but still promote client empowerment. The screen consists of seven considerations: protection of life, equality and inequality, autonomy and freedom, least harm, quality of life, privacy and confidentiality, and truthfulness and full disclosure.

In life-modeled practice, social workers' personal values and beliefs are acknowledged and respected. What may first appear to be an ethical dilemma may in fact reflect an *incongruence of values* (Winter et al., 2016): Workers' personal beliefs conflict with those of their clients. Social workers learn to appreciate the difference between the world of *should* and the world of *is*.[1] The first is the world that workers believe is best for their clients, based on their views of right and wrong and good and bad. "It is not necessarily a 'wrong' vision for . . . clients, but it reflects what [the worker] want[s], not necessarily what [clients] want" (Gitterman et al., 2021101). In contrast, the world of *is* "is the one that is inhabited by . . . clients. It reflects *their* social reality, *their* perspectives, *and their* lived experiences" (Gitterman et al., 2021 102). This is the world in which life-modeled social workers practice.

Cultural Humility, Diversity-Sensitive, and Culturally Competent Practice

The life model presumes that social workers are always in the process of understanding the worldviews and internalized identities of their clients and how these shape their clients' ways of coping and their views of life stressors; the worker; and the help that is sought, proffered, or mandated. The life model distinguishes three aspects of diversity-sensitive and culturally competent practice (Gitterman et al., 2021; Sue et al., 2015).

Appreciate Clients' Internalized Identities

A Euro/American-centric worldview predominates in the United States and emphasizes "rugged individualism." This perspective is endemic and ingrained, which requires social workers to understand the ways in which this majority perspective influences their views of self and others, right and wrong, just and unjust, and the like.

Social workers continuously seek to understand the social realities of their clients and recognize that diversity exists within groups that share similar identities. Practitioners look beyond clients' identities to the complex ways in which these identities are rewarded or denigrated. *Microaggressions*, which can take the form of microinsults and microinvalidations, represent the subtle and often unintentional ways that individuals from minority groups are disparaged (Grant & Naish, 2016; Seelman et al., 2017).

Life-modeled practice requires social workers to appreciate the multiple identities that many individuals occupy, known as *intersectionality* (Jani et al., 2011; Lum, 2010). Some social positions and identities may exacerbate powerlessness and stigmatization, whereas others place individuals in the contradictory position as both privileged and marginalized (e.g., a professional social worker who is a member of the LGBTQ+ community).

The assumptions associated with critical race theory assist social workers in recognizing the ways in which racial groups of color are systematically disenfranchised (Kolivoski et al., 2014). Race is less a biological phenomenon than it is a social, economic, and political one that defines power relationships and contributes to the privileged status of some and the marginalization of others.

---

1. We thank Lawrence Shulman for first introducing this insightful conceptualization.

Appreciate One's Own Social Identity and Position

The life model requires that social workers understand their identities and the social positions they occupy as well as the assumptions and biases they may hold about others. Research indicates that dominant, majority views of "others" continue to influence social workers' assessments regarding client strengths and the meaning of client behaviors (Araten-Bergman & Werner, 2017; Gaston et al., 2016). In the most recent edition to the life model textbook, the authors expand upon the concept of *white privilege* (Nicotera & Kang, 2009) to reflect the reality that positions of privilege and power are determined by more than just race (Gitterman et al., 2021). The different identities and positions social workers and clients occupy and identify with advantage and/or disadvantage them. *Social privilege* may be earned, as in the case of being a professional social worker, but in many cases, a privileged status is unearned and results from structural, social, and economic forces that protect some individuals and groups and afford them power at the expense of others (Conley et al., 2017).

Rather than feeling guilty about the privileged status(es) they may enjoy, life-modeled social workers adopt a position of *cultural humility* (Rosen et al., 2017), which is rooted in an acceptance of the structural inequality that is endemic in U.S. society. Guilt can be immobilizing, whereas humility spurs social workers to action, consistent with the "cause" aspect of the profession. Cultural humility also presumes that social workers are always in the process of being curious about people's cultural backgrounds.

Embrace Diversity in One's Personal Life

Research indicates that people, including social workers, associate with others who are—or whom they perceive to be—like them. When social workers move "beyond the familiar and enter the world of 'others,' [their] understanding of the impact of social privilege, prejudice, and discrimination is enhanced" (Gitterman et al., 2021136). Social workers' direct experience with the social realities of others with different social identities and occupying differing social positions complements the knowledge derived from their work with clients and their education.

Evidence-Guided Practice

We are intentional in our use of the term evidence-*guided* practice rather than the more commonly employed term evidence-*based* practice (Gitterman & Knight, 2013; Gitterman et al., 2021). Life-modeled practice relies on research findings, but it also requires social workers to rely on theoretical constructs and a repertoire of professional competencies and skills. Social workers employ the science of social work but recognize that clients are the experts in their lives. Evidence-guided practice also respects the role that the individual social worker's intuition and distinctive style play (Gitterman & Knight, 2013).

Theory and research findings provide social workers with general guidance rather than a clear-cut prescription for action. "[Social workers] cannot assume a linear relationship between 'knowing' and 'doing' and mechanically apply a concept or a research finding. . . . Knowledge is essential, but not sufficient" (Gitterman et al., 2021 47). Life-modeled practice requires social workers to use knowledge gleaned from research, theory, and practice creatively and flexibly in a way that reflects their unique personality and style as well as the unique needs, personality, and style of their clients.

Social Work Practice as Art

Practitioner style and creativity are indispensable in life-modeled practice. Social workers utilize the same core skills and rely on the same knowledge and value base, but the way in which they use this "science" will be unique to each practitioner, client, and the distinctive qualities and context of their working relationship. Workers' genuine reactions such as humor and displays of empathy and understanding reduce the distance between clients and them.

Professional education and socialization can restrict workers' spontaneity, discouraging purposeful and genuine reactions such as humor and displays of empathy and understanding, increasing rather than reducing the distance between workers and clients. Clients do not need social workers to be infallible. What they need are professionals "who are willing to reveal their humanness, vulnerability, and spontaneity" (Gitterman et al., 2021 103).

Social workers' ability to use themselves in ways that are helpful to clients epitomizes the blending of art and science. Use of self includes workers' mannerisms and natural ways of interacting and also is conveyed through dress and office décor. It is most obviously reflected in workers' use of self-disclosure. Appropriate use of self requires social workers to consistently reflect on their own thoughts, feelings, and reactions as they surface in their work to ensure that their personal values and beliefs do not interfere with their ability to be with clients in the world of *is*.

Promoting Client Empowerment and Social Justice

In life-modeled practice, the professional relationship is conceived as a partnership. The working relationship is characterized by mutuality and reciprocity. Workers minimize social distance and differences in power between themselves and their clients by maintaining openness, honesty, and authenticity in the relationship.

Helping in life-modeled practice is based on a process of mutual assessment that results in shared definitions of life stressors and agreement between worker and client on foci and priorities. This respects clients' individuality, enhances self-directed problem-solving, and strengthens coping skills. The process of assessment provides structure and focus to the work, decreases anxiety associated with the unknown and the ambiguity inherent in beginnings, and mobilizes workers' and clients' energy for work.

The emphasis in life-modeled practice is on identifying, mobilizing, and building on clients' strengths and promoting resilience by integrating solution-focused strategies (DeJong & Cronkright, 2011; Oliver & Charles, 2015). Many clients will struggle to identify their strengths because they are consumed with life stressors. When social workers ask clients the *miracle question*, they convey that change is possible. Coping questions and asking about exceptions encourage clients to identify strategies they have successfully used—even if they are unaware of them—to manage life stressors. Asking about between-session change allows clients to see the progress they are making.

Life-modeled practice considers clients' motivation for change, recognizing that behaviors labeled as "resistant," "hostile," and "unmotivated" often reflect clients' views about the possibility of change. Many clients—particularly those who are members of marginalized and disenfranchised groups—view the world with an external locus of control, believing that they have little or no control over their fate and the circumstances within which they find themselves. This leads to a sense of psychological impotence (Gitterman et al., 2021), with clients questioning, "Why should I try because nothing I do will make a difference?"

In addition to considering clients' views regarding the possibility for change, social workers recognize that the goals that they or their agency have established for clients may not be the goals that clients have for themselves, particularly when they are mandated to receive services. The transtheoretical model and its stages of change (Prochaska & DiClemente, 1984; Prochaska et al., 1995) help social workers realistically appraise clients' level of motivation and then help clients progress through them: precontemplation, contemplation, determination, action, maintenance, and relapse. Beginning with clients' definition of the problem (which often is the mandate that requires them to receive services), the worker helps clients identify what needs to happen for them to get what they want. When the worker truly "starts where their clients are," this is both validating and empowering (Gitterman & Heller, 2011).

The life model's emphasis on client empowerment extends to broader social systems and forces that lead to the marginalization and disenfranchisement of certain client groups. Whereas some social workers specialize in macro practice and focus their attention on legislative and regulatory, community, and organizational change, the life model requires that *all* social workers identify steps they can take to promote social justice.

Life-modeled social workers recognize they have an obligation to address organizational policies that disenfranchise clients and are unresponsive to clients' needs and interests. They also understand they have a responsibility to empower communities to work collectively to resolve stressors. Finally, social workers engaged in direct practice with clients simultaneously engage in "policy practice" (Jansson, 2008; Weiss, 2016), as they seek to improve opportunities and resources for those living in poverty and other vulnerable and marginalized populations by advocating for more effective legislative and regulatory responses to human needs (Gitterman et al., 2021).

Trauma-Informed Practice

In 2001, Harris and Fallot introduced an approach to practice that recognized the unique needs of trauma survivors and that was characterized by five principles: trust, safety, collaboration, choice, and empowerment. Social workers create a working relationship with clients that emphasizes these principles (trauma-informed practice) and create and sustain an organizational environment that promotes these same principles for clients and staff (trauma-informed care). The life model promotes and epitomizes this approach to practice.

A disproportionate number of clients seen by social workers have histories of trauma (Becker-Blease, 2017; Branson et al., 2017). In many settings—such as child welfare, mental health, correctional/criminal justice, and schools—social workers will work with clients on present-day challenges that reflect experiences with past trauma. In other settings, such as rape crisis and disaster relief, they encounter clients in the immediate aftermath of trauma exposure. Whether problem- or trauma-focused, a trauma-informed lens is essential to responding to the unique needs of clients who are trauma survivors in ways that are empowering and lessen the risk of retraumatization (Knight, 2015).

The Helping Process and Core Skills

Life-modeled practice encompasses six modalities: work with individuals, families, groups, and communities; organizational intervention; and legislative advocacy and political action (Gitterman et al., 2021). Social work practice is conceptualized as occurring in four phases of work: preparatory, initial, ongoing, and ending. Workers and clients often move back and forth between the phases in response to changing circumstances and clients' needs and goals. Skills primarily associated with one phase often are used at other points in practitioners' work with clients.

Preliminary Phase

The preliminary phase of work requires workers to consider and anticipate clients' views and perceptions, including those associated with seeing—or being forced to see—them. Social workers prepare themselves to enter people's lives by reflecting on available data concerning potential clients' objective reality, using anticipatory empathy to then identify clients' perceptions and feelings.

In preparing to meet with families and groups, the worker has additional preparatory tasks. With group practice, for example, the worker has to formulate the group's purpose, compose the group to maximize the potential for mutual aid, and develop a plan to recruit group members.

Initial Phase

The initial phase focuses on how clients and workers define a life stressor(s) because this will determine what they will do. An important consideration in this phase is clients' degree of choice in engaging in the working relationship. Services may be sought, offered/proffered, or mandated; each context shapes workers' and clients' beginning transactions. Two skill sets initiate this phase: (1) clarifying role and purpose and the nature of the services available to clients and (2) soliciting their feedback.

The worker uses empathy skills to convey understanding of clients' concerns, including those associated with being mandated to seek help and with the worker's ability to help based on cultural differences and differences in social identities and positions. Responding directly to clients' direct and indirect communications enhances clients' trust in the worker and the worker's understanding of clients' concerns and social reality.

Assessment is both a process and a product. The worker collects relevant information about clients' exchanges with their environment using clarifying and elaborating skills. This process results in mutually developed and agreed upon decisions regarding how workers' and clients' efforts can be helpful. In some instances, intervention may be directed more

toward clients or toward their environment, but workers never lose sight of the fact that both are important and interdependent.

Ongoing Phase

Social workers employ six skill sets to help clients manage stressful life transitions, traumatic experiences, and environmental pressures, each of which is intended to support and strengthen adaptive capacities and problem-solving abilities. *Enabling skills* reinforce clients' motivation to deal with the difficult life stressors and the stress it arouses. *Exploring and clarifying skills* provide focus and direction to the work and ensure that social workers develop an accurate understanding of clients' circumstances and what they would like to accomplish. "[These skills] help [social workers] to 'be on the same page' as [their] clients . . . [thereby] deepening the working alliance" (Gitterman et al., 2021 110).

Mobilizing skills strengthen client's motivation to deal with difficult life stressors and overcome feelings of hopelessness and powerlessness that can undermine efforts to change. Clients often need help identifying and building upon strengths and positive attributes within themselves and their environment. These skills provide clients with hope that change is possible.

Guiding skills help clients develop problem-solving skills needed for coping with life stressors. Social workers appreciate and respect clients' unique learning style and provide them with opportunities to be successful in their change efforts, through behavioral rehearsal, role play, and discussion and exchange of ideas.

Facilitating skills encourage clients to remain committed to the work. Many clients are reluctant to examine and work on difficult issues, even those who willingly sought social work services. Social workers directly address manifestations of avoidance by making supportive demands, commenting on the avoidance pattern, challenging illusions of mutual agreement, and identifying discrepant messages. These interventions can stimulate and mobilize clients' energy for the work. However, they may lead to client defensiveness and withdrawal if a strong working alliance is absent.

Coordinating skills assist both worker and client in deciding on and pursing a plan for work. They include monitoring clients' progress and the quality of the working alliance to ensure that it is supporting clients' work. When necessary, this may lead to revising the working agreement.

Working with Clients' Environment

Social workers often must connect clients with needed resources in the external environment and ensure that they can access those resources. When clients are unsuccessful in their interactions with their environment, the worker uses *mediating skills* to foster connections between clients and the people and systems that matter to them. The worker identifies points of commonality between clients and their social environment. This involves helping both sides to negotiate and compromise, requiring the worker to appreciate differing points of view.

When mediation does not lead to improved communication and relationship patterns, the worker may need to employ *advocacy skills*. These can involve teaching clients to advocate for themselves, but often social workers must directly advocate for their clients' interests. Advocacy may or may not require an adversarial stance. Workers assess what strategies are most likely to be persuasive as well as gauge the potential risks to both themselves and their clients associated with advocacy efforts. Ethical practice may require that the worker adopt a more adversarial position when essential entitlements are denied or client rights are violated, regardless of risks.

Working with Families, Groups, and Communities

In addition to the skills previously noted, the life model identifies skills that social workers employ when they work with families and groups. Maladaptive patterns of interaction and communication compromise families', groups', and communities' ability to work collectively to address life stressors and challenges. In families, groups, and communities, maladaptive patterns may themselves be the source of stress.

The social worker assists members in recognizing obstacles and communicating more openly and directly and helps them develop a sense of mutuality and concern for one another's well-being. Internal mediating and advocating skills include identifying and commenting on problematic patterns, challenging collective resistance, inviting and exploring alternative points of view, establishing protective ground rules, lending support, and crediting work.

Working in the Broader Social Environment

Many of the same skills employed in direct work with and on behalf of clients are necessary when workers turn their attention to influencing organizations, policymakers, and regulatory bodies. These skill sets include coordinating, mediating, advocating, organizing, innovating, and influencing. Additional skill sets and tasks come into play.

Influencing the organization begins with establishing a receptive climate for introducing the problem and its proposed solution. The worker then decides on methods of intervention, which may include demonstrating and presenting, collaborating, persuading, and creating conflict (Brager & Holloway, 2002). Social workers, particularly those in lower ranking positions, must carefully consider the use of conflict-oriented strategies because of their vulnerability to reprisals. Yet certain situations, such as violations of clients' rights, will require more adversarial actions, especially in the face of marked dissent over goals and methods.

After a desired outcome is adopted, it needs to be put into action because initial acceptance does not ensure implementation. To maintain administrators' cooperation, the innovation has to be experienced as being in their self-interest.

Influencing legislation and the legislative process requires social workers to engage in seven tasks. The social worker begins by *gathering information*, including the views of key players and constituency groups and the status and procedural history of proposed or existing legislation. The worker then *builds an agenda* and crafts a position statement to be presented to key legislators. The social worker develops strategies to persuade an important decision-maker(s) to place the issue on the agenda of other decision-makers in the legislative setting.

The effectiveness of political advocacy requires social workers to *engage legislators* and *influence key players*. The worker is prepared to address what is likely to be legislators' primary concerns: "Who is for it?" "Who is against it?" "What's it going to cost?" "What's in it for me?" and "Does this help or hurt my chances of re-election?" *Networking* and *building coalitions* of organizations and groups reflect the benefits associated with "power in numbers" and enhance the social worker's influence. Finally, *testifying* at hearings provides social workers with the opportunity to have their perspectives heard by the public and amplified through the media.

Influencing community life can take the form of social action, locality development, and social planning approaches (Rothman, 2007; Thomas et al., 2011). Social planning approaches rely on information and data to document the existence of a social problem and suggest solutions.

Locality development and social action require workers to mobilize community members for action and involve three tasks and skill sets. Social workers must gain members' willingness to participate in collective action and *develop a stake in the work*. The worker also assists members in *creating a structure for work*. This often requires that social workers use group work skills. Participants often need guidance to learn how to conduct their own meetings, engage in democratic group decision-making, reach out and build constituencies, deal with differences and disagreements, and build consensus. Social workers also assist community members in *identifying and implementing change strategies*.

Ending Phase

The ending phase makes specific demands of workers and clients to explore feelings and thoughts aroused by the ending; review accomplishments and what remains to be achieved; plan for the future, including transfer to another worker or referral to another agency; and evaluate the service provided.

When endings are planned, four phases may be distinguished. Each phase has its own tasks, but not every client will go through each phase in the order outlined in the life model. The more satisfactory the relationship, the more likely clients are to ward off anxiety by avoiding its reality. Frequent reminders are often necessary so that the painful reality remains on the agenda.

Avoidance gives way to the reality of termination through the social worker's empathic support. Clients' reactions often begin with anger, which may be expressed directly or more subtly. Some may turn their anger inward and experience the ending as a reflection of their unworthiness and/or the worker's disappointment with them. Social workers must remain sufficiently detached to invite and pursue the expression of negative reactions and feelings about themselves and the service.

Anger gives way to feelings of sadness at separating. Social workers encourage and support client expressions and respond to them by sharing their own sense of loss.

Once workers and clients have addressed their affective responses to ending, they are able to realistically tackle the tasks that remain in the final stage, release—recognition of gains and specification of remaining work; development of plans for the future, such as transfer, referral, or self-directed tasks; and final goodbyes and disengagement.

When encounters between workers and clients are brief, endings may occur in the same session as beginnings. Time limits on services may lead to feelings on the part of both workers and clients that their work is unfinished. To minimize this likelihood, workers should—from the beginning—adapt the pacing and focus of their work to reflect the imposed time limits.

References

Addams, J. (1910). *Twenty years at Hull House.* Macmillan.

Araten-Bergman, T., & Werner, S. (2017). Social workers' attributions towards individuals with dual diagnosis of intellectual disability and mental illness. *Journal of Intellectual Disability Research, 61,* 155–167.

Becker-Blease, K. A. (2017). As the world becomes trauma-informed, work to do. *Journal of Trauma & Dissociation, 18,* 131–138.

Brager, G., & Holloway, S. (2002). *Changing human service organizations: Politics and practice.* Free Press.

Branson, C. E., Baetz, C. L., Horwitz, S. M., & Hoagwood, K. E. (2017, February). Trauma-informed juvenile justice systems: A systematic review of definitions and core components. *Psychological Trauma, 9*(6), 635–646. http://dx.doi.org/10.1037/tra0000255

Conley, C. L., Deck, S. M., Miller, J. J., & Borders, K. (2017). Improving the cultural competency of social work students with a social privilege activity. *Journal of Teaching in Social Work, 37*(3), 234–248.

DeJong, P., & Cronkright, A. (2011). Learning solution-focused interviewing skills: BSW student voices. *Journal of Teaching in Social Work, 31,* 21–37.

Dolgoff, R., Harrington, D., & Lowenstein, F. M. (2012). *Ethical decisions for social work practice* (8th ed.). Brooks/Cole.

Gaston, G. B., Earl, T. R., Nisanci, A., & Glomb, B. (2016). Perception of mental health services among Black Americans. *Social Work in Mental Health, 14,* 676–695.

Germain, C. B., & Gitterman, A. (1980). *The life model of social work practice.* Columbia University Press.

Germain, C. B., & Gitterman, A. (1996). *The life model of social work practice: Advances in theory and practice* (2nd ed.). Columbia University Press.

Gitterman, A., & Germain, C.B. (2008). *The life model of social work practice: Advances in theory and practice* (3rd ed.). Columbia University Press.

Gitterman, A., & Heller, N. (2011). Integrating social work perspectives and models with concepts, methods, and skills with other professions' specialized approaches. *Clinical Social Work Journal, 39,* 204–211.

Gitterman, A., & Knight, C. (2013). Evidence-guided practice: Integrating the science and art of social work. *Families in Society, 94,* 70–78.

Gitterman, A., Knight, C., & Germain, C. B. (2021). *The life model of social work practice: Advances in theory and practice* (4th ed.). Columbia University Press.

Grant, A., & Naish, J. (2016). Depathologising sexualities in mental health services. *Mental Health Practice, 19,* 26–31.

Harris, M., & Fallot, R. (2001). *Using trauma theory to design service systems: New directions for mental health services.* Jossey-Bass.

Jani, J. S., Pierce, D., Ortiz, L., & Sowbel, L. (2011). Access to intersectionality, content to competence: Deconstructing social work education diversity standards. *Journal of Social Work Education, 47,* 283–301.

Jansson, B. S. (2008). *Becoming an effective policy advocate: From policy practice to social justice* (5th ed.). Brooks/Cole.

Knight, C. (2015). Trauma-informed social work practice: Practice considerations and challenges. *Clinical Social Work Journal, 43,* 25–37.

Kolivoski, K., Weaver, A., & Constance-Huggins, M. (2014). Critical race theory: Opportunities for application in social work practice and policy. *Families in Society, 95,* 269–276.

Lee, P. R. (1929). Social work as cause and function. In *Social work cause and function: Selected papers of Porter R. Lee* (pp. 3–24). Columbia University Press.

Lum, D. (2010). *Culturally competent practice: A framework for understanding diverse groups and justice issues* (4th ed.). Cengage.

Nicotera, N., & Kang, H. K. (2009). Beyond diversity courses: Strategies for integrating critical consciousness across social work curriculum. *Journal of Teaching in Social Work, 29,* 188–203.

Oliver, C., & Charles, G. (2015). Which strengths-based practice? Reconciling strengths-based practice and mandated authority in child protection work. *Social Work, 60,* 135–143.

Prochaska, J. O., & DiClemente, C. C. (1984). *The transtheoretical approach: Crossing traditional boundaries of therapy.* Dow Jones-Irwin.

Prochaska, J. O., Norcross, J. C., & DiClemente, C. C. (1995). *Changing for good.* Avon Books.

Richmond, M. E. (1917). *Social diagnosis.* Russell Sage Foundation.

Rosen, D., McCall, J., & Goodkind, S. (2017). Teaching critical self-reflection through the lens of cultural humility: An assignment in a social work diversity course. *Social Work Education, 36,* 289–298.

Rothman, J. (2007). Multi modes of intervention at the macro level. *Journal of Community Practice, 15,* 11–40.

Seelman, K. L., Woodford, M. R., & Nicolazzo, Z. (2017). Victimization and microaggressions targeting LGBTQ college students: Gender identity as a moderator of psychological distress. *Journal of Ethnic & Cultural Diversity in Social Work, 26,* 112–125.

Sue, D. W., Rasheed, M. N., & Rasheed, J. M. (2015). *Multicultural social work practice: A competency based approach to diversity and social justice* (5th ed.). Wiley.

Thomas, M. L., O'Connor, M. K., & Netting, F. E. (2011). A framework for teaching community practice. *Journal of Social Work Education, 47,* 337–355.

Weiss, G. I. (2016). Policy practice in social work education: A literature review. *International Journal of Social Welfare, 25,* 290–303.

Winter, V. R., Kattari, S. K., Begun, S., & McKay, K. (2016). Personal and professional values: Relationships between social workers' reproductive health knowledge, attitudes, and ethical decision-making. *Journal of Social Work Values and Ethics, 13,* 35–46.

The Biopsychosocial–Spiritual Perspective

Melissa D. Grady and Randall O'Toole

The biopsychosocial–spiritual (BPSS) perspective is deeply rooted in the history of social work and embodies the values of social work as a profession and how social workers practice (Brekke, 2014). Because it is a perspective rather than a discrete model of practice, it can be operationalized in many different ways based on the particular setting, goals of the intervention, level of practice, and theoretical orientation of the practitioner. In this chapter, the domains within the BPSS are defined and its use in practice with different client systems is demonstrated using two case examples, illustrating how social workers use the BPSS framework in their practices.

Social Work Practice

Social work practice involves knowledge of human development and behavior, the psychology of providing and receiving help from another, understanding multiple modes of communication, appreciating the reciprocal relationship between groups and individuals, acknowledging the influence of culture and social context on various levels of client systems, recognizing the interactional nature of relationships, recognizing the importance of the community and the available social services in the lives of people, and recognizing that social workers must monitor their own emotions and reactions in order to be of service to the client (Bartlett, 2003, p. 269).

Although there are potentially endless ways to define social work practice, this description captures the essential elements of the holistic and person-in-environment perspectives held by the social work profession (Kondrat, 2008). Given the breadth of knowledge Bartlett (2003) considers necessary for effective social work practice, it is possible that social workers could be overwhelmed by the scope of information they need to gather when working with any client system ("client system" throughout this chapter refers to an individual, couple, family, group, organization, or community). In light of these expansive responsibilities, the BPSS framework can be utilized to organize and prioritize the information, thereby informing the worker's understanding of the clients' issues as well as how to think about intervention strategies moving forward (Corcoran & Walsh, 2006; Grady & Dombo, 2016; Hutchinson, 2017). Because the BPSS perspective can be flexibly used across multiple contexts, levels of practice, and types of client systems, it has been employed in social work and other fields to address issues such as diabetes and other health conditions, substance use disorders, and cross-cultural practice (Aamar et al., 2015; Al Ghaferi et al., 2017; Bolton & Gillett, 2019; Corcoran & Walsh, 2006; Zittel et al., 2002).

Defining the BPSS Perspective in Social Work

Social work is often described as an integrative discipline that draws on multiple sources of knowledge to inform our understanding of human behavior and guide our interventions (Brekke, 2014). As such, social workers' methods for gathering and organizing information include synthesizing information from a multitude of sources. Any and all information gathered in an assessment is considered in the context of all of the other information gathered, meaning that all client data, facts, or information is continuously interacting with and influencing our understanding of other known data. This view that all data have a reciprocal relationship with all elements of the clients' identity, background, and context is consistent with the first aspect of Barlett's (2003) definition and an essential feature of the BPSS perspective. Because it is not possible to hold all sources of information about a client system simultaneously, social workers have developed the BPSS perspective as a way to organize their knowledge into a unified framework divided by domains: biological, psychological, social, and spiritual (Corcoran & Walsh, 2006; Grady & Dombo, 2016; Hutchinson, 2017). Within each domain, there are numerous factors or areas

that social workers should consider in their assessments and interventions with their clients. Which ones are most relevant for clients will depend on the unique needs and strengths of each client system.

Domains of the BPSS

As outlined by Grady and Dombo (2016), the specific items within each domain are presented in Table 22.1. Each of these individual elements is important for social workers to explore within a comprehensive assessment (Corcoran & Walsh, 2006; Grady & Drisko, 2014; Hutchinson, 2017) and to consider when planning for an intervention.

Reciprocal Nature of the BPSS

Although it is easy to ask clients about and explore each of the individual factors listed in Table 22.1 as stand-alone issues to consider, as noted previously, what sets this perspective apart from other perspectives is the attention paid to the reciprocal relationship that the various factors have with one another. For example, health conditions are listed under the biological domain. Yet, ample research discusses the connection between health and mental health issues (Bolton & Gillett, 2019). This research indicates that health conditions can lead to mental health conditions and that the reverse is true—mental health issues can lead to health issues. As such, the BPSS perspective recognizes that mental health conditions must be explored as a singular piece of information for a client and in conjunction with health issues. The BPSS perspective holds that social workers must ask about and explore any issue, such as mental health, that falls under the psychological domain in the context of the other domains, including the meaning that the person makes of their psychological struggles (spiritual domain), as well as how their culture may view any mental health issue (social) and whether there are health conditions and/or

TABLE 22.1 Domains of the BPSS Perspective

Physical	Psychological	Social	Spiritual
Bodily elements	Gender	Roles	Spiritual beliefs
Diagnoses	Sexuality	Culture	Organized religion
Health concerns	Personal experiences	Values	Values
Genetic predispositions	Significant others	Economic elements	Meaning making
Prescribed physical characteristics, including sex and race	Habits/behaviors	Race and ethnicity	
Abilities and disabilities	Relational patterns	Community connections	
Timing such as aging process	Language	Stereotypes	
Neurobiology	Personal history	Physical spaces	
		Access to services	
		Historical events	
		Agency setting	
		Political situation	
		Institutions	
		Legal status	
		National origin	

BPSS, biopsychosocial–spiritual.
Source: Grady and Dombo (2016, p. 51).

medication issues that may be contributing to or exacerbating the existence of the identified mental health issues (biological domain).

Case Example

Mr. J is a 51-year-old single client who identifies as cisgender, heterosexual, and comes from a mixed racial/ethnic background (Latino and Caucasian). He has recently experienced a major depressive episode (psychological), and this depression manifests in him overeating and staying in bed. If Mr. J also has a genetic predisposition for developing diabetes (biological domain), the current coping behaviors he is using to manage the depressive symptoms may lead to him developing diabetes if he does not adopt alternative coping strategies to manage his depressive symptoms. Furthermore, Mr. J's home community is unsafe (social domain) due to high rates of community violence. As

a result, he does not want to exercise because he does not have access to parks where he could go for walks or get other forms of physical activity. In addition, Mr. J has limited financial resources (social domain), so, among other things, he does not have access to a gym or other health care resources that could provide other venues for exercise or for getting the health care he needs. Furthermore, Mr. J holds a spiritual or philosophical belief that only "weak people" experience mental illness (spiritual), and now he has developed unhelpful thinking patterns (psychological domain) that deepen his experiences of depression as he begins to blame himself further for his current state of being.

The example of Mr. J highlights that no one factor exists in isolation. Rather, each factor has a relationship or multiple relationships with other factors in the same domain or across the other domains outlined in the BPSS perspective. Consistent with social workers' holistic and person-in-environment perspectives (Kondrat, 2008), social workers' utilization of the BPSS perspective means that all issues must be considered in the context of the others.

How the BPSS Is Used in Social Work Practice

The BPSS perspective is used in social work practice in several key ways. The first is to guide the assessment *process*, as discussed previously. By using the BPSS perspective during an assessment, social workers will explore key aspects of human functioning that are essential to consider as they work to understand the strengths and needs of their clients. It is especially important that when used during an assessment, social workers consider the reciprocal nature of their clients' experience, as shown previously with Mr. J. No one factor about a client exists in isolation from another. When used as part of the fact-gathering phase of the work with clients, the BPSS is considered a process.

The second way BPSS is referred to in social work is as a *product.* It is common for social workers to refer to the document that they have created after they have completed their assessment as the BPSS, meaning the written summary of the information they have gathered about their client. In fact, many social work students are often assigned in their practice courses to write a BPSS about a client that is then graded as part of a practice course. With these assignments, professors are attempting to determine whether students are able to gather, organize, synthesize, and present client information in a cohesive, comprehensive, and professional manner. When used as a product, the BPSS becomes part of the medical or other official record for clients. Therefore, it is critical that social workers learn how to create a well-written product based on their BPSS process.

A third way that the BPSS perspective is used in social work is during the intervention phase. Although the BPSS does not offer a specific intervention road map as a model of intervention would, such as cognitive–behavioral therapy (Beck, 2011) or mentalization-based therapy (Bateman & Fonagy, 2013), considering this perspective during the intervention phase increases the likelihood that the interventions will be consistent with the profession's emphasis on the importance of considering the whole person as well as Bartlett's (2003) eight principles of practice. In addition, the BPSS perspective helps social workers consistently balance micro and macro factors while not privileging either area of focus. When social workers consider all of the BPSS domains and their reciprocal nature of the various factors within them, then they are more likely to consider both how and where to intervene to help clients achieve their goals.

When using the BPSS perspective during the assessment phase, social workers will identify the primary issues facing their clients as well as their strengths. In addition, as social workers gather their information, they will begin to develop a theory or hypothesis as to why the clients present as they do. These case-based theories are formulated using their clinical expertise (Graybeal, 2014), paired with their knowledge of various empirically driven theories, which depending on the client system could be individual, family, organizational, and/or macro or structural theories (Walsh, 2013). Social workers should also refer to the research that has been published on interventions with client systems similar to theirs and work with the client to create an intervention plan (Drisko & Grady, 2019). However, in which domain the social worker should intervene, the timing of when to address which factor, and whether to address one issue at a time or simultaneously address multiple issues are determined by the social worker who is continuously balancing the art and the science of their work with clients (Graybeal, 2014; Weinberger & Rasco, 2007). In this way, the BPSS perspective offers a guide while serving as a reminder for social workers regarding the complexities of their clients' lives. Exactly what those interventions should entail is left up to the expertise of the social worker.

Social workers are trained to consider both the individual and the contextual factors that lead to clients' struggles. As such, they should remember that they can design and implement interventions that consider *simultaneously* individual and contextual factors in order to help clients reach their goals (Berlin, 1982). The person-in-environment perspective views clients holistically and is central to the social work perspective (Kondrat, 2008). In practice, the BPSS perspective reminds social workers of the importance of attending to their clients' internal and external worlds concurrently.

Case Applications
Case of Mr. J—Micro Intervention

Returning to the case of Mr. J, who is struggling with symptoms of depression, in planning the interventions, the social worker has several issues to consider based on the BPSS assessment process. The social worker could consider using a psychotherapeutic model of intervention, such as cognitive–behavioral therapy (Beck, 2011). With this approach, the social worker would seek to address Mr. J's unhelpful thinking patterns, which may stem from a combination of his spiritual and family teachings, in order to address any patterns of thinking that maintain his depression.

Using a case management approach, the social worker could also consider making referrals and identifying supports for Mr. J to get proper medical care, which could potentially (1) help him learn about his risk factors

for health-related illnesses, such as diabetes; (2) provide him with psychoeducation about nutrition and diet in order to prevent those illnesses; and (3) design an exercise program that would both address his health issues and address his depression as he produces more endorphins that could help counter depression (Cooney et al., 2013). Such interventions would address both the biological and the social domains within the BPSS, which would in turn address the psychological issues with which he is struggling.

In fact, research has shown that when providers use a BPSS approach in the treatment of diabetes, patients report improvements in not just their diabetes or within the biological domain but also their mental health (Aamar et al., 2015). In this research, "patients reported strengths, concerns, and goals that were related to multiple aspects of their health (i.e., biological, psychological, social, and spiritual)" (p. 33), and the authors recommended that "to promote best practices in treating diabetes, providers should focus on each of these areas of health during treatment planning" (p. 33). In the case of Mr. J, the direct practice social worker may not develop interventions focused on reducing the community violence because the work is focused on an individual client system. However, by using the BPSS perspective to orient her work, the social worker would consider how this context impacts Mr. J and work with him to find other options to help him reach his health and mental health goals. It is possible for social workers to work simultaneously across multiple client systems. However, time and other resources may not allow for such comprehensive interventions. If not possible, social workers should at a minimum use the BPSS perspective to better understand their clients' needs within the context of the other factors identified in the BPSS domains.

The ABC Neighborhood— Macro Intervention

As stated previously, social workers may intervene in different ways depending on the system with which they are working. On a macro level, social workers are working with systems (Hill et al., 2017) rather than individuals. However, just like with micro work or direct practice, all client systems must be considered in the context of the other systems that surround them (Bronfenbrenner, 1992). Therefore, in macro interventions, social workers must simultaneously consider the individuals within the system as well as the larger context that surrounds the system in which the system of interest exists. Here again, by using the BPSS perspective, social workers are able to keep all of these systems in mind.

For example, Mr. J's community is the ABC Neighborhood. A group of neighbors who are frustrated with the amount of community violence they have witnessed contacted a local community action network to help them improve the safety of the ABC Neighborhood. In using the BPSS perspective, the social worker, Ms. R, who is working with the members of this neighborhood group, noted in her assessment that many of the residents are in poor health (biological), which has impacted their energy levels and their motivation (psychological) to address the issue of community violence (social). In addition, as she entered into the residences of the community members, Ms. R saw that the housing conditions were poor (social), with broken or misshapen windows that allowed dust and other pollutants to enter the homes. These poor living conditions (social) may have contributed to the residents' current health conditions (biological). Outside of the residences, she also noted that there was poor lighting and the one playground had not been maintained by the city (social). She also explored what community resources, including places of worship, are currently available to the residents (social), as well as what messages/teaching these institutions communicate to their members regarding who they are and their roles in creating change (spiritual/social). Furthermore, Ms. R asked the residents about their levels of psychological trauma (psychological), which she believes may influence their levels of trust of Ms. R and any individuals whom they encounter in their neighborhood (psychological). These are just a few examples to demonstrate how the BPSS perspective can be used to assess a larger system.

In her intervention planning, Ms. R needs to consider which of the previously assessed factors may have the greatest impact on the safety of the community. As with micro or direct practice level interventions, social workers who work in macro practice develop their own theory or theories as to what the cause(s) of the problems is based on their practice experience, their knowledge of explanatory theories, and the research. This case theory based on the BPSS assessment then informs how and where to intervene. In the case of the ABC Neighborhood, Ms. R determined that one of the primary causes of the neighbors not feeling safe is the condition of their residences, as well as the lack of lighting and the lack of a safe space where they can gather, such as the playground. She hypothesized that these factors contributed to the residents staying inside and away from each other. This avoidance of gathering outside, she believes, has also contributed to their health conditions by preventing opportunities to exercise and forcing them to remain inside, which creates additional negative effects.

Based on her assessment and subsequent case theory, her first priority in her intervention plan was to help the residents advocate with the local housing authority and city government to come to the ABC Neighborhood and add/repair lighting and complete an upgrade on the neighborhood playground. She also worked with the authorities to do inspections of the residences to begin to identify which units needed repairs. It was hoped that by creating homes and surrounding spaces that felt safer, more residents would venture outside. As more residents came outside, they would develop a stronger sense of community and be more active and engaged in their communities, which would in turn help their health and mental health, as well as decrease the likelihood that violence would occur because more people were aware of and invested in the activities outside their front doors.

Although Ms. R's plan focused primarily on only the social domain of the BPSS perspective, as a social worker, she held the belief that all of the domains are connected and have a multidirectional relationship with each other. In this case, as residents felt safer and more connected to their neighbors, their mental health would improve. In addition, as they went outside more and engaged with others, they would become more physically active, which would improve their overall health. This appreciation for and attention to the reciprocal nature of how all client factors interact with each other and must be considered in the context of the others is consistent with the teachings and practice of social work (Bartlett, 2003; Bronfenbrenner, 1992; Kondrat, 2008).

Limitations of the BPSS Perspective

Although there are many strengths of the BPSS perspective, it is not a panacea for social work practice. As the case examples show, the BPSS perspective helps identify areas for assessment and intervention, but an assessment of the factors under each domain must then be paired with the social worker's practice expertise, theoretical knowledge, and the best available research in order to develop a case theory and intervention plan (Drisko & Grady, 2019; Grady & Drisko, 2014). It is for this reason that the BPSS is referred to as a perspective or framework; it helps organize

information rather than provide a precise road map for an intervention (Hutchinson, 2017). Social workers will need to use other sources of knowledge in their work, including theories of human development and practice theories.

Another limitation is the number of factors that fall within each domain. The sheer number of factors to consider in an assessment and places in which to intervene could potentially be overwhelming. How can any single social worker address each and every factor within all four domains? The answer is that they cannot. However, because the BPSS perspective recognizes the reciprocal nature of the factors within the domains, by addressing some of the factors, the others in turn may be impacted as one part of the system changes. Using their clinical, empirical, and theoretical knowledge, social workers can then systematically prioritize which aspects within the BPSS perspective to target and in what order.

Conclusion

The BPSS perspective provides a framework that emphasizes the holistic perspective of assessment and intervention. This perspective is consistent with social work's values, through its attention to and recognition of the multiple systems in which clients are embedded. Social workers can use the BPSS perspective as a part of the assessment process than can be turned into a formal document that is part of the case record for clients. Furthermore, it is used by social workers to inform interventions within multiple levels of social work practice—micro, mezzo, and macro. The reciprocal nature of the domains within the BPSS perspective ensures that as social workers intervene in any one area, the other domains will also be impacted. As such, the BPSS perspective provides a useful tool to help social workers frame their work with multiple levels of client systems in their efforts to help clients reach their goals.

References

Aamar, R., Lamson, A., & Smith, D. (2015). Qualitative trends in biopsychosocial–spiritual treatment for underserved patients with type 2 diabetes. *Contemporary Family Therapy, 37*(1), 33–44. doi:10.1007/s10591-015-9326-x

Al Ghaferi, H., Bond, C., & Matheson, C. (2017). Does the biopsychosocial–spiritual model of addiction apply in an Islamic context? A qualitative study of Jordanian addicts in treatment. *Drug and Alcohol Dependence, 172,* 14–20.

Bartlett, H. M. (2003). Working definition of social work practice. *Research on Social Work Practice, 13*(3), 267–270. doi:10.1177/1049731503013003002

Bateman, A., & Fonagy, P. (2013). Mentalization-based treatment. *Psychoanalytic Inquiry, 33*(6), 595–613. doi:10.1080/07351690.2013.835170

Beck, J. S. (2011). *Cognitive behavior therapy: Basics and beyond* (2nd ed.). Guilford.

Berlin, S. B. (1982). Cognitive behavioral interventions for social work practice. *Social Work, 27*(3), 218–226.

Bolton, D., & Gillett, G. (2019). *The biopsychosocial model of health and disease: New philosophical and scientific developments.* Springer.

Brekke, J. S. (2014). A science of social work, and social work as an integrative scientific discipline: Have we gone too far, or not far enough? *Research on Social Work Practice, 24*(5), 517–523. doi:10.1177/1049731513511994

Bronfenbrenner, U. (1992). *Ecological systems theory.* Kingsley.

Cooney, G. M., Dwan, K., Greig, C. A., Lawlor, D. A., Rimer, J., Waugh, F. R., McMurdo, M., & Mead, G. E. (2013). Exercise for depression. *Cochrane Database of Systematic Reviews, 2013*(9):CD004366.

Corcoran, J., & Walsh, J. (2006). *Clinical assessment and diagnosis in social work practice* (2nd ed.). Oxford University Press.

Drisko, J. W., & Grady, M. D. (2019). *Evidence-based practice in clinical social work* (2nd ed.). Springer.

Grady, M. D., & Dombo, E. A. (2016). *Moving beyond assessment: A practical guide for beginning helping professionals.* Oxford University Press.

Grady, M. D., & Drisko, J. W. (2014). Thorough clinical assessment: The hidden foundation of evidence-based practice. *Families in Society, 95*(1), 5–14. doi:10.1606/1044-3894.2014.95.2

Graybeal, C. (2014). The art of practicing with evidence. *Clinical Social Work Journal, 42*(2), 116–122. doi:10.1007/s10615-013-0462-1

Hill, K., Erickson, C. L., Linda, P. D., Fogel, S. J., & Ferguson, S. M. (2017). Perceptions of macro social work education: An exploratory study of educators and practitioners. *Advances in Social Work, 18*(2), 522–542. doi:10.18060/21455

Hutchinson, E. D. (2017). *Essentials of human behavior: Integrating person, environment, and the life course* (2nd ed.). Sage.

Kondrat, M. E. (2008). Person-in-environment. In T. Mizrahi & L. E. Davis (Eds.), *Encyclopedia of social work.* NASW Press and Oxford University Press.

Walsh, J. (2013). *Theories for direct social work practice* (3rd ed.). Cengage.

Weinberger, J., & Rasco, C. (2007). Empirically supported common factors. In S. G. Hofman & J. Weinberger (Eds.), *The art and science of psychotherapy* (pp. 103–129). Routledge.

Zittel, K. M., Lawrence, S., & Wodarski, J. S. (2002). Biopsychosocial model of health and healing: Implications for health social work practice. *Journal of Human Behavior in the Social Environment, 5*(1), 19–33. doi:10.1300/J137v05n01_02

Person-Centered Therapy

Tara Bohley

The person-centered therapy used in social work practice today traces its origins to psychologist Carl Rogers (1902–1987), who came to notoriety during the heyday of Freudian psychoanalysis. Rogers and his contemporary, Abraham Maslow, developed the humanistic perspective of psychology as a response to what they perceived as pessimistic and problem-focused tenets innate to psychoanalysis and the simplistic and mechanical tenets of behaviorism. Roger's unique theory blends humanistic, phenomenological, and experiential ideals into an approach supporting people in actualizing their potential. As Rogers' theory evolved, so did the terminology used to describe it— first "nondirective therapy" became "client-centered therapy," and then eventually it matured to "person-centered theory." Shifting the terminology from *patient* to *client* and ultimately to *person*, Rogers recognized that this was more an approach to life and living than an approach to therapy.

This chapter provides an overview of person-centered therapy and its principles, identifies many of the models that developed around it, provides examples for its applicability in various social work settings, and discusses the contemporary challenges to implementation.

Overview of Person-Centered Therapy

Although all social work educational and training programs likely incorporate a basic Rogerian approach to counseling, person-centered therapy had largely been marginalized to the realm of technique rather than model during the latter decades of the 20th century. This was primarily due to the increasing focus on evidence-based models targeting identified problems and the critique that person-centered therapy was too general in approach and not specific to a particular disorder; therefore, outcomes could not be shown to reduce symptoms associated with a diagnosis as is the expectation within the predominant medical model. However, during the civil rights movement in the 1970s, the values identified by Rogers were reignited among advocates, with a focus on recovery for persons with disabilities. The embers of person-centered theory have remained burning since that time, with more widely adopted practices in Europe (Miller et al., 2017), Australia, and New Zealand (World Association for Person-Centered & Experiential Psychotherapy & Counseling, n.d.). In the United States, the flame has been especially bright during the 21st century, in which person-centered principles are closely aligned with recovery-oriented approaches to care.

Congruence

Particularly important to person-centered therapy are the many elements to the concept of congruence. Congruence is demonstrated on the following levels: intrapersonal within the client, intrapersonal within the therapist, interpersonal between the client and others, and interpersonal between the client and the therapist (Cornelius-White et al., 2013). Specifically, the hypothesis is that mental ill health is created by incongruence between how the person experiences themself and how others perceive them and treat them. This interpersonal incongruence contributes to (or causes) incongruence within the person between how the person experiences their own emotions and how they express them. It is only through present-moment encounters with a therapist who themself is intrapsychically congruent that a client can create new experiences in which their own feelings, being heard and reflected by an empathic therapist, are accepted by another human being without judgment. Within this positive therapeutic alliance, the client can internalize the acceptance offered by the therapist and therefore become more intrapsychically congruent themself.

The Therapeutic Alliance

The premise of person-centered theory is that human beings have an inherent tendency toward growth and development (i.e., an inherent growth principle) and the capacity to actualize their own possibilities (i.e., an actualizing tendency). The primary intervention for all psychological suffering is the therapeutic

relationship. It is through the encounter of an empathic, genuine, and unconditional relationship that a person moves toward their full potential. In order for person-centered therapy to be effective, there must be a strong therapeutic alliance, and the stronger the alliance, the greater the person-centeredness in this reciprocal relationship (Hamovitch et al., 2018). In fact, evidence strongly supports that the strength of the therapeutic alliance is a better predictor of a positive outcome in therapy than any technique or modality used (Ardito et al., 2011).

From a pure Rogerian interpretation, and as published in Rogers' seminal article, "The Necessary and Sufficient Conditions of Therapeutic Personality Change" (1957), there are six circumstances that any beneficial therapeutic encounter must include:

1. Two persons are in psychological contact.
2. The client is in a state of incongruence, being vulnerable or anxious.
3. The therapist is congruent or integrated within the relationship.
4. The therapist experiences unconditional positive regard for the client.
5. The therapist experiences an empathic understanding of the client's internal frame of reference and endeavors to communicate this experience to the client.
6. The communication to the client of the therapist's empathic understanding and unconditional positive regard is achieved.

Hence, the defining features of person-centered therapy are that (1) it focuses on the hypothesis of the inherent growth principle; (2) the conditions for a client's improvement in functioning are based on the quality of the therapeutic attitudes and alliance; (3) the primary tool used is empathic understanding response as an expression of the therapist's genuine attitudes of congruence, acceptance, and empathic understanding; and (4) it maximizes a nondirective approach by the therapist (Brodley, 2019).

Empathic Listening

The skill of empathic listening is vital for the development of a therapeutic alliance. The listening skill is demonstrated in therapist responses to convey to the client that the therapist is listening with intent to understand. The following are examples of common types of empathic understanding responses: literal responses; restatements; summaries; statements that point toward the felt experience of the client but do not name or describe the experience; interpretive or inferential guesses concerning what the client is attempting to express; metaphors; questions that strive to express understandings of ambiguous experience of the client; gestures of the therapist's face, hands, and body; and vocal gestures (Brodley, 2019). The goal of empathic listening is to understand the person's internal frame of reference in such a way as to facilitate the person's own understanding of it, through communication of their thoughts and feelings.

Techniques

Through the therapist's conveyance of congruence, acceptance, and empathy, and their adoption of a nondirective approach, the client can experience the therapist (who has an inherent authoritarian role) as distinctly non-authoritarian, freeing the client from feeling judged or evaluated for expressing their true thoughts and feelings. Techniques that can be applied by a social worker using a person-centered approach include the following (Hayes, 2015):

- Nondirectiveness: Allow the client to lead the therapy session; therapists refrain from giving advice or structuring their sessions.
- Reflection of feelings: Repeat what the client has shared, with an emphasis on the emotions involved, giving them an opportunity to further explore their feelings.

- Open questions: Ask questions that lead to more than a "yes" or "no" response. These questions typically begin with "who," "what," "when," "how," and "where."
- Paraphrasing: Use your own words to repeat back to the client the feelings shared. This can also aid the therapeutic alliance in checking to make sure the therapist fully understands the client's perspective.
- Encouragers: Words or phrases such as "uh-huh," "go on," and "what else?" encourage the client to continue; these can be especially useful for a client who is introverted or otherwise having trouble expressing themself.

A person-centered approach can be very difficult to fully learn because it does not come with a manual or follow any particular course of treatment. Rather, the approach relies on the unique qualities of the social worker to build an empathic and genuine relationship with each individual client.

Person-Centered Principles in Contemporary Models

Social workers using the person-centered approach must value the primacy of experience and the importance of presence (Cornelius-White et al., 2013). Within those foci, one can clearly see the footings of mindfulness, which can assist both the therapist and the client in awareness of their present-moment thoughts and feelings (Jooste et al., 2015). Indeed, elements of person-centered theory have formed the premise of many contemporary models, especially motivational interviewing, with its focus on empathic listening and a strong therapeutic alliance. Additional examples include narrative therapy, emotionally focused therapy, feedback-informed treatment, and positive psychology. Furthermore, many modalities and allied disciplines have been heavily influenced by these principles, such as interpersonal relationships and group work, cross-cultural communication, parenting, care for persons with special needs, learner-centered education, technology-enhanced learning environments, human relations leadership training, life coaching, and patient-centered medicine (Cornelius-White et al., 2013).

A social worker using person-centered therapy may also find it possible to utilize techniques identified with other therapies such as those applied in behavioral therapy, cognitive therapy, gestalt therapy, hypnosis, focusing, relaxation, and meditation. In such an occurrence, these techniques would only be introduced upon the request of the client or when the interaction itself causes the client to become aware of unmet needs that could be alleviated by such techniques. In this situation, the social worker does not have any preconceived notions nor treatment plans identifying what the client needs without the client's approval. The social worker is not imposing these techniques, and the client remains in control of their use in a truly self-directed manner (Brodley, 2019).

Uses in Social Work Settings

Social workers use person-centered practices in a variety of settings and with a range of populations. Examples include the following:

> Older adults: Person-centered practices are increasingly being incorporated into adult day care, home- and community-based long-term services and supports, and nursing homes. Social workers are uniquely equipped to practice in these settings, with their focus on supporting self-determination; individual, cultural, and ethnic differences; and the right of each person to define their own needs and goals (Washburn & Grossman, 2017).

> People with learning disabilities: Person-centered planning is widely used in the United Kingdom (Sanderson et al., 2006) and is incorporated into national policy, ensuring that it is available for all people with learning disabilities who want it (Martin, 2001).

> People with different intellectual and physical abilities; people with mental illness and people with substance use challenges- along with the release of the New Freedom Commission on Mental Health in the United States (*President's New Freedom Commission on MH: Report to the President: Roster of Commissioners*, 2003), came a mandate that recovery be integrated into all aspects of mental health policy. The Substance Abuse and Mental Health Services Administration furthered this mandate to officially designate person-centeredness as a fundamental component of recovery (*National consensus statement on mental health recovery*, 2004). As a result, many states have adopted person-centered principles and approaches into their models of care.

> Social work in medical settings: Person-centered care (alternatively known as patient-centered care) continues to evolve in various medical settings, with a new focus on its potential for cost savings in the United States in particular. Evidence supports that patient-centered practice, as measured by patient-perceived scores of professional empathy, correlates with reduced discomfort and concern, better mental health, fewer diagnostic tests, and fewer referrals (Stewart et al., 2000). In addition, person-centered and patient-centered approaches are being widely incorporated into primary care and

mental health services provided by the U.S. Department of Veterans Affairs (The National Academies of Sciences, Engineering, and Medicine, 2018).

One can clearly see that this is a varied list of settings—and a list that continues to expand along with the growing evidence for valuing the voice and preferences of the person being served.

Case Example

Kathy is a 71-year-old woman recovering from a stroke. She is in an inpatient rehabilitation setting, and this is the third meeting with the social worker to discuss discharge planning. The family has requested a psychological evaluation and is considering incorporating antidepressant medication for her. Although Kathy wants to return home at discharge, her family is concerned that she needs more assistance than can be provided at home.

Kathy: I've heard that they want me to have a psychological evaluation. You know, I'm really not depressed. I've been depressed, so I know what that's like. It's just that everyone keeps telling me to push myself, to work harder. But they don't understand, I *am* working hard. Everything I do is hard. They just don't understand. It's not depression. I just can't do what I used to do. And I'm tired.

Social Worker: It sounds like you have a clear sense of your current struggles, but others are characterizing them differently. You are working hard and feel tired, and maybe a little defeated? (*Here the social worker is summarizing, restating, and checking emotions.*)

Kathy: Yes. Like my daughter, I know she loves me and wants what she believes is best for me. She keeps saying

"You have to push yourself." I *am* pushing myself. They have no idea what it's like to be in this body. I don't have control over my body anymore. What used to be so easy—tying my shoes, putting on makeup, taking a shower—those things are exhausting, and they take an enormous amount of time.

Social Worker: Your physical abilities are impaired and it's hard for you to perform basic daily activities. You feel you don't have control and your daughter is having a hard time accepting your new normal.

Kathy: And I am, too! I can't do anything for myself, it seems. They say I'm doing so much better than I was, but I don't see it.

Social Worker: Mmmm. I can understand how frustrating and disappointing that must be—to feel kind of helpless, that you have to rely on others for so many things you are used to doing independently. You don't feel the progress that others are seeing.

Kathy: And you know, I'm really tired of having to go to the dining room for meals. The staff come to my room at 6:30 every morning to get me to come to breakfast. I tell them every day, as I have said for 2 months that I've been here, "I don't eat breakfast. I have never eaten breakfast," but they keep coming, every day. I hate going to that dining room. It's depressing and I don't like being served. I don't like the small talk chit-chat that goes on and the gossip among the people at my table. I'd rather just not be a part of any of it. I just want to stay in my room and wish people would leave me alone.

Social Worker: It sounds like you are in many situations now in which your preferences are secondary to other's schedules or worries. For someone who was previously so independent—living alone, taking care of others, making all of your own decisions, what is this like for you now, to not have that same level of autonomy? (*Here the social worker uses an open question to assist Kathy in exploring her emotions.*)

Kathy: I don't like it. But truthfully, since the stroke, things don't bother me the way they used to. I just don't feel things emotionally like I did before, which is probably a good thing. If people would just leave me alone, acknowledge that I am doing the best that I can, and let me make the decisions around what's best for me, I would be just fine. I know that I need to be here. I could not take care of myself at home the way I am now.

Social Worker: You make sense, Kathy. Let me see if I understand this correctly: Since the stroke, you've noticed that your emotions are a bit numbed, making you behave and feel differently than the person you were before the stroke. This change concerns your family, and they fear this is a symptom of depression. You miss your independence and are still learning how to adjust to your physical limitations. While you yearn for your old life, you also realize that returning to it is not really feasible right now. Is that accurate? (*Here the social worker is reflecting Kathy's feeling and posing a question that strives to understand Kathy's ambiguous experience.*)

Kathy: Yes, that's it. I want to go home. But I realize I'm not ready. I hate it, but I know I need more help than I can get at home.

In this interchange, the social worker is working through the therapeutic alliance to help Kathy clarify her feelings about her current situation, using restatements, making inferential guesses at her felt emotion, and, most important, listening with the intent to understand. The goal of the intervention is aiding Kathy to make her own decisions about her care.

Implementation Challenges

Even as person-centered care has been written into state and national policy, implementation within the predominant medical model systems is challenging, particularly around billable codes requiring "medical necessity" thresholds and diagnoses for reimbursement by public and private insurers in the United States (Miller et al., 2017). Even in countries with nationalized health care systems, such as the United Kingdom, social workers are met with the same hierarchical challenges, with psychiatric power at the top, and priorities focused on clinical tasks, professional language, and medicalization—all of which serve as barriers to the person achieving an identity of recovery (Le Boutillier et al., 2015). The person-centered approach is in direct opposition to the key features of the disease-oriented medical model, which (1) focuses on the individual, (2) positions the practitioner as the expert, and (3) emphasizes distress and dysfunction within the person. In contrast, person-centered therapy (1) focuses on the person within the context of family, community, and other social systems; (2) positions the client as the expert; and (3) emphasizes the strengths and healthy potential of the person (Joseph, 2017). In a person-centered approach, the social worker does not use the language of the medical model, with its focus on symptoms, diagnosis, and disease, nor make assumptions that specific conditions require specific treatments (Joseph, 2017).

A study by Lodge et al. (2017) revealed 12 barriers to person-centered recovery planning across public mental health organizations in Texas, and it identified that half of those barriers were within the organizations. These barriers included lack of time and resources, noncollaborative planning, software and treatment plan structure barriers, leadership barriers, dissemination barriers, and cultural resistance to change (Lodge et al., 2017).

The tension social workers experience as they transition from a traditional model of care to a more person-centered approach is polarizing, positioning autonomy of the client versus compliance with treatment, freedom to be ambitious with goals versus structure to implement treatment, focusing on strengths of the person versus symptoms of mental illness, and individualized and unique care versus a one-size-fits-all approach for the masses (Doherty et al., 2020). Lisbeth Sommerbeck (2017) describes the duality felt by therapists who practice person-centered therapy while working within a medical model setting, necessitating the therapist to switch between the roles of the two worlds while balancing the natural tendency to advocate for one side over the other. The therapist in this seemingly contradictory situation must resist the pull to take on the role of expert over the client's condition and course of treatment and also the pull to become the advocate or spokesperson for the client's will or viewpoint. The therapist may be more effective in expressing the client-centered values and perspectives outside of the therapy room and inside the staff meetings and in professional interactions with members of the multidisciplinary team, which can have a macro impact on the organizational culture and the uptake of person-centered practices that could be applied to all clients within the organization.

Conclusion

In a study published in 2016, Blanchard and Farber found that 93% of respondents reported having lied to their therapists. The majority of the lies were about the quality of the therapeutic relationship, and one-third concerned their perception of the effectiveness of therapeutic intervention. Blanchard and Farber conclude that the field in general would benefit from a renewed emphasis on fostering, and checking in on, the therapeutic alliance. Person-centered practice is the prescription for the impaired therapeutic alliance. Yet in actuality, it is often merely values espoused, trainings attended, and language used on the treatment plan to be in compliance with external regulations. In order for the true principles to be comprehensively applied, it requires a cultural shift toward the client and away from the expert/professional.

Helpful Resources

Association for the Development of the Person Centered Approach: https://www.adpca.org/content/welcome-adpca

National Center for Advancing Person-Centered Practices and Systems: https://ncapps.acl.gov/about-ncapps.html

The Person-Centred Association: https://www.the-pca.org.uk

World Association for Person Centered & Experiential Psychotherapy & Counseling: https://www.pce-world.org

References

Ardito, R. B., Rabellino, D., & Simpson, S. G. (2011, October 18). Therapeutic alliance and outcome of psychotherapy: Historical excursus, measurements, and prospects for research. *Frontiers in Psychology.* https://doi.org/10.3389/fpsyg.2011.00270

Blanchard, M., & Farber, B. A. (2016). Lying in psychotherapy: Why and what clients don't tell their therapist about therapy and their relationship. *Counselling Psychology Quarterly, 29*(1), 90–112. https://doi.org/10.1080/09515070.2015.1085365

Brodley, B. T. (2019). Client-centered therapy—What is it? What is it not? *The Person Centered Journal, 24*(1).

Cornelius-White, J. H. D., Motschnig-Pitrik, R., & Lux, M. (Eds.). (2013). *Interdisciplinary handbook of the person-centered approach: Research and theory.* Springer. https://doi.org/10.1007/978-1-4614-7141-7

Doherty, M., Bond, L., Jessell, L., Tennille, J., Stanhope, V., & Doherty, A. L. (2020). Transitioning to person-centered care: A qualitative study of provider perspectives. *Journal of Behavioral Health Services & Research, 47,* 399–408. https://doi.org/10.1007/s11414-019-09684-2

Hamovitch, E. K., Choy-Brown, M., & Stanhope, V. (2018). Person-centered care and the therapeutic alliance. *Community Mental Health Journal, 54*(7), 951–958. https://doi.org/10.1007/s10597-018-0295-z

Hayes, K. (2015). *Person-centred therapy: A guide to counselling therapies.* J & S Garrett.

Jooste, J., Kruger, A., Steyn, B. J. M., & Edwards, D. J. (2015). Mindfulness: A foothold for Rogers's humanistic person-centred approach. *Journal of Psychology in Africa, 25*(6), 554–559. https://doi.org/10.1080/14330237.2015.1124619

Joseph, S. (Ed.). (2017). *The handbook of person-centered therapy and mental health.* PCCS Books.

Le Boutillier, C., Chevalier, A., Lawrence, V., Leamy, M., Bird, V. J., Macpherson, R., Williams, J., & Slade, M. (2015). Staff understanding of recovery-orientated mental health practice: A systematic review and narrative synthesis. *Implementation Science, 10*(1). https://doi.org/10.1186/s13012-015-0275-4

Lodge, A. C., Kaufman, L., & Stevens Manser, S. (2017). Barriers to implementing person-centered recovery planning in public mental health organizations in Texas: Results from Nine Focus Groups. *Administration and Policy in Mental Health and Mental Health Services Research, 44*(3), 413–429. https://doi.org/10.1007/s10488-016-0732-7

Martin, G. (2001). "Valuing people"—A new strategy for learning disability for the 21st century: How may it impinge on primary care? *British Journal of General Practice, 51*(471), 788–790.

Miller, E., Stanhope, V., Restrepo-Toro, M., & Tondora, J. (2017). Person-centered planning in mental health: A transatlantic collaboration to tackle implementation barriers. *American Journal of Psychiatric Rehabilitation, 20,* 251–267. https://doi.org/10.1080/15487768.2017.1338045

President's New Freedom Commission on Mental Health. (2003). *Report to the President: Roster of commissioners.* https://govinfo.library.unt.edu/mentalhealthcommission/reports/FinalReport/downloads/downloads.html

Rogers, C. R. (1957). The necessary and sufficient conditions of therapeutic personality change. *Journal of Consulting Psychology, 21*(2), 95–103.

Sanderson, H., Thompson, J., & Kilbane, J. (2006). The emergence of person-centred planning as evidence-based practice: The impact of PCP on the life experiences of people with learning disabilities. *Journal of Integrated Care, 14*(2), 18–25.

Sommerbeck, L. (2017). Complementarity between client-centred therapy and psychiatry: The theory and the practice. In S. Joseph (Ed.), *The handbook of person-centered therapy and mental health* (pp. 121–132). PCCS Books.

Stewart, M., Brown, J. B., Donner, A., McWhinney, I. R., Oates, J., Westin, W. W., & Jordan, J. (2000). The impact of patient centered care on outcomes. *Journal of Family Practice, 49*(9), 796–804.

Substance Abuse and Mental Health Services Administration. (2004). *National consensus statement on mental health recovery.*

The National Academies of Sciences, Engineering, and Medicine. (2018). *Evaluation of the Department of Veterans Affairs Mental Health Services: A consensus study report.* https://doi.org/10.17226/24915

Washburn, A. M., & Grossman, M. (2017). Being with a person in our care: Person-centered social work practice that is authentically person-centered. *Journal of Gerontological Social Work, 60*(5), 408–423. https://doi.org/10.1080/01634372.2017.1348419

World Association for Person-Centered & Experiential Psychotherapy & Counseling. (n.d.). *WAPCEPC chapters.* Retrieved May 29, 2020, from https://www.pce-world.org/chapters.html

Principles of Attachment Theory for Social Work Practice

Shelley Cohen Konrad

Background
Attachment Theory

Attachment theory focuses on the development and impacts of relational bonds. Sigmund Freud, an Austrian neurologist and originator of psychoanalytic theory, was one of the first theorists to formally recognize the importance and influence of early relational connections, especially the mother–infant bond. He speculated that these earliest attachments set indelible relational patterns that resonated throughout the life course. According to Freud (1977), how well or how poorly mothers responded to their infants set the stage for secure or insecure attachment, the latter assumed to be the source of lifelong emotional/relational disorders.

Like Freud, British practitioner-researcher Donald Winnicott, a pediatrician and psychoanalyst, believed early bonds to be central to the growing child's ongoing health and secure development. Unlike Freud, he considered the formation of human bonds to be interactional and bidirectional, consisting of parallel engagement and responsivity between mother/caregiver and infant. Variations in relational behaviors contributed to what Winnicott (1986) called "good enough mothering." He concluded that mothers' responses were tailored to their infant's individual physical, temperamental, and emotional needs. Met needs resulted in secure attachments that paved the way for the development of independence and lifelong emotional well-being. Inconsistency or unmet needs challenged a child's relational and behavioral stability.

John Bowlby (1951), a British psychiatrist, advanced attachment research and popularized its tenets. Sometimes referred to as the "father" of attachment theory, Bowlby believed that to achieve secure attachment, an infant required a primary attachment figure, most notably the birth mother. He postulated that during the first 5 years of life, the relationship between the infant and the primary attachment figure instilled an internal, cognitive framework that influenced how the child would later understand the self (identity), others (relationships), and the world (sociocultural beliefs) (Bretherton & Mulholland, 1999).

Bowlby (1969) identified four tenets of attachment relationships:

1. Proximity maintenance—the desire to be close to those we feel attached to

2. Safe haven—internalization of relational security especially when faced with uncertainty, threat, or fear
3. Secure base—the reliable presence of a stable, comforting primary carer when the child seeks to explore their world
4. Separation distress—anxiety or stressful behaviors in the absence of a primary attachment figure(s)

Bowlby was drawn to the work of researchers William Goldfarb (1943) and René Spitz and Kathryn Wolf (1946), whose studies concentrated on the impacts of long-term institutionalization on infants. Their findings suggested that infants who were denied contact and affection developed lasting physical and behavioral problems, and at the most extreme, they became severely depressed. These findings have been critiqued throughout the years as narrowly conceived and with no consideration for environmental or social factors.

Bowlby's thoughts on attachment evolved over time, influenced by his contemporaries and experiences working directly with children and families. Later in his career, he supported a less deterministic standpoint to attachment (van der Horst et al., 2008), suggesting that relational health could evolve over time (Mirick & Steenrod, 2016), a theory now substantiated by contemporary neuroscience research. Bowlby's broadened conceptualization of attachment resonates with social work's person-in-environment framework (Kondradt, 2013) and underscores the intersectionality between the individual, environmental factors, and health.

Attachment Patterns

Bowlby's work coincided with that of Mary Salter Ainsworth, whose early studies focused on the variability and intergenerational nature of attachment patterns. The most famous of these, "the Strange Situation" procedure (SSP), examined whether maternal relational styles were consistently associated with specific patterns of attachment (Ainsworth et al., 1978). Ainsworth and her colleague Sylvia Bell (1970) identified three patterns of attachment: *Secure attachment*, characterized by attuned parent–child responsivity, and two patterns of *insecure attachment*—ambivalent (indiscriminately seeks connection; may be clingy/inconsolable) and avoidant (avoid/reject relational connection), both viewed as resulting from factors such as parental inconsistency, volatility, and disrupted parent–child bonding.

A fourth attachment pattern, *disorganized attachment*, was later identified by Mary Main and Judith Solomon (1990). Disorganized attachment develops when caregivers are chronically disengaged from their infants and, at times, create unsafe physical and emotional environments (Rees, 2007). Factors such as child maltreatment, emotional abuse, and chronic neglect are thought to contribute to children's disorganized attachments. Interpersonal violence, parental mental illness, or substance use disorders may also be factors. For these children, relationships are perceived as untrustworthy.

Pervasive relational disconnection in early childhood is thought to contribute to reactive attachment disorder (RAD). Children diagnosed with RAD are assumed to lack relational trust and thus do not seek nurturance from the people in their worlds. Failure to develop social relatedness results in an array of behaviors that are alternately dissociated, contradictory, and sometimes aggressive even without provocation. Main and Solomon (1990) hypothesized that fear was the primary source of disorganized attachment patterns. Fearing loss, abandonment, harm, or parental retribution, children develop unpredictable responses to survive perceived hostile relational encounters. As children grow and engage with the outside world, these responses impede critical relationships and affect learning and social agency.

Psychoanalyst and researcher Selma Fraiberg explored intergenerational attachment patterns—what she referred to as "ghosts in the nursery" (Fraiberg et al., 1975). Fraiberg and colleagues noticed that new mothers repeated unconscious patterns of caregiving that they had experienced in childhood. These researchers were pioneers in recognizing that parents who themselves had insufficient or disrupted early attachments required nurturing and early parenting intervention to effectively rear their dependent infants. Fraiberg's (1987) collective work is recognized as foundational to the infant mental health (IMH) field. IMH focuses on factors that enhance or inhibit the young child's capacities to "experience, regulate, and express emotions, form close and secure relationships, and explore the environment and learn" (Zeanah & Zeanah, 2009, p. 6).

Allan Schore, an IMH psychologist and neuropsychology researcher, has advanced the work begun by Fraiberg and colleagues. His interdisciplinary inquiry integrates neurobiology, psychobiology, and attachment theory revealing critical interconnections between the brain and infant social/emotional/relational development and growth. This applied research is used to inform prevention, intervention, and treatment of attachment disorders, offering more "detailed psychoneurobiological understandings of attachment and a broader model of normal and adaptive infant mental health" (A. Schore, 2001, p. 203).

Classifying patterns of attachment is meant to help practitioners understand factors that contribute to common relational styles. However, not every parent–child bonding experience can be easily sorted by attachment classifications; circumstances, culture, context, and congenital capacities affect early and ongoing relationships. According to A. Schore (2001), the quality of attachment is best understood as a unique and interactional product of "genetic endowment with a particular environment" (p. 203). Schore and other neuroscience

and attachment researchers have produced volumes of scientific information linking brain development, environmental factors, and social determinants with attachment theories. Positive aspects of brain science suggest that although early attachment experiences have potent implications, attuned therapeutic and other relationships can transform relational connection throughout life.

Enduring Bonds and Ambiguous Losses

Child–parent separations in early childhood occur for many reasons and can be of variable duration. Causes include parental death; termination of parental rights; and children being placed in permanent foster care, which sometimes results in adoption by foster families. Separations may also be temporary. Parental incarceration, military deployments, hospitalization, or other disruptions affect the continuity of parent–child ties. Even brief separations may affect attachment, especially when they occur early or are frequent in nature (van der Horst et al., 2008).

Children experience complicated responses to ambiguous parental disconnections. Pauline Boss and Janet Yeats (2014) define ambiguous loss as "a loss that remains unclear and without resolution" (p. 63). These losses can occur when a parent is psychologically absent yet physically present, distracted by addiction, physical or mental illness, post-partum depression, or post-traumatic stress. Struggling parents move between being loving and present and being distracted and unresponsive. In these circumstances, the presence of a consistent parent or other adult carer can mediate the impact of ambiguous relational loss.

Children may also experience ambiguous loss when they remain psychologically bonded to a parent whose whereabouts are unknown. Children in foster care, for example, may fantasize about their relationship with an absent biological parent. A child adopted at birth may wonder why they were unwanted. Unrequited desires to reconnect to a birth parent create a pall of sadness that the child cannot voice. The psychological bond to the wished-for parent can further cause relational strains between the child and those who care for the child.

For children who experience multiple separations, disruptions, and transitions, the pile up of ambiguous losses and associated grief may be substantial. These losses are not always recognized as grief. When left unacknowledged, they can have significant short- and long-term impacts on the child's emotional well-being and their capacity to form trusting relationships.

Disrupted early bonds also influence identity development (Anderson & Gedo, 2013; Siu & Hogan, 1989). Attachment behaviors convey messages that are absorbed and integrated into the child's evolving sense of self. Securely attached children feel affirmed in their strengths and are able to take risks because they know that missteps and mistakes will be forgiven. When attachments are unreliable, children live with relational uncertainty that undermines efficacy and self-worth. Early relationships that result in physical or emotional harm may cause the child to be in continuous survival mode, overly reactive to potential threats of abandonment. Disconnection in infancy challenges the growing child to discover their capabilities and worthiness. For these youngsters, the road to developmental success is difficult but not impossible; they need patience, understanding, time, and tolerance.

Family ties represent the child's history of belonging. Bonds with others serve as protective factors buffering people from the expected and unexpected rigors of life. When early attachments are secure, relationships can withstand separations, relocations, disagreements, and losses. When bonds are marred by neglect, abuse, abandonment, or adversity, it is challenging to understand clients' persistent yearning for relational reunion. Some

may have never consciously known their birth parents, yet they are drawn to find them. Reunion for some may be rewarded and family ties renewed. However, hopes for reconnection are often disappointing, rejected, or the parent cannot be found.

Social workers are often perplexed by the tenacity of children's ties to parents who they have never met or by whom they have been mistreated or abandoned. The strength and endurance of children's family ties, however, should not be minimized. Whether relational ties are real or idealized, social workers should acknowledge and recognize their importance to the child.

Case Example: Ambiguous Loss

Sarina's story (Cohen Konrad, 2019) encapsulates the durability of early bonds, ambiguous loss, and the tenaciousness of family ties. Her initial foster placement occurred at age 4 years following a fire that destroyed the family's trailer. Sarina and her 6-year-old sister were placed in separate homes after it was determined that their mother was unable to safely care for them. By age 15 years, she had lived in and left five different homes. After multiple failed family reunions, the mother's parental rights were terminated. Sarina and her sister were never reunited.

Sarina's workers remembered her as a sad and unsettled youngster, consumed with finding her mother. The reunion, however, never took place. At age 19 years, Sarina had a baby of her own, a little girl named for her mother. Workers engaged with youngsters such as Sarina are frequently frustrated by the youths' attachment to parents who neglect, abandon, or abuse. But the meaning of these early ties has enduring significance even when the reality of reconnection is out or reach and never comes to fruition.

Attachment Critique

Attachment theories had many early critics, including from the field of social work. Although most agreed with the importance of these earliest relationships, theoretical criticisms focused on pressures placed on mothers as sole arbiters of children's relational health. They argued that person-in-environment factors such as material insecurities, discrimination, trauma, gender bias, and environmental factors were equally influential to children's attachments as were fathers and other carers.

Feminist scholars such as Jean Baker Miller (1976) revisited the scientific and developmental tenets of attachment theory. They deconstructed previously unquestioned developmental concepts such as autonomy, independence, and emotional separateness as markers of adult health. They proposed that ongoing connection to caregivers was necessary for children to achieve independence.

Miller (1976) and others revised and expanded essential tenets of attachment theory, integrating them into the broader relational–cultural theory (RCT). RCT conceptualizes relational bonds as psychologically mutual, participatory, and central to human functionality and survival. Relational disconnection is viewed as a major source of human suffering (Miller & Stiver, 1997). Successful development is understood by RCT theorists as a lifelong balancing and rebalancing of connection, interdependence, and autonomy.

RCT's standpoint explicitly considers the person-in-environment (Kondradt, 2013), viewing relationships as shaped by myriad life circumstances and by social, racial, political, and economic factors, including discrimination and inequities. RCT posits that resiliency and positive connection are possible for all people of all ages through interventions that foster restorative and mutual relationships even after years of attachment failures, losses, and trauma. Such therapies help rebuild attachments through changes in the brain's essential neurological architecture (Hartling, 2008).

Attachment and Brain Science

Freud, Bowlby, and others firmly believed that future discoveries would reveal associations between attachment, relationship, regulatory functioning, and neurological development. They would be astounded by neuroscientific advancements that not only affirmed their hunches but also illuminated them via neuroimaging innovations. Interdisciplinary longitudinal studies such as those in the *From Neurons to Neighborhoods* (FNTN; Shonkoff & Phillips, 2000) report confirmed Bowlby's assumption that children's brains were born wired for connection. There is no longer speculation about the utility of person-in-environment frameworks because FNTN research confirmed the critical role of context, circumstance, and the environment in children's early relational development. Studies such as the CDC–Kaiser Permanente Adverse Childhood Experiences (ACE) study (Felitti et al., 1998) suggest that adverse early life experiences including differing forms of direct abuse, trauma, family disruption, and parental illness have immediate and long-term negative consequences on attachment, brain development, and adult physical health (Björkenstam et al., 2013; Dong et al., 2003; Shonkoff et al., 2009).

Research and brain imaging link neurobiology with the growing child's brain architecture, which regulates emotional, social, and interactional functionality (Banks, 2011; Mitchell, 2018). The right side of the brain responds to affect regulation and perception, contributing to developing capacities to organize stress and harness resiliency (Cohen Konrad, 2019; Montgomery, 2013; see also Chapter 33, this volume). From a neuroscience standpoint, the primary carer's responses offer feedback to the developing brain and central nervous system, in effect teaching infants how to regulate. Mirick and Steenrod (2016) explain that secure attachments help children "develop cause-and-effect thinking and understand and regulate feelings such as hunger, fatigue, stress or sadness" (p. 550).

While parental responses effectively instruct infants to regulate their needs, so too do infants' responses influence and reinforce caregivers' neurological patterning. Fraiberg et al. (1975) were some of the earliest attachment researchers to recognize the importance of relational reciprocity for successful infant–parent bonding. Parents need to feel loved by their infants. When infants are chronically unresponsive, parents may lose hope or feel rejected. Nurturance and support help these parents build or rebuild neurological pathways responsive to their infants' relational cues.

Goodness of fit describes the synchrony between parent and child temperament that contributes to the quality of attachment (Thomas & Chess, 1977). When parents are responsive and attuned to their infant, they feel loved and secure. Alternately, infants may make brave but unsuccessful attempts to bring a parent into relationship. When infants and caregivers are relationally out of sync, they experience distressing states of uncertainty. When regulatory problems persist or remain therapeutically unaddressed, they have the potential to negatively impact the child's present and future cognition, behavior, relational capacities, and social–emotional acuity.

Attachment and infant brain research further suggest that vulnerable parents—those affected by early, cumulative, and persistent hardships—may be especially taxed by caregiving. As Bell (1970) observed, people carry "ghosts" of their own attachment failures into their parenting styles and capacities. Brain research finds that early adversity has enduring impacts on the brain, affecting abilities to nurture, sustain relationships, cope with stress, and regulate emotions (A. Schore, 2001). Although

many parents overcome early relational hurdles to become loving and nurturing parents, some do not.

IMH theory and associated practices underscore the importance of knowing and applying attachment theory and infant brain research to social work practice providing insight into why some children skillfully manage the rigors of early childhood while others fail. They explain why many clients struggle throughout their lives with building and maintaining relational trust. Perhaps most important, neuroscience and attachment research offer scientific, rather than judgmental, assessment of difficult behaviors across the life span. Understanding the brain as a source of social and behavioral problems increases the likelihood of compassion rather than judgment and blame.

Viewing the brain as repairable and responsive to psychotherapeutic intervention is a relatively new concept—one that is trauma-informed (Substance Abuse and Mental Health Services Administration, 2014) and offers hope for building resilience and change. It challenges the long-held belief that emotional and relational health are decidedly fixed in childhood. Relationally based therapies show promise, including improvements in adult clients' regulatory and relational capacities (Bryant, 2016; J. Schore & Schore, 2008). Social workers informed by attachment theory and brain research believe that resilience and relational growth are possible for all people when supported by responsive relationships (Mackey Andrews et al., 2017).

Attachment and Atypicality

The formation of relational bonds is dynamic and interactive, affected by many factors, including the infant's developmental capacities and, in some cases, delays and disabilities. For example, Fraiberg and co-workers (1975) studied unique attributes of attachment behaviors between visually impaired infants and their parents. Parents of children with autism spectrum disorders (ASD) may similarly locate untraditional methods to establish relational bonds. Youngsters with ASD, a neurodevelopmental disorder, struggle with social communication, restricted and repetitive behaviors, and sensory sensitivities (Martínez-Pedraza & Carter, 2009). Parents understandably become frustrated when their nurturance is met with irritability, avoidance, or inconsolability. Social workers, in collaboration with teachers and peer mentors, can support parents as they reconfigure relational hopes and establish attachment patterns specifically geared to their child's special needs.

Case Example: Autism Spectrum Disorder

When Cameron was born, Jane and Bob were excited by the prospect of raising their beautiful infant son. But their pleasure was tempered by Cameron's unrelenting irritability and the futility of their efforts to soothe him. Family and friends assured them that his behaviors were normal; things would become easier over time. Rather than improving, however, Cameron became increasingly detached. Bob and Jane blamed themselves and each other for Cameron's problems.

At age 4 years, Cameron was diagnosed with ASD and was referred for social work services because of heightened frustration and aggressive outbursts in school. Services for Cameron's family focused on autism education and identifying sources of peer and professional support. The couple came to understand that what they had assumed to be attachment failures were expectable challenges due to Cameron's neurodevelopmental communication differences. Knowledge of ASD eased the couple's feelings of parental inadequacy, replacing it with fervor to find ways to become attuned to Cameron's world.

Attachment as a Human Right

Attachment theory is commonly applied to the biopsychosocial lives of children and families, mostly in clinical, social service, and health care settings. However, the imperative of attachment for human health is also viewed as an essential right. In 1989, the United Nations Convention on the Rights of Children (UNCRC) human rights treaty codified children's rights to be nurtured, to belong, and to be loved by their primary and extended carers (Melton, 2010). The U.S. government was active in drafting the UNCRC and was a signatory by 1995; however, a vote to ratify it has yet (as of 2020) to be put before Congress.

Bowlby called attachment a primary human necessity in helping people survive in a challenging world. Neuroscientific and infant attachment research has since validated the critical and enduring effects of relationship on human health and well-being. The FNTN report (Shonkoff & Phillips, 2000) recommended that governments and policymakers integrate knowledge about the centrality of early relationships for children and their families, noting that existing brain and attachment science are underutilized for helping children, families, and child-serving systems negotiate 21st-century challenges.

Public health, education, physical/behavioral health, and welfare policymakers have responsibilities to be informed decision-makers, raising awareness and identifying and investigating the influences of early attachment. Knowledge exchange between legislators, institutional leaders, and neuroscience experts, among others, must ensure that policies reflect the intersectionality between attachment, early adversity, social determinants, and the population dimensions of problems that are often viewed as individual or family failings (Shonkoff & Phillips, 2000). Insufficient early attachments result in large-scale human and economic costs, which can

be mediated by well-developed and sufficiently resourced services to prevent and address them. Social work activists are poised
to raise such awareness not only because we
value relational connection but also because
as a profession we are committed to human
rights, social inclusion, equity, justice, and
actions that effect change (Council on Social
Work Education, 2015).

Conclusion

Attachment theory offers ways to conceptualize
the multilevel impacts of early and ongoing
human relationships. Its principles suggest
strategies that enable social workers to identify
strengths and patterns of early relational bonds
and use them to address challenges faced when
attachments are insufficient, unreliable, or
broken by life circumstance. Along with individual impacts, attachment theory also speaks
to the effects that cultural and community disconnection has on people who have been soci-
etally marginalized or disenfranchised. Infant
mental health and brain science have advanced
knowledge about what is necessary to achieve
successful attachments and set forth therapeutic methods that can ameliorate relational
disconnection in early childhood and beyond.
Such knowledge brings hope and possibility
to those who have experienced early adversity, trauma, and other circumstances that have
left them mistrustful of or without benefit of
human relationship.

It is equally incumbent on legislators
and policymakers to use advancements in
neuroscience research to inform policies that
help people negotiate the evolving and ever-
complicated demands of life in the 21st century (Shonkoff & Phillips, 2000). The drafters
of the UNCRC codified protection of children's
primary ties to their families and communities
as a human right. They underscored relational
attachments as "critical to purpose in life,
sense of personal fulfillment, and identity as
both an individual and a member of a family
or a clan, a religious community, and a nation or an ethnic group—in effect, the ingredient in personhood" (Melton, 2010, p. 165).
Social workers are committed to safeguarding
the right to relational health and advocate for
evidence-informed programs that foster support, provide opportunities, and empower
vulnerable families to thrive and participate in
their communities.

References

Ainsworth, M. D. S., & Bell, S. M. (1970). Attachment, exploration, and separation: Illustrated by the behavior of one-year-olds in a strange situation. *Child Development, 41*, 49–67.

Ainsworth, M. S., Blehar, M. C., Waters, E., & Wall, S. (1978). *Patterns of attachment: A psychological study of the Strange Situation.* Erlbaum.

Anderson, S., & Gedo, M. (2013). Relational trauma: Using play therapy to treat a disrupted attachment. *Bulletin of the Menninger Clinic, 77*(3), 250–268.

Banks, A. E. (2011). Developing the capacity to connect. *Zygon, 46*(1), 168–182.

Bell, S. M. (1970). The development of the concept of object as related to infant-mother attachment. *Child Development*, 291–311.

Björkenstam, E., Hjern, A., Mittendorfer-Rutz, E., Vinnerljung, B., Hallqvist, J., & Ljung, R. (2013). Multi-exposure and clustering of adverse childhood experiences, socioeconomic differences and psychotropic medication in young adults. *PLoS One, 8*(1), e53551. https://journals.plos.org/plosone/article?id=10.1371/journal.pone.0053551

Boss, P., & Yeats, J. (2014). Ambiguous loss: A complicated type of grief when loved ones disappear. *Bereavement Care, 33*(2), 63–69.

Bowlby, J. (1951). Maternal care and child health. *Bulletin of the World Health Organization, 3*(3), 355–533.

Bowlby, J. (1969). *Attachment and loss: Vol. 1. Attachment.* Basic Books.

Bretherton, I., & Mulholland, K. A. (1999). Internal working models revisited. In J. Cassidy & P. R. Shaver (Eds.), *Handbook of attachment: Theory, research, and clinical applications* (pp. 89–111). Guilford.

Bryant, A. (2016). Social attachments and traumatic stress. *European Journal of Psychotraumatology, 7*(1), 29065–29067. https://www.tandfonline.com/doi/full/10.3402/ejpt.v7.29065

Cohen Konrad, S. (2019). Child and Family Practice: A Relational Perspective. New York: Oxford Press.

Council on Social Work Education. (2015). *Educational policy and accreditation standards.* https://cswe.org/Accreditation/Standards-and-Policies/2015-EPAS

Dong, M., Anda, R. F., Dube, S. R., Giles, W. H., & Felitti, V. J. (2003). The relationship of exposure to childhood sexual abuse to other forms of abuse, neglect, and household dysfunction during childhood. *Child Abuse & Neglect, 27*(6), 625.

Felitti, V. J., Anda, R. F., Nordenberg, D., Williamson, D. F., Spitz, A. M., Edwards, V., Koss, M. P., & Marks, J. S. (1998). Relationship of childhood abuse and household dysfunction to many of the leading causes of death in adults: The Adverse Childhood Experiences (ACE) study. *American Journal of Preventive Medicine, 14*(4), 245–258.

Fraiberg, S. (1987). The muse in the kitchen: A case study in clinical research. In L. Fraiberg (Ed.), *Selected writings of Selma Fraiberg* (pp. 65–99). The Ohio State University Press.

Fraiberg, S., Adelson, E., & Shapiro, V. (1975). Ghosts in the nursery: A psychoanalytic approach to the problems of impaired infant–mother relationships. *Journal of the American Academy of Child Psychiatry, 14*(3), 387–421.

Freud, S. (1977). *Introductory lectures on psychoanalysis.* Norton.

Goldfarb, W. (1943). Infant rearing and problem behaviour. *American Journal of Orthopsychiatry, 13,* 249–265.

Hartling, L. M. (2008). Strengthening resilience in a risky world: It's all about relationships. *Women & Therapy, 31*(2–4), 51–70.

Kondradt, M. E. (2013). Person-in-environment. Encyclopedia of *social work online.* https://oxfordre.com/socialwork/view/10.1093/acrefore/9780199975839.001.0001/acrefore-9780199975839-e-285

Mackey Andrews, S., Belisle, A., Hoffmann Frances, R., Cohen Konrad, S., Pérez, A., Redding, J., & Taglienti, R. (2017). *Maine Trauma Informed Network Planning Grant: Disseminating trauma-informed knowledge for practice: The blueprint.* John T. Gorman Foundation.

Main, M., & Solomon, J. (1990). Procedures for identifying infants as disorganized/disoriented during the Ainsworth Strange Situation. In M. T. Greenberg, D. Cicchetti, & E. M. Cummings (Eds.), *Attachment in the preschool years* (pp. 121–160). University of Chicago Press.

Martínez-Pedraza, F. de L., & Carter, A. S. (2009). Autism spectrum disorders in young children. *Child Adolescent Psychiatric Clinics of North America, 18*(3), 645–663. https://doi:10.1016/j.chc.2009.02.002

Melton, G. B. (2010). It's all about relationships! The psychology of human rights. *American Journal of Orthopsychiatry, 80*(2), 161–169.

Miller, J. B. (1976). *Toward a new psychology of women* (2nd ed.). Beacon.

Mirick, R., & Steenrod, S. (2016). Using attachment theory to guide child welfare intervention. *Child & Adolescent Social Work Journal, 33*(6), 547–557.

Mitchell, A. (2018). *Attached, addicted, & adrift: Understanding the rural opioid crisis.* Unpublished paper.

Montgomery, A. (2013). *Neurobiology essentials for clinicians: What every therapist needs to know.* Norton.

Rees, C. (2007). Childhood attachment. *British Journal of General Practice, 57*(544), 920–922.

Schore, A. N. (2001). The effects of early relational trauma on right brain development, affect regulation, and infant mental health. *Infant Mental Health Journal, 22*(1–2), 201–269.

Schore, J. R., & Schore, A. N. (2008). Modern attachment theory: The central role of affect regulation in development and treatment. *Clinical Social Work Journal, 36*(1), 9–21.

Shonkoff, J. P., Boyce, W. T., & McEwen, B. S. (2009). Neuroscience, molecular biology, and childhood roots of health disparities: Building a new framework for health promotion and disease prevention. *JAMA, 301*(21), 2252.

Shonkoff, J. P., & Phillips, D. (Eds.). (2000). *From neurons to neighborhoods: The science of early childhood development.* National Academies Press.

Siu, S., & Hogan, P. T. (1989). Public child welfare: The need for clinical social work. *Social Work, 34*(6), 423–428.

Spitz, R. A., & Wolf, K. M. (1946). Anaclitic depression: An inquiry into the genesis of psychiatric conditions in early childhood. *Psychoanalytic Study of the Child, 2*(1), 313–342.

Substance Abuse and Mental Health Services Administration. (2014). *SAMHSA's concept of trauma and guidance for a trauma-informed approach.* HHS Publication No. (SMA) 14-4884.

Thomas, A., & Chess, S. (1977). *Temperament and development.* Brunner/Mazel.

van der Horst, F. C. P., LeRoy, H. A., & van der Veer, R. (2008). "When strangers meet": John Bowlby and

Harry Harlow on attachment behavior. *Integrative Psychological and Behavioral Science, 42,* 370–388. https://doi.org/10.1007/s12124-008-9079-2

Winnicott, D. W. (1986). The theory of parent–infant relationship. In P. Buckley (Ed.), *Essential papers on object relations* (pp. 233–253). New York University Press.

Zeanah, C. H., Jr., & Zeanah, P. D. (2009). The scope of infant mental health. In C. H. Zeanah, Jr. (Ed.), *Handbook of infant mental health* (pp. 5–21). Guilford.

Fundamentals of Brief Treatment

Jan Ligon

Brief, time-limited treatment has evolved from a model previously seen as the antithesis of the proper way to help people to being viewed as a mainstream approach. Indeed, brief interventions have a long history and have been found to be useful for a wide range of problems.

History and Overview

A time-limited perspective has been dated to the work of psychiatrists with World War II veterans in the mid-1940s (Budman & Gurman, 1988), although more contemporary approaches can be traced to the work of Milton Erickson in the 1950s (de Shazer et al., 1986). Many of the theoretical approaches, assumptions, and techniques of brief work, as it is practiced today, are grounded in the endeavors of two centers—Mental Research Institute's (MRI) Brief Therapy Center in Palo Alto, California, and the Brief Family Therapy Center (BFTC) in Milwaukee, Wisconsin, which provided training and resources for 25 years (1982–2007).

MRI began in 1959 and approached working with clients from a theoretical perspective that differed from the more common approaches of that time in several ways:

1. Problems were viewed as normal occurrences in life. This stance was a radical departure from theories grounded in pathology, deficits, and dysfunction.
2. The purpose of treatment was to make changes, preferably small ones. Insight and meaning, the cornerstone of some treatment, were not the goal of working with clients.
3. The role of the clinician was to be an active and engaged participant who works with what the client brings.
4. The model explicitly limited clients to a maximum of 10 sessions based on the assumption that "a time limit on treatment has some positive influence on both therapists and patients" (Weakland et al., 1974, p. 144).

Unlike MRI, the BFTC approach did not specify a number of sessions, and the focus was on developing solutions to problems (de Shazer et al., 1986). Both MRI and BFTC note the importance of shifting how the therapist views people, their problems, and solutions.

Milton Erickson, a psychiatrist, was an important influence on those involved in the development of brief approaches to treatment.

Although he claimed to not have a theoretical basis for his work (O'Hanlon & Weiner-Davis, 1989), two of his terms are fundamental to brief work. The first is *expectancy*; simply stated, this is the social worker's belief that people and situations can change and the lives of people can be better. This concept is deceptively simple; it is one thing to understand the term and another to embrace the concept to the extent that one's practice connotes this sincere belief. Clients pick up on this very quickly, and the effective social worker truly knows that things can be better; it may not happen, but it can. The object is to set the client up for a positive self-fulfilling prophecy. The second term is *utilization*; the work is conducted with what the client brings (O'Hanlon & Weiner-Davis, 1989). In fact, clients bring vast resources with them, including their past successes, survival skills, life wisdom, and stories that are used extensively in brief treatment models (Saleebey, 2012).

Core Practice Skills and Techniques

Numerous authors have published detailed accounts of many techniques and strategies that can be employed in brief practice models (Budman & Gurman, 1988; de Shazer et al., 1986; de Shazer & Dolan, 2007; Dewan et al., 2004; Franklin, 2012; Hudson & O'Hanlon, 1991; Miller et al., 1996; O'Hanlon & Weiner-Davis, 1989; Walter & Peller, 2000; Weakland et al., 1974). There are, however, five core areas of practice that are common to most approaches: (1) the use of time, (2) the approach to problems and solutions, (3) the use of language, (4) the development and measurement of goals, and (5) the use of a strengths perspective.

Use of Time

Obviously, time is a key concern in brief work, and given that most clients complete fewer than eight sessions, the use of time is a very manageable task. It is important to not view time as only that which occurs in the therapy session. Many clients arrive early, and this time can be used to complete not only initial paperwork but also tools that can be helpful in a session, such as rapid assessment instruments to measure problems (Corcoran & Fischer, 2013). Next, clients can be asked about pretreatment change; that is, What has changed since the time the client made the appointment for the first session and the occurrence of the first session? Weiner-Davis found that when asked this question, "two-thirds of the clients noticed changes" (de Shazer et al., 1986, p. 215). By inquiring about what is now different and how the client was able to get those pretreatment changes to occur, the social worker can begin to hear information that will help uncover client and family strengths and form solutions for change.

Approach to Problems and Solutions

The therapist's approach to problems is critical. First, it is important to acknowledge and validate clients' problems. If the social worker moves immediately into developing goals and solutions without acknowledging and hearing the client's problems and issues, the client may not move forward (Hudson & O'Hanlon, 1991). However, to get stuck in a repetitive cycle of only acknowledging the problems will impede forward movement. Next, it is important to ask clients whether they have had a similar problem before and to inquire about how they handled it. This information is essential for use in further identifying client strengths, developing goals, and beginning to view potential solutions. Finally, it is important to not get bogged down in the details of the problem but, rather, to find out when the problem does not happen—that is, which are the times noted as the "exceptions to their problems" (de Shazer & Dolan, 2007, p. 4). This is particularly helpful when working with couples; it is easy to find that an entire session's time has been consumed with accusations about the other partner and pleas for understanding about how it really is in the relationship. The brief therapist cannot afford to lose precious time in this manner, and ultimately it is not helpful to the clients. Therefore, it is important to acknowledge, find the exceptions, and move on (Hudson & O'Hanlon, 1991).

Use of Language

The choice of words in brief treatment is critical; language needs to connote movement, openness, the future, and a feeling that is action-oriented. For example, the early works of MRI (Weakland et al., 1974) noted the importance of discussing *what* is happening or *how* things could be changed. The choice of the word *why*, however, seeks deeper understanding or may imply the need to delve into history; this is not helpful in brief work. O'Hanlon and Weiner-Davis (1989) note that the use of *yet* is helpful; "you haven't found the right job *yet*." Similarly, *when* can keep the dialogue moving forward, which is of key importance in developing solutions; "*when* you are working again" implies hope and a future.

Development and Measurement of Goals

At the core of brief work is the development, implementation, and measurement of goals. De Jong and Miller (1995) note that a well-formed goal is one that is important to the client, framed in the client's language, small, concrete, specific, behavioral, seeks the presence rather than the absence of something, is realistic, worthy, and a step toward an end. Clients often do not accomplish goals because the goals are more of a vision than goals. For example, "to become independent" or "to live a clean and sober life" are admirable desires for a client, but both are too big. Such goals can be overwhelming and a setup for failure;

both are only attainable through steps leading toward each goal. Therefore, if goals are carefully developed with the client, the likelihood of follow-through is improved, and clients may even accomplish more than the goal once they find that they are able to experience some initial success. Once measurable goals have been developed, it is important to look at outcomes assessment.

Like all service providers, social workers and agencies are increasingly required to document the outcomes of interventions and programs. Two common methods, self-anchored scales and rapid assessment instruments (RAIs), are helpful and simple ways to quantify outcomes. A self-anchored scale is very easy to develop by merely asking the client to rate a problem or situation by scoring it from low to high (1 to 5 or 1 to 10). RAIs for use in assessing a wide range of problems are available from a two-volume sourcebook (Corcoran & Fischer, 2013). Such measures can be repeated at the beginning and end of treatment to establish change from pretest to post-test; measures may also be taken at established increments, with the scores plotted to illustrate change over time. RAIs are particularly helpful during the assessment process to determine the severity of such problems as depression, anxiety, or substance use. Some instruments are also available at no cost from the internet, including the Zung Self-Rating Depression Scale, which can be used as a screening tool for depression (see Helpful Resources).

Strengths Perspective

Working from a strengths perspective (DeJong & Miller, 1995; Saleebey, 2012) is the opposite of the approach used by many large human services systems that are based on pathology, dysfunction, symptoms, diseases, and the assignment of diagnoses. Inherent in these approaches, such as the medical model, is an assumption that the service provider is the expert, and the patient is advised what needs to be done by the expert. Social work practice from a strengths perspective recognizes that resources can be tapped within both the social worker and the client, as well as within the community. Therefore, the relationship is approached as collaborative and avoids hierarchy; the intent is to empower the client to collaborate actively in the change process. A strengths perspective acknowledges that the client possesses knowledge, abilities, resilience, coping, and problem-solving skills that are there to be employed. Certainly, people get stuck, become overwhelmed, or experience events that render them unable to make full use of their strengths. It is important to identify and amplify strengths so that the client can go back and rediscover what has already worked for them in the past. Therefore, the role of the social worker is to facilitate the process, serve as a bridge to the client's own resources, move ahead, and seek solutions.

Usefulness and Limitations

Brief interventions have been found to be useful in working with inpatient mental health clients (Durrant et al., 2007; Lamprecht et al., 2007), for the prevention and treatment of substance abuse (Substance Abuse and Mental Health Services Administration, 2017), working with couples (Abusaidi et al., 2018; Davidson & Horvath, 1997), working with children and adolescents (Monroe & Kraus, 2005; Newsome, 2005; Tripodi et al., 2007; Valdez et al., 2013), in medical settings (Yaxi et al., 2018; Zhang et al., 2018), for gambling problems (Larimer et al., 2011; Petry et al., 2016), in suicide prevention (Lamprecht et al., 2007; Petrakis & Joubert, 2013), and working with families who have been affected by substance abuse (Ligon, 2004; Velleman et al., 2011). Indeed, clients have been found to be satisfied with only one, two, or three sessions (Ligon, 1996).

However, no single model is universal, and brief therapy is not suitable for all client situations. Although brief approaches view problems in a different manner than some other methods, they do not excuse the social worker from ethical and competent practice, including the assessment of mental status; medical concerns; and risk for suicide, homicide, child abuse, or situations that involve safety concerns. Brief approaches may not be sufficient when working with clients who have experienced trauma or emotional or sexual abuse and those who have experienced domestic or intimate partner violence.

Looking Ahead

It is common in social work for terms, interventions, and techniques to evolve and change over time. When managed care quickly moved behavioral health services to a time-limited model, the interest in brief techniques escalated. Now the use of this approach is a common method from which a social worker may choose, depending on the situation. Social workers are likely to continue to operate in environments that are tight on financial and human resources. Therefore, it will be important to continue to master the basic skills of brief practice. Used appropriately by qualified and trained social workers, brief therapy models offer an approach that has been found to be helpful to a wide range of clients across many problem areas. Brief social work practice fits well with the profession's values of being with the client, self-determination, empowerment, and respect and dignity for the value and worth of each individual.

Helpful Resources

Substance Abuse and Mental Health Services Administration. (2012). *TIP 34: Brief interventions* and brief therapies for substance abuse. https://store.samhsa.gov/product/TIP-34-Brief-Interventions-and-Brief-Therapies-for-Substance-Abuse/SMA12-3952

Substance Abuse and Mental Health Services Administration's National Helpline: 1-800-662-HELP (4357)

U.S. Department of Veterans Affairs, South Central Mental Illness Research, Education, and Clinical Center. (2008). *A provider's guide to brief cognitive behavioral therapy.* https://www.mirecc.va.gov/visn16/docs/therapists_guide_to_brief_cbtmanual.pdf

Zung Self-Rating Depression Scale (SDS): https://psychology-tools.com/test/zung-depression-scale

References

Abusaidi, E., Kianoosh, A., & Farshad, M. (2018). Effect of solution-focused brief couple therapy in improvement of communication patterns and marital intimacy in women. *Journal of Research & Health, 8*(5), 555–564.

Budman, S. H., & Gurman, A. S. (1988). *Theory and practice of brief therapy.* Guilford.

Corcoran, K., & Fischer, J. (2013). *Measures for clinical practice and research.* Oxford University Press.

Davidson, G. N. S., & Horvath, A. O. (1997). Three sessions of brief couples therapy: A clinical trial. *Journal of Family Psychotherapy, 11,* 422–435.

De Jong, P., & Miller, S. D. (1995). How to interview for client strengths. *Social Work, 6,* 729–736.

de Shazer, S., Berg, I. K., Lipchik, E., Nunnally, E., Molnar, A., Gingerich, W., & Weiner-Davis, M. (1986). Brief therapy: Focused solution development. *Family Process, 25,* 207–221.

de Shazer, S., & Dolan, Y. (2007). *More than miracles: The state of the art of solution-focused brief therapy.* Haworth.

Dewan, M. J., Steenbarger, B. N., & Greenberg, R. P. (2004). *The art and science of brief psychotherapies.* American Psychiatric Publishing.

Durrant, C., Clarke, I., Tolland, A., & Wilson, H. (2007). Designing a CBT service for an acute inpatient setting: A pilot study. *Clinical Psychology and Psychotherapy, 14,* 117–125.

Franklin, C. (2012). *Solution-focused brief therapy: A handbook of evidence-based practice.* Oxford University Press.

Hudson, P., & O'Hanlon, W. (1991). *Rewriting love stories: Brief marital therapy.* Norton.

Lamprecht, H., Laydon, C., McQuillan, C., Wiseman, S., Williams, L., Gash, A., & Reilly, J. (2007). Single-session solution-focused therapy and self-harm: A pilot study. *Journal of Psychiatric & Mental Health Nursing, 14,* 601–602.

Larimer, M. E., Neighbors, C., Lostutter, T. W., & Whiteside, U. (2011). Brief motivational feedback and cognitive behavioural interventions for prevention of disordered gambling: A randomized clinical trial. *Addiction, 107,* 1148–1158.

Ligon, J. (1996). Client satisfaction with brief therapy. *EAP Digest, 16*(5), 30–31.

Ligon, J. (2004). Six "Ss" for families affected by substance abuse: Family skills for survival and change. *Journal of Family Psychotherapy, 15,* 95–99.

Miller, S. D., Hubble, M. A., & Duncan, B. (Eds.). (1996). *Handbook of solution-focused brief therapy.* Jossey-Bass.

Monroe, B., & Kraus, F. (Eds.). (2005). *Brief interventions with bereaved children.* Oxford University Press.

Newsome, W. S. (2005). The impact of solution-focused brief therapy with at-risk junior high students. *Children and Schools, 29,* 83–90.

O'Hanlon, W., & Weiner-Davis, M. (1989). *In search of solutions: A new direction in psychotherapy.* Norton.

Petrakis, M., & Joubert, L. (2013). A social work contribution to suicide prevention through assertive brief psychotherapy and community linkage: Use of the Manchester Short Assessment of Quality of Life (MANSA). *Social Work in Health Care, 52,* 239–257.

Petry, N. M., Rash, C. J., & Alessi, S. M. (2016). A randomized controlled trial of brief interventions for problem gambling in substance abuse treatment patients. *Journal of Consulting and Clinical Psychology, 84*(10), 874–886.

Saleebey, D. (2012). *The strengths perspective in social work practice* (6th ed.). Allyn & Bacon.

Substance Abuse and Mental Health Services Administration. (2017). *Screening, brief intervention, and referral to treatment (SBIRT).* https://www.samhsa.gov/sbirt

Tripodi, S. J., Springer, D. W., & Corcoran, K. (2007). Determinants of substance abuse among incarcerated adolescents: Implications for brief treatment and crisis intervention. *Brief Treatment and Crisis Intervention, 7,* 34–39.

Valdez, A., Cepeda, A., & Parrish, D. (2013). An adapted brief strategic family therapy for gang-affiliated Mexican American adolescents. *Research on Social Work Practice, 23*(4), 383–396.

Velleman, R., Orford, J., Templeton, L., Copello, A., Patel, A., Moore, L., Macleod, J., & Godfrey, C. (2011). 12-Month follow-up after brief interventions in primary care for family members affected by the substance misuse problem of a close relative. *Addiction Research and Theory, 19*(4), 362–374.

Walter, J. L., & Peller, J. E. (2000). *Recreating brief therapy: Preferences and possibilities*. Norton.

Weakland, J. H., Fisch, R., Watzlawick, P., & Bodin, A. M. (1974). Brief therapy: Focused problem resolution. *Family Process, 13,* 141–168.

Yaxi, L., Solomon, P., Zhang, A., Franklin, Ji, Q., & Chen, Y. (2018). Efficacy of solution-focused brief therapy for distress among parents of children with congenital heart disease in China. *Health & Social Work*, 43(1), 30–40.

Zhang, A., Franklin, C., Currin-McCulloch, J., Park, S., & Kim, S. (2018). The effectiveness of strength-based, solution-focused brief therapy in medical settings: A systematic review and meta-analysis of randomized controlled trials. *Journal of Behavioral Medicine, 41*(2), 139–151.

Solution-Focused Brief Therapy

Anao Zhang and Cynthia Franklin

The late Steve de Shazer, one of the inventors of solution-focused brief therapy (SFBT), informally referred to it as a way of conversation with clients. With SFBT, the conversation is directed toward developing and achieving the client's vision of solutions through the process of co-construction (De Jong et al., 2013). SFBT practitioners intentionally use a set of techniques/skills to promote change while holding the "not-knowing" stance, which puts their clients in the position of being experts about their own lives. This intrinsic "strength-based perspective" of SFBT, from its historical development to its underlying change theories, sets it apart from many other approaches in clinical social work.

History and Development

Solution-focused brief therapy originated from systemic family therapy and was largely developed inductively through careful observation of therapy sessions, using the one-way mirror by an interdisciplinary team of colleagues, led by two social workers, Steve de Shazer and Insoo Kim Berg at the Brief Family Therapy Center in Milwaukee, Wisconsin (Franklin et al., 2012). The interdisciplinary team approach became very important to the development and practice of SFBT. The team focused on the question of what appeared to work effectively in brief therapy practice. During live therapy sessions, de Shazer, Berg, and their interdisciplinary team of colleagues attempted to set aside past assumptions about client change and pay attention to which clients seemed to be making progress and what the practitioner might be doing that was useful (de Shazer et al., 1986). During this process, they made several discoveries about therapy and invented related techniques (e.g., exceptions and miracle question), which they continued to refine through ongoing use and observation.

Clients came to the Brief Family Therapy Center with a complexity of difficulties, such as child abuse, mental illnesses, and substance use, and several clients were referred from social services and court systems. It soon became clear that the clients who made progress could discuss with the therapist clearer visions of what they wanted to be different (goals) and could identify times in their lives when problems were not occurring or were less serious (exceptions).

Consequently, more time in therapy sessions was spent on questioning techniques about changes in the future, and new assumptions about therapy and client change developed around the importance of focusing on strengths, goal formulation, exception finding, and focusing on the future. The use of language and the co-construction of goals and solutions between clients and therapists later became very important to understanding how the SFBT techniques work with clients (Franklin, Streeter, et al., 2018). Over time, researchers improved and studied the therapeutic techniques of SFBT and also developed several research studies that support the change techniques of SFBT.

SFBT Assumptions

- The "not knowing" stance with which the clinician works *with* the clients through co-construction.
- Clients are the experts about their own lives and have the solution to their life challenges.
- There are always strengths and resilience among clients, and the clinician focuses only on clients' strengths and resilience.

Solution-Focused Co-construction

Based on the previously mentioned assumptions, SFBT practitioners use core SFBT techniques (described later) to intentionally set up a therapeutic process/conversation wherein practitioners (first) *listen for* and (then) *select out* the words and phrases from the client's own language that are indications (initially, often only small hints) of some aspect of a solution, such as what a client really wants or what a past success looks like. After having listened and made the selection, the practitioner then composes a next question or other response (e.g., a paraphrase or summary) that connects to the client's exact language (i.e., frame of reference) and invites the client to build toward a clearer and more detailed version of some aspect of a solution. As the client responds from their own frame of reference, the practitioner continues to listen, select, and compose the next solution-focused question or response—one that is built on what the client has said so far in the conversation. It is through this continuing process of listening, selecting, and building on the client's language that practitioners and clients together co-construct new meanings and new possibilities for solutions.

Previous and ongoing research on the change process of SFBT (e.g., microanalysis) is adding empirical details to the understanding of how solution-focused co-construction occurs (Choi, 2019; De Jong et al., 2013; Froerer & Jordan, 2013). A systematic review and meta-summary of SFBT's change process (Franklin, Zhang, et al., 2018) found that SFBT practitioners apply "the purposeful use of language in the form of the co-construction of meaning in a unique way that is different from some other therapies" (p. 26). Specifically, SFBT practitioners use questions and responses (paraphrases and summaries) that are not neutral or objective but contain embedded SFBT assumptions about clients and their situations. In answering the questions and accepting SFBT practitioners' paraphrases and summaries, clients are co-constructing new common ground (i.e., shared understandings) about themselves and (potential solutions for) their situations. Through such non-neutral, and thus directional, conversational exchanges with the client, SFBT practitioners lead from one step behind, and this metaphor means that therapists ask questions to set in motion a dialogue in which clients actively participate in solution building as persons who possess abilities and resources that they can use to improve their life challenges.

The Change Theory of SFBT

Co-construction is the core clinical process of SFBT, and recently researchers have proposed SFBT's possible change theory explaining how the co-construction process creates therapeutic growth. Note that it is still debated whether SFBT is atheoretical or not, especially given the significant role of clinical observation in its development (Franklin et al., 2012). However, evaluating and understanding the change theory of any psychotherapy are critical to effectively train clinicians and to deliver the intervention, including SFBT (Wampold, 2010). Among other efforts (e.g., Blundo et al., 2014; Kelch & Demmitt, 2010), Kim and Franklin (2015) argued that SFBT practitioners invoke clients' positive emotions such as hope through SFBT's co-construction process to create more openness and efficacy toward change. Grounded in Fredrickson's (2004) broaden-and-build theory of positive emotions, SFBT practitioners use various techniques, such as the miracle question or the exception question, to invoke clients' positive emotion. With these positive emotions, clients are expected to also broaden their thought-action repertoires, which consequently undoes their lingering negative emotions, increases resiliency, and promotes more creative problem-solving and positive coping behaviors. Although SFBT developers and therapists have not shown agreement on a key SFBT change theory, there is accumulating evidence that supports the use of SFBT techniques to invoke positive emotion and coping during the co-construction process with clients as potentially one of the effective practices of SFBT (e.g., Franklin, Zhang, et al., 2018; Wheeler, 2018).

SFBT Techniques

SFBT practitioners use a variety of techniques to co-construct solutions with clients and to invoke positive emotion to create therapeutic progress. Some of these techniques are SFBT-specific, meaning these techniques are created by SFBT developers and are primarily used among SFBT practitioners. Other techniques are common across different therapeutic approaches, but SFBT practitioners utilize these common techniques differently.

SFBT-Specific Techniques

(Future-Oriented) Goal-Formulation Question

After the client briefly describes a problem, practitioners begin to co-construct goal setting by asking the following:

- When this challenge becomes less of one, what will be different?
- What would have to be different by the end of our session for you so that you would walk out of the session and think "that session was useful and not a waste of time"?

Miracle Question

The miracle question is the best known of SFBT's goal formulation questions. In addition, it is a signature SFBT technique that facilitates positive emotion among clients by asking the them to envision a preferred future. The miracle question can be asked in many ways, depending on a clinician's clinical style and the client's characteristics; however, its overall structure reads similar to the following:

> I have a question for you, and this may take some imagination. [brief pause] So, after today's session, you go home and finish the rest of your day as usual and then go to bed. Suppose while you are sleeping tonight, a miracle happens. The miracle is that the problem that has brought you here today is solved—just like that! Only you don't know it because you're sleeping. So, when you wake up

next morning, what is the first thing you will notice that is different and will tell you: Wow! Things are really different, a miracle must have happened.

The miracle is an opener for a series of follow-up questions formulated around the client's beginning answer to what will be different when the miracle happens. These follow-ups use who, what, when, and where questions to get details about the client's preferred future. ("Why" questions are not asked because they have not been proven useful in promoting client change.) For example, to the depressed client who starts out by saying the first difference they will notice is "feeling better," the practitioner continues by asking: "So, when you are feeling better, who will be the first to notice?" "When might [that person] notice?" "What will [that person] do when they notice you feeling better?" "What will you do then?" And so forth.

Exception Question

As a strength-based intervention approach, SFBT practitioners often use exception questions to discover and amplify client strengths and resources. SFBT practitioners use exception questions to intentionally solicit clients' past successes and inner resources that have already worked for them. Exception questions are most useful for building solution. The following are examples of exception questions:

- Are there times when you are even a little bit "less discouraged" (client's words)?
- Are parts of the miracle you described to me happening already?

Once the client identifies an exception, the interviewer follows up with several who, what, when, and where questions for details to further build solutions.

What's Better Question

Many other approaches begin second and subsequent sessions of therapy with a review of assigned suggestions or the client's estimate of progress. In SFBT, practitioners simply ask "What's better?" or "What's been working so far?" This question is sometimes used as another form of exception question that most readily elicits mention of successes that occurred since the last session. When given time to think and answer, most clients can identify something better and positive, which the practitioner then invites the client to amplify through additional questions.

General Techniques (That Are Used Differently by SFBT Practitioners)

Scaling Question

Scaling is an effective way to help clients express complex, intuitive observations about their past experiences and future possibilities in concrete terms. In addition to this common utility of scaling questions across approaches, SFBT practitioners use scaling questions for the following purposes: (1) to positively reinforce the client's existing strengths and (2) to explicitly identify and amplify the client's coping skills and inner resources. For example, after inviting a client to rate their depression state on a scale of 0 (absolutely the worst depression) to 10 (not depressed at all), the SFBT practitioner will follow up any non-zero score by asking "What's making you give yourself a score of 1.5 rather than 0? Would you tell me more about that 1.5 score of strengths?" If a client responds with a score of 0, an SFBT practitioner will not focus on the 0 score (which may occur in other approaches) but instead ask, "Even with a 0 score, you still manage to come to today's session. I am curious to hear more on what's supporting you to come to the session?"

Coping Question

The coping question is a form of questioning technique used when clients seem overwhelmed and discouraged beyond the point of trying. It can also be used flexibly in conjunction with other SFBT techniques. The following are examples:

- I am amazed! With all that has happened to you, I don't know how you make it. How do you do it?
- Ah, so you do it by reminding yourself that "my children need me." You must love your children very much! So, when you remind yourself that "my children need me," how does that help you?

SFBT Treatment Manual

Clinicians, researchers, and SFBT trainers throughout the world have proposed different versions of SFBT protocols (e.g., De Jong & Berg, 2013; de Shazer et al., 2007; Franklin et al., 2012). To our knowledge, the Research Committee at the Solution Focused Brief Therapy Association (SFBTA) in the United States holds the most elaborative version of SFBT's treatment manual (Bavelas et al., 2013). Although existing versions of an SFBT treatment manual and/or protocol vary slightly, they are highly consistent regarding the overall between- and within-session structure.

For all sessions, SFBT practitioners should consistently keep a positive, collegial, and solution-focused stance and should focus on searching for previous solutions and exceptions. SFBT practitioners use language intentionally (i.e., conversations, questions, and responses) so that they tend to make no interpretations of clients' language. Instead, SFBT practitioners often use clients' own words (frame of reference) to form conversations with clients and invite them to come up with (pieces or ingredients of) solutions to their current challenges. The

SFBTA treatment manual provides a detailed descriptive on the specific use of SFBT techniques within the larger session structure (Bavelas et al., 2013).

Research Evidence Supporting SFBT

As SFBT continues to gain popularity across practice settings, outcome studies evaluating SFBT's effectiveness have made significant progress during the past 30 years. Considering that SFBT is still a relatively young approach compared with other well-established interventions, such as cognitive–behavioral therapy, SFBT has received satisfactory support from the research community, evidenced by several systematic review and/or meta-analysis studies. Stams and colleagues (2006) and Kim (2008) are among the first to report meta-analytic studies of SFBT. Notably, the two studies revealed overall small-to-moderate treatment effect sizes with equivalent outcomes to other psychotherapeutic approaches over a lower average number of sessions. Meta-analytic review studies have also reported SFBT's effectiveness across various settings, including schools (Franklin et al., 2009; Kim & Franklin, 2009), families (Bond et al., 2013), and hospital settings (Zhang et al., 2018).

Furthermore, studies have supported SFBT's effectiveness across various populations, especially among Chinese (Gong & Hsu, 2017; Kim et al., 2015) and Latino clients (Gonzalez Suitt et al., 2016). For most published SFBT meta-analyses, although evidence remains preliminary with regard to the effectiveness of SFBT for externalizing and social relational outcomes, consistent and strong support has been established for SFBT's treatment effect for internalizing disorders such as depression and anxiety (Schmit et al., 2016). Considering all the available empirical evidence, it is reasonable to consider SFBT as an emerging empirically supported, strengths-based intervention approach.

SFBT for Social Work Practitioners

Many inherent characteristics of SFBT make this approach suitable for social work practitioners. First, SFBT is nondiagnostic and is not problem specific. It is very functional in its approach to building solutions and focuses on behaviors that need to be changed and social interactions that need to be altered for solutions to happen. SFBT is an approach to having conversations with clients about change built around their definitions of what they want different in their lives and drawing on their past successes and other relevant resources. Second, the not-knowing stance and no-assumption principle comport well with core professional values of social work, such as respecting human dignity, advocating for clients, building on strengths, and maximizing self-determination. Finally, SFBT practitioners often refrain from interpreting client's meaning but, rather, use the client's own frame of reference and ask questions in ways that return the choice to clients. Like most therapies, SFBT does not specifically focus on structural societal changes that are often associated with supporting equity and inclusion; rather, SFBT helps therapists show an empathetic respect for clients within their social and cultural contexts. The deep respect for a client's words and meanings may explain why SFBT has been successfully used across many cultural groups.

Helpful Resources

European Brief Therapy Association: http://blog.ebta.nu

Institute for Solution-Focused Therapy: https://solutionfocused.net

Solution Focused Brief Therapy Association: http://www.sfbta.org

References

Bavelas, J., De Jong, P., Franklin, C., Froerer, A., Gingerich, W., Kim, J., Korman, H., Langer, S., Lee, M. Y., McCollum, E. E., Jordan, S. S., & Trepper, T. S. (2013). *Solution focused therapy treatment manual for working with individuals.* https://irp-cdn.multiscreensite.com/f39d2222/files/uploaded/Treatment%20Manual%20Final%2C%20Update%203-17-18.pdf

Blundo, R., Bolton, K. W., & Hall, J. C. (2014). Hope: Research and theory in relation to solution-focused practice and training. *International Journal of Solution-Focused Practices, 2*(2), 52–62.

Bond, C., Woods, K., Humphrey, N., Symes, W., & Green, L. (2013). Practitioner review: The effectiveness of solution focused brief therapy with children and families: A systematic and critical evaluation of the literature from 1990–2010. *Journal of Child Psychology and Psychiatry, 54*(7), 707–723.

Choi, J. J. (2019). A microanalytic case study of the utilization of "solution-focused problem talk" in solution-focused brief therapy. *American Journal of Family Therapy, 47*(4), 244–260.

De Jong, P., Bavelas, J. B., & Korman, H. (2013). An introduction to using microanalysis to observe co-construction in psychotherapy. *Journal of Systemic Therapies, 32*(3), 17–30.

De Jong, P., & Berg, I. K. (2013). *Interviewing for solutions* (4th ed.). Brooks/Cole.

de Shazer, S., Berg, I. K., Lipchik, E., Nunnaly, E., Molnar, A., Gingerich, W., & Weiner-Davis, M. (1986). Brief therapy: Focused solution development. *Family Process, 25,* 207–221.

de Shazer, S., Dolan, Y. M., Korman, H., Trepper, T. S., McCollum, E. E., & Berg, I. K. (2007). *More than miracles: The state of the art of solution focused therapy.* Haworth.

Franklin, C., Kim, J. S., & Tripodi, S. J. (2009). A meta-analysis of published school social work practice studies: 1980–2007. *Research on Social Work Practice, 19*(6), 667–677.

Franklin, C., Streeter, C. L., Webb, L., & Guz, S. (2018). *Solution focused brief therapy in alternative schools: Ensuring student success and dropout prevention.* Routledge.

Franklin, C., Trepper, T. S., McCollum, E. E., & Gingerich, W. J. (Eds.). (2012). *Solution-focused brief therapy: A handbook of evidence-based practice.* Oxford University Press.

Franklin, C., Zhang, A., Froerer, A., & Johnson, S. (2018). Solution focused brief therapy: A systematic review and meta-summary of process research. *Journal of Marital and Family Therapy, 43*(1), 16–30.

Fredrickson, B. L. (2004). The broaden-and-build theory of positive emotions. *Philosophical Transactions of the Royal Society of London. Series B: Biological Sciences, 359*(1449), 1367–1377.

Froerer, A., & Jordan, S. S. (2013). Identifying solution-building formulations through microanalysis. *Journal of Systemic Therapies, 32*, 61–75.

Gong, H., & Hsu, W. (2017). The effectiveness of solution-focused group therapy in ethnic Chinese school settings: A meta-analysis. *International Journal of Group Psychotherapy, 67*(3), 383–409.

Gonzalez Suitt, K., Franklin, C., & Kim, J. (2016). Solution-focused brief therapy with Latinos: A systematic review. *Journal of Ethnic & Cultural Diversity in Social Work, 25*(1), 50–67.

Kelch, B. P., & Demmitt, A. (2010). Incorporating the stages of change model in solution focused brief therapy with non-substance abusing families: A novel and integrative approach. *The Family Journal, 18*(2), 184–188.

Kim, J. S. (2008). Examining the effectiveness of solution-focused brief therapy: A meta-analysis using random effects modeling. *Research on Social Work Practice, 18*, 107–116.

Kim, J. S., & Franklin, C. (2009). Solution-focused brief therapy in schools: A review of the outcome literature. *Children and Youth Services Review, 31*(4), 464–470.

Kim, J. S., & Franklin, C. (2015). Understanding emotional change in solution-focused brief therapy: Facilitating positive emotions. *Best Practices in Mental Health, 11*(1), 25–41.

Kim, J. S., Franklin, C., Zhang, Y., Liu, X., Qu, Y., & Chen, H. (2015). Solution-focused brief therapy in China: A meta-analysis. *Journal of Ethnic & Cultural Diversity in Social Work, 24*(3), 187–201.

Schmit, E. L., Schmit, M. K., & Lenz, A. S. (2016). Meta-analysis of solution-focused brief therapy for treating symptoms of internalizing disorders. *Counseling Outcome Research and Evaluation, 7*(1), 21–39.

Stams, G. J., Dekovic, M., Buist, K., & de Vries, L. (2006). Effectiviteit van oplossingsgerichte korte therapie: een meta-analyse [Efficacy of solution focused brief therapy: A meta-analysis]. *Gedragstherapie, 39*, 81–95.

Wampold, B. E. (2010). *The basics of psychotherapy: An introduction to theory and practice (theories of psychotherapy)*. American Psychological Association.

Wheeler, J. (2018). Ways of knowing: Extending the possibilities for solution focused practice. In K. Manakandan, K. R. Santhosh, J. Koorankot, & P. K. Raheemudheen, (Eds.), *Solution focused practices in behavioural sciences*, (pp. 12–21). University of Calicut. http://asfpindia.org/wp-content/uploads/2018/05/Proceedings-ICSFP2016.pdf#page=12

Zhang, A., Franklin, C., Currin-McCulloch, J., Park, S., & Kim, J. (2018). The effectiveness of strength-based, solution-focused brief therapy in medical settings: A systematic review and meta-analysis of randomized controlled trials. *Journal of Behavioral Medicine, 41*(2), 139–151.

Fundamental Principles of Behavioral Social Work

Denise E. Bronson

Traditional behavioral methods, derived from the experimental analysis of behavior and learning theory in psychology, were introduced to social work in the mid-1960s (Thomas, 1967) and quickly became one of the most widely used interventions in social work practice (Bronson & Thyer, 2001; Gambrill, 1995; Thyer, 2012). Behavior therapy, or behavior modification, is a broad umbrella term used to cover various strategies that examine the antecedent and consequential conditions that support and maintain problematic behavior, as well as how to change those conditions to promote desirable behavior (Gambrill, 1977). Whereas the first generation of behavioral methods focused on changing overt behavior, subsequent generations of behavioral methods have expanded the role of maladaptive cognitive patterns in treatment (e.g., cognitive–behavioral therapy) and incorporated concepts such as mindfulness, emotions, acceptance, and commitment into behavioral interventions (Dobson & Dozois, 2019; Gonzalez-Prendes et al., 2019; Hayes et al., 2004; Hayes & Hofmann, 2018).

Although behavioral interventions have evolved since being introduced to social work practice, all behaviorally based methods share the following characteristics that distinguish them from other treatment approaches:

- Behavioral methods based on extensive empirical work in basic and applied settings and ongoing empirical evaluation of service are an integral part of behavioral practice.
- Behavioral interventions are highly individualized and address the unique learning history of each client. An individualized behavioral assessment (functional behavioral assessment) is therefore extremely important and focuses on identifying the environment in which the problem behavior occurs (antecedents), the behavior itself (response), and what happens afterwards (consequences).
- Principles of learning are applied to understand how behaviors are acquired and maintained. This occurs at all levels—individual, family, group, societal, and cultural.
- Behavioral interventions are time-limited and focus on the presenting problems.

- Identified outcomes are clinically and socially meaningful to the client and significant others.
- Maintenance and generalization of changes are not assumed to occur automatically once the desired goals are obtained. Instead, the conditions for ensuring maintenance and generalization are carefully assessed and become an important consideration in developing a successful intervention.

Within these parameters, contemporary behavior therapy has been used to address a variety of issues in diverse social work settings. Systematic reviews and other outcome studies have demonstrated the effectiveness of behavioral strategies to address individual issues (e.g., anxiety disorders and phobias, anger management, depression, academic performance, employment skills, and substance abuse), family concerns (e.g., family violence, parent training, communication, and decision-making), and community/social needs (e.g., ecological behavior, seat belt usage, littering, and recycling). Systematic reviews examining the effectiveness of behavioral interventions are readily available from numerous websites and professional journals listed in the Helpful Resources section. With all the developments in behaviorally based interventions, it is easy to lose sight of the fundamental principles that are the foundation of all behavioral methods. This chapter uses two case examples to review these principles and illustrate the use of behavior therapy in social work.

Case Example 1

Sally Adams developed a fear of driving over or under bridges following the collapse of an interstate highway bridge in Minneapolis. She lives in a city with many bridges, and this phobia has escalated to the point that she is unable to drive without planning long, time-consuming routes to her destination. This has interfered with her ability to get to work on time, and she is in danger of losing her job.

Case Example 2

John and Mary Brown's 4-year-old daughter Megan has become unmanageable. Bedtime is especially problematic, and it can take up to 3 hours to get Megan into bed. Megan pleads with her parents to stay up later and then throws temper tantrums when she is told that she must go to bed. This has started to cause problems between her parents, who argue over how to handle their daughter.

Key Concepts in Behavioral Social Work

Several key concepts and technical terms are important in behavioral assessment and intervention (Cooper et al., 2019; Martin & Pear, 2019; Spiegler, 2015). Behaviorists generally classify behavior into two broad categories— respondent behaviors and operant behaviors. *Respondent behaviors* are elicited by stimuli in the environment and involve the autonomic nervous system (i.e., blood pressure, heart rate, rapid breathing, or changes in the glandular system). Cognitions can be part of the antecedents that trigger a respondent response. For example, Sally Adams' fear of bridges in Case Example 1 triggers several physiological reactions (rapid heart rate, heightened alertness, sweating, etc.) whenever she approaches a bridge. *Operant behaviors*, on the other hand, are those that "operate" on the environment and are controlled by the environmental consequences that follow. Most overt, observable behaviors fall into this category, including language. For example, in Case Example 2, if Megan is praised by a parent for going to bed on time, she is more likely to go to bed on time in the future; conversely, if her parents attend to her temper tantrums, it is likely that the tantrums will increase in frequency or intensity. Furthermore, parents are more likely to use praise in the future if it increases the probability that their child will comply with parental requests. Historically, it was believed that respondent behaviors were controlled by antecedent stimuli and that operant behaviors were controlled by consequential stimuli. Although this distinction is still useful, recent research has demonstrated considerable overlap in the processes described by these concepts. In addition, genetic and biological factors will set limits on the range and type of respondent and operant behaviors that are possible.

Respondent and operant behaviors are learned in two ways—respondent conditioning and operant conditioning. In *respondent conditioning*, a neutral stimulus [conditioned stimulus (CS)] is repeatedly paired with an eliciting stimulus [unconditioned stimulus (UCS)]. Eventually, the neutral stimulus will also elicit a similar response, which is now referred to as the conditioned response (CR). For example, the sudden bright light of a flashbulb (UCS) elicits an eye blink (unconditioned response). Unfortunately, the camera (CS), through its repeated pairing with the flash (UCS), can also begin to elicit an eye blink (CR), often resulting in family pictures in which the subject's eyes are closed in "anticipation" of the flash. Or in Sally Adams' case, repeatedly viewing the images of the interstate bridge collapse in Minneapolis elicited emotional reactions that were associated with a previously neutral stimulus, namely bridges. In this way, phobias are acquired through respondent conditioning when neutral stimuli begin to elicit physiological or fear responses.

Operant conditioning refers to the process of learning in which the future likelihood of the behavior will either increase or decrease depending on the *contingencies* associated with that behavior. Contingencies refer to both the *consequences* that follow the behavior

and the *antecedents* that precede the behavior indicating the type of consequence that is likely. For example, telling a joke at a party will probably be followed by a friend's laughter. If the same joke is told to the same friend during a lecture, however, the friend might respond with "sshhhh" rather than laughter. In this case, the antecedent conditions associated with a party signal that a positive response (a positive reinforcer) will follow telling a joke, whereas the same behavior in class will receive a negative reaction (a punisher). Our jokester soon learns to *discriminate* the conditions under which jokes will be reinforced. Similarly, in Case Example 2, it is important to conduct a functional analysis to determine the antecedents (e.g., parental request to go to bed), the behavior (e.g., Megan's temper tantrums), and the consequences that follow Megan's outbursts, which might be increasing the future probability of those tantrums (e.g., parents acquiesce and let her stay up or parental attention).

Behaviorists refer to four types of consequences—positive reinforcers, negative reinforcers, positive punishers, and negative punishers. Any consequence that increases the future probability of the behavior it follows is a *reinforcer*. Positive reinforcers are stimuli that are presented contingent on the occurrence of the behavior (e.g., receiving an allowance for household chores). The termination or removal of an aversive stimulus (negative reinforcement) will also increase the behavior it follows (e.g., putting on a sweater when you feel cold). Conversely, any consequence that decreases the future probability of the behavior it follows is a *punisher*. Positive punishment is the presentation of an aversive stimulus contingent on a behavior (e.g., saying "no" to a child who asks for cookies before dinner), whereas negative punishment is the removal of a reinforcer contingent on a behavior (e.g., turning off the television when children fight about which program to watch). What serves as reinforcers and punishers is highly individualized and varies according to one's learning history, biological and genetic characteristics, and the setting. The only way to determine which stimuli are reinforcers and punishers is to observe the effect of those stimuli on future behavior.

The *schedule of reinforcement* is another important concept that refers to the frequency with which a behavior is reinforced. Often when new behaviors are being acquired, they are reinforced after every occurrence; this is called a continuous reinforcement schedule. Usually in the natural environment, however, behaviors are reinforced only intermittently depending on the number of times the behavior is performed (ratio schedules of reinforcement), the amount of time that passes (interval schedules of reinforcement), or the rate of responding (differential reinforcement of high or low rates). Intermittent schedules of reinforcement are most resistant to periods of *extinction* when reinforcement that was previously available is withdrawn.

Finally, operant behaviors are often preceded by antecedent stimuli (*discriminative stimuli*) that cue which behavior will be reinforced in a particular setting. Through a process of discrimination training in which a behavior is consistently reinforced only in the presence of specific stimuli, individuals learn which behaviors are likely to be reinforced in each setting. To illustrate, consider Megan in Case Example 2. When Megan's request to stay up later is made to her mother, permission is usually given; when the request is made to the father, it is usually refused. Megan learns quickly to discriminate those situations (i.e., the presence of mother) in which requests to stay up late (behavior) are likely to be reinforced (permission granted) from those situations in which the behavior will not be reinforced.

Engaging in Behavioral Social Work

Behavioral Assessment

Assessment in behavioral social work is an extremely important process that is closely linked to decisions about which intervention strategy to use. During assessment (also referred to as a *functional analysis*), the social worker collects information to determine the antecedents and consequences of the problem behavior, specifies the desired outcomes (the *target behavior*), and selects the most appropriate therapeutic technique. Clients and significant others are an important part of this process. A summary of the steps used by behavioral social workers during assessment is presented in Table 27.1.

Intervention Strategies

Following the assessment and collection of baseline data, behavioral social workers (1) specify the desired target behavior, antecedents, and consequences; (2) identify a data collection strategy for monitoring changes in the target behavior; and (3) develop an intervention plan. Maintenance and generalization of changes, once they are obtained, are not assumed to occur naturally, and strategies for ensuring lasting change are included in the intervention planning.

Generally, behavioral interventions can be categorized according to whether the primary activity focuses on modifying the stimulus conditions preceding the behavior, developing the behavior itself, or altering the consequences of the behavior. In many cases, one or more strategies from these three categories are employed simultaneously to address the target problem. Table 27.2 presents examples of commonly used intervention techniques for modifying stimulus conditions (antecedents). These strategies are used when the assessment shows that the client is able to perform the desired behavior but

TABLE 27.1 Steps in Behavioral Assessment

Step	Activities
1. Identify the problem areas and priorities.	Obtain a list of problem areas from the client(s) using interviews, observation, and standardized assessment questionnaires. Determine priorities for service. Select the problem(s) to be addressed and the desired outcome (target behavior).
2. Specify the target behaviors.	Describe the problem and target behaviors in observable and measurable terms. Determine whether the problem is one of behavioral excesses or behavioral deficits. Determine whether the problem is primarily operant or respondent in nature. Begin collecting pretreatment (baseline) data, if possible, using direct observation, client self-reports on internal states or emotions (using rating scales or standardized questionnaires), and physiological measures.
3. Assess the controlling conditions (antecedents and consequences).	Collect information about the environmental antecedents that precede the problem behavior. Collect information about the consequences that immediately follow the problem and target behavior. Determine whether the problem is primarily one of: Poor stimulus control (i.e., lack of cues for the appropriate behavior, poor discrimination training, or the presence of stimuli that elicit inappropriate respondent and emotional behaviors) Behavioral deficits (i.e., client lacks skills to perform the desired behavior) Inadequate or inappropriate consequences (i.e., client has the necessary skills but reinforcers for the desired behavior are missing, the reinforcers are conflicting or delayed, or the reinforcers consist of inappropriate personal reinforcers that cause harm to others or are culturally disapproved)

unable to discriminate the appropriate time/place for the behavior or that environmental stimuli elicit problematic emotional states (e.g., phobias).

In some cases, the assessment indicates that the client has not learned the desired behavior and is therefore unable to perform it. The behavioral social worker will select an

TABLE 27.2 Interventions for Modifying Stimulus Conditions

Discrimination training	Procedure in which the desired behavior is reinforced in the presence of appropriate stimuli and not reinforced in the presence of inappropriate stimuli to teach when/where to perform target behavior. Fading can be used to gradually change dimensions of the stimulus to teach difficult discrimination.
Prompting	Cues to remind or guide client to engage in the desired behavior; can be combined with fading to eventually remove prompt
Respondent extinction	Process of breaking the connection between the conditioned stimulus (CS) and the unconditioned stimulus (UCS) by repeatedly presenting the CS without the UCS until it no longer elicits the conditioned response
Systematic desensitization	Method used to treat phobias by gradually exposing client to increasingly anxiety-producing stimuli while engaging in responses incompatible with the anxiety (usually relaxation)

TABLE 27.3 Interventions for Developing New Behaviors

Shaping	Teaching a new behavior through gradually reinforcing increasingly complex or precise approximations to the final desired behavior
Chaining	Procedure used when the final behavior consists of several steps needed to complete the action (e.g., dressing). Chaining can begin at the beginning or end of the sequence to train each of the stimulus–response sequences needed for the desired behavior.
Modeling	Presenting a live or filmed demonstration of the desired behavior in which the client learns which behaviors are desired and the contingencies under which they occur

intervention designed to teach or train a new behavior. Table 27.3 presents examples of some of the commonly used strategies.

The assessment may also indicate that the desired behavior does not occur because the consequences of the behavior are faulty. For example, the environment might not reinforce the desired behavior or could be reinforcing an incompatible, inappropriate behavior. Interventions to modify the consequential contingencies can be grouped into two types of strategies—those that focus on increasing the desired behavior and those that focus on decreasing an undesirable behavior. Frequently, behavioral social workers will use techniques from both groups simultaneously. Table 27.4 presents examples of both types of strategies designed to alter the consequences following a behavior. The effectiveness of interventions to modify the consequences of

a behavior will depend on several factors, including the immediacy of the consequence, the salience of the reinforcer or punisher, and the schedule of reinforcement. The behavioral social worker will assess each of these factors and address them in deciding how to intervene.

The Future of Behavioral Social Work

Although the previously discussed fundamental principles and methods still guide behavioral social work practice, the concepts have expanded and now encompass a variety of intervention methods that are also widely used by social workers. These interventions have been referred to as "second-wave" and "third-wave" behavioral methods (Hayes & Hofmann, 2018). Although a detailed description of these interventions is

TABLE 27.4 Interventions for Modifying Response Consequences

Increasing Desired Behavior	*Positive & Negative Reinforcement*	Presenting a reinforcing stimulus or removing an aversive stimulus, respectively, immediately following the performance of the desired behavior
	Escape & Avoidance Conditioning	Similar to negative reinforcement in that an aversive stimulus is removed (escape) or prevented (avoidance) after the occurrence of a response
Decreasing Undesired Behavior	*Operant Extinction*	Process in which a reinforcer is withheld following an operant response that had previously produced that reinforcer
	Positive & Negative Punishment	Presenting an aversive stimulus or removing a reinforcer immediately following the performance of the undesirable behavior
	Differential Reinforcement	Manipulating the schedule of reinforcement to decrease behavior by reinforcing low rates of responding, zero responding, or incompatible responding

TABLE 27.5 Examples of Current Behaviorally Based Interventions

Intervention	Description
Cognitive–behavioral therapy	Combines social learning theory and cognitive appraisal theory to guide assessment and intervention
Rational emotive behavior therapy	Attempts to change rigid, irrational beliefs to bring about behavior change
Dialectical behavior therapy	Developed as a treatment for borderline personality disorder, depression, self-harm, and suicidality
Acceptance and commitment training	Based on a theory of language and relational frame theory to use acceptance, mindfulness, values, and commitment to change to bring about change

beyond the scope of this chapter, Table 27.5 provides a listing of some of the most widely used behaviorally based approaches (Dobson & Dozois, 2019; Hayes et al., 2004; Rizvi & King, 2019).

The efficacy and effectiveness of traditional behavioral methods, as well as later behaviorally based treatment models, are strongly supported by systematic reviews that examine the use of these techniques to address various presenting problems and populations. Easy access to systematic reviews of the research literature in electronic, online databases makes these treatment methods more accessible to practitioners and is consistent with advances in evidence-based practice for social work. In addition, the behavioral approach offers empirically tested, change-focused, client-centered, and environmentally based social work interventions that are highly consistent with the values and objectives of social work practice (Thyer, 2012).

Helpful Resources

Organization	Website	Focus
American Psychological Association	https://www.div12.org/psychological-treatments/treatments	Listing of empirically supported treatments
California Evidence-Based Clearinghouse for Child Welfare	https://www.cebc4cw.org	Tool for identifying, selecting, and implementing evidence-based child welfare practices
Cambridge Center for Behavioral Studies	http://www.behavior.org	Online tutorials and publications
Campbell Collaboration	http://www.campbellcollaboration.org	Library of relevant systematic reviews
Cochrane Collaboration	http://www.cochrane.org	Library of relevant systematic reviews

Journal	Focus
Behavior Analysis in Practice	Science-based, best-practice information relevant to service delivery in behavior analysis
Behavior Analysis: Research and Practice	Experimental and translational research, and applications of behavioral analysis, to improve human behavior in all contexts
Behavior and Social Issues	Applying science of behavior to social justice, human rights, and environmental sustainability
Behavior Modification	Research, reports, and reviews on applied behavior modification
Behavior Therapy	Application of the behavioral and cognitive sciences to the assessment and treatment of psychopathology and related clinical problems

Organization	Website	Focus
Journal of Applied Behavior Analysis		Research about applications of the experimental analysis of behavior to problems of social importance
Research on Social Work Practice		Empirical research about assessment methods and outcomes of social work practice

References

Bronson, D. E., & Thyer, B. A. (2001). Behavioral social work: Where has it been and where is it going? *The Behavior Analyst, 2*(3), 192–195.

Cooper, J. O., Heron, T. E., & Heward, W. L. (2019). *Applied behavior analysis* (3rd ed.). Pearson.

Dobson, K. S., & Dozois, D. J. A. (Eds.). (2019). *Handbook of cognitive–behavioral therapies.* Guilford.

Gambrill, E. (1977). *Behavior modification: Handbook of assessment, intervention, and evaluation.* Jossey-Bass.

Gambrill, E. (1995). Behavioral social work: Past, present, and future. *Research on Social Work Practice, 5*(4), 460–484.

Gonzalez-Prendes, A., Hicks, L., Mathews, T., & Domke, D. (2018). Cognitive–behavioral therapy. *Oxford Bibliographies.* doi:10.1093/obo/9780195389678-0149

Hayes, S. C., & Hofmann, S. G. (Eds.). (2018). *Process-based CBT: The science and core clinical competencies of cognitive behavioral therapy.* New Harbinger.

Hayes, S. C., Strosahl, K. D., Bunting, K., Twohig, M., & Wilson, K. G. (2004). What is acceptance and commitment therapy? In S. C. Hayes & K. D. Strosahl (Eds.), *A practical guide to acceptance and commitment therapy* (pp. 1–30). Springer. doi:10.1007/978-0-387-23369-7_1

Martin, G., & Pear, J. (2019). *Behavior modification: What it is and how to do it* (11th ed.). Routledge.

Rizvi, S. L., & King, A. M. (2019). Dialectical behavior therapy: A comprehensive cognitive–behavioral treatment for borderline personality disorder, emotion dysregulation, and difficult-to-treat behaviors. In K. S. Dobson & D. J. A. Dozois (Eds.), *Handbook of cognitive–behavioral therapies* (pp. 297–317). Guilford.

Spiegler, M. D. (2015). *Contemporary behavior therapy* (6th ed.). Wadsworth.

Thomas, E. J. (1967). *The socio-behavioral approach and applications to social work.* Council on Social Work Education.

Thyer, B. (2012). Behavioral social work practice. *Oxford Bibliographies.* doi:10.1093/OBO/9780195389678-0040

Cognitive–Behavioral Therapy

Theresa J. Early and M. Elizabeth Vonk

Cognitive–behavioral therapy (CBT) is a widely used psychotherapy with ample empirical support of its efficacy and effectiveness for a number of mental health conditions and problem areas. CBT is based on the interplay among thoughts, feelings, and behavior. People often believe that something that happens (an event) causes them to feel a certain way, but in reality, what they think about themselves and about the event intervenes to bring about emotional and behavioral responses.

The term CBT refers to a number of related therapies that focus on cognition as the mediator of emotional distress and behavioral dysfunction. As the name implies, CBT combines the theoretical and practical approaches of behavior therapy, dating to the 1950s, and cognitive therapy, dating to the 1960s work of Beck and Ellis (Ledley et al., 2018). Behavior therapy, as developed in the United States from the work of Skinner, redefined various mental illnesses as behavioral problems that had arisen from a type of learning called conditioning or reinforcement. Treatment from a behavioral perspective is directed at relearning. In contrast, treatment from a cognitive perspective is directed at identifying and changing thoughts, attributions, and beliefs

that affect emotional, physiological, and behavioral responses to an experience (Ledley et al., 2018).

This chapter presents a concise description of the practice of CBT, illustrated by a case study of its application; resources for further study; and a brief overview of computer-assisted CBT and mobile apps. We begin with an introduction to our client.

Case Example

John, a 38-year-old European American man, sought counseling at his wife's urging. John was experiencing significant anxiety about his work and was moody and withdrawn at home. John described having been in the office supply business for 15 years and having worked his way up to a recent promotion to a management position. Along with new responsibilities, John has new worries that he will not be able to handle his new role. He is "extremely worried" that he will fail and lose his job. He now thinks he "can't do anything right" at work. He is particularly worried about the monthly and quarterly reports he must complete. Despite John's best efforts, his supervisor has caught minor errors on two occasions. John worries that he will lose his job and become unable to support his family if this continues.

At home, John's anxiety is interfering in his relationship with his wife, who has told him that she is irritated by his absence while he works long hours. She has also complained that when he is home, he is "off in his own world fretting." John wishes his wife would be less critical about his need to work longer hours and spend a lot of time thinking about work. He also worries, however, that he may be "a lousy husband and father"—just like he always feared. He describes a history of anxiety, particularly about work matters, with the current level of anxiety higher than at any previous time. Exploration of early history reveals that John was raised in an intact family in the rural Midwest. He describes his mother as "loving, but always trying to please my father." He describes his father as "mean-spirited and never satisfied with anything, no matter how much I tried." John would like to be less worried and to feel better about his relationship with his wife.

Basic Concepts of Cognitive–Behavioral Therapy

The cognitive model at its core consists of thoughts and beliefs giving rise to emotional and behavioral responses to an event or situation. A change in one of these systems (thoughts/beliefs/emotion/behavior) brings about change in the other systems. Three elements of cognitive activity are important in addressing emotional and behavioral problems: the actual content of thoughts, or "automatic thoughts"; core beliefs; and assumptions, attitudes, or rules. We are most aware of the content of automatic thoughts or the thoughts and images that come into our minds as we experience events. The other levels of thoughts and beliefs, more hidden from our awareness, are the rules or assumptions through which we interpret our experiences. For example, upon receiving critical feedback at work, John may automatically think, "I can't handle this situation." If he were able to identify a rule related to the situation, it might be "I must be perfect at everything I do."

The second area of cognitive focus, core beliefs, refers to global, durable beliefs about the self and the world that are formed through early life experiences. Core beliefs are maintained through attending to information that supports the belief while disregarding information that is contrary to it (Beck, 2011). As a child, John experienced intense criticism from his father and seems to have formed a core belief that "I am totally inadequate." As an adult, he seems to ignore his career successes and instead focuses on the few instances at work when he has made a mistake or was unsure of himself. At home, he focuses on his wife's current irritation and discounts a 14-year history of marriage that has been "mostly good for both of us."

The third element of cognition involves assumptions and rules of processing information; when these are maladaptive, they are referred to as cognitive distortions. Many types of distortions exist (Beck, 2011; Wright, et al., 2017); a few of these are applied to John in the following examples:

- Catastrophizing: "If my boss criticizes a piece of my work, I will lose my job, be unable to support my family, my wife will leave me, and I will end up homeless."
- Emotional reasoning: "I feel horribly anxious about this report I just completed, so that proves I must have done a terrible job on it."
- Minimization: "I got the employee-of-the-year award purely from luck; it has nothing to do with how well I performed."

Many emotional and behavioral disorders have been characterized by specific cognitive content, schema, and information-processing styles (Dienes et al., 2011). As previously mentioned, people with anxiety disorders perceive themselves as inadequate and the world as dangerous and threatening. Regarding information processing, those with anxiety pay greater attention to anxiety-provoking stimuli than they do to neutral stimuli. In panic disorder, the attentional bias is toward bodily sensation, with sufferers more acutely aware of their heart rates compared with other people. People with social phobia, on the other hand, attend to and make negative evaluations of their own social behavior.

Depression also has been specified in terms of cognitive content and processing styles. People who are depressed have a negative view of the self, the world, and the future (Beck, 2011). For example, someone who is depressed may think, "I never do anything right; people are never there for me; things will never get better." Core beliefs are most often related to perceptions of self-defect, and attention is directed to experiences that focus on loss and failure (Dienes et al., 2011).

Practitioners of CBT employ understanding of the elements of cognition and their relation to specific disorders, as described previously, in a therapeutic relationship with well-specified roles for both the practitioner and the client. The hallmark of the therapeutic relationship in CBT is collaboration, and roles of both the client and the practitioner are active. The role of the practitioner most closely resembles that of a supportive teacher or guide who holds expertise in cognitive and behavioral therapeutic methods, as well as possesses interpersonal skills (Ledley et al., 2018). The practitioner helps the client learn to identify, examine, and alter maladaptive thoughts and beliefs and increase coping skills. Although the practitioner lends methodological expertise, the client is the source of information and expertise about their own idiosyncratic beliefs and assumptions. The client and practitioner thus work together to define goals, set agendas for sessions, and uncover and explore attitudes and beliefs that are significant to the client's well-being. Successful replacement of maladaptive cognitions depends on collaboration between client and practitioner, for the client can provide the most lasting and effective cognitive replacements.

Applications of Cognitive–Behavioral Therapy

The most prominent models of CBT are Beck's cognitive therapy (Beck, 2011), Meichenbaum's cognitive behavior therapy (Meichenbaum, 1994), and Ellis' rational emotive behavior therapy (Ellis, 1996). Although there are differences among them related to, for instance, the therapist's level of direction and confrontation, all of the models share basic elements. All rely on identifying the content of cognitions, including assumptions, beliefs, expectations, self-talk, or attributions. The cognitions are then examined to determine their current effects on the client's emotions and behavior. Some models also include exploration of the development of the cognitions to promote self-understanding. This is followed with use of techniques that encourage the client to adopt alternative and more adaptive cognitions. The replacement cognitions, in turn, produce positive affective and behavioral changes. Other similarities of the models include the use of behavioral techniques, the time-limited nature of the interventions, and the educative component of treatment.

It is useful to consider the application of CBT in steps. At each step, a great number of specific techniques are available. Only a few are reviewed here due to space limitations.

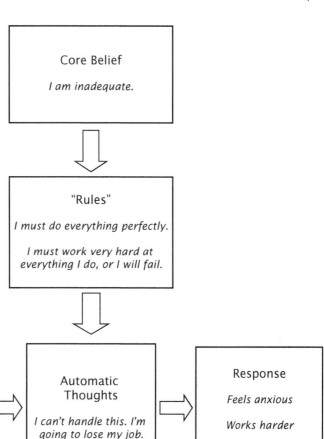

FIGURE 28.1 Cognitive formulation for John.

Assessment

As in many clinical social work assessment processes, cognitive–behavioral assessments may result in a case formulation that includes psychiatric diagnosis; definition of the client's problem in terms of duration, frequency, intensity, and situational circumstances; description of client's strengths; and treatment plan. Cognitive analysis of a client's problem, however, is unique to cognitive–behavioral assessments. Assessment and case formulation include many of the previously mentioned items, in addition to a prioritized problem list and working hypothesis that encompass a cognitive analysis of the problems (Ledley et al., 2018). Problems are described very briefly and are accompanied by the client's related thoughts, emotions, and behaviors. The working hypothesis, unique to each client, proposes specific thoughts and underlying beliefs that have been precipitated by the client's current experiences. Formulations may also include an examination of the origin of the maladaptive cognitions and information processing style in the client's early life. The working hypothesis is then directly related to treatment planning. As an example, we have created a cognitive conceptualization for John, shown in Figure 28.1.

Teaching the ABC Model to the Client

Concurrent with assessment, the cognitive–behavioral therapist educates the client about the relationship of thoughts, emotions, and behaviors. Leahy (2017) suggests contrasting the client's usual way of describing the relationship of thoughts, emotions, and behaviors with the alternative ABC model. For most people, the usual way to think about it is that an activating event (A) causes an emotional or behavioral consequence (C). For example, John states that because he received criticism on his report (A), he is feeling anxious (C). The ABC model proposes that in actuality, a thought or image representing a belief or attitude (B) intervenes between A and C. Using the same example, following the criticism (A), John may think that he will lose his job (B), resulting in anxiety (C). Clients need to become very familiar with the model through presentation of and practice with personal illustrations.

Teaching the Client to Identify Cognitions

Once the client understands the ABC model, the therapist helps the client learn to identify thoughts and beliefs. Clients may find that many types of cognitions are relevant for analysis, including those related to expectations, self-efficacy, self-concept, attention, selective memory, attribution, evaluations, self-instruction, hidden directives, and explanatory style (McMullin, 2000). A great variety of useful techniques for the purpose of identifying cognitions are described by McMullin (2000), DeRubeis et al. (2010), and Leahy (2017). The daily thought record is a written method involving a form made up of columns within which clients record activating events (column A), corresponding emotional reactions (column C), and immediate thoughts related to the events (column B). In the case example, John would be taught to identify and record on the form an anxiety-provoking situation from the previous week, such as hearing from his boss that a report needed correction. Next, he would be asked to identify his feelings when the situation occurred. Then he would be

prompted to remember what went through his mind at the moment his boss spoke with him. In this instance, he would record his thought, "I can't handle this" in between the situation and the anxious feelings. Another method, the downward arrow technique, is a verbal way to discover the underlying meaning of conscious thoughts through the use of questions such as "What would it mean to you if the [thought] were true?" Through the use of the downward arrow technique, the client may discover a core belief. John might provide an answer such as "It would mean I'm incapable." People generally are unaware of their core beliefs that are, nonetheless, very fundamental to the way they feel and behave.

Teaching the Client to Examine and Replace the Maladaptive Cognitions

After identifying thoughts and beliefs, the client is ready to begin examining evidence for and against the cognitions. In addition, the client is encouraged to replace maladaptive cognitions with more realistic or positive ones. Replacement requires frequent repetition and rehearsal of the new cognitions. Again, McMullin (2000), DeRubeis et al. (2010), and Leahy (2017) provide a wealth of information about specific techniques, a few of which are briefly describe here.

Many of the techniques are verbal, relying on shifts in language to modify cognitions. In one technique, the client is taught to identify maladaptive thoughts as particular cognitive distortions. Cognitive distortions are maladaptive thinking styles that commonly occur during highly aroused affective states, making logical thinking difficult. Identifying the use of a distortion allows for the possibility of substituting more rational thinking. Thought stopping, a behavioral means to draw attention to the need for substitution, might involve snapping an elastic band. Another technique involves asking questions to evaluate the truth, logic, or function of beliefs (Beck, 2011; Leahy, 2017). Such questions include the following:

- What is the evidence for and against the belief?
- What are alternative interpretations of the event or situation?
- What are the advantages and disadvantages of keeping this belief?

Imagery and visualization are also used to promote cognitive change. For example, clients may be encouraged to visualize coping effectively in difficult situations or visualize an idealized future to provide insight into current goals. McMullin (2000) suggests that imagery techniques are particularly useful to encourage perceptual shifts, whereas verbal techniques help facilitate change in more specific thoughts and beliefs. A combination of the two types of techniques is often useful.

Other Techniques

Cognitive–behavioral therapy incorporates a wide variety of behavioral techniques, according to clients' needs. These include relaxation training, assertion training, problem-solving, activity scheduling, and desensitization (Beck, 2011; Wright et al., 2017). More recently, mindfulness has been incorporated into cognitive–behavioral therapies, such as mindfulness-based stress reduction (Stahl et al., 2010), dialectical behavior therapy (Koerner & Linehan, 2012), and acceptance and commitment therapy (Hayes et al., 2012). Most likely, both relaxation and mindfulness training would be useful for John.

- Relaxation training involves teaching the client to relax muscles systematically and to slow breathing. The client learns to discriminate between tension and relaxation. Through practice, the relaxation response can be activated easily.

- Assertion training provides clients with interpersonal skills that allow for appropriate self-expression. Often, these skills are taught and practiced in small groups.
- Problem-solving involves teaching the client to solve personal problems through a process of specifying the problem and then devising, selecting, implementing, and evaluating a solution.
- Activity scheduling allows clients to plan for activities that will provide pleasure, socialization, or another identified need during the time between contacts with the practitioner.
- Desensitization provides clients with graduated exposure to anxiety-provoking objects or situations while engaged in behaviors that compete with anxiety, such as relaxation. The exposure may be imaginary or real.
- Mindfulness training allows clients to purposefully attend to the experience of the present moment without judging or fighting against what is occurring. Such awareness is thought to reduce emotional reactivity and suffering.

In addition, cognitive–behavioral therapists often assign homework to their clients for the purpose of extending learning beyond the therapy session. Homework assignments vary according to the idiosyncratic needs of the client and generally are designed collaboratively. One common assignment is the use of a form such as the daily thought record.

Strengths of Cognitive–Behavioral Therapy

Various features of CBT fit well with social work. The collaborative nature of the therapeutic relationship is consistent with the social work value of self-determination. In addition, the client's active involvement in the change process is consistent with an empowerment approach. CBT's use within an integrative framework that allows for specification of techniques to match individuals' needs is consistent with the ideal of individualizing treatment. More recently, those who have proposed integrative therapy models have examined the role of the client's idiosyncratic meaning in CBT, noting a close kinship with constructive models of therapy (Dienes et al., 2011).

Many characteristics of CBT lend themselves to the demands of current practice settings. The structure of CBT and the extensive description of its methods in many sources make it an accessible therapy for both novice and experienced practitioners. Because the methods of therapy require initial and ongoing recording of thoughts and behaviors, mechanisms for evaluation are built in, lending support to the use of CBT by clinicians with interest in or need to document the outcomes of their work with clients. Because part of the practice of CBT is teaching the client the intervention, CBT is useful for relapse prevention. In addition, CBT targets specific problems, thus lending itself to a short-term approach, which is consistent with the desires of both many clients and their third-party payers. Another feature of CBT that is attractive to managed care entities is the well-supported efficacy of the approach, particularly for the treatment of depression and anxiety (Wright et al., 2017).

Mounting evidence attests to the versatility of CBT. Specific cognitive–behavioral treatments have been designed for a variety of disorders, including some that have been considered complex or difficult to treat, such as borderline personality disorder. Depression, generalized anxiety disorder, post-traumatic stress disorder, substance misuse, eating disorders, grief and bereavement, and personality disorders are among those conditions for which CBT interventions have been developed (Wright et al., 2017).

Computer-Assisted Cognitive–Behavioral Therapy and Mobile Apps

Computer-assisted CBT (CCBT) is a rapidly developing innovation in delivering treatment for emotional disorders such as depression and anxiety. Effectiveness is supported by multiple randomized clinical trials for a number of programs (Wright et al., 2019). A therapist often is involved in the treatment as well, through email, in person, or via phone. Not surprisingly, more frequent and more direct (e.g., in person or phone) therapist support was associated with better outcomes (Wright et al., 2019). Little evidence is available for the efficacy of mobile apps, but carefully selected apps may be useful for augmenting treatment through providing access to coping strategies (see the Helpful Resources section). Researchers who study CCBT and mobile apps recommend a number of steps practitioners should take before recommending use to a client, including trying the CCBT program or app yourself first; evaluating the program/app for its implementation of CBT; and selecting programs/apps that provide confidentiality and security of private information, including health information (Wright et al., 2019).

The Future

As we look toward the future, CBT promises to remain vital to the treatment of emotional and behavioral disorders. In fact, it appears that the use of CBT will continue to expand as more is learned about specifying treatments and integrating additional techniques for particular problem areas and populations. At the same time, more treatment providers will apply wide-ranging techniques from CBT into integrative treatment models that include newer interventions such as mindfulness training. The versatility of this treatment will enable its continued use in the changing environment of treatment settings, telehealth, computer-assisted treatment, and mobile apps. Finally, the fact that CBT has been used successfully across a variety of cultural groups from China to Sweden (Dienes et al., 2011) demonstrates that it will be able to serve the rapidly changing needs of the increasingly diverse population of people who are served by social workers.

Helpful Resources

Websites

American Institute for Cognitive Therapy: http://www.cognitivetherapynyc.com

Beck Institute for Cognitive Behavior Therapy: http://beckinstitute.org

National Association of Cognitive–Behavioral Therapists: http://www.nacbt.org

The Linehan Institute: http://marieinstitute.org

UMass Memorial Health Center for Mindfulness: http://www.umassmed.edu/cfm/index.aspx

Apps

Day to Day and Thought Challenger, two apps from the suite Intellicare, Northwestern University: https://intellicare.cbits.northwestern.edu

PTSD Coach, U.S. Department of Veterans Affairs: https://mobile.va.gov/app/ptsd-coach

References

Beck, J. S. (2011). *Cognitive therapy: Basics and beyond* (2nd ed.). Guilford.

DeRubeis, R. J., Tang, T. Z., Webb, C. A., & Beck, A. T. (2010). Cognitive therapy. In K. S. Dobson (Ed.), *Handbook of cognitive–behavioral therapies* (3rd ed., pp. 277–316). Guilford.

Dienes, K. A., Torres-Harding, S., Reinecke, M. A., Freeman, A., & Sauer, A. (2011). Cognitive therapy. In S. B. Messer & A. S. Gurman (Eds.), *Essential psychotherapies* (3rd ed., pp. 143–183). Guilford.

Ellis, A. (1996). *Better, deeper, and more enduring brief therapy: The rational emotive behavior therapy approach.* Brunner/Mazel.

Hayes, S. C., Strosahl, K. D., & Wilson, K. G. (2012). *Acceptance and commitment therapy: The process and practice of mindful change* (2nd ed.). Guilford.

Koerner, K., & Linehan, M. (2012). *Doing dialectical behavior therapy: A practical guide.* Guilford.

Leahy, R. L. (2017). *Cognitive therapy techniques: A practitioner's guide* (2nd ed.). Guilford.

Ledley, D. R., Marx, B. P., & Heimberg, R. G. (2018). *Making cognitive-behavioral therapy work* (3rd ed.). Guilford.

McMullin, R. E. (2000). *The new handbook of cognitive therapy techniques.* Norton.

Meichenbaum, D. (1994). *A clinical handbook/practical therapist manual: For assessing and treating adults with post-traumatic stress disorder.* Institute Press.

Stahl, B., Goldstein, E., Kabat-Zinn, J., & Santorelli, S. (2010). *A mindfulness-based stress reduction workbook.* New Harbinger.

Wright, J. H., Brown, G. K., Thase, M. E., & Basco, M. R. (2017). *Learning cognitive-behavioral therapy* (2nd ed.). American Psychiatric Publishing.

Wright, J. H., Mishkind, M., Eells, T. D., & Chan, S. R. (2019). Computer-assisted cognitive–behavior therapy and mobile apps for depression and anxiety. *Current Psychiatry Reports, 21,* article No. 62. https://doi.org/10.1007/s11920-019-1031-2

Task-Centered Practice

Anne E. Fortune, Blanca Ramos, and William J. Reid

Task-centered practice is a short-term, problem-solving approach to social work practice (Epstein & Brown, 2001; Marsh & Doel, 2005; Reid, 1992, 2000; Reid & Epstein, 1972). It was developed by Laura Epstein (1914–1996) and William J. Reid (1928–2003) using an empirical research and development (R & D) approach that tested interventions, assessed results, refined the interventions, tested them again, and so on, repeating the cycle with new clients and new problems (Reid, 1997; see also Fortune, 2012). In an era that emphasizes evidence-based practice, it is one of the few "homegrown" intervention models developed through systematic research within social work.

The task-centered model has been used worldwide in most types of social work settings, as a stand-alone, as part of a bundle of services, or integrated into multilevel, multisystems generalist practice (Fortune et al., 2010; Hepworth et al., 2016; Jagt, 2008; Tolson et al., 1994; Trotter, 2015). It has been used with voluntary and involuntary clients; with individuals, groups, and families; as a method of case management; as a system for agency management; as a model for clinical supervision; and as an approach to community work (Caspi & Reid, 2002; Holosko, 2018). Its emphasis on client-defined problems, client decision-making, and client action in the environment is compatible with strengths-based and empowerment approaches. It was developed empirically with disenfranchised and disadvantaged clients and in many cultural settings. Thus, it is a flexible approach to practice with many applications.

Task-centered practice is simultaneously highly individualized—client-identified problems and action to resolve them—and structured, with distinguishable stages over time (beginning, middle, and end), an agenda for each interview, and overall strategies for resolving common problems.

Basic Characteristics and Principles

A combination of key characteristics defines the task-centered model: a focus on client problems, problem-solving actions, integrative theoretical stance, planned brevity, a collaborative relationship, an empirical orientation, and structured interventions.

Focus on Client Problems

Task-centered practice is highly individualized in that the focus of service is on specific problems that clients explicitly acknowledge as being of concern to them. These problems in living usually involve personal and interpersonal difficulties, but contextual and environmental change may also be a focus.

Problem-Solving Actions (Tasks)

Change in problems is brought about primarily through problem-solving actions (tasks) undertaken by clients outside of the session in their own environment. The primary function of the treatment session is to lay the groundwork for such actions through systematic steps and structure. In addition, tasks by practitioner and others provide a means of effecting environmental change in the client's interest.

Integrative Theoretical Stance

The task-centered model developed initially from psychosocial casework and now draws selectively on theories and methods from compatible approaches—for example, problem-solving, cognitive–behavioral, family structural, and interpersonal approaches. It also provides a framework and strategies that can be used with other approaches. For example, a core intervention—the task planning and implementation sequence—can be used with any intervention model.

Planned Brevity

Service is generally planned short term by design (6–12 weekly sessions within a 4-month period). The short time limits capitalize on the "goal gradient effect," where individuals are motivated by deadlines and clear goals. Extensions beyond these limits are possible.

Collaborative Relationship

Relationships between clients and practitioners are both caring and collaborative. The practitioner avoids hidden goals and agendas. Extensive client input to develop intervention strategies makes tasks more effective and develops the clients' problem-solving abilities. Good practitioner interpersonal and relationship skills enhance task-centered practice, but the primary medium of change is client action to resolve problems.

Empirical Orientation

Within task-centered practice, methods and theories tested and supported by empirical research are preferred. Hypotheses and concepts about the client system are grounded in case data. Speculative theorizing about the client's problems and behavior is avoided. Assessment, process, and outcome data are systematically collected. Numerous studies, including eight controlled experiments, have been used to test and improve the model (Fortune et al., 2010; Reid, 1997).

Structured Intervention

Within the model framework of individualized client-defined problems and tasks, task-centered sessions and intervention processes are structured. Each session has a specific agenda that guides the client and practitioner work. In addition, some intervention processes are semi-standardized; for example, the task implementation sequence includes steps appropriate for any client or practitioner task. Finally, because tasks are usually interim steps to a broader goal, task strategies are a series of tasks or a meta-approach to deal with specific common problems, such as depression, bullying, or social isolation (Naleppa & Reid, 2003; Reid, 2000).

Structured Activities at Three Stages of Task-Centered Practice

Sessions in task-centered practice are structured, although the content of each session is individualized for clients and their problems.

I. Initial phase (sessions 1 and 2). To engage clients and develop consensus on future work, the initial session(s) includes the following:

1. Discussion of reasons for referral, especially with nonvoluntary client(s) (Rooney & Mirick, 2018; Trotter, 2015).

2. Exploration and assessment of client-acknowledged problems in living that will be the focus of future work.

3. Negotiation and agreement on a service contract, including problems and goals to be addressed, explanation of treatment methods, and agreement on duration.

4. Development and implementation of initial tasks (see phase II.3).

II. Middle phase (each middle-phase session). Each session in the middle phase of task-centered practice includes the following activities, listed in logical order. Whereas task and problem review should occur early to give focus to the session, other activities are often interwoven with each other.

1. *Problem and task review.* Problem status and accomplishment of tasks developed in previous sessions are reviewed in each session to determine progress. The task review includes how the task has gone and whether it affected the problem. It is the basis for most other discussion and intervention.

2. *Identification and resolution of obstacles to task accomplishment.* If the client has or may have difficulty with the task, internal and external obstacles are reviewed and plans made to resolve them. If the obstacles cannot be resolved, an alternative task is developed to overcome or avoid the obstacle.

3. *Task planning and implementation sequence.* The task planning and implementation sequence is central to completing tasks and resolving problems (Fortune, 2012). The order of activities varies for each client and situation.

- *Task selection.* Clients are more likely to agree to and implement tasks if they are involved in planning the tasks. Tasks are not "assigned" unilaterally by the practitioner. The practitioner instead elicits and builds on the client's ideas. Practitioners, caregivers, and other service providers may also take on tasks.

- *Task agreement.* The client's explicit agreement on task(s) is important.

- *Planning specifics of implementation.* Tasks are customized and fleshed out in collaboration between practitioner and clients. Normally, the task is implemented prior to the next session. The task plan should have a high probability of success because successful performance creates a sense of mastery, which can augment problem-solving efforts. For the task plan to work, the client must have a clear notion of what is to be done.

- *Establishing incentives and rationale.* To help establish motivation, the practitioner and client develop a rationale for carrying out the task. The practitioner reinforces the client's realistic perception of benefits or points out positive consequences.

- *Identifying and resolving anticipated obstacles.* An important practitioner function in task planning is to help the client identify potential obstacles to the task and to shape plans so as to avoid or minimize these obstacles. The emphasis on identifying and resolving obstacles—both before and after they are encountered—is generally absent in other social work approaches (Rooney, 2010).

- *Guided practice, rehearsal.* To improve client skills or confidence, the social worker may model possible task behavior or ask clients to rehearse what they are going to say or do. Guided practice is the performance of the actual (as opposed to simulated) task behavior by the client during the interview. Guided practice can also be extended to real-life situations, such as accompanying a fearful client to the doctor (guided practice) and asking questions of medical staff (modeling).
- *Summarizing and recording the task plan.* Summaries of task plans allow review and clarification of the plan and enhance the expectation that the task will be carried out and that the client's efforts will be reviewed. Writing tasks down is also useful, especially when tasks are complex.

4. *Implementation of tasks between sessions.* Clients, practitioners, and others carry out tasks in the environment. The completion (or not) of these tasks and their results on the problems become the topics of the review that starts the next interview in middle sessions.

III. Terminal phase (final or last two sessions).

1. *Assessment of current status problems and overall problem situation.*
2. *Identification of successful problem-solving strategies used by client(s).* Emphasis is on establishing client's success in problem-solving and using strategies in similar situations.
3. *Discussion of other ways to maintain client gains.* Maintenance may include "fail-safe planning" (what to do if a problem crops up), self-reinforcement,

practicing new behaviors in additional situations (generalization), etc.

4. *Discussion of what can be done about remaining problems*, including possible task strategies.
5. *Acknowledge reactions to ending.* Because ending is expected, reactions to termination are more likely to be ambivalent—mixed satisfaction and regret—than negative. These reactions are acknowledged as normal and healthy but not as reasons to prolong treatment. In many circumstances, a termination ritual helps bring closure—for example, a memento of the relationship, a review of clients' accomplishments, etc.
6. *Making decisions about extensions.* Decisions are jointly made by client and practitioner. Extensions are usually time-limited and focused on particular problems or goals. The critical consideration is what can be accomplished by extending service. Often, cases that show little progress by the 12th visit will show no more progress by the 20th.

Task Strategies

Task strategies are *sequences* of tasks that have empirical support for resolving particular problems (Naleppa & Reid, 2003; Reid, 1992). First developed by cumulation of evidence during task-centered R & D research process, task strategies can also draw on current evidence-based practice for specific problems. Plans generated from task strategies are handled like other task plans: The client must agree to the strategy and to each task at the appropriate time, and planning tasks takes into account the individual details of each client's situation—for example, the context for implementation, obstacles, possible collaborations, etc.

Task-Centered Practice with Families

Task-centered practice is easily adapted to work with families, in constellations from single-parent to multigenerational and nonkin families. The work may be framed within a specific family theory—for example, intervening to re-align the generational balance in a family. Or there may be no additional systems concepts used to define the problems and interventions. Either way, work must take into account multiple participants and the family dynamics. For example, all family members define and agree to target problems, which may be shared (mother and father disagree about household expenditures) or interrelated (father believes he has no authority, son believes father is over-bearing and punitive) or framed within a particular theoretical framework (the women are repeating a pattern of abdicating responsibility for child-rearing). Although there may be individual problems (daughter needs to improve her school record), problems should be balanced among family participants and should not represent one part of the family scape-goating another part. In families, even more than other situations, client participation and commitment to problem resolution hinge on accurate identification of meaningful target problems.

Similarly, tasks may evolve and be completed differently in families. "Session tasks" such as negotiating family rules, building marital skills, or practicing new ways of talking to one another are conducted during sessions as part of a strategy that progresses to environmental tasks such as implementing rules or holding breakfast conversations. Tasks, too, are better accepted if they are balanced; each individual has a fair "task load," and an individual's tasks may benefit others as well as the individual—for example, reciprocal tasks to help out on each other's schoolwork or a shared "date night" during which a husband and wife create time together to stimulate caring feelings for each other.

Task-Centered Practice in Small Groups

The task-centered model is readily used in group treatment of individual (or family) problems (Fortune, 1985). Small groups—usually from four to eight persons—are formed around problems that are similar, such as school failure or issues in caregiving. Members specify problems and undertake tasks related to them, as in individual work. Sessions follow the same structured agenda outlined previously. However, in group treatment, members assist one another in formulating problems and in work on tasks, including task planning and review. Group members may act as "buddies" between meetings.

Group norms are shaped to encourage task-centered work—for example, the expectation that clients will take action and reinforcement of successes. Group processes are used to enhance intervention. For example, when members have similar problems, group cohesion can occur more quickly and members have multiple role models and ideas for task strategies. Reviewing task progress in pairs makes each individual accountable for their own progress as well as aides others' progress.

Considerations for Work with Organizations and Other Contexts

The task-centered model has been adapted for use in clinical and educational supervision, case management, organizational management, and community organization. In these uses, the problems in living are replaced by other types of problems or goals—for example, by skills to be mastered by a supervisee, by an organization's unclarity about its mission, or by a community's need to develop stronger norms against violence. Once a problem/goal is negotiated among participants, the task-centered problem-solving steps are used to develop strategies and tasks to achieve the goals. Tasks are implemented, their accomplishment is evaluated, and the situation is reviewed systematically as in individual task-centered practice. Time limits are also used to increase motivation and participant action. The primary differences from individual practice lie in the dynamics of the unit. For example, in supervision, the employee is (we hope) motivated to improve competence, whereas the supervisor holds authority to enforce organizational rules to protect clients; the employee's choice of skill development may be constrained by rules about legally acceptable interventions. In interdisciplinary case management teams, disagreement about values and approaches from the different disciplines may inadvertently overshadow the client's perspective. In organizational management, problems may be readily identified, but getting the key organizational players to collaborate may require more effort than generating task strategies.

Summary

Task-centered practice is one of the few empirical clinical practice models developed in social work. It has demonstrated its applicability to a wide range of problems, clients, modalities, and worldviews. It can be used like an all-purpose tool, adapted to the immediate need or embedded in other interventions. It now appears so well-embedded in social work that one critic suggested that it is "simply good social work practice . . . [whose major contribution is] a sturdy yet flexible practice technology that contains enough rigor to be consistently effective but also enough space to be adapted creatively to an incredible number of social work practice contexts" (Kelly, 2008, p. 199).

Case Example

Ana, 66 years old, was recently diagnosed with mild depression. A year ago, she emigrated from Chile, where she was heavily involved in her church and had an active social life. She lives with her daughter, Liz, and a teenage granddaughter, Sofia, with whom she rarely interacts. Ana resents Liz, blaming her for "forcing" her to leave behind her family and friends whom she fears she will never see again. This has strained the relationship to the point where Ana prefers not to ask Liz for help and support when needed. Ana describes her current life as 'lonely,' "meaningless," and "unhappy." She longs to be back in Chile and cries "all the time."

Initial Phase

Ana and the practitioner identified two target problems: her loneliness and limited support system. They tentatively agreed on three intervention strategies: expanding her social network, increasing contact with family in Chile, and improving her relationships with Sofia and Liz. They contracted to meet weekly for 3 months.

The practitioner mentioned a church near Ana's house that offered Spanish Mass and educational and social activities daily for Latino seniors. For an initial task, Ana suggested with little enthusiasm she would go to the church and give it a try. With prompting, she agreed to ask Liz to drive her to the church on Liz's way to work and to pick her up after work. Ana would go to the church at least three times a week.

Middle Phase

At the beginning of the next session, Ana reviewed her task: As agreed, she went to the church three times. She shared with some enthusiasm how she met other Latina immigrants to whom she could relate and found spiritual comfort attending Mass and talking to the priest. Ana was not sure she could continue working on this task because it was difficult getting to the church. She struggled waking up so early and worried about making Liz late to work.

When prompted for ways to overcome this obstacle, Ana recalled befriending Tina, who goes to the church daily and lives a block away. She agreed to ask Tina if she could stop by on her way to the church so they could go together. Ana would discuss this idea with Liz, emphasizing her own concern about making Liz late for work.

The practitioner suggested another task: to ask Sofia to show her how to use email to communicate with her loved ones in Chile. This task was also intended to facilitate closer interactions with Sofia.

During each session in the middle phase, Ana and the practitioner reviewed task progress, problem status, and obstacles to task accomplishment. Ana continues going to the church, sometimes more than three times a week, and participates actively. She walks to the church with Tina, and during bad weather Liz gives them both a ride. Even with Sofia's help, electronic communication is challenging and frustrating, but Ana is highly motivated.

Terminal Phase

In the last few sessions, the practitioner reminded Ana how many sessions remained. At first, Ana wanted to continue, but she agreed that their work was almost completed and they would end when they had initially planned.

In the final session, Ana and the practitioner reviewed the status of the target problems. Ana did not feel as lonely: She talked enthusiastically about the positive changes in her life since she began attending the church. She has new friends, participates in meaningful activities, and benefits spiritually. Ana still misses her family and life in Chile and cries from time to time. She continues trying

to use email and, as a result, spends more time bonding with Sofia.

Ana and Liz have grown closer. They often go grocery shopping after taking Tina home, and they prepare meals together. Ana enjoys teaching Liz the "old dishes," while Liz likes hunting ingredients in the bodega. Ana now views Liz as a supportive, caring daughter who had good intentions inviting her to live with her in this country.

The practitioner pointed out Ana's strengths, including her tremendous problem-solving abilities and resilience. They discussed how Ana could use these personal resources to continue working on her current and new problems. Ana plans to go to the church more often and even get there on her own when needed. She and the practitioner rehearsed what Ana would do if she found herself feeling lonely, crying when longing for her family and friends in Chile, or needing nurturing from Liz and Sofia.

Ana thanked the practitioner profusely, stating with sadness she would greatly miss their weekly sessions. The practitioner praised Ana for her accomplishments and acknowledged the sad nature of this ending and transition. Ana timidly, with teary eyes, gave the practitioner a small vase from Chile. This was graciously accepted and proudly placed on the practitioner's desk. They both contemplated it and gave each other warm smiles before Ana left the room.

References

Caspi, J., & Reid, W. J. (2002). *Educational supervision in social work: A task-centered model for field instruction and staff development.* Columbia University Press.

Epstein, L., & Brown, L. B. (2001). *Brief treatment and a new look at the task-centered approach* (4th ed.). Pearson.

Fortune, A. E. (Ed.). (1985). *Task-centered practice with families and groups.* Springer.

Fortune, A. E. (2012). Development of the task-centered model. In T. L Rzepnicki, S. G. McCracken,

& H. E. Briggs (Eds.), *From task-centered social work to evidence-based and integrative practice: Reflections on history and implementation* (pp. 15–39). Lyceum.

Fortune, A. E., McCallion, P., & Briar-Lawson, K. (Eds.). (2010). *Social work practice research for the 21st century* (pp. 181–249). Columbia University Press.

Hepworth, D. H., Rooney, R. H., Dewberry-Rooney, G., & Strom-Gottfried, K. (2016). *Direct social work practice: Theory and skills* (10th ed.). Brooks/Cole.

Holosko, M. J. (2018). *Social work case management: Case studies from the frontlines*. Sage.

Jagt, L. J. (2008). Van Richmond naar Reid: Bronnen en ontwikkeling van taakgerichte. Bohn Stafleu van Logham.

Kelly, M. (2008). Task-centered practice. In T. Mizrahi & L. Davis (Eds.), *Encyclopedia of social work* (20th ed., pp. 197–199). NASW Press/Oxford University Press.

Marsh, P., & Doel, M. (2005). *The task-centred book*. Routledge, with Communitycare.

Naleppa, M. J., & Reid, W. J. (2003). *Gerontological social work: A task-centered approach*. Columbia University Press.

Reid, W. J. (1992). *Task strategies: An empirical approach to social work practice*. Columbia University Press.

Reid, W. J. (1997). Research on task-centered practice. *Social Work Research, 21,* 132–137.

Reid, W. J. (2000). *The task planner*. Columbia University Press.

Reid, W. J., & Epstein, L. (1972). *Task-centered casework*. Columbia University Press.

Rooney, R. H. (2010). Task-centered practice in the United States. In A. E. Fortune, P. McCallion, & K. Briar-Lawson (Eds.), *Social work practice research for the 21st century* (pp. 195–202). Columbia University Press.

Rooney, R. H., & Mirick, R. G. (Eds.). (2018). *Strategies for work with involuntary clients* (3rd ed.). Columbia University Press.

Tolson, E. R., Reid, W. J., & Garvin, C. D. (1994). *Generalist practice: A task-centered approach*. Columbia University Press.

Trotter, C. (2015). *Working with involuntary clients* (3rd ed.). Taylor & Francis.

Crisis Intervention
Frameworks for Social Worker Practice

Yvonne Eaton-Stull

In the midst of the coronavirus pandemic, we begin this chapter on crisis intervention. All social work practitioners will encounter crises—it is just a matter of time. An individual facing interpersonal violence, a family who lost a loved one, or a group displaced by a tornado are just a few examples of crises social workers will be faced with. Social workers are employed in a variety of settings in which they will encounter people in crisis, including emergency rooms, crisis agencies, and mental health facilities. Despite the need for skill in de-escalating and resolving crises, very few have had specialized training in crisis intervention. This chapter summarizes essential skills and several frameworks and tools for responding to crises so that practitioners can successfully respond and resolve these challenging situations.

occurs when individuals are exposed to crises. Lindemann viewed individual's reactions as acute but normal, temporary responses to a crisis (James & Gilliland, 2017). Caplan expanded the concept that individuals have difficulty coping and overcoming the situation with normal strategies, thereby leading to upset and difficulty coping and problem-solving (James & Gilliland, 2017). Rather than adopting a pathologizing view of the person, Lindemann and Caplan believed crises were the outcome or state of disequilibrium resulting from an event and able to be addressed with early intervention (Jackson-Cherry & Erford, 2014). These valuable contributions formed the foundation for what is helpful following crises and what practitioners can do to assist those who have experienced a traumatic event.

Theoretical Foundation

Crisis intervention theory is based on the ideas and work of founders Erich Lindemann and Gerald Caplan. Disequilibrium is the foundational theoretical belief about what

Essential Crisis Skills

Effective crisis intervention can be enhanced when the social worker practitioner possesses some specific characteristics and traits. James and Gilliland (2017) indicate that poise is a beneficial trait. Poise refers to the crisis worker's ability to remain calm and professional when confronted with a host of scary and volatile situations. Being creative and flexible is another useful trait because the crisis worker may need to develop innovative solutions to complex problems (James & Gilliland, 2017). Cavaiola and Colford (2018) stress the importance of other traits, including tenacity, optimism, and confidence. Crises are often long and involved situations that require the social worker to persist and maintain a positive attitude along with a belief in their ability to assist those in need. These personality traits are often present in the most successful crisis interventionists.

Although one cannot easily modify a personality, there is consensus regarding the type of training and knowledge that should be taught and practiced for those who frequently respond to crises. Suicide and homicide risk, interpersonal violence, substance abuse, psychiatric crises, and grief and loss are all essential content in crisis intervention texts. Practitioners are encouraged to obtain continuing education in these critical areas. The Substance Abuse and Mental Health Services Administration Evidence-Based Practices Resource Center (n.d.) provides valuable information on treatment for these crises. The Center of Excellence for Integrated Health Solutions (National Council for Behavioral Health, 2020) offers useful information on screening tools to use for suicide and substance abuse. The National Center on Domestic and Sexual Violence (n.d.) provides trainings, webinars, and events throughout the country. Finally, professionals can obtain valuable online training in grief and loss through the National Alliance for Grieving Children (2020) or The Center for Complicated Grief (n.d.). In addition to seeking training to enhance one's competence, adopting a useful framework to guide interventions is helpful in ensuring that necessary steps are taken to address the client's needs. Next, numerous frameworks are outlined and explained to offer practitioners options for responding to crises.

Frameworks for Individual Crisis Intervention

ABC Model

The ABC model (Kanel, 2015) is one of the briefest and easiest to recall frameworks. According to Kanel, this framework includes three steps:

> A = Attending and active listening to develop and maintain rapport: The first step in this model is to develop and maintain rapport by demonstrating interest, warmth, and empathy while using skills including questioning, paraphrasing, emotion labeling, and summarizing.
>
> B = Identify the problem: This step refers to identifying the nature of the problem, exploring the client's cognitions, level of distress, and impairment, such as behavioral, academic, social, and occupational. It is during this step that practitioners identify what further assessments are critical, such as suicide risk.
>
> C = Coping strategies: Finally, this step explores past and present coping strategies along with considering other options the client can utilize. Knowledge of referral agencies and resources is essential in helping the client resolve their crisis.

L-A-P-C Model

This easy-to-remember model includes four steps (Cavaiola & Colford, 2018):

> L = Listen: Listening is at the core of all crisis intervention because one must

gain a real understanding of the crisis from the client's perspective in order to establish rapport, gain their trust, and assist them in developing a plan of action. According to Cavaiola and Colford, this first step involves actively listening to the client's explanation of their situation.

A = *Assess*: This step involves determining how the client is responding to the situation, specifically evaluating their emotions, behaviors, and thoughts.

P = *Plan*: The planning step involves generating options that may include identification of supports and resources the client can utilize.

C = *Commit*: The commitment step involves the client employing the agreed upon strategies to resolve their crisis.

SAFER-R Model

The SAFER-R model (Everly & Mitchell, 2008) offers a useful mnemonic device to recall the steps of this intervention, as each letter of this framework corresponds to the first letter of the appropriate action:

S = *Stabilize*: This model starts off with an essential step not addressed in previous models. This step includes active strategies to address environmental stressors (Everly & Mitchell, 2008)—for example, removing clients from volatile others who may be exacerbating the situation or even calling for emergency medical services or police to secure an unsafe scene.

A = *Acknowledge*: This step refers to using active listening and communication to determine what happened and the impact on thoughts, emotions, and behavior.

F = *Facilitate understanding*: In this step, the cognitions are evaluated in more detail. For example, is the client experiencing normal feelings that can be validated or is there something more serious happening?

E = *Encourage effective coping*: This step includes facilitating self-coping within the client, such as strategies they have used in the past, or implementing treatment interventions to assist.

R = *Recovery or referral*: The final step is to restore the client's functioning, but often this involves referral. Referral to a higher level of care, such as inpatient psychiatric treatment, may be necessary.

Greenstone and Leviton Model

The following six-step process has been proposed by Greenstone and Leviton (2011):

Step 1: Immediacy: According to Greenstone and Leviton, this step is critical in ensuring that clients do not harm themselves or others. Potential actions such as enlisting the assistance of emergency personnel, police, or other supports may be useful during this step.

Step 2: Control: This step is a more directive process. The social worker will attempt to assess the surrounding and individuals present. The purpose of this step is to help lessen the current chaos as the practitioner maintains a calm, supportive demeanor while attempting to establish structure. One key element during this step often includes separating the client from others who may be fuelling an already intense situation.

Step 3: Assessment: During this step, the social worker obtains helpful information. Unlike typical social work sessions that involve a complete biopsychosocial history, a crisis assessment is more focused on the current struggle and recent precipitants. Greenstone and Leviton suggest the worker attempt to gain recent information about what happened to the client, why they are having difficulty coping, and what type of intervention is needed. This step also requires a thorough safety risk assessment. Taking time to hear the client's stressors thoroughly helps the worker determine what areas need immediate attention and, as such, what must be included in the disposition.

Step 4: Disposition: Greenstone and Leviton indicate that this step includes the decision about how to handle the crisis situation. Key skills necessary for this step include creative thinking, problem-solving, and considering various options. Based on information gained in the previous step, it is hoped the social worker will have identified existing resources that may be helpful to include in the decision-making process.

Step 5: Referral: Almost all crises involve making referrals. Often, this may include referrals to emergency services or hospitals with inpatient mental health care; thus, it is important to have knowledge of local resources. Greenstone and Leviton suggest that practitioners take steps to build relationships with these crisis providers before being faced with an actual crisis—for example, visiting other agencies, making a resource list, and investigating transportation options.

Step 6: Follow-up: This is an important step many practitioners fail to complete; however, it can be potentially helpful in preventing another crisis. Greenstone and Leviton note that it is important to determine whether the client has connected with the referrals provided or if assistance or re-referrals are needed.

Roberts' Seven-Stage Model

A similar step model as that of Greenstone and Leviton (2011) was proposed by the late Al Roberts (2005):

Stage 1: Plan and conduct a crisis assessment: The first step involves a quick assessment of risk and dangerousness, including suicide and homicide/violence risk assessment, need for medical attention, and current drug or alcohol use (Roberts, 2005). There are a variety of formal assessments for risk of suicide/ homicide, but these tools should always be accompanied by a thorough clinical assessment with information from the individual as well as other relevant sources of information. Answers to assessment questions will help the social worker determine the appropriate next steps. Substance use is an important factor to evaluate because it can contribute to impulsively acting on thoughts of suicide/homicide. In addition, a substance assessment should include information about drugs used, amount used, last use, and any withdrawal symptoms the client is experiencing (Eaton & Roberts, 2002). If possible, a medical assessment should include a brief summary of the presenting problem, any medical conditions, current medications (including dosages and last dose), and allergies (Eaton & Roberts, 2002). This medical information is essential to relay to medical responders attempting to treat problems, such as overdoses, if they are in progress.

Stage 2: Rapid establishment of rapport: This often occurs simultaneously with Stage 1. Conveying respect and acceptance are key skills in this stage. Workers must display a nonjudgmental attitude as well, ensuring that their personal opinions and values are not apparent or stated (Roberts, 2005). Roberts and Yeager (2009) also note that creativity, flexibility, and a positive attitude are additional strengths in successful crisis workers.

Stage 3: Identify the major problems: Use of open-ended questions will enable the social worker to hear more from the client's perspective—for example, asking a client what happened to bring them to this point. This provides the crisis worker with valuable insights into the nature of the presenting problem and potential precipitating events.

Stage 4: Deal with feelings and emotions: Active listening skills are essential during this stage. Clients should be encouraged to share their story as the practitioner listens intently in order to understand their situation better (Roberts & Yeager, 2009).

Stage 5: Generate and explore alternatives: Ideally, the ability of the worker and the client to work collaboratively during this stage should yield the widest array of potential resources and alternatives (Eaton & Roberts, 2002). According to Roberts (2005), individuals in crisis have untapped resources and coping skills, which can be utilized to help them resolve the crisis. At this point in the intervention, the social worker should use solution-focused questions to explore strategies the client has used previously to help them through rough times. These may potentially be useful in formulating the action plan.

Stage 6: Develop an action plan: The crisis worker should assist the client in the least restrictive manner, enabling them to feel empowered (Eaton & Roberts, 2002). Important steps at this stage include providing coping mechanisms and identifying persons and referral sources to be contacted (Roberts, 2005). According to Jackson-Cherry and Erford (2014), action plans should include (1) information about restricting access, such as removing guns; (2) strategies for self-care/stress management; (3) family supports; and (4) mental health resources. Writing such a plan on a carbon-copy form allows a quick way for both the social worker and the client to agree and document the process.

Stage 7: Follow-up: Crisis workers should follow up with the client after the initial intervention to ensure the crisis has been resolved (Roberts & Yeager, 2009). This allows an opportunity to determine whether the client has followed through with recommendations and continued care. If indicated, additional referrals can be made at this time.

Tools for Providing Group Support

Psychological First Aid

According to expert consensus, psychological first aid (PFA) is the recommended intervention for groups impacted by disasters (Kaul & Welzant, 2005; Watson et al., 2011). PFA is also endorsed by the North Atlantic Treaty Organization (NATO) as the evidence-informed approach to decreasing distress and fostering adaptive functioning and coping (NATO Joint Medical Committee, 2008). PFA includes the following actions—to be provided by the practitioner: (1) making contact and engaging with survivors, (2) enhancing safety and comfort, (3) calming and stabilizing survivors, (4) gathering information, (5) providing practical assistance, (6) connecting with social supports, (7) giving information on coping, and (8) linking with collaborative services (National Child Traumatic Stress Network & National Center for PTSD, 2006). Free Web-based training in PFA is available for social workers to enhance their knowledge and skills in this area.

Animal-Assisted Crisis Response

Another innovative crisis intervention strategy, animal-assisted crisis response (AACR), involves specially trained teams of a canine handler and experienced therapy/comfort dog. These highly trained and evaluated dogs offer comfort and support to individuals impacted by crises (HOPE AACR, 2020). They receive intense training, both initially and ongoing, and are equipped to respond to intense, chaotic, and crowded environments. These dogs are also accepting and responsive to a variety of human emotions that are common during crises and disasters. HOPE AACR teams are the only responder of this kind in the National Voluntary Organizations Active in Disasters and are trained in PFA, have background checks, and carry $1 million liability insurance. These teams do not self-deploy but, rather, partner with social workers and other response organizations to better meet the post-crisis needs of those served.

Conclusion

Responding to crisis situations can be a daunting and dangerous task social workers will ultimately face. However, developing personal traits and enhancing one's competence through specialized training help ensure effective crisis intervention. In addition, adopting

a useful framework to guide necessary crisis steps provides practitioners with a valuable tool to help those in need. Finally, becoming familiar with group interventions such as PFA and AACR can lead to the creation of valuable partnerships in resolving crises.

Helpful Resources

Apps
Crisis Go App: https://www.crisisgo.com/download
Jason Foundation: A Friend Asks: https://apps.apple.com/us/app/jason-foundation-a-friend-asks/id585429140
Suicide Safe Mobile App: https://store.samhsa.gov/product/suicide-safe
Suicide Safety Plan: https://apps.apple.com/us/app/suicide-safety-plan/id1003891579

Websites
HOPE Animal-Assisted Crisis Response: http://www.hopeaacr.org
National Child Traumatic Stress Network: http://www.nctsn.org
National Center for PTSD: http://www.ptsd.va.gov

References

Cavaiola, A. A., & Colford, J. E. (2018). *Crisis intervention: A practical guide.* Sage.
Eaton, Y. M., & Roberts, A. R. (2002). Frontline crisis intervention: Step-by-step practice guidelines with case applications. In A. R. Roberts & G. J. Greene (Eds.), *Social workers' desk reference* (pp. 89–96). Oxford University Press.
Everly, G. S., & Mitchell, J. T. (2008). *Integrative crisis intervention and disaster mental health.* Chevron Publishing.
Greenstone, J. L., & Leviton, S. (2011). *Elements of crisis intervention: Crises and how to respond to them* (3rd ed.). Brooks/Cole.
HOPE Animal-Assisted Crisis Response. (2020). Home page. https://www.hopeaacr.org
Jackson-Cherry, L. R., & Erford, B. T. (2014). *Crisis assessment, intervention, and prevention* (2nd ed.). Pearson.
James, R. K., & Gilliland, B. E. (2017). *Crisis intervention strategies* (8th ed.). Cengage.
Kanel, K. (2015). *A guide to crisis intervention* (5th ed.). Cengage.

Kaul, R. E., & Welzant, V. (2005). Disaster mental health: A discussion of best practices as applied after the Pentagon attack. In A. R. Roberts (Ed.), *Crisis intervention handbook: Assessment, treatment, and research* (pp. 200–220). Oxford University Press.

National Alliance for Grieving Children. (2020). *Online learning.* https://childrengrieve.org/education/online-learning

National Center on Domestic and Sexual Violence. (n.d.). *Upcoming trainings, webinars, and events around the country.* http://www.ncdsv.org/ncd_upcomingtrainings.html

National Child Traumatic Stress Network & National Center for PTSD. (2006). *Psychological first aid: Field operations guide* (2nd ed.). Available at http://www.nctsn.org and http://www.ncptsd.va.gov

National Council for Behavioral Health. (2020). *Center of Excellence for Integrated Health Solutions.* https://www.thenationalcouncil.org/integration

North Atlantic Treaty Organization Joint Medical Committee. (2008). *Psychosocial care for people affected by disasters and major incidents.*

Roberts, A. R. (2005). Bridging the past and present to the future of crisis intervention and crisis management. In A. R. Roberts (Ed.), *Crisis intervention handbook: Assessment, treatment, and research* (3rd ed., pp. 31–34). Oxford University Press.

Roberts, A. R., & Yeager, K. R. (2009). *Pocket guide to crisis intervention.* Oxford University Press.

Substance Abuse and Mental Health Services Administration. (n.d.). *Evidence-Based Practices Resources Center.* https://www.samhsa.gov/ebp-resource-center

The Center for Complicated Grief. (n.d.). *Training.* https://complicatedgrief.columbia.edu/professionals/training

Watson, P. J., Brymer, M. J., & Bonanno, G. A. (2011). Post disaster psychological intervention since 9/11. *American Psychologist, 66*(6), 482–494.

Narrative Therapy

Mark Smith

With the publication of Michael White and David Epston's seminal text, *Narrative Means to Therapeutic Ends* (1990), narrative therapy (NT) entered the scene as a direct challenge to existing therapeutic practices and concepts. Narrative practice was quickly recognized as an important development in contemporary social work practice because the two founders, White and Epston, both emerged from social work backgrounds rather than psychiatry, psychology, or counseling. Their clinical approach arose in the late 1980s as a result of the collaboration of White, a social worker/family therapist from South Australia, and Epston, a social worker/family therapist from New Zealand, and integrated both a new approach to clinical practice and engagement in community organization and practice. NT was among the first clinical practices thoroughly grounded in ideas of postmodernism, post-structuralism, and critical theory (Freedman & Combs, 1996; Nichols, 2014). Like other postmodernist perspectives, NT challenges modernist ideas of a solitary or singular truth while emphasizing that each person's experiences are linguistically constructed from one's unique sociocultural and political contexts, biases, and individual conditioning. Essentially, NT suggests that we

inhabit the stories we are telling about ourselves, as well as the stories being told about us. NT developed within the context of the social constructionist and second-order cybernetic movements, which began influencing the field of family therapy in the 1970s and 1980s. In addition to positioning themselves within the epistemological perspective of social constructionism, White and Epston also drew from the ideas of constructivism; the work of Foucault; and the fields of sociology, anthropology, race/gender/queer critical theory, and literary criticism (Kelley & Murty, 2003). A primary influence for White and Epston was the thinking of Michel Foucault (1972, 1984, 1994), whose analysis of power dynamics inherent in social discourse and related social structures provided the foundation for NT's focus on dominant social narratives and their impact on personal narratives that may have been diminished, silenced, or subjugated. Although NT began in the family therapy movement, its influence has spread to work at individual, group, organizational, and community levels.

Constructivism focuses on an individual's perceptions and cognitions as the primary factor shaping one's view of reality, whereas social constructionism focuses more on the social and cultural narratives that individuals internalize and take for granted as constituting "reality." Both views deny the existence of an objective reality, believing that one's view of reality is linguistically constructed based on selected social interactions. White and Epston's early therapeutic work incorporated both social constructionism and constructivism, believing that people create stories of their lives to make sense of lived experiences. The stories people develop about themselves are heavily influenced by the dominant social and cultural stories of identity, gender, ethnicity, and power, along with the set of personal stories co-constructed in interaction with others (family, friends, and professional helpers). These stories constitute the knowledge people have about themselves and their worlds. As in postmodern literary criticism, the narrative therapist helps clients "deconstruct" the story lines around which they have organized their lives, assessing the plot, characters, and timeline for relevance and meaning, and looking for other alternative "truths" that may exist.

The goal of NT in clinical social work practice is to help clients first understand the relational impact of the stories around which they have organized their lives and then deconstruct, challenge, and broaden these stories, thus creating new realities that are more consonant with preferred lives (Freedman & Combs, 1996). These discoveries can help clients see alternatives to how things have seemed and ways of being not previously realized. They can also help clients see aspects of themselves that have become forgotten or suppressed, such as strengths and coping skills they already have, and which can be mobilized to fight the effects of the problems they are facing. Therapy is viewed as a form of mutual conversation in which language and connection construct a preferred reality (Madigan, 2019). In other words, through social discourse, reality (including one's history) is socially reconstructed (created). While focusing on the stories clients are telling, NT is more than storytelling; it is story *changing* or *re-storying*. The narrative therapist does not deny the harsh realities facing clients, such as poverty, racism, or illness, but rather challenges the power given to these adverse aspects of their lives and the control the problems have over their lives.

Using a Narrative Approach

Narrative therapy takes a collaborative approach in working with clients, in which clients are the experts on their lives. As the client's story lines unfold and are told in richer detail, the client and social worker together discover other possible realities and join in fighting the effects of the problem depiction. Key concepts of NT are as follows:

- *Problem-saturated stories.* These are the one-dimensional or *thin* stories clients have about themselves and their life situations that act to restrict or limit them. These problem-saturated stories have been co-constructed in interaction with others and are influenced by sociocultural forces. These stories are examined in therapeutic conversations as clients are challenged to expand their limited views of self.
- *Double-listening.* This is also referred to as attending to the *absent but implicit.* Therapists listen to both the explicit expressions of client complaints/distress and what is absent from the expression but implicit in its meaning. This practice can help elicit a range of intentional or historical understandings for clients and set the stage for them to become more active agents in countering disabling narratives.
- *Externalizing the problem.* In conversation with clients, the problem is externalized, or separated from the person, whereby the problem, not the person, becomes the target

of change. The externalized problem is given a name so that the client and others in their life can join in mobilizing against the influence of the problem story.

- *Mapping the problem's domain.* The effects of the problem narrative over time (past, present, and possible future) and across many situations are examined. In so doing, the client is encouraged to assess what might be done to counteract the impact of the present problem description. In addition to mapping practices, clients are often enlisted to undertake an "archeology of the present," which acknowledges helpful influences that have been important as well as evidence of historical precursors of the client's present resolve to seek help in restoring a preferred sense of self. This reinforces client readiness and motivation to enact change behaviors.
- *Unique outcomes.* This refers to those times the client can identify when they were not overcome by their problems but may have had the strength or resources to resist. For clients, these times may represent new truths and discoveries about themselves that are often indicators of hidden or unrecognized strengths. These episodes are highlighted and shifted into positions of prominence in descriptions of the client's situation.
- *Outsider witness practices.* Problems are viewed as being situated relationally; therefore, clients are encouraged to call upon individuals who may have unique understandings of the client that contrast, challenge, provide insight, or add perspective to the problem-saturated story. These outsider witnesses may be present in one's life, may be imaginary characters, or may even be dead, but they provide confirmation and support for intentions and preferred actions.
- *Re-membering/praxis.* Once clients start experiencing some positive change, they are encouraged to let others know about their intentions and subsequent successes in fighting the effects of the problems or

in not giving in to the problems. This may involve celebrations, certificates, awards, letter writing, or even talking to groups of others facing similar problems. Rather than positioning the client as victim or even a survivor of difficulties, client *insider expertise* regarding experience with this kind of problem is acknowledged, and therapists often encourage clients to join with others in forming new memberships of community engagement and advocacy.

What distinguishes narrative practitioners from those utilizing other approaches is that workers utilizing the previously presented processes refrain from initiating interventions in order to do something "to" a client. Neither does the clinician assume that a problem or symptom serves an important psychological function for the individual (as in psychodynamic approaches) or for the family (as in family systems approaches). There are no presumptions about clients. Clients are carefully listened to so therapists can more fully understand clients' perceptions of the problem and the meanings they ascribe to it. Then, through respectful listening and deconstructive questioning, problems are externalized and problem-saturated stories examined through mapping and questioning (White, 2007). In the reconstruction or *re-storying* stage, some assumed "truths" are gently challenged through questioning, and *unique outcomes* (when the problem was not dominant) are explored. Therapy is ended by mutual agreement, and worker and client consider plans for *spreading the news* of the realizations, often with celebrations or awards and with engagement in community education or advocacy.

Narrative therapy contains many "wondering" questions to help clients think about and reflect on their interpretations and beliefs about their lived experiences. Through such reflections, they consider other interpretations and other meanings, which act to expand their view of self. NT is usually short term, with a few sessions spread over a longer period. The concepts and interventions of NT bear some similarity to solution-focused therapy (SFT) (de Shazer & Berg, 1993) and the strength perspective (Saleebey, 2013) in that they all are empowerment-based approaches (Lee, 2017) aimed at mobilizing clients' inherent strengths and resources. However, these approaches also have some distinct differences:

- The "unique outcomes" of NT are different from SFT's "exceptions" in that they are not asked for but, rather, discovered through careful listening.
- In NT, the discussion of possible futures does not focus solely on the hoped for (positive) future but also assesses the potential future if the problem continues to dominate clients' lives.
- Because clients come into the relationship with a specific problem to solve, ameliorate, or cope with, narrative therapists do not avoid discussing problems that clients present with but, rather, attend to them as part of a broader, more extensive story.

Case Example

Family therapy sessions were held for a blended family consisting of a mother who had married before; her 14-year-old daughter, Mary Ann; and her second husband, who had never married before and had no previous children. A younger daughter born of both parents, aged 7 years, was not brought to the sessions. The family was concerned that Mary Ann had become rebellious and dropped her previous friends to run with an older boyfriend and his crowd who engaged in dangerous and illegal activities and did not attend school. These activities represented a dramatic shift from her previous good behavior. Her mood had changed from happy and helpful to surly and disrespectful. In addition, her grades had dropped dramatically.

Mary Ann discussed how she believed she was living in a house designed for little girls, with little accommodation for her to grow up and achieve independence. She also believed that her stepfather did not love her, was mean to her, and favored the younger daughter. The mother discussed how she lived in terror, fearing what might happen to Mary Ann if the illegal and dangerous activities continued. She mourned the loss of her close relationship with Mary Ann, and she felt torn between loyalty to husband and oldest daughter. After listening intently to the different stories of the problem as viewed by the various family members who were present, the therapist attempted to articulate the different perceptions and descriptions offered about the situation and then asked for corrections or clarifications. The stepfather was asked to imagine Mary Ann was not present in the session and how he would introduce Mary Ann to the therapist. Following the stepfather's introduction, the therapist asked mother and Mary Ann what seemed left out or missing in the father's description. As expected, Mary Ann protested that the descriptions offered by both mother and stepfather were inaccurate and that neither parent seemed to really understand her. When Mary Ann described herself in less troubling ways, the therapist asked the family to speculate about how the present family situation seemed to be getting in the way of Mary Ann being viewed in the way she would prefer. Each family member described their own struggles with being misunderstood, and they agreed that this was something they all wanted. The stepfather discussed sometimes feeling left out of the family given the close relationship between the mother and daughter and admitted being overly strict sometimes out of his frustration at not being allowed to join the family. The mother wanted the others to know how difficult she was trying to get everyone to just get along with each other and how afraid she was for Mary Ann. After each member had heard the stories of fear and frustrations of the others, the meanings they made of family events shifted. Double-listening helped the family recognize that close relationships and feeling love and understanding were values the family shared. Stepfather's attempts to establish control and his strictness were viewed as attempts at loving and caring, and Mary Ann's rebelliousness was perceived as familiar adolescent struggles to change and grow and establish identity. Adolescence and its expected emotional storms were externalized as a major new "member" entering their family life. They discussed ways they might welcome the new member into the family (Mary Ann stated that she was not giving up her bedroom to this intruder!), how they might understand this new member better, and how they might help it become a positive force in the family instead of a negative one. As the family developed more empathy and understanding for each other, they began laughing as they talked about how to welcome the new member; how changes and compromises were to be expected; and how emerging needs for independence could be earned without having to resort to rebelliousness, defiance, and dangerous behaviors. Family meetings to agree on the rules were set up in which Mary Ann's development of a preferred self would be supported. Many old beliefs were deconstructed, and new ways to deal with problems emerged.

Narrative Therapy and Social Work

Narrative therapy is compatible with the traditional social work methods and values of viewing each client as unique, respecting each client's story, respecting cultural differences, and separating one's own beliefs and values from those of clients through self-understanding and conscious use of self. Social work values are demonstrated through the following methods:

Respectful listening. By taking a "nonexpert, not knowing" position about the clients' lives, we show respect for their knowledge, and we listen carefully to their ideas. This stance is not the same as neutrality, because some stories are clearly less useful or even harmful (e.g., violence) than others, but here the therapist assesses the outcomes and consequences with the client and may challenge the story through deconstruction and by assessing its origins.

Avoidance of labels. The use of labels, diagnoses, and categories for totalizing clients as to who they are is avoided, and through externalization clients are viewed as being afflicted with a problem but not constituted of it. For example, persons may be afflicted with a particular medical condition, such as cancer or a serious mental illness, but that affliction is just one part of who they are, not their total being. Thus, a person would not be viewed as a schizophrenic but as a person contending with the influences of schizophrenia and the effects of social discourses in regard to having such a diagnosis.

Fostering empowerment. The political nature of NT, wherein clients are "liberated" from dominant familial and cultural stories that have restricted them, and instead are urged to take a stand on their own behalf, makes it especially compatible with social work practice.

Emphasis on social justice. NT also takes a stand on social justice issues, as exemplified in the work of New Zealanders Waldegrave, Tamasese,

Tuhaka, and Campbell (2003), who developed their own version of NT called "just therapy" because it focuses on social justice. White and Epston (1992), Madigan (2007), and Denborough (2008, 2019) have all engaged in social justice projects and have worked with oppressed communities to challenge dominant narratives that act to oppress them. Beginning in 1999, White and others at the Dulwich Family Therapy Training Centre in Adelaide, South Australia, organized international narrative therapy conferences that have focused on work with families, communities, trauma, discrimination, and other social justice issues.

Extensions beyond the office. The bridge between micro and macro practice is useful for social workers and fits in with newer community practice approaches. Narrative therapists work beyond office walls to advocate for policy transformation and social justice issues by engaging in such practices as fostering communities of support and empowering clients and direct social action.

Potential Concerns

Although NT seems consistent with good social work practice, some problems regarding it have been raised. Compared with other "evidence-based" approaches, there continues to be less empirical research supporting NT. Its foundation in postmodernism and critical theory de-emphasized the essentialist perspectives that are at the core of most empiricism. Other research approaches, such as qualitative methods and case studies, have addressed this concern to some degree. Kelley (1998) noted that two major trends in clinical practice, postmodernism and managed care, seem at odds with each other. Managed care demands DSM-5 and ICD-9 diagnoses with preapproved treatment plans designed by the clinician and based on empirically proven methods, whereas in NT the emphasis is on the therapist and client co-constructing new realities through dialogue rather than conducting problem-solving activities designed by the therapist.

Future Practice Applications

Questions regarding NT and its perceived lack of established research evidence have not diminished its impact. As Minuchin et al. (2007) note, "Narrative therapy . . . is a perfect expression of the postmodern revolution" (p. 2). The approach that was once considered revolutionary has now become more mainstream, as evidenced by inclusion in major social work texts (e.g., Turner, 2017) and family therapy texts (Nichols, 2014), and numerous books and articles on the subject, as reviewed by Walther and Carey (2009). A book by Freedman and Combs (1996) has long been considered a classic in the field. Until his death in 2008, Michael White continued to develop narrative ideas and publish (White, 2007). David Epston continues to add to the NT literature. Changes have developed over time as NT broadened its scope to more community and group work (Carey & Russell, 2011; Kelley & Murty, 2003; Vodde & Gallant, 2003), further decreasing the distinction between micro and macro practice. Applications of NT in work with specific populations and circumstances include work with children and in play therapy (Castan, 2020; Fife & Hawkins, 2019; Freeman et al., 1997), work with the elderly and grief work (Nozari et al., 2019; Rodriguez-Vega et al., 2014), work with those who have encountered significant trauma or witnessed violence or genocide (Denborough, 2008; Farzad et al., 2019; Garo & Lawson, 2019; Gómez et al.,

2017; Waldegrave et al., 2003), and a recent impetus to integrate new discoveries in neurology and brain science with narrative processes (Denborough, 2019; Lainson, 2019; Young, 2019; Zimmerman, 2017).

Helpful Resources

Dulwich Centre: http://www.dulwichcentre.com.au

SickKids Centre for Community Mental Health: https://sickkidscmh.ca/

Planet Therapy (online mental health learning community): http://www.planet-therapy.com

Victoria Dickerson (narrative therapy): http://www.victoriadickerson.com

Vancouver School for Narrative Therapy:: http://www.therapeuticconversations.com

References

Carey, M., & Russell, S. (2011). Pedagogy shaped by culture: Teaching narrative approaches to Australian aboriginal health workers. *Journal of Systemic Therapies, 3*(3), 26–41.

Castan, L. (2020). Child-centered play therapy and narrative therapy: Consilience and synthesis. *International Journal of Narrative Therapy and Community Work,* (1), 24–33.

de Shazer, S., & Berg, I. K. (1993). Constructing solutions. *Family Therapy Networker, 12,* 42–43.

Denborough, D. (2008). *Collective narrative practice: Responding to individuals, groups, and communities who have experienced trauma.* Dulwich Center Books.

Denborough, D. (2019). Travelling down the neuropathway: Narrative practice, neuroscience, bodies, emotions, and the affective turn. *International Journal of Narrative Therapy & Community Work* (3), 13–53.

Farzad, J., Alireza, H., & Fatemah, H. S. (2019). Narrative therapy for depression and anxiety among children with imprisoned parents: A randomised pilot efficacy trial. *Journal of Child & Adolescent Mental Health, 31*(3), 189–200.

Fife, S. T., & Hawkins, L. G. (2019). Doctor, snitch, and weasel: Narrative family therapy with a child suffering from encopresis and enuresis. *Clinical Case Studies, 18*(6), 452–467.

Freedman, J., & Combs, J. (1996). *Narrative therapy: The social construction of preferred realities.* Norton.

Freeman, J., Epston, D., & Lobovits, D. (1997). *Playful approaches to serious problems: Narrative therapy with children and their families.* Norton.

Foucault, M. (1972). *The archeology of knowledge: And the discourse on language.* Pantheon.

Foucault, M. (1984). *The Foucault reader* (P. Rabinow, Ed.). Pantheon.

Foucault, M. (1994). *The birth of the clinic.* Pantheon.

Garo, L. A., & Lawson, T. (2019). My story, my way: Conceptualization of narrative therapy with trauma-exposed Black male youth [Special issue]. *Urban Education Research & Policy Annuals,* 2164–6406.

Gómez, A. M., Cerezo, A., & Ajayi Beliard, C. (2017, October). Deconstructing meta-narratives: Utilizing narrative therapy to promote resilience following sexual violence among women survivors of color. *Journal of Sex & Marital Therapy,* 282–295.

Kelley, P. (1998). Narrative therapy in a managed care world. *Crisis Intervention, 4*(2–3), 113–123.

Kelley, P., & Murty, S. (2003). Teaching narrative approaches in community practice. *Social Work Review (of New Zealand), 15*(4), 14–20.

Lainson, C. (2019). Narrative therapy, neuroscience and anorexia: A reflection on practices, problems and possibilities. *International Journal of Narrative Therapy and Community Work* (3), 80–95.

Lee, M. Y. (2017). Solution-focused therapy. In F. J. Turner (Ed.), *Social work treatment: Interlocking theoretical approaches* (6th ed., pp. 513–531). Oxford University Press.

Madigan, S. (2007). Anticipating hope within written and naming domains of despair. *Hope and despair in narrative and family therapy: Adversity, forgiveness and reconciliation,* 100–112.

Madigan, S. (2019). *Narrative therapy* (2nd ed.). American Psychological Association.

Minuchin, S., Nichols, M., & Lee, M. Y. (2007). *Assessing families and couples: From symptom to system.* Allyn & Bacon.

Nichols, M. P. (2014). *The essentials of family therapy* (6th ed.). Pearson.

Nozari, Z., Mo'tamedi, A., Eskandari, H., & Ahmadivand, Z. (2019). Narrative group therapy to improve aging perceptions and reduce thanatophobia (death anxiety) in older adults. *Elderly Health Journal, 5*(2), 117–123.

Rodriguez-Vega, B., Bayon, C., Paleaotarrio, A., Liria, A. F., & Ferdosi, F. (2014). Mindfulness-based narrative therapy for depression in cancer patients. *Clinical Psychology Psychotherapy, 21,* 411–419.

Saleebey, D. (2013). *The strengths perspective in social work practice* (6th ed.). Allyn-Bacon.

Turner, F. J. (Ed.). (2017). *Social work treatment: Interlocking theoretical approaches* (6th ed.). Oxford University Press.

Vodde, R., & Gallant, J. (2003). Bridging the gap between micro and macro practice: Large scale change and a unified model of narrative–deconstructive practice. *Social Work Review (of New Zealand), 15*(4), 4–13.

Waldegrave, C., Tamasese, K., Tuhaka, F., & Campbell, W. (2003). *Just therapy—A journey: A collection of papers from the Just Therapy Team.* Dulwich Centre Publications.

Walther, S., & Carey, M. (2009, October). Narrative therapy, difference and possibility: Inviting new becomings. *Contexts,* 3–8.

White, M. (2007). *Maps of narrative practice.* Norton.

White, M., & Epston, D. (1990). *Narrative means to therapeutic ends.* Norton.

White, M., & Epston, D. (1992). *Experience, contradiction, narrative and imagination: Selected papers of David Epston & Michael White, 1989–1991.* Dulwich Center Publications.

Young, K. (2019). Reflections on narrative, neuroscience and social engagement. *International Journal of Narrative Therapy & Community Work* (3), 54–56.

Zimmerman, J. (2017). Neuro-narrative therapy: Brain science, narrative therapy, poststructuralism, and preferred identities. *Journal of Systemic Therapies, 36*(2), 12–26.

A Family Resilience Framework

Froma Walsh

In recent decades, the field of family therapy has refocused attention from family deficits to family strengths. The therapeutic relationship is collaborative and empowering of client potential, recognizing that successful interventions depend more on tapping into family resources than on therapist techniques. Assessment and intervention are directed to how problems can be solved, identifying and amplifying existing and potential competencies. Therapist and clients work together to find new possibilities in a problem-saturated situation and overcome roadblocks to change and growth. This positive, future-oriented direction shifts the emphasis from what went wrong to what can be done for optimal functioning and well-being of families and their members.

A family resilience approach builds on these developments to strengthen family abilities to overcome adversity. A basic premise guiding this approach is that serious life crises, disruptive transitions, and persistent adversity have an impact on the whole family, and in turn, key family processes influence the adaptation and resilience of all members, their relationships, and the family unit. As families gain mastery of their immediate difficulties, they also increase their resourcefulness to meet future challenges. Thus, in strengthening family resilience, each intervention is also a preventive measure.

The Concept of Family Resilience: Crisis and Challenge

Resilience—the capacity to withstand and rebound from adversity—has become an important concept in mental health theory, research, and practice. Countering the deterministic assumption that early, severe, or persistent adversity inevitably damages lives, research has amply documented the potential to rise above serious life challenges (Rutter, 1987). For instance, most children who suffered abuse did not become abusive parents. What makes the difference?

Early studies, in the 1980s, focused on individual traits for hardiness, reflecting the dominant cultural ethos of the "rugged individual." Resilience was viewed as inborn or acquired on one's own, as "the invulnerable child" seen as impervious to stress owing to inner fortitude. An interactive perspective emerged, recognizing that the impact of initial risk conditions or traumatic events may be outweighed by mediating environmental influences that foster resilience. Major studies of resilient children and adults noted the crucial influence of significant relationships, with extended family members and mentors such as coaches or teachers who supported them, believed in their potential, and encouraged them to make the best of their lives (Rutter, 1987; Werner & Smith, 2001). However, the skewed clinical focus on family dysfunction blinded many to the kinship resources that could be found and strengthened, even in troubled families.

A family resilience orientation fundamentally alters that traditional deficit-based lens, shifting the perspective from viewing families as *damaged* to viewing them as *challenged*. Rather than rescuing so-called survivors from dysfunctional families, this approach affirms the family's reparative potential, based on the conviction that both individual and relational healing and growth can be forged out of adversity.

The concept of family resilience has valuable potential as a framework for intervention, prevention, research, and social policy aimed at supporting and strengthening families facing adversity (Walsh, 2003, 2016a). Although some families are shattered by crisis or persistent stresses, others surmount their challenges and emerge stronger and more resourceful. For instance, the death of a child poses a heightened risk for parental divorce, yet couple and family bonds are strengthened when members pull together and support each other in dealing with their tragedy. The concept of resilience extends beyond coping and adaptation to recognize the enhanced strengths and growth that can be forged out of adversity. A crisis often leads to reappraisal of life priorities and greater investment in meaningful relationships and pursuits. Many find new purpose in efforts to prevent similar tragedies or help others who are suffering or struggling (Lietz, 2013; Walsh, 2016b).

A family resilience practice approach aims to identify and build key relational processes to overcome stressful life situations, with the conviction that collaborative efforts best enable families and all members to thrive. The approach is grounded in family systems theory, combining ecological and developmental perspectives to view the family as an open system that functions in relation to its broader sociocultural context and evolves over the multigenerational life cycle.

Ecological Perspective

A biopsychosocial systems orientation views problem situations and their solutions as involving multiple recursive influences of individuals, families, larger systems, and sociocultural variables. A family resilience approach recognizes that most problems involve an interaction of individual and family vulnerability with the impact of stressful life experiences and social contexts.

- Difficulties may be primarily biologically based, as in serious illness or disability, yet are largely influenced by interpersonal and sociocultural variables.
- Family distress may be fueled by external events, such as a major disaster, or by ongoing stressors, such as persistent conditions associated with poverty, racism, heterosexism, or other forms of discrimination.
- Family distress may result from unsuccessful attempts to cope with a pileup of stressors that overwhelm resources.

Developmental Perspective: Family Coping, Adaptation, and Resilience

A family resilience approach attends to adaptational processes over time, from ongoing interactions to family life cycle passage and multigenerational influences. Life crises and persistent stresses have an impact on the functioning of a family system, with ripple effects to all members and their relationships (Patterson, 2002). Family processes in preparedness and response are crucial for coping and adaptation; one family may falter, whereas another rallies with similar life challenges. How a family confronts and manages a disruptive or threatening experience, buffers stress, effectively reorganizes, and reinvests in life pursuits influences adaptation for all members.

As one example, the presumption that divorce inevitably damages children is not supported by empirical data that indicate that most children fare reasonably well over the long term and nearly one-third flourish. We need to take into account the multiple variables in risk and resilience over time that make a difference in children's adaptation, including the predivorce climate, postdivorce financial strains, reorganization of households, transitions with remarriage/repartnering and stepparenting, and persistent parental conflict or cutoff (Coleman et al., 2013; Greene et al., 2012). Research identifying family processes that distinguish those who are resilient can inform therapeutic and collaborative divorce efforts for optimal postdivorce child and family adaptation.

In resilience-oriented practice, family functioning is assessed in the context of the multigenerational system moving forward over time.

- A genogram and family timeline (McGoldrick et al., 2019) are useful tools to schematize relationship information and track system patterns to guide intervention planning, noting strengths and resources—past, current, and potential—as well as problems and limitations.
- Linkages are noted between the timing of symptoms and recent or impending stress events that have disrupted or threatened the family, such as a son's drop in school grades following his father's job loss and family financial strain.
- Frequently, symptoms coincide with stressful developmental transitions. Each poses particular challenges, as new developmental priorities emerge, boundaries shift, and roles and relationships are redefined. Families must deal with both predictable, normative stresses, such as becoming parents, and unpredictable, disruptive events, such as the untimely death of a young parent or birth of a child with disabilities.
- Families are more resilient when they are able to balance intergenerational continuity and change and maintain links between their past, present, and future, especially with immigration (Falicov, 2012).
- Family history, stories, and patterns of relation and functioning transmitted across the generations influence response to adversity and future expectations, hopes, dreams, and catastrophic fears.
- The convergence of developmental and multigenerational strains affects family coping ability. Distress rises when current stressors reactivate past vulnerable issues or painful losses, particularly when similar challenges are confronted, such as life-threatening illness (McGoldrick et al., 2014; Rolland, 2018).
- It is important to inquire about models and stories of resilience and of extended family, cultural, and spiritual resources in overcoming past family adversity that might inspire coping strategies in the current situation.

Advantages of a Family Resilience Framework

Postmodern perspectives have heightened awareness that views of family normality, pathology, and health are socially constructed (Walsh, 2012). Clinicians and researchers bring their own assumptive maps into every evaluation and intervention, embedded in cultural norms, professional orientations, and personal experience.

In recent decades, along with global social and economic transformations, the very concept of the family has been expanded. Cultural diversity, economic and racial disparities, more fluid gender identity and role relations, and varied family forms and household arrangements require a broad, inclusive, and flexible view of family life (Cherlin, 2010; Walsh, 2012). Over a lengthening life course, children and their parents often move in and out of varied and complex family constellations. Resilience is needed with disruptive transitions posing new adaptational challenges. Yet, a substantial body of research finds that most children and families thrive in a variety of kinship arrangements and with gay or straight parents (Green, 2012). What matters most are relational *processes* for effective family functioning and the quality of caring, committed bonds for stability, nurturing, guidance, and protection.

Systems-based research on family functioning in recent decades has offered empirical grounding to identify and facilitate key processes in intervention with distressed families (Lebow & Stroud, 2012). However, studies based on White, middle-class, intact families that are not under stress contribute to faulty assumptions that family distress and differences from the norm are pathological. Furthermore, static and acontextual family typologies fail to attend to a family's social influences and emerging challenges over time.

A family resilience framework offers several advantages:

- By definition, it focuses on strengths under stress.
- It is assumed that no single model fits all family situations. Functioning and resilience

must be assessed in context—relative to each family's values, structure, resources, and life challenges.
- There are many, varied pathways in resilience. Processes for optimal functioning and the well-being of members will vary over time, as challenges unfold and families evolve across the life cycle.
- This approach to practice is grounded in a deep conviction in the potential for family repair, recovery, and growth out of adversity.

Key Processes in Family Resilience

The Walsh Family Resilience Framework identifies nine key processes and subcomponents for resilience (Walsh, 2016b). It is informed by three decades of research in the social sciences and clinical field on resilience and well-functioning family systems. The framework synthesizes major findings in three domains of family functioning: family belief systems, organizational patterns, and communication processes.

- Family belief systems support resilience when they help members (1) make meaning of their adverse experience; (2) sustain a hopeful, positive outlook, fueling active initiative and perseverance; and (3) draw on transcendent or spiritual values and purpose, inspiring transformation and positive growth.
- Family organization bolsters resilience by (1) flexibility to adapt, with strong leadership; (2) connectedness for mutual support and teamwork; and (3) extended kin, social, and community resources.
- Communication processes facilitate resilience through (1) information clarity; (2) sharing of both painful and positive emotions; and (3) collaborative problem-solving, with a proactive approach to future challenges.

Applications of Family Resilience Approaches

Family resilience–oriented practice shares principles and techniques common among strengths-based approaches but attends more centrally to links between presenting problems and family stressors, focusing on family coping and adaptational strategies. Interventions are directed to strengthen relational bonds and tap resources to reduce vulnerability and master challenges. The family resilience framework is designed to guide assessment, interventions, and prevention to identify and strengthen key processes that foster recovery and growth.

A family resilience framework has been usefully applied in a wide range of adverse situations (Walsh, 2016a, 2016b):

- Healing from crisis, trauma, and loss (e.g., family bereavement, relational trauma, war-related and refugee trauma, and disaster recovery)
- Navigating disruptive transitions (e.g., migration, separation/divorce, stepfamily formation, and foster/kinship care)
- Mastering multistress challenges with chronic conditions (e.g., illness/disability, unemployment/financial strain, community violence, and discrimination)
- Supporting positive development of at-risk youth (e.g., family–school partnerships and gang prevention programs)

Efforts to foster family resilience can benefit all family members, not just those currently in distress. A systemic assessment may lead to multilevel approaches to risk reduction, problem resolution, and individual/family well-being. Putting an ecological view into practice, interventions often involve community collaboration and change; peer groups and social networks; and workplace, school, health care, and other larger systems. Programs for youth mentoring, skill-building, parenting and caregiving, and creative expression through the arts are important components of many resilience-oriented interventions.

Family resilience–oriented intervention approaches are increasingly being developed for situations of collective trauma and loss, as in war-related trauma, refugee displacement/resettlement, and major disasters or catastrophic events (e.g., Landau, 2007; MacDermid, 2010; Saul, 2013; Walsh, 2007). In contrast to individual symptom-focused treatment programs, multilevel systemic approaches build collaborative networks that facilitate individual, family, and community resilience. Programs create a safe haven for family and community members to support each other in sharing both deep pain and positive strivings. They expand a shared vision of what is possible through collective efforts, not only to survive trauma and loss but also to regain their spirit to thrive.

Resilience-oriented family interventions can be adapted to a variety of formats:

- Family consultations, brief counseling, or more intensive family therapy may combine individual and conjoint sessions, including members affected by stressors and those who can contribute to resilience.
- Multifamily groups, workshops, and community forums offer social support and practical strategies for stress reduction, crisis management, problem-solving, relational support, and enhanced functioning as families navigate stressful challenges.
- Brief, cost-effective periodic "resilience checkups" can be timed around critical transitions or emerging challenges in long-term adaptation processes—for example, in a chronic illness, disaster recovery, or refugee resettlement.

Conclusion

Crisis and challenge are inherent in the human condition. Beyond the rhetoric of promoting family strengths, research and practice priorities must support efforts of vulnerable families to deal with highly stressful life challenges. Conceptual and research advances have laid important groundwork for understanding and facilitating family resilience in a wide range of adverse situations (Walsh, 2016b). Further mixed-method research is needed, combining qualitative and quantitative methods (Card & Barnett, 2015).

A research-informed family resilience framework can guide clinical and community-based practice by assessing family functioning on key system variables as they fit each family's values, structure, resources, and life challenges and then targeting interventions to strengthen family resilience as presenting problems are addressed.

With recognition of multilevel systemic influences in risk and resilience, better integration of child and family approaches is called for (Masten & Monn, 2015). Efforts must also be directed to transform larger systemic/structural policies and programs to address economic, racial, and gender disparities and to restructure workplace, health care, child care, and elder care to support resilience in all families.

Helpful Resource

Chicago Center for Family Health: http://www.ccfhchicago.org

References

Card, N., & Barnett, M. (2015). Methodological considerations in studying individual and family resilience. *Family Relations, 64*(1), 120–133.

Cherlin, A. J. (2010). Demographic trends in the United States: A review of research in the 2000s. *Journal of Marriage and Family, 72,* 403–419.

Coleman, M., Ganong, L., & Russell, R. (2013). Resilience in stepfamilies. In D. Becvar (Ed.), *Handbook of family resilience* (pp. 85–103). Springer.

Falicov, C. (2012). Immigrant family processes: A multi-dimensional framework (MECA). In F. Walsh (Ed.), *Normal family processes: Growing diversity and complexity* (4th ed., pp. 297–323). Guilford.

Green, R.-J. (2012). Gay and lesbian family life: Risk, resilience, and rising expectations. In F. Walsh (Ed.), *Normal family processes: Growing diversity and complexity* (4th ed., pp. 172–195). Guilford.

Greene, S., Anderson, E., Forgatch, M., deGarmo, D., & Hetherington, M. (2012). Risk and resilience after divorce. In F. Walsh (Ed.), *Normal family processes: Growing diversity and complexity* (4th ed., pp. 102–127). Guilford.

Landau, J. (2007). Enhancing resilience: Families and communities as agents for change. *Family Process, 46*(3), 351–365.

Lebow, J., & Stroud, C. B. (2012). Assessment of effective couple and family functioning: Prevailing models and instruments.

Lietz, C. (2013). Family resilience in the context of high-risk situations. In D. Becvar (Ed.), *Handbook of family resilience* (pp. 153–172). Springer.

MacDermid, S. M. (2010). Family risk and resilience in the context of war and terrorism. *Journal of Marriage and Family, 72,* 537–556.

Masten, A., & Monn, A. R. (2015). Child and family resilience: A call for integrating science, practice, and training. *Family Relations, 64*(1), 5–21.

McGoldrick, M., Garcia-Preto, N., & Carter, B. (Eds.). (2014). *The expanded family life cycle: Individual, family, and social perspectives* (5th ed.). Allyn & Bacon.

McGoldrick, M., Gerson, R., & Petry, S. (2019). *Genograms: Assessment and intervention* (4th ed.). Norton.

Patterson, J. (2002). Integrating family resilience and family stress theory. *Journal of Marriage and the Family, 64*(2), 349–360.

Rolland, J. S. (2018). *Helping couples and families navigate illness and disability.* Guilford.

Rutter, M. (1987). Psychosocial resilience and protective mechanisms. *American Journal of Orthopsychiatry, 57,* 316–331.

Saul, J. (2013). *Collective trauma, collective healing: Promoting community resilience in the aftermath of disaster* (Vol. 48). Routledge.

Walsh, F. (2003). Family resilience: A framework for clinical practice. *Family Process, 42*(1), 1–18.

Walsh, F. (2007). Traumatic loss and major disasters: Strengthening family and community resilience. *Family Process, 46,* 207–227.

Walsh, F. (Ed.). (2012). *Normal family processes: Growing diversity and complexity* (4th ed.). Guilford.

Walsh, F. (2016a). Applying a family resilience framework in training, practice, and research: Mastering the art of the possible. *Family Process, 55,* 616–632.

Walsh, F. (2016b). *Strengthening family resilience* (3rd ed.). Guilford.

Werner, E., & Smith, R. (2001). *Journeys from childhood to midlife: Risk, resiliency, and recovery.* McGraw-Hill.

Family Systems

Tara Bohley and Michael E. McGuire

From a systems perspective, "mental health" can be seen as relationship health.
—Becvar and Becvar (2018, p. 66)

Presenting problems and symptoms do not manifest in a vacuum but are systemic in nature. Family therapy seeks to address problems through the activation of change within the family system, thereby encouraging quicker and more lasting results than sometimes seen when working with clients individually. Researchers and practitioners have pioneered a host of principles and models that social workers can adopt and adapt to support efforts in treating the system as opposed to the symptom.

Genesis of Family Systems

For millennia, families have served as protective institutions, having distinct variations based on the family's need to adapt to their particular culture, economy, and social structure (Hill, 2012). The family often yields greater influence on a person's development and trajectory than any other social system, including work, school, and church (Becvar & Becvar, 2018). Early indicators of this understanding can be seen, for example, in

pioneer social worker Mary Richmond's book *Social Diagnosis* (1917), in which she advises outreach workers to assess "the trend of the family" and inquire as to "the attitude of the members of the family toward one another. Do they hang together through thick and thin or is there little cohesion?" Richmond, taking a forward-looking posture, prompts the worker to ask, "What are the family's plans and ambitions for the future?" (pp. 379–381). The dominant approach to therapy during this era and through the first half of the 20th century was psychoanalysis (Samuel, 2013), which considered the dynamic forces of family interaction as central to the intrapsychic struggles of their patients. It was not until the mid-1900s, however, that a new approach to therapy began to view family members as not only causal to the problems but also curative to the solutions (Weinstein, 2013). Early pioneers influencing the field of family therapy include Alfred Adler (birth order), John Bowlby (attachment), Murray Bowen (intergenerational), Virginia Satir (communications), Carl Whitaker (experiential), Gregory Bateson and Milton Erickson (meta-communication), Jay Haley and Cloe Madanes (strategic), and Salvador

Minuchin (structural). Although each offered a unique perspective to family systems theory, all facilitated a shift of focus in therapy from the inner world to the outer world, from intrapersonal to interpersonal, from individual to system. As Janet Malcolm wrote in her 1978 *New Yorker Magazine* article, "Psychoanalysis is a nineteenth century concept . . . it is about man out of context. Today we are in a historical period in which we cannot conceive of nonrelated things" (as cited in Becvar & Becvar, 2018, p. 2).

Here, Malcolm speaks to the profound shift from a Freudian, intrapsychic approach exploring instinctual urges and unconscious drives to an interactional, person-in-environment model. Consequentially, this novel systems perspective situated the therapist from that of a detached observer to an active participant and, quite literally, shifted the position of the client from couch to chair as they worked together in co-creating a new reality. Expanding on this logic, therapists look to the systemic, bidirectional influences beyond that of the immediate family and consider the broader environment, including other families, church, neighborhood, school, work, human service providers, cultural values, societal laws and norms, and other ecological considerations as conceptualized in the work of Urie Bronfenbrenner (Hertler et al., 2018).

However, this bidirectional approach soon drew criticism from early feminist and postmodern scholars for failing to acknowledge how the inherent inequities in social systems impact family roles and power dynamics and because of the implicit power the therapist has over the family (Hare-Mustin, 1978). This wave of critique pushed the field into a new direction of second-order systems thinking. When the therapist "joins" the family, the therapist brings their own context, values, and ethnocentric viewpoint into the system. The influence over the family impacts the dynamics and can serve to perpetuate the values of the dominant culture (Hoffman, 1985). Taking this concept even further, post-structuralists such as Michael White expanded the focus on social context that considers the family narrative within the context of varying societal narratives which incorporate race, socioeconomics, trauma, and sexual and gender identities and recognized that problematic systems not only influence difficulties in families but also at times create the troubles (Dickerson, 2014). As noted by Dadras and Daneshpour (2018), "a systemic thinker and therapist must expand his/her conceptualizations to understand complexity of the Other's life circumstances" (p. 8).

Contemporary Approaches

The most commonly practiced family therapies are integrative approaches—combining the work of the aforementioned pioneers with influences of a second generation of systems practitioners–researchers such as Insoo Kim Berg and Steven de Shazer (solution-focused brief therapy), Evan Imber-Black (families and larger systems), and Michael White (narrative family therapy) (Lebow, 2019). Although there are many model-specific tools, interventions, and even manuals unique to the practices used today, across all of them are four common factors: (1) conceptualizing difficulties in relational terms, (2) disrupting dysfunctional relational patterns, (3) expanding the direct treatment system, and (4) expanding the therapeutic alliance (Sprenkle et al., 2009).

Two seminal articles published in *Family Process* by Allen Carr (2019a, 2019b) summarize the evidence supporting the use of family systems models and interventions for a wide range of presenting problems:

- Problems in infancy and early childhood
  - Family-based behavioral programs for problems with infant feeding and sleeping

- Child–parent psychotherapy for helping primary caregivers form secure attachment bonds with their infants by addressing their own adverse childhood experiences and everyday stressors
- Attachment and biobehavioral catch-up, video-feedback intervention to promote positive parenting, and circle of security for attachment disorders in infancy and early childhood
- Child abuse and neglect
  - Cognitive–behavioral family therapy, parent–child interactional therapy, and multisystemic therapy for child physical abuse and neglect
  - Trauma-focused cognitive–behavioral therapy for childhood sexual abuse
  - Multidimensional treatment foster care for foster families
- Problems in adolescence
  - Multisystemic therapy for juvenile delinquency and substance use disorders
  - Brief strategic family therapy, multidimensional family therapy, and functional family therapy for youth problem behaviors
  - Family-based treatment for child and adolescent eating disorders, also known as the Maudsley method
- Adult mental health and chronic physical illness
  - Emotionally focused couples therapy for relationship distress, depression, post-traumatic stress disorder, and chronic physical illness
  - Behavioral, cognitive–behavioral, and solution-focused couple therapy for depression
  - Partner-assisted cognitive–behavioral exposure therapy for anxiety disorders
  - Family-focused treatment for bipolar disorder
  - Psychoeducational family therapy and multiple family group therapy for psychosis
- Relationship distress and psychosexual problems
  - Behavioral, cognitive–behavioral, and solution-focused couple therapy for mild to moderate intimate partner violence
  - Masters and Johnson's sex therapy and cognitive–behavioral interventions for psychosexual problems

Although this is not an exhaustive list, it offers social workers a broad view of how these models are used across the family life cycle. As practice-informed literature continues to grow, it will be increasingly important to stay abreast of new models used for contemporary problems.

Family Systems Concepts

A family systems therapist views the family as the client, focusing on the family context as a whole rather than individual family member in isolation. Therapists tend more to the immediate rather than historical context of interpersonal interactions, recognizing it is the relationship sequences that both drive and limit the behavior of an individual. All behavior is viewed as communicative, necessitating the family therapist to focus on elements of nonverbal communication and interaction; hence, the *process* of communication is valued equivalent to, or more than, the *content* of what is said. The interactional position of the speakers is viewed by the therapist in terms of closeness and distance, and autonomy and control, while noting patterns that move the system either toward change (positive feedback loops) or toward consistency and stability, thereby minimizing change (negative feedback loops). A systems lens is nonjudgmental in that causality is circular—no one behavior simply causes another. Instead, each behavior is linked to a preceding and subsequent behavior, with no particular starting or ending point. It is this circularity that perpetuates the homeostasis, with the pull of each family member's behavior on the others to reinforce familiar patterns.

General systems theory concepts guide the therapist in problem formulation and goal development. Specifically, families interact in predictable, organized ways that have produced stability and coherence, and there is a natural, if unconscious, desire to maintain that stability and to resist change (morphostasis). A system has the ability to restore itself according to its own internal structure and operating procedures following any disturbance to the system, whether originating from within or without. This natural tendency of the family system can be construed as problematic to a therapist, who is, by definition, a perturber of the system. However, rather than labeling this as resistance, the family therapist views this tendency as both natural and often vital to the well-being of a family.

In addition, the therapist encourages change on two levels: (1) a change in the way elements within a system relate to one another (first-order change) and (2) a change in the way the system is organized (second-order change). Although first-order change is an indicator of progress, the goals for therapy are to achieve second-order change, which is necessary for the system to develop lasting and self-maintaining new patterns of interaction (Watzlawick et al., 2011).

Embedded within the family system are smaller systems such as the sibling subsystem and the marital/couple/parental subsystem. Most systems include a hierarchy—an understood vertical arrangement of authority among family members. Boundaries serve as the figurative borders of a system or subsystem, delineating what or whom is inclusive and exclusive to the system. Boundaries can be on a spectrum from diffuse to rigid, and they contribute to the health and/or dysfunction within the system. Particular models of therapy, such

as structural and strategic, aim to reorganize the system by restructuring interactions and realigning boundaries.

The successful family therapist *joins* the family system by establishing an alliance of trust and rapport with individual members as well as with the family as a whole. Different theorists view the level of joining across a spectrum, with some, such as Bowen, preferring to maintain a level of detached centrality, and others, such as Whitaker, joining the systems as an additional family member (Minuchin & Fishman, 1981). In either approach, the challenge is to maintain a balance of neutrality versus alignment with particular members while preserving a strong therapeutic alliance with the entire system.

Immediate Application

The following are 16 systems-oriented interventions social workers may readily apply:

- Redefine family—Broaden the definition of family to include anyone the family considers close to the problem and as a useful resource toward a solution.
- Recruit—Discuss with the client the importance/relevance of bringing their immediate support system (i.e., their family) into the counseling process (see Case Example).
- Offer parity—Create space for each member to express their view of both the problem and the ideas for a solution. *Example*: "I'd like to hear from each of you about any concerns you have for your family."
- Avoid speeding tickets—Use caution when shifting the focus of treatment from the identified patient to the family system; otherwise, the family may prematurely end treatment. *Example*: "Parents dealing with behaviors like those of your daughter often experience stress. How has your daughter's behavior affected your relationship?"

- Add or subtract—When feeling "stuck," change the composition of the session by adding members or segmenting. *Example*: Meet with only the children, or only the parents, or only the mother and daughter, etc.
- Become less central—Find ways to encourage family members to speak directly to one another and not through you. *Example*: "Let me step aside while your family discusses this issue."
- Circular questioning—Help members check their assumptions about what other members think about a subject. *Example*: "What do you think your father thinks about this problem?" (Note: allow for the response to generate productive conversation.)
- Be experiential—Augment talk therapy with more tactile experiences. Examples include Draw Your Family, Family Sculpting, and Alter Ego (Edwards, 2012).
- Reframe the problem—Offer opportunities for members to view the problem as relational. *Example*: When a father says his son never talks to his parents, offer "You'd like better communication with your son."
- Hold process over content—Rather than give attention to the *problem du jour*, explore the interactional patterns the family relies on for addressing and resolving disturbances. *Example*: "When things like this happen, how does the family talk about the event?"
- Develop family goals—Broaden the view of both the problem and the solution by developing an interactional, systems-oriented goal. *Example*: "The family will make time to check in with one another by eating supper together at least three times each week."
- Develop individual family goals—Allow each member to identify one thing they would like to change about themselves that, when successful, will also help the family. Example of a parent's individual family goal: "I will not drink alcohol until after tucking the children to bed."
- Consider multigenerational trends— *Example*: Use a genogram to help family members and social worker contextualize the current challenges.
- Expand the system—Explore the family's interconnectedness with broader systems such as school, work, and community. *Example*: Create an ecomap.
- Develop a systems-congruent premise— Ensure your working hypothesis of the case highlights systems theory. *Example*: "To the degree Partner A becomes more emotionally available, Partner B will become less angry. And to the degree Partner B becomes less angry, Partner A will become more emotionally responsive."
- Examine biases—Consider how your values, beliefs, and understanding of family may interfere with the family seeking treatment. *Example*: How does your paradigm around gender roles manifest in your work with this family?

Case Example

The parent of a 10-year-old calls with concerns about her son's behavior, including talking back, persistent complaining, and not following rules. The parent is told, in summary, "The way we work is to see the whole family so we can get a full picture of the problem. We find this approach leads to greater success than seeing only a part of the family." For the initial family session, all members of the family living in the home are in attendance: two parents, son (the identified patient), two additional children, and the sister of one of the parents. After a brief introduction, each member is given the opportunity to offer any concerns they have for the family. Beyond the behavior of the son, there were concerns noted about the parents' conflict over parenting styles.

By the end of the session, the family agrees to a goal for how they would like the family to look different, and each member develops a strategy of how they can help toward this goal. For example, the father chooses a goal of spending more time on the weekends with his children, and one of the children sets a goal of not yelling as much. The session ends with the social worker reflecting family strengths, offering confidence in the family's ability to find a solution, and scheduling the next appointment, being sure to discuss potential barriers to attendance. During the next few weeks, the social worker continues to meet with the entire family, while at times segmenting and meeting with subsystems (e.g., parents), and uses the family's in-session interactions to experientially effect the desired second-order change(s). The social worker's hypothesis for the case is, "To the degree that the parents present a unified front regarding discipline, the child's behavior will improve. To the degree the child's behavior improves, the parents will feel effective and build a closer bond with each other."

Using a family systems approach, the social worker conceptualized both the genesis of the problem and the prospect of a solution as reliant on the communication, interplay, reciprocity, and circularity between the members of the family. The ReSPECT model (Edwards, 2012) offers a systems-oriented guide for an initial family session, some of which can be seen utilized in the previous case example. The model offers the following six stages for an initial family session:

Re—Recruitment: At a minimum, request that everyone living in the home attend the first session.

S—Social: Offer space for sharing interests and hobbies, and find out about other key members of the system not in attendance.

P—Problem: Encourage each family member to offer their view of the problem(s).

E—Exploration: Encourage family members to talk about the problem(s) while you observe, listen, and support.

C—Closing: Support family strengths; offer hope; and, if appropriate, discuss referrals and/or schedule the next session.

T—Talk to a colleague: Discuss the case with a professional colleague or supervisor.

These simple and practical components of an initial family session ensure a systems-oriented start to services and help the social worker join the family by creating space for each member, noting family strengths, and instilling hope. As the developer of structural family therapy, Salvador Minuchin (2017), wrote, "The individual patient is not the patient. The patient is the relational patterns that are created by belonging to a subsystem" (pp. 95–96).

Administrative Considerations

The unique nature of working with families often requires special attention to a variety of administrative and clinical processes. To optimize success using the family systems model, social workers are encouraged to consider the following:

- The medical model widely in use today typically requires a singular identified patient and diagnosis. This convention may be antithetical to systems principles and create challenges in confidentiality, billing, and organization of client files.
- Studies pointing to the efficacy of family therapy often obscure the real-world challenges of engaging families in therapy, including child care, travel expense, and time.
- Family therapy can, at times, be counterindicated for issues such as severe interpersonal violence, existential reflection, or significant marital discord. Referrals to

individual counseling, couples counseling, group counseling, and multiple family group counseling should be considered.

- In certain evidence-based models, the use of family therapy is considered a component of a multimodal approach, which includes the use of psychopharmacology (e.g., with psychosis and eating disorders as presenting issues).

Conclusion

A systems approach to counseling offers the opportunity to work within the structure of the family and the context of the broader societal environment. Rather than treating the client as primarily responsible for presenting problems and subsequent solutions, the family systems social worker explores and targets cyclical and interdependent patterns of behavior under the prism of ecological factors. This approach offers a wide range of potential points of intervention and utilizes the inherent influence of individual members of the system as well as the system as a whole. As carbon atoms under enormous pressure become a diamond, so too is a family, even under enormous pressure, greater than the sum of its individual members.

Helpful Resources

American Association for Marriage and Family Therapy: https://www.aamft.org

Family Therapy Training Institute of Miami: https://brief-strategic-family-therapy.com

Functional Family Therapy: https://www.fftllc.com

Multidimensional Family Therapy: http://www.mdft.org/MDFT-Program/What-is-MDFT

National Council on Family Relations: https://www.ncfr.org

The Bowen Center: https://www.thebowencenter.org/theory

The Center for Family Systems Theory: http://www.familysystemstheory.org/history

References

Becvar, D. S., & Becvar, R. J. (2018). *Systems theory and family therapy: A primer* (3rd ed.). Hamilton Books.

Carr, A. (2019a). Couple therapy, family therapy and systemic interventions for adult-focused problems: The current evidence base. *Journal of Family Therapy, 41*(4), 492–536. https://doi.org/10.1111/1467-6427.12225

Carr, A. (2019b). Family therapy and systemic interventions for child-focused problems: The current evidence base. *Journal of Family Therapy, 41*(2), 153–213. https://doi.org/10.1111/1467-6427.12226

Dadras, I., & Daneshpour, M. (2018). Social Justice Implications for MFT: The Need for Cross-Cultural Responsiveness. In *Cross-Cultural Responsiveness & Systemic Therapy* (pp. 1–20). Springer, Cham.

Dickerson, V. C. (2014). The advance of poststructuralism and its influence on family therapy. *Family Process, 53*(3), 401–414. https://doi.org/10.1111/famp.12087

Edwards, J. (2012). *Working with families: Guidelines and techniques* (2nd ed.). Wiley.

Hare-Mustin, R. T. (1978). A feminist approach to family therapy. *Family Process, 17*(2), 181–194. https://doi.org/10.1111/j.1545-5300.1978.00181.x

Hertler, S. C., Figueredo, A. J., Peñaherrera-Aguirre, M., Fernandes, H. B. F., & Woodley of Menie, M. A. (2018). Urie Bronfenbrenner: Toward an evolutionary ecological systems theory. In S. C. Hertler, A. J. Figueredo, M. Peñaherrera-Aguirre, H. B. F. Fernandes, & M. A. Woodley of Menie (Eds.), Life history evolution: A biological meta-theory for the social sciences (pp. 323–339). Springer. https://doi.org/10.1007/978-3-319-90125-1_19

Hill, S. (2012). *Families: A social class perspective*. Sage. https://doi.org/10.4135/9781483349374

Hoffman, L. (1985). Beyond power and control: Toward a "second order" family systems therapy. *Family Systems Medicine, 3*(4), 381–396. https://doi.org/10.1037/h0089674

Lebow, J. L. (2019). Current issues in the practice of integrative couple and family therapy. *Family Process, 58*(3), 610–628. https://doi.org/10.1111/famp.12473

Minuchin, S. (2017). Deconstructing Minuchin. *Journal of Systemic Therapies, 36*(4), 95–97. https://guilfordjournals.com/doi/pdf/10.1521/jsyt.2017.36.4.95

Minuchin, S., & Fishman, H. C. (1981). *Family therapy techniques*. Harvard University Press.

Richmond, M. E. (1917). *Social diagnosis*. Russell Sage Foundation.

Samuel, L. R. (2013). *Shrink: A cultural history of psychoanalysis in America.* University of Nebraska Press.

Sprenkle, D. H., Davis, S. D., & Lebow, J. L. (2009). *Common factors in couple and family therapy: The overlooked foundation for effective practice.* Guilford.

Watzlawick, P., Weakland, J. H., & Fisch, R. (2011). *Change: Principles of problem formulation and problem resolution.* Norton.

Weinstein, D. (2013). *The pathological family.* Cornell University Press. https://doi.org/https://doi.org/10.7591/9780801468155

Critical Theories for Social Work Practice

Travis J. Albritton, William J. Hall, and L. B. Klein

Perhaps social work is unique among the human service professions because its mission is explicitly focused on "the needs and empowerment of people who are vulnerable, oppressed, and living in poverty" (National Association of Social Workers, 2017). This mission assumes that clients are living in a society with systems of oppression that stratify people into groups based on particular factors (e.g., race, gender, and sexual orientation) and use institutional resources and processes (e.g., norms, ideals, laws, preferential treatment, policing, and violence) to advantage and disadvantage groups of people (e.g., White people and people of color). These systems result in exploitation, marginalization, disempowerment, and human suffering. Social workers respond to presenting problems such as depression, anxiety, addiction, food insecurity, neglect, and homelessness with theoretically and evidence-informed interventions; however, social workers cannot address these problems with individuals without considering the broader context of social oppression.

Given the pervasiveness of oppression, its human consequences, and the mission of social work, social workers must use a critical lens to understand and address clients' concerns, and critical theories can provide this framework. *Critical theories* are focused on understanding how individual problems are shaped by broad social systems of oppression, consciousness-raising about inequities and injustices, critiquing social work that leads to social control, centering voices and empowerment of minoritized clients and communities, and building alliances to transform society. This chapter focuses on three of those theories: critical race theory (CRT), feminist theory, and queer theory. Additional critical theories include Latinx critical race theory, Asian American critical race theory, American Indian critical race theory, critical disability theory, and critical gerontology.

Critical Race Theory
Historical Roots of Critical Race Theory
The origins of CRT can be traced to early critical legal scholars such as Derrick Bell,

Richard Delgado, and Alan Freeman, who argued that the law is neither neutral nor objective with respect to issues of race and racial discrimination (Brown & Jackson, 2013; Delgado & Stefancic, 2012; Ladson-Billings, 1998). Bell, Delgado, and Freeman's emphasis on the centrality of race challenged "colorblind" applications of the law that ignore how racism negatively impacts the lives of people of color. Their centering of race was foundational to the development of CRT as they worked to ensure that the United States did not lose the gains made during the civil rights movement.

In 1989, Delgado and Bell, along with 22 critical legal scholars of color, met at a conference organized by Kimberlé Crenshaw where they discussed what they viewed as "new developments in CRT" (Crenshaw, 2011; Delgado & Stefancic, 2012). It was at this conference that CRT began to take shape.

Critical Race Theory Tenets

Although much has been written about CRT since its early development, scholars agree that the theory does not have a set of formally agreed upon tenets (Daftary, 2018; Ladson-Billings, 1998; McDowell & Jeris, 2004). A review of relevant literature, however, reveals six central principles used by those who employ CRT in their work: the permanence of racism, interest convergence, the critique of liberalism, intersectionality and anti-essentialism, whiteness as property, and the use of counternarratives.

The *permanence of racism* refers to the fact that racism exists in every aspect of our society. CRT scholars see racism as inescapable "and, because it is so enmeshed in the fabric of our social order, it appears both normal and natural to people in this culture" (Ladson Billings, 1998, p. 11).

Interest convergence, a principle first asserted by Derrick Bell, is the idea that any civil rights gains for people of color only occur when converging with the interests of Whites (Bell, 1980). For example, critical race theorists argue that the Supreme Court's 1954 *Brown v. Board of Education* decision had little to do with a desire to see Black people receive an equal education but, rather, served as a response to international pressure that called into question the country's treatment of African Americans (Kolivoski et al., 2014).

CRT rejects the liberal notion of a colorblind society, one in which everyone is afforded the same opportunities. Notions of equality and equal opportunity are interrogated, and there is recognition that "only aggressive, color conscious efforts to change the way things are" will address the systemic racism experienced by people of color (Delgado & Stefancic, 2012, p. 27).

Intersectionality, discussed in further detail later in this chapter, recognizes that no one person holds a singular identity. Race intersects with gender, gender identity, class, sexual orientation, and a whole host of identities. CRT examines the interplay of these identities and resists attempts to reduce individuals to a singular identity. Critical race theorists ask questions about what it means to be Black and male; Black, female, and queer; Black, trans, and poor.

Whiteness as property as explained by Cheryl Harris (1993) can be traced to the early racialization of Black people and Native Americans in the United States. Harris points out that "the hyper-exploitation of Black labor was accomplished by treating Black people themselves as objects of property" (p. 1716). She goes on to write that "the conquest, removal, and extermination of Native American life and culture were ratified by conferring and acknowledging the property rights of whites in Native American lands" (p. 1716). As a result, whiteness functions as a mechanism that bestows privilege on those who are deemed White. This privilege is transferable to individuals who conform to the values and ideals associated with whiteness (Kolivoski et al., 2014).

The *use of counter stories* centers the voices of people of color and acknowledges their lived experiences as important and valuable (Ortiz & Jani, 2010; Yosso, 2005). Counter stories provide an alternative to the majoritarian narratives perpetuated by White culture. The use of counter stories recognizes people of color as experts on their lives and gives them the opportunity to control how and when their stories are told (Daftary, 2020).

Critical Race Theory and Social Work Practice

As the United States becomes increasingly racially diverse, it is important that social workers use frameworks that appreciate the racial diversity of the clients they serve (Pew Research Center, 2019). CRT offers social workers one such framework. Specifically, CRT offers a lens for practitioners to "analyze the institutional arrangements of society, assess how they are shaped by dominant cultural assumptions, and recognize how they may disadvantage members of nondominant cultural groups" (Ortiz & Jani, 2008, p. 189). Whether used to examine practices that lead to disproportionality in child welfare, disparities in health care, or the underutilization of mental health services by people of color, CRT gives social workers a set of tools to constantly engage in practice that asks important questions about how race impacts service provision. The use of CRT can also impact how policies are written and implemented and can help ensure that communities of color are viewed through a lens of equity and justice.

Feminist Theory

Feminist theory, often described as a feminist approach or perspective, is used to examine societal gender inequity and its impact on individuals, families, and communities

(Brabeck & Brown, 1997). Historically, feminist theorists sought to critique dominant sociological theories that did not include gendered hierarchies and the experiences of women (Acker, 1973). Feminist theory provides a gender analysis of power relations, particularly between men and women, and proposes that society is constructed and controlled by men (*patriarchy*) to benefit men (Gardiner, 1999). Under patriarchy, there is a gendered division of labor (Chafetz, 1988), and women are controlled through violence perpetrated by men inside and outside of their homes (Stanko, 1995).

Feminisms

There are multiple forms of feminism that further critique and expand feminist theory. For example, feminist theory has been further critiqued for its adherence to gender as a binary as well as its focus on women who were assigned female at birth (i.e., cisgender women). Transfeminism has emerged to cultivate a feminist analysis that is more inclusive of transgender women and nonbinary people (Koyama, 2003). This is just one example of how there are multiple feminisms. Other branches of feminism include intersectional (discussed later in this chapter), liberal, Marxist, radical, and eco-feminism.

Feminist Standpoint Theory

Feminist standpoint theory is particularly relevant to social work practice because it posits that objectivity is not possible and that those who are minoritized know more about systems of oppression that harm them than do the dominant groups that benefit from those systems (Harding, 2004). Simply stated, people are the best experts on their own lives and communities. Therefore, social work practice with both individuals and communities should involve iterative processes that are driven by marginalized people's perspective and wisdom.

A Feminist Approach to Social Work Practice

Social workers have highlighted the need for feminist critiques of the role that social welfare systems often play in perpetuating oppression, including against women seeking support (Eyal-Lubling & Krumer-Nevo, 2016). Feminist social work practice often involves group therapy that provides a space for people, especially women, to share their experiences and to have them normalized and validated by others who share similar experiences (Kammer et al., 2011; Saulnier, 2000). Relational–cultural therapy may be of particular interest to social workers seeking a feminist approach because it is rooted in helping clients establish connections and develop mutual empathy through a focus on empowerment and consideration of societal context and cultural factors (Jordan, 2010). Both relational–cultural therapy and feminist group modalities relied on the idea that consciousness raising is crucial not only for personal change but also to engender societal transformation and ending women's marginalization (Carr, 2003; Jordan, 2010).

Queer Theory

Queer theory is a theoretical perspective that challenges normative assumptions about sexuality and gender to transform social norms and deconstruct oppressive systems. Queer theory rests on several key concepts and principles: (1) Gender is a performance; (2) sex, gender, and sexual identities are socially constructed; (3) identities and social norms concerning gender and sexuality should be resisted and critiqued; and (4) oppression in the form of homophobia, biphobia, transphobia, heterosexism, and cisgenderism should be opposed and dismantled. Although queer theory continues to evolve, its foundation was shaped by Judith Butler, Michel Foucault, and Eve Sedgwick, among others.

Key Themes of Queer Theory

Judith Butler (1990) challenged commonly accepted notions of gender as a natural and fixed identity. Butler forwarded that a person's gender is a performance characterized by repeated acts, gestures, and expressions. People come into the world and are given a sex label of male or female, raised as boys and girls who become men and women, and taught that these identities are fixed and associated with acceptable ways of behaving—social norms governing gender expression and sexuality. Girls and women are bound to feminine gender expectations and boys and men to masculine expectations, which include personality traits (e.g., women should be nurturing, men should be assertive), professional roles (e.g., women should be nurses, men should be engineers), and relationship roles (e.g., women should marry men and be good wives, men should marry women and provide for their family). Queer theory challenges such social constructions of sex, gender, and sexuality, especially binary constructions (e.g., male/female, man/woman, masculine/feminine, and heterosexual/homosexual). Indeed, science and research have documented substantial variation and fluidity in sex, gender, and sexuality (Affected by Intersex/Differences of Sex Development, 2017; Hall, 2019; Kimmel, 2016; Teich, 2012), which refute binary categories.

Michel Foucault (1978) rebuked sexually repressive practices of Western society that stigmatized sexual expressions outside of traditional heterosexual marriage. These so-called perversions included homosexuality. Foucault also asserted that the social construction of sexuality was fueled by efforts in the biomedical and behavioral sciences to study human sexuality, which included identifying types of sexual people (e.g., homosexuals and heterosexuals). These identity labels were constructed in ways to restrict the rich diversity of sexual desires, attractions, behaviors, and relationships that characterizes human sexuality. Foucault also analyzed how sexually repressive social constructions led to asymmetric power relations and social control.

Eve Sedgwick (1990) critiqued ideologies and social practices regarding heterosexuality and homosexuality that oversimplify and regulate bodies, thoughts, desires, acts, identities, and relationships—resulting in the oppression of minoritized individuals (e.g., gay people) and loss of understanding the diversity and nuance of human sexuality. Sedgwick also discussed the construction and function of "the closet" for people with nonheterosexual identities and its connection with *heteronormativity*, the idea that heterosexuality is the natural and normal expression of human sexuality. Sedgwick advanced that "queer" was an "open mesh of possibilities" (p. 110) and that the socially marginalized position of queer identities can be used for unification and empowerment to contest and subvert sociosexual norms. Indeed, many queer theorists, including Sedgwick (1990) and Seidman (1997), have advocated for sociopolitical action to confront sexuality- and gender-based oppression.

Applying Queer Theory to Social Work Practice

Queer theory can enhance social work practice with all clients—not just gay, lesbian, bisexual, and transgender clients. Practitioners should not assume a client's sex, gender, and sexual orientation, and binaries should not be reinforced (e.g., people are gay or straight). A person may appear or behave in a way that fits social definitions about a particular sex, gender, or sexual identity; however, that person may not align with practitioner assumptions or identify with any identity. Furthermore, clients who wish to explore their gender or sexuality do not have to conclude the process by choosing an identity. Questioning, exploring, or resisting labels do not signify an intrapsychic conflict or stunted

psychosexual development. If clients do identify in particular ways, practitioners can ask them what their identities mean to them and how they shape their life experiences, perhaps in enriching and challenging ways (e.g., facing discrimination). Any two clients may use the same identity label (e.g., bisexual), but what the identity means to each client may vary. Social workers should also be mindful of how gender and sexual identities intersect with other socially constructed identities (e.g., race, class, ability/disability, and age group) and with associated systems of social oppression (e.g., racism, classism, ableism, and ageism). Finally, clients' presenting problems may be connected with internalization and performance of oppressive social expectations regarding sex, gender, and sexuality. It may be helpful to explore and change core beliefs and behavior patterns that feel stifling and invalidating to clients who desire lives spanning the spectrum possibilities.

Critical Theories and Intersectionality

The notion that we all hold intersectional identities is a thread that is woven into multiple critical theories. Coined by Kimberlé Crenshaw, intersectionality considers how individual and group statuses overlap to shape experiences of oppression (Collins, 2000; Crenshaw, 1989). Intersectionality posits that oppression is not simply additive but is shaped by all the social identities someone holds. For example, Black women do not experience the same discrimination as either Black men or White women but, rather, discrimination specific to being Black women (Bowleg, 2008). The examination of the interplay of multiple identities resists attempts to reduce individuals to a singular identity and encourages a more nuanced recognition of how those individuals experience the world (Daftary, 2020).

The use of an intersectional analysis fits with the social work profession's emphasis on client-centered approaches. Intersectionality acknowledges and celebrates how people are different, and it is precisely this difference that calls for services and interventions that ask questions about how the confluence of race, gender, sexual orientation, class, and other social identities impacts how one experiences discrimination and oppression.

No matter their area of practice, social workers can use an intersectional approach and apply critical theories to fulfill social work's mission of empowering those who are most harmed by systems of oppression.

Helpful Resources

Websites

3 Women 3 Ways (podcast on feminist multicultural approaches to counseling): https://www.stitcher.com/podcast/blogtalkradio/3-women-3-ways/e/55231386

The Urgency of Intersectionality (Crenshaw): https://www.ted.com/talks/kimberle_crenshaw_the_urgency_of_intersectionality?language=en

University of Birmingham, Critical Race Theory: https://www.birmingham.ac.uk/research/crre/critical-race-theory/index.aspx

App

Hollaback!: https://www.ihollaback.org/take-action/get-app

Readings

Argüello, T. (Ed.). (2019). *Queer social work: Cases for LGBTQ+ affirmative practice*. Columbia University Press.

McCann, H., & Monaghan, W. (2020). *Queer theory now: From foundations to futures*. Red Globe Press.

Turner, S. G., & Maschi, T. M. (2015). Feminist and empowerment theory and social work practice. *Journal of Social Work Practice, 29*(2), 151–162. https://www.tandfonline.com/doi/abs/10.1080/02650533.2014.941282

References

Acker, J. (1973). Women and social stratification: A case of intellectual sexism. *American Journal of Sociology, 78*, 936–945.

Affected by Intersex/Differences of Sex Development. (2017). What is intersex and/or DSD? https://interconnect.support/what-is-intersex/

Bell, D. A. (1980). *Brown v. Board of Education* and the interest–convergence dilemma. *Harvard Law Review, 93*, 518–533.

Brabeck, M., & Brown, L. (1997). Feminist theory and psychology practice. In J. Worrell & N. G. Johnson (Eds.), *Shaping the future of feminist psychology: Research and practice* (pp.15–35). American Psychological Association.

Brown, K., & Jackson, D. (2013). The history and conceptual elements of critical race theory. In M. Lynn & A. Dixson (Eds.), *Handbook of critical race theory in education* (pp. 9–22). Routledge.

Butler, J. (1990). *Gender trouble: Feminism and the subversion of identity*. Routledge.

Carr, E. S. (2003). Rethinking empowerment theory using a feminist lens: The importance of process. *Affilia, 18*(8), 8–20.

Chafetz, J. S. (1988). The gender division of labor and the reproduction of disadvantage: Toward an integrated theory. *Journal of Family Issues, 9*(1), 108–131. https://doi.org/10.1177/019251388009001006

Collins, P. H. (2000). Gender, Black feminism, and the Black political economy. *Annals of the American Academy of Political and Social Science, 568*(1), 41–53. https://doi.org/10.1177%2F000271620056800105

Crenshaw, K. W. (1989). Demarginalizing the intersection of race and sex: A Black feminist critique of antidiscrimination doctrine, feminist theory, and antiracist politics. *University of Chicago Legal Forum, 1*(8). http://chicagounbound.uchicago.edu/uclf/vol1989/iss1/8

Crenshaw, K. W. (2011). Twenty years of critical race theory: Looking back to move forward. *Connecticut Law Review, 43*, 1255–1346.

Daftary, A. H. (2020). Critical race theory: An effective framework for social work research. Journal of Ethnic & Cultural Diversity in Social Work, 29(6), 439–454.

Delgado, R., & Stefancic, J. (2012). *Critical race theory: An introduction*. New York University Press.

Eyal-Lubling, R., & Krumer-Nevo, M. (2016). Feminist social work: Practice and theory of practice. *Social Work, 61*(3), 245–254. https://doi.org/10.1093/sw/sww026

Foucault, M. (1978). *The history of sexuality, Vol. 1: An introduction* (R. Hurley, Trans.). Vintage Books.

Gardiner, J. (1999). Patriarchy. In A. Harrington, B. L. Marshall, & H. Muller (Eds.), *Encyclopedia of social theory* (pp. 420–22). Routledge.

Hall, W. J. (2019). Sexual orientation. In C. Franklin (Ed.), *Oxford research encyclopedia of social work.* NASW Press and Oxford University Press.

Hall, W. J. (2019). Sexual orientation. In C. Franklin (Ed.), Oxford research encyclopedia of social work. Washington, DC: National Association of Social Workers Press and Oxford University Press. doi:10.1093/acrefore/9780199975839.013.1271

Harris, C. I. (1993). Whiteness as property. *Harvard Law Review, 106*(8), 1707–1791.

Jordan, J. (2010). *Relational cultural therapy.* American Psychological Association.

Kammer, R., Turner, S., & Bowdin, K. (2011). Treating women right. *Affilia, 25*(1), 83–86.

Kimmel, M. S. (2016). *The gendered society* (6th ed.). Oxford University Press.

Kolivoski, K. M., Weaver, A., & Constance-Huggins, M. (2014). Critical race theory: Opportunities for application in social work practice and policy. *Families in Society, 95*(4), 269–276.

Koyama, E. (2003). The transfeminist manifesto. In R. Dicker & A. Pipmeier (Eds.), *Catching a wave: Reclaiming feminism for the twenty-first century* (pp. 244–259). Northeastern University Press.

Ladson-Billings, G. (1998). Just what is critical race theory and what's it doing in a nice field like education? *International Journal of Qualitative Studies in Education, 11*(1), 7–24.

McDowell, T., & Jeris, L. (2004). Talking about race using critical race theory: Recent trends in the *Journal of Marital and Family Therapy. Journal of Marital and Family Therapy, 30*(1), 81–94.

National Association of Social Workers. (2017). *Code of ethics of the National Association of Social Workers.* NASW Press.

Ortiz, L., & Jani, J. (2010). Critical race theory: A transformational model for teaching diversity. *Journal of Social Work Education, 46*(2), 175–193.

Pew Research Center. (2019). *Americans see advantages and challenges in country's growing racial and ethnic diversity.* https://www.pewsocialtrends.org/2019/05/08/americans-see-advantages-and-challenges-in-countrys-growing-racial-and-ethnic-diversity

Saulnier, C. F. (2000). Incorporating feminist theory into social work practice: Group work examples. *Social Work with Groups, 23*(1), 5–29. https://doi.org/10.1300/J009v23n01_02

Sedgwick, E. K. (1990). *Epistemology of the closet.* University of California Press.

Seidman, S. (1997). *Difference troubles: Queering social theory and sexual politics.* Cambridge University Press.

Stanko, E. A. (1995). Women, crime, and fear. *Annals of the American Academy of Political and Social Science, 539,* 46–58. https://doi.org/10.1177/0002716295539001004

Teich, N. M. (2012). *Transgender 101: A simple guide to a complex issue.* Columbia University Press.

Yosso, T. J. (2005). Whose culture has capital: A critical race theory discussion of community cultural wealth. *Race Ethnicity and Education, 8*(1), 69–91.

The Neurobiology of Toxic Stress
Implications for Social Work

Julie M. Rosenzweig and Stephanie A. Sundborg

Social workers are committed to serving the most vulnerable individuals, families, and communities that are disproportionately affected by historical trauma and structural inequities. Many of these individuals and families are also involved with and overrepresented in human service organizations such as social services, homeless shelters, child welfare, juvenile justice, adult criminal justice, mental health centers, and substance abuse programs (Edalati & Nicholls, 2019; Jäggi et al., 2016; Klein & Merritt, 2014). Studies indicate that social service clients and incarcerated individuals are more likely to have experienced adverse conditions and trauma, including historical trauma, compared to the general population (Paul et al., 2017; Srivastav et al., 2020; Troutt, 2017). Without an integration of scholarship about the neurobiological underpinnings of psychological trauma into social policy and social work practice at both the organizational and practitioner levels, service delivery to vulnerable, traumatized populations will unknowingly fail to recognize clients' trauma-based survival behaviors and exacerbate their existing physiological and emotional trauma sequelae. Social workers employed within these organizations may also be negatively impacted by agency cultures that minimize the effects of secondary trauma exposure and vicarious traumatization (Ashley-Binge & Cousins, 2020).

Researchers are working to identify the biological mechanisms that embed adversity/trauma in the mind–body system, disrupt brain architecture, and transmit epigenetic changes (Berens et al., 2017; Farah, 2017; Lehrner & Yehuda, 2018). Such studies contribute to a greater appreciation of our nervous system's innate bias toward safety and survival and our need for trusting connectedness with others. Understanding the neurobiological response to trauma and adversity is also essential to developing, implementing, and sustaining trauma-informed policy and practice.

Without an understanding of how trauma exposure shifts both physical structures and neurochemical functioning of our neural networks that respond to threat, reshapes our perceptions of what is dangerous and what is safe, and informs implicit responses that seek protection from harm, practitioners are more likely to misinterpret behaviors and motives of clients who are using automatic (nonconscious) survival-based coping strategies and are responding to perceptions of threat that are neurobiologically embedded from prior and ongoing trauma experiences (Rosenzweig, 2015). In addition, practitioners are susceptible to vicarious traumatization through secondary exposure to client narratives of adversity, and they may experience similar neurobiological changes that need to be recognized and responded to by supportive organizational policies and practices, supervisors, and co-workers (Yatchmenoff et al., 2017).

Infusion of scholarship on the neurobiological underpinnings of psychological trauma is a crucial update to our knowledge base on human development and behavior, one that will sharpen our lens for understanding adaptive transactions between individuals and social environments and institutional systems and will align our organizations with trauma-informed principles and trauma-specific interventions. Social work academic institutions that provide classroom and field education are among those organizations that can become leaders in professional education, including continuous learning, about psychological trauma for social workers and allied professions.

The primary intent of this chapter is to provide social workers with foundational knowledge about the neurobiological changes brought about by exposure to adversity and psychological trauma. We begin by defining *toxic stress* as an expansion of traumatic stress and a neurophysiological adaptation from adversity. An overview of brain architecture activated and changed by toxic stress is presented, followed by a description of the mind–body stress response systems, including polyvagal theory.

What Makes Stress Toxic?

The human stress response is fundamentally intended to promote safety (physical and psychological) and survival. In the presence/perception of threat, or in the absence of safety cues, the brain coordinates a neurochemical response in the body that automatically mobilizes our bodies for fight or flight, to promote survival. In some cases, when actions of fight or flight are not options, our bodies will automatically shift to a state of immobilization or shutdown as a means of survival (Porges & Carter, 2017). Survival-based mobilization and immobilization behaviors are initiated without our conscious awareness. For the most part, we are not cognizant of our stress response, and not all experiences that we believe are stressful are considered toxic. Stressful challenges, when buffered by supportive others, can and do promote healthy brain architecture and allow us to expand our adaptive capacity and build resilience. When our stress response is beyond adaptive or tolerable, it is by comparison considered toxic (B. McEwen, 2012). In situations of extreme, repeated, or prolonged survival threats (e.g., poverty, child abuse and neglect, and domestic violence), our brain–body marshals a continuous response of flooding the body with stress hormones, particularly cortisol. This response keeps our body in a perpetual state of fight or flight, and the structures and functioning of the brain–body neural circuits regulating our stress response become impaired (B. McEwen, 2017). These changes in the brain architecture are the basis of disrupted neurodevelopment and its sequelae as described in numerous adverse childhood experiences studies (for a review, see Hughes et al., 2017).

Research and scholarship have continued to deepen our knowledge of toxic stress. For example, bridging neuroscience, epidemiology, developmental psychology, and ecology, the Center on the Developing Child at Harvard University proposed a biodevelopmental framework that underscores the significance of the mind–body's stress response system and the concept of toxic stress (Shonkoff, 2010). In contrast to traumatic stress, toxic stress is a more inclusive concept that comprehensively acknowledges the intricate intersection between biology (genetics) and environmental conditions, as well as the lifelong consequences of a child's stress response system being relentlessly activated (van der Kolk, 2014). C. McEwen and McEwen (2017) advanced this framework by proposing a model of toxic stress that combines both the biological processes and the mechanisms through which social inequalities become embodied. Accordingly,

> Toxic stress is the central biological mechanism in an emerging neuroscientific theory of the ways in which social circumstances, experiences, and relationships shape and reshape brain and body development, especially in early childhood, with resultant effects on later educational and occupational attainment as well as on health. Toxic stress involves the frequent or sustained activation of the biological stress system and is prompted by chronic social conditions and repeated or accumulating adverse events when social support systems are weak and when early-life experiences acting epigenetically have impaired the development of neural circuits involved in self-regulation of emotions and behavior. (p. 448)

Brain Architecture That Responds to Threat

Learning more about the brain structures and their functions specific to threat detection and response provides the policymaker and practitioner with a more complete understanding of emotional regulation, cognition systems, memory formation, and meaning-making processes, all fundamental to creating trauma-informed care systems and working with individuals, families, and communities affected by psychological trauma and toxic stress. A comprehensive review of brain anatomy is beyond the scope of this chapter; interested readers are encouraged to pursue the references included in this chapter for additional information. To facilitate understanding, Figure 35.1 shows the brain with key areas identified.

Hemispheric Specialization

The cerebral cortex has two halves, a right hemisphere (RH) and a left hemisphere (LH).

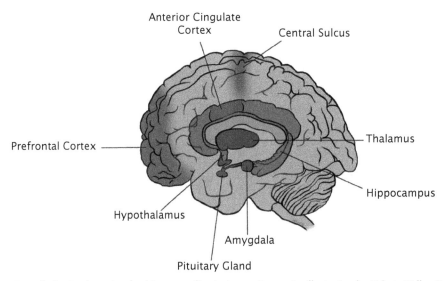

FIGURE 35.1 Brain structures involved in responding to traumatic events. Illustration by Halorie Walker-Sands.

Although these two halves appear identical in size and structures, there are important differences in function and processing style. The RH is dominant at birth (Dehaene-Lambertz & Spelke, 2015) and continues to be the primary hemisphere for the first 3 years of life, with its functions focused on survival, attachment patterns, emotional regulation, and sensory experiences (Schore, 2015). The RH uses several pathways to process emotion, often occurring prior to conscious awareness. One of the brain areas that is involved in the subconscious processing of fearful emotion is the amygdala (Tyler et al., 2011).

The RH is the relational hemisphere, mapping the emotional terrain of our earliest attachment experiences through cycles of dysregulation and regulation as infant and caregiver engage in reciprocity of attunement and resonance. These imprints, or internal working models of self and the world, serve as signposts for safety and promote or inhibit exploration (Beebe et al., 2012; Sherman et al., 2015).

The LH develops more slowly than the RH, not becoming fully wired-up (myelinated) until 18–24 months. Compared with the RH, the LH tends to be more logical, analytical, and sequential, and it focuses on details in order to construct complex theories and narratives (Gazzaniga et al., 2019). The LH, or *interpreter* (Gazzaniga et al., 1996), makes meaning of events in order to guide behavior (Gazzaniga et al., 2019) and regulate emotion (Shobe, 2014).

The two hemispheres each contribute uniquely to communication. The LH is understood to be primary in producing and comprehending language, in the traditional sense; however, the RH plays an important role in understanding emotion-based nonverbal cues such as body language and facial expressions (Schirmer & Adolphs, 2017). Both are important not only for communicating with others but also as a way of maintaining a sense of order. Meaning-making is the way individuals interpret their worlds and give explanation to events that happen. Whereas the RH is dominant for emotions and relationships, the LH provides the narrative to emotional experiences, expanding on what is known in the present; making inferences based on past experience; and contributing to the development of a worldview, against which events are scanned to provide explanation (Karaduman et al., 2017). Individuals with traumatic histories, especially early childhood experiences, are more likely to have a worldview of self-as-bad and others-dangerous and filter relationships and experiences through this lens. This is particularly applicable for early caregiver attachments that become neural guides for future relationships.

The Amygdales

Responding to traumatic events and toxic stress involves many brain regions, and of primary importance are the amygdales (one in each hemisphere). Acting as a first responder, this small, almond-shaped area processes input from our sensory systems, including tactile, visual, olfactory, auditory, and gustatory stimuli, determining if the incoming information is life-sustaining or life-threatening. The amygdala automatically coordinates with brain areas involved in long-term memory (hippocampus) and inhibitory control (prefrontal cortex) through elaborate neural networks and, when warranted, participates in initiating survival-based responding.

All sensory input associated with a dangerous or threatening situation is encoded by the amygdala as a threat to survival and is formed into memory. Before the development of language, the encoding of memories is automatic and outside of conscious awareness. These implicit-type memories do not contain autobiographical or chronological references and thus are devoid of a sense of self, time, or place and cannot be recalled voluntarily. Implicit memory encoding continues throughout the life span and is fundamental to encoding traumatic experiences (Packard et al., 2014). The amygdales and the implicit memory-making processes build a database of all information associated with the threat. This database is used to anticipate and respond to danger, both actual and perceived.

The Hippocampi

The hippocampi (one in each hemisphere) are also key brain areas involved in processing traumatic experiences, and they are highly susceptible to the damaging effects of toxic stress. Named appropriately for its seahorse-like shape, the hippocampus is critical for learning and long-term memory processing. The explicit type of memory, processed by the hippocampus, differs in several ways from the implicit memory formed and stored by the amygdala. First, explicit memories can be voluntarily recalled and explained using language, which is why it is often referred to as declarative memory. Second, the information encoded is factually based and represents details of people, places, and events, giving these memories a sense of self, time, and place (Moscovitch et al., 2016). Together, the amygdala and the hippocampus contribute to the rich, detailed autobiographical story of our lives (Joëls et al., 2006).

The Hypothalamus and Pituitary

Located in an area between the cerebrum and the brain stem, essentially above the roof of the mouth, is the hypothalamus. The priority of this area is to regulate behavior in order to maintain the body's internal consistency or homeostasis (Kandel et al., 2013). In particular, the hypothalamus works to maintain life-essential functions, such as the regulation of blood pressure, body temperature, thirst, hunger, and reproductive behaviors (Saper & Lowell, 2014). Although much of this activity engages the "rest and digest" system, under

threatening conditions, the hypothalamus co-ordinates with the brain stem and the pituitary gland to initiate the body's stress response system, preparing for fighting, fleeing, or shutting down. The pituitary, considered to be the master gland, lies beneath the hypothalamus and acts as the "mouthpiece through which the hypothalamus speaks to the body" (Bear et al., 2007, p. 485). When activated under stress, the pituitary releases a cascade of stress hormones.

The Medial Prefrontal Cortex and Anterior Cingulate Cortex

The brain areas discussed thus far act reflexively and subconsciously, for the most part, and are involved in what can be termed *bottom-up* processing. Areas of the brain involved in *top-down* processing are located in the frontal lobe. The frontal lobe offers comparatively slower processing by filtering reactions, inhibiting responses, regulating emotions, engaging in problem-solving, directing attention, making plans, and integrating information. It is within these brain circuits that the feeling of fear is consciously understood (LeDoux & Pine, 2016). In the case of a threatening situation, areas of the frontal lobe, specifically the medial prefrontal cortex (mPFC) and anterior cingulate cortex (ACC), help interpret threat, evaluate emotional conflict, and distract from fearful stimuli (Etkin et al., 2011). Segments of these brain frontal lobe areas focus on immediate threat, whereas others plan responses to anticipated threat (Etkin et al., 2011). The mPFC and ACC also monitor bodily changes—for instance, increased heart rate and breathing—insight referred to as interoceptive awareness (Garfinkel et al., 2015). After interpreting the situation, these frontal lobe areas may promote a stress reaction, or they may quiet reactive areas such as the amygdala and hypothalamus (Schore, 2014, 2015). As discussed in the next section, when threat is consistently present or perception of danger sensitized, bottom-up processing becomes normative, and the involvement of the frontal lobe in threat assessment is bypassed and, thus, emotional regulation impaired.

Seeking Safety: Stress Responses of Social Connection, Fight or Flight, and Collapse

The most well-recognized stress reaction is fight or flight, the neurochemical changes and behaviors associated with the hypothalamic–pituitary–adrenal (HPA) axis response. After receiving a message of threat by the amygdala, the hypothalamus releases corticotropin-releasing hormone (CRH). This signals the pituitary gland to release adrenocorticotropic hormone, which prompts the adrenal gland to release cortisol (Ehlert, 2013). All types and levels of stress, whether physical, psychological, or emotional, can initiate a release of cortisol (Kandel et al., 2013). Although a dysregulated cortisol level can be problematic, an adequate amount of this hormone is necessary for motivating activity as well as turning off the stress response (B. McEwen, 2019). When the stress system is continually activated by threat in a person's environment, the brain adapts to this environment by resetting the norm to a consistently fired-up state. As noted previously, this heightened, persistent level of stress response becomes toxic to the mind and body (Lapp et al., 2019).

Porges' (2011) polyvagal theory describes a three-tiered hierarchical response to danger that has also become a map for psychological trauma interventions (Dana, 2018; Porges, 2018). Polyvagal theory expands on the well-established role of the two main branches of the autonomic nervous system—the sympathetic nervous system (SNS) and the parasympathetic nervous system (PNS)—in scanning for what is safe and not safe in our surroundings and driving survival responses. Our fight-or-flight response to danger (hyperarousal),

as described previously, is part of the SNS. Specifically, fight or flight involves the midsection of the spinal cord and acts quickly, first releasing adrenaline (Fink, 2016) and then, minutes later, cortisol.

The PNS, associated with the vagus nerve, branches from the brain stem and communicates in two directions. The ventral vagal pathway supports our need for social engagement and social connection as a resource for safety and survival (Dana, 2018; Porges, 2017). This vagal pathway connects above the diaphragm to lungs, heart, larynx, inner ear, and facial muscles around the mouth and eyes. The connections with facial expressions and sounds are particularly important in signaling safe and not safe social interactions. The other pathway, the dorsal vagal, which connects below the diaphragm and is unmyelinated, assists in regulating heart, lungs, and digestion. When there is detection of extreme threat or danger, a dorsal vagal state of collapse or shutdown (hypoarousal) is activated as a means of preserving life.

Porges (2011, 2017) proposes that these three survival-based responses to danger are hierarchically anchored in our human evolutionary history. Our innate drive to connect with others as a survival strategy is our most recent development and is specific to mammals. This concept is supported by both the social brain hypothesis (Dunbar, 2009) and the neurobiological attachment system of the right hemisphere. According to polyvagal theory, we are neurobiologically hardwired to first seek safety with others; this is our ventral vagal strategy. When our safe social connections are not available or we have interpersonal trauma that has disrupted our capacity for secure attachment, the SNS fight-or-flight survival strategy is automatically activated in threatening situations. Finally, our oldest pathway, which we hold in common with our ancient vertebrate ancestors, the dorsal vagal shutdown strategy, is activated as a last resort when there is detection of life threat. This is often the process that is activated in infancy and childhood, given that trauma is most frequently interpersonal and fight and flight are not options. Hence, individuals with developmental trauma frequently experience dissociation.

Cues associated with the threat, such as visual prompts, smells, ambient sounds, and time of the day, which ordinarily do not cause a stress response, are automatically associated with the threat itself and the information stored in the amygdala's implicit memory file as a warning of potential harm. As a result, negative affective states (fear, shame, rage, numbing, dissociation, etc.) and physical sensations (muscle tension, increased heart rate, rapid breathing, etc.) are easily activated to cues even in seemingly nonthreatening environments (Lanius et al., 2017; Rabellino et al., 2016). This is essentially the experience of most clients involved with human service systems.

The amygdala stores only implicit-type memories and relies on the hippocampus for contextual information about its perception of threat and emotional memories (Desmedt et al., 2015; Squire & Dede, 2015) to determine the "realness" of the danger. For example, an individual may initially experience a racing heart and the emotion of fear at the sound of scratching on a window in the night because the stress response system has been activated by the amygdala's perception of threat (Rosenzweig, 2015). However, the hippocampus, based on contextual memory, sends a message that it is a tree brushing up against the house and the stress response shuts off, restoring emotional and physiological regulation. In order to not be frightened by every shadow or unknown object, this coordination between the reflexive (amygdala) and rational (frontal cortex and hippocampus) brain areas is essential (Schore, 2014). In addition to the hippocampus, the mPFC and ACC offer interpretation and regulation (Aupperle et al., 2012; Shin & Liberzon, 2009).

Altered for Adaptation

Understanding that toxic stress changes brain architecture and functioning in service of survival necessitates integrating the concept of adaptive functioning into service design and delivery. Toxic stress profoundly impairs the HPA system and alters the structure and functioning of brain areas. A number of studies have demonstrated that the HPA system becomes highly sensitive and overreactive when exposed to unmitigated chronic stress (Chen et al., 2017; Dieleman et al., 2015; B. McEwen, 2019), particularly in developing brains (Gunnar & Loman, 2010; Herzberg & Gunnar, 2020). Closely aligned with the HPA processes, the hippocampus appears exceptionally vulnerable to the effects of stress. When there is chronic overactivation of the stress response system resulting in the brain being flooded with excess cortisol, hippocampal-dependent learning and memory processes become impaired (Joëls et al., 2006). Excessive cortisol causes a reduction in hippocampal dendrite density, reducing the overall volume of the hippocampus and impacting function (Anacker et al., 2013; Lupien et al., 2018). When altered by toxic stress, the hippocampus has a significantly reduced capacity to provide important contextual information to the amygdala about which conditions represent danger and which represent safety. When the hippocampus is compromised, it is not effective in sending messages to the hypothalamus to stop producing CRH and turn off the stress response (B. McEwen & Gianaros, 2010). Many individuals who suffer from post-traumatic stress disorder (PTSD) show low baseline levels of cortisol, suggesting an exhausted HPA system, which accounts for the intrusive memories they experience (Yehuda et al., 2015).

The amygdala, working in concert with the hippocampus and the HPA system, is also changed structurally and functionally by toxic stress. In contrast to the hippocampus, the overactivation of the amygdala increases its volume, creating a greater sensitivity to emotional stimulation, increasing the probability of mood disorders (B. McEwen et al., 2016). The amygdala is central to relational processes and development of attachment strategies, making it extremely sensitive to excessive activation in early life (Lyons-Ruth et al., 2016). Infants, children, and youth are particularly sensitive to toxic stress and impairment in regulatory functioning in the PFC and the ACC. Again, excessive activation in the areas that respond to emotions and an underactivation in areas involved in cognitive processes of assessment and evaluation lead to developmental disruptions.

Epigenetic Transmission

The question of whether or not exposure to adversity and toxic stress alters genetics and transmits resilience and vulnerability to stress in subsequent generations is a topic of significant importance for practitioners and researchers alike (Lehrner & Yehuda, 2018; Zannas et al., 2015). Epigenetic adaptation is a complex process that involves an interaction between environmental variables and genetics that changes gene expression in succeeding generations. Although much of the current research is based on laboratory studies with mice, Rachel Yehuda's multiyear studies of holocaust survivors and their children suggest the transmission does take place across generations in humans. Yehuda et al. (2016) found differences across the generations in stress hormone levels, suggesting epigenetic changes in gene functions that are linked to PTSD. The role of this interaction related to toxic stress is beginning to be better understood and will contribute significantly to understanding intergenerational transmission trauma (Jiang et al., 2019) and potentially influencing trauma interventions.

Historical and cultural trauma effects through the lens of epigenetic transmission expand our understanding of collective and systematic trauma. In addition to a shared physical and psychological experience, the effects are also shared biologically across generations, increasing vulnerability for negative health and mental health consequences (Stringhini et al., 2015). This fundamental notion is at the core of health and mental health disparities in historically subjugated communities. Not only is the direct experience of toxic stress likely to create epigenetic changes but also it is probable that secondary exposure to effects of toxic stress, such as a child's experience of their primary caregiver's anxiety and depression, does so as well (Conching & Thayer, 2019; Gone et al., 2019).

A Note About Resilience

Throughout this chapter, we have identified social–cultural and historical vulnerabilities to adversity and toxic stress consequences for individuals and communities. As the neuroscience of toxic stress becomes better understood, researchers also strive to unpack the concept and biology of resilience as it relates to adversity (Osório et al., 2017). Knowledge about the neural underpinnings of resilience is slowly emerging as the neuroscience of toxic stress becomes clearer. Currently, scholarship on resilience lacks a shared definition of the construct, making measurement and implementation into service delivery challenging. There are promising emerging examinations of resilience as an ecological construct as well as an individual characteristic (Shaw et al., 2016; Ungar, 2013). We are hopeful that research on resilience will take lessons from research on toxic stress and continue to examine neuroscience in the context of structural inequities and diversity.

Conclusion

There is still much to learn about how toxic stress affects the structures and functions of the brain, mind, and body and the resultant consequences on emotions, cognitions, behaviors, and sensory and somatic experiences; and, moreover, how the social ecology promotes, inhibits, or exacerbates these effects. It is in the implementation and application of this knowledge by social workers that will create systemic changes in organizations, human interactions, and individual neurobiologies.

We recognize the overwhelming need for substantial changes in social, economic, and political structures that contribute to adversity and psychological trauma in order to prevent the life-altering neurobiological changes discussed in this chapter. The demand for practitioners with education and training to provide trauma-specific therapy and advocate for systems' change continues to grow and exceed the capacity of human service organizations. As we write this chapter, the world is suffering from the COVID-19 pandemic. We know too well that this suffering includes widespread trauma and grief that will continue to unfold for a long time and that epigenetic changes are already in motion. We hope this chapter inspires the reader to learn more about the psychological trauma and help bridge the gap between demand and capacity.

References

Anacker, C., Cattaneo, A., Luoni, A., Musaelyan, K., Zunszain, P. A., Milanesi, E., Rybka, J., Berry, A., Cirulli, F., Thuret, S., Price, J., Riva, M. A., & Gennarelli, M. (2013). Glucocorticoid-related molecular signaling pathways regulating hippocampal neurogenesis. *Neuropsychopharmacology, 38*(5), 872–883.

Ashley-Binge, S., & Cousins, C. (2020). Individual and organisational practices addressing social workers' experiences of vicarious trauma. *Practice, 32*(3), 191–207.

Aupperle, R. L., Melrose, A. J., Stein, M. B., & Paulus, M. P. (2012). Executive function and PTSD: Disengaging from trauma. *Neuropharmacology, 62*(2), 686–694.

Bear, M. F., Connors, B. W., & Paradiso, M. A. (2007). *Neuroscience: Exploring the brain* (3rd ed.). Lippincott Williams & Wilkins.

Beebe, B., Lachmann, F., Markese, S., & Bahrick, L. (2012). On the origins of disorganized attachment and internal working models: Paper I. A dyadic systems approach. *Psychoanalytic Dialogues, 22*(2), 253–272. doi:10.1080/10481885.2012.666147

Berens, A. E., Jensen, S. K., & Nelson, C. A. (2017). Biological embedding of childhood adversity: From physiological mechanisms to clinical implications. *BMC Medicine, 15*(1), 135–147.

Chen, X., Gianferante, D., Hanlin, L., Fiksdal, A., Breines, J. G., Thoma, M. V., & Rohleder, N. (2017). HPA-axis and inflammatory reactivity to acute stress is related with basal HPA-axis activity. *Psychoneuroendocrinology, 78,* 168–176.

Conching, A. K. S., & Thayer, Z. (2019). Biological pathways for historical trauma to affect health: A conceptual model focusing on epigenetic modifications. *Social Science & Medicine, 230,* 74–82.

Dana, D. A. (2018). *The polyvagal theory in therapy: Engaging the rhythm of regulation* (Norton Series on Interpersonal Neurobiology). Norton.

Dehaene-Lambertz, G., & Spelke, E. S. (2015). The infancy of the human brain. *Neuron, 88*(1), 93–109.

Desmedt, A., Marighetto, A., Richter-Levin, G., & Calandreau, L. (2015). Adaptive emotional memory: The key hippocampal–amygdalar interaction. *Stress, 18*(3), 297–308.

Dieleman, G. C., Huizink, A. C., Tulen, J. H., Utens, E. M., Creemers, H. E., van der Ende, J., & Verhulst, F. C. (2015). Alterations in HPA-axis and autonomic nervous system functioning in childhood anxiety disorders point to a chronic stress hypothesis. *Psychoneuroendocrinology, 51,* 135–150.

Dunbar, R. I. (2009). The social brain hypothesis and its implications for social evolution. *Annals of Human Biology, 36*(5), 562–572.

Edalati, H., & Nicholls, T. L. (2019). Childhood maltreatment and the risk for criminal justice involvement and victimization among homeless individuals: A systematic review. *Trauma, Violence, & Abuse, 20*(3), 315–330.

Ehlert, U. (2013). Enduring psychobiological effects of childhood adversity. *Psychoneuroendocrinology, 38*(9), 1850–1857.

Etkin, A., Egner, T., & Kalisch, R. (2011). Emotional processing in anterior cingulate and medial prefrontal cortex. *Trends in Cognitive Sciences, 15*(2), 85–93.

Farah, M. J. (2017). The neuroscience of socioeconomic status: Correlates, causes, and consequences. *Neuron, 96*(1), 56–71.

Fink, G. (2016). Stress, definitions, mechanisms, and effects outlined: Lessons from anxiety. In G. Fink (Ed.), *Stress: Concepts, cognition, emotion, and behavior* (pp. 3–11). Academic Press.

Garfinkel, S. N., Seth, A. K., Barrett, A. B., Suzuki, K., & Critchley, H. D. (2015). Knowing your own heart: Distinguishing interoceptive accuracy from interoceptive awareness. *Biological Psychology, 104*, 65–74.

Gazzaniga, M. S., Eliassen, J. C., Nisenson, L., Wessinger, C. M., Fendrich, R., & Baynes, K. (1996). Collaboration between the hemispheres of a callosotomy patient: Emerging right hemisphere speech and the left hemisphere interpreter. *Brain, 119*(4), 1255–1262.

Gazzaniga, M. S., Ivry, R. B., & Mangun, G. R. (2019). *Cognitive neuroscience: The biology of the mind* (5th ed.). Norton.

Gone, J. P., Hartmann, W. E., Pomerville, A., Wendt, D. C., Klem, S. H., & Burrage, R. L. (2019). The impact of historical trauma on health outcomes for Indigenous populations in the USA and Canada: A systematic review. *American Psychologist, 74*(1), 20–35.

Gunnar, M. R., & Loman, M. M. (2010). Early experience and the development of stress reactivity and regulation in children. *Neuroscience and Biobehavioral Reviews, 34*, 867–876.

Herzberg, M. P., & Gunnar, M. R. (2020, April 1). Early life stress and brain function: Activity and connectivity associated with processing emotion and reward. *NeuroImage, 209*, 116493.

Hughes, K., Bellis, M. A., Hardcastle, K. A., Sethi, D., Butchart, A., Mikton, C., Jones, L., & Dunne, M. P. (2017). The effect of multiple adverse childhood experiences on health: A systematic review and meta-analysis. *Lancet Public Health, 2*(8), e356–e366.

Jäggi, L. J., Mezuk, B., Watkins, D. C., & Jackson, J. S. (2016). The relationship between trauma, arrest, and incarceration history among Black Americans: Findings from the National Survey of American Life. *Society and Mental Health, 6*(3), 187–206.

Jiang, S., Postovit, L., Cattaneo, A., Binder, E. B., & Aitchison, K. J. (2019). Epigenetic modifications in stress response genes associated with childhood trauma. *Frontiers in Psychiatry, 10*, 808.

Joëls, M., Pu, Z., Wiegert, O., Oitzl, M. S., & Krugers, H. J. (2006). Learning under stress: How does it work? *Trends in Cognitive Sciences, 10*(4), 152–158.

Kandel, E. R., Schwartz, J. H., Jessell, T. M., Siegelbaum, S. A., & Hudspeth, A. J. (2013). *Principles of neural science* (5th ed.). McGraw-Hill.

Karaduman, A., Göksun, T., & Chatterjee, A. (2017). Narratives of focal brain injured individuals: A macro-level analysis. *Neuropsychologia, 99*, 314–325.

Klein, S., & Merritt, D. H. (2014). Neighborhood racial & ethnic diversity as a predictor of child welfare system involvement. *Children and Youth Services Review, 41*, 95–105.

Lanius, R. A., Rabellino, D., Boyd, J. E., Harricharan, S., Frewen, P. A., & McKinnon, M. C. (2017). The innate alarm system in PTSD: Conscious and subconscious processing of threat. *Current Opinion in Psychology, 14*, 109–115.

Lapp, H. E., Ahmed, S., Moore, C. L., & Hunter, R. G. (2019). Toxic stress history and hypothalamic–pituitary–adrenal axis function in a social stress task: Genetic and epigenetic factors. *Neurotoxicology and Teratology, 71*, 41–49.

LeDoux, J. E., & Pine, D. S. (2016). Using neuroscience to help understand fear and anxiety: A two-system framework. *American Journal of Psychiatry, 173*(11), 1083–1093.

Lehrner, A., & Yehuda, R. (2018). Trauma across generations and paths to adaptation and resilience. *Psychological Trauma, 10*(1), 22–29.

Lupien, S. J., Juster, R. P., Raymond, C., & Marin, M. F. (2018). The effects of chronic stress on the human brain: From neurotoxicity, to vulnerability, to opportunity. *Frontiers in neuroendocrinology, 49*, 91–105.

Lyons-Ruth, K., Pechtel, P., Yoon, S. A., Anderson, C. M., & Teicher, M. H. (2016). Disorganized attachment in infancy predicts greater amygdala volume in adulthood. *Behavioural Brain Research, 308*, 83–93.

McEwen, B. S. (2012). Brain on stress: How the social environment gets under the skin. *Proceedings of the National Academy of Sciences of the USA, 109*(Suppl. 2), 17180–17185.

McEwen, B. S. (2017). Neurobiological and systemic effects of chronic stress. *Chronic Stress, 1*, 1–11.

McEwen, B. S. (2019). What is the confusion with cortisol? *Chronic Stress, 3*, 2470547019833647 .doi:10.1177/2470547019833647

McEwen, B. S., & Gianaros, P. J. (2010). Central role of the brain in stress and adaptation: Links to socioeconomic status, health, and disease. *Annals of the New York Academy of Science, 1186*, 190–122.

McEwen, B. S., Nasca, C., & Gray, J. D. (2016). Stress effects on neuronal structure: Hippocampus, amygdala, and prefrontal cortex. *Neuropsychopharmacology, 41*(1), 3–23.

McEwen, C. A., & McEwen, B. S. (2017). Social structure, adversity, toxic stress, and intergenerational poverty: An early childhood model. *Annual Review of Sociology, 43*, 445–472.

Moscovitch, M., Cabeza, R., Winocur, G., & Nadel, L. (2016). Episodic memory and beyond: The hippocampus and neocortex in transformation. *Annual Review of Psychology, 67*, 105–134.

Osório, C., Probert, T., Jones, E., Young, A. H., & Robbins, I. (2017). Adapting to stress: Understanding the neurobiology of resilience. *Behavioral Medicine, 43*(4), 307–322.

Packard, P. A., Rodríguez-Fornells, A., Stein, L. M., Nicolás, B., & Fuentemilla, L. (2014). Tracking explicit and implicit long-lasting traces of fearful memories in humans. *Neurobiology of Learning and Memory, 116*, 96–104.

Paul, T. M., Lusk, S. L., Becton, A. B., & Glade, R. (2017). Exploring the impact of substance use, culture, and trauma on American Indian adolescents. *Journal of Applied Rehabilitation Counseling, 48*(1), 31–39.

Porges, S. W. (2011). *The polyvagal theory: Neurophysiological foundations of emotions, attachment, communication, and self-regulation* (Norton Series on Interpersonal Neurobiology). Norton.

Porges, S. W. (2017). *The pocket guide to the polyvagal theory: The transformative power of feeling safe.* Norton.

Porges, S. W. (2018). Polyvagal theory: A primer. In S. W. Porges & D. Dana (Eds.), *Clinical applications of the polyvagal theory: The emergence of polyvagal-informed therapies* (pp. 50–72). Norton.

Porges, S. W., & Carter, C. S. (2017). Polyvagal theory and the social engagement system: Neurophysiological bridge between connectedness and health. In P. L. Gebarg, P. R. Muskin, & R. P. Brown (Eds.), Complementary and *integrative treatments in psychiatric practice* (pp. 221–240). American Psychiatric Association Publishing.

Rabellino, D., Densmore, M., Frewen, P. A., Théberge, J., & Lanius, R. A. (2016). The innate alarm circuit in post-traumatic stress disorder: Conscious and subconscious processing of fear- and trauma-related cues. *Psychiatry Research: Neuroimaging, 248*, 142–150.

Rosenzweig, J. M. (2015). Neurobiological underpinnings for trauma-informed care: A primer. *Focal Point: Youth, Young Adults, and Mental Health, 29*, 7–9.

Saper, C. B., & Lowell, B. B. (2014). The hypothalamus. *Current Biology, 24*(23), R1111–R1116.

Schirmer, A., & Adolphs, R. (2017). Emotion perception from face, voice, and touch: Comparisons and convergence. *Trends in Cognitive Sciences, 21*(3), 216–228.

Schore, A. N. (2014). Dysregulation of the right brain: A fundamental mechanism of traumatic attachment and the psychopathogenesis of PTSD. *Neuroscience and Psychoanalysis*, 197–245.

Schore, A. N. (2015). *Affect regulation and the origin of the self: The neurobiology of emotional development.* Routledge.

Shaw, J., McLean, K. C., Taylor, B., Swartout, K., & Querna, K. (2016). Beyond resilience: Why we need to look at systems too. *Psychology of Violence, 6*(1), 34.

Sherman, L. J., Rice, K., & Cassidy, J. (2015). Infant capacities related to building internal working models of attachment figures: A theoretical and empirical review. *Developmental Review, 37*, 109–141.

Shin, L. M., & Liberzon, I. (2009). The neurocircuitry of fear, stress, and anxiety disorders. *Neuropsychopharmacology, 35*(1), 169–191.

Shobe, E. R. (2014). Independent and collaborative contributions of the cerebral hemispheres to emotional processing. *Frontiers in Human Neuroscience, 8*, 230.

Shonkoff, J. P. (2010). Building a new biodevelopmental framework to guide the future of early childhood policy. *Child Development, 81*(1), 357–367.

Squire, L. R., & Dede, A. J. (2015). Conscious and unconscious memory systems. *Cold Spring Harbor Perspectives in Biology, 7*(3), a021667.

Srivastav, A., Richard, C. L., Kipp, C., Strompolis, M., & White, K. (2020). Racial/ethnic disparities in health care access are associated with adverse childhood experiences. *Journal of Racial and Ethnic Health Disparities, 7*(6), 1225–1233.

Stringhini, S., Polidoro, S., Sacerdote, C., Kelly, R. S., Van Veldhoven, K., Agnoli, C., Grioni, S., Tumino, R., Giurdanella, M. C., Panico, S., Mattiello, A., Palli, D., Masala, G., Gallo, V., Castagne, R., Paccaud, F., Campanella, G., AgnoliChadeau-Hyam, M., & Vineis, P. (2015). Life-course socioeconomic status and DNA methylation of genes regulating inflammation. *International Journal of Epidemiology, 44*(4), 1320–1330.

Troutt, D. D. (2017). Trapped in tragedies: Childhood trauma, spatial inequality, and law. *Marquette Law Revue, 101*, 601.

Tyler, L. K., Marslen-Wilson, W. D., Randall, B., Wright, P., Devereux, B. J., Zhuang, J., Papoutsi, M., & Stamatakis, E. A. (2011). Left inferior frontal cortex and syntax: Function, structure and behaviour in patients with left hemisphere damage. *Brain, 134*, 415–431. doi:10.1093/brain/awq369

Ungar, M. (2013). Resilience, trauma, context, and culture. *Trauma, Violence and Abuse, 14*(3), 255–266.

van der Kolk, B. A. (2014). *The body keeps the score: Brain, mind, and body in the healing of trauma.* Penguin.

Yatchmenoff, D. K., Sundborg, S. A., & Davis, M. A. (2017). Implementing trauma-informed care: Recommendations on the process. *Advances in Social Work, 18*(1), 167–185.

Yehuda, R., Daskalakis, N. P., Bierer, L. M., Bader, H. N., Klengel, T., Holsboer, F., & Binder, E. B. (2016).

Holocaust exposure induced intergenerational effects on FKBP5 methylation. *Biological Psychiatry, 80*(5), 372–380.

Yehuda, R., Hoge, C. W., McFarlane, A. C., Vermetten, E., Lanius, R. A., Nievergelt, C. M., Hobfoll, S. E., Koenen, K. C., Neylan, T. C., & Hyman, S. E. (2015). Post-traumatic stress disorder. *Nature Reviews Disease Primers, 1*(1), 1–22.

Zannas, A. S., Provençal, N., & Binder, E. B. (2015). Epigenetics of posttraumatic stress disorder: Current evidence, challenges, and future directions. *Biological Psychiatry, 78*(5), 327–335.

Harm Reduction for Problematic Substance Use

Michael E. McGuire

A harm reduction approach, as the name implies, seeks to minimize the adverse consequences of behaviors without necessarily reducing or eliminating the behavior. An example of this approach being broadly applied is evident in laws requiring motorists to wear seat belts. Although seat belt regulations are not expected to eliminate traffic accidents, they are a policy-level attempt to minimize the harm of being involved in an automobile accident. Automobile accidents continue to kill thousands of people each year, but seat belts have saved nearly 400,000 lives in the United States since 1976 (National Safety Council, n.d.). Harm reduction policies have been initiated for a wide range of public health challenges throughout the world, including carbon exchange programs to combat air pollution, food labels to encourage healthier eating habits, access to condoms to reduce sexually transmitted infections, and directives to minimize large social gatherings to avoid contagion during the COVID-19 pandemic. For each of these examples, the first priority is to mitigate physical, psychological, and economic harm for individuals, families, and communities.

There have been considerable developments in harm reduction policies and practices aimed at reducing negative public health effects associated with the use of licit and illicit drugs (including alcohol). Notably, in response to the HIV epidemic in the 1980s, the Netherlands was the first to deploy the use of syringe services programs (SSPs; commonly referred to as needle exchange programs), with numerous countries soon adopting comparable policies. Similarly, in 1986, Switzerland opened the first government-sanctioned overdose prevention sites (OPSs; commonly referred to as safe injection sites), which have since demonstrated effectiveness in reducing lethal opioid overdose as well as reducing comorbid public health outcomes (Kreit, 2019). Despite the evidence supporting the effectiveness of SSPs and OPSs, the United States continues to lag far behind in adopting these politically charged programs, resulting in significant loss of lives (Drucker & Crofts, 2017; Saloner et al., 2018). Many states, however, have adopted harm reduction initiatives including drug law reformation to reduce the iatrogenic effects from the "war on drugs" (e.g., mass incarceration). In addition, in response to the opioid epidemic, there have been local and federal harm reduction efforts to make medications for treatment and overdose reversal more easily accessible.

Problematic Substance Use

According to the 2018 National Survey on Drug Use and Health, 3 out of 5 people older than age 11 years used substances (tobacco, alcohol, or illicit drugs) within the past month. Of these 164 million people, 20 million had a substance use disorder for either alcohol or illicit drugs, with 1 in 5 receiving treatment [Substance Abuse and Mental Health Services Administration (SAMHSA), 2019]. In addition, the harm caused by substance use that falls short of the threshold of diagnostic criteria for a disorder often lacks consideration. According to the Williams (2018),

> The bulk of the societal, personal, and health care related costs are not a result of addiction but of excessive substance use. Until such time as we acknowledge this fact, and address it appropriately, we are unlikely to make significant progress towards a solution.

Indeed, the *Surgeon General's Report on Alcohol, Drugs, and Health* reported problematic substance use costing the United States $442 billion annually in crime, health care, and lost productivity (SAMHSA, 2016).

Harm Reduction for Problematic Substance Use

Harm reduction is a paradigm-shifting idea that has the potential to significantly improve the treatment of problem

substance users. The essence of harm reduction is the recognition that treatment must start from the client's needs and personal goals and that all change that reduces the harms associated with substance use can be regarded as valuable.
—Tatarsky (2003, p. 249)

In contrast to the medical model viewing addiction as a chronic disease (American Society of Addiction Medicine, 2019), or the moral model viewing addiction as the result of personal shortcomings (Lassiter & Culbreth, 2018; Marlatt, 1996), the harm reduction model does not promote a particular etiology of problematic substance use (PSU). Similarly, whereas the medical and moral models historically hold abstinence as the singular goal for treatment, harm reduction seeks to ameliorate adverse consequences of using drugs through a wide continuum of options, including abstinence, moderation, and substitution. Although abstinence-based models have helped countless people reach and maintain recovery, critics suggest that the sustained cessation of use emphasized by these programs deters many people from seeking treatment or other support. Moreover, the prevailing punitive and abstinence-required approaches to substance use intervention often aggravate the overall negative repercussions of substance use for people who use drugs and society at large (Drucker et al., 2016).

A harm reduction approach, on the other hand, may be more inviting to people who use drugs and who would otherwise not seek treatment or other support. The harm reduction model, in effect, lowers the threshold for those seeking help who may be unable or unwilling to abstain from use. Harm reductionists recognize that people with PSU are a remarkably diverse population and develop problematic patterns of substance use for widely divergent reasons (Tatarsky & Marlatt, 2010) and therefore require an equally wide range of solutions.

According to Foy (2017), harm reduction features pragmatism, humanistic values, a focus on harms, and the analysis of costs and benefits of harm reduction initiatives. In addition, this approach tends to be less concerned with requiring clients to meet diagnostic criteria for a substance use disorder or other specific conceptualizations of addiction. The harm reduction approach to PSU emphasizes client autonomy and the right to self-determination. In doing so, this approach may be more congruent with social work values than more conventional approaches that require abstinence (Vakharia & Little, 2017).

Current Trends

Medication-Assisted Treatment

Prescribing opioids to treat opioid addiction has been a point of controversy in the United States dating back to the late 19th century (Musto, 1999). The current opioid epidemic, which in the United States claimed more than 46,000 lives in 2018 alone (Centers for Disease Control and Prevention, 2020), brought about a renewed urgency to make medication available for treating opioid use disorder (OUD). The medications for OUD work in two primary ways: (1) as an agonist that, through a more controlled administration, activates the same receptors as opioids such as heroin, oxycodone, and morphine; and (2) as an antagonist that blocks opioid receptors. Currently, there are three prevalent medications used for the treatment of OUD in the United States, with each offering help with cravings, withdrawal, or both:

Methadone—a full opioid agonist with a slower release than other opioids
Buprenorphine—a partial opioid agonist working in a similar way but with less

activation of the receptors, thereby minimizing euphoric effects
Naltrexone—an opioid antagonist used to block opioid receptors, thereby negating the euphoric effects of opioids

Medication-assisted treatment (MAT) consists of medications in combination with psychosocial treatment. However, there is a growing preference to use the phrase *medication for opioid use disorder* (MOUD) as opposed to MAT, particularly from the lens of harm reductionists, who maintain that these medications are viable stand-alone interventions and need not be "assisted" by other interventions such as psychotherapy. In addition, it is important to keep in mind that many OUD treatment programs and recovery groups adhering to an abstinence model prohibit participants from "substituting one drug for another." Considering that more than 750,000 people in the United States died from drug overdose from 1999—2018 (Centers for Disease Control and Prevention, 2020), any barriers to the use of medications to manage addiction may be considered a deterrent to improved outcomes.

Medication is also prescribed for treating alcohol use disorder (AUD) and tobacco use disorder. For AUD, there are three prominent medications:

Disulfiram—an alcohol-aversive drug causing significant unpleasant physical reactions when alcohol is consumed
Acamprosate—used post-detoxification to stabilize chemical signaling in the brain
Naltrexone—which blocks the euphoric effects of alcohol

Smoking cessation treatment includes the controlled use of nicotine administered as a transdermal patch, spray, gum, inhaler, or lozenges. In addition to these nicotine replacement therapies (NRTs), bupropion and varenicline are two U.S. Food and Drug Administration–approved medications that do not contain nicotine and are used to target specific brain receptors in an effort to curb nicotine cravings and mitigate withdrawal. The use of e-cigarettes (vaping) is not approved for smoking cessation by the FDA, although studies suggest it can be as effective as NRTs (e.g., Borrelli & O'Connor, 2019; Rahman et al., 2015) for cessation and useful in mitigating harm as a substitute for smoking cigarettes (Warner, 2018).

Today's social worker needs to be prepared to engage in discussions with clients, their families, and other professionals regarding potential benefits and drawbacks of using medications for treating substance use disorders.

Controlled Approach

The use of agonist medications for the treatment of PSU is a narrowly targeted harm reduction approach generally reserved for people with substantial opioid addiction. A more generalized harm reduction intervention is that of controlling or moderating the use of a substance. This approach has been widely accepted for a range of harmful behaviors outside of the addiction field. For example, patients at risk of cardiovascular complications may be encouraged to reduce their health risk by modifying their diet toward consuming less salt, fat, and refined sugar, as opposed to being told to completely eliminate these substances. These same patients may be encouraged to begin a simple exercise regimen such as walking two times a week rather than being told they must attend 90 aerobics classes in 90 days. Everyday lives are replete with harm reduction strategies. Consider attempts to moderate, versus eliminate, time spent on social media or on cell phones, binging on streaming videos, or going on shopping sprees, just to name a few.

Although substance use addictions may have a greater sense of urgency than some of these examples, the principle remains the same—that is, change is not easy, and at times people may be more willing to attempt incremental change rather than acute change such as abstinence. Harm reductionists aim to support the client's current motivation and goals rather than prescribing a one-size-fits-all treatment plan.

Screening, Brief Intervention, and Referral to Treatment

Screening, Brief Intervention, and Referral to Treatment (SBIRT) is an evidence-based model used to identify and reduce harms related to substance use (Aldridge et al., 2017). Although not specifically presented as a harm reduction intervention, SBIRT's client-centered and nonjudgmental approach reflects harm reduction principles (Institute for Research, Education & Training in Addictions, 2019). SBIRT may be considered a low-threshold model through addressing both "risky" substance use behaviors and behaviors meeting the diagnostic criteria for a substance use disorder.

Application of a Harm Reduction Approach

Social workers are employed in a vast array of settings conducive to a harm reduction approach, including schools, colleges, hospitals, child welfare services, mental health clinics, housing, and private practice. Targets for harm reduction include virtually any behavior that may cause harm, such as binge drinking, unprotected sex, poor diet, lack of physical activity, aggressive behavior, and excessive time spent on social media. Broad suggestions for applying a harm reduction model are presented here.

Incorporate the principles of harm reduction: The Harm Reduction Coalition, a leading voice in the harm reduction field, offers the following eight principles for working from a harm reduction stance (Harm Reduction Coalition, n.d.):

- Accepts, for better and for worse, that licit and illicit drug use is part of our world and chooses to work to minimize its harmful effects rather than simply ignore or condemn them.
- Understands drug use as a complex, multifaceted phenomenon that encompasses a continuum of behaviors from severe abuse to total abstinence and acknowledges that some ways of using drugs are clearly safer than others.
- Establishes quality of individual and community life and well-being—not necessarily cessation of all drug use—as the criteria for successful interventions and policies.
- Calls for the nonjudgmental, noncoercive provision of services and resources to people who use drugs and the communities in which they live in order to assist them in reducing attendant harm.
- Ensures that drug users and those with a history of drug use routinely have a real voice in the creation of programs and policies designed to serve them.
- Affirms drugs users themselves as the primary agents of reducing the harms of their drug use and seeks to empower users to share information and support each other in strategies that meet their actual conditions of use.
- Recognizes that the realities of poverty, class, racism, social isolation, past trauma, sex-based discrimination, and other social inequalities affect both people's vulnerability to and capacity for effectively dealing with drug-related harm.
- Does not attempt to minimize or ignore the real and tragic harm and danger associated with licit and illicit drug use.

Develop a strong therapeutic alliance: With pervasive stigma associated with PSU, social workers need to pay particular attention to the working relationship by meeting the client where they are along with a nonjudgmental stance. Harm reduction psychotherapy (Tatarsky, 2003) promotes

> an empathic resonance between clinician and client, deepening the identification and understanding of what is distressing to the client (that is, what is harmful about substance use and other issues), setting harm reduction goals that can be hypothesis tested to determine if they are realistic for the client, and working toward change with strategies that meet the client's unique needs and strengths. (p. 252)

Harm reduction psychotherapy becomes a dressing room in which clients are free to try on different versions of themselves, explore their values and priorities, and test their own theories of the change process.

Share information: Harm reductionists offer clients information to reduce the negative effects stemming from drug use, including education around safer ways to procure drugs (e.g., practicing safer sex if trading sex for drugs), use drugs (e.g., avoiding infections when injecting), and survive an overdose (e.g., administering naloxone). Connecting these clients to services such as health clinics, treatment, support groups, and housing and employment not predicated on abstinence is an essential part of the harm reduction model.

Integrate harm reduction with other treatment models: The principles and features of harm reduction compliment a wide range of evidence-based treatment models (Futterman et al., 2005; Hertler et al., 2018; Tatarsky & Kellogg, 2010), including motivational interviewing (Gallagher & Bremer, 2018), mindfulness (Bayles, 2014), cognitive-behavioral therapy (Logan & Marlatt, 2010), solution-focused brief therapy (Foy, 2017), family therapy (Denning, 2010), and psycho-analysis (Denning & Little, 2011). Each of these models, used in conjunction with harm reduction, promotes a nonjudgmental experience that measures success based on the client's goals as opposed to the provider's goals.

Case Example

This case example is from a newly graduated MSW student reflecting on her field placement experience.

I got a crash course in harm reduction in my field placement this year. I was working with a client who had hepatitis C and severe endocarditis as a result of drug use. She also lived in a home with no electricity or running water and could not be accessed by car because there were no paved roads. At the time I met the client, her doctor stated she only had 10% use of her heart and poor lung functioning. Through the use of suboxone, the client had successfully stopped using heroin, but her medical doctor stated, "This patient is going to die. We are just trying to extend her life and improve her quality of life until that happens." I was shocked and somewhat unsure about my role moving forward.

In our second session, the client reported she remained abstinent from heroin but that she was smoking crack cocaine and marijuana daily. She reported when she smoked crack, she was using copper wire stripped from an old lamp as a makeshift filter and that the copper was charred and brittle from repeated use. She also reported she was using book pages to roll joints. She noted she had quite a bit of chest pain when she smoked, and she had visible burns on her lips from smoking a hot pipe. I was really concerned about the effects of this on her lungs, and I spoke to my supervisor and her doctor about the ethics of focusing my sessions on harm reduction rather than abstinence. I knew a bit already about safer marijuana use and asked if it was okay for me to learn more about safer crack smoking practices to share with the client. We all agreed that she was in a dire situation and that harm reduction was the most ethical avenue. I found myself googling "how to smoke crack" in order to learn as much as I could about the process and the materials. I then reached out to the Harm Reduction Coalition and was able to acquire a safer crack smoking kit to provide the client, which included fresh Chore Boy, a small wire mesh filter, several Pyrex glass pipes, and thick tape to wrap the pipe in to protect her lips and fingertips. I provided the patient with the material and spoke with her about using new Chore Boy with each smoke. Also, I asked if she had a water pipe she could use to smoke weed and she acknowledged she had a bubbler that she never uses. I taught her how to clean her water pipe and explained how the water filters the smoke and cools the temperature, which can make it smoother on her lungs. I also let her know she can add ice to the water in her pipe to further cool the temperature of the smoke. She was enthusiastic to try these interventions because she was having so much pain with smoking.

Of all the interventions I've ever done with a client, this one felt the most practical, useful, and effective. I actually think it would have been unethical for me to not provide this patient with harm reduction information and supplies. A big part of my practice philosophy is remembering that we are not operating in an ideal world and that we have to meet our clients where they're at. Perhaps harm reduction is not indicated for every case, but it would be unethical for us to ignore an approach useful to our patients just because of social or political pressure.

The student's retelling of her experience exemplifies the compassionate, pragmatic, and often unconventional nature of harm reduction. Although this example revolves around a person in particularly dire straits, harm reduction may be used with any client experiencing adverse consequences from their substance use.

Conclusion

There are a multitude of barriers to the practice of harm reduction in the United States, including the prevailing zero-tolerance, punitive drug policies; an abstinence-centric paradigm toward PSU; lack of resources and funding; and the omnipresent stigma associated with substance use. Nonetheless, an alternative public health perspective for addressing the harms associated with drug use continues to gain momentum, adding greater choice, opportunity, connection, and dignity for people who use drugs. In the end, the harm reduction model neither condemns nor condones drug use, and instead concerns itself with the quality of life for individuals, community, and society.

Helpful Resources

American Addiction Centers: https://americanaddictioncenters.org/harm-reduction

Harm Reduction for Alcohol: https://hams.cc

Harm Reduction International: https://www.hri.global

Harm Reduction Therapy Center: https://harmreductiontherapy.org

Institute for Research, Education & Training in Addictions: https://ireta.org/resources/how-harm-reduction-fits-into-the-sbirt-model

National Harm Reduction Coalition: https://harmreduction.org

Substance Abuse and Mental Health Services Administration: https://www.samhsa.gov/medication-assisted-treatment

U.S. Food and Drug Administration: https://www.fda.gov/drugs/information-drug-class/information-about-medication-assisted-treatment-mat

References

Aldridge, A., Linford, R., & Bray, J. (2017). Substance use outcomes of patients served by a large US implementation of Screening, Brief Intervention and Referral to Treatment (SBIRT). *Addiction, 112*(S2), 43–53. https://doi.org/10.1111/add.13651

American Society of Addiction Medicine. (2019). *Definition of addiction.* https://www.asam.org/Quality-Science/definition-of-addiction

Bayles, C. (2014). Using mindfulness in a harm reduction approach to substance abuse treatment: A literature review. *International Journal of Behavioral Consultation and Therapy, 9,* 22–25. https://doi.org/10.1037/h0100995

Borrelli, B., & O'Connor, G. T. (2019). E-cigarettes to assist with smoking cessation. *New England Journal of Medicine, 380*(7), 678–679. https://doi.org/http://dx.doi.org/10.1056/NEJMe1816406

Centers for Disease Control and Prevention. (2020, March 18). *New data show significant changes in drug overdose deaths.* CDC Online Newsroom. https://www.cdc.gov/media/releases/2020/p0318-data-show-changes-overdose-deaths.html

Denning, P. (2010). Harm reduction therapy with families and friends of people with drug problems. *Journal of Clinical Psychology, 66*(2), 164–174. https://doi.org/https://doi.org/10.1002/jclp.20671

Denning, P., & Little, J. (2011). *Practicing harm reduction psychotherapy, second edition: An alternative approach to addictions.* Guilford.

Drucker, E., Anderson, K., Haemmig, R., Heimer, R., Small, D., Walley, A., Wood, E., & van Beek, I. (2016). Treating addictions: Harm reduction in clinical care and prevention. *Journal of Bioethical Inquiry, 13*(2), 239–249. https://doi.org/10.1007/s11673-016-9720-6

Drucker, E., & Crofts, N. (2017). Are we anywhere near there yet? The state of harm reduction in North America in 2017. *Harm Reduction Journal, 14.* https://doi.org/http://dx.doi.org/10.1186/s12954-017-0155-0

Foy, S. (2017). *Solution focused harm reduction: Working effectively with people who misuse substances.* Palgrave Macmillan.

Futterman, R., Lorente, M., & Silverman, S. W. (2005). Beyond harm reduction: A new model of substance abuse treatment. *Journal of Psychotherapy Integration, 15*(1), 3–18. https://doi.org/10.1037/1053-0479.15.1.3

Gallagher, J. R., & Bremer, T. (2018). A perspective from the field: The disconnect between abstinence-based programs and the use of motivational interviewing in treating substance use disorders. *Alcoholism Treatment Quarterly, 36*(1), 115–126. https://doi.org/10.1080/07347324.2017.1355223

Harm Reduction Coalition. (n.d.). *Principles of harm reduction.* Retrieved May 20, 2020, from https://harmreduction.org/about-us/principles-of-harm-reduction

Hertler, S. C., Figueredo, A. J., Peñaherrera-Aguirre, M., Fernandes, H. B. F., & Woodley of Menie, M.

A. (2018). Urie Bronfenbrenner: Toward an evolutionary ecological systems theory. In S. C. Hertler, A. J. Figueredo, M. Peñaherrera-Aguirre, H. B. F. Fernandes, & M. A. Woodley of Menie (Eds.), *Life history evolution: A biological meta-theory for the social sciences* (pp. 323–339). Springer. https://doi.org/10.1007/978-3-319-90125-1_19

Institute for Research, Education & Training in Addictions. (2019). *How harm reduction fits into the SBIRT model.* https://ireta.org/resources/how-harm-reduction-fits-into-the-sbirt-model

Kreit, A. (2019). Safe injection sites and the federal "crack house" statute. *Boston College Law Review, 60*(2), 412–468.

Lassiter, P. S., & Culbreth, J. R. (2018). *Theory and practice of addiction counseling.* Sage. https://doi.org/10.4135/9781071800461

Logan, D. E., & Marlatt, G. A. (2010). Harm reduction therapy: A practice-friendly review of research. *Journal of Clinical Psychology, 66*(2), 201–214. https://doi.org/10.1002/jclp.20669

Marlatt, G. A. (1996). Harm reduction: Come as you are. *Addictive Behaviors, 21*(6), 779–788.

Musto, D. F. (1999). *The American disease: Origins of narcotic control.* Oxford University Press.

National Safety Council. (n.d.). *Injury facts.* https://injuryfacts.nsc.org/motor-vehicle/occupant-protection/seat-belts

Rahman, M. A., Hann, N., Wilson, A., Mnatzaganian, G., & Worrall-Carter, L. (2015). E-cigarettes and smoking cessation: Evidence from a systematic review and meta-analysis. *PLoS One, 10*(3), e0122544. https://doi.org/10.1371/journal.pone.0122544

Saloner, B., McGinty, E. E., Beletsky, L., Bluthenthal, R., Beyrer, C., Botticelli, M., & Sherman, S. G. (2018). A public health strategy for the opioid crisis. *Public Health Reports, 133*(1 Suppl), 24S–34S. https://doi.org/10.1177/0033354918793627

Substance Abuse and Mental Health Services Administration. (2016). *Highlights of the Surgeon General's report on alcohol, drugs, and health: At-a-glance.* https://addiction.surgeongeneral.gov/sites/default/files/surgeon-generals-report.pdf

Substance Abuse and Mental Health Services Administration. (2019). *Key substance use and mental health indicators in the United States: Results from the 2018 National Survey on Drug Use and Health.* HHS Publication No. PEP19-5068, NSDUH Series H-54, Vol. 170, pp. 51–58. https://www.samhsa.gov/data/sites/default/files/cbhsq-reports/NSDUHNationalFindingsReport2018/NSDUHNationalFindingsReport2018.pdf

Tatarsky, A. (2003). Harm reduction psychotherapy: Extending the reach of traditional substance use treatment. *Journal of Substance Abuse Treatment, 25,* 249–256.

Tatarsky, A., & Kellogg, S. (2010). Integrative harm reduction psychotherapy: A case of substance use, multiple trauma, and suicidality. *Journal of Clinical Psychology, 66*(2), 123–135. https://doi.org/10.1002/jclp.20666

Tatarsky, A., & Marlatt, G. A. (2010). State of the art in harm reduction psychotherapy: An emerging treatment for substance misuse. *Journal of Clinical Psychology, 66*(2), 117–122. https://doi.org/10.1002/jclp.20672

Vakharia, S. P., & Little, J. (2017). Starting where the client is: Harm reduction guidelines for clinical social work practice. *Clinical Social Work Journal, 45*(1), 65–76. https://doi.org/10.1007/s10615-016-0584-3

Warner, K. E. (2018). How to think—not feel—about tobacco harm reduction. *Nicotine & Tobacco Research, 21*(10), 1299–1309. https://doi.org/10.1093/ntr/nty084

Williams, J. (n.d.). *SBIRT training of trainers.* Retrieved May 26, 2020, from https://ireta.org/resources/sbirt-training-of-trainers

Fundamental Principles of Trauma Interventions

Joan M. Blakey

Introduction: What Is Trauma?

Trauma is known by many names, including hysteria, shell shock, and combat fatigue (DeCandia et al., 2014; Herman, 1992). The increased attention to trauma has led to confusion about what is considered traumatic within the context of mental and physical health. Trauma is "a single event, multiple events, or a prolonged event that is harmful or threatening often leading to intense feelings of helplessness, hopelessness, and fear and has lasting adverse effects on the individual's physical, social, emotional, or spiritual well-being" [Substance Abuse and Mental Health Services Administration (SAMHSA), 2014, p. 7]. Trauma leaves an imprint on individuals' minds, bodies, and brains (van der Kolk, 2014). Trauma often affects individuals' worldviews, relationships with others, and their ability to trust people and the world. Trauma can affect individuals long after the traumatic experience occurred (van der Kolk, 2014).

Rarely do people experience a single traumatic event; rather, they experience multiple or chronic traumatic events commonly known as complex trauma (SAMHSA, 2014). *Complex trauma* refers to repeated and prolonged traumatic events that accumulate over time (Courtois, 2004; Herman, 1992). Complex trauma has wide-ranging, long-term effects that often result in severe, pervasive, and difficult-to-treat symptoms that disrupt individuals' lives and put them at risk for additional traumatic experiences and impairment (Courtois, 2004; van der Kolk, 2014).

Case Example

Farah is a 33-year-old African American mother of one child and the youngest of four daughters.[1] Farah's family was very wealthy. Farah's father was a neurosurgeon, and her mother was a model. Farah's father was physically abusive toward her mother. Farah described her mother as neglectful and an alcoholic. Farah's father sexually molested her and her three sisters. Farah had a strained relationship with her mother because she blamed her mother for letting the abuse happen. Farah also was sexually abused by her uncle. The sexual abuse from her father occurred from when

---

1. Some details regarding Farah's identity have been slightly altered to ensure her identity remains anonymous.

Farah was 6 years old until she left home at age 16 years for Harvard University. Her uncle's abuse was periodic, starting when Farah was age 9 years and lasting until she was 12 years old, when she refused to be around him.

School was always Farah's safe haven. She graduated from high school at the age of 16 years. She received a full ride to Harvard University and moved to Boston, far away from her family. After her undergraduate degree, Farah received a full ride to Tulane University's Medical School, which was cut short by Hurricane Katrina. Farah did not evacuate because by the time she finished her shift, it was too late to leave. She remained at the hospital for 3 days until she was rescued.

Farah lost everything in Hurricane Katrina. Medical students were dispersed. Farah finished her medical degree at Yale School of Medicine. Farah received her PhD in molecular biology and her medical degree. She did her residency at the Mayo Clinic College of Medicine and Science in Jacksonville, Florida, where she trained to become a cardiothoracic surgeon. During her residency, she met her husband. Although he was married at the time, they started dating, she fell in love with him, and she ignored all the signs of abuse.

She described her husband "as one of the best surgeons in the country with a God complex." They were very wealthy and lived a lavish lifestyle. Farah's husband was verbally and emotionally abusive. Soon after finishing her residency, she became pregnant but had a miscarriage at 4 months. Farah was devastated. She hoped the baby would save her failing marriage and stop her husband's infidelity, which he blamed on her inability to give him children. She had three more miscarriages; with each miscarriage, she became more depressed. Instead of tending to her mental health, she threw herself into her work. She worked nonstop so she would not have to think about her life and how unfulfilled she felt.

One night, she left the hospital just after midnight. While walking to her car, she was raped. Farah never told anyone she was raped.

The next day, she went to work like nothing ever happened. Months later, Farah found out she was 4 months pregnant. She was in shock and disbelief. Her periods had always been sporadic because of her bulimia nervosa, with which she had struggled since the age of 12 years. She had mixed feelings because she was unsure if the baby was her husband's or the rapist's. Because she wanted a baby so badly, she decided it did not matter.

Farah began seeing a therapist after she had a nervous breakdown because one of her patients died on the operating table. Her patient reminded her of her dad. He smelled like her dad. He looked like her dad. The way the man's daughter responded to her dad's touch reminded her of when she was young. Farah was convinced the daughter was being molested by her father. While Farah was cleared of all wrongdoing, she was not sure if, unconsciously, she killed him. While performing the man's surgery, she kept having flashbacks of her dad molesting her. She does not remember exactly what went wrong or exactly what led to this man's death. Farah has been unable to return to work because she is fearful of killing another patient (Table 37.1).

Farah's Case Formulation

Farah presents with post-traumatic stress disorder (PTSD) with delayed expression, which appears to be precipitated by the death of a patient. Farah has a history of depression due to emotional and verbal abuse as an adult, prior history of sexual abuse from ages 9 to 16 years by her father and uncle, rape, and being evacuated after being trapped in the hospital for 3 days due to Hurricane Katrina. The current problem is maintained by shame, guilt, fear, and believing she can handle everything on her own. Her protective and positive factors include her education, career as a doctor, financial stability, and faith in God. Farah's overall disability score is 37.22%, which is on the lower end. Areas in which she experiences the most problems are self-care, getting along with people,

TABLE 37.1 Complex Trauma Chart by Age (Farah, Aged 33 Years)

Types of Trauma Experienced (by Age)	0	5	9	10	11	12	14	15	16	20	25	30	31	32	33
Impaired caregiver—mother (substance abuse)	■	■	■	■	■	■	■	■	■						
Witnessed domestic violence	■	■	■	■	■	■	■	■	■						
Neglect by her mother		■	■	■	■	■	■	■	■						
Childhood sexual abuse by father			■	■	■										
Childhood sexual abuse by uncle					■	■	■								
Hurricane Katrina											■				
Miscarriages												■	■		
Intimate partner violence—emotional and verbal abuse						■	■	■	■		■	■	■	■	■
Raped (possible pregnancy)														■	
Patient died while she was performing heart surgery															■
Racial-based trauma and oppression	■	■	■	■	■	■	■	■	■	■	■	■	■	■	■
Bulimia			■	■	■	■	■	■	■						
Total types of trauma	3	4	6	6	7	7	7	6	6	1	3	3	3	3	3

and participation in society. Farah meets criteria for the following DSM-5 diagnoses:

- 309.81 PTSD with delayed expression (principal diagnosis)
- 300.4 persistent depressive disorder (dysthymia), moderate, with pure dysthymic syndrome, with peripartum onset
- 307.51 bulimia nervosa, moderate

Trauma Intervention Continuum

Trauma-informed practice, trauma-specific services, and trauma-focused interventions often are used interchangeably because they all are intended to improve the experiences of people who have histories of trauma (DeCandia et al., 2014); however, they are different. Trauma interventions (e.g., trauma-specific services, trauma-informed practice, and trauma-informed organizations) are on a continuum (Figure 37.1). These approaches vary with respect to the area of focus and how they are intended to help trauma survivors.

Trauma-specific services or *trauma-focused interventions* are on one end of the continuum and directly address and reduce individuals' trauma symptoms (SAMHSA, 2014). Trauma-specific services are clinical treatments used with individuals and families to reduce

Specific Interventions — Broad Interventions

Trauma-Specific Services　　Trauma-Informed Practice　　Trauma-Informed Organizations

FIGURE 37.1 Illustration of the Trauma Interventions Continuum.

PTSD symptomology and improve functioning (DeCandia et al., 2014). *Trauma-informed practice* refers to a set of practices individual practitioners use to increase effectiveness of services and minimize the possibility of inadvertently retraumatizing individuals whose trauma histories may not be known (DeCandia et al., 2014). Trauma-informed practice focuses on service providers and the extent to which they change their practice to more effectively meet the needs of individuals with histories of trauma (Elliot et al., 2005; SAMHSA, 2014). Finally, *trauma-informed care* refers to the ways organizations and systems of care focus on changing the entire system, including staff, policies, and procedures, and any other aspects that affect clients' experiences within the system so every interaction aids recovery and reduces any possibility of retraumatization (Elliot et al., 2005). This chapter focuses on trauma-specific interventions and trauma-informed practice.

Trauma-Specific Services/Interventions

Trauma-specific services/interventions refer to evidence-based and promising prevention, intervention, or treatment services that address PTSD and any co-occurring disorders, including substance use and mental disorders, that develop during or after trauma (DeCandia et al., 2014). Trauma-specific interventions improve clients' interpersonal functioning, enhance emotion regulation, increase resiliency, and facilitate trauma recovery (SAMHSA, 2014). Trauma-specific interventions often are either present- or past-focused in their approach (Torchalla et al., 2012). Trauma-specific interventions include psychoeducational groups about trauma and its impact, services that teach safety skills, ways to manage trauma symptoms, psychoeducation, cognitive–behavioral therapy, psychotropic medication, and individual or group counseling in which

trauma is the primary focus (Cohen et al., 2000). Trauma-specific interventions focus on reducing the cumulative and tangential effects resulting from trauma, such as job loss and loss of relationships (Kira et al., 2015). Finally, trauma-specific interventions, which focus on individuals' recollection of the traumatic event, PTSD symptoms, and co-occurring disorders, have been found to be cost-effective and better suited to meet clients' needs [National Center for PTSD (NCP), 2020; Torchalla et al., 2012].

Different Types of Trauma-Specific Services/Interventions

There are a variety of efficacious trauma-specific interventions with the strongest supporting evidence: (1) prolonged exposure (Foa & Kozak, 1986), (2) cognitive processing therapy (Monson et al., 2006), (3) eye movement desensitization and reprocessing (Shapiro, 1995), and (4) trauma-focused cognitive–behavioral therapy. Many of these interventions involve the use of visualization, prolonged exposure that requires individuals to think and talk about the event, and talk therapy focused on changing unproductive beliefs and behaviors (NCP, 2020). Many of these treatments also have empirical support with children and adolescents, communities of color, and specialized populations, such as refugees and individuals with histories of trauma who also have substance use disorders (Cohen et al., 2012; Murray et al., 2008). A variety of other types of therapies, services, and interventions—such as yoga and meditation—have little empirical research but have been found to be helpful with individuals who have been diagnosed with PTSD.

Although there are myriad trauma-specific interventions, there is not consensus on which trauma-specific intervention is best to treat PTSD (Wagner et al., 2007). van der Kolk (2014) wrote,

There is no one treatment of choice for trauma, and any therapist who believes that his or her particular method is the only answer to [clients'] problems is suspect of being an ideologue rather than somebody who is interested in making sure that [clients] get well. No therapist can possibly be familiar with every treatment, and he or she must be open to your exploring options other than the ones they offer. He or she must also be open to learning from the [client]. (p. 212)

Trauma-Informed Practice

Trauma-informed practice posits that because trauma is widespread among clinical and non-clinical populations, there is a need for practices, policies, procedures, and environments that reduce the likelihood of retraumatizing clients, particularly because individuals' histories of trauma may or may not be known (Knight, 2018). Whereas trauma-specific interventions/services are intended to address and treat past traumas, trauma-informed practice is a lens through which practitioners understand clients' traumatic experiences are present and could be part of the presenting problem (van der Kolk, 2014). Trauma-informed practice is based on awareness, sensitivity, understanding, and responsiveness to the role trauma plays in the physical, psychological, and emotional well-being of individuals who have histories of trauma (Hopper et al., 2010).

Trauma-informed practice provides opportunities for healthy relationships with others, corrective emotional experiences for clients, and partnerships with clients that lead to the restoration of their sense of self-control and empowerment (Hopper et al., 2010; Levenson, 2017). According to Knight (2019),

"Practitioners who do not attend to survivors' past, and the relationship it plays in the present, undermine their ability to deal with the underlying trauma and the present day challenges that brought them to [you] in the first place" (p. 25).

Although there are no set guidelines for what trauma-informed practice looks like, there are core principles that should be included in a trauma-informed approach: safety, trustworthiness, choice, collaboration, and empowerment (Fallot & Harris, 2009).

1. Listen to what individuals tell you and to what they do not say (*choice*). What prompted clients to come see you may not actually be the presenting problem. Through the course of your assessment, you may have an indication or an inclination that your client has a history of trauma. Honor their choice to be selective about what and when they reveal things about them or their traumatic past.

   When Farah first came to the agency, she was impeccably dressed. She appeared very cool, calm, and collected. The presenting problem was she was having trouble sleeping and concentrating. During the assessment, she carefully chose her words. It was apparent she was trying to say all the right things. It was evident there was so much more to discover.

2. Be patient. Focus on building therapeutic relationship (*trustworthiness*). Clients often will not reveal trauma histories until they have some modicum of safety and trust. As you build trust with clients, they often feel comfortable revealing more about their history. As you build a stronger relationship and rapport with clients, you may be able to probe a little more. If you sense any hesitation or resistance, ease up. Agency policies and procedures, insurance restrictions/limitations, and impatient family members

can make social workers feel pressured to move faster than clients are ready. Trauma-informed practice means clients set the pace regarding your work together.

> *When Farah first came for help, she blamed her job and stress for her sleeplessness. Remember there is much more to the story, keep focusing on the relationship. Right before the session ended one day, Farah opened up about the death of her patient. Even still, she slowly revealed more details over time.*

3. Understand that getting to the trauma history can take months, even years (*empowerment*). The treatment process may depend on whether practitioners are working for an agency or are in private practice. To the extent possible, let clients set the pace.

> *It took Farah 2 months before she could talk about why she was not sleeping. It took Farah years before she was able to share her entire trauma story.*

4. Keep in mind that there are different types of safety (*safety*). You must attend to them all. *Physical safety*—sometimes trauma survivors like to sit near the door so they can easily leave. Let them choose where they would like to sit. *Psychological safety* is where clients feel comfortable taking risks, telling their truth, and letting others know what they need without fear of retribution or retaliation. Sometimes trauma survivors reveal pieces of the story so they can see how you react. Your reaction will let them know whether they can trust you with more. *Emotional safety* is where all emotions, no matter how raw, vile, or disturbing, are safe to display without fear of judgment.

> *In terms of physical safety, Farah needed to sit so she could see the door. This made her feel safe and less anxious.*

5. You are partners and co-collaborators. Do not allow your relationship to become simply a transactional process (*collaboration*). For many trauma survivors, transactional processes are predictable and safe. They do not require a person to give of themselves, often because they have already determined what they need to give to get what they want. To survive, individuals with histories of trauma had to become good at reading people and situations. It is not manipulation—it is survival. When you partner with them, it shifts the relationship from hierarchical (transactional) to partnership (collaboration), where both people have to give to make the relationship work. Both have to be willing to take risks. Both have to take responsibility if the relationship does not work.

> *When Farah came for help, she was waiting for the "expert" to fix her. She kept trying to make the relationship transactional versus collaborative. A large part of the work was constantly reminding her there was no magic wand that could be waived to make all her problems disappear. She had to do the work if she wanted to get better and the therapist is there to assist.*

Conclusion

Trauma-informed practice is contextual and looks different depending on the clients and the types of trauma they have experienced. It is dependent on the staff, their educational level, and their openness to trauma as a viable explanation that can shed light on clients' behavior, which is why there are principles but no specific how-to steps. There are a variety of ways to intervene with individuals who have trauma histories. With regard to trauma-specific interventions, there is no treatment that is right for everyone (van der Kolk, 2014). Sometimes clinicians must try different treatments until they find one that works for their client. The client and social worker must work together to decide which treatment(s) is best based on the strengths, drawbacks, and side effects of each.

Trauma-informed practice is a broad intervention that requires practitioners have increased awareness of trauma and recognize the possible impact that different types of trauma can have on individuals' behavior, mental health, and overall well-being. Trauma-informed practitioners allow safety, choice, empowerment, trustworthiness, and collaboration to guide their work with clients. Using trauma interventions can improve symptoms, enhance personal and professional relationships, and increase individuals' quality of life (DeCandia et al., 2014).

References

Cohen, J. A., Mannarino, A. P., Berliner, L., & Deblinger, E. (2000). Trauma-focused cognitive behavioral therapy for children and adolescents: An empirical update. *Journal of Interpersonal Violence, 15*(11), 1202–1223. https://doi.org/10.1177/088626000015011007

Cohen, J. A., Mannarino, A. P., Kliethermes, M., & Murray, L. A. (2012). Trauma-focused CBT for youth with complex trauma. *Child Abuse & Neglect, 36*(6), 528–541. https://doi.org/10.1016/j.chiabu.2012.03.007

Courtois, C. A. (2004). Complex trauma, complex reactions: Assessment and treatment. *Psychotherapy, 41*(4), 412–425. https://doi.org/10.1037/0033-3204.41.4.412

DeCandia, C. J., Guarino, K., & Clervil, R. (2014). *Trauma-informed care and trauma-specific services: A comprehensive approach to trauma intervention.* National Center on Family Homelessness.

Elliot, D. E., Bjelajac, P., Fallot, R. D., Markoff, L. S., & Reed, B. G. (2005). Trauma-informed or trauma-denied: Principles and implementation of trauma-informed services for women. *Journal of Community Psychology, 33*(4), 461–477. https://doi.org/10.1002/jcop.20063

Fallot, R. D., & Harris, M. (2009). *Creating Cultures of Trauma-Informed Care (CCTIC): A self-assessment and planning protocol.* Community Connections.

Foa, E. B., & Kozak, M. J. (1986). Emotional processing of fear: Exposure to corrective information. *Psychological Bulletin, 99*(1), 20–35. https://doi.org/10.1037/0033-2909.99.1.20

Herman, J. (1992). Trauma and recovery. Basic Books.

Hopper, E. K., Bassuk, E. L., & Olivet, J. (2010). Shelter from the storm: Trauma-informed care in homeless service settings. *The Open Health Services and Policy Journal, 3,* 80–100. https://www.homelesshub.ca/sites/default/files/cenfdthy.pdf

Kira, I. A., Ashby, J. S., Omidy, A. Z., & Lewandowski, L. (2015). Current, continuous, and cumulative trauma-focused cognitive behavior therapy: A new model for trauma counseling. *Journal of Mental Health Counseling, 37*(4), 323–340. https://doi.org/10.17744/mehc.37.4.04

Knight, C. (2018). Trauma-informed supervision: Historical antecedents, current practice, and future directions. *The Clinical Supervisor, 37*(1), 7–37. https://doi.org/10.1080/07325223.2017.1413607

Levenson, J. (2017). Trauma-informed social work practice. *Social Work, 62*(2), 105–113. https://doi.org/10.1093/sw/swx001

Monson, C. M., Schnurr, P. P., Resick, P. A., Friedman, M. J., Young-Xu, Y., & Stevens, S. P. (2006). Cognitive processing therapy for veterans with military-related posttraumatic stress disorder. *Journal of Consulting and Clinical Psychology, 74*(5), 898–907. https://doi.org/10.1037/0022-006X.74.5.898

Murray, L. K., Cohen, J. A., Ellis, B. H., & Mannarino, A. (2008). Cognitive behavioral therapy for symptoms of trauma and traumatic grief in refugee youth. *Child and Adolescent Psychiatric Clinics of North America, 17*(3), 585–604. https://doi.org/10.1016/j.chc.2008.02.003

National Center for PTSD. (2020, March 12). *PTSD: National Center for PTSD.* https://www.ptsd.va.gov

Shapiro, F. (1995). *Eye movement desensitization and reprocessing: Basic principles, protocols and procedures.* Guilford.

Substance Abuse and Mental Health Services Administration. (2014). SAMHSA's concept of trauma and guidance for a trauma-informed approach (HHS Publication No. 14–4884). https://ncsacw.samhsa.gov/userfiles/files/SAMHSA_Trauma.pdf

Torchalla, I., Nosen, L., Rostam, H., & Allen, P. (2012). Integrated treatment programs for individuals with concurrent substance use disorders and trauma experiences: A systematic review and meta-analysis. *Journal of Substance Abuse Treatment, 42*(1), 65–77. https://doi.org/10.1016/j.jsat.2011.09.001

van der Kolk, B. (2014). *The body keeps the score: Mind, brain and body in the transformation of trauma.* Penguin.

Wagner, A. W., Zatzick, D. F., Ghesquiere, A., & Jurkovich, G. J. (2007). Behavioral activation as an early intervention for posttraumatic stress disorder and depression among physically injured trauma survivors. *Cognitive and Behavioral Practice, 14*(4), 341–349. https://doi.org/10.1016/j.cbpra.2006.05.002

PART IV

Assessment in Social Work Practice: Knowledge and Skills

Use of Rapid Assessment Instruments (RAIs) in Clinical Social Work Practice

Michael O. Killian and David W. Springer

Need for Assessment
Assessment in Services

Much of evidence-based practice (EBP) in social work services and practice-based research centers on assessment of client problems, accurate quantification of these experiences, and examining evidence to improve effectiveness of services (Gibbs & Gambrill, 2002; Thyer, 2004). EBP includes professional knowledge and experience of the social work practitioner and alignment with client values. Identifying answerable questions and critically evaluating practice become a vital part of this process, requiring social workers to reliably and validly measure aspects of practice and client outcomes (Hudson, 1978). The integration of paper-and-pencil or computer-based testing into the daily schedule and tasks of social work practice can be a challenge. The need for concise, accurate, and easily completed measures is then obvious and requires striking a balance between intrusiveness and client burden of completing measures and the value of generating data and evidence of progress during services.

Connect Evidence-Based Assessment with Evidence-Based Practice

Fortunately, social work practitioners have access to a number of concise, client self-report, and easily scored measures across a range of social work practice settings (Corcoran & Fischer, 2013a, 2013b). These relatively short tools, assessments, or measures, which are easily integrated into practice to provide validated and reliable insight into practice, are often referred to as rapid assessment instruments (RAIs). RAIs often have a smaller number of questions all centering on a central idea or concept to be assessed in a client or group. They should be easily completed by a client and easily integrated into the flow of practice by the social worker. Their simplicity allows practitioners to repeatedly give the assessment to a client to monitor change over time and perhaps progress during services. Scores or valuations produced through their completion and scoring should easily and quickly inform practice. Measurement in social work practice allows social workers to gain valuable and quantitative information about client behaviors, thoughts, attitudes, cognitions, and other qualities and the ability to monitor potential changes over time and during services. Evidence-based assessment allows for an important first step into EBP.

Evidence-Informed Services and Rapid Assessment Instruments

The important use of RAIs in social work has historical roots to the earliest periods of the profession. Abraham Flexner (1915/2001) critiqued the nascent vocation of social work practice by asserting that social work did not yet qualify as a true profession, primarily due to a lack of generating its own "professional learnings" and a sustained body of knowledge. Essentially, social work was deemed at that time as an evidence-less, admirably well-intentioned, volunteer, and philanthropic service. Mary Richmond was among the first and most notable social workers who pushed the profession toward the development and quantification of the experiences of clients and the outcomes of services (Richmond, 1917/1935; Thyer, 2008). The use of RAIs in social work practice continues this important endeavor and tradition of quantifying client experiences and demonstrating evidence of our work.

External and internal pressures for social workers to take an evidence-based approach to services have increased in recent times. Beginning with Joel Fischer's seminal article in 1973 about the lack of evidence of effectiveness in casework through to today's emphasis on managed-care models, social work practitioners must consider the quantification and evidence behind their services. RAIs are integral in these efforts (Springer et al., 2002). RAIs can offer details on clients' feelings, attitudes, thoughts, beliefs, and cognitions that can be extremely difficult to observe directly as a practitioner. RAIs can be easily included and found valuable during the assessment period when working to tailor services to the needs of a client. Once services have been initiated, RAIs can provide an operationalized and objective metric of client progress over time. RAIs can be repeatedly given to a client to complete because their brevity reduces respondent burden and also reduces the effect on scores on subsequent administrations (i.e., a client remembering how they answered the last time, which influences their current responses). Scores from these instruments, when presented to a client, family, or group, can be a powerful visual to inform them of progress, engage them in the process, and motivate them toward future goals. RAIs and scores collected from a number of clients can be a powerful tool for advocacy and consideration of policy change. Agencies and organizations often search for evidence to substantiate their work and advocate for continued or future funding. Perhaps most important, a commitment to integrating RAIs into practice allows social work practitioners, agencies, and organizations to assess critically and insightfully whom they serve effectively and who remains underserved.

Fortunately, social work practitioners have an ever-increasing number of RAIs from which to select a tool that coincides with their evidence and evaluation goals. Increasingly, social work practitioners are graduating degree programs with a better knowledge of how to collect evidence and evaluate practice and a better understanding of basic research methodologies of assessment. There has been greater integration of research methods and scientific standards for demonstrating the quality of services and programs carrying out the general mission of social work. All of these advancements and refinements generate the persistent need for measurement in social work practice. Our ability to quantify client experiences and the effectiveness of services is central to the National Association of Social Workers' Code of Ethics (2017). The challenge for any social work practice is the integration of measurement in the client–provider relationship and process. This chapter focuses on understanding the development and refinement of any RAI tool as a guide to their consideration, selection, and utilization in social work practice.

Development of RAIs

A basic understanding of the development of RAIs is necessary for their selection, use, and interpretation in social work practice. Social workers dedicated to practice and work with clients, families, agencies, organizations, and communities are not likely to engage in research efforts to develop, pilot, and refine an RAI or similar instrument. Simply stated, their expertise, efforts, and passion are better spent serving those vulnerable individuals and groups. In the process of quantifying practice and evaluating these efforts, knowledge of measurement development, validation, and psychometric properties is vital to the selection and use of RAIs in social work practice. Understanding the basics of measurement and psychometrics can better inform RAI selection, use, interpretation, and implementation of findings back into practice. Social work practitioners intending to use an RAI should examine the possible measure through the same thinking and framework used to develop the RAI initially. Examining the underpinnings and development of the measure can offer key insights as to the applicability and utility of an RAI to a particular social work practice setting aiming to quantify aspects of practice and client experience. Here, topics of RAI development, piloting, determination of reliability, testing of validity, and other cultural and translational considerations for unique populations are reviewed.

Initial Qualitative Work and Refinement of the Conceptual Definition for Measurement

Social workers beginning to search for an RAI for use in client or program evaluation should first identify the exact definition of the concept being measured within the RAI. When initially being developed, an RAI will have defined the concept of interest intending to be measured and the exact purpose of that measurement. . Concepts to be measured, such as stress, depression, post-traumatic growth, resilience, or social capital, can be difficult to define, and often a definition may change depending on the intended use of the RAI.

Social workers interested in selecting a measure should pay careful attention to the definition of the concept originally used as the basis for development of the measure. Social science theories may lend clarity to the definition of the concept. Practitioners should identify these theories and definitions in the development of the RAI and ensure that they are compatible with the intended use of the RAI in their client, program, or organizational evaluation.

Item Development

Determining a precise definition of the concept to be measured is followed by the development of items or questions. Often, researchers and practitioners will meet with focus groups or key stakeholders to discuss the definition of the key concept to be measured, determine its suitability for the individuals or groups to be measured, and generate a pool of questions that adequately define and encompass the target concept. Practitioners should scrutinize items of an RAI to determine if all items or sets of items (i.e., "factors" or "subscales") are addressing some facet of the same underlying idea. Ideally, for any concept, the items should provide adequate coverage of the breadth of the concept without introducing other possible ideas that are not representative of that same concept. An important consideration here is the intended use of the measure because some practitioners may want to have a broad or overall measure of a concept and others may want a more targeted and specific measure. Practitioners should examine items of an RAI with the intended purpose of the measure in mind.

The scaling of items is important during this state of RAI development and an important consideration for social work practitioners when reviewing possible RAIs for use in practice. Most commonly, as evidenced by the common use of the term, items on RAIs are Likert scaled, meaning that response options are given in order based on varying degrees of the concept. Practitioners can see this on everything from customer service satisfaction surveys to longer self-report instruments included in psychological evaluations. The following is a common form of Likert scaling: "strongly disagree," "somewhat disagree," "slightly disagree," "neither agree or disagree," "slightly agree," "somewhat agree," and "strongly disagree." Often, these phrases accompany a numerical value used later when tallying a final RAI score for the overall measure. Response options should allow a client the opportunity to express fully their level of endorsement of the item. If the response options are truncated, or the item is extreme in some positive or negative manner, the answers to items will be artificially skewed toward one end of the possible response options. The number and nuance of response options should also be considered based on the developmental ability of the intended respondent. Younger children and those populations with cognitive deficits may have difficulty distinguishing between two unique response options when the range of possible responses is large. For example, younger children may be able to report their feelings more accurately when 3 or 4 response options are offered, possibly accompanied with pictures. Adults are likely to feel comfortable with 7, 10, or more response options because they have greater developmental ability to understand nuance and differentiate response options.

A common misconception by practitioners is that an RAI and its items are intended to generate a dichotomous outcome such as a diagnostic measure. Although certainly this can be the case with measures used for client or family assessment, client completion of other RAI measures may result in an overall score within a range of possible scores. This variation in scores allows practitioners to gain a more nuanced view of a client belief, attitude, feeling, thought, or behavior.

Expert and Service User Reviews

When selecting items to include within an RAI, consultation with expert researchers, experienced practitioners, and informed stakeholders is important. Each of these authorities brings different expertise able to inform the wording and scope of items included in a pool for possible inclusion in the final RAI. These individuals are often asked about item clarity, wording, readability, and whether items are worded appropriately for the target client population (DeVellis, 2016). Perhaps more important than a cursory review of item clarity and applicability is the invaluable input of content experts, experienced practitioners, and service users regarding how an RAI would be perceived and used in practice. Focus groups of experts who have studied a concept, treated clients struggling with it, or experienced it can provide feedback on all aspects of an RAI (Gilgun, 2004). Social work practitioners assessing an RAI for use in evaluation of practice should follow a similar process. Examining the RAI for use in concert with other practitioners and even asking opinions of clients can provide insight as to whether a particular RAI is a good option.

Initial Development and Testing

Researchers often publish an initial study on the development and original validation of an RAI. These initial studies often provide information on the guiding theory or framework on which the RAI was developed. How the RAI was developed, for whom the tool was intended, and how the final version was conceptualized are important to understand and consider. Samples used in the development of an RAI are important. RAIs that have been studied in both community samples (i.e., the general population) and clinical samples (e.g., those normally encountered during provision of services) are likely to have stronger evidence towards their validity. These initial reports will often provide descriptive statistics and a range of scores reported in a particular sample. Means and standard deviation values reported for particular samples provide a useful basis of comparison for social workers to understand how normal or extreme clients are from their practice or agency.

Factor Validity

Unidimensional and Multidimensional Measures

Longer psychometric measures and shorter RAIs can be considered measures of a concept that is often not directly observable. These concepts may be multifaceted or begin to be associated with a number of related ideas. A quality RAI should be able to capture a singular idea, or at least a few ideas, very concisely for numerous reasons mentioned previously. When developing an RAI, researchers will test if the RAI contains questions that capture single or multiple ideas and if these questions all "cluster" together. Factor analysis is a statistical method for testing if an RAI contains multiple ideas or facets of a concept. Factors within measurement are often referred to as dimensions or subscales. Measures can contain one dimension or factor, called unidimensional measures, or multiple dimensions, called multidimensional measures. A multidimensional instrument is nothing more than a collection of two or more unidimensional scales that work together to measure different domains

of a construct. Factor analysis allows us to determine the number and nature of factors or dimensions that may exist in sets of questions within an overall measure (DeVellis, 2016). Exploratory factor analysis (EFA) is used initially to explore the number and nature of possible factors in a set of questions. Once an RAI has a developed and supported "factor structure" with a hypothesized number of factors, future studies may use scores from new research samples to determine if these new data still support the hypothesized number and structure of the factors. Essentially, a strong theoretical and empirical basis exists for explaining the number of factors and which items belong to each factor. In this case, researchers will use confirmatory factor analysis (CFA) to examine if the same number of factors and the questions within these factors are still supported. Researchers will often refer to this examination of factors and their constituent questions as a "test of model fit," meaning they are testing if the hypothesized nature and number of factors still provide a good model of new data. Both EFA and CFA are important analytic techniques for establishing and reaffirming the factor validity of an RAI and its questions.

CFA is especially important for the construction and consideration of RAIs. Often, researchers will create an RAI from a longer questionnaire. The goal is to shorten the questionnaire while still maintaining the nature of the questionnaire and its ability to measure the key concept. In this regard, CFA is a useful technique in determining if a shortened RAI version of the longer questionnaire maintains the same factor validity. In a study, researchers will report a number of indices of model fit, and social work practitioners should read interpretations of these fit indices closely. RAIs with excellent or supported factor structures based on these reported values of fit indices are suggested. More information about factor analysis, various approaches to assessing factors, and more in-depth explanations of these indices of factor model fit are available for interested social work practitioners (see Abell et al., 2009; Costello & Osborne, 2005).

Reliability

Reliability is simply the ability of an RAI to produce consistent scores across a number of conditions and contexts. There are primarily three types of reliability that are tested during the development of an RAI, and practitioners will want determine if an RAI meets at least some of these standards.

Internal Consistency Reliability

The most commonly considered and reported form of reliability is internal consistency reliability, which tests the degree of covariation among the set of items within an RAI. When a sample of individuals answer a set of items within a measure, internal consistency reliability quantifies the degree to which all answers tend to vary together. Essentially, a reliable RAI that cleanly measures some psychosocial phenomena of interest to social work researchers and practitioners will contain items that are all "consistent among themselves." If an individual provides responses with a greater degree on several items, it is hoped that similarly high responses will be found for other items. All responses to items are correlated with each other, hence the name "internal consistency reliability." This ensures that all items are sharing a significant amount of their variation, which in theory is being driven by the degree of the underlying idea being measured by the RAI.

Often, researchers test this by reporting Cronbach's alpha (α) coefficient, with values ranging from 0 to 1. Practitioners considering using an RAI in clinical practice or for overall program evaluation must pay particular attention to the reported Cronbach's α coefficients from prior studies in which the RAI was

used. In larger samples, RAIs with Cronbach's α coefficients of .80 or higher are considered appropriate for use. There is an important caveat with Cronbach's α coefficients when using RAIs with individuals in repeated clinical assessment: Because of the difficulty of measuring a single idea in a single individual, RAIs with a Cronbach's α coefficient of .90 or higher are recommended (Abell et al., 2009; Nunnally & Bernstein, 1994). Due to the difficulty of measuring any psychosocial concept in an individual, higher Cronbach's α coefficients help reduce the possible error and misrepresentation of that concept in the individual.

Interrater Reliability

Interrater reliability is the ability of an RAI to produce similar results when two or more individuals provide answers on the RAI when viewing or assessing the same psychosocial phenomena or event. There are many examples of interrater reliability in practice, but each centers on multiple individuals rating some shared concept or event using the same RAI. Two behavioral analysts might use the same RAI to assess a child's behavior in the classroom. If the RAI has high interrater reliability, both behavioral analysts assessing the child's behavior will obtain similar scores on the RAI, which together may better represent the child's externalizing behaviors in the classroom. Another example is in health social work contexts in which an RAI measures health-related quality of life of a child diagnosed with a chronic health condition. A health social worker may ask the child and parent to each rate the child's health-related quality of life. Scores of the child and parent should be similar on the RAI with good interrater reliability. Regardless of the context, interrater reliability is consistency between two individuals assessing the same shared concept.

Social work practitioners should consider what "agreement" between raters means for a selected RAI. When an RAI has fewer response options or is intended to reach a conclusion of "diagnosis or not diagnosis" based on a cutoff score, basic agreement between raters means that both provide the same "yes/no" answer. When an RAI includes fewer response options, then agreement between raters may be sufficient as basic "absolute agreement." Here, absolute agreement presented as a percentage is the appropriate metric of interrater reliability.

Sometimes simple agreement may misrepresent interrater reliability on an RAI intended to produce a score on a possible range. For example, consider two raters who each used the same RAI to rate several children's behaviors during a 15-minute period in a classroom. The RAI had a possible range of scores from 1 to 100 available to the raters. For each child assessed, each rater reported only a 1-point difference. Although these raters may have demonstrated extraordinary consistency (i.e., only 1-point difference each time over a range of 100 possible answers), they also displayed no absolute agreement on the RAI when rating the children.

In cases in which RAIs are intended to produce a score from a larger possible range, absolute agreement is not the correct form of interrater reliability to consider for the RAIs. In these instances, intraclass correlation (ICC) is the most commonly reported statistical value. Higher ICC values indicate greater interrater reliability. ICC values range from -1 to 1, with 1 indicating perfect consistency and agreement between raters, -1 indicating perfect disagreement, and 0 indicating only random agreement. Generally, ICC scores less than 0.40 are considered to have poor interrater reliability, scores between 0.40 and -.59 are considered to be fair, scores between 0.60 and 0.74 are considered good, and scores higher than 0.75 indicate excellent interrater reliability (Cicchetti, 1994).

Test–Retest Reliability

Test-retest reliability is the ability of an RAI to produce consistent scores over time for an individual. An RAI with good test–retest reliability will allow an individual to provide similar answers over time when it is assumed that the underlying concept has not changed over time. Test–retest reliability is especially important when progress or changes over time are assessed with repeated use of the same RAI.

There are several considerations when examining the test–retest reliability of an RAI that should be of concern by both a researcher developing a RAI and a social worker selecting one for use in practice. To adequately examine the consistency of an RAI over two points in time, it must be assumed that the score of interest in the individual has not changed over time. In other words, the intervening period of time between two administrations of the RAI should be short enough that the individual can be assumed not to have changed over time or had something external potentially affect their score. Conversely, the intervening period of time cannot be too short wherein the first administration of the RAI affects the subsequent score. Therein lies the challenge of examining and considering test–retest reliability. It is important that enough time, but not too much time, has lapsed between the two administrations of the RAI. A sufficient period of time needs to have lapsed so that an individual does not remember how they completed the measure the first time. On the other hand, if too much time has passed, changes in their responses on the RAI might be due to natural progression or some other factor in their life.

Correlation coefficients such as Pearson's r and Spearman's rho (ρ) are used to examine and report test–retest reliability. Researchers examining the psychometric properties of an RAI should report these correlations in RAI scores between two defined points in time. Social work practitioners should review these correlations and how suitable the defined time points are to their intended use of the RAI. Practitioners wanting a weekly and brief assessment of a client's anxiety would ideally select an RAI with demonstrated test–retest reliability and strong correlations in scores obtained from similar client samples over a period of a week. Pearson's *r* and Spearman's ρ each range from –1.00 to 1.00, but correlation coefficients 0.70 or higher are considered generally to demonstrate acceptable test–retest reliability. This is not always the case because changes in the period of time tested, context, concept of interest being measured, and individual circumstances may all affect the resulting correlation between scores. Ultimately, social work practitioners should be mindful of the purpose and context of the RAI and select an RAI that has demonstrated test–retest reliability in similar clients and practice settings and situations.

Measurement Validity

The psychometric and measurement validity of an RAI is the confidence that scores produced by the RAI are reflective of the underlying concept. This is a challenging and interesting aspect to the development of an RAI and its selection for use in social work practice. Measurement validity is the confidence that an RAI instrument measures exactly what it intends to measure. Whereas reliability implies consistency over time and context, measurement validity implies the accuracy of the measure. Is the underlying concept being measured the sole reason why an individual would answer higher or lower for each item on the RAI? If so, this points to the accuracy of the RAI when a score is produced. Establishing the measurement validity of an RAI involves providing evidence that the scores on the RAI are associated with aspects of the underlying concept it intends to measure. This is a challenging and multifaceted concept, and the criteria for measurement validity are germane and unique to the concept of interest. There are primarily four types of measurement validity: face validity, content validity, criterion-related

validity, and construct validity. We review each here.

Face and Content Validity

Face and content validity are often assessed together because they are both determined by the opinion of research experts, clinical authorities, and other stakeholders able to inform the wording and content of items in an RAI. Those developing and validating an RAI will select panels of experts and stakeholders to assess the items to determine if they appear to address the concept of interest (i.e., face validity) and if they appear to provide adequate cover of the breath of the concept (i.e., content validity). Face validity is achieved when experts and stakeholders agree the items all measure the concept or appear to be applicable at face value. Basically, do the items look correct? Content validity is slightly more complex in that a concept an RAI is purporting to measure should be fully covered in the items. An example of poor content validity is a depression RAI that only asks questions about social isolation or only about anhedonia. Items solely focusing on social isolation or anhedonia would leave an RAI measuring depression with poor content validity because depression is a cluster of symptomologies including many more facets. Social work practitioners should similarly inspect the items and their wording within an RAI to assess the applicability of each item to the concept to be measured and if the concept is fully covered by the items.

Criterion-Related Validity

Testing of an RAI against expected standards for a measure of that concept is called criterion-related validity. The defining feature of criterion-related validity is that an RAI is tested on criteria of that same concept. For scores from an RAI to have criterion-related validity, these scores might correlate with other known measures of the same concept (known-instruments validity), differ between groups of individuals known to have or not have various amounts of the concept (known-groups validity), and must be useful in the prediction of later events involving this concept (predictive validity). All of these standards rely on an empirical determination that scores from an RAI should be significantly associated with an important feature of the concept.

Known-Instruments Validity

Known-instruments criterion-related validity is established when a newly developed RAI correlates highly and significantly with a "gold standard" measure of the same concept. Scores from a newly developed RAI serving as a short and effective measure of anxiety might be compared to scores from the Beck Anxiety Inventory (BAI; Beck et al., 1988). The BAI is an established and well-regarded assessment of anxiety, yet this 21-item self-report questionnaire might be too long or burdensome for integration into weekly contact with a client. However, an RAI with 7 self-report items would be considered to have excellent known-instruments criterion-related validity if these scores highly correlated with the longer BAI when both were completed by a client. Often, a shortened form of a longer version of the same measure is developed. The shortened version acting as an RAI should very highly correlate with the original longer version. The RAI could then provide very similar scores with reduced respondent burden and could be a valuable tool in clinical social work practice.

Known-Groups Validity

Scores completed from an RAI should significantly differ between groups of individuals known to have varying degrees of the concept of interest. Known-groups criterion-related validity is this empirical standard. If a measure is valid, in that it captures the concept it is intending to measure, then scores should differ significantly between particular groups. Children diagnosed and managing a chronic condition should report significantly lower health-related quality of life compared to otherwise healthy children sampled from schools, as is the case with the PedsQL Generic Core 4.0 measure, an RAI measuring this health-related quality of life (Varni et al., 2001). The scores obtained from the Adolescent Concerns Evaluation (ACE) RAI have been shown to vary significantly between groups of adolescents in a runaway shelter, detained in a juvenile justice setting, or attending school and living at home (Springer, 1998). ACE measures the risk of running away in adolescents. Known-groups validity is a very basic and necessary aspect of the validity of this measure. What use would this measure be, or could this measure claim to be valid, if runaway risk scores did not differ between these groups of adolescents? Social work practitioners should examine RAIs for this form of criterion-related validity to determine if scores from a measure differ when given to a population of interest compared to other groups of non-social work clients.

Predictive Validity

An RAI that has utility when predicting future events has good predictive criterion-related validity. A common example in social work is the use of a child maltreatment risk assessment tool. If a family reports or is rated to have a particular risk score, is that score predictive of a maltreatment outcome such as likelihood of allegations of child maltreatment in the next 6 months or removal of the children from the home based on safety concerns in that same period? RAIs with demonstrated predictive criterion-related validity are clinically valuable in social work practice if scores reported by individuals or families translate into the likelihood of a poor outcome. The Concise Health Risk Tracking (CHRT) is a self-report measure assessing suicidal severity and risk in adolescents (Mayes et al., 2018) and in various samples of adults (Ostacher et al., 2015; Reilly-Harrington et al., 2016; Trivedi et al., 2011). Recently, a shortened and revised version was completed by 251 high-risk adolescents enrolled in a suicide-prevention intensive outpatient program in a large children's medical center in the southwestern United States (Mayes et al., 2020). Adolescent self-reported scores on the revised 14-item CHRT were predictive of suicidal events in later weeks while the adolescents were in these outpatient programs. Often, predictive validity is assessed statistically when using scores from an RAI to test their association with the likelihood of an outcome happening later (logistic regression) or test the ability of these scores to classify individuals accurately to high-risk and low-risk groups. The accuracy of this classification is reported as a value called area under the curve (AUC), often calculated along with the receiver operating characteristic curve. An RAI with scores that cannot be used to classify individuals as low or high risk for an outcome no better than chance would have an AUC of 0.50, which is indicative of a predictively useless measure. Commonly accepted AUC values and their indication for predictive criterion-related validity are the following: 0.50–0.60, no predictive validity; 0.60–0.70, poor predictive validity; 0.70–0.80, fair predictive validity; 0.80–0.90, good predictive validity; and 0.90 or higher, excellent predictive validity.

Construct Validity

An RAI that truly captures a concept should have scores that are correlated with other theoretically related concepts. If an RAI is claimed to measure depression accurately, then scores from it should be strongly associated with scores produced from a known measure of anxiety when both are completed by clients. Given the well-known association between the two mood disorders of depression and anxiety, an RAI measuring depression should be correlated with anxiety scores to be considered a valid measure. This is construct validity for a measure. A measure of any psychosocial

concept should be correlated with theoretically similar or associated concepts to have construct validity. There is an important distinction here from criterion-related validity. Criterion-related validity is based on the association of an RAI with the same concept (e.g., an association with a different measure of the same concept, differences in groups of individuals classified by the same concept, and prediction of an outcome involving that same concept). By contrast, construct validity is evident when an RAI exhibits expected relationships with different yet conceptually associated ideas. With construct validity, there are two types that should be considered: convergent construct validity and discriminant construct validity.

Convergent Construct Validity

Convergent construct validity is the most often considered and assumed type of construct validity. The example of an RAI measuring depression being correlated with a known measure of anxiety is evidence of convergent construct validity. Scores from the RAI should correlate to theoretically associated ideas. Essentially, the ideas converge, providing evidence that the RAI may measure what it ostensibly measures. A study of the Working Alliance Inventory–Short Form (WAI-S; Horvath, 1981; Horvath & Greenberg, 1986, 1989) and its use in child protection services provides an example of convergent construct validity (Killian et al., 2017). WAI-S measures the quality and strength of the therapeutic relationship between a client and a therapist by assessing perceptions around shared goals, tasks to reach those goals, and their shared sense of bond. The WAI-S has never been used in research and program evaluation of child protection services, so the researchers included a measure of client engagement during these services. Although work relationship and engagement are different concepts, they were theorized to be highly associated. Results from the study demonstrated the significant correlation between WAI-S and scores of engagement in services; thus, the researchers concluded that WAI-S had convergent construct validity within child protection services research. WAI-S is a well-known measure developed in psychological counseling and services, but researchers evaluated the RAI for potential use in social work research and practice in child welfare. For social work practitioners assessing an RAI, convergent construct validity might be an important aspect of the tool to be considered. An RAI demonstrating conceptual alignment and association with key concepts targeted by an intervention, a particular modality of treatment, or a program overall would be valuable and a good choice for selection in practice.

Discriminant Construct Validity

Discriminant construct validity of an RAI is found when scores from the measure are not associated with conceptually dissimilar ideas. A measure should be correlated with similar concepts (convergent) and be uncorrelated with different and unrelated concepts (divergent). Divergent construct validity provides evidence that the RAI produces scores that do not begin to measure other ideas or that the measure does not unnecessarily capture other concepts. The study evaluating the use of WAI-S in children protection services found WAI-S scores correlated with other measures of engagement in services (convergent construct validity) and not associated with the social workers' degree of safety concerns about the family in the areas of alcohol problems, drug use, domestic violence, previous receipt of child protection services, and other aspects of the family environment (Killian et al., 2017). Social work practitioners, as a basic principle and following a code of ethics, should have positive regard for all clients. That WAI-S scores did not vary by levels of social work concern and evaluation of risk in these domains provides important

divergent construct validity evidence for WAI-S. Combined with the evidence of convergent construct validity, this evidence of divergent construct validity for WAI-S supports the use of the measure in children protection services evaluation of practice.

Cultural Appropriateness and Cultural Validity

Cultural differences can have an important impact on social work services and research. Cultural differences arise from a number of social, geographic, racial, ethnic, and other differences that can lead individuals or communities to have varying views on what a particular construct means to them. For example, Hispanics may present with distinct profiles of depression that indicate varying clinical presentations and reporting of depression, as found in a sample of Hispanic women seeking depression treatment in primary care (Killian et al., 2021). The Patient Health Questionnaire–9 was used as the RAI in the study, but significant variation was found among these women with regard to particular questions, especially concerning somatization symptoms such as "feeling tired or having little energy" and "trouble falling asleep or staying asleep, or sleeping too much." This is important because the manifestation and experience of depression may vary between Hispanic and non-Hispanic populations. Hispanic patients with depression may report disproportionately high experiences of somatic symptoms (Chong et al., 2010). Selecting an RAI with a higher or lower number of somatic questions when attempting to measure depression may produce scores that do not accurately represent the experience of depressive symptoms in a Hispanic client.

The central issue for measurement is making certain the RAI is capturing and measuring what the construct means in a particular sociocultural context. "Is that what it means to them?" is a fundamental question. Selecting a quantitative RAI for use in practice and in research is rife with these qualitative assumptions about what this construct means to an individual or group and how this construct is manifested or perceived by them. Risk of scores from an RAI misrepresenting a construct within a particular sociocultural context can be reduced when examining a tool for use in practice. Much of these efforts can be taken during the initial examination of the questions within an RAI. Have experts, experienced practitioners, and other stakeholders, such as service users, review a measure and how differing individuals may perceive particular questions. Search for RAIs that have been informed or developed by informants with expertise in that culture and focus groups (Van de Vijver & Tanzer, 2004).

Differences in languages and translated versions of RAIs should also be examined thoroughly by social workers before integrating RAIs into practice. Selecting an RAI that has been properly translated into the desired language is important. Social work practitioners can enlist bilingual colleagues or clients to assess the accuracy and applicability of translated questions. The gold-standard process is to translate questions from an RAI into a desired language and then use another group of bilingual experts to translate the questions back to the original language. The Parental Self-Care Scale and Family Responsibility Scale were each developed and validated to assess caregivers of people living with HIV/AIDS about their experiences as caregivers and challenges as heads of household (Abell, Ryan, & Kamata, 2006a; Abell, Ryan, Kamata, & Citrolo, 2006). Due to validating the measure using English- and Spanish-speaking individuals, translation and back-translation were used. Importantly, the back-translation was conducted by two Spanish-speaking individuals, one of Mexican and the other of Puerto Rican

descent. Translation and back-translation can be a powerful tool to identify nuanced changes in meaning of items, alteration in the intended meaning, and possible problems introduced by colloquial terms or idioms. Social worker practitioners should carefully examine translated RAIs for these issues.

Conclusion

The use of RAIs in social work practice has a long and important history in our profession. EBP relies on quantification and assessment of client problems and the examination of our efforts. RAIs offer the opportunity to integrate evidence collection and consideration into the challenging practice environment. An important consideration throughout the process for any social work practitioner is to view the RAI and its completion through the eyes of their clients or families completing the measure. Clinical intuition and experience can be a powerful guide to examine how appropriate a particular RAI will be for quantifying a particular concept within a particular population of clients. Knowledge of measure development and validation allows social workers to be insightful and considerate of which RAIs are chosen to quantify the needs and progress of clients, families, communities, organizations, and agencies. Social work practice deserves our reexamination of old practices, finding evidence of our and our clients' success, and using trustworthy data to identify those still underserved by our efforts.

References

Abell, N., Ryan, S., & Kamata, A. (2006). Assessing capacity for self-care among HIV-positive heads of household: Bilingual validation of the parental self-care scale. *Social Work Research, 30*(4), 233–243.

Abell, N., Ryan, S., Kamata, A., & Citrolo, J. (2006). Bilingual validation of the Family Responsibility Scale: Assessing stress among HIV+ heads of household. *Journal of Social Service Research, 32*(3), 195–212.

Abell, N., Springer, D. W., & Kamata, A. (2009). *Developing and validating rapid assessment instruments*. Oxford University Press.

Beck, A. T., Epstein, N., Brown, G., & Steer, R. A. (1988). An inventory for measuring clinical anxiety: Psychometric properties. *Journal of Consulting and Clinical Psychology, 56*, 893–897.

Chong, J., Reinschmidt, K. M., & Moreno, F. A. (2010). Symptoms of depression in a Hispanic primary care population with and without chronic medical illnesses. Primary Care Companion to *the Journal of Clinical Psychiatry, 12*(3), PCC.09m00846.

Corcoran, K., & Fischer, J. (2013a). *Measures for clinical practice: A sourcebook* (Vol. 1). Oxford University Press.

Corcoran, K., & Fischer, J. (2013b). *Measures for clinical practice: A sourcebook* (Vol. 2). Oxford University Press.

Costello, A. B., & Osborne, J. (2005). Best practices in exploratory factor analysis: Four recommendations for getting the most from your analysis. *Practical Assessment Research & Evaluation, 10*(7). https://scholarworks.umass.edu/pare/vol10/iss1/7

DeVellis, R. F. (2016). *Scale development: Theory and applications* (4th ed.). Sage.

Flexner, A. (2001). Is social work a profession? *Research on Social Work Practice, 11*(2), 152–165. doi:10.1177/ 104973150101100202 (Original work published 1915)

Gibbs, L., & Gambrill, E. (2002). Evidence-based practice: Counterarguments to objections. *Research on Social Work Practice, 12*(3), 452–476.

Gilgun, J. F. (2004). Qualitative methods and the development of clinical assessment tools. *Qualitative Health Research, 14*(7), 1008–1019.

Horvath, A. O. (1981). *An exploratory study of the working alliance: Its measurement and relationship to therapy outcome*. Unpublished doctoral dissertation, University of British Columbia.

Horvath, A. O., & Greenberg, L. S. (1986). The development and validation of the working alliance inventory. In L. S. Greenberg & W. M. Pinsof (Eds.), *The psychotherapeutic process: A research handbook* (pp. 529–556). Guilford.

Horvath, A. O., & Greenberg, L. S. (1989). Development and validation of the Working Alliance Inventory. *Journal of Counseling Psychology, 36*, 223–233. doi:10.1037/0022-0167.36.2.223

Hudson, W. W. (1978). First axioms of treatment. *Social Work, 23*(1), 65–66.

Killian, M. O., Forrester, D., Westlake, D., & Antonopoulou, P. (2017). Validity of the Working Alliance Inventory within child protection services. *Research on Social Work Practice, 27*, 704–715. doi:10.1177/1049731515596816

Killian, M. O., Sanchez, K., Eghaneyan, B. H., Cabassa, L., & Trivedi, M. H. (2021). Psychometric properties of the Patient Health Questionnaire–9 (PHQ9) and profiles of depression in a treatment seeking Hispanics. *International Journal of Methods in Psychiatric Research, 30*(1), e1851. doi:10.1002/mpr.1851. Epub 2020 Aug 30. PMID: 32862484; PMCID: PMC7992282.

Mayes, T. L., Kennard, B. D., Killian, M. O., Carmody, T., Granneman, B., Emslie, G. J., & Trivedi, M. H. (2018). Psychometric properties of the Concise Health Risk Tracking (CHRT-SR) in adolescents with suicidality. *Journal of Affective Disorders, 235*, 45–51. doi:10.1016/j.jad.2018.03.007

Mayes, T. L., Killian, M. O., Rush, A. J., Emslie, G. J., Carmody, T., Kennard, B. D., Jha, M. K., King, J., & Trivedi, M. H. (2020). Predicting future suicidal events in adolescents using the Concise Health Risk Tracking Self-Report (CHRT-SR). *Journal of Psychiatric Research, 126*, 19–25. https://doi.org/10.1016/j.jpsychires.2020.04.008

National Association of Social Workers. (2017). *The NASW code of ethics*. https://www.socialworkers.org/about/ethics/code-of-ethics/code-of-ethics-english

Richmond, M. (1935). *Social diagnosis*. Russell Sage. (Original work published 1917)

Springer, D. W. (1998). Validation of the Adolescent Concerns Evaluation (ACE): Detecting indicators of runaway behavior in adolescents. *Social Work Research, 22*, 241–250.

Springer, D. W., Abell, N., & Hudson, W. W. (2002). Creating and validating rapid assessment instruments for practice and research: Part 1. *Research on Social Work Practice, 12*(3), 408–439. doi:10.1177/1049731502012003005

Thyer, B. (2004). What is evidence-based practice? *Brief Treatment and Crisis Intervention, 4*(2), 167–176.

Thyer, B. A. (2008). The quest for evidence-based practice? We are all positivists! *Research on Social Work Practice, 18*, 339–345.

Van de Vijver, F., & Tanzer, N. K. (2004). Bias and equivalence in cross-cultural assessment: An overview. *European Review of Applied Psychology, 54*(2), 119–135. doi:10.1016/j.erap.2003.12.004

Varni, J. W., Seid, M., & Kurtin, P. S. (2001). PedsQL 4.0: Reliability and validity of the Pediatric Quality of Life Inventory Version 4.0 generic core scales in healthy and patient populations. *Medical Care, 39*, 800–812.

Using Assessment Tools with Children

Craig Winston LeCroy

Assessment instruments play a vital role in both the clinical and programmatic aspects of social service delivery. Upon referral, these tools help guide effective treatment choices by providing insight into the client's presenting problem. Broadly speaking, these tools illuminate knowledge, attitudes, beliefs, behaviors, or conditions that are symptomatic and/or impede successful functioning. Instruments that track changes in these domains can assist in establishing the effectiveness of an intervention. These tools have become the central mechanism for program leadership to articulate and substantiate the positive impacts of their program to their stakeholders.

Until fairly recently, the majority of high-quality assessment tools were developed exclusively for adult populations. Unfortunately, the developmental differences between adults, youth, and children means that instruments designed for one group do not necessarily translate to other groups. To complicate matters further, the actual process of administering assessment instruments with children is far more nuanced than with adult populations. In addition to communication and comprehension issues, the uniquely vulnerable status of children as dependents adds new levels of complexity when making assessments. Very rarely, if ever, do children admit themselves for treatment. Consequentially, the adults in their lives—those who voiced "the complaint" or need for services—inevitably play a major role in the assessment process and often serve as a "proxy reporter" for the indicated child. The inclusion of caregivers, siblings, mentors, school personnel, or case managers can create a rich, multifaceted understanding of the presenting problem; however, it can also raise difficult questions in terms of reliability and confidentiality. There is evidence that children's perceptions of their conditions do not highly correlate with those of their caregivers, particularly in social or emotional domains (Sherifali & Pinelli, 2007; Van der Ende et al., 2012), suggesting the need for a multidimensional approach. Table 39.1 presents various factors that should be considered in an assessment.

As the demand for short-term and effective treatment services for children and adolescents' increases (LeCroy, 2008, 2011), so does the need for developmentally appropriate

TABLE 39.1 Three Factors That Influence Assessment

The Source of Data	The Setting	The Method
Parents or caregivers	Home	Observation
Child	School	Self-report
Other informant (e.g., teacher)	Community	Rating scale

assessment instruments. There must also be an emphasis on guiding practitioners to administer the instruments in sensitive, engaging, and ethical ways. This chapter reviews the fundamentals of the construction and utility of child assessment tools and discusses strategies to implement them successfully in social work practice.

Basic Typologies

Assessment tools crystallize information into a useful summary for analysis and comparison. The client's individual scores can be contrasted to normative data sets (i.e., other children at similar developmental stages) or compared to the results before the intervention was put into place (i.e., pre-/post-testing). Two of the most common forms of assessment tools are behavior rating scales and standardized interviews.

Behavior rating scales are widely used with children because they are brief, they can be filled out by multiple reporters, and they generally do not require significant training to administer. Another benefit of rating scales is that they provide reporters with a more anonymous context than, for example, face-to-face interviews. This decreases the pressure on the child to report in socially desirable ways. Common examples of behavior rating scales include the Child Behavior Checklist, Conner's Rating Scales, and Children's Depression Inventory. Conversely, the simplicity of a rating scale can lend itself to bias, especially across ethnic groups. One example of ethnic bias is that Hispanic Americans have been

found to choose the extreme ends of 5-point rating scales more than Caucasian Americans (Tyson, 2004). Optimally, a program should use measures that have been validated for their target population in terms of age, gender, ethnicity, and region.

A second typology is the standardized interview. This method refers to an in-person assessment of the child or family wherein the administrator is trained to use the same questions, procedures, and scoring of responses. In this format, clients respond to statements indicating a frequency of occurrence of a behavior, or they rate themselves on scaled items in terms of "a little" or "a lot" or "true" and "false" (for an example, see Table 39.2). The Diagnostic Interview Schedule for Children (DISC) uses software to adapt the interview as the responses are entered. The Child Assessment Schedule, although still standardized, is more qualitative. The benefit of the structured interview is increased engagement and the opportunity to include clinical observation in the process. These strategies, however, can be significantly more time-intensive and complex to analyze. There is no single "best" assessment typology; rather, the aim is to find a good fit between a given instrument and the needs of the program.

TABLE 39.2 Sample Items from the Hopelessness Scale for Children

True or false	I want to grow up because I think things will be better.
True or false	I might as well give up because I can't make things better for myself.
True or false	When things are going badly, I know they won't be as bad all the time.
True or false	I can imagine what my life will be like when I'm grown up.
True or false	I have enough time to finish the things I really want to do.
True or false	Some day I will be really good at doing the things I really care about.

Source: Kazdin (1983).

Additional Uses for Assessment Tools

The main objective of assessment tools is to describe and classify a presenting problem. Additional uses for instruments include screening for early intervention, evaluation of treatment effectiveness, and diagnosis using *Diagnostic and Statistical Manual of Mental Disorders* (DSM) criteria.

Screening for Prevention/Early Intervention

Assessment tools are increasingly being used to screen children who are in the early stages of developing behavioral, social, or emotional problems (Whitcomb, 2017). Early screening minimizes the adverse outcomes associated with psychological disorders and "at-risk" environmental situations by initiating appropriate interventions at critical developmental stages. Screening instruments can be used to predict individuals who are at "high risk" by offering a score that qualifies for preventive intervention. In general, there is a need for further evaluation when children score one or more standard deviations above a normative mean on an instrument.

Assessment of Treatment

Assessment instruments can also be useful for assessing changes over time and treatment effectiveness. Typically, these tools incorporate a Likert-scale format (e.g., "strongly disagree" to "strongly agree" or "seldom" to "always") to evaluate the frequency or extent of behavioral, social, or emotional symptoms. To properly function as a gauge of an intervention, the same instrument should be administered at least twice in order to create a standard of comparison. Pre/post assessments contrast the outcome at the end of treatment against a baseline assessment before treatment began. Assessments can also be more frequently administered at various points throughout treatment in order to build a progressive picture of change. This approach is commonly done when evaluating client change using a single system design. Frequent assessment throughout treatment can improve the clinical relationship and has been shown to contribute to a significant decrease in dropout rates (Miller et al., 2006). Used in this manner, assessment instruments track progress while providing clients with a forum for active participation and feedback. Examples of these types of tools include the Child and Adolescent Functional Assessment Scale, the Eyberg Child Behavior Inventory, and the Healthy Families Parenting Inventory.

Diagnosis

Assessment tools can be used to determine the presence of major categorical psychiatric disorders in children (Prinstein et al., 2019). Typically, these tools are in the form of structured or semistructured interviews, in which certain responses from the child, adolescent, parent, or teacher will determine the interview questions leading to a specific diagnosis. Examples of these interview schedules include DISC and the Anxiety Disorders Interview Schedule for DSM-V (TR): Child Version ADIS for DSM-V. A frequent challenge to consider when diagnosing children according to the DSM is that the time frames for establishing chronicity have not always been structured to account for the rapid nature of growth and change that occurs in children (Whitcomb, 2017). Regular application of assessment tools becomes especially important to help distinguish between transient and permanent conditions.

Selecting Assessment Tools

Assessment instruments are widely used with children in educational, child welfare, and juvenile justice settings. Often, these assessments inform life-changing placement decisions for the child. In many cases, children have not received the appropriate care or placement as a result of clinicians using unreliable and invalid assessments (Tyson, 2004). Numerous assessment tools are available for purchase, and many more are accessible free of charge. However, not all instruments are of equivalent quality or utility, so considerable thought must be dedicated to selecting the correct measurement for a given setting. The main selection criteria are scientific acceptability, relevance, and ease of use.

The scientific acceptability of a measure is described in terms of reliability and established validity. *Reliability* refers to the stability and consistency of the results produced by an instrument. *Validity*, on the other hand, refers to how well the instrument measures what it claims to measure. If a measure is not reliable or valid, the benefits of a good intervention could be masked or the harmful impacts of a poor intervention could go undetected (LeCroy, 2019). Practitioners may need to refer to a standard research text to interpret both reliability and validity data. As a general rule, however, a reliability of 0.80 is considered acceptable for most purposes.

Although documented scientific credibility is beneficial, in this developing field some helpful instruments many fall short of the ideal standard of evidence. In these cases, thoughtful analysis of the individual items on an instrument can help practitioners decide on the *face validity* of a tool. Do the questions appear to be measuring the concept in a clear and logical manner? Has the measure been tested with the target demographics of a program? Does the measure test similar items in a similar way to the better known instruments for this outcome? Finally, is the instrument sensitive enough to detect meaningful changes over time?

An instrument's relevance—how well a given instrument correlates to a desired outcome—may seem like an obvious selection criterion. Yet, relevance can be easily misunderstood by practitioners and administrators. The most common error is to select an instrument that is conceptually related to a desired change but not in itself a direct indicator. For example, if a group program is designed to increase children's social skills, it could seem reasonable to track self-esteem because of an assumption that the two are linked. A clearer and more direct approach is to use a measure that has been validated for demonstrating change in *social skills*, such as the Matson Evaluation of Social Skills with Youngsters. Granted, there are outcomes that do not yet have a validated measurement instrument. In these cases, it is possible to use a proxy outcome measure, although the proxy measure should be supported by literature that draws a strong correlation between the proxy and the desired outcome. In assessing relevance, keep in mind this primary question: To what extent does the measure tap into whether the person is improving or deteriorating so that intervention changes can be made?

Ease of use is an important criterion for real-world use of instruments. Instruments that are time-intensive, costly, or require a high level of specified training to administer may not be practical in many settings. Instruments should be well designed graphically, have clear directions, and have clear scoring procedures. Some instruments require software to score, which can delay results. Many rapid assessment scales—fewer than 20 questions and can be scored in minutes—are widely available. The trade-off for using brief scales is that they have less specific and detailed information, which must also be weighed. High-quality assessment tools are relatively accessible in print and online resources. Some well-known resources include Fischer et al. (2020), Sperry (2011), McLeod et al. (2013), and Whitcomb (2017). Online resources include those listed in the Helpful Resources section.

Administering Child Measures in Practice

One of the most important developments in the field of assessment has been the recognition that the child's voice must be central in the process (Smith & Handler, 2006). As children are more regularly included in the assessment process, new types of instruments have been adapted. Table 39.3 lists the various assessment methods that practitioners use to conduct assessments with children and youth. The techniques range from more traditional checklists to more interactive tools such as role-play interviews.

In contrast to standard adult practice, with children it is critical to use multiple instruments that draw from multiple reporters (Achenbach, 2011). It is not advisable to rely solely on a parent's report of a particular behavior without eliciting information from another adult (ideally from a distinct setting, such as school) and from the child. This method is

TABLE 39.3 Examples of Different Types of Assessment Measures

Type of Assessment	Example
Clinical interview	Psychosocial history
Semistructured interview	Child Assessment Schedule
Behavioral observation	Playground observation of behavior
Role-play test	Behavioral Assertiveness Test for Children
Parent reports	Healthy Families Parenting Inventory
Teacher reports	Walker Problem Behavior Identification
Peer assessment	Peer rating of status
Self-reports	Children's Depression Inventory
Client logs	Journal of critical incidents
Nonreactive measure	School records of days absent
Cognitive measure	Preschool Interpersonal Problem-Solving Test
Performance measure	Matching Familiar Figures Test

more time-intensive and does demand more sophisticated practitioner discernment; there are, however, two central reasons for taking the additional steps.

First, child behaviors are often environmentally contingent. Children are under the social control of others and, as a consequence, children's behavior can be situationally specific (Achenbach, 2011). For example, hyperactive behavior in the classroom may not predict overactivity in the home. Specifying exactly when, where, and to what degree the behavior exists helps create a multidimensional understanding of the problem, which in turn illuminates the most strategic intervention plan. Using the previous example, if hyperactivity is reported only in the classroom, then the focus can shift from exploring attention-deficit/hyperactivity disorder to possible environmental factors or learning problems.

A second consideration is that administering instruments to children requires particular clinical sensitivity. Many children may lack insight into their behaviors, or they may fear consequences for telling the truth. The inherent pressure of assessment can be distressing. Under duress, children are susceptible to answering according to what they believe to be socially desirable. High-quality instruments have likely been specifically designed to mitigate this effect (Achenbach, 2011), yet the onus remains on the administrator to help the child feel more comfortable. The administrator must ensure that children understand exactly why they are being asked to complete instruments, what the information will be used for, and with whom the results will be shared. Failing to do so is not only unethical but also undermines accuracy. Simple verbal reminders throughout the process, such as "there are no right or wrong answers," can also help improve authenticity.

For certain topics—such as suicidal ideation, substance use, sexual experiences, or abuse—the administration of the measure is nearly as important as the content of the measure. In these areas, clients rarely spontaneously self-disclose (Lawrence et al., 2010). Tracking outcomes for sensitive content continues to be problematic; however, the use of touchscreen and computer-based technology has demonstrated promise as a more effective and accurate assessment format. Both adults and children are more likely to disclose sensitive information when using computer-based assessment instruments (Lawrence et al., 2010). Many children are comfortable with technology and may be more engaged in the process as a result. Opting for audio voice commands through headsets can help when literacy is a concern. Technology opens the possibility for ever more innovative and user-friendly measurement instruments. Manassis and colleagues (2009) found that traditional measures for anxiety could not be validated with children younger than age 8 years because of vocabulary barriers. This is problematic because the onset of anxiety can occur as early as preschool. Nonverbal assessments, such as visual "thermometer" scales, are helpful but are also heavily contingent on cognitive ability (Shields et al., 2003). The Mood Assessment via Animated Characters (MAAC) developed by Manassis et al. uses a computer-based program with animated cartoon characters to help young children identify symptoms in a way that is developmentally adapted. Emerging measurement instruments, such as the MAAC, highlight that in clinical practice with children it is vital to select the correct instruments but also critical to implement them in engaging and thoughtful ways.

Helpful Resources

Websites

Health and mental health status measures: https://www.mirah.com/why-mirah?gclid=Cj0KCQiAsvTxBRDkARIsAH4W_j-UcBJqHCIAe-Yr582_OcbhycioY5ly9lC3KyNsfLlSxNBeMm8WVfsaAjbfEALw_wcB

Measurement Instrument Database for the Social Sciences: http://whitakerinstitute.ie/infrastructure-item/ measurement-instrument-database-social-sciences

Ontario Centre of Excellence for Child and Youth Mental Health: https://www.cymh.ca/Modules/MeasuresDatabase/en

Readings

King, R. (1997). Practice parameters for the psychiatric assessment of children and adolescents. *Journal of the American Academy of Child and Adolescent Psychiatry, 36*, 4–20.

LaGreca, A. (1990). *Through the eyes of the child: Obtaining self reports from children and adolescents.* Allyn & Bacon.

Prinstein, M. J., Youngstrom, E. A., Mash, E. J., & Barkley, R. A. (2019). *Treatment disorders in childhood and adolescence.* Guilford.

References

Achenbach, T. (2011). Commentary: Definitely more than measurement error: But how should we understand and deal with informant discrepancies? *Journal of Clinical Child & Adolescent Psychology, 40*(1), 80–86.

Fischer, J., Corcoran, K., & Springer, D. W. (2020). *Measures for clinical practice and research: A sourcebook* (6th ed., Vols. 1–2). Oxford University Press.

Lawrence, S., Willig, J., Crane, H., Ye, J., Aban, I., Lober, W., Nevin, C., Batey, D. S., Mugavero, M. J., McCullumsmith, C., Wright, C., Kitahata, M., Raper, J. L., Saag, M. S., & Schumacher, J. (2010). Routine, self-administered, touch screen, computer-based suicidal ideal assessment linked to automated response team notification in an HIV primary care setting. *Clinical Infectious Diseases, 50*, 1165–1173.

LeCroy, C. W. (2008). *Handbook of evidence-based child and adolescent treatment manuals.* Oxford University Press.

LeCroy, C. W. (2011). *Parenting mentally ill children: Faith, hope, support, and surviving the system.* Praeger.

LeCroy, C. W. (2019). Mismeasurement in social work practice: Building evidence-based practice one measure at a time. *Journal of the Society for Social Work & Research, 10*, 301–318.

Manassis, K., Mendowitz, S., Kreindler, D., Lumsden, C., Sharpe, J., Simon, M., Woolridge, N., Monga, S., & Adler-Nevo, G. (2009). Mood assessment via animated characters: A novel instrument to evaluate feelings in young children with anxiety disorders.

Journal of Clinical Child & Adolescent Psychology, 38(3), 380–389.

McLeod, B. D., Jensen-Doss, A., & Ollendick, T. H. (2013). *Diagnostic and behavioral assessment in children and adolescents: A clinical guide.* Guilford.

Miller, W., Sorensen, J., Selzer, J., & Brigham, G. (2006). Disseminating evidence-based practices in substance abuse treatment: A review with suggestions. *Journal of Substance Abuse Treatment,* 31, 25–39.

Prinstein, M. J., Youngstrom, E. A., Mash, E. J., & Barkley, R. A. (Eds.). (2019). *Treatment of disorders in childhood and adolescence.* Guilford Press.

Sherifali, D., & Pinelli, J. (2007). Parent as proxy reporting: Implications and recommendations for quality of life research. *Journal of Family Nursing,* 13(1), 83.

Shields, B., Palermo, T., Powers, J., Grewe, S., & Smith, G. (2003). Predictors of a child's ability to use a visual analogue scale. *Child Care, Health & Development,* 29, 281–290.

Smith, S., & Handler, L. (2006). *The Clinical assessment of children and adolescents: A practitioners' guide.* Routledge.

Sperry, L. (2011). *Family assessment* (2nd ed.). Routledge.

Tyson, E. (2004). Ethnic differences using behavior rating scales to assess the mental health of children: A conceptual and psychometric critique. *Child Psychiatry and Human Development,* 34(3), 167–201.

Van der Ende, J., Verhulst, F. C., & Tiemeier, H. (2012). Agreement of informants on emotional and behavioral problems from childhood to adulthood. *Psychological Assessment,* 24, 293–300.

Whitcomb, S. A. (2017). *Behavioral, social, and emotional assessment of children and adolescents* (3rd ed.). Routledge.

Assessment Protocols and Rapid Assessment Instruments with Adolescents

David W. Springer, Stephen J. Tripodi, and Stephanie Kennedy

Adolescents present a set of unique challenges and opportunities to social work practitioners. Although there are clearly similarities between conducting assessments with adolescents and conducting them with either children or adults, there are also distinct differences that warrant special consideration. Adolescents are negotiating specific developmental tasks, such as transitioning from the family to the peer group, developing their sexual identity, managing encounters with drugs and alcohol, and navigating the use of social media. Anyone who has worked with adolescents will certainly agree that they bring a unique (and often refreshing) perspective to the helping relationship that a competent practitioner integrates into a thorough assessment protocol.

In addition to the importance placed on recognizing the developmental tasks of adolescence during the assessment process, this chapter is grounded on the assumptions about assessment presented by Jordan and Franklin (1995, p. 3): "(1) Assessment is empirically based, (2) assessment must be made from a systems perspective, (3) measurement is essential, (4) ethical practitioners evaluate their clinical work, and (5) well qualified practitioners are knowledgeable about numerous assessment methods in developing assessments." These assumptions serve as a guide for social workers when determining what type of assessment protocol to implement with adolescents (and their families).

The first of these assumptions, that assessment is empirically based, was first comprehensively addressed in 2005 when the *Journal of Clinical Child and Adolescent Psychology* devoted a special section to developing guidelines for the evidence-based assessment of child and adolescent disorders, where evidence-based assessment is "intended to develop, elaborate, and identify the measurement strategies and procedures that have empirical support on their behalf" (Kazdin, 2005, p. 548). In this special issue, Mash and Hunsley (2005) emphasized how assessment is a critical facet of intervention and acknowledged that the development of evidence-based assessment has not kept up with the increased emphasis on evidence-based treatment. More than 15 years later, a disconnect between evidence-based assessment and evidence-based treatment still exists. This gap is amplified for adolescents who are struggling to manage the symptoms of multiple mental health disorders.

Coexisting Disorders

The terms *comorbid disorders* and *coexisting disorders* are frequently used interchangeably to describe adolescents who are struggling with several mental health issues, such as depressive and anxiety disorders or post-traumatic stress and obsessive–compulsive disorder. The term *dual diagnosis*, on the other hand, refers to individuals who are diagnosed with both a mental health and a substance use disorder. Although the fifth edition of the *Diagnostic and Statistical Manual of Mental Disorders* (DSM-5; American Psychiatric Association, 2013) has moved away from the multiaxial system and reframes mental disorder and substance misuse categories as dimensions, the terminology mentioned here is retained in this chapter to improve clarity. A substantial percentage of adolescents seen by social workers in the United States will be diagnosed with coexisting disorders or be given a dual diagnosis. Rather than comprising a special population, adolescents seeking treatment services are likely to be experiencing both mental health and substance use disorder issues (Brewer et al., 2017; Roberts & Corcoran, 2005). Thus, many adolescents seeking services today are likely to have substance use problems, mental health diagnoses, as well as myriad social, behavioral, and familial problems (Bender et al., 2006; Conway et al., 2016; Heller & Gitterman, 2010; Tripodi et al., 2006).

Given the prevalence of coexisting disorders in clinical settings and the long-term consequences of making false-positive or false-negative diagnoses, it is critical that social work practitioners assess for the presence of coexisting disorders in a deliberate manner rather than making "on-the-spot" diagnoses. A social worker's assessment often helps guide treatment planning. Misdiagnosing an adolescent as not having (or having) a certain set of problems (e.g., mistaking acting out behaviors related to poverty as conduct disorder or confusing symptoms of attention-deficit/hyperactivity disorder with bipolar disorder) can negatively affect the course of treatment (e.g., the wrong medications may be prescribed or adolescents and their families may be turned off to treatment due to repeated treatment "failures"). Using sound assessment methods can help eliminate such pitfalls.

Assessment Methods

Various methods of assessment are available to social work practitioners that can be used with adolescents. These include, but are not limited to, interviews, individualized rating scales, rapid assessment instruments, and standardized assessment tools. Although the focus of this chapter is primarily on the use of standardized assessment tools and rapid assessment instruments with adolescents, the importance and clinical utility of other available assessment methods, such as conducting a thorough interview, are also underscored.

Interviews

The assessment process typically starts with a face-to-face interview (e.g., psychosocial history) alone with the adolescent so they do not feel restricted disclosing information in the presence of their family. The family, however, should also be interviewed, both separately and together with their teen. This allows the practitioner to hear the perspectives of, and establish rapport with, all key players in the system and gain a deeper understanding of the adolescent's life. In addition, separate interviews enable the social worker to triangulate information, determining whether and how each version of the story differs. (It is important to note that the practitioner must negotiate how to maintain the confidentiality of the adolescent client if also working with the family system.) Consider the following case for illustration purposes.

Case Example

Robert, a 14-year-old White male, is brought to your agency by his parents because he is "failing most of his classes and is totally withdrawn." The week before, Robert's parents had discovered large quantities of marijuana and pills in his bedroom and note that he has made several recent comments about wanting to end his life. In addition to obtaining information from Robert's parents typically covered in a psychosocial history (e.g., medical, developmental, social, and family history), some areas that the social worker may cover with family members during an initial interview are as follows:

- Presenting problem and specific precipitating factor (e.g., "Tell me in your own words what prompted you to bring Robert in for help at this point in time?")
- Attempts to deal with the problem (e.g., "How has your family tried to deal with this problem[s]? What have you tried that has worked?")
- Hopes and expectations (e.g., "What do you hope to get out of coming here for services? If you could change any one thing about how things are at home, what would it be?")
- Exceptions to the problem (e.g., "When was the problem not evident in your recent past? What was different then?")

In addition to these areas of inquiry (with variations of the corresponding sample questions), consider some questions that the social worker may ask Robert individually:

- Peer relationships (e.g., "Tell me about your friends. What do you like to do together?")
- School (e.g., "What are your favorite [and least favorite] classes at school? What about those classes do you like [or not like]?")
- Suicide risk (e.g., "When you feel down, do you ever have any thoughts of hurting/ killing yourself? Do you ever wish you were dead? How would you end your life?")
- Substance use (e.g., "What do you drink or use? When was the last time you had a drink or used? How much did you have? Have you ever tried to reduce your substance use but found you could not?")
- Targeted behavior/goal setting (e.g., "If there was anything that you could change about yourself/your life, what would it be? What do you like most about yourself?")

Of course, the questions in the case example are meant only to illustrate the range of issues that one might address during an interview. A complete psychosocial history needs to be conducted. Information gathered from the face-to-face interview can subsequently be used to inform a more in-depth assessment in targeted areas, which in turn will guide treatment planning. Individualized rating scales, rapid assessment instruments, and other standardized assessment protocols may prove useful for this purpose.

Individualized Rating Scales

Individualized rating scales are nonstandardized assessment tools that the client and the social work practitioner develop and tailor to specifically meet the client's needs and measure the client's unique targeted outcomes (Bloom et al., 2009). These scales are used to measure change during the course of treatment; before, during, and after an intervention; or to track the strength or magnitude of a specific problem for one client across time.

Individualized rating scales can be an especially potent tool to show clients how they are progressing toward a goal. For example, imagine a client who comes to you for help managing severe panic attacks that occur at seemingly random intervals throughout the day. After conducting a thorough interview and obtaining a psychosocial history, you could ask the client to begin tracking the total number of panic attacks per day, the time the attacks occurred, and what they were doing immediately preceding the attacks. By the second session, you and the client would have a reference point, or baseline, of the problem (in this case, panic attacks) and a wealth of information about when and under what circumstances attacks are most likely to occur (Bloom et al., 2009). If treatment is successful, the client will be able to see the total number of panic attacks per day drop, reinforcing the good work they are doing. If, on the other hand, treatment is unsuccessful, it will be readily apparent in the client's rating scales, allowing you and your client to discuss new strategies to tackle this problem. Individualized rating scales are often used in conjunction with standardized scales as an additional, and more personal, form of assessment.

Rapid Assessment Instruments and Standardized Assessment Tools

Rapid assessment instruments (RAIs; Levitt & Reid, 1981) are short-form, pencil-and-paper assessment tools that are used to assess and measure change for a broad spectrum of client problems (Bloom et al., 2009; Corcoran et al., 2020; Hudson, 1982). RAIs are used as a method of empirical assessment, are easy to administer and score, are typically completed by the client, and can help monitor client functioning over time. Both RAIs and standardized tools have proliferated in recent years, and there are a wealth of assessments to measure various areas of adolescent functioning. Because it can be an overwhelming task to select a tool for use

with an individual client, we provide guidelines to help integrate these assessments into social work practice.

The social work practitioner needs to take several factors into consideration when choosing an RAI or standardized protocol for use with clients, such as the tool's reliability, validity, clinical utility, directness, availability, and so on (Corcoran et al., 2020). To the extent that an RAI has sound psychometric properties, it helps practitioners measure a client's problem consistently (reliability) and accurately (validity). Using reliable and valid tools becomes increasingly critical as one considers the complexities surrounding assessment with adolescents who (potentially) have comorbid disorders. A brief overview of reliability and validity is provided next; however, the reader is referred to other sources for a more detailed exposition on these topics (e.g., Abell et al., 2009; Corcoran et al., 2020; Hudson, 1982; Springer, Abell, & Hudson, 2002; Springer, Abell, & Nugent, 2002).

Reliability

A measurement instrument is reliable to the extent that it consistently yields similar results over repeated and independent administrations. There are several types of reliability, including interrater, test–retest, and internal consistency. All three types of reliability are designed to assess, and ideally minimize, measurement error. Interrater reliability refers to the degree of agreement between or among observers. When raters agree about how they would assess a client or behavior, then the researcher can be more confident that the outcomes observed are "real" and not purely a function of measurement error. Test–retest reliability is a measure of a tool's consistency over time. Using a stable measure helps the researcher attribute changes in score to the intervention or treatment rather than variations in measurement. Internal consistency is a measure of how strongly the items on a standardized scale correlate to one another. This information is represented through reliability coefficients, which range from 0.0 to 1.0. What constitutes a satisfactory level of reliability depends on how a measure is to be used. For use in research studies and scientific work, a reliability coefficient of 0.60 or greater is typically considered acceptable (Hudson, 1982). However, for use in guiding decision-making with individual clients, a higher coefficient is needed. Springer et al. (2002) provide the following guidelines for acceptability of reliability coefficients for use with individual clients:

- <0.70 = unacceptable
- 0.70–0.79 = undesirable
- 0.80–0.84 = minimally acceptable
- 0.85–0.89 = respectable
- 0.90–0.95 = very good
- >0.95 = excellent

The greater the seriousness of the problem being measured (e.g., suicidal risk), and the graver the risk of making a wrong decision regarding a client's level of functioning, the higher the standard that should be adopted.

Validity

Whereas reliability represents an instrument's degree of consistency, validity represents how accurately an instrument measures what it is supposed to measure. There are various ways to determine an instrument's validity: face validity, content validity, criterion-related validity, construct validity, and factorial validity.

Face validity refers to whether the concepts in an assessment tool align with common perceptions of those concepts. For example, if we designed a depression measure, respondents should be asked about sadness and thoughts of suicide rather than given math problems to solve. Content validity takes face validity one step further by evaluating whether a measure covers all aspects of a concept. In our depression measure example, we would

want to be sure the assessment tool did not ignore key features of how depression is experienced by many people.

Criterion-related validity and construct validity, on the other hand, assess how a measure relates to some external concept. That is, individuals who score high on our depression measure should also score high on other standardized depression measures. Likewise, if our measure suggests a person might be struggling with depression, then other facets of their life should not suggest otherwise. We would not expect a person with depression to state that they feel great, have plenty of energy, and are excited for the future.

Finally, factorial validity has to do with how many concepts an assessment tool measures. For instance, if our scale measures both the physical and the emotional experience of depression, we would expect a statistical factor analysis to show two distinct factors. The items about the emotional side of depression should group together, and the items assessing the physical experience of depression should group together. If they group differently than we expected them to, or if a factor analysis suggested that only 1 construct (or 10 constructs) was actually being measured on our scale, we would have to go back to our items and consider if our content really was measuring depression in the way we intended. In addition, the social worker must make decisions about a measure's validity in relation to its intended use. In other words, they must determine if the measure is valid for that particular client in a particular setting at a given time. A measure may be valid for one client but not for another.

Examples of Standardized Assessment Tools

The number of standardized tools developed specifically for use with adolescents has grown considerably in recent years, and it is impossible to review them all here. However, two selected standardized tools that may be useful in assessing for comorbid disorders in adolescents are briefly reviewed next. Each tool has sound psychometric properties and can be used to help guide treatment planning and monitor client progress over the course of treatment.

Child and Adolescent Functional Assessment Scale

The Child and Adolescent Functional Assessment Scale (CAFAS; Hodges, 2000; Hodges et al., 2004) is a validated standardized instrument used to measure the degree of impairment in youth aged 7–17 years (Bates et al., 2006; Boydell et al., 2005). It is a clinician-rated measure covering eight areas of functioning: school/work, home, community, behavior toward others, moods/emotions, self-harmful behavior, substance use, and thinking. In each of these domains, the practitioner chooses behavioral indicators about the youth's functioning. The following are sample items:

- Frequent display of anger toward others; angry outbursts
- Talks or repeatedly thinks about harming self, killing self, or wanting to die
- Frequently intoxicated or high (e.g., more than two times a week)
- Frequently fails to comply with reasonable rules and expectations within the home

The youth's level of functioning in each domain is then scored as severe (score of 30), moderate (score of 20), mild (score of 10), or minimal (score of 0). These scores are graphically depicted on a one-page scoring sheet that provides a profile of the youth's functioning in each area. The CAFAS also contains optional strengths-based and goal-oriented items (e.g., good behavior in classroom and obeys curfew) that are helpful in guiding treatment planning. A computerized software program is available that scores the CAFAS, generates a treatment plan, and produces outcome reports

to help practitioners track client progress (Hodges, 2000).

Behavioral and Emotional Rating Scale, Second Edition

The Behavioral and Emotional Rating Scale, Second Edition (BERS-2; Epstein & Sharma, 2004) is a strengths-based suite of three instruments that measure functioning in youth across five different areas: interpersonal strength, family involvement, intrapersonal strength, school functioning, and affective strength. A key feature that distinguishes the BERS-2 from other standardized tools (e.g., Achenbach's widely used Child Behavior Checklist) is that it is truly based on a strengths perspective (in contrast to a deficit model), and the wording of the items reflects this outlook. The Teacher Rating Scale (TRS) has 52 items and is one of the three measures in the BERS-2 package. The following are sample items from the TRS:

- Maintains positive family relationships
- Accepts responsibility for own actions
- Pays attention in class
- Identifies own feelings

The strengths perspective makes this tool particularly appealing to parents, adolescents, and social workers who strive for a helping relationship that centers on client strengths and empowerment. The BERS-2 has been validated with many different populations, including Hispanic and African American adolescents in the United States, and both Spanish- and Arabic-language versions of the scale have been validated (Farmer et al., 2005; Gonzalez et al., 2006; Mooney et al., 2005; Mutairi & Khurinej, 2008; Sharkey et al., 2009).

Additional Rapid Assessment Instruments

In addition to the CAFAS and BERS-2, there are numerous RAIs that can be used with adolescents to measure functioning across various areas, such as risk of running away (e.g., Adolescent Concerns Evaluation), suicidal tendencies (e.g., Multi-Attitude Suicide Tendency Scale), post-traumatic symptoms (e.g., Child and Parent Report of Post-traumatic Symptoms), conduct-problem behaviors (e.g., Eyberg Child Behavior Checklist), family functioning (e.g., Family Assessment Device and the Index of Family Relations), and peer relations (Index of Peer Relations) (Corcoran et al., 2020). There are also standardized general behavior rating scales (e.g., Louisville Behavior Checklist, Child Behavior Checklist, and Conners Rating Scales) and tools that are useful for measuring the degree of functional impairment (e.g., Children's Global Assessment Scale) (Shaffer et al., 1999).

Conclusion

The field continues to make progress in developing user-friendly standardized assessment tools with sound psychometric properties that can be used to facilitate assessment with adolescents. Although these tools should not take the place of a face-to-face psychosocial history, they can complement the assessment process and be used to track progress in client functioning over the course of treatment. It is important to also emphasize that a standardized tool is not a substitute for a solid therapeutic helping relationship. Social workers should take care to build rapport with adolescent clients prior to administering standardized assessments or RAIs. Establishing a relationship and explaining why and how assessments will be used ensure that treatment decisions are not based solely on the score of an assessment tool and that adolescents are able to actively participate in their own treatment. After all, the goal is to help adolescents make desired changes and develop agency and healthy habits as they move forward into adulthood.

Social workers have an ethical obligation to use empirical assessment protocols and standardized tools whenever possible, rather than relying solely on gut feelings when conducting assessments with adolescents. The potential consequences of misdiagnosing an adolescent can be severe. Thus, social work practitioners are encouraged to make use of available empirically based assessment tools within a systems framework to guide treatment planning, monitor client functioning, and evaluate the effectiveness of their interventions.

References

Abell, N., Springer, D. W., & Kamata, A. (2009). *Developing and validating rapid assessment instruments*. Oxford University Press.

American Psychiatric Association. (2013). *Diagnostic and statistical manual of mental disorders* (5th ed.). American Psychiatric Publishing.

Bates, M. P., Furlong, M. J., & Green, J. G. (2006). Are CAFAS subscales and item weights valid? A preliminary investigation of the Child and Adolescent Functional Assessment Scale. *Administration and Policy in Mental Health and Mental Health Services Research, 33*(6), 682–695. http://dx.doi.org/10.1007/s10488-006-0052-4

Bender, K., Springer, D. W., & Kim, J. S. (2006). Treatment effectiveness with dually diagnosed adolescents: A systematic review. *Brief Treatment and Crisis Intervention, 6*(3), 177–205.

Bloom, M., Fischer, J., & Orme, J. (2009). *Evaluating practice: Guidelines for the accountable professional* (6th ed.). Allyn & Bacon.

Boydell, K. M., Barwick, M., Ferguson, H. B., & Haines, R. (2005). A feasibility study to assess service providers' perspectives regarding the use of the Child and Adolescent Functional Assessment Scale in Ontario. *Journal of Behavioral Health Services & Research, 32*(1), 105–109.

Brewer, S., Godley, M. D., & Hulvershorn, L. A. (2017). Treating mental health and substance use disorders in adolescents: What is on the menu? *Current Psychiatry Reports, 19*(1), 5.

Conway, K. P., Swendsen, J., Husky, M. M., He, J. P., & Merikangas, K. R. (2016). Association of lifetime mental disorders and subsequent alcohol and illicit drug use: Results from the National Comorbidity Survey–Adolescent Supplement. *Journal of the American Academy of Child & Adolescent Psychiatry, 55*, 280–288.

Corcoran, K., Fischer, J., & Springer, D. W. (2020). *Measures for clinical practice and research* (6th ed., Vols. 1–2). Oxford University Press.

Epstein, M. H., & Sharma, J. M. (2004). *Behavioral and Emotional Rating Scale: Examiner's manual* (2nd ed.). Pro-ED.

Farmer, T. W., Clemmer, J. T., Leung, M., Goforth, J. B., Thompson, J. H., Keagy, K., & Boucher, S. (2005). Strength-based assessment of rural African American early adolescents: Characteristics of students in high and low groups on the Behavioral and Emotional Rating Scale. *Journal of Child and Family Studies, 14*(1), 57–69. http://dx.doi.org/10.1007/s10826-005-1113-0

Gonzalez, J. E., Ryser, G. R., Epstein, M. H., & Shwery, C. S. (2006). The Behavioral and Emotional Rating Scale–Second Edition: Parent Rating Scale (BERS-II PRS): A Hispanic cross-cultural reliability study. *Assessment for Effective Intervention, 31*(3), 33–43.

Heller, N. R., & Gitterman, A. (Eds.). (2010). *Mental health and social problems: A social work perspective.* Routledge.

Hodges, K. (2000). *The Child and Adolescent Functional Assessment Scale: Self training manual.* Department of Psychology, Eastern Michigan University.

Hodges, K., Xue, Y., & Watring, J. (2004). Use of the CFAS to evaluate outcome for youths with severe emotional disturbance served by public mental health. *Journal of Child and Family Studies, 13,* 325–339.

Hudson, W. W. (1982). *The clinical measurement package: Field manual.* Dorsey.

Jordan, C., & Franklin, C. (1995). *Clinical assessment for social workers: Quantitative and qualitative methods* (3rd ed.). Lyceum.

Kazdin, A. E. (2005). Evidence-based assessment for children and adolescents: Issues in measurement development and clinical application. *Journal of Clinical Child and Adolescent Psychology, 34*(3), 548–558.

Levitt, J., & Reid, W. (1981). Rapid-assessment instruments for practice. *Social Work Research and Abstracts, 17*(1), 13–19.

Mash, E., & Hunsley, J. (2005). Evidence-based assessment of child and adolescent disorders: Issues and challenges. *Journal of Clinical Child and Adolescent Psychology, 34*(3), 362–379.

Mooney, P., Epstein, M. H., Ryser, G., & Pierce, C. D. (2005). Reliability and validity of the Behavioral and Emotional Rating Scale–Second Edition: Parent Rating Scale. *Children & Schools, 27*(3), 147–155.

Mutairi, H. A., & Khurinej, A. A. (2008). The psychometic properties of the Arabic version of the Behavioral and Emotional Rating Scale (BERS). *DOMES: Digest of Middle East Studies, 17*(2), 54–65.

Roberts, A., & Corcoran, K. (2005). Adolescents growing up in stressful environments, dual diagnosis, and sources of success. *Brief Treatment and Crisis Intervention, 5*(1), 1–8.

Shaffer, D., Lucas, C. P., & Richters, J. E. (Eds.). (1999). *Diagnostic assessment in child and adolescent psychopathology.* Guilford.

Sharkey, J., You, S., Morrison, G., & Griffiths, A. (2009). Behavioral and Emotional Rating Scale–2 Parent Report: Exploring a Spanish version with at-risk students. *Behavioral Disorders, 35*(1), 53–65.

Springer, D. W., Abell, N., & Hudson, W. W. (2002). Creating and validating rapid assessment instruments for practice and research: Part 1. *Research on Social Work Practice, 12,* 408–439.

Springer, D. W., Abell, N., & Nugent, W. R. (2002). Creating and validating rapid assessment instruments for practice and research: Part 2. *Research on Social Work Practice, 12,* 768–795.

Tripodi, S. J., Kim, J. S., & DiNitto, D. M. (2006). Effective strategies for working with students who have co-occurring disorders. In C. Franklin, M. B. Harris, & P. Allen-Meares (Eds.), *School social work and mental health workers training and resource manual* (pp. 165–174). Oxford University Press.

Using Standardized Tests and Instruments in Family Assessments

Jacqueline Corcoran

Definitions and Descriptions

A *measure* helps determine the existence of certain behaviors, attitudes, feelings, or qualities—and their magnitude—in clients when they come to a social work practitioner for assistance. The first rule for using measures is to employ an already established measure—one that has been standardized—rather than devise and test a new one. An inventory (the words "measure," "inventory," and "instrument" are used interchangeably) is standardized when it has been tested (normed) on a relevant group of people, a process that results in psychometric data—specifically, information about reliability and validity—that have to meet certain acceptable standards. *Reliability* refers to the consistency and the accuracy of the measure, and *validity* involves the extent to which the instrument measures what it purports to measure. For the different methods of determining reliability and validity, see a social work research text such as Rubin and Babbie (2016).

Standardization of an instrument also means there are certain procedures for its administration. Items are completed in the order they appear, and certain items cannot be taken out at the administrator's discretion, nor can only certain items be chosen, because items are considered to be a set. A certain procedure for scoring the measure has also been developed (Fischer et al., 2020a).

Standardized measures can be completed by the client (self-report); by an important collateral person who can make key observations about the client's behavior, attribute, or attitude (e.g., a parent, teacher, or spouse); or by the practitioner using an observational measure. This discussion concentrates on either client self-report measures or inventories completed by parents of children because the emphasis here is on family assessment.

Rationale for Use of Measures

Why should social workers use family assessment measures? After all, they take time away from service delivery, clients may resent filling them out and fail to see their relevance, and they require some effort for the practitioner to find and to figure out how to score. However, the use of instruments in family assessment offers several potential benefits (Fischer et al., 2020a):

- They provide detailed information about feelings—attitudes and qualities, and their magnitude—information that may be difficult to observe overtly.
- They aid in the assessment process, helping the practitioner determine the specific issues to address and to select appropriate services.
- They track client progress to ascertain whether interventions are proceeding in the necessary direction.
- Positive changes may motivate the client to continue to participate in services and to make progress.
- If gathered in sufficient numbers, measures can provide information about the effectiveness of a particular approach or intervention with a group of individuals for an agency, funding source, or dissemination of knowledge to the field.
- They provide evidence to third-party payers for reimbursement or to establish the need for continued services.

Selecting Measures

Selection of measures depends on the purpose for which measurement is targeted (screening, assessment, or monitoring progress), the nature of the client's problem, practicality issues, and the psychometric capacities of the instrument (Fischer et al., 2020b). For example, if the purpose of the measurement is to assess progress, is the instrument sensitive to clinical change (Johnson et al., 2008)? Issues of practicality include the length of the instrument and the ability of the client to complete it. Fischer et al. (2020a) suggest that a scale should take no longer than 10–15 minutes to complete. Some measures have both a longer and a shorter version. For instance, the Parenting Stress Index (Abidin, 2012) has a 120-item version and a 36-item version. Other issues of practicality specifically relevant to supervisors and managers include the cost of purchasing measures; the resources involved in training social work staff; the length of time required to score and interpret measures (Johnson et al., 2008); and, if it is necessary to compile the results of multiple scores, the resources involved with finding a usable database system, the construction of a database, data entry, and data analysis.

Psychometric standards for selecting instruments include established validity and reliability. Many agency personnel rely on instruments they have created to assess client functioning and to measure client change. This is ill-advised, despite the prevalence of this practice; without established reliability and validity, "various alternative explanations for the findings (e.g., examiner bias, chance, and effects of maturation) cannot be ruled out, which seriously restricts the usefulness of findings" (Johnson et al., 2008, p. 7).

Another question related to psychometrics is how similar the client population is to the characteristics of the sample on which the instrument was normed. Many psychological inventories have been normed on undergraduate samples, traditionally from White and middle- to upper-class populations, which may differ in significant ways from high school–educated, low socioeconomic status, and/or minority clients. Although a measure may not necessarily be rejected because it has been normed on a sample dissimilar from the characteristics of a particular client or client group, some care must then be taken with regard to the interpretation of scores.

Several publications have compiled various family assessment instruments. Fischer et al. (2020a) focus on children, couples, and families. For child and adolescent problems, the interested reader is urged to consult Youngstrom et al. (2020), which provides a comprehensive discussion of various self-report instruments, rating scales for teachers and parents, and behavioral observational measures. Corcoran (2000) compiled instruments organized by type of problems for which families may receive services. Corcoran and Walsh (2016) delineate measures that involve child and adolescent *Diagnostic and Statistical Manual of Mental Disorders*–defined diagnoses, and Early and Newsome (2005) discuss measures that emphasize strengths for families. Finally, Johnson et al. (2008) specifically address family assessment in relation to child welfare.

The following section details information on family assessment measures—specifically family functioning, parenting practices, and marital functioning—with demonstrated validity and reliability that have been reviewed by Corcoran (2000).

Family Assessment Measures

Family Functioning

Stemming from the field of family therapy and a family systems theoretical approach, three main self-report measures are widely used to assess the family as the unit of attention (Johnson et al., 2008): the McMaster Family Assessment Device, the Family Environment Scale, and the Family Adaptability and Cohesion Evaluation Scale. These instruments are highly correlated with one another and may be used interchangeably (Olson, 2000; Beavers & Hampson as cited in Johnson et al., 2008).

The McMaster Family Assessment Device (Epstein et al., 1983) is a 60-item, Likert-type self-report measure that assesses overall health/pathology in a general score, as well as six areas of family functioning: (1) problem-solving, (2) communication, (3) roles, (4) affective responsiveness, (5) affective involvement, and (6) behavior control.

The Family Environment Scale (FES; Moos & Moos, 1981) is a 90-item, true–false questionnaire assessing 10 dimensions of family life in three general areas: (1) relationship dimensions, which involve cohesion, expressiveness, and conflict; (2) personal growth dimensions, which involve independence, achievement orientation, intellectual/cultural orientation, moral–religious emphasis, and active–recreational orientation; and (3) system maintenance dimensions, which involve organization and control. There are three different forms of the FES: the real form, which assesses members' perceptions of their families; the ideal form, measuring members' preferred family environments; and the expectations form, which assesses members' expectations about family environments.

The Family Adaptability and Cohesion Evaluation Scales, Version IV (FACES IV; Olson & Gorrall, 2003), is a 62-item self-report measure in which members rate their families on two different dimensions: (1) adaptability (ability of a family system to alter structure, roles, and rules in response to situational and developmental stress) and (2) cohesion (emotional bonding). FACES IV also assesses family communication and satisfaction.

Parenting Assessment

Measures of parenting often stem from the field of developmental psychology, with the caregiver-child dyad as the unit of analysis (Johnson et al., 2008). We focus on the Child Abuse Potential Inventory and the Parenting Stress Index as prime examples of these types of instruments.

The Child Abuse Potential Inventory (Milner, 1986), a 160-item self-report survey, includes a 77-item physical child abuse scale with six descriptive factor scales: (1) distress, (2) rigidity, (3) unhappiness, (4) problems with child and self, (5) problems with family, and (6) problems from others. The Child Abuse Potential Inventory can be completed by those with a third-grade reading level.

The Parenting Stress Index (Abidin, 2012) is a 120-item self-report inventory for parents of children ages 1 month to 12 years. It not only yields a total score of parenting stress but also indicates whether sources of stress may be related to child characteristics (child's adaptability, reinforcing qualities, demandingness, activity level, mood, and acceptability to the parent) or parental functioning (the parent's sense of competence, isolation, depression, attachment to the child, parent health, perceived restrictions of role, depression, and spousal and social system support). The short form (36 items) has the following subscales: (1) total stress, (2) parental distress, (3) parent–child dysfunctional interaction, and (4) difficult child (Abidin, 2012).

Partner Relational Functioning

Several instruments are designed to assess marital functioning. The Marital Adjustment Test (Locke & Wallace, 1959) is a 15-item self-report assessing the accommodation of partners to each other. The Dyadic Adjustment Scale (Spanier, 1999) is a 32-item self-report inventory measuring marital adjustment with four subscales: (1) dyadic consensus (agreement regarding marital issues), (2) dyadic cohesion (the extent to which partners are involved in joint activities), (3) dyadic satisfaction (overall evaluation of relationship and level of commitment), and (4) affectional expression (the extent of affection and sexual involvement). The 20-item O'Leary–Porter Scale (Porter & O'Leary, 1980) measures the frequency of various forms of overt marital hostility (e.g., quarrels, sarcasms, and physical abuse) witnessed by children.

Intimate partner violence can be measured by the Revised Conflict Tactics Scales (Straus et al., 1996). This 78-item self-report instrument assesses psychological and physical attacks on a partner, as well as the use of negotiation, in a marital, cohabiting, or dating relationship. The following subscales are included: (1) physical assault, (2) psychological aggression, (3) negotiation, (4) injury, and (5) sexual coercion. The items are asked in the form of questions (what the participant did and what the partner did). They are written at a sixth-grade reading level.

Guidelines for Using Measures

The following are guidelines for the administration of measures:

When will the measure be completed?
Preferably, before services have begun (so the social worker can assess the impact of intervention), during intake, or at the first contact with the social worker.
Where will the measure be completed?
A quiet place, free of distractions, with a hard writing surface available— a desk or a clipboard— and appropriate writing utensils.
Why should the social worker be present if all family members are completing measures?
Members might start discussing items among themselves, and the more powerful people in the family might influence others' responses. Children are particularly vulnerable because they often have difficulty reading and understanding items. If parents start reading the measure to their children, either the children may respond in a way they think is desirable to the parents or the parents may more actively influence the children's responses (e.g., "You don't feel sad, do you?").
What procedure should the worker follow in the administration of measures?

- Explain the purpose of the measure (see the Rationale for Use of Measures section).
- Read aloud the directions, which include how the client should respond to items.
- Check the instrument over.
- Score the instrument (in front of the client, if possible, so immediate feedback can be provided).
- Repeat the measure at a later date (e.g., every month, at the termination of services, and possibly as a follow-up to services) using similar procedures each time.
- Track scores over time and provide feedback to the client on progress.

What if clients seem unable to complete measures?

If individuals are unsure of an answer, they should be encouraged to provide what they think is the best answer. The social worker should avoid interpreting the items or questions.

If a child seems to be struggling to complete an instrument or complains about not being able to understand the items, the practitioner can separate the child from other family members and the measure can be read aloud to the child.

Adults will not usually volunteer that they cannot read, but if a person seems to be struggling, then the social worker may ask whether the client would prefer that items were read aloud with the worker recording responses.

For non–English-speaking clients, the best source of information on the availability of measures written in other languages is the author of the inventory or the publishing house.

If a client complains about difficulties completing a measure, perhaps they could agree to come earlier for subsequent sessions so that completion of an instrument can occur in the waiting area and does not interfere with session time. Other alternatives include selecting a measure with fewer items.

What should the practitioner be checking for when the instrument is completed?

Items left blank, which can be pointed out to the client, so the measure is fully completed.

Bias in terms of social desirability (i.e., clients responding in a way that they think pleases the worker or in a way to suggest that services are either not necessary or should not be terminated) or a response set bias— that is, clients answering items in a particular pattern (e.g., all 4's on a 6-point scale) (Fischer et al., 2020b). Inquiring about a particular pattern may provide information about the client's level of comprehension of items or the level of cooperation.

Conclusion

The use of measurement instruments for assessment and evaluation will, in all likelihood, increase due to the demands of managed care. The information provided will not only assist the social worker in choosing appropriate measures for use in family assessment but also aid the worker in gaining familiarity with some of the practical matters involved so that the clinical utility of measurement instruments will be maximized.

Helpful Resource

UCLA Subscales of McMaster Family Assessment Device: http://chipts.ucla.edu/wp-content/uploads/downloads/2012/02/McMaster-FAD-Subscales.pdf

References

Abidin, R. R. (2012). *Parenting stress index* (4th ed.). Psychological Assessment Resources.

Corcoran, J. (2000). *Evidence-based social work practice with families: A lifespan approach*. Springer.

Corcoran, J., & Walsh, J. (2016). *Clinical assessment and diagnosis in social work practice* (3rd ed.). Oxford University Press.

Early, T., & Newsome, S. (2005). Measures for assessment and accountability in practice with families from a strengths perspective. In J. Corcoran (Ed.), *Building strengths and skills: A collaborative approach to working with clients* (pp. 359–393). Oxford University Press.

Epstein, N., Baldwin, L., & Bishop, D. (1983). The McMaster Family Assessment Device. *Journal of Marital and Family Therapy, 9*, 171–180.

Fischer, J., Corcoran, K., & Springer, D. (2020a). *Measures for clinical practice and research: A sourcebook, Volume 1: Couples, families, and children* (6th ed.). Oxford University Press.

Fischer, J., Corcoran, K., & Springer, D. (2020b). *Measures for clinical practice and research: A sourcebook, Volume 2: Adults* (6th ed.). Oxford University Press.

Johnson, M., Stone, S., Lou, C., Vu, C., Ling, J., Mizrahi, P., & Austin, M. (2008). Family assessment in child welfare services: Instrument comparisons. *Journal of Evidence-Based Social Work, 5*, 57–90.

Locke, H., & Wallace, K. (1959). Short marital-adjustment and prediction tests: Their reliability and validity. *Marriage and Family Living, 21*, 251–255.

Milner, J. S. (1986). *The Child Abuse Potential Inventory: Manual* (2nd ed.). Psytec.

Moos, R. H., & Moos, B. S. (1981). *Family Environment Scale manual*. Consulting Psychologists Press.

Olson, D. H. (2000). Circumplex model of marital and family systems. *Journal of Family Therapy, 22*, 144–167.

Olson, D. H., & Gorrall, D. (2003). Circumplex model of marital and family systems. In F. Walsh (Ed.), *Normal family processes: Growing diversity and complexity* (3rd ed., pp. 514–548). Guilford.

Porter, B., & O'Leary, D. (1980). Marital discord and childhood behavior problems. *Journal of Abnormal Child Psychology, 8*, 287–295.

Rubin, A., & Babbie, E. (2016). *Research methods for social work* (9th ed.). Brooks/Cole.

Spanier, G. B. (1999). *Dyadic Adjustment Scale manual*. Multi-Healthsystems.

Straus, M., Hamby, S., Boney-McCoy, S., & Sugarman, D. (1996). The revised Conflict Tactics Scales (CTS2). *Journal of Family Issues, 17*, 283–316.

Youngstrom, E., Prinstein, M., Mash, E. J., & Barkley, R. A. (2020). *Assessment of disorders in childhood and adolescence* (5th ed.). Guilford.

Using Genograms to Map Family Patterns

Monica McGoldrick

During the past several decades, genograms increasingly have been used by health care and human service professionals as a practical tool for mapping family patterns (McGoldrick et al., 2020). They are becoming a common language for tracking family history and relationships (Figure 42.1). Genograms map family information graphically, providing a quick gestalt of complex family patterns. They are a rich source of hypotheses about the evolution of both clinical problems and the family contexts within which problems develop and are generally resolved. The video, *Harnessing the Power of Genograms in Psychotherapy* (McGoldrick, 2013) demonstrates my first interview with a client, showing questioning around the presenting problem while gathering relevant genogram information, drawing it on the genogram, and helping the client see its value. The video and a follow-up 10 years later with the same family (*Couples Therapy: A Family Systems Approach*; McGoldrick, 2019a) are available from http://www.psychotherapy.net. Other demonstrations of the use of genograms in clinical practice available at that website include *The Legacy of Unresolved*

Loss (McGoldrick, 2001), which illustrates the use of a genogram approach throughout the therapy of a remarried family; *Racism, Family Secrets and the African American Experience* (McGoldrick, 2019b) about the genogram research of Elaine Pinderhughes; *Assessment and Engagement in Family Therapy* (McGoldrick, 2019d), which illustrates the use of genograms in early sessions with a remarried immigrant family; and *Freeing Ourselves from the Ghosts of Our Past* (McGoldrick, 2005), which offers a powerful discussion of the use of genograms in understanding a multigenerational traumatic pattern of murder and suicide.

Families are organized within biological, legal, cultural, and emotional structures, as well as by generation, age, gender, and other factors. Where one fits in the family structure can influence functioning, relational patterns, and the type of family one forms in the next generation. Gender and birth order are key factors shaping sibling relationships and characteristics. Family configurations mapped on a genogram allow clinicians to hypothesize about possible personality characteristics and relational compatibilities. Cultural issues

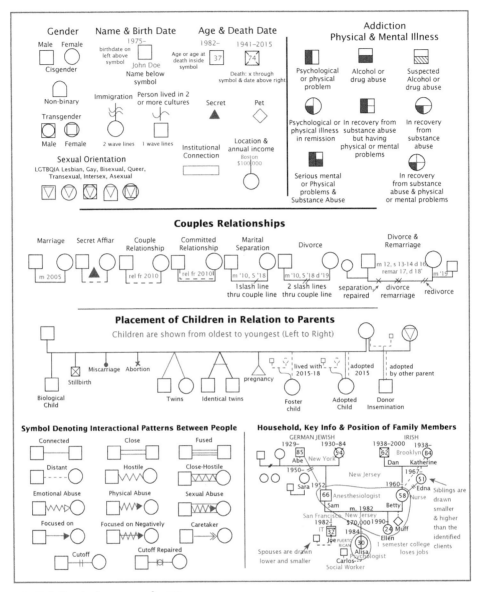

FIGURE 42.1 Standard genogram format.

including ethnicity, race, religion, migration, class, and other socioeconomic factors, as well as a family's time and location in history, also influence a family's structural patterns (Congress, 1994; Hardy & Laszloffy, 1995; McGoldrick, 2011, 2016; McGoldrick et al., 2005, 2015; Walsh, 2009). These factors, too, become part of the genogram map.

Genograms are tangible and graphic representations of complex family patterns. They allow clinicians to map the family structure

clearly and track and update the family picture as it emerges. For a clinical record, the genogram provides an efficient summary, allowing a clinician unfamiliar with a case to quickly grasp a large amount of information about a family and view potential problems. Whereas notes written in a chart or questionnaire tend to become lost in the record, genogram information is immediately recognizable and can be added to and corrected at each clinical visit as more is learned about a family.

Genograms make it easier for clinicians to keep in mind the complexity of a family's context, including family history, patterns, and events that may have ongoing significance for patient care. Just as our spoken language potentiates and organizes our thought processes, genograms, which map relationships and patterns of family functioning and cultural history, help clinicians think systemically about clients' problems in the context of their lives and history.

Gathering genogram information should be an integral part of any comprehensive clinical assessment. It cannot be used cookbook fashion to make clinical predictions, but it is a rich factual and interpretive tool, enabling clinicians to generate hypotheses in a family assessment. Typically, genograms are constructed from information gathered in an assessment and revised as new information becomes available. Thus, the initial assessment forms the basis for treatment. Of course, we cannot compartmentalize assessment and treatment. Each interaction with a case informs our assessment and thus influences the next intervention. *Harnessing the Power of Genograms in Psychotherapy* (McGoldrick, 2013) demonstrates the back and forth necessary in learning about a client's history while remaining relevant to the client's specific presenting problem.

Genogram Format

Genograms are an important way of engaging and getting to know clients. They promote a systemic perspective, which helps track individual and family issues through space and time. They enable an interviewer to reframe, detoxify, and normalize emotion-laden issues. Because genogram interviewing provides a ready vehicle for systemic questioning, it begins to orient clients to a systemic perspective as well. The genogram thus helps both clinician and client see the larger picture, viewing problems in their current and historical context

and evaluating the client's strengths, resilience, and vulnerabilities in relation to their overall situation.

We include on a genogram nuclear and extended family members, as well as significant non-blood kin, friends, and pets who have lived with or played a major role in the family's life. We can also note significant events and problems. Current behavior and problems of family members can be traced from multiple perspectives. It allows us to view the index person (IP)—the person with the problem or symptom—in the context of various subsystems, such as siblings, triangles, reciprocal relationships, multigenerational patterns, and life cycle stages and transitions, as well as in relation to the broader community, social institutions (schools, courts, etc.), and the sociocultural context.

Genograms "let the calendar speak," suggesting possible connections between family events over time. By scanning the family system culturally and historically and by assessing previous life cycle transitions, the clinician can place present issues in the context of the family's evolution over time. We include on a genogram cultural and demographic information about at least three generations of family members to clarify repetitive patterns, themes, myths, rules, and emotionally charged issues. Patterns of illness and shifts in family relationships brought about through changes in family structure and other critical life changes can easily be noted on the genogram, providing a framework for hypothesizing about factors influencing the current crisis. In conjunction with genograms, we also create a family chronology, which depicts the family history on a timeline, while the genogram itself maps first the structure and then the chronology of generations. We also often create a sociogram or eco-map (Hartman, 1978), which shows how clients are emotionally connected to family and to other resources in their lives.

344 | Part IV Knowledge and Skills

The Family Information Net

The process of gathering family information can be thought of as casting out an information net in progressively larger circles, spreading in a number of different directions:

- From the presenting problem to the larger context of the problem
- From the immediate household to the extended family and broader social systems
- From the present family situation to relevant events in the family's history
- From easy, nonthreatening queries to difficult, anxiety-provoking questions
- From obvious facts to judgments about functioning and relationships to hypotheses about family patterns

The Presenting Problem and the Immediate Household

In health care situations, genogram information is often recorded as it emerges during medical visits. In family therapy and social service situations, specific problems may be identified, which provide the clinician's starting point. At the outset, families are told that some basic background information is needed to understand their situation. Exploration of the presenting problem and its impact on the immediate household usually grows naturally, starting from the name, age, gender, and occupation of immediate family members and the context in which the problem occurs:

- Who lives in the household?
- How is each person related?
- Where do other family members live?

Other relevant information is then elicited about the problem:

- Who knows about the problem?
- How do they each view it and how have they responded?

- Has anyone in the family ever had similar problems?
- What solutions were attempted by whom in those situations?
- When did the problem begin? Who noticed it first? Who is most concerned about the problem? Who is least concerned?
- Have family relationships changed since the problem began? Have other problems developed?
- Has the problem changed? If so, how?

It is important to inquire about previous efforts to get help for the problem, including names of previous therapists, medications, hospitalizations, and the name of the current referring person.

The Current Situation and Recent Life Transitions

Next, the clinician expands to any other recent or anticipated changes in the family (e.g., people coming or leaving, illnesses, job problems, births, marriages, divorces, deaths, health, and behavioral or legal problems).

The Wider Family Context

The clinician looks for an opportunity to explore the wider family context, asking about the extended family and cultural background of all the adults involved, inquiring about each side of the family separately. For example, the clinician may state, "Let's begin with your mother's family. Your mother was which one of how many children? When and where was she born? Is she alive? If not, when and how did she die? If alive, where is she now? What does she do? Is she retired? If so, since when? How did your parents meet? When did they marry? Had she been married before? If so, when? Did they have children by other relationships? Did they separate or divorce or did the spouse die? If so, when was that?" And so on. The goal is to get information about at least three generations, including grandparents, parents, aunts, uncles, siblings, spouses, and children of the

IP, as well as important nonfamily kin, friends, and sources of support.

Dealing with a Family's Resistance to Doing a Genogram

When family members react negatively to questions about the extended family or complain that such matters are irrelevant, it may help to redirect the focus to the immediate situation until the connections between it and other family experiences can be established. An example of such a genogram assessment for a remarried family whose teenage daughter's behavior was the presenting problem has been produced in the videotape *The Legacy of Unresolved Loss* (McGoldrick, 2001). This video also illustrates, as does *Harnessing the Power of Genograms in Psychotherapy* (McGoldrick, 2013), how to manage a client's resistance to revealing genogram information (for details on genogram interviewing, see McGoldrick, 2016). Gentle persistence over time will usually result in obtaining the information and demonstrating its relevance to the family.

Ethnic and Cultural History

It is essential to learn something about the family's socioeconomic, political, and cultural background to place presenting problems and relationships in context. Exploring ethnicity and migration history helps establish the cultural context in which the family is operating and offers the therapist an opportunity to understand family attitudes and behaviors determined by such influences (McGoldrick et al., 2005). It is important to learn what the family's cultural traditions are for health care and dealing with problems, in addition to where the current family members stand in relation to those traditional values and their cultural expectations about relationships with health care professionals.

Differences in social class background among family members or between family members and the health care professional often create discomfort and need to be attended to.

The family's current income, education, and social status within their community are relevant to understanding their situation. Once you see how these factors may be influencing the family, you can begin to raise delicate questions geared to helping the family identify behaviors that—even if culturally sanctioned in their original context—may be keeping them stuck (McGoldrick et al., 2005; McGoldrick & Hardy, 2019).

The Informal Kinship Network

The information net extends beyond the biological and legal structure of the family to cohabiting relationships, miscarriages, abortions, stillbirths, foster and adopted children, and anyone else who is an important support—godparents, teachers, neighbors, friends, parents of friends, clergy, caretakers, doctors, and the like who are then included on the genogram. Pets are often a primary source of support to family members and should be included on the genogram as well. In exploring outside supports for the family, the clinician might ask the following:

- To whom could you turn for financial, emotional, physical, and spiritual help?
- What roles have outsiders played in your family?
- What is your relationship to your community?
- Who outside the family has been important in your life?
- Did you ever have a nanny, caretaker, or babysitter to whom you felt attached? What became of them?
- Has anyone else ever lived with your family? When? Where are they now?
- What has been your family's experience with doctors and other helping professionals or agencies?

For particular clients, certain additional questions are appropriate. For example, the following questions would be important in working with LGBTQ clients (Burke & Faber, 1997; Green, 2008):

- Who was the first person you told about your sexual orientation?
- To whom on your genogram are you out?
- To whom would you most like to come out?
- Who would be especially easy or difficult to come out to?
- Who is in your social network? (These people should always be added to the genogram.)

Tracking Family Process

Tracking shifts that occurred around births, deaths, and other transitions can help the clinician hypotheses about the family's adaptive style. Particularly critical are untimely or traumatic deaths and the deaths of pivotal family members (Walsh & McGoldrick, 2004). We search for specific patterns of adaptation or rigidification following such transitions. Assessment of past adaptive patterns, particularly after losses and other critical transitions, may be crucial in helping a family in the current crisis. The relationship family members have to the past provides important clues about their rules, expectations, strengths, resources, and sources of resilience (Walsh, 2016).

Helping the family view itself in historical perspective involves linking past, present, and future and noting the family's flexibility in adapting to changes. It may help to inquire how they see the future of the problem as well. Questions may include the following:

- What will happen in the family if the problem continues? What will happen if it goes away?
- What does the future look like?
- What changes do family members imagine are possible in the future?

Difficult Questions About Individual Functioning

Family members may function well in some areas but not in others, and they may cover up their dysfunction. Often, it takes careful questioning to reveal the true level of functioning. A family member with a severe illness may show remarkable adaptive strengths, and another may show fragility in response to slight apparent stress. Clients may have difficulty answering questions about their functioning, and sensitivity and tact are always required, especially about issues of alcohol abuse, chronic unemployment, severe symptomatology, or trauma. The clinician will need to judge the degree of pressure to apply if the family resists questions that may be essential to dealing with the presenting problem.

Clinicians need to exercise extreme caution about when to ask questions that could put a family member in danger. For example, if violence toward a wife is suspected, she should never be asked about her husband's behavior in his presence because the question assumes she is free to respond, which may not be the case. It is the clinician's responsibility to be sure their questions do not put a client in jeopardy. The following questions reflect issues of relevance but not necessarily a format for ascertaining the information, which could require delicate and diplomatic interviewing.

Serious problems
- Has anyone in the family had a serious medical or psychological problem? Been depressed? Had anxieties? Fears? Lost control?
- Has there been physical or sexual abuse?
- Are there any other problems that worry you? When did that problem begin? Did you seek help for it? If so, when? What happened? What is the status of that problem now?
Work

- Have there been any recent unemployment, job changes, or job problems?
- Do you like your work? Do other family members like their work?

Finances

- How much income does each member generate? Does this create any imbalance in family relationships? How does the economic situation compare with that of relatives or neighbors?
- Is there any expected inheritance? Are there family members who may need financial help or caretaking?
- Are there any outstanding debts? What is the level of credit card debt?
- Who controls the money? How are spending decisions made? Are these patterns different from the ways money was handled in the families of origin?

Drugs and alcohol

- Do any family members routinely use medication? What kind and for what? Who prescribed it? What is the family's relationship with that physician?
- Do you think any members drink too much or have a drug problem? Has anyone else ever thought so? What drugs? When? What has the family attempted to do about it?
- How does the person's behavior change under the influence of the drug? How does the behavior of others change when a member is drug involved?

Trouble with the law

- Have any family members ever been arrested? For what? When? What was the result? What is that person's legal status now?
- Has anyone ever lost their driver's license?

Physical or sexual abuse

- Have you ever felt intimidated in your family? Have you or others ever been hit? Has anyone in your family ever been threatened with being hit? Have you ever threatened anyone else in your family or hit them?
- Have you or any other family members ever been sexually molested or touched inappropriately by a member of your family or someone outside your family? By whom?

Setting Priorities for Organizing Genogram Information

One of the most difficult aspects of genogram assessment remains setting priorities for inclusion of family information on a genogram. Awareness of basic genogram patterns can help the clinician set such priorities. As a rule of thumb, the data are scanned for the following:

- Repetitive symptoms, relationships, or functioning patterns across the family and over the generations; repeated cutoffs, triangles, coalitions, patterns of conflict, and over- and underfunctioning
- Coincidences of dates—for example, the death of one family member or anniversary of this death occurring at the same time as symptom onset in another, or the age at symptom onset coinciding with the age of problem development in another family member
- Changes, particularly in functioning or relationship, that correspond with critical family life events or untimely life cycle transitions—such as births, marriages, or deaths that occur "off schedule"

Missing information about important family members, events, or discrepancies in the information offered frequently reflects charged emotional issues in the family. The clinician should take careful note of the connections family members make or fail to make to various events.

A Family Systems Perspective

A family systems perspective views families as inextricably interconnected. Neither people nor their problems or solutions exist in a vacuum. Both are interwoven into broader interactional systems, the most fundamental of which is the family. The family is the primary and, except in rare instances, most powerful system to which we humans belong. In this framework, "family" consists of the entire kinship network of at least three generations, both as it currently exists and as it has evolved through time (McGoldrick et al., 2015). By our definition, family is those who are tied together through their common biological, legal, cultural, and/or emotional history and their implied future together. The physical, social, and emotional functioning of family members are profoundly interdependent, with changes in one part of the system reverberating in other parts. In addition, family interactions and relationships tend to be highly reciprocal, patterned, and repetitive. These patterns allow us to make tentative predictions from the genogram.

Historical or concurrent events in different parts of a family may be interconnected systemically, although the connections may be hidden (McGoldrick, 2016). In addition, key family relationship changes seem more likely to occur at certain times than at others. They are especially likely at points of life cycle transition. Symptoms tend to cluster around such transitions in the family life cycle, when family members face the task of reorganizing their relations with one another to go on to the next phase (McGoldrick et al., 2015). The symptomatic family may become stuck in time, unable to resolve its impasse by

reorganizing and moving on. The history and relationship patterns revealed in a genogram assessment provide important clues about the nature of this impasse—how a symptom may have arisen to preserve some relationship pattern or to protect some legacy of previous generations.

Of particular interest are family patterns of relational distance and closeness. At one extreme are family members who do not speak or are in constant conflict with each other. The family may be in danger of cutting off entirely. At the other extreme are families who seem almost stuck together in "emotional fusion." Family members in fused or poorly differentiated relationships are vulnerable to dysfunction, which tends to occur when the level of stress or anxiety exceeds the system's capacity to deal with it. The more closed the boundaries of a system become, the more immune it is to input from the environment, and consequently, the more rigid the family patterns become. Family members in a closed, fused system react automatically to one another and may be impervious to events outside the system that require adaptation to changing conditions. Fusion may involve either positive or negative relationships—that is, family members may feel very good about each other or experience almost nothing but hostility and conflict. In either case, there is an overly dependent bond that ties the family together. Genograms can map family boundaries and indicate which subsystems are fused and thus likely to be closed to new input about changing conditions.

As Bowen (1978) notes, two-person relationships seem to be unstable, under stress tending to draw in a third person. They tend to stabilize their relationship by forming a coalition of two in relation to the third. The basic unit of an emotional system thus tends to be the triangle. Genograms can help us identify key triangles in a family system, see how triangular patterns repeat from one generation to the next, and design strategies for changing them (Fogarty, 1973; Guerin et al., 1996). For an introductory video to the concepts of triangles and detriangling, see *Triangles and Family Therapy: Strategies and Solutions* (McGoldrick, 2019b).

The members of a family tend to fit together as a functional whole, their behaviors of being complementary or reciprocal. This does not mean that family members have equal power to influence relationships, as is obvious from the power differentials between men and women, parents and children, the elderly and younger family members or between family members of different cultures, classes, or races (McGoldrick & Hardy, 2019). What it does mean is that belonging to a system opens people to reciprocal influences and involves them in one another's behavior in inextricable ways. They come to expect a certain interdependent fit or balance, involving give and take, action and reaction. Thus, a lack (e.g., irresponsibility) in one part of the family may be complemented by a surplus (overresponsibility) in another part. The genogram helps the clinician pinpoint the contrasts and idiosyncrasies in families that indicate this type of complementarity or reciprocal balance.

Clearly, a genogram is limited in how much information it can display at one time. It is hoped that computer programs will be developed that will allow clinicians to examine the genogram with multiple levels of detail and explore different aspects one at a time: illness, cultural patterns, education and job history, couple relationships, and so on. Clinicians gather a great deal more important information on people's lives than can ever appear on a genogram, which is just one part of an ongoing clinical investigation and must be integrated into the total family assessment. But the genogram is the best map we have for coordinating basic demographic, functioning, and relationship information about clients.

Mapping the Genograms of Those Who Grow Up in Multiple Settings: The Meaning of Home

An individual's sense of "home" or what some have referred to as "homeplace" (Burton et al., 2004) can be a crucial aspect of developing a healthy identity. The more clearly clinicians track the actuality of a person's history, however complex, the better able they are to validate the person's actual experience and multiple forms of belonging and to understand their sense of home. Such a map can begin to make order out of the sometimes chaotic or sudden placement changes a child must go through because of illness, trauma, or other loss. It can also help validate for a child the realities of their birth and life connections that vary from traditional norms.

Many children grow up in multiple settings because their parents divorce, remarry, migrate, die, or have other special circumstances that require the children to live for a while or even permanently in a different place. Genograms can greatly facilitate tracking children in these multiple living arrangements—biological, legal, foster, adoptive, or informal kin relationships—in which their many different family constellations are otherwise extremely difficult to hold in mind. Indeed, genograms are an exceptionally useful tool to track children's experiences through the life cycle, taking into account the multiple family and other institutional contexts to which they have belonged (McGoldrick et al., 2015).

When children have lived as part of several families—biological, foster, and adoptive—it may help to create separate genograms to depict their multiple "homes" over time. Although many situations are very complicated, creativity and a commitment to validate all of a child's connections facilitate our mapping and tracking a child's family and kin connections. Sometimes the only feasible way to clarify where children were raised is to take chronological notes on each child in a family and then transform them into a series of genograms that show the family context as it evolves. Especially when children have experienced many losses and changes, such a series of genograms can both validate the losses and offer a rich picture of all the people to whom they have belonged. It can be an important clinical tool to help put children in context and to acknowledge both the traumas and the resilience of such children and families.

Of course, to more completely track the history of children in a family, we might need to do genograms for each child, including who they lived with as they were growing up, along with mapping their caregivers, friends, mentors, and other support systems, especially in cases in which children have experienced significant losses. Mapping out all these particulars seems the best way to assess each person's sense of home or homeplace and belonging, which is a crucial aspect of any clinical assessment.

Lines are then drawn to encircle various households when children have grown up in several households. This is especially important in multinuclear families, in which children spend time in different households. *Genograms: Family Assessment and Intervention* (McGoldrick et al. 2020) offers examples of such complex families with multiple colors illustrating the different households of the families.

When the "functional" family is different from the biological or legal family, such as when children are raised by a grandparent or in an informal adoptive family, it can help to create a separate genogram to show the functional structure (Watts-Jones, 1997).

The complexities of LGBTQ families are also important to indicate on a genogram. A child may be born to one spouse with a sperm donor and adopted by the other. And as Burke and Faber (1997) suggest, it can be important to depict the liaisons, long-term bonds, communities, and social networks of such families.

Genograms are also important for children in adoptive care. Fortunately, the policy of closed adoption is increasingly shifting to one of open adoption, in which both the biological family and the adoptive family may be involved with a child as they grow up. Using the information from genograms, child care workers can also help adoptive children create scrapbooks about their lives, with information, photos, and stories about both biological and adoptive families and others involved in their lives, from teachers and sitters to neighbors and friends, who may be especially important to validate their belonging and connections. In this way, children can be doubly enriched by having connections with all those who have cared about them, rather than these people being pitted against each other in terms of whoever "failed" to meet all the children's needs.

The accepted practice of severing family ties—whether biological, adopted, foster, or blended—is, in our view, extremely detrimental and disrespectful. It has led to clinicians being expected to "replace" relationships in a person's natural system. Cutoffs may leave practitioners depressed, bereft, weakened, and with a "hole" in their hearts. A cutoff of one person tends to potentiate cutoffs of other family members and losing other potentially enriching relationships, however limited. Cutoffs weaken the entire fabric of a family. Even where there has been abuse, we must beware of cutting children off from others who have been part of their support system, whether extended family members related to the abuser, teachers as children are moved from school to school, or caretakers and friends. Social workers' use of genograms can help counter this tendency by making clear the enormity of such losses and validating the connection, meaning, and richness of all parts of a child's "home."

Conclusion

The physical genogram, which is a highly condensed map of a rich and complex family, can provide an awesome lesson for anyone unable to see beyond the cutoffs that too often occur in a family (McGoldrick, 2011, 2016; McGoldrick et al., 2020). We believe that no relationship is to be disregarded or discounted. All our relationships inform the wholeness of who we are and where we come from and, more important, can help us make constructive, conscious choices about who we will be in the future.

One of the most powerful aspects of genograms is the way they can steer people to the rich, ongoing possibilities of complex kin relationships, which are sources of connection and life support. It is not just a shared history that matters but also the spiritual power of our survival and our current connections that strengthen us and can enrich our future.

Helpful Resources

GenoPro, genealogy software: http://www.genopro.com
Multicultural Family Institute: http://www.multiculturalfamily.org

References

Bowen, M. (1978). *Family therapy in clinical practice.* Aronson.

Burke, J. L., & Faber, P. (1997). A genogrid for couples. *Journal of Gay and Lesbian Social Services, 7*(1), 13–22.

Burton, L. M., Winn, D. M., Stevenson, H., & Clark, S. L. (2004). Working with African American clients: Considering the "homeplace" in marriage and family therapy practices. *Journal of Marital and Family Therapy, 30*(4), 397–410.

Congress, E. P. (1994, November). The use of culturegrams to assess and empower culturally diverse families. *Families in Society, 75,* 531–540.

Fogarty, T. (1973). *Triangles: The family.* Center for Family Learning.

Green, R. (2008). Gay and lesbian couples: Successful coping with minority stress. In M. McGoldrick & K. V. Hardy (Eds.), *Revisioning family therapy: Race, culture and gender in clinical practice* (2nd ed., pp. 300–310). Guilford.

Guerin, P., Fogarty, T. F., Fay, L. F., & Kautto, J. G. (1996). *Working with relationship triangles.* Guilford.

Hardy, K. V., & Laszloffy, T. A. (1995). The cultural genogram: Key to training culturally competent family therapists. *Journal of Marital and Family Therapy, 21*(3), 227–237.

Hartman, A. (1978, October). Diagrammatic assessment of family relationships. *Social Casework, 79,* 465–476.

McGoldrick, M. (2001). The legacy of unresolved loss [Video]. https://www.psychotherapy.net

McGoldrick, M. (2005). Freeing ourselves from the ghosts of our past [Video]. https://www.psychotherapy.net

McGoldrick, M. (2011). *The genogram journey: Reconnecting with your family.* Norton.

McGoldrick, M. (2013). Harnessing the power of genograms in psychotherapy [Video]. https://www.psychotherapy.net

McGoldrick, M. (2016). *The genogram casebook.* Norton.

McGoldrick, M. (2019a). Couples therapy: A family systems approach [Video]. https://www.psychotherapy.net

McGoldrick, M. (2019b). Racism, *family secrets* and the African American *experience* [Video]. https://www.psychotherapy.net

McGoldrick, M. (2019c). Triangles and *family therapy*: Strategies & *solutions* [Video]. https://www.psychotherapy.net.

McGoldrick, M. (2019d). Assessment and *engagement* in *family therapy* [Video]. https://www.psychotherapy.net

McGoldrick, M., Carter, B., & Garcia-Preto, N. (2015). *The expanded family life cycle: Individual, family, and social perspectives* (5th ed.). Allyn & Bacon.

McGoldrick, M., Gerson, R., & Petry, S. (2020). *Genograms: Assessment and intervention* (4th ed.). Norton.

McGoldrick, M., Giordano, J., & Garcia-Preto, N. (2005). *Ethnicity and family therapy* (3rd ed.). Guilford.

McGoldrick, M., & Hardy, K. V. (Eds.). (2019). *Revisioning family therapy: Culture, class, race, and gender* (3rd ed.). Guilford.

Walsh, F. (2009). *Spiritual resources in family therapy* (2nd ed.). Guilford.

Walsh, F. (2016). *Strengthening family resilience* (3rd ed.). Guilford.

Walsh, F., & McGoldrick, M. (2004). *Living beyond loss: Death and the family* (3rd ed.). Guilford.

Watts-Jones, D. (1997). Toward an African American genogram. *Family Process, 36*(4), 373–383.

Assessment for Child Trafficking Victims

Javonda Williams, Chris Lim, and Valerie Trull

Case Example

Jai, a child welfare social worker, rushes out of the office to meet her 15-year-old client Tammy at a fast food restaurant just on the outskirts of town. Tammy has been on "runaway status" for the past 2 weeks. Tammy's runaways usually span from a few weeks to a little over a month. The story is often the same. Jai drops Tammy off at a new foster home, and within days the foster parents call to report Tammy missing. Tammy ends up calling after a few weeks, and they have the same conversation:

Jai: Why did you run away?
Tammy: (shrugs)
Jai: Do you need to go to the hospital? Are you hurt?
Tammy: No.
Jai: Where did you go and how did you get there?
Tammy: I moved in with in my new boyfriend. He is 27 and lives with his momma in the next city.
Jai: How did you meet a 27-year-old? Didn't his mother care that you were staying there? Did she know you were underage?
Tammy: I'm hungry.

Jai: Let's get you something to eat. You have to promise me you will try to stay in the next home until the end of the school year. You have missed most of the school year.
Tammy: Yeah whatever.

Assessing and identifying human trafficking in child victims requires a combination of an in-depth understanding of trauma, knowledge about key signs of human trafficking, and empathetic interviewing skills. The story in the case example is very common. Often, human trafficking victims are described as being "hidden in plain sight." This seems paradoxical because it seems it would be difficult to hide 200,000 children (the estimated number of child trafficking victims in the United States by the Human Trafficking Center), and yet research shows that human trafficking is one of the most underreported crimes because victims are so challenging to assess (National Research Council, 2013). In fact, the U.S. Department of Health and Human Services indicated in their July 2017 bulletin that several studies show that "50 to more than 90 percent of children who were victims of child sex trafficking had been involved with child welfare services" (Child Welfare Information Gateway, 2017).

An assessment of a minor victim of human trafficking should balance the need to ascertain information for the development of an effective treatment plan with the needs of the minor for safety and stability. An assessment can feel sterile, intrusive, or coercive to a minor survivor of human trafficking, and if not conducted in a victim-centered and trauma-informed manner, it can result in an ineffective treatment plan at best and further harm to the minor at worst. The Office of Justice Programs' Office for Victims of Crime (2020) has summarized promising practices on its website, which offers many helpful tips and tools for conducting intakes and assessments, both formally and through informal assessments. This chapter highlights recent research and best practices for assessing child victims of human trafficking.

Trauma-Informed Approach

Effective assessment methods for intervention with child victims of human trafficking begin and end with understanding the effects of trauma and specifically complex trauma. Courtois (2004) defined complex trauma as "a type of trauma that occurs repeatedly and cumulatively, usually over a period of time and within specific relationships and contexts" (p. 412). Courtois suggested that complex trauma has a distinctive symptomology that includes (1) difficulty with emotional regulation and self-destructive self-soothing behaviors; (2) dissociative episodes and depersonalization; (3) chronic sense of guilt, shame, and responsibility for the abuse; (4) altered perception of the perpetrator; (5) difficulty with trust and intimate relationships; (6) psychosomatic and chronic medical conditions; and (7) a sense of hopelessness and despair. These sequelae of symptoms are often contributing factors to common outcomes associated with child trafficking, such as depression,

anxiety, post-traumatic stress disorder, substance use disorder, and suicidal ideations (Hopper, 2017).

Assessments for child victims for human trafficking need to reflect sensitivity to the unique needs of human trafficking victims versus other forms of child abuse (Busch-Armendariz et al., 2011). Palines et al. (2020) found that child victims of human trafficking demonstrated increased mental health disorders in comparison to children in other high-risk groups, including runaways and foster youth. These findings suggest more specialized assessments and treatment interventions for trafficked youth may yield results that are more efficacious than those of assessments that are designed for other high-risk youth groups.

Johnson (2020) included empathy training as a component in training counselors in assessing child trafficking victims. A victim-centered empathic approach is necessary given the barriers to intervention to all human trafficking victims. The developmental challenges of appropriately assessing children are magnified in child victims of human trafficking. Assessments for human trafficking must account for the fact that intake screenings and case management software or assessment tools alone will typically not be sufficient to assess for human trafficking.

Assessment Methods

Both formal and informal assessment methods can be useful in working with victims of human trafficking. Building trust, however, is the first step to effective assessment for human trafficking victims (Simich, 2014). Practitioners can build trust by creating a sense of safety through the incorporation of victim-centered approaches (i.e., avoiding the use of professional jargon and speaking directly to the victim in the presence of other service providers). Service providers can also work on meeting immediate needs first, including food, shelter, and medical assistance. Other more long-term needs, such as legal and case management assistance, can also bolster trust and support after the immediate needs have been met.

Identifying Victims Through Formal Assessments

The use of assessment and screening tools and/or well-crafted intake processes can be useful to structure the assessment process and to clearly document the connections between the assessment and interventions with client systems. McIntyre (2014) cautioned that formal assessments should not replace sound clinical judgment but found the combination of formal assessments and clinical judgment could provide an effective assessment process for child trafficking victims. Employing an ecological approach, McIntyre used a formal assessment that included two domains:

1. The trafficking experience
   Initial vulnerability
   Recruitment
   Primary trafficking process
   Intended exploitation
2. Social environment of the trafficking victim
   The child survivor
   Family
   Community

This multisystemic approach provides an opportunity to triangulate data and decrease bias, and it offers a comprehensive perspective of the environment of the victim. The assessment is a process of multiple interviews with the victim as opposed to one comprehensive interview. McIntyre also used additional assessment tools such as genograms, ecomaps, and social histories. Rigby and Whyte (2015) found that the ecological framework best supported assessments with child trafficking victims. They emphasized the centrality of the child's narrative in the process of screening and assessment.

Tips:

- Make sure you understand how to use the chosen tool.
- Warmly introduce yourself.
- Properly set the child's expectations.
- Be careful to not coach the answers.
- Try to be conversational.

Identifying Victims Through Informal Assessments

By "informal," we are not suggesting the assessment lacks rigor or objectivity but, rather, that the process for collecting the assessment data is informal as opposed to formal.

Because of the presence of trauma in victims of human trafficking, and the corresponding trauma responses, the indications of human trafficking often emerge over time through informal conversations. This is in part because as a child who has been a victim of human trafficking begins to build trust in their case manager, they will slowly disclose information, often subtly, to test their ability to trust the case manager with such information. This is also in part because many of the indicators observed in isolation may not cause suspicion of human trafficking, but the aggregate of multiple indicators building up over time may provide a strong indication of the presence of human trafficking.

Conducting Informal Assessments

Conducting informal assessments requires vigilance of the case manager to always be mindful of human trafficking indicators. In addition, the case manager must be able to easily enter assessment data into the child's profile from anywhere at any time.

A case manager might identify human trafficking indicators through conversation with the minor. Often, as the minor begins to trust the case manager, they will subtly introduce an indicator into their conversation to determine if the case manager will pick up the hint and to see how the case manager responds. Sometimes, after trust between the survivor and the case manage has been established, the minor might disclose the trafficking. However, self-disclosure is infrequent because of the effects of trauma on the victims and because the victim often does not have the language to formally identify their victimization as human trafficking.

The conversation might follow a pattern like the following:

Tammy: I hate Marcus (her 27-year-old boyfriend)

Jai: Why?

Tammy: He makes me do things I'm not comfortable with.

Jai: What types of things?

Tammy: Nasty stuff with his friends . . . I feel like I have to though . . . he's helped me so much, and he really does love me . . . and I love him.

This type of disclosure most likely will not come up in the case manager's office or in the minor's placement. These conversations happen when the case manager is driving the minor to an appointment or when they are eating lunch at a restaurant. As a result, the case manager needs to have the ability to easily enter assessment data into the child's profile from anywhere at any time. Promising practices are beginning to emerge with case management software that can be accessed in the field or through apps that are secure and can be uploaded to the system at a later time.

When a disclosure is made, the caseworker should follow all mandated reporting procedures and notify the local law enforcement agency and the National Human Trafficking Hotline. The National Human Trafficking Hotline can also suggest additional resources to the case manager to assist with treatment and service provision. The hotline is available 24 hours a day and can facilitate more than 200 languages; it can be accessed through the National Human Trafficking Hotline's website (https://humantraffickinghotline.org), by phone (1-888-373-7888), or by text (233733).

Helpful Resources

Center for the Human Rights of Children, Loyola University Chicago, Rapid Screening Tool (RST) for Child Trafficking—a short 1-page form used to make an initial assessment: http://www.ocwtp.net/pdfs/ht/rapid%20screening%20tool.pdf

National Human Trafficking Hotline: https://humantraffickinghotline.org; phone: 1-888-373-7888; text: 233733; TTY: 711

Office of Justice Programs. *Human Trafficking Task Force e-guide: Victim service provider intake & needs assessment:* https://www.ovcttac.gov/taskforceguide/eguide/4-supporting-victims/42-victim-service-provider-intake-and-needs-assessment

U.S. Department of Health and Human Services, Children's Bureau. *Human trafficking and child welfare: A guide for caseworkers:* https://www.childwelfare.gov/pubs/trafficking-caseworkers

Westcoast Children's Clinic. *Commercial Sexual Exploitation Identification Tool (CSE-IT):* https://www.westcoastcc.org/cse-it

References

Busch-Armendariz, N. B., Nsonwu, M. B., & Heffron, L. C. (2011). Human trafficking victims and their children: Assessing needs, vulnerabilities, strengths, and survivorship. *Journal of Applied Research on Children, 2*(1), article 3.

Child Welfare Information Gateway. (2017). *Human trafficking and child welfare: A guide for caseworkers.* U.S. Department of Health and Human Service, Children's Bureau.

Courtois, C. (2004). Complex trauma, complex reactions: Assessment and treatment. *Psychotherapy: Theory, Research, Practice, Training, 41*(4), 412–425.

Hopper, E. K. (2017). Polyvictimization and developmental trauma adaptations in sex trafficked youth. *Journal of Child & Adolescent Trauma, 10*(2), 161–173.

Johnson, B. C. (2020, February). Featured counter-trafficking program: Trauma recovery for victims of sex trafficking. *Child Abuse & Neglect, 100,* 104153.

McIntyre, B. L. (2014). More than just rescue: Thinking beyond exploitation to creating assessment strategies for child survivors of commercial sexual exploitation. *International Social Work, 57*(1), 39–63.

National Research Council. (2013). *Confronting commercial sexual exploitation and sex trafficking of minors in the United States.* National Academies Press. http://www.nap.edu/catalog.php?record_id=18358

Office for Victims of Crime. (2020). Victim service provider intake & needs assessment. Office of Justice Programs. https://www.ovcttac.gov/taskforceguide/eguide/4-supporting-victims/42-victim-service-provider-intake-and-needs-assessment

Palines, P. A., Rabbitt, A. L., Pan, A. Y., Nugent, M. L., & Ehrman, W. G. (2020). Comparing mental health disorders among sex trafficked children and three groups of youth at high-risk for trafficking: A dual retrospective cohort and scoping review. *Child Abuse & Neglect, 100,* 104196.

Rigby, P., & Whyte, B. (2015). Children's narrative within a multi-centred, dynamic ecological framework of assessment and planning for child trafficking. *British Journal of Social Work, 45*(1), 34–51.

Simich, L. (2014). *Out of the shadows: A tool for identification of human trafficking victims.* Research summary, Vera Institute of Justice.

Spiritual Assessment

Chris Stewart

There is a growing body of literature suggesting that client spirituality may be beneficial for numerous client outcomes. Several reviews have supported the positive impact of client spirituality on depression, suicide, anxiety, and substance use (Koenig, 2010, 2012). Similarly, there is evidence to support the role of spirituality to health outcomes, including hypertension, Alzheimer's disease, and even mortality (Koenig, 2012; Seeman et al., 2003).

Clearly, such extant evidence supports the inclusion of client spirituality in any holistic assessment and subsequent intervention planning. This is especially true as many clients continue to request spiritual components in treatment (Lietz & Hodge, 2013; Oxhandler et al., 2018). In response, spiritual assessment is often discussed in professions such as medicine and psychology (Paloutzian & Park, 2014; Saad et al., 2017; Sulmasy, 2002). Client spirituality also fits extremely well within the biopsychospiritual, person-in-environment framework and use of evidence-based practices promulgated by the social work profession (Drisko & Grady, 2019). The National Association of Social Workers' Code of Ethics (2017) requires sensitivity to client religious and spiritual diversity. This practice standard is also echoed by the Council on Social Work Education's Educational Policy and Accreditation Standards, Competency 2 (2015), addressing respect for client diversity.

How Do We "Measure" Spirituality?

In assessment of any client issues, it is important to utilize psychometrically sound measures. For example, if a practitioner is interested in assessing or tracking a client's progress with depression, it would be critical to employ a measure that consistently (reliably) and accurately (validly) evaluates depression. One difficulty in assessing client spirituality is the complicated process of conceptualizing and operationalizing spirituality. In other words, what exactly do we mean by "spirituality"? Without a clear definition of spirituality for guidance, any subsequent measurement and assessment runs the risk of producing inaccurate results. Similarly, poorly developed assessments, regardless of spiritual perspective, may not elucidate the complicated relationship between spirituality and other important behaviors or clinical factors.

The study of spirituality has a long history and its' development has created an overwhelming number of empirical perspectives. Currently, there are numerous definitions of spirituality in the literature, and the use of these various conceptualizations and subsequent operationalizations significantly influences not only the interpretation of individual research studies on client outcomes but also comparing these effects across studies.

In reviewing available spirituality conceptualizations and their related assessment procedures, there are several important factors for clinicians to consider when choosing both an assessment method and a particular spirituality measure. First is the relationship between spirituality and religiosity. Generally, the current approach is to conceptually differentiate between religiosity and spirituality, although there is strong evidence to suggest there is an interaction between spiritual and religious dimensions (López et al., 2017; MacDonald et al., 2015; Miller, 2012; Saroglou, 2012). Second, although the consensus is that spirituality should be conceptualized as multidimensional, the exact nature and number of dimensions are still debated (Hill & Pargament, 2003; MacDonald, 2000). MacDonald (2009) has identified numerous multidimensional models utilizing as few dimensions as two and as many as nine.

The third factor concerns the possibility that spirituality may be more accurately conceptualized as a feature or result of other individual characteristics such as well-being or personality. However, current research provides evidence that spirituality is distinct from personality traits (Ashton & Lee, 2013; MacDonald, 2009). A fourth consideration is the cultural universality of spirituality. It has been suggested that the cultural uniqueness of spirituality prevents an accurate general or comprehensive conceptualization (Belzen & Lewis, 2010; Rich & Cinamon, 2007). Recent investigation, however, suggests that although spirituality as currently understood is not universal, it might be considered a comparable construct cross-culturally (López et al., 2017; MacDonald et al., 2015). Furthermore, evidence indicates that the effects of spirituality may be similar across cultures (Saroglou, 2011; Saroglou & Cohen, 2013). With these general factors in mind, there are several general approaches from which to choose when selecting a spiritual assessment.

Scale Measures

Any far-reaching discussion of scales devoted to the measurement of spirituality is well beyond the scope of this chapter. One volume created by two well-known researchers contains more than 200 instruments (Hill & Hood, 1999). Generally, these scales are developed for research purposes and address a single dimension of spirituality, such as religious attachment, private practices, or spiritual coping (Hill, 2013). For example, one popular scale is the RCOPE (and Brief RCOPE), developed to measure how people use spiritual resources to deal with adversity (Pargament et al., 2000, 2011).

These scales have been primarily developed within the psychology field to further the overall study of religion and spirituality. A strength of these measures is that there has been a great deal of attention spent on the psychometric soundness (or lack thereof) of the measures. Many are also fairly brief, which might be helpful in clinical settings that do not allow great amounts of time with clients (e.g., hospitals). Conversely, some scales are quite lengthy in the quest for psychometric strength. Furthermore, many of these scales have not been tested multiculturally.

Although many of these measures are appropriate for use in clinical practice (e.g., Brief RCOPE), it would require that the practitioner be familiar enough with the study of spirituality to choose a scale addressing the desired spiritual dimension(s) and interpret the results.

There are several examples of scales that may be helpful in assessing overall spirituality.

One such scale was developed to measure religious involvement. The Duke University Religion Index is a readily available measure that contains only five items that measure organizational religiousness, non-organizational religiousness, and both intrinsic and extrinsic spirituality (Koenig & Bussing, 2010). This measure has been thoroughly tested in many languages and has very good psychometric properties for a short measure (Koenig & Büssing, 2010).

Another scale is the Expressions of Spirituality Inventory–Revised (ESI-R) (MacDonald, 2000). This 32-item measure was developed to produce a five-dimensional model of spirituality. The domains include Cognitive Orientation Toward Spirituality—the importance of spirituality in daily life (e.g., "Spirituality gives life focus and direction"); existential Well-Being—meaning and purpose in facing the existential adversities in life (e.g., "I seldom feel tense about things"); Paranormal Beliefs—belief in the existence of paranormal phenomena and activities (e.g., "It is possible to communicate with the dead"); Experiential/Phenomenological Dimension—spiritual or mystical experiences, including perceptions of the divine (e.g., "I have had an experience in which I seemed to transcend space and time"); Religiousness—an intrinsic belief in religious values and practice (e.g., "I practice some form of prayer").

MacDonald (2000, 2009) created the ESI-R to carefully address the well-known spirituality measurement issues. This approach allows for a distinctiveness of both religiosity and spirituality while acknowledging an interrelatedness. The measure was created through a comprehensive factor analytic study to ensure no significant domain of spirituality was omitted. Finally, the ESI-R has been rigorously tested in many cultures (López et al., 2017; MacDonald et al., 2015; Silva, MacDonald, Cunha, & Ferreira, 2017).

If time is not a limiting factor, the Multidimensional Measurement of Religiousness/Spirituality (MMRS) can be used (Fetzer Institute, 2003; downloadable from https://fetzer.org/resources/multidimensional-measurement-religiousnessspirituality-use-health-research). This multidimensional measure was created by a working group from the Fetzer Institute and the National Institute on Aging. The long version is an 88-item instrument that measures spirituality and religiousness through 12 domains: daily spiritual experiences, meaning, values, beliefs, forgiveness, private religious practices, religious/spiritual coping, religious support, religious/spiritual history, commitment, organizational religiousness, and religious preferences.

The inclusion of 12 spiritual domains allows the MMRS to provide a quite comprehensive spiritual assessment. Although many of the questions are standard ordinal scales (e.g., rated from 1 to 5), there are several open-ended questions that could help facilitate further discussion and more of a mixed method approach to spiritual assessment. Because the MMRS includes some well-known scales, such as the Daily Spiritual Experience Scale and the RCOPE, the psychometric properties appear to be acceptable (Fetzer Institute, 2003).

The short form of this measure, which contains 38 items, also measures the identical 11 dimensions (except meaning) of spirituality as the longer version. Because these domains use only portions of their parent scales, the psychometric characteristics may not be as strong but still may facilitate a useful discussion with clients (Piedmont et al., 2006).

Semistructured Qualitative Measures

Several semistructured spiritual assessment tools are available for various professions, including physicians, nurses, and chaplains.

These measures were developed specifically to assist professionals in assessing the importance of spirituality in the lives of those for whom they care (Cadge & Bandini, 2015). These measures often use acronyms to guide the assessment. Two important considerations are that (1) these tools may have been developed within a specific profession, such as nursing; and (2) the measures may have been developed for specific populations, such as children or cardiac patients. These factors may influence the assessment results or limit generalizability (Cadge & Bandini, 2015).

Also, although many of the tools follow a semistructured approach, they do not necessarily specify questions within framework domains. So, if example questions are offered, the practitioner may need to revise them for their unique client profile. As with most qualitative methodology, without careful use it may be possible to interpret results incorrectly or introduce practitioner bias. The advantages to this more "qualitative" approach is that it may allow the client to define individually important spiritual concepts and domains that may help with further assessment or personalizing treatment options. Because of these advantages, some researchers believe that a qualitative approach is the most appropriate route for spiritual assessment (Hodge, 2001).

One well-known assessment from the medical field (Puchalski & Romer, 2000) uses the acronym FICA to help guide the assessment process. Open-ended questions are posed for the following domains: *Faith and Belief*—those factors that bring meaning to life; *Importance:* How important are the client's beliefs? *Community*—the role of a spiritual community; *Address in Care*—how the individual would like to incorporate their spiritual beliefs in their treatment. There are no predetermined questions for these domains, but examples are often provided in many FICA presentations. An example of a Faith domain question is, "Do you consider yourself a religious or spiritual person?"

Another assessment tool also developed from the field of medicine uses the mnemonic HOPE (Anandarajah & Hight, 2001). This tool follows a similar, open-ended approach and asks questions in the following domains: *H:* sources of meaning and comfort, "What are your sources of comfort and peace?"; *O:* role of organized religion, "Do you consider yourself to be part of an organized religion?"; *P:* personal spiritual practices, "Do you have spiritual practices outside of an organization?"; *E:* effects of spirituality and beliefs on medical care, "Is there anything I can do to help you address your spiritual needs?"

Social Work Spiritual Qualitative Assessments

Although many of the discussed measures for spiritual assessment have been developed in disciplines such as psychology and medicine, several tools have been developed specifically from the social work perspective. Hodge (2001, 2005, 2006) has written extensively on the qualitative approach to spiritual assessment. Traditional assessment measures such as genograms and ecomaps can be successfully utilized for spiritual assessment. Practitioners are encouraged to review this material (see Chapter 123, this volume) for further information.

A wide variety of tools and approaches are available to practitioners interested in assessing their client's spirituality. These measures range from very brief scales to comprehensive interviews. In some cases, a practitioner may only have time to ask, "Do you consider yourself a spiritual or religious person?" whereas in other instances it may be important to understand a full spiritual history. A carefully selected spiritual assessment tool can greatly benefit both an understanding of the client's unique perspective and enhance the chances for successful treatment outcomes.

References

Anandarajah, G., & Hight, E. (2001). Spirituality and medical practice: Using the HOPE questions as a practical tool for spiritual assessment. *American Family Physician, 63*(1), 81.

Ashton, M. C., & Lee, K. (2013). Personality and religiousness. In V. Saroglou (Ed.), *Religion, personality, and social behavior* (pp. 41–55). Psychology Press.

Belzen, J. A., & Lewis, C. A. (2010). Towards cultural psychology of religion: Principles, approaches and applications. *Mental Health, Religion and Culture, 13*(4), 327–328.

Cadge, W., & Bandini, J. (2015). The evolution of spiritual assessment tools in healthcare. *Society, 52*(5), 430–437.

Council on Social Work Education. (2015). *Curriculum policy statement for baccalaureate and master's degree programs in social work education.*

Drisko, J. W., & Grady, M. D. (2019). *Evidence-based practice in clinical social work.* Springer.

Fetzer Institute. (2003). *Multidimensional measurement of religiousness/spirituality for use in health research: A report of the Fetzer Institute/National Institute of Aging Working Group.* Fetzer Institute.

Hill, P. C. (2013). Measurement assessment and issues in the psychology of religion and spirituality. *Handbook of the Psychology of Religion and Spirituality, 2,* 48–74.

Hill, P. C., & Hood, R. W. (Eds.). (1999). *Measures of religiosity* (pp. 119–158). Religious Education Press.

Hill, P. C., & Pargament, K. I. (2003). Advances in the conceptualization and measurement of religion and spirituality: Implications for physical and mental health research. *The American Psychologist, 58*(1), 64–74.

Hodge, D. R. (2001). Spiritual assessment: A review of major qualitative methods and a new framework for assessing spirituality. *Social Work, 46*(3), 203–214.

Hodge, D. R. (2005). Developing a spiritual assessment toolbox: A discussion of the strengths and limitations of five different assessment methods. *Health & Social Work, 30*(4), 314–323.

Hodge, D. R. (2006). A template for spiritual assessment: A review of the JCAHO requirements and guidelines for implementation. *Social Work, 51*(4), 317–326.

Koenig, H. G. (2010). Spirituality and mental health. *International Journal of Applied Psychoanalytic Studies, 7*(2), 116–122.

Koenig, H. G. (2012). Religion, spirituality, and health: The research and clinical implications. *Psychiatry, 2012,* 1–34.

Koenig, H. G., & Büssing, A. (2010). The Duke University Religion Index (DUREL): A five-item measure for use in epidemiological studies. *Religions, 1*(1), 78–85.

Lietz, C. A., & Hodge, D. R. (2013). Incorporating spirituality into substance abuse counseling: Examining the perspectives of service recipients and providers. *Journal of Social Service Research, 39,* 498–510. doi:10.1080/01488376.2012.676023

López, E., Jódar, R., & MacDonald, D. A. (2017). Psychometric properties of a Spanish adaptation of the Expressions of Spirituality Inventory–Revised (ESI-R). *International Journal of Transpersonal Studies, 36*(1), 110–121.

MacDonald, D. A. (2000). Spirituality: Description, measurement, and relation to the five factor model of personality. *Journal of Personality, 68*(1), 153–197.

MacDonald, D. A. (2009). Identity and spirituality: Conventional and transpersonal perspectives. *International Journal of Transpersonal Studies, 28*(1), 86–106.

MacDonald, D. A., Friedman, H. L., Brewczynski, J., Holland, D., Salagame, K. K. K., Mohan, K. K., Gubrij, Z. O., & Cheong, H. W. (2015). Spirituality as a scientific construct: Testing its universality across cultures and languages. *PLoS One, 10*(3), e0117701.

Miller, L. J. (Ed.). (2012). *The Oxford handbook of psychology and spirituality.* Oxford University Press.

National Association of Social Workers. (2017). *Code of ethics of the National Association of Social Workers.*

Oxhandler, H. K., Polson, E. C., & Achenbaum, W. A. (2018). The religiosity and spiritual beliefs and practices of clinical social workers: A national survey. *Social Work, 63*(1), 47–56.

Paloutzian, R. F., & Park, C. L. (Eds.). (2014). *Handbook of the psychology of religion and spirituality.* Guilford.

Pargament, K. I., Feuille, M., & Burdzy, D. (2011). The Brief RCOPE: Current psychometric status of a short measure of religious coping. *Religions, 2*(1), 51–76.

Pargament, K. I., Koenig, H. G., & Perez, L. M. (2000). The many methods of religious coping: Development and initial validation of the RCOPE. *Journal of Clinical Psychology, 56*(4), 519–543.

Piedmont, R. L., Mapa, A. T., & Williams, J. E. (2006). A factor analysis of the Fetzer/NIA Brief Multidimensional Measure of Religiousness/Spirituality (MMRS). *Research in the Social Scientific Study of Religion, 17,* 177.

Puchalski, C., & Romer, A. L. (2000). Taking a spiritual history allows clinicians to understand patients more fully. *Journal of Palliative Medicine, 3*(1), 129–137.

Rich, Y., & Cinamon, R. G. (2007). Conceptions of spirituality among Israeli Arab and Jewish late adolescents. *Journal of Humanistic Psychology, 47*(1), 7–29.

Saad, M., de Medeiros, R., & Mosini, A. C. (2017). Are we ready for a true biopsychosocial–spiritual model? The many meanings of "spiritual." *Medicines, 4*(4), 79–84. https://doi.org/10.3390/medicines4040079

Saroglou, V. (2011). Believing, bonding, behaving, and belonging: The big four religious dimensions and cultural variation. *Journal of Cross-Cultural Psychology, 42*(8), 1320–1340.

Saroglou, V. (2012). Are we born to be religious? *Scientific American Mind, 23*, 53–57.

Saroglou, V., & Cohen, A. B. (2013). Cultural and cross-cultural psychology of religion. In R. F. Paloutzian & C. L. Park (Eds.), *Handbook of the psychology of religion and spirituality* (2nd ed., pp. 330–353). Guilford.

Seeman, T. E., Dubin, L. F., & Seeman, M. (2003). Religiosity/spirituality and health: A critical review of the evidence for biological pathways. *The American Psychologist, 58*(1), 53.

Silva, L. X. D. L., MacDonald, D. A., Cunha, D. P. D., & Ferreira, A. L. (2017). Psychometric examination of a Brazilian adaptation of the expressions of Spirituality Inventory-Revised. *Estudos de Psicologia (Natal), 22*(2), 132–143.

Sulmasy, D. P. (2002). A biopsychosocial–spiritual model for the care of patients at the end of life. *The Gerontologist, 42*(Suppl. 3), 24–33.

Identification, Screening, and Referral for Treatment of Problematic and Disordered Gambling

Jody Bechtold and Alyssa N. Wilson

"Do you gamble?" asked the social worker.

"No!" said the client.

"Oh, do you play the lottery?"

"Every day!" said the client with a smile.

Gambling is a socially acceptable form of entertainment that has seen exponential expansion throughout the United States and the world. Although traditional forms of brick-and-mortar gambling establishments, such as casinos and racetracks, are often attributed to "gambling," recent advancements in technology and accessibility of the internet have resulted in an alarming expansion of online gambling options throughout the world.[1] From social gaming on Facebook to sports betting on smartphones, it is becoming increasingly difficult to see a hard line differentiation between playing games for entertainment (i.e., gaming) and gambling. Given this fallout, it is easy for social workers to ask the wrong question, and when the wrong question is asked, we get a wrong answer. The answer to "Do you gamble?" is contingent upon how you define *gambling*.

Gambling, at a basic level, can be defined as playing a game for a chance to take home more money or possessions than what is started with. A more refined version may be reconfigured to consider gambling as any wager (regardless of commodity or size of the wager), for self or others, where the outcome is uncertain or depends on chance or skill (see Gamblers Anonymous, 2000). Depending on how gambling is defined, numerous examples in everyday life could be considered gambling but may not necessarily be endorsed as such during the reporting process. For example, playing the stock market, putting money on the 18th hole of one's own golf game, and creating a spread among friends or colleagues to determine who gets closest to a new baby's

---

1. A similar discussion as that in this chapter is provided in the book by Bechtold and Wilson (2021). Although the entire book is dedicated to the assessment and treatment of gambling disorder, substantial discussion and research overview are provided in the first two chapters on the transformation of the gambling industry with technology, video and internet gaming, internet accessibility throughout the world, etc.

birth date or height/weight are all forms of gambling under the second definition.

The purpose of this chapter is to give social workers a thoroughgoing overview of problem and disordered gambling. Whereas discussions about treatment for disordered gambling exist elsewhere (e.g., Bechtold & Wilson, 2021; Petry, 2005), this chapter seeks to provide an in-depth analysis and discussion about problem gambling for social workers. In this way, social workers will learn how to

- define problematic and disordered gambling, including all forms of gambling;
- screen for gambling across a range of clients and settings;
- provide education about gambling as a potential problematic behavior;
- modify therapy/treatment processes to include language for gambling and when to refer to a specialist; and
- learn how to get training and certification for treating problem and disordered gambling as a social work profession.

Global Gambling Expansion and Accessibility

Gambling is everywhere! We are experiencing a surge in gambling activities, especially through the use of technology with electronic devices accessing the internet. We can no longer consider gambling to mean going to a casino in Las Vegas or Atlantic City or even in our own community. It now also includes online sports betting, online casino slots and other games of chance, as well as online lottery tickets and scratch-offs. We even expect to encounter gambling opportunities at truck stops, gas stations, restaurants, and airports. When the Supreme Court overturned the Professional and Amateur Sports Protection Act (PASPA) in 2018, it allowed each state to

decide if it wanted to legalize sports betting. Before this, Nevada and Oregon were the only two states with legalized sports betting. Most sports betting was done illegally, either with a bookie or an offshore betting site. Within months of the PASPA ruling, several states were ready to offer sports betting in brick-and-mortar settings (i.e., sports books) as well as online for residences in their jurisdiction. The Supreme Court decision can be viewed as a major event that transformed the gambling scene as well as the problem gambling treatment field into another level of access, opportunity, and availability.

In early 2020, the global pandemic halted all gambling activities for the first time in history. There were no casinos, sporting events, or other in-person gambling opportunities, both legal and illegal. Casinos in Las Vegas had to figure out how to lock their doors (which had no locks), as they never were closed before the pandemic (Rovell, 2020). Sports betting sites such as FanDuel and DraftKings had no sports or fantasy sports, globally, to promote. Within weeks, these online sports betting sites began to offer games of chance, such as slots, as well as simulated sports through video games, with marked increases in online revenue (Parry, 2020). Now, more than ever before, prevention and treatment professionals in the field of problem gambling need to develop and implement strategies to address the 24/7 instant access gambling explosion and blurred lines between gambling and gaming.

Forms of gambling are classified into two categories: games of *chance* and games of *skill*. Examples of games of chance are the lottery, scratch-offs, bingo, slots, roulette, and fundraiser activities such as the 50/50. Examples of games of skill are card games (e.g., blackjack and poker), sports, and board games. But all games of skill still have an element of chance; they are not 100% skill. With the accessibility of online and other forms of easy-to-use technology (i.e., smartphone applications or "apps"), we see an increase in the market for free-to-play gambling-themed activities across a range of social media sites and applications (Market.US, 2019; for similar discussion, see also Bechtold & Wilson 2021). So it can quickly become confusing when we attempt to differentiate between in-person and virtual gambling because almost all forms of gambling now exist online. With the increased presence of social media, many people are playing games online for free, until they reach a barrier, and they can pay to move to the next level (e.g., Candy Crush) knowing that they will never receive a cash payout.

Problem and Disordered Gambling

Gambling behavior exists on a continuum from recreational or social gambling to at-risk to problematic and disorder gambling behavior. It has often been referred to as the *hidden addiction* because people can keep it hidden for such a long time compared to other addictions, especially substances. For example, you cannot smell a gambling problem on someone's breath like you can with alcohol. You cannot conduct a urine analysis to determine if someone has relapsed on gambling. And you cannot tell from other physical markers such as pinned or glassy eyes. Yet it is similar to substance use behaviors and disorders in tolerance, frequency, denial, dishonesty, and eventually crossing moral and legal boundaries to continue the compulsive behaviors.

With the release of the fifth edition of the *Diagnostic and Statistical Manual of Mental Disorders* (DSM-5; American Psychiatric Association, 2013), gambling disorder was reclassified under the substance use disorders, behavioral addictions subsection. Gambling addiction and compulsive gambling are terms also used to describe a gambling disorder. For the diagnosis of gambling disorder, the DSM-5 requires at least four of nine criteria to be met in the past year. Criteria include tolerance, withdrawal symptoms, preoccupation, chasing, increased consequences, and bailouts; the previously included criterion of committing illegal acts (e.g., fraud or theft) to financially support gambling was omitted. Whereas substance use disorders have two levels that distinguish abuse from addiction, there is no diagnosis code for problem gambling, or a score 1 or more but less than 4. The move in the DSM-5 further legitimized that gambling behaviors are more similar to addictive disorders than impulse control disorders.

Research continues to measure and examine prevalence rates of problem and disorder gambling. We can expect these numbers to change and possibly increase with the expansion of online access in the next few years. Currently, problem and disordered gambling prevalence rates have been reported between 2.2% and 5.8% of adults in the United States and globally (United States: Calado & Griffiths, 2016; Kessler et al., 2008; Williams et al., 2012). Studies (e.g., Molinaro et al., 2014) indicate that despite adolescent gambling being an illegal activity, youth engage in gambling with a prevalence rate higher than that of adults (Gupta & Derevensky, 2000; Volberg et al., 2010). The findings showed that 0.2–12.3% of youth meet criteria for problem gambling, notwithstanding differences among assessment instruments, cutoffs, and time frames (Calado et al., 2017).

To date, researchers have identified common demographic features that are associated with problem and disordered gambling, across a range of psychosocial factors. From a whole person perspective, it is imperative to consider age, gender, race/ethnicity, co-occurring mental health disorders and histories (including trauma, military, etc.), medications consumed, and geographical accessibility. A brief synthesis of a handful of such factors is presented next.

Males are more likely than females to develop a problem with gambling (Hing et al., 2016; Kessler et al., 2008), with different levels of gambling engagement and problems compared to females (Stoletenberg et al., 2007). Similarly, research on gambling and older adults has shown that approximately 3% of adults older than age 65 years may engage in gambling (Ariyabuddhiphongs, 2012). Gambling is often considered a socially acceptable activity to address any or all of the following age-specific risk factors: isolation, boredom, inactivity, increased health issues, and the need to find new activities to support aging.

Furthermore, research has long shown that racial and ethnic minority groups have higher rates of problem gambling compared to Whites (e.g., Caler et al., 2017; Ellenbogen et al., 2007). For example, some estimate that African American adults are up to two times more likely to develop a gambling problem (Alegria et al., 2009), but that is not to overshadow similar findings of disproportionate prevalence rates of Hispanic (Caler et al., 2017) and Asian (Marshall et al., 2009; Petry et al., 2003) individuals. Most studies have variations in socioeconomic, gender, and geographical location of respondents, so it is important for clinicians to consider the whole person, including the intersection of the client's socially perceived and lived experience.

Military and veteran servicemen and -women represent another at-risk population for problem and disordered gambling. According to Gallaway et al. (2019), prevalence of frequent gambling in the military (8%) is nearly twice the U.S. prevalence (5%). Problem gambling also correlates with depression, alcohol use, and legal problems in the military. Etuk et al. (2020) found gambling disorders often co-occur with trauma-related conditions, substance use, and suicidality, which can complicate treatment outcomes. Shame, stigma, and difficulty asking for help can negatively impact active duty and veteran military personnel from receiving help until the consequences are too severe to ignore. As social workers working with the military, it is important to conduct routine screening for potential at-risk and problematic gambling activities to ensure the military population receives proper treatment.

Co-occurrences with psychiatric disorders and disordered gambling have been observed in both clinical and community-based research. However, the nature of the co-occurrences between problem and disordered gambling and psychiatric disorders remains incompletely understood. Research has found increased rates of gambling and co-occurring depression/anxiety (Barrault & Varescon, 2013), mood disorders (Lister et al., 2015), co-occurring substance use (Cowlishaw et al., 2014; Potenza, 2008), and impulsivity (Potenza, 2007). Self-control and individual decision-making are important in the treatment of gambling disorders, and interventions are targeted to increase self-control over desires to gamble and to make decisions to engage in nongambling behaviors. In the field of psychiatry, there has also been a substantial increase in neurobiological studies investigating pathological gambling. The research primarily investigates the neurotransmitters of serotonin, dopamine, norepinephrine, and opioids. The research hypothesizes that these systems are particularly important for various aspects of disordered gambling: serotonin underlying impulse control, dopamine differential reward and reinforcement, norepinephrine arousal and excitement, and opioids pleasure and urges (Potenza, 2008). Additional research continues to investigate the noradrenergic systems and the role of glutamates. Social workers will do well to continue to stay updated on the effectiveness (or not) of medications in clinical practice.

The association between suicidality and problem and disordered gambling has been researched since the late 1990s. However, there continues to be very little research identifying individuals at risk or which factors contribute to nonfatal suicidal behavior (Karlsson & Håkansson, 2018). Social workers need to conduct thorough suicide risk assessments not only during the initial evaluation but also throughout treatment, regardless of treatment setting. Risk factors can include depression, cluster B personality disorders, substance use disorders, attention-deficit/hyperactivity disorder, and even poor physical health. Regardless of the primary diagnosis, social workers need to assess for suicide continuously, especially if an individual also shows signs of at-risk or problematic gambling behavior.

The medications consumed by a person may also impact the extent to which they develop a gambling problem. Dopamine receptor agonists, for instance, have been implicated in some cases. For example, in 2016, the U.S. Food and Drug Administration (FDA) released a safety warning on the association of aripiprazole (Abilify) and increased urges for gambling, binge eating, hypersexuality, and increased spending and also on the association of Requip and Mirapex (restless leg syndrome) and increased compulsive gambling. These drugs are believed to impact dopamine receptor agonists, which may cause impulse control problems given the imbalances to the dopamine (reward) system. As such, it is important to review medication additions or changes as part of the diagnostic evaluation to determine if an individual is experiencing problematic gambling behaviors due to a medication side effect. This can directly impact the course of treatment.

Effective Screening for Gambling Disorders

Social workers need to consider what underlying issues may be the cause or source of individuals' presenting problems. Many individuals will seek help for relationship issues, financial problems, domestic violence/intimate partner violence, or work/school performance issues when the underlying cause is problematic or disordered gambling. Others will seek help for a gambling problem when gambling has become a symptom of a deeper problem. Screening, therefore, must be sensitive enough to identify both types of individuals who seek help. Given a lack of accessibility for providers, several open-sourced screening tools have been shown to effectively screen for problem gambling.

Lie–Bet Questionnaire

The Lie–Bet screen (Johnson et al., 1988) is a two-question survey:

1. Have you ever felt the need to bet more and more money?
2. Have you ever lied to people important to you about how much you gambled?

If the client responds "yes" to one or both questions, a further evaluation is conducted.

Brief Biosocial Gambling Screen

The Brief Biosocial Gambling Screen (BBGS; Gebauer et al., 2010) is a three-question brief screening instrument:

1. During the past 12 months, have you become restless, irritable, or anxious when trying to stop or cut down on gambling?
2. During the past 12 months, have you tried to keep your family or friends from knowing how much you gambled?
3. During the past 12 months, did you have such financial trouble as a result of your gambling that you had to get help with living expenses from family friends or welfare?

If the answer is "yes" to one or more questions, a further evaluation is needed.

Gambling Brief Intervention and Referral to Treatment

The Gambling Brief Intervention and Referral to Treatment (GBIRT) was developed using the DSM-5, BBGS, and the Screening, Brief Intervention, and Referral to Treatment (SBIRT) model (Illinois DG_SPS and Elizabeth Hartney, PhD). GBIRT is designed to help professionals in various settings, including clinical practice, screen, conduct a brief intervention, and refer to treatment, like the SBIRT for substance use and abuse. GBIRT was developed in part by comparison analyses that highlighted the utility of SBIRT for problem gambling.

Another approach for social workers is to simply ask open-ended questions that clients can easily answer, yet these questions can help surface any potential at-risk or problematic behaviors. Then the social worker can provide education or psychoeducation in response to reducing at-risk and harmful gambling behaviors. For example, ask a person during intake or early in the therapeutic relationship, "How do you like to celebrate your birthday?" "What do you do to calm down, relax, or unwind?" and "What do you do when you are bored?" Often, clients will talk about how the entire family goes to the casino to celebrate birthdays, or they will comment on playing games on their tablet or smartphone.

Gambling Treatment and Treatment Referrals

In practice settings, social workers can effectively screen and provide feedback and education about gambling with little training. Gambling disorders often exist with other co-occurring disorders, so social workers need to know about at-risk and problematic gambling. Physical health, mental health, and substance use all represent opportunities to treat the whole person with effective screening and brief interventions. During the evaluation, regardless of setting, the following are key indicators to also explore gambling behavior and activities: risk for suicide; possible mental health issues of depression, anxiety, or impulsivity; physical injuries such as traumatic brain injury; emotional injuries such as trauma and sexual abuse; and early age of tobacco and cannabis use. Social workers need to incorporate gambling-related screens and questions in all intake evaluations.

Given the complex nature of problem and disordered gambling, there is a clear need to consider gamblers as a heterogeneous population (Ladouceur et al., 2001) and develop ways for clinicians to target the causes of their clients' gambling addiction. Blaszcynski and Nower's (2002) pathways model provides a synthesis between biological, psychological, sociocultural, and spiritual determinants of problem gambling (Milosevic & Ledgerwood, 2010) and also provides a way for social workers to consider characteristics and emotional and biological vulnerabilities as a way to develop a gambler profile, while taking a whole person approach during treatment (Valleur et al., 2016). Three pathways are conceptualized and categorized across one of three subtypes. Behaviorally conditioned gamblers develop a problem given the known residuals of operant and classical conditioning, such as habituation, chasing losses (or wins), etc. Psychologically vulnerable gamblers are similar in that they too are impacted by the same behavioral conditioning factors as the first subgroup, while also experiencing emotional vulnerabilities toward mental health disorders (anxiety, mood disorders, etc.). Finally, antisocial and impulsive gamblers are impacted by the behavioral conditioning, psychological vulnerabilities, as well as vulnerabilities toward impulsivity, antisocial personality, and attention deficit (Blaszcynski & Nower, 2002).

When providing education about gambling, social workers can employ active and/or passive education and awareness stances. Active stance takes the approach of having direct conversations with clients about gambling, using gambling screens, and providing specific and targeted education about warning signs and at-risk behaviors of gambling activities. In passive stance, social workers can passively educate people about gambling, warning signs, and where to seek help, without having a direct conversation or discussion about it.

Active Stance

Social workers can provide psychoeducation to clients when they endorse gambling activities, whether at-risk or problematic. This education can be delivered in a conversation style with a person-in-environment perspective. Social workers can start by discussing the definition of gambling and how playing the stock market is an example. Then, they can ask clients to talk more about their preferred gambling activities whether they are games of chance or games of skill. Discussing the 10 Rules of Responsible Gambling is very useful and encourages clients to gamble safely when choosing to gamble. The discussion can then easily move to understanding the warning signs or when gambling is becoming problematic.

Passive Stance

This approach is modeled after the domestic violence/intimate partner violence awareness approaches that suggest placing information on the back of bathroom stalls in public places or including information in packets that everyone receives. Having handouts, brochures, and information sheets in the waiting room, offices, and incorporated into any therapy-related materials will make it easier for clients to passively learn more about problem gambling without having to admit to having a problem first. In substance use settings, adding examples of gambling to all discussions, materials, videos, and other handouts will help clients learn more about it and also reduce potential risk of switching from one addiction to another in early recovery. Also, offering to hold Gamblers Anonymous meetings in addition to the already scheduled Alcoholics Anonymous and Narcotics Anonymous meetings will increase knowledge about the similarities with substance use disorders. In primary care settings, patients should be asked whether they have had mental health or substance use treatment in the past. If they have, they should be provided education about the warning signs of problematic gambling along with a 10 Rules of Responsible Gambling handout.

A combination of both active and passive messaging about gambling is useful when people are engaging in any type of gambling activity. For example, the senior retirement center organizes a bus trip for its seniors to go to the local casino. By giving everyone a handout about the rules of responsible gambling as they get on the bus, social workers are actively providing education. On the back side of the handout, the warning signs about problematic gambling and the helpline provide a passive approach to educating without having a direct conversation.

Advancing the Field to Include a Focus on Problem Gambling

University Training

With the rapid expansion of gambling access and opportunity, we expect the field of social work to advocate for the need to include problematic and disordered gambling in social work curricula, particularly within schools and programs that emphasize substance abuse training and concentration coursework. Currently, Rutgers University is the only university in the United States that has a gambling center (founded in 2007) within its school of social work. Interestingly, Engel et al. (2012) examined whether gambling disorder was included in graduate curricula at 86 schools of social work. Sixty-one percent of accredited Master of Social Work (MSW) programs did not include gambling-related content in their curricula, whereas 38% reported having gambling-related content in the MSW curricula. The schools with gambling-related content were located in states with casino gambling (28 total, representing 93%). With gambling now online and internet-based, all social work programs need to include gambling in their curriculum to keep pace with the normalization of gambling in society.

Postgraduate Training and Gambling-Specific Certification

Although gambling disorder is a behavioral health condition, the treatment of this disorder may not be within the scope of practice for licensed clinical social workers and other licensed mental health professionals without additional education and training. In the National Association of Social Workers (NASW) Code of Ethics (2017), the value of competence and the ethical principle, "Social workers practice within their areas of competence and develop and enhance their professional expertise," requires social workers to practice within their scope of training and education. It is recommended that social workers conduct routine screenings, regardless of practice, and then refer to a qualified social worker. The Association of Problem Gambling Service Administrators has developed and maintains a list of approved problem gambling programs and/or certified providers by state and may often provide access to problem gambling treatment funding to qualified providers.

NASW has advanced practice specialty certifications for addictions, gerontology, clinical, case management, health care, military, and youth and family (NASW, n.d.). The National Association for Alcoholism and Drug Abuse Counselors has several types of certifications for all levels of education (https://www.naadac.org/types-eligibility). However, none of these certifications include gambling disorders. As such, the International Gambling Counselor Certification Board was established to provide voluntary certifications to ensure a body of qualified professionals in the field of clinical treatment for individuals and their families impacted by at-risk, problematic, and disordered gambling (https://www.igccb.org). There are several levels of certification, and each requires specific hours of training, direct contact hours, passing an examination, and consultation oversight by a board-approved clinical consultant. All certifications can take more than a year to obtain, which is expected for a certification that demonstrates expertise.

Conclusion

Social workers at all education levels and in all practice settings are equipped to screen and advocate for problem gambling awareness, but there is an ever-growing need within the discipline to increase the workforce of qualified social workers ready to assist problem gamblers. Quality gambling training and even hierarchical certifications can and should become more widely available for both incoming social work students and those currently in practice. With the ever-expansive gambling opportunities, access, and availability, the social worker profession will continue to be in a position to effectively screen, intervene, and/or refer for gambling-specific treatment.

Helpful Resources

Association of Problem Gambling Service Administrators: http://www.apgsa.org
Gam-Anon: http://www.gam-anon.org
Gambler Anonymous: http://www.gamblersanonymous.org

International Gambling Counselor Certification Board: http://www.igccb.org

National Council on Problem Gambling: http://www.ncpgambling.org

References

Alegria, A. A., Petry, N. M., Hasin, D. S., Liu, S. M., Grant, B. F., & Blanco, C. (2009). Disordered gambling among racial and ethnic groups in the US: Results from the National Epidemiologic Survey on Alcohol and Related Conditions. *CNS Spectrums, 14*(3), 132–142.

American Psychiatric Association. (2013). *Diagnostic and statistical manual of mental disorders* (5th ed.). https://doi.org/10.1176/appi.books.9780890425596

Ariyabuddhiphongs, V. (2012). Older adults and gambling: A review. *International Journal of Mental Health and Addiction, 10*(2), 297–308.

Barrault, S., & Varescon, I. (2013). Cognitive distortions, anxiety, and depression among regular and pathological gambling online poker players. *Cyberpsychology, Behavior, and Social Networking, 16*(3), 183–188. doi:10.1089/cyber.2012.0150

Bechtold, J., & Wilson, A. N. (2021). *The gambling disorder treatment handbook*. Kingsley.

Blaszczynski, A., & Nower, L. (2002). A pathways model of problem and pathological gambling. *Addiction, 97*(5), 487–499.

Calado, F., Alexandre, J., & Griffiths, M. D. (2017). Prevalence of adolescent problem gambling: A systematic review of recent research. *Journal of Gambling Studies, 33*(2), 397–424.

Calado, F., & Griffiths, M. D. (2016). Problem gambling worldwide: An update and systematic review of empirical research (2000–2015). *Journal of Behavioral Addictions, 5*(4), 592–613.

Caler, K. R., Garcia, J. R. V., & Nower, L. (2017). Problem gambling among ethnic minorities: Results from an epidemiological study. *Asian Journal of Gambling Issues and Public Health, 7*(1), 7.

Cowlishaw, S., Merkouris, S., Chapman, A., & Radermacher, H. (2014). Pathological and problem gambling in substance use treatment: A systematic review and meta-analysis. *Journal of Substance Abuse Treatment, 46*(2), 98–105.

Ellenbogen, S., Gupta, R., & Derevensky, J. L. (2007). A cross-cultural study of gambling behaviour among adolescents. *Journal of Gambling Studies, 23*(1), 25–39.

Engel, R. J., Bechtold, J., Kim, Y., & Mulvaney, E. (2012). Beating the odds: Preparing graduates to address gambling-related problems. *Journal of Social Work Education, 48*, 321–335.

Etuk, R., Shirk, S. D., Grubbs, J., & Kraus, S. W. (2020). Gambling problems in US military veterans. *Current Addiction Reports, 7*, 210–228.

Gallaway, M. S., Fink, D. S., Sampson, L., Cohen, G. H., Tamburrino, M., Liberzon, I., Calabrese, J., & Galea, S. (2019). Prevalence and covariates of problematic gambling among a US military cohort. *Addictive Behaviors, 95*, 166–171.

Gamblers Anonymous. (2000). *GA: A new beginning*. Gamblers Anonymous International Service Office.

Gebauer, L., LaBrie, R., & Shaffer, H. J. (2010). Optimizing DSM-IV-TR classification accuracy: A brief biosocial screen for detecting current gambling disorders among gamblers in the general household population. *Canadian Journal of Psychiatry, 55*(2), 82–90.

Gupta, R., & Derevensky, J. L. (2000). Adolescents with gambling problems: From research to treatment. *Journal of Gambling Studies, 16*, 315–342.

Hing, N., Russell, A., Tolchard, B., & Nower, L. (2016). Risk factors for gambling problems: An analysis by gender. *Journal of Gambling Studies, 32*, 511–534. doi:10.1007/s10899-015-9548-8

Johnson, E. E., Hamer, R., Nora, R. M., Tan, B., Eistenstein, N., & Englehart, C. (1988). The Lie/Bet Questionnaire for screening pathological gamblers. *Psychological Reports, 80*, 83–88.

Karlsson, A., & Håkansson, A. (2018). Gambling disorder, increased mortality, suicidality, and associated comorbidity: A longitudinal nationwide register study. *Journal of Behavioral Addictions, 7*(4), 1091–1099. doi:10.1556/2006.7.2018.112

Kessler, R. C., Hwang, I., Labrie, R., Petukhova, M., Sampson, N. A., Winters, K. C., & Shaffer, H. J. (2008). DSM-IV pathological gambling in the National Comorbidity Survey Replication. *Psychological Medicine, 38*(9), 1351–1360.

Ladouceur, R., Gosselin, P., Laberge, M., & Blaszczynski, A. (2001). Dropouts in clinical research: Do results reported in the field of addiction reflect clinical reality? *The Behavior Therapist, 24*, 44–46.

Lister, J. J., Milosevic, A., & Ledgerwood, D. M. (2015). Psychological characteristics of problem gamblers with and without mood disorder. *Canadian Journal of Psychiatry, 60*(8), 369–376. doi:10.1177/070674371506000806

Market.US. (2019). Social media statistics and facts. https://market.us/statistics/social-media

Marshall, G. N., Elliott, M. N., & Schell, T. L. (2009). Prevalence and correlates of lifetime disordered gambling in Cambodian refugees residing in Long Beach, CA. *Journal of Immigrant and Minority Health, 11*(1), 35–40.

Milosevic, A., & Ledgerwood, D. M. (2010). The subtyping of pathological gambling: A comprehensive review. *Clinical Psychology Review, 30*(8), 988–998.

Molinaro, S., Canale, N., Vieno, A., Lenzi, M., Siciliano, V., Gori, M., & Santinello, M. (2014). Country-and individual-level determinants of probable problematic gambling in adolescence: A multi-level cross-national comparison. *Addiction, 109*(12), 2089–2097.

National Association of Social Workers. (2017). *Code of ethics.* https://www.socialworkers.org/about/ethics/code-of-ethics

National Association of Social Workers. (n.d.). *Apply for NASW social work credentials.* https://www.socialworkers.org/Careers/Credentials-Certifications/Apply-for-NASW-Social-Work-Credentials

Parry, W. (2020, January 15). Internet, sports bets spur AC to $3.3B take. Newark Star-Ledger, A15.

Petry, N. M. (2005). *Pathological gambling: Etiology, comorbidity, and treatment* (Vol. 2). Washington, DC: American Psychological Association.

Petry, N. M., Armentano, C., Kuoch, T., Norinth, T., & Smith, L. (2003). Gambling participation and problems among South East Asian refugees to the United States. *Psychiatric Services, 54*(8), 1142–1148.

Potenza, M. R. (2007). Impulsivity and compulsivity in pathological gambling and obsessive–compulsive disorder. *Revista Brasileira de Psiquiatrai, 29,* 105–106.

Potenza, M. R. (2008). The neurobiology of pathological gambling and drug addiction: An overview and new findings. *Philosophical Transactions: Biological Sciences, 363*(1507), 3181–3189.

Rovell, D. (2020, March 18). *Sin city shutdown: What happens in Vegas when the casinos are forced to close their doors.* Retrieved June 4, 2020, from https://www.actionnetwork.com/news/las-vegas-casinos-sportsbook-shutdown-coronavirus-darren-rovell

Stoletenberg, S., Batien, B., & Birgenheir, D. (2007). Does gender moderate associations among impulsivity and health-risk behaviors? *Addictive Behaviors, 33,* 252–265.

U.S. Food and Drug Administration. (2016, June 7). *FDA drug safety communication: FDA warns about new impulse-control problems associated with mental health drug aripiprazole (Abilify, Abilify Maintena, Aristada).* Retrieved June 4, 2020, from https://www.fda.gov/drugs/drug-safety-and-availability/fda-drug-safety-communication-fda-warns-about-new-impulse-control-problems-associated-mental-health#:~:text=The%20U.S.%20Food%20and%20Drug,%2C%20Aristada%2C%20and%20generics

Valleur, M., Codina, I., Vénisse, J. L., Romo, L., Magalon, D., Fatséas, M., Chéreau-Boudet, I., Gorsane, M. A., Guilleux, A., Groupe, J. E. U., Grall-Bronnec, M., & Challet-Bouju, G. (2016). Towards a validation of the three pathways model of pathological gambling. *Journal of Gambling Studies, 32*(2), 757–771.

Volberg, R., Gupta, R., Griffiths, M. D., Olason, D., & Delfabbro, P. H. (2010). An international perspective on youth gambling prevalence studies. *International Journal of Adolescent Medicine and Health, 22,* 3–38.

Williams, R. J., Volberg, R. A., & Stevens, R. M. (2012). *The population prevalence of problem gambling: Methodological influences, standardized rates, jurisdictional differences, and worldwide trends.* Ontario Problem Gambling Research Centre.

Identification, Screening, and Referral for Gaming Disorder

Stephanie Diez and Jody Bechtold

Playing video games, also known as computer games or electronic games, is a nearly universal behavior among adults and youth. Due to internet advancements and related technologies that have contributed to new platforms for video game playing, the prevalence of this behavior continues to increase (Lenhart, 2015; Pew Research Institute, 2018). Previous research has demonstrated that youth may be particularly susceptible to spending increasing amounts of time playing video games. The Kaiser Family Foundation found that more than 90% of U.S. youth play video games and report spending extensive amounts of time video gaming (Gentile et al., 2017). Video gaming is a behavior that has been seen in 54% of males and 46% females (Entertainment Software Association, 2019). In addition, 83% of U.S. adolescent females and 96% of U.S. adolescent males report they play video games regularly (Pew Research Institute, 2018). Historically, research indicates that prolonged and extensive video game playing can cultivate compulsive and/or addictive behavior for some individuals (Shek & Yu, 2012). Thus, further research has been conducted on problematic

video game playing and the implications on biopsychosocial factors among youth and adults.

As video games continue to evolve and play a pivotal role in the lives of youth, it is imperative to detect potential problematic behaviors early to reduce the risk of addiction. Similar to substance-related and addictive disorders, one of the first warning signs of internet gaming disorder (IGD) is isolation from family and social events (Young, 2009). Associated negative consequences of IGD include mood changes, irritability, anger, depression, anxiety, suicide risk, sleep disturbances, financial issues, social isolation, psychosocial conflict, and academic issues. Across different samples and approaches to measurement, between 3% and 10% of adolescents are impacted by signs and symptoms of IGD that parallel those experienced by people with substance-related and addictive disorders (Griffiths, Kuss, et al., 2016a). These signs and symptoms include dimensions of preoccupation, tolerance, withdrawal, loss of control, and negative psychosocial consequences (Festl et al., 2013; Griffiths et al., 2016b).

Video gaming, online gaming, gaming, computer gaming, and electronic gaming are interchangeable terms used to describe playing video games. Nowadays, video games are rarely a solo experience. Most video gaming is played with multiple players, in person and/or virtually, from immediate friends and family to people throughout the world. When immersed in online video games, the user is in a globally connected environment in which cooperation with other players is essential to achieve advancement. This often leads to video gamers having collaborative experiences with other players, whom they may not have met in person, and forming a social support system of online friends to achieve their collective goal of advancement in a game. Accordingly, one of the cultural components of online gaming is that often a virtual social environment is developed that is part of the immersive experience and may reinforce video gaming behaviors.

Internet gaming disorder is also referred to as gaming or internet use disorder, gaming or internet addiction, gaming or internet dependence, pathological or problematic video gaming, and anecdotally as video game addiction. IGD first appeared in the fifth edition of the *Diagnostic and Statistical Manual of Mental Disorders* (DSM-5) in Section III, "Conditions for Further Study" appendix [American Psychiatric Association (APA), 2013]. The APA has proposed criteria for the condition of IGD; however, by placing IGD in Section III of the DSM-5, the APA is acknowledging IGD and stating that further research is needed before IGD can be categorized as a formal disorder.

Current State of the Disorder

The study of IGD has grown rapidly since 2013, when IGD was included in the appendix of the DSM-5 (Torres-Rodriguez et al., 2019).

Thus far, much of the research includes examining the validity of screening tools, treatment approaches, pharmacotherapy, co-occurring disorders, prevention education, implications, and at-risk groups. Despite its name, online video games are not exclusively a criterion for IGD (Gentile et al., 2017). The DSM-5 states that video game playing must produce clinically significant impairment in an individual's life (APA, 2013). Problematic use can occur offline and online, although most excessive and problematic video gaming is often online. Research found that online video games have a higher addictive potential than offline games in part because online video games are constructed with a reward-based systems approach that reinforces game playing (Kuss & Griffiths, 2012). Yet, research has found that playing video games online may not be an indicator of problematic video gaming behaviors because immersive video games played offline also pose a potential for IGD (Griffiths, Kuss, et al., 2016; Lemmens & Hendriks, 2016). Due to the ubiquitous nature of the internet, most video games include an online component and generally tend to be more immersive, intensive, and time-consuming. It is worth noting the lack of consensus and ongoing discussion among scientists regarding a universal definition of IGD and its relation to problematic internet use (Kuss et al., 2017). Problematic internet use (PIU), also termed internet use disorder or internet addiction, refers to general problematic or addictive use of the internet and is not limited to video gaming. Historically, PIU and similar terminology were used interchangeably for IGD prior to the DSM-5's inclusion of IGD in 2013. Nevertheless, PIU and IGD are dissimilar concepts, and as such the psychometric properties and measures used to quantify and assess these behaviors should be different. Accordingly, identifying, screening, and assessing for IGD is a process that requires extensive understanding of the current and historical contexts of this disorder.

The DSM-5 criteria suggestions for IGD include (1) preoccupation with games; (2) withdrawal symptoms; (3) tolerance; (4) unsuccessful attempts to control or reduce participation; (5) loss of interest in real-life relationships; (6) continued excessive use despite problems; (7) deceiving family, therapist, or others regarding amount of gaming; (8) use of games to escape or relieve a negative mood; and (9) jeopardized or lost significant relationship, job, or educational opportunity (APA, 2013). The APA proposes that individuals must meet five or more of the nine criteria within a 12-month period for this diagnosis (APA, 2013). Other diagnostic features of IGD include (1) a pattern of excessive and prolonged internet gaming that results in a cluster of cognitive and behavioral symptoms and (2) continued behavior despite negative consequences. The essential feature of IGD is persistent and recurrent excessive participation in video gaming (APA, 2013). Behaviors that are currently excluded from the IGD diagnosis include excessive use of social media, online pornography, and excessive internet use without gaming. As we continue to see a convergence with gaming, gambling, and internet use, research will need to determine whether separate diagnosis or modified diagnosis is superlative.

In 2018, gaming disorder (GD) received official recognition as a mental condition in the 11th revision of the *International Classification of Diseases* (ICD-11) (World Health Organization, 2020). This recognition generated concern that this inclusion would pathologize highly involved albeit not problematic gamers (Billieux et al., 2019). Gaming disorder is characterized by a pattern of persistent or recurrent gaming behavior (i.e., "digital gaming" or "video-gaming"), which may be online or offline, manifested by (1) impaired control over gaming (e.g., onset, frequency, intensity, duration, termination, and context); (2) increasing priority given to gaming to the extent that gaming takes precedence over other life interests and daily activities; and (3) continuation or escalation of gaming despite negative consequences. In addition, GD is a behavioral pattern of sufficient severity resulting in impairment of personal, family, social, educational, occupational, or other important areas of biopsychosocial functioning.

Prevalence of Internet Gaming Disorder

The DSM-5 provided very little prevalence data and reported that prevalence is unclear due to varying questionnaires, criteria, and assessment thresholds (APA, 2013). The prevalence rates of IGD reported in representative samples in the United States have ranged from approximately 1% to 8% (Gentile et al., 2017). Internationally, the prevalence rates of IGD using national samples vary drastically by country and region, and rates tend to be higher for males than females and higher for youth than adults. For example, with German adolescents, the prevalence is reported at 1.2% (Rehbein et al., 2015); among Dutch adolescents, it is 5.5%, with a rate of 5.4% for Dutch adults (Lemmens et al., 2015); the prevalence rate is 4.3% among Hungarian adolescents (Király et al., 2014); and there is a combined prevalence rate of 1.6% among European adolescents from seven varying countries (Müller et al., 2015). The discrepancy in prevalence rates is mainly due to the reliance on nonrepresentative samples, varying assessment, and conceptual heterogeneity (Kircaburun et al., 2020). Previous research reports that the discrepancy in prevalence of IGD found in different studies is partly due to diverse measurements (i.e., different measurements used to quantify IGD) and their usage among different cultures and samples (Kuss, 2013). These diverse measurements examine dissimilar constructs (i.e., computer dependency, internet gaming dependence, problematic video gaming, and excessive video gaming) and have also been used with different cultures and samples (e.g., children, adolescents, and video gamers). Culture is an essential component to consider because higher prevalence of video gaming has been reported in East-Asian countries, where there is a higher societal acceptance for video gaming and internet access compared to many Western countries (King et al., 2013). However, Kuss (2013) suggests that a lack of acceptance for video gaming may lead to more distress and stigmatization of the behavior, which in turn might increase problematic video gaming behaviors because youth may engage in video gaming to cope with stress.

Screening and Diagnostic Evaluation

Numerous screening tools have been developed in recent years for IGD and related heterogeneous concepts. King et al. (2020) conducted an extensive review of 32 measures from empirical studies and reported the measures where not optimal. Of the 32 measures reviewed, each measure was methodically scored based on inclusion of dimensions and items aligning with the DSM-5 criteria, the ICD-11 criteria, and the shared criteria of a behavioral pattern of sufficient severity resulting in impairment with the individual's life (King et al., 2020). Results from this scientific review found the following measures fulfilled most scoring criteria: Game Addiction Scale–7, Internet Gaming Disorder Scale–Short-Form (IGDS9-SF), Ten-Item Internet Gaming Disorder Test (IGDT-10), Young Diagnostic Questionnaire, and Internet Gaming Disorder Scale–9. The IGDS9-SF and IGDT-10 were the only tools that provided total coverage of the DSM-5 and ICD-11 criteria (King et al., 2020; Király et al., 2017; Pontes et al., 2017). It is recommended that a standard international tool would best advance the IGD field and enable more

consistent estimates of prevalence across countries (King et al., 2020). Due to past and ongoing international debate for assessment and conceptualization of IGD, a universal measure for screening and diagnosis of IGD would best support clinical practices.

In conducting thorough screening and evaluation, social workers are trained to consider possible co-occurring disorders. Thus, it is essential to consider all possible associations and correlations between signs and symptoms across two or more mental health disorders. As social workers, we are taught to utilize various theories and frameworks, such as a person-in-environment perspective, when assessing clients. The person-in-environment perspective is that an individual and their behavior cannot be understood adequately without consideration of various facets and systems of the individual's environment (e.g., social, political, familial, temporal, spiritual, economic, and physical). Therefore, social workers and clinicians should consider contributing, co-occurring, or correlating factors when screening for IGD.

Research that examines the relationship between GD and symptoms of other psychiatric disorders is needed to identify co-occurring tools for screening. Andreassen et al. (2017) evaluated the relationship between addictive use of video games and mental health disorders and concluded that symptoms of attention-deficit/hyperactivity disorder (ADHD), obsessive–compulsive disorder, anxiety, and depression need to be thoroughly assessed because these symptoms are found within IGD treatment. Nakayama et al. (2017) researched treatment and risk factors of internet use disorders and determined that being male, suffering from ADHD, and exhibiting deteriorating psychiatric symptoms can impact the severity of the disorder. Previous studies found IGD is associated with depression, anxiety, autism spectrum disorder, ADHD, and conduct disorders (Torres-Rodriquez et al., 2019). Therefore, to adequately provide best clinical practices when screening and diagnosing IGD, knowledge of the relationship between IGD and the pathology of the aforementioned mental health disorders is needed.

Treatment Issues

Treatment approaches for IGD have largely been adopted from substance-related addiction treatment models (King & Delfabbro, 2020). Reviews of literature regarding effective treatment approaches indicate most studies utilize similar scientific design, with very few including a randomized or well-controlled study design for IGD. There is a need for robust and reliable evidence-based treatment approaches because internationally many clinicians and agencies are already providing IGD treatment (Przybylski et al., 2017). Approaches that have been studied and applied include cognitive–behavioral therapy (CBT); family therapy; and motivational interviewing, which is also applied in conjunction with CBT. King and Delfabbro (2020) determined that there are two crucial components of effective treatment: (1) strategies that modify the client's maladaptive beliefs about gaming behavior and (2) techniques that aid in reducing psychological and physical symptoms of withdrawal and other unpleasant feelings, emotions, and moods that occur when not gaming. Billieux et al. (2020) classified cognitive factors that should be considered when treating IGD into two categories: cognitive deficits and cognitive biases. Impaired decision-making, executive functioning impairments, and deliberative processes are cognitive deficits. Attentional biases, cognitive distortions, and dysfunctional cognitions are cognitive biases. In addition, there are particular cognitive factors that may be directly associated with IGD. Some of these potential cognitions include beliefs about game reward value and tangibility, maladaptive and inflexible rules about gaming, need for gaming to increase self-esteem, and gaming for

gaining social acceptance (King & Delfabbro, 2014). For decreasing the frequency, duration, and intensity of video game playing, using harm reduction strategies is a public health approach to viewing gaming as a normalized behavior and helping individuals engage in gaming activities that reduce harm and promote moderation.

The merging of video gaming and gambling-related cognitions also affects treatment considerations. *Gamblification* is a term used to describe the convergence between gambling and video gaming (King et al., 2010; Lopez-Gonzalez & Griffiths, 2016; Macey & Hamari, 2018). Although gambling is often a chance-based activity and video gaming may be considered a more skill-based activity, there are several components of video gaming that apply a chance-based system within the game playing. Gamblification is often found in e-sports (Gainsbury et al., 2017), virtual items and currencies (e.g., loot boxes; Hamari & Keronen, 2017; Lehdonvirta, 2009), and free-to-play games (Gainsbury et al., 2017). Due to the direct psychosocial impact gamblification components can have on individuals, and the mezzo and macro implications related to gambling restrictions and legalities with minors, the moral, ethical, and legal status of gamblification products and services are highly debated and vary internationally (Griffiths et al., 2017).

As discussed throughout this chapter, there are multiple facets associated with gaming disorder that must be considered when identifying IGD. These considerations, among others, add to the complexity and competence of properly diagnosing and treating an individual with IGD. Therefore, making referrals to appropriate treatment resources is crucial for gaming disorder. As is often seen with treating addictions, there are multiple possible approaches, including self-help models; peer recovery support; and clinically specialized assessment, diagnosis, and treatment. Founded in the United States, Reboot and Recover is a nonprofit organization that specializes in clinical assessment, treatment, and prevention of IGD (https://www.rebootandrecover.org). This organization can serve as a referral for clinical expertise, assessment, diagnosis, treatment, education, and prevention for children and families regarding gaming disorder and related problematic technology use (e.g., problematic internet use, problematic social media use, and co-occurring disorders). Online Gamers Anonymous (OLGA) is a community-based support group that offers group meetings both in a face-to-face setting and online for IGD (https://www.olganon.org). OLGA is structured with the Alcoholics Anonymous (AA) 12-step model, meaning it is part of a mutual-help organization whose aim is to assist those suffering from addiction. At the core of the program are the 12 steps (Anon, 1939/1985), which discuss aspects of the individual's psychological and spiritual orientation to life (Anon, 1952). In addition to OLGA, which focuses on the individual who is experiencing problematic video gaming, OLG-Anon is a community-based support group providing information and shared experiences from friends, family, and loved ones of those with a gaming disorder. Another community resource is self-help via peer support that is offered through Game Quitters (https://gamequitters.com). The founder of the organization is an individual who identifies as being in recovery from IGD.

Because this chapter serves as a reference for IGD, the aforementioned resources are not all encompassing of nationally and internationally available resources. With additional training, social workers can gain knowledge and understanding for working with IGD. As defined by the National Association of Social Workers' Code of Ethics (2017), social workers practice in accordance with professional values and ethics, including developing competence to enhance their professional expertise when treating clients. As such, training is available to cultivate clinical knowledge and expertise in gaming disorder via the International Gaming Disorder Certificate. This training focuses on utilizing evidence-based approaches and best practices for addressing IGD with clients. More information on this certificate can be found via the International Gambling Counselor Certification Board website (https://www.igccb.org/igdc-certification).

Future Recommendations

Given this disorder is relatively new, there is a dearth of research and evidence-based approaches. Hence, it is important for social workers as clinicians and mental health providers to view themselves as "first responders" for many children, adolescents, and young adults who are immersed in increasing amounts of digital media use. School counselors and child, youth, and family workers should inquire about digital use and assess for co-occurring disorders, including depression, anxiety, and ADHD. Exploring hobbies and how to cope with boredom or unpleasant feelings, emotions, or moods as additional screening and assessment strategies can uncover potential at-risk and problematic gaming behaviors. Social workers should consider how to provide education for parents and guardians about the potential risks and effects of excessive video gaming as well as behavior modification strategies for rewards and punishments that are age appropriate.

Social workers have a duty to advocate at the micro, mezzo, and macro levels. When we think of IGD as an addiction, it does not currently have representation with the Substance Abuse and Mental Health Services Administration (SAMHSA) for education, prevention, and treatment. There is no federal oversight for IGD with SAMHSA or the

National Institute of Mental Health; thus, we are missing opportunities to enhance research efforts, inform best treatment practices, and determine insurance reimbursement. Social workers in the education system have an opportunity to include at-risk and problematic gaming behaviors in their current programs that educate about substance use, sexual health, and gambling. As with other potentially addictive behaviors, poor school performance, truancy, and alcohol and cannabis use are indicators that screening, assessment, and referral for treatment should be conducted. Because schools are requiring increased use of the internet both in and out of class for educational purposes, they should also be providing education about warning signs and symptoms of gaming disorder to students and their families in an effort to prevent and reduce IGD among youth.

Helpful Resources

Game Quitters: https://gamequitters.com
International Gambling Counselor Certification Board. International Gaming Disorder Certificate: https://www.igccb.org/igdc-certification
Internet Gaming Disorder Scale–Short-Form (IGDS9-SF): https://www.halleypontes.com/igds9sf
Online Gamers Anonymous: https://www.olganon.org
Reboot & Recover: https://www.rebootandrecover.org
Ten-Item Internet Gaming Disorder Test (IGDT-10):https://pubmed.ncbi.nlm.nih.gov/30589307

References

American Psychiatric Association. (2013). *Diagnostic and statistical manual of mental disorders* (5th ed.).
Andreassen, C. S., Pallesen, S., & Griffiths, M. D. (2017). The relationship between addictive use of social media, narcissism, and self-esteem: Findings from a large national survey. *Addictive behaviors, 64*, 287–293.
Anon. (1952). *The twelve steps and twelve traditions.* Alcoholics Anonymous/World Services.
Anon. (1985). *Alcoholics Anonymous—The story of how many thousands of men and women have recovered from alcoholism.* Alcoholics Anonymous/World Services. (Original work published 1939)
Billieux, J., Flayelle, M., Rumpf, H. J., & Stein, D. J. (2019). High involvement versus pathological involvement in video games: A crucial distinction for ensuring the validity and utility of gaming disorder. *Current Addiction Reports, 6*(3), 323–330.
Billieux, J., Potenza, M. N., Maurage, P., Brevers, D., Brand, M., & King, D. L. (2020). Cognitive factors associated with gaming disorder. In A. Verdejo-Garcia (Ed.), *Cognition and addiction* (pp. 221–230). Academic Press.
Entertainment Software Association. (2019). 2019 Essential facts about the computer and video game industry. https://www.theesa.com/wp-content/uploads/2019/05/2019-Essential-Facts-About-the-Computer-and-Video-Game-Industry.pdf#:~:text=The%20Entertainment%20Software%20Association%20%28ESA%29%20released%202019%20Essential,about%20their%20video%20game%20playing%20habits%20and%20attitudes
Festl, R., Scharkow, M., & Quandt, T. (2013). Problematic computer game use among adolescents, younger and older adults. *Addiction, 108*(3), 592–599.
Gainsbury, S. M., Abarbanel, B., & Blaszczynski, A. (2017). Intensity and gambling harms: Exploring breadth of gambling involvement among esports bettors. *Gaming Law Review, 21*(8), 610–615.
Gentile, D. A., Bailey, K., Bavelier, D., Brockmyer, J. F., Cash, H., Coyne, S. M., Doan, A., Grant, D. S., Green, C. S., Griffiths, M., Markle, T., Petry, N. M., Prot, S., Rae, C. D., Rehbein, F., Rich, M., Sullivan, D., Woolley, E., & Young, K. (2017). Internet gaming disorder in children and adolescents. *Pediatrics, 140*(Suppl. 2), S81–S85.
Griffiths, M. D., Kuss, D. J., Lopez-Fernandez, O., & Pontes, H. M. (2017). Problematic gaming exists and is an example of disordered gaming: Commentary on: Scholars' open debate paper on the World Health Organization ICD-11 Gaming Disorder proposal (Aarseth et al.). *Journal of Behavioral Addictions, 6*(3), 296–301.
Griffiths, M. D., Kuss, D. J., & Pontes, H. M. (2016a). A brief overview of internet gaming disorder and its treatment. *Australian Clinical Psychologist, 2*(1), 20108.
Griffiths, M. D., Van Rooij, A. J., Kardefelt-Winther, D., Starcevic, V., Király, O., Pallesen, S., Muller, K, Dreier, M., Carras, M., Prause, N., King, D. L., Aboujaoude, E., Kruss, D. J., Pontes, H. M., Fernandez, O. L., Nagygyorgy, K., Achab, S., Billieux, J., Quandt, T., Carbonell, X., . . . Demetrovics, Z. (2016b). Working towards an international consensus on criteria for assessing internet gaming

disorder: A critical commentary on Petry et al. (2014). *Addiction (Abingdon, England), 111*(1), 167.

Hamari, J., & Keronen, L. (2017). Why do people buy virtual goods: A meta-analysis. *Computers in Human Behavior, 71,* 59–69.

King, D. L., Chamberlain, S. R., Carragher, N., Billieux, J., Stein, D., Mueller, K., Potenza, M. N., Juergen, R., Saunders, J., Starcevic, V., Demetrovics, Z., Brand, M., Lee, H. K., Spader, M., Lemenager, T., Pallesen, S., Achab, S., Kyrios, M., Higuchi, S., . . . Delfabbro, P. H. (2020). Screening and assessment tools for gaming disorder: A comprehensive systematic review. *Clinical Psychology Review, 77,* 101831.

King, D. L., & Delfabbro, P. H. (2014). The cognitive psychology of internet gaming disorder. *Clinical Psychology Review, 34*(4), 298–308.

King, D. L., & Delfabbro, P. H. (2020). Video game addiction. In C. Essau & P. Delfabbro (Eds.), *Adolescent Addiction* (pp. 185–213). Academic Press.

King, D. L., Delfabbro, P., & Griffiths, M. (2010). The convergence of gambling and digital media: Implications for gambling in young people. *Journal of Gambling Studies, 26*(2), 175–187.

King, D. L., Delfabbro, P. H., & Griffiths, M. D. (2013). Trajectories of problem video gaming among adult regular gamers: An 18-month longitudinal study. *Cyberpsychology, Behavior, and Social Networking, 16*(1), 72–76.

Király, O., Griffiths, M. D., Urbán, R., Farkas, J., Kökönyei, G., Elekes, Z., Tamas, D., & Demetrovics, Z. (2014). Problematic internet use and problematic online gaming are not the same: Findings from a large nationally representative adolescent sample. *Cyberpsychology, Behavior, and Social Networking, 17*(12), 749–754.

Király, O., Sleczka, P., Pontes, H. M., Urbán, R., Griffiths, M. D., & Demetrovics, Z. (2017). Validation of the Ten-Item Internet Gaming Disorder Test (IGDT-10) and evaluation of the nine DSM-5 internet gaming disorder criteria. *Addictive Behaviors, 64,* 253–260.

Kircaburun, K., Pontes, H. M., Stavropoulos, V., & Griffiths, M. D. (2020). A brief psychological overview of disordered gaming. *Current Opinion in Psychology, 36,* 38–43.

Kuss, D. J. (2013). Internet gaming addiction: Current perspectives. *Psychology Research and Behavior Management, 6,* 125.

Kuss, D. J., & Griffiths, M. D. (2012). Internet gaming addiction: A systematic review of empirical research. *International Journal of Mental Health and Addiction, 10*(2), 278–296.

Kuss, D. J., Griffiths, M. D., & Pontes, H. M. (2017). Chaos and confusion in DSM-5 diagnosis of internet gaming disorder: Issues, concerns, and recommendations for clarity in the field. *Journal of Behavioral Addictions, 6*(2), 103–109.

Lemmens, J. S., & Hendriks, S. J. (2016). Addictive online games: Examining the relationship between game genres and internet gaming disorder. *Cyberpsychology, Behavior, and Social Networking, 19*(4), 270–276.

Lemmens, J. S., Valkenburg, P. M., & Gentile, D. A. (2015). The internet gaming disorder scale. *Psychological Assessment, 27*(2), 567.

Lenhart, A. (2015). *Teens, social media & technology overview 2015.* Pew Research Center. http://www.pewinternet.org/2015/04/09/teens-social-media-technology-2015

Lehdonvirta, V. (2009). ARTICLE ONE. *Sarja/Series A-11: 2009,* 101. https://www.utupub.fi/bitstream/handle/10024/98536/Ae11_2009lehdonvirta.pdf?sequence=2&isAllowed=y#page=101

Lopez-Gonzalez, H., & Griffiths, M. D. (2016). Is European online gambling regulation adequately addressing in-play betting advertising? *Gaming Law Review and Economics, 20*(6), 495–503.

Macey, J., & Hamari, J. (2018). Investigating relationships between video gaming, spectating esports, and gambling. *Computers in Human Behavior, 80,* 344–353.

Müller, K. W., Janikian, M., Dreier, M., Wölfling, K., Beutel, M. E., Tzavara, C., Richardson, C., & Tsitsika, A. (2015). Regular gaming behavior and internet gaming disorder in European adolescents: results from a cross-national representative survey of prevalence, predictors, and psychopathological correlates. *European Child & Adolescent Psychiatry, 24*(5), 565–574.

Nakayama, H., Mihara, S., & Higuchi, S. (2017). Treatment and risk factors of internet use disorders. *Psychiatry and Clinical Neurosciences, 71*(7), 492–505.

National Association of Social Workers. (2017). *Code of ethics.* https://www.socialworkers.org/About/Ethics/Code-of-Ethics/Code-of-Ethics-English

Pew Research Institute. (2018). *5 facts about Americans and video games.* https://www.pewresearch.org/fact-tank/2018/09/17/5-facts-about-americans-and-video-games

Pontes, H. M., Stavropoulos, V., & Griffiths, M. D. (2017). Measurement invariance of the Internet Gaming Disorder Scale–Short-Form (IGDS9-SF) between the United States of America, India and the United Kingdom. *Psychiatry Research, 257,* 472–478.

Przybylski, A. K., Weinstein, N., & Murayama, K. (2017). Internet gaming disorder: Investigating the clinical relevance of a new phenomenon. *American Journal of Psychiatry, 174*(3), 230–236.

Rehbein, F., Kliem, S., Baier, D., Mößle, T., & Petry, N. M. (2015). Prevalence of internet gaming disorder in German adolescents: Diagnostic contribution of the nine DSM-5 criteria in a state-wide representative sample. *Addiction, 110*(5), 842–851.

Shek, D. T., & Yu, L. (2012). Internet addiction phenomenon in early adolescents in Hong Kong. *The Scientific World Journal, 2012,* 104304.

Torres-Rodríguez, A., Griffiths, M. D., Carbonell, X., Farriols-Hernando, N., & Torres-Jimenez, E. (2019). Internet gaming disorder treatment: A case study evaluation of four different types of adolescent problematic gamers. *International Journal of Mental Health and Addiction, 17*(1), 1–12.

World Health Organization. (2020).*6C51 gaming disorder.* https://icd.who.int/browse11/l-m/en#/http%3a%2f%2fid.who.int%2ficd%2fentity%2f1448597234

Young, K. (2009). Understanding online gaming addiction and treatment issues for adolescents. *American Journal of Family Therapy, 37*(5), 355–372.

PART V

Developing and Implementing Treatment Plans with Specific Groups and Disorders

Treatment Planning for Attention-Deficit/Hyperactivity Disorder

Schuyler C. Cunningham and Tim Norman

In many cases, a client seeks a diagnosis of attention-deficit/hyperactivity disorder (ADHD) from a family doctor. Although doctors are licensed to diagnose ADHD, it is becoming best practice for a prescriber to refer to a mental health expert, such as a social worker, to complete an assessment and form a treatment plan that may include medication as an option for treating ADHD. In other words, social workers are becoming increasingly more engaged in the diagnosis of ADHD, with prescribers referring clients for the mental health assessment prior to prescribing medications. Moreover, with this interdisciplinary approach, social workers are able to make additional recommendations for treatments that could help the client, such as neurofeedback, counseling, and group support. It is hoped that this will contribute to a change in the considerable controversy concerning ADHD being overdiagnosed, leading to overprescribing ADHD medications. As social workers become more capable of assessing for ADHD and the *Diagnostic and Statistical Manual of Mental* *Disorders* (DSM) criteria evolve, social workers have the opportunity to further establish themselves as the providers of choice to assess clients and develop suitable treatment plans for ADHD in conjunction with prescribers, parents, and clients.

Many clients seek treatment for ADHD to improve their quality of life, productivity, organization, social relations, and ego strength. To support their courage in seeking these improvements, rendering a diagnosis requires a robust and valid assessment process. Following an assessment and a diagnosis, an evidenced-based informed treatment plan is developed. Consider the following case example as a frame of reference for conducting an assessment and making a treatment plan that includes evidence-based interventions.

Case Example

Nicole is a 27-year-old location scout for film and television production companies. She lives in New York City and identifies herself

386 | Part V Treatment Plans with Specific Groups and Disorders

as a White, female, cisgender, bisexual. She was initially diagnosed with ADHD as a child. Currently, she is seeking help with her executive functions, including focus/attention, motivation to start/finish tasks, and emotional regulation (anger management). Nicole has difficulty starting on tasks and maintaining effort and motivation to complete tasks—especially if the tasks evoke fear or boredom. She gets easily sidetracked by less important activities, often switching to doing something lower on her list of priorities because it is more stimulating. Nicole is anxious in social situations, in which she worries about "being too much" for people or doing and saying awkward things that make others feel uncomfortable. She is very sensitive to criticism from others, feeling the sting of criticism more deeply and for a longer time than average. This can cause her to become irritated easily, with a short fuse, leading to sudden outbursts of anger. Her last boyfriend broke up with her because she was, as he said, "always raging" on him, like yelling at him in public and harassing him with unnecessarily angry texts. Once her anger subsides, she sometimes feels guilty and embarrassed about her actions, as well as about past failed relationships. Nicole also suffers from time myopia, causing her to be late to most events. She tested positive for comorbidity, with depression and anxiety. In college, she tried a dialectical behavior therapy (DBT) group for several months, but she has had no formal psychotherapy otherwise. These symptoms have been present since childhood and continue to disrupt her life today.

Assessment Considerations

Assessing for ADHD is essential to the validity of the diagnosis and therefore to the recommended treatments. Although there are assessment batteries, or a group of questionnaires,

intended to be administered as a cohesive whole to make an assessment and form a diagnosis, these far exceed what social workers are licensed to administer. However, there are plenty of useful assessment tools that can produce an elegant and effective battery for a full assessment in which a social worker can confidently render an ADHD diagnosis (American Psychological Association, 2020).

There are also controversies in the field about the quality of an evaluation a social worker can conduct. This is likely due to ignorance regarding the scope of a social work license, traditional "turf wars" between mental health and medical professionals, and social workers' not leveraging their license and training to create a robust assessment process.

The independent clinical social work license is a powerful tool. It enables those who hold it to render mental health diagnoses to clients the same as any other professional afforded the same privilege. Although the nuances between licenses across jurisdictions vary, social workers are empowered to diagnose a mental health condition. Ensuring that colleagues know this capability is essential, and fighting for it is even more so. Without this autonomy, social workers could not bill insurance companies, support clients in the use of evidenced-based interventions, or train the next generation of mental health providers. However, the privilege to render a diagnosis must be supported with continued training and diligence and a robust assessment process.

One often-cited area of contention by colleagues in the mental health field who are not social workers is that the assessment battery a social worker can provide is not as robust as what a clinical psychologist or medical doctor or equivalent could administer. Although social workers are not able to conduct assessments with instruments deemed suitable only for interpretation by psychologists or psychiatrists, this misaligned thinking leads to the conclusion that social workers should not perform these assessments because they should know that something "better" is available to their clients. In addition to being flat wrong, this gives the impression that social workers will be doing a disservice to their clients by conducting a valid and reliable assessment that will lead to a valid and reliable diagnosis.

The 2018 report, "The Mental Health Workforce: A Primer," prepared by the Congressional Research Service, reports that "estimates show that clinical social workers are the most abundant of the mental health professions." Not only are social workers the most numerous but also their training affords a unique person-in-environment perspective that allows social workers to assess for elements of a specific client's milieu that may be related to or contributing to the reason for their assessment. In other words, social workers are the most numerous fully empowered mental health providers in the United States to provide reliable and valid assessments, render their diagnostic opinions, and build treatment plans for clients. In cases in which additional assessment is required, such as learning disability, IQ, and visual or auditory processing, a social worker can simply include recommendations for further testing in their treatment plan and still render a diagnosis. This ensures the client knows what other options they have to rule out other possible complications related to their presentation.

Assessments

A thorough assessment is likely to include the following (Gualtieri & Johnson, 2005):

1. A comprehensive clinical interview
2. A mental status exam of the client
3. A medical evaluation
4. Questionnaires with self-report from the client
5. Questionnaires completed by interested third parties, such as parents, teachers, etc.

6. Report evaluations from adjunct interested parties, such as speech and language therapists, occupational therapists, school counselors, etc.

Including an interdisciplinary approach is key to obtaining accurate information for the assessment and therefore leads to a more informed diagnosis and treatment recommendations. Using interdisciplinary team members, such as doctors, speech and language therapists, teachers, and occupational therapists, can add insight that might explain or further explain a client's experience of their presenting problem.

Note that assessing children is different than assessing adults, despite the fact that rendering a diagnosis of ADHD for an adult case requires substantial evidence of symptoms before the age of 12 years (American Psychiatric Association, 2013). When assessing for ADHD in adults, be sure to include assessment tools for other comorbid diagnoses, such as disorders of mood, anxiety, personality, and substance use (Katzman et al., 2017). It may be difficult for them to recall their symptoms when they were younger, but good training in clinical interviewing can aid that process. On the other hand, in children, seeking input from guardians, teachers, and others directly involved in the child's day-to-day activities can provide important information that a child may be less likely to include in their report. Also, screening for common comorbid disorders such as conduct disorder or oppositional defiant disorder in children will be helpful (Cuffe et al., 2020). The inclusion of assessment tools for comorbid disorders will allow for a more thorough assessment, which will lead to a more informed diagnosis and treatment recommendations.

An effective assessment should include sound psychological questionnaires that have been normed in the ADHD population; a clinical interview; and, if possible, a continuous performance test (CPT). The questionnaires

TABLE 47.1 Questionnaires to Assess ADHD

	Self-Report	Child Client[a]	Adult Client[b]	Third Party[c]	CPT
Adult ADHD Clinical Diagnostic Scale (ACDS)	Y	N	Y	N	N
Adult ADHD Self-Report Scale 5 (ASRS)	Y	N	Y	Y	N
Barkley Deficits in Executive Functioning Scale–Children and Adolescents (BDEFS-CA)	Y	Y	N	Y	N
Barkley Deficits in Executive Functioning Scale–Other (BDEFS-Other)	Y	N	Y	Y	N
Barkley Deficits in Executive Functioning Scale (BDEFS)	Y	N	Y	N	N
Behavior Assessment System for Children (BASC-3)	Y	Y	Y	Y	N
Brown Executive Functioning and Attention Scales (BEFAS)	Y	Y	Y	Y	N
Child Behavior Checklist	Y	N	N	Y	N
Conners Comprehensive Behavior Rating Scale (Conners CBRS)	Y	Y	N	Y	N
Conners Continuous Performance Test (Conners CPT)	N	Y	Y	N	Y
Conners Adult ADHD Rating Scales (CAARS)	Y	N	Y	Y	N
Integrated Visual and Auditory (IVA) Continuous Performance Test	N	Y	Y	N	Y
Integrated Visual and Auditory (IVA) Continuous Performance Test–2	N	Y	Y	N	Y
NICHQ Vanderbilt Assessment Scales	Y	Y	N	Y	N
Swanson, Nolan, and Pelham Teacher and Parent Rating Scale (SNAP)	Y	Y	N	Y	N
Test of Variables of Attention (TOVA)	N	Y	Y	N	Y
Weiss Functional Impairment Rating Scale (WFIRS)	Y	Y	N	Y	N
Wender Utah Rating Scale (WURS)	Y	N	Y	N	N

[a]Refers to clients who are older than age 6 years and younger than age 18 years.
[b]Refers to clients aged 18 years or older.
[c]Includes parents, teachers, and other third parties to the client.
ADHD, attention-deficit/hyperactivity disorder; CPT, continuous performance test; N, no; Y, yes.

will make up the bulk of the battery. Table 47.1 provides an illustrative list of valid ADHD questionnaires for both children and adult clients. It is organized in alphabetical order so as to neutralize the impression of endorsement of one or another tool. The table also indicates type of tool (e.g., self-report or CPT), which population it is for (e.g., child or adult client), and whether it includes tools for third parties (parents/primary caregivers, partners, teachers, etc.). It is by no means an exhaustive list but provides enough tools for a social worker to establish their own battery. It is important to obtain additional training to administer, score, and interpret these instruments, and that training is usually widely available. Consultation with a more experienced provider is also a form of training that will ensure social workers are practicing within their scopes of expertise.

The clinical interview will add vital insight by allowing the client to report information about the history of their symptoms in various domains of their life. Although it can be difficult for adults to recall specific details about their life before age 12 years, which is required to make a diagnosis, using open- and closed-ended questions, asking similar questions in different ways, and asking about potential repercussions of the symptoms may lead to memories more easily being recalled. For example, if attempting to assess the hyperactivity profile of an adult who is now middle-aged, it might be helpful to ask the following: "Were you ever assigned a special seat in class?" "Did you really enjoy recess or gym?" and/or "Were you the class clown?" The goal of these questions is to help jog their memory. If a kid was assigned a seat in class, it might suggest that they were a bit rambunctious or needed to be separated from their friends to concentrate—all important elements to considering an adult ADHD diagnosis.

Similarly, it can be difficult for children to be reliable reporters of their symptoms. This might be driven by their desire to build rapport through approval seeking, priming from someone outside the assessment room, or fear of a stigma associated with an ADHD diagnosis. This is why it is important to include parents, teachers, guardians, and others involved in the child's care and academic life. This also allows for an assessment across multiple domains of social functioning, which is consistent with DSM-5 guidelines.

If administered, a CPT will add an additional level of objectivity to the assessment. This not only leads to confirming or ruling out a diagnosis of ADHD but also aids the clinician in making more targeted recommendations, including referring for additional testing for learning disorders or auditory or visual learning deficits. CPTs have been used in the field of ADHD assessing for decades and are generally well regarded (Losier et al., 1996). What prevents many social workers from utilizing them is the additional cost and training associated with interpretation and using them. Cost to enhance the validity of an assessment should not be a barrier, and many of the CPTs can be used to support other interventions as effective pre- and post-test to an intervention, such as neurofeedback.

Treatment Goals

Developing both micro and macro goals for the client is essential to creating an effective treatment plan. Setting smaller goals the client can easily achieve, such as "Client will go to bed by 11:00 p.m. every night," will help keep the momentum of task completion going (Prevatt et al., 2017). At the same time, broader goals, such as "Client will develop emotional regulation tools," offer the client guideposts by which to improve skills and adjust thoughts and behavior slowly over time. A discussion about strategies for incorporating both in the client's treatment plan is presented next.

Several acronyms have been created to inform goal-setting. Here, the SMART goals method, developed by George Doran (1981), is highlighted for its simplicity and ubiquitousness. Doran suggests that every goal should follow five guidelines:

> Specific: Detailed, not too broad.
> Measurable: There's a way to measure progress.
> Achievable: There's a way to finish the goal.
> Realistic: It's possible to achieve given my ability and resources.
> Time-bound: There's a time limit to the goal.

Returning to the case example presented previously, Nicole's goals will address the specific issue(s) she is dealing with—difficulty following through on tasks that should be manageable. But even that may be too broad, so being more specific allows for more clarity for the client. For example, regarding building organizational skills, a goal for Nicole could be "to demonstrate proficiency using two separate organizational skills: calendaring and to-do list."

To measure her progress "demonstrating proficiency by using calendaring and a to-do list," Nicole will keep a daily log of whether or not she spends 10 minutes each day practicing calendaring, and perhaps show a 90% success rate. A lofty goal, indeed. And, in fact, she was able to complete it—a great accomplishment. Yet, for someone with ADHD, this goal will most likely not sound very fun. Introducing creativity into goal-setting and encouraging the client to offer creative suggestions and uniquely tailored solutions can improve efficiency of goal completion (Boot et al., 2020). In this case, perhaps it means allowing Nicole to determine a creative time of day to practice calendaring, a creative reward once complete, or spending 9 minutes a day instead of 10, with an 82% success rate. Anything to lend excitement or foster creativity to goal-setting can help improve client outcomes.

Although it is possible for Nicole to achieve a 90% success rate with practicing calendaring and a to-do list every day, it may not be realistic. At this time, as throughout the goals and treatment planning process, the social worker should check in with the client to assess if the goal is realistic. When asked, Nicole says "no," she does not believe a 90% success rate is realistic for this goal. So the social worker discusses a more realistic goal with her, and they determine that 80% is a more reasonable goal. It is important that the goal is not so unattainable that the client barely has a chance to succeed. Good goals are those that are challenging enough to stretch the client out of their comfort zone but not so demanding that the client loses motivation or gives up. The priority is to set the client up for "a win" so they have a high probability to achieve their goal with less than maximum effort. Note that this is not cheating or lowering their expectations—something clients tend to fiercely defend. Instead, it is using goal-setting as an intervention to provide the client a positive accomplishment.

Setting a time frame for Nicole's organizational goals is key to her success. Without a deadline, progress can extend indefinitely, and the client can more easily lose momentum. The first deadline for Nicole should be 1 or 2 weeks after the goal is set. This way, she can chart her progress between therapy sessions, and not too much time passes before she discusses her progress with the social worker. If her success rate is greater than 80%, all criteria stay the same and she tries for another successful week. If her success rate is less than 80% (which is likely), the social worker discusses strategies with the client and they choose another deadline to practice again, perhaps for another week. This is how we set up small "wins" for our clients and help them improve their progress over time by discussing what worked and what did not work, all the while making adjustments during sessions. After several weeks, we should start to see Nicole increasing her success rate toward 80% and eventually higher. Her sense of accomplishment and engagement in treatment may also increase due to her success and the positive and desired impacts it has on her life.

Objectives/ Interventions

In order to implement a treatment plan, the plan must describe the objectives—or interventions—the social worker plans to implement to support the client in achieving their treatment goals. For ADHD clients with symptoms similar to those of Nicole, it is typical to incorporate a combination of cognitive–behavioral therapy and psychoeducation. Referring Nicole to a DBT group may also be beneficial for her treatment to support in the development of coping skills.

Evidenced-Based Treatment Plan

Creating the treatment plan starts with describing the client's presenting problem, goals, objectives, interventions, and finally the termination criteria. Devised with the client at the beginning of treatment, the termination criteria contain the broad goals the client intends to accomplish in order to "graduate" from treatment. The treatment plan should be completed within 30 days of the initial interview with the client. After the initial treatment plan, a new treatment plan is created every 90 days (Table 47.2).

Helpful Resources

Apps
Phone applications and utility websites that can help people with ADHD are vast and varied. Some are free to use, and others have costs associated with the different tiers of functionality. In addition, they come and go quickly, which requires diligence on the clinician's part to ensure recommendations to clients are up-to-date and accurate. Nonetheless, here is a list of helpful applications and websites that can be utilized to support managing ADHD:

Task and Reminder functions on webmail applications such as gmail or yahoo: Many email and calendar services offer reminders. Setting up reminders that notify you of an upcoming deadline or task can be an effective way to manage symptoms of ADHD.

Anydo—organized to-do list

Due—provides a task reminder system and persistent alerts, making it difficult to ignore

Remember the Milk—a to-do application for busy people

Self-Control—allows you to prevent yourself from accessing distracting websites for a period of time that you set

Evernote—a multimedia note-taking app

TABLE 47.2 Treatment Plan for Nicole

Presenting Problem(s)
Client has difficulty with focus and attention, motivation to start/finish tasks, and emotional regulation (anger management). She reports social anxiety and high sensitivity to criticism from others, becoming irritated easily with sudden outbursts of anger. History of past failed relationships. Time myopia, causing chronic lateness. Comorbid with depression and anxiety.

Goals
1. Client will create and maintain use of two different daily organizing tools.

2. Client will learn and demonstrate anger management skills.

Objectives
a. Demonstrate proficiency using a calendaring app/planner.

b. Demonstrate proficiency using a to-do list.

a. Daily meditation, breathing, exercise, nutrition.

b. Cognitive restructuring of anger habits and triggers.

Interventions
Cognitive–behavioral therapy
Psychoeducation
Motivational interviewing

Cognitive–behavioral therapy
Psychoeducation
Dialectical behavior group

Termination Criteria
a. Client will demonstrate organizational maintenance using a calendar and to-do list to prioritize and follow through with 80% of tasks attempted each week.

b. Client will regularly utilize emotional regulation techniques for anger management, demonstrating self-care skills through daily habits of mediation, mindfulness, nutrition, and exercise.

RescueTime—provides a "productivity pulse" based on how much or little you are using your phone and for what purposes throughout the day

focus@will—provides personalized music to help you stay focused

Asana—a work management platform

Trello—for organization and prioritization of tasks

Websites

Attention Deficit Disorder Association: https://add.org

Centers for Disease Control and Prevention: https://www.cdc.gov/ncbddd/adhd/index.html

Children and Adults with Attention-Deficit/Hyperactivity Disorder: https://chadd.org

National Institute of Mental Health: https://www.nimh.nih.gov/health/topics/attention-deficit-hyperactivity-disorder-adhd/index.shtml

References

American Psychiatric Association. (2013). *Diagnostic and statistical manual of mental disorders* (5th ed.). https://doi.org/10.1176/appi.books.9780890425596

American Psychological Association. (2020). Test battery. In *Dictionary of psychology*. Accessed April 10, 2020, from https://dictionary.apa.org/test-battery

Boot, N., Nevicka, B., & Baas, M. (2020). Creativity in ADHD: Goal-directed motivation and domain specificity. *Journal of Attention Disorders, 24*(13), 1857–1866.

Congressional Research Service. (2018). *The mental health workforce: A primer.* https://fas.org/sgp/crs/misc/R43255.pdf

Cuffe, S. P., Visser, S. N., Holbrook, J. R., Danielson, M. L., Greryk, L. L., Wolraich, M. L., & McKeown, R. E. (2020). ADHD and psychiatric comorbidity: Functional outcomes in a school-based sample of children. *Journal of Attentional Disorders, 24*(9): 1345–1354.

Doran, G. T. (1981). There's a S.M.A.R.T. way to write management's goals and objectives. *Management Review, 70*(11), 35–36.

Gualtieri, C. T., & Johnson, L. G. (2005). ADHD: Is objective diagnosis possible? *Psychiatry, 2*(11), 44–53.

Katzman, M. A., Bilkey, T. S., Chokka, P. R., Fallu, A., & Klassen, L. J. (2017). Adult ADHD and comorbid disorders: Clinical implications of a dimensional approach. *BMC Psychiatry, 17*(1), 302. https://doi.org/10.1186/s12888-017-1463-3

Losier, B .J., McGrath, P. J., & Klein, R. M. (1996). Error patterns on the continuous performance test in non-medicated and medicated samples of children with and without ADHD: A meta-analytic review. *Journal of Child Psychology and Psychiatry, 37*, 971–987. doi:10.1111/j.1469-7610.1996.tb01494.x

Prevatt, F., Smith, S. M., Diers, S., Marshall, D., Coleman, J., Valler, E., & Miller, N. (2017). ADHD coaching with college students: Exploring processes involved in motivation and goal completion. *BMC Psychiatry, 31*(2), 93–111.

Play Therapy

Nancy Boyd Webb

We live in a world in which violence, terror, abuse, and neglect are everyday occurrences in families, schools, and communities, and no one of any age is immune to the possibility of exposure and to the associated stress and anxiety related to concerns about personal safety. Some children may suffer abuse by their parents, and others may experience bullying in school and on the internet. Even if not targeted personally, children observe many instances of violence in the world around them. The reality is that childhood is not a blissful safe time for many or most children growing up in the 21st century. Many anxious young people develop symptoms that interfere with their normal development and adjustment at home and in school. Some children, due to temperamental or other factors, have delayed or compromised development that causes problems in their daily lives. The tension and fear associated with all these stressors can result in clinging behaviors, aggression, or withdrawal. Regardless of the cause, when these symptomatic children come to the attention of adult professionals, they may be referred for play therapy, with the expectation that this will help the child attain or return to "normalcy." This chapter presents an overview of play therapy and discusses a range of play therapy theories and interventions for use with troubled children. A detailed case example illustrates a variety of play therapy methods, many of which have been studied and found to be evidence-based.

Play Therapy: Definition and Rationale

Play therapy refers to a theoretically based helping interaction between a trained adult therapist and a child that aims to relieve the child's emotional distress through the deliberate use of the therapeutic powers of play to help prevent or resolve psychosocial difficulties and achieve personal growth [adapted from the Association of Play Therapy (APT), 2018]. Play therapy is the treatment of choice in helping children with emotional difficulties because it permits them to communicate through child-friendly play rather than verbally. Children are at a disadvantage when adults expect them to interact with them verbally because most are not proficient in using words. Whereas adults talk out their worries to try to understand them and experience relief from stress, children express their fears and anxieties by playing them out. Landreth (2012) refers to play as "the language of childhood." The child identifies with the toy doll or other object and displaces their feelings onto the toy and then may talk through the toy. The assumption of play therapy is that when children understand that the therapist's role is to help them, they express their emotional conflicts within the metaphor of play. Often, play therapy not only alleviates the presenting symptoms (important as this may be to the parents and the child) but also helps remove impediments to the child's ongoing growth, thereby enhancing their future development. In other words, the child's relief from anxiety frees them to proceed more comfortably with their daily interactions at home and at school (Crenshaw, 2006; Webb, 1996, 2007, 2019).

Some of the specific elements inherent in play that make it valuable have been identified as its communication power, its abreaction power (permitting the expression of past stress and the associated negative emotions), and its rapport-building power (Reddy et al., 2005). It has been recognized as an evidence-based practice (Yee et al., 2019). Each child's situation is unique; therefore, therapy with individual children will have different emphases, depending on the assessment of the child's problem situation and their specific responses. In summary, the primary purpose of play therapy is to help troubled children express and obtain relief from their conflicts and anxieties symbolically through play in the context of a therapeutic relationship with a trained mental health therapist.

Different Play Therapy Approaches

Play therapy has its roots in the work of child psychoanalysts Anna Freud and Melanie Klein, who adapted methods of adult psychoanalysis to helping children in the 1930s and 1940s. Both analysts agreed about the importance of the therapeutic relationship with the child and about using play as the primary method of communication. Since that time, many variations of play therapy have been developed and promoted by child therapists. The numerous approaches include (1) child-centered play therapy (Cochran et al., 2010; Landreth, 2012), (2) psychodynamic child therapy (Bromfield, 2007; Mordock, 2015), (3) cognitive–behavioral treatment (Cavett, 2015; Cohen et al., 2010; Friedberg & McClure, 2015), and (4) integrated child therapy (Drewes et al., 2011; Gil, 2006; Shelby & Felix, 2005). This is not a comprehensive list, and it is not possible to provide a detailed comparison and analysis of these different types of therapy here. Readers who wish to learn more about the different forms of play therapy may consult Weisz and Kazdin (2010) and Crenshaw and Stewart (2015). A basic difference between the methods depends on the overall emphasis of each about the extent to which the therapist actively guides the child and suggests various play therapy activities. The directive method, as its title suggests, follows a planned protocol with the therapist making suggestions and encouraging the child to complete certain tasks. This is the approach in cognitive–behavioral treatment, which is the recommended treatment for traumatized children (Cavett, 2015). By contrast, in nondirective treatment (the hallmark of child-centered therapy), the therapist encourages the child to make their choices about their play and express themself freely (Pester et al., 2019). The psychodynamic model (Bromfield, 2007; Mordock, 2015) employs elements of both directive and nondirective methods, as does the integrated approach (Gil et al., 2015). According to Kenny-Noziska et al. (2012), both directive and nondirective play interventions have been found to be equally effective in producing therapeutic change. However, nondirective interventions work best for certain disorders, whereas directive approaches work best for others, thereby making the case that play therapists should be able to employ both. This argument is the basis for promoting an integrative model of play therapy to best meet the needs of the diverse population of children who require play therapy (Drewes, 2009; Gil, 2006; ; Kenny-Noziska et al., 2012). It has been noted that throughout the history of child trauma therapy, there has been debate about how best to intervene (Shelby & Felix, 2005). In view of the lack of agreement (and lack of conclusive empirical research findings), it seems understandable that few child therapists currently rely on either a purely directive or nondirective treatment approach. Therefore, this chapter strongly concurs with an article in the *International Journal of Play Therapy* that states that both directive and nondirective skills should be in the repertoire of all play therapists (Kenney-Noziska et al., 2012).

APT was established in 1982 to foster communication among professionals who provide services to children and to encourage and train them in the use of play therapy (APT, 2018). APT monitors therapists who wish to become "registered play therapists" and designates the necessary hours of training and supervised experience. Certification as a play therapist requires post-master's-level training.

A 2020 issue of the journal *Play Therapy* stated that there were currently 7,518 "registered play therapists" worldwide who have met the criteria of APT that qualify them to practice play therapy. They include therapists from a variety of disciplines, including social work, psychology, counseling, and others. Of these, more than 4,000 are registered supervisors who train new therapists to use play therapy methods with children.

The Assessment Process

It is essential for the social worker who is doing play therapy to take a history related to the child's symptom development and any associated trauma. Although an extensive psychosocial history usually is not feasible because of the pressure of time, the worker needs to have a general sense of the child's overall functioning as well as a description and history of onset of the child's current symptomatic behaviors and about how these are interfering with the child's current life.

There are three parts to any assessment of a symptomatic child. I refer to this as the tripartite assessment (Webb, 2007, 2019). The specific groups of factors in each part include

- factors related to the individual child;
- factors related to the support system; and
- factors related to the problem.

The first set of data refers to the nature of the child's overall adjustment, the second part describes the nature of the child's surrounding environment, and the third set of data relates to the nature of the problem. The play therapist must obtain pertinent information from the parents and other sources regarding these matters to establish appropriate treatment goals. Space does not permit full discussion of the assessment process here, and readers who wish more detailed information about using this assessment tool and the accompanying forms may consult detailed descriptions in Webb (2004, 2007, 2011, 2019). The process of assessment and treatment is illustrated in the case of Anna, later in this chapter.

Setting Goals

The focus of treatment following referral is to return the child to their previous adjustment when that was satisfactory and, in all cases, to remediate the factors that have contributed to the child's symptomatic behavior. When the child's behavior appears to be rooted in developmental delays or interruptions, it is helpful to learn when the difficulty first began and to find out how the family and others have responded. The treatment goals flow directly from the assessment. For example, if a child is waking up every night and going into the parents' room for comfort, the goal may be to help the child feel comfortable enough to stay in their own bed. Sometimes the child becomes emotionally stronger after some play therapy sessions because the child now identifies themselves as having overcome the past difficulties. Involving the child in setting the goals usually increases the child's motivation to achieve them. Depending on the child's age, it is often desirable also to have the parent involved with the assessment process and with the treatment plan that evolves from the assessment. Rewarding the child for small gains increases their motivation to persist.

Case Example

Note: A brief discussion of this case appears in Webb (1996).

This case illustrates the value of timely play therapy intervention following a traumatic event. Anna, age 5 years, became preoccupied and inattentive in school following a fire that caused a middle-of-the-night evacuation from her apartment. Although Anna, her parents, and her brother had been safely relocated to a new apartment, she was waking every night, and during the day when at home she always wanted to be in her mother's presence. Anna was disconsolate because she had lost her beloved stuffed bunny with which she used to sleep every night. Her mother did not comprehend the meaning and degree of her daughter's loss and Anna's need to mourn this.

In play therapy over four sessions with the mother and child together, the therapist used directive methods to encourage Anna to re-create her traumatic experience in drawing and in play with blocks and toy furniture. Typically, the play therapist tells the young child that the therapist intends to help the child with any troubles or worries and then invites the child to relate specific concerns either verbally or in play or drawings. When using a directive approach as recommended in trauma-focused cognitive–behavioral therapy (TF-CBT; Cohen et al., 2010), the therapist may ask the child to "show me what happened" with the puppets or dolls or in a drawing. During this process with Anna, the therapist acknowledged the child's loss in her mother's presence and validated the child's pain, thereby stimulating the mother's awareness of her child's grief. After four sessions, the child's symptoms of anxiety and accompanying school inattention were significantly reduced.

Specific Play Therapy Interventions

The play therapist began by telling Anna that she intended to help her with any troubles or worries and then invited Anna to relate specific concerns either verbally or in play. This conveyed to Anna that it was not necessary to talk. The play therapy with Anna consisted of several drawing and block play activities in which the child re-created the traumatic event and revealed her ongoing fears of the possibility of a fire in her new apartment.

Initially, the therapist asked Anna to draw a picture of her current bedroom, and after she had done so, the therapist invited her to use blocks to duplicate this. As Anna created her room, using a toy bed and tiny bendable dolls, she said, "Behind the wall is the kitchen, and there is a fire in the stove." After questioning further and with the mother's input, it became evident that Anna was referring to the pilot light in the stove, which she worried could cause a fire. Their previous apartment had had an electric stove, so the pilot light was a new factor that was contributing to Anna's current fears. Both the mother and the therapist assured Anna that the light in the stove was "only for cooking" and that it would not spread and burn down this new apartment. In the first session, the therapist invited Anna to draw a picture of her old apartment before the fire. Anna drew the apartment and spontaneously inserted a drawing of her bunny in the corner of the paper. The picture of the bunny was quite distorted, and as she drew it, Anna kept talking about how much she missed her bunny. In response to this, the mother said rather dismissively, "I'll get you a new bunny." The play therapist said in response that there will never be another bunny like the one Anna had before. Subsequent sessions included more block play and drawings; in the third session, the therapist believed that Anna was sufficiently comfortable, so she asked her to draw a picture of her apartment in the fire. As the child did this, she kept repeating her wish that they had been able to save her bunny. The therapist then suggested that Anna write a letter to her bunny stating her feelings. Because Anna did not yet have sufficient writing skills, the therapist wrote the child's dictated message on her drawing. Her message was brief and said only "I love you and miss you." The therapist suggested that she add the word "good-bye" to help Anna realize that she would not see her bunny again. This activity seemed to have great meaning for Anna. Her mother reported in the next session that Anna had stopped her nighttime waking and was behaving more appropriately in school. At this point, the therapist asked Anna to draw a picture of how she wants to remember her bunny now. Anna drew an intact bunny with a smile on its face, which was in sharp contrast to the disjointed drawing she had made before.

Obviously, several factors contributed to Anna's rapid alleviation of anxiety. First, there was clarification about the child's current safety once the reassurances about the "fire in the stove" were made. Second, the mother picked up from the therapist the need to acknowledge the pain of Anna's loss of her beloved toy bunny. Most important, the therapist acknowledged the child's feelings of sadness, which the mother had tended to dismiss. Finally, Anna was able to "say goodbye" to her bunny, thereby acknowledging that she will not see it again.

Specific Intervention Techniques

Play therapy methods cover a wide range of activities, including the following:

- Art activities: Including drawing, painting, and use of clay and Play-Doh. See Malchiodi (2011) and Malchiodi and Crenshaw (2014) for more information about art and play therapy.
- Doll play: The use of bendable family dolls, doll furniture, army dolls, rescue personnel and vehicles, fantasy figures such as witches and fairies, stuffed animals, and dinosaurs. See Webb (2007, 2019) for cases involving the use of dolls in play therapy.
- Puppet play: With a variety of friendly and wild animals, family puppets, and worker puppets in the form of both hand puppets and finger puppets. Inclusion of several "adult" puppets and "child" puppets of the same species encourages displacement of family dynamics onto the toys. See Baggerly (2007) for an illustration using puppet play with children following a natural disaster.
- Storytelling: Sometimes the therapist initiates this by beginning a story and asking the child to complete it. See Gil (1991) for examples.
- Sand play: This involves making scenes in a sandbox using a variety of miniature toys.

See Carey (2006) for an example of sand play therapy with a traumatized boy.

- Board games: These may be either specifically "therapeutic" games or regular games that the therapist selects because of themes that resemble the child's experience. See Schaefer and Reid (2001) for numerous examples of the use of board games in play therapy.

The assumption in the use of these materials is that the child identifies with the toy and projects and displaces their own feelings onto the play figures. The therapist's responses may include curiosity (so the child will give more details), expression of feelings (so the child feels validated), or statements of closure and conclusion (so the child can put the experience behind them).

The Anna case illustrated the use of directive play therapy with a child who had experienced a traumatic event. A version of directive play therapy with traumatized children, TF-CBT, has been referred to as a "hybrid model" (Cohen et al., 2010) because it incorporates both directive and nondirective methods. This approach emphasizes the importance of play re-enactment of the stressful/traumatic experience, as well as the mental reworking or cognitive restructuring of the event. Rooted in the belief that it is crucial for the individual to be able to review their crisis/traumatic experience and develop a narrative about it, this verbal review involves repeated guided interactions in which the therapist directs the child to imagine and describe a different desired outcome to the stressful event. After ensuring that the child is comfortable with the therapist, the therapist then guides the child gently in giving details of what happened, including the "worst moment." Subsequent sessions encourage the child to process this experience with the goal of putting it in the wider context of the child's whole life and to reframe it as "something bad that happened." This brings about a changed outlook regarding the experience. Conjoint parent–child sessions are held later, during which the child shares the story and receives support from the parent. In summary, some specific methods in the cognitive approach include the use of calming and relaxation techniques, guided imagery, psychoeducation, positive self-talk, and instruction that the child should rely on parents and other competent adults in dangerous situations. There is a complete discussion of this method in Cohen et al. (2009).

Conclusion

Social workers should obtain training in the use of both directive and nondirective treatment to relieve children's distress following crisis or traumatic experiences and/or to help them cope with the stresses of their everyday lives. Play therapy is the treatment of choice because it offers multiple methods to help symptomatic children overcome anxiety, obtain relief, and feel more competent to carry on with their daily activities.

Helpful Resources

Association for Play Therapy: http://a4pt.org
Child Trauma Academy: https://www.childtrauma.org/
Childswork/childsplay: http://www.childcrafteducation.com
International Society for Traumatic Stress Studies: http://www.istss.org
National Institute for Trauma and Loss in Children: https://tlcinstitute.wordpress.com/about/#:~:text=The%20National%20Institute%20for%20Trauma%20and%20Loss%20in,over%2060%2C000%20trauma%20professionals%2C%20thousands%20have%20given%20testimony.
National Child Traumatic Stress Network: https://www.nctsn.org/
Play Therapy Training Institute: http://www.ptti.org
Self-Esteem Shop: http://www.selfesteemshop.com
Trauma-Focused Cognitive Behavioral Therapy: http://www.musc.edu/tfcbt
University of North Texas Center for Play Therapy: https://cpt.unt.edu/ or http://www.centerforplaytherapy.org

References

Association for Play Therapy. (2018). *About APT.* https://a4pt.site-ym.com/page/AboutAPT

Baggerly, J. (2007). International interventions and challenges following the crisis of natural disasters. In N. B. Webb (Ed.), *Play therapy with children in crisis: Individual, family, and group treatment* (3rd rev. ed., pp. 345–367). Guilford.

Bromfield, R. (2007). *Doing child and adolescent psychotherapy: Adapting psychodynamic treatment to contemporary practice.* Wiley.

Carey, L. (Ed.). (2006). *Expressive and creative arts methods for trauma survivors.* Kingsley.

Cavett, A. (2015). Cognitive–behavioral play therapy. In D. A. Crenshaw & A. L. Stewart (Eds.), *Play therapy: A comprehensive guide to theory and practice* (pp. 83–98). Guilford.

Cochran, N., Nordling, W., & Cochran, J. (2010). *Child-centered play therapy: A practical guide to developing therapeutic relationship with children.* Wiley.

Cohen, J. A., Mannarino, A. P., & Deblinger, E. (2010). Trauma-focused cognitive–behavioral therapy for traumatized children. In J. R. Weisz & A. E. Kazdin (Eds.), *Evidence-based psychotherapies for children and adolescents* (2nd ed., pp. 295–311). Guilford.

Cohen, J. A., Mannarino, A. P., Deblinger, E., & Berliner, L. (2009). Cognitive–behavioral therapy for children and adolescents. In E. B. Foa, T. M. Keane, M. J. Friedman, & J. A. Cohen (Eds.), *Effective treatments for PTSD* (2nd ed., pp. 223–244). Guilford.

Crenshaw, D. A. (2006). *Evocative Strategies in Child and Adolescent Psychotherapy.* Jason Aronson.

Crenshaw, D. A. & Stewart, A. L. (Eds.) (2015) *Play therapy: A comprehensive guide to theory and practice.* Guilford.

Drewes, A. A. (2009). *Blending play therapy with cognitive behavioral therapy.* Wiley.

Drewes, A. A., Bratton, S. C., & Schaefer, C. E. (2011). *Integrative play therapy.* Wiley.

Friedberg, R. D., & McClure, J. M. (2015). *Clinical practice with children and adolescents: The nuts and bolts* (2nd ed.). Guilford.

Gil, E. (1991). *The healing power of play.* Guilford.

Gil, E. (2006). *Helping abused and traumatized children: Integrating directive and nondirective approaches.* Guilford.

Gil, E., Konrath, E., Shaw, J., Goldin, M., & Bryan, H. M. (2015). Integrative approach to play therapy. In D. A. Crenshaw & A. L. Stewart (Eds.), *Play therapy: A comprehensive guide to theory and practice* (pp. 99–113). Guilford.

Kenney-Noziska, S., Schaefer, C. E., & Homeyer, L. E. (2012). Beyond directive or nondirective: Moving the conversation forward. *International Journal of Play Therapy, 21*(4), 244–252.

Landreth, G. (2012). *Play therapy: The art of the relationship* (3rd ed.). Routledge.

Malchiodi, C. A. (2011). *Handbook of art therapy* (2nd ed.). Guilford.

Malchiodi, C. A., & Crenshaw, D. A. (Eds.). (2014). *Creative arts and play therapy for attachment problems.* Guilford.

Mordock, J. B. (2015). Psychodynamic play therapy. In D. A. Crenshaw & A. L. Stewart (Eds.), *Play therapy: A comprehensive guide to theory and practice* (pp. 66–82). Guilford.

Pester, D., Lenz, S. A., & Dell'Aquila, J. (2019). Meta-analysis of single-case evaluations of child-centered play therapy for treating mental health symptoms. International Journal of Play Therapy, 28(3), 144–156.

Reddy, L., Files-Hall, T., & Schaefer, C. (2005). *Announcing empirically based play interventions for children.* American Psychological Association.

Schaefer, C. E., & Reid, S. E. (Eds.). (2001). *Game play* (2nd ed.). Wiley.

Shelby, J. S., & Felix, E. D. (2005). Posttraumatic play therapy: The need for an integrated model of directive and nondirective approaches. In L. A. Reddy, T. M. Files-Hall, & C. E. Schaefer (Eds.), *Empirically-based interventions for children* (pp. 79–103). American Psychological Association.

Webb, N. B. (1996). *Social work practice with children.* THE ANNA CASE: p. 139. Guilford.

Webb, N. B. (Ed.). (2004). *Mass trauma and violence: Helping families and children cope.* Guilford.

Webb, N. B. (Ed.). (2007). *Play therapy with children in crisis* (3rd ed.). Guilford.

Webb, N. B. (2011). *Social work practice with children* (3rd ed.). Guilford.

Webb. N. B. (2019). *Social work practice with children* (4th ed.). Guilford.

Weisz, J. R., & Kazdin, A. E. (2010). *Evidence-based psychotherapies for children and adolescents* (2nd. ed.). Guilford.

Yee, T., Ceballos, P., & Swan, A. (2019). Examining the trends of play therapy articles. A 10-year content analysis. *International Journal of Play Therapy, 28*(4), 250–260.

Dating Violence

Victoria A. Anyikwa

Dating violence is a form of intimate partner violence, referring to abuse in close relationships among dating partners or boyfriends/girlfriends, where the behaviors of one or both partners are harmful to the other [Centers for Disease Control and Prevention (CDC), 2020]. Dating violence in adolescence to young adulthood is referred to as teen dating violence (TDV). Dating violence occurs in many forms: *physical*, where one partner uses hitting and other types of physical force against the other; *sexual*, where one partner forces the other into sexual acts without their consent, ranging from touching to kissing and intercourse; *stalking*, where one partner induces fear through various intimidation methods; and *psychological aggression*, where one partner uses various types of aggressive behaviors to bring emotional harm to the other. Psychological aggression is more difficult to measure because there are no visible scars. Very often, it precedes physical and sexual abuse (Breiding et al., 2015). Dating violence can be traumatizing for many of its victims, particularly adolescents who are naive when it comes to romantic relationships. Even more devastating is the fact that violence inflicted by a dating partner is rarely a one-time event; it is repetitive in nature and often perpetrated in the various forms, simultaneously.

This chapter discusses the prevalence and various forms of TDV among teens and young adults, with attention to young adults on college campuses. It discusses the psychological distress outcomes of dating violence and ways in which social workers can intervene in clinical and other settings in which social workers are found. A list of helpful resources is provided, including information on programs that social workers can use to further their knowledge in providing services to this population. The term TDV is the primary term used throughout; it is used interchangeably with dating violence. The terms adolescents and teens are also used interchangeably.

Prevalence

Teens

The CDC (2020) has declared TDV a public health problem, with 1 in 11 adolescent girls reporting physical violence and 1 in 9 reporting dating sexual violence. Among males, 1 in 15 report physical violence and 1 in 26 report dating sexual violence. In a national study, the Youth Risk Behavior Surveillance, of more than 14,000 adolescents, comprising 9th–12th graders, 69% reported violence in a dating relationship in the past 12 months (Kann et al., 2018). Dating violence through psychological aggression occurs at an even greater rate in TDV because adolescence and young adults communicate primarily through digital means—that is, texting, email, Instagram, Facebook, and other social media platforms. Much of this form of abuse occurs in digital dating violence. Other terms used in reference to this type of violence include cyber dating violence, cyber aggression, cyber bullying, and cyber stalking. With digital dating violence, even after the abuse is thought to be over, negative information and images are often shared online to humiliate and discredit the victim. Studies show that teens who are victimized face-to-face or offline by their dating partners have a greater chance of being victimized online. In addition, experiencing TDV in high school leads to greater risks of dating violence in college. TDV is often underreported because adolescents do not always understand certain behaviors as abusive. They may view some behaviors as playful and signs of love, thus missing the warning signs.

College Students

College students are among the highest risk groups for dating violence, including sexual violence. In a review of more than 60 articles on dating violence among college students, Murray and Kardatzke (2007) found that both physical and sexual dating violence were common and that in most studies, psychological aggression was more common than all other forms and perpetrated by both males and females. In addition, they found that it often co-occurred with both physical and sexual abuse. In another study, Bonomi et al. (2012)

collected retrospective data among 271 college students, having them reflect back to age 13 years, where they assessed physical, sexual, and psychological dating violence. In their sample, more than 60% of both males and females, slightly higher among females (64.7%) than males (61.7%), reported dating violence beginning as early as age 13 years through age 19 years, and for many of the students, this experience occurred with more than one partner.

Perpetrators and Victims

There has been controversy in the broader research on intimate partner violence about reciprocal violence, also known as gender symmetry. Some researchers have reported females perpetrating as much physical violence as males. They have received tremendous criticism, citing a lack of context in which women might be defending themselves and that women are physically incapable of causing the same degree of harm. The controversy exists in TDV research as well, but more studies on TDV reveal that adolescent girls engage in as much or even more physical violence as adolescent boys (Wincentak et al., 2017). Studies on psychological aggression reveal that although both males and females report use of psychological aggression against their partners, adolescent females tend to engage in this form of violence more so than adolescent males. Hughes et al. (2016) conducted a qualitative study among college women on their reasons for engaging in psychological abuse and found six themes in women's responses. The most common response dealt with being angry and frustrated, followed by their partner cheating or being hurtful toward them. Other reasons included getting their partners to pay attention, to retaliate against a partner, to soothe themselves, and saying things that were meant as jokes.

Consequences/Impact of Dating Violence

Teen dating violence has been linked to a host of physical and psychological distress outcomes, including low self-esteem; depression; anxiety; eating disorders; substance use, drug abuse, and other self-destructive behaviors; aggressive and victimizing behaviors such as sexual promiscuity; and suicide attempts. The CDC (Niolon et al., 2017) reports suicide attempts as being five times more likely among women who have experienced dating violence than those who have not, and suicide is the second leading cause of death in those aged 15–34 years. The numbers are significant for both males and females but are greater among females. Depression and anxiety are more prevalent among those who are abused through digital means and other forms of psychological aggression. Among college students, TDV impacts their social and academic functioning, placing them at risk of failure. Dating violence victims often seek help from their peers as opposed to campus counseling offices, and although peers can be helpful, they are sometimes harmful as well.

Risk and Protective Factors for Teen Dating Violence

Peer influence is among the many risk factors for TDV, with peers often serving in an enabling role in both helping their friends to begin romantic relationships and creating tensions through rumors and other tactics among their peer groups. Risk factors cut across the social ecology. They include *individual factors* beyond the friends one keeps, such as self-esteem, communication style, age (where being an adolescent or young adult increases the risk of TDV), attitudes and beliefs that

condone violence, and mental health and substance abuse issues; *family-level factors* that include family upbringing and poor parenting, where children are abused and neglected or where children witness parental violence; and *community- and societal-level factors* such as poverty, cultural norms, and strict adherence to gender roles for men and women.

Among college students, alcohol abuse is reportedly the greatest risk factor for dating violence. A major part of college life for many young people is having a sense of belonging. Sororities and fraternities become attractive pathways to that sense of belonging, and alcohol plays a major role in being initiated in these groups. In these settings, having helpful peers can serve as a protective factor for teens and young adults who may become impaired as a result of substance use, whether voluntarily or involuntarily.

Protective factors include, but are not limited to, social support; good parenting; good problem-solving skills; and connectedness to family, friends, and communities. Many adolescents and young adults lack the important protective factors that mediate the risks of TDV, particularly young college students who are far removed from their support systems and the protection of parents and families. When working with this population, it is important to strengthen protective factors, which also serve to empower teens with the tools needed to reduce the risk of TDV.

Implications for Interventions

The prevalence of TDV has led to tremendous efforts to prevent and curb this problem among teens and young adults in the United States, with the aim of preventing intimate partner violence in adult relationships. Teens who perpetrate abuse and teens who are abused by dating partners have a higher likelihood of engaging in unhealthy relationships as adults, often leading to abuse in adult relationships. Traditional intimate partner violence interventions are at three levels of prevention: primary prevention, aimed at education to stop the violence before it happens; secondary prevention, aimed at reducing the prevalence rate; and tertiary prevention, which focuses on reducing the impacts of intimate partner violence on victims, thereby promoting healing to survivors.

Recognizing the many factors that place adolescents at risk for TDV, the CDC has adopted a public health approach that focuses on primary prevention strategies through the use of a four-level social ecological model (see https://www.cdc.gov/violenceprevention/publichealthissue/social-ecologicalmodel.html). The levels address (1) individual risk factors, with preventive strategies aimed at changing attitudes, beliefs, and behaviors surrounding violence, through such approaches as conflict resolution and life skills training; (2) relationship factors, targeting peers and families who are influential factors in the behaviors relating to TDV, through approaches such as mentoring, peer, parenting, and family programs; (3) community, addressing neighborhood concerns, improving areas such as housing, and policies impacting schools and the workplace; and (4) societal-level factors and cultural beliefs around gender roles and policies that promote issues such as discrimination and oppression, broadening disparities across groups. It is at this level where governmental policies and laws are implemented to hold individuals, such as perpetrators of violence, accountable for their actions; and addressing inequalities across groups.

What Can Social Workers Do?

Social work practitioners are in unique positions to provide interventions at all three prevention levels, beginning at the tertiary or the client-centered level as they are often on the front lines where adolescents and young adults seek counseling services. Mental health problems such as depression, anxiety, binge eating, low self-esteem, and other disorders are common among this population, and the social worker must be adept in understanding teens and young adults in ways that will allow them to ask the right questions. Social workers with knowledge of TDV risk factors and consequences can tailor their assessment and intervention skills when working with adolescents and young adults. Having knowledge of a trauma-informed approach to care (TIC) is also valuable in these instances in terms of engagement and assessment that lead to appropriate interventions. The social worker must first understand the importance of the therapeutic alliance in building trust that leads to healing for this population, particularly if they are survivors of dating violence. Other key variables to be addressed include safety at the core of all interventions, including questions that may trigger TDV memories; being mindful not to retraumatize the adolescent or young adult; and empowerment—equipping them with the tools they need to make decisions regarding their treatment, always recognizing their choice (for further discussion of the TIC approach, see Anyikwa, 2016).

Assessment

Assessment is the key to intervention. The social worker should go beyond the general information gathered in a standard intake form or biopsychosocial and incorporate some behaviorally specific questions to assess for TDV and risk and protective factors. These questions should center around (1) whether or not they are dating, using TDV definitions as a guide but clarifying their meaning because dating may be interpreted differently for this population; (2) feelings of safety in relationships; (3) alcohol and drug use, particularly for college students; and (4) feelings of fearfulness both online and offline, addressing the forms of violence as age appropriate and bearing in mind that adolescents may interpret behaviors differently and not report them as abusive. Research from the National Institutes of Health also shows that adolescents respond more positively if the information is presented as pervasive across youth and young adult. Therefore, it is important to explain why you are asking the questions. Integrating screening questions is a good beginning step to assess and address TDV. It also allows for information on context that is not often found in quantitative measures. However, social workers may also consider screening instruments, keeping in mind the adolescent's age because some scales for older teens may not be appropriate for younger teens. Information on accessing these instruments is provided in the Helpful Resources section. Some may require permission from the creators.

Teen Dating Violence Instruments

The Youth Behavior Survey, which can be accessed online, asks questions relating mainly to physical violence. Another instrument is the Conflict in Adolescent Dating Relationships Inventory, which assesses violence across five domains: threatening, verbal/emotional, relational, physical, and sexual. A newer instrument designed for teens and young adults aged 13–21 years and that appears to capture a broad range of information on TDV is the Teen Screen for Dating Violence (TSDV; Emelianchik-Key et al., 2018). The TSDV consists of five scales that may be used as a full screen or as separate subscales based on the presenting problem or concern. The scales include (1) Perception of Violence scale, which measures knowledge and understanding of violence; (2) Experience of Violence scale, which allows for assessment of victimization of physical, emotional, and sexual forms of TDV; (3)

Perpetration of Violence scale, measuring the three forms of TDV as well; (4) Exposure to Violence scale, be it within the family of origin or exposed in peer relationships; and (5) Support scale, revealing help-seeking strategies among teens. According to the authors, this screening instrument addresses all aspects of dating violence, considers all genders and sexual orientations, and can be used for intervention for all levels of prevention. Another widely used instrument, which might be more appropriate for college-age youth or adults, is the Revised Conflict Tactics Scale. This instrument measures the various forms of violence, incorporating cultural aspects as well.

Interventions

Individual- and group-level strategies should address the various risk factors, including alcohol use and consequences, ensuring protective factors such as positive peer influences at vulnerable times, and empowerment strategies. Cognitive–behavioral therapy (CBT) is one evidence-based approach used to work with individuals of all ages presenting with depression and post-traumatic stress disorder. Cognitive processing theory (Resick & Schnicke, 1992), a form of CBT, has been used with much success for sexual assault victims in both individual and group treatment, focusing on faulty cognitions and stuck points, challenging negative ways of thinking. Other trauma-specific approaches include prolonged exposure (Foa et al., 2009) and eye movement sensitization and reprocessing (Shapiro, 2018), each using different strategies to reprocess early trauma. Additional training is generally required for appropriately implementing these approaches.

The social worker is also able to teach adolescents about the dynamics of healthy and unhealthy relationships, including signs of abuse, particularly those in the form of psychological aggression in both online and offline face-to-face interactions. This can also be done in either modality, depending on whether the client is a teenage or a young adult. Groups may be more suited for younger adolescents. There are various programs and tool kits that social workers can access—for example, Love Is Respect and Dating Matters—through the CDC, which provides frameworks for implementing these interventions. These programs can be implemented at the three prevention levels discussed previously, beginning at middle school, before dating violence occurs.

Programs

One major comprehensive approach is the CDC's Dating Matters program. This program provides education to middle and high school students on healthy relationships. There are separate training modules geared toward parents, schools, and communities. These are accessible online resources aimed at creating prevention programs to stop TDV and, ultimately, intimate partner violence in adulthood.

Bystander intervention programs have also been instituted across communities, primarily across college and universities. These programs teach peers and the overall community intervention strategies aimed at stopping a perpetrator's behaviors that lead to sexual violence and other forms of dating violence. These programs focus on issues such as power and control, attitudes and behaviors toward sexual and other forms of dating violence including stalking, accountability across levels going beyond the perpetrator to peers and community members who stand by and allow sexual violence to happen and to college administrators who must have policies in place to prevent sexual assaults on campus. Colleges and institutions of higher education are now required to report dating and sexual violence on campus as a condition for receiving federal funding. The social worker working with college students should learn about programs in their area that provide services to this population.

Conclusion

Dating violence is one pathway by which both micro and macro roles of social workers are visible. Primary and secondary prevention of teen dating violence requires collaboration among social workers across micro and macro levels—educators, domestic violence advocates, and other health care providers working with adolescents and young adults. Ending TDV is the work of all these professionals.

Helpful Resources

Social workers interested in tool kits and other resources for programs and interventions targeting middle and high school students, parents, college students, and community programs are encouraged to access the various sites listed here.

- CDC's website, Violence Educational Tools Online (VetoViolence). This site provides links to various TDV training programs and evidence-based practices to reduce and/or eliminate dating violence. Among the trainings are Adverse Childhood Experiences—administration and strategies to reduce the impacts; and Dating Matters, with tool kits for engaging groups and communities. https://www.cdc.gov/violenceprevention/communicationresources/veto.html
- The Love Is Respect program is a product of the National Domestic Violence Hotline, aimed at teens and young adults. The organization has rich resources and tool kits for social workers, clients, educators, and all involved in ending teen violence. http://www.loveisrespect.org
- Cumulative list of training on various aspects of dating violence, including male survivor series, trauma-informed advocacy, and native youth and domestic violence: https://vawnet.org/type/training-tools
- The Child Welfare Information Gateway to various TDV prevention programs: https://www.childwelfare.gov/topics/systemwide/domviolence/prevention/teen-dating

Instruments

Conflict in Adolescent Dating Relationships Inventory (CADRI): https://pubmed.ncbi.nlm.nih.gov/30589276/?from_term=conflict+in+adolescent+dating+relationships+measure&from_pos=1

Dating Violence Scale for youth: https://www.ncbi.nlm.nih.gov/pmc/articles/PMC6236324

Revised Conflict Tactics Scale: https://pubmed.ncbi.nlm.nih.gov/?term=revised+conflict+tactics+scale

Youth Risk Behavior Surveillance Survey: https://www.cdc.gov/healthyyouth/data/yrbs/index.htm

References

Anyikwa, V. (2016). Trauma-informed approach to survivors of intimate partner violence. *Journal of Evidence-Informed Social Work, 13*(5), 484–491. https://doi.org/10.1080/23761407.2016.1166824

Bonomi, A. E., Anderson, M. L., Nemeth, J., & Bartle-Haring, S. (2012). *Dating violence victimization across the teen years: Abuse frequency, number of abusive partners, and age of first occurrence. BMC Public Health, 12,* article 637. http://www.biomedcentral.com/1471-2458/12/637

Breiding, M. J., Basile, K. C., Smith, S. G., Black, M. C., & Mahendra, R. R. (2015). *Intimate partner violence surveillance: Uniform definitions and recommended data elements, Version 2.0.* National Center for Injury Prevention and Control, Centers for Disease Control and Prevention.

Centers for Disease Control and Prevention. (2020). *Preventing teen dating violence.* https://www.cdc.gov/violenceprevention/intimatepartnerviolence/teendatingviolence/fastfact.html

Emelianchik-Key, K., Hays, D. G., & Hill, T. (2018). Initial development of the teen screen for dating violence: exploratory factor analysis, rasch model, and psychometric data. *Measurement and Evaluation in Counseling and Development, 51*(1), 16–31.

Foa, E. B., Chrestman, K. R., & Gilboa-Schechtman, E. (2009). Programs that work. Prolonged exposure therapy for adolescents with PTSD: Emotional processing of traumatic experiences: Therapist guide. Oxford University Press.

Hughes, H. M., Massura, C. E., Anukem, O. V., & Cattage, J. S. (2016). Women college students' reasons for engaging in psychological dating aggression: A qualitative examination. *Journal of Family Violence, 31,* 239–249. doi:10.1007/s10896-015-9758-y

Kann, L., McManus, T., Harris, L., Shanklin, S. L., Flint, K. H., Queen, B., Lowry, R., Chyen, D., Whittle, L., Thornton, J., Lim, C., Bradford, D., Yamakawa, Y., Leon, M., Brener, N., & Ethier, K. A. (2018). Youth risk behavior surveillance—United States, 2017. MMWR Surveillance Summaries; 67(8), 1–114.

Murray, C. E., & Kardatzke, K. N. (2007). Dating violence among college students: Key issues for college counselors. *Journal of College Counseling, 10,* 79–89.

Niolon, P. H., Kearns, M., Dills, J., Rambo, K., Irving, S., Armstead, T., & Gilbert, L. (2017). *Preventing intimate partner violence across the lifespan: A technical package of programs.* National Center for Injury Prevention and Control, Centers for Disease Control and Prevention.

Resick, P. A., & Schnicke, M. K. (1992). Cognitive processing therapy for sexual assault victims. *Journal of Consulting and Clinical Psychology, 60*(5), 748–756.

Shapiro, F. (2018). *Eye movement desensitization and reprocessing (EMDR) therapy.* Guilford.

Wincentak, K., Connolly, J., & Card, N. (2017). Teen dating violence: A meta-analytic review of prevalence rates. *Psychology of Violence, 7*(2), 224–241.

Social Anxiety Disorder

Bruce A. Thyer

Contemporary social workers helping clients who experience significant problems with social anxiety disorder (SAD) are in a very fortunate position indeed. The diagnostic conceptualizations of clinical anxiety have been considerably refined during the past five iterations of the *Diagnostic and Statistical Manual of Mental Disorders* [DSM; American Psychiatric Association (APA), 2013], and the newer nomenclature in the DSM-5 is closer to nature's truth about how clients experience pathological anxiety than the system described in previous editions. Clinicians are also fortunate in that considerable effectiveness and efficacy research involving very sophisticated randomized controlled clinical trials has demonstrated that selected psychosocial treatments are genuinely helpful in ameliorating SAD, a condition that, if left untreated, is typically chronic and unremitting, causing significant distress and impaired functioning. There are relatively few psychosocial problems facing social workers wherein the outcomes are so potentially favorable. Given this positive state of affairs, it is incumbent upon social work practitioners who wish to practice both ethically and accountably to become familiar with research-supported methods of assessment and intervention found to be useful for socially anxious clients. This chapter focuses on diagnosis, assessment, research-based interventions, and treatment goals and planning for clients with SAD.

Diagnostic Criteria and Prevalence of Social Anxiety Disorder

The term social anxiety disorder is often used interchangeably with the term social phobia, with the former now the primary label used in the DSM-5. Many clinical researchers and consumer advocacy organizations are encouraging the use of the term SAD because it promotes recognition of the problem as a serious, treatable condition rather than something to be stoically endured. The DSM-5 lists approximately a dozen distinct disorders that may apply to children and adults seeking help and who present with the prominent features of anxiety, fear, avoidance, or increased arousal. The diagnostic criteria for social phobia first appeared in the third edition of the DSM, were revised somewhat in DSM-III-R, again in DSM-IV and DSM-IV-TR, and now most recently in

DSM-5 and renamed social anxiety disorder (APA, 2013). Currently, SAD is defined by the following diagnostic criteria (APA, 2013):

> A. Marked fear or anxiety about one or more social situations in which the individual is exposed to possible scrutiny by others. Examples include social interactions (e.g., having a conversation, meeting unfamiliar people), being observed (e.g., eating or drinking), and performing in front of others (e.g., giving a speech).
>
> The individual fears that he or she will act in a way or show anxiety symptoms that will be negatively evaluated (e.g., will be humiliating or embarrassing; will lead to rejection or offend others).
>
> The social situations almost always provoke fear or anxiety.
>
> The social situations are avoided or endured with intense fear or anxiety.
>
> The fear or anxiety is out of proportion to the actual threat posed by the social situation and to the sociocultural context.
>
> The fear, anxiety, or avoidance is persistent, typically lasting six months or more.
>
> The fear, anxiety, or avoidance causes clinically significant distress or impairment in social, occupational, or other important areas of functioning. (pp. 202–203)

It addition, the features of SAD cannot be better explained by another mental disorder, a substance, or a medical condition. There is one specifier for SAD, *performance only*, that applies if the fear is centered around speaking or performing in public. Research seems to support the nosological merits of this specifier (Fuentes-Rodriguez et al., 2018).

SAD is the fourth most common psychiatric disorder in the United States, with a lifetime prevalence of approximately 12%, exceeded only by major depression, specific phobia, and alcohol dependence (Kessler et al., 2005). The 12-month prevalence rate for SAD in the United States is approximately 7% (APA, 2013, p. 204). The mean age of onset is during the teenage years (Thyer et al., 1985), although some research has shown a bimodal distribution, with the onset for some individuals, who may have a more generalized form of social phobia, occurring earlier in childhood. Alcohol abuse can be a consequence of individuals with social phobia drinking to self-medicate symptoms, often prior to speaking engagements, parties, or performances (Oliveira et al., 2018; Thyer et al., 1986), and a careful assessment of possible alcohol and drug abuse is advisable in its own right. SAD has also been shown to be highly comorbid with major depressive disorder and appears to have a negative impact on its course and outcome. The personal and societal ramifications of SAD can be profound. For example, Tolman et al. (2009) found that SAD can be a significant impediment to returning to work among women welfare recipients. The disorder is more prevalent among women (Asher & Aderker, 2018).

Further Assessment of Social Anxiety Disorder

Arriving at a DSM-5 diagnosis of SAD is only a part of a comprehensive social work assessment, which should involve an array of quantitative and qualitative methods of appraisal: the clinical interview; structured client self-reports (e.g., narrative diaries and logs of out-of-home social/public activities); rapid assessment instruments; structured clinical interviews centered around anxiety disorders; medical checkups to rule out organic causes, including the possible role of medication effects and drug interactions; and, possibly, interviews with other family

---

BOX 50.1 Recommended Assessment Tools for Social Phobia[a]

Interaction and Audience Anxiousness Scales

Liebowitz Social Anxiety Scale

Social Anxiety Questionnaire for Adults

Social Anxiety Scale for Children

Social Anxiety Thoughts Questionnaire

Social Avoidance and Distress Scale

Social Fear Scale

Social Interaction Anxiety Scale

Social Interaction Self-Statement Test

Social Phobia and Anxiety Inventory for Children

Social Phobia Endstate Functioning Index

Social Phobia Scale

Simulated Social Interaction Test

[a]Readily found in Fischer et al. (2020), De Sousa et al. (2018), and on the Society of Clinical Psychology's website (https://www.div12.org/diagnosis/social-anxiety-disorder-and-public-speaking-anxiety).

---

members. There are highly specific rapid assessment instruments and rating scales developed for assessing aspects of SAD and related client functioning (De Sousa et al., 2018). A partial list of frequently recommended clinical tools is provided in Box 50.1. Pretreatment assessment should involve using one or more of these reliable and valid outcome measures, ideally encompassing a rapid assessment instrument, as well as direct measures of behavior, perhaps systematically recorded by the client or a significant other. Some measures may be administered daily or weekly. Other, more global, outcome indicators, such as a quality-of-life scale, a measure of family functioning, or a measure of overall health, simply could be administered pre- and post-treatment.

Once it has been determined that clients meet the DSM-5 criteria, it is essential to carefully isolate the parameters or boundaries of their anxiety-evoking stimuli because various types of social phobias can be quite diverse. A well-established way of accomplishing this is for client and social worker to construct a rank-ordered list of specific social situations that lead to anxiety for the client. Such a list can then be incorporated into a treatment plan that will is described later in the chapter. Find out, for example, if a fear of talking to someone of the opposite gender is impacted by the age or attractiveness of the listener. If younger or less attractive people generate minimal anxiety, initial sessions of exposure therapy could involve such individuals rather than people who make the client exceedingly uncomfortable. If a musician has severe performance anxiety, find out if this varies by context (e.g., solo performance versus playing in a quartet versus playing in a full-sized orchestra), as this too can help in the arrangements for treatment.

Research-Based Interventions

A large body of research exists in support of effective psychosocial interventions for SAD, based on various combinations of behavioral and cognitive–behavioral approaches (Pelissolo et al., 2019). Components of these interventions include exposure to feared stimuli, social skills training, relaxation training, and cognitive restructuring. These interventions have been successfully conducted in both group and individual therapy settings.

An important component of successful psychosocial treatment is graduated exposure to feared situations. The first step of the process is for the social worker and client to put together a rank-ordered list, from least to most frightening, of social situations that produce anxiety. Exposure can be accomplished by imagining fearful scenes, usually narrated by the therapist (imaginal exposure); role playing with the therapist or others who resemble people the client fears; and using virtual reality technology. In addition, direct real-life exposure to the feared situation can be employed. The client agrees to remain in the anxiety-evoking situation with the therapist's support until the anxiety considerably diminishes. Imaginal rehearsal, prolonged exposure in fantasy or via virtual reality, can be conducted in situations in which real-life exposure is not possible (e.g., an upcoming once-in-a-lifetime solo performance by a musician at Carnegie Hall), although real-life exposure is usually preferable when possible. This is due to the fact that imaginal exposure is considerably removed from the real thing and generally less effective at either inducing anxiety or helping the client develop genuinely effective coping and performance skills in real life. Exposure can be carried out in individual or group therapy settings, and clients are usually given exposure exercises as homework, to carry out on their own between sessions, sometimes recruiting helpful family or friends for support and homework practice.

Social skills training (SST) is based on the premise that a lack of social skills, such as poor eye contact or poor conversation skills, can result in a negative reaction from others, thus causing unpleasant and anxiety-provoking social interactions with others. Although there is still some debate as to whether all clients need SST, this approach has been shown to be effective as both a stand-alone intervention and in conjunction with exposure-based approaches (Herbert et al., 2005).

Relaxation training can be used in conjunction with exposure therapy, although relaxation training alone has not been shown to be helpful and has sometimes been used as a control condition in studies. The most commonly used form of relaxation training is progressive muscle relaxation, which is employed in a process called applied relaxation. It has been shown to be effective for SAD when clients are trained in it and then use it while confronting feared situations (Ost, 1987). Systematic reviews and meta-analyses of the intervention research on SAD have shown medium-to-large effect sizes, indicating clinically significant results for exposure therapy with or without the relaxation component (Acarturk et al., 2008).

Because some clients are not helped by the previously mentioned treatments and others achieve only partial symptom reduction, the search for ways to improve existing interventions and conduct research on innovative treatments continues. When using any innovative treatment, it is crucial to provide full informed consent to the client on the state of the evidence and to try the interventions with the greatest empirical support first. One newer approach of interest to researchers is acceptance and commitment therapy (ACT; Herbert et al., 2018). ACT is based on behavior therapy, with the addition of mindfulness and acceptance components. Pilot studies have shown promising results (Ossman et al., 2006). ACT is based on the idea that the primary reason people suffer from psychological disorders is not negative emotions per se but, rather, the struggle to control and avoid experiencing such emotions. Unlike many conventional therapies, the explicit goal of ACT is not to eliminate negative emotions or reduce symptoms (although the pilot studies show that this can often occur) but instead to assist the client in giving up the struggle against emotions and thus promote a nondefensive acceptance (not mere tolerance) of emotions, including anxiety. The identification of client values and helping the client take committed value-directed action are also an important element of ACT. ACT alone has also been shown to increase a person's willingness to engage in necessary exposure-based procedures (Herbert et al., 2018).

Considerable research has also gone into investigating the effectiveness of various medications to help clients with SAD, and the general consensus of reviews on this topic is that selected medications are indeed helpful in temporarily reducing symptomatology (Dias, 2018; Williams et al., 2017). However, unlike psychosocial treatments, the effects of drug therapy are ameliorative, not usually curative, and relapse is high following the discontinuation of medication. Furthermore, medication treatment provides no behavioral benefits to clients whose SAD is related to a skills deficit (e.g., initiating and maintaining conversations or underassertiveness), in terms of helping them develop such functional behaviors.

Treatment Goals

Ideally, the goal mutually arrived at with a client with SAD is the complete alleviation of pathological anxiety—in other words, a cure. Realistically, the goal is more enhanced functioning and some relief of symptoms, not necessarily a complete remission of the difficulty. Enhanced quality of life, improved relationship and family functioning, more effective vocational functioning, and increased ability to function in other areas of life valued by the client (e.g., hobbies, recreation, social activities, and volunteer work) are all amenable to reliable and valid qualitative and quantitative measurement before, during, and at the completion of treatment, and sometimes thereafter. Such data should be routinely gathered and shared with clients (and perhaps their family members) as appropriate. Graphing relevant data and including these in client records is also a recommended practice using single case research designs (Thyer, 2020).

Treatment Planning

Newer treatment modalities for the socially anxious include exposure therapy augmented using virtual reality technology (Nason et al., 2020), therapy conducted via the internet (Gershkovitz et al., 2017), and therapy conducted through the use of mobile apps (Stolz et al., 2018). For public speaking anxiety, a very friendly, supportive, and low-cost organization called Toastmasters International, devoted to helping individuals improve public speaking and leadership skills, can be very helpful. The Toastmasters program is, in effect, a lay-developed program of graduated exposure therapy sessions. Other viable options are various self-books with an evidence-based perspective written by mental health professionals. Antony and Swinton (2017) is one such resource. More can be found on the website called Research-Based Psychological Treatments prepared by the Division of Clinical Psychology of the American Psychological Association, under the link for social anxiety disorder (https://www.div12.org/diagnosis/social-anxiety-disorder-and-public-speaking-anxiety).

A triaged or stepped approach to helping the client with SAD, following an accurate assessment, could involve an initial recommendation to read and follow one of the available self-help books, with weekly one-on-one consultations by telephone to monitor adherence and outcomes. Clients with the so-called bashful bladder syndrome, a variant of SAD, could make use of an excellent science-based self-help book specific to this condition (Soifer et al., 2001). Somewhat more intensive would be recommending the use of the available research-based mobile phone apps or internet-based self-help programs, also with regular therapist monitoring. Clients specifically with public speaking phobias could be referred to the local Toastmasters groups found in most cities. Clients with more idiosyncratic anxiety-evoking stimuli may require therapist-assisted exposure therapy right away—for instance, clients fearful of performing music in public. If real-life exposure, even beginning with very modest levels of exposure, is unacceptable to the client, referral to a specialized clinic with virtual reality technology available may prove to be a more tolerable way to begin the exposure process. Generally, however, the innovative therapist can find ways of introducing elements of life exposure to socially phobic situations with the client that are not overwhelming and allow treatment to proceed. If giving a speech to a crowd of unfamiliar adults is overwhelming, arranging for the client to address a smaller group of nonthreatening children may prove to be an acceptable place to begin real-life exposure. Or speaking with the client's back to the audience may attenuate their anxiety enough to proceed. But if the ultimate goal is for the client to place themself in public spaces, exposed to the possibly critical scrutiny of others, without debilitating anxiety, then at some point actual engagement with this real-life situation is a necessary part of successful care. Exposure in fantasy alone, or using virtual reality, may help get to that point, but by themselves these methods are not usually sufficient to provide adequate symptom relief. Nor are office-based traditional counseling methods usually useful.

If the client with public speaking fears is not benefited by participation in Toastmasters, or from following one of the various self-help books, exposure therapy conducted in small groups can be an effective medium. By introducing the novice client to other individuals with similarly debilitating speaking fears, some initial relief is obtained by learning that they are not alone and that many other apparently "normal-looking" persons similarly suffer. Also, by listening to the stories of the more experienced clients who have made some progress, hopeful expectations can be promoted. Initially, the newer client is welcome to sit quietly and listen. Then, if comfortable, the client can introduce themself and share stories of how their life has been negatively impacted by their social fears. The client can observe more seasoned clients giving small talks to the group, provide feedback, and eventually reach the point of being willing to deliver a brief formal presentation themself. If the size of the group is too large for comfort, other members are usually willing to wait outside while the newer client speaks to one or just a few other members. With practice, the size of the group can be increased and the type of speech exercises intensified (longer, louder, more dramatic presentations, etc.). The evidence in support of exposure therapy for social phobia conducted in small groups is substantial (e.g., Fogarty et al., 2019).

Helpful Resources

Anxiety and Depression Association of America: http://www.adaa.org
Social Anxiety Institute: https://socialanxietyinstitute.org
Toastmasters International: https://www.toastmasters.org

References

Acarturk, C., Cuijpers, P., van Straten, A., & de Graaf, R. (2008). Psychological treatment of social anxiety disorder: A meta-analysis. *Psychological Medicine, 39,* 241–254.

American Psychiatric Association. (2013). *Diagnostic and statistical manual of mental disorders* 5th ed.).

Antony, M. M., & Swinton, R. P. (2017). *The shyness and social anxiety workbook: Proven, step-by-step techniques for overcoming your fear* (3d ed.). New Harbinger.

Asher, M., & Adeker, I. M. (2018). Gender differences in social anxiety disorder. *Journal of Clinical Psychology, 74,* 1730–1741.

De Sousa, D. A., Moreno, A. L., & Osorio, F. (2018). Assessment of social anxiety disorder: A current overview of instruments. In F. L. Osorio & M. F. Donadon (Eds.), *Social anxiety disorder: Recognition, diagnosis and management* (pp. 45–64). Nova Biomedical.

Dias, M. M. (2018). Pharmacotherapy for social anxiety disorder. *Issues in Mental Health Nursing, 39,* 1047–1048.

Fischer, J., Corcoran, J., & Springer, D. (Eds.). (2020). *Measures for clinical practice and research: A sourcebook.* Oxford University Press.

Fogarty, C., Hevey, D., & McCarthy, O. (2019). Effectiveness of cognitive behavioural group therapy for social anxiety disorder: Long-term benefits and aftercare. *Behaviour Research and Therapy, 47,* 501–513.

Fuentes-Rodriguez, G., Garcia-Lopez, L.-J., & Garcia-Trujillo, V. (2018). Exploring the role of the DSM-5 performance-only specifier in adolescents with social anxiety disorder. *Psychiatry Research, 270,* 1033–1038.

Gershkovitz, M., Herbert, J. D., Forman, E. M., Schumacher, L. M., & Fischer, L. E. (2017). Internet-delivered acceptance-based cognitive–behavioral intervention for social anxiety disorder with and without therapist support: A randomized trial. *Behavior Modification, 41,* 583–608.

Herbert, J. D., Forman, E. M., Kaye, J. L., Gershckovitch, M., Goetter, E., Yuen, E. K., Glassman, L., Goldstein, S., Hitchcock, P., Shaw Tronieri, J., Berkowitz, S., & Marando-Blanck, S. (2018). Randomized controlled trial of acceptance and commitment therapy versus traditional cognitive behavior therapy for social anxiety disorder: Symptomatic and behavioral outcomes. *Journal of Contextual Behavioral Science, 9,* 88–96.

Herbert, J. D., Gaudiano, B. A., Rheingold, A. A., Myers, V. H., Dalrymple, K., & Nolan, E. M. (2005). Social skills training augments the effectiveness of cognitive behavioral group therapy for social anxiety disorder. *Behavior Therapy, 36,* 125–138.

Kessler, R. C., Berglund, P., Demler, O., Jin, R., Merikangas, R., & Walters, E. E. (2005). Lifetime prevalence and age-of-onset distributions of DSM-IV disorders in the National Comorbidity Survey Replication. *Archives of General Psychiatry, 62,* 593–602.

Nason, E., Trahan, M., Smith, S., Metsis, V., & Selber, K. (2020). Virtual treatment for veterans social anxiety disorder: A comparison of 360-degree video and 3D virtual reality. *Journal of Technology in Human Services, 38*(3), 288–308.

Oliveira, L. M., Bermudez, M. B., de Ameorim Macedo, M. J., & Passos, I. C. (2018). Comorbid social anxiety disorder in patients with alcohol use disorder: A systematic review. *Journal of Psychiatric Research, 106,* 8–14.

Ossman, W. A., Wilson, K. G., Storaasli, R. D., & McNeill, J. W. (2006). A preliminary investigation in the use of acceptance and commitment therapy in group treatment for social phobia. *International Journal of Psychology and Psychological Therapy, 6,* 397–416.

Ost, L. G. (1987). Applied relaxation: Description of a coping technique and review of controlled studies. *Behaviour Research and Therapy, 25,* 397–409.

Pelissolo, A., Abou Kassm, S., & Delhay, L. (2019). Therapeutic strategies for social anxiety disorder: Where are we now? *Expert Review of Neurotherapeutics, 19,* 1179–1189.

Soifer, D., Zgourides, G. D., Himle, J., & Pickering, N. (2001). *Shy bladder syndrome: Your step by step guide to overcoming aruesis.* New Harbinger.

Stolz, T., Schultz, A., Krieger, T., Vincent, A., Urech, A., Moser, C., Westerman, S., & Berger, T. (2018). A mobile app for social anxiety disorder: A three-arm randomized controlled trial comparing mobile and PC-based guided self-help interventions. *Journal of Consulting and Clinical Psychology, 86,* 493–504.

Thyer, B. A. (2020). Evaluating social work practice with single system research designs. In L. Joubert & M. Webber (Eds.), *The Routledge handbook of social work practice research* (pp. 127–145). Routledge.

Thyer, B. A., Parrish, R. T., Curtis, G. C., Nesse, R. M., & Cameron, O. G. (1985). Ages of onset of DSM III anxiety disorders. *Comprehensive Psychiatry, 26,* 113–122.

Thyer, B. A., Parrish, R. T., Hirnle, J., Cameron, O. G., Curtis, G. C., & Nesse, R. M. (1986). Alcohol abuse among clinically anxious patients. *Behaviour Research and Therapy, 24,* 357–359.

Tolman, R. M., Himle, J., Bybee, D., Abelson, J. L., Hoffman, J., & Van Etten-Lee, M. (2009). Impact of social anxiety disorders on employment among women receiving welfare benefits. *Psychiatric Services, 60,* 61–66.

Williams, T., Hattingh, C. J., Kariuki, C. M., Tromp, S. A., van Balkom, A. J., Ipser, J. C., & Stein, D. J. (2017). Pharmacotherapy for social anxiety disorder (SAnD). *Cochrane Database of Systematic Reviews, 2017*(10), CD001206. doi:10.1002/14651858.CD001206.pub3

Adult Oncology Social Work

Sarah F. Kurker

A cancer diagnosis can produce physical and emotional trauma that patients and families endure for the rest of their lives. Following a diagnosis, a patient's psychosocial needs may change throughout their care and survival. In turn, oncology social workers must develop a specialty for providing effective evidence-based interventions to their patients and their families. Zebrack et al. (2016) state,

> These evidence-based interventions include cognitive behavioral therapy, crisis management, conflict resolution, brief mental health interventions, progressive muscle relaxation, structured psychoeducational interventions for problem solving, and supportive expressive therapy. In addition to administrating these interventions, social workers are also responsible for resource referral, case management, community outreach and education, behavioral health management, and provision of assistance with insurance, finances, housing, transportation and legal resources. (p. 1938)

Social workers provide a variety of interventions to patients and families. They also communicate pertinent family psychosocial needs to the oncology team to ensure appropriate care for patients. Oncology social workers can facilitate counseling, case management, and support groups. Needs vary from patient to patient, but in every case, certain critical considerations must be taken into account.

Psychosocial Assessment
Significance

In oncology settings, every new patient must be assessed by a social worker. During this vital interaction, the social worker explains their role on the oncology team and outlines how they will assist patients and their families throughout the patients' care.

Keeping in mind the dynamic shifts in oncology care and accreditation, "social workers in health care are continually challenged to adapt to new models of patient care, education and advocacy as trends in illness change and health care technology evolves" (Burg et al.,

2010, p. 39). Oncology social workers must remain current on technology, trends, and best practices when providing evidence-based support for patients.

Educating the Patient About the Role of the Social Worker

When a social worker takes the time to explain their role and the questions they will pose, the patient might feel more comfortable and less stressed during the initial assessment. If the social worker's initial questions are answered with hesitation, the social worker can use clinical skills, such as active listening, to connect with the patient during the initial contact.

Baseline Assessment and Relationship Building

Although the assessment is personal, there are several strategies for building rapport throughout the interview. First, if the social worker is experienced, they might share with the patient how long they have been working in clinical oncology settings; this strategy might lend credibility and authority to the social worker and could engender trust with the patient. Second, allowing for permission and HIPAA (Health Insurance Portability and Accountability Act of 1996) compliance, the social worker might share another patient's experience that illustrates positive outcomes from treatment and interventions. Third, the social worker should establish an open dialogue that encourages active listening and asking questions by both parties. Overall, the social worker must remember that throughout the initial interview, they must take steps to ensure the comfort of patients and their families.

Consistency of Support

Oncology social workers have the incredible opportunity to see patients and families on a daily or weekly basis for an extended period of time. The social worker's physical and emotional labor varies significantly; on some occasions, they might hold long psychosocial support sessions, whereas on other days they might simply greet a family member during a visit. Other times, the social worker supports the patient when they are experiencing the negative physical or emotional side effects of treatment. The sporadic and inconsistent nature of this work requires the social worker to check in with patients on a regular basis to demonstrate that they are available whenever the patients need them.

The Psychosocial Framework

As in any assessment, this assessment consists of open-ended questions. This assessment should be guided by the social worker. Some clients share significant detailed information, whereas others need more guidance or direction. The social worker's comfort level with conducting these assessments will develop with time. See Table 51.1 for an example of an initial psychosocial assessment.

The Quality of Life Instrument

The City of Hope National Medical Center and Beckman Research Institute have developed the Quality of Life Instrument that can be useful in a clinical and research setting as a benchmark for patient's psychosocial well-being (see Helpful Resources). The instrument can be a tool for continued assessment. It can complement psychosocial support and serve as a continual self-reporting apparatus for patients. It can also be used as an intervention evaluation to chart patient progress. Overall, this instrument enables the collaboration between oncology specialists who work hard to support one another to provide the best care for all patients.

TABLE 51.1 Oncology Social Work—Initial Psychosocial Assessment

Date: _____

Patient Name: _____

Patient's Family _____
Members Present: _____

Oncology Psychosocial Assessment

Question #1:	**Please tell me about your family** (immediate, extended)
	How are the relationships within the family? Family strengths? Happiest memories/traditions?
	How have you dealt with change/challenges?
	Have you experienced death within the family? What was this like?
Notes:	
Question #2:	**Please share with me details about your career** Highlights? Challenges?
Notes:	
Question #3:	**Please share about your diagnosis** Emotions? Supports?
Notes:	
Question #4:	**Previous health concerns**? Cancer treatment thus far? Mental health issues? Chronic illness?
Notes:	
Question #5:	**Understanding of treatment?** Concerns? Questions? How has or will your treatment affect your family?
Notes:	
Question #6:	**Coping skills?** How have you coped in the past? How have you dealt with stress?
Notes:	
Question #7:	**Financial concerns?**
Notes:	
Question #8:	**Experiences with social worker? Mental health specialists? Things you found helpful? Things that did not help you?**
Notes:	
Question #9:	**Your religion or spiritual views?**
Notes:	
Question #10:	**Your cultural considerations? What culture do you identify with?**
Notes:	

Additional Notes

Open-ended: Anything else to share?

Notes on Interview Experience:

Referrals and Collaboration

Oncology social workers must maintain currency with regard to their institutions' supports, community supports, and online supports for their patients. Whenever possible and appropriate, social workers should connect patients with resources such as support groups, financial supports, and online cancer support communities. Additional referral or collaboration opportunities may emerge throughout the patient's care. For example, the social worker might refer a patient to a support group in the early stages of care, but the patient might not be interested or ready to utilize this resource until 6 months after the referral. Therefore, the social worker must keep abreast of the patient's evolving care needs throughout their treatment in order to make timely and appropriate referrals to (or partnerships with) relevant stakeholders.

Oncology Education

Join Professional Networks

As an oncology social worker, connecting with other oncology professionals is beneficial to one's social work practice. First, the social worker can learn from others and share their experiences in kind. This networking also connects the oncology team to new ideas and treatments to better support patients. For more information about networking opportunities, refer to the Helpful Resources section.

Active Oncology Team Member

The social work profession contributes to the care team's understanding of patients on a deep personal level. Social workers gain insight into the behavioral, psychological, and social dimensions of a patient and how these characteristics will affect their coping during treatment. While sharing this information with the care team, the social worker must respect the patient's right to privacy by revealing only those personal details relevant to the treatment plan or by obtaining prior authorization from the patient to share certain information with the team.

Individual Specialists in Social Work

While the oncology social worker specializes in caring for patients in clinical settings, communities have social work supports that can supplement this care. Mental health and financial nonprofit agencies in the community can provide home visits or specialized oncology social work care. Knowing current community supports is vital for the oncology social worker, and collaborating with them on patient care is essential to providing comprehensive care. In treatment with patients, social workers can give referrals as well as share information about what these agencies can offer them.

Daily Rounds

Performing daily rounds provides the oncology social worker numerous opportunities for connection and outreach. From a patient and family perspective, daily rounds demonstrate the social worker's vital role on the care team. For the oncology team, the social worker's presence during daily rounds positions psychosocial issues as an integral part of the treatment plan and healing. For the oncology social worker, daily rounds provide additional insight into the medical and pharmaceutical aspects of cancer treatment. Each of these dimensions supports the necessity and benefits of conducting daily rounds.

Treatment Knowledge

It is the obligation of the oncology social worker to be educated on their specialty of cancer as well as side effects of various treatments. It is imperative for social workers to understand the side effects of specific medications in order to distinguish between medicinal side effects and mental health reactions to cancer and its treatment. Knowing about the protocols of treatment also improves the social worker's ability to support patients through their diagnosis. When the oncologist meets with a patient, they often invite the social worker to provide additional support during these consultations. Thus, oncology social workers should familiarize themselves with treatments, therapies, and their side effects in order to contribute meaningfully to the care team's work.

Social Work Interventions

Psychosocial Support

Conducted during the initial contact, the required psychosocial evaluation establishes rapport and trust between the oncology social worker and the patient. Issues identified during this evaluation will be revisited during treatment as needed. Also, the oncology social worker will provide regular check-ins and offer support. "Other interventions involved communication skills training, patient education, patient navigation, identifying and addressing psychological distress such as depression and coping or providing emotional support and interventions addressing a particular group of patients or specific symptom using a multidisciplinary team" (Pockett et al., 2015, p. 597). Because each visit offers unique opportunities for social work interventions, the social worker draws from any of the aforementioned support techniques to meet the patient's and their family's needs.

Providing social work interventions to the caregivers is another dimension of oncology social work. It is evident that the patient is not the only client of the social worker. Caregivers provide significant support toward ensuring the health and well-being of the patient. Therefore, oncology social workers also

provide support to caregivers. "Caregivers are often faced with an overwhelming amount of clinical information and rely heavily on healthcare providers to help understand complex information" (Shin et al., 2020, p. 63). It is therefore important to acknowledge that caregivers can have the same psychosocial distress as patients. It allows for better communication between the caregiver and the patient. When there is conflict, it can negatively affect the health of the patient.

Case Management

Oncology social workers provide case management in collaboration with the team. For example, social workers need to know the process of approving durable medical equipment. Another common responsibility is working with insurance providers to procure additional supports for patients. When evaluating each case, the oncology social worker must take into account the treatment's financial impacts on the patient, their caregivers, and their family and provide essential financial resources when necessary. In summary, the oncology social worker must remain flexible and adaptable in their approach to case management.

Referrals

Oncology social workers contribute to their patients' comprehensive care by referring patients to hospital services (e.g., support groups) and community agencies designed specifically for oncology patients and their families. It is therefore the oncology social worker's responsibility to identify and collaborate with these agencies, either by visiting these community resources in-person with clients or by connecting clients with online supports that explain these services. "Online interventions enable caregivers to easily access useful resources and participate in a variety of simple activities using their devices" (Shin et al., 2020, p. 61). It is often helpful for the oncology social worker to develop a list of these resources to hand out to patients and their families. These materials are especially critical for this population because they are often immune suppressed and unable to be around people, so online supports are critical for their physical health.

Addressing Anxiety, Depression, and Grief

Following a cancer diagnosis, a client often grieves for their former life. Seemingly overnight, they are forced to make an extraordinary adjustment in their worldview and outlook, typically without time to process their emotions. Therefore, the oncology social worker must complete ongoing screenings for mental health reactions to the cancer diagnosis or treatment. Although the social worker can in some cases address issues that are identified, they can also refer patients to internal or external psychotherapists. Because oncology centers recognize that cancer diagnoses can produce significant psychological stress, oncology center protocols are beginning to "implement screening programs for psychosocial distress as new criterion for accreditation" (Pirl et al., 2014, p. 2946).

Post-Traumatic Growth

During or after treatment, some patients might express a desire to mentor other cancer patients, either one-on-one or in a support group of their own design. Contributing to someone else's treatment gives these patients a sense of purpose and might improve their overall well-being. The oncology social worker can use the patient's philanthropic activities as an opportunity to assess the patient's post-traumatic growth and to intervene when necessary. Equally important, the patient who shares their experiences might give hope to new patients, enabling them to see beyond their present circumstances to a potentially brighter future.

Acknowledging Patient Wishes

At times, the oncology social worker must serve as an intermediary between the patient, the care team, and, occasionally, the family. Sometimes, patients share that they want to stop treatment or feel uncomfortable discussing a side effect of treatment with the medical team. In those cases, it is the oncology social worker's responsibility to communicate this information (when permissible) with the team. Other times, the oncology social worker must facilitate communication between the patient and their family regarding complex or emotionally sensitive aspects of treatment. Whatever the case, the oncology social worker facilitates communication between stakeholders in ways that respect the patient's wishes and preserve their right to privacy.

"Unrelated Social" Work Support

Because life is complicated by multiple layers of family and interpersonal dynamics, patients undoubtedly come to treatment with prior issues and concerns. It is the responsibility of the social worker to address these issues, even if that means making an outside referral. "Patients with cancer have different motives for seeking psychological counseling, not all of which are related to cancer distress" (Lilliehorn et al., 2019, p. 495). A cancer diagnosis can trigger multiple layers of dysfunction with families that predate the diagnosis; if unaddressed, these layers of dysfunction can interfere with the patient's treatment. Acknowledging the social and emotional context of these additional issues is part and parcel of providing holistic patient support.

Being Present

Simply being present during difficult times is a powerful contribution to the patient's care. Sometimes, oncologists deliver difficult news, and the oncology social worker steps in to counsel the patient when the oncologist leaves the room. Other times, the social worker simply listens to the patient's disclosures of distress without interrupting or trying to make the situation better; they listen and acknowledge the patient's feelings and experiences, ensuring that the patient feels heard before attempting to intervene or make recommendations. Active listening and being present in the moment are two of the most basic yet impactful skills in the oncology social worker's skill set.

Bright IDEAS: Problem-Solving Skills Training for Everyday Living

Problem-solving is an effective intervention in social work practice. The Children's Oncology Group has researched, developed, and published the Bright IDEAS (Identify, Define, Evaluate, Act, and See) intervention; the creators of Bright IDEAS have made all of the information and resources public and accessible online (see the Helpful Resources section). By incorporating the Bright IDEAS intervention into their social work practice, oncology social workers help increase the independence and confidence of their patients, who often struggle with decision-making.

The stress of a patient's diagnosis and treatment, coupled with other life pressures, can overwhelm the patient and make even the smallest decision quite challenging. The simplicity of the Bright IDEAS intervention complements oncology social work in several ways. First, it can be used with patients and their caregivers. It can also be used in individual and group settings. The Bright IDEAS format is a step-by-step approach that patients feel comfortable using with a social worker as well as on their own. Following the psychosocial assessment, the oncology social worker can implement the Bright IDEAS intervention to support patients during their cancer treatment,

giving them a tool that they can use in other facets of their lives as well.

Facilitate Support Groups

Cancer can be both physically and mentally isolating. Many patients' social connections are severed or compromised as their cancer treatment progresses; for example, some patients cannot work, attend school, or engage in social activities. Also, family and friend connections might wane for a variety of reasons at a time when patients most need these support systems. Fortunately, evidence suggests that participation in a support group can provide patients the much-needed social support from people who truly understand the impact of a cancer diagnosis. For this reason, referrals to cancer support groups are beneficial to many patients.

An oncology social worker who personally facilitates a support group gains insight into the myriad dynamics and effects of cancer and its treatment. Running open-ended or closed-group sessions provides the oncology social worker with a deep understanding of factors that might not be gleaned from individual sessions. These benefits are best illustrated in Donald L. Rosenstein and Justin M. Yopp's *The Group* (2018), which brilliantly depicts the powerful therapeutic healing that can occur in group therapy. Their book is an invaluable resource for oncology social workers in particular.

Helpful Resources

American Psychosocial Oncology Society: https://apos-society.org
Association of Oncology Social Workers: https://aosw.org
Association of Pediatric Oncology Social Workers: https://aposw.org
Bright Ideas: https://www.childrensoncologygroup.org/index.php/bright-ideas
National Cancer Institute: https://www.cancer.gov
National Cancer Institute. NCI Fact Sheets: https://www.cancer.gov/publications/fact-sheets

The Quality of Life Instrument: https://www.midss.
    org/sites/default/files/qol-cs.pdf
Stupid Cancer: https://stupidcancer.org
The Samfund: http://www.thesamfund.org

References

Burg, M. A., Zebrack, B., Walsh, K., Maramaldi, P., Lim, J., Smolinski, K. M., & Lawson, K. (2010). Barriers to accessing quality health care for cancer patients: A survey of members of the Association of Oncology Social Work. *Social Work in Health Care*, *49*(1), 38–52. https://doi.org/10.1080/00981380903018470

Lilliehorn, S., Isaksson, J., & Salander, P. (2019). What does an oncology social worker deal with in patient consultations? An empirical study. *Social Work in Health Care*, *58*(5), 494–508. https://doi.org/10.1080/00981389.2019.1587661

Pirl, W. F., Fann, J. R., Greer, J. A., Braun, I., Deshields, T., Fulcher, C., Harvey, E., Holland, J., Kennedy, V., Lazenby, M., Wagner, L., Underhill, M., Walker, D. K., Zabora, J., Zebrack, B., & Bardwell, W. A. (2014). Recommendations for the implementation of distress screening programs in cancer centers: Report from the American Psychosocial Oncology Society (APOS), Association of Oncology Social Work (AOSW), and Oncology Nursing Society (ONS) joint task force. *Cancer, 120*(19), 2946–2954. https://doi.org/10.1002/cncr.28750

Pockett, R., Dzidowska, M., & Hobbs, K. (2015). Social work intervention research with adult cancer patients: A literature review and reflection on knowledge-building for practice. *Social Work in Health Care*, *54*(7), 582–614. https://doi.org/10.1080/00981389.2015.1046577

Rosenstein, D. L., & Yopp, J. M. (2018). *The group*. Oxford University Press.

Shin, J. Y., & Choi, S. W. (2020). Interventions to promote caregiver resilience. *Current Opinion in Supportive and Palliative Care, 14*(1), 60–66. https://doi.org/10.1097/SPC.0000000000000481

Zebrack, B., Kayser, K., Padgett, L., Sundstrom, L., Jobin, C., Nelson, K., & Fineberg, I. C. (2016). Institutional capacity to provide psychosocial oncology support services: A report from the Association of Oncology Social Work. *Cancer, 122*(12), 1937–1994. https://doi.org/10.1002/cncr.30016

Animal-Assisted Interventions

Diane Scotland-Coogan and Elizabeth Ruegg

Animal-assisted interventions and research pertaining to their effectiveness have flourished in the past 20 years, but both have been hampered by inconsistencies in classifying the different types of interventions that are applied and even by the descriptions and terms that are used to describe therapeutic interactions between humans and animals (LaJoie, 2003). Labels such as "pet therapy," "animal-assisted therapy in counseling," and "canine-assisted interactions" have proliferated with the growth of the field, causing confusion for providers, recipients of service, and researchers alike.

Fine and Mackintosh (cited in Fine, 2015) employ the term *animal-assisted interventions* as an overarching umbrella that encompasses animal-assisted activities, animal-assisted education, and animal-assisted therapy. This terminological framework is consistent with that used by the American Veterinary Medical Association ("Service, emotional support and therapy animals"; n.d.) as well as by the International Association of Human–Animal Interaction Organizations, which created a task force composed of academics, veterinary specialists, and clinicians from other medical and mental health disciplines for the purpose of standardizing and defining the many facets of

animal-assisted interventions and developing ethical standards around them (Jegatheesan et al., 2014).

Animal-assisted interventions utilize the human–animal bond in order to aid people with their social, physical, emotional, or educational needs. The animals involved in this work are typically personal pets that have been trained by their guardian handlers to display predictable behavior and perform specific tasks in response to particular cues. They are specifically selected for their affiliative nature; that is, they appear to enjoy and seek out social contact with humans beyond their immediate family group (McConnell & Fine, 2015). This affiliation characteristic is important because it minimizes the risk that the animal will ignore the target of the visit (the hospitalized adult, the child in school, and so on) in favor of its guardian handler.

Animal-assisted activities include social visits made by volunteer handlers and their therapy dogs to patients in hospitals, nursing homes, rehabilitation facilities, and other institutional settings. In order to earn the "therapy dog" designation, the animal must demonstrate through testing that it has a trusting, cooperative relationship with its guardian handler, impeccable obedience skills, a relaxed and friendly disposition, and a temperament that is suited to both the amount and type of interaction which commonly occur during a visit (Butler, 2013). The general purpose of an animal-assisted activity is to provide enjoyment, offer pleasant distraction, stimulate social interaction, and reduce stress (Howie, 2015). Although they typically work in non-emergent situations, volunteer "comfort dog" crisis response teams are specially trained to work at the sites of man-made and natural disasters for the purpose of providing calming comfort to survivors and first responders (Stapf, 2017). Whether animal-assisted activities occur in emergent or non-emergent situations, the human handler is not responsible for rendering professional services, working with the person being visited on specific therapeutic goals and objectives, or completing clinical documentation.

Fine and Mackintosh (cited in Fine, 2015) define *animal-assisted education* as the inclusion of animals to facilitate the provision of humane education as well as animal-assisted reading programs that take place in schools, libraries, and other learning centers. These programs are designed to encourage struggling or reluctant young readers by pairing them with amiable therapy dogs that provide nonjudgmental companionship while the child reads aloud, which has been found to improve the acquisition of reading skills as well as to increase students' enthusiasm for reading (Kirnan et al., 2016).

Animal-assisted therapy, according to Fine and Mackintosh (cited in Fine, 2015), includes animal-assisted psychotherapy, animal-assisted social work, and animal-assisted occupational and physical therapy, among other professional services. In these modalities, appropriately credentialed medical and mental health providers, working within their professional scope of practice, utilize the principles of the human–animal bond to facilitate treatment with their patients/clients (Gammonley et al., 1997). This process includes the development of clinical documentation that reflects treatment planning with clearly articulated goals for change, objectives that are specific and measurable, and the expectation of identifiable progress toward the treatment goals.

Animal-Assisted Therapy in Generalist Social Work Practice

In a national study of social workers in clinical practice, Risley-Curtiss (2010) found that 23% of the randomly sampled social workers included animals in some aspect of their practice, such as making visits to institutional settings or engaging in animal-assisted psychotherapy. Those who reported including animals in their professional interventions with clients were almost twice as likely to work with dogs than with cats, and smaller animals such as birds and hamsters were also represented. The social workers who included therapy animals in their client interactions were most likely to involve their personal therapy animals in the visits, whereas a smaller percentage encouraged or allowed clients to bring their own pets to the appointments.

Of the social workers who reported including animals in some aspect of their practice, 82% reported no specialized training in animal-assisted therapy (Risley-Curtiss, 2010). This may be due to the relative paucity of professional animal-assisted therapy training programs in the United States and the absence of standardized guidelines for social workers who practice animal-assisted therapy. The National Association of Social Workers Code of Ethics (2017) promotes diversity, the ecological person-in-environment perspective, and contextual sensitivity in understanding and responding to human behavior. However, despite the fact that 67% of American households had at least one pet in 2019 (Bedford, 2020), the Code of Ethics is silent on the ethical considerations of the human–animal bond, the link between animal abuse and interpersonal violence (Boat, 1999), or the steadily increasing integration of animals into the provision of professional social work services. By contrast, the American Counseling Association has published counseling competencies for animal-assisted therapy that are designed to guide professional counselors who include animals in their clinical practice (Stewart et al., 2016).

Animal-Assisted Psychotherapy: The Therapeutic Triad

Social workers who engage in animal-assisted psychotherapy establish a therapeutic triad in the consultation room. The change process of individual psychotherapy has traditionally depended on a dyadic relationship between the therapist and the client. Animal-assisted psychotherapy, by contrast, involves an animal— typically a dog or, less commonly, a "therapy zoo" with multiple animals—that serves as a therapeutic third (Parish-Plass, 2013). The inclusion of the animal in the psychotherapy process results in the development of a triadic relationship between the therapist, the client, and the animal. This complex triad offers the client the potential for a rich psychotherapeutic experience and provides a framework around which the client can explore thoughts and feelings, resolve intrapsychic conflicts, correct unrealistic and/or negativistic self-referencing beliefs, and practice relationship-building and other healthy skills and behaviors.

Animal-assisted psychotherapy as an interventional approach is sufficiently flexible that treatment providers who operate from a broad range of theoretical perspectives may involve animals in therapy activities in order to

assist their clients with the process of change (Bruneau & Johnson, 2011). For example, psychodynamic therapists who are grounded in attachment theory may include an animal in their work with a client in order to encourage the development of a positive bond between the client and the animal. The establishment of that bond can be especially fruitful for the client whose experiences with insecure early attachments have resulted in trust aversion. The introduction of an affable dog or other animal within the context of psychotherapy may reduce the client's abandonment fears and encourage the establishment of a secure base that can be generalized to the therapist and, later, to other people; this may eventually pave the way for deeper and more fulfilling relationships than the client has previously experienced (Zilcha-Mano et al., 2011b). Because therapy dogs are selected for their high degree of affiliation, meaning that they themselves are motivated to create connections with humans, the rejection risk threshold for the client is reduced.

Animal-assisted psychotherapy facilitates the exploration of thoughts, feelings, and behaviors—the three main spheres of focus in the psychotherapy process. Scholarly literature further supports the approach due to the unique and specific benefits it provides, such as comforting physical contact that is difficult to offer within the ethical parameters of the traditional psychotherapy relationship (Parish-Plass, 2013); reduced autonomic arousal (Lefkowitz et al., 2005); and increased motivation to attend and participate in treatment, especially for those who had previous negative experiences in therapy or those who have not before been in therapy and who are anxious about or resistant to the process (Lange et al., 2007). An additional advantage of animal-assisted psychotherapy is that treatment plan goals and objectives that involve animal-assisted activities can be developed for clients who experience a wide array of psychiatric illnesses and can result in beneficial skill development across a variety of domains.

Emotional Support Animals and Service Dogs

Therapy dogs are often invited to make visits to organizations that are not generally pet-friendly, such as hospitals and schools, but they do not have any special legal protections or rights of public access. Emotional support animals, by contrast, are permitted under the Fair Housing Act to reside in no-pet housing, and under the Air Carrier Access Act, they are permitted to fly in the main cabin of an aircraft with their guardian handlers at no charge. (Bourland, 2009). Beyond housing and transportation, however, emotional support animals do not have rights of public access to stores, restaurants, and other businesses. They may be any species and are not required to have any obedience training or to perform specific tasks, beyond offering emotional support or comfort to their guardian handlers. In order to qualify for an emotional support animal, the guardian handler must have a psychiatric diagnosis that results in disability and must obtain documentation from a health care professional, such as a physician or social worker, that attests to the individual's need for the animal in order to alleviate some aspect of the disability (Younggren et al., 2020).

Service dogs have special legal protections under the Americans with Disabilities Act, along with rights of public access that are not afforded to companion animals, therapy dogs, emotional support animals, or other pets. They work for and on behalf of their guardian handlers to the exclusion of all others, and they are expected to ignore environmental distractions, including humans other than their guardian handlers, while performing their tasks. They may be owner trained or professionally trained to perform specific tasks that mitigate the disability of their individual handler. For example, the service dog working for a deaf handler is trained to alert to audible signals such as a crying baby or a doorbell; the guide dog for the blind is trained to lead its handler; and the service dog working for a mobility impaired handler is trained to retrieve items, open or close doors, or push buttons. In order to earn their designation as working dogs that enjoy legal protection and rights of public access, service dogs must be task-trained to perform at least one skill that meets the specific needs of their guardian handler, as well as to demonstrate advanced obedience so that they do not become a nuisance (e.g., by barking or soiling) in areas of public accommodation, such as stores and restaurants (Mills & Yeager, 2012). Service dogs work on behalf of people with a wide variety of disabilities and medical needs, including those with sensory, developmental, mobility, or psychiatric impairments.

Animal-Assisted Intervention for Post-Traumatic Stress Disorder

Post-traumatic stress disorder (PTSD) is a debilitating disorder experienced by many veterans returning from combat. Unfortunately, half or more of all military members and veterans with deployment-related trauma responses resist participating in more traditional treatments such as prolonged-exposure therapy and cognitive processing therapy (Monson et al., 2006; Scotland-Coogan et al., 2020). Reports of veterans' participation in these programs state a 50% early dropout rate, and many veterans decline any involvement (O'Brien, 2015; Scotland-Coogan et al., 2020). Reported reasons for this resistance to participate and early termination of treatment include time limitations, client hesitancy to talk about their trauma experiences, disconnects with the therapist, a perceived stigma of asking for help, and a desire to not be viewed as "weak" when acknowledging their symptoms (O'Brien, 2015; Scotland-Coogan et al., 2020). There are increasingly more complementary alternative treatments for PTSD that may address these barriers to treatment, one of which is service dogs. Statistically significant benefits have been found to support veterans attending programs to train their own service dog (Scotland-Coogan et al., 2020; Whitworth et al., 2019).

Veterans Training Their Own Service Dogs

Service dogs "are individually trained to do work or perform tasks for people with disabilities" (U.S. Department of Justice, 2011). Research on veterans training their own dogs has shown clinically significant decreases in PTSD-related symptoms, such as anxious arousal, anxiety, hyperarousal, intrusive experiences, and defensive avoidance, that appear to contribute to gains in their social and relational functioning (Seal et al., 2007; Scotland-Coogan et al., 2020; Whitworth et al., 2019). These relational gains may include getting along with others, decreased insecure attachment, relational avoidance, and rejection sensitivity (O'Haire & Rodriguez, 2018; Renaud, 2008; Scotland-Coogan et al., 2020). Research also provides support for the use of attachment theory as a primary means of understanding the underlying mechanisms on how these service dog training programs help veterans with PTSD (O'Haire et al., 2015; Renaud, 2008; Scotland-Coogan et al., 2020; Vitztum & Urbanik, 2016). Developing a close bond with their service dog, being able to attach to their service dog, may provide a "relationship bridge" that may assist these veterans to reconnect with family members, partners,

and friends. The veteran's bonding relationship with their service dog may nurture development of a more positive perception of themselves and of their relationship partners. Connecting with and forming a "grounding relationship" with their canine also appears to remind these veterans that they are currently not in a threat environment, which then likely decreases relational and social avoidance (O'Haire et al., 2015; Scotland-Coogan et al., 2020; Zilcha-Mano et al., 2011a). Their relationship with their service dog could improve veterans' positive concept of self as well as their concept of their relationship partners. Improved relationship capacity may foster a decrease in suicidality given that relational difficulties are associated with increased risk for suicide among military veterans (Rozanov & Carli, 2012), which has been supported by research on service dog programs (Scotland-Coogan, 2017). Still another consideration is that the supportive service animal that is almost solely focused on their owner may increase the veteran's secretion of oxytocin, which leads to improvements in mood and relational and social engagement (Beetz et al., 2012; Rodriquez et al., 2018; Scotland-Coogan, 2019; Scotland-Coogan et al., 2020).

Case Example

John served in Operation Enduring Freedom and Operation Iraqi Freedom in special forces. He was proud of what he had done for his country. Serving two tours, John decided it was time to leave the military and join his family back home. Since being home, he has found he is struggling with issues that never plagued him in the past. He is angry much of the time, he does not like to leave the house, people in general frustrate him, he cannot relate to his wife or children anymore, and he prefers to be alone. He finds it difficult to sleep, walking the house at night checking doors and windows to make sure his family is safe and secure. His children seem to be afraid of him, and he and his wife fight frequently. He has also noticed his balance is off. He knew he had injured his back but tried to ignore this; however, now he could tell it was getting worse. He felt weak and broken both emotionally and physically. Eventually, depression also set in. He started drinking alcohol to numb himself both physically and mentally. Finally, John's wife gave him an ultimatum of getting help or she and the children would leave.

John decided to reach out for help and participate in traditional therapies. He first tried medication, which made him feel as if he was moving in slow motion, in almost a "zombie-like" state. This led to cognitive–behavioral therapy, prolonged exposure, and attending groups. None of these seemed to significantly relieve the depression, anger, or anxiety he was dealing with. He heard from a friend about a program in which he would train his own service dog. His friend told him that it had helped with his symptoms, and he believed his relationships had improved. Not truly believing this would help, John thought he would give it a try. He thought this was much less embarrassing than going to therapy.

Once paired with his new service dog, John started the 19-week training program. During each weekly session, he worked on a new obedience technique and then practiced this during the following week. He noticed immediately that he felt emotion for the dog, something he had not experienced for a very long time. When the dog began to respond to his commands, he started to feel a little more in control of his world. His sleep improved; he felt comfortable closing his eyes and relaxing because he believed his dog would alert him to any threats. His dog would also wake him from nightmares soon after they started, and he noticed these nightmares became less frequent and less violent. In addition, his dog alerted him if anyone was coming up behind him, which helped diminish his startle reflex.

John felt safer in public with his dog, and when he was losing his balance the dog would lean into him to help him regain his equilibrium. Over time, John noticed his anger, anxiety, and depression had lifted significantly. He also found that his relationships with his family and friends greatly improved.

The changes John experienced are typical responses of veterans who train their own service dogs. Research demonstrates the significant reduction in PTSD symptom severity and improved relationships. This suggests that this type of intervention should be a consideration for veterans with PTSD.

Assessment Considerations and Instruments

Many instruments are available to test for post-traumatic stress symptom severity. One such instrument, the Trauma Symptom Inventory-2 (Briere, 2011), is a 136-item evidence-based measure used in the evaluation of acute and chronic post-traumatic symptomatology, including the effects of physical assault, combat experiences, major accidents, and natural disasters. It was designed to assess post-traumatic stress and other psychological sequelae of traumatic events. Having the veterans complete this at the beginning of the first class, and again after the last class, will provide information on the change in PTSD symptom severity. Another instrument is the World Health Organization Disability Assessment Schedule 2.0 (WHODAS 2.0). This questionnaire asks about difficulties due to health conditions, including both physical and mental health. It also examines problems associated with alcohol and drugs (World Health Organization, 2020). The domains covered by WHODAS 2.0 include cognition (understanding and communicating), mobility (moving and getting around), self-care (hygiene, dressing, eating, and staying alone), getting along (interacting with others), life activities (domestic responsibilities, leisure, work, and school), and participation (joining in community activities). Having this completed before the first class and after the last class will provide information about the veterans' perception of their quality of life.

Having a veteran train their own service dog is a strength-based and evidence-based treatment that may be used as a stand-alone treatment or as a gateway to participate more fully in other forms of treatment. For those who struggle with stigma issues, this may be viewed as less stigmatizing than most traditional forms of treatment. With the goal of lessening the severity of PTSD symptoms and improving quality of life, this should be a consideration for veterans struggling with this debilitating disorder.

Conclusion

Animal-assisted interventions are steadily increasing in our culture, and the body of research on their utility and effectiveness continues to grow. Social workers may be professionally involved in animal-assisted activities, animal-assisted education, and animal-assisted therapy, and they will likely benefit from the development of social work–specific guidelines for practice with all these animal-assisted interventions. In addition, social workers should strive to become knowledgeable about emotional support animals and service dogs in order to advocate for their clients who could obtain benefit from them.

Helpful Resources

American Kennel Club Therapy Dog Program: https://www.akc.org/sports/title-recognition-program/therapy-dog-program

Service Dogs for America: https://www.servicedogsforamerica.org/#:~:text=At%20Service%20Dogs%20for%20America,religion%2C%20gender%20or%20sexual%20orientation

Equine Assisted Growth and Learning Association: https://www.eagala.org

Professional Association of Therapeutic Horsemanship International: https://www.pathintl.org

References

American Veterinary Medical Association. (n.d.). *Service, emotional support and therapy animals.* https://www.avma.org/resources-tools/animal-health-welfare/service-emotional-support-and-therapy-animals

Bedford, E. (2020). *Number of pet owning households in the United States in 2019/20, by species.* https://www.statista.com/statistics/198095/pets-in-the-united-states-by-type

Beetz, A., Uvnäs-Moberg, K., Julius, H., & Kotrschal, K. (2012). Psychosocial and psychophysiological effects of human–animal interactions: The possible role of oxytocin. *Frontiers in Psychology, 3,* 234.

Boat, B. (1999). Abuse of children and abuse of animals: Using the link to inform child assessment and protection. In F. R. Ascione & P. Arkow (Eds.), *Child abuse, domestic violence, and animal abuse: Linking the circles of compassion for prevention and intervention* (pp. 83–100). Purdue University Press.

Bourland, K. M. (2009). Advocating change within the ADA: The struggle to recognize emotional-support animals as service animals. *University of Louisville Law Review, 48*(1), 197–220.

Bruneau, L., & Johnson, A. (2011). *Fido and Freud meet: Integrating animal-assisted therapy into traditional counseling theories.* Paper presented at the ACA Conference, March 27.

Butler, K. (2013). *Therapy dogs today: Their gifts, our obligation.* Funpuddle Publishing Associates.

Fine, A. H. (2015). *Handbook on animal-assisted therapy: Foundations and guidelines for animal-assisted interventions* (4th ed.). Academic Press.

Gammonley, J., Howie, A. R., Kirwin, S., Zapf, S. A., Frye, J., Freeman, G., Stuart-Russell, R. (1997). *Animal-assisted therapy: Therapeutic interventions.* Delta Society Press.

Howie, A. R. (2015). *Teaming with your therapy dog.* Purdue University Press.

Jegatheesan, B., Beetz, A., Ormerod, E., Johnson, R., Fine, A., Yamazaki, K., Dudzik, C., Garcia, R. M., Winkle, M., Choi, G. (2014). *IAHAIO white paper: Definitions for animal assisted intervention and guidelines for wellness of animals involved.* International Association of Human–Animal Interaction Organizations.

Kirnan, J., Siminerio, S., & Wong, Z. (2016). The impact of a therapy dog program on children's reading skills and attitudes toward reading. *Early Childhood Education Journal, 44*(6), 637–651.

LaJoie, K. R. (2003). An evaluation of the effectiveness of using animals in therapy. *Dissertation Abstracts International: Section B: The Sciences and Engineering, 64*, 424–431.

Lange, A. M., Cox, J. A., Bernert, D. J., & Jenkins, C. D. (2007). Is counseling going to the dogs? An exploratory study related to the inclusion of an animal in group counseling with adolescents. *Journal of Creativity in Mental Health, 2*, 17–31.

Lefkowitz, C., Paharia, I., Prout, M., Debiak, D., & Bleiberg, J. (2005). Animal-assisted therapy for prolonged exposure: A treatment for survivors of sexual assault suffering from posttraumatic stress disorder. *Society and Animals, 13*, 275–295.

McConnell, P. B., & Fine, A. (2015). Understanding the other end of the leash: What therapists need to understand about their co-therapists. In A. Fine (Ed.), *Handbook on animal-assisted therapy: Theoretical foundations and guidelines for practice* (pp. 103–113). Elsevier.

Mills, J. T., & Yeager, A. F. (2012). Definitions of animals used in healthcare settings. *U.S. Army Medical Department Journal*, 12–17.

Monson, C. M., Schnurr, P. P., Resick, P. A., Friedman, M. J., Young-Xu, Y., & Stevens, S. P. (2006). Cognitive processing therapy for veterans with military-related posttraumatic stress disorder. *Journal of Consulting and Clinical Psychology, 74*(5), 898–907.

National Association of Social Workers. (2017). *Code of ethics.* https://www.socialworkers.org/about/ethics/code-of-ethics

O'Brien, B. (2015, August 11). *Seeking and studying alternative PTSD treatments.* WLRN Miami–South Florida. http://wlrn.org/post/seeking-and-studying-alternative-PTSD-treatments

O'Haire, M. E., McKenzie, S. J., Beck, A. M., & Slaughter, V. (2015). Animals may act as social buffers: Skin conductance arousal in children with autism spectrum disorder in a social context. *Developmental Psychobiology, 57*(5), 584–595.

O'Haire, M. E., & Rodriguez, K. E. (2018). Preliminary efficacy of service dogs as a complementary treatment for posttraumatic stress disorder in military members and veterans. *Journal of Consulting and Clinical Psychology, 86*(2), 179.

Parish-Plass, N. (2013). *Animal-assisted psychotherapy: Theory, issues, and practice.* Purdue University Press.

Renaud, E. F. (2008). The attachment characteristics of combat veterans with PTSD. *Traumatology, 14*(3), 1–12.

Risley-Curtiss, C. (2010). Social work practitioners and the human–companion animal bond: A national study. *Clinical Social Work, 55*(1), 38–46.

Rozanov, V., & Carli, V. (2012). Suicide among war veterans. *International Journal of Environmental Research and Public Health, 9*, 2504–2519.

Scotland-Coogan, D. E. (2017). Receiving and training a service dog: The impact on combat veterans with posttraumatic stress disorder. Doctoral dissertation, Capella University.

Scotland-Coogan, D. E. (2019). Relationships, socialization and combat veterans: The impact of receiving and training a service dog. *The Qualitative Report, 24*(8), 1897–1914.

Scotland-Coogan, D. E., Whitworth, J. D., & Wharton, T. (2020, January 21). Outcomes of participation in a service dog training program for veterans with PTSD. *Society and Animals*, 1–22.

Seal, K. H., Bertenthal, D., Miner, C. R., Sen, S., & Marmar, C. (2007). Bringing the war back home: Mental health disorders among 103,788 US veterans returning from Iraq and Afghanistan seen at Department of Veterans Affairs facilities. *Archives of Internal Medicine, 167*(5), 476–482. https://doi.org/10.1001/archinte.167.5.476

Stapf, J. (2017). *A beginner's guide to comfort dogs.* https://www.hopeaacr.org/2016/fema-offers-a-beginners-guide-to-comfort-dogs/

Stewart, L. A., Chang, C. Y., Parker, L. K., & Grubbs, N. (2016). *Animal-assisted therapy in counseling competencies.* American Counseling Association, Animal-Assisted Therapy in Mental Health Interest Network.

U.S. Department of Justice. (2011). *Service animals.* https://www.ada.gov/service_animals_2010.htm

Vitztum, C., & Urbanik, J. (2016). Assessing the dog: A theoretical analysis of the companion animal's actions in human–animal interactions. *Society & Animals, 24*(2), 172–185.

Whitworth, J. D., Scotland-Coogan, D., & Wharton, T. (2019). Service dog training programs for veterans with PTSD: Results of a pilot-controlled study. *Social Work in Health Care, 58*(4), 412–430.

World Health Organization. (2020). *WHO Disability Assessment Schedule 2.0 (WHODAS 2.0).* https://apps.who.int/iris/bitstream/handle/10665/43974/9789241547598_eng.pdf;jsessionid=4DC61B1EB092C96364FF0DDF264475E0?sequence=1#:~:text=The%20World%20Health%20Organization%20Disability%20Assessment%20Schedule%20%28-WHODAS,for%20measuring%20health%20and%20disabil-%20ity%20across%20cultures

Younggren, J. N., Boness, C. L., Bryant, L. M., & Koocher, G. P. (2020). Emotional support animal assessments: Toward a standard and comprehensive model for mental health professionals. *Professional Psychology, 51*(2), 156–162.

Zilcha-Mano, S., Mikulincer, M., & Shaver, P. R. (2011a). An attachment perspective on human–pet relationships: Conceptualization and assessment of pet attachment orientations. *Journal of Research in Personality, 45*(4), 345–357.

Zilcha-Mano, S., Mikulincer, M., & Shaver, P. R. (2011b). Pet in the therapy room: An attachment perspective on animal-assisted therapy. *Attachment & Human Development, 13*(6), 541–561.

Dementia and Family Caregiving

Noelle L. Fields and Joanna Glover

The number of older adults aged 65 years or older in the United States is projected to roughly double from 52 million in 2018 to 95 million in 2060 (Mather et al., 2019). This growth represents a significant demographic trend that brings both challenges and opportunities to the social work profession. As the population ages, the need for social workers with knowledge and skills related to working with older adults and their families is relevant to the profession across all practice specialty areas. In particular, social workers will find that they are increasingly serving persons with dementia and their families in a variety of settings.

Dementia is not an inevitable and/or normal part of aging; however, its prevalence and incidence increase as people age (Qiu & Fratiglioni, 2018). The neurocognitive disorders category in the fifth edition of the *Diagnostic and Statistical Manual of Mental Disorders* (DSM-5; American Psychiatric Association, 2013) covers the group of disorders (referred to in the DSM-IV as dementia, delirium, amnestic, and other cognitive disorders) in which the primary clinical problem is acquired, impaired cognition (i.e., not been present since birth or very early life) and a

decline from previous levels of functioning. The DSM-5 uses *dementia* as the common term for degenerative dementia disorders that typically affect older adults. However, it is important to note that dementia is not a specific disease but, rather, the overall term for a group of symptoms. The primary symptoms of dementia are difficulties with memory, language, problem-solving, and other cognitive skills that impact a person's ability to independently perform everyday activities (Alzheimer's Association, 2020). Although some cognitive functioning may slow as people grow older, these changes do not necessarily mean that a person has dementia. Many conditions (e.g., delirium, depression, and infections) can cause dementia-like symptoms that, once treated, may be reversed.

Alzheimer's disease is the most common cause of dementia, accounting for roughly 60–80% of cases, and it is the sixth leading cause of death in the United States (Alzheimer's Association, 2020). Alzheimer's disease is progressive, meaning that it gets worse over time. Currently, there are medications that can help slow symptoms of Alzheimer's disease, but there are no medications to prevent or stop the disease (i.e., there is no cure) (National

Institutes of Health, 2018). People aged 65 year or older can live an average of 4–8 years after a diagnosis of Alzheimer's disease; however, some individuals may live as long as 20 years after the diagnosis (Alzheimer's Association, 2020). In 2020, approximately 5.8 million Americans aged 65 years or older were living with Alzheimer's disease—a number that is projected to grow to 13.8 million by 2050 unless a cure is found (Alzheimer's Association, 2020). With an increase in the number of racial and ethnic minorities in the United States aged 65 years or older, there is also a projected increase in Alzheimer's disease and related dementias among older persons belonging to diverse racial and ethnic groups. In particular, the negative physical and cognitive outcomes associated with Alzheimer's disease may have a greater impact on African Americans because they are twice as likely to be diagnosed with the disease compared with other racial and ethnic groups (Alzheimer's Association, 2020).

The challenges associated with Alzheimer's disease are not limited to the person with the diagnosis. The vast majority of care for older adults with Alzheimer's disease in the United States is provided by family members, friends, and/ or other unpaid caregivers. Family caregivers are faced with a myriad of challenges when providing help and assistance to a person with Alzheimer's disease. A large body of research suggests that the challenges associated with managing memory impairment, functional decline, and behavioral problems of care recipients with Alzheimer's disease pose considerable emotional, psychological, and physical health risks for family caregivers. However, the experience of dementia caregiving varies based on the unique background and culture of each family. For example, African American dementia family caregivers often report more positive aspects of caregiving compared with White caregivers (Roth et al., 2015). African American older adults also historically experience health

disparities and limited access to resources, which may negatively impact conditions such as dementia (Epps et al., 2018).

Case Example

Valerie is a 75-year-old African American woman who lives with her husband, Joe, who is 80 years old. They have lived together in their home of more than 40 years. They have one grown daughter who lives and works full-time nearby. Early in 2018, Valerie noticed that Joe started to frequently repeat questions and misplace items. Their daughter also commented that her father seemed to be forgetting conversations that had taken place between them. Over the next several months, other friends and family began commenting that Joe used to be "really sharp" but that during the past year he seemed to have difficulty learning and remembering short-term information. Valerie began to sleep only a few hours at night because Joe was up and down at night with restlessness. She was extremely tired during the day and began seeing increasingly less of her church friends and neighbors. Joe did not want to meet with his church friends either due to embarrassment that he would lose his train of thought during a conversation.

As time went on, Valerie became increasingly involved in Joe's care. She began to help him with dressing and grooming. She took care of all the meal preparation and paying the bills. Joe's symptoms (forgetfulness, confusion, and memory loss) began increasing in frequency and intensity. Valerie declined outside help, saying that she preferred to take care of him herself. When she needed help, she reached out to her daughter, who would come over when she could. She also relied on her friends from her women's church group. Valerie began worrying at night that Joe would wander out of the house, and the lack of sleep began to take its toll on her. Valerie was exhausted, and her daughter observed that Valerie's physical and mental well-being had declined significantly during the past few months. Over the next several months, Valerie found that Joe was "forgetting the way" to places that they went frequently, including the church that they had attended for the past 25 years. Due to increasing concerns about Joe's memory and behavior, Valerie makes an appointment at the nearest community health clinic. You are assigned as Joe's social worker.

Assessment Considerations for the Case

As Joe's social worker, you will help collect information as to whether the change in his mental status was rapid or gradual. In this case, Joe's cognitive and behavioral symptoms, as described by the family, occurred over a time span of nearly 2 years. This is important because Alzheimer's disease tends to develop slowly and gradually worsen over time (Mayo Clinic, 2019). When the symptoms appear abruptly, other conditions should be ruled out by a physician or other health care provider, including delirium. A comprehensive medical evaluation is needed with Joe because he is presenting with signs of Alzheimer's disease or related dementia. The physician's interview with Joe is a fundamental component of this medical evaluation. However, Joe's assessment of his own functioning may be insufficient, and the observations of the family may be needed to corroborate the information provided by Joe, preferably with his permission and knowledge (McInnis-Dittrich, 2020).

One of your important roles will be to promote open communication between Joe, Valerie, and the treatment team. A person-centered approach to care for a person with dementia (Fazio et al., 2018) emphasizes the importance of working with Joe and Valerie together, rather than separately. You recognize and support Valerie as an expert in Joe's care. This relationship-based care approach will help you better assess Valerie's need for support, resources, and information. Person-centered dementia care assessment provides an opportunity for relationship building in an effort to reduce the stigma and fear that sometimes occur with referrals to outside support (Fazio et al., 2018). This is important because African American dementia caregivers may be more reluctant to accept support from outside community resources.

Cultural values, attitudes, and beliefs about caregiving are critical for you to consider in this case. The literature related to African American caregivers points to the importance of familial values such as maintaining family continuity, reciprocity, and role-modeling (Apesoa-Varano et al., 2016). African American family caregivers often rely on a system of both blood relatives and fictive kin for informal support as part of dementia caregiving. African American dementia caregivers may be reluctant to use formal services and supports due to perceptions that service providers are biased or will minimize their cultural background and experiences (Collins & Hawkins, 2016). African American families may also generally mistrust formal systems of care due to a history of institutional and systemic racism resulting in unequal or inadequate treatment. In addition, the stigma (and sometimes shame) associated with dementia may pose as a barrier to African American families from seeking and receiving services (Epps et al., 2018). As the social worker, you should consider a multidimensional assessment approach that considers the ways that race and ethnicity, as well as cultural traditions, beliefs, and values, affect African American dementia caregivers (Richardson et al., 2019).

Assessment Tactics for the Case

Social workers are involved in the screening for, rather than the diagnosing of, cognitive impairment. The usual areas of assessment for the social workers include cognitive abilities, activities of daily living, instrumental activities of daily living, risk/safety, mood and behavior, environmental demands/resources, and the status/needs of the family caregiver(s) (Cox, 2007). Direct observation and the use of standardized screening instruments are key to a social worker's assessment. However, these instruments should never take the place of the social worker's professional judgment and in-person interaction with the older adult. In the case of Joe, as well as with other older clients, these instruments may elicit fear of being tested and losing independence.

Alzheimer's disease is often characterized by a progressive decline in both activities of daily living (e.g., bathing, dressing, toileting, eating, and grooming) and instrumental activities of daily living (e.g., money management, shopping, food preparation, and using the telephone). The most noticeable losses in functioning usually happen in the activities in which an individual has to complete a series of tasks, such as Joe's difficulties managing money and paying bills. For functional assessment, the Katz Index of Daily Living (Katz, 1983) and the Lawton Instrumental Activities of Daily Living Scale (Lawton & Brody, 1969) are two of the most widely accepted instruments. These tools can be used in addition to direct observations. The instruments most frequently used in assessing cognitive functioning with older adults are the Mini-Mental Status Exam (Folstein et al., 1975), the Mini-Cog (Borson et al., 2003), and the Brief Interview for Mental Status (Chodosh et al., 2008).

In your role as the social worker, it is important to assess the availability of Joe's personal and community supports at home through a family caregiver assessment (Anderson et al., 2018). A family caregiver assessment includes seven conceptual domains (Family Caregiver Alliance, 2012):

1. Care providers should consider the background of the caregiver and the caregiving situation.
2. Caregiver's perception of the health and functional status of the care recipient.
3. Caregiver's values and preferences with respect to everyday living and care provision.
4. Health and well-being of the caregiver.
5. Consequences of caregiving.
6. Skills, abilities, and knowledge of the caregiver to provide the care that is needed.
7. Potential resources a caregiver might need.

The following social work treatment goals and objectives are pertinent to the case (adapted from Gitlin & Hodgson, 2018):

Treatment goal 1: Symptom management
- Objective: Assess for and prevent, reduce/minimize behavioral and psychological symptoms (BPSDs)
  - Provide caregiver education, recommend the establishment of daily routines, and recommend strategies for caregiver communication with Joe.

Treatment goal 2: Care planning
- Objective: Care coordination/care management
  - Identify and discuss care goals with Joe and his family.
  - Provide referrals to community agencies supporting family caregivers and dementia family caregivers.

Treatment goal 3: Quality of life
- Objective: Identify needs of and provide education and support for family caregivers
  - Evaluate social support network.
  - Provide education and support.
- Objective: Promote aging in place at home
  - Refer to opportunities for social engagement, caregiver respite, and social connectivity of Joe and his family.
  - Refer to home- and community-based services and supports to enable Valerie to continue caring for Joe at home.

Evidence-Based Programs

There are a variety of evidence-based programs and approaches that you may utilize and/or recommend for Joe and his family, including nonpharmacological practices to address the behavioral and psychological symptoms of dementia, education and information, and respite care. It is important to keep in mind that in addition to possible differences in perceptions of and responses to dementia caregiving challenges, African American caregivers may also have different patterns of health-seeking behavior and responses to caregiver interventions (Samson et al., 2016). Overall, evidence-based interventions that are culturally informed and culturally tailored are generally linked to better dementia caregiver outcomes, particularly among African American families.

A range of evidence-based nonpharmacological practices exist to address BPSDs, including sensory practices, psychosocial practices, and structured care protocols (Scales et al., 2018). Sensory practices include aromatherapy, massage, multisensory stimulation, and light therapy. Psychosocial practices include validation therapy; reminiscence therapy; music therapy; pet therapy; and the provision of individualized, meaningful activities. Structured care protocols for mouth care and bathing may also help minimize pain and other behavioral triggers that may arise with personal care activities.

Education and information about Alzheimer's disease are effective for dementia family caregivers when presented with other targeted evidence-based strategies (Selwood et al. 2007). Education and information about dementia may encompass a range of topic areas, including information about the progression of Alzheimer's disease, medication options, genetic and environmental risk factors, stress management, available and appropriate services, and addressing the future needs of persons with dementia as the disease progresses (Whitlatch & Orsulic-Jeras, 2018). As the social worker, one of your roles is to help provide education and information that are well-supported by the latest research. It is also most useful to provide information that targets the current needs and situation of the person with dementia and their family caregiver, rather than presenting a "one-size-fits-all" approach to education (Van Mierlo et al., 2012).

Respite care is primarily designed to give caregivers a "break" and allow them time for relief from their caregiving tasks and responsibilities. Respite provides caregivers the opportunity to rest at home and/or have the chance to run errands, exercise, visit other friends and family, or engage in other well-being activities. Although more research related to respite care is needed, studies show that respite may improve caregiver burden and anxiety (Walter & Pinquart, 2020). Respite may be provided in several ways, including by volunteers through programs such as the Senior Companion Program. The Senior Companion Program is funded by the Corporation for National and Community Service and matches peer older adults with other frail older adults to serve as companions and to provide respite care for families. Research related to the Senior Companion Program suggests that it is a promising platform for culturally informed dementia caregiver interventions (Fields et al., 2021). Respite care may also be provided in adult day service settings, which research suggests may benefit dementia family caregivers through the provision of caregiver education, support groups, case management, and individual counseling (Anderson et al., 2015).

Finally, there is growing evidence that family caregivers' religion and/or faith are important aspects of dementia family caregiving in the African American community. Historically, the church has served as a key spiritual and community support for African American families. Interventions for African American dementia caregivers that are linked to religious organizations such as churches may help build coping skills for caregiving-related stress (Epps et al., 2019), and attending worship services can potentially promote happiness and social engagement for persons with dementia (Epps & Williams, 2020).

Helpful Resources

Apps

Alzheimer's Association Science Hub: https://www.alz.org/help-support/resources/the-alzheimer-s-association-science-hub

Care Zone: https://carezone.com/home

Caring Village: https://www.caringvillage.com

Websites

Alzheimer's Association: https://www.alz.org

American Association of Retired Persons: https://www.aarp.org/home-family/caregiving

Care Zone: https://carezone.com/home

Family Caregiver Alliance: https://www.caregiver.org

myALZteam: https://www.myalzteam.com

Rosalynn Carter Institute for Caregivers: http://www.rosalynncarter.org

References

Alzheimer's Association. (2020). *2020 Alzheimer's disease facts and figures.* https://www.alz.org/media/Documents/alzheimers-facts-and-figures.pdf

American Psychiatric Association. (2013). *Diagnostic and statistical manual of mental disorders* (5th ed.).

Anderson, K. A., Dabelko-Schoeny, H., & Fields, N. L. (2018). *Home- and community-based services for older adults: Aging in context.* Columbia University Press.

Anderson, K. A., Dabelko-Schoeny, H. I., Fields, N. L., & Carter, J. R. (2015). Beyond respite: The role of adult day services in supporting dementia caregivers. *Home Health Care Services Quarterly, 34*(2), 101–112.

Apesoa-Varano, E., Tang-Feldman, Y., Reinhard, S. C., Choula, R., & Young, H. M. (2016). Multicultural caregiving and caregiver interventions: A look back and a call for future action. *Generations, 39*(4), 39–48.

Borson, S., Scanlan, J. M., Chen, P. J., & Ganguli, M. (2003). The Mini-Cog as a screen for dementia: Validation in a population based sample. *Journal of the American Geriatrics Society, 21*, 349–355.

Chodosh, J., Edelen, M. O., Buchanan, J. L., Yosef, J. A., Ouslander, J. G., Berlowitz, D. R., Streim, J. E., & Saliba, D. (2008). Nursing home assessment of cognitive impairment: Development and testing a brief instrument of mental status. *Journal of the American Geriatric Association, 56*, 2079–2075.

Collins, W. L., & Hawkins, A. D. (2016). Supporting caregivers who care for African American elders: A pastoral perspective. *Social Work and Christianity, 43*(4), 85.

Cox, C. B. (Ed.). (2007). *Dementia and social work practice: Research and interventions.* Springer.

Epps, F., Rose, K. M., & Lopez, R. P. (2019). Who's your family? African American caregivers of older adults with dementia. *Research in Gerontological Nursing, 12*(1), 20–26.

Epps, F., Weeks, G., Graham, E., & Luster, D. (2018). Challenges to aging in place for African American older adults living with dementia and their families. *Geriatric Nursing, 39*(6), 646–652.

Epps, F., & Williams, I. C. (2020). The importance of religiosity to the well-being of African American older adults living with dementia. *Journal of Applied Gerontology, 39*(5), 509–518.

Family Caregiver Alliance. (2012). *Selected caregiver assessment measures: A resource inventory for practitioners* (2nd ed.). https://www.carealliance.ie/userfiles/file/SelCGAssmtMeas_ResInv_FINAL_12_10_12.pdf

Fazio, S., Pace, D., Maslow, K., Zimmerman, S., & Kallmyer, B. (2018). Alzheimer's Association dementia care practice recommendations. *Gerontologist, 58*(Suppl. 1), S1–S9.

Fields, N. L., Xu, L., Richardson, V. E., Parekh, R., Ivey, D., & Calhoun, M. (2021). Utilizing the Senior Companion Program as a platform for a culturally informed caregiver intervention: Results from a mixed methods pilot study. *Dementia, 20*(1), 161–187. doi:10.1177/1471301219871192

Folstein, M. F., Folstein, S. E., & McHugh, P. R. (1975). Mini-mental state: A practical method for grading the cognitive state of patients for the clinician. *Journal of Psychiatric Research, 12,* 189–198.

Gitlin, L., & Hodgson, N. (2018). *Better living with dementia: Implications for individuals, families, communities, and societies.* Elsevier.

Katz, S. (1983). Assessing self-maintenance: Activities of daily living, mobility and instrumental activities of living. *Journal of the American Geriatrics Society, 31*(12), 721–726.

Lawton, M. P., & Brody, E. M. (1969). Assessment of older people: Self-maintaining and instrumental daily living. *The Gerontologist, 9*(3), 179–186.

Mather, M., Scommegna, P., & Kilduff, L. (2019). *Fact sheet: Aging in the United States.* https://www.prb.org/resources/fact-sheet-aging-in-the-united-states/

Mayo Clinic. (2019). *Alzheimer's stages: How the disease progresses.* https://www.mayoclinic.org/diseases-conditions/alzheimers-disease/in-depth/alzheimers-stages/art-20048448

McInnis-Dittrich, K. (2020). *Social work with older adults: A biopsychosocial approach to assessment and intervention* (5th ed.). Pearson.

National Institutes of Health, National Institute on Aging. (2018). *How is Alzheimer's disease treated?* https://www.nia.nih.gov/health/how-alzheimers-disease-treated

Qiu, C., & Fratiglioni, L. (2018). Aging without dementia is achievable: Current evidence from epidemiological research. *Journal of Alzheimer's Disease, 62*(3), 933–942.

Richardson, V. E., Fields, N., Won, S., Bradley, E., Gibson, A., Rivera, G., & Holmes, S. D. (2019). At the intersection of culture: Ethnically diverse dementia caregivers' service use. *Dementia, 18*(5), 1790–1809.

Roth, D. L., Dilworth-Anderson, P., Huang, J., Gross, A. L., & Gitlin, L. N. (2015). Positive aspects of family caregiving for dementia: Differential item functioning by race. *Journals of Gerontology Series B: Psychological Sciences and Social Sciences, 70*(6), 813–819.

Samson, Z. B., Parker, M., Dye, C., & Hepburn, K. (2016). Experiences and learning needs of African American family dementia caregivers. *American Journal of Alzheimer's Disease & Other Dementias, 31*(6), 492–501.

Scales, K., Zimmerman, S., & Miller, S. J. (2018). Evidence-based nonpharmacological practices to address behavioral and psychological symptoms of dementia. *The Gerontologist, 58*(Suppl. 1), S88–S102.

Selwood, A., Johnston, K., Katona, C., Lyketsos, C., & Livingston, G. (2007). Systematic review of the effect of psychological interventions on family caregivers of people with dementia. *Journal of Affective Disorders, 101*(1–3), 75–89.

Van Mierlo, L. D., Meiland, F. J., Van der Roest, H. G., & Dröes, R. M. (2012). Personalised caregiver support: Effectiveness of psychosocial interventions in subgroups of caregivers of people with dementia. *International Journal of Geriatric Psychiatry, 27*(1), 1–14.

Walter, E., & Pinquart, M. (2020). How effective are dementia caregiver interventions? An updated comprehensive meta-analysis. *The Gerontologist, 60*(8), 609–619.

Whitlatch, C. J., & Orsulic-Jeras, S. (2018). Meeting the informational, educational, and psychosocial support needs of persons living with dementia and their family caregivers. *The Gerontologist, 58*(Suppl. 1), S58–S73.

Geriatric Depression

Assessment and Treatment

Zvi D. Gellis and Bonnie Kenaley

Depression is a serious health issue among older adults, with estimates of 9–14% diagnosed with major depressive disorder. Late-life depression is associated with cognitive and functional decline, suicidal risk, and increased health care utilization. In this chapter, we provide an evidence-based plan of assessment and treatment protocols for social work service delivery.

Assessment of Late-Life Depression

As with any clinical assessment, the older client should first be interviewed individually to establish a rapport and a trusting climate to share valuable information. When assessing for late-life depression, particular attention should be given to assessing for possible sensory impairment, including hearing and visual difficulties resulting in the tailoring and accommodation to gather vital information (Glover & Srinivasan, 2017). In addition, after gaining the client's permission, collateral sources of historical information should be explored.

Biopsychosocial Assessment

Biological Assessment

A comprehensive biopsychosocial assessment is standard to develop a clinical and critical synthesis of the client's condition. The assessment should focus on past and present medical history and medical conditions that may increase the client's risk or indicate the presence of depression or suicide ideation, including HIV/ADIS, chronic obstructive pulmonary disease, genital disorders, liver disease, heart disease (congestive heart failure and myocardial infarction), renal disease, rheumatoid disorders, cancer, chronic pain, cerebrovascular disease, and neurological diseases (Huntington's disease, Parkinson's disease, multiple sclerosis, seizure disorder, and spinal cord injury) (Conejero et al., 2018). Ascertaining a list of current prescribed and over-the-counter medications, recent hospitalizations, as well as allergies and interactions to medications is advised. The client should be assessed for independence in activities of daily living (ADLs; e.g., bathing, dressing, grooming, toileting, feeding, and self-transferring) and instrumental ADLs (e.g., driving, shopping for groceries, preparing meals, managing finances, using the telephone, and safely administering their medications). The client's biological assessment should expand to a discussion of their nutritional status; disability; and past and current physical trauma, including physical self-neglect and abuse.

Psychological Assessment

A formal psychological assessment for depression encompasses the client's sensorium and orientation, general appearance and behavior, mood and affect, speech, thought process and content, perception, cognition, insight, and judgment. This is important: Because older adults often experience a "depression without sadness syndrome" or "depletion syndrome," clients may not demonstrate the hallmark symptom of sadness but will demonstrate withdrawal, apathy, amotivation, fatigue, and a lack of vigor (Glover & Srinivasan, 2017). In contrast, other clients may experience restlessness and delusions with the thematic content of guilt, sin, or hypochondriasis. Therefore, psychological assessment should be modified to reflect these plausible client presentations with a focus on the onset, duration, and severity of presenting symptomatology. In addition, the psychological assessment should entail components that include a history of past psychiatric illness(es), current psychiatric medications, adverse interactions of psychiatric medications, and allergies to psychiatric medications. When exploring past psychiatric history, the occurrence of similar symptoms or episodes and the response to previous treatment modalities should be determined. A family history of mood or cognitive impairment should be ascertained, including the course of the disorder, medication history, and response to treatment. Resiliency factors for coping with late-life depression, such as temperament, personality (i.e., perseverance, passion, and grit), positive

relationships, and the presence and use of humor, should be evaluated as well (Laird et al., 2019).

Although the suicide rate for older adults is lower compared with that of other age cohorts, older adults who have a mood disorder or have a history of suicide attempts are at higher risk of committing suicide (K. Rudd et al., 2019). Older adults who have risk factors for suicide should be frequently assessed because they may vary in feelings, thoughts, and behaviors across time. The mnemonic IS PATH-WARM helps assess for suicide and reviews for elements of *i*deations (suicidal), *s*ubstance use, *p*urposelessness (no reason to live or having no sense of purpose), *a*nxiety, *t*rapped (feeling like there is no way out), *h*opelessness, *w*ithdrawal (from family, friends, and society), *r*ecklessness (reckless activity), and *m*ood changes (M. Rudd et al., 2012). An evaluation of thought content should include exploration of thoughts of self-harm and suicidal ideations or plans. "Suicidal thoughts may range from passive (thoughts of hopelessness or that life is not worth living), in the absence of intent to self-harm, to active thoughts of self-harm or suicidal ideation" (Glover & Srinivasan, 2013, p. 551). In addition, the client and family members should be evaluated for the access to weapons or other lethal means (i.e., the presence of firearms or poison and hoarding of medications).

Social Assessment

A thorough social assessment for late-life depression explores the client's past education and current or past work history; retirement history (i.e., forced retirement); current and past marital status and intimate relationships; sexual activity/functioning; history of interpersonal violence; hoarding; living arrangements; social support networks; and religious/spiritual affiliations. Clients should be assessed for recent and current stressors, including changes in marital status; losses in financial status (e.g., loss of funds and exploitation of funds); changes in the home environment (e.g., recent/future move, eviction, or relocation to and from a shared home or long-term care); social isolation; recent loss or death of family members, caregiver, friends, or pets; loss of societal roles and goals; and social support networks (Glover & Srinivasan, 2013). When assessing for these stressors, it is imperative to evaluate for their magnitude, the client's perceived controllability, and the availability of external and interpersonal resources. Maladaptive methods of coping with past and current stressors should be evaluated, such as present or past use of alcohol, use of prescribed medications, or use of illegal substances. In addition, a thorough exploration of healthy coping strategies may assist in treatment planning.

Depression Assessment Scales for Older Adults

In conjunction with the psychiatric interview, the use of standardized depression screening tools and rating scales significantly aids in identification of late-life depression and its severity, as well as the monitoring of treatment outcomes (Glover & Srinivasan, 2017). The most commonly used validated standardized screening and rating scales for late-life depression include the Geriatric Depression Scale–Short Form (GDS-S), the Hamilton Depression Rating Scale (HAM-D), and the Patient Health Questionnaire–9 (PHQ-9). Depression tools are now available via mobile phone apps. However, inadequate reporting of organization and content source increases the difficulty to assess the credibility and reliability of the apps; thus, these must be used with caution.

Geriatric Depression Scale–Short Form

The GDS-S is a subset of 15 items from the original GDS 30-item version (Sheikh & Yesavage,

1986). The items focus on domains related to cognition, loss, and self-image. The scale takes 5–7 minutes to administer in written or verbal form. The items are formatted "yes/no," with 10 of the 15 items indicating the presence of depression with positive responses and the remaining 5 items indicating depression with negative responses. Total scores range from 0 to 10; scores of 0–5 indicate a normal score, scores higher than 5 suggest the presence of depression, and scores of 10 or higher are almost always indicative of depression. The target population includes healthy, medically ill, and mild to moderately cognitively impaired older adults, including community-dwelling adults and those living in long-term care settings. It is reliable and has proven sensitivity in differentiating between depressed and nondepressed clients.

Hamilton Depression Rating Scale

The HAM-D is a clinician-administered scale that consists of 21 items, with the first 17 items identifying symptoms of depression and the remaining 4 items assessing for subtypes of depression (Hamilton, 1960). The scale takes 15–20 minutes to administer. Of the first 17 items, 8 are scored on a 5-point scale, ranging from 0 = not present to 4 = severe, and 9 are score from 0 to 2. The HAM-D has proven reliability and validity across many different populations (Mottram, Wilson, & Copeland, 2000) and has been translated into several languages.

Patient Health Questionnaire–9

The PHQ-9 is a clinician or self-administered 9-item scale that corresponds with the fifth edition of the *Diagnostic and Statistical Manual of Mental Disorders* (American Psychiatric Association, 2013) criteria for major depressive disorder (Spitzer et al., 1999). It provides a severity score, a provisional diagnosis, and takes less than 3 minutes to administer. Each item is scored on the frequency of occurrence over the preceding 2-week period (from 0 = not at all to 3 = nearly every day). A score of less than 5 indicates no depression, a score of 5–9 indicates mild depression, a score of 10–14 indicates moderate depression, a score of 15–19 indicates moderate to severe depression, and a score of 20–27 indicates severe depression. A score of 10 or higher is considered clinically significant and requires further evaluation. The questionnaire has proven specificity, sensitivity, and reliability and can be administered in different settings.

Problem-Solving Therapy : Viable Depression Option for Older Adults

Problem-solving therapy (PST) is an easily delivered evidence-based treatment for community-based and cognitively intact older adult clients/patients. It is a derivative of the cognitive–behavioral and social problem-solving model. It has robust scientific evidence of effectiveness among depressed older adults, particularly those who reject antidepressant medication, are unable to manage their daily living problems, are not coping well with chronic medical conditions, or are experiencing limited social support (Frost et al., 2018). Studies demonstrate that PST is feasible and acceptable to community-based older adults (Cuijpers et al., 2018; Gellis & Nezu, 2011; Gellis et al., 2014; Jonsson et al., 2016), easily integrated by social workers, and transferable to telemedicine (Gellis et al., 2012) and other health settings (Erdley-Kass et al., 2018).

PST helps reduce depression by increasing an individual's problem-solving skill levels, optimism, self-efficacy, and coping skills with stressful problems. In addition, it focuses on a more realistic (compared to catastrophic) appraisal and evaluation of specific daily living problems linked to depression. The PST therapist empowers the older client to collaboratively develop and choose the best possible solution options and implement action plans to solve identified problems. PST can also address anhedonia and psychomotor retardation through increased exposure to daily pleasurable activities (behavioral activation). Scheduling and implementation of daily pleasurable activities can be used as a pathway to problem-solving strategies and skill acquisition.

Problem-Solving Therapy Treatment Components with Case Example

Case Example

Mrs. Darrell is a 67-year-old female who has an appointment at the local hospital outpatient clinic to meet with a social worker about her low mood. The client was referred to the social worker by the clinic physician, who offered Mrs. Darrell medication, but she refused. Mrs. Darrell reported that she preferred to talk with someone instead. Mrs. Darrell has diabetes and osteoarthritis, and she was recently hospitalized for a fall but is now mobile. She has home-health nursing for diabetes disease management and physical therapy for balance and walking exercise. According to the referral, she exhibits low mood and does not appear to be interested in too many things. Apparently, Mrs. Darrell believes that her depressed mood is due to her health problems, and she is reluctant to take antidepressant medication. However, she is willing to talk with a social worker about her depression but does not want to be in a group with older people. The client scored 22 (high) on the PHQ-9 depression scale.

PST treatment involves a series of clinical phases: (1) clearly define the nature of the daily living problem and develop a realistic outcome/goal, (2) generate a wide range of alternative solutions, (3) systematically evaluate the potential consequences of each solution (i.e., exam advantages and disadvantages of each potential solution option), (4) select an optimal solution to implement based on decision criteria (effort, realistic, cost, and achievability), and (5) monitor and evaluate a solution outcome after its implementation. Table 54.1 provides an outline of the PST treatment session skills sets and content for older adults.

An important initial component of PST is preparing the older adult for depression treatment by socializing the client to problem-solving (i.e., asking how they solved problems in the past and what they want to put on the agenda). The PST therapist advocates for a positive optimistic outlook toward solving daily

TABLE 54.1 Problem-Solving Treatment Sessions

Session	Content
1 Adopt positive attitude *Skill set* Identify problems Develop goal	Orient and introduce PST for depression (client adopts positive attitude toward problem-solving); explain connections between daily problems, stress, mood, and pleasurable events; review causes, symptoms, medications, and treatments for depression; identify and define nature of stressful problems in daily living; identify client coping responses; realistic goal-setting for problem; orient to and choose two pleasurable activities (daily scheduling); empower client to develop and review an action plan for the week.
2 *Skill set* Brainstorm alternative solutions	Review client action plan, including performance outcome for chosen solution; review log of pleasurable activities; review symptoms; review coping responses to problem; identify problem-solving style; review goals; generate alternative solutions; identify/choose one or two solutions based on criteria—realistic, achievable, cost, effort (predict outcome effectiveness and consequences); instruct client to try out chosen solutions with action plan and monitor outcome; troubleshoot any difficulties; develop new weekly action plan; choose/schedule two pleasurable activities each day.
3 *Skill set* Review pros and cons	Review action plan; review performance outcome for chosen solution; teach client to reward self for efforts in attempted problem-solving; review log of pleasurable activities; review symptoms; review goal and alternative solutions if solution was less than successful, or examine new problem and renew goals; brainstorm alternative solutions; choose one or two solutions (predict consequences—pros/cons); try solutions with action plan, monitor, and evaluate outcome for next session; troubleshoot any difficulties; set new action plan; choose two pleasurable activities.
4 *Skill set* Decide and choose solution(s)	Review action plan; review performance outcome for chosen solution; client rewards self for efforts in attempted problem-solving; review log of pleasurable activities; review symptoms; review goal if solution was less than successful, or examine new problem and renew goals; generate alternative solutions; choose a solution (predict consequences) based on criteria—realistic, achievable, cost, effort; try solution with action plan, monitor, and evaluate outcome; set new action plan; troubleshoot any difficulties; choose two pleasurable activities.
5 *Skill set* Try out chosen solution(s) Action plan	Review action plan; review performance outcome for chosen solution; client rewards self for efforts in attempted problem-solving; review log of pleasurable activities; review symptoms; review goal if solution was less than successful, or examine new client problem and renew goals; generate alternative solutions; choose a solution (predict consequences); set new action plan; troubleshoot any potential difficulties; choose two pleasurable activities; prepare client for clinical termination; review PST steps; empower client to try solution with action plan, monitor, and evaluate outcome.
6 *Skill set* Evaluate Review skills Closure	Review action plan—review performance outcome for chosen solution; client rewards self for efforts; review log of pleasurable activities; review symptoms; review goal if solution was less than successful, or examine new problem and renew goals; generate alternative solutions; choose a solution (predict consequences); try out solution with new action plan, monitor, and evaluate outcome; set homework; troubleshoot any difficulties; choose two pleasurable activities; clinical termination with client; review PST steps and wrap-up; review progress with client.

PST, problem-solving therapy.

stressful problems because this will help with treatment outcomes. Psychoeducation on depression and the basics of solving daily problems is provided in the initial session and can also be reviewed over the duration of therapy. Basically, the therapist educates the client on what is known about the causes of depression, depressive symptoms, known effective treatments, and links to problem-solving and behavioral activation.

Sessions 1 and 2 involve an introduction, structure, and orientation to the PST treatment that includes developing a positive attitude toward solving one's problems, problem identification and establishing a realistic measurable goal, brainstorming and evaluating solution options, and trying out a solution during the week. Sessions 3 and 4 involve continued psychoeducation and practice in the problem-solving skills. Sessions 5 and 6 provide for an applied integration of the PST model and continued practice in the various problem-solving skill components.

To identify the client's stressful life problems, the PST therapist uses a problem list form (Box 54.1). For example, in the case of Mrs. Darrell, the PST therapist uses the problem list form and prioritizes which problem to start with based on the empowered client expressed needs. This form delineates various older client problem domains: (1) personal health, health care system/providers; (2) emotional/psychological; (3) finances; (4) living arrangements; (5) transportation; (6) relationships; (7) activities of daily living; (8) house management; and (9) socialization. The PST therapist identifies the client's problems and develops a priority list to work on over

---

BOX 54.1 PENN-PST Problem List Form

CASE: Example (Mrs. Darrell)

Problems with health problems, health care, obstacles:

Client concerned about falling, has numerous health problems, refuses to take antidepressant medication

Problems with emotional/psychological, loneliness, isolation, coping with stress, etc.:

Client has little contact with others, isolated, depressed, possibly related to health conditions

Problems with money and finances:

Unknown

Problems with living arrangements:

Living alone, daughter lives in another city, some telephone contact

Problems with transportation:

None according to client

Problems with relationships:

Spouse or partner; family members: children, grandchildren; friends; other:

Unknown

Problems with doing activities around the house:

Possibly needs assistance with house cleaning

Problems with ADLs: shopping, cooking, bathing, taking meds, grooming, dressing, walking:

Possibly needs assistance with meal preparation

ADLs, activities of daily living.

a potential range of 6–10 sessions. One of the primary goals of the therapy is to teach the older person problem-solving skills to deal with daily life stresses in a rational and planned way in order to prevent depressive symptoms from reoccurring.

The therapist itemizes the type of problems reported by the older client into identified life stress domains. The PST therapist uses a reflective style to engage the older client and develop a therapeutic alliance as well as a directive approach to engage in problem-solving. To ascertain the nature and extent of the problems identified, the therapist orients the older client to the importance of developing a positive attitude toward solving their problems. The therapist gains insight into the problems identified by asking W-5 questions (who, what, where, when, and why) in order for the older client to gain awareness of why a certain problem persists. The therapist can identify the client's problem-solving coping style using items from the Social Problem-Solving Inventory (D'Zurilla & Nezu, 1999) to understand past coping attempts to resolve problem.

The PST therapist uses a PST session worksheet (Table 54.2) in each session as a guide to cover the problem-solving skills delineated in Table 54.1. The PST therapist completes the worksheet based on the client's assessed needs for the week. The

TABLE 54.2 PENN PST Worksheet

Name:	**Action Plan Review from Previous Session**	
Date:	PHQ-9 Score	**Pleasant Activity Level Score** (PALS)
Session #:	20–27	Severe HOW PLEASANT, ENJOYABLE, OR
	15–19	Moderately severe HOW REWARDING was the activity?
	10–14	Moderate 0 This was not pleasurable
	5–9	Mild 1 This was somewhat pleasurable
	1–4	Minimal 2 This was pleasurable
	3	This was very pleasurable

PENN-PST SESSION WORKSHEET

Step1. **Socialize and Orient to Problem-Solving (Positive Attitude)**
Step 2. **Problem Identified in Session**:
Step 2a. **Specify Goal** (realistic, measurable):

Step 3. **Brainstorm Solutions** (to identified problem below)	Step 4a. **Evaluate Each Solution Option** (based on effort, time needed, achievable, etc.)	
	Pros ✓ (advantages)	Cons ☒ (disadvantages)
Solution option 1	1	1
Solution option 2 (etc.)	2	2

Step 4b. **Choose Solution** (based on Step 4a)	Step 5. **Steps to Achieve Solution** (reduce barriers)	Try out Solution/Evaluate Outcome

Homework/Activity Schedule for Week:
Pleasant activities:
Solution(s) to try out:
Use of Coping Cards, positive statements, stop-and-think rule, etc. as examples

PHQ-9, Patient Health Questionnaire–9; PST, problem-solving therapy.

therapist helps the older client rate problems from highest to lowest priority. The client is then asked to choose a priority problem that they would like to resolve, and then a short-term goal is developed that must be realistic and measurable. Once these tasks are completed, the older client is oriented to the skill of "brainstorming" alternative solutions to solve the identified problem without judging each solution option. Once the older client has completed this phase, the PST therapist directs the client to examine each potential solution option for its advantages (i.e., Pros) and disadvantages (i.e., Cons) on the PST worksheet. This process assists the client in shaping decisions about the solution options based on several decision-making criteria: (1) Is the solution option realistic? (2) Is the solution option achievable (i.e., can I do it)? (3) How much effort do I have to expend? and (4) is there an emotional or time cost. Based on the older client's responses in the decision-making process, the client can make an effective solution choice from the options list as an attempt to reach the goal and solve the identified problem.

During treatment sessions, emphasis is placed on psychoeducation about depression and scheduling daily pleasurable activities chosen from a list developed by the client. The PST therapist empowers the older client to develop a personal tailored list of pleasurable activities during each session as part of the weekly action plan (homework) activity. During session discussion of the action plan, the PST therapist encourages the older person to choose and complete one or two pleasurable activities each day until the next PST session. The pleasant activity scheduling builds on simple and graduated activities that target depressive symptoms. The older client is provided with a pleasant activities weekly scheduling form to keep track of the type and frequency of activities. The older client is asked to rate each completed activity using

the Pleasant Activity Level Score (Gellis & Nezu, 2011) on a scale from 0 (*this was not pleasurable*) to 3 (*this was very pleasurable*) to reinforce behavioral activation and problem-solving success. The PST therapist monitors and reviews the action plans and pleasant activity schedule at the beginning of each session to evaluate the outcomes of the attempted solution.

PST therapists assess for late-life depressive symptoms at each session by administering the PHQ-9 (Spitzer et al., 1999). The PST therapist completes this process because (1) it assists in tracking treatment progress; (2) it helps the older client monitor their own symptoms each week; (3) it provides a connection between how the client feels and their level of pleasurable activity, thus counteracting anhedonia; (4) the PHQ-9 outcomes can be graphically illustrated with the client to interpret and explain progress; and (5) this process empowers the older client to take more control of their mood and engage in their recovery from depression.

PST therapists are asked to administer the interventions in a flexible manner, reviewing all skills for each client but allocating different amounts of time, depending on the older person's needs. Flexibility is recommended in the use of terminology, mode of presentation, and action plan format to fit individual difference in educational background, cognitive skills, and sensory capacity. PST therapists are encouraged to be flexible with the schedule and length of sessions based on client needs and preferences.

References

American Psychiatric Association. (2013). *Diagnostic and statistical manual of mental disorders* (5th ed.).
Conejero, I., Olié, E., Courtet, P., & Calati, R. (2018). Suicide in older adults: Current perspectives. *Clinical Interventions in Aging, 13,* 691–699.
Cuijpers, P., de Wit, L., Kleiboer, A., Karyotaki, E., & Ebert, D. (2018). Problem-solving therapy for adult

depression: An updated meta-analysis. *European Psychiatry, 48,* 27–37.

D'Zurilla, T. J., & Nezu, A. M. (1999). *Problem-solving therapy: A social competence approach to clinical intervention* (2nd ed.). Springer.

Erdley-Kass, S., Kass, D., Gellis, Z. D., Bogner, H., Berger, A., & Perkins, R. M. (2018). Using problem-solving therapy to improve problem-solving orientation, problem-solving skills and quality of life in older hemodialysis patients. *Clinical Gerontologist, 41*(5), 424–437

Frost, R., Bauernfreund, Y., & Walters, K. (2018). Non-pharmacological interventions for depression/anxiety in older adults with physical comorbidities affecting functioning: Systematic review and meta-analysis. *International Geriatrics, 31*(8), 1121–1136.

Gellis, Z. D., Kenaley, B., McGinty, J., Bardelli, E., Davitt, J, & Ten Have, T. (2012). Impact of telehealth intervention on heart and chronic respiratory failure medically ill patients. *The Gerontologist, 52*(4), 541–552.

Gellis, Z. D., Kenaley, B., & Ten Have, T. (2014). Randomized trial of integrated telehealth care for chronic illness and depression in geriatric homecare patients: The I-TEAM study. *Journal of the American Geriatrics Society, 62*(5), 889–895.

Gellis, Z. D., & Nezu, A. T. (2011). Integrating depression treatment for homebound medically ill older adults: Using evidence-based problem-solving therapy. In K. Sorocco & S. Lauderdale (Eds.), *Cognitive behavior therapy with older adults: Innovations across care settings* (pp. 391–420). Springer.

Glover, J., & Srinivasan, S. (2013). Assessment of the person with late-life depression. *Psychiatric Clinics, 36*(4), 545–560.

Glover, J., & Srinivasan, S. (2017). Assessment and treatment of late-life depression. *Journal of Clinical Outcomes Management, 24*(3), 135–144.

Hamilton, M. (1960). A rating scale for depression. *Journal of Neurology, Neurosurgery, and Psychiatry, 3,* 56–62.

Jonsson, U., Bertilsson, G., Allard, P., Gyllensvard, H., Soderlund, A., Tham, A., & Andersson, G. (2016). Psychological treatment of depression in people aged 65 years and over: A systematic review of efficacy, safety, and cost-effectiveness. *PLoS One, 11*(8), e0160859. doi:10.1371/journal.pone.0160859

Laird, K. T., Krause, B., Funes, C., & Lavretsky, H. (2019). Psychological factors for resilience and depression in late life. *Translational Psychiatry, 9,* 1–18.

Mottram, P., Wilson, K., & Copeland, J. (2000). Validation of the Hamilton Depression Rating Scale and Montgommery and Asberg Rating Scales in terms of AGECAT depression cases. *International Journal of Geriatric Psychiatry, 15*(12), 1113–1119.

Rudd, K., Breen, R., Srinivasan, S., & Hrisko, S. (2019). Suicide in late-life: Collaborative approaches for assessment, prevention, and treatment. *American Journal of Geriatric Psychiatry, 27*(3), S13–S14.

Rudd, M. D., Berman, A. L., Joiner, T. E., Jr., Nock, M. K., Silverman, M. M., Mandrusiak, M., Van Orden, K., & Witte, T. (2012). Warning signs for suicide: Theory, research and clinical applications. *Suicide Life Threat Behavior Journal, 36*(3), 255–262.

Sheikh, J. I., & Yesavage, J. A. (1986). Geriatric Depression Scale (GDS): Recent evidence and development of a shorter version. In T. L. Brink (Ed.), *Clinical gerontology: A guide to assessment and intervention* (pp. 165–174). Haworth Press.

Spitzer, R. L., Kroenke, K., & Williams, J. B. (1999). Validation and utility of a self-report version of PRIME-MD: The PHQ primary care study. Primary Care Evaluation of Mental Disorders. Patient Health Questionnaire. *Journal of the American Medical Association, 282,* 1737–1744.

Treatment Planning with Families

An Evidence-Based Approach

Catheleen Jordan and Cynthia Franklin

Managed behavioral health care and other accountability and cost-containment approaches have encouraged the move toward formalized family treatment planning and the trend toward efficacious, brief family therapy interventions. A formalized social work treatment plan identifies measurable goals, objectives, and outcomes as well as evidence-based treatments known to be effective with specific client problems and populations. A family treatment plan (see Box 55.1 for an example) can be understood as a road map that can be used to guide a family's pursuit of its shared goals. The plan should specify the overarching treatment goal, along with objectives and interventions. It is crucial that during the treatment planning process, the social worker devise a plan for ongoing measuring and monitoring of progress on each objective over the course of treatment (Hepworth et al., 2016). This means that a treatment plan is not a one-time snapshot of the family's goals but, rather, a document that guides the progress of the family over time and may also be revised over the treatment process. Treatment plan content, for example, may be modified as the family's goals are achieved or

change. If a treatment team is providing services to the family, the treatment plan should specify which provider is responsible for each specified intervention.

Special challenges in treatment planning with families include selecting problems, goals, and outcomes that are meaningful to all family members. For instance, the parents may desire their child to become more compliant; the child, on the other hand, may desire an end to constant parental nagging! Also, goals should be selected and interventions selected with consideration to issues of diversity (Gehart, 2018). For example, the social worker should select interventions that best match the client, their culture, preferences, and circumstances. Whereas individual treatment planning requires careful consideration of client characteristics (e.g., ethnicity, sexual orientation, religious beliefs, and physical health) and life circumstances (e.g., income, transportation, employment, and parenting demands) (Antony & Barlow, 2011), family treatment planning requires consideration of these factors for each member of the family unit. Another challenge in family treatment planning is that problem-focused

BOX 55.1 Treatment Plan Example

Brief history: Jordan, age 9, lives with her grandmother, Iris. This is a temporary arrangement during the COVID-19 pandemic in 2020. Jordan's mother, Mary, works at the hospital, thus is at increased risk of acquiring the virus and passing it along to others. Also, Jordan must be home schooled, and Mary works during the day while Jordan would ordinarily be at school. But schools are closed during the pandemic, so Iris is home schooling the 9-year-old in addition to her own university teaching job, which she is doing from home as well. Mary asked Iris if she would keep Jordan until the danger has passed. Iris and Jordan are on day 31 of this new living arrangement and Jordan is not happy and has been rebelling against the new arrangement. She recently screamed at Iris, "You are too strict! My mother is much more relaxed. You are mean!" Iris responds to these comments by begging and pleading for Jordan's cooperation. Both Jordan and Iris agreed to speak to an online social worker with expertise in family therapy, Dr. Lloyd.

Problem definition: Dr. Lloyd suggested that Iris and Jordan address two problems: (1) dissatisfaction between Jordan and Iris; (2) Jordan's reluctance to do her online schoolwork.

Goal: Improve the relationship between Jordan and Iris, as well as improve Jordan's compliance with her online schoolwork.

Measurable objective 1: Improve Jordan and Iris' relationship as measured by the Hudson Parent–Child Relationship Inventory. This simple measure covers seven scales, including parent support, satisfaction with parenting, involvement, communication, and limit setting. It is used weekly to monitor treatment. Available here: https://www.wpspublish.com

Intervention 1:

Communication skills training. For example, see Kristin Zolten, MA, and Nicholas Long, PhD, Department of Pediatrics, University of Arkansas for Medical Sciences. Artwork by Scott Snider © 1997, 2006, https://extension.tennessee.edu/centerforparenting/TipSheets/Parent%20Child%20Communication.pdf

Measurable objective 2: Improve Jordan's compliance with completing daily homework as measured by daily checklist completed by both Jordan and Iris. Check when a homework assignment is completed on time. For examples of checklists, see here: https://www.teacherspayteachers.com

Intervention 2: Reward system for timely homework completion. For example, see "How to Use Rewards" here: https://www.cdc.gov/parents/essentials/consequences/rewards.html

Diagnosis: V 61.20(Z62.820) (Grand)parent–child relationship problem.

treatment planning is sometimes at odds with the systems approaches that are used in family intervention and the social work strengths-based approach, which is also used to work with families. Hepworth and colleagues (2016) advocate stating goals in positive terms. For instance, rather than stipulating that an adolescent will *reduce* noncompliance, one can indicate that the adolescent will *increase* instances of compliance with household rules.

Steps of Treatment Planning with Families

Treatment planning requires the social worker to think through the therapeutic process from assessment to intervention and evaluation. Today's focus on brief, manualized interventions is perfect for this type of planned approach because it requires the problem to be measured. Standardized measures are instruments completed by the client and/or social worker that provide a score indicating the extent or severity of a client problem. For example, a couple may complete the Hudson Index of Marital Satisfaction; each receives a score indicating the level of satisfaction with the marriage. A score more than 25 indicates a clinically significant problem. Standardized scales should be administered repeatedly over the course of treatment so that scores can be graphed to assess, track, and evaluate client progress (Hepworth et al., 2016). Dattilio et al. (2015) identify six steps of treatment planning: problem selection, problem definition, goal development, objective construction, intervention creation, and diagnosis determination.

Step 1: Problem Selection

Problem selection in family treatment requires the social worker to assess client problems and then prioritize them in a way meaningful to the family. Jordan and Franklin (2021) recommend a problem selection and specification process guided by a person-in-environment perspective. Problem assessment moves from a global, systems view to an operationalized view of specific problems. For example, a global assessment technique, such as an ecomap, is used to obtain a global view of the family in the context of their important environmental systems. From the map, the social worker is able to conclude that problems stem from a relationship pattern between an adolescent and parent, where the parenting and communication is not working well and the adolescent is having behavioral problems. Data specific to a problem or behavior (e.g., parent–child arguments) may be collected via standardized measures. In Box 55.1, the treatment plan example, the problem is the (grand)parent–child relationship. We further specify the meaning of the problem in Step 2, the problem definition.

Step 2: Problem Definition

After the problem(s) is selected, it must be defined. Use of the fifth edition of the *Diagnostic and Statistical Manual of Mental Disorders* (DSM-5; American Psychiatric Association, 2013) is the most agreed upon way of categorizing or defining problems but is not always the most meaningful to family social workers, especially considering the controversies regarding its' limitations and usefulness for social work practice. The DSM-5 V codes may be most helpful; these address relationship and environmental issues. As mentioned previously, standardized measures have gained popularity in social work and may be used to quantify client problems. Examples of problems that may be measured in this way include family relationships and satisfaction, marital satisfaction, sexual abuse and family violence, dual-career relationship, and child–parent relationships. Individual problems such as depression, self-esteem, or anxiety, which may be a part of a family's problem, can also be easily measured using standardized instruments.

Other ways of measuring problems include counting discrete behaviors (e.g., number of family arguments or number of child tantrums) or developing goal-attainment or self-anchored scales. Goal-attainment scales, developed by the social worker, are used to identify outcomes and to operationalize categories indicating successive approximations toward 100% goal completion. Numbers are assigned to each category, with minus signs indicating lack of progress or deterioration. A typical scale range is from –2 to +2. Self-anchored scales are developed by the social worker in conjunction with the family. The targeted behavior—for example, family satisfaction—is rated from 1 to 5. A rating of 1 may indicate "the most satisfied" and 5 "the least satisfied" that the family can imagine. Anchors, indicating specific family behaviors, are then matched with each numerical ranking. For instance, the family may describe a category 1 ranking, the "most satisfied," as a time when they were having dinner together as a family, engaged in pleasant conversation with no fighting, and so on.

In addition to a focus on problems, the value of a strengths-based approach is that it encourages social workers to measure and intervene by building on client strengths (e.g., number of positive family communications or family outings). These positive behavioral objectives may be incorporated into the treatment plan. In the treatment plan example shown in Box 55.1, the problem is defined as disregard for household rules. We then develop a goal statement in Step 3.

Step 3: Goal Development

Dattilio et al. (2015) recommend specifying one goal statement for each problem. The goal statement is a broadly stated description of what successful outcome is expected. Goals are not necessarily operationalized in measurable terms, as are objectives. Instead, they may be broad statements of the overall anticipated positive outcome. In the sample treatment plan (Box 55.1), the overall goal is to improve communication and increase compliance with house rules. We could specify additional goals, such as improving parenting skills or increasing the amount of quality time the family spends together. Goals may be long-term expectations. We further operationalized the goal by specifying objectives in Step 4.

Step 4: Objective Construction

Objectives are the measurable steps that must occur for the goals to be met. Each goal should have at least two objectives that are operationalized in measurable terms and provide the short-term steps necessary to achieve the goal. In the sample plan (Box 55.1), the social worker may measure the objective of "reduce number of weekly arguments between child–parent." The objective is measurable by keeping a daily log and making a checkmark when an argument occurs. Target dates should be assigned to each objective to focus treatment sessions and to ensure brief treatment and problem resolution (Hepworth et al., 2016). As families progress through treatment, they may add additional objectives. The next step moves the treatment plan from defining and operationalizing problems to specifying the intervention.

Step 5: Intervention Creation

Interventions, the clinicians' tools for treating the problem, should be matched with each objective. Although interventions are selected according to the social worker's theoretical clinical orientation and clinical expertise, it is important to note that the trend in family social work is toward brief, evidence-based methods that have proven efficacy for specific families or family problems. When selecting interventions, social workers are advised to consider family characteristics, the target problems and diagnoses, and the evidence base for potential interventions for those problems/diagnoses, respective to client family characteristics.

Another trend in treatment is toward manualized interventions and treatment planners that provide guidelines to the social worker as to how to proceed with specific problems. Manualized interventions involve greater operationalization of the treatment, which heightens the social worker's ability to attribute positive changes to the intervention. Meanwhile, treatment planners are designed to provide all the elements necessary to proficiently develop treatment plans that satisfy the demands of third-party payers and accrediting agencies. These elements include prewritten treatment goals, objectives, and interventions, organized around common presenting problems (Dattilio et al., 2015). In Box 55.1, a skills-oriented intervention is identified to help communication between the clients. Finally, the treatment concludes with a DSM diagnosis.

Step 6: Diagnosis Determination

Treatment planning assumes that an appropriate diagnosis will be determined based on the overall client family picture. As mentioned previously, the diagnostic approach has not been favored by many family social workers due to its' limitations (Jongsma, 2004) and also to social workers' value of strengths-based treatment and a systems approach to assessment (Jordan & Franklin, 2021). Nevertheless, due to the demands of third-party payers, family therapy treatment planning is primarily based on a symptom-focused medical model (Gehart, 2018). Social workers face the reality of needing to know the characteristics of DSM criteria as part of a complete assessment picture. Fortunately, the DSM-5 has responded to some criticisms and requires a more thorough assessment of a client's biopsychosocial presentation, including cultural and life span issues across specific diagnosis. In Box 55.1, the diagnosis is a V code, favored by social workers. The V codes identify interpersonal and environmental goals and fit with a social work perspective. In this case, the child and her grandmother are having family relationship issues.

Treatment Planning Resources for Family Social Workers

Dattilio et al. (2015) emphasize the importance of developing an individualized treatment plan for each client family, based on its own uniqueness. This section discusses references helpful to the social worker, proceeding through each step of the treatment plan.

Problem Selection and Definition

Jordan and Franklin (2021) provide a framework for assessment that teaches the social work practitioner to move from a global, person-in-environment family picture to a more specific, measurable focus on target problems and strengths. Specific standardized instruments for measuring child and family problems are presented by Corcoran and Fischer (2013). Bloom et al. (2009) discuss a variety of ways available to measure problems, including goal-attainment scaling and behavioral measurement mentioned previously. Finally, prewritten treatment goals, objectives, and interventions and a sample treatment plan that conforms to the requirements of most third-party payers and accrediting agencies are available from Dattilio et al. (2015).

Goal and Objective Development

Jongsma (2004) discusses goal- and objective-setting for general practice and for family practice. Social work research practitioners, Bloom and colleagues (2009), discuss goal- and objective-setting from a single subject design perspective. Their text describes not only how to measure problems but also how to set up a system for tracking therapeutic progress. Finally, Gehart (2018) provides a guide to writing useful client goals that includes a goal-writing worksheet that walks the practitioner through a process of identifying the linkages between the presenting problem, family dynamics, and client symptoms before identifying the most appropriate intervention, based on evidence and theory.

Intervention Construction and Differential Diagnosis

Lambert (2021) reviews the efficacy of clinical interventions, including child, family, and marital therapy. Several texts written by social workers review methods available for treating families and children (Collins et al., 2012; Nichols & Davis, 2020). In addition, Reid's (2000) tried-and-true text provides a step-by-step guide for the practitioner in intervention task planning, including tasks for family social workers. Finally, Bloom and colleagues (2009) include software called Singwin, a computerized data analysis program for the ideographic data provided by single case analysis.

Future Applications for Treatment Plans

Treatment plans help ensure a positive future for client families. They help social workers set goals and objectives for clients that are measurable and offered in a brief and timely manner. Treatment planning requires that social workers specify what they will do in the way of helping. It provides a structure for an evidence-based approach to treatment, which is strongly encouraged and, in some cases, mandated. Finally, treatment planning requires that social workers document what is done to ensure accountability and to monitor progress through the treatment process. Family treatment plans further ensure that social workers offer the best possible social work treatment based on consideration of the family's culture, socioeconomic status, preferences, and values.

Helpful Resources
Websites

Center of Excellence for Integrated Health Solutions: https://www.integration.samhsa.gov/about-us/esolutions-newsletter/esolutions_september_2015

Evidence-based treatment planners from Dr. Arthur Jongsma: https://jongsma.com

NIDA/SAMHSA Blending Initiative: https://www.drugabuse.gov/nidasamhsa-blending-initiative

Simplepractice. *Wiley treatment planners*: https://www.simplepractice.com/wiley-treatment-planners/?utm_source=google&utm_medium=cpc&utm_campaign=rc-search-non-brand-dsa&utm_term=&gclid=EAIaIQobChMIo-7kutuO6QIVkIjICh3FSgjhEAAYASAAEgLHYvD_BwE

Apps

Family5—Activities, Goals and Parenting Tips: Family5 aims to improve the quality of today's busy family life. Parents and caretakers of children aged 1–12 years will find inspiration for fun and development-boosting activities to do together, in the real world. They can also set goals for the family to create healthy new habits.

In Love While Parenting (couples): This app grants you access to cutting-edge research and tips that will help you build a strong, loving relationship with your partner while you raise happy, well-adjusted children. Years of groundbreaking research and findings in psychology, neuroscience and relationships have been curated into one easy-to-use app.

Lasting (marriage counseling): Lasting helps you and your partner nurture your emotional connection and repair relationship issues. Each session creates the space for you to reflect, unpack your thoughts, and discuss them with your partner. This enables you to understand one another better, work through disagreements, and connect in healthy ways. And it's all based on decades of research.

References

American Psychiatric Association. (2013). *Diagnostic and statistical manual of mental disorders* (5th ed.).

Antony, M. M., & Barlow, D. H. (2011). *Handbook of assessment and treatment planning for psychological disorders* (2nd ed.). Guilford.

Bloom, M., Fischer, J., & Orme, J. G. (2009). *Evaluating practice: Guidelines for the accountable professional* (6th ed.). Allyn & Bacon.

Collins, D., Jordan, C., & Coleman, H. (2012). *Brooks/Cole empowerment series: An introduction to family social work* (4th ed.). Cengage.

Corcoran, K., & Fischer, J. (2013). *Measures for clinical practice and research, Volume 1: Couples, families, and children* (Vol. 1). Oxford University Press.

Dattilio, F. M., Jongsma, A. E., Jr., & Davis, S. D. (2015). *The family therapy treatment planner with DSM-5 updates*. Wiley.

Gehart, D. R. (2018). *Mastering competencies in family therapy: A practical approach to theory and clinical case documentation* (3rd ed.). Cengage.

Hepworth, D. H., Rooney, R. H., Rooney, G. D., Strom-Gottfried, K., & Larsen, J. A. (2016). *Direct social work practice: Theory and skills* (10th ed.). Brooks/Cole.

Jongsma, A. E. J. (2004). Psychotherapy treatment plan writing. In G. P. Koocher, J. C. Norcross, & S. S. Hill, III (Eds.), *Psychologist's desk reference* (2nd ed.). Oxford University Press.

Jordan, C., & Franklin, C. (2021). *Clinical assessment for social workers: Quantitative and qualitative methods* (5th ed.). Oxford University Press.

Lambert, M. J. (2021). *Bergin and Garfield's handbook of psychotherapy and behavior change* (7th ed.). Wiley.

Nichols, M. P., & Davis, S. D. (2020). *Family therapy: Concepts and methods* (12th ed.). Pearson.

Reid, W. J. (2000). *The task planner: An intervention resource for human service professionals*: Columbia University Press.

Developing and Facilitating Mutual Aid Groups

Carolyn Knight and Alex Gitterman

Group work remains a powerful force for client empowerment and social change. This chapter discusses the benefits of this modality and considerations associated with group formation and identify core group work skills, integrating relevant theoretical and empirical literature.

Mutual Aid and Its Benefits

Five interdependent advantages are associated with mutual aid (Gitterman, 2006, 2017; Gitterman et al., 2021). Individuals often struggle to resolve life stressors because they assume that they are the only one, resulting in feelings of isolation and stigmatization. When members discover they are not alone, they are freed up to address the challenges they face (Kunikata et al., 2016). Variously known as *all-in-the-same-boat* (Shulman, 2012) or *universality* (Yalom & Leszcz, 2008), this is the defining characteristic of mutual aid. Social workers can normalize and universalize individual clients' experiences and concerns.

However, their reassurance has less impact and less credibility than that provided by those who have "walked in the same shoes" (Knight & Gitterman, 2014, p. 7).

Group membership provides participants with the opportunity to assist and support one another, a phenomenon known as *altruism* (Yalom & Leszcz, 2008). The experience is uniquely available in group work and promotes feelings of self-efficacy as members realize they have something to offer others (Sanger et al., 2019).

In individual practice, workers offer reassurance and support to clients; they also encourage clients' growth and challenge signs of avoidance. In a group, members' shared experiences mean that the *mutual support* they offer and *mutual demands* they make of one another have greater credibility. Both factors foster members' self-understanding and lead to a more realistic perception of themselves and their difficulties (Wendt & Gone, 2017).

Members' collective efforts are likely to have a greater impact on their social environment than if each acted alone, because there is "power in numbers" (Shulman, 2012). Working together also is empowering and enhances members' feelings of self-efficacy.

Social Worker Role and Purpose

In group work, social workers' primary task is to "help members use each other, exploit each other's strengths . . . and enlist each other in the performance of the common tasks that brought them together" (Schwartz, 1994, p. 579). Group workers have a dual focus: The group as a whole and each individual member. When workers lack an understanding of mutual aid, they risk engaging in "casework in the group" (Kurland & Salmon, 2005). This denies members the opportunity to support and learn from one another, obscures the commonalities that reduce feelings of isolation and stigmatization, and minimizes the impact that mutual demand has on members' willingness and ability to change.

Although there appears to be a preference for co-led over solo-led groups, research suggests that neither model is more effective. Two leaders may be better able to pick up on and respond to members' interactions and can serve as role models of adaptive communication (Toseland & Rivas, 2017). However, co-leadership can have a disruptive influence when the leaders have differing perspectives on their role and the purpose of the group (Toseland & Rivas, 2017).

Group Formation Tasks

The mutual aid potential of a group will be more fully realized when a group's purpose, type, composition, and structure complement one another. Four tasks associated with group formation have been found to facilitate the group's development, enhance members' commitment, and reduce the likelihood of dropout

(Browne et al., 2021; Firth et al., 2020; Pozza & Dèttore, 2017).

Establish Group Purpose

Groups can be formed to assist participants with mastering life transitions that are routine, such as a group for first-time parents; less expected but still relatively common, such as groups for separated/divorced individuals; or atypical for members' phase in the life cycle, such as grandparents raising grandchildren (Gitterman & Knight, 2019). Groups help members manage traumatic life events, such as survivors of interpersonal violence and human-made and natural disasters, and empower individuals who occupy stigmatized or marginalized social identities, such as individuals living with mental illness and those who identify as LGBTQ+.

Group members' collective efforts also may be directed toward stressors in their environment. A group formed to help parents better understand and adapt to their child's diagnosis of autism might also address the public school system's lack of responsiveness to their children's needs. Or, a group may be formed specifically to address broader social injustices.

Determine Group Type

In most cases, social workers will facilitate one of three broad group types, although groups often possess elements of one, two, or all three. In a *psychoeducational group*, the worker provides information, clarifies misinformation, and encourages members to learn from and process the information with one another. In a *support group*, the worker facilitates members' expressions of understanding and promotes mutual learning and problem-solving. In a group focused on *social action*, the worker helps members identify common concerns and develop strategies for collective action.

In some cases, the appropriate group type may be clear-cut. A job-readiness group for women in a homeless shelter will have a strong educational component, helping members prepare for job interviews and write a resume. The emphasis in a group for survivors of childhood sexual abuse will be on members supporting one another by capitalizing upon their shared experiences, although they also will learn from one another and the worker.

In other situations, determining the appropriate group type is less straightforward. A group for parents of infants born with significant genetic problems could be psychoeducational, in which members learn about their child's difficulties and prognosis, or it could be a support group in which members share their sadness, fear, and loss and help each other with day-to-day stressors, or it could be both. The worker's decision will reflect agency and practical considerations as well as members' sense of urgency and felt need.

Research suggests that clients may benefit from beginning in a group that has an educational focus and then "graduating" into a support group (McLaughlin et al., 2017; Schwartze et al., 2019). Psychoeducational groups often operate with predetermined curricula and provide members with a degree of structure that is reassuring; support groups operate with less structure and therefore may be less comfortable for some members.

In any group, the worker may employ activity to foster mutual aid. Activities can be used as icebreakers to help members develop comfort with one another. Groups for children and adults with developmental, intellectual, and emotional challenges often rely on art, music, and movement activities and also on life and social skills training to fulfill their purpose. In social action groups, members will—by definition—engage in activities such as boycotts and demonstrations.

Decide on Group Composition

When members share personal characteristics such as age, gender, race, and ethnicity, and

possess similar interpersonal and behavioral styles, they tend to quickly develop a sense of cohesiveness (Burlingame et al., 2018). It is important that workers strive to balance the degree of homogeneity and heterogeneity. "Excessively homogeneous groups can limit the . . . vitality essential to . . . create the necessary tension for change, and to provide models for alternative attitudes and behaviors" (Gitterman et al., 2021, p. 199). However, groups in which there is too much diversity may have difficulty developing a sense of "we-ness" (Burlingame et al., 2018).

Research findings indicate that *screening of members* to determine goodness of fit enhances the development of cohesion and decreases dropout (Berke, et al., 2019). The "Noah's Ark" (Yalom & Leszcz, 2008) principle suggests that each member should share with at least one other member characteristics considered central to the group's work. The "not the only one" principle (Gitterman et al., 2021) suggests that no one should "stand out as the sole member with a characteristic that is relevant to the group's work" (p. 201). Determining salient characteristics can be difficult. Consider the following examples:[1]

Example 1: The social worker developed a grief group for adults. The following potential members, all of whom identified as African American or Black, expressed interest:
  • Three mothers and one father in their 30s and 40s who had lost sons to gun violence
  • A 40-year-old woman, Mavis, whose husband died of cancer
  • A 22-year-old man whose twin brother died after being knifed in a robbery
  • A 30-year-old woman whose younger sister was a victim of domestic violence

---

1. Earlier versions of these examples appear in Gitterman et al. (2021).

- A 50-year-old man whose wife had been raped and murdered

The worker determined that members' differences in age, race, and gender were likely to be overridden by the shared commonality of losing a loved one to violence. Mavis shared the commonality of loss, but hers was the "only one" that resulted from natural causes. Because this was the only grief group being offered, the worker discussed the advantages and potential challenges to Mavis, who decided to join the group. The worker recognized that she might need to use skills that would connect Mavis to the group and the group to her (discussed later).

Example 2: The social worker in a youth diversion program offered a group for adolescents who also were survivors of childhood sexual abuse. The worker received seven referrals for youth between the ages of 15 and 17 years. Four were African American, two were Puerto Rican, and one was Caucasian. All seven had been convicted of similar crimes involving assault and had been sexually abused by a father or other male caregiver. Six potential members were young men, but one was a young woman. The worker decided that members' shared sense of urgency would override the likelihood that the sole Caucasian teenage boy would feel like "the only one." However, the worker believed the only female might struggle with identifying and connecting with the other members given its purpose and decided the group was not a good fit for her.

Research suggests that advance preparation increases the likelihood that potential members will commit to the group experience and lowers the risk of dropouts (Baker et al.,

2013). This may take the form of an in-person individual interview, small cluster sessions, or phone calls.

Decide on Group Structure: Timing, Size, and Physical Space

Most group offerings are short term and time-limited, and members start and finish together. Although time limits may be arbitrary, evidence suggests that when the number of sessions is known at the outset, members' commitment and motivation are enhanced and dropout is reduced (Paquin, 2017). A group offering may consist of only one session in settings in which client turnover is high and motivation or ability to commit to an extended time frame is limited.

Longer term groups tend to be open-ended, with new members joining when another member has departed. These groups are responsive to clients with chronic, intractable personal and environmental stressors but may lead the worker and members to lose sight of their original sense of purpose. Open-ended groups may be the only option when client turnover is high and therefore may rely on a drop-in format, with members attending the group if they are at the agency on the day it meets.

Decisions regarding session length should reflect members' developmental needs, attention span, and ability to focus on collective tasks (Burlingame et al., 2018). Groups for children and individuals with intellectual, emotional, and behavioral challenges will be shorter (20–30 minutes), whereas those for adolescents and adults may be longer (60–90 minutes). Weekly meetings provide continuity and promote cohesiveness (Lo Coco et al., 2019), but other options—such as biweekly or monthly—may be necessary for practical reasons.

For many of the groups that social workers will facilitate, size may range from as many as 12–15 members to as a few as 4 or 5. Moderately sized groups (6–8 members) are likely to be beneficial for most client populations because they provide opportunities for intimacy as well as for distance. Large groups may be threatening or confusing for some clients, resulting in feelings of isolation and increasing the risk of dropout. Smaller groups offer greater opportunity for individualization, but they also can be threatening. A group with 3 or 4 members risks becoming a dyadic session if a member is absent, whereas groups exceeding 20 participants may become a class. Groups with an educational focus can be larger, whereas groups that emphasize support are most helpful when they are smaller. Social action groups depend on large numbers, which will require the worker to help members develop a structure for work.

The room arrangement should promote discussion and member interaction and should ensure privacy. Anticipating members' spatial needs can be difficult, so the worker should have the ability to modify the space as needed.

Managing Agency Constraints on Social Work Practice with Groups

The previous considerations reflect "best practices" when forming a group. In agency-based practice, a group's composition and structure may be predetermined, requiring social workers to adjust the group's purpose and type accordingly. Consider the following example:[2]

> The worker in a shelter for homeless families facilitated a weekly group for any adult residents who were in

the shelter when the group was held. Residents were typically women, and most had experienced numerous traumas, including childhood abuse and domestic violence. The worker wanted to lead a support group focused on members' past and present trauma. Rapid turnover in membership, the typically large number of members who attended, and the drop-in nature of the group precluded this. The group's purpose was ever changing in response to members' shared sense of urgency. At times the group became more psychoeducational as members learned how to access resources in the community. At others, it became more of a support group, as members disclosed the many challenges they faced. It also took on elements of a social action group when members expressed their dissatisfaction with the quality of food and the leader helped them develop a strategy to present their concerns to the shelter's director.

Core Group Work Skills and Tasks

In this section, for ease of discussion, core group work skills are associated with four phases of work. In fact, these will be employed throughout the group's life. In groups that are open and have a revolving membership, preparation/beginnings skills will predominate.

Group Work Skills in the Preparation Phase

The formation tasks are essential aspects of the preparation phase. In addition, when social workers engage in *preparatory empathy*, they consider how members are likely to approach the first session. They may understand that

---

2. An earlier version of this example appears in Gitterman et al, (2021).

they will be with others experiencing similar challenges, but they also are likely to experience ambivalence—hope that their participation will be reassuring and fear that others will not understand and accept them.

Group Work Skills in the Beginning Phase

Eight professional skill sets help members develop a system of mutual aid. The worker begins by clarifying the role and purpose of the group and the role and purpose of the leader. The worker answers the question that is likely to be uppermost in participants' minds, "How can being with others like me *possibly* be helpful?" which requires the worker to put into words the advantages of mutual aid and clarify that their role will be to help members help one another.

Social workers' explanation is accompanied by an explanation of the expectations that will guide members' interactions with one another and that help members achieve their collective goals. Ground rules are reassuring and reduce members' fears of the unknown. When they are used punitively to address problematic group dynamics, this undermines the mutual aid process. In the next section, skills that address these challenges are identified.

The worker may establish basic expectations prior to the group's start or work with members to develop expectations for how they will work together. Basic ground rules typically address confidentiality, the stipulation that one member talks at a time, attendance and absence, and members' contact with one another outside of the group. Additional expectations will reflect specific needs of clients and the practice context; for example, in some groups, members will need to be reminded they cannot hurt one another or themselves physically or verbally.

Explicitly stated expectations are not equivalent to group *norms*, which inevitably develop out of members' interactions with one another and reflect what "should and should not" take place. However, when there is an inconsistency between the two, norms will exert the more powerful influence.

In a first session, the worker encourages members to engage in a "problem swap" in which members introduce and provide relevant information about themselves (Shulman, 2012). The worker assures members that *they* control their narrative, sharing as much or as little as they wish. The specific information that members share depends on the purpose and type of group and members' developmental, social, and emotional needs. The leader of a psychoeducational group for patients newly diagnosed with cancer might ask members to share their diagnosis, prognosis, and identify any questions they may have. The leader of a support group for this same client population might also ask members to share their affective reactions to their diagnosis.

Beginning in the first session, social workers constantly monitor members' reactions, allowing them to identify and comment on significant nonverbal behaviors. This skill also encourages individual members to talk to one another because the worker's attention is focused on the reactions of others. Even with this subtle encouragement, workers may have to direct and redirect members to talk to one another.

The worker employs five interrelated connecting skills to create a system of mutual aid (Gitterman et al., 2021):

1. *Point out members' underlying commonalities* based on information gleaned from the problem swap.
2. *Identify and focus on collective themes* that surface as members share information with one another.
3. *Reframe individual members' comments, experiences, and reactions* in a way that resonates with others in the group and

helps members recognize their underlying commonality.

4. *Invite members to build on one another's contributions* based on members' verbal and nonverbal communication.
5. *Connect the individual to the group and the group to the individual* based on the worker's use of the previous four skills.

In a group with revolving membership, the worker will employ these skills anytime a new member joins.

Group workers also may employ two differentiating skills (Gitterman et al., 2021), which convey to members that independence of thought and action is acceptable:

1. *Invite expressions of difference* when members reveal differing points of view.
2. *Reach for contradictory perceptions and opinions* when members' nonverbal and indirect communication suggests they have differing points of view.

A final skill requires the social worker to *directly address power and privilege* (Gitterman et al., 2021). In mandated groups, members' resentment may impede their ability to connect with one another and with the leader. Differences in social identities and positions between the worker and members may lead members to assume that the worker cannot understand the challenges they face. Sociocultural differences between members also can present barriers, based on assumptions they make about one another. When the group worker employs three connecting skills—point out members' underlying commonalities, identify and focus on collective themes, and connect the individual to the group and the group to the individual—members are helped to see beyond perceived differences to their underlying similarities. In groups in which members' sense of urgency is high, the potentially disruptive impact of sociocultural differences is lessened (Gitterman, 2006).

Group Work Skills in the Middle/Work Phase

Members' interactions will change over time as their comfort with one another increases. Five additional skill sets will come into play. The social worker continues to *monitor the group to ensure that its normative structure supports members' work*. As noted previously, when norms and expectations are inconsistent, norms will exert the greatest influence on members' actions. Consider the following scenario:[3]

> The social worker facilitates a support group for women sexually abused in childhood. The group is ongoing and operates with a closed membership. The group worker expressed concern about members' silence and their seeming unwillingness to talk about their past, even though members were explicitly encouraged to engage in open and honest discussion. She also expressed frustration at the frequent absences, despite the expectation that members needed to attend to maximize benefits of their participation. As the worker processed the group with a colleague, she realized that when sensitive topics like members' molestation surfaced, she and the members became uncomfortable. She recognized that when a member *did* try to disclose sensitive information, the topic swiftly changed to something less painful. Rather than tackling members' abuse directly, the group norm became one of avoidance, which the leader unwittingly reinforced.

---

3. This example first appeared in Knight (2016, p. 27).

Once the social worker recognized that the *norm* of avoidance preempted the *stated expectation* that members could talk openly about their past and present challenges, she employed another skill, *renegotiating with members' expectations for participation*:

> Over the last couple of weeks some of you have missed group and I've noticed a lot of uncomfortable silence. When we started, I suggested that one of the ways that the group would be helpful was for you to talk openly about your experiences and feelings. Yet, I get the feeling that this has been difficult. It is painful to hear others' stories and to tell your own. How about we spend some time talking about how we can make it easier to share your experiences? I sense that you *want* to do this, but are afraid to because it is so hard, and it hurts so much.

In this example, the worker employs a third skill, *holding members to the agreed upon focus and challenging avoidance*, by reframing members' actions—in this case, their absences and changing the focus of discussion—as manifestations of their desire to avoid painful topics.

One of the most challenging aspects of facilitating groups is the emergence of internal dynamics that undermine the group's mutual aid potential. Maladaptive processes include member roles such as the silent member, the monopolist, the scapegoat, and the defensive member. In order to understand and manage these processes when they surface, the social worker first *develops a transactional definition of the maladaptive process* (Gitterman et al., 2021). In addition to connecting skills, five skills assist workers in managing maladaptive processes when the surface:

1. Identify for members the maladaptive pattern.

2. Re-identify for members the maladaptive pattern if needed.
3. Search for and identify common definitions and perceptions.
4. Acknowledge the role they may have played in creating and/or sustaining the pattern.
5. Search for and sustain the expression of strong feelings.

The following example illustrates a common error made by workers when they fail to appreciate the transactional nature of maladaptive patterns, in this case scapegoating:[4]

> Frank is an intellectually challenged member of a group for high school males with high rates of truancy. He exhibits poor self-control and occasionally engages in childish clowning. One member, Stanley, described the challenges he faced in the classroom: "The work is too hard, and my teacher calls on me when I don't know the answers." Frank responded, "Yeah, in dancing class, all the kids laugh at me." He then began dancing around the room. Billy said, "Frank, you are so damn stupid." Angelo added, "You don't even know how to read, write, or do math." All the boys laughed and joined in attacking Frank. The worker responded by reprimanding the members who made fun of Frank, reminding them of the "rule" that they should respect one another.

The worker's "either/or" approach to members' scapegoating of Frank leads him to side with Frank and chastise members. This serves only to distance Frank even further from the group. (In other cases, the worker might side with the group, experiencing frustration at the scapegoat.)

---

4. An earlier version of this example appears in Gitterman et al. (2021).

A more helpful intervention would be to identify and reframe the maladaptive pattern and employ connecting skills to help members see their underlying commonality, which in this case is members' academic struggles. The worker would need to begin by acknowledging the role he played, saying, for example, "When you guys started making fun of Frank, I started to feel like I had to protect him." The worker could continue with

> You guys are laughing, but I'm thinking that maybe it's easier to laugh than it is to talk about what Stanley and Frank brought up, about how difficult school is for you guys. That's tough to talk about it, isn't it? Each of you guys struggles in the classroom, and maybe that's why you skip school? Because it's embarrassing and frustrating?

Group Work Skills in the Ending Phase

In time-limited groups, particularly more long-term ones, skills associated with four phases of termination help members end with another and with the leader (Gitterman et al., 2021). In an ongoing group, this phase may not exist, although departing members and the group will need to say their mutual good-byes. Endings can bring out strong feelings in both clients and workers. Therefore, workers must continuously *reflect on their own feelings*. Because members may struggle to put their feelings into words, workers also will need to *look for indirect manifestations* such as members skipping sessions and the group as a whole reverting to earlier themes.

Initially, members may avoid the prospect of ending and may even claim to "forget" that this is going to occur. The following strategies assist members in moving through this phase:

1. Provide sufficient time to allow for period of avoidance.

2. Offer frequent and persistent reminders of ending date.
3. Share worker's feelings about ending.
4. Validate members' avoidance and reasons behind it.

The worker explores members' unwillingness to acknowledge the group's ending. Constant reminders, coupled with pointing out the pattern, assist the group in moving through this stage.

As members begin to accept the inevitability of ending, negative reactions such as anger and resentment are likely to surface, requiring workers to use the following skills:

1. Pursue and accept members' negative feelings.
2. Sustain expression of client anger.
3. Avoid premature reassurance and power struggles.
4. Connect individual and collective behaviors and actions to unexpressed feelings.
5. Convey faith in members and their collective efforts.

Members' feelings may be directed toward the leader, underscoring the need for workers to de-personalize members' reactions and encourage their expression.

Anger often gives way to sadness as members appreciate the loss that the group's ending will mean for them. To help members move through this phase, workers must do the following:

1. Encourage and support expression of sadness and regret.
2. Share their own sadness and regret.
3. Avoid escape into happy activities.

Because members' reactions in this phase may produce feelings of guilt and sadness in workers, they must manage their own feelings so that they do not collude with members in avoidance.

Once members move through their affective reactions to ending, they can take stock of their work together to achieve *release*. The following skills assist members in working through this final phase of ending:

1. Invite review of collective work.
2. Emphasize strengths and gains.
3. Elicit discussion of remaining areas of difficulty, if needed.
4. Consider next steps, including contracting for another time-limited group and referral for additional services.
5. Provide opportunity for final goodbye.

Conclusion

The group modality exemplifies the strength- and empowerment-based orientation of the social work profession. If groups are going to reach their mutual aid potential, social workers must understand the unique benefits provided by this modality and how to create and maintain a culture that supports members helping, supporting, and making demands from one another.

References

Baker, E., Burlingame, G. M., Cox, J. C., Beecher, M. E., & Gleave, R. L. (2013). The Group Readiness Questionnaire: A convergent validity analysis. *Group Dynamics, 17,* 299–314.

Berke, D. S., Kline, N. K., Wachen, J. S., McLean, C. P., Yarvis, J. S., Mintz, J., Young-McCaughan, S., Peterson, A. L., Foa, E., Resick, P. A., & Litz, B. T. (2019). Predictors of attendance and dropout in three randomized controlled trials of PTSD treatment for active duty service members. *Behaviour Research and Therapy, 118,* 7–17.

Browne, K. C., Chen, J. A., Hundt, N. E., Hudson, T. J., Grubbs, K. M., & Fortney, J. C. (2021). Veterans self-reported reasons for non-attendance in psychotherapy for posttraumatic stress disorder.

Psychological Services, 18(2), 172–185. https://www.ncbi.nlm.nih.gov/pmc/articles/PMC7147996/

Burlingame, G. M., McClendon, D. T., & Yang, C. (2018). Cohesion in group therapy: A meta-analysis. *Psychotherapy, 55,* 384–398.

Firth, N., Delgadillo, J., Kellett, S., & Lucock, M. (2020). The influence of socio-demographic similarity and difference on adequate attendance of group psychoeducational cognitive behavioural therapy. *Psychotherapy Research, 30*(3), 362–374.

Gitterman, A. (2006). Building mutual support in groups. *Social Work with Groups, 28*(3–4), 91–106.

Gitterman. A. (2017). The mutual aid model. In C. Garvin, L. Gutierrez, & M. Galinsky (Eds.), *Handbook of social work with groups* (2nd ed., pp. 113–132). Guilford.

Gitterman, A., & Knight, C. (2019). Non-death loss: Grieving for the loss of familiar place and for precious time and associated opportunities. *Clinical Social Work Journal, 47,* 147–155.

Gitterman, A., Knight, C., & Germain, C. B. (2021). *The life model of social work practice* (4th ed.). Columbia University Press.

Knight, C. (2016). Group work practice: Phases of work and associated skills and tasks. In G. Greif & C. Knight (Eds.), *Group work with populations at risk* (3rd ed., pp. 17–36). Oxford University Press.

Knight, C., & Gitterman, A. (2014). Groups for bereaved individuals: The power of mutual aid. *Social Work, 59,* 5–12.

Kunikata, H., Yoshinaga, N., & Nakajima, K. (2016). Effect of cognitive behavioral group therapy for recovery of self-esteem on community-living individuals with mental illness: Non-randomized controlled trial. *Psychiatry & Clinical Neurosciences, 70,* 457–468.

Kurland, R., & Salmon, R. (2005). Group work versus case work in the group: Principles and implications for teaching and practice. *Social Work with Groups, 28,* 133–148.

Lo Coco, G., Melchiori, F., Oieni, V., Infurna, M. R., Strauss, B., Schwartze, D., Rosendahl, J., & Gullo, S. (2019). Group treatment for substance use disorder in adults: A systematic review and meta-analysis of randomized-controlled trials. *Journal of Substance Abuse Treatment, 99,* 104–116.

McLaughlin, B., Ryder, D., & Taylor, M. F. (2017). Effectiveness of interventions for grandparent caregivers: A systematic review. *Marriage & Family Review, 53,* 509–531.

Paquin, J. D. (2017). Delivering the treatment so that the therapy occurs: Enhancing the effectiveness of time-limited, manualized group treatments. *International Journal of Group Psychotherapy, 67*(Supp. 1), S141–S153.

Pozza, A., & Dèttore, D. (2017). Drop-out and efficacy of group versus individual cognitive behavioural therapy: What works best for obsessive–compulsive disorder? A systematic review and meta-analysis of direct comparisons. *Psychiatry Research, 258,* 24–36.

Sanger, S., Bath, P. A., & Bates, J. (2019). "Someone like me": User experiences of the discussion forums of non-12-step alcohol online support groups. *Addictive Behaviors, 98,* 106028.

Schwartz, W. (1994). The classroom teaching of social work with groups: Some central problems. In T. Berman-Rossi (Ed.), *The collected writings of William Swartrz* (pp. 574–582). Peacock.

Schwartze, D., Barkowski, S., Strauss, B., Knaevelsrud, C., & Rosendahl, J. (2019). Efficacy of group psychotherapy for posttraumatic stress disorder: Systematic review and meta-analysis of randomized controlled trials. *Psychotherapy Research, 29,* 415–431.

Shulman, L. (2012). *The skills of helping individuals, families, groups, and communities* (8th ed.). Cengage.

Toseland, R. W., & Rivas, R. F. (2017). *Introduction to group work practice* (8th ed.). Pearson.

Wendt, D. C., & Gone, J. P. (2017). Group therapy for substance use disorders: A survey of clinician practices. *Journal of Groups in Addiction & Recovery, 12,* 243–259.

Yalom, I., & Leszcz, M. (2008). *The theory and practice of group psychotherapy.* Basic Books.

PART VI

Guidelines for Specific Techniques

Introduction to Direct Practice from a Technique Perspective

Francis J. Turner and Susan P. Robbins

In preparing the update of this section on clinical techniques, originally written by the eminent scholar, the late Francis J. Turner, a dilemma quickly surfaced in trying to distinguish between techniques, methods, procedures, skills, therapies, models, and other terms that are used to describe exactly what we do in social work practice. Unfortunately, there is little in the social work literature that clarifies the differences in these terms, which are often used interchangeably. Turning to a dictionary description (The Free Dictionary, n.d.), a technique is defined as

> 1) the manner and ability with which an artist, writer, athlete, etc. employs the technical skills of a particular art or field of endeavor; 2) the body of specialized procedures and methods used in any specific field, esp. in an area of applied science, 3) any method used to accomplish something; and 4) technical skill; degree to which one is able to apply procedures or methods. (para. 3)

The confusion involved in clearly defining a technique is only amplified by these descriptors, which equate techniques with application of skills, or procedures, and methods. One textbook specifically devoted to techniques for social work practice (Sheafor & Horejsi, 2015) covers basic communication and helping skills such as verbal and nonverbal communication; skills for agency practice such as client records and documentation; techniques for all phases of the planned change process, including engaging the mandated client; and techniques for direct practice that focus primarily on assessment. Although the distinction between a skill and a technique is never clarified in this book, they are not identical. In the simplest terms, a skill is the ability to do something well, and it generally requires practice. A technique, on the other hand, refers to a specific way of executing a task or specific practice. What they share in common, however, is that both are learned and not innate.

What drives our choice of technique in a particular case? To answer this query, we first have to consider what we mean by technique. For those of us in social work, this is not an easy question to answer—or at least to answer with any degree of consistency. Although we have frequently used the term "technique" in our clinical literature throughout the decades, we have not been precise in what we mean by the term. Thus, we have used it to describe various different things. There have been very few efforts to define technique in an agreed upon way. We seem to presume that we all understand what we mean by the term. One attempt to be precise about the term can be found in Howard Goldstein's excellent book, *Social Work Practice: A Unitary Approach* (1973).

Several years later, Joel Fischer (1978) brought into focus the importance of technique when he reminded us that everything we do with, to, and for clients constitutes the application or utilization of a cluster of actions for which we need to take responsibility and upon which we need to build our theoretical base. This comes close to the idea of technique. Only when we can be precise and cognizant about what specifically we are doing in practice with, to, and for clients, and only when we are committed to understanding the different effects of these various activities on our clients, can we begin to understand the differential importance of our rich range of theories. In this way, we can search out richer and more effective ways of putting our theories to use. A greater attention to technique helps us understand how various techniques can bring about different ways of helping our clients and, of at least equal importance, also help us identify more precisely areas and situations in which our theories can be harmful to some or all clients. This reminds us that with the intensity of the impacts we have, or will have, on clients, an inappropriate use of some techniques can be harmful. Thus, we need to understand the element of risk that is introduced into our use of various techniques.

If we move to greater interest in technique, we should work to agree on a definition of technique that will assist us in moving toward a more precise use of the concept. Turner and Rowe (2013) offer two definitions that provide us with further precision in the use of the term. The first states that "technique refers to the spectrum of actions we consciously do for, with, and to clients in the process of a professional intervention" (p. xv). Although not generally recognized as a technique, Turner and Rowe hold that this "presumes that almost everything we do in working with a client in a psychosocial intervention is a technique" (p. xv). The second definition states that

> a technique is the artistic use of some practical object or activity by a social worker as a component of treatment aimed at achieving an identified outcome. Such action or object is replicable by others, is ethical, has a level of professional approbation and is understandable from a relevant theoretical perspective. (p. 5)

One of the difficulties for those of us in social work in dealing with the technique component of our practice in a conceptual way is that so many of our techniques are quite mundane in nature and lack the attractiveness of techniques in other disciplines. An example of this is something as mundane as a handshake. The question of whether we shake hands with a client is not a simple question. Among other concerns, it involves such things as gender, values, customs, religion, age, and occasion. When properly assessed and utilized, a handshake can provide considerable positive impact for a client. But a handshake can also be totally inappropriate, even to the point of offending a client who might well misunderstand the action to such an extent that it will affect the relationship in a negative way. A handshake also could be viewed as a very positive gesture on our part, one that the client perceives as very supportive. Similar issues arise in regard to many of our techniques.

As we begin to appreciate that virtually everything we do in relationship with our clients can and frequently does have an impact on them, we can appreciate just how important it is that many of our apparently mundane actions be examined with care. It is very important that we pay much more attention to all the things we do with, to, and for clients and seek to understand on an ongoing basis the significance of how we interact with them. We also need to learn to identify our differential actions to assess their impact, both positive and possibly negative. That is, we need to ask ourselves on an ongoing basis whether what we are doing is the most effective and helpful way to achieve our therapeutic goals.

Of course, much of this assessment takes place outside of the interview, as we sit back and engage in a process of evaluation. We do not want to take away from the essential spontaneity of a therapeutic process, which is so essential to the effective engagement of our clients. But we do want to learn to view our interviewing partly as a wide assortment of discrete actions. This requires us to engage in an ever-continuing process of examining what techniques we use and how we interact. We must ask ourselves, "What are the risks in making various uses of my technique repertoire?" and "Can I better serve this client by a shift in my technique repertoire?" Or by trying something from my own repertoire with this client?"

If we begin to analyze technique in our individual practices, then as a profession, we will expand our available data, which will help us understand and make fruitful use of the relationships among technique, theory, assessment, and diagnosis. Also, in the long term, we will begin to develop patterns of theory and technique so that we can begin to differentiate among our clients based on who we are, who they are, and how we can best help them. We also will develop a better understanding of how some of the things we do are, in some cases, not helpful.

Of course, an obvious and appropriate response to this stream of thought would be to say, "But this is what I have always done and do in all my interviews with clients." We all are highly skilled interviewers and we can draw a client into a meaningful positive helping situation quickly and effectively. We can even transform the most troubled and hostile of situations into relationships that are at least minimally helpful and at best enormously helpful. But what we do not do is identify how we do this, what techniques we use to accomplish this, and what we would have done differently, given a choice. "What could I have done to be more helpful?" we might ask. "What can I do to improve the effectiveness of many of my techniques?" Of course, we all do this to some extent already. What is different or novel about this train of thought is that we have not been sufficiently precise to ourselves, or to our profession, in defining the term "technique." Without that, and without a commitment to precision, we cannot make full use of our rich body of knowledge and bring this abundance to our clients so that we can better serve them.

One way we can start down this trail is to work from a categorization of our techniques, as was done in Turner and Rowe's book, *101 Social Work Clinical Techniques* (2013). Obviously, many different ways of categorizing techniques could be used. Then, we would have to develop or work from an agreed-upon list. This latter effort is an interesting process, as Turner and Rowe discovered. From their work on this project, Turner and Rowe were convinced that there are many more techniques used in social work practice that need to be identified and added to our repertoire. We need also to begin a process of considering whether some techniques better fit some theories more than others or whether all techniques fit all theories. At the same time, we need to continue the process of assessing the risk involved in making use of various techniques. On the other hand, we might ask ourselves whether matters of effectiveness are related to inherent client strengths rather than something inherent in the technique or skill of the practitioner.

References

Fischer, J. (1978). *Effective casework practice: An eclectic approach*. McGraw-Hill.

Goldstein, H. (1973). *Social work practice: A unitary approach*. University of South Carolina Press.

Sheafor, B. W., & Horejsi, C. R. (2015). *Techniques and guidelines for social work practice* (10th ed.). Pearson.

The Free Dictionary. (n.d.). *Technique*. https://www.thefreedictionary.com/technique

Turner, F. J., & Rowe, W. S. (2013). *101 social work clinical techniques*. Oxford University Press.

Cognitive Restructuring Techniques

Bruce A. Thyer

From a cognitive–behavioral perspective, human functioning is conceptualized as the product of the reciprocal interaction of cognition, behavior, emotion, personal factors (emotion, motivation, physiology, and physical phenomena), and social environmental influences. As social worker Harold Werner (1982) stated, "The primary determinant of emotion and behavior is thinking" (p. 3), reflecting a perspective similar to that of social worker James Lantz (1978): "The primary concept held by cognitive practitioners is that most human emotion is the result of what people think, tell themselves, assume, or believe about themselves and their social situations" (p. 361).

From a *behavior analytic* perspective, overt actions, thoughts, and feelings are all viewed as forms of behavior, without any causal relations among them. This is in keeping with the definition of behavior provided in the National Association of Social Workers *Social Work Dictionary*: "Any action or response by an individual, including observable activity, measurable physiological changes, cognitive images, fantasies, and emotions" (Barker, 2014, p. 38). Unlike the cognitive–behavioral perspective,

however, behavior analysis does *not* posit that thinking causes behavior, or even has primacy in explaining overt behavior. Rather, the behavior analyst contends that overt actions, thoughts, and feelings are all largely originating in the person's environmental experiences and biology. This is an important distinction. If one theorizes that thinking causes overt behavior, then to change overt behavior one should focus on changing cognition. This is, of course, the conventional view of most psychotherapies, including cognitive–behavioral therapies. However, if one theorizes that thoughts, overt behavior, and feelings are all caused by one's person-in-environment transactions (and biology), the social worker largely will focus on providing new and different environmental experiences in order to bring about changes in thoughts, feelings, and actions. This is much more of an *environmentalist* orientation, as opposed to a mentalist one, and has important treatment ramifications. Cognitive–behavioral therapy would focus more on office-based consultations and therapies, whereas the behavior analyst would view cognitive change efforts as more real-world based, with change efforts occurring outside the office. Both approaches can be effective for cognitive restructuring. Next, we discuss various ways of changing thinking, derived from these two orientations.

Techniques for Changing Thoughts

Socratic Dialogue

Cognitive restructuring is the term used for a variety of procedures focused on the modification of cognitions and cognitive processing. Many approaches to cognitive restructuring use the Socratic method to guide the client in the identification, exploration, modification, and elaboration of cognitions. Other approaches use imagery, guided discovery, and real-life behavioral procedures to "test out" and modify beliefs. The goal of cognitive restructuring is to guide the client in the exposure of cognitions influencing untoward, unappealing, discomforting, or dysfunctional outcomes and modify them through further exploration, disputation, or elaboration. Clients are guided in the use of logic or evidence to examine and modify their exaggerated, distorted, or ill-founded beliefs. The first task is to elicit the thoughts, cognitive processing errors, or images contributing to the client's unhappiness or distress. Wells (1997) recommends a Socratic sequence combining general questions with more specific probe questions. Probe questions are useful in gaining clarification and greater detail. The use of reflection and expressions of empathy and affirmation may promote relationship development and client awareness that the therapist clearly understands. The following dialogue illustrates early intervention with a client experiencing high anxiety (Wells, 1997, p. 53):

> Therapist: What did you feel in the situation? (general question)
> Client: I felt scared and couldn't stop shaking.

> T: When you felt scared and shaky (reflection) what thoughts went through your mind?
> C: I don't know. I just felt awful.
> T: Did you think anything bad could happen when you felt like that? (probe)
> C: Yes. I thought I looked stupid.
> T: What do you mean by stupid? (probe)
> C: I thought everyone would notice and think I was an alcoholic or something.

After gaining an understanding of the client's thinking and associated emotional responses, the focus shifts to modification efforts. The following is a list of questions for potential use in modifying thoughts:

- Where is the evidence?
- Is there any evidence to the contrary?
- How strongly do you believe that?
- Could you see yourself . . . with more positive views of self . . . having more trust in your partner's dedication to you . . . having greater purpose in life?
- What is the worst that could happen?
- Could you look at it another way?
- What other meanings can you identify?
- What are the consequences of looking at it this way?
- How do you feel when you think _____ _____?
- Would it be possible to _____?
- What images or sensations do you experience when you think _____?
- What other thoughts flow from that thought (image)?
- Given your current understanding of the impact that our meanings have on the way we think, feel, and are motivated to act, what is your best advice to yourself?
- What if?

Socratic dialogue uses questions such as the foregoing to probe for the logic or evidence supporting the client's thinking and explore the consequences of the belief or beliefs. As beliefs fail to demonstrate validity or viability, cognitive restructuring proceeds with the generation of alternative meanings and their consequences (J. Beck, 1995; Granvold, 1994).

Therapist Modeling Adaptive Thinking

It is important that the therapist model desirable cognitive processing in the questions asked. For example, "How did that make you feel?" promotes an external locus of control thinking. Such thinking places the power over one's well-being with other people or with one's life circumstances. This violates the cognitive therapy principle that, with a few exceptions, each of us is responsible for our feelings and ultimately our mental health. The question can be rephrased easily as "How did you feel when . . .?" Another therapist trap easily avoided is the use of expressions in which information processing errors are evident. For example, to avoid modeling dichotomous thinking, the therapist can ask such questions as "What factors influenced your decision to divorce?" and "When you got angry in traffic, what thoughts were going through your mind?"

Case Example

The following is an illustration of cognitive restructuring with a client who is going through a contentious divorce. By temporary court order, her husband has been given custody of their children. Her relationship with her children has been troubled largely due to past episodes of depression and a demanding work schedule. Following the recent separation, she has felt extremely depressed and hopeless, along with feelings of hurt, sadness, loss, and anger. She admits to suicidal ideation but has no plan to do so, nor can she see herself actually committing suicide. Socratic dialogue has identified a web of strong beliefs that undermine her

emotional well-being and promote negative views of self. In the following excerpt, one of the most powerful beliefs from this matrix of meanings is identified and explored for change. The probing is focused on uncovering evidence to support or negate her belief.

Client: I have moved out of the house into an apartment. I've lost everything. I don't have my house. My husband doesn't love me. I don't have my kids anymore. I've lost my children (crying).

Therapist: You have experienced a lot of loss with the separation, and I feel badly that you are going through this. You just said that you have lost your children. Could you tell me more about that thought?

C: I don't see them each night when I come home from work. I've lost them. I'm not a mother anymore.

T: When you think the thought, "I've lost my children," how do you feel?

C: I feel empty and sad . . . and hurt.

T: So the thought, "I've lost my children" promotes some pretty unpleasant feelings.

C: Yes (softly crying).

T: You may recall our past discussions about the role our thoughts tend to play in our feelings. You have expressed the thought that you have lost your children. As evidence to support this thought, you indicated that you don't see them each evening as you did prior to the separation. Let's explore this statement. Have you seen them at all since you moved out 3 weeks ago?

C: Oh, yes, I see them one or two nights a week and on Saturday or Sunday, sometimes both days.

T: So despite not seeing them daily, you do spend time with them several times a week.

C: Yes, that's right.

T: Although it is not the same as when you were living in the same household with them, are you their mother when you are spending time with them?

C: Well, yes I am, but it doesn't feel the same.

T: In what ways does it feel different?

C: I guess it's different because I know that I am going to my apartment alone, without them.

T: Would you conclude from our discussion that although it isn't the same, you haven't actually lost your children?

C: Yea, I guess that's more accurate.

T: So, you're still their mother, and you are continuing to be actively involved in their lives. Earlier you said that you feel sad, empty, and hurt in relation to the thought that you've lost your children. Would you conclude that shifting your thought from, "I've lost my children" to "It isn't the same" is really a more accurate statement of your situation?

C: Yes, it is, I guess.

T: You have reported feeling sad, empty, and hurt in relation to the thought that you've lost your children. Though it would be unrealistic to expect these feelings to go away completely, can you detect feeling any *less* sad, empty, and hurt as you think, "Parenting isn't the same," rather than "I've lost my children?"

C: It's really hard to tell, but I suppose I don't feel as badly.

T: Perhaps you will be able to detect greater change in your feelings over time. Each time you think, "I've lost my children," would you be willing to answer that thought with, "No, I haven't lost my children, it [parenting] just isn't the same?"

C: Yes, I'll try it.

The therapist guided the client in revising a powerful statement presumably influential in promoting strong feelings. The client realized that the evidence contradicted the meaning she attached to the post-separation change in parenting. She arrived at an alternative meaning that was more consistent with her recent experience as a parent. She also considered the connection between her thoughts and feelings. Based on the awareness that effective cognitive restructuring requires repetition, the client was asked to repeat the reframing whenever the faulty thought occurred. This practice was reviewed at several subsequent sessions. As noted previously, the thought addressed in this excerpt is one of a web of beliefs contributing to her current views about her children, herself, and her emotional state. She also believed that her children no longer cared for her (e.g., "They never call me"; "They could care less whether I call them or not"; "When we are together, it's all about them"). These and other beliefs were similarly isolated for cognitive restructuring with the focus on the identification of supportive evidence and evidence to the contrary.

Therapist Modeling of Adaptive Performance

Observing another person engage in desired behavior can be an effective method of inducing behavioral, affective, and cognitive changes (Bandura, 1977). For example, in the behavioral technique of exposure therapy and response prevention, which often is used to treat clients with phobias, a therapist will model all behaviors to be subsequently asked of the client, such as touching a harmless snake, holding it, and verbalizing aloud realistic and adaptive thoughts. Similarly, role-playing exercises for nonassertive persons may involve a therapist displaying various ways of acting appropriately assertive with a confederate while the client observes. The exercises may involve gradually escalating scenarios wherein the therapist/model demonstrates increasingly greater levels of assertiveness and changed thinking.

Use of Scaling to Assess Change

Cognitive restructuring may not produce a complete change in the client's beliefs. Thoughts and beliefs determined to strongly contribute to distress, disturbance, self-downing, and unrest may remain active following cognitive restructuring efforts. It is more realistic to expect a reduction in the strength of the view rather than complete eradication of the belief. To evaluate the effectiveness of the specific cognitive restructuring effort, the therapist may ask the client to rate the current strength of the belief under scrutiny:

> Therapist: How much do you believe that your husband is trying to take everything from you?
>
> Client: About 50 percent, I guess.
>
> T: How have you managed to drop from 95 to 50 percent?
>
> C: I looked over the proposed property settlement and I can see that he's trying to be fair in that area. I can't let go of the idea completely though, because he's the one with the children (i.e., custody).
>
> T: And now how angry do you feel toward him?
>
> C: Oh, I'm still pretty upset. I guess about a 60 (percent).
>
> T: I see. Although you're still upset, you are making meaningful change in your views and feelings.

Scaling is used in a variety of psychotherapies, including behavioral and cognitive behavioral therapy, solution-focused brief treatment, and many others (Harris et al., 2019; Kim, 2014; Miller et al., 2003; Thyer et al., 1984). Apart from being useful to evaluate any changes, the mere act of scaling seems capable of inducing some positive changes on the part of the client.

Guided Imagery

Guided imagery is another method to use to restructure cognitions. An early approach to the use of imagery was developed by Maultsby (1975) in the form of rational emotive imagery (REI). Other cognitive–behavioral therapy leaders have also employed the use of imagery as a cognitive restructuring method (A. Beck & Emery, 1985; A. Beck & Weishaar, 2008; Ellis, 1977). Edwards (1989) notes that "the main techniques for obtaining an image from which to begin are the visualization of a life event or theme, the reinstatement of a dream or daytime image, and feeling focusing" (p. 286). Images, dreams, and fantasies may be drawn from the client's history or current imagination. Alternatively, the therapist may generate content for use in guided imagery. In the example that follows, guided imagery is used with a Vietnam veteran suffering from nightmares about a specific combat experience in which two men under his leadership were killed. The client feels responsible for their deaths and believes he should have acted to save them. He is a decorated veteran known for his leadership in combat situations. When he awakens from these recurrent nightmares about combat more than 40 years ago, he feels extreme sadness and intense self-reproach. On these occasions, he subsequently acts cold and distant toward his wife and his employees.

> Therapist: You said that when you think back on the firefight in Vietnam in which two of your men were killed, you feel responsible, that you should have acted to save them.
>
> Client: That's right. I have vivid dreams about them being torn apart by bullets.
>
> T: Close your eyes. Imagine that you did little to prepare your men for combat and that you are out on patrol. The patrol is attacked, and your men go down beside you. You and your remaining men fight off the enemy and the shooting ends. As you attend to the casualties, how are you feeling?
>
> C: First, I would never act this way. But I'll go along with this thinking . . .

I feel angry with myself, a lot of self-loathing . . . and ashamed for being so irresponsible.

T: So when you think of yourself as failing to prepare your men for combat and casualties result, you feel anger with yourself, self-loathing, and shame. Now this time, imagine that you have prepared your men extremely well for combat. By your instruction, they have become highly skilled soldiers, but you recognize that war is war. Each man knows that he may die in battle. You enter the firefight as before, and men are lost. The patrol is attacked, and your men go down beside you. You and your remaining men fight off the enemy and the shooting ends. As you attend to the casualties, how are you feeling?

C: I feel pretty empty inside over the loss of these men, but I don't feel as upset with myself. I did what I could do . . . but war is war, as you just said.

In this example, the client was asked to consider himself performing his responsibilities unconscionably by failing to prepare his men for battle (a legitimate basis for accepting responsibility for casualties of war). After identifying the associated feelings, he imagined the same combat scene with the awareness that he *had* prepared his men well for battle. This process resulted in a reduction in the degree to which he felt upset and reinforced the thought "war is war." The latter thought is one that the client had expressed in a previous session. The client was a strong candidate for the use of imagery inasmuch as he was experiencing powerful imagery (both nightmares and daydreams) outside therapy sessions.

The early behavior therapy called systematic desensitization asks clients to imagine themselves being exposed to phobic or upsetting situations, moving up a hierarchy from minimally upsetting scenarios to more distressing ones. This too is another form of

guided imagery that has been described in the social work literature (e.g., Fischer, 1978; Himle & Shorkey, 1973; Shorkey & Himle, 1974). Prolonged exposure in imagination is also useful to help people overcome phobic behavior, physiological arousal, and distressing thinking patterns related to upsetting situations. This guided imagery technique may be used as an initial approach to exposure, prior to transitioning to real-life situations, or as the primary treatment method when real-life exposure may not be feasible (thunderstorms, an anticipated airplane flight, etc.).

Skills Building and Real-Life Experiments

Behavioral experiments may be used to identify and modify beliefs, assumptions, and expectations. As A. Beck and Weishaar (2008) note, the client and therapist collaboratively develop a plan for the client to

> test out the veracity or viability of his or her views. In the behavioral experiment, the client may "predict" an outcome based on personal automatic thoughts, carry out the agreed-upon behavior, and then evaluate the evidence in light of the new experience. (p. 286)

Ellis (1977) introduced his famous "shame attacking" exercises early in the development of Rational Emotive Therapy (RET) In these exercises, clients exposed themselves to negative attention, typically with little or no actual disconcerting consequences. Several iterations of the experiment often resulted in cognitive and emotive change.

Behavioral experiments may be enacted in real-life settings or take place in the therapist's office as role-playing exercises. In some cases, the simple gathering of information may suffice (J. Beck, 1995). The following are illustrations of clients' evaluation of their beliefs in actual life experiences. A client experiencing social phobia tested the hypothesis that "no one will speak to me" at a singles' Sunday school class. By attending the class, she disproved the hypothesis and actually experienced a warm reception by many. Another client viewed himself as extremely unappealing and consequently no one would be willing to go out with him on a date. He further believed that if he *was* successful, he would not find the woman desirable. We agreed that this experiment might take several iterations. He went online and made contact with several people. After developing ongoing correspondence with several women, he began arranging dates. His first few efforts actually supported his original hypothesis. On the fourth outing, however, he met a woman whom he found to be highly attractive. They dated for a time. Although their relationship was not sustained, he modified his self-view as a consequence of this experience.

Through behavioral experimentation, clients modify their views as actual life experiences provide evidence that contradicts their conceptualizations. Some clients may approach behavioral experimentation with marked skepticism and strong beliefs that they are "right" in their conceptualizations. For those clients, a review of their personal life experience may be persuasive. Attempt to identify prior life experiences in which anticipation failed to match realized experience (e.g., aerobics classes are for athletic people only). These experiences may serve as useful points of reference in dispelling client reluctance and in developing openness to behavioral experiments.

The author was once consulted by an older woman who had developed a severe phobia to dogs following her being savagely attacked by a large dog 4 years earlier (see Thyer, 1981). She wished to become less afraid of dogs (change her feelings), think less anxious thoughts about them (change her cognitions), and stop unrealistically avoiding them (change her actions). The social worker realized that purely cognitive interventions such as Socratic dialogue, cognitive elaboration, scaling, and guided imagery would likely be less effective at helping her achieve her goals compared with more direct experiences in real life. This is in keeping with Bandura's (1977) admonition that

> it is performance-based procedures that are proving to be most powerful for effecting psychological changes. As a consequence, successful performance is replacing symbolically based experiences as the principle vehicle of change. . . . Cognitive processes mediate change but . . . cognitive events are induced and altered most readily by experience of mastery arising from successful performance. (p. 191)

Accordingly, with full client-informed consent, the therapist arranged a series of real-life encounters with live dogs, initially small and cute and then large and intimidating ones, with the client in the therapist's office—the behavioral experiment called real-life exposure therapy. Although she was initially made highly anxious during these sessions, with the passage of time within each session she calmed down, felt less anxious, avoided the dogs less, and had less distressing thoughts. Office-based sessions were replaced with real-life interactions with dogs, including a visit to the local humane society. A complete remission of all symptoms, overt behavior avoidance, distressing cognitions about dogs, and fear was achieved after five such sessions, in approximately 1 month. Close contact without anything untoward happening, being repeatedly licked and jumped on, and her mastery of commanding the trained dogs to sit, "speak," and lay down all worked at inducing not only cognitive restructuring but also therapeutic changes in feelings and actions. This form of experiential behavior therapy also makes use of therapist modeling desired behavior, which is another valuable way to induce changes in cognitions, feelings, and overt actions.

Conclusion

Humans are no strangers to the process of cognitive restructuring in some form. We develop and modify beliefs automatically as part of life span development. Beliefs operate rather inflexibly, and cognitive processing patterns become routine. When modification of these phenomena is indicated, cognitive restructuring procedures such as those presented in this chapter provide a methodology for effective change. Clinicians engaged in cognitive restructuring efforts are invited and encouraged to draw on their creativity individually and collaboratively with their clients in developing efficacious cognitive restructuring strategies. More detailed reviews of cognitive restructuring methods can be found via the internet links provided in the Helpful Resources section and in Garland and Thyer (2013), Granvold (1994), and Thyer (2020).

Helpful Resources

Academy of Cognitive and Behavioral Therapies: https://www.academyofct.org
Association for Behavioral and Cognitive Therapies: http://www.abct.org/home
Beck Institute for Cognitive Behavior Therapy: https://beckinstitute.org
Rational Emotive Behavior Therapy Network: http://www.rebtnetwork.org

References

Bandura, A. (1977). Self-efficacy: Toward a unifying theory of behavioral change. *Psychological Review, 84,* 191–215.

Barker, R. L. (Ed.). (2014). *The social work dictionary* (6th ed.). NASW Press.

Beck, A. T., & Emery, G. (1985). *Anxiety disorders and phobias: A cognitive perspective.* Basic Books.

Beck, A. T., & Weishaar, M. E. (2008). Cognitive therapy. In R. J. Corsini & D. Wedding (Eds.), *Current psychotherapies* (8th ed., pp. 263–294). Thomson.

Beck, J. S. (1995). *Cognitive therapy: Basics and beyond.* Guilford.

Edwards, D. J. A. (1989). Cognitive restructuring through guided imagery: Lessons from Gestalt therapy. In A. Freeman, K. M. Simon, L. E. Beutler, & H. Arkowitz (Eds.), *Comprehensive handbook of cognitive therapy* (pp. 283–297). Plenum.

Ellis, A. (1977). The rational–emotive approach to sex therapy. In A. Ellis & R. Greiger (Eds.), *Handbook of rational–emotive therapy* (pp. 198–215). Springer.

Fischer, J. (1978). *Effective casework practice: An eclectic approach.* McGraw-Hill.

Garland, E., & Thyer, B. A. (2013). Cognitive-behavioral approach. In M. Gray & S. Webb (Eds.), *Social work theories and methods* (2nd ed., pp. 159–172). Sage.

Granvold, D. K. (1994). Concepts and methods of cognitive treatment. In D. K. Granvold (Ed.), *Cognitive and behavioral treatment: Methods and applications* (pp. 3–31). Brooks/Cole.

Harris, R., Murphy, M., & Rakes, S. (2019). The psychometric properties of the Outcome Rating Scale used in practice: A narrative review. *Journal of Evidence-Based Social Work, 16,* 347–362.

Himle, D., & Shorkey, C. (1973). The systematic desensitization of a car phobia and the recall of a related memory. *Journal of Biological Psychology, 15*(1), 4–7.

Kim, J. (Ed.). (2014). *Solution-focused brief therapy: A multicultural approach.* Sage.

Lantz, J. (1978). Cognitive theory and social casework. *Social Work, 23,* 361–366.

Maultsby, M. C. (1975). *Help yourself to happiness.* Institute for Rational Living.

Miller, S. D., Duncan, B. L., Brown, J., Sparks, J. A., & Claud, D. A. (2003). The Outcome Rating Scale: A preliminary study of the reliability, validity and feasibility of a brief visual analog measure. *Journal of Brief Therapy, 2*(2), 91–100.

Shorkey, C., & Himle, D. (1974). Systematic desensitization treatment of a recurring nightmare and related insomnia. *Journal of Behavior Therapy and Experimental Psychiatry, 5,* 97–98.

Thyer, B. A. (1981). Prolonged in vivo exposure therapy with a 70-year-old woman. *Journal of Behavior Therapy and Experimental Psychiatry, 12,* 69–71.

Thyer, B. A. (2020). Behavioral and cognitive theories. In J. R. Brandell (Ed.), *Theory and practice in clinical social work* (3rd ed., pp. 21–38). Cognella.

Thyer, B. A., Papsdorf, J. D., Davis, R., & Vallecorsa, S. (1984). Autonomic correlates of the Subjective Anxiety Scale. *Journal of Behavior Therapy and Experimental Psychiatry, 15,* 3–7.

Wells, A. (1997). *Cognitive therapy of anxiety disorders: A practice manual and conceptualization guide.* Wiley.

Werner, H. D. (1982). *Cognitive therapy: A humanistic approach.* Free Press.

Motivational Interviewing

Jean Paul Hare, Kirk von Sternberg, Shannon Johnson, and Mary M. Velasquez

Motivational interviewing (MI) is a collaborative, client-centered style of communication designed to strengthen personal motivation for and commitment to behavior change. A clinician using MI guides a client in exploring reasons for change within an atmosphere of acceptance and compassion (Miller & Rollnick, 2013). MI provides an alternative approach to counseling styles that attempt to educate, scare, or persuade clients to change unhelpful behaviors. MI pays attention to the language of change, underscoring a client's values, shepherding the conversation toward overcoming ambivalence and enhancing readiness (Miller & Rose, 2009).

MI arose in the field of addictions during the 1980s. Since then, it has been supported by a myriad of empirical studies, and due to its efficacy with a variety of behaviors, MI holds widespread appeal across a number of disciplines. MI is appealing to social workers because it is applicable to the range of settings in which they work. The tenets of MI also dovetail with the ethical standards of the social work profession (Hohman, 2012).

MI is characterized by a distinct spirit, guiding principles, processes, and core strategies. This chapter provides an overview of these components as well as an introduction to their value to social work. It also provides a brief case example and resources to learn more about MI and some recent developments describing the use of technology in its delivery. This chapter discusses the role of technology, addressing an increased need to deliver and train MI from a distance.

The Motivational Interviewing Spirit

Although it is purposive, MI is not about fixing people; it is about encouraging change that is consistent with a client's values and desires. MI originators William Miller and Stephen Rollnick (2013) explain the spirit of MI with the acronym PACE: *partnership*, *acceptance*, *compassion*, and *evocation*.

Partnership describes the relationship between practitioner and client. This concept is not unique to MI. In this approach, the re-lationship is particularly egalitarian. The MI practitioner does not enter the partnership to provide solutions, remedies, or the wisdom to change but instead serves as a collaborative guide. The practitioner neither leads nor fol-lows the client but, rather, walks alongside and gently reinforces movement in the direction of change.

Acceptance is central to MI. Accepting clients where they are does not equate to ap-proval, especially of behaviors that are illegal or unhelpful for the client. Acceptance means that the MI practitioner affirms the client's ab-solute worth and offers unconditional positive regard. Regardless of their behaviors, clients are respected and valued, and the practitioner con-veys this through both nonverbal and verbal messages. Acceptance also requires attempting to actively understand the client and their cir-cumstances through empathic listening, sup-porting autonomy, and affirming the client's inherent strengths.

Compassion is a fundamental value in MI. Compassion is actively promoting the client's welfare and prioritizing their needs. This means removing the interests of the practitioner from the therapeutic process in favor of the client's prerogatives. The promotion of others' welfare is an important premise in social work; indeed, it is compassion that allows the social worker to respect and prioritize a client's well-being.

Evocation refers to the elicitation of the client's wisdom, goals, and solutions about change (Miller & Rollnick, 2013). Rather than focusing on deficits, MI is a strength-based model; it does not presume clients to be sick, broken, or lacking some quality that helping professionals need to install in them (Hohman, 2012). The potential for change belongs to the client, who is already equipped and capable to do so. The role of the MI practitioner is to evoke or bring out an inherent ability to change. At the inception of MI, this concept was un-common among substance use treatments,

which generally assumed clients incapable or unmotivated toward healthful decisions (Miller & Rose, 2009).

Processes of Motivational Interviewing

Four key client-centered processes are used throughout an MI session to help a client de-fine goals and begin to move toward them. The four processes are engaging, focusing, evoking, and planning (Miller & Rollnick, 2013). The processes are loosely conceptualized as se-quential, although they may overlap and recur in practice.

Engaging is the process of establishing an effective therapeutic connection with the client. This is tantamount regardless of ser-vice, setting, or population. Engaging is the relational foundation of MI, and positive en-gagement has been shown to predict client outcomes (Project MATCH Research Group, 1997). Successful engagement is characterized by developing a shared vision about the pur-pose of the work. Engagement also requires trust and respect within the partnership. This is made possible through collaboration that em-phasizes the client's own knowledge, strength, wisdom, and values.

Focusing is the process of establishing a trajectory in the conversation toward change. It is about helping the client determine what is truly important and using that information to set the tone for the work ahead. The practi-tioner and client mutually agree upon the goals established during this focusing phase, and cli-ents identify their own areas of ambivalence and begin to work in the direction of change.

Evoking is the process of eliciting a client's thoughts and motivations to change. An as-sumption of MI is that human beings are in-herently driving toward their own survival, health, and success. The humanist lineage of MI regards behavior as purposeful. The wisdom to change lies within the client rather than the practitioner. A skillful MI practitioner listens carefully for clients to use language that communicates desire, ability, and reasons to change. Practitioners reinforce these utterances through strategic reflections and affirmations.

Planning is a process with two distinct components: (1) solidifying the client's commitment to change and (2) mapping out tangible, concrete steps to action the change. Planning is always dependent on the expressed permission of the client, and practitioners resist the urge to move to planning prematurely. Some clients will enter the session with content ready to work on, whereas others will move more slowly. An effective MI practitioner will follow the client's lead, assessing readiness and matching strategies consistent with the client's stage of change along the way (DiClemente & Velasquez, 2002).

Core Strategies

Four essential communication skills facilitate the principals and processes of MI described previously. These skills are the cornerstone of MI and can be easily remembered by using the acronym OARS: asking *o*pen questions, *a*ffirming, *r*eflecting, and *s*ummarizing.

Open questions facilitate dialogue and allow clients to elaborate on their responses. Open questions cannot be answered with a simple word or phrase; they are a means of soliciting information in a neutral way. Clients do most of the talking while the practitioner listens for and reinforces change talk.

Affirming is to recognize, support, and encourage the client. When done sincerely, it supports and promotes self-efficacy. Affirmation is distinct from praise—a judgment made by the practitioner. Affirmation is an observation about something positive that the client can feel proud about. One subtle distinction is that statements starting with "you" affirm, whereas statements beginning with "I" imply an imbalance of power in which the practitioner bestows approval. Affirming may also entail reframing otherwise negative content in the client's dialogue. Affirming reduces defensiveness, which increases alliance and openness to change. This strategy also serves to keep clients invested in treatment and therefore more likely to complete it.

Reflective listening entails making testable assumptions about the meaning of client dialogue. It is a fundamental skill in MI. Reflective listening can vary from simple repetition of client language to a more complex synthesis or interpretation of the underlying meaning. This serves several purposes, including verification of shared understanding, maintaining momentum, building accurate empathy, and ultimately guiding conversation toward change talk. Reflective listening allows practitioners to participate without usurping the client's ownership of the dialogue. Good reflective listening is a skill that takes a great deal of practice, much like becoming proficient at a sport or playing a musical instrument.

Summarizing serves the role of connecting separate sections of the client's narrative. A good summary can link pertinent information between sessions or within a single conversation. It serves as a tool to transition from one task to another or bookend the session. Summarizing differs from reflection in that it ties several ideas together across time.

Strategies and Tools

Motivational interviewing can be understood as a way of communicating. A skilled MI practitioner becomes proficient at listening and purposefully moving the dialogue toward change, listening for *change talk*. As mentioned previously, client language reflecting positive movement toward change is characterized by elements of desire, reasons, abilities, or needs for change (DARN). Client verbiage such as "wish," "need to," "want to," "change," and "tired" often signals dissatisfaction with the status quo and movement toward change.

The opposite of change talk is *sustain talk*, which reflects the client's desire to maintain the existing behavior. The presence of sustain talk is not a negative indicator in and of itself; sustain talk can reflect the client's lack of readiness to change, or ambivalence, and should be respected. A skillful practitioner understands the difference between change talk and sustain talk and gently guides the client away from sustain talk and toward change talk. When MI is practiced effectively, clients often literally talk themselves into change (Miller & Rollnick, 2004).

Another aspect of change talk is *commitment language*. Commitment language occurs when a client voices intentions, obligations, or agreements to change. Linguistic research suggests that commitment language predicts behavior change; specifically, it is the strength of the commitment language that is most predictive of change (Miller et al., 2006; Moyers et al., 2009).

A variety of strategies can be used to facilitate change talk. For example, a series of scaling questions and rulers are often employed to evaluate importance, confidence, or readiness to change. MI practitioners offer a numerical scale and encourage clients to quantify their response. An example is ranking on a scale of 0 to 10 how ready a client is to change a behavior. Practitioners can remark on the significance of that value and ask why the client did not select a lower number or explore the circumstances that might make the value larger in the future. This elicits change talk that often, in turn, increases a client's motivation to change and sense of confidence in doing so.

Motivational Interviewing in Groups

Motivational interviewing has been adapted for diverse modalities in part because it has been successful in individual addiction counseling (Project MATCH Research Group, 1997). MI is used in the treatment of psychopathology, improving athletic performance, and as a primer for training general health care professionals. MI has proved effective in group settings (D'Amico et al., 2012; Velasquez et al., 2013; Wagner & Ingersoll, 2013).

When delivering MI in a group format, the spirit and principles of MI remain ostensibly the same as in individual work. Co-facilitators model these components and encourage the group to do the same. In group formats, however, the group becomes the de facto client. Attention to group processes takes precedence over the focus on the individuals within the group. Several empirically supported group MI formats have been manualized and outline the structures and milestones facilitators can follow (Velasquez et al., 2015; Wagner & Ingersoll, 2013).

Applications in Social Work Practice

From its inception, MI has been well received by many professions, including social work (Hohman, 2012). Given the consistency of MI principals with the core values of the social work profession, the National Association of Social Workers has several ongoing initiatives to incorporate MI into social work practice settings (Hohman, 2012). Further appeal lies in the cost-effectiveness of MI treatments. MI interventions have demonstrated equal effectiveness in treating substance use in half the number of patient contacts compared with other manualized approaches (Project MATCH Research Group, 1997).

Cross-cultural efficacy of MI has also been established in meta-analysis, which contributes to its popularity with social workers. Systematic reviews have demonstrated even larger effect sizes for minority groups compared with European American clients (Hettema et al., 2016). MI has been translated into 18 languages, and expert trainers in MI who are members of the Motivational Interviewing Network of Trainers (MINT) represent more than 40 languages, operating worldwide (Hohman, 2012). This underscores the applicability of MI for diverse groups, making it well suited for social work.

How to Learn Motivational Interviewing

Many resources are available to learn the technical skills of MI. The third edition of Miller and Rollnick's foundational text, *Motivational Interviewing: Helping People Change* (2013), provides an excellent starting point. MI mastery takes practice, supervision, and feedback from an experienced guide (Martino et al., 2011; Moyers et al., 2005). The *Motivational Interviewing Treatment Integrity Scale Coding Manual* (MITI) version 4.2.1 offers the framework for assessing fidelity when applying MI in research studies or in clinical practice (Moyers et al., 2015). The MITI is a helpful tool in navigating the stages of learning MI. A useful workbook for practitioners who wish to build their MI skills is provided by Rosengren (2017). Links to the MINT website and other educational resources are provided in the Helpful Resources section. These resources provide routes to supervision, workshops, professional affiliation, and distance learning opportunities for MI practitioners.

Delivering Motivational Interviewing Using Technology

Motivational interviewing is being adapted to technology-delivered formats for intervention and practitioner training. A systematic review by Hai et al. (2019) established the efficacy of technology-based interventions in preventing

and reducing substance use among women of childbearing age. The review considered 15 randomized controlled trials, two-thirds of which reported use of MI principles and included 3,488 participants dating back to 2007.

The COVID-19 pandemic accelerated the use of technology-based MI interventions and virtual training of practitioners. MI trainers worldwide quickly adapted to the use of digital platforms to teach MI skills. This training has typically been taught over multiday in-person workshops. Many trainers and professors who teach MI in person are moving to distance learning. Technology-based, distance MI training will likely have continued application, particularly in social work programs.

Virtual training offsets the high cost and logistical difficulties of in-person MI trainings. Although MI training in a virtual format promises standardization, empirical data for online MI training are forthcoming. Preliminary studies point to the pedagogical potential of virtual trainings. A pilot study of a virtual MI training for health care professionals is promising (Mitchell et al., 2011). A study by Gavarkovs (2019) tested immersive virtual simulations as an approach to virtual MI training. In immersive virtual simulations, the learner's sense of presence within the virtual environment can enhance the ability to develop empathy. A growing body of research has provided a glimpse of potential innovations in the future of virtual MI treatment and training.

Case Example

The following brief example demonstrates the core strategies utilized in MI to facilitate the processes and the guiding principles of the approach:

> Counselor: It is nice to meet you Steve. What brings you here today? (open question)

Client: I've never done anything like this before so I'm not sure what I'm supposed to say.

Counselor: This goes differently for everybody, so I would like to start today talking about where you are, and where you would like to be. (engaging)

Client: There is so much going on it feels overwhelming. I've been working at the same company for 6 years and it seems like every success just leads to more work. There is no real appreciation from the boss, just threats. It's a grind. Really stressful, you know?

Counselor: You are a hard worker. You have tremendous commitment. (affirming)

Client: Yea. Long days, big commute, late nights with no overtime. The last year was especially rough. It started to wear on me and my marriage.

Counselor: Your marriage is important to you as well. (reflecting)

Client: Yea. We have been together for 10 years now, God bless her. She knew who I was when she married me though. I work hard, I play hard, just like all the men in my family. But if there is a roof over our heads and food on the table then I did my part, am I right?

Counselor: You do your best to be a good partner and provider, but it has its challenges too, like meeting all the expectations your partner has. (complex reflecting)

Client: I wish it had not gotten to this point though. (change talk)

Counselor: You would like some things to be different. What would you change? (reflecting/open question)

Client: Well I'm not sure I can do anything; it's just been really hard since I got the DUI. The wife seems angry and distrustful of me. We have to watch every dollar we spend now because of the legal fees and fines. I've been late to work a few times and the boss keeps bringing it up. When he finds out about the DUI, there are going to be a new batch of problems. Transportation is an issue now too. I feel really alone in this mess.

Counselor: Things are really challenging right now, in part because of an incident involving alcohol. What are your thoughts about making some changes with alcohol in your life? (reflection/open question)

Client: Well I don't think alcohol is the problem. I'm not a drunk, I just enjoy it. (resistance)

Counselor: It seems like alcohol has almost been a tool for maintaining the challenging pace of your life. What else does drinking do for you? (rolling with resistance/open question)

Client: Well I guess it helps me sleep when I'm anxious and relax when I'm uncomfortable. I notice my back pain less, at least for a while, although lately it seems worse the next morning. I feel 70 years old when I get up now. But I know drinking is not the solution and my family constantly bothers me about it. (change talk/ambivalence)

Counselor: It seems like the stability of your family and your health are important and drinking sometimes challenges those things. (reflecting discrepancies between values and behaviors)

Client: Yea it's frustrating.

Counselor: If it is okay with you, I'd like to ask you a question about your future and alcohol. (seeking permission)

Client: Yea.

Counselor: On a scale of 0 to 10, 10 being the most, how ready are you to reduce your drinking behavior? (evaluating readiness to change with a ruler)

Client: I don't know, maybe a four?

Counselor: Wow, four is a significant number, tell me why is it a four and not a two? (open question to elicit change talk)

Client: I guess I can remember times that were better, where drinking wasn't such a big part of my life. I have also accomplished difficult things in the past. Between the tight income and the issues with my wife it's a concession I'd consider. I cannot imagine giving it up though with everything else going on, but maybe less of it for a while. So, I feel like that is a four. If some of the stresses in my life somehow where lessened, it might even be higher. (change talk)

Counselor: You work very hard to support your family and feel that doing so has taken a toll on you and your marriage. You noticed that with increasing stress you drank more and while you aren't completely comfortable with all the consequences, you also understand that it serves some purposes for you. Considering all of this you are thinking about a change to your drinking. (summarizing)

Conclusion

Motivational interviewing is an empirically supported treatment backed by 40 years of research. More than 300 critically appraised studies and more than 100 systematic reviews suggest the efficacy of MI in a variety of behaviors in diverse settings. MI is well-suited for social work and many other professions in which clients collaborate to change behavior and overcome ambivalence to do so.

Helpful Resources

An Expanded Bibliography of Motivational Interviewing: https://www.guilford.com/add/miller2/biblio.pdf?t

Center for Excellence for Integrated Health Solutions: https://www.integration.samhsa.gov/clinical-practice/motivational-interviewing

Dr. Miller and Dr. Rollnick official and websites: https://www.williamrmiller.net and https://www.stephenrollnick.com

Health Behavior Research and Training Institute: https://sites.utexas.edu/hbrt/training

Motivational Interviewing Network of Trainers: www.motivationalinterviewing.org

Motivational Interviewing Series: https://www.guilford.com/browse/psychology-psychiatry-social-work/applications-motivational-interviewing-series

References

D'Amico, E. J., Osilla, K. C., Miles, J. N. V., Ewing, B., Sullivan, K., Katz, K., & Hunter, S. B. (2012). Assessing motivational interviewing integrity for group interventions with adolescents. *Psychology of Addictive Behaviors, 26*(4), 994–1000. https://doi.org/10.1037/a0027987

DiClemente, C. C., & Velasquez, M. M. (2002). Motivational interviewing and the stages of change. In W.R. Miller & S. Rollnick (Eds.), *Motivational interviewing* (2nd ed., pp. 201–216). Guilford.

Gavarkovs, A. G. (2019). Behavioral counseling training for primary care providers: Immersive virtual simulation as a training tool. *Frontiers in Public Health, 7*, 116. https://doi.org/10.3389/fpubh.2019.00116

Hai, A. H., Hammock, K., & Velasquez, M. M. (2019). The efficacy of technology-based interventions for alcohol and illicit drug use among women of childbearing age: A systematic review and meta-analysis. *Alcoholism, 43*(12), 2464–2479. https://doi.org/10.1111/acer.14203

Hettema, J. E., Wagner, C. C., Ingersoll, K. S., & Russo, J. M. (2016). Brief interventions and motivational interviewing. In K. J. Sher (Ed.), *The Oxford handbook of substance use and substance use disorders* (Vol. 2, pp. 513–530). Oxford University Press. https://dx.doi.org/10.1093/oxfordhb/9780199381708.013.007

Hohman, M. (2012). *Motivational interviewing in social work practice*. Guilford.

Martino, S., Ball, S. A., Nich, C., Canning-Ball, M., Rounsaville, B. J., & Carroll, K. M. (2011). Teaching community program clinicians motivational interviewing using expert and train-the-trainer strategies. *Addiction, 106*(2), 428–441. http://dx.doi.org/10.1111/j.1360-0443.2010.03135.x

Miller, W. R., Moyers, T. B., Amrhein, P. C., & Rollnick, S. A. (2006). Consensus statement on defining change talk. *MINT Bulletin, 13*, 6–7. https://motivationalinterviewing.org/mint-bulletin-volume-13-issue-2

Miller, W. R., & Rollnick, S., (2004). Talking one-self into change: Motivational interviewing, stages of change, and therapeutic process. *Journal of Cognitive Psychotherapy,* 18(4), 299–308. http://dx.doi.org/10.1891/jcop.18.4.299.64003

Miller, W. R., & Rollnick, S. (2013). *Motivational interviewing: Helping people change* (3rd ed.). Gilford.

Miller, W. R., & Rose, G. S. (2009). Toward a theory of motivational interviewing. *American Psychologist,* 64(6), 527–537. https://doi.org/10.1037/a0016830

Mitchell, S., Heyden, N., Schroy, P., Andrew, S., Sadikova, E., & Wiecha, J. (2011). A pilot study of motivational interviewing training in a virtual world. *Journal of Medical Internet Research,* 13(3), e77. http://dx.doi.org/10.2196/jmir.1825

Moyers, T. B., Manuel, J. K., & Ernst, D. (2015). *Motivational Interviewing Treatment Integrity coding manual 4.2.1.* Center on Alcoholism, Substance Abuse, and Addictions. https://casaa.unm.edu/download/MITI4_2.pdf

Moyers, T. B., Martin, T., Houck, J. M., Christopher, P. J., & Tonigan, J. S. (2009). From in-session behaviors to drinking outcomes: A causal chain for motivational interviewing. *Journal of Consulting and Clinical Psychology,* 77(6), 1113–1124. http://dx.doi.org/10.1037/a0017189

Moyers, T. B., Martin, T., Manuel, J. K., Hendrickson, S. M., & Miller, W. R. (2005). Assessing competence in the use of motivational interviewing. *Journal of Substance Abuse Treatment,* 28(1), 19–26. http://dx.doi.org/10.1016/j.jsat.2004.11.001

Project MATCH Research Group. (1997). Matching alcoholism treatments to client heterogeneity: Project MATCH posttreatment drinking outcomes. *Journal of Studies on Alcohol,* 58(1), 7–29. https://doi.org/10.1080/09652149934152

Rosengren, D. B. (2017). *Building motivational interviewing skills: A practitioner workbook* (2nd ed.). Guilford.

Velasquez, M. M., Crouch, C., Stephens, N. S., & DiClemente, C. C. (2015). *Group treatment for substance abuse, second edition: A stages-of-change therapy manual* (2nd ed.). Guilford.

Wagner, C. C., & Ingersoll, K. S. (2013). *Motivational interviewing in groups.* Guilford.

Neurofeedback

An Evidence-Based Nonmedication Intervention

Schuyler C. Cunningham, Tim Norman, and
Steven Warner

What Is Neurofeedback Training?

Neurofeedback (NFB) training is a way to pro-actively and directly influence brain wave activity. Through this process, brain waves are modified to reflect more of a neurotypical brain wave pattern, which is consistent with reduction or elimination of mental health symptoms and modification of some physical disorders. A neurotypical brain can be determined by an average based on large normative databases. And neurofeedback is much more than simply a mental health intervention. It is a way to influence desired internal emotional states through brain wave training.

NFB fits squarely within the category of biofeedback. The Biofeedback Certification International Alliance approved the following definition of biofeedback on May 18, 2008:

> Biofeedback is a process that enables an individual to learn how to change physiological activity for the purposes of improving health and performance. Precise instruments measure physiological activity such as brainwaves. . . . These instruments rapidly and

accurately "feedback" information to the user. The presentation of this information—often in conjunction with changes in thinking, emotions, and behavior—supports desired physiological changes. Over time, these changes can endure without continued use of an instrument.

Although there are many forms of biofeedback, NFB is the primary intervention that targets the central nervous system and specifically cortical brain waves.

NFB works by providing the brain with spontaneous feedback during a training session. The feedback is focused on altering specific brain waves that might be expressing themselves too strongly or insufficiently, thereby having a negative impact on the client. The International Society for Neurofeedback & Research (ISNR), in January 2009, adopted the following definition of NFB:

> NFT [neurofeedback training] uses monitoring devices to provide moment-to-moment information to an individual on the state of their physiological functioning. The

characteristic that distinguishes NFT from other biofeedback is a focus on the central nervous system and the brain. Neurofeedback training has its foundations in basic and applied neuroscience as well as data-based clinical practice. It takes into account behavioral, cognitive, and subjective aspects as well as brain activity.

Whereas many medical professionals, including doctors and neurologists, focus mainly on electroencephalogram (EEG) brain waves that signify seizures or other serious neurological conditions, NFB leverages the subtler expression of brain waves that influence mental health conditions.

NFB training is ideally preceded by a quantitative EEG (qEEG), which is an assessment tool for brain wave activity and is summarized into a graphical representation known as a brainmap. See Figure 60.1 for an example summary brainmap. A brainmap summarizes the raw qEEG data in a useful way such that a social worker can determine an NFB training treatment protocol. Although a qEEG is not required before determining an NFB training protocol, it is recommended. If a social worker is trained in NFB but not qEEG collection or brainmap interpretation, they can partner with a provider who can administer a qEEG and interpret it for them.

Through NFB training sessions, clients learn to retrain their brains through a reward system. They learn to keep their brain wave activity in the optimal spectrum ranges, resulting in gradual relief from their mental health symptoms. NFB training is as natural as watching a movie or television show or playing a video game, while the software and clinician modulate rewards and inhibit specific brain waves the client produces, over a number of training sessions, thereby achieving a desired result. The results from this treatment tend to be long-lasting, and side effects are minimal compared to those of many other treatment forms.

Brief History of Neurofeedback

The following discussion is an illustrative and brief history of the development of NFB. There are too many contributors to list them all here. Nonetheless, this should provide an introduction to the development of NFB in clinical practice.

NFB is based on the EEG. Evidence of electrical activity in brains was reported by Richard Caton to the British Medical Association in Edinburgh in July 1875. Caton

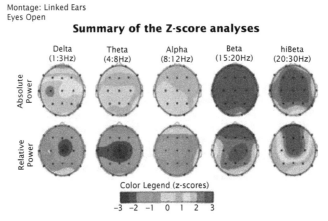

FIGURE 60.1 Example of a brain map. *Source:* © 2020 Washington DC Center for Neurocognitive Excellence, LLC.

reported that he used a galvanometer and observed electrical impulses from the surface of the brains of animals. Similarly, Adolf Beck, in 1875, reported event-related EEG desynchronization in the German publication *Centralblatt für Physiologie*. Hans Berger conducted the first studies that observed EEG in humans in 1929, and his work was validated by Edgar Douglas Adrian and B. H. C. Matthews in 1934 (Berger, 1929). Adrian's work was published in numerous journals as well as in his books, *The Basis of Sensation*, *The Mechanism of Nervous Action*, and *The Physical Basis of Perception*.

The first documented case of humans controlling their own brain waves was provided in 1958 by Joe Kamiya, a professor at the University of Chicago. Kamiya published his findings in which he detailed humans' altering their own brain waves, specifically alpha waves (Spilker et al., 1969). He showed that humans could intentionally alter their brain waves, thereby changing the paradigm from one of observation to intervention.

In the late 1960s, Barry Sterman at the University of California, Los Angeles investigated how pathological conditions could be treated with NFB (Sterman, 1977; Sterman & Friar, 1972). After partnering with NASA, he found that typical laboratory cats experienced seizures when exposed to rocket fuel, like NASA test pilots, whereas cats that received brain training suffered no adverse effects from the fuel. He concluded that NFB had stabilized the brains of the unaffected animals, allowing them to endure exposure to the fuel without incident. Sterman later used NFB to virtually eliminate seizures in a patient who experienced at least two seizures a month for 15 years (van der Kolk, 2014).

The first article written about the connection between NFB and hyperactivity was by Joel Lubar. With the help of his wife, Judy, Lubar devised a training protocol to increase beta brain waves while decreasing theta waves. This approach was based on the fact that excess theta wave activity caused a lack of mental vigilance.

On the other hand, increased beta waves led to improved cognitive processing and diminished inattention and hyperactivity.

Robert Thatcher spent 20 years as a psychiatry professor at the University of Maryland. He was instrumental in developing what has become the "gold standard normative database" for qEEG and created NeuroGuide, a software program for NFB and qEEG.

Siegfred Othmer and his wife, Susan, started NFB training in 1985 because their son had a seizure disorder and they hoped NFB would help. This led the Othmers to study and train others in NFB. They pioneered new applications of and instrumentation. Recently, they developed infra-low NFB, which trains brain waves at or below 0.5 Hz.

Thomas Collura has more than 40 years of experience as a neurophysiologist, biomedical engineer, and, more recently, a mental health professional. Currently, his interests and research are focused on automated feedback systems, evoking potential NFB and low-cost qEEG. Collura's seminal book, *Technical Foundations of Neurofeedback*, was published in 2013. He founded BrainMaster Technologies, Inc., one of the leading providers of NFB equipment, software, and training through Stress Therapy Solutions.

Mark Smith, a social worker practicing in New York City, was one of the first clinicians to utilize *z* score training, working closely with Thomas Collura and Robert Thatcher. *z* score training is a multivariate proportional approach based on the normative database. Smith also developed the software for infra-slow fluctuation (ISF) NFB.

Neuroplasticity and the Process of Neurofeedback

Advances in the scientific understanding of brain plasticity, or neuroplasticity, have provided the foundational opportunities NFB promises through brain wave regulation and re-training. Neuroplasticity refers to the ability of the central nervous system to change and adapt, based on its response to environmental and physiological changes. It should not be thought of as a temporary brain state but, rather, as an ongoing state of change to the genetic, cellular, and body-regulation systems. This culminates in a gain or loss of the client's behavior or function (Orndorff-Plunkett et. al., 2017).

The delivery process by which NFB is administered begins with brain events. The delivery process of NFB uses EEG to monitor brain events, then feeds the brain's own data back to itself using external feedback, such as audio, visual, and/or tactile feedback. The brain events can be regulated toward externalized expressions of behavior and/or internalized regulations of thought. These feedback loops regulate brain waves through operant conditioning, as set in the specific NFB training protocol administered by the clinician (Smith et al., 2014). The Brodmann areas, or international 10–20 sites, are the industry standard for charting location for applying the electrodes to the scalp for training.

Basic Instrumentation/ Hardware and Software

Neurofeedback involves multiple pieces of equipment and software. The main hardware component is the amplifier and the associated equipment, such as electrodes. Many companies sell the hardware, software, and training to administer NFB.

Another major hardware component required is a computer and displays. The computers used for NFB must meet the specifications of the NFB training platform the social worker utilizes to administer NFB. Displays are needed for the client to watch the visual and auditory feedback.

Various software programs exist to run NFB applications, the most popular of which is BrainMaster's BrainAvatar. This interface allows for several types of NFB to be practiced using the same software interface, such as alpha–theta training, ISF, and sensory motor rhythm NFB. Third-party NFB applications can be used through primary software interfaces such as BrainAvatar, including Bio-Explorer, LENS, NeuroGuide, and sLORETA.

Client Assessment

In addition to the standard client assessment, the NFB assessment must include a more detailed medical history. Because NFB may influence non–mental health symptoms, asking clients to provide a more detailed health history is highly recommended. Many NFB trainings will provide education about salient domains of assessment for NFB. Of note, items to consider include seizure, stroke history, traumatic brain injuries, migraines, bruxism, chronic pain, fibromyalgia, heart issues, tinnitus, syncope, tremors, and visual issues. A rubric may be offered to allow the client to rate the severity of their presenting problems, first identifying which conditions the client associates with, then asking the client to rate the severity of their symptoms from 1 to 3 (1 = mild, 2 = moderate, and 3 = severe). It is also typical for social workers to request a self-report from a client approximately 24 hours after receiving NFB. In other words, an ongoing assessment process is important during the administration of NFB.

Psychopharmacological Considerations

Neurofeedback training is impacted by medications that clients are prescribed (Saletu et al., 2010). Medication refers to prescription medications but also substances clients might be taking such as medical marijuana, street drugs, and even alcohol use. It is important to determine how much of a medication was used and how close to the date of training and within a

TABLE 60.1 Illustrative List of Influence of Medications on Brain Waves (Stress Therapy Solutions, 2019)

Drug	Increases	Decreases
Adderall	Beta between 12 and 26 Hz	Delta and theta
Ativan	Beta between 20 and 30 Hz	Alpha
Haldol	Delta, theta, and beta above 20 Hz	Alpha and beta below 20 Hz
Lithium	Theta and mild increase in beta	Mild decrease in alpha
Opiates	High-amplitude slow alpha in 8 Hz	None reported
Prozac	Mild increases in beta at 18–25 Hz	Frontal alpha
Seroquel	Global beta	Alpha and beta below 20 Hz
THC	Frontal alpha	Beta and high beta
Vyvanse	Beta between 12 and 26 Hz	Delta and theta
Xanax	Beta between 20 and 30 Hz	Alpha
Zoloft	Mild increases in beta at 18–25 Hz	Frontal alpha

© 2020 Washington DC Center for Neurocognitive Excellence, LLC.

window of time following training. An ongoing assessment process must be utilized to ensure the clinician is continuously assessing for changes that might impact NFB.

Table 60.1 provides an illustrative list of some of the more frequently used substances and their potential impact on EEG and therefore NFB training.

As with any form of social work practice, medications should be used with the consultation of a prescriber. NFB may allow a client to reduce their medication dose or discontinue use entirely as NFB reduces or eliminates their need for medications. Likewise, clients who self-medicate with substances, such as caffeine, marijuana, or alcohol, might be advised to reduce their use of substances so as not to negatively impact the gains of training.

Ethics and Professional Conduct

Often, NFB is an element of a therapeutic relationship and is adjuvant to traditional mental health counseling. Therefore, the same ethical, legal, and professional standards apply. Specifically, most ethical issues the clinician will encounter during NFB training will be the same as those encountered by practitioners using other types of biofeedback.

Because NFB is an emerging science and practice, it is wise for the clinician to treat NFB with extra caution, especially during the informed consent process. Such additional ethical and legal precautions may greatly support the clinician to avoid unnecessary and costly legal conflict. Because NFB has yet to be accepted by a multitude of insurance providers, additional commitment to adherence of ethics is necessary for protection of the client and clinician (Striefel, 2009).

The ISNR released a Code of Ethics for NFB practitioners in 2002. The nine main tenets are responsibility, competence, ethical standards, multiculturalism and diversity, public statements, confidentiality, protection of client rights and welfare, professional relationships, and research with humans and animals. In order to become a member of ISNR, the social worker must adhere to this Code of Ethics.

Research Base for Neurofeedback

Neurofeedback has been extensively researched across many different populations and with different modalities. The results are very promising and are worthy of inclusion in clinical practice, psychoeducation, and printed educational materials for clients and providers. The following discussion is an illustrative summary of specific studies that show very promising use of NFB in mental health conditions as well as limitations to the use of NFB. Refer to ISNR (2020) for a more robust bibliography of the use of NFB.

Is Neurofeedback Real or Just Placebo?

A debate in the literature regarding the efficacy of NFB training exists. Thibault et al. (2018) and others have published articles suggesting that NFB is "neurosuggestion" and is a very strong placebo-based intervention. However, numerous studies that control for "sham neurofeedback" show that NFB not synced to a subject's EEG will not have the desired change, providing support to the idea that feedback is subject specific. This is also why the administering clinician is not subject to the client's feedback during training. Pigott et al. (2021) responded to Thibault et al. and concluded that NFB, compared to "fake-feedback," is viable and that learning methodology matters, and they made a plea to adhere to best practices when administering NFB.

Neurofeedback for Attention-Deficit/ Hyperactivity Disorder

Monastra (2005) published a paper that details the rationale and empirical foundations for using NFB to treat attention-deficit/hyperactivity disorder (ADHD) as an alternative to medication treatment only. This is a groundbreaking idea because it positions NFB as a highly effective treatment for those seeking nonmedication interventions for ADHD.

Building on Monastra's work, Arns et al. (2009) published a meta-analysis that reported on the efficacy of NFB in the treatment of ADHD. They concluded that "neurofeedback treatment

for ADHD can be considered 'efficacious and specific' (Level 5) with a large [effect size] for inattention and impulsivity and a medium [effect size] for hyperactivity" (p. 10). This is consistent with the ISNR guidelines for rating clinical efficacy. Furthermore, Arns et al. (2020) published a paper that concluded that NFB is a viable treatment for ADHD with a medium to large effect size and "32–47% remission rates and sustained effects after 6–12 months were achieved" (p. 39). These studies provide strong research support for the use of NFB as a viable alternative to medication in the treatment of ADHD.

Neurofeedback and Depression

Walker and Lawson (2013) reported the findings of a study that included 183 patients with drug-resistant depression. They found that after six NFB sessions, a remission was achieved in 84% of participants, with results retained for a year or longer in all but 3 subjects.

Neurofeedback and Post-Traumatic Stress Disorder

Van der Kolk et al. (2016) conducted a randomized controlled study of the effect of NFB on people with chronic post-traumatic stress disorder (PTSD). They found that after 24 NFB sessions over 12 weeks, "the effect size of NF (neurofeedback) is comparable to those reported for the most effective evidence-based treatments for PTSD" (p. 12). Further supporting these findings, Chiba et al. (2019) published a systematic review on the status of NFB in the treatment of PTSD. They found that NFB treatment may allow for clients to forgo exposure therapy and produce desired changes in the symptoms of PTSD after using NFB training. In addition, Sebern Fisher published a groundbreaking book about the treatment of developmental trauma disorder with NFB, as described in van der Kolk et al.'s (2016) work on developmental trauma.

Current Trends in Neurofeedback

The field of brain-based interventions, including NFB, is exploding within the mental health community. Although there are too many fascinating trends to report here, an illustrative survey of current trends is provided next.

LORETA and sLORETA

Pasqual-Marqui (2002) introduced the field to low-resolution electromagnetic tomography (LORETA) and standardized LORETA (sLORETA) training, which provides a three-dimensional image of the brain during training with a more precise focus on specific regions of the brain. This is done by using a variable resolution electromagnetic tomography algorithm to estimate the probability that each voxel is contributing to the data received by surface electrodes. See Figure 60.2 for an example summary sLORETA brainmap. LORETA and sLORETA NFB training allows the clinician to target regions of interest in subcortical structures. A voxel allows for a visualization of brain waves that includes volume and surface placements (Pascual-Marqui, 2002). sLORETA includes assumptions allowing for smoothing and weighting in the algorithm, thereby producing zero localization error, making it less sensitive and more specific (Pascual-Marqui, 2002).

Integrating Clinical Hypnosis with Neurofeedback

Over the years, several theorists and practitioners have combined NFB of various types (amplitude and z score, etc.) with cognitive tasks (Thompsons & Thompson, 2003; Tinius, 2009), visual tasks, (Nash, 2014), and the integration of hypnotic suggestions (Hammond, 2019).

There is a significant body of research demonstrating the overlap between hypnotic neurophenomenology and "deep state training" NFB (alpha–theta training). Rewarding deep state responsivity has been found to have a significant remediation impact on substance abuse, anxiety, PTSD, etc. (Peniston et al., 1993). Offering healing, solution-oriented ego-strengthening hypnotic suggestions during training may strengthen positive expectancy and clinical improvement. It is taking the best of clinical hypnosis and integrating it with NFB.

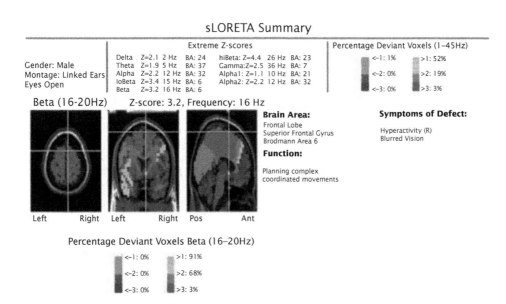

FIGURE 60.2 Example of an sLORETA brain map. *Source:* © 2020 Washington DC Center for Neurocognitive Excellence, LLC.

Conclusion

Neurofeedback is a viable and reliable mental health intervention that meets high standards for safety and effectiveness. Social workers can safely and ethically administer NFB. Furthermore, it has an extensive history of rigorous research and decades of application. NFB is a skill that takes a significant commitment to master. Offering clients an effective nonmedication-based intervention is a benefit that can help social workers add more value to the field and improve the client's mental health.

Helpful Resources

Biofeedback Certification International Alliance: https://www.bcia.org

EEG Education and Research: http://www.eegspectrum.com

EEGInfo: https://www.eeginfo.com

International Society for Neurofeedback & Research: https://isnr.org

Stress Therapy Solutions: http://stresstherapysolutions.com

References

Arns, M., Clark, C. R., Trullinger, M., deBeus, R., Mack, M., & Anifto, M. (2020). Neurofeedback and attention-deficit/hyperactivity disorder (ADHD) in children: Rating the evidence and proposed guidelines. *Applied Psychophysiology and Biofeedback, 45,* 39–48. https://doi.org/10.1007/s10484-020-09455-2

Arns, M., de Ridder, S., Strehl, U., Breteler, M., & Coenen, A. (2009). Efficacy of neurofeedback treatment in ADHD: The effects on inattention, impulsivity and hyperactivity: A meta-analysis. *Clinical EEG and Neuroscience, 40*(3), 180–189. https://doi.org/10.1177/155005940904000311

Berger, H. (1929). Über das elektrenkephalogramm des menschen. *Archiv für Psychiatrie und Nervenkrankheiten, 87,* 527–570.

Biofeedback Certification International Alliance. (2008). *Biofeedback.* Retrieved February 10, 2020 from https://www.bcia.org/i4a/pages/index.cfm?pageid=3524

Chiba, T., Kanazawa, T., Koizumi, A., Ide, K., Taschereau-Dumouchel, V., Boku, S., Hishimoto, A., Shirakawa, M., Sora, I., Lau, H., Yoneda, H., &

Kawato, M. (2019). Current status of neurofeedback for post-traumatic stress disorder: A systematic review and the possibility of decoded neurofeedback. *Frontiers in Human Neuroscience, 13,* 233. doi:10.3389/fnhum.2019.00233

Hammond, D. C. (2019). Integrating clinical hypnosis and NFB. *American Journal of Clinical Hypnosis, 61*(4), 302–321.

International Society for Neurofeedback & Research. (2009). *What is neurofeedback.* Retrieved February 10, 2020, from https://isnr.org/what-is-neurofeedback

International Society for Neurofeedback & Research. (2020). *The ISNR comprehensive bibliography of neurofeedback research.* https://isnr.org/isnr-comprehensive-bibliography

Monastra, V. J. (2005). Electroencephalographic biofeedback (neurotherapy) as a treatment for attention deficit hyperactivity disorder: Rationale and empirical foundation. *Child and Adolescent Psychiatric Clinics of North America, 14*(1), 55–82. https://doi.org/10.1016/j.chc.2004.07.004

Nash, J. (2014). Vision therapy as a complementary procedure during neurotherapy. In D. S. Cantor & J. R. Evans (Eds.), *Clinical neurotherapy: Applications of techniques for treatment* (pp. 383–396). Academic Press.

Orndorff-Plunkett, F., Singh, F., Aragón, O. R., & Pineda, J. A. (2017). Assessing the effectiveness of neurofeedback training in the context of clinical and social neuroscience. *Brain Science, 7,* 95.

Pascual-Marqui, R. D. (2002). Standard low-resolution brain electromagnetic tomography (sLORETA): Technical details. *Methods and Findings in Experimental & Clinical Pharmacology, 24*(Suppl. D), 5–12.

Peniston, E. G., Marrinan, D., Deming, W., & Kulkosky, P. (1993). EEG alpha–theta brainwave synchronization in Vietnam theater veterans with combat-related post-traumatic stress disorder and alcohol abuse. *Advances in Medical Psychotherapy, 6,* 37–50.

Pigott, H. E., Cannon, R., & Trullinger, M. (2021). The fallacy of sham-controlled neurofeedback trials: A reply to Thibault and Colleagues (2018). *Journal of Attention Disorders, 25*(3), 448–457. https://doi.org/10.1177/1087054718790802

Saletu, B., Anderson, P., & Saletu-Zyhlarz, G. M. (2010). EEG mapping and tomography in drug evaluation. *Medicographia, 32*(2), 190–200.

Smith, M., Collura, T. F., & Tarrant, J. (2014). *Neurofeedback.* Taylor & Francis.

Spilker, B., Kamiya, J., Callaway, E., & Yeager, C. L. (1969). Visual evoked responses in subjects trained to control alpha rhythms. *Psychophysiology, 5,* 683–695.

Sterman, M. B. (1977). Sensorimotor EEG operant conditioning: Experimental and clinical effects. *Pavlovian Journal of Biological Science, 12,* 63–92. https://link.springer.com/article/10.1007/BF03004496

Sterman, M. B., & Friar, L. (1972). Suppression of seizures in an epileptic following sensorimotor EEG feedback training. *Electroencephalography and Clinical Neurophysiology, 33,* 89–95.

Striefel, S. (2009). Ethics in neurofeedback practice. In J. Evans, T. Budzynski, H. Budzynski, & A. Abarbanel (Eds.), *Introduction to quantitative EEG and neurofeedback: Advanced theory and applications* (pp. 473–492). Academic Press.

Stress Therapy Solutions. (2019). *Neurofeedback bootcamp for beginners: Psychopharmacological considerations.* PowerPoint presentation.

Thibault, R. T., & Raz, A. (2017). The psychology of neurofeedback: Clinical intervention even if applied placebo. *American Psychologist, 72*(7), 679–688. doi:10.1037/amp0000118

Thibault, R. T., Veissière, S., Olson, J. A., & Raz, A. (2018). Treating ADHD with suggestion: Neurofeedback and placebo therapeutics. *Journal of Attention Disorders, 22*(8), 707–711. https://doi.org/10.1177/1087054718770012

Thompson, M., & Thompson, L. (2003). *The neurofeedback book: An introduction to basic concepts in applied psychophysiology.* Association for Applied Psychophysiology and Biofeedback.

Tinius, T. (2009). The combination of cognitive training exercises and neurofeedback. In J. R. Evans (Ed.), *Handbook of neurofeedback, dynamics and clinical applications* (pp. 137–153). Haworth.

Van der Kolk, B. A. (2014). *The body keeps the score: Brain, mind, and body in the healing of trauma.* Viking.

van der Kolk, B. A., Hodgdon, H., Gapen, M., Musicaro, R., Suvak, M. K., Hamlin, E., & Spinazzola, J. (2016). A randomized controlled study of neurofeedback for chronic PTSD. *PLoS One, 11*(12), e0166752. https://doi.org/10.1371/journal.pone.0166752

Walker, J. E., & Lawson, R. (2013). FP02 beta training for drug-resistant depression—A new protocol that usually reduces depression and keeps it reduced. *Journal of Neurotherapy, 17*(3), 198–200. doi:10.1080/10874208.2013.785784

Mindfulness-Based Social Work Techniques

Kielty Turner

What Is Mindfulness?

Mindfulness, the central tenet of Buddhist meditation, has been described by Kabat-Zinn (1994) as "paying attention in a particular way, on purpose, in the present moment and non-judgmentally" (p. 4). My own introduction to mindfulness was at yoga classes approximately 25 years ago. I immediately noticed the benefits of a heightened awareness of my thoughts, feelings, and body as a result of these gentle stretches. Meditation, one of the many contemplative practices, is most often identified with the "mindfulness movement." Both concentrative (samatha) meditation and mindfulness (vipassana) meditation practices are associated with Buddhist tradition. In samatha meditation, the practitioner focuses the mind on a single internal or external object, such as the breath or a "mantra." In vipassana meditation, the practitioner notices moment by moment their thoughts, sensations, and emotions as they come and go, visualizing them like fluffy clouds, floating into and out of awareness. In addition to meditation, other contemplative practices that can be relevant to social work practice include yoga, visualization, journaling, deep listening, and forms of activism, all rooted in the intentions of developing awareness, communion,

and connection (Center for Contemplative Mind in Society, n.d.). Contemplative practices have been deemed "transformative" for social work students "because of the potential skills they cultivate, such as insight, awareness, acceptance, stress reduction and information processing" (Wang et al., 2020, p. 58).

Mindfulness-Based Techniques

Fisher (as cited in Turner, 2015, p. 621) referred to a social work technique as what "we do with, to and for our clients" in order to help them. Mindfulness skills training provides a variety of social work techniques that can both be taught to clients and be learned by social workers. Germer (2005) described two general approaches to the application of mindfulness in clinical work as mindfulness-based psychotherapy and mindful presence in psychotherapy. Hick (2009) conceptualized that mindfulness can occur at three levels in social work practice: as an intervention to support clients (individuals, families, and groups), at the mezzo/macro level, and within the worker. Mindfulness-based social work interventions and mindful presence in social workers are explored in this chapter as important social work techniques.

Mindfulness-Based Interventions

There are many mindfulness-based psychotherapies in which the worker explicitly teaches the client skills derived from contemplative traditions in order to achieve their clinical goals. Each mindfulness-based modality has specific training and practice requirements in order to be considered a certified clinician. The four major modalities are mindfulness-based stress reduction (MBSR) (Kabat-Zinn, 1990), mindfulness-based cognitive therapy (MBCT) (Segal et al., 2002), dialectical behavior therapy (DBT) (Miller et al., 2007), and acceptance and commitment therapy (ACT) (Hayes et al., 1999). A systematic review and meta-analysis of mindfulness-based interventions of psychiatric disorders (Goldberg et al., 2018) found consistent evidence in support of mindfulness-based interventions, especially for depression, pain conditions, smoking, and addictive disorders. A comprehensive discussion of the empirical findings for mindfulness-based interventions is beyond the scope of this chapter.

MBSR was initially developed by Kabat-Zinn (1990) as an 8-week pain management program for chronically physically ill patients. The focus of MBSR is the development of mindfulness skills through meditation and mindful yoga. MBCT (Segal et al., 2002) was developed to treat chronically depressed clients who learn and practice skills to accept and let go of their ruminative thoughts. Linehan (1993) developed DBT to treat women with borderline personality disorder and suicidal behavior. In addition to weekly individual sessions, clients attend a 2½-hour group skills training session in which mindfulness, focusing on one thing in the moment without judgment, is presented as the "core skill." ACT (Hayes et al., 1999) utilizes the Buddhist tradition of teaching through metaphor to enable clients to accept and reduce their physical or emotional pain. All four of these mindfulness-based approaches are being studied with populations such as youth, "demonstrating much promise" when they are adapted to the clients' developmental needs (Zack et al., 2014, p. 52).

In addition to the four approaches identified previously, there has been a proliferation of mindfulness-based approaches to the specific issues with which clients present. Mindfulness-based cancer recovery is based on MBSR and adapted for cancer care (Schellekens et al., 2017). Mindfulness-based resilience training (MBRT) incorporates skills from MBSR and ACT with stress management and resilience training (Stonnington et al., 2016) for transplant patients and their caregivers. In addition, MBRT has been explored as a method to reduce aggression in law enforcement officers (Ribeiro et al., 2020). Mindfulness-based addiction treatment (MBAT) incorporates mindfulness into cognitive–behavioral relapse prevention, teaching people to bring present-focused, nonjudgmental awareness to cravings (Bowen & Marlatt, 2009). Mindfulness-based feminist therapy (MBFT) (Crowder, 2016), based on MBSR with a feminist framework, emphasizes self-compassion exercises as a group modality for women who have experienced intimate partner violence.

Applications of Mindfulness Techniques in Practice

Mindfulness practices are techniques to foster present moment acceptance. It is easy to be drawn into sadness over the past and worry about the future. Mindfulness training can assist a client to notice when they are going to the past or future. Then they can label the thought without judgment and bring the attention back to the present moment. One powerful and simple tool is focused breathing. There are many resources for a 3-minute breathing space on the apps listed in the Helpful Resources section.

I find breathing meditation to be useful early in the introduction of mindfulness to clients, encouraging them to focus on their breath even as the session starts, as a form of grounding in the present moment. This technique also assists as the client is thinking about their "intention" for the session. We spend approximately 3 minutes, centering on where we are and what we want in our time together. For example, after greeting the client and taking our seats, I might say,

> As we are getting started, I would like to suggest that we take a few moments to go inside, closing your eyes if that is OK with you today. Now notice your breath. There is no need to change anything, simply start to notice that you are breathing. Focus your attention on the rise and fall of your belly, expanding as you inhale and contracting when you exhale. You will notice that your mind will wander. When this happens, this is perfectly OK. Just notice that your mind wandered and bring your attention back to the breath. [After 2 minutes] Now, as you are centered in your breath, ask yourself what your intention is for today's session; what would you like to work on in our time together today? Accepting whatever comes to mind, being grateful for your inner wisdom. Now as you are ready, preparing yourself to return to the room prepared to honor that intention.

The body scan is a lying-down meditation in which each part of the body (starting at the big toe of the left foot) is attended to in a systematic and nonjudgmental manner. The body scan builds the client's ability both to focus attention and to notice where the mind habitually wanders. The instructions for a body scan vary. The MBSR body scan on the Insight Timer app is 43 minutes. This and shorter body scan meditations are available through apps listed in the Helpful Resource section. In these and similar exercises, Siegel (2007) suggests that mindful awareness permits the "decoupling of automaticity" (p. 144), leading to a potential "lasting change in observable traits such as flexibility of affect and cognitive styles and patterns of interaction with others" (p. 158).

Many of our clients are disconnected from their bodies. Mindful yoga can provide a palatable introduction to mindfulness. Clients do not need to be fit or flexible to start a yoga practice. Specific yoga positions can reinforce some of the goals clients aim to achieve. For example, a client who wants to gain strength and stability can benefit from the mountain pose, in which the client is grounded, envisioning themself to be strong and rooted like a mountain. Balance poses such as the tree pose are useful to train attention and the ability to tolerate frustration. There are poses to open up the heart, which are useful as a client is developing loving-kindness. If a social worker is experienced in yoga (and the client is receptive), one or two of these postures can be useful within a therapy session. Other clients might attend yoga as an adjunctive to their therapy. My own personal experience was that going to my therapy sessions directly after an hour of yoga prepared me to be more open in my therapy sessions, and I made deeper and more rapid progress on my goals.

Clients with post-traumatic stress disorder (PTSD) often have impaired body awareness. However, mainstream yoga classes may have a triggering effect on these clients. Van Der Kolk and Colleagues (2014) have designed Trauma Center Trauma-Sensitive Yoga (TCTSY) with promising results in the reduction of PTSD symptomology. Special accommodations for clients with PTSD increase the sense of safety and predictability in the yoga intervention. In TCTSY, there are two facilitators (one yoga instructor and one mental health worker/social worker) who rarely leave their mats and never give any physical assistance to the participants (Neukirch et al., 2019). In this yoga intervention, the participants learn to trust their bodies, "making choices to modify a posture, to stay in a particular posture, or to let the posture go" (van der Kolk et al., 2014, p. e2).

Emotion regulation is one of the key deficits with which many of our clients present. They find themselves buffeted around by anger, sadness, and worry. When practicing meditation, one technique is to imagine the emotion or triggering thought as a puffy cloud floating in the sky. Using this visualization, the client can be taught to watch the cloud with the worry on it float gently away. What tends to exacerbate troubling emotions is the revulsion of that feeling. For example, I have had clients who worry about their worrying. I have used the "Chinese handcuff" (Germer, 2005) metaphoric technique with clients who resist their painful affects. This finger trap toy demonstrates that the more you pull (try to escape the worry), the tighter the handcuff (worrying) becomes, whereas if you stop resisting, you can escape the handcuff.

Craving is another form of suffering that clients come to us with. Mindful urge surfing (Bowen & Marlatt, 2009) can be a useful technique in which the client practices noticing the mental and physical triggers of urges as well as discerning the coming and going of the urge. This technique, based on the Buddhist principle of impermanence, emphasizes that all experiences are transient and that our suffering is often due to clinging to pleasure. Clients learn to notice their clinging (attachment) and to ride the wave of the urge.

I had been working with Tom in both group (four per week) and individual sessions (two per week) in an outpatient drug treatment center utilizing mindfulness skills training as well as psychoeducation and mutual support. Tom was abstinent, although he reported a persistent urge to get high. He shared very little

beyond superficial sarcasm, resisting an exploration of these urges. Increasingly aware of my own frustration, I took a few minutes before meeting with him to close my eyes, breathe, and sit with my concern that Tom would relapse. Then I became aware of my curiosity about his urges. We started our session that day with Tom saying, "All I can think about is getting high." I was more keenly aware that Tom felt tormented. I said, "Every day, you talk about these urges. It must feel like torture. I just wonder what triggers them. I think it would help if we knew how they get started." At first, Tom still claimed that the urges came from nowhere. Silence ensued, then defiantly, Tom stated, "My daughter told me that she hates me." Tom said with tears in his eyes, "They'd be better off without me. You know, I wish all the time that I could just run away." Applying mindful acceptance of thoughts, we explored his self-judgment, Tom said, "I'm just so messed up. I think that it would have been better if I died last time I OD'd [overdosed]." By the end of the session that day, Tom gained insight that he had been trying to run away (or die) for the past 20 years. Now we were able to identify that thoughts of how his family has been harmed by his addiction triggered his urge to use. Next, Tom was able to learn to surf the wave of the urge, first noticing his self-blaming thoughts and then the urge to use, which rises (intensifies) and recedes (dissipates).

These techniques are not exclusive to addictive disorders. They can also enable clients to learn to make behavioral change in externalizing disorders such as aggression. Singh and colleagues (2019) studied the use of urge surfing techniques with adolescents with autism spectrum disorder for the self-management of aggression. Participants were taught to ride out the urges to be physically or verbally aggressive. These adolescents were able to learn that urges arise like waves, increase and peak, finally slowly dissipating. Attention to the breath is taught to be like a surfboard to ride out the waves of urges by observing each urge with a nonjudgmental attitude of equanimity and curiosity.

Shame and self-loathing are common in our clients. Mindfulness skills provide methods to both explore and reduce these tendencies. The previously described techniques for self-awareness can be used with clients to explore their harsh self-criticism. Instead of hiding or judging themselves for their negative thoughts about themselves, clients can develop a kind curiosity about this tendency, noticing thoughts with a mindset of "isn't it interesting." I worked with one young woman who recognized that she was judging herself for coming to treatment rather than staying at home with her mother. The 3-minute breathing meditation enabled her to make conscious what had been fueling much of her drug use: the belief that she was "a lousy daughter." Once the self-judgment was explored, then the client was able to identify and take steps to reduce her self-judgment, using a loving-kindness meditation (LKM) both in session and at home. LKM is an important technique to use with clients that can enable them to develop self-compassion and compassion for others. As clients gain awareness of their judgment of self and others, this type of meditation increases nonjudgmental acceptance. Many variations of LKM are available. Most include words such as "May I enjoy happiness and the root of happiness," "May I be safe," and "May I be healthy, peaceful, and strong." LKM practice usually involves wishing these "kindnesses" on a friend, on someone for whom you feel neutral, on someone whom you find difficult or offensive, and on all beings.

Negativity is a habitual pattern that causes much suffering and yet it is the default thinking pattern for many of our clients. Mindful awareness of that "negative" thinking and gratitude meditation can be useful techniques for clients to practice in and out of sessions. Scripts for gratitude meditations vary. They tend to focus on the positive people and things in our lives

that we frequently overlook. This technique can be useful after the client has explored those thoughts and has identified the intention to think and feel more positive. In DBT, this is one of the "dialectics," acceptance of the negatives in life *and* change of focus to the positive, developing new thinking patterns.

In addition to the previously discussed uses of mindfulness training with clients, contemplative skills training is a resilience-focused approach that is more acceptable for clients who might be wary of more formalized therapy modalities. Tools such as online apps make it accessible to clients who are poor or who live in remote locations. Contemplative practices are congruent with many spiritual and religious ideologies, emphasizing finding meaning in the present moment. Conversely, mindfulness training can be stressful at first. Rather than experiencing relaxation, a new practitioner is often disturbed to discover the persistent thoughts, feelings, and sensations uncovered through mindfulness. Caution is required when using mindfulness techniques with clients who have difficulty with dissociation or symptoms of psychosis. In addition, clients from some cultural or religious groups might be reluctant to engage in mindfulness, associating the practices with specific religious or "new age" groups. Workers want to consider the context in which they work when using contemplative practices. Mindfulness techniques have been widely utilized in medical and educational settings. However, they are newer in systems such as prisons and the military.

Mindful Presence in Social Work

Mindful presence in psychotherapy is the development of therapeutic worker qualities through training in mindfulness skills (Germer, 2005). Four of the qualities that mindfulness can foster in social workers are attention, affect regulation, attunement, and empathy (Turner, 2009). It is vital that workers focus on the client(s) in front of them. Meditation trains attention, establishing a pattern of returning the practitioner to the present moment. Mindful social workers attend to both internal and external experiences when at work, presenting as focused and aware. Social workers can develop affect regulation skills in order to *be with* clients who are suffering. Brenner and Homonoff (2004) found that social workers who practice mindfulness could be "in the midst of suffering and not be overwhelmed by the magnitude of distress" (p. 267). Mindful social workers develop an attitude of friendly curiosity with their own affective experience with clients. The worker notices their thoughts, physical experiences, and emotions without judgment in the practice setting. Mindfulness practice in social work can be a vehicle to explore the relational process with the client in the "here and now," developing nonjudgmental attunement with clients. Finally, mindfulness skills provide a method for social workers to increase their empathy. LKM (described previously) is one method for social workers to build empathic skills. I often do the following brief meditation before meeting with a client (Morgan & Morgan, 2005, p. 89):

1. Take a moment and feel the rise and fall of your breath before rising to meet your next patient.
2. As you walk to the door, imagine that on the other side of the door another human being is waiting.
3. The human being is someone who is suffering, who has hopes and dreams, who has tried to be happy and only partially succeeded, and who is coming to you, believing that you can relieve his or her suffering.
4. Now open the door and say "hello."

In addition to providing techniques to increase social worker effectiveness, mindfulness training has been identified as a method to increase worker subjective well-being (SWB). Shier and Graham (2011) found that mindful social workers self-reported higher SWB. In order to be helpful to clients, social workers need to remain in the profession with their passion for social justice and social change intact. The practice of mindfulness can enable social workers to "think about and negotiate within their personal and work lives" (Shier & Graham, 2011, p. 41), thus reducing burnout.

How to Learn Mindfulness

My own path of incorporating mindfulness into my work with clients and into my "self" as a social worker has been gradual. First, I practiced yoga. Then I started a meditation practice. I attended conferences and read books and articles on mindfulness-based therapies. I began to slowly incorporate the elements of mindfulness into my techniques with clients and social work students. I added training (the 8-week MBSR training), using and referring others to meditation apps. It is now easier than ever to have online access to meditations and education on contemplative practices. There is no right way to learn mindfulness. You can "start where you are" (Chödrön, 1994), developing acceptance and nonjudgment, finding what works for you and for your clients. Mindfulness techniques enable clients to improve their lives and, for us as social workers, "to enhance human well-being and help meet the basic human needs of all people" (National Association of Social Workers , 2020, preamble).

Helpful Resources

Apps
Insight Timer
Mindfulness Coach
Smiling Mind

Websites

Mindful: https://www.mindful.org

Mindful Experience: https://www.mindfulexperience.com

UCLA Mindful Awareness Research Center: https://www.uclahealth.org/marc

References

Bowen, S., & Marlatt, A. (2009). Surfing the urge: Brief mindfulness-based intervention for college student smokers. *Psychology of Addictive Behaviors, 23*(4), 666–671. doi:10.1037/a0017127

Brenner, M. J., & Homonoff, E. (2004). Zen and clinical social work: A spiritual approach to practice. *Families in Society, 85,* 261–269. doi.org/10.1606%2F1044-3894.315

Center for Contemplative Mind in Society. (n.d.). *The tree of contemplative practices.* https://www.contemplativemind.org/practices/tree

Chödrön, P. (1994). *Start where you are: A guide to compassionate living.* Shambala.

Crowder, R. (2016). Mindfulness based feminist therapy: The intermingling edges of self-compassion and social justice. *Journal of Religion & Spirituality in Social Work: Social Thought, 35,* 24–40. doi:10.1080/15426432.2015.1080605

Germer, C. K. (2005). Teaching mindfulness in therapy. In C. K. Germer, R. D. Siegel, & P. R. Fulton (Eds.), *Mindfulness and psychotherapy* (pp. 55–73). Guilford.

Goldberg, S. B., Tucker, R. P., Greene, P. A., Davidson, R. J., Wampold, B. E., Kearney, D. J., & Simpson, T. L. (2018). Mindfulness-based interventions for psychiatric disorders: A systematic review and meta-analysis. *Clinical Psychology Review, 59,* 52–60. doi.org/10.1016/j.cpr.2017.10.011

Hayes, S. C., Strosahl, K. D., & Wilson, K. G. (1999). *Acceptance and commitment therapy: An experiential approach to behavior change.* Guilford.

Hick, S. F. (2009). Mindfulness and social work: Paying attention to ourselves, our clients and society. In S. E. Hick (Ed.), *Mindfulness and social work* (pp. 1–30). Lyceum.

Kabat-Zinn, J. (1990). *Full catastrophe living: Using the wisdom of your body and mind to face stress, pain and illness.* Dell.

Kabat-Zinn, J. (1994). *Mindfulness meditation for everyday life.* Hyperion.

Linehan, M. M. (1993). *Skills training manual for treating borderline personality disorder.* Guilford.

Miller, A. L., Rathus, J. H., & Linehan, M. M. (2007). *Dialectical behavior therapy with suicidal adolescents.* Guilford.

Morgan, W. D., & Morgan, S. T. (2005). Cultivating attention and empathy. In C. K. Germer, R. D. Siegel, & P. R. Fulton (Eds.), *Mindfulness and psychotherapy* (pp. 73–90). Guilford.

National Association of Social Workers. (2020). *Preamble to the code of ethics.* Retrieved May 27, 2020, from https://www.socialworkers.org/About/Ethics/Code-of-Ethics/Code-of-Ethics-English

Neukirch, N., Reid, S., & Shires, A. (2019). Yoga for PTSD and the role of interoceptive awareness: A preliminary mixed-methods case series study. *European Journal of Trauma & Dissociation, 3*(1), 7–15. doi.org/10.1016/j.ejtd.2018.10.003

Ribeiro, L., Colgan, D. D., Hoke, C. K., Hunsinger, M., Bowen, S., Oken, B. S., & Christopher, M. S. (2020). Differential impact of mindfulness practices on aggression among law enforcement officers. *Mindfulness, 11,* 734–745. doi.org/10.1007/s12671-019-01289-2

Schellekens, M. P. J., Tamagawa, R., Labelle, L. E., Speca, M., Stephen, J., Drysdale, E., Sample, S., Pickering, B., Dirkse, D., Savage, L. L., & Carlson, L. E. (2017). Mindfulness-based cancer recovery (MBCR) versus supportive expressive group therapy (SET) for distressed breast cancer survivors: Evaluating mindfulness and social support as mediators. *Journal of Behavioral Medicine, 40,* 414–422. doi.org/10.1007/s10865-016-9700-6

Segal, Z. V., Williams, M. G., & Teasdale, J. D. (2002). *Mindfulness-based cognitive therapy for depression: A new approach to preventing relapse.* Guilford.

Shier, M. L., & Graham, J. R. (2011). Mindfulness, subjective well-being, and social work: Insight into their interconnection from social work practitioners. *Social Work Education, 30*(1), 29–44. doi.org/10.1080/02615471003763188

Siegel, D. J. (2007). *The mindful brain: Reflection and attunement in the cultivation of well-being.* Norton.

Singh, N. N., Lancioni, G. E., Karazsia, B. T., Myers, R. E., Kim, E., Chan, J., Jackman, M. M., McPherson, C. L., & Janson, M. (2019). Surfing the urge: An informal mindfulness practice for the self-management of aggression by adolescents with autism spectrum disorder. *Journal of Contextual Behavioral Science, 12,* 170–177. doi: 10.1016/j.jcbs.2018.10.003

Stonnington, C. M., Darby, B., Santucci, A., Mulligan, P., Pathuis, P., Cuc, A., Hentz, J. G., Zhang, N., Mulligan, P., & Sood, A. (2016). A resilience intervention involving mindfulness training for transplant patients and their caregivers. *Clinical Transplantation, 30*(11), 1466–1472. doi.org/10.1111/ctr.12841

Turner, F. J. (2015). Practice from a technique perspective. In K. Corcoran & A. R. Roberts (Eds.),

Social workers' desk reference (3rd ed., pp. 621–622). Oxford University Press.

Turner, K. (2009). Mindfulness: The present moment in clinical social work. *Clinical Social Work Journal, 37,* 95–103. doi.org/10.1007/s10615-008-0182-0

van der Kolk, B. A., Stone, L., West, J., Rhodes, A., Emerson, D., Suvak, M., & Spinazzola, J. (2014). Yoga as an adjunctive treatment for PTSD. *Journal of Clinical Psychiatry, 75,* e559–e565. doi:10.4088/JCP.13m08561

Wang, D. S., Perlman, A., & Temme, L. J. (2020). Utilizing contemplative practices in social work education, *Journal of Religion & Spirituality in Social Work: Social Thought, 39*(1), 47–61. doi:10.1080/15426432.2019.1635063

Zack, S., Saekow, J., Kelly, M., & Radke, A. (2014). Mindfulness based interventions for youth. *Journal of Rational-Emotive & Cognitive-Behavioral Therapy, 32,* 44–56. doi.org/10.1007/s10942-014-0179-2

The Miracle and Scaling Questions for Building Solutions

Mo Yee Lee, Ray Eads, and Erica Magier

The miracle question and the scaling question are integral parts of solution-focused brief therapy (SFBT), which was originally developed at the Brief Family Therapy Center in Milwaukee, Wisconsin, by Steve de Shazer, Insoo Kim Berg, and their associates (de Shazer et al., 1986). SFBT begins as atheoretical with a focus on finding "what works in therapy" (Berg, 1994) and postulates that positive and long-lasting change can occur in a relatively brief period of time by focusing on "solution talk" instead of "problem talk" (de Shazer, 1986; Lee, 2013; Nelson & Thomas, 2007). A growing body of research supports SFBT as an evidence-based practice for a range of emotional, behavioral, and interpersonal problems (Kim et al., 2019). Furthermore, process research indicates that the active ingredients of SFBT include focusing on strengths and co-constructing meaning through therapeutic dialogue (Franklin et al., 2017). Miracle questions and scaling questions, in many ways, synthesize the treatment orientation and practice characteristics of SFBT. Its conversational- and solution-based characteristics are intimately related to three definitive assumptions and practice principles of SFBT:

1. *The power of language in creating and sustaining reality.* SFBT views language as the medium through which personal meaning and understanding are expressed and socially constructed in conversation (de Shazer, 1994).
2. *A focus on solutions, strengths, and health.* SFBT assumes that clients have the resources and have the answer.
3. *Solutions as clients' constructions.* Solutions are not objective "realities" but, rather, private, local, meaning-making activities by an individual (Miller, 1997).

Solution-Focused Questions

The primary purpose of solution-focused interventions is to engage the client in a therapeutic dialogue that is conducive to a solution-building process. Evidence suggests that in comparison to problem-focused questioning, solution-focused questioning improves client self-efficacy and helps clients generate more actionable ideas to help them reach their goals (Grant, 2012). In this dialogue, the clinician invites the client to be the "expert" by listening and exploring the meaning of the client's perceptions of their situation. The SFBT treatment manual endorsed by the Solution-Focused Brief Therapy Association (Bavelas et al., 2013) provides a detailed description of this co-constructive therapeutic process through the steps listen, select, *and* build (De Jong & Berg, 2013; de Shazer, 1994; de Shazer et al., 2007). The therapist first *listens* for and *selects* out the words and phrases from the client's language that are indications of some aspect of a solution, including past successes, exceptions to the problem pattern, and resources. *Building* on the client's descriptions and using their language, the therapist composes another question to invite the client to elaborate on the solution further. Based on the principle that "what is noticed becomes reality" (Lee et al., 2003, p. 32), solution-focused questioning aims to generate detailed descriptions of the client's life without the problem and to identify small positive steps they have already taken. It is through this continuing process of listening, selecting, and building that therapists and clients co-construct new meanings and possibilities for solutions (Bavelas et al., 2013).

Miracle Question

The miracle question is a solution-focused technique that can help clients create a detailed vision of their future lives without the identified problem (Berg, 1994; Stith et al., 2012). The development of the miracle question was inspired by Milton Erickson's work on the "crystal ball" technique (de Shazer, 1985). A major challenge encountered by most clients in social work treatment is that they know when they have a problem but they do not know when the problem has been successfully addressed. Helping clients to develop a clear vision of their future without the problem promotes successful treatment because it establishes indicators of change and helps gauge clients' progress toward their desired future (De Jong & Berg, 2013; Lee, 2003). The miracle question also helps identify specific areas in which change would be beneficial, and it promotes a collaborative and empowering client–worker alliance (Franklin et al., 2017; Oliver & Charles, 2016; Toros, 2019).

The miracle question is intended to accomplish the following:

1. Allow clients to distance themselves from problem-saturated stories so that they can be more playful in creating a beneficial vision of their future
2. Facilitate a clear vision about a desirable future without the problem
3. Establish indicators of change that help clients to gauge success and progress
4. Increase clients' awareness of their choices and offer them an opportunity to play an active role in their treatment (De Jong & Berg, 2013)
5. Encourage clients to be hopeful about their lives and the possibility of change
6. Empower clients to self-determine a desirable future for themselves

Table 62.1 outlines steps for asking the miracle question, with examples of statements a therapist could use. Using the process listen, select, *and* build, the therapist carefully listens to the client's response to the miracle question, selects descriptions that are indicative of the client's goal, and uses solution-focused questions to help the client build and expand the solution picture continuously. Note that the focus is on small signs of change. It is also important to invite clients to describe their solution picture in greater detail and to determine how it differs from their current behaviors, feelings, and thinking. A more detailed description yields clearer indicators of change, which will increase the likelihood that clients will actualize their solution picture.

TABLE 62.1 Process and Techniques for Asking the Miracle Question

Process and Techniques	Rationale	Sample Dialogue
Express curiosity about the person's primary concerns.	SFBT does not need to understand problems to co-construct a solution, but allowing clients to express their concerns shows respect, builds rapport, and helps the therapist frame the miracle.	What brings you here today? How can I be helpful to you? What needs to change in your life for this to be worth your time?
Assess for the best time to open a solution-building dialogue.	Although it is important to respect the client's need to communicate their problem, too much focus on the problem is counterproductive to SFBT.	It sounds like your main concern right now is _____. Is that correct?
Suggest trying something new and ask for the person's permission.	This helps build the client's curiosity and prepares them to engage creatively, while still giving the client control of the therapeutic process.	I wonder if we might try something a little different, it might even seem strange at first, but it could help us come up with some new ideas. Would you like to give it a try?
Build the premise of an event that has solved the person's problems and ask about the changes they would notice first.	The idea of the miracle question is to get the client out of their problem-saturated thinking and to imagine their life without the problem. Using specific details about the client's life can help them visualize the scene as though it is really happening.	Suppose that when you go home tonight, you get ready for bed as you usually do [restate details person has given as applicable], and you fall asleep. But, while you are sleeping, a miracle happens. All of the problems you've told me about are gone. When you wake up, I wonder what would you might notice first to tell you something was different?
Explore in detail what the person will be doing differently after the problem is gone.	Expressing the effects of the miracle in terms of the client's own behavior helps point to what the client could start doing now.	Tell me more. What will you be doing differently now that the miracle has happened?
Ask about others in their life who would notice the person acting in a different way.	Relationship questions add depth to life after the miracle and connect the client's own behavior to the reactions of others.	Who will be the first person to see the change in you? What will they notice about you that will tell them that you are different?
Agree on small steps that the person can take toward the life they described.	Connecting goals to the miracle can be inspiring, but solving the problem all at once will likely overwhelm the client. Smaller goals can be manageable and realistic.	You mentioned once the problem is gone you would like to _____. Is that something you could try doing at least once in the next week to see what it's like?
Use scaling questions to help build the person's motivation and confidence.	Scaling the client's motivation, confidence, or progress toward the miracle is a useful tool for highlighting strengths and progress, and it can also help identify ways to move up on each scale.	On a 1-to-10 scale, where 1 is no confidence and 10 is complete confidence, how confident are you that you can do that this week? What could you do that would make that a [one number higher]?

SFBT, solution-focused brief therapy.

Scaling Questions

Scaling questions ask clients to rank their situation and/or goal on a 1-to-10 scale (Berg, 1994). Usually, 1 represents the worst scenario that could possibly be, and 10 represents the most desirable outcome. Scaling questions provide a simple tool for clients to quantify and evaluate their situation and progress so that they can establish clear indicators of progress (De Jong & Berg, 2013). More important, this is a self-anchored scale with no objective criteria. The constructivist characteristic of the scaling question honors clients as the "knowers" and the center of the change process. Scaling can be used to help clients rate their perception of their progress, their motivation for change, and confidence to engage in solution-focused behaviors. Scaling questions are also helpful in assisting clients to establish small steps and indicators of change in their solution-building process. The following are common examples of scaling questions:

1. Problem severity/progress: On a 1-to-10 scale, with 1 being the worst the problem could possibly be and 10 being the most desirable outcome, where would you place yourself on the scale? What would be some small steps that you could take to move from a "4" to a "5"?

2. Motivation: On a 1-to-10 scale with 1 being you have no motivation to work on the problem and 10 being you would do whatever is necessary, where would you place yourself on the scale? How would your wife (or other significant persons) rank your motivation to change on a 1-to-10 scale?

3. Confidence: On a scale of 1 to 10, how confident are you that you could do that? On a scale of 1 to 10, how confident are you that this will be helpful?

As with other solution-focused questions, the therapist carefully listens to the client's responses, selects descriptions that are connected with hints of solutions, and then helps clients build on desirable change and solutions.

Case Example

Linda is a 47-year-old woman who suffers chronic back pain since being involved in a car accident. The therapist (SWR) uses the miracle question to help her envision a more hopeful future.

SWR: Suppose that after our meeting today, you go home, do your things and go to bed. While you are sleeping, a miracle happens and the problem that brought you here is suddenly solved, like magic. When you wake up tomorrow morning, you will be different. How will you know a miracle has happened? What will be the first small sign? (*Use the miracle question to engage the client in a solution-building process.*)

Linda: I won't be as cranky as an immoveable mountain.

SWR: Instead of being like an immoveable mountain, how do you see yourself being? (*Help client move from a negatively stated description to a positively stated description.*)

Linda: Be a little more upbeat and cheerful. Get my mind off of it, not on the mountain of pain.

SWR: So you want to be more upbeat, cheerful, and distract yourself from the mountain of pain and do something different? (*Select positive description and use client's language.*)

Linda: So when I am around people they are not affected by it and dragged down by it.

SWR: When you wake up after this miracle happens, what would be the first small thing that you would do, that you are not doing now? (*Build and expand solution picture.*)

Linda: I don't know. Maybe I would get up and open the curtain and turn my computer on, open a book, anything besides lying in bed and staring at the wall.

SWR: When this miracle happens, you would get out of bed, open the curtain. What else would you do? (*Select and further build solution-picture.*)

Linda: Get out of bed and do something.

SWR: Do something? (*Invite a more detailed description.*)

Linda: Maybe sweep, dust, or mop.

SWR: And who would notice the change? (*Relationship question*)

Linda: My neighbors, friends.

SWR: *How* would they notice? (*Invite an observable description.*)

Linda: I would respond to them, not giving them dirty looks when it is not their fault.

SWR: Who would be most affected by this change? (*Invite a description of the expected effect.*)

Linda: I suppose that would help other people as well as me.

SWR: How so? (*Invite further elaboration of the effect of change.*)

Linda: You know it would help me because I don't want to be a big drag. That way I won't be dragging people down and it won't be dragging me down. I want to get over it, I want to get over the top of the mountain and go on from here.

SWR: Tomorrow, you can do this. On a 1-to-10 scale, 10 being likely that you can do this, and 1 being no chance at all, where would you think you are? (*Scaling question regarding feasibility of the change efforts; timing of scaling question is good because client has just articulated desire and motivation for change.*)

Linda: I am at a 6 right now.

SWR: So you are saying getting out of bed in the morning, opening the curtains, and turning on the computer is quite doable because you are at a 6?

Linda: It is doable. I can do that.

SWR: Using the same scale, 10 being you are motivated to do this because it would improve your life, and 1 being you are wishy-washy about it, where would you put yourself on the scale? (*Scaling question regarding motivation of change.*)

Linda: I would say an 8, because I don't want to be cranky anymore.

Adapting Solution-Focused Techniques

The purpose of the miracle question in SFBT is to help clients envision a future without their problems. However, the co-construction process of SFBT is grounded in the life context of each client, so the miracle question must make sense within the client's own view of the world. For example, research has indicated the need to adapt solution-focused techniques—including the miracle question—to a client's cultural frame. In particular, the concept of the miracle and the future-focused time orientation may not translate well across cultures (Liu et al., 2015; Meyer & Cottone, 2013), and the linguistic techniques of SFBT may need to be adapted for other languages (González Suitt et al., 2019). Furthermore, SFBT with persons with intellectual disabilities may require changes to aid comprehension, such as using a 3-point scale for scaling questions instead of 10 (Roeden et al., 2009). Finally, the word "miracle" may simply not fit the preferences or belief system of an individual client, in which case the therapist should consider using alternate wording such as "fresh start, dreams, at your best, harmony with people and life, click your fingers, something big is possible, and on track" (Kayrouz & Hansen, 2020, p. 1). Consequently, social work professionals should use creativity to adapt the miracle question as appropriate, using the language and values that fit their client best. Examples include the following:

- Suppose you were to experience harmony with all people and things, what would that look like? How would you be different? (Meyer & Cottone, 2013)
- "Let us suppose that your family finds counseling helpful, and every member here has contributed to the well-being of the whole family. How will you know that things have gotten better? What is the first thing you will notice that tells you that the family is different?" (Cheung & Jahn, 2017, p. 174)

- Imagine that while you are sleeping tonight you have a dream, and in that dream you find the answers to your problems. You don't remember the dream when you wake up, but something is different about you. What would be the first sign to tell you that had found the answer to the problem? (Greene et al., 1998)

Conclusion

Solution-focused questions such as the miracle and scaling questions help clients envision and gauge progress toward their desired future. Through listen, select, *and* build (Bavelas et al., 2013), the therapist and client can co-construct a solution-building process that is grounded in clients' personal reality and cultural strengths (Lee, 2013). The therapeutic process is thus collaborative and egalitarian, and one in which the client's self-determination is fully respected (De Jong & Berg, 2013). Adaptations of the miracle and scaling questions can be used to further integrate and acknowledge a client's cultural frame and personal perspective (Kayrouz & Hansen, 2020; Meyer & Cottone, 2013). Using these solution-focused techniques and principles, therapists can harness the power of language and empower clients to build their desired solutions.

Helpful Resources

European Brief Therapy Association: http://ebta.eu
Solution Focused Brief Therapy Association: https://www.sfbta.org

References

Bavelas, J., De Jong, P., Franklin, C., Froerer, A., Gingerich, W., Kim, J., Korman, H., Langer, S., Lee, M. Y., McCollum, E. E., Smock Jordan, S., & Trepper, T. S. (2013). *Solution focused therapy treatment manual for working with individuals (2nd version)*. Solution Focused Brief Therapy Association.

Berg, I. K. (1994). *Family based services: A solution-focused approach*. Norton.

Cheung, C. W., & Jahn, S. A. B. (2017). Closing the acculturation gap: A solution-focused approach with East Asian American families. *The Family Journal, 25*(2), 170–178.

De Jong, P., & Berg, I. K. (2013). *Interviewing for solutions* (4th ed.). Brooks/Cole.

de Shazer, S. (1985). *Keys to solutions in brief therapy*. Norton.

de Shazer, S. (1994). *Words were originally magic*. Norton.

de Shazer, S., Berg, I. K., Lipchik, E., Nunnally, E., Molnar, A., Gingerich, W., & Weiner-Davis, M. (1986). Brief therapy: Focused solution development. *Family Process, 25*(2), 207–221.

de Shazer, S., Dolan, Y. M., Korman, H., Trepper, T. S., McCollum, E. E., & Berg, I. K. (2007). *More than miracles: The state of the art of solution-focused brief therapy*. Routledge.

Franklin, C., Zhang, A., Froerer, A., & Johnson, S. (2017). Solution focused brief therapy: A systematic review and meta-summary of process research. *Journal of Marital and Family Therapy, 43*(1), 16–30.

González Suitt, K., Franklin, C., Cornejo, R., Castro, Y., & Smock Jordan, S. (2019). Solution-focused brief therapy for Chilean primary care patients: Exploring a linguistic adaptation. *Journal of Ethnicity in Substance Abuse, 18*(1), 103–128.

Grant, A. M. (2012). Making positive change: A randomized study comparing solution-focused vs. problem-focused coaching questions. *Journal of Systemic Therapies, 31*(2), 21–35.

Greene, G. J., Lee, M. Y., Mentzer, R., Pinnell, S., & Niles, D. (1998). Miracles, dreams, and empowerment: A brief practice note. *Families in Society, 79*, 395–399.

Kayrouz, R., & Hansen, S. (2020). I don't believe in miracles: Using the ecological validity model to adapt the miracle question to match the client's cultural preferences and characteristics. *Professional Psychology: Research and Practice, 51*(3), 223–236.

Kim, J., Jordan, S. S., Franklin, C., & Froerer, A. (2019). Is solution-focused brief therapy evidence-based? An update 10 years later. *Families in Society, 100*(2), 127–138.

Lee, M. Y. (2003). A solution-focused approach to cross-cultural clinical social work practice: Utilizing cultural strengths, *Families in Society, 84*, 385–395.

Lee, M. Y. (2013). Solution-focused therapy. In C. Franklin (Ed.), *The 23rd encyclopedia of social work*. Oxford University Press.

Lee, M. Y., Sebold, J., & Uken, A. (2003). *Solution-focused treatment with domestic violence offenders: Accountability for change*. Oxford University Press.

Liu, X., Zhang, Y. P., Franklin, C., Qu, Y., Chen, H., & Kim, J. S. (2015). The practice of solution-focused brief therapy in mainland China. *Health & Social Work, 40*(2), 84–90.

Meyer, D. D., & Cottone, R. R. (2013). Solution-focused therapy as a culturally acknowledging approach with American Indians. *Journal of Multicultural Counseling and Development, 41*(1), 47–55.

Miller, G. (1997). *Becoming miracle workers: Language and meaning in brief therapy*. Aldine de Gruyter.

Nelson, T. S., & Thomas, F. N. (Eds.). (2007). *Handbook of solution-focused brief therapy: Clinical applications*. Routledge.

Oliver, C., & Charles, G. (2016). Enacting firm, fair and friendly practice: A model for strengths-based child protection relationships? *British Journal of Social Work, 46*(4), 1009–1026.

Roeden, J. M., Bannink, F. P., Maaskant, M. A., & Curfs, L. M. (2009). Solution-focused brief therapy with persons with intellectual disabilities. *Journal of Policy and Practice in Intellectual Disabilities, 6*(4), 253–259.

Stith, S. M., Miller, M. S., Boyle, J., Swinton, J., Ratcliffe, G., & McCollum, E. (2012). Making a difference in making miracles: Common roadblocks to miracle question effectiveness. *Journal of Marital and Family Therapy, 38*(2), 380–393.

Toros, K. (2019). Miracle question promotes open communication and positive interaction between clients and practitioners. *International Social Work, 62*(2), 483–486.

Eye Movement Desensitization and Reprocessing Therapy

Tonya Edmund and Molly M. McLay

In 1989, Francine Shapiro published the first study on what she initially described as eye movement desensitization (EMD), reporting positive outcomes in reducing trauma symptoms across an array of traumatic events in adults. The following year, she expanded the name of the treatment approach to eye movement desensitization and reprocessing (EMDR) to reflect her observation that the treatment did more than desensitize; it facilitated an adaptive reprocessing of traumatic memories (Shapiro, 2001). By 1993, Shapiro had launched the EMDR Institute as a driving mechanism for conducting national and international workshops and formal trainings in the proper implementation of this novel trauma treatment. Access to EMDR training was further enhanced by the development of the EMDR Humanitarian Assistance Program in 1995 to provide rapid disaster response training in the United States and globally. The EMDR International Association (EMDRIA), also formed in 1995, aids therapists in becoming certified in EMDR, which currently requires 2 years of experience as a licensed mental health professional, completion of an EMDRIA-approved training, 50 hours using EMDR in clinical sessions, and 20 hours with an approved consultant (EMDRIA, 2020).

EMDR therapy is intended to be utilized by experienced, trained mental health professionals with populations and clinical issues they are trained to treat. A strength of EMDR therapy is that its unique characteristics lend themselves well to therapists practicing from a variety of theoretical frameworks (Shapiro & Laliotis, 2011). EMDR can and should be tailored toward the client's needs. This may involve variation in session length, number of sessions, and pacing of sessions. EMDR experts and trainers encourage therapists to use their best judgment on these determinations. However, 50–90 minutes is viewed as a typical session length (EMDRIA, 2020).

Eight-Phase Process, Three-Pronged Approach

EMDR therapy involves eight phases. As treatment moves through these phases, three main prongs are addressed: past traumatic experiences, current triggers, and future potential challenges (Shapiro, 2001). These three prongs are crucial touchstones throughout the eight phases of EMDR, as discussed next.

History Taking

Like in many therapeutic processes, obtaining a client history is important and a key feature of the first phase. The therapist and client work together to develop a treatment plan containing elements of the three-pronged approach: specific events or memories the client would benefit from processing, current triggers activating those memories, and future challenges and needs the client may have.

Preparation

During the second phase, the therapist helps the client understand their symptoms and, when appropriate, any diagnoses that may be warranted and works collaboratively with the client to develop a treatment plan. The therapist provides the client with psychoeducation about trauma, information explaining how EMDR works, and the available evidence on the effectiveness of EMDR therapy. In addition, the therapist addresses client concerns and fears, equipping the client with tools to self-soothe and regulate, and gaining an understanding of their available internal and external supports.

Assessment

Phase 3 involves identifying the target issue that needs to be addressed in treatment. Components of the target that need to be identified include the presenting problem, an image of the memory associated with the problem, the distressing emotions the memory generates, a negative self-belief associated with the memory, a preferred and more adaptive positive self-belief, and any associated physical sensations the client experiences when picturing the memory. Two rating scales are used in this process to track the progress of the trauma

processing work: the Subjective Units of Distress (SUD) scale (1–10) to track the intensity of the emotions expressed and the Validity of Cognitions (VOC) scale (1–7) to assess the positive self-belief.

Desensitization

The fourth phase involves (1) decreasing the client's level of distress around the target memory, in order to reprocess this experience; (2) weakening linkages to it; and (3) strengthening linkages to adaptive experiences. It is this phase in which the unique element of bilateral stimulation comes into play. The client is asked to hold the target memory components in mind while experiencing bilateral stimulation, which can be induced through eye movements, hand taps or vibrations, and audio. The client does not need to walk through a coherent narrative in this process; the focus is on the image and noticing thoughts and feelings as they emerge. After each set of bilateral stimulation, the client reports whatever has come up for them, and periodically their distress rating on the 10-point SUD scale is assessed. The goal is to continue this process until the client's distress regarding the target memory is decreased down to a 0 or 1.

Installation

The fifth phase involves "installing" the client-identified positive self-belief after desensitization has been achieved. Bilateral stimulation is used with this positive self-belief, while periodically assessing how true it feels to the client through the VOC scale. This stage is finished when the client indicates that the desired positive self-belief feels mostly or completely true as illustrated with a rating of a 6 or 7 on the VOC scale.

Body Scan

In the sixth phase, the therapist asks the client to re-access both the target memory and the positive self-belief while scanning their body to notice any physical sensations that may be present. If negative sensations emerge, the therapist returns to phases 3–5 for further processing through bilateral stimulation.

Closure

The seventh phase, closure, is completed at the end of each EMDR session, even if the preceding stages have not all been completed in that session. This stage involves aiding the client in identifying their need for self-soothing, accessing internal and external support, and assessing emotional stability to move on from the session. The therapist typically asks the client to keep a log of any cognitions, emotions, and bodily sensations that come up between sessions to identify potential associated traumatic material that remains unresolved and in need of processing.

Reassessment

This eighth and final phase involves the client reevaluating the target memory to determine if it has been adequately reprocessed. This can involve examining the client log and anything else that has come up for the client. The three prongs are expressly explored, as the therapist assesses distress regarding past experiences, current triggers, and future challenges once more. If any distress remains, phases 3–8 take place again.

Theoretical Underpinnings of EMDR Therapy

The primary working explanation for EMDR therapy is Shapiro's (2001) adaptive information processing model, which posits that humans contain an internal information processing system that integrates life experiences into networks of memory. When a person is experiencing distress, this processing system may be disrupted because of changes that the brain and body endure. As a result, memories may not encode properly into the memory networks. In particular, processing of both external stimuli (e.g., sights and sounds) and internal stimuli (e.g., thoughts, affect, and bodily sensations) may be impacted (Shapiro & Laliotis, 2011). As a result, later stimuli resembling elements of the distressing situation can trigger these improperly coded memories, which can lead to additional distress and mental health issues.

EMDR aims to activate the neural network storing these memories and reinitiate the encoding process (EMDRIA, 2020; Shapiro & Laliotis, 2011). By engaging with past experiences, current triggers, and future potential challenges across its eight-phase process (Shapiro, 2001), the processing of these distressing memories may resume, but in a much more emotionally safe environment than during the original distress. The trauma processing allows for resolution of the memories, this time encoding them into the neural network properly.

Despite significant advances in research on the psychological, psychophysiological, and neurobiological models that have been used to hypothesize the underlying mechanisms of change associated with EMDR, conclusive explanations remain elusive (Landin-Romero et al., 2018).

Bilateral Stimulation

From its inception and emphasized in its name, eye movements have been presented as an essential component of EMDR therapy. This has been an ongoing source of both intrigue and consternation. Eye movements are facilitated either by following the therapist's hand motions or with assistance of a light bar. In both laboratory and clinical studies, the use of eye movements increased effectiveness of EMDR in reducing trauma symptoms (Lee & Cuijpers, 2013). The inclusion of eye movements in EMDR has been credited with generating a faster response in symptom reduction compared with other psychotherapies and a greater reduction in vividness of targeted traumatic memories, which has implications for treating intrusive images and flashbacks in survivors with PTSD (Lee & Cuijpers, 2013). Current research efforts are exploring the relationship between the speed of eye movements and working memory capacities, with mixed results (van Schie et al., 2016; van Veen et al., 2015). Bilateral stimulation is not limited to eye movements. Adaptations to bilateral stimulation have included the use of alternating (left—right) hand taps or handheld vibrating pods, or use of headphones that produce alternating sounds in the left–right ear. There is also a technique called the butterfly hug, wherein the client uses crossed arms to self-induce bilateral stimulation just under the (left–right) collarbone (Jarero & Artigas, 2012). Research suggests that eye movements may produce quicker results than other forms of bilateral stimulation (Landin-Romero et al., 2018).

Evidence of Effectiveness

Francine Shapiro, the developer of EMDR, was a staunch advocate for EMDR research. From its inception, she insisted on the need for scientific investigation of the effectiveness of EMDR, initially for the treatment of PTSD and related trauma symptoms and then for the underlying mechanisms facilitating trauma resolution, as well as to advance knowledge on the parameters of effectiveness across other clinical conditions. The need for research was intensified by the early and enduring levels of skepticism and controversy related to the use of eye movements and other forms of bilateral stimulation. As a consequence, in the past 30 years, more than 300 studies have been conducted on EMDR (Landin-Romero et al., 2018), including more than 76 randomized controlled trials and numerous systematic reviews and meta-analyses (Cuijpers et al., 2020). There has been variance in quality across these

studies and reviews, with warranted scientific critique (Opheim et al., 2019), but the consistency of positive outcomes and increased rigor over time have led to recognition of EMDR as an evidence-based trauma treatment.

The evidence base of its effectiveness is very strong, generated from an array of trauma types from single incident to complex and chronic traumas that originated in childhood. After a rigorous scientific review process, the International Society for Traumatic Stress Studies (ISTSS) PTSD guidelines (2019) gave a "strong recommendation" for use of EMDR in treating PTSD in adults. This designation is the strongest endorsement available, based on "quality of evidence and the highest certainty of effect" (p. 7). It is the same designation that other well-established evidence-based trauma treatments received, including cognitive therapy, cognitive processing therapy (CPT), prolonged exposure (PE), and cognitive–behavioral therapy (CBT) with a trauma focus. This also aligns with recommendations for use of EMDR for PTSD treatment from numerous other national and international bodies that provide guidelines for best practices, including the National Registry of Evidence Based Programs and Practices of the Substance Abuse and Mental Health Services Administration, the National Institute of Health and Clinical Excellence (United Kingdom), and the World Health Organization.

EMDR therapy has a few advantages over other evidence-based trauma treatments that clinicians and their clients may find compelling. EMDR has achieved comparable outcomes to other effective interventions with a fewer number of sessions (Stanbury et al., 2020), less homework (Lewey et al., 2018), and a lower rate of treatment dropouts compared to CPT and PE (Lewis et al., 2020). This suggests that EMDR may be more efficient, and therefore cost-effective, which could be beneficial for clients with limited mental health coverage through their insurance plans, low-income clients without insurance coverage, and low-resourced agencies with limitations on the number of therapy sessions they can provide.

Applicability of EMDR Therapy

A critical assessment for any trauma therapist is determining the applicability of a given evidence-based treatment to the unique presenting clinical concerns of their clients. It is essential that there be a good fit between the intervention and its ability to address specific diagnoses, trauma symptoms, desired treatment outcomes, client characteristics, and client preferences. Often, clinical trials on the effectiveness of psychotherapies are evaluated with predominately White, middle-class, well-educated women and assumed to be equally effective across other populations with differing social identities. The multiple identities that clients hold profoundly impacts their experiences of trauma, including historical trauma, the trauma of racism, and differential access to evidence-based trauma treatment. Social workers have an ethical obligation to "promote sensitivity to and knowledge about oppression and cultural and ethnic diversity . . . [and to] strive to ensure access to needed information, services, and resources; equality of opportunity; and meaningful participation in decision making for all people" (National Association of Social Workers, 2017). EMDRIA offers similar standards for working with clients and provides cultural competence and anti-racism resources on its website (EMDRIA, 2020). Furthermore, EMDR clinician networks are beginning to bring their skills into community settings to address systemic racism and other civil rights issues (Rosenblum et al., 2017).

A major strength of EMDR therapy is that it is clinically effective in reducing PTSD and other trauma symptoms across a diverse array of clients from various nationalities and ethnicities, males and females, across the life span, and for those with low incomes and education levels (Acaturk et al., 2016; Allon, 2015; Naseh et al., 2019). Within the United States, although the majority of research participants have been White, the second most frequent ethnic group represented has been Hispanics, followed by African Americans (Edmond & Lawrence, 2015). In a small number of studies, samples have included participants who self-identified as Asian Pacific Islanders, Native American, and Alaskan Natives. The diversity of participants within studies has consistently demonstrated effectiveness in reducing PTSD and other trauma symptoms, suggesting good generalizability of effectiveness across social identities.

Children and Adolescents

Although the EMDR research on children and adolescents lags behind that on adults, evidence is mounting to illustrate its effectiveness in treating PTSD and related trauma symptoms in those populations. de Roos and colleagues (2017) demonstrated that after receiving EMDR for the treatment of a single trauma incident, 92.5% of participants (aged 8–18 years) no longer met PTSD criteria. Furthermore, this was accomplished in an average of four sessions. In a comparison between EMDR and trauma-focused cognitive–behavioral therapy (TF-CBT), Lewey and colleagues (2018) found TF-CBT to be slightly more effective, but they suggest that EMDR may be advantageous for children who have language difficulties because there are fewer elements involving reading and writing. Meta-analyses have compared the effectiveness of different trauma-focused interventions commonly used with children and adolescents and found EMDR to be as effective as various CBT interventions (Mavranezouli et al., 2020). The ISTSS PTSD guidelines (2019) gave EMDR a "strong recommendation" (its highest rating), and the California Evidence-Based Clearinghouse for Child Welfare (2019) gave EMDR a rating of "1: Well-supported by research evidence."

Therapists can be creative and flexible when it comes to using EMDR therapy with children and adolescents. Adler-Tapia and Settle (2017) present a number of ways therapists can bring in modifications that maintain EMDR treatment fidelity, are developmentally appropriate, and involve play. Therapists can integrate psychoeducation on understanding and recognizing emotions, expressive arts, play therapy, and sand tray work. They can offer alternatives in bilateral stimulation, such as using shorter sets of eye movements with a stuffed animal instead of fingers, and having the child march, drum, or clap as audio or tactile alternatives. They can use a magnifying glass as a metaphor to signify the scanning process. These approaches should only be utilized by therapists trained to work with traumatized children and adolescents, with inclusion of safe parents/caregivers as appropriate to provide collateral information and support.

Areas with Emerging Evidence of Treatment Effects

As therapists saw the positive effects of EMDR therapy in treating PTSD and related trauma symptoms, they understandably explored the potential benefits of using EMDR to treat other mental health conditions, particularly when these seemed connected to a traumatic event. The broad application of EMDR therapy has outpaced the corresponding research, and as a consequence, there is a sparsity of evidence of effectiveness for most of these other treatment concerns. Areas with promising results, but limited evidence, include the following: anxiety, phobias, and panic (Cuijpers et al., 2020; Horst et al., 2017; Yunitri et al., 2020); depression (Dominguez et al., 2021; Jahanfar et al., 2020); borderline personality disorder (De Jongh et al., 2020); bipolar disorder (Valiente-Gomez et al., 2019); psychosis (Adams et al., 2020); substance abuse (Markus et al., 2020); eating disorders (Balbo et al., 2017); suicidal ideation (Proudlock & Peris, 2020); and neurological disorders (Cope et al., 2018).

Group Approaches to EMDR

EMDR therapy was originally designed to be delivered in the context of individual psychotherapy. However, in some settings, particularly those with limited resources, it can be advantageous to have the option of delivering treatment in a group format. Jarero and Artigas (2012) introduced the group EMDR format, called EMDR-Integrative Group Treatment Protocol (ITGP), which utilizes the eight-phase EMDR treatment in a group with art therapy and the butterfly hug bilateral stimulation option. A pilot of EMDR-IGTP with female cancer patients showed reduction in PTSD symptoms post-treatment (Jarero et al., 2015). However, Allon's (2015) work with sexual assault survivors in the Congo found that individual EMDR therapy was more effective than EMDR-IGTP in reducing PTSD symptoms.

Integrated and Intensive Treatment

Van Woudenberg and colleagues (2018) offered adults with multiple traumas and diagnoses an integrated approach to treating PTSD by combining PE and EMDR. Participants received 2 hours of psychoeducation about PTSD and 8 consecutive days of PE in the morning (90 minutes) and EMDR in the afternoon (90 minutes). Four times per day, participants could also engage in structured physical activity at their own pace. At the conclusion of the 2-week program, "more than 80% of the patients with severe PTSD and multiple comorbidities showed a clinically meaningful response, while more than half of the patients lost their PTSD diagnosis" (p. 8). It was the first study to combine EMDR with PE in this intensive format, and the dropout rate was less than 3%.

Early Treatment Intervention: Single and Multiple Sessions

In the trauma treatment field, efforts are underway to develop and evaluate treatments for use within the first 3 months of a traumatic event in the hope of preventing the development of PTSD. Based on the few currently available early intervention studies using a single session of EMDR, the ISTSS PTSD guidelines (2019) have designated it as an "intervention with emerging evidence" of effectiveness for preventing PTSD in adults. For multiple-session early treatment interventions with children, EMDR received a "standard recommendation" for preventing PTSD, made when there is "at least reasonable quality of evidence and low certainty of effect" (p. 7).

Conclusion

In 2019, EMDRIA held a ceremony honoring the 30th anniversary of EMDR therapy and paid tribute to its founder, Francine Shapiro, who had recently died. She cared deeply about alleviating human suffering and believed strongly in the critical role that research could play in advancing our understanding of the underlying mechanisms of change and the parameters of effectiveness of EMDR therapy. She frequently extolled the virtues of research to therapists, encouraging them to use their clinical observations to write case studies or to partner with researchers to support evaluation of EMDR in various countries, cultural contexts, types of trauma, and clinical conditions. As fruitful as the past 30 years have been in researching the effectiveness of EMDR therapy, she would be laser-focused on the work that still remains.

Helpful Resources

EMDR humanitarian assistance programs: https://www.emdrhap.org

EMDR Institute. *Networking groups*: http://www.emdr.com/networking-groups

EMDR International Association: http://www.emdria.org

References

Acarturk, C., Konuk, E., Cetinkaya, M., Senay, I., Sijbrandij, M., Gulen, B., & Cuijpers, P. (2016). The efficacy of eye movement desensitization and reprocessing for post-traumatic stress disorder and depression among Syrian refugees: results of a randomized controlled trial. *Psychological medicine, 46*(12), 2583–2593.

Adams, R., Ohlsen, S., & Wood, E. (2020). Eye movement desensitization and reprocessing (EMDR) for the treatment of psychosis: A systematic review. *European Journal of Psychotraumatology, 11*(1), 1711349. http://doi.org/d2wf

Adler-Tapia, R., & Settle, C. (2017). *EMDR and the art of psychotherapy with children: Infants to adolescents* (2nd ed.). Springer.

Allon, M. (2015). EMDR group therapy with women who were sexually assaulted in the Congo. *Journal of EMDR Practice and Research, 9*(1), 28–34. http://doi.org/d2wg

Balbo, M., Zaccagnino, M., Cussino, M., & Civilotti, C. (2017). Eye movement desensitization and reprocessing (EMDR) and eating disorders: A systematic review. *Clinical Neuropsychiatry: Journal of Treatment Evaluation, 14*(5), 321–329.

California Evidence-Based Clearinghouse for Child Welfare. (2019, June). *CEBC program: Eye movement desensitization and reprocessing.* https://www.cebc4cw.org

Cope, S. R., Mountford, L., Smith, J. G., & Agrawal, N. (2018). EMDR to treat functional neurological disorder: A review. *Journal of EMDR Practice and Research, 12*(3), 118–131. http://doi.org/d2wh

Cuijpers, P., van Veen, S. C., Sijbrandij, M., Yoder, W., & Cristea, I. A. (2020). Eye movement desensitization and reprocessing for mental health problems: A systematic review and meta-analysis. *Cognitive Behaviour Therapy, 49*(3), 165–180. http://doi.org/ggmnrw

De Jongh, A., Groenland, G. N., Sanches, S., Bongaerts, H., Voorendonk, E. M., & Van Minnen, A. (2020). The impact of brief intensive trauma-focused treatment for PTSD on symptoms of borderline personality disorder. *European Journal of Psychotraumatology, 11*(1), 1721142. http://doi.org/gg2fz5

de Roos, C., van der Oord, S., Zijlstra, B., Lucassen, S., Perrin, S., Emmelkamp, P., & de Jongh, A. (2017).

Comparison of eye movement desensitization and reprocessing therapy, cognitive behavioral writing therapy, and wait-list in pediatric posttraumatic stress disorder following single-incident trauma: A multicenter randomized clinical trial. *Journal of Child Psychology and Psychiatry, 58*(11), 1219–1228. http://doi.org/ggtrjk

Dominguez, S., Drummond, P., Gouldthorp, B., Janson, D., & Lee, C. W. (2021). A randomized controlled trial examining the impact of individual trauma-focused therapy for individuals receiving group treatment for depression. *Psychology and Psychotherapy: Theory, 94*(1), 81–100. http://doi.org/d2wj

Edmond, T., & Lawrence, K. (2015). Eye movement desensitization and reprocessing. In *Encyclopedia of social work*. Oxford University Press.

EMDR International Association. (2020). *EMDR International Association home/EMDR practitioners*. EMDR International Association. https://www.emdria.org

Horst, F., Den Oudsten, B., Zijlstra, W., de Jongh, A., Lobbestael, J., & De Vries, J. (2017). Cognitive behavioral therapy vs. eye movement desensitization and reprocessing for treating panic disorder: A randomized controlled trial. *Frontiers in Psychology, 8*, 1409. http://doi.org/gbtm96

International Society for Traumatic Stress Studies. (2019). *Posttraumatic stress disorder prevention and treatment guidelines: Methodology and recommendations*.

Jahanfar, A., Fereidouni, Z., Behnammoghadam, M., Dehghan, A., & Bashti, S. (2020). Efficacy of eye movement desensitization and reprocessing on the quality of life in patients with major depressive disorder: A randomized clinical trial. *Psychology Research and Behavior Management, 13*, 11–17. http://doi.org/d2wm

Jarero, I., & Artigas, L. (2012). The EMDR integrative group treatment protocol: EMDR group treatment for early intervention following critical incidents. *European Review of Applied Psychology, 62*(4), 219–222. http://doi.org/d2wn

Jarero, I., Artigas, L., Uribe, S., Evelyn Garcia, L., Alicia Cavazos, M., & Givaudan, M. (2015). Pilot research study on the provision of the eye movement desensitization and reprocessing integrative group treatment protocol with female cancer patients. *Journal of EMDR Practice and Research, 9*(2), 98–105. http://doi.org/d2wp

Landin-Romero, R., Moreno-Alcazar, A., Pagani, M., & Amann, B. L. (2018). How does eye movement desensitization and reprocessing therapy work? A systematic review on suggested mechanisms of action. *Frontiers in Psychology, 9*, 1395. http://doi.org/gd387b

Lee, C. W., & Cuijpers, P. (2013). A meta-analysis of the contribution of eye movements in processing emotional memories. *Journal of Behavior Therapy and Experimental Psychiatry, 44*(2), 231–239.

Lewey, J. H., Smith, C. L., Burcham, B., Saunders, N. L., Elfallal, D., & O'Toole, S. K. (2018). Comparing the effectiveness of EMDR and TF-CBT for children and adolescents: A meta-analysis. *Journal of Child & Adolescent Trauma, 11*(4), 457–472. http://doi.org/ggtrkj

Lewis, C., Roberts, N. P., Gibson, S., & Bisson, J. I. (2020). Dropout from psychological therapies for post-traumatic stress disorder (PTSD) in adults: Systematic review and meta-analysis. *European Journal of Psychotraumatology, 11*(1). http://doi.org/ggw2wb

Markus, W., Hornsveld, H. K., Burk, W. J., de Weert-van Oene, G. H., Becker, E. S., & DeJong, C. A. J. (2020). Addiction-focused eye movement desensitization and reprocessing therapy as an adjunct to regular outpatient treatment for alcohol use disorder: Results from a randomized clinical trial. *Alcoholism, 44*(1), 272–283. http://doi.org/d2wv

Mavranezouli, I., Megnin-Viggars, O., Daly, C., Dias, S., Stockton, S., Meiser-Stedman, R., Trickey, D., & Pilling, S. (2020). Research review: Psychological and psychosocial treatments for children and young people with post-traumatic stress disorder: A network meta-analysis. *Journal of Child Psychology and Psychiatry, 61*(1), 18–29. http://doi.org/d2wx

Naseh, M., Macgowan, M. J., Wagner, E. F., Abtahi, Z., Potocky, M., & Stuart, P. H. (2019). Cultural adaptations in psychosocial interventions for post-traumatic stress disorder among refugees: A systematic review. *Journal of Ethnic & Cultural Diversity in Social Work, 28*(1), 76–97. http://doi.org/d2w3

National Association of Social Workers. (2017). *NASW code of ethics*. https://www.socialworkers.org/About/Ethics/Code-of-Ethics

Opheim, E., Andersen, P. N., Jakobsen, M., Aasen, B., & Kvaal, K. (2019). Poor quality in systematic reviews on PTSD and EMDR: An examination of search methodology and reporting. *Frontiers in Psychology, 10*, 1558. http://doi.org/d2w4

Proudlock, S., & Peris, J. (2020). Using EMDR therapy with patients in an acute mental health crisis. *BMC Psychiatry, 20*(1), 14. http://doi.org/d2w5

Rosenblum, R. E., Dockstader, D. J., & Martin, S. A. (2017). EMDR, community psychology, and innovative applications of a trauma recovery network as a tool for social change. *Journal of EMDR Practice and Research, 11*(4), 206–216. http://doi.org/d2w7

Shapiro, F. (2001). *Eye movement desensitization and reprocessing: Basic principles, protocols and procedures* (2nd ed.). Guilford.

Shapiro, F., & Laliotis, D. (2011). EMDR and the adaptive information processing model: Integrative treatment and case conceptualization. *Clinical Social Work Journal, 39*(2), 191–200.

Stanbury, M. M., Drummond, D., & Lee, W. (2020). Efficiency of EMDR and Prolonged Exposure in Treating Posttraumatic Stress Disorder: A Randomized Trial. *Journal of EMDR Practice and Research, 14*(1), 3.

Valiente-Gomez, A., Moreno-Alcazar, A., Gardoki-Souto, I., Masferrer, C., Porta, S., Royuela, O., Hogg, B., Lupo, W., & Amann, B. L. (2019). Theoretical background and clinical aspects of the use of EMDR in patients with bipolar disorder. *Journal of EMDR Practice and Research, 13*(4), 307–312. http://doi.org/d2w8

van Schie, K., van Veen, S. C., Engelhard, I. M., Klugkist, I., & van den Hout, M. A. (2016). Blurring emotional memories using eye movements: Individual differences and speed of eye movements. *European Journal of Psychotraumatology, 7*(1), 29476. http://doi.org/f8wxvq

van Veen, S. C., van Schie, K., Wijngaards-de Meij, L. D. N. V., Littel, M., Engelhard, I. M., & van den Hout, M. A. (2015). Speed matters: Relationship between speed of eye movements and modification of aversive autobiographical memories. *Frontiers in Psychiatry, 6,* 45. http://doi.org/d2w9

Van Woudenberg, C., Voorendonk, E. M., Bongaerts, H., Zoet, H. A., Verhagen, M., Lee, C. W., Minnen, A. V., & De Jongh, A. (2018). Effectiveness of an intensive treatment programme combining prolonged exposure and eye movement desensitization and reprocessing for severe post-traumatic stress disorder. *European Journal of Psychotraumatology, 9*(1), 1487225. http://doi.org/d2xb

Yunitri, N., Kao, C.-C., Chu, H., Voss, J., Chiu, H.-L., Liu, D., Shen, S.-T. H., Chang, P.-C., Kang, X. L., & Chou, K.-R. (2020). The effectiveness of eye movement desensitization and reprocessing toward anxiety disorder: A meta-analysis of randomized controlled trials. *Journal of Psychiatric Research, 123,* 102–113. http://doi.org/d2xc

Developing Successful Relationships

The Therapeutic and Group Alliances

Lawrence Shulman

A middle-aged mother of three comes to a counseling agency for help dealing with her young children. She has just separated from her husband of 20 years. Her main concern is her children, who are upset and have been acting out since their father moved out. At the first interview with her 25-year-old, recently graduated social worker, she asks, "Do you have any children?" The worker responds, "We are here to talk about you, not me." For the balance of the interview, the client appears distracted, providing minimal responses to the worker's effort to obtain a social history. The worker's notes describe the client as "depressed and resistant."

Putting ourselves in the shoes of the client, we can see that she may be asking, "Since you don't have children, how can you understand my situation, how can you help me?" Because of the norm against directness, she raised her concerns indirectly. Feeling defensive, the worker responded in a way that closed off discussion.

In another example, we have a first session of a court-mandated "anger management"

group with African American teenagers. One member angrily confronts the two Caucasian, middle-class suburban female group leaders and says, "Why should I talk about my problems? What am I going to learn from two old White women like you?" The group leaders, in their mid-twenties, report that it was the "old women" comment that hurt the most. Periods of silence mark the rest of the session. When conversation does take place, it consists of an "illusion of work" with no real emotion or significance (Shulman, 2018).

The leaders open the next session by referring back to the comment from the confrontational member. They realize she was an internal leader stating what other group members might have thought as well. They address the authority theme, the relationship between the group members and the workers. "We don't blame you for feeling this way. Not only are we older but we are also White and we live in the suburbs. No wonder you do not trust us or think we can ever understand what you go through. But how can we understand and help if you won't tell us?" The intervention asking the clients to describe their life experiences is an example of a solution-focused intervention (Corey, 2008), an evidenced-based practice (EBP) in which the workers put the group members in the position of being the experts in their own lives.

The workers' directness raising race and class begins the development of a "working relationship," now more commonly referred to as the therapeutic alliance (Shulman, 2018). In the third session, the same member discloses she experienced sexual abuse in her family. Other group members share similar traumatic experiences as one of the underlying sources of their anger. As the group members share these painful life experiences, they are simultaneously strengthening the underlying group alliance.

The Therapeutic and Group Alliances

Skillful interventions in the beginning phase can increase the possibility of establishing an effective working relationship with the client. Elements of the relationship include rapport ("I get along with my worker"), trust ("I can tell my worker anything on my mind"), and caring ("My worker cares as much about me as he/she cares about my children") (Shulman, 2018).

In situations with more than one client, there are often unstated concerns about the other clients in the session. Experience indicates that clients must first create a positive therapeutic alliance with the social worker and then address issues of group alliance.

Although the concept of the "therapeutic alliance" has been found to have a positive impact on outcomes, alliance to the group as a whole has not been as widely studied. Lindgren et al. (2008), citing their own research, suggest, "In treatment formats in which the group process is predicted to be a curative factor, it is counterintuitive to emphasize only the relationship between an individual patient and therapists" (p. 164). In a study of group alliance and cohesion, Joyce et al. (2007) examined the impact of each on outcomes in short-term group therapy. They found group alliance variables were more consistently associated with improved outcomes.

When these relationship issues, also referred to as the authority theme and the intimacy theme (Shulman, 2018), are added to ambivalence about accepting that a problem exists, one can understand the complexities associated with beginnings. This phase of work requires the client to make a "first decision" to engage in the process. A skillful worker can influence that decision but cannot make it for the client.

The skills identified in this chapter are those that increase the possibility that the client will take that first step. Although the focus of this chapter is on the impact of the core skills and constant elements, the helping relationship also includes variant elements. For example, the nature of the problem or the setting of practice can have an influence. Working in a high school dealing with violence prevention and bullying might look different from working in a hospital dealing with mental illness. Factors such as gender, race, ethnicity, sexual orientation, physical ability, and so on can all affect how the client perceives the offer of help.

For example, Elze (2006) described how a school social worker could be GLBTQQ (gay, lesbian, bisexual, transgendered, queer, and questioning) sensitive in practice. This is a crucial stage during which students attempt to come to grips with their sexual orientation. Elze suggests that the social worker needs to demonstrate that he or she is an "askable" person in response to all students using such strategies as employing gender-neutral language when exploring a youth's dating interests, sexual behaviors, and so on. In describing best practices in group work with these clients, Horne et al. (2014) suggested that group leaders begin with an examination of "their own biases and assumptions regarding sexual and gender orientation prior to working with this population" (p. 254).

Strategies appropriate for one population may be ineffective with another. Working interculturally (e.g., a Caucasian worker with a client of color) as well as working intraculturally (e.g., a Hispanic worker with a Hispanic client) may modify the dynamics and the strategies employed. Practice with voluntary, involuntary, or semivoluntary clients may also look quite different. A first session of a voluntary parenting group requires a different strategy than one with a court-mandated group of men convicted of driving while intoxicated (DWI).

In an example of a first session of a men's DWI group, the "deviant member" crumples the paper listing the topic for discussion each week and throws it into a wastebasket. The young female leader does not fall into the trap of using the authority of the court to demand compliance. Drawing on the EBP motivational interviewing (MI) model stages of change concept (Mason, 2009; Miller & Rollnick, 1991; Wahab, 2010), and recognizing that these men are in the "precontemplation stage of change," her first effort is to help them move into the "contemplation" stage.

She recognizes that building a therapeutic alliance is best achieved by exploring the resistance. She says, "I can see you are not happy at being forced to attend this group. I don't think you are the only one feeling this way. How about it? Are others also upset?" Members immediately respond with comments such as "I don't want to be called an alcoholic or made to feel guilty," "Everyone drinks on weekends; I just got caught," etc.

The leader writes on a board "Don't Want" and lists under this the concerns raised by the members. She then points out that these issues are on the agenda she has handed out and will be the topics of discussion. The tone of the meeting changes as her skillful response to the denial begins the development of the therapeutic alliance.

Finally, practice is influenced by the worker's theoretical orientation and underlying assumptions. The model of understanding practice against the backdrop of time—the preliminary, beginning, middle, and ending/transition phases of work—and the skills identified are proposed as core elements in all of the variations. Schwartz (1961) described the importance of these phases of work, adding a preliminary phase to beginnings, middles, and endings/transitions phases first identified in social work by Taft (1942, 1949).

The Phases of Work: The Preliminary and Beginning Phases

Schwartz (1961) suggested that because clients often raise many of their concerns in an indirect manner, workers need to prepare to hear the client's indirect cues by developing a preliminary empathy. The skills of the preliminary phase are discussed next.

Tuning In

Tuning in is an exercise in which the worker develops a tentative empathy with the client's feelings and concerns. The worker also tunes in to their own emotional state because it will affect the worker's moment-by-moment responses to the client. The previous example of the teenage girls "anger management" group is an example of tuning in between sessions.

Responding Directly to Indirect Cues

Responding directly to indirect cues is the skill of articulating a client's thoughts and feelings in response to indirect communications in the first session. A common illustration of the importance of this skill and that of tuning in is the vignette that began this chapter. The recently divorced mother of three children asks the unmarried social worker, a recent graduate of a school of social work, the question, "Do you have children?" Unless the worker has tuned in both to her own feelings of inadequacy because she does not have a child and the real feelings of the mother, it is not uncommon for the worker to respond defensively—for example, "We are here to talk about you, not me!" or, alternatively, "I don't have children but I have taken courses on child development at the school of social work." These responses miss what might be the underlying questions: "Can you understand my situation?" "Will you be able to help me?" and "Can I trust you?"

It is important to understand that a successful direct response will meet three conditions: (1) It must be genuine with the worker trying to experience the emotion; (2) the client has to be ready to hear it; and (3) each worker must find a way to respond that reflects their own personality and artistry. With these conditions in mind, one response to the indirect cue might be,

> I'm not married, and I don't have any children. Why do you ask? Are you concerned I may not understand what it is like for you? I am worried about that as well. For me to help, I need to understand. For me to understand, you will have to tell me.

In addition to illustrating the power of tuning in and responding directly, this example also illustrates a number of skills identified in the middle or work phase. In my research, these skills were found to be associated with a positive working relationship when used in the beginning phase of practice (Shulman, 2011, 2018). The importance of expression of genuine empathy in developing a positive relationship was supported by Truax (1966) and in the work of Hakansson and Montgomery (2003).

It is important to note there is an artistry to practice and that the words used by workers may differ although the intent and impact of the intervention are the same. The worker's empathic responses must be genuine and not a phrase that is recited without feelings. Clients know when a worker is "reflecting" and not experiencing their feelings. Expressions such as "I hear you saying . . ." with no real affect attached can be experience by clients as artificial.

Another crucial element of the beginning phase is the development of a contract (working agreement) between the worker and the client(s). This contract establishes a structure creating the freedom to proceed. Note the following:

- A contract may not be fully developed in the first session, and this working agreement can change over time (re-contracting).
- The client must feel an investment in the work or the sessions will constitute an "illusion of work."
- The worker must make clear the purpose and their role in nonjargonized terms that the client can understand.

Specific contracting skills are as follows (Shulman, 2018):

> *Clarifying purpose*: The skill of making a brief opening statement that clarifies the purpose of the session. This skill is used when initiating a service (e.g., a first group meeting) or responding to a client's request for service (e.g., "Can you let me know what brought you in today so we can see how I might be able to help?").
>
> *Clarifying role*: The skill of describing in a brief, no jargon manner the kind of help the social worker can provide. For example, "I can't give you the right answer for dealing with your husband. I can help you examine how you deal

with him now, your feelings about the relationship, and how you see yourself in the future. Perhaps if we work together I can help you find the answer that is right for you."

Reaching for feedback: The skill of encouraging clients to explain their perceptions of the problem and the areas in which they wish to receive help.

Clarifying mutual expectations: Developing an agreement on what the client may expect of the worker as well as defining the client's obligations (e.g., regular attendance at group sessions).

Discussing authority issues: Dealing with issues that concern the authority of the worker (e.g., the mandated nature of the service, the limits of confidentiality, and the worker's responsibility as a mandated reporter).

Although contracting is initiated in the first sessions, it is not unusual to have to re-contract as the work develops. The client may not have fully understood the implications of the contract. It is also common for clients to begin with near problems, which are real to the client but not at the core of the work. As clients begins to understand their issues more clearly, they are better able to articulate them. The client may have been in the MI precontemplation stage (DiClemente et al., 1991). For example, clients in substance abuse counseling, such as in the DWI vignette shared previously, may not have accepted that they have a problem with alcohol.

The Phases of Work: The Middle Phase

As the work continues, the client makes the transition from the beginning to the middle or work phase. This change is dependent on having developed the therapeutic alliance and the group alliance in the beginning phase.

When clients experience rapport, trust, and caring from their social worker, and from each other, they feel safer in moving onto more difficult issues making the "second decision."

The client may still be embarrassed to raise a difficult issue. Some examples include taboo areas such as sex, dependency, finances, health, or death. Alternatively, the client may not be consciously aware of the existence of the problem. The skills presented in the following list are designed to assist clients in telling their stories and telling them with feelings. These skills also assist clients in examining their cognitions or thought patterns related to their self-perception or perception of the problem or of others. An underlying assumption is that how one feels affects how one thinks, which affects how one acts, which in turn affects how one feels, and so on. It is the feeling, thinking, and doing connection that is explored in the middle phase of practice.

The following skills can be helpful in this transition phase (Shulman, 2018).

Sessional tuning in: The skill of developing a tentative, preliminary empathy for issues that may emerge at the start of a specific session. Examples include the impact of a traumatic event in a client's life, issues left over from the previous session, and a traumatic community event such as an armed attack on a school or church.

Sessional contracting: Skills designed to determine the issues or concerns facing clients at a particular session. Examples include remaining tentative at the start of the session while listening for indirect cues, asking a client what is on their mind, and checking in with group members at the start of a session.

Elaborating skills: The skills for helping clients tell their story (e.g., listening, containment, questioning, and reaching inside of silences).

Empathic skills: Skills that address the emotional content of the client's experiences (e.g., reaching for feelings, acknowledging feelings, and articulating the client's feelings).

Sharing worker's feelings: The skill of sharing appropriate worker affect in response to the productions of the clients. Boundaries need to be respected so that the sharing of worker affect is professional and responsive to the needs of the clients. Issues of countertransference, client stereotyping, inappropriate worker frustration, and so on need to be considered and closely monitored. However, a general prohibition on sharing worker affect reflects a false dichotomy between the personal and professional selves mandating that the worker mistakenly chose between the two.

Making a demand for work: A facilitative confrontation in which the worker asks a client to engage in the agreed upon work. Specific skills include confronting denial, reaching inside of a silence, directly raising a taboo issue, and challenging the illusion of work.

Providing data: Providing relevant, unavailable information the client needs to deal with the task. Data can include facts, values, beliefs, and so on. Data should be provided in a manner leaving the information open to challenge.

Sessional endings and transitions: The skills involved in ending a session. These skills may include summarizing, evaluating progress, and discussion of transition issues (e.g., the client's next step and role-play of anticipated future conversations).

It is common for a client to disclose a powerful issue at the end of the session. This is called "doorknob therapy," with the image of the client dropping a bombshell with his or her hand on the office doorknob as he or she is about to leave the session. For example, a female college student may hint at a difficult time at a party the previous weekend. She may talk at the beginning of a session about being concerned that she drank too much. This could be a "first offering." The worker responding to the issue of concern over drinking starts to explore the question of substance use in the student's life. As the interview proceeds, the student drops hints of how rowdy the party became and her increasing feelings of concern. This could be the "second offering." The worker may begin to respond to issues of safety in a situation in which alcohol is consumed. Almost at the end of the session, the "third offering" emerges as the student describes having passed out, perhaps being drugged, and waking up in a bedroom in a state of undress with evidence that she had been raped.

In a situation such as this, the social worker may have to extend the session or arrange a later appointment that same day to deal with this powerful issue. The worker also has to consider reporting the incident to the authorities or helping the client to do so. When the issue is addressed, it would be important for the worker to explore why it was so difficult to raise the incident directly in the beginning of the session. As the client discusses her feelings that may include shame, self-blame, and so on, which made it difficult to discuss the sexual assault, she is actually beginning the discussion of the assault itself.

With this last example, we complete the discussion of the engagement phase of practice and the transition to the middle phase. For a more complete discussion, see Shulman (2018). The middle (work) phase of practice and the ending and transition phase are discussed in detail. The use of interventions drawn from the EBP and EIP research is included with an integrative approach suggesting less prescriptive strategies and room for practitioner artistry. The integration of science and art by the worker contributes significantly to the development of the therapeutic alliance in individual practice and serves as the precursor of the group alliance.

Helpful Resources

Green, R.-J. (2004). *Therapeutic alliance, focus, and formulation: Thinking beyond the traditional therapy orientations.* Pyschotherapy.net: http://www.psychotherapy.net/article/Therapeutic_Alliance

Mahaffey, B. A., & Granello, P. F. (2007). Therapeutic alliance: A review of sampling strategies reported in marital and family therapy studies. *The Family Journal, 15*(3), 207–216: http://tfj.sagepub.com/cgi/content/abstract/15/3/207

References

Corey, G. (2008). *Theory and practice of counseling and psychotherapy* (8th ed.). Belmont, CA: Brooks/Cole.

DiClemente, C. C., Prochaska, J. O., Fairhurst, S. K., Velicer, W. F., Velasquez, M. M., & Rossi, J. S. (1991). The process of smoking cessation: An analysis of precontemplation, contemplation, and preparation stages of change. *Journal of Consulting and Clinical Psychology, 59*(2), 295.

Elze, D. (2006). Working with gay, lesbian, bisexual and transgender students. In C. Franklin, M. B. Harris, & P. Allen-Meares, (Eds.), *The school services sourcebook: A guide for school-based professionals* (pp. 861–870). Oxford University Press.

Hakansson, J., & Montgomery, H. (2003). Empathy as an interpersonal phenomenon. *Journal of Social and Personal Relationships, 20,* 267–284.

Horne, S. G., Levitt, H. M., Reeves, T., & Wheeler, E. E. (2014). Group work with gay, lesbian, bisexual, transgender, queer, and questioning clients. In J. L. Delucia-Waack, C. R. Kalodner, & M. T. Riva (Eds.), *Handbook of group counseling & psychotherapy* (2nd ed., pp. 253–263), Sage.

Joyce, A. S., Piper, W. E., & Ogrodniczuk, J. S. (2007). Therapeutic alliance and cohesion variables as predictors of outcome in short-term group psychotherapy. *International Journal of Group Psychotherapy, 57*(3), 269–296.

Lindgren, A., Barber, J. P., & Sandahl, C. (2008). Alliance to the group-as-a-whole as a predictor of outcome in psychodynamic group therapy. *International Journal of Group Psychotherapy, 58*(2), 142–163.

Mason, M. J. (2009). Rogers redux: Relevance and outcomes of motivational interviewing across behavioral problems. *Journal of Counseling & Development, 87*(3), 357–362.

Miller, W. R., & Rollnick, S. S. (1991). *Motivational Interviewing.* New York: Guilford.

Schwartz, W. (1961). The social worker in the group. In *New perspectives on services to groups: Theory, organization, practice.* National Association of Social Workers.

Shulman, L. (2018). *The skills of helping individuals, families, groups, and communities* (8th ed., enhanced). Cengage.

Taft, J. (1942). The relational function to process in social casework. In V. P. Robinson (Ed.), *Training for skill in social casework* (pp. 206–226). University of Pennsylvania Press.

Taft, J. (1949). Time as the medium of the helping process. *Jewish Social Service Quarterly, 26,* 230–243.

Truax, C. B. (1966). Therapist empathy, warmth, genuineness and patient personality change in group psychotherapy: A comparison between interaction unit measures, time sample measures, and patient perception measures. *Journal of Clinical Psychology, 71,* 1–9.

Wahab, S. (2010). Motivational interviewing and social work practice. In K. van Wormer & B. Thyer (Eds.), *Evidence-based practice in the field of substance abuse* (pp. 197–210). Thousand Oaks, CA: Sage.

Best Practices

Parenting Techniques

Carolyn Hilarski

This chapter describes the current empirical thinking regarding the possible etiology and outcomes for parent–child non-helpful interactions and "best practice parenting approaches" to help professional social workers empower family systems and their members toward resilience and self-efficacy.

Constructive Parenting

Children's first teachers are parents, and there is abundant empirical evidence that parents who practice constructive parenting strategies positively support their personal self-efficacy and their children's social–emotional development that includes self-esteem, resilience, and autonomy (Hajihashemi et al., 2019).

Constructive parenting is understood, in this chapter, as parent interactions with a child in a milieu that embodies respect, safety, and genuineness, while attending to the parent's parenting style and both the parent's and the child's temperament, goodness of fit, and level of attachment. Research documents that this parenting attitude and the resulting behaviors

are crucial to the overall well-being of children and the family system (Ryan & Ollendick, 2018). To elaborate, a child's social competence level is highly associated with academic achievement, and because the parent–child early interactions and resulting relationship initially shape the child's worldview and social proficiency, the quality of this relationship (e.g., both are able to share thoughts and emotions in an appropriate manner) is profoundly influencing for the child. Several factors are thought to act on the level of parent–child attachment: the child's temperament, goodness of fit with the parent, and environment (e.g., the parent's style of parenting and temperament) (Ryan & Ollendick, 2018).

The Influence of the Child's Temperament on Parenting Behaviors

There appears to be consensus that the concept of temperament involves the early presentation of patterned responses to others and situations urged by biological systems influenced by attention, emotion, and self-regulation. Parents will frequently describe their infants as easy (e.g., generally cheerful, adaptable, or unproblematic), difficult (e.g., often irritable, emotional, and/or highly resistance to change), or slow-to-warm (e.g., denoting a relatively inactive or indifferent child who may show moderate resistance to new situations) (Sanson et al., 2018). Moreover, these descriptors appear to remain relatively stable, with some moderation due to the goodness or poorness of fit between the child and their environment. It is essential for parents to understand that their child's temperament can influence their level of attachment with the primary caregiver, which can then mediate parent disciplining strategies (Cassiano et al., 2020). The following case is meant to illustrate this concept.

Case Example

Juan, a healthy Hispanic 5-year-old male, can be disruptive and antagonistic, according to his parents Mateo and Elena, who are expecting a new baby and fearful of how Juan will respond. Juan's mother relates that he does not handle change agreeably and will often engage in outburst-type behaviors when faced with new or perceived disagreeable situations. According to his mother,

> Juan has always been demanding. He is not like my husband and me. I don't understand why he insists on fighting or stubbornly disobeying. I sometimes find it difficult to sit and play with him because he is so aggressive. I often become frustrated and use a harsh tone and/or punish him, which makes me feel guilty.

There seems to be a mismatch of temperaments between mother and child. Elena does not understand Juan's behavior and is puzzled why

punishing does not remedy the situation. She feels inept as a parent. This may be a time when parent self-reflection might be helpful (Box 65.1). If parents can empathize with their children and accept that they are unique individuals with potentially different temperaments, parenting behaviors often modify (Ryan & Ollendick, 2018). For example, parents may be more selective about shared activities, choosing ones that "fit" their child's temperament to increase the likelihood that the mother–child interactions are more positive and increasing both the parent's and the child's self-esteem.

Parent–Child Goodness of Fit and Parenting Behaviors

Children who perceive their caregivers as warmly attentive in early life are more likely to comply with directives later in their development. Indeed, the effectiveness of the child's socialization attempts (e.g., aggressive or non-aggressive peer interactions) is associated with the parent–child relationship (attachment) and a caregivers' style of interaction that is responsive (e.g., taking the child's perspective), supportive (e.g., accepting, encouraging, and affectionate), attentive (e.g., listening and encouraging conversation), guiding (e.g., providing information), and receptive (e.g., inviting emotional expression). These parenting practices provide a safe environment in which the child can develop emotional coping and self-regulation strategies associated with higher self-esteem and positive life outcomes (Ryan & Ollendick, 2018).

Parenting Philosophy and Parenting Behaviors

The environment provided to an individual during childhood is generally dynamic and

BOX 65.1 Parent Self-Reflection Questions

Parents: Ask yourself. . . .

1. When my child exhibits unhelpful behaviors, what are my thoughts?
2. What are my resulting feelings from those thoughts?
3. What is my behavior toward the child in response to these thoughts and feelings?
    a. Is negative labeling being used?
    b. Am I overcontrolling?
    c. Am I choosing harsh punishment or belittling words?
4. How does my child respond to my behavior?
5. How might I constructively change a negative interchange with my child?

Keeping in mind . . . .

a. My child's temperament: Ask yourself, What is my child's . . .
    1. General activity level?
    2. Overall quality of mood?
    3. Level of flexibility, determination, and focus?
b. My temperament
Is there a mismatch in how my child and I respond to experiences?
c. My child's biological development (e.g., their abilities to take on a task)?
d. My child's maturity level (e.g., how prepared is my child to accept responsibility, move through setbacks, delay gratification—self-control, listen . . .)?

highly influenced by family and community socioeconomics along with the parents' history, personality traits, and philosophy on parenting. These factors impact the overall parent–child relationship (e.g., attachment) and the child's well-being. The most powerful of these environmental factors is suggested to be the parenting philosophy or style (Uka & Berisha, 2019).

The parenting style is the approach a parent takes to parenting. It is described by Baumrind (1966, pp. 889–892) as follows:

Permissive: Parents, desiring love at all costs, tend not to set clear and consistent limits with their children, and blurred or nonexistent consequences, responsibilities, and boundaries flourish. Their children find themselves on their own, which is anxiety-producing and may promote a view of the world as a scary and difficult place where not accepting responsibility and overstepping boundaries interfere with relationships and the rights of others.

Authoritarian: Parents tend to fear losing control. Discipline is commonly reward or harsh punishment (accusing, blaming, argumentative, and rigid). Children may comply and struggle with independence or rebel.

Authoritative: Parents have clear, consistent, and respectful expectations for their children and persistently and empathically enforce reasonable limits. Parents actively listen and focus on encouragement and acknowledgment of child helpful behaviors. Children are given limited choices to help them learn and experience the consequences of their choices. A child's self-esteem rises, and the child is more cooperative when there is a perception of control and ownership of their life path.

The associated child outcomes of permissive and authoritarian parental interactions are related to child depression and acting-out behavior (Pinquart, 2017). However, parenting styles are adjustable with training and practice (Smetana, 2017).

Child Development and Parenting Behavior

Parents with basic knowledge of child development are better equipped to understand their child's behavior and respond constructively to the child's psychological and physical needs. This has many benefits. For example, the parent may enjoy perceived competency in parenting and the child may profit from academic and social success. Moreover, a child's psychosocial maturity seems to be related to parents appreciating the child's place on the maturity spectrum, which may not necessarily correspond to the child's biological age, in their parenting response (i.e., considering the child's need for psychological autonomy and maintaining a rational level of control) (Kuay et al., 2017). Children in the beginning phases of maturity (no matter what the age) may present as self-absorbed, with argumentative and uncooperative behaviors. In this case, it is suggested that behavioral consequences that are not tied to cooperation are the most helpful parental response to encourage the child's progression on the maturity scale. As the child advances on the maturity timeline, a parent might notice the child using respect and compromise for win–win outcomes and later value responsibility and ethical and empathic behaviors. Once a child understands the benefits and uses for "respectful compromise," parents may wish to include these behaviors in

their parent–child negotiations. Parents with unrealistically high or low expectations may find themselves frustrated and their parent–child relationship compromised (Curran et al., 2020).

Why Children Might Choose Non-Helpful Behaviors

A Child's Desire to Belong

Children are social beings. They strive to find their place first in their family and then in society. From infancy, a child's earliest attempts are finding ways to belong, contribute, and be needed. Their behavior is goal-oriented and trial and error. They continue behaviors that results in goal attainment and abandon behaviors that do not.

Children as Misguided Observers

Although children are very good observers, they can easily misinterpret their observations, drawing mistaken conclusions. These misunderstandings often motivate their unhelpful behaviors. The following description elucidates:

> Four-year-old Kadina watches intently as her mother is busy with her new baby sister. She correctly observes that the new baby takes much of mother's time and there is less attention for her. But she mistakenly interprets that to get mother's attention she must be helpless like the baby. Kadina regresses to soiling herself after having been toilet trained for more than a year.

Parents who choose to remain calm in the face of their child's regressive behavior are available for self-reflection and empathic tuning-in to understand their child's behavior along with considering the child's level of development and maturity. In Kadina's case, the current family transition from one child to two may lead to an intervention that includes or adds to "shared time with Kadina."

Four Misdirected Child Behaviors

Special attention: All children desire and request attention, but a child who equates attention with their goal of being accepted, needed, and loved may resort to behaviors that, as perceived by others, demand special attention. In response to this perception, parents may feel frustrated, anxious, and/or guilty and reprimand and/or withdraw from the child, who may feel satisfied in the moment (even though the attention was negative), but the gratification does not linger.

Power: Some children believe that being in charge or the "boss" will ensure their goal of being loved, needed, and accepted. The message they often send with their behavior is "I am in control." They perceive that if they are "top dog," things will go their way, such as being accepted and loved (their consummate goal). However, in response, parents often feel angry, confronted, bullied, and/or defeated, leading to some level of fear. To reduce these negative feelings, parents will often find themselves in power struggles with their children that frequently end with "defensive withdrawal" (feeling helpless and hopeless) by both parties. The child may initially perceive the parent's withdrawal as "winning the conflict" on some level. However, it does not take long for the parent's retreat to be framed as rejection by the child, and the child's requirement for love urges the non-helpful behavioral approaches, meant to ensure acceptance, to begin again. It is best if the parent forgoes the power struggle and chooses to initiate a family meeting, in which the house members may all help problem-solve the child's need to control.

Revenge: This method is used when children feel hurt and/or defeated. They may decide that the only way to belong and be loved (their goal) is to turn the tables so others may know how "hurt" feels. This behavior frequently reaches its goal, as parents or caregivers often feel wounded, saddened, incredulous, dismayed, and/or rejected. Parents will find that using self-reflection (see Box 65.1), listening, and sharing help problem-solve this situation.

Assumed inadequacy: Disengaging may be the child's perceived best option for being loved and accepted. They may conclude that if they retreat, no harm is being done by them; moreover, while in withdrawal, they are given no expectations, so they are unable to disappoint others. Withdrawing is often used because of feelings of helplessness and may be displayed by not doing homework or other required activities. Parents, in response to seeming peacefulness, may join the child and withdraw with helpless/hopeless feelings **or** try overcompensating (overhelping) due to internal conflict, which can lead to resentment. Parent active listening can be effective here. Also, there are many books for children related to self-esteem—reading together is fun!

These four non-helpful behavioral modes, by both parent and child, are significant signs that bidirectional interfaces need modifications. Parents/caregivers must be self-aware and persistent and not accept that their or others' non-helpful behavior be allowed to continue, or they may withdraw and support the unwanted behavior by labeling the child as "deficient" and thus relinquishing parent responsibility for change. There is generally a reason that children use non-helpful behaviors. Parents who remain calm, self-reflect, and courageously use their toolbox of skills are likely to find the answer.

Constructive Parenting Toolbox

Considering Parent/Child Feelings

Helping children choose and engage in beneficial behaviors begins with the parent/caregiver first becoming aware of their response to the child's behavior (see Box 65.1) (Weisleder et al., 2019). Then, they must decide on the appropriate (developmentally, respectful, and empathetic) response. Children have beliefs about, for example, how they belong, and from these assumptions arise emotions and actions. It is important that the child's impressions be respected because these perceptions are genuine to the child and influenced by the child's unique temperament and evolving worldview. Parent/caregivers who choose to engage in self-reflection (see Box 65.1) and are agreeable, if deemed necessary, to modifying their response to a specific experience or empathic response display a strong sense of self-efficacy, which makes a significant difference in influencing their child's emotional and behavioral life (Noyan Erbaş et al., 2021). Empathy and humility are helpful behaviors to model for children and

are suggested protective factors (Del Vecchio et al., 2020).

Encouragement

Everyone desires approval. And the way we often receive it is in the form of praise. An example is stating, "Your drawing is great!" This well-intentioned phrase is usually given as encouragement. However, it is commonly received as a judgment. A different kind of statement, "I am noticing that you mixed red and blue and made purple in that drawing!" describes the observation that a new color was made. The child is genuinely encouraged with the facts. Praise statements inspire children to look outside of themselves for self-worth because their acceptance is dependent on the judgment of others. This can lead to unhealthy anxiety, low levels of self-efficacy, and poor motivation because the child feels discounted and powerless. Encouragement, on the other hand, acknowledges the child's participation and effort rather than results, thus encouraging perseverance, resilience, and self-efficacy (Gillison et al., 2017).

Listening and Sharing

Learning how to really (actively) listen not only works with children but also with anyone. When someone feels "heard," it can modify their feelings and actions. Often, when someone is speaking to us, we are thinking of something else or how we might respond. Effective listening builds trusting relationships and can aid the listener in discovering the speaker's underlying concerns and/or emotions. Let's return to Kadina as our example. She might say, "I want a bottle like the baby." An active listening reply might be, "Oh, you want something to drink. Let's get some milk and share some time together. Ok?" Accepting the child's needs and/or feelings without judgment, along with a desire to understand and empower, sends a message of respect, which helps build self-esteem in both parents and child (MacPherson, 2020).

Sharing your thoughts and feelings with your child begins with respectful language. Using "you-messages" tends to be heard as blaming or judging. Using "I-messages" shows that you own your feelings, and you are telling your child(ren) how you feel without blame or put-downs. If we think about Juan as an example, he might say, "I don't want a baby." A sharing reply might be, "Before my sister was born, I was afraid my mom would like the baby better. Do you ever feel that way?" This might also be a good time to share a book about fear.

Problem-Solving

Is the issue/problem before the parent/child considered a puzzle, a threat, or an opportunity? How the parent/caregiver frames the issue/problem makes a difference. To illustrate, if the parent immediately perceives the issue as a threat from beliefs such as "My job is to make sure my child completes homework! If they do not, failure might be the consequence!" the biological response might be fight-or-flight mode, offering communication such as "Anne, you didn't do your homework, so you can't go out for 2 weeks." On the other hand, if parents take a moment to breathe, calm the mind, and engage empathic listening and tuning-in to determine if their immediate response is indeed correct, this might lead to an alternate outcome with a different type of thinking and communication for all concerned. For example, does the consequence "not going out for 2 weeks" relate to not doing homework? Perhaps learning why Anne is not doing her homework and working together on a solution might be more helpful. Furthermore, setting a positive expectation can add to the learning opportunity—for example, "Anne, I know we can solve this problem together" (Stenason et al., 2020).

Who Owns the Problem?

An excellent way to help children build self-esteem is to empower them to handle their own problems—keeping in mind the child's actual need, not what others may think. First, decide, as a team, who belongs to the problem. Then, continuing as a team, determine the next course of action. The benefits are empowering to both child and parents. When children live irresponsibly and parents step in to handle any resulting consequences, the self-esteem and well-being of both the children and the parents suffer (Ryan & Ollendick, 2018).

Family Meetings

Adding family meetings to the household calendar is a supportive self-esteem–building parenting behavior. Everyone meets at a predetermined time to discuss problems, concerns, and plans (for fun?) together. All family members are invited to respectfully share, negotiate, and offer suggestions. Choices are made in a democratic way, and members may each take on a task with a deadline (Corwin et al., 2020).

Timing and Benefits of Parenting Education

There are several ideal conditions for parent education. For example, it is quite helpful if parents are interested and consider it a priority to learn effective parenting strategies. If they perceive that they have little influence over their children's lives, the first task for them is to understand that "reality" is quite the opposite. It is also important for parents to have the time, energy, and each other's support to participate in such education. As far as when parent education should happen, some researchers suggest the earlier the better, even suggesting that parents will benefit prior to the birth of their child. However, parents with very young children enjoy several paybacks. First, the child's undesirable behaviors tend to be less ingrained. Second, parental interventions are usually more effective because preschoolers tend to lack strong peer influences. Third, a younger child is generally more accepting of changes in behavioral consequences. Finally, young children, even aggressive ones, tend to continue to show and desire affection with their caregivers. In summary, parenting classes structured in a group format offer parents the added benefit of socialization, while sharing frustrations and child-rearing strategies, in addition to increasing supportive networks (Hajihashemi et al., 2019).

Helpful Resources

Pacific Spirit Play Resources. https://www.pacificspiritplay.com/

The Gottman Institute. *Mindful parenting: How to respond instead of react*: https://www.gottman.com/blog/mindful-parenting-how-to-respond-instead-of-react

Zero to Three. *Mindfulness for parents*: https://www.zerotothree.org/resources/2268-mindfulness-for-parents

References

Baumrind, D. (1966). Effects of authoritative parental control on child behavior. *Child Development, 37*(4), 887–907.

Cassiano, R. G. M., Provenzi, L., Linhares, M. B. M., Gaspardo, C. M., & Montirosso, R. (2020). Does preterm birth affect child temperament? A meta-analytic study. *Infant Behavior and Development, 58,* 101417. https://doi.org/10.1016/j.infbeh.2019.101417

Corwin, T. W., Maher, E. J., Merkel-Holguin, L., Allan, H., Hollinshead, D. M., & Fluke, J. D. (2020). Increasing social support for child welfare-involved families through family group conferencing. *British Journal of Social Work, 50*(1), 137–156.

Curran, T., Hill, A. P., Madigan, D. J., & Stornæs, A. V. (2020). A test of social learning and parent socialization perspectives on the development of perfectionism. *Personality and Individual Differences, 160,* 109925. https://doi.org/10.1016/j.paid.2020.109925

Del Vecchio, T., Rhoades, K. A., Mitnick, D. M., Heyman, R. E., & Smith Slep, A. M. (2020). In K. Wampler (Ed.), *The handbook of systemic family therapy: Systemic family therapy with children and adolescents* (Vol. 2, pp. 163–189). Wiley.

Gillison, F. B., Standage, M., Cumming, S. P., Zakrzewski-Fruer, J., Rouse, P. C., & Katzmarzyk, P. T. (2017). Does parental support moderate the effect of children's motivation and self-efficacy on physical activity and sedentary behaviour? *Psychology of Sport and Exercise, 32,* 153–161.

Hajihashemi, M., Mazaheri, M. A., & Hasanzadeh, A. (2019). Assessment of educational intervention in enhancing parenting self-efficacy in parents of primary school students. *Journal of Education and Health Promotion, 8*(1), 43. https://www.ncbi.nlm.nih.gov/pmc/articles/PMC6432816/

Kuay, H., Tiffin, P., Boothroyd, L., Towl, G., & Centifanti, L. (2017). A new trait-based model of child-to-parent aggression. *Adolescent Research Review, 2*(3), 199–211. https://doi.org/10.1007/s40894-017-0061-4

MacPherson, H. A. (2020). More than medication: The importance of family treatments for pediatric bipolar disorder. *Brown University Child and Adolescent Behavior Letter, 36*(1), 1–6.

Noyan Erbaş, A., Özcebe, E., & Cak Esen, T. (2021). Investigation of the effect of Hanen's "More Than Words" on parental self-efficacy, emotional states, perceived social support, and on communication skills of children with ASD. *Logopedics Phoniatrics Vocology, 46*(1), 17–27.

Pinquart, M. (2017). Associations of parenting dimensions and styles with externalizing problems of children and adolescents: An updated meta-analysis. *Developmental Psychology, 53*(5), 873–932. https://doi.org/10.1037/dev0000295

Ryan, S., & Ollendick, T. (2018). The interaction between child behavioral inhibition and parenting behaviors: Effects on internalizing and externalizing symptomology. *Clinical Child and Family Psychology Review, 21*(3), 320–339. https://doi.org/10.1007/s10567-018-0254-9

Sanson, A. V., Letcher, P. L. C., & Havighurst, S. S. (2018). Child characteristics and their reciprocal effects on parenting. In M. R. Sanders & A. Morowska (Eds.), *Handbook of parenting and child development across the lifespan* (pp. 337–370). Springer.

Smetana, J. G. (2017). Current research on parenting styles, dimensions, and beliefs. *Current Opinion in Psychology, 15,* 19–25. https://doi.org/10.1016/j.copsyc.2017.02.012

Stenason, L., Moorman, J., & Romano, E. (2020). The experiences of parents and facilitators in a positive parenting program. *The Qualitative Report, 25*(1), 1–13.

Uka, V., & Berisha, H. (2019). The influence of parenting styles on social behavior and competence in function of student learning success. *Prizren Social Science Journal, 3*(3), 91–95. https://doi.org/10.32936/pssj.v3i3.123

Weisleder, A., Cates, C. B., Harding, J. F., Johnson, S. B., Canfield, C. F., Seery, A. M., Raak, C. D., Alonso, A., Dreyer, B. P., & Mendelsohn, A. L. (2019). Links between shared reading and play, parent psychosocial functioning, and child behavior: Evidence from a randomized controlled trial. *Journal of Pediatrics, 213*, 187–195.e1. https://doi.org/10.1016/j.jpeds.2019.06.037

Grief, Loss, and Trauma

A Strengths-Based Approach

Elizabeth C. Pomeroy, Renée Bradford Garcia, and Kathleen A. Hill

Loss is a universal experience, and the death of a loved one can be especially devastating. This type of grief causes significant disruption in a person's functioning both internally (physically and emotionally) and externally (socially and occupationally). Historically, mental health practitioners received little training related to grief and loss interventions. Today, practitioners are more experienced in helping bereaved individuals. Yet, there is a growing need for understanding the individual's grieving process within the context of the environment rather than just examining the intrapsychic experience of the individual.

Early interventions with loss were based on a problem-oriented model and validated that grief is a negative, painful, and disruptive experience for the mourner. This approach views a person experiencing grief as someone suffering from an illness that must be cured. As a result, this approach may de-emphasize the mourners' strengths and resiliencies that can be brought to bear on their unique experience of loss. The strengths-based framework of grief assists practitioners in building on the inherent strengths of individuals while they navigate the grieving process. It encourages mourners to use their positive coping abilities and environmental resources. Furthermore, the strengths-based approach to grief is grounded in the view that grief in response to the death of a loved one is a natural, normal, and potentially health-producing process that aids the individual in adjusting to the absence of the loved one.

The Strengths-Based Framework for Grief

The strengths perspective of social work practice developed by Saleebey (1996, 2013) and Rapp (1998) views all clients as having assets and resources that enhance their ability to cope with life events. These assets and resources can be categorized into individual strengths and environmental strengths. Individual strengths include aspirations, competencies, and confidence (Rapp & Goscha, 2012). Although strengths are present in every individual, some people are able to capitalize on their strengths more than others. This may be due to a combination of biological, psychological, and social factors. Environmental strengths include resources, social relations, and opportunities. Together, a person's individual and environmental strengths influence one's sense of well-being, empowerment, and life satisfaction (Rapp & Goscha, 2012).

The strengths-based perspective is particularly salient for grieving clients. It builds on previous theories of grief with an emphasis on the health-producing aspects that are intrinsic to the mourner as well as the process of grief. Focusing on client strengths rather than deficits provides the practitioner with a valuable tool and aids in assessment and intervention. It effectively highlights aspects of the person and their environment that can be used and enhanced to assist in the grieving process and promote positive growth. The basic tenets of the strengths-based framework of grief are as follows (Pomeroy & Garcia, 2009):

1. Grief is a natural, expectable, and potentially health-producing process that aids the person in adjusting to the absence of the loved one.
2. The symptoms, emotions, and behaviors associated with expected grief reactions represent a process of healthy adaptation and are not inherently pathological.
3. Mourners benefit by knowing that life-enhancing grief reactions facilitate healing within the mourner and are productive and beneficial.
4. All persons have individual and environmental strengths that can assist them as they experience grief. The reinforcement and application of those strengths promote healthy grieving.
5. Environmental conditions can either help or hinder the mourner's ability to adapt to the loss and enhance the person's life.
6. Many uncomfortable symptoms of grief that are commonly regarded as negative

symptoms are also healthy coping mechanisms that facilitate the process of separation, adaptation to change, and integration of the loss.
7. Life-enhancing grief reactions to loss facilitate the process of adaptation and psychological separation from the deceased.
8. Life-enhancing grief symptoms should be allowed expression while being carefully monitored so that they remain helpful to the mourner's process of adaptation. Grief may be considered life-depleting when the symptoms it produces significantly weaken the mourner's aspirations, competencies, and confidence.
9. Life-depleting grief reactions are those responses and circumstances that act as impediments to the expected grieving process and interfere with the mourner's ability to live a fulfilling life.
10. Life-depleting grief reactions thwart the process of adaptation and lead to entropy.
11. Life-enhancing and life-depleting grief reactions exist on a continuum of intensity.
12. The experience of grief evolves over a person's lifetime, and grief is experienced with varying levels of conscious awareness.
13. The process of grief is fertile ground for personal growth and the development or enhancement of the mourner's strengths.

A strengths-based model of grief calls for a shift from problems and pathology to a more holistic view that includes the client's strengths and resources. However, there is still the need for empirical research and the development of evidence-based criteria for strengths-based practice as well as a shared language of resilience (Rapp et al., 2005).

Bereavement in the DSM-5

Historically, bereavement has received minimal attention from the American Psychiatric Association (APA) and was included in the *Diagnostic and Statistical Manual of Mental*

Disorders (DSM-III, DSM-IV and DSM-IV-TR) as a V code under "Other Conditions That May Be a Focus of Clinical Attention." Uncomplicated bereavement remains in the DSM-5 as a V code and is considered a normal expression of grief over the loss of a loved one and not a mental disorder (APA, 2013). The duration of a normal grief reaction is not specified in the DSM-5, with an acknowledgment that culture may play a significant role in the length of the grief process.

However, the DSM-5 removed the bereavement exclusion for the diagnosis of major depression, and it allows for a person experiencing a severe grief reaction and depression to be diagnosed with a major depressive disorder (APA, 2013).

Bereavement is also noted in the DSM-5 in the Trauma and Stressor-Related Disorders chapter under "Other Specified Trauma and Stressor-Related Disorder." The official diagnostic criteria allow for "severe and persistent grief and mourning reactions" to be classified as a persistent complex bereavement disorder (APA, 2013, p. 289). A specifier of "with traumatic bereavement" can be included if the death was of a traumatic nature, such as homicide or suicide. Persistent complex bereavement disorder is also being considered as a unique diagnosis; however, currently it is in the Appendix under "Conditions for Further Study." Therefore, to diagnose a client who is experiencing these symptoms, a practitioner would have to use the "other trauma and stressor-related disorder" classification (APA, 2013).

Finally, bereavement can also be found in the DSM-5 (APA, 2013) under adjustment disorders. In the case of the death of a loved one, the grief reaction must surpass what is customary in that person's environment and culture. In addition, the developmental level of the person must be taken into consideration (APA, 2013). Despite these limitations in the DSM-5, the World Health Organization (2018) has classified prolonged grief disorder in the 11th revision of the *International Classification of Diseases* as a medical diagnosis.

Grief Reactions from a Strengths-Based Framework

According to the strengths-based framework of grief, the term *expected grief* describes the predictable grief experience that reflects the healthy process of separation from the deceased individual. This type of grief may present diversely and is what the practitioner would expect to see with someone who has lost a loved one. Expected grief leads to health-producing growth. The term *complex grief* describes symptoms that interfere with the health-producing growth process of expected grief. If complex grief is not addressed appropriately, it can lead to life-depleting responses (Pomeroy & Garcia, 2009). Complex grief responses can further be classified as traumatic or nontraumatic. Complex grief that is traumatic occurs because the circumstances surrounding the loss overwhelm the mourner's ability to process the event. Complex grief without trauma occurs when the circumstances are not traumatic but for other reasons the grief becomes stalled, delayed, maladaptive, or prolonged. As noted by Shear et al. (2013), sufferers of complex grief experience

> frequent intense yearning, intense sorrow and emotional pain, preoccupation with the deceased and/or circumstances of the death, excessive avoidance of reminders of the loss, difficulty accepting the death, feeling alone and empty, and feeling that life has no purpose or meaning without the deceased person. (p. 3)

Complex mourning results in the bereaved feeling "stuck" between efforts to avoid the pain associated with life without their loved one and also holding on to the loved one and protesting the reality of the loss. The result is an inability to integrate the loss and obtain renewed fulfillment in life (Shear et al., 2013; Solomon, 2019).

Strengths-Based Assessment and Interventions with Individual Clients

Intervening with bereaved clients from the strengths-based framework involves several skills that originate from a comprehensive understanding of the strengths-based model. As clients present their story of loss and experience with grief, each retelling can offer new insight. The practitioner listens for information that will complete a preliminary assessment of the client's internal and external strengths, resources, and social supports. Some of the skills that the practitioner uses include active and empathetic listening, nonjudgmental acceptance of intense emotions, normalizing and educating the client about the grief process, assisting the client with coping skills and resources, and helping the client develop life-enhancing strategies to re-engage fully in life. Finally, practitioners assist clients in using their experience as fuel for personal growth.

Strengths-Based Group Interventions for Adults

In addition to individual counseling, group counseling has been used as a primary vehicle for working with the bereaved (Worden, 2018). Psychoeducational group interventions have been shown to improve well-being and grief resolution, increase social support, and decrease the risk of psychopathology related to unresolved grief issues (Pomeroy & Holleran, 2002). The power of group support and shared, mutual concerns can ameliorate the loneliness and isolation associated with loss. The potential benefit of being with others who share a common experience with grief is far-reaching (Brown, 2018).

The authors have found bereavement groups that combine the strengths-based framework with a psychoeducational format can greatly enhance mourners' feelings of competency in relation to managing grief. The provision of both information and emotional support serves to alleviate some of the painful symptoms associated with loss and allows participants to understand the process of grief in a context that includes not only themselves but also others. This approach helps dispel some of the myths and unrealistic expectations associated with the grieving process. In addition, the mutual sharing of common experiences creates a community from which participants can draw strength. These dynamics assist mourners in developing the internal and external resources that are necessary for the healing process to progress. Psychoeducational groups are not only effective but also economically feasible for clients who cannot afford individual counseling as well as for agencies with limited resources (Pomeroy & Garcia, 2009). Online self-help psychoeducational bereavement groups have also been found to be very useful in providing information and support (Dominick et al., 2009). The following discussion outlines a psychoeducational group design that uses the strengths-based framework of grief.

The Strengths-Based Psychoeducational Group Design

Group Goals

The goals for this group are to provide individuals with a safe and structured environment to facilitate healthy adjustment to the absence of the loved one. This is accomplished by building an understanding of the life-enhancing aspects of grief, processing the mourner's adaptation to the loss, promoting awareness about life-depleting grief reactions, and enhancing the mourner's coping skills and resources to engage in a life separate from the loved one. These goals underlie the content of the group sessions (Pomeroy & Garcia, 2009).

Time-limited psychoeducational groups based on the strengths-based framework of grief have been found to be practical and productive because of the structured discussion topics, the life-enhancing coping strategies that are encouraged between group sessions, and the trusting relationships that develop among members. Although the first two sessions focus on the participants' losses, subsequent sessions guide the participants in the strengths-based coping model outlined previously. The group meets for 6–8 weeks and is compatible with agencies that specialize in end-of-life care, such as hospice or community outpatient clinics. The facilitator of this type of group also serves as a conduit between participants and community resources (Pomeroy & Garcia, 2009).

Group Content

The content of a grief group will be somewhat dependent on the composition of the group members. For example, in a group composed of parents who have lost a child, discussions may focus on the need for communication between the surviving parents. However, regardless of the specific issues that the members bring to the group, there is certain content that is covered in all groups using the strengths-based psychoeducational approach. These topics include expected grief reactions, adjustment to the loss, navigating transitions, family concerns, using community resources, and engaging in outside activities (Pomeroy & Garcia, 2009).

A Strengths-Based Traumatic Grief Group Intervention

Group intervention can also be effective for mourners experiencing traumatic grief reactions, particularly when membership includes others whose loved ones died in a similar manner. Interventions used in these types of groups are highly specific to the population of survivors. These groups can also provide a buffer from isolation and stigmatized loss (e.g., suicide, drug use, HIV/AIDS, and COVID-19).

The authors have found that traumatic grief reactions can be more effectively addressed in a group setting after the mourner has had some individual counseling or has had time to process the trauma associated with the death. An individual assessment prior to entering a traumatic grief group is recommended and considers the degree of trauma and level of crisis, as well as the person's overall mental health status (Pomeroy & Garcia, 2009).

Assessment and Intervention in Children and Adolescents

An accurate assessment of grieving children and adolescents must include information from a variety of sources. Although the ability to obtain detailed information from a young child is limited, collaborative resources can provide important and accurate information about the loss and the problems the child may be experiencing. Relevant data can be gleaned from parents or caregivers, medical and school personnel, and other adults who have central involvement in the child's life. Although older children and adolescents may be able to provide salient information, the involvement of caregivers is still important to providing quality care.

Three primary elements in grief assessment of a child identified by Webb (2010) are the individual child's level of functioning, the factors related to the death, and the child's support system. If the youth is complaining of physical symptoms, a physician's referral is warranted prior to the beginning of therapy. For example, a young child who presents with encopresis may have a medical problem and should be thoroughly assessed by a physician before determining that it may be regression associated with loss.

Conducting an assessment with children younger than age 12 years requires an understanding of the child's developmental functioning (Ener & Ray, 2018). Most often, this involves play therapy techniques to access and observe the child's feelings and behaviors. Through various activities such as drawing pictures of family, home, or a favorite activity, the practitioner opens the door for conversation regarding the child's experiences and relationships (Landreth, 2012). Drawing on play therapy resources, practitioners may utilize a variety of approaches to elicit the child's feelings and perceptions.

Older children often possess a great deal of insight and understanding of their experience of loss. Practitioners should assess adolescents for levels of distress, anxiety, and depression; degree of loneliness; anger; and their interpretation of the loss (Balk, 2000; Webb, 2010). Teens may converse more easily when simultaneously involved in another activity such as walking, playing games, or making something with their hands.

Grief Group Interventions with Children and Adolescents

Group interventions with children and teens can be beneficial to youth who are grieving. One benefit of group counseling is that it provides a place for bereaved youth to find relief from the feeling of being different from their peers because of the loss. Group interventions may take many forms, including multifamily counseling, community- or school-based groups, youth camps, and online support groups. Important components of group intervention with children and teens include sharing the story of the loss, educating and normalizing grief responses, expressing feelings associated with grief, identifying life-enhancing coping mechanisms, addressing feelings of guilt associated with the loss, and memorializing the deceased (Garcia, 2017).

Group Interventions with Grieving Older Adults

The elderly encounter numerous losses that come with advanced age, ranging from the loss of loved ones and friends to personal losses such as being out of the workforce, changes in health status and physical abilities, and, for some, the ability to live independently. Ageism and social devaluation further complicate the grief experience for the elderly. Older adults are at high risk for complex grief (Lundorff et al., 2017). In addition, chronic complicated grief has been associated with physical and mental illness as well as suicidality (Supiano & Luptak, 2013). Older adults can benefit greatly from grief support groups, which provide needed social support and outside activities for those who are vulnerable to intense loneliness and isolation.

Grief and Persons with Special Circumstances

Although there are many commonalities among bereaved persons regardless of the type of loss they have experienced, there are also some deaths that are unique in the way they impact the mourner and the healing process. Counselors require specialized knowledge and understanding to be most effective with these types of mourners. Examples include the grief experience for persons with disabilities, immigrant populations, veterans of war, GLBT populations, mourners of perinatal loss, and victims of crime and domestic abuse. Many persons within these groups have developed a reservoir of resiliency due to their encounters with adversity and discrimination. Because their special circumstances often involve additional stigma and ostracism from society, it is especially important that practitioners help them identify life-enhancing strategies for navigating the grief process.

Practice Implications for the Professional

Working with bereaved individuals from a strength-based approach is a powerful and moving experience. It is important for practitioners to build on the strengths and resources that the client brings to bear and to differentiate expected from complex grief. The act of being emotionally present for someone who is mourning may trigger the practitioner's personal loss experiences. Although these experiences enable practitioners to relate to their clients, care must be given to ensure appropriate detachment and attunement. In addition, the work of grief counseling involves regular and intimate contact with the prevalence, probability, and impact of death—a reality that society encourages us to ignore. Awareness of how the counseling process affects the practitioner is essential to competent and ethical practice with grieving clients.

Self-awareness, quality professional social work supervision, and an ability to tolerate the expression of intense emotional distress and ambiguity are all necessary components of being a professional grief counselor (Kosminsky & Jordan, 2016). Understanding, implementing, and upholding the National Association of Social Workers Code of Ethics (2017) is essential for social workers involved with grieving individuals, groups, and families. Finally, social workers practicing in this area benefit from

using positive self-care methods, including professional and personal support when needed. Developing an expertise in grief and loss is a rewarding and worthwhile endeavor.

Helpful Resources

Dougy Center: https://www.dougy.org
Friends for Survival: https://friendsforsurvival.org
The Compassionate Friends: https://www.compassionatefriends.org

References

American Psychiatric Association. (2013). *Diagnostic and statistical manual of mental disorders* (5th ed.). https://doi.org/10.1176/appi.books.9780890425596

Balk, D. E. (2000). Adolescents, grief, and loss. In K. Doka (Ed.), *Living with grief: Children, adolescents, and loss* (pp. 35–50). Hospice Foundation of America.

Brown, N. (2018). *Psychoeducational groups: Process and practice* (4th ed.). Routledge. https://doi.org/10.4324/9781315169590

Dominick, S. A., Irvine, B., Beauchamp, N., Seeley, J. R., Nolen-Hoeksema, S., Doka, K. J., & Bonanno, G. A. (2009). An internet tool to normalize grief. *OMEGA, 60*(1), 71–87. https://doi.org/10.2190/OM.60.1.d

Ener, L., & Ray, D. C. (2018). Exploring characteristics of children presenting to counseling for grief and loss. *Journal of Child and Family Studies, 27*(3), 860–871. https://link.springer.com/article/10.1007/s10826-017-0939-6

Garcia, R. B. (2017). Using grief support groups to support bereaved students at school. In J. A. Brown & S. R. Jimerson (Eds.), *Supporting bereaved students at school* (pp. 115–129). Oxford University Press.

Kosminsky, P. S., & Jordan, J. R. (2016). *Attachment-informed grief therapy: The clinician's guide to foundations and applications*. Routledge.

Landreth, G. L. (2012). *Play therapy: The art of relationship* (3rd ed.). Routledge/Taylor & Francis.

Lundorff, M., Holmgren, H., Zachariae, R., Farver-Vestergaard, I., & O'Connor, M. (2017). Prevalence of prolonged grief disorder in adult bereavement: A systematic review and meta-analysis. *Journal of Affective Disorders, 212*, 138–149. https://doi.org/10.1016/j.jad.2017.01.030

National Association of Social Workers. (2017). *Code of ethics*. https://www.socialworkers.org/about/ethics/code-of-ethics

Pomeroy, E. C., & Garcia, R. B. (2009). *The grief assessment and intervention workbook: A strengths perspective.* Cengage.

Pomeroy, E. C., & Holleran, L. (2002). Tuesdays with fellow travelers: A psychoeducational HIV/AIDS-related bereavement group. *Journal of HIV/AIDS in Social Services, 1,* 61–77. https://doi.org/10.1300/J187v01n02_05

Rapp, C. A. (1998). *The strengths model: Case management with people suffering from severe and persistent mental illness.* Oxford University Press.

Rapp, C. A., & Goscha, R. J. (2012). *The strengths model: A recovery-oriented approach to mental health services* (3rd ed.). Oxford University Press.

Rapp, C. A., Saleebey, D., & Sullivan, W. P. (2005). The future of strengths-based social work. *Advances in Social Work, 6*(1), 79–90. https://doi.org/10.18060/81

Saleebey, D. (1996). The strengths perspective in social work practice: Extensions and cautions. *Social Work, 41*(3), 296–305. https://doi.org/10.1093/sw/41.3.296

Saleebey, D. (2013). *Strengths perspective in social work practice* (6th ed.). Pearson.

Shear, M. K., Ghesquiere, A., & Glickman, K. (2013). Bereavement and complicated grief. *Current Psychiatry Reports, 15*(11). https://doi.org/10.1007/s11920-013-0406-z

Solomon, R. M. (2019). The utilization of EMDR therapy with grief and mourning. Poster presentation, Compassion Works, April 12–13, Dallas, TX.

Supiano, K., & Luptak, M. (2013). Complicated grief in older adults: A randomized controlled trial of complicated grief group therapy. *The Gerontologist, 54*(5), 840–856. https://doi.org/10.1093/geront/gnt076

Webb, N. B. (2010). Assessment of the bereaved child. In N. B. Webb (Ed.), *Helping bereaved children: Social work practice with children and families* (3rd ed., pp. 22–50). Guilford.

Worden, J. W. (2018). *Grief counseling and grief therapy: A handbook for the mental health practitioner* (5th ed.). Springer.

World Health Organization. (2018). *ICD-11: Prolonged grief disorder.* https://icd.who.int/browse11/l-m/en#/ http://id.who.int/icd/entity/1183832314

Working with Clients Who Have Recovered Memories

Susan P. Robbins

One of the most controversial and divisive issues among mental health professionals and researchers in the past two decades has been the delayed recovery of memories of traumatic events. During the 1990s, major social work journals published a handful of articles on this topic (Benatar, 1995; Robbins, 1995; Stocks, 1998). In contrast, well-respected journals in psychology, psychiatry, and law published numerous articles and special issues dedicated to the debate about the nature, veracity, and accuracy of recovered memories, particularly memories of childhood sexual abuse (CSA). More recently, continued research in this area has focused on laboratory experiments in word memorization, cognitive processes involved in both remembering and motivated forgetting, Vietnam veterans with post-traumatic stress disorder, source monitoring, the effects of misinformation in real-world settings, and neuroimaging of cognitive processes that give rise to true and false memories, among others (Belli, 2012; McNally, 2005). In 2005, McNally held that the debate about recovered memory "is unresolved, but not irresolvable" (p. 26).

At the heart of this debate is whether it is possible to repress or dissociate all memory of CSA and later accurately recall the trauma as an adult. Two related questions pertain to the actual prevalence of abused children who completely forget their early abuse and the specific mechanisms responsible for the absence of memory. These became contentious issues because some believe that early memories of traumatic events that are inaccessible to the conscious mind can nonetheless affect one's social and psychological functioning throughout life.

During the 1980s and 1990s, thousands of people, primarily White middle-class women, were diagnosed by mental health practitioners such as social workers, psychologists, psychiatrists, and substance abuse and other counselors as having been victims of sexual abuse in their childhood, despite a total lack of recall of any such event. Others, who had continuous memories of early abuse, were told that they were victims of additional episodes of CSA, often horrific in nature, which they did not recall, such as satanic ritual abuse (SRA). Recovered memories of SRA most typically included being drugged, brainwashed, and forced to watch or participate in satanic rituals that often included murder or rape by multiple perpetrators. Seeking mental health and counseling services for a broad array of problems that included depression, eating disorders, marital difficulties, substance abuse, and bereavement (among others), clients began to allegedly "recover" memories of CSA and SRA with the help of their therapists, spontaneously, or upon reading books for sexual abuse survivors and attending self-help groups.

Clinicians who strongly advocated the use of memory recovery techniques believed that it was necessary for their clients to retrieve their previously forgotten memories of CSA in order to heal and recover from what they believed to be a forgotten but unresolved trauma. Concepts such as repression, dissociation, traumatic amnesia, and multiple personality disorder [later renamed dissociative identity disorder in the fourth edition of the *Diagnostic and Statistical Manual of Mental Disorders* (DSM-IV); American Psychiatric Association (APA), 1994] were used to explain why memory of the alleged trauma was not available to the conscious mind. In the quest to assist clients in recovering these memories, a variety of therapeutic techniques were used that included, but were not limited to, hypnosis, truth serum, guided imagery, dream interpretation, age regression, free association, journaling, psychodrama, reflexology, massage and other forms of "body work" to recover "body memories," primal scream therapy, attending survivor groups, and reading books on recovering from sexual abuse. Clients were often encouraged by their therapists and self-help groups to believe in the veracity of their newly recovered memories, define themselves as "survivors," and interpret their current-day problems and symptoms in terms of their early unresolved trauma. Although reports of recovered memories began to wane by the late 1990s, largely due to the refusal of insurance

companies to pay for diagnoses that supported its use, recovered memory therapy (RMT) continued to be practiced by those who remained convinced of its utility, despite research that found such techniques to be both questionable and harmful.

Therapy of this sort had consequences not only for the clients but also for their families. As the retrieval of recovered memories came to be viewed as the path to healing, many clients were also encouraged to confront their alleged perpetrators and break off all contact with anyone in the family who questioned the veracity of their newly recalled memories. Further complicating this issue were criminal and civil charges that clients were encouraged to file against family members as part of their recovery process. Over the years, a large number of cases involving claims of recovered memory reached the appellate courts and raised serious issues related to discovery rules, statutory limitations, and rules of scientific evidence.

Beginning in 1992, a small group of parents who claimed to have been falsely accused joined together with sympathetic professionals to form a support and advocacy organization, the False Memory Syndrome Foundation (FMSF). In addition to sponsoring scientific and medical research on memory, suggestibility, and repression, the FMSF disseminated research to the media, the public, and the legal and mental health professions. Their final newsletter was published in 2011, as a mounting body of research on memory cast serious doubt on the ability of people to totally forget and later remember traumatic events (McNally, 2005) and new claims of recovered memories dramatically declined. A growing number of people have since recanted their accusations of abuse, accusing their therapists of pressure, suggestion, and coercion.

Eventually, the existence of multiple personality disorder (MPD)/dissociative identity disorder, one of the underlying mechanisms used to explain repressed memory, came under serious scrutiny. In a well-researched expose of Sybil, one of the most famous cases of MPD that is credited with launching the multiple personality craze, Nathan (2011) documented the ways in which otherwise well-meaning but misguided therapy led to the total fabrication of Sybil's multiple personality "alters." Supporting this position, Allen Francis (2014), Chair of the DSM-IV Task Force, questioned not only the suggestive therapeutic techniques used to create such alters but also the validity of the diagnosis itself.

Although this has strongly bolstered the position that such memories are the product of unethical therapy rather than events rooted in reality, recovered memory advocates are skeptical that suggestive techniques can create false memories of CSA. To date, there are no accepted standards for determining the veracity of reports of abuse that are based solely on recovered memories, and most agree that it is impossible to determine the validity of recovered memories without external corroboration.

This supports the thorough previous review of the literature on RMT, in which Stocks (1998) examined the various techniques and therapeutic interventions that were commonly used to assist in the recovery of abuse memories as well as the impact of such therapy on client outcomes. Noting the historical ambivalence toward sexual abuse that was prevalent until the latter part of the 20th century, Stocks also provided a discussion and critique of the initial studies that led some clinicians and researchers to conclude that CSA memories were frequently repressed. In doing so, he cautioned that the reality of abuse should not be confused with skepticism about recovered memories of abuse. This echoed Loftus and Ketcham's (1994) earlier position that the disagreement about memory is not a debate about CSA.

According to Stocks (1998), the research on RMT shows that such techniques are not reliable in recovering valid memories. Although some recovered memories may be accurate, many are partly or totally confabulated, and there is no way to reliably distinguish between those that are real and those that are not. Furthermore, he found no conclusive evidence that memories of this sort have any clinical utility. In fact, the few existing outcome studies suggest that RMT is likely to lead to deterioration rather than improved functioning. Based on this, Stocks warned that the risks of RMT far outweigh the perceived benefits, discussed the necessity of informed consent for therapy that is unreliable and potentially harmful, and concluded that social workers should avoid using such techniques in their practice. Subsequent letters to the editor in response to his article reflected the professional division concerning the nature of recovered memories and the utility of RMT.

A similar split can be seen in the 1996 final report of the American Psychological Association Working Group on Investigation of Memories of Childhood Abuse. The clinicians in the group differed from the researchers on several points, including the mechanisms that are responsible for delayed recall, the frequency of the creation of false memories, and the rules of evidence for testing hypotheses about memory and the consequences of trauma. They concluded that their failure to reach consensus was due in part to "profound epistemological differences" between the researchers and the clinicians. Contentious issues related to recovered memories have not abated and continue, despite attempts at reconciliation (Belli, 2012). This basic disagreement is reflected in the field of social work as well.

There is, however, an underlying professional consensus in four basic areas, as summarized in Table 67.1 (APA, 1996; Knapp & VandeCreek, 2000, p. 336; London et al., 2005; Robbins, 2019). Despite these significant areas of consensus, it is the ongoing areas of disagreement that continue to divide professionals in the field (Belli, 2012). This division is not merely an academic debate inasmuch

TABLE 67.1 Consensus on Recovered and False Memories

Child abuse	Child abuse is harmful and prevalent.
	The degree of harm relates to the type of abuse and the relationship to the perpetrator.
	Satanic or ritual abuse is rare.
Memory and the creation of memories	Most people who were sexually abused remember all or part of what happened to them.
	Adults with continuous memories of being abused are likely to have accurate memories.
	Although it is rare, some memories of past traumas can be forgotten and later remembered.
	Memories from infancy are highly unreliable.
	False or pseudo-memories can be created.
	Magnification and minimization are better ways to conceptualize memories than the dichotomy of "true" or "false."
	It is difficult to ascertain the accuracy of memories recovered by suggestive "memory recovery" techniques.
	It is impossible to distinguish a true memory from a false one without other corroborative evidence.
Diagnosis of and psychotherapy with patients with memories of abuse	Child abuse, in and of itself, is not a diagnosis.
	Child abuse cannot be assessed from a set of current symptoms or a checklist of symptoms.
	Mental illness and mental disorders have many causes.
	Psychotherapists should ask patients about past childhood abuse if it is clinically indicated or as part of an overall psychosocial assessment that focuses on both negative and positive events in a patient's life.
	Memory recall of abuse is not necessary for effective therapy to occur.
	The focus of treatment should be on the current functioning of the patient.
	Treatments should be tailored to the individual needs of each patient.
	At times, patients may need to learn to live with ambiguity about the veracity of memory or memory fragments.
Role of psychotherapists	Psychotherapists need to respect and promote patient autonomy.
	Psychotherapists need to scrupulously maintain professional boundaries.
	Psychotherapists need to maintain therapeutic neutrality on the issues of litigation and confrontation.
	Although psychotherapists have no primary legal duty to third parties, they should not be oblivious to the impact of their actions on those third parties.

as it directly affects the theories and practice techniques that are used with clients. By the mid-1990s, most of the major professional organizations had issued warnings concerning suggestibility and false memories. One of the strongest cautionary statements came from the American Medical Association (AMA, 1994) in its position that "the AMA considers recovered memories of childhood sexual abuse to be of uncertain authenticity, which should be subject to external verification. The use of recovered memories is fraught with problems of potential misapplication" (p. 4).

Most early organizational statements on recovered memory therapy urged the use of caution, with the acknowledgment that recovered memories may or may not be true. Many of the later statements more explicitly warn against the use of memory recovery techniques as a method or focus of practice. Although these statements no longer appear on most professional websites, a good chronology of statements and positions on RMT made by professional organizations can be found on the internet at http://www.religioustolerance.org/rmt_prof.htm.

Subsequently, professional concerns focused on informed consent and, as noted by the American Academy of Psychiatry and the Law (1999), in light of the warnings given by most professional organizations, "Few would currently argue against informing patients about the fallibility of memory and the dangers involved with recovering memories of sexual abuse" (p. 2). Given the unproven clinical utility of RMT, coupled with the lack of evidence that the benefits of such therapy outweigh the risks, the issue of informed consent is critical for social workers inasmuch as this is also mandated by the National Association of Social Workers (NASW) Code of Ethics (1996a).

A specific practice statement addressing the evaluation and treatment of adults with the possibility of recovered memories of childhood sexual abuse, developed by the NASW National Council on the Practice of Clinical Social Work, was published in June 1996. In this statement, social workers are cautioned to (1) establish and maintain an appropriate therapeutic relationship with careful attention to boundary management; (2) recognize that the client may be influenced by the opinions, conjecture, or suggestions of the therapist; (3) not minimize the power and influence they have on a client's impressions and beliefs; (4) guard against engaging in self-disclosure and premature interpretations during the treatment process; (5) guard against using leading questions to recover memories; (6) be cognizant that disclosure of forgotten experience is a part of the process but not the goal of therapy; and (7) respect the client's right to self-determination (NASW, 1996b, p. 2).

Despite the fact that the use of recovered memory therapy has declined dramatically since the 1990s, the debate about memory in academic circles, dubbed by Frederick Crews (1995) as the "memory wars," has not abated. A recent bibliometric analysis of articles and citations about repressed/recovered memories published from 2001 to 2018 found that these issues are still currently being debated by both proponents and opponents in multidisciplinary fields (Dodier, 2019). Current research demonstrates continued differences in beliefs about recovered memories between therapists, lay individuals, students, and memory researchers (Brewin, 2021; Dodier et al., 2020; Ost et al., 2017; Patihis et al., 2014, 2018; Patihis & Pendegrast, 2019). Although, in general, there is more skepticism about recovered memories than in the 1990s, the belief in repression continues to be held by therapists and the general public. Not surprisingly, therapists were more likely to believe that memories can be repressed and retrieved in therapy, whereas researchers and memory experts were dubious and concerned about the dangers of memory distortion and the iatrogenic nature of RMT (Ost et al., 2017; Patihis et al., 2014, 2018).

However, due to the prevalence of RMT during the 1980s and 1990s and the sensationalized media coverage of recovered memories, social workers are still likely to encounter clients who were previously, or even recently, subjected to a variety of RMT techniques, abuse survivor groups and literature, or who spontaneously recovered abuse memories. Some clients may still believe in the veracity of these memories, whereas others may have come to question them. Still others may have fully recanted their abuse allegations upon realizing that their memories were inaccurate or iatrogenically induced in therapy. Working with such clients can prove to be a challenge for social workers because most typically receive little or no formal education regarding the nature of memory or the suggestive techniques that can create false memories.

As noted elsewhere (Robbins, 1997), it is critical that social workers adhere to NASW guidelines when working with clients who have possibly recovered memories of childhood sexual abuse. Neutrality about the veracity of such memories is critical because it is impossible to determine the accuracy of memories without external corroboration. This is especially true when RMT techniques have been used. The NASW guidelines caution that "enthusiastic belief or disbelief can and will have an effect on the treatment process" (NASW, 1996b, p. 2). Personal biases may result in incorrect diagnosis and inadequate or inappropriate treatment.

Social workers should always follow accepted professional standards when diagnosing and treating clients. Information about abuse and other negative childhood experiences should be gathered in the course of obtaining a complete psychosocial history, but this should only be one part of a holistic assessment that includes an evaluation of the client's "total clinical picture including symptoms and level of functioning" (NASW, 1996b, p. 2).

It is also important to remember that CSA is an event in a person's life; it is not a diagnosis and should not be treated as such. In addition, CSA should not be inferred from any specific symptoms or cluster of symptoms (APA Working Group, 1996). Social workers should also be cognizant of the fact that most victims of CSA either completely or partially remember their abuse. Although delayed recall is possible, the frequency of abuse memories that are forgotten and later recalled is not known (Belli, 2012; Knapp & VandeCreek, 2000).

Treatment should always be based on a complete assessment, informed by the scientific literature, designed to meet the individual client's needs, and the emphasis should be on the client's current functioning (Knapp & VandeCreek, 2000). According to NASW (1996b), the social worker's responsibility is to "maintain the focus of treatment on symptom reduction or elimination and to enhance the ability of the client to function appropriately and comfortably in his or her daily life" (p. 2).

In accordance with this, archeological reconstruction of one's past and placing a focus on working through painful emotions should not be the primary goal of treatment. If a client enters treatment with the desire to discuss or examine recovered memories, NASW (1996b) recommends that social workers "explore the meaning and implication of the memory for the client, rather than focusing solely on the content or veracity of the report" (p. 2). In addition, it is the responsibility of the social worker to inform the client that their memory may be "an accurate memory of an actual event, an altered or distorted memory of an actual event, or the recounting of an event that did not happen" (p. 2).

Clients who have recanted memories of abuse may need assistance in understanding the dynamics that led them to believe in recovered memories of events that never happened. A psychoeducational approach can assist them in understanding the nature of memory, memory reconstruction, and the specific techniques that can lead to false memories. They may also need help in resolving issues of guilt and self-blame and in re-establishing relationships within their families. This is particularly true if their abuse memories resulted in accusations, angry confrontation, legal action, or alienation among family members.

Social workers should also be cognizant of legal issues related to recovered memories and be fully informed about issues related to risk management. Although the social worker's primary responsibility is to the client, the social worker should also be concerned about the effect of false allegations on the accused, many of whom are family members. The guidelines developed by NASW (1996b) discuss this in detail, with specific recommendations related to record keeping, informed consent, client self-determination, and requisite knowledge of state and federal laws.

Finally, it is incumbent on social workers to have adequate training and maintain current skills and knowledge in the areas of trauma and memory if they are working with clients who have histories of abuse or recovered memories of abuse. Scientific research in this area is constantly emerging, and social workers must be able to critically assess new findings and be open to incorporating new evidence-based knowledge into practice.

Helpful Resources

False Memory Syndrome Foundation: http://www.fmsonline.org

Madeline Kearns. (2018). "False memories" are more common than you think. *National Review*: https://www.nationalreview.com/2018/09/cognitive-science-false-memories-more-common-than-you-think

Science Direct. *False memory syndrome*: https://www.sciencedirect.com/topics/neuroscience/false-memory-syndrome

Sybil: A brilliant hysteric? (2014). *The New York Times*: https://www.nytimes.com/video/us/100000003250377/sybil-a-brilliant-hysteric.html

References

American Academy of Psychiatry and the Law. (1999, April). Recovered memories of sexual abuse: Informed consent. *American Academy of Psychiatry and the Law Newsletter, 24* (2), 5–6.

American Medical Association. (1994, July 14). *Report of the Council on Scientific Affairs* (CSA Report 5-A-94).

American Psychiatric Association. (1994). *Diagnostic and statistical manual of mental disorders* (4th ed.).

American Psychological Association Working Group on Investigation of Memories of Childhood Abuse. (1996). *Final report.*

Belli, R. F. F. (Ed.). (2012). *True and false recovered memories: Toward a reconciliation of the debate* (Nebraska Symposium on Motivation). Springer.

Benatar, M. (1995). Running away from sexual abuse: Denial revisited. *Families in Society, 76*(5), 315–320. https://doi.org/10.1177/104438949507600505

Brewin, C. R. (2021). Tilting at windmills: Why attacks on repression are misguided. *Perspectives on Psychological Science, 16*(2), 443–453. https://doi.org/10.1177/1745691620927674

Crews, F. (1995). *The memory wars: Freud's legacy in dispute.* New York Review of Books.

Dodier, O. (2019). A bibliometric analysis of the recovered memory controversy in the 21st century. *Applied Cognitive Psychology, 33*(4), 571–584. https://doi.org/10.1002/acp.3498

Dodier, O., Gilet, A., & Colombel, F. (2020, July 24). What do people really think of when they claim to believe in repressed memory? Methodological middle ground and applied issues. https://doi.org/10.31234/osf.io/4qrny

Francis, A. (2014, January 28). Sex and satanic abuse: A fad revisited. *Huffington Post Science.* https://www.huffpost.com/entry/sex-and-satanic-abuse-a-f_b_4680605

Knapp, S., & VandeCreek, L. (2000). Recovered memories of childhood abuse: Is there an underlying professional consensus? *Professional Psychology: Research and Practice, 31*(4), 365–371. https://doi.org/10.1037/0735-7028.31.4.365

Loftus, E. F., & Ketcham, K. K. (1994). *The myth of repressed memory: False memories and accusations of sexual abuse.* St. Martin's Press.

London, K., Bruck, M., Ceci, S. J., & Shuman, D. W. (2005). Disclosure of child sexual abuse: What does the research tell us about the ways that children tell? *Psychology, Public Policy, and Law, 11*(1), 194–226. https://doi.org/10.1037/1076-8971.11.1.194

McNally, R. J. (2005). *Remembering trauma.* Belknap.

Nathan, D. (2011). *Sybil exposed: The extraordinary story behind the famous multiple personality case.* Free Press.

National Association of Social Workers. (1996a). National Association of Social Workers Code of Ethics. *NASW News, 41* (10), Insert 1–4.

National Association of Social Workers. (1996b). *Practice statement on the evaluation and treatment of adults with the possibility of recovered memories of childhood sexual abuse.* National Association of Social Workers Office of Policy and Practice.

Ost, J., Easton, S., Hope, L., French, C. C., & Wright, D. B. (2017). Latent variables underlying the memory beliefs of chartered clinical psychologists, hypnotherapists and undergraduate students. *Memory, 25*(1), 57–68. https://doi.org/10.1080/09658211.2015.1125927

Patihis, L., Ho, L. Y., Tingen, I. W., Lilienfeld, S. O., & Loftus, E. F. (2014). Are the "memory wars" over? A scientist–practitioner gap in beliefs about repressed memory. *Psychological Science, 25*(7), 519–530. https://doi.org/10.1177/0956797613510718

Patihis, L., Lavina, L., Ho, Y., Loftus, E., & Herrera, M. E. (2018). Memory experts' beliefs about repressed memory. *Memory.* https://doi.org/10.1080/09658211.2018.1532521

Patihis, L., & Pendegrast, M. H. (2019). Reports of recovered memories of abuse in therapy in a large age-representative U.S. national sample: Therapy type and decade comparisons. *Clinical Psychological Science, 7*(1), 3–21. doi:10.1177/2167702618773315

Robbins, S. P. (1995). Wading through the muddy waters of recovered memory. *Families in Society, 76,*(8), 478–489. https://doi.org/10.1177/104438949507600804

Robbins, S. P. (1997). Cults (update). In *Encyclopedia of social work* (19th ed. on CD ROM). National Association of Social Workers Press.

Robbins, S. P. (2019). Child sex abuse and recovered memories of abuse: Looking back, looking ahead. *Families in Society, 100*(4), 367–380. https://doi.org/10.1177/1044389419879590

Stocks, J. T. (1998). Recovered memory therapy: A dubious practice technique. *Social Work, 43*(5), 423–436. https://doi.org/10.1093/sw/43.5.423

PART VII

Guidelines for Specific Interventions

Individual Interventions

Cognitive–Behavioral Therapy
Techniques for Youth and Adults

Skyler Milligan LeCroy

An Overview of Cognitive–Behavioral Therapy Techniques

Cognitive–behavioral therapy (CBT) offers many techniques and interventions that are valuable in treating a variety of mental health issues. Techniques can be selected to best fit the individual, and often multiple tools are utilized in the treatment. One major benefit of CBT is the ability for the therapist to better customize their treatment plan to each individual seeking therapy. The goal with each intervention is to help clients identify their maladaptive thinking and work to change the behaviors associated with their thinking. Having the individual increase their awareness of their emotional state and the triggers for their maladaptive behavior is a key mechanism through which CBT works. As a result, CBT requires an effort on behalf of the client to be motivated for change and enact the chosen CBT techniques in everyday life. What separates CBT from other talk therapies is the focus on the present, skill building, and the addition of take-home assignments to further progress. CBT is a collaborative effort

between therapist and client, and the best results will be found with motivated individuals willing to commit their time to implementing the chosen CBT techniques.

CBT is a very common approach, and many people may already be familiar with some CBT techniques. CBT is more than just a toolbox of techniques to utilize with clients; rather, it is an entire framework for approaching cognitive–behavioral issues. Over time, individuals can build and reinforce maladaptive and negative behaviors, and some of these behaviors, as they are reinforced in the environment, overwhelm the individual's personality, contributing to clinical disorders. Similarly, in Axis I disorders, we can often see self-reinforcing negative ideas and behaviors such as in the case of depression, in which the feeling of "I'm no good" may evolve to problems with speaking and confidence, such as "I'm no good, no one wants to hear my ideas." CBT targets the negative perceptions and behaviors so patients can view them from a positive adaptive mindset. Often, patients are interpreting negative perceptions from everyday normal activities, and it is the therapist's goal in CBT to help them realize that they are incorrectly analyzing situations and teach them how to reframe and substitute positive or coping thoughts with these activities.

When to Use Cognitive–Behavioral Therapy?

Cognitive–behavioral therapy is an excellent candidate for initial treatment sessions, especially among individuals or clients looking to try a simple therapy before exploring medications. CBT has been shown to be effective for a wide variety of conditions (David et al., 2018; Hofmann et al., 2012) but is generally considered most effective for patients with less severe mental illness. However, CBT is increasingly being used in the treatment of severe mental disorders (Thase et al., 2014; Wright et al., 2009). Table 68.1 presents a common list of uses for CBT; however, this therapy is highly adaptable to many client circumstances and is even used with clients with no mental illness, such as in the case of life coaching. CBT may not be appropriate or effective for clients with complex mental health issues and learning disabilities. CBT is often the treatment of choice for short-term interventions or when the number of sessions is limited; however,

TABLE 68.1 Common applications for CBT

Depression	Anxiety
Borderline personality disorder	Eating disorders
Panic disorder	Phobias
Post-traumatic stress disorder	Psychosis
Schizophrenia	Insomnia/sleep problems
Substance abuse	Coping with long-term health conditions

CBT, cognitive–behavioral therapy.

the importance of clients continuing to practice their CBT skills after therapy sessions have concluded must be emphasized.

What Are the Key Factors for Successful Cognitive–Behavioral Therapy Treatment?

Cognitive–behavioral therapy is a highly collaborative treatment between therapist and client. Often, as with any therapy, the most critical success factor is a strong positive relationship between therapist and client. Having frequent check-ins and communication to build and maintain the therapist–client relationship is essential. Having a clear understanding of the client's psychological makeup and needs will help you better tailor the CBT sessions and tools to be most effective.

It is important to consider if your client is a good fit for CBT treatment by examining if they meet success factors for CBT. CBT requires learning and frequent reflection, so a key factor in successful CBT treatment is that the client must be self-motivated and able to work independently after sessions (Renaud et al., 2014). Patients need to be able to effectively set and maintain goals for their treatment along with maintaining the time commitment to CBT treatment "homework." Consistency and discipline in applying the CBT tools and homework are often the difference in creating successful outcomes.

CBT can have limited success for people with vague or unclear feelings of unhappiness. Although CBT can be an effective treatment for management of long-term health issues such as irritable bowel syndrome or chronic fatigue syndrome, it is important to note these improvements are generally related to better coping mechanisms rather than curing physical symptoms. In addition, for clients with complex mental issues or long-standing emotional traumas, CBT can often be a good first step in providing relief, but additional therapy may be needed to target more intractable difficulties.

An Introduction to Leading Cognitive–Behavioral Therapy Sessions

Developing and growing a strong, trusting interpersonal relationship between therapist and client should always be the priority in CBT sessions. Being an effective CBT therapist relies on being able to have clear and honest discussions about the client's feeling, progress, and challenges. CBT is a highly reflective therapy, so creating a comfortable environment for sharing and self-evaluation of issues is a good first step in understanding your client and the best CBT tools and techniques to apply. CBT should always be personalized to the client, and spending ample time reflecting on progress and what worked or did not work can help direct the therapist on how to shape future sessions. Creating a high degree of client involvement and collaboration will help clients gain agency in their personal development. However, it is important to ensure you have a clear agenda and ideas for the session if the client cannot or does not feel like contributing in a given session. Generally, a CBT session will last approximately 60 minutes, with the initial 15 minutes or more spent on check-in and review of homework or activities since last session. On average, people who receive CBT will do so for an average of 16 sessions (National Association of Cognitive Behavioral Therapists, 2016). As a therapist, being flexible with regard to what the client wants to spend their time on is valuable because the specific situations and examples clients are facing are critical to integrate into your sessions. The therapist role is to better

help the client understand concerns rather than advise clients on the choices to make.

Basic Structure of a Cognitive–Behavioral Therapy Session

The following is the basic structure of CBT sessions (Beck, 2007; Cully & Teten, 2008):

1. Mood check: How are you doing?
2. Updates on anything that has happened since last session (the bridge)
3. Follow up on the action plan or homework activities
4. Collaboratively setting the agenda
5. Setting up out-of-session work for experiments and action plans for next week
6. Conclude the session: What today is going to be most helpful next week? Feedback: What can we do better?

CBT sessions are educational and generally work through a sequence of lessons or learning over time, rather than using a static talk therapy structure. Initial sessions are typically focused on thoughts and mood. Often, clients are assigned a workbook or reading to assist them in applying CBT principles to their life (Greenberger & Padesky, 2015; Knaus & Carlson, 2014). Therapists should provide guidance and exercises to help the client understand how one's perceptions and thoughts influence one's mood. The Socratic method is a good framework to use with clients because as a CBT therapist you need to create a collaborative reflective dialogue to help them think through challenges and issues. The goal of these sessions is to help the client reflect on their potential thinking errors and dysfunctional thoughts. Some examples of this type of thinking are overgeneralizing, excessive responsibility, selective abstraction, and dichotomous thinking (Ackerman, 2020). Once clients have learned to self-reflect and understand how their thoughts and moods are connected, the therapist can start providing strategies and techniques for generating positive thoughts and decreasing unhealthy negative thinking. Learning about thoughts and thinking processes can be the focus of therapy sessions for the first several sessions (1–5). During this period, it is valuable to have clients start applying self-reflection tools such as journaling, thought logs, or mindfulness mediation.

Once the therapist believes that the client has established a better understanding of their thinking processes and developed a mindset for self-reflection, the therapist should introduce the concept of how activities and actions affect one's mood. The discussion should be reflective and examine how the participant can better increase control over their life and have more freedom surrounding choices. For example, a discussion may center around how the client's depression is limiting their participation in positive activities, which in turn could be increasing their depressive symptoms. In collaboration with the therapist, clients will work to set goals and activities that will improve the patient's mood or experience, and then the client will set out to test these theories outside of therapy sessions. Helping patients identify positive and negative activities and associated obstacles is a key goal. Some common tools that are applied during this stage of therapy are behavioral activation (scheduling of pleasant activities), the "pie" technique (for goal setting), and exposure (Beck, 2011). CBT therapists need to be aware of how clients can use cognitive distortions in their daily thinking. The following are some of the most common distortions (Ackerman, 2020):

> Filtering—Focusing on the negative, ignoring the positive
> Catastrophizing—Expecting the worst-case scenario, minimizing the positive
> Polarized thinking—All-or-nothing thinking, ignoring complexity

Heaven's reward fallacy—Expecting self-sacrifice to be rewarded
Control fallacies—Assumes only others to blame or assumes only self to blame
Always being right—Being wrong is unacceptable, being right supersedes everything
Fallacy of fairness—Assumes life should be fair
Personalization—Always assuming self-responsible
Overgeneralization—Assumes a rule from one experience
Jumping to conclusions—Makes assumptions based on little evidence
Emotional reasoning—"If I feel it, it must be true."
Blaming—Assumes everyone else at fault
Fallacy of change—Expects other to change
Global labeling—Extreme generalization
"Shoulds"—Holds tight to personal rules or behavior, judges self and other if rules broken

Later sessions often focus on relationships and support systems, helping the patient to better understand how their relationships are affecting their moods and behaviors. Therapists will often focus on strategies such as behavioral rehearsal to give patients practice engaging and developing a healthy relationship. The focus might be on learning skills such as how to start a conversation or how to ask someone to lunch. Reflecting on social supports and the client's ability to succeed in difficult situations should be a focus here as well, but it is also important to examine how our social relationships can be a trigger for dysfunctional thinking or behaviors. Therapists should focus activities and homework around how to better develop assertive communication skills along with how to properly maintain and develop healthy relationships.

Working progressively with the client's internal thoughts and dialogue and then expanding to activities, and finally moving into relationships, is a powerful strategy that allows the therapist to build on the strengths and challenges the client is facing as they move toward situations that they have less control over (most control: thoughts; least control: relationships). With all cognitive therapy approaches, this progression should be highly personalized because some clients will inevitably find certain areas in which it is more challenging to make progress. Therapists should ensure that clients have a strong ability to reflect on their thoughts and moods before moving on to more complex topics. Ensuring that the core concept of how our thoughts influence behaviors will assist the client in learning new ways to behave.

What Tools and Techniques Can Be Used in Cognitive–Behavioral Therapy Sessions?

Cognitive–behavioral therapy is a methodology that encompasses a wide variety of approaches. Thus, therapists must be mindful in selecting the appropriate tools and techniques to best fit the needs of their clients. Initial sessions should build a strong rapport and focus on understanding the nature of the client's problems; this will allow the therapist to select the best tools tailored for each client and session. If a participant is having trouble with a specific technique, it is worth examining why and if there is a better tool to accomplish the same goal.

Homework is an essential component of a successful CBT approach. Selecting the correct practices, reading, or writing assignments helps reinforce therapy ideas and makes the client an active participant in their treatment. In addition, building these habits is critical to helping the client continue to manage their symptoms after therapy ends.

Descriptions of Common Cognitive Therapy Techniques and Tools

Journaling

- A simple and effective way to introduce clients to the core idea of self-reflection.
- Easy to implement—most people have a basic understanding of journaling.
- Encourage the patient to reflect on each day; have them write about whatever they want or provide them prompts if they need support.
- Recording and reflecting can help patients better direct session agendas and goals.
- Used to gather information about thoughts and feelings and observe how thoughts can influence feelings and behaviors.
- Present the idea of a mood thermometer, tracking and recording how they are feeling every day.
- Effective homework activity.

Mindfulness Mediation

- Helps people disengage from obsessive or negative thoughts and connect to the present moment.
- Many available training and self-help resources for practicing mindfulness.
- Have the client try progressive muscle relaxation, mediation, and deep breathing to determine what works best.
- Helps people learn how to respond to distressing situations in new ways and think more rationally.
- Can be used as an active response to stress (e.g., deep breathing for anxiety) and as a reflection and training tool.
- Effective homework activity.

The SOLVED Process

- Provide people with a memorable problem-solving tool to address issues as they face them.

- Can be a great tool in session to address challenges; be sure to follow up to determine if the plan was successful.
- Encourages patients to think before they act.
- S—*S*elect a problem that the client wants to solve.
- O—*O*pen your mind to all solutions—brainstorm all the options with your client.
- L—*L*ist the potential advantages and disadvantages of each potential solution.
- V—*V*erify the best solution—decide which choices are practical or desirable.
- E—*E*nact the plan.
- D—*D*ecide if the plan worked (Cully & Teten, 2008).

Successive Approximation

- Help people tackle overwhelming goals/tasks by breaking them down into smaller steps.
- Use smaller tasks to practice skills and move toward accomplishing the larger goal.
- Can be used as a take-home activity within session follow-up and support.

Behavioral Rehearsal or Role Play

- Role play can be useful for exploring and helping the patient train for various situations, activities, and relationships.
- Best used in session to help the patient get clarity or understanding on a specific topic.
- Powerful as a skill-building tool in a comfortable environment, especially for clients who have difficulty in social situations.
- Helps uncover automatic thoughts and processes.
- Gives patients an opportunity to test out new ways to respond to situations.

Exposure/Desensitization

- Have patients approach their fears and anxiety in a controlled way to instill understanding that the sensations are not dangerous.
- Requires a high level of trust to have patient agree to expose themselves to their fear or anxiety triggers.

- Can be highly effective for phobias, anxiety, and fear reduction.
- Exposure techniques are best utilized as part of a therapeutic intervention with a therapist who is well trained in their use.
- Situation exposure hierarchies aim to have patients rate their fear or distress as the therapist goes through an increasingly challenging list of situations.
- Flooding technique works by starting with the most difficult scenarios to help show that even in the worst situations the patient is okay. Flooding can elicit strong responses, so caution is advised, and it is best used in a therapeutic intervention setting.
- Systemic desensitization combines relaxation techniques with exposure to feared object or situations to create reassociations to relaxation rather than negative feelings.
- Exposure can also be used as a home assignment or experiment—for example, having a person with agoraphobia go jogging outside to test their fear and see that they are okay.

Cognitive Restructuring

- Help clients identify negative thinking patterns such as catastrophizing, overgeneralizing, all-or-nothing thinking, labeling, mind reading, and negative filtering.
- Worksheets and take-home assignment can pair well with journaling.
- Five "thought challenges" (from the National Health Service, Fife Department of Psychology, 2013):
  1. What are the chances . . .?
  2. What is the worst thing . . .?
  3. Am I right to think that . . .?
  4. Five years from now will it really matter?
  5. What is this worth?

Activity Scheduling

- Help patients plan and engage in behaviors they would normally avoid.
- Identify and encourage rewarding low-frequency behaviors, assisting the client to

find time to increase the frequency of these activities.

- Highly effective for depression to re-introduce positive behaviors into the routing.
- Effective to plan in session and follow up in the next session to ensure scheduled activities were accomplished.

Functional Assessment Antecedents, Behaviors, Consequences

- Helpful to establish patterns of behavior for discussion.
- Focus on analyzing the antecedents, behaviors, and consequences of a situation.
- Useful framework for session check-ins when client is describing a situation they think went wrong.

Conclusion

Cognitive–behavioral therapy is a broad technique that every social worker should be familiar with. It provides an adaptive tool chest that can be effectively used to treat many conditions. There is no "right" way to conduct a CBT session; rather, therapists should use a clearly defined structure that works for their process and allows them to personalize the therapy program to the client's specific challenges and needs.

Case Example
Client Description

Ray is a 55-year-old architect who has lost confidence in his abilities to design and execute drawing plans. He was also diagnosed with a sleep disorder and has had difficulties maintaining consistent sleep. Ray says that his work is the only thing "that gives me purpose in life" and is worried about not being able to continue to work. He states that he "feels like a failure" and "is terrible at what he does," and feels like this is the end of his career. Ray says that he is usually a very active person, but he has lost interest in his outside activities, is lacking in overall energy, and feels down a lot of the time.

Case Conceptualization

Ray is experiencing depression that is related to his work performance and suffering from a sleep disorder. He is unsure how to get his life back in order, and he clearly has negative thoughts that are impacting his quality of life. Therapy will aid his adjustment by targeting dysfunctional and irrational thoughts about being a "failure" and his black-and-white thinking. Treatment will also focus on helping him obtain a sense of achievement from his work. CBT will also be used to help him develop a routine, relaxation techniques, and techniques to calm his mind to assist him in obtaining better sleep.

Helpful Resources

Association for Behavioral and Cognitive Therapies: http://www.abct.org/Home

National Association of Cognitive–Behavioral Therapists: https://www.nacbt.org

References

Ackerman, C. E. (2020). *25 CBT techniques and worksheets for cognitive–behavioral therapy*. Retrieved May 13, 2020, from https://positivepsychology.com/cbt-cognitive-behavioral-therapy-techniques-worksheets/

Beck, J. S. (2007). *Setting the agenda in session* [Blog post]. Retrieved March 8, 2007, from https://beckinstitute.org/setting-the-agenda-in-session-judith-s-beck-writes-in/

Beck, J. S. (2011). *Cognitive behavior therapy: Basics and beyond*. Guilford.

Cully, J. A., & Teten, A. L. (2008). *A therapist's guide to brief cognitive behavioral therapy*. Department of Veterans Affairs, South Central Mental Illness Research, Education and Clinical Center.

David, D., Cristea, I., & Hofmann, S. G. (2018). Why cognitive behavioral therapy is the current gold standard of psychotherapy. *Frontiers in Psychiatry, 9*, 4. https://doi.org/10.3389/fpsyt.2018.00004

Greenberger, D., & Padesky, D. A. (2015). *Mind over mood: Change how you feel by changing the way you think* (2nd ed.). Guildford.

Hofmann, S. G., Asnaani, A., Vonk, I. J., Sawyer, A. T., & Fang, A. (2012). The efficacy of cognitive behavioral therapy: A review of meta-analyses. *Cognitive Therapy and Research, 36,* 427–440. https://doi.org/10.1007/s10608-012-9476-1

Knaus, W. J., & Carlson, J. (2014). *The cognitive behavioral workbook for anxiety: A step-by-step program.* New Harbinger.

National Association of Cognitive–Behavioral Therapists. (2016). *What is cognitive–behavioral therapy (CBT)?* Retrieved May 13, 2020, from https://www.nacbt.org/whatiscbt-htm

National Health Service, Fife Department of Psychology. (2013). *Negative thinking: CBT tools.* Retrieved May 8, 2020, from https://www.moodcafe.co.uk/media/19118/Negative%20Thinking.pdf

Renaud, J., Russell, J. J., & Myhr, G. (2014). Predicting who benefits most from cognitive-behavioral therapy for anxiety and depression. *Journal of Clinical Psychology, 70*(10), 924–932.

Thase, M. E., Kingdon, D., & Turkington, D. (2014). The promise of cognitive behavior therapy for treatment of severe mental disorders: A review of developments. *World Psychiatry, 13,* 244–250. doi:10.1002/wps.20149

Wright, J. H., Turkington, D., Kingdon, D. G., & Basco, M. R. (2009). *Cognitive behavioral therapy for severe mental illness.* American Psychiatric Publishing.

Dialectical Behavior Therapy

Andre Ivanoff, Laura Miller, and Claire A. Cunningham

History

Cited by *Time* magazine (2017) as one of the top 100 scientific discoveries of recent decades, dialectical behavior therapy (DBT) was developed by Marsha Linehan and colleagues at the University of Washington between 1981 and 1990. Originally designed to treat the problems of chronically suicidal women, DBT was, in fact, the first treatment demonstrated as empirically effective at treating characteristics of borderline personality disorder (BPD). DBT was also the first cognitive–behavioral treatment model to incorporate mindfulness.

What does DBT add to standard cognitive–behavioral therapy? There are nine elements distinguishing DBT that improve upon standard cognitive–behavioral therapy:

1. A model for understanding suicidal behavior
2. A synthesis of acceptance and change
3. Principle based integration of evidence-based treatments
4. A focus on in-session behaviors
5. "Stages" of treatment targeting by severity and threat
6. The Linehan Risk Assessment and Management Protocol—a suicide risk and assessment protocol
7. Skills based on evidence-based treatments and mindfulness skills
8. Definition of "team" as part of therapy
9. Therapist self-disclosure

Dialectical and Biosocial Foundations of Treatment

The practice of DBT is guided by three overarching theories: the biosocial model, dialectics, and behavior therapy—also referred to as behaviorism. Each theory informs and influences all aspects of the intervention. The goal of DBT is to assist the client in creating a "life worth living." It is a principle-based, rather than protocol-driven, treatment guided by these theories. The "art" and skill in administering DBT are knowing when and in what measure to apply these various principles. Strong knowledge of the theoretical foundations is required to apply the treatment principles effectively.

The Biosocial Model

The biosocial model (Linehan, 1993a) explains how pervasive emotion dysregulation is both developed and maintained over time.

Emotion dysregulation arises from a transactional relationship between biologically based vulnerability or emotional dysfunction and an invalidating environment. Biological dysfunction may cause a heightened sensitivity to emotions, an intense reactivity to emotions, and a slower return to an emotional baseline. Emotion dysregulation is further escalated by a social environment that invalidates the individual's experience and often punishes expression of private emotional experience. For example, expressed emotions may be completely ignored, or the environment may respond in a way that communicates that the emotion is inaccurate. Invalidating environments may also intermittently reinforce emotional expression by only responding to extreme arousal and ignoring other emotional expression. Invalidating environments do not model appropriate emotional expressions nor teach individuals how to regulate their emotions effectively. This transaction between the biological vulnerability and an invalidating environment leads to pervasive emotion dysregulation. If an individual cannot trust their own emotional experience, they do not learn to understand, label, tolerate, or regulate emotions. Furthermore, the transactional nature of the theory suggests that each factor affects the others, such that higher dysregulation leads to a higher likelihood of environmental invalidation, leading to even higher emotional reactivity.

Dialectics

Dialectics is "the art of investigating or discussing the truth of opinions" and usually refers to opposing tensions that, when considered together, create a new perspective and synthesis greater than the sum of the two (Linehan & Schmidt, 1995, p. 554). DBT evolved from an inherently necessary dialectical dilemma—that of acceptance and change (Linehan & Schmidt, 1995). In DBT, this dialectic promotes the balance of acceptance and change, and it is a response to the often extreme and polarized behavior patterns that arise in treatment with individuals suffering from extreme emotion dysregulation. Dialectics are used to help the therapist navigate polarization within the client–therapist relationship; the therapist and the client can search for the kernel of truth in both poles and together move toward synthesis.

Behavior Therapy and Theories of Behavior

Behavior therapy and theories of behavior drive DBT. Behavior is anything an individual does—thoughts, emotions, and actions; any and all are targets for change. Behavior therapy requires a specific definition of behaviors. Assessment of behavior includes specifying what the behavior actually looks like—identifying intensity, frequency, antecedents, and consequences. This is also referred to as the *operational definition* of the behavior. These specifics inform how a problem is defined and also guide treatment decisions.

Interventions used in DBT focus on increasing the frequency of adaptive behaviors and decreasing the frequency of maladaptive behaviors. These interventions assume that all behaviors can be conceptualized according to the principles of operant conditioning (i.e., learning through rewards and punishment) and modeling. Behavior change occurs by identifying the factors that contribute to the development and maintenance of the behavior and then changing the consequences of the behavior. Behavior therapy recognizes that all behavior is caused and serves a function, and therefore makes sense in context. It is also understood that problem behaviors may persist due to skills deficits, problematic environmental contingencies, deficiencies in emotional processing, and cognitive factors. DBT interventions that address these factors include skills training, contingency management, exposure, and cognitive restructuring.

Treatment Overview: Structure and Modes of Treatment

Comprehensive Dialectical Behavior Therapy

Comprehensive DBT is delivered through four primary modes: individual therapy, skills training, "phone coaching" (including other generalization strategies; Rizvi & Roman, 2019), and consultation team (Linehan, 1993a). DBT is a modularized program of treatment (Lungu & Linehan, 2017) rather than a single intervention delivered by one practitioner in isolation. There are five functions that must be met to qualify DBT as comprehensive treatment: (1) motivating clients, (2) increasing client capabilities (i.e., teaching skills, (3) generalizing these skills to the client's natural environment and improving client's motivation, (4) maintaining and enhancing therapist capabilities and motivation, and (5) structuring the environment (Linehan et al., 2001). These functions are carried out by the four modes of treatment.

Structural Strategies

Within DBT, structural strategies are used to guide the individual psychotherapy, informing how both treatment as a whole and each individual session begin and end.

The first four individual sessions are structured so that the therapist and client can collaboratively decide to work together and then are subsequently used to build commitment to DBT. These sessions are referred to as pretreatment (Linehan, 2015a).

As individual sessions continue, therapists must attend to the beginning and ending of each session and address behaviors according to the DBT target hierarchy (Linehan, 1993a). Suicidal and life-threatening behaviors are at the top of the target hierarchy and are always addressed first. It is essential within each session to target decreasing suicidal behaviors before any other behaviors are targeted. The individual psychotherapy hierarchy is further discussed later in this chapter.

When ending sessions, therapists should be aware that therapy frequently brings up negative emotions for the clients. The therapist should strive to return the clients to their environments close to, if not at, their emotional baseline. Here, therapists may use structural strategies such as allowing sufficient ending time, summarizing the session, and soothing and "cheerleading" the client (Linehan, 1993a). Structural strategies should also be considered during the termination process. Termination should be introduced at the first session, particularly if there are known limits to program length. Tapering session frequency rather than stopping abruptly is also useful for many clients. Ultimately, termination is done knowing that a DBT goal is to enable clients to live life skillfully, without relying on therapists (Linehan, 1993a).

Modes of Treatment

Individual Psychotherapy

In individual psychotherapy in DBT, each client has a primary therapist with whom they generally meet once per week. Session times range from 45 to 120 minutes, and session length should be matched to the tasks at hand. For example, prolonged exposure sessions may require 90–120 minutes (Linehan, 1993a). Individual therapy sessions are conducted to help the patient inhibit maladaptive behaviors and replace them with adaptive, skillful responses. Individual therapists intervene with both personal and environmental factors that prevent maladaptive behaviors from occurring, and they continuously elicit and reinforce adaptive behaviors.

Skills Training

"Skills" in DBT are the client's cognitive, emotional, and behavioral responses to situations or events. Individuals who have not learned, for whatever reason, to use specific skills to effectively respond to situations arising in their everyday lives may respond with maladaptive behaviors, worsening situations (Linehan, 1993a). The overarching aim of DBT is to replace ineffective behaviors with skillful responses. Three procedures are necessary in skills training: skills acquisition (instructions and modeling), skill strengthening (behavioral rehearsal and practice), and skill generalization (extension of skills into the natural environment through homework assignments).

DBT teaches skills in four modules: mindfulness, emotion regulation, interpersonal effectiveness, and distress tolerance. *Mindfulness skills* help individuals increase attentional control and develop a nonjudgmental awareness and more positive understanding of themselves. *Emotion regulation skills* help individuals understand emotions and their functions, increase positive emotions, manage and decrease vulnerability to negative emotions, as well as accept negative emotional experiences as they arise. *Interpersonal effectiveness skills* help individuals improve relationships by teaching a balance of communication that is both assertive and maintains self-respect. *Distress tolerance skills* help individuals manage highly distressing or crisis situations without acting impulsively to make the situation worse. Radical acceptance of reality is also taught as part of distress tolerance. Recently, there has been more research on skills-only interventions, with good success for clients who do not need comprehensive DBT (McMain et al., 2017).

In comprehensive DBT, skills training is generally conducted over 6 months to 1 year in groups or "classes" of approximately 6–12 members with a leader and co-leader. First published with the original treatment manual (Linehan, 1993b), a long-awaited two-volume skills training manual update was recently published (Linehan, 2015a, 2015b). Now handouts and worksheets may be duplicated for client use through a cooperative agreement between Linehan and Guilford Press.

Phone Coaching and Other Generalization Modes

Generalizing skills to the client's natural environment capabilities is a critical component in all behavior therapies. Learning and practicing new skills only once a week in a skills group is insufficient to build these skills into the client's behavioral repertoire. DBT places explicit emphasis on helping clients transfer the skills learned in skills groups to their daily lives. Linehan (1993a) describes that generalization can occur through recording sessions for client review, in vivo behavior rehearsal, phone or text coaching, and structuring the environment to promote skill use.

Phone coaching is the term often most associated with generalization approaches. DBT clients are encouraged to call their individual therapists and ask for help applying skills before a crisis occurs. In addition, phone coaching offers the opportunity to repair any relationship ruptures between sessions (Linehan, 1993a). Phone coaching is a brief intervention to assist in the moment; it is time-limited and goal-oriented, not a remote therapy session. Most clients require orientation to the purpose of phone coaching and direct feedback and practice in how best to use it.

Since DBT was developed, there has been substantial development in technology and communication methods. Therapists and clients may choose to contact over phone, email, text messaging, social media, or mobile apps. Rizvi and Roman, (2019) warn that with these many options readily available, therapists need to remember that the primary function of phone coaching is generalization. Therapists must consider which medium is most likely to lead to generalization and increase flexibility where needed.

Consultation Team

Consultation team is known as "therapy for the therapist." The purpose of the DBT consultation team is to help the team apply DBT principles, speak a common language, enhance and maintain therapist capabilities, increase adherence to the DBT model, and prevent therapist burnout. Although delivering DBT to multiproblematic patients can be highly rewarding, treating clients who may engage in high-risk behaviors can also be stressful for therapists. All DBT therapists and skills trainers should participate in this regular weekly meeting to receive validation from colleagues as well as problem-solve for the complex situations that may arise in treatment.

Consultation team meetings begin with a mindfulness exercise, followed by reading one of the consultation team agreements. Consult team agreements are the cardinal principles that team members implement in the DBT framework (dialectical thinking, fallibility, consultation to the patient, consistency, observing limits, etc.). Although the exact structure may vary, this is usually followed by team members describing their challenges implementing the model. The focus is on the clinicians' challenges applying the model effectively, not on the clients' problems per se.

Structuring Treatment: A Hierarchy of Target Behaviors

As discussed previously, DBT is principle driven, with the selection and meaning and application of individual intervention techniques based on the therapist's best judgment of the appropriate intervention in each situation. Treatment is also structured according to a hierarchy stipulating how target behaviors should be prioritized for intervention.

Individual Therapy Hierarchy

In the first stage of DBT, it is the therapist's goal to help clients reduce behavioral dyscontrol and gain basic skills to replace maladaptive coping patterns with skillful means. In this stage, treatment targets decrease (1) "life-threatening" behaviors, (2) therapy-interfering behaviors, and (3) behaviors that interfere with the quality of life (in this order). The positive corollary of this hierarchy is the overall increase in behavioral skills.

Stage 2 DBT attends to feelings of misery, desperation, and traumatic stress that arise more intensely once Stage 1 behaviors are under control. In this stage, clinicians attend to "secondary targets," such as emotional vulnerability, active passivity, apparent competence, inhibited grieving, and unrelenting crises. Stage 3 addresses more ordinary problems of daily living, helping clients increase their self-respect and achieve individual goals. Finally, Stage 4 DBT focuses on treatment, helping clients achieve greater awareness of themselves, attend to any feelings of incompleteness, and work toward spiritual fulfillment.

Across all stages, diary cards, including daily ratings of emotions, problem behaviors, and skills used, are used to monitor targets. The treatment hierarchy should be used to organize sessions and set agendas. DBT therapists should note that although these stages of treatment are discussed here in a linear fashion, stages of treatment may overlap.

Basic Treatment Strategies

Dialectical behavior therapy treatment strategies include activities, tactics, and procedures that therapists employ while targeting maladaptive behaviors (Linehan, 1993a). For example, therapists may identify current dialectical dilemmas, balance their use of acceptance and change, and use different styles of communicating. The individual therapist determines when and how much each strategy should be used; not all strategies are necessary for every session.

Dialectical Strategies

Dialectical strategies acknowledge the tensions that are generated in therapy and help therapists facilitate change by responding to polarized viewpoints skillfully. Therapists should be alert to dialectical tensions as they occur and move back and forth between acceptance and change to maintain a collaborative relationship. Therapists should also teach and model dialectical behavior patterns to emphasize that truth is not absolute. Therapists can also "enter the paradox" and highlight contradictions of the patient's own behavior, the therapeutic process, and reality in general. Dialectical strategies include using metaphors to promote dialectical and flexible thinking, playing "devil's advocate" to argue an opposing point of view, or even taking the client more seriously than they take themself by "extending" the seriousness of a client's communication. Therapists should also continuously activate the client's wise mind, assess all situations dialectically, and allow for natural change to occur (Linehan, 1993a).

Core Strategies

Core strategies include problem-solving and validation and are at the heart of DBT and used across all client interactions. Validation communicates to clients that their behavior makes sense and is understandable in context. Direct validation involves the therapist identifying and reflecting the wisdom of the patient's response.

Problem-solving strategies are used as an active approach to counteract the sometimes passive nature that DBT clients employ when approaching problems. Problem-solving is thought of as a two-stage process: (1) understanding and accepting the problem and (2) attempting to generate, evaluate, and implement alternative solutions for use in future

situations (Linehan, 1993a). Acceptance strategies include behavioral analysis, insight strategies, and didactic strategies. Change strategies include solution analysis, orienting patients to the process and requirements of DBT, and increasing commitment. Contingency management targets problematic contingencies in the patient's environment, and exposure and cognitive modification of maladaptive thinking patterns are also used when necessary.

Stylistic Strategies

Stylistic strategies are specific interpersonal and communication styles used in DBT. There are two primary stylistic strategies in DBT: reciprocal and irreverent communications. Reciprocal communication is intended to connect with the client and pull the client closer to the therapist. A therapist using reciprocal communication is responsive, warm, genuine, and uses self-disclosure. On the contrary, an irreverent communication style is unorthodox in manner and used to unsettle or throw a client off balance. This style includes using a confrontational tone, calling a client's bluff, "plunging in where angels fear to tread," oscillating intensity, and using silence. The opposing styles are meant to be both balanced and synthesized in DBT, as therapists should move back and forth between the two with such speed and flow that this blend itself creates its own communication style (Linehan, 1993a).

Case Management Strategies

Case management strategies identify how therapists should interact with and respond to clients' environments. One of the primary goals in DBT is to help clients achieve a more active role in solving their own life problems. In DBT case management, rather than directly intervening on the client's behalf, the DBT therapist consults with patients on how to interact effectively with their environments. However, at times when an issue is critically important and/or patients' ability to intervene on their own behalf is limited, therapists may intervene with the client's environment on their behalf to avoid harm to the client. In these situations, except in emergencies, it is necessary to inform patients prior to intervention and to obtain client consent.

Research Support and Adaptations

An established body of empirical support demonstrates the efficacy of DBT for suicidal individuals with BPD. Twenty-seven randomized controlled trials of comprehensive DBT demonstrate efficacy, and 18 randomized controlled trials demonstrate the efficacy of DBT skills only. Current research trends suggest that there are many more patients with BPD and related emotion regulation disorders seeking DBT than there are trained providers, demanding increased training by qualified training entities. As DBT continues to expand, researchers are tasked with developing systematic ways to optimize DBT treatment, including promoting clinician fidelity and adherence as well as identifying which clients are likely to most benefit from DBT. It is critical for beginning DBT therapists to seek DBT intensive training because delivering DBT with adherence not only reduces suicide attempts in patients but also increases treatment retention (Harned, 2019).

In addition to this research on standard comprehensive DBT, there are also several randomized controlled trials adapting DBT to a broad range of client populations and problems, albeit all characterized by emotion dysregulation. The earliest adaptations include DBT-SUD (substance use disorders; Linehan et al., 1999), DBT for college students (Pistorello, 2012), DBT-A (adolescents; McCauley et al., 2018; Mehlum, 2014), DBT-PE (prolonged exposure) for PTSD (Harned et al., 2014), and DBT-C (children; Perepletchikova et al., 2017). DBT has also been applied quasi-experimentally in multiple forensic settings (for a review, see Ivanoff & Marotta, 2019) and schools (Mazza & Mazza, 2019). These adaptations underscore the ability of clinicians from across mental health disciplines to implement DBT.

Helpful Resources
Remote Training
Developed over the past two decades, remote DBT training options of increasing sophistication are now widely available. Training has been carried out with Behavioral Tech, owned by the nonprofit Linehan Institute, now in collaboration with Psychwire. Many other smaller organizations and practices also offer training and remote consultation. In addition, individuals and groups have worked to develop DBT apps. Diary cards, skills teaching, and coaching, even in near crisis situations, have proliferated. Some of these resources, such as those through Dialexis in the Netherlands and through Shireen Rizvi's laboratory at Rutgers University, are outstanding.

Apps
Author. (Jan. 1, 2017). TIME MAGAZINE 100 NEW SCIENTIFIC DISCOVERIES 2017 SPECIAL EDITION Single Issue Magazine.

Dialexis Advises B.V. DBT Travel Guide: https://apps.apple.com/us/app/dbt-travel-guide/id959541436

Durham DBT. DBT Diary Card & Skills Coach: https://apps.apple.com/us/app/dbt-diary-card-skills-coach/id479013889

Psychwire. DBT Skills–Behavioral Tech: https://psychwire.com/linehan/dbt-skills

WTF Happened chain analysis tool: https://www.youtube.com/watch?v=iXhan9h4y70

https://www.talkgood.org/

References

Harned, M. (2019). *Annual update on DBT research.* Presentation at the International Society for the Improvement and Teaching of Dialectical Behavior Therapy, Atlanta, GA.

Harned, M. S., Korslund, K. E., & Linehan, M. M. (2014). A pilot randomized controlled trial of dialectical behavior therapy with and without the dialectical behavior therapy prolonged exposure protocol for suicidal and self-injuring women with borderline personality disorder. *Behaviour Research and Therapy, 55,* 7–17.

Ivanoff, A., & Marotta, P. (2019). DBT in forensic settings. In M. Swales (Ed.), *The Oxford handbook of dialectical behaviour therapy* (pp. 615–643). Oxford University Press.

Linehan, M. (1993a). *Cognitive–behavioral treatment of borderline personality disorder*. Guilford.

Linehan, M. (1993b). *Skills training manual for treating borderline personality disorder*. Guilford.

Linehan, M. M. (2015a). *DBT skills training manual*. Guilford.

Linehan, M. M. (2015b). *DBT skills training handouts and worksheets*. Guilford.

Linehan, M. M., Cochran, B. N., & Kehrer, C. A. (2001). Dialectical behavior therapy for borderline personality disorder. In D. H. Barlow (Ed.), *Clinical handbook of psychological disorders: A step-by step treatment manual* (3rd ed., pp. 470–522). Guilford.

Linehan, M., & Schmidt, H. (1995). The dialectics of effective treatment of borderline personality disorder. In W. T. O'Donohue & L. Krasner (Eds.), *Theories of behavior therapy: Exploring behavior change* (pp. 553–584). American Psychological Association.

Linehan, M., Schmidt, H., Dimeff, L., Craft, J., Kanter, J., & Comotois, K. (1999). Dialectical behavior therapy for patients with borderline personality disorder and drug dependence. *American Journal of Addiction, 8*(4), 279–292.

Lungu, A., & Linehan, M. (2017). Dialectical behavior therapy: Overview, characteristics, and future directions. In S. Hofmann & G. Asmundson (Eds.), *The science of cognitive behavioral therapy* (pp. 429–259). Elsevier.

Mazza, J. J., & Mazza, E. T. (2019). DBT skills in schools: Implementation of the DBT STEPS—A social emotional curriculum. In M. Swales (Ed.), *The Oxford handbook of dialectical behaviour therapy* (pp. 719–733). Oxford University Press.

McCauley, E., Berk, M. S., Asarnow, J. R., Adrian, M., Cohen, J., Korslund, K., Avina, C., Hughes, J.,

Harned, M., Gallop, R., & Linehan, M. M. (2018). Efficacy of dialectical behavior therapy for adolescents at high risk for suicide: A randomized clinical trial. *JAMA Psychiatry, 75*(8), 777–785.

McMain, S. F., Guimond, T., Barnart, R., Habinski, L., & Streiner, D. L. (2017). A randomized trial of brief dialectical behaviour therapy skills training in suicidal patients suffering from borderline disorder. *Acta Psychiatrica Scandinavica, 135,* 138–148.

Mehlum, L. (2014). Dialectical behavior therapy for adolescents with repeated suicidal and self-harming behavior: A randomized trial. *Journal of the American Academy of Child Adolescent Psychiatry, 53*(10), 1082–1091.

Perepletchikova, F., Nathanson, D., Axelrod, S., Merrill, C., Walker, A., Grossman, M., Rebta, J., Scahill, L., Kaufman, J., Flye, B., Mauer, E., & Walkup, J. (2017). Randomized clinical trial of dialectical behavior therapy for preadolescent children with disruptive mood dysregulation disorder: Feasibility and outcomes. *Journal of the American Academy of Child and Adolescent Psychiatry, 56*(10), 832–840.

Pistorello, J., Fruzzetti, A. E., MacLane, C., Gallop, R., & Iverson, K. M. (2012). Dialectical behavior therapy (DBT) applied to college students: a randomized clinical trial. *Journal of consulting and clinical psychology, 80*(6), 982.

Rizvi, S. L., & Roman, K. M. (2019). Generalization modalities: Taking the treatment out of the consulting room—Using telephone, text, and email. In M. Swales (Ed.), *The Oxford handbook of dialectical behaviour therapy* (pp. 201–215). Oxford University Press.

Sayrs, J., & Linehan, M. (2019). Modifying CBT to meet the challenges of treating emotion dysregulation: Utilizing dialectics. In M. Swales (Ed.), *The Oxford handbook of dialectical behaviour therapy* (pp. 107–120). Oxford University Press.

Acceptance and Commitment Therapy

Danielle L. DeMailo

Acceptance and commitment therapy (ACT) is designed to assist clients in distress, regardless of their diagnosis or psychosocial circumstances. Considered a third-wave cognitive–behavioral therapy, ACT teaches clients that they can make behavioral choices based on their values and not the content of their internal or private events to include thoughts, emotions, physical sensations, behavioral urges, and memories (Hayes et al., 2011). The structure of ACT both in individual and in group therapy combines didactics with metaphors, illustrations, experiential exercises in which the therapist is often a participant, and in-between session practice activities. Based on the premise that we do not have to rid ourselves of painful symptoms or experiences in order to act in accordance with our values, ACT requires clients to first unlearn previously formed assumptions about the goal of psychotherapy and expected outcomes. The two critical goals in ACT are to assist the client in developing psychological flexibility and living a life of vitality or meaning. ACT is typically provided weekly for approximately 12–16 sessions.

Case Example

Judy is a 35-year-old single African American female with no children. She works from home as a computer software engineer for a small business that designs social media applications. She lives alone with her dog, has a few friends, and talks to her mother regularly. Her father passed away from lung cancer when she was 12 years old. She is confident in her career; however, she is insecure about entering into romantic relationships. Longing for a relationship but believing she is unlovable leads her to feeling isolated, lonely, and depressed. Judy reports to the therapist that when she was young, her father used to berate her and her mother. She indicates that her father used to tell her she was ugly and that "no man would ever love her." Her mother did not defend her and often said to her that she is fortunate to even know her father. Judy often wonders why there were few dolls made that looked like her, and she has really started to believe her father's words.

Assessment and Treatment Planning

Continuing the case example, the first one or two individual therapy sessions focus on assessing suicide risk and discussing confidentiality and limits, conducting a comprehensive biopsychosocial assessment, and then determining if ACT therapy is appropriate for Judy. In addition to assessing her symptoms of depression by utilizing a standardized assessment instrument (e.g., the Beck Depression Inventory–II; Beck et al., 1996), it is important to assess her current psychological flexibility (e.g., using the Acceptance and Action Questionnaire–II; Bond et al., 2011). Questions focus on one's ability to separate their emotions, memories, and other private events from their behaviors and overall quality of life. Note that other assessment measures can be used at the therapist's clinical discretion and may assess other diagnostic symptoms such as anxiety or post-traumatic stress disorder, the working therapeutic alliance, or the client's current quality of life.

After the assessment, the therapist asks Judy to identify what she would like to accomplish in therapy. Judy indicates she would like to be "happier" and to stop thinking poorly of herself. It is at this time that informed consent about the structure and function of ACT is discussed. The therapist informs Judy that ACT is different from traditional cognitive and/or behavioral-based therapies in that it focuses on the acceptance of thoughts, emotions, and other private events rather than challenging or changing them. The change occurs in the actions that are driven by one's values. The therapist encourages Judy to carve out space for this process and recognize that viewing problems and solutions in this way may take time and patience. A metaphor can be utilized to assist Judy in understanding this process. The therapist can validate Judy's desire to feel happy and help her recognize that happiness is not a constant state. The goal of therapy is not to get rid of unwanted thoughts and emotions, replacing them with pleasant emotions, but rather to gain improved control over her life. In that process, the experience may seem like a rollercoaster ride, with ups and downs and times when she may want to give up or believe that making this change is not worth it (Walser et al., 2012). The therapist asks Judy to hang in there, especially for the first four to six sessions, and the therapist continues to check in with her regarding ACT's workability for her.

The next one or two sessions begin with a brief mindfulness exercise. A recommended first mindfulness exercise is one that focuses on general awareness and breathing (Walser & Westrup, 2007). This will assist Judy in becoming fully present for the session. After each mindfulness exercise, the therapist inquires about Judy's reactions to the experience or challenges to staying present. The therapist normalizes the tendency for our minds to wander into the future or past and notes that with consistent practice, we can develop the skill of becoming present to that distraction and then bring our focus back to the present moment.

Judy expresses challenges not judging herself when completing the exercise, thinking she is likely doing it wrong and fearing that the therapist will be upset with her. The therapist normalizes this experience as well, especially in the context of Judy's presenting concerns. The therapist explains that mindfulness is a foundational process in ACT because it allows the client to be in tune with the present moment, become aware of their private events without judgment (thoughts, emotions, physical sensations, behavioral urges, and memories), and practice giving their attention a specific focus. Because the skill of mindfulness can assist Judy with developing the other ACT skills, daily mindfulness practice and tracking mindfulness and her effectiveness with it are assigned to Judy for homework. Judy is then directed

TABLE 70.1 Valued Living Questionnaire

No.	Life Domain	Level of Importance	Behavioral Consistency
1	Family (other than marriage or parenting)	4	3
2	Marriage, couples, intimate relations	10	1
3	Parenting	9	1
4	Friends, social life	5	4
5	Work	9	10
6	Education/training	5	9
7	Recreation/fun	6	4
8	Spirituality	8	9
9	Citizenship, community life	4	5
10	Self-care (diet, exercise, sleep)	6	4

to the Valued Living Questionnaire (Wilson & Groom, 2002), in which she is asked to think about her life now and identify how important each of the 10 different life domains are to her on a scale of 1–10 (with 10 being "extremely important") and then to what extent her actions are consistent with her currently assigned level of importance (Table 70.1). Note that in a group setting, this is typically administered in the latter sessions, along with values and committed actions.

Judy reports she would very much like to be in a relationship, get married, and become a parent, but she avoids dating because she does not believe anyone would want to be in a relationship with her. This inconsistency with values and actions guides Judy's treatment plan. The therapist works with her to identify that although she cannot control the outcome of a romantic relationship, her actions can demonstrate a greater desire to seek romantic relationships and perhaps start a family. In addition, because Judy loves children, engaging in activities to mentor children could serve to move her in the direction of values around parenting. Judy maintains that she does not believe she could meet these goals. In addition to practicing and tracking mindfulness exercises, the therapist asks Judy to identify other barriers that interfere with her living a valued-driven life.

Creative Hopelessness

After assessment measures, a mindfulness exercise, and review of homework, in the third to fifth session the therapist gives Judy a dry erase board and asks her to identify all of the problems she has been struggling with that led her to see the therapist in one column. The therapist then asks Judy to identify everything she has tried so far to get rid of those unwanted symptoms, experiences, and behaviors in another column (Table 70.2).

The therapist acknowledges and praises Judy for her ability to recognize and verbalize both problems and attempted solutions and also for her hard work in trying to solve her problems. Judy indicates that it has been unsuccessful and that some of her solutions have been either unhealthy or resulted in making her problems worse. The therapist then asks her to reflect upon the two lists on the dry erase board and asks Judy what comes to mind. Judy says she feels frustrated and hopeless, which are added to the problems list. The therapist identifies that there is something not right with this process, in that Judy has tried very hard, to no avail, and that her efforts have resulted in costs. Judy indicates that maybe she needs to try harder, and the therapist adds this to the solutions list. Judy says that some of her attempts, such as avoidance, have made her feel even

TABLE 70.2 Problems and Solutions

Problems I've Been Trying to Get Rid Of	Attempted Solutions to My Problems
Feeling isolated and unlovable	Sleeping too much
Not liking being African American	Eating too much
Discrimination	Overworking
Feeling "less than"/not liking myself	Trying to ignore my feelings
Loneliness, sadness, depression	Talking with a friend
Fear, anxiety, low self-esteem	Journaling
Anger at myself, anger at others	Exercising
Sleeping too much	Drinking too much (sometimes)
Eating too much	Staying at home
Drinking too much (sometimes)	Avoidance
Envy of others in relationships	Trying to better understand my culture
Grief about dad	Just getting over it
Memories of verbal abuse by dad	Getting angry with God
Nervousness with new people	Reading self-help books

more lonely and more unattractive. The therapist asks Judy if it is possible that getting rid of what she is struggling with is not the solution, or not even possible.

The therapist pauses and then introduces the "person-in-the-hole" metaphor (Hayes et al., 2011), asking Judy to imagine being blindfolded, picked up by a helicopter, and dropped into a large field with nothing but a bag of tools and then asked to live her life. The therapist tells Judy that in the field are large holes and she falls into one of them. After removing the blindfold, Judy opens the bag and discovers a shovel. She tries to dig her way out, but this just makes the hole bigger, so digging is not the answer. The therapist compares this scenario to Judy's experience with problems and solutions and invites Judy to see if this is confirmed with her own experiences outside of therapy. The therapist gives Judy a homework assignment. The worksheet asks her to identify private events triggered by situations, how long she has been struggling with these events, strategies she has used in attempts to resolve the events, and how well they worked for her.

Control as the Problem

After standard agenda items are conducted as in the previous session, in approximately the fourth to sixth sessions, the therapist expands upon the notion that attempts to get rid of problems deplete energy and often exacerbate the problems. Judy shares an experience of feeling depressed after seeing a reminder on the internet about Valentine's Day approaching and deciding to hide in her bed most of the day. She indicates that this attempt to stop feeling depressed actually led her to feel more depressed. The therapist asks Judy to explore the idea that control may be the problem instead of the solution. Judy maintains that she does not believe she could go to a party or consider online dating until she stops feeling depressed.

The therapist invites Judy to stand up and face the therapist, imagining they are a physiological representation of her depression and to describe what that would look like. Judy reports it would be like a large black cloud that is hovering over her and intimidating her. Judy notes that she hates that she associates the color black with something monstrous. The therapist then presents a rope and tells Judy to imagine that she and her depression are engaged in a tug-of-war (Hayes et al., 2011), with the object being to pull each other into the bottomless pit that is between them. The therapist and Judy continue to tug at the rope. The more Judy tugs, the more her depression tugs, and the closer she gets to the bottomless pit.

The therapist eventually asks Judy what it would be like to drop the rope and also asks if Judy would have more energy if she drops the rope in order to engage in activities such as going to work or church. Judy pretends to go to work, and the therapist follows her with the rope. This serves to demonstrate that Judy can have depression while still engaging in activities she values. Alternative or additional experiential exercises can be utilized to illustrate this process, such as the polygraph metaphor (Hayes et al., 2011) and Don't Think About Vanilla Ice Cream (Walser & Westrup, 2007). When Judy asks the therapist how to drop the rope in real life, the therapist directs her to her next homework assignment. This activity enables Judy to check in with her own experience with regard to control moves she makes, what symptoms she is trying to control, how effective she is at doing so, and if there are costs to her control attempts.

Acceptance and Willingness

Following the weekly agenda items, in approximately the fifth to seventh sessions, the therapist focuses on engaging in what ACT considers an alternative to control: willingness. Willingness is neither a behavior nor an emotion but, rather, a stance. Willingness is the ability to experience and hold uncomfortable thoughts, emotions, and other private events while engaging in something of value. Willingness also implies acceptance not only of the present experience of distressing symptoms but also that these experiences may not be permanently eliminated from one's life. Acceptance also denotes the understanding that experiencing unwanted thoughts, emotions, sensations, urges, and memories is a part of being human. After the introductory and standard agenda items are complete, the therapist introduces this concept of willingness and then asks Judy to participate

in an exercise called "eyes on" (Walser et al., 2012). Mindfulness exercises such as Welcome Anxiety and Recognizing Mind Quality Mindfulness (Walser & Westrup, 2007) can be supplemented in shepherding clients to experience willingness.

The therapist asks Judy to pull her chair closer and face the therapist directly. The therapist then asks Judy to simply look at the therapist directly in the eyes without speaking or trying to communicate. The therapist does not share how long the exercise will last and encourages Judy to just regard the therapist and notice what comes up for her. Judy initially expresses concern that this would be very uncomfortable, considering she does not like to be this close to others because it makes her feel self-conscious. She also said she did not know how to do this given that she considers the therapist an authority figure and also Caucasian. Judy says she was taught that this was disrespectful and could get her into trouble. The therapist maintains the same directions and encourages Judy to start. The exercise lasts for approximately 3 minutes, with the therapist remaining silent. Afterwards, they process the experience.

Judy shares that the experience was terrifying, and she spent much of the time telling herself not to feel anxious and some of the time also trying to distract herself from the exercise by thinking about what she was going to have for dinner. She indicates that at one point she was not thinking of much at all and actually felt a connection with her therapist. The therapist reveals this was a demonstration of willingness. The therapist also reminds Judy that there was no mandate or report of negative consequences should Judy stop the exercise and yet she was able to participate throughout the duration of the 3 minutes. Judy recognizes this accomplishment; however, she wonders if she could do something like this outside of the therapist's office.

The homework assignment shifts from mere insight into Judy's current experience to asking her to make behavioral changes that reflect increased willingness. She is asked to identify at least one action per week that moves in the direction of what she values; to recognize what uncomfortable thoughts, emotions, or other private events she would be willing to have in order to engage in this activity; and then to take a willing stance. She is then to describe, if successful, what it was like to be willing. If not successful or partially successful, she is to describe barriers to her willingness. Judy agrees to start slow and says she is going to sign up for an online dating site. She recognizes this will remind her of everything her father said to her about being unlovable and the messages society has given her about the undesirability of her race. She also identifies feeling sad about her father's death and wishing he were still alive.

Cognitive Defusion

The next several sessions (estimated to be sessions 6–10) focus on the ACT-created term and concept known as *cognitive defusion* (Hayes et al., 2011). As part of the standard weekly agenda items, Judy shares that she opened up her computer, logged on to a dating site, and started to create her personal profile. When she started writing about herself, she started thinking about how no one is going to choose her, how she should use a fake picture in order to be selected, and how she will never meet anyone. She then thought, 'Why bother with this, I'm unwanted.' She discontinued her profile and left the website. The therapist recognizes that Judy is fused with the thought that she is not going to meet anyone, and this thought dictates her choice to refrain from spending further energy in efforts to seek a romantic partner.

The therapist then presents the dry erase board again and draws a picture of two identical computers (Walser et al., 2012). Judy recognizes this immediately and is excited because she understands computers. The therapist adds the following message to both

screens: "I'm unwanted." However, when the person is added to the pictures, the person to the left has their head literally in the computer, and the person to the right is sitting back just a bit from the computer. The therapist explains that everyone collects programming that shows up on the screen throughout their lives, and some of this programming is judgmental and unhelpful.

The therapist inquires how the person away from the screen would handle this programming differently that the person attached to the screen. Judy retorts that the person connected to the screen would stay away from everyone, and the person to the right may do something differently. The therapist confirms that the person to the right is demonstrating cognitive defusion, which means separating the content of our programming from our behavioral responses. The person to the right could even do something seemingly opposed to their programming, such as call a friend or go to a party. Additional mindfulness and/or experiential exercises applied to illustrate cognitive defusion include the leaves on a stream exercise (Hayes et al., 2011) and the lemon exercise (Zettle, 2007).

Encouraging Judy to practice this skill, the therapist assigns Judy to the Taking Inventory worksheet (Zettle, 2007). This instructs Judy to identify a triggering event or circumstance and then identify her thoughts, emotions, physical sensations, memories, and other reactions such as impulses or urges. However, instead of just recording this in the typical fashion, Judy is instructed to defuse from the content of her private events by prefacing each thought, emotion, etc. with "I have that thought that . . ." and "I have the feeling that . . . ." Manipulating words and sentence structure is one technique to defuse the self from the content of their minds, particularly when these thoughts or feelings are recurrent and counterproductive. A similar language-dissection assignment is the thoughts on cards exercise (Zettle, 2007).

Self-as-Context

The next several sessions (estimated to be sessions 8–12) concentrate on the concept of self-as-context. Sessions begin as always with mindfulness exercises that are often related to the concepts being illustrated, assessment measures, general check-ins regarding safety, and homework review. When Judy reviews her homework, she identifies a triggering event of talking to her mother on the phone and her mother mentioning her father. She immediately reports thoughts of being berated and told she was ugly, dirty, and disgusting. She also thought of his death and how he died tragically. Judy demonstrates some difficulty prefacing each thought with "I have the thought that . . .," and the therapist asks her to repeat each statement using the defusion technique and discuss any reactions to this shift.

Judy recognizes how much she is fused with these experiences and how she automatically believes them. Judy asks the therapist how she can separate from her thoughts, which are a part of her. The therapist validates this question and adds that the thoughts are not all of her. There is a Judy that does not solely consist of her thoughts, feelings, or other private events. This is the Judy who was once a small child, a teenager, and a young adult and now who she is today. This concept of the self is a continuous stream of consciousness throughout one's life, despite transforming physically and gathering an array of experiences and memories over time. In addition to the self being continuous, there is an ability for the self to observe one's experiences such as their own breath in a mindfulness exercise.

The ability to step away from one's experiences, in a similar way as in cognitive defusion, allows one to become an observer rather than an active participant in struggle. The therapist pulls out a chessboard and a number of blue and red pieces. Asking Judy if she has ever played chess, which she has, the therapist indicates that they are going to utilize the pieces and general game of chess to illustrate self-as-context (Hayes et al., 2011). Additional experiential exercises and metaphors include the passengers on the bus metaphor (Luoma et al., 2007) and the continuous "you"/observer self (Zettle, 2007). Judy is asked to identify several unwanted thoughts, emotions, physical sensations, memories, and urges. As she names them, the therapist places blue chess pieces on one side of the board. She then identifies several pleasant private events, and the therapist places red chess pieces on the other side of the board. The therapist indicates that typically the red and blue pieces battle each other and then knocks several pieces off the board. Then the pieces return. Some pieces stay for a long time, similar to Judy's feeling of loneliness and thought of being unwanted.

The therapist asks Judy to identify herself within the game. Judy begins to understand that she is separate from the pieces and is also a constant in her life. She chooses the board, and her therapist congratulates her. The board is the context, not the content that holds all of the content of one's mind. The content fluctuates, whereas the context remains consistent. Being able to recognize that Judy can allow herself to have unwanted thoughts and emotions, without becoming them, is comforting to her. She is asked to test this out at home by exploring how her experiences fluctuate throughout the day and as she engages in distinct life roles.

Values and Committed Actions

The remaining sessions in therapy (typically the final four sessions) focus on identifying values from the previously ascertained life domains in the earlier sessions, developing goals or committed actions, following through with these actions outside of therapy, and identifying barriers or challenges to this follow-through. After the standard introductory items are completed, Judy reviews her homework to understand firsthand how she is both continuous and an observer. She identifies completing a project for her work, feeling proud, delighted, and prominent. She holds thoughts that she is satisfied with her work and has excelled. She recognizes how significantly different these experiences are when faced with interpersonal interactions. Judy also recognizes that she does not have to believe her programming about her worth in romantic relationships. Her desire to improve her relationships and the pain she encounters when thinking about her lack of relationships cues her into how much she values this in her life. The therapist reminds Judy that she recognized that she has refrained from nurturing her needs to be intimate with others as well as taking on a parental role.

The therapist assists Judy with modifying these life domains to become values. The therapist uses a compass to demonstrate that values are not ever truly achieved or completed, like the way we do not ever reach true north (Walser & Westrup, 2007). The skiing metaphor (Hayes et al., 2011) connects clients with the process rather than outcome as the value. Committed actions are then extensions of values; however, they are similar to treatment goals in the sense that they are specific, measurable, and time-bound. Both values and committed actions maintain a focus on what an individual can actively practice, regardless of the actions of others (Table 70.3).

Final Session

In addition to reviewing and identifying the status of treatment goals and any unfinished business, administering closing instruments to measure unwanted symptoms, psychological flexibility, and vitality, and reviewing any fears about terminating the therapeutic relationship, the final session is designed to encourage clients to commit to continuing to practice the principles learned and experienced in therapy so that they can engage in a values-based life. Judy is able to demonstrate this by a written commitment, with a focus on willingness to continue to move in the direction of intimate relationships, regardless of internal and external barriers. In group therapy, members can stand and commit (Walser et al., 2012) by sharing their most prominent values and declaring their intentions in moving forward with their lives.

Efficacy

The Substance Abuse and Mental Health Services Administration listed ACT as an empirically supported treatment on its National Registry of Evidence-Based Programs and Practices. The American Psychological Association, Division 12, identifies ACT as an empirically supported treatment for chronic pain, depression, mixed anxiety, obsessive–compulsive disorder, and psychosis. In addition, initial clinical trials have tested the efficacy of focused acceptance and commitment

TABLE 70.3 Life Domain, Values, and Committed Actions

No.	Life Domain	Value	Committed Action
1	Marriage, couples, intimate relations	To be an active participant in seeking and maintaining intimate relationships	1. Join a meet-up group before next week. 2. Participate in at least one meet-up group per week for 3 weeks. 3. Invite one member of the meet-up group to meet outside of group within 4 weeks.
2	Parenting	To provide parental caregiving and mentoring to others	1. Contact children's grief organization within 1 week. 2. Submit volunteer application within 2 weeks.

therapy, a 4-week group conducted in a U.S. Department of Veterans Affairs primary care setting (Glover et al., 2016).

Helpful Resources

ACT Coach (phone app): https://mobile.va.gov/app/act-coach

Association for Contextual Behavioral Science: https://contextualscience.org

PESI: https://www.pesi.com

PRAXIS: https://www.praxiscet.com

Psychotherapy.net. *ACT in action: 6-Video series*: https://www.psychotherapy.net/video/steven-hayes-act

Society of Clinical Psychology Division 12 of the APA: https://www.div12.org

References

Beck, A. T., Steer, R. A., & Brown, G. K. (1996). *Manual for the Beck Depression Inventory–II.* Psychological Corporation.

Bond, F. W., Hayes, S. C., Baer, R. A., Carpenter, K. M., Guenole, N., Orcutt, H. K., Waltz, T., & Zettle, R. D. (2011). Preliminary psychometric properties of the Acceptance and Action Questionnaire–II: A revised measure of psychological inflexibility and experiential avoidance. *Behavior Therapy, 42,* 676–678.

Glover, N. G., Sylvers, P. D., Shearer, E. M., Kane, M. C., Clasen, P. C., Epler, A. J., Plumb-Vilardaga, J. C., Bonow, J. T., & Jakupcak, M. (2016, May). The efficacy of focused acceptance and commitment therapy in VA primary care. *Psychological Services, 13*(2), 156–161.

Hayes, S. C., Strosahl, K., & Wilson, K. G. (2011). *Acceptance and commitment therapy: An experiential approach to behavior change* (2nd ed.). Guilford.

Luoma, J. B., Hayes, S. C., & Walser, R. D. (2007). *Learning ACT.* New Harbinger.

Walser, R. D., Sears, K., Chartier, M., & Karlin, B. E. (2012). *Acceptance and commitment therapy for depression in veterans: Therapist manual.* U.S. Department of Veterans Affairs.

Walser, R. D., & Westrup, D. (2007). *Acceptance and commitment therapy for the treatment of posttraumatic stress disorder and trauma-related problems.* New Harbinger.

Wilson, K. G., & Groom, J. (2002). *The Valued Living Questionnaire.* Available from Kelly Wilson.

Zettle, R. D. (2007). *ACT for depression: A clinician's guide to using acceptance & commitment therapy in treating depression.* New Harbinger.

Exposure Therapy

Keith Bredemeier and Edna B. Foa

Exposure therapy involves systematically and repeatedly confronting stimuli that cause significant distress, whether these stimuli are external (e.g., situations and objects) or internal (e.g., thoughts and mental images). In doing so, the goal is to reduce reactivity and distress in response to these stimuli, as well as counter developed habits of avoiding them. Exposure therapy can be traced back to work on classical conditioning in the early 1900s. Mary Cover Jones is credited with the first formal use of exposure to treat an individual with a fear of rabbits, based on presumptive extinction of conditioned associations (Jones, 1924). Later (beginning in the 1950s), Joseph Wolpe helped advance the use exposure techniques in behavior therapy with his work on "systematic desensitization" (Wolpe et al., 1973); this work helped pave the way for many current methods and applications of exposure (although coupling exposure with relaxation techniques is no longer considered to be necessary for therapeutic benefit). Today, exposure therapy is among the most widely studied and well-established forms of psychotherapy (Abramowitz et al., 2019; Foa & McLean, 2016; Hofmann et al., 2012). As a result, exposure techniques are a core behavioral component of many established cognitive–behavioral therapy (CBT) protocols, particularly for the treatment of anxiety-related problems (which are the focus of this chapter). The essence of exposure therapy techniques is the elicitation of emotional responses followed by processing of corrective information, with the aim of altering the client's mental representation of the situation or stimuli (e.g., all dogs are dangerous) by developing new competing (i.e., inhibitory) associations (e.g., some dogs can be dangerous but most are not; see Foa & Kozak, 1986, Foa & McLean, 2016; Craske et al., 2008, 2014). At a more basic level, a key goal of exposure therapy is to counter the maladaptive use of avoidance coping that is aimed at minimizing short-term distress but can maintain unhelpful emotional reactions, thoughts, and beliefs (Barlow, 2002).

Planning and Preparing for Exposure Sessions

The first part of this chapter focuses on key details and considerations about the process of using exposure techniques—in essence, the "nuts and bolts" of exposure therapy. We begin with an introduction to general types of exposure that therapists may plan and use in treatment.

Types of Exposure

There are three general types of exposure. *In vivo exposure* involves systematically confronting feared situations or stimuli "in real life." This is not inherently limited to situations involving actual risk that a feared outcome will occur; rather, reminders or simulations of those situations/fears can often be salient and effective in vivo exercises (e.g., pictures, videos, arranged situations with "confederates," and virtual reality). *Imaginal exposure* involves confronting feared situations or outcomes by carefully imagining them happening. This approach is generally used when a particular situation that is critical to target in exposure would either be inappropriate to engage in during therapy (e.g., committing a serious legal violation or contracting an illness) or is not possible (e.g., is in the distant future). To facilitate engagement in imaginal exposure, clients are encouraged to first generate ideas for the imaginal scenario or script, which they may write down, and then close their eyes and use present-tense language when telling the "story" to facilitate imagining. Finally, *interoceptive exposure* involves confronting and experiencing specific bodily sensations, often with a focus on those sensations directly linked with experiences of anxiety, fear, or panic or perceptions of threat (e.g., increased heart rate and stomach discomfort). Although all types of exposure exercises arguably elicit prominent bodily changes and sensations, the goal and purpose of interoceptive exposure are to experience these symptoms in isolation (i.e., not in the context of feared situations or outcomes), often through elicitation by engaging in specific physical or sensory exercises (e.g., running in place or hyperventilating). This form of exposure is thought to be helpful (and possibly critical) when working with clients who have developed strong associations and/or beliefs about the bodily sensations alone; thus, these sensations begin to serve as salient triggers of emotional reactions.

Before Starting Exposure— Initial Session(s)

Presenting a Rationale and Discussing the Treatment "Contract"

Before starting exposure therapy, an important step in preparation for this work is to present and discuss the rationale for it. This can include a general discussion about the relation between avoidance and anxiety/distress (focused on how avoidance leads to short-term relief but ultimately maintains emotional reactivity), a more detailed discussion about the cognitive–behavioral model of the problem(s) to be address in treatment through exposure, or both. Discussion of the treatment rationale/model is a common component of CBT, supporting the collaborative nature of CBT; nevertheless, it may be particularly important for fostering engagement and motivation in more difficult or distressing therapy exercises such as exposure. A useful follow-up to this is to discuss the plans for treatment and the importance of making a commitment to treatment (i.e., the treatment "contract"), because inconsistent follow-through and/or regular revisiting of plans during exposure therapy can slow or even prevent progress.

Introducing a Metric for Communicating Severity of Distress During Exposures

Typically, a metric for communicating severity of distress is introduced as subjective units of distress (SUDs), which range on a scale from 0 (*no distress at all*) to 100 (*the most intense distress the client could imagine*). This scale can be adjusted to a client's needs or preferences (e.g., making the scale 0–10)—the key is to have an agreed upon way for the client to (quickly) communicate the intensity of their distress in a given moment. As the name implies, this scale is subjective, so it can be helpful for clients to reflect on personal experiences that align with different points on the scale and to emphasize that these will vary across individuals (and over time). Although the primary function of the SUDs scale is to provide a simple way to discuss the client's level of distress during an exposure (without creating a significant distraction from the exposure stimuli), SUDs can also be a useful way to rate anticipated levels of distress that an exposure will lead to before partaking in it, which can be an important part of initial planning (when building the exposure "hierarchy"—discussed in the next section) and can also be helpful to discuss just before engaging in a specific exposure (e.g., as a way to make "expectancy violation" during an exposure more salient—discussed later).

Building the Exposure Hierarchy

A last but essential step in preparing for exposure therapy is to make a detailed list of the exposure exercises that that will be part of the treatment plan, along with estimates of how difficult each one will be (typically using the SUDs scale, as noted previously). Then, these exposure plans can be arranged in order of difficulty. In doing so, it is important to consider and include any details that might facilitate planning the exposure, as well as predicting how difficult it will be. Client's should be encouraged to specify any detail that might have a significant impact on the anticipated SUDs, and it can sometimes be helpful to include different variations of the same exposure that will be at different levels of difficulty (e.g., riding the subway at midday may be a 70, whereas riding it at rush hour is an 85). Also, in generating these ideas, work on identifying key themes of feared outcomes (e.g., pain and uncertainty); doing so can help generate ideas for more effective exposures, especially at the higher end of the hierarchy. It is important for the client to be actively engaged in this process of generating

hierarchy items. The therapist may certainly make suggestions for possible exposures, but the client should feel they have a choice about what to include (and take on in treatment).

During Exposure Sessions

Preparation for Each Exposure Session

Once you begin exposure work with a client, preparation is important. Ensure that you plan and allocate your time for each session effectively and have whatever items are needed or have the necessary arrangements made for the exposure to be implemented successfully. Many exposures will necessitate some preparation, such as finding appropriate pictures/videos (e.g., of feared stimuli) or a "confederate" who will participate, and having plans in place before the session can ensure these are optimal. To do so, discussion of which item of the hierarchy you will be tackling next is also helpful. In doing so, clients should be told that it is not essential to progress sequentially "up" the hierarchy—they can choose the pace in which to proceed and what to do next (to support self-efficacy and help them master CBT skills). Note that starting very high up on the hierarchy (sometimes referred to as "flooding") can be effective, but it is generally not preferred by clients. Preemptive plans, even if tentative, can prevent you from spending time in session deciding on an exposure. Duration of the exposure is an important consideration. Generally, it is advisable to allow up to 45 minutes for most exposures (although this amount of time is not always necessary, if the client's anxiety diminishes significantly before that point). Planning for less time runs the risk of having to end an exposure when the client is still highly distressed, which can inadvertently reinforce escape behavior. Dedicating this much time for exposure during a 50- or 60-minute session is inherently difficult, and it requires efficiently addressing other agenda items (e.g., homework review and scheduling).

What Clients Should Do—and Pay Attention to—During the Exposure

Once the client has begun an exposure, there are a few important things the therapist should do. First, the therapist must monitor and record the client's level of distress throughout; this can be done using the SUDs scale, typically every 5–10 minutes. This is helpful for tracking changes in distress over time (within and between sessions) and concretely illustrating these changes for clients. Second, the therapist should ensure that the client is sufficiently engaged. A key is to look for signs of overt attentional focus consistent with the planned exposure (e.g., looking directly at the feared stimulus). Attending to the client's visible signs of affect (and potential discrepancy with reported level of distress) can also be helpful. In some instances, when a client appears "overengaged" to a degree that may detract from emotional processing (e.g., crying hysterically), subtle "distancing" techniques can be used to titrate the difficulty of the exposure (e.g., opening eyes during imaginal exposure). Finally, the therapist should attend any possible "safety behaviors" that the client may be (intentionally or unintentionally) engaging in—that is, any behaviors (overt or internal) that may function to reduce their distress and/or prevent an undesirable outcome. Examples of safety behaviors include sitting in the "safest" location (e.g., near an exit) and not making eye contact during a conversation. Reducing/eliminating safety behaviors can improve exposure therapy outcomes (Piccirillo et al., 2016). If the therapist notices a safety behavior, this should be discussed (during or after the exposure, based on clinical judgment), and plans should be made to resist these in future exposures. Relatedly, novice exposure therapists often ask "What should I say during the exposure?" Although certain statements may facilitate "leaning into the anxiety" (sometimes called "exposure statements"), the simplest and safest options (to avoid disengaging

or reassuring the client) are to offer brief statements of encouragement (e.g., "Keep it up" and "You are doing a great job") or to say nothing at all (other than probing about SUDs).

After the Exposure

At the end of each exposure session, time (ideally at least 5–10 minutes) is dedicated to discussing (i.e., "processing") the exposure experience—in particular, what the experience was like and what the client learned from it. In doing so, it is usually helpful to explicitly highlight and praise the client's commitment and effort ("You did it—great job!"). From there, the therapist should prioritize asking questions to foster reflection so that the client can come up with their own observations and conclusions rather than the therapist directly offering specific ideas or insights (although some clients benefit from a more directive approach). It is often helpful to begin with more broad, open-ended questions (e.g., "What was that experience like for you?"), followed by more pointed questions following from the client's response aimed at "guiding" the discussion in helpful directions (e.g., "If it was easier this time compared to last time, what do you think will happen if you practice doing this even more?"). Here again, timing and planning are key—otherwise, you may not have sufficient time to process the exposure afterwards, which may undermine some of the potentially learning that results.

The Importance of Repetition

A very important part of the exposure therapy process, beyond the initial difficulty of facing a new and distressing situation, is continuing to face the distressing situation. In other words, repetition of these exposures is critical—this is considered important for fostering habituation (a reduction in reaction to the same experience over time, which is often considered a sign of learning). Furthermore, repetition should help facilitate changes in conscious perceptions or beliefs because the client will have more experiences from which to draw helpful conclusions (e.g., a client with a fear of dogs may think one exposure to a dog that does not result in harm is due to "luck" but may change their perceptions of how dangerous dogs are after many exposures). The importance of repetition in exposure therapy should be emphasized to clients early and often, especially as a rationale for why homework will involve regular (ideally, daily) exposure practice. Generally, homework will simply entail repetition of exposures already completed in session (with tracking of SUDs to monitor progress). However, as clients advance in treatment, it may be appropriate and helpful for them to take on new items from the hierarchy on their own (usually only if they have become progressively more independent and skilled in navigating exposures). For imaginal exposure, clients can facilitate independent practice by recording the imaginal narrative and then listen to this for homework (often repeatedly, especially for shorter narratives).

Expectancy Violation

Research on exposure therapy techniques has increasingly highlighted the important role of expectancy violation for fostering learning from exposure (Craske et al., 2014); in other words, exposures are more beneficial to the extent that the client's experience is different from what they expected. There are a number of ways that a client's expectations can be "violated," including when a client strongly expects a feared outcome to occur but it does not and when a client expects a particular experience to be particularly difficult and/or distressing but it is easier than anticipated. Arguably, all exposures involve some degree of expectancy violation because perceived danger or threat is thought to drive strong reactions of fear, anxiety, and avoidance. Still, planning exposures that will explicitly challenge the client's expectations can be important when generating the exposure hierarchy, especially for identifying the most salient and

difficult hierarchy items (for which their negative expectations are likely strongest). Expectancy violation can also be addressed during processing by drawing the client's attention to ways that the exposure experience may have differed from their expectations (e.g., asking "How was this experience different than you expected it to be?"). These efforts can be bolstered by explicitly assessing expectancies before the start of each exposure—for example, by discussing expected SUDs, feared outcomes, how likely those feared outcomes seem, and how bad those outcomes would be (if they do occur). When discussed beforehand, expectancies can be treated as hypotheses to be tested during the exposure. Then, the therapist and client analyze the data (e.g., "You said that you were afraid that someone would laugh at you. Did that happen?").

Tracking Progress

There are helpful ways to track progress during the course of treatment, some of which are not unique to exposure therapy (e.g., periodic symptom severity assessments). One important and unique way to track progress during exposure therapy is to look for evidence for between-session habituation—this means that the intensity of the client's distress throughout an exposure decreases over successive sessions (reflected in a lower starting SUDs, lower peak SUDS, or earlier/sharper decline in SUDs). Studies suggests that this type of habituation can be helpful in predicting later changes in symptoms and functioning (Rupp et al., 2017; Sripada & Rauch, 2015). Thus, this approach may be particularly useful in brief or intensive treatment formats (when change in some symptoms may be difficult to observe). When tracking this type of habituation, keep in mind that the client's SUDs during each practice may be impacted by factors other what is being targeted in exposure treatment (e.g., sleep and stress). Thus, it can be more helpful to average over a few "data points" rather than draw strong inferences from one. Another option for tracking progress can be to assess evidence for belief change (based on standardized belief measures or discussions during exposure processing). For this approach to be suitable, it is necessary to have a conceptualization of the types of beliefs that may be contributing to the maintenance of the problem [e.g., beliefs about dangerousness of the world in post-traumatic stress disorder (PTSD)] and thus are a salient treatment target.

Applications of Exposure Therapy for Anxiety-Related Disorders

The remainder of this chapter is dedicated to brief overviews of how exposure therapy techniques are commonly used in some established CBT protocols for anxiety-related disorders (for adults): social anxiety disorder, obsessive–compulsive disorder, and PTSD. Exposure is also one of the core components of CBT protocols for most other anxiety-related disorders, including specific phobias (typically focused on in vivo exposure, which can be effective in as little as one session; Zlomke & Davis, 2008), panic disorder (focused on interoceptive exposure to address "fear of fear"), agoraphobia (in vivo exposure to avoided situations), and even general anxiety disorder (emphasizing imaginal exposure to counter "cognitive avoidance"). Note that the following discussions are intended to orient readers to potential uses of exposure therapy techniques for relevant clients and should not replace protocols/manuals (or formal training in these). Although exposure therapy has historically been emphasized and studied most for the treatment of anxiety, exposure has increasingly been tested and used in treatments for other clinical populations [e.g., eating and body image disturbances (Griffen et al., 2018), alcohol misuse (Byrne et al., 2019), and prolonged grief (Bryant et al., 2014)]. Finally, the treatment of anxiety-related

disorders with exposure therapy for clients with comorbid problems has been studied in many cases (e.g., PTSD and substance use disorders; Coffey et al., 2005), but this generally warrants careful consideration and attention to relevant treatment literature before deciding on treatment plans.

Social Anxiety Disorder

Like other phobias, the treatment of social anxiety disorder with exposure is highly effective (even as a stand-alone treatment; Feske & Chambless, 1995), and it often relies heavily on in vivo exposure. Notably, consideration and inclusion of in vivo exercises that do not involve typical "risks" (e.g., role-playing situations or conversations with the therapist or a "confederate," or giving a practice speech or presentation alone or with a selected audience) can be very helpful, typically as a way to "titrate" (and ultimately work toward) more difficult hierarchy items. Imaginal exposure can also be considered and potentially useful for this, as can other situations that may be helpful to include on the hierarchy (e.g., having a disagreement with a boss or growing old alone). Beyond these standard exposure approaches, a few specialized (in vivo) exposure techniques have been developed and tested for treating social anxiety, including (1) clients videotaping and then watching themselves, either during standard in vivo exercises or during designed experiments (e.g., while using safety behaviors or not), in order to provide an external vantage point (and, potentially, a more objective view) of performance (Rapee & Hayman, 1996); and (2) intentionally engaging in feared outcomes ("social cost" exposures; Fang et al., 2013), such as drawing attention to oneself in public, making a mistake during a presentation, or doing something embarrassing. These exposures provide systematic experiences with the occurrence of these outcomes and how "bad" they are (to inform/correct their expectations about them).

Obsessive–Compulsive Disorder

Exposure therapy for individuals with obsessive–compulsive disorder utilizes a combination of in vivo exposure and imaginal exposure (and, in some cases, interoceptive exposure), which leads to the best outcomes when coupled with resistance or prevention of compulsive behaviors or "rituals" (Abramowitz, 1996). When generating in vivo exposure ideas, the therapist and client should work together to identify salient triggers of obsessive thoughts, including external triggers (e.g., situations and stimuli) and internal triggers (e.g., initial thoughts or worries and bodily sensations), as well as situations and circumstances that the client has begun to avoid altogether or that involve proactive ritualizing (e.g., showering immediately upon returning home or other daily "routines"). This is sometimes accomplished most effectively by conducting some in vivo exposure exercises in the real world, including the client's home when indicated. Imaginal exposure is typically important to utilize with these clients as well, often to address deeper or more distal feared outcomes (e.g., living with intense guilt if responsible for a "disaster"). In addition to being helpful for addressing these sorts of feared consequences (and assessing feared consequences, when these are not known), imaginal exposure can address concerns about perceived risk of simply thinking about these outcomes coming true (referred to as thought–action fusion; Gillihan et al., 2012).

Post-Traumatic Stress Disorder

Exposure-based protocols for PTSD generally focus on imaginal exposure. Notably, imaginal exposure is used in a different manner in PTSD treatment because it focuses on exposure to memories of past experiences (traumatic events) rather than hypothetical situations/outcomes. Nevertheless, the basic theory behind this is the same because cognitive–behavioral models of PTSD emphasize that avoidance of trauma memories and reminders maintains reactivity to them, which can be addressed through exposure. Imaginal exposure to trauma memories can be conducted in different formats, including repeated retelling and imagining of the full memory followed by more focused retelling of the most difficult parts (in prolonged exposure therapy; Foa et al., 2007) or writing of the trauma "narrative" followed by reading and revising this (e.g., in cognitive processing therapy; Resick et al., 2016). Some PTSD treatment protocols also include in vivo exposure to situations that the person began avoiding after their trauma, usually because these serve as reminders of the thoughts or feelings associated with the trauma.

Conclusion

Exposure therapy has been used, studied, and refined over many decades, resulting in a set of specialized techniques that require training and practice to master. The goal of this chapter was to provide an overview of these techniques, as well as an introduction to how they are applied for the treatment of certain anxiety-related disorders. These exposure therapy techniques are very effective and widely used for many problems, particularly difficulties with fear and anxiety, and thus are an important and valuable skill set for any therapist who is new to the field and/or learning to conduct CBT.

Helpful Resources

Apps

MindShift—CBT resources for individuals with anxiety disorders, including social anxiety

noCD—support for individuals with obsessive–compulsive disorder at different stages of the treatment process

PE Coach—support for individuals undergoing prolonged exposure therapy (for PTSD)

Websites

Anxiety & Depression Association of America. *Myths & realities: Generalized anxiety disorder (GAD):* https://adaa.org/understanding-anxiety/myth-conceptions

Association for Behavioral and Cognitive Therapies: http://www.findcbt.org/FAT

International OCD Foundation. *How is OCD treated?*: https://iocdf.org/about-ocd/ocd-treatment

Ivanhoe. *Exposure therapy for kids*: https://www.ivanhoe.com/family-health/exposure-therapy-for-kids

Oxford University Press: *Treatments that work series*: https://www.oxfordclinicalpsych.com/page/ttwseries/treatments-that-work-series

The Anxiety Coach. *Exposure therapy for fears and phobias*: https://www.anxietycoach.com/exposuretherapy.html

U.S. Department of Veterans Affairs. *PTSD: National Center for PTSD*: https://www.ptsd.va.gov/professional/treat/txessentials/index.asp

References

Abramowitz, J. S. (1996). Variants of exposure and response prevention in the treatment of obsessive–compulsive disorder: A meta-analysis. *Behavior Therapy, 27*, 583–600.

Abramowitz, J. S., Deacon, B. J., & Whiteside, S. P. (2019). *Exposure therapy for anxiety: Principles and practice*. Guilford.

Barlow, D. H. (2002). *Anxiety and its disorders: The nature and treatment of anxiety and panic* (2nd ed.). Guilford.

Bryant, R. A., Kenny, L., Joscelyne, A., Rawson, N., Maccallum, F., Cahill, C., Hopwood, S., Aderka, I., & Nickerson, A. (2014). Treating prolonged grief disorder: A randomized clinical trial. *JAMA Psychiatry, 71*, 1332–1339.

Byrne, S. P., Haber, P., Baillie, A., Giannopolous, V., & Morley, K. (2019). Cue exposure therapy for alcohol use disorders: What can be learned from exposure therapy for anxiety disorders? *Substance Use & Misuse, 54*, 2053–2063.

Coffey, S. F., Schumacher, J., Brimo, M., & Brady, K. T. (2005). Exposure therapy for substance abusers with PTSD: Translating research to practice. *Behavior Modification, 29*, 10–38.

Craske, M., Kircanski, K., Zelikowsky, M., Mystkowski, J., Chowdhury, N., & Baker, A. (2008). Optimizing inhibitory learning during exposure therapy. *Behaviour Research and Therapy, 46*, 5–27.

Craske, M., Treanor, M., Conway, C., Zbozinek, T., & Vervliet, B. (2014). Maximizing exposure therapy: An inhibitory learning approach. *Behaviour Research and Therapy, 58*, 10–23.

Fang, A., Sawyer, A. T., Asnaani, A., & Hofmann, S. G. (2013). Social mishap exposures for social anxiety disorder: An important treatment ingredient. *Cognitive and Behavioral Practice, 20*, 213–220.

Feske, U., & Chambless, D. L. (1995). Cognitive behavioral versus exposure only treatment for social phobia: A meta-analysis. *Behavior Therapy, 26*, 695–720.

Foa, E. B., Hembree, E., & Rothbaum, B. O. (2007). *Prolonged exposure therapy for PTSD: Emotional processing of traumatic experiences—Therapist guide*. Oxford University Press.

Foa, E. B., & Kozak, M. J. (1986). Emotional processing of fear: Exposure to corrective information. *Psychological Bulletin, 99*, 20–35.

Foa, E. B., & McLean, C. P. (2016). The efficacy of exposure therapy for anxiety-related disorders and its underlying mechanisms: The case of OCD and PTSD. *Annual Review of Clinical Psychology, 12*, 1–28.

Gillihan, S. J., Williams, M. T., Malcoun, E., Yadin, E., & Foa, E. B. (2012). Common pitfalls in exposure and response prevention (EX/RP) for OCD. *Journal of obsessive–compulsive and related disorders, 1*, 251–257.

Griffen, T. C., Naumann, E., & Hildebrandt, T. (2018). Mirror exposure therapy for body image disturbances and eating disorders: A review. *Clinical Psychology Review, 65*, 163–174.

Hofmann, S. G., Asnaani, A., Vonk, I. J., Sawyer, A. T., & Fang, A. (2012). The efficacy of cognitive behavioral therapy: A review of meta-analyses. *Cognitive Therapy and Research, 36*, 427–440.

Jones, M. C. (1924). A laboratory study of fear: The case of Peter. *Journal of Genetic Psychology, 31*, 308–315.

Piccirillo, M. L., Dryman, M. T., & Heimberg, R. G. (2016). Safety behaviors in adults with social anxiety: Review and future directions. *Behavior Therapy, 47*, 675–687.

Rapee, R. M., & Hayman, K. (1996). The effects of video feedback on the self-evaluation of performance in socially anxious subjects. *Behaviour Research and Therapy, 34*, 315–322.

Resick, P. A., Monson, C. M., & Chard, K. M. (2016). *Cognitive processing therapy for PTSD: A comprehensive manual*. Guilford.

Rupp, C., Doebler, P., Ehring, T., & Vossbeck-Elsebusch, A. N. (2017). Emotional processing theory put to test: A meta-analysis on the association between process and outcome measures in exposure therapy. *Clinical Psychology & Psychotherapy, 24*, 697–711.

Sripada, R. K., & Rauch, S. A. (2015). Between-session and within-session habituation in prolonged exposure therapy for posttraumatic stress disorder: A hierarchical linear modeling approach. *Journal of Anxiety Disorders, 30*, 81–87.

Wolpe, J., Brady, J. P., Serber, M., Agras, W. S., & Liberman, R. P. (1973). The current status of systematic desensitization. *American Journal of Psychiatry, 130*, 961–965.

Zlomke, K., & Davis, T. E., III. (2008). One-session treatment of specific phobias: A detailed description and review of treatment efficacy. *Behavior Therapy, 39*, 207–223.

An Introduction to Problem-Solving Therapy

Elizabeth S. Phillips and Hannah M. Thomson

Problem-solving therapy (PST) is a brief cognitive–behavioral intervention that provides clients with a set of strategies to approach and solve problems inherent in everyday living (D'Zurilla & Nezu, 2007). PST can fundamentally change our clients' life circumstances while building in them a sense of empowerment, self-confidence, and agency over their own lives (Nezu et al., 2007). This evidence-based intervention has broad application. It has been effectively implemented with multiple populations, including, but not limited to, people with depression, anxiety, substance use and psychotic disorders; people with a variety of medical diagnoses; those with relationships problems (D'Zurilla & Nezu, 2007); and adolescents and young adults (Hoek et al., 2012; Siu & Shek, 2010).

People generally approach problems in habitual ways, only vaguely aware that their "strategies" can exacerbate the very situations that are causing them distress. D'Zurilla and Nezu (2007) identify the following three problem-solving styles: avoidant, impulsive, and rational. Avoidant and impulsive styles usually lead to greater problems. Consider two scenarios. First, a client who cannot afford to pay her rent handles the situation by hiding from the apartment manager until she gets served with an eviction notice. Forced to live in her car, her distress escalates, and she becomes less able to manage the cascade of problems that follow. Second, a client in a similar situation impulsively writes his rent check hoping that there is enough money in his bank account to cover it. This strategy has sometimes worked for him, but he has experienced the inevitable miscalculations that have resulted in even more serious problems.

People also tend to have either a positive or a negative relationship to problems (D'Zurilla & Nezu, 2007), with those on the positive end of the spectrum approaching them as challenges or opportunities, and those at the other end experiencing them as threatening to their well-being. The former believe they are able to solve problems and are generally unruffled by them; the latter become upset, frustrated, and overwhelmed when problems arise, and they doubt their ability to solve them (D'Zurilla & Nezu, 2007).

According to D'Zurilla and Nezu (2007), the goal of PST is to help clients develop a more positive orientation to problems and become rational in their approach. Rational problem-solvers employ a deliberate and systematic approach wherein they gather facts and information about a problem, set meaningful and realistic problem-solving goals, and identify any obstacles toward achieving those goals. They generate a variety of options, compare the advantages and disadvantages of each, and devise a realistic action plan based on the information gathered (D'Zurrilla & Nezu, 2007). Clients who carefully apply this combination of skills can set into motion a new trajectory imbued with hope and opportunity.

The Orientation

Hegel and Areán (2011) have developed a manual for use with people with depression in primary care. They recommend beginning treatment with an orientation phase that, they assert, is critical to building a trusting, therapeutic relationship. It also provides the social worker an opportunity to instill hope that a client can experience significant improvement in their quality of life through this relatively straightforward PST process. The orientation should take approximately 30 minutes and cover the following topics: the structure of the sessions, the rationale for using PST, problems as a normal part of life, a brief review of the client's symptoms, a brief description of the seven steps, and an overview of the client's pressing problems. For the remainder of the chapter, we use a case example along with explanatory text to demonstrate the application of PST.

Case Example
The Structure of the Sessions

Social worker: Hi Peter, tell me what brings in today?

Peter (42-year-old African American male): Well, I was referred by my doctor. I have been feeling down and

the Doc gave me Zoloft. It is helping me feel better, but she said that this problem-solving therapy might also help me. I guess I'm still a little confused though, about what I am signing up for exactly.

Social worker: Of course, yes, you need some more information. Let me tell you a little bit about PST before we get started, and then you can decide. How about that? (Peter nods.) First of all, if you decide to move forward, we'll meet once a week for about 8 weeks. Sessions will take about 30 minutes. Today, however, we'll take a bit longer so I can share with you what PST is all about. Our focus will be on the here and now as opposed to taking a deep dive into your past. That doesn't mean you can't talk about things that happened previously, but I will likely direct you to think about how that presents a problem for you currently. Our intent will be to work through one problem each session; however, if a problem is more challenging, we can spend more time on it as needed. An important piece of PST is an activity you will be doing between sessions. This will be a task that you create each week during our sessions that's designed to move you toward your goal. What questions do you have for me so far? (Peter indicates he understands and has no questions.)

The Rationale for PST

Social worker: Now I'd like to share with you the rationale for using PST. First of all, it's an evidence-based intervention, which means it's been rigorously studied and found to be effective in helping people feel better. You said that you have been struggling with depression.

Peter: Yes, most of my adult life.

Social worker: So, you probably know from personal experience that depression, as well as anxiety and a host of other negative feelings, is caused, or at least exacerbated by, problems of everyday living. Think about this: What happens when you are really depressed, and a new problem comes up. Say, for example, your car starts leaking oil. How might this affect your depression and your ability to solve this problem?

Peter: I would be overwhelmed and probably ignore the leak.

Social worker: Yes, and that would create another problem and your depression would likely get worse, creating a downward spiral that's difficult to get out from under. What's remarkable about PST is that it teaches a set of skills that reverses that spiral. Solving one problem at a time can improve our mood, which makes us much more able to face the next problem that arises. Also, taking action—even if it doesn't result in the outcome we had hoped for—very often improves mood.

Problems Are a Normal Part of Life

Social worker: Problems are a part of life. Everybody has them. I don't say that in any way to minimize the problems you are going through. It's more to help you understand that problems don't occur because you are inherently deficient, or not "good enough" in some way. If you are alive, you have problems. What fundamentally affects our quality of life is what we do to address the problems we have. And fortunately for us, these skills can be learned.

A Brief Review of the Client's Symptoms

The acronym SIGECAM, which stands for *s*leep, *i*nterest, *g*uilt, *e*nergy, *c*oncentration, *a*ppetite, and *m*ood, can be used to assess for symptoms of anxiety and depression. It is important not to get too detailed when discussing symptoms because this can take away from the valuable time allotted to working through the steps. Once troubling symptoms are known, the social worker may choose to focus on those in future sessions rather than ask about each symptom at every meeting.

Social worker: A major benefit of PST is that it promises to relieve symptoms of anxiety and depression. We want to monitor those that are causing you the most difficulty throughout our time together to make sure that this intervention is working for you. I'm going to go over a list of common symptoms and I want you to tell me on a scale of 1 to 10, with 1 being no problem at all, and 10 being a serious problem, which number applies to you. Let's start with sleep. How would you rate your ability to have a good night's sleep?

Peter: About a 7.

Social worker: Do you have trouble falling asleep, staying asleep? Maybe both?

Peter: I wake up in the middle of the night and can't get back to sleep.

Social worker: Let me ask you—when you are lying in bed trying to get back to sleep, what do you generally think about?

Peter: How I'm dreading going to work in the morning.

Social worker: So, work is a big problem for you. (Client nods.) Okay. We'll make sure to monitor your sleep over time. Hopefully, through PST a good bit of your work stress can be reduced. How's your interest level when it comes to things outside of work?

A Brief Description of the Seven Steps

Social worker: I am going to tell you a bit about the seven steps of PST. The first and second steps include identifying the problem and developing a realistic and meaningful goal. In the third step, you will brainstorm options to achieve the goal. This is where you get to be very creative. In the fourth step we will look at the pros and cons of each of your options, and then, step 5, you select the best option based on your analysis. Step 6 is creating an action plan which you will carry out between sessions. Finally, step 7 is where we'll review how the action plan worked, and decide if we need to revise it or move on to solve another problem. Don't worry if you don't remember everything I just said. These steps will become clearer as we get into the actual process of applying them.

An Overview of Pressing Problems

Social worker: I'd like to get a general idea of the problems you'd like to resolve over the next few weeks. You mentioned work. Is there any other area of your life that you'd like to focus on?

Peter: Yes, I am bored a lot. I feel really lonely. I also don't like where I live, I think I want a nicer apartment. I want to go to the gym.

Social worker: This is a good list. What do you think we should prioritize to work on first?

The Seven Steps of Problem-Solving Therapy

After the orientation, the remainder of the session is spent working through the steps of problem-solving therapy. As is often true in therapy encounters, the fairly straightforward steps of PST are sometimes challenging in application. A social worker needs to "meet the client where they are" by starting the conversation with problems the client readily identifies with, even if the social worker believes the focus should be different. Sometimes, a client's problems may even seem superficial but are really indicative of a larger underlying issue the client may not be ready to address (Phillips et al., 2020). Clients often have negative assumptions (Hegel & Areán, 2011; Nezu et al., 2007) and may feel shame, embarrassment, ambivalence, and frustration over not being able to deal with a situation on their own. A social worker's ability to be flexible, encourage active client participation, and use clinical skills to engage and redirect to the tasks of problem-solving will keep the steps of PST from feeling mechanistic or impersonal (D'Zurilla & Nezu, 2007).

This section introduces a seven-step approach, similar to what Hegel and Areán (2011) developed in their manual for PST for depression and Phillips et al. (2020) further adapted. Nezu et al. (2007) outline a five-step model; however, the general progression of problem-solving is consistent between sources. The authors' own practice experience with PST was used to further address common concerns and develop the vignette.

Step 1: Identifying the Problem

It is not possible to effectively conduct PST without a clearly identified problem. For the purpose of this text, a problem is defined as a situation a person desires to change but some obstacle (internal or external) stands in the way (Hegel & Areán, 2011; Phillips et al., 2020). Sometimes a client will identify a problem, but when asked about barriers, the client does not identify any. For example, the client may need a ride to work, but when questioned, they know plenty of people to ask—they just have not gotten around to it. A social worker may briefly help with Step 6, developing an action plan, but may encourage the client to select another problem that is more complex (Hegel & Areán, 2011).

If a client is feeling unsure of what topics to address, a social worker can utilize a common problems checklist (Hegal & Areán, 2011). These types of lists can easily be found in a general internet search, and they usually include major life domains such as relationships, health, work, sexuality, and aging. Once a general area has been identified, the clinician and client work together to make the problem specific. Clinicians are encouraged to ask their client to "think like a detective"—identifying the who, what, when, where, and how of the problem (Hegel & Areán, 2011; Nezu et al., 2007). It is also important to work with clients to tease out facts from assumptions (Nezu et al., 2007). For example, let's say a client describes her problem as work-related. Further query reveals that her boss, who is normally quite communicative, has not emailed in several weeks. The client worries that her boss is disappointed in her work performance.

While the client has identified a work problem, further investigation has shown this to also potentially be an interpersonal problem (e.g., "My boss is disappointed in me"). The "who" of the situation is the client and her boss. The "what" is the lack of emails. The "when" is the last several weeks. The "where" is at work. The "how" in this case is how often this occurs. These are the facts. The major assumption the client is making is that the lack of

communication is related to her work performance. As part of PST, the social worker may help the client weigh the evidence by asking questions such as "What other explanations might there be for the lack of emails?" Once the client's assumptions are dispelled (or possibly confirmed), the problem is then defined specifically. In this instance, the client recognized that she might be assuming the worst about her boss but was concerned about whether she was meeting objectives for a new work project.

Sometimes what first appears to be one large complex problem is actually a number of smaller, interrelated problems (Hegel & Areán, 2011). A client who says, "I have low self-esteem," clearly believes they have a problem, and exploration would reveal multiple barriers. However, this problem is emotionally based and is not clear or specific. Again, a social worker can help the client be a detective and clarify what contributes to this statement. In this case, the client said they felt low self-esteem because of lack of connection with friends, lack of engagement in daily work, and limited financial resources. Each of these problem areas can be targeted to work on individually, with goals that can be evaluated for successful outcomes.

Problem identification is vital in order for the rest of the PST steps to proceed smoothly. If a social worker realizes a problem has not been well-defined, it is important to return to Step 1 until it is understood clearly by both parties (Hegel & Areán, 2011). Although this sometimes happens with even very experienced social workers, valuable time can be saved by not rushing this part of the conversation and remembering that "a problem well-defined is a problem half-solved" (John Dewey, as cited in Nezu et al., 2007, p. 43).

In the first session with his social worker, Peter said his problem was that he was lonely. "Being lonely" is a feeling state, so the social worker took some time to help clarify the problem. Some exploration around the who, what, when, where, and how revealed that Peter felt like he didn't know anyone with common interests. He felt this most often when he wanted to discuss a book or movie he had recently read or watched, or when he wanted to go out for coffee or dinner.

Step 2: Creating a Goal

A goal should be directly linked to the identified problem. The goal should be achievable and realistic (Phillips et al., 2020). It is important that the goal be framed in behavioral terms that are within the client's control and ability to complete, within a reasonable time, and with the resources available to them (Hegel & Areán, 2011; Nezu et al., 2007). A goal to "feel better about myself" is not specific or measurable, whereas a goal to "increase pleasurable activities every day" allows for brainstorming and behavioral change.

One good way to begin establishing a goal is to ask the client, "What would you be doing differently if the problem didn't exist anymore?" (Phillips et al., 2020). A client who wants to "feel less depressed by getting out more" may say if they felt better, they would "travel more." This creates an entrance point for discussion about goals. One point of caution is to avoid jumping to a solution: "Great, let's plan a weekend trip to get you traveling!" Instead, there is an interplay between problem identification and goal development. The problem is clarified when the client defines "getting out more" as "travel." The therapist and client can then work on short- and mid-term goals that will support this lifestyle change. Like with problem identification, breaking down goals into smaller achievable steps, often referred to as the "simplification rule," will help the client feel successful (D'Zurilla & Nezu, 2007).

Peter decided that his goal was to meet some friends he could spend time with. He felt specifically that if he had people he could call

on the phone and go on outings with, he would feel less lonely and isolated.

Step 3: Brainstorming Options

The third step of PST offers a client the opportunity to employ their creative thinking by generating a list of ideas to solve their problem. The social worker encourages the client to suspend judgment, emphasizing that quantity increases the chances of finding something that will work (Hegel & Areán, 2011; Nezu et al., 2007). It is okay for the client to modify and combine ideas; however, the goal is to not evaluate or disqualify any listed options in this phase, no matter how unrealistic they may seem (Hegel & Areán, 2011).

The challenge for both the client and the social worker is to allow the struggle that comes with the creative process of brainstorming (Hegel & Areán, 2011). Clients will often ask the social worker, "What do you think?" Social workers may believe they have great potential solutions to the identified problem based on what they know about the client's history and problem-solving style (Hegel & Areán, 2011; Phillips et al., 2020). However, the goal of PST is for the client to develop their problem-solving skills, and the social worker wants to avoid the client becoming dependent on the social worker for answers (Phillips et al., 2020).

So, what do you do if the client is really stuck? Several techniques can be used to help generate ideas without the social worker coming to the rescue. Sometimes, it helps the client when they are reminded of the underlying "teaching paradigm" of PST (Hegel & Areán, 2011); the social worker can explain how to paint a picture, but it is up to the client to generate the actual artwork. A reminder that the client is the best judge of what is best for them and using silence while the client thinks can often stimulate new ideas (Hegel & Areán, 2011).

An additional way to help a "stuck" client is to ask them to think of all the ideas they are sure would fail or to share the silliest ideas they can think of (Hegel & Areán, 2011; Nezu et al., 2007). Social workers may also ask the client to think from a third-person perspective, possibly incorporating a fictional character, famous personality, or someone the client just admires (Nezu et al., 2007; Phillips et al., 2020).

Peter, with prompting from his social worker, was able to generate a list of potential ways to meet people. The list included the following:

> Join a gym and talk to people as he worked out at the various stations.
> Approach people in the science fiction section of the bookstore or library because he knew they would share an interest in reading material.
> Volunteer at an animal shelter.
> Find an Alcoholics Anonymous meeting and connect with the "regulars."
> Ask his case manager about depression support groups.

Step 4: Weighing the Advantages and Disadvantages

If brainstorming is about quantity, weighing advantages and disadvantages is about quality. Step 4 of PST asks the client to strategically think about options and compare the relative merits of each in terms of time, effort, needed resources, financial constraints, cooperation of others, etc. (Hegel & Areán, 2011). A framework of advantages and disadvantages can be helpful in considering potential options; however, sometimes a benefit or drawback may have more significance to a client, and the "weight" of that must also be acknowledged (Hegel & Areán, 2011; Phillips et al., 2020). Again, the social worker facilitates this process by asking open-ended questions such as

"What would the advantages/disadvantages be . . .?" The social worker wants to continue to avoid adding their own judgments to the evaluation process. The only exception to this is if the client is overlooking a negative consequence to an action that might be extreme (Hegel & Areán, 2011; Phillips et al., 2020). For example, cutting the neighbor's electricity in order to turn off a motion sensor light that is keeping the client awake at night could result in jail time and fines. It is also okay for the social worker to remind the client of a benefit or drawback they mentioned in any of the earlier phases of treatment. In this case, the social worker is not offering any new information but is simply reminding the client in case they want to include it in the process (Hegel & Areán, 2011).

Peter was able to see there were benefits and drawbacks to all of his ideas. For example, he believed that although he was very passionate about animals, he maybe would have more opportunities for interaction with four-legged creatures than two-legged ones if he were to volunteer at a shelter. He got a little stuck on the "joining the gym" idea because he liked the benefit of "getting two things, my workout and meeting people, done at once." However, in talking it through with his social worker, he realized he would not get the kind of workout he wanted if he was distracted by trying to socialize, and it may be better to keep those two tasks separated.

Step 5: Evaluating and Choosing the Solution(s)

As the social worker and client weigh the benefits and drawbacks of potential options, the more appealing solutions often become apparent. However, it is important not to rush the evaluation because this is part of the process of the client developing critical thinking skills (Hegel & Areán, 2011). The client may want to choose more than one solution, which is supported when the ideas remain feasible with time, money, and resources (Phillips et al.,

2020). In this stage, social workers are helping the client clarify their thinking and address negative cognitions that may be preventing them from moving forward.

Ultimately, Peter decided that he was going to try to approach one person at the bookstore and another person at the library. He believed that it would be easy to start a conversation with someone showing a similar reading interest. If it went well, he could ask the person to join him at the coffee shop (both locations had coffee options), and it was minimal risk if the person was not interested in talking to him.

Step 6: Developing an Action Plan

During this stage, the clinician and client identify the details necessary to execute the chosen solution, including dates, times, who will be involved, and what resources are needed. Specific steps are outlined, and any potential barriers are discussed (Hegel & Areán, 2011).

It can sometimes be tempting to rush through this stage and assume the client's ability to generate ideas and choose a solution means they also know what tasks need to happen. Making sure the client is comfortable and has confidence to proceed is critical to this step and the overall success of implementing PST. If the client lacks confidence, the social worker can talk through concerns and divide the task into smaller steps if necessary (Hegel & Areán, 2011). Social workers can also gently remind clients that although an outcome cannot be guaranteed, there is value in moving from talking about solutions to trying them (D'Zurilla & Nezu, 2007; Phillips et al., 2020).

Peter's action plan was pretty straightforward. He was able to identify with his social worker that he would try the library on Tuesday (his regular day to check out books). He decided to go to the bookstore on Saturday afternoon because he believed the store would be busier and there would be in increased likelihood of several people being in the science

fiction section. He rehearsed his introduction in session. Peter was realistic in his expectation that this approach would not immediately lead to friendship, but it would help him meet people with common interests.

Step 7: Evaluating the Outcome

The final step of PST, evaluating the outcome, happens at the beginning of the session following the implementation of the action plan (Hegel & Areán, 2011). The social worker and client review efforts to complete the action plan. The social worker praises success and perseverance demonstrated by the client (Hegel & Areán, 2011). The social worker then asks about any unexpected barriers or difficulties, normalizing that sometimes things do not go as planned (Phillips et al., 2020). If there was a failure to complete the task, the client and social worker examine what new information there may now be about the problem that can be used toward future success (Hegel & Areán, 2011). The social worker helps the client explore what they learned from the experience and how they could implement these lessons of success (or difficulty) in the future (Hegel & Areán, 2011).

The social worker may also do a quick check on reported SIGECAM symptoms and, if observed, share positive changes they are noticing about a client's mood as they engage in problem-solving efforts (Phillips et al., 2020). Evaluating the outcome creates an opportunity to look back on how all the steps of PST led to overall client learning and growth (Hegel & Areán, 2011).

Peter reported to his social worker that he was able to follow through on their outlined action plan. He introduced himself to two people in the bookstore, and although he did not think he would see either party again, he enjoyed the conversations. He was especially pleased with his experience at the library, as he learned there was a book club for science fiction fans. He thought this would be an even better venue to meet "regulars."

Despite these successes, Peter reported his mood was still down, and his affect in this session was also observed to be low. The social worker asked Peter what he thought of this discrepancy. Peter paused, and then he said the problem he brought up last week was not really the "biggest" problem with being lonely. He explained what he really wanted was to start dating again, but his antidepressant was causing problems with erection. He was embarrassed to tell the social worker at the first meeting because he "didn't really know her or how this PST stuff worked." The social worker acknowledged the concern and normalized that sometimes it takes trying PST to see how the process works and that, as with any therapy, it takes a little time to build trust in the therapy relationship. The social worker then suggested that she and the client revisit the steps of PST with this new problem as the focus of that day's session.

Conclusion

Problem-solving therapy is a systematic process that can be fairly quickly learned and applied. However, as Nezu et al. (2012) caution, PST should never be conducted in a mechanistic manner. Building the relationship through warmth and compassion is critical to this intervention, as is true in any therapeutic setting. A social worker's ability to be enthusiastic, optimistic, and provide reassurance can transform a client's relationship to problems and their approach to solving them (Nezu et al., 2012). PST is a widely beneficial evidence-based intervention in the context of social work practice. Problems are, after all, a part of life. How we manage them can either exacerbate or mitigate their effects and profoundly change the way we feel.

References

D'Zurilla, T. J., & Nezu, A. M. (2007). *Problem-solving therapy: A positive approach to clinical intervention.* Springer.

Hegel, M., & Areán, P. A. (2011). *Problem-solving treatment for primary care (PST-PC): A treatment manual for depression.* https://pstnetwork.ucsf.edu/sites/pstnetwork.ucsf.edu/files/documents/Pst-PC%20Manual.pdf

Hoek, W., Schuurmans, J., Koot, H. M., & Cuijpers, P. (2012). Effects of internet-based guided self-help problem-solving therapy for adolescents with depression and anxiety: A randomized controlled trial. *PLoS One, 7*(8), e43485.

Nezu, A. M., Nezu, C. M., & D'Zurilla, T. J. (2007). *Solving life's problems: A five-step guide to enhanced well-being.* Springer.

Nezu, A. M., Nezu, C. M., & D'Zurilla, T. (2012). *Problem-solving therapy: A treatment manual.* Springer.

Phillips, E. S., Brekke, J., & Supranovich, R. (2020). Problem-solving therapy: Training workbook [Unpublished student manual]. Suzanne Dworak-Peck School of Social Work, University of Southern California.

Siu, A. M., & Shek, D. T. (2010). Social problem solving as a predictor of well-being in adolescents and young adults. *Social Indicators Research, 95*(3), 393–406.

Educational Interventions
Principles for Practice

Kimberly Strom

Social workers frequently serve as faculty members or field instructors, but the opportunity to teach also occurs in other settings and interventions. Perhaps the most prominent example is Brené Brown, whose expertise on uncomfortable emotions has reached millions via podcasts, Tedx talks, speeches, and a Netflix special (MacDonnell, n.d.; Ugwu, 2020). Although others in the profession may lack her global impact, many social workers also teach—via psychoeducational groups, volunteer training, professional or community education workshops, educational supervision, or as part of their interventions with clients (Brown, 2018; Jivanjee et al., 2015; Proctor, 2017). However, practitioners may not view these activities as teaching, thus missing valuable frameworks to assist in their practice. In order to encourage systematic attention to this role, this chapter summarizes the key elements of an education framework. It is intended to help social workers in a variety of settings to consider the educational aspects of their practice and to more effectively use teaching interventions.

Effective educational practice relies on six essential components:

1. Developing clear and appropriate objectives
2. Understanding the learners' needs and abilities
3. Developing an atmosphere that is conducive to learning
4. Being knowledgeable about the material to be conveyed
5. Selecting and using teaching methods appropriately
6. Evaluating one's performance and the learners' acquisition of educational outcomes

Whether one is teaching distress tolerance to an individual teenager, conducting a psychoeducational group for parents of mental health consumers, or presenting a course on crisis intervention to a group of volunteers, these steps comprise the necessary components of an effective educational program. Steps 1–6 are ongoing but typically begin well before the worker and learners come together. Step

6 should take place throughout the duration of educational contact and be done retrospectively as well.

Developing Clear and Appropriate Objectives

"No wind is favorable if you don't know your destination." This quote, attributed to the Roman philosopher Seneca, aptly addresses the first step in any form of social work intervention. Workers must be clear about their purpose in using an intervention or technique, the goals they hope to accomplish, and the intended outcomes their clients expect. Specific to educational interventions, the worker should have some sense of what capabilities the learners already possess and what skills, knowledge, or attitudes they hope the learners will have as a result of the intervention (Anastas, 2010). Even incidental teaching during the course of therapy depends on knowing the client, how best to educate them, and particular triggers or barriers to the material (Meyers, 2014). Because a program's marketing, participant recruitment, location, topic selection, teaching methods, and evaluation all flow from its purpose, it is imperative that the goals are clearly articulated and appropriate for the needs and interests of the end users.

Goals are sometimes an outgrowth of existing work with a client or group (Johnson & Johnson, 1997). For example, clinicians may find that their clients diagnosed with medical conditions can benefit from education about the course and management of their diseases as well as strategies to manage daily activities and relationships in light of the illnesses. At other times, educational programs are developed independently, after which participants choose (or are chosen) to participate. The development of Web-based continuing education to meet the needs of professionals desiring continuing education credits in ethics is one such example.

Needs may also be determined through formal surveys, past enrollment data or program evaluations, interviews with service providers from social work and other disciplines, and from meetings or focus groups with potential consumers or representative groups.

Learning objectives typically fall into three broad categories: those geared to achieving knowledge or understanding, those geared to achieving skills or abilities, and those geared to achieving insight or attitudinal change (The Second Principle, 2021). Within a given content area, interventions may have one focus ("Learn about diabetes and the diet plan to manage the disease"—*knowledge goal*) or several ("Learn about the diabetes diet plan and be able to plan meals that fit in the diet"—*knowledge and skills goals*). Clarity about the type of learning expected is especially important when workers select their teaching methods because teaching strategies are better suited to some educational goals than others. For example, skill building is better done through simulations or role-plays than a strictly lecture-based teaching format, experiential exercises can effectively lead to understanding and self-examination, and webinars or podcasts address knowledge goals (Ko & Rossen, 2010). In creating continuing education or staff development programs, administrators may consider whether growth in knowledge, skills, or attitudes is most needed. Some learning objectives (improving identification of implicit bias, developing empathy, and understanding countertransference) may be better handled through educational supervision than group processes (Kadushin & Harkness, 2014).

Clear objectives are also important when marketing an educational program. The dangers of launching a program with an ambiguous purpose include drawing participants with too broad a range of abilities or interests or discouraging appropriate people from enrolling at all because they cannot determine if the program is "for them." Finally, particularly in programs in which learners and teachers are evaluated on the outcomes they have achieved, goals must be clearly specified in order to adequately assess attainment (Congress, 2012; Riley-Tillman et al., 2020).

Understanding Learners' Needs and Abilities

Determining the need for and the purpose of an educational endeavor requires consideration of the prospective learners. Actually developing the educational intervention requires taking this understanding a step further and examining the particular life space of the learners, including their abilities, knowledge, and attitudes and what motivation or reluctance they may possess with regard to the content. It involves "tuning-in" to the "feelings and concerns that the client may bring to the helping encounter" (Shulman, 1992, p. 56). It may also involve understanding ethnocultural, developmental, and other issues and the way that teaching dynamics are affected by differences among teachers and learners (Anastas, 2010). An accurate understanding of learners will facilitate the selection and sequencing of content and the training methods used. Inadequate tuning-in may lead to learners' resentment and resistance; may affect enrollment and attendance; and may lead to the selection of material that is variously rudimentary, irrelevant, or too complex (Anastas, 2010; Bain, 2004).

A number of teaching principles are predicated on "knowing the learner" both as an aggregate group and as individuals. These include understanding sources of intrinsic and extrinsic motivation, making the material relevant and meaningful for each individual, building on the learner's existing knowledge, sequencing material from the familiar to the unfamiliar, identifying learning styles, and expressing appropriate confidence in the learner's abilities (Kadushin & Harkness, 2014). The ability to individualize learning makes it more potent, as does forging a relationship in which the participant feels known and valued. Both require actively anticipating and understanding the individual-as-learner (Hogan & Sathy, 2020; Sathy & Hogan, 2019).

Developing a Learning-Conducive Atmosphere

This component of teaching refers to both the physical environment and the emotional environment in which learning is to take place. Clearly, all educational opportunities carry with them the risk of mistakes or failure. As Kadushin (1985) has noted regarding educational supervision,

> We learn best when we can devote most of our energies in the learning situation to learning. Energy needed to defend against rejection, anxiety, guilt, shame, fear of failure, attacks on autonomy or uncertain expectations, is energy deflected from learning. (p. 149)

In keeping with this admonition, educators should inform learners about the purposes, processes, and structures for the learning activity. Learners must know what will be expected from them and what they can expect from the teacher (Lemov, 2010). The teacher should acknowledge and support the learner's risk-taking in pursuit of change and establish a climate of trust and safety. When teaching in a group format, guidelines should be established and articulated that will yield a supportive environment for all involved, and the leader should be aware of any dynamics that are impinging on an individual's participation (Brooks, 2011; Gregory, 2013; Ko & Rossen, 2010). Co-created group norms and ground rules facilitate collective investment in the group learning environment. Sample agreements include, "Use 'I statements,'" "Don't be afraid to share differences," "Respect one another's privacy," "Learn to sit with discomfort," and "Let everyone have a chance to speak" (Linabary, 2020).

Some class members may pose challenges to the safety and efficacy of the learning environment. Participants who are hostile, monopolizing, inattentive, unprepared, or fawning may alienate both the instructor and fellow class members (Royse, 2001). It is up to the leader to determine the basis for the problematic behaviors and craft an effective response. Some problems arise from poorly specified expectations or norms, and thus the resolutions may be structural in nature. Problems that arise from behavioral, psychological, or interpersonal issues will likely require an individualized intervention (McKeachie & Svinicki, 2014). As with other challenges arising in social work practice, supervision and consultation are essential to assist the worker in managing their personal responses to the difficulty and the difficulty itself.

When training is offered in person, the physical climate must be considered, even if it is not in the teacher's control. Ideally, the facilities should be well-suited for the purposes and characteristics of the learners. The literature on group work is relevant here as we consider, for example, the needs of a group of adults in a day-long didactic presentation compared to those of teenagers in an experiential learning program. The very setting of the educational program should be determined with the purpose and audience in mind. The location, accessibility, safety, parking, available hours, and "reputation" or message carried by the site will influence learner attendance, comfort, and safety. Keeping the nature of the training and trainees in mind, attention must also be paid to room size; temperature; arrangement; the use of tables or chairs without tables; other furnishings; and the availability of parking,

audiovisual equipment, restrooms, and refreshments. Creating the appropriate levels of physical and emotional comfort for learners is a planning task and an ongoing management responsibility for the educator.

Knowledge of Content

Implied in accepting the role of educator is the notion that one has some knowledge that can be taught to or shared with another. Yet a stumbling block for many would-be educators is the fear that they do not have a sufficient command of the material to put themselves forth as instructors. This section addresses how much knowledge of content is needed, what sources can be used to enhance or supplement the instructor's knowledge, and how the fear of not knowing enough can be overcome.

How much knowledge is required depends on the needs of the learners and the purposes and structure of the educational program (Anastas, 2010). A single fact about normative child development may be sufficient to inform a client in an incidental intervention around parenting, but a good deal more knowledge will be required if providing an adult education course on the subject. As noted previously, clarity about the goals of the educational program will be a vital guide. As educators begin to tune in to the program and learners, they get a sense of the depth and breadth of information needed. Reviewing curricula and online resources or discussing ideas with colleagues and clients will help further identify content needs even prior to the training. These steps often remind facilitators that they know more than they think they do. Where further knowledge of content is needed, presenters can supplement their knowledge through traditional sources such as texts and journals, interviewing subject experts, or viewing videos and films. In the classroom, presenters can augment the content they have to offer by using educational media, handouts, case discussions, bibliographies, videos, or outside speakers.

Despite these steps, educators often feel vulnerable about their command of the course content. Such feelings may stem from the mistaken impression that the teacher must be "the sage on the stage" rather than "the guide on the side." This misconception not only places an unrealistic burden on the worker but also can deprive all participants of the richness that comes from shared responsibility for learning. Sometimes referred to as student-centered learning, this model encourages the instructor to set the stage and provide the foundation through which all class members can contribute and learn from one another. This approach is consonant with theories of adult education, mutuality, and empowerment-based practice. Even if instructors cannot wholly utilize such a model, they must address the fear of not knowing. Learners do not expect that instructors will have all the answers, and in fact, they will have a greater respect for those who are able to say "I don't know. I'll check and get back to you" or "I hadn't heard about that. What do you know?" Similarly, the ability to catch and acknowledge mistakes conveys important messages about the authenticity of the instructor and the acceptability of errors. Conversely, the need to be correct or know it all often sets up an adversarial learning environment in which genuine learning is sacrificed for gamesmanship and defensiveness (Lang, 2012).

Although there is no definitive answer to "How much content is enough?" there are multiple strategies for adjusting content in the event of over- or underestimation. When planning a program, instructors should anticipate the amount of time they will devote to certain material, and they should think about how they might be able to cut or add as necessary. In multisession groups, instructors

can retool between sessions as content needs become apparent. Discussions, experiential exercises, and case studies can be used to take content to a deeper level of application if presenters move through their material more quickly than anticipated. If too much material has been planned, instructors can re-examine the objectives and eliminate less crucial information, or outside work or reading can supplement in-class time. In addition, the dilemma can be shared with learners, and their input can be used to prioritize the content to address with limited time.

Selecting and Using Teaching Techniques

Many people teach the way they have been taught. Unfortunately, many people have been taught in ways that stifle learner involvement, enthusiasm, and critical thinking. Having sat through mind-numbing slide shows, tangential discussions, and fun-but-pointless exercises, they may believe that these are the only available means of conveying information. In fact, there exists an array of teaching approaches; The challenge is not only in finding them but also in selecting them to appropriately meet the needs of the learners and the objectives of the intervention.

Certain structures and teaching techniques are particularly well-suited for different teaching goals (B. Davis, 2009; Knowles, 1975; Strom-Gottfried, 2006):

Lectures
- Convey complex material
- Highlight important facts and concepts
- Create a cognitive map for future applications

Exercises, demonstrations, role plays, and simulations
- Build group cohesion

- Foster skill acquisition and rehearsal
- Generate insight
- Model techniques and concepts
- Facilitate problem-solving

Cases, discussions, and debates
- Apply concepts
- Foster new perspectives and tolerance for ambiguity
- Bring energy and excitement
- Encourage decision-making in complex scenarios
- Facilitate team problem-solving

Web-based and other instructional technologies
- Convey complex material
- Allow self-paced and self-timed learning, review, and repetition
- Allow archiving of content, assignments, and discussions for sharing or future use

Each teaching method has its own promises and pitfalls. The following are suggestions for effectively using instructional strategies (Ambrose et al., 2010; Carnes, 2011; B. Davis, 2009; Filene, 2005; Lang, 2016; McKeachie & Svinicki, 2014; Royse, 2001; Sweet, 2010):

Lectures
- Limit length or break up with discussions, examples, question-and-answer sessions, or activities.
- Vary vocal intonations, facial expressions, gestures, and movement about the room.
- Initiate with a compelling question or scenario to be addressed by the lecture content.
- Do not read the lecture, but do read the audience.
- Provide scaffolding for content in outline form through handouts or PowerPoint presentations.

Exercises, demonstrations, role plays, and simulations
- Link to learning goals or course material.

- Choose judiciously.
- Clearly explain the objectives and directions; post on slides or board.
- Be alert to emotional reactions among participants.
- Promote skill development with modeling, videotaped examples, or discussion of strategies for effective practice.
- Demonstrate enthusiasm for the exercise and support for moving out of comfort zones.
- Debrief to identify strengths, weaknesses, and links to learning objectives.

Cases, discussions, and debates
- Choose compelling prompts and questions.
- Use handouts or slides to display necessary information.
- Create a supportive, caring, and respectful atmosphere.
- Develop clear learning points.
- Establish ground rules for discussions.
- Allow time for participants to think before responding.
- Encourage or structure alternative perspectives.
- Summarize key outcomes.

Web-based and other instructional technologies
- Carefully sequence educational modules.
- Make sure materials and directions are clear, thorough, and accurate.
- Design should be visually compelling and user-friendly.
- Anticipate technological glitches.
- Incorporate varied teaching strategies, including real-time meetings, discussion boards, video clips, question-and-answer sessions, and other interactive opportunities.

When selecting strategies to support various learning objectives, educators must also keep in mind their learners' capacities, the size of their group, and the amount of time they have for instruction. Such variables will affect the mix of teaching strategies employed, the time needed to carry them out, the learners' ability to benefit from the technique, the facilities needed, and the sequencing of material (Anastas, 2010).

Evaluating Teaching Performance and Learners' Acquisitions

Most evaluations address two questions: "Were the learning objectives achieved?" and "How effective was the instructor in helping them to be met?" Both elements of evaluation are important. Evaluating satisfaction without having some measure of the benefit of the content is referred to as "popularity polling" (L. Davis & McCallon, 1974, p. 275). Evaluating attainment without determining what was effective and what was not in terms of delivery does not help the instructor generalize the effort to future situations. A variety of measures can be used for each form of evaluation, and to some extent, the measure chosen depends on how the information gleaned will be used (Unrau et al., 2018). If the information will be quantified—for example, to give the learner a grade or to rate the instructor—precise numerical measures will be called for. For other purposes, less precise measures are adequate and sometimes preferable. For example, in measuring what people learned in a social skills training program, observed change or self-reported change may be adequate, whereas a CPR training program would require more definitive measures of competency. Post-tests are commonly required at the conclusion of webinars, online trainings, or self-directed programs to gauge knowledge acquisition before the participant is approved for education credits. Used alone or in combination with quantifiable ratings, open-ended questions

or narrative evaluations at periodic intervals can provide feedback with valuable depth and context (B. Davis, 2009). For example, the instructor may find that an inadvertent comment quelled class discussion or the instructions or timing of an exercise was ineffective, not the exercise itself. Open-ended questions invite examples, elaborations on how course material is being applied in practice, and enduring memories from the course.

In addition to the form of evaluation, timing must also be considered. In general, periodic formal or informal check-in types of evaluation will help both learners and educators reassess their progress toward achieving the objectives and reprioritize material or alter teaching strategies accordingly (B. Davis, 2009; Unrau et al., 2018). Methods for this include brief self-reports at the end of a session about insights and information achieved and "minute cards" or online surveys where participants provide written feedback on the meeting.

Effective and ethical instruction arises from the conscientious use of various forms of evaluation to inform practice. In addition to utilizing incremental and cumulative verbal and written feedback from participants, social workers can utilize peer observers, coaching, and videotaped sessions to continually improve and refine teaching performance.

Conclusion

Teaching is an integral part of social work practice, done in a variety of settings with a range of populations. This chapter offers guidance for the creation and delivery of educational interventions and offers resources for further study. It encourages the examination of social work activities from an education framework, advocating that as this function is better defined, models can be further developed, teaching challenges examined, and the necessary knowledge and skills for effective practice specified.

Helpful Resources

Websites

American Psychological Association. *10 tips for speaking like a TED Talk pro*: https://www.apa.org/monitor/2017/02/tips-speaking

International Association for Social Work with Groups, Inc.: http://www.iaswg.org

International Association for the Study of Cooperation in Education: https://uia.org/s/or/en/1100011230

International Association of Facilitators: http://www.iaf-world.org

Jisc. *Using digital media in new learning models*: https://www.jisc.ac.uk/full-guide/using-digital-media-in-new-learning-models

Sacramento State University Library. *Social work* (collection of videos and podcasts): https://csus.libguides.com/c.php?g=768302&p=5510331

staffdevelop.org. *How teachers learn new technologies*: http://www.staffdevelop.org

The Second Principle: https://thesecondprinciple.com

Apps

Educreations: Like an interactive whiteboard, this app lets users use animations, diagrams, and audio to share ideas and knowledge.

KahootKahoot: This app facilitates the creation and delivery of quizzes, games, and homework.

Keynote: This presentation app allows design, collaboration, and observation; accessible from mobile devices.

Poll Everywhere: This versatile app facilitates class management and interaction. It is an audience response system that lets trainers track attendance and comprehension, encourage participation, and solicit input.

Speeko: The "public speaking coach" provides practice exercises, instructional videos, and feedback to help build confidence and competence in various forms of verbal communication.

References

Ambrose, S. A., Bridges, M. W., & DiPietro, M. (2010). *How learning works: Seven research-based principles for smart teaching.* Jossey-Bass.

Anastas, J. W. (2010). *Teaching in social work: An educators' guide to theory and practice.* Columbia University Press.

Bain, K. (2004). *What the best college teachers do.* Harvard University Press.

Brooks, D. (2011). Getting students to talk. *Chronicle of Higher Education.* https://www.chronicle.com/article/getting-students-to-talk/

Brown, N. (2018). *Psychoeducational groups* (4th ed.). Routledge.

Carnes, M. C. (2011, March 6). Setting students' minds on fire. *Chronicle of Higher Education.* http://chronicle.com/article/Setting-Students-Minds-on/126592

Congress, E. P. (2012). Guest editorial continuing education: Lifelong learning for social work practitioners and educators. *Journal of Social Work Education, 48*(3), 397–401. https://doi.org/10.5175/JSWE.2012.201200085

Davis, B. G. (2009). *Tools for teaching* (2nd ed.). Jossey-Bass.

Davis, L. N., & McCallon, E. (1974). *Planning, conducting, and evaluating workshops.* Concepts.

Filene, P. (2005). *The joy of teaching: A practical guide for new college instructors.* University of North Carolina Press.

Gregory, C. (2013). Love the one you're with: Creating a classroom community. Faculty Focus. http://www.facultyfocus.com/articles/effective-classroom-management/love-the-one-youre-with-creating-a-classroom-community

Hogan, K. A., & Sathy, V. (2020, April 7). 8 ways to be more inclusive in your Zoom teaching. *Chronicle of Higher Education.* https://www.chronicle.com/article/8-Ways-to-Be-More-Inclusive-in/248460

Jivanjee, P., Pendell, K., Nissen, L., & Goodluck, C. (2015). Lifelong learning in social work: A qualitative exploration with practitioners, students, and field instructors. *Advances in Social Work, 16*(2), 260–275.

Johnson, D. W., & Johnson, F. P. (1997). *Joining together: Group theory and group skills* (6th ed.). Allyn & Bacon.

Kadushin, A. (1985). *Supervision in social work.* Columbia University Press.

Kadushin, A., & Harkness, D. (2014). *Supervision in social work* (5th ed.). Columbia University Press.

Knowles, M. S. (1975). *Self-directed learning.* Association Press.

Ko, S., & Rossen, S. (2010). *Teaching online: A practical guide* (3rd ed.). Routledge.

Lemov, D. (2010). *Teach like a champion: 49 techniques that put students on the path to college.* Jossey-Bass.

Lang, J. M. (2012, October 22). Teaching what you don't know. *Chronicle of Higher Education.* http://chronicle.com/article/Teaching-What-You-Dont-Know/135180

Lang, J. M. (2016). *Small teaching: Everyday lessons from the science of learning.* Jossey-Bass.

Linabary, J. (2020). Establishing and Maintaining Group Norms. *Small Group Communication.* https://smallgroup.pressbooks.com/chapter/norms/

MacDonnell, O. (n.d.). With 32 million views of her TED Talk, we must learn from Brene Brown about becoming a confident presenter. Confident Speak. https://www.confidentspeak.com/brene-browns-confidence-become-a-confident-powerful-presenter

McKeachie, W., & Svinicki, M. (2014). *McKeachie's teaching tips: Strategies, research, and theory for college and university teachers* (14th ed.). Cengage.

Meyers, L. (2014). Connecting with Clients. *Counseling Today.* https://ct.counseling.org/2014/08/connecting-with-clients/#

Proctor, E. (2017). The pursuit of quality for social work practice: Three generations and counting. *Journal of the Society for Social Work and Research, 8*(3), 335–353. https://doi.org/10.1086/693431

Riley-Tillman, T. C., Burns, M. K., & Kilgus, S. P. (2020). *Evaluating educational interventions: Single-case design for measuring response to intervention.* Guilford.

Royse, D. (2001). *Teaching tips for college and university instructors: A practical guide.* Allyn & Bacon.

Sathy, V., & Hogan, K. A. (2019, July 22). How to make your teaching more inclusive. *Chronicle of Higher Education.* https://www.chronicle.com/interactives/20190719_inclusive_teaching

Shulman, L. (1992). *The skills of helping: Individuals, families, and groups.* Peacock.

Strom-Gottfried, K. J. (2006). Managing human resources. In R. L. Edwards & J. A. Yankey (Eds.), *Effectively managing nonprofit organizations* (pp. 141–178). NASW Press.

Sweet, M. (2010, November 5). Group work that works. *Chronicle of Higher Education.* http://chronicle.com/blogs/profhacker/group-work-that-works-even-in-large-classes/28459

The Second Principle. (2021). *Three domains of learning: Cognitive, affective, psychomotor.* https://thesecondprinciple.com/instructionaldesign/threedomainsoflearning

Ugwu, R. (2020, April 24). Brené Brown is rooting for you, especially now. *The New York Times.* https://www.nytimes.com/2020/04/24/arts/brene-brown-podcast-virus.html

Unrau, Y. A., Gabor, P. A., & Grinnell, R. M., Jr. (2018). *Evaluation in social work: The art and science of practice* (8th ed.). Oxford University Press.

The Interface of Psychiatric Medications and Social Work Revisited

Kia J. Bentley and Joseph Walsh

Psychiatric medications are regularly used to help treat clients at mental health agencies who present with a variety of mental, emotional, and behavioral symptoms and challenges. Social workers, representing the largest number of professionals in outpatient mental health settings, and who often have the most extensive face-to-face interactions with clients, are increasingly called upon to be a resource for clients with respect to issues related to medication use. However social workers *across settings*, including in private practice, schools and child welfare agencies, jails and other forensic settings, and hospitals, clinics, hospices and other health care settings, also work with closely with clients using these medications on a regular basis. This suggests that social workers who want to be responsive to the complex and comprehensive concerns of clients need to develop a competence and comfort in addressing their medication-related dilemmas. That is, social workers should learn how to both use what they already know, as well as develop new skills and strategies to partner with clients and their families to help

them, for example, make informed decisions about psychiatric medication use, deal with accompanying issues of meaning and identity, design strategies to assist with adherence problems when relevant, build referral highways, and sometimes advocate for access to affordable medications. This chapter provides some context to the role of social workers related to psychiatric medication, outlines the major classes of medication and briefly reviews relevant controversies within each class, presents two overarching goals with respect to psychiatric medications and social work practice, and offers six specific role categories through which to meet those goals and a case example demonstrating their implementation. Finally the chapter identifies future issues in psychopharmacotherapy that will likely influence the roles of social workers in the coming decade.

The introduction of chlorpromazine (Thorazine) in the 1950s is most often associated with stimulating the modern era in psychopharmacology, and today psychiatric medications are routinely used with mental and emotional disorders and challenges. The explosion of brain research in the past few decades, and the renewed emphasis by NIH and others on etiological models of mental illness emphasizing genetics and neurotransmission, no doubt had a defining influence on pharmacological research and development. Medications were characterized as "fixing" the chemical imbalances in the brain thought by some to be the cause of mental illness. Others have harshly criticized that simplistic explanation and have pointed to flaws in the clinical research often cited to support these generalizations. Indeed while psychopharmacologists theorize much about why psychiatric medications "work," precise causes of action are typically not fully known. Social workers instead commonly embrace a more complex biopsychosocial model of causation for all aspects of human behavior, including mental illness. And while psychiatric medications, similar to other medical interventions, are generally presented to be about 70% effective for consumers, that fact does not mean that mental illness is actually initially or solely caused by problems in the electrochemical processes in the brain. Indeed we are learning more and more each day about the impact of psychosocial and behavioral events like trauma and stress on the brain and even on our genes. The arrows of causation do not seem to go one way. Listed below are the five classes of medications with some key examples of each, although, as will be seen, there is much overlap among categories in their use. In fact, a key idea around the classes of medication, seemingly named for the disorders they often treat, are chosen based on their effect on symptoms, not underlying disorders:

Antipsychotics

First-generation medications, those developed before the mid-1980s, include, as examples, fluphenazine (Prolixin), haloperidol (Haldol), perphenazine (Trilafon), thiothixene (Navane),

and trifluoperazine (Stelazine). The second-generation medications, at one time thought to be associated with fewer side effects, include risperidone (Risperdal), Olanzapine (Zyprexa), aripiprazole (Abilify), clozapine (Clozaril), and quietapine (Seroquel). Although other medications discussed later are used for treating some symptoms of psychosis, antipsychotic drugs are considered to be the main line of intervention for people with psychosis, including people with schizophrenia. This class of medication is thought to be most effective, for example, with the "positive symptoms" of schizophrenia (hallucinations, delusions, and disordered thinking) and less effective with the "negative symptoms" (flat affect and avolition). Considered by some to be among the riskiest medications, given the seriousness of some of the side effects of long-term use (e.g., neuroleptic malignant syndrome and agranulocytosis), attention in recent years has focused on the controversial use of antipsychotics with children and with older adults. Prescriptions for children diagnosed with oppositional defiant disorder and bipolar disorder have risen dramatically, and garnering particular attention is the perceived overuse of medication for children in the foster care system—an issue that has caught the attention of social work practitioners and researchers alike. Likewise, the high rate of use of antipsychotics in long-term care facilities to address behavioral issues associated with dementia is considered by many to be problematic.

Antidepressants

Antidepressants are the third most commonly prescribed medication of all types, and some reports suggest that approximately 1 in 10 people currently take them. Four different types of antidepressant medications include the monoamine oxidase inhibitors such as phenelzine (Nardil) and tranylcypromine (Parnate); cyclic drugs such as amilriptyline (Elavil), nortriptyline (Pamelor), doxepin (Sinequan), and imipramine (Tofranil); the selective serotonin reuptake inhibitors (SSRIs) including fluoxetine (Prozac), citapropam (Celexa), paroxetine (Paxil), sertraline (Zoloft), and fluvoxamine (Luvox); and the serotonin/norepinephrine reuptake inhibitors (SNRIs) such as desvenlafaxine (Pristiq), duloxetine (Cymbalta), and venlafaxine (Effexor). Other antidepressants that do not fit neatly into any of the previous categories include bupropion (Wellbutrin), buspirone (Buspar), and maprotilene (Ludiomil). The SSRI drugs are most commonly prescribed and are known to often take several weeks before a therapeutic effect is experienced. Recently, significant attention has been given to the large placebo effect in clinical trials of antidepressants as well as withdrawal symptoms upon discontinuation.

Mood Stabilizers

For decades, lithium, a naturally occurring salt, has been the most widely prescribed medication for the symptoms of bipolar disorder. A major concern with lithium is its narrow therapeutic window—that is, the amount needed to achieve a meaningful effect is relatively close to levels of toxicity, necessitating close monitoring. However, anticonvulsant drugs including valproate (Depakote), lamotrigine (Lamictal), and carbamazepine (Tegretol) have emerged since the late 1970s as acceptable alternatives. The hope of these medications is that they reduce both the frequency and the severity of manic episodes as well as address depressive symptoms. Controversies related to mood stabilizers include their off-label use with children as well as their use in conjunction with antidepressants.

Antianxiety Medications

In the past 25 years, antidepressant medications, especially the SSRIs and SNRIs, have emerged as drugs of first choice in treating long-term symptoms of anxiety. The cyclic antidepressants, due to their sedative properties, are often prescribed for persons whose anxiety prevents them from sleeping soundly. The benzodiazepines are the largest category of strictly antianxiety drugs, including diazepam (Valium), alprazolam (Xanax), lorazepam (Ativan), clonazepan (Klonopin), and triazolam (Halcion). However, there is concern about these drugs' potential for dependence and abuse, and a literature and practice are developing on how to successfully withdraw from these medications.

Stimulants

The use of natural stimulants dates back more than 1,000 years with the discovery of the energy-producing effects of caffeine found in coffee beans, tea leaves, and cocoa. Chemical stimulants created in the laboratory arrived in the mid-1800s. The stimulants, now especially used to treat symptoms of attention-deficit/hyperactivity disorder, include amphetamine (Adderall), pemoline (Cylert), methylphenidate (Ritalin and Concerta), and dextro-methylphenidate (more active than its counterpart; Focalin). Nonstimulants used to treat attention difficulties include atomoxetine (Strattera) and guanfacine (Intuniv XR). Some of these medications are available in extended-release form. There is long-standing controversy about the overuse of these medications with children, as well as concern about its stunting impact on their physical development. More recently, attention has focused on the misuse of these drugs by college students to enhance academic performance.

Toward Responsiveness and Collaboration

As noted previously, almost all social workers work at least occasionally with clients who use psychotropic medications as part of their intervention plans. In many service settings, social workers assess mental status and inquire about psychiatric medication use as part of a client's biopsychosocial assessment. However, social workers have recently begun to elaborate a more complete range of professional roles with regard to psychiatric medication. They are more frequently expected by clients and other professionals to possess sound knowledge of medications and their consequences for clients' lives, not merely to complement the prescriber's role but, rather, because they have important insights, techniques, and a special appreciation of client self-determination. A social work perspective includes a person-in-environment perspective (viewing people within a larger context of systems and in cultural and historical context), a social justice perspective (awareness of sociopolitical dimensions of situations with a special sensitivity to inequities in the distribution of rights and privileges), and a strengths and empowerment perspective (putting client self-determination at the center of practice and using client capacities to reach goals). Contemporary practice requires the social worker to strive for two related and overarching goals with respect to psychiatric medication:

Goal 1: Be an effective collaborator with clients, families, and other providers. To do this well, social workers should subscribe to the following philosophical practice principles:

- Embrace a client-centered "partnership" perspective around the range of medication-related dilemmas and issues that emerge in practice. This suggests working toward a nonthreatening alliance, a demystification of the helping process, and a mutual sharing of respective expertise. Clients want clinicians to create an attentive helping milieu in which collaborative problem-solving

can happen in a nonjudgmental and authentic space.
- Maintain a balanced perspective about psychiatric medication in the face of admittedly complex issues related to human rights and professional roles and also the "costs" and "benefits" of medication use. This means that social workers should likely neither be a cheerleader nor a naysayer for the use of psychiatric medication. Social workers are aware of the encouraging data about their effectiveness and the improved lives of many who use them but are also aware of their limitations in terms of effectiveness, the negative side effects, and the vast differences in client lived experiences with respect to medication.
- Work toward the successful integration of psychosocial interventions and psychopharmacology. Social workers should recognize the intrinsic power of both kinds of interventions and stay abreast of clinical outcome research that typically supports the superiority of combined treatments. However, client preferences also strongly influence actual treatment choices.
- Work toward interdisciplinary relationships characterized by equality of input and mutual respect, flexibility, decreased professional control, mutual understanding and shared goals, and also appreciate the challenges that emerge in managing parallel treatment. A desire to be understood as a profession must follow from knowledge of the professional domains of other providers and a deep appreciation of their own roles with clients.
- Appreciate both the strengths and the limits of clients and their families. Interventions should center on clients' and families' unique strengths and aspirations and away from symptoms

or weaknesses. Yet barriers to progress, such as a lack of skills or inadequate resources, must be appreciated and addressed whenever possible.

Goal 2. Be a meaningful resource to clients, families, and other providers with regard to medication-related issues and dilemmas. Social workers can do this by engaging in a range of general activities:

- Being a valuable source of whatever information, support, or "supplies" are called for in reaching specific "wants" and goals of clients with respect to their medication.
- Focusing first on assessing and clarifying medication-related issues, which can occur on psychological, social, strategic, practical, and informational levels.
- Being creative in applying skills and techniques drawn from evidence-based practice theories and models to medication-related issues, and emphasizing the use of both individual and environmental supports and resources.
- Encouraging the client and family to share their own experiences and emotions about medication use, provide input to the helping process, generate and weigh options, negotiate, and offer feedback as decisions are made.

Roles and Competencies in Medication Management

There are six specific and often overlapping contemporary roles for social workers with relevance for psychopharmacotherapy.

The Consultant

The social worker takes on an active role while maintaining a non-adversarial position with the provider. The social worker performs preliminary screenings to determine clients' possible need and desire for medication, makes referrals to prescribers, assists in information sharing and shared decision-making, and consults with clients and providers as needed. The social worker prepares clients for active participation in the medication assessment. Related responsibilities might include articulating the rationale for the referral, addressing the client's attitude toward prescribers, discussing the client's expectations and fears about medications, assessing the client's ability to access and pay for medication, and addressing issues of adherence. The worker monitors the client's subjective experience as well, particularly the meaning and impact of the referral to the client.

The Counselor

In the context of shared decision-making, the social worker helps clients articulate goals, understand the range of options, weigh numerous alternatives, plan and practice tasks, and take action steps to solve problems and reach personal goals related to psychiatric medication. Counseling can also involve sharing data on a specific medication's typical effectiveness and sharing experiences of other clients who have used it. It might mean the express use of a decision aid to guide the process. Offering advice based on the literature and professional experiences only works if the client knows it can be rejected without compromising the relationship. The counselor recognizes the importance of empathy, especially with regard to the client experience of side effects or impatience with therapeutic effect. For example, the counselor listens to the lived experiences of clients and provides opportunities for clients to share the impact of medication on their sense of self and identity. Social workers need to deeply listen to how medication, both positive effects and adverse effects, and self-definitions of mental illness or emotional distress are intertwined.

The Advocate

Social workers perform two essential tasks that relate to their ethical mandate to advocate for clients: (1) advocating directly for clients and families and (2) empowering and facilitating clients to advocate for themselves. Examples of advocacy in psychopharmacotherapy include trying to increase client access to the newest types of medication, helping a client obtain free medication from a drug company, discussing potential overmedication with the client's prescriber, challenging a hospital's termination of a clinical trial, or appealing an insurance company that declines coverage of a psychiatric drug. Advocacy is linked with client and family rights, particularly regarding access to quality treatment.

The Monitor

The social worker can help sustain the client's maintenance on medication by advising them about how to reliably keep track of both positive and negative effects of medication so that prompt prescriber action may be summoned when indicated. This function is supported when social workers have a basic understanding of pharmacokinetics (effects of the body on a drug) and pharmacodynamics (effects of a drug on the body). In addition, monitoring adverse psychological effects involves watching for any changes in the client's self-image and identity that emerge as a result of using medications. For example, clients may come to view themselves as "sick" people or become overly dependent on medication as a solution to perceived problems. Adverse social effects include any potentially negative consequences that go beyond the individual to consider how medication use affects one's employment, family relationships, or standing with certain social institutions. Finally, social workers can be creative in using existing rapid assessment measures or devising systematic procedures to evaluate each medication's effectiveness and a client's response over time.

The Educator

The social worker performs as a teacher and coach for clients, families, and perhaps other providers regarding issues including drug actions, benefits, risks, common side effects, dosing regimens, routes of administration, withdrawal, toxicity, and adherence. In addition, social workers teach and practice the steps in problem-solving, and in collaboration with nurses, pharmacists, and others, they offer practical suggestions to help clients take medication appropriately. Teaching clients skills in assertiveness and negotiation can help clients maximize their relationship with prescribers and other providers.

The Researcher

Using case reports, single-case designs, or more elaborate designs, the social worker documents how medications impact the lives of clients and families, how medications interact with other interventions, and how interdisciplinary relationships can be best coordinated.

Figure 74.1 summarizes the social worker's application of the roles described previously, followed by a clinical illustration.

Case Example

Rebecca was a 40-year-old divorced attorney with no children, living alone, with a diagnosis of schizoaffective disorder, characterized by delusions of persecution and agitated behavior. While representing her law firm overseas, she confronted associates about their inappropriate "spying" on her and threatened lawsuits in retaliation. She was hospitalized against her will by her parents and sister. Although she took injectable medication and quickly stabilized in the hospital, she remained angry and paranoid.

FIGURE 74.1 Roles of the social worker.

She refused to take medication as an outpatient, threatening to sue the social worker if he tried to convince her otherwise. The family was concerned about additional problematic behavior on Rebecca's part, which could ruin her already damaged legal career.

The social worker learned during his assessment that the client perceived medication use as evidence that she was "crazy," and taking it would have a devastating effect on her self-image as an independent woman succeeding in a male-dominated profession. Furthermore, Rebecca believed that the medication represented efforts of others to "control her mind" and "sabotage" her important legal advocacy work. Clearly, the idea of medications had strong, negative meanings to Rebecca's self-image. Rather than refer her directly to a prescriber, the social worker spent several weeks getting to know the client, validating her successes and empathizing with her trials, and not "pushing" her use of medications (counselor role). He was able to share several examples of clients with whom he had worked who similar symptoms and were helped by medication, but he also noted that effectiveness was not guaranteed and use likely would come with some side effects. The balanced perspective helped the client gradually develop trust in the social worker, and she agreed to a trial of "minimal-dose" medications that would serve to "help me

relax and deal with the stress of my persecution." With the client's assent, the social worker met with the prescriber before Rebecca's first session to let him know of her history and her attitudes about medication (consultant). He also arranged for Rebecca to receive free medications for 3 months from the agency's funding pool, even though she did not strictly qualify for it (advocate). The client admitted that, with her level of ambivalence, she would not take medications if she had to pay for them. With the social worker's encouragement, the prescriber also validated Rebecca's concerns about the medications and agreed to be available, through the social worker, should her ambivalence become more pronounced (monitor). With the social worker's patient intervention, Rebecca eventually accepted the medication and benefited from it. The social worker continued to emphasize its role in helping her remain calm (educator), and the client took it regularly. He also maintained contact with the client's family, with Rebecca's permission, to teach them about the hoped for effects and possible limitations of the medication and answer their questions about what is known and not known about these types of medications (educator). He was also able to offer strategies on how the family could support adherence without being coercive or becoming frustrated themselves.

Future Directions

Issues of importance to the fields of psycho-pharmacology and social work practice in the coming years include the following:

- *Integrated care* and other new models of health care delivery and financing that may reduce stigma and influence drug use, availability, and access to psychosocial interventions
- Increased interest and research related to *psychopharmacogenomics* and the hope this will lead to renewed interest in the develop-ment of new psychiatric drugs
- The fuller exploration of the use of *microdoses of psychedelic drugs* in psychiatry
- The discovery of and experimentation with *unique delivery routes and new technologies* such as smart drugs, brain implants, skin patches, or under-the-tongue medications
- More sophisticated *research on diverse popu-lations* of people (age, gender, race, ethnicity, religion, and health status) and the differ-ential physical and psychological effects of medications
- More findings about the *placebo effect* and how to harness it for good
- More research on the *additive or interactive effects of combining psychosocial interven-tions*, including new approaches such as mo-tivational interviewing, mindfulness, and acupuncture
- *Uncertainties about the lasting popularity of herbs, vitamins, nutritional interventions, and holistic alternatives*
- *The continuing expansion of prescription privileges* among nonphysician health care providers

- *Increased public scrutiny and criticisms* of psychiatric medications, clinical drug trials, drug companies, and advertising agencies
- *Greater mandate to learn how to evaluate in-formation from websites* and maintain up-to-date knowledge base through professional development offerings

Ideal practices for social workers with regard to psychiatric medications will always feature a collaborative helping environment in which the work is comfortably paced but action-oriented, and relationships are charac-terized by honesty, genuineness, and warmth. More attention should be paid to the eth-ical dimensions of medication management, such as avoiding subtle coercion of clients, respecting clients' decisions not to take med-ication, being vocal about concerns related to over- or undermedication, and long waiting lists for medication evaluation. Whereas a medical model of intervention suggests that the goals of care are symptom reduction and compliance, the goals of care in a social work–focused partnership perspective are quality of life; self-determination; and collaborative, compassionate care.

Helpful Resources

Mad in America: https://www.madinamerica.com
Mayo Clinic: https://www.mayoclinic.org
Mental Health America: https://www.mhanation.org
Mental Health Information Center: https://www.mentalhealth.org
National Alliance on Mental Illness: https://www.nami.org
National Institute of Mental Health. *Mental health medications*: https://www.nimh.nih.gov/health/topics/mental-health-medications/index.shtml
Physicians' desk reference: https://www.pdr.net

Trauma-Focused Therapy for Children and Adolescents

Alison Salloum and Melissa A. Thompson

Common types of traumatic events among children presenting for treatment include traumatic loss, domestic violence, impaired caregiver, emotional abuse, physical abuse, neglect, sexual abuse, and community violence. However, there are many other types of traumatic events, such as medical trauma, disasters, war, terrorism, serious injuries, and school violence, with children experiencing exposure to multiple traumatic events (Greeson et al., 2014). Approximately 16% of youth who are exposed to traumatic events will develop post-traumatic stress disorder (PTSD); rates vary based on gender and type of trauma, with the rate higher (32.9%) for girls exposed to interpersonal trauma (Alisic et al., 2014). During the first 1–6 months post trauma, there may be a decline in post-traumatic stress symptoms for some children. However, without effective treatment, PTSD will persist for a substantial percentage of children (Hiller et al., 2016). If left untreated, childhood trauma is associated with negative long-term mental health (Curran et al., 2018) and health consequences that can last a lifetime (Hughes et al., 2017).

Many children who present with PTSD may also have other emotional and behavioral problems. Children exposed to traumatic events are at an increased risk for depression. Approximately one-fourth of children exposed to trauma will also meet criteria for clinically significant depression or diagnosis (Vibhakar et al., 2019). Children exposed to trauma may also present with anxiety disorders and behavioral disorders (Briggs-Gowan et al., 2010). In a study consisting of clinical interviews with parents of young children (284 children aged 3–6 years) who had experienced single trauma, repeated trauma, and exposure to a hurricane, non-PTSD disorders arose in the presence of PTSD for 95% of the children, suggesting that when comorbidities are present, clinicians should target PTSD, especially when resources are limited (Scheeringa, 2019). When disruptive behavioral disorders are present and/or parents' coping capacities are limited, treatments need to incorporate strategies for behavioral management and parental support. Most trauma-focused treatments allow flexibility to tailor treatment to the child's and parent's needs while remaining focused on decreasing traumatic stress, which often is accompanied by decreases in associated childhood disorders and parental stress. However, an assessment with standardized trauma-focused assessment measures is needed to plan, tailor, monitor, and evaluate treatment.

Screening and Assessment

Screening and assessment tools may be used in various settings, such as schools, health clinics, and mental health clinics, to screen children for potentially traumatic events and traumatic stress symptomatology. Checklists of types of traumas with response formats of yes or no may be used for a rapid screening to identify children who have experienced traumatic events. There are also several parent and child self-reports that can be used to assess for PTSD symptomatology and likely PTSD. Due to weak associations between parent and child reports of trauma exposure and symptomology (Stover et al., 2010), assessing both parent and child is recommended, as well as using a standardized clinical interview. Last, it is important to include broadband measures that assess for other psychopathologies as well as strengths. There are several considerations for selecting well-validated and reliable measures, such as age of the child (there are different measures for children aged 6 years or younger), language availability, cost, training, scoring ease, and time administrating measures. Table 75.1 lists websites for measures.

Evidence-Based Treatment for Childhood Trauma

There are several trauma-focused evidence-based treatments for children and adolescents, including trauma-focused cognitive–behavioral therapy (TF-CBT; Cohen et al., 2017) and eye movement desensitization and reprocessing (Karadag et al., 2020), and for young children, including Preschool PTSD Treatment (Scheeringa, 2016) and Child–Parent Psychotherapy (Thomas et al., 2017). Research suggests that evidence-based treatments that help children in a direct way process the traumatic events and include some types of CBT strategies are effective (Mavranezouli et al., 2020).

To date, TF-CBT has the largest evidence base with widespread dissemination efforts. TF-CBT is for children ages 3–18 years and their caregivers. TF-CBT has demonstrated effectiveness with diverse populations and a wide range of traumatic events. Although TF-CBT utilizes common CBT methods, other theories, such as systems theory and attachment theory, also guide the intervention. TF-CBT is a trauma-focused components-based treatment in which the child and caregiver participate in all of the PRACTICE components: psychoeducation; parenting skills; affect modulation; cognitive coping; trauma narrative and cognitive processing of the traumatic event; in vivo mastery of trauma reminders, if needed; conjoint child–parent sessions; and enhancing safety and future development. Importantly, gradual exposure to the child's traumatic events occurs in all components, with the most exposure occurring during the trauma narrative sessions (Cohen et al., 2017). All of the components of TF-CBT are also included in nine domains identified as common practices across evidence-based practice (EBP) for childhood trauma. Social workers and other behavioral health professionals should address these core components and practices when providing trauma-focused treatment (Layne et al., 2014; see Table 75.1).

Caregiver participation is recommended in TF-CBT because the treatment involves a parallel process in which both child and

TABLE 75.1 Core Trauma-Focused Components and Practices for Childhood Trauma

Trauma-Focused Component	Trauma-Focused Practice and Websites
Assessment	Presence of trauma-related symptoms and impairment, risk factors, and protective factors. Use of standardized measures for trauma-specific symptoms and broadband assessments. *Websites* International Society for Traumatic Stress Studies: https://istss.org/home National Center Traumatic Stress Network. *Measures review database*: https://www.nctsn.org/treatments-and-practices/screening-and-assessments/measure-reviews National Center for PTSD. *List of all measures*: https://www.ptsd.va.gov/professional/assessment/list_measures.asp
Safety	Assess safety throughout treatment and intervene as needed. *Websites* Child Welfare Information Gateway. *Safety planning in child protection*: https://www.childwelfare.gov/topics/responding/child-protection/safety-planning-in-child-protection National Institute of Mental Health. *Ask Suicide-Screening Questions (ASQ) toolkit*: https://www.nimh.nih.gov/research/research-conducted-at-nimh/asq-toolkit-materials/index.shtml
Engagement	Engagement might involve listening and understanding the child's and parent's perspective of concerns to be address, problem-solving and addressing barriers to meeting goals, and building therapeutic alliance, including psychoeducation (educating, normalizing, and validating).
Attachment/ strengthening relationships	Strengthen the parent–child and/or family relationships through activities that foster "attunement, communication and problem-solving capacities" (Layne, 2014, p. 9).
Social context	Understand the environmental influences that may hinder or support the child and family. Identify the secondary adversities and plan collaboratively. Advocate and engage case management as needed.
Core treatment interventions	Teach, practice, and promote self-regulation skills. These are typically the PRAC skills (i.e., psychoeducation, parenting skills, affect modulation, and cognitive coping) that occur before the trauma narrative. *Websites* Medical University of South Carolina. *TF-CBT web training*: https://tfcbt2.musc.edu Child–Parent Psychotherapy: https://childparentpsychotherapy.com/about
Trauma processing	Help the child tell their story about what happened in a coherent manner (beginning, middle, and end) with identifying thoughts and feelings (including feeling in the body). As part of TF-CBT, there is a cognitive processing of the trauma narrative after the trauma narrative is shared as well as a conjoint parent–child session in which the child shares their trauma narrative with the parent (or caregiver).
Consolidation/ post-traumatic growth	Consolidation entails placing the traumatic event in the larger context of the child's life while engaging in meaning-making. This component may also focus on coping strategies when trauma reminders in the future occur, awareness on current progress, and future development.
Self-care	Clinicians focus on their own self-care strategies as well as assessment of burnout and secondary trauma reactions. While personal self-care strategies are promoted so are environmental practices and resources that recognize the impact of trauma on the clinicians and within the practice context. *Websites* Professional Quality of Life measure: https://proqol.org/ProQol_Test.html Trauma-Informed Self-Care measure: http://intra.cbcs.usf.edu/PersonTracker/common/cfm/Unsecured/socialwork/bio.cfm?ID=118

Note. The nine core components are from Layne et al. (2014), as are the trauma-focused practices; additional information has been added to the practices.
PTSD, post-traumatic stress disorder; TF-CBT, trauma-focused cognitive–behavioral therapy.

caregiver are learning and practicing the components, although there may be situations in which caregiver participation is not possible. A review of caregiver involvement in TF-CBT found preliminary support for caregiver's distress related to the child's trauma, PTSD, and depression decreasing pre- to post-TF-CBT and that child improvements were not as strong with children who had parents with high depression (Martin et al., 2019). Given caregiver involvement in the child's trauma-focused treatment, social workers and other behavioral health professionals should use standardized tools to assess parent distress related to the child's trauma, PTSD, and depression prior to, during, and after treatment.

Training and Implementation

Learning how to implement a trauma-focused EBP takes training, practice implementing the treatment, and consultation from a trained clinician. For example, certification in TF-CBT requires a master's degree in a mental health discipline, professional licenses, taking a Web-based TF-CBT course, attending a 2-day training in TF-CBT, completing at least three TF-CBT cases with at least two of these involving a caregiver, using standardized measures to track progress, and passing a certification test.

Research on implementation and dissemination is providing lessons learned in terms of barriers and facilitators of successful implementation. Some barriers may include cases not appropriate for specific trauma-focused treatment, management not supportive, therapists resistant to implementing EBP, therapist avoidance of processing the trauma with the child, not having trainers within the organization, staff turnover, and time constraints. There are several facilitators to help therapists implement a trauma-focused EBP such as TF-CBT.

Organizational factors that can help with successful implementation of a trauma-focused EBP include assessing the organization's readiness to implement the practice, having leadership "buy-in" and support, ensuring that the community and those making referrals know the importance of using EBP for trauma-focused treatment so that they advocate for the use of such treatment for their clients, and partnering with state agencies or others who can assist with additional funding that will be needed for training and consultations. Factors that may contribute to therapists successfully implementing the trauma-focused EBP include having expert coaching and consultation available as well as face-to-face consultation and training throughout the learning process, utilizing an application process in which therapists who want to implement the treatment document their willingness and capacity to participate, and incentives or stipends (Sigel et al., 2013).

Trauma-Focused Self-Care

One of the core components in evidence-based treatment programs is self-care. The impact of one's own trauma and/or the effects of working with people who have experienced trauma may lead to burnout or secondary trauma. Helping survivors can be very rewarding and satisfying, but clinicians must practice self-care. As noted by Salloum et al. (2015), trauma-informed self-care (TISC) consists of

> being aware of one's own emotional experience in response to exposure to traumatized clients and planning and engaging in positive coping strategies, such as seeking supervision, attending trainings on secondary trauma, working within a team, balancing caseloads, and work–life balance. (p. 54)

Clinicians are encouraged to practice TISC to buffer against burnout and secondary trauma. In addition to assessing one's own TISC practices, it is important to assess burnout, secondary trauma, and comparison satisfaction to maintain one's own well-being and to mitigate worker burnout, secondary trauma, and/or PTSD resulting from trauma work (Salloum et al., 2019).

Future Directions for Trauma-Focused Treatment for Children and Youth

Future directions for trauma-focused treatments for childhood trauma need to address sustainability of effective treatments for improved access for all children in need, increasing the number of trained clinicians, the development of accurate feasible assessment tools, and the development of effective treatment of multiple problems for which there is high treatment participation and low attrition. Future treatments may be delivered utilizing new service delivery methods such as parent-led therapist-assisted stepped care treatment (Salloum et al., 2017) and/or that incorporate technology that improves access to treatment in various settings. New assessment and treatment monitoring methods that include technology and/or biomarkers rather than relying solely on self-reports are needed. Future treatment may also include transdiagnostic treatments that target core mechanisms of change that address trauma-related symptomatology and prior emotional and behavioral problems. Transdiagnostic approaches address the burden of clinicians learning multiple EBPs and the burden on children and their families needing different treatments for different problems. When children experience traumatic events, treatments must be available, efficient, and effective to change the trajectory from a lifetime of suffering to a resilience path.

References

Alisic, E., Zalta, A. K., van Wesel, F., Larsen, S. E., Hafstad, G. S., Hassanpour, K., & Smid, G. E. (2014). Rates of post-traumatic stress disorder in trauma-exposed children and adolescents: Meta-analysis. *British Journal of Psychiatry, 204*(5), 335–340. https://doi.org/10.1192/bjp.bp.113.131227

Briggs-Gowan, M. J., Carter, A. S., Clark, R., Augustyn, M., McCarthy, K. J., & Ford, J. D. (2010). Exposure to potentially traumatic events in early childhood: Differential links to emergent psychopathology. *Journal of Child Psychology and Psychiatry, 51*(10), 1132–1140. https://doi.org/10.1111/j.1469-7610.2010.02256.x

Cohen, J. A., Mannarino, A. P., & Deblinger, E. (2017). *Treating trauma and traumatic grief in children and adolescents.* Guilford.

Curran, E., Adamson, G., Rosato, M., De Cock, P., & Leavey, G. (2018). Profiles of childhood trauma and psychopathology: US national epidemiologic survey. *Social Psychiatry and Psychiatric Epidemiology, 53*(11), 1207–1219. https://doi.org/10.1007/s00127-018-1525-y

Greeson, J. K., Briggs, E. C., Layne, C. M., Belcher, H. M., Ostrowski, S. A., Kim, S., Lee, R. C., Vivrette, R. L., Pynoos, R. S., & Fairbank, J. A. (2014). Traumatic childhood experiences in the 21st century: Broadening and building on the ACE studies with data from the National Child Traumatic Stress Network. *Journal of Interpersonal Violence, 29*(3), 536–556. https://doi.org/10.1177/0886260513505217

Hiller, R. M., Meiser-Stedman, R., Fearon, P., Lobo, S., McKinnon, A., Fraser, A., & Halligan, S. L. (2016). Research review: Changes in the prevalence and symptom severity of child post-traumatic stress disorder in the year following trauma—A meta-analytic study. *Journal of Child Psychology and Psychiatry, 57*(8), 884–898. https://doi.org/10.1111/jcpp.12566

Hughes, K., Bellis, M. A., Hardcastle, K. A., Sethi, D., Butchart, A., Mikton, C., Jones, L., & Dunne, M. P. (2017). The effect of multiple adverse childhood experiences on health: A systematic review and meta-analysis. *Lancet Public Health, 2*(8), e356–e366. https://doi.org/10.1016/s2468-2667(17)30118-4

Karadag, M., Gokcen, C., & Sarp, A. S. (2020). EMDR therapy in children and adolescents who have post-traumatic stress disorder: A six-week follow-up study. *International Journal of Psychiatry in Clinical Practice, 24*(1), 77–82. https://doi.org/10.1080/13651501.2019.1682171

Layne, C. M., Strand, V., Popescu, M., Kaplow, J. B., Abramovitz, R., Stuber, M., Amaya-Jackson, L., Ross, L., & Pynoos, R. S. (2014). Using the core curriculum on childhood trauma to strengthen clinical knowledge in evidence-based practitioners. *Journal of Clinical Child and Adolescent Psychology, 43*(2), 286–300. https://doi.org/10.1080/15374416.2013.865192

Martin, C. G., Everett, Y., Skowron, E. A., & Zalewski, M. (2019). The role of caregiver psychopathology in the treatment of childhood trauma with trauma-focused cognitive behavioral therapy: A systematic review. *Clinical Child and Family Psychology Review, 22*(3), 273–289. https://doi.org/10.1007/s10567-019-00290-4

Mavranezouli, I., Megnin-Viggars, O., Daly, C., Dias, S., Stockton, S., Meiser-Stedman, R., Trickey, D., & Pilling, S. (2020). Research review: Psychological and psychosocial treatments for children and young people with post-traumatic stress disorder: A network meta-analysis. *Journal of Child Psychology and Psychiatry, 61*(1), 18–29. https://doi.org/10.1111/jcpp.13094

Salloum, A., Choi, M. J., & Stover, C. S. (2019). Exploratory study on the role of trauma-informed self-care on child welfare workers' mental health. *Children and Youth Services Review, 101*, 299–306. https://doi.org/10.1016/j.childyouth.2019.04.013

Salloum, A., Kondrat, D. C., Johnco, C., & Olson, K. R. (2015). The role of self-care on compassion satisfaction, burnout and secondary trauma among child welfare workers. *Children and Youth Services Review, 49*(2), 54–61. https://doi.org/10.1016/j.childyouth.2014.12.023

Salloum, A., Small, B. J., Robst, J., Scheeringa, M. S., Cohen, J. A., & Storch, E. A. (2017). Stepped and standard care for childhood trauma. *Research on Social Work Practice, 27*(6), 653. http://ezproxy.lib.usf.edu/login?url=http://search.ebscohost.com/login.aspx?direct=true&db=edb&AN=125196953&site=eds-live

Scheeringa, M. S. (2016). *Treating PTSD in preschool: A clinical guide.* Guilford.

Scheeringa, M. S. (2019). Development of a brief screen for symptoms of posttraumatic stress disorder in young children: The Young Child PTSD Screen. *Journal of Developmental and Behavioral Pediatrics, 40*(2), 105–111. https://doi.org/10.1097/dbp.0000000000000639

Sigel, B. A., Benton, A. H., Lynch, C. E., & Kramer, T. L. (2013). Characteristics of 17 statewide initiatives to disseminate trauma-focused cognitive–behavioral therapy (TF-CBT). *Psychological Trauma, 5*(4), 323–333. https://doi.org/10.1037/a0029095

Stover, C. S., Hahn, H., Im, J. J. Y., & Berkowitz, S. (2010). Agreement of parent and child reports of trauma exposure and symptoms in the early aftermath of a traumatic event. *Psychological Trauma, 2*(3), 159–168. https://doi.org/10.1037/a0019156

Thomas, R., Abell, B., Webb, H. J., Avdagic, E., & Zimmer-Gembeck, M. J. (2017). Parent–child interaction therapy: A meta-analysis. *Pediatrics, 140*(3). https://doi.org/10.1542/peds.2017-0352

Vibhakar, V., Allen, L. R., Gee, B., & Meiser-Stedman, R. (2019). A systematic review and meta-analysis on the prevalence of depression in children and adolescents after exposure to trauma. *Journal of Affective Disorders, 255*, 77–89. https://doi.org/10.1016/j.jad.2019.05.005

Family Interventions

Effective Couple and Family Treatment for Client Populations

Cynthia Franklin, Catheleen Jordan, and Laura M. Hopson

The practice and research on couple and family treatment are supported by several disciplines, including social work, psychology, family science, and marriage and family therapy. As a result of this interdisciplinary participation, a number of effective therapeutic methods have evolved. This chapter offers a review of couple and family therapies and their effectiveness for social work practitioners, followed by selection guidelines for using these interventions with diverse client populations.

Couple and Family Practice Methods and Research

The 1950s and 1960s ushered in the development of specific family therapy models, still popular today. These are grounded in systems theory that views individual problems in relation to other family members and significant others in the social environment. This approach began at the Mental Research Institute (MRI) in Palo Alto, California, co-founded in 1959 by psychiatrist Don Jackson and social worker Virginia Satir. Other influential family

therapists were trained at the MRI, including social workers Steve de Shazer and Insoo Kim Berg (solution-focused brief therapy) and Jay Haley (strategic family therapy). Other systems models were developed by Murray Bowen (family systems), Salvador Minuchin (structural family therapy), and by Gerald Patterson (parenting). Further information about these models is provided in Jordan and Franklin's *Clinical Assessment for Social Workers* (2020).

Practice Methods

All family systems approaches have in common a focus on making changes in the family as a means of creating therapeutic change. In addition, different approaches have increasingly been integrated in couple and family practice to develop empirically supported treatments for high-risk groups. Cognitive–behavioral therapy is often integrated with family systems approaches to create the most efficacious interventions for couple and family treatment. In addition to integration of multiple approaches, technical eclecticism (selected use of techniques from different models) and common factors are also used (Sprenkle et al., 2009). Common factors include therapeutic alliance, empathy, goal consensus and collaboration, positive regard and affirmation, mastery, and congruence/genuineness.

Finally, the field has moved toward evidence-based practice. Many evidence-based couple and family approaches also share common characteristics or core components. For example, parent management training is one of the primary components of effective treatment programs (Kazdin & Whitley, 2003). Effective interventions typically include educational components and opportunities to practice new skills, such as communication and problem-solving skills. Practitioners model new behaviors and provide feedback to family members on their ability to implement the behaviors. Intervening on multiple ecological levels is also important, and many effective approaches intervene with family members, school staff, and providers in the community (Jordan & Franklin, 2020). Couple and family approaches may also integrate feminist, postmodern, critical race, and multicultural theory into systems perspectives because these viewpoints are very significant to understanding how relationships in diverse family systems function (Boyd-Webb, 2013).

Research

Several reviews of couple and family therapy approaches show effective applications of the different family interventions (e.g., Carr, 2009; Sprenkle, 2012). Sprenkle's (2012) review suggests that family therapies are most effective for conduct disorder; drug abuse; psychoeducation with mental illness; alcoholism; relationship distress, including relationship education; and child and adolescent disorders. The following guidelines for classifying evidence-based treatments in couple and family therapy, developed by Sexton et al. (2011), may be useful in selecting interventions:

Category 1: Some evidence for the model compared with reasonable alternatives (i.e., treatment as usual)

Category 2: Promising model; has some verification

Category 3: Effective model with strong scientific evidence of effectiveness; shows change with various problems and populations

The strongest studies have relevant comparison groups, random assignment, treatment fidelity measures, and use multiple measures to measure outcomes. As mentioned previously, a trend in family therapy is to integrate techniques from more than one family therapy model and to operationalize these using clinical manuals and protocols.

Selecting Couple and Family Interventions

Across family therapy models, characteristics of the therapeutic relationship are important factors moderating the effectiveness of family interventions. One meta-analysis indicates that therapeutic relationship variables are good predictors of family therapy outcomes (Karver et al., 2006), and the use of self in couple and family interventions is particularly important because these therapies are directive and rely on the therapist in the change processes. It is also important to keep in mind that although all couple and family practice models show potential effectiveness, certain models produce better outcomes. Evidence indicates that these couple and family treatments show clinical efficacy or considerable promise when applied to certain client groups (Sprenkle, 2012). Currently, behavioral, cognitive–behavioral, functional, psychoeducational, and ecostructural and strategic models, including multisystemic, emotion-focused, and solution-focused models, have been shown to be effective with client groups. Each of these approaches also has well-developed clinical protocols, procedures, and treatment manuals to help social workers and other therapists learn how to perform the interventions.

Behavioral family therapies have shown effectiveness with child and adolescent issues and couple's distress. A number of studies support behavioral parent training intervention; these studies show statistically significant findings for treating hyperactivity, parenting problems, behavior problems, and developmental and speech disorders (Franklin, Harris, et al., 2012; Sexton et al., 2021). Skills training approaches based on behavioral therapies are also effective for the treatment of substance use and antisocial behaviors.

Functional family therapy has also shown empirical support for treating sexual or physical or verbal abuse (Sexton et al., 2021). It integrates systems theory and behavioral methods into its own unique relationship therapy for juvenile offenders and their families. Evidence shows that functional family therapy reduces arrests in younger siblings (Sexton, 2010). Garland et al. (2017) reports that treatment programs for child maltreatment incorporate several behavioral methods, including family preservation programs and several successful child maltreatment prevention programs. These are family-focused, utilize home visits and a strengths-based approach, and aim to increase social supports; they have been found to decrease abuse and neglect as well as to improve child adjustment and overall family functioning. Two other family interventions that are integrated programs which use behavioral interventions and have shown success with youth behavior problems are Incredible Years and Triple P Positive Parenting (Sexton et al., 2011).

Behavioral couple therapies are among the most well-researched and effective treatments for distressed couples and also for the treatment of alcohol problems (Johnson & Lebow, 2000; Lebow et al., 2012; O'Farrell & Clements, 2012; Perissutti & Barraca, 2013). Behavioral couples therapy has been shown to improve family relationships, decrease relationship dissatisfaction, decrease substance abuse and depression, and improve relationships in cases of infidelity (Garland et al., 2017; O'Farrell & Clements, 2012; Sexton et al., 2021). Integrated behavioral family therapy further integrates family systems theory and cognitive–behavioral therapy and demonstrates positive outcomes with substance-abusing youth (Barrett Waldron et al., 2001) .

Family psychoeducation is also associated with behavioral interventions and has been used in mental health and hospital settings with chronic illnesses (Lefley, 2009). It has also been found to be a useful approach in the treatment of families with a member who has a mental illness, such as schizophrenia, or a chronic health condition, such as diabetes. Psychoeducation uses multifamily group interventions and provides education and social support. It is the family treatment of choice when working with chronic health conditions. Research also demonstrates that participation in psychoeducation is associated with increased social supports and improved ability to manage social conflicts (Magliano et al., 2006).

Ecostructural and strategic interventions are successful interventions for youth with conduct disorders, eating disorders, substance abuse disorders, and attention-deficit/hyperactivity disorder. For example, the Maudsley method for treating anorexia and bulimia was influenced by Minchin's structural family therapy and added elements from strategic interventions and employs its own unique methods for empowering parents to help adolescents resume normal eating. The Maudsley method has been investigated in clinical trials research and has become an important treatment for adolescents with eating disorders (Loeb & le Grange, 2009). Brief strategic family therapy (BSFT) integrates concepts from systemic, structural, and strategic models in addressing issues of delinquency, substance abuse, and family relationship problems. The BSFT model has been evaluated repeatedly over the course of 30 years and has shown effectiveness in clinical trials research treating minority and nonminority adolescents with behavior problems including drug use (Robbins et al., 2011). Other integrated treatments that use ecostructural and strategic approaches that show promising results include multisystemic therapy (MST; Henggeler & Sheidow, 2012) and multidimensional family therapy (Henderson et al., 2010). The multidimensional approach also integrates a developmental approach to assessment and treatment. All of these family programs have repeatedly been shown to be effective for treating youth exhibiting delinquent behavior and substance use.

Multisystemic therapy, which uses ecological approaches, intensive family preservation, and structural family therapy, has also demonstrated positive outcomes with juvenile delinquents and substance abusers (Henggeler & Sheidow, 2012). In addition, this approach offers sophisticated protocols for engaging difficult-to-reach clients and manuals for maintaining the treatment adherence of therapists. Past controversies regarding the effectiveness of MST, however, illustrate the challenges of identifying effective evidence-based interventions. Researchers are not in agreement with regard to which therapies are most effective. MST, for example, is a widely accepted evidence-based intervention by federal funding organizations and private institutions (Franklin & Hopson, 2007). Yet a systematic review conducted by the Nordic Campbell Center of the Campbell Collaboration concluded that the intervention is not consistently more effective than alternative treatments (Littell et al., 2005).

Another efficacious intervention is emotion-focused therapy for couples, which emphasizes the importance of attachment and emotional processes (Basham & Miehls, 2004; Greenberg & Goldman, 2008; Lebow et al., 2012). Research studies on emotion-focused therapy are rapidly progressing, and there is evidence for its effectiveness with distressed couples, including those who experience trauma (Denton et al., 2000; Lebow et al., 2012). A meta-analysis indicates that emotion-focused therapy may be more effective than behavioral models for treatment of marital distress (Wood et al., 2005), and the revised behavioral couples therapy that includes components of emotion-focused interventions has also been shown to be effective with distressed couples (Lebow et al., 2012). Integrative couples therapy uses acceptance strategies that reframe hard emotions, such as anger, into soft emotions, such as sadness. Discussions about attachment patterns learned in one's family of origin help couples gain insight, empathy, and acceptance of each other's behavior (Christensen et al., 2006; Jacobson & Christensen, 1996).

Solution-focused brief therapy (SFBT) is a strengths-based approach that was developed within brief family therapy and can be applied to individuals or families. Research on this approach has progressed significantly during the past 15 years. Several experimental and quasi-experimental studies have shown SFBT to be a promising model for use with a wide range of problems, including adult depression and child and family issues (Franklin, Trepper, et al., 2012; Gingerich & Peterson, 2013; Kim, 2008; Kim & Franklin, 2008; Newsome, 2004). Kim and Franklin (2008) conducted a systematic review of studies of SFBT in school settings and found that one experimental design study, six quasi-experimental design studies, and one single-case design study on SFBT had been published since 2000. The effect sizes calculated by the authors and reported in the individual studies also show SFBT to be a promising intervention for work with children and families within school settings, with most studies having medium and some large effect sizes.

Conclusion

Family therapies based on systems theory emerged in the 1950s and 1960s and have become useful treatment approaches for many different client issues. Consistent support for the effectiveness of couple and family therapies exists, although research on the efficacy of specific approaches with various client populations is stronger. Behavioral, ecostructural, and strategic family approaches appear to have considerable experimental and clinical support for their effectiveness. They also have a long history of applications within the field. Newer models, such as emotion-focused couples therapy, are also building a solid empirical base for their effectiveness. Other promising models, such as SFBT, are developing a growing experimental research base. Family therapy has come a long way in developing an understanding of the common factors shared by all effective approaches. A trend in family therapy is to integrate techniques from more than one family therapy model and to also operationalize these using clinical manuals and protocols, making it possible for practitioners to apply these treatment manuals in their practices. Evidence-based approaches to family treatment share core components and are integrative by design. As we move into the future, it is important for social workers to continuously appraise the changing evidence for different approaches to couple and family treatment and to stay abreast of new developments in the field, as well as evaluate the effectiveness of their own practices using appropriate outcome measures.

Helpful Resources

American Association for Marriage and Family Therapy: http://www.aamft.org

Mental Research Institute: http://mri.org

Minuchin Center for the Family: http://minuchincenter.org

Solution Focused Brief Therapy Association: http://www.sfbta.org

References

Basham, K., & Miehls, D. (2004). *Transforming the legacy: Couple therapy with survivors of childhood trauma.* Columbia University Press.

Boyd-Webb, N. (2013). *Culturally diverse parent, child and family relationships.* Columbia University Press.

Carr, A. (2009). The effectiveness of family therapy and systemic interventions for adult-focused problems. *Journal of Family Therapy, 31*(1), 46–74.

Christensen, A., Atkins, D. C., Yi, J., Baucom, D. H., & George, W. H. (2006). Couple and individual adjustment for two years following a randomized clinical trial comparing traditional versus integrative behavioral couple therapy. *Journal of Consulting and Clinical Psychology,74*(6), 1180–1191.

Denton, W. H., Burleson, B. R., Clark, T. E., Rodriguez, C. P., & Hobbs, B. V. (2000). A randomized trial of emotion-focused therapy for couples in a training clinic. *Journal of Marital and Family Therapy, 26*(1), 65–78.

Franklin, C., & Hopson L. M. (2007). Facilitating the use of evidence-based practices in community organizations. *Journal of Social Work Education, 43*(3), 377–404.

Franklin, C., Harris, M. B., & Allen-Meares, P. (2012). *School services source book.* Oxford University Press.

Franklin, C., Trepper, T. S., Gingerich, W., & McCollum, E. (2012). *Solution-focused brief therapy: A handbook of evidence-based practice.* Oxford University Press.

Garland, A. F., Lebensohn-Chialvo, F., Hall, K. G., & Cameron, E. (2017). Capitalizing on scientific advances to improve access to and quality of children's mental health care. *Behavioral Sciences & the Law, 35*(4), 337–352.

Gingerich, W. J., & Peterson, L. T. (2013). Effectiveness of solution-focused brief therapy: A systematic qualitative review of controlled outcome studies. *Research on Social Work Practice, 23*(3), 266–283.

Greenberg, L. S., & Goldman, R. N. (2008). *Emotion-focused couples therapy: The dynamics of emotion, love, and power.* Washington DC: American Psychological Association.

Henderson, C. E., Dakof, G. A., Greenbaum, P. E., & Liddle, H. A. (2010). Effectiveness of multidimensional family therapy with higher severity substance-abusing adolescents: Report from two randomized controlled trials. *Journal of Consulting and Clinical Psychology, 78*(6), 885–897.

Henggeler, S. W., & Sheidow, A. J. (2012). Empirically supported family-based treatments for conduct disorder and delinquency in adolescents. *Journal of Marital and Family Therapy, 38*(1), 30–58.

Jacobson, N. S., & Christensen, A. (1996). *Integrative couple therapy: Promoting acceptance and change.* Norton.

Johnson, S. M., & Lebow, J. (2000). The "coming of age" of couple therapy: A decade review. *Journal of Marital and Family Therapy, 26*(1), 23–38.

Jordan, C., & Franklin, C. (2020). *Clinical assessment for social workers: Quantitative and qualitative methods* (5th ed.). Oxford University Press.

Karver, M. S., Handelsman, J. B., Fields, S., & Bickman, L. (2006). Meta-analysis of therapeutic relationship variables in youth and family therapy: The evidence for different relationship variables in the child and adolescent treatment outcome literature. *Clinical Psychology Review, 26*(1), 50–65.

Kazdin, A. E., & Whitley, M. K. (2003). Treatment of parental stress to enhance therapeutic change among children referred for aggressive and antisocial behavior. *Journal of Consulting and Clinical Psychology, 71*(3), 504–515.

Kim, J. S. (2008). Examining the effectiveness of solution-focused brief therapy: A meta-analysis. *Research on Social Work Practice, 18*(2), 107–116.

Kim, J. S., & Franklin, C. (2008). Solution-focused brief therapy in schools: A review of the outcome literature. *Children and Youth Services Review, 31*(4), 464–470.

Lebow, J., Chambers, A., Christensen, A., & Johnson, S. (2012). Research on the treatment of couple distress. *Journal of Marital and Family Therapy, 38*(1), 145–168.

Lefley, H. (2009). *Family psychoeducation for serious mental illness: Evidence-based practices.* Oxford University Press.

Littell, J., Campbell, M. Green, S., & Toews, B. (2005). Multi-systemic therapy for social, emotional, and behavioral problems in youth aged 10–17. *Campbell Collaboration Review, 2.* https://www.cochranelibrary.com/cdsr/doi/10.1002/14651858.CD004797.pub4/full?highlightAbstract=multisystem%7Cmultisystemic%7Ctherapy%7Ctherapi

Loeb, K. L., & le Greange, D. (2009). Family-based treatment for adolescent eating disorders: Current status, new applications and future directions. *International Journal of Child and Adolescent Health, 2*(2), 243–254.

Magliano, L., Fiorillo, A., Malangone, C., De-Rosa, C., & Maj, M. (2006). Patient functioning and family burden in a controlled, real-world trial of family psychoeducation for schizophrenia. *Psychiatric Services, 57*(12), 1784–1791.

Newsome, S. (2004). Solution-focused brief therapy (SFBT) group work with at-risk junior high school students: Enhancing the bottom-line. *Research on Social Work Practice, 14*(5), 336–343.

O'Farrell, T. J., & Clements, K. (2012). Review of outcome research on marital and family therapy in treatment for alcoholism. *Journal of Marital and Family Therapy, 38*(1), 122–144.

Perissutti, C., & Barraca, J. (2013). Integrative behavioral couple therapy vs. traditional behavioral couple therapy: A theoretical review of the differential effectiveness. *Clínica y Salud, 24*, 11–18.

Robbins, M., Feaster, D., Horigian, V., Bachrach, K., Burlew, K., Carrion, I., Schindler, E., Rohrbaugh, M., Shoham, V., Miller, M., Hodgkins, C., Vandermark, N., Werstlein, R., & Szapocznik, J. (2011). Brief strategic therapy versus treatment as usual: Results of a multisite randomized trial for substance using adolescents. *Journal of Consulting and Clinical Psychology, 79*(6), 713–727.

Sexton, T. L. (2010). *Functional family therapy in clinical practice.* Routledge.

Sexton, T. L., Coop Gordon, K., Gurman, A., Lebow, J., Holtzworth-Munroe, A., & Johnson, S. (2011). Guidelines for classifying evidence-based treatments in couple and family therapy. *Family Process, 50*(3), 377–392.

Sexton, T. L., Datchi, C., Evans, L., LaFollette, J., & Wright, L. (2021). The effectiveness of couple and family-based clinical interventions. In M. J. Lambert (Ed.), *Bergin and Garfield's handbook of psychotherapy and behavior change* (7th ed., pp. 587–639). Wiley.

Sprenkle, D. H. (2012). Intervention research in couple and family therapy: A methodological and substantive review and an introduction to the special issue. *Journal of Marital and Family Therapy, 38*(1), 3–29.

Sprenkle, D. H., Davis, S. D., & Lebow, J. L. (2009). *Common factors in couple and family therapy: The overlooked foundation for effective practice.* Guilford.

Wood, N., Crane, D., Schaalje, G., & Law, D. (2005). What works for whom: A meta-analytic review of marital and couples therapy in reference to marital distress. *American Journal of Family Therapy, 33*(4), 273–287.

Family Psychoeducation for Families of Children and Adults with Serious Mental Illnesses

Mary C. Acri and Mary M. McKay

In the United States, approximately 11.2 million people (4.5% of the adult population) are estimated to have a serious mental illness (SMI), a category of disorders characterized by significant impairments in one or more areas of functioning (National Institute of Mental Illness, n.d.). The care of adults with SMIs usually defaults to the family, who provide emotional support, information about resources and services, and financial assistance; advocate and make decisions about their relative's care; and schedule treatment appointments, provide transportation to and from them, and in some cases attend appointments on behalf of their loved one (Dewi et al., 2019; Dixon et al., 2000).

Family members are often unaware of the responsibilities associated with their relative's serious mental illness, and they report feeling overwhelmed and ill-prepared to manage their complex needs (Dewi et al., 2019; Shamsaei et al., 2015). In addition, families lack needed information about mental illness, its course, and how it will impact their lives (Shamsaei et al., 2015). Moreover, stigma about mental illness often results in social isolation from family, friends, and social networks (Shamsaei et al., 2015). Not surprisingly, family carers often feel alone (Dewi et al., 2019); experience high rates of stress, strain, anxiety, and depression (Brady et al., 2017; Dewi et al., 2019); report physical ailments, including headaches, insomnia, high blood pressure, and migraines (Dewi et al., 2019; Shamsaei et al., 2015); and incur financial strain and missed work days, or they leave their jobs altogether because of the demands associated with caring for their relative (Brady et al., 2017; Shamsaei et al., 2015). The stressors that families incur, compounded by a lack of social support, information, and resources, sends a clear directive to the mental health field to both support family members for their own health and well-being and support their relative with serious mental health problems.

Family Psychoeducation

One of the most common and effective models for family members of individuals with SMIs is family psychoeducation (FPE). Developed in the 1970s, FPE provides supports and resources to family members and, in some cases, the consumer in order to support their recovery and reduce the risk of relapse (Goldstein & Miklowitz, 1995). Originally, PFE was designed for families of individuals with schizophrenia (Goldstein & Miklowitz, 1995; Lyman et al., 2014). As evidence of the effectiveness of this approach grew, FPE was adapted for families of relatives with bipolar disorder, depression, and other serious mental illnesses (Brady et al., 2017).

There are variations across FPE models regarding format (e.g., whether the intervention involves one family or a multiple family group), length (some models have as few as two sessions, but most span across months or years), location (e.g., FPE has been conducted in hospitals, day hospitals, outpatient clinics, the community, or the family's home); and inclusion, with some models involving the consumer and the family for all or some of the sessions, whereas other models are only open to the family (Lyman et al., 2014; U.S. Department of Health and Human Services, n.d.). Furthermore, although FPE was originally designed to be delivered by mental health professionals, several established models are delivered by peers, who are caregivers or family members of a child or adult with a serious mental illness (Lyman et al., 2014). For example, the family-led organization National Alliance on Mental Illness (NAMI) developed Family-to-Family, a 12-session FPE program co-delivered by two trained family members of individuals with SMIs. Currently, more than 300,000 family members have participated in Family-to-Family, making it the largest FPE program in the United States (National Alliance on Mental Illness, n.d.).

Theoretical Underpinnings

Theoretically, FPE is based on the premise that being in a stressful environment in which family members have high expressed emotion, such as overly critical and hostile interactions and being overinvolved emotionally, increases the risk of relapse for individuals with SMIs (McFarlane, 2016; Shimazu et al., 2011). To this point, a meta-analysis consisting of 27 studies found that high expressed emotion was a significant predictor of relapse for schizophrenia, mood disorders, and other serious mental illnesses (Butzlaff & Hooley, 1998). Critically, FPE does not assume that there is pathology in the family (Brady et al., 2017; Goldstein & Miklowitz, 1995). Rather, it operates on the premise that families may need education, information, and other supports to manage their relative's serious mental illness (Lyman et al., 2014) and that these resources will strengthen the family to manage their relative's mental health difficulties and reduce emotionally charged and negative interactions that may put their loved one's recovery at risk (McFarlane, 2016).

Core Components

Despite considerable variability in factors such as length, format, and inclusion, most FPE models have the following five core components (Brady et al., 2017; Lyman et al., 2014; U.S. Department of Health and Human Services, n.d.):

1. Education about serious mental illnesses, their course, prognosis, and treatment and therapeutic options
2. Information about additional supports and resources
3. Skill building, including communication and coping skills, and self-care so that family members can better manage their relative's illness
4. Problem-solving to enable family members to deal with any issues that arise
5. Social support/developing social networks with other families or in general to decrease

social isolation and foster effective solutions to problematic situations

Evidence for Family Psychoeducation

More than 100 studies have examined the effectiveness of FPE; the majority have focused on outcomes associated with schizophrenia and other psychotic disorders, with a lesser number targeting bipolar disorder and depression. With respect to schizophrenia, results consistently support the effectiveness of FPE for reducing time to relapse and rehospitalization (Dixon et al., 2000; Lyman et al., 2014), which are the primary goals in managing schizophrenia (Motlova et al., 2006). Specifically, rates of relapse among consumers of families who participate in FPE are between 50% and 60% lower than those among individuals receiving usual services (McFarlane, 2016). Some evidence suggests the maintenance of these outcomes over time as well; for example, Motlova et al. (2006) found that individuals whose families participated in FPE were less likely to be rehospitalized and had a substantially shorter readmission length of stay (5.89 days) compared to those who did not receive FPE (17.78 days) 1 year post-discharge. Because of the number of studies and their consistent and positive findings, FPE is considered to be a best practice for the treatment of schizophrenia (Dixon et al., 2000).

Although lesser in number, studies have associated FPE with reduced rates of relapse for consumers with bipolar disorder (Miklowitz et al., 2003) and depression (Brady et al., 2017; Shimazu et al., 2011). For example, Shimazu et al. (2011), who randomized families of adults with depression to either a four-session FPE intervention or services as usual, found that the number of relapses was signifcanly lower and the length of time to relapse was significantly longer among families who participated in the FPE intervention in comparison to consumers of families in the control group.

Although originally focused on the consumer, research has expanded to examine the potential benefits of FPE for family members. To this end, studies have shown FPE to be associated with reductions in stress and burden and improvements in communication and coping skills, problem-solving, and knowledge about schizophrenia (Devaramane et al., 2011; Dixon et al., 2011; Lyman et al., 2014; Pitschel-Walz et al., 2001). For example, in a pre/post study, Family-to-Family was associated with significant reductions in perceived burden and depression and improvements in empowerment, as well as gains in knowledge about SMIs, the mental health system, and self-care (Dixon et al., 2004). In a subsequent randomized controlled trial, it was associated with significant improvements in knowledge about SMIs and empowerment (which was a measure of coping) (Dixon et al., 2011).

Children and Adolescents

Although originally designed for adult consumers with SMI and their families, FPE has been broadened for use with caregivers of children with mental health disorders, including psychotic disorders (Gearing, 2008), mood disorders (Fristad et al., 2002; Ong & Caron, 2008), anorexia (Geist et al., 2000), and disruptive behavior disorders. For example, McKay and colleagues developed the 4 Rs and 2 Ss Program for Strengthening Families, a multiple family group model for children aged 7–11 years (Chacko et al., 2015; Franco et al., 2008; Gopalan et al., 2015; McKay et al., 2002, 2011). Typically, two generations of families, including the child, their primary caregivers (e.g., parents or grandparents), and siblings older than age 8 years, constitute each group.

Group content focuses on strengthening family processes implicated in the onset and perpetuation of behavior problems, including communication difficulties, inconsistent and/or harsh discipline, and strained caregiver–child relationships (Montague et al., 2010; Patterson, Crosby, et al., 1992; Patterson, Reid, et al., 1992). In addition, sessions address low social support and high stress, which are both known to impede engagement and retention in services, particularly among poverty-impacted families (Kazdin & Whitley, 2003). Accordingly, through the group process, families receive education about family processes (establishing *rules*, identifying *responsibilities* of each family member, fostering *relationships*, and *respectful* communication between family members) and threats to the family (lack of *social* support and high *stress*); information about resources; and emotional support (e.g., normalizing difficulties and validating family experiences providing mutual aid).

The research for FPE models for families of children and adolescents is not as plentiful as for adult consumers with SMIs and their families; nonetheless, there is evidence of their effectiveness. As a case in point, an evaluation of NAMI Basics, a peer-delivered FPE program for families of children aged 22 years or younger with serious mental health problems, was conducted in 2012 and found significant improvements among the 36 caregivers in perceived empowerment, self-care, and incendiary family communication (e.g., yelling and losing control when having a disagreement) from pretest to post-test (Brister et al., 2012).

Encouraging results have also emerged from a set of studies that examined the 4 Rs and 2 Ss Program for Strengthening Families; in comparison to services as usual, one study found that families receiving the 4 Rs and 2 Ss evidenced significant improvements in oppositional behaviors among youth peer relationships and impairment at post-test and 6-month follow-up (Chacko et al., 2015; Gopalan et al.,

2015). In addition, caregivers with clinically significant levels of depression and stress evidenced significant reductions in both at 6 months' follow-up in comparison to caregivers who received services as usual (Gopalan et al., 2018). Collectively, these findings are optimistic and suggest child FPE models are associated with critical outcomes for children with serious mental health problems and their families.

Conclusion and Future Directions

Family psychoeducation is an established model associated with important benefits to adults, and there is a growing evidence base that FPE conveys important benefits for youth with serious mental health problems as well. Theoretically, improvements among consumers hinge upon changes in caregiver outcomes. To this end, research has shown positive outcomes for families, including reductions in stress and depression. What is less clear, and an area of future inquiry, is how caregiver and consumer outcomes are related. The research specific to schizophrenia suggests reduced levels of expressed emotion are associated with positive consumer outcomes; how and if these findings generalize to other mental health problems are less clear. Understanding the mechanisms by which FPE is effective for different SMIs and age groups will advance the field's knowledge of this approach and its variations.

References

Brady, P., Kangas, M., & McGill, K. (2017). What works in family psychoeducation for depression? A component analysis of a six-week program for family-carers of people with depression. *The Australian Community Psychologist, 28*(2), 67–84.

Brister, T., Cavaleri, M. A., Olin, S. S., Shen, S., Burns, B. J., & Hoagwood, K. E. (2012). An evaluation of the NAMI Basics program. *Journal of Child & Family Studies, 21*, 439–442.

Butzlaff, R. L., & Hooley, J. M. (1998). Expressed emotion and psychiatric relapse: A meta-analysis. *Archives of General Psychiatry, 55*(6), 547–552.

Chacko, A., Gopalan, G., Franco, L. M., Dean-Assael, K. M., Jackson, J. M., Marcus, S., Hoagwood, K., & McKay, M. M. (2015). Multiple family group service model for children with disruptive behavior disorders: Child outcomes at post-treatment. *Journal of Emotional and Behavioral Disorders, 23*(2), 67–77.

Devaramane, V., Pai, N. B., & Vella, S. L. (2011). The effect of a brief family intervention on primary carer's functioning and their schizophrenic relatives' levels of psychopathology in India. *Asian Journal of Psychiatry, 4*(3), 183–187.

Dewi, A. R., Daulima, N. H. C., & Wardani, I. Y. (2019). Managing family burden through combined family psychoeducation and care decision without pausing therapies. *Enfermeria Clinica, 29*, 76–80.

Dixon, L., Adams, C., & Lucksted, A. (2000). Update on family psychoeducation for schizophrenia. *Schizophrenia Bulletin, 26*(1), 5–20.

Dixon, L., Lucksted, A., Medoff, D., Burland, J., Stewart, B., & Lehman, A. (2011). Outcomes of a randomized study of a peer-taught family-to-family education program for mental illness. *Psychiatric Services, 62*(6), 591–597.

Dixon, L., Lucksted, A., Stewart, B., Burland, J., Brown, C. H., Postrado, L., McGuier, C., H., & Hoffman, M. (2004). Outcomes of the peer-taught 12-week family-to-family education program for severe mental illness. *Acta Psychiatrica Scandinavica, 109*(3), 207–215.

Franco, L. M., Dean-Assael, K. M., & McKay, M. (2008). Multiple family groups to reduce youth disruptive difficulties. In C. W. LeCroy (Ed.), *Handbook of evidence-based treatment manuals for children and adolescents* (pp. 546–590). Oxford University Press.

Fristad, M. A., Goldberg–Arnold, J. S., & Gavazzi, S. M. (2002). Multifamily psychoeducation groups (MFPG) for families of children with bipolar disorder. *Bipolar Disorders, 4*, 254–262.

Gearing, R. E. (2008). Evidence-based family psychoeducational interventions for children and adolescents with psychotic disorders. *Journal of the Canadian Academy of Child and Adolescent Psychiatry, 17*(1), 2.

Geist, R., Heinmaa, M., Stephens, D., Davis, R., & Katzman, D. K. (2000). Comparison of family therapy and family group psychoeducation in adolescents with anorexia nervosa. *Canadian Journal of Psychiatry, 45*(2), 173–178.

Goldstein, M. J., & Miklowitz, D. J. (1995). The effectiveness of psychoeducational family therapy in the treatment of schizophrenic disorders. *Journal of Marital and Family Therapy, 21*(4), 361–376.

Gopalan, G., Bornheimer, L. A., Acri, M., Winters, A., O'Brien, K. H., & Chacko, A. (2018). Multiple family group service delivery model for children with disruptive behavior disorders: Impact on caregiver depressive symptoms. *Journal of Emotional and Behavioral Disorders, 26*(3), 182–192.

Gopalan, G., Chacko, A., Franco, L. M., Rotko, L., Marcus, S., & McKay, M. M. (2015). Multiple family groups service delivery model to reduce childhood disruptive behavioral disorders: Outcomes at 6-months follow-up. *Journal of Child and Family Studies, 24*(9), 2721–2733.

Kazdin, A. E., & Whitley, M. K. (2003). Treatment of parental stress to enhance therapeutic change among children referred for aggressive and antisocial behavior. *Journal of Consulting and Clinical Psychology, 71*(3), 504–515.

Lyman, D. R., Braude, L., George, P., Dougherty, R. H., Daniels, A. S., Ghose, S. S., & Delphin-Rittmon, M. E. (2014). Consumer and family psychoeducation: Assessing the evidence. *Psychiatric Services, 65*(4), 416–428.

McFarlane, W. R. (2016). Family interventions for schizophrenia and the psychoses: A review. *Family Process, 55*(3), 460–482.

McKay, M. M., Gopalan, G., Franco, L., Dean-Assael, K., Chacko, A., Jackson, J. M., & Fuss, A. (2011). A collaboratively designed child mental health service model: Multiple family groups for urban children with conduct difficulties. *Research on Social Work Practice, 21*(6), 664–674.

McKay, M. M., Harrison, M. E., Gonzales, J., Kim, L., & Quintana, E. (2002). Multiple-family groups for urban children with conduct difficulties and their families. *Psychiatric Services, 53*(11), 1467–1468.

Miklowitz, D. J., George, E. L., Richards, J. A., Simoneau, T. L., & Suddath, R. L. (2003). A randomized study of family-focused psychoeducation and pharmacotherapy in the outpatient management of bipolar disorder. *Archives of General Psychiatry, 60*(9), 904–912.

Montague, M., Cavendish, W., Enders, C., & Dietz, S. (2010). Interpersonal relationships and the development of behavior problems in adolescents in urban schools: A longitudinal study. *Journal of Youth and Adolescence, 39*(6), 646–657.

Motlova, L., Dragomirecka, E., Spaniel, F., Goppoldova, E., Zalesky, R., Selepova, P., Figlova, Z., & Höschl, C. (2006). Relapse prevention in schizophrenia: Does group family psychoeducation matter? One-year prospective follow-up field study. *International Journal of Psychiatry in Clinical Practice, 10*(1), 38–44.

National Alliance on Mental Illness. (n.d.). *NAMI Family-to-Family*. Retrieved December 28, 2019, from https://www.nami.org/find-support/nami-programs/nami-family-to-family

National Institute of Mental Illness. (n.d.). *Mental illness*. Retrieved December 26, 2019, from https://www.nimh.nih.gov/health/statistics/mental-illness.shtml

Ong, S. H., & Caron, A. (2008). Family-based psychoeducation for children and adolescents with mood disorders. *Journal of Child and Family Studies, 17*(6), 809–822.

Patterson, G. R., Crosby, L., & Vuchinich, S. (1992). Predicting risk for early police arrest. *Journal of Quantitative Criminology, 8*(4), 335–355.

Patterson, G. R., Reid, J. B., & Dishion, T. J. (1992). *A social learning approach: IV. Antisocial boys*. Castalia.

Pitschel-Walz, G., Leucht, S., Bäuml, J., Kissling, W., & Engel, R. R. (2001). The effect of family interventions on relapse and rehospitalization in schizophrenia—A meta-analysis. *Schizophrenia Bulletin, 27*(1), 73–92.

Shamsaei, F., Cheraghi, F., & Esmaeilli, R. (2015). The family challenge of caring for the chronically mentally ill: A phenomenological study. *Iranian Journal of Psychiatry and Behavioral Sciences, 9*(3), e1898.

Shimazu, K., Shimodera, S., Mino, Y., Nishida, A., Kamimura, N., Sawada, K., Fujita, H., Furukawa, T. A., & Inoue, S. (2011). Family psychoeducation for major depression: Randomised controlled trial. *The British Journal of Psychiatry, 198*(5), 385–390.

U.S. Department of Health and Human Services. (n.d.). *Evidence-based practices KIT: Knowledge informing transformation*. https://store.samhsa.gov/sites/default/files/d7/priv/howtouseebpkits-act_0.pdf

Functional Family Therapy for Youth Behavioral Problems

John A. Cosgrove and Helen Hauser Midouhas

An estimated 17% of children and adolescents in the United States experience psychological disorders (Whitney & Peterson, 2019). This rate is strikingly higher among youth involved with public social service systems, with an estimated 50–75% of youth in the juvenile justice system (Underwood & Washington, 2016) and half in the child welfare system (Bronsard et al., 2016) meeting criteria for diagnosable disorders. Externalized behavioral disorders, such as disruptive and conduct disorders, are the most common diagnoses in youth involved with these systems (Bronsard et al., 2016; Underwood & Washington, 2016). Despite its prevalence, youth with behavioral disorders often do not receive the care that they need, particularly those involved with public service systems such as juvenile justice and child welfare who have increased behavioral health needs (Alegria et al., 2010; American Psychological Association Task Force on Evidence-Based Practice for Children and Adolescents, 2008). Delivering effective behavioral health services to youth remains a pressing concern for social work practice and policy.

Behavioral disorders are multifaceted, with many intersecting individual, relational, and environmental risk factors (Wasserman et al., 2003). The family dynamic has been shown to play a key role in youth behavior. Family communication, family distress and conflict, parenting practices and supervision, and family structure are well-established correlates of youth behavioral problems (Clark & Shields, 1997; Kapetanovic et al., 2019; Wasserman et al., 2003), and youth involved with the juvenile justice and child welfare systems experience increased levels of family dysfunction. Therefore, modifying intrafamilial risk and protective factors could help mitigate youth behavioral problems, particularly among youth involved with these systems.

Functional Family Therapy

Functional family therapy (FFT; Alexander et al., 2013) is a short-term, structured, and intensive family therapy intervention that draws upon the family dynamic as a key mechanism for change in reducing adolescent problem behaviors. The target population for FFT includes youth ages 11–18 years presenting with behavioral and emotional problems, often referred by juvenile justice, child welfare, and other public service systems. An average full course of FFT consists of 12–14 therapy sessions delivered over 3–5 months by FFT-trained therapists in home- or clinic-based treatment settings.

FFT uses a belief system of core principles, values, and therapist attributes that promote successful treatment of at-risk youth and their families. The core principles that anchor therapists to the FFT model include a relational (versus problem) focus, the use of a phase-based intervention to bring about change, the necessity of transmitting respectfulness, and accountability to model fidelity. The core values of FFT therapists can be translated into a particular "attitude" that embodies traditional therapist qualities without assuming expertise about any particular family's strengths, challenges, or dynamics. Therapists are respectful of family form and culture, are nonjudgmental of how that family form or culture works, and are strength-based in their approaches. Working with clients from a family-based perspective entails understanding the presenting problems in relational terms and, as such, creating a balanced working alliance among all family members in therapy. Therapist traits of humility, compassion, warmth, and flexibility are used to maintain a relational, rather than individual, problem focus. The core principle of accountability lends itself to the therapist characteristic of being "fearless" in their advocacy for families and commitment to helping each family achieve change (Alexander et al., 2013).

Functional Family Therapy Treatment Phases

The FFT model consists of five phases of treatment: (1) engagement, (2) motivation, (3) relational assessment, (4) behavior change, and (5) generalization (Alexander et al., 2013). The phases are developmental and synergistic in that each subsequent phase builds on the last, although the timing of some phases can overlap (e.g., relational assessment and motivation phases, and behavior change and generalization phases). The logic model in Figure 78.1 (EPISCenter, 2015) describes the objectives and activities of each phase and illustrates how they work to reduce risk factors and enhance protective factors in the individual, family, and community, which are important mediators of change for achieving immediate and long-term outcomes.

Prior to starting the intervention with a family, there is a pretreatment phase. In this phase, the therapist collaborates with the referral source (e.g., a juvenile probation officer or foster care case manager) to not only receive the referral but also understand the presenting problem(s) that the referral source expects to be addressed. The therapist is viewed as embedded in the referral systems and assumes responsibility for understanding system expectations, processes, culture, resources, etc.

Engagement

Engagement starts at the first contact with the family. The goal of the engagement phase is to "maximize the family's expectation of positive change" (Alexander et al., 2013, p. 9). Engagement establishes the therapists as responsive and credible. Engagement activities primarily involve therapist outreach and availability to family members, with sensitivity to their cultural perspectives and values, to initiate a working relationship.

Risk factors addressed in this phase include perceptions—particularly negative ones—about treatment, negative agency reputation, transportation issues, and early dropout. Protective factors are enhanced during this phase through therapist qualities that promote credibility, such as warmth, flexibility, and responsiveness. Effective engagement often involves multiple contacts with multiple family

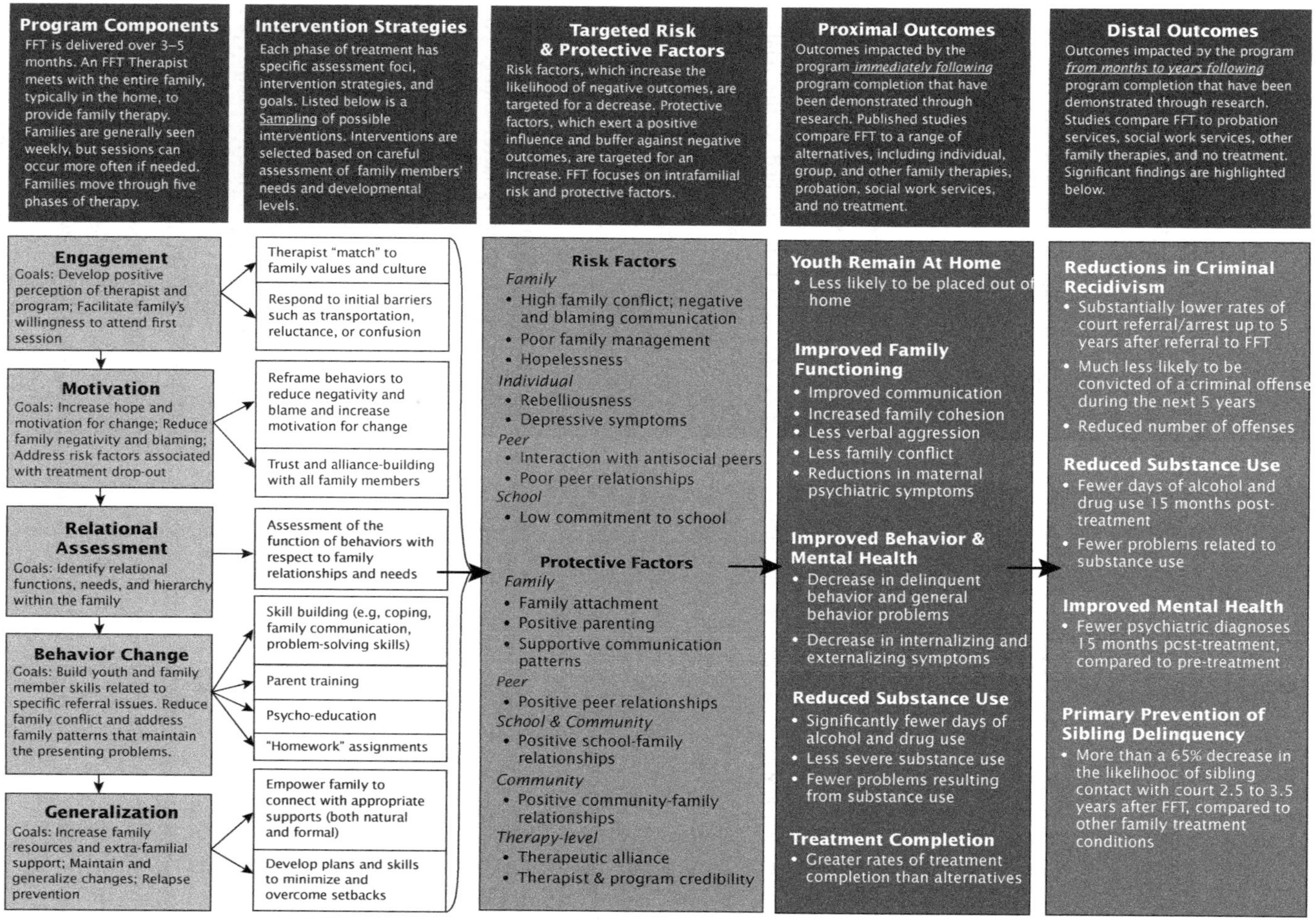

Program Components

FFT is delivered over 3–5 months. An FFT Therapist meets with the entire family, typically in the home, to provide family therapy. Families are generally seen weekly, but sessions can occur more often if needed. Families move through five phases of therapy.

Intervention Strategies

Each phase of treatment has specific assessment foci, intervention strategies, and goals. Listed below is a *Sampling* of possible interventions. Interventions are selected based on careful assessment of family members' needs and developmental levels.

Targeted Risk & Protective Factors

Risk factors, which increase the likelihood of negative outcomes, are targeted for a decrease. Protective factors, which exert a positive influence and buffer against negative outcomes, are targeted for an increase. FFT focuses on intrafamilial risk and protective factors.

Proximal Outcomes

Outcomes impacted by the program *immediately following* program completion that have been demonstrated through research. Published studies compare FFT to a range of alternatives, including individual, group, and other family therapies, probation, social work services, and no treatment.

Distal Outcomes

Outcomes impacted by the program *from months to years following* program completion that have been demonstrated through research. Studies compare FFT to probation services, social work services, other family therapies, and no treatment. Significant findings are highlighted below.

Engagement
Goals: Develop positive perception of therapist and program; Facilitate family's willingness to attend first session

- Therapist "match" to family values and culture
- Respond to initial barriers such as transportation, reluctance, or confusion

Motivation
Goals: Increase hope and motivation for change; Reduce family negativity and blaming; Address risk factors associated with treatment drop-out

- Reframe behaviors to reduce negativity and blame and increase motivation for change
- Trust and alliance-building with all family members

Relational Assessment
Goals: Identify relational functions, needs, and hierarchy within the family

- Assessment of the function of behaviors with respect to family relationships and needs

Behavior Change
Goals: Build youth and family member skills related to specific referral issues. Reduce family conflict and address family patterns that maintain the presenting problems.

- Skill building (e.g. coping, family communication, problem-solving skills)
- Parent training
- Psycho-education
- "Homework" assignments

Generalization
Goals: Increase family resources and extra-familial support; Maintain and generalize changes; Relapse prevention

- Empower family to connect with appropriate supports (both natural and formal)
- Develop plans and skills to minimize and overcome setbacks

Risk Factors

Family
- High family conflict; negative and blaming communication
- Poor family management
- Hopelessness

Individual
- Rebelliousness
- Depressive symptoms

Peer
- Interaction with antisocial peers
- Poor peer relationships

School
- Low commitment to school

Protective Factors

Family
- Family attachment
- Positive parenting
- Supportive communication patterns

Peer
- Positive peer relationships

School & Community
- Positive school-family relationships

Community
- Positive community-family relationships

Therapy-level
- Therapeutic alliance
- Therapist & program credibility

Youth Remain At Home
- Less likely to be placed out of home

Improved Family Functioning
- Improved communication
- Increased family cohesion
- Less verbal aggression
- Less family conflict
- Reductions in maternal psychiatric symptoms

Improved Behavior & Mental Health
- Decrease in delinquent behavior and general behavior problems
- Decrease in internalizing and externalizing symptoms

Reduced Substance Use
- Significantly fewer days of alcohol and drug use
- Less severe substance use
- Fewer problems resulting from substance use

Treatment Completion
- Greater rates of treatment completion than alternatives

Reductions in Criminal Recidivism
- Substantially lower rates of court referral/arrest up to 5 years after referral to FFT
- Much less likely to be convicted of a criminal offense during the next 5 years
- Reduced number of offenses

Reduced Substance Use
- Fewer days of alcohol and drug use 15 months post-treatment
- Fewer problems related to substance use

Improved Mental Health
- Fewer psychiatric diagnoses 15 months post-treatment, compared to pre-treatment

Primary Prevention of Sibling Delinquency
- More than a 65% decrease in the likelihood of sibling contact with court 2.5 to 3.5 years after FFT, compared to other family treatment conditions

FIGURE 78.1 FFT logic model. *Source:* EPISCenter (2015), created in collaboration with FFT, Inc.

members to ensure that each family member views that they have something to gain by participating in the treatment process.

Motivation

For many families, the presenting referral behaviors may, on the surface, seem unamenable to change. The motivation phase is critical to FFT's model of change because the therapist must create a context for change within the family that fosters hope by disputing feelings of hostility and blame and building balanced alliances with all family members. During motivation, treatment activities include disrupting negative interactions and conflict and reframing the presenting problem behaviors in a manner that provides a more positive (and potentially noble) motive for disruptive behaviors.

Risk factors addressed during the motivation phase involve the negativity and blame that indicate a lack of hope for change and can further preempt early dropout and hopelessness. The spacing of sessions can help with this. Sessions may be provided more often in the early phases, particularly if the risk of dropout is high. Protective factors include working diligently to create a balanced alliance so that all family members feel heard and accepted (Alexander et al., 2013). Giving the family a new frame for understanding the problem (i.e., one that is relational and hopeful for change) protects the family from giving up early on.

Relational Assessment

The relational assessment phase is contemporaneous with motivation. Relational assessment involves identifying interactive patterns among family members to understand the functions of individual behaviors in the context of the broader family unit (e.g., relational payoffs). The therapist listens to and observes statements, interactions, and descriptions of behaviors to decipher which increase and/or decrease connection and contact and which have influence on others. Risk factors addressed during this phase are individual behaviors that are associated with the presenting problems. Protective factors include individual and familial behaviors that are constructive for meeting family members' needs.

Behavior Change

The main goal of the behavior change phase is to improve family functioning by reducing or eliminating the maladaptive behaviors of individual family members that contribute to family dysfunction and, thereby, the presenting problems. The therapist addresses the risk factors that lead to the presenting problems through strategies that match the family's relational assessment. These strategies involve improving family communication and teaching new skills to achieve more positive interaction through domain-specific interventions (problem-solving, anger management, depression, anxiety, substance use, etc.) that are tied to the relational assessment. Therapists introduce tasks or skills to the family by providing the rationale for the exercise; coaching, modeling, and rehearsing techniques; and giving feedback along with homework for the family to practice outside of the session (Alexander et al., 2013). Youth temperament and parental pathology are also factors to consider during the behavior change phase. Caregiver beliefs and values, developmental mismatch with youth, lack of parenting skills, low conflict resolution skills, and poor negotiation skills are all risk factors that can lead to presenting behaviors. Protective factors will depend on how the family reframed the presenting behaviors relationally during the motivation phase.

Generalization

Finally, during the generalization phase, the changes made during the behavioral change phase are extended into other systems. Activities during the generalization phase include connecting the family with community resources that support positive changes, developing a plan with the family to prevent recurrence of the presenting problems, and improving the family's ability to manage relapse. Therapists must develop an extensive knowledge of professional and natural supports in the communities in which they work so that plans can be generalizable. Risk and protective factors addressed during this phase can entail both the amount of social support that the family has and the family's access to this support. The therapist's development of resources, along with creativity in fostering community linkages, can help sustain the change the family has experienced.

Post-treatment, therapist relationships with referral sources (e.g., juvenile justice and child welfare) will be essential to communicate outcomes of the intervention, along with plans for relapse (e.g., the generalization plan) and recommended support linkages for families. FFT utilizes booster sessions, which are brief sessions that occur after the successful completion of FFT. The goal of these sessions is to help the family "get back on track" with the positive changes achieved during FFT, and this involves a review of generalization phase goals. Booster sessions can be planned—for situations that the therapist is aware of at the end of formal treatment that may occur and present risk to sustained change—or not planned, such as when the family or referral source encounters disruption to the change achieved during FFT.

Case Example

The following describes a pseudonymous successful FFT case to illustrate how FFT's treatment phases work to address intrafamilial risk and protective factors and improve the presenting problem behaviors.

Background and Presenting Problems

Alex is a 17-year-old female who was mandated into therapy by a court judge. She lives with her mother, Anna, and her father, Joseph, and a younger sibling, Ava, age 8 years. When she was 15 years old, Alex was found guilty for possession of a criminal weapon (gun) that was involved in a shooting. Before she started FFT, she attempted other programs over the prior 2 years but failed them for testing positive for marijuana, having a "bad attitude," and poor attendance. Her specific referral behaviors were curfew violations, fighting at school, alleged gang involvement, verbal and physical conflict with her mother, and marijuana use. Alex also struggled with generalized anxiety disorder linked to her referral behaviors and her strained relationship with her family.

Pretreatment activities involved immediate outreach to the probation officer on the case to gather additional referral information, confirm contact information, and learn about the probation officer's specific expectations for Alex. The therapist engaged the family through timely contact (within 24 hours of getting the referral). This involved reaching out to Alex directly, in addition to her parents, which aided the therapist's credibility with all of them. The first session was scheduled within the first week of the contact. The therapist demonstrated flexibility by accommodating later appointment hours requested by Joseph given his work schedule.

Effective Motivation Techniques

The therapist utilized multiple interventions to disrupt negative family interactions and change their negative views about one another by introducing more positive themes about what might be driving their behaviors.

Building a Relational Focus

Anna did not attend the first session. Joseph and Alex stated that Anna was the root of all their problems and that it would be difficult to get her to attend. The therapist acknowledged their negativity and pointed out the areas in which the two of them agreed and shared common concerns about Anna, thereby creating a relational focus around concern rather than blame. To further create a focus on the relationships rather than problem behaviors, the therapist also noted how all of their behaviors were interconnected.

In between sessions, the therapist addressed the failure to engage Anna by reaching out to her directly. By the second session, Anna had joined, and her involvement made all the difference in treatment. Once Anna was in session, the therapist was able to create a discussion that focused on the linked sequences of behaviors of individual family members, and Anna and Joseph were able to see the link between family conflict and Alex smoking marijuana in a nonblaming way.

Themes

What seemed to engage and motivate this family most was the use of building a theme around fear. Doing this allowed the family to view one another in a different, more vulnerable light that also linked and gave meaning to their interactions with one another. This theme is demonstrated by the following example of a therapist statement:

> I have been really thinking about you guys since we last met, and something that came to me is that I believe you all struggle with some serious fear. And I think that you all react to that fear in a very different way. Anna, as I said last session, when you see that your baby girl, the girl that you carried for 9 months and gave birth to is getting into trouble, you become extremely scared and you show it through becoming angry mama bear and screaming and yelling. Joseph, for you when you begin to feel this fear that your daughter could end up in prison or even on the streets and homeless as you experienced, you set rules and high expectations. And Alex I think for you, you really struggle with fear. Fear that you do not trust yourself to be able to turn your life around and fear that if you tell your parents that you are not

going to school or smoking that maybe they're going to give up on you so you lie to them. Not because you want to be deceptive but because you are so fearful of losing your parents' love and support at a time where you are struggling even supporting yourself.

Relational Assessment

Relational Functions

Anna was contacting; however, she did not know how to achieve the contact other than to yell at both Joseph and Alex. This triggered Alex to act out and instigate a fight with her father that ultimately resulted in Anna not getting her needs met. Joseph was contacting with both Anna and Alex; however, he became distant with Anna when she yelled at him and became overly contacting with Alex when he feared she was getting into trouble. Alex was mid-pointing where she needed autonomy and alone time; however, she needed positive contact with both parents, which allowed her to feel positive connection and minimized her need to act out as a sign of help. Anna was one up in the relational hierarchy. She set the tone for the family, and many of the behaviors exhibited by Joseph and Alex suggested they were one down or symmetrical, responding in ways to address Anna's needs.

Behavior Change Plan

Communication Skills

The relational assessment revealed that Anna and Alex struggled with high verbal conflict. Joseph also struggled with his ability to communicate with Anna.

Impact Statements

Anna struggled with her ability to express her vulnerable feelings and instead reverted to yelling loudly at both Joseph and Alex. Teaching Anna how to utilize impact statements while also focusing on tone of voice and congruency would stop Alex from being triggered to leave the home and smoke marijuana. Alex struggled with her ability to express her emotions and reverted to yelling hurtful things to get Anna's attention. Impact statements were taught to aide Alex to achieve her emotional needs without starting a fight with her parents or sister.

Specificity and Directness

Joseph struggled with his ability to deal with Anna when she became angry. Teaching Joseph how to directly advocate for himself with specific statements that were supportive to Anna but allowed him to communicate his needs would be helpful for him. Alex struggled with her ability to be honest and specific about her negative behaviors out of fear her parents would give up on her. Teaching Alex how to utilize honest and specific statements to open communication with her parents would allow her to be supported and for them to be informed. Joseph would also learn how to use specific and direct statements to address the increased contacting behavior, per the relational assessment, that would still allow him to connect with his daughter but not disconnect from Anna.

Identifying Triggers

Anna and Alex both struggled with anger management. Teaching the dyad how to identify their triggers and hold one another accountable would aide them in their struggle with escalation and explosions that could become physical. The relational assessment revealed that their fighting often led to Alex leaving the home in a dysregulated state, which increased the likelihood of poor decision-making and impulsive acting-out in the community.

Conflict Resolution

Alex and Anna achieved connectedness through yelling at one another and each escalating until one left or things got physical. The message was often lost between the

two, and Anna became focused on the past, using "you" statements that were negative and blaming. Teaching the dyad effective skills to come to resolutions would reduce conflict, detriangulate Joseph, and also increase relationship building.

Parenting Skills
Reward System

Alex was always punished when she broke the rules but felt as though she did not receive recognition for when she did the right thing. Having her parents put a reward system in place would allow Alex to receive positive praise and motivate her to continue positive behaviors. In addition, it would enable her parents to be more aware of the positive changes Alex was making. The effective implementation of rewards would also provide a nurturing context within the family that reduced the time Alex spent with deviant peers.

Monitoring

Anna and Joseph were currently skilled at monitoring Alex; however, they did so from a blaming and paranoid stance that shut Alex down and then raised their anxiety. Teaching them how to monitor her through asking questions about her day would increase relationship bonding. This was essential because it would create a context in which Alex could feel appreciated and then she would be more willing to share details about where she was going and who she was with. This created a two-way street between Alex and her parents, with respect flowing in both directions.

Negotiating

Alex was not skilled at negotiating with her parents, which resulted in fights or lying. Equipping her with skills to effectively negotiate for her needs would reduce conflict and also allow her to feel more respected by her parents, which was of high value to her. Negotiation was essential for Alex in getting more time to spend with friends without all of the negativity and paranoia that had dominated the family's interactions prior to entering treatment.

Generalization Plan

Generalization of Skills

The therapist worked with the family to draw upon skills they had learned in the behavior change phase to (1) identify Alex's triggers for smoking external to the family and specifically build plans to fight these triggers together; (2) engage and communicate with persons in the community such as those at school and especially the probation officer; (3) encourage Anna and Alex to use cognitive–behavioral therapy (CBT) techniques to fight their cognitive distortions that fuel anxiety outside of the family context and generalize these skills into Anna's workplace and Alex's school and work environment; and (4) use co-parenting skills to remain a united front when communicating with probation, school, and other important systems in Alex's life.

Maintenance for Change

The family will continue to apply the relational perspectives and coping techniques they developed during FFT in the following ways:

1. The family will schedule weekly activities that allow Alex personal attention and space to feel her parents' support and love to prevent her from acting out to get attention.
2. When Alex experiences triggers for relapse (within the family, community, the legal system, and relationships), she will follow a specific plan tailored to fighting each trigger through relational support and CBT coping mechanisms.
3. Joseph's biggest trigger for relapse was when he felt out of touch with Anna and Alex, which caused him to feel the need to give advice or compare. To prevent this trigger, the family will maintain ongoing contact with Joseph through text or verbal check-ins.

Conclusion

Functional family therapy frames youth behavioral problems relationally and modifies them through intrafamilial risk and protective factors unique to each family. The effects of FFT on reducing emotional and behavioral symptoms, delinquency, out-of-home placement, and associated public costs have been established by more than 40 years of peer-reviewed research (Robbins et al., 2016). The FFT model has been effectively transported across diverse community-based settings throughout the United States and internationally. It has been adopted by many juvenile justice, child welfare, and other public service systems, helping make quality behavioral health treatment available to youth with the greatest needs. Please see the websites listed in the Helpful Resources section for additional information on FFT's extensive evidence base, training and implementation protocol, and model adaptations, along with other FFT resources.

Acknowledgment

We acknowledge Michael Robbins, PhD, of the Oregon Research Institute and Functional Family Therapy, LLC for reviewing and providing feedback on this chapter.

Helpful Resources

Blueprints for Healthy Youth Development. *Functional family therapy (FFT)*: https://www.blueprintsprograms.org/programs/28999999/functional-family-therapy-fft

California Evidence-Based Clearinghouse for Child Welfare. *Functional family therapy (FFT)*: https://www.cebc4cw.org/program/functional-family-therapy

Functional Family Therapy: https://fftllc.com

Functional Family Therapy. *FFT research*: https://www.fftllc.com/about-fft-training/fft-research.html

Functional Family Therapy. *FFT training*: https://www.fftllc.com/about-fft-training/implementing-fft.html

Title IV-E Prevention Clearinghouse. *Functional family therapy*: https://preventionservices.abtsites.com/programs/154/show

U.S. Department of Justice, Office of Justice Programs. *Program profile: Functional family therapy (FFT)*: https://www.crimesolutions.gov/ProgramDetails.aspx?ID=122

References

Alegria, M., Vallas, M., & Pumariega, A. J. (2010). Racial and ethnic disparities in pediatric mental health. *Child and Adolescent Psychiatric Clinics of North America, 19*(4), 759–774. https://doi.org/10.1016/j.chc.2010.07.001

Alexander, J. A., Waldron, H. B., Robbins, M. S., & Neeb, A. (2013). *Functional family therapy for adolescent behavior problems*. American Psychological Association.

American Psychological Association Task Force on Evidence-Based Practice for Children and Adolescents. (2008). *Disseminating evidence-based practice for children and adolescents: A systems approach to enhancing care*. American Psychological Association.

Bronsard, G., Alessandrini, M., Fond, G., Loundou, A., Auquier, P., Tordjman, S., & Boyer, L. (2016). The prevalence of mental disorders among children and adolescents in the child welfare system: A systematic review and meta-analysis. *Medicine, 95*(7), e2622. https://doi.org/10.1097/MD.0000000000002622

Clark, R. D., & Shields, G. (1997). Family communication and delinquency. *Adolescence, 32*(125), 81.

EPISCenter. (2015). *Functional family therapy model information: Logic model*. Retrieved March 4, 2020, from https://evidencebasedassociates.com/wp-content/uploads/2020/11/FFT-Logic-Model.pdf

Kapetanovic, S., Boele, S., & Skoog, T. (2019). Parent–adolescent communication and adolescent delinquency: Unraveling within-family processes from between family differences. *Journal of Youth and Adolescence, 48,* 1707–1723. https://doi.org/10.1007/s10964-019-01043-w

Robbins, M. S., Alexander, J. F., Turner, C. W., & Hollimon, A. (2016). Evolution of functional family therapy as an evidence-based practice for adolescents with disruptive behavior problems. *Family Process, 55*(3), 543–557. https://doi.org/10.1111/famp.12230

Underwood, L. A., & Washington, A. (2016). Mental illness and juvenile offenders. *International Journal of Environmental Research and Public Health, 13*(2), 228. https://doi.org/10.3390/ijerph13020228

Wasserman, G. A., Keenan, K., Tremblay, R. E., Cole, J. D., Herrenkohl, T. I., Loeber, R., & Petechuk, D. (2003, April). *Risk and protective factors of child delinquency*. Child Delinquency Bulletin Series. Office of Juvenile Justice and Delinquency Prevention. Retrieved March 3, 2020, from https://www.ncjrs.gov/pdffiles1/ojjdp/193409.pdf

Whitney, D. G., & Peterson, M. D. (2019). US national and state-level prevalence of mental health disorders and disparities of mental health care use in children. *JAMA Pediatrics, 173*(4), 389–391. https://doi.org/10.1001/jamapediatrics.2018.5399

Integrative Behavioral Couple Therapy

Katherine J. W. Baucom, Felicia De La Garza-Mercer, Monique C. Aguirre, and Andrew Christensen

Case Example

Janelle, a 32-year-old African American woman, and Adam, a 36-year-old Caucasian man, presented for treatment in a local clinic. The middle-class, dual-earner, interracial couple had been in a relationship for 8 years and married for 4 years. They had two young children, a 2½-year-old son and a 1-year-old daughter. Janelle and Adam were in the dissatisfied range of relationship functioning and reported arguments up to twice a day surrounding the amount of time Adam spent away from home. The couple reported that their arguments had steadily increased after the birth of their son; Janelle thought Adam did not give household tasks and their family enough time, and Adam was upset with Janelle's tendency to express her concern with criticism and anger. Janelle and Adam requested therapy after an argument resulted in Adam spending the night at a hotel. Both partners worried they could not overcome the difficulties they were currently facing. Their progress through therapy is used throughout this chapter as an illustration of integrative behavioral couple therapy (IBCT).

Integrative behavioral couple therapy, developed by Andrew Christensen and the late Neil S. Jacobson (Christensen et al., 2020; Jacobson & Christensen, 1998), integrates interventions aimed at increasing emotional acceptance with change techniques from existing behavioral couple therapies (Jacobson & Margolin, 1979).

Assessment and Feedback

In IBCT, couples typically participate in three assessment sessions as well as a feedback session. The goal of these sessions is to orient the couple to IBCT, determine whether they are appropriate for the treatment, identify a core issue(s), develop a formulation of the issue(s), and lay out a general plan for treatment.

The formulation of a couple's relationship problems includes a "DEEP understanding" that conceptualizes the presenting problems for therapist and the couple. DEEP is an acronym that stands for *d*ifferences or incompatibilities between partners; *e*motional reactions, sensitivities, and vulnerabilities of each partner; *e*xternal circumstances or stressors; and the destructive *p*attern of interaction in which the couple often becomes engaged in as they struggle with their problems. The purpose of the assessment sessions is to develop rapport with the couple, gather the information necessary to develop a DEEP formulation, and learn of the existing strengths of the couple.

The first assessment session of IBCT is a joint session with both partners of the couple. During this session, the therapist orients the couple to IBCT, learns about the presenting concerns and history of the relationship, and begins to gather information for the formulation. In the discussion of current relationship problems, the therapist attends to the emotional and behavioral reactions of each partner and the typical interaction pattern that the couple enacts around issues in the relationship. To learn more about the couple's background, the therapist facilitates a discussion of the history of the relationship, including how the couple met, how their relationship developed, and how their presenting problems came about. The therapist also inquires about reported cultural/ethnic differences between the partners and whether the couple views these differences as connected to their ongoing concerns. If relevant, the therapist explores how the couple feels about working with a therapist from a different cultural background. The therapist seeks to learn about positive aspects of their relationship and the areas in which the couple has particular strengths, in addition to the current problems facing them in their relationship. Finally, couples are introduced to *Reconcilable Differences* (Christensen et al., 2014), a text written for couples participating in IBCT, and are encouraged to read it during treatment.

In the first meeting with Janelle and Adam, the therapist identified their core issue as work–relationship balance and discovered some important differences between them. As is often the case, these differences were qualities that had initially attracted them to one another: Janelle was spontaneous and liked to make decisions on the fly, whereas Adam valued predictability and liked to have a plan for doing things. They also differed in the emphasis they placed on the relationship versus work, with Janelle more focused on the former and Adam on the latter. The couple was able to effectively navigate these differences early in their relationship and marriage, but they began to struggle when they became parents and were presented with many new demands. Despite the joys Janelle and Adam experienced as parents, this transition functioned as an *external* stressor that increased the salience of their differences.

At the end of the first assessment session, the IBCT therapist typically gives partners objective measures to provide information about important areas of the relationship. The most common areas assessed with these measures are relationship quality (e.g., the Couples Satisfaction Index; Funk & Rogge, 2007), intimate partner violence (e.g., Revised Conflict Tactics Scale; Straus et al., 1996), and target behaviors (e.g., the Frequency and Acceptability of Partner Behavior Inventory; Doss & Christensen, 2006). The freely available Couple Questionnaire (Christensen, 2009) is a screening tool that broadly assesses each of these areas. It is critical that therapists assess for intimate partner violence prior to beginning treatment; IBCT therapists do not treat couples whose problems include either (1) violence leading to injury in the past year or (2) ongoing fear of physical reprisal for voicing one's views (Christensen et al., 2020). If a partner reports either of these, the therapist should recommend treatment that focuses on the violence rather than on the relational distress only.

The second and third assessment sessions are individual sessions with each partner. They typically begin with a confidentiality caveat that the therapist does not withhold information discussed in the individual sessions in joint sessions unless the partner explicitly asks the therapist to do so. In the event that a partner reveals private information to the therapist that is relevant to the couple's relationship (e.g., an ongoing affair), the therapist stresses the importance of working together to share that information with the partner or to quickly resolve the issue (e.g., end the affair). IBCT therapists do not continue therapy if a partner discloses current infidelity to the therapist and is unwilling to stop the affair or reveal it to the partner.

The goal of these individual sessions is to gain better knowledge of the current relationship problems and of each partner's personal history, with an eye toward the *emotional vulnerabilities* that each partner brings to the relationship, and the typical *pattern of inter-action* that the couple enacts around problem areas. Often, the therapist begins by focusing on material that came up in the joint session as well as inquiring about particular items endorsed on the questionnaires. In the discussion of an individual's personal history, the therapist learns about the partner's relationships with close family members, their cultural identities and values, the overall atmosphere in the partner's home during childhood, and previous romantic relationships. In the individual sessions, the therapist learned that Janelle grew up in an upper middle-class African American family. Her parents traveled for their jobs and spent much of the time they were at home working. Thus, Janelle was sensitive to disconnection from Adam, often feeling abandoned and lonely as she completed an increasing number of child care and household tasks. Adam grew up in a low-income family and watched his father spend a great deal of time outside the home to make ends meet while his mother took care of him and his siblings. Thus, having grown up in a family with traditional gender roles, and being intimately aware of the consequences of limited resources, Adam was committed to ensuring that his family had the opportunities he did not have as a child. This contextual information, most relevant to the emotional vulnerabilities component of the

formulation, helped the therapist make sense of *why* child care and time at home were so difficult for Adam and Janelle in particular. In Adam and Janelle's case, knowledge about partners' families of origin also provided a framework for understanding Adam and Janelle's differences: The qualities of spontaneity and need for predictability were adaptive for Janelle and Adam in their respective families of origin.

Discussion of individual emotional vulnerabilities led to additional discussion in individual sessions with Janelle and Adam about the typical pattern of interaction that the partners played out around problem areas: Janelle, feeling anxious and abandoned, often criticized Adam for not being at home more, whereas Adam, feeling ashamed as well as anxious, tended to throw himself further into work so as to better provide for the family. This pattern is referred to as the polarization process. As the term suggests, partners' attempts to change one another often serve to increase the conflict and distance between them, even when often the purpose of trying to change one another is to facilitate intimacy or closeness. The result of this polarization process is a mutual trap in which both partners' efforts to solve the problem just make it worse. For example, the conflict that ensues from Janelle's frequent criticism of Adam for not being at home led him to feel more insecure about the future of their relationship. His insecurity about the relationship served to deepen his fear that he will be unable to provide his family with necessary financial support, and he increased the time he spent at work. The more time he spent at work, the less time Janelle had to criticize him, which reinforced his spending time away from home. Janelle criticized Adam to right the child care imbalance between them, but she found the imbalance increasing rather than decreasing. Thus, Janelle and Adam found themselves in a vicious cycle of interaction.

In addition to the development of the case formulation, another important function of the individual sessions is to evaluate the level of violence in the relationship as well as each partner's level of commitment. Therapists trained in IBCT explicitly ask about intimate partner violence, commitment, and extradyadic affairs, often by focusing on relevant questionnaire items the client may have endorsed. Neither Janelle nor Adam reported any violence or affairs; both reported a high level of commitment to their relationship despite their distress.

In the feedback session, the therapist makes explicit the level of distress of partners, their commitment to the relationship, and individual and couple strengths that may aid the course of therapy. However, the main focus of the feedback session is to present the DEEP formulation of the couple's problems, which is the foundation on which the course of IBCT treatment is built.

During the feedback session, the therapist also presents the treatment plan. The goals of treatment include both acceptance and change for various factors in the DEEP analysis, with acceptance being appropriate for the natural differences between partners and the enduring emotional sensitivities that each brings to the relationship; with change being appropriate for the patterns of interaction that frustrate them; and with acceptance and/or change being appropriate for their external stressors, depending on the nature of those stressors. The therapist describes how treatment will work by introducing the Weekly Questionnaire (Christensen, 2010), which will be the basis of treatment. In this brief questionnaire designed to be completed shortly before the session, partners rate their satisfaction with each other during the week, describe any major changes that have occurred, identify the most positive and most difficult interactions they had with each other during the week, and identify what incident or issue they wish to focus on in the session. The therapist describes how a typical session will proceed. Assuming there were no major changes, the therapist would normally review the most positive events between the couple and then focus on the incident or issue that partners have identified as being of most importance to discuss, with the therapist being an active facilitator of these discussions. At the end of the feedback session, the couple should have a clear idea of how the therapist views their concerns and how these concerns will be addressed in therapy. The couple is asked to consider whether they want to proceed with treatment and make a joint decision as to whether to do so. The treatment phase of IBCT does not begin unless all parties commit to move forward with the treatment plan.

Treatment

Beginning with the first treatment session (following the feedback session), and in most subsequent treatment sessions, the therapist focuses on emotionally salient incidents and issues related to the formulation that are identified in the Weekly Questionnaire. In addition to this focus on incidents and issues, the therapist pays attention to the emotions of the partners within the session and often finds that examples of their problematic patterns of communication unfold in the session. These examples provide an ideal opportunity for the therapist to help the couple alter their pattern of interaction. For instance, when Janelle and Adam began to argue about Adam's work in a therapy session, the therapist began the following intervention:

> Janelle: [angrily crying, looking down] If you cared about our family, you would at least make it home in time for dinner.
>
> Adam: I do care, Janelle. I just have a lot of responsibilities at work.
>
> Therapist: I'd like you two to step back for one second and look at what is happening here. Janelle, it seems that

you are feeling quite hurt right now, and Adam that you feel pretty put on the spot.

Emotional Acceptance Techniques

Therapists trained in IBCT often begin treatment with acceptance interventions to help partners understand and accept differences between them and their individual emotional vulnerabilities. IBCT therapists do this through three acceptance techniques: empathic joining, unified detachment, and tolerance building.

Empathic Joining

In facilitating empathic joining, the therapist works to reformulate relationship discord in terms of differences between rather than deficiencies within partners and in terms of the emotional sensitivities that such differences often trigger, thus allowing partners to empathize with one another's experience. The therapist also focuses on eliciting more vulnerable disclosures of "soft emotions" (e.g., sadness and fear) rather than "hard emotions" (e.g., anger and blame) from partners by suggesting soft emotions as a potential basis of behavior. In the previous example, the therapist suggested that Janelle was feeling hurt when she expressed the harder emotion of anger.

Rather than attempting to increase the amount of time Adam spent at home, the therapist involved the couple in a discussion of what time at work means to Adam by eliciting his thoughts and feelings around work. In addition, the therapist invited Janelle to talk about her emotional reactions to the time Adam spends at work and what that meant to her. This discussion facilitated empathic joining in that it allowed Adam to better understand the impact of his actions on Janelle, and it allowed Janelle to better understand Adam's emotion-based reasons for spending so much time at work. In this case, Janelle was surprised to find that her

husband worried their family would end up in a similar financial situation to that of his family when he was growing up.

Ideally, such conversations help modify the emotional reaction of one partner to the other's behavior. The conversations Adam and Janelle had in therapy helped Janelle see that Adam's long hours at work were fueled by his anxiety about money, which allowed her to offer support to her husband rather than criticizing him for not spending adequate time at home. Adam began to seek support and connection from Janelle when he was anxious about their finances, and they worked to establish a savings account with a "prudent reserve" only to be used for emergencies. As sometimes is the case, this focus on acceptance actually created a paradoxical effect: Adam began to work less once he felt less pressure and more understanding from Janelle, and they worked together to reduce the anxiety underlying Adam's late nights.

Unified Detachment

Therapists using IBCT techniques help partners discuss problems with unified detachment—that is, help partners step back, take a nonjudgmental stance, and consider relationship problems in descriptive, behavioral terms rather than with blame and accusation. The goal is to create a kind of dyadic mindfulness in which partners change their view of the problem from a "you" or a "them" to an "it" that the partners can join around. A common strategy is to help partners describe the sequence of interaction between the two of them during emotionally provocative incidents, identifying the "triggers" or "buttons" that activate each of them and elaborating the pattern of escalation between the two of them. Often, IBCT therapists help the couple give their interaction pattern or "dance" a name, which serves to further distance the partners from the difficult emotions of (and often bring humor to) the pattern. For example, Adam and Janelle labeled their interactional pattern their "cat and mouse game" in which Janelle, the cat, pursued Adam, the mouse. The emotional distance created through unified detachment allows partners to understand better the behaviors and reactions of one another.

Tolerance Building

IBCT therapists also use tolerance building to help partners cope with the other's unwelcome but nondestructive behavior. If one partner is not willing or initially resistant to change, then working with the other partner to face and ultimately tolerate the behavior is likely the only way for them to maintain a happy, harmonious relationship. When one partner begins to demonstrate some acceptance of the specific behavior, the other partner's appreciation of this tolerance may lead to increased closeness (and sometimes even change of the behavior).

An IBCT therapist uses a number of strategies to build tolerance: positive re-emphasis, highlighting the complementarity of partners' differences, preparing couples for backsliding, helping them achieve alternative means of support, and faking bad behavior. Through positive re-emphasis, an IBCT therapist points out the positive functions of behaviors thought by one partner to be solely negative, while often still validating the negative qualities of such behavior. For example, Adam and Janelle's therapist highlighted how Adam's long hours at work are a result of his commitment to his job, and although it is distressing for Janelle to feel alone with home responsibilities, he demonstrates a similar commitment to his family: When he says he will finish something, Janelle can count on him to do it.

Regardless of whether the change is one partner's behavior or the other partner's understanding of it, there will be times when the couple lapses into their typical pattern of interaction. Because they frequently engaged in this pattern when they entered therapy, these lapses are expected and common. Thus, IBCT therapists help partners plan responses to such lapses prior to their occurrence, helping them tolerate lapses when they do happen. In addition, the therapist encourages each partner to consider alternative means of support (e.g., from friends) and ways of self-soothing (e.g., taking a warm bath or listening to enjoyable music) when in difficult times. When individuals learn to care more for themselves, they may put less pressure on their partners to meet their emotional needs and be less susceptible to perceptions that their partners are at fault for needs not being met. Finally, the IBCT therapist may ask the couple to re-enact or fake their problematic interaction patterns in the session to help them observe more carefully their dynamics when they are not emotionally invested in the interaction.

Change Techniques

Often, as in the case of Janelle and Adam, acceptance techniques bring about adequate, spontaneous change in behavior and perception, and traditional change techniques are not necessary. However, as needed, IBCT uses several direct behavior change techniques in treatment to alter the dysfunctional pattern of interaction: redirection and replay, behavior exchange, communication training, and problem-solving training. Typically, these interventions and the rules underlying them are adapted maximally to the needs and idiosyncrasies of the couple.

Redirection and Replay

When the couple gets into a dysfunctional pattern of interaction in the session, which often occurs, the IBCT therapist will interrupt that pattern of interaction and redirect the couple, prompting them to interact differently. A common IBCT tactic is that the therapist may ask each partner to talk first to the therapist rather than to the partner and, with the therapist's help, fashion the message they would like the partner to hear. The therapist would then direct them to say this message to their partner. Another common tactic is to have the couple replay difficult interactions that occurred during the week and determine if they can improve them in the session, with the therapist's assistance.

Behavior Exchange

In behavior exchange, the therapist seeks to increase positive behaviors in the relationship by first identifying those behaviors, then instigating those behaviors, and finally debriefing the occurrence of those behaviors. In a typical treatment scenario, the couple is first asked to identify positive behaviors that each partner could engage in that would increase the other partner's satisfaction in the relationship. This may be a homework assignment that the couple is asked to bring to their next session. Then the therapist asks the couple to increase the daily frequency of one or more behaviors on their list, with the only guideline being that partners not tell one another which behaviors they will enact. Finally, the therapist debriefs the couple on giving and receiving positive behaviors. In these discussions, partners may provide one another with feedback about specific behaviors so that the couple has a better idea of which behaviors truly do increase perceived satisfaction.

Communication Training

Couples can be taught speaker and listener skills in communication training (CT), with the aim being to help partners become more effective communicators with one another. The partners first practice the skills in sessions with corrective feedback and direction from the therapist, and then they are encouraged and sometimes given assignments to practice the skills at home. Speaker effectiveness skills include focusing on the self (i.e., using "I" statements), expressing emotional reactions, and highlighting specific behaviors of their partner that lead to emotional reactions (e.g., "I feel hurt when you stay late at work and forget to call to let me know"). Listener effectiveness skills include paraphrasing and reflecting what one's partner says. This ensures that partners understand one another without the misinterpretation common to distressed couples.

Problem-Solving Training

It is expected that there will be times when, regardless of how effectively partners communicate about an issue, they have difficulty reaching a solution. Thus, couples are also taught ways of problem-solving that keep them from entering into the mutual trap of dysfunctional problem discussion. As with CT, the IBCT therapist first works with the couple during therapy sessions to use problem-solving skills and then recommends that they practice at home to find solutions to problems.

Couples are taught three sets of skills in problem-solving training: problem definition, problem solution, and structuring skills. They first learn how to define problems in terms of specific behavior and the environment in which it occurs. IBCT therapists often ask that partners disclose emotional reactions to also work toward emotional acceptance. Finally, each partner defines their role in the problem.

Next, partners learn problem solution skills. The first step in problem solution is brainstorming—the couple is asked to come up with all possible solutions, whether realistic or unrealistic. They then delete unrealistic solutions from the list until they are left with possible solutions to the problem. Partners then agree on a solution, write down and sometimes sign the agreement, and discuss things that might get in the way of instituting the solution. The couple is instructed to post the agreement where both partners will be aware of it, and the therapist checks in with the couple about the agreement for several sessions. If necessary, the agreement may be renegotiated.

The final skills couples are taught are structuring skills. Couples are encouraged to structure their problem-solving interactions so that they set aside a specific time and place to discuss the problem, ideally outside of the immediate problem situation. During their discussion, they are instructed to use skills from CT as well as problem-solving skills and to avoid negative verbal and nonverbal behavior.

Other IBCT Therapist Guidelines

Therapists trained in IBCT seek to remain flexible throughout the intervention techniques. They tailor interventions to the specific areas of deficiency of the couple and sometimes use failed change techniques as indication that relying more on acceptance interventions may be beneficial for the couple. Therapists should attend to in-session interactions and help facilitate in-session repair between partners when necessary. IBCT therapists remain nonjudgmental and accepting of partners and the outcome of the relationship. The goal of IBCT is to help partners have a different type of interaction around difficult issues and allow them to make the most informed decisions for the two individuals within the relationship.

Efficacy of Integrative Behavioral Couple Therapy

One of IBCT's strengths, in addition to its clinical value, is its empirically demonstrated efficacy. In a random assignment of 8 couples to a group format of IBCT and 9 couples to a wait-list control group, Wimberly (1998) found significantly favorable results for the IBCT couples. In a preliminary clinical trial, 21 distressed couples were randomly assigned to either IBCT or traditional behavioral couple therapy (TBCT) (Jacobson et al., 2000). Results indicated that 80% of IBCT couples evidenced clinically significant improvement in relationship satisfaction compared to 64% of TBCT couples. Finally, in

the largest randomized clinical trial of couple therapy to date (Christensen et al., 2004), 134 seriously and chronically distressed married couples were randomly assigned to either IBCT or TBCT and provided with approximately 26 sessions with trained therapists. TBCT couples improved more rapidly at the onset of treatment than did IBCT couples but also plateaued more quickly than IBCT couples. In contrast, IBCT couples made steadier change throughout the course of therapy, suggesting that IBCT's tendency to immediately focus on central issues, rather than small, overt behavioral change, may foster an important environment of emotional acceptance and safety that permits continual, stable improvement. Doss et al. (2005) found that although TBCT facilitated greater change in the frequency of targeted behaviors early in therapy, IBCT facilitated greater acceptance of target behaviors throughout the course of therapy and that acceptance of target behaviors had a stronger link with satisfaction later in therapy than did change in the frequency of these behaviors. In addition to these primary studies, other research has explored IBCT's applicability to specific couple-related issues. For example, IBCT may be an efficacious treatment for couples in which one or both partners experience chronic pain (Leonard et al., 2006) and for couples experiencing infidelity (Atkins et al., 2005). Other studies have documented gains at long-term follow up periods (Baucom et al., 2011; Christensen et al., 2010; Sevier et al., 2008).

IBCT has been disseminated in many venues. The U.S. Department of Veterans Affairs (VA) chose IBCT as an evidence-based treatment to be implemented in facilities nationwide. Couples who received IBCT at VA facilities had gains in relationship functioning from pre- to post-treatment, with effect sizes in the small to moderate range but larger effect sizes associated with more sessions of IBCT (Christensen & Glynn, 2019). In addition, OurRelationship, an 8-hour online self-help program based on IBCT principles, has been evaluated in three randomized controlled trials (e.g., Doss et al., 2016) and a sample of more than 700 low-income distressed couples (Doss et al., 2020), with positive results maintained at 1-year follow-up in both studies (Doss et al., 2019; Roddy et al., 2021). In addition to increasing access to IBCT-based intervention to more couples, this program may be a useful supplement to traditional IBCT (Christensen et al., 2020).

Helpful Resources

American Psychological Association. *Integrative behavioral couple therapy*: https://www.apa.org/pubs/videos/4310904.aspx

American Psychological Association. *Integrative behavioral couple therapy with gay men*: http://www.apa.org/pubs/videos/4310939.aspx

Integrative Behavioral Couple Therapy: https://ibct.psych.ucla.edu

Our Relationship: http://www.ourrelationship.com

References

Atkins, D. C., Eldridge, K., Baucom, D. H., & Christensen, A. (2005). Infidelity and behavioral couple therapy: Optimism in the face of betrayal. *Journal of Consulting and Clinical Psychology, 73,* 144–150.

Baucom, K. J. W., Sevier, M., Eldridge, K. A., Doss, B. D., & Christensen, A. (2011). Observed communication in couples 2 years after integrative and traditional behavioral couple therapy: Outcome and link with 5-year follow-up. *Journal of Consulting and Clinical Psychology, 79,* 565–576.

Christensen, A. (2009). *Couple questionnaire.* Unpublished questionnaire. To obtain this freely available measure, contact Andrew Christensen, PhD, UCLA Department of Psychology, Los Angeles, CA 90095. https://ibct.psych.ucla.edu/questionnaires

Christensen, A. (2010). *Weekly questionnaire.* Unpublished questionnaire. To obtain this freely available measure, contact Andrew Christensen, PhD, UCLA Department of Psychology, Los Angeles, CA 90095. https://ibct.psych.ucla.edu/questionnaires

Christensen, A., Atkins, D. C., Baucom, B. R., & Yi, J. (2010). Marital status and satisfaction five years following a randomized clinical trial comparing traditional versus integrative behavioral couple therapy. *Journal of Consulting and Clinical Psychology, 78,* 225–235.

Christensen, A., Atkins, D. C., Berns, S., Wheeler, J., Baucom, D. H., & Simpson, L. E. (2004). Traditional versus integrative behavioral couple therapy for significantly and chronically distressed married couples. *Journal of Consulting and Clinical Psychology, 72,* 176–191.

Christensen, A., Doss, B. D., & Jacobson, N. S. (2014). *Reconcilable differences* (2nd ed.). Guilford.

Christensen, A., Doss, B. D., & Jacobson, N. S. (2020). *Integrative behavioral couple therapy: A therapist's guide to creating acceptance and change.* Norton.

Christensen, A., & Glynn, S. (2019). Integrative behavioral couple therapy. In B. H. Fiese (Editor-in-chief), *APA handbook of contemporary family psychology: Vol. 3. Family therapy and training* (pp. 275–290). American Psychological Association.

Doss, B. D., & Christensen, A. (2006). Acceptance in romantic relationships: The frequency and acceptability of partner behavior inventory. *Psychological Assessment, 18,* 289–302.

Doss, B. D., Cicila, L. N., Georgia, E. J., Roddy, M. K., Nowlan, K. M., Benson, L. A., & Christensen, A. (2016). A randomized controlled trial of the Web-based OurRelationship program: Effects on relationship and individual functioning. *Journal or Consulting and Clinical Psychology, 84,* 285–296.

Doss, B. D., Knopp, K., Roddy, M. K., Rothman, K., Hatch, S. G., & Rhoades, G. K. (2020). Online programs improve relationship functioning for distressed low-income couples: Results from a nationwide randomized controlled trial. *Journal of Consulting and Clinical Psychology, 88,* 283–294.

Doss, B. D., Roddy, M. K., Nowlan, K. M., Rothman, K., & Christensen, A. (2019). Maintenance of gains in relationship and individual functioning following the online OurRelationship program. *Behavior Therapy, 50,* 73–86.

Doss, B. D., Thum, Y. M., Sevier, M., Atkins, D. C., & Christensen, A. (2005). Improving relationships: Mechanisms of change in couple therapy. *Journal of Consulting and Clinical Psychology, 73,* 624–635.

Funk, J. L., & Rogge, R. D. (2007). Testing the ruler with item response theory: Increasing precision of measurement for relationship satisfaction with the Couples Satisfaction Index. *Journal of Family Psychology, 21,* 572–583.

Jacobson, N. S., & Christensen, A. (1998). *Acceptance and change in couple therapy: A therapist's guide to transforming relationships.* Norton.

Jacobson, N. S., Christensen, A., Prince, S. E., Cordova, J., & Eldridge, K. (2000). Integrative behavioral couple therapy: An acceptance-based, promising new treatment for couple discord. *Journal of Consulting and Clinical Psychology, 68,* 351–355.

Jacobson, N. S., & Margolin, G. (1979). *Marital therapy: Strategies based on social learning and behavior exchange principles.* Brunner/Mazel.

Leonard, M. T., Cano, A., & Johansen, A. B. (2006). Chronic pain in a couples context: A review and integration of theoretical models and empirical evidence. *Journal of Pain, 7,* 377–390.

Roddy, M. K., Knopp, K., Georgia Salivar, E., & Doss, B. D. (2021). Maintenance of relationship and individual functioning gains following online relationship programs for low-income couples. *Family Process, 60,* 102–118.

Sevier, M., Eldridge, K., Jones, J., Doss, B., & Christensen, A. (2008). Observed changes in communication during traditional and integrative behavioral couple therapy. *Behavior Therapy, 39,* 137–150.

Straus, M. A., Hamby, S. L., Boney-McCoy, S., & Sugarman, D. B. (1996). The revised Conflict Tactics Scales (CTS2): Development and preliminary psychometric data. *Journal of Family Issues, 18,* 283–316.

Wimberly, J. D. (1998). An outcome study of integrative couples therapy delivered in a group format (Doctoral dissertation, University of Montana, 1997). *Dissertation Abstracts International: Section B: The Sciences and Engineering, 58*(12-B), 6832.

Parent Management Training

Randy Magen

Parent management training (parent training) comprises interventions designed to increase a parent's knowledge and skills to more effectively deal with child behavior. The empirical literature in this area is extensive; the Cochrane Library lists more than 5,800 controlled trials, and there are many meta-analyses and systematic reviews. Much of the focus in the empirical literature has been training parents to successfully change child behavior, in particular to prevent or eliminate disruptive child behavior whether from preschoolers or teenagers. However, many other child issues have been targeted with parent management training, including asthma, autism spectrum disorder, cerebral palsy, chronic illnesses, cystic fibrosis, infectious diseases, nocturnal enuresis, obesity, and preterm birth. By equipping parents with knowledge, support, and specific skills, parents become agents of change in their children's lives.

In some of the empirical literature, it is the parent's identity or behavior that is the pathway to parent management training. For example, parent management training has been offered for expectant parents, foster parents, and custodial grandparents. In other instances, parents suspected of child maltreatment are often referred for parent management training. Parent management training has been one component of a multicomponent intervention for parents experiencing psychosocial distress (e.g., depression and relationship distress). Finally, some parents come to parent management training with subclinical problems, simply wanting to be better parents.

Whatever the identified problem, for parents there is no shortage of advice on bookshelves, the internet, from friends, or from professionals. Parents can find parenting advice in the Bible as well as in a book that for several years was second to the Bible in sales, Dr. Benjamin Spock's, common sense book, *Baby and Child Care* (Spock & Needlman, 2012). However, not all parenting advice is helpful, usable, or culturally appropriate. For some parents, the absence of role models while growing up or deviations from average expected development in their child present challenges to successful parenting. Social workers frequently work in settings where parents seek or are referred for assistance around parenting. Fortunately, evidence-based programs are readily available. Two parent management programs that are backed by extensive literature and substantial internet-based tools are the Positive Parenting Program (Triple P) and the Incredible Years (see Helpful Resources).

Assessment

Assessment prior to initiating parent management training typically involves the use of scales and inventories, interviews, and perhaps observation or simulation of parent–child interactions. Practitioners typically collect information on the parent's perception of the child's behavior, parenting practices, the parent's psychosocial functioning, and spousal relationship (if applicable). A *Diagnostic and Statistical Manual of Mental Disorders* (American Psychiatric Association, 2013) diagnosis may not be a necessary part of the assessment, unless one is needed for reimbursement purposes. Fathers are underrepresented in the parent training literature because they are prone to not engage in these interventions (Panter-Brick et al., 2014). Therefore, it is likely that assessment data will be provided by the mother, which has proven adequate in most circumstances.

There are a number of scales that are easily administered and scored to understand the parents' perception of child behavior. One such scale is the Eyberg Child Behavior Checklist (ECBI; Eyberg & Robinson, 2000), which measures conduct problems in children aged 2 years to adolescents aged 16 years. The 36-item inventory is available in both English and Spanish and has a sixth-grade reading level. The ECBI measures the presence (yes/no) as well as the intensity of common behaviors. Another scale is the Strengths and Difficulties Questionnaire (SDQ), which has 25 items related to emotional symptoms, conduct problems, hyperactivity/inattention, peer relationships, and prosocial behavior. The SDQ has been used for children between the ages of 3 and 16 years.

Parenting practices can be assessed through scales, with data collected in interviews,

and through simulation or observation. Assessment of parenting through scales can be done through the publicly available Parenting Scale (Arnold et al., 1993), which is a 30-item questionnaire that asks parents how they would react to different child behaviors. The Parenting Practices Inventory (PPI), also in the public domain, is a 73-item questionnaire that can be either self-administered or integrated into an interview. The PPI is scored into seven subscales: appropriate discipline, harsh and inconsistent discipline, positive verbal discipline, monitoring, physical punishment, praise and incentives, and clear expectations.

Observation of parenting practices can take place in a home environment, office, and even virtually using a tool such as Zoom. Observations overcome the limitations of interviews and scales by showing the social worker a small sample of how parents and children interact. Home observation, as an assessment tool, has been widely used in home visiting programs. One approach to the observation of parent–child interactions in the home or office setting has been to structure the session around a meal, bedtime, or problem-solving or some other task that is more likely to elicit disruptive behavior. Observation used in assessment has been criticized as lacking validity and for being time-consuming (Aspland & Gardner, 2003). Simulated observation, used infrequently, can be done in role play with the social worker or through a role-play test (Magen & Rose, 1998).

The Incredible Years has an extensive interview protocol available on its website. As might be expected, the protocol is a comprehensive psychosocial interview with several sections devoted to understanding both the parent and the child. In any interview, the social worker will want to seek data on the parent's experience with their own parent, their beliefs about parenting, and their sources of stress and strengths. Because the majority of parent management interventions are delivered in group settings, assessment for fit with a group and ability to function at the same level as other group members is important. Most, if not all, of the evidence-based parent management training interventions have a foundation in a behavioral approach; for this reason, as well as for evaluation purposes, it is often helpful to obtain specific behavioral assessment data. For example, in the interview, the social worker may want to obtain a functional analysis of the parent's or child's behaviors (frequency, expression, duration, and effect). Another approach to assessment is to document the antecedents and consequences associated with the behaviors. As Patterson and colleagues (Reid et al., 2002) have demonstrated, understanding and rearranging the antecedents or consequences of behavior in a parenting context can have powerful effects.

Treatment

A meta-analysis by Wyatt Kaminski et al. (2008) identified five aspects of parent training programs associated with successful outcomes: (1) coaching parents on how to positively interact with their child, (2) requiring parents to practice skills at home with their child, (3) teaching parents emotional communication skills, (4) training parents how to use the skill of time-out, and (5) teaching parents to discipline consistently. It is interesting that only two of these aspects (time-out and consistency) are related to discipline, whereas promoting positive interactions and increasing emotional communication focus on the quality of parent–child interactions. Other aspects of the programs, such as teaching parents about child development, training in problem-solving, and promoting children's academic skills, appeared to be less crucial to program success. This does not mean that these aspects of the programs should be abandoned; rather, they did not produce strong statistical associations with outcome. It seems likely that in a clinical setting,

some parents may benefit from these aspects of the parent training programs.

Two manualized evidence-based parent training interventions are the Positive Parenting Program (Triple P) and the Incredible Years (IY). Triple P has been used internationally with published peer-reviewed research involving Iranian, Chinese, Japanese, Swiss, Indigenous Australian, and American families. Triple P is best thought of as a series or suite of interventions. The developers describe the program as having five levels:

> Level 1: Universal Triple P, which is a social marketing intervention for communities.
>
> Level 2: Described as "light touch," which is a one-time intervention delivered through seminars or brief consultation in person or over the telephone.
>
> Level 3: This level is for parents of children whose behavior is categorized as mild or moderately difficult and consists of four individual consultations supplemented by small group discussion.
>
> Level 4: This is an 8- to 10-session program delivered in a variety of formats (group, Web-based, or individually) for parents who want in-depth training and/or whose children have severe behavioral difficulties.
>
> Level 5: This is an intensive and enhanced program for parents with complex issues, including child maltreatment.

The Triple P program focuses on two age ranges in the delivery of parent training: birth to age 12 years and teenagers up to age 16 years. In addition, the Triple P program has adaptations for parents whose children have developmental disabilities, for families experiencing separation or diverse, and for Indigenous families. Training is available, at a cost, for practitioners who want full access to the Triple P materials and support.

Similar to the Triple P program, IY is a multicomponent intervention that at its core is a parent management program. Although IY has programs for children and teachers, the focus here is on the parent program. IY has separate programs based on the child's age: birth to 1 year, 1–3 years, 3–6 years, and 6–12 years. This parent training intervention is primarily group based (12–20 weekly sessions). In addition, IY has an optional home visiting coaching program to supplement the group training. IY has been delivered to Asian, Hispanic, African American, Caucasian, Maori, Korean, and Native American populations. Like Triple P, IY has training programs and materials at a cost for social workers; however, much of the program material is available for free from the IY website (see Helpful Resources).

Outcomes

A meta-analysis by Piquero et al. (2008) reported that across 55 studies, the weighted effect size was .35 (a medium effect size) and that early parent training (for children younger than age 6 years) produced few negative side effects. Epstein et al.'s (2015) meta-analysis found that parent training either alone or as part of a larger multipart intervention was more effective than interventions focused solely on the child. Across these studies, there were consistent results showing changes in child behavior toward less disruptive and more prosocial behaviors.

Delivery of parent management training has been shown to be effective in group settings as well as via the internet (Breitenstein et al., 2014). Adaptations to existing programs have been made for different cultural groups (Van Mourik et al., 2016) and have also shown positive outcomes. In addition to changes in parent knowledge and skills, short-term effects have also included improvements in parent psychosocial health (Barlow et al., 2012).

Conclusion

Considerable research has accumulated regarding effective parent management training. Most parent training is behaviorally based and teaches parents skills in emotional communication, positive interactions with their child, the use of time-out, consistent discipline, and skill practice at home. Many programs include manuals for social workers' use with families, groups, schools, and communities, and a wide variety of programs can be located online (see Helpful Resources). Two very effective programs that impact child behavior were highlighted in this chapter, namely Triple P and the Incredible Years.

Helpful Resources

Agency for Healthcare Research and Quality. *Effective health care program: Child behavior disorders*: https://effectivehealthcare.ahrq.gov/health-topics/child-behavior-disorders

Blueprints for Healthy Youth Development: https://www.blueprintsprograms.org

Child Welfare Information Gateway: https://www.childwelfare.gov/

Cochrane Library—provides high-quality, accessible, systematic reviews and synthesizes current research for health care professionals: https://www.cochranelibrary.com

Positive Parenting Program (Triple P): https://www.triplep.net/glo-en/home

The Incredible Years: http://www.incredibleyears.com/programs

References

American Psychiatric Association. (2013). *Diagnostic and statistical manual of mental disorders* (5th ed.).

Arnold, D. S., O'Leary, S. G., Wolff, L. S., & Acker, M. M. (1993). The Parenting Scale: A measure of dysfunctional parenting in discipline situations. *Psychological Assessment, 5*(2), 137–144. http://dx.doi.org/10.1037/1040-3590.5.2.137

Aspland, H., & Gardner, F. (2003). Observational measures of parent–child interactions: An introductory review. *Child and Adolescent Mental Health, 8*(2), 136–143. https://doi.org/10.1111/1475-3588.00061

Barlow, J., Smailagic, N., Huband, N., Roloff, V., & Bennett, C. (2012). Group-based parent training programmes for improving parental psychosocial health. *Campbell Systematic Reviews, 15,* 1–197. https://doi.org/10.4073/csr.2012.15

Breitenstein, S. M., Gross, D., & Christophersen, R. (2014). Digital delivery methods of parent training interventions: A systematic review. *Worldviews on Evidence-Based Nursing, 11*(3), 168–176. https://doi.org/10.1111/wvn.12040

Epstein, R. A., Fonnesbeck, C., Potter, S., Rizzone, K. H., & McPheeters, M. (2015). Psychosocial interventions for child disruptive behavior disorders: A meta-analysis. *Pediatrics, 136*(5), 947–960. https://doi.org/10.1542/peds.2015-2577

Eyberg, S. M., & Robinson, E. A. (2000). *Dyadic parent–child interaction coding system: A manual.* School of Nursing, University of Washington. http://www.incredibleyears.com/download/research/dpics-manual.pdf

Magen, R. H., & Rose, S. D. (1998). Assessing parenting skills through role-play: Development and reliability. *Research on Social Work Practice, 8*(3), 271–285. https://doi.org/10.1177/104973159800800302

Panter-Brick, C., Burgess, A., Eggerman, M., McAllister, F., Pruett, K., & Leckman, J. F. (2014). Practitioner review: Engaging fathers—Recommendations for a game change in parenting interventions based on a systematic review of the global evidence. *Journal of Child Psychology and Psychiatry, 55*(11), 1187–1212. https://doi.org/10.1111/jcpp.12280

Piquero, A. R., Farrington, D. P., Welsh, B. C, Tremblay, R., & Jennings, W. G. (2008). Effects of early family/parent training programs on antisocial behavior & delinquency. *Campbell Systematic Reviews, 4*(1), 1–122. https://doi.org/10.4073/csr.2008.11

Reid, J. B., Patterson, G. R., & Snyder, J. J. (2002). *Antisocial behavior in children and adolescents: A developmental analysis and model for intervention.* American Psychological Association.

Spock, B., & Needlman, R. (2012). *Dr. Spock's baby and child care* (11th ed.). Gallery Books.

Van Mourik, K., Crone, M. R., de Wolff, M. S., & Reis, R. (2016). Parent training programs for ethnic minorities: A meta-analysis of adaptations and effects. *Prevention Science, 18,* 95–105. https://doi.org/10.1007/s11121-016-0733-5

Wyatt Kaminski, J., Valle, L. A., Filene, J. H., & Boyle, C. L. (2008). A meta-analytic review of components associated with parent training program effectiveness. *Journal of Abnormal Child Psychology, 36,* 567–589. https://doi.org/10.1007/s10802-007-9201-9

Group Interventions

Best Practices in Social Work with Groups

Foundations

Mark J. Macgowan and Alice Schmidt Hanbidge

Social work with groups should be based on best practices within the profession gained through a career-long commitment to a systematic process of critical reflection, inquiry, application, and practice evaluation, defined as evidence-based group work (EBGW; Macgowan, 2008). EBGW is a process of the judicious and skillful application in group work of the best evidence using evaluation to ensure desired results are achieved (Macgowan, 2008). It is operationalized through a critical four-stage process model in which group workers (1) formulate an answerable practice question; (2) search for evidence; (3) undertake a critical review of the evidence for rigor, impact, and applicability yielding "best available evidence"; and (4) apply the evidence in practice with concern for relevance and appropriateness for the group and its diverse members, utilizing evaluation to determine if desired outcomes are achieved. EBGW is a process that can incorporate different theories and models of practice, if there is best evidence that they will be helpful to all group members. Failure to engage in this process can

lead to stagnation in practice, reliance on what is popular and not effective, practices that are not attentive to diversity, and group processes and outcomes that are iatrogenic but avoidable. EBGW incorporates (1) empirically supported group interventions and processes/structures, (2) evidence-supported guidelines, and (3) practice evaluation.

Empirically Supported Group Interventions and Processes

Systematic reviews continue to demonstrate that group work is an effective modality (Burlingame & Jensen, 2017). Empirically supported *group interventions* (including preventive interventions) (ESGIs) have been shown to be efficacious for specific diagnostic groups (e.g., depression and anxiety) or populations through randomized clinical trials and meta-analyses. ESGIs are typically well-defined, often manualized, and structured (Burlingame

& Jensen, 2017). Group workers would use such interventions if they are determined to be "best available evidence" as defined previously.

Empirically supported *group processes and structures* are what research has demonstrated to be associated with positive outcomes in groups. The empirically strongest example is cohesion, which consists of two parts: (1) a structural dimension representing the member–leader, member–member, and member–whole group relationships; and (2) an affective dimension consisting of interpersonal and emotional support (Burlingame et al., 2018). A meta-analysis of 55 studies (Burlingame et al., 2018) reported that cohesion is significantly associated ($r = .26$, $d = .56$) with reductions in symptom distress or improvements in interpersonal functioning across different types of group work (e.g., cognitive–behavioral, psychodynamic, and supportive), settings (inpatient and outpatient), and diagnoses. The relationship between cohesion and outcomes is powerful and consistent so that group workers should "seriously consider routinely assessing, monitoring, and enhancing group cohesion for optimal patient outcomes" (Burlingame et al., 2018, p. 394).

Evidence-Supported Best Practice Guidelines

The second element that EBGW critically incorporates is evidence-supported group work standards and practice guidelines developed by panels of experts to promote appropriate and effective practices (best practice guidelines). All group workers must become familiar with the standards and guidelines, and particularly those within their professions. Such standards and guidelines incorporate the best practices, values, and ethics of the respective professions. There are practice guidelines from the American Group Psychotherapy Association (AGPA, 2007; Burlingame et al., 2006; Leszcz & Kobos, 2008), best practice guidelines and

standards from the Association for Specialists in Group Work (ASGW, 2000, 2008), and emerging standards in international group analytic psychotherapy (Voyatzaki, 2015).

Within social work, there are standards for the practice of social work with groups developed by the International Association for the Advancement of Social Work with Groups (IASWG, 2015; see also Cohen et al., 2013). The Standards "represent the perspectives of the [IASWG] on the value and knowledge and skill base essential for professionally sound and effective social work practice with groups and are intended to serve as a guide to social work practice with groups" (IASWG, 2015, p. 1). A reliable and valid measure has been developed to assess group workers' perceptions of the importance of the items in the Standards and their confidence in doing them (Macgowan, 2012; Macgowan et al., 2018; contact the first author for a copy of the measure). Teachers have used the measure to help learners use the Standards in education and practice (Lee, 2018; Macgowan & Vakharia, 2012; Macgowan & Wong, 2017; Shera et al., 2013). Using the measure, one study (Macgowan, 2012) identified the top items in the Standards that respondents ($n = 426$) were least confident in doing. Two top items were promoting group exploration of nonproductive norms when they arise and helping members mediate conflict within the group. This chapter includes specific practice ideas/techniques to manage those two issues. Knowing how to use the IASWG Standards is an essential foundation for social work with groups.

In addition, ASGW (2012) developed best practice principles for multicultural group work and social justice. The principles fall into three areas: (1) awareness of self and group members; (2) use of strategies and skills that reflect multicultural and social justice advocacy competence in group planning, performing, and processing; and (3) social justice advocacy (Singh et al., 2012). A group worker with a multicultural orientation and social justice perspective has cultural humility, seeks opportunities to highlight diversity in the group, and strives for equal distribution of power and eliminates oppression within the group (Kivlighan & Chapman, 2018; Ortega & Garvin, 2019).

Technology-based group work has grown throughout the years, but it has surged as the global pandemic related to the coronavirus (COVID-19) forced many into technology-assisted services (e.g., telehealth and telebehavioral health). The IASWG Standards (IASWG, 2015, pp. 17–18) advocates that group workers seek adequate training in the practical aspects of the technologies and unique ethical issues with technology in group work. Working remotely, group workers in the United States should become familiar with the National Association of Social Workers (NASW), Association of Social Work Boards, Council on Social Work Education, and the Clinical Social Work Association Standards for Technology in Social Work Practice (NASW, 2017). Group workers in Canada should consult their province's Standards of Practice available through the Canadian Association of Social Workers (2020).

Practice Evaluation

The third area of EBGW is practice evaluation. According to the IASWG Standards (2015), group workers should include in their practice "monitoring and evaluation of success of group in accomplishing its objectives through personal observation, as well as collecting information in order to assess outcomes and processes" (p. 5). Practice evaluation needs appropriate assessment measures and a suitable research design.

Assessment

Assessment may focus on (1) member-related outcomes, (2) group-related outcomes, and (3) group processes/structures. Assessing

member-related outcomes focuses on the original concern that led to the member's referral (e.g., aggression, depression, and social competence). An excellent resource for member-related assessment instruments is Corcoran et al.'s *Measures for Clinical Practice and Research* (2020). Assessing *group-related outcomes* focuses on collecting information about the group experience from group members and group workers. Examples of such measures include the Post-Session Questionnaire (Rose, 1984), the Group Evaluation Scale (Hess, 2006), and the Evaluation of the Group Experience (Corey et al., 2010). Assessing *group processes* emphasizes areas such as cohesion and engagement, which are related to positive group outcomes. For cohesion, the Group Questionnaire (Burlingame, McClendon, et al., 2011) or the Cohesiveness Scale (Burlingame et al., 2006) can be used, and the Group Engagement Measure can be used for engagement (Macgowan, 1997, 2006; Macgowan & Newman, 2005). To assess group members' perceptions about how a multicultural orientation is experienced within the group, Kivlighan and Chapman developed the Multicultural Orientation Inventory–Group Version (Kivlighan & Chapman, 2018; Kivlighan et al., 2019). The inventory measures within-group processes of cultural humility, cultural comfort, and cultural missed opportunities (for additional group outcome and process measures, see Burlingame et al., 2006; Garvin et al., 2016; Sodano et al., 2014). Assessment instruments should be carefully selected for their rigor, impact, and applicability (Macgowan, 2008). In particular, they should be appropriate for the sex and racial and ethnic group with which they will be used (Macgowan, 2008; Singh et al., 2012).

Research Design

To determine if the group work service helps group members, assessment is accompanied by a suitable research design. There are different approaches to evaluating whether an intervention is successful (Garvin et al., 2016). One informal approach is to use goal attainment scaling (Kiresuk et al., 1994; Toseland & Rivas, 2017). Goals may target the problems of individual group members (member-related outcomes) or something within the group itself (group-related outcomes), such as level of cohesion or engagement. A more formal approach is to use a single-case design (Macgowan & Wong, 2014). A basic A–B single-case design can be used consisting of taking several baseline measurements ("A") before the group begins, followed by repeated measurements over the course of the group ("B"). In addition to the quantitative single-case design, group workers may use a qualitative method, such as a focus group to gather detailed information about the group work service (Garvin et al., 2016; Toseland & Rivas, 2017).

All three elements of EBGW—empirically supported group interventions and processes, evidence-supported best practice guidelines, and practice evaluation—are incorporated in this chapter. We describe how social work with groups incorporates the best available evidence through a generic developmental stage model of group work of planning, beginnings, middles, and endings. The pre-group planning stage is described next, and the stages in which group members and the group work meet together are described in Chapter 82.

Planning

Northen and Kurland (2001) defined planning as including "the thinking, preparation, decision-making, and actions of the social worker prior to the first meeting of the group" (p. 109). Best practice guidelines (AGPA, ASGW, and IASWG) and many empirical research studies (Burlingame et al., 2013) refer to the importance of pre-group planning and preparation. The IASWG Standards (2015) include 15 tasks and skills that group workers should master in the planning stage related to

recruiting, screening, and selecting members; provisions and limits for informed consent; and identifying group purposes and goals. Of the 15 areas, 3 that social workers have felt least confident doing are (1) selecting the group type, structure, processes, and size that will be appropriate for attaining the purposes of the group; (2) selecting members for the group in relationship to principles of group composition (assuming one has a choice); and (3) preparing members for the group (Macgowan, 2012). These areas are addressed in the following sections on screening, purpose, composition, structure, and content.

Screening

Best practice guidelines (AGPA, ASGW, IASWG) recommend that group members should be selected and screened to assess their suitability for group work and to determine how the proposed group work may meet those needs. The first consideration is to determine if the prospective member is suitable and prepared for group work. Systematic reviews have shown that there are no statistical differences in outcomes between group and individual formats when identical treatments, clients, and doses are compared (Burlingame & Jensen, 2017; Burlingame et al., 2016). Although we can be confident in group work for most people, some may not benefit or may not engage well. Research-based screening tools can be helpful, such as the Group Readiness Questionnaire (Baker et al., 2013) and the Group Therapy Questionnaire (GTQ) (Burlingame et al., 2006; MacNair-Semands, 2004). The GTQ may be used to evaluate client expectancies for group work, which "may identify clients that could be 'at risk' for premature dropout, allowing more effective preparation of the client prior to group participation" (Burlingame, Cox, et al., 2011, p. 71). Although these measures are research-based (rigorous), they should also be evaluated by each group worker for their applicability for the intended group members (Macgowan, 2008).

Purpose

The group's purpose determines many factors about the group, such as "the group type, structure, processes, and size" (IASWG, 2015, p. 6). A clear statement of purpose reflects member needs and agency mission and goals (IASWG, 2015). It is essential to have a preliminary purpose statement that is succinct and that captures the essentials of the group work service. So that it is clearly understood, the purpose statement should ideally be one sentence, such as "to help sixth-grade pupils make a satisfactory adjustment to junior high school," followed by goals that "would be related clearly to the needs of particular members of the group" (Northen & Kurland, 2001, p. 125).

In discussing the purpose of the group, group workers should ideally meet in person with prospective members. Although it may not always be feasible, the meeting is recommended because it (1) helps prepare members for the group service, (2) can establish the empirically supported therapeutic alliance that lays the foundation for group cohesion (Burlingame et al., 2018), and (3) may improve retention (Burlingame et al., 2003; Piper & Ogrodniczuk, 2004). Sometimes such sessions are done in an orientation group session, in which suitability for the prospective group can be assessed in vivo. This orientation session would also include (1) obtaining informed consent, which aids group member commitment; (2) a discussion of member rights and a professional confidentiality disclosure outlining the limits of confidentiality; and (3) dealing with any potential concerns or questions.

Composition

The function of screening is to determine members' suitability to participate in the life of the group and to not distract others from that ability. Composition in groups is the planned mix of individuals who have already been screened. Unlike screening, for which there are clearer guidelines, the research on how to compose groups has mixed findings: "The diversity of findings regarding composition suggests that there is no simple rule to follow, requiring group leaders to be conversant with relevant research findings" (Burlingame et al., 2013, p. 669). Thus, what follows are tentative guidelines for composition. In many cases, composition cannot be predetermined, but where it can, members should be selected based on principles of group composition, which is part of the IASWG Standards (2015).

The first and foremost principle is that the group's purpose will guide who should be included (Northen & Kurland, 2001; Toseland & Rivas, 2017). All members must share the common purpose, although not necessarily common objectives. A second principle is that composition is less important with groups that are briefer and more structured, such as task- and training-oriented groups, rather than groups that are relationally oriented and interactional (Yalom & Leszcz, 2005). A third principle is if the group work is focusing on a specific issue, group members should be similar with respect to that issue. This is so with group interventions that may be specifically related to race and culture ("culture-specific groups"; see Merchant, 2009), such as bicultural skills training with Latino immigrant families (Bacallao & Smokowski, 2005). A meta-analysis (Griner & Smith, 2006) reported that interventions provided for same-race participants were four times more effective than interventions provided for mixed-race groups. Interventions delivered in clients' own language were twice as effective as interventions delivered in English. A fourth general principle is to avoid having one person with little in common with other members (Northen & Kurland, 2001; Ortega & Garvin, 2019). A fifth principle is that even in groups in which there is homogeneity with respect to certain variables (e.g., race and ethnicity), heterogeneity with respect to life experience, level of expertise, and coping skills is desirable so that members may benefit from each other's different strengths. Such differences "can provide multiple opportunities for support, validation, mutual aid, and learning" (Toseland & Rivas, 2017, p. 173).

Structure

Structure includes many things, two of which are group size and the amount of time the group will meet. Both of these vary depending on the purpose of the group and the population involved. For example, closed groups that meet for more than 12 sessions and involve nonmandated involuntary clients may need to have larger group sizes to compensate for attrition. However, as a general guide, cohesion is strongest when a group has more than 12 sessions and includes five to nine members (Burlingame, McClendon, et al., 2011). With respect to the number of sessions, there are different standards depending on the type of group. Ideally, psychoeducational groups meet for 12–16 sessions, and counseling groups meet for 10–15 sessions (or more) (DeLucia-Waack & Nitza, 2014). To effectively have time to integrate therapeutic factors into adult groups, psychoeducational and counseling groups are typically 1 to 1½ hours in duration (DeLucia-Waack & Nitza, 2014). Groups for mandated members often vary in the number of sessions that they meet and are focused on the development of skills. Anger management, problem-solving, or offender groups often meet for 8–12 sessions (Morgan, 2004).

Content

Empirically supported group interventions have been shown to be efficacious for persons with specific diagnoses through randomized trials, meta-analyses, or consensus of experts based on a critical review of the best research evidence. Systematic reviews throughout the years support the efficacy (tightly controlled studies) and effectiveness (real-world settings) of small group interventions (Burlingame & Jensen, 2017; Burlingame et al., 2003, 2013). A systematic review of more than 250 studies across 12 problem areas/client populations

concluded that there is "clear support for group treatment with good or excellent evidence for most disorders reviewed (panic, social phobia, OCD [obsessive–compulsive disorder], eating disorders, substance abuse, trauma related disorders, breast cancer, schizophrenia, and personality disorders) and promising for others (mood, pain/somatoform, inpatient)" (Burlingame et al., 2013, p. 664).

With respect to change theories, there is very good to excellent evidence of the following (Burlingame & Jensen, 2017; Burlingame et al., 2013, 2014; Magill et al., 2019):

- Cognitive–behavioral group therapy (CBGT) is effective with social phobia and comorbid depression, bulimia nervosa, binge-eating disorders, panic disorder, schizophrenia, trauma symptoms and secondary outcomes.
- Psychoeducation, time-limited therapy, and support groups are effective for cancer patients.
- CBGT and dialectical behavior therapy are effective for treating suicidality, parasuicidality, depression, and hopelessness associated with borderline personality disorder.
- A range of models (e.g., cognitive–behavioral, motivational, contingency management, psychoeducational, integrative group therapy, and interactional, 12-step) are effective for reducing substance use.

The efficacy of group work delivered remotely has been examined in many studies. Overall, the research evidence suggests the modality is promising, but many studies suffer from lack of rigor. Systematic reviews have reported generally beneficial results with technology-assisted group work with outcomes comparable to in-person groups (Banbury et al., 2018; Burlingame et al., 2013). Systematic reviews of online peer support group studies have reported a dearth of high-quality studies, suggesting that although the evidence indicates some benefits, online peer support groups are best used as an adjunct to other forms of help (Ali et al., 2015; Griffiths et al., 2009; McCaughan et al., 2017; Robinson & Pond, 2019).

Group workers should critically examine the studies included in systematic reviews for rigor, impact, and applicability to ensure they are providing the best available evidence (Macgowan, 2008). An ESGI may be "efficacious," but it may not be appropriate for the group. This is particularly important when considering the use of ESGIs with populations that are culturally different from those in the original studies. To be more effective, such interventions may need to be adapted or tailored for race and ethnicity (Benish et al., 2011; Chen et al., 2008; Macgowan & Hanbidge, 2014). To be a skillful multicultural group worker (ASGW, 2012), it is important to develop "a repertoire of culturally relevant group work interventions" (DeLucia-Waack, 2004, p. 167).

Conclusion

The EBGW model and the planning stage are important foundations for when group members meet together with the group worker through the beginning, middle, and ending stages of group development, which are described in Chapter 82.

Helpful Resources

American Group Psychotherapy Association. *Connecting online*: https://www.agpa.org/home/practice-resources/connecting-online

Evidence-Based Group Work (includes links to group work journals and group work organizations): http://www.evidencebasedgroupwork.com

International Association for Social Work with Groups. *Teaching group work*: https://www.iaswg.org/teaching-group-work

References

Ali, K., Farrer, L., Gulliver, A., & Griffiths, K. M. (2015). Online peer-to-peer support for young people with mental health problems: A systematic review. *JMIR Mental Health, 2*(2), e19. https://doi.org/10.2196/mental.4418

American Group Psychotherapy Association. (2007). *Practice guidelines for group psychotherapy.* Retrieved June 1, 2020, from http://www.agpa.org/home/practice-resources/practice-guidelines-for-group-psychotherapy

Association for Specialists in Group Work. (2000). *Professional standards for the training of group workers.* Retrieved June 1, 2020, from https://asgw.org/wp-content/uploads/2020/06/ASGW-Professional-Standards-for-the-Training-of-Group-Workers.pdf

Association for Specialists in Group Work. (2008). *Association for Specialists in Group Work: Best practice guidelines 2007 revisions.* Retrieved June 1, 2020, from https://asgw.org/wp-content/uploads/2020/06/usgw297284-111.117.pdf

Association for Specialists in Group Work. (2012). Association for Specialists in Group Work: Multicultural and social justice competence principles for group workers. *Journal for Specialists in Group Work, 37*(4), 312–325. https://doi.org/10.1080/01933922.2012.721482

Bacallao, M. L., & Smokowski, P. R. (2005). "Entre dos mundos" (between two worlds): Bicultural skills training with Latino immigrant families. *Journal of Primary Prevention, 26*(6), 485–509. https://doi.org/10.1007/s10935-005-0008-6

Baker, E., Burlingame, G. M., Cox, J. C., Beecher, M. E., & Gleave, R. L. (2013). The Group Readiness Questionnaire: A convergent validity analysis. *Group Dynamics: Theory, Research, and Practice, 17*(4), 299–314. https://doi.org/10.1037/a0034477

Banbury, A., Nancarrow, S., Dart, J., Gray, L., & Parkinson, L. (2018). Telehealth interventions delivering home-based support group videoconferencing: Systematic review. *Journal of Medical Internet Research, 20*(2), e25. https://doi.org/10.2196/jmir.8090

Benish, S. G., Quintana, S., & Wampold, B. E. (2011). Culturally adapted psychotherapy and the legitimacy of myth: A direct-comparison meta-analysis. *Journal of Counseling Psychology, 58,* 279–289. https://doi.org/10.1037/a0023626

Burlingame, G. M., Cox, J. C., Davies, D. R., Layne, C. M., & Gleave, R. (2011). The Group Selection Questionnaire: Further refinements in group member selection. *Group Dynamics: Theory, Research, and Practice, 15*(1), 60–74. https://doi.org/10.1037/a0020220

Burlingame, G. M., Fuhriman, A., & Mosier, J. (2003). The differential effectiveness of group psychotherapy: A meta-analytic perspective. *Group Dynamics: Theory, Research, and Practice, 7*(1), 3–12.

Burlingame, G. M., & Jensen, J. L. (2017). Small group process and outcome research highlights: A 25-year perspective. *International Journal of Group Psychotherapy, 67*(Suppl. 1), S194–S218. https://doi.org/10.1080/00207284.2016.1218287

Burlingame, G. M., McClendon, D. T., & Alonso, J. (2011). Cohesion in group therapy. *Psychotherapy, 48,* 34–42. https://doi.org/10.1037/a0022063

Burlingame, G. M., McClendon, D. T., & Yang, C. (2018). Cohesion in group therapy: A meta-analysis. *Psychotherapy, 55*(4), 384–398. https://doi.org/10.1037/pst0000173

Burlingame, G. M., Seebeck, J. D., Janis, R. A., Whitcomb, K. E., Barkowski, S., Rosendahl, J., & Strauss, B. (2016). Outcome differences between individual and group formats when identical and nonidentical treatments, patients, and doses are compared: A 25-year meta-analytic perspective. *Psychotherapy, 53*(4), 446–461. https://doi.org/10.1037/pst0000090

Burlingame, G. M., Strauss, B., & Joyce, A. (2013). Change mechanisms and effectiveness of small group treatments. In M. J. Lambert (Ed.), *Bergin and Garfield's handbook of psychotherapy and behavior change* (6th ed., pp. 640–689). Wiley.

Burlingame, G. M., Strauss, B., Joyce, A., MacNair-Semands, R., MacKenzie, K. R., Ogrodniczuk, J., & Taylor, S. (2006). *CORE Battery–Revised: An assessment toolkit for promoting optimal group selection, process, and outcome.* American Group Psychotherapy Association.

Burlingame, G. M., Whitcomb, K., & Woodland, S. (2014). Process and outcome in group counseling and psychotherapy. In J. L. DeLucia-Waack, C. R. Kalodner, & M. Riva (Eds.), *Handbook of group counseling and psychotherapy* (pp. 55–67). Sage.

Canadian Association of Social Workers. (2020). Virtual counselling resources. https://www.casw-acts.ca/en/resources/virtual-counselling-resources

Chen, E. C., Kakkad, D., & Balzano, J. (2008). Multicultural competence and evidence-based practice in group therapy. *Journal of Clinical Psychology, 64,* 1261–1278. https://doi.org/10.1002/jclp.20533

Cohen, C. S., Macgowan, M. J., Garvin, C., & Muskat, B. (Eds.). (2013). *IASWG standards for social work with groups: Research, teaching and practice.* Social Work with Groups, 36 [Special issue].

Corcoran, K., Fischer, J., & Springer, D. W. (2020). *Measures for clinical practice and research: A sourcebook* (6th ed.). Oxford University Press.

Corey, M. S., Corey, G., & Corey, C. (2010). *Groups: Process and practice* (8th ed.). Brooks/Cole.

DeLucia-Waack, J. L. (2004). Multicultural groups: Introduction. In J. L. DeLucia-Waack, D. A. Gerrity, C. R. Kalodner, & M. Riva (Eds.), *Handbook of group counseling and psychotherapy* (pp. 167–168). Sage.

DeLucia-Waack, J. L., & Nitza, A. (2014). *Effective planning for groups.* Sage.

Garvin, C. D., Tolman, R. M., & Macgowan, M. J. (2016). *Group work research.* Oxford University Press.

Griffiths, K. M., Calear, A. L., & Banfield, M. (2009). Systematic review on internet support groups (ISGs) and depression (1): Do ISGs reduce depressive symptoms? *Journal of Medical Internet Research, 11*(3), e40. https://doi.org/10.2196/jmir.1270

Griner, D., & Smith, T. B. (2006). Culturally adapted mental health intervention: A meta-analytic review. *Psychotherapy, 43*(4), 531–548. https://doi.org/10.1037/0033-3204.43.4.531

Hess, H. (2006). Group Evaluation Scale. In G. M. Burlingame, B. Strauss, A. Joyce, R. MacNair-Semands, K. R. MacKenzie, J. Ogrodniczuk, & S. Taylor (Eds.), *CORE Battery–Revised: An assessment tool kit for promoting optimal group selection, process, and outcome* (pp. 78, 88–89, 106). American Group Psychotherapy Association.

International Association for Social Work with Groups. (2015). *Standards for social work practice with groups* (2nd ed.). Retrieved June 2, 2020, from https://www.iaswg.org/standards

Kiresuk, T. J., Smith, A., & Cardillo, J. E. (1994). *Goal attainment scaling: Applications, theory, and measurement.* Erlbaum.

Kivlighan, D. M., III, Adams, M. C., Drinane, J. M., Tao, K. W., & Owen, J. (2019). Construction and validation of the Multicultural Orientation Inventory–Group Version. *Journal of Counseling Psychology, 66*(1), 45–55. https://doi.org/10.1037/cou0000294

Kivlighan, D. M., III, & Chapman, N. A. (2018). Extending the multicultural orientation (MCO) framework to group psychotherapy: A clinical illustration. *Psychotherapy, 55*(1), 39–44. https://doi.org/10.1037/pst0000142

Lee, C. D. (2018). Social work with groups' practice ethics and standards: Student confidence and competence. *Research on Social Work Practice, 28*(4), 475–481. https://doi.org/10.1177/1049731516655456

Leszcz, M., & Kobos, J. C. (2008). Evidence-based group psychotherapy: Using AGPA's practice guidelines to enhance clinical effectiveness. *Journal of Clinical Psychology, 64*(11), 1238–1260. https://doi.org/10.1002/jclp.20531

Macgowan, M. J. (1997). A measure of engagement for social group work: The Groupwork Engagement Measure (GEM). *Journal of Social Service Research, 23*(2), 17–37. https://doi.org/10.1300/J079v23n02_02

Macgowan, M. J. (2006). The Group Engagement Measure: A review of its conceptual and empirical properties. *Journal of Groups in Addiction and Recovery, 1*(2), 33–52.

Macgowan, M. J. (2008). *A guide to evidence-based group work.* Oxford University Press.

Macgowan, M. J. (2012). A standards-based inventory of foundation competencies in social work with groups. *Research on Social Work Practice, 22*(5), 578–589. https://doi.org/10.1177/1049731512443288

Macgowan, M. J., Dillon, F., & Spadola, C. (2018). Factor structure of a standards-based inventory of competencies in social work with groups. *Journal of Evidence-Informed Social Work, 15*(4), 403–419. https://doi.org/10.1080/23761407.2018.1464996

Macgowan, M. J., & Hanbidge, A. S. (2014). Advancing evidence-based group work in community settings: Methods, opportunities, and challenges. In J. L. DeLucia-Waack, C. R. Kalodner, & M. Riva (Eds.), *The handbook of group counseling and psychotherapy* (2nd ed., pp. 303–317). Sage.

Macgowan, M. J., & Newman, F. L. (2005). The factor structure of the Group Engagement Measure. *Social Work Research, 29,* 107–118. https://doi.org/10.1093/swr/29.2.107

Macgowan, M. J., & Vakharia, S. P. (2012). Teaching standards-based group work competencies to social work students: An empirical examination. *Research on Social Work Practice, 22*(4), 380–388. https://doi.org/10.1177/1049731512442249

Macgowan, M. J., & Wong, S. (2014). Single-case designs in group work: Past applications, future directions. *Group Dynamics, 18*(2), 138–158. https://doi.org/10.1037/gdn0000003

Macgowan, M. J., & Wong, S. E. (2017). Improving student confidence in using group work standards: A controlled replication. *Research on Social Work Practice, 27*(4), 434–440. https://doi.org/10.1177/1049731515587557

MacNair-Semands, R. (2004). *Manual for Group Therapy Questionnaire–Revised.* University of North Carolina at Charlotte.

Magill, M., Ray, L., Kiluk, B., Hoadley, A., Bernstein, M., Tonigan, J. S., & Carroll, K. (2019). A meta-analysis of cognitive–behavioral therapy for alcohol or other drug use disorders: Treatment efficacy by contrast condition. *Journal of Consulting and Clinical Psychology, 87*(12), 1093–1105. https://doi.org/10.1037/ccp0000447

McCaughan, E., Parahoo, K., Hueter, I., Northouse, L., & Bradbury, I. (2017). Online support groups for women with breast cancer. *Cochrane Database of Systematic Reviews, 3*(3), CD011652. https://doi.org/10.1002/14651858.CD011652.pub2

Merchant, N. M. (2009). Types of diversity-related groups. In C. F. Salazar (Ed.), *Group work experts share their favorite multicultural activities: A guide to diversity-competent choosing, planning, conducting and processing* (pp. 13–24). Association for Specialists in Group Work.

Morgan, R. D. (2004). Groups with offenders and mandated clients. In J. L. DeLucia-Waack, D. A. Gerrity, C. R. Kalodner, & M. Riva (Eds.), *Handbook of group counseling and psychotherapy* (pp. 388–400). Sage.

National Association of Social Workers. (2017). *NASW, ASWB, CSWE, & CSWA standards for technology in social work practice.* Retrieved June 2, 2020, from https://www.socialworkers.org/includes/newIncludes/homepage/PRA-BRO-33617.TechStandards_FINAL_POSTING.pdf

Northen, H., & Kurland, R. (2001). *Social work with groups* (3rd ed.). Columbia University Press.

Ortega, R. M., & Garvin, C. D. (2019). *Socially just practice in groups.* Sage.

Piper, W. E., & Ogrodniczuk, J. S. (2004). Brief group therapy. In J. L. DeLucia-Waack, D. A. Gerrity, C. R. Kalodner, & M. Riva (Eds.), *Handbook of group counseling and psychotherapy* (pp. 641–650). Sage.

Robinson, C., & Pond, D. R. (2019). Do online support groups for grief benefit the bereaved? Systematic review of the quantitative and qualitative literature. *Computers in Human Behavior, 100,* 48–59. https://doi.org/https://doi.org/10.1016/j.chb.2019.06.011

Rose, S. D. (1984). Use of data in identifying and resolving group problems in goal oriented treatment groups. *Social Work with Groups, 7*(2), 23–36.

Shera, W., Muskat, B., Delay, D., Quinn, A., & Tufford, L. (2013). Using a group work practice standards inventory to assess the impact of a "social work practice with groups" course. *Social Work with Groups, 36*(2–3), 174–190. https://doi.org/10.1080/01609513.2012.745110

Singh, A. A., Merchant, N., Skudrzyk, B., & Ingene, D. (2012). Association for Specialists in Group Work: Multicultural and social justice competence principles for group workers. *Journal for Specialists in Group Work, 37*(4), 312–325. https://doi.org/10.1080/01933922.2012.721482

Sodano, S., Guyker, W., DeLucia-Waack, J. L., Cosgrove, H., Altabef, D., & Amos, B. (2014). Measures of group process, dynamics, climate behavior, and outcome: A review. In J. L. DeLucia-Waack, C. R. Kalodner, & M. Riva (Eds.), *Handbook of group counseling and psychotherapy* (pp. 159–177). Sage.

Toseland, R. W., & Rivas, R. F. (2017). *An introduction to group work practice* (8th ed.). Allyn & Bacon.

Voyatzaki, Z. (2015). International standards network. *Group Analysis, 48*(3 Suppl.), 12–17. https://doi.org/10.1177/0533316415597662d

Yalom, I. D., & Leszcz, M. (2005). *The theory and practice of group psychotherapy* (5th ed.). Basic Books. http://www.loc.gov/catdir/toc/ecip055/2005000056.html

Best Practices in Social Work with Groups

Beginnings to Endings

Mark J. Macgowan and Alice Schmidt Hanbidge

The evidence-based group work model, empirically supported group interventions and processes, evidence-supported best practice guidelines, and practice evaluation were discussed in Chapter 81. Best available evidence is incorporated through the group developmental stages of planning, beginnings, middles, and endings. Pre-group planning was illustrated in Chapter 81. This chapter continues with exploration of best practices in the group developmental stages of beginnings, middles, and endings.

Beginnings

The beginning of a group is often characterized by caution and tentativeness, and it is common for group members to enter the group with mixed emotions—excitement and hope that the group can be beneficial mixed with concerns about trusting strangers with personal information and fears that the group could be a negative experience. The role of the group worker in establishing the group is now central. There are many areas that must be addressed at

this stage, and the International Association for Social Work with Groups (IASWG) Standards (2015) include tasks and skills related to beginnings. We focus on what the Standards highlight as important; namely cultivating mutual aid and building cohesion.

Cultivate Mutual Aid

One of the early tasks as the group begins is for the worker to invite members to introduce themselves and to say what brought them to the group. This activity helps members begin to share mutual concerns and interests in a trusting environment to develop universality ("all in the same boat"), which is an essential ingredient of mutual aid (Steinberg, 2010). Creating mutual aid is a core part of social work with groups (IASWG, 2015). Schwartz (1961/1994) defined mutual aid as "an alliance of individuals who need each other, in varying degrees, to work on certain common problems" (p. 266). The group work serves a "mediating" function (Schwartz, 1976) connecting individuals with each other and with the worker to create a helping system.

The IASWG Standards (2015) include numerous items related to helping build mutual aid in groups, such as "helps members establish relationships with one another"; "highlights member commonalities"; "encourages direct member to member communication"; "clarifies and interprets communication patterns among members, between members and worker, and between the group and systems outside the group"; "models and encourages honest communication and feedback among members and between members and workers"; and "links members to one another." In particular, linking is an important technique for fostering mutual aid. Middleman and Wood (1990) discuss two ways in which members may be linked: a feeling link and an information link. A feeling link asks members "to connect with a feeling being expressed" (p. 120), whereas an information link asks members "to connect with a statement or question that someone has expressed" (p. 122). Reaching for an information link not only connects members but also allows the worker to "give back their assumed power to others by signaling that they are the ones best able to respond to their issues out of their own experiences" (p. 123).

Build Cohesion

Cohesion is an essential part of effective group work. Research studies have reported that cohesion is most strongly associated with client improvement in groups using an interpersonal, psychodynamic, or cognitive–behavioral orientation, and it contributes to outcomes regardless of inpatient and outpatient or diagnostic classifications (Burlingame et al., 2011, 2018). To build cohesion, the group worker should (Burlingame et al., 2001, 2018)

- conduct pre-group preparation to establish treatment expectations;
- introduce structured activities in early sessions, which reduces anxiety and leads to higher levels of disclosure and cohesion

later in the group (but reduce structure over time);
- facilitate member interaction;
- model effective interpersonal feedback, and maintain a moderate level of control and affiliation;
- time the delivery of feedback based on the developmental stage of the group and the readiness of members;
- handle conflict when it arises;
- effectively manage their own emotional presence to be warm, accepting, and empathic, which not only affects relationships with individuals in the group but also affects all group members as they see the worker's way of relating with others; and
- facilitate group members' emotional expression (e.g., empathy, support and caring, and acceptance) and the responsiveness of others to that expressiveness.

Ongoing assessment of group processes is essential for measuring the optimal functioning of the group and for moving the group toward desired outcomes. Best practice guidelines [American Group Psychotherapy Association (AGPA), 2007; Burlingame et al., 2006] recommend assessing group processes such as cohesion to determine if strategies are needed to improve processes linked to positive outcomes. Group workers can monitor the effectiveness of the previously discussed cohesion-building strategies using the Group Psychotherapy Intervention Rating Scale (Chapman et al., 2010).

Middles

The journey to the middle stage may not be smooth. The group may go through what has been described as a time of "uncertainty-exploration" characterized by "storming" or "power and control" (Garland et al., 1965; Northen & Kurland, 2001; Tuckman, 1965). During that time, workers help the group discuss and manage negative expressions of feelings, hostility, and conflict that might occur. Encouraging members to express negative feelings creates an environment of openness and gives opportunity to address behaviors that are incongruent with the group's purpose.

The middle (or working) stage of the group is often characterized by an increased level of self-disclosure, cohesion, mutual aid, problem-solving, a willingness to work on personal issues, and individual and group growth (Toseland & Rivas, 2017). The leader's role shifts from active to less directive, encouraging greater group ownership and shared leadership within the group [an important value of the IASWG Standards (2015)]. There are many areas that workers attend to in the middle stage, including maintaining cohesion, empowering group members, acknowledging cultural diversity, assessing progress, and continuing to promote the process of mutual aid and to "use that process as a vehicle for work on personal, interpersonal, group, and environmental problems" (Northen & Kurland, 2001, p. 353). The IASWG Standards include 21 tasks and skills in the middle stage. Two skills that group workers find most challenging (Macgowan, 2012) are managing disruptive norms and dealing with conflict in the group, which are discussed here.

Manage Nonproductive Norms

The IASWG Standards (2015) note that unproductive norms and conflict are to be explored with the group rather than addressed exclusively by the group worker. Processing interpersonal and group-related factors with members is "a major source of learning for both members and leaders" (Ward & Ward, 2014, p. 40) and an essential part of social work with groups. Norms are shared expectations about ways to act in the group, may be explicit or implicit, and develop through the interactions of group members (Toseland & Rivas, 2017). A single action is not usually evidence of a norm,

but the repeated pattern of actions (behavior) over time and/or by a number of members is an indication. Given that norms are developed through group interactions, the group must be involved in the process to manage norms. Group workers have the primary responsibility to guide the group to create and reinforce productive group norms in the planning and beginning stages, and they have the responsibility to guide the group to explore nonproductive norms when they arise in any stage (Bernard et al., 2008; IASWG, 2015). Examples of nonproductive norms include group members using "you" and "we" language, speaking in the third person, resistance, rescuing, and challenging the leader (Sklare et al., 1990).

The IASWG Standards (2015) note that group members are to participate in the process of change. The group worker points out the unproductive norm and puts it back to the group to work it out, such as "How have we let the repeated tardiness continue to today?" If successful, this may lead to the group managing other norm disruptions without prompting (Bernard et al., 2008). Techniques for promoting group exploration of nonproductive norms as they arise include (partly based on IASWG, 2015)

- solicit group members' feedback on the norm;
- discuss or demonstrate how the norm will affect the group's ability to fulfill its purpose;
- help the group develop a new productive response; and
- help members reflect on the process of norm adjustment.

If these measures fail, the worker may need to directly intervene or have an external member work with the group to change its norms.

Work with Conflict

Conflict is "behavior in which there is disagreement between two or more persons" and is "a natural, necessary, and important component of group process" (Northen & Kurland, 2001, p. 214). A worry of group workers, particularly those with limited group work education and training, is that conflict will spiral out of control and ruin the group experience (Northen & Kurland, 2001). As with exploring unproductive norms, the IASWG Standards (2015) expect that group workers help "members mediate conflict within the group" (p. 13) rather than resolving it unilaterally or solving it exclusively outside the group. The role as mediator "resolves disputes, conflicts, or opposing views within the group or between a member and some other person or organization; takes a neutral stand and helps members arrive at a settlement or agreement that is mutually acceptable" (Toseland & Rivas, 2017, p. 287). The most important task of the group worker is to help group members work through the conflict in a constructive manner: "When conflict is constructively discussed, members learn that their relationships are strong enough to withstand an honest level of challenge, which is what many people want to achieve in their outside relationships" (Corey & Corey, 2006, p. 187). The role as mediator in the group, described previously as part of the function of the group worker (Schwartz, 1976), helps model for group members the effective management of conflict.

There are practices that can help members mediate conflict within the group. The first is to help members understand that the role of mediator is of one between the persons involved and not the unilateral decision-maker of solving the conflict. Toseland and Rivas (2017) offer a number of suggestions for handling conflict in group, such as

- view conflict as normal and helpful;
- identify conflict;
- encourage members to listen to the entire group discussion before judging;
- help members avoid personal differences and stick to facts and preferences;
- promote consensus;

- pre-plan a problem-solving model and follow it, using agreed-upon decision criteria;
- clarify and summarize discussion regularly, while remaining neutral in the conflict; and
- be sensitive to group members' preferences and concerns.

Endings

The ending stage is an essential but often neglected part of group work. Best practice guidelines [AGPA, Association for Specialists in Group Work (ASGW), and IASWG] discuss the critical importance of preparing members in advance for endings (also known as termination, adjourning, separation, and transition). The ending stage should be viewed as a "unique stage with its own goals and processes" (AGPA, 2007, p. 64). The work on endings should ideally begin in the planning stage, when the parameters for termination are initially discussed (Yalom & Leszcz, 2005). Endings also occur each session as individuals leave open groups and with the entire group if the group is closed. If the group is closed, the work on endings should occur a few sessions before the final session (Toseland & Rivas, 2017). Workers should be attuned to any cultural variations among members in endings (ASGW, 2012). Rituals such as ceremonies and celebrations may be used, "which aid the members in learning through the leave taking process" (AGPA, 2007, p. 64).

The group worker manages both instrumental and affective tasks related to endings. Instrumental tasks relate to assessing problem reduction and goal achievement, discussing maintenance of gains, and reducing reliance on the group. The group worker should complete the following instrumental tasks (AGPA, 2007; Bernard et al., 2008; IASWG, 2015; Northen & Kurland, 2001; Toseland & Rivas, 2017):

- Review and reinforce individual and group change (preferably through systematic

evaluation methods; see the discussion on evaluation in Chapter 81).
- Discuss unfinished individual work.
- Help members apply knowledge and skills to environments outside of the group.
- Anticipate situations that might be stressful and practice coping skills developed in the group.
- Refer members to other services and, if appropriate, involve significant others in referral decisions.
- Prepare record material (e.g., progress notes; see the discussion on assessment in Chapter 81) as required.

The group worker also helps members manage their feelings about endings and separation. The amount of time spent doing this will depend on the structure and type of group. For example, in unstructured therapy and support groups, feelings about endings may be more intense compared to those in educational or task groups. Both positive and negative feelings are solicited, and both direct and indirect signs of members' reactions to endings are monitored and discussed. Indirect expressions may be tactics to delay or avoid discussing endings, such as late or missed sessions, denial, acting out, and changing topics (IASWG, 2015; Toseland & Rivas, 2017). Feelings of transference, countertransference, and "unfinished business" may arise in the final phase of group work for both the worker and the group members, and sharing these feelings in the group is encouraged. Best practice guidelines and the literature (AGPA, 2007; ASGW, 2012; Bernard et al., 2008; IASWG, 2015; Northen & Kurland, 2001; Shulman, 2011; Toseland & Rivas, 2017) identify the following tasks the group worker should complete in dealing with emotional aspects of endings:

- Be aware of and manage one's own feelings related to separations.
- Share own feelings about endings with the group.
- Explore, support, and clarify the range of emotional expressions related to endings.
- Appreciate the possible wide range of emotions that may be expressed, being aware of cultural differences in endings.
- Use empathy as members struggle to share feelings related to success, loss, or failure.
- Particularly in therapy groups, help members "resolve conflicted relationships with one another and the leader" (AGPA, 2007, p. 64).

Helpful Resources

American Group Psychotherapy Association. *Connecting online*: https://www.agpa.org/home/practice-resources/connecting-online
Evidence-Based Group Work (includes links to group work journals and group work organizations): http://www.evidencebasedgroupwork.com
International Association for Social Work with Groups. *Teaching group work*: https://www.iaswg.org/teaching-group-work

References

American Group Psychotherapy Association. (2007). *Practice guidelines for group psychotherapy*. Retrieved June 1, 2020, from http://www.agpa.org/home/practice-resources/practice-guidelines-for-group-psychotherapy
Association for Specialists in Group Work. (2012). Association for Specialists in Group Work: Multicultural and social justice competence principles for group workers. *Journal for Specialists in Group Work, 37*(4), 312–325. https://doi.org/10.1080/01933922.2012.721482
Bernard, H., Burlingame, G., Flores, P., Greene, L., Joyce, A., Kobos, J. C., Leszcz, M., Semands, R. R. M., Piper, W. E., Slocum McEneaney, A. M., & Feirman, D. (2008). Clinical practice guidelines for group psychotherapy [Special issue]. *International Journal of Group Psychotherapy, 58*(4), 455–542. https://doi.org/10.1521/ijgp.2008.58.4.455
Burlingame, G. M., Fuhriman, A., & Johnson, J. E. (2001). Cohesion in group psychotherapy. *Psychotherapy, 38*(4), 373–379.

Burlingame, G. M., McClendon, D. T., & Alonso, J. (2011). Cohesion in group therapy. *Psychotherapy, 48,* 34–42. https://doi.org/10.1037/a0022063

Burlingame, G. M., McClendon, D. T., & Yang, C. (2018). Cohesion in group therapy: A meta-analysis. *Psychotherapy, 55*(4), 384–398. https://doi.org/10.1037/pst0000173

Burlingame, G. M., Strauss, B., Joyce, A., MacNair-Semands, R., MacKenzie, K. R., Ogrodniczuk, J., & Taylor, S. (2006). *CORE Battery–Revised: An assessment toolkit for promoting optimal group selection, process, and outcome.* American Group Psychotherapy Association. http://www.agpa.org

Chapman, C. L., Baker, E. L., Porter, G., Thayer, S. D., & Burlingame, G. M. (2010). Rating group therapist interventions: The validation of the Group Psychotherapy Intervention Rating Scale. *Group Dynamics, 14*(1), 15–31. https://doi.org/10.1037/a0016628

Corey, M. S., & Corey, G. (2006). *Groups: Process and practice* (7th ed.). Thomson Brooks/Cole.

Garland, J. A., Jones, H. E., & Kolodny, R. L. (1965). A model for stages of development in social work groups. In S. Bernstein (Ed.), *Explorations in group work: Essays in theory and practice* (pp. 12–53). Boston University School of Social Work.

International Association for Social Work with Groups. (2015). *Standards for social work practice with groups* (2nd ed.). Retrieved June 2, 2020, from https://www.iaswg.org/assets/docs/Resources/2015_IASWG_STANDARDS_FOR_SOCIAL_WORK_PRACTICE_WITH_GROUPS.pdf

Macgowan, M. J. (2012). A standards-based inventory of foundation competencies in social work with groups. *Research on Social Work Practice, 22*(5), 578–589. https://doi.org/10.1177/1049731512443288

Middleman, R. R., & Wood, G. G. (1990). *Skills for direct practice in social work.* Columbia University Press.

Northen, H., & Kurland, R. (2001). *Social work with groups* (3rd ed.). Columbia University Press.

Schwartz, W. (1976). Between client and system: The mediating function. In R. W. Roberts & H. Northen (Eds.), *Theories of social work with groups* (pp. 171–197). Columbia University Press.

Schwartz, W. (1994). The social worker in the group. In T. Berman-Rossi (Ed.), *Social work: The collected writings of William Schwartz* (pp. 257–276). Peacock. (Reprinted from *The Social Welfare Forum: Proceedings of the National Conference on Social Welfare,* 1961, Columbia University Press)

Shulman, L. (2011). *Dynamics and skills of group counseling.* Brooks/Cole.

Sklare, G., Keener, R., & Mas, C. (1990). Preparing members for "here-and-now" group counseling. *Journal for Specialists in Group Work, 15*(3), 141–148. https://doi.org/10.1080/01933929008411924

Steinberg, D. M. (2010). Mutual aid: A contribution to best-practice social work. *Social Work with Groups, 33*(1), 53–68. https://doi.org/10.1080/01609510903316389

Toseland, R. W., & Rivas, R. F. (2017). *An introduction to group work practice* (8th ed.). Allyn & Bacon.

Tuckman, B. W. (1965). Developmental sequence in small groups. *Psychological Bulletin, 63*(6), 384–399.

Ward, D. E., & Ward, C. A. (2014). *How to help leaders and members learn from their group experience.* Sage.

Yalom, I. D., & Leszcz, M. (2005). *The theory and practice of group psychotherapy* (5th ed.). Basic Books.

Mutual Aid Groups

Olga Molina

History of the Interactionist Approach

A mutual aid group is defined as a group in which the priority for the worker is to help the members learn how to help one another (Steinberg, 2014). Mutual aid has been a constitutive aspect of social group work practice since the beginning of the profession in the United States (Addams, 1910/2008). The antecedents to mutual aid group work can be found in the settlement house movement and its use of democratic principles with groups (Addams, 1902/2001, 1910/2008).

Moreover, researchers observed that members could learn new skills more effectively through experiential learning that engages auditory, visual, and kinesthetic learning pathways (Coyle, 1939/1980; Jacinto, et al., 2017). In keeping with the democratic ethos of social group work, William Schwartz (1976/1994a, 1961/1994b) coined the term "interactionist approach" to describe the group worker's engagement with members as they focus on holistic elements of their life circumstances. The interactionist approach built directly on the values of group work's roots in the settlement, recreation, and progressive education movements (Cohen & Graybeal, 2007).

Schwartz was concerned about the complex interaction between the members and the group with their neighborhoods and societal institutions. Schwartz described the group worker as a mediator between the members, group, and society.

Using the democratic approach to group work, the group worker is one among equals assisting members in the discovery of pathways and solutions to problems (Molina et al., 2020). Schwartz (1961) wrote, "This is a helping system in which the clients need each other as well as the worker. This need . . . to create not one but many helping relationships is a vital ingredient of the group process" (p. 19). Schwartz used the term "interactionist" to emphasize interactions between people and external systems (Gitterman, 2005). He was the major proponent of the use of "mutual aid" in social group work and the first to introduce the term into social work (Cohen & Graybeal, 2007; Steinberg, 2014).

Mutual aid encompasses democratic values and humanistic assumptions regarding human nature (Jacinto, et al., 2017).

The Mutual Aid Model

The interactionist approach is now called the mutual aid model; the concept of mutual aid is central to social work with groups. Mutual aid refers to people helping one another as they work together to develop solutions to problems (Steinberg, 2014). The mutual aid model is a psychosocial approach to group work. It is a holistic approach that is a strength-based practice. The model is based on the belief that we work with groups because of their potential for mutual aid (Molina & Chapple, 2017; Steinberg, 2014). Group members both receive and give help to one another, and in helping others, they also help themselves (Steinberg, 2014). Mutual aid groups help members cope with stressful life circumstances and improve coping abilities. According to Steinberg (2014), mutual aid groups have three main functions: helping the group identify the strengths of each member, helping it use members' strengths to build a community based on mutual aid, and teaching group members the process of purposeful use of self so that they engage in mutual aid. When group members begin sharing with each other and realize they are not alone, their sense of isolation decreases, and they can start managing the challenges they face (Beggs et al., 2018; Knight & Gitterman, 2014).

Steinberg (2014) describes mutual aid as being both a process and an outcome. She states that mutual aid does not happen automatically in groups; it requires communication and a climate of risk-taking, cooperation, and creativity. Shulman (2011) says that the role of the worker in the group is to help group members recognize obstacles to mutual aid and work through these obstacles. Shulman (2006) and Steinberg (2014) further discuss the dynamics of mutual aid and their implications for group work practice. According to them, recognizing the dynamics of mutual aid can help us realize when it is taking place (Steinberg, 2014).

There are nine dynamics of mutual aid: sharing data, dialectical process, discussing a taboo area, all in the same boat phenomenon (a universal perspective), mutual support,

mutual demand, individual problem-solving, rehearsal, and strength in numbers (Steinberg, 2014). For example, when members share information (data) and feedback with each other, they help each other by sharing their knowledge and understanding (Cohen & Graybeal, 2007). The group worker encourages this dynamic as a helping process that takes place among group members, and members start to appreciate the strengths they bring to the group.

Purpose of Mutual Aid Groups

The purpose of mutual aid groups is to help members cope with stressful life events and revitalize coping abilities (Toseland & Rivas, 2017). Mutual aid groups effectively build support, mutuality, and connection among group members (Cohen & Graybeal, 2007). Moreover, mutual aid groups contribute to group members' mental well-being by enhancing a sense of control, increasing resilience, and facilitating participation (Seebohm et al., 2013). Seebohm et al. (2013) explored the contribution of mutual aid groups to mental well-being by interviewing 21 group facilitators in the United Kingdom. This qualitative study concluded that group members gained self-esteem, knowledge, and confidence through the mutual aid system they created. According to Matto (2014), group members in mutual aid groups benefit in important ways from their participation, particularly in receiving instrumental and emotional support from other members.

Benefits of Mutual Aid Groups

Mutual aid groups allow group members to find common ground that leads to group cohesiveness and achieving a sense of personal, interpersonal, and environmental control over their lives (Gitterman & Shulman, 2005; Hyde,

2013). Mutual aid groups encourage members to use their collective resourcefulness and creativity in a peer support group. Mutual aid is a process in which group members can develop collaborative, trustworthy, and supportive relationships; identify existing strengths and develop new strengths; and work together toward both individual and collective goals (Hyde, 2013). Mutual aid groups can assist group members in terms of feeling less isolated, more empowered, better able to acquire effective coping strategies, and achieving a new level of self-efficacy (Knight & Gitterman, 2014). This is because mutual aid groups allow members to share similar experiences and gain social support from others who have been through the same experience (Hyde, 2013).

Mutual aid groups have been found to help adolescent survivors of parental intimate partner violence feel less alone because the groups offer a form of social support. The support and connections that adolescents obtain from the mutual aid groups are beyond any support that individual therapeutic counseling could provide for an individual client (Molina, 2013). Mutual aid groups meet the treatment needs of trauma survivors and reduce the symptoms associated with trauma, enhance self-esteem, and reduce depression and isolation (Jacinto et al., 2017; Knight, 2009).

Mutual aid groups help normalize and validate the members' experiences and increase the mutual aid benefits of members believing they are "all in the same boat." The members' sense of isolation decreases when they realize they are not alone. Groups provide an opportunity for members to connect with others who have similar experiences, and this helps build the members' self-esteem and self-efficacy (Knight & Gitterman, 2014). In addition, mutual aid groups that are more structured and time-limited and have an educational component are more effective with socially isolated

members (Molina et al., 2020). Kurland and Salmon (1996) distinguish the practice of "case work in a group," in which the worker encourages each group member to talk about issues of concern, and group work, in which the worker maximizes mutual aid and group interaction (Cohen & Graybeal, 2007).

Solution-Focused Mutual Aid Groups

Group work scholars are beginning to merge other theoretical approaches with the mutual aid group model. For example, Cohen and Graybeal (2007) introduced the emergence of the solution-focused mutual aid group model. The incorporation of solution-focused techniques in the group encourages members to ask one another questions, listen, and be empathetic. The emphasis in solution-focused mutual aid groups is on the present and future and builds on the strengths of group members. The model is effective in moving away from problem-saturated member stories to focusing on solutions. According to Cohen and Graybeal (2007), this focus builds on the strengths and resilience that Schwartz (1961/1994b) described as central to the mutual aid process.

Mutual Aid Groups and Resiliency

Schwartz emphasized the strengths and resiliency of group members in his writings (1961/1994b), pointing to the multiplicity of the helping relationships found in mutual aid groups. Contemporary group work scholars expanded further on the concept referring to "the strengths in numbers" inherent in groups (Abels & Abels, 2002; Berman-Rossi & Cohen, 1988; Dean, 1998; Gitterman & Shulman, 2005; Lee & Swenson, 2005; Steinberg, 2014).

Mutual Aid and Evidence-Based Practice

Steinberg (2010) has written about mutual aid being a contribution to best practice social work. She presents five characteristics of mutual aid practice that reflect best practice social work: mutual aid as a strengths-driven process; mutual aid practice as inherently holistic; mutual aid as a psychosocial process; mutual aid practice as antioppressive social work; and mutual aid as evidence. Steinberg argues that the group helping process takes place with perceptions of its participants. For example, group workers always encourage feedback from group members, and this process of evaluation increases the evidence-based practice knowledge in the field of group work.

Research on Mutual Aid Groups

A number of research studies have examined the effectiveness of mutual aid groups. For example, White et al. (2013) studied the co-participation in 12-step mutual aid groups and methadone maintenance treatment of a sample of 322 patients in an urban community in the northeastern United States. Survey results found a high rate of past-year Narcotics Anonymous/Alcoholics Anonymous (NA/AA) participation (66%) and high rates of reported helpfulness of AA and NA (88–89%).

In addition, Mogro-Wilson et al. (2015) assessed the effectiveness of mutual aid groups for high school students. The study evaluated the influence of mutual aid groups in decreasing the perceived risk of substance use. The researchers used a quasi-experimental design with a sample of 242 adolescents. The findings indicated mutual aid groups significantly reduced favorable attitudes toward drug use

and decreased alcohol and marijuana usage compared to the control group. The authors conclude that the study supports the effectiveness of mutual aid groups for reducing alcohol use and increasing group engagement for high school students.

In addition to quantitative research, qualitative studies have also been conducted. For example, Calcaterra and Raineri (2020) assessed a peer supervision group with facilitators of mutual aid groups. Four meetings of a peer supervision group were analyzed. The group consisted of 11 individuals (5 women and 6 men). The researchers found that peer supervision groups help members better assume the role of facilitator in mutual aid groups. The group helped the participants better understand, address, and cope with difficulties in leading mutual aid groups.

Mutual Aid Groups and Diverse Populations

Currently, mutual aid groups are successfully used in a wide variety of settings with diverse populations, such as children experiencing bereavement and loss (Knight, 2005a), parents grieving children (Beggs et al., 2018), LGBT youth (DeLois, 2003), Latinx adolescent survivors of parental intimate partner violence (Molina & Chapple, 2017), divorced women (Molina et al. 2009), people with HIV/AIDS (Getzel, 2005; Shulman, 2005b), women in violent interpersonal relationships (Cohen, 2003), men who abuse intimate partners (Blalock, 2003), survivors of sexual abuse (Knight, 2005b; Schiller & Zimmer, 2005), homeless persons (Lee, 2005), refugees and immigrants (Breton, 1999), older persons and their caregivers (Berman-Rossi, 2005); substance abusers (White et al., 2013), Rwandan women trauma survivors (Jacinto et al., 2017), and many others (Cohen & Graybeal, 2007).

The International Association for Social Work with Groups

The International Association for Social Work with Groups (IASWG) is an international association for social workers and other helping professionals engaged in group work. The purpose of this nonprofit, member-driven organization is to promote excellence in group work practice, education, field instruction, research, and publication. The goals of IASWG are to develop a program of action and advocacy at both local and international levels. IASWG's practice committee has written the *Standards for Social Work Practice with Groups* (2015). These standards serve as a guide to professionals on the value, knowledge, and skill base needed for effective social work practice with groups. The standards are divided into several sections: core values and knowledge, pre-group phase, group work in the beginning phase, group work in the middle stage, group work in the ending phase, and ethical considerations. The standards apply to group work practice in general; however, they are useful to mutual aid group workers as well. The standards are taught in group work practice courses throughout the United States as well as in many other countries to identify the variety of skills that group workers need to practice throughout the stages of group development.

Limitations of Mutual Aid Groups

The mutual aid model has two known limitations. First, it is not effective for people who have an extreme need for privacy. Second, it is not effective for people whose behavior is so alien to others that it results in negative, rather than positive, interactions that can lead to other group members discontinuing the group (Toseland & Rivas, 2017).

Conclusion

Despite the previously mentioned limitations, it is clear that the mutual aid model has had considerable endurance. It has maintained currency with contemporary social issues and client presenting problems. The variety of current settings and topics that lend themselves to the mutual aid model is considerable (Cohen & Graybeal, 2007).

Finally, Cohen and Graybeal (2007) note,

> Schwartz's legacy lives on in the work of the group work scholars who followed him, many of whom he mentored. These authors, including Gitterman, Shulman, Berman-Rossi, Northen, Kurland, Salmon, Steinberg, Middleman, Breton, and others, added their own contributions to the mutual aid model, keeping it timely and relevant to current practice issues and settings. (p. 44)

Helpful Resource

International Association for Social Work with Groups: https://www.iaswg.org

References

Abels, P., & Abels, S. (2002). Narrative social work with groups: Just in time. In S. Henry, J. East, & C. Schmitz (Eds.), *Mining the gold in social work with group* (pp. 57–73). Haworth.

Addams, J. (2001). *Democracy and social ethics.* University of Chicago Press. (Original work published 1902)

Addams, J. (2008). *Twenty years at Hull House: With autobiographical notes.* Dover. (Original work published 1910)

Beggs, J. J., Molina, O., & Jacinto, G. A. (2018). Mutual aid groups for grieving parents. *International Journal of Childbirth Education, 33*(3), 31–35.

Berman-Rossi, T. (2005). The group as a source of hope: Institutionalized older persons. In A. Gitterman & L. Shulman (Eds.), *Mutual aid groups, vulnerable and resilient populations, and the life cycle* (3rd ed., pp. 73–110). Columbia University Press.

Berman-Rossi, T., & Cohen, M. B. (1988). Group development and shared decision-making: Working with homeless mentally ill women. *Social Work with Groups, 11*(4), 63–78.

Blalock, N. (2003). Gender awareness and the role of the groupworker in programmes for domestic violence perpetrators. In M. B. Cohen & A. Mullender (Eds.), *Gender and groupwork* (pp. 66–79). Routledge.

Breton, M. (1999). The relevance of the structural approach to group work with immigrant and refugee women. *Social Work with Groups, 22*(4), 11–29.

Calcaterra, V., & Raineri, M. L. (2020). Helping each other: A peer supervision group with facilitators of mutual aid groups. *Social Work with Groups, 43*(2–3), 351–364. doi:10.1080/01609513.2019.16428294

Cohen, M. B. (2003). Women in groups: The history of feminist empowerment. In M. B. Cohen & A. Mullender (Eds.), *Gender and groupwork* (pp. 32–40). Routledge.

Cohen, M. B., & Graybeal, C. T. (2007). Using solution-oriented techniques in mutual aid groups. *Social Work with Group, 30*(4), 41–58.

Coyle, G. L. (1980). Education for social action. In A. Alissi (Ed.), *Perspectives on social group work practice: A book of readings.* Free Press. (Original work published 1939)

Dean, R. (1998). A narrative approach to groups. *Clinical Social Work Journal, 26*(1), 23–36.

DeLois, K. (2003). Genderbending: Reflections on group work with queer youth. In M. B. Cohen & A. Mullender (Eds.), *Gender and groupwork* (pp. 107–115). Routledge.

Getzel, G. (2005). No one is alone during the AIDS pandemic. In A. Gitterman & L. Shulman (Eds.), *Mutual aid groups, vulnerable and resilient populations, and the life cycle* (3rd ed., pp. 249–265). Columbia University Press.

Gitterman, A. (2005). Group formation. In A. Gitterman & L. Shulman (Eds.), *Mutual aid groups, vulnerable and resilient populations, and the life cycle* (3rd ed., pp. 73–110). Columbia University Press.

Gitterman, A., & Shulman, L. (Eds.). (2005). *Mutual aid groups, vulnerable and resilient populations, and the life cycle* (3rd ed.). Columbia University Press.

Hyde, B. (2013). Mutual aid group work: Social work leading the way to recovery-focused mental health practice. *Social Work with Groups, 36*(1), 43–58.

International Association for Social Work with Groups. (2010). *Standards for social work practice with groups.*

Jacinto, G. A., Chapple, R. L., Nyiransekuye, H., & Molina, O. (2017). Women trauma survivors of the Rwandan genocide: A seven-week group building exercise. *Groupwork, 27*(1), 49–65.

Knight, C. (2005a). Healing hearts: A bereavement group for children. In A. Gitterman & L. Shulman (Eds.), *Mutual aid groups, vulnerable and resilient populations, and the life cycle* (3rd ed., pp. 114–138). Columbia University Press.

Knight, C. (2005b). From victim to survivor: Group work with men and women who were sexually abused. In A. Gitterman & L. Shulman (Eds.), *Mutual aid groups, vulnerable and resilient populations, and the life cycle* (3rd ed., pp. 321–351). Columbia University Press.

Knight, C. (2009). Trauma survivors. In A. Gitterman & R. Salmon (Eds.), *Encyclopedia of social work with groups* (pp. 240–243). Routledge.

Knight, C., & Gitterman, A. (2014). Group work with bereaved individuals: The power of mutual aid. *Social Work, 59*(1), 5–12.

Kurland, R., & Salmon, R. (1996). Making joyful noise: Presenting, promoting, and portraying group work to and for the profession. In B. Stempler, M. Glass, & C. Savinelli (Eds.), *Social group work today and tomorrow: Moving from theory to advanced training and practice* (pp. 19–33). Haworth.

Lee, J. A. B. (2005). No place to go: Homeless women and children. In A. Gitterman & L. Shulman (Eds.), *Mutual aid groups, vulnerable and resilient populations, and the life cycle* (3rd ed., pp. 373–397). Columbia University Press.

Lee, J. A. B., & Swenson, C. (2005). Mutual aid: A buffer against risk. In A. Gitterman & L. Shulman (Eds.), *Mutual aid groups, vulnerable and resilient populations, and the life cycle* (3rd ed., pp. 573–596), Columbia University Press.

Matto, H. C. (2014). Mutual aid support groups: Benefits and recommendations. *Journal of Groups in Addiction & Recovery, 9*(3), 197–198.

Mogro-Wilson, C., Letendre, J., Toi, H., & Bryan, J. (2015). Utilizing mutual aid in reducing adolescent substance use and developing group engagement. *Research on Social Work Practice, 25*(1), 129–138.

Molina, O. (2013). Latino adolescent survivors of child abuse and parental intimate partner violence: How group work can help [Special issue]. *NASW, Child Welfare Section Connection,* 5–7.

Molina, O., & Chapple, R. (2017). A mutual-aid group for Latino and Latina adolescent survivors of parental intimate partner violence. *Groupwork, 27*(1), 66–86.

Molina, O., Lawrence, S. A., Azhar-Miller, A., & Rivera, M. (2009). Divorcing abused Latina immigrant women's experiences with domestic violence support groups. *Journal of Divorce and Remarriage, 50*(7), 459–471.

Molina, O., Nyiransekuye, H., & Jacinto, G. A. (2020). Use of the labyrinth in mutual-aid group work. *Groupwork, 28*(3), 70–87.

Schiller, L. Y., & Zimmer, B. (2005). Sharing the secrets: The power of women's groups for sexual abuse survivors. In A. Gitterman & L. Shulman (Eds.), *Mutual aid groups, vulnerable and resilient populations, and the life cycle* (3rd ed., pp. 290–319). Columbia University Press.

Schwartz, W. (1994a). Between client and system: The mediating function. In T. Berman-Rossi (Ed.), *Social work: The collected writings of William Schwartz* (pp. 171–197). Peacock. (Original work published 1976)

Schwartz, W. (1994b). The social worker in the group. In T. Berman-Rossi (Ed.), *Social work: The collected writings of William Schwartz* (pp. 7–34). Peacock. (Original work published 1961)

Seebohm, P., Chaudhary, S., Boyce, M., Elkan, R., Avis, M., & Munn-Giddings, C. (2013). The contribution of self-help/mutual aid groups to mental well-being. *Health & Science Care in the Community, 21*(4), 391–401.

Shulman, L. (2005). Persons with AIDS in substance-abusing recovery. In A. Gitterman & L. Shulman (Eds.), *Mutual aid groups, vulnerable and resilient populations, and the life cycle* (3rd ed. pp. 266–289). Columbia University Press.

Shulman, L. (2006). *The skills of helping individuals, families, and groups* (5th ed.). Brooks/Cole.

Steinberg, D. M. (2010). Mutual aid: A contribution to best-practice social work. *Social Work with Groups, 33*(1), 53–68.

Steinberg, D. M. (2014). *A mutual-aid model for social work with groups.* Routledge.

Toseland, R. W., & Rivas, R. F. (2017). *An introduction to group work practice* (8th ed.). Pearson.

White, W. L., Campbell, M. D., Shea, C., Hoffman, H. A., Crissman, B., & DuPont, R. L. (2013). Coparticipation in 12-step mutual aid groups and methadone maintenance treatment: A survey of 322 patients. *Journal of Groups in Addiction & Recovery, 8*(4), 294–308.

Social Skills Training and Behavioral Groups

Craig Winston LeCroy

An increasing emphasis is being placed on learning social skills for understanding, preventing, and remediating problems. This conceptualization asserts that problem behavior can be understood in terms of individuals not having acquired skills appropriate to meet situational demands. Individuals may fail to develop appropriate social skills for many reasons; however, a deficit in skills can lead to problems in successful adaptation to life tasks.

Social skills therapy or education teaches prosocial skills that substitute for problem behaviors such as being aggressive or excessively shy or communicating poorly. Interpersonal skills can be taught to enhance communication with friends, family members, work associates, and authority figures. Stress management and coping skills can be taught to help prevent future problems. Numerous opportunities exist for the implementation of various skills-based programs that can help facilitate successful problem resolution. Social skills training groups have been used to address a wide variety of issues in daily living, such as communicating empathically, giving constructive feedback, listening, speaking up in a group, making friends, making job presentations, controlling aggression, and resolving conflict.

Ravenscraft (2020) wrote a popular *New York Times* article, "An Adult's Guide to Social Skills, for Those Who Were Never Taught," which resonated with many people. His point was simply that many people have not been taught the basics on the best way to interact constructively with others.

Research strongly suggests that social skills are essential for healthy normal development (Ashford et al., 2019). It is through our interactions with peers that many of life's necessary behaviors are acquired. For example, sexual socialization, control of aggression, expression of emotion, and caring in friendships develop through interaction with peers. When adults fail to acquire such social skills, they are beset by problems such as inappropriate expression of anger, friendship difficulties, and inability to assert themselves. It is this understanding that has led to the current focus on changing interpersonal behavior. Because many problem behaviors develop in a social

---

BOX 84.1 Considerations When Using a Group Approach

Promotes mutual support between members

Cost-effective and efficient treatment strategy

Can be implemented with clear guidelines following a group treatment manual

Promotes cohesion among group members

Strengthens the social support and reinforcement that members can obtain from each other

Provides feedback that can reflect "real-life" issues

Provides an interpersonal context that can facilitate learning skills

Provides models and rehearsal opportunities for group members

---

context, the teaching of social skills is one of the most promising approaches in remediating social difficulties and is often done in groups.

Using Groups to Teach Social Skills

One of the clear advantages to group work is that clients work together. Furthermore, the experience of being together in a group for mutual support is itself an important therapeutic factor. An important group leader skill is being able to encourage group members to help each other. Other advantages include the interactions that can take place as group members provide feedback and modeling for each other. Also, group members can obtain reinforcement and encouragement that are often needed to encourage new behavior changes. The group setting is interactive, real, and often becomes an environment that mimics issues in the real world. In this environment, the group leader can use information that can help group members bring about new awareness and opportunities to try different ways of thinking or behaving in interactions with others.

Group-based treatment may be the treatment of choice depending on the nature of the problem being treated (Tolman & LeCroy, 2017). In particular, a group-based model may be ideally suited for individuals with multiple

behavior problems and who experience some "rigidity" regarding their orientation to change (Shaffer, 1976). An additional advantage of group work is that program models are available that provide a manualized set of guidelines for the practitioner. For example, there are group manuals for depression, social skills training, trauma, divorce, substance abuse, and others (LeCroy, 2008). Box 84.1 summarizes the key considerations of working with groups from a cognitive–behavioral perspective.

Defining and Conceptualizing Social Skills

Social skills can be defined as a complex set of skills that facilitate successful interactions between others. "Social" refers to interactions between people; "skills" refers to making appropriate discriminations—that is, deciding what would be the most effective response and using the verbal and nonverbal behaviors that facilitate interaction (LeCroy, 2008, 2013).

Social skills training uses two key elements in addressing social adaptation of individuals: knowledge and skilled performance. In order to respond appropriately to situational demands, a person must have knowledge of appropriate interpersonal behavior. However, that knowledge must be translated into skilled performance or social skills. Social skills training programs or therapy use methods to enhance a person's knowledge of social situations and enhance effective performance in those situations. An additional consideration is to plan for generalization so that any new skills learned are translated into different environments that have to do with friendships, work settings, family interactions, and so forth.

The conceptualization of social skills as training suggests that problem behaviors can be viewed as remediable deficits in the person's response repertoire. This focuses on building prosocial responses or skills as opposed to an emphasis on the elimination of behaviors such as excessive antisocial responses. A large part of treatment is having individuals learn new options to problem situations. Learning how to respond effectively to new situations produces more positive consequences than past behaviors used in similar situations. This model focuses on the teaching of skills and competencies for day-to-day living rather than focusing on the understanding and elimination of defects. It is an optimistic view and is implemented in an educative remedial framework.

Developing Program or Therapy Goals and Selecting Skills

Social skills training can be conducted as a program of skills using a group format or as a treatment plan for an individual. The first step in the development of a successful social skills training program is to identify the goals of the program based on the needs of the target population or individual. What specific skills does the person need to learn? For example, a program goal for a shy or withdrawn person is to be able to initiate positive social interactions (Antony, 2004). Once the goals of the program are clearly defined, the next step is to select the specific skills that need to be learned.

Some key problems that can be addressed with a social skills approach are shown in Table 84.1, translating presenting problems into skills.

Assertiveness training, often offered in groups, was conceptualized as a social skills training intervention designed to reduce anxiety (Antony & Swinson, 2000; Speed et al., 2018). It was an intervention that could help individuals who lacked the skills needed to adapt to their everyday lives. Lazarus (1971) promoted assertive training as a key therapy and identified four key aspects to help individuals: (1) learning how to present one's desires and needs to others, (2) learning to say no to requests that are not acceptable, (3) communicating one's feelings to others, and (4) establishing social support and developing friendships. Although assertiveness training is not recognized today as much as it was in the past (Speed et al., 2018), it has been incorporated into many well-known approaches to cognitive–behavioral therapy, including behavioral rehearsal, modeling, and dialectical behavior therapy. Patterson (2000) presents a program for implementing assertiveness training with adults. Lowndes (2003) discusses how to develop social skills for relationships with others.

In promoting social skills for success in everyday life, Sethi (2019) created the ultimate guide to social skills and he emphasizes five skills that he considers critical for any successful person: learning how to be interesting, learning how to make small talk, learning to overcome shyness, learning how to master conversations, and learning how to be more likeable.

Sander (2020) lists 14 skills that are helpful to adults:

1. How to start a conversation with anyone as an adult
2. How to stop being nervous
3. How to be more outgoing as an adult
4. How to approach intimidating people
5. How to deal with hate and criticism

TABLE 84.1 Translating Presenting Problems into Skills

Problem	Skills
Withdrawn, moody, and irritable	Being aware of one's feelings Getting pleasure from interaction with others Controlling one's mood Behavioral activation
Anxious behavior	Relaxing Deep breathing Being more mindful Being assertive Reducing negative self-statements Getting pleasure from social interactions
Depression	Developing pleasant activities (behavioral activation) Obtaining support from others Developing assertiveness
Difficult relationships	Being independent Accepting disapproval of others Handling rejection Being likeable Anger control Expressing empathy
Feeling unloved, showing no outside enjoyment in life, bored	Getting pleasure from loving acts toward others Getting pleasure from exploration Anticipating pleasure and fun from activities Celebrating one's accomplishments and successes Accepting compliments from others Getting pleasure from positive attention
Substance abuse	Identifying problem situations Using effective refusal skills Making friends with non-using friends General problem-solving for risky situations Managing leisure time

6. How to have more meaningful, deep conversations with friends
7. What to do when people get bored with what you have to say
8. How to improve your social skills
9. How to stop worrying about what others think
10. How to be confident (without coming off as arrogant)
11. How to stop being uncomfortable at parties
12. How to improve your self-esteem
13. How to be more charismatic
14. How to make people respect you

The process of social skills training requires continual attention to refining each skill that is to be taught. After identifying the broad social skills, it is important to divide each broad skill into its component parts so that they can be more easily learned. For example, LeCroy (2008, p. 136) breaks down the skill "beginning a conversation" into seven component parts:

1. Look the person in the eye and demonstrate appropriate body language.
2. Greet the person, saying one's own name.
3. Ask an open-ended question about the person. Listen attentively for the response.
4. Make a statement to follow up on the person's response.
5. Ask another open-ended question about the person. Listen attentively to the response.
6. Make another statement about the conversation.
7. End the conversation by letting the person know you have to leave.

Guidelines for Using Social Skills Training Methods

After program goals are defined and skills are selected, various methods can be used for teaching social skills. These methods of influence are the ways in which the learning of such skills is promoted. There are three main methods of influence used in social skills training: skills-based behavioral rehearsal, group-based social skills treatment, and behavior modification. Many variations exist within these three main methods—for example, using reinforcement of selected skills during therapy sessions, producing narrative stories with clients that reinforce selected skills, conducting audio or video models of the selected skills being taught, and using covert modeling as a means of rehearsal and reinforcement of skills. The most widely used social skills training techniques include the following:

- *Instruction* is the educational component of social skills training that involves the modeling of appropriate social behaviors.
- *Behavioral rehearsal*, or role-play, involves practicing new skills during therapy in simulated situations.
- *Corrective feedback* is used to help improve social skills during practice.
- *Modeling* is having the person see the skill being taught so they can learn it.
- *Positive reinforcement* is used to reward improvements in social skills.
- *Weekly homework assignments* provide the chance to practice new social skills outside of therapy.

When conducting behavioral rehearsal, practitioners should follow the basic principles established in modeling theory. Guidelines include the following:

1. Use multiple characters to provide exposure to multiple models.

2. Have a role model experience reinforcing consequences of their action.
3. Design a character that is viewed as desirable and appropriate to the cultural context.
4. Use a coping model whereby the character struggles some but then overcomes those initial difficulties.
5. Practice using self-talk demonstrating the use of good coping skills.

Group-Based Social Skills Treatment

Social skills training is often conducted in a group format, which provides support and a reinforcing context for learning new responses and appropriate behaviors in a variety of social situations. The group is a natural context for social skills training because of the peer interactions that take place as the group members work together. In addition, the group allows for extensive use of modeling and feedback, which are critical components of successful skills training.

The following seven basic steps delineate the process that group leaders can follow when teaching social skills training (based on LeCroy, 2008). Box 84.2 presents these steps and outlines the process for teaching social skills. In each step, there is a request for group member involvement. This is because it is critical that group leaders involve the participants actively in the skill training. Also, this keeps the group interesting and fun for the group members.

1. *Present the social skill being taught.* The first step for the group leader is to present the skill. The leader solicits an explanation of the skill—for example, "Can anyone tell me what it takes to start a conversation with someone you don't know?" After group members have answered this question, the leader emphasizes the rationale for using the skill—for example, "You would use this skill when you're in a situation where you want to

---

BOX 84.2 Summary of the Steps in Teaching Social Skills Training

1. Present the social skills being taught.
    A. Solicit an explanation of the skill.
    B. Get group members to provide rationales for the skill.
2. Discuss the social skill.
    A. List the skill steps.
    B. Get group members to give examples of using the skill.
3. Present a problem situation and model the skill.
    A. Evaluate the performance.
    B. Get group members to discuss the model.
4. Set the stage for role-playing the skill.
    A. Select the group members for role-playing.
    B. Get group members to observe the role-play.
5. Group members rehearse the skill.
    A. Provide coaching if necessary.
    B. Get group members to provide feedback on verbal and nonverbal elements.
6. Practice using complex skill situations.
    A. Teach accessory skills (e.g., problem-solving).
    B. Get group members to discuss situations and provide feedback.
7. Train for generalization and maintenance.
    A. Encourage practice of skills outside the group.
8. Get group members to bring in their problem situations.

---

get to know someone better or you are at an informal work setting and you are supposed to 'network.'" The leader then requests additional reasons for learning the skill.

2. *Discuss the social skill.* The leader presents the specific skill steps that constitute the social skill. For example, the skill steps for starting a conversation are good nonverbal communication (includes eye contact, posture, and voice volume), greet the person, ask an open-ended question, make a follow-up statement to the person's response, ask another open-ended question, listen carefully, reflect on what was said or make a statement about the conversation, and end the discussion. Leaders then ask group members to share examples of when they used the skill or examples of when they could have used the skill but did not.

3. *Present a problem situation and model the skill.* The leader presents a problem situation. For example, the following is a problem situation for starting a conversation:

> You are at a work event and there is a person there that you would like to get to know better. You have met this person before but want to show some interest in that person.

The group leader chooses members to role-play this situation and then models the skills. Group members evaluate the model's performance. Did the model follow all the skill steps? Was the model's performance successful? The group leader may choose another group member to model if the leader believes they already have the requisite skills. If you know beforehand the skills being taught, another alternative is to present to the group videotaped models. This has the advantage of following the recommendation by researchers that the models be similar to the trainee in age, gender, and social characteristics.

4. *Set the stage for role-playing of the skill.* For this step, the group leader needs to construct the social circumstances for the role-play. Leaders select group members for the role-play and give them their parts to play. The leader reviews with the role players how to act out their role. Group members not in the role-play observe the process. It is sometimes helpful if they are given specific instructions for their observations. For example, one member may observe the use of nonverbal skills, and another member may be instructed to observe what questions are used to start the conversation.

5. *Group members rehearse the skill.* Rehearsal or guided practice of the skill is an important part of effective social skills training. Group leaders and group members provide instructions or coaching before and during the role-play and provide praise and feedback for improvement. Following a role-play rehearsal, the leader will usually give instructions for improvement, model the suggested improvements, or coach the person to incorporate the feedback in the subsequent role-play. Often, the group members doing the role-play will practice the skills in the situation several times to refine their skills and incorporate feedback offered by the group. The role-plays continue until the trainee's behavior becomes increasingly more similar to that of the model. It is important that "overlearning" takes place, so the group leader should encourage many examples of effective skill demonstration followed by praise. Group members should be taught how to give effective feedback before the rehearsals. Throughout the teaching process, the group

leader can model desired responses. For example, after a role-play, the leader can respond first and model feedback that starts with a positive statement.

6. *Practice using complex skill situations.* This phase deals with more difficult and complex skill situations. Complex situations can be developed by extending the interactions and roles in the problem situations. Most social skills groups also incorporate the teaching of problem-solving abilities. Problem-solving is a general approach to helping young people gather information about a problematic situation, generate a large number of potential solutions, evaluate the consequences of various solutions, and outline plans for the implementation of a particular solution. Group leaders can identify appropriate problem situations and lead members through the previous steps. The problem-solving training is important because it prepares people to make adjustments as needed in a given situation. It is a general skill with large-scale application. For a more complete discussion on the use of problem-solving approaches, see Chapter 72, this volume).

7. *Train for generalization and maintenance.* The success of the social skills program depends on the extent to which the skills that individuals learn transfer to their day-to-day lives. Practitioners must always be planning for ways to maximize the generalization of skills learned and promote their continued use after training. Several principles help facilitate the generalization and maintenance of skills. The first is the use of overlearning. The more that overlearning takes place, the greater likelihood of later transfer of skills. Therefore, it is important that group leaders insist on mastery of the skills. Another important principle of generalization is to vary the stimuli as skills are learned. To accomplish this, practitioners can use a variety of models, problem situations, role-play actors, and trainers. The

different styles and behaviors of the people used as role-play actors produce a broader context in which to apply the skills learned. Perhaps most important is to require that people use the skills in their real-life settings. Group leaders should assign and monitor homework to encourage transfer of learning. This may include the use of written contracts to do certain tasks outside of the group. Group members should be asked to bring to the group examples of problem situations in which the social skills can be applied. Last, practitioners should attempt to develop external support for the skills learned. One approach to this is to set up a buddy system in which group members work together to perform the skills learned outside the group.

Conclusion

As social workers work toward the goal of enhancing the social competence of individuals, social skills training has much to offer. Social workers can make an important contribution in their work with individuals through preventive and remedial approaches such as those described in this chapter. As previously discussed, a person's social behavior is a critical aspect of positive mental health and successful adaptation in society. The strategy of social skills training provides a clear methodology for providing remedial and preventive services to individuals. This direct approach has been applied in numerous problem areas and with many behavior problems. It is straightforward in application and has been adapted so that social workers, supervisors, teachers, and peers have successfully applied the methodology. It can be applied in individual, group, or classroom settings. Research supports the efficacy of social skills training; it is a promising new treatment model that should be more widely used.

Helpful Resources

Burns, D. D. (1985). *Intimate connections*. Signet (Penguin).

McKay, M., Davis, M., & Fanning, P. (1995). *Messages: The communication skills book*. New Harbinger

Paterson, R. (2000). *The assertiveness workbook: How to express your ideas and stand up for yourself at work and in relationships*. New Harbinger

References

Antony, M. (2004). *10 simple solutions to shyness*. New Harbinger.

Antony, M., & Swinson, R. (2000). *Shyness and social anxiety workbook: Proven techniques for overcoming your fears*. New Harbinger.

Ashford, J. B., LeCroy, C. W., & Williams, L. (2019). *Human behavior and the social environment: A multidimensional perspective*. Cengage.

Lazarus, A. A. (1971). *Behavior therapy and beyond*. McGraw-Hill.

LeCroy, C. W. (2013). Designing and facilitating groups with children. In C. Franklin, M. B. Harris, & P. Allen-Meares (Eds.), *The school services handbook: A guide for school-based professionals* (pp. 611–618). Oxford University Press.

LeCroy, C. W. (2008). *Handbook of evidence-based child and adolescent treatment manuals*. Oxford University Press.

Lowndes, L. (2003). *How to talk to anyone: 92 little tricks for big success in relationships*. McGraw-Hill.

Ravenscraft, E. (2020, January 23). An adult's guide to social skills, for those who were never taught. *New York Times*. https://www.nytimes.com/2020/01/23/smarter-living/adults-guide-to-social-skills.html

Sander, D. A M. (2020). *Social skills for adults: 14 best guides to be better socially*. https://socialpronow.com/blog/social-skills-training-adults

Sethi, R. (2019). *The ultimate guide to social skills: The art of talking to anyone*. Retrieved June 1, 2020, from https://www.iwillteachyoutoberich.com/guides/ultimate-guide-to-social-skills

Shaffer, W. F. (1976). *Heuristics for the diagnostic interview*. ERIC.

Speed, B. C., Goldstein, B. L., & Goldfried, M. R. (2018). Assertiveness training: A forgotten evidence-based treatment. *Clinical Psychology, 25,* e12216. doi:10.1111/cpsp.12216

Tolman, R., & LeCroy, C. W. (2017). Cognitive–behavioral group work. In C. D. Garvin, L. M. Gutiérrez, & M. J. Galinsky (Eds.), *Handbook of social work with groups* (pp. 133–151). Guilford.

PART VIII

Evidence-Based Practice

What Is Evidence-Based Practice?

Bruce A. Thyer

The process of evidence-based practice (EBP) was introduced to the social work literature more than two decades ago (Gambrill, 1999) and represented the extrapolation of the emerging principles of evidence-based medicine to the purposes of our discipline. EBP is fundamentally quite different from precursor perspectives that addressed the potential of applying scientific methods to social work practice: predecessor movements such as psychoanalytic theory and its variants, behavioral social work (BSW) and its cognitive offshoots, and empirical clinical practice (ECP; Jayaratne & Levy, 1979; Reid, 1994; Siegel, 1984). BSW and ECP shared the ideas that social workers should select their choice of interventions from those best supported by empirical research and also the recommendation that when feasible, social workers should evaluate the outcomes of their clinical practice using single-system research designs (SSRDs). The former idea is difficult to criticize, but it does leave out many important considerations, such as whether the clinician is adequately trained to deliver the empirically supported treatment, the availability of resources required to provide the indicated treatment, the ethical appropriateness of the intervention, an assessment of environmental considerations and client preferences and values, and other factors that bear on the possibility of delivering scientifically supported interventions. The recommendation concerning the use of SSRDs to evaluate outcomes at the level of the individual case has been written about extensively and even successfully applied to a limited extent, but lacking any external reinforcers to support the efforts, busy social workers have not adopted SSRDs on a widespread scale.

The process of inquiry known as EBP has received considerable attention within the field of social work during the past two decades (Drisko & Grady, 2019; Okpych & Yu, 2014), so much so that this fourth edition of the *Social Worker's Desk Reference* continues to contain a large section devoted to it. In early 2020, as I prepared this chapter, my Google search of the term "evidence-based practice" found more than 1 billion and 80 million hits. A PsycINFO search of the terms "evidence-based practice" and "social work" obtained more than 2,000 citations. Further searching will readily disclose the application of EBP in various helping fields such as psychology, nursing, public health, policy practice, dentistry, public administration, management, and even extending to evidence-based government. Clearly, EBP has gained considerable influence throughout the world.

There is some confusion as to what is meant by the term EBP (Drisko & Freidman, 2019; Drisko & Grady, 2019, Grady et al., 2018; Rubin & Parrish, 2007), and this initial descriptive chapter will help set the stage for understanding the succeeding chapters. Here is the brief definition from the original book in the field of evidence-based medicine (now in its fifth edition), the definition from which most extrapolations to other fields, such as social work, are derived: "Evidence-based medicine (EBM) requires the integration of the best research evidence with our clinical expertise and our patient's unique values and circumstances" (Straus et al., 2019, p. 1).

By replacing the medically laden term "patients" with the more encompassing word "clients," the foregoing definitions potentially can be seen to apply readily to all the helping professions, including social work. What is also conspicuous in these definitions is the equal weight given to the core factors of scientific evidence, clinical expertise, patient preferences, and the client's unique values and circumstances. No one factor is implied to be more important than the others—all are important and each can potentially trump the others. This definitional egalitarianism is important to realize from the outset because some professionals erroneously believe that in EBP research evidence is accorded greater weight than other factors (see Gitterman & Knight, 2013). Straus et al. (2019, p. 1) go on to operationally define what is meant by "best research evidence," "clinical expertise," "patient values," and "patient circumstances" and describe the five steps that comprise the clinical decision-making process of EBP (pp. 4–5):

> *Step 1*: Converting the need for information (about prevention, diagnosis, prognosis, therapy, causation) into an answerable question.

> *Step 2*: Tracking down the best evidence with which to answer that question.
> *Step 3*: Critically appraising that evidence for its validity, impact, and applicability.
> *Step 4*: Integrate the critical appraisal with our clinical expertise and the client's unique . . . values and circumstances.
> *Step 5*: Evaluating our effectiveness and efficiency in executing Steps 1–4 and seeing ways to improve them both for next time.

The other entries comprising this part of the *Social Worker's Desk Reference* address each of these five steps. Again, EBP does not privilege scientific research findings about other considerations in making practice decisions, but it does insist that such factors be accorded their due weight. It is worth repeating this principle because a common misconception of EBP is that it gives primacy (if not sole attention) to research findings and ignores other crucial elements of practice decision-making. As Straus et al. (2019) unambiguously state, "Evidence, strong or weak, is never sufficient to make clinical decisions. Individual values and preferences must balance this evidence to achieve optimal shared decision-making and highlight that the practice of EBM is not a 'one size fits all approach'" (p. 9).

So, envision the following practice situation. A social worker encounters a client for the first time (client could mean an individual, a couple, a family, an organization, etc.), and the client presents a situation for which they are seeking help. Using traditional relationship building and clinical skills, the social worker comes to know the client and their situation. The issue may be a problem, such as a diagnosis, or a situation, such as excessive absenteeism among the students attending a given school. Or the situation may not involve a problem to be reduced per se but, rather, a goal involving enhancing some aspect of existing client's, organization's, or system's functioning. Satisfactory high school graduation rates can always be improved, or a healthy person may wish help in exercising more. There is certainly nothing about EBP that is incompatible with the strengths perspective, and the application of EBP does not depend on having a formal diagnosis, medical or psychiatric.

In Step 1, the client and social worker build up a clear understanding of what is being sought, and this is formulated as a potentially answerable question, such as "What psychosocial interventions have been shown to be effective in regulating the mood swings of clients like mine who meet the criteria for bipolar disorder?" or "How can a given political party enhance the numbers of voters to cast a ballot in a forthcoming election?" or "What interventions can be effective in reducing face-touching during an epidemic?" Good answerable questions often revolve around the acronym of PICO, which involves stating the population, intervention, comparison condition, and outcome. With a satisfactory answerable question in hand, Step 2 is undertaken.

Step 2 involves searching for credible evidence that might answer the question. Currently, this is usually done via internet searches, first searching for high-quality systematic reviews that have already answered your question. Useful sources in this regard are the websites of the Cochrane and Campbell Collaborations (see Helpful Resources). One typical Cochrane review dealt with the topic of *Family Intervention for Schizophrenia* and a recent Campbell review addressed *The Promotion of Well-Being Among Children Exposed to Intimate Partner Violence*. Reports such as these, known as systematic reviews (SRs), represent state-of-the-art, inclusive summaries of the best available evidence addressing each issue. They can be of inestimable value for the busy practitioner. One can always search for more recent primary studies on one's answerable question, with a focus on high-quality intervention research, as opposed to descriptive, correlational, or epidemiological studies. The former has more direct application to practice.

With this best and most recent evidence in hand, Step 3 involves the social worker critically appraising this evidence along all of the dimensions important in EBP and attempting to draw conclusions as to what the best research studies show which course of action seems most likely to benefit the client. This segues into Step 4, providing an honest summary of what you have learned to the client, perhaps giving them some reading material to digest, and attempting to develop a treatment plan agreeable to the client based on high-quality effectiveness studies showing that the intervention has worked with people similar to your client, is not too expensive, is ethical, is acceptable to the client, and will be supported by other people important in the client's environment. It should also indicate that the practitioner has the requisite skills needed to implement the intervention (or can refer the client to someone with the needed expertise). This step, of course, is completely consistent with traditional sound social work practice, with the added emphasis on consulting high-quality recent and pertinent empirical research. This intervention plan is then implemented, leading to Step 5.

This final step of the EBP model involves the social worker evaluating, ideally using reliable and valid measures, the outcomes for the client, as well as an introspective appraisal of their own skills in helping. Foremost is empirically evaluating the outcomes of our intervention, or at least determining, using credible data, if the client clinically and significantly improved. There are many ways to do this, but the methodology known as single-case or within-client research designs is perhaps the most extensively developed (Thyer, 2020). The model of EBP includes appropriately using selected forms of single-case studies to evaluate practice outcomes at the level of the individual client (Straus et al., 2019), and these have been used by social workers since the late 1960s. Apart from the clinician self-reflecting on how the process went, it is an excellent idea to ask the client something like "So, how did I do? Can you think of anything I could have done to make our time together more pleasant or effective? Is there anything I did which was off-putting or otherwise did not make sense or was offensive? Are you pleased with the outcome?" By engaging in Step 5, the clinician is better prepared to assist the next client who asks for help with this type of situation or problem.

Given the previous discussion, it is crucial to recognize that EBP is a *process* for assisting the client and practitioner to make decisions about what course of treatment to pursue. It is a joint, respectful endeavor—a shared responsibility. The clinician brings their expertise to the table and listens to the client's equally crucial information. Action is directed from a "bottom-up" process. Contrast this to another model, often confused with EBP. An agency director, a state official, or a federal grant funder decides that a particular model of practice should be uniformly adopted by its agency. A supposedly research-based treatment is selected, agency practitioners are trained in that model, and the agency may even go so far as to become a licensed provider of that treatment. Most clients coming through the door seeking help are told what treatment they will get, and the clinicians have little choice in the matter. Treatment can be of any type—the Duluth model, 12-step programs, multisystemic therapy, Triple-P, eye movement desensitization and reprocessing, play therapy, insight-oriented psychotherapy, etc.—and this approach exemplifies the one-size-fits-all model decried by real EBP. This is a top-down approach and affords neither the client treatment options nor the clinician any professional latitude as to what services to provide. It tends to be resented and bitterly resisted by practitioners, and some have labeled this approach managerialism (Rogowski, 2011). Even if the chosen treatment is very well supported by high-quality research, to impose this one approach on service providers and clients is the antithesis of EBP. In real EBP, there are no such things as evidence-based *practices*

because such a label devalues the other equally important factors that go into clinical decision-making (Thyer & Pignotti, 2011).

This valuing of scientific research is not an unfamiliar concept to professional social work and indeed has been a defining characteristic of the formal discipline, something that set it aside from impulsive altruism, the efforts of faith-based social missionaries, or unsystematic secular efforts aimed at helping others. Consider the quotes presented in Box 85.1, selected as representative of the century-long perspective that science and empirical research must be integrated into social services. Indeed, scientific charity and scientific philanthropy were the original names for the social casework movement in the United States (Bremmer, 1956).

The assertions found in Box 85.1 clearly indicate that the principles of EBP are congruent with central core descriptions of social work as a science-based discipline, dating back to the beginnings of our field. There is much to learn and nothing to fear from adopting the model of EBP. The original phrase "evidence-based medicine" as currently conceived first appeared in 1992 in an article authored by Gordon Guyatt and colleagues (Evidence-Based Medicine Working Group, 1992), and several concurrent developments and issues led to its widespread acceptance within medicine and then rapidly through the other helping professions. Among these developments was the recognition that practitioners needed valid information about the causes and possible effective treatments for the problems clients bring to them. Another was the recognition that books, traditional journals, conferences, and other usual sources of information were comparatively inefficient ways to acquire this knowledge. Another motivational factor was an increasing awareness that as our clinical expertise is enhanced with years of experience, our knowledge about contemporary developments related to assessment and intervention research often declines. Many

BOX 85.1 Illustrative Quotations Documenting the Close Linkage Between Science and Social Work

"Charity is a science, the science of social therapeutics, and has laws like all other sciences" (Kellogg, 1880, cited in Germain, 1970, p. 9).

"Many of the leaders of the conference [the 1884 meeting of the National Conference on Charities] accepted the implications of a scientific approach to social work problems. They acted on the tacit assumption that human ills—sickness, insanity, crime, poverty—could be subjected to the study and methods of treatment. . . . This attitude raised these problems out of the realm of mysticism and into that of a science. . . . As a result of the adoption of this scientific attitude, conference speakers and programs looked forward toward progress. They believed in the future; that it was possible by patient, careful study and experimentation to create a society much better than the one they lived in" (Bruno, 1964, pp. 26–27).

"To make benevolence scientific is the great problem of the present age" (Toynbee, 1912, p. 74).

"Social work is not merely a question of enthusiasm, sympathy, self-sacrifice or money, but it is a question of wisdom, discretion, and the scientific interpretation and comparison of facts" (Professor Peabody, c.f., Curtis, 1916, p. 271).

"The scientific spirit is necessary to social work whether it is a real profession or only a go-between craft. . . . The elements of scientific approach and scientific precision must be back of all social reform. . . . It is almost superfluous to ask why social work should take on the character of science. It is hardly a question of 'may or may not.' Rather, should we say, it is a matter of the categorical must" (Todd, 1920, pp. 66, 75).

Social work is defined as "all voluntary efforts to extend benefits which are made in response to a need, are concerned with social relationships, and avail themselves of scientific knowledge and methods" (Cheney, 1926, p. 24).

"The faculty and students of a professional school of social work should together be engaged in using the great method of experimental research which we are just beginning to discover in our professional educational programme, and which should be as closely knit into the work of a good school of social work as research has been embodied into the programme of a good medical school. . . . Social workers must be so trained scientifically that they belong in the social science group" (Abbott, 1931, pp. 55, 148).

"The difference between the social work of the present and of all preceding ages is the assumption that human behavior can be understood and is determined by causes that can be explained . . . any scientific approach to behavior supposes that it is not in its nature incomprehensible by sensory perception and inference therefrom" (Bruno, 1936, pp. 192–193).

"[In German social work] everywhere the belief in science, in learning and in the scientific spirit is in evidence" (Salomon, 1937, p. 33).

"Employment of scientifically approved and tested techniques will ensure the profession the confidence and respect of clients and the public, for increasingly the social casework process will operate more certainly for known and desired ends in the area of social adjustment" (Strode, 1940, p. 142).

"The scientific approach to unsolved problems in the only one which contains any hope of learning to deal with the unknown" (Reynolds, 1942, p. 24).

"Social work must develop its 'own science,' with its 'own field of knowledge,' tested in its own research laboratories" (Eaton, 1956, p. 22).

"I believe that it is possible to understand scientifically the movement of social and economic forces and to apply our strength in cooperation with them" (Reynolds, 1963/1991, p. 315).

practitioners simply do not have much discretionary time to track down clinically useful information through traditional but cumbersome methods, such as reading professional journals or attending continuing education workshops. Although these limiting factors are operative in the lives of most social workers, other developments in technology and professional infrastructure pointed to some possible solutions. Among these were the increasing usefulness of the internet as a means of locating valid information rapidly, the creation of the Cochrane and Campbell Collaborations as international and interdisciplinary organizations devoted to crafting comprehensive systematic reviews for answering commonly asked questions related to practice, and the emergence of journals focused on publishing much more practice-relevant research studies (e.g., *Research on Social Work Practice*). The concatenation of these events and development set the stage for the emergence of EBP.

There is some concern that EBP is primarily oriented toward clinical practice, but this is a misconception. There are many organizations and interest groups interested in applying the principles of EBP to macro levels of practice. The empirical literature devoted to EBP and macro-level social work is growing (e.g., Thyer, 2001, 2009), so much so that an entire journal, *Evidence and Policy* (see Helpful Resources), deals with this topic. A literature search of various social science research databases using key words such as "evidence-based management," "evidence-based supervision," and "evidence-based administration" will also reveal a burgeoning body of literature.

Another misconception is that EBP is somehow a development unique to the United States. In reality, the major authors in the field of evidence-based medicine were British and Canadian; the Cochrane Collaboration is headquartered in England, and the Campbell Collaboration is based in Norway, with local centers located in the United States and Canada. Thyer and Kazi's (2004) book describes EBP-related developments not just in the United States, Canada, and Great Britain but also in Israel, Hong Kong, Finland, South Africa, and Australia. The protocols developed by the Cochrane and Campbell Collaborations for the development of systematic reviews explicitly call for using international teams of experts to ensure that relevant non-English literature is not overlooked. EBP is not scientism, nor is it another example of U.S. hegemony in the realm of social work education and practice. It is the natural fruition and maturation of professional tendencies that have existed in our discipline worldwide since its inception in the late 1880s.

Evidence-based practice is not a medical model. It is atheoretical with respect to the causes of problems or conditions, neutral with respect to the types of interventions that are appropriate (e.g., psychosocial treatments vs. medications), and silent as to the disciplinary training required to deliver care (physicians are not assumed to be the service providers). EBP did originate among physicians, but the five-step decision-making model of this approach is a template that is almost universally applicable across the human services and health care disciplines.

Nor does EBP tell social workers what to do with their clients. It does not develop lists of scientifically approved treatments, nor does it prepare practice guidelines. It does lay out a systematic process for the social worker seeking information to help them make important practice decisions related to choosing assessment and intervention methods. It provides guidance in locating and critically appraising this information. It helps integrate research-based data into other critical domains—such as one's clinical skills; the clients' values, preferences, situation, and available resources; and professional ethical guides—to then arrive at a decision. It also guides us in evaluating effectiveness in delivering services. EBP helps us find out what we need to know to arrive at practice decisions. What we choose to do remains the prerogative of the individual social worker, working with the client. It may be that a clinician seeks guidance about possibly effective treatments for someone who is severely depressed. A review of the literature may disclose some interventions shown to generally be quite helpful for depressed persons, such as cognitive–behavioral therapy or interpersonal psychotherapy. But if the client is also intellectually disabled, the social worker may well choose not to provide one of these empirically supported interventions if it is judged that the client lacks the cognitive abilities to be successfully engaged in these treatments. In such a case, the social worker could still be said to be operating within the EBP framework.

More than 85 years ago, John Dewey (1927) said, "Men have got used to an experimental

method in physical and technical matters. They are still afraid of it in human concerns" (p. 179). The emergence and adoption of EBP within social work suggest that we are overcoming such fears. It is hoped that the reader finds that the following chapters more fully describe what EBP really is, and it is recommended that one consult further primary sources (Straus et al., 2019) describing this approach in greater detail. Third- and fourth-hand descriptions of EBP commonly found in the social work literature are rife with distortions, incorrect information, and false inferences.

Helpful Resources

Campbell Collaboration: http://www.campbell collaboration.org
Cochrane Collaboration: http://www.cochrane.org
Evidence & Policy: https://www.ingentaconnect.com/content/tpp/ep

References

Abbott, E. (1931). *Social welfare and professional education*. University of Chicago Press.
Bremner, R. H. (1956). Scientific philanthropy: 1873–93. *Social Service Review, 30*, 168–173.
Bruno, F. (1936). *The theory of social work*. Health.
Bruno, F. (1964). *Trends in social work: 1874–1956*. Columbia University Press.
Cheney, A. (1926). *The nature and scope of social work*. Health.
Curtis, H. (1916). The functions of social service in state hospitals. *Boston Medical and Surgical Journal, 175*, 271–275.
Dewey, J. (1927). *The public and its problems*. Swallow Press.
Drisko, J. W., & Friedman, A. (2019). Let's clearly distinguish evidence-based practice and empirically supported treatments. *Smith College Journal of Social Work, 89*(3-4), 264–281.
Drisko, J. W., & Grady, M. D. (2019). *Evidence-based practice in clinical social work* (2nd ed.). Springer.
Eaton, J. W. (1956). Whence and whither social work: A sociological perspective. *Social Work, 1*(1), 11–26.
Evidence-Based Medicine Working Group. (1992). Evidence-based medicine: A new approach to teaching the practice of medicine. *JAMA, 268*, 2420–2425.

Gambrill, E. (1999). Evidence-based practice: An alternative to authority-based practice. *Families in Society, 80,* 341–350.

Gitterman, A., & Knight, C. (2013). Evidence-guided practice: Integrating the science and art of social work. *Families in Society, 94,* 70–78.

Grady, M. D., Wike, T., Putzu, C., Field, S., Hill, J., Bledsoe, Bellamy, J., & Massey, M. (2018). Recent social work practitioners' understanding and use of evidence-based practice and empirically supported treatments. *Journal of Social Work Education, 54*(1), 163–179.

Jayaratne, S., & Levy, R. L. (1979). *Empirical clinical practice.* Columbia University Press.

Okpych, N., & Yu, J. (2014). A historical analysis of evidence-based practice in social work: The unfinished journey towards an empirically grounded profession. *Social Service Review, 88*(1), 3–58.

Reid, W. J. (1994). The empirical practice movement. *Social Service Review, 68,* 165–184.

Reynolds, B. C. (1942). *Learning and teaching in the practice of social work.* Farrar & Rinehart.

Reynolds, B. C. (1991). *An uncharted journey.* NASW Press. (Original work published 1963)

Rogowski, S. (2011). Managers, managerialism and social work with children and families: The deformation of a profession? *Practice: Social Work in Action, 23*(3), 157–167.

Rubin, A., & Parrish, D. (2007). Views of evidence-based practice among faculty in masters of social work programs: A national survey. *Research on Social Work Practice, 17,* 110–122.

Salomon, A. (1937). *Education for social work.* Verlag fur Recht und Gessellscaft.

Siegel, D. (1984). Defining empirically based practice. *Social Work, 29,* 325–329.

Straus, S. E., Glasziou, P., Richardson, W. S., & Haynes, R. B. (2019). *Evidence-based medicine: How to practice and teach EBM* (5th ed.). Elsevier.

Strode, H. (1940). *Introduction to social casework.* Harper & Brothers.

Thyer, B. A. (2001). Evidence-based approaches to community practice. In H. Briggs & K. Corcoran (Eds.), *Social work practice: Treating common client problems* (pp. 54–65). Lyceum.

Thyer, B. A. (2009). Evidence-based macro-practice: Addressing the challenges and opportunities for social work education. *Journal of Evidence-Based Social Work, 5,* 453–472.

Thyer, B. A. (2020). Evaluating social work practice with single system research designs. In L. Joubert & M. Webber (Eds.), *The Routledge handbook of social work practice research* (pp. 127–145). Routledge.

Thyer, B. A., & Kazi, M. F. (Eds.). (2004). *International perspectives on evidence-based practice in social work.* Venture Press.

Thyer, B. A., & Pignotti, M. (2011). Evidence-based practices do not exist. *Clinical Social Work Journal, 38,* 328–333.

Todd, A. J. (1920). *The scientific spirit and social work.* Macmillan.

Toynbee, A. (1912). *Lectures on the industrial revolution in eighteenth century England.* Longmans, Green.

Posing Well-Structured Questions for Evidence-Informed Practice

Step 1

Eileen Gambrill

Those in the helping professions are expected to possess knowledge and skills to help clients attain outcomes they value. The balance of knowledge and ignorance changes over time. Interventions assumed to be effective may later be found to be harmful (Herrera-Perez et al., 2019). Keeping up-to-date requires self-learning skills to identify gaps in knowledge that may compromise outcomes for clients. The process of evidence-based practice (EBP) is designed to help practitioners keep up-to-date. Translating information needs (knowledge gaps) related to decisions into wellstructured questions that facilitate a search for relevant research is the first step in the process of EBP (Straus et al., 2019). Key decisions include whether to search, when to search, where to search, what resources to use, and when to stop.

Background questions concern general knowledge about a problem, process, situation, and intervention. This includes knowledge of psychological, biological, or sociological factors related to a concern. Such questions include "a question root (who, what, when,

where, how, why) with a verb" (Straus et al., 2019, p. 21) as well as some aspect of care, such as an assessment measure or intervention. The following are examples: "What factors are related to hoarding behavior?" and "What circumstances increase risk of further child abuse?" Foreground questions concern specific knowledge to inform clinical/policy decisions. (See later discussion of four-part questions.) Such questions usually concern a specific client or population. Background knowledge informs foreground knowledge. Straus et al. (2019) suggest that as experience regarding a concern increases, need for background knowledge decreases, and need for foreground knowledge increases (p. 23).

Some questions require immediate answers; others do not. Recurring questions are especially important to pose and attempt to answer. If we do not recognize our knowledge gaps and pose related questions, we are less likely to seek and discover helpful research to guide decisions; we may harm clients or offer clients ineffective methods. Recognizing information needs is a countermeasure to overconfidence and confirmation biases that hinder learning and the integration of practice and research. Most research regarding posing and answering questions concerns physicians. Ely et al. (1999) found that physicians answered only a small percentage of questions that arise by consulting relevant research. Del Fiol et al. (2014) reported that approximately 50% of questions are not pursued. Ely et al. (2007) found that 48 physicians readily answered 166 (28%) of 585 questions via the very first fast electronic resource used. To my knowledge, there is no such information in psychology, psychiatry, and social work.

Awareness of Information Needs

We may or may not be aware of what we do not know that is important to know to help clients (Straus et al., 2019). We are unlikely to search for information if we are unaware of our ignorance. This highlights the importance of accurate views of our ignorance and applies to all players in the system of care that affect client outcomes, including direct line staff, supervisors, administrators, policymakers, and researchers. Sources of uncertainty include limitations in current knowledge due, for example, to poor quality research, lack of familiarity with knowledge available, and difficulties distinguishing between personal ignorance and lack of competence and actual limitations of knowledge (Fox, 1959). Awareness of ignorance is key to the process and philosophy of EPB. Information needs may concern the following (adapted from Straus et al., 2019, p. 25):

> *Description*: gathering and accurately interpreting information concerning client characteristics and circumstances that may influence clients and outcomes, including agency structure, public

policies, legislation, and community characteristics

Etiology/risk: identifying causes or risk factors regarding concerns

Indicators of specific concerns: identifying these and using this knowledge to make informed decisions

Setting priorities: for example, when considering causes, selecting those that are likely, serious, and responsive to intervention

Assessment measures: selecting and accurately interpreting assessment measures that contribute to understanding clients and their concerns attending to accuracy, acceptability, safety, and expense

Prognosis: estimating a client's likely course over time and anticipating likely complications

Intervention: selecting services that do more good than harm and are worth the effort and cost of using them

Prevention: reducing the likelihood of concerns by identifying and modifying related risk factors, and identifying concerns early through screening

Experience and meaning: learning how to empathize with clients, appreciating the meanings they find in their experiences and understanding how these influence outcomes

Self-improvement: keeping up-to-date; improving skills; and providing a better, more efficient care system

Straus et al. (2019) state,

> No matter who initiates the questions, we count finding relevant answers as one of the ways we serve our [clients], and to indicate this responsibility, we call these questions "ours." When we can manage to do so, we find it helpful to negotiate explicitly with our [clients] about which

questions should be addressed, in what order, and by when. And, increasingly, our [clients] want to work with us on answering some of these questions. (p. 25)

Four-Part Questions

Straus ct al. (2019) suggest posing four-part PICO questions that describe the population of clients (P), the intervention of concern (I), what it may be compared to (including doing nothing) (C), and hoped-for outcome (O). An assessment question might be the following (Gibbs, 2003): If elderly nursing home residents who may be depressed or have Alzheimer's disease or dementia complete a depression screening test compared to a short mental examination test, which test most reliably discriminates between depression and dementia? As Straus et al. (2019) note, "Good questions are the backbone of both practicing and teaching [EBP], and [clients] serve as the starting point for both" (p. 28). Well-structured questions guide an electronic search for related research findings. The process of forming a specific question often begins with a vague general question and then is crafted into a wellstructured one. Synonyms can be used to facilitate a search. For example, if abused children are of concern, other terms for this may be "maltreated children," "neglected children," and "mistreated children." Posing clear questions contributes to efficient use of scarce learning time and focuses on information relevant to clients' well-being. Related core competencies identified by Albarqouni et al. (2018) in a systematic review included the following:

- Explain the difference between the two types of questions.
- Identify the different types of clinical questions, such as questions about treatment, diagnosis, prognosis, and etiology.
- Convert clinical questions into structured answerable client questions. This competence includes the following:

- Recognize the importance of and strategies for identifying and prioritizing uncertainties and knowledge gaps in practice.
- Understand the rationale for using structured clinical questions.
- Identify the elements of PICO questions and use variations when appropriate.

In a study of hospital clinicians, Cheng (2004) reported that the majority of questions posed were not PICO questions and that well-built questions were no more likely to be answered than those that were not so structured. As Ely et al. (2007) note, finding answers to questions may be affected by many other factors, including search skills.

Different Kinds of Questions

Different kinds of practice/policy questions (about assessment, prognosis, harm, effectiveness, prevention, risk, and description) may require different research methods to critically test them. Many questions may arise with one client or family. Consider a social worker employed in a hospice who counsels grieving parents who have lost a child. Descriptive questions include the following: "What are the experiences of parents who lose a young child?" "How long do these last?" and "Do they change over time and if so, how?" Both survey data and qualitative research such as focus groups and in-depth interviews, as well as observation studies, can be used to explore such questions. Research may be available describing experiences of grieving parents based on a large randomly drawn sample. Questions concerning risk may arise, such as "In parents who have lost a young child, what is the risk of depression?" as may questions about effectiveness: "For parents who have lost a young child, is a support group compared to individual counseling most effective in decreasing depression?" Prevention questions include the following: "For parents who have lost a young child, is brief counseling compared to a support group more effective in preventing depression which interferes with care of other children?" Searching for related research can be facilitated by use of quality filters related to question type. For example, if a question concerns risk, relevant methodological filters include sensitivity, specificity, and predictive validity. The terms "systematic review" and "meta-analysis" are valuable in all searches because such reports, if well done, provide a rigorous review of all related research. However, as always, skepticism is warranted by the abundance of poor quality reviews (Ioannidis, 2016).

Effectiveness Questions

Many questions concern the effectiveness of service methods. An example is "For disoriented elderly persons who reside in a nursing home, does reality orientation therapy compared to validation therapy result in better orientation to time, place, and person?" We may discover number needed to treat—how many clients would have to receive an intervention for one to be helped. We may locate number needed to harm (NNH)—how many clients have to receive a treatment for one to be harmed. Quality filters when searching include the words "randomized controlled trials" and "systematic review."

Prevention Questions

Prevention questions direct attention to the future. These include questions about the effectiveness of early childhood visitation programs in preventing delinquency. An example is "In families with young children, do early home visitation programs, compared with no service, decrease future child neglect?" Here, too, a high-quality systematic review of well-designed randomized controlled trials would be sought.

Prediction (Risk/Prognosis) Questions

Professionals often attempt to estimate risk, for example, of future child maltreatment. We may ask, "What is the validity of a risk assessment measure?" and "What is the false positive rate [clients incorrectly said to have a characteristic such as being suicidal] and false negative rate [clients inaccurately said not to have this characteristic; e.g., not being suicidal]?" A well-built risk prognosis question is "In abused or neglected children placed in foster care, will an actuarial risk assessment measure, compared to a consensus-based model, provide the most accurate predictions regarding reabuse when children are returned to their biological parents?" Quality filters here include sensitivity and specificity.

Assessment Questions

Clinicians use a variety of assessment measures and draw on related theories. For example, out-of-control behavior on the part of a child may be assumed to be due to "mental illness." Measures are related to a particular theory that may or may not be accurate. Assessment measures differ in their reliability (e.g., consistency of responses over time) and validity (whether they measure what they purport to measure). The sample used to gather data and provide "norms" on a measure (scores of a certain group of individuals) may be quite different than clients of concern, so these norms may not apply. A well-built assessment question is "In frail elderly people who appear depressed, is the Beck Depression Inventory or the Pleasant Events Schedule most accurate in detecting depression?" Quality filters here include validity and reliability.

Description Questions

Clients, direct line staff, administrators, supervisors, and policymakers may seek descriptive information, such as resources needed by and experiences of caregivers of frail elderly relatives. A related question may be "In those who care for dying relatives, what challenges arise and how are they handled?" Some description questions call for qualitative research. For example, questions concerning experiences such as loss of an infant or living in a nursing home call for research methods that can provide such accounts—for example, in-depth interviews and focus groups. Other kinds of description questions require data involving large samples—for example, about problem prevalence and causes. Survey data in a local community may provide information about the percentage of grieving parents who continue to grieve in certain ways with certain consequences and thus provide useful information for planning services. Here, too, we should consider the quality of related research.

Questions About Harm

Any intervention, including assessment methods, may harm as well as help. How many people have to receive an assessment measure or service for one to be harmed? This is known as NNH. Related questions include "How many people would have to be screened to identify one person who could benefit from help?" and "How many of these would be harmed by simply taking the test who are not at risk?"

Questions About Costs and Benefits

Limited resources highlight the importance of cost–benefit analyses. What is the cost of offering service A compared to service B, and how many people benefit from each? Criteria for reviewing cost–benefit studies can be found in many sources, such as Guyatt et al. (2015).

Questions Related to Lifelong Learning

Integrating practice and research requires lifelong learning. A question here is "For newly graduated professionals, will a journal club, compared to a 'buddy system' be most effective in maintaining practice-related skills?"

Selecting and Saving Questions

There will always be more questions than time to answer them. Which questions are most important to pose for client well-being? Which recur often? Which questions are most feasible to answer in the time available and which ones are most vital to self-learning needs? Straus et al. (2019) recommend saving questions so that answers to recurring questions can be retrieved. Options they suggest for doing so include writing questions down on a three- or four-column form (client, intervention, comparison, and outcome), dictating into a pocket-sized recorder, or using a personal digital assistant. Questions and answers can be prepared as critically appraised topics (CATs). These consist of brief (1-page) descriptions of a clinical question, clinical bottom line, evidence summary, comments, citations, and name of appraiser (Straus et al., 2019). Critical appraisal guides for assessing the validity and usefulness of different kinds of studies can be drawn on in preparing CATS. (See, for example, the Centre for Evidence-Based Medicine, https://www.cebm.net.) CATs can be prepared for journal club presentations (Aronson, 2017). Posing questions related to information needs that frequently arise and sharing these with colleagues in the form of CATs offer continuing learning opportunities.

Evaluating Your Progress

Related self-evaluation questions suggested by Straus et al. (2019) include the following:

- Am I asking any practice questions at all?
- Am I asking well-informed (four-part) questions?
- Am I using a "map" to locate my knowledge gaps and articulate questions?

- Can I get myself "unstuck" when answering questions?
- Do I have a working method to save my questions for later answering?
- Is my success rate of asking questions increasing?
- Am I modeling the asking of answerable guidelines for others?

Common Errors

Errors that may occur when posing questions include having more than one question in a question and trying to answer a question before stating it clearly. Students may not distinguish between a practice or policy question useful to guide a search and a research question specific to answering a question by collecting data (Gibbs, 2003). Leading or loaded questions may imply that only a particular answer is acceptable, such as "For persons who may be at risk for suicide, who receive the Brief Psychiatric Rating Scale or the Beck Depression Scale, how much higher will the positive predictive value of the former be for predicting suicide?" (It may be lower.) Vague questions are so unspecific that they net nothing useful. A lack of assessment knowledge may result in overlooking important individual differences in a client's circumstances or characteristics that should be included in a question. For example, posing an effectiveness question before discovering factors that contribute to depression (e.g., "In adults who are depressed, is cognitive–behavioral therapy, compared to medication, most effective in decreasing depression?") may overlook the fact that for this client recent losses in social support are uppermost, which suggests a different question, such as "In adults who are depressed because of recent losses in social support, is a support group or individual counseling more effective in decreasing depression?" Novices may pose different questions compared to experts in an area who are familiar with practice-related research regarding a concern and the complexity of related factors. A lack of assessment knowledge may result in overlooking important individual differences in a client's circumstances or characteristics that should be included in a question.

Obstacles

Literature concerning EBP suggests that posing well-structured questions can be difficult. This may be hampered by educational practices that "do not reward us for sharing our ignorance" (Straus et al., 2019, p. 24). Posing questions about the effectiveness of services may be viewed as a threat. Questions are not benign, as illustrated by the fate of Socrates. Staff who pose questions may be viewed as troublemakers who are disloyal to the agency or profession (Gambrill, 2020). Supervisors may not have experience in posing well-built questions and may wonder why it is of value.

Ely et al. (2002) conducted a qualitative study investigating obstacles to answering physicians' questions about patient care with evidence. Participants included 9 academic/generalist doctors, 14 family doctors, and 2 medical librarians. They identified 59 obstacles. Those related to forming clear questions included the following:

- Missing client data concerning, for example, client characteristics and circumstances may require an unnecessarily broad search for information. Ely et al. (2002) suggest that questions which include demographic or clinical information and information about client preferences may help focus the search. They note that the kind of information that would be of value will vary depending on the question and may not be clear until the search is underway.
- Inability to answer specific questions with general resources. A question such as "What is this rash?" and vague cries for help, "I don't know what to do with this client," cannot be answered by a general resource.
- Uncertainty about the scope of the question and unspoken ancillary questions. For example, it may not be apparent that the

original question should be expanded to include many ancillary questions.

Obstacles related to modifying a question include the following:

- Uncertainty about changing specific words in the question.
- Unhelpful modifications resulting from flawed communication.
- The need for modifications is apparent only after the search has begun.
- Difficulty modifying questions to fit a four-part question format.
- Trying to answer too many questions at once.
- Trying to answer a question while posing it.

Practice questions may be confused with research questions. Words selected may not facilitate a search; they may be too narrow or too broad. Valuable quality filters may not be used. Questions may be too vague. Barriers reported in a systematic review included individual, organizational, and systemic factors (Scurlock-Evans & Upton, 2015). Individual barriers included lack of time, training, and supervision and a suspicion of research. Organizational barriers included lack of resources such as unreliable access to the internet; organizational culture included lack of interest in making evidence-informed decisions and a blame culture. Corrective feedback may not be available via ongoing coaching. Administrators and supervisors may not be supportive. Systemic barriers included poor match between a practice setting and research findings (Manuel et al., 2009).

Other barriers include comorbidities, contexts, the volume of available information, not knowing which resource to search, doubt that anything will be located, difficulty recalling questions for later review, and complex questions (Cook et al., 2013). Research barriers include conflicting results and limited references. Self-learning skills may be absent. There may be financial barriers, lack of teamwork, and lack of incentives and models (Despard,

2016; Sadeghi-Bazargani et al., 2014). A lack of understanding of contextual influences on services may result in overlooking factors that affect implementation of services, including overburdened staff and lack of money to offer evidence-informed services. Science is often misrepresented and misunderstood in social work, as is the process of EBP (Gambrill, 2019). The process of EBP is often confused with provision of interventions deemed as EPBs.

Still Missing: Harvesting Questions

After decades, we still do not have lists of questions that arise in different social work settings and those that have been answered and not. As in medicine, questions from frontline staff could inform research priorities (Fenton et al., 2009). For example, those that arise frequently but for which related research is scarce could be used to set research priorities. Are social workers' information needs less? Is there less information available related to questions that arise in social work settings? In some areas, such as parent training, there is an extensive literature showing that some methods are more effective than others. Are there so few resources to offer evidence-informed services that inquiry is viewed as a waste of time? Social work clients are often poor and their needs linked to social policies and related political differences that influence availability of effective, timely services. The poor have less access to effective advocacy, including less money to pursue lawsuits, and are less informed about important questions to raise regarding quality of services (Knighton et al., 2017). (*Health literacy* refers to the extent to which someone can obtain, communicate, process, and understand basic health information and services to make appropriate health decisions). Informed consent, in which clients are fully informed regarding the evidentiary status of services to which they are referred, is more the exception than the rule; that is, clients are not fully informed about the likelihood that services they receive will help them attain hoped-for outcomes.

Decreasing Challenges

Options for addressing challenges include providing repeated guided experience with corrective feedback in posing wellstructured practice and policy questions during professional education programs, continuing education opportunities, and ongoing coaching. Learning by doing is emphasized in the process of EBP. The more we use a skill, the more facility we gain with it, if we have access to corrective feedback. Unless we try to perform a skill, we cannot determine our competency level. Posing well-structured practice/policy questions and searching for related research may sound easy, but it can be difficult due to both personal and environmental obstacles, including lack of encouragement to recognize ignorance. Searchers may forget to use valuable quality filters. We still do not know the questions that arise in different social work settings and what percentage are answered. Given the slowness on the part of social workers to pose client-focused questions about services and the reluctance of administrators to facilitate this, change will require pursuit of other routes, including increasing the health literacy of clients and advocating for greater transparency concerning the evidentiary status of services provided, for example, on agency websites. Ethical obligations to help and not harm clients are a compelling guide to encourage posing and pursuing answers to questions that affect clients' lives and involving clients as informed participants, including the related mandate to press for altering circumstances that prevent this.

References

Albarqouni, L., Hoffman, T., Straus, S., Olsen, N. R., Young, T., Illic, D., Shaneyfelt, T., Haynes, R. B., Guyatt, G., & Glasziou, P. (2018). Core competencies in evidence-based practice for health professionals: Consensus statement based on a systematic review and Delphi Survey. *JAMA Network Open, 1*(2):e180281. doi:10.1001/jamanetworkopen.2018.0281

Aronson, J. K. (2017). Journal clubs: Why and how to run them and how to publish them. *BMJ Evidence-Based Medicine, 22*, 232–234.

Cheng, G. Y. T. (2004). A study of clinical questions posed by hospital clinicians. *Journal of the Medical Library Association, 92*, 444–458.

Cook, D. A., Sorenson, K. J., Wilkinson, J. M., & Berger, R. A. (2013). Barriers and decisions when answering clinical questions at point of care: A grounded theory study. *JAMA Internal Medicine, 25*, 1962–1969.

Del Fiol, G., Workman, E., & Gorman, P. N. (2014). Clinical questions raised by clinicians at the point of care: A systematic review. *JAMA Internal Medicine, 174*, 710–718.

Despard, M. R. (2016). Challenges in implementing evidence-based practices and programs in nonprofit human service organizations. *Journal of Evidence-Informed Social Work, 13*(6), 505–522.

Ely, J. W., Osheroff, J. A., Ebell, M. H., Bergus, G. R., Levy, B. T., Chambliss, M. L., & Evans, E. R. (1999). Analysis of questions asked by family doctors regarding patient care. *British Medical Journal, 319*, 358–361.

Ely, J. W., Osheroff, J. A., Ebell, M. H., Chambliss, M. L., Vinson, D. C., Stevermer, J. J., & Pifer, E. A. (2002). Obstacles to answering doctors' questions about patient care with evidence: Qualitative study. *British Medical Journal, 324*, 710–718.

Ely, J. W., Osheroff, J. A., Maviglia, S. M., & Rosenbaum, M. E. (2007). Patent-care questions that physicians are unable to answer. *Journal of the American Medical Information Association, 14*, 407–414.

Fenton, M., Brice, A., & Chalmers, I. (2009). Harvesting and publishing patients' unanswered questions about the effects of treatment. In P. Littlejohns & M. Rawlins (Eds.), *Patients, the public and priorities in healthcare* (pp. 165–180). Radcliffe.

Fox, R. C. (1959). *Experiment perilous: Physicians and patients facing the unknown*. Free Press.

Gambrill, E. (2019). The promotion of avoidable ignorance in the *British Journal of Social Work. Research in Social Work Practice, 29*(4), 455–469.

Gambrill, E. (2020). Avoidable ignorance and the politics and ethics of whistleblowing in mental health. *Journal of Ethics in Mental Health, 11*, 1–39.

Gibbs, L. E. (2003). *Evidence-based practice for the helping professions*. Brooks/Cole.

Guyatt, G., Rennie, D., Meade, M. O., & Cook, D. J. (2015). *Users' guide to the medical literature: Essentials of evidence-based clinical practice* (3rd ed.). McGraw-Hill and JAMA Evidence.

Herrera-Perez, D., Haslam, A., Crain, T., Gill, J., Livingston, C., Kaestner, V., Hayes, M., Morgan, D., Cifu, A. S., & Prasad, V. (2019). Meta research: A comprehensive review of randomized clinical trials in three medical journals reveals 396 medical reversals. *eLife Sciences, 8,* e45183. doi:10.7554/elife.45183

Ioannidis, J. P. A. (2016). The mass production of redundant, misleading and conflicting systematic reviews and meta-analyses. *Milbank Quarterly, 94,* 485–514. doi:10.1111/1468-0009.1221

Knighton, A. J., Brunisholz, K. D., & Savitz, S. T. (2017). Detecting risk of low health literacy in disadvantaged populations using area-based measures. *eGEMS, 5*(3), 7. doi:10.5334/egems.191

Manuel, J., Mullen, E., Fang, I., Bellamy, J., & Bledsoe, S. (2009). Preparing social work practitioners to use evidence-based practice: A comparison of experiences from an implementation project. *Research on Social Work, 19,* 613–627.

Sadeghi-Bazargani, H., Tabrizi, J. S., & Azami-Aghdash, S. (2014). Barriers to evidence-based medicine: A systematic review. *Journal of Evaluation in Clinical Practice, 20,* 793–802.

Scurlock-Evans, L., & Upton, D. (2015). The role and nature of evidence: A systematic review of social workers evidence-based practice orientation, attitudes, and implementation. *Journal of Evidence-Informed Social Work, 12,* 369–399.

Straus, S. E., Glasziou, P., Richardson, W. S., & Haynes, R. B. (2019). *Evidence-based medicine: How to practice and teach EBM* (5th ed.). Elsevier.

Locating Research Results for Evidence-Based Practice

Step 2

James Drisko and Melissa D. Grady

Starting Points

After completing a thorough assessment (Grady & Drisko, 2014; Straus et al., 2019) and defining an orienting question, the second step of the evidence-based practice (EBP) process is to efficiently locate the best available research relevant to your client's needs and specific circumstances (Thyer, 2004). A curious and questioning attitude is useful in this endeavor. One may search for specific foreground sources for disorders that are familiar to the social worker and commonly seen in practice. For novel and unfamiliar disorders, background information may be needed to orient the practitioner and sharpen practice questions.

Background and Foreground Information for Practice

The first choice is often between background information and very specific or foreground information. If you are already familiar with a disorder or problem, its diagnosis, and its treatments, a good starting point is to search for specific outcome research information. This is called foreground information. On the other hand, if the issue is new and unfamiliar, or if a social worker has reason to think their knowledge may be old or limited, starting with background information may be a better choice. Background information in this context focuses on the diagnosis, prevalence, prognosis, and course of a disorder. It generally orients professionals to help clarify the most appropriate and inclusive research questions for practice. Reviewing background materials will take longer but will also prepare you for other future clients with similar needs, and it offers a learning opportunity. In many ways, establishing background information is the role of degree granting and continuing education programs and textbooks. Once broad and comprehensive background is established, specific client-based foreground questions may be framed. Background information may be dated quickly, so checking on timeliness of these materials is important.

Print or Online Materials: Ensuring Information Is Up-to-Date

Foreground information sources in evidence-based medicine (EBM)/EBP address more specific practice outcome research knowledge

(Bronson & Davis, 2012; Sands & Gellis, 2011). An initial choice will be between using print or online resources. Both have assets and liabilities. Both can also have significant infrastructure costs, which users often must pay. Books and print articles are expensive, often very specialized, and must be updated as new editions are printed. Computers, internet access, and database access can also have significant costs for individuals and agencies (Drisko, 2010; Kreuger & Stretch, 2000). On the plus side, agencies and practices with electronic record systems may have much of the needed infrastructure on-site.

Print resources may include useful information but can quickly become outdated (Bronson & Davis, 2012). Some major medical sources simply advise to avoid textbooks and most print resources. Straus et al. (2019) state, "Should traditional textbooks be treated like garbage? . . . They should be handled as dangerous waste" (p. 39). This overstatement points out the care needed to use up-to-date knowledge in practice. Straus et al. suggest only using textbook and other print materials offering recommendations for care when they include in-line citations (i.e., linked directly to the specific text) giving both source and date for each recommendation. If sources are more than 2 or 3 years old, they suggest seeking newer materials. This suggestion fits the medical literature well, but materials in social work and psychology may not be updated so frequently. Still, we seek the best and most current information to guide practice. Print texts and materials need careful review for up-to-date recommendations.

Even online textbooks require such critical evaluation. Straus et al. (2019) suggest in-line and dated citations for all recommendations, which allow one to determine how recent is the reported evidence. They continue that online texts should have a clear policy stating the criteria for appraising evidence and link these criteria to each specific recommendation. There are several standards for grading research

evidence, although all sources have limitations and critics. (This topic is more fully addressed in the next section.) Furthermore, Straus et al. argue that each chapter should be date stamped and that the policy for updating each chapter should be clearly stated. In this way, readers can determine if the materials they read are out-of-date and learn how ratings of evidence are determined. Finally, readers should be able to sign up for "push" electronic update alerts from the author/publisher to keep current. Straus et al.'s analysis indicates that even online medical journals, which are more widely read than social work journals, vary widely in timeliness, breadth, and quality. All materials used in EBP should be based on transparent quality standards and should be clearly dated and regularly updated.

Preappraised Summaries or Appraise It Yourself Individual Studies?

As Gambrill (2001), Soydan and Palinkas (2014), and others have advocated in social work, Straus et al. (2019) challenge authority-based recommendations, promoting instead the use of explicit, high-quality, best evidence resources. With no sense of irony, Straus et al. argue for use of "evidence-based, regularly updated, online texts and preappraised evidence services" (p. 40). What is ironic here? Expert authorities create the preappraised evidence resources. Generally, these are carefully and rigorously done. On the other hand, Littell (2008, 2013) found that some evidence summaries which claim to follow clear guidelines end up distorting evidence within the summary. Other reviews do not fully apply widely recognized research quality standards. This is not to say that use of evidence-based and regularly updated, preappraised sources of evidence should be avoided. Such sources generally do make up the best current state of the art in practice research. Still, further careful review may lead to identification of shortcomings even within such resources.

Alper and Haynes (2016) present a five-stage hierarchy of preappraised evidence for practice. (Note: Preappraised means that some experts have summarized other people's work, so dates and research methods must be clearly stated for each recommendation offered.) At best, they argue for a *system* in which electronic medical records should "push" the best and most current research results to practitioners as part of intake and ongoing contact notes. Yet such systems do not yet exist in full, although some parts of such a system are beginning to appear in medical settings. Second best is a *synthesized summary* for clinical reference that combines some background information with detailed recommendations for practice. A synthesized summary must incorporate practice guidelines tied to specific research evidence for which dates are also provided. Synthesized summaries are available for some very common concerns but not for all practice needs.

Third best are *practice guidelines* with a specific focus such as suicide prevention or treatment for generalized anxiety disorder. Many such guidelines are now available online but are created by different experts. Alper and Haynes (2016) state that each practice guideline recommendation should be linked to specific sources of evidence and separately dated. In addition, the method for rating recommendations must be clearly stated. Practice guidelines often include expert recommendations with very little evidence to support them other than years of experience. Readers must critically appraise all practice guidelines. Fourth in Alper and Haynes' hierarchy are *systematic reviews*. Systematic reviews, such as from the Cochrane Collaboration or the Campbell Collaboration, exhaustively search the literature on the topic and provide a transparent synopsis of multiple studies. Most systematic reviews provide plain-language summaries with fewer technical terms as well as separate, more detailed summaries of the literature. On the other hand, they rarely include specific practice guidelines or the specific steps of the treatments they summarize. In psychiatry, psychology, and social work, such systematic reviews may be quickly dated by new findings. Additional searches for more current studies may also be needed to supplement systematic reviews. Fifth in the Alper and Haynes hierarchy are *individual studies* that require careful critical evaluation by the consumer. Individual studies may take considerable time to locate and appraise, and they obligate the consumer to integrate multiple studies to create their own practice recommendations. This is why many EBP authors argue for use of preappraised research summaries. Yet individual studies are often the best, most up-to-date source of practice research knowledge.

There are limitations to preappraised research summaries. When the client has co-occurring difficulties, summaries may not be available for the specific combination of challenges the client faces. Up-to-date summaries may be lacking. Information regarding the sample from which recommendations or practice guidelines are developed may not be provided in detail. This leaves consumers unclear if cultural or other human diversity differences may limit the relevance of results for the specific client need and situation. Experimental studies are purposefully highlighted, although quasi-experimental or cohort studies may be included in EBM/EBP systematic review summaries. There are also methods for systematically reviewing qualitative studies (Drisko, 2020). Results from qualitative studies may be difficult to locate and are generally omitted from practice guidelines and EBP summaries.

Online Information Resources

There are not yet well-developed "push" systems or online synthesized summaries automatically sent to social workers with up-to-date electronic evidence resources at the point of contact with clients. Some online practice guidelines are available, but many lack citations for each recommendation made and/or dates for the evidence on which guidelines are based. The best developed evidence resources are heavily weighted to medical concerns and research. Straus et al. (2019) point to several widely used medical sources for EBP evidence summaries. We summarize some of these online resources, their focus, and their costs.

Bear in mind that some paid online resources are available through public libraries, although specific holdings and access vary widely. You may also find theses paid resources accessible through local colleges and universities.

Locating Practice Guidelines

BMJ Best Practice (https://bestpractice.bmj.com/info/us) is an institutionally based, paid subscription resource that offers "step by step guidance on diagnosis, prognosis, treatment, and prevention" that is "updated daily using robust evidence based methodology and expert opinion" (2020, para 2). BMJ Best Practice replaces the discontinued BMJ Clinical Evidence website. The change emphasizes point-of-care information needs, guideline summaries, and up-to-date practice evidence.

UpToDate (https://www.uptodate.com/home) is a database offering graded, evidence-based recommendations that it claims are associated with improved patient care outcomes. It offers some free search options by clicking the UpToDate tab. An asset is that UpToDate offers both background and foreground information, which is helpful when one is new to a topic area.

DynaMed (https://www.dynamed.com), from EBSCO health, offers some free background and current paid foreground information on many medical disorders. Its methods of grading recommendations are fully detailed for paid users. Issues of diagnosis, treatment, and prevention are included for paid users. It costs

$199 per year for licensed practitioners and $99 per year for students.

Essential Evidence Plus (http://www.essentialevidenceplus.com) is another paid service by John Wiley and Sons Publishers. It provides access to more than 13,000 medical topics, guidelines, and decision support tools. It has 42 sections listed under Psychiatry covering major disorders and substance use.

Locating Social Work, Mental Health, and Substance Misuse Resources

The National Association of Social Workers (https://www.socialworkers.org/newhomepage) appears to have no specific resources for EBP, although it has listed several in prior years.

The Social Work Policy Institute https://www.naswfoundation.org/Our-Work/Social-Work-Policy-Institute offers a lengthy and varied set of resources (both paid and free), but links may be dated.

The American Psychiatric Association (https://www.psychiatry.org/psychiatrists/practice/clinical-practice-guidelines) offers links to some preappraised practice guidelines for schizophrenia and psychotic disorders and alcohol abuse disorder. Also available are links to older legacy summaries addressing a somewhat wider range of mental health concerns.

The American Psychological Association (APA), Division 12, Clinical Psychology (https://www.div12.org/psychological-treatments) provides information about effective treatments (empirically supported treatments) for many diagnoses. One can browse treatments by diagnosis or browse a specific treatment list. The listing includes APA rating of the strength of research support for each listed treatment. A strong rating reflects that multiple studies support a treatment, a modest rating reflects that only a single study supports the treatment, and a controversial rating reflects that some research supports effectiveness while other studies do not. The site also links to relevant case study research based on signs and symptoms rather than diagnosis.

The American Academy of Family Physicians (https://www.aafp.org/patient-care/clinical-recommendations/all/ADHD.html) offers detailed practice guidelines for children and adolescents who have attention-deficit/hyperactivity disorder (ADHD) or attention-deficit disorder. Note that dates of sources are not clearly stated, but methods for evaluating evidence are plainly stated.

Humana Behavioral Health (https://www.humanabehavioralhealth.com/providers/tools/clinical-guidelines) offers links to adult and child and adolescent resources for practice from psychiatry. Links to practice guidelines on bipolar disorder, schizophrenia, major depressive disorder, substance abuse, and ADHD are included. These resources were developed by major professional organizations, but dates for each recommendation are not consistently provided, nor is all included evidence from recent studies.

The U.S. Department of Veterans Affairs (https://www.healthquality.va.gov/HEALTHQUALITY/guidelines/MH/index.asp) provides access to its own guidelines for post-traumatic stress disorder, bipolar disorder, major depressive disorder, and substance abuse. Reviews are carefully vetted for quality of the included research studies by experts, but dates for the evidence supporting each recommendation are not provided.

The U.S. Substance Abuse and Mental Health Services Administration https://www.samhsa.gov/ offers links to external guidelines (created by other organizations) on a wide range of concerns. Work in acute emergency settings is well highlighted. Both the timeliness and evidence base of linked resources vary widely and may be minimal.

Locating Systematic Reviews

To ensure access to current best evidence, several sources provide access to summaries of the best available research through systematic reviews. A systematic review includes a comprehensive and transparently stated search of the literature, followed by a review of the quality of research and a quantitative meta-analysis aggregating multiple study results. These lead to a statistical comparison of the effectiveness of different treatments for a specific disorder. The large scope and large samples that make up a systematic review enhance its usefulness for practice. The results of a systematic review report the effectiveness of treatment using a number of effect size statistics. From these statistics, comparisons of the effectiveness of various treatment for a single disorder are generated. Summaries for professionals and summaries in "plain language" are also included in systematic reviews.

Two major sources of systematic reviews for social work practice are found in the Cochrane Collaboration and the Campbell Collaboration. These are international, multidisciplinary organizations that seek to determine the best available evidence for practice. Of course, evidence may not be available on some topics, and evidence may be quickly dated by new research.

The Cochrane Library (https://www.cochranelibrary.com) is a database of high-quality systematic reviews on single medical topics. The Cochrane Library includes psychiatry and substance misuse. Abstracts (which are often adequate for practice) are available without cost, but the full reviews are available for a fee to users in the United States. Cochrane reviews are widely considered to be the best sources of EBP research knowledge. This is because the Cochrane Collaboration includes working groups that set the most rigorous and transparent standards for systematical reviews of clinical research in medicine and psychiatry. Cochrane reviews also tend to be conservative and may find less clear support for treatments than do other reviewing organizations.

The Campbell Collaboration Library (https://campbellcollaboration.org/campbell-library.html) is a database of high-quality program reviews focusing on social welfare, education, and criminal justice topics. It is organized by general topic area. Both abstracts and full reviews are available for free. The Campbell Collaboration Library is widely considered to be the best source for research knowledge about the effectiveness of programs. The Campbell Collaboration's systematic reviews follow the rigorous guidelines set by the Cochrane Collaboration. Campbell reviews tend to be conservative and thorough. The database is growing but may prove to be limited for any specific social need.

Locating Individual Studies

When systematic reviews or treatment guidelines are not available for a disorder of interest, the next step is to search for individual articles. For the multiproblem concerns of social work clients, and to include attention to the client's situation, individual articles often provide more specific targeted information than do systematic reviews. The offset is that searching and locating individual research studies can require the expertise of a reference librarian—expertise not held by all social workers. Some key online resources for EBP are described next.

PubMed (https://pubmed.ncbi.nlm.nih.gov) is a useful interface to MEDLINE, the vast online database of medical research articles maintained by the U.S. National Library of Medicine. Many, but not all, PubMed citations include links to full text articles for free as well as abstracts. This is a major asset for clinicians. PubMed also includes prominent and easy-to-use search features that allow users to shift from a specific topic, such as borderline personality disorder, to a higher order topic, such as personality disorders in general. PubMed also has online help guides to help improve your search skills. PubMed Internet Help is found at https://www.ncbi.nlm.nih.gov/books/NBK3827.

PubMed has been updated and offers links under the "Find" option for both "Advanced Search" and "Clinical Queries." Both options are specially designed to aid in EBP searches. Advanced searches can be limited to specific "fields" such as author, date, title, and topic. This allows combining multiple search terms to aid precision in the located results. This option is very useful for clients with unique needs and situations. Clinical queries are similar but allow selection of "clinical study categories" such as diagnosis, therapy, etiology, and prognosis. The "systematic review" option under clinical queries searches specifically for systematic reviews. Review types may be further specified using the filter list. Both advanced searches and clinical queries may be created using Boolean search parameters such as "OR" to search for publications addressing either search term, "AND" for only those publications that include both search terms, and so on. These allow for very targeted and specific searches for clinical information. (There are several online tutorials on Boolean searches. Most social work programs offer such library-use tutorials. One good Boolean search tutorial is available from the New York University Libraries at https://guides.nyu.edu/boolean.

PsychINFO is a database resource for abstracts and citations of behavioral and social science research. Its coverage includes more psychological, social work, and social service studies than does PubMed, but it is a paid database. PsychINFO may be available in public libraries and through many hospitals and educational institutions. Individual subscriptions are also available for $139 per year through PsychNet.

CINAHL (Cumulative Index to Nursing and Allied Health Literature) is the nursing profession's online database that includes many publications of interest to social workers. This paid resource is available through many hospitals and educational institutions.

Google and Google Scholar offer very comprehensive access to both free and paid online materials and books. The strength is the scope and variety of studies, but the disadvantage is a complete lack of vetting for practice. Our experience shows that Google searches can be overwhelming in terms of the numbers of results displayed, yet the links often lead to useful publications, which may then be difficult to access in full. Google searches may also be combined using Boolean search operations.

The limitation of individual articles is that the consumer must personally evaluate their research rigor. This takes solid expertise in both clinical practice (to determine if the measures truly capture the disorder under study and measure progress that is relevant to your client's needs) and research methods (to determine if the study was designed, implemented, and reported rigorously). On the other hand, being exposed to the details of each study can better educate the user on what exactly was studied, who was studied or omitted, and how the study was done. This can be of great help when your client is from a vulnerable and understudied group or has unique personal values and preferences.

Practice Considerations

For many social workers, the realities of practice include large caseloads, busy schedules, limited access to professional journals and paid online materials, as well as supervision that is often focused on administrative issues rather than clinical ones (Wike et al., 2014). These realities mean that for many social workers, there is not much time to search for and review multiple sources of information to keep abreast of the most current research and practice guidelines. For these reasons, it is tempting to focus only on discrete preappraised models that are neatly packaged and easy to follow. However, clients do not present as simple packages and may need interventions to be modified and tailored to their unique needs. Therefore, when reviewing research summaries, social workers should examine them with a critical lens focusing on the research but also on how appropriate any intervention is for *each* client. Client values and preferences and the clinician's expertise combine with the best available research evidence in the EBP process. Many research summaries are focused on certain types or profiles of clients in order to carefully test the efficacy of a particular treatment model based on research with strong internal validity. Individual studies, on the other hand, may explore how a particular model applies to different client populations (i.e., age group, racial identity, and other diversity factors) and therefore may be of particular interest to the worker. When available, reviewing both aggregated sources and individual studies is often the best way to ensure that one is current and making the best clinical decisions based on the needs of the client.

Conclusion

Decisions about clinical interventions in EBP should consider the client's needs based on a thorough clinical assessment, the client's values and preferences, as well as the best available research (Drisko & Grady, 2019; Rubin & Bellamy, 2012; Straus et al., 2019). Social workers then must integrate these components using their expertise and clinical knowledge along with active collaboration with their clients. Together, these steps make up the EBP process. Such expertise should include knowing the types of information that are needed, where and how to obtain them efficiently, and the capacity to critically appraise what is located and relevant. Armed with such knowledge, social workers can work collaboratively with their clients to develop and implement the most appropriate intervention for each individual client that is well-grounded in clinical and empirical knowledge. This is a key objective of EBP.

References

Alper, B., & Haynes, R. B. (2016). EBHC pyramid 5.0 for accessing preappraised evidence and guidance. *BMJ Evidence-Based Medicine, 21,* 123–125.

Bronson, D., & Davis, T. (2012). *Finding and evaluating evidence.* Oxford University Press.

Drisko, J. (2010). Technology in teaching. In J. Anastas (Ed.), *Teaching in social work: An educator's guide to theory and practice* (pp. 115–150). Columbia University Press.

Drisko, J. (2020). Qualitative research synthesis: An appreciative and critical introduction. *Qualitative Social Work, 19,* 736–753. https://doi.org/10.1177/1473325019848808

Drisko, J., & Grady, M. (2019). *Evidence based practice in clinical social work* (2nd ed.). Springer.

Gambrill, E. (2001). Social work: An authority-based profession. *Research on Social Work Practice, 11,* 166–175.

Grady, M., & Drisko, J. (2014). Thorough clinical assessment: The hidden foundation of evidence-based practice. *Families in Society, 95,* 5–14.

Kreuger, L., & Stretch, J. (2000). How hypermodern technology in social work bites back. *Journal of Social Work Education, 36,* 103–114.

Littell, J. (2008). Evidence-based or biased? The quality of published reviews of evidence-based practices. *Children and Youth Services Review, 30*(11), 1299–1317.

Littell, J. (2013). The science and practice of research synthesis. *Journal of the Society for Social Work and Research, 4,* 292–299.

Rubin, A., & Bellamy, J. (2012). *Practitioner's guide to using research for evidence-based practice* (2nd ed.). Wiley.

Sands, R., & Gellis, Z. (2011). *Clinical social work practice in behavioral mental health: Toward evidence based practice* (3rd ed.). Pearson.

Soydan, H., & Palinkas, L. (2014). *Evidence based practice in social work.* Routledge.

Straus, S., Glasziou, P., Richardson, W. S., & Haynes, R. B. (2019). *Evidence-based medicine: How to practice and teach EBM* (5th ed.). Elsevier.

Thyer, B. (2004). What is evidence-based practice? *Brief Treatment and Crisis Intervention, 4,* 167–176.

Wike, T. L., Bledsoe, S., Manuel, J., Despard, M., Johnson, L, Bellmay, J., & Killian-Farrell, C. (2014). Evidence-based practice in social work: Challenges and opportunities for clinicians and organizations. *Clinical Social Work Journal, 42,* 161–170.

Critically Appraising Evidence for Its Validity and Applicability

Step 3

Danielle E. Parrish and Allen Rubin

This chapter focuses on the third step of the evidence-based practice (EBP) process, which involves critically appraising the evidence gathered in Step 2 with regard to its validity and applicability to answer the EBP question posed in Step 1. Perhaps the best place to start is to define the term *evidence* and what it means in the context of EBP. According the *Cambridge Dictionary* (n.d.), evidence is "one or more reasons for believing something is or is not true." Although there may be various ideas or perspectives of what one might deem evidence, EBP specifically integrates the best available *research evidence* with practice expertise and the client's values, preferences, unique circumstances, and background (Straus et al., 2019). According to Straus and colleagues, the best research evidence is defined as

> clinically relevant research, sometimes from the basic sciences of medicine, but especially from patient-centered clinical research into the accuracy and precision of diagnostic tests (including

the clinical examination), the power of prognostic markers, and the efficacy and safety of therapeutic, rehabilitative, and preventative strategies. (p. 1)

When translated to social work, this broad definition encompasses practically relevant, valid research that answers a variety of practice-related questions regarding issues ranging from conducting valid, reliable assessments to the prevention of societal factors that lead to social or health disparities to the efficacy of various approaches for reducing symptoms or suffering.

The scientific method offers key features that ensure that the research informing EBP decisions is valid and trustworthy. This method views all professional knowledge as tentative and subject to refutation (Rubin & Babbie, 2017). Therefore, science does not prove or declare the results from studies as forever facts; instead, the results of research studies add to a knowledge base that is always open to question and that may change based on newly emerging empirical research. Consequently, social workers should stay current with the most recent research as it emerges. The scientific method also requires that planned systematic and comprehensive observations are made. Steps should be planned prior to starting the study to minimize the bias of the observations, and there should be transparency in the final reporting of procedures. *Transparency* requires that all study procedures are clearly identified so that others can come to their own conclusions about the nature and implications of the results. Finally, although complete research objectivity may be difficult to obtain, the *pursuit of objectivity* is important. Thus, researchers should take steps to minimize potential biases (which lead to systematic deviations from the truth) and demonstrate how this was done when transparently reporting their results (Rubin & Babbie, 2017; Straus et al., 2019). EBP practitioners are tasked with evaluating the degree to which research studies have achieved these important aims.

Kinds of Evidence for Evidence-Based Practice

The emphasis on the kinds of research evidence most highly valued as a part of EBP has been contentious and highly debated yet greatly misunderstood by many in recent decades, leading to many misconceptions about EBP in social work. This is unfortunate because it was never meant to be controversial. *Evidence-Based Medicine* by Sackett (1997) clearly laid out the differences between background and foreground EBP questions and the varied kinds of research evidence needed to answer such questions. Evidence that answers *background questions* focuses on obtaining general knowledge about a particular condition, experience, assessment tool, or other aspect of practice for which more information is needed (Straus et al., 2019). Therefore, the kind of

empirical evidence used to answer these kinds of questions is varied, deriving from qualitative studies, instrument validation studies, and cross-sectional or longitudinal studies. Evidence generated from *foreground questions* is used to guide or inform practice decisions or actions (Straus et al., 2019). This evidence, in contrast to the evidence from background questions, focuses on what the most effective course of action would be with a client or target population. Given the need to better understand cause and effect with regard to the impact of an intervention, program, or policy, the best research evidence for answering these questions comes from studies with high levels of internal validity, such as randomized controlled trials, rigorous quasi-experimental designs, and systematic reviews or meta-analyses of such studies that permit causal inferences.

Validity and Applicability in Evidence-Based Practice

Validity has to do with the degree to which research is objective and systematic, thus minimizing sources of bias that reduce the truthfulness or trustworthiness of the research. *Applicability*, on the other hand, is the degree to which the research is clinically or substantially important to practice. When critiquing research, practitioners should ask both of the following questions (Straus et al., 2019): (1) Is this research valid and trustworthy? and (2) Is this research clinically and substantively important for my client(s)? If research is not valid, it does not matter if it clinically or substantially important, because it does not provide trustworthy, unbiased information to inform or guide practice. If the research is not practically or clinically important for practice, it does not matter how well it is done or how valid it is, because it does not have the capacity to truly help achieve the goals set with a client or client population.

The substantive or clinical importance of a study has to do with its practical application to practice. In other words, what do the findings really mean for what you are hoping to learn or accomplish? In this case, if the study is valid, it is important to consider several aspects of the study. First, what is the strength of the relationships between the variables studied or the magnitude of impact made by the policy, program, or intervention? Studies with large samples are more likely to obtain statistically significant findings—for example, differences between study groups or among variables— but the strength of the relationships between variables can be weak or inconsequential. So, it is essential to identify the effect sizes and get a sense of the weakness or strength of these relationships.

The next step it to determine if the relationships identified in the study are meaningful given the kinds of measures being used and what these relationships might mean, practically. For example, perhaps the goal is to identify an effective intervention to treat post-traumatic stress disorder symptoms for a 38-year-old Hispanic female client with a history of interpersonal violence with her spouse or partner. Hypothetically, suppose a study involving a very similar situation focused on the same outcomes being targeted in this practice setting, and the results demonstrated a statistically significant difference, with the recipients of an adapted cognitive–behavioral therapy intervention scoring 5 points lower on a trauma symptom questionnaire than those in a control group receiving treatment as usual. This statistically significant difference means that the difference between the two groups was not likely due to statistical chance or sampling error. Typically, in social sciences research, we are comfortable with being 95% confident that the difference between groups is not due to chance but instead represents a true difference between the groups. Therefore, if the probability of the differences between the groups being due to chance is less than 5% (or $P < .05$), the authors will reject the null hypothesis (or that chance is responsible for the group

differences) and report the findings as statistically significant. However, closer inspection of the measures and their scores might reveal that the results show both groups continue to have severe trauma symptoms and the 5-point reduction is actually not particularly meaningful from a clinical perspective. The lack of clinical significance can then temper any excitement generated by finding significant differences between the two groups. In turn, the lack of clinical significance limits the applicability of the findings for guiding practice. Thus, even if a research study is done quite well and with statistically significant results, it is important to remember the findings might lack practical importance. In each case, it is up to the reader of each study to think critically about its applicability.

Evidence for Informing Assessment

Evidence-based assessment (EBA) has been defined as "the use of research and theory to inform the selection of targets, the methods and measures used in the assessment, and the assessment process itself" (Hunsley & Mash, 2007, p. 29). Specifically, when engaging in EBA, one examines the existing research to find the very best research evidence to guide the selection on instruments (assessment tools, rapid assessment instruments, protocols, etc.) that fit best with the client's situation, culture, values, and preferences. Primary factors to consider when engaging in EBA include psychometric adequacy (reliability, validity, and sensitivity of measures or assessment protocols), their fit with the client or target population characteristics, their applicability to the culture and preferences of the client or target population, and the clinical or practical utility of their use (Parrish et al., 2015). An in-depth discussion of how to critique measures is beyond the focus of this chapter; however, many research methods texts provide excellent guidance for appraising measurement instruments.

Evidence for the Effectiveness of Interventions, Programs, or Policy

Research designed to answer whether an intervention, program, or policy is efficacious or effective must be able to demonstrate causation between the intervention and the measured outcomes of the study. Three criteria must be met in order to establish causation. First, there must be correlation or a relationship between the receipt of the intervention and a measure of outcome. For example, recipients of treatment for anxiety should score better on an anxiety measure than a comparable group of nonrecipients. Second, time order must be established, indicating change in the outcome measure from before to after implementation of the intervention. Finally, various confounding factors must be controlled to ensure it is the intervention and not something else causing the change in the outcome variable.

There are various confounding factors—called threats to internal validity—that can be alternative explanations for the change in the outcome variable. Two such threats are history and maturation. *History* is not like it sounds; it is not something in the past. Rather, it is something contemporaneous that occurs at the same time the intervention is delivered and that could explain the change in the outcome variable. For example, if the duration of the COVID-19 pandemic coincided with the period during which people were receiving a new treatment for depression, better post-test scores (after treatment) on a measure of depression might have been caused more by the lifting of the pandemic than by the treatment. Using a control group would help determine whether the threat of history could be ruled out as an

alternate explanation for the improvement. This could be done by randomly assigning a pool of depressed people to the new treatment intervention or to a wait-list or treatment-as-usual group. Then, if the new treatment group improves significantly more than the control group, it can be inferred that the new intervention was effective and that the pandemic did not explain the results.

A control group can also control for *maturation* (or passage of time). Imagine that, like the contemporaneous events, it is also possible that individuals may grow out of the outcome you are measuring just due to the passage of time or by growing out of it developmentally. For example, adolescents receiving an intervention to reduce vaping might reduce their use not because of an intervention but, rather, because they have grown out of the developmental phase that fostered such experimentation. Again, randomly assigning a group of vaping adolescents to a prevention intervention group and a control group would determine whether the maturation possibility can be ruled out.

A more in-depth discussion of all the aspects of internal validity is beyond the scope of this chapter and can be found in a variety of research methods textbooks (e.g., Rubin & Babbie, 2017). The most important features for outcome studies are those we have already mentioned—valid and meaningful measurement and random assignment to at least one intervention group and a control group. In addition, it is important that the same measures be administered at each data point (pre, post, and follow-up) and in the most objective way. The objectivity of the data collection procedures can be appraised by considering the following questions: Who collected the data and were they blind to the condition of the participants? Were they well trained? Is it possible that they had a vested interest in the outcome, and how might that have affected the results? Were the data collected in a way that exacerbated a *social desirability bias* among participants, thus increasing their proclivity to act or respond in a way that made the outcome appear better than it actually was? Finally, it is important to examine attrition rates—how many participants drop out of each group. For example, if only 60% of those in the intervention group and 100% in the control condition complete a post-test or follow-up measure, the groups are no longer comparable. It may be that the intervention was too demanding and only those willing to stick it out were retained. In all cases, the study should report on the completion of all parts of the study using a CONSORT chart (http://www.consort-statement.org/consort-statement/flow-diagram). If there is differential attrition, an intent-to-treat analysis should be conducted whereby those dropping out are counted as an outcome failure or given the same pretest score at post-test.

As each kind of outcome study is described briefly in the following sections, additional key considerations are mentioned, and evidence appraisal checklists (CASP: https://casp-uk.net/casp-tools-checklists) are referenced that have been designed to walk consumers of research through the important aspects of each study. Those who consume and conduct research are also encouraged to become familiar with the Journal Article Reporting Standards (American Psychological Association, 2020).

Randomized Controlled Trials

Randomized controlled trials (RCTs) are individual studies that have random assignment and a control group. In the social sciences, for ethical reasons, a control group is typically set up to receive treatment as usual or serve as a wait-list control. Treatment as usual (sometimes also referred to as conventional care) includes the services usually provided in a social services setting, whereas a wait-list control utilizes individuals waiting for services to serve in the control condition while they wait to utilize services. This is considered more ethical than a no treatment control option because treatment that would be readily available is being provided or treatment is not yet available. Some studies will extend upon these RCTs to examine *mediation*, where they study whether the proposed mechanisms of change impacted the change in the outcome variable. Or they may study *moderation* to examine with whom the intervention works best within a diverse sample. These are important analyses to better understand how to apply the intervention. There are a variety of checklists—both for authors and for research consumers—that outline expectations for RCTs, including the CASP RCT checklist and the CONSORT-SPI 2018 (Grant et al., 2018).

Quasi-Experimental Designs

The "quasi" in quasi-experimental designs means "partly, but not quite" because they are very similar to RCTs with the exception of random assignment. For various reasons, in social settings, randomization may not be feasible, possible, or perceived by an organization as ethical. There may also be issues with treatment diffusion or contamination—or having the intervention provided to those in the intervention group affect those in the comparison intervention—when it is provided to students in the same school or youth in an inpatient setting, for example. In these cases, it may be better to select matched sites where individuals do not interact to compare those receiving the intervention in specific sites to those who are receiving treatment as usual in other sites. Those receiving treatment as usual or the wait-list control are referred to as those in the *comparison group*. Given the lack of random assignment, these designs are not quite as good at demonstrating cause and effect as RCTs. However, with the exception of random assignment, these designs are very similar to RCTs.

Given the lack of random assignment, the onus is on the author(s) of the study to provide a convincing argument regarding the comparability of the groups to start. They should provide statistical comparisons of the intervention and comparison groups on important background and demographic variables, as well as the outcome variables at pretest. If there are any differences between groups to start, these are possible confounding factors that may explain the outcomes of the study. Although CASP has a case–control checklist that can be referenced, the TREND list for nonrandomized designs (http://www.cdc.gov/trendstatement) is quite detailed and useful (Des Jarlais et al., 2004).

Systematic Reviews and Meta-Analyses

Systematic reviews summarize and synthesize the available research literature. They use "explicit methods to systematically search, critically appraise, and synthesize the evidence base on a specific issue" (Straus et al., 2019, p. 112). Systematic reviews also seek to minimize the bias that may be present in only published studies by drawing on both the published and the gray literature (e.g., unpublished reports and dissertations). In some cases, a systematic review might also be a meta-analysis, whereby the results of the studies are statistically synthesized to identify an overall effect size for an intervention for each outcome of interest. Systematic reviews are quite useful for busy practitioners. When done well, they reduce the time necessary to appraise the evidence. Two widely trusted sources of systematic reviews in the helping professions are the Cochrane Collaboration and the Campbell Collaboration (see Chapter 87). These sources provide plain-language summaries that provide useful interpretations for the evidence and its application to practice. Although the aforementioned evidentiary checklists provide detailed guidance for appraising these studies, there are a few key questions that may also be helpful for guiding your reading of a systematic review (Straus et al., 2019): (1) Does the systematic review cover randomized trials only? (2) Does it describe a comprehensive and detailed search of relevant trials? (3) Are the results consistent across studies? (4) What is the magnitude of the treatment effect (the effect size)? and (5) Do the authors provide a statement indicating that they had no conflict of interest in conducting the review? Checklists from CASP and PRISMA (http://www.prisma-statement.org) are useful for both producers and consumers of these reviews.

One-Group or One-Arm Studies

When evidence from an RCT or a quasi-experimental group design is not available, the best available evidence may be from a one-group or one-arm study. This type of study includes only an intervention group, and the outcome measure is assessed before and after the intervention to determine if there is improvement in the desired direction. These studies are typically used as a first step to assess whether a larger RCT is feasible and worth funding. Without a control group and random assignment, however, these studies are unable to minimize the following confounding factors or threats to internal validity: history, maturation, and statistical regression to the mean. *Statistical regression* occurs when those with the worst scores—or those who are perceived to be most in need of an intervention based on a pretest score—are assigned to a treatment condition. Without rigorous random assignment to a control group—where such matching of worst scores to a treatment group would be controlled—it is possible that some of those with the worst scores on the day they were tested were having an unusually bad day and reported that day as such. In fact, on a more typical day, their pretest score would be much better. Because of this, when you give them the post-test, this does not represent improvement but, rather, simply the fact that their score regressed back to their typical or average day.

Practice Guidelines

Straus and colleagues (2019) list practice guidelines above systematic reviews and individual studies in their "evidence-based health care pyramid" (p. 41). These practice guidelines include *systematically derived recommendations* focused on a specific practice area, such as the treatment of anxiety disorders in youth. The National Association of Social Workers also produces practice guidelines (https://www.socialworkers.org/Practice/Practice-Standards-Guidelines). Another example of potentially relevant practice guidelines is the American Psychological Association's APA Professional Practice Guidelines (https://www.apa.org/practice/guidelines). These are placed higher on the pyramid of evidence sources because the evidence has been synthesized and translated into actionable practice guidelines by experts in the field. However, as with all sources of evidence, it is important to appraise the quality of these practice guidelines.

As with individual studies and systematic reviews, there are guides for assessing the validity of practice guidelines. The AGREE Collaboration, for example, has developed a checklist for appraising such practice guidelines (https://www.agreetrust.org). This checklist provides guidance in assessing the scope and purpose of the guidelines; the involvement of stakeholders (including those who developed the practice guidelines and the intended target users); the rigor of guideline development; and the clarity of presentation/recommendations, applicability, and editorial independence (Brouwers et al., 2016).

The reviews should include a synthesis of all relevant strategies for managing the practice issue (e.g., assessment, diagnosis, screening, prognosis, and treatment options) and the full range of possible outcomes—both good and bad (Straus et al., 2019). In addition, because the degree of evidence may vary for various guidelines, authors should grade the supporting evidence by specific levels or quality. One commonly adopted approach is the GRADE system (https://www.gradeworkinggroup.org/). This system first indicates whether the recommendation is for or against a practice option, and then it designates the quality of evidence as high, moderate, low, or very low (Guyatt et al., 2008). Additional important questions to ask of each practice guideline include the following (Straus et al., 2019): (1) Did the developers of the guideline carry out a comprehensive, reproducible literature review within the past 12 months? (2) Is each recommendation connected directly to a specified level of evidence (based on a systematic rating procedure) and linked to one or more specific citations? and (3) Is the guideline applicable to my client, practice orientation, practice setting, and community?

Qualitative Studies— Evidence for Understanding Meaning, Experiences, and Processes

Qualitative research can be useful and important for helping EBP practitioners better understand the experiences of their clients—in terms of both life experience and reactions to the ways that we try to help through various interventions, programs, and policies. However, given the potential for bias inherent in studies using the researcher to collect data and as the source of data analysis, this research should be rigorous and trustworthy if it is to guide practice. A detailed description of these methods is beyond the scope of this chapter; however, the CASP website provides guidelines for appraising the trustworthiness of qualitative research (https://casp-uk.net/wp-content/up-loads/2018/03/CASP-Qualitative-Checklist-2018_fillable_form.pdf).

Self-Evaluation

It seems fitting to conclude this chapter with self-appraisal questions posed by Straus and colleagues (2019): (1) Am I critically appraising external evidence at all? (2) Are the critical appraisal guides becoming easier for me to apply? (3) Am I becoming more accurate and efficient in applying some of the critical research appraisal skills? and (4) Am I creating any appraisal summaries? It is hoped that this chapter provides useful information for critically appraising practice-relevant research and making such appraisal more feasible. One of the challenges identified broadly in the EBP literature is the time required and the learning curve involved in learning how to efficiently critique the available research evidence (Wike et al., 2019). Some potential solutions involve developing a journal club within one's practice network or agency (Straus et al., 2019), where the work, the learning, and the results of the EBP process are shared. The benefit of persistence through this process, although it is initially challenging, is that once a reasonable number of EBP questions have been answered and the related evidence is appraised, there is only the need to stay on top of newly emerging research. The process also becomes easier as one practices it.

References

American Psychological Association. (2020). *Publication manual of the American Psychological Association* (7th ed.).

Brouwers, M. C., Kerkvliet, K., Spithoff, K., on behalf of the AGREE Next Steps Consortium. (2016). The AGREE Reporting Checklist: A tool to improve reporting of clinical practice guidelines. *BMJ, 352,* i1152. https://www.bmj.com/content/352/bmj.i1152

Cambridge Dictionary. (n.d.). Cambridge University Press. https://dictionary.cambridge.org/us

Des Jarlais, D. C., Lyles, C., Crepaz, N., & the Trend Group. (2004). Improving the reporting quality of nonrandomized evaluations of behavioral and public health interventions: The TREND statement. *American Journal of Public Health, 94,* 361–366.

Grant, S., Mayo-Wilson, E., Montgomery, P., Macdonald, G., Michie, S., Hopewell, S., Moher, D., on behalf of the CONSORT-SPI Group. (2018). CONSORT-SPI 2018 explanation and elaboration: Guidance for reporting social and psychological intervention trials. *Trials, 19,* 406. https://doi.org/10.1186/s13063-018-2735-z

Guyatt, G. H., Oxman, A. D., Vist Gunn, E., Kunz, R., Falck-Ytter, Y., Alonso-Coello, P., Schunemann, H. J., for the GRADE Working Group. (2008). GRADE: An emerging consensus on rating quality of evidence and strength of recommendations. *BMJ, 336,* 924. https://doi.org/10.1136/bmj.39489.470347.AD

Hunsley, J., & Mash, E. (2007). Evidence-Based Assessment. *Annual Review of Clinical Psychology, 3.*

Parrish, D., Springer, D., & Franklin, C. (2015). Standardized assessment measures and computer-assisted technologies for evidence-based practice. In C. J. Jordan & C. Franklin (Eds.), *Clinical assessment for social workers: Quantitative and qualitative methods* (4th ed., pp. 81–120). Oxford University Press.

Rubin, A., & Babbie, E. (2017). *Research methods for social work* (9th ed.). Cengage.

Sackett, D. L. (1997, February). Evidence-based medicine. In *Seminars in perinatology* (Vol. 21, No. 1, pp. 3–5). WB Saunders.

Straus, S. E., Glasziou, P., Richardson, W. S., & Haynes, R. B. (2019). *Evidence-based medicine: How to practice and teach EBM* (5th ed.). Elsevier.

Wike, T. L., Grady, M., Massey, M., Bledsoe, S. E., Bellamy, J. L., Stim, H., & Putzu, C. (2019). Newly educated MSW social workers' use of evidence-based practice and evidence-supported interventions: Results from an online survey. *Journal of Social Work Education, 55,* 504–518, doi:10.1080/10437797.2019.1600444

Integrating Information from Diverse Sources in Evidence-Based Practice

Step 4

Eileen Gambrill

Evidence-based practice (EBP) "requires the integration of the best research evidence with our clinical expertise and our [client's] unique values and circumstances" (Straus et al., 2011, p. 1). This entails integrating information concerning external research findings related to client concerns with client circumstances and characteristics, including their values and expectations, and available resources, and, together with the client, deciding what to do. Decisions are made about what characteristics of clients and their contexts to attend to and how to weigh them and what information to gather and how to do so. This process is typically burdened with uncertainties, including the extent to which external research findings apply to a given client. Lack of important background and/or foreground knowledge on the part of practitioners may compromise decisions. Background questions refer to general knowledge about problems/outcomes, tests, or interventions; foreground questions concern specific knowledge regarding clients,

populations, and problems (Straus et al., 2019). The time and effort devoted to making a decision should depend on the potential consequences and what is needed, based on external research findings and prior experience.

Clinical expertise refers to using clinical knowledge and skills including past experience to identify each (client's) unique concerns and "their individual risks and benefits of potential interventions, and their personal values and expectations" (Straus et al., 2011, p. 1). Sackett et al. (1997) note,

> Increased expertise is reflected in many ways, but especially in more effective and efficient [assessment] and in the more thoughtful identification and compassionate use of individual [clients'] predicaments, rights and preferences in making clinical decisions about their care.... Without clinical expertise, practice risks becoming tyrannized by external evidence, for even excellent

external evidence may be inapplicable to or inappropriate for an individual [client]. Without current best external evidence, practice risks becoming rapidly out of date, to the detriment of [clients]. (p. 2)

Client preferences and circumstances are considered as well as access to needed resources. Relevant questions include the following: Do research findings apply to my client? That is, is a client similar to clients included in related research? Can I use this method in my setting (e.g., are needed resources available)? If not, is there some other access to effective programs? What alternatives are available? Will the benefits of service outweigh the harms for this client? Are interventions acceptable to my client? What if I do not find anything? Many application barriers may compromise the quality of decisions and related actions. Gathering information about their frequency and nature is useful in planning how to decrease them. Examples include chaotic work environments, being overwhelmed by problems/issues due to large caseloads, lack of resources, poor education, and poor interagency communication and collaboration. Information may be available about certain kinds of clients, but these clients may differ greatly, so findings may not apply. (Much of the literature on implementation concerns use of practices deemed as evidence-based (EBPs) rather than the process of EBP (Bertram et al., 2015).

Do Research Findings Apply to My Client?

The unique characteristics and circumstances of a client may suggest that a method should not be used because negative effects are likely or because such characteristics would render an intervention ineffective. For example, referring clients who have a substance abuse problem to parent training programs may not be effective. Problems such as lack of income

and/or housing may influence the effectiveness of a method, as may the unique factors associated with distress, such as depression. Claims regarding a practice guideline may not apply to a particular client, agency, or community. Norms on assessment measures may be available but not for people like your client. (Note, however, that norms should not necessarily be used as a guideline for selecting outcomes for individual clients because outcomes they seek may differ from normative criteria and norms may not be optimal, such as low rates of positive feedback from teachers to students in classrooms.) Knowledge of behavior and how it is influenced provides helpful information (Borsboom et al., 2018; Madden, 2013). Sheldon et al. (1998) suggests that the following questions should be asked regarding whether a particular intervention applies to a client: (1) Is the risk reduction attributed to an intervention likely to be different because of client characteristics? (2) What is the client's absolute risk of an adverse event without the intervention (see later discussion)? (3) Is there some other problem or a contraindication that might reduce the benefit? (4) Are there social or cultural factors that might affect the suitability of a practice or policy or its acceptability? and (5) What do the client and the client's family want?

Are Research Findings Important? The "So What" Question

If external research findings apply to a client, are they important? Would they make a difference in decisions made? Were all important outcomes considered? Were surrogate outcomes relied on—those that are not of direct practical relevance but assumed to reflect vital outcomes? The acronym POEMS refers to patient-oriented evidence that matters. Grandage et al. (2002) suggest the following formula for judging usefulness: usefulness = (validity × relevance)/work.

How Definitive Are the Research Findings?

Reviews may be high-quality systematic reviews or incomplete, unrigorous (haphazard) reviews (Ioannidis, 2016). In the former, there may be strong evidence not to use a method (e.g., harmful effects have been found) or strong evidence to use one (e.g., critical tests show the effectiveness of a program). Often, there will be uncertainty about what is most likely to be effective. Different views of the quality of evidence related to programs abound (Littell, 2008).

What If Experts Disagree?

Depending on the views of experts is not without risk, as illustrated by studies comparing recommendations of clinical experts to suggestions based on results of carefully controlled research (Antman et al., 1992). It depends on whether the expert is informed (Norman et al., 2017). Seeking and reviewing the quality of evidence for ourselves may not be possible due to time constraints, for example. Indicators of honesty of experts include (1) accurate description of controversies, including methodological and conceptual problems with preferred positions; (2) accurate description of well-argued disliked views; (3) critical appraisal of both preferred and well-argued alternative views; and (4) inclusion of references regarding claims so readers can examine these for themselves.

Will Potential Benefits Outweigh Potential Risks and Costs?

Every intervention, including assessment measures, has potential risks and benefits—for example, false-positive or -negative results.

Will the benefits of an intervention outweigh potential risks and costs? We can estimate this in a number of ways: relative risk reduction (RRR), absolute risk reduction (ARR), and number needed to treat (NNT). Relative risk (e.g., "There is a 50% benefit of taking chemotherapy") is very misleading. Absolute risk should be given to clients (e.g., "Of 100 women, there are 6 recurrences of cancer in 10 years without chemotherapy compared to 3 among those who take chemotherapy"). Schwartz et al. (2009) describe a "drug fact box to communicate drug benefits and harms" (p. 516). A nomogram can be used to calculate NNT based on absolute risk in the absence of treatment (Guyatt et al., 2008). How many clients have to receive a harm reduction program to help one person? Is there information about number needed to harm? This refers to the number of individuals who would have to receive a service to harm one person. ARR should always be given; RRR is highly misleading. Accurately communicating risk to clients is much easier using frequencies rather than probabilities (Wegworth & Gigerenzer, 2011).

How Can Practitioners Help Clients Make Decisions?

How decisions are framed (in terms of gains or losses) influences choices; different surface wordings of identical problems influence judgments (framing effects). Gains or losses that are certain are weighed more heavily than those that are uncertain. Clients differ in how risk-averse they are and in the importance given to particular outcomes. It is important to know client preferences when (1) options have major differences in outcomes or complications, (2) decisions require trade-offs between short- and long-term outcomes, (3) one choice can result in a small chance of a grave outcome, and (4) there are marginal differences in outcomes between options (Kassirer, 1994). Presentation of risks and benefits by professionals is often quite misleading (Gigerenzer, 2002). Thus, a key step in helping clients make a decision is for practitioners to be aware of errors they make in estimating risk and presenting options.

Helping clients identify their beliefs and preferences may require involving them in a decision analysis. Decision aids can be used to inform clients about risks and benefits of different options. Such aids can "personalize" information by allowing clients to ask questions important to them. They can highlight vital information often overlooked, such as absolute risk. Benefits include reducing the proportion of clients who are uncertain about what to choose; increasing clients' knowledge of problems, options, and outcomes; creating realistic expectations; improving the match between choices and a client's values; and increasing informed participation in decision-making (Stacey et al., 2017). In social work areas such as child welfare, clients are often nonvoluntary. Whether voluntary or not, the evidentiary status of proposed interventions should be accurately described to clients.

Can This Method Be Implemented Effectively in My Agency?

Can a plan be carried out in a way that maximizes success? Are needed resources available? Are services matched to client assessment? Lack of access to effective services is common (Marsh et al., 2009). Do providers have the skills required to carry out plans with required fidelity? Can needed resources be created? Differences in provider adherence to intervention requirements may influence effectiveness. Barriers may be so extensive that Straus et al. (2005, p. 167) refer to them as "killer B's":

1. The burden of concern (the frequency of a concern may be too low to warrant offering a costly program with high integrity)

2. Beliefs of individual clients and/or communities about the value of services or their outcomes may not be compatible with what is most effective.
3. Bad bargain in relation to resources, costs, and outcome.
4. Barriers such as geographic, organizational, traditional, authoritarian, or behavioral.

Problems may have to be redefined from helping clients attain needed resources to helping them withstand the strain of not having the resources or involving clients with similar concerns in advocacy efforts to acquire better services. Sackett et al. (1997) suggest the following questions be considered to decide whether to implement a guideline (p. 182):

1. What barriers exist to its implementation? Can they be overcome?
2. Can you enlist the collaboration of key colleagues?
3. Can you meet the educational, administrative, and economic conditions that influence the success or failure of implementing the strategy? These include
   - credible synthesis of the evidence by a respected body;
   - respected, influential local exemplars already using the strategy;
   - consistent information from all relevant sources;
   - opportunity for individual discussions about the strategy with an authority;
   - user-friendly format for guidelines;
   - implementable within target group of clinicians (without the need for extensive outside collaboration); and
   - freedom from conflict with economic and administrative incentives and client and community expectations.

Implementation concerns have received increased attention. Auschra (2018) identified 20 types of barriers to integration of care categorized into six groups—administration and regulations, funding, interorganization domains, organizational domain, service delivery, and clinical practice—some of which they suggest are set up deliberately. Creation of a learning environment and ongoing coaching may be needed to maintain important skills. Successful implementation may require attention to the total context that influences individual decisions.

Are Alternative Options Available?

Are other options available, perhaps another agency to which a client could be referred? Self-help programs may be available. Here, too, familiarity with practice-related research can facilitate decisions.

What If Clients Prefer Untested, Ineffective, or Harmful Methods?

The acceptability of plans must be considered. This will influence adherence to important procedural components associated with success. Most interventions used by professionals in the interpersonal helping professions have not been tested; we do not know whether or not they are effective or harmful. Untested methods are routinely offered (Pignotti & Thyer, 2009). Methods critically tested and found to be ineffective or harmful should certainly not be offered. Untested methods that continue to be preferred and used should be tested to determine whether they do more good than harm.

What If a Search Reveals No Related Research?

The discovery of ignorance is just as important as the discovery of knowledge in accurately informing clients. Evidence-informed practice involves sharing ignorance and uncertainty as well as knowledge in a context of ongoing support. A review of research findings related to questions may reveal that little or nothing is known. Ethical obligations to involve clients as informed participants and to consider their preferences provide a guide; limitations of research findings should be shared with clients, and empirically grounded theory as well as client preferences should be used to guide work.

What If Related Research Is of Poor Quality?

A search will often reveal uncertainty regarding the effectiveness of a method. Critical appraisal of peer-reviewed literature reveals this to be deeply flawed (Ioannides, 2005, 2016), calling for vigilance. The term *best practice* is used to describe a hierarchy of evidence (Straus et al., 2011, p. 127) in which related research differs greatly in the extent to which claims are critically tested. If there are no randomized controlled trials regarding an effectiveness question, then we move down the list. This is often what must be done because most interventions used in psychiatry, psychology, and social work have not been critically tested. Instead of well-designed randomized controlled trials regarding the effectiveness of an intervention, only pre/post studies may be available, which are subject to many rival explanations regarding change. Some guidelines are described as "well established" if two well-designed randomized controlled trials show positive outcomes. It is less misleading to say that a claim has been critically tested in two wellcontrolled trials and has passed both tests. This keeps uncertainty in view. Whatever is found is shared with clients, and practice theory as well as client preferences are used to fill in the gaps. (See, for example, Database of Uncertainties About the Effects of Treatments.) Published uncertainties come from "patients, carers, and clinicians' questions about the effects of treatment, research recommendations in reports of systematic reviews of existing research and in clinical guidelines in which knowledge gaps are revealed and ongoing research" (Teachers of Evidence-Based Health Care, n.d.). It is assumed that "patients and the public have a right to expect that research funders, researchers, and health professionals are aware of uncertainties about the effects of treatments. . . . Ignoring treatment uncertainties puts [clients] at risk" (Teachers of Evidence-Based Health Care, n.d.).

What If Research Is Available but It Has Not Been Critically Appraised?

One course of action is to critically appraise this literature. However, the realities of practice may not allow time for this. Perhaps an expert in the area can be contacted. If the question concerns a problem that occurs often, interested others can be involved in critically appraising related research. Routine collection of questions regarding information needs allows setting priorities for research and preparation of critical appraisal topics. After three decades, we still do not have this information in social work.

Balancing Individual and Population Perspectives

One of the most challenging aspects of practice is considering both individuals and populations. There are only so much money and time. Decisions made about populations may limit options of individuals. Ethical issues regarding the distribution of scarce resources are often overlooked.

Common Errors

Common errors in integrating information are related to cognitive biases such as overconfidence, hindsight bias, confusing naming and explaining, status quo bias, wishful thinking, influence by redundant information, and confirmation biases (Gambrill, 2019). Availability

biases including influence by vivid case examples are common, as are biases based on representativeness (influence by misleading associations). Eagerness to help clients may encourage unfounded confidence in methods. Lack of reliability and validity of assessment measures may be ignored, resulting in faulty inferences. The environment circumstances in which clients live may be unknown and/or ignored. Jumping to conclusions may result in oversimplifications regarding client concerns. Or, the opposite may occur, as in suggesting obscure complex causes, none of which have intervention implications. Poor question posing and search skills may compromise what is found. Lack of evidence for preferred methods may be shared with clients in an unempathetic manner.

Ongoing Challenges and Evolving Remedies

As discussed previously, obstacles include both personal and environmental characteristics. Organizational cultures may discourage raising questions regarding services offered; needed tools, such as access to important databases, may not be available. Ongoing challenges include encouraging practitioners to be honest with clients about uncertainties in a supportive manner, ensuring practitioners offer high-quality common factors such as empathy that contribute to positive outcomes (Wampold, 2015), minimizing cognitive biases in integrating data, and critically appraising claims in the professional literature about "what works" and what accounts for client concerns. Biases intrude both on the part of researchers when conducting research and preparing research reviews (Ioannidis, 2005, 2016) and on the part of practitioners when making decisions. Many components in the process of EBP are designed to minimize biases, such as jumping to conclusions—for example, using "quality filters" (terms relevant to different kinds of studies) when seeking research related to questions (Gambrill & Gibbs, 2017). EBP highlights the play of bias and uncertainty in helping clients and encourages helpers and clients to seek available knowledge to handle this honestly and constructively. Consider the attention given to helping both clients and practitioners to acquire critical appraisal skills in reviewing research findings related to practice and policy questions (see http://www.testingtreatments. org). Availability biases, including preferred practice theory and preconceptions regarding certain kinds of people, as well as representative biases, including stereotypes, may interfere with judicious integration of external research findings with client values, preferences, and unique circumstances and characteristics. We tend to overestimate what "we know" (Dunning, 2011). Helping professionals to learn from their experiences in ways that improve the accuracy of future decisions is a key priority.

We can draw on literature concerning judgment, problem-solving, and decision-making to discover common biases and how to avoid them. We can take advantage of literature investigating components of expertise, such as specialized knowledge (Monteiro & Norman, 2013; Norman et al., 2017), as well as guidelines described in the decision-making and critical thinking literature to minimize biases such as encouraging active open-minded thinking (Baron, 2017). Use of handheld computers to guide decisions may be of value in decreasing errors and biases. Such aids can be used to prompt valuable behaviors, critique a decision such as purchasing services from an agency that offers ineffective services, match a client's unique circumstances and characteristics with a certain service, suggest options, and interpret different assessment pictures (Guyatt et al., 2008). Just as the narratives of clients are valuable in understanding how we can improve services, those of practitioners are valuable in identifying challenges and opportunities to

integrate information (Greenhalgh & Hurwitz, 1998), including questions of concern to different parties (Fenton et al., 2009). We can attend to and try to minimize gaps that compromise integration and minimize avoidable distraction (Gambrill, 2015).

Related Ethical Issues

Challenges in integrating data and making decisions illustrate the close connection between ethical and evidentiary issues. These include the obligation to accurately inform clients regarding uncertainties involved in making decisions including the evidentiary status of recommended methods and their risks and benefits together with the risks and benefits of alternative options. This requires honesty and accuracy regarding the likely effectiveness of different services. This in turn is related to the accuracy of providers' beliefs about their background and foreground knowledge, highlighting the importance of accurate appraisals of one's own knowledge and ignorance because this affects questions posed in the first step in the process of EBP.

References

Antman, E. M., Lau, J., Kupelnick, B., Mosteller, F., & Chalmers, T. C. (1992). A comparison of results of meta-analyses of randomized controlled trials and recommendations of clinical experts: Treatments for myocardial infarction. *JAMA, 268*(2), 240–248.

Auschra, C. (2018). Barriers to the integration of care in inter-organizational settings: A literature review. *International Journal of Integrative Care, 18*(1), 5. doi:05334/ijic.3068

Baron, J. (2017, August 27). Assessment of actively open-minded thinking. *Brown Bag Talks.* https://www.sas.upenn.edu/~baron/papers/aotwrefs.pdf

Bertram, M., Blase, K. A., & Fixen, D. L. (2015). Improving programs and outcomes: Implementation frameworks and organizational change. *Research on Social Work Practice, 25*, 477–487.

Borsboom, D., Cramer, A. O. J., & Kalis, A. (2018). Brain disorders? Not really: Why network structures block reductionism in psychopathology research. *Behavioral and Brain Sciences, 42*, 1–54. doi:10.1017/50140525X17002266

Dunning, D. (2011). The Dunning–Kruger effect: On being ignorant of one's own ignorance. *Advances in Experimental Social Psychology, 44,* 247–262. doi:10.1016/B978-0-12-385522-0.00005-6

Fenton, M., Brice, A., & Chalmers, I. (2009). Harvesting and publishing patients' unanswered questions about the effects of treatments. In P. Littlejohns & M. Rawlins (Eds.), *Patients, the public and priorities in healthcare* (pp. 165–180). Radcliffe.

Gambrill, E. (2015). Integrating research and practice: Distractions, controversies, and options for moving forward. *Research on Social Work Practice, 25,* 510–522.

Gambrill, E. (2019). *Critical thinking and the process of evidence-based practice.* Oxford University Press.

Gambrill, E., & Gibbs, L. (2017). *Critical thinking for helping professionals: A skills-based workbook* (4th ed.). Oxford University Press.

Gigerenzer, G. (2002). *Calculated risks: How to know when numbers deceive you.* Simon & Schuster.

Grandage, K. K., Slawson, D. C., Barnett, B. L., Jr., & Shaughnessy, A. F. (2002). When less is more: A practical approach to searching for evidence-based answers. *Journal of the Medical Library Association, 90,* 298–304.

Greenhalgh, T., & Hurwitz, B. (1998). *Narrative based medicine: Dialogue and discourse in clinical practice.* BMJ Press.

Guyatt, G., Rennie, D., Meade, M. O., & Cook, D. J. (2008). *Users' guides to the medical literature: A manual for evidence-based clinical practice.* American Medical Association.

Ioannidis, J. P. A. (2005). Why most published research findings are false. *PLoS Medicine, 2,* e124.

Ioannidis, J. P. A. (2016). The mass production of redundant, misleading and conflicting systematic reviews and meta-analyses. *Milbank Quarterly, 94,* 485–514. doi:10.1111/1468-0009.12210

Kassirer, J. P. (1994). Incorporating patient preferences into medical decisions. *New England Journal of Medicine, 330,* 1895–1896.

Littell, J. (2008). Evidence-based or bias? The quality of published reviews. *Children and Youth Services Review, 30,* 1299–1317.

Madden, G. J. (2013). *APA handbook of behavior analysis.* American Psychological Association.

Marsh, J. C., Cao, D., & Shin, H.-C. (2009). Closing the needs–service gap: Gender differences in matching services to client needs in comprehensive substance abuse treatment. *Social Work Research, 33,* 183–192. doi:10.1093/swr/33.3.183

Monteiro, S. M., & Norman, G. (2013) Diagnostic reasoning: Where we've been, where we're going. *Teaching and Learning in Medicine, 25,* S26–S32. doi:10.1080/10401334-2013.842911

Norman, G. R., Monteiro, S. D., Sherbino, J., Illgen, J. S., Schmidt, H. G., & Marmede, S. (2017). The causes of error in clinical reasoning: Cognitive biases, knowledge deficits, and dual process thinking. *Academic Medicine, 92,* 23–90.

Pignotti, M., & Thyer, B. A. (2009). The use of novel unsupported and empirically supported therapies by licensed clinical social workers. *Social Work Research, 33,* 5–17.

Sackett, D. L., Richardson, W. S., Rosenberg, W., & Haynes, R. B. (1997). *Evidence-based medicine: How to practice and teach EBM.* Churchill Livingstone.

Schwartz, L. M., Woloshin, S., & Welch, H. G. (2009). Using a drug facts box to communicate drug benefits and harms: Two randomized trials. *Annals of Internal Medicine, 150*(8), 516–527.

Sheldon, T. A., Guyatt, G. H., & Haines, A. (1998). Getting research findings into practice: When to act on the evidence. *British Medical Journal, 317,* 139–142.

Stacey, D., Légaré, F., Lewis, K., Barry, M. J., Bennett, C. L., Eden, K. B., Holmes-Rovner, M., Llewellyn-Thomas, H., Lyddiatt, A., Thomson, R., & Trevena, L. (2017). Decision aids for people facing health treatment or screening decisions [Review]. *Cochrane Database of Systematic Review, 4*(4), CD001431.

Straus, D. L., Glasziou, P., Richardson, W. S., & Haynes, R. B. (2011). *Evidence-based medicine: How to practice and teach EBM* (4th ed.). Churchill Livingstone.

Straus, D. L., Glasziou, P., Richardson, W. S., & Haynes, R. B. (2019). *Evidence-based medicine: How to practice and teach EBM* (5th ed.). Elsevier.

Straus, S. E., Richardson, W. S., Glasziou, P., & Haynes, R. B. (2005). *Evidence-based medicine: How to practice and teach EBM* (3rd ed.). Churchill Livingstone.

Teachers of Evidence-Based Health Care (n.d.). *Learning resources database.* https://teachingebhc.org

Wampold, B. E. (2015). How important are the common factors in psychotherapy? An update. *World Psychiatry, 14,* 270–277.

Wegworth, O., & Gigerenzer, G. (2011). Statistical illiteracy in doctors. In G. Gigerenzer & J. A. M. Gray (Eds.), *Better doctors, better patients, better decisions* (pp. 137–151). MIT Press.

Evaluating Effectiveness in Carrying out Evidence-Based Practice

Step 5

Bruce A. Thyer

Having completed Steps 1–4 of the evidence-based practice (EBP) model of decision-making, there remains the final step—evaluating how well one did during this particular clinical encounter. This involves asking some first-person questions while retrospectively reviewing the previous four steps. How did I do in formulating an answerable question? How did I do in tracking down relevant current credible information with which to answer that question(s)? How well did I do in critically appraising that information? And, how well did I integrate the information I found with the client's preferences and values, their current situation, potential costs and benefits, professional ethics, available resources, etc.? One useful benchmark to judge one's success is the clinical outcome. In short, is the client's situation, condition, or disorder clinically significantly improved? Going through the four prior steps successfully absent a positive and identifiable outcome is akin to saying the operation was a success but the

patient died. Sometimes, in the case of dichotomous outcomes, evaluating success is easy, as in "Is the formerly unemployed client now working?" or "Does my client no longer meet the DSM criteria for major depression?" But often client outcomes are much more complex, and more subtle evaluation tools are needed.

There are several sources of help in conducting this self-evaluation. One can begin with oneself, working through the steps of EBP. For example, one can ask, How long did it take me to come up with an appropriate answerable question? (Step 1). Did I have any false starts, or was I successful the first time? Was my question efficiently worded, avoiding double-barreled phrases, for example, or did I follow the PICO format (problem, intervention, comparison condition, and outcome)? Was I successful in locating clinically relevant studies that helped answer my question? (Step 2). Ideally, these studies would be well-designed empirical outcome reports involving clients similar to mine as opposed to solely theoretical papers, correlational or epidemiological studies, or clinical opinions. If I was unable to locate a systematic review involving a meta-analysis via the websites of the Cochrane Collaboration or the Campbell Collaboration, did I find such studies via other credible outlets? Did I find recent well-designed randomized controlled trials (RCTs)? If not, did any well-designed quasi-experimental studies emerge, or any case–control or cohort studies? Were there any experimental single-subject studies published that were useful? Did I use any Facebook pages or other social media involving people interested in my client's type of problem and ask about any recent studies they could direct me to?

The next step in your self-evaluation, Step 3, assimilating the information, can be greatly facilitated if you have located a recent high-quality systematic review (SR) on the treatment of your client's condition. These may be found on the websites of the Cochrane Collaboration and the Campbell Collaboration and are sometimes published independently of these organizations. In such SRs, the authors have already tracked down the latest information, systematically appraised it, and summarized any legitimate conclusions. While writing this chapter, an SR on the topic of "the promotion of well-being among children exposed to intimate partner violence" could be found on the Campbell Library website. If one has a child client who had been exposed to parental violence, this would be an exceptionally useful resource, augmented by a further search for publications that appeared more recently than the years covered by this particular SR (publications that appeared until April 2018). Help in appraising studies can be found in many locations, including training materials available on the Cochrane website (https://training.cochrane.org/search/site/training), so if you do not understand the nuances of a particular study you found, you can learn more about it

(enhancing your own critical appraisal skills for use with future clients). In addition, you may wish to speak with a colleague or supervisor who has more familiarity with these types of resources.

Step 4, integration and collaborative action with the client, is outlined very well in Drisko and Grady (2019, pp. 177–199). Review the ethical appropriateness of potential interventions, and discuss these with your client, being alert for potential cultural issues that may arise. Client non-cooperation may be due to a misunderstanding or a religious, systemic familial, or other issue. The client may have better ideas for what will or will not be acceptable to them than what you bring to the table, so listening to their suggestions is important. Be sure the proposed intervention is affordable and not too time-consuming. Ask about contacting significant others in the client's life to gain their perspectives. I once suggested to a Muslim couple in which the wife was agoraphobic that I pay home visits and go on outings with her during the day (a common practice in treating persons with agoraphobia). This did not sit well with the husband because of religious and cultural traditions, and they did not return from the initial consultation visit with me, much to my shame. This type of cultural misstep or oversight can be avoided if and when we create a space in which our clients can inform us of their personal belief systems. Clients' preferences and wishes must be elicited and accommodated, to a point. I will not provide a requested therapy that research has shown to essentially be a placebo, even if the client requests it. I can refer them to practitioners with fewer scruples than I have, freeing my time to provide empirically supported treatments whose effects exceed those of placebo therapy. The evidence-based social worker also has an obligation to avoid potentially harmful interventions, such as conversion therapy, recovering supposed memories of childhood sexual abuse via hypnosis, or holding therapies (there are many of these harmful treatments).

Soliciting feedback from the client and significant others in their life is often helpful to the review of one's conduct of EBP. If one has a formal supervisor familiar with the EBP model, they may be another useful resource to consult in this review. One's professional peers may also be able to lend insight into how you did and how you could improve the process.

Evaluating Clinical Practice Outcomes

From the inception of EBP, authorities in this field have advocated that clinicians consider undertaking a type of experimental study they labeled the $n = 1$ RCT. The primary reference book, *Evidence-Based Medicine: How to Practice and Teach EBM* (Straus et al., 2019), includes a positive description of this type of design:

> The *n-of-1* trial applies the principles of rigorous clinical trial methodology to . . . determine the best treatment for an individual patient. It randomizes time, and assigns the patient . . . to active therapy or placebo at different times, so that the patient undergoes cycles of experimental and control treatment, resulting in multiple crossovers (within the same patient) to help us to decide on the best therapy. (p. 146)

The experimental logic of the $n = 1$ RCT can be illustrated with an example. Let us say that a child has been diagnosed with hyperactivity, and a physician has prescribed a medication to help calm the child. The parents doubt that the drug will be helpful and are resistant to following this treatment recommendation. However, with the helpful intervention of a social worker, they agree to give it a try for several

weeks on an experimental basis. Two identical bottles of pills are prepared. One bottle is labeled A and contains (unknown to the parents, the teacher, or the child) the active medicine, whereas bottle B contains similar-looking pills lacking any active ingredient (i.e., a placebo). The social worker arranges for the teacher to rate the child's behavior in school at the end of each day, using a valid behavior rating scale. Flipping a coin, the social worker assigns the child to receive either pill A (heads) or pill B (tails) each day for a 2-week period. The social worker prepares a simple line graph, with behavior ratings scored on the vertical axis and the days of the week on the horizontal one. The ratings for the days pill A is administered are plotted and connected, and the ratings for pill B are similarly portrayed. If there is no overlap in the two sets of lines and the ratings during the days the child received the active medication are unambiguously those in which behavior was improved, then clear and compelling evidence of a genuinely experimental nature has demonstrated the superiority of the active drug over placebo.

This type of demonstration has several functions. First, there is empirical proof that the drug is helpful with this individual client, which is, after all, a highly desirable outcome of practicing EBP. Second, the evidence may alleviate the parents' reservations about using medication and help them decide to continue its use. This example presupposes that the medication has no significant side effects, is not unreasonably expensive, that taking it is not prohibited by the family's religious beliefs, and so on. If the two sets of lines connecting the two different treatment conditions had significant overlap, then the effects of the active drug versus placebo would be less dear. Completely overlapping lines would suggest that the medicine was little better than placebo and need not be used at all. This is also good to know.

Within the field of psychotherapy, this type of design is called the alternating treatments design (ATD; Barlow & Hayes, 1979). In May 2020, a search of the PsycINFO database using "alternating treatments design" as key words appearing anywhere in an article found more than 580 published examples of its use across a wide array of disciplines, including social work, audiology, medicine, education, and psychology. An ATD was used by social worker Steven Wong to help determine empirically how the immediate environmental situation affected the psychotic-like behavior of a person suffering from chronic mental illness (Wong et al., 1987). The client, Tom, was a 37-year-old man with a diagnosis of chronic schizophrenia who was experiencing his fourth hospitalization. Systematic assessments of Tom's psychotic-like mumblings were tape recorded via a wireless microphone attached to his shirt for five sessions of unstructured free time in the hospital day room where he had access to usual recreational materials (e.g., television, stereo, magazines, books, table games, and cards) but was otherwise left alone. The subsequent experimental phase consisted of randomly alternating between two interventions—a 40-minute session in the day room begun by prompting the client to read articles or to build a model he found interesting from an assortment of novel magazines and models offered to him versus spending 40 minutes in the room without any reading prompting or access to novel magazines or models (identical to the original baseline condition). These two treatments were randomly alternated for 18 consecutive sessions, and the percentage of time Tom spent engaged in stereotypic laughter and mumbling, reliably recorded, was the dependent variable (outcome measure). It was very clear that when Tom was given something interesting to do (e.g., reading new magazines or model building), his psychotic-like speech was markedly reduced, relative to having unstructured free time. There was no overlap in the two sets of data, providing compelling evidence that the simple intervention was causally

responsible for these behavioral differences. Because a clear causal inference is possible via the intentional manipulation of the intervention and control conditions, this $n = 1$ RCT can be legitimately classified as a true experiment at the level of the individual client, and it provides useful treatment applications (e.g., regularly providing an interesting activity for patients to do may reduce psychotic-like behavior). Wong also used this type of design to demonstrate experimentally that a checklist could be used effectively to help a memory-impaired woman with diabetes successfully undertake regular checking of her own blood sugar levels using a glucometer (Wong et al., 2000).

Within the field of EBP, $n = 1$ RCTs are held in such high esteem that it has been claimed that these studies provide a *stronger* foundation for making decisions about the care of individuals than does the evidence derived from systematic reviews, meta-analyses, individual RCTs, and other evidentiary sources (Guyatt et al., 2002, p. 12). This certainly turns the usual apex of the evidentiary hierarchy on its head! But note the original definition of EBP: "The conscientious, explicit, and judicious use of current best evidence in making decisions about the care of *individual patients*" (Sackett et al., 1996, p. 71, emphasis added). What better evidence regarding the appropriateness of a given intervention than a clear and compelling demonstration that it really seems to work with *our client*? Large-scale group studies very rarely make use of true probability samples, a prerequisite for generalizing findings, and in any case probability theory only permits inferences upward from sample to population, not downward from a sample (as in an RCT) to one's individual client. Within the social work research literature, the term *experiment* is almost exclusively reserved for nomothetic studies involving relatively large groups of clients who are randomly assigned to receive an experimental psychosocial intervention, to receive no treatment, to treatment as usual, or to a placebo control group. Pretreatment assessments may be used, and post-treatment assessments are essential to make any inferences about possible differential effects of the conditions to which the clients were exposed. Any post-treatment differences may be plausibly ascribed to their assigned condition (e.g., to the active or experimental treatment) as opposed to some rival explanation (e.g., passage of time, regression to the mean, or concurrent history). Such designs have the potential to possess high internal validity in that any conclusions drawn about the relative effects of the experimental conditions can be viewed as quite credible, with the random assignment feature controlling for other possibilities. Such designs are called RCTs and can indeed be quite powerful. Contrary to popular myth, social workers have published more than 1,000 RCTs (see the bibliography by Thyer, 2015), illustrating their value.

However, traditional RCT methodology is often required in social work intervention research only because of the large amount of variance present in our studies. Frequently, the independent variable (e.g., treatment) exerts modest effects at best and may be quite labile, readily influenced by client idiosyncratic or environmental contextual factors. In other words, our interventions are often not robust. Dependent variables (e.g., outcome measures) may lack precision, being subject to various forms of bias, and contain a large amount of noise or unexplained variation as well. These factors essentially require the use of sophisticated inferential statistics to separate out the "real" effects of treatment from the noise and also necessitate studies having sufficiently large sample sizes to possess adequate statistical power to accomplish this task. But keep in mind that nomothetic research designs and inferential statistics are just one set of tools to accomplish experimental demonstrations. Extremely powerful treatments do not require such sophisticated controls because their effects are obvious and compelling, swamping

the sometimes unwanted variance caused by client and context.

Other Forms of Experimental $n = 1$ Design

The $n = 1$ RCT or ATD is not the only type of within-client research design that can be applied to evaluate the effects of interventions with individual clients. Other selected $n = 1$ designs may also permit robust conclusions using the same logic applied with the ATD, namely repeated demonstrations of an effect, following the introduction or removal of a treatment. In the ATD, this introduction or removal of a treatment condition is dictated by the toss of a coin. If the outcome measure reliably fluctuates in a manner closely consistent with the manipulation of the treatment, we have increasing confidence that these outcome fluctuations can be attributed to the treatment itself or to its removal. The greater the number of such demonstrations, the greater the internal validity.

Similar simple logic is the basis for causal inference in a type of $n = 1$ study called the A–B–A–B design. Here, A refers to a period of time when the client received no formal treatment. The time period could conceivably be hours, days, weeks, or months, depending on the nature of the problem and circumstance surrounding it. During this A or baseline phase, a credible outcome measure is administered a number of times, and the data are plotted on a line graph, with time on the horizontal axis and the outcome measure scaled on the vertical axis. Ideally, the first baseline is long enough to obtain enough individual data points that are visually stable and show that the client is not obviously getting better (it is okay if they are getting worse, in terms of causal inference). Then the treatment is introduced, and the outcome measure continues to be assessed. Ideally, one sees an immediate improvement after the treatment begins during this second, or B, phase. The data continue to be plotted, and these improvements themselves stabilize. Thus far, one has completed an A–B $n = 1$ study—one that possesses only one apparent demonstration of a functional relationship between the introduction of a treatment and client improvement.

Unfortunately, only one such demonstration does not usually qualify a study to be labeled as a true experiment. A number of rival explanations cannot be ruled out with this simple design—for example, concurrent history, regression, placebo, a cyclic nature to the problem, and so on. To help rule out such threats, the intervention, B, is deliberately withdrawn or removed, and the baseline condition is reinstated (the second A phase). Ideally (in an experimental, not clinical sense), the client's functioning deteriorates during this second A phase. If it does not, the inferential logic breaks down. With deterioration, however, we now enjoy two demonstrations of an apparent functional relationship between the treatment and the problem—one when the treatment was introduced (the client got better) and the second when the treatment was removed (the client got worse).

The second A phase is then followed by the reintroduction of the treatment for a period of time, comprising the second B phase. Ideally (in both an experimental and a clinical sense), the client improves once again, leaving the social worker with three solid demonstrations of experimental control of outcome by the treatment—twice when the treatment was introduced (and the client got better) and once when the treatment was removed (and the client got worse). When graphically depicted, with obvious demarcations in the data between the four phases of the study, this is usually a very convincing demonstration of the effects of treatment. The inferential logic remains the same between the A–B–A–B design and the ATD, repeatedly introducing the treatment or

its removal. Strong effects are evident to practitioners, clients, and neutral observers alike. Absent strong effects (e.g., in the case of only minor changes in the data or considerable overlap in the range of data between adjacent phases), the same conservative principles suggest that one conclude the intervention is not clinically valuable. Again, Type II error is more likely (you will miss minor but reliable effects) and Type I error minimized (you are very unlikely to conclude that a strong effect is present, when it is really not).

The possible permutations of these simple principles are numerous. A further demonstration may be possible, as in the A–B–A–B–A–B design. One may try to compare the relative efficacy of two interventions, as in the A–B–A–C design, with the C phase reflecting the client's receiving a treatment different from B. These types of $n = 1$ designs, relying on changes in the data coincident with the introduction of the treatment and its *removal*, are obviously only possible for interventions with short-lived effects. If a treatment can be expected to produce a durable improvement, then the A–B–A–B design will not be useful because the relapse anticipated during the second B phase will not be forthcoming. Examples of such interventions may include teaching the client a social or intellectual skill, the attainment of personal insight (perhaps via psychotherapy), personal growth or strengthening of psychological resources, the removal of phobic fears or obsessive–compulsive behaviors, or acquiring a cognitive coping skill (e.g., rational self-talk). Discontinuing such an intervention will not necessarily obliterate any clinical gains made by the client, and thus the A–B–A–B design, or another $n = 1$ study that depends on client relapse occurring following the removal of a treatment for causal inferences to be made, is not usually a suitable $n = 1$ design in such circumstances.

When one is applying a treatment that is expected to produce not only immediate but also durable effects, another form of $n = 1$

740 | PART VIII EVIDENCE-BASED PRACTICE

experiment called the multiple baseline (MBL) design may be possible. The MBL also relies on the same logic as other experimental clinical research designs—repeatedly demonstrating that an effect is observed when a treatment is applied. There are various types of MBL designs, and one of the more common is the *MBL across clients*. This design requires that you have two or more clients seeking treatment at approximately the same point in time, with a similar problem, for which you believe a particular treatment is appropriate. Let us use as an example two clients who present for help in overcoming a specific phobia. You begin with a baseline phase for both clients, having searched the literature and located one (or more) credible outcome measure(s). When each client has stability in their baseline data (the A phase), you begin treatment (e.g., gradual real-life exposure therapy) for Client 1 (transitioning into the B phase) but not for Client 2 (who remains in the A phase). The internal validity of this design depends on seeing rapid improvements in Client 1 but not in Client 2. Some time passes, Client 1 continues to improve, and you then begin treating Client 2 with a similar program of exposure therapy (the B phase). Imagine two A–B designs stacked atop each other, with the lower one having a longer baseline, but each having stable baseline data and showing marked improvement only when treatment begins during the B phase. This approach in effect permits two possible demonstrations of experimental control, each time when the treatment was applied to two different clients. Two demonstrations are much better than one (as in a simple A–B design), and three such demonstrations, as in an MBL design across three clients, approach the internal validity of the A–B–A–B design (which also can yield three demonstrations).

A second form of MBL is called the *MBL across settings design*, and it may be used to determine the effects of one particular therapy on one problem experienced by one client

in different contexts. For example, suppose a child client displayed hyperactive behavior at home and at school, and this was posing a significant problem for the child. In the MBL across settings design, baselines would be taken of hyperactive behavior in the two settings and displayed on two stacked A–B-type graphs. When the baseline data are stable in both settings, an intervention (e.g., a point system to reward calm behavior) is initiated in one setting only—for example, the school—whereas the baseline condition is maintained in the other setting (the home). Experimentally, one hopes to see immediate improvements in the first setting and stable, problematic conditions continuing in the second. Then, after some time, the same intervention is applied in the other setting, with, it is presumed, a similar positive effect. This design also constitutes providing two demonstrations of experimental control, an improvement over only one demonstration, and adding a third setting for baselining and intervention enhances internal validity even further.

A third form of MBL design is the *MBL across problems* design. It may be useful in clinical situations in which one client presents with two or more problems potentially amenable to treatment by the same intervention. Imagine a child doing poorly in two subjects at school, arithmetic and reading. With the cooperation of the teacher, the social worker gets regular reports of the child's grades in each of these two subjects. These grades are baselined separately, and then an intervention, such as tutoring, is provided in one subject but not in the second, which continues to be baselined. Experimentally, one wishes to see that for the first academic subject (for which tutoring was provided), the child displays immediate and marked improvements in grades, whereas for the second subject, the child remains stable (with poor grades). Then the same intervention, tutoring, is provided for the second subject, and the child immediately displays a sharp improvement in grades. Again, the logic is the same, with two or more demonstrations of an effect: The problem is stable, an intervention is applied, and the problem is significantly improved. The MBL across three or more problems is even more convincing than that with only two. In certain circumstances—for example, clear data, a valid outcome measure, and treatments that can be deliberately introduced—the social worker is capable of providing genuinely experimental results—outcomes so compelling that most doubts are removed as to the effectiveness of the intervention.

In any research design—a large group RCT or an $n = 1$ study—poor results mean that experimental control has not been demonstrated, and internal validity is low. But if powerful effects are exerted by the treatment, these can be compellingly disclosed in $n = 1$ studies. The ATD is one $n = 1$ study with the potential to demonstrate internally valid conclusions. $n = 1$ studies using withdrawal designs, such as the A–B–A–B, or the various forms of MBL designs are also capable of permitting causal inferences. There is no claim that the experimental $n = 1$ studies can be applied in every clinical situation, but certainly their versatility permits far greater use than they have heretofore enjoyed as a method of evaluating clinical outcomes in social work practice. And $n = 1$ designs of lesser internal validity, such as the B, A–B, or A–B–A types (Thyer, 2020), are even more readily applicable in everyday practice. The use of $n = 1$ studies within social work is not hypothetical. A bibliography on the topic (Thyer & Thyer, 1992) prepared almost 30 years ago found more than 200 published examples, and Wong (2010) provides an excellent overview of the use of these designs in social work practice.

EBP has long advocated that practitioners evaluate the effects of their interventions using experimental $n = 1$ research designs. Thus far, the EBP literature in this regard has given limited attention to one type of $n = 1$ study, the alternating treatments design. However, a more diverse array of $n = 1$ designs have the potential to yield truly experimental results, and these deserve serious consideration by the social worker seeking to practice within the model known as EBP.

The evidence-based model described in this section on evaluating the effects of intervention presents a perspective that has long been present in social work (McIver, 1931).

> The social worker can throw light on social causation. It is sometimes said that the sociologist, unlike other scientists, cannot engage in experiments. But that is what the social worker does all the time . . . he does, and must, experiment. . . . Practical necessity compels the social worker to seek an answer to the questions of causation. (pp. 83–84)

> What we want to discover, whether as social scientists or as social workers, is the causes of things, the dependence of one phenomenon on another. . . . The social worker, being always engaged in making experiments, can advance the far too neglected study of social causation. (p. 89)

> The question of social causation is so crucial for the social worker that it should determine his whole approach. (p. 93)

Single-case experimental designs provide a robust methodology to fulfill these laudable aspirations of many years ago. When combined with the five-step decision-making process of EBP, the potential for improvements in the delivery of social work services is immense.

Helpful Resources

Campbell Collaboration: https://campbell collaboration.org
Cochrane Collaboration: https://www.cochrane.org

Evidence-Based Medicine Toolbox: https://ebm-tools.knowledgetranslation.net

References

Barlow, D. H., & Hayes, S. C. (1979). Alternating treatments design: One strategy for comparing the effects of two treatments in a single subject. *Journal of Applied Behavior Analysis, 12,* 199–210.

Drisko, J. W., & Grady, M. D. (2019). *Evidence-based practice in social work* (2nd edition). Springer.

Guyatt, G., Haynes, B., Jaeschke, R., Cook, D., Greenhalgh, T., Meade, M., Green, L., Naylor, A., Wilson, M., McAlister, F., & Richardson, W. (2002). Introduction: The philosophy of evidence-based medicine. In G. Guyatt & D. R Rennie (Eds.), *Users' guides to the medical literature* (pp. 5–71). AMA Press.

McIver, R. M. (1931). *The contribution of sociology to social work.* Columbia University Press.

Sackett, D. L., Rosenberg, W. M., Gray, J. A., Haynes, R. B., & Richardson, W. S. (1996). Evidence based medicine: What it is and what it isn't. *BMJ, 312*(7023), 71–72.

Straus, S. E., Glasziou, P., Richardson, W. S., & Haynes, R. B. (2019). *Evidence-based medicine: How to practice and teach EBM* (5th ed.). Elsevier.

Thyer, B. A. (2015). A bibliography of randomized controlled experiments in social work (1949–2013): *Solvitur ambulado. Research on Social Work Practice, 25,* 753–793.

Thyer, B. A. (2020). Evaluating social work practice with single system research designs. In M. Joubert & M. Webber (Eds.), *The Routledge handbook of social work practice research* (pp. 137–155). Routledge.

Thyer, B. A., & Thyer, K. B. (1992). Single-system research designs used in social work practice: A bibliography from 1965–1990. *Research on Social Work Practice, 2,* 99–116.

Wong, S. E. (2010). Single-case evaluation designs for practitioners. *Journal of Social Service Research, 36,* 248–259.

Wong, S. E., Seroka, P. L., & Ogisi, J. (2000). Effects of a checklist on self-assessment of blood glucose level by a memory-impaired woman with diabetes mellitus. *Journal of Applied Behavior Analysis, 33,* 251–254.

Wong, S. E., Terranova, M. D., Bowen, L., Zarate, R., Massei, H. K., & Liberman, R. P. (1987). Providing independent recreational activities to reduce stereotypic vocalizations in chronic schizophrenics. *Journal of Applied Behavior Analysis, 20,* 77–81.

PART IX

Case Management Guidelines

Strengths-Based Case Management

David C. Kondrat

Strengths-based case management (SBCM) is a uniquely social work form of case management that originated at the University of Kansas in the 1980s. The original model was rooted in the pioneering work of Saleebey (1992) and colleagues, who developed an approach to practice that focused on positive qualities that clients bring to the practice setting and not on pathology. The approach challenged practitioners to view their clients from a different lens—one of client strengths. The focus on strengths can be defined as follows (Glicken, 2004):

> [A] way of viewing the positive
> behaviours of all clients by helping them
> see that problem areas are secondary to
> areas of strengths and that out of what
> they do well can come helping solutions
> based upon the successful strategies they
> use daily in their lives to cope with a
> variety of important life issues, problems,
> and concerns. (p. 3)

The SBCM model was designed specifically to mirror strength-based practice. Furthermore, the original case management model was designed to work with people with serious mental illness (Rapp & Wintersteen, 1989). However, SBCM is currently used in more settings with different populations, from child welfare (Grube & Mendenhall, 2016) to geriatric social work (Fast & Chapin, 2000). Although the focus of this chapter is on the contribution of SBCM to persons with mental illness, the model is adaptable to different populations.

Assumptions and Principles of Strengths-Based Case Management

Strengths-based case management is guided by a set of assumptions that guide the case manager in work with their clients. The assumptions focus practitioners away from clients' pathologies and on to what the client is doing well or has in their environment that can help them be successful. Specifically, these assumptions are as follows (Saleebey, 2013, pp. 17–20):

- Every individual, group, family, and community has strengths.
- Trauma, abuse, illness, and struggle may be injurious, but they may also be sources of challenge and opportunity.
- Assume that you do not know the upper limits of the capacity to grow and change and take individual, group, and community aspirations seriously.
- We best serve clients by collaborating with them.
- Every environment is full of resources.
- Caring, caretaking, and context.

The assumptions push the practitioner to consider the client as a whole person, capable of change and growth. The client is to be viewed through a lens of the possible and not the pathological. Furthermore, these assumptions challenge the practitioner to be on equal footing with clients. Rather than viewing the case manager as the expert, SBCM holds that the client is capable of fully contributing to their own success. These basic assumptions are the foundation from with the case management model is articulated.

These assumptions are buttressed by a set of principles that guide the helping process. These principles direct practitioners to focus on strengths and represent the overarching philosophy of the practice of SBCM. These principles are outlined by Kisthardt (2013, pp. 59–65):

1. The initial focus of the helping process is on the strengths, interests, abilities, knowledge, and capabilities of each person and not on their diagnosis, deficits, symptoms, and weaknesses as defined by another (Kisthardt, 2013, p. 59). Clients are often focused on the problems that bring them to case management. By focusing on strengths, clients are encouraged to see themselves outside of the pathologies and problems that brought them to case management. Focusing on deficits can have a deleterious effect on clients. Using mental illness as an example, clients who hold negative beliefs about mental illness tend to have more negative outcomes (Link, 1987). Therefore, focusing on strengths can potentiate positive change in and of itself.

2. The helping relationship becomes one of collaboration, mutuality, and partnership. Power with another, not power over another (Kisthardt, 2013, p. 60). Rather than being hierarchical, with the case manager making decisions for clients, SBCM holds that the relationship should be mutual, with each person in the relationship having equal power.

3. All human beings have the inherent capacity to learn, grow, and transform. People have the right to try, the right to succeed, and the right to fail (Kisthardt, 2013, p. 62). Rather than merely maintaining clients in a stable state, SBCM seeks to improve clients and help them achieve their desired goals.

4. Helping activities in naturally occurring settings in the community are encouraged (Kisthardt, 2013, p. 64). SBCM is not office based. Rather, the helping process occurs in the community in which the client lives.

5. The entire community is viewed as an oasis of potential resources to enlist on behalf of service participants. Naturally occurring resources are considered as a possibility first, before segregated or formally constituted "mental health" or "social services" (Kisthardt, 2013, p. 65). Often, the community is viewed as a desert of resources. SBCM seeks to help consumers find available resources in the community. Focus is placed on finding resources that are nontraditional. For example, a client's friendship network contains a plethora of resources to help the client achieve goals.

The SBCM Model

The foundation of the SBCM model is the relationship that is developed by the case manager and the client. Rapp and Goscha (2006) delineate a series of elements that make the SBCM different from other client and practitioner relationships. First, the relationship should be purposeful. All work should be done with the purpose of helping the client, including helping the client recognize and actualize their own strengths. Next, the relationship should be reciprocal. As Rapp and Goscha write,

> The role of the case manager should resemble being more like a travel companion with the person on their recovery journey rather than as a travel agent. Both parties should learn from each other and enjoy the time spent together. (pp. 74–75)

The relationship should be friendly. Rather than approaching the relationship from a hierarchical detached stance, the case manager should work with the client in an atmosphere that is warm and accepting. The case manager relationship should be empowering, helping the client achieve their full potential. The relationship should also be trusting. Both the client and the case manager need to develop a relationship built on trust. Finally, the relationship should be hope-inducing, helping the client see their path forward. The case manager needs to believe that the client can and will get better and needs to convey this message to the client.

The Strengths Assessment

A foundational tool of SBCM is the strengths assessment. The strengths assessment sets the stage for the work of case management and is the purposeful assessment of strengths instead of pathologies and problems. A strength is anything in the client or their environment that has the potential to create growth or change (Saleebey, 2009). In terms of individuals, strengths can be aspirations, competencies, and confidence; in terms of communities,

strengths can be opportunities, social networks, resources, and tangible service (Rapp & Goscha, 2012).

The strengths assessment provides a unique opportunity to focus on what the client is doing well and resources and their community. Clients often come to the case management relationship with a view of their self that is ridden with the negative. They are often keenly aware of what is going wrong in their life. Focusing on strengths, through the strengths assessment, clients can counter the narrative that their lives are a pathology. The strengths assessment is the springboard for developing goals. Goals should follow from what the client is doing well. Strengths should be incorporated into the assessment whenever possible. Using a SBCM approach, goals utilize strengths identified in the strengths assessment.

The Language of Strengths

The adage that "language matters" is true in SBCM. Case managers need to purposefully speak in the language of strengths and not deficits. One way for this to be accomplished is to utilize questions and language from solution-focused therapy (SFT; Greene et al., 2006). SFT has many of the same assumptions about utilizing the positive as does SBCM. In addition, SFT has sets of questions that can be used to elicit client strengths in a way that is in concert with SBCM. Although a full discussion of the use of SFT in SBCM is beyond the scope of this chapter, one example will suffice. Outcome questions can be used to identify goals. For example, a case manager may ask a client, "Suppose we are sitting here 6 months from now, what will you be telling me is different?"

The Structure of SBCM Services

Rapp (1998) provides what he has called the active ingredients of SMCM. Individual case managers provide services to clients. Case managers work in teams under a supervisor.

Although the case manages do work in teams, the individual case manager is responsible for their client caseload. The purpose of managers keeping their own caseload is to maximize the benefit of the client and case manager relationship. Weekly supervision meeting happens in teams. The team and the team supervisor provide necessary guidance for working with clients. In addition, these meetings are a time to celebrate the successes of clients. Services are provided in the community and not in office settings. Case managers have up to 20 clients on their caseload. Services providers on a team are available 24 hours a day for emergencies. There is no time limit to services; clients can continue to receive services if they believe it is necessary. Fukui et al. (2012) explored the relation between the extent to which adherence to the SBCM model was faithfully followed and positive outcomes. They found that being more faithful to the model was associated with better outcomes, including fewer psychiatric hospitalizations and more frequent independent living.

Research on Strengths-Based Case Management

Research on SBCM has been mixed, although to date, no randomized clinical trials of SBCM have been conducted. Early studies focused on the degree to which clients were achieving their goals, using goal attainment as the outcome. For example, Rapp and Wintersteen (1989), using a pretest/post-test design, explored the extent to which clients achieved their goals. The authors found that clients achieved approximately 70% of their goals. In their meta-analysis, Ibrahim et al. (2014) explored six quasi-experimental studies of SBCM. They found that SBCM was as effective as treatment as usual with regard to functioning and quality of life. Taken as a whole, the research on SBCM is mixed.

Case Example

Susan is a 36-year-old woman living with schizoaffective disorder. She lives in an apartment that her father found for her. She has been living with mental illness for more than 10 years. Susan does very little in life. She spends her days watching television and smoking cigarettes. Susan's psychiatrist referred her to the SBCM program for assistance

The case manager called Susan to find out if she was interested in meeting. Susan agreed, but not at her house. She wanted to meet at the food court of the local mall. The case manager agreed, wanting Susan to be comfortable in the relationship. For 3 weeks, the case manager and Susan met in the mall. They would get lunch and walk. During this time, the case manager asked Susan what she wanted from life. Susan wanted to work for a business that allowed her to use her skills in English. Susan had gone to the local university to study English and has always wanted to find a job that will allow her to utilize her skills. The case manager reflected this desire back to Susan and explained that this desire was a strength.

After 3 weeks, Susan agreed to have the case manager meet in her house. The case manager worked with Susan on conducting a strengths assessment. During this process, the case manager learned that Susan is a very good copy editor. The case manager also learned that Susan has a friend who oversees the production of an academic journal at the local university. In discussing goals with the case manager, Susan stated that she wanted to work for her friend.

The case manager and Susan developed a plan for Susan to contact her friend to find out if she could use Susan's skill with the English language. Fortunately, the journal needed someone to serve as the manager of the journal, taking care of the day-to-day tasks of moving manuscripts in and out for review. Her friend agreed to give Susan a chance. Susan thrived in this environment. Her friend stated that the journal never ran so smoothly. Over time, her friend gave Susan more responsibilities, including copyediting some of the manuscripts. Susan was equal to the task.

Susan stated that she was happy in her new world of work. She felt as if she no longer needed the help of the case manager. The case manager agreed, but told Susan that she could still use the services of the case management agency at any time.

Conclusion

Strengths-based case management represents one form of case management that is based on the principles and assumptions of strengths-based practice and is uniquely social work in origin. These principles and assumptions of SBCM guide the practitioner in their work with clients. Fundamental to SBCM is the strengths assessment, which provides a platform from moving clients from a focus on their pathologies to a focus on their possibilities. The strengths assessment provides the groundwork for developing goals with clients. In addition, the relationship that a case manager has with a client is fundamental. Case management teams follow a formalized structure. Clients do better when the model is more faithfully followed.

References

Fast, B., & Chapin, R. K. (2000). *Strengths-based care management for older adults.* Health Professions Press.

Fukui, S., Goscha, R., Rapp, C. A., Mabry, A., Liddy, P., & Marty, D. (2012). Strengths model case management fidelity scores and client outcomes. *Psychiatric Services, 63*(7), 708–710. doi:10.1176/appi.ps.201100373

Glicken, M. D. (2004). *Using the strengths perspective in social work practice: A positive approach for the helping professions.* Pearson.

Greene, G. J., Kondrat, D. C., Lee, M. Y., Clement, J., Siebert, H., Mentzer, R. A., & Pinnell, S. R. (2006). A solution-focused approach to case management and recovery with consumers who have a severe mental disability. *Families in Society, 87*(3), 339–350.

Grube, W., & Mendenhall, A. N. (2016). Adolescent mental health case management: Provider perspectives. *Social Work in Mental Health, 14,* 583–605. doi:10.1080/15332985.2015.1089971

Ibrahim, N., Michail, M., & Callaghan, P. (2014). The strengths based approach as a service delivery model for severe mental illness: A meta-analysis of clinical trials. *BMC Psychiatry, 14,* 243. doi:10.1186/s12888-014-0243-6

Kisthardt, W. E. (2013). Integrating the core competencies in strengths-based, person-centered practice. In D. Saleebey (Ed.), *The strengths perspective social work practice* (pp. 23–78). New Jersey: Pearson.

Link, B. G. (1987). Understanding labeling effects in the area of mental disorders: An assessment of the effects of expectations of rejection. *American Sociological Review, 52,* 96–112. doi:10.2307/2095395

Rapp, C. A. (1998). The active ingredients of effective case management: A research synthesis. *Community Mental Health Journal, 34*(4), 363–380.

Rapp, C. A., & Goscha, R. J. (2012). *The strengths model: A recovery-oriented approach to mental health services* (3rd ed.). Oxford University Press.

Rapp, C. A., & Wintersteen, R. (1989). The strengths model of case management: Results from twelve demonstrations. *Psychosocial Rehabilitation Journal, 13*(1), 23–32.

Saleebey, D. (1992). *The strengths perspective in social work practice.* Longman.

Saleebey, D. (2009). *The strengths perspective in social work practice* (5th ed.). Allyn & Bacon.

Saleebey, D. (2013). *The strengths perspective in social work practice* (6th ed.). Pearson.

Case Management in Child Welfare

Khalilah L. Caines and Jayson Caines

Social work case managers work in a variety of settings to coordinate services in collaboration with and on behalf of clients [National Association of Social Workers (NASW), 2013a]. The process of case management includes "identifying, planning, accessing, advocating for, coordinating, monitoring, and evaluating resources, support, and services" (NASW, 2013a, p. 11). Frequently utilized as an intervention in child welfare, case management is a strategic approach to service coordination designed to support and strengthen families receiving child welfare services (NASW, 2013b). Child welfare organizations provide a range of services to children and families impacted by maltreatment, including prevention, diversion, investigative, protective, foster care, adoption, and independent living services (Child Welfare Information Gateway, 2018). Although the specific tasks within these categories may vary, the role of the case manager is the same—to coordinate services on behalf of children and families to promote safety, well-being, and permanency.

As outlined in the NASW case management standards, case management functions follow the generalist intervention model and provide a framework for common child welfare case management duties that can include the following (NASW, 2013a):

1. Identification
   a. Understand and identify signs of abuse and/or neglect
   b. Identify family causes or issues that contribute to child safety concerns
   c. Identify strengths and protective factors and capacities of families
   d. Strengths-based child and family assessments
2. Planning
   a. Collaborate with families and organizations to develop a plan to address risk factors
   b. Develop case plan to achieve permanency goals
   c. Provide service referrals to meet identified needs
3. Monitoring
   a. Conduct home visits and parent visits
   b. Supervise visitation
   c. Maintain regular contact with service providers and caregivers
   d. Attend judicial hearings and staffings to monitor progress

  e. Documentation of all efforts and communication
4. Coordination
   a. Coordinate and link families to services
   b. Collaborate with service providers to assess progress
   c. Documentation of all efforts
5. Evaluation
   a. Attend judicial hearings and staffings
   b. Preparation for case closure
   c. Identify appropriateness of permanency goal
6. Termination
   a. Attend judicial hearing and staffings
   b. Documentation of progress and outcomes

Professional Competence: Knowledge, Skills, and Values

Professional social work competence is defined as "the ability to integrate and apply social work knowledge, values, and skills to practice situations in a purposeful, intentional, and professional manner to promote human and community well-being" (Council on Social Work Education, 2015, p. 6). Utilizing this definition, this chapter reviews the knowledge, skills, and values pertinent for effective child welfare case management.

Knowledge

Social workers engaged in child welfare case management must possess general social work knowledge as well as specialized knowledge about child protection, the judicial dependency process, trauma-informed care, and evidence-based practices.

Child Protection

The federal goals of child protection are to promote the safety, permanency, and well-being of children (Adoption and Safe Families Act, 1997). Child protection principles are child-centered, drawing on the strengths of families to provide family-focused and culturally competent services to promote permanency (Child Welfare League of America, 1999; DePanfilis, 2018). The philosophical underpinnings of child protection are rooted in family preservation, with an emphasis on strengthening families to meet the needs of the child (McCroskey, 2001). Federal legislation and research support maintaining a child within the family and suggest that children do best if they are able to safely remain with their family or in a family-like setting [Families First Prevention Services Act (FFPSA), 2017; Proctor & Dubowitz, 2014]. The FFPSA was signed into law in 2018 and is aimed to invest in prevention and family services, ensure necessity of a placement that is not a foster family home, support child and family services, and provide incentives to states to promote adoption and legal guardianship (FFPSA, 2017). This landmark legislation demonstrates a shift in the government's approach to funding for child protection that impacts child welfare service provision.

Case management within child protection is child-centered, family-focused, strengths-based, culturally competent, and aimed toward permanency (DePanfilis, 2018). Assessing for safety is a primary goal of child protection, and case managers must be prepared to assess for safety of children wherever they are placed throughout the life of a case. In addition, case managers must be aware of court orders and stipulations when preparing safety plans to ensure safety and compliance. This is an ongoing process that requires continuous planning, monitoring, coordination, and evaluation. Case managers must also attend to the well-being of children. The framework for understanding well-being relates to healthy development, which includes social, emotional, biological, and academic development; this often requires coordination with youth, families, and various service providers (Child

Welfare Information Gateway, n.d.; NASW, 2013b).

The Dependency System

Child welfare case managers must also understand basic federal, state, and agency rules that guide efforts to achieve child protection goals. Case managers may engage in preventive or protective efforts to promote safety on behalf of children and families. In cases in which the courts deem it necessary to remove the child from the home to ensure safety, additional judicial hearings are held to determine further court involvement, visitation rights, case planning efforts, service provision, and permanency planning (Child Welfare Information Gateway, 2013). Case managers must be prepared to engage in this judicial process and participate in permanency planning efforts on behalf of children (NASW, 2013b). Permanency goals can include reunification, legal guardianship, and adoption, each of which involves a unique set of services to achieve the permanency goal. Within the dependency system, case managers may be involved in the initial reporting and investigation of child maltreatment, conduct comprehensive assessments to understand family strengths and needs, and collaborate with families to develop a plan to mitigate risk factors to strengthen and protect children and families. Coordination of these services requires an understanding of legal court orders and stipulations to ensure safety and compliance.

Trauma-Informed Care

Trauma-informed care was established as a framework for organizations and systems to understand and recognize the impact and signs of trauma while incorporating this knowledge in all interactions to avoid revictimization (U.S. Department of Health & Human Services, n.d.). An understanding of trauma and its impact on functioning is one of the major tenets of a trauma-informed approach to care that is vital

to child welfare organizations. The National Child Traumatic Stress Network (NCTSN, n.d.) identifies seven elements of a trauma-informed child welfare system that ensures physical and psychological safety, identifies trauma-related needs, enhances the well-being of children and families and child welfare professionals, while partnering with children and families and child-serving agencies. In addition to online training resources, the NCTSN has developed a Child Welfare Training Toolkit to promote a trauma-informed approach to child welfare case management (Walsh et al., 2019). FFPSA now mandates child welfare organizations to utilize trauma-informed programs and services, which requires case managers to incorporate this approach in their work with children and families. Case managers within a child welfare context are a crucial component of a trauma-informed system. A trauma-informed perspective guides how case managers engage and understand a child's needs in order to identify appropriate services (NCTSN, 2013).

Evidence-Based Practices

Knowledge about child welfare services that are supported by research is crucial to effective case management (NASW, 2013b). The prevalence of childhood traumatic stress has garnered national attention, with Congress establishing the National Child Traumatic Stress Initiative designed to improve treatment and services for children and families that have experienced traumatic events (Substance Abuse and Mental Health Services Administration, 2015). In addition to an increased focus on trauma-informed services and treatment models within child welfare organizations, FFPSA promotes the use of evidence-based practices (EBPs) to improve child welfare outcomes (FFPSA, 2017). EBPs are "practices supported by a substantial body of outcomes-based research" (Myers et al., 2006, p. 374). For states and programs to be eligible to receive Title-IV E funding, FFPSA now mandates the use of EBPs that are promising, supported, and well-supported for prevention and family services. The Title IV-E Prevention Services Clearinghouse was established as an electronic registry for review of research on programs and services considered promising, supported, and well-supported practices (U.S. Department of Health and Human Services, 2019). This clearinghouse is one of many designed to evaluate research about services and practices commonly used in child welfare. A list of additional child welfare clearinghouses can be found in the Helpful Resources section.

Skills

States are responsible for the provision of child welfare services with an increase in partnerships with private and nongovernment organizations for service delivery (Hubel et al., 2013; Kahn & Kamerman, 1999; Westat & Chapin Hall Center for Children, 2002). This public–private partnership, known as privatization, allows states to contract with private organizations for service provision (Cohen & Eimicke, 1998). Increased collaboration with public and private organizations requires case managers to develop a specialized skill set with engagement, interviewing, and interdisciplinary collaboration.

Engagement and Interviewing

A basic understanding of human development will allow case managers to utilize developmentally appropriate engagement strategies with children and families. Engagement and interviewing skills are crucial to the helping process, particularly within case management practice, and have been found to promote positive outcomes (Altman, 2008; Cheng & Lo, 2016; Damiani-Taraba et al., 2017). Involvement with child welfare systems can be challenging for children and families due to the nature of the relationship and potential resistance by family members (Forrester et al., 2012). Case managers must be prepared to engage both youth and families to achieve permanency

outcomes (NASW, 2013b). A strengths-based approach to case management allows case managers to find a delicate balance between empathy and authority through collaborative partnerships with families to promote safety, identify family strengths, and establish common goals (Oliver & Charles, 2016). Case managers must also be skilled in engagement and interviewing in order to collect valuable information for planning, coordination, and monitoring of services.

Interdisciplinary Collaboration

In order to effectively address the multifaceted needs of children and families, case managers must collaborate with a variety of groups, organizations, and disciplines. Historically utilized within health care settings, interdisciplinary collaboration involves two or more disciplines working together to achieve a common goal and has been found to impact providers and clients (Houldin et al., 2004; Petri, 2010). With an emphasis on collaboration and information sharing, interdisciplinary collaboration in child welfare allows case managers to develop a holistic understanding of families' needs, develop a comprehensive service plan, and improve child and family outcomes (Altshuler, 2003; Woodside-Jiron et al., 2019).

Child welfare case managers are members of interdisciplinary teams that can include relatives, service providers, court-appointed volunteers, juvenile probation officers, attorneys, and more. Interdisciplinary collaboration requires strong communication and negotiation skills to initiate and monitor services on behalf of children and families (Magnuson et al., 2012). As a result, it is important for case managers to understand their role and the roles of other disciplines to collaboratively work toward common goals (NASW, 2013b). In addition, case managers are responsible for documentation of efforts and progress through case notes and judicial documentation. These responsibilities require an ability to navigate and communicate with various disciplines and organizations to promote child safety, permanency, and well-being.

Values

Both the social work profession and child protection efforts are guided by a set of core values to promote well-being (DePanfilis, 2018; NASW, 2017). Child welfare case managers must be culturally competent, strengths-based, and collaborative in their work with children and families.

Families receiving child welfare service are diverse in composition, need, and culture; therefore, case management services should reflect this diversity through individualized service provision (DePanfilis, 2018). Training in cultural competence has been associated with improving engagement for child welfare workers and is important in understanding and honoring family values to improve family outcomes (Chen & Lo, 2018). Utilizing a strengths-based approach, case managers recognize that each family possesses strengths and protective capacities and the role of a case manager is to help families identify and maximize these strengths to improve family functioning (NASW, 2013b). Engaging families as collaborative partners in identifying and meeting their needs increases participation and has been found to improve outcomes (Child Welfare Information Gateway, 2016; Platt, 2012).

The Role of Technology in Child Welfare Case Management

An increase in the complexity of the needs of children and families requires child welfare organizations to find new and innovative approaches to promote child safety. Technology is increasingly being leveraged as a tool to improve child welfare outcomes (Cahalane et al., 2012; Collins-Camargo et al., 2019;

Hughes, 2018). Recent funding incentives encourage states to transition from a Statewide/Tribal Automated Child Welfare Information System to a Comprehensive Child Welfare System (Children's Bureau, 2016). This allows for a centralization of information technology used for data collection, analysis, and information sharing among child serving organizations. This approach to information sharing will help case managers effectively and efficiently identify and address the needs of children and families they serve. In addition, child welfare organizations are using technology to facilitate case management responsibilities through video-assisted visitation, communication resource referrals, and predictive analytics (Cuccaro-Alamin et al., 2017; Quinn et al., 2015; Weiner et al., 2019). Last, many organizations are incorporating simulation in child welfare training to equip case managers with engagement skills necessary for working with vulnerable populations (Bogo et al., 2014; Rawlings & Blackmer, 2019). Ultimately, case managers in child welfare must be flexible to incorporate available technology resources into their daily practice to promote safety, well-being, and permanency.

Helpful Resources

Annie E. Casey Foundation: https://www.aecf.org
California Evidenced-Based Clearinghouse for Child Welfare: https://www.cebc4cw.org
Casey Family Programs: https://www.casey.org
Child Welfare Information Gateway: https://www.childwelfare.gov
Child Welfare Information Gateway Podcast Series: https://www.childwelfare.gov/more-tools-resources/podcast
Child Welfare League of America: https://www.cwla.org
Children's Bureau: https://www.all4kids.org
Congressional Coalition on Adoption Institute: http://ccainstitute.org
Foster Care to Success: https://www.fc2success.org/knowledge-center/groups-and-support
National Child Traumatic Stress Network: https://www.nctsn.org

Title IV-E Prevention Services Clearinghouse: https://preventionservices.abtsites.com

Youth.gov: https://www.youth.gov

References

Adoption and Safe Families Act of 1997, Pub. L. 105–89, 111 Stat. 2115 (1997).

Altman, J. C. (2008). A study of engagement in neighborhood-based child welfare services. *Research on Social Work Practice, 18*(6), 555–564. https://doi.org/10.1177/1049731507309825

Altshuler, S. J. (2003). From barriers to successful collaboration: Public schools and child welfare working together. *Social Work, 48*(1), 52–63. https://doi.org/10.1093/sw/48.1.52

Bogo, M., Shlonsky, A., Lee, B., & Serbinski, S. (2014). Acting like it matters: A scoping review of simulation in child welfare training. *Journal of Public Child Welfare, 8*(1), 70–93. https://doi.org/10.1080/15548732.2013.818610

Cahalane, H., Fusco, R., & Rauktis, M. B. (2012). *Maximizing current and future mobile technology in Pennsylvania's public child welfare system.* University of Pittsburgh School of Social Work.

Cheng, T. C., & Lo, C. C. (2016). Linking worker–parent working alliance to parent progress in child welfare: A longitudinal analysis. *Children and Youth Services Review, 71*, 10–16. https://doi.org/10.1016/j.childyouth.2016.10.028

Child Welfare Information Gateway. (2013). *How the child welfare system works.* U.S. Department of Health and Human Services, Children's Bureau.

Child Welfare Information Gateway. (2016). *Family engagement: Partnering with families to improve child welfare outcomes.* U.S. Department of Health and Human Services, Children's Bureau.

Child Welfare Information Gateway. (2018). *What is child welfare? A guide for educators.* U.S. Department of Health and Human Services, Children's Bureau.

Child Welfare League of America. (1999). *CWLA standards of excellence for services for abused and neglected children and their families* (Rev. ed.).

Children's Bureau. (2016). *The Comprehensive Child Welfare Information System final rule: Overview,* https://www.acf.hhs.gov/cb/resource/ccwis-final-rule-overview

Cohen, S., & Eimicke, W. (1998). *Tools for innovators.* Jossey-Bass.

Collins-Camargo, C., Strolin, J., & Akin, B. (2019). Use of technology to facilitate practice improvement in trauma-informed child welfare systems. *Child Welfare, 97*(3), 85–108.

Council on Social Work Education. (2015). *Educational policy and accreditation standards.* https://www.cswe.org/getattachment/Accreditation/Accreditation-Process/2015-EPAS/2015EPAS_Web_FINAL.pdf.aspx

Cuccaro-Alamin, S., Foust, R., Vaithianathan, R., & Putnam-Hornstein, E. (2017). Risk assessment and decision making in child protective services: Predictive risk modeling in context. *Children and Youth Services Review, 79,* 291–298. https://doi.org/10.1016/j.childyouth.2017.06.027

Damiani-Taraba, G., Dumbrill, G., Gladstone, J., Koster, A., Leslie, B., & Charles, M. (2017). The evolving relationship between casework skills, engagement, and positive case outcomes in child protection: A structural equation model. *Children and Youth Services Review, 79,* 456–462. https://doi.org/10.1016/j.childyouth.2017.05.033

Families First Prevention Services Act, Public Law 110–351, 113–183, 122 & 128 Stat. (2017).

Forrester, D., Westlake, D., & Glynn, G. (2012). Parental resistance and social worker skills: Towards a theory of motivational social work. *Child & Family Social Work, 17*(2), 118–129. https://doi.org/10.1111/j.1365-2206.2012.00837.x

Houldin, A. D., Naylor, M. D., & Haller, D. G. (2004). Physician–nurse collaboration in research in the 21st century. *Journal of Clinical Oncology, 22*(5), 774–776. https://doi.org/10.1200/JCO.2004.08.188

Hubel, G. S., Schreier, A., Hansen, D. J., & Wilcox, B. L. (2013). A case study of the effects of privatization of child welfare on services for children and families: The Nebraska experience. *Children and Youth Services Review, 35,* 2049–2058. https://doi.org/10.1016/j.childyouth.2013.10.011

Hughes, K. (2018). *SACHS research summary: Innovative technologies in child welfare services.* Academy for Professional Excellence.

Kahn, A. J., & Kamerman, S. B. (1999). *Contracting for child and family services: A mission-sensitive guide.* Annie E. Casey Foundation.

Magnuson, D., Patten, N., & Looysen, K. (2012). Negotiation as a style in child protection work. *Child & Family Social Work, 17,* 296–305. https://doi.org/10.1111/j.1365-2206.2011.00780.x

McCroskey, J. (2001). What is family preservation and why does it matter? *Journal of Family Strengths, 5*(2), Article 4.

Myers, S. M., Smith, H. P., & Martin, L. L. (2006). Conducting best practices research in public affairs. *International Journal of Public Policy, 1*(4), 367–378.

National Association of Social Workers. (2013a). *NASW standards for social work case management.* https://www.socialworkers.org/LinkClick.aspx?fileticket=acrzqmEfhlo%3D&portalid=0

National Association of Social Workers. (2013b). *NASW standards for social work practice in child welfare.* https://www.socialworkers.org/LinkClick.aspx?fileticket=zV1G_96nWoI%3D&portalid=0

National Association of Social Workers. (2017). *NASW code of ethics.* https://www.socialworkers.org/About/Ethics/Code-of-Ethics/Code-of-Ethics-English

National Child Traumatic Stress Network. (n.d.). Essential elements, https://www.nctsn.org/trauma-informed-care/trauma-informed-systems/child-welfare/essential-elements

National Child Traumatic Stress Network, Child Welfare Committee. (2013). *Child welfare trauma training toolkit: Comprehensive guide* (3rd ed.). National Center for Child Traumatic Stress.

Oliver, C., & Charles, G. (2016). Enacting firm, fair, and friendly practice: A model for strengths-based child protection relationships? *British Journal of Social Work, 46*(4), 1009–1026. https://doi.org/10.1093/bjsw/bcv015

Petri, L. (2010). Concept analysis of interdisciplinary collaboration. *Nursing Forum, 45,* 73–82. https://doi.org/10.1111/j.1744-6198.2010.00167.x

Platt, D. (2012). Understanding parental engagement with child welfare services: An integrated model. Child & Family Social Work, 17, 138–148. doi:10.1111/j.13652206.2012.00828.x

Proctor, L. J., & Dubowitz, H. (2014). Child neglect: Challenges and controversies. In J.E. Korbin & R.D. Krugman (Eds.), *Handbook of child maltreatment* (pp. 27–62). Springer.

Quinn, A., Sage, K., & Tunseth, P. (2015). An exploration of child welfare workers' opinions of using video assisted visitation (VAV) in the family reunification process. *Journal of Technology in Human Services, 33*(1), 5–15. https://doi.org/10.1080/15228835.2014.998573

Rawlings, M. A., & Blackmer, E. R. (2019). Assessing engagement skills in public child welfare using OSCE: A pilot study. *Journal of Public Child Welfare, 13*(4), 441–461. doi:10.1080/15548732.2018.1509760

Substance Abuse and Mental Health Services Administration. (2015). *National Child Traumatic Stress Initiative: understanding child trauma.* https://www.samhsa.gov/child-trauma/understanding-child-trauma

U.S. Department of Health and Human Services. (2019). Title IV-E Prevention Services Clearinghouse, 2018–2023, https://www.acf.hhs.gov/opre/research/project/title-iv-e-prevention-services-clearinghouse

Walsh, C. R., Conradi, L., & Pauter, S. (2019). Trauma-informed child welfare: From training to practice and policy change. *Journal of Aggression, Maltreatment & Trauma, 28*(4), 407–424. doi:10.1080/10926771.2018.1468372

Weiner, D., Navalkha, C., Abramsohn, E., DePumpo, M., Paradise, K., Stiehl, M., & Lindau, S. T. (2019). Mobile resource referral technology for preventive child welfare services: Implementation and feasibility. *Children and Youth Services Review, 107,* 104499. https://doi.org/10.1016/j.childyouth.2019.104499

Westat & Chapin Hall Center for Children, University of Chicago. (2002). State innovations in child welfare financing. https://aspe.hhs.gov/pdf-report/state-innovations-child-welfare-financing

Woodside-Jiron, H., Jorgenson, S., Strolin-Goltzman, J., & Jorgenson, J. (2019). "The glue that makes the glitter stick": Preliminary outcomes associated with a trauma-informed, resiliency-based, interprofessional graduate course for child welfare, mental health, and education. *Journal of Public Child Welfare, 13*(3), 307–324. https://doi.org/10.1080/15548732.2019.1600630

Case Management and Persons with Intellectual and Developmental Disabilities

Richard S. Glaesser

Developments during the past century in public health programs, medical care, and institutional and residential settings have led to increased life span for persons with intellectual and developmental disabilities (IDD) (Braddock et al., 2017). But disparities in health have led to this group's lower life expectancy compared to that of the general population (Coppus, 2013; Williamson, 2015). Persons with IDD are a unique group given their complex medical needs and requirements for lifetime supports (The ARC, 2016). This chapter provides an overview of features related to persons with IDD and their families, and it focuses on key competencies of social work case management that underpin a best practice intervention for supporting this population's needs.

Intellectual disability (formerly titled mental retardation) is defined as a neurodevelopmental disability, occurring before age 18 years, involving limitations in adaptive skills (i.e., practical, social, and conceptual abilities) and intellectual functioning [i.e., limitations in problem-solving, learning, and reasoning; assessed at intelligence quotient (IQ) of 70 or below] (American Psychiatric Association, 2013). Developmental disability is a chronic, severe disability due to a physical and/or mental impairment, diagnosed prior to age 22 years (Developmental Disabilities Act of 2000; PL 106-402). Examples of developmental disabilities include cerebral palsy, autism, epilepsy, and intellectual disabilities. Causes of IDD include preterm birth, substance abuse during pregnancy (e.g., alcohol or drugs), infectious disease, and/or chromosomal or genetic abnormalities (Centers for Disease Control and Prevention, 2019).

Prevalence

More than 7 million persons with IDD reside in the United States (Braddock et al., 2017). Approximately 1.2 million (17%) receive state-provided long-term services and supports (LTSS), and more than 200,000 persons are on a waiting list for government services (Larson et al., 2019). Fifty-eight percent of persons with

IDD live with a family member; 25% reside in a group home, intermediate care facility, or other group setting; 12% live independently; and 5% live in a host home (i.e., foster home for adults with IDD) (Braddock et al., 2017). More recent trends show increased rates of IDD among children (aged 3–17 years) from 12.8% in 1997–1999 to 17.8% in 2015–2017, likely indicating improvements in diagnostic criteria and identifying the condition (Jenco, 2019). Regarding gender, more boys (8.15%) than girls (4.29%) are diagnosed with a developmental disability (Zablotsky et al., 2017).

Persons with Intellectual and Developmental Disabilities and Their Families

Families (mostly parents) are the main caregivers to persons with IDD who need lifetime supports in daily living (Heller et al., 2017). Caregiving, in this regard, is a lifelong commitment that can last upwards of 60 years compared to an average of 4 years for caregivers in the general population (Haley & Perkins, 2004; National Alliance for Caregiving & AARP, 2015). Most families adjust well to having a member with IDD, but the cumulative effect of lifetime care provision puts families at risk of social isolation, psychological and physical exhaustion, and care recipient mistreatment (e.g., psychological, sexual, physical, and/or financial abuse/neglect) (Heller & Factor, 2008; Orfila et al., 2018; Perkins, 2009). Furthermore, many parental caregivers have fewer resources to offset a financial emergency such as job loss, health problems, or other crisis (Parish et al., 2010). Currently, both state and federal funding for services and supports do not properly meet the financial needs of parental caregivers.

A large percentage of parents of persons with IDD are aged 60 years or older (Coyle et al., 2014). Thus, typical (i.e., referring to no disability) adult siblings are the likely choice to assume future caregiving when parents are not able (Burke et al., 2015). This transition of care, however, usually occurs during a crisis when parents are sick, aging, or have died (Vanhoutteghem et al., 2014). Furthermore, 40% of families have not planned for the future of their member with IDD and do not involve their typical children in long-term planning yet expect them to provide financial support and legal guardianship (Lauderdale & Huston, 2012). If formal supports (e.g., government services and supports) are unavailable, the typical sibling caregiver may be required to provide residence (Glaesser, 2018). Co-residence can have a major impact on the quality of life for sibling caregivers and their families. The post-transitional outcome for typical siblings who assume the caregiving role can affect well-being, family functioning, and career growth (Glaesser, 2018). Social work case managers can assist families of persons with IDD to plan for the future of their loved one by assessing, coordinating, and linking persons to LTSS.

Comorbidities and Health Disparities

Although adults with IDD are experiencing longer lives and have greater access to medical care, they have inadequate access to quality and preventive care (Williamson, 2015). Women with IDD are less likely to receive needed screenings and may postpone care (Parish & Huh, 2006; Parish & Saville, 2006). But children and older adults with IDD also experience higher levels of health inequities compared to children and older adults with no disabilities (The Ohio State University Wexner Medical Center, 2017). Children with IDD use more health services than typical children but experience more unmet health needs (Lindly et al., 2016). Unmet health needs in childhood can lead to poor health and lower functioning in adulthood (Lindly et al., 2016). Older adults with IDD are also disproportionately at higher risk for secondary conditions such as asthma, high cholesterol, obesity, diabetes, heart disease, arthritis, and high blood pressure (Franklin et al., 2019).

Limited access to health care can have a financial and employment consequence for families who must pay more to support a member's medical services or stop working to support their activities of daily living (e.g., cleaning, cooking, bathing, laundry, and transportation to medical appointments) (The ARC, 2016). A major concern among adolescents with IDD (aged 12–19 years) is the rate of obesity (38–42%) compared to typically developing adolescents (20.9%); causes of obesity include poor diet, sedentary behavior, and disability type (Franklin et al., 2019).

Barriers to proper health care include challenges among persons with IDD to understand information and/or communicate their health care needs (Greenwood et al., 2014; Williamson, 2015), health care providers' inability to understand and assess patients (Tyler et al., 2010), and health care providers ill-equipped and poorly trained to work with persons with IDD (Warfield et al., 2015). Social determinants of health care inequalities include age, race/ethnicity, social isolation, lower education, lower socioeconomic status, and poor health education (Bodde & Seo, 2009; Krahn et al., 2006).

Services and Supports

Approximately 90% of persons with IDD receive LTSS at home—that is, through natural supports (e.g., unpaid, family caregiving) or through community-based supports (formal supports such as paid caregiving). Most persons with IDD depend on formal services and supports to work and live in the community (Larson et al., 2019). But many individuals with IDD require lifetime supports due to limitations in self-care (The ARC, 2016; Glaesser, 2018). There are many legislative and funding efforts, but these have strict eligibility requirements. Medicaid (i.e., the health services program administered by the Centers for

Medicare and Medicaid Services) remains the main source of LTSS funding for persons with IDD (Williamson, 2015). Programs include Children's Health Insurance Program (CHIP; i.e., program for children with IDD containing financial eligibility requirement; provides diagnosis, treatment, and behavioral and physical services) (Musumeci & Chidambaram, 2019), Intermediate Care Facilities for Individuals with Intellectual Disabilities (ICF/IDD; i.e., program providing bundled service package including physician, nursing, dental, pharmacy, nutritional, and rehabilitative care) (Centers for Medicare and Medicaid Services, 2016), and Home and Community-Based Waiver [HCBS; i.e., fee-for-service program in which persons with IDD can select services based on funding allotment, including case management, family caregiver stipend (in some states), respite, behavioral and medical supports, residential/group home services, employment and community participation, environmental modifications, and transportation] (Larson et al., 2019).

Social Work Case Management and Persons with Intellectual and Developmental Disabilities

The roots of social work case management date back to the profession's origin. Social work case management is a multifaceted role that involves applying key competencies for efficiency in program and service delivery to individuals and their families. These competencies involve community outreach (identifying persons requiring supports), functional assessment (assessing persons for needed services), coordination and linkage (coordinating and linking persons to services), monitoring and evaluating (monitoring and evaluating for services' effectiveness), and advocacy (advocating for additional services when gaps are exposed).

Influence of Disability on Developmental Stages Across the Life Course

Social work case management for persons with IDD can be challenging given this population's many distinctive, lifelong needs for health care and LTSS. A person's disability can affect their developmental stages (Smart, 2012). Case management must consider stages of development throughout the life course to understand persons' health care and service needs at different life stages. For instance, childhood developmental disabilities can have lifelong consequences that affect expected future transitions regarding the social, biological, and psychological milestones typical children experience. As persons with IDD age, the loss in physical and mental acuity associated with having a developmental disability increases, resulting in even greater challenges. Families remain the primary support to persons with IDD. Unfortunately, these families also experience emotional, physical, and financial challenges associated with providing lifelong care to their member with IDD. Depending on the setting, social work case managers may encounter persons with IDD and their families at their home, hospital, group home, assisted living facility, intermediate care facility, and/or through a public or private service provider.

Key Competencies of Social Work Case Management for Persons with Intellectual and Developmental Disabilities

Social work case managers for persons with IDD may work independently, as a contracted Medicaid service (i.e., Medicaid Targeted Case Management), through an agency, or as part of a larger multidisciplinary team in various settings. The following key competencies outline the actions of case management for organizing services and supports:

- Community outreach: Identifying persons with IDD and their families within the community (e.g., at home, hospital, school, group home, assisted living facility, intermediate care facility, and/or long-term care facility) who have little knowledge of and access to case management services that can provide information and coordinate important resources.
- Functional assessment: Assessing overall functionality of the person with IDD and their family at different stages throughout the life course to determine services and supports required. Functional assessments focus on activities of daily living (ADLs); instrumental activities of daily living (IADLs); safe home environment; physical functioning; cognitive, psychological, and behavioral functioning; family functioning; legal status; and circle of supports.
  - ADLs: Evaluating individual's skills to perform tasks in self-care (e.g., ambulating, toileting, and bathing). ADLs are measured to assess the individual's adaptive functioning.
  - IADLs: Measure of individual's ability to live independently in the community based on different tasks (e.g., housekeeping, managing medication, and shopping).
  - Safe home environment: Evaluating home environment safety for risk of falls, hygiene and nutrition, and cleanliness.
  - Physical functioning: Regular examination of individual's primary and secondary health conditions to determine medical and preventive care needs at all life course stages.
  - Cognitive, psychological, and behavioral functioning: For children, conduct initial diagnosis to determine primary and

secondary physical and mental health condition(s), between 3 and 6 years of age (healthychildren.org, 2015; Logsdon, 2019). Testing involves assessing IQ, adaptive behavior, and blood panel (Gentile et al., 2019). From childhood throughout adulthood, ongoing, annual testing must be performed to assess cognitive functioning, including memory loss, impaired decision-making or judgment, signs of anxiety or depression, changes in behavior, interpersonal functioning, mental status, and/or signs of delirium.

- Family functioning: Observe family dynamics for positive or negative transactional patterns between members to assess for cohesion and adaptability within the family caregiving unit. Positive family functioning includes open communication, high levels of affection, and greater presentation of self-esteem among all family members. Negative family functioning exposes poor communication, lower levels of affection, and less ability to adapt, leading to greater conflict and dysfunction.
- Legal status: Determining the legal status of persons with IDD as related to self-guardianship or guardianship through a family member or court-appointment guardian ad litem. As mandated by law, within the scope of self-determination and person-centered practices, all programs, services, and supports must involve the individual's choice, recommendation, and/or agreement, no matter the person's legal status.
- Coordination and linkage: After assessing a person with IDD and their family, the types of services needed can be determined. Typically, a treatment or support plan is developed that outlines all services decided on by the person with IDD (with the support of family, the social work case manager, and,

possibly, the service provider representative and state agency representative). This process involves educating persons with IDD and their families about eligibility, availability, and types of service supports. The final step includes coordinating and linking persons to programs (e.g., CHIP, ICF/IDD, HCBS waiver, Social Security Disability Income, and Supplemental Security Income).
- Monitor and evaluation: At predetermined time intervals, it is important for social work case managers to monitor and evaluate the services' efficacy to determine whether they are achieving their intended objective. If a service does not achieve its goal, case managers must source other service options.
- Advocacy: Advocate on behalf of persons with IDD and their families for services and supports due to assessed needs, waiting lists, and/or service gaps. Educate and empower persons with IDD, families, and other key stakeholder groups to push for needed services.

Best Practice Considerations and Key Competencies

There is limited evidence regarding the effectiveness of case management for persons with IDD. However, existing disparities in health and long waiting lists for services and supports may provide evidence of this deficiency. Successful case management involves best practice approaches, rooted in key competencies, that consider the person's biopsychosocial status and transactional influence at the micro and macro levels. Based on these key competencies, the following items are suggested as a best practice approach to case management:

- Micro level
  - Biopsychosocial assessment: This assessment forms the basis for any case management process that reviews

the following features: personal data, health status, emotional status, cognitive functioning, functional status, cultural issues, circles of supports (i.e., family members, social work case manager, and service provider representative), caregiver support system, financial status, and vocational status.

- Functional assessment: Employ case management skills for ongoing evaluation of functionality regarding physical status; safe home environment; and cognitive, psychological, and behavioral status to identify at-risk persons.
- Individual therapeutic engagement: Engage individual in therapeutic relationship to understand goals and desires for independence, including potential for living independently, furthering education (e.g., higher education for persons with IDD), and/or future employment.
- Family/caregiver support: Engage family caregivers with crisis management to help cope with unplanned transitions such as aging parental caregivers unable to fulfill the caregiving role, transition of care to adult sibling caregivers, or difficulties managing their member with IDD. Implement family treatment interventions to reduce the stress and burden of care provision through positive interactions and functioning between family members.
- Macro level
  - Community-based supports: Become familiar with extent of services and supports available, including home and community-based services and eligibility requirements for attaining benefits/funding supports that can reduce the economic and social challenges of caregiving. Continuing advocacy for sourcing a variety of services through different agencies.

- Circle of support (multidisciplinary team approach): Collaborate with key stakeholders [e.g., natural supports (family members), social work case manager, service provider representative, and/or state agency representative] and person with IDD to discuss results of biopsychosocial assessment and determine service needs that reflect the decision of the person supported. Educate all stakeholders on self-determination and person-centered decision-making, ensuring all final decisions include the goals and desires of the person supported.

Status of Medicaid Programs

Currently, legislative and funding challenges to Medicaid programs have a direct impact on service provision, reducing service dollars spent per person (Larson et al., 2019). Persons with IDD incur the greatest per capita spending of all Medicaid beneficiaries, comprising 15% of all recipients but spending 42% of the total Medicaid budget (Connolly & Paradise, 2012). Currently, service demands exceed supply, and greater numbers of persons await services. To reduce waiting lists and curb spiraling Medicaid costs, privatized managed care long-term services and supports (MLTSS) has emerged as a potential panacea (Larson et al., 2019). Within the MLTSS model, service recipients receive a similar scope of services (as within the HCBS fee-for-service model) but through a singular provider [i.e., managed care organization (MCO)] on a per-member per-month rate (Gifford et al., 2011). Reported challenges include limited cost savings, stakeholders skeptical of managed care, and MCO's lack of experience with this population (Lewis et al., 2018). Currently, growth of managed care is slow, and there are few persons enrolled in MLTSS (Saucier et al., 2012).

Conclusion

Persons with IDD and their families continue to face many challenges. Service limitations and poor funding have created great strain on families who must provide for their member with IDD (Larson et al., 2019). Although persons with IDD are enjoying longer lives, many have secondary physical and mental health conditions yet experience broad inequities in health care. Most persons with IDD and their families (e.g., parental and sibling caregivers) depend on LTSS to survive. However, fragmented service delivery, long waiting lists for services, and reduced funding have negatively impacted family caregivers. Providing care to a person with IDD is a lifelong commitment that can be socially isolating as well as physically, psychologically, and financially overwhelming. As the needs of this population continue, social work case managers will be tasked to identify and advocate for policies and services. In the context of persons with IDD and their families, it is the role of the social work case manager to enhance the emotional, cognitive, social, and physical functioning to improve the overall well-being of this group.

Helpful Resources

Association of University Centers on Disabilities—Research group providing information on individuals with intellectual and developmental disabilities, their families, and the community: https://www.aucd.org/template/index.cfm

Case Management Society of America— National group providing practice and policy resources and standards of practice for case management: https://www.cmsa.org

Centers for Medicare and Medicaid Services—Information and guide to Medicaid funding programs: https://www.cms.gov

Family Caregiver Alliance—National group providing information, support, and resources for family caregivers: https://www.caregiver.org/about-family-caregiver-alliance-fca

National Association of Councils on Developmental Disabilities—National advocacy group and information resource representing state and local developmental disabilities councils throughout the United States: https://www.nacdd.org

Sibling Leadership Network—National advocacy group providing information, resources, and networking for sibling caregivers of persons with disabilities: https://siblingleadership.org/about

The ARC—Advocacy and information source regarding persons with intellectual and developmental disabilities: https://thearc.org

References

American Psychiatric Association. (2013). *Diagnostic and statistical manual of mental disorders* (5th ed.). American Psychiatric Publishing.

Bodde, A. E., & Seo, D. C. (2009). A review of social and environmental barriers to physical activity for adults with intellectual disabilities. *Disability and Health Journal, 2*(2), 57–66.

Braddock, D., Hemp, R., Tanis, E. S., Wu, J., & Haffer, L. (2017). *The state of the states in intellectual and developmental disabilities* (11th ed.). The American Association for Intellectual and Developmental Disabilities.

Burke, M. M., Fish, T., & Lawton, K. (2015). A comparative engagement analysis of adult siblings' perceptions toward caregiving. *Intellectual and Developmental Disabilities, 53,* 143–157.

Centers for Disease Control and Prevention. (2019, September 26). *Facts about developmental disabilities.* https://www.cdc.gov/ncbddd/developmentaldisabilities/facts.html

Centers for Medicare and Medicaid Services. (2016, November 22). *Intermediate care facilities for individuals with intellectual disabilities (ICF/IID).* https://www.cms.gov/Medicare/Provider-Enrollment-and-Certification/CertificationandComplianc/ICFIID

Connolly, J., & Paradise, J. (2012). *People with disabilities and Medicaid managed care: Key issues to consider.* http://kaiserfamilyfoundation.files.wordpress.com/2013/01/8278.pdf

Coppus, A. M. W. (2013). People with intellectual disability: What do we know about adulthood and life expectancy? *Developmental Disabilities Research Reviews, 18*(1), 6–16.

Coyle, C. E., Kramer, J., & Mutchler, J. E. (2014). Aging together: Sibling carers of adults with intellectual and developmental disabilities. *Journal of Policy and Practice in Intellectual Disabilities, 11,* 302–312.

Franklin, M. S., Beyer, L. N., Brotkin, S. M., Maslow, G. R., Pollock, M. D., & Docherty, S. L. (2019). Health care transition for adolescent and young adults with intellectual disability: Views from the parents. *Journal of Pediatric Nursing, 47,* 148–158.

Gentile, J. P., Cowan, A. E., & Dixon, D. W. (Eds.). (2019). *Guide to intellectual disabilities: A clinical handbook*. Springer.

Gifford, K., Smith, V. K., Snipes, D., & Paradise, J. (2011). *A profile of Medicaid managed care programs in 2010: Findings from a 50-state survey*. https://kaiserfamilyfoundation.files.wordpress.com/2013/01/8220-es.pdf

Glaesser, R. S. (2018). *Transition of persons with developmental disabilities from parental to sibling co-residential care: Effects on sibling caregiver well-being and family functioning*. Doctoral dissertation, University of South Florida. http://scholarcommons.usf.edu/etd/7155

Greenwood, N. W., Dreyfus, D., & Wilkinson, J. (2014). More than just a mammogram: Breast cancer screening perspectives of relatives of women with intellectual disability. *Intellectual and Developmental Disabilities, 52*(6), 444–455.

Haley, W. E., & Perkins, E. A. (2004). Current status and future directions in family caregiving and aging people with intellectual disabilities. *Journal of Policy and Practice in Intellectual Disabilities, 1*, 24–30.

healthychildren.org. (2015, December 18). *Children with intellectual disabilities*. https://www.healthychildren.org/English/health-issues/conditions/developmental-disabilities/Pages/Intellectual-Disability.aspx

Heller, T., & Factor, A. (2008). Family support and intergenerational caregiving: Report from the State of the Science in Aging with Developmental Disabilities Conference. *Disability and Health Journal, 1*, 131–135.

Heller, T., Scott, H., & Janicki, M. (2017). *Caregiving and intellectual and developmental disabilities and dementia: Report of the pre-summit workgroup on caregiving and intellectual and developmental disabilities*. National Task Group on Intellectual Disabilities and Dementia Practices. http://rrtcadd.org/wp-content/uploads/2017/08/NIH-Presummit-on-IDD-Brief-FINAL-8-12-17_v2a.pdf

Jenco, M. (2019, September 26). Study: 1 in 6 children has developmental disability. *AAP News*. https://www.aappublications.org/news/2019/09/26/disabilities092619

Krahn, G. L., Hammond, L., & Turner, A. (2006). A cascade of disparities: Health and health care access for people with intellectual disabilities. *Mental Retardation and Developmental Disabilities, 12*, 70–82.

Larson, S., Eschenbacher, H., & Pettingell, S. L. (2019). Housing: A place to call home. In A. S. Hewitt & K. M. Nye-Lengerman (Eds.), *Community living and participation for people with intellectual and developmental disabilities* (pp. 53–68). American Association on Intellectual and Developmental Disabilities.

Lauderdale, M., & Huston, S. J. (2012). Financial therapy and planning for families with special needs children. *Journal of Financial Therapy, 3*(1), 3.

Lewis, S., Patterson, R., & Alter, M. (2018, June 11). *Current landscape: Managed long-term services and supports for people with intellectual and developmental disabilities*. ANCOR. https://www.ancor.org/sites/default/files/ancor_mltss_report_-_final.pdf

Lindly, O. J., Chavez, A. E., & Zuckerman, K. E. (2016). Unmet health services needs among US children with developmental disabilities: Associations with family impact and child functioning. *Journal of Developmental and Behavioral Pediatrics, 37*(9), 712–723.

Logsdon, A. (2019, November 7). *Common developmental disabilities in children*. Verywell Family. https://www.verywellfamily.com/what-are-developmental-disabilities-2162827

Musumeci, M., & Chidambaram, P. (2019, June 12). *Medicaid's role for children with special health care needs: A look at eligibility, services, and spending*. Kaiser Family Foundation. https://www.kff.org/medicaid/issue-brief/medicaids-role-for-children-with-special-health-care-needs-a-look-at-eligibility-services-and-spending

National Alliance for Caregiving & AARP. (2015). *2015 report: Caregiving in the U.S.* https://www.aarp.org/content/dam/aarp/ppi/2015/caregiving-in-the-united-states-2015-report-revised.pdf

Orfila, F., Coma-Solé, M., Cabanas, M., Cegri-Lombardo, F., Moleras-Serra, A., & Pujol-Ribera, E. (2018). Family caregiver mistreatment of the elderly: Prevalence of risk and associated factors. *BMC Public Health, 18*(1), 167.

Parish, S. L., & Huh, J. (2006). Health care for women with disabilities: Population-based evidence of disparities. *Health and Social Work, 31*(1), 7–15.

Parish, S. L., Rose, R. A., & Swaine, J. G. (2010). Financial well-being of US parents caring for coresident children and adults with developmental disabilities: An age cohort analysis. *Journal of Intellectual and Developmental Disability, 35*, 235–243.

Parish, S. L., & Saville, A. W. (2006). Women with cognitive limitations in the community: Evidence of disability-based disparities in health care. *Mental Retardation, 44*(4), 249–259.

Perkins, E. A. (2009). *Caregivers of adults with intellectual disabilities: The relationship of compound caregiving and reciprocity to quality of life*. Doctoral dissertation. Available from ProQuest Dissertations and Theses database (UMI No. 3420612).

Saucier, P., Kasten, J., Burwell, B., & Gold, L. (2012). *The growth of managed long-term services and supports (MLTSS) programs: A 2012 update*. https://www.medicaid.gov/medicaid/downloads/mltssp_white_paper_combined.pdf

Smart, J. (2012). Major demographics changes and ways in which disabilities interact with stages of development. In *Disabilities across the developmental lifespan: For the rehabilitation counselor* (pp. 105–128). Springer.

The ARC. (2016). Medicaid issues for people with disabilities. http://www.thearc.org/what-we-do/public-policy/policy-issues/medicaid

The Ohio State University Wexner Medical Center. (2017, September 11). *Study: Individuals with developmental disabilities experience health disparities.* . https://wexnermedical.osu.edu/mediaroom/pressreleaselisting/study-individuals-with-developmental-disabilities-experience-healthcare-disparities

Tyler, C. V., Jr., Schramm, S., Karafa, M., Tang, A. S., & Jain, A. (2010). Electronic health record analysis of the primary care of adults with intellectual and other developmental disabilities. *Journal of Policy and Practice in Intellectual Disabilities, 7*(3), 204–210.

Vanhoutteghem, I., Hove, G., D'haene, G., & Soyez, V. (2014). "I never thought I would have to do this": Narrative study with siblings-in-law who live together with a family member with a disability. *British Journal of Learning Disabilities, 4,* 315–322.

Warfield, M. E., Crossman, M. K., Delahaye, J., Der Weerd, E., & Kuhlthau, K. A. (2015). Physician perspectives on providing primary medical care to adults with autism spectrum disorders (ASD). *Journal of Autism and Developmental Disorders, 45*(7), 2209–2217.

Williamson, H. J. (2015). *Implementation of Medicaid managed long-term services and supports for adults with intellectual and/or developmental disabilities: A state's experience.* Doctoral dissertation, University of South Florida. http://scholarcommons.usf.edu/etd/6053

Zablotsky, B., Black, L. I., & Blumberg, S. J. (2017, November). *Estimated prevalence of children with diagnosed developmental disabilities in the United States, 2014-2016.* National Center for Health Statistics, Centers for Disease Control and Prevention. https://www.cdc.gov/nchs/products/databriefs/db291.htm

Case Management with Refugees and Asylum Seekers

Leticia Villarreal Sosa and Suhad Tabahi

According to the United Nations High Commissioner for Refugees (UNHCR; 2019), we are witnessing an unprecedented 70.8 million people worldwide who have been forced to leave their home as a result of persecution or violence. Of those, 41.3 million are internally displaced, 25.9 million are refugees, and 3.5 million are asylum seekers. The largest share of refugees (46.5%) to the United States came from Africa, followed by 16.9% from Near East/South Asia, 16.3% from East Asia, 16.1% from Europe, and 4.2% from Latin America and the Caribbean (American Immigration Council, 2020). In terms of asylum applications to the United States, as of 2018, the countries with the highest number were El Salvador, Guatemala, Venezuela, Honduras, and Mexico (UNHCR, 2018).

Despite the growing number of people who have become displaced in the past 10 years, refugee resettlement has dropped to historic lows in the United States. The United States is no longer the leading country in refugee admissions (Krogstad, 2019), even though the capacity to do so far exceeds that of most other countries. The decrease in numbers of refugees received in the United States has also led to reduced funding for refugee services because resettlement agencies are provided a lump sum per refugee to fund services (National Immigration Forum, 2019). The decline in funding, and other policies such as not authorizing agencies serving less than 100 refugees to assist new arrivals, has led to the closure of more than 100 agencies and the dismantling of the refugee resettlement infrastructure that cannot be easily rebuilt (Karas, 2019). It is within this context of uncertainty and reduced funding that case management is taking place, necessitating an approach that includes assuming multiple roles.

Shared Language

Before continuing to discuss case management with refugees and asylum seekers, it is important to define several key terms:

- *Refugee*: A refugee is someone who has experienced a natural disaster, political disturbance, or had to flee their country of origin because they are at risk of human rights violations or persecution. Under U.S. law, a refugee is someone who cannot return to their homeland due to a "well-founded fear of persecution" due to membership in a particular social group or their political opinions. This legal definition is based on The Refugee Act of 1980.[1]

- *Migrant*: Migrant refers to a person who changes their country of residence regardless of the reason or legal status. It is important to note that migrants are still entitled to have their human rights protected. Distinctions between voluntary and involuntary migration are not clear-cut. This distinction can conceal the complexities and causes of migration, and it can lead to migrants who may be "unrecognized" refugees and therefore not eligible for services (Hugo & Kwok Bun, 1990).

- *Asylum seeker*: An asylum seeker is an individual who is targeted for persecution or abuse in the country of origin based on race, ethnicity, religion, or political opinion. An asylum seeker claims to be a refugee, but their claim has not yet been determined by the country in which they are seeking asylum. According to Amnesty International (2020), "Not every asylum seeker will ultimately be recognized as a refugee, but every refugee is initially an asylum seeker" (para. 1).

- *Asylee*: An asylee is an individual who meets the definition of refugee and is already present in the United States or is seeking admission at a port of entry. Asylees may apply for green card status 1 year after their asylum status is approved [U.S. Department of Homeland Security (DHS), n.d.].

refugee status and resettlement in the United States, the resettlement process begins. The U.S. Refugee Resettlement Program (USRAP) has been lauded as one of the most successful humanitarian programs in the United States, settling more than 3 million refugees since it was established in 1980 (Kerwin, 2018). The primary measure of success for resettlement programs has been self-sufficiency through employment, which is overwhelmingly met (Kerwin, 2018).

However, Shaw and Poulin (2015) note that the general goal of resettlement to help incoming refugees achieve economic self-sufficiency is not enough and argue that there is a need for attention to increased well-being as a critical outcome of the resettlement process. Furthermore, they find that standard resettlement case management, lasting for only 6 months, is not as effective at improving outcomes compared to case management over a 24-month period. Finally, in the resettlement process, it is important to note that public–private partnerships have been instrumental in service provision by providing substantial in-kind and financial support complementing federal dollars, and these should be strengthened (Kerwin, 2015). Despite the overall successful integration of refugees, barriers to economic success include factors such as food insecurity, social isolation, mental health challenges, and lack of access to health care. Thus, case management is a critical component of refugee resettlement that can assist with addressing these factors.

Resettlement Process

Once a refugee undergoes a rigorous screening process, including a security screening, and it is determined that they are eligible for both

Case Management

As refugees begin the process of starting their lives in a new country, caseworkers are critical in the resettlement process. Having roots in the

---

1. The Refugee Act of 1980 was passed unanimously and signed into law by President Jimmy Carter. This law established a clear and flexible policy for refugee resettlement, raised the ceiling on the number of refugees, and provided flexibility for an increase in numbers in times of emergencies. This law changed the definition to a person with a "well founded fear of persecution," which was standard established by the United Nations protocols. This act also created an Office of Refugee Resettlement.

19th and 20th centuries, casework has evolved over time, such as shifting to a more active client role and in partnership with the service provider. Despite these changes in casework, the legacies of a needs-based approach remain. A needs-based approach is based on a deficit model with outcomes set by the professional, and the process is laden with values of the service provider rather than the service user. In contrast, a rights-based approach focuses on human rights and the importance of active participation in decision-making, places equal value on process and outcomes, and holds that all persons have a right to safety.

A human rights approach applies to casework with refugees in two specific areas. First, all people have basic human rights, such as the right to safety; the right to worship based on their religious beliefs; the right to access to education, health care, and food; and the right to privacy. Thus, pre- and post-arrival services are designed to help service users meet these basic needs. Second, a human rights approach emphasizes the collaborative nature of the relationship and participation in decision-making. It is important to remember that refugees are semi-voluntary service users in that they often do not have choices about where to receive services. Thus, it is important to spend time clearly explaining consent for services, that they can refuse your services, and what might happen if they do so.

Case Management Role

In order to best serve the refugee community, case managers must understand social work principles and ethics and apply them to the everyday situations encountered. Case managers provide individualized planning and counseling, but they also identify additional services to best meet mental health needs to address trauma and other health-related issues refugees experience. The role of a case manager is complex, encompassing being a broker, an advocate, a teacher/educator, and a social change agent. According to Klimek (2011), as a case manager working with refugees and asylum seekers, functions include the following:

Client assessment: This phase includes assessing needs, the situation, and resources. When working with refugees, it is imperative that this assessment be conducted with humility and sensitivity, recognizing the stigma and taboos often associated with sharing personal information and seeking assistance.

Service planning: This phase includes collaboratively identifying services and resources that are accessible and designing and implementing a holistic intervention plan focused on resettlement.

Linkage and service coordination: In this phase, the service user is connected with services that are accessible and meet their needs. This may entail working with clients to set up the appointments and ensuring that they understand the logistics of accessing and receiving services. Interpretation services should be explored if needed.

Follow-up and monitoring service delivery: This phase involves ensuring that service users and their families receive the intended services and are getting their needs met. The case worker checks in to determine if new circumstances need to be addressed.

In this process of navigating the complex role, a useful approach is that of accompaniment. Accompaniment is collaborative, based on mutual respect and equality in the relationship, and focuses on the outcomes deemed important by the service user. Accompaniment is also about being present with another's emotional and spiritual pain, without an emphasis on "fixing." Accompaniment centers the relationship, which is critical for case management with refugee populations. Villarreal Sosa et al. (2019) found that service users "felt respected, empowered, and reported less isolation and stress" (p. 18) after receiving accompaniment services.

Family Case Management

A family case management approach provides more holistic services. One promising model considers a two-generation, whole family strategy grounded in the recognition that supporting children is key to successful adaptation in the United States. In this whole family approach, families are provided with 2 years of holistic case management services, which may include regular assessments and identification of family needs for services such as microloans and mental health services. A second model is family case management funded by the U.S. Immigration and Customs Enforcement and used between 2016 and 2017 to address the needs of families seeking asylum at the border as an alternative to detention (Obser, 2019). Despite documenting success with government goals (99% appearance rate at immigration hearings) and being a humane alternative to detention at only a fraction of the cost, the program was terminated after only a year and half as part of the Trump administration's increased use of family separation and detention (Obser, 2019). Family case management has been a successful approach to meeting the needs of asylum seekers, refugees, and government goals. Even if not formally using a family case management model, it is important for case managers to consider the whole family in service provision for most effective results.

Peer Support

In many cases, agencies who offer resettlement services utilize a peer-support approach to case management. Peers play an important role as brokers between cultures and systems, often serving as "bridge builders" (Shaw, 2014, p.

288). Peers also provide reassurance and are a source of empowerment by demonstrating the possibilities for the future. In addition, use of peer case managers can result in fewer delays in accessing services and can be cost-effective due to eliminating the language barrier and the need for translators. Although utilizing peers can provide many benefits, they run the risk of burnout due to the intensity of vicarious trauma (Shaw, 2014). In addition, stress and cultural conflict are common when caseworkers share ethnic, cultural, and linguistic backgrounds (Shaw, 2014). Utilizing peer case managers can be an important source of support for refugees; however, peer case managers must be provided with adequate support, supervision, and capacity-building to help them effectively manage this complex role.

Refugee Populations

Three key groups that have been both targeted in this xenophobic context and make up a large share of either the refugee population or asylum applicants are discussed in this section. Beyond these particular groups, we encourage case managers to have basic information about the refugee population they serve, including the dynamics between the country of origin of the refugees and the United States.

Unaccompanied Minors

Unaccompanied minors are children younger than age 18 years who enter the United States with an unauthorized status and do not have a parent or legal guardian with them. According to UNHCR (2018), there were 136,600 unaccompanied children worldwide in 2018. There continues to be an increase in numbers of unaccompanied minors apprehended along the U.S.–Mexico border, with the largest numbers from Mexico, El Salvador, Guatemala, and Honduras (Amuedo-Dorantes & Puttitanun, 2016). Children apprehended at the border are detained by DHS and then transferred to the

Office of Refugee Resettlement. Those who escape apprehension often work in agriculture, manufacturing, restaurants, or as domestic workers and are highly vulnerable to exploitation. For those who remain in custody, the shortage of space and resources has left children in deplorable conditions along the border in ICE facilities not meant to house children. Caseworkers should be aware of the trauma children have experienced and work transnationally in connecting youth with their families.

Central Americans

In the 1980s and 1990s, the numbers of Guatemalans, Salvadorians, and Nicaraguans in the United States increased dramatically (Gonzalez, 2011). Civil wars in these countries and the continued instability led to people fleeing their homes. In Guatemala, for example, an international truth commission confirmed that acts of genocide and mass extermination of Mayan communities had occurred (Rothenberg et al., 2012). Furthermore, this violence was a direct result of U.S. involvement in those countries, both militarily and economically (Gonzalez, 2011). U.S. policy can be discriminatory based on the United States' political interests and ideology. For example, the Immigration and Naturalization Service (INS)[2] frequently detained and routinely denied refugee status to Guatemalans and Salvadorians. In these countries, the U.S. provided military aid to right-wing leaders even though government-sponsored terrorism was documented in the region by human rights groups. Both the Reagan and Bush administrations refused to aid those coming across the border escaping terrorism in what they claimed was an effort to stop communism (Gonzalez, 2011). Although civil war is no longer taking place in Central America, the legacy of social

disorganization remains in the form of poverty, gang violence, and internal displacement. Case managers working with those who are granted asylum or are in the process of their application, such as unaccompanied minors, must have a basic understanding of this complex history and its legacy as they work with service users from this region. Finally, because many may not be recognized as refugees, encountering such families in other contexts as case managers is possible.

Middle East and North Africa

Approximately two-thirds of all refugees worldwide are from countries identified under the Middle East and North African (MENA) group: Syria, South Sudan, and Somalia. Between 2005 and 2015, the number of displaced persons increased from 5 million to 23 million and was primarily driven by conflicts in three main MENA countries: Syria, Yemen, and Iraq (Connor, 2016). The U.S. invasion of Iraq in 2003 marked a stark transformation in the landscape of the MENA region. The Iraqi diaspora has been noted as the largest of modern times and is considered a humanitarian crisis (Global Policy Forum, 2017). It is estimated that by the end of 2015, 4.4 million Iraqis had been internally displaced and more than a quarter million were refugees abroad (UNHCR, 2016). Similarly, since the Syrian civil war began in 2011, roughly 6 million Syrians have been internally displaced; 6 million people have fled to neighboring countries; 1 million have sought refuge in Europe; and approximately 100,000 live outside of Europe, the MENA region, and Africa (Connor, 2018).

Of the 6 million who fled Syria, only 18,000 Syrians were resettled in the United States between 2011 and 2016. Despite the widespread displacement caused by the Yemini

---

2. INS no longer exists. INS was part of the U.S. Department of Justice. In 2003, the functions of INS were transferred to the newly formed DHS. There are now three components under DHS: U.S. Citizenship and Immigration Services, U.S. Immigration and Customs Enforcement, and U.S. Customs and Border Protection.

civil war, the United States accepted only 61 refugees from Yemen between 2011 and 2016. Executive orders and the travel ban[3] under the Trump administration greatly affected the inflows of MENA migrants and refugees in 2017. Furthermore, in fiscal year 2019, the U.S. accepted a far greater number of Christian refugees (79%) than Muslim refugees, which is in stark contrast to previous years that saw the highest number of Muslims admitted (Krogstad, 2019). Case managers working with refugees from the MENA region should understand the religious, cultural, and linguistic diversity that exists within the region while also acknowledging the xenophobic social and political challenges that many Muslim refugees experience during the resettlement process.

Mental Health Needs
Trauma and Resilience

Refugees experience significant trauma during pre-migration, migration, and resettlement. People who have fled their country endure factors such as war, political upheaval, structural violence, forced displacement, and exposure to human right violations, leaving them vulnerable to higher rates of trauma-related mental health disorders (Im et al., 2020). Case managers are generally not considered to be clinicians; however, supporting refugees can be complex and access to other services may be limited, leaving case managers in the role of providing mental health support. Although refugees experience a great deal of hardship,

they also demonstrate incredible resilience. Identifying sources of strength and honoring traditional methods of healing can help foster healthy and positive adjustment. It is imperative that case managers acknowledge struggles that refugees experience while affirming their fortitude, will, and strength. The model discussed next could be useful in supporting refugees.

The Multi-tier Model of Refugee Mental Health and Psychosocial Support

Western clinical approaches to working with refugees often lack cultural, religious, and linguistic considerations, and they pathologize [Im et al., 2020; Inter-Agency Standing Committee (IASC), 2007]. The mental health needs of refugees are complex and require acknowledgment of the U.S. political climate that promotes hostility toward refugee populations. Im and colleagues (2020) propose a multitier mental health and psychosocial support (MHPSS)[4] model as a holistic approach to the resettlement process. The MHPSS has four tiers:

1. Case managers assist with social adjustment and integration with services such as vocational training, housing, and school enrollment. Assessment at this stage can determine if services at a higher tier are needed.
2. Family and community support systems focus on healthy coping and include groups around shared issues.

---

3.   U.S. President Donald Trump signed Executive Order 13769, formally titled Protecting the Nation from Foreign Terrorist Entry into the United States and popularly known as the "Muslim ban" in 2017. This ban decreased the number of refugees admitted into the United States, banning foreign nationals from seven Muslim-majority countries; suspended USRAP; and suspended entry of all Syrian refugees indefinitely. Since then, two other Muslim bans were enacted. See the American Civil Liberties Union's timeline of the bans and political/legal responses at https://www.aclu-wa.org/pages/timeline-muslim-ban.

4.   The generic term mental health and psychosocial support (MHPSS) has frequently been used to incorporate into refugee programs in a variety of humanitarian settings. This model was first developed by IASC in the Guidelines on MHPSS in Emergency Settings. The model discussed in this chapter is one that has been adopted from the IASC's MHPSS 2007 model. See https://www.who.int/mental_health/emergencies/guidelines_iasc_mental_health_psychosocial_june_2007.pdf.

3. Bereavement and trauma healing, which can include community-based psychosocial support.
4. Specialized mental health treatment, a two-pillar (culture- and trauma-informed) approach that can be applied in the context of refugee resettlement from the time of arrival through social integration.

MHPSS programs operate under a community-wide collaborative partnership that aligns with the proposed 30- to 90-day resettlement services along with 8-month Medicaid eligibility (IASC, 2007). Such an approach builds on individual capacity and strength as well as community resilience.

Practice Tips for Case Managers

The following practice tips may assist case managers to provide culturally responsive services to promote a successful transition:

- *Check biases*: Cultural humility promotes the idea of lifelong learning and taking a reflective stance. Case managers should engage in reflective practice that acknowledges implicit and explicit biases. Assessment of privilege and power should be an ongoing process.
- *Recognize language and dialects*: Recognize between- and within-group diversity. For example, although the official language of Syria is Arabic, some refugees may be Assyrian and prefer to speak Assyrian. There are also differences in dialects that case managers must be aware of in order to provide the most linguistically appropriate services. It is critical to be sensitive to Indigenous languages, which are often mistaken for dialects and therefore unintentionally devalued.
- *Honor status/professional background*: Caseworkers should remember that although refugees may be seeking assistance in the United States, they may be professionals, highly educated, and have high social status in their country of origin. Caseworkers should respect the service user's skills, knowledge, and resources.
- *Understand routes of migration*: Every refugee has their unique story of how they arrived in the United States. These routes often present refugees with extreme challenges and trauma. Case managers should work to understand the challenges that they overcame, underscore their resilience, and address issues of loss.
- *Be aware of legacies of colonialism*: Case managers should be aware of and understand the context of U.S. interference in the country of origin, often directly or indirectly causing the forced migration.
- *Be a mythbuster*: Contrary to xenophobic rhetoric surrounding refugees, refugees contribute to the success and welfare of the U.S. economy and educational system. Refugees pay on average $20,000 more in taxes than they receive in benefits (Evans & Fitzgerald, 2017), are equally or more educated than U.S.-born citizens, are less likely to access welfare benefits, and have a higher workforce participation rate than native-born citizens (Henry et al., n.d.).
- *Willingness to expand role*: Being a case manager requires one to take on multiple roles, such as an advocate, teacher, counselor, and an informal ambassador to the United States. Successful resettlement and integration require the case manager to be versatile, resourceful, and informed.

Acknowledgments

We acknowledge our graduate assistants, Douglas Barge and Isabel Palencia, for their support and contributions to this chapter.

References

American Immigration Council. (2020, January). Fact sheet: An overview of U.S. refugee law and policy. https://www.americanimmigrationcouncil.org/research/overview-us-refugee-law-and-policy

Amnesty International. (2020). Refugees, asylum-seekers, and migrants. https://www.amnesty.org/en/what-we-do/refugees-asylum-seekers-and-migrants

Amuedo-Dorantes, C., & Puttitanun, T. (2016). DACA and the surge in unaccompanied minors at the U.S.–Mexico border. *International Migration, 54*(4), 102–117. doi:10.1111/imig.12250

Connor, P. (2016, October 18). *Middle East's migrant population more than doubles since 2005: Regional conflict and economic opportunity boost numbers of migrants from 25 million to 54 million.* Pew Research Center. https://www.pewresearch.org/global/2016/10/18/conflicts-in-syria-iraq-and-yemen-lead-to-millions-of-displaced-migrants-in-the-middle-east-since-2005

Connor, P. (2018, January 29). *Most displaced Syrians are in the Middle East, and about a million are in Europe.* Pew Research Center. https://www.pewresearch.org/fact-tank/2018/01/29/where-displaced-syrians-have-resettled

Evans, W., & Fitzgerald, D. (2017, June). *The economic and social outcomes of refugees in the United States: Evidence from the ACS.* National Bureau of Economic Research Working Paper No. 23496. www.nber.org/papers/w23498?utm_campaign=ntw&utm_medium=email&utm_source

Global Policy Forum. (2017). War and occupation in Iraq. https://www.globalpolicy.org/en/publication/war-and-occupation-iraq

Gonzalez, J. (2011). *Harvest of Empire: A history of Latinos in America.* Penguin.

Henry, B. F., Ringler-Jayanthan, E., Brubaker, D., Darling, I., & Wilson, M. (n.d.). *Challenges of refugee resettlement: Policy and psychosocial factors.* National Association of Social Workers. https://www.socialworkers.org/LinkClick.aspx?fileticket=X2QaNfEuJUk%3D&portalid=0

Hugo, G., & Kwok Bun, C. (1990). Conceptualizing and defining refugee and forced migrations in Asia. *Southeast Asian Journal of Social Science, 18*(1), 19–42. https://www.jstor.org/stable/24491752

Im, H., Rodriguez, C., & Grumbine, J. M. (2020). A multitier model of refugee mental health and psychosocial support in resettlement: Toward trauma-informed and culture-informed systems of care. *Psychological Services.* http://dx.doi.org/10.1037/ser0000412

Inter-Agency Standing Committee. (2007). IASC guidelines on mental health and psychosocial support in emergency settings. https://www.who.int/publications/i/item/9789953026275

Karas, T. (2019). US refugee agencies whither as Trump administration cuts numbers to historic lows. Public Radio International. https://www.pri.org/stories/2019-09-27/us-refugee-agencies-wither-trump-administration-cuts-numbers-historic-lows

Kerwin, D. (2015). The US refugee protection system on the 35th anniversary of the 1980 Refugee Act. *Journal on Migration and Human Security, 3*(2), 205–254. https://journals.sagepub.com/doi/pdf/10.1177/233150241500300204

Kerwin, D. (2018). The US refugee resettlement program—A return to first principles: How refugees help to define, strengthen, and revitalize the United States. *Journal on Migration and Human Security, 6*(3), 205–225. https://doi.org/10.1177/2331502418787787

Klimek, B. (2011). *USCCB/MRS refugee resettlement case management manual: The application of social work principles, ethics, and the case management approach in service delivery to refugees.* Department of Migration and Refugee Services, United States Conference on Catholic Bishops. https://www.ritaresources.org/wp-content/uploads/2018/04/USCCB-RMS-Refugee-Resettlement-Case-Management-Manual.pdf

Krogstad, J. M. (2019, October). Key facts about refugees to the U.S. Pew Research Center. https://www.pewresearch.org/fact-tank/2019/10/07/key-facts-about-refugees-to-the-u-s

National Immigration Forum. (2019). Fact sheet: U.S. refugee resettlement. https://immigrationforum.org/article/fact-sheet-u-s-refugee-resettlement

Obser, K. (2019). The family case management program: Why case management can and must be part of the US approach to immigration. Women's Refugee Commission. https://reliefweb.int/sites/reliefweb.int/files/resources/The-Family-Case-Management-Program.pdf

Rothenberg, D., & Comisión para el Esclarecimiento Histórico (Guatemala). (2012). *Memory of silence: The Guatemalan Truth Commission report.* Palgrave Macmillan.

Shaw, S. A. (2014). Bridge builders: A qualitative study exploring the experiences of former refugees working as caseworkers in the United States. *Journal of Social Service Research, 40*(3), 284–296. doi:10.1080/01488376.2014.901276

Shaw, S. A., & Poulin, P. (2015). Findings from an extended case management U.S. refugee resettlement program. *Journal of International Migration and Integration, 16*(4), 1099–1120. https://doi.org/10.1007/s12134-014-0374-0

United Nations High Commissioner for Refugees. (2016). Global trends: Forced displacement in 2016. https://www.unhcr.org/576408cd7.pdf

United Nations High Commissioner for Refugees. (2018). Global trends: Forced displacement in 2018. https://www.unhcr.org/globaltrends2018

United Nations High Commissioner for Refugees. (2019). Figures at a glance. https://www.unhcr.org/en-us/figures-at-a-glance.html

U.S. Department of Homeland Security. (n.d.). *Refugees and asylees.* https://www.dhs.gov/immigration-statistics/refugees-asylees

Villarreal Sosa, L., Diaz, S., & Hernandez, R. (2019). Accompaniment in a Mexican immigrant community: Conceptualization and identification of biopsychosocial outcomes. *Journal of Religion & Spirituality in Social Work: Social Thought, 38,* 21–42. https://doi.org/10.1080/15426432.2018.1533440

Social Work Case Management in Medical Settings

Michael Campbell and Roberta Restaino

In 1992, Karls and Wandrei championed the notion that the individual does not exist in isolation but, moreover, they live as a person in their environment (PIE), which has become a formative theoretical structure in social work education and an evolving framework for the way care is rendered in medical settings. More than a decade later, Reid et al. (2005) published a call to action for health care systems. They argued for a similar systemic approach to caring for patients in medical settings. The PIE model found standing in the health care literature and serves to reinforce the alignment of social work case management (SWCM) in the medical team. This focus nested systems in care for medical and social problems remains a primary focus for SWCM (Michailakis & Schirmer, 2014).

Social workers leverage the concept of nested systems at both a macro and a micro level in their work. At the macro level, social workers view the patient and their family as a nested member of what Bronfenbrenner argues is a theory of ecological system with interconnected subsystems (Eriksson et al., 2018). Furthermore, public health literature has started to explore treatment of communities and not simply the individual in the context of population-level health, and SWCM has been uniquely positioned to deliver on this model (Rose et al., 2016).

One area for social workers to advocate for change in case management and health care delivery can be found in ongoing debate regarding health care reform (Harkey, 2017). Existing programs, such as Medicare and Medicaid, have continuously served as a health care safety net for the most vulnerable populations, and social workers remain a prominent voice for change with these programs (Bachman et al., 2017). Similarly, the broader debate about the Affordable Care Act and the evolution of the model for health care delivery in North America has strong roots in social work efforts to advocate for equity and access (Andrews et al., 2013; McCabe & Wahler, 2016).

At the patient care or micro level, the social work case manager operates from a model that embraces all clients and their families as inexorably interconnected with the myriad of social and communal systems that intersect their lives. One such example can be found in the ambulatory integration of the medical and social (AIMS) model (Rizzo et al., 2016). The AIMS model follows a four-step process (engagement, assessment, case management, and maintenance) to assist adult patients in caring for chronic and complex medical conditions.

The social work case manager engages health care provision across the four levels of care in the application of micro to macro social work practice. These levels of health care escalate from primary care to secondary care, with an elevation to tertiary care, and finally quaternary care. These levels escalate from less to more invasive care provision, and all of these levels incorporate various direct engagement with SWCM. This chapter leverages the case study approach to map one family's care journey across these four levels of care.

Case Study Application

The case study presented in this chapter illustrates the complexity of interdisciplinary care and highlights both the roles and the skills needed for the effective implementation of SWCM in medical settings. The vignette focuses on the medical journey of the Rivera family and how the social work case manager assists them with navigation across the four levels of this care. The Rivera family includes Johnny (age 67 years) and his wife Sarah (age 64 years) and their three adult children. Johnny and Sarah have been married 25 years and have been relatively healthy throughout that time. The narrative of this family's complex journey through the medical system will bridge multiple episodes of care, with attention paid to the role the social work case manager can play in improving outcomes such as the quality of care received and quality of life.

Social Work Case Management in Primary Care

Primary care is sometimes referred to as ambulatory care and is the least restrictive option for health care delivery. At this level of care, the patient and their family work with their primary care provider (PCP) and team for well visits to maintain health and to manage routine health concerns (Sacco et al., 2018). Most of the health care is offered in this level. The role of the social work case manager in primary care is to assist with alleviating the psychological, social, and financial hardships caused by chronic or acute illness. The medical social worker connects patients and families to the appropriate resources to improve their quality of life and health care experience.

In this case presented in this chapter, the skills that the medical social worker, Mary, uses during meetings with the Riveras include active listening and validation of feelings. The tasks include the use of a psychosocial assessment, intervention to educate, creating a plan, and empowering the couple to problem-solve (Putney et al., 2017).

Case Study Narrative

During a routine visit with her PCP when Sarah is in her early 40s, she talks about the financial stressors resulting from Johnny's intermittent employment. She explains that Johnny has spent the past two decades working as a construction foreman and has had several work-related accidents that have impacted his back. He is in constant pain and has evolved from alcohol use on just the weekends to daily use of alcohol and other drugs to "get through the day." They share the same PCP, and she coordinates an appointment for the couple to discuss these concerns and the need for treatment, and they also consult the onsite social work case manager, Mary.

Mary meets with the PCP to review the concerns about the Rivera family. She reviews Johnny's chart and them meets with Johnny and Sarah in her office. Mary builds rapport with the couple by inviting them to express their feelings and concerns regarding Johnny's back injury and how it has impacted their relationship, their finances, and his ongoing difficulty working with chronic pain. Mary assesses the concerns about the reported use of drugs and/or alcohol daily, and with their permission, she educates the couple on the signs and symptoms of substance use disorders (SUDs).

Sarah begins by sharing her feelings with Mary. Sarah expresses ongoing stress that she feels because she is the one who is handling the finances and is frustrated with the lack of change. Johnny is reserved at first and then states that he feels guilty that his illness is impacting the family's finances and to isolate himself to use drugs and alcohol has been his only way to find comfort and relief. After both have relayed their feelings and concerns to Mary, she validates their feelings and provides recommendations. Mary explains the role of outpatient counseling for treating SUDs, and based on the couples' interest in seeking treatment, she coordinates with the couple's insurance carrier and refers Johnny for outpatient counseling. She also knows the importance of peer supports to treat SUDs and recommends a 12-step program to both Johnny and Sarah as well as a local support group that focuses on coping with the chronic pain.

Johnny agrees to go to outpatient counseling as well as attend a 12-step program, and the couple agrees to meet with Mary at Johnny's next PCP appointment in 6 weeks. In between these visits, Mary calls the couple to check on their progress and Sarah confirms that they have made a connection with the counselor for the SUD treatment. She confirms that Johnny has a sponsor and actively attends the 12-step groups weekly, and she sees a positive change in Johnny with his ability to manage pain without using drugs and alcohol. Mary encourages the couple to continue with treatment and makes plans to see them at their next visit to the PCP.

Social Work Case Management in Secondary Care

When the care needs of a patient exceed the ability of the PCP to deliver, a patient is referred

to a specialist and the care moves from primary to secondary in nature. In secondary care, the patient and their PCP are coordinated in care delivery, and the patient often needs more invasive tests, assessment, and treatment than is typical in primary care. Sometimes this care is offered as an outpatient service, such as in primary care, or as a residential service, which requires additional support and structure. The role of the social work case manager in secondary care is to continue to assist with alleviating the psychological, social, and financial hardships caused by chronic or acute illness but to do so with a deeper knowledge of treatments and supports for a specific condition. The skills Mary used during follow-up meetings with Johnny and Sarah involve a more targeted assessment of SUD using Screening, Brief Intervention, and Referral to Treatment (SBIRT) (Committee on Substance Use & Prevention, 2016; Sacco et al., 2017), referrals for residential treatment, and coordination with a community psychiatrist who specializes in addiction medicine. The tasks include the use of a standardized assessment(s) and techniques in motivational interviewing to educate and empower the couple to problem-solve (Hohman, 2012).

Case Study Narrative

Johnny and Sarah continue to see the PCP for ongoing care. The couple report that, during the next several years, Johnny has had consistently reduced pain and is feeling much better about his physical and mental health. They talk with their PCP and Mary about the struggles of recovery, and Mary reminds them that small relapses are likely but recovery is a process and so they must continue to engage their supports even if there is a slight slip. Johnny and Sarah are working through is SUD treatment plan, with support from his children, and he remains sober for 9 years.

When Johnny turned age 50 years, they had a surprise party at their home, and he was surrounded by family, friends, and co-workers. They served food and alcohol to the guests, but Johnny did not have any alcohol, and he felt a sense of pride in his choice. Unfortunately, one of his co-workers consumed too much alcohol and chose to drive home from the party. On the drive home, the co-worker lost control of his vehicle and was killed in an automobile accident. Johnny blamed himself for the accident and was struck with profound guilt and sadness. When the Riveras return to meet with the PCP and Mary, they talk about the aftermath from the 50th birthday party and report that Johnny did not complete the outpatient program, does not attend Alcoholics Anonymous, and his drinking and self-medicating with drugs has gotten worse. Sarah states that she has tried everything and nothing works, so in her exhaustion, she has decided she is leaving Johnny if he does not get help now.

Mary asks Johnny what he thinks about more aggressive treatment, and he is initially resistant. Mary employs her motivational interviewing skills to help Johnny and Sarah talk through the benefits and risks associated with his SUD to help the family develop a sense of discrepancy between what they want to achieve and how their current behavior is working to get them there. After a few similar discussions, Johnny reports he is willing to get further treatment. Mary provides them with names of local facilities and helps them chose one. Mary sends a referral online to the facility. The medical records are faxed, with Johnny's signed consent, and the plan is for Johnny to go directly to the facility from the PCP office.

Social Work Case Management in Tertiary Care

Tertiary care is synonymous with hospital-based care and is needed when primary and secondary care options are not able to improve outcomes or when there is a need for resource-intensive care to stabilize or assess a complex patient need. This section discusses how tertiary care is used in support of the family. SWCM in tertiary care involves many areas in the hospital system. The social work case manager can work in the emergency department to screen and assess for a range of issues, from domestic violence and abuse to traumatic events such as automobile accidents (Edmonds et al., 2015). The social work case manager can also be found working on intensive care units and the medical/surgical floors to assist the medical team in caring for acute and chronic conditions (Bronstein et al., 2015). Often, the social work case manager serves a vital function to translate the patient's psychosocial condition to the treatment team to help make linkages to improve the patient's adherence to treatment (Kim & Ko, 2014). Essentially, they help the treatment team better understand the cultural context of the patients they serve (Watters et al., 2016). At times, they help translate the complexity of the medical plan to patients to help them determine how they will implement the plan in their home setting and document the plan to aid in adherence and reduce risk (Reamer, 2014).

Case Study Narrative

At age 64 years, Johnny presents to his PCP for an annual physical and to review his routine blood work. He has completed residential treatment for SUD and has been sober for the past 14 years and feels a sense of pride in his recovery. He reports feeling the typical aches and pains of aging but nothing out of the ordinary. The PCP reports that his liver enzymes continue to be stable, and they celebrate his continued sobriety. However, the PCP is concerned about other blood levels in Johnny's complete blood count and orders repeated blood work and additional tests that may indicate another underlying concern, namely cancer. After undergoing the additional testing, Johnny and Sarah have another joint meeting with their PCP to review the results, the combination of which is highly suspicious of a cancer. They are referred to an oncologist, a specialist for treating cancer, for additional testing to explore the diagnosis.

When they visit the oncologist, Johnny and Sarah are introduced to the oncology social worker, Jazmin, at the outpatient oncologist office. At this point, they have already met with the oncologist and received the news confirming Johnny has advanced stage leukemia, which impacts the body's blood-forming tissues. The oncologist has recommended that Johnny be admitted to the hospital to receive inpatient chemotherapy treatments. Jazmin provides an assessment and intervention of support. During this visit, Jazmin calls the social work case manager who works in the hospital, Edwin, and they all speak over the phone about how they will coordinate their efforts into and out of the hospital admission. Johnny and Sarah are understandably scared, so Jazmin helps the family write down important contact numbers for the clinic and the social work team so the family has a simple way to connect when needed.

Once in the hospital, Johnny contacts Edwin, the social work case manager who works on the oncology floor, and it is easy to speak with him because Johnny had previously spoken with him on the phone. Edwin is focused on Johnny's ongoing care after discharge from the hospital. He provides an assessment to complete a safe discharge and reinforces the recommendation Jazmin made that getting connected with the American Cancer Society will be very beneficial for additional education and support and provides Johnny with the contact information. He remains available to meet with Johnny and/or Sarah should any psychosocial needs arise during Johnny's 4-day admission, and he checks in on Johnny every few days to discuss his progress. Edwin helps Johnny and his family review the steps needed for ongoing treatment and obtaining any durable medical equipment such as a bedside commode that are arranged to be delivered to the home. He also provides key contact information needed to continue treatment.

Social Work Case Management in Quaternary Care

Quaternary care is viewed as an extension of tertiary care and offers a more specialized level of care. Quaternary care delivery is highly specific to a small number of patients in a geographic region and as such not every medical center offers it. It is often the case that medical centers will offer a coordinated patchwork of quaternary care options to reduce costs but to ensure that a region has access to that level of care (Lukersmith et al. 2016). In this level of care, the social work case manager employs all the skills that are needed in the lower levels of care. Despite the challenges, many social work case managers report that being on a connected team that is mission driven to serve its clients brings them immense job satisfaction (Marmo & Berkman, A. 2018).

Case Study Narrative

Upon discharge, ongoing chemotherapy is provided at the oncologist's office in the outpatient infusion suite, where intravenous medications are delivered in a secure and safe place. Johnny has a family member with him for these treatments, and his blood counts make a slow and steady improvement. One day in the middle of February, Johnny catches a cold. Typically, a common cold is not a significant concern, but for a patient who takes chemotherapy, their immune system is artificially low. The oncologist shares that Johnny's blood work is getting dramatically worse and that they have maximized his chemotherapy protocol.

Johnny is made aware that the chemotherapy was not successful and that his disease stage and prognosis are poor. Johnny and Sarah meet with Jazmin, and she provides them the time and space to process the life-changing news. They talk about how they feared this news would come but not so soon. Jazmin provides support and validation of feelings, which is a critical first step (Rine, 2018). Previously, during one of the numerous hospitalizations, they worked with Edwin to draft their advanced directives to spell out exactly how they wanted care to proceed should Johnny's condition progress to a terminal state.

Jazmin talks with the Rivera family about the oncologist's recommendations for palliative care and hospice services (Reinhardt et al., 2017), and they reluctantly agree. She provides Johnny and Sarah with education on the hospice philosophy and services and informs them that Johnny is able to receive these services in their home. Jazmin calls Mary in the PCP office to provide an overview of their care and the plan of care transition back to the PCP with hospice support. Mary provides Johnny with the names of two hospices in his area. Johnny gives Mary permission to send a referral to the hospice of his choice to establish care.

Dora, the hospice social worker, meets with Johnny and Sarah in their home to conduct a full psychosocial assessment in order to assess how hospice can best serve the Rivera family. Dora helps the family coordinate care in the home and provides anticipatory guidance by opening up discussions on difficult subjects such as advanced directives and funeral arrangements (Reinhardt et al., 2017). The social worker does this with the goal of helping to offer support and empower the family to take care of the necessary preparations in his final hours. In his death, Johnny is surrounded by his family and a supportive hospice team that helps the family through the difficult process

of grieving and in moving toward their own recovery.

Conclusion

The social work case manager is an integral part of most interdisciplinary medical teams throughout the various levels of health care provision. The case study of the Rivera family provides an overview of how the social work case manager works to provide psychosocial and resource support and is a critical element in maintaining continuity of care to patients and their families. Evidence-based approaches to interdisciplinary medical care increasingly call for the active inclusion of SWCM across many health care settings and with a widening variety of patient populations in primary, secondary, tertiary, and quaternary care. Nested within those sectors are highly targeted areas for the social work case manager to help with care provision. Social work case managers are visible in most hospital emergency rooms and hospital units, such as neurosurgery, trauma, labor and delivery, and neonatal intensive care units, as well as many other areas of patient care.

As the practice of Western medicine continues to grow in complexity and scope, there is a constant call for the holistic treatment of patients that seeks to address issues that impact not only the body but also the mind and spirit. These holistic aspects of treatment call for competent professionals who are trained in interdisciplinary practice to deliver seamless care. SWCM in medical settings continues to grow and be recognized as necessary for patients as well as their families to successfully navigate the health care system and various health challenges. The Council of Social Work Education's annual survey of the social work profession (*From Social Work Education to Social Work Practice*) consistently ranks social work in health care practice in the top areas of growth and need. The Helpful Resources section lists websites to give resources and direction to anyone interested in joining this growing area of social work practice.

Helpful Resources

America Case Management Association: https://www.acmaweb.org

Case Management Society of America: https://www.cmsa.org

Centers for Medicare & Medicaid Services. *Medicaid definition of covered case management services clarified*: https://www.cms.gov/newsroom/fact-sheets/medicaid-definition-covered-case-management-services-clarified

Centers for Medicare & Medicaid Services. *Care management fact sheet*: https://www.cms.gov/Medicare/Medicare-Fee-for-Service-Payment/PhysicianFeeSched/Care-Management

Commission for Case Manager Certification: https://ccmcertification.org

Medicare.gov. *Chronic care management services*: https://www.medicare.gov/coverage/chronic-care-management-services

Substance Abuse and Mental Health Services Administration. *Case management*. https://www.samhsa.gov/homelessness-programs-resources/hpr-resources/case-management

Substance Abuse and Mental Health Services Administration. *Comprehensive case management for substance abuse treatment*. https://store.samhsa.gov/system/files/sma15-4215.pdf

References

Andrews, C. M., Darnell, J. S., McBride, T. D., & Gehlert, S. (2013). Social work and implementation of the Affordable Care Act. *Health Social Work, 38*(2), 67–71.

Bachman, S. S., Wachman, M., Manning, L., Cohen, A. M., Seifert, R. W., Jones, D. K., & Riley, P. (2017). Social work's role in Medicaid reform: A qualitative study. *American Journal of Public Health, 107*(Suppl. 3), S250–S255.

Bronstein, L. R., Gould, P., Berkowitz, S. A., James, G. D., & Marks, K. (2015). Impact of a social work care coordination intervention on hospital readmission: A randomized controlled trial. *Social Work, 60*(3), 248–255.

Committee on Substance Use & Prevention. (2016). Substance use screening, brief intervention, and referral to treatment. *Pediatrics, 138*(1), e20161211.

Edmonds, A., Moore, E., Valdez, A., & Tomlinson, C. (2015). Social work and the HIV care continuum: Assisting HIV patients diagnosed in an emergency department. *Social Work, 60*(3), 238–246.

Eriksson, M., Ghazinour, M., & Hammarstrom, A. (2018). Different uses of Bronfenbrenner's ecological theory in public mental health research: What is their value for guiding public mental health policy and practice? *Social Theory & Health, 16*, 414–433.

Harkey, J. (2017). Case management at the intersection of social work and health care. *Social Work Today, 17*(1), 20.

Hohman, M. (2012). *Motivational interviewing in social work practice*. Guilford.

Karls, J. M., & Wandrei, K. E. (1992). PIE: A new language for social work. *Social Work, 37*(1), 80–85.

Kim, K., & Ko, J. (2014). Attitudes toward interprofessional health care teams scale: A confirmatory factor analysis. *Journal of Interprofessional Care, 28*(2), 149–154.

Lukersmith, S., Millington, M., & Salvador-Carulla, L. (2016). What is case management? A scoping and mapping review. *International Journal of Integrated Care, 16*(4), 2.

Marmo, S., & Berkman, C. (2018). Social workers' perceptions of job satisfaction, interdisciplinary collaboration, and organizational leadership. *Journal of Social Work End Life Palliative Care, 14*(1), 8–27.

McCabe, H. A., & Wahler, E. A. (2016). The Affordable Care Act, substance use disorders, and low-income clients: Implications for social work. *Social Work, 61*(3), 227–233.

Michailakis, D., & Schirmer, W. (2014). Social work and social problems: A contribution from systems theory and constructionism. *International Journal of Social Welfare, 23*(4), 431–442.

Putney, J. M., O'Brien, K. H. M., Collin, C.-R., & Levine, A. (2017). Evaluation of alcohol Screening, Brief Intervention, and Referral to Treatment (SBIRT) training for social workers. *Journal of Social Work Practice in the Addictions, 17*(1–2), 169–187.

Reamer, F. G. (2014). Clinical social work in a digital environment: Ethical and risk-management challenges. *Clinical Social Work Journal, 43*(2), 120–132.

Reid, P. P., Compton, D., Grossman, J. H., & Fanjiang, G. (2005). *Building a better delivery system: A new engineering/health care partnership*. National Academies Press.

Reinhardt, J. P., Downes, D., Cimarolli, V., & Bomba, P. (2017). End-of-life conversations and hospice placement: Association with less aggressive care desired in the nursing home. *Journal of Social Work End Life Palliative Care, 13*(1), 61–81.

Rine, C. M. (2018). Is social work prepared for diversity in hospice and palliative care? *Health Social Work, 43*(1), 41–50.

Rizzo, V. M., Rowe, J. M., Shier Kricke, G., Krajci, K., & Golden, R. (2016). AIMS: A care coordination model to improve patient health outcomes. *Health Social Work, 41*(3), 191–195.

Rose, S. M., Hatzenbuehler, S., Gilbert, E., Bouchard, M. P., & McGill, D. (2016). A population health approach to clinical social work with complex patients in primary care. *Health Social Work, 41*(2), 93–100.

Sacco, P., Ting, L., Crouch, T. B., Emery, L., Moreland, M., Bright, C., Frey, J., & DiClemente, C. (2017). SBIRT training in social work education: Evaluating change using standardized patient simulation. *Journal of Social Work Practice in the Addictions, 17*(1–2), 150–168.

Sacco, P., Unick, G. J., & Gray, C. (2018). Enhancing treatment access through "safe stations." *Journal of Social Work Practice in the Addictions, 18*(4), 458–464.

Watters, A., Bergstrom, A., & Sandefer, R. (2016). Patient engagement and meaningful use: Assessing the impact of the EHR incentive program on cultural competence in healthcare. *Journal of Cultural Diversity, 23*(3), 114–122.

Case Management with Persons with Severe Mental Illness

David C. Kondrat and Theresa J. Early

Case management is a foundational treatment modality for persons with severe mental illness (SMI). SMI involves having a mental illness that interferes in at least one area of daily living, such as the ability to care for oneself or the ability to maintain employment. Diagnoses that tend to fall into these categories include mood, thought, and anxiety disorders. Roughly 2.6% of persons in the United States have a lifetime prevalence of SMI (Goldman & Grob, 2006).

Deinstitutionalization and the subsequent unpreparedness of the community for release of persons with SMI from hospitals led to the development of case management. Clients left the hospital with many unmet needs into a fragmented service system (Stein & Test, 1980). Case management was designed to help clients navigate the community and fragmented service system. According to Thornicroft (1991), the basic components of case management include continuity of services, accessibility, case manager–client relationship, services tailored to meet client needs, encouraging independence, and patient and systems advocacy. Brokered case management, which focuses on assessment and referral, was not found to

be particularly helpful to persons with SMI (Ziguras & Stuart, 2000). That is, basic case management services were not enough to help clients maintain in the community (Stein & Test, 1980).

Assertive Community Treatment

Programs of Assertive Community Treatment (PACT) was designed to provide clients with SMI intensive services to help them meet their multiple and complex needs. PACT, which was later renamed assertive community treatment (ACT), was developed in Madison, Wisconsin, in the 1970s. The original name of PACT was Training in Community Living (Marx et al., 1973). Stein and Test (1980) developed a team-based model of care that recognized that providing services in the community was superior to the standard treatment practices of the day. What was learned in hospitals by clients was not generalizable to the community. The researchers saw a revolving door of clients to the community and back to the psychiatric hospital. For persons with SMI to be successful in the community, some of the services that hospitals offered needed to be provided in the community. Early results indicated that this approach was superior at reducing hospitalizations (Stein & Test, 1980); the model was cost-effective (Weisbrod et al., 1980); and the model was associated with reduced arrests, suicide attempts, and emergency room care (Test & Stein, 1980).

ACT was designed for the most severely disabled persons with SMI. Therefore, the focus has been on providing ACT treatment to individuals who often find themselves in crises or with multiple psychiatric hospitalizations. Clients for whom ACT is most clinically profitable are those who use the most services.

The model was formed based on a set of assumptions and practices about care for persons with SMI in the community (Bond & Drake, 2015). The first of these is in vivo services. Services are provided where clients live. One of the realizations that the originators of ACT identified was that learning to live independently in the hospital was not as beneficial as learning daily living in the community (Stein & Test, 1980). Providing services in the community increased the clients' view of and satisfaction with mental health services (Bond et al., 2001). Therefore, treatment was conducted in the community. Another principle is assertive outreach. Clients are sometime hesitant to keep appointments or comply with treatment requirements or requests. So, not only do the teams meet the persons in the community but also they actively find the clients in order to provide needed services, such as medication management. According to Salyers and Tsemberis (2007), "ACT teams utilize engagement and retention strategies that include repeated attempts to contact consumers despite their refusals, close monitoring or medication compliance, behavioral contracting, use of outpatient commitment, and representative payeeship" (p. 622). The assertive outreach

component often leaves consumers with the belief that ACT is paternalistic.

The ACT team provides a holistic approach to treatment. According to Bond and Drake (2015), the ACT team, and not outside service providers, delivers all needed services to clients, "helping with illness management, medications management, housing, finances, and anything else that is critical to an individual's community adjustment" (p. 441). The ACT team supports the client in all activities of daily living. No activity is too small. For example, members of the ACT team work with clients on activities such as cleaning an apartment, going shopping, or learning to ride the bus.

The ACT team is a multidisciplinary team (Bond & Drake, 2015). The team is made up of all professionals who can help meet the needs of clients. For example, teams will have social workers, psychiatrists, nurses, and therapists. The leader of the team is a clinical supervisor who monitors the progress of the team. More recently, employment specialists have been added to the team (Bond et al., 2008), as have former clients as providers (Salyers & Tsemberis, 2007). As recovery in mental illness has become ubiquitous with mental health care, peer specialists have been added to teams (Dixon et al., 1997). In addition, teams may add other specialists as needed based on the specific population with which the team works. For example, housing specialists are provided for teams whose focus is on working with the homeless, and teams that focus on working with dual-diagnosed individuals will have substance abuse specialists. Although the teams are multidisciplinary, the exact composition of each team is based on the specific population with which the team is working. Furthermore, although the teams utilize a team approach, one member of the team takes on primary responsibility for a client, which allows for the development of a working relationship between the client and the member of the team responsible for the client's care.

Another critical ingredient of the ACT team is that the team uses a direct service model. As previously stated, the ACT team provides for all the needs of clients. That is, the team does not refer clients to other agencies unless it cannot provide the services itself. Therefore, the team takes care of most of the biopsychosocial needs of clients. Along with this commitment to being a direct service model, the teams also integrate services. One of the complaints about treatment before ACT was developed was that the service setting was fragmented (Intagliata, 1982). Service providers from different agencies were not communicating with one another. Thus, clients might receive duplicate or incongruent services. The ACT team ensures that clients receive all needed services and that these services are coordinated. This leads to the principle of integrated services: Services are provided by the team.

An important feature of ACT is the low client-to-staff ratio. The model calls for one act team member for every 10 clients. The purpose of this requirement is to ensure that clients are met with multiple times during the week. High-need clients may be met every day for medication management. In addition, multiple providers get to know each client, which enables continuity of care should one member of the client's team leave or become sick. Another feature of ACT is continuous coverage. Staff are available 24 hours a day, 7 days a week. Any client emergency is handled by the ACT team. Last, the team provides long-term and continuous care. Persons who receive ACT services can receive them for a lifetime. There is no time limit on how long services are offered.

Additional Services

Over time, ACT models have become specialized to meet the demands of different client groups. Persons with SMI have a higher rate of arrest compared with members of the public (Morrissey et al., 2007). This fact has led to the development of forensic assertive community treatment (FACT) teams. Members of FACT teams have specialized knowledge in working with this population. These teams work in a variety of forensic settings and have as one of their goals the reduction in recidivism of clients. For example, these teams are often embedded in mental health courts to serve clients of the court. Some persons with SMI have co-occurring substance use disorders or other psychiatric condition (Frisman et al., 2009). Integrated dual-disorder treatment (IDDT) was designed to meet the needs of persons with comorbid mental health or substance abuse needs. IDDT includes an ACT component. Tsemberis and colleagues (2004) developed the Housing First program, which provides housing to homeless clients. As part of this program, ACT services are made available to consumers.

Case Manager–Client Relationship

Often misunderstood is the relationship between the client and the case manager. Ryan and colleagues (1994) argue that although programs of care such as ACT are highly prescriptive, the workers are responsible for operationalizing the model. So, the models may be more or less faithful to the ideal model dependent on the case manager. For example, Ryan et al. (1994) found that case managers accounted for roughly 15% of the variation in the amount of time that a consumer was in treatment. Researchers have shown that case managers in ACT programs influence client views of their quality of life (Kondrat & Early, 2011). The working alliance with case managers is important and accounts for positive outcomes (Kondrat & Early, 2010; Solomon et al., 1995). However, case manager beliefs about the recovery chances of persons with SMI are also important. For example, Goscha et al. (2013) found that case manager beliefs about what it takes to be ready to work strongly influenced the extent to which clients were engaged in work-related activities, such as receiving supported employment or going on job interviews. The more stringent the case managers' beliefs about what it takes to be ready for work, the less likely that the case managers' clients were engaged in work-related activities. Thus, attitudes about recovery are an important ingredient in developing strong, recovery-focused case manager–client relationships.

Empirical Support for Assertive Community Treatment

Assertive community treatment is considered an evidence-based treatment by the U.S. Substance Abuse and Mental Health Services Administration (2008) and other mental health professional associations, based on results of a number of research studies dating to the 1970s. One review of well-designed and executed research found that the strongest finding across 25 studies was that people with serious mental illness who were served by ACT had greater reduction in psychiatric hospitalization compared to similar persons not served by ACT (Bond et al., 2001). Other common findings are that participation in ACT increases housing stability and moderately improves symptoms and subjective quality of life, but it has little impact on social functioning (Bond et al., 2001). One area in which ACT has been particularly effective is engaging consumers with SMI in treatment, increasing their 1-year retention in mental health treatment (Bond et al., 2001).

Whereas evidence indicates that ACT is superior to other forms of case management and other mental health treatments in reducing hospitalization in the United States, research in the United Kingdom has found little difference (Burns et al., 2007). However, more detailed analysis of the usual treatment in the United

Kingdom found that it shares some of the important elements of ACT (Burns et al., 2007). These analyses confirmed that some of the main components of ACT (multidisciplinary teams and extensive outreach to engage consumers) influenced reduction in hospitalization and also that the practices were not exclusive to ACT in the UK context (Burns, 2010).

Assertive Community Treatment Fidelity

In developing an ACT program, model fidelity is important (Salyers et al., 2003). Salyers et al. (2003) evaluated a fidelity measurement tool, the Dartmouth Assertive Community Treatment Scale (DACTS), that allowed for programs to be measured against the model program. The scale consists of 25 items. DACTS was able to discriminate between ACT and other forms of case management, meaning that the use of DACTS can detect the degree to which a program is being faithful to the ACT model of care. Research into fidelity and program outcomes has been mixed. For example, Bond and Salyers (2004) found that although fidelity scores did not significantly predict lower rates of hospitalization, the top performers on the DACTS did, in fact, have lower rates of hospitalization. In contrast, McHugo et al. (1999) found that higher rates of fidelity were associated with lower rates of hospitalization. Despite these inconsistent findings, DACTS can be used to help organize services and ensure that teams are in concert with the ideal ACT model.

Recovery in Mental Illness and Assertive Community Treatment

Recovery in mental illness has become the clarion call of most mental health programs. Recovery in mental illness is a treatment philosophy in which persons with mental illness are viewed as active and capable participants in their own treatment. Persons with SMI can and do live satisfying lives despite the limitations imposed on them by their illness (Anthony, 2000). Critical to recovery are hope, coping skills, empowerment, and a supportive social network (Greene et al., 2006). In total, the work of recovery in mental illness is based on personal responsibility and choice of services (Salyers & Tsemberis, 2007). In terms of service provision, recovery means moving away from a clinical-driven model to full participation with clients and members of their social network.

ACT is a highly prescriptive, and sometimes coercive, form of treatment (Salyers & Tsemberis, 2007). Clinicians assertively engage clients in the community to ensure treatment adherence, including medication treatment adherence. With its focus on individual responsibility, recovery in mental illness seems at odds with ACT. However, Salyers and Tsemberis (2007) argue that recovery and ACT are not diametrically opposed. They outline four principles that can bring ACT services in line with recovery in mental illness. First is the integration of evidence-based practices to allow consumers more choice in services. For example, offering Illness Management and Recovery and Wellness Recovery Action Plans can provide greater service choice to consumers. Second is to monitor the recovery orientation of clinical staff. Higher recovery orientations have been associated with increased clinical benefits to clients. Therefore, teams should monitor how well their staff comport with the ideas and tenants of recovery in mental illness. Third, the agency must provide staff with training and supervision in recovery-oriented work. The goal is to move practitioners away from a symptom-focused view of mental illness to a holistic view, which sees the person with SMI as capable of making decisions. Finally, ACT teams need to hire former consumers to be fully participating members of the team.

Case Example

John is a 25-year-old male with schizophrenia. He hears voices telling him to hurt himself and to hurt others. He has never acted on these voices. John has lived with his parents since he dropped out of college at age 22 years during his senior year. John's parents have worked hard to help him, including getting John onto Social Security, Medicare, and Medicaid. During the past year, John has been hospitalized four times because he has been fearful of acting on his voices telling him to end his life. John's parents find it difficult to know how best to help him. They are tired of trying to get John to take his medication, which he takes sporadically. John is fearful that the medication will cause long-lasting and debilitating side effects, even though the medication helps him with his voices.

During his most recent hospital visit, John was referred to the local ACT team for help. Although at first John did not want to meet with these professionals for fear of being controlled, after discharge he agreed to meet with a member of the ACT team, a social worker, at his house. The team member discussed with John the services that the ACT team could provide, including helping him live independently and find employment. John agreed to work with the ACT team on a trial basis.

A few days later, the ACT team's psychiatrist and psychiatric nurse visited John. The psychiatrist had reviewed John's medical records and worked with John on putting together a medication plan for him. John agreed to take the medication. Following the plan, the nurse brings medication to John every day and supervises him taking the medication. Although John is usually home when the medications are delivered, he sometimes forgets his appointment with the nurse. When this occurs, the nurse looks for John at his local hangout, the river near his house where he likes to go fishing. The nurse witnesses John taking his medication. The psychiatrist meets with

John monthly to ensure that the medication is helping John with his symptoms and also to ensure that the side effects are not bothering John. John reports that the medication appears to be helping with his symptoms.

The team, in collaboration with John, has agreed to help John move toward three goals: finding independent living (the team wants to take over care of John from his parents), helping him develop independent living skills, and helping him find employment. In order to help John meet his needs, the team has agreed to be John's payee for his Social Security checks. They provide John with a weekly stipend. John receives this stipend every Friday when the nurse brings his medication.

The ACT team works with a local landlord who is willing to house persons on their team. Within a month of connecting with the ACT team, John is moved into his own apartment. In addition to receiving medication every day, a consumer provider of the ACT team visits John to help him learn to take care of his house and other independent living skills. John has never lived alone, and his parents have always taken care of his basic needs. Over time, John begins to take care of his own apartment without help. Early in his tenure in his new apartment, John felt scared at night because his voices were telling him to take his life. He decided to call the ACT team's emergency contact number. The team member on call was able to work with John on strategies to stay home. The next day, John reported that the crisis call helped him get through a rough patch with his voices.

After 6 months of working with the ACT team, John believed he was ready to start working. John's primary case manager, a social worker, agreed and introduced John to the team's employment specialist. John began by taking some work preparation classes. Within a year, John was ready to work. John was assigned to work at a local supermarket. John loves his work because he gets to interact with people outside of his home. John only works one day a week. His goal is to move to full-time employment. Ultimately, John wants an "office" job in which he can utilize what he learned in his 3 years of college studying accounting. John continues to see an ACT worker daily for medications and is working with the employment specialist on moving to a new position.

Conclusion

Case management for persons with SMI is ubiquitous with community treatment for this population. ACT and variants of this model are among the most common forms of case management for persons with SMI. ACT is a highly structured, team-based approach for working with this population. This model can be adapted for working with special populations. Research suggests that this model is successful at reducing hospitalizations. Although its highly prescriptive approach to treatment may conflict with the idea of recovery in mental illness, adaptations can be made to make the model more recovery focused.

References

Anthony, W. A. (2000). A recovery-oriented service system: Setting some system level standards. *Psychiatric Rehabilitation Journal, 24,* 159–169.

Bond, G. R., & Drake, R. E. (2015). The critical ingredients of assertive community treatment. *World Psychiatry, 14*(2), 240–242.

Bond, G. R., Drake, R. E., & Becker, D. R. (2008). An update on randomized controlled trials of evidence-based supported employment. *Psychiatric Rehabilitation Journal, 31*(4), 280–290. doi:10.2975/31.4.2008.280.290

Bond, G. R., Drake, R. E., Mueser, K. T., & Latimer, E. (2001). Assertive community treatment for people with severe mental illness: Critical ingredients and impact on patients. *Disease Management and Health Outcomes, 9*(3), 141–159.

Bond, G. R., & Salyers, M. P. (2004). Prediction of outcome from the Dartmouth Assertive Community Treatment Fidelity Scale. *CNS Spectrums, 9*(12), 937–942. doi:10.1017/s1092852900009792

Burns, T. (2010). The rise and fall of assertive community treatment? *International Review of Psychiatry, 22*(2), 130–137. https://doi.org/10.3109/09540261003661841

Burns, T., Catty, J., Dash, M., Roberts, C., Lockwood, A., & Marshall, M. (2007). Use of intensive case management to reduce time in hospital in people with severe mental illness: Systematic review and meta-regression. *British Medical Journal, 335,* 336–340. https://doi.org/10.1136/bmj.39251.599259.55

Dixon, L., Hackman, A., & Lehman, A. (1997). Consumers as staff in assertive community treatment programs. *Administration and Policy in Mental Health and Mental Health Services Research,* 25(2), 199–208.

Frisman, L. K., Mueser, K. T., Covell, N. H., Lin, H.-J., Crocker, A., Drake, R. E., & Essock, S. M. (2009). Use of integrated dual disorder treatment via assertive community treatment versus clinical case management for persons with co-occurring disorders and antisocial personality disorder. *Journal of Nervous and Mental Disease, 197*(11), 822–828. doi:10.1097/NMD.0b013e3181beac52

Goldman, H. H., & Grob, G. N. (2006). Defining "mental illness" in mental health policy. *Health Affairs, 25*(3), 737–749. doi:10.1377/hlthaff.25.3.737

Goscha, R., Kondrat, D. C., & Manthey, T. J. (2013). Case managers' perceptions of consumer work readiness and association with pursuit of employment. *Psychiatric Services, 64*(12), 1267–1269. doi:10.1176/appi.ps.201200537

Greene, G. J., Kondrat, D. C., Lee, M. Y., Clement, J., Siebert, H., Mentzer, R. A., & Pinnell, S. R. (2006). A solution-focused approach to case management and recovery with consumers who have a severe mental disability. *Families in Society, 87*(3), 339–350.

Intagliata, J. (1982). Improving the quality of community care for the chronically mentally disabled: The role of case management. *Schizophrenia Bulletin, 8*(4), 655–674. doi:10.1093/schbul/8.4.655

Kondrat, D. C., & Early, T. J. (2010). An exploration of the working alliance in mental health case management. *Social Work Research, 34*(4), 201–211.

Kondrat, D. C., & Early, T. J. (2011). Battling in the trenches: Case managers' ability to combat the effects of mental illness stigma on consumers' perceived quality of life. *Community Mental Health Journal, 47*(4), 390–398. doi:10.1007/s10597-010-9330-4

Marx, A. J., Test, M. A., & Stein, L. I. (1973). Extrohospital management of severe mental illness: Feasibility and effects of social functioning. *Archives of General Psychiatry, 29*(4), 505–511. doi:10.1001/archpsyc.1973.04200040051009

McHugo, G. J., Drake, R. E., Teague, G., & Xie, H. (1999). The relationship between model fidelity and client outcomes in the New Hampshire Dual Disorders Study. *Psychiatric Services, 50,* 818–824.

Morrissey, J., Meyer, P., & Cuddeback, G. (2007). Extending assertive community treatment to criminal justice settings: Origins, current evidence, and future directions. *Community Mental Health Journal, 43*(5), 527–544. doi:10.1007/s10597-007-9092-9

Ryan, C. S., Sherman, P. S., & Judd, C. M. (1994). Accounting for case manager effects in the evaluation of mental health services. *Journal of Consulting and Clinical Psychology, 62*(5), 965–974. doi:10.1037//0022-006x.62.5.965

Salyers, M. P., Bond, G. R., Teague, G. B., Cox, J. F., Smith, M. E., Hicks, M. L., & Koop, J. I. (2003). Is it ACT yet? Real-world examples of evaluating the degree of implementation for assertive community treatment. *Journal of Behavioral Health Services & Research, 30*(3), 304–320. doi:10.1007/BF02287319

Salyers, M. P., & Tsemberis, S. (2007). ACT and recovery: Integrating evidence-based practice and recovery orientation on assertive community treatment teams. *Community Mental Health Journal, 43*(6), 619–641. doi:10.1007/s10597-007-9088-5

Solomon, P., Draine, J., & Delaney, M. A. (1995). The working alliance and consumer case management. *Journal of Mental Health Administration, 22*(2), 126–134. doi:10.1007/Bf02518753

Stein, L. I., & Test, M. A. (1980). Alternative to mental hospital treatment: I. Conceptual model, treatment program, and clinical evaluation. *Archives of General Psychiatry, 37*(4), 392–397. http://www.ncbi.nlm.nih.gov/pubmed/7362425

Substance Abuse and Mental Health Services Administration. (2008). *Assertive community treatment: The evidence.* DHHS Publication No. SMA-08-4344. Center for Mental Health Services, Substance Abuse and Mental Health Services Administration, U.S. Department of Health and Human Services. Retrieved July 31, 2020, from https://store.samhsa.gov/product/Assertive-Community-Treatment-ACT-Evidence-Based-Practices-EBP-KIT/SMA08-4344

Test, M. A., & Stein, L. I. (1980). Alternative to mental hospital treatment: III. Social cost. *Archives of General Psychiatry, 37*(4), 409–412.

Thornicroft, G. (1991). The concept of case management for long-term mental illness. *International Review of Psychiatry, 2*(1), 125–132.

Tsemberis, S., Gulcur, L., & Nakae, M. (2004). Housing First, consumer choice, and harm reduction for homeless individuals with a dual diagnosis. *American Journal of Public Health, 94*(4), 651–656. doi:10.2105/ajph.94.4.651

Weisbrod, B. A., Test, M. A., & Stein, L. I. (1980). Alternative to mental hospital treatment: II. Economic benefit–cost analysis. *Archives of General Psychiatry, 37*(4), 400–405. http://www.ncbi.nlm.nih.gov/pubmed/6767462

Ziguras, S. J., & Stuart, G. W. (2000). A meta-analysis of the effectiveness of mental health case management over 20 years. *Psychiatric Services, 51*(11), 1410–1421. doi:10.1176/appi.ps.51.11.1410

Case Management for Human Trafficking Child Victims

Javonda Williams, Chris Lim, and Valerie Trull

Case Example

Jenny never imagined that she would end up here. Everything seemed to go wrong since she was placed in foster care after her parents died. Jenny was moved to three different homes during the first year and half in the system. She was angry, hurt, and heartbroken, but all of that changed when she met Danny at a local mall. Although he was almost 24 years old when they first met, he always treated Jenny as if she mattered, and that felt good. He took her to eat at nice restaurants and told her he would help her pay for her to enroll in a nail tech program so that she could work in a fancy salon downtown as a manicurist. Once Jenny ran away from her foster home to live with Danny, everything changed. He yelled at her for spending money on small things such as groceries and magazines. Danny was no longer the sweet and kind boyfriend that she had grown to love and trust. One day, Danny asked her to do him a "favor"; he asked Jenny to have sex with some friends of his to help him make ends meet. Danny promised it would be just the one time, but nothing could have been further from the truth. Now at age 17 years, here she is pregnant, again, with no education, no family, and no other options.

Definition of Child Trafficking

Jenny's story is representative of many youth throughout the world who are entangled in the vicious world of human trafficking. The globally accepted definition of human trafficking, found in what is commonly called the Palermo Protocol, defines child trafficking as the act of recruitment, transportation, transfer, harboring, or receipt of a child for the purpose of exploitation regardless of the use of force, deception, or coercion. There are two primary categories of trafficking: sex trafficking and labor trafficking. In the United States, the Trafficking Victims Protection Act of 2000 defines sex trafficking as "the recruitment, harboring, transportation, provision, or obtaining of a person for the purposes of a commercial sex act, in which the person induced to perform such an act has not attained 18 years of age" [22 USC § 7102 (9–10)]. Labor trafficking is defined as the "the recruitment, harboring, transportation, provision, or obtaining of a person for labor or services, through the use of force, fraud, or coercion for the purposes of subjection to involuntary servitude, peonage, debt bondage, or slavery" [22 USC § 7102(9)].

There is great debate on the reliability of estimates of prevalence and incidence of child trafficking victims. This is in part due to the difficulty in identifying victims and perpetrators, which is associated with low arrest and prosecution rates. In addition, there is also extreme variability in legislation and policies designed to address child trafficking. Despite these limitations, several global organizations have provided what most consider modest estimates. In 2017, the International Labour Organization estimated that 5.7 million children were victims of human trafficking worldwide (International Labour Office & Walk Free Foundation, 2017, p. 10). Although exact numbers are elusive, according to Ernie Allen, former chief executive officer of the National Center for Missing & Exploited Children, between 100,000 and 300,000 children are estimated to be victims of sex trafficking each year (Smith et al., 2009).

Victims of Child Trafficking

Although any child can become a victim of human trafficking, the primary common factors are unhealthy family relationships, racial/sexual minority status, and poverty. Within those broad categories, the specific groups of children discussed in this section are more vulnerable to human trafficking.

Homeless or Runaway Youth

Homeless or runaway youth are at the greatest risk for exploitation and trafficking (Gibbs et al., 2015). One in three teens on the street will be lured into prostitution within 48 hours of leaving home (Hammer et al., 2017). One study found that almost one-fourth (24.1%) of homeless youth have agreed to sexual activity with someone in exchange for money, and 27.5% have agreed to sexual activity in exchange for a place to spend the night (Administration for Children and Families, 2014).

Youth Involved with the Child Welfare System

Reports indicate that a large number of child sex trafficking survivors in the United States were at one time in the foster care system. Many children enter the child welfare system because of activities associated with trafficking such as lack of parental supervision (Biehal & Wade, 2000; Fong & Berger-Cardoso, 2010). Youth who have had contact with child welfare agencies, especially those who have been in the foster care system, present increased vulnerabilities, making them targets for human traffickers (Smith et al., 2009).

Racial, Ethnic, and Sexual Minority Youth

Racial, ethnic, and sexual minority youth are disproportionately represented as victims of trafficking and exploitation (National Research Council, 2013). The Federal Bureau of Investigation reports that African American and Latino youth are disproportionately represented in child trafficking cases. Similarly, LGBTQIA + youth are disproportionately represented in homeless youth populations and consequently overrepresented in trafficking cases (Administration for Children and Families, 2014).

Identification of Child Victims of Human Trafficking

Human trafficking victims may be identified at any time, in any place. This may include instances when a client is receiving case management services for other needs (e.g., foster care or domestic violence) when they are recognized as a victim of trafficking or disclose a trafficking situation. Because human trafficking has so many overlapping components with other crimes, it can be difficult to recognize that trafficking is taking place. It is imperative that social workers are trained to recognize the signs of trafficking and ensure every potential trafficking case is investigated properly.

The Trafficking Victims Protection Act of 2000 and its subsequent reauthorizations define human trafficking as follows:

(a) Sex trafficking in which a commercial sex act is induced by force, fraud, or coercion, or in which the person induced to perform such act has not attained 18 years of age; or

(b) The recruitment, harboring, transportation, provision, or obtaining of a person for labor or services, through the use of force, fraud, or coercion for the purpose of subjection to involuntary servitude, peonage, debt bondage, or slavery. [22 U.S.C. § 7102(9)]

Understanding this definition and applying it to the identification of potential victims of trafficking are two distinct undertakings. In application, the signs of trafficking become very important and must be considered on a broad scale. Whereas some indicators may be immediate verification of trafficking, such as a minor engaged in commercial sex, others may require putting multiple indicators together, like pieces of a puzzle, to equate to trafficking. These indicators might be seemingly minor, such as a child who is often too exhausted to stay awake through school combined with talk of a job that may be incompatible with the age of the child. A sex abuse case may have no mention of trafficking, but a witness may disclose that a third party dropped the victim off at the location of the incident.

The most important piece to identifying victims of trafficking is to pay attention to all of the details and fill in those that are missing. Side comments may carry significant information that could differentiate between an abuse situation and a trafficking case. Learn the signs of trafficking available in the Helpful Resources section, utilize the strategies provided in Chapter 43 of this volume, build strong relationships with law enforcement in your area, and keep your eyes and ears open at all times.

Effects of Human Trafficking on Children

Human trafficking has serious deleterious and long-term effects on child survivors. Child victims of human trafficking have increased chronic health problems, including heart disease, sexually transmitted diseases, and dental problems (Muraya & Fry, 2016). Child victims are also at higher risk for serious mental health disorders, including post-traumatic stress disorder, depression, and substance use disorders. There are also psychosocial effects associated with human trafficking, including a higher incidence of relationship dysfunction, poorer educational and job performance, and lower wage earnings compared to those of non-trafficked counterparts. Victims often experience wage theft ; suffer substantial economic costs due to physical, sexual, and psychological abuse (Busch-Armendariz et al., 2016); and, due to a lack of legal work histories, face diminished economic opportunity (Bocinski, 2017). Families and communities suffer in terms of lost wages; poor family relationships; and difficulty with community engagement, which is common among survivors of human trafficking.

Case Management Models

The term case management has been widely applied to describe a professional process of assessment, planning, implementation, coordination, monitoring, and evaluation of the options and services required to meet an individual's needs (Commission for Case Management Certification, n.d.). Frankel et al. (2019) state that case management has two essential purposes: (1) improving the quality of care to vulnerable populations and (2) controlling the costs of such care. They note that these purposes often conflict with each other. Specifically, there is a recognizable tension in most case management models between efficacy (best quality) and efficiency (low cost). The case management literature features many models and approaches typically based on the needs and functioning of the clientele, the service setting, the direct services available, and the tasks associated with the case manager.

Comprehensive case management services are arguably one of the most vitally important elements of aftercare services for child trafficking victims (Muraya & Fry, 2016). The multifaceted effects of human trafficking typically result in multiagency and multidisciplinary interventions, including medical, dental, mental health, legal, educational/vocational, and housing services. The case manager often serves as the consistent link between the survivor and all of these service providers. In addition, case managers can serve as a consistent source of encouragement and support that can bolster healing for child survivors. Pesso (2014) found that case management services supported resiliency and empowerment in child trafficking survivors.

Trauma-Based Case Management

The most effective case management models for addressing the needs of child victims of trafficking emphasize a trauma-informed approach. A trauma-informed case manager can recognize the signs and indicators of trauma in their population and integrate that knowledge into their practice with a focus on mitigating retraumatization.

Cyclical Nature of Healing and Restoration

It is essential to understand the cyclical nature of healing and restoration for victims of trauma. Without understanding this and the various ways trauma presents in minors who are survivors of human trafficking, indicators can be overlooked and trauma responses misinterpreted. Many practitioners working with victims of human trafficking are familiar with the transtheoretical model created by James O. Prochaska of the University of Rhode Island and Carlo Di Clemente in 1977 through studying the recovery process of people overcoming addictive behaviors. The model describes a client moving through sequential stages during their recovery, beginning in a state of being unaware of their need for change, followed by stages in which they consider their need for change, make perpetrations and take action toward change, and ultimately attempt to maintain their healthy lifestyle until the inevitable relapse happens.

The transtheoretical model has been adapted by many fields working with populations struggling with returning to the behaviors they are trying to mitigate. Recently, researcher Chris Lim has improved on that model, adapting it to make it empowering and more accurate to the experience of the survivor of human trafficking. In his Introduction to Human Trafficking class in the School of Social Work at the University of Alabama, Lim introduced the revised model shown in Figure 97.1 (Lim, 2020).

FIGURE 97.1 The cycle of healing and restoration.

TABLE 97.1 Cycles of Healing and Restoration

Stages of Change	Cycles of Healing and Restoration	Distinction
Precontemplative	Challenge	Rather than being in a state of ignorance, this adaptation begins with a point of tension requiring a decision.
Contemplative	Awareness	In this stage, the person is identifying the need for change and their options.
Preparation	Motivation	In this stage, the person is evaluating their reason to change and making a decision passively or actively.
Action	Action	In this stage, the person takes action.
Maintenance	Improvement	In this stage, the person is engaged in the process of continuing the restorative and healing action, motivated by their reason for their need to change.

This adaptation begins with the individual encountering a challenge that must be addressed rather than with a state of being unaware or uninformed about the consequences of their behavior. The important distinction is not merely psychological but also frames the need for personal healing and growth rather than simply improving one's condition or situation. In the second stage, the adaptation expands the person's focus from only internal to both internal and external. Likewise, in the third stage the individual is not just making a decision to better themselves through something such as counseling, exercise, or mitigating substance use but also examining and evaluating the reasons why this change is necessary. This essential step provides the defenses that will be needed when they encounter their next challenge in life, thus beginning the cycle again. Taking action is the same in both models, but the final state considers another key distinction for survivors of human trafficking. Instead of experiencing a time of maintenance punctuated with temptations of relapse, the cycles of healing and restoration acknowledge and celebrate the victories and improvements resulting from their decisions and actions. This affirmation emboldens them as they face their next challenge with the confidence that they can overcome whatever difficulties they face. And when that cycle restarts, it is not a failure resulting in the inevitable lapse or relapse but, rather, a new challenge, for which they are better prepared. Because of their past successes, they know that even if their response results in the continued presence of the challenge, they are not in a position of ignorance or weakness resulting in harm reduction strategies, but, rather, of empowerment, resulting in increased awareness and motivation.

It is important to understand that as a social worker when you engage a survivor of human trafficking, you are encountering them as they are experiencing one of the stages of this cycle. When attempting to provide effective case management, the social worker will need to quickly ascertain which stage the survivor is in and engage with them appropriately (Table 97.1).

The Trauma Response and Case Management

Understanding trauma response will provide insight into some behaviors that may make your engagements with minors challenging. Their reactions to trauma, or trauma response, will vary from individual to individual but will often appear to be inappropriate responses to external stimuli. Like someone who has been attacked by a swarm of bees in the past might overreact to the sight or sound of a nearby bee, a survivor of human trafficking might overreact when exposed to something apparently mundane. Conversely, using the bee attack victim as the simile, the survivor might appear to be apathetic while the bee lands on their arm, stating "Oh well, if it's going to sting me, there's nothing I can do." Either way, the affect does not correspond to the experience, and it could be their trauma response.

Trauma may present in many different ways with a multitude of nuances as it relates to your work with the child: fear and anxiety; anger; apathy; hypervigilance; hyperarousal; avoidance of relationships, places, activities, situations, and attachment; and so on. When the case manager recognizes a response that appears to be in some way inappropriate given the circumstance, they should identify that as a potential trauma response and begin to work with the minor to help them develop a healthy response. This is an opportunity for the case manager to ask the minor clarifying questions to identify why they responded the way they did. What is learned from this will allow the case manager to more effectively provide care and make appropriate service referrals for the child, and it is an opportunity for the case manager to safety plan with the minor to prepare them for future triggering events.

Whenever possible, it is best to offer service provision through individuals and/or agencies that have been trained on human trafficking and operate from a trauma-informed and victim-centered framework.

Safety Planning and Goal Setting

The safety planning process is a psychoeducational opportunity for the case manager to help the survivor identify dangers and triggers and explore options to manage them when they arise. This empowers the survivor to both control their healing experience

and retrain cognitive processes that are suppressed from their trauma.

The options to mitigate triggers and dangers they have identified can be turned into goals and tracked to indicate progress and to celebrate successes. For example, the case manager can work with Jenny (from the case example) to identify options in the event that she finds herself to be housing insecure. If her immediate thought is to return to Danny, her trafficker, because it is a known situation, the case manager and Jenny can make a list of alternative solutions for housing. They then set a goal for Jenny that the next time she has the fear of housing insecurity, she will go to her list and call through the housing options instead of calling Danny. When Jenny follows through with those calls, thus achieving her goal, her success is acknowledged and celebrated by the case manager.

Clinical Case Conference Reviews

Case reviews can involve the case manager, the minor, a supervisor, and/or a licensed social worker. This time can incorporate an analysis of the progress of the survivor, evaluation of their safety plan, and a celebration of goals reached. The team can then strategize around future goals, service needs, and interventions. Involving the survivor gives them a voice in their treatment plan and allows them to see the collaborative and caring team working to support their healing process.

Individual and Group Supervision

The case manager should have regular supervision to evaluate their management of the case and identify strengths and opportunities for growth. The team of case managers should also participate in regular group supervision. This allows for the sharing of different ideas, strategies, and approaches that other case managers have implemented. These group supervision sessions can also facilitate beneficial mental health sessions and team-building or group-care activities.

Helpful Resources

Blue Campaign—U.S. Department of Homeland Security's public awareness campaign and resources: https://www.dhs.gov/blue-campaign

Guardian Group—anti-trafficking organization for the hotel industry: https://guardiangroup.org

Office for Victims of Crime—promising practices for the case management of survivors of human trafficking: https://www.ovcttac.gov/taskforceguide/eguide/4-supporting-victims/43-the-vital-role-of-case-management-service-planning

Shared Hope International—annual state report cards; training resource: https://sharedhope.org

Truckers Against Trafficking—anti-trafficking organization for the transportation industry: https://truckersagainsttrafficking.org

References

Administration for Children and Families. (2014). *Street Outreach Program Data Collection Project, 2014* [Executive summary]. U.S. Department of Health and Human Services. https://www.acf.hhs.gov/archive/fysb/report/resource/sop-executive-summary

Biehal, N., & Wade, J. (2000). Going missing from residential and foster care: Linking biographies and contexts. *British Journal of Social Work, 30*(2), 211–225.

Bocinski, S. G. (2017). *The economic drivers and consequences of sex trafficking in the United States.* Institute for Women's Policy Research.

Busch-Armendariz, N., Nale, N. L., Kammer-Kerwick, M., Kellison, J. B., Torres, M. I., Cook-Heffron, L., & Nehme, J. (2016). *Human trafficking by the numbers: The initial benchmark of prevalence and economic impact for Texas.* Institute on Domestic Violence and Sexual Assault (IDVSA), The University of Texas at Austin.

Commission for Case Management Certification. (n.d.). *Definition of case management.*

Fong, R., & Berger Cardoso, J. (2010). Child human trafficking victims: Challenges for the child welfare system. *Evaluation and Program Planning, 33*(3), 311–316.

Frankel, A. J., Gelman, S., & Pastor, D. K. (2019). *Case management: An introduction to concepts and skills* (4th ed.). Oxford University Press.

Gibbs, D. A., Walters, J. L. H., Lutnick, A., Miller, S., & Kluckman, M. (2015). Services to domestic minor victims of sex trafficking: Opportunities for engagement and support. *Children and Youth Services Review, 54,* 1–7.

Hammer, H., Sedlak, A. J., & Finkelhor, D. (2017). *National Incidence Studies of Missing, Abducted, Runaway, and Thrownaway Children (NISMART), 1999* Version 2017-12-12. https://doi.org/10.3886/ICPSR04566.v2

International Labour Office & Walk Free Foundation. (2017). *Global estimates of modern slavery.* https://www.ilo.org/wcmsp5/groups/public/@dgreports/@dcomm/documents/publication/wcms_575540.pdf

Lim, C. (2020). *An introduction to human trafficking.* University of Alabama.

Muraya, D. N., & Fry, D. (2016). Aftercare services for child victims of sex trafficking: A systematic review of policy and practice. *Trauma, Violence, & Abuse, 17*(2), 204–220.

National Research Council. (2013). *Confronting commercial sexual exploitation and sex trafficking of minors in the United States.* National Academies Press. http://www.nap.edu/catalog.php?record_id=18358

Pesso, L. (2014). Supporting human trafficking survivor resiliency through comprehensive case management. In L. Simich & L. Andermann (Eds.), *Refuge and resilience: Promoting resilience and mental health among resettled refugees and forced migrants* (Vol. 7, pp. 195–209). Springer.

Smith, L. A., Healy Vardaman, S., & Snow, M. A. (2009). *The national report on domestic minor sex trafficking: America's prostituted children.* Shared Hope International.

Trafficking Victims Protection Act of 2000, 22 USC § 7102(9).

Case Management with Older Adults

Daniel S. Gardner and Aaron Rooney

Medical and public health advances during the past half-century have reduced the burden of disease, extended life expectancy, and significantly accelerated the aging of the population. In 2016, more than 49.2 million people—approximately 15% of Americans—were aged 65 years or older (National Center for Health Statistics, 2016). By 2060, this number is expected to grow to 94.7 million, representing more than 20% of the population (U.S. Census Bureau, 2019). Although older adults are living longer, healthier lives, more than two-thirds live with chronic illnesses or conditions such as diabetes, cancer, cardiovascular disease, depression, or dementia (Centers for Disease Control and Prevention, 2013).

The growing prevalence of chronic and disabling conditions in later life poses considerable challenges for older adults, their families, and caregivers. Chronic conditions typically increase disability, medication use, frailty, and hospitalizations; require ongoing medical monitoring and care; and can negatively affect quality of life (Benjamin, 2010). More than 41% of older adults report some type of disability that is associated with difficulties in walking,

hearing, vision, or self-care that require assistance from others in order to live independently (Okoro et al., 2016). Approximately 39 million Americans—representing 19% of all adults—care for someone aged 50 years or older with a chronic, disabling condition; an estimated 15 million adults care for a family member living with Alzheimer's disease or other dementias (National Alliance for Caregiving and AARP Public Institute, 2015).

The human and economic costs associated with these changes are substantial. In 2017, the economic value of uncompensated family care was estimated to be more than $470 billion (Reinhard et al., 2019). In response to ever-increasing expenditures, Congress passed the Omnibus Budget Reconciliation Act of 1981 (Public Law No. 97-35, Sec. 2176), authorizing the funding of demonstration projects under the Medicaid Home and Community-Based Waiver that integrate health care, personal care, and case management for community-dwelling older adults and people living with disabilities who might otherwise require institutionalization (Anderson et al., 2018; Duckett & Guy, 2000). To further support older adults in the community and control Medicare and Medicaid costs, Title III of the Older Americans Act funds geriatric case management programs throughout the country through the Aging Services Network (i.e., State Units on Aging and Area Agencies on Aging).

Despite the complex health and service needs of older adults, home- and community-based long-term services and supports are often fragmented and difficult to access (Anderson et al., 2018). Geriatric case management (GCM) responds to these barriers by providing person-centered assessment and care planning; facilitating access to critical resources; and coordinating health, mental health, and long-term services and supports that enhance quality of life and promote the health and functional independence of community-dwelling elders. The geriatric case manager's specific role is shaped by agency function (e.g., assisting with financial, housing, health, nutritional, or mental health needs), care setting, and population served (Morano et al., 2015; Tahan et al., 2015). An array of case management approaches have emerged in the past several decades, including care coordination, patient navigation, and transitional care models. Although these terms are often used interchangeably, they represent distinct models of care, goals, and functions. GCM is a cross-disciplinary practice specialty, and certified geriatric case managers have backgrounds in social work, nursing, or rehabilitative medicine. The case manager's professional discipline, skill set, and care setting further frame the focus of practice (Tahan et al., 2015).

Case management is a foundational method in clinical social work dating back to the roots of the profession in the late 19th century [Frankel & Gelman, 1998; National Association of Social Workers (NASW), 2013]. Social work case management is grounded in professional values of enhancing individual autonomy and dignity, advancing social justice, working across systems of care to link resources, and challenging oppression and ending inequities systems (NASW, 2013). Although their goals and functions vary by setting, social work case managers share a commitment to holistic client- and family-centered practice, maintain a strengths perspective, and attend to the sociocultural and relational contexts of individual and social functioning (Darnell, 2013; NASW, 2013). Case management with older adults aims to enhance health and well-being and support independent functioning in the community.

Components of Geriatric Case Management

Geriatric case managers work independently or as members of interdisciplinary teams, in a variety of institutional-, home-, and community-based settings—including Aging Service Network agencies (e.g., case management agencies, naturally occurring retirement communities, or senior centers), hospitals, home health care organizations, long-term care institutions, and other human service organizations (Morano et al., 2015). The past several decades have seen the growth of private GCM providers with older adults to meet the growing demand of families seeking information, assistance, and advocacy around accessing resources, coordinating services, and making current and long-term care decisions (Morano et al., 2015; Tahan et al., 2015).

Although operationalized differently by practice setting and professional background, geriatric case managers share a set of core service components that include the following:

1. Community outreach: Identifying and focusing on at-risk older adults in the community who lack access to case management services or community resources and supports.
2. Comprehensive geriatric assessment: Conducting systematic, thorough, multidimensional assessments of older adults and their home environments. A core

component of all case management with older adults, comprehensive geriatric assessment (CGA), is the foundation of a care plan that addresses the client's unique needs, strengths, and challenges. CGA addresses the following domains:

- Activities of daily living (ADLs): The ability to perform daily self-care (i.e., bathing, toileting, and ambulating) within one's place of residence. ADLs represent a well-documented measure of client's functional status and capacity to live independently.
- Instrumental activities of daily living (IADLs): Tasks that, when performed independently, enable the adult to live in the community. IADLs include shopping, housekeeping, and medication management.
- Pharmacological profile: Medications list (prescription and over-the-counter) and daily protocols. Identify and address gaps in access and care, drug interactions, adverse effects, medication adherence, and use of herbal remedies or alternative treatments.
- Cognitive, psychological, and psychiatric functioning: Diagnostic workup, including evaluation of mental status, memory loss, signs of delirium, dementia, and impairment in judgment or decision-making. Includes assessing client's psychological state and mental health history, signs of depression or anxiety, and interpersonal functioning, as well as making referrals for further evaluation and treatment when indicated.
- Home environment: Adequacy of living situation and extent of person–environment fit. Assessment of home safety, fall risk, and adequate nutrition and hygiene. Identification of eviction risk due to rent/mortgage/maintenance arrears or unsafe living conditions (i.e., cluttering/hoarding problems). Obtaining and coordinating in-home supports or assistance seeking an alternative living situation.
- Financial stability: Evaluation of client's income, resources, and monthly expenses. Identification of gaps in a client's monthly budget and implementation of interventions to close these gaps and ensure financial needs are met on an ongoing basis. Interventions include referrals for money management/bill payer programs, referrals for benefit and entitlement programs, private grants and stipends, access to banking/checking accounts, and financial counseling and literacy training.
- Long-term care planning and legal concerns: Client's care preferences and goals, including views about medical treatment, settings of care, and the decision-making process. Facilitate client–family and client–provider conversations about care preferences and advance care planning; client income and assets; and securing legal assistance with wills, power of attorney, guardianship, and advanced directives.
- Family/caregiver supports: Client's social and familial supports, and social and family functioning. Identify clients experiencing social isolation and loneliness, and assess clients for adequate caregiving and other supports needed to live independently.

3. Benefits and entitlement navigation: Educate older adults and their caregivers about the continuum of community-based services, and help them navigate complex health systems and benefits (e.g., Medicare and Medicaid and assistance with income subsidies, housing, and utilities). Identify and access personal care services, assistance with chores, homemaking, medical care and chronic illness management,

nutritional services and home-delivered meals programs, transportation services and escorting older clients to appointments, financial management and budgeting, and legal assistance. Identify eligibility and assist in accessing food stamp programs, cell phone assistance, and other public benefits when eligible.

4. Interagency coordination and advocacy: Facilitate communication between the institutions and systems with which clients interface to ensure continuity of care and address lack of communication and care coordination. Collaborate with other mental health and community health care providers involved in the client's care to advocate for resources and ensure continuity of care. Plan, facilitate, and monitor care transitions between hospital and home, home and assisted living, or acute care and skilled nursing facilities. Partner with constituent services of local elected officials on behalf of clients in order to advocate for housing, public benefits, or other community needs.

Practice Considerations and Essential Competencies

Research evaluating the effectiveness of GCM has been limited by the lack of shared definitions, goals, and outcomes of different case management models (Peikes et al., 2009). Although there is evidence that case management reduces hospitalizations and health care costs for frail elders, the lack of accepted definitions and diversity of models, aims, and settings makes overall assessment difficult. A survey of Medicare-funded demonstration programs, for example, found that only 3 of 15 care coordination projects were successful in reducing rehospitalization rates (Peikes et al., 2009). The lack of consistent evidence may also reflect the prevalence of complex needs

among case management-eligible elders (Ferry & Abramson, 2006).

Successful community-based case management programs share several components, including targeted outreach to at-risk elders in the community (e.g., those who were recently hospitalized or had multiple emergency room visits), personal contact (including face-to-face and telephone) between the case manager and client, and the use of interdisciplinary teams in which nurses focus on health promotion and illness management and social workers facilitate and coordinate supportive services and resources (Brown et al., 2012). Targeted outreach entails in-depth research about the community being served, including ongoing community needs assessment to remain up-to-date with demographic changes, language needs, generational shifts, environmental conditions such as deteriorating infrastructure, and prevalent health concerns.

Drawing on established geriatric competencies in social work (Naito-Chan et al., 2005), we consider the following knowledge, skills, and attitudes essential to working effectively with older adults and their families:

1. Biopsychosocial and spiritual needs of older adults: Knowledge of age-related physical, functional, and cognitive changes and the impact of comorbid chronic illnesses, geriatric syndromes, frailty, and medication effects in later life. Understanding developmental concerns and tasks of older adults and family caregivers, normative life events and stressors (e.g., retirement, widowhood, and multiple losses), and family life cycle development. Awareness of cultural differences regarding aging, and understanding the biopsychosocial and economic effects of institutional oppression and disparities on African American, Latino, immigrant, LGBT, poor, and economically insecure elders.

2. Engagement, assessment, and planning: Skills in conducting initial and ongoing assessments with older adults; identifying

at-risk clients; prioritizing needs; and evaluating cognitive and functional status, person–environment fit, and the home environment. Familiarity with standardized measures of geriatric health, mental health, and physical functioning. Ability to develop and modify care plans with measurable, mutually established goals that meet the client's goals and maximize independent functioning.

3. Continuum of community-based supports: Familiarity with range of supportive services for older adults, from home- and community-based health and social services to institutional long-term care settings, and knowledge of current eligibility requirements for accessing benefits (e.g., income supports, health insurance, and services). Ability to determine which community program is the right fit for the specific needs of the client (e.g., knowing which bill payer program provides services in Mandarin or which meals program serves the client's community). Skills in negotiating multiple complex systems (e.g., medical, long-term care, and housing) and advocating to best meet the needs of vulnerable older adults and their families. Ability to build strong community partnerships and collaborations, with a focus on expeditious mutual referrals and access.

4. Client- and family-centered interventions: Skills in providing crisis intervention when needed and ensuring access to short- and long-term psychotherapeutic and psychopharmacological treatment for older adults coping with stressful life events or mental health or substance use disorders. Knowledge of evidence-based interventions for older adults (e.g., cognitive–behavioral and interpersonal therapy for elders with depression and functional adaptation skills training for older adults with severe mental illness) and their caregivers (Patterson et al., 2006). Family counseling skills in working with family members and caregivers to improve client supports, alleviate caregiver burden, and access supportive services. Knowledge of psychosocial dynamics of grandparents raising grandchildren, a population that experiences higher rates of depression, anxiety, and are less likely to tend to their own chronic health conditions (Beltran, 2016).

5. Interdisciplinary team care: Seamless transdisciplinary collaboration is an essential component of efforts to assess the needs and enhance the health and well-being of older adults and their families (Hintenach & Howe, 2020). Skills in collaboration, advocacy, and leadership with other team members or supportive contacts around meeting the biopsychosocial and spiritual needs of older clients and their family caregivers. Geriatric case managers must be able to educate and advocate on behalf of clients in order to ensure access to essential supportive services.

6. Cultural competence and humility: Reflexivity about one's own background and values, mindful of cultural differences, and ability to interact effectively with clients from diverse cultures and social groups. Understanding the impact of racism and other systems of oppression as social determinants of health and well-being in later life. Recognizing that most theories on aging and many aging services do not adequately account for non-heteronormative sexual and gender identities and relationships. Openness to the unique experiences of individuals over the life span, including those undergoing gender transitions in later life (Fabbre, 2014).

Case Example

Ms. S is a 75-year-old woman who worked closely with a case management program to address issues related to financial management, housing stability, and health. Ms. S owns a co-op apartment in New York City and has lived there alone for many years. She receives a minimal Social Security income, approximately $820 a month, that makes it difficult to stay abreast of her monthly rent. Her case manager helped Ms. S apply to a private foundation that approved her for a monthly stipend of $330 to help keep her bills up-to-date and keep enough food in the apartment. The case manager also helped her access SNAP (Supplemental Nutrition Assistance Program) benefits for food, the Medicare Savings Program, Medicaid, and SCHE (Senior Citizens Homeowners Exemption in New York City). Her SCHE program nearly lapsed this year when she missed several notices, but active advocacy efforts by her case manager in collaboration with her doctor and NYC Department of Finance representatives led her renewal to be approved retroactively, and her home was protected.

In the course of their work together, the case manager learned that Ms. S is a resourceful and resilient woman with a long trauma history, who works continuously to manage symptoms of anxiety disorder and major depressive disorder. She has a severe hoarding/cluttering issue in her home that can be a barrier in accessing needed services. For example, if work needs to be done on her phone or a plumber is needed, Ms. S's anxiety and hoarding often impede and sometimes prevent her case manager's strategies for resolving the problem. Ms. S also has a fear of opening mail, and despite systems in place to open mail with her social worker to alleviate anxiety, mail can easily be missed. The case manager referred her to a program specializing in hoarding disorder and collaborated with the program to address the issue in Ms. S's apartment. She has made a commitment to herself to declutter and has allowed these workers to enter her home, taking a major step forward in dealing with her problems.

As is clear in the case of Ms. S, engaging with older clients and establishing a trusting working relationship can be a critical challenge for geriatric case managers. Older adults are often wary of "strangers" and choose to interact with smaller circles of friends and family (Carstensen et al., 1999; Lang, 2000). Some older adults present with psychosocial concerns that can create barriers to service, such as prior mental and behavioral health concerns, a history of difficulties with service providers, or family conflict and dysfunction (Ferry & Abramson, 2006). Geriatric case managers must demonstrate authentic empathy and respect for client autonomy, take the time to establish trust, and be persistent while respecting boundaries in order to develop successful working alliances with older case management clients.

The Changing Context

During the past several decades, trends toward community-based services, consumer direction, and care coordination have been significant drivers of the field of GCM (Anderson et al., 2018). Sweeping changes set in motion by passage of the Patient Protection & Affordable Care Act of 2009 (ACA; Public Law 111–148) have had a far-reaching impact on older adults, caregivers, and case managers. In addition to extending insurance coverage to an estimated 27 million uninsured people (Nardin et al., 2013), the ACA expanded Medicaid coverage to millions of individuals living near the poverty line, encouraging greater use of home- and community-based services, and incentivizing the use of case management and care coordination to increase access to and use of home- and community-based long-term care services for older adults and people with disabilities (Andrews et al., 2013).

Building on the successes of Medicare demonstration projects that integrated medical and social services for community-dwelling older adults (e.g., Program for All-Inclusive Care of the Elderly and social health maintenance organizations), the ACA promoted Medicare innovations in long-term services and supports and care for older adults living with multiple complex chronic conditions (Anderson et al., 2018; Blumenthal & Abrams, 2016). The ACA created incentives for greater use of electronic medical records to reduce medical error and increase systems communication, and it models new payment structures that seek to reward efficiency and quality. The goal of these reforms is to reduce health care costs and fragmentation of medical and social services and supports and to promote health, function, and independence among community-dwelling older adults (Schore, 2009). Continued investment and innovation in community-based supports are critical to ensuring the health and well-being of the nation's aging population.

Conclusion

Case management with older adults has evolved in response to demographic, epidemiologic, and economic changes of the past half century, including (1) a rapidly aging population; (2) the growing prevalence of chronic illnesses in later life; (3) system-wide changes in health care financing and delivery; and (4) an increasingly fragmented, costly, and difficult-to-access system of health and social service supports for vulnerable older adults. As is demonstrated by the work of the case manager and Ms. S, our work must be founded on sincere respect for the dignity and work of older adults; an appreciation of their lives and distinct situations; and individual, familial, and community resources.

Our ability to meet the complex needs of older adults and their families is constrained by a critical shortage of social workers, nurses, and other direct service workers who are trained in the competencies of working with older adults and their caregivers (Institute of Medicine, 2008). As the baby boom generation ages and life expectancies grow over the next several decades, there will be an increasing need for all social workers to be skilled in working with older adults and their families. Social workers will be called upon to evaluate and advocate

for innovative health and long-term care policies and services that more effectively meet the needs of community-dwelling older adults. And geriatric case managers will continue to enhance their clients' physical, emotional, cognitive, and social functioning while ensuring autonomy, choice, and dignity for older adults and their caregivers.

Helpful Resources

AARP—national nonprofit member organization for people older than age 50 years: resources, research, and advocacy for older Americans and gerontologists: http://www.aarp.org

Administration for Community Living, U.S. Department of Health & Human Services—home of federal policy affecting older adults; guide to programs and policies, and consumer guide: http://www.aoa.gov

American Case Management Association—training, networking, and advocacy for case managers in health care: http://www.acmaweb.org

Case Management Society of America—national membership organization providing policy and practice resources, including case management standards of practice: http://www.cmsa.org

Centers for Medicare & Medicaid Services—information and guide to the primary public health care programs covering older adults: http://www.cms.gov

Eldercare Directory—resources for caregivers of older adults in all 50 states: http://www.eldercaredirectory.org/state-resources.htm

National Association of Area Agencies on Aging—membership organization of Aging Network programs; Eldercare Locator; resources and news about elder services: http://www.n4a.org

National Council on Aging—nonprofit service and advocacy organization; resources for elders, caregivers, and organizations: http://www.ncoa.org

U.S. Department of Health and Human Services—lists resources and provides information about health and support-related resources for older adults: https://health.gov/myhealthfinder

References

Anderson, K. A., Dabelko-Schoeny, H., & Fields, N. L. (2018). *Home and community-based services for older adults: Aging in context*. Columbia University Press.

Andrews, C. M., Darnell, J. S., McBride, T. D., & Gehlert, S. (2013). Social work and implementation of the Affordable Care Act. *Health & Social Work, 38*(2), 67–71.

Beltran, A. (2016). The state of grandfamilies in America: 2015. *Child Law Practice Today, 35*(1). https://www.americanbar.org/groups/public_interest/child_law/resources/child_law_practiceonline/child_law_practice/vol-35/january-2016/the-state-of-grandfamilies-in-america--2015

Benjamin, R. M. (2010). Multiple chronic conditions: A public health challenge. *Public Health Reports, 125*(5), 626–627.

Blumenthal, D., & Abrams, M. K. (2016). Tailoring complex care management for high-need, high-cost patients. *JAMA, 316*(16), 1657–1658.

Brown, R. S., Peikes, D., Peterson, G., Schore, J., & Razafindrakoto, C. (2012). Six features of Medicare coordinated care demonstration programs that cut hospital admissions of high-risk patients. *Health Affairs, 31*(6), 1156–1166.

Carstensen, L. L., Isaacowitz, D. M., & Charles, S. T. (1999). Taking time seriously: A theory of socioemotional selectivity. *American Psychologist, 54*(3), 165.

Centers for Disease Control and Prevention. (2013). *The state of aging and health in America 2013.*

Darnell, J. S. (2013). Navigators and assisters: Two case management roles for social workers in the Affordable Care Act. *Health & Social Work, 38*(2), 123–126.

Duckett, M., & Guy, M. (2000). Home and community-based services waivers. *Health Care Financing Review, 63*, 123–125.

Fabbre, V. D. (2014). Gender transitions in later life: The significance of time in queer aging. *Journal of Gerontological Social Work, 57*(2–4), 161–175.

Ferry, J., & Abramson, J. (2006). Toward understanding the clinical aspects of geriatric case management. *Social Work in Health Care, 42*(1), 35–56.

Frankel, A., & Gelman, S. (1998). *Case management: An introduction to concepts and skills.* Lyceum.

Hintenach, A. M., & Howe, J. L. (2020). Interprofessional care: Why teamwork matters. In A. Chun (Ed.), *Geriatric practice* (pp. 491–500). Springer.

Institute of Medicine. (2008). *Retooling for an aging America: Building the health care workforce.* National Academies Press.

Lang, F. (2000). Endings and continuity of social relationships: Maximizing intrinsic benefits within personal networks when feeling near to death. *Journal of Social and Personal Relationships, 17*(2), 155–182.

Morano, C., Gardner, D., & Swerdlow, S. (2015). Geriatric care management settings. In B. Berkman & D. Kaplan (Eds.), *Handbook of social work in health and aging* (2nd ed., pp. 191–202). Oxford University Press.

Naito-Chan, E., Damron-Rodriguez, J., & Simmons, W. J. (2005). Identifying competencies for geriatric social work practice. *Journal of Gerontological Social Work, 43*(4), 59–78.

Nardin, R., Zallman, L., McCormick, D., Woolhandler, S., & Himmelstein, D. (2013, June 6). The uninsured after implementation of the Affordable Care Act: A demographic and geographic analysis. *Health Affairs Blog.* http://healthaffairs.org/blog/2013/06/06/the-uninsured-after-implementation-of-the-affordable-care-act-a-demographic-and-geographic-analysis

National Alliance for Caregiving and AARP Public Institute. (2015). *Caregiving in the U.S. 2015.*

National Center for Health Statistics. (2016). *Older Americans 2016: Key indicators of well-being: Federal Interagency Forum on Aging Related Statistics.* U.S. Government Printing Office.

Okoro, C. A., Hollis, N. D., Cyrus, A. C., & Griffin-Blake, S. (2016). Prevalence of disabilities and health care access by disability status and type among adults—United States, 2016. *MMWR Morbidity & Mortality Weekly Report, 67*, 882–887. http://dx.doi.org/10.15585/mmwr.mm6732a3

Patterson, T. L., Mausbach, B. T., McKibbin, C., Goldman, S., Bucardo, J., & Jeste, D. V. (2006). Functional adaptation skills training (FAST): A randomized trial of a psychosocial intervention for middle-aged and older patients with chronic psychotic disorders. *Schizophrenia Research, 86*(1–3), 291–299.

Peikes, D., Brown, R., Chen, A., & Schore, J. (2009) Effects of care coordination on hospitalization, quality of care, and health care expenditures among medicare beneficiaries: 15 randomized trials. *JAMA, 301*(6), 603–618.

Reinhard, S., Feinberg, L. F., Houser, A., Choula, R., & Evans, M. (2019). *Valuing the invaluable: 2019 update charting a path forward.* AARP Public Policy Institute.

Schore, J. (2009). *The promise of care coordination: Models that decrease hospitalizations and improve outcomes for Medicare beneficiaries with chronic illnesses.* AARP National Health Policy Council, Health and Long-Term Care Committee.

Tahan, H. M., Watson, A. C., & Sminkey, P. V. (2015). What case managers should know about their roles and functions: A national study from the Commission for Case Manager Certification: Part I. *Professional Case Management, 20*(6), 271–296.

U.S. Census Bureau. (2019). National population projections. http://www.census.gov/programs-surveys/popproj.html

Community Practice

Consensus Organizing

Facilitating Community Change

Mary L. Ohmer

Community organizing is the process of helping communities work together to identify and solve problems (Ohmer & Brooks, 2013). Social work scholars Rubin and Rubin (2005) broadly define community organizing as "people coming together to fight shared problems" (p. 189). Most organizing approaches focus on empowering and strengthening communities to solve their own problems. There are multiple approaches to community organizing; however, most are connected to the original three organizing models developed by social work scholar Jack Rothman (1968, 1996): locality development, social planning, and social action.

Locality development is a neighborhood-based organizing approach to engage a broad range of key stakeholders in developing goals and taking civic action (Rothman, 1996). Organizers build community capacity and create social connections and relationships among diverse people (Rothman, 1996). Social planning uses technical experts to help residents solve problems (Rothman, 1996). Organizers engage experts to help residents design formal plans and policies to deliver goods and services to people who need them

(Rothman, 1996). Social action focuses on making demands on the larger community for increased resources and power on behalf of an aggrieved or disadvantaged segment of the population (Rothman, 1996).

Although community organizing approaches have evolved considerably during the past century (Weil, Reisch, & Ohmer, 2012), Saul Alinsky (1946;1971) is considered the founder of community organizing in the United States. Alinsky used an approach to organizing called conflict organizing, which continues to be practiced today. Alinsky believed that self-interest was a motivating factor for resident and community engagement. His goal was to create "people's organizations" that regular citizens with similar self-interests could join to make demands on people in power to improve communities.

What Is Consensus Organizing?

Consensus organizers incorporate the concept of self-interest as motivator for change; but they harness the diverse self-interests of both residents and members of the power structure (Beck & Eichler, 2000; Ohmer & DeMasi, 2009). Consensus organizers practice parallel organizing by developing "deep, authentic relationships and partnerships among and between community residents and stakeholders, and members of the external power structure to facilitate positive and tangible community change" (Ohmer & DeMasi, 2009, p. 13). Gamble and Weil (2010) argue that community organizing is one of the most fundamental processes for community social work practice. Their definition of organizing resonates well with consensus organizing: "efforts to engage citizens in developing their local leadership capacity and to equip them with the knowledge, skills, and organizational power to make positive decisions affecting their social, emotional, environmental, and economic conditions" (p. 10).

How and Why Was Consensus Organizing Started?

Consensus organizing was started by Mike Eichler (2007), a community organizer who was trained in conflict organizing approaches. Eichler created consensus organizing after seemingly "successful" conflict approaches left residents feeling less empowered. A neighborhood in Pittsburgh, Pennsylvania, faced the effects of blockbusting by realtors who were using racially motivated scare tactics to turn over and sell the houses, causing Whites to flee the neighborhood (Eichler, 2007; Ohmer & DeMasi, 2009). Eichler, who was trained in the Saul Alinsky model of organizing, "responded the way conflict organizers are trained to respond: He organized residents to direct their hostility and put pressure on the real estate company responsible for the blockbusting" (Ohmer & DeMasi, 2009, p. 20).

Eichler worked with residents to implement several conflict organizing tactics,

including targeting the real estate broker causing the problem with picketing and a legal lawsuit (Beck & Eichler, 2000; Ohmer & DeMasi, 2009). Despite winning the lawsuit, the real estate company was only charged a $5,000 fine, a small fraction of the actual proceeds it was getting from the sale of neighborhood properties (Beck & Eichler, 2000). Eichler began to seriously question conflict tactics when residents responded with disappointment despite winning the lawsuit. So, Eichler began to think of alternative ways the neighborhood could have a "win." He worked with residents to become real estate agents, partnering with the "target" they had fought against—the real estate industry. Eichler taught residents collaborative strategies to join forces with another real estate company that saw an opportunity to generate business and help residents build capacity to take control of the real estate market in their neighborhood (Beck & Eichler, 1995; Eichler, 2007; Ohmer & DeMasi, 2009). Neighborhood homes began to be sold again at "respectable prices" and the neighborhood was stabilized (Eichler, 2007).

Comparing Consensus Organizing to Other Organizing Approaches

Similar to locality development, consensus organizers focus on community assets and resources, and they engage a broad range of stakeholders from the community, including residents, local churches and businesses, schools, and other organizations. However, consensus organizers also engage members from the external power structure who can support the community (Ohmer & DeMasi, 2009). Consensus organizers develop leadership among a broad and diverse group of residents who are respected but may not currently hold leadership positions, whereas conflict organizers primarily recruit leaders from established organizational networks, such as churches

(Ohmer & DeMasi, 2009). Consensus organizers focus on capacity building and creating locally controlled community organizations that represent the diversity of the communities they serve.

Similar to Alinsky and social action, consensus organizers motivate people around their self-interests; however, consensus organizers also engage external players around their self-interests for the benefit of the community (Beck & Eichler, 2000; Ohmer & DeMasi, 2009). Consensus organizers believe in the creation of power versus taking power from others. They do not force people to share power and resources but, rather, focus on ways to engage everyone to support social justice (Beck & Eichler, 2000; Ohmer & DeMasi, 2009).

The Process of Consensus Organizing

Consensus organizing focuses on five key strategic principles and nine basic steps (Ohmer & DeMasi, 2009). Box 99.1 lists the five strategic principles that consensus organizers adhere to in all aspects of their work (Ohmer & DeMasi, 2009). These principles are similar to those used by social workers, and they also reflect the social work Code of Ethics [National Association of Social Workers (NASW), 2017].

The first principle of consensus organizing is strongly related to the social worker's ethical responsibility to clients around self-determination. According to NASW (2017), self-determination means that "social workers respect and promote the right of clients to self-determination and assist clients in their efforts to identify and clarify their goals." In consensus organizing, self-determination means that people are the experts of their own lived experiences, and those experiences should be at the center of solutions to local problems (Ohmer & DeMasi, 2009). Consensus organizers believe that everyone who shares mutual interests with residents has something to contribute. Although partnerships with external resources and those in power are important for community change initiatives, the solutions are created by neighborhood residents.

According to the Code of Ethics (NASW, 2017), social workers also respect the inherent dignity and worth of the person. This means that "social workers seek to enhance clients' capacity and opportunity to change and to address their own needs" (NASW, 2017). Moreover, social work's focus on the strengths of individuals and communities is directly related to this ethical principle. The idea that all people have worth and capacities is also central to consensus organizing. A consensus organizer views the world through a glass that is "half-full," focusing on the strengths people

---

BOX 99.1 Strategic Principles for Consensus Organizing

- Solutions to local problems should come from affected communities.
- Pragmatic leadership is present in communities, although not always recognized.
- Self-interest can be harnessed as a motivation for improving the welfare of communities.
- If a project achieves its short-term goals without positioning the participants to make even greater gains in the future, then an opportunity has been missed.
- Building relationships and strategically positioning leaders to make a program work require time, care, and finesse.

Source: Ohmer and DeMasi (2009).

bring to the table rather than their deficiencies (Ohmer & DeMasi, 2009).

Consensus organizers also recognize the power of self-interest, which is not the same as being selfish. People are motivated by what they care about—for example, their family's safety, their children's education, having access to healthy food, and being able to afford housing in their own communities. Central to consensus organizing is marrying the self-interests of people in the community with the self-interests of those who can contribute resources and connections to promote social justice and community change. According to the social work Code of Ethics (NASW, 2017), "Social workers challenge social injustice . . . and pursue social change, particularly with and on behalf of vulnerable and oppressed individuals and groups of people."

The achievement of short-term goals motivates people to continue their struggle toward social and community change. However, a consensus organizer positions people to continue to make these changes. Consensus organizers build capacity by strengthening and building on the assets and skills people bring to the table. Once residents become confident that their skills and abilities can contribute to short-term changes, this motivates them to tackle more difficult issues. Consensus organizers help residents learn how to solve problems, resolve conflict, and work with those in power to develop their neighborhoods (Ohmer & DeMasi, 2009).

According to the social work Code of Ethics (NASW, 2017),

> Social workers recognize the central importance of human relationships. Social workers understand that relationships between and among people are an important vehicle for change. Social workers engage people as partners in the helping process. Social workers seek to strengthen relationships among

people in a purposeful effort to promote, restore, maintain, and enhance the well-being of individuals, families, social groups, organizations, and communities.

Consensus organizers understand how "well-meaning" helping professionals and outsiders may have not engaged the community in ways that respect people's dignity and worth. Prior encounters with outsiders may have created mistrust, suspicion, and hostility (Ohmer & DeMasi, 2009). A consensus organizer realizes that trust must be built over time by engaging residents as true partners and recognizing the damage that has been done in the past by other organizers, social workers, and helping professionals. Consensus organizers act as brokers of relationships and bridge builders between people who have similar interests (Ohmer & DeMasi, 2009).

The Basic Steps in Consensus Organizing

The basic consensus organizing steps, listed in Box 99.2, are not necessarily meant to be linear; however, some of these steps naturally occur before others. In Step 1, a consensus organizer conducts a community analysis, which has three components: (1) understanding a neighborhood's history, culture, characteristics, strengths, and demographics; (2) understanding and building relationships with the internal resources in a neighborhood—the people who live, work, provide services, and operate businesses in the neighborhood; and (3) understanding and building relationships with external resources—the corporate interests, government officials and bureaucrats, institutions, and philanthropists who can contribute to community change (Ohmer & DeMasi, 2009).

Although social workers often conduct assessments, it is important to understand that

BOX 99.2 Basic Steps of Consensus Organizing

Step 1: Conduct a community analysis
Step 2: Build relationships
Step 3: Design and implement win–win
projects
Step 4: Disseminate information
Step 5: Strengthen and solidify a
core group
Step 6: Develop strategies
Step 7: Identify internal and external
resource partners
Step 8: Develop and implement
action plans
Step 9: Develop sustainable
neighborhood

Source: Ohmer and DeMasi (2009).

a community analysis is not a needs assessment. Low-income communities have been studied for decades by outside agencies and government. Sometimes residents are part of the process, and other times they are not. Although needs assessments can be important tools to identify issues, they often focus on community weaknesses versus strengths. Community needs assessments and surveys are also often used by agencies to support or justify the status quo and their programs or demonstrate needs so that they can secure funding. Consensus organizers use an in-depth community analysis to find out "how a community works" and to build relationships and engage residents and other community stakeholders (Ohmer & DeMasi, 2009). The analysis helps identify people's self-interests, including what they care about and the community problem-solving efforts they might be motivated to get involved in. A needs assessment may be part of this process; however, these tools are developed and implemented with a community once an organizer has built relationships with residents.

Step 2 focuses on the deliberate process of building and strengthening relationships with residents and internal and external stakeholders identified in Step 1 (Ohmer & DeMasi, 2009). During the community analysis, the organizer begins to understand the common concerns and interests among a broad spectrum of residents and institutions and who is and is not currently connected to address these concerns. Through their initial relationships, the organizer begins to identify opportunities for group action (Ohmer & DeMasi, 2009). Building relationships requires reciprocity, honesty, trust, and transparency. People may feel isolated and believe that no one else cares. An organizer connects people with others who care about the same issues. Ohmer and DeMasi (2009) note that

> a functioning core group is built on strong, in-depth relationships based on mutual self-interest. When people realize they share similar goals and dreams, they feel empowered and want to work together. Relationships are the key to everything else that happens and the most important job of a consensus organizer. (p. 79)

During Step 3, consensus organizers bring people together with common interests to do something to address one of their more immediate concerns. These projects are "winnable, meaning that they address an issue or problem many people care about, they can be achieved readily, have broad roles for people to play, are seen as a positive action by many, and can solve immediate problems" (Ohmer & DeMasi, 2009, p. 80). They provide an opportunity for people to use their skills and strengths and to develop working relationships, including defining norms for how they will work together in the future. Win–win projects instill hope that something can be done to create community change and motivate people to continue working together (Ohmer & DeMasi,

812 | P<small>ART</small> X C<small>OMMUNITY</small> P<small>RACTICE</small>

2009). Leaders often emerge from these efforts, and relationships are strengthened between residents and external stakeholders who can also make contributions to these projects.

Step 4 focuses on disseminating information; however, this is something that a consensus organizer should also continually do. An organizer will begin to understand how information is communicated in the neighborhood during the early steps. During Step 4, the organizer works with residents to strengthen communication and information sharing. An organizer must be familiar with in-person and remote communication outlets (e.g., email and social media) and determine how each audience in the neighborhood receives or could receive information. When residents believe information is transparently shared, this builds trust and keeps people connected.

Working with groups is central to social work practice as well as consensus organizing. During Step 5, a consensus organizer brings together a core group of people who have demonstrated the most interest, leadership, and commitment to working together (Ohmer & DeMasi, 2009). The organizer seeks people who are open and willing to share power with others but who are also trusted and respected. These individuals do not need to be existing leaders; they can be ordinary people who may be quietly working to solve problems in their neighborhood. Members of this group share common interests that sustain their engagement over time.

During Step 6, a consensus organizer works with the core group to develop strategies to address their common interests. The organizer helps residents analyze potential issues and solutions that are likely to gain the most support from both residents and external stakeholders (Ohmer & DeMasi, 2009). Then, during Step 7, a consensus organizer works with the core group to identify the self-interest of potential partners inside and outside the neighborhood and ways to engage them around common goals and solutions. This helps ensure that the issues are important to most of the people in the community

and the potential solutions are achievable. In Step 8, a consensus organizer facilitates the development of written action plans related to the issues and potential solutions developed in Step 7. These plans are similar to other types of plans social workers develop (e.g., strategic plans); however, the goal is to build on the momentum created through the win–win project and visioning process conducted in Steps 6 and 7. Action plans are based on the support and approval of the community, and they are connected to the interests, resources, and support of external players. Committees can be formed to develop plans around specific goals, including potential projects. At various steps in the process, large community meetings are also helpful to engage a wider group of people and build momentum and support. A successful action plan has four major ingredients (Ohmer & DeMasi, 2009, p. 86):

- Community support and buy-in
- Real and tangible roles for residents in the implementation of the plan
- Criteria to evaluate progress toward meeting the goals of the plan
- Internal and external resources engaged and invested in the plan's success

The goal of this process is to help residents create sustainable neighborhoods in which they can advocate for themselves (Step 9). Forming a credible and respected group of residents builds community power that can be harnessed to influence the issues they care about. Consensus organizers build organized and credible groups that are in a better position to be heard (Chaskin et al., 2001, as cited in Ohmer & DeMasi, 2009).

> While consensus organizing aims to solve real problems, the ultimate contribution of consensus organizing is leaving behind the capacity for neighborhoods to be able to continually solve problems and build and sustain effective relationships and

partnerships. The consensus organizing process should leave behind capable leaders who can break down complex community problems in a way that is understandable and leads to effective strategies and solutions. (p. 87)

How Has Consensus Organizing Been Used?

There are several examples of how consensus organizing has been used to engage residents and build their capacity to create community change in community development, family services, violence prevention, and equitable development. After its creation by Eichler (2007), consensus organizing was used to develop community-controlled development corporations in cities throughout the country. For example, Eichler worked with local corporate leaders to engage residents and community stakeholders after the devastating losses caused by the collapse of the steel industry in Pittsburgh (Beck & Eichler, 2000; Eichler, 2007; Ohmer & DeMasi, 2009). Consensus organizing was also used to create community development corporations where local capacity was lacking through a program called the Development Team under a national intermediary called Local Initiatives Support Corporation (Eichler, 2007; Ohmer & DeMasi, 2009). Consensus organizers also assisted family service agencies in several cities to become more community-centered through a national initiative sponsored by the Alliance for Children and Families (now called the Alliance for Strong Families and Communities). Eichler also created the Consensus Organizing Center at San Diego State University School of Social Work. The center provides consensus organizing training to high school and university youth to partner with community organizations around justice, safety, and youth empowerment.

More recently, consensus organizing has been used to address community and youth violence prevention and equitable development.

Youth and adult residents were trained in consensus-organizing strategies to build collective efficacy for the prevention of crime and violence in a low-income neighborhood in Atlanta, Georgia (Ohmer, 2016; Ohmer & Owens, 2013). Collective efficacy includes the relationships of trust among residents and their willingness to intervene to address neighborhood problems, which helps prevent community violence (Ohmer et al., 2016; Sampson et al., 1997). Consensus organizing was used to strengthen relationships among youth and adult residents; build trust among residents and external stakeholders, including the police; and develop residents' skills in identifying common interests, solutions, and points of intervention to prevent and address crime and violence in their neighborhood. Participants worked with one another and the wider community on a win–win project to address a community-identified issue related to crime and violence. The results showed that participants increased neighborhood engagement and connections; strengthened relationships with their neighbors; were significantly more likely to intervene in neighborhood problems; and improved their attitudes, norms, and values about intervening (Ohmer, 2016; Ohmer & Owens, 2013). This project translated the evidence on collective efficacy into tangible action by residents to address the crime and violence issues they cared about the most.

Consensus organizing was also used in a project to increase youth and adult resident civic engagement around equitable development, which is becoming increasingly important in communities facing pressures from neighborhood change and gentrification. Consensus organizing was first used to build resident capacity to conduct community-led development and equip residents to revitalize their neighborhoods. However, some of these same communities are now facing pressures that can lead to displacement. Nationally, gentrification is occurring at twice the rate of the 1990s (Maciag, 2015; Pendall & Hedman, 2015), and Pittsburgh is facing similar pressures. In fact,

Pittsburgh is the eighth most gentrifying city in the United States based on data from 2000 to 2013 (Richardson et al., 2019).

Consensus-organizing strategies were used to engage residents around equitable development, which is "a positive development strategy that ensures everyone participates in and benefits from the region's economic transformation—especially low-income residents, communities of color, immigrants, and others at risk of being left behind" (Treuhaft, 2016, p. 4). The project engaged more than 30 youth and adult residents in a series of community conversations about how to increase civic engagement and activism around equitable development. Residents were taught consensus organizing as a vehicle for civic engagement, including ways to find common ground and mutual interests, engage and influence external stakeholders, and develop and engage a core group of people who cared about equitable development. External stakeholders who influence equitable development through affordable housing, community planning, and local equity plans and policies were invited to speak with and engage residents in learning more about local efforts and ways to effectively influence equitable development plans to ensure they are implemented. The community conversations resulted in an *Equitable Development Playbook* that other residents can use to influence positive community change. Results showed that youth and adult participants knew how to influence people who made decisions about their neighborhood, understood the importance of equitable development and how to influence it, and understood the importance of civic engagement in their community.

Why Is Consensus Organizing Important Today?

Consensus organizing is a vehicle through which social workers can address contemporary issues that continue to impact the individuals, families, groups, and communities with which we work, including racial injustices, police brutality, as well as health, housing, food, and other equity issues exacerbated by the COVID-19 pandemic. Consensus organizing can help people build and strengthen relationships, break down myths and misunderstandings between people, and identify common ground and work together to develop viable solutions.

For example, active engagement in communities can break down barriers between residents and the police. A Black law enforcement official said he looks for people with community service when he hires officers because it shows their willingness to become active community members and build relationships with residents (Evans, 2020). He said this helps break down perceptions officers and residents have of one another. Research shows that volunteerism increases residents' sense of community and ability to work together to solve problems (Ohmer, 2007). In the violence prevention project discussed previously, residents worked alongside police officers and external stakeholders to redevelop a vacant lot that was a source of crime and blight, which helped change perceptions and strengthen relationships (Ohmer & Owens, 2013).

Consensus organizers engage in advocacy and peaceful protests around inequity and racial injustices. However, they also work to create mutual interests and solutions around these long-term problems, authentically engaging residents and those affected by problems to lead the creation of solutions to some of society's most pressing issues.

Helpful Resources

Consensus Organizing Center at San Diego State University School of Social Work: https://consensus.sdsu.edu

Study site for *Consensus organizing: A community development workbook* (Ohmer & DeMasi, 2009): https://studysites.sagepub.com/ohmerstudy

University of Pittsburgh School of Social Work and Homewood Children's Village. *Equitable development playbook*: https://www.canva.com/design/DADmZ_Qp9rk/Gy5-ULHasxMhkgley5_zCQ/view?utm_content=DADmZ_Qp9rk&utm_campaign=designshare&utm_medium=link&utm_source=publishsharelink#1

References

Alinsky, S. D. (1946). *Reveille for radicals*. Chicago: University of Chicago Press.

Alinsky, S. (1971). *Rules for Radicals: Practical Primer for Realistic Radicals*. Random House, New York.

Beck, E. L., & Eichler, M. (2000). Consensus organizing: A practice model for community building. *Journal of Community Practice, 8*(1), 87–102.

Chaskin, R. J., Brown, P., Venkatesh, S., & Vidal, A. (2001). Building community capacity. Aldine de Gruyter.

Eichler, M. (2007). Consensus organizing: Building communities of mutual self-interest. Sage.

Evans, E. (2020, June 15). Can volunteering help heal our country's racial divide? *Deseret News*. https://www.deseret.com/indepth/2020/6/15/21286935/george-floyd-volunteering-community-service-racial-divide-racism-united-states-healing

Gamble, D., & Weil, M. (2010). Community practice skills: Local to global perspective. New York: Columbia University Press.

Maciag, M. (2015, February). Gentrification in America Report. Governing the Future of States and Localities. http://www.governing.com/gov-data/gentrification-in-cities-governing-report.html

National Association of Social Workers. (2017). *Code of ethics*. https://www.socialworkers.org/about/ethics/code-of-ethics

Ohmer, M. L. (2007). Citizen participation in neighborhood organizations and its relationship to volunteers' self- and collective efficacy and sense of community. *Social Work Research, 31*(2), 109–120.

Ohmer, M. L. (2016). Strategies for preventing youth violence: Facilitating collective efficacy among youth and adults. *Journal of the Society for Social Work and Research, 7*(4), 681–705.

Ohmer, M. L., & Brooks, F. (2013). The practice of community organizing. *The Handbook of Community Practice*, 233–248.

Ohmer, M. L., & DeMasi, K. (2009). *Consensus organizing: A community development workbook: A comprehensive guide to designing, implementing, and evaluating community change initiatives*. Sage.

Ohmer, M. L., & Owens, J. (2013). Using photovoice to empower youth and adults to prevent crime. *Journal of Community Practice, 21*(4), 410–433.

Ohmer, M. L., Teixeira, S., Booth, J., Zuberi, A., & Kolke, D. (2016). Preventing violence in disadvantaged communities: Strategies for building collective efficacy and improving community health [Special issue]. *Journal of Human Behavior in the Social Environment, 26*(7–8), 608–621.

Pendall, R., & Hedman, C. (2015). *Worlds apart: Inequality between America's most and least affluent neighborhoods*. The Urban Institute.

Richardson, J., Mitchell, B., & Franco, J. (2019). *Shifting neighborhoods: Gentrification and cultural displacement in American cities*. National Community Reinvestment Coalition.

Rothman, J. (1968). Three models of community organization practice. In F. Cox, J. Erlich, J. Rothman & J. Tropman (Eds.), *Strategies of Community Organization*. F.E. Peacock, Itasca, IL.

Rothman, J. (1996). The interweaving of community intervention approaches. *Journal of Community Practice, 3*(3-4), 69–99.

Sampson, R. J., Raudenbush, S. W., & Earls, F. (1997). Neighborhoods and violent crime: A multilevel study of collective efficacy. *Science, 277*, 918–924.

Truehaft, S. (2016). Equitable development: A path to an all-in Pittsburgh. PolicyLink. https://www.policylink.org/sites/default/files/report_pittsburgh_FINAL_PDF_0.pdf

Weil, M., Reisch, M. S., & Ohmer, M. L. (Eds.). (2012). *The handbook of community practice*. Sage Publications.

Community Organizing Principles and Practice Guidelines

Terry Mizrahi

This chapter is based on my practice experiences over 40 years. It is both a condensed and an updated version of this chapter as it appeared in the third edition of this volume (2015). Examples and actions related to these principles can be found at https://sssw.hunter.cuny.edu/emeritus-faculty/mizrahi-terry-msw-phd/ under Links.

Principle 1: Effective Organizing Balances Process and Product

A key assumption is that there never is sufficient time, staff, and other resources to involve people in making change (the process) and in accomplishing a specific goal or task (the product) simultaneously. The question is how to operationalize and balance them. Process means enough discussion to achieve a consensus in order to move ahead and keep participants engaged. Consensus does not mean unanimity but, rather, a "sense of the body" informally or alternatively by a more formal voting procedure. Where there is disagreement, there must be a mechanism to ascertain its intensity as well as its extensiveness and to determine whether moving ahead means a permanent division or dissolution among the members or constituents. There needs to be "enough" process to gauge people's interest in and commitment to the task, and there must be enough time to create a sense of investment and to build trust among participants. That can be done by working on the task while stopping to reflect periodically on the process, asking: "How we are doing?" "Whose voices do we still need to hear from?" "Are we ready to move to the next step?"

The solutions to managing time so that the product/outcome is achieved without sacrificing the process are (1) calculate a more complete and realistic timetable, (2) modify expectations if necessary, (3) prioritize what is essential, and (4) ascertain who else can assist with the project. Organizing means planning for contingencies, allowing more time than appears necessary at first, and anticipating opposition (Principle 11).

Principle 2: Planning Is a Complex Value-Based Sociopolitical and Technical Process

Planning is not just about data collection, setting goals, creating strategies, and timelines. It is not just about finding someone who can write a clear, internally consistent proposal. What underlies all planning processes is a value base or ideology. This includes basic assumptions about why a problem exists, who or what is "to blame," and why conditions are not optimal or needs are not being met. Social work values are informed by principles of social and economic justice and democratic, participatory decision-making. Planning as part of organizing is also a sociopolitical process, meaning that power and resources inform the way constituents define the problem and select the solutions. Power means understanding that some*body* (with a small or capital B)—that is, some individual or entity—has the ability to make decisions about how resources are allocated and whether to implement a program or change a policy. Resources include creating, increasing, or redistributing assets (social and economic capital) that address the planning outcomes. Hence, the goals and strategies selected by a group are done within a value-based and sociopolitical context.

Principle 3: There Is No Such Thing as "Rational" and "Irrational" from the Perspective of How Problems Are Defined or Resources Allocated

Be alert when someone says, "It does not make sense" or "It's irrational" with respect to why a policy has been created or has been changed. When that statement is made, consider reframing the question by instead asking "To whom does it make sense?" "For whom is it functional and working?" "Why hasn't that policy been changed, even though it is not working for clients or constituents of an agency?" Usually what is uncovered as to the reasons why conditions or attitudes have remained in place is that it does make sense to those in power or to a privileged constituency. In other words, it is not irrational for groups that may be affected adversely to attempt to maintain the status quo. Understanding this means that the group seeking change needs to identify the covert as well as overt reasons for why those who control the decision-making may resist change. This does not mean that there are instances in which resisting change is not deliberate or intentional.

Often, the term "rationality" is invoked by those resisting change, in contrast to the term "ideology," such as, for example, when opponents of a plan state that the other side is not being rational or that those seeking change are biased. The group needs to consider whether, when hearing somebody propose a "rational" solution, it is being used to prevent deliberations on policies and programs that invoke values such as fairness, equality, and justice.

Nevertheless, political and ideological arguments about rationality should not obfuscate the need to be logical, systematic, and problem-focused. It is necessary to anticipate the steps, activities, people, and resources needed to produce a coherent plan from beginning to end, implement it, and evaluate it, as well as to identify contingencies beyond the control of a constituency that could impede a preferred solution.

Principle 4: Know and Make Your Case

Evaluation and assessment are a critical part of social work practice, including community organizing and planning. It is essential to ask the following questions: "How does one know there is a problem?" "How does one know there is a need for a particular intervention?" "Who asserts that there is a problem/need?" "Who is defining the problem/need?" "Why at this time?" "How serious and pervasive is the problem?" and "How will the participants, policymakers, and funders know if the goals were achieved?" —that is, "How will success be measured?"

Remember, the way a problem is defined will determine the proposed solution(s).

Once an issue is defined as a problem (or moves from a private issue to a public problem), the next step in the planning process is to document the problem. This entails gathering quantitative and qualitative data, sometimes called empirical (objective) and perceptual (subjective) information.

Next, after documentation comes the presentation of the data to various communities, also known as strategic outreach. Consider the ways in which to convey that information to make the strongest, most convincing case. Different audiences require different spokespersons. Outreach is a strategic campaign of many steps, processes, and deliberation; it is not just an activity.

Principle 5: The "Community" Is Not Monolithic

When various people say "Lets involve 'the community,'" the question must always be "Which community?" "Community" has multiple definitions (based on geography, identity, and/or interest and issue). Most people belong to multiple communities and will lead with one or the other depending on where and who asks. For example, for some political and strategic purposes, someone may identify as part of a general constituency (e.g., Latinx, seniors, or Asian Americans). Still, it is important to recognize that within those large categories, there usually are differences according to other identities, such as gender, country of origin, culture, and other attributes, that may segment the group. In engaging in a change effort, or in trying to build the influence of a constituency or community (however defined), the organizer must pay attention to historic tensions, intra- and interpersonal conflicts, and interorganizational and interdisciplinary differences, as well as structural inequalities within specific communities and between them. These often prevent people from working together effectively and focusing on what they have in common.

In working to obtain a policy or community goal, organizers should be paying attention to the ways they can bring a diverse set of actors/stakeholders to the table. This may be in the form of a task force or coalition, or just an ad hoc meeting. Recognize that there are segments within and between communities of all kinds that have had little contact with each other and/or past contacts may have been negative. When bringing groups with different amounts and types of power and privilege together, it will almost always require additional time, sensitivity, and intentionality. Historical and current differences by class, race, gender, ethnicity, status, generation, or sexual orientation should be factored in from the beginning. Anticipate tensions if new partners from different backgrounds are coming together for the first time or if groups that distrust each other are returning to a new table.

The relationship between an organization that is leading a campaign (whether at a grassroots or coalition level) and the constituencies it wishes to reach is the important factor in how organizing proceeds. Is the founding organization trustworthy and competent? Are the organization and organizer from that community (however defined) or from outside? The organizer is not a free agent. The auspices and background of the organizers are critical factors in the role they play in organizing a campaign.

Principle 6: Know the Decision-Making Structures of the Target System— Who Holds Formal Power (Authority) as Critical Actors and Who Holds Informal Power (Influence) as Facilitating Actors

Understanding and utilizing the concept of power is an essential component of organizing. Power has two faces—authority and influence. Those with authority are labeled "critical" actors. They are the actual legitimate decision-makers—that is, those with the sanctioned formal authority to grant the request, make the change, and allocate the resources. Those with influence are those who wield power based on attributes or position other than authority. They are labeled "facilitating" actors who can influence the critical actors because of their relationship to them and status in the community. Often, people do not know who has the formal power to make the desired change happen because it is hidden or because the institutional system is complicated.

The best approach is to do a power analysis beforehand. Who are the people and organizations who control the systems needed to make change? The formal system of authority is usually found on some version of an organizational chart. These are usually in the form of a diagram that shows the chain of command, who reports to whom in the hierarchy, who controls certain subparts of the organization (span of control), and to whom they are accountable internally. Do not be surprised if the organizational chart is difficult to obtain, even from one's own organization. Many organizations do not want to reveal the formal authority; they may conceal differences between those designated to make decisions and those who actually make them. Often, groups will be told that the organizational table is in transition or not current. Persist.

Knowing someone's formal position can help decide the level of intervention in the system. If someone says they cannot make a certain decision, ascertain whether they are being accurate or "buck passing." It is essential to ask that person, "Who *can* make that change or grant the request?" The persons or department initially approached may be a facilitating actor in the process of making change if they reveal their relationships to the critical actor(s). There are many instances in which organizers and their constituencies are at the wrong door as a result of ignorance or deceit.

There is also a need to know and possibly use the informal structures of influence—that is, people who are able to amass power to make change by virtue of being able to influence the decision-making bodies (the critical actors). There are many ways groups can be powerful when they are not in a position to command "Just do it!" People have power through the positions they hold, their past history of action, longevity in a system, perceived effectiveness and expertise, connections to the decision-makers, ability to control a large constituency, and characteristics such as persistence and willingness to take risks. There are powerful "subordinates" in organizations because of certain functions they perform or access they could provide (e.g., janitors, secretaries, and technical staff).

Organizing power by using strategies of influence is an essential skill set. Organizers use these strategies to bring pressure to bear on the structures of authority to convince them to make the needed changes, fund programs, reallocate resources, and so on. Different tactics will be needed for confronting public/government versus private/corporate power. Depending on the issue, many changes can be made at lower levels in both public and private bureaucracies.

It is not always necessary or wise to start with or go to the top of the chain of command.

Principle 7: Do Not Assume that the Target of Change Is a Unified, Monolithic System

When focusing on a target of change, search for internal strains, divisions, and vulnerability within that system, organization, or institution. Seek out colleagues and allies from within. Most organizations try to create a culture of unity among their staff and clients/constituents; at the very least, they attempt to present a unified front to the public. However, that does not mean that there is unanimity in relation to their positions, policies, or programs, especially in large bureaucracies. In analyzing the system to be influenced, it is essential to ascertain who on the inside of that system feels similarly about the issue as does the group/constituency seeking change. Those inside actors can provide information if courted, including the identification of critical and facilitating actors within. They know the organization's past and current policies, formal and informal leaders, procedures, and culture. Conversely, those insiders may need support, legitimacy, and resources from outside groups, and they may even want outsiders to pressure the organization/institution. (Principle 12 provides more detail for those on "the inside.")

Principle 8: Assume Nobody Knows Anything, Anytime

For political and strategic purposes, organizers work from the assumption that those in charge of the system or institution are ignorant of the problem or need. Therefore, the first step is to define and document the need in a way that

gives the decision-makers a chance to respond (see Principle 3). This step is vital even if it is well known that those in control already have the requisite information on which to act.

Allowing decision-makers/critical actors to save face is essential. Do not underestimate the value of this human principle to be gracious rather than shaming—at least in the beginning of the change process before the latter is strategically used as a tactic. In the best case scenario, those with the power will do something about the issue (i.e., clean up the park, fund a program, pass legislation, allocate staff time for an activity, etc.). In the worst case scenario, they will delay or oppose the solution openly. If they do not respond, there is greater legitimacy for moving ahead and escalating the pressure—to move from presenting additional information to using more intense and persistent persuasive tactics, including taking the issue to the media and threatening additional more conflictual actions. The important point is to document all the steps taken in this process of organizing for change and keep the relevant people, constituents, and organizations informed and involved.

This principle also applies to educating the clients/constituents (e.g., members, tenants, and residents) about the root causes of the identified issue and the power structure that needs to be confronted. This must be done in a way that respects their views even if misinformed or incomplete. Starting where the client is, a social work principle, does not mean ending there.

Principle 9: Assume Goodwill and Common Cause on the Part of Those Who Control and Operate the System

This may seem to contradict Principle 7, but in reality, both tensions have to be managed at the same time—both are truths.

In beginning any campaign with an organizational target, it makes sense to assume that the system is not intentionally out to harm or hurt the clients/constituents but, rather, is attempting to do the job it was given with inadequate resources and incomplete information. Hence, there is value in framing the problem in consensus terms, at least initially. A critique of the status quo should not be presented or perceived as a "win/lose" situation (see Principle 8). A goal of a campaign can be stated in ways that recognize that all involved have a similar mission; for example, they all want to help the children, provide quality health care, have a clean environment, keep a neighborhood safe, and so on. In addition, the organizers could convey an understanding of the difficulties that the agency/system has in meeting the needs of its clients/constituents. Then the strategy becomes one of demonstrating and documenting to the leadership, staff, and the public how the agency/system is interfering with or defeating its own goals or mission. Where possible, appeals should be made to their self-interest as well as to their altruism: "What we are asking is good for the individual and good for the community!"

Assuming common cause does not mean letting people off the hook or giving them a "pass." As conveyed in Principle 8, it means alerting them to the inadequacy or deleteriousness of their program or policy in a systematic, sustained, and easily understood manner and giving them a chance to respond.

Principle 10: Assume the Principle of Least Contest—Escalate the Process Only as Needed

Following from Principle 9, in order to have credibility and to gain the broadest support, the organizers and leaders should not antagonize the target of their change prematurely or unnecessarily. Intervene just high enough to gain recognition to achieve their goals. Strategies of influence exist on a continuum of social change from consensus to contest and conflict tactics. These range from education of the target and public to tactics of persuasion; negotiation and bargaining processes; offering incentives; more conflictual tactics including threats; and, finally, using social action strategies of mass mobilization, protest, peaceful resistance, and disruption.

In general, and in accordance with Principle 8, adversarial and confrontational tactics should be considered only after those in authority position have (or had) been given a reasonable chance to make the demanded changes voluntarily. Beginning with consensus does not assume that information alone will be sufficient to produce major change. The strategic question to answer is "What will it take to have an issue seriously addressed?" A well-thought-out strategy will determine the process and timing of moving from the least to the most conflictual strategies. The cogent questions are "How long have those organizing been waiting for change to occur?" "How long can they wait?" "How serious are the consequences of inaction?" "What is the group prepared to do if their demands are not granted?" and "What resources and contributions are needed to successfully escalate the strategies without losing too many allies and supporters?"

In intensifying the pressure on those with authority, ethical considerations come to the forefront. Not alienating potential allies unnecessarily or prematurely includes the principle of "no surprises." This means not going above or around a facilitating or critical actor without first giving them a chance to enact the change, and then warning them of the consequences of resisting the change. If there is a need to catch an opponent or adversary off guard because of the seriousness of the issue, anticipate the fallout and possible backlash and discuss it with those engaging in the process. Don't be caught off guard.

Among the essential ethical practices based on social work values is to inform the constituents about the tactics in which they are being asked to engage. If there is a chance of provocation or serious repercussions at an event or due to certain actions, participants must have the ability to make an informed choice in advance, even at the risk of losing some of them, to the extent that the risks can be anticipated. As noted in Principle 11 next, organizers need to anticipate the opposition and consider countermeasures. A key question to pose is "What's the worst that could happen if . . .?" Organizers cannot promise their constituents immunity from the consequences of their actions. Even when they may be legally correct, people can still be harmed emotionally, financially, and even physically when they confront powerful targets of social change. It is essential to uncover any perceived fears, even if not grounded in reality, so these can be addressed by the group. People are often caught short when they have not thought through potential consequences of their actions or calculated a risk–benefit ratio.

Collectively, participants need to know the consequences of moving from lawful protest to nonviolent civil disobedience. This is especially important around tactics that have legal ramifications—for example, events that need police permits, trespassing on private property, and so on. Some people are privileged to take more risks than others (e.g., getting arrested, being sued, or being fired). Organizers informed by social work principles need to seriously weigh whether to ever use undemocratic or deceitful tactics—for sure, never to do so without consulting colleagues, allies, and superiors.

Principle 11: There Will Always Be Opposition to Change at Some Level, Be It Active or Passive Resistance

Assuming that some*body*/Body will be opposed to the change a group wants to make means anticipating the range of responses to its goal. This may be articulated as "It can't be done," "We've tried it before, and it doesn't work," "We can't afford it," and so on. As much as possible, analyze in advance those who may be opposed to the identified solutions and why. Play out the opposing side's arguments in advance by testing the waters with the facilitating actors who can influence those decision-makers. Learn from their media and publications how they have responded in the past, while not assuming they will not be persuaded to change their minds.

Effective organizers develop strategies to counter or neutralize opposition where they can, as well as identify those elements in the change process that they or the group cannot control. In identifying supporters, it is essential not to write off potential allies, even if they have been adversaries on other issues. Some commenters believe that there is no such thing as a permanent ally or adversary. Short of intense ideological battles in which there is usually little room for compromise (e.g., abortion rights and affirmative action), appeals for support can be made to most sectors of society. Appeals may be made to factors such as reputation, pride, and professional expertise to gain or keep people on the side of the proposed change. Ask for the advice of would-be supporters, and ask would-be adversaries to put themselves in the shoes of their opponents.

Sometimes the opposition may not be apparent because the implications of the change may not be visible until the change process is underway. Do not assume that all the opposition is external or, conversely, that it is being orchestrated from the target of change. Remember that communities and systems are not monolithic. There may be division and difference within a community as between "the community" and the target of change (see Principles 5 and 7). Sometimes the opposition may just be passivity or inertia rather than visible and organized differences. Would-be supporters may not have been convinced of the urgency or seriousness of the campaign. Opponents may merely delay or avoid a response in hopes of outlasting the group.

Understand that groups engaged in social change are not obligated to come up with one or more solutions just because they identify an issue. In a democratic society, citizens have the right to raise questions, make demands, and hold those in charge accountable for outcomes. The latter have the authority, resources, and expertise to fix the deficiencies or demonstrate why those cannot be fixed. Any individual or group has a right to point out that things are not working without knowing how to right the ship.

Anticipating the opposition includes being able collectively to answer the following questions: How much is the group willing to negotiate? What is the bottom line? What happens if the target says no? Is the answer to retreat or escalate? What happens if the target says yes? What happens if those in charge ask the group to come up with a proposal or to join a task force? That would mean moving from the outside "protesting at the door" to moving on the inside "being at the table." Is the group willing to do that or to identify allies who would? The best chance of making major change happen is when there are organized groups on both the inside and the outside that respect each other's strategy and communicate respectfully with each other.

Principle 12: In Making Change from Inside, Assess Risks Realistically—Identify and Weigh Costs Against Gains

Engaging successfully in major change efforts from within one's own system or agency is possible if one strategically assesses their role and is prepared for possible controversy. There are several positive aspects to initiating or participating in change from within. Those

persons already have a foot in the door. They have the legitimacy to ask for and obtain information; they generally know who makes decisions and how the system "really" works—that is, they have an understanding of its informal as well as formal structure (See Principle 6); they know the history of past efforts to engage in change; and, most important, presumably they have some credibility, longevity, and allies within that structure. Working to improve an organization from within is not disloyal. As noted in the National Association of Social Workers Code of Ethics, it may be the only ethical course to pursue. Timing and tactics are part of the equation as to when and how to act—not whether.

There is a long continuum from doing nothing to getting fired. The importance of keeping one's own house in order cannot be stressed enough. Rarely will employees be directly sanctioned for their organizing activities. They are more likely to be called to task for not doing their paid job or carrying out assigned responsibilities. Pay attention and do not be caught off guard when engaged in internal organizing. Staff members are reprimanded for not turning in reports on time, for leaving early, and for not following up. To minimize any criticism, the opposite may be called for—for example, taking on additional responsibilities, demonstrating one's value to the organization or agency, and becoming a mentor or trainer of others within.

There are, however, two conundrums in working from within. Those on the outside may not know of the efforts of the insiders behind the scenes and might assume that they have been co-opted. In addition, it takes courage and commitment to speak in opposition to traditional policies and practices.

There will be some risk for every action taken. It is important to anticipate actual or perceived repercussions (as per Principle 11) from peers, line or support staff, supervisors, managers, and clients/constituents. Therefore, if a major change is needed, or if the required action includes an implied criticism of the agency or system, one needs to also employ Principles 8–10.

Principle 13: Record Keeping and Note Taking Are Political, Not Clerical Functions

If information is power, then obtaining and recording information is a political process. The persons or groups in charge of those processes are among the most powerful players in their organization or system. Experienced organizers always want to be involved in those note-taking processes. Leaders and others active in the organization should discuss and decide which records to maintain and how records are kept. Documentation includes taking, reviewing, and storing minutes (the records of meetings held); correspondence; keeping supporters and allies informed; and reminding people of past decisions and future plans through letters, emails, and social media. Technology allows for myriad methods of storing data, but the bottom line is to have it permanently stored and available in multiple ways.

Minute taking is a critical skill, value, and process. Minutes help gauge and set the tone for the way a group makes decisions as well as what decisions are made and by whom. These documents are accountability tools; they help keep processes and outcomes transparent, and they keep the people involved focused and honest. They also provide a historical account by preserving the institutional memory, and their availability allows most disputes about past actions to be resolved. It should not be surprising that there are memory lapses (intentional or not) and different interpretations with regard to issues addressed and promises made. If those are absent or incomplete, then denial or disruption of progress may occur unnecessarily.

One can often assess the seriousness, effectiveness, and cohesiveness of a group/organization by whether minutes are taken and reviewed and how engaged participants are in their production, review, and storage. Minutes can also be a diagnostic tool to assess an organization's culture, structure, and history. Experience has demonstrated that if there are no minutes of a meeting or group process, chances are rarely will there be substantial change. When organizations spend an inordinate amount of time reviewing and refuting minutes, one can infer that there is distrust and dissention among those involved in that process which will usually result in an inability to move ahead effectively. Conversely, when minutes are viewed as pro forma without much attention paid to them, one can infer that there is not much investment or involvement of its participants in the organization's operation.

Experience has shown that those in charge of a system or the target of change will often resist the formal recording of a meeting. In those instances, the organization's leaders attending such a meeting must create a paper trail that includes agreements and timetables to be shared among its constituents, regardless of whether the person in charge agrees to have notes taken. The notes can be assembled after a meeting and sent to everyone who attended for review and comment.

Principle 14: The Media Are Unpredictable and Amoral—Proceed with Caution

Given the importance of communicating with a variety of constituencies and publics, understanding the role of the media as a powerful sector of society, and knowing the types and functions of various print and electronic media outlets, is an essential part of the organizer's job.

As part of an outreach campaign, the first step is to identify the various communities that need to be reached and then decide how they are best reached. How do they receive their information? What mainstream, ethic, or community media do they read, watch, and listen to? How many and which social media platforms do they use? Who are the media personalities that influence them? Second is to identify and cultivate a person or persons fluent with each of those outlets, a generic term used here for the different types of media.

In addition, one should identify the reporters and commentators who write and talk about the topic or issue of concern. Be proactive with them. Send them background materials about the organization and the issue. Invite those reporters or opinion-makers or the staff to the organization to meet with the constituency. Determine who may be more friendly and who may be less friendly to the organization and/or issue. (The same principle applies to the involvement of elected officials/political actors.) Next is to craft a message so that the relevant media will want to publish or cover the issue. The story must be told in compelling ways.

It is at this juncture in the process of outreach to media that organizers and most media part ways; hence, the "amoral assertion" made in stating the principle.

Understand that the media, including social media platforms, as a sector of society have the same biases as other institutions in the United States. Those in control usually reflect the "isms" of the greater society (racism, sexism, ageism, etc.) regardless of their politics. Recognition of this fact will temper expectations about receiving a sympathetic or compatible outcome. There are many examples of media coverage that reflect these institutional inequalities. First, when covering a "story," with few exceptions, media people will reach out to the professionals and high-status individuals instead of focusing on those with "lived experience," unless that is unique or special in some way. They will most likely seek out males more than females; they will gravitate more to White people rather than people of color. Therefore,

practically speaking, if the group wants to downplay those disparities and help ensure a unified and accurate message, it must identify and prepare spokespersons in advance.

Conclusion

The principles discussed in this chapter are meant as guides to action and will apply differentially, depending on the auspices of the group or organization, the goals it identifies, the political and economic context of its various communities, the issues in question, and the system driving the organizing. Organizers cannot control all the variables, but acquiring these competencies along with a commitment for the long haul will go a long way. Finally, remember to incorporate the four H's into the work: humanity, humility, honesty, and humor.

Helpful Resources
Websites
Association for Community Organization and Social Action: https://acosa.clubexpress.com/
Community Toolbox: http://www.ctb.ku.edu
COMM.ORG: The Community Organizing Website: http://www.comm-org.wisc.edu

Publications
Bobo, K., Kendall, J., & Max, S. (2009). *Organizing for social change: Midwest academy manual for activists* (4th ed.). Seven Locks Press.
Burghardt, S. (2014). *Macro practice in social work for the 21st century* (2nd ed.). Sage.
Eichler, M. (2007). *Consensus organizing: Building communities of mutual self-interest.* Sage.
Hardcastle, D. A., with Powers, S. R., & Wenocur, S. (2011). *Community practice: Theories & skills for social workers* (3rd ed.). Oxford University Press.
Hardina, D. (2013). *Interpersonal social work skills for community practice.* Springer.
Homan, M. S. (2015). *Promoting community change: Making it happen in the real world* (6th ed.). Cengage.
Kirst-Ashman, K. K., & Hull, G. H. (2017). *Generalist practice with organizations and communities* (7th ed.). Cengage.
Netting, F. E., Kettner, P. M., & McMurtry, S. L. (2017). *Social work macro practice* (6th ed.). Pearson.

Pyles, L. (2014). *Progressive community organizing: Reflective practice in a globalizing world* (2nd ed.). Routledge.

Reisch, M. (2019). *Macro social work practice: Working for change in a multicultural society.* Cognella.

Rothman, J., Erlich, J., & Tropman, J. (Eds.). (2007). *Strategies of community intervention* (7th ed.). Peacock.

Staples, L. (2016). *Roots to power: A manual for grassroots organizing* (3rd ed.). Praeger.

Weil, M., & Gamble, D. N. (2010). *Community practice skills workbook.* Columbia University Press.

Weil, M. O., Reisch, M., & Ohmer, M. (Eds.). (2012). *Handbook of community practice* (2nd ed.). Sage.

Principles and Practices in African American Community Development

Colita Nichols Fairfax

African American community development is an important model of cultural tradition, resiliency, creativity, and economic sustainability, coupled with skill sets of economic and people development processes. It has an important place in African American life and sustainability because America as a country has consistently ignored and neglected this community through a myriad of systemic barriers, violent racism, overpolicing, regulatory and repressive policy, and institutional discriminatory behaviors. Thus, African American community development transcends professional practice, which has often framed community development as follows: "Community development emphasizes self-help and voluntary cooperation among members or residents of disadvantaged communities or sectors of society . . . working on behalf of disadvantaged citizens, community development strives to further the acquisition or redistribution of resources" (Estes, 1997, p. 45); it has also been defined as "a procedure of social capital development" (Koutra, 2015, p. 185). By analysis of

African-centered principles, this chapter explores how social workers should understand, encourage, and sustain African American community development skills and processes in a model of social action. Explicitly, the learner of this subject matter must also be a student of history because the social conditions of African Americans post-Civil War are the genesis of models and skills to transcend, uplift, transform, and develop the full potential of African American people in community, for "to leave the history of social work almost completely to others might challenge the very reproduction of the profession" (Fisher & Dybicz, 2015, p. 117).

Unlike the history of community development taught in higher education, that "community development in America as an organized, purposeful, self-help activity has its roots in late nineteenth century rural life" (Phifer, 1990, p. 18), as reflected in examinations of largely White populations, the African American community development model differs from a person-in-environment model because it is a cultural social action model of people advancement, interdependence, and resilience. The model is birthed within an African-centered intellectual critique, which is also related to African philosophy, rooted within philosophies, cultures, and principles that analyze and apply theories to praxis, unique locally and globally (Fairfax, 2017, p. 74), because "Progressive-era African American social workers' community practice was essentially 'race work,' which personalized problems to alleviate human suffering and concurrently organized and developed private organizations to change the system" (Carlton-LaNey, 1999, p. 311). As Davis et al. (2010) note, an African-centered intellectual critique or an Afrocentric critique of

> historical events, policies, and behaviors has similar goals as other contextualizing forms of research (i.e., feminist research, participatory research, empowerment research, and appreciative inquiry). The difference is that African American experiences and culture are placed at the center of the research question, which allows culturally meaningful constructs to emerge and become part of the research agenda. (p. 340)

When developing African American community development practice, the principles must be developed within an African-centered intellectual or Afrocentric framework that is critiqued by principles that inform practice steps. There are many historical and contemporary development models reflective of this framework in which we find cultural resiliency, mutual aid and cooperation, socialization and education, asset development and capital, such as the Universal Improvement Negro Association (Harvey, 1994), community development credit unions (Nembhard, 2013), settlement houses (Hansan, 2011), missions (Carlton-LaNey, 1997), clinics (Wells-Wilbon,

2015), educational institutions (Fairfax, 2014), and mutual beneficial societies (Marlowe, 2003) such as the Independent Order of St. Luke (Schiele et al., 2005).

Principles

"Community-defined practice gives credence to the perspectives of, and reflects the values of the community, as beneficial to the members of the group" (Goddard et al., 2014, p. 5). Communities are developed by people who use their cultural traditions, histories, and resources to influence the development and potentiality of people. "Communities are an open system influenced by their environment as well as by their internal structures, because the development of community (like human development) is inseparable from its environment" (Chavis & Wandersman, 2002, p. 76). Community development practice is effective when African-centered philosophy and principles are used to shape the practice. "African-centered research is rooted within philosophies, cultures, and principles that analyze and apply theories to praxis, unique locally and globally" (Fairfax, 2017, p. 74), providing "an African-centered or Afrocentric approach that is a culturally competent alternative to respond" (Bent-Goodley, 2005, p. 198) to systemic diseases that are disruptive in the trajectory of culture in African American families and communities and community development. The manifestation or principles of African-centered/Afrocentric framework are found in the Egyptian system, Ma'at, as a social, religious, and moral code of authentic African behaviors through 42 declarations that tutor justice, order, and morality among one another and with systems: "Ma'at provides a useful reflection point on human justice and relationship to nature and the environment" (Ferguson, 2016, p. 2). As a conceptual system utilized to organize thinking, behavior, and society, Ma'at was used to dispel disorder and chaos. Each declaration directs how the person should comport themself. Another value system applied that was developed by Maulana Karenga (creator of the celebration of Kwanzaa) is the Nguzo Saba of the Kawaida theory that reinforces family, culture, and community. These values are as follows (Kalonji, 2014):

> (1) Umoja (Unity), i.e., to strive for and maintain unity in the family, community, nation, and race; (2) Kujichagulia (Self-Determination), i.e., to define ourselves, name ourselves, create for ourselves, and speak for ourselves; (3) Ujima (Collective Work and Responsibility), i.e., to build and maintain our community together and make our brothers and sisters' problems our problems and to solve them together; (4) Ujamaa (Cooperative Economics), i.e., to build and maintain our own stores, shops, and other businesses and to profit from them together; (5) Nia (Purpose), i.e., to make our collective vocation the building and development of our community in order to restore our people to their traditional greatness; (6) Kuumba (Creativity), i.e., to do always as much as we can, in the way we can, in order to leave our community more beautiful and beneficial than we inherited it; and (7) Imani (Faith), to believe with all our heart in our people, our parents, our teachers, our leaders, and the righteousness and victory of our struggle. (p. 203)

With regard to community well-being of African Americans, Ma'at and the Nguzo Saba have been applied in analyzing organic behaviors and cultural institutions of people of African descent, with a special emphasis on "healing, transformation, spiritual, self-determination (Davis et al., 2010, p. 344) and "fundamental goodness, self-knowledge, communalism, interconnectedness, spirituality, [group] reliance,

language and the oral tradition, and thought and practice" (Bent-Goodley, 2005, p. 199). There is continuity among scholars about African American cultural values. As Goodard et al. (2014) note, they are

> grounded in both environmental conditions and a complex structure of cultural precepts, virtues, values, customs, themes and prerequisites. Traditional African American cultural values alone consist of respect for elders, race pride, collective responsibility, restraint, devotion, reciprocity, patience, cognitive flexibility, courage, resilience, defiance, integrity, self-mastery, persistence, and productivity. (p. 9)

Principles that have been highlighted from this framework have been culled into frameworks in order to identify optimal and healthy functioning, such as "interconnectedness and authenticity (e.g., kinship) and harmony (e.g., spirituality)" (Jones, 2007, p. 128). The importance of African principles in African American community development is that not only is the model applied in crisis but also it is a sustainable life thrust, for "Africentric principles are part of the microsystem for African Americans" (Jones, 2007, p. 145). Finally, Ma'at and Nguzu Saba underscore the importance of place. Community is a revered place where one's intimate network is located, the fondest memories are made, and the patterns of life begin. "Everyday places sustain or undermine access to resources and opportunities, connections to others, emotional and physical health, spirituality, identities, and memories" (Kemp, 2010, p. 114). It may also be a place that becomes a painful vessel of disorganization, abuse, and the unimaginable suffering of a dessert. There should be no demarcation of place with any study of people in community development.

In order to cohesively respond to and ameliorate systemic barriers, and maintain cultural solvency, African American community development models of best practices are culled from these principles. Foundational for creating a model of practice responses from the microsystem of African Americans, based on ancient cultures and traditions, these models provide the practitioner with invaluable and purposeful approaches to attend to community needs. "Attending to the landscape means that social workers should acknowledge not only the dearth of economic development in certain communities, but also the absence of cultural development and the presence of practiced African behaviors" (Fairfax, 2017, p. 75). When applying these principles, social workers should attend to transforming the landscape and sensibilities of the population who (1) stayed for generations because of ancestral settlement after enslavement, (2) migrated there due to economic and family choices, and (3) aligned themselves with the neighborhood due to political choices. Terms such as the home place, family home, or "my block" or "the hood" speak more to spaces in which people first understood their humanity and their cultural reality and are visceral indicators of the landscape of belonging and being. The landscape should inhabit safe spaces such as museums, foundations, churches, businesses, people development programs (rites of passage programs, cotillions, drill teams, etc.), historically Black colleges/universities, and independent schools and agencies. Community development should not be confused with outreach practices, which entail providing resources when there are gaps, or community mobilization efforts, which stimulate engagement and participation.

Community Development Practices

African American community development practice is not an isolated practice of economic, civic, housing, political, or artistic activities. It involves practices that transform people to engage with their own intimate network and wider societal network in a manner that advances and sustains all systems and processes in the family/community that represent and serve the family/community and are organic to communities. Goddard et al. (2014) state,

> African American community based practices should, at a minimum, demonstrate in their philosophy, structure, function and relational outcomes a recognizable linkage between the meaning of being human and the contours of its cultural manifestations as represented in the behaviors, beliefs, values, attitudes, customs and traditions it engenders. (p. 15)

The presence of these behavioral traits is tantamount to recognizing traditional African cultural orientation in African American communities, where interventions and treatment programs are enabled for transformative change. Social workers should create experiential scenarios for cultural brokers to reinforce cultural norms (Levy et al., 2018), in practices to engage spirituality and healing rituals (Monteiro & Wall, 2011), use collective creativity (Whitehead, 2018), infuse kinship/interconnectedness, expose fundamental goodness (Bent-Goodley, 2005), and develop group reliance skills, for economic sustainability/vertical integration (Anderson, 2001; Harvey, 1994). Suitable scenarios include having cultural brokers use journaling to observe and document cultural-oriented behaviors and discuss these behaviors with identifiable local leaders who are not aware of cultural-oriented behaviors (Fairfax, 2017). True development of community is about restoration and healing through "traditional African healing methods and cures [that] focus on realignment of the individual with the material, social and spiritual worlds" (Monteiro & Wall, 2011, p. 237).

Organic institutions such as churches, benevolent organizations, museums, and development programs, which are already attending to sustainable efforts and people development, are appropriate environments for these practices.

The time is always ripe for African American community development because there has been "persistent opposition to African American survival and advancement has compelled African Americans to coalesce and work toward common goals of racial equality and justice, and created considerable tension among African Americans to sustain a collective focus" (Schiele, 2005, pp. 807–808) and/or refocus best practices when conditions present themselves. The presence of these best practices working in tandem optimally represents the African American community development model. Table 101.1 explains seven African American community development model practices and approaches that are presented for social workers to incorporate within cultural values and traditions and "protects African Americans from the adverse effects of Eurocentric domination and allow them to freely express their unique human particularity" (Schiele, 2005, p. 821). Applying these best practices simultaneously in the environment buttresses a synergy that continues cultural traditions, customs, and practices while attending to conditions that undermine people development and transformation. "Place matters in socially-just social work practice" (Kemp, 2010, p. 139). The practices presented in Table 101.1 should be utilized in the revered space of community, reflective of conceptual principles, Ma'at, and the Nguzo Saba.

Conclusion

The lack of racial empathy in all systems in American society has created gaps of cultural sustainability and resiliency in impoverished communities in which African Americans reside. Social workers can take advantage of residentially segregated communities to apply community development model practices that are conceptualized within traditional customs, traditions, and values of African culture. Since post-Civil War, African American community development practices have been a necessary aspect of cultural sustainability, traditions, socialization practices, political engagement, and economic survival, "particularly as strategies to save costs, provide quality goods and services, increase income, combat racial discrimination, and increase economic stability and self-sufficiency" (Nembhard, 2004, p. 318). This practice model is most impactful and effective within African-centered philosophy and principles of justice, order, morality, interdependence, relationships, creativity, and economic sustainability, in the special revered place of community.

The profession of social work should support and sponsor funding streams for the application of African American community development practices. This practice model affirms cultural identity in one's intimate network and the wider societal network organic to all systems and processes in the family/community. Social workers should create experiential scenarios for cultural brokers to reinforce cultural norms; engage in practices of spirituality, healing rituals, and collective creativity; infuse kinship/interconnectedness; expose fundamental goodness; and develop group reliance skills, economic sustainability, and vertical integration. Localities have defined community development as housing redevelopment or business/corporation development. These efforts do not represent the model that has been used for generations by African American social reformers post-Civil War. Given the recalcitrant nature of America's social institutions to discriminate and deny equal access and opportunities to African Americans, it is necessary to apply the African American community development model to transcend, uplift, transform, and develop the full potential of African Americans.

TABLE 101.1 African American Community Development Model Practices

Practice	Definition of Use
Apply experiential scenarios	Locate optimally productive examples in which there is the presence of four or more community development practices in place, working in tandem to sustain one community.
Engage spirituality and healing rituals	Apply sacred ritual dances and movements that include prayer, fasting, meditative singing, poetry, and prose in the traditions of the family that specifically highlight the area of trauma and pain in churches, temples, mosques, and other sacred spaces.
Use collective creativity	Research and receive the community's creative preference of how the community model is manifested in epistemology, affect, and motion.
Infuse kinship/ interconnectedness	Locate extended family connections and relationships through institutional and group affiliation, and highlight relationships that exemplify interdependence, sharing, and mutual aid in communities that may be used to attend to conditions that create isolation and emotional vulnerability.
Expose fundamental goodness	Create exercises that help people reflect upon the positive, meaningful, and contributory actions they conduct in their families and communities that counterbalance past wrongs. It provides spaces of forgiveness, redemption, and healing, and it transcends living community memories so communities may move forward together.
Develop group reliance skills	Examine each institution to reveal tangible contributions of resources, experts, events, and activities that showcase functionality not only in events of crisis but also day-to-day functions, showing how institutions instinctively work together for the greater good, modeling optimal marital and family behavior.
Include economic sustainability/ vertical integration	Evaluate cost–benefit–profit outcomes of institutions and businesses that are interdependent economic engines within the community, developed and sustained by the community through goods, services, and human capital, such as community development credit unions, museums, schools, cultural centers, think tanks, mobile clinics, agencies, foundations, grocers, religious institutions, farms, etc., that may alleviate poverty.

Helpful Resources

African American Community Service Agency: http://www.sjaacsa.com

African American Planning Commission: https://aapci.org/site

Bethel LA Community Development Corporation: https://bethellacdc.com

Black Community Development Corporation: https://www.blackcdcky.org

Black Community Resource Directory: https://blackcommunityresource.com

National Association of Community Development Extension Professionals: https://www.nacdep.net/

Tanner Community Development Corporation: https://www.tcdccorp.org

References

Anderson, C. (2001). *PowerNomics: The national plan to empower Black America*. Powernomics Corporation of America.

Bent-Goodley, T. B. (2005). An African-centered approach to domestic violence. *Families in Society, 86*(2), 197–206.

Carlton-LaNey, I. (1997). Elizabeth Ross Haynes: An African American reformer of womanist consciousness. *Social Work, 42*(6), 573–583.

Carlton-LaNey, I. (1999). African American social work pioneers' response to need. *Social Work, 44*(4), 311–321.

Chavis, D. M., & Wandersman, A. (2002). Sense of community in the urban environment: A catalyst for participation and community development. In T. A. Revenson, A. R. D'Augelli, S. E. French, D. L. Hughes, D. Livert, E. Seidman, M. Shinn, & H. Yoshikawa (Eds.), *A quarter century of community psychology* (pp. 265–292). Springer.

Davis, S. K., Williams, A. D., & Akinyela, M. (2010). An Afrocentric approach to building cultural relevance in social work research. *Journal of Black Studies, 41*(2), 338–350.

Estes, R. (1997). Social work, social development, and community welfare centers in international perspective. *International Social Work, 40*(1), 43–55.

Fairfax, C. N. (2014). A historical account of community mobilization in public education in early twentieth-century African America: Introducing Miss Virginia Estelle Randolph, master-teacher and community mobilizer. *Women's History Review, 23*(1), 1–17.

Fairfax, C. N. (2017). Community practice and the Afrocentric paradigm. *Journal of Human Behavior in the Social Environment, 27*(1–2), 73–80.

Ferguson, R. J. (2016). *The ancient Egyptian concept of Maat: Reflections on social justice and natural order.* CEWCES Research Paper No. 13. Centre for East West Cultural and Economic Studies.

Fisher, R., & Dybicz, P. (2015). The place of historical research in social work. *Journal of Sociology & Social Welfare, 26*(3), Article 7. http://scholarworks.wmich.edu/jssw/vol26/iss3/7

Goddard, L., Haggins, K. L., Nobles, W. W., Rhett-Mariscal, W., & Williams-Flournoy, D. (2014). *Redefining the definition of an African American community-defined practice: A supplemental report to the African American Population Report for the California Reducing Disparities Project: We ain't crazy! Just coping with a crazy system: Pathways into the Black population for eliminating mental health disparities.* https://www.cibhs.org/post/refining-definition-african-american-community-defined-practice

Hansan, J.E. (2011). *Locust Street Settlement House.* Social Welfare History Project. http://socialwelfare.library.vcu.edu/settlement-houses/locust-street

Harvey, A. R. (1994). A Black community development model: The Universal Negro Improvement Association and African Communities League 1917–1940. *Journal of Sociology & Social Welfare, 21*(1), Article 10. http://scholarworks.wmich.edu/jssw/vol21/iss1/10

Jones, J. M. (2007). Exposure to chronic community violence: Resilience in African American children. *Journal of Black Psychology, 33*(2), 125–149.

Kalonji, T. (2014). The Nguzo Saba & Maat, a path for self-reconstruction and recoveredness: Exploring a Kawaida paradigm for healing addiction in the Black community. *Journal of Pan African Studies, 7*(4), 195–210.

Kemp, S. P. (2010). Place matters: Toward a rejuvenated theory of environment for direct social work practice. In W. Borden (Ed.), *Reshaping theory in contemporary social work: Toward a critical pluralism in clinical practice* (pp. 114–145). Columbia University Press.

Koutra, K. (2015). Community development: A challenging strategy for social capital, health promotion, and community social work. In C. D. Johnson (Ed.), *Social capital: Global perspectives, management strategies and effectiveness economic issues, problems and perspectives series* (pp. 179–196). Nova Science.

Levy, I., Emdin, C., & Adjapong, E. S. (2018). Hip-hop cypher in group work. *Social Work with Groups, 41*(1–2), 103–110.

Marlowe, G. W. (2003). *A right worthy grand mission: Maggie Lena Walker and the quest for black economic empowerment.* Howard University Press.

Monteiro, N. M., & Wall, D. J. (2011). African dance as healing modality throughout the diaspora: The use of ritual and movement to work through trauma. *Journal of Pan African Studies, 4*(6), 234–252.

Nembhard, J. G. (2004). Cooperative ownership in the struggle for African American economic empowerment. *Humanity & Society, 28*(3), 298–321.

Nembhard, J. G. (2013). Community development credit unions: Securing and protecting assets in Black communities. *Review of Black Political Economy, 40*(4), 459–490.

Phifer, B. M. (1990). Community development in America: A brief history. *Sociological Practice, 8*(1), Article 4. http://digitalcommons.wayne.edu/socprac/vol8/iss1/4

Schiele, J. H. (2005). Cultural oppression and the high-risk status of African Americans. *Journal of Black Studies, 35*(6), 802–826.

Schiele, J. H., Jackson, M. S., & Fairfax, C. N. (2005). Maggie Lena Walker and African American community development. *Affilia, 20*(1), 21–38.

Wells-Wilbon, R. (2015). Family planning for low-income African American families: Contributions of social work pioneer Ophelia Settle Egypt. *Social Work, 60*(4), 335–342.

Whitehead, M. M. (2018). Applying Afrocentric theory to mezzo practice with African-Americans. *Journal of Human Behavior in the Social Environment, 28*(2), 125–141.

The Fair Food Program

A Worker-Led Model for Human Rights in Practice

Vitina L. P. Monacello

A fundamental goal of social work is to transform society through the promotion of individual and societal well-being (National Association of Social Workers, 2017). One profound example of a successful, evidenced-based approach to meeting this goal is the Fair Food Program (FFP). Created by the Coalition of Immokalee Workers (CIW), the FFP was identified as one of 15 social movements "that defied the odds and achieved life-changing results" along with the anti-apartheid movement, car seats, and marriage equality (Ditkoff & Grindle, 2017). This program and the model to which it gave rise have transformed the lives of individual workers and their families, strengthened the social fabric by forging unprecedented partnerships, and created a more just society through eradicating human rights abuses ranging from sexual violence to modern-day slavery. This program did not grow out of academia, a legislative campaign, or a progressive urban center. It was created by migrant farmworkers and first flourished in conservative, rural, southwest Florida. To understand this remarkable feat—how an internationally lauded, revolutionary human rights program was created out of thin air in Immokalee—it is necessary to start with the context: understanding the community.

The Community

Immokalee, a small unincorporated town located north of the Everglades in southwest Florida, is the heart of Florida's 619-million-dollar tomato industry. Annually, Florida produces approximately 50% of all fresh tomatoes in the United States and virtually all domestically grown fresh commercial tomatoes in the winter (Florida Tomato Committee, n.d.). The population of Immokalee can nearly double with migrant workers during the tomato season (Bowe, 2008). Each season, 33,000 workers are hired to pick the fruit by hand (Florida Tomato Committee, n.d.). Immokalee has long been an agricultural labor reserve, and thus its demographics have shifted dramatically along with the overall demographics of farmworkers during the past 50 years. In the 1970s, farmworkers in South Florida were predominantly African American and Puerto Rican, with a minority of White workers

(Bowe, 2008). In recent years, farmworkers in Immokalee have become an immigrant workforce composed predominately of workers from Mexico, Central America, and Haiti (Marquis, 2017).

Farmworker populations are notoriously vulnerable. The International Labour Organization (2015) lists agriculture as one of the top three most dangerous professions, with workers in agriculture at double the risk of workplace fatalities compared to those in other industries. In addition to occupational hazards, workers are subject to poverty wages, wage theft, verbal and physical abuse, sexual violence, and poor housing conditions (Estabrook, 2018; Lindgren, 2016; Marquis, 2017; Murrow, 1960; Oxfam America, 2004). In the United States, farmworkers have been excluded from labor laws; workplace protections; and common benefits such as health insurance, overtime pay, and paid time off (Asbed & Hitov, 2017a; Lindgren, 2016). As a predominately immigrant workforce, many farmworkers lack access to social safety-net programs (Hernandez & Gabbard, 2018).

In 1993, farmworkers in Immokalee began meeting in a small community room at the local Catholic church and formed CIW. Many of those who gathered had experience with peasant movements and community organizations in their home countries that had utilized Popular Education (Asbed & Hitov, 2017a; Marquis, 2017). Popular Education relies on dialogue and mutual learning from experience to generate critical analysis and collective action (Castelloe et al., 2002). This became the foundation of CIW's organizing philosophy: consciousness + commitment = change, or C + C = C (Bell, 2007). Utilizing storytelling, drawings, fliers, theater performance, and songs, farmworkers transcended differences in language, literacy, culture, race, ethnicity, and place of origin to create a shared identity as a community (Marquis, 2017). As workers shared their experiences and identified common problems—low wages, dangerous

and exploitative working conditions, and violence in the fields—they collectively built an understanding that this was not a matter of individual abuses but, rather, a systemic denial of farmworkers' dignity and basic human rights (Marquis, 2017). In addition to consciousness building, early members of CIW fostered broad-based leadership through leadership training and development, and they instituted an emphasis on consensus and collective decision-making (Marquis, 2017). All members had an active role to play—all farmworkers were leaders. This not only fostered commitment among participants but also addressed the challenge of constant turnover in a migrant farmworker community and created organizational strength (Marquis, 2017).

Commitment was also fostered through taking action. Early actions included work stoppages, a 30-day hunger strike, protests, and marches. Through public pressure, CIW won modest raises from growers, ending years of declining wages in the industry (CIW, n.d.-a). The final piece of CIW's equation, change, was ultimately achieved after CIW collectively decided on a new strategy to tackle the endemic problems.

The Campaign for Fair Food

The CIW's vision was clear: fair wages; dignity and respect from employers; real power in the industry to ensure safe and healthy working conditions; and enforcement for those who violate farmworkers' rights, particularly the most basic human right to live and work free from slavery (Marquis, 2017). The map for arriving at that vision was still coming into focus.

Early organizing had focused on confronting growers, but gains were limited. In approximately 1999, CIW widened its analysis beyond growers to consider larger systems at work in keeping farmworkers poor (Sellers & Asbed, 2013). This led to an economic examination of the food industry and the impact of multi-billion-dollar corporations' unmatched purchasing power. CIW concluded that this immense downward pressure on the supply chain was the driving force eroding wages and working conditions (Alliance for Fair Food, n.d.). In short, companies such as Taco Bell—which would become the first focus and success of the campaign—were able to demand the lowest possible price because of the volume at which they purchased tomatoes (CIW, n.d.-a). Growers in turn would cut their labor expenses in an effort to harvest the same product at a cheaper price and protect shrinking profit margins, passing down the cost and risks to farmworkers (Oxfam America, 2004). Corporate buyers may not have intended to perpetuate farmworker poverty and create dangerous, degraded working conditions in their supply chain, but it was an undeniable outcome of their volume purchasing (Asbed & Sellers, 2013).

This insight, that market power could incentivize and impact conditions in the supply chain, particularly at the bottom of the supply chain, led CIW to launch the Campaign for Fair Food in 2001 (CIW, n.d.-b). The goal was to get corporations to sign legally binding agreements with CIW to utilize the companies' purchasing power to demand a fairly harvested product instead of the cheapest one possible, the latter of which resulted in worker exploitation and enslavement (Marquis, 2017). The campaign had three demands (Alliance for Fair Food, n.d.):

1. Corporate buyers pay an additional surcharge of a penny per pound for tomatoes; this surcharge would go directly into farmworkers' paychecks to improve economic security.
2. Corporations agree to require compliance with the Fair Food Code of Conduct from growers to ensure humane labor standards and working conditions on the farms from which they purchase.

3. Workers have a seat at the table in monitoring and enforcing their rights through these agreements.

The launch of the campaign also marked a new chapter in CIW's organizing efforts. The farmworker community recognized that to produce change in the supply chain, they needed allies (Marquis, 2017). CIW once again employed popular education to build consciousness among consumers. Through presentations, retreats, online organizing, and creative actions, CIW built a powerful narrative to enlist the public's help in achieving a solution.

The success of the campaign is reflected in the 14 Fair Food agreements that were signed with CIW between 2005 and 2015. CIW forged partnerships with the largest fast-food companies and food services providers, as well as major grocery retailers (CIW, n.d.-b). Today, the campaign continues with a focus on fast-food industry and supermarket holdouts, such as Wendy's and Publix (Alliance for Fair Food, n.d.).

In addition to corporate agreements, at the end of 2010, CIW achieved what it had been seeking since its earliest organizing efforts: an agreement with the Florida Tomato Growers Exchange (FTGE). This landmark agreement paved the way for the implementation of CIW's Fair Food Code of Conduct on more than 90% of the Florida tomato industry and marked the birth of FFP (CIW, n.d.-a).

The Fair Food Program

In 2011, soon after the FTGE agreement, the Fair Food Standards Council (FFSC) was formed. As an independent, third-party monitoring body, the sole mission of FFSC is to oversee implementation and enforcement of the FFP on participating farms (FFSC, n.d.).

The FFP, as a new human rights program, quickly established a track record as a comprehensive, verifiable, transparent, enforceable, and sustainable initiative (Asbed & Sellers, 2013). At the heart of the program is a human rights-based Code of Conduct, informed by farmworkers, that lays out the new labor standards for the industry. Participating growers agree to implement the Fair Food Code of Conduct on their farms, ensuring workers' right to labor in a safe and healthy environment, free of violence, sexual harassment, and modern-day slavery (Asbed & Hitov, 2017b; FFSC, 2019). Participating buyers—the corporate partners that have signed Fair Food agreements with CIW—agree to direct all possible purchases to participating farms in good standing with the program and pay a penny surcharge to growers that is distributed directly to farmworkers through their paychecks in the form of a bonus (Asbed & Hitov, 2017a, 2017b). Growers that violate standards in the FFP Code of Conduct are suspended from the program and cannot sell to participating buyers (FFSC, 2019).

In documenting the tremendous impact of the FFP, *New York Times* reporter Steven Greenhouse (2014) observed, "The Fair Food Program's standards go far beyond what state or federal law requires" (para. 15). It is also worth noting that as a private regulatory system, the FPP can operate more quickly, thoroughly, and effectively to address abuses on behalf of workers than the country's legal system ever could (Asbed & Hitov, 2017a). Comprehensive compliance with the FFP Code of Conduct is ensured through essential and overlapping mechanisms: worker-to-worker education, complaint resolution, auditing, and market-based enforcement (FFSC, 2019).

Worker-to-Worker Education

On participating farms, every worker receives training on their rights under the FFP Code of Conduct. This education is reinforced twice throughout the harvest season—once with educational booklets and a farmworker-authored popular education video and again through interactive sessions conducted by CIW

farmworker staff to ensure that workers can be effective frontline monitors (FFSC, 2019).

Complaint Resolution

Once workers are educated on their rights, they need a way to enforce them. When workers encounter a potential violation of the FFP Code of Conduct, they have access to a toll-free hotline, which is staffed 24 hours a day, 7 days a week by FFSC investigators who work quickly to investigate and resolve complaints. Strict enforcement of the FFP's prohibition on retaliation ensures a safe context to report abuse for workers (FFSC, 2019).

Audits

The FFSC uses in-depth field, payroll, and management audits to monitor and enforce compliance within the program. Audits, both announced and unannounced, include thorough interviews with management, supervisors, and at least half the workers across all farms—a percentage of the workforce that is far above the industry standard (FFSC, 2019). In addition to interviews, FFSC investigators have full access to farm operations and payroll records to ensure rigorous compliance with the Code of Conduct (FFSC, 2019). These audits uncover problematic conduct that may be invisible to individual workers, such as improper accounting practices, and also complement the complaint hotline, recognizing that even after workers are trained on their rights, they may not trust the system based on their previous experiences outside the FFP (Asbed, 2016).

Enforcement

Whether through audit findings or an investigation following a hotline complaint, farms that are found to be out of compliance with the Code of Conduct, or fail to implement corrective actions, are placed on probation or suspended (FFSC, 2019). During a suspension, growers lose the business of participating buyers. Namely, human rights become the price of doing business when market-based consequences are imposed (Asbed & Sellers, 2013).

The program has also transformed once-adversarial relationships between workers and growers into collaborative partnerships (Damico & Sellers, 2018). One manifestation of this is the FFP working group, a body composed of representatives from participating growers and CIW, which meets regularly to discuss and adapt program policy (FFSC, 2019).

The rigor and effectiveness of the program are self-evident in the annual report produced by FFSC. The following is an illustrative snapshot based on data from FFSC's (2019) report, which covers the first seven seasons of the program between November 2011 and October 2018:

- The average compliance score for participating growers was 89 out of 100 in the program's seventh season (2017–2018), up from merely 10 in the first season (2011–2012).
- 58,861 workers have been trained through 775 CIW education sessions.
- There have been 2441 hotline complaints, only 5% of which could not be investigated. More than half of the complaints were resolved in less than 2 weeks, and 80% were resolved within 1 month.
- FFSC investigators have conducted 23,630 worker interviews during 260 operations audits. These audits yielded 7,738 audit findings, which were addressed through 189 corrective action plans.
- During the program's seventh season, no Participating Growers were suspended, and only five were placed on probation.
- The program has uncovered 13 cases of sexual harassment with physical contact, and all offenders were terminated. In addition, nine supervisors have been banned from any FFP farm for use of violence or threats of violence.
- Financial auditors tracked the distribution of $29,008,992.10 of Fair Food Premium to qualifying workers.

The success of the FFP in Florida has led to its expansion to cover the existing participating growers' operations in Georgia, North and South Carolina, Virginia, Maryland, and New Jersey (WSR Network, 2019). The FFP has also started pilot programs to expand coverage into a variety of fruit and vegetable crops across Florida.

Another stark example of the program's effectiveness came in its fifth season (2015–2016) when a forced labor case was reported over the hotline. Slavery is a scourge that has long plagued U.S. agriculture, and it continues to persist unfettered outside of the FFP (Asbed & Hitov, 2017a; Bowe, 2008; Marquis, 2017; Murrow, 1960). The FFP is designed to prevent modern-day slavery with the threat of market-based consequences, and its oversight and enforcement mechanisms are designed to swiftly identify and thoroughly redress any problems that may nevertheless arise (Asbed & Hitov, 2017a). In this case, in February, less than 2 weeks after the abuse began, workers called FFSC, which immediately conducted an investigation that resulted in the perpetrators and overseeing manager being summarily fired and an automatic suspension of the grower, despite senior management having no knowledge of the abuse (Estabrook, 2018). Within 2 weeks of the initial call, FFSC handed the case to law enforcement, and days later, the perpetrators, Augustin Mendez and Ever Mendez, were arrested and charged under forced labor statutes (Estabrook, 2018). Finally, 11 months later, these men had pled guilty and were serving prison sentences (Estabrook, 2018). Whereas previous cases had taken years to bring to justice, from start to finish the response to this case was handled in less than 1 year.

The Model: Worker-Driven Social Responsibility

The FFP is the first manifestation of a new model, Worker-driven Social Responsibility

(WSR; Asbed & Hitov, 2017a, 2017b). WSR provides a framework for ensuring human rights in global supply chains rather than simply viewing those rights as an aspirational goal. It is a unique alternative to traditional efforts to ensure fair and humane labor practices, and it is the obverse of corporate social responsibility, which is intrinsically corporate self-regulation (WSR Network, 2017).

In a study of labor standards in international supply chains, Fordham Law professor James Brudney (2016) concluded that "neither the [International Labour Organization] conventions and accompanying national government enforcement machinery nor the private codes of social responsibility have adequately addressed substandard working conditions in the global supply chains" (p. 359). He observed two fundamental shortcomings of these approaches: insufficient worker participation and weak monitoring and enforcement (Brudney, 2016). WSR not only addresses these shortcomings but also is more adept at responding to workers' rights violations compared to government enforcement mechanisms, which are limited by political borders. As illustrated by the FFP, WSR—which is built on robust, independent enforcement mechanisms—is less dependent on the legal system, thus allowing for solutions that span jurisdictions, and it provides a unified response within global supply chains (Asbed & Hitov, 2017a, 2017b).

In 2015, the Worker-driven Social Responsibility Network was formed to spearhead the mission of advancing and adapting the WSR model in other industries throughout the world. Based on the FFP, the network defined six key principles of the WSR model (WSR Network, 2017):

1. Labor rights initiatives must be worker-driven.
2. Obligations for global corporations must be binding and enforceable.
3. Buyers must afford suppliers the financial incentive and capacity to comply.
4. Consequences for noncompliant suppliers must be mandatory.
5. Gains for workers must be measurable and timely.
6. Verification of workplace compliance must be rigorous and independent.

The promise of the WSR model has only just begun to be realized. Many communities in the United States and abroad remain mired in a world like Immokalee before the FFP, and they are searching for effective solutions. From Arkansas' poultry workers and New York's fashion models to Bangladesh's seamstresses and Lesotho's garment producers, workers from many corners of the globe look to the FFP as a model (WSR Network, n.d.). They do not seek to photocopy the FFP; rather, they seek to replicate the process: engage the worker community most affected, analyze the problems workers are facing, craft a vision for the solution, and map out the players in the supply chain with the power to make that solution real. Then they commit to the often long, challenging path to winning meaningful power and overturning decades, if not centuries, of precedent in the world's most abusive and underpaid industries.

Discussion and Conclusion

For the past 25 years, despite the exponential growth in the scope of the organization's work, CIW has remained rooted in its worker-led model. Farmworkers continue to crowd into CIW's community center every Wednesday evening to participate in regular meetings, replete with Popular Education drawings or theater pieces, unpacking the everyday experiences in workers' lives and collectively arriving at a conclusion for how to move the FFP or the Campaign for Fair Food forward. For social workers, this embodies the profession's principal value of responsiveness, namely the dynamic interconnectivity between individuals in a community and an organization seeking to amplify the collective power and voices of those individuals in the service of creating a more just society. Specifically, the story of CIW illustrates the ways in which responsiveness cannot be treated as aspirational but, rather, must be fundamental, in order to successfully analyze and uproot the underlying social ills that give rise to poverty, abuse, and oppression.

Built on the foundation of that responsiveness, CIW's success is a powerful example for social workers of how community organizing can translate into radically successful policy and transformative social change. In her book *I Am Not a Tractor!*, Susan Marquis (2017), Dean of the Pardee RAND Graduate School, observes that "paying attention to the end-game details, continuously learning and recalibrating, are essential if an idea is to result in actual change. This is where many ideas, public policies, and programs fail" (p. 102). She concludes that CIW's unwavering focus on implementation, making its vision of change real, was vital to the program's success (Marquis, 2017).

Marquis (2017) draws five lessons from CIW's work that made systemic change possible: (1) Change must be initiated from within the system, (2) change must encompass a holistic understanding of the system, (3) compelling narratives drive change, (4) change is measured through effective enforcement, and (5) change is driven by the commitment and creativity of the people leading the effort. For social workers, these lessons are broadly applicable for those seeking to address systemic change. Above all, the story of CIW illustrates the social work mission of seeking to enhance the capacity of all people to address their own needs—both collectively and individually—in the immediate moment and for the long term.

Helpful Resources

Alliance for Fair Food: http://www.allianceforfairfood.org

Coalition for Immokalee Workers: http://ciw-online.org

Fair Food Program: https://www.fairfoodprogram.org

Fair Food Standards Council: http://www.fairfoodstandards.org

Worker-Driven Social Responsibility: https://wsr-network.org

References

Alliance for Fair Food. (n.d.). Our history. https://www.allianceforfairfood.org/our-history

Asbed, G. (2016). The Coalition of Immokalee Workers' Fair Food Programme. *Security Community, 4,* 20–21. https://www.osce.org/magazine/292926?download=true

Asbed, G., & Hitov, S. (2017a). Preventing forced labor in corporate supply chains: The Fair Food Program and worker-driven social responsibility. *Wake Forest Law Review, 52,* 497–531.

Asbed, G., & Hitov, S. (2017b). Clean supply chains are possible: The Fair Food Program approach. *CHTCS, 2*(3), 1–9.

Asbed, G., & Sellers, S. (2013). The Fair Food Program: Comprehensive, verifiable and sustainable change for farmworkers. *University of Pennsylvania Journal of Law & Social Change, 16,* 39–48. https://scholarship.law.upenn.edu/jlasc/vol16/iss1/3/

Bell, B. (2007). Florida farmworkers build unity through education and action. *Race, Poverty & the Environment, 14*(2), 39–41.

Bowe, J. (2008). *Nobodies: Modern American slave labor and the dark side of the new global economy.* Random House.

Brudney, J. J. (2016). Decent labour standards in corporate supply chains: The Immokalee Workers model. In J. Howe & R. Owens (Eds.), *Temporary labour migration* in the *global era: The regulatory challenges* (pp. 351–376). Hart Publishing.

Castelloe, P., Watson, T., & White, C. (2002). Participatory change: An innovative approach to community practice. *Journal of Community Practice, 10*(4), 7–32.

Coalition of Immokalee Workers. (n.d.-a). About CIW. http://ciw-online.org/about

Coalition of Immokalee Workers. (n.d.-b). Campaign for fair food. https://ciw-online.org/campaign-for-fair-food

Damico, N., & Sellers, S. (2018, February 14). *Now the fear is gone: Advancing gender justice through worker-driven social responsibility.* Worker-Driven Social Responsibility Network. https://wsr-network.org/resource/now-the-fear-is-gone

Ditkoff, S. W., & Grindle, A. (2017, September–October). Audacious philanthropy. *Harvard*

Business Review, 110–118. https://hbr.org/2017/09/audacious-philanthropy

Estabrook, B. (2018). Tomatoland: From harvest of shame to harvest of hope (3rd ed.). Andrews McMeel.

Fair Food Standards Council. (2019, October 3). Fair food: 2018 update [PDF file]. https://www.fairfoodprogram.org/wp-content/uploads/2019/10/Fair-Food-Program-2018-SOTP-Update-Final.pdf

Fair Food Standards Council. (n.d.). About. http://www.fairfoodstandards.org/about

Florida Tomato Committee. (n.d.). Tomato 101 [PDF file]. https://www.floridatomatoes.org/wp-content/uploads/2013/01/Tomato_1011.pdf

Greenhouse, S. (2014, April 24). In Florida tomato fields, a penny buys progress. *The New York Times.* https://www.nytimes.com/2014/04/25/business/in-florida-tomato-fields-a-penny-buys-progress.html

Hernandez, T., & Gabbard, S. (2018). *Findings from the National Agricultural Workers Survey (NAWS) 2015–2016: A demographic and employment profile of United States farmworkers* (Vol. 13). JBS International. https://www.doleta.gov/naws/research/docs/NAWS_Research_Report_13.pdf

International Labour Organization. (2015, March 23). Agriculture: A hazardous work. http://www.ilo.org/global/topics/safety-and-health-at-work/areasofwork/hazardous-work/WCMS_356550/lang--en/index.htm

Lindgren, K. (2016). *Justice in the fields: A report on the role of farmworker justice certification and an evaluation of the effectiveness of seven labels.* Fair World Project. https://fairworldproject. org/resources/certifier-analysis/farmworker-certification-analysis

Marquis, S. L. (2017). *I am not a tractor! How Florida farmworkers took on the fast food giants and won.* Cornell University Press.

Murrow, E. R. (1960). Harvest of shame. CBS News. https://www.cbsnews.com/video/1960-harvest-of-shame

National Association of Social Workers. (2017). Code of ethics. https://www.socialworkers.org/About/Ethics/Code-of-Ethics/Code-of-Ethics-English

Oxfam America. (2004). Like machines in the fields: Workers without rights in American agriculture [PDF file]. https://s3.amazonaws.com/oxfam-us/www/static/oa3/files/like-machines-in-the-fields.pdf

WSR Network. (2017, July 11). Fact sheet: What is WSR [PDF file]. https://wsr-network.org/what-is-wsr

WSR Network. (2019, March 1). Fact sheet: Fair Food Program. https://wsr-network.org/resource/fact-sheet-fair-food-program

WSR Network. (n.d.). Success stories. Retrieved May 1, 2020, from https://wsr-network.org/success-stories

Social Media

Maximizing the Power of Online Activism

Randy Shaw

Have you tweeted to all media? What about those who covered our last protest? We should email both news stations and individual reporters. Who's hitting the Facebook groups? Have we asked people if they are willing to promote the event on their personal Facebook and Instagram accounts? Who's taking pictures? We need to be sending out photos as the protest is occurring as that attracts media and public attention. Have we checked out the most popular Twitter and Instagram hashtags? Do we have a list of people and groups to tag? We also should be live tweeting to build interest and excitement. And who's in charge of monitoring responses and issuing replies?

Anything we've missed?

If these comments are unfamiliar to you, this chapter may prove a revelation. Social media has become a busy and complicated place. It is also an essential tool for winning social change. As much as some activists "don't like Twitter" or "get tired of Facebook," social media is a key part of the activist toolbox. Social media may not be indispensable for every local campaign, but why engage in a citywide, state, national, or international struggle without it? Winning major social change requires using all of the tools at one's disposal. Campaigns that do not use Twitter, Facebook, or Instagram are not maximizing their chances for success.

If you remain hesitant about social media, your opponents are unlikely to be. Social media is no longer just used by edgy hipsters on the cutting edge of technology; powerful and moneyed interests use social media to the max to defend and advance their interests. Consider that in the 2016 presidential election the Trump campaign and Russian government used Facebook to reach millions. And in the 2020 race for the Democratic presidential nomination, Michael Bloomberg's campaign used part of its $900 million budget to hire more than a dozen Instagram "influencers" to get his message out. When old-school activists talk about Martin Luther King, Jr., Cesar Chavez, the anti-Vietnam War movement, and the women's movement of the 1970s never using Twitter or Facebook, they are describing a very different media era. In the 1960s and 1970s, coverage by even one of the three national television networks effectively meant "the whole world is watching." Activists chanted that because a good portion of the nation actually was watching. But those days are gone. Today, the public is subdivided into so many news and information outlets—on top of what people learn from "friends" on social media—that relying exclusively on traditional media to gain broad public attention is a fool's errand.

Social media is a two-edged sword. It subdivides your audience but facilitates reaching your campaign's targets. That is because today's news media lack the "gatekeepers" of the past. Powerful interests no longer solely decide what stories become "news." They can still screen out coverage of activist campaigns from major newspapers and television stations, but today's information world is much broader. In my own work, social media's ability to provide coverage of tenant struggles otherwise ignored by mainstream media has been a huge asset. I even created a website in 2004, BeyondChron.org, to ensure campaigns I support get coverage. But eliminating gatekeepers has a disadvantage: It has boosted the proliferation of "fake news." Social media has led millions to trust information they get from Facebook "friends" as much as news in *The Washington Post*. Faith in social media posts has promoted the very questioning of facts themselves.

Social media also fits perfectly into a media world always in a rush and desperate for content. Many online reporters have production quotas. They need to build relationships with advocates who can regularly feed them new content. The life cycle of "breaking news" is shorter, increasing pressure on reporters to find new story lines. The combination of the lack of gatekeepers, the 24-hour news cycle, and a constant need for new content means that activists have more media options than ever before. The challenge is navigating this more receptive media landscape to achieve your goals.

This chapter explains how to most effectively use social media. My overriding message is that social media is a means to an end. It can help bring victories or contribute to defeats. Social media is most effective in combination with traditional organizing and mobilizing strategies. I cannot emphasize this strongly enough. A campaign that limits its activism

to sending emails, tweeting, or posting on Facebook or Instagram is unlikely to succeed. Social media is not a substitute for public engagement. Twitter, Instagram, and Facebook make it easy for people to wrongly think they are making a difference via social media posts alone. But social media complements, not replaces, traditional activism.

Tweeting for Change

Activists need to be on Twitter. Twitter is activists' most essential social media tool. If you are running a national presidential campaign, have unlimited funding, and need to microtarget voters throughout the nation, Facebook is your go-to social media platform. Otherwise, Twitter is more essential. Here's why:

Activists' most common media and political targets are either active on Twitter or have someone monitoring their Twitter feed.

If there were ever a time when most politicians were not active on Twitter, that ended with the constant tweeting of @realDonaldTrump. Now virtually all politicians tweet. They (or their staff) also monitor what others are tweeting about them or their issues. Pre-Twitter, politicians were only directly reachable by email. And that was true only if you had their personal address, as emails sent to state or national elected officials at their public addresses were invariably reviewed by staff. Other targets of activist campaigns, such as corporate CEOs, are also best reached via Twitter.

Twitter Rapidly Expands Public Knowledge of Activist Campaigns

There are times when speed matters. Consider the March 2020 federal coronavirus stimulus package. Prospects for a multi-billion-dollar stimulus package emerged virtually overnight. Advocates for funding homelessness prevention and affordable housing had to quickly build political support for a package addressing these goals. Housing/homelessness had been excluded from Congress' first stimulus plan and could easily have been ignored again but for a concerted campaign.

Twitter offered the quickest way for Washington, DC–based groups such as the National Low Income Housing Coalition (NLIHC) and the National Alliance to End Homelessness to inform their constituents. Twitter also provided the fastest and most direct way for groups to let their allies know how to support the cause. Although traditional lobbying was still required, there was no time for local or national rallies—and social distancing requirements then in place prevented these even if time were not of the essence.

NLIHC's leader, Diane Yentel, continually tweeted updates on the housing/homelessness funding plans. Tweets went to intermediaries such as me, who then used their Twitter accounts to enlist new groups to the campaign. These groups then tweeted urgent messages to their supporters. Time was of the essence, which made Twitter essential. The deal on the $2 trillion stimulus package was reached on March 25. Housing and homelessness secured at least $12 billion, with another $150 billion available to states for housing purposes. Email or phone calls could not have generated such a quick national campaign. There were too many people to contact, too many funding details, and too short a time frame. Unlike mass emails, tweets do not go to spam folders. And reaching enough key people by phone would be difficult under normal circumstances but was near impossible with most working at home due to shelter-in-place orders.

I asked Yentel about Twitter's role in the campaign. She responded (email from Diane Yentel to author, April 21, 2020),

> Twitter is valuable for policymakers and reporters since it shares information in real-time. When mobilizing, it's helpful

to first share key action items and backgrounds. Users can easily search a repository of information using a hashtag or keyword. This was especially helpful during the stimulus mobilization because it allowed me to quickly share a summary of a complicated piece of legislation. My network appreciated the breakdown of information and in turn, shared it with others, including people outside their immediate network.

Twitter Offers Quick Feedback on Activist Branding and Framing of Issues

In early 2019, New York Congressmember Alexandria Ocasio-Cortez (AOC) labeled her climate change plan a "Green New Deal." AOC had more than 2.6 million Twitter followers and more than 2.1 million on Instagram. "Green New Deal" began as only a working title. AOC later said (Chavez, 2019),

> I wasn't 1,000 percent sure on that kind of branding, if you will, or how we would talk about that. But it kept leaking, and catching, and people just started writing articles calling it a Green New Deal before we even said anything or called it that ourselves. And so because of that, that was in a moment where it was listening, and I was like OK let's not try to force our own thing on this, if this is building traction, if it's easily being communicated, then let's just run with it.

Seemingly overnight, the #GreenNewDeal hashtag was everywhere. And Green New Deal policies became central to the nation's progressive agenda (Chavez, 2019).

Twitter Expands Public Participation

In *Generation Priced Out: Who Gets to Live in the New Urban America*, I describe how local land use policies are often decided in weekday afternoon or late night meetings (Shaw, 2020). The scheduling makes it difficult for working people and/or parents with children with less flexible schedules to participate. As a result, in city after city, land use meetings are dominated by a demographic that is older, Whiter, and more likely to be homeowners than the city or political district as a whole. Forums that disproportionately hear from boomer homeowners while excluding younger tenants have a predictable impact: city policies that stop the construction of new multi-unit buildings that existing homeowners oppose but younger millennials need. This undemocratic approach to land use hearings worsens the urban housing crisis.

Twitter has helped change this in two key ways. First, "live tweeting" of public meetings is now common. People can follow public meetings and offer comments to the city officials from home. This makes a huge difference in many ways. It provides a far more diverse set of views than are gained from in-person attendees. In addition, it lets decision-makers know that a broader section of the city is paying attention to how they vote; this raises the political stakes behind making decisions that benefit an upscale demographic but negatively affect most residents.

Second, Twitter can publicly expose critical testimony during these public meetings. In Minneapolis, Minnesota, John Edwards has used @WedgeLIVE! to publicize testimony about land use hearings to approve apartments. Thanks to Edwards, the public was able to see an April 11, 2016, zoning and planning committee hearing that featured truly gripping testimony from neighbors opposing a project. Opponents pleaded with the committee about "saving our children" and urged them to stop a project that would see "couches and mattresses" being dumped on the street. One speaker broke down crying over the city's alleged plan to "destroy" their community. I did not know what exactly was being proposed, but from the testimony I assumed it was a halfway house or affordable

housing project planned for a homeowner-dominated neighborhood. But it was actually a 10-unit market apartment building proposed for a majority renter neighborhood. Thanks to Edwards' use of Twitter, the broader public got to see the racism and classism underlying the opposition. And that makes it easier for city officials to approve future housing (Shaw, 2020). Edwards describes Twitter's importance (conversation with author, April 15, 2020):

> Twitter is where I get the most reach for posts, including video. I think that's the effort I put into it, but also because of the political and pro-housing culture that exists on the platform. Twitter also has more than its share of government types and policymakers. So if you can be compelling or entertaining enough to direct the conversation [and when it comes to local politics, often there is not much competition], it can really amplify the power of your message.

Expanding Access for People with Disabilities

Alice Wong, founder of the Disability Visibility Project and co-founder of the #CripTheVote hashtag, explains why she took to Twitter to expand electoral participation for people with disabilities. In her 2016 article titled "Disability Advocacy and Twitter: Why Use It?" Wong cites several benefits of running an online campaign that prioritizes Twitter, including the much greater resources needed to organize in-person events and the ability to converse with a wide spectrum of people with disabilities by using the #CripTheVote hashtag. Wong also cites the ability to have organized Twitter chats on specific issues and the ease of using social media because it requires no special training. Wong views Twitter as a strong vehicle for allowing disabled persons to "insert ourselves into the broader policy/election discussion without any interference" (Wong, 2016).

Getting Started

It's easy to get a Twitter "handle." It's more difficult to expand your Twitter "followers" so your tweets reach their targets. The first step is sending tweets to media and political people who can help your campaigns succeed. Reporters are trying to get the latest stories. If you can provide them new story angles/ideas via Twitter, they will follow you. Politicians are in the business of knowing what's happening within their purview. They follow people and groups providing such information. Activists should also "follow" all media and political targets relevant to your campaigns and reciprocate when a media or political target becomes a follower. This shows both groups that you value their work. Following reporters on Twitter also ensures you are up to speed when they do stories connected to your campaign. Activists can also build positive relationships with reporters by retweeting or "liking" their tweets and/or stories; this is particularly helpful for activists who do not regularly tweet to stay on the media's radar.

Overcoming Roadblocks

Every Activist Strategy Meets Resistance: Social Media Is No Exception

Using Twitter or Facebook for policy campaigns opens your "feed" to opponents. Some may engage in vicious personal attacks that rise to the level of harassment; in fact, this has led some women activists to avoid social media. That is why it is important to remember that Facebook and Twitter allow you to ban people from your feed. Use this feature! And do so without hesitation. Using social media to achieve your policy goals does not require providing an open forum for others. Some activists enjoy back-and-forth arguments on social media. But unless such arguments will move your policy goals—which is rarely the case—why spend the time? I have

never experienced a politician or other campaign target whose position changed after dialoguing on Twitter or Facebook. Targets can be swayed by what they read on social media, but discussions of issues are better left to phone calls or personal meetings.

Social Media World Is Not Real World

The other chief roadblock is confusing your campaign's place in the social media world with the actual political environment. This becomes an obstacle by giving a misleading sense of your campaign's progress. Here's an example from 2019; names are not included so as not to criticize the well-intentioned groups involved.

A coalition of groups issues a report. The coalition includes representatives of multiple cities throughout the nation but is heavily tilted to the East Coast. Although the report is solely a product of the participating groups, the coalition announces it as offering a path-breaking solution to a long-standing crisis. Rallies accompanying the report's release make for great photos on Instagram, Facebook, and Twitter. The coalition promotes the report on social media, and it dominates the Twitter feed in the policy area. Overall, it seemed like a major step forward in addressing a crisis had occurred. I was encouraged that the report involved a coalition of groups that had not previously been involved in the issue. I viewed it as broadening a political base, and I joined in promoting the report on social media.

But I soon realized that the larger grassroots world involved with the issue knew nothing about the report. The nation's leading stakeholders on the issue had not even been consulted. Substantively, the report was great. But it lacked connection to the real political world that would determine its future implementation. The report made a big splash in a small segment of social media but never broke through to get much, if any, coverage outside that narrow world.

The problem here is that social media gave the coalition promoting the report a misleading sense of what it had accomplished. The social media coverage became "proof" of the report's impact when in the real political world—and among the longtime grassroots groups in the policy field—it had little or no influence. This is not akin to an "astroturf" campaign where powerful interests create fake "grassroots" groups to propel their agenda. The coalition groups are real people doing important work. But there was clearly no effort made to build an actual campaign for implementation. And there lacked the level of outreach required for the current or a future Congress to ever consider enacting the report's recommendation. Social media helped create a false impression of the report's importance. Its issuance became an end in itself rather than a means to an end.

In the old school, pre-social media days of 1999 and 2000, I co-authored two major housing reports. Like the 2019 coalition, we connected to local housing groups that held rallies around the reports' release. The difference with our approach is that we knew that to impact targeted politicians, we needed traditional media. The combination of the newsworthiness of our study and local groups' media connections generated newspaper and television news coverage throughout the nation. Many of the stories included quotes from targeted politicians responding to media inquiries asking for a response to our reports. When U.S. senators, congressmembers, and even the President are publicly explaining their position on your issue—as occurred with our reports—you are operating in the real political world.

I cannot say what would have happened had social media been available back then except that our rally photos would have been shared much more widely. But our assessment of "success" was based entirely on forcing our targets to respond, not on the number of retweets or likes on social media. Social media offers documented proof that people know about the work being promoted, but that can be a misleading measure of a campaign's progress.

The Big Picture

I stated at the outset that social media is most effective in combination with traditional organizing and mobilizing strategies. Social media is not a substitute for personal outreach. Activists still must build the personal relationships with fellow activists, politicians, and others crucial to uniting for successful campaigns. Social media can expand your base of allies and help build broad coalitions. But social workers know best of all that developing personal skills and ability to work with people are key. Activists can be phenomenal at posting Instagram photos and drafting tweets, but if they cannot connect to people on a personal level, they are not going to build a successful campaign. Social media builds upon the infrastructure created by traditional organizing and outreach; if used effectively, it can mean the difference between victory and defeat.

Helpful Resources
Publications

Marantz, A. (2019). *Antisocial: Online extremists, techno-utopians, and the hijacking of the American conversation*. Viking.

Shaw, S. (2013). *The activist's handbook: Winning social change in the 21st century*. University of California Press.

Vaidhyanathan, S. (2018). *Antisocial media: How Facebook disconnects us and undermines democracy*. Oxford University Press.

Websites

BeyondChron: The Voice of the Rest: http://beyondchron.org

Disability Visibility Project: https://disabilityvisibilityproject.com

National Low Income Housing Coalition: https://nlihc.org

Sunrise Movement. *What is the Green New Deal?*: https://www.sunrisemovement.org/green-new-deal

References

Chavez, A. (2019, February 2). How the Green New Deal became the Green New Deal. *The Intercept*. https://theintercept.com/2019/02/02/green-new-deal-aoc

Shaw, S. (2020). *Generation priced out: Who gets to live in the new urban America*. University of California Press.

Wong, A. (2016, May 7). *Disability advocacy and Twitter: Why use it?* Disability Visibility Project. https://disabilityvisibilityproject.com/2016/05/07/disability-advocacy-and-twitter-why-use-it

Asset-Based Community Development

John L. McKnight and Cormac Russell

In 1993, the Asset-Based Community Development Institute was established by two faculty colleagues, John McKnight and Jody Kretzmann, at the Center for Urban Affairs at Northwestern University. The Center was an urban policy research group of 24 faculty members, largely social scientists. Although the faculty was dedicated to social justice and urban change, their implicit view of neighborhoods was that they were full of problems and victimized people. Like nearly all other universities, their work focused on policies that would alleviate poverty and discrimination. Their understanding of the appropriate actors to implement their policies were government, health and social welfare agencies, and other large institutions. Their unstated assumption was that "fixing" neighborhoods was the job of outsiders. McKnight and Kretzmann recognized that this academic and policy framework rarely included neighbors. At that time, almost none of the policy research recognized that a principal party in neighborhood change was local residents and their inventiveness and problem-solving capacities. Nor did the researchers conceive that there were local resources that represented the wealth in local places.

Because of this policymaking blind spot, McKnight and Kretzmann undertook research to make visible the multiple resources in neighborhoods. Over 4 years, they gathered resident stories (called case studies in universities) in several hundred neighborhoods, asking, "Can you tell us what residents in this neighborhood have done together that made things better?" The responses provided four key findings that became the core of asset-based community development (ABCD) practice.

The first finding is that scale is a critical factor in effective neighborhood work. ABCD stories came from small neighborhoods and towns. Therefore, the three findings that follow are based on information gathered in small space-bound places. The essence of ABCD is lost when neighborhood-based personal relationships are not the basic connective tissue.

Second, the analysis of the hundreds of neighborhood stories enabled the Institute to identify the principal local resources that generate productive neighborhoods. These resources became the classic six assets that are the core of ABCD practice: individual resident capacities; local associations; neighborhood institutions—business, not-for-profit, and government; physical assets—the land and everything on it and beneath it; exchange between neighbors—giving, sharing, trading, bartering, exchanging, buying, and selling; and stories. The Institute published a book titled *Building Communities from the Inside out: A Path Toward Finding and Mobilizing a Community's Assets* (Kretzmann & McKnight, 1993). This text described each of the assets and their uses. Very soon, thousands of copies of the book were sold, and an "asset-based" movement emerged in many neighborhoods and some universities and agencies. This movement was manifested in a paradigm shift in the organizing and policy fields in which the importance of local resources provided a new framework for analyzing and implementing community change. The rapid spread of the ABCD paradigm was largely the result of the following three critical characteristics of the ABCD framework: It is simple; it is eminently usable; and it has universal applications, as the worldwide movement has demonstrated.

The third core finding was that the most common method used by the groups to implement their collective activity involved three steps. First, local assets were identified. Second, assets that were unconnected were connected. Third, a group or individual usually acted as the initiating connector. Central to this process is the connective function. In fact, the hundreds of stories could be understood as descriptions of how unconnected local assets got connected. This understanding emphasizes the importance of ABCD work focused on connectors in contrast to leaders. Some leaders are connectors, but most connectors are not thought of as leaders. Although there are thousands of leadership development programs, the Institute has developed a unique role in enhancing the capacity of people who are connectors and expanding the understanding of this function.

A fourth finding was the method used by effective local groups that engaged outside institutions. The process emerges when local groups undertake a more comprehensive initiative. In planning such an initiative, the following three questions are most frequently involved: (1) What can we produce with assets in our neighborhood? (2) What can we produce with our assets and some supportive outside resources? (3) What will our assets not be able to produce so that outside resources will have to do the entire function? The sequence here is critical because "you don't know what you need from outside until you know what you have inside." Therefore, ABCD work always starts with "What do we have in the neighborhood that can produce what we want?" The answer, of course, requires a thorough understanding of what local resources are available. This is why the "map" of the six assets has been so universally useful. In summary, the work of ABCD is to enhance and support local residents' capacity to make visible their assets and to support and enhance the connection of those assets. These two essential roles are the way we undergird productive citizenship. We emphasize the word "productive." The basic standard for determining whether local activity is ABCD work is to ask who was the producer of the outcome. If it is a group of local citizens, then it qualifies. And to be the producer does not mean to be a client, advisor, or advocate. It means to be the implementer—a person with the power to act. Alexis de Tocqueville wrote that "the health of a democratic society may be measured by the quality of functions performed by private citizens." This is why the ABCD work that enhances citizens and their associations is critical to the future of democracy. Citizens and their associations have a different place in democracy than institutions. In the 20th century, there were two great tyrannies and both had excellent institutions. They were tyrannies because they stamped out all freestanding associations and the free expression of citizens. They knew that they could control institutions but they could not control citizens, so they outlawed the basic power-making tools of citizens—freedom of expression and association. This is why the essential home of ABCD is with citizens, their gifts, and their local associations.

Assets

Asset-based community development offers a description of what happens when citizens act effectively together and what assets they use to build their preferred futures. This section details the six key local assets that we have found communities of place across the world recurrently identify, connect, and mobilize to enhance local well-being in every sense of the term: associational, cultural, environmental, etc. These assets are abundant (there is enough/sufficient amount for everyone and when productively shared they do not run out), universally available (every community has them without exception), and extremely useful to communities eager to get things done to enhance community well-being. The six assets are the contributions of individual residents, local associations, and neighborhood institutions to community well-being, and the physical assets (built and natural environment), exchange between neighbors, and stories that are the carriers of various cultures and heritages.

Contributions of Residents

This category of assets includes the gifts, skills, passions, and knowledge of residents, which are contributed toward the collective well-being of their community. Gifts are innate; people are born with them. Skills are what people practice, learn, and can teach or share with others, whereas passions are what people care about enough to take action on. We are particularly interested in civic passions. Passions need not necessarily be rooted in either a given person's gift or skill but simply a deeply held care, concern, or interest. When a person contributes a gift, skill, passion, or knowledge, or a combination of all four, to a neighbor, they are engaging in a foundational form of citizenship.

Contributions of Local Associations

Associations are clubs, groups, and networks of unpaid citizens who create the vision and implement the actions required to make their vision visible and of consequence. They can be formal, such as a chamber of commerce, or informal, such as a book reading club. An association is the collective word for citizen. As a bird is to a flock, citizen is to an association, and it is within this domain that an individual's gifts, skills, passions, and knowledge, when joined with those of their neighbors, can be amplified and multiplied so that the whole becomes greater than the sum of its parts.

Contributions of Neighborhood Institutions

Neighborhood institutions, whether for profit, nonprofit/nongovernmental organization, or governmental, show up in the civic realm in one of two ways: institutionally or community oriented. The nature of an institution that is community oriented is that it acts as a resource toward community well-being and aims to be supportive rather than directive. The goal of such supportive institutions is to enable citizenship and interdependence at the center of community life. Supportive institutions consider citizens to be the primary inventors of community well-being in a democracy, and they view their role as cheering on that inventiveness and serving while walking backwards. Institutions can precipitate collective vision-making and citizen production through the following actions:

- Organizing their supports the way people organize their lives—small and local
- Putting institutional assets at the service of community-building efforts and investing in community alternatives to their traditional ways of working
- Being clear about what they are not going to do to/for/with communities because to do

so would be to take power from the people they serve

- In the case of government institutions, creating a dome of protection against outside forces that could harm community life

Physical Assets

The main stage on which the previously discussed three human resources/assets are revealed, connected, and brought into productive collective action is the built and natural environment. Small, local, bounded places that people relate to as their shared place (neighborhood, village, town, etc.) provide an optimal threshold within which these resources can be brought into right relationship with each other to become connected and mobilized. As well as providing an ideal context for gift exchange, hospitality, and revealing abundance, local bounded places are replete with all manner of practical resources that are essential to community life. From the air we breathe to the community gardens we tend, to the places we casually bump into our neighbors or gather in deep fellowship, our shared places root our community experiences.

Exchange Between Neighbors

In the nonmonetary world, there are three forms of exchange: the exchange of intangibles, the exchange of tangibles, and use of alternative currencies. In the commercial world, there is a fourth form of exchange in the form of money.

Exchanging Intangibles

Through the long history of human exchange between kin, clan, and neighbors, exchanges have primarily been about the circulation of gifts. It is said that a gift is not a gift until it is given; it is also true to say it is not a gift until it is received. Hence, this is why abundant communities nurture a culture of giving and receiving: Such exchanges tend to be entered into in a relational rather than a transactional way.

Exchanging Tangibles

Exchange can involve the bartering or swapping of tangible resources—for example, a pig for five chickens, or sharing one lawnmower between six households on a street.

Alternative Currencies

Like the previous two forms of exchange, alternative currencies enable local choice and control. During the Great Depression, for instance, many small towns created alternative ways of paying their debt by introducing their own local currencies as an alternative to the beleaguered U.S. dollar. A popular modern example of this is time banking, in which members of a timebank use their time as a form of currency: Each hour of contribution is equal to all others regardless of what is contributed.

Money-Based Exchange

All three types of exchange described previously occur within and strengthen the commons (shared civic space) in that they increase gift exchange, deepen associational life, and encourage hospitality. The final form of exchange is money-based, and although it is an important feature of community life, we consider it to be the least useful of the four exchanges in producing collective well-being because it operates on the basis of scarcity, not abundance. Money is viewed as a scarce resource because it is about debt; in effect, it is a promissory note or an IOU. It also tends to operate outside the commons (civic realm) in the realm of private property, in that it does not promote gift exchange, associational life, or hospitality in the way the other three forms of exchange do. Money can often undermine them. However, money exchanges, when kept local, can play a powerful role in nurturing community well-being. Credit union schemes, worker-owned cooperatives, and shop local initiatives are all examples of this. We also know—based on what we have learned from our friend and faculty member Judith Snow and others vulnerable to not having their gifts recognized and received—that when people have income in place of services and programs (e.g., personal budgets), they can use that resource to enable them to become more interdependent at the center of their communities and have more choice and control over their own lives.

Stories

Local culture or "the community way" often finds expression within stories of the people and the "ways" they have learned through time to survive and thrive within their home places. Hence, the sixth resource that enables shared visioning and productivity is community stories. We are all creatures of narrative, and when we cooperate with our neighbors in creating and exchanging stories of a more compelling future that respects our traditions, we ensure our culture (our way) prevails. Stories enable us to pass on important life lessons and traditions to the further generations. Stories also act as powerful connection points between older and younger generations within a community. Local stories, therefore, are treasure maps that help us discover the hidden bounty that weaves our cultural assets together like a tapestry. Our cuisines, spiritual beliefs, ways of raising our children, local dialects, and arts are the threads that combine to form this community tapestry. Each tapestry is unique and particular to the place that created it and to that place alone. And, as strangers become friends, it takes the shape of a mosaic reflecting beauty in diversity.

Community Building

Having addressed the question of what communities use to co-create their own well-being, the second question we consider here is "How do communities go about making those resources productive in a communal sense?" In answer to this question, we note that abundant communities use methods that involve identifying and productively connecting unconnected local

resources. In keeping with our fourth finding, the following three steps are noted. First, start with what residents can do themselves as an association of citizens, without any outside help. Second, determine what they can do with a little outside help. Finally, once these local assets have been fully connected and mobilized, citizens decide collectively on what they want outside agents to do for them. The order is critical. When we start with the third step, as often is the case in traditional helping endeavors, we preclude citizen power. The methods that are used vary widely, but at their heart they are focused on bringing resources that were previously disconnected together and supporting them to become mobilized through collective citizen action. There are countless methods by which communities can connect and mobilize their resources. Suffice to say, ABCD approaches are iterative and emergent.

Although there are no methods that we can prescribe, there are a number of practices that communities throughout the world have found helpful. These practices include discover, welcome, portray, share, celebrate, and vision.

Discover

Discover local resident connectors who naturally weave their community together through neighbor-to-neighbor and associational relationship building. Convening a table of connectors who represent the diversity of an entire neighborhood can be a powerful means of building community throughout that neighborhood.

Welcome

Actively welcome neighbors and those who are pushed to the margins through inclusive learning conversations and listening campaigns. Learning conversations and listening campaigns surface what people care about enough to act upon with their neighbors. Some communities find it helpful to have a community organizer (called community builders/

animators in Europe) to support these processes. It is important to remember that if a paid practitioner is supporting a community, this is a backseat role. Local citizens must remain in the lead. Community organizers can be helpful with regard to identifying tactics for deep inclusion and addressing issues of conflict and power imbalance alongside a range of other important functions. They can help build the ship, but they must never become the ship's captain.

Portray

As people discover what they care about enough to take collective action, creating dynamic portraits of the local resources that they can use is a helpful way of making assets visible to everyone. No one person can hold a full picture of all the resources that a community has, so creating a shared and evolving portrait (what some call an asset map) is a powerful method of enabling citizens to discover what resources they already have and to determine how best to connect unconnected resources.

Share

Intentionally doing things together, from sharing meals to tending a community garden, brings us into a radical presence with our neighbors. Sometimes we also create "shareable moments," in which we intentionally create the conditions for neighbors to become friends. Such shareable moments can include skills exchanges, seed swaps, and repair cafes. They create a community on-ramp for people who may be unsure about how to get into community life. The more these moments enable gift exchange, hospitality, and association, the more likely they will become part of a community's way.

Celebrate

Celebrating neighborliness and community life, through food, fun, songs, and dance, is one of the best and most natural ways to honor our past achievements and dream up new community possibilities.

Vision

Creating a collective vision that both sets down the priorities and reveals the possibilities for the shared future of a community is a powerful community-building method. It ensures that the community owns the process and is the primary producer of it and the actions that flow from it.

Conclusion

The Asset-Based Community Development Institute is at the center of a large and growing movement that considers local assets as the primary building blocks of sustainable community development. Building on the skills of local residents, the power of local associations, and the supportive functions of local institutions, asset-based community development draws upon existing community strengths to build stronger, more sustainable communities for the future (Russell, 2018).

Where Does Social Work Fit Within Such an Approach?

In this chapter, we have noted that there are certain issues that are best addressed interdependently by citizens within the context of their families and communities. The role of social work—with the appropriate assistance of allied professionals when required—is to adopt subsidiary functions that supplement community capacities.

Social work practice has changed significantly over the course of the past four decades, with an apparent shift in emphasis from community social work to an assessment and case management-based approach, in which the focus is too often on supposed individual and family pathologies, conditions, and deviances. The problem here is that labels that emerge from standard assessment processes obscure people's stories and stifle the creativity of social workers to respond in nonprescriptive ways.

The costs of this practice migration (since the 1980s) away from community-oriented and capacity-focused approaches that precipitate the identification, connection, and mobilization of the assets of individuals, families, and communities have been incredibly high (McKnight, 1995). They include the following:

- People we wish to help become known by their deficits and labels, instead of their capacities and narratives.
- Resources flow to those providing ameliorative, one-sided compensatory programs and services, which often separate individuals from their networks, and not to low-income families.
- Active citizenship retreats in the face of expertise, and civic functions become outsourced to professionals.
- Entire communities become mapped and defined by their deficits and in turn internalize that map so fully that they come to believe that they are powerless to change anything themselves and/or in association with their family and community. They come to believe that the only way things will get better is if an expert from outside comes in to make them so.

In the final analysis, we believe a better social order will be achieved when people who have been defined as the problem secure the power to redefine the problem and gain greater interdependence at the center of community life (Russell, 2020). It is our sincere hope that social workers—who serve marginalized people as well as provide services that supplement community capacities—can more regularly become key precipitators towards more community-driven asset-based social change. And, toward that end, we hope that asset-based community development may offer a useful vista on this rich, largely untapped reservoir of potential.

Helpful Resources
Publications

Block, P. (2008). *Community: The structure of belonging*. Berrett-Koehler.

Block, P., Bruggeman, W., & McKnight, J. (2016). *An other kingdom: Departing the consumer culture*. Wiley.

Green, M., Moore, H., & O'Brien, J. (2006). *ABCD in action: When people care enough to act*. Inclusion Press.

Kretzmann, J. P., McKnight, J. L, Dobrowolski, S., & Puntenney, D. (2005). *Discovering community power: A guide to mobilizing local assets and your organization's capacity*. Asset-Based Community Development Institute, Northwestern University.

McKnight, J., & Block, P. (2010). *The abundant community*. Berrett-Koehler.

Russell, C. (2010). Making the case for an asset-based community development (ABCD) approach to probation: From reformation to transformation. *Irish Probation Journal, 7*, 119–132.

Russell, C. (2011). Pulling back from the edge: An asset-based approach to ageing well. *Working with Older People, 15*, 96–105. https://doi.org/10.1108/13663661011176642

Russell, C. (2018). Does more medicine make us sicker, Ivan Illich revisited. *Gaceta Sanitaria Public Health Journal, 33*, 579–583. https://doi.org/10.1016/j.gaceta.2018.11.006

Websites

ABCD in Action: https://abcdinaction.org

Asset-Based Community Development Institute: https://resources.depaul.edu/abcd-institute/publications/Pages/default.aspx

Nurture Development: https://www.nurturedevelopment.org

References

Kretzmann, J. P., & McKnight, J. L. (1993). *Building communities from the inside out: A path toward finding and mobilizing a community's assets*. ACTA Publications.

McKnight, J. L. (1995). *The careless society: Community and its counterfeits*. Basic Books.

Russell, C. (2018). *Asset-based community development—Looking back to look forward: In conversation with John McKnight about the intellectual and practical heritage of ABCD and its place in the world today*. Cormac Russell.

Russell, C. (2020). *Rekindling democracy, a professional's guide to working in citizen space*. Wipf & Stock.

Sport Social Work

Stacy E. Kratz and Stephanie E. Rosado

Described as a profession of "power, passion, and purpose" (Bent-Goodley, 2014, p. 197), social work promotes individual and societal change and development. With a primary purpose to "promote social justice and social change with and on behalf of clients" (National Association of Social Workers, 2017, p. 1) and a mission to enhance human well-being, social work focuses on individual well-being in a social context and the well-being of society. Sport too embodies a spirit of individual and societal welfare and provides a robust platform for the manifestation of well-being and change (United Nations, 2009; Young & Okada, 2014).

Sport in society dates back millennia of course, as does the difficulty of defining sport (Klein, 2017). What qualifies as sport continues as an ever-evolving controversial discussion—just think esport or cornhole: sport or not? Debates rage on, but most definitions of sport include words such as athleticism, activity, entertainment, physical exertion, players, teams, skill, and competition (Jenny et al., 2017). Relational to social work, the Council of Europe (2001) European Sports Charter provides a useful definition: "Sport means all forms of physical activity, which through casual or organized participation, aim

at expressing or improving physical fitness and mental well-being, forming social relationships or obtaining results in competition at all levels" (p. 1). Components of this definition expose how sport and social work naturally intersected in the early days of the profession and how contemporary social work is well situated to continue the work.

From Early to Contemporary Sport Social Work

The social work profession emerged in the late 19th century from three major social change strategies of the era: the Charity Organization Society movement, the child welfare movement, and the settlement house movement (Suppes & Wells, 2018). Although all three approaches focused on searching for solutions to crippling poverty, exploitation, and oppression, it was the settlement house movement that explicitly included sport in its approach to societal change (Ehrenreich, 2014; Reynolds, 2017). Settlement house movement leader and social work pioneer, Jane Addams, recognized as the most prominent of the American settlement theoreticians, founded Chicago's Hull House to manifest large-scale societal change. From the beginning, her vision of reform included organized community sport as a tool focusing on the power of personal development and community cohesion to harness progress (Addams, 1910; Reynolds, 2017).

Addams enmeshed social work and sport from the nascence of the profession with a vision of progress in which individuals and communities build "enthusiasms which are so mysteriously aroused by athletics," recognizing strength through a "fellowship which athletics . . . affords more easily than anything else" (Addams, 1910, p. 442). Opening Chicago's first public playground in 1893, Addams went on to found the National Playground Association and became an advocate for playgrounds and organized sport nationwide (Bachrach, 2012). With a desire to further grow the positive impact of sport in communities, Addams brought recreational and sport-based programmatic training to social work curriculum as early as 1918 (Reynolds, 2017). Although not identified as such at the time, scholars bringing this practice knowledge into the field helped birth the practice subspecialty of sport social work. The work has continued across decades, and since 2015, with the development of the Alliance of Social Workers in Sports (ASWIS), a professional member organization, the subspecialty has been well-documented (ASWIS, 2020). Moore and Gummelt (2019) define sport social work as "the practice subfield of social work that promotes social justice and social change by focusing on the unique needs of athletes at both the individual and environmental level" (p.1). A more complete definition of sport social work is the practice subfield of social work that promotes social justice and social change by focusing on the unique needs of athletes, their allies, and the communities in which they live, at both the individual and the environmental level, promoting human and community well-being. The contemporary role of sport

social workers is framed within the profession's continued commitment to address the *Grand Challenges for Social Work*, as well as the United Nations' *2030 Agenda for Sustainable Development* (Lubben et al., 2018; United Nations, 2015). Joining these frameworks thus allows for sport social work practice to appear across the life span.

Sport Social Work Across the Athlete's Life Span

Sport has the capability to penetrate each stage of the life span as well as systems therein, at the micro, mezzo, and macro levels (Moore et al., 2018). Therefore, a brief but robust exploration of how sport social work can manifest at different stages is necessary. This section explores four distinct high-impact stages: youth, high school, collegiate, and professional sport.

Youth Sports

The developmental and social advantages of youth participation in sport is well-documented (Newman et al., 2017). As licensed professionals, many clinical social workers provide mental health therapies to youth athletes—some even utilizing sport to enhance therapeutic practices among non-athletes. Doc Wayne Youth Services, employing several sport social workers, integrates two therapeutic frameworks—attachment, regulation, and competency and dialectical behavior therapy—fusing both approaches with sports to improve mental health of at-risk youth (Doc Wayne Youth Services, 2020). Other organizations use sport as a mechanism to drive large-scale change and address youth-related systemic issues in society. In an effort to diminish gender inequality, Women Win serves girls and young women by partnering with a variety of sport organizations utilizing the game of soccer to develop leadership capabilities and self-advocacy skills (Women Win, n.d.). A final example of sport social work impacting youth is Mission 89, a global-reaching nonprofit dedicated to protecting young athletes from trafficking in the name of sport (Mission 89, 2020). All three of these organizations utilize social work strategies and youth sport to reduce the vulnerability of athletes and their communities.

Challenges and Considerations with Youth Sports

Although data reporting the rate of youth participation in organized sport are limited, in 2013 there were roughly 45 million youth in organized sport (Merkel, 2013). Sport social workers serving youth, their families, and the communities in which they live recognize the athlete's social environment is multifaceted and can be even more complex than those of non-athletes (Moore, 2016). Social work interventions must be flexible because every youth athlete's experience is unique, even if playing the same sport on the same team (Moore et al., 2018). Some challenges social workers address in the youth athletic arena include sport's impact on the family unit, parental roles in the sport arena, financial burdens in an increasingly privatized system, issues related to sex and gender, identity (personal and athletic identities), general medical issues, problematic psychosocial behaviors, pressure to perform well, and player–coach relationships (Bean et al., 2014; Kerr & Stirling, 2008). Regardless of life span stage, the focus of the sport social worker must fall back to the important social work core principle—maintaining a person-centered or athlete-centered approach that focuses on the person-in-environment (Kerr & Stirling, 2008).

High School Sports

Nearly 8 million American high school students play in organized athletics (National Federation of State High School Associations,

2017). High school coaches often are not adequately trained to effectively support a high school youth's overall well-being (Newman et al., 2017). However, coaches are often the main point of contact for emotional support. More effective intervention can be accomplished if athletic departments appropriately utilize the skill set that sport social workers bring to the table (Dean & Rowan, 2014). An example of effective collaboration can be seen in the work of Ms. Natalie Graves, licensed clinical social worker and owner of Natalie Graves Athletic Counseling (NGAC). Specializing in therapy for high school athletes, coaches, and families, NGAC provides behavioral health services to help families understand and navigate the commitment and pressures of sport. For coaches, she offers counseling sessions to help build understanding of team dynamics and how sport and coaching intertwine and affect day-to-day life (NGAC, n.d.). A sport social worker at the high school level can help alleviate and prevent issues from multiple dimensions of the sporting environment.

Challenges and Considerations with High School Sports

In addition to some of the challenges mentioned previously (i.e., pressure to perform, athletic identity, sexuality, etc.), more complex issues come into play during high school. For student–athletes, often preoccupied with securing an athletic college scholarship, college infiltrates the high school experience extremely early, and thus college recruiting and all of the nuances surrounding athletic scholarship attainment become reality for young athletes (Moore & Gummelt, 2019). Sport social work professionals need to be well-versed in National Association of Intercollegiate Athletics (NAIA) and National Collegiate Athletic Association (NCAA) rules, recruiting, eligibility, and best practice standards. In addition, support is needed for athletes when aspirations of becoming a collegiate athlete are not realized (i.e., via injury or lack of interest by college athletic programs). Best practices demand a continuum of services offered to student–athletes so that they can explore their other strengths, interests, and capabilities present off the court or playing field. Social workers are well-equipped to help high school youth navigate through such an exploratory and uncertain time in their development before transitioning to college.

Collegiate Sports

The two largest collegiate sport governing bodies, the NCAA and the NAIA, regulate more than 500,000 student–athletes and as such share greatly in responsibility for academic and athletic well-being (NCAA, 2020). Collegiate athletes experience unique challenges and are at risk for increased levels of vulnerabilities in many areas. High levels of depression, suicidality, substance misuse, eating disorders, and perpetration or victimization of serious misconduct including sexual violence exist throughout collegiate sport programming (ESPN, 2018; Moore, 2016). To address many of these issues, the NCAA Sport Science Institute (2016) partnered with several mental health providers, including licensed clinical social workers, and released a mental health best practices guide to encourage understanding and implementation of mental health interventions among college athletic departments.

In response to the 2020 coronavirus (COVID-19) pandemic and the 2020 Black Lives Matter movement, ASWIS past president, Dr. Emmett Gill, created a nonprofit organization Athletes & Advocates for Social Justice in Sport and wrote a letter to implore the NCAA to re-examine what the organization is doing to support the reintegration of Black, Indigenous, and People of Color (BIPOC) athletes back to campus (Gill, 2020). Gill's letter, co-signed by dozens of sport social workers and other allies, helped influence the NCAA Office of

Inclusion to develop a Student–Athlete Mental Health and Well-Being Task Force to address the mental health disparities affecting athletes of color (Gill, 2020). Social work professionals also intervene at the individual level and provide and coordinate student–athlete academic support services; mental health treatment; career counseling; and coaching on financial aid assistance, performance enhancement strategy, and other areas (Moore et al., 2018).

Challenges and Considerations with Collegiate Sports

Although historically present, sport social work in the collegiate arena remains an emerging field. Numbers of master's-level field interns and employed social workers in college sports are on the rise, with promising job outlooks. Still, social workers must position themselves strongly and advocate for opportunities (Moore & Gummelt, 2019). As examples of success, many large universities employ social workers throughout their programs, including Tulane University, The University of Texas, the University of Tennessee, Wayne State University, and the University of Michigan. The University of Michigan employs five licensed clinical social workers within their athletic counseling team, some of whom are also involved with the university's Athletes Connected Program, strategizing best practices to normalize mental health treatment and wellness programming within athletics (University of Michigan Athletics, 2020). Provisioning of services to student–athletes, however, remains challenging.

Persistent issues remain in working with collegiate athletes. Stigma associated with accessing treatment continues, and cultural and religious perceptions that amplify negative mental health symptoms endure (Moore et al., 2018). In addition, deep systemic racism and exploitation continue (Murty & Roebuck, 2015). As evidence, football and basketball are the most profitable teams in collegiate sports, with many athletes coming from low-socioeconomic backgrounds, and yet student–athletes are not compensated and therefore economically exploited (Murty & Roebuck, 2015). Furthermore, athletes may speak out, act, and use their platform to advocate for change or reform, at times jeopardizing their eligibility to play. A current example of this is athlete advocates in the Black Lives Matter movement using their platform to speak out about racial injustice (NCAA, 2020). Social work professionals are well-positioned to successfully navigate these challenges with the athletes and their allies, including activism and policy change efforts.

Professional Sports

The Bureau of Labor and Statistics (2020) reports that in 2018, American corporations employed 13,500 athletes and sports competitors. Although typically glorified in American society, and most often portrayed as benefitting from participation, professional athletes experience multiple levels of vulnerability. Purcell et al. (2019) describe an athlete's well-being in terms of a spectrum of risk factors, such as financial management, social support maintenance (family, team, coaches, or others), media portrayal, self-image/identity, injury, and transitions to life after sports, which all may negatively impact mental health and interpersonal relationships and lead to performance issues. Sport social workers can and do play a vital helping role for professional athletes and their teams, which has led to professional sporting organizations increasing employment opportunities. For example, the Carolina Panthers hired Tish Guerin, LCSW, as Director of Player Wellness, situating the team as one of the first football franchises to secure an internal mental health provider (Rodrique, 2018). Also, the Las Vegas Raiders hired Devon Lewis-Buchanan, MSW, as their Alumni Relations Director;

and Jarrod Barnes, MSW, serves as Manager of Former Player Marketing and Services for the Los Angeles Rams (D. Lewis-Buchanan, personal communication, February 5, 2020; J. Barnes, personal communication, February 5, 2020). Increased recognition of professional athletes as a vulnerable population is creating more opportunities for sport social workers and therefore increased positive outcomes for the athletes, their families, and the communities in which they live.

Challenges and Considerations with Professional Sports

Like other areas of sport across the life span, challenges and considerations for social workers serving professional athletics remain. Many professional sports exist on the international stage, requiring some professional athletes to compete overseas, unprepared for immersion in foreign cultural life. In addition, many college athletes also compete internationally in the professional-level sector while representing their respective national teams. This international aspect of sport carries with it inconsistency among rules and policies for participation, as well as other unique challenges specific to athlete adjustment (Hester, 2017). Also, sport social workers must be prepared to aid professional athletes who carry trauma from their collegiate experiences. Two hallmark examples of detrimental college scandals and abuse in the past decade are the Sandusky scandal of 2011, in which former assistant football coach at Penn State University, Jerry Sandusky, was convicted of 52 counts of child molestation, and the 2018 USA Gymnastics scandal brought about by Michigan State University athletic physician and national team doctor, Larry Nassar, in which he sexually abused hundreds of female athletes under the façade of treating injuries (Fuller, 2020; Rosado, 2018). These examples further stress the idea alluded to previously in the chapter that systemic issues are imbedded in sport, but sport is also often used at a means to perpetuate systemic injustices as well. Nonetheless, the enmeshed nature of college and professional sports along with the urgent need to safeguard elite athletes create a call to action for change and for sport social workers to lead the charge (Mountjoy et al., 2016).

Conclusion

As change agents, sport social workers assist athletes, their families, allies, athletic organizations, and communities to enhance well-being. The practice subspecialty is poised for growth and continued impact. Membership in ASWIS has grown year after year, field placements in athletics have increased in schools of social work, pertinent academic journal publications continue, international interest is spreading, and employment opportunities are flourishing (M. Moore, personal communication, July 2020). Despite this success, unknowns still exist, and further collaborations with other athlete-serving professions are needed to continue the impact trajectory. Probably the most famous words about sport came from Nelson Mandela in 2000 when he stated, "Sport has the power to change the world" (as cited in Laureus, 2020). Jane Addams lived this philosophy more than a century prior, and contemporary sport social workers allow those words to live on.

Helpful Resources

Alliance of Social Workers in Sports: https://www.aswis.org
Beyond Sport: https://www.beyondsport.org
Doc Wayne: http://docwayne.org
Laureus: https://www.laureus.com
Sport and Dev: https://www.sportanddev.org
Sport and Social Change: https://sportsandsocialchange.org
Women Win: https://www.womenwin.org

References

Addams, J. (1910). *Twenty years at Hull House.* Macmillan.

Alliance of Social Workers in Sports. (2020, July). History. https://www.aswis.org/history

Bachrach, J. (2012, May 14). Chicago playgrounds: A history. Time Out Chicago. https://www.timeout.com/chicago/kids/activities/chicago-playgroundsa-history

Bean, C. N., Fortier, M., Post, C., & Chima, K. (2014). Understanding how organized youth sport may be harming individual players within the family unit: A literature review. *International Journal of Environmental Research and Public Health, 11*(10), 10226–10268. https://doi.org/10.3390/ijerph111010226

Bent-Goodley, T. (2014). Social work: A profession of power, passion, and purpose [Editorial]. *Social Work, 59*(3), 197–199.

Council of Europe. (2001). European sports charter (adopted by the Committee of Ministers on 24 September 1992 at the 480th meeting of the Ministers' Deputies and revised at their 752nd meeting on 16 May 2001). https://rm.coe.int/16804c9dbb

Dean, C., & Rowan, D. (2014). The social worker's role in serving vulnerable athletes. *Journal of Social Work Practice, 28*(2), 219–227.

Doc Wayne Youth Services. (2020). 2018–19 *annual* report. http://docwayne.org/2018-19-annual-report

Ehrenreich, J. H. (2014). *The altruistic imagination: A history of social work and social policy in the United States.* Cornell University Press.

ESPN. (2018). *Brenda Tracy shares powerful story of survival* [Video]. YouTube. https://www.espn.com/video/clip/_/id/24455009

Fuller, L. (2020). Sport sex scandals: A comparison between Penn State and USA Gymnastics. *Democratic Communiqué, 29*(1), 116–123.

Gill, E. L. (2020, December 7). *2020 Power five conference Behavioral/Mental Health Providers race & gender report card.* Athletes & Advocates for Social Justice in Sports. https://socialjusticeinsports.org/report-cards%2Ftestimonies

Hester, S. L. (2017). *Out of bounds: The bodies, borders, and voices of female athletes.* Doctoral dissertation, The University of Memphis. ProQuest Dissertations Publishing.

Jenny, S. E., Manning, R. D., Keiper, M. C., & Olrich, T. W. (2017). Virtual(ly) athletes: Where eSports fit within the definition of "sport." *Quest, 69*(1), 1–18.

Kerr, G. A., & Stirling, A. E. (2008). Child protection in sport: Implications of an athlete-centered philosophy. *Quest, 60*(2), 307–323.

Klein, S. E. (2017). Introduction. In S. E. Klein (Ed.), *Defining sport: Conceptions and borderlines* (pp. xi–xviii). Lexington Books.

Laureus. (2020). Sport has the power to change the world. https://www.laureus.com

Lubben, J. E., Barth, R. P., Fong, R., Flynn, M. L., Sherraden, M., & Uehara, E. (2018). Grand Challenges for social work and society. In R. Fong, J. E. Lubben, & R. P. Barth (Eds.), *Grand Challenges for social work and society* (pp. 1–19). Oxford University Press.

Merkel, D. L. (2013). Youth sport: Positive and negative impact on young athletes. *Open Access Journal of Sports Medicine, 4,* 151–160. https://doi.org/10.2147/OAJSM.S33556

Mission 89. (2020). About us. https://mission89.org/about-us

Moore, M., Ballesteros, J., & Hansen, C. J. (2018). The role of social work values in promoting the functioning and well-being of athletes. *Journal of Social Work Values and Ethics, 15*(2), 48.

Moore, M., & Gummelt, G. (2019). *Sport social work: Promoting the functioning and well-being of college and professional athletes.* Cognella.

Moore, M. A. (2016). Taking a timeout to ensure well-being: Social work involvement in college sports. *Social Work, 61*(3), 267–269. https://doi.org/10.1093/sw/sww020

Mountjoy, M., Brackenridge, C., Arrington, M., Blauwet, C., Carska-Sheppard, A., Fasting, K., Kirby, S., Leahy, T., Marks, S., Martin, K., Starr, K., Tivas, A., & Budgett, R. (2016). International Olympic Committee consensus statement: Harassment and abuse (non-accidental violence) in sport. *British Journal of Sports Medicine, 50*(17), 1019–1029.

Murty, K. S., & Roebuck, J. B. (2015). Deviant exploitation of Black male student athletes on White campuses. *Deviant Behavior, 36*(6), 429–440.

Natalie Graves Athletic Counseling. (n.d.). Services. http://www.nataliegraves.com/services

National Association of Social Workers. (2017). *Code of ethics.* NASW Press.

National Collegiate Athletic Association. (2020, July). *Listen, learn and act: The voices of NCAA student–athletes.* https://www.ncaa.com/ncaa/listen-voices-ncaa-student-athletes

National Collegiate Athletic Association Sport Science Institute. (2016). *Mental health best practices: Inter-association consensus document: Best practices for understanding and supporting student–athlete mental wellness.* https://ncaaorg.s3.amazonaws.com/ssi/mental/SSI_MentalHealthBestPractices.pdf

National Federation of State High School Associations. (2017). *High school sports participation increases for 28th straight year, nears 8 million mark.* https://www.nfhs.org/articles/high-school-sports-participation-increases-for-28th-straight-year-nears-8-million-mark

Newman, T. J., Alvarez, M. A. G., & Kim, M. (2017). An experiential approach to sport for youth development. *Journal of Experiential Education, 40*(3), 308–322.

Purcell, R., Gwyther, K., & Rice, S. M. (2019). Mental health in elite athletes: Increased awareness requires an early intervention framework to respond to athlete needs. *Sports Medicine—Open, 5,* 46. https://doi.org/10.1186/s40798-019-0220-1

Reynolds, J. (2017, July 17). Jane Addams' forgotten legacy: Recreation and sport. *Journal of Issues in Intercollegiate Athletics,* 11–18.

Rodrique, J. (2018, September 28). Everybody is dealing with something, so Panthers invest in mental health of players. *The Charlotte Observer.* https://www.charlotteobserver.com/sports/nfl/carolina-panthers/article219058125.html

Rosado, S. (2018, March 18). Student athletes deserve mental health care access. *The Journal Gazette.* https://www.journalgazette.net/opinion/columns/20180313/student-athletes-deserve-mental-health-care-access

Suppes, M. A., & Wells, C. C. (2018). *The social work experience: A case-based introduction to social work and social welfare* (7th ed.). Pearson.

United Nations. (2009). Building a peaceful and better world through sport and the Olympic ideal. https://undocs.org/A/RES/64/4

United Nations. (2015). Transforming our world: The 2030 agenda for sustainable development. https://www.un.org/ga/search/view_doc.asp?symbol=A/RES/70/1&Lang=E

University of Michigan Athletics. (2020). Michigan athletics counseling team. https://mgoblue.com/sports/2017/6/16/athletics-counseling.aspx#team

Women Win. (n.d.). About us. https://www.womenwin.org/about

Young, K., & Okada, C. (2014). Introduction: Sport, social development and peace: Acknowledging potential, respecting balance. In K. Young & C. Okada (Eds.), *Sport, social development and peace* (pp. ix–xxix). Emerald.

Community Resilience to Natural Disasters

A Social Capital Approach

Grace L. Whaley, Lenore Arlee, Heather Baker, and Betty Pfefferbaum

Communities are increasingly complex, and so are the challenges they face. Natural disasters are more frequent and costlier. Factors such as climate change and increased urbanization can expose more people to disasters. Disasters impact not only physical structures but also health, mental health, education, employment, relationships, and leisure activities. From an ecological systems perspective, it is intuitive that the healing capacities of a community lie largely in the relationships between entities, individuals, groups, and networks and the benefits they provide: social capital.

Due to the unpredictable nature of disasters, it is imperative that social workers become familiar with the response networks in their immediate locale, region, and state as well as how these organizations interface with the federal government. Disasters disproportionately affect socioeconomically disadvantaged and minority populations [Institute of Medicine (IOM), 2015]; thus, it is important for social workers to participate in social justice efforts to empower vulnerable community members and ensure equitable access to resources throughout recovery. Knowledge and social capital can assist social workers in responding effectively and efficiently when the community needs support most.

Resilience

Resilience, whether referring to an individual or other entity, is a dynamic process of successfully adapting to adversity (Norris et al., 2008), which fluctuates based on resource availability and accessibility (Ungar, 2011). Ungar (2011) defines a community's resilience as its "social capital, physical infrastructure, and culturally embedded patterns of interdependence that give it the potential to recover from dramatic change, sustain its adaptability, and support new growth that integrates the lessons learned during a time of crisis" (p. 1742).

Individual and community resilience are interconnected and influenced by state and federal policy. Current research seeks to understand individual differences in patterns of resilience (Bonanno et al., 2010), but the resilience of individuals rarely exceeds that of their community (Ungar, 2011). Communities with the capacity to care for their most vulnerable members day-to-day are more likely to demonstrate resilience when facing significant adversity (IOM, 2015; Ungar, 2011).

Social Capital

Social capital, a key component of individual and community resilience, refers to the benefits gained through the relationships between individual entities, groups, and networks, including emotional support, tangible support, shared information and learning, sense of belonging, and economic benefits (Sadri et al., 2018). Social capital is conceptualized as a three-prong model of bonding, bridging, and linking (Aldrich & Meyer, 2015). Bonding social capital refers to strong, personal ties between close friends or family, characterized by emotional connection and similarities among members. Bridging social capital refers to a broader, typically more diverse network of acquainted individuals and groups that may work on civic projects or participate in interest groups together. Bridging relationships facilitate information and resource sharing and greater access to and awareness of available resources and opportunities. Linking social capital connects community members to people and entities in positions of power, such as government representatives or agencies (Aldrich & Meyer, 2015).

Social workers and community leaders should manage, maintain, strengthen, and leverage social capital of all three types. Multiple studies have observed faster post-disaster recovery among those with higher levels of social capital, based on markers such as a higher level of trust in government, "denser personal networks" (i.e., close personal ties/relationships), geographic closeness to networks, and assistance from neighbors (Sadri et al., 2018). Communities with higher social capital also have reported greater satisfaction with community rebuilding (Aldrich & Meyer, 2015).

Pre-Disaster: Laying the Foundation

Bonding, bridging, and linking relationships need to be initiated and strengthened prior to a disaster to enable prompt, efficient mobilization when needed (Norris et al., 2008). Government, nonprofit, and private sectors should coordinate preparedness, response, and recovery plans and be prepared to work as a team [Federal Emergency Management Agency (FEMA), 2011].

Building the Network

All three types of social capital should be cultivated in communities to increase the likelihood of resilience should a disaster strike. Of primary concern is building and strengthening social networks within the community. Social workers can increase bonding social capital by encouraging community gatherings, volunteer work, and community problem-solving (Aldrich & Meyer, 2015), all of which also enhance a sense of ownership and belonging in a community.

Community organizations of various kinds contribute to bridging and linking relationships that yield social capital. Organizations that build upon principles of bridging and linking include chambers of commerce, nonprofit networks, public and community health organizations, parent–teacher organizations, and interfaith coalitions [U.S. Department of Homeland Security (DHS), 2016]. Representatives from these or similar sources of social capital may also partner with disaster-focused organizations such as Voluntary Organizations Active in Disaster

(VOAD) at the national or state level or Community Organizations Active in Disaster in local communities. VOAD is a hub of organizations that fosters preparedness by planning and building social capital through cooperation, communication, coordination, and collaboration (National Voluntary Organizations Active in Disaster, 2020). When existing organizations and networks are able to connect, collaborate, and problem-solve efficiently prior to a disaster, they are positioned to respond rapidly to a crisis when needed; the foundation of community response and recovery has been laid.

Community Assessment and Strategic Planning

Each community's cohesion, social capital, demographics, location, economy, resources (FEMA, 2011), cultures, and history make it unique. Each community's disaster response will be unique as well (B. Pfefferbaum et al., 2017a). Assessing not only preparedness plans but also the daily functioning of a community is vital to resilience because disasters compound existing vulnerabilities (IOM, 2015), whereas existing strengths can be maximized to fuel recovery.

One publicly available and evidence-informed resource for community assessment is the Communities Advancing Resilience Toolkit (CART) Assessment Survey, which gathers information from key informants in the community regarding five interrelated community resilience domains: connection and caring, resources, transformative potential, disaster management, and information and communication (R. Pfefferbaum et al., 2015). The results of the CART Assessment Survey or a similar tool can illuminate disparities in a community and inform goals and strategies to improve resilience (IOM, 2015; R. Pfefferbaum et al., 2015). In addition, the assessment process in itself can unite community members for a common purpose and contribute to social capital.

Communities with large vulnerable populations are likely to recover more slowly and are less likely to be resilient (IOM, 2015). Populations identified as particularly vulnerable to disasters by IOM (2015) include children, the elderly, people with disabilities, the medically vulnerable, people experiencing mental illness, the financially fragile, the uninsured or underinsured, the unhoused, and those in foster care. Ungar (2011) describes the community's ability to care for its most vulnerable as a measure of resilience. Thus, a key element of disaster preparedness is addressing social and economic inequity (IOM, 2015).

Disaster Preparedness

Whereas the principles of community resilience are applicable to a wide range of hazards or unexpected challenges, strategies to mitigate losses vary by disaster. Thus, disaster preparedness education should be tailored to a community or region based on the relative risk of particular disasters (B. Pfefferbaum et al., 2015). National organizations such as the American Red Cross and FEMA offer comprehensive resources to guide preparedness for many aspects of various disasters. In addition to adults, FEMA (2011) recommends involving children and youth in disaster preparedness education programs, which may be delivered at schools or in other community settings. Children may then help disseminate information, educate their families, and raise enthusiasm about preparedness (B. Pfefferbaum et al., 2018). However, disseminating disaster preparedness recommendations and response plans alone is insufficient; communities must also recognize the need for critical reflection, flexibility, and efficient collective problem-solving (Norris et al., 2008).

Disaster Event and Immediate Response

The period of time during and immediately following a disaster is a chaotic one, characterized by fear and urgency. The immediate response phase involves reducing or preventing human, property, and environmental loss (B. Pfefferbaum et al, 2015). Formal teams and informal networks are critical during this time.

Communication

Clear, consistent, timely, and trusted communication is essential. Individuals tend to act on information from the sources they trust most, often friends and family (Aldrich & Meyer, 2015), especially in crisis situations in which little time is available to evaluate sources (Norris et al., 2008). When available, social media and text messages help spread warning and response information rapidly. Media portrayals influence the way a disaster is perceived (Norris et al., 2008), which may influence protective action and/or initial responses.

Social Support

Social connectedness affects the resilience of individuals and the community as a whole (IOM, 2015). The bonding form of social capital is often the first line of defense in a crisis (Aldrich & Meyer, 2015). Close friends, family, and neighbors may provide information or warning, emotional support, shelter, supplies, or physical rescue, whereas those with limited social ties are less likely to be rescued, evacuate, or receive assistance from others (Aldrich & Meyer, 2015). These relationships may be strained if the disaster is widespread, requires evacuation, or displaces members of a bonded group (Aldrich & Meyer, 2015). As much as possible, existing social support systems should be sustained and strengthened throughout the recovery process (IOM, 2015; Norris et al., 2008).

Social support is most helpful when reciprocal, to avoid depleting resources or generating feelings of helplessness or incapability (Norris et al., 2008). In research on social support, perceived support is often distinguished from received support. Perceived support, which is a stronger predictor of resilience (Bonanno et al., 2010; Norris, Friedman, Watson, et al., 2002), refers to the general belief that resources are available and accessible if/when they are needed (Norris, Friedman, Watson, et al., 2002; Norris et al., 2008), as opposed to received support, which may be in part a reflection of the degree of experienced devastation and need (Bonanno et al., 2010).

Coordination

A disaster demands rapid, harmonious assistance from a wide range of agencies. Existing social and professional networks communicate and begin to mobilize even prior to an anticipated or imminent disaster. Immediate responders when disaster strikes might include law enforcement agencies, firefighters, and emergency medical services. Organizations designated to serve as shelters can begin activating volunteer networks and coordinating with other involved organizations. Ideally, these roles and responsibilities are determined and outlined prior to a disaster.

People from unaffected areas may be moved to help in the aftermath of a disaster but unsure what to do. Untrained, spontaneous volunteers can be a valuable asset, but those with prior coordination and guidance (e.g., American Red Cross volunteer training or search and rescue training) may prove more effective at this stage. Aside from volunteering, well-meaning donations from surrounding communities may create a burden for the affected community without coordinated and timely communication among community stakeholders (Gurwitch et al., 2007).

Post-Disaster: Long-Term Recovery

The post-disaster phase begins when the immediate threat to safety has ended and attention shifts to rebuilding and resuming daily activities (B. Pfefferbaum et al., 2017a). This phase can last for years following an event, depending on the extent and severity of damages and available resources. Immediate and long-term post-disaster phases can overlap (DHS, 2016). For example, some families may still be housed in emergency shelters when many others have settled into at least semi-permanent housing. Community cohesion and helping behavior organically emerge in the immediate aftermath of a crisis, but the urgency and sense of unity wane over time (Norris et al., 2008). A successful and sustained post-disaster phase relies on community leadership, participation, and ownership (Norris et al., 2008), contributing to a sense of communal purpose and hope.

Empowerment

Community engagement and participation are vital to a community's recovery and are consistently posed as a resilience strategy (IOM, 2015; B. Pfefferbaum et al., 2015). FEMA's "Whole Community Approach to Emergency Management" (2011) recommends as a core principle to "engage and empower all parts of the community" (p. 4). Community members from diverse backgrounds, agencies, professional affiliations, and community groups should be represented in long-term recovery planning in order to accurately conceptualize and consider the perspectives, cultures, and needs of the whole community (FEMA, 2011; B. Pfefferbaum et al., 2015 , 2017a).

Mentoring and support from disaster-experienced professionals in other communities may be invaluable, but long-term recovery efforts must be led by trusted members of the affected community (Norris et al., 2008). Community leaders earn the trust of constituents by listening to, understanding, and responding to the needs and concerns of community members (FEMA, 2011).

Similarly, the American Red Cross offers ongoing comprehensive training programs to prepare and build a network of invaluable trained volunteers, but the ideas and input

that shape growth and development should emerge from empowered community members (FEMA, 2011). This type of local ownership improves the likelihood that community members will remain engaged even after the energy of the immediate aftermath fades (FEMA, 2011).

Children and adolescents should also participate in community healing. Involving children and adolescents in developmentally appropriate ways serves the youth through development of skills, knowledge, social responsibility, and social interaction, and the community benefits from the projects implemented and from a youth population with enhanced capacities (B. Pfefferbaum et al., 2017b).

Strong community cohesion is an asset in many ways, but it can also contribute to discriminatory exclusion in particularly tight-knit and homogeneous communities, neighborhoods, or groups (Aldrich & Meyer, 2015; IOM, 2015; Ungar, 2011). Mitigation of potential discrimination aligns with social work's core value of social justice: "Social workers pursue social change, particularly with and on behalf of vulnerable and oppressed individuals and groups of people" (National Association of Social Workers, 2017). One role of the social worker and community builder is to cultivate relationships with groups that may be viewed as peripheral in a community and encourage their involvement in the community recovery process (Aldrich & Meyer, 2015).

Collaboration

Services within a community often overlap, but in order to make the most efficient use of post-disaster resources, duplication of services should be minimized. Community leaders and representatives from recovery-involved organizations may form an interdisciplinary team or long-term recovery group (LTRG) to coordinate services, determine best use of resources, and assess and adapt to the changing needs of the community for months to years following a disaster. Subcommittees may be formed to carry out tasks or focus on a more specific piece of recovery, such as crisis counseling/spiritual care, unmet needs, community assessment, disaster case management, donations management, volunteer coordination, government coordination, or communications/public relations (Center for Disaster Philanthropy, 2020).

Coordination and cooperation are significant challenges reported by many professionals with disaster experience (Norris, Friedman, & Watson, 2002). Stakeholders cannot promote their own agenda; for the sake of the whole, they must set differences and private interests aside to focus on the common goal of supporting their community. Rather than attempting to enforce rigid plans, an LTRG should create space for trust, openness, teamwork, and creative problem-solving even in the most trying of circumstances (IOM, 2015).

Community Growth

Disasters can bring new resources and opportunities to a community, which can be leveraged to improve long-term community resilience (IOM, 2015). This may include furthering community improvement efforts that are already envisioned or initiated (IOM, 2015), enhancing relationships in the community, rethinking infrastructure, and/or bolstering community pride. Through the healing and rebuilding process, communities may benefit from developing a meaningful community narrative that tells the story of the experience, response, and growth associated with the disaster (Norris et al., 2008; Ungar, 2011).

Adjustment and Self-Care

As with any major change, adjustment can be difficult, and aspects of previously "normal" life must be grieved. This process will take time and vary for each person. Community members will find themselves on a collective journey through growth and struggle, hope and loss, gratitude and sorrow, at times simultaneously.

In the context of social capital, it is especially important to consider the impact of this intense and prolonged experience on professionals involved in disaster recovery (IOM, 2015). Many professionals may take on additional duties or volunteer. Their participation in LTRGs may be in addition to regular professional duties and their own personal stress from the disaster. (Norris, Friedman, Watson, et al., 2002). Burnout and compassion fatigue are rampant in the months to years following a disaster (IOM, 2015). Patience, self-care, and safe and supportive relationships could not be more critical.

Conclusion

A community's post-disaster resilience will reflect its capacity to equitably integrate and support all members of the community on a regular basis. Communities should reduce systemic barriers to opportunity to improve overall resilience. Building social capital prior to a disaster is a widely supported resilience strategy for communities, which in turn supports the resilience of individual members. Recovery should be guided by diverse and representative members and trusted leaders of the affected community and should be orchestrated to use resources as efficiently as possible.

Helpful Resources
Websites

211: https://www.211.org

American Red Cross: https://www.redcross.org

Department of Homeland Security: https://www.disasterassistance.gov

National Voluntary Organizations Active in Disaster: https://www.nvoad.org

Substance Abuse and Mental Health Services Administration: https://www.samhsa.gov/disaster-preparedness

The National Child Traumatic Stress Network: https://www.nctsn.org

United Way: https://www.unitedway.org

Apps

Federal Emergency Management Agency (FEMA) Psychological First Aid (PFA)

Red Cross apps: Emergency!, Tornado, Hurricane, Flood, Earthquake

References

Aldrich, D. P., & Meyer, M. A. (2015). Social capital and community resilience. *American Behavioral Scientist, 59*(2), 254–269. https://doi.org/10.1177/0002764214550299

Bonanno, G. A., Brewin, C. R., Kaniasty, K., & La Greca, A. M. (2010). Weighing the costs of disaster: Consequences, risks, and resilience in individuals, families, and communities. *Psychological Science in the Public Interest, 11*(1), 1–49. https://doi.org/10.1177/1529100610387086

Center for Disaster Philanthropy. (2020). Long term recovery groups. https://www.disasterphilanthropy.org/issue-insight/long-term-recovery-groups

Federal Emergency Management Agency. (2011). *A whole community approach to emergency management: Principles, themes, and pathways for action.* U.S. Department of Homeland Security. https://www.fema.gov/sites/default/files/2020-07/whole_community_dec2011__2.pdf

Gurwitch, R. H., Pfefferbaum, B., Montgomery, J. M., Klomp, R. W., & Reissman, D. B. (2007). *Building community resilience for children and families.* Terrorism and Disaster Center at the University of Oklahoma Health Sciences Center.

Institute of Medicine. (2015). *Healthy, resilient, and sustainable communities after disasters: Strategies, opportunities, and planning for recovery.* National Academies Press. https://doi.org/10.17226/18996

National Association of Social Workers. (2017). Code of ethics. https://www.socialworkers.org/about/ethics/code-of-ethics

National Voluntary Organizations Active in Disaster. (2020). About us. https://www.nvoad.org/about-us

Norris, F. H., Friedman, M. J., & Watson, P. J. (2002). 60,000 disaster victims speak: Part II. Summary and implications of the disaster mental health research. *Psychiatry, 65*(3), 240–260. https://doi.org/10.1521/psyc.65.3.240.20169

Norris, F. H., Friedman, M. J., Watson, P. J., Byrne, C. M., Diaz, E., & Kaniasty, K. (2002). 60,000 disaster victims speak: Part I. An empirical review of the empirical literature, 1981–2001.

Psychiatry, 65(3), 207–239. https://doi.org/10.1521/psyc.65.3.207.20173

Norris, F. H., Stevens, S. P., Pfefferbaum, B., Wyche, K. F., & Pfefferbaum, R. L. (2008). Community resilience as a metaphor, theory, set of capacities, and strategy for disaster readiness. *American Journal of Community Psychology, 41,* 127–150. https://doi.org/10.1007/s10464-007-9156-6

Pfefferbaum, B., Pfefferbaum, R. L, & Van Horn, R. L. (2015). Community resilience interventions: Participatory assessment-based, action-oriented processes. *American Behavioral Scientist, 59*(2), 238–253. https://doi.org/10.1177/0002764214550298

Pfefferbaum, B., Pfefferbaum, R. L., & Van Horn, R. L. (2018). Involving children in disaster risk reduction: The importance of participation. *European Journal of Psychotraumatology, 9*(2), 1–6. https://doi.org/10.1080/20008198.2018.1425577

Pfefferbaum, B., Van Horn, R. L., & Pfefferbaum, R. L. (2017a). A conceptual framework to enhance community resilience using social capital. *Clinical Social Work Journal, 45*(2), 102–110. https://doi.org/10.1007/s10615-015-0556-z

Pfefferbaum, B., Van Horn, R. L., & Pfefferbaum, R. L. (2017b). Involving adolescents in building community resilience for disasters. *Adolescent Psychiatry, 7,* 253–265. https://www.eurekaselect.com/159004/article

Pfefferbaum, R. L., Pfefferbaum, B., Nitiéma, P., Houston, J. B., & Van Horn, R. L. (2015). Assessing community resilience: An application of the expanded CART survey instrument with affiliated volunteer responders. *American Behavioral Scientist, 59*(2), 181–199. https://doi.org/10.1177/0002764214550295

Sadri, A. M., Ukkusuri, S. V., Lee, S., Clawson, R., Aldrich, D., Nelson, M. S., Seipel, J., & Kelly, D. (2018). The role of social capital, personal networks, and emergency responders in post-disaster recovery and resilience: A study of rural communities in Indiana. *Natural Hazards, 90,* 1377–1406. https://doi.org/10.1007/s11069-017-3103-0

Ungar, M. (2011). Community resilience for youth and families: Facilitative physical and social capital in contexts of adversity. *Children and Youth Services Review, 33,* 1742–1748. https://doi.org/10.1016/j.childyouth.2011.04.027

U.S. Department of Homeland Security. (2016). *National disaster recovery framework* (2nd ed.). https://www.fema.gov/media-library/assets/documents/117794

Truth and Reconciliation Commissions and Community Practice

David K. Androff

What can social workers do to heal divided societies haunted by trauma? The United States' unresolved painful histories of colonialism, slavery, and repression echo through contemporary health disparities, civil and political disenfranchisement, inequality and poverty, and stigmatization and discrimination. Truth and reconciliation commissions (TRCs) are an innovative way for community practitioners to respond to traumatic legacies and their consequences. TRCs are community-based restorative justice interventions that aim to transform communities recovering from violence and injustice. This chapter shows how practitioners can use TRCs to advance human rights and social justice.

Evolution and Evidence

In the 1970s and 1980s, TRCs were first used in Africa and Latin America by recently democratized governments to investigate mass human rights violations (Hayner, 2011). South Africa had the most famous TRC as part of the peaceful transition of power from apartheid; it may have prevented widespread racial conflict predicted by many (Gibson, 2004). Since then, TRCs have become widespread across the Global South in countries rebuilding after violent conflict, such as Liberia, Peru, Sierra Leone, and Timor-Leste.

More recently, TRCs have been applied in the Western democracies of the United States and Canada to combat the social damage of racial discrimination and violence (Androff, 2012a). These examples demonstrate that community practitioners in the United States can use TRCs to address historical and contemporary racial injustice. In Greensboro, North Carolina, a grassroots coalition of churches, activists, and other community groups conducted the first TRC in North America in 2004. The Greensboro TRC (GTRC) investigated the 1979 Greensboro Massacre, when Ku Klux Klan and American Nazi Party members murdered five activists at an anti-racism rally. The GTRC focused on this one incident to engage the community beyond the social trauma of the massacre to the intersecting issues of racism, labor exploitation, and violence.

The Canadian TRC in 2008 and the Maine Wabanaki-State Child Welfare TRC in 2012 addressed legacies of colonialism in Indigenous communities, specifically the forced schooling of children through the child welfare system (Androff, 2012a). Inspired by these examples, others in the United States have organized TRC efforts on issues ranging from national poverty to racial discrimination in federal housing policy in Detroit; the legacies of race riots, lynching, and other hate crimes in South Carolina, Georgia, and Mississippi; and Hurricane Katrina in New Orleans.

A core strength of the TRC intervention is that it can be adapted to any historical and cultural context, and increasingly to a growing range of issues. Originally, TRCs focused on civil and political rights; TRCs in Argentina and Chile, for example, investigated the disappearances, imprisonment, torture, and extrajudicial killings by military dictatorships. The South African TRC focused on political violence during the apartheid era, yet apartheid dimensions of economic exploitation and social segregation led to discussion of Black South Africans' exclusion from education, health care, and social services. Later TRCs such as the Timor-Leste TRC included a more explicit focus on economic and social crimes such as domicide, forced starvation, destruction of roads and infrastructure, and the extraction of natural resources. These have also more commonly focused on gender-based violence, especially the Sierra Leone TRC. The Canada and Maine TRCs have expanded the intervention's application to cultural violations as well, including the colonial schools' prohibition of Indigenous children speaking their native language and practicing their native religion, in addition to physical and sexual abuse.

Practitioners can apply the TRC model to other issues faced by their communities. There have been calls for a TRC in the United States to address the War on Terror, police brutality, the legacy of slavery, and the Trump administration's pandemic response. Scholars also advocate for using TRCs to address climate justice (Klinsky & Brankovic, 2018).

Evidence on the effectiveness of TRCs is mixed; there are few rigorous evaluations. The South African TRC was found to build legitimacy for the new democratic state (Gibson, 2004). The Greensboro TRC was found to contribute to some interpersonal reconciliation (Androff, 2010a) and community reconciliation (Androff, 2012d). Most TRCs, however, are judged on their political outcomes and are typically criticized for failing to deliver justice, either by granting perpetrators amnesty or by not supporting their criminal prosecution. Yet often such perpetrators are former government officials, and coexisting with them is a price of reconciliation and peace. Other TRCs have been criticized for failing to address economic crimes; yet when TRCs give reparations to the families of victims, they are criticized for buying off the victims.

Theoretical Underpinning and Model of Community Practice

Truth and reconciliation commissions are based on the theory of restorative justice; they are often used where traditional retributive justice systems are inadequate, corrupt, or lack jurisdiction (Androff, 2013). The failure of legal systems to deliver justice often compounds community trauma, furthering social division and distrust of institutions. Community practitioners can use restorative justice interventions to combat systems of oppression that cannot be overcome solely in court. Restorative justice holds that violence and trauma damage not just victims but the wider community, and therefore it aims to repair relationships through engaging with perpetrators, victims, and communities. Typical interventions include dialogue between offenders and victims and engaging community stakeholders to repair social harm. The goal is community well-being and recovery from trauma, not punishment.

From a social work perspective, TRCs are trauma-informed and rights-based interventions (Androff, 2019). In responding to community or national trauma, TRCs offer recovery, resiliency, and, it is hoped, reconciliation and justice through truth-seeking and -telling. TRCs are trauma-informed and rights-based in that they respond to social traumas and seek to respond to the needs of victims whose rights have been violated. Truth-seeking can facilitate individual recovery from trauma; reconciliation can facilitate recovery on a macro level. TRCs advance social repair through promoting mutual tolerance among formerly antagonistic groups and thus the prevention of future violence. TRCs can also educate communities about trauma and human rights violations. Through telling victims' stories, TRCs lead to their (re)humanization.

Although TRCs have not been explicitly tied to social work, social workers have played a role in TRCs by providing support and services to victims (Androff, 2010b). And yet, TRCs share many goals and processes with community practice models, such as empowerment; development; capacity building; and healing from social injustice, violence, and oppression. In fact, TRCs have significant overlap with established models of community practice. TRCs represent a form of community capacity development that seeks to empower communities; encourage civic participation and action; and build social cohesion through coalitions across racial, ethnic, religious, social, and class groups (Rothman, 2008). TRCs also fit the model of neighborhood and community organizing in that they are place-based and cater to improving the quality of life for that geographic location's residents (Weil & Gamble, 2005). TRCs' foci on

dialogue and public forums for social change are related to community study circles, peacemaking circles, and restorative justice dialogue circles (Beck et al., 2011).

TRCs incorporate a range of community practice elements, such as diversity, citizen participation, empowerment, collective problem-solving, and public forums (Weil & Gamble, 2005). TRCs can be participatory interventions through community engagement and social interactions across diverse racial, ethnic, and class divisions. TRCs can build social capital and trust, the goal of many community practice interventions (Rothman, 2008). When started by local community members, they represent a bottom-up approach to social change. In these ways, TRCs can build the capacity of community members to overcome traumatic legacies through social action, reform civic institutions, and increase tolerance of diversity.

How Truth and Reconciliation Commissions Work

A major benefit of the TRC intervention for community practitioners is that it can be adapted to a wide variety of contexts and be made to fit local communities' specific history, religion, politics, and culture. Each TRC differs in its origin, relationship to government, focus on certain human rights violations or injustice, and incorporation of local culture. For example, TRCs have been created by legislation, judicial decisions, or community mobilization by diverse actors such as politicians, religious leaders, victims' rights groups, and community organizers. Some government-sponsored TRCs have subpoena power, others can offer amnesty from prosecution, whereas community-based TRCs without legal or political sanction have a social authority or community mandate. However, all TRCs share a common focus on the past, which can range from a single incident to decades of conflict and oppression. TRCs are always only temporary by design, structured to conduct specific investigatory and reconciliation activities with a certain time frame that concludes by producing a final report with recommendations. TRCs have used First Nations' aboriginal healing ceremonies in Canada, animist shamans in village-level ceremonies in Timor-Leste, and churches in Greensboro (Androff, 2008, 2018).

TRCs seek the truth to unearth information about injustices and abuses. TRCs investigate the scale and scope of human rights violations with research methods such as interviews with victims and key informants; community surveys; analyses of official documents and census data; and public hearings featuring testimony from victims, perpetrators, witnesses, and community members. If they have subpoena power, TRCs can access records and obtain testimony from those otherwise unwilling. The findings are released in a final report at the TRC's conclusion.

Interviews with victims serve to document human rights violations, which may in turn be used for potential prosecutions. Truth-seeking is a vital tool for public education so that communities can learn about the nature of injustice affecting their welfare. Ignorance about human rights violations abounds, usually due to silencing of victims and deliberate misinformation by perpetrators. Truth-seeking can reveal who did what to whom and combat the lies and stigmatization that often accompany social injustice. Ideally, these findings are incorporated into school curricula, museums, and monuments. Raising the public consciousness can lead to new attitudes, behaviors, and social norms. This is important when social groups are stigmatized for contemporary problems such as poverty or substance abuse without understanding these issues as connected to their historical trauma.

Reconciliation, as an outcome of TRCs, is poorly defined and often has idealistic overtones. A more realistic concept of reconciliation is the mutual, peaceful coexistence of perpetrators and victims, achieved through their testimony and community dialogue. Yet many critics believe that any accommodation of perpetrations is a betrayal of victims. Reconciliation occurs on both micro and macro levels. Micro-level reconciliation can be thought of as changes in individuals' thoughts or feelings (cognitive affective reconciliation), behaviors (behavioral reconciliation), or interpersonal relationships (social reconciliation) (Androff, 2010a). Macro-level reconciliation occurs between groups at local, regional, or national levels (Androff, 2012d).

Community Practice Steps for Implementing Truth and Reconciliation Commissions

Truth and reconciliation commissions employ common community practice techniques such as framing, strategic planning, outreach, recruitment, fundraising, research and investigation, public hearings, media campaigns, and issuing reports. Through these steps, TRCs advance the human rights-based principles for social work of human dignity, nondiscrimination, participation, transparency, and accountability (Androff, 2016). This section describes the steps that community practitioners can take to implement TRCs to respond to episodes of violence and legacies of systematic injustice.

Framing and Strategy

The first step for community practitioners considering using a TRC model is to determine its framing. Framing in community practice refers to how interventions are connected to a community's shared morals and values (Weil & Gamble, 2005). Truth as a frame invokes values of objectivity and honesty, reconciliation invokes values of dialogue and peace, and the

TRC itself invokes the values of human rights. By addressing issues faced by those who have been historically marginalized, harmed, and traumatized, community practitioners can advance the human rights-based principle of nondiscrimination.

Practitioners should first assess communities' histories of social change to identify opportunities and barriers to social change. Next, they should pick a focal point to organize the TRC around. It should be something that is widely felt, represents an unsettled injustice, can motivate community engagement, and is still relevant to contemporary issues faced by local populations. These questions should be explored in-depth with community stakeholders and partners in order to assess various choices. For example, the Greensboro TRC used the incident of the 1979 shooting massacre to address legacies of racism, labor exploitation, and violence that were pervasive in the U.S. South, as well as traditions of resistance to oppression.

Community practitioners must adopt a strategy of inclusiveness in organizing a TRC. After identifying and engaging stakeholders, the next step is to implement an inclusive selection process for choosing commissioners. TRCs have approximately seven commissioners who act as neutral volunteer supervisors of the process. Therefore, their selection benefits from transparency and wide community participation to ensure high investment. Diverse stakeholders should be invited to nominate and select the commissioners, with the intention that all community residents would feel represented by at least one of the participants of the selection process. For example, a selection committee could include representatives from government offices; universities; and prominent community, labor, religious, and political groups.

Practitioners should endeavor to include participants from multiple sides of issues or conflicts. In the case of conflict, both victims and perpetrators should be invited to participate in the selection process, give testimony, and attend public hearings. Although social injustice and human rights violations are often politically contested, a transparent and objective selection process can imbue the TRC with legitimacy, particularly where victims have been stigmatized. If framed appropriately and sufficiently inclusive, a TRC can facilitate communities' construction of a new meaning of their past and a new vision for their future.

Outreach and Fundraising

Successful community practice depends on the participation of community members. Similarly, TRCs involve significant outreach and recruitment. Although TRCs have varying legal and political authority, most rely on grassroots support for the public credibility to be viewed as legitimate. If a community trusts the TRC process, then the work can have major impact. Door-to-door canvassing and other outreach tactics can raise awareness, recruit volunteers and participants, and gather community members' perceptions and feedback about the TRC. Many TRCs that were started by national governments have been criticized for focusing on political elites rather than victims in the community. TRCs without public credibility can lead to the whitewashing of, rather than meaningful engagement with, painful histories.

Practitioners can seek funding to support TRCs from social justice philanthropic foundations; private individual grassroots donations; and in-kind donations of meeting space, food, and technical assistance from individuals and corporations. Community members should be encouraged to get involved in the TRC process through volunteering or offering testimony of their own. Individuals may experience validation and healing from telling their story, which provides data for the TRC and contributes to its findings. In this way, TRCs can embrace the human rights-based principle of participation.

Truth-Seeking and Transparency

The truth-seeking steps include research and investigation by reviewing government records, media coverage, and evidence from the legal trials that may have taken place. In addition to documentary sources, TRCs conduct semistructured interviews with key informants, including both victims and their families, perpetrators, witnesses, community members, residents, leaders, media personnel, and anyone who can add to the overall story (Androff, 2012b). Hundreds, thousands, or even hundreds of thousands of testimonial statements are collected in these interviews and in public hearings. This massive data collection effort can be used by community practitioners to assess community strengths, assets, needs, and traumas. The goal is to discover as comprehensively as possible not only the details of who did what to whom but also the impact and cost of injustice throughout multiple generations and populations. Publicizing this information advances the human rights-based principle of transparency.

The public hearings are among the major events of the TRC. In addition to eliciting testimony, they are also an opportunity to turn out the community, to use volunteers, and to garner media attention. The hearings, as live events before large audiences, imbue the TRC with dramatic action. TRCs can incorporate symbolic gestures into the public hearings, such as opening with prayer, having a moment of silence in remembrance, and having empty chairs to represent victims. TRCs can hold multiple public hearings, each one organized around different themes or periods. The commissioners preside over the hearings, asking follow-up questions to the participants once they have given prepared testimonies. TRCs can use other events such as a formal empaneling of the commissioners to mark the beginning of the TRCs' work and a closing ceremony in which the findings are released in a final report. Community dialogue meetings can also be held to reflect on the testimony and consider reconciliation strategies.

Truth-seeking contributes to individual and community healing through cathartic relief for participants and public validation (Androff, 2012c). Through their testimony, victims can gain control over their traumatic past and work to repair their self-identity by telling their story. By doing so in front of the supportive audience of a public commission, the victims can receive a measure of acknowledgment and validation. This is significant; official denials of injustice and silencing victims exacerbate their traumas. However, care should be taken with victims who may risk retraumatization in recounting their stories. Victims should be supported by trained clinical interviewers and culturally appropriate counseling; all parties should receive training, support, and long-term follow-up to mitigate the risk of secondary traumatization. TRCs are not therapeutic interventions; although they can facilitate healing, they cannot substitute for more intensive and individual services.

In raising victims' stories, TRCs enable their rehumanization and the human rights-based principle of human dignity. Human rights violations frequently rely on the dehumanization of the victim by the offender, often in the form of stigmatization, discrimination, and scapegoating. Human dignity is uplifted by the way that TRCs seek the truth about traumatic human rights violations; validate the harm caused to victims; and bring victims, perpetrators, and community members together to rebuild relationships.

Accessibility and Resistance

Community practitioners should ensure that their TRC is accessible to as many community members as possible. Like many social change initiatives, TRCs often meet with public apathy and, in some cases, resistance from those invested in maintaining the status quo.

Publicizing its work as widely as possible can combat this apathy and resistance and help the TRC reach a greater audience.

Community practitioners should develop a media campaign for the TRC. They should aim to have dedicated communications staff who can maintain an active website that can distribute a newsletter and archive the testimony. They can work with local, national, and social media. The staff should consider a public access television program. TRCs can use town hall meetings to facilitate community discussions of the final report and its recommendations.

Recommendations and Accountability

A TRC's final step is the release of its final report. The final report should contain sets of recommendations for policy changes and reforms for a broad range of institutional and organizational actors. These usually include implications for acknowledging the injustice; memorializing and disseminating the TRC's findings; and promoting justice, reconciliation, and a human rights culture. Acknowledgment is an important goal for TRCs, especially apologies from responsible parties such as perpetrators and enabling institutions, often governments. Public recognition of the ongoing negative impact of the traumatic incident and related injustice from local and national leaders can facilitate reconciliation and healing. TRCs can promote the human rights-based principle of accountability through supporting prosecution for the perpetrators and reparations for the victims.

TRCs can also offer recommendations for community development and organizing for social justice. For example, volunteers and others engaged by the TRC could be mobilized into community oversight and watchdog groups to monitor the police and media and to engage in continued dialogue, reconciliation, and civic participation efforts. Such engagement can increase victims' collective efficacy

as they become involved in lobbying and advocacy. Upon creating the political will, the goal should be to confront the crimes of the past. The final report is an opportunity to further the TRC's outreach. The report can be formally released at a public ceremony before invited guests. Partnering organizations should be asked to serve as final report receivers who agree to promote readings and discussion groups based on the findings.

The recommendations should call for structural reform in areas beyond the TRC's focal incident. TRCs should use their findings to indicate where investments should be made in health care, social services, a living wage for workers, and sustainable development. The goal of these implications for structural change should be reforming corrupt organizations, agencies, policies, and institutions; promoting open, transparent, and democratic norms; and improving communities' social welfare. In this way, TRCs can rebuild social trust between communities affected by trauma and their governments and institutions.

The TRC recommendations should also promote awareness-raising and educational reforms that adjust public perception and revise the historical narrative in a way that highlights the harm done to the community. TRCs can call for anti-racism trainings, reports on racial disparities, and a community justice center from local and national governments. TRC findings can be incorporated into museums and public monuments. The historical information should be used in school curricula. Public education campaigns based on the TRC can publicize who was responsible for the human rights violations and encourage reflection on everyone, perpetrators and bystanders, who played a role in facilitating social injustice. Through raising awareness about the nature and extent of human right violations, the victims' experiences, and the steps that should be taken to prevent future violations, TRCs promote a human rights culture.

Conclusion

Community practitioners can use TRCs to advance human rights and recovery from trauma. Through a restorative justice approach, TRCs can engage communities, repair broken relationships, foster new relationships, and build capacity for further social justice initiatives. TRCs contribute to participatory democracy, civic engagement, and community practice. And yet TRCs are not the only solution for responding to past injustice. TRCs alone are not sufficient for social transformation. TRCs are best understood as one instrument within a larger toolbox of community practice interventions to remedy and prevent human rights violations. With TRCs, community practitioners can lead the way in confronting the shameful legacies of oppression, imagine a new path forward, and engage people to do the work required to realize a new world.

Helpful Resources

Closer to the Truth Project. *Facilitation and* dialogue guide: https://greensborothemovie.com/project/resources/links_resources/CloserToTheTruthProject_FacilitationAndDialogueGuide_final(low_res).pdf

International Center for Transitional Justice: https://www.ictj.org

Racial Equity Tools. *Racial reconciliation*: https://www.racialequitytools.org/act/strategies/racial-reconciliation-and-racial-healing

References

Androff, D. (2008). Working in the mud: Community reconciliation and restorative justice in Timor-Leste. In K. van Wormer (Ed.), *Restorative justice across the East and West* (pp. 123–144). Casa Verde.

Androff, D. (2010a). "To not hate": Reconciliation among victims of violence and participants of the Greensboro Truth and Reconciliation Commission. *Contemporary Justice Review, 13*(3), 269–285.

Androff, D. (2010b). Truth and reconciliation commissions (TRCs): An international human rights intervention and its connection to social work. *British Journal of Social Work, 40*(6), 1960–1977.

Androff, D. (2012a). Adaptations of truth and reconciliation commissions in the North American context: Local examples of a global restorative justice intervention. *Advances in Social Work, 13*(2), 408–419.

Androff, D. (2012b). Can civil society reclaim the truth? Results from a community-based truth and reconciliation commission. *International Journal of Transitional Justice, 6*(2), 296–317.

Androff, D. (2012c). Narrative healing among victims of violence: The impact of the Greensboro Truth and Reconciliation Commission. *Families in Society, 93*(1), 10–16.

Androff, D. (2012d). Reconciliation in a community based restorative justice intervention: Victim assessments of the Greensboro Truth and Reconciliation Commission. *Journal of Sociology and Social Welfare, 39*(4), 73–96.

Androff, D. (2013). Truth and reconciliation commissions and transitional justice in a restorative justice context. In K. van Wormer & L. Walker (Eds.), *Restorative justice today: Practical applications* (pp. 205–213). Sage.

Androff, D. (2016). *Practicing rights: Human rights-based approaches to social work practice*. Routledge.

Androff, D. (2018). A case study of a grassroots truth and reconciliation commission from a community practice perspective. *Journal of Social Work, 18*(3), 273–287.

Androff, D. (2019). Truth and reconciliation commissions, human rights, and trauma. In L. Butler, F. Critelli, & J. Carello (Eds.), Trauma and *human rights* (pp. 265–286). Palgrave Macmillan.

Beck, E., Kropf, N., & Leonard, P. (2011). *Social work and restorative justice: Skills for dialogue, peacemaking, and reconciliation*. Oxford University Press.

Gibson, J. (2004). *Overcoming apartheid: Can truth reconcile a divided nation?* Russell Sage Foundation.

Hayner, P. (2011). *Unspeakable truths: Transitional justice and the challenge of truth commissions* (2nd ed.). Routledge.

Klinsky, S., & Brankovic, J. (2018). *The global climate regime and transitional justice*. Routledge.

Rothman, J. (2008). Multi modes of community intervention. In J. Rothman, J. Erlich, & J. Tropman (Eds.), *Strategies of community intervention* (pp. 141–170). Bowers.

Weil, M., & Gamble, D. (2005). Evolution, models, and the changing context of community practice. In M. Weil (Ed.), *Handbook of community practice* (pp. 117–149). Sage.

Community Recovery from Mass Shootings

Rob Gordon, Estelli Ramos, and Julie A. Steen

Mass shootings have become an increasing phenomenon in the United States, creating community-level trauma that impacts not only individuals but also the community in which the violence occurs. The community is the environment for personal reactions and supports recovery from tragedy or causes painful isolation and disrupts healing. The community impact must be recognized, understood, and managed as a resource for recovery. Social workers seeking to meet this goal may find guidance in the community recovery model developed by Gordon (2004). In this chapter, we present Gordon's (2004) model and apply it to our experience in Orlando, Florida, following the Pulse Nightclub shooting, providing readers with an example of how the community passes through the recovery phases and how one might support community recovery during each phase.

Pulse Nightclub Shooting

The Pulse Nightclub was more than just a gay club on a Saturday night for Orlando's LGBTQ Latinx community. It was a safe place for Spanish-speaking members of Del Ambiente (Puerto Rican code word meaning "from the LGBTQ environment") to come together and celebrate the lifestyle within their own culture. Central Florida has a large Latin community, but at the time, for those who were gay, the Pulse was the only nightclub to go on a weekend night with one's lover or friends. The salsa, merengue, bachata, and reggaeton music provided the ambience to dance the night away. Same-sex dance couples would fill the dance floor making salsa turns and bachata moves that can only be rivaled in the motherland of Borinquen. African Americans and Black Islanders would also join in as the rhythms of the night reminded them of mother Africa through the calling of the conga.

During the early morning hours of June 12, 2016, a gunman, Omar Mateen, age 29 years, entered the Pulse Night Club and shot 102 people. Fifty-three individuals survived the shooting and 49 victims were killed (Rothaus, 2016). Although proclaimed as a terrorist attack and hate crime on Orlando's LGBTQ population, the shooting was a direct assault on Orlando's Latinx and Puerto Rican LGBTQ community (Kline & Cuevas, 2018).

The experience following the shooting was one marked by opposing forces, both a coming together and a pulling apart. A week after the shooting, the community held a candlelight vigil attended by approximately 50,000 people. The vigil was marked by the chants of "One Orlando," "Orlando United," and "Somos Orlando" ("Orlando Attack," 2016). The city's mayor, Buddy Dyer, addressed the crowd, saying "We can't wait to show the world that joy and love conquers hate. . . . Hate will not define us. Hate will not defeat us. Because we are One Orlando" (Miller, 2016). This coming together was also seen in the faith community, which united and expressed support for Orlando's LGBTQ community (Segal & Regan, 2017). At the same time, an anti-LGBT hate group called Westboro Baptist Church traveled to Orlando to protest at the funerals of people killed in the shooting. The group was met by community members dressed as angels who blocked it from the view of mourners (Stelloh, 2016).

Although the community experienced great moments of solidarity, it also experienced conflict. The national media descended on Orlando and raised overarching voices as to what was significant to the attack. Messages of gun control, hate crimes, anti-Muslim sentiments, and political pundits using the incident to help exemplify their positions were voiced through the national media. Few voices raised issue with the fact that the incident was a direct attack on the Latino-Latina/Puerto Rican LGBTQ community (Lawrence, 2016). Leaders within the community quickly became aware that they were speaking for a population they knew very little about (Sullivan & Hernandez, 2016). Latinx community activists started to raise voices within the community to challenge both political and community leaders to become aware of such behaviors (Sifuentes, 2016). They started to question the lack of Latinx representation the moment health and human service providers continually mispronounced Spanish names and gave little acknowledgment to the fact that the Latin community had

just witnessed its most tragic event in LGBTQ Latinx history (Page, 2016).

Cleavages also developed within social networks. Some wanted to honor their loved ones through political change, whereas others wanted a quiet solemn event to remember and mourn their loved ones. Occasionally, these two desires conflicted with one another, as some believed that political activity was disrespectful and others believed that political inactivity was disrespectful. In addition, some LGBTQ individuals who were not strongly connected with the LGBTQ community felt more isolated following the shooting, particularly when their social networks avoided discussions of the event.

The shooting also impacted the city's human service sector. Prior to the shooting, this sector included multiple agencies that provided counseling, including specialized services for survivors of violent crimes and population-specific providers. LGBTQ individuals had access to a wide range of services through organizations that were created for and led by the LGBTQ community. Likewise, Latinx individuals had access to a similar set of services through organizations created for and led by the Latinx community. The City of Orlando set up an assistance center several days following the shooting that included many of these providers. Agencies and associations that previously had little interaction with one another were suddenly providing services to the same clients. This unexpected shift would have been difficult in any situation, but the change was especially difficult due to the diversity of norms across the organizations. Eventually, the Family Assistance Center closed, and the City of Orlando transitioned to a new system called the Orlando United Assistance Center (Hughes, 2019). Meanwhile, many service providers conducted counseling sessions through home visits because some survivors were wary of leaving their homes (Molina et al., 2019). Although several years have passed since the shooting, the professional and organizational connections built through the response remain, resulting in a stronger system of providers with a higher level of cultural competence.

Gordon's Recovery Model

Gordon's (2004) model of community recovery, which can serve as a framework for understanding Orlando's experience, is based on 30 years of observations of large and small disasters and traumas and of the role the social world plays in them. Through these observations, Gordon found that many communities pass through six phases representing pre-impact community structure, disaster impact, rebounding, cleavage planes, constructive differentiation, and a new complex social structure. Each phase presents unique challenges and opportunities for the social worker seeking to promote and support recovery.

Phase 1: Pre-Impact Community Structure

Communities are a medium for life. Their members are attached to each other in multiple ways and to the community (Miami Theory Collective, 1991). A web of attachments from the individual perspective constitutes a complex, multidimensional social system from the social perspective (Luhmann, 1995). The relationships prescribe consistent patterns of interaction that confer security, predictability, and identity on the members (Dyke & Dyke, 2002). There are many dimensions to this web of relationships, from locality to occupational, political, cultural, and religious affiliations bringing people together in different ways so similarities and differences can coexist.

Preparedness for disaster needs relationships established before the event, not improvised in the aftermath. Key personnel need to be familiar with each other because familiarity overrides formal relationships in emergencies

(Drabek, 1986, 2010). This challenge can be seen in the example of Orlando's pre-impact community structure, which included population-specific service networks that lacked strong connections to other networks and the resources within those networks. The result was a response system that lacked full access to Spanish materials and Spanish-speaking counselors. Thus, before an emergency occurs, social workers should take the following steps:

1. Create communication networks among all agencies likely to be involved.
2. Ensure each service's plans include recognition of the roles of others.
3. Build appropriate liaison relationships between agencies into operating procedures.
4. Establish links with networks representing vulnerable or marginalized groups and ensure their representatives understand the systems and provide local knowledge to authorities.
5. Practice together and use desktop exercises with emergency service exercises.
6. Develop communication mechanisms to provide clear, timely information to the community, especially minority groups.

Phase 2: Disaster Impact

A disaster erupts into the normal pattern of life and cannot be delegated to authorities but must be responded to immediately by community members. Pre-existing roles and relationships are momentarily irrelevant. Surviving the immediate physical situation is the only consideration. In that moment, people describe their lives and relationships receding into the background, leaving the focus on immediate survival. Normal attachments are replaced by action. The person drops out of the web of relationships into an individual survival state. Intense concentration on the situation excludes self-awareness so they are often unable to describe what happened at that moment (Gordon, 2006).

The state of survival can be expressed as momentary *debonding* from the normal fabric of relationships into a new, improvised response to the disaster. It involves changes in instinctive systems in brain and mind, shattering previously held assumptions and expectations when in a moment, a lifetime of consistent experiences is torn apart (Kauffman, 2002). Relationships and connections are ruptured, especially if people prepare to die (Gordon, 2006). Debonding is loss of communicational connection with others, physically separated or lying together hoping not to be shot. There is an aloneness without words. Friends and family also go into high arousal with anxiety when they fear their loved one's death in an intense, instinctive, imaginative state, which disrupts the foundations of their attachments. Debonding involves not only a detachment from the normal social fabric of everyday life but also far-reaching changes to relationships for those who survive.

Recovery begins when those affected come out of high arousal, reenter support systems and begin to incorporate the trauma. As seen in Orlando, some individuals became isolated following the shooting and needed outreach to bring them into community support networks and service systems. Noting this issue, social workers can take the following steps to strengthen networks and systems and connect individuals to these supports:

1. When the scene is safe, ensure personnel trained in psychological first aid and early intervention in trauma support those affected who do not require medical attention.
2. Provide time to settle and receive support and reassurance about services available.
3. Support reunion with family or return home. Family are also traumatized and need psychological first aid and information about how to help their family member.
4. Ensure everyone understands the recovery system and follow up, many who leave the scene need sensitive outreach to recruit them into the recovery system.
5. Ensure continuity with initial contacts after the event for the initial engagement period.
6. Psychological first aid and early intervention reduce arousal by restoring safety and security, reconnecting to personal networks and facilitating decisions to restore control. Formal mental health interventions are reserved for those in mental health crisis.

Phase 3: Rebound

When the threat is no longer the focus of attention, community representatives, emergency services, helpers, family and friends appear. The person focuses their arousal state onto social roles and relationships that carry community values of care, protection and healing. Hunger for attachment to whomever offers care replaces the isolation of survival mode, then they attach to family, friends and community members. Those seeking loved ones are also in high arousal, and when they unite, a different arousal occurs. The whole community is aroused with complex emotions; they want to do something; they gather where they can. This drive for connection can be seen in Orlando when large numbers of people donated blood and attended vigils.

An intense need to attach to each other is expressed as emotive communication which does not conform to previous social codes or roles. Strangers hug, help each other and share the most intense moment in their lives. Communication of similar emotions creates a state of social *fusion*. It is the rebound from debonding, but high arousal is maintained and prevents return to pre-disaster roles and relationships and disrupts the return to the previous social structure. Affected people fuse with highly aroused helpers and family by the most elementary human attachment – identification. People identify with each other because they had the same experience or belong to the same hurt community. Building on the common elements, it assumes everyone has been through the same thing.

The unity of the fused community is inconsistent with the complexity of normal community life. It is formed by shared high arousal and survival instincts and only sustainable in the emergency. The bonds need gradually to be loosened and allow complex structures of normal society to reappear. The change from unity to complexity is a process of *differentiation* of the fusion back into a complex network. The social task for recovery is to conduct the community from fusion into a new, multidimensional normal structure supporting its members.

However, the fusion has contradictory features. A *positive fusion* is marked by sympathy, altruism, volunteering, self-sacrifice and pro-social values motivating heroic assistance. It is not confined by social structure, and empathy and social values unite people with each other around the tragedy, which is owned by the community.

Fusion communication is intense, not organized by the boundaries of normal social structures and rumors and myths hamper recovery activity. When the system stabilizes, it becomes evident that contrary to the initial experience, everyone has not been through the same thing. Those who experienced the same tragedy, wounds, terror, trauma, loss of loved ones come to realize they each have their own unique loss or pain. It becomes apparent that *no one has had the same experience*. This awareness introduces the *negative fusion*. In the fused community there are simplistic communications about who deserves sympathy or assistance. Because everything carries high emotion, these differences cause stress in fused relationships, based on identification around common experiences (Kaniasty & Norris, 1999).

The greatest recovery asset is the community. The positive fusion provides the opportunity to form core recovery systems and discourage the negative fusion to come. To address this situation, social workers should:

1. Define the affected community widely and ensure different impacts are given equal respect and support, to discourage tensions, cleavages and damage to social capital.
2. Preserve norms and social roles within the fused community, supporting affected people to make their own decisions and provide the mutual care as they would normally.
3. Repeat information about the recovery system and services to counter rumors and myths.
4. Provide structured information to media to cover all aspects of recovery.
5. Form community representative and advocacy groups to participate in government and city recovery planning.
6. Ensure mental health services are community based and integrated with local networks.

Phase 4: Cleavage Planes

Awareness of the varied impacts emerges in an atmosphere of tension and readily leads to conflict. Strong emotions create boundaries between groups and bring them into conflict amplified by social media. The emotional atmosphere quickly polarizes for or against issues, with sympathy or blame. The fused community develops rifts or *cleavage planes* that form at any difference in the impact on groups: those who were there and those not, those who escaped and those not, those wounded and those not, those helped and those not, those eligible for financial assistance and those not. It also activates preexisting cleavages around social groups, minorities and disadvantage. Cleavages are mobilized by media reports, rumors, personal emotions, feelings of missing out and all the emotions of trauma and tragedy. The strongest cleavage planes are often between authorities tasked with managing recovery and the community they endeavor to serve.

Cleavages of social systems occur throughout case studies of disaster recovery. A long-standing finding in social theory is that groups lacking boundaries for their members tend to establish them through conflict and negative emotion (Coser, 1956). Cleavage planes serve a function to establish necessary boundaries in a fused social system, but by destructive emotions and conflict that undermine the cooperation and support needed for recovery. Lack of organized communication and problem-solving results in conflict as the issue gathers importance. Its inevitability points to an important function as communities transition from fusion back to a complex social system. It is a mechanism for differentiating the fused unity in the absence of a constructive process of differentiation.

Orlando's experience exemplifies the cleavage planes that can develop between and among segments of the community and human service sector. Social workers must work to identify possible cleavage planes and mitigate conflict through inclusion and representation. The following steps are important components of these efforts:

1. Using community representative and advocacy groups, provide clear, authoritative statements to address myths, rumors, and tensions.
2. Convene carefully planned meetings and gatherings to bring people together across cleavages to promote understanding and work through tensions and conflicts.
3. Highlight commonalities to unite opposing groups across cleavages and mobilize broader identities based on the whole community.
4. Publicize anecdotes and examples that humanize different groups and describe the range and complexity of impacts.

5. Define procedures for flexibility, adjusting regulations to provide equity. A program to address inequalities and needs not fitting formal criteria brings the community together.
6. With community consultation, promote symbols and rituals to give meaning to aspects of the tragedy and promote communal identity.

Phase 5: Constructive Differentiation

Although the fusion blindly differentiates through conflict, a *constructive differentiation* process is also seen in new organization of the community around unique aspects of the event, the people involved, and what is important in recovery. Support, advocacy, and representative groups emerge in the affected community, assisted by professionals, to negotiate with authorities about the many issues inherent in recovery. A sense of ownership of their community develops as community members increasingly take control of the community healing process. The boundary between personal and social identities is often a cleavage plane and that between community and state or municipal authorities when legal, financial, or political issues sideline community sentiments.

Strategies for constructive differentiation need to commence while the fusion is forming and not leave it to be organized by emotion. Temporary systems can provide assistance, inform policymakers and service providers about community priorities, coordinate emerging needs, and claim a voice in decision-making. As affected groups stabilize and more of the community members feel involved, temporary systems evolve toward formal structures and continue representation, facilitate self-help groups and supports, but need official validation. Formation of community-based self-help, information, and advocacy groups is the best predictor of the speed and quality of recovery (Aldrich, 2012, 2019).

Forming a transitional coordination system to implement constructive differentiation and manage cleavages in the fusion needs to be a deliberate strategy. It promotes forward planning to work with officials to determine how the recovery program will bring about recovery. Thus, social workers should engage in the following tasks:

1. Establish liaison between authorities and community leaders and representatives.
2. Form representative groups that validate existing and emerging groups, integrating them into structures with a voice in emergency management and recovery.
3. Ensure important information about services is repeated. Affected people become available to use these services at all stages of recovery.
4. Coordinate and integrate community networks. Trusted local people supported by professionals are preferred sources of assistance.
5. Provide services to assist people to understand their needs and make decisions about how to manage their own recovery. These tasks are unfamiliar for most people.
6. Create disaster-specific media and communication channels to ensure dissemination of authoritative information.

Phase 6: The New Complex Social Structure

The goal of recovery is not to return to the structure before the disaster. The essence of trauma is that it changes things forever. The future based on history is gone; the tragedy has swept away assumptions on which the old life was based; and new values and assumptions must be built up over time to become the foundation for new goals, hopes, and aspirations. This is done gradually, but the vision of this task must be created by all the members of the community. It takes time and requires a system of groups

representing interests and needs that can work through issues around anniversaries, memorials, creating history, and leaving a legacy of learning to ensure the community is also benefited as well as the wounded. Some of this work can be seen in the example of the onePULSE Foundation, which coordinates a memorial, a museum, legacy scholarships, and community events. The new future takes as long as it takes. It is the process of bringing people together to think about their community and life together that forms a new community.

As formal recovery subsides, those most affected continue to be affected for many years before they find a "new normality," but if recovery transitions into community development, a more therapeutic and resilient community forms. The following steps promote this goal:

1. Convene opportunities for representatives of the affected community to participate in considering the future—how the event is remembered or recorded. These processes cannot be rushed; they integrate the community and heal cleavages.
2. Use memorials, anniversaries, and other seasonal events to create new traditions.
3. Support artists to represent the event constructively toward a better community.
4. Support reviews to develop stronger, more resilient systems, including planning or cultural innovations reflecting the values arising out of the tragedy.
5. Consider formalizing community representational and mutual aid groups to broaden their function beyond disaster recovery to general community welfare.
6. Recovery activity provides opportunities for participation in community for many people who have not done so in the past.

Conclusion

Overall, the phenomenon of mass shootings demonstrates the need for social workers to consider the community as an important area of focus and effort. As social workers begin the journey of responding to these events, they should understand these phases and anticipate the challenges that come with each one. Their response will require an emphasis on inclusion, representation, and connection. Throughout the phases, social workers should ask, "Who is missing and how can we invite them in?" This process has the potential to not only address immediate needs but also lay the groundwork for a stronger network of community members and service agencies.

Helpful Resources

Keep the Pulse: The One Orlando Collection: http://oneorlandocollection.com

onePULSE Foundation: https://onepulsefoundation.org

Orlando United Assistance Center: https://orlandounitedassistancecenter.org

U.S. Department of Health and Human Services. *Post-mass shooting programs and resources overview*: https://files.asprtracie.hhs.gov/documents/post-mass-shooting-programs-and-resources-overview.pdf

U.S. Department of Justice, Office for Victims of Crime: https://www.ovc.gov/pubs/mvt-toolkit/lessons-learned.html

References

Aldrich, D. (2012). *Building resilience: Social capital in post-disaster recovery*. University of Chicago Press.

Aldrich, D. (2019). *Black wave: How networks and governance shaped Japan's 3/11 disasters*. University of Chicago Press.

Coser, L. (1956). *The functions of social conflict*. Free Press.

Drabek, T. (1986). *Human systems responses to disaster*. Springer-Verlag.

Drabek, T. (2010). *The human side of disaster*. CRC Press.

Dyke, C., & Dyke, C. (2002). Identities: The dynamical dimensions of diversity. In P. Alperson (Ed.), *Diversity and community: An interdisciplinary reader* (pp. 65–87). Blackwell.

Gordon, R. (2004). Community process and the recovery environment following emergency. *Environmental Health, 4*, 19–34.

Gordon, R. (2006). Acute responses to emergencies: Findings and observations of 20 years in the field. *Australian Journal of Emergency Management, 21*, 17–23.

Hughes, T. S. (2019). 2016 Pulse Night Club shooting in Orlando, FL. In J. Halpern, A. Nitza, & K. Vermeulen (Eds.), *Disaster mental health case studies: Lessons learned from counseling in chaos* (pp. 122–129). Routledge.

Kaniasty, K., & Norris, F. (1999). The experience of disaster: Individuals and communities sharing trauma. In R. Gist & B. Lubin (Eds.), *Response to disaster: Psychosocial community and ecological approaches* (pp. 25–62). Bruner/Mazel.

Kauffman, J. (Ed.). (2002). *Loss of the assumptive world: A theory of traumatic loss*. Brunner-Routledge.

Kline, N., & Cuevas, C. (2018). Resisting identity erasure after Pulse: Intersectional LGBTQ(+) Latinx activism in Orlando Florida. *Chiricu Journal, 2*(2), 68–71.

Lawrence, T. (2016). Life and death on the Pulse dance floor: Translogical politics and erasure of the Latinx in the history of Queer dancing. *Journal of Electronic Dance Music and Culture, 8*(1), 1–25.

Luhmann, N. (1995). *Social systems*. University of California Press.

Miami Theory Collective. (1991). *Community at loose ends*. University of Minnesota Press.

Miller, Z. (2016, June 14). Thousands gather in Orlando for somber vigil. *Time*. https://time.com/4367738/orlando-shooting-vigil

Molina, O., Yegidis, B., & Jacinto, G. (2019). The Pulse Nightclub mass shooting and factors affecting community resilience following the terrorist attack. *Best Practices in Mental Health, 15*(2), 1–15.

Orlando attack: City pauses to remember one week after Pulse nightclub shooting. (2016, June 20). The Guardian. https://www.theguardian.com/us-news/2016/jun/20/orlando-nightclub-shooting-city-pauses-to-remember-one-week-after-pulse-massacre

Page, E. (Director). (2016). *Gaycation: Orlando* [Documentary]. Vice TV.

Rothaus, S. (2016, June 12). Pulse Orlando shooting scene a popular LGBT club where employees, patrons "like family." *The Miami Herald*.

Segal, C., & Regan, M. (2017, June, 11). *After Pulse shootings, Orlando faith and LGBTQ groups opened dialogue*. PBS News Hour. https://www.pbs.org/newshour/nation/pulse-shooting-orlando-faith-lgbtq-groups

Sifuentes, F. (2016, June 21). A preemptive strike: Cannibalizing Queer People of Color in the aftermath of the Orlando massacre. *The Feminist Wire*. https://thefeministwire.com/2016/06/cannibalizing-queer-people-color-aftermath-orlando-massacre/

Stelloh, T. (2016, June 19). *Angels quietly block Westboro protesters at Orlando funeral*. NBC News.

Sullivan, K., & Hernandez, A. (2016, June 12). Orlando's Latino community hit hard by massacre at night club. *The Washington Post*.

PART XI

Working with Vulnerable Populations and Persons at Risk

The Legacy of Racism for Social Work Practice Today and What to Do About It

Margaret E. Pittman, Elizabeth Perryman, Deidre McDaniel, and M. Taqi Tirmazi

The social and political unrest during the past few years not only illustrates the history of racism in the United States but also demonstrates the discrete, distinct, and insidious racism that African Americans, Black, Indigenous, People of Color (BIPOC), and other minority groups have faced since birth. These precarious times, exacerbated by the COVID-19 pandemic and illuminated by the use of contemporary personal technology (Pittman, 2017), highlight the travesty of society that the world did its best to hide: Systematic racism exists in all facets of our lives and overt racism has regained its power behind veils of nationalism and patriotism embedded in slogans such as "All Lives Matter" and "Make America Great Again." For social workers to practice in accordance with the National Association of Social Workers (NASW) Code of Ethics (2017), Miller and Garnan (2017) explain the importance of social workers understanding how racism shapes lives, constrains and constricts opportunity for some, and confers privileges to others based on the social construction of race. Social work practice is not immune to racism, whether systemic or overt. Racism has been and continues to be rooted in discriminatory hiring, research, and racist practices and agendas. Social work continues to promote the *savior complex* for the less fortunate in that the higher education administration continues to be heavily populated with people whose experiences are vastly different from those of the people they are teaching to and about in schools of social work. Social work has contributed to the enormous gains in the advancement of historically oppressed, underserved, and marginalized communities. Despite these contributions, collective professional critical reflection and growth continue to be necessary to advance the profession.

Racism claims many victims. Individuals who are discriminated against and experience inequality are joined by those who carry out the transgressions themselves, as they are accountable for internalizing racist values and belief systems. Furthermore, society suffers due to racism's divisiveness. As social workers, we are not immune to this experience. It is our responsibility to commit to anti-racism work in support of NASW's Code of Ethics (2017) in three main areas: (1) uphold the inherent dignity and worth of BIPOC; (2) challenge the social injustices of race-based oppression; and (3) enhance professional competence around understanding racism. White privilege and BIPOC disadvantages must be explored in order to contribute more wholly and diversely to the knowledge base of the social work profession.

Racism: A Social Work Perspective

Historically, social welfare has served two main purposes: social treatment and social control (Day & Schiele, 2013). During the late 19th century, as the United States transitioned from an agricultural to an urban society, formerly enslaved African Americans began to migrate from the South to the North, placing great demands on resources such as jobs, housing, and social services (Bowles et al., 2016; Day & Schiele, 2013). In response to this demand, social work practices were established on philosophies such as worthy versus unworthy poor, inequality, and racialized dominance, with White social workers functioning in service provision roles such as friendly visitors, caseworkers, and agents of social control (Day & Schiele, 2013; Edmonds-Cady & Wingfield, 2017; Maurer, 2016). White social workers were given charge to develop a system of service provisions to those deemed the worthy poor, and to control those deemed the unworthy poor. Void of input from communities of color, deemed as the unworthy poor, inherent power dynamics of the Eurocentric ideology of deservingness of service provision were solidified and perpetuated discriminatory and exclusionary practices (Maurer, 2016).

In response to the oppressive and repressive policies and practices of White social workers, communities of color relied heavily on their internal networks for support to maintain important cultural values and traditions of spirituality and helping (Bowles et al., 2016; Martin & Martin, 2002; Schiele, 2020). However, as social work became more secularized in the 20th century, social workers of color were forced to assimilate to the norms of the White dominant group and began to adhere to more of the Eurocentric values of social work practice and scholarship in an effort to gain legitimacy within the profession (Martin & Martin, 2002). Unfortunately, this assimilation toward Whiteness further propelled the field of social work into a Eurocentric value-neutral epistemology that favored theories and practices that were "universally applicable" and void of diverse cultural values and viewpoints (Martin & Martin, 2002; Schiele, 2007).

The creation of professional social work organizations such as the Council on Social Work Education (CSWE), which accredits educational institutions, and NASW, which develops ethical practice standards, also addressed the concerns and interests of marginalized groups in an effort to somewhat quell some of the historical damage created by racist service provision and practice. However, these efforts fell and continue to fall short by using models and theories that merely call for more diversity, or multicultural micro-level interventions, as opposed to developing strategies to address racism within social work education, practice, and scholarship (CSWE, 2015; Kiehne, 2016; NASW, 2008; Schiele, 2007; Varghese, 2016). The adoption and promotion of theories and concepts such as cultural competence, diversity trainings, and the equality of oppression are problematic because they are intended to be all-inclusive. However, such theories dilute academia's ability to conduct an extensive analysis on the oppression of individualized groups, and therefore social workers are ill-equipped to understand the intensity and prevalence of oppression and racism (Schiele, 2007). When interventions at the micro level focus on behavior change and subtle changes at the mezzo and macro levels focus on healing during the aftermath, rather than focusing on political action to dismantle and eradicate systemic racism, there is a disservice to the cause (Corley & Young, 2018; Kiehne, 2016; Schyett, 2019). This ambivalence toward racism by default or exclusion further contributes to the permanence of racism in social work. Laissez-faire approaches to racism within social work practice and "invisible enactments of Whiteness" have contributed to the perpetuation of racist structures and oppressive clinical practices (Maurer, 2016; Varghese, 2016).

As it relates to scholarship, Eurocentric epistemology, resistance to overcoming White privilege, and the marginalization of race and racism in social work education are contributors to the lack of literature on racism in social work as publications in the field are dominated by White researchers and academicians (Corley & Young, 2018; Edmonds-Cady & Wingfield, 2017; Kiehne, 2016; Salsberg et al., 2017; Sowell, 1983). As social workers continue to grapple with the definition of racism, White privilege, and power structures, this discourse presents itself in the classroom and the social work literature in a watered-down version of discussions and research as it relates to racism in social work (Edmonds-Cady & Wingfield, 2017; Hoyt, 2012). Furthermore, academia has a history of excluding the works and contributions of BIPOC and historically Black colleges and universities (HBCUs) in the social sciences. For example, HBCUs incorporated standards inclusive of the "biopsychosocial-spiritual perspective" decades prior to the CSWE's 2008 Educational Policy and Accreditation Standards that included spirituality as a standard in social work education for the first time. Furthermore, much of the literature on BIPOC in social work reinforces negative stereotypes of poverty and family dynamics as opposed to a strength-based perspective of resilience and resistance despite the racism (Corley & Young, 2018). In order for social work to progress as a profession, it is imperative that a more deliberate and inclusive mezzo and macro plan of action is developed, incorporating the voices and scholarship of BIPOC, to address the ongoing historically ingrained institution of racism on which the United States was founded.

Racism Today

Racial and ethnic differences within a country have the capacity to lead to unstable governments or governments that use racial tensions to repress groups (Sowell, 1983). The rise of extremist and political groups during the past 30 years has created and continues to create environments of violence and fear mongering in an effort to undermine movements of resistance and give permission for violence and racist attacks without repercussion (Scheyett, 2019; Sowell, 1983). McGranahan (2019) asserts that the normalizing of racist actions and speech in the United States is polarizing the nation. This in turn rationalizes oppression while also vilifying and negating the humanity of the oppressed, which leads to "othering" (Kiehne, 2016; Perez Huber, 2016). Specifically, McGranahan (2019) contends that

> President Donald Trump's actions consolidates several cultural logics in motion in the United States: anti-Muslim sentiment since 9/11; the mainstreaming of nativist, anti-immigrant sentiment in U.S. public discourse; and support for both of these is a joint claim about who is American (White people) and who cannot ever truly be American in quite the same way (most others). (p. 3176)

Perez Huber (2016) explains that racist nativism and all forms of racism are symptoms of a much larger ideological construct that allows covert and overt expressions of oppression as socially acceptable concepts. Whereby, ideologies such as racism and White supremacy are fundamental principles of a preponderance of hate groups in America (Stack, 2019). According to *The New York Times* (Stack, 2019), the number of hate groups in America has increased by 30% since 2014 and continues to rise. Moreover, in 2018, hate groups rose by 7% overall and 50% among White nationalist groups (Stack, 2019). From 2015 to 2017, there has been a 30% increase in the number of hate crimes reported to the Federal Bureau of Investigation (Stack, 2019), and in 2017 there were 5,060 victims of racially motivated hate crimes, of which 48.6% were committed by anti-Black or anti-African American groups (Federal Bureau of Investigation, n.d.). Furthermore, approximately 73% of all extremist-related deaths during the past decade can be linked to extremist groups in America (Anti-Defamation League, 2019).

Because racism is not empyrean in creation but, rather, a creation of humanity sustained by false narratives and oppressive indoctrination of people, the hope in its dismantling is that it was in essence "created" and therefore can be eradicated (Kendi, 2016; Williams, 1983). Forces of resistance have served as mechanisms to provide scholarship and leadership in providing truth to the lies of racial superiority, built upon corruption and systemic prosecution and the devolution of BIPOC. In recent years, activists and BIPOC groups have been working diligently to change the account of what racism is and is not and how to eradicate it. However, post-racial discourse and strategies to delegitimize efforts of resistance, such as Black Lives Matter (BLM) and MeToo movements, are used to distract from issues of systemic racism by elevating notions of "good" and "bad" BIPOC citizenship and protest (Banks, 2018)—for example, promotion of "peaceful protests" of the civil rights movement compared to "race hustling and rioting" of the BLM movement

(Banks, 2018) or the prioritization of sexual violence against White women and devaluing of sexual violence against women who are BIPOC (Foster, 2020; Kiehne, 2016; "Our Pain," 2019). Moreover, the impact of systemic racism traverses every aspect of the lives of BIPOC, creating disparities in education, income, incarceration, and health. BIPOC have lower graduation rates of primary and secondary education (Libassi, 2018), lower incomes (McIntosh et. al., 2020), experience three to six times higher rates of incarceration (Gramlich, 2019), and have higher rates of disparities across all domains of health. Even during the 2020 coronavirus pandemic, BIPOC in the United States were contracting and dying from the virus at disproportionate rates (Mein, 2020).

As it stands, the present that we are now faced with was built on a history of false ideologies that we refused to contest (McGranahan, 2019). Bent-Goodley (2015) asserts that as activists, social workers are called to recognize and incorporate the strengths in the communities in which they serve; be proactive and politically grounded in addressing racial issues, even before debates are sparked; and serve as "thought leaders and change agents who are able to mobilize communities" (p. 102). At what point do we build a future on the truths of resistance and radical thought that provide "transformative possibilities for research and action" (McGranahan, 2019)? Yet, in pursuit of a vision of a more benevolent society, Perez Huber (2016) states that it is White supremacy that plagues our legal, social, and economic structures and we must continue to remain vigilant and proactive in identifying what we know we see.

Racism in Social Work Practice and Education

Race was once thought to be biological in origin and evolved to serve as a social construct to designate social groups (Varghese, 2016). However, race became weaponized as racism by those with white skin privilege, to make harmful generalizations about the worth and treatment of groups of people based on notions of superior and inferior races. Subsequently, racism limits social mobility and opportunity, further alienating and impacting the overall health and mental health of BIPOC while also creating conflict within one's own ethnic identity. Here, we take a closer look at the nature of internalized and interpersonal racism and their effects within social work practice and education.

Internalized racism is the "internalization of racial oppression by the racially subordinated" (Pyke, 2010, p. 1). Racial oppression captures the essence of what it is to be a person of color living within a dominantly White society and the incorporation of negative self-views and prejudices about one's own abilities and intrinsic worth (Jones, 2000; Pheterson, 1986). It is important to note, however, that internalized racism is not meant to examine the contributions or accountability of the oppressed; it serves as a description of the cause, experience, and effects of systemic racism on the psyche and overall experiences of BIPOC individuals. Interpersonal racism, on the other hand, occurs between individuals; is divisive by nature; perpetuates feelings of anger, humiliation, retribution, and domination; and can lead to power-seeking behaviors and violence among Whites (Demosthenous, 2013). It is a discriminatory practice and takes many forms through stigmatization, social exclusion, unfair treatment, and threats or harassment (Brondolo et al., 2005; Contrada et al., 2001). Aversive racism is based on prejudice, appears benign on the surface, and is subtle and indirect. Aversive racists may support racial equality, sympathize with acts of injustice, and believe they are nonprejudiced; however, they still maintain conflicting, nonconscious, and negative feelings and beliefs about BIPOC (Dovidio et al., 2017). A White male who supports the BLM movement and still sees an unarmed Black man in his neighborhood as a threat is an example of an aversive racist.

Although a principled field, social work is not exempt from the blights of internalized and interpersonal racism or the insufficient strategies social workers have developed to combat them. Social work has a long relationship with social reform and advocacy for vulnerable populations—incorporating race, racism, and BIPOC in educational curriculum since the 1960s (Lum, 2000). In line with its long history of advocacy, the current stance on social work education is more inclusive and holistic in its views on the intersectionality of multiple factors impacting oppression than it has ever been, and the CSWE Educational Policy and Accreditation Standards (2015) for engaging diversity and difference in practice at the baccalaureate and master's level reflect that. However, these standards do not explicitly address racism. This lack of recognition extends beyond educational policies into the realm of practice, supervision, and research. Thomas's (2000) concept of "anything but race" contends that Whites view issues BIPOC face as due to other ailments, such as social class, or that BIPOC themselves are to blame for the problems they experience. This notion is furthered by the literature within social work regarding racism and the call to action or lack thereof.

Social workers have been criticized as being standoffish in the fight for racial equality. Clinical social work has been accused of not aligning with the larger mission of addressing needs of marginalized and oppressed groups (Maschi & Killian, 2011) and engaging in desertion of social justice through alignment with psychotherapy, which treats only the individual (Specht & Courtney, 1994). Furthermore, a qualitative study conducted by Varghese in 2016 highlights social work faculty members' insufficient knowledge of race by understanding the construct as an individual ethnic or cultural identity, lacking "conceptual, historical, and sociological knowledge about racism and its links to other forms of oppression" (p. 1) to correctly understand and teach students about racism or white skin privilege.

Another study found that social work educators emphasized the role of self-awareness and cultural awareness through teaching cultural competency from the 1960s ideology of multiculturalism rather than teaching more recent or anti-racism curriculum (Feize et al., 2018). Whereas social work embraces cross-cultural perspectives, most diversity-related education (including multiculturalism) fails to mention oppression, privilege, and racism (Cordero & Rodriguez, 2009; Dessel et al., 2006; Garran & Werkmeister Rozas, 2013; Sisneros et al., 2008). Social work instructors are also culpable because many prefer to discuss safer and more comfortable subjects than racism, discrimination, and oppression (Lum, 2007; McMahon & Allen-Meares, 1992). Moreover, students bring their own biases and experiences with race and racism to their education. Abrams and Moio (2009) explain that students who learn about the dynamic of oppression and privilege for the first time may "deny their own role in occupying privileged or more powerful social identity positions, and it may even take the form of outward anger, resentment, or an overwhelming sense of guilt" (p. 248). Clinical supervision is an arena in which these discussions can occur to prepare these up and coming clinicians; however, the training and standardization for this process are nonexistent. O'Neill and del Mar Fariña (2018) contend that there is a need for "critical dialogue in social work supervision regarding dynamic of sameness, differences, intersectional identities, power and privilege" (p. 298) in order for students to succeed in truly addressing race-based oppression through understanding White privilege and BIPOC disadvantage.

Organizational and Institutional Racism

Racial inequalities are not "naturally occurring" in society; they are a result of patterns of covert and overt action over time that lead to institutional or organizational racism (Carmichael & Hamilton, 1967). Systemic racism includes the intersections of conscious and unconscious forms of racism through prejudice and microaggressions as well as through multiple systems of domination by Whites (Padilla, 2001). Having unfavorable attitudes toward someone based on race alone is prejudiced thinking. Microaggressions transform these negative views into action—they are unintentional and intentional insults in the form of verbal, behavioral, or environmental transgressions (Sue et al., 2000). Examples of these types of injuries include assumptions of criminal status, BIPOC treatment as second-class citizens, assignment of intelligence based on race, denial that a White person does not see race, and assertions that race plays a minor role in life success (Sue et al., 2000). These experiences ultimately lay the foundation for overarching institutional or multidomain racism to take hold.

The United States has a deep and strong relationship with structural inequities, as evidenced by the racial disparities in systems of education, employment, health care, housing, criminal justice, and immigration (Apollon & Sawyer, 2011; Esposito & Murphy, 2010). These patterns are in the form of power differentials, unjust policies and procedures that produce unequal outcomes for BIPOC, and ultimately create and maintain a "racialized social order" (Ballard, 2008, p. 28). Examples of such discrimination include Blacks being more likely to be discriminated against relative to Whites when economic conditions require layoffs (Elvira & Zatzick, 2002) and significant differences in the delivery of health care that have been attributed to racism by health providers, independent of access to health insurance (Smedley et al., 2003).

Combatting Racism

Racism, left unchecked, festers and pervades social systems, relationships, and our own self-view. As social workers, we have a responsibility to understand the conditions of the vulnerable—racial oppression being no exception. It is through learning about the work that is being done to eliminate racism that we can be more effective change agents. It is imperative that anti-racism education is acknowledged, supported, and properly disseminated in order to more effectively combat inequality. Anti-racism is an "educational and organizing framework that seeks to confront, eradicate and/or ameliorate racism and privilege" (Bonnett, 2000, p. 3). This can be achieved through a variety of means, and we make several recommendations for social work students, educators, and practitioners to adopt into practice, teaching, and supervision. However, the greatest recommendation we can make is not to shy away from these difficult and uncomfortable discussions, as that is where genuine growth and change happen.

Social work educators must find ways to engage meaningful lifelong learning occasions that not only include discourse around race and racism but also include anti-racism discussions and activities. For example, if you are a White man who has held a position of power on an HBCU campus for years, what do your anti-racist practices versus "I am not a racist" practices resemble? How are they different? Do you have the uncomfortable talks about what privilege means in the classroom of BIPOC? If on a traditionally White campus, would you even have the conversation about privilege and racism and anti-racist practices? We hope the answer is yes. We also hope that the long-held practice of inviting guest speakers who are experts and entrenched in the community makes a resurgence so we, the educators, can be educated by the people for the people. A successful example of this kind of education by community experts would be the BLM movement. Furthermore, educators can create a classroom environment in which students are encouraged and compelled to hold critical conversations

on race and racism. Educators can facilitate this process by (1) furthering their own competence in the areas of critical race frameworks, racism, and anti-racism work prior to engaging with students on the subject; (2) instituting curriculum that explores the nature of White privilege, oppression, power, and injustice; and (3) having the competence and confidence to challenge White students' denial and resistance to race-based oppression.

Field practicum supervisors, practitioners, and clinicians must maintain a certain number of continuing education units every couple of years in specific categories (e.g., ethics, HIV, and diversity) depending on the state. Racism is a local, regional, and national crisis that deserves to be addressed on its own. We suggest adding a 3-hour category of training focused on racism and racist and anti-racist practices. This type of training requirement would ensure that students are gaining field experience in examining interactions and services through the lens of racist and anti-racist practices. In addition, field practicum supervisors and clinicians can initiate and support conversations with students and clients by explicitly discussing race (sameness and differences) as a recurring agenda topic and highlighting the voices of BIPOC through learning experiences when possible. Students must also critically reflect on themselves and their positions of power relative to clients.

Community and social service organizations would do well to collaborate with social work researchers to conduct community participatory-based research to determine the deleterious practices that have been institutionalized and oppressive to BIPOC for decades. Qualitative data collected would tell the painful, raw, and lived experiences resulting from overt and covert racism and give historically marginalized people an opportunity to formally document their years of racist mistreatment, oppression, and stress. Both qualitative and quantitative data could be used to tell the story and to advocate for policy and social change. Furthermore, community and social service organizations can address racism by building community capacity through skills development and sharing knowledge about the effects of racism in the community, ways to seek help for health and mental health, as well as how to advocate for social justice through community leaders and grassroots initiatives and legislative efforts to address issues such as police and criminal justice reform. These organizations can also partner with agencies and institutions that support BIPOC, take responsibility for responding to racism, and can provide fruitful partnerships (Dreher, 2006). The ultimate goal of social justice is achieved by building "on the culturally responsive framework and critical race frameworks with an emphasis on intersectionality and multilevel analysis" (Varghese, 2016, p. S137). All marginalized and oppressed groups, including BIPOC, must continue to tell, write, and share our own story. We must follow in the steps of the pioneers who told, wrote, and shared their stories. For example, we must continue compilations that are written by, for, and about BIPOC that speak to both the risks encountered and resilience developed living in urban areas (Wells-Wilbon et al., 2017). Moreover, we must create new inclusive spaces and support existing exclusive spaces such as the Association of Black Social Workers that give a platform for racism, racist, and anti-racist dialogue.

References

Abrams, L. S., & Moio, J. A. (2009). Critical race theory and the cultural competence dilemma in social work education. *Journal of Social Work Education, 45*(2), 245–261.

Anti-Defamation League. (2019, January 23). Right-wing extremism linked to every 2018 extremist murder in the U.S., ADL finds. https://www.adl.org/news/press-releases/right-wing-extremism-linked-to-every-2018-extremist-murder-in-the-us-adl-finds

Apollon, D., & Sawyer, M. Q. (2011). *From the interpersonal to the institutional to the intersectional: How millennials understand race and racism in post-racial United States.* Paper presented at the Western Political Science Association 2011 annual meeting. San Antonio, Texas.

Ballard, K. (2008). *Teaching in context: Some implications of a racialised social order.* Paper presented as keynote address at the Te Kotahitanga Voices Conference 2008, Hamilton, New Zealand.

Banks, C. (2018). Disciplining Black activism: Post-racial rhetoric, public memory and decorum in news media framing of the Black Lives Matter movement. *Journal of Media & Cultural Studies, 32*(6), 709–720.

Bent-Goodley, T. (2015). A call for social work activism [Editorial]. *Social Work, 60*(2), 101–103.

Bonnett, A. (2000). *Anti-racism.* Psychology Press.

Bowles, D. D., Hopps, J. G., & Clayton, O. (2016). The impact and influence of HBCUs on the social work profession. *Journal of Social Work Education, 52*(1), 118–132.

Brondolo, E., Thompson, S., Brady, N., Appel, R., Cassells, A., Tobin, J. N., & Sweeney, M. (2005). The relationship of racism to appraisals and coping in a community sample. *Ethnicity and Disease, 15*(4), S5.

Carmichael, S., & Hamilton, C. V. (1967). *Black power: Politics of liberation in America.* Random House.

Contrada, R. J., Ashmore, R. D., Gary, M. L., Coups, E., Egeth, J. D., Sewell, A., Ewell, K., Goyal, T. M., & Chasse, V. (2001). Measures of ethnicity-related stress: Psychometric properties, ethnic group differences, and associations with well-being 1. *Journal of Applied Social Psychology, 31*(9), 1775–1820.

Cordero, A., & Rodriguez, L. N. (2009). Fostering cross-cultural learning and advocacy for social justice through an immersion experience in Puerto Rico. *Journal of Teaching in Social Work, 29*(2), 134–152.

Corley, N. A., & Young, S. M. (2018). Is social work still racist? A content analysis of recent literature. *Social Work, 63*(4), 317–326.

Council on Social Work Education. (2015). *2015 educational policy and accreditation standards.* https://www.cswe.org/getattachment/Accreditation/Accreditation-Process/2015-EPAS/2015EPAS_Web_FINAL.pdf.aspx

Day, P. J., & Schiele, J. H. (2013). *A new history of social welfare* (7th ed.). Pearson.

Demosthenous, H. T. (2013). Social structures and processes linking anger, humiliation power and violence in racist societies. In *Third International Conference on Racisms in the New World Order: Realities of culture, colour and identity* (p. 69). The Cairns Institute, James Cook University.

Dessel, A., Rogge, M. E., & Garlington, S. B. (2006). Using intergroup dialogue to promote social justice and change. *Social Work, 51*(4), 303–315.

Dovidio, J. F., Gaertner, S. L., & Pearson, A. R. (2017). Aversive racism and contemporary bias. In C. G. Sibley & F. K. Barlow (Eds.), *Cambridge handbook of the psychology of prejudice* (pp. 267–294). Cambridge University Press.

Dreher, T. (2006). *Whose responsibility? Community anti-racism strategies in NSW after September, 11, 2001*. UTSePress.

Edmonds-Cady, C., & Wingfield, T. T. (2017). Social workers: Agents of change or agents of oppression? *Social Work Education, 36*(4), 430–442.

Elvira, M. M., & Zatzick, C. D. (2002). Who's displaced first? The role of race in layoff decisions. *Industrial Relations, 41*(2), 329–361.

Esposito, L., & Murphy, J. W. (2010). Post-civil rights racism and the need to challenge racial/ethnic inequality beyond the limits of liberalism. *Theory in Action, 3*(2).

Federal Bureau of Investigation. (n.d.). *2017 hate crime statistics*. Retrieved February 10, 2020, from https://ucr.fbi.gov/hate-crime/2017/topic-pages/victims

Feize, L., & Gonzalez, J. (2018). A model of cultural competency in social work as seen through the lens of self-awareness. Social Work Education, 37(4), 472–489.

Foster, A. (2020, June 25). *Does the #MeToo movement even apply to women of color?* SWAAY. https://swaay.com/women-of-color-metoo-movement

Garran, A. M., & Werkmeister Rozas, L. (2013). Cultural competence revisited. *Journal of Ethnic and Cultural Diversity in Social Work, 22*(2), 97–111.

Gramlich, J. (2019, April 23). *The gap between the number of Blacks and Whites in prison is shrinking*. Pew Research Center. https://www.pewresearch.org/fact-tank/2019/04/30/shrinking-gap-between-number-of-blacks-and-whites-in-prison

Hoyt, C., Jr. (2012). The pedagogy of the meaning of racism: Reconciling a discordant discourse. *Social Work, 57*(3), 225–234.

Jones, D. (2000). Physical attractiveness, race and somatic prejudice in Bahia, Brazil. In Adaptation and *human behavior: An anthropological perspective* (pp. 133–152). Routledge.

Kendi, I. X. (2016). *Stamped from the beginning: The definitive history of racist ideas in America*. Nation Books.

Kiehne, E. (2016). Latino critical perspective in social work. *Social Work, 61*(2), 119–127.

Libassi, C. J. (2018, May 23). *The neglected college race gap: Racial disparities among college completers*. Center for American Progress. https://www.americanprogress.org/issues/education-postsecondary/reports/2018/05/23/451186/neglected-college-race-gap-racial-disparities-among-college-completers

Lum, D. (2000). *Social work practice and people of color: A process-stage approach* (4th ed.). Brooks/Cole.

Lum, D. (2007). *Culturally competent practice: A framework for growth and action* (3rd ed.). Brooks/Cole.

Martin, E., & Martin, J. (2002). *Spirituality and the Black helping tradition in social work*. NASW Press.

Maschi, T., & Killian, M. L. (2011). The evolution of forensic social work in the United States: Implications for 21st century practice. *Journal of Forensic Social Work, 1*(1), 8–36.

Maurer, K. (2016). The invisibility of Whiteness in clinical practice: Case commentary on "becoming visible: The case of Colette." *Clinical Social Work Journal, 44*, 351–356.

McGranahan, C. (2019). A presidential archive of lies: Racism, Twitter, and a history of the present. *International Journal of Communication, 13*, 3164–3182.

McIntosh, K., Moss, E., Nunn, R., & Shambaugh, J. (2020, February, 27). Examining the Black–White wealth gap. The Brookings Institute. https://www.brookings.edu/blog/up-front/2020/02/27/examining-the-black-white-wealth-gap

McMahon, A., & Allen-Meares, P. (1992). Is social work racist? A content analysis of recent literature. *Social Work, 37*(6), 533–539.

Mein, S. (2020). COVID-19 and health disparities: The reality of "the great equalizer." *Journal of General Internal Medicine, 35*(8), 2439–2340.

Miller, J., & Garran, A. M. (2017). *Racism in the United States: Implications for the helping professions*. Springer.

National Association of Social Workers. (2008). *Code of ethics*. NASW Press.

National Association of Social Workers. (2017). Code of ethics. https://www.socialworkers.org/About/Ethics/Code-of-Ethics/Code-of-Ethics-English

O'Neill, P., & del Mar Fariña, M. (2018). Constructing critical conversations in social work supervision: Creating change. *Clinical Social Work Journal, 46*(4), 298–309.

Our pain is never prioritized. #MeToo founder Tarana Burke says we must listen to "untold" stories of minority women. (2019, April 23). *Time Magazine*. https://time.com/5574163/tarana-burke-metoo-time-100-summit

Padilla, L. M. (2001). But you're not a dirty Mexican: Internalized oppression, Latinos & law. *Texas Hispanic Journal of Law & Policy, 7*, 59.

Perez Huber, L. (2016). Make America great again: Donald Trump, racist nativism and the virulent adherence to White supremacy amid US demographic change. *Charleston Law Review, 10*, 215–248.

Pheterson, G. (1986). Alliances between women: Overcoming internalized oppression and internalized domination. *Signs: Journal of Women in Culture and Society, 12*(1), 146–160.

Pittman, M. E. (2017). Student use of technology and academic activities in community colleges. Doctoral dissertation, Morgan State University.

Pyke, K. (2010). What is internalized racial oppression and why don't we study it? Acknowledging racism's hidden injuries. *Sociological Perspectives, 53*(4), 551–572.

Salsberg, E., Quigley, L., Mehfoud, N., Acquaviva, K., & Sliwa, S. (2017). *Profile of the social work workforce.* Council on Social Work Education & National Workforce Initiative Steering Committee. https://www.cswe.org/Centers-Initiatives/Initiatives/National-Workforce-Initiative/SW-Workforce-Book-FINAL-11-08-2017.aspx

Scheyett, A. (2019). Social work in fractured times: The both/and of weaving and resisting. *Social Work, 64*(3), 185–187.

Schiele, J. H. (2007). Implications of the equality-of-oppressions paradigm for curriculum content on people of color. *Journal of Social Work Education, 43*(1), 83–100.

Schiele, J. H. (2020). *Social welfare policy: Regulation and resistance among people of color* (2nd Ed.). Cognella.

Sisneros, J., Stakeman, C., Joyner, M. C., & Schmitz, C. L. (2008). *Critical multicultural social work.* Oxford University Press.

Smedley, B. D., Stith, A. Y., & Nelson, A. R. (2003). Racial and ethnic disparities in diagnosis and treatment: A review of the evidence and a consideration of causes. In B. D. Smedley, A. Y. Stith, & A. R. Nelson (Eds.), *Unequal treatment: Confronting racial and ethnic disparities in health care* (1st ed., pp. 125–159). National Academies Press.

Sowell, T. (1983). *The economics and politics of race: An international perspective.* Quill.

Specht, H., & Courtney, M. E. (1994). *Unfaithful angels: How social work has abandoned its mission.* Free Press.

Stack, L. (2019, February 20). Over 1,000 hate groups are now active in United States, civil rights group says. *The New York Times.* https://www.nytimes.com/2019/02/20/us/hate-groups-rise.html

Sue, D. W., Capodilupo, C. M., Torino, G. C., Bucceri, J. M., Holder, A., Nadal, K. L., & Thomas, M. (2000). Anything but race: The social science retreat from racism. *African American Research Perspectives, 6*(1), 79–96.

Varghese, R. (2016). Teaching to transform? Addressing race and racism in the teaching of clinical social work practice. *Journal of Social Work Education, 52*(Suppl. 1), S134–S147.

Wells-Wilbon, R., McPhatter, A. R., & Vakalahi, H. F. (Eds.). (2015). *Social work practice with African Americans in urban environments.* Springer.

Williams, C. (1983). *The destruction of Black civilization: Great issues of a race from 4500 B.C. to 2000 A.D.* Third World Press.

Anti-Oppressive Social Work Practice

Altaf Husain and Katie Ishizuka

The Council on Social Work Education's (CSWE, 2015) Education Policy and Accreditation Standards (EPAS) includes "advance human rights and social, economic and environmental justice" (p. 7) as one of the nine competencies. It is therefore expected that

> social workers understand that every person regardless of position in society has fundamental human rights such as freedom, safety, privacy, an adequate standard of living, health care, and education. Social workers understand the global interconnections of oppression and human rights violations, and are knowledgeable about theories of human need and social justice and strategies to promote social and economic justice and human rights. Social workers understand strategies designed to eliminate oppressive structural barriers to ensure that social goods, rights, and responsibilities are distributed equitably and that civil, political, environmental, economic, social, and cultural human rights are protected. (p. 7)

Social workers have a professional mandate to identify and challenge the ways in which oppression is upheld, both within and outside the field, across individual, organizational, and systemic domains (Maidment & Cooper, 2002). Mitigating the ways in which social, economic, and political systems, and the profession itself, perpetuate oppression and applying models of empowerment and liberation to institutions, relationships, and values are known as anti-oppressive practice (AOP; Brown & Mistry, 2005).

AOP in social work is not an established, monolithic framework but, rather, an evolving variety of different practice approaches and theories oriented toward a social justice perspective. This chapter provides a snapshot of AOP along with practical tools, guidance, and considerations for its use across a diverse range of practice settings. The chapter is informed by a review of the literature; the authors' experiences across the spectrum of direct social work practice, macro social work practice, and social work academia; and our insights as members of oppressed groups.

The chapter is composed of five sections. The first section provides a brief history of AOP in social work to situate its current approaches within the field. The next two sections present critical theories and key concepts for AOP. The fourth section discusses possible barriers toward actualizing anti-oppressive work in practice, and the final section concludes with considerations for advancing AOP within the profession.

History of Anti-Oppressive Practice in Social Work

Since its origins in the late 19th century, social work has wrestled with its contradictory roles in maintaining the status quo as a function of the state and challenging oppression (Abramovitz, 1999). Both internal and external political struggles have shaped the profession's relationship to social change (Abramovitz, 1999). Although the profession has been concerned with oppression since its inception, its contemporary role in social reform was ignited in the mid-1960s by the civil rights movement (CSWE, 2009). Prior to the mid-1960s, social work practice and education were characterized by ethnocentrism and assimilation, in which not only were the norms and values of dominant culture applied universally to all client groups but also there was an expectation that they were to be adopted wholesale by the client groups in place of their own traditions and culture (Schiele, 2007).

Between the mid-1960s and the mid-1970s, social workers of color and White advocates challenged the Eurocentric bias in social work teaching and practice and the deficit-oriented view of Black, Indigenous, People of Color (BIPOC) (Abrams & Moio, 2009). Activism prompted increased attention to the history of racism in social work and the CSWE to mandate content on race and racism in social work education (Abrams & Moio, 2009).

Starting in the mid-1970s, activism and analysis of additional oppressed groups

(CSWE, 2009) created a more intersectional approach that was inclusive of, and made connections with, other forms of oppression (Crenshaw, 1989; Keating, 2000). Since then, social work education has broadened its conceptualization and coverage of oppression content. Between 1975 and 1984, CSWE established a commission on women and mandated content on gender issues, including feminist practice theories and methods (Schiele, 2007). Between 1985 and 1995, CSWE championed sexual orientation issues and established a Commission on Gay, Lesbian, Bisexual and Transgender Issues (Schiele, 2007). Since 1995, CSWE has continued to broaden its content on diversity and oppression issues. In 2015, CSWE expanded EPAS to include 16 dimensions of diversity that are understood as the intersectionality of multiple factors, including, but not limited to, age, class, color, culture, disability and ability, ethnicity, gender, gender identity and expression, immigration status, marital status, political ideology, race, religion/spirituality, sex, sexual orientation, and tribal sovereign status.

In addition to changes in the way that oppression is conceptualized, the profession has also made changes to the way it engages with issues of oppression and members of oppressed groups. In the 1960s, the cultural competence model was employed, which focused on changing the beliefs and behaviors of individual practitioners to promote cross-cultural sensitivity and understanding (Abrams & Moio, 2009). Critiques of this framework are that it only focuses change efforts at the level of the individual and not the institutional and systemic levels; it assumes that increased cultural knowledge and skills will enhance practice, without questioning whether the practices and interventions are appropriate; and it has limited empirical evidence (Abrams & Moio, 2009). In contrast, the AOP model targets change efforts at the individual, institutional, and systemic levels (Abrams & Moio, 2009).

Critical Theories for Anti-Oppressive Practice

Anti-oppressive practice encompasses a range of practices and theories, as opposed to one practice approach. An anti-oppressive framework may include, but is not limited to, the critical theories discussed next.

Anti-Racist and Anti-Oppressive Theories

An anti-racist approach recognizes the structural nature of racism (Maiter, 2009). It questions and critiques White supremacy; the marginalization and DE legitimization of the voices, experiences, and knowledge of BIPOC; and that BIPOC can only access power as White society dictates (Maiter, 2009). An anti-racist framework challenges individuals in power, including social workers, for their role in perpetuating racism, and it calls for change at all levels of social work practice (Abrams & Gibson, 2007). Intersectionality is central to anti-oppressive theories. According to Kimberley Crenshaw (as cited in Guardia, 2018),

> Intersectionality is simply a prism to see the interactive effects of various forms of discrimination and disempowerment. It looks at the way that racism, many times, interacts with patriarchy, heterosexism, classism, xenophobia—seeing that the overlapping vulnerabilities created by these systems actually create specific kinds of challenges. (para. 6)

The theory posits that an understanding of a client's experience based on their social location within these systems will capture the complexity, individuality, and nuances of their actions, choices, and outcomes (Murphy et al., 2009).

Critical Theory

Critical theory is concerned with practices that will eliminate domination, exploitation, and oppression (Fook, 2002). It is interested in understanding how social constructions and power structures are used to dominate and in leveraging this knowledge to disrupt dominant structures (Fook, 2002). Practitioners understand social problems as the result of these societal structures and cultural norms rather than individual factors or deficits.

Critical Race Theory

Critical race theory is interested in the relationship between race, law, policy, social context, and power (Bell, 1992/2018; Gordon, 1999; Yosso, 2005). It identifies racism as permanent and pervasive (Bell, 1992/2018). Practitioners engage in active opposition to structural and institutional oppression (Abrams & Moio, 2009).

Empowerment Theory

Empowerment theory explores the structural context of social problems and focuses on individual and community strengths, resiliencies, and resources (Perkins & Zimmerman, 1995). Practitioners are engaged as collaborators in increasing individual and community power and facilitate client involvement in all decisions impacting their lives (Morgaine & Capous-Desyllas, 2014). An empowerment approach fosters critical consciousness in clients through engagement and education on issues of structural oppression and forms of resistance (Morgaine & Capous-Desyllas, 2014).

Feminist Theory

The feminist approach focuses on understanding and addressing the oppression of women, including the ways women experience political, social, and economic marginalization (Morgaine & Capous-Desyllas, 2014). Practice models are grounded in a feminist analysis of social problems and prioritize social change and social justice for women (Dominelli & McLeod, 1989).

Radical and Structural Theories

The radical approach to social work seeks structural and revolutionary transformation, as opposed to social workers functioning as "caretakers" while working with, rather than against, oppressive systems (Dreikosen, 2009). This approach is informed by a class analysis and critique of capitalism. The structural approach situates social problems within a specific societal context and does not attribute them to individual failures (Mullaly, 1997). It promotes empowerment, consciousness-raising, an understanding of issues from a global perspective, and an awareness of capitalism's impact on shaping conditions and relationships (Mullaly, 1997).

Key Concepts of Anti-Oppressive Practice

Engage in Critical Reflection

The personal, social, and professional dimensions of a practitioner are intertwined and influence the social worker's own experience as well as the client's experience of the social worker (Mandell, 2008). Social workers need to be aware of the ways in which their own positionality, experiences, biases, self-concept, cultural background, and values shape their perception, judgment, emotions, and behavior and how that impacts every client interaction (Mandell, 2008). Practitioners also need to understand professional power in practice and the power imbalance between social worker and client (Mandell, 2008). It is important to be cognizant of which actions are for the benefit of oneself and one's position, versus the benefit of the client, and the ways in which practitioners can use their power to harm and further disenfranchise clients. In addition, social workers should be aware of the ways in which they themselves are oppressed or experience oppression and how that impacts their work. The reflective process may entail asking questions

of oneself and then analyzing those answers critically (Mandell, 2008). Examples of questions that can be asked include the following: In what ways did I stereotype and make conscious or unconscious assumptions about this client and how did that impact my interactions and treatment of the client? What part about my interactions with the client met my own needs versus met the client needs? Did I impose my notion of what was "right" and what the client "should" do, or did I value and foster the client's self-determination? Did I maintain, exacerbate, or improve the situation the client is in? How would I do it differently next time? Are there systemic changes or changes in agency policy that could be made to better meet the needs of this client or group?

Assess Client Experiences of Oppression: Apply Knowledge of How Structural Oppression Shapes Individual Outcomes

Clients cannot be separated from their social context and the ways in which their social identities have shaped their experiences with oppression. Baines (1997) describes the importance of understanding client challenges as the result of structural and systemic forces and seeking "solutions that [go] beyond those just for individual cases" (p. 314). Social work is a profession and a social institution with the capacity to either perpetuate or transform oppressive social relations (Campbell, 2003). Social workers should be aware of the multitude of forms and effects of oppression (Mulally, 2002) and examine their own role in maintaining privilege and oppression in their own environments and the environments of the people they serve (Nicotera & Kang, 2009). Although an analysis of oppression is necessary, it is insufficient to enact social change. Knowledge of the structural dynamics of oppression, as well as one's own role in maintaining it, should then be translated into social change and social justice initiatives (van Wormer & Snyder, 2007).

Social workers should be equipped to apply anti-oppressive frameworks to all aspects of practice at the micro, mezzo, and macro level.

Work in Partnership with Clients

A key step in avoiding practice-based oppression is to treat clients as experts. Clients should be engaged in all decisions that affect themselves, their families, and their communities. Rather than social workers imposing their perspectives of what a client needs, client input should be meaningfully involved in all areas of practice, including assessment, treatment planning, and treatment evaluation (A. Barnes, personal communication, July 19, 2013). Social workers should avoid assuming paternalistic "knowing" positions (Butler et al., 2003) or the role of "expert," and they should value the insights and agency that clients have into their own lives (van Wormer & Snyder, 2007).

Empower Clients

Social workers should identify ways in which power can be operationalized and channeled constructively (Bundy-Fazioli et al., 2013) to empower the client and transform practices and institutions rather than destructively to sustain oppressive practices (Keating, 2000). Practitioners need to know where their power lies, within and outside of their organizations, and how to channel it to facilitate client empowerment (Dustin & Montgomery, 2010). Client power can be developed by highlighting client strengths; expanding client networks and linkages to resources; and asserting the ways in which the client has agency, choice, and privileges, both within and outside the professional relationship (Rankin, 2006).

Maintain Minimal Intervention

Social workers should reflect critically on the impact that actions, assumptions, and values have on the client and how they can serve to either reproduce or disrupt structures of oppression (Campbell, 2003). Interventions should be as least disruptive to clients as possible. Each client and situation is unique, so meeting client needs may require creativity and flexibility (Dustin & Montgomery, 2010). There is no "universal formula" or "one-size-fits-all" approach. It is important to be able to apply and adapt social work theories and best practices to best suit the needs of each individual situation, context, and client. It is critical to question traditional assumptions, practices, and policies that are not working (Mulally, 2002). Employing active listening in all clinical interactions promotes understanding of the client's unique perspective, context, background, cultural values, and current situation (Graham et al., 2009). It also provides insight that can be used to tailor interventions to individual values, comfort levels, and needs.

Barriers to Successful Anti-Oppressive Practice

Practitioners' Awareness of Power, Privilege, and Positionality and Impacts on Practice

Many people are unaware of forms of oppression that are not overt and/or resist acknowledgment of the positions of privilege they occupy. Nearly 70% of the social workers in the United States are White (Salsberg et al., 2017), and multiple research studies have shown that White social workers who maintain racist attitudes and beliefs may not perceive themselves as racist (Schiele, 2007). A 2001 study found that highly educated White women who considered themselves opponents of racism enacted racism through stereotypical images and paternalistic assumptions (Trepagnier, 2001). Trepagnier (2001) suggests that people should view themselves on a continuum from "less racist" to "more racist," and never "not racist," because racism is so habitual, systemic, and ingrained. A separate study of Master of Social Work students by Garcia & Van Soest (1997) found that the majority (71%) of White students identified their own privilege as being a barrier to acknowledging and learning about oppression. Once one does become aware of their own relationship with racism and other forms of oppression, it is a long and dedicated process to unlearn years of conditioning and socialization (Abrams & Gibson, 2007).

Insufficient Time and Resources

The funding constraints of social services mean that agencies are often understaffed and practitioners are often overworked and underpaid (Mulally, 2002). It leaves little opportunity for social workers to connect the day-to-day focus on individual change with larger social and political change efforts. The time and resource constraints can also impede the ability of practitioners to optimize the well-being of clients, critically reflect on their practice, and foster their own well-being. Research has found that when social workers become burnt out or emotionally exhausted, they depersonalize and distance themselves from their clients, which clients in turn experience as dehumanizing (Mandell, 2008). Practitioners need to take responsibility for, and be supported in, their emotional and professional capacity and well-being.

Not Establishing Coalitions of Like-Minded Colleagues

Social work literature and practitioners suggest that the most crucial aspect of carrying out AOP and protecting oneself from the risks inherent in resisting oppression is to establish and maintain coalitions with like-minded colleagues (Mulally, 2002). Having access to such support can alleviate the tremendous mental and emotional burden associated with reflection and introspection while also providing a forum to discuss and process possible challenges in carrying out AOP.

Contradiction Between Anti-Oppressive Practice and Sustaining the Field of Social Work

Social work is often funded by, and a function of, the government. Many agencies are also reliant upon funding from corporate-based foundations. Being involved in social and political change initiatives can be opposed to government and corporate interests, which poses a challenge for the profession.

Effective Analysis Does Not Always Translate into Effective Action

Although there has been significant research and intellectualizing over oppression and anti-oppression, it is questionable how much this information has been applied within the field. The language and rhetoric appear to have changed more than anything else (Butler et al., 2003). Within social work education, for example, despite CSWE's mandate to include content on oppression, challenges arise in transmitting content into meaningful learning (Phan et al., 2009) and then translating learning into social action (Hancock et al., 2012).

Division Among Social Work Professionals Due to a History of Exclusion of the Voices and Needs of Marginalized Social Workers

The National Association of Black Social Workers (NABSW) was created as a separate entity from the National Association of Social Workers during the civil rights movement in the 1960s (NABSW, 2013). NABSW became dedicated to issues impacting the Black community, including White supremacy, racism, and Eurocentric-focused human services and social welfare systems (NABSW, 2013). NABSW was compelled to create its own space to become a leading advocacy group for the Black community because it did not have that space within NASW. More than half a century later, NABSW remains a separate entity. A critical, ongoing focus on AOP will be imperative to its sustainability and effectiveness within the field. Some of the future directions for AOP within the profession might include transforming the Eurocentric framework of social work pedagogy; "centering" diverse ways of knowing; creating space for marginalized voices; evaluating the implementation and effectiveness of AOP; and defining quality assurance standards, clear outcome goals, and measurement tools.

References

Abramovitz, M. (1999). Social work and social reform: An arena of struggle. *Social Work, 44*(6), 512–527.

Abrams, L. S., & Gibson, P. (2007). Reframing multicultural education: Teaching White privilege in the social work curriculum. *Journal of Social Work Education, 43*(1), 147–160.

Abrams, L. S., & Moio, J. (2009). Critical race theory and the cultural competence dilemma in social work education. *Journal of Social Work Education, 45*(2), 245–261.

Baines, D. (1997). Feminist social work in the inner city: The challenges of race, class, and gender. *Affilia, 12*(3), 297–317.

Bell, D. (2018). *Faces at the bottom of the well: The permanence of racism.* Basic Books. (Original work published 1992)

Brown, A., & Mistry, T. (2005). Group work with "mixed membership" groups: Issues of race and gender. *Social Work with Groups, 28*(3/4), 133–148.

Bundy-Fazioli, K., Quijano, L. M., & Bubar, R. (2013). Graduate students' perceptions of professional power in social work practice. *Journal of Social Work Education, 49*, 108–121.

Butler, A., Elliott, T., & Stopard, N. (2003). Living up to the standards we set: A critical account of the development of anti-racist standards. *Social Work Education, 22*(3), 271–282.

Campbell, C. (2003). Anti-oppressive theory and practice as the organizing theme for social work education: The case in favour. *Canadian Social Work Review/Revue canadienne de service social, 20*(1), 121–125.

Council on Social Work Education. (2009). *Advanced social work practice in clinical social work.* https://www.cswe.org/getattachment/Accreditation/Other/EPAS-Implementation/ClinicalSocialWork_FINAL.pdf.aspx

Council on Social Work Education. (2015). *2015 educational policy and accreditation standards.* https://www.cswe.org/getattachment/Accreditation/Accreditation-Process/2015-EPAS/2015EPAS_Web_FINAL.pdf.aspx

Crenshaw, K. (1989). Demarginalizing the intersection of race and sex: A Black feminist critique of antidiscrimination doctrine, feminist theory and antiracist politics. *University of Chicago Legal Forum, 1989,* Article 8.

Dominelli, L., & McLeod, E. (1989). *Feminist social work.* Macmillan.

Dreikosen, D. (2009). Radical social work: A call to link arms. *Journal of Progressive Human Services, 20*(2), 107–109.

Dustin, D., & Montgomery, M. R. (2010). The use of social theory in reflecting on anti-oppressive practice with final year BSc social work students. *Social Work Education, 29*(4), 386–401.

Fook, J. (2002). *Social work: Critical theory and practice.* Sage.

Garcia, B., & Van Soest, D. (1997). Changing perceptions of diversity and oppression: MSW students discuss the effects of a required course. Journal of Social Work Education, 33, 119–130.

Gordon, L. R. (1999). A short history of the "critical" in critical race theory. *American Philosophy Association Newsletter, 98*(2), 1.

Graham, J. R., Bradshaw, C., & Trew, J. L. (2009). Adapting social work in working with Muslim clients. *Social Work Education, 28*(5), 544–561.

Guobadia, O. (2018). *Kimberlé Crenshaw and Lady Phyll talk intersectionality, solidarity, and self-care.* https://www.them.us/story/kimberle-crenshaw-lady-phyll-intersectionality

Hancock, T. U., Kledaras, C. G., & Waites, C. (2012). Facing structural inequality: Students' orientation to oppression and practice with oppressed groups. *Journal of Social Work Education, 48*(1), 5–25.

Keating, F. (2000). Anti-racist perspectives: What are the gains for social work? *Social Work Education, 19*(1), 77–87.

Maidment, J., & Cooper, L. (2002). Acknowledgement of client diversity and oppression in social work student supervision. *Social Work Education, 21*(4), 399–407.

Maiter, S. (2009). Using an anti-racist framework for assessment and intervention in clinical practice with families from diverse ethno-racial backgrounds. *Clinical Social Work Journal, 37,* 267–276.

Mandell, D. (2008). Power, care and vulnerability: Considering use of self in child welfare work. *Journal of Social Work Practice, 22*(2), 235–248.

Morgaine, K., & Capous-Desyllas, M. (2014). *Anti-oppressive social work practice.* Sage.

Mullaly, B. (1997). *Structural social work: Ideology, theory and practices.* Oxford University Press.

Mullaly, B. (2002). *Challenging oppression: A critical social work approach.* New York, NY: Oxford University Press.

Murphy, Y., Hunt, V., Zajicek, A. M., Norris, A. N., & Hamilton, L. (2009). *Incorporating intersectionality in social work practice, research, policy and education.* Port City Press.

National Association of Black Social Workers. (2013). History. https://www.nabsw.org/page/History

Nicotera, N., & Kang, H. (2009). Beyond diversity courses: Strategies for integrating critical consciousness across social work curriculum. *Journal of Teaching in Social Work, 29,* 188–203.

Perkins, D. D., & Zimmerman, M. A. (1995). Empowerment theory, research, and application. *American Journal of Community Psychology, 23*(5), 569–579.

Phan, P., Vugia, H., Wright, P., Woods, D. R., Chu, M., & Jones, T. (2009). A social work program's experience in teaching about race in the curriculum. *Journal of Social Work Education, 45*(2), 325–333.

Rankin, P. (2006). Exploring and describing the strength/empowerment perspective in social work. *IUC Journal of Social Work Theory and Practice,* 14.

Salsberg, E., Quigley, L., Mehfoud, N., Acquaviva, K. D., Wyche, K., & Silwa, S. (2017). *Profile of the social work workforce.* https://www.cswe.org/Centers-Initiatives/Initiatives/National-Workforce-Initiative/SW-Workforce-Book-FINAL-11-08-2017.aspx

Schiele, J. H. (2007). Implications of the equality-of-oppressions paradigm for curriculum content on people of color. *Journal of Social Work Education, 43*(1), 83–100.

Trepagnier, B. (2001). Deconstructing categories: The exposure of silent racism. *Symbolic Interaction, 24*(2), 141–163.

Van Wormer, K., & Snyder, C. (2007). Infusing content on oppression into the social work curriculum. *Journal of Human Behavior in the Social Environment, 16*(4), 19–35.

Yosso, T. J. (2005). Whose culture has capital? A critical race theory discussion of community cultural wealth. *Race Ethnicity and Education, 8*(1), 69–91.

Understanding the Risks and Vulnerabilities African American Children Face Due to Racism

The Critical Role of Race-Relevant Responses

Eric Kyere

The United States has a long and turbulent history of racism, which has produced an uneven and difficult access to resources that optimize and actualize potential for people of color. Among those groups are African Americans, who have endured centuries of struggles against cascading racial subordinating forces, including slavery, domestic terrorism, Jim Crow segregation, racialized mass incarceration, and conscious social and economic oppression that have threatened the livelihood of African American communities and families. Although progress has been made, and African Americans have made significant strides in several domains of life, including education, economics, housing, and health, very visible and vexing struggles continue, in particular as evidenced by the current events of police brutality and residential and community segregation where African Americans are positioned in most underresourced neighborhoods. The disproportionate impacts of COVID-19 on African Americans have highlighted the costs associated with inequalities that are rooted in a historical legacy of oppression and that continue through modernized mechanisms and self-perpetuating forces.

Because of these inequities (Darling-Hammond, 2007; Orfield et al., 2012), many Black lives may be classified as schizoid, frustrated, and restricted (Wilson, 1978), making Black children one of the most vulnerable populations in American society (Adams-Bass et al., 2014; McAdoo, 2002). As a racial minority, African American children experience unique ecological circumstances—racism, stereotypes, discrimination, and stigmatization (García Coll et al., 1996; Spencer, 1999). Racism—the beliefs, attitudes, practices, institutional arrangements, and acts that denigrate individuals or groups on the basis of phenotypic characteristics or racial and ethnic group affiliation (Clark et al., 1999)—is a significant stressor with pernicious effects on the development of African American children and youth.

Racial discrimination—systematic treatment of the minoritized group that results in differential and negative effects on racial minorities—is one cardinal mechanism by which racism as an ideology manifests to shape the psychological and material conditions, and it is normative and pervasive for minority youth such as African Americans across various developmental trajectories (Umaña-Taylor, 2016; Witherspoon et al., 2016). These discrimination experiences have been associated with poorer mental health outcomes; behavioral problems such as substance use, physical aggression, and risky sexual behaviors; and poor academic adjustments (Seaton & Douglass, 2014; Umaña-Taylor, 2016).

Racism is toxic and can be very traumatic for African American children and youth through several pathways (Williams & Mohammed, 2013). For example, racism works through development planning, housing, and residential segregation to concentrate African American families to materially deprived and highly disadvantaged neighborhoods (Erickson, 2016; Shapiro, 2017; Sharkey & Elwert, 2011; Wilson, 1978). Living in such material- and resource-deprived neighborhoods, African American families and their children are exposed to several health-related risks, including lack of or limited access to healthy food and water, exposure to environmental hazards, neighborhood violence and crimes, and underfunded public schools (Erickson, 2016; Williams et al., 2019). Although these experiences affect African American children and youth directly, they also affect them indirectly through their parents, the neighborhoods, and the schools they attend. Together, they suggest that racism has compounding and cascading effects on African American children and youth, which in turn determine their future opportunities relative to long-term educational attainment,

employment potential, incarceration, health status and access to health care services, and family formation. Thus, racism works to confer intergenerational disadvantages on African Americans, making Black children one of the most vulnerable populations in the United States.

Racism and Wealth in African American Families and Communities

One mechanism by which African American children are structured to be most disadvantaged and vulnerable group is through the racial wealth gap. Wealth provides a realistic estimate of an individual's, a family's, or a community's current and future well-being. It provides ample opportunities for families to engage in a variety of activities without the stress of financial insecurity. Wealth enables families to seamlessly relocate to a new residential location, adapt well in times of emergencies, and transition well between jobs. In addition, wealth allows parents to pay for children's education (Hanks et al., 2018). In the United States, there is a large racial wealth gap, with Blacks or African Americans disproportionately having far fewer opportunities for generating and sustaining wealth, even after accounting for education and the hard work ethic (Hanks et al., 2018). African Americans are positioned in a vicious cycle due to the long history of racism and discriminatory practices in several domains of society (e.g., employment, housing, and mortgage and banking loans) that restrict their access to tax-advantaged savings and benefits that support wealth accumulation and its maintenance (Hanks et al., 2018; Shapiro, 2017). In 2016, the median and mean wealth of White families was $171,000 and $933,700, respectively. In comparison, Black families' median and mean wealth was $17,600 and $138,200, respectively

(Dettling et al., 2017). This racial wealth disparity that is disproportionately felt by African Americans can be traced to both explicit and implicit racist policies and practices: (1) from slavery to Jim Crow, (2) from redlining to segregations in residential and schooling, and (3) from mass incarceration to environmental and employment racism. These practices have consistently restricted African Americans efforts to access opportunities that make the American dream a reality (Alexander, 2012; Battalora, 2013; Hanks et al., 2018; Wilder, 2013). The United States was built on a system that concentrates power and wealth on Whites and oppression and suppression on Blacks.

Although some strides have been made, and African Americans have seen improvement in several domains of life in American society, racism continues to affect these families' ability to generate and maintain wealth through limited opportunity for education and employment, racial discrimination in hiring decisions, and racial discrimination with regard to health (Pattillo, 2013; Shapiro, 2017; Sharkey & Elwert, 2011; Williams et al., 2019). These in turn can affect African American communities' and families' ability to competently provide for the developmental needs of their children in a holistic manner. For example, research by the Brooking Institute using the household pulse survey from the Census Bureau shows that in June 2020, approximately 16% of households with children indicated that "their children were not eating enough over the last week due to lack of resources" (Bauer, 2020). Although this study shows an increase in the rate of food insecurity for all children in the United States, Black children's experiences of food insecurity due to lack of family resources was higher compared to those of children from other racial backgrounds.

The limited resources predicting higher rates of food insecurity in Black families can be attributed to the racial wealth gap discussed previously. Compared to Whites, racial minority families have fewer resources to provide for their children, although Blacks and Hispanics are highly disadvantaged compared to Asians (Bauer, 2020). This indicates how racism conditions racial minorities, African Americans in particular, to violent conditions. Yet, when the violent conditions that racism creates to shape many African American families manifest in parenting practices and behaviors of children, these families are more likely to be blamed. Moreover, state intervention punishes them by taking away their children or prescribing individual-level interventions with limited attention to the structural forces operating through the state itself (Sarri & Finn, 1992). Family-level characteristics such as parenting are critical to understanding and addressing children's health and well-being (Grogan-Kaylor & Woolley, 2010). However, when viewed at the superficial level that only assesses families' choices and decisions to the exclusion of the structural factors interacting with the internal dynamics of families, researchers, practitioners, and policymakers may exaggerate or overestimate the role of families and underestimate or ignore the significant impact of the structural conditions within which Black families are embedded.

Racism and Health of African American Families

Disparate health inequities exist in the United States in that the prevalence of disease and death rates are higher for persons of color such as African Americans, Latinos, Asians, and Native Americans compared to Whites. Specific to African Americans, racism (structural racism in particular) has been identified as the fundamental driver of negative health and health inequities that African Americans confront (Bailey et al., 2017). Scholarship on medical racism and segregated health care that characterized colonial America and both the 18th and 19th centuries shows that in the same way that racism has evolved through slavery to contemporary forms of anti-Blackness, it has also evolved into a racialized health care system (Hammonds & Reverby, 2019; Owens & Fett, 2019). Under slavery, racist ideas and practices relied on public health to justify and strengthen racial subordination of the enslaved Africans. Enslaved Africans were considered to be in need of White control through harsh treatments and segregation into unhealthy and unhygienic living conditions that resulted in outbreak of diseases and death at rates higher than those of Whites (Bronson & Nuriddin, 2014). After slavery, this medical racism was carried over and continues to affect African American families (Owens & Fett, 2019). For example, the Centers for Disease Control and Prevention's (CDC, 2020) surveillance of hospitalizations due to COVID-19 showed that Blacks were impacted by the pandemic at a disproportionate rate compared to Whites and Hispanics. One central explanation that research suggests can explain African Americans' higher risk of infection to COVID-19 is structural or institutional racism. The critical pathway by which structural racism drives the disparities in COVID-19–related impact is through racial residential segregation (CDC, 2020). This coupled with the police killings of African Americans such as George Floyd, Ahmaud Arbery, Breonna Taylor, and several others killed throughout colonial America (for a review, see Moore et al., 2018) to date suggest the varying degrees of vulnerabilities and risks that characterize African American children growing up in the United States. Even in instances in which individuals killed by police may not be directly related to racism, research shows that hearing or seeing the killing of Blacks has serious and adverse mental health effects on Blacks in the general population (Bor et al., 2018).

Drawing on the biopsychosocial model of minority health, researchers have indicated that stress originating from racial discrimination generates physiological, social, and psychological effects that influence the health and academic well-being of African American children and youth (Huynh & Fuligni, 2010; Neblett, 2006; Utsey, 1998; Witherspoon et al., 2016).

Racism and Mental Health

Specific to mental health, research has shown that racial discrimination has adverse direct and indirect mental health effects on African American children (Reynolds & Gonzales-Backen, 2017). In a longitudinal study of youth over a 5-year period, Brody et al. (2006) report that racial discrimination experiences were associated with behavior problems (e.g., anger, aggression, and violence) and depressive symptoms. These symptoms in turn were associated with poor academic achievement and school dropout (Brody et al., 2006). Furthermore, racial discrimination has been associated with suicidal and morbid ideations for both African American boys and girls through depression, and anxiety for girls only, over time (Walker et al., 2017).

Racism and Education

In addition to racism's indirect impact on the academic adjustment and outcomes of African American youth through health and mental health, there is a direct impact on education to produce racial inequalities in education (Diamond & Lewis, 2019; Kyere et al., 2020). Although some scholars have argued that the racial disparities in education are more of a class issue, even in affluent schools in which African American students and students in other racial groups, particularly Whites, may have similar socioeconomic backgrounds, disparities in test scores, grades, and course-taking still exist (Diamond, 2006; Diamond & Lewis, 2019; Hartney & Flavin, 2013; Mickelson et al., 2013). Black youth in schools negotiate racialized terrain (Diamond, 2006; DeCuir-Gunby, 2007).

According to Diamond (2006), this racialized context affects Black youth in three ways:

> (1) by institutionally limiting their access to valued educational resources outside of school, (2) institutionally, by being positioned systematically at the most disadvantaged learning locations inside the school; and (3) ideologically, by having their intellectual capacity questioned and their cultural styles devalued within the school and the broader social discourse. (p. 496)

Overall, it is evident that growing up as an African American child in the United States is associated with tremendous consequences with regard to race. Racism affects the development of the African American child through multiple pathways, including inequalities in wealth-generating and wealth maintenance opportunities, health and mental health as well as health resources, racial residential segregation, underresourced educational systems, community and neighborhood violence, as well as direct racism in school and the criminal justice system and indirectly through their families or significant adults in their lives. These children are growing up in a society whose institutions have been historically structured to foster racial discrimination through mutually reinforcing systems, beliefs, and practices to adversely affect the health and overall well-being of children and youth of color (Bailey et al., 2017; Williams et al., 2019).

Potential Race-Relevant Mechanism for Responding to Racial Stress and Vulnerabilities

Within the strange social paradox of subordination and opportunities, African American parents are expected to raise children with functional competencies. These parents and caretakers have the arduous task of preparing children with the cognitive and psychological resources to navigate adverse social forces such as persistent racial stigmatization and discrimination that undermine the expectations and opportunities for actualizing their potential for productive lives. Scholarship on the best practice approach for optimal family functioning including child-rearing in African American communities has documented culturally unique adaptation strategies that parents devise and integrate into their parenting practices to help themselves and their children navigate their racialized social and institutional spaces to achieve developmental goals.

One such culturally responsive approach is racial/ethnic socialization, a process whereby African American parents/caretakers instill in their children messages relative to their racial identity and its social significance in U.S. society (Hughes et al., 2006; Huguley et al., 2019; Kyere & Huguley, 2020). These messages generally include (1) themes of positive racial heritage and pride in the racial group; (2) messages that equip children for racial biases they may encounter, both proactively and also in reaction to racialized experiences in their social ecology, including the media; and (3) skills for engaging in interaction with members of other racial groups. For example, Murry et al. (2014) examined the long-term impact of vigilant-involved and race-specific parenting practices that prepare youth for potential discrimination and foster pride in African American heritage on positive behavioral outcomes. These parenting approaches promoted futuristic orientation, which in turn was associated with youth's prosocial peer affiliation. Prosocial peers were also linked to self-regulation in the context of stressful events to influence prosocial norms that keep youth from engagement in risky behaviors such as alcohol and drug use and risky sexual behaviors that predispose youth to HIV/AIDS.

Racial–ethnic socialization predicts racial–ethnic identity—the significance and subjective meaning that is attributed to race in one's conceptualization of self (Hughes et al., 2006; Huguley et al., 2019; Kyere & Huguley, 2020). Although the link between racial–ethnic identity and African American youth developmental outcomes is mixed, a substantive body of work has established that racial–ethnic identity acts as a promotive factor and buffer against the negative impact of racial discrimination to allow African American youth to achieve healthy psychosocial development (Neblett et al., 2012, 2016).

Conclusion

Because of the pervasiveness of racism and its pernicious impact on African American families, Black children are arguably one of the most vulnerable populations in the United States today. It is critical for helping professionals to understand that without race-specific interventions that can help African American youth respond to racial stress, racism's impact may continue unabated. From an equity standpoint, social workers and other helping professionals interested in addressing racial disparities in both health and education need to give considerable attention to racial–ethnic socialization and racial identity.

References

Adams-Bass, V. N., Stevenson, H. C., & Kotzin, D. S. (2014). Measuring the meaning of Black media stereotypes and their relationship to the racial identity, Black history knowledge, and racial socialization of African American youth. *Journal of Black Studies, 45*(5), 367–395.

Alexander, M. (2012). *The new Jim Crow: Mass incarceration in the age of colorblindness*. New Press.

Bailey, Z. D., Krieger, N., Agénor, M., Graves, J., Linos, N., & Bassett, M. T. (2017). Structural racism and health inequities in the USA: Evidence and interventions. *Lancet, 389*(10077), 1453–1463.

Battalora, J. (2013). *Birth of a White nation: The invention of White people and its relevance today*. Strategic Book Publishing.

Bauer, L. (2020). *About 14 million children in the US are not getting enough to eat*. Brooking Institute. https://www.brookings.edu/blog/up-front/2020/07/09/about-14-million-children-in-the-us-are-not-getting-enough-to-eat

Bor, J., Venkataramani, A. S., Williams, D. R., & Tsai, A. C. (2018). Police killings and their spillover effects on the mental health of Black Americans: A population-based, quasi-experimental study. *Lancet, 392*(10144), 302–310.

Brody, G. H., Chen, Y. F., Murry, V. M., Ge, X., Simons, R. L., Gibbons, F. X., . . . & Cutrona, C. E. (2006). Perceived discrimination and the adjustment of African American youths: A five-year longitudinal analysis with contextual moderation effects. *Child Development, 77*(5), 1170–1189.

Bronson, J., & Nuriddin, T. (2014). "I don't believe in doctors much": The social control of health care, mistrust, and folk remedies in the African American slave narrative. *Journal of Alternative Perspectives in the Social Sciences, 5*(4), 706–732.

Centers for Disease Control and Prevention. (2020). *COVID-19 in racial and ethnic minority groups*. https://www.cdc.gov/coronavirus/2019-ncov/community/health-equity/racial-ethnic-disparities/index.html

Clark, R., Anderson, N. B., Clark, V. R., & Williams, D. R. (1999). Racism as a stressor for African Americans: A biopsychosocial model. *American Psychologist, 54*(10), 805.

Darling-Hammond, L. (2007). Race, inequality and educational accountability: The irony of "No Child Left Behind." *Race Ethnicity and Education, 10*(3), 245–260.

DeCuir-Gunby, J. T. (2007). Negotiating identity in a bubble: A critical race analysis of African American high school students' experiences in an elite, independent school. *Equity & Excellence in Education, 40*(1), 26–35.

Dettling, L. J., Hsu, J. W., Jacobs, L., Moore, K. B., & Thompson, J. P. (2017, September 27). Recent trends in wealth-holding by race and ethnicity: Evidence from the Survey of Consumer Finances. *FEDS Notes*. https://doi.org/10.17016/2380-7172.2083

Diamond, J. B. (2006). Still separate and unequal: Examining race, opportunity, and school achievement in "integrated" suburbs. *Journal of Negro Education, 75*(3), 495–505.

Diamond, J. B., & Lewis, A. E. (2019). Race and discipline at a racially mixed high school: Status, capital, and the practice of organizational routines. *Urban Education, 54*(6), 831–859.

Erickson, A. T. (2016). *Making the unequal metropolis: School desegregation and its limits.* University of Chicago Press.

García Coll, C., Lamberty, G., Jenkins, R., McAdoo, H. P., Crnic, K., Wasik, B. H., & Vázquez García, H. (1996). An integrative model for the study of developmental competencies in minority children. *Child Development, 67*(5), 1891–1914. http://doi.org/10.2307/1131600

Grogan-Kaylor, A., & Woolley, M. E. (2010). The social ecology of race and ethnicity school achievement gaps: Economic, neighborhood, school, and family factors. *Journal of Human Behavior in the Social Environment, 20*(7), 875–896.

Hammonds, E. M., & Reverby, S. M. (2019). Toward a historically informed analysis of racial health disparities since 1619. *American Journal of Public Health, 109*(10), 1348–1349.

Hanks, A., Solomon, D., & Weller, C. (2018). *Systematic inequality: How America's structural racism helped create the Black–White wealth gap.* Center for American Progress. Retrieved https://cdn.americanprogress.org/content/uploads/2018/02/20131806/RacialWealthGap-report.pdf

Hartney, M. T., & Flavin, P. (2013). The political foundations of the Black–White education achievement gap. *American Politics Research, 42*(1), 3–33.

Hughes, D., Rodriguez, J., Smith, E. P., Johnson, D. J., Stevenson, H. C., & Spicer, P. (2006). Parents' ethnic–racial socialization practices: A review of research and directions for future study. *Developmental Psychology, 42*(5), 747–770. http://doi.org/10.1037/0012-1649.42.5.747

Huguley, J. P., Wang, M. T., Vasquez, A. C., & Guo, J. (2019). Parental ethnic–racial socialization practices and the construction of children of color's ethnic–racial identity: A research synthesis and meta-analysis. *Psychological Bulletin, 145*(5), 437–458.

Huynh, V. W., & Fuligni, A. J. (2010). Discrimination hurts: The academic, psychological, and physical well-being of adolescents. *Journal of Research on Adolescence, 20*(4), 916–941.

Kyere, E., & Huguley, J. P. (2020). Exploring the process by which positive racial identity develops and influences academic performance in Black youth: Implications for social work. *Journal of Ethnic & Cultural Diversity in Social Work, 29*(4), 286–304.

Kyere, E., Karikari, I., & Teegen, B. C. (2020). The associations among teacher discrimination, parents' and peer emotional supports, and African American youth's school bonding. *Families in Society, 101*(4), 469–483.

McAdoo, H. P. (Ed.). (2002). *Black children: Social, educational, and parental environments.* Sage

Mickelson, R. A., Bottia, M. C., & Lambert, R. (2013). Effects of school racial composition on K–12 mathematics outcomes: A metaregression analysis. *Review of Educational Research, 83*(1), 121–158.

Moore, S. E., Robinson, M. A., Clayton, D. M., Adedoyin, A. C., Boamah, D. A., Kyere, E., & Harmon, D. K. (2018). A critical race perspective of police shooting of unarmed Black males in the United States: Implications for social work. *Urban Social Work, 2*(1), 33–47.

Murry, V. M., Berkel, C., Simons, R. L., Simons, L. G., & Gibbons, F. X. (2014). A twelve-year longitudinal analysis of positive youth development among rural African American males. *Journal of Research on Adolescence, 24*(3), 512–525.

Neblett, E. W. (2006). African American adolescents' discrimination experiences and academic achievement: Racial socialization as a cultural compensatory and protective factor. *Journal of Black Psychology, 32*(2), 199–218. http://doi.org/10.1177/0095798406287072

Neblett, E. W., Rivas-Drake, D., & Umaña-Taylor, A. J. (2012). The promise of racial and ethnic protective factors in promoting ethnic minority youth development. *Child Development Perspectives, 6*(3), 295–303. http://doi.wiley.com/10.1111/j.1750-8606.2012.00239.x

Neblett, E. W., Sosoo, E. E., Willis, H. A., Bernard, D. L., Bae, J., & Billingsley, J. T. (2016). Racism, racial resilience, and African American youth development: Person-centered analysis as a tool to promote equity and justice. Advances in Child Development and Behavior, 51, 43–79. http://doi.org/10.1016/bs.acdb.2016.05.004

Orfield, G., Kucsera, J., & Siegel-Hawley, G. (2012). *E pluribus . . . separation: Deepening double segregation for more students.* The Civil Rights Project, University of California, Los Angeles.

Owens, D. C., & Fett, S. M. (2019). Black maternal and infant health: Historical legacies of slavery. *American Journal of Public Health, 109*(10), 1342–1345.

Pattillo, M. (2013). *Black picket fences: Privilege and peril among the Black middle class.* University of Chicago Press.

Reynolds, J. E., & Gonzales-Backen, M. A. (2017). Ethnic–racial socialization and the mental health of African Americans: A critical review. *Journal of Family Theory & Review, 9*(2), 182–200.

Sarri, R., & Finn, J. (1992). Child welfare policy and practice: Rethinking the history of our certainties. *Children and Youth Services Review, 14*(3–4), 219–236.

Seaton, E. K., & Douglass, S. (2014). School diversity and racial discrimination among African-American adolescents. *Cultural Diversity and Ethnic Minority*

Psychology, 20(2), 156–165. http://doi.org/10.1037/a0035322

Shapiro, T. M. (2017). *Toxic inequality: How America's wealth gap destroys mobility, deepens the racial divide, and threatens our future.* Basic Books.

Sharkey, P., & Elwert, F. (2011). The legacy of disadvantage: Multigenerational neighborhood effects on cognitive ability. *American Journal of Sociology, 116*(6), 1934–1981.

Spencer, M. B. (1999). Social and cultural influences on school adjustment: The application of an identity-focused cultural ecological perspective. *Educational Psychologist, 34*(1), 43–57.

Umaña-Taylor, A. J. (2016). A post-racial society in which ethnic–racial discrimination still exists and has significant consequences for youths' adjustment. *Current Directions in Psychological Science, 25*(2), 111–118.

Utsey, S. O. (1998). Assessing the stressful effects of racism: A review of instrumentation. *Journal of Black Psychology, 24*(3), 269–288.

Walker, R., Francis, D., Brody, G., Simons, R., Cutrona, C., & Gibbons, F. (2017). A longitudinal study of racial discrimination and risk for death ideation in African American youth. *Suicide and Life-Threatening Behavior, 47*(1), 86–102

Wilder, C. S. (2013). *Ebony and ivy: Race, slavery, and the troubled history of America's universities.* Bloomsbury.

Williams, D. R., Lawrence, J. A., & Davis, B. A. (2019). Racism and health: Evidence and needed research. *Annual Review of Public Health, 40,* 105–125.

Williams, D. R., & Mohammed, S. A. (2013). Racism and health I: Pathways and scientific evidence. *American Behavior Science, 57*(8), 1152–1173.

Wilson, A. N. (1978). *The developmental psychology of the Black child.* Africana Research Publications.

Witherspoon, D. P., Seaton, E. K., & Rivas-Drake, D. (2016). Neighborhood characteristics and expectations of racially discriminatory experiences among African American adolescents. *Child Development, 87*(5), 1367–1378. http://doi.org/10.1111/cdev.12595

Social Work Practice with Indigenous and Native Peoples

Andrea G. Tamburro and Paul-René Tamburro

Terminology and Demographics

American Indian is the term used by the U.S. federal government in all policies and treaties and for government services. Legal and descriptive terms for Indigenous peoples of North America include AmerIndian, Native American, and American Indian/ Alaska Native (AI/AN). Status and Non-Status Indian, Native, Inuit, and Métis and metis are terms used in Canada and have legal and descriptive meanings. Also, many people from Latin America identify as Indigenous rather than solely Hispanic or Latinx; they speak an Indigenous language along with Spanish. Most Indigenous people prefer to use their specific nation's name. Many have more than one tribal or ethnic affiliation. The respectful approach is to ask clients to describe their identity (Brown et al., 2016; Weaver & Brave Heart, 1999).

Context for Practice

Millions of Indigenous peoples have lived on Turtle Island for thousands of years. Only 500 years ago, 100% of what is now Mexico, the United States, and Canada belonged to Indigenous peoples. Colonization destroyed Indigenous social and environmental systems, resulting in economic poverty and multigenerational, historical, and ongoing trauma (Duran et al., 1998). Until the late 20th century, federal policies focused on assimilation and destroying Indigenous cultures and languages. Slavery, disease, removals from homelands, and relocations to reservations in the 1800s and to urban centers in the 1900s all led to destruction of traditional support systems and historic trauma. The leadership roles of women in matriarchal cultures were reduced (Burnette, 2015). Children were forced to assimilate into Eurocentric culture by attending residential schools and later placed in foster homes, away from their communities, languages, ceremonies, and cultures.

Tribal Sovereignty

Recently the number of federally recognized tribes has increased to 574 ("Indian Entities," 2018). This includes 277 federally recognized village groups in Alaska (National Conference of State Legislatures, 2020). According to the Administration for Native Americans (2014), there are also approximately 70 state-recognized tribes in 16 states in the United

States. There are more than 100 terminated tribes and unrecognized tribes, which self-identify with no formal government recognition (Goldberg & Champagne, 1996).

Because little information is provided through public or university education, including field practicum, or the media, many social workers need to know more about Indigenous peoples and resources that are available (Clark et al., 2010; Johnson et al., 2012). Social workers must learn about tribal sovereignty, the rights of Indigenous people, and the resources stemming from those unique treaty rights. Also, it is essential to understand the extensive diversity among various Indigenous cultures and among rural, reservation, urban, government-*recognized* and -*unrecognized* people who may need specific services. Indigenous people living and working in urban communities may still have strong ties to their home communities (U.S. Census Bureau, 2006).

Forms of government in the United States include federal, tribal, state, and local. The federal government and federally recognized tribes have a government-to-government relationship that was established in the U.S. Constitution, supported by treaties, and confirmed through cases by the U.S. Supreme Court in the 1830s (Prucha, 1990; Wilkins, 1997). Through treaties, in exchange for land and resources, the federal government agreed to provide in perpetuity food, health care, education, and financial support to federally recognized tribes. The acknowledgment of tribal sovereignty and self-determination reestablished the rights that had been suppressed. The right to citizenship and for tribes to practice their religions, develop their own form of government, tax their members, and enforce policies and laws established by the tribes was acknowledged. The Council on Social Work Education's (CSWE) 2015 Educational Policy and Accreditation Standards, under Competency 2: Engage Diversity and Difference, acknowledged for the first time the importance of understanding tribal sovereign status. Self-determination is supported by the National Association of Social Workers Code of Ethics (2017) and focuses social work away from deficits toward a strengths-based approach with Indigenous peoples (Red Horse & Limb, 2004; Weaver, 2003). Canada has a system that recognizes Indian, Métis, and Inuit status and has treaties in most provinces and territories.

Issues Facing Indigenous Peoples: Research and Advocacy Needed

During the COVID-19 pandemic, conditions on a few reservations were reported on the national news. Lack of running water on some reservations, people living far from adequate medical facilities, undistributed governmental funds, lack of broadband internet, and already underresourced medical infrastructure caused a rapid COVID-19 infection rate. On May 18, 2020, the Navajo Nation had a higher per capita rate of COVID-19 than New York state, with significantly less resources (Silverman et al., 2020).

Missing and murdered Indigenous people, especially women in the United States and Canada, constitute an ongoing crisis that has gone unnoticed by the media. Addington (2019) states that AI/AN people are 2.5 times more likely to experience violence compared to other diverse groups. Human trafficking, communication and data gaps, and enforcement are ongoing issues.

As social workers identify the importance of environmental justice (CSWE, 2015), advocacy for sustainability has become a pressing issue. For Indigenous peoples, traditional territory is a cradle of the culture and spirituality, it provides a sense of home, and it is a place to protect. Climate change has had a major impact on the land, communities, and cultures of Indigenous peoples. Coastal erosion and rising sea levels have impacted Indigenous communities. With traditional knowledge of the earth's ecosystems, Indigenous people can play a role in solutions to climate change (Koppel Maldonado et al., 2014). Therefore, social workers need to support social action, such as the recent Silent No More movement or the Water Keepers, on resource rights and climate change.

While government administrations continue to perpetuate multigenerational trauma on Indigenous families from Latin America at the U.S. border, social workers are recognizing the importance of working toward change. For more than 20 years, the impact of historical or multigenerational trauma on the health and well-being of Indigenous peoples has been explicitly identified (Brave Heart, 1999a, 1999b, 2000; Brave Heart & DeBruyn, 1998; Evans-Campbell, 2008). Brave Hart et al. (2011) described historical trauma as a psychological wound that passes from one generation to the next and is carried throughout life. This study identified responses to historical trauma among Lakota people, similar to the experiences of Jewish Holocaust survivors, including feelings of guilt, numbness, anger, and depression; repeatedly remembering the loss of ancestors and land; and intrusive dreams. These multigenerational experiences are exacerbated by current experiences of colonization, including disease, violence, illness, and poverty (Tjaden & Thoennes, 2000); suicide (Olson & Wahab, 2006); child abuse and neglect (Cross et al., 2000); poor health and mental health (Fong et al., 2006; Walters et al., 2002); high rates of incarceration (Waldram, 1997); and experiences of constant microaggressions and racist stereotypes.

Indigenous North Americans: Impact on Social Work Interventions

Indigenous professional social workers have always been a minority within the social work profession. In 1973, there were less than 20 Native American social workers in the United States (Mackey, 1973). Most services are still provided by non-native practitioners (Cross et al., 2009). Professional Indigenous social workers have published important resource material that all social workers should read. Learning about the discrimination and racism experienced by any diverse group must be counterbalanced with an understanding of the strengths of that group. In the United States, approximately 6.9 million people self-identify with American Indian ancestry (U.S. Census Bureau, 2018).

Indigenous Americans are also part of a political and cultural group. They represent an important identity, a connection to a tribe or community of Indigenous people, sometimes recognized by a government and sometimes not. Clients who are Indigenous may appear stereotypically Indigenous, Black, White, Hispanic, Asian, or any mixture of these stereotyped groups. Citizens of federally recognized communities are often eligible for specific services and benefits through their respective governments. These services include health care, employment assistance, protections under the Indian Child Welfare Act (ICWA), annual annuities, and other specific services. However, the majority of these are unavailable to Indigenous people who are not eligible for membership in a recognized tribe (United States) or status community (Canada). There are many nonstatus and nonrecognized people in the United States and Canada who are unable to access benefits. This may also be true for eligible clients due to distance from services on a reservation or reserve community. During the termination and relocation era (1953–1969), many cities developed American Indian Centers. In Canada, Friendship Centers were developed (Stanford School of Medicine, n.d.). These organizations provide direct assistance such as referrals, housing, food, and community support in urban areas.

Social workers are the first line of defense of the ICWA. Ongoing, disproportionate child removals assisted by social workers have led to extreme distrust of social agencies by many Indigenous peoples. Social work practitioners, educators, and students are often unaware of the safety net provided by ICSW [National Indian Child Welfare Association (NICWA), 2017]. ICWA requires states to notify the tribes as soon as interventions with Indian children are initiated. Many Indigenous children are not specifically covered by ICWA because they are not eligible for membership in a recognized tribe, but they still need support to connect to Indigenous-centered services. Negative labeling of Indigenous people who were more closely tied to their culture has led to mental health labels and practices of intervention that made matters worse. ICWA has helped stop overt government removals of children, but states have been out of compliance with implementation. Child welfare workers must know and follow through with the protections ICWA provides to tribal communities and children who are enrolled or could be enrolled in federally recognized tribes (NICWA, 2020). Social workers must support policies and funding that underpin ICWA (Limb, 2004).

The disproportionate rates of Indigenous child placement in Canada require social workers to know policies to keep connections to communities. Therefore, most social workers need to research the social situations of their Indigenous clients. Information is available, but it takes persistence to find because Indigenous data are often omitted from comparisons with other diverse groups. On many issues, Indigenous people fare worse than any other ethnic group in terms of poverty, access to housing and health care, rates of incarceration and out-of-home child placement, alcoholism, substance abuse, death rate, health, and youth suicide (Substance Abuse and Mental Health Services Administration, 2018).

Social workers need to discuss Indigenous background with all clients, even if they do not "look" Indigenous. Ask clients if they are enrolled or can be enrolled in a federally or state-recognized tribe. If they are Canadian, ask if they are part of a status community; if they are Latin American, ask their Indigenous Nation. Next, determine which services they may want and are eligible to receive. Because they may not know or may not be willing to talk about it initially, it is important to continue to ask about their tribal status and who in their family might know if they are eligible for or have tribal enrollment (Gonzalez & Gonzalez-Santin, 2014).

Practitioner- and Evidence-Based Culturally Focused Interventions

Long before the profession of social work, members of Indigenous communities helped each other (Tamburro & Tamburro, 2014). Today, these communities have had extensive historical and ongoing trauma resulting from government interventions (Tamburro, 2013). Clients respond differently to services based on their Indigenous identity connection to community (Walters, 1999). Utilizing a more culturally centered worldview may be essential to services with diverse Indigenous clients, depending on their interests and perspectives. For example, NICWA offers workshops on positive Indian parenting to help parents identify family and child needs and strengthen connections to their cultural community. They also offer training for child welfare workers. Utilizing elders, circle talks, ceremonies, and community-specific healing practices can enhance interventions (BigFoot, 2007). Incorporating the extended family into interventions expands the support network. Elders can unify Indigenous families and keep alive a worldview in which intergenerational interdependence, interconnectedness, and caring are essential (Red Horse et al., 2000). Cultural programs help youth and young adults form healthy lives and provide important buffers for drug and alcohol addiction (Brown et al., 2016; Jacobs, 2015). Motivational interviewing has been integrated with traditional practices to impact urban Indigenous youth dealing with drugs and alcohol (Dickerson et al., 2015). Storytelling has supported a resilience model for urban elders (Reinschmidt et al., 2016). Healing takes place by restoring the balance among genders, including two-spirit, women, and men in Indigenous communities (Anderson & Lawrence, 2003). Helping Indigenous people find balance and harmony to reconnect with spirituality can enhance healing (Hodge et al., 2009). To reduce substance abuse and chemical dependency, community organizing at Esketemc (Alkali Lake, British Columbia, Canada) has been successful (Bopp & Bopp, 2011). Inpatient programs have combined 12-step with traditional healing and ceremonies (Round Lake Treatment Center in British Columbia, Canada, and the Native American Rehabilitation Association in Portland, Oregon).

Practical Way Social Workers Can Help

Members of federally recognized tribes are eligible for Indian Health Service and benefits that differ based on treaties and their tribe, pueblo, or community. When working with Indigenous peoples, navigating Indian Country is complex and takes patience. Developing an understanding of the unique circumstances of each client system is essential.

Culturally competent social workers need to assess the sociocultural location of their client system (Weaver, 2003, 2004). Best practice begins where the client is. Throughout the relationship, situations may help build trust, and it can take time to achieve a sense of connection and support. An eco-map, including items that help assess connections to a physical community such as a reservation or a support network such as a Friendship or Indian Center, is very helpful. Also, determine if they are or

could become a member of a government-recognized community, giving them access to services. If they have a Certificate of Degree of Indian Blood card in the United States, they are eligible for Indian Health Service (IHS) with hospitals, mental health services, and clinics. A client may not meet the criteria of eligibility, or the nearest IHS facility could be far away. It is also important for social workers to research resources focusing on the specific communities and resources identified by clients. Most tribes or Native Alaskan communities (United States) and bands (Canada) have websites, so additional assistance from their community can be found. Services to Indigenous Latin Americans may also be available, especially in cities. Be aware of anti-Indigenous racism within Latin American counties. Social workers also need to advocate for Indigenous Latin Americans specific needs—for example, translation in an Indigenous language.

Social and Situational Assessment and Intervention

Understanding an Indigenous worldview enhances the trust and discussion of an individual client's identity, cultural practices, strengths, and ways to support their growth and healing through traditional and Western approaches. Discussing current and historic trauma experienced by the client system is essential (Brave Heart et al., 2011). Assessment goals include helping clients explore their situation, discussing their cultural identity, affiliations, and treatment preferences. The length, severity, and possible sources of their concerns need to be unpacked. Exploring positive aspects of their life, including individual, family, and community strengths and potential support networks, is critical. Gaining an understanding of the timeline of life events and trauma (historic and ongoing) is essential. Culturally sensitive assessment tools can be utilized (Congress & Kung,

2013; Hodge & Limb, 2011). Consider the intersection of oppressions experienced by an individual, couple, family, or community. Focus on the goals selected by the client, family, group, or community that support self-determination. Enhance positive ways to cope with anger, stress, and anxiety. Build on the strengths and resilience in the family and community (Goodluck, 2002). Support clients' choices about how to incorporate traditional approaches in their healing (Limb & Hodge, 2008; Waldram, 1997). Locate local Indigenous resources and social and cultural activities in the area.

Conclusion

To enhance cultural competence and decolonize social work practice, social workers must support tribal sovereignty and address the historic and ongoing trauma experienced by Indigenous peoples. By addressing issues in Indigenous communities and enhancing self-determination and advocacy, social workers can become allies with Indigenous communities. Social workers can find or support clients seeking assistance to support their cultural, spiritual, and physical needs, thus enhancing the evidence-based and practitioner-based approaches to helping Indigenous people.

Helpful Resources

Indian Country Child Trauma Center: http://www.icctc.org
Indian Health Service: http://www.ihs.gov
National Indian Child Welfare Association: http://www.nicwa.org

References

Addington, C. (2019) *Missing and murdered Indigenous women crisis*. Bureau of Indian Affairs Report to House Committee on Natural Resources Subcommittee for Indigenous Peoples of the US. https://www.doi.gov/ocl/mmiw-crisis

Administration for Native Americans. (2014). American Indians and Alaska Natives: What are state recognized tribes. https://www.acf.hhs.gov/ana/fact-sheet/american-indians-and-alaska-natives-what-are-state-recognized-tribes

Anderson, K., & Lawrence, B. (2003). *Strong women stories*. Sumach Press.

BigFoot, D. (2007). Evidence-based practices in Indian country. Presentation at the Institute for Indigenous Wellness Research, Seattle, WA.

Bopp, M., & Bopp, J. (2011). *The Esketemc (Alkali Lake) community story: A case study*. Four Winds Press. https://sjiedmonton.files.wordpress.com/2013/12/alkali-lake-cs.pdf

Brave Heart, M. Y. H. (1999a). Gender differences in the historical trauma response among the Lakota. *Journal of Health and Social Policy, 10*(4), 1–21.

Brave Heart, M. Y. H. (1999b). Oyate Ptayela: Rebuilding the Lakota Nation through addressing historical trauma among Lakota parents. *Journal of Human Behavior in the Social Environment, 2*(1–2), 109–126.

Brave Heart, M. Y. H. (2000). Wakiksuyapi: Carrying the historical trauma of the Lakota. *Tulane Studies in Social Welfare*, 245–266.

Brave Heart, M. Y. H., Chase, J., Elkins, J., & Altschul, D. B. (2011). Historical trauma among Indigenous peoples of the Americas: Concepts, research, and clinical considerations. *Journal of Psychoactive Drugs, 43*(4), 282–290.

Brave Heart, M. Y. H., & DeBruyn, L. M. (1998). The American Indian holocaust: Healing historical unresolved grief. *American Indian and Alaska Native Mental Health Research, 8*, 56–78.

Brown, R. A., Dickerson, D. L., & D'Amico, E. J. (2016). Cultural identity among urban American Indian/Alaska Native youth: Implications for alcohol and drug use. *Prevention Science, 17*(7), 852–861. https://doi.org/10.1007/s11121-016-0680-1

Burnette, C. E. (2015). Indigenous women's resilience and resistance to historical oppression: A case example from the United States. *Affilia, 30*(2), 253–258. https://doi.org/10.1177/0886109914555215

Clark, N., Drolet, J., Mathews, N., Walton, P., Tamburro, P., Derrick, J., & Arnouse, M. (2010). Decolonizing field education: Melq'ilwiye coming together: An exploratory study in the interior of British Columbia. *Critical Social Work, 11*(1).

Congress, E. P., & Kung, W. W. (2013). Using the culturagram to assess and empower culturally diverse families. In E. P. Congress & M. J. Gonzalez (Eds.), *Multicultural perspectives in social work practice with families* (3rd ed., pp. 1–20). Springer.

Council on Social Work Education. (2015). *2015 educational policy and accreditation standards*. https://

www.cswe.org/Accreditation/Standards-and-Policies/2015-EPAS

Cross, S. L., Brown, E. F., Day, P., Limb, G. E., Pellebon, D., Proctor, E. C., & Weaver, H. N. (2009). Task force on Native Americans in social work education: Status of Native Americans in social work higher education. https://www.cswe.org/getattachment/Centers-Initiatives/Scholarships-and-Fellowships/ Scholars-Program/ Past-CSWE-Scholars/ 10-TaskForceonNativeAmericansin SocialWorkEducation.pdf.aspx

Cross, T. A., Earle, K. A., & Simmons, D. (2000). Child abuse and neglect in Indian country: Policy issues. *Families in Society, 81*(1), 49–58.

Dickerson, D. L., Brown, R. A., Johnson, C. L., Schweigman, K., & D'Amico, E. J. (2015). Integrating motivational interviewing and traditional practices to address alcohol and drug use among urban American Indian/Alaska Native youth. *Journal of Substance Abuse Treatment, 65*, 26–35. https://doi.org/10.1016/j.jsat.2015.06.023

Duran, B., Duran, E., & Brave Heart, M. Y. B. (1998). Native Americans and the trauma of history. In R. Thornton (Ed.), *Studying Native America* (pp. 60–76). University of Wisconsin Press.

Evans-Campbell, T. A. (2008). Historical trauma in American Indian/Alaska Native communities: A multilevel framework for exploring impacts on individuals, families and communities. *Journal of Interpersonal Violence, 23*, 316–338.

Fong, R., McRoy, R., & Hendricks, C. O. (2006). *Intersecting child welfare, substance abuse, and family violence: Culturally competent approaches.* CSWE Press.

Goldberg, C., & Champagne, D. (1996). Status and needs of unrecognized and terminated California Indian tribes. In *A second century of dishonor: Federal inequities and California tribes.* American Indian Studies Center, UCLA. https://www.aisc.ucla.edu/ca/Tribes.htm

González, T., & González-Santin, E. (2014). ICWA: Legal mandate for social justice and preservation of American Indian/Alaska Native heritage. *Social Issues in Contemporary Native America: Reflections from Turtle Island, 129.*

Goodluck, C. (2002). *Native American children and youth well-being indicators: A strengths perspective.* National Indian Child Welfare Association.

Hodge, D. R., & Limb, G. E. (2011). Spiritual assessment and Native Americans: Establishing the social validity of a complementary set of assessment tools. *Social Work, 56*(3), 213–223.

Hodge, D. R., Limb, G. E., & Cross, T. L. (2009). Moving from colonization toward balance and harmony: A Native American perspective on wellness. *Social Work, 54*(3), 211–219.

Indian entities recognized and eligible to receive services from the United States Bureau of Indian Affairs. (2018, January 30). *Federal Register.* https://www.federalregister.gov/documents/2018/07/23/2018-15679/indian-entities-recognized-and-eligible-to-receive-services-from-the-united-states-bureau-of-indian

Jacobs, M. R. (2015). Urban American Indian identity: Negotiating Indianness in northeast Ohio. *Qualitative Sociology, 38*(1), 79–98. https://doi.org/10.1007/s11133-014-9293-9

Johnson, S., Tamburro, P. R., & Clark, N. (2012). Indigenous field education: Protocols and practices. In J. Drolet, N. Clark, & H. Allen (Eds.), *Shifting sites of practice: Field education in Canada* (pp. 137–158). Pearson.

Koppel Maldonado, J., Colombi, B., & Pandya, R. (2014). *Climate change and Indigenous peoples in the United States: Impacts, experiences, and actions.* Springer. https://doi.org/10.1007/978-3-319-05266-3

Limb, G. (2004). Foster care and permanency issues for American Indian/Alaska Native families and children. In National Indian Child Welfare Association (Ed.), *Impacts of child maltreatment in Indian Country: Preserving the seventh generation through policies, programs, and funding streams* (pp. 256–284) [Congressional report]. National Indian Child Welfare Association.

Limb, G., & Hodge, D. (2008). Developing spiritual competency with Native Americans: Promoting wellness through balance and harmony. *Families in Society, 89*(4), 615–622.

Mackey, J. E. (1973). *American Indian: Task force report.* Council on Social Work Education.

National Association of Social Workers. (2017). *Code of ethics.* https://www.socialworkers.org/About/Ethics/Code-of-Ethics/Code-of-Ethics-English

National Conference of American Indians. (2020). Demographics. http://www.ncai.org/about-tribes/demographics

National Indian Child Welfare Association. (2017). Disproportionality. https://www.nicwa.org/wp-content/uploads/2017/09/Disproportionality-Table.pdf

National Indian Child Welfare Association. (2020). About ICWA. https://www.nicwa.org/about-icwa

Olson, L. M., & Wahab, S. (2006). American Indians and suicide: A neglected area of research. *Trauma, Violence, and Abuse, 7*(1), 19–33.

Prucha, F. P. (Ed.). (1990). *Documents of United States Indian policy* (2nd ed.). University of Nebraska Press.

Red Horse, J., & Limb, G. (2004). Sovereignty, cultural competency, and family preservation. In National Indian Child Welfare Association (Ed.), *Impacts of child maltreatment in Indian Country: Preserving the seventh generation through policies, programs,* and funding streams (pp. 235–255) [Congressional report]. National Indian Child Welfare Association.

Red Horse, J. G., Martinez, C., Day, P., Day, D., Poupart, J., & Scharnberg, D. (2000). Family preservation concepts in American Indian communities. National Indian Child Welfare Association.

Reinschmidt, K. M., Attakai, A., Kahn, C. B., Whitewater, S., & Teufel-Shone, N. (2016). Shaping a stories of resilience model from urban American Indian elder's narratives of historical trauma and resilience. American Indian & Alaska Native Mental Health Research, 23(4), 63–85. https://doi.org/10.5820/aian.2304.2016.63

Silverman, H., Toropin, K., Sidner, S., & Perrot, L. (2020). Navajo Nation surpasses New York state for the highest Covid-19 infection rate in the US. CNN. https://www.cnn.com/2020/05/18/us/navajo-nation-infection-rate-trnd/index.html

Stanford School of Medicine. (n.d.). Ethnogeriatrics: Termination. https://geriatrics.stanford.edu/ethnomed/american_indian/learning_activities/learning_1/termination_relocation.html

Substance Abuse and Mental Health Services Administration. (2018). National Survey on Drug Use and Health: American Indians and Alaska Natives. https://www.samhsa.gov/data/sites/default/files/reports/rpt23246/1_AIAN_2020_01_14_508.pdf

Tamburro, A. (2013). Including decolonization in social work education and practice. Journal of Indigenous Social Development, 2(1), 1–15.

Tamburro, A., & Tamburro, P. R. (2014). Social services and Indigenous peoples of North America: Pre-colonial to contemporary times. In H. N. Weaver (Ed.), Social issues in contemporary Native America: Reflections from Turtle Island Native America (pp. 45–58). Ashgate.

Tjaden, P., & Thoennes, N. (2000). Full report on the prevalence, incidence and consequences of violence against women (NCJ 183781). National Institutes of Justice.

U.S. Census Bureau. (2006). We the people: American Indians and Alaska Natives in the US. https://www.census.gov/prod/2006pubs/censr-28.pdf

U.S. Census Bureau. (2018). American Indian and Alaska Native heritage month. Retrieved November 2019 from https://www.census.gov/newsroom/facts-for-features/2019/aian-month.html

Waldram, J. (1997). The way of the pipe: Aboriginal spirituality and symbolic healing in Canadian prisons. Broadview Press.

Walters, K. L. (1999). Urban American Indian identity attitudes and acculturation styles. In H. Weaver (Ed.), Voices of First Nations people: Human services considerations (pp. 163–178). Haworth.

Walters, K. L., Simoni, J. M., & Evans-Campbell, T. (2002). Substance use among American Indians and Alaska Natives: Incorporating culture in an "indigenist" stress-coping paradigm. Public Health Reports, 117(1), 104–117.

Weaver, H. (2003). Cultural competence with First Nations peoples. In D. Lum (Ed.), Culturally competent practice: A framework for understanding diverse groups and justice issues (pp. 223–247). Brooks/Cole.

Weaver, H. (2004). The elements of cultural competence: Applications with Native American clients. Journal of Ethnic and Cultural Diversity in Social Work, 13(1), 19–35.

Weaver, H. N., & Brave Heart, M. Y. H. (1999). Examining two facets of American Indian identity: Exposure to other cultures and the influence of historical trauma. In H. N. Weaver (Ed.), Voices of First Nations people: Human services considerations (pp. 19–33). Haworth.

Wilkins, D. E. (1997). American Indian sovereignty and the U.S. Supreme Court. University of Texas Press.

Social Work Practice with Latinas/Latinos/Latinx

Susana E. Mariscal, Michelle Johnson-Motoyama, and Alan J. Dettlaff

Engaging in culturally sensitive social work practice with Latinx has never been more critical than it is in the current sociopolitical climate. This chapter provides an overview of Latinx social and demographic characteristics and a model for culturally sensitive social work practice that draws on decades of seminal work in the field of social work.

Diverse Heritage and Identities: Hispanic Versus Latinas/Latinos/Latinx

The term *Hispanic* includes individuals with family origins in Spain or in a country that was a former colony of Spain, including Mexico, Central or South America, and the Spanish Caribbean (Vidal-Ortiz & Martínez, 2018). The term *Latino* includes the same group of people, except those with ancestry in Spain (Morin, 2009). The term Latino emerged in the 1980s as an expression of resistance to

obscuring historical and social differences between Spain and Latin American countries, its former colonies, and emphasizes the rich and diverse legacy of Indigenous and other cultures. The term *Latina/o* emerged as a term of resistance to the androcentrism of Spanish language, reclaiming the female space. The term *Latinx* is more recent and inclusive of gender nonconforming and sexual minorities and non-Whiteness. However, the term Latinx still faces some opposition from those who consider it an academic imposition and may reflect Latinx gender sexual minorities' struggle to be included (Vidal-Ortiz & Martínez, 2018).

Many Latinas/Latinos prefer to identify themselves by their heritage (e.g., country of origin), and then as Latino/Hispanic, rather than trying to fit in a U.S.-government single racial category (Morin, 2009). Latinx use a variety of terms, such as *trigueno*, *moreno*, and *mestizo*, to refer to mixed races (Delgado, 2007). Considering these different labels, in practice, it is important that Latinx have the opportunity to clarify how they identify and define themselves.

Demographic Characteristics

In 2017, the approximately 60 million Latinx people in the United States represented approximately 18% of the U.S. population and the largest minority group (Noe-Bustamante & Flores, 2019). Latinxs are projected to represent 30% of the total population by 2050 (U.S. Census Bureau, 2010), and their relevance for social work practice cannot be overstated. At a median age of 29 years, the Latinx population is younger than the overall U.S. population at a median of 38 years (U.S. Census Bureau, 2017a). Most Latinx are U.S. citizens (77%), with many residing in mixed-status families (Taylor et al., 2011). Nearly 80% of Latinx immigrants have resided in the United States for at least 10 years (Noe-Bustamante, 2019).

Latinxs have diverse heritages, each with different economic and demographic profiles (Noe-Bustamante, 2019). In 2017, Mexicans (62%) and Puerto Ricans (10%) were the largest groups, followed by Salvadorans (4%), among many others (24%). The Latinx population grew 16% from 2010 to 2017, with Venezuelan, Dominican, and Guatemalan groups growing the fastest (Noe-Bustamante, 2019). The Spanish language facilitates Latinx connections with cultures of origin and within communities. Approximately 70% of Latinxs are proficient in English (Noe-Bustamante, 2019), whereas 60% of those aged 5 years or older speak Spanish at home (U.S. Census Bureau, 2017a). However, there are local differences in Spanish vocabulary, diction, and speech patterns, and many Indigenous Latinx immigrants speak different languages and dialects. More than half of Latinx adults in the United States are Catholic (55%), but this percentage is declining (Pew Research Center, 2014), and some Latinx hold folk beliefs.

Approximately 32 million Latinx were estimated to be eligible to vote in 2020, the largest minority group in the electorate, and although the 116th Congress is the most racially/ethnically diverse, Latinx are still underrepresented at 9.2% (Krogstad & Noe-Bustamante, 2019). Despite some improvements, U.S. Latinxs are still poorly understood by the general population and the government and its institutions. Latinx history in the United States is largely absent from school texts and curricula, which prevents Latinx youth from learning about themselves and their culture, history, and identity. Furthermore, a great share of news stories about Latinxs focus on crime and illegal immigration, which increases public misperceptions and leads to prejudice, discrimination, and, thus, injustice (Morin, 2009). Although Latinx representation in the media has increased in recent years, particularly in children's programming, there is much more work to do.

Disparities/ Disproportionality Among Latinx Populations

Consistent with other historically marginalized populations, Latinx children and families are at disproportionate risk of experiencing a number of problems. The rapid growth of the Latinx population is evident as Latinx represent 22.7% of all people enrolled in school (U.S. Census Bureau, 2017b). Although Latinx high school dropout rates have declined to 12% and college enrollment has increased to 35%, a gap persists in college completion (Krogstad, 2016; U.S. Census Bureau, 2017b). Only 15% of Latinx had a bachelor's degree in 2014 compared to 41% of Whites (Krogstad, 2016). As of 2017, 18.3% of the Latinx population lived in poverty compared to 8.7% of the non-Hispanic White population. Although high, this represents a decrease in poverty since 2010 (26.6%) (Fontenot et al., 2018).

Consistent with the high rate of poverty, Latinxs are disproportionately overrepresented in a number of systems. For example, Latinx youth are 65% more likely to be detained in a juvenile justice facility compared to their White peers (Sentencing Project, 2017). In the child welfare system, Latinx children are slightly underrepresented at the national level, as they represent 21% of children in foster care although they make up 25% of the general child population. However, Latinx children are overrepresented in 20 states, with the highest overrepresentation occurring in Maine, where they are represented in foster care at a rate of nine times their proportion of the general population (National Council of Juvenile and Family Court Judges, 2017).

Latinx also experience differential access to health services. Latinx health care utilization is low: Only 75% of Latinx adults reported seeing a doctor in the past year compared to 90% of White adults (Kaiser Family Foundation, 2019). Similarly, 25% of Latinxs report not having a regular health care provider compared to only 14% of their White counterparts (Kaiser Family Foundation, 2019). This may be partly related to disparities in health insurance coverage. Among racial groups, Latinxs are three times as likely as White adults and nearly twice as likely as Black adults to be uninsured (Hostetter & Klein, 2018).

Latinx and COVID-19

Latinx have tested positive for COVID-19 at disproportionally higher rates than the White population throughout the United States, corroborating persistent social and economic inequities (New York City Health, 2020; "The Virus Doesn't Discriminate," 2020). Latinx COVID-19 rates may be higher than reported because many Latinx are uninsured and less likely to seek medical care due to financial strains and/or fear of deportation. Latinx simultaneously

represent a large share of the essential workforce as well as those most impacted by pay cuts and job losses due to COVID-19 (Pew Research Center, 2020). Furthermore, although undocumented Latinx make tax contributions, they will not receive unemployment assistance or stimulus checks, nor will their U.S. citizen spouses if married and filing taxes jointly. Therefore, the economic impact of COVID-19 is hitting Latinx communities disproportionally hard with negative long-term consequences in today's charged sociopolitical climate.

It Is Getting More Difficult to Be Latinx in the United States

The sociopolitical climate in the United States continues to negatively impact the well-being of the Latinx community, and 54% of Latinxs report that it is more difficult to be a Latino in the United States today compared to past reports (Pew Research Center, 2018). Some Latinx experience fear and anxiety related to immigration and border control policies, including deportation, family separation, and the delayed reunification of children and families (Cowger et al., 2017). For example, recent policy changes have led to the highest numbers of migrant children detained at the border in U.S. history (Dickerson, 2018). The majority of these children are unaccompanied teenagers from Central America who crossed the border alone seeking asylum and have not been released to live with families or other sponsors. Recent policy changes have also affected the number of sponsors coming forward to claim children for fear of deportation, creating a humanitarian crisis (Meissner et al., 2018). Although nearly half of Latinxs have serious concerns about their place in the post-President Trump United States, the majority continue to be proud to be American and Latinx (Pew Research Center, 2018).

Culturally Sensitive Social Work Practice

What does it mean to be culturally sensitive in social work practice? It means that a practitioner considers cultural influences alongside human behavior theories and knowledge about Latinx social, cultural, and historical experiences. Culturally sensitive social work practice also recognizes within-group differences and the potential influence of the social worker's own culture and values (Furman et al., 2009).

Strengths-Based Culturally Sensitive Social Work Practice with Latinx Populations

The strengths-based culturally sensitive social work practice model integrates literature on culturally sensitive practice and practice models with Latinx people (Calvo et al., 2016; Delgado, 2007; Furman et al., 2009; Gelman, 2004; Organista, 2009), the principles and practice model of the strengths perspective (Rapp & Goscha, 2011; Saleebey, 2013), and the socioecological

resilience framework (Ungar, 2013). As Figure 113.1 shows, the helping relationship is primary and at the heart of the model, in which the client's dreams and aspirations provide direction; the client's voice and uniqueness guide the process and pace; and the client's assets, community resources, and cultural strengths promote transformation, resilience, and ethnic identity integration (client dimensions). The practitioner dimensions include the practitioner's knowledge and skills, such as professional use of self, and flexibility to make adaptations to meet client needs. The practitioner's commitment to ongoing professional development enhances the overall quality of the services provided.

The Quality of the Relationship Is Critical: Developing Trust, Respeto, and Personalismo

The vital importance of the quality of the helping relationship depends on the presence of three key elements: empathy, genuineness, and unconditional positive regard (Rogers, 1961). This relationship is purposeful, friendly, trusting, empowering, and client-centered (Mariscal, 2014). The ability to build a working therapeutic alliance is one of the most critical skills in the provision of culturally sensitive services

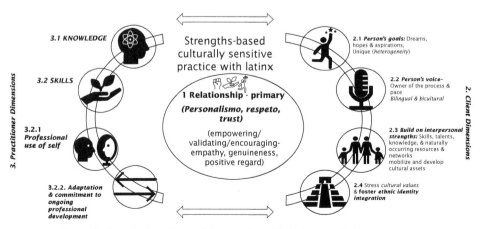

FIGURE 113.1 Strengths-based culturally sensitive practice with Latinx populations.

to Latinx. Given the current sociopolitical climate, it is important to spend the first session building trust and conveying warmth and personal connection, *personalismo*. The first session should also discuss the process to decrease stigma around mental health services, which is common among Latinx (Furman et al., 2009).

Core Elements of a Strengths-Based Culturally Sensitive Relationship with Latinx

1. The relationship is a collaboration in pursuit of the client's aspirations, hopes, and dreams (Rapp & Goscha, 2011). The client's uniqueness as a human being is honored (Rapp & Goscha, 2011).
2. The client guides the process and pace, and their voice is respected (Rapp & Goscha, 2011). The client has a choice regarding their language of preference. Thus, the ideal practitioner would be bilingual and bicultural.
3. Active listening to the client's narratives, stories, and lore allows a practitioner to discover the client's strengths, talents, resources, and cultural assets beyond concerns (Mariscal, 2014). When examining community resources, the practitioner creates opportunities for the client to reclaim their personal power and make decisions that impact their life (Rapp & Goscha, 2011). Build on Latinx cultural assets and naturally occurring resources and social support networks, such as

extended family systems, *compadres* (a child's godparent or co-parent), and other close relationships (Delgado, 2007).
4. A practitioner can foster Latinx identity integration by identifying and highlighting cultural values and assets; considering what is meaningful to a client (Ungar, 2013); and determining what values they want to adopt, transform, or discard.

Client Dimensions
Person's Hopes and Aspirations

The practitioner explores the client's dreams, hopes, and aspirations and seeks to capture a holistic portrait of the client and their environment from the client's perspective (Rapp & Goscha, 2011). The practitioner recognizes the uniqueness of the client and avoids stereotypes and generalized Latinx perceptions; gains knowledge of the role of class and culture for this particular client; and integrates important concerns for the client, such as family and immigration (Gelman, 2004).

Person's Voice and Ownership of the Process

The client is the owner of the process and their voice, in their preferred language, guides the practitioner's work. Bilingual and bicultural practitioners are ideal in their ability to navigate both languages and cultures. The practitioner's recognition that the client guides the process and focuses the relationship on achieving the client's aspirations communicates the practitioner's belief that the client is capable of changing their own reality and supports the possibility of a different future (Saleebey, 2013), empowering the client.

Build on Interpersonal Strengths

Each individual, family, and community has strengths and assets that can support pursuit of the client's goals. The practitioner discovers and mobilizes the client's strengths, assets, skills, and talents as the client describes their experiences, stories, cultural lore, wisdom, and assets (Mariscal, 2014). The practitioner identifies and attains resources and supports to promote resilience and transformation (Rapp & Goscha, 2011). To identify interpersonal strengths and resources, it is important to ask how the client managed to overcome barriers in the past, who/what helped, and what resources are available now. This process typically takes place in the community, allowing the practitioner to tap into the client's natural social support networks, resources, and cultural assets, which from the strengths perspective represent an oasis of resources (Saleebey, 2013). The Latinx support network typically consists of caring individuals, including close and extended family and friends; merchants and social clubs; members of the religious community; and folk healers. Connecting with Latinx cultural assets in the community involves trust, patience, skills, mutual respect and interdependence, and the willingness to share power with the community, which has the capacity to help itself (Delgado, 2007).

Fostering Client's Ethnic Identity Integration

Racial/ethnic identity can also be a source of pride and strength (Delgado, 2007). Considering the socioecological framework of resilience, fostering the client's ethnic identity integration requires a co-construction process in which cultural values and assets are passed down to youth and youth adopt, discard, or change what is meaningful to them (Ungar, 2013). Some strategies to foster Latinx identity include contacting and visiting family and friends left in the country of origin as well as activities such as folk music and tales, art, drama, literature, historic events, and creative writing

about ancestral heritage (Delgado, 2007). In this model, the practitioner focuses on the cultural values that are meaningful to the client, identifying from the client's multiple cultural backgrounds values that the client may choose to adopt, keep, transform, or reinvent in their lives. Considering Latinx diversity, the ethnic identity of a client will be unique, resulting from the integration of selected generic Latinx values, Indigenous traditions and beliefs, African heritage, and/or mainstream culture.

Practitioner Dimensions
Knowledge

Practitioner knowledge includes both informal and formal information regarding Latinx social, cultural, and historical experiences, such as the information presented in the first section of this chapter. It also includes the content presented in this section, which can be applied to improve assessment, develop interventions, and advance social justice–oriented practice. Importantly, this knowledge enhances awareness of the Latinx heterogeneity and diversity.

ACCULTURATION AND ACCULTURATIVE STRESS

Acculturation refers to immigrants' internal process of change upon their exposure to a new culture (Padilla & Perez, 2003) and involves several challenges for Latinx (Calvo et al., 2016; Delgado, 2007; Dettlaff et al., 2014; Furman et al., 2009; Gelman, 2004; Organista, 2009). Acculturative stress results from the acculturative process. Examples of sources of acculturative stress include language barriers, unemployment, financial strains, discrimination in the new culture (e.g., immigration policies), and social isolation (Dettlaff et al., 2014), which may take a toll on well-being. Considering that behavior, language, knowledge, values, and cultural identity are indicators of the acculturation process, they are key considerations in practice (Furman et al., 2009; Organista, 2009). Strategies to enhance the quality of services for clients with limited

English proficiency include providing trained interpreters, hiring bilingual and ideally bicultural staff, developing culture- and language-specific assessment tools (e.g., normed with Latinx samples), and providing materials and resources in Spanish (Delgado, 2007).

ASSIMILATION, INTEGRATION, AND ETHNIC IDENTITY

Integration refers to a process that depends on immigrants' initiative to incorporate themselves into the host society and, at the same time, on the host society's opportunities for newcomers and the community of origin's level of acceptance (Calvo et al., 2016). This approach is different from assimilation, in which the newcomer conforms to the American cultural norms. Ethnic identity, identifying with one's ethnic group, plays a role in identity formation and can affect psychosocial adjustment (Delgado, 2007; Organista, 2009).

OPPRESSION AND SOCIAL JUSTICE

Knowledge of structural theories forms the basis for culturally sensitive practice and advocacy on behalf of Latinx clients and communities, including theories of oppression and social justice (e.g., exploring conscious and unconscious attitudes and behaviors across societal levels) and social stratification (e.g., structured inequality of societal resources and power) (Organista, 2009). Practitioners who fight oppression and advocate for social justice on behalf of Latinx clients and communities can help facilitate integration. Calvo and colleagues (2016) propose to use immigrants' cultural capital (e.g., bilingualism) and advocate for structural opportunities for immigrants.

ACCESSIBILITY TO QUALITY SERVICES

Practitioners must be attuned to multiple dimensions of client access to services. Delgado (2007) proposes an interdependent model, including *geographical/physical* (e.g., Can the client get to the space where services are offered?), *psychological* (e.g., Does the client feel safe?), *cultural* (e.g., Are services in Spanish?), and *operational* accessibility (e.g., Do we offer services to clients when they need them?).

CULTURAL ASSETS

Delgado (2007) defines cultural assets as

> beliefs, traditions, principles, knowledge, and skills that effectively help people, particularly those who have been marginalized economically and socially by a society, to perceive and succeed in spite of immense odds against them. (p. 20)

Cultural values are assets that help Latinx navigate adversity (Delgado, 2007). For example, the value of cooperation or collectivism entails mutual empathy and a sense of belonging and respect (Furman et al., 2009). *Familismo* refers to the attachment to one's nuclear and extended family and to strong lifelong interdependence between family members. The value of *personalismo* highlights the importance of personal contact and individualized attention when receiving services, and it attempts to minimize professional distance, like *simpatía* (sympathy), which values pleasantry and warmth (Calvo et al., 2016; Delgado, 2007; Welland & Ribner, 2008). *Respeto* (respect) reflects the quality of the relationship, which could refer to close family relationships or professional deference due to authority and/or social status.

Skills

Practitioner skills correspond to the ongoing development of culturally sensitive engagement, assessment, and intervention aptitudes and competencies, including social work's core values and competencies (Delgado, 2007; Furman et al., 2009; Organista, 2009). Some of the most important skills include the ability to build a helping relationship, use one's self, and modify and adapt practices to meet the client's unique needs.

PROFESSIONAL USE OF SELF

Practitioner self-awareness is fundamental in social work practice with Latinx (Furman et al., 2009). Social workers need to understand how their own cultural heritage, worldviews, biases, race, social class, and overall privilege impact their perceptions and practice with Latinx (Furman et al., 2009). Thus, examination of the self is of utmost importance. Cultural sensitivity can be enhanced by developing self-awareness of personal biases and accepting their existence. Indeed, practitioners who acknowledge their privilege and power differential are likely to be able to build stronger relationships (Furman et al., 2009). In addition, because Latinx value respeto, they may initially adopt a distant "doctor–client" relationship, which could be improved through personalismo. For instance, some Latinx clients may ask about the social worker's family life. The practitioner's appropriate personal disclosure allows the client to view the social worker as a person, as part of a family, and thus enhances trust (Furman et al., 2009; Gelman, 2004). Practitioners may also need to increase appropriate physical contact and their comfort level in accepting gifts when working with Latinx clients (Gelman, 2004).

ONGOING COMMITMENT TO PROFESSIONAL DEVELOPMENT

Cultural sensitivity requires the practitioner's commitment to ongoing professional development of cultural awareness, knowledge, and skills (Organista, 2009), including expressing openness and demonstrating commitment to language and cultural expertise (Calvo et al., 2016). Commitment to providing culturally sensitive services involves refusing "one-size-fits-all" models and adapting and modifying practices according to the client's cultural values, beliefs, and expectations (Delgado, 2007; Gelman, 2004). It also involves keeping up with innovations in practice with diverse groups.

Conclusion

This chapter reviewed key social and demographic information about Latinx populations and introduced the strengths-based culturally sensitive social work practice model. However, a single chapter cannot capture all of the information needed to practice effectively with Latinx clients. To provide culturally sensitive social work practice in the context of today's dynamic sociopolitical climate, it is critical for social workers to engage in "perpetual" learning (Delgado, 2007), including learning from the communities they serve.

References

Calvo, R., Ortiz, L., Padilla, Y. C., Waters, M. C., Lubben, J., Egmont, W., Rosales, R., Figuereo, V., Cano, M., & Villa, P. (2016). *Achieving equal opportunity and justice: The integration of Latino/a immigrants into American society*. American Academy of Social Work and Social Welfare.

Cowger, S., Bolter, J., & Pierce, S. (2017). The first 100 days: Summary of major immigration actions taken by the Trump administration. *Migration Policy Institute*.

Delgado, M. (2007). *Social work with Latinos: A cultural assets paradigm*. Oxford University Press.

Dettlaff, A. J., Johnson-Motoyama, M., & Mariscal, E. S. (2014). Latino children and families. In R. Fong, A. J. Dettlaff, J. James, & C. Rodriguez (Eds.), *Addressing racial disproportionality and disparities: Multisystemic approaches* (pp. 109–152). Columbia University Press.

Dickerson, C. (2018, September 12). Detention of migrant children has skyrocketed to highest levels ever. *The New York Times*. https://www.nytimes.com/2018/09/12/us/migrant-children-detention.html

Fontenot, K., Semega, J., & Kollar, M. (2018). *Income and poverty in the United States 2017*. U.S. Census Bureau.

Furman, R., Negi, N. J., Iwamoto, D. K., Rowan, D., Shukraft, A., & Gragg, J. (2009). Social work practice with Latinos: Key issues for social workers. *Social Work, 54*(2), 167–174.

Gelman, C. R. (2004). Empirically-based principles for culturally competent practice with Latinos. *Journal of Ethnic and Cultural Diversity in Social Work, 13*(1), 83–108.

Hostetter, M., & Klein, S. (2018). *In focus: Identifying and addressing health disparities among Hispanics.* The Commonwealth Fund.

Kaiser Family Foundation. (2019). *Health and health care for Hispanics in the United States.*

Krogstad, J. M. 2016. "5 Facts about Latinos and Education." Pew Research Center, July 28. http://www.pewresearch.org/fact-tank/2016/07/28/5-facts-aboutlatinos-and-education/

Krogstad, J. M., & Noe-Bustamante, L. (2019, October 14). 7 facts for National Hispanic Heritage Month. Pew Research Center. https://www.pewresearch.org/fact-tank/2019/10/14/facts-for-national-hispanic-heritage-month

Mariscal, E. S. (2014). The strengths perspective and the strengths model of case management: Enhancing the recovery of people with psychiatric disabilities. In A. Francis, V. Pulla, M. Clark, E. S. Mariscal, & I. Ponnuswami (Eds.), *Advancing social work in mental health through strengths based practice* (pp. 118–144). Primrose Hall.

Meissner, D., Hipsman, F., & Aleinikoff, A. (2018). *The U.S. asylum system in crisis: Charting a way forward.* Migration Policy Institute.

Morin, J. L. (2009). *Latino/a rights and justice in the United States.* North Carolina Academic Press.

National Council of Juvenile and Family Court Judges. (2017). *Disproportionality rates for children of color in foster care (fiscal year 2015).*

New York City Health. (2020). Rates of cases, hospitalizations, and deaths by race/ethnicity group. https://www1.nyc.gov/assets/doh/downloads/pdf/imm/covid-19-deaths-race-ethnicity-04162020-1.pdf

Noe-Bustamante, L. (2019). Key facts about U.S. Hispanics and their diverse heritage. Pew Research Center. https://www.pewresearch.org/fact-tank/2019/09/16/key-facts-about-u-s-hispanics

Noe-Bustamante, L., & Flores, A. (2019). Facts on Latinos in the U.S. Pew Research Center. https://www.pewresearch.org/hispanic/fact-sheet/latinos-in-the-u-s-fact-sheet

Organista, K. C. (2009). New practice model for Latinos in need of social work services. *Social Work, 54*(4), 297–305.

Pew Research Center. (2014). *The shifting religious identity of Latinos in the United States.* https://www.pewforum.org/2014/05/07/the-shifting-religious-identity-of-latinos-in-the-united-states

Pew Research Center. (2018). *More Latinos have concerns about their place in America under Trump.* https://www.pewresearch.org/hispanic/2018/10/25/latinos-have-become-more-pessimistic-about-their-place-in-america

Pew Research Center. (2020). *U.S. Latinos among hardest hit by pay cuts job losses due to coronavirus.* https://www.pewresearch.org/fact-tank/2020/04/03/u-s-latinos-among-hardest-hit-by-pay-cuts-job-losses-due-to-coronavirus

Rapp, C. A., & Goscha, R. J. (2011). *The strengths model: A recovery-oriented approach to mental health services.* Oxford University Press.

Rogers, C. (1961). *On becoming a person.* Houghton Mifflin.

Saleebey, D. (Ed.). (2013). *The strengths perspective in social work practice* (6th ed.). Pearson.

Sentencing Project. (2017). *Latino disparities in youth incarceration.*

Taylor, P., Lopez, M. H., Passel, J. S., & Motel, S. (2011). *Unauthorized immigrants: Length of residency, patterns of parenthood.* Pew Hispanic Center. https://www.pewresearch.org/hispanic/2011/12/01/unauthorized-immigrants-length-of-residency-patterns-of-parenthood

"The virus doesn't discriminate but governments do": Latinos disproportionately hit by coronavirus. (2020, April 18). *The Guardian.* https://www.theguardian.com/us-news/2020/apr/18/the-virus-doesnt-discriminate-but-governments-do-latinos-disproportionately-hit-by-coronavirus

Ungar, M. (2013). Resilience, trauma, context, and culture. *Trauma, Violence, & Abuse, 14*(3), 255–266.

U.S. Census Bureau. (2010). Facts for features: Hispanic heritage month 2010. https://www.nrcs.usda.gov/Internet/FSE_DOCUMENTS/nrcs142p2_015178.pdf

U.S. Census Bureau. (2017a). Facts for features: Hispanic heritage month 2017. https://www.census.gov/newsroom/facts-for-features/2017/hispanic-heritage.html

U.S. Census Bureau. (2017b). *School enrollment of the Hispanic population: Two decades of growth.* https://www.census.gov/newsroom/blogs/random-samplings/2017/08/school_enrollmentof.html

Vidal-Ortiz, S., & Martínez, J. (2018). Latinx thoughts: Latinidad with an X. *Latino Studies, 16*, 384–395.

Welland, C., & Ribner, N. (2008). *Healing from violence: Latino men's journey to a new masculinity.* Springer.

Social Work Practice with African American Families

An Afrocentric Intergenerational Solidarity Model

Cheryl Waites Spellman

Multigenerational family networks have been a source of strength for African American families. Multigenerations providing support and care for family members and fictive kin (non-blood relatives) across the life course have been well documented (Billingsley, 1992; Hill, 1971, 1999; Martin & Martin, 1985; McAdoo, 1998; Schiele, 1996, 2000, 2017). Born out of African traditions and adaptation to a harsh environment, multigenerational families have persevered in the face of disparity and oppression spanning 400 years of slavery; years of "Jim Crow"; and decades of segregation, marginalization, and intentional and unintentional racism (Christian, 1995) and economic, educational, and health disparity. Despite these obstacles, people of African descent have a legacy of intergenerational kinship, resilience, spirituality, and hope (Bagley & Carroll, 1998).

As our society ages, multigenerational families will be more common, resulting in longer years of "shared lives" across generations (Bengtson, 2001). It has been predicted that there will be almost equal bands of older adults, middle-generation adults, young adults, adolescents, and children as the 21st century progresses (U.S. Census Bureau, 2010). This statistic holds true for African Americans. The numbers of African American elders, aged 65 years or older, are increasing. In 2017, this group totaled 4,587,094, and it is projected to expand to 12.1 million by 2060 (Administration for Community Living, 2018). Individuals are now more likely to grow older in four-, or even more, generation families; spend an unprecedented number of years in family roles such as grandparent, great-grandparent, great aunt, and great uncle; and remain part of a network of intergenerational family ties (Bengtson, 2001). Kin and non-kin will be available to provide care and assistance to younger families (Silverstein et al., 1995) and caregiving for dependent elders. In view of the changing demographics, it is important to revisit cultural values regarding how families interact across generations.

Historically, cultural values, family practices, and strengths such as special care for children and elders, kinship ties, and collectivism have been part of African American life (Barnes, 2001). Hill (1971, 1999) wrote eloquently about five strengths of African American families: strong achievement orientation, strong work orientation, flexible family roles, strong kinship bonds, and strong religious orientation. Hill (1999) and others have pointed to strengths that are linked to history, culture, values, and cultural adaptations and suggested that building on these strengths is a good strategy for working with African American families (McCullough-Chavis & Waites, 2004).

The challenges individuals and families face today warrant use and revitalization of cultural strengths. Problems such as the following are complex and impactful: drug and alcohol addiction; overrepresentation of African American children in foster care; education, economic, and health disparities; high rates of incarceration; employment and housing insecurity; food deserts; and exposure to violence. Effective strategies to help families as they contend with pressing issues are rooted in African American cultural strengths. Cultural values and practices that sustained families in the past can be used to empower families today.

Other practice approaches have been proposed for culturally competent practice with African Americans and other ethnic and racial groups. However, there is a need for an approach that builds on and restores the strengths and resilience of multigenerational families and intergenerational kinship. This approach may include restoring the influence of the extended family's multigenerational network so that relatives and fictive kin are encouraged to remain involved with family members and step forward to provide support and care. An Afrocentric, intergenerational solidarity approach that acknowledges family networks, as well as the values and traditions that have sustained people of African descent, is a mechanism for promoting family support.

Embracing the legacies and wisdom of past generations and the hope and promise of the future is a framework for best practice.

An Intergenerational Perspective: Theoretical Foundations for Practice

An intergenerational model that provides support and assistance to African American families was first presented by Waites (2008). It brings attention to kinship, intergenerational relationships, and multigenerational families. Strengths, values, and practices that are transmitted across generations, family life cycle stages, intergenerational support, and current cultural context are central to this perspective (Waites, 2008). It provides a framework for understanding the past, exploring the current environment, and using culturally relevant strategies and practices to empower families.

Intergenerational Solidarity

Bengtson (2001) states that "intergenerational bonds are more important than nuclear family ties for well-being and support over the life course" (p. 7). With increased longevity, parents, grandparents, great aunts and great uncles, and other relatives can be available to serve as resources for younger generations. Kin, across several generations, are increasingly called on to provide essential family functions and intergenerational support and care over time.

Bengtson and Schrader (1982) provide a multidimensional construct for understanding intergenerational relationships. Derived from classical social theory, social psychology, and family sociology, their intergenerational solidarity model examines social cohesion between generations. The construct evolved from a longitudinal study consisting of a cross-sectional survey with 2,044 participants from three generational families. Data from 279 participants were collected at three intervals, including the great-grandchild generation. From this research, Bengtson and Schrader constructed an intergenerational solidarity taxonomy containing six elements for understanding intergenerational relationships.

Afrocentric Paradigm

An Afrocentric paradigm fits well with the intergenerational solidarity framework because it affirms human capacities and family and cultural strengths and promotes intergenerational connections (Waites, 2008). It presents a worldview that highlights traditional African philosophical assumptions, which emphasize a holistic, interdependent, and spiritual conception of people and their environment (Schiele, 2000, 2017). The Afrocentric paradigm affirms that there are universal cultural strengths and a spirit of resilience that survived the generational devastations caused by the transatlantic slave trade, bondage, and the oppression and racism that followed. As a result, it is important to understand and respect the customs, practices, and values that are central to African American families and communities.

Family Life Cycle

Families are at the heart of the intergenerational perspective. Families have shared history and futures (McGoldrick et al., 2016); they move through time together. This is often referred to as family life cycle stages. Theses stages have been identified as leaving home, single young adults, joining of families through marriage, the new couple/partners, families with young children, families with adolescents, launching children and moving on, and families in later life (McGoldrick et al., 2016). Multiple family units are formed, and all are a part of the larger multigenerational family. There is a temporal reality associated with multigenerational families, and the family life cycle provides some descriptive information regarding how families move across time.

The stages described by McGoldrick et al. (2016) laid a foundation for understanding African American families and family life cycle stages. African cultural traditions, environmental realities, resiliency, and the diversity of family forms—which evolved from cultural traditions and adaptations to hardships, racism, and inequality—are also relevant. A legacy of strong intergenerational kinship, multigenerational families, and extended family networks is reflected in Hill's (1999) flexible family roles. For example, caregiving is an important value for African American families. Grandparents may step in to assist or raise a grandchild. A single parent may depend on support from parents or grandparents. African American children raised by grandparents often feel filial obligations to care for parents and grandparents (Ruiz & Carlton-LaNey, 1999). Multigenerations may live in the same residence and pool their resources. For African American families, the family life cycle stages have significant intergenerational patterns of assistance and care that are reciprocal over time. These intergenerational supports, in some cases, may be in need of validation, nurturing, and revitalization to strengthen and support troubled families (Waites, 2008).

Afrocentric Intergenerational Practice

The Afrocentric intergenerational practice model presented here builds on the solidarity construct and the Afrocentric paradigm. It acknowledges the diversity and flexibility of the family life cycle and brings attention to traditions and cultural influences. This practice model's basic principles promote a society that values all generations and (1) recognizes that each generation has unique strengths; (2) recognizes the roles of youths, middle generations, and elders in families and communities;

(3) acknowledges conflicts that may occur in intergenerational relationships; (4) encourages collaboration and support across generations; (5) fosters intergenerational kinship and interdependence; (6) fosters public policy that recognizes and addresses the needs of all generations; and (7) supports and nurtures family and cultural strengths. This model is culturally responsive and transforms knowledge and cultural awareness into interventions that support and sustain healthy family functioning (Waites et al., 2004).

Afrocentric Intergenerational Solidarity Model

The Afrocentric intergenerational solidarity model consists of six elements and provides indicators of intergenerational cohesion. The infusion of an Afrocentric paradigm provides culturally relevant issues, questions, and empowerment-oriented strategies. The first element, *associational solidarity*, focuses on the type and frequency of contact between generations. Within an Afrocentric paradigm, assessing family traditions and history regarding communication is important. Once information is obtained, a process of nurturing, reinforcing, and revitalizing contact and communication among family members can be undertaken. Intergenerational communication may go beyond phone calls; traditions such as Sunday dinners, family reunions, and other celebrations are mechanism for connections. Use of FaceTime and social media to share updates can also lead to useful intergenerational communication, strong supportive networks, and enhance the frequency and quality of contact.

The second element, *affectional solidarity*, addresses the expressed closeness, warmth, and trust found in intergenerational kinships. The indicators call for the practitioner to examine emotional ties to family and community, signs of intergenerational conflict, and the overall reciprocity of positive sentiment among

family members and across generations. With an Afrocentric paradigm, affiliations with and sentiments toward the extended family, and the African American community as a whole, must also be explored. The goal is to assess and address the issues of affection, trust, and closeness and to support and nurture relational understanding and reciprocity across generations.

The third element, *consensual solidarity*, examines agreements of values and beliefs. The indicators call for an assessment of intrafamilial concordance—Afrocentric values, beliefs, and traditions, as well as the cultural strengths, enhance the cultural relevance of practice. Understanding family members' generational differences and their willingness to build dialogue, respect, and collaboration is also important. The model suggests that practitioners encourage the understanding of cultural strengths, resilience, as well as contemporary perspectives. Attempts should be made to support the family and extended family as they engage in history reminding; consciousness raising; and intergenerational understanding, respect, and helping.

The fourth element, *functional solidarity*, addresses the frequency of intergenerational exchanges of assistance and resources. The indicators direct the assessment of help-giving and -receiving and how families assist and support each other. The roles of collectivism, extended family support, and community support from churches, lodges, fraternal orders, and so forth are also assessed. Mechanisms to support equitable intergenerational care and the use of formal and informal resources are suggested.

Normative solidarity, the fifth element, addresses filial responsibility and obligations. The indicators are family roles and the strength of obligation to those roles. The Afrocentric paradigm expands this sense of obligation not only to parents, grandparents, children, and grandchildren but also to the extended family, fictive kin, and the community as a whole.

Intergenerational family and extended family support and the use of community programs and formal resources are encouraged.

The sixth and last element, *structural solidarity*, highlights the opportunity for intergenerational interaction as it relates to residential propinquity, environmental conditions, and access to supportive resource. The indicators address family structure in the form of number and types of relations, family proximity, and environmental supports and factors. The practitioner is charged with employing strategies to help families rethink how to address structural barriers. This could take the form of family members organizing and sharing transportation and communication resources or forming a family support network for respite, support, and celebration.

Using the Model

The Afrocentric intergenerational solidarity model can be used in harmony with other approaches. Practitioners are directed to explore each of the intergenerational solidarity elements with family members using the six identified practice strategies. Associational solidarity is explored by asking family members questions about their family traditions and how they keep in touch with each other. Family solidarity is enhanced when there are traditions, activities, and history that serve to keep family members connected—for example, Sunday dinners at a relative's home, regular phone calls, church or religious service attendance, family reunions, celebrations, or holiday activities. The practitioner encourages family members to reach out to each other or participate in family events.

Affectional solidarity questions are posed to family members by exploring whom they feel particularly close to and why. Helping family members understand family roles and relationships and how they influence affectional solidarity is an important practice strategy. Affectional solidarity can be nurtured by encouraging a sense of intergenerational

kinship—that is, affection for and appreciation of family and extended family members. The practitioner role is to aid family members in identifying and developing closer ties.

Consensual solidarity can be explored by discussing family values and by affirming a shared vision for family life. Exploring family members' perceptions and generational differences and similarities provides information regarding family solidarity. Gauging the family's sense of cultural pride and their African American identify is also pertinent. Cultural pride can serve as a unifying force for family solidarity. History reminding to facilitate appreciation of family cultural strengths is appropriate as a practice strategy and might include providing information about cultural history, supporting family opportunities to share thoughts and information about cultural values and beliefs, and engaging family members in activities that will enhance cultural pride. Communities and families often have Kwanzaa celebrations, festivals, and religious-related programs; enjoy movies together; share family pictures; participate in relevant community causes; or engage in other culturally inspired activities. These resources can serve to connect the family and facilitate consensual solidarity.

Functional solidarity is assessed by identification of the "go-to" family members when someone needs assistance. It is also important to identify family roles and resources and how support and care are exchanged across the family and the generations. The practice strategy is to create or restore the family helping network and involves supporting family members as they embrace a collective responsibility and intergenerational support and care for all family members.

Normative solidarity is assessed by exploring expectations regarding family roles. It is also crucial to discuss what happens when someone is not able to perform the designated role. What are the family norms for who should step in? The practice strategy is to explore, affirm, strengthen, and formalize the family members' commitment to one another. This may take the form of encouraging the development of multigenerational networks in which children, parents, grandparents, aunts, uncles, and fictive kin all play a role in supporting and caring for family members. Because this responsibility can be demanding, connecting families with community resources such as family support programs, support groups for caregivers, food security programs, housing assistance programs, financial assistance, and other programs that serve to strengthen families and extended family helping is crucial.

Structural solidarity is explored by assessing family composition and proximity, as well as exploring environmental conditions and access to resources. The role of the practitioner is to help family members identify issues and overcome barriers to a helpful intergenerational operating structure. This might include completing a genogram to fully identify and locate family members and then exploring environmental challenges (safety, affordability, and access) and resources.

Use of this model involves the exploration of all solidarity elements. Family members and families may show strengths in a specific area. If not, the practitioner can use one or all of the suggested practice strategies. A case example presents contemporary family issues and suggested strategies.

Case Example

Denise is a 32-year-old African American single, divorced mother who is trying to cope with caregiving for her son, daughter, and grandmother. Denise's 9-year-old son, David, has been referred to the school social worker due to excessive absences. The family living arrangement has recently changed. Denise's 71-year-old grandmother had a stroke 6 months ago and is now residing with Denise and her son and 14-year-old daughter in a two-bedroom apartment. Denise is distraught because her maternal grandmother was the caretaker and "the strong one in the family," and no other family members have stepped forward to help. All solidarity elements must be assessed. However, there is a pressing need for support and assistance for Denise and her family. This calls for focusing first on normative and functional solidarity. The worker can help Denise examine her current caregiving roles. It is also important for the worker to discuss Denise's decision to care for her grandmother. What is her sense of obligation and commitment to this role and other family resources? Once Denise has explored her caregiving values, beliefs, the realities of her situation, and her intentions, she and the practitioner can develop a plan. This might include identifying family resources, discussing the availability of other family and extended family members for support and caregiving, and other community and more formal resources.

Conclusion

In view of contemporary issues facing families and the significance of multigenerational families, culturally relevant models of practice are called for. The Afrocentric intergenerational solidarity model is a strengths-based approach that works to empower multigenerational families and intergenerational relationships. It facilitates an understanding of how intergenerational relationships can be supported and provides multidimensional guidance. The intergenerational model considers generational transmission from a strengths perspective, examining not only problems but also the assets that multiple generations may provide. It is a framework that taps into the power, resilience, and capital from past and current traditions and relationships. Application of the Afrocentric intergenerational practice model, in conjunction with other empowerment-oriented approaches, is a best practice method especially relevant for work with vulnerable

African American families in need of nurturance and care.

Helpful Resource

Waites, C. (2009). Building on strengths: Intergenerational practice with African American families. *Social Work, 54*(3), 278–287. doi:10.1093/sw/54.3.278

References

Administration for Community Living. (2018). 2018 profile of African Americans age 65 and over. U.S. Department of Health and Human Services. https://acl.gov

Bagley, C. A., & Carroll, J. (1998). Healing forces in African-American families. In H. I. McCubbin, E. A. Thompson, A. I. Thompson, & J. A. Farrell (Eds.), *Resiliency in African-American families* (pp. 117–143). Sage.

Barnes, S. (2001). Stressors and strengths: A theoretical and practical examination of nuclear single parent, and augmented African American families. *Families in Society, 85,* 449–461.

Bengtson, V. L. (2001). Beyond the nuclear family: The increasing importance of multi-generational bonds. *Journal of Marriage and the Family, 63,* 1–16.

Bengtson, V. L., & Schrader, S. (1982). Parent–child relationships. In D. Mangen & W Peterson (Eds.), *Handbook of research instruments in social gerontology* (Vol. 2, pp. 115–185). University of Minnesota Press.

Billingsley, A. (1992). *Climbing Jacob's ladder: The enduring legacy of African-American families.* Simon & Schuster.

Christian, C. M. (1995). *Black age: The African American experience.* Houghton Mifflin.

Hill, R. B. (1971). *The strength of Black families.* Emerson-Hall.

Hill, R. B. (1999). *The strengths of African American families: Twenty-five years later.* University Press of America.

Martin, J., & Martin, E. (1985). *The helping tradition in the Black family and community.* NASW Press.

McAdoo, H. P. (1998). African-American families: Strengths and realities. In H. I. McCubbin, E. A. Thompson, A. I. Thompson, & J. A, Futrell (Eds.), *Resiliency in African-American families* (pp. 17–30). Sage.

McCullough-Chavis, A., & Waites, C. (2004). Genograms with African American families: Considering cultural context. *Journal of Family Social Work, 8*(2), 1–19.

McGoldrick, M., Preto, N. G., & Carter, B. (2016). *Expanding family life* (5th ed.). Pearson.

Ruiz, D., & Carlton-LaNey, I. (1999). The increase in intergenerational African American families headed by grandmothers. *Journal of Sociology & Social Welfare, 26*(4), 71–86.

Schiele, J. H. (1996). Afrocentricity: An emerging paradigm in social work practice. *Social Work, 41,* 284–294.

Schiele, J. H. (2000). *Human services and the Afrocentric paradigm.* Haworth.

Schiele, J. H. (2017). The Afrocentric paradigm in social work: A historical perspective and future outlook. *Journal of Human Behavior in the Social Environment, 27*(1–2), 15–26.

Silverstein, M., Parrott, T. M., & Bengtson V. L. (1995). Factors that predispose middle-aged sons and daughters to provide social support to older parents. *Journal of Marriage and the Family, 57,* 465–476.

U.S. Census Bureau. (2010, May). The next four decades: The older population in the United States: 2010 to 2050. Population estimates and projections.

Waites, C. (2008). *Social work practice with African-American families: An intergenerational perspective.* Routledge.

Waites, C., Macowan, M. J., Pennell, J., Carlton-LaNey, I., & Weil, M. (2004). Increasing the cultural responsiveness of family group conferencing. *Social Work, 49,* 291–300.

Social Work Practice with Asians and Pacific Islanders

Jessica Euna Lee and Khadija Khaja

Asians and Pacific Islanders in the United States are a heterogeneous group representing diverse ethnic groups, countries of origin, national identities, and political histories. This population is the nation's fastest growing racial and ethnic category and includes more than 24 million people (U.S. Census Bureau, 2020; Pew Research Center, 2020). The Asia–Pacific region spans multiple continents and is divided into subregions as depicted in Figure 115.1.

In this chapter, the United Nations' classification of subregions is used: Central Asia, East Asia, South Asia, Southeast Asia, and Pacific Islands. *Asian and Pacific Islander* (API) is used as an inclusive term to refer to the diverse people with origins in countries, states, territories, and jurisdictions (or of the diaspora) in the identified Asia–Pacific geographic region.

Demographics and Definitions

Asians and Pacific Islanders in the United States originate from more than 26 different countries, and the API population in the United States is estimated to be more than 24 million (U.S. Census Bureau, 2020).[1] There are many ethnicities, hyphenated identities, and national identities among APIs, who represent the nation's fastest growing racial group (U.S. Census Bureau, 2020). APIs include immigrants, refugees, U.S.-born citizens, naturalized citizens, undocumented immigrants, asylum-seekers, native communities in U.S. jurisdictions, non-immigrants (e.g., international students and fiancées), and single- or multiracial individuals.

Racial classifications of APIs in the United States have changed throughout history and continue to vary in political meaning. Currently, the U.S. Census Bureau (2020) defines "Asian" to include people with origins in "the Far East, Southeast Asia, or the Indian subcontinent." The Asian population is estimated as 22.6 million according to 2018 Census data (U.S. Census Bureau, 2020). The category "Native Hawaiian or other Pacific Islander" is classified as individuals having origins

---

1. This figure includes 2018 Census population estimates for "Asian alone or in combination" in addition to "Native Hawaiian and other Pacific Islander alone or in combination with one or more races" categories (U.S. Census Bureau, 2020).

Central Asia
East Asia
Pacific Islands
South Asia
Southeast Asia

FIGURE 115.1 The Asia–Pacific region.

in "Hawaii, Guam, Samoa, or other Pacific Islands." Approximately 1.6 million Native Hawaiians/Pacific Islanders reside within the United States (U.S. Census Bureau, 2020).

The largest percentage of APIs in the United States are from China, the Philippines, India, Vietnam, Korea, and Japan (U.S. Census Bureau, 2020). Census data show that the growth rate of the Asian population from 2010 to 2018 was 27.4% (Frey, 2019). The metropolitan areas of New York City, San Francisco, and Los Angeles house the largest Asian populations in the United States. During the past decade, metropolitan areas experiencing the largest growth in API populations in Midwest and Northeast states (Frey, 2019; U.S. Census Bureau, 2018).

Social Considerations

There are substantial differences in income, poverty rates, education, acculturation, and other social factors among the API population in the United States. Income inequality is now the highest among Asians relative to all racial groups according to studies by Pew Research Center (Kochhar & Cilluffo, 2018). Increasing diversity in education and income among API subgroups reflects structural conditions such as changing immigration trends and geopolitics. Since the 1980s, API groups arriving in the United States have diversified—highly educated API immigration grew through the H-1B visa program, and resettlement of refugees fleeing political violence from Southeast Asian countries also increased (Refugee Processing Center, 2020).[2] Asian households in the United States have a median income of $81,331, which is higher than the national median household income for all races of $61,372 (U.S. Census Bureau, 2018). Yet, most APIs' household incomes fall below both medians. Indians and Filipinos have the highest median household incomes in the United States. Poverty rates are highest among Burmese and Bhutanese groups, which are primarily composed of recently resettled refugees (Kochhar & Cilluffo, 2018; U.S. Census Bureau, 2018). Educational attainment among the total API population is higher than that of the overall national population.

API families and households may be mixed-status and/or multicultural because

2. These trends refer to the years 1980–2017, prior to immigration policy changes that occurred during the Trump Administration and the COVID-19 pandemic.

family members across generations may hold different immigration statuses, carry different ethnic and national identities, or speak different languages. Nearly 74% of APIs speak a language other than English at home (U.S. Census Bureau, 2018). Because API subgroups reside in diverse contexts in the United States, it is vital to understand their unique processes of acculturation and assimilation. Acculturation is theorized to be a lifelong process for immigrants and ethnic minorities, which results when people of different cultures come into contact and undergo changes in culture patterns (Berry, 1997). Berry (1997) theorized that in the acculturation process, a trade-off occurs between retention of heritage cultural identity and adoption of that of dominant/ mainstream society. Portes and Zhou (1993) considered structural perspectives of ethnic disadvantage to formulate the theory of segmented assimilation. Segmented assimilation suggests that outcomes of individual-level assimilation are influenced by macro-level social conditions. This framework recognizes that American society is increasingly diversifying and stratifying, resulting in different "segments" into which new immigrants may assimilate (Portes & Zhou, 1993).

Racialization in the United States occurs along a continuum, which reflects longstanding systems of racial categorization and oppression. These systems present varying challenges for APIs who may experience different degrees of racism and forms of oppression. As more API immigrant families integrated into U.S. society after 1965, the "model minority" stereotype emerged. This stereotype maintains a standard of achievement for APIs and suggests that Asian immigrants have assimilated into American culture by abiding by the values of the majority group (Chou & Feagin, 2015). The model minority myth and accompanying "achievement paradox" present complex privileges and challenges for APIs, particularly younger APIs

(Lee & Zhou, 2015). The model minority myth is limiting—not just for APIs but also for other racial minorities—because it reinforces a hegemonic standard while masking differential experiences among API groups. The COVID-19 pandemic presents sociopolitical challenges for APIs with the emergence of Sinophobia (Kambhampaty, 2020). Stop AAPI Hate has been tracking anti-Asian incidents in the United States since March 2020. According to their August 2020 report, there were 2,583 anti-Asian incidents across 47 states. These incidents included various types of discrimination, such as verbal harassment, deliberate avoidance, and physical assault, and potential civil rights violations, such as workplace discrimination (Stop AAPI Hate, 2020).

Research on API populations in the United States demonstrates that immigrants and refugees receive significantly less health and mental health care than native-born populations, even though APIs' health needs may be greater (Chu & Sue, 2011; Grabovschi et al., 2013). It is important to note that APIs represent a substantial aging population, with nearly 25% of the API population in 2018 being older than age 55 years (U.S. Census Bureau, 2018). Mental health conditions are a significant challenge for APIs. National data indicate that 21.1% of the Native Hawaiian and Pacific Islander population and 14.7% of the Asian population experienced mental illness in 2018 [Substance Abuse and Mental Health Services Administration (SAMHSA), 2019]. Yet, only 10.9% of Native Hawaiians and Pacific Islanders and 6.3% of Asian American adults received mental health services that year (SAMHSA, 2019). Suicide was the leading cause of death for APIs aged 10–24 years [Centers for Disease Control and Prevention (CDC), 2018]. National data indicate that suicidality among Asian American young women is higher than that of other racial categories in the United States (CDC, 2018). The trends in underutilization of services may be attributed to barriers to health access, stigma, and differences in help-seeking (Abe-Kim et al., 2007; Augsberger et al., 2015).

East Asians

East Asia includes China, Hong Kong, Macao, North Korea, South Korea, Japan, Mongolia, and Tibet. East Asians are the largest API subgroup in the United States, with the largest percentage of individuals having origins in China, followed by Korea and Japan. The Immigration Act of 1965 resulted in large waves of East Asian immigrants during the 20th century. East Asians possess substantial social capital through long-standing co-ethnic communities, religious institutions, and ethnic organizations. Sinophobia and anti-Asian discrimination proliferated during the COVID-19 pandemic (Gover et al., 2020). Chinese were often the targeted ethnic group during these incidents; however, 60% of respondents were not Chinese (Stop AAPI Hate, 2020).

A substantial body of literature demonstrates that East Asian populations in the United States underutilize health and mental health services; in particular, Koreans have the lowest rates (Lee et al., 2015; Li et al., 2016). Health insurance and a usual source of care are among the main factors driving health care utilization among East Asians (Li et al., 2016). Data indicate that East Asian families demonstrate the lowest rates of parent and child English language usage among API groups (Huang et al., 2012). Especially underserved East Asian subgroups in the United States include older, less educated, and newer female immigrants (Li et al., 2016). Studies connect the model minority stereotype to misconceptions that East Asian Americans have less health and mental health problems relative to other ethnic groups (Huang et al., 2012). However, East Asian groups exhibit higher risk of mental health conditions relative to other racial groups (SAMSHA, 2019).

East Asian cultures are traditionally marked by collectivism, social harmony, and interdependence (Yoon & Lau, 2008). Researchers suggest that this carries social and psychological implications for East Asians, particularly the children of immigrants, because it influences family dynamics, parenting, and outcomes for children (Huang et al., 2012; Yoon & Lau, 2008). East Asian immigrant parents may bring a "success frame" and family pressure may be concentrated on younger generations. Scholars describe traditional East Asian parenting practices as "harsher, more intrusive and less collaborative" than U.S. native-born parenting behaviors (Hwang & Wood, 2009, p. 126). Parenting strategies among East Asian families may not align with dominant U.S. constructions of parenting styles. Data indicate that this may correspond to differences in experiences with child welfare services (Zhai & Gao, 2009). Decision-making in East Asian families may occur collectively or be directed more by the parents and the older generation rather than individually. Social workers should therefore be mindful of family dynamics and issues pertaining to confidentiality and clients' autonomy.

South Asians

It is speculated that by 2065, Asian Americans will be the largest immigrant population in the United States. The South Asian population grew exponentially at 40% in 7 years, from 3.5 million in 2010 to 5.4 million in 2017. This includes people coming from countries such as India, Pakistan, Bangladesh, Sri Lanka, Nepal, Afghanistan, Bhutan, and Maldives. Many South Asians have also sought asylum in the United States during the past 10 years, with U.S. Immigration and Customs Enforcement detaining 3,013 South Asians since 2017 and U.S. Customs and Border Patrol arresting 17,119 South Asians from 2014 to 2018 due to border enforcement (AsAm News, 2019). South

Asians who immigrate to the United States will bring their diverse traditions, beliefs systems, and religions while usually trying to maintain their rich South Asian "identities, family ties, and loyalties" back in their home country (Chandras et al., 2013, p. 2). The Asian population is "the fastest growing in the United States, and Asian Indians are the second largest group (after the Chinese), about 18% of Asians in the United States" (Bhandari, 2018, p. 2; U.S. Department of Commerce, Bureau of the Census, 2010).

Social Services

Like other Asian American communities, the South Asian community has long been described as a model minority due to its members' increasing socioeconomic status and vast educational achievements in the United States (Dasgupta & Warrier, 1996). Yet research shows that many South Asians are still "careful about publicly acknowledging social problems including but not limited to homelessness, drug addiction, sexual assault, and domestic violence" or mental health issues, concerned about stigma and saving face in their communities (Bhandari, 2018, p. 2). Diverse sexual and gender identities are still often stereotyped in many South Asian families, which could lead to adolescents being careful in the "coming out" process, exhibiting caution or hesitancy in where they seek support. A culture of shame and silence and keeping things within the nuclear or extended family still permeates many South Asian families, although this is starting to improve.

One gap in cultural-appropriate intervention regards South Asian older adults because "only 35% of older people (aged over 65 years) can speak English and only 21% can read and write English" (Blakemore et al., 2018, p. 2). Many rely on their first language of Hindi, Urdu, Punjabi, etc., which creates challenges for completion of screening tools and diagnostic tests, with more education needed on

dementia to ensure more help-seeking so that early intervention and treatment reduce the "burden of dementia for patients and family caregivers (Blakemore et al., 2018, p. 2). More culturally responsive assistance in nursing homes or long-term health facilities has also been recommended.

Among South Asians, "domestic violence is as high as 40% for physical and sexual abuse and about 50% if emotional and psychological abuse is also included" (Bhandari, 2018, p. 2; Mahapatra, 2012; Raj & Silverman, 2007). As Bhandari (2018) notes,

> The South Asian women experiencing domestic violence are at the intersection of disadvantages that range from their immigrant status, insensitivity of the mainstream services, perceptions of maintaining the family honor including the pressure created by the construction of their community as a "model minority." (p. 3)

Numerous studies have found that many South Asian women tend to reach out more to "familial support and friends in the non-kin group when reaching out for help" rather than community social service supports (Bhandari, 2018, p. 4; Yoshioka et al., 2003).

Cultural Adaptation of Services

Numerous studies have found key areas in which South Asians can be assisted to feel comfortable to access mainstream social service supports. Terragni et al. (2018) identified the following critical areas to ensure cultural adaptation of services for South Asians: (1) "approaching the community in the right way (i.e. build relation of trust, overcome fear, create door opener, involve community where applicable, use team workers from the same community, and capitalize on desire for change)"; (2) "intervention as a place for social relations (i.e. create opportunities for building networks, mobilize existing resources, make participants feel at ease"; (3) increase "support from public authorities/other relevant actors (i.e. build alliances with local institutions and find creative solutions)"; and (4) "be reflexive and flexible (i.e. acknowledge different values/practices and adapt to participants' pace)" (p. 54). They also suggested that main challenges that service providers still face and need to improve when working with South Asians include language and communication, cultural adaptation, lack of long-term investment and commitment, limitation of using ethnicity to define groups, differences in acculturations, differences in social class, and the influence of paternalism in many South Asian families. Faith-based intervention can be an important component in assisting South Asian families; considering this intervention in practice can be helpful if a client requests to do so.

Violence against South Asians continues to be a problem—for example, a "White supremacist neo-Nazi gunman stormed a Sikh temple in Oak Creek, Wisconsin, killing six worshippers" (Caswell, 2015, abstract). Since September 11, 2001, many violent attacks, arsons, bullying, and vandalism of South Asian temples, mosques, or other venues have taken place, with hate crimes increasing dramatically against this community.

Southeast Asians

Southeast Asia includes the geographic region from eastern India to China and is divided into Mainland and Maritime (or island) zones (Figure 115.2). Countries in Mainland Southeast Asia include Cambodia, Burma/Myanmar, Laos, (West) Malaysia, Thailand, and Vietnam. Countries in Maritime Southeast Asia include Brunei, Indonesia, (East) Malaysia, the Philippines, Singapore, and Timor-Leste. Southeast Asians represent the majority of refugees resettled in the United States.

Refugee groups include Burmese, Cambodian, Hmong, Indonesian, and Vietnamese peoples. Filipino and Vietnamese Americans are two of the largest ethnic groups among the API population currently residing in the United States (Chen & Lewis, 2018). Filipinos were among the first Southeast Asians to migrate to the United States, the earliest arriving in the late 19th century and then larger waves arriving after 1965 (Gallardo & Batalova, 2020). Mass migration of Southeast Asian refugees began in 1975 as Cambodian, Hmong, and Vietnamese refugees fled political violence, including the Khmer Rouge genocide, mass bombings of Laos, and the Vietnam War.

Southeast Asian refugees began arriving prior to the U.S. Refugee Act of 1980, during a time when the country lacked an infrastructure for refugee resettlement. Thus, the first Southeast Asian refugees were "resettled ad hoc" throughout the United States (Southeast Asian Resource Action Center & Asian Americans Advancing Justice, 2020). The advocacy work of early Southeast Asian mutual assistance associations and ethnic community-based organizations was instrumental to the passage of the Refugee Resettlement Act of 1980 (Southeast Asian Resource Action Center & Asian Americans Advancing Justice, 2020), which led to the formation of the U.S. system for humanitarian resettlement. Southeast Asian refugees have continued to arrive in the United States since 1980, with Burmese refugees representing some of the most recent arrivals (Refugee Processing Center, 2020). Due to their premigration experiences, many Southeast Asian refugees have experienced political violence and complex trauma. An extensive body of literature on the mental health of Southeast Asian refugees indicates high incidents of post-traumatic stress disorder (PTSD), depression, and psychiatric disorders among the community (Gonzalez Benson et al., 2020; Hsu et al., 2004; Kim & Kim, 2014). Studies and national data report as many as 60–70%

FIGURE 115.2 Southeast Asia.

of Southeast Asians have been diagnosed with PTSD (Wagner et al., 2013). Data demonstrate that Southeast Asian families have significantly poorer physical health and mental health outcomes compared to other API groups and that Southeast Asian children are at higher risk for mental health problems (SAMHSA, 2019).

There are considerable disparities among Southeast Asian ethnic groups (Kochhar & Cilluffo, 2018). Data demonstrate that Southeast Asian refugees are more likely to experience poverty compared to other Asian subgroups and also more likely to live in disadvantaged contexts (Huang et al., 2012). However, Filipinos have the second highest median household incomes among API subgroups and are more likely to be naturalized citizens and insured (Gallardo & Batalova, 2020). Vietnamese and Burmese groups in the United States, like other Asians, exhibit high academic achievement and a "success frame" trope as demonstrated by other groups (Lee &

Zhou, 2015). Family support and social support among co-ethnic ties are found to be integral to the positive outcomes for Southeast Asians (Singh et al., 2015).

Pacific Islanders

Pacific Islanders in the United States refer to people with origins in Melanesian Islands, Micronesian Islands, and Polynesian Islands (Mokuau et al., 2008). The Pacific Islands geographic region includes more than 15 countries and territories across thousands of islands in the Pacific Ocean (Godinet et al., 2019). Native Hawaiians and Pacific Islanders are classified as a distinct racial category by the U.S. Census Bureau and are one of the smallest groups in the United States, with an estimated population of 1.6 million (Godinet et al., 2019; U.S. Census Bureau, 2018). The Pacific Islands consist of the subregions Melanesia, Micronesia, and

Polynesia. Polynesia includes Hawai'i, Samoan Islands, Tonga, Tahiti, Aotearoa, and Tokelau. Micronesia includes Guam, Mariana Islands, Saipan, Palau, Caroline Islands, Kosrae, Pohnpei, Chuuk, Yap, Marshall Islands, and Kiribati. Melanesia includes Fiji, Papua New Guinea, Vanuatu, and Solomon Islands. The Pacific Islands embody complex political histories, with several islands and nations holding relationships with the United States. Pacific Islanders often hold transnational and multi-cultural identities and vary in citizenship and immigration status (Godinet et al., 2019).

Native Hawaiians, Samoans, and Chamorros comprise the majority of Pacific Islanders in the United States. Native Hawaiians are First Nations people and are indigenous to Hawai'i (Braun et al., 2015). Samoans include people from American Samoa and Samoa, the former being a U.S. territory and the latter an independent nation. *Chamorros* refers to Indigenous peoples of Guam, a U.S. territory. The 2019 article by Godinet et al. describes social work practice implications of transnationalism among Pacific Islanders. Pacific cultures, including Native Hawaiian, Samoan, and Chamorro, traditionally carry deep ties to the land and place importance on family, community, interdependence, inclusivity, nature, and spirituality (Godinet et al., 2019). Pacific Islanders may experience complex acculturation experiences due to colonization- and immigration-based issues (Braun et al., 2015; Godinet et al., 2019).

Pacific Island nations may face geographic isolation, vulnerability to climate change, and a limited economy. Extreme poverty is not pervasive among all Pacific Islands; however, "multidimensional poverty" attributed to lack of access to resources may be a significant concern (Executive Board of the United Nations Development Programme, 2017). Pacific Islanders exhibit poorer health outcomes and shorter life expectancies relative to Asians and the overall U.S. population. Native Hawaiians

and Samoans also have shorter life expectancies than other ethnic groups residing on the same islands. Native Hawaiians and Pacific Islanders have the second highest rates of mental illness out of all racial categories in the United States (SAMSHA, 2019). Data indicate that in the state of Hawai'i, the prevalence of depression among Native Hawaiians and Pacific Islanders is nearly twice that of the overall state prevalence (Braun et al., 2015).

Elders are valued among Pacific cultures and bear responsibility for the transmission of traditions and language to younger generations. Pacific families are more likely to care for elder relatives compared to the U.S. population (Braun et al., 2015). However, Pacific Islander older adults are a particularly vulnerable population because they have some of the lowest incomes and highest poverty rates among ethnic groups. Integrating native languages into service delivery, establishing personal connections, and respecting spirituality and family dynamics are vital (Godinet et al., 2019; Mokuau et al., 2008).

Conclusion

Asians and Pacific Islanders represent a vibrant population in the United States. APIs overall demonstrate successful social outcomes in educational attainment and participation in the U.S. labor market. Heterogeneity and disparities among APIs are not fully understood due to the dearth of ethnic-specific studies. Policy decisions and systems such as the model minority myth may not fully consider the historic trauma and social challenges that some APIs may face, which warrants social workers to take actively anti-oppressive approaches to practice.

Social workers should be mindful of the diverse political, colonization, and immigration histories of API clients to fully consider the person in their environment. Responding to cultural diversity is essential to promote health equity and wellness. A CDC report states that disparities in the quality of care among minoritized racial and ethnic groups are correlated with poorer health and higher mortality rates (Terlizzi et al., 2019). Factors that are associated with these disparities include lack of a diverse service provider workforce and biases and perceptions of clients and providers (Jones et al., 2019; Terlizzi et al., 2019). APIs exhibit underutilization of health and mental health services while experiencing higher rates of mental health conditions (SAMHSA, 2019). Help-seeking behaviors, health literacy, cultural constructions of illness, competing needs, language, stigma, and insurance status all have an impact on health and well-being. As studies convey the significance of social support among API families and communities, interventions that harness stakeholder strengths would enable culturally salient care. Throughout the United States, API groups have established strong social networks, communities, and mutual assistance associations. Effective practice with APIs may be strengthened by integrating cultural humility and Indigenous frameworks of understanding (Fisher-Borne et al., 2015; Tervalon & Murray-Garcia, 1998).

References

Abe-Kim, J., Takeuchi, D. T., Hong, S., Zane, N., Sue, S., Spencer, M. S., Appel, H., Nicdao, E., & Alegria, M. (2007). Use of mental health-related services among immigrant and US-born Asian Americans. *American Journal of Public Health, 97*(1), 91–98. doi:10.2105/AJPH.2006.098541

AsAm News. (2019). South Asians grew 40% in the U.S. in just 7 years. https://asamnews.com/2019/05/16/south-asians-grew-40-in-the-u-s-in-just-7-years

Augsberger, A., Yeung, A., Dougher, M., & Hahm, H. C. (2015). Factors influencing the underutilization of mental health services among Asian American women with a history of depression and suicide. *BMC Health Services Research, 15*, 542. https://doi.org/10.1186/s12913-015-1191-7

Berry, J. (1997). Immigration, acculturation, and adaptation. *Applied Psychology, 46*(1), 5–34.

Bhandari, S. (2018). South Asian women's coping strategies in the face of domestic violence in the United States.

Health Care for Women International, 39(2), 220–242. https://doi.org/10.1080/07399332.2017.1385615

Blakemore, A., Kenning, C., Mirza, N., Daker-White, G., Panagioti, M., & Waheeed, W. (2018). Dementia in UK South Asians: A scoping review of the literature. *BMJ Open Access, 8*(4), e020290. doi:10.1136/bmjopen-2017-020290

Braun, K. L., Kim, B. J., Kaʻopua, L. S., Mokuau, N., & Browne, C. V. (2015). Native Hawaiian and Pacific Islander elders: What gerontologists should know. *The Gerontologist, 55*(6), 912–919. https://doi.org/10.1093/geront/gnu072

Caswell, M. (2015). *Documenting South Asian American struggles against racism: Community archives in a post-9/11 world.* https://link.springer.com/chapter/10.1057/9781137032720_10

Centers for Disease Control and Prevention. (2018). *CDC WISQARS Fatal Injury Data Visualization Tool.* https://wisqars-viz.cdc.gov:8006/explore-data/home

Chandras, K. V., Chandras, S. V., & DeLambo, D. A. (2013). *Counseling Asian–American Indians from India: Implications for training multicultural counselors.* https://www.counseling.org/docs/default-source/vistas/counseling-asian-american-indians-from-india---implications-for-training-multicultural-counselors.pdf?sfvrsn=dfac6309_10

Chen, H. M., & Lewis, D. C. (2018). Working with Asian American individuals, couples and families: A Toolkit for stakeholders. National Resource Center for Healthy Marriage and Families. Retrieved from: https://www.healthymarriageandfamilies.org/sites/default/files/Resource%20Files/AsianAm_Toolkit_RevSep2018.pdf

Chou, R. S., & Feagin, J. R. (2015). *The myth of the model minority: Asian Americans facing racism.* Paradigm.

Chu, J. P., & Sue, S. (2011). Asian American mental health: What we know and what we don't know. *Online Readings in Psychology and Culture, 3*(1), 1–18.

Dasgupta, S., & Warrier, S. (1996). In the footsteps of "Arundhati": Asian Indian women's experience of domestic violence in the United States. *Violence Against Women, 2*, 238–259. doi:10.1177/1077801296002003002

Executive Board of the United Nations Development Programme. (2017). *Subregional programme document for the Pacific Island countries and territories (2018–2022).* https://open.undp.org/download/CPD/pacific_island2018_2022.pdf

Fisher-Borne, M., Cain, J. M., & Martin, S. L. (2015). From mastery to accountability: Cultural humility as an alternative to cultural competence. *Social Work Education, 34*(2), 165–181.

Frey, W. H. (2019). Report: Six maps that reveal America's expanding racial diversity. Brookings. https://www.brookings.edu/research/americas-racial-diversity-in-six-maps

Gallardo, L. H., & Batalova, J. (2020). Filipino immigrants in the United States. *Migration Information Source.*

Godinet, M. T., Vakalahi, H. O., & Mokuau, N. (2019). Transnational Pacific Islanders: Implications for social work. *Social Work, 64*(2), 113–122.

Gonzalez Benson, O., Wachter, K., Lee, J., Nichols, D., & Hylton, E. (2020, August 31). Social work scholarship on forced migration: A scoping review. *British Journal of Social Work,* bcaa081. https://doi.org/10.1093/bjsw/bcaa081

Gover, A. R., Harper, S. B., & Langton, L. (2020). Anti-Asian hate crime during the COVID-19 pandemic: Exploring the reproduction of inequality. *American Journal of Criminal Justice, 45,* 647–667. https://doi.org/10.1007/s12103-020-09545-1

Grabovschi, C., Loignon, C., & Fortin, M. (2013). Mapping the concept of vulnerability related to health care disparities: A scoping review. *BMC Health Services Research, 13*(94).

Hsu, E., Davies, C. A., & Hansen, D. (2004). Understanding mental health needs of Southeast Asian refugees: Historical, cultural, and contextual challenges. *Clinical Psychology Review, 24*(2), 193–213.

Huang, K. Y., Calzada, E., Cheng, S., & Brotman, L. M. (2012). Physical and mental health disparities among young children of Asian immigrants. *Journal of Pediatrics, 160*(2), 331–336.e1. https://doi.org/10.1016/j.jpeds.2011.08.005

Hwang, W. C., & Wood, J. J. (2009). Acculturative family distancing: Links with self-reported symptomology among Asian Americans and Latinos. *Child Psychiatry and Human Development, 40,* 123–138.

Jones, N., Breen, N., Farhat, T., Das, R., & Palmer, R. (2019). Cross-cutting themes to advance the science of minority health and health disparities. *American Journal of Public Health, 109*(Suppl. 1), S48–S55.

Kambhampaty, A. P. (2020). "I will not stand silent." *Time.* https://time.com/5858649/racism-coronavirus

Kim, I., & Kim, W. (2014). Post-resettlement challenges and mental health of Southeast Asian refugees in the United States. *Best Practices in Mental Health, 10*(2), 63–77.

Kochhar, R., & Cilluffo, A. (2018). *Income inequality in the U.S. is rising most rapidly among Asians.* Pew Research Center. https://www.pewsocialtrends.org/2018/07/12/income-inequality-in-the-u-s-is-rising-most-rapidly-among-asians

Lee, J., & Zhou, M. (2015). *The Asian American achievement paradox.* Russell Sage Foundation.

Li, J., Maxwell, A. E., Glenn, B. A., Herrmann, A. K., Chang, L. C., Crespi, C. M., & Bastani, R. (2016). Healthcare access and utilization among Korean Americans: The mediating role of English use and proficiency. *International Journal of Social Science Research, 4*(1), 83–97.

Mahapatra, N. (2012). South Asian women in the U.S and their experience of domestic violence. *Journal of Family Violence, 27,* 381–390. doi:10.1007/s10896-012-9434-4

Mokuau, N., Garlock-Tuiali'i, J., & Lee P. (2008). Has social work met its commitment to Native Hawaiians and other Pacific Islanders? A review of the periodical literature. *Social Work, 53,* 115–121.

Pew Research Center. (2020). Pew Research Center Analysis of 2018 American Community Survey Integrated Public Use Microdata Series.

Portes, A., & Zhou, M. (1993). The new second generation: Segmented assimilation and its variants. *Annals of the American Academy of Political and Social Science, 530,* 74–96.

Raj, A., & Silverman, J. G. (2007). Domestic violence help-seeking behaviors of South Asian battered women residing in the United States. *International Review of Victimology, 14*(1), 143–170. doi:10.1177/026975800701400108

Refugee Processing Center. (2020). *Admissions and arrivals: Interactive reporting.* https://ireports.wrapsnet.org

Substance Abuse and Mental Health Services Administration. (2019). *2018 National Survey on Drug Use and Health: Detailed tables.* https://www.samhsa.gov/data/report/2018-nsduh-detailed-tables

Southeast Asian Resource Action Center & Asian Americans Advancing Justice. (2020). *Southeast Asian American journeys.* https://www.searac.org/wp-content/uploads/2020/02/SEARAC_NationalSnapshot_PrinterFriendly.pdf

Singh, S., McBride, K., & Kak, V. (2015). Role of social support in examining acculturative stress and psychological distress among Asian American immigrants and three sub-groups: Results from NLAAS. *Journal of Immigrant and Minority Health, 17,* 1597–1606. https://doi.org/10.1007/s10903-015-0213-1

Stop AAPI Hate. (2020). *Stop AAPI Hate national report March 19, 2020–August 5, 2020.* http://www.asianpacificpolicyandplanningcouncil.org/wp-content/uploads/STOP_AAPI_Hate_National_Report_3.19-8.5.2020.pdf

Terlizzi, E. P., Connor, E. M., Zelaya, C. E., Ji, A. M., & Bakos, A. D. (2019, October). Reported importance and access to health care providers who understand or share cultural characteristics with their patients among adults by race and ethnicity. *National Health Statistics Reports,* No. 130, 1–12.

Terragni, L., Beune, E., Stronks, K., Davidson, E., Qureshi, S., Kumar, B., & Diaz, E. (2018). Developing culturally adapted lifestyle interventions for South Asian migrant populations: A qualitative study of the key success factors and main challenges. *Public Health, 161*, 50–58.

Tervalon, M., & Murray-Garcia, J. (1998). Cultural humility versus cultural competence: A critical distinction in defining physician training outcomes in multicultural education. *Journal of Health Care for the Poor and Underserved, 9*(2), 117–125.

U.S. Census Bureau. (2018). *2018 American community survey 1-year estimates.* https://www.census.gov/programs-surveys/acs/data.html

U.S. Census Bureau. (2020). *Asian and Pacific Islander population in the United States.* https://www.census.gov/library/visualizations/2020/demo/aian-population.html

U.S. Department of Commerce, Bureau of the Census. (2010). *The Asian population: 2010.* http://www.census.gov/prod/cen2010/briefs/c2010br-11.pdf

Wagner, J., Burke, G., Kuoch, T., Scully, M., Armeli, S., & Rajan, T. V. (2013). Trauma, healthcare access, and health outcomes among Southeast Asian refugees in Connecticut. *Journal of Immigrant and Minority Health, 15*(6), 1065–1072. https://doi.org/10.1007/s10903-012-9715-2

Yoon, J., & Lau, A. S. (2008). Maladaptive perfectionism and depressive symptoms among Asian American college students: Contributions of interdependence and parental relations. *Cultural Diversity and Ethnic Minority Psychology, 14*(2), 92–101.

Yoshioka, M. R., Gilbert, L., El-Bassel, N., & Baib-Amin, M. (2003). Social support and disclosure of abuse: Comparing South Asian, African American, and Hispanic battered women. *Journal of Family Violence, 18*(3), 171–180. doi:10.1023/A:1023568505682

Zhai, F., & Gao, Q. (2009). Child maltreatment among Asian Americans: Characteristics and explanatory framework. *Child Maltreatment, 14*(2), 207–224. https://doi.org/10.1177/1077559508326286

Social Work Practice with LGBTQ+ Populations

Richard A. Brandon-Friedman

The modern gay rights movement is considered to have begun with the Stonewall riots in June 1969. Since that time, lesbian, gay, bisexual, transgender, queer, and other sexual and/or gender minority individuals (LGBTQ+) have made significant progress in obtaining legal rights, but they have also dealt with many setbacks. Understanding LGBTQ+ communities requires attention not only to the individuals themselves but also to the history of the community.

The first pride marches were held on the 1-year anniversary of the Stonewall riots. These small commemorative events were held in New York, Chicago, and Los Angeles and would form the basis of what is now often celebrated as gay pride month in June. It was 3 years later in 1973 that the American Psychiatric Association voted to remove homosexuality from the third edition of the *Diagnostic and Statistical Manual of Mental Disorders*. Four years later, Harvey Milk was elected to the San Francisco Board of Supervisors after running as an openly gay man. Unfortunately, he was assassinated less than 1 year later.

In 1979, the first National March on Washington was held in order to draw national attention to the drive for equality and encourage passage of civil rights legislation; an estimated 75,000–125,000 people participated in the march (Ghaziani, 2008). The AIDs epidemic during the 1980s dealt a strong blow to the movement as people began associating the deadly virus with gay men (Shilts, 1987). During this time, militancy groups such as AIDS Coalition to Unleash Power (ACT UP) began to demand greater attention to the needs of queer people. The 1990s saw the passage of Don't Ask, Don't Tell, a compromise between the U.S. Congress and President Clinton that allowed gays and lesbians to serve in the military as long as they did not disclose their sexual orientation. In 2000, Virginia became the first state to legalize same-sex unions, followed by Massachusetts legalizing same-sex marriage in 2004. Don't Ask, Don't Tell was repealed in 2010, allowing gay and lesbian individuals to openly serve in the U.S. military for the first time. A U.S. Supreme Court ruling in 2015 legalized same-sex marriage throughout the United States.

LGBTQ+ Terminology and Symbols

To understand the modern LGBTQ+ communities, it is necessary to recognize the importance of language and symbols. The terms *sexual orientation* and *sexual orientation identity* refer to the gender of the individual to whom a person is sexually or romantically attracted. *Gender identity* refers to the gender with which an individual identifies. Those who identify with the sex they were assigned at birth are referred to as *cisgender*, whereas those who identify with a gender that does not correspond to the sex they were assigned at birth are referred to as *gender-diverse* or *transgender*. Both sexual orientation identity and gender are social constructs and are fluid, leading to a large variety of sexual orientation identities and gender identities.

Additional definitions for terms related to sexual orientation identity and gender identity are listed in Table 116.1. It is important to note that genders and sexualities are self-defined, and they represent both individuals' experiences and their identities. In other words, people may experience themselves as a gender but not identify with the identity often associated with that experience or engage in sexual and/or romantic relationships with others but not identify with the identity often associated with those sexual interactions. For example, a man may have sex with another man and identify himself as heterosexual or a person assigned male at birth may identify as female but not as transgender. Furthermore, a person may identify as polyamorous but be in a long-term monogamous relationship.

The main symbol of LGBTQ+ communities, the rainbow flag, originated in San Francisco in 1978. The contemporary rainbow flag has six colors—red, orange, yellow, green, blue, and violet—whereas the original had eight colors, including pink and indigo and replacing blue with turquoise. Although the rainbow flag was intended to represent all sexual minorities, many subgroups under the LGBTQ+ umbrella have their own flags used to represent their identities. For example, there are flag designs for lesbian, bisexual, pansexual, transgender, and nonbinary individuals, to name just a few. A rainbow flag with a large letter A on it is often used to represent allies to LGBTQ+ communities. Other important symbols of LGBTQ+ communities include the upside-down pink triangle, a symbol reclaimed by the community from its use of representing homosexuals in Nazi concentration camps. Interlocking gender symbols are also often used to represent same-gender unions. Displaying symbols such as these indicates support for LGBTQ+ communities.

Mental Health Within the LGBTQ+ Communities

Aside from within their personal lives, many social workers will first meet members of LGBTQ+ communities to address mental health concerns. As a result of the stigma, discrimination, and harassment many LGBTQ+ individuals face, they have elevated rates of mental health and substance use disorders and suicidality (Plöderl & Tremblay, 2015). Although many of these concerns can be addressed using the same techniques as those used with any population, such as cognitive–behavioral therapy, acceptance and commitment therapy, and mindfulness, special attention must be paid to the place of stigma in the lives of LGBTQ+ individuals.

Minority stress theory (Meyer, 2003) emphasizes the additive effects of stigma and discrimination on individuals' mental health. Many LGBTQ+ people face stigma, harassment, and discrimination in multiple settings, such as home, employment, and typical social interactions. Furthermore, when these negative experiences permeate multiple areas, LGBTQ+

TABLE 116.1 Definitions

Term	Definition
Agender	An individual who identifies as having no gender
Ally	An individual who identifies as supports LGBTQ+ individuals, often in a public and actionable manner
Aromantic	An individual who does not experience romantic attraction to anyone or who has a lack of interest in romantic relationships
Asexual	An individual who does not experience traditional forms of sexual attraction to anyone or who has a lack of interest in sexual activity
Assigned female at birth (AFAB) or female assigned at birth (FAAB)	An individual who was assigned as female by a medical provider based on their genital presentation when they were born
Assigned male at birth (AMAB) or male assigned at birth (MAAB)	An individual who was assigned as male by a medical provider based on their genital presentation when they were born
Assigned sex at birth (ASAB) or sex assigned at birth (SAAB)	The sex an individual was assigned by a medical provider when they were born
Bigender	An individual who identifies as both male and female
Bisexual	An individual sexually and/or romantically attracted to both men and women
Cisgender	An individual whose gender identity corresponds with the gender roles associated with the sex they were assigned at birth
Demisexual	An individual who experiences sexual attraction to another individual after having a strong romantic and/or emotional connection
Female to male (FtM or F2M)	An individual assigned female at birth who identifies as male; a transgender man
Gay	A man (cisgender or transgender) who is sexually and/or romantically attracted to other men (cisgender or transgender men); this may also be used as an umbrella term for the LGBTQ+ community
Gender-diverse or gender variant or gender expansive	An individual who does not identify as either male of female; an individual who may alternate identification with specific genders over time
Gender fluid or genderfluid	An individual whose sense of their gender fluctuates over time
Heterosexual	An individual sexually and/or romantically attracted to individuals with a binary gender that differs from their own; generally used to refer to a woman who is sexually and/or romantically attracted to men (cisgender or transgender men) or vice versa; also known as "straight"
Homosexual	An individual sexually and/or romantically attracted to individuals with a binary gender that corresponds with their own
Intersex	An individual born with sex characteristics and/or genitalia that do not correspond with socially standard definitions of male or female; an individual with ambiguous genitalia
Lesbian	A woman (cisgender or transgender) who is sexually and/or romantically attracted to other women (cisgender or transgender women)
Male to female (MtF or M2F)	An individual assigned male at birth who identifies as female; a transgender woman
Men who have sex with men (MSM)	Cisgender men who have sex with cisgender men; requires both parties to have a penis; may or may not identify as gay; often used in medical literature to describe sexual behaviors rather than sexual orientation/identities

TABLE 116.1 Continued

Term	Definition
Monogamy or monogamous	A practice of having only one romantic and/or sexual relationship at a time
Nonbinary or non-binary or enby	An individual who does not identify as exclusively a man or woman, which includes genderfluid, genderqueer, bigender, among many more
Pangender	An individual who identifies with many or all genders
Pansexual	An individual who is sexually and/or romantically attracted to people of any gender
Polyamorous or polyromantic or poly	A practice of having more than one consensual romantic and/or sexual relationship simultaneously; an individual who engages in polyamory
Queer	A reclaimed term that can represent anyone within the LGBTQ+ umbrella; an individual who resists traditional sex and/or gender roles; an identity of someone who resists forms of heteronormativity and cisnormativity
Questioning	An individual who is questioning their sexual orientation identity or gender identity
Same gender loving (SGL)	An individual who loves and/or is sexually attracted to a person of the same gender
Skoliosexual	An individual primarily attracted to individuals outside the gender binary, transgender individuals, or those who do not identify exclusively as a man or woman
Transgender	An individual whose gender identity is different than the gender roles associated with the sex they were assigned at birth; this is sometimes used as an umbrella term that can represent everyone in the gender expansive community
Two-Spirit	An Indigenous North American term used to describe an individual who has both genders within them
Women who have sex with women (WSW)	Cisgender women who have sex with cisgender women; requires both parties to have a vagina; may or may not identify as lesbian; often use in medical literature to describe sexual behaviors rather than sexual orientation/identities

individuals may not have access to the common sources of support that help build resilience. The impact of these experiences is greater than the impact of any one on its own and can lead to many of the mental health disparities noted previously.

Within minority stress theory, stressors are evaluated at various levels. Distal stressors include prejudice, social judgments, and negative messaging from the media and other social institutions. Two powerful distal stressors are *heteronormativity* and *cisnormativity*, which refer to the assumptions that all individuals are heterosexual and cisgender, respectively. These assumptions can be harmful to LGBTQ+ individuals because they may believe their identities are not recognized or valued. They further reinforce the idea that those who identify as LGBTQ+ are not normal. More proximal stressors include experiences of victimization, harassment, and discrimination. These experiences serve to personalize distal stressors as they come to impact the individuals' lives. For example, experiencing discrimination based on one's sexual orientation translates the general concept of social judgments to an actual experience.

Fully proximal stressors are those that occur internally. Expectations of harassment or judgment may lead LGBTQ+ individuals to remain at a heightened level of awareness and vigilance, leading to chronically high stress levels. Furthermore, social judgments can lead to internalized homophobia or internalized homonegativity—that is, when LGBTQ+ individuals internalize the negative social messaging directed toward them. When present within gender-diverse individuals, this internalization is referred to as internalized transphobia or internalized transnegativity. Combating this type of experience requires attention to the person as well as to societal reactions so that the negative and personal social messaging can be challenged and new narratives developed. Given the heightened role of stress in their lives and their greater likelihood of having experienced trauma, trauma-informed therapeutic techniques may be warranted when working with LGBTQ+ individuals.

Conversion therapies, also known as reparative therapies, are attempts to change individuals' sexual orientation to heterosexual or gender identity to cisgender. Some techniques include mental health therapy, medical interventions, aversion therapy, sexual violence, and/or religious therapy. Conversion therapies are considered harmful and go against the National Association of Social Workers Code of Ethics (National Association of Social Workers, 2015).

Working with LGBTQ+ Youth

Working with LGBTQ+ youth requires attention to the development of their sexual orientation and gender identity and its impact on their lives. Throughout the years, many models of sexual orientation identity development have been proposed, largely based on Cass (1979). Although the original models focused on gay men, they are often accepted as applicable to all LGBTQ+ individuals. The model posits six stages that sexual minorities go through as they develop an understanding of themselves:

Identity confusion—a time when individuals begin to consider their sexual orientation/gender identity and connect discussion about sexuality and gender diversity to themselves

Identity comparison—when individuals begin to accept they may be LGBTQ+ and compare their identities to those of others in their lives

Identity tolerance—when individuals having begun tolerating the idea that they may be LGBTQ+

Identity acceptance—when individuals have fully identified as LGBTQ+ and accept this identification

Identity pride—when individuals openly identify as LGBTQ+ to others in an unashamed manner

Identity synthesis—when individuals incorporate their LGBTQ+ identities into their global identity or as a part of their lives

Troiden (1989) developed a four-step model that largely followed Cass' (1979) model and built on her previous work but that also focused on three aspects of LGBTQ+ identity. The internal self represents how individuals identify, whereas the perceived self is when individuals feel others identify them as LGBTQ+. The final aspect, the presented self, is when LGBTQ+ publicly present themselves as LGBTQ+. In general, it is considered best if all three aspects of the self are aligned, although this is not required and there are many reasons an individual may choose to not align them, such as in a situation that they perceive presenting themselves as LGBTQ+ may be dangerous or harmful. In terms of gender, Devor (2004) published a model of transsexual (*sic*) identity development, but it is not as widely used.

As youth progress through these stages and become more comfortable with themselves, they are confronted with questions about to whom and when to reveal their sexual orientation or gender identity or "come out of the closet." Although many families are supportive of their LGBTQ+ family member, others can ostracize the youth. Youth who are supported in their coming out often can successfully integrate their sexual orientation into the rest of their identities, resulting in positive psychosocial functioning (Sadowski et al., 2009). However, many youth may still be exploring their sexual orientation after coming out, leading to fluidity in labels and self-understanding, and they should be supported in this process.

When working with LGBTQ+ youth, it is important that the youth remember their own process of coming out and the struggles they went through because many youth expect their families to be open and supportive immediately when they come out. Even supportive family members often require some time to adjust their new knowledge of the youth's sexual orientation or gender identity and the impact it will have on them and the rest of the family. Encouraging youth to be patient with family members can enhance familial functioning.

Some youth suffer harassment from those within their families or close circle of friends. Familial rejection based on youths' LGBTQ+ identity is the number one cause of homelessness among LGBTQ+ youth (Ray, 2006). Professionals working with youth need to be aware of the possibility that youths' family members or friends may be rejecting and assist youth with realistically examining the possible effects of such a disclosure. Youth should always have a plan available to ensure their own safety and security if such an experience were to occur.

LGBTQ+ youth often struggle in schools, with many reporting discrimination, victimization, and forced isolation (Kosciw et al., 2018). As a result of the victimization many experience, LGBTQ+ youth have higher rates of mental health disorders and substance use compared to their heterosexual peers (Plöderl & Tremblay, 2015). Fortunately, having a

supportive family or engaging with supportive professionals or organizations such as gay–straight alliances, gender and sexuality alliances, or LGBTQ+ community centers has been shown to reduce the negative impact of these occurrences (Asakura, 2010; Walls et al., 2013).

Sexual education and sexual health are important areas to address with LGBTQ+ youth. Most sexual education curricula are heavily heteronormative, ignoring LGBTQ+ youths' sexuality and preventing them from receiving important sexual health information. Parents are similarly unprepared, with many reporting discomfort or lack of adequate knowledge on how to address these areas with their LGBTQ+ youth (Newcomb et al., 2018). Advocating for the inclusion of LGBTQ+ content in sexual education curricula or being willing to speak about it with LGBTQ+ youth is an important area for social work practitioners (McCave et al., 2014).

Working with LGBTQ+ Adults and Older Adults

LGBTQ+ adults have unique challenges. Although they have more freedom to choose their environment compared to youth, their mobility may be limited by finances or social ties. Furthermore, many have experienced years of harassment and discrimination as well as years of questioning themselves. The lack of legal recognition of same-sex relationships nationally until 2015 led to many believing their relationships were discredited and limiting their connection to some social safety nets. Chronic stress can also be a factor, especially for older adults, leading to higher mental health and social service needs.

There are many reasons why individuals might wait until they are adults to come out. Common precipitating factors include the death of a parent, feelings of emotional and social stagnation, meeting other LGBTQ+

individuals for the first time, or finding a supportive peer or professional. Prior to coming out, many have been involved in heterosexual relationships, sometimes for many years, and many have children. These situations lead to many concerns, such as losing established relationships, concerns about custody of children, fear of being accused of having lied to others for years, losing a sense of self, and losing the safety and security of existing relationships (Rickards & Wuest, 2006). For LGBTQ+ parents, there is a constant process of coming out as they meet new people and encounter experiences such as doctor appointments, school registrations, and meeting their child(ren)'s friends.

Among LGBTQ+ older adults, there can be further experiences of isolation. Many faced higher levels of stigma, harassment, and discrimination when growing up than youth do today with the increased acceptance of LGBTQ+ individuals. Loss of social connections can occur at this age, reducing social supports at a difficult time. Furthermore, factors such as having lived through the HIV/AIDs crisis may limit their willingness to engage with medical and social service providers, leading to increased risk of health problems, as well as reducing their social circle. Assisted living facilities, nursing homes, and community centers can be particularly stressful because they may not be well-attuned to the needs of LGBTQ+ individuals. Many report feeling the need to go back into the closet prior to joining a retirement community, possibly leading to a loss of sense of self and further isolation (Johnson, 2013). All of these experiences can further contribute to psychosocial concerns among LGBTQ+ adults—a vicious cycle for a group that may be resistant to seeking services.

Gender Diversity

Gender-diverse individuals are important constituents of the LGBTQ+ communities. It is important to differentiate gender, or an individual's sense of themself as a gendered person, from sexual orientation, which refers to the sex or gender of the individuals a person finds sexually attractive. Transgender refers to an individual whose gender identity, or the gender with which they identify, is different than the sex they were assigned when they were born. Alternatively, cisgender individuals are those whose gender identity matches the sex they were assigned at birth. Because many view the term transgender as too binary, gender-diverse or gender-expansive are used more expansively to represent all gender identities other than cisgender. Gender identity examples include nonbinary, pangender, and genderfluid. In 2016, more than 1.4 million adults in the United States identified as transgender (Flores et al., 2016).

Name and pronouns can be a particular areas of importance to gender-diverse individuals. Many gender-diverse individuals choose a name that corresponds with their gender identity rather than their legal name. They often also use pronouns of their identified gender rather than the sex they were assigned at birth. Those who identify as nonbinary or outside the gender binary or who reject the gendered nature of the he/him/his and she/her/hers binary may utilize a singular form of they. This type of singular usage of "they" dates back to the Middle Ages, even though many view it as a new occurrence. In such a case, standard grammar protocols should be followed—for example, "They are coming with me to the store," even if there is only one person coming along. Other pronouns may include "ze" or "xe." Table 116.2 shows singular pronoun usage rules.

Although many LGTBQ+ individuals face stigma, gender-diverse individuals face greater amounts due to their perceived affront to gender norms. Such is the stigma that during the latter half of the 2010s, many states sought to enact laws that are discriminatory and to enforce social adherence to the sex individuals

TABLE 116.2 Singular Pronoun Usage Rules

	Subject	Object	Possessive Adjective	Possessive Pronoun	Reflexive
Feminine	She	Her	Hers	Hers	Herself
Masculine	He	Him	His	His	Himself
Gender neutral	They	Them	Theirs	Theirs	Themselves
Gender neutral	Ze or Xe	Zir or Hir	Zirs or Hirs	Zirs or Hirs	Zirself or Hirself

were assigned at birth. Several states were successful in their attempts to pass these bills even though many major corporations were against them.

LGBTQ+ People of Color

Intersectionality is an essential aspect of the lives of LGBTQ+ people of color (POC). Many LGBTQ+ POC experience a significant disconnect between their racial/ethnic identity and their LGBTQ+ identity, leading to what has been referred to as a conflict of allegiance in which they must choose which identity to foreground at different times (Sarno et al., 2015). Contributing factors to these conflicts include racism within LGBTQ+ communities and homonegativity/transnegativity within racial/ethnic communities. These dual stigmatized identities can further exacerbate psychosocial concerns through additional layers of minority stress. Feeling connected to others can partially mitigate the impact of these stressors, especially if individuals are able to form a community with other LGBTQ+ POC (Ghabrial, 2016).

Professional Tips

Recommendations for working with LGBTQ+ individuals in social work practice include the following:

- Seek training on best practices for working with LGBTQ+ individuals.
- Examine your own beliefs about LGBTQ+ individuals, the bases for those beliefs, and the ways in which they may affect how you work with these individuals.
- Explore means to visibly show support for LGBTQ+ individuals through displaying LGBTQ+ symbols or participating in LGBTQ+ community events.
- Develop, publicly post, and enforce nondiscrimination policies that explicitly mention LGBTQ+ individuals, including intolerance of jokes about gender and sexuality.
- Politely ask clients what name and pronouns they use and ensure individuals refer to clients using the proper pronouns and proper chosen name (rather than legal name).
- Review agency paperwork and forms to ensure inclusivity through language, such as asking for the names of each parent rather than the names of mother and father and avoiding checkboxes that limit gender options (when in doubt, use a write-in line).
- Recognize that although important, sexuality and gender are only pieces of individuals' identities and avoid making them the centerpiece of services if not warranted.

Helpful Resources

Brill, S., & Kenney, L. (2016). *The transgender teen: A handbook for parents and professionals supporting transgender and non-binary teens.* Cleis Press.

Dentato, M. P. (Ed.). (2017). *Social work practice with the LGBTQ community: The intersection of history, health, mental health, and policy factors.* Oxford University Press.

Erickson-Schroth, L. (2014). *Trans bodies, trans selves: A resource for the transgender community.* Oxford University Press.

Kattari, S., Kinney, M. K., Kattari, L., & Walls, N. E. (Eds.). (2020). *Social work and health care practice with transgender and nonbinary individuals and communities: Voices for equity, inclusion, and resilience*. Routledge.

Mallon, G. P. (Ed.). (2017). *Social work practice with lesbian, gay, bisexual, and transgender people* (3rd ed.). Routledge.

Nealy, E. C. (2017). *Transgender children and youth: Cultivating pride and joy with families in transition*. Norton.

References

Asakura, K. (2010). Queer youth space: A protective factor for sexual minority youth. *Smith College Studies in Social Work, 80*(4), 361–376.

Cass, V. C. (1979). Homosexual identity formation: A theoretical model. *Journal of Homosexuality, 4*(3), 219–235. https://doi.org/10.1300/J082v04n03_01

Devor, A. H. (2004). Witnessing and mirroring: A fourteen stage model of transsexual identity formation. *Journal of Gay and Lesbian Psychiatry, 8*(1–2), 41–67.

Flores, A. R., Herman, J. L., Gates, G. J., & Brown, T. N. T. (2016). *How many adults identify as transgender in the United States?* Williams Institute.

Ghabrial, M. A. (2016). "Trying to figure out where we belong": Narratives of racialized sexual minorities on community, identity, discrimination, and health. *Sexuality Research and Social Policy, 14*(1), 42–55. https://doi.org/10.1007/s13178-016-0229-x

Ghaziani, A. (2008). *The dividends of dissent: How conflict and culture work in lesbian and gay marches on Washington*. University of Chicago Press.

Johnson, I. (2013). Gay and gray: The need for federal regulation of assisted living facilities and the inclusion of LGBT individuals. *Journal of Gender, Race & Justice, 16*(1), 293–321.

Kosciw, J. G., Greytak, E. A., Zongrone, A. D., Clark, C. M., & Truong, N. L. (2018). *The 2017 National School Climate Survey: The experiences of lesbian, gay, bisexual, transgender, and queer youth in our nation's schools*. GLSEN.

McCave, E., Shepard, B., & Winter, V. R. (2014). Human sexuality as a critical subfield in social work. *Advances in Social Work, 15*(2), 409–427.

Meyer, I. H. (2003). Prejudice, social stress and mental health in lesbian, gay and bisexual populations: Conceptual issues and research evidence. *Psychological Bulletin, 129*(5), 674–697. https://doi.org/10.1037/0033-2909.129.5.674

National Association of Social Workers. (2015). *Sexual orientation change efforts (SOCE) and conversion therapy with lesbians, gay men, bisexuals, and transgender persons*. NASW Press.

Newcomb, M. E., Feinstein, B. A., Matson, M., Macapagal, K., & Mustanski, B. (2018). "I have no idea what's going on out there": Parents' perspectives on promoting sexual health in lesbian, gay, bisexual, and transgender adolescents. *Sexuality Research & Social Policy, 15*(2), 111–122. https://doi.org/10.1007/s13178-018-0326-0

Plöderl, M., & Tremblay, P. (2015). Mental health of sexual minorities: A systematic review. *International Review of Psychiatry, 27*(5), 367–385. https://doi.org/10.3109/09540261.2015.1083949

Ray, N. (2006). *An epidemic of homelessness: Lesbian, gay, bisexual and transgender youth*. National Gay and Lesbian Task Force Policy Institute and the National Coalition for the Homeless.

Rickards, T., & Wuest, J. (2006). The process of losing and regaining credibility when coming-out at midlife. *Health Care for Women International, 27*(6), 530–547. https://doi.org/10.1080/07399330600770254

Sadowski, M., Chow, S., & Scanlon, C. P. (2009). Meeting the needs of LGBTQ youth: A "relational assets" approach. *Journal of LGBT Youth, 6*(2–3), 174–198. https://doi.org/10.1080/19361650903013493

Sarno, E. L., Mohr, J. J., Jackson, S. D., & Fassinger, R. E. (2015). When identities collide: Conflicts in allegiances among LGB people of color. *Cultural Diversity and Ethnic Minority Psychology, 21*(4), 550–559. https://doi.org/10.1037/cdp0000026

Shilts, R. (1987). *And the band played on*. St. Martin's Press.

Troiden, R. R. (1989). The formation of homosexual identities. *Journal of Homosexuality, 17*(1–2), 43–74. https://doi.org/10.1300/J082v17n01_02

Walls, N. E., Wisneski, H., & Kane, S. B. (2013). School climate, individual support or both? Gay–straight alliances and the mental health of sexual minority youth. *School Social Work Journal, 37*(2), 88–111. https://doi.org/10.1177/0044118X09334957

Best Practices for Refugee Resettlement

Bret Weber, Carenlee Barkdull, Isaac Karikari, and Reginald Tarr

Refugees resettled in the United States represent incredible diversity in terms of socioeconomics, educational levels, language, religious, and cultural traditions. Social workers' ecological, person-in-environment practice orientation, respect for diversity and inclusion, strengths perspective, and grounding in both trauma and resiliency are foundational in effective practice with refugees. This chapter summarizes refugee resettlement in the United States and integrates theory and practice in the context of the resettlement journey across levels of practice.

Historical and Policy Context

Since the passage of the Refugee Act of 1980, the United States has accepted nearly 3 million of the 4 million refugees resettled globally (Connor & Krogstad, 2018). Immigration restriction has been a cornerstone of U.S. President Donald Trump's administration, including curtailed refugee admissions and a planned all-time low admission of only 18,000 refugees for fiscal year 2020 (Krogstad, 2019). In response, the National Association of Social Workers (2018) updated its policy brief recommending both domestic and international concerns regarding the humanitarian plight of immigrants and refugees.

A refugee is "someone who is unable or unwilling to return to their country of origin owing to a well-founded fear of being persecuted for reasons of race, religion, nationality, membership of a particular social group, or political opinion" [UN High Commissioner on Refugees (UNHCR), 2019]. Refugees are distinguished from migrants, who may have moved for myriad reasons, and from immigrants, who may have moved to the United States with or without legal documentation.

The number of people displaced globally by the end of 2018 was estimated to be higher than at any other time in human history (UNHCR, n.d.). Among the world's approximately 71 million displaced individuals, the UNHCR estimates that approximately 30 million are refugees, nearly half of which are children and youth younger than age 18 years (UNHCR, n.d.).

Immigration is a defining aspect of the American experience, and social workers have worked closely with immigrants since the dawn of the profession. New Americans provide infusions of labor, talent, and vibrancy to the cultural tapestry, although fear of immigrants periodically strains the nation's political and social fabric. U.S. refugee policy, like all other immigrant policy, has historically been impacted by nativism, racism, and national security fears. Nonetheless, after World War II, the United States began implementing, and led the world in, humanitarian refugee-specific immigration policies. Those early policies have since been altered by reactions to the Vietnam War; the terrorist attacks on American soil on September 1, 2001 (9/11); and the Trump administration.

The first refugee-specific legislation, the Displaced Persons Act of 1948, allowed the admission of 400,000 refugees. In 1965, President Lyndon Johnson signed a new Immigration Act that abolished previous restrictive national-origin and religion-based quotas and opened the door to immigrants from "Third World (and all) countries" (Segal et al., 2010, p. 30). Then, following the Vietnam War, many refugees migrated from Southeast Asia. In response, American altruism, racism, and recognition of the difficulties and costs associated with resettlement led to the Refugee Act of 1980, which raised the limit on the number of refugees admitted annually and established flexible protocols to address emergencies requiring even higher admission levels (Lee, 2006). This act continues to direct contemporary resettlement policy.

Despite these gains in support of universal human rights, refugee policy decisions continued to be dominated by U.S. foreign policy and domestic political considerations, with resulting reductions in admittances (Waibsnaider, 2006). This was particularly evident after 9/11 when legislation undermined refugee protections with questionable

contributions to public safety (Keith & Holmes, 2009). The 2001 Patriot Act defined any person taking up arms against any government as a terrorist, including, ironically, groups actively *supporting* U.S. policy (Pasquarella & Cohen, 2006), and thousands were denied protection for having provided "material support" to designated terrorist groups even when their support was minimal or "provided" under coercion, including robbery, forced labor, and rape (Stein, 2007).

The combined effects of homeland security legislation were dramatic. Table 117.1 draws from the U.S. government's Office of Refugee Resettlement (U.S. Department of Health and Human Services, n.d.). Refugee admissions slowed considerably between 2000 and 2009, dropping in 2003 to less than half (42%) of 2000 levels.

The overreaching nature of post-9/11 national security legislation increased the dangers and hardships for fleeing war-torn regions and denied protection to credible asylum-seekers (Hughes, 2009; Lombardo et al., 2006; Stein, 2007). Increased suspicion of refugees further inflamed domestic attitudes, increased arrests of hundreds of Arabs and Muslims on suspicion of terrorist affiliation (Barkdull, Khaja, et al., 2011; Johnson, 2004), and many state legislatures passed new restrictive policies toward immigrants while weakening support for the agencies assisting refugees (Chang-Muy & Congress, 2009).

Despite Congressional inertia during the Obama administration, by 2016 admissions had nearly regained their pre-9/11 levels. Then, from the beginning of his presidential campaign, anti-immigrant rhetoric served as a cornerstone of Donald Trump's election and presidency. On January 27, 2017, by executive order, the Trump administration banned foreign nationals from seven predominantly Muslim countries from entering the United States for 90 days, indefinitely denied entry of Syrian refugees, and suspended admittance of

TABLE 117.1 Number of Refugees Admitted to the United States from 2000 to June 30, 2020

Fiscal Year	No. of Refugees Admitted to the United States (All Countries)
2000	94,222
2001	87,104
2002	45,793
2003	39,201
2004	73,858
2005	53,738
2006	41,053
2007	48,281
2008	60,193
2009	74,654
2010	73,311
2011	56,424
2012	58,238
2013	69,926
2014	69,987
2015	69,933
2016	84,994
2017	53,716
2018	22,501
2019	30,000
2020	7,754

all other refugees for 120 days. Globally, the Trump administration closed 50 of the 350 resettlement offices and set the lowest annual refugee ceiling since 1980, resulting in record low admittances (Pierce, 2019).

The Resettlement Process

Resettlement in the United States starts with refugees fleeing their homes due to experiencing oppression, violence, torture, and even genocide. An estimated two-thirds of refugees will spend a number of years in a refugee camp, where they are often separated from family members and live in housing intended to be temporary. By 2019, fewer than 5%

were resettled, and the median length of time refugees spend in exile is 5 years, with many languishing generationally (Devictor, 2019). The UNHCR supports resettlement for those with urgent medical needs, women and girls at risk, children and adolescents at risk, and survivors of violence or torture (USA for UNHCR, n.d.). Criminals and those deemed to pose a security risk are ineligible for resettlement (U.S. Citizenship and Immigration Services, 2020).

Host countries decide who they will consider for resettlement from among those designated by the UNHCR. Those considered for resettlement in the United States undergo an additional vetting process conducted by resettlement support centers and then interviews by the Department of Homeland Security and U.S. Citizenship and Immigration Services; applications may be accepted or rejected without explanation or appeal. This process precedes medical examinations and multiple, additional security checks (Refugee Council USA, 2019).

After completing the previously described process, a designated U.S. resettlement agency [from nine designated voluntary agencies (VOLAGs)] coordinates travel arrangements (Barkdull, Weber, et al., 2011; U.S. Office of Refugee Resettlement, 2012). For the first 90 days, the VOLAG ensures individuals receive food, housing, transportation, English language instruction, orientation to their new communities, help finding employment, and referral to other supportive services. VOLAGs receive a one-time payment of $975 per refugee from the federal government, with the majority of funds generally spent before refugees even arrive in the community. This often results in agencies needing to raise funds to make up the difference (Lutheran Immigration and Refugee Service, n.d.). This public–private partnership persists as the foundation of the refugee resettlement program. Refugees receive 8 months of modest financial assistance from the federal government, but the cost of their travel to the

United States must be paid back within 3 years (Refugee Council USA, 2019).

Services in the Context of the Resettlement Journey

The refugee experience is generally discussed in terms of preflight, flight, and resettlement (Ludwig, 2016; Mott, 2010). Most refugees experience trauma and loss within each of these stages, but many do not share Westernized conceptualizations of health or mental health (Murray et al., 2010). Accordingly, utilization of a holistic model that spans life domains, such as the Ecological Acculturation Framework (Salo & Birman, 2015), is recommended to shift the focus from individual deficits and strengths to an assessment of adjustment and adaptation across life domains. Such models are congruent with social work's focus on empowering vulnerable populations while actively addressing social justice needs.

To offer a sense of stability and normalcy, agency caseworkers generally make arrangements for airport pickups, help newly arrived refugees settle into rental housing, and orient them to the community. There are pressures to quickly attain financial self-sufficiency because refugees are generally eligible to receive only 8 months of modest cash assistance and temporary access to medical care.

In designated resettlement communities in the United States, state and local governments, VOLAGs, and other nongovernmental organizations partner to facilitate refugees' successful integration into host communities. In addition to housing, cultural orientation, English acquisition skills, psychoeducational groups, and programs to promote access to education and employment, refugees require supports to navigate unfamiliar medical, legal, social service, and occupational systems; those with children must also be oriented to public school settings, as well as norms and laws related to child welfare.

Many refugees will have underlying conditions related to the lack of adequate health care in refugee camps. The resettlement process includes medical screenings by certified health officers, including physical examinations soon after arrival. Differences in cultural conceptions and the need for culturally and linguistically competent care make health care systems challenging both for refugees to navigate and for providers seeking to offer care.

Language barriers significantly affect the capacity for social, cultural, and economic engagement. Therefore, ready access to programs such as English Language Learner and English for Speakers of Other Languages must be prioritized (Cort, 2010). Language barriers often constitute a key source of insecurity and economic hardship, and they sometimes pose one of the most difficult barriers to overcome, especially for older adults (Tshabangu-Soko & Caron, 2011).

In the hierarchy of resettlement needs, employment follows language. Employment facilitates integration into mainstream society and greater self-sufficiency (Kerwin, 2018). Resettlement workers strive to connect refugees with work, but many, especially women, end up with low-paying jobs that keep them below the federal poverty level. Hostile political rhetoric, and the belief among some U.S.-born workers that refugees are taking jobs from them, can elevate stress and anxiety (Minor & Cameo, 2018; Yakushko et al., 2008). Social workers must maintain awareness that employment is a significant achievement, but it is not the endpoint of the resettlement journey.

Acculturation opportunities are more readily available for younger children due to their engagement in the public school system and the resulting immersion in American culture. Accordingly, children may adapt more easily to the norms of the host nation, and studies indicate that school belonging was positively associated with higher perceived self-efficacy (Kia-Keating & Ellis, 2007). However, this also means a child's acculturation path will likely be distinct from that of other family members, creating a complicated sense of identity. At home, their often-superior English language skills may lead adults to rely on them for roles they would not normally assume or for which they may not be developmentally ready, whereas at school they are often viewed as having behavior problems, which affects attendance and achievement (Xu, 2005). Helping professionals must coordinate and collaborate across multiple systems in order to develop linkages to developmentally appropriate school and community supports.

The acculturation process includes other challenges and pitfalls for those whose religious worldview does not easily align with that of the host community (Mott, 2010). Social workers must assess acculturation challenges on an ongoing basis and identify sources of psychological, emotional, social, and spiritual strength and support from extended family members and from others within their heritage cultures (Salo & Birman, 2015).

Some acculturation challenges derive from experiences in camps, including unique survival skills. Behaviors appropriate in the resource-starved environment of a refugee camp often lead to friction in the more resource-abundant environment of the host community. For instance, in the camp, insufficient rations create an urgent response to procure items, which manifests survival behaviors among refugee children which appear different from non-refugee children. Similarly, the inevitable dependence on others that cannot be avoided in the camp tends to be frowned upon in mainstream American culture, where individualism is a highly valued trait. Caseworkers might perceive refugees as demanding or unable to understand the rules, but they need to understand the broader context of the refugees' lived experiences and educate the host community

about camp experiences and the transition to vastly changed material conditions.

Supporting resilience requires helping refugees acculturate over time while validating pride in their cultural identities and traditions. A focus on individual and family adjustment must be situated in the context of structural and regulatory barriers. Acculturation is a two-way process requiring conscious effort from both newcomers and long-standing members of the host community. Most refugees achieve self-sufficiency and near economic parity with the U.S.-born population within 5–10 years, and host communities can enjoy tremendous economic and cultural benefits. Healthy acculturation processes include the establishment of beneficial ecological networks, broad inclusion of refugees in policy decisions, and intentional linkages with formal organizations (Darrow, 2018; Koyoma, 2017; Phillimore, 2011; Soller et al., 2018). Social workers can support these gains and mitigate challenges through active and intentional engagement at the mezzo and macro levels, directing intervention efforts at both newcomers and members of the host community.

Refugees, even if from the same country and even the same camp, are never homogeneous and must be considered within an intersectional framework across a spectrum of diversity in terms of age, language, gender identification, religion, education, trauma, and other defining characteristics (Darrow, 2018; Koyoma, 2017). This impacts individual acculturation processes and must inform policy and practice. Elderly refugees may acquire only limited English proficiency, whereas infants may grow up with English as their dominant language. Some individuals will be illiterate in their own language, whereas others may possess advanced degrees. Within this array, social workers must address practical needs such as language and job training, job acquisition, helping people adapt to new climatic conditions, food sources, the infrastructure, and even such mundane matters as learning how to drive.

The major U.S. refugee resettlement agencies address these issues, but often for only the initial 8-month settlement period before funding runs out. Also, they tend to do so from Eurocentric perspectives. Those communities most successful in their acculturation processes, and most likely to retain new community members, often do so by establishing processes that reach across local government, employers, the faith community, and educational institutions. To be successful, these processes must foster the informal networks that provide the sense of security and belonging that comes from community attachment and support, and they must do so in culturally appropriate ways that include and empower New Americans (Haidar, 2017; Soller et al., 2018). There is no one-size-fits-all approach. Instead, processes must consider the unique characteristics of both the refugees and the host communities.

Social workers, community organizers, social justice advocates, elected officials, and members from across the New American community must collaborate on community-led efforts, such as Welcoming America (WA), and more refugee-led efforts, such as the National Network for Arab American Communities (NNAAC) and South Asian Americans Leading Together (SAALT).

The WA approach emphasizes the need for the established community to welcome and embrace diversity and cultural vibrancy. The NNAAC/SAALT approach more readily embraces the generational, cultural, and other divides that exist in most communities but which are uniquely vulnerable in this situation (Iyer, 2015). Most important, neither approach requires formal professionalism as long as there are multiple opportunities for interaction. In addition, it is beneficial if informal networks engage in some degree of service provision rather than just social interaction (Haidar,

2017). Social workers need to advocate for innovative structures including flexible financing (especially with Muslim communities, in which receiving or paying interest is eschewed), facilitate leadership growth among the refugee community, and work toward a public narrative of a mutually enriching future. Successful acculturation embraces and accommodates differences across cultures by promoting an orientation of learning to live and thrive together among people. Social workers' unique training and social justice orientation help develop leaders and foster self-determination by shifting from advocating *for* to advocating *with* New Americans.

Conclusion

Overall, resettlement is complicated by the rich variety of cultures within refugee populations, across and within host communities, the dynamics of U.S. domestic and foreign policies, and a myriad of other complicating factors. Social workers need to avoid assumptions that host systems are generally adequate and that the solution lies with "fixing" individuals by helping them cope within host communities.

In relation to refugee policy, the United States is experiencing an unprecedented administration that has enacted policies to curtail all immigration, including that of formally designated refugees. The rhetoric has harmed immigrants throughout the country, with documented reports of widespread increases in hate crimes against historically marginalized groups (Cohen, 2017) and record growth in hate groups, and it has raised awareness of the harmful impacts of micro-aggression to a public health concern (Torino, 2017). Social workers must be aware of this context, learn about its impact on refugee communities, and seek ways to ameliorate harm while advocating for change.

Finally, social workers need to understand the increasingly urgent intersections of economic, social, and environmental crises. Climate change, income inequality, persistent poverty, famine, and war intersect and complicate the nuanced definitional differences between immigrants, migrants, and refugees (United Nations, n.d.). Thus, global politics play out in terms of the changing populations requiring resettlement, and the political priorities of the countries who accept them, requiring alliances of social workers across national boundaries to seek solutions and opportunities for effective advocacy and intervention.

References

Barkdull, C., Khaja, K., Queiro-Tajali, I., Swart, A., Cunningham, D., & Dennis, S. (2011). Experiences of Muslims in four Western countries post-911. *Affilia, 26*(2), 139–153.

Barkdull, C., Weber, B., Swart, A., & Phillips, A. (2011). *Refugee resettlement policy and programs: A social work call for action. Journal of Ethnic and Cultural Diversity in Social Work, 1*(1), 107–119.

Chang-Muy, F., & Congress, E. P. (2009). *Social work with immigrants and refugees: Legal issues, clinical skills and advocacy.* Springer.

Cohen, R. (2017, November 13). *Hate crimes rise for second straight year: Anti-Muslim violence soars amid President Trump's xenophobic rhetoric.* Southern Poverty Law Center. https://www.splcenter.org/news/2017/11/13/hate-crimes-rise-second-straight-year-anti-muslim-violence-soars-amid-president-trumps

Connor, P., & Krogstad, J. M. (2018, July 5). For the first time, U.S. resettles fewer refugees than the rest of the world. Pew Research Center. https://www.pewresearch.org/fact-tank/2018/07/05/for-the-first-time-u-s-resettles-fewer-refugees-than-the-rest-of-the-world

Cort, D. A. (2010). What happened to familial acculturation?. *Ethnic and Racial Studies, 33*(2), 313–335.

Darrow, J. H. (2018). Administrative indentureship and administrative inclusion: Structured limits and potential opportunities for refugee client inclusion in resettlement policy implementation. *Social Service Review, 92*(1), 36–68.

DeVictor, X. (2019, December 9). *2019 update: How long do refugees stay in exile?* To find out, beware of averages. World Bank Group. https://blogs.worldbank.org/dev4peace/2019-update-how-long-do-refugees-stay-exile-find-out-beware-averages

Haidar, A. (2017). Social workers and the protection of immigrant and refugee rights. *Advocates' Forum,* 25–38.

Hughes, A. (2009). *Denial and delay: The impact of the immigration law's "terrorism bars" on asylum seekers and refugees in the United States.* Human Rights First.

Iyer, D. (2015). *We too sing America: South Asian, Arab, Muslim, and Sikh immigrants shape our multiracial future.* New Press.

Johnson, K. R. (2004). *The "huddled masses" myth: Immigration and civil rights.* Temple University Press.

Keith, L. C., & Holmes, J. S. (2009). A rare examination of typically unobservable factors in US asylum decisions. *Journal of Refugee Studies, 22*(2), 224–241.

Kerwin, D. (2018). The US refugee resettlement program—A return to first principles: How refugees help to define, strengthen, and revitalize the United States. *Journal on Migration and Human Security, 6*(3), 205–225.

Kia-Keating, M., & Ellis, B. H. (2007). Belonging and connection to school in resettlement: Young refugees, school belonging, and psychosocial adjustment. *Clinical Child Psychology and Psychiatry, 12,* 29–43. doi:10.1177/1359104507071052

Koyoma, J. (2017). For refugees, the road to employment in the United States is paved with workable uncertainties and controversies. *Sociological Forum, 32*(3), 501–521. doi:10.1111/socf.12346 501-521

Krogstad, J. M. (2019, October 7). *Key facts about refugees to the U.S.* Pew Research Center. https://www.pewresearch.org/fact-tank/2019/10/07/key-facts-about-refugees-to-the-u-s/

Lee, E. (2006). A nation of immigrants and a gatekeeping nation: American immigration law and policy. In R. Ueda (Ed.), *A companion to American immigration* (pp. 5–35). Blackwell.

Lombardo, M. L., Buwalda, A. J., & Lyman, P. B. (2006). Terrorism, material support, the inherent right to self-defense, and the US obligation to protect legitimate asylum seekers in a post-9/11, post-PATRIOT Act, post-REAL ID Act world. *Regent Journal of International Law, 4,* 237.

Ludwig, B. (2016). "Wiping the refugee dust from my feet": Advantages and burdens of refugee status and the refugee label. *International Migration, 54*(1), 5–18.

Lutheran Immigration and Refugee Service. (n.d.). *The real cost of welcome: A financial analysis of local refugee reception.* Lutheran Immigration and Refugee Service.

Minor, O. M., & Cameo, M. (2018). A comparison of wages by gender and region of origin for newly arrived refugees in the USA. *Journal of International Migration and Integration, 19*(3), 813–828.

Mott, T. E. (2010). African refugee resettlement in the US: The role and significance of voluntary agencies. *Journal of Cultural Geography, 27*(1), 1–31.

Murray, K. E., Davidson, G. R., & Schweitzer, R. D. (2010). Review of refugee mental health interventions following resettlement: Best practices and recommendations. *American Journal of Orthopsychiatry, 80*(4), 576–585. doi:10.1111/j.1939-0025.2010.01062.x

National Association of Social Workers. (2018, January). *Social work speaks* (11th ed.). NASW Press.

Pasquarella, J., & Cohen, M. F. (2006). Victims of terror: Stopped at the gate to safety. *Immigration Law Today, 16,* 16–25.

Phillimore, J. (2011). Refugees, acculturation strategies, stress and integration. *Journal of Social Policy, 40*(3), 575–593. doi:10.1017/S0047279410000929

Pierce, S. (2019). *Immigration-related policy changes in the first two years of the Trump administration.* Migration Policy Institute.

Refugee Council USA. (2019, January). *The United States handpicks and stringently screens and vets refugees before they enter the country.* https://rcusa.org/wp-content/uploads/2019/10/Screening-and-Vetting-Procedures.pdf

Salo, C. D., & Birman, D. (2015). Acculturation and psychological adjustment of Vietnamese refugees: An ecological acculturation framework. *American Journal of Community Psychology, 56,* 395–407. doi:10.1007/s10464-015-9760-9

Segal, U. A., Elliott, D., & Mayadas, N. S. (2010). *Immigration worldwide: Policies, practices, and trends.* Oxford University Press.

Soller, B., Goodkind, J. R., Greene, R. N., Browning, C. R., & Shantzek, C. (2018). Ecological networks and community attachment and support among recently resettled refugees. *American Journal of Community Psychology, 61,* 332–343. doi:10.1002/ajcp.12240

Stein, K. B. (2007). Female refugees: Re-victimized by the material support to terrorism bar. *McGeorge Law Review, 38,* 815–842.

Torino, G. (2017, November 10). *How racism and microaggressions lead to worse health.* Center for Health Journalism. https://www.centerforhealthjournalism.org/2017/11/08/how-racism-and-microaggressions-lead-worse-health

Tshabangu-Soko, T. S., & Caron, R. M. (2011). English for speakers of other languages (ESOL): Improving English language acquisition for preliterate and nonliterate adult African refugees. *Journal of Immigrant & Refugee Studies, 9*(4), 416–433.

United Nations. (n.d.). *Refugees.* https://www.un.org/en/global-issues/refugees

United Nations High Commissioner on Refugees. (2019, February 19). *Less than 5 per cent of global refugee resettlement needs met last year.* https://www.unhcr.org/en-us/news/briefing/2019/2/5c6bc9704/5-cent-global-refugee-resettlement-needs-met-year.html

U.S. Citizenship and Immigration Services. (2020) *Refugee security screening fact sheet.* Retrieved September 15, 2020, from https://www.uscis.gov/sites/default/files/document/fact-sheets/Refugee_Screening_and_Vetting_Fact_Sheet.pdf

U.S. Department of Health and Human Services, Administration for Children and Families, Office of Refugee Resettlement. (n.d.). *Refugee arrival data: By country of origin and state of initial resettlement.* Retrieved June 4, 2011, from https://www.acf.hhs.gov/archive/orr/data/refugee-arrival-data

U.S. Office of Refugee Resettlement. (2012, July 17). *Resettlement agencies.* https://www.acf.hhs.gov/orr/resource/resettlement-agencies

USA for UNHCR. (n.d.). *Information on UNHCR resettlement.* https://www.unhcr.org/en-us/information-on-unhcr-resettlement.html

Waibsnaider, M. (2006). How national self-interest and foreign policy continue to influence the U.S. refugee admissions program. *Fordham Law Review, 75*(1), 209–258.

Xu, Q. (2005). In the best interest of immigrant and refugee children: Deliberating on their unique circumstances. *Child Welfare, 84,* 747–770.

Yakushko, O., Backhaus, A., Watson, M., Ngaruiya, K., & Gonzalez, J. (2008). Career development concerns of recent immigrants and refugees. *Journal of Career Development, 34*(4), 362–396.

White Nationalism

Aniko Felix, Khadija Khaja, and Jeremy F. Price

White supremacy has generally been focused on oppression of people of color, diverse sexual and gender identities, reproductive rights of women, and minoritized religions (Ward, 2017), whereas White nationalism takes the step further to an even greater extreme, advocating for the complete removal of all minority groups, creating a pure White ethno-state. These beliefs are employed for the purpose of prolonged cruel social stratification, unjust treatment, repression, brutality, injustice, subjugation, exploitation, tyranny, persecution, and genocide that stem from far-right movements that started many years ago. Historically, such beliefs have been used for unequal and unjust land appropriation, imperial conquests, labor exploitation, and repressive cultural alienation (Lozenski, 2018; Robinson, 1983).

The White nationalist label is associated with a "fringe minority of emboldened US citizens—the alt-right," "socially positioned as White, conservative, and rural," and "portrayed as adhering to supremacist ideologies with regard to race, religion, and sexuality" (Lozenski, 2018, p. 3). Currently, White nationalism ideology is gaining greater support in large populated cities and suburbs throughout the United States. The growth of protests to support the Black Lives Matter movement in the United States, especially after the deaths of numerous Black men and women during interactions with law enforcement, has been used by White nationalists to stoke fearmongering to gain greater support.

In 2020, the United States experienced large Black Lives Matter protests that were mostly peaceful, but some outside small fringe groups and individuals engaged in vandalism and violence, destroyed businesses and police stations, set fires, and even committed homicide. White nationalists used these events to create fear and hate of non-Whites to recruit more support. President Trump's participation in stoking fears about the Black Lives Matter movement by his numerous statements on Twitter and during rallies and interviews have been described as sowing "fresh racial divisions among Americans (Wilkie, 2020, p. 1). This chapter addresses the history of far-right movements, radicalization, the growth of hate groups, and social work practice implications.

History of Far-Right Movements

From the beginning of time, scapegoating mechanisms, prejudice, discrimination, marginalization, oppression, exploitation, and persecution have been used to create divisions in minoritized groups (Linder, 2008). Radical-right, far-right, and the extreme-right (Mudde, 2014a) are just a few names that political scientists have used to describe organizations, groups, and political parties that operate with exclusionary ideologies that promote racist and xenophobic beliefs. The core ideology of these rapidly growing organizations throughout the world is nationalism, welfare chauvinism, law and order, and xenophobia (Mudde, 2000). Right-wing ideologies have also been linked with populism, distinguishing the in-group and the out-group (Mudde, 2014b). Globally and within the United States, far-right groups are gaining support due to online recruitment efforts and disinformation campaigns, and they have become more brazen and used violence against targeted groups. Jews, communities of color, religious–cultural minorities, immigrants, refugees, and diverse sexual/gender identities have become more openly targeted.

Historical and Global Context

Most experts agree that right-wing groups and political parties emerged directly after World War II, mostly characterized by Nazi and Fascist ideologies, tied to people such as Mussolini and Hitler (Tucker, 2018). The spread of right-wing extremism continued into a second wave during the 1950s and 1960s. The second wave of right-wing movements was named the "middle-class extremists" (Lipset, 1960, p. 3). According to some, these waves occurred around the same time in different countries (Buijs & Van Donselaar, 1994), whereas others believe that these occurrences were more country-specific (Veen, 1997). During the 1980s and 1990s, right-wing groups continued to grow. Supporters were mostly termed the "losers of modernization," who could not adapt to the challenges of the modern world and were known as the third wave of far-right

ideology (Betz, 1994). Scholars mostly described the typical supporter of right-wing parties during this time as low-skilled, undereducated men, mostly working in blue-collar jobs (Ibid). During this time, two different directions of right-wing movements could be distinguished: the radical-right parties, which combined nativism and authoritarianism; and the populist radical-right that also added populism to their belief system (Mudde, 2000). With regard to regional differences, there was significant difference between Western Europe and the United States and Eastern Europe in the development of far-right movements. In Western Europe and the United States, they engaged in anti-immigrant rhetoric and were concerned about the changing demographics as Whites were perceived as becoming a minority. In Eastern Europe, far-right groups targeted the Jews and Roma (Mudde, 2000).

The fourth wave of far-right movements started in the 2000s and has been spreading at an alarming rate globally and nationally in the United States. Many new political parties and groups have emerged worldwide supporting far-right ideology, with some leaders elected now to prominent political positions in power. As far-right movements have grown, their supporters now come from diverse socioeconomic backgrounds. As a result of these factors, simplistic explanations that people who vote for or support far-right groups are just "losers" or "frustrated, angry people" does not stand anymore; they have a far more sophisticated look and blend in easily.

The Far Right

Far-right ideology originated in Europe and mostly focused on cultural differences (Spektorowski, 2003) and on three main directions: populist radical right, extreme right, and new/alternative right. Whereas populist radical right-wing organizations operated within strong beliefs around nativism, authoritarianism, and populism (Mudde, 2014 b), the extreme-right

TABLE 118.1 Far-Right Organizations

	Type of Organization			
Ideology of Organization	Organization and ideology	Populist radical right	Extreme right	New right Alternative right
	Parties	Populist radical right parties	Extreme right (anti-democratic) parties	Extreme political parties
	Movement	Movements directly linked to populist radical right parties (counter-jihad movements, etc.)	Paramilitary Neo-Nazi Skinheads	Identitarians Alternative right White supremacist White nationalist
	Sociocultural milieu, other organizations	Background institutes, festivals	Smaller anti-democratic organizations, smaller festivals	Communities, intellectual centers that relate to the new right or alternative right ideology

groups rejected pluralism and the protection of minority rights (Mudde, 2014a). In the United States, terms such as alternative-right or alt-right are more frequently used to describe this phenomenon (Hawley, 2017).

There are different types of far-right organizations and groups. Minkenberg (2015, p. 5) describes these as parties, movements, and sociocultural milieus. Table 118.1 provides examples (Félix, 2019).

Causes of Growth in Far-Right Groups

Some scholars have started to examine structural and societal problems as explanatory factors that have created socioeconomic inequalities leading to radicalization into far-right groups, including growing fear that countries which used to have predominantly White populations will change due to influx of immigrants/refugees and growing birth rates of non-Whites (Félix, 2019). The quantity and diversity of the supporters regarding their age (Mudde, 2014), gender (Félix, 2015), class (Betz, 1994), education (Rippeyoung, 2007), and level of engagement oblige scholars to avoid generalizations and examine the phenomenon by using

evidence-based research. The growing presence of far-right ideology support on college and university campuses is deeply concerning. Although studies have shown that unemployment status (Bay & Blekesaune, 2014) and inherited values (Grasso et al., 2017) can have some impacts on far-right orientation of young people, more research is needed to examine what causes students and younger generations to be affiliated with far-right ideas and groups (Bessant, 2018). Research has shown that in some cases, one of the strongest factors in decisions of people to support the far right is the need for belonging to a community (Félix & Gregor, 2014). Other research indicates that resentment stemming from changing demographics has led to fears by some Whites that they will soon be in the minority due to migration of many other diverse ethnic–religious groups (Khaja & Alhajri, 2019). In addition, studies on women who have joined far-right groups have shown that these groups offer a community through some sort of "caring" discourse, especially for women who believe they only have a "national identity" left (Mulinari & Neergard, 2017). Other research has found that the neo-Nazi scene has been used as a "rite of passage" for young males who feel emasculated (Kimmel, 2007).

Refugee Crises

After 2015, an unprecedented refugee crisis occurred throughout the world due to civil conflicts. Far-right populist leaders took advantage of this and came into power or strengthened extremist political positions engaging in fear-mongering about the dangers that immigrants, refugees, and non-Whites posed. This took place largely in Brazil, Hungary, the United States, and France. This harsh rhetoric against immigration and simplistic forms of nativism called for a "pure" ethnic White state, which led to the troubling growth of White nationalism movements that we are witnessing throughout the world. What is troubling is that some of the political leaders who espouse such views define themselves as conservatives or Republicans in the United States, yet their ideological stance is closer to far-right ideology, which often supports false conspiracy theories such as the denial of climate change, anti-Semitism, Islamophobia, racism, and xenophobia (Barna & Félix, 20217). Deeply troubling is that some of the political leadership throughout the world that espouses White nationalism is making more questionable connections with the "real" far-right formal and informal alliances that espouse racist, xenophobic, anti-Semitic, and Islamophobic sentiments (Turner, 2019). This has led to White nationalism acceptance becoming more mainstream, gaining wider open support.

Radicalization

Although there is not one ultimate definition of radicalization, most scholars define it as a process in which both ideological and sociopsychological factors create opportunities for people to become susceptible to it. Bjørgo (1997, pp. 201–207) suggests that the following factors can lead to radicalization: sympathy for the underdog position of the extreme right in relation to radical and violent opponents, protection against enemies and perceived threats, curiosity, search for excitement, opposition to a previous generation or to parents, search for an alternative to family or parents, search for friends or a community, search for status or identity, and tendency to be docile in friendships. Other factors that can lead to radicalization include feelings of insecurity, perceived injustice, and threats (van der Valk & Wagenaar, 2010). *Deradicalization* is the process in which someone who was previously radicalized leaves the radical ideology or goes through "disengagement," which refers more to leaving a radical environment, organization, or group. *Counterradicalization* describes efforts that aim at preventing or responding to radicalization and/or extremism (Eggert, 2018).

White Nationalism Trends in the United States

As mentioned previously, far-right movements are complex with a mix of diverse ideology (Jacobs, 2017; Tucker, 2018). Tucker (2018) notes that White nationalism

> ideology is founded on the notion that European culture, specifically White Anglo-Saxon culture has a right to exist just like any other culture and social programs like affirmative action measures as well as the removal of Confederate icons represent the slow replacement of White culture. (p. 4)

Deeply concerning is that many supporters of White nationalism may not belong to organized groups, yet they "still hold values of these groups" under a shadow (Tucker, 2018, p. 4). President Trump's campaign in his presidential election win in 2016 widely used campaign rhetoric on border security and otherization of various minority groups under the backdrop of an agenda referring to many non-White groups as "invaders," which White nationalists took as support of their ideology. Many are concerned that "Trump's attitude and policies seems to give encouragement to these individuals and their affiliated groups, a troublesome fact for many on both sides of the isle" (Tucker, 2018, p. 3).

Hate Groups

Globally, the rise of hateful acts in the context of authoritarian-leaning, populist-oriented heads of states is on a marked increase (Anti-Defamation League (ADL), 2018a; Hornback, 2018; ; Simon & Sidner, 2018). One country in which right-wing populism and far-right ideology have long-standing popularity is Hungary. Some politicians in both Hungary and America also have troubling relationships with some far-right groups.

Currently, there are at least 900 hate groups in the United States, with many of them espousing beliefs associated with White nationalism; in the past two decades, the number of hate groups in the United States has doubled (Meltzer & Dokoupil, 2017). The increase of racist ideologies that have led to bullying, vandalism, and violence in school, colleges, and universities, in addition to synagogues, mosques, Black churches, Latinx venues, and ethnic cultural organizations throughout the country, has been deeply frightening (Tareen, 2017). Extremism and explicit hate, particularly emanating from the political far right, are on the rise in the United States and throughout the world and have led to deadly consequences (ADL, 2018b). In August 2017, groups affiliated with White nationalism gathered in Charlottesville, Virginia, outside the University of Virginia. Sadly, "(tiki) torch-wielding men grimaced with anger, shouting slogans like "White lives matter!" "Jew will not replace us!" and "blood and soil" (Lozenski, 2018, p. 2). One person was run over by a car and killed during the protest. The president's statement after the incident was "there are good people on both sides," which infuriated many people working to end racism, anti-Semitism, Islamophobia, and xenophobia.

On August 3, 2019, a massacre left 22 people dead and dozens wounded in a Walmart in Texas, with the shooter posting an anti-immigrant message on an anonymous extremist online message board making reference to the Christchurch, New Zealand, mosque shooter who left 51 dead as his inspiration (Fieldstadt & Kilanian, 2019). In April 2019, a man opened fire in a San Diego, California, synagogue, murdering 1 person. The shooter also posted a message online that was almost identical to that of the Christ Church shooter, with anti-Semitic language praising White supremacy and praising the 2018 killing of 11 people in a Pittsburgh, Pennsylvania, synagogue. Six people were killed at a Sikh temple in Wisconsin in 2012, 3 people were gunned down at a Jewish community center in Kansas in 2013, and 9 people were killed at a Black church in South Carolina in 2015 (Fieldstadt & Kilanian, 2019).

Social Work Role in Dealing with White Nationalism

It is deeply concerning that, as Fieldstadt and Kilanian (2019) state,

> extremist related murders spiked 35 percent from 2017 to 2018, making them responsible for more deaths than in any year since 1995, according to the Anti-Defamation League (ADL). Last year, every one of those extremist-related murders was carried out by a right-wing extremist. Meanwhile, White supremacist propaganda distribution nearly tripled from 2017 to 2018, according to the ADL, which also

documented a rise in racist rallies and demonstrations. (p. 1)

Social workers, mental health/health providers, and advocacy and community building/development organizations need to play a more active and vocal role in condemning and addressing White nationalism head on. Social work professionals, practitioners, educators and researchers, and clinicians can benefit from direct partnerships with individuals and institutions in other countries that face similar situations and challenges to learn how they are addressing White nationalism proactively. Social workers must play a leading role in the development of mental health and trauma counseling for communities that have been impacted by the trauma of White nationalism rhetoric, vandalism, and violence. Social justice education in public schools, colleges, and universities on how to counter White nationalist ideology must be an area to which social workers commit. Social workers and those in other interdisciplinary fields must develop educational materials that can be used in public and private school classrooms and college/university face-to-face and online courses to educate students on White nationalism and its oppressive and racists beliefs. More training for the social work profession via webinars on how to identify radicalization and on effective intervention design is critical. Social workers must also play an active role in advocating against online forums that promote hate; these often operate in anonymity but serve as prime recruit areas for White nationalists. The National Association of Social Work Code of Ethics calls for us to fight for social justice, speak up, engage in activism, and address oppression. Thus, our profession must play a key role in addressing White nationalism.

References

Anti-Defamation League. (2018a). *Anti-Semitic incidents surged nearly 60% in 2017, according to new ADL report*. Retrieved November 11, 2018, from https://www.adl.org/news/press-releases/anti-semitic-incidents-surged-nearly-60-in-2017-according-to-new-adl-report

Anti-Defamation League. (2018b). Audit of anti-*Semitic* incidents. https://www.adl.org/media/11174/download

Barna I., & Félix A. (eds.) (2017). *Modern Antisemitism in the Visegrád countries*. Budapest: Tom Lantos Institute.

Bay, A.-H., & Blekesaune, M. (2014). Youth, unemployment and political marginalization. In C. Mudde (Ed.), *Youth and the extreme right* (pp. 21–35). IDebate.

Bessant, J. (2018). Right-wing populism and young "stormers": Conflict in democratic politics. In S. Pickard & J. Bessant (Eds.), *Young people regenerating politics in times of crises: Palgrave studies in young people and politics* (pp. 139–159). Palgrave Macmillan.

Betz, H. (1994). Radical right-wing populism and the challenge of global change. In H. Betz (Ed.), *Radical right-wing populism in Western Europe* (pp. 1–35). Palgrave Macmillan.

Bjørgo, T. (1997). *Racist and right-wing violence in Scandinavia: Patterns, perpetrators and responses*. Tano Aschehoug.

Buijs, F. J. and J. Van Donselaar (1994), Extreme-right: aanhang, geweld en onderzoek, Leiden, LISWO

Eggert, J. (2018). *The roles of women in counter-radicalization and disengagement (CRaD) processes: Best practices and lessons learned from Europe and the Arab World. Input Paper*. Berghof Foundation.

Fieldstadt, E., & Kilanian, K. (2019). White nationalism-fueled violence is on the rise, but FBI is slow to call it domestic terrorism. https://www.nbcnews.com/news/us-news/white-nationalism-fueled-violence-rise-fbi-slow-call-it-domestic-n1039206

Félix, A. (2015). Old missions in new clothes: The reproduction of the nation as women's main role perceived by female supporters of golden dawn and jobbik. *Intersections: East European Journal of Society and Politics, 1*(1), 166–182.

Félix, A. (2019). *"I was a catalyst": An analysis of the (changing) Hungarian far right from a gender perspective*. PhD dissertation (in Hungarian). https://edit.elte.hu/xmlui/handle/10831/44522

Félix, A., & Gregor, A. (2014). Kell egy csapat? –A Jobbik és fiatal támogatóinak vizsgálata különös tekintettel a társadalmi nemekre. In Á. Nagy & L. Székely (Eds.), *Másodkézből–Magyar Ifjúság 2012* (pp. 263–291). Iszt Alapítvány-Kutatópont.

Grasso, M. T., Farrall, S., Gray, E., Hay, C., & Jennings, W. (2017). Thatcher's children, Blair's babies, political socialization and trickle-down value change: An age, period and cohort analysis. *British Journal of Political Science, 49*(1), 17–36.

Hawley, G. (2017). *Making sense of the alt-right*. Columbia University Press.

Hornback, R. (2018). Afterword: White Nationalism, Trolling Humor as Propaganda, and the "Renaissance" of Christian Racism in the Age of Trump. In *Racism and Early Blackface Comic Traditions* (pp. 271–293). Palgrave Macmillan, Cham.

Jacob, H. (2017). Former neo-Nazi: Here's why there's no real difference between alt-right, White nationalism, and White supremacy. *Business Insider*. https://www.businessinsider.com/why-no-difference-alt-right-white-nationalism-white-supremacy-neo-nazi-charlottesville-2017-8

Khaja, K., & Alhajri, W. (2019). *Bullying experiences of Muslim students in the United States*. Indiana University Press.

Kimmel, M. (2007). Racism as adolescent male rite of passage. *Journal of Contemporary Ethnography, 36*(2), 202–218.

Linder, A. (2008). The legal status of Jews in the Roman Empire. In S. Katz (Ed.), *Judaism* (Vol. 4, pp. 128–173). Cambridge University Press.

Lipset, S. M. (1960). Party systems and the representation of social groups. *European Journal of Sociology/Archives Européennes de Sociologie, 1*(1), 50–85.

Lozenski, B. (2018). On the mythical rise of White nationalism and other stranger things. Journal of Language and Literacy Education. http://jolle.coe.uga.edu/wp-content/uploads/2018/03/SSO-March-2018_Lozenski_Final.pdf

Meltzer, L., & Dokoupil, T. (2017, August). *Hate rising: White supremacy's rise in the U.S.* https://www.cbsnews.com/news/hate-rising-cbsn-on-assignment/

Minkenberg, M. (2015). *Pattern, process, policies: Conceptualizing radical right impact*. Working paper.

Mudde, C. (2000). *The ideology of the extreme right*. Manchester University Press.

Mudde, C. (2014a). *Youth and the extreme right*. IDEBATE Press.

Mudde, C. (2014b). Fighting the system? Populist radical right parties and party system change. *Party Politics, 20*(2), 217–226.

Mulinari, D., & Neergaard, A. (2017). Theorising racism: Exploring the Swedish racial regime. *Nordic Journal of Migration Research, 7*(2), 88–96.

c, C. J. (1983). *Black Marxism: The making of the Black radical tradition*. University of North Carolina Press.

Rippeyoung, P. L. F. (2007). When women are right. *International Feminist Journal of Politics, 9*(3), 379–397.

Simon, M., & Sidner, S. (2018). In 2008, there was hope. In 2018, there is hurt. This is America's state of hate. CNN.

Spektorowski, A. (2003). The New Right: Ethno-regionalism, ethno-pluralism and the emergence of a neo-fascist Third Way. *Journal of Political Ideologies, 8*(1), 111–130

Tareen, S. (2017, November). From graffiti to Snapchat, schools react to racial incidents. https://apnews.com/article/7bb08c22ccb84ccdaec3815a23edb55e

Tucker, G. A. (2018). MAGA, memes, and magnificent hair: How have alt-right, White supremacy, and White nationalism become rooted in American history? *Op-Ed Pieces: Augustana Digital Commons*, 1–36. https://digitalcommons.augustana.edu/polsoped/20

Turner, F. (2019): Machine Politics. The Rise of the Internet and a New Age of Authoritarianism. In: Harper's Magazine. Available online at http://harpers.org/archive/2019/01/machine-politics-facebook-political-polarization/

Van der Valk, I., & Wagenaar, W. (2010). *The extreme right: Entry and exit*. Anne Frank House.

Veen, H. J. (1997). Rechtsextremistische und Rechtspopulistische Parteien in Europa (EU) und in Europarlament, Texte zur Inneren Sicherheit, I, 63–79.

Ward, E. K. (2017). *As White supremacy falls down, White nationalism stands up*. https://popcollab.org/white-supremacy-falls-white-nationalism-stands

Wilkie, C. (2020, June 25). *Trump cranks up attacks on the Black Lives Matter movement for racial Justice*. https://www.cnbc.com/2020/06/25/trump-attacks-black-lives-matter-racial-justice-movement.html

Islamophobia

Khadija Khaja and Wafa Alhajri

Religion is one form of "cultural identity that defines difference from the dominant culture" (Dupper et al., 2015, p. 37). Although the population in the United States is becoming more culturally and ethnically diverse, 8 in 10 adults represent various forms of Christianity, 5% are of other faiths, and approximately 1 in 6 people is not necessarily aligned with any religion. In 2011, the Federal Bureau of Investigation hate crime statistics indicated "1,480 anti-religious hate crimes incidents" (Dupper et al., 2015, p. 37). Deeply troubling is that "hatred toward people who are affiliated with minority religions" is increasing in the United States, with some saying the growth of White nationalism is leading to far more hate crimes against religious minorities such as Jews, Sikhs, Muslims, Hindus, etc. (Dupper et al., 2015, p. 37). A Gallup poll found that 43% of Americans shared being prejudiced toward Muslims and were twice as likely to perceive Muslims more negatively than Buddhist, Christians, or Jews (Gallup Center for Muslim Studies, 2010). In September 2015, then presidential candidate Ben Carson told NBC's *Meet the Press* host that he would "not advocate that we put a Muslim in charge of this nation" in response to a question (Cherkaoui, 2016, p. 3). Also, then presidential candidate Donald Trump reported that

he wanted "a total and complete shutdown of Muslims entering the United States," and soon after he became president, he "signed an executive order banning most travelers from several Muslim-majority countries" ("Hate Crimes Against Muslims," 2018, p. 1), citing national security concerns. In addition, "Trump has long stoked the idea that Obama might be a 'secret follower' of Islam and he was not born a U.S. citizen" (Cherkaoui, 2016, p. 5). The Pew Research Center (2017) reports 82% of Republicans are "very concerned" about the rise of Islamic extremism in the world compared with 60% of political independents and 51% of Democrats. Similarly, two-thirds of Republicans (67%) say that Islam is more likely than other religions to encourage violence among its believers compared with 47% of independents and 42% of Democrats (Cherkaoui, 2016, p. 8). Acts of terrorism committed by a very small minority of Muslims have led to Islam being generalized as hostile and violent, otherized, and feared by many mainstream Americans. Deepak (2017) states that "Islamophobia is a form of racism because it is embedded in systems, policies, laws, and stereotypes, and it is racialized. Those who are perceived to be Muslim are the targets, and this perception is shaped by racialized stereotypes" (p. 1).

Demographics

There are approximately 1.8 billion Muslims throughout the world, comprising almost one-fourth of the world population. In more than 50 countries, Muslims comprise the majority of the population; 20% of Muslims reside in countries in which other faith groups are more prevalent (Barkdull et al., 2011). Approximately 65% of Muslims living in the United States were born in other countries, but the majority (84%) have lived in the United States since 1980 (Barkdull et al., 2011). The Pew Research Center (2016) estimates that there were approximately 3.3 million Muslims of all ages living in the United States in 2015, comprising approximately 1% of the total U.S. population, and that this is expected to double by 2050. Mohamed (2016) reports that "over half of the projected growth of the American Muslim population from 2010 to 2015 is due to immigration" (p. 1). The Pew Research Center (2017) reports that

> among U.S. Muslim adults who were born abroad, more come from South Asia (35%) than any other region. An additional 23% were born in other parts of the Asia–Pacific region (such as Iran, Indonesia, etc.), 25% come from the Middle East–North Africa region, 9% come from sub-Saharan Africa, 4% were born in Europe and 4% come from elsewhere in the Americas. (p. 1)

Black Muslims make up one-fifth of Muslims living in the United States, and approximately half are converts to Islam (Pew Research Center, 2019).

Islamophobia Defined

Ali (2012) reports the term Islamophobia was coined by European scholars during the 1990s in Great Britain to describe fear or dislike of Muslims (Runnymede Trust, 1997).

Historically, "Arabs and Muslims living in the United States have long faced negative stereotypical portrayals in the media and popular culture" and stigmatization of "Arabs and Muslims, dates back to black-and-white silent movies" (Almontaser, 2018, p. 99). Islamophobia's key traits include "Islam viewed as static and unresponsive to new realities," "not having values similar to other cultures," the Islamic religion "seen as inferior to the West—barbaric, irrational, primitive and sexist," and "Islam seen as violent, aggressive, threatening, supportive of terrorism" and "engaged in a clash of civilizations" (Ali, 2012, p. 1034).

The sociopolitical environment since 19 al-Qaeda terrorists hijacked four planes with the aim "to destroy American landmarks and inflict massive loss of life" on September 11, 2001 (9/11), created a troubling aftermath of growing anti-Islamic sentiment toward Muslims (Tankle, 2013, p. 273). Hate crimes, stereotypes, and stigma faced by Muslims and Arabs increased tremendously post 9/11 in the United States. People who were perceived as being Muslim, even if they were not, also experienced verbal or physical assaults, in addition to homicide.

The "fear and hatred of Islam in the United States reached a symbolic precipice when the mere belief that, then presidential candidate, Barack Obama, was a 'secret Muslim' threatened his viability as a candidate" (Tankle, 2013, p. 274). Former Speaker of the House Newt Gingrich added that "Islamic law is a mortal threat to the survival of freedom in the United States and in the world as we know it" (Tankle, 2013, p. 274). The Pew Research Center, CAIR, and individual researchers have reported that Muslim experiences of stigma and discrimination increased dramatically after 9/11; the invasion of Iraq; the growth of ISIS; and during recent election cycles due to heated rhetoric that was used by some politicians and hate groups against Muslims. This fearmongering continues at an alarming rate with numerous disinformation campaigns against Muslims. As Ali (2012) notes, "Despite the fact that the term Islamophobia was formally constructed during the 1990s, American Muslims prior to 9/11 were largely able to practice their religion freely" and were for the most part "unrestricted in their day-to-day activities" (p. 1040). Currently, however, the level of intolerance and bigotry faced by Muslims in the United States and throughout the world is increasing at an alarming rate.

Effects of Religious Discrimination

Blank (1998, p. 2) reports that according to polling data, even before 9/11, more than 50% of Americans believed that Islam was "inherently anti-American, anti-Western or supportive of terrorism," even though only 5% of Americans reported little or no contact with a Muslim person (Blank, 1998, p. 2; Barkdull et al., 2011). Human Rights Watch (2002) estimated a 1,700% increase in Muslim hate crimes in the United States in 2001. Abadi (2018) notes that hate crimes

> against Muslims or people who look as if they may be Muslim are at an all-time high. According to the Southern Poverty Law Center, from 2015 to 2016 the number of anti-Muslim hate groups in the United States grew 197 percent and anti-Muslim hate crimes surged 67 percent. From January to July 2017, there were 63 attacks on mosques. (p. 5)

Currently, Muslims face growing verbal and physical assaults, in addition to homicide. In 2019, a White supremacist gunman murdered 51 Muslims in a New Zealand mosque.

One study by CAIR (2014) found that 50% of Muslim students in public schools in California experience some form of religious bullying, but more evidence-based studies are needed on religious bullying experiences of Muslims in public schools in other states, especially rural areas (Baadarani, 2016). Another smaller study in New York found that 85% of Muslim students experienced discrimination due to their religious background (Sirin & Fine, 2007). A small study showed that "bullying and cyberbullying among Muslim students is more prevalent than it is among ethnic majority groups and that it is predominantly based on religious differences" (Baadarani, 2016, p. 13). Other studies have found that many Muslims believe that inaccurate media depictions and stereotypes may contribute to more prejudiced views of Muslims living in the United States (Baadarani, 2016). The recent American policy of banning visitors from predominantly Muslim countries from entering the United States has also exacerbated the situation, with many Muslim families believing their faith is under attack. Research shows that the growing suspicion of Muslims is starting to be normalized. Schwartz (2010) describes Islamophobia as America's new fear industry, and others have reported that it has created a second-class citizenry (Ali, 2012). Muslim Advocates (n.d.) reports that cases of vandalism, threats, and arson against mosques are at "an all-time high" (p. 1). Muslim women have been mocked for wearing hijabs and have even had their hijab pulled off in public. A few case studies have illustrated increased bullying incidents faced by students in schools due to their "minority religious group affiliation" (Dupper et al., 2015, p. 37). CAIR (2002) has documented increases in harassment against Muslims, denial of religious accommodations, job termination, unequal treatment, profiling at airports, and even being spit upon.

Islamophobia has "reached an intractable point as it continues to grow without any sign of possible decline," continuously being spread by "wide scale of negative narratives against Islam" and targeted vandalism and arson incidents, including bombing plots that have been uncovered against mosques or Islamic centers, particularly in the United States and Europe (Ariyanto, 2018, p. 83).

Social Work Practice in Countering Islamophobia

Social workers can play an important role in assisting the Muslim community to address Islamophobia. Barkdull et al. (2011) state that social workers must act to eradicate stereotyping, fearmongering, and discrimination toward Muslims. Key tenets of the profession of social work are to eradicate social injustice and address oppression and racism. Social workers can contribute in many ways to challenge social conditions that create social exclusion and subjugation. Khalifa (2018, p. 112) recommends seven ways to do so. First, they can attend community events of Muslims to build trust, coalitions, and relationships. Second, they can arrange to have meetings with mosque leaders to learn more about the community and its needs, concerns, and recommendations to address Islamophobia. Third, social work agencies can hold informational sessions about how they can help. Fourth, social workers can recruit Muslims to work in mainstream agencies, illustrating a commitment to diverse communities. Fifth, social workers can review social media of their organizations or agencies to determine if they are inclusive to Muslim needs. Sixth, social workers can leverage the strengths and assets of Muslim communities. Seventh, social workers can attend interfaith events and create a Muslim advisory team to assist them in developing counseling services to address discrimination and trauma faced due to experiencing Islamophobia. Almontaser (2018) recommends "hiring of culturally competent counselors who understand diverse Muslim communities, incorporating culturally responsive training, helping mosques to become a community resource for non-Muslims via open houses and interfaith engagement" (p. 101). Educators in social work can create Muslim community service projects for social work field placement students so that they learn how to culturally sensitively work with diverse groups. More social workers should work collaboratively with Muslim mental health counselors, cosponsoring public service announcement campaigns on diversity and issues statements when Muslims are attacked to show "Muslims are an integral part of their community" (p. 101). Almontaser (2018) also suggests more people should propose "anti-Islamophobia bills, and encourage elected officials to call out Islamophobes, and deter bigotry in the media by holding producers accountable who rely on self-proclaimed experts on the Middle East and Islam who pass false information that stigmatizes Muslims" (p. 101).

Ariyanto (2018) suggests that we should "engage in a constructive and meaningful dialogue (interreligious, intercultural, and intercivilizational) toward cohesive and harmonious societies" to counter racism and discrimination (p. 87). Ariyanto notes, "Finding a comprehensive solution to Islamophobia relies on collective work and active contributions from stakeholders, including governments, international organizations, nongovernmental organizations, civil societies, religious leaders, and communities" (p. 83). Deepak (2017) states,

> Our professional ethics and commitment to social justice and human rights require that we work to understand, dismantle, and address Islamophobia and the consequences of it in our own lives and the lives of our clients. By educating ourselves and examining our own preconceived notions—as well as examining the impact of it on individuals, families, and children—we can become stronger practitioners, educators, and allies both within and outside of our respective agencies and systems. (p. 1)

Learning about human right inequities to ensure social justice is also critical (Barkdull et al., 2011). The social work profession must take a leadership role in addressing the stigmatization of Muslims as a social justice issue and take action to ameliorate its causes and consequences on individuals, families, and groups.

References

Abadi, H. (2018). *Countering the Islamophobia industry: Toward more effective strategies.* The Carter Center. https://www.cartercenter.org/resources/pdfs/peace/conflict_resolution/countering-isis/cr-countering-the-islamophobia-industry.pdf

Ali, Y. (2012). Shariah and citizenship—How Islamophobia is creating a second-class citizenry in America. *California Law Review, 100*(4), 1027–1068.

Almontaser, D. (2018). *Islamophobia: From challenge to opportunity.* https://www.oic-oci.org/upload/islamophobia/2018/Carter_Center_Countering_The_Islamophobia_Industry.pdf

Ariyanto, D.(2018). Multilayered Approaches to Islamaphobia: A contribution toward developing a Susatainable and Strategic Response. https://www.oic-oci.org/upload/islamophobia/2018/Carter_Center_Countering_The_Islamophobia_Industry.pdf

Baadarani, D. (2016). *The bullying experiences of Muslim–American youth in U.S. public schools.* Oregon State University Press.

Barkdull, C., Khaja, K., Queiro-Tajalli, I., Swart, A., Cunningham, D., & Dennis, S. (2011). Experiences of Muslims in four Western countries post-911. *Affilia, 26*(2), 139–153.

Blank, J. (1998, July 20). The Muslim mainstream. *U.S. News and World Report, 125*(3), 22–25.

Cherkaoui, M. (2016, November 10). *Part 2: The mediatized Islamophobia in America: What is beyond othering Muslims.* Al Jazeera Center for Studies.

Council on American–Islamic Relations. (2002). *Civil rights reports: The status of Muslim civil rights in the United States 2002.*

Council on American–Islamic Relations. (2014). Mislabeled: The impact of school bullying and discrimination on California Muslim students.

Deepak, A. C. (2017). Interrupting Islamophobia: It takes a social work village. *The New Social Worker.* https://www.socialworker.com/feature-articles/practice/interrupting-islamophobia-it-takes-a-social-work-village

Dupper, D. R., Forrest-Bank, S., & Lowry-Carusillo, A. (2015). Experiences of religious minorities in public school settings: Findings from focus groups involving Muslim, Jewish, Catholic and Unitarian Universalist Youth. *Children and School, 37*(1), 37–45.

Gallup Center for Muslim Studies. (2010, January 21). *In U.S., religious prejudice stronger against Muslims.* https://news.gallup.com/poll/125312/religious-prejudice-stronger-against-muslims.aspx

Hate crimes against Muslims rose 15 percent last year. (2018, April 23). *New York Post.* https://nypost.com/2018/04/23/hate-crimes-against-us-muslims-rose-15-percent-last-year

Human Rights Watch. (2002). *We are not the enemy: Hate crimes against Arabs, Muslims, and those perceived to be Arab or Muslim after September 11.* https://www.hrw.org/report/2002/11/14/we-are-not-enemy/hate-crimes-against-arabs-muslimsand-those-perceived-be-arab-or

Khalifa, S. (2018). *Turning challenges into opportunities in our current environment.* https://www.oic-oci.org/upload/islamophobia/2018/Carter_Center_Countering_The_Islamophobia_Industry.pdf

Mohamed, B. (2016, January 6). A new estimate of the U.S. Muslim population. Pew Research Center. https://www.pewresearch.org/fact-tank/2016/01/06/a-new-estimate-of-the-u-s-muslim-population

Muslim Advocates. (n.d.). *Threats and violence in mosques.* https://muslimadvocates.org/advocacy/threats-and-violence-against-mosques

Pew Research Center. (2016). *A new estimate of the U.S. Muslim population.* https://www.pewresearch.org/fact-tank/2016/01/06/a-new-estimate-of-the-u-s-muslim-population

Pew Research Center. (2017). *Demographic portrait of Muslim Americans.* https://www.pewforum.org/2017/07/26/demographic-portrait-of-muslim-americans

Pew Research Center. (2019). *Black Muslims account for a fifth of all U.S. Muslims, and about half are converts to Islam.* https://www.pewresearch.org/fact-tank/2019/01/17/black-muslims-account-for-a-fifth-of-all-u-s-muslims-and-about-half-are-converts-to-islam

Runnymede Trust. (1997). *Islamophobia: A challenge for us all.*

Schwartz, S. (2010). Islamophobia: America's new fear industry. *Phi Kappa Forum,* 19–21.

Sirin, S. R., & Fine, M. (2007). Hyphenated selves: Muslim Americans youth negotiating identities on the fault lines of global conflict. *Applied Developmental Science, 11*(3), 151–163.

Tankle, L. (2013). The only thing we have to fear is fear itself: Islamophobia and the recently proposed unconstitutional and unnecessary anti-religion laws. *William and Mary Bill of Right Journals, 21,* 273–302.

Rural Social Work Practice

Barb Pierce and Stephanie Boys

The U.S. Census Bureau (Ratcliffe et al., 2016) defines rural as "what is not urban—that is, after defining individual urban areas, rural is what is left," yet population density thresholds (e.g., 1,000 people per square mile for an urban area), land use, and distance factor into the equation. Other federal agencies define rural slightly differently in terms of land that is not within proximity to urban centers, which are more densely populated with highly developed land; rural areas are less dense and less developed and have fewer people living on more land masses more distant from each other. Rural social work is practiced in U.S. Census–defined rural areas and in small towns and frontier areas (including Native American lands) throughout the United States. According to the U.S. Census Bureau (2017), 97% of the Country's land is considered to be rural but only 19.3% of the population lives there. Although some rural counties are quite wealthy, many of the poorest people in the United States live in rural counties such as Oglala Lakota County, South Dakota, or Holmes County, Mississippi. In fact, the Deep South, southern Texas, New Mexico, and Native American lands in various states comprise lands where many of the poorest people live (Guzman et al., 2018).

Rural people tend to have many of the same diversities as urban populations but with the added diversity of being from a rural community, and social workers who work with them require deep knowledge of the communities in which they live. For many rural families, they and their ancestors have lived in their town or on their land for generations. In fact, scholars studying rural communities describe them using the term *gemeinschaft*, which was coined in 1887 by Tönnies to denote communities that are built on tradition, with affective bonds and long-term relationships. Rural communities do have the strengths of tradition, relationships, informal resources, stability, and access to the natural environment, but they also have the challenges that come from living away from services and highly paid work. Riebschleger et al. (2015) identified the following areas of knowledge and skill competence for rural social work practice: poverty, resources, cultural competency, generalist competence, autonomy/need for support, dual relationships, and leadership.

Poverty

Poverty is an ongoing nuanced social problem in rural communities. Guzman et al. (2018)

report that based on U.S. Census data, between 2013 and 2017, U.S. poverty for completely rural counties was 17.2% and that for mostly rural counties was 16.3%, whereas the percentage for all U.S. counties combined was only 14.6% (2013) and 14.3% (2017) for mostly urban counties. This does in fact leave many rural communities at least above the poverty line, but percentages do remain higher in rural communities. The median household income in the United States is approximately $57,652, whereas in completely rural counties it is $44,020–$47,020 for mostly rural counties. Demographic shifts reveal that urban and suburban areas of the country have grown dramatically as populations move for work opportunities. Many people living in rural areas may travel to small cities or towns for necessary health care or other services. Social workers in both urban and rural areas must understand the public and private programs that can assist their clients or the rural community population in general. Often, private, informal, or faith-based resources are quite helpful and abundant in rural areas. Some rural communities can grow their own food. In addition, federal grants are available to nonprofit groups in rural areas to help them partner on building community gardens. Many land grant universities also have agricultural extension services that can help with these efforts. On a systemic level, it is ironic that the population that grows food and harvests meat and poultry for the nation experiences more poverty than the rest of the country. Agriculture has become a corporate entity and small family farms have dwindled throughout the years.

Other expressions of poverty in rural areas include substandard housing, deficiencies in utility and internet infrastructure, and contaminated water wells. Another systemic effect of rural poverty is the lack of opportunity for jobs in these areas, which contributes to increased enlistment in the military. In fact, the percentage of military recruits from rural America is disproportionate to the percentage of the total population. Rural Americans also comprise 11% of the veteran populations, leading to more need for veteran benefit services in those areas (U.S. Department of Agriculture, 2013). Hence, it is important for rural social workers to have some knowledge of military and veteran benefits and ways to access services for these clients. In addition, some communities may be so remote that social workers may have to arrange transportation or other means of accessing federal and state benefits. Given the lack of internet access in some rural areas, social workers may be the lifeline for families to access internet applications for SNAP, housing, or Medicaid/CHIP benefits.

Contrary to clear increased poverty in rural areas, many rural areas are experiencing increased economic activity and increases in the tax base because of the oil and natural gas industries. Without debating their relative merits and environmental impact, they do bring a positive economic impact to small towns and rural areas. Some remote communities have experienced economic and population growth as workers move rurally to work in those industries. In addition, the logging industry in many cases has developed sustainable practices and provides jobs, increasing the economy and tax base. Rural social work agencies often address needs for housing, food security, and mental health and addiction services as itinerant workers move to work in these industries.

Generalist Practice

Overall, due to a lack of social workers in rural areas, the social workers who do live and/or work in these areas must be generalist in their practice. They are often called upon to provide assistance and usually use an ecosystems approach in order to understand person in environment. Rural social workers may be the frontline eyes and ears for state child and adult protection services, provide information on health and home health needs, assist families to access resources for poverty or transportation, link veterans to services using their military benefits, provide support to families whose loved ones are deployed, and provide frontline mental health and addiction screenings or services. They interface with other frontline professionals to become an integral part of the medical and social service array of services needed for clients in these areas. Social workers become trusted members of the professional community, and a new social worker in a rural community would do well to make positive connections with other professionals, including police officers, firefighters, ambulance services, physicians, nurses, and other therapists already there (Norris, 2018). Although there have been many good attempts at integrating telehealth services into rural communities, social workers sometimes have to help families be creative in order to access these services due to poor internet access or computing access issues. Given that a rural social worker may be the sole provider of services in a community, developing partnerships with other professionals, writing grants, administering agency services, and providing leadership skills within organizations are critical to success.

Practice Issues

Practice in rural areas can be rewarding but also presents some professional challenges. There might be challenges to obtaining supervision and consultation with other social workers. Hence, rural practitioners usually develop relationships outside of their communities in order to obtain consultations when necessary. In addition, it is important to develop relationships with other social workers and mental health providers to find the best evidence-based care for clients. Issues that might necessitate referral include eating disorders, addiction treatment,

ongoing mental health counseling, and services for autism and other developmental disabilities. Having a sufficient understanding of the evidence-based treatments necessary for such issues and having available handy resources, especially personal relationships with others at the closest referral center, are valuable. A client who trusts the local worker may be more willing to follow through with the referral if the local worker knows the referral worker.

Another professional challenge occurs because of living and working in the same geographic area. It may be difficult for the social worker and their family to keep their lives private in small towns and rural areas. Inevitably, children attend the same schools or families shop at the same food stores, potentially leading to confidentiality and privacy issues. This also leads to the possibility of dual relationships, especially if children are in the same class or families attend the same church or have the same family physician. It is important for the worker to understand that it is their responsibility to keep all information confidential and understand the effect of power on professional relationships given all potential community contacts (Halverson & Brownlee, 2010). If workers do live and work in separate communities, this helps avoid dual relationships, but it is not always possible, particularly in completely rural and frontier areas of the country. Other ways to ensure confidentiality include having an unlabeled office if the worker has a private practice or having agency offices in areas where there are multiple other professional offices so others in the community do not know that a family is seeking social work or mental health services. It also helps to decrease the stigma of obtaining services, which is still an issue (Crawford & Brown, 2002; Rost et al., 1993). In many rural communities, families seek mental health care from their family doctor, which helps decrease stigma, and it is often the family doctor who refers families to local social workers (Komiti et al., 2006).

Cultural Competence

Gaining cultural competence ultimately becomes an important issue if the worker did not grow up in the rural community. Communities differ also by geography, remoteness, and services available. Rural areas hold long-term and even generational relationships. Developing trust with clients and other professionals can be quite difficult. Listening more than talking and respecting and honoring rural practices are important to developing trust. There are also practical aspects of cultural competence, such as understanding that people live far apart from each other. Home visiting, providing transportation, and navigating rural roads are critical, as is understanding the weather patterns to remain safe from tornados or snowstorms while on the roads. A key reminder is that people who live in and identify as rural sometimes experience discrimination and bias because they are a minority in the population and are frequently made fun of by people in the dominant culture and by media representations (Murray, 2019; Wendell, 2002). Cultivating a deep respect and cultural humility toward all persons with whom we work allows social workers to work most effectively with all persons.

Rural practice can be a solitary and difficult task, but it can also be rewarding, allowing the social worker to use a vast array of skills, including leadership and advocacy skills. One area of great need and concern in rural areas is the lack of resource availability, particularly for domestic violence programs/shelters and reproductive health needs. Health equity, although a major issue in the country, is particularly concerning in rural America.

Policy Advocacy for Rural Community Health Care Equity

All social workers have a professional responsibility to advocate for social justice and equitable distribution of resources (National Association of Social Workers, 2018). Whether the government has a duty to provide access to affordable, high-quality health care is one of the most divisive issues of the 21st century. Social workers must have strong voices in the health policymaking arena to ensure the populations we serve can live with dignity and to their full potential.

There is broad consensus that many differences are evident in health care access between rural and urban areas (Douthit et al., 2015). Most governmental regulation of public health occurs at the federal and state levels, which often results in a lack of consideration of rural areas. Several barriers to health care access for rural residents arise when their needs are not accounted for in federal and state policy; these include cultural barriers, transportation barriers, and barriers to accessing telehealth services (Douthit et al., 2015). Obstacles to accessing care exist in all areas of mental and physical health for persons living in rural communities. In this section, women's reproductive health is used to demonstrate the practical challenges and policy solutions.

Cultural Barriers

The highly interconnected nature of rural communities can be a cultural obstacle to residents seeking preventative or reactive health care. Often, local doctors are within a patient's social ecosystem, which raises patient concerns about whether they might experience stigma or discrimination from providers, as well as whether their information will remain confidential (Douthit et al., 2015). In small communities, boundaries can be lax, with community members viewing local medical practitioners as neighbors rather than professionals bound by ethical duties (Brems et al., 2006).

Concerns regarding potential stigma and confidentiality of information are particularly salient for women seeking services for sensitive reproductive health issues, such as treatment of sexually transmitted infections, access to birth control, or abortion procedures if they are even available in the local community. Social workers must perform advocacy in the form of education by providing information to community members on the ethical standards necessary for credentialing of various health care professionals. With additional education on the importance of preventative care, social workers can alter community attitudes toward seeking care and confidence in the privacy of client information. In addition, social workers should advocate for funding of public service announcements regarding the need for regular medical examinations.

Transportation Barriers

Transportation is another barrier to accessing health care in rural areas. Rural communities suffer from a shortage of medical resources at all levels, including trained medical professionals, hospitals and clinics, and diagnostic technologies; thus, extensive travel may be necessary to obtain care (Brems et al., 2006). Transportation, travel time, and the associated expenses are a significant obstacle for rural residents to obtaining a wide variety of health care services (Pathman et al., 2006).

The specialty of women's reproductive health care provides a primary example of how transportation can hinder access to health care, particularly with regard to the declining number of labor and delivery units and abortion clinics in rural areas. During the past decade, the United States has experienced a significant decline in the number of rural obstetric units as hospitals have ceased providing labor and delivery services due to "low birth volume, private hospital ownership, a limited supply of family physicians and location in a lower income county" (Hung et al., 2016, p. 1555). Extended travel times for labor and delivery services in rural areas are associated with an increased number of home births, induced labor, and cesarean deliveries (Pearson et al., 2018).

Lack of abortion access in rural areas due to travel-related challenges often reaches the public spotlight. In 2017, Bearak et al. found that although the majority of American women would not have to travel a significant distance to access abortion services, "a sizable minority of women would have to travel 80 miles or more, and variation between counties is greater than between states" (p. 498). Thus, any state legislation impacting the number of clinics is more likely to adversely affect women in rural communities (Bearak et al., 2017). Many current state laws require women to wait 24–72 hours between seeing a provider and receiving an abortion procedure. Waiting time policies exponentially increase travel costs, with the potential need for multiple trips, hotel expenses, and/or increased time off work (Jerman et al., 2016). The consequence of these costs is that distance from a clinic has a significant impact on whether a woman can access an abortion (Cunningham et al., 2017).

Social workers must advocate for scope-of-practice regulations, medical licensing requirements, and certificate-of-need (CON) laws that will ensure equitable access to all forms of health care in the rural areas of their state. First, scope-of-practice laws regulate functions that can be performed by medical professionals such as nurse practitioners, physician assistants, and midwives. Laws that expand the scope of practice of these professionals will alleviate some rural challenges of attracting doctors and patient travel for procedures. Second, CON laws are state regulations that require new medical expenses, particularly facilities, be approved by the state. Currently, 35 states have CON programs in place (Pitsor, 2019). CON laws are generally established to reduce costs by preventing duplication of services (Pitsor, 2019). Social workers must advocate against any reduction in services that will reduce access to health care for rural communities. Finally, state medical licensing requirements can hinder doctors from practicing across states lines. Many rural communities are on the border between states and could benefit from cross-state agreements. In addition, state licensing requirements prevent expansion of telehealth services across state lines.

Barriers to Accessing Telehealth Services

The availability of telehealth services could provide a solution to the two barriers to health care previously discussed. If rural residents could access health care services through telehealth providers, it would clearly reduce transportation challenges, and it would also reduce cultural barriers because patients could connect with health care professionals from outside their region. However, current legal regulations maintain barriers to access of online health services. Telehealth policy is set at the state level, and each state has a unique policy in place [Center for Connected Health Policy (CCHP), 2019]. Most regulations surrounding telehealth focus on reimbursement policy, which varies by Medicaid and private payer insurance. All states and Washington, DC, require some level of Medicaid reimbursement for real-time video telehealth services, although they vary greatly by amounts and limits of service. Currently, 22 states require Medicaid reimbursement for remote patient monitoring, or using technology to collect health data on a patient from a distance; 14 states reimburse for store-and-forward services, in which medical providers can securely share patient data. Only 8 states reimburse all three types of the aforementioned telehealth services: real-time video, remote patient monitoring, and store-and-forward services (CCHP, 2019). With respect to private payer insurance reimbursement, 40 states and Washington, DC, require reimbursement for telehealth services, and parity with in-person health care can vary greatly across states (CCHP, 2019).

Telehealth services could break down barriers to rural health equity in many areas of medical practice. For example, the past decade has seen a boom in telehealth options for women to access birth control online (Zuniga et al., 2020). For persons living in rural areas, telehealth could potentially help women comply with state laws on abortion waiting periods. Travel costs would be greatly reduced if practitioners could provide consultation online and the procedure in person after the waiting period has lapsed. For social work policy advocates, the time is ripe for advocacy for fair telehealth reimbursement because the coronavirus pandemic has placed a spotlight on even the urban area need for telehealth services and has accelerated research on the best practice standards of what can safely and effectively be provided via telehealth.

Conclusion

Practice in rural communities and with people who live in rural communities is rewarding but takes specialized knowledge, values, and skills encompassing all aspects of generalist practice and policy skills. Learning to engage with rural communities allows the social worker to provide a full array of services to children, families, adults, and elders in these communities.

References

Bearak, J.M., Lagasse Burke, K., & Jones, R. K. (2017). Disparities and change over time in distance women would need to travel to have an abortion in the USA: A spatial analysis. *Lancet Public Health, 2,* 493–500.

Brems, C., Johnson, M. E., Warner, T. D., & Roberts, L. W. (2006). Barriers to healthcare as reported by rural and urban interprofessional providers. *Journal of Interprofessional Care, 20,* 105–118.

Center for Connected Health Policy. (2019, Fall). *State telehealth law & reimbursement policies: A comprehensive scan of the 50 states & the District of Columbia.* https://www.cchpca.org/sites/default/files/2019-10/50%20State%20Telehalth%20Laws%20and%20Reibmursement%20Policies%20Report%20Fall%202019%20FINAL.pdf

Crawford, P., & Brown B. (2002). "Like a friend going round": Reducing the stigma attached to mental health care in rural communities. *Health and Social Care in the Community, 10* (4), 229–238.

Cunningham, S., Lindo, J. M., Myers, C., & Schlosser, A. (2017). *How far is too far? New evidence on abortion clinic closures, access, and abortions.* National Bureau of Economics Research.

Douthit, N., Kiv, S., Dwolatzky, T., & Biswas, S. (2015). Exposing some important barriers to health care access in the rural USA. *Public Health, 129*(6), 611–620.

Guzman, G., Posey, K. G., Bishaw, A., & Benson, C. (2018). *Differences in income growth across U.S. counties.* https://www.census.gov/library/stories/2018/12/differences-in-income-growth-across-united-states-counties.html

Halverson, G., & Brownlee, K. (2010). Managing ethical considerations around dual relationships in small rural and remote Canadian communities. *International Social Work, 53*(2), 247–260. https://journals.sagepub.com/doi/10.1177/0020872809355386

Hung, P., Kozhimannil, K. B., Casey, M. M., & Moscovice, I. S. (2016). Why are obstetric units in rural hospitals closing their doors? *Health Services Research, 51*(4), 1546–1560.

Jerman, J., Jones, R. K., & Onda, T. (2016). *Characteristics of US abortion patients in 2014 and changes since 2008.* Guttmacher Institute.

Komiti, A., Judd, F., & Jackson, H. (2006). The influence of stigma and attitudes on seeking help from a GP for mental health problems: A rural context. *Social Psychiatry and Psychiatric Epidemiology, 41*, 1–8.

Murray, J. D. (2019). *Op-ed: Rural stereotypes in reality TV serve up skewed views.* Advance Local Media. https://www.pennlive.com/opinion/2013/01/op-ed_rural_stereotypes_in_reality_tv_serve_up_skewed_views.html

National Association of Social Workers. (2018). *Code of ethics of the National Association of Social Workers.*

Norris, D. (2018). Poverty, pavement, and paying attention: Rural child welfare practice in the American Great Plains. In J. Riebschleger & B. Pierce (Eds.), *Rural child welfare practice: Stories from the field* (pp. 32–46). Oxford University Press.

Pathman, D. E., Ricketts, T. C., & Konrad, T. R. (2006). How adults' access to outpatient physician services relates to the local supply of primary care physicians in the rural southeast. *Health Services Research, 41,* 79–102.

Pearson, J., Friedrichsen, S., & Olson, L. (2018). Changes in labor and delivery patterns and outcomes after rural obstetrical service closure. *Journal of Regional Medical Campuses, 1*(4). https://pubs.lib.umn.edu/index.php/jrmc/article/view/1379/1318

Pitsor, J. (2019). States modernizing certificate of need laws. *Legisbrief, 27*(41), 1–2.

Ratcliffe, M., Burd, C., Holder, K., & Fields, A. (2016). *Defining rural at the U.S. Census Bureau* (ACSGEO-1). U.S. Census Bureau.

Riebschleger, J., Norris, D., Pierce, B., Pond, D., & Cummings, C. (2015). Preparing social work students for rural child welfare practice: Emerging curriculum competencies. *Journal of Social Work Education, 51,* S209–S224. https://doi.org/10.1080/10437797.2015.1072422

Rost, K., Smith, G. R., & Taylor, J. L. (1993). Rural–urban differences in stigma and the use of care for depressive disorders. *Journal of Rural Health, 9*(1), 57–62. doi:10.1111/j.1748-0361.1993.tb00495.x

Tönnies, F. (1887). *Gemeinschaft und gesellschaft.* Fues's Verlag. (Translated in 1957 by C. Price Loomis as *Community and Society,* Michigan State University Press)

U.S. Department of Agriculture. (2013). *Rural veterans at a glance.* Economic Brief 25. https://www.ers.usda.gov/webdocs/publications/42891/40612_eb25.pdf?v=4049.6

U.S. Census Bureau (2017). *One in Five Americans live in rural Areas.* https://www.census.gov/library/stories/2017/08/rural-america.html

Wendell, B. (2002). The prejudice against country people. *Progressive, 66*(4), 21.

Zuniga, C., Grossman, D., Harrell, S., Blanchard, K., & Grindlay, K. (2020). Breaking down barriers to birth control access: An assessment of online platforms prescribing birth control in the USA. *Journal of Telemedicine and Telecare, 26*(6), 322–331. https://doi.org/10.1177/1357633X18824828

PART XII

Behavioral and Mental Health

Substance Use Disorders

Overview, Special Populations, and Treatment Considerations

Sara Beeler-Stinn, Autumn Asher BlackDeer, and
David A. Patterson Silver Wolf

Substance use disorders (SUDs) are the most prevalent psychiatric disorders and are highly comorbid with other mental health diagnoses (McGue & Irons, 2013). There are 20.3 million individuals aged 12 years or older currently meeting diagnostic criteria for SUDs, with alcohol being the foremost substance, followed by illicit drugs including marijuana and nonprescription pain medicine (opioids). An estimated 2.7 million individuals are polydrug users and meet diagnostic criteria for both alcohol use disorders and SUDs [Substance Abuse and Mental Health Services Administration (SAMHSA), 2019]. Historically, many terms have been used to describe what is currently known as SUDs, including, but not limited to, addiction, abuse, misuse, problem drinking/use, and dependence. The term most used and understood in the general public, addiction, is not just specific to alcohol and drug use but may also include harmful behaviors related to sex, food, gambling, video games, social media, etc. This variance of terminology impacts how SUDs are measured and understood.

The fifth edition of the *Diagnostic and Statistical Manual of Mental Disorders* [American Psychiatric Association (APA), 2013] introduced the most current term, substance use disorder. SUDs are diagnosed on a tier of mild, moderate, or severe depending on the number of impairment criteria met, which is two or three, four or five, and six or more, respectively. Criteria are based on the following symptoms [APA, 2013; U.S. Department of Health and Human Services, Office of the Surgeon General (DHHS OSG), 2016]:

- Using larger quantities or using longer than intended
- Wanting to cut down/stop, but unable to
- A lot of time dedicated to obtain, use, and/or recover from use
- Cravings

- Unable to manage commitments
- Continuing to use, despite problems
- Quitting important activities due to use
- Using even when it puts you in danger
- Using even when there are physical or psychological consequences to continued use
- Increased tolerance
- Withdrawal

Risk Factors

Adolescence is a critical stage for the etiology of SUDs (DHHS OSG, 2016; McHugh et al., 2018). Most individuals reporting a SUD in their lifetime were diagnosed by the time they turned age 25 years, with use typically starting in adolescence (DHHS OSG, 2016). Risk factors contribute to the development of persistent and problematic drug and alcohol use in adolescence or SUDs in early adulthood (Hawkins et al., 1992).

SUD risk factors fall within three broad categories: biological, environmental, and developmental [DHHS OSG, 2016; National Institute on Drug Abuse (NIDA), 2018b]. Biological factors refer to predispositions to the development of SUDs from genetics (McGue & Irons, 2013). At an environmental level, these are known as determinants that include societal and cultural norms (e.g., negative views/opinions on drug and alcohol use), legal systems (e.g., harsh drug and alcohol policies, arrests), and economic structures (e.g., taxing and high alcohol availability; Stone et al., 2012). Environmental factors also include interpersonal variables such as peer and familial substance use and exposure to traumatic events and/or violence (DHHS OSG, 2016; Stone et al., 2012). Developmental risk factors refer not only to the impact of early drug use on the body and changes in the brain but also to the interaction of genetic and environmental factors (Hawkins et al., 1992; McGue & Irons, 2013).

Special Populations
People in the Criminal Justice System

Special Considerations

Rates of SUDs among inmates are often 10–12 times higher than seen within the general population (NIDA, 2018c). Statistics of SUDs prevalence in the criminal justice system from 2007 and 2008/2009 reported 58% of state prison populations and 63% of sentenced individuals in jails met diagnostic criteria for either drug dependence or abuse per the DSM-IV (Bronson et al., 2017). Prevalence of alcohol use disorders has been documented as high as 51% among prisoner populations (Fazel et al., 2017). Given the illegal nature of illicit drug use and the propensity of committing crimes while under the influence of drugs or alcohol (Bronson et al., 2017), the high risk of involvement with the criminal justice system is clear.

Treatment Options

The most common and oldest SUD treatment offered in prisons is known as therapeutic communities (TCs), which are often cited as the most effective prison treatment [Center for Substance Abuse Treatment (CSAT), 2005; Messina et al., 2010]. TCs typically last approximately 6 months at a minimum and are set up like typical community-based residential, inpatient SUD treatment systems (Shapiro, 2001). Traditional TCs mostly target outcomes such as rearrest, incarceration, substance use, and/or enrollment in aftercare, and sometimes treatment completion and retention (Malivert et al., 2012; Perry et al., 2015). Other options available for treatment within prisons include cognitive–behavioral treatment and 12-step peer support groups such as Alcoholics Anonymous (CSAT, 2005). Unlike prisons, health care is not mandated in jails, and given the high rates of population turnover, Screening, Brief Intervention, and Referral to Treatment is a better option for intervention (Belenko et al., 2013).

Barriers to Treatment

Institutional budget constraints and inadequate spatial capacity are often the primary reasons why individuals with SUDs are not able to receive services in criminal justice institutions (CSAT, 2005). There is not adequate space for separate treatment wings within the institutions, and participants reside among the general incarcerated population (CSAT, 2005). Similarly, given the high need for treatment for SUDs among incarcerated populations (Fazel et al., 2017; Tsai & Gu, 2019), existing treatment resources may not be able to meet demand (Cropsey et al., 2012). In addition, upon release, formerly incarcerated persons may find a lack of coordination or treatment available from incarceration into the community (Priester et al., 2016). Fragmented service delivery systems along with an increased risk for stigma are critical barriers for formerly incarcerated persons accessing needed SUD treatment (Baillargeon et al., 2010; Begun et al., 2016).

Women

Special Considerations

Unique differences exist between men and women that impact the likelihood of developing SUDs as well as access to/utilization of treatment. Although men account for the majority of treatment admissions (SAMSHA Center for Behavioral Health Statistics and Quality (CBHSQ), 2017), women have higher drinking and illicit drug use rates (NIDA, 2018c). Furthermore, women diagnosed with SUDs report higher rates of psychological distress (SAMHSA CBHSQ, 2017). This is likely due to women also experiencing higher rates of emotional, physical, and sexual abuse (Covington, 2008) and subsequently using

drugs and alcohol to self-medicate or cope with the emotional or physical pain (Chesney-Lind & Pasko, 2013). Women are shown to have a faster progression of substance use to SUDs, a process known as "telescoping" (McHugh et al., 2018, p. 14). In addition, women often present with more severe symptoms and impairment in medical and social domains when they enter SUD treatment, even when they have used substances for a shorter period (Greenfield et al., 2010).

Treatment Options

Standard community-based SUD treatments available include residential and outpatient treatment (DHHS OSG, 2016); however, it is important to recognize that most treatment options available are based on male models of treatment (Saxena et al., 2014). There are six principles of care to consider when treating and/or finding care for women with SUDs: (1) Offer gender-specific groups/treatment; (2) have comprehensive and integrated treatment that addresses addiction, mental health, parenting, relationships, culture, employment, and other care management; (3) ensure it is a trauma-informed environment; (4) offer a variety of therapy options that address the whole person; (5) use approaches and perspectives that are strengths-based; and (6) offer individualized treatment (Covington, 2002). Similarly, effective programming for women has included social and peer supports as well as activities that build their coping and decision-making skills through empowerment (Austin et al., 1992).

Barriers to Treatment

Women have unique service needs that may contribute to lack of utilization and/or dropout. Unless prison treatment is modified to include gender-responsive programming, trauma and other mental health issues are likely to remain unaddressed, threatening overall success. This is problematic given the prevalence of trauma and other mental health diagnoses among women in prison, in addition to the fact that psychological distress has been linked as a key recidivating factor for formerly incarcerated women (Messina et al., 2006). Treatment that fails to address the unique needs of women can lead to poor coping post-release (CSAT, 2005), increasing the likelihood of relapse and/or re-arrests. Most women who enter treatment are mothers of young children (Greenfield et al., 2010) and often experience disproportionate rates of stigma compared to their male counterparts, which often presents mothers with two options: seek treatment or retain custody of children (Chesney-Lind & Pasko, 2013). Given this, lack of onsite child care is a major barrier to treatment for women (Priester et al., 2016). This is further complicated for pregnant women with SUDs or using drugs and/or alcohol; pregnant women will often not seek treatment for fear of prosecution (McHugh et al., 2018).

People with Opioid Use Disorders

Special Considerations

Opioids are inclusive of illegal drugs (i.e., heroin and fentanyl) and legal prescription drugs (i.e., oxycodone, hydrocone, codeine, morphine, etc.; NIDA, n.d.). Overprescribing of pain medicine in the 1990s spurred the opioid crisis (DHHS OSG, 2016) that represents the roughly 2 million individuals aged 12 years or older diagnosed with an opioid use disorder (OUD; SAMHSA, 2019). Drug overdose has been the long-standing leader in accidental deaths (NIDA, 2018a; NIDA, 2018b), with 70% of these fatalities involving an illicit or prescription opioid (Centers for Disease Control and Prevention, 2020). Another concern is the growing incidence of neonatal abstinence syndrome among infants exposed to drugs, specifically opioids, while in utero, which impacts long-term overall health (DHHS OSG, 2018).

Treatment Options

Like other SUDs, OUDs can be treated with community-based treatments including residential and outpatient treatment, which is more broadly referred to as psychotherapy treatment (Marsch & Dallery, 2012). Evidence suggests that the best treatment for long-term recovery (i.e., abstinence) for individuals living with OUDs is utilizing both psychotherapy and medication-assisted treatment (MAT; i.e., methadone, buprenorphine, or naltrexone) (Sordo et al., 2017; Volkow et al., 2014). MAT medications are approved by the U.S. Food and Drug Administration and are designed to help with craving and withdrawal and block the effects of the drug and/or alcohol (SAMHSA, 2020). All MAT medications have their respective administration route, dosage, side effects, and optimal phase of treatment for efficiency (Lee et al., 2015; SAMHSA, 2020). OUD MAT includes methadone, buprenorphine, and naltrexone and the overdose preventative naloxone (SAMHSA, 2020). Given the psychosocial treatment needs of individuals with SUDs (e.g., emotional, relational, and housing needs), a combination of MAT and psychosocial treatment is beneficial (Aletraris et al., 2016; SAMHSA, 2020).

Barriers to Treatment

In addition to other barriers mentioned previously, there are several specific barriers to MAT for OUDs. Access to prescribers with MAT expertise, lack of medical staff onsite to qualify for MAT administration, and lack of funding are among the most reported barriers to implementing/accessing MAT from treatment administrators (Knudsen et al., 2011). Although most insurance providers and Medicaid cover some MAT options, there are still restrictions, such as limited dosing and/or annual or lifetime administration limits that prevent ongoing care (Volkow et al., 2014). Stigma, which is a common barrier across all SUD treatments, can also contribute to OUD availability because it may prevent eligible providers from adopting/ getting certified to implement MAT (Getz, n.d.); this further impacts access, particularly for rural populations (Cole et al., 2019).

Conclusion

Criminalization has historically been the way addictive behavior has been approached. Society's enactment of policy often dictates what is legal versus illegal and fuels mixed ideologies of SUDs at a family, treatment, and societal level (DiClemente, 2018). Like other chronic diseases, SUDs benefit from long-term comprehensive care. SUDs have complex treatment issues that require a collaborative continuum of care, including behavioral health, medical, and other social and community services (SAMHSA, 2020). Considering the needs of special populations and availability of effective interventions is critical to individualized treatment, which is key to long-term recovery (Hilton & Pilkonis, 2015).

Helpful Resources

HealthMeasures: https://www.healthmeasures.net
National Institute on Alcohol Abuse and Alcoholism: https://www.niaaa.nih.gov
National Institute on Drug Abuse. *Publications*: https://www.drugabuse.gov/publications
Substance Abuse and Mental Health Services Administration: https://www.samhsa.gov
Substance Abuse and Mental Health Services Administration. *Treatment Improvement Protocol (TIP) series*: https://store.samhsa.gov/?f%5B0%5D=series%3A5557

References

Aletraris, L., Edmond, M. B., Paino, M., Fields, D., & Roman, P. M. (2016). Counselor training and attitudes toward pharmacotherapies for opioid use disorder. *Substance Abuse, 37*(1), 47–53. https://doi.org/10.1080/08897077.2015.1062457

American Psychiatric Association. (2013). *Diagnostic and statistical manual of mental disorders* (5th ed.). American Psychiatric Publishing.

Austin, J., Bloom, B., & Donahue, T. (1992). *Female offenders in the community: An analysis of innovative strategies and programs.* National Council on Crime and Delinquency.

Baillargeon, J., Hoge, S. K., & Penn, J. V. (2010). Addressing the challenge of community reentry among released inmates with serious mental illness. *American Journal of Community Psychology, 46*(3), 361–375. https://doi.org/10.1007/s10464-010-9345-6

Begun, A. L., Early, T. J., & Hodge, A. (2016). Mental health and substance abuse service engagement by men and women during community reentry following incarceration. *Administration and Policy in Mental Health and Mental Health Services Research, 43*(2), 207–218. https://doi.org/10.1007/s10488-015-0632-2

Belenko, S., Hiller, M. L., & Hamilton, L. (2013). Treating substance use disorders in the criminal justice system. *Current Psychiatry Reports, 15*(11), 1–7. https://doi.org/10.1007/s11920-013-0414-z

Bronson, J., Stroop, J., Zimmer, S., & Berzofsky, M. (2017). *Drug use, dependence, and abuse among state prisoners and jail inmates, 2007–2009.* Bureau of Justice Statistics.

Center for Disease Control and Prevention. (2020, May 5). *Drug overdose*. Retrieved May 24, 2020, from https://www.cdc.gov/drugoverdose/index.html

Center for Substance Abuse Treatment. (2005). *Substance abuse treatment for adults in the criminal justice system. Treatment improvement protocol (TIP) series 44* [HHS Publication No. (SMA) 13-4056]. Substance Abuse and Mental Health Services Administration. https://store.samhsa.gov/system/files/sma13-4056.pdf

Chesney-Linda, M., & Pasko, L. (2013). *The female offender: Girls, women, and crime* (3rd ed.). Sage.

Cole, E. S., DiDomenico, E., Cochran, G., Gordon, A. J., Gellad, W. F., Pringle, J., Warwick, J., Chang, C.-C. H., Kim, J. Y., Kmiec, J., Kelley, D., & Donohue, J. M. (2019). The role of primary care in improving access to medication-assisted treatment for rural Medicaid enrollees with opioid use disorder. *Journal of General Internal Medicine, 34*(6), 936–943. https://doi.org/10.1007/s11606-019-04943-6

Covington, S. S. (2002). Helping women recover: Creating gender-responsive treatment. In S. L. A. Straussner & S. Brown (Eds.), *The handbook of addiction treatment for women: Theory and practice* (pp. 52–72). Jossey-Bass.

Covington, S. S. (2008). Women and addiction: A trauma-informed approach. *Journal of Psychoactive Drugs, 5*, 377–385.

Cropsey, K. L., Binswanger, I. A., Clark, C. B., & Taxman, F. S. (2012). The unmet medical needs of correctional populations in the United States.

Journal of the National Medical Association, *104*(11–12), 487–492. https://doi.org/10.1016/S0027-9684(15)30214-5

DiClemente, C. C. (2018). *Addiction and change. How addictions develop and addicted people recover.* Guilford.

Fazel, S., Yoon, I. A., & Hayes, A. J. (2017). Substance use disorders in prisoners: An updated systematic review and meta-regression analysis in recently incarcerated men and women. *Addiction, 112,* 1725–1739. doi:10.1111/add.13877

Getz, L. (n.d.). Medication-assisted treatment: Tool tackling opioid crisis faces stigma, other barriers. *Social Work Today, 18*(4), 10. Retrieved May 24, 2020, from https://www.socialworktoday.com/archive/JA18p10.shtml

Greenfield, S. F., Back, S. E., Lawson, K., & Brady, K. T. (2010). Substance abuse in women. *Psychiatric Clinics of North America, 3*(2), 339–355. https://doi.org/10.1038/jid.2014.371

Hawkins, J. D., Catalono, R. F., & Miller, J. Y. (1992). Risk and protective factors for alcohol and other drug problems in adolescence and early adulthood: Implications for substance abuse prevention. *Psychological Bulletin, 112*(1), 64–105.

Hilton, T. F., & Pilkonis, P. A. (2015). The key to individualized addiction treatment is comprehensive assessment and monitoring of symptoms and behavioral change. *Behavioral Sciences, 5*(4), 477–495. https://doi.org/10.3390/bs5040477

Knudsen, H. K., Abraham, A. J., & Oser, C. B. (2011). Barriers to the implementation of medication-assisted treatment for substance use disorders: The importance of funding policies and medical infrastructure. *Evaluation and Program Planning, 34*(4), 375–381. https://doi.org/10.1016/j.evalprogplan.2011.02.004

Lee, J., Kresina, T. F., Campopiano, M., Lubran, R., & Clark, H. W. (2015). Use of pharmacotherapies in the treatment of alcohol use disorders and opioid dependence in primary care. *BioMed Research International,* 2015, Article ID 137020. https://doi.org/10.1155/2015/137020

Malivert, M., Fatséas, M., Denis, C., Langlois, E., & Auriacombe, M. (2012). Effectiveness of therapeutic communities: A systematic review. *European Addiction Research, 18*(1), 1–11. doi:10.1159/000331007

Marsch, L. A., & Dallery, J. (2012). Advances in the psychosocial treatment of addiction: The role of technology in the delivery of evidence-based psychosocial treatment. *Psychiatric Clinics of North America, 35*(2), 481–493. https://doi.org/10.1016/j.psc.2012.03.009

McGue, M., & Irons, D. E. (2013). Etiology. In B. S. McCrady & E. E. Epstein (Eds.), *Addictions: A comprehensive guidebook* (pp. 36–72). Oxford University Press.

McHugh, R. K., Votaw, V. R., Sugarman, D. E., & Greenfield, S. F. (2018). Sex and gender differences in substance use disorders. *Clinical Psychology Review 66,* 12–23.

Messina, N., Burdon, W., & Prendergast, M. (2006). Prison-based treatment for drug-dependent women offenders: Treatment versus no treatment. *Journal of Psychoactive Drugs, 3,* 333–343. doi:10.1080/02791072.2006.10400597

Messina, N., Grella, C. E., Cartier, J., & Torres, S. (2010). A randomized experimental study of gender-responsive substance abuse treatment for women in prison. *Journal of Substance Abuse Treatment, 38*(2), 97–107.

National Institute on Drug Abuse. (2018a). *Understanding drug use and addiction.* https://www.drugabuse.gov/publications/drugfacts/understanding-drug-use-addiction

National Institute on Drug Abuse. (2018b). *Overdose death rates.* https://www.drugabuse.gov/related-topics/trends-statistics/overdose-death-rates

National Institute on Drug Abuse. (2018c). *Substance use in women.* https://www.drugabuse.gov/publications/research-reports/substance-use-in-women

National Institute on Drug Abuse. (n.d.). *Opioids.* Retrieved May 23, 2020, from https://www.drugabuse.gov/drugs-abuse/opioids

Perry, A. E., Neilson, M., Martyn-St. James, M., Glanville, J. M., Woodhouse, R., & Hewitt, C. (2015). Interventions for female drug-using offenders. *Cochrane Database of Systematic Reviews, 2015*(6), CD010910. doi:10.1002/14651858.CD010910.pub2

Priester, M., Browne, T., Iachini, A., Clone, S., DeHard, D., & Seay, K. D. (2016). Treatment access barriers and disparities among individuals with co-occurring mental health and substance use disorders: An integrative literature review. *Journal of Substance Abuse Treatment, 61,* 47–59. https://www.ncbi.nlm.nih.gov/pmc/articles/PMC4695242/

Saxena, P., Messina, N. P., & Grella, C. E. (2014). Who benefits from gender-responsive treatment? Accounting for abuse history on longitudinal outcomes for women in prison. *Criminal Justice and Behavior, 41*(4), 417–432. doi:10.1177/0093854813514405

Shapiro, B. (2001). A view from the line. The therapeutic community movement in corrections. *Corrections Today, 63*(1), 24–32.

Sordo, L., Barrio, G., Bravo, M. J., Indave, B. I., Degenhardt, L., Wiessing, L., Ferri, M., &

Pastor-Barriuso, R. (2017). Mortality risk during and after opioid substitution treatment: Systematic review and meta-analysis of cohort studies. *British Medical Journal, 357,* j1550. https://doi.org/10.1136/bmj.j1550

Stone, A. L., Becker, L. G., Huber, A. M., & Catalano, R. F. (2012). Review of risk and protective factors of substance use and problem use in emerging adulthood. *Addictive Behaviors, 37,* 747–775. doi:10.1016/j.addbeh.2012.02.014

Substance Abuse and Mental Health Services Administration. (2019). *Key substance use and mental health indicators in the United States: Results from the 2018 National Survey on Drug Use and Health* (HHS Publication No. PEP19-5068, NSDUH Series H-54). Center for Behavioral Health Statistics and Quality, Substance Abuse and Mental Health Services Administration. https://www.samhsa.gov/data

Substance Abuse and Mental Health Services Administration. (2020). *Medications for opioid use disorder.* Treatment Improvement Protocol (TIP) Series 63. Publication No. PEP20-02-01-006. https://store.samhsa.gov/product/TIP-63-Medications-for-Opioid-Use-Disorder-Full-Document/PEP20-02-01-006

Substance Abuse and Mental Health Services Administration, Center for Behavioral Health Statistics and Quality. (2017). *Treatment Episode Data Set (TEDS): 2005–2015. State admissions to substance abuse treatment services* [BHSIS Series S-95, HHS Publication No. (SMA) 17-4360]. https://www.samhsa.gov/data/data-we-collect/teds-treatment-episode-data-set

Tsai, J., & Gu, X. (2019). Utilization of addiction treatment among U.S. adults with history of incarceration and substance use disorders. *Addiction Science & Clinical Practice, 14*(1), 9. https://doi.org/10.1186/s13722-019-0138-4

U.S. Department of Health and Human Services, Office of the Surgeon General. (2016). *Facing addiction in America: The Surgeon General's report on alcohol, drugs, and health.*

U.S. Department of Health and Human Services, Office of the Surgeon General. (2018). *Facing addiction in America: The Surgeon General's spotlight on opioids.*

Volkow, N. D., Frieden, T. R., Hyde, P. S., & Cha, S. S. (2014). Medication-assisted therapies—Tackling the opioid-overdose epidemic. *New England Journal of Medicine, 370*(22), 2063–2066. https://doi.org/10.1056/NEJMp1402780

Treatment of Tobacco Use Disorder

Susan B. Trout, Michael H. Baca-Atlas, and Stefani N. Baca-Atlas

After 400 years of cultivation and commercialization of tobacco in the United States, the 1964 Surgeon General's *Report on Tobacco* warned "cigarette smoking is a health hazard of sufficient importance in the United States to warrant appropriate remedial action" (Public Health Service, 1964, p. 33). Today, the causal links between tobacco use and cancer are well established, and smoking increases the likelihood of cardiovascular disease, lung disease, fertility and pregnancy-related problems, and dental and oral issues across all populations [Centers for Disease Control and Prevention (CDC), n.d.c]. Social workers may be the first and only point of contact with marginalized populations. As such, social workers must be cognizant of systemic inequities that increase the burden of tobacco use among marginalized groups, including people of color, people with mental illness, veterans, and immigrants (Creamer, 2019). Social workers are trained to work with diverse clients affected by interpersonal and systemic issues that may contribute to tobacco use uptake, delayed help-seeking, and limited access to evidence-based treatment (Acquavita, 2020).

Background

Although tobacco use disorder (TUD) may be most commonly associated with cigarettes, new mechanisms for delivering nicotine to the brain are constantly emerging on the market. Tobacco companies continue to develop tobacco products, in part to attract new users (Office of the Commissioner, 2016; Soneji et al., 2016). Targeted advertisements, federal policy, and availability contribute to the differential impact of certain products on particular groups, including youth and marginalized groups (J. J. Prochaska et al., 2017). A general understanding of tobacco products on the market can assist with screening and identifying appropriate interventions. Table 122.1 provides an overview of tobacco products.

TUD is a chronic disease that may contain multiple periods of remission and relapse and require as many interventions (Joseph et al., 2011). Tobacco treatment and control measures are effective and can significantly increase rates of long-term abstinence leading to positive health and behavioral health outcomes, including improving abstinence from other addictive substances (J. J. Prochaska et al., 2004). Social workers are encouraged to meet clients where they are and collaborate with clients to assess readiness for change and choose strategies to maintain their goals. Approximately 70% of adult cigarette smokers want to quit, and social workers are well equipped to support clients' cessation efforts (J. J. Prochaska & Benowitz, 2016).

change theories used with clients coping with substance use (Whitelaw et al., 2000). This theory emphasizes the stages are not linear: A client may move among the stages multiple times and experience relapses (DiClemente et al., 1991; DiClemente & Prochaska, 1998). Table 122.2 provides a description of each stage, clients' corresponding characteristics, and strategies for intervention.

Transtheoretical Model of Behavior Change

The transtheoretical model, also known as the stages of change model, may provide a framework for identifying a client's readiness for change and subsequently developing strategies for working with the client (J. O. Prochaska & DiClemente, 1983; Whitelaw et al., 2000). This is among the most commonly used behavior

Tobacco Use Assessment

The U.S. Preventive Services Task Force recommends that all clinicians ask clients if they use tobacco and, if so, to advise clients to stop using tobacco and provide behavioral interventions (Siu, 2015). This recommendation is vital because social workers may be the only point of contact for marginalized populations

TABLE 122.1 Overview of Common Tobacco Products

Products	Description
Cigarette, cigar, cigarillo, little cigar	Cigarettes most commonly used (13.7% of U.S. adults); highest among Indigenous/Native Americans. Higher rates among lesbian/gay/bisexual vs. heterosexual. "Low," "light," or "mild" products are not safer than regular cigarettes. Cigars may be modified by clients (adding cannabis, cocaine). Combination nicotine replacement therapy and varenicline most effective medications + behavioral interventions (*Cochrane Review*).
Hookah, water pipe	Used in group settings, common among youth. Similar health risks to cigarettes. 7.8% high school students in 2018; 12.3% young adults (aged 19–30 years) in 2018.
Smokeless	Examples: chewing tobacco, snuff, snus. Increased risk of head, neck, and gastrointestinal cancers. Varenicline, lozenges, and behavioral interventions.
ENDS	E-cigarette, e-pen, vape, e-hookah. Look like regular tobacco products or USB flash drives or pens. Top selling brand: JUUL. Nicotine in one "pod" is equivalent to that of approximately one pack of cigarettes. Common among youth through age 24 years. Nicotine can harm the developing brain. Increases likelihood youth will smoke. Long-term health effects of ENDS still unknown.

ENDS, electronic nicotine delivery systems.

Sources: Centers for Disease Control and Prevention (n.d.a, n.d.b, n.d.c, 2016), Creamer (2019), Lichtenberg (2017), Office of Population Affairs (2016), and Stead et al. (2016).

TABLE 122.2 Transtheoretical Model/Stages of Change

Stage	Client Characteristics	Strategies for Intervention
Precontemplation	Denies problem. Currently uses tobacco and has no intention of change.	Discuss and educate client on the risks versus benefits of continued tobacco use and the potential positive outcomes of behavior change. Motivational interviewing. "What if" statements.
Contemplation	Aware of the need to change behavior, but no commitment to action. Weighs advantages and disadvantages.	Identify barriers and misconceptions; address concerns; work with client to identify support system. May create cognitive dissonance around client's current behavior and what they desire. Motivational interviewing.
Preparation	Intent on making change. Begins to form goals and plan.	Develop SMART goals. Create specific timeline. Positively reinforce. Help prepare optimal conditions for success.
Action	Implemented behavior modifications.	Positively reinforce (and avoid other forms of reinforcement).
Maintenance	Maintaining behavior change; the client actively remains tobacco-free.	Positive feedback and support. Review relapse prevention strategies/plans.

Note: Clients are likely to move up and down through stages. Although there is not a stage for "relapse," social workers should remember that when the client is in precontemplation, they are actively using tobacco. Social workers are nonjudgmental and allow clients to explore tobacco use and ambivalence as they relate to their personal values and goals.

Sources: Davidson (1998), J. O. Prochaska and DiClemente (1983), and Sorensen et al. (2009).

(Acquavita, 2020). Two tools are commonly used to directly assess levels of nicotine addiction.[1] The Fagerstrom Test for Nicotine Dependence consists of six questions to determine the level of physical nicotine dependence (Heatherton et al., 1991). The History of Nicotine Checklist captures quantitative data on the level of nicotine addiction and loss of autonomy among adolescents (DiFranza et al., 2002). Biochemical assessments of tobacco use provide objective data that can be beneficial in discussing a client's tobacco use and treatment plan (Goldstein et al., 2018).

Tobacco Use Treatment

Less than 3% of unaided adult smokers succeed in quitting tobacco use, and they experience high relapse rates (Miller et al., 2019). A combination of pharmacotherapy with behavioral support has a higher rate of efficacy than pharmacotherapy or support alone (Stead et al., 2016). Multiple modalities and techniques are available to support clients, and ongoing support is key to long-term abstinence (Lunden et al., 2019). Social workers are responsible for identifying and adapting approaches and tools that will best serve their population.

Tobacco Cessation Medications

Pharmacotherapy can help reduce physical symptoms of nicotine withdrawal so that clients can focus their attention and energy on establishing new life patterns, managing various emotional states, and participating in social activities without nicotine (Jackson et al., 2015). Long-acting medications (i.e., nicotine patch, bupropion, and varenicline) reduce nicotine withdrawal symptoms and urges, whereas

---

1. Nicotine's highly addictive properties are the basis for TUD.

immediate-release medications (i.e., nicotine gum, lozenge, inhaler, and nasal spray) help manage urges that occur throughout the day due to triggers and physical withdrawal.

Brief Interventions

Five A's

The 5 A's intervention (*ask*, *advise*, *assess*, *assist*, and *arrange*) incorporates screening and assessment into the brief intervention. The 5 A's is ideal for addressing tobacco use with clients in health care settings and is particularly useful for social workers who do not have expertise in substance use disorder treatment (Dixon et al., 2009). Modified versions of the 5 A's may prove beneficial based on the setting and needs of social workers and clients.

Motivational Interviewing

Motivational interviewing (MI) is based on a collaborative relationship between the clinician and client (Davidson, 1998). Social workers use open-ended and nonjudgmental questions that help clients assess their motivations for and barriers to becoming tobacco-free (Sorensen et al., 2009). This technique is especially useful for clients who appreciate a nonhierarchical alliance and who are in precontemplative stages (Grobe et al., 2020; Heckman et al., 2010). See the Helpful Resources section for resources related to MI.

Behavioral Interventions and Techniques

Cognitive–Behavioral Therapy

A range of emotions may trigger tobacco cravings and use (Ussher et al., 2009). Cognitive–behavioral therapy (CBT) can be used to help clients identify and change unhelpful patterns (e.g., all-or-nothing thinking and catastrophizing) (Collins et al., 2013). CBT is the most common behavioral therapy for tobacco cessation (Lunden et al., 2019).

Problem-Solving and Skills Training

The goal of problem-solving and skills training is to provide alternative ways of coping without tobacco (Fiore et al., 2008). The core components are (1) recognize triggers for relapse, (2) develop coping skills, and (3) provide basic information related to tobacco use (Fiore et al., 2008; Patnode et al., 2015).

Acceptance and Commitment Therapy

Acceptance and commitment therapy (ACT) can help clients learn strategies for coping with everyday emotions, cravings, and urges. ACT may be especially beneficial for clients with mental illness (J. J. Prochaska et al., 2017).

Mindfulness and Alternative Therapies

Mindfulness can reduce stress and anxiety, and it promotes self-awareness related to tobacco use, cravings, and urges. This technique can be used as a first-line treatment (Chiesa & Serretti, 2014; Hick & Furlotte, 2009). Exercise also has an immediate effect on cravings and urges and is recommended as a supplement to pharmacological and/or counseling therapies (Ussher et al., 2009). Some alternative treatments, such as acupuncture and hypnosis, are not as efficacious as traditional therapies, but they may be used in conjunction with traditional therapies in order to respect client's autonomy and to promote resolve to remain tobacco-free (Steinka-Fry et al., 2017).

Conclusion

Tobacco use is a global public health problem that affects diverse populations in the United States. In addition, social workers may be the first and only point of contact for marginalized groups seeking health and social services. Social workers are trained to work in multiple settings with diverse clients; they are equipped to collaborate with clients to identify interventions and strategies that will promote long-term tobacco cessation. This chapter provided an overview of TUD assessment and treatment as well as resources for more information necessary for social workers to provide services that are congruent with the profession's principles and values, including dignity and worth of a person and social justice (National Association of Social Workers, 2017).

Helpful Resources

Cessation Mobile Apps	Additional Cessation and Abstinence Apps
SmartQuit—Google Play Craving to Quit!—Google Play Quit Guide—Google Play quitSTART—Apple Store, Google Play Quit Tracker—Google Play SmokeFree—Apple Store	Mindfulness Apps UCLA Mindful App—free meditation app Insight Timer—free meditation app Exercise Apps Couch to 5k—free beginner running app Zombies, Run!—free beginner running app 7-Minute Workouts Charity Miles—exercise for donations
Federal, State, and Local Resources	**Special Populations**
Centers for Disease Control and Prevention Smoking and Tobacco Use 1-800-232-4636 National Cancer Institute Risk Factors > Tobacco 1-800-422-6237 UCSF Schools of Pharmacy & Medicine Medicine Rx for Change (comprehensive training for health professionals) Motivational Interviewing—MINT website	Pregnant women/mothers SmokefreeMOM or text MOM to 222888. At least 6 weeks, 3–5 texts/day You Quit Two Quit Veterans SmokefreeVET: 6–8 weeks, 3–5 texts/day Quitline – 1-(855)-QUITVET Spanish-speakers SmokefreeEspañol: 6–8 weeks, 3–5 texts/day Youth SmokefreeTEEN or text QUIT to 47848. Age 60+ SmokeFree 60+
Quitlines and Textlines	
National Cancer Institute 1-877-448-7848 1-877-44U-QUIT	Smokefree.gov 1-800-784-8669 1-800-QUITNOW 1-855-784-8838	SmokeFreeTXT Text QUIT to 47848

References

Acquavita, S. P. (2020). How social work can address the tobacco epidemic. *Journal of Social Work Practice in the Addictions, 20*(1), 82–87. https://doi.org/10.1080/1533256X.2020.1702348

Centers for Disease Control and Prevention. (n.d.a). Hookahs. https://www.cdc.gov/tobacco/data_statistics/fact_sheets/tobacco_industry/hookahs/index.htm

Centers for Disease Control and Prevention. (n.d.b). Smokeless tobacco: Health effects. https://www.cdc.gov/tobacco/data_statistics/fact_sheets/smokeless/health_effects/index.htm

Centers for Disease Control and Prevention. (n.d.c). Smoking & tobacco use. https://www.cdc.gov/tobacco/data_statistics/fact_sheets/index.htm?s_cid=osh-stu-home-spotlight-00

Centers for Disease Control and Prevention. (2016). Introduction, conclusions, and historical background relative to e-cigarettes. In *E-cigarette use among youth and young adults: A report of the Surgeon General*. U.S. Department of Health and Human Services, Centers for Disease Control and

Prevention. http://www.ncbi.nlm.nih.gov/books/NBK538684/

Chiesa, A., & Serretti, A. (2014). Are mindfulness-based interventions effective for substance use disorders? A systematic review of the evidence. *Substance Use & Misuse, 49*(5), 492–512. https://doi.org/10.3109/10826084.2013.770027

Collins, S. E., Eck, S., Torchalla, I., Schröter, M., & Batra, A. (2013). Understanding treatment-seeking smokers' motivation to change: Content analysis of the decisional balance worksheet. *Addictive Behaviors, 38*(1), 1472–1480. https://doi.org/10.1016/j.addbeh.2012.08.008

Creamer, M. R. (2019). Tobacco product use and cessation indicators among adults—United States, 2018. *MMWR Morbidity and Mortality Weekly Report, 68*(45), 1013–1019. https://doi.org/10.15585/mmwr.mm6845a2

Davidson, R. J. (1998). The treatment of substance abuse and dependence. In A. S. Bellack & M. Hersen (Eds.), *Comprehensive clinical psychology* (pp. 567–606). Pergamon. https://doi.org/10.1016/B0080-4270(73)00234-0

DiClemente, C. C., & Prochaska, J. O. (1998). Toward a comprehensive, transtheoretical model of change: Stages of change and addictive behavior. In W. R. Miller & N. Heather (Eds.), *Treating addictive behaviors* (2nd ed., pp. 3–24). Plenum.

DiClemente, C. C., Prochaska, J. O., Fairhurst, S., Velasquez, M., & Rossi, J. (1991). The process of smoking cessation: An analysis of precontemplation, contemplation, and preparation. *Journal of Consulting and Clinical Psychology, 59*(2), 295–304. https://doi.org/10.1037/0022-006X.59.2.295

DiFranza, J. R., Savageau, J. A., Fletcher, K., Ockene, J. K., Rigotti, N. A., McNeill, A. D., Coleman, M., & Wood, C. (2002). Measuring the loss of autonomy over nicotine use in adolescents: The Development and Assessment of Nicotine Dependence in Youths (DANDY) study. *Archives of Pediatric Adolescent Medicine, 156*, 397–403.

Dixon, L. B., Medoff, D., Goldberg, R., Lucksted, A., Kreyenbuhl, J., DiClemente, C., Potts, W., Leith, J., Brown, C., Adams, C., & Afful, J. (2009). Is implementation of the 5 A's of smoking cessation at community mental health centers effective for reduction of smoking by patients with serious mental illness. *American Journal on Addictions, 18*(5), 386–392. https://pubmed.ncbi.nlm.nih.gov/19874158/

Fiore, M. C., Jaén, C. R., Baker, T. B., Bailey, W. C., Benowitz, N. L., Curry, S. J., Dorfman, S. F., Froelicher, E. S., Goldstein, M. G., Healton, C. G., Henderson, P. N., Heyman, R. B., Koh, H. K., Kottke, T. E., Lando, H. A., Mecklenburg, R. E., Mermelstein, R. J., Mullen, P. D., Orleans, C. T., . . . Leitzke, C. (2008). *Treating tobacco use and dependence: 2008 update.* U.S. Department of Health and Human Services.

Goldstein, A. O., Gans, S. P., Ripley-Moffitt, C., Kotsen, C., & Bars, M. (2018). Use of expired air carbon monoxide testing in clinical tobacco treatment settings. *CHEST, 153*(2), 554–562. https://doi.org/10.1016/j.chest.2017.11.002

Grobe, J. E., Goggin, K., Harris, K. J., Richter, K. P., Resnicow, K., & Catley, D. (2020). Race moderates the effects of motivational interviewing on smoking cessation induction. *Patient Education and Counseling, 103*(2), 350–358. https://doi.org/10.1016/j.pec.2019.08.023

Heatherton, T. F., Kozlowski, L. T., Frecker, R. C., & Fagerstrom, K. O. (1991). The Fagerstrom Test for Nicotine Dependence: A revision of the Fagerstrom Tolerance Questionnaire. *British Journal of Addiction, 86*, 1119–1127.

Heckman, C. J., Egleston, B. L., & Hofmann, M. T. (2010). Efficacy of motivational interviewing for smoking cessation: A systematic review and meta-analysis. *Tobacco Control, 19*(5), 410–416. https://doi.org/10.1136/tc.2009.033175

Hick, S. F., & Furlotte, C. (2009). Mindfulness and social justice approaches: Bridging the mind and society in social work practice. *Canadian Social Work Review, 26*(1), 5–24.

Jackson, K. J., Muldoon, P. P., De Biasi, M., & Damaj, M. I. (2015). New mechanisms and perspectives in nicotine withdrawal. *Neuropharmacology, 96*(Part B), 223–234. https://doi.org/10.1016/j.neuropharm.2014.11.009

Joseph, A. M., Fu, S. S., Lindgren, B., Rothman, A. J., Kodl, M., Lando, H., Doyle, B., & Hatsukami, D. (2011). Chronic disease management for tobacco dependence. *Archives of Internal Medicine, 171*(21), 1894–1900. https://doi.org/10.1001/archinternmed.2011.500

Lichtenberg, K. (2017). E-cigarettes: Current evidence and policy. *Missouri Medicine, 114*(5), 335–338.

Lunden, S. E., Pittman, J. C., Prashad, N., Malhotra, R., & Sheffer, C. E. (2019). Cognitive, behavioral, and situational influences on relapse to smoking after group treatment for tobacco dependence. *Frontiers in Psychology, 9*, Article 2756. https://doi.org/10.3389/fpsyg.2018.02756

Miller, S. C., Fiellin, D. A., Rosenthal, R. N., Saitz, R., & American Society of Addiction Medicine. (Eds.). (2019). *The ASAM principles of addiction medicine* (7th ed.). Wolters Kluwer.

National Association of Social Workers. (2017). Code of ethics. https://www.socialworkers.org/About/Ethics/Code-of-Ethics/Code-of-Ethics-English

Office of Population Affairs. (2016, September 23). Adolescents and tobacco: Trends. U.S. Department of Health and Human Services, Office of Population Affairs. https://www.hhs.gov/ash/oah/adolescent-development/substance-use/drugs/tobacco/trends/index.html

Office of the Commissioner. (2016). *Recognize tobacco in its many forms.* U.S. Food and Drug Administration. https://www.federalregister.gov/documents/2016/05/10/2016-10685/deeming-tobacco-products-to-be-subject-to-the-federal-food-drug-and-cosmetic-act-as-amended-by-the

Patnode, C. D., Henderson, J. T., Thompson, J. H., Senger, C. A., Fortmann, S. P., & Whitlock, E. P. (2015). Behavioral counseling and pharmacotherapy interventions for tobacco cessation in adults, including pregnant women: A review of reviews for the U.S. Preventive Services Task Force. *Annals of Internal Medicine, 163,* 608–621. http://www.acpjournals.org/doi/10.7326/m15-0171

Prochaska, J. J., & Benowitz, N. L. (2016). The past, present, and future of nicotine addiction therapy. *Annual Review of Medicine, 67,* 467–486. https://doi.org/10.1146/annurev-med-111314-033712

Prochaska, J. J., Das, S., & Young-Wolff, K. C. (2017). Smoking, mental illness, and public health. *Annual Review of Public Health, 38*(1), 165–185. https://doi.org/10.1146/annurev-publhealth-031816-044618

Prochaska, J. J., Delucchi, K., & Hall, S. M. (2004). A meta-analysis of smoking cessation interventions with individuals in substance abuse treatment or recovery. *Journal of Consulting and Clinical Psychology, 72*(6), 1144–1156. https://doi.org/10.1037/0022-006X.72.6.1144

Prochaska, J. O., & DiClemente, C. C. (1983). Stages and processes of self-change of smoking: Toward an integrative model of change. *Journal of Consulting and Clinical Psychology, 51*(3), 390–395. https://doi.org/10.1037/0022-006X.51.3.390

Public Health Service. (1964). *Smoking and health: Report of the Advisory Committee to the Surgeon General of the Public Health Service* (No. 1103). U.S. Department of Health, Education, and Welfare, Public Health Service.

Siu, A. L. (2015). Behavioral and pharmacotherapy interventions for tobacco smoking cessation in adults, including pregnant women: U.S. Preventive Services Task Force recommendation statement. *Annals of Internal Medicine, 163*(8), 622–634. https://doi.org/10.7326/M15-2023

Soneji, S., Sargent, J., & Tanski, S. (2016). Multiple tobacco product use among US adolescents and young adults. *Tobacco Control, 25*(2), 174–180. https://doi.org/10.1136/tobaccocontrol-2014-051638

Sorensen, J. L., Hettema, J. E., & Larios, S. (2009). What is evidence-based treatment? In P. M. Miller (Ed.), *Evidence-based addiction treatment* (pp. 1–20). Academic Press. https://doi.org/10.1016/B978-0-12-374348-0.00001-X

Stead, L. F., Koilpillai, P., Fanshawe, T. R., & Lancaster, T. (2016). Combined pharmacotherapy and behavioural interventions for smoking cessation. *Cochrane Database of Systematic Reviews, 3,* CD008286. https://www.cochranelibrary.com/cdsr/doi/10.1002/14651858.CD008286.pub3/full

Steinka-Fry, K. T., Tanner-Smith, E. E., Dakof, G. A., & Henderson, C. (2017). Culturally sensitive substance use treatment for racial/ethnic minority youth: A meta-analytic review. *Journal of Substance Abuse Treatment, 75,* 22–37. https://doi.org/10.1016/j.jsat.2017.01.006

Ussher, M., Cropley, M., Playle, S., Mohidin, R., & West, R. (2009). Effect of isometric exercise and body scanning on cigarette cravings and withdrawal symptoms. *Addiction, 104*(7), 1251–1257. https://doi.org/10.1111/j.1360-0443.2009.02605.x

Whitelaw, S., Baldwin, S., Bunton, R., & Flynn, D. (2000). The status of evidence and outcomes in stages of change research. *Health Education Research, 15*(6), 707–718. https://doi.org/10.1093/her/15.6.707

Spiritual Assessment and Intervention

David R. Hodge

Spiritual assessment is the process of gathering, analyzing, and synthesizing information about clients' spirituality and religion into a working, malleable template that provides the basis for subsequent clinical decisions. *Spirituality* commonly refers to an individual's subjective relationship with God (Snider & McPhedran, 2014) or, more broadly, the sacred or the transcendent (Hodge, 2015). *Religion* refers to a shared set of beliefs and practices that have been developed over time by those who hold similar understandings of spirituality (Praglin, 2004). For the purposes of this chapter, spirituality is typically used as an umbrella term that encompasses both personal spirituality and communal religion, although it is important to note that many different understandings of these two constructs exist among social work clients, practitioners, and scholars (Canda et al., 2020).

Why Assessment Is Important in Behavioral Health Settings

At least two rationales exist for administering spiritual assessments in behavioral health settings, which are related to cultural competence and the strengths perspective. Regarding the former, spirituality is often expressed in culturally distinct religious worldviews or value systems. Examples of populations that tend to have distinctive value systems include American Indians, evangelical Christians, Hindus, Latter-day Saints, Muslims, and Orthodox Jews (Richards & Bergin, 2014). Clients from these cultures may hold values that directly or indirectly intersect service provision. Muslims, for example, may be uncomfortable discussing intimate issues with practitioners of the opposite sex, taking medications containing pork by-products, and engaging in certain types of pet therapy. Spiritual assessment provides insight into these value systems, equipping social workers with the knowledge they need to tailor services in a manner that addresses clients' spiritual needs. In turn, adapting services so that they convey respect for clients' value systems tends to enhance clinical effectiveness (Sue et al., 2019), which leads to the second rationale.

A substantial body of research has emerged during the past few decades linking spirituality to a wide array of mental health outcomes (Koenig et al., 2012; Koenig & Al Shohaib, 2019; Oman & Lukoff, 2018; Oman & Syme, 2018). For instance, spirituality is typically inversely related to depression. Although it is important to note the results are not univocal, spirituality is typically a strength that is associated with diverse salutary health outcomes. Moreover, the importance of spirituality tends to be disproportionately affirmed among traditionally disadvantaged populations, such as women, older adults, and Latinos (Newport, 2012). For example, 90% of African Americans report that prayer is very important in dealing with stressful situations (Chatters et al., 2008). Assessment provides a method of identifying these assets, and once identified, they can often be operationalized in treatment and discharge planning to facilitate health and wellness (van Weeghel et al., 2019).

Due to these and other reasons, the importance of spiritual assessment is widely affirmed as a routine component of behavioral health care (Milner et al., 2020). The Joint Commission (2018)—the nation's most prominent health care accrediting body—recommends an assessment for clients receiving treatment for substance use and other behavioral and emotional disorders. Likewise, the Statement of Ethical Principles of the International Federation of Social Workers (2018) enjoins social workers to formulate spiritual assessments and interventions, a process discussed in more depth in the following sections.

Brief Assessment

As illustrated in Table 123.1, spiritual assessment is commonly conceptualized as a multistep process that begins with the administration of a brief assessment with all clients (Hodge, 2015). The purpose of a short, preliminary assessment—such as the iCARING model depicted in Table 123.1—is threefold: (1) to save valuable therapeutic time; (2) to help legitimize the topic of spirituality in clinical settings; and (3) to determine if a more extensive, comprehensive assessment is needed.

The assessment aims to understand how spirituality shapes functioning. In other words, the goal is not to determine the veracity of clients' beliefs but, rather, to understand how the beliefs influence functioning related to the presenting problem. If the results of the brief assessment reveal that clients' spirituality is likely unrelated to service provision, then the process ends. Conversely, if the results raise the possibility that spirituality is related to the presenting problem, then a comprehensive assessment may be warranted. Take, for instance, the case of a devout American Indian facing a possible diagnosis for schizophrenia who reports hearing voices external to himself. In such situations, a comprehensive assessment is called for to determine whether the voices are an indicator of mental illness or a normative expression of spirituality, and perhaps even a strength that may facilitate wellness (van der Watt et al., 2018).

Comprehensive Assessment

The purpose of a comprehensive spiritual assessment is twofold: (1) to obtain a more detailed understanding of clients' spiritual beliefs, practices, and experiences; and (2) to determine how these various characteristics may be operationalized to help ameliorate the challenges currently encountered. Toward this end, several conceptually distinct comprehensive spiritual assessment approaches or methods have been developed. Both clients and practitioners have a variety of needs and interests in any given clinical setting. Factors that can vary from case to case include the nature of the presenting behavioral health problem; clients' personality characteristics, communication styles, and cultural backgrounds; and the amount of time available for assessment. Developing familiarity with different approaches positions

TABLE 123.1 Moving from Spiritual Assessment to Spiritual Intervention: A Multistep Process

Step 1. Brief assessment—typically administered to all clients

iCARING Brief Assessment model: Sample preliminary assessment with malleable, working questions

Importance	*I was wondering how important spirituality is to you?*
Community	*Do you happen to participate in a church or some other type of religious community?*
Assets and resources	*Are there certain spiritual beliefs, practices, or rituals you find helpful in dealing with problems, perhaps especially in the past?*
Influence	*I was curious how your spirituality has shaped your understanding of your current situation?*
Needs	
Goals	*I was interested in knowing if there are any spiritual needs I could address?*
	Looking ahead, I was wondering if you were interested in incorporating your spirituality into our work together? And if so, what that might look like from your perspective?

Step 2. Comprehensive assessment—administered if clinically warranted based on the brief assessment

The choice of a comprehensive assessment options is based on a variety of factors, including the nature of the presenting problem; clients' personality characteristics, communication style, and cultural background; the setting and the amount of time available for assessment; and practitioners' theoretical orientation.

Five conceptually distinct options for conducting comprehensive assessments and associated strengths

Spiritual history	A good fit with clients who are verbal, comfortable with face-to-face interaction, or from cultures that value oral knowledge transmission (storytelling). Relatively nonstructured, nonlinear format creates space for client-directed narratives. Relatively easy to understand conceptually, administer, and incorporate into a broader assessment of functioning.
Spiritual lifemap	May appeal to clients who are artistic, creative, or uncomfortable with verbal expression and enjoy drawing. Readily understood conceptually and may be assigned as homework, saving valuable therapeutic time. Client-constructed, which implicitly communicates important competencies, and the construction process can foster new insights, including the development of new, salutary scripts.
Spiritual genogram	Can be helpful when the family system plays a significant role in the presenting problem or with clients who desire a very structured approach. Implicitly communicates respect for family members and illustrates spiritual patterns across generations, helping identify previously unrecognized strengths in the family system.
Spiritual eco-map	Relatively easy to understand and quick to administer (approximately 20–30 minutes) and can be integrated into a broader assessment (by added additional systems to the map—i.e., work). The map's emphasis on relationships can shift the focus away from clients and their problems, facilitating rapport. Can be used to document salutary changes and reinforce treatment gains.
Spiritual ecogram	Provides a holistic picture, illustrating the interconnected nature of reality. As is the case with all diagrammatic methods, the visual depiction can foster fresh insights about potential barriers as well as spiritual assets that might be leveraged to solve problems. But ecograms are especially suited to illustrating current and historical strengths as well as the connections between these variables.

Step 3. Spiritual intervention—based on the information obtained through the assessment process

Factors that guide the formulation of interventions include clients' interest in a given therapeutic strategy, its effectiveness in ameliorating a specific disorder, practitioners' level of expertise in the proposed modality, and the behavioral health setting. For instance, practitioners competent in CBT might use the information obtained from the assessment to construct spiritually modified CBT protocols; if clients are interested in this approach, and sufficient evidence exists to suggest such an approach might be effective in problem amelioration.

CBT, cognitive–behavioral therapy.

Adapted from Hodge and Reynolds (2019).

social workers to select the method that provides the best fit for each client's unique situation in the context of practitioners' theoretical orientation. As can be seen in Table 123.1, this assessment "toolbox" consists of a verbally based approach, spiritual histories, and four diagrammatically based approaches—spiritual lifemaps, spiritual genograms, spiritual eco-maps, and spiritual ecograms (Hodge, 2015).

Spiritual histories use a semistructured interview protocol to explore clients' spiritual narratives. In a manner analogous to conducting a family history, practitioners interface questions into the conversation to help unpack clinically relevant information. These questions help ensure the clinical conversation remains focused on the intersection between clients' spirituality and service provision.

Spiritual lifemaps can be viewed as a diagrammatic alternative to spiritual histories, in which pens, markers, and diverse media are used to depict clients' spiritual stories on a large sheet of paper. The delineation of spiritually significant events provides an illustrated account of clients' relationship with God or the sacred over their life course. Much like road maps, lifemaps illustrate where clients have come from, where they are now, and where they are going in the future.

Spiritual genograms portray spiritual information across at least three generations. Building upon the structure of a basic genogram, colors are used to represent religious affiliations of individuals across the family system. Symbols drawn from clients' belief system can be added to the genogram to indicate spiritual significant events (baptisms, confirmations, visions, etc.). The end result is a color snapshot of the overall spiritual composition of the family system that depicts complex intergenerational spiritual interactions.

Spiritual eco-maps, or environmental maps, depict clients' relationships to key spiritual systems in their current surroundings. The client, represented by a circle in the center of the paper, is surrounded by significant spiritual systems near the borders of the paper (the Creator, rituals, elders, small groups, scripture reading, etc.). Diverse types of lines are drawn between the client and the spiritual systems, which communicate information about the strength and character of the client's relationships with the respective spiritual systems. In contrast to spiritual histories, lifemaps, and genograms—which all survey clients' spiritual stories as they exist through time—spiritual eco-maps provide a diagrammatic illustration of clients' relationships with spiritual systems that are viewed as meaningful in their current environments.

Spiritual ecograms incorporate the strengths of spiritual genograms and eco-maps in a single approach. With the client placed in the center of the paper, the top half of the paper features a spiritual genogram, and the bottom half features a spiritual eco-map. Accordingly, spiritual ecograms depict clients' relationship to current spiritual systems—like a spiritual eco-map—while also charting the flow of spirituality across three generations—like a spiritual genogram. In addition, connections between past and present functioning can be illustrated by conceptualizing the larger family system as an interconnected set of spiritual systems.

In addition to listing the assessment approaches, Table 123.1 also lists the common strengths associated with each method. Understanding the various assessment approaches and their associated strengths helps optimize service provision. This knowledge aids in selecting an approach that can help identify barriers that can be eliminated so that they do not impede service provision while concurrently identifying spiritual assets that can be used to formulate therapeutic strategies that enhance coping, recovery, and wellness.

Spiritual Interventions

Spiritual interventions are therapeutic strategies that incorporate a spiritual dimension as a key component of the intervention (Hai et al., 2019). Spiritual interventions can take many forms. Factors that impact the formulation of interventions include clients' interest in a given strategy, its effectiveness in ameliorating a specific disorder, practitioners' level of expertise in the proposed modality, and the behavioral health setting.

Systematic reviews suggest that spiritual interventions are effective in ameliorating problems in both individual and group therapy settings (Viftrup et al., 2013; Worthington et al., 2011). Meta-analyses of randomized clinical trials have consistently found that spiritual interventions are at least as effective as traditional interventions (Captari et al., 2018; Gonçalves et al., 2015). Spiritual interventions have been used to address a variety of problems, including anxiety (Paukert et al., 2011), depression (Anderson et al., 2015), post-traumatic stress disorder (Smothers & Koenig, 2018), and substance abuse (Hai et al., 2019). However, the methodological rigor of the studies in these areas can vary significantly.

Perhaps most research has been conducted on spiritually modified cognitive–behavioral therapy (CBT). At a fundamental level, CBT posits that behavioral health problems stem from cognitive distortions. Clinical work consists of helping clients identify maladaptive scripts and replacing them with more salutary schema. Spiritually modified CBT replicates this same basic process, but the maladaptive scripts are replaced with salutary schema drawn from clients' spiritual narratives. This approach has been successfully used to treat a variety of mood disorders, particularly anxiety and depression, with reviews indicating it is at least as effective as traditional CBT (Anderson et al., 2015; Lim et al., 2014; Paukert et al., 2011). CBT protocols have been adapted to incorporate schema from a variety of worldviews, including Christianity, Judaism, Islam, Taoism, and generic spiritual value systems. These findings suggest that spiritually modified CBT may be an appropriate intervention with many clients, especially given the wider body of research on the effectiveness of CBT in tandem

with the fact that many practitioners are proficient in CBT.

It is also possible to conceptualize spiritual interventions in more simplified forms. Consider, for example, clients in residential treatment facilities. In such settings, practitioners might facilitate access to scripture, clergy, or various sacred practices or rituals (van der Watt et al., 2018). Likewise, social workers operating in multidisciplinary teams can play an important role alerting other helping professionals to potential treatment barriers as well as spiritual resources that might be leveraged to promote wellness.

It is important to note that incorporating spiritual interventions into treatment can reduce health disparities among disadvantaged populations (Maura & Weisman de Mamani, 2017). As noted previously, spirituality tends to be an especially salient factor among disadvantaged groups. Increasing the cultural relevance of treatment by adapting service to incorporate clients' spiritual values can increase their social validity. Interventions that are perceived to be relevant within the context of clients' worldview are more likely to be adopted and implemented. Likewise, framing more traditional treatments within the context of clients' spiritual value system can also help facilitate client engagement and retention, which in turn leads to better outcomes.

References

Anderson, N., Heywood-Everett, S., Siddiqi, N., Wright, J., Meredith, J., & McMillan, D. (2015). Faith-adapted psychological therapies for depression and anxiety: Systematic review and meta-analysis. *Journal of Affective Disorders, 176*, 183–196. https://doi.org/10.1016/j.jad.2015.01.019

Canda, E. R., Furman, L. D., & Canda, H.-J. (2020). *Spiritual diversity in social work practice: The heart of helping* (3rd ed.). Oxford University Press.

Captari, L. E., Hook, J. N., Hoyt, W., Davis, D. E., McElroy-Heltzel, S. E., & Worthington, E. L. (2018). Integrating clients' religion and spirituality within psychotherapy: A comprehensive meta-analysis. *Journal of Clinical Psychology, 74*(11), 1938–1951. https://doi.org/10.1002/jclp.22681

Chatters, L. M., Taylor, R. J., Jackson, J. S., & Lincoln, K. D. (2008). Religious coping among African Americans, Caribbean Blacks and non-Hispanic Whites. *Journal of Community Psychology, 36*(3), 371–386. https://doi.org/10.1002/jcop.20202

Gonçalves, J. P. B., Lucchetti, G., Menezes, P. R., & Vallada, H. (2015). Religious and spiritual interventions in mental health care: A systematic review and meta-analysis of randomized controlled clinical trials. *Psychological Medicine, 45*(14), 2937–2949. https://doi.org/10.1017/S0033291715001166

Hai, A. H., Franklin, C., Park, S., DiNitto, D. M., & Aurelio, N. (2019). The efficacy of spiritual/religious interventions for substance use problems: A systematic review and meta-analysis of randomized controlled trials. *Drug and Alcohol Dependence, 202*, 134–148. https://doi.org/10.1016/j.drugalcdep.2019.04.045

Hodge, D. R. (2015). *Spiritual assessment in social work and mental health practice.* Columbia University Press.

Hodge, D. R., & Reynolds, C. (2019). Spirituality among people with disabilities: A nationally representative study of spiritual and religious profiles. *Health & Social Work, 44*(2), 75–86.

International Federation of Social Workers. (2018). Global social work statement of ethical principles. https://www.ifsw.org/global-social-work-statement-of-ethical- principles/

Joint Commission. (2018). Body, mind, spirit, Part 2. *The Source, 16*(2), 1–6.

Koenig, H. G., & Al Shohaib, S. S. (2019). Religiosity and mental health in Islam. In H. Moffic, J. Peteet, A. Hankir, & R. Awaad (Eds.), *Islamophobia and psychiatry* (pp. 55–65). Springer.

Koenig, H. G., King, D., & Carson, V. B. (2012). *Handbook of religion and health* (2nd ed.). Oxford University Press.

Lim, C., Sim, K., Renjan, V., Sam, H. F., & Quah, S. L. (2014). Adapted cognitive–behavioral therapy for religious individuals with mental disorder: A systematic review. *Asian Journal of Psychiatry, 9*, 3–12. https://doi.org/10.1016/j.ajp.2013.12.011

Maura, J., & Weisman de Mamani, A. (2017). Mental health disparities, treatment engagement, and attrition among racial/ethnic minorities with severe mental illness: A review. *Journal of Clinical Psychology in Medical Settings, 24*(3–4), 187–210. https://doi.org/10.1007/s10880-017-9510-2

Milner, K., Crawford, P., Edgley, A., Hare-Duke, L., & Slade, M. (2020). The experiences of spirituality among adults with mental health difficulties: A qualitative systematic review. *Epidemiology and Psychiatric Sciences, 29*, e34. https://doi.org/10.1017/S2045796019000234

Newport, F. (2012). *God is alive and well: The future of religion in America.* Gallup Press.

Oman, D., & Lukoff, D. (2018). Mental health, religion, and spirituality. In D. Oman (Ed.), *Why religion and spirituality matter for public health* (pp. 225–243). Springer.

Oman, D., & Syme, S. L. (2018). Weighing the evidence: What is revealed by 100+ meta-analyses and a systematic reviews of religion/spirituality and health? In D. Oman (Ed.), *Why religion and spirituality matter for public health* (pp. 261–281). Springer.

Paukert, A. L., Phillips, L. L., Cully, J. A., Romero, C., & Stanley, M. A. (2011). Systematic review of the effects of religion-accommodative psychotherapy for depression and anxiety. *Journal of Contemporary Psychotherapy, 41*(2), 99–108. https://doi.org/10.1007/s10879-010-9154-0

Praglin, L. J. (2004). Spirituality, religion, and social work: An effort towards interdisciplinary conversation. *Journal of Religion & Spirituality in Social Work: Social Thought, 23*(4), 67–84.

Richards, P. S., & Bergin, A. E. (Eds.). (2014). *Handbook of psychotherapy and religious diversity* (2nd ed.). American Psychological Association.

Smothers, Z. P. W., & Koenig, H. G. (2018). Spiritual interventions in veterans with PTSD: A systematic review. *Journal of Religion and Health, 57*(5), 2033–2048. https://doi.org/10.1007/s10943-018-0680-5

Snider, A.-M., & McPhedran, S. (2014). Religiosity, spirituality, mental health, and mental health treatment outcomes in Australia: A systematic literature review. *Mental Health, Religion & Culture, 17*(6), 568–581. https://doi.org/10.1080/13674676.2013.871240

Sue, D. W., Sue, D., Neville, H. A., & Smith, L. (2019). *Counseling the culturally diverse: Theory and practice* (8th ed.). Wiley.

van der Watt, A. S. J., Nortje, G., Oladeji, B. D., Seedat, S., & Gureje, O. (2018). The perceived effectiveness of traditional and faith healing in the treatment of mental illness: A systematic review of qualitative studies. *Social Psychiatry and Psychiatric Epidemiology, 53*(6), 555–566. https://doi.org/10.1007/s00127-018-1519-9

van Weeghel, J., van Zelst, C., Boertien, D., & Hasson-Ohayon, I. (2019). Conceptualizations, assessments, and implications of personal recovery in mental illness: A scoping review of systematic reviews and meta-analyses. *Psychiatric Rehabilitation Journal, 42*(2), 169–181. https://doi.org/10.1037/prj0000356

Viftrup, D. T., Hvidt, N. C., & Buus, N. (2013). Spiritually and religiously integrated group psychotherapy: A systematic literature review. *Evidence-Based Complementary and Alternative Medicine, 2013*, 1–12. https://doi.org/10.1155/2013/274625

Worthington, E. L., Hook, J. N., Davis, D. E., & McDaniel, M. A. (2011). Religion and spirituality. *Journal of Clinical Psychology, 67*(2), 204–214. https://doi.org/10.1002/jclp.20760

Assessment and Treatment of Specific Phobia

Bruce A. Thyer

The fifth edition of the *Diagnostic and Statistical Manual of Mental Disorders* [DSM-5; American Psychiatric Association (APA), 2013] categorizes human dysfunctional behavior into a number of groupings. One such section deals with what are called anxiety disorders (pp. 189–233), and we are told that these reflect behaviors characterized by excessive fear in response to imminent or real threats and/or anxiety, which occurs when anticipating a future threat. Many conditions fall under this large category called anxiety disorders, and one of the most common diagnoses is labeled specific phobia (SP). A client with an SP experiences severe fear or anxiety that is evoked by specific objects or situations. Typically, fears of objects can involve various animals (dogs, cats, snakes, spiders, etc.), and situational fears usually relate to circumstances such as flying, the sight of blood or trauma, heights, and small or enclosed spaces. In this chapter, these objects and situations are labeled anxiety-evoking stimuli (AES). When an AES is encountered, the person actively tries to avoid it or to escape; if neither of these is possible, the situation is endured with great fear. In general, the fearful

or anxious behaviors are out of proportion to the reality of the situation, but most persons with an SP acknowledge the irrational nature of their fears and that they are not really in actual danger. Anxiety evoked in situations or with objects that are objectively dangerous would not meet the criteria for an SP.

To qualify for a diagnosis of an SP, the client needs to experience clinically significant distress or impairment in some important life role—for example, familial, occupational, or social. The miner who develops claustrophobia, the butcher with a newly developed fear of the sight of blood, and the vet tech who acquires a fear of dogs are examples of how one's functioning could be impaired by an SP. The issue of a differential diagnosis is important. Some more complex conditions may initially present like an SP, but the AES may be part of a larger, initially unrecognized, issue. An example might be someone with undiagnosed agoraphobia whose major impairment is an inability to drive over a long bridge. The superficial presentation might appear to be an SP of bridges, but a more detailed clinical interview might identify the occurrence of irregular panic attacks and a host of other avoided situations (e.g., grocery stores, hair salons, and banks), all secondary to the primary diagnosis of panic disorder with agoraphobia. In this case, the latter diagnosis would supersede that of SP. There are some specifiers that may qualify the SP, such as a fear centered around certain animals; aspects of the natural environment such as thunderstorms; certain situations such as small spaces or heights; or fears centered around blood, injury, or illness. The latter is unusual in that patients with fears of blood or trauma may actually faint, whereas fainting is very rare among the other presentations of SP (Thyer, Himle, et al., 1985). Sometimes the same individual has multiple AES, in which case careful interviewing is needed to ensure that a differential diagnosis is not more appropriate (e.g., a fear of germs and an inability to be around religious symbols may both be caused by obsessive–compulsive disorder).

The degree of impairment may vary according to the ubiquitousness with which the AES is encountered. Someone living in Michigan with a fear of bees may feel completely fine during the winter, but the spring and summer months may be a torment of fear when bees are buzzing around outside or of anticipatory anxiety when faced with going on a family picnic. Generally, the closer the proximity in terms of distance, and the shorter the time until an anticipated encounter with one's AES, the more severe the fear. Acute fear can almost be turned on or off as with a switch by suddenly encountering or fleeing one's AES.

The 12-month community prevalence for adults with SP is approximately 7–9%, which makes it a relatively common diagnosis (APA, 2013, p. 199). A fairly early age of onset is common, and by the time one reaches middle age, newly emerging SPs are rare (Thyer, Parrish, et al., 1985). This sometimes does happen, however, such as in the case in which an older person has a traumatic event that does not rise to the level of post-traumatic stress disorder (for a case example, see Thyer, 1983). Apart from impairments centered around the SP, most such individuals function fairly well, with little co-morbid conditions. The risk of suicide related to SP is rare, but it has been known to happen (Pergeron et al., 1986).

Assessment

The foundation for assessing a client presenting with a presumptive SP is the clinical interview. There are not usually any medical conditions presenting as an SP, and there are no blood tests or other clinical benchmarks useful for arriving at the diagnosis. There is an Anxiety and Related Disorders Interview Schedule formatted using the DSM-5 criteria (Brown & Barlow, 2021), but usually the diagnosis is not difficult to arrive at without supplements such as this. A number of anxiety disorder rapid assessment instruments are available, as well as some very specific ones such as a spider phobia questionnaire, a claustrophobia scale, etc., but these too are rarely necessary given the relative ease of diagnosis. The APA offers a free scale to measure the severity of an SP (https://www. psychiatry.org/psychiatrists/practice/dsm/ educational-resources/assessment-measures), but I do not think it affords any additional information that the clinical interview does not disclose. It might use useful as a pretest–post-test measure, at the beginning and end of therapy, to assist in the empirical evaluation of clinical outcomes with each case.

Sometimes the etiology of an SP is relatively easy to pinpoint, such as the client having directly experienced a frightening event (e.g., being scared by an exploding balloon). Other times the fear is acquired by modeling from significant others (e.g., a mother displaying a severe fear of heights to her child) or more vicariously, such as developing a clown phobia after seeing a frightening movie about a murderous clown or developing a phobia of dogs after reading a terrifying book about a large rabid dog that kills people. The client may not be able to recall the onset of their fear, but asking them to consult with parents or significant others may often reveal the apparent cause. Adverse widespread cultural or newsworthy events may initiate the onset of SPs, with severe fears of flying increasing after a horrific plane crash, for example. It is not uncommon for the etiology to remain hidden after considerable examination, but because etiology does not usually bear on the course of treatment, this is not problematic (Fyer, 1998). In common parlance, many types of SPs are given unique names, such as claustrophobia, arachnophobia, etc. These are not used in the DSM and are persiflage, of little value in clinical practice and not recommended. Ruling out potential differential diagnoses is important. Treating someone who presents only with a fear of loud noises as an instance of SP is not likely to yield a favorable outcome if the underlying condition is post-traumatic stress disorder but the client is reluctant to discuss their other symptoms linked to the true underlying condition.

Treatment

The most generally effective treatments for clients with SPs are variants of graduated exposure to the AES in real life. It is preferred that treatment be conducted in real life because the clients are generally afraid of their real-life AES, not imaginary dogs, needles, heights, etc. Treatment gains obtained from therapy conducted via exposure in imagination, virtual reality, or other artificial circumstances usually need to be replicated in the real-life contexts in order to ensure the consolidation, maintenance, and generalization of improvements. Real-life exposure therapy (ET) begins by describing the approach as one possible way to help the client. There are a number of resources that can be provided to the client to help them learn about this approach, with various books, internet resources, and YouTube videos demonstrating it.

Emphasize that if undertaken, ET will be done slowly, that the client will have control of the situation, and that the client can ask to slow down or terminate the procedure at any time. This obviously requires the establishment of a trusting relationship between the client and social worker. In the first session, discuss an array of ways the AES could be presented to the client. For example, a client with a severe fear of dogs may agree to enter a room containing a small caged puppy 12 feet away. If this is too intense, use a smaller dog or increase the distance. Assure the client that the puppy will remain caged until the client consents otherwise. If this is still too intense, see if using a stuffed but realistic dog or watching a movie of a dog would be acceptable, if these induce severe fear.

Before beginning treatment, teach the client to self-rate their fear on a 0 (no fear) to 100 (maximum fear, panic) scale. This simple assessment method is widely used in the treatment of clients with anxiety disorder and has good validity with physiological measures of fear (Thyer et al., 1984). When they enter the room and see their AES, ask for their immediate anxiety rating. Ask them to sit and simply observe the puppy, snake, bug, etc. while you engage the client in conversation. Every few minutes, ask them to self-rate their fear. When self-rating declines slightly, ask permission to intensify the situation mildly—for example, by asking if you can move and sit next to the caged puppy, have the puppy lick your fingers, etc. As the client's fear ratings decline, ask them to come closer. Anxiety will likely increase and then subside after a few minutes. Repeat. When the client is close to the cage watching the puppy lick your fingers, encourage the client to touch the puppy themselves through the cage. Provide a glove to the client if unprotected touch is too scary. Get them to let the puppy lick them. In due course, ask if you can take the puppy out of the case and hold it securely in your lap. Assure the client you will not let it go. If they refuse, see if they will agree after they back away a few feet. Put the puppy on a short leash if need be.

Allow the client to adapt to your holding the uncaged puppy and then encourage the client to come closer, touch the puppy, get licked, and ask permission to transfer the dog to the client's lap, etc. Sessions should last at least 1 hour, preferably 2, and the exposure exercise should be terminated on a high note, when the client is calmer.

The second and subsequent sessions can be similarly arranged. Expect some regression at the beginning of session 2 compared to the end of session 1. This will usually be quickly regained, and more progress will be made. Substantial relief from the phobia can be obtained in most cases by approximately 10 hours of real-life ET. Gains made in the office should be replicated outside in the real world and amid varying contexts and AES. For example, use larger dogs or several dogs. Home visits for real-life guided exposure can be very useful. If a snake-phobic client is unable to walk about their yard freely, office-based improvements can be enhanced by replicating sessions sitting on the grass at the client's home, even using larger than usual docile species, such as ball pythons borrowed from an obliging pet store. Asking clients to practice exposure exercises in real life outside of therapy sessions moves progress along more rapidly.

Modification of the previously discussed regimen can be undertaken for situational SPs, such as small spaces, heights, etc. Use modeling behavior to demonstrate what you ask the client to do, reinforce small gains with verbal praise, and ask the client what they are observing about the AES and about what they are feeling and thinking. Use reality testing during and after exposure sessions to help them realize the faulty perceptions they had—for example, snakes are not slimy and they did not faint while confronting the dog. Vivid but not necessarily upsetting dreams related to the AES sometimes occur after intense exposure sessions. Videotaping sessions can be useful to demonstrate the substantial progress the client

made within or across sessions. Encourage family members or other significant persons to practice with the client during homework. Additional resources describing the conduct of ET are common (e.g., Thyer, 1983, 1985, 1987; Vonk & Thyer, 1995), and properly conducted therapy of this nature is also highly effective and well tolerated by children and adolescents (Raggi & Samson, 2018).

Evaluation

Within sessions, you can clinically observe what the client does and says, and afterwards a debriefing session to process the experience can be helpful. Periodically asking the client to self-rate their fear during exposure is a very useful adjunct to observing their behavior and listening to their narrative. Consider asking the client to wear a fingertip heart rate monitor during the sessions, and glance at it when the client tells you their anxiety level. Note the time, fear rating, and heart rate concurrently; do so periodically, such as every 5 minutes, and consider graphing these data to prepare a visual display of progress within and across sessions. "Fear" has three elements—behavior, subjective feelings, and physiological responses. With exposure, these do not necessarily decline in a synchronous manner. Usually, behavior avoidance declines earliest, followed by reductions in the self-report of fear, then a normalized heart rate. As mentioned previously, end individual sessions with self-report of fear relatively low— do not halt a session immediately after you have increased the intensity of the exposure and the client is tachycardic and terrified.

An added element to augment evaluation is to conduct a standardized behavioral approach test (BAT) at the beginning of a session and again at the end. This requires preparation in advance but is easy to implement and takes only a few minutes. Consider a client with a fear of snakes. With the client's consent, set up in advance a snake in a cage or terrarium in another room, behind a closed door. Before beginning the formal exposure session, ask the client to stand outside the door, knowing there is a securely caged snake in the next room, and to give you a subjective rating of their fear (0–100). Note their heart rate if you have a monitor available. Then, with consent, open the door and ask them to look at the live snake. Repeat the measures. You then step into the room—for example, 2 feet closer—and ask the client to follow you. If they do, repeat the measures, noting the data on a data collection sheet you have prepared. Step 2 feet closer and ask the client to follow you. Continue this until the client refuses to approach their AES any closer. Your pretest BAT is complete. You now have three measures of fear: a way of quantifying the client's "phobia," through a measure of behavior (how close they were willing to come); a measure of subjective fear (the 0–100 ratings at various distances from the AES); and a measure of physiological arousal—their heart rate at various distances. You can see how this is an excellent way of operationalizing the social work dictum of "beginning where the client is at"!

Take the client from the room, rearrange items for your exposure session, and conduct treatment as described previously. When you finish a given session, escort the client to another area and set up the BAT situation again. Then repeat the behavioral approach test again.

Doing a BAT at the beginning and end of a single session usually shows significant improvements within a given session. Then if you repeat this across sessions, to the end of treatment, you have completed a powerful evaluation of your own practice—one ideally documenting substantial improvements. This approach to evaluation is called the repeated pretest–post-test single-subject experiment (Thyer & Curtis, 1983) and is of course completely consistent with what the National Association of Social Workers Code of Ethics (2017) states about evaluating the outcomes of our own practice. Clinically, it is also a powerful

tool to share this information with the client to help them appreciate how their hard work is paying off.

When do you terminate formal treatment? Pragmatically, I believe this should be done when the client is no longer experiencing any significant functional limitations in their life due to their phobia; when exposure sessions demonstrate that behaviorally, subjectively, and physiologically the client is not fearful; and when office-based gains mediated by the social worker have been consolidated by the client working independently in their real-world settings. Follow up with the client by phone or text every 3 months for approximately 1 year to be certain the client is doing well. Long-term follow-up studies on ET for SP reveal that improvements are usually long-lasting, without relapse, and that if relapse does happen, most clients have been taught how to treat themselves when needed (Wolitzky-Taylor et al., 2006).

There are an array of self-help books, computer-assisted therapies, and cell phone apps available to help the client with an SP. A triaged approach may be adopted by busy practices in that after the clinical intake the client can be offered a self-help book and asked to read it and try to undertake some of the therapy themselves, with the social worker checking in by phone or text approximately once a week. If satisfactory improvements are not forthcoming, then offer one-to-one live sessions in the office or real life.

There are many specialty programs offering help for persons. The University of Michigan's program where I was trained, housed in the Department of Psychiatry, is one of the oldest (https://medicine.umich.edu/dept/psychiatry/programs/anxiety-disorders-program-adult#:~:text=The%20Anxiety%20Disorders%20Program%20has,a%20leading%20anxiety%20research%20center). Boston University's Center for Anxiety and Related Disorders offers a

1-week intensive treatment program for persons with SPs (https://medicine.umich.edu/dept/psychiatry/programs/anxiety-disorders-program-adult#:~:text=The%20Anxiety%20Disorders%20Program%20has,a%20leading%20anxiety%20research%20cente). This might be considered for persons who have not benefited from less intensive treatment or for people facing an experience in the near future involving unavoidable encounters with their AES (e.g., an imminent vacation involving a long airplane trip for someone with a fear of flying).

Challenges

Sometimes the client's AES is difficult to re-create in real life—for example, thunderstorms, overseas flights, or fear of vomiting (don't ask!). Surrogate AES may have to be used—for example, movies or soundtracks of terrible storms or episodes of emesis—perhaps with the sound very low and the screen minimized at the beginning. Think outside the box. The client with a fear of flying can be taken, with permission and prearranged, to a local airport where a small plane and pilot have been hired. The hired pilot agrees to follow instructions. Get seated, with the client up front next to the pilot. Let them sit there for a few minutes before asking permission to close the door. Wait. Ask permission from the client for the pilot to start the motor, but do not move the plane. Wait. Ask permission to taxi slowly along the taxiway. Then a little faster. Then to go down the runway but *not* take off. Repeat as needed going faster. Ask permission to take off, remain approximately 10 feet above the ground for approximately 100 feet, and then return to the ground. Repeat. Go a little higher. Repeat. Then ask the client for permission to do a go-around—to take off, circle the airport once, and then land. Repeat. Within an hour or so of this process, I have seen the formerly terrified client laughing as they steer the plane themself

and make turns several thousand feet in the air miles from the airport. After intense sessions such as these, flying an hour in a comfortable jet is much easier. Having the pilot explain how the airplane flies and the built-in safety features can be helpful.

Sometimes clients absolutely refuse to be exposed to their real-life AES. Again, think outside the box. Improvise. Faced with a new client with a severe fear of snakes (she made her husband screen all newspapers and magazines in the home and cut out any pictures of stories of snakes), she was adamant about not seeing a small live snake. I asked about a rubber snake? Nope! A photograph of a live snake? No! A cartoon of a snake? Nein! I finally got her to agree to my putting a cartoon of a snake on my desk and to cover the cartoon with a postcard. She came into the room, and, with her permission, I slowly slid the postcard along the cartoon until a quarter inch of the snake's tail was visible. Bingo. Working from this very miniscule beginning, I spent half an hour or so slowly revealing the entire cartoon. Each new quarter inch of exposure increased her anxiety substantially, but this would subside, and with her permission I disclosed another quarter inch. I promised her no tricks, no surprises, and I kept my word. At the end of the first session, she agreed to take my cartoon home and leave it where she could see it all day. Her spouse could not believe this. She returned for future sessions and we resumed, moving to photos, movies, rubber snakes (she took these home, too, to leave around the house and eventually have her husband hide them in unexpected places where she would encounter them), and eventually to ET with live snakes (notice the plural).

Titrating the dose of exposure takes some skill. Moving too rapidly risks overwhelming the client and having them drop out. Moving too slowly becomes boring and means you can treat fewer clients in need. You need the equivalent of Goldilocks' porridge to get it just right.

Client attrition with real-life exposure is, surprisingly, equivalent to that of more conventional verbal psychotherapies not involving such intense demands on client fortitude. The generally rapid improvements seen in the first sessions encourage continuance, and it is common for clients to state after a few hours something along the lines of "I cannot believe I am doing this!" as they comfortably hold a formerly terrifying cat in their lap. Or rat.

Sometimes people do not make significant gains. When this happens, I look for potential environmental contingencies of reinforcement that may be inadvertently maintaining the phobic behavior. When there are loud and repeated demands to check the house or expel someone's anxiety-evoking stimulus (e.g., Get rid of the spider! Cut out pictures of snakes from the newspaper), a cycle of positive and negative reinforcement (the phobic complainer gets what they want, and the spouse finds that compliance reduces aversive nagging) maintains such phobic-centric behavior. Sometimes people claim to be unable to hold a job because of their phobia and, rarely, get a disability pension for their fears. I once had a client who worked as a butcher. After he developed an SP to the sight of blood, which sometimes led to fainting, he qualified for a social security disability pension. It is very difficult to make enduring clinical gains when significant improvement means one will lose a monthly government check. Also make sure you have not overlooked a differential diagnosis. An apparent SP that is secondary to panic disorder, post-traumatic stress disorder, or obsessive–compulsive disorder is very difficult to resolve when treated in isolation.

Other Resources

The Anxiety and Depression Association of America is an excellent resource for clinical social workers and for persons with specific phobias (https://adaa.org/understanding-anxiety/ additional-disorders/phobias). It offers much information for professionals; therapy guides and self-help materials; blogs; webinars; an online store for books; a professional journal; continuing education programs for LCSWs and others; support groups; and an annual conference open to clinicians, researchers, and the public alike.

There are various phone applications intended to help persons with SPs self-treat. The app Zero-Phobia, for example, is intended for people with a severe fear of heights (https://www.zerophobia.app). Clear-Fear is aimed at SPs in general (https://play.google.com/store/apps/details?id=uk.org.stem4.clearfear&hl=en_US), and there are many fear of flying apps (https://www.thefearofflying.com/articles/conquer-your-flying-phobia-with-the-top-6-fear-of-flying-apps). A little searching can locate others.

Conclusion

Most people with SPs can be significantly benefited by embarking upon a program of treatment involving graduated real-life exposure therapy. Although intense affect can occur during sessions, many forms of therapy often produce similar reactions. The demonstrable gains that typically occur within just a few hours of therapy encourage the client to persevere. ET is very well supported with dozens of well controlled randomized trials demonstrating its efficacy over many decades of clinical research. Positive outcomes initially obtained in research contexts have been widely replicated in agency-based contexts with more "typical" clients. Its results are superior to the passage of time, credible placebo treatments, and purely office-based verbal psychotherapies. The substantial improvements are typically well-maintained over long follow-up periods. Considerable clinical resources are available for LCSWs to draw upon in learning about this powerful research-supported intervention.

References

American Psychiatric Association. (2013). *Diagnostic and statistical manual of mental disorders* (5th ed.). American Psychiatric Publishing.

Brown, T. A., & Barlow, D. H. (2021). *Anxiety and Related Disorders Interview Schedule for DSM-5 (ADIS-5)–Adult Version.* Oxford University Press.

Fyer, A. J. (1998). Current approaches to etiology and pathophysiology of specific phobia. *Biological Psychiatry, 12,* 1295–1304.

National Association of Social Workers. (2017). *Code of ethics.* https://www.socialworkers.org/about/ethics/code-of-ethics

Pergeron, J. P., Curtis, G. C., & Thyer, B. A. (1986). Simple phobia leading to suicide: A case report [Letter]. *The Behavior Therapist, 9,* 134–135.

Raggi, V. L., & Samson, J. G. (2018). *Exposure therapy for treating anxiety in children and adolescents: A comprehensive guide.* New Harbinger.

Thyer, B. A. (1983). Treating anxiety disorders with exposure therapy. *Social Casework, 64,* 77–82.

Thyer, B. A. (1985). The treatment of phobias in their natural contexts. *Journal of Applied Social Sciences, 9*(1), 73–83.

Thyer, B. A. (1987). *Treating anxiety disorders: A guide for human service professionals.* Sage.

Thyer, B. A., & Curtis, G. C. (1983). The repeated pretest–posttest single-subject experiment: A new design for empirical clinical practice. *Journal of Behavior Therapy and Experimental Psychiatry, 14,* 311–315.

Thyer, B. A., Himle, J., & Curtis, G. C. (1985). Blood–injury–illness phobia: A review. *Journal of Clinical Psychology, 41,* 451–459.

Thyer, B. A., Papsdorf, J. D., Davis, R., & Vallecorsa, S. (1984). Autonomic correlates of the Subjective Anxiety Scale. *Journal of Behavior Therapy and Experimental Psychiatry, 15,* 3–7.

Thyer, B. A., Parrish, R. T., Curtis, G. C., Nesse, R. M., & Cameron, O. G. (1985). Ages of onset of DSM-III anxiety disorders. *Comprehensive Psychiatry, 26,* 113–122.

Vonk, M. E., & Thyer, B. A. (1995). Exposure therapy in the treatment of vaginal penetration phobia: A case study. *Journal of Behavior Therapy and Experimental Psychiatry, 29,* 359–363.

Wolitzky-Taylor, K. B., Horowitz, J. D., Powers, M. B., & Telch, M. L. (2008). Psychological approaches in the treatment of specific phobias: A meta-analysis. *Clinical Psychology Review, 28,* 1021–1037.

Assessment, Prevention, and Intervention with Suicidal Youth

Jonathan B. Singer, Hannah Szlyk,
and Kimberly H. McManama O'Brien

Risk and Protective Factors

Although there is no single pathway to suicide, there are factors that increase the risk of suicidal thoughts and behaviors (STB). The role of gender is important to consider because female youth (ages 10–24 years) attempt suicide more than two times as often as male youth [Centers for Disease Control and Prevention (CDC), 2020c], but male youth die by suicide at more than three times the rate of female youth (CDC, 2020a). With respect to ethnicity, youth suicide rates (per 100,000) are highest for American Indians/Alaskan Natives (17.79), followed by Whites (10.98), Asian/Pacific Islanders (8.01), and Blacks (7.55) (ages 10–24 years for the year 2018) (CDC, 2020a). The suicide rate is lower for youth who identify as Hispanic (3.98 per 100,000) than non-Hispanic youth (8.20 per 100,000) (CDC, 2020a). Youth who identify as gay, lesbian, or bisexual attempt suicide at nearly a fivefold greater rate than their heterosexual peers (21.8 vs. 4.6 per 100,000, respectively) (Kann et al., 2018; see also the Trevor Project report at https://www.thetrevorproject.org/survey-2020). Last, youth who live in rural areas compared to youth in urban areas are less likely to report suicidal ideation or attempt but die by suicide at nearly twice the rate as youth in urban areas (Goldman-Mellor et al., 2018).

The strongest psychosocial risk factor for STB is a prior suicide attempt. Psychiatric diagnosis and comorbidity greatly increase risk for youth STB. Mood-related psychological factors that contribute to risk include hopelessness, elevations in suicidal ideation, higher levels of affect dysregulation, and recent self-injurious behaviors. Although nonsuicidal self-injury (NSSI) is by definition not suicidal behavior (and should be treated as distinct), some studies suggest NSSI may be a precursor and/or correlate with STB or a coping strategy for suicidal ideation. Substance use, especially alcohol use, is consistently associated with risk for youth STB. The disinhibition and interaction with depressive symptoms caused by alcohol intoxication may facilitate suicidal ideation and increase the likelihood of acting on suicidal thoughts (O'Brien et al., 2014).

Among youth with no clear psychopathology or histories of suicidality, a critical risk factor for suicide is access to a loaded firearm in the home. Other psychosocial factors that increase the risk for STB include chronic physical illness; the presence of a disability; low peer and/or parental support; family history of a suicide attempt; and having been a victim, perpetrator, or victim–perpetrator of bullying or sexual or physical abuse. Perceived discrimination, including racial, ethnic, and homophobic microaggressions, may also contribute to youth STB (Madubata et al., 2019).

Essential to risk assessment and treatment planning is identifying protective factors, or skills and resources that act as a buffer from youth suicide risk. There are two types of protective factors: internal factors and external factors. Internal factors include problem-solving skills, proactive emotional regulation, and feelings of self-efficacy. External factors include positive therapeutic relationships; social supports (peers and family); high family functioning; supportive school environments; and engagement in meaningful activities, including religious and/or spiritual practices and hobbies (Szlyk, 2020).

Suicide Risk Assessment

The suicide risk assessment must be conducted within a biopsychosocial evaluation. Information gathered from a suicide risk assessment provides guidance regarding what preventive measures need to be put into place to ensure short-term safety and long-term hope. Social workers should have knowledge of next steps before starting a suicide risk assessment and assess for suicide in the context of other individual and family factors. Individual factors to consider include mental status, risk and protective factors, supports in place, ability of the youth to employ coping strategies, future orientation, and willingness to engage in treatment. Family factors to consider include family structure and dynamics, willingness of family to engage in treatment, supports available to the family, culture, ethnicity, religion, immigration status, family history of mental illness and treatment, family's ability to identify strengths within the system, coping strategies, and flexibility in considering treatment options. Because

youth STB is especially episodic, assessment should be a part of a social worker's routine practice, and findings should be shared with the systems that influence the youth.

To conduct an effective suicide risk assessment, parents and the youth must be interviewed separately. Because of shame, stigma, or fear of punishment, youth are often hesitant to express the full extent of their suicidal ideation and intent. Social workers should be well-versed in the content of a suicide risk assessment and techniques designed to elicit suicidal ideation and intent, such as shame attenuation, behavioral incident, gentle assumption, and symptom amplification (Shea, 2002). These techniques will help social workers respond when the client says "no" or "I don't know." It is critical to ask open-ended and detailed questions about suicide, including the "who, what, when, where, why, and how." If the youth endorses suicidal ideation, the social worker must screen for plan, intent, and access. If the youth endorses having made a plan to attempt suicide, the social worker must ask about the timing and location of the act, the lethality and availability of means, and whether there are acts currently in preparation. To assess for intent, the social worker must inquire about the extent of the youth's plan and how much the youth believes the plan to be lethal versus as self-injurious.

It is always critical to ask about access to lethal means. Firearm access is a key risk factor for suicide because of the lethality of the method. In 2018, firearms accounted for 37% of suicide deaths in youth aged 10–24 years (CDC, 2020a; CDC, 2020b). Poisoning also represents a common suicide attempt method. Social workers must assess for the youth's access to over-the-counter medications, household cleaning supplies, and the youth's prescription medications. Similarly, the parent(s) and child should be interviewed separately about access to lethal means. Getting a description of the current problem and precipitants to the STB involves understanding symptoms and their severity and also recent STB, plans, notes, etc. The social worker must also ask about precipitating events (e.g., an argument with a friend) and stressors and whether or not they are acute (e.g., recent humiliation) or chronic (e.g., illness, poverty, or abuse/neglect). Prior suicide attempts and current substance use must also be assessed.

Safety Planning

After conducting a suicide risk assessment and determining if the youth can return to the community, the social worker must develop a safety plan with the youth and family prior to discharge. Safety plans are not the same as no-suicide contracts, which are not proven to be effective because they do not provide a reasonable and agreed upon plan (Wortzel et al., 2013). Safety plans include engaging the youth in the planning, identifying strategies they can complete alone, places they can go, and contacts that can help them decrease distress. Next, the clinician asks the youth to rank order strategies and discuss how confident they feel to follow the plan the next time they are suicidal. Last, safety planning should include limiting access to means, increasing positive coping strategies and supports, and keeping caregivers involved in the safety plan. Safety plans are increasingly embedded in smartphone applications to facilitate ease of use (Melia et al., 2020). Participation in safety planning and a structured follow-up phone call after discharge from an emergency department are clinically proven to reduce suicidal behaviors and increase engagement in additional mental health services compared with usual care (Stanley et al., 2018).

Prevention Strategies

Suicide prevention takes a public health perspective in which targets for prevention efforts can be universal, selective, or indicated (Singer et al., 2019). *Universal* prevention programs target an entire population to reduce risk factors or enhance protective factors. *Selective* prevention programs target youth who demonstrate risk factors associated with STB but who have not yet reported suicidal ideation or an attempt. *Indicated* prevention programs are designed to intervene with youth who have already displayed STB. Schools are a widely used setting for youth suicide prevention programs, which include suicide awareness and education, screening, gatekeeper training, peer leadership training, and skills training (Erbacher & Singer, 2018; Singer et al., 2019).

Intervention Strategies
Hospital-Based Interventions

Inpatient Psychiatric Units

Suicidal thoughts and behaviors are a common problem for youth admitted to an inpatient psychiatric hospital, which represents the most restrictive level of care available to suicidal youth. Inpatient hospitalization is necessary if the suicidal youth's behavior is so unstable and unpredictable that there is serious short-term risk (Shaffer & Pfeffer, 2001). The primary goals of short-term inpatient psychiatric care typically include safety and containment, mood stabilization, and follow-up care coordination.

Emergency Departments

Before admission to inpatient psychiatric hospitals, many youth are evaluated in a hospital emergency department (ED). The ED represents an ideal environment for a brief intervention with suicidal youth and their families, such as the Family Intervention for Suicide Prevention (FISP; Asarnow et al., 2017). Major goals of FISP are to improve continuity of care between the ED and community mental health services and to decrease the risk of short-term repeated suicidal behavior. FISP is implemented after the youth has been evaluated and determined ready for discharge. During FISP, the suicidal crisis is reframed as maladaptive coping skill within the context of a family crisis. FISP has demonstrated success in connecting youth to follow-up care but not reducing STB (Asarnow et al., 2017).

Community-Based Interventions

Community-based practices for suicidal youth include crisis assessment and intervention, individual and family therapy, integrated interventions, and psychopharmacotherapy. There is mixed evidence about the clinical effectiveness of group therapy. The Youth-Nominated Support Team–Version II (YST-II) is an innovative social network intervention in which suicidal youth identify a supportive adult. YST-II improves mental health service use and medication management 12 months following hospitalization, and it reduces self-injury and overall mortality (King et al., 2009, 2019).

Dialectical Behavior Therapy for Adolescents

Dialectical behavior therapy for adolescent (DBT-A; Mehlum et al., 2019) was adapted from DBT, which was initially developed to address self-harm among women with borderline personality disorder (Linehan et al., 1991). The goal of DBT is to improve a person's ability to regulate emotions by reducing distress associated with moving between opposing, or dialectical, thoughts, emotions, and behaviors. DBT-A combines weekly individual therapy with a multifamily skills group and between-session therapist check-ins. Although DBT-A has demonstrated significant reductions in suicide attempts, NSSI, and self-harm compared to other therapies, evidence supporting the long-term advantages of DBT-A is mixed (McCauley et al., 2018; Mehlum et al., 2019).

Attachment-Based Family Therapy

Attachment-based family therapy (ABFT) utilizes family and individual sessions to address depression and STB via an attachment-based, emotion-focused psychotherapy model (Diamond, Russon, et al., 2019). ABFT strengthens the parent–child relationship and reestablishes the family as a source of strength and support during suicidal and other crises. ABFT has demonstrated effectiveness in reducing suicidal ideation and depressive symptoms among youth with a history of trauma, sexual minority youth, and Black and Latino families with complex needs. A recent trial comparing ABFT to a family-enhanced nondirective therapy found that although youth in both groups demonstrated significant decreases in suicidal ideation, there was no significant difference in the rate of change in suicidal ideation or depressive symptoms between groups (Diamond, Kobak, et al., 2019).

Integrated Interventions

Integrated Cognitive–Behavioral Therapy

Integrated cognitive–behavioral therapy (I-CBT; Esposito-Smythers et al., 2019) combines individual and family CBT and parent training to target the common maladaptive behaviors and beliefs that underlie STB and substance abuse. Individually, I-CBT addresses issues with cognitive distortions, coping, and communication. A parent training and/or family session is added in which the mental health and substance abuse treatment goals of the adolescent are addressed and parents learn monitoring, emotion regulation, communication, and behavioral contracting skills. Research suggests that I-CBT improves functioning and decreases STB, nonsuicidal self-injury, hospitalizations, emergency department visits, substance use, and depressive symptoms up to 19 months post treatment (Esposito-Smythers et al., 2019).

Safe Alternatives for Teens and Youths

Safe Alternatives for Teens and Youths (SAFETY; Asarnow et al., 2017) is a 12-week intervention for youth with a recent suicide attempt or self-harm that is family-centered and informed by CBT and DBT. Sessions allow for parents and the youth to practice coping skills, identify issues that could impact future STB, and enhance access to community-based supports. Research found that compared to enhanced treatment as usual, youth who received SAFETY were significantly less likely to attempt suicide, but between-group differences weakened after completion of treatment and SAFETY did not have a significant impact on NSSI (Asarnow et al., 2017).

Conclusion and Future Directions

In this chapter, we identified and described current assessment, prevention, and intervention strategies with suicidal youth. The existing empirical literature suggests that few intervention programs (YST-II, DBT-A, and SAFETY) have been shown to reduce STB in youth over time, highlighting the need for continued research on effective youth interventions. Promising advancements in suicide prevention and intervention have emerged related to the development and adaptation of interventions for diverse youth populations. Historically, youth suicide prevention and intervention programs have been designed with White, English-speaking, heteronormative samples from middle-class communities. More programs are being developed for youth and include more individuals who do not meet this narrow description (Humensky et al., 2017). There is still tremendous work to be done to ensure that available prevention and intervention programs meet the needs of vulnerable youth groups, especially as the United States experiences increases in STB among Black and sexual and gender minority youth.

The integration of technology in suicide prevention and intervention programs is one strategy to address barriers to mental health service access (i.e., transportation, limited hours, and clinical settings) and personalize care (i.e., using a smartphone application to practice coping skills). Technology-enhanced prevention and interventions are not without drawbacks. Not all insurance companies cover telehealth sessions, many smartphone applications do not meet the minimum requirements for effectiveness with suicidal populations (i.e., lack of direct access to emergency resources or do not contain a safety plan), and access to technology (i.e., smartphones or tablets) and the internet is still variable within the United States (Szlyk et al., 2020). Although many youth may feel more comfortable communicating via phone or texting, some may feel wary of the possible breaches of privacy that may arise with telehealth services. It is important that social workers weigh the advantages and disadvantages of available services and treatments to address youth STB and advocate for their clients' unique strengths and issues when adaptations are needed.

Helpful Resources

American Association Suicidology: https://suicidology.org
American Foundation for Suicide Prevention: https://afsp.org
Speaking of Suicide, Stacey Freedenthal, PhD, LCSW: https://www.speakingofsuicide.com/about-stacey-freedenthal/stacey-freedenthal-phd-lcsw

References

Asarnow, J. R., Hughes, J. L., Babeva, K. N., & Sugar, C. A. (2017). Cognitive–behavioral family treatment for suicide attempt prevention: A randomized controlled trial. *Journal of the American Academy of Child & Adolescent Psychiatry, 56*(6), 506–514. https://doi.org/10.1016/j.jaac.2017.03.015
Centers for Disease Control and Prevention, National Center for Injury Prevention and Control. (2020a). *WISQARS—Web-based Injury Statistics Query and Reporting System: Fatal injury reports, 1999–2018, for national, regional, and states*. Retrieved June 10, 2020, from http://www.cdc.gov/injury/wisqars

Centers for Disease Control and Prevention, National Center for Injury Prevention and Control. (2020b). *WISQARS—Web-based Injury Statistics Query and Reporting System: Leading causes of death reports, 1981–2018*. Retrieved June 10, 2020, from http://www.cdc.gov/injury/wisqars

Centers for Disease Control and Prevention, National Center for Injury Prevention and Control. (2020c). *WISQARS—Web-based Injury Statistics Query and Reporting System: Non-fatal injury data 2001–2018*. Retrieved June 10,2020, from http://www.cdc.gov/injury/wisqars

Diamond, G. S., Kobak, R. R., Ewing, E. S. K., Levy, S. A., Herres, J. L., Russon, J. M., & Gallop, R. J. (2019). A randomized controlled trial: attachment-based family and nondirective supportive treatments for youth who are suicidal. *Journal of the American Academy of Child & Adolescent Psychiatry, 58*(7), 721–731.

Erbacher, T. A., & Singer, J. B. (2018). Suicide risk monitoring: The missing piece in suicide risk assessment. *Contemporary School Psychology, 22*(2), 186–194. https://doi.org/10.1007/s40688-017-0164-8

Esposito-Smythers, C., Wolff, J. C., Liu, R. T., Hunt, J. I., Adams, L., Kim, K., Frazier, E. A., Yen, S., Dickstein, D. P., & Spirito, A. (2019). Family-focused cognitive behavioral treatment for depressed adolescents in suicidal crisis with co-occurring risk factors: A randomized trial. *Journal of Child Psychology and Psychiatry, 60*(10), 1133–1141. https://doi.org/10.1111/jcpp.13095

Goldman-Mellor, S., Allen, K., & Kaplan, M. S. (2018). Rural/urban disparities in adolescent nonfatal suicidal ideation and suicide attempt: A population-based study. *Suicide and Life-Threatening Behavior, 48*(6), 709–719. https://doi.org/10.1111/sltb.12390

Humensky, J. L., Coronel, B., Gil, R., Mazzula, S., & Lewis-Fernández, R. (2017). Life is Precious: A community-based program to reduce suicidal behavior in Latina adolescents. *Archives of Suicide Research, 21*(4), 659–671. https://doi.org/10.1080/13811118.2016.1242442

Kann, L., McManus, T., Harris, W. A., Shanklin, S. L., Flint, K. H., Queen, B., Lowry, R., Chyen, D., Whittle, L., Thornton, J., Lim, C., Bradford, D., Yamakawa, Y., Leon, M., Brener, N., & Ethier, K. A. (2018). Youth risk behavior surveillance—United States, 2017. *MMWR Surveillance Summaries, 67*(8), 1–114. https://doi.org/10.15585/mmwr.ss6708a1

King, C. A., Arango, A., Kramer, A., Busby, D., Czyz, E., Foster, C. E., & Gillespie, B. W., for the YST Study Team. (2019). Association of the Youth-Nominated Support Team intervention for suicidal adolescents with 11- to 14-year mortality outcomes: Secondary analysis of a randomized clinical trial. *JAMA*

Psychiatry, 76(5), 492. https://doi.org/10.1001/jamapsychiatry.2018.4358

King, C. A., Klaus, N., Kramer, A., Venkataraman, S., Quinlan, P., & Gillespie, B. W. (2009). The Youth-Nominated Support Team–Version II for suicidal adolescents: A randomized controlled intervention trial. *Journal of Consulting and Clinical Psychology, 77*(5), 880–893. https://doi.org/10.1037/a0016552

Linehan, M. M., Armstrong, H. E., Suarez, A., Allmon, D., & Heard, H. L. (1991). Cognitive–behavioral treatment of chronically parasuicidal borderline patients. *Archives of General Psychiatry, 48*(12), 1060–1064.

Madubata, I., Spivey, L. A., Alvarez, G. M., Neblett, E. W., & Prinstein, M. J. (2019). Forms of racial/ethnic discrimination and suicidal ideation: A prospective examination of African American and Latinx Youth. *Journal of Clinical Child & Adolescent Psychology, 1–*9. https://doi.org/10.1080/15374416.2019.1655756

McCauley, E., Berk, M. S., Asarnow, J. R., Adrian, M., Cohen, J., Korslund, K., Avina, C., Hughes, J., Harned, M., Gallop, R., & Linehan, M. M. (2018). Efficacy of dialectical behavior therapy for adolescents at high risk for suicide: A randomized clinical trial. *JAMA Psychiatry, 75*(8), 777–785. https://doi.org/10.1001/jamapsychiatry.2018.1109

Mehlum, L., Ramleth, R., Tørmoen, A. J., Haga, E., Diep, L. M., Stanley, B. H., Miller, A. L., Larsson, B., Sund, A. M., & Grøholt, B. (2019). Long term effectiveness of dialectical behavior therapy versus enhanced usual care for adolescents with self-harming and suicidal behavior. *Journal of Child Psychology and Psychiatry, 60*(10), 1112–1122. https://doi.org/10.1111/jcpp.13077

Melia, R., Francis, K., Hickey, E., Bogue, J., Duggan, J., O'Sullivan, M., & Young, K. (2020). Mobile health technology interventions for suicide prevention: Systematic review. *JMIR MHealth and UHealth, 8*(1), e12516. https://doi.org/10.2196/12516

O'Brien, K. H. M., Becker, S. J., Spirito, A., Simon, V., & Prinstein, M. J. (2014). Differentiating adolescent suicide attempters from ideators: Examining the interaction between depression severity and alcohol use. *Suicide & Life-Threatening Behavior, 44*(1), 23–33. https://doi.org/10.1111/sltb.12050

Shaffer, D., & Pfeffer, C. R. (2001). Practice parameter for the assessment and treatment of children and adolescents with suicidal behavior. *Journal of the American Academy of Child & Adolescent Psychiatry, 40*(Suppl. 7), 24S–51S.

Shea, S. C. (2002). *The practical art of suicide assessment: A guide for mental health professionals and substance abuse counselors*. Mental Health Presses.

Singer, J. B., Erbacher, T. A., & Rosen, P. (2019). School-based suicide prevention: A framework for evidence-based practice. *School Mental Health, 11*(1), 54–71. https://doi.org/10.1007/s12310-018-9245-8

Stanley, B., Brown, G. K., Brenner, L. A., Galfalvy, H. C., Currier, G. W., Knox, K. L., Chaudhury, S. R., Bush, A. L., & Green, K. L. (2018). Comparison of the safety planning intervention with follow-up vs. usual care of suicidal patients treated in the emergency department. *JAMA Psychiatry, 75*(9), 894–900. https://doi.org/10.1001/jamapsychiatry.2018.1776

Szlyk, H. S. (2020). Resilience among students at risk of dropout: Expanding perspectives on youth suicidality in a non-clinical setting. *School Mental Health, 12,* 567–579. https://doi.org/10.1007/s12310-020-09366-x

Szlyk, H. S., Berk, M., Peralta, A. O., & Miranda, R. (2020). Coronavirus disease 2019 takes adolescent suicide prevention to less charted territory. *Journal of Adolescent Health,* S1054139X20303025. https://doi.org/10.1016/j.jadohealth.2020.05.046

Wortzel, H. S., Matarazzo, B., & Homaifar, B. (2013). A model for therapeutic risk management of the suicidal patient. *Journal of Psychiatric Practice, 19*(4), 323–326. https://doi.org/10.1097/01.pra.0000432603.99211.e8

Adolescent Mental Health

Craig Winston LeCroy

Adolescents in today's society face significant risks that can compromise their mental health and well-being. The developmental period of adolescence is recognized as more difficult and dangerous than it has been in the recent past. A significant difference is that modern adolescents are exposed to risky behavior, such as cigarette use and sex, at a much earlier age compared to adolescents of the past (Carr, 2002). It has been estimated that half of all youth are at moderate to high risk of engaging in problem behaviors (Ashford et al., 2018). Carr (2002) estimates that between 10% and 20% of adolescents will suffer from psychological problems serious enough to warrant treatment. Complicating their health is that almost half of adolescents with mental health issues do not receive any mental health services (Center for Behavioral Health Statistics and Quality, 2013). The following are important facts about adolescent mental health: At least one in four youth suffers from a current developmental, emotional, or behavioral problem; half of all lifetime cases of mental disorders begin by age 14 years (Lipari et al., 2016); and mental health services are delivered across a variety of settings, complicating the service delivery model (Lipair et al., 2016). Even adolescents who are not considered to be at risk must navigate through adolescence, and this is a period easily characterized as a playing field of obstacles and barriers to healthy development.

Interventions being used with adolescents have become increasingly focused on programs that can promote positive youth development, reduce risk factors, and remediate adolescent problem behaviors and disorders. Better assessment tools and better interventions have paved the way for improving the quality of the mental health and well-being of adolescents. An increasing emphasis on best practices, research-based practice, and evidence-based practice is being supported and promoted by various groups of professionals, such as the Society for Social Work Research, the American Psychological Association, the Office of the Surgeon General, American Family Physicians, and the Substance Abuse and Mental Health Services Administration. Furthermore, advocacy groups, parents, and local governments are also placing a renewed emphasis on effective interventions for adolescents.

The purpose of this chapter is to review current issues and problems facing adolescents and examine prevention and intervention strategies and programs designed to promote adolescent mental health and well-being. The central concern is best practices when working with adolescents and evidence-based programs specific to adolescents.

Overview of Problems Facing Adolescents

Adolescent development is an important consideration in the design and implementation of effective interventions. During early adolescence, physical changes occur more rapidly than at any other time in the life span except infancy (Ashford et al., 2018). The production of sex hormones, puberty, and the appearance of secondary sex characteristics are significant changes that take place in adolescence. During adolescence, young people begin to think more abstractly and shift from concrete to formal operational thinking. This has significance for the design of interventions because young adolescents or troubled adolescents often have difficulty linking thoughts, feelings, and behaviors. Identity formation and self-development are central to adolescents and can lead to positive or negative behaviors. Peers provide support; however, pressure by peers for approval and conformity is directly related to engagement in risky behaviors. Last, emotional development is maturing, and adolescents experience a wide fluctuation of emotional reactions. Coping with negative emotions is important in developing a positive sense of well-being. An important skill in working with adolescents is being able to identify common developmental problems, issues needing closer observation, and developmental observations requiring attention (Ashford et al., 2018). For example, routine observations when working with adolescents should include assessing peer groups, body image, sense of morality, sexual identity, focus on physical appearance, and hormonal changes. Common developmental issues that practitioners should be aware of include

concern with body image, spending too much time alone, negative peer influence, decreased interest in school, moodiness, sexual behavior, parent conflict, and risky behaviors. Finally, developmental observations that require attention include eating disorders, depression, pregnancy, sex abuse and rape, violent behaviors and exposure to violence, firearm exposure, and conduct disorder and delinquency.

Although adolescence is a time of significant development, it is also the time when many of the major mental disorders begin. Furthermore, after onset, many of these disorders persist into adulthood, leading to significant impairment in adulthood. Beyond mental disorders, many adolescents engage in risky behavior or are exposed to social conditions that impact their development. These high-risk behaviors often pave the way for dysfunctional adult behavior such as substance use and unprotected sex.

It is now understood that many problem behaviors and mental disorders are common in adolescence. Epidemiological studies of adolescents have provided a better understanding of the likelihood of occurrence of such behaviors and disorders. Table 126.1 presents some of the more common behavior problems and mental disorders that occur in adolescence.

The prevalence of mental disorders in children and adolescents has been increasing throughout the years. Better assessment and detection account for some of these observations. However, the stressful and difficult environments that adolescents experience are also a contributor. Furthermore, adolescence is now considered to last longer than it did in the past. Emergent adulthood is recognized as a new stage and is also considered to be part of adolescence (Arnett, 2004). This coupled with the availability of potentially harmful environments (exposure to drugs, poverty, and homelessness) can take a toll on young people.

Adolescent interventions can be categorized according to two main types. The

TABLE 126.1 Common Behavior Problems and Mental Disorders Occurring in Adolescence

Drug use	Past 30 days have been drunk
	21% for 10th graders
	33% for 12th graders
	By high school graduation
	54% have used illicit drugs
Sexual behavior	Birth rate for girls aged 15–19 years
	57 per 1,000
	Pregnancy rate per year
	Approximately 10% of girls aged 15–19 years
	Approximately half of adolescents are sexually active before they graduate from high school.
School dropout	Status dropout rate: the percentage of an age group that is not enrolled in school and has not earned a high school diploma
	Approximately 11% of 16- to 24-year-olds (who were out of school without a high school diploma)
Suicide	Overall suicide rate of 8–9%, with 2–3% of the attempts requiring medical attention
Depression	Depression rates range from 1% to 6%.
	When all kinds of depressive disorders are included, the rate is approximately 10%.
Anxiety disorders	Overall rate for all kinds of anxiety disorders ranges from 6% to 15%.
Eating disorders	Approximately 3–4% of the adolescent female population suffer from eating disorders.
	Anorexia
Autism spectrum disorder	Prevalence rates have shown increases during the past 30 years.
	Recent estimates are
	16.8 per 10,000 for autism
	45.8 per 10,000 for other pervasive developmental disorders

first refers to the absence of dysfunction in psychological, emotional, behavioral, and social spheres (Kazdin & McWhinney, 2018). Dysfunction is defined as impairment in everyday life. Mental health disorders such as anxiety disorder, depression, and autism are examples of dysfunctions. Adolescent who suffer from a disorder such as this are impaired in their everyday functional abilities (e.g., social relationships and school performance), and their dysfunction is likely to influence their well-being (e.g., suicide attempts and substance abuse). As Kazdin (1993) notes, it is important to recognize that

> a variety of behaviors in which adolescents engage (e.g. substance use, antisocial acts, school dysfunction) and conditions to which they are exposed (e.g. poverty, homelessness, physical abuse) are dysfunctional because they impede the quality of current functioning and often portend deleterious physical and psychological consequences. (p. 128)

The second main type of adolescent intervention focuses on optimal functioning or well-being in psychological or social domains (Kazdin, 2018). Well-being is the presence of strengths that promote optimal functioning—it is not just the absence of impairment. The strengths perspective and positive psychology promote social competence, coping skills, and positive attachments to significant others—all of which are a part of optimal functioning. Social competence is considered a key concept that directs attention to adolescents' ability to cope with the demands of the environment by using cognitive and social skills to achieve positive outcomes.

These two approaches are part of a continuum of interventions with adolescents but suggest different conceptualizations, models of treatment, and intended outcomes. Promoting optimal functioning or positive mental health is fundamentally based on promoting certain competencies. The goal of these interventions is to build strengths, teach coping skills, and teach new social skills to enhance everyday functioning. In addition to being more socially competent, adolescents may benefit from these approaches because they limit the development of clinical problems. In contrast, interventions designed to address dysfunction are based on diagnosis of disorders and the administration of certain interventions to reduce impairment. More intensive interventions, such as long-term therapy, residential treatment, hospitalization, and medication, are often needed. Box 126.1 lists some of the major at-risk problems and clinical disorders in adolescence.

Key Evidence-Based Treatment Programs for Adolescents

There is growing demand for practitioners to use evidence-based treatment with children and adolescents. Perhaps for good reason, as Kazdin (2000) lists hundreds of available

---

BOX 126.1 Common Adolescent At-Risk Problems and Diagnoses

Anxiety disorder

Conduct disorder and delinquency

Depression

Eating disorders

Substance use and abuse

Sexual behavior

Running away from home, homelessness

Oppositional defiant disorder

School problems and dropout

Cutting behavior

Suicide risk

---

treatments for children and adolescents, raising the question: How does one select the best treatment for a given child's problem? Determining which treatments are evidence-based is becoming increasingly complicated. Review articles list treatments with evidence, meta-analytic studies examine statistics to determine which treatments have the most impact, and websites provide lists (based on unknown criteria) from which "evidence-based" programs can be selected. Many sources provide contradictory information; for example, some reviews may claim a program is evidence-based and other reviews may claim there is insufficient evidence. The design and quality of the research that support the interventions are evaluated inconsistently; for example, some reviews will only accept randomized controlled trials and other reviews accept quasi-experimental designs. The number of studies that support different evidence-based treatments varies greatly from 2 (usually thought of as the minimum) to more than 20. Also complicating the picture is the criteria or measures that are being used to assess the outcomes (LeCroy, 2019)—different criteria or measures may lead to different conclusions. An important task of the contemporary practitioner is to sort through information and make informed decisions about evidence when selecting treatments. Within the realm of adolescent mental health, Box 126.2 provides some generally accepted treatments used primarily with adolescents that many reviews consider evidence-based. Chorpita et al. (2011) provide a comprehensive analysis of more than 750 studies in examining the evidence for child and adolescent interventions. When collapsed across categories (attention deficit disorder, depression, etc.), most of the evidence-based treatments are included in Box 126.2.

Considerations in Service Delivery

A fundamental issue in service delivery with adolescents is their ability to find and accept help when they deem it necessary. In addition to adolescence being a time during which serious problems can emerge, it is also a time when adolescents face acute barriers to accessing the help they need. Adolescents often do not know where to go for help or who they can trust to get help. Consider the following scenarios: the adolescent girl who is raped but too ashamed to tell her friends or parents, an adolescent trapped in a sexually intimate relationship with no birth control or protection from sexually transmitted diseases, an adolescent who has depressed moods and feels hopeless, or an adolescent who feels trapped by a gang and is now involved in illegal behavior.

Most adolescents underutilize the systems of care created to assist them. Adolescents seek care less than any other age group (Lipari et al., 2016). In general, adolescents seek care through a variety of settings, such as school and outpatient clinics. Regardless of the setting, approximately 50% of adolescents reported they received services because they felt depressed (Lipari et al., 2016). The key factors in this underutilization of services are cost, poor organization of services,

---

BOX 126.2 Evidence-Based Interventions for Adolescents

Cognitive–behavior therapy (e.g., coping with depression course)

Multisystemic therapy, functional family therapy, family checkup

Problem-solving and social skills training

Multidimensional foster care

Multigroup psychoeducation

Dialectical behavior therapy, acceptance and commitment therapy

Assertiveness training, anger replacement therapy

Parent management training and contingency management

Exposure therapy, relaxation training

---

lack of availability, and concerns regarding confidentiality (LeCroy, 2011). Furthermore, treatment for many of the serious problems confronted by adolescents, such as mental disorders, sexually transmitted diseases, and abuse, is not covered by many health insurances plans or the coverage is so restrictive and complex that access to help is impeded.

To improve effectiveness, interventions must become more sensitive to adolescents' concerns about their privacy and confidentiality (LeCroy & Daley, 2001). Survey results reveal that under conditions in which medical treatment would be confidential, adolescents would be significantly more likely to seek care for depression, birth control, sexually transmitted diseases, and drug use (National Research Council, 1993). Kobocow et al. (1983) administered personal interviews requiring substantial self-disclosure to a group of 195 seventh- and eighth-grade students and found that "56.8% of females and 38.6% of males listed assurance of confidentiality as the most important statement made to the interviewer prior to the interview" (p. 422). These results illustrate the high value that adolescents place on confidentiality, as well as the need for increased sensitivity to adolescents' strong concerns about their privacy. If we want to help young people in trouble or at risk, we need to pave a road for them that is easy to follow and will lead to a successful outcome. Access to professionals who are specifically trained in helping adolescents is only one component of successful intervention for youth in trouble. Youth who need help must feel cared for and respected by a network of people.

Interventions for adolescents form a continuum from brief structured treatments to longer ongoing treatment strategies. These longer ongoing interventions are designed for adolescents with persistent and long-term conditions. Typically, multimodal interventions are directed at youth and include residential treatment, ongoing family treatment, medication management, and special education. An important aspect of intervention at this level is the awareness and understanding that the problems being confronted are serious and chronic. In many respects, the mental health system has not adapted to an approach to intervention that acknowledges and responds to these chronic conditions.

Motivation for Treatment

A distinguishing feature of interventions with adolescents, compared with adults, is that often the client has not sought help on their own accord. Many adolescents end up in treatment because they were arrested, a parent found drugs in their room, or a teacher reported behavior problems. Although we have stressed promising or evidence-based interventions with adolescents, all are dependent on engagement in the treatment. Engagement is a significant issue for adolescents in individual and group therapy and also for those in family therapy.

The popularity of motivational interviewing (Miller & Rollnick, 2002) is related to awareness of the need for proper engagement in treatment. The stages of change model (Prochaska & DiClemente, 1986) has also helped focus intervention efforts on motivation. These are critical concepts for work with adolescents. Change takes place when individuals are in the proper stage of change and motivated to take action toward solving their problem. Dishion and Kavanagh (2003) discuss initial strategies for engaging adolescents in treatment. Table 126.2 presents a summary of these ideas.

TABLE 126.2 Strategies for Engaging Adolescents in Treatment

Respect privacy and space	Adolescents often begin treatment with a sense of mistrust. Empathize with their reluctance to participate in the treatment.
Normalize experiences	Try to normalize the adolescent's need for help—for example "This can be a difficult time and a lot of young people have found talking with someone helpful."
Advocate the adolescent's interest	Be clear about your relationship with the adolescent. Communicate about how you perceive their situation and describe what the benefit is for their involvement.
Link interests and services	Adolescents are more engaged if they see the connection between their concerns, the assessment, and the intervention.
Create optimistic reframes	The extent of an adolescent's engagement in treatment is related to the use of positive reframes.
Keep it brief, start slow	Do not make the mistake of being too friendly or too confrontive or both too early in treatment. Adolescents may be better helped in a brief time period such as 30 minutes rather than the standard 50-minute session.

Based on Dishion and Kavanagh (2003).

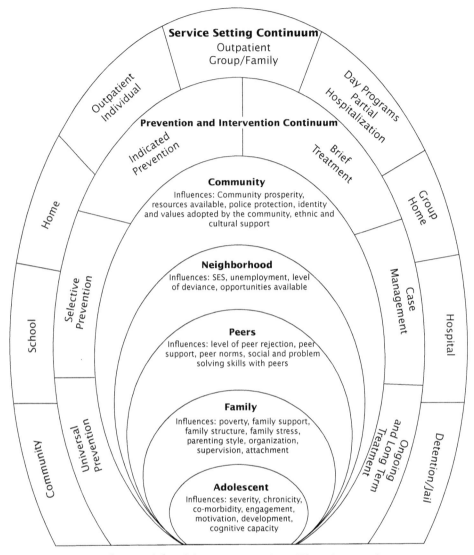

FIGURE 126.1 Ecological framework for adolescent interventions. SES, socioeconomic status.

Context and Focus of Treatment

When an adolescent is identified as needing help, the most common provision of treatment is the individual adolescent. This may be appropriate for many situations; however, focusing only on the adolescent ignores the context—the various ecosystems that can influence the adolescent's functioning. Environmental factors play an important role in understanding and intervening in adolescent problem behaviors. The adolescent's individual and cognitive

functioning are important, interpersonal relationships and peer relationships are considered critical in adolescence, the school system provides an important context for understanding difficulties, and the community and neighborhood can have a direct influence of functioning.

Many adverse ecosystem features have a direct impact on adolescent functioning and clinical disorders. For example, factors such as sexual abuse or participation in a peer drug culture directly impact an adolescent's behavior. As a contextual factor, poverty limits access, participation, and the effectiveness of interventions. These multiple influences raise the question, To whom should the treatment be directed? Interventions can occur at the individual, family, peer, school, and neighborhood level. Figure 126.1 presents an ecological perspective on prevention and intervention for adolescent mental health. A common error is to limit the intervention to just the individual level (LeCroy, 1992). Research has shown that family and peer interventions are sometimes needed to produce desired outcomes. Many of the evidence-based programs reviewed in this chapter stress a multidimensional approach to treatment. At the prevention level, neighborhoods and communities are reasonable targets for change. Increasingly, researchers and practitioners are embracing the value of a multifaceted perspective for intervention.

References

Arnett, J. J. (2004). *Emerging adulthood: The winding road from the late teens through the twenties.* Oxford University Press.

Ashford, J., LeCroy, C., & Williams, L. (2018). *Human behavior in the social environment: A multidimensional perspective* (6th ed.). Cengage.

Carr, A. (2002). *Prevention: What works with children and adolescents? A critical review of psychological prevention programs for children, adolescents and their families.* Taylor & Francis.

Center for Behavioral Health Statistics and Quality. (2013). *Results from the 2012 National Survey on Drug Use and Health: Mental health findings* (HHS Publication No. SMA 13-4805, NSDUH Series H-47). Substance Abuse and Mental Health Services Administration.

Chorpita, B. F., Daleiden, E. L., Ebesutani, C., Young, J., Becker, K. D., Nakamura, B. J., Phillips, L., Ward, A., Lynch, R., Trent, L., Smith, R. L., Okamura, K., & Starace, N. (2011). Evidence-based treatments for children and adolescents: An updated review of indicators of efficacy and effectiveness. *Clinical Psychology: Science and Practice, 18,* 154–172.

Dishion, T. J., & Kavanagh, K. (2001). *Intervening in adolescent problem behavior.* Guilford.

Kazdin, A. E. (1993). Psychotherapy for children and adolescents: Current progress and future research directions. *American Psychologist, 48,* 644–657.

Kazdin, A. E. (2000). *Psychotherapy for children and adolescents: Directions for research and practice.* Oxford University Press.

Kazdin, A. E., & McWhinney, E. (2018). Therapeutic alliance, perceived treatment barriers, and therapeutic change in the treatment of children with conduct problems. *Journal of Child and Family Studies, 27*(1), 240–252.

Kobocow, B., McGuire, J. M., & Blau, B. I. (1983). The influence of confidentiality conditions on self-disclosure of early adolescents. *Professional Psychology: Research and Practice, 14,* 435–475.

LeCroy, C. W. (1992). Enhancing the delivery of effective mental health services to children. *Social Work, 37,* 225–233.

LeCroy, C. W. (2011). *Parenting mentally ill children: Faith, caring, support and surviving the system.* Praeger.

LeCroy, C. W. (2019). Mismeasurement in social work practice: Building evidence-based practice one measure at a time. *Journal of the Society for Social Work and Research, 10,* 301–318.

LeCroy, C. W., & Daley, J. (2001). *Empowering adolescent girls: Building skills for the future with the Go Grrrls program.* Norton.

Lipari, R. N., Hedden, S., Blau, G., & Rubenstein, L. (2016). Adolescent mental health service use and reasons for using services in speciality, educational, and general medical settings. *The CBHSQ Report.* Substance Abuse and Mental Health Service Administration. Retrieved May 5, 2016, from https://www.samhsa.gov/data/sites/default/files/report_1973/ShortReport-1973.html

Miller, W. R., & Rollnick, S. (2002). *Motivational interviewing: Preparing people for change* (2nd ed.). Guilford.

National Research Council. (1993). *Losing generations: Adolescents in high-risk settings.* National Academies Press.

Prochaska, J. O., & DiClemente, C. C. (1986). Toward a comprehensive model of change. In W. Miller & N. Heather (Eds.), *Treating addictive behaviors: Processes of change* (pp. 3–27). Plenum.

The Physical Health of People with Serious Mental Illness

Mark R. Hawes and Leopoldo J. Cabassa

This chapter describes why people with serious mental illnesses (SMI) die at an earlier age than people in the general population and what social workers can do to address this deadly health disparity. SMI encompasses a range of mental disorders (e.g., schizophrenia spectrum disorders and bipolar disorder) that cause serious functional impairments and limit major life activities (e.g., work and family relationships). In 2018, approximately 4.6% of adults in the United States, approximately 11.4 million people, reported an SMI in the past year [Substance Abuse and Mental Health Services Administration (SAMHSA), 2019]. People with SMI are overrepresented among low-income populations, those that rely on disability and Medicaid programs, and are mostly served in the public mental health system (SAMHSA, 2017).

Although life expectancy increased in the general population during the past several decades, people with SMI have not realized these gains. People with SMI die 10–25 years earlier than people in the general population largely due to chronic medical conditions (Correll et al., 2015). For instance, the leading cause of death in people with SMI is cardiovascular disease (CVD), which has a prevalence two or three times higher than in the general population (Janssen et al., 2015).

Behavioral risk factors (e.g., smoking), cardiometabolic side effects of psychiatric medications, poor health care, and structural factors are largely responsible for the chronic diseases and excess mortality that disproportionately impact people with SMI (Janssen et al., 2015; Figure 127.1). In the following sections, we discuss the impact these factors have on the health of people with SMI, the interventions available to improve the health of this population, and the role that social workers can play in developing and delivering these interventions.

Behavioral Risk Factors

Behavioral risk factors, such as unhealthy diets, physical inactivity, tobacco smoking, and substance use, disproportionally impact people with SMI. Understanding the interplay of these risk factors can inform intervention programs and policies aimed at improving the health of people with SMI.

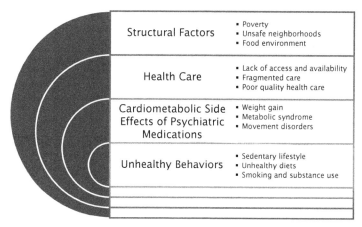

FIGURE 127.1 Factors that are largely responsible for the chronic diseases that disproportionately impact people with serious mental illness.

Diet and Physical Activity

Compared to the general population, people with SMI consume more calories per day, eat more obesogenic foods (i.e., energy dense and nutrient poor), and are more sedentary and less likely to meet physical activity guidelines (Firth et al., 2019). These dietary and physical activity patterns are concerning because they increase the risk of developing metabolic abnormalities and are two primary drivers for obesity, which is present in up to 55% of people with SMI (Janssen et al., 2015). Metabolic abnormalities and obesity are risk factors for many of the health conditions linked to premature mortality among people with SMI, particularly CVD, cancer, and diabetes (Firth et al., 2019).

Smoking

The leading causes of death in people with SMI are causally linked to tobacco smoking, and smoking is associated with lower quality of life, poorer mental health, and worse functional outcomes (e.g., financial and personal care skills) in people with SMI (Bennett et al., 2015). Approximately 50% of people with SMI use tobacco. Smokers with SMI tend to be heavy smokers (i.e., smoke 25 cigarettes or more per day) and to extract more nicotine with each cigarette than those without SMI, further exacerbating the negative health effects (Peckham et al., 2017).

The high prevalence of smoking among people with SMI is multicausal (Bennett et al., 2015). Historically, smoking cessation treatment was not routinely delivered to people with SMI, smoking was an accepted part of behavioral health settings, and the tobacco industry targeted this population. Furthermore, medications that help people quit smoking (e.g., bupropion and varenicline) are an important component of smoking cessation interventions but are underprescribed in people with SMI. Quitting without appropriate supports may be more difficult for people with SMI because evidence suggests that nicotine briefly normalizes cognitive deficits and temporarily lowers blood levels of antipsychotic medications, thus reducing medication side effects (Firth et al., 2019). Despite these challenges, many people with SMI want to quit smoking, and combined pharmacotherapy and behavioral interventions can be equally as effective as they are in the general population (Peckham et al., 2017).

Substance Use

In 2018, an estimated 3.2 million adults in the United States had a past year co-occurring SMI and substance use disorder (SUD), corresponding to 28% of people with SMI (SAMHSA, 2019). Having co-occurring SMI and SUD increases the risk for incarceration, homelessness, suicide, poorer course of illness, hospitalizations, relapse, comorbidities, and premature mortality compared to those with an SMI alone (SAMHSA, 2017). Co-occurring disorders increase the risk of CVD mortality by 25% and the risk for contracting HIV compared to SMI alone (Bruckner et al., 2017; Janssen et al., 2015).

Cardiometabolic Side Effects of Antipsychotic Medications

Antipsychotic medications are a key treatment for people with SMI because they help restore and improve functioning, reduce relapses and hospitalizations, and may reduce early mortality (Firth et al., 2019). However, antipsychotic medications are associated with side effects that can contribute to chronic disease and lower quality of life (Correll et al., 2015). Weight gain is often the most distressing concern of people taking antipsychotics and can lead to poor adherence. Although all antipsychotic medications are associated with weight gain, second-generation antipsychotics (e.g., clozapine) have the highest propensity for weight gain. The first year of antipsychotic use is when the largest percentage of weight gain is observed. Antipsychotics may also cause serious cardiometabolic side effects (e.g., hypertension and dyslipidemia) that increase the risk for CVD, stroke, and diabetes. Prolonged use of antipsychotics can lead to movement disorders (e.g., tardive akathisia), which are more prevalent among people taking first-generation antipsychotics (e.g., haloperidol), but second-generation antipsychotics are not immune from these effects (Correll et al., 2015).

Health Care Factors

Premature mortality in people with SMI is also driven by inequities in the availability, access, delivery, and quality of health care (Firth et al., 2019). People with SMI are less likely to receive routine screening of medical conditions (e.g., diabetes and cancer), and when conditions are identified, they are less likely to receive treatment. Patients with SMI are also less likely to receive standard medications (e.g., beta blockers and statins) after a heart attack, even though these medications reduce morbidity and mortality (Firth et al., 2019). Some evidence suggests health care disparities may be more pronounced for racial/ethnic minorities with SMI. Research indicates that racial/ethnic minorities with SMI are less likely to receive treatment for dyslipidemia, hypertension, and diabetes compared to non-Hispanic Whites with SMI (Mangurian et al., 2016). More studies are need to understand these racial/ethnic health care disparities in people with SMI.

Health care disparities for people with SMI are partially driven by fragmented care, stigmatization of people with SMI, and mistrust of providers (Corrigan et al., 2014). Fragmented care is a product of unintegrated mental and physical health care systems resulting in less communication between providers and less preventative health care services. Stigma often results in diagnostic overshadowing, in which health care providers attribute patients' physical symptoms to their mental illness rather than a physical health condition, which may result in unequal distribution of testing and diagnostic services. Societal stigma causes a lack of resource allocation for public health systems, resulting in overcrowded clinics, long wait times, and high staff turnover, all of which may discourage people from seeking and engaging in medical care. In addition, mistrust of medical providers due to stigma and prior negative experiences can cause people with SMI to avoid or delay seeking care, resulting in worse medical outcomes (Corrigan et al., 2014).

Structural Factors

Disparities in social conditions also have deleterious impacts on the health of people with

SMI. People with SMI are overrepresented in neighborhoods of lower socioeconomic status, which are less likely to have resources that promote health (Henwood et al., 2013). For instance, people with SMI report that eating a healthy diet is impeded by living in areas with a high density of fast-food restaurants and corner stores with limited healthy food options, and their neighborhoods have fewer bike lanes, pedestrian walkways, and safe parks for recreation. Limited financial resources among people with SMI is a barrier to affording healthy foods and resources such as gym memberships (Cabassa et al., 2014). Furthermore, unstable housing and homelessness are associated with food insecurity, which promulgates unhealthy dietary patterns (Henwood et al., 2013).

Evidence-Based Interventions

This section focuses on some of the solutions being deployed to improve the health of people with SMI. We discuss three main interventions: healthy lifestyle interventions targeting improvements in diet and physical activity, smoking cessation interventions, and health integration models designed to decrease fragmentation of care.

Healthy Lifestyle Interventions

Healthy lifestyle interventions are a first-line strategy for improving the physical health of people with SMI and have shown some promise in achieving weight loss, increasing physical activity, and improving cardiometabolic indicators (e.g., blood pressure) (Naslund et al., 2017). The most successful healthy lifestyle interventions tend to be intensive manualized programs that last for at least 1 year and offer a package of services that employ behavioral techniques (e.g., problem-solving and action planning) to help people engage in healthy

behaviors. These interventions are delivered in a variety of settings (e.g., outpatient clinics) by a range of providers, including case managers, peer specialists (i.e., people with lived experiences recovering from SMI), social workers, nurses, dieticians, and fitness instructors (Naslund et al., 2017).

For example, the Individualized Self Health Action Plan for Empowerment (InSHAPE) is a 12-month healthy lifestyle intervention for people with SMI delivered by a health mentor with certification as a fitness trainer (Bartels et al., 2015). InSHAPE participants collaborate with their health mentor to create an individualized tailored diet and fitness plan. InSHAPE includes free access to a local gym, group and individual fitness and nutritional classes, and incentives (e.g., prizes) for meeting goals. Participants can also attend group cooking classes and grocery store visits during which healthy eating habits are taught and reinforced. Health mentors meet weekly with participants to review progress toward goals, problem-solve, and encourage continued involvement in health behavior change. Consistent with a recovery model, InSHAPE takes place in mainstream community settings, which encourages social inclusion and community integration. Two randomized clinical trials of InSHAPE have demonstrated improvements in diet and fitness, helping people lose weight, and reductions in CVD risk (Bartels et al., 2015).

Smoking Cessation Interventions

Programs designed to help people quit smoking are critical for improving the health of people with SMI. Smoking cessation medications (nicotine replacement therapy, bupropion, and varenicline) used in combination with behavioral interventions are effective at helping people with SMI quit smoking (Peckham et al., 2017). There is some variability in the types of behavioral smoking cessation strategies used (e.g., contingency reinforcement and carbon monoxide feedback), and the most effective components have not been determined.

For example, Bennett et al. (2015) evaluated the effectiveness of a behavioral smoking cessation intervention compared to a supportive smoking cessation program (i.e., active comparison group) for people with SMI. Both conditions took place during 24 twice-weekly group sessions, offered 2 weeks of engagement-focused outreach (i.e., reminder calls and transportation assistance), provided education on smoking cessation medications, and encouraged participants to set a quit date. The supportive condition's weekly meetings provided support for quitting and education on a range of smoking cessation topics (e.g., consequences of smoking and barriers to cessation). Meetings started with participants taking a carbon monoxide breath test to assess recent (i.e., previous 6 hours) smoking status, but no feedback was provided.

In the behavioral condition, participants met individually with a trained interventionist to discuss both how smoking negatively affected them and their motivations for quitting (Bennett et al., 2015). Participants were offered assistance in obtaining smoking cessation medications from their prescriber. In each group session, participants were administered a carbon dioxide breath test to assess recent smoking status; if the test was negative (<10 ppm), they received $1.50 in contingency rewards. This amount was increased by $0.25 for each negative test (maximum of $3.50) and reset to $1.50 if the participant tested positive. Carbon dioxide feedback provided reinforcement by offering tangible rewards and praise from peers and therapists for smoking cessation or reduction. Group sessions discussed goal setting and taught participants how to recognize triggers and to cope with quitting, cravings, and high relapse risk situations (e.g., how to refuse cigarettes). Although this study did not find significant differences between study

conditions, participants in both behavioral and supportive conditions significantly reduced nicotine dependence scores and reduced the number of cigarettes smoked per day from 15 to 7. At the end of the trial, 73% of participants had made at least one quit attempt, and 12% achieved abstinence. These findings indicate that if delivered in line with best practices, a range of smoking cessation interventions can help people with SMI quit smoking.

Integrating Physical and Mental Health Care for People with Serious Mental Illness

An important component of managing multimorbidity and reducing physical health disparities for people with SMI is providing integrated holistic care in which services for mental health, physical health, and social needs are coordinated. Physical and mental health conditions should be addressed in tandem due to their bidirectional interaction and common risk factors (Firth et al., 2019). This can be accomplished through behavioral health homes and health care manager interventions.

The behavioral health home model builds on the chronic care model and integrates primary medical care into community mental health settings (Fortuna et al., 2020). This model facilitates communication between primary care providers (PCPs) and mental health providers, provides case management, emphasizes patient activation through education and collaborative goal setting, and helps people with SMI navigate what are often disjointed systems of care while also receiving a range of other services (e.g., housing and employment). Behavioral health homes have the potential to increase the receipt of diagnostic and primary care services but have shown mixed results in improving cardiometabolic outcomes (Fortuna et al., 2020).

In a randomized trial, Druss et al. (2017) tested the effectiveness of a behavioral health home versus usual care. The behavioral health home clinic was established within the community mental health center (CMHC) by the Federally Qualified Health Center. Clinic staff—a part-time nurse practitioner and full-time nurse care manager—provided care for cardiometabolic risk factors and comorbid medical conditions. The clinic took a treat-to-target approach in which objective clinical measures were taken and treatments were adjusted based on test results. Clinic staff held weekly meetings to discuss patients with abnormal test results. The clinic provided wellness education (e.g., smoking and diet) and support to ensure patients could attend medical appointments. To facilitate integration, clinic staff attended weekly rounds at the CMHC. The study found that the behavioral health home model resulted in improvements in the quality of general medical and cardiometabolic care and an increase in preventative care services and PCP visits compared to usual care. Although many clinical outcomes (e.g., blood pressure) improved over the course of the trial, they did not differ between the behavioral health home and usual care.

A second strategy for integrating care is through the use of health care managers. Health care managers located in CMHCs coordinate care for patients treated across fragmented health systems while providing education and logistical support to facilitate improved primary care services (Cabassa et al., 2018). Health care manager interventions have the advantage of being less expensive than integration through co-location of services, which makes these interventions more feasible for smaller sites with less resources, and existing mental health case managers can be retrained to provide these services (Cabassa et al., 2018).

Bridges to Better Health and Wellness (B2BHW) is an example of a health care manager intervention adapted for Hispanics with SMI and master's-level social workers (Cabassa et al., 2018). B2BHW was delivered by trained master's-level social workers employed in an outpatient mental health clinic. The two core components of B2BHW were patient activation for physical health issues and care coordination. The health care manager served as an advocate and coach to clients who might have otherwise had trouble navigating what are often disparate health systems. Each health care manager met with patients monthly for 12 months. Health care managers helped patients develop the knowledge, skills, and confidence to actively participant in their health care. Health care managers also helped coordinate care between primary and mental health care teams by sharing information about changes in medications or medical status. A small pilot study of 34 Hispanics with SMI found that participating in B2BHW was associated with significant increases in patient activation, self-efficacy for communicating with their PCP, and self-efficacy for managing their chronic condition. B2BHW was also associated with significant increases in the receipt of preventive primary care services (e.g., vaccination and health screening) over the course of a 12-month period (Cabassa et al., 2018).

Role of Social Workers in Improving the Health of People with Serious Mental Illness

Social workers can play important roles in reducing health disparities among people with SMI. First, social workers can deliver psychosocial components of healthy lifestyle interventions using their therapeutic skills to employ motivational interviewing, problem-solving, and behavioral techniques (e.g., goal setting and action planning). Second, social workers can deliver psychosocial smoking cessation interventions by leading group and individual therapy sessions that incorporate psychoeducation and skills training. Third, as discussed for B2BHW, social workers can take on the role of health care managers, helping people with SMI become more engaged and activated in their own health care, helping them navigate fragmented health care systems, and providing care coordination by acting as a bridge between mental health and primary care providers. Finally, social workers can work in research roles developing and testing the impact of psychosocial interventions central to mental health services that address the physical health and well-being of people living with SMI.

Conclusion

In this chapter, we discussed the prevalence and determinants of premature mortality in people with SMI and presented several interventions that can help improve the health of this at-risk population. Efforts to reduce these deadly health disparities should focus on improving the management of cardiometabolic side effects of antipsychotic medications, increasing the reach and accessibility of healthy lifestyle interventions and smoking cessation programs, and supporting the integration of physical and mental health services. More work is needed to develop, test, and implement structural interventions and policies that increase access to affordable fitness facilities and healthy foods, stable housing, and ways to make neighborhoods more conducive to physical activity and overall health. Because premature death among people with SMI is a multifaceted problem, we need multifaceted solutions that address these issues simultaneously. Social workers are uniquely situated to be at the forefront of reducing these health disparities in people with SMI given the profession's deep understanding of the needs and strengths of vulnerable communities; our commitment to social justice; our emphasis on applying a person-in-environment approach; and our focus on changing systems of care to improve the access, quality, and outcomes of health care for all.

Helpful Resources

Center of Excellence for Integrated Health Solution: https://www.thenationalcouncil.org/integrated-health-coe
Healthy Active Lives (HeAL) Initiative https://www.iphys.org.au

References

Bartels, S. J., Pratt, S. I., Aschbrenner, K. A., Barre, L. K., Naslund, J. A., Wolfe, R., Xie, H., McHugo, G. J., Jimenez, D. E., Jue, K., Feldman, J., & Bird, B. L. (2015). Pragmatic replication trial of health promotion coaching for obesity in serious mental illness and maintenance of outcomes. *American Journal of Psychiatry, 172*(4), 344–352. https://doi.org/10.1176/appi.ajp.2014.14030357

Bennett, M. E., Brown, C. H., Li, L., Himelhoch, S., Bellack, A., & Dixon, L. (2015). Smoking cessation in individuals with serious mental illness: A randomized controlled trial of two psychosocial interventions. *Journal of Dual Diagnosis, 11*(3–4), 161–173. https://doi.org/10.1080/15504263.2015.1104481

Bruckner, T. A., Yoon, J., & Gonzales, M. (2017). Cardiovascular disease mortality of Medicaid clients with severe mental illness and a co-occurring substance use disorder. *Administration and Policy in Mental Health and Mental Health Services Research, 44*(2), 284–292. https://doi.org/10.1007/s10488-016-0722-9

Cabassa, L. J., Manrique, Y., Meyreles, Q., Camacho, D., Capitelli, L., Younge, R., Dragatsi, D., Alvarez, J., & Lewis-Fernández, R. (2018). Bridges to better health and wellness: An adapted health care manager intervention for Hispanics with serious mental illness. *Administration and Policy in Mental Health and Mental Health Services Research, 45*(1), 163–173. https://doi.org/10.1007/s10488-016-0781-y

Cabassa, L. J., Siantz, E., Nicasio, A., Guarnaccia, P., & Lewis-Fernández, R. (2014). Contextual factors in the health of people with serious mental illness. *Qualitative Health Research, 24*(8), 1126–1137. https://doi.org/10.1177/1049732314541681

Correll, C. U., Detraux, J., De Lepeleire, J., & De Hert, M. (2015). Effects of antipsychotics, antidepressants and mood stabilizers on risk for physical diseases in people with schizophrenia, depression and bipolar disorder. *World Psychiatry, 14*(2), 119–136. https://doi.org/10.1002/wps.20204

Corrigan, P. W., Druss, B. G., & Perlick, D. A. (2014). The impact of mental illness stigma on seeking and participating in mental health care. *Psychological Science in the Public Interest, 15*(2), 37–70. https://doi.org/10.1177/1529100614531398

Druss, B. G., von Esenwein, S. A., Glick, G. E., Deubler, E., Lally, C., Ward, M. C., & Rask, K. J. (2017). Randomized trial of an integrated behavioral health home: The Health Outcomes Management and Evaluation (HOME) study. *American Journal of Psychiatry, 174*(3), 246–255. https://doi.org/10.1176/appi.ajp.2016.16050507

Firth, J., Siddiqi, N., Koyanagi, A., Siskind, D., Rosenbaum, S., Galletly, C., Allan, S., Caneo, C., Carney, R., Calvalho, A. F., Chatterton, M. L., Correll, C. U., Curtis, J., Gaughran, F., Heald, A., Hoare, E., Jackson, S. E., Kisely, S., Lovell, K., . . . Stubbs, B. (2019). The *Lancet Psychiatry* Commission: A blueprint for protecting physical health in people with mental illness. *Lancet Psychiatry, 6*(8), 675–712. https://doi.org/10.1016/S2215-0366(19)30132-4

Fortuna, K. L., DiMilia, P. R., Lohman, M. C., Cotton, B. P., Cummings, J. R., Bartels, S. J., Batsis, J. A., & Pratt, S. I. (2020). Systematic review of the impact of behavioral health homes on cardiometabolic risk factors for adults with serious mental illness. *Psychiatric Services, 71*(1), 57–74. https://doi.org/10.1176/appi.ps.201800563

Henwood, B. F., Cabassa, L. J., Craig, C. M., & Padgett, D. K. (2013). Permanent supportive housing: Addressing homelessness and health disparities? *American Journal of Public Health, 103*(S2), S188–S192. https://doi.org/10.2105/AJPH.2013.301490

Janssen, E. M., McGinty, E. E., Azrin, S. T., Juliano-Bult, D., & Daumit, G. L. (2015). Review of the evidence: Prevalence of medical conditions in the United States population with serious mental illness. *General Hospital Psychiatry, 37*(3), 199–222. https://doi.org/10.1016/j.genhosppsych.2015.03.004

Mangurian, C., Newcomer, J. W., Modlin, C., & Schillinger, D. (2016). Diabetes and cardiovascular care among people with severe mental illness: A literature review. *Journal of General Internal Medicine, 31*(9), 1083–1091. https://doi.org/10.1007/s11606-016-3712-4

Naslund, J. A., Whiteman, K. L., McHugo, G. J., Aschbrenner, K. A., Marsch, L. A., & Bartels, S. J. (2017). Lifestyle interventions for weight loss among overweight and obese adults with serious mental illness: A systematic review and meta-analysis. *General Hospital Psychiatry, 47*(4), 83–102. https://doi.org/10.1016/j.genhosppsych.2017.04.003

Peckham, E., Brabyn, S., Cook, L., Tew, G., & Gilbody, S. (2017). Smoking cessation in severe mental ill health: What works? An updated systematic review and meta-analysis. *BMC Psychiatry, 17*(1). https://doi.org/10.1186/s12888-017-1419-7

Substance Abuse and Mental Health Services Administration. (2017). *Interdepartmental Serious Mental Illness Coordinating Committee full report. The way forward: Federal action for a system that works for all people living with SMI and SED and their families and caregivers* (HHS Publication No. PEP17-ISMICC-RTC).

Substance Abuse and Mental Health Services Administration. (2019). *Key substance use and mental health indicators in the United States: Results from the 2018 National Survey on Drug Use and Health* (HHS Publication No. PEP19-5068, NSDUH Series H-54).

Reducing Harmful Alcohol Use

Integrating a Screening and Brief Interventions into Routine Social Work Practice

Sara Beeler-Stinn, Autumn Asher BlackDeer, and David A. Patterson Silver Wolf

According to the National Institute on Alcohol Abuse and Alcoholism (NIAAA, 2020), at-risk alcohol consumption and alcohol problems are common throughout the United States, killing 88,000 Americans yearly. This is nearly double the number of yearly opioid overdose deaths (National Academies of Science, 2019). Although much effort and funded services go into treating alcohol use disorder, alcohol use remains a significant problem. Historical research has determined that heavy drinkers have a greater risk of hypertension, gastrointestinal bleeding, sleep disorders, major depression, hemorrhagic stroke, cirrhosis of the liver, and several cancers. The Institute of Medicine states that if alcohol problems are to be significantly reduced, the foremost focus of interventions should be with people who have a mild or moderate alcohol problem (Finn et al., 2018).

Most people who drink at high-risk levels seek some type of consultation within medical health care or other social services more frequently than addiction-specific treatment services (Finn et al., 2018). Unfortunately, when alcohol-related services are rendered by these nonspecialists, they consist mainly of referring the problem drinker to an alcohol-specific service. There is a plethora of research indicating that when the problem drinker is referred to addiction-specific services, they do not follow through with that referral (Bien et al., 1993).

Bien and colleagues' (1993) review of brief interventions for alcohol problems indicated that the earliest health services research on brief interventions for problem drinkers, beginning in the 1960s, focused on dealing with problems of facilitating referrals after an emergency room visit. This comprehensive review of research provided findings on the application of brief interventions for alcohol problems in general health care settings, along with methodological strengths and weaknesses of studies (Bien et al., 1993). One of the earliest studies found that of the 1,200 individuals diagnosed with an alcohol use disorder entering an emergency room and recommended to seek alcohol treatment, less than 5% followed through (Chafetz et al., 1962). A study conducted 30 years later found a similar 5% referral follow-through in a veteran's health care facility (Luckie et al., 1995).

Community-based behavioral and mental health organizations are in a prime position to screen and intervene on large numbers of individuals and their harmful alcohol use. It is up to the social workers stationed on the front lines of these facilities to screen and intervene on this national problem (National Association of Social Workers, 2020). Unfortunately, heavy and high-risk drinking often goes undetected throughout community-based mental health organizations. If questions do arise during usual biopsychosocial assessments, responses that might indicate a problem are not professionally addressed (Patterson Silver Wolf, 2015).

Possible Reason Why Social Workers Fail to Intervene on Addiction

Social work caseloads, regardless of agency type, have always included problem drinkers (Wechsler & Rohman, 1982). The limited educational and training experiences received by students coming out of schools of social work may result in barriers to conducting assessments of patients with alcohol or other drug problems (Gilbert & Terrell, 2005). Because alcohol drinkers present with various and multiple issues, untrained social workers lack the insight to recognize symptoms of alcohol problems, often resulting in missed cues to harmful drinking or a misdiagnosis.

Alcohol-related knowledge is positively related to a social worker's ability to identify problem drinking and their willingness to work with this population (Richardson, 2008). It is not the unwillingness of the professional social worker to intervene on specific patient issues but, rather, often a lack of knowledge that blocks proven practices. In order to overcome this barrier, social workers need to be equipped with an easy-to-use and effective intervention tool that can be used with every patient entering professional mental and behavioral health services.

Effective Components of a Brief Screening and Intervention

The most effective way to introduce any kind of alcohol intervention is to emphasize an empathic, respectful, and caring counseling style. This approach has been well studied, validated, and proven to significantly increase patients' openness to discuss alcohol use as well as consider a subsequent appointment (Claunch et al., 2015; Demone, 1963). Bien and colleagues' (1993) note that brief interventions in health care facilities have been tested against untreated control trials in 14 nations. Of the 12 studies designed to increase referral follow-up to alcohol specialists, all but 1 found significant effects (Bien et al., 1993).

Most primary care patients who screen positive for heavy drinking or alcohol use disorders show some motivational readiness to change, with those who have the most severe symptoms being the most ready (Williams et al., 2006). Clinical trials have demonstrated that brief interventions can advance significant, lasting reductions in alcohol consumption for those who have high-risk drinking levels. Many drinkers evaluated as being alcohol dependent will better accept referral to addiction treatment programs as the result of integrating a screening into standard care (Fleming et al., 2002). Even for patients who do not accept a referral to further alcohol services, repeated alcohol-focused visits with a health provider can lead to significant health improvement (Willenbring & Olson, 1999).

With research showing that screening and intervening on harmful drinking are effective in lowering risks associated with alcohol consumption, the primary goal for frontline social workers is to leverage these effective tools during their routine services.

A Proven, Free Online Tool for Alcohol Screening and Brief Intervention: Rethinking Drinking

The NIAAA (n.d.) developed a clinician's guide for helping people with alcohol problems. This online tool was created and tested with primary care providers in order to integrate an alcohol intervention into standard medical care services. Its overall goal is to assist medical professionals in screening for at-risk alcohol consumption and provide a brief intervention. Frontline social workers are ideal users of this tool because it is free, simple to use, and beneficial for patients being seen for various behavioral health reasons. Social workers should familiarize themselves with the information and tools included on the tool's website. This discussion follows the flow and information of the online tool, with the hope of fully informing frontline social workers on incorporating this tool with their patients. The headings of this section follow the online tabs and headings of the NIAAA tool.

The step-by-step clinician guide begins with a simple question: "Do you enjoy a drink now and then?" If answered no, the intervention is over. If the patient indicates they do sometimes drink alcohol, the next step is to educate and collect more information.

How Much Is Too Much?

This section provides important information about how much patients are drinking, the harm it causes, and ways to reduce overall risks.

What counts as a drink? It is important to understand and be able to explain to patients what counts as a common, standard drink. This page explains what consists of a standard drink as well as visuals.

- *What's a standard drink?* Asking a patient how many drinks they have, without an agreed understanding of what a drink really

is, results in possible miscommunication and misdiagnosis. This page shows exactly what a "standard" drink is.
- *How many drinks are in common containers?* This page includes information about how many drinks are in a common container. Patients should understand that one 40-ounce can of beer does not equal one drink but, rather, 3.3 drinks.

At the bottom of the page, there is a calculator link that helps patients quantitatively understand how their drinking impacts other parts of their lives. The calculator, also listed in the Tools tab, includes the following:

- *Cocktail content calculator*: This shows how the number of standard drinks and the alcohol content of a cocktail can vary depending on the type of alcohol and the cocktail's recipe.
- *Drink size calculator*: This shows the alcohol content of different types of beer and other alcohol beverages.
- *Alcohol calorie calculator*: Because alcohol delivers calories with few nutrients, drinking contributes to unwanted weight gain. This tool shows the calories consumed per week.
- *Alcohol spending calculator*: This calculator helps determine the average amount of spending on drinking per week, month, and year.
- *Blood alcohol concentration (BAC) calculator*: This educational calculator offers insights into BAC, which helps those who drink understand the risks of drinking and driving.

What's Your Pattern?

This section educates the patients on safe drinking levels and why women face higher risk factors. The overall goal is to offer education to the patient.

- *What are the different drinking levels?* This educational page includes information on safe, moderate alcohol drinking levels along with when these levels might still be harmful. It also describes both binge and heavy drinking measures.

- *Why do women face higher risks?* This page offers education on biological differences between males and females that may contribute to women experiencing alcohol-related problems much earlier than men.

What's the Harm?

Once patients understand what counts as an actual drink and their own drinking patterns, this section provides information on the harmful effects of alcohol, symptoms of a disorder, and how patients can reduce their risks.

- *What are the risks?* This page provides information on alcohol-related injuries, health problems, birth defects, and alcohol use disorders.
- *What are symptoms of alcohol use disorder?* This important page allows the social worker and patient to click boxes of certain symptoms resulting from alcohol use. Although it is not a formal diagnosis tool, it creates a tailored feedback form that the patient can use to address any harm that could result from their drinking symptoms.
- *How can you reduce your risks?* This page provides detailed options for reducing alcohol-related risks. Clicking through the Next buttons will lead you to the next top tab, Thinking About Change, which helps patients lower their alcohol-related harms.

Thinking About Change

These pages are a combination of motivational interviewing techniques and cognitive–behavioral therapy worksheets (Coull & Morris, 2011; Miller & Rollnick, 1991). They also provide helpful information and tools that help patients address harmful alcohol use.

- *It's up to you*: This section includes the advantages and disadvantages of changing drinking behaviors, helpful information for

patients who are ready to change and those who are not, guides for when the patient is interested in reducing their drinking or quitting altogether, and a goals-orientated tool for patients who are ready to change their drinking levels.
- *Strategies for cutting down*: This section includes tips for small changes and strategies for being reminded of the change plan.
- *Support for quitting*: This section lets the patient choose their own approach for quitting, self-help strategies, social supports needed when trying to stop drinking, and professional help information.

The remaining two tabs on this page present questions and answers with help links. The overall goal of this interactive website is to help behavioral health and health care professionals address the harmful effects of alcohol use (NIAAA, n.d.). Because most Americans do not understand the risks associated with drinking, providing them with some basic information that is grounded in science and helpful strategies and tools for lowering their risks will greatly decrease alcohol's consequences.

Conclusion

Most frontline behavioral health professions are social workers. By employing an easy-to-use, understandable, and effective tool such as Rethinking Drinking during routine services, their patients are less likely to end up with a diagnosed alcohol use disorder. Significantly lowering high-risk drinking may further decrease many other health and wellness conditions caused by alcohol consumption.

Helpful Resources

Al-Anon: https://al-anon.org
Alcohol Treatment Navigator: https://alcoholtreatment.niaaa.nih.gov
Alcoholics Anonymous: https://www.aa.org
Center of Excellence for Integrated Health Solutions. *Screening, Brief Intervention, and Referral to*

Treatment (SBIRT): https://www.integration.samhsa.gov/clinical-practice/sbirt

Substance Abuse and Mental Health Services Administration. *Behavioral health treatment services locator*: https://findtreatment.samhsa.gov

Substance Abuse and Mental Health Services Administration. *TIP 35: Enhancing motivation for change in substance use disorder treatment*: https://store.samhsa.gov/product/TIP-35-Enhancing-Motivation-for-Change-in-Substance-Use-Disorder-Treatment/PEP19-02-01-003

References

Bien, T. H., Miller, W. R., & Tonigan, S. J. (1993). Brief interventions for alcohol problems: A review. *Addiction, 88*, 315–336.

Chafetz, M. E., Blane, H. T., Abram, H. S., Golner, J., Lacy, E., McCourt, W. F., Clark, E., & Meyers, W. (1962). Establishing treatment relations with alcoholics. *Journal of Nervous and Mental Disease, 134*(5), 395–409. https://doi.org/10.1097/00005053-196205000-00001

Claunch, K., Marlow, S., Ramsey, A. T., Drymon, C., & Patterson Silver Wolf, D. A. (2015). Therapeutic alliance in substance abuse treatment. *Counselor, 16*, 42–47.

Coull, G., & Morris, P. G. (2011). The clinical effectiveness of CBT-based guided self-help interventions for anxiety and depressive disorders: A systematic review. *Psychological Medicine, 41*(11), 2239–2252.

Demone, H. W. (1963). Experiments in referral to alcoholism clinics. *Quarterly Journal of Studies on Alcohol, 24*, 495–502.

Finn, S. W., Hammarberg, A., & Andreasson, S. (2018). Treatment for alcohol dependence in primary care compared to outpatient specialist treatment—A randomized controlled trial. *Alcohol and Alcoholism, 53*(4), 376–385. https://doi.org/10.1093/alcalc/agx126

Fleming, M. F., Mundt, M. P., French, M. T., Manwell, L. B., Staauffacher, E. A., & Barry, K. L. (2002). Brief physician advice for problem drinkers: Long-term efficacy and cost–benefit analysis. *Alcoholism, Clinical and Experimental Research, 26*, 36–43.

Gilbert, N., & Terrell, P. (2005). *Dimensions of social welfare policy* (6th ed.). Pearson Allyn & Bacon.

Luckie, L. F., White, R. E., Miller, W. R., Icenogle, M. V., & Lasoski, M. C. (1995). Prevalence estimates of alcohol problems in a Veterans Administration outpatient population: AUDIT vs. MAST. *Journal of Clinical Psychology, 51*(3), 422–425.

Miller, W. R., & Rollnick, S. (1991). *Motivational interviewing: Preparing people to change addictive behavior*. Guilford.

National Academies of Science. (2019). *Medications for opioid use disorder save lives*. National Academies Press. https://doi.org/10.17226/25310

National Association of Social Workers. (2020). *About social workers*. Retrieved May 30, 2020, from https://www.socialworkers.org/News/Facts/Social-Workers

National Institute on Alcohol Abuse and Alcoholism. (2020). *Alcohol facts and statistics*. Retrieved May 30, 2020, from https://www.niaaa.nih.gov/publications/brochures-and-fact-sheets/alcohol-facts-and-statistics

National Institute on Alcohol Abuse and Alcoholism. (n.d.). *Rethinking Drinking: Alcohol & your health*. Retrieved May 30, 2020, from https://www.rethinkingdrinking.niaaa.nih.gov/Default.aspx

Patterson Silver Wolf, D. A. (2015). Factors influencing the implementation of a brief alcohol screening and educational intervention in social settings not specializing in addiction services. *Social Work in Health Care, 54*(4), 345–364. https://doi.org/10.1080/00981389.2015.1005270

Richardson, M. A. (2008). Social work education: The availability of alcohol-related course curriculum and social workers' ability to work with problem drinkers. *Journal of Social Work Practice, 22*(1), 119–128. https://doi.org/10.1080/02650530701872470

Wechsler, H., & Rohman, M. (1982). Future caregivers' views on alcoholism treatment: A poor prognosis. *Journal of Studies on Alcohol, 43*(9), 939–955. https://doi.org/10.15288/jsa.1982.43.939

Willenbring, M. L., & Olson, D. H. (1999). A randomized trial of integrated outpatient treatment for medically ill alcoholic men. *Archives of Internal Medicine, 13*(159), 1946–1952.

Williams, E. C., Kivlahan, D. R., Saitz, R., Merrill, J. O., Achtmeyer, C. E., McCormick, K. A., & Bradley, K. A. (2006). Readiness to change in primary care patients who screened positive for alcohol misuse. *Annals of Family Medicine, 4*(3), 213–220. https://doi.org/10.1370/afm.542

Understanding and Treating Autism

Annette L. Becklund

The only way to treat Autism is
with respect.
　　　　—Unknown

What Is Autism?

According to the online *Merriam-Webster
Dictionary* (Merriam-Webster, n.d.), autism is

> a variable developmental disorder that
> appears by age three and is characterized
> especially by difficulties in forming
> and maintaining social relationships,
> by impairment of the ability to
> communicate verbally or nonverbally,
> and by repetitive behavior patterns and
> restricted interests and activities.

According to the Centers for Disease Control
and Prevention (2020), on data analysis
from 2016,

> One in 54, 8-year-old children are
> diagnosed with autism in the United
> States. Boys were more than four times
> as likely to be identified as having autism
> than girls. There was no differential

between Black or White children.
Hispanic children have lower rates
compared to White or Black children.
Both Black and Hispanic children are
receiving evaluations at an older age
than White children. This may be due
to the availability and access of services
in any given area and not to the actual
numbers of children receiving an
autism diagnosis. The younger a child
is identified with autism, the sooner
services can be made available. This
improves overall outcomes and quality of
life for the child and his/her family. (p. 1)

Defining autism is likened to the parable
of the blind men and the elephant in which
each man is exposed to a different part of the
elephant and, therefore, each man's perception
of what the elephant consists of is different. To
truly define autism, however, as an effective social worker, begin where the client is (Goldstein,
1983). A parent's definition would differ from
that of a grandparent, a friend, a spouse, a
teacher or a college professor, a physician (psychiatrist, neurodevelopmental pediatrician,
neurologist, primary care, gastroenterologist,
endocrinologist, etc.), a therapist (psychologist,

neuropsychologist, psychotherapist, occupational therapist, speech and language therapist, physical therapist, ABA behaviorist, music therapist, art therapist, etc.), an employer, a self-advocate, the "helping" organizations, etc. Most important, the definition, over time, is decided upon by the individual themself. Often, that definition has the potential to be explored in therapy.

According to Temple Grandin, a professor at Colorado State University, an individual with autism, an advocate, author, and speaker, autism is "a continuum of traits" (Grandin, 2020). There are varying degrees of intellectual abilities as well as verbal abilities. There are some on the autism spectrum who have been labeled "low functioning" and "mentally retarded" or cognitively impaired because they are nonverbal, yet their command of the English language by use of communication devices might put some English teachers to shame. Mel Baggs, formerly known as Amanda Baggs, is one such self-advocate. They (a nonbinary individual) published numerous blogs and videos to educate society about autism. One such YouTube video, which has been used in numerous training sessions, delivers a powerful message with the use of facilitated communication (Baggs, 2007). In the video, Mel, known as Amanda at the time, says,

> The way that I move is described as being in a world of my own . . . the thinking of people like me is only taken seriously if we learn your language. My language is not about designing words or visual symbols for the human mind to interpret. . . . I would honestly like to know how many people, if you met me on the street would believe I wrote this. I find it interesting, by the way, that failure to learn your language is seen as a deficit, but failure to learn my language is seen as so natural that people like me are officially described as mysterious and

puzzling rather than anyone admitting that it is themselves who are confused, not autistic people or other cognitively disabled people who are inherently confusing.

Therefore, it is important to understand the terminology, but utilize caution in the use of this terminology to not offend an individual with autism. Unfortunately, some professionals make the mistake of assuming those who do not speak are "lower functioning." A more effective mantra in the treatment of autism is "Always presume intellect" (Stillman, 2006, 2007). By presuming intellect, the individual is treated with dignity and respect, and there are no incorrect assumptions made about lack of ability to think or feel or be in on decisions that affect one's life. In the fifth edition of the *Diagnostic and Statistical Manual of Mental Disorders* (DSM-5; American Psychiatric Association, 2013), there are several labels that fall under the neurodevelopmental disorders umbrella. These labels fall into the categories of intellectual disabilities, communication disorders, autism spectrum disorder, attention-deficit/hyperactivity disorder (ADHD), specific learning disorders, motor disorders, tic disorders, and, of course, the unspecified—or physician did not decide, which possibly means a combination of several or combined disorders. The term "Asperger's" will sometimes still be utilized interchangeably with "high functioning autism." Although advocates fought to keep Asperger's in the DSM-5, it is no longer included. The DSM-5 is utilized in the United States for clinical diagnostic purposes and insurance reimbursement, but in 2016, the coding for the same insurance was changed to utilize the *International Classification of Diseases*, 10th revision (ICD-10; American Psychiatric Association, 2016). There is still a diagnosis for Asperger's syndrome, but only in the ICD-10-CM. There is no diagnosis for Asperger's syndrome in the DSM-5, which utilizes ICD-10-CM codes. That was meant to sound confusing because it is. In the United States, Asperger's is no longer recognized as a diagnosis, yet it is still important to know what it is because the term is still utilized. Asperger's has also become important as a cultural identity to some individuals.

What Causes Autism?

Autism is a neurobiological disorder, which means it affects the brain (Minshew & Williams, 2007). Theories vary on what causes autism—genetic links, vaccines, maternal age at conception, etc. Autism is a multi-million-dollar business with "crazes" for everyone. As social workers, our job is not to judge but, rather, to support the family's choices to self-determine, no matter what those choices happen to be. Currently, there is no cure, and given the opportunity, many individuals with autism might state that they are not interested in a cure. Instead, the desire is to be understood and, most important, to be accepted, validated, and respected.

The Neurodiversity Movement

The term *neurodiversity* was first coined in the 1990s by Australian social scientist Judy Singer, a woman with autism ("Neurodiversity," 2020). It is a term adapted by advocates among the Autism community along with accompanying terms such as *neurotypical* or someone who is not autistic (sometimes referred to as NT). According to NeuroDiversity Connect (2016), "Neurodiversity means the diversity of human brains and minds. Neurodivergent means having a brain that works in ways that are significantly different (divergent) from our society's standard of 'normal.'" Neurological differences are respected, then, as any other human variation. Examples include, but are not limited to,

dyslexia, ADHD, Tourette syndrome, autism, and dyspraxia (ADHD Aware, 2019).

The neurodiversity movement has its own culture, its own heroes, and its own trailblazers (e.g., Mel Baggs, Ari Neeman, Temple Grandin, Michael John Carley, John Elder Robison, William Stillman, Stephen Shore, Donna Williams, and Jim Sinclair). If you were to go to an Autism Self Advocacy Network gala event, for example, protocol requires you to be autism friendly by not wearing any fragrances that might cause discomfort to those on the spectrum. The idea is to maintain a sensory friendly environment.

Creating the Environment for Effective Treatment: Be Aware of Sensory Needs

It is said that individuals with autism have a deficit in "theory of mind" or in perspective taking (Richman & Bidshahari, 2018). Some of the literature references challenges with empathy (Russ et al., 2020). The challenge, then, as an effective social worker is to adapt to the issue of theory of mind and to develop a sense of empathy for individuals with autism to treat various mental health conditions. Theory of mind, ergo, is a two-way street. Rather than putting the onus on the individual with autism to take on a neurotypical perspective, the challenge is for the clinician to develop a sense of empathy. A considerably basic place to start is in the five senses. This addresses the environment in which you are providing treatment.

Some individuals prefer dimly lit rooms as opposed to bright lights. Florescent lights that are common in offices and schools sometimes make annoying hums that not only cause problems for those with auditory processing challenges but also are overstimulating for the eyes (they also make one's makeup look bad) (Diffuser Specialist, 2014). Utilizing soft lighting in one's office rather than florescent lighting is one way to make the environment more autism friendly. Accept that some individuals may wear sunglasses or visors to compensate for the inability to tolerate bright lighting. Do not force eye contact. It is too intense. There will be so much focus and distraction that any communication might be lost. It will cause anxiety. Individuals with autism may eventually look in your direction. If you are teaching job skills and a person is choosing not to disclose their autism, you can teach to look at the top of the head or at a person's nose. But that is a matter of choice.

Sound for some individuals can be overwhelming. The hum of florescent lights may cause distraction. Sounds from the outdoors during a therapy session may sound like a freight train (e.g., the landscaper with the leaf blower). Fireworks have been described as "painful." Think about the last time you cringed at someone scraping their teeth on their fork or even the mere thought of the sound of nails on a chalkboard. Noise-canceling headphones or earplugs purchased at a drug store can sometimes remedy this situation (Autism: Growing up Taylor, 2019). White noise may be helpful. It is up to the preference of the individual. For example, one young man had his mother drive him to a baseball game each Wednesday night—fireworks night—after the ninth inning and they parked in the adjoining parking lot. He was determined to tolerate fireworks. Each week, they stayed a little longer. But this was his choice and the issue was not forced. Finally, by season's end, the young man attended a baseball game on the night there were fireworks. He was enormously proud of his accomplishment.

Taste can be challenging at times to some individuals on the spectrum, whereas others have diets full of variety. As a result, there may be children whose diets are limited and are high in carbohydrates. One therapist purchased food from a fast-food restaurant before a teen social skills group only to find that the teenagers would not eat most of the food. There were pickles on the cheeseburgers and ketchup on the hamburgers; the only items that were consumed were the plain French fries and chicken nuggets. Some individuals have such a high sensitivity to taste that they can tell the difference between iced tea brands. One occupational therapist told a story about a child who stopped eating (a concern because this child's diet was very limited), and when they followed up with the company that manufactured the pasta that the child ate, they discovered that there was one ingredient that was now purchased from a different source. The child tasted the difference.

There may be sensory-based feeding disorders with aversions to certain textures or sometimes colors (Nadon et al., 2011). From a neurotypical perspective, think of the first time you may have had a raw clam or oyster. Some people would grimace at the thought. There are eating disorders such as avoidant/restrictive food intake disorder, formerly known as selective feeding disorder (Leader et al., 2020). Referrals in young children may be made to feeding teams, which can perform more proper diagnostic work. There are some who are sensory seeking and prefer extraordinarily strong tastes such as hot sauces or sour pickles.

A child was learning about his autism in a social skills group and the topic of a strong sense of smell was introduced. "What does that mean?" asked the child. The clinician answered, "You can probably tell me what I had for lunch just by smelling my breath." The inquisitive 8-year-old boy lifted his head, took a quick whiff, and correctly answered, "A cheeseburger." Individuals may be adversely affected by strong fragrances. Some women who are pregnant, for example, report that they are unable to tolerate the smell of coffee. Certain scents have also proved to have a calming effect for some individuals, such as lavender (Alexa, 2018).

The sense of touch affects each person in a unique way. Individuals may or may not be open to handshaking. This may be cultural, or it may be preferential. One young man was walking in a hallway at school. The principal approached from behind and gave him an "attaboy" tap on the shoulder to let him know he was doing a great job. The young man responded by punching the principal in the stomach. It could be that the "attaboy" tap felt like a brick being slammed on his shoulder. Unfortunately, the young man was suspended. The principal was the one at fault. Some individuals may prefer strong hugs, which may have a calming effect, whereas others recoil in disgust at the thought of being touched. This can be tough on affectionate parents. The social work role, then, becomes that of instructor and sometimes arbitrator.

Comorbidity with Autism

Many mental health conditions are comorbid with autism. This makes sense because autism is a neurobiological disorder (Minshew & Williams, 2007). Neurobiology has to do with the brain. The most common disorders that occur with autism are anxiety disorders and ADHD (Collins & Siegel, 2019). Other mental health conditions also affect those with autism, including mood disorders such as depression and bipolar disorder, eating disorders, substance abuse and dependence disorders, psychosis, post-traumatic stress disorder, etc. An effective clinician is not treating a disorder; they are treating a person. Along with mental health conditions, there are also physical conditions. These may include, but are not limited to, gastrointestinal problems, obesity, sensory-based feeding disorders, seizure disorders, muscle or joint pain, central auditory processing disorder, and sleep disorders (Salamon, 2014). These challenges, along with sensory integration challenges, may or may not lead to emotional deregulation, which in children may cause tantrums and in adults may cause "meltdowns," aggression, self-injury, escape/runaway behavior, emotional outbursts, etc. (Kring et al., 2010). Carefully assessing the reason for a behavior can lead to helping an individual cope with environmental and emotional concerns and perhaps remedy behaviors that are unproductive in some way. Finding the reason for an outburst, for example, may be key in referring to an occupational therapist or a gastroenterologist versus a psychiatrist.

When treating any of the previously mentioned comorbid conditions, it is important to ensure proper diagnosis. This may mean a referral for further evaluation to get to the root cause of the challenge an individual may face. As a clinical social worker, you are treating the mental health condition within the context of autism. A social worker, in this instance, may work in tandem with several other professionals, such as occupational therapists, speech therapists, physical therapists, and psychiatrists.

Individuals are often at first misdiagnosed with ADHD, bipolar disorder, depression, schizoaffective disorder, obsessive–compulsive disorder, and borderline personality disorder because of either misdiagnosis or symptom overlap (Kaim, 2016). During a 12-month period from July 2018 through June 2019, approximately 50% of patients in an inpatient mental health facility were screened using the AQ10, which screens for autism (Allison et al. 2012). The results indicated that 8–18.67% of the patients had "autism-like" features. Further evaluation would need to be done to determine if these adults could possibly be misdiagnosed or have a comorbid autism condition.

What Can You Do as a Social Worker?

Individual and family therapy and group social skills, including psychoeducation, are helpful when working with people who have autism. Refer to appropriate professionals and work as a team with these professionals. Provide or refer for recreational opportunities, including acting lessons, music lessons, and the arts when possible. Individuals with autism want to have friends and want to be included. They may not initiate; coaching and encouraging may be needed. Cognitive–behavioral therapy (CBT) is useful if an individual is motivated to work on a behavior (Wood et al., 2015). Of course, this depends on the presenting issues of the individual. You do not have to be an expert in the field of autism to provide services. You can seek supervision. Individual therapy may also include techniques that help reduce anxiety, such as mindfulness or a combination of mindfulness and CBT (Sizoo & Kuiper, 2017). It is safe to focus on the individual's special interest to assist in reducing anxiety during a session. Individuals with autism often have special interests. It is not detrimental to utilize those interests as rewards or to discuss these interests in therapy. You are providing what Carl Rogers' calls "unconditional, positive regard" (McLeod, 1970). Because you are the person's therapist, you may be the only one who listens for a significant amount of time about a special interest; a family sometimes has difficulty giving full, undivided attention.

Social skills groups provide opportunities to socialize with like-minded individuals. The goals and topics of the groups vary. If running groups is not something you are interested in, you can refer out. However, you are missing an opportunity to grow, learn, and be challenged. Sometimes these groups can take the form of clubs—for example, history clubs, writers' clubs, Pokémon clubs, cooking clubs, art clubs, drama clubs, etc. This allows individuals to socialize, and it is an excellent way for a social worker to embark on the use of self. Remember that humor is therapeutic, and it can be utilized once you are trusted in opportunities of "teachable social moments." Here is a chance to utilize your own creativity to help others.

You need not go to school for applied behavioral analysis (ABA; unless of course you want to do so). ABA therapy focuses on specific behaviors. "With Autism, ABA is most successful when intensely applied for more than 20 hours a week and prior to the age of 4" ("Applied Behavioral Analysis," 2020). ABA does not address emotional needs.

Conclusion

Utilizing the five senses is an excellent way to assist you in directing your treatment, in whatever the individual and their family needs. As a social worker who is culturally competent, of the upmost importance is to respect and honor the individual's culture. This includes the culture of autism.

When deciding which treatment approach to utilize, there is not a "one-size-fits-all" approach to autism. You must utilize your clinical "bag of tricks" with all those excellent training classes you have attended on therapeutic techniques. Remember to presume intellect, and also remember what Stephen Shore says: "If you met one person with autism, you met one person with autism."

References

ADHD Aware. (2019, April 2). *Neurodiversity and other conditions*. Retrieved May 16, 2020, from https://adhdaware.org.uk/what-is-adhd/neurodiversity-and-other-conditions

Alexa, M. (2018, June 26). *11 essential oils for autism and ADHD that are super effective—full list*. Retrieved May 16, 2020, from https://www.autismmag.org/news/11-essential-oils-for-autism-and-adhd-that-are-super-effective

Allison, C., Auyeung, B., & Baron-Cohen, S. (2012). Toward brief "red flags" for autism screening: The Short Autism Spectrum Quotient and the Short Quantitative Checklist in 1,000 cases and 3,000 controls. *Journal of the American Academy of Child & Adolescent Psychiatry, 51*(2), 202–212.e7. doi:10.1016/j.jaac.2011.11.003

American Psychiatric Association. (2013). *Diagnostic and statistical manual of mental disorders* (5th ed.). American Psychiatric Publishing.

American Psychiatric Association. (2016). New ICD–10–CM coding updates at a glance. Retrieved May

16, 2020, from https://www.psychiatry.org/psychi-atrists/practice/dsm/updates-to-dsm-5/coding-updates/2016-coding-updates

Applied behavior analysis. (2020). *Psychology Today*. Retrieved May 16, 2020, from https://www.psychologytoday.com/us/therapy-types/applied-behavior-analysis

Autism: Growing up Taylor. (2019, June 23). *Noise canceling headphones*. Retrieved May 16, 2020, from https://www.autismgrowinguptaylor.com/sensory-toys-and-resources/noise-canceling-earphones

Baggs, A. [silentmiaow]. (2007, January 14). In *My Language* [Video]. YouTube. Retrieved May 16, 2020, from https://www.youtube.com/watch?v=JnylM1hI2jc&t=16s

Centers for Disease Control and Prevention. (2020, April 16). *Autism prevalence rises in communities monitored by CDC*. Retrieved May 7, 2020, from https://www.cdc.gov/media/releases/2020/p0326-autism-prevalence-rises.html

Collins, H. C., & Siegel, M. S. (2019, August 29). *Recognizing and treating comorbid psychiatric dis-orders in people with autism*. Retrieved May 16, 2020, from https://www.psychiatrictimes.com/special-reports/recognizing-and-treating-comorbid-psychiatric-disorders-people-autism

Diffuser Specialist. (2014, December 10). *Why do fluo-rescent lights make that "buzzing" sound?* Retrieved May 16, 2020, from https://diffuserspecialist.com/why-do-fluorescent-lights-make-that-buzzing-sound

Goldstein, H. (1983). Starting where the client is. *Social Casework, 64*(5), 267–275. doi:10.1177/104438948306400502

Grandin, T. (2020, February 2). *Temple Grandin on au-tism: The world needs all kinds of minds*. Retrieved May 7, 2020, from https://ed.ted.com/lessons/the-world-needs-all-kinds-of-minds-temple-grandin

Kaim, N. (2016, August 15). *Autism spectrum and mental illness: Misdiagnosis or co-occurring condi-tion?* Retrieved May 16, 2020, from https://www.aane.org/misdiagnosis-co-occurring-condition

Kring, S. R., Greenberg, J. S., & Seltzer, M. M. (2010). The impact of health problems on behavior prob-lems in adolescents and adults with autism spec-trum disorders: Implications for maternal burden. *Social Work in Mental Health, 8*(1), 54–71. https://doi.org/10.1080/15332980902932441

Leader, G., Tuohy, E., Chen, J. L., Mannion, A., & Gilroy, S. P. (2020). Feeding problems, gastrointes-tinal symptoms, challenging behavior and sensory issues in children and adolescents with autism spec-trum disorder. *Journal of Autism & Developmental Disorders, 50*(4), 1401–1410. https://doi.org/10.1007/s10803-019-04357-7

McLeod, S. (1970, January 1). *Carl Rogers theory*. Retrieved May 16, 2020, from https://www.simplypsychology.org/carl-rogers.html

Minshew, N. J., & Williams, D. L. (2007, July). The new neurobiology of autism: Cortex, connectivity, and neuronal organization. *Archives of Neurology, 64*(7), 945–950. Retrieved May 16, 2020, from https://www.ncbi.nlm.nih.gov/pmc/articles/PMC2597785

Nadon, G., Feldman, D. E., Dunn, W., & Gisel, E. (2011). Association of sensory processing and eating problems in children with autism spec-trum disorders. *Autism Research & Treatment*, 1–8. https://doi.org/10.1155/2011/541926

Neurodiversity. (2020). *Psychology Today*. Retrieved May 16, 2020, from https://www.psychologytoday.com/us/basics/neurodiversity

NeuroDiversity Connect. (2016, January 11). *About NeuroDiversity Connect*. Retrieved May 16, 2020, from http://neurodiversityconnect.org.au/about

Richman, K. A., & Bidshahri, R. (2018). Autism, theory of mind, and the reactive attitudes. *Bioethics, 32*(1), 43–49. https://doi.org/10.1111/bioe.12370

Russ, V., Kovshoff, H., Brown, T., Abbott, P., & Hadwin, J. A. (2020). Exploring the role of empathy in under-standing the social–cognitive profile for individuals referred for autism spectrum disorders assessment in adulthood. *Journal of Autism & Developmental Disorders, 50*(5), 1470–1478. https://doi.org/10.1007/s10803-018-3693-8

Salamon, M. (2014, May 14). *Adults with autism at risk for many health problems: Study*. Retrieved May 16, 2020, from https://www.webmd.com/brain/autism/news/20140514/adults-with-autism-at-risk-for-many-health-problems-study#2

Sizoo, B. B., & Kuiper, E. (2017). Cognitive behavioural therapy and mindfulness based stress reduction may be equally effective in reducing anxiety and de-pression in adults with autism spectrum disorders. *Research in Developmental Disabilities, 64*, 47–55. https://doi.org/10.1016/j.ridd.2017.03.004

Stillman, W. (2006). *Autism and the God connection*. Sourcebooks.

Stillman, W. (2007). *Presuming intellect: 10 ways to enrich our relationships through a belief in compe-tence*. Retrieved May 16, 2020, from https://www.williamstillman.com/archive/presuming-intellect.php

Wood, J. J., Ehrenreich-May, J., Alessandri, M., Fujii, C., Renno, P., Laugeson, E., Piacentini, J. C., De Nadai, A. S., Arnold, E., Lewin, A. B., Murphy, T. K., & Storch, E. A. (2015). Cognitive behavioral therapy for early adolescents with autism spectrum disorders and clinical anxiety: A randomized, con-trolled trial. *Behavior Therapy, 46*(1), 7–19. https://doi.org/10.1016/j.beth.2014.01.002

Identification, Diagnosis, and Treatment of Depression in Primary Care

Katherine Sanchez, Alan Kunz-Lomelin, and Marisol Vargas Vilugron

Clinical depression is the leading cause of medical disability, health burden, and increased medical costs in the United States and the world. One in six Americans will be diagnosed with depression in their lifetime, costing an estimated $83–$125 billion in the United States each year, and more than half these expenses are publicly funded (Kessler et al., 2009). High rates of depression and anxiety are common in people with chronic medical disease, which often impairs self-care and treatment of their disease (Unutzer et al., 2006). For example, in patients with diabetes, depression severity is associated with diabetes complications, greater anxiety, dysthymia, financial worries, social stress, and poorer quality of life (Ell et al., 2009). In primary care, depression increases perception of medical symptoms, causing additional impairment in functioning (Unutzer et al., 2006). Many patients with depression and chronic disease delay treatment of mental health concerns, which can not only make depression remission difficult but also make treatment of the physical condition challenging (Kravitz & Ford, 2008).

Depression also appears to increase the risk for developing a chronic disease. One longitudinal study found that major depressive disorder predicted the onset of chronic disease (Kravitz & Ford, 2008). Because chronic medical conditions affect nearly half of the people in the United States, and two-thirds of encounters with health professionals are for the management of those conditions, the incidence of depression in primary care is high (Vogeli et al., 2007). The presence of multiple health conditions, and their predisposing risks, has become the norm in the general population, increases significantly with age, and represents the rule rather than the exception in primary care (Fortin et al., 2005). Often, in primary care, the problems identified by patients are nonspecific, span long periods of time, and require a breadth of services (Rosen et al., 2003).

The majority of people with depression are served in primary care, without referral

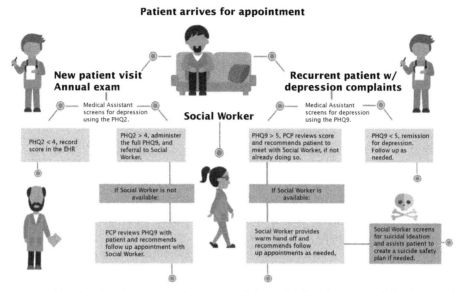

Patient arrives for appointment

New patient visit Annual exam

Medical Assistant screens for depression using the PHQ2.

Social Worker

Recurrent patient w/ depression complaints

Medical Assistant screens for depression using the PHQ9.

PHQ2 < 4, record score in the EHR

PHQ2 > 4, administer the full PHQ9, and referral to Social Worker.

PHQ9 > 5, PCP reviews score and recommends patient to meet with Social Worker, if not already doing so.

PHQ9 < 5, remission for depression. Follow up as needed.

If Social Worker is not available:

If Social Worker is available:

PCP reviews PHQ9 with patient and recommends follow up appointment with Social Worker.

Social Worker provides warm hand off and recommends follow up appointments as needed,

Social Worker screens for suicidal ideation and assists patient to create a suicide safety plan if needed.

FIGURE 130.1 Identification, diagnosis, and treatment of depression in primary care. EHR, electronic health record; PCP, primary care physician.

to specialty mental health. And although effective treatment exists, only a minority of people with diagnosed mental health disorders receive appropriate treatment (Kessler et al., 2005; Young et al., 2001). Treatment in primary care is typically brief, and even well-trained providers are limited in what they can address in a 15-minute office visit during which they also must address more pressing medical problems (Unutzer et al., 2006). The time constraints of primary care physicians have resulted in redesigned practices and use of social workers in the management of depression (Oxman et al., 2003).

Low use of antidepressant medication, poor doctor–patient communication, and persistent stigma around issues of mental illness are key barriers to the treatment of depression. Common concerns about depression treatments include fears about the addictive and harmful properties of antidepressants, worries about taking too many pills, and the stigma attached to taking psychotropic medications (Cabassa et al., 2008; Ell et al., 2011). Somatic presentation of depressive symptoms, especially in the context of comorbid illness, impedes accurate and timely detection by primary

care providers. In settings in which depression screening is absent, barriers to treatment are further amplified (Vega et al., 2010). Figure 130.1 provides an example of clinical workflow for the identification, diagnosis, and treatment of depression in primary care.

Clinical Presentation of Depression in Primary Care

The most comprehensive guide for categorizing, diagnosing, and treating mental health disorders is the fifth edition of the *Diagnostic and Statistical Manual of Mental Disorders* (DSM-5; American Psychiatric Association, 2013). In the DSM-5, mood disorders are categorized based on the presentation and severity of major depressive, manic, and hypomanic episodes (Table 130.1). The DSM-5 provides an exhaustive explanation of each type of mood disorder currently recognized by the American Psychological Association. For the purpose of this chapter, we limit our discussion to mood disorders most commonly found in the patient population in primary care settings.

TABLE 130.1 Diagnostic Criteria for Depression

Major depressive episode	*Onset of symptoms*: 2 or more weeks *Symptoms*: eating and/or sleeping more/less than usual, feelings of guilt, low energy, trouble concentrating, and/or thoughts about death
Manic episode	*Onset of symptoms*: 1 or more weeks *Symptoms*: Patient may feel elated, irritable, grandiose, talkative, hyperactive, distractible, and/or may show bad judgment in decision-making, which leads to impairment in relationships and/or work. Manic episodes may require hospitalization.
Hypomanic episode	Similar to a manic episode but is brief and less severe

Clinical presentations of depression commonly found in primary care settings are often associated with a patient's background, socioeconomic status, health, and availability to resources. The most used diagnosis in primary care is major depressive disorder (MDD). The Patient Health Questionnaire–9 (PHQ-9; Kroenke & Spitzer, 2002) is a nine-question assessment that can be used to diagnose MDD and identify the severity of symptoms (Table 130.2). Scores can range between 0 and 27. Table 130.3 describes the different severity categories than can be identified with the PHQ-9.

Clinicians should pay special attention to the ninth question in the PHQ-9, "In the past 2 weeks, how often have you been bothered by thoughts that you would be better off dead or of hurting yourself in some way"? This question helps measure suicide risk, ideation, and/or intent. However, this question only raises a red flag; it is then up to the clinician to further explore a patient's suicidal ideation or intent. A patient's suicidality often falls into one of two categories—passive or active suicidal ideation. Passive suicidal ideation is associated with thoughts of wanting to go to

TABLE 130.2. PHQ 9 depression screening tool

PHQ9- Over the *last 2 weeks*, how often have you been bothered by any of the following problems?	Not at all	Several days	More than half of the days	Every day
1. Little interest or pleasure in doing things	0	1	2	3
2. Feeling down, depressed, or hopeless	0	1	2	3
3. Trouble falling/staying asleep, sleeping too much	0	1	2	3
4. Feeling tired or having little energy	0	1	2	3
5. Poor appetite or overeating	0	1	2	3
6. Feeling bad about yourself or that you are a failure or have let yourself or your family down	0	1	2	3
7. Trouble concentrating on things, such as reading the newspaper or watching television.	0	1	2	3
8. Moving or speaking so slowly that other people could have noticed. Or the opposite; being so fidgety or restless that you have been moving around a lot more than usual.	0	1	2	3
9. Thoughts that you would be better off dead or of hurting yourself in some way.	0	1	2	3
If you checked off any problem on this questionnaire so far, how difficult have these problems made it for you to do your work, take care of things at home, or get along with other people?	Not difficult at all	Somewhat difficult	Very difficult	Extremely difficult

TABLE 130.3 Depression Severity Scores

PHQ-9 Score	Severity	Clinical Recommendation
0–4	Minimal depression	Patient may not need depression treatment.
5–9	Mild depression	Patient may benefit from depression treatment.
10–14	Moderate depression	Clinical judgment will be required to develop treatment plan.
15–19	Moderately severe depression	Clinical judgment will be required to develop treatment plan.
20–27	Severe depression	Clinician should provide depression treatment and identify comorbidities and other influencing factors (e.g., substance abuse).

sleep and not wake up, wishing they could go away, wishing they could disappear, etc. In contrast, patients with active suicidal ideation may have these thoughts but also have a plan, intent, or desire to harm themselves or take their own life.

Clinicians can use the Columbia-Suicide Severity Rating Scale (Posner et al., 2011) as a follow-up questionnaire to asses suicide risk. This assessment helps clinicians identify a patient's suicide risk and take appropriate action, such as creating a safety plan, contacting relatives/friends, and/or hospitalizing the patient. If the risk is high, it is best to consult with a colleague or supervisor before hospitalizing a patient (especially if it is involuntary) to avoid unnecessary distress and discomfort to the patient, as well as to protect the therapeutic alliance.

Although the PHQ-9 is an effective and useful tool that clinicians can use to identify and diagnose depression, it does not always provide a complete picture of a patient's behavioral health needs. Therefore, the PHQ-9 is often delivered in conjunction with the Generalized Anxiety Disorder Scale–7 (GAD-7), the Alcohol Use Disorders Identification Test (AUDIT; Reinert & Allen, 2002), and the Drug Abuse Screening Test (DAST; Skinner, 1982) questionnaires. GAD-7 (Spitzer et al., 2006) is a questionnaire used for diagnosing generalized anxiety disorder, AUDIT measures alcohol use, and DAST measures drug use.

Clinicians benefit from administering all four assessments during a behavioral health intake appointment because together they provide a clear picture of the patient's behavioral health needs, possible comorbidities, and other factors that might be contributing to their diagnosis.

Other types of depression commonly found in primary care settings include dysthymia, reactive depression, and substance/medication-induced depressive disorder. A fourth category worth mentioning is depressive disorders, which are more complex, less common, and often associated with another mental health diagnosis (e.g., post-traumatic stress disorder, bipolar disorder, or schizophrenia). Table 130.4 provides brief descriptions of the distinguishing characteristics and special considerations when diagnosing and treating each of these types of depression.

Treatment Modalities

Clinicians can help clients best when following a multidimensional approach in their practice, which individualizes the treatment plan to the specific needs and challenges of the patient. Clinicians have access to a variety of treatment modalities that allow them to customize their treatment plan and identify the approach and techniques that will be most effective in achieving the behavioral health goals of their patients. For this chapter, we briefly review the most common treatment modalities and

TABLE 130.4 Mood Disorder Characteristics and Considerations

Clinical Presentation	Mood Episodes and Special Considerations
Major depressive disorder	Defining characteristics Does not have manic or hypomanic episodes. Must have one or more major depressive episodes. It can be a single episode or recurrent. Special considerations Not all patients may be able to identify these symptoms on their own. The PHQ-9 can be administered by the clinician and completed by the patient as a self-report measure. However, the clinician must be mindful of a patient's cultural, socioeconomic, and educational background to better assess the patient's ability to comprehend and answer the questions accurately.
Dysthymia (persistent depressive disorder)	Defining characteristics Depressive symptoms that last longer but are less severe than major depressive episodes. Special considerations This type of patient may never reach a PHQ-9 score less than 5. It is likely that they will always score positive for mild depression.
Reactive depression (depressive disorder due to another medical condition)	Defining characteristics Depressive symptoms do not have to meet criteria of the previous categories to be diagnosed. This depressive state can be a result of physical illness or neurological disorders. Special considerations In primary care settings, this is often associated with new medical diagnoses and chronic health conditions. These may include, but are not limited to, diabetes, hypertension, and chronic pain. Patients experiencing grief may also fall into this category. Patients feel depressed because of a loss—loss of a loved one, their independence, work, financial stability, autonomy, etc.
Substance-/medication-induced depressive disorder	Defining characteristics Depressive symptoms do not have to meet criteria for the previous categories to be diagnosed. Depressive symptoms resulting from the use or withdrawal of alcohol and/or drugs. Special considerations The most common substances that patients use to cope with and that may result in depression are alcohol, marijuana, and medications that were not prescribed or are being taken in a way that was not prescribed.
Other presentations of depressive symptoms	Defining characteristics Post-traumatic stress disorder: Patients who experience depressive symptoms due to reliving a traumatic event from their past repeatedly. Bipolar: Patient has had at least one major depressive episode in addition to one or more manic or hypomanic episodes. Schizophrenia: Patients diagnosed with schizophrenia often have experienced one or more major depressive episodes. Special considerations The resources available to a clinician in primary care settings may not be enough to treat post-traumatic stress disorder, bipolar disorder, and schizophrenia. Therefore, it may warrant a referral to a higher level of care in a mental health treatment facility and/or a referral to psychiatry.

techniques used in practice. The most commonly used approaches by clinicians in primary care are cognitive–behavioral therapy (CBT), acceptance and commitment therapy (ACE), behavioral activation, and psychoeducation. These approaches are particularly well-suited to primary care due to their brevity and the conduciveness to positive change.

Cognitive–Behavioral Theory and Practice

Cognitive–behavioral theory's primary focus is on altering a patient's behavior and ways of thinking in ways that will lead to positive change in their relationships, work, and life satisfaction. CBT theorists believe there is a strong and interconnected relationship between an individual's way of thinking and subsequent behavior. They posit that a person's behavior can affect their mood; similarly, one's mood and state of mind may influence the way an individual behaves. Because of this interconnectedness, it is important for clinicians to focus not just on one of these areas. By working with patients to simultaneously change their behavior and ways of thinking, clinicians are able to bring about positive changes in their patients.

Challenging Irrational Thinking

Clinicians should validate patients' feelings while simultaneously challenging irrational or maladaptive ways of thinking, often referred to as thinking traps. Thinking traps are thoughts that patients believe to be true despite lacking evidence that this is the case. Some of the most common thinking traps include all-or-nothing thinking, catastrophizing, minimizing, jumping to conclusions, overgeneralizing, fortune-telling, "should" statements, and filtering. In CBT, a clinician's role is to help patients challenge thinking traps and find more accurate and adaptive ways of interpreting their circumstances. Table 130.5 presents common thinking traps.

TABLE 130.5 Common Thinking Traps and Their Definitions

Thinking Trap	Definition
All or nothing	Black-and-white thinking *Example*: "Making a mistake makes me a bad person" (instead of "I made a mistake, but I'm not a bad person").
Catastrophizing	Thinking that a problem is larger than it truly is *Example*: "If I lose my job, I will lose everything I have and will never be happy."
Minimizing	Thinking that a problem is smaller than it truly is *Example*: "I've been taking drugs my whole life and I am completely healthy."
Mind reading	Guessing what other people are thinking about you *Example*: "I don't go out because people make fun of my weight behind my back."
Fortune-telling	Predicting what will happen *Example*: "If I start a new relationship, they will hurt me again."
Overgeneralizing	Viewing one situation as representative of all other similar situations *Example*: "All men are abusive and dominant."
Should statements	Confusing things that a person wants with things that they need Example: "I should find someone to marry or I will never be happy."
Filtering	Only seeing the negative and disregarding the positive *Example*: "My life is over because I was diagnosed with diabetes and hypertension" (ignoring the fact they can afford treatment, have a good job, and have a supportive family).

Bringing About Behavioral Change

Similarly, in CBT, clinicians have a variety of strategies for helping patients achieve behavioral change. A common strategy is behavioral activation or the use of pleasurable activities to improve a patient's mood. Clinicians also focus on teaching patients to set aside time in their day for self-care. Patients often prioritize responsibilities and disregard self-care activities. Clinicians must not only motivate patients to practice self-care but also potentially help them brainstorm some self-care activity ideas. Bringing about behavioral change also involves practicing healthy coping strategies, exercising, and improving a patient's diet. Tobacco, alcohol, drugs, and/or sex can become unhealthy coping strategies that prevent positive behavioral change. Healthy, more adaptive coping strategies include daily exercise, a nutritious diet, arts and crafts, reading, mindfulness, relaxation exercises, time with family, time with friends, church attendance, etc. Due to a patient's emotional state, they may not always be able to develop solutions on their own. Therefore, clinicians must educate patients about the importance of self-care and healthy coping strategies; motivate them to put these into practice; and help them identify the ones that will best fit their needs, interests, and schedule.

Acceptance and Commitment Theory and Practice

Acceptance and commitment therapy is a novel therapeutic approach that incorporates components of CBT, mindfulness, and solution-focused therapy. ACT is a behavioral approach that focuses on helping patients take guided action toward goals that align with their values. Through the use of mindfulness, ACT helps patients follow values-guided actions that lead them to the person they want to be, how they want to feel, and what they want to accomplish.

Harris (2009) has helped shape ACT practice into what it is today. He identifies the six core therapeutic processes of ACT as contact with the present moment, diffusion, acceptance, self as context, values, and committed action. Table 130.6 provides a detailed description of the ACT therapeutic processes.

Harris (2009) also created a training manual for clinicians that provides more detailed descriptions of each core process in ACT, as well as a variety of ACT exercises for use with patients. Clinicians are strongly encouraged to read the handbook or complete other types of ACT training before attempting to implement ACT strategies with their patients.

Behavioral Activation

Individuals with depression commonly report lack of motivation, energy, and interest to do their daily activities. This inactivity often leads to feelings of guilt and ineffectiveness, causing the person with depression to feel stuck and in a never-ending cycle of depression, fatigue, unproductivity, and guilt.

Behavioral activation is a simple and effective, evidenced-based therapeutic intervention that helps patients feel better. Behavioral activation simply consists of assisting patients to break the depression cycle, as they seek to engage in activities that have the potential to produce positive feelings of pleasure, sense of purpose, and achievement. Those activities can be simple, such as making one's bed, or more complex, such as volunteering once a week. It is helpful to assist patients to select a combination of pleasant and productive activities or activities that can be both pleasant and productive at the same time. Table 130.7 provides examples of pleasant and productive activities.

In addition, remind patients to start small and slowly increase their activity levels until they return to their normal levels of functioning. Ideas to assist patients to overcome inactivity and the urge to do nothing

TABLE 130.6 Detailed Description of the ACT Therapeutic Processes

Core Therapeutic Process	Definition
Contact with the present moment	The first four core processes are inspired by the principles of mindfulness. Contact with the present moment focuses on being attentive to the world around and within us by allowing ourselves to be fully present in the moment—carrying a compassionate and curious attitude toward our surroundings, thoughts, and emotions.
Defusion	This is the ability to step back and watch our thoughts, emotions, and memories with compassion and curiosity. We avoid getting tangled up, absorbed, or caught up in these by seeing them for what they are—pictures and words that do not necessarily have to influence our behavior.
Acceptance	This is when we open up and make room for unwanted thoughts, emotions, and feelings. Instead of fighting them, hiding them, or trying to push them away, we make space for them. We allow these to flow through us at their own time and speed. We do not try to rush through them or allow them to linger longer than they should.
Self as context	ACT views the mind as having two parts—one that thinks and the other that notices the thinking. This concept is referred to as the noticing mind. The noticing mind is the part of us that is aware that there is thinking, judgment, memories, and emotions happening in our mind. Being aware of the noticing mind will help patients through the other processes.
Values	Values are physical or psychological qualities that serve as a compass. Our values can guide our actions in a direction that will lead to the person we want to be, the way we want to feel, and what we want to accomplish. ACT aims to help patients engage in values-driven actions that will lead to positive changes in their lives.
Committed action	This process refers to the ability of patients to take effective physical and/or psychological action, guided by their values, in order to live a more full and meaningful life. Clinicians must motivate patients to engage in values-driven actions, despite unpleasant thoughts and feelings that may show up for them during this process.

ACT, acceptance and commitment therapy.

are presented later. Table 130.8 presents self-activation techniques (Burns, 2008).

Important Note on Psychoeducation

Psychoeducation is not a therapeutic approach but, rather, is a useful tool that clinicians can utilize to enhance their practice. A patient's depression symptoms are often exacerbated by receiving a new unfamiliar medical diagnosis, by what they eat or drink, or by other habits in their lives that may be inadvertently impacting their health. Therefore, it is often useful for clinicians to spend a session or two

TABLE 130.7 Examples of Behavioral Activation Activities

Pleasant Activities	Productive Activities	Pleasant and Productive Activities
Watching a movie	Do the dishes	Take a shower
Call a close friend	Go to work	Take a walk
Drink a cup of coffee or tea	Pay bills	Cook a meal
Play with pet	Organize closet or garage	Water plants
Listen to music	Plan day using an agenda or calendar	Read a book
	Buy groceries	Play an instrument
		Volunteer

TABLE 130.8 Self-Activation Techniques and Examples

Target Symptoms	Self-Activation Technique	Purpose of the Method	Examples
You feel disorganized. You have nothing to do. You get lonely and bored on weekends.	Daily activity schedule	Plan things 1 hour at a time and record the amount of mastery and pleasure. Virtually any activity will make you feel better than lying in bed and will undercut your sense of inadequacy.	8 a.m. Take a shower 9:30 a.m. Walk dog 2 p.m. Call sister 5 p.m. Cook 7 p.m. Watch a movie
You feel overwhelmed by the urge to do nothing.	Daily record of dysfunction thoughts	You expose the illogical thoughts that paralyze you. You learn that motivation follows action, not vice versa.	Nothing I do can make me feel better. ("That's not true, I usually feel better when I do almost anything.") I have no energy. ("I have some energy, I am not dead.")
You feel overwhelmed by the magnitude of everything you have to do.	Little steps for little feet	Break the task down into its tiny component parts, and do these one step at a time.	Task: Do the dishes. Step 1: Empty dish washer. Step 2: Pile dishes. Step 3: Fill the dishwasher. Take breaks between steps, if necessary.
You feel guilty, oppressed, obliged, and duty-bound.	Motivation without coercion	You eliminate "shoulds," "musts," and "oughts" when you give yourself instructions.	"I *should* exercise every day for 60 minutes." Instead, say "I can take a 20-minute walk in the afternoons."

Adapted from Burns (2008).

educating patients about medical diagnoses they may have or could be at risk of getting, as well as discussing habits in their lives that may be impacting their health. The most common types of psychoeducation that a clinician will utilize in primary care settings are discussing mental health diagnoses and treatment options and conducting psychoeducation on the negative effects of alcohol, tobacco, and drugs on a patient's emotional and physical well-being. By investing time in psychoeducation, clinicians can help normalize symptoms, demystify diagnoses, provide encouragement, and possibly diminish depression symptoms that may be resulting from these. Figure 130.2 shows a patient education infographic.

Barriers to Treatment

Depression is one of the most common conditions in the United Stated, affecting more than 264 million people worldwide (World Health Organization, 2020). Although depression is a highly treatable condition in most cases, only one in four people with depression receives treatment. Among those who receive treatment, more than half will discontinue their treatment prematurely, increasing chances of a relapse (Olfson et al., 2006). The following factors affect access and compliance to depression treatment:

- Social barriers
  - *Stigma* remains a significant barrier to depression treatment. Often, people are embarrassed or afraid to tell others about their depression due to fear of judgments such as "You should be stronger," "You should be more grateful," "It is all in your mind," and "Just think positive." Others avoid acknowledging and seeking treatment for depression

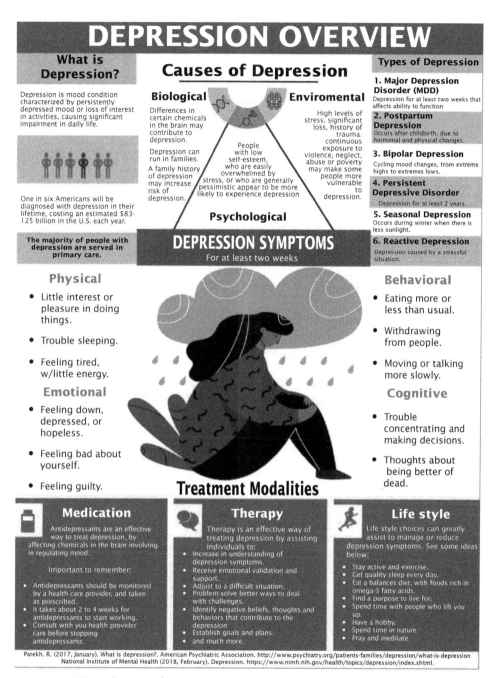

FIGURE 130.2 Patient education infographic.

due to the fear that a depression diagnosis might affect their employment and relationship prospects.

- *Socioeconomic barriers* such as lack of income, transportation barriers, and immigration status.

- Personal barriers
  - *Self-reliance*: Many people believe or are told that if they try harder or try to be stronger, they will feel better; therefore, they do not need antidepressants or professional health.

- *Lack of information* about what psycho-therapy entails.
- *Addiction concerns*: Some patients might refuse pharmacological treatment, such as antidepressants, due to concerns about dependency and that they will become addicted to the drug for the rest of their lives or that the antidepressant will change them to the point that they will not be able to feel like themselves.

Depression Treatment Plan Example		
Patient's Personal Information	**Medical Information**	
Patient's Name: Richard Davis	**MRN:** 12345678	**PCP:** Dr. Robert Jones
Date of Birth: 11/17/1975	**Date:** 08/27/2020	
Diagnosis: Major Depression Disorder (MDD). **Current PHQ9:** 17- moderately severe depression.	**Currently prescribed antidepressant/ psychotropic?** 20 mg of Citalopram once per day.	
Prior Psychiatric Hospitalizations: None.	**Current Suicidal Ideation:** Passive suicidal ideation, with no plans or means.	
History of trauma/ abuse: None.	**History of substance abuse:** None	
Symptoms Complaint: Loss of interest, anhedonia, hypersomnia and passive suicidal ideation with no plans or means.	**Presenting Problem:** Patient was recently laid off from work and is experiencing financial problems, depression and conflicts with his wife and children. Patient feels demoralized for not being able to provide financially for his family. Patient feels easily annoyed and is having daily anger outbursts.	
Therapy Goals and Objectives: **Projected completed date:** 09/09/2020.		
Long-term goals: Reduce depression (PHQ9 < 10), find new employment and increase in emotional regulation.	**Short-term goals**	
1. Manage depression by using Behavior Activation, Cognitive Behavior Therapy and Solution Focused principles and techniques.	1. Increase understanding of depression feelings. 2. Increase activity level by scheduling daily activities using an agenda. 3. Identify and replace automatic negative thoughts.	
2. Apply for unemployment benefits and new employment.	1. Update resume within a week. 2. Apply for unemployment benefits within one week. 3. Apply for five jobs per week. 4. Reach out to professional network for job leads.	
3. Eliminate anger outbursts by using anger management principles and self-soothing skills.	1. Increase understanding of anger feelings. 2. Address causes of anger feelings. 3. Learn three self-soothing skills. 4. Learn three anger management skills.	
Therapy modalities: Cognitive Behavior Therapy/Behavior Activation and Solution Focused Therapy.		
Support system: Wife, children, siblings and best friend (Jonny).	**Strengths:** Able to work, able to express emotions, receptive and motivated to treatment.	
Barriers: Lack of employment, lack of emotional regulation and apprehension regarding taking antidepressants.		
Estimated number of sessions needed: 6		

FIGURE 130.3 Sample treatment plan.

- Health care delivery barriers
  - Lack of access to treatment
  - Lack of communication with health providers
  - Lack of coordination and collaboration between health providers

Conclusion

Effective treatment of depression requires a proactive and direct approach to education and treatment. Social workers advocate for a biopsychosocial approach to treatment planning that focuses on meeting patients' behavioral health needs and promoting functioning from a comprehensive whole person perspective. An integrative evaluation of the patient's needs is essential, followed by a plan to address those needs within the context of the individual's unique history and current circumstances and in a manner designed to maximize treatment effectiveness. The treatment plan should be developed in conjunction with the patient, with goals identified by the patient. Finally, a copy of the treatment plan should be provided to the patient, with short- and long-term goals identified and timelines established. Figure 130.3 shows a sample of a completed treatment plan.

Helpful Resources

ACT Mindfully Workshops with Russ Harris: https://www.actmindfully.com.au/free-stuff
Black Dog Institute: https://www.blackdoginstitute.org.au
Commonly prescribed psychotropic medications: http://aims.uw.edu/sites/default/files/Psychotropics%20Medications_2018.pdf
Therapist Aid. *Essential tools for mental health professionals*: https://www.therapistaid.com

References

American Psychiatric Association. (2013). *Diagnostic and statistical manual of mental disorders* (5th ed.). American Psychiatric Publishing.

Burns, D. (2008). *Feeling good: The new mood therapy*: Harper.

Cabassa, L. J., Hansen, M. C., Palinkas, L. A., & Ell, K. (2008). Azucar y nervios: Explanatory models and treatment experiences of Hispanics with diabetes and depression. *Social Science & Medicine, 66*(12), 2413–2424.

Ell, K., Katon, W., Cabassa, L. J., Xie, B., Lee, P. J., Kapetanovic, S., & Guterman, J. (2009). Depression and diabetes among low-income Hispanics: Design elements of a socio-culturally adapted collaborative care model randomized controlled trial. *International Journal of Psychiatry in Medicine, 39*(2), 113–132.

Ell, K., Xie, B., Kapetanovic, S., Quinn, D. I., Lee, P. J., Wells, A., & Chou, C. P. (2011). One-year follow-up of collaborative depression care for low-income, predominantly Hispanic patients with cancer. *Psychiatric Services, 62*(2), 162–170.

Fortin, M., Bravo, G., Hudon, C., Vanasse, A., & Lapointe, L. (2005). Prevalence of multimorbidity among adults seen in family practice. *Annals of Family Medicine, 3*(3), 223–228.

Harris, R. (2009). *ACT made simple: An easy-to-read primer on acceptance and commitment therapy.* New Harbinger.

Kessler, R. C., Aguilar-Gaxiola, S., Alonso, J., Chatterji, S., Lee, S., Ormel, J., Ustun, T. B., & Wang, P. S. (2009). The global burden of mental disorders: An update from the WHO World Mental Health (WMH) surveys. *Epidemiologia E Psichiatria Sociale, 18*(1), 23–33.

Kessler, R. C., Demler, O., Frank, R. G., Olfson, M., Pincus, H. A., Walters, E. E., Wang, P., Wells, K. B., & Zaslavsky, A. M. (2005). Prevalence and treatment of mental disorders, 1990 to 2003. *New England Journal of Medicine, 352*(24), 2515–2523.

Kravitz, R. L., & Ford, D. E. (2008, November). Introduction: Chronic medical conditions and depression—The view from primary care. *American Journal of Medicine, 121*(11 Suppl. 2), S1–S7.

Kroenke, K., & Spitzer, R. L. (2002). The PHQ-9: A new depression diagnostic and severity measure. *Psychiatric Annals, 32*(9), 509–515.

Olfson, M., Marcus, S. C., Tedeschi, M., & Wan, G. J. (2006). Continuity of antidepressant treatment for adults with depression in the United States. *American Journal of Psychiatry, 163*(1), 101–108.

Oxman, T. E., Dietrich, A. J., & Schulberg, H. C. (2003). The depression care manager and mental health specialist as collaborators within primary care. *American Journal of Geriatric Psychiatry, 11*(5), 507–516.

Posner, K., Brown, G. K., Stanley, B., Brent, D. A., Yershova, K. V., Oquendo, M. A., Currier, G. W.,

Melvin, G. A., Greenhill, L., Shen, S., & Mann, J. J. (2011). The Columbia-Suicide Severity Rating Scale: Initial validity and internal consistency findings from three multisite studies with adolescents and adults. *American Journal of Psychiatry, 168*(12), 1266–1277.

Reinert, D. F., & Allen, J. (2002). The Alcohol Use Disorders Identification Test (AUDIT): A review of recent research. *Alcoholism, 26*(2), 272–279.

Rosen, A. K., Reid, R., Broemeling, A. M., & Rakovski, C. C. (2003). Applying a risk-adjustment framework to primary care: Can we improve on existing measures? *Annals of Family Medicine, 1*(1), 44–51.

Skinner, H. (1982). The Drug Abuse Screening Test. *Addictive Behaviors, 7*(4), 363–371.

Spitzer, R. L., Kroenke, K., Williams, J. B. W., & Lowe, B. (2006). A brief measure for assessing generalized anxiety disorder—The GAD-7. *Archives of Internal Medicine, 166*(10), 1092–1097.

Unutzer, J., Schoenbaum, M., Druss, B. G., & Katon, W. J. (2006). Transforming mental health care at the interface with general medicine: Report for the President's Commission. *Psychiatric Services, 57*(1), 37–47.

Vega, W. A., Rodriguez, M. A., & Ang, A. (2010). Addressing stigma of depression in Latino primary care patients. *General Hospital Psychiatry, 32*(2), 182–191.

Vogeli, C., Shields, A. E., Lee, T. A., Gibson, T. B., Marder, W. D., Weiss, K. B., & Blumenthal, D. (2007, December). Multiple chronic conditions: Prevalence, health consequences, and implications for quality, care management, and costs. *Journal of General Internal Medicine, 22*(Suppl. 3), 391–395.

World Health Organization. (2020). *Depression.* https://www.who.int/news-room/fact-sheets/detail/depression

Young, A. S., Klap, R., Sherbourne, C. D., & Wells, K. B. (2001). The quality of care for depressive and anxiety disorders in the United States. *Archives of General Psychiatry, 58*(1), 55–61.

Pseudoscientific Behavioral and Mental Health Treatments

Bruce A. Thyer

At the beginning of the 20th century, social work continued its evolution from being a field practiced primarily by well-meaning volunteers with a good heart, guided by practice wisdom, intuition, common sense, authority, and tradition, to a more professionalized field. Advances along these lines occurred on many fronts, and one strong orientation that continues to today is a growing reliance on the empirical findings of behavioral, social, and biological sciences to help inform our understanding of the etiologies of psychosocial problems and larger scale societal ills and also to help us create effective behavioral and mental health treatments for practice. Without abandoning earlier ways of knowing, we began to incorporate sophisticated research methods better capable of answering important questions for our field, such as "Is a given treatment genuinely helpful?" Half a century ago, there were few credible answers to such questions. As our science moved beyond a primary reliance on anecdote, case history, survey, and correlational investigations, we, as well as other health care providers, began making use of stronger intervention methodologies such as single-system research designs,

quasi-experimental studies, randomized experiments, meta-analyses, and systematic reviews. Indeed, the first randomized controlled experimental outcome study in social work was published in 1949, roughly parallel to the adoption of this powerful method for making causal inferences within related fields such as clinical psychology and medicine (Thyer, 2015).

We are now in a position in which a very large number of psychosocial treatments have been shown to be genuinely effective, above and beyond placebo value, with long-lasting impacts, and there are many places where social workers can locate this information (e.g., Nathan & Gorman, 2015; Thyer et al., 2017). This has facilitated the widespread adoption of the five-step clinical decision-making process known as evidence-based practice, which requires that social workers seek out information about research-supported treatments, and the reader is directed to Part VIII in this volume to learn more about this process.

Advances in the science-based foundations of social work are of course a wonderful feature of contemporary practice. The *Social Work Dictionary* published by the National

Association of Social Workers (NASW; Barker, 2014) describes social work as "the *applied science* of helping people achieve an effective level of psychosocial functioning and effecting society changes to enhance the well-being of all people" (p. 402, italics added). Florida's definition of clinical social work begins by defining the field as "the use of *scientific and applied knowledge*, theories, and methods" (Florida Legislature, n.d., italics added), and most states' legal definitions include similar language embracing the scientific foundations of our field. The accreditation standards of the Council on Social Work Education (2015) state that a fundamental competency of social workers is that they "understand quantitative and qualitative research methods and their respective roles in advancing a *science of social work* and in evaluating their practice." The idea that social work is founded on the basis of science and scientific research could not be clearer.

Less laudable, however, is the practice of a very large segment of our profession who engage in pseudoscientific treatments—treatments that seemingly have scientific support but in reality lack such a foundation (Pignotti & Thyer, 2015; Thyer & Pignotti, 2010). The advocates of pseudoscientific therapies (PTs) fall into several camps. One consists of naive practitioners who have learned about some therapy that they are told is well supported by research and accept these claims without having thoroughly investigated them prior to getting trained in the pseudoscientific treatment and providing it to their clients. Another group consists of the equivalent of the old-fashioned snake oil salesperson, who knows about the falsity of their claims to having an effective treatment, and knows that the scientific foundations are lax to nonexistent, but promotes the treatment via offering trainings in the technique (for a fee) or sells books, audiovisual materials, or equipment supposedly needed to deliver the therapy. Some even provide certificate programs,

diplomas, or other practice credentials attesting that the certificant is a registered/certified/accredited practitioner of the treatment in question. This is done to produce income, reputation, and prestige. Few accomplishments are more professionally significant than to establish a new theory and apparently an effective therapy. A third type of practitioner of PT consists of individuals who believe that it really makes no difference what therapy is provided so long as it is acceptable and plausible to the client. Advocates of this "all psychotherapies are equally effective" hypothesis dismiss compelling evidence that some interventions really are more effective than others (Reid, 1997; Reid et al., 2004). This also dismisses any notion that we as professionals need to keep up with the latest developments in new treatments or the changing evidentiary status of existing therapies or that we have an ethical obligation to provide clients with research-supported treatments, where these are known to exist, as first-choice option (Myers & Thyer, 1997). This gives rise to the quaint notion that being honest with clients is not important. For example, one noted psychotherapy researcher, Wampold (2007), has argued the following:

> I argue here that the truth of the
> explanation is unimportant to the
> outcome of psychotherapy. The power
> of the treatment rests on the patient
> accepting the explanation rather
> than on whether the explanation
> is "scientifically" correct. . . . What
> is critical to psychotherapy is
> understanding the patient's explanation
> of it (i.e., the patients folk psychology)
> and modifying it to be more adaptive. . . .
> I hypothesize that effective explanations
> in psychotherapy must be different
> from presently held explanations for
> a patient's troubles but not sufficiently
> discrepant from the patient's intuitive
> notions of mental functioning as to

be rejected. . . . Effective therapists are skilled at monitoring acceptance of the explanation and will modify the delivery of an explanation as necessary. (pp. 863–864)

This seemingly diminishes all effective psychotherapies to essentially being placebo treatments (remember, they are all said to be equivalent) and implies that formal training in research-supported treatments is a waste of time. So long as the explanation for the therapy is plausible to the client, and they believe it, even if the therapist knows the explanation they provide to be false, treatments will be equally curative! Thus, it would be viewed as legitimate, for example, for an LCSW to dwell compellingly on the role of eye movements in the effectiveness of eye movement desensitization and reprocessing (EMDR), and how the brain processes information differently on the two side of the brain, *knowing this information is false*, if the client believes it, and placebo factors are accordingly activated, producing some relief.

How do such views square with principles from our Code of Ethics, such as "*Value of Integrity*—Social workers act honestly and responsibly" and "*Dishonesty, Fraud, or Deception*—Social workers should not participate in, condone, or be associated with dishonesty, fraud, or deception" (NASW, 2017)? The solution is to dismiss the equivalence of all psychotherapies hypothesis (it is very likely false), to keep abreast of the latest research-supported treatments suitable for the clients you see, and to adopt the model of evidence-based practice in our professional lives. And never be content with being a purveyor of a treatment that is merely a psychosocially dressed-up placebo. We are not worthy of the name "professional" if what we have to offer is little more than magic, shamanism, or snake oil.

Unfortunately, surveys of the practices of modern social workers disclose that the use

of PTs remains widespread (Pignotti & Thyer, 2009a, 2012). Holden and Barker (2018) provide an extensive listing of pseudoscientific treatments that social workers can deliver, and the generous and all-embracing notions of what constitutes acceptable social work practice provide little leverage to discourage the proliferation of PTs. Our leading textbooks on acceptable social work theory (e.g., Turner, 2017) promote pseudoscience by including chapters on interventions such as neurolinguistic programming (NLP), even though the fundamental principles of NLP are wrong and there is little evidence that it is a useful therapy, beyond placebo value (Kotera & Sweet, 2019). This has been known for many years, but a simple Google search linking "LCSW" and "NLP" discloses members of our discipline offering this PT. Some PTs are favorably written about in our professional journals (e.g., Robb, 2003). Our approved continuing education programs required for licensure renewal regularly promote pseudoscientific treatments (Thyer & Pignotti, 2016) such as so-called energy therapies. Energy therapies involve social workers moving their hands near a client's body, and examples of such practices include thought field therapy, emotional freedom techniques, reiki, polarity therapy, therapeutic touch, and various ways to tap on a client's body. This supposedly transfers energies unknown to science that have never been shown to exist, and available evidence suggests they do not exist (Pignotti, 2005; Rosa et al., 1998). Our approved continuing education programs teach about practices alien to social work training and expertise, such as acupuncture, which itself lacks a plausible theory or a credible research foundation demonstrating it is effective for the types of problems clients bring to social workers (Thyer & Pignotti, 2016).

The field of mental health has long been bedeviled by pseudoscientific practitioners. The works of Lawrence (1910) and Walsh (1924) provide excellent early descriptions of this problem, and Steiner (1945) is a social worker who similarly bewailed the proliferation of bogus therapies. She wrote about the use of tarot cards as a method of counseling, and today you can Google "Tarot" and "LCSW" and find clinical social workers engaging in this practice under the auspices of their social work license.

Characteristics of Pseudoscientific Treatments

Pseudoscientific therapies have been defined by Bunge (1998) as "a body of beliefs and practices whose practitioners wish, naively or maliciously, pass for science although it is alien to the approach, the techniques, and the fund of knowledge of science" (p. 41). Pseudoscientific treatments sometimes used by social workers often possess a number of characteristics that can serve as "red flags" for the practitioner or student interested in learning more about a given treatment. Some of these red flags are discussed next.

Implausible Theory

Implausible theory occurs when a theoretical mechanism of action for the PT posits something not currently accepted by mainstream science or which has been convincingly refuted. Wilhelm Reich's orgone energy is an example (see Spitzer, 2005), as is Mesmer's animal magnetism and also the life force of therapeutic touch (Rosa et al., 1998). A Google search using "LCSW" and "orgone" or "therapeutic touch" will return a number of clinical social workers using these methods. The bilateral eye movements supposed hemispheric specialization of the brain postulated by Francine Shapiro in her explanation of how eye movement desensitization and reprocessing was supposed to work has been shown to not be crucial to the treatment's value (Hill, 2020)—that is, the

original theory was wrong. The implausibility of early EMDR theory led many critics to label it as pseudoscientific (Herbert et al., 2000).

Overreliance on Anecdotes

Although anecdotes, often in the form of case studies, can be an important impetus to more formal scientific investigations, by themselves anecdotes are not typically considered strong evidence. In part, this is due to the next problem.

Selective Attention to Confirmatory Evidence

Whether it be searching for people with a positive response to a new treatment or a researcher searching the literature, it is crucial to locate and evaluate *all* the evidence, not just successful clinical outcomes or published studies that support one's point of view. This is also known as cherry picking the evidence.

Use of Jargon or Neologisms

Jargon refers to using scientific-sounding language in an effort to enhance the credibility or support of a given therapy. Saying that primal scream therapy (invented by an MSW, Arthur Janov) is supported by three randomized controlled trials (it is not, by the way) published in peer-reviewed journals ignores the possibility that the three randomized controlled trials may have been poorly designed or misreported. Also, some periodicals are predatory journals that rapidly publish submissions in return for paying a high fee and not using rigorous blind peer review. Readers may not realize that the *International Journal of Case Studies* is a predatory journal, whereas *Clinical Case Studies* is a very reputable periodical. *Neologisms* are made-up words or phrases, often nonsensical and, in the case of pseudoscientific treatments, designed to provide the aura of scientific respectability about a new therapy. Orgone energy, meridians, neurolinguistic programming, electropsychometer, bioresonance therapy, energy toxins, archetypes, ennegram, past-life regression, sensory-motor integration, perturbations, thought field, facilitated communication, epigenetic molecular wounds, holotropic breathwork, and muscle memory are all neologism terms used to describe various pseudoscientific theories or treatments. But they sound like . . . science!

Here is an example of pseudoscientific jargon from a book co-authored by a licensed social worker who uses crystals to heal clients from addictions (Cunningham & Ramer, 1988):

> Some crystals are concentrated aspects of earth-energy. Each one vibrating on and resonating with a different frequency. . . . By holding two different crystals in your hands and deepening your awareness into them, letting their energy wash through you and move you, you can create excellent substitutes for addictive substances. The cerebrum of the brain is composed of two hemispheres. Each has slightly different ways of processing information. The right hemisphere, which controls the left side of the body, is more fluid, spatial, and visually oriented. The left hemisphere, which controls the right side of the body, is more linear, time-oriented, and verbal. By holding a different stone in each hand and working with the pair, you can subtly alter your brain functions and initiate different states of consciousness. . . . Feel that when you hold your crystal you can breathe in its energy through your hands into your body. Because of their structure and nature, crystals are able to retain energy put into them, and can carry energy from outside sources. (p. xiii)

There is no evidence for any of this nonsense, beginning with the myth that the two sides of the brain operate in fundamentally different ways (they do not; see Lilienfeld et al., 2010). The idea that crystals emit vibrations, that these vary somehow and have specific healing properties, and can transfer energy to or from an individual, are all myths, demonstrated by double-blind studies comparing how people respond when they are wearing wrapped real crystals, versus identically wrapped plain pebbles (there is no difference!).

Reversed Burden of Proof

In scientific inquiry, the burden of proof rests with the person making an unusual claim. Often, the advocates of PT respond, when challenged to produce evidence, along the lines of "Well, you can't prove it is not true!" If a company marketing psychotherapy conducted over the internet claims that its services are effective, the public expects credible evidence to support this claim. If an upscale drug rehabilitation center states that 95% of its clients stay sober 12 months after discharge, professional ethics demands that it provide the evidence to support that claim.

Extravagant Claims

This occurs when the proponents of the PT assert that the treatment is effective for a wide array of psychosocial and health problems, some of which are seemingly disconnected. Thought field therapy is said to be effective for depression, anxiety, phobias, addictions, post-traumatic stress disorder (PTSD), swollen joints pain, stress disorders, cancer, headaches, heart disease, and arthritis (see http://www.rogercallahan.com/callahan.php)! This bewildering array of conditions, lacking any evident common substrate or etiology, suggests either that thought field therapy is truly a panacea-like treatment or, just perhaps, its advocates are seeking to broaden their potential client base so as to earn additional income. Parsimony suggests the latter. Another form of extravagant claim is to assert that the PT works exceedingly rapidly and regardless of the problem's duration or severity. Here is an example of this type of claim, found on the previously cited website: "What's fascinating about TFT is it's quick, painless and its success rate is almost unheard of in the field of mental health in any type of treatment over this whole century."

Substantial Financial Incentives

Although it is understandable that LCSWs wish to be reasonably compensated for their professional expertise, the originators and other advocates of PT also financially benefit from the substantial fees they earn training practitioners in the PT and then perhaps additional courses to train the trainer to enable the approved LCSW to charge for teaching the PT to other practitioners. Sometimes there are certifications to be earned in various PTs. For $425, one can become certified in biofeedback. After this entry-level qualification has been earned, one must pay much more money to become certified in neurofeedback and separately in pelvic muscle dysfunction biofeedback (see https://www.bcia.org/i4a/pages/index.cfm?pageid=3816). One can become a certified trauma professional by undergoing training in, among other modalities, various somatic therapies (see https://www.evergreencertifications.com/evg/detail/1000/certified-clinical-trauma-professional-cctp). There are dozens of bogus credentials one can earn to become an approved provider of various PTs. These credentials are united only by their lack of legal or enforceable standing. Apart from various certifications, diplomats, and other qualifications of dubious value, the promoters of PT can sell their books, audiovisual training materials, and sometimes various forms of ancillary equipment. For more than $600, one can purchase a light bar that features a light which travels back and forth while the client's eyes follow it, obviating the EMDR therapist from the labor of physically moving their fingers during tedious sessions. The ethics of selling (and using) a light bar in EMDR practice, when it has been shown that the eye movements are not needed for the treatment's success, is questionable. Someone is making a lot of money from these practices.

The NASW published a book titled *Person-in-Environment Manual* (Karls & O'Keefe, 2008), billed as an alternative to traditional systems of diagnosing mental disorders and other health problems. Unfortunately, no research suggests that this person-in-environment (PIE) system of assessment has credible reliability and validity, as acknowledged by the developers of PIE themselves (Karls et al., 1997). One would have hoped that such studies with positive results would have been published before marketing PIE and earning money from naive practitioners who assume that it must be legitimate because is it published by their major professional association. Just as there are PTs, there are also bogus methods of assessment, and the ethical practitioner avoids both (Thyer & Pignotti, 2011, 2015).

Misuse of Legitimate Research

This occurs when the advocates of a PT unjustifiably extrapolate from prior research and claim these findings support their treatment when, in fact, they do not. We can see how claiming that a drug that improved survivability in mice infected with cancer should be adopted now for use with human beings is an unreasonable application from the finding in mice. Similarly, claiming that a PT which proved useful in reducing stress among college students not diagnosed with any mental disorder proves it will help combat veterans with PTSD would be an overreach. Yet this is frequently done. A similar practice is engaged in when energy therapists claim that some phenomena observed in quantum physics experiments supports their contention that their treatments are effective due to these subatomic observations on energy and matter (Pignotti & Thyer, 2009b). The reality is that experimental findings in the field of quantum physics have no analogy to the macro world in which we and our clients live. They only apply (for now anyway) in the subatomic world.

Conclusion

The use of pseudoscientific behavioral and mental health treatments, and methods of assessment, continues to be an embarrassment to the profession of social work. Remedies include asking the purveyors of PT to stop offering such services in their role as LCSWs and to file ethics complaints with NASW (if the offender is a member) and with the state licensing board (if the offender is licensed). Sometimes this works. Reamer (2012) describes how one LCSW using so-called aura therapy had a complaint filed against him by a disgruntled client, and the state licensing board found him to have indeed exceeded his scope of practice. Perhaps we can be inspired by the words of one of our profession's founders, Mary Richmond: "The cure for the pseudo-science of much of our present investigation" (Mary Richmond claimed) is "more investigation" and a willingness to use "our best brains, time and strength upon [the] delicate task of finding out the right thing to do" (cited in Agnew, 2004, p. 106). Critical thinking about all claims for therapy effectiveness is an essential tool to protect oneself from the siren songs of pseudoscientific treatments (Hupp et al., 2019).

References

Agnew, E. N. (2004). *From charity to social work: Mary Richmond and the creation of an American profession.* University of Illinois Press.

Barker, R. (2014). *The social work dictionary* (6th ed.). NASW Press.

Bunge, M. (1998). *Philosophy of science: From problem to theory* (Vol. 1, rev. ed.). Transaction Publishers.

Council on Social Work Education. (2015). *2015 educational policy and accreditation standards.* https://www.cswe.org/getattachment/Accreditation/Standards-and-Policies/2015-EPAS/2015EPASandGlossary.pdf.aspx

Cunningham, D., & Ramer, A. (1988). *Further dimensions of healing addictions.* Cassandra Press.

Florida Legislature. (n.d.). *The 2020 Florida statutes.* http://www.leg.state.fl.us/statutes/index.cfm?App_mode=Display_Statute&Search_String=&URL=0400-0499/0491/Sections/0491.003.html

Herbert, J. D., Lilienfeld, S. O., Lohr, J. M., Montgomery, R. W., O'Donohue, W. T., Rosen, G. T., & Tolin, D. F. (2000). Science and pseudoscience in the development of eye movement desensitization and reprocessing: Implications for clinical psychology. *Clinical Psychology Review, 20,* 945–971.

Hill, M. D. (2020). Adaptive information processing theory: Origins, principles, applications, and evidence. *Journal of Evidence-Based Social Work, 17,* 317–331.

Holden, G., & Barker, K. (2018). Should social workers be engaged in these practices? *Journal of Evidence-based Social Work, 15*(1-3), 1–13.

Hupp, S., Mercer, J., Thyer, B. A., & Pignotti, M. (2019). Critical thinking about psychotherapy. In S. Hupp (Ed.), *Pseudoscience in child and adolescent psychotherapy: A skeptical field guide* (pp. 1–13). Cambridge University Press.

Karls, J. M., Lowery, C. T., Mattaini, M. A., & Wandrei, K. E. (1997). Use of the PIE (person-in-environment) system in social work education. *Journal of Social Work Education, 33,* 49–58.

Karls, J. M., & O'Keefe, M. (2008). *Person-in-environment system manual* (2nd ed.). NASW Press.

Kotera, Y., & Sweet, M. (2019). Comparative evaluation of neuro-linguistic programming. *British Journal of Guidance and Counseling, 47,* 744–756.

Lawrence, R. M. (1910). *Primitive psycho-therapy and quackery.* Houghton-Mifflin.

Lilienfeld, S. O., Lynn, S. J., Ruscio, J., & Beyerstein, B. L. (2010). *50 great myths of popular psychology.* Wiley-Blackwell.

Myers, L. L. & Thyer, B. A. (1997). Should social work clients have the right to effective treatment? *Social Work, 42,* 288–298.

Nathan, P. E., & Gorman, J. M. (Eds.). (2015). *A guide to treatments that work* (4th ed.). Oxford University Press.

National Association of Social Workers. (2017). *Code of ethics.* https://www.socialworkers.org/about/ethics/code-of-ethics

Pignotti, M. (2005). Thought field therapy voice technology vs random meridian point sequences: A single-blind controlled experiment. *Scientific Review of Mental Health Practice, 4,* 38–47.

Pignotti, M., & Thyer, B. A. (2009a). The use of novel unsupported and empirically supported therapies by Licensed Clinical Social Workers: An exploratory study. *Social Work Research, 33,* 5–17.

Pignotti, M., & Thyer, B. A. (2009b). Some comments on *Energy Psychology: A Review of the Evidence*: Premature conclusions based on incomplete evidence? *Psychotherapy, Theory, Research, Practice, Training, 46*, 257–261.

Pignotti, M., & Thyer, B. A. (2012). Novel unsupported and empirically supported therapies: Patterns of usage among Licensed Clinical Social Workers. *Behavioural and Cognitive Psychotherapy, 40*, 331–349. doi:10.1017/S135246581100052X

Pignotti, M., & Thyer, B. A. (2015). New Age and related novel unsupported therapies in mental health practice. In S. O. Lilienfeld, S. J. Lynn, & J. M. Lohr (Eds.), *Science and pseudoscience in clinical psychology* (2nd ed., pp. 191–209). Guilford.

Reamer, R. (2012, June 28). The boundaries of alternative therapies in clinical social work. *Social Work Today*. https://www.socialworktoday.com/news/eoe_062912.shtml

Reid, W. J. (1997). Evaluating the dodo's verdict: Do all interventions have equivalent outcomes? *Social Work Research, 21*, 5–16.

Reid, W. J., Kenaley, B. D., & Colvin, J. (2004). Do some interventions work better than others? A review of comparative social work experiments. *Social Work Research, 28*, 71–81.

Robb, M. (2003, December). Thought field therapy at your fingertips. *Social Work Today*, 20–23.

Rosa, L., Rosa, E., Sarner, L., & Barrett, S. (1998). A close look at therapeutic touch. *JAMA, 279*, 1005–1010.

Spitzer, R. L. (2005). An examination of Wilhelm Reich's demonstration of orgone energy. *Scientific Review of Mental Health Practice, 4*(1). https://www.srmhp.org/0401/reich.html

Steiner, L. R. (1945). *Where do people take their troubles?* Houghton-Mifflin.

Thyer, B. A. (2015). A bibliography of randomized controlled experiments in social work (1949–2013): *Solvitur ambulando. Research on Social Work Practice, 25*, 753–793.

Thyer, B. A., Babcock, P., & Tutweiler, M. (2017). Locating research-supported interventions for child welfare practice. *Child and Adolescent Social Work Journal, 34*, 85–94.

Thyer, B. A., & Pignotti, M. (2010). Science and pseudoscience in developmental disabilities: Guidelines for social workers. *Journal of Social Work in Disability and Rehabilitation, 9*, 110–129.

Thyer, B. A., & Pignotti, M. (2011). Pseudoscience in clinical assessment. In C. Jordan & C. Franklin (Eds.), *Clinical assessment for social workers: Quantitative and qualitative approaches* (2nd ed., pp. 163–178). Lyceum.

Thyer, B. A., & Pignotti, M. (2015). *Science and pseudoscience in social work practice.* Springer.

Thyer, B. A., & Pignotti, M. G. (2016). The problem of pseudoscience in social work continuing education. *Journal of Social Work Education, 52*, 136–146.

Turner, F. (2017). *Social work treatment: Interlocking theoretical approaches* (6th ed.). Oxford University Press.

Walsh, J. J (1924). *Cures: The story of cures that fail.* Appleton.

Wampold, B. (2007). Psychotherapy: The humanistic (and effective) treatment. *American Psychologist, 62*, 857–873.

The Importance of Empathy to Social Work Practice

Melanie Reyes, Elizabeth A. Segal, and Cynthia A. Lietz

Empathy is essential in all aspects of life. Human beings seek relationships to build a sense of belonging and to create a shared understanding of our experiences and emotions (de Waal, 2009). Empathic understanding involves one's ability to perceive accurately the position of another. It is through empathic understanding that social connections are forged and maintained. Despite its importance, empathy as a concept is often vaguely defined. The eminent social psychologist C. Daniel Batson, who has studied empathy for more than 40 years, concluded the concept "empathy" is described in the literature in eight different ways. Although there are variations, all share the view that empathy is a process in which "one person can come to know the internal state of another and be motivated to respond with sensitive care" (Batson, 2011, p. 11). Despite varying definitions, most agree that empathy involves achieving an understanding of another that informs our desire and ability to respond effectively, which speaks to the importance of empathy to social work practice.

The Professional Imperative for Empathy in Social Work

From a social work perspective, both interpersonal and social empathy remain essential. Interpersonal empathy involves the ability to understand accurately the perspective of an individual and is important for developing micro-level insight needed to build rapport with individual clients. Social empathy offers macro-level insight to meet the needs of groups, communities, and the greater society (Segal, 2018).

The connection between social work and empathy is strong, given the importance of social interactions and relationships in our society and the great impact of developing and communicating an empathic response to client populations (Frankel, 2017). There is broad recognition that empathy is a fundamental principle for the profession of social work as a central and potentially unifying theoretical tenet (King, 2011). With the mission of the social work profession centered on enhancing well-being, self-determination, and respect for others, empathy is an active construct at the heart of social work. Empathy is a central part of social work practice on the micro and macro levels, reflecting interpersonal empathy and social empathy.

The National Association of Social Workers (NASW) Code of Ethics (2017) focuses on the enhancement of well-being, the needs and empowerment of all with an emphasis on serving those most in need, the well-being of society, and the environmental forces that pertain to social justice. The Code emphasizes ethical principles that relate directly to empathy, including the challenge of social injustices, respect for human inherent dignity and worth, recognition of the central importance of human relationships, focus on clients' interests and self-determination, as well as cultural awareness and social diversity. Social workers are called to treat colleagues with respect, cooperate with a focus on client well-being, and maintain a responsibility to the general welfare of society seeking to realize social justice (NASW, 2017). Social workers strive to prevent and eradicate discrimination, oppression, exploitation, and power differences while engaging with social and political action (NASW, 2017). These principles are built on successful engagement in interpersonal and social empathy.

Defining Empathy

Based on the integration of years of research, we have identified seven components that together describe interpersonal and social empathy, which together comprise the full process of empathy. By understanding each distinct element, we can recognize our strengths and areas of growth as we work to enhance our capacity to understand the micro- and macro-level interactions that are a part of social work practice. The overall goal is to engage competently

in all of these components to display the full depth and breadth of empathy.

The Five Components of Interpersonal Empathy

Interpersonal empathy is composed of five major components: affective response, affective mentalizing, self–other awareness, perspective taking, and emotion regulation (Segal et al., 2017). Each component is an individual psychological phenomenon that together comprise the full experience of interpersonal empathy.

Affective response is an automatic unconscious mirroring response from sensory and imaginative input transmitted along neurological pathways. Considered to be a lower order empathic reflex, affective response incorporates mimicry of others' expressions and movements to trigger similar responses in the observer (Debes, 2010). Mirror reflexes build a contagious state that may generate the responsive sharing in the empathy target's emotions (Carroll, 2014; Decety & Jackson, 2006). From this unconscious aspect, empathy moves to conscious efforts.

Affective mentalizing bridges between the affective creation of a mental image and the cognitive awareness of experiences and emotions to support behavior predictions (Decety & Jackson, 2006). Mentalizing may be defined as understanding another person's social and emotional perspective as separate from one's own perspective that is a neurologically observable phenomenon both physiologically and cognitively (Baird & Roellke, 2017; Segal, 2014).

Self–other awareness is the cognitive ability to discriminate between the experiences of another person and one's own experiences, in the observation of another person's emotional state (Neumann et al., 2009). Through observation, the observer identifies partially with the person being observed, as influenced by identified similarities, familiarities, and affection (Neumann et al., 2009). When self–other awareness is absent, there is a risk of emotional contagion due to the lack of distinction between what is one's experience and the experience of someone else (Singer & Klimecki, 2014).

Perspective taking brings cognitive processing and intentionality into the process of assuming another's point of view (Decety, 2015). This involves imagining the narrative of the other person, along with that person's emotional and cognitive state, while recognizing the individuality of the other as distinct from oneself (McFee, 2014). The perspective-taking aspect of empathy is an elevated sophisticated response that engages cognitive processing and interpretation of what another person's motivations and emotional state may be (Eisenberg & Eggum, 2009).

The final component, *emotion regulation*, provides cognitive control as a mediating factor to connect and temper affective response, self–other awareness, perspective taking, and affective mentalizing (Segal et al., 2017). With a strong core of emotional regulation, social work professionals can integrate all components in a balanced and productive manner. With strong emotion regulation, vicarious reactions are mitigated, thereby lowering the possibility for personal distress to replace empathy (Eisenberg, 2002). When there is complete overlap between oneself and the empathy target, personal distress and compassion fatigue may develop (Thomas, 2013). The empathy component of emotion regulation helps minimize this overlap and allows the emergence of empathic concern (Thomas, 2013).

The Two Components of Social Empathy

Social empathy builds on interpersonal empathy to incorporate *contextual understanding* and *macro perspective taking* on the systemic level (Segal & Wagaman, 2017). It is the "ability to more deeply understand people by perceiving or experiencing their life situations and as a result gain insight into structural inequalities and disparities" (Segal, 2011, p. 266). The examination of cultural and societal barriers, historical discrimination, inequalities, and oppressive acts expands empathic understanding toward social responsibility (Segal & Wagaman, 2017).

Macro perspective taking builds on the interpersonal empathy component of perspective taking to expand the ability to step into someone else's perspective on a broader level—that is, to understand different groups. Macro perspective taking relies on contextual understanding to ensure congruence with cultural and historical context, expand awareness of how external factors impact group experiences, and decrease stereotyping and prejudice (Segal, 2011). The key to social empathy remains embedded in the powerful blend of the awareness of life situations of other groups with a deeper understanding of the root of historical experiences; this combination may present as a call to social justice action (Segal, 2018).

Practice Implications

Empathy promotes understanding and working with clients. Empathy in social work is characterized by an open attitude of learning about others' experiences, suspension of judgment and personal bias, ability to step into the emotional world of another individual while regulating our own emotions, and aptitude to generate empathic responses demonstrating understanding of the other person's feelings (Birkenmaier et al., 2014).

Research has shown empathy to be the factor that lowers client resistance and influences client responsiveness and information sharing (Forrester et al., 2007). Empathy has been identified as playing a role in positive counseling relationships (Sale et al., 2008). Empathy, in particular, has been studied as a predictor of levels of marital satisfaction and marital functioning (Waldinger et al., 2004). Other research demonstrated that the expression of empathy and understanding supported children in talking about their emotions and working toward solutions (Green & Christensen, 2006). Research has explored perspective taking with regard to valuing someone's well-being as an antecedent for empathic concern when we perceive that person to be in need (Batson et al., 2007).

Social workers are tasked with understanding the client in the environment, creating case plans based on client strengths, holding clients accountable, and having difficult conversations—all at the same time. Social workers are in the roles of investigator, support system, system navigator, resource connector, and clinician. Empathy is key for navigating these roles while maintaining a relationship with the client. Through empathic listening, social workers can understand the client's emotional state and constructed meaning of life experiences to identify alternatives and interventions that honor cultural preferences (King, 2011).

In addition, empathy can help train clients in empathic interventions that inhibit aggression and antisocial behavior (Segal, 2014). Research showed that empathy is linked with increased prosocial behavior, and both empathy and prosocial behavior may be full mediators for the association between attachment and self-esteem (Laible et al., 2004).

Empathy in the social work profession fosters a heightened critical consciousness, ethical thinking, and a radical orientation toward social justice (Gair, 2017; King, 2011; NASW, 2017). Equipped with a strong commitment to social justice, social workers understand structural barriers and historical oppression, the importance of advocacy, and the significance of macro perspective taking in effective work with communities and populations (Segal & Wagaman, 2017). Social workers are uniquely positioned to work as change agents to challenge the status quo.

Empathy Can Prevent Burnout

Social work can be emotionally demanding. There is an assumed connection between empathy and compassion fatigue (Nilsson, 2014). Social workers may be at higher risk of secondary trauma if they experienced trauma in their pasts and then work with clients in similar trauma situations (Grant, 2014). Emotional overarousal and compassion fatigue may occur when professional stress becomes personal distress, resulting in the diminishing of empathy and the elevation of social and psychological issues (Nilsson, 2014; Thomas, 2013).

On a positive note, research has found that empathy may be a mitigating factor to avoid compassion fatigue, burnout, and secondary traumatic stress (Wagaman et al., 2015). Emotion regulation and self-awareness are essential to understanding the client's experience and context while keeping a balance between empathic engagement and the avoidance of emotional distress (Gibbons, 2011; Nilsson, 2014). Social workers benefit from establishing professional boundaries and paying careful attention to signs of compassion fatigue, transference, and burnout to avoid overly engaging emotionally with clients (Gair, 2011). The skill of emotion regulation is key to prevention of burnout.

Best Practices to Cultivate Empathy in Social Work

Social workers should be able to empathize fully, a skill that requires the ability to understand the context of another person's emotions (Hoffman, 2000). Forms of empathy employed in work with client systems include empathic mirroring, invitational empathy encouraging clients to articulate their emotions, and inferred empathic hypotheses regarding client emotions

(Birkenmaier et al., 2014). Expressed therapeutic empathy communicates to clients that they have value in the eyes of the practitioner and that they are not alone (Howe, 2008). The most powerful tool for engaging with a client exhibiting anger may be empathy, communicating calm recognition of the emotion and availability to help (Birkenmaier et al., 2014).

Empathic displays reflect the ability to recognize and respond to another person's affective cues (Neumann et al., 2009). Clinical tools such as discourse and positioning support the presence of empathy as a potentially significant positive determinant of therapeutic success (Sinclair & Monk, 2005). Discursive empathy requires therapists to examine the dominant messages that impact their relationships with clients while heightening awareness of cultural assumptions (Sinclair & Monk, 2005). Similarly, clients benefit from practicing mindfulness, identifying their own ideologies, and engaging in critical discussion that involves active listening to learn from another person's perspective (Rosenwald et al., 2012).

Possible options that can be used to increase the presence of empathy in relationships include role plays, simulations, videos viewing, emotion recognition exercises, vignettes, and intergroup meditation (Weisz & Zaki, 2017). These activities offer opportunities for affective mentalizing, which may stimulate growth in cognitive reasoning, an exploration of racism and privilege, and critical reflection (Gair, 2017). In addition, social–psychological interventions may assist in increasing empathy through the introduction of a growth mindset and expanding perceptions of group membership (Weisz & Zaki, 2017). These techniques may cultivate macro perspective taking through the exposure to the lives and situations of oppressed populations (Segal & Wagaman, 2017).

Social workers can promote social empathy by increasing proximity between groups and opportunities for cross-cultural exchanges (Segal, 2011). We are positioned to promote volunteerism, community service, and democratic values to protect the public interest, while exposing people to those from different backgrounds to increase mirroring opportunities, perspective taking, and self–other awareness. Contextual understanding may be learned through exploration of historical poverty, systems, structural oppression, and policy advocacy strategies that combine the understanding of contextual factors with the skills necessary to advocate and implement social change (Wagaman et al., 2018).

Supervisors may benefit from maintaining a direct client caseload to understand their supervisees' experiences and perspectives (Wagaman et al., 2015). Mindfulness and self-awareness training, boundary creation and maintenance, and positive self-talk can mitigate and prevent burnout that results from being exposed to the distress of clients (Neumann et al., 2009). Social workers benefit from professional socialization, experiential learning in the workplace, and clinical supervision to integrate their professional training into empathic practice (Gibbons, 2011).

Empathy as an Organizing Framework for Social Work

Despite varying definitions of empathy, it remains clear that empathy involves a process of understanding the position of another to inform our action moving forward. This process offers implications for micro and macro social work practice. In fact, it is difficult to identify any social work interaction that would not require empathic understanding and action. It is our contention that empathy serves as an overarching framework that can guide all levels of practice. Understanding and developing the components of interpersonal and social empathy may be one of the most important ways that we prepare social workers to effectively advance our mission.

References

Baird, A. A., & Roellke, E. V. (2017). Girl uninterrupted: The neural basis of moral development among adolescent females. In J. Decety & T. Wheatley (Eds.), *The moral brain* (pp. 157–179). MIT Press.

Batson, C. D. (2011). These things called empathy: Eight related but distinct phenomena. In J. Decety & W. Ickes (Eds.), *The social neuroscience of empathy* (pp. 3–15). MIT Press.

Batson, C. D., Eklund, J. H., Chermok, V. L., Hoyt, J. L., & Ortiz, B. G. (2007). An additional antecedent of empathic concern: Valuing the welfare of the person in need. *Journal of Personality and Social Psychology, 93*(1), 65–74.

Birkenmaier, J., Berg-Weger, M., & Dewees, M. P. (2014). *The practice of generalist social work* (3rd ed.). Routledge.

Carroll, N. (2014). On some affective relations between audiences and the characters in popular fictions. In A. Coplan & P. Goldie (Eds.), *Empathy: Philosophical and psychological perspectives* (pp. 162–184). Oxford University Press.

de Waal, F. B. M. (2009). *The age of empathy*. Random House.

Debes, R. (2010). Which empathy? Limitations in the mirrored "understanding" of emotion. *Synthese, 175*, 219–239.

Decety, J. (2015). The neural pathways, development and functions of empathy. *Current Opinion in Behavioral Sciences, 3*, 1–6.

Decety, J., & Jackson, P. L. (2006). A social-neuroscience perspective on empathy. *Current Directions in Psychological Science, 15*(2), 54–58.

Eisenberg, N. (2002). Empathy-related emotional responses, altruism, and their socialization. In R. J. Davidson & A. Harrington (Eds.), *Visions of compassion: Western scientists and Tibetan Buddhists examine human nature* (pp. 131–164). Oxford University Press.

Eisenberg, N., & Eggum, N. D. (2009). Empathic responding: Sympathy and personal distress. In J. Decety & W. Ickes (Eds.), *The social neuroscience of empathy* (pp. 71–83). MIT Press. https://doi.org/10.7551/mitpress/9780262012973.003.0007

Forrester, D., Kershaw, S., Moss, H., & Hughes, L. (2007). Communication skills in child protection: How do social workers talk to parents? *Child and Family Social Work, 13*, 41–51.

Frankel, R. M. (2017). The many faces of empathy: Biological, psychological, and interactional perspectives. *Journal of Patient Experience, 4*(2), 55–56.

Gair, S. (2011). Exploring empathy embedded in ethics curricula: A classroom inquiry. *Advances in Social Work, 12*(1), 329–344.

Gair, S. (2017). Pondering the colour of empathy: Social work students' reasoning on activism, empathy and racism. *British Journal of Social Work, 47*, 162–180.

Gibbons, S. B. (2011). Understanding empathy as a complex construct: A review of the literature. *Clinical Social Work Journal, 39*(3), 243–252. https://doi.org/10.1007/s10615-010-0305-2

Grant, L. (2014). Hearts and minds: Aspects of empathy and wellbeing in social work students. *Social Work Education, 33*(3), 338–352.

Green, E. J., & Christensen, T. M. (2006). Elementary school children's perceptions of play therapy in school settings. *International Journal of Play Therapy, 15*(1), 65–85.

Hoffman, M. L. (2000). *Empathy and moral development: Implications for caring and justice*. Cambridge University Press.

Howe, D. (2008). *The emotionally intelligent social worker*. Palgrave Macmillan.

King, S. H., Jr. (2011). The structure of empathy in social work practice. *Journal of Human Behavior in the Social Environment, 21*(6), 679–695. https://doi.org/10.1080/10911359.2011.583516

Laible, D. J., Carlo, G., & Roesch, S. C. (2004). Pathways to self-esteem in late adolescence: The role of parent and peer attachment, empathy, and social behaviours. *Journal of Adolescence, 27*, 703–716.

McFee, G. (2014). Empathy: Interpersonal vs artistic? In A. Coplan & P. Goldie (Eds.), *Empathy: Philosophical and psychological perspectives* (pp. 185–208). Oxford University Press.

National Association of Social Workers. (2017). *Code of ethics*. https://www.socialworkers.org/about/ethics/code-of-ethics

Neumann, M., Bensing, J., Mercer, S., Ernstmann, N. Ommen, O., & Pfaff, H. (2009). Analyzing the "nature" and "specific effectiveness" of clinical empathy: A theoretical overview and contribution towards a theory-based research agenda. *Patient Education and Counseling, 74*, 339–346.

Nilsson, P. (2014). Are empathy and compassion bad for the professional social worker? *Advances in Social Work, 15*(2), 294–305.

Rosenwald, M., Wiener, D. R., Smith-Osborne, A., & Smith, C. M. (2012). The place of political diversity within the social work classroom. *Journal of Social Work Education, 48*(1), 139–158.

Sale, E., Bellamy, N., Springer, J. F., & Wang, M. Q. (2008). Quality of provider–participant relationships and enhancement of adolescent social skills. *Journal of Primary Prevention, 29,* 263–278.

Segal, E. A. (2011). Social empathy: A model built on empathy, contextual understanding, and social responsibility that promotes social justice. *Journal of Social Service Research, 37*(3), 266–277.

Segal, E. A. (2014). Social empathy. *Encyclopedia of Social Work* [Online publication]. https://doi.org/10.1093/acrefore/9780199975839.013.1152

Segal, E. A. (2018). *Social empathy: The art of understanding others.* Columbia University Press.

Segal, E. A., Gerdes, K. E., Lietz, C. A., Wagaman, M. A., & Geiger, J. M. (2017). *Assessing empathy.* Columbia University Press.

Segal, E. A., & Wagaman, M. A. (2017). Social empathy as a framework for teaching social justice. *Journal of Social Work Education, 53*(2), 201–211.

Sinclair, S. L., & Monk, G. (2005). Discursive empathy: A new foundation for therapeutic practice. *British Journal of Guidance & Counseling, 33*(3), 333–349. https://doi.org/10.1080/03069880500179517

Singer, T., & Klimecki, O. M. (2014). Empathy and compassion. *Current Biology, 24*(18), R875–R878.

Thomas, J. (2013). Association of personal distress with burnout, compassion fatigue, and compassion satisfaction among clinical social workers. *Journal of Social Service Research, 39*(3), 365–379. https://doi.org/10.1080/01488376.2013.771596

Wagaman, M. A., Compton, K. S., & Segal, E. A. (2018). Social empathy and attitudes about dependence of people living in poverty on government assistance programs. *Journal of Poverty, 22*(6), 471–485.

Wagaman, M. A., Geiger, J. M., Shockley, C., & Segal, E. A. (2015). The role of empathy in burnout, compassion satisfaction, and the secondary traumatic stress among social workers. *Social Work, 60*(3), 201–209.

Waldinger, R. J., Hauser, S. T., Schulz, M. S., Allen, J. P., & Crowell, J. A. (2004). Reading others' emotions: The role of intuitive judgments in predicting marital satisfaction, quality, and stability. *Journal of Family Psychology, 18* (1), 58–71.

Weisz, E., & Zaki, J. (2017). Empathy-building interventions: A review of existing work and suggestions for future directions. In E. M. Seppala, E. Simon-Thomas, S. L. Brown, M. C. Worline, C. D. Cameron, & J. R. Doty (Eds.), *The Oxford handbook of compassion science* (pp. 205–217). Oxford University Press.

Multifamily Behavioral Treatment for Obsessive–Compulsive Disorder

Barbara Van Noppen

Clinicians who use this guide are presumed to have solid experience in providing cognitive–behavioral therapy (CBT) for obsessive–compulsive disorder [OCD; that includes exposure and response prevention (ERP) as a foundation] and have a basic knowledge of family-based treatments for OCD. Clinicians are encouraged to be familiar with the following workbooks that outline ERP and complementary CBT interventions for OCD. One of these resources may be "required" reading assigned to participants prior to beginning the multifamily behavioral treatment (MFBT) to augment the psychoeducation provided during treatment: *The OCD Workbook* (Hyman & Pedrick, 2010), *Overcoming Obsessive–Compulsive Disorder: A Behavioral and Cognitive Protocol for the Treatment of OCD* (Steketee, 1999), and *Getting over OCD: A 10-Step Workbook for Taking Back Your Life* (Abramowitz, 2009).

Family-based recommended reading includes Sassano et al. (2015) and Thompson-Hollands et al. (2014). For a review of expressed emotion implications for OCD family treatment, see Steketee et al. (1998) and Berardis

et al. (2008). For a full description of the clinical application of MFBT, see Van Noppen (2002) and Van Noppen and Steketee (2003). Familiarity with self-help books about OCD, Web resources, podcasts, blogs, and other electronic resources (for a full listing, see https://IOCDF.org) is helpful. This treatment guide builds upon theoretical foundations and outcome studies of multifamily psychoeducational groups originally developed for schizophrenia. It is recommended that the clinician be familiar with Anderson et al. (1986) and McFarlane (1983). During the past three decades, the concept of family accommodation (FA) has received exponentially growing attention, and replicated studies identify FA as one of the most robust predictors of OCD treatment outcome in both adults and children/adolescents (for comprehensive review, see Shimshoni et al., 2019).

The concept of FA was first published in the clinical literature in 1990 (Livingston-Van Noppen et al., 1990). It is recommended to use one of the three validated versions of the Family Accommodation Scale pre and post MFBT to measure change in FA: FAS–Interview Rated (Calvocoressi et al., 1999), FAS–Self-Rated (FAS-SR; Pinto et al., 2013), and FAS–Patient Version (FAS-PV; Wu et al., 2016). These three versions of FAS have been translated in more than 15 languages and are available in the public domain at https://publichealth.yale.edu/familyaccommodationocd.

This guide is intended to instruct clinicians on the implementation of MFBT for OCD; it is not a substitute for clinical training and ongoing supervision. MFBT differs considerably from traditional family therapy in that the clinician takes a very active role in providing information, facilitating problem-solving, participating in direct and imaginal exposure, making suggestions directly to families, and assigning homework exercises in a family group modality that includes the individual with OCD (Van Noppen & Steketee, 2009). This may not be customary for dynamically trained clinicians. For MFBT to be effective, the clinician should be clear about and comfortable with the role described. This MFBT is written for adult patients (aged 18 years or older); it can be adapted to be suitable for adolescents and children (children as young as age 8 years have successfully participated in MFBT outcome studies). MFBT has demonstrated efficacy in reducing OCD symptoms comparable to individual ERP with slightly more durable effects than individual group ERP (Van Noppen, Steketee, et al., 1997).

Features and Procedures of Multifamily Behavior Treatment

Features

Multifamily behavior treatment treats five to seven families (no more than 16 total participants are recommended), including the individual diagnosed with OCD and identified significant others who are in considerable daily contact (at least 1 hour a day) with the identified patient.

Co-leaders are optimal. At least one of the leaders should have an advanced degree and license in social work, psychology, or certified counseling; experience in clinical work with individuals, families, and groups; and proficiency in CBT with extensive experience in an OCD population.

Each of the 18 sessions is approximately 2 hours, and the time-limited nature of this treatment program serves to motivate patients and helps the program be time-efficient, cost-effective, and follow a specific agenda. Leaders and participants (unless refusal) participate in the in vivo and imaginal exposures and response prevention (RP) during the group. An active therapeutic ingredient in the MFBT is therapist and participant modeling. Teaching families to tolerate their loved one's discomfort with support of others who are afflicted by OCD is essential to successful outcome.

Treatment Procedure

Following is a manual for an 18-session MFBT and one 90-minute intake session conducted with each OCD patient and their family members.

Information Gathering and Pre-Group Screening (90 Minutes)

1. Take a general biopsychosocial history and collect information about OC symptoms for treatment planning (20 minutes). Use the Yale–Brown Obsessive–Compulsive Checklist and Severity Scale (YBOCS; Goodman et al., 1989a, 1989b) to indicate primary obsessions and major compulsions and rate symptom severity.
2. Discuss onset of OCD and efforts to cope (10 minutes).
3. Begin exposure hierarchy, as in individual ERP (15 minutes).
4. Teach the patient and family how to rate anxiety according to the Subjective Units of Distress Scale (SUDS) and estimate at which treatment session the trigger will be introduced. See hierarchies in Table 133.1

TABLE 133.1 Exposure Hierarchies

Situation	Discomfort (1–100)	Treatment Session
Hierarchy 1: Fears of Contamination—"Cancer" from Brother and Cigarettes		
Holding unopened cigarette pack	45	1
Touching doorknobs at home	55	2
Holding opened cigarette pack	55	2
Touching "dirty" clothes (basement)	85	5
Touching cigarette filter	90	6
Stepping barefoot on a cigarette	95	7
Hierarchy 2: Fear of Contamination—Cancer from "Chemical" Contact		
Touching microwaved food	30	1
Holding batteries	40	2
Touching sand at beach	65	5
Eating food items "scanned" at checkout	75	6
Drinking diet soda	85	7
Eating chicken	100	8

5. Describe ERP (10 minutes). Offer treatment rationale.

6. Description of MFBT program and review of overall goals (5 minutes).

7. Discuss the degree of family accommodation and response styles (20 minutes). Administer the FAS-SR in the group (Pinto et al., 2013).

8. Homework assignment (5 minutes): read Hyman and Pedrick (2010), Chapters 1, 2, 5, and 6.

9. Wrap up (5 minutes). Address concerns and questions.

Session 1: Building Cohesion and Trust: "We're Not Alone!" Psychoeducational Phase: "What Is Obsessive–Compulsive Disorder?" (2 hours)

1. Welcome (5 minutes). The group leaders and participants introduce themselves and group leaders outline the agenda for all 12 sessions.

2. Administrative issues (10 minutes). Review scheduling of sessions, cancelation policy, group guidelines about confidentiality, and therapist availability.

3. Definition of OCD (1 hour). Review Chapters 1 and 2 in Hyman and Pedrick (2010) on the biological and learned bases of OCD. Distribute YBOCS symptom checklist (self-rated version). Go over each example provided, with group members volunteering to read. Encourage disclosure by asking for examples from patients' or family members' experiences. Introduce concepts of ERP.

4. Administer the FAS in the groups (FAS-SR for family, FAS-PV for patients. Discuss and encourage feedback among group members (15 minutes).

5. Homework (30 minutes). Go-round: Each patient chooses a specific ERP challenge to practice daily for homework. Distribute self-rating exposure homework form, and explain how to use it (Hyman & Pedrick, 2010, p. 93). If there is time during the session, ask patients to volunteer an ERP and all participants model it.

Session 2: Psychoeducational Phase: "How Do You Treat Obsessive–Compulsive Disorder?"

1. Check-in (10 minutes). Review the previous group session.
2. Go-round (10 minutes). Each patient reports on homework completed during the week, including SUDs. If the homework is inadequately completed or reported, discuss problems identified and encourage group feedback.
3. Overview of behavior therapy (30 minutes). Define in vivo and imaginal exposure.

Include a few statements about tolerating initial high anxiety that will decrease over time with repeated, systematic use of ERP (habituation). The following is a case example of the sequences of in vivo and imaginal exposure and RP for a patient with contamination fears.

Case Example

The patient, Steve, felt contaminated by feces, urine, sweat, and contact with others. He feared contracting a debilitating disease. The following hierarchy was constructed for Steve: feces, 100 SUDs; urine, 90 SUDs; toilet seats in public bathrooms, 80 SUDs; sweat, 75 SUDs; newspapers, 60 SUDs; and doorknobs, 50 SUDs.

> *Session 1*—Steve and group members walked with the therapist through the building touching doorknobs, especially those of the public restrooms. No handwashing.
> *Session 2*—Steve and group members held newspapers in the waiting room. No washing.
> *Session 3*—Steve held newspapers and doorknobs. Contact with sweat was introduced by asking him to place one hand under his arm and the other in his shoe.
> *Session 4*—Exposure began with newspapers and sweat. Toilet seats were added by coaching the patient to stand next to the toilet and place his hands on the seat.
> *Session 5*—Exposure began with contact with sweat and toilet seats. Urine was then introduced by encouraging Steve to hold a paper towel dampened in his own urine.
> *Session 6*—Exposure included urine, toilet seats, and sweat repeatedly until SUDS decreased by at least 50%.
> *Sessions 7–12*—Daily exposure to urine and sweat.

Homework focused on the objects used during that day's treatment session.

> *Imaginal exposure*: First written, then read aloud in the group, and then recorded. This should be followed by in vivo exposure to objects or situations related to that scene and provoke similar levels of discomfort.
> *Response prevention*: Remind participants of the specific instructions periodically during treatment. Give a copy of the rules to each patient and their family, modeling the instructions after the following example for washers:

Washers: During the response prevention period, patients are not permitted to use water on their body—that is, no handwashing, no rinsing, no wet towels, washcloths, wet wipes, or antibacterial gels except as negotiated with the therapist. Supervised showers are permitted every day for target time, including hair washing. Ritualistic washing of specific areas of the body (e.g., genitals and hair) is prohibited. If prevention of washing feels unbearable, patients may wash briefly and immediately re-contaminate with the items currently being exposed in treatment.

At home, relatives may be available to the patient should the patient have difficulty controlling a strong urge to wash. If the patient reports such concerns, family members can coach the patient to delay the urge until it decreases to a manageable level. Family members may attempt to stop such violations through firm verbal insistence, but no physical force should be used, and arguments should be avoided. Relatives can turn off faucets if the patient gives prior consent to such a plan. Showers can be timed by family, with no direct observation of showering behavior.

4. Homework go-round. ERP (60 minutes). Each patient chooses a behavioral homework task. Use feedback and support from group members to develop the optimal homework assignment, and then try to practice in the group. For example,
   - For harming obsessions with reassurance seeking and checking, the group leader and patients dampen their hands and touch light switches; other group members follow by touching the same switches. No reassurance seeking or checking is allowed. Level of anxiety is discussed and rated. This is repeated several times to model the homework assignment and to begin the process of habituation. Another exposure challenge is to pass a pair of scissors around the group, point first, and say, "I'm a killer."
   - For contamination obsessions with washing and/or passive avoidance, fear of being responsible for something bad happening and checking, hoarding, ordering and arranging, and other obsessions and compulsions, devise in vivo ERP accordingly.
5. Family role (10 minutes). Instruct family members to offer support and encouragement for patient's completion of ERP

homework. No changes in family responses should be made without prior negotiation.

Session 3: Psychoeducation: Family Responses to Obsessive–Compulsive Disorder and Family Guidelines: "What Should We Do?"

1. Check-in (10 minutes).
2. Go-round (10 minutes).
3. Psychoeducational lecture on neurobiology of OCD (15 minutes). (If a psychiatrist is not able to be present, a previously videotaped discussion on the neurobiology of OCD by an MD psychiatrist is viewed in the group.)
4. ERP (60 minutes). In the group, each patient selects exposure items with SUD level of approximately 50–60; continue with in vivo ERP.
5. Family guidelines (15 minutes). Distribute *Learning to Live with OCD* guidelines for families available at https://iocdf.org/expert-opinions/expert-opinion-family-guidelines/ (Van Noppen, Pato, et al., 1997) and read and discuss as a group. Identify and label family response styles (accommodating, antagonistic, split, and oscillating).
6. Homework selection (10 minutes). Each patient reassesses behavioral homework task with family guidelines in mind and adds another challenge.

Session 4: Intensive Treatment Phase: Managing the Symptoms: "Out with Doubt!"

1. Check-in and go-round (20 minutes). Proceed as previously described.

2. Explain family behavioral contracting (20 minutes); see Steketee et al. (1998); Van Noppen (2002).
   - One at a time, each family identifies problem areas. How does the family accommodate? Is there a lot of hostile criticism directed toward the patient by family? Review the FAS-SR as a group and facilitate discussion.
   - Guide the family to focus on one problem area at a time and define it.
   - Using feedback from the group, family members explore behavioral response options and the possible consequences of each.
   - Patient selects an ERP, and leaders elicit response options from the family and group. For example, if a patient is practicing exposure to leaving the house without checking appliances, the behavioral contract might be that the family gives a 10-minute "warning" when preparing to depart for an outing, then a 5-minute "warning," and if the patient is still checking, the agreement is that the family departs without the patient and without argument.

   To address reassurance seeking, a behavioral contract includes that the family's first responses are "What do you think I will say?" "What have I told you before?" and "What would the therapist say?" thereby placing the decision back on the patient and interrupting the reassurance compulsion cycle.
   - The leaders facilitate a negotiation process among family members.
   - When possible, the family rehearses the ERP and behavioral contract during the treatment session in vivo, thereby beginning to implement a new solution.

   As described, the group leaders actively guide one family at a time through the process of negotiating a behavioral contract, including all patients and family members

in the exercise. Families are instructed to renegotiate the contract if they find it too stringent.

3. Homework (10 minutes). Each patient selects individual exposure homework, and each family commits to a written behavioral contact homework.

Session 5: Behavioral Family Treatment Phase: "We Can Make a Difference!"

1. Check-in and go-round (30 minutes).
2. Continue behavioral contracting (80 minutes). Each family practices behavioral contracting in vivo. ERP with therapist and participant modeling should be used extensively. Each family is allotted 10–15 minutes.
3. Homework (10 minutes). Patients and relatives commit to ERP homework and family contracts.

Sessions 6–11: "Practice! Practice! Practice!" and "We Can Take Charge!"

The group leaders follow the previously described format for the remaining weekly sessions. Progressively, patients are increasingly responsible for devising the in vivo ERP task challenges and family contracts, an expectation cultivated by the leaders.

Session 12: Exposure, Contracting, and Termination: "We Have Tools to Do This on Our Own!" (Last Weekly Multifamily Session)

1. Check-in (30 minutes).
2. Go-round (45 minutes). Each family modifies or adds to existing contracts. Group members devise in vivo ERP tasks.

Each family presents the ERP plan for the next month.

3. Dealing with termination (25 minutes). Remind the group of the self-instructional nature of behavioral treatment. Review the steps that were taught: create hierarchy, assess distress levels, select exposure situation (either internal or external trigger), devise ERP challenge, record this on a form, and practice it repeatedly for long periods of time until anxiety decreases.
   - Initial anxiety will increase while using ERP.
   - Habituation takes time and practice.
   - Long-term gains are made through perseverance and commitment to treatment.
   - Encourage patients to refer to self-help workbooks.
   - Leaders are available to patients between monthly sessions.

4. Complete self-rated YBOCS and FAS-SR in the group (15 minutes).

5. Discuss monthly check-in sessions (5 minutes). Schedule dates and describe this as a trial period to develop confidence for independent individual ERP and family behavioral contracting.

Sessions 13–18: Monthly Check-in Sessions: "We Have the Tools to Beat Obsessive–Compulsive Disorder" (2 Hours)

The main purpose of these six sessions is to assist patients and their families in the transition from the leader-directed behavioral treatment to the self-instruction form of therapy. Check-in sessions ensure maintenance of treatment gains in the vulnerable period directly following the weekly 12 sessions. They also provide motivation.

Each session begins in typical fashion with the check-in and go-round, but no in vivo exposure takes place. Patients and family members report on homework tasks, contracts, successes, pitfalls, and general life events that may be influencing the OCD or interfering with behavioral therapy. Leaders are more passive, facilitating the group process and answering questions that require clinical clarification. Clinician-rated YBOCS are collected at each session for pre- and post-treatment comparisons.

At the last monthly session, issues related to treatment termination are acknowledged, and referrals are made for continued behavior therapy or medication if necessary. The FAS for each family in the group is completed. A post-treatment YBOCS under 16 is optimal.

Conclusion

Multifamily behavior treatment offers several advantages over standard individual behavioral treatment. It is cost-effective by allowing for the simultaneous treatment of five to seven patients and their family members with one or two therapists for 2 hours a week, compared to the same families treated individually requiring 10–14 hours of therapist time per week. This is a savings of up to 12 hours of therapist time per week.

As typically practiced, individual behavioral treatment offers little structured psychoeducation, support, or guidance for the family members who have to cope with the symptoms and demands imposed by OCD. MFBT can be modified to conduct family behavioral treatment with one patient and family members. In this age of managed care and short-term treatments, it makes sense to mobilize natural supports such as family systems. Once families understand OCD symptoms and are taught behavioral strategies, they can participate effectively in ERP with the OCD patient. This treatment offers a marked decrease in both cost for treatment and therapist time, as well as the possibility of improving long-term outcome.

References

Abramowitz, J. (2009). *Getting over OCD: A 10-step workbook for taking back your life.* Guilford.

Anderson, C., Reiss, D., & Hogarty, G. (1986). *Schizophrenia and the family.* Guilford.

Berardis, D., Campanella, D., Serroni, N., Ganbi, F., Carano, R., Nardella, E., Pizzorno, A., Cotellessa, C., Salerno, R., & Ferro, F. (2008). Insight and expressed emotion among adult outpatients with obsessive-compulsive disorder. *Journal of Psychiatric Practice, 14*(3), 154–159.

Calvocoressi, L., Mazure, C. M., Kasl, S. V., Skolnick, J., Fisk, D., Vegso, S. J., Van Noppen, B. L., & Price, L. H. (1999). Family accommodation of obsessive-compulsive symptoms: Instrument development and assessment of family behavior. *Journal of Nervous and Mental Disease, 187,* 636–642.

Goodman, W. K., Price, L. H., Rasmussen, S. A., Mazure, C., Delgado, P., Heninger, G. R., & Charney, D. S. (1989a). The Yale–Brown Obsessive Compulsive Scale: II. Validity. *Archives of General Psychiatry, 46*(11), 1012–1016.

Goodman, W. K., Price, L. H., Rasmussen, S. A., Mazure, C., Fleischmann, R. L., Hill, C. L., & Charney, D. S. (1989b). The Yale–Brown Obsessive Compulsive Scale: I. Development, use, and reliability. *Archives of General Psychiatry, 46*(11), 1006–1011.

Hyman, B., & Pedrick, C. (2010). *The OCD workbook.* New Harbinger.

Livingston-Van Noppen, B., Rasmussen, S. A., McCartney, L., & Eisen, J. L. (1990). Family function treatment in obsessive compulsive disorder. In M. Jenike, L. Baer, & W. Minichiello (Eds.), *Obsessive compulsive disorder: Theory and management* (pp. 325–341). Year Book.

McFarlane, W. R. (1983). *Family therapy in schizophrenia.* Guilford.

Pinto, A., Van Noppen, B., & Calvocoressi, L. (2013). Development and preliminary psychometric evaluation of a self-rated version of the Family Accommodation Scale for Obsessive–Compulsive Disorder. *Journal of Obsessive-Compulsive and Related Disorders, 2,* 457–465.

Sassano, S., Sapp, F., & Van Noppen, B. (2015). Cognitive behavior therapy for obsessive compulsive disorder. *APA Journal Focus, 13*(3), 148–161.

Shimshoni, Y., Shrinivasa, B., Cherian, A., & Lebowitz, E. R. (2019). Family accommodation in psychopathology: A synthesized review. *Indian Journal of Psychiatry, 61*(7), 93–103.

Steketee, G. (1999). *Overcoming obsessive-compulsive disorder: A behavioral and cognitive protocol for the treatment of OCD.* New Harbinger.

Steketee, G., Van Noppen, B., Lam, J., & Shapiro, L. (1998). Expressed emotion in families and the treatment of OCD. *In Session: Psychotherapy in Practice, 4*(3), 73–91.

Thompson-Hollands, J., Edson, A., Thompson, M., & Comer, J. (2014). Family involvement in the psychological treatment of obsessive–compulsive disorder. *Journal of Family Psychology, 28*(3), 287–298

Van Noppen, B. (2002). Multifamily behavioral treatment (MFBT) for OCD: A step-by-step model. *Brief Treatment and Crisis Intervention, 2*(2), 107–122.

Van Noppen, B., Pato, M., & Rasmussen, S. (1997). *Learning to live with OCD.* Obsessive Compulsive Foundation.

Van Noppen, B., & Steketee, G. (2003). Family responses and multifamily behavioral treatment of obsessive compulsive disorder. *Brief Treatment and Crisis Intervention, 3*(2), 231–248.

Van Noppen, B., & Steketee, G. (2009). Testing a conceptual model of patient and family predictors of obsessive compulsive disorder (OCD) symptoms. *Behavior Research and Therapy, 47,* 18–25.

Van Noppen, B., Steketee, G., McCorkle, B., & Pato, M. (1997). Group and multifamily behavioral treatment of obsessive compulsive disorder: A pilot study. *Journal of Anxiety Disorders, 11*(4), 431–446.

Wu, M. S., Pinto, A., Horng, B., Phares, V., McGuire, J. F., Dedrick, R. F., Van Noppen, B., Calvocoressi, L., & Storch, E. A. (2016). Psychometric properties of the Family Accommodation Scale for Obsessive–Compulsive Disorder–Patient Version. *Psychological Assessment, 2*(3), 251–262.

PART XIII

School Social Work

Evidence-Based Practice and School Social Work

Robert Lucio and James C. Raines

The field of school social work has come a long way during the past 100 years, from starting as "visiting teachers" in the early 1900s to becoming part of federal Individuals with Disabilities Education Act (IDEA) legislation in 1997 and developing professional organizations, all while unifying and expanding the profession. School social workers continue to demonstrate the ways in which they are vital as part of the school team to this day.

Brief History

School social work is rooted in two concurrent social policy movements following the industrial revolution of the 19th century. The first was child labor laws; the second was compulsory education (Butler, 1899; Mulkeen, 1986). These developments had an unforeseen effect: They brought incorrigible children into an educational system with needs the schools were ill-equipped to handle (Johanningmeier, 1986). Special classes had to be created for children who were "slow in mind and often defective in body, poor in family background, and lazy but defiant in school" (Richardson & Parker, 1993, p. 365). Social work in schools

began during the 1906–1907 school year in four major cities throughout the United States: Boston, Massachusetts; Hartford, Connecticut; New York, New York; and Chicago, Illinois (McCullagh, 1993, 2000, 2002a, 2002b). Until 1942, these social workers were known as visiting teachers (Shaffer & Fisher, 2017).

Legal Authority

School social work was recognized nationally when the Education for All Handicapped Children Act (P.L. 42-142) was passed in 1975. The federal definition of school social work services includes five broad activities:

> (i) Preparing a social or developmental history on a child with a disability; (ii) Group and individual counseling with the child and family; (iii) Working in partnership with parents and others on those problems in a child's living situation (home, school, and community) that affect the child's adjustment in school; (iv) Mobilizing school and community resources to enable the child to learn

as effectively as possible in his or her educational program; and (v) Assisting in developing positive behavioral intervention strategies. (Sec. 300.34(b) (14), p. 46761)

The latest regulations for IDEA indicated that these five services were meant to be illustrative, not exhaustive (U.S. Department of Education, 2006). When Congress passed the No Child Left Behind Act (NCLB; P.L. 107-110) in 2002, school social workers were also listed under one of three types of school-based mental health providers, which also includes school counselors and school psychologists. The current Every Student Succeeds Act (ESSA; P.L. 114-95), passed in 2015, left this situation intact.

School Social Work Association of America's National Model

The School Social Work Association of America's (SSWAA) national model was established in 2011 to meet two goals: (1) to provide a framework that delineates the knowledge and skills that can be reasonably expected from school social workers; and (2) to promote a consistent model for school social work services throughout the country for pre-service education, professional development, credentialing, and professional practice (Frey, et al., 2017). The three practice features identified were (1) provide evidence-based educational, behavioral, and mental health services; (2) promote a school climate and culture conducive to learning; and (3) maximize access to school-based and community-based resources.

Evidence-Based Practice

Evidence-based practice in schools began with the reauthorization of IDEA in 1997. Schools were expected to write "measurable

annual goals" for students with Individualized Education Programs. This expectation was increased under NCLB, which mentioned "scientifically based" interventions 122 times in 670 pages (Raines, 2008). This extremely rigorous standard was relaxed in ESSA to a more nuanced approach to "evidence-based" interventions with four levels of evidence (Raines, 2019):

- Strong evidence (based on randomized controlled trials)
- Moderate evidence (based on quasi-experimental designs)
- Promising evidence (based on correlational studies)
- Rationales (based on related research)

School social workers must be able to implement multi-tiered system of supports (MTSS) for students. This perspective requires school social workers to be familiar with universal prevention programs, targeted short-term or group interventions for at-risk youth, and intensive interventions for students with serious emotional or behavioral disorders. This MTSS approach also requires social workers know how to monitor students' response to interventions using objective measures (Avant & Swerdlik, 2016), such as school-wide screening or rapid assessment instruments (see Helpful Resources). Figure 134.1 provides a visual model of MTSS that shows each tier to be permeable based on student need.

School Climate

School social workers take a person-in-environment approach to student learning while also recognizing that a trauma-informed approach means taking an environment-in-person perspective because students often internalize past childhood traumas and exhibit their continuing reactions to adverse childhood experiences in a school setting (Dombo & Sabatino, 2019). Accordingly, school social workers (1) advocate for school policies and

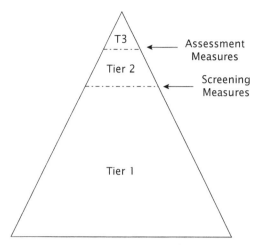

FIGURE 134.1 Multi-tiered system of supports.

procedures that provide safe and structured environments; (2) work to build capacity where school resources are thin or absent; and (3) establish supportive relationships between and within students, families, school staff, and community providers (Frey et al., 2017).

Maximizing Access

School social workers are called on to engage in macro practice (Brake & Roth, 2017; Thiede, 2005). This requires extensive knowledge with community resources, coordinating care between community providers and school, and identifying gaps in the social service delivery system. Furthermore, it means that school social workers challenge barriers to service delivery and work to creatively fill in cracks in an often-fragmented social service system. This can mean addressing ethnic and racial disparities in education and advocating for equal access to educational resources (Becerra, 2012).

Professionalization of School Social Work and School Mental Health

In 2009, Altshuler and Webb examined the professionalization of school social work compared to school counselors and school psychologists. They found that the requirements varied tremendously from state to state and even with districts within states. In fact, only 20 states required a Master of Social Work (MSW), 12 required a Bachelor of Social Work(BSW)/ Bachelor of Arts (BA), and 18 did not specify requirements at all. They surmised that one of the ways school social work could be considered more equal to the other professions in school mental health delivery was to achieve comparable certification standards across all states. Furthermore, they also believed that the school social work profession should identify relevant standards based on clinical practice with students and their families, professional collaboration with teachers and staff, and changing systemic barriers.

Since 2009, there has been a 50% increase in the number of states requiring an MSW (Table 134.1). Among states that did not have specific requirements, 6 now require an MSW. Nine states changed from requiring a bachelor's degree (BA or BSW) to requiring an MSW. Unfortunately, 30% of states still have no requirement specified. Of the states that require an MSW, 12 also require a state license to be held, 12 mandate that state universities certify the candidate, and 10 have specific courses that school social workers must complete.

Role of School Social Work

Several studies of school social workers have examined how they spend their time (Bye et al., 2009; Kelly et al., 2010; Whittlesey-Jerome, 2013). It was found that almost all school social workers engage in individual counseling, group counseling, and classroom groups. A majority of school social workers perform psychosocial evaluations and case management services. School social workers reported that more than 60% of their time is spent on secondary and tertiary prevention, whereas only 30% is spent on primary prevention. Prevention activities focused on school attendance, discipline problems, school climate, academic achievement, school violence, dropout prevention, and teen pregnancy (Bye et al., 2009).

TABLE 134.1 School Social Work Degree Requirement by State

State	2010	2020			
Alabama	NA	NA	Montana	NA	NA
Alaska	BSW	MSW	Nebraska	NA	NA
Arizona	NA	MSW	Nevada	MSW	MSW
Arkansas	NA	NA	New Hampshire	BSW	MSW
California	MSW	MSW	New Jersey	BSW	MSW
Colorado	MSW	MSW	New Mexico	BSW	BSW
Connecticut	MSW	MSW	New York	BA	MSW
Delaware	BSW	MSW	North Carolina	BSW	BSW
Florida	BSW	MSW	North Dakota	NA	NA
Georgia	BSW	MSW	Ohio	MSW	MSW
Hawaii	BSW	NA	Oklahoma	NA	NA
Idaho	MSW	MSW	Oregon	NA	MSW
Illinois	MSW	MSW	Pennsylvania	NA	MSW
Indiana	BSW	MSW	Rhode Island	NA	MSW
Iowa	MSW	MSW	South Carolina	NA	NA
Kansas	MSW	NA	South Dakota	NA	NA
Kentucky	MSW	MSW	Tennessee	NA	BSW
Louisiana	MSW	MSW	Texas	MSW	NA
Maine	NA	NA	Utah	MSW	MSW
Maryland	NA	MSW	Vermont	NA	MSW
Massachusetts	MSW	MSW	Virginia	MSW	MSW
Michigan	MSW	MSW	Washington	MSW	MSW
Minnesota	BSW	BSW	West Virginia	NA	NA
Mississippi	NA	NA	Wisconsin	MSW	MSW
Missouri	NA	NA	Wyoming	MSW	MSW

BSW, Bachelor of Social Work; MSW, Master of Social Work; NA, not applicable.

School social workers reported wanting more administrative decision-making and a lack of understanding of their roles and responsibilities by others as the most frequently cited survey responses (Peckover et al., 2013). When roles are not clear, there can be confusion about what school social workers do, and this can lead to duties being assigned to social workers that do not fit with their skills and training.

The current state of social work practice in schools points to a focus on clinical services for students already identified as at risk. Currently, school social workers have taken limited roles as leaders in prevention; improvement of school culture; and policy change at the local, state, and national levels (Kelly et al., 2010). Although there is no doubt that case management and attendance are valuable work, a shift in focus to a prevention model and school mental health creates an opportunity for school social workers to be leaders in this movement and affect both the broader systemic influences and student-level outcomes.

It has been suggested that school social workers can start by engaging teachers in a collaborative process by offering training and in-service opportunities to empower teachers; providing support for school personnel in dealing with academic and behavior problems; and being advocates for helping children, families, schools, and communities (Bye et al., 2009).

School Social Work and School Mental Health

Approximately one in five youth experiences a mental health disorder with severe distress or impact during their lifetime (Merikangas et al., 2010; Raines, 2019). Unfortunately, even among primary-age children, it is estimated that one in six will have a mental, behavioral, or developmental disorder (Cree et al., 2018; Whitney & Peterson, 2019). Anxiety disorders were most prevalent, reported in almost one in three (31.9%), followed by behavioral disorders (19.1%) and mood disorders (14.3%) (Merikangas et al., 2010). The mean age of onset was earliest for anxiety at 6 years; the mean age of onset was 11 years for behavioral problems and 13 years for mood disorders. Approximately 40% of youth meet the criteria for more than one disorder. The rate of mental health disorders is also rising among school-aged youth, with the rates of depression increasing by nearly 30% in the past decade (Mojtabai et al., 2016). School social workers have identified key issues that students face, including adjustment, behavioral problems, emotional issues, mental health problems, and traumatic experiences (Kelly & Frey, 2015). For instance, Kelly and Frey (2015) reported that with regard to mental health, 95.4% of social workers reported that they worked with youth who had eating disorders, followed by sexual identity issues (94.9%), substance use (79.2%) and suicidal ideation (74.2%).

Unfortunately, students with mental health needs do not always receive treatment. Between 25% and 50% of youth with a mental health need have received treatment in the previous year (Burns et al., 2004; Whitney & Peterson, 2019). When youth do receive treatment, approximately 80% of that treatment occurs in schools (Atkins et al., 2010). Traumatic experiences and mental health issues can impact academics, social and emotional well-being, and even lead to suicide (DeSocio & Hootman, 2004; Guzman et al., 2011; Larson et al., 2017; Murphy et al., 2015).

Research has shown that youth who identify as gay, lesbian, or bisexual are up to four times more likely to attempt suicide (Kann et al., 2018). Youth who are low income, youth of color, or have a disability are at higher risk of a mental health disorder (Alegria et al., 2010; Chandra & Minkovitz, 2006; Strang et al., 2012). Whether it is a lack of prevention programs, lack of access to care, lack of stable living conditions, or other related issues, school social workers are equipped to address both the students' needs and underlying barriers to care.

The SSWAA (n.d.) recognizes the need for school social workers to address these critical issues. The need for specialized skills is paramount in being able to provide evidence-based mental health services, promote a culture that supports student learning, and maximize access to resources in schools and communities. Fully addressing the mental health needs of youth requires school social workers to effectively work across all three levels of an MTSS.

Conclusion

The ability to identify students who are most at risk allows for the most efficient use of time and resources by school social workers. Targeting interventions to students who need them most enables school social workers to direct services where they are most vital, optimizing resources and allowing for school social workers to differentiate between individual and system concerns. This shift in thinking continues to build on the path that is being paved with evidence-based practice. Understanding the factors that help make students successful allows school social workers to partner with families and other systems in order to address those areas that present as a risk for academic and behavioral success.

Helpful Resources

Rapid Assessment Instruments

BERS-2: Behavioral and Emotional Rating Scale–Second Edition: https://www.proedinc.com/Products/11540/bers2-behavioral-and-emotional-rating-scalesecond-edition.aspx

Child and Adolescent Needs & Strengths (CANS): https://praedfoundation.org/tcom/tcom-tools/the-child-and-adolescent-needs-and-strengths-cans/

Fischer, J., & Corcoran, K. (2020). *Measures for clinical practice and research: A sourcebook. Volume 1: Couples, families, and children*. Oxford University Press. ISBN:9780190655792

Level of Stability Index for Children (LSIC): McMillan, J. D., & Abell, N (2006). Validating the Level of Stability Index for Children. *Research on Social Work Practice, 16*(3), 326–337.

Solution Focused Recovery Scale (SFRS): Kruczek, T., & Ægisdóttir, S. (2005). Adaptive coping in adolescent trauma survivors: A preliminary study of the Solution Focused Recovery Scale. *Traumatology, 11*(1), 41–55.

Universal Screeners

Behavioral and Emotional Screening System (BASC-3: BESS): https://www.pearsonassessments.com/store/usassessments/en/Store/Professional-Assessments/Behavior/Comprehensive/BASC-3-Behavioral-and-Emotional-Screening-System/p/100001482.html

Devereux Students Strengths Assessment–Mini: https://store.apperson.com/specialty-products/dessa-paper-forms?page=1

School Success Profile: https://schoolsuccessprofile.net

Social, Academic, & Emotional Behavior Risk Screener (SAEBRS): http://ebi.missouri.edu/?p=1116

Social Skills Improvement System: https://www.pearsonassessments.com/store/usassessments/en/Store/Professional-Assessments/Behavior/Social-Skills-Improvement-System-Performance-Screening-Guide/p/100000356.html

Strengths and Difficulties Questionnaire: https://www.sdqinfo.org/a0.html

Student Risk Screening Scale—Internalizing/Externalizing: http://www.ci3t.org/screening#srssie

Systematic Screening for Behavior Disorders: https://ancorapublishing.com/product/ssbd-classroom-screen-packet-grades-1-9

References

Alegria, M., Vallas, M., & Pumariega, A. J. (2010). Racial and ethnic disparities in pediatric mental health. *Child and Adolescent Psychiatric Clinics of North America, 19*(4), 759–774. https://doi.org/10.1016/j.chc.2010.07.001

Altshuler, S. J., & Webb, J. R. (2009). School social work: Increasing the legitimacy of the profession. *Children & Schools, 31*(4), 207–218.

Atkins, M. S., Hoagwood, K. E., Kutash, K., & Seidman, E. (2010). Toward the integration of education and mental health in schools. *Administration & Policy in Mental Health, 37*(1–2), 40–47.

Avant, D. W., & Swerdlik, M. E. (2016). A collaborative endeavor: The roles and functions of school social workers and school psychologists in implementing multi-tiered system of supports/response to intervention. *School Social Work Journal, 41*(1), 56–72.

Becerra, D. (2012). Perceptions of educational barriers affecting the academic achievement of Latino K–12 students. *Children & Schools, 34*(3), 167–177.

Brake, A., & Roth, B. (2017). Contemporary federal policy and school social work. In L. Villarreal Sosa, M. Alvarez, & T. Cox (Eds.), *School social work: National perspectives on practice in schools* (pp. 83–97). Oxford University Press.

Burns, B. J., Phillips, S. D., Wagner, H. R., Barth, R. P., Kolko, D. J., Campbell, Y., & Landsverk, J. (2004). Mental health need and access to mental health services by youths involved with child welfare: A national survey. *Journal of the American Academy of Child and Adolescent Psychiatry, 43*(8), 960–970.

Butler, A. W. (1899). Indiana [Reports from states]. In I. C. Barrows (Ed.), *Proceedings of the National Conference of Charities & Corrections at the 25th annual session held in the city of New York, May 18–25, 1898* (pp. 45–47). Ellis.

Bye, L., Shepard, M., Partridge, J., & Alvarez, M. (2009). School social work outcomes: Perspectives of school social workers and school administrators. *Children & Schools, 31*(2), 97–108.

Chandra, A., & Minkovitz, C. S. (2006). Stigma starts early: Gender differences in teen willingness to use mental health services. *Journal of Adolescent Health, 38*(6), 754.e751–754.e758.

Cree, R. A., Bitsko, R. H., Robinson, L. R., Holbrook, J. R., Danielson, M. L., Smith, C., Kaminski, J. W., Kenney, M. K., & Peacock, G. (2018). Health care, family, and community factors associated with mental, behavioral, and developmental disorders and poverty among children aged 2–8 years—United States, 2016. *Morbidity and Mortality Weekly Report, 67*(50), 1377–1383.

DeSocio, J., & Hootman, J. (2004). Children's mental health and school success. *Journal of School Nursing, 20*(4), 189–196.

Dombo, E. A., & Sabatino, C. A. (2019). *Creating trauma-informed schools: A guide for school social workers and educators*. Oxford University Press.

Frey, A., Raines, J. C., Sabatino, C. A., Alvarez, M., Lindsey, B., McInerney, A., & Streeck, F. (2017). The National School Social Work practice model. In L. Villarreal Sosa, M. Alvarez, & T. Cox (Eds.), *School social work: National perspectives on practice in schools* (pp. 27–38). Oxford University Press.

Guzman, M. P., Jellinek, M., George, M., Hartley, M., Squicciarini, A. M., Canenguez, K. M., Kuhlthau, K. A., Yucel, R., White, G. W., Guzman, J., & Murphy, J. M. (2011). Mental health matters in elementary school: First-grade screening predicts fourth grade achievement test scores. *European Child & Adolescent Psychiatry, 20*(8), 401–411. https://doi.org/10.1007/s00787-011-0191-3

Johanningmeier, E. V. (1986). Compulsory education in the United States: Its development and some recent considerations. In G. Genovesi (Ed.), *Compulsory education: Schools, pupils, teachers, programs and methods. Conference papers for the 8th session of the International Standing Conference for the History of Education (Parma, Italy, September 3–6, 1986).* Vol. IV, pp. 161–170. ERIC document ED 279–101.

Kann, L., McManus, T., Harris, W. A., Shanklin, S. L., Flint, K. H., Queen, B., Lowry, R., Chyen, D., Whittle, L., Thornton, J., Lim, C., Bradford, D., Yamakawa, Y., Leon, M., Brener, N., & Ethier, K. A. (2018). Youth Risk Behavior Surveillance—United States, 2017. *Morbidity and Mortality Weekly Report, 67*(8), 1–114.

Kelly, M. S., Berzin, S. C., Frey, A., Alvarez, M., Shaffer, G., & O'Brien, K. (2010). The state of school social work: Findings from the National School Social Work Survey. *School Mental Health Journal, 2*(3), 132–141.

Kelly, M. S., & Frey, A. J. (2015). The state of school social work: Revisited. *School Mental Health, 7*(3), 174–183.

Larson, S., Chapman, S., Spetz, J., & Brindis, C. (2017). Chronic childhood trauma, mental health, academic achievement, and school-based health center mental health services. *Journal of School Health, 87*(9), 675–686.

McCullagh, J. G. (1993). The roots of school social work in New York City. *Iowa Journal of School Social Work, 6*(1–2), 49–74.

McCullagh, J. G. (2000). School social work in Chicago: An unrecognized pioneer program. *School Social Journal, 25*(1), 1–15.

McCullagh, J. G. (2002a). The inception of school social work in Boston: Clarifying and expanding the historical record. *School Social Work Journal, 26*(2), 58–67.

McCullagh, J. G. (2002b). School social work in Hartford, Connecticut: Correcting the historical record. *Journal of Sociology and Social Welfare, 29*(2), 93–103.

Merikangas, K. R., He, J.-P., Burstein, M., Swanson, S. A., Avenevoli, S., Cui, L., Benjet, C., Georgiades, K., & Swendsen, J. (2010). Lifetime prevalence of mental disorders in U.S. adolescents: Results from the National Comorbidity Survey Replication–Adolescent Supplement (NCS-A). *Journal of the American Academy of Child and Adolescent Psychiatry, 49*(10), 980–989. https://doi.org/10.1016/j.jaac.2010.05.017

Mojtabai, R., Olfson, M., & Han, B. (2016). National trends in the prevalence and treatment of depression in adolescents and young adults. *Pediatrics, 138*(6), e20161878.

Mulkeen, T. A. (1986). The compulsory curriculum in industrial America: Connections between past and present. In G. Genovesi (Ed.), *Compulsory education: Schools, pupils, teachers, programs and methods. Conference papers for the 8th session of the International Standing Conference for the History of Education (Parma, Italy, September 3–6, 1986).* Vol. III, pp. 189–201. ERIC document ED 279-100.

Murphy, J. M., Guzmán, J., McCarthy, A. E., Squicciarini, A. M., George, M., Canenguez, K. M., Dunn, E. C., Baer, L., Simonsohn, A., Smoller, J. W., & Jellinek, M. S. (2015). Mental health predicts better academic outcomes: A longitudinal study of elementary school students in Chile. *Child Psychiatry and Human Development, 46*(2), 245–256. https://doi.org/10.1007/s10578-014-0464-4

Peckover, C. A., Vasquez, M. L., Van Housen, S. L., Saunders, J. A., & Allen, L. (2013). Preparing school social workers for the future: An update of school social workers' tasks in Iowa. *Children & Schools, 35*(1), 9–17.

Raines, J. C. (2008). *Evidence-based practice in school mental health: A primer for school social workers, psychologists, and counselors.* Oxford University Press.

Raines, J. C. (Ed.). (2019). *Evidence-based practice in school mental health: Addressing DSM-5 disorders in schools.* Oxford University Press.

Richardson, J. G., & Parker, T. L. (1993). The institutional genesis of special education: The American case. *American Journal of Education, 101*(4), 359–392.

School Social Work Association of America. (n.d.). *School social workers' role in addressing students' mental health needs and increasing academic achievement.* https://www.sswaa.org/copy-of-about-school-social-work

Shaffer, G. L., & Fisher, R. A. (2017). History of school social work. In L. Villarreal Sosa, T. Cox, & M. Alvarez (Eds.) *School social work: National perspectives on practice in schools* (pp. 7–26). Oxford University Press.

Strang, J. F., Kenworth, L., Daniolos, P., Case, L., Willis, M. C., Martin, A., & Wallace, G. L. (2012).

Depression and anxiety symptoms in children and adolescents with autism spectrum disorders without intellectual disability. *Research in Autism Spectrum Disorders, 6*(1), 406–412.

Thiede, C. E. (2005). A macro approach to meet the challenge of No Child Left Behind. *School Social Work Journal, 29*(2), 1–24.

U.S. Department of Education. (2006). Assistance to states for the education of children with disabilities and preschool grants for children with disabilities: Final rule. *Federal Register, 71*(156), 46540–46845.

Whitney, D. G., & Peterson, M. D. (2019). US national and state-level prevalence of mental health disorders and disparities of mental health care use in children. *JAMA Pediatrics, 173*(4), 389–391.

Whittlesey-Jerome, W. (2013). Results of the 2010 statewide New Mexico school social work survey: Implications for evaluation the effectiveness of school social work. *School Social Work Journal, 37*(2), 76–87.

Trauma-Informed Schools

Eileen A. Dombo and Christine Anlauf Sabatino

We are currently in the midst of a storm of national challenges, including the COVID-19 pandemic, racism, and educational disparities. State and local school officials struggle to address the intersection between social constructions of health, race, ethnicity, class, and ability with issues of educational advantage and disadvantage. Add to this mix collective trauma, historical trauma, and complex trauma that "leave traces on our minds and emotions, on our capacity for joy and intimacy, and even our biology and immune system" (Van der Kolk, 2014, p. 1) and today's students bring to school deeply disturbing experiences that interfere with school success in many different ways.

According to Atkins et al. (2010), schools have become the default mental health provider for children and adolescents. This thesis was recognized in 2015 with passage of the Every Student Succeeds Act (P.L. 114-95). Under Title I, Specialized Instructional Support Personnel were authorized to improve relevant student skills outside academic subject matter with school-based mental health services. Under Title II, these mental health services were expected to provide "in-service training of school personnel to educate their colleagues about specific topics" (Raines, 2019, p. 30).

School social workers are trained to work with students with mind-numbing experiences; wounds from previous generations; and occurrences of child maltreatment, including emotional abuse and neglect, sexual abuse, physical abuse, and witnessing domestic violence. More important, school social workers' ecological and holistic approach uniquely positions them to work with colleagues to create a multi-tiered supportive school climate that incorporates factors of diversity, equity, and inclusion in comprehensive school programs.

This chapter is a brief guide for creating trauma-informed school environments for children. It discusses the impact of trauma on development and academic learning; the connection between trauma, learning disorders, and special education placement; pillars of a safe school environment and principles of trauma-informed services; and developing a theory of change to demonstrate accountability. For more detail, see Dombo and Sabatino (2019).

The Impact of Trauma on Learning

Every adult who engages with children in schools must understand that one of the risk factors to school success is the impact of trauma on the child's ability to learn. Although individual factors of strengths and resilience can help a child overcome this risk factor, school systems must work to become a protective factor for the child. The defining aspect of trauma is that the experiences overwhelm the child's capacity to cope so that the aftereffects of the event (referred to as sequelae), create behavioral, emotional, psychological, and social problems in functioning. Roughly 50% of children and adolescents who experience trauma develop post-traumatic stress disorder (Afifi & Macmillan, 2011). The type, duration, and severity of the traumatic experiences are the factors that inform the experience turning into a disorder. It is also important to note that rates of revictimization are high; there is a 69% chance for children with trauma to experience additional forms of maltreatment (Lawson, 2009; Pears et al., 2008). Typically, traumatic experiences are divided into two categories: those that are interpersonal in nature (neglect, physical abuse, and sexual abuse) and those that are not (natural disasters and accidents). Interpersonal trauma, with the experience of abuse coming from someone a child is supposed to be able to trust and rely on, can create sequelae know as complex trauma and betrayal trauma. These experiences impact the child's ability to manage emotions and develop safe and secure relationships (Cook et al., 2005). Annually, there are approximately 1 million substantiated childhood abuse reports in the United States (D'Andrea et al., 2012).

Sequelae of Trauma in Children and Adolescents

Each individual experience of trauma is unique; however, there are some general sequelae that are helpful to understand. They are presented here in the areas of biological, psychological, behavioral, social, and spiritual dimensions for children and adolescents.

Biological Sequelae

Traumatic experiences activate the brain's natural "alarm" systems, and these natural stress responses create fight/flight/freeze reactions. Over time, sustained trauma reactions can lead to somatic expressions of trauma such as stomachaches, immune disorders, and other physical issues (De Bellis & Zisk, 2014). Because neurological development continues throughout childhood and adolescence, trauma can have negative impacts on developmental milestones and processes, depending on the timing of these experiences. Earlier traumatic experiences will impact neurological developmental functions, which in turn influence later developmental milestones (Davis et al., 2015). Particular effects are seen in attention, executive functioning, and IQ, especially when the trauma occurs before age 9 years (Pears et al., 2008). Because the child's environment can provide protective factors, a negative trajectory is not inescapable (Afifi & Macmillan, 2011). Many of the behaviors seen in children who have experienced trauma have a brain component. Being curious about why a child is acting hypervigilant or emotionally dysregulated is a good place to start. This requires a shift in the questions that schools ask about children. Instead of asking a child "What's wrong with you?" the question becomes "What happened to you?" Understanding the connections between trauma, neurobiology, and academic success is particularly important for those in school settings.

Psychological and Behavioral Sequelae

Children who experience abuse and neglect often lack the opportunity to develop safe and secure attachments with adults. This means they often lack skills necessary to navigate their environment and develop constructive coping mechanisms to employ when there is a negative experience. Without these essential foundations, the child can develop problematic coping mechanisms and is at higher risk of developing mental health disorders (Milot et al., 2010). They often show symptoms of re-experiencing, avoidance, and hyperarousal that may not be easily identifiable as trauma reactions (D'Andrea et al., 2012). Approximately 40% of children with trauma histories have mood and anxiety disorders (Copeland et al., 2007). In young children, this can present in a generalized fear, regression to earlier developmental stages, separation anxiety, irritability, hypervigilance, and rumination. These are referred to as *internalizing disorders* and are often not seen as part of trauma symptoms. In addition, they are often not flagged as problems in school settings if they do not present as behavioral issues in the classroom. *Externalizing disorders* are more disruptive in classroom environments and are more commonly the focus of attention. Children who are disruptive in classroom settings due to not paying attention, being hyperactive, being defiant and oppositional, and being aggressive with peers tend be the ones who get more attention (O'Hare, 2016).

Trauma can also be expressed through aggression, social isolation, and somatic symptoms such as head- and stomachaches. These issues may develop along with problems concentrating and learning (Hunt et al., 2017). Flat affect, explosive anger, and inappropriate affect are also common indicators of a deficit in self-regulation (D'Andrea et al., 2012). As children become adolescents, unaddressed trauma may lead to acting out behaviors that are dangerous and coping behaviors that are self-harming, as well as detachment from others, increased shame and guilt, and intense emotions (Peh et al., 2017). Sleep and eating disorders, personality-related problems, confusion around sense of self and identity, increased dissociation, sexual difficulties, mood and anxiety disorders, suicidal thoughts and impulses, and hyperactivity and hyperarousal are common challenges as well (Lawson, 2009).

Many adolescents in this situation can develop substance use disorders if they turn to alcohol and other drugs to cope (Alvarez-Alonso et al., 2016).

Educators and school social workers must learn to view undesirable behaviors as coping strategies. Understanding that children and adolescents who act out behaviorally do so because they lack the skills to control their behavior, not because they are choosing to "be bad," is crucial to being trauma-informed.

Social and Spiritual Sequelae

When trauma is caused by someone who is supposed to care for a child, the boundaries of that relationship have been violated. Boundaries are the foundation of healthy social relationships. Key social skills such as understanding how to engage in social situations, read social cues, and perceive the perspective of another person have been found to be inhibited in, and lead to social isolation for, children who experience trauma (D'Andrea et al., 2012; G. Elliott et al., 2005). Although we understand that children who can be socially inappropriate may be socially off-putting, it is important to view this behavior as communication that the child needs help learning how to navigate social situations.

Childhood trauma can also impact trust in God or a higher power (Gall et al., 2007), and this aspect is often overlooked. Religion and spirituality can serve as protective factors for mental health disorders (Howell & Miller-Graff, 2014) because many practices offer help coping with adversity (Farley, 2007). However, children and adolescents may turn away from family traditions and practices after trauma (Feinson & Meir, 2015). Spirituality has also been shown to be connected to social supports, particularly for adolescents, who can benefit from a community, especially when family connections are not safe (Howell & Miller-Graff, 2014). This has particular implications for those in faith-based school settings. Children who are socially isolated, have difficulty forming friends, or have sudden changes in spirituality or religiosity may have experienced trauma.

Adverse Childhood Experiences

In their groundbreaking study examining more than 17,000 children in Southern California using physical examinations and surveys concerning childhood experiences, current health status, and behaviors, the Centers for Disease Control and Prevention and Kaiser Permanente explored whether negative childhood experiences affect an individual's health and well-being throughout their life. They discovered what are now referred to as adverse childhood experiences (ACEs) that pose strong risk factors regarding health and overall functioning throughout a person's life (U.S. Department of Health and Human Services, 2016). Initially, there were 10 types of ACEs a child could be exposed to in their home: emotional abuse, emotional neglect, physical abuse, sexual abuse, physical neglect, witnessing the mother being treated violently, the presence of substance abuse, mental illness of a family member, parental separation or divorce, and the incarceration of a family member.

The ACEs study indicated that two out of three participants lived through at least one ACE, and one in four reported having three or more (U.S. Department of Health and Human Services, 2016). An additional finding is that the higher number of adverse experiences, the higher the chance of health and mental health problems, such as disrupted neurological development; impaired social, emotional, and cognitive functioning; risky health behaviors; poorer health outcomes; and early death. Later work on ACEs found that community trauma also plays a significant role, with adverse experiences occurring in a collective, not solely individual, experience, such as poverty, racism, and other forms of structural violence (Pinderhughes et al., 2015). For children in schools, this exposure to trauma can negatively influence their ability to function successfully in traditional learning environments. In addition to the 10 ACEs categories, children can be exposed to the trauma experienced by parents while still developing in utero (Sandman et al., 2012). Other types of traumatic experiences not addressed in the ACEs study include traumatic loss, medical trauma, natural disasters, immigration and refugee experiences, terrorism, and human trafficking.

Relationship Between Trauma, Learning Disorders, and Special Education Placement

Children who have experienced childhood trauma are more likely to have learning disorders, higher rates of school absences, increased likelihood to drop out of school, and more suspensions and expulsions (Perfect et al., 2016). Traumatic events, especially chronic trauma, can adversely affect a child's ability to concentrate and organize information and can impact memory and cognition (National Child Traumatic Stress Network Schools Committee, 2008). Often, these children go unnoticed and underserved in our education system, based on criteria outlined in the Individuals with Disabilities in Education Act (IDEA). One in five children have mental health conditions that cause educational impairment. However, only 1% of the school-age population receive special education supports under the "emotional disturbance" classification in IDEA (Barnett, 2012). As a result, many traumatized children go undetected and are not referred for special education services to address their academic needs, which can have long-term impacts on their education and future (Winder, 2015).

Children who have high ACEs scores are more likely to have an increased number of mental health diagnoses, less likely to be engaged in school, and more likely to be retained in grade and have an Individualized Educational Plan (Porche et al., 2016). Both cognitive and behavioral functioning are impacted by trauma, as research shows that these children have lower IQ scores, lower verbal functioning, and difficulty with memory, as well as problems with discipline, poor attendance rates, and high dropout rates (Perfect et al., 2016). For example, a child who is overwhelmed by emotions and has difficulty concentrating in class may be misidentified as "explosive" or "inattentive." Because research indicates that there is a positive association between children's mental health services and academic outcomes (Becker et al., 2014), social workers in schools have a clear rationale for assessing trauma as part of special education evaluations and championing the creation of trauma-informed schools.

Creating Safe Environments: The Pillars and Principles of Trauma Care in Schools

Central to creating a trauma-informed school is ensuring that three pillars of trauma-informed care are present in all interactions: safety, connection, and regulation (Bath, 2008). Safety a subjective "felt sense" that can often be difficult to describe. It is felt through connections with people who have a calm and focused presence. In schools, this means remaining attuned to the child's actions, words, and nonverbal communications and respecting their boundaries and rights. Safety is also about feeling in control and having power. The child is allowed to make their own decisions as much as is developmentally appropriate. When adults use their power to punish, children do not feel safe. When searching for safe people, children look for predictability and consistency. Following through on what you say you will do and avoiding unsafe behaviors are essential. To establish safety, stay calm, self-regulated, and attuned when the child is dysregulated, aggressive, or out of control (Dombo & Sabatino, 2019).

Traumatic experiences can teach children that connection with others is unsafe. Although connection may feel risky for some, it is an important pillar for trauma-informed work (Bath, 2008). Power struggles or imbalances can drive disconnection, and school environments create many situations in which children and adults grapple over who is in charge. These dynamics can unwittingly re-enact traumatic experiences for children when adults have negative reactions to safety-seeking behaviors (van der Kolk, 2005). Avoiding power struggles, honoring the need for safety and respect, establishing predictable routines and clear rules and boundaries, and paying close attention to behavior will help with connection. When a child acts in a dysregulated manner, responding with a curious and neutral stance while noticing the behavior will help foster connection (Dombo & Sabatino, 2019).

The third pillar of trauma-informed care is emotional regulation, which is the ability to manage feelings and impulses. Difficulty tolerating distress, identifying emotions, and engaging in self-soothing actions are common for children who have experienced trauma (van der Kolk, 2005). Many of these skills will need to be taught in the school setting because they were not learned at home. Modeling these behaviors is a good starting point, as are other opportunities to teach about emotions as if they were a new language, because they are (Dombo & Sabatino, 2019). Co-regulating, or working with the child to calm down, is also very effective (Bath, 2008). The three pillars of trauma-informed care can be applied to schools in many creative ways.

In addition to the pillars of trauma care with children and adolescents, clinicians and researchers generally agree on the following set of principles necessary to create trauma-informed environments (D. Elliott et al., 2005):

- Recognize the impact of trauma on development and coping behaviors.
- Place recovery from trauma as a primary goal.

- Use an empowerment model.
- Maximize the individual's control over their recovery process.
- Use relational collaboration.
- Address need for safety, acceptance, and respect.
- Focus on adaptation and resilience in a strengths-based manner.
- Minimize potential for more traumatic experiences.
- Strive for cultural competence.
- Involve consumers in program design and evaluation.
- Address vicarious trauma.

Each principle is explored in more detail in Dombo and Sabatino (2019).

Evaluation: Demonstrating Accountability

In an era of financial constraint, school systems are forced to curtail their budgets and sometimes view school social work services as an area to cut expenditures. Hence, it is critically important to provide demonstrably effective benefits, especially with new or innovative programs such as trauma-informed school social work services.

There are two important resources that help school social workers think through the critical elements for establishing compelling evidence for the school system. The Kellogg Foundation's (2004) *Logic Model Development Guide* teaches practitioners and researchers how to articulate the theory of change or logic model, which is a visual statement of the activities and the results you expect to obtain. It is a conceptual framework for describing, planning, implementing, and evaluating trauma-informed practices in schools.

The process begins by bringing together all stakeholders, including administrative

leadership, school personnel, community collaborators, and parents and students, to increase their knowledge of trauma and motivate their interest in tackling the issue of trauma and its effect on the teaching–learning process. The value of this work at the start of an initiative cannot be underestimated, and social workers are the natural choice to lead it. Developing this tool helps create consensus and generates support through its declaration of what is to be accomplished and how.

An approach by Fixsen et al. (2005) expanded the movement for evidence-based programs and practice to discuss the unaddressed issue of fidelity when implementing programs for high-quality outcomes. Implementation is defined as "a specified set of activities designed to put into practice an activity or program of known dimensions" (p. 5). They discuss core components and stages of implementation to confirm effective and efficient methods to evaluate innovative mental health programs and practices.

Following the recommendations outlined in the two previously mentioned resources is a tall order, and not all components of a logic model or elements of implementation fidelity will be fully realized. Even so, the fact that deliberation was given to the key components of each approach and they are considered and reported serves to identify gaps that need to be filled, provides data for necessary improvement, and suggests future directions for the school.

Conclusion

As Sabatino (2014) notes, "Schools experience enormous pressure from public officials and community stakeholder to develop effective school programs that address the needs of at-risk populations and demonstrate value for tax dollars" (p. 44). The healing power of school is real. School social workers have an unambiguous and clear role in helping school personnel understand how integrated trauma-informed prevention and early intervention programs ameliorate major human, interpersonal, and social barriers to behavioral and academic success.

Human growth and development are located not just within an individual but also in the collective effort of society. Trauma-informed schools provide a bridge that connects the lived experience of abused children and adolescents with their local school environment. An important pathway to school success for wounded students lies in the fusion of multi-tiered systems of school social work services with knowledge about child and adolescent trauma.

Helpful Resources

Child Mind Institute: https://childmind.org
Conscious Discipline Model: https://consciousdiscipline.com
National Child Traumatic Stress Network: https://www.nctsn.org
School Social Work Association of America: https://www.sswaa.org
Trauma Sensitive Schools: https://traumasensitiveschools.org

References

Afifi, T. O., & Macmillan, H. L. (2011). Resilience following child maltreatment: A review of protective factors. *Canadian Journal of Psychiatry, 56,* 266–272.

Alvarez-Alonso, M. J., Jurado-Barba, R., Martinez-Martin, N., Espin-Jaime, J. C., Bolaños-Porrero, C. Ordoñez-Franco, A., & Rubio, G. (2016). Association between maltreatment and polydrug use among adolescents. *Child Abuse & Neglect, 51,* 379–389.

Atkins, M. S., Hoagwood, K. E., Kutash, K., & Seidman, E. (2010). Toward the integration of education and mental health in schools. *Administration & Policy in Mental Health, 37*(1–2), 40–47.

Barnett, D. (2012). A grounded theory for identifying students with emotional disturbance: Promising practices for assessment, intervention, and service delivery. *Contemporary School Psychology, 16*(1), 21–31.

Bath, H. (2008). The three pillars of trauma-informed care. *Reclaiming Children and Youth, 17*(3), 17–21.

Becker, K., Brandt, N., Stephan, S., & Chorpita, B. (2014). A review of educational outcomes in the children's mental health treatment literature. *Advances in School Mental Health Promotion, 7*(1), 5–23.

Cook, A., Spinazzola, J., Ford, J., Lanktree, C., Blaustein, M., Cloitre, M., & Van der Kolk, B. (2005). Complex trauma. *Psychiatric Annals, 35*(5), 390–398.

Copeland, W. E., Keeler, G., Angold, A., & Costello, E. J. (2007). Traumatic events and posttraumatic stress in childhood. *Archives of General Psychiatry, 64,* 577–584.

D'Andrea, W., Ford, J., Stolbach, B., Spinazzola, J., & van der Kolk, B. A. (2012). Understanding interpersonal trauma in children: Why we need a developmentally appropriate trauma diagnosis. *American Journal of Orthopsychiatry, 82*(2), 187–200.

Davis, A. S., Moss, L. E., Nogin, M. M., & Webb, N. E. (2015). Neuropsychology of child maltreatment and implications for school psychologists. *Psychology in the Schools, 52*(1), 77–91.

De Bellis, M. D., & Zisk, A. (2014). The biological effects of childhood trauma. *Child and Adolescent Psychiatric Clinics of North America, 23*(2), 185–222.

Dombo, E. A., & Sabatino, C. A. (2019). *Creating trauma-informed schools: A handbook for school social workers and educators.* Oxford University Press.

Elliott, D., Bjelajac, P., Fallot, R., Markoff, L., & Reed, B. (2005). Trauma-informed or trauma-denied: Principles and implementation of trauma-informed services for women. *Journal of Community Psychology, 33*(4), 461–477.

Elliott, G. C., Cunningham, S. M., Linder, M., Colangelo, M., & Gross, M. (2005). Child physical abuse and self-perceived social isolation among adolescents. *Journal of Interpersonal Violence, 20,* 1663–1684.

Farley, Y. R. (2007). Making the connection: Spirituality, trauma, and resilience. *Journal of Religion and Spirituality in Social Work, 26*(1), 1–15.

Feinson, M., & Meir, A. (2015). Exploring mental health consequences of childhood abuse and the relevance of religiosity. *Journal of Interpersonal Violence, 30*(3), 499–521.

Fixsen, D. L., Naoom, S. F., Blase, K. A., Friedman, R. M., & Wallace, F. (2005). *Implementation research: A synthesis of the literature* (FMHI Publication No. 231). University of South Florida, Louis de la Parte Florida Mental Health Institute, the National Implementation Research Network.

Gall, T. L., Basque, V., Damasceno-Scott, M., & Vardy, G. (2007). Spirituality and the current adjustment of adult survivors of childhood sexual abuse. *Journal for the Scientific Study of Religion, 46,* 101–117.

Howell, K. H., & Miller-Graff, L. E. (2014). Protective factors associated with resilient functioning in young adulthood after childhood exposure to violence. *Child Abuse & Neglect, 38*, 1985–1994.

Hunt, T. K. A., Slack, K. S., & Berger, L. M. (2017). Adverse childhood experiences and behavioral problems in middle childhood. *Child Abuse & Neglect, 67*, 391–402.

Lawson, D. M. (2009). Understanding and treating children who experience interpersonal maltreatment: Empirical findings. *Journal of Counseling & Development, 87*(2), 204–215.

Milot, T., Éthier, L. S., St.-Laurent, D., & Provost, M. A. (2010). The role of trauma symptoms in the development of behavioral problems in maltreated preschoolers. *Child Abuse & Neglect, 34*(4), 225–234.

National Child Traumatic Stress Network Schools Committee. (2008). *Child trauma toolkit for educators*. National Center for Child Traumatic Stress.

O'Hare, T. (2016). *Essential skills of social work practice: Assessment, intervention, and evaluation*. Oxford University Press.

Pears, K. C., Kim, H. K., & Fisher, P. A. (2008). Psychosocial and cognitive functioning of children with specific profiles of maltreatment. *Child Abuse & Neglect, 32*(10), 958–971.

Peh, C. X., Shahwan, S., Fauziana, R., Mahesh, M. V., Sambasivam, R., Zhang, Y., Ong, S., Chong, S., & Subramaniam, M. (2017). Emotional dysregulation as a mechanism linking child maltreatment exposure and self-harm behaviors in adolescents. *Child Abuse & Neglect, 67*, 383–390.

Perfect, M., Turley, M., Carlson, J., Yohanna, J., & Gilles, M.P.S. (2016). School-related outcomes of traumatic event exposure and traumatic stress symptoms in students: A systematic review of research from 1990-2015. *School Mental Health, 8*(1), 7–43.

Pinderhughes, H., Davis, R., & Williams, M. (2015). *Adverse community experiences and resilience: A framework for addressing and preventing community trauma*. Prevention Institute.

Porche, M., Costello, D., & Rosen-Reynoso, M. (2016). Adverse family experiences, child mental health, and educational outcomes for a national sample of students. *School Mental Health, 8*(1), 44–60.

Raines, J. C. (2019). *Evidence-based practices in school mental health: Addressing DSM-5 disorders in schools* (2nd ed.). Oxford University Press.

Sabatino, C. A. (2014). *Consultation theory and practice: A handbook for school social workers*. Oxford University Press.

Sandman, C. A., Davis, E. P., Buss, C., & Glynn, L. M. (2012). Exposure to prenatal psychobiological stress exerts programming influences on the mother and her fetus. *Neuroendocrinology, 95*(1), 8–21.

U.S. Department of Health and Human Services, National Center for Injury Prevention and Control, Division of Violence Prevention. (2016). About the CDC–Kaiser ACE study. https://www.cdc.gov/violenceprevention/acestudy/about.html

van der Kolk, B. A. (2005). Developmental trauma disorder: Toward a rational diagnosis for children with complex trauma histories. *Psychiatric Annals, 35*(5), 401–408.

van der Kolk, B. A. (2014). *The body keeps the score: Brain, mind, and body in the healing of trauma*. Viking Press.

W. K. Kellogg Foundation. (2004). *Logic model development guide*. https://www.wkkf.org/resource-directory/resources/2004/01/logic-model-development-guide

Winder, F. (2015). Childhood trauma and special education: Why the "IDEA" is failing today's impacted youth. *Hofstra Law Review, 44*(2), 601.

Violence Prevention in Schools

Matthew J. Cuellar

School safety has become a priority for the people of the United States. Resultantly, a growing trend in today's schools is the implementation of violence prevention strategies and policies designed to reduce the occurrence of school-based violence. This chapter provides an overview of the prevalence of violence in schools, what violence prevention looks like in schools today, and the role social workers can play in violence prevention in schools moving forward.

Prevalence of Violence in Today's Schools

Based on results from the most recent School Survey on Crime and Safety (SSOCS), a nationally representative database from school administrators throughout the United States, schools are generally safe places for youth. In fact, literature suggests trends in school violence are heading in a desirable direction. For example, between 2001 and 2017, the percentage of students aged 12–18 years who reported being victimized at school decreased from 6% to 2%.

Although data suggest the trend in occurrence of lethal violence in school is declining, it is still a serious concern that must be addressed. According to SSOCS, there were 38 reported cases of school-associated violent deaths during the 2015–2016 school year. A total of 18 of the 1,478 homicides involving school-aged youth (ages 5–18 years) in the United States occurred at school during the same school year. Finally, during the same period, 3 of the 1,941 total suicides of school-age youth occurred at school (Musu et al., 2019).

Current research suggests educators might perceive homicides and lethal school violence as among the most common threats to daily student safety (Ewton, 2014). However, nonfatal day-to-day violence is much more common, particularly in inner-city school districts and in schools that serve older youth (Cuellar & Coyle, 2020). In fact, school-aged students experienced approximately 827,000 nonlethal victimizations (i.e., theft and nonfatal violent victimization) at school and 503,800 total victimizations away from school, representing a victimization rate of roughly 33 victimizations per 1,000 students at school (Musu et al., 2019). Elementary school serving professionals, male students, and public school systems report the highest degree of violence and victimization in school (Musu et al., 2019).

What Is Violence Prevention in Schools?

Violence prevention in schools broadly refers to any proactive approach to reducing the occurrence of maladaptive and harmful student behavior in school. Violence prevention methods can vary by school. These methods have been classified a number of ways. Nickerson and Spears (2007) provide the most parsimonious framework for classifying violence prevention strategies in schools. They assert that school safety strategies can be grouped into two categories: authoritarian and educational/therapeutic. The authoritarian approach assumes the use of restricted autonomy to prevent school violence, often involving the deployment of police or the application of security hardware (e.g., metal detectors, security cameras, school policing, and zero-tolerance policies). In contrast, educational and therapeutic approaches aim to improve school climate by increasing communication between students and school personnel. Educational and therapeutic interventions often include counseling, conflict resolution training, peer mediation programs, and parent–community programs (Nickerson & Spears, 2007).

Authoritarian Violence Prevention

Research on authoritarian strategies is dominated by cross-sectional self-report survey data sources and qualitative data, frequently capturing perceptions of students, school personnel, and school administrators as they concern school safety and school connectedness. The most researched of these strategies is metal detectors and school policing. Little empirical research exists on the use and effectiveness of surveillance cameras, locked doors, and monitored gates in school.

In a systematic literature review, Hankin et al. (2009) identified seven studies focused on effects of metal detectors on students, all of which utilized data from self-report surveys, and found that only one study provided limited support for their use in reducing the number of weapons brought into schools. Research by Gastic and Johnson (2015) suggests that metal detectors compromise students' feelings of safety in U.S. schools and that metal detectors are used disproportionally in U.S. schools characterized by more violence and a large percentage of minority students enrolled.

Research on school policing is more mixed but similar in that primary sources of data are secondary self-report or qualitative. Research suggests students generally perceive school police as an effective tool in preventing school violence and believe that their work is beneficial to maintaining safety (Brown, 2006). However, research in the past decade paints a different picture. For example, Perumean-Chaney and Sutton (2013) found among a nationally representative sample of U.S. school-aged youth that the number of visible security measures used in schools (e.g., metal detectors, security cameras, and locked gates) was negatively associated with students' feelings of safety.

Complementing this body of research is a large body of theoretical literature that argues a number of authoritarian practices can be detrimental to students and school personnel, although these effects have not been tested. This literature provides detailed hypotheses that students' rights can be violated when strategies such as security cameras (Braggs, 2004; Warnick, 2007), student searches (Beger, 2003; Essex, 2003; Finley, 2006), and zero-tolerance policies (Skiba & Peterson, 2000) are implemented, particularly when no consideration is given to how these strategies might affect students prior to their implementation (Theriot & Cuellar, 2016). Without evidence as to the effectiveness of these strategies, it is difficult to draw conclusions about whether they play a role in reducing the occurrence of school violence.

This writer is unaware of any experimental research on the effects of different types of authoritarian approaches and the occurrence of school-based violence. This lack of experimental and longitudinal research in an area dominated by self-report survey data suggests there are insufficient data on authoritarian strategies to draw conclusions as to their effectiveness in reducing school violence. Regardless, they remain the centerpiece of school safety at the federal, state, and local levels (Musu et al., 2019).

Educational/Therapeutic Violence Prevention

Similar to authoritarian strategies, educational/therapeutic strategies have seen widespread implementation in the past decade due to the push by federal legislation and funding initiatives to incorporate evidence-based approaches into mental health care in U.S. schools. These strategies encourage student–student and staff–student communication and promote students' feelings of school connectedness. It is important to note that many of these strategies vary in their labels, but a common theme across these interventions is that they are preventative (e.g., Tier 1) practices. These include conflict resolution, student mentoring, individual and group counseling, encouraging anonymous student reporting, and promoting student connectedness.

Conflict resolution training and peer mediation are composed of a series of techniques that promote positive interactions among students in an attempt to informally resolve the effects of student crime or violence. The primary objective of conflict resolution training and peer mediation is to provide students with a framework for effectively addressing student conflicts among themselves and their peers (Daunic et al., 2000). These practices are grounded in developmental and social psychology theory, centered around promoting the significance of peer relationships and their contribution to student well-being. Research supports the effectiveness of conflict resolution and peer mediation in schools of different education levels throughout the world (Bickmore, 2001; Haskvoort, 2010; Latipun et al., 2012). Many of these programs vary by school, and therefore it can be challenging for school personnel to adapt their fundamental principles.

Educational and therapeutic prevention methods have seen widespread growth in schools throughout the United States as a result of federal legislation and nationally recognized multi-tiered practice frameworks that aim to incorporate evidence-based practices in schools. Unlike research on authoritarian strategies, educational and therapeutic prevention methods have received rigorous research attention that has demonstrated many benefits of its use.

Both peer mediation and conflict resolution have been found to be efficient and effective tools for reducing the occurrence of school violence. For example, in a longitudinal study of youth in sixth through eighth grades, 30 students were trained in peer mediation, which was in turn found to be associated with an increase in student resolution and a decrease in the number of disciplinary referrals resulting in suspensions across a student body of 796 (Bell et al., 2000). The relationship between these types of programs and school violence is not new. Research on conflict resolution, peer mediation, student mentoring, and counseling programs suggests a positive association between their use and reducing school violence (Bell et al., 2000; Benson & Benson, 1993; Daunic et al., 2000; DuBois et al., 2011; Smith et al., 2002).

Trends in Violence Prevention Research

Literature on violence prevention in schools within the United States during the past two decades depicts a continuously evolving area with a number of common themes, many of which have emerged during the past 15 years. Current research suggests a number of associations among commonly implemented authoritarian strategies and students and school personnel. These relationships include the disproportional use of authoritarian safety strategies, the possibility for authoritarian strategies to violate students' rights, and increased arrest rates as a product of authoritarian strategies for school-based offenses that pose no legitimate threat to school safety.

Disparities in Exposure to Violence Prevention Practices

Much of the research concerning the disproportional use of authoritarian approaches was conducted using large, publicly available secondary data sets originating from self-report surveys at the student or school level (e.g., Gastic & Johnson, 2015). At the between-school level, these studies suggest the use of authoritarian prevention methods in U.S. schools is disproportional in larger secondary schools characterized by a greater percentage of students who are of low socioeconomic status or majority–minority. Within-school differences in exposure to school safety have received less attention due to methodological limitations, although research suggests that children of color are less likely to engage in educational/therapeutic interventions such as peer mediation but much more likely to be searched for contraband during school or feel like they are within eyesight of a security camera (Cuellar & Coyle, 2020).

Protecting Students' Rights

The hypothesis that students' rights are compromised by various authoritarian prevention methods has virtually no empirical examination. However, there is an extensive body of literature that uses theoretical research to explore the hypothesis. This research suggests that a number of authoritarian approaches have legal implications and might violate ethical principles and compromise students' rights and feelings of safety in schools (Steketee, 2012). For example, Theriot and Cuellar (2016) discuss a number of studies and court cases to explain how, without careful consideration, school policing and affiliated practices can compromise students' rights and negatively affect student outcomes. Others suggest that the use of student searches such as those facilitated by metal detectors, security cameras, and school policing is detrimental to students and can adversely affect student outcomes (Finley, 2006; Warnick, 2007).

Criminalization of Student Behavior

The criminalization hypothesis is a topic of debate [American Civil Liberties Union (ACLU), 2017] and has been empirically supported through the use of secondary data sets such as the School Survey on Crime and Safety (Na & Gottfredson, 2013) and research that uses survey data across schools (e.g., Theriot, 2009). Stronger support for the criminalization hypothesis exists in the study by Na and Gottfredson (2013), who highlight a positive association between the deployment of school police and arrest rates for nonserious student offenses in U.S. schools; however, due to the research design, it is unclear whether school policing actually caused increased arrest rates. Theriot (2009) compared schools that had school resource officers with schools that did not use trained school resource officers and found an increased arrest rate for disorderly conduct offenses in schools without these officers. Although there are not enough data to determine if criminalization occurs due to authoritarian practices, current literature suggests associations between the use of certain authoritarian methods and increased arrest rates for less serious student misconduct.

Trauma-Informed Practices

Because many violence prevention practices are applied in a general sense (i.e., as Tier 1 interventions), many fail to consider the way in which experienced trauma effects the manifestation of threats to school safety. It is estimated that more than half of students in today's schools experience one or more traumatic events before reaching adulthood (McLaughlin et al., 2013; Saunders & Adams, 2014). It is suggested that the risk for violence perpetration in schools increases nearly four-fold for each additional adverse childhood event reported among students in one state-representative sample in the Midwest (Duke et al., 2010). The psychological and physiological reactions to trauma are well documented and include student inability to effectively respond to stressors, aggression, behavior problems, and acts of violence at home and in school (Davis et al., 2015; Debellis & Zisk, 2014). Therefore, research calls on practitioners and educators to continually evaluate the effects of exposure to and exacerbation of traumatic experiences around violence prevention programming in schools.

Active Shooter Drills

Although there are extremely limited data regarding the long-term effects of these interventions, they have become commonplace in U.S. schools. In fact, it is estimated that approximately 95% of schools in the United States currently drill students on a lockdown procedure, and 76% report drilling students on shelter-in-place procedures (Musu et al., 2019). The requirement for drilling differs across states. For example, in New Jersey, schools "are required to have at least one fire drill and one school security drill each month within the school hours" (N.J.S.18A:41-1). Practitioners much consider the potentially adverse effects of these drills, which are currently almost entirely unknown. As schools increasingly adopt these practices, needs assessments and program evaluations must take place to determine their cost:benefit ratio.

The Role Social Workers Play in Violence Prevention in Schools

Social workers are in a position in which they can share a unique perspective concerning violence prevention practices employed in their schools. Typically trained in violence prevention and in the ability to use research to inform their practice, school social workers have the tools to develop and oversee violence prevention strategies that have minimal adverse effects on students and the school environment. Their professional preparedness and multidisciplinary collaborative approach contribute to an ability to identify school safety needs and advocate for change in policies and practices that potentially harm students and school personnel. Social workers in school settings can take several actions to inform school violence prevention planning in schools today.

First, social workers must take on leadership roles to advocate for person-in-environment perspective and data-informed decision-making in violence prevention programming. Researchers have recently pushed for advocating for and advancing social work leadership in school settings. This is a promising way to incorporate social work input in case management and planning, assessment, program development and implementation, and program evaluation efforts around violence prevention initiatives. Qualitative data on social work leadership indicate that school social workers perceive leadership as an avenue for promoting educational and therapeutic interventions in the school setting through multidisciplinary collaboration and coordination in case planning meetings, among other tasks (Elswick et al., 2019).

Second, social workers can help students and school personnel understand and effectively handle the effects of trauma among students. School social workers are in a unique position to advocate for trauma-informed programs and practices when working with students. Estimates suggest more than half of students in today's schools have experienced one or more traumatic events before the age of 17 years (McLaughlin et al., 2013; Saunders & Adams, 2014). Social workers have a clear responsibility to help address trauma, whether it is endured during or exacerbated by violence prevention in schools. Moreover, social workers must assess the extent to which trauma has been endured for the youth they serve before developing targeted interventions to reduce perpetration of violence. Such approaches could ultimately assist practitioners and educators in preventing more serious threats to school safety. For example, research suggests that traumatized students have a higher likelihood of committing school-based homicides (Langman et al., 2018). In a historical analysis of 593 U.S. school shootings since 1960, approximately 87% of school shooters indicated that they had been victims of bullying or other traumatic events (Lee, 2013).

Third, school social workers must adapt and help school-based personnel apply multi-tiered systems of support in school violence prevention programs. School workers are in a unique position to advocate for the utilization of multi-tiered systems of support. These support systems can be applied in violence prevention planning to avoid letting mental health concerns in this planning "fall between the cracks." Within the context of school safety, these systems allow the practitioner to consider a "tiered" approach to address the severity of needs among students. School social workers must teach their colleagues the importance of following frameworks to isolate students who are in need of more intensive levels of care. This is critical in reducing the potential escalation of violence in youth who have a higher propensity of engaging in violence in and around school.

Fourth, social workers and mental health care providers must advocate for policy to include more mental health care providers in schools. In addition to understanding the nuances and effects of trauma through a multi-tiered system of support, social workers must acknowledge there are simply not enough mental health care providers in schools today. Professionals must be prepared to advocate for change in current policy and ultimately an increase is state and federal funding to increase the presence of school-based mental health care providers in schools. Current research suggests approximately 10 million students are in a school with a police officer but no social worker employed; 14 million students are in a school with police but no counselor, nurse, psychologist, or social worker employed. Moreover, many states report two or three times more police officers in schools in comparison to social workers (ACLU, 2019). Although there is no way of knowing parameters for the overall population of school social workers in the United States, yet another dire need for this subspecialty of social work, it is imperative that social workers take every step possible to effectively advocate for an increase in school social work presence in schools.

Directions for Future Work

Several gaps in the violence prevention literature currently exist. Future research must seek to identify best practices for protecting the rights of vulnerable populations and the extent to which school-based policies and programs such as drilling and exclusionary discipline exacerbate trauma among youth in schools. In the long term, research must also aim to better understand how school social workers can engage in multidisciplinary collaboration with school security personnel to improve safety outcomes. This is critical because emerging research suggests increased collaboration between these professionals can lead to more holistic programing for youth and a perceived safer climate. Finally, researchers must also make efforts to determine the cost:benefit analysis of violence prevention measures in school, a major gap in the literature that can help practitioners and educators determine what is most effective within the context of budgeting limited resources.

References

American Civil Liberties Union. (2017). Bullies in blue: The *origins and consequences of school policing* [White paper]. https://www.aclu.org/report/bullies-blue-origins-and-consequences-school-policing

American Civil Liberties Union. (2019). *Cops and no counselors* [Report]. https://www.aclu.org/issues/juvenile-justice/school-prison-pipeline/cops-and-no-counselors

Beger, R. (2003). The "worst of both worlds": School security and the disappearing fourth amendment rights of students. *Criminal Justice Review, 28*(2), 336–354.

Bell, S. K., Coleman, J., Anderson, A., & Whelan, J. (2000). The effectiveness of peer mediation in a low-SES rural elementary school. *Psychology in the Schools, 37*(6), 505–516.

Benson, A. J., & Benson, J. M. (1993). Peer mediation: Conflict resolution in schools. *Journal of School Psychology, 31*(3), 427–430.

Bickmore, K. (2001). Student conflict resolution, power "sharing" in schools, and citizenship education. *Curriculum Inquiry, 31*(2), 137–162.

Braggs, D. (2004). Webcams in classrooms: How far is too far? *Journal of Law & Education, 33*(2), 275–282.

Brown, B. (2006). Understanding and assessing school police officers: A conceptual and methodological comment. *Journal of Criminal Justice, 34*(6), 591–604.

Cuellar, M. J., & Coyle, S. (2020, July 25). Assessing inequalities in school safety: Roles and recommendations for mental health care practitioners. *Security Journal.* https://doi.org/10.1057/s41284-020-00254-2

Daunic, A., Smith, S., Robinson, T., Miller, M., & Landry, K. (2000). School-wide conflict resolution and peer mediation programs: Experiences in three middle schools. *Intervention in School and Clinic, 38*(2), 94–100.

Davis, A. S., Moss, L. E., Nogin, M. M., & Webb, N. E. (2015). Neuropsychology of child maltreatment and implications for school psychologists. *Psychology in the Schools, 52*(1), 77–91.

Debellis, M. D., & Zisk, A. (2014). The biological effects of childhood trauma. *Child and Adolescent Psychiatric Clinics of North America, 23,* 185–222. doi:10.1016/j.chc.2014.01.002

DuBois, D. L., Portillo, N., Rhodes, J. E., Silverthorn, N., & Valentine, J. C. (2011). How effective are mentoring programs for youth? A systematic assessment of the evidence. *Psychological Science in the Public Interest, 12*(2), 57–91.

Duke, N. N., Pettingell, S. L., McMorris, B. J., & Borowsky, I. W. (2010). Adolescent violence perpetration: Associations with multiple types of adverse childhood experiences. *Pediatrics, 125,* 778–786. doi:10.1542/peds.2009-0597

Elswick, S. E., Cuellar, M. J., & Mason, S. E. (2019). Leadership and school social work in the United States: A qualitative assessment. *School Mental Health, 11,* 535–548. https://doi.org/10.1007/s12310-018-9298-8

Essex, N. (2003). Intrusive searches can prove troublesome for school personnel. *The Clearing House, 76*(4), 195–197.

Ewton, M. (2014). Student safety: Parents' and school principals' perceptions. *New Waves—Educational Research & Development, 17*(1), 109–125.

Finley, L. L. (2006). Examining school searches as systemic violence. *Critical Criminology, 14*(2), 117–135.

Gastic, B., & Johnson, D. (2015). Disproportionality in daily metal detector student searches in U.S. public schools. *Journal of School Violence, 14*(3), 299–315. doi:10.1080/15388220.2014.924074

Hankin, A., Hertz, M., & Simon, T. (2009). Impacts of metal detector use in schools: Insights from 15 years of research. *Journal of School Health, 81*(2), 100–106.

Haskvoort, I. (2010). The conflict pyramid: A holistic approach to structuring conflict resolution in schools. *Journal of Peace Education, 7*(2), 157–169.

Langman, P., Petrosino, A., & Persson, H. (2018). *Five misconceptions about school shootings.* WestEd. https://www.wested.org/wp-content/uploads/2018/08/JPRC-Five-Misconceptions-Brief.pdf

Latipun, S., Nasir, R., Zainah, A. Z., & Khairudin, R. (2012). Effectiveness of peer conflict resolution focused counseling in promoting peaceful behavior among adolescents. *Asian Social Science, 8*(9), 8–16.

Lee, J. H. (2013). School shootings in the U.S. public schools: Analysis through the eyes of an educator. *Review of Higher Education and Self-Learning, 6,* 88–120.

McLaughlin, K. A., Koenen, K. C., Hill, E. D., Petukhova, M., Sampson, N. A., Zaslavsky, A. M., & Kessler, R. C. (2013). Traumatic event exposure and posttraumatic stress disorder in a national sample of adolescents. *Journal of the American Academy of Child and Adolescent Psychiatry, 52,* 780–783.

Musu, L., Zhang, A., Wang, K., Zhang, J., & Oudekerk, B. A. (2019). *Indicators of school crime and safety: 2018* (NCES 2019-047/NCJ 252571). National Center for Education Statistics, U.S. Department of Education, and Bureau of Justice Statistics, Office of Justice Programs, U.S. Department of Justice.

Na, C., & Gottfredson, D. C. (2013). Police officers in schools: Effects on school crime and the processing of offending behaviors. *Justice Quarterly, 30*(4), 619–650.

Nickerson, A., & Spears, W. (2007). Influences on authoritarian and educational/therapeutic approaches to school violence prevention. *Journal of School Violence, 6*(4), 3–31. doi:10.1300/J202v06n04_02

N.J.S.18A:41-1: P.L.2016, Chapter 80, approved December 5, 2016; Assembly, No. 3349.

Perumean-Chaney, S. E., & Sutton, L. M. (2013). Students and perceived school safety: The impact of school security measures. *American Journal of Criminal Justice, 38*(4), 570–588.

Saunders, B. E., & Adams, Z. W. (2014). Epidemiology of traumatic experiences in childhood. Child and Adolescent Psychiatric Clinics of *North America, 23*(2), 167–184. doi:10.1016/j.chc.2013.12.003

Skiba, R., & Peterson, R. (2000). School discipline at a crossroads: From zero tolerance to early response. *Exceptional Children, 66*(3), 335–347.

Smith, S. W., Daunic, A. P., Miller, M. D., & Robinson, R. T. (2002). Conflict resolution and peer mediation in middle schools: Extending the process and outcome knowledge base. *Journal of Social Psychology, 142*(5), 567–586. doi:10.1080/00224540209603919

Steketee, A. (2012). *The legal implications of security cameras.* District Administration. https://eric.ed.gov/?id=EJ969969

Theriot, M. T. (2009). School resource officers and the criminalization of student behavior. *Journal of Criminal Justice, 37*(3), 280–287.

Theriot, M. T., & Cuellar, M. J. (2016). School resource officers and students' rights. *Contemporary Justice Review, 19*(3), 1–17. doi:10.1080/10282580.2016.1181978

Warnick, B. (2007). Surveillance cameras in schools: An ethical analysis. *Harvard Law Review, 77*(3), 317–343.

Solution-Focused Brief Therapy Interventions for At-Risk Students in Schools

Cynthia Franklin, Xiao Ding, Johnny S. Kim, Michael S. Kelly, and Stephen J. Tripodi

Solution-focused brief therapy (SFBT) is a useful approach in school settings for working with student behavioral and emotional issues, academic problems, and attendance and dropout prevention (Bond et al., 2013; Franklin et al., 2001, 2007, 2008; Franklin & Hopson, 2009; Kim & Franklin, 2009; Newsome, 2004). At-risk students often have academic struggles that coincide with unstable living arrangements, socioeconomic and cultural stress, behavioral health challenges, and school dropout (Franklin et al., 2018). SFBT is a practice that has been specifically used for dropout prevention in schools with at-risk youths and can be effectively implemented with underrepresented and diverse student populations (Kelly & Bluestone-Miller, 2009; Newsome, 2004). Because of its brief nature and flexibility in working with different problems, SFBT is a practical intervention approach for school social workers to use to address a variety of student issues and risk factors that can lead to school failure (Franklin et al., 2001; Jordan et al., 2013; Kim et al., 2017). This chapter describes SFBT and its usefulness in school settings with at-risk students, covering the research evidence available and the steps and skills involved in implementing this approach, including an interview format that school practitioners can use. A detailed case is also presented to demonstrate SFBT skills.

SFBT Practice in Schools

SFBT focuses on client strengths and resources, previous successes, goals, building on competencies, and future actions as ways to help clients solve problems. Regardless of the practice setting, the following assumptions guide SFBT:

- The "not knowing" stance with which the practitioner works *with* the clients through co-construction.
- Clients are the experts about their own lives and have the solutions to their life challenges.

- There are always strengths and resiliencies among clients, and the practitioners focus only on clients' strengths and resiliencies.

A systematic review and meta-summary of SFBT's change process (Franklin et al., 2017) studied SFBT skills and how the intervention works to help clients change. According to this review, "the purposeful use of language in the form of the co-construction of meaning is a unique way that SFBT works differently from some other therapies" (p. 11). This means that SFBT school practitioners use questions and responses (paraphrases and summaries) that are not neutral or objective but contain embedded assumptions about clients and their situations. Co-construction and other core communication processes used in SFBT are described in detail in Chapter 26 of this volume and also in a treatment manual that is available online from the Solution Focused Brief Therapy Association (SFBTA; http://www.sfbta.org/our-impact). The SFBTA treatment manual is currently also available in Spanish, and this translation broadens its applications to students of color who do not speak English.

School Practice Examples

Practitioners started to use the SFBT skills in schools during the 1990s, and both conceptual and practice research studies appeared in print (e.g., Kral, 1995; LaFountain & Garner, 1996; Metcalf, 1995; Murphy, 1996). Since that time, the SFBT literature in schools has grown exponentially across disciplines (Berg & Shilts, 2005; Franklin et al., 2018; Franklin & Gerlach, 2007; Kim et al., 2017; Metcalf, 2008; Murphy, 2015; Murphy & Duncan, 2007; Wallace et al., 2020) and among different countries (Fong & Urban, 2013; Hsu & Wang, 2011; Kim, 2013). The fast-growing literature, for example, demonstrates that SFBT interventions and programs have been successfully transferred and implemented in schools in the United States, Canada, Europe, Australia, Latin America, South Africa, Korea,

and in the provinces of Mainland China and Taiwan (Daki & Savage, 2010; Fitch et al., 2012; González et al., 2017; Kim et al., 2017; Liu et al., 2015). SFBT can be applied to Tier 1–3 interventions by teachers, school social workers, and other mental health professionals, but systematic reviews of the SFBT school research have shown that SFBT is usually delivered in Tier 2 and 3 interventions by school social workers and other mental health professionals. SFBT can be delivered in different modalities, including individual, group, classroom, and family, and at different grade levels, but studies on school-based practices have shown that SFBT is more often delivered in a group modality within schools (Franklin et al., 2020).

The practice literature is filled with helpful examples of the different ways that SFBT is practiced in schools. For example, the techniques of SFBT have been used to

- help at-risk students in individual, group, and family interventions (Murphy, 2015);
- coach teachers in a classroom (e.g., the WWOW program; Kelly & Bluestone-Miller, 2009; Kim et al., 2017);
- change interactions among parents, teachers, and students, such as parent–teacher meetings (Metcalf, 1995, 2008); and
- change the school culture, such as when an entire school adopts the solution-focused change philosophy and trains all staff (including teachers and principals) in SFBT techniques (Franklin & Streeter, 2003; Franklin et al., 2018).

The Growing Research on SFBT in Schools

During the past 30 years, research studies on SFBT have revealed that it is an effective and promising approach to work with at-risk children and adolescents in school settings. One of the advantages of SFBT is that all school staff can be trained in SFBT to work with at-risk students and achieve desirable outcomes (Kim et al., 2017). One systematic review and one meta-analysis have reviewed the studies within the United States (Franklin et al., 2020; Kim & Franklin, 2009), and other SFBT reviews also exist from Taiwan and China (Franklin et al., 2020; Gong & Hsu, 2017. Table 137.1 draws on these reviews and demonstrates some examples of the studies on SFBT in schools with at-risk youths. These reviews summarize some of the positive findings of solution-focused approaches in schools:

- SFBT can be used in kindergarten through grade 12 (K–12), college, and alternative schools, but it is most frequently used with adolescents.
- SFBT is an efficacious intervention that improves internalizing problems, such as depression and anxiety, and academic and interpersonal problems.
- The intervention is most effectively applied within schools in a group modality, and evidence shows the group modality may work better than other modalities.
- SFBT is effective in diverse settings and with different ethnic groups.
- SFBT is a flexible approach that is used by social workers and counselors in individual, group, and family interventions and by teachers in classrooms; it can also be used within interprofessional teams. This makes it an excellent approach for transportability into school situations that require different mental health interventions to meet changing and variable crises and presenting problems.

SFBT Interview Process

Franklin et al. (2006) suggest that in schools, interviews may last for shorter periods of time—for example, 20–30 minutes. The SFBT interviews and conversations with students may be thought of as being a continuous set of brief elements that are structured in process sequences and can move back and forth but have a beginning and an ending. Thinking of student interviews in this way may help the school social worker guide the client toward a purposeful solution-building conversation and offer a framework for how to apply the various skills of the solution-focused approach. Table 137.2 provides a guide concerning conversations using the SFBT session structure, including ways to use various solution-focused skills in the interview process.

Following this structure, social workers know how to begin interviews, proceed to explore solutions while assessing progress, and proceed to offer reflections and end the interviews with a goal direction. Next, we discuss the types of solution-focused questions to ask and skills to use while facilitating the school interview (adapted from Franklin et al., 2006).

SFBT Questions and Skills

Exception Questions

Exception questions explore past experiences in a student's life when the student's problem might reasonably have been expected to occur but somehow did not or was less severe.

- *When does the problem not occur?*
- *What was different about those times when things were better between you and your teacher?*
- *Even though this is a very bad time, in my experience, people's lives do not always stay the same. I will bet that there are times when the problem of being sent to the principal's office is not happening, or at least is happening less. Please describe those times. What is different? How did you get that to happen?*

Relationship Questions

Relationship questions allow students to discuss their problems from a third person point

TABLE 137.1 Solution-Focused Brief Therapy Studies in Schools

Study	Design	Outcome Measure	Sample Size	Sample Population	Tiers of Intervention	Results
Ates (2016)	RCT	School Burnout Scale	30	High school students	Tier 2 intervention for high school students challenged by school burnout	Solution-focused group counseling was effective in treatment of high schoolers' struggles with school burnout across gender.
Boyer et al. (2014)	RCT	Disruptive Behavior Disorder Rating Scale—Parent Version; four neuropsychological tests: tower test, trail making test, key search test, and zoo map test; Child Depression Inventory; Child Behavior Check List; Screen for Child Anxiety Related Emotional Disorders; Disruptive Behavior Disorder Rating Scale; School Attitude Questionnaire; Homework Problems Checklist; Conflict Behavior Questionnaire Parent Version; Conflict Behavior Questionnaire—Adolescent Version; Impairment Rating Scale (IRS) Parent Version; Disruptive Behavior Disorder Rating Scale—Teacher Version; medication use	159	Adolescents with ADHD	Tier 3 of intervention with parent sessions	Adolescents improved greatly between pre- and post-test, with large effect sizes on all domains. ADHD symptoms and coexisting problems improved from baseline to 3 months after treatment. Planning-focused CBT exhibited marginal additional beneficial effects to SFBT.
Corcoran (2006)	Quasi-experimental	Conner's Parent Rating Scale; Feelings, Attitudes, and Behaviors Scale for Children	239	Children with behavior problems	Tier 3 of intervention with family sessions	Although both the SFBT and comparison groups improved at post-test, no significant differences were found between groups on both measures.
Franklin et al. (2001)	Single case	Conners' Teacher Rating Scale	7	Middle school students aged 10–12 years	Tier 2 intervention with students who displayed learning disabilities and classroom behavioral problems	Five of seven (71%) improved per teachers' report.

Study	Design	Outcome Measure	Sample Size	Sample Population	Tiers of Intervention	Results
Franklin et al., (2007)	Quasi-experimental	Grades; attendance	85	At-risk high school students	Tier 1 of intervention with students enrolled in an SFBT alternative high school. The alternative high school was a public choice option for students with 10 or more credits.	SFBT sample had statistically significant higher average proportion of credits earned to credits attempted than the comparison sample. Both groups decreased in the attendance mean per semester; the comparison group, however, showed a higher proportion of school days attended for the semester.
Froeschle et al. (2007)	RCT	American Drug & Alcohol Survey Substance Abuse; Subtle Screening Inventory Adolescent–Version 2; Knowledge exam on physical symptoms of drug use; Piers–Harris Children's Self-Concept Scale version 2; Home & Community Social Behavior Scales; School Social Behavior Scales, 2nd edition; GPA	65	8th grade females	Tier 2 intervention with students who display challenging behavior at school and/or home	Statistically significant differences were found favoring the SFBT group on drug use, attitudes toward drugs, knowledge of physical symptoms of drug use, and competent behavior scores as observed by both parents and teachers. No group differences were found on self-esteem, negative behaviors as measured by office referrals, and GPs.
Green et al. (2007)	RCT	Trait Hope Scale; Cognitive Hardiness Scale; Depression Anxiety and Stress Scale–21	56	Female senior high school students	Tier 3 of intervention with female students who were not identified as vulnerable or at-risk	Students in the solution-focused groups reported significant increases in hope and cognitive hardiness and also significant decreases in depression but not the control group.
Indriúnienė (2017)	Quasi-experimental	Students' self-evaluations; teachers' behavioral evaluations; students' self-rated motivation (all weighted on a 0- to 10-point scale)	192	Senior students challenged by physical education classes	Tier 3 intervention of students with challenges participating in physical education classes	The majority of students in SFBC reported medium or great progress in dealing with a severe problem related to physical activity; and positive behavioral changes were observed in physical education classes.
Joker and Ghaderi (2015)	RCT	Self-Conception Questionnaire	30	High school students	Tier 2 intervention of students with challenges related to self-concept	Solution-based group counseling group showed significant increase in self-conception, self-respect, and self-admission measurements.

(continued)

TABLE 137.1 Continued

Study	Design	Outcome Measure	Sample Size	Sample Population	Tiers of Intervention	Results
Kvarme et al. (2010)	Quasi-experimental	General Self-Efficacy scale; domain-specific self-efficacy	144	Schoolchildren aged 12 or 13 years and identified as socially withdrawn	Tier 2 of intervention of students with a socially withdrawn presentation and low self-efficacy	The general self-efficacy scores increased significantly among girls in the SFBT group but not the control group. From pretest to 3-month follow-up, general self-efficacy increased for both sexes in the SFBT group and the control group.
LaFountain & Garner (1996)	RCT	Index of Personality Characteristics; Student Goal (counselor reported on a 1–5 scale)	311	Mixed grades students	Tier 2 of intervention of students school counselors selected for SFBT groups	Students in solution-focused groups reported significantly higher levels of self-esteem in self-perception scores and areas outside of academics. No significant differences were found in academic scale, possibly because most students chose to work on non-academic goals.
Littrell et al. (1995)	Quasi-experimental	Goal Attainment (joint student–teacher evaluation scale ranging from 0% to 100%); Intense Feeling Scale (student report on a 1–7 scale); Student Concern Scale (student report on a 1–7 scale)	61	High school students from an urban setting	Tier 3 of intervention for self-referred students working toward self-identified goals	All brief approaches were effective in enabling achievement of goals. SF group was more efficient.
Marinaccio (2001)	Quasi-experimental	Behavioral Assessment System for Children (BASC); Parent Rating Scale; BASC-Teacher Rating Scale; BASC-Self-Report of Personality	48	Mixed grades students	Tier 3 of school-based family sessions with the student as the primary client	Significant differences were found between the control group and the SF group. Students did not report increased positive perceptions of self, but teachers and parents reported SF effectiveness in reducing anxiety, aggression, and conduct problems.

Study	Design	Outcome Measure	Sample Size	Sample Population	Tiers of Intervention	Results
Newsome (2004)	Quasi-experimental	GPA; school attendance	52	Middle school students	Tier 2 intervention to examine the effect of SFBT on GPA and attendance	Statistically significant results, with SFBT group increasing mean grade scores while grades for the comparison group decreased. No difference on attendance measure.
Wallace (2020)	RCT	Teachers' Sense of Efficacy Scale; Student–Teacher Relationship Scale–Short Form; Student Internalizing Behavior Teacher/Staff Version; Community and Youth Collaborative Institute School Experience Surveys Student Externalizing Behavior Teacher/Staff Version; behavioral referrals (school records)	413	General population of 4th and 5th grade students	Tier 1 intervention at the classroom level	SFBT showed feasibility for therapists to use in both public and private school settings and potential to improve student attendance and classroom performance.

ADHD, attention-deficit/hyperactivity disorder; CBT, cognitive-behavioral therapy; GPA, grade point average; RCT, randomized controlled trial; SFBT, solution-focused brief therapy.

Sources: Kim and Franklin (2009) and Franklin et al. (2020).

TABLE 137.2 Structure of Solution-Focused Brief Therapy Interviews

	Begin Session →	Exploring Solutions →	Assessing Progress →	Reflection Break →	End Session
Goals of the stage	Rapport building. Shift focus toward strengths and away from problem talk. Support student.	School social worker and student build solution together. Have student take responsibility for their own solutions. Discussion is on possible solutions in concrete behavioral details.	Continue to provide compliments. Create small, attainable, concrete goals. Explore steps to achieving the goals.	Continue supporting student. Reflect on student's strengths and resources. Identify future steps.	Assess whether to schedule another appointment. Lay groundwork for future sessions.
Questions To ask	What has to happen while talking with me today that will make it worth your time to come?	What kinds of things have you done in the past that have worked for you? What would be different about the problem in your life? When is the problem better? Even a little bit?	What would your parents say about your progress? Who would be the most surprised if you did well on that test? What would your friends say is the biggest change they've noticed in you?	I'd like to take a minute to think about what we've discussed. Would that be all right with you?	Has this been helpful? What has been helpful for you about our meeting? Would you like to meet again?
Keys points to remember and SFBT techniques	Use student's words and metaphors. Focus on student's definition of the problem.	Use exception questions. Use miracle question to elicit details of student's goals. Focus on strengths.	Elicit incidents of small changes students have made. Use scaling questions. Use relationship questions.	Formulate four or five genuine compliments for student. Formulate tasks toward the solution. Formulate possible homework assignment.	Client and school social worker both determine whether to meet again.

SFBT, solution-focused brief therapy.

of view. This sequence of questions makes the problem less threatening and allows the school social worker, counselor, or teacher to assess the student's viewpoints and allows the student to practice thinking about the problem from the viewpoint of others.

- *What would your teacher say about your grades?*
- *What would your mother say?*
- *If you were to do something that made your teacher very happy, what would that be?*

Scaling Questions

Scaling questions are a sequence of questions used to determine where students are in terms of achieving their goals. The school social worker has the option to use scaling questions to quantify and measure the intensity of internal thoughts and feelings along with helping a student anchor reality and move forward from their goals (Franklin & Nurius, 1998; Pichot & Dolan, 2003). Numerous variations of this technique can be used, such as asking for percentages of progress or using smiling and frowning faces for small children.

- *On a scale from 1 to 10, with 1 being the lowest and 10 being the highest, where would you rate yourself in terms of reaching your goals that you identified last week?*
- *On a scale from 1 to 10, with 1 being that you never go to class and 10 being that you have perfect attendance, where would you put yourself on that scale? What would it take to move up two numbers on the scale?*
- *On a scale of 1 to 10, with 1 being that you are getting into trouble every day in the class and 10 being that you are doing all your school-work and not getting into trouble, where would you be on that scale?*

Other uses of the scaling questions in SFBT include asking for exceptions to problems, such as asking "What are you doing so you are not a 1?" or "How did you manage to keep yourself at a 5?" and harnessing the scale to discover solutions or construct "miracles" (Franklin et al., 2018). For example, the counselor could ask the student to imagine what will happen if the student moves from a 1 rating to a 3 rating, or what new behaviors did the student employ, or what positive changes did the student notice from a 4 to a 5? Using scaling techniques provides an opportunity for the counselor and the student to work together to construct new meanings of the current situation. SFBT practitioners might also express their surprise that the problem is not worse on the scale as a way of complementing to encourage the students to start from where they are and change their negative views on the problem nature.

The Miracle Question

The miracle question strengthens the student's goals by allowing them to reconstruct their story, imagining a future without the student's perceived problem (Berg & De Jong, 1996; De Jong & Berg, 2001). In addition, the school social worker uses the miracle question to help

students identify ways that the solution may already be occurring in their lives.

- *Now, I want to ask you a strange question. This is probably a question no one has asked you before. Suppose that while you are sleeping tonight a miracle happens and the problem that brought you here is solved. However, because you are sleeping, you don't know that the miracle has happened. So, when you wake up tomorrow morning, what will be the first thing you notice that is different—that will tell you a miracle has happened and the problem that brought you here is solved?*

Goal Setting/Goaling

The act of setting goals is used as a verb in SFBT and is sometimes referred to in the literature as "goaling." Goals are considered the beginning of behavior change, not the end. The school social worker and the student negotiate small, observable goals, set within a brief time frame, that lead to a new story for the student. A goal should describe what a student is to do instead of describing the problem behavior. The negotiation of goals should start immediately between the school social worker and the student.

Break for Reflection

A break is taken near the end of the session to help formulate a positive ending to the session.

Compliments and a Set of Take-Away Tasks

These consist of continuous affirmation of the student's strengths and character and suggested behavioral tasks that reinforce client solutions.

- *You did that?*
- *I am amazed.*
- *How did that make you feel?*
- *I bet your mother was pretty proud of you!*
- *That seemed to work! Do you think you could do that again?*

The SFBT session structure, questions asked, and skills used must be flexible enough to adapt to the individual needs of each student but also structured enough to provide guidance to school social workers who need to be able to apply the solution-focused questions and skills with the interview process to help clients change. A case example follows.

School Case Study

As discussed previously, the solution-focused school interview can be divided into distinct elements. The first part usually is spent building rapport and exploring strengths with the student to find out a little bit about the student's life. During this first part, the school social worker may be seeking to understand the student's interests, motivations, competencies, and belief systems. The following case of a school social worker and a student illustrates the structure of a solution-focused session in schools and several core techniques.

> Social Worker: Hello, Tina. I understand your teacher Mrs. Jones sent you here to see me because your attendance and grades are keeping you from making progress at the school. But I'd like to hear from you. What are the reasons for you to be here today? [Allows student to state the problem.]
>
> Tina: I don't know. I just want to get it over with so that my teacher and my mom can stop bugging me and leave me alone! There's a bunch of problems in my family and I don't know why everyone is blaming me. I hated this place and I wish I could just drop out so that I can get to do what I want.
>
> SW: So, if I understand you correctly, you're here to see me because there are a lot of things going on in your family and you felt unjust about how you're treated. But it sounds like you also

cared about what your mom and Mrs. Jones' thought and want them and the school to give you more personal space so that you can do more things that you like?

> T: Yeah. I guess so.
>
> SW: So, what sorts of things do you like to do?
>
> T: Ummm, I like to hang out with my friends. And I like to do my art projects.
>
> SW: Wow. That is very cool. What type of art do you do? Do you and your friends do art projects together?
>
> T: Well, thanks. I draw and paint. My friends usually like music and stuff but we sometimes work on things together. You know the sketch, the charcoal one outside of the makerspace? I did that.
>
> SW: Wow. Now I have to go and see it after our meeting. You're very talented Tina.
>
> [Social worker will continue to develop rapport and try to find out student's interests and belief systems.]

The second part of the session, which takes up the bulk of the time—approximately 40 minutes in traditional sessions but may be shorter in school interviews—is spent discussing the issues that emerged, looking for exceptions, searching for instances of success, and formulating goals. One of the key components to SFBT that has been emphasized in this chapter is working with the student to identify the problem, look for times when the problem is absent, look for ways the solution is already occurring, and develop attainable goals to help resolve the problem. This second part follows the rapport building and is usually initiated with questions such as "How can this meeting be of help to you?" or "What is your best hope from our meeting today?" (establish a goal that is observable and practical rather than a goal stated in the absence of some undesirable situations) (Sklare, 2014).

SW: OK, so how can I help you or what can you get out of our meeting today so that you know it's been worth your time to see me?

T: I want my teachers and my parents to stop bugging me about coming back to classes and work harder on math so that I won't keep failing the tests or dropout whatsoever. This school is just a waste of my time, and my classes are stupid. They don't know how hard it is.

SW: I hear you. Mrs. Jones told me that actually you were once very good at math. When was that?

[Instead of dwelling on the problem, use the information that has already been gathered to inquire about previous success.]

T: Well, last year. I got some A's in Mrs. Jones' math class last year. But that was when Mrs. Jones only teaches math for our class. But now she has to cover two classes and I never get to spend personal time with her ever. Last year, we also had Mr. Johnson [a para teacher who Tina trusted but left the school recently] to sit with me and give me instructions to help me. The math got way harder in 10th grade! And no one is here to help me. No one! No one has time for me, my teacher, or my family.

SW: I see. Well, Tina, I heard you say that even though you "failed math," you kept going to the class. What I noticed about you is that you are able to keep trying even though it is so frustrating for you. How did you learn to be so persistent? [Constructs positive new meanings for the problematic situation.]

T: I don't know. I kinda like Mrs. Jones and wished Mr. Johnson were still here.

SW: So, would you say that more one-on-one time for you in Mrs. Jones' math class would help you to catch up?

T: Yeah. I think so. I'd like that.

[The social worker has to be an astute observer and listener to catch the potential solutions tied to the student's expressed needs. The client–therapist coalition can usually identify a solution by visiting what worked in the past.]

SW: What about the other classes? Is there a class that you didn't think was stupid or a waste of time? [Example of looking for exceptions.]

T: The computer science class is cool.

SW: What made the computer science class good?

T: I don't have a computer at home. But I am like a natural. I mean, to me, it's easy. It won't take up a lot of effort and there's no need to bother other people to explain a whole bunch to me.

SW: You said you hated this school, but yet you haven't dropped out yet. How have you managed to do that? [Allows student to identify possible solutions and possible successes she had already achieved; meanwhile, actively listen to the client's narratives and select and build upon the solutions that already exist.]

T: Well, I'm still going to some of my classes, but at this point I just don't care anymore.

SW: Tina, for those classes that you do attend, what would your teacher say about your academic work? [Example of relationship question.]

T: I guess they might say that I don't pay attention in class, that I don't do my homework, and that I'm not trying.

SW: Do you agree with that?

T: I guess, but it's just hard to concentrate when I have to go back home to hear my parents fighting and arguing every night.

SW: I'd like to ask you an unusual question. It's probably something no one has ever asked you before. Suppose, after we're done and you leave my office, you go to bed tonight and a miracle happens. This miracle solves all the problems that brought you here today but because you were sleeping, you didn't know it occurred. So, the next morning you wake up and you sense something is different. What will be the first thing you notice that is different that lets you know your problems are solved? [Example of the miracle question.]

T: I guess my parents would go back to normal. Mr. Johnson would still be here and I would probably get better grades. I would hope that people still care about me. And I can feel good about myself.

SW: I am sure that people still love you and care about you and that's why your mom and Mrs. Jones referred you to me to have this meeting. What will you be doing differently to get better grades?

T: I would probably stop cutting so many classes.

SW: Do you think that would make the situation better? What will happen if you sit through your classes and started paying more attention? [Let the student take the initiative. Continue to probe and elicit more details and examples.]

T: I'd probably start to catch things up.

SW: What else will you be doing differently when you're getting better grades?

T: Probably finishing my homework and not stepping out of classes to upset Mrs. Jones.

SW: So, what will you being doing instead of walking out of the classroom?

T: Listen and sit there and take notes, I guess.

SW: So, on a scale from 1 to 10, with 1 being "I'm ready to throw in the towel and give up ever doing well in school" and 10 being that "I am ready to keep on trying," where would you say you are right now? [Example of asking motivation questions using the scales.]

T: Eh . . . 3.

SW: What sorts of things prevent you from giving it a 2 or a 1?

T: Well, I kinda know Mrs. Jones cares about me and I need to get my high school diploma because I always want to apply to an art school to design anime and eventually maybe work at Pixar or some big studios to be an artist.

SW: Wow! That sounds terrific Tina! You are really ambitious. So, you need to finish school for that. So, what would need to happen for you to be a 4 or a 5?

T: I'd need to find a way to be, you know, be less sad about my family. And coming to classes and finishing the work, I guess.

[After the coping and motivation question, the social worker needs to assess and reflect on (1) if the identified problem is too overwhelming to the student, (2) how much self-efficacy and hope the student possesses toward the resolution, (3) the degree of commitment of the student, and (4) if the problem that has been identified is a priority for her (Franklin et al., 2018, p. 18).]

SW: Are those things you'd like to start trying to do?

T: I think so.

[Social worker would continue searching for solutions that are already occurring in Tina's life and collaborate on identifying and setting small, attainable goals.]

The final part of the session lasts approximately 5–10 minutes. It involves giving the student a set of compliments, homework, and determining whether to continue discussing this topic at another time. In school settings, practitioners such as teachers and social workers have separated this last part from the rest of the conversation. The break, for example, might be extended, and the conversation might pick up in different class periods or at different times of the day (e.g., before and after lunch).

SW: I'd like to take a minute to write down some notes based on what we've talked about. Is there anything else you feel I should know before I take this quick break?

T: No.

SW: [After taking a break] Well, Tina, I'd like to compliment you on your commitment to staying in school despite your frustrations. And I really admire your ambitions. You seem like a bright student and understand the importance of finishing high school. I'd like to meet with you again to continue our work together. Would that be all right with you?

T: Sure.

SW: So, for next week, I'd like you to try on those small steps that we've agreed upon today and notice when things are going a little bit better both in your classes and back at home and what you're doing differently during those times.

T: Ok.

SW: Great. I will see you next week then.

Future Applications

SFBT has been applied with all ages of students and in different types of schools from K–12 to college and in alternative schools with high-risk adolescents. Studies have shown that it is used most often in schools with adolescents and may be particularly efficacious for internalizing, interpersonal, and academic problems. Social workers using SFBT in schools help students build solutions acting as a coach, facilitator, and mental health therapist. As the case example illustrated, SFBT offers an interview structure and a set of counseling skills that help social workers successfully facilitate the solution-building process to prevent school dropout and other problems. In the future, SFBT school training protocols and materials need to be developed with the aims of providing better training on the co-construction and structure of interviews and on the specific SFBT skills and interventions needed for different tiers of interventions. To obtain favorable results in schools with SFBT, it is essential for school social workers to learn how to practice SFBT well, and for this to happen, fidelity measures are needed. Better training on how to deliver SFBT in groups and in interpersonal interventions is also needed, along with guidance on skills and interview processes. SFBT has been shown to work well with diverse ethnic groups, but its effectiveness with different populations requires further study in practice.

Helpful Resources

Austin Independent School District. *Garza High School: A solution-focused high school*. http://www.garzahighschool.com/

Simply Focus Podcast. *The good life approach. Solution focus in schools works: From Garza High School to the worldwide evidence with Professor Cynthia Franklin*: https://podcasts.google.com/feed/aHR0cHM6Ly93d3cuc2ZvbnRvdXIuY29tL2ZlZWQvcG9kY2FzdC8/episode/aHR0cDovL3d3dy5zZm9udG91ci5jb20vP3Bvc3RfdHlwZT1wcm9qZWN0JnA9NjU5MA?hl=en&ved=2ahUKEwissIGBh93qAhUF5awKHdwEDCIQieUEegQICxAS&ep=6

Solution Focused Brief Therapy Association: http://www.sfbta.org

Solution Focused Schools Unlimited. *The solution focused school conference*. https://solutionfocusedschoolconference.wordpress.com

References

Ates, B. (2016). Effect of solution focused group counseling for school students in order to struggle with school burnout. *Journal of Education and Training Studies, 4*(4), 27–34.

Berg, I. K., & De Jong, P. (1996). Solution-building conversation: Co-constructing a sense of competence with clients. *Families in Society, 77,* 376–391.

Berg, I. K., & De Jong, P. (1996). Solution-building conversation: Co-constructing a sense of competence with clients. *Families in Society, 77,* 376–391.

Berg, I. K., & Shilts, L. (2005). *Classroom solutions: WOWW approach.* Brief Family Therapy Center.

Bond, C., Woods, K., Humphrey, N., Symes, W. & Green, L. (2013). Practitioner review: The effectiveness of solution focused brief therapy with children and families: A systematic and critical evaluation of the literature from 1990–2010. *Journal of Child Psychology & Psychiatry, 54*(7), 707–723

Boyer, B. E., Geurts, H. M., Prins, P. J., & Van der Oord, S. (2016). One-year follow-up of two novel CBTs for adolescents with ADHD. *European Child & Adolescent Psychiatry, 25*(3), 333–337.

Corcoran, J. (2006). A comparison group study of solution-focused therapy versus "treatment-as-usual" for behavior problems in children. *Journal of Social Service Research, 33*(1), 69–81.

Daki, J., & Savage, R. S. (2010). Solution-focused brief therapy: Impacts on academic and emotional difficulties. *Journal of Educational Research, 103*(5), 309–326. doi:10.1080/00220670903383127

De Jong, P., & Berg, I. K. (2001). Co-constructing cooperation with mandated clients. *Social Work, 46,* 361–381.

Fitch, T., Marshall, J., & McCarthy, W. (2012). The effect of solution-focused groups on self-regulated learning. *Journal of College Student Development, 53*(4), 586–595. doi:10.1353/csd.2012.0049

Fong, R., & Urban, B. (2013). Solution-focused approach with Asian immigrant clients. In J. S. Kim (Ed.), *Solution-focused brief therapy: A multicultural approach* (pp. 122–132). Sage.

Franklin, C., Biever, J., Moore, K., Clemons, D., & Scamardo, M. (2001). The effectiveness of solution-focused therapy with children in a school setting. *Research on Social Work Practice, 11,* 411–434.

Franklin, C., & Gerlach, B. (2007). Solution-focused brief therapy in public school settings. In T. S. Nelson & F. N. Thomas (Eds.), *Handbook of solution-focused therapy: Clinical applications* (pp. 167–190). Haworth.

Franklin, C., Guz, S., Zhang, A., Kim, J., Zheng, H., Hai, A. H., Cho, Y. J., & Shen, L. (2020). Solution-focused brief therapy for students in schools: A comparative meta-analysis of the English and Chinese literature. *Journal of the Society for Social Work and Research.* University of Chicago Press. doi:10.1086/712169

Franklin, C., Harris, M. B. E., & Allen-Meares, P. E. (2008). *The school practitioner's concise companion to preventing violence and conflict.* Oxford University Press.

Franklin, C., & Hopson, L. (2009). Involuntary clients in public schools: Solution-focused interventions. In R. Rooney (Ed.), *Strategies for work with involuntary clients* (2nd ed.). (pp. 478–493) Columbia University Press.

Franklin, C., Kim, J. S., & Tripodi, S. J. (2006). Solution-focused brief therapy interventions for students at-risk to drop out. In C. Franklin, M. B. Harris, & P. Allen-Meares (Eds.), *The school services sourcebook* (pp. 691–704). Oxford University Press.

Franklin, C., & Nurius, P. (1998). Distinction between social constructionism and cognitive constructivism: Practice applications. In C. Franklin & P. Nurius (Eds.), *Constructivism in practice: Methods and challenges* (pp. 57–94). Families International.

Franklin, C., & Streeter, C. L. (2003). *Creating solution-focused accountability schools for the 21st century: A training manual for Garza High School.* University of Texas, Hogg Foundation for Mental Health.

Franklin, C., Streeter, C. L., Webb, L., & Guz, S. (2018). *Solution focused brief therapy in alternative schools: Ensuring student success and preventing dropout.* Routledge.

Franklin, C., Streeter, C. L., Kim J. S., & Tripodi, S. J. (2007). The effectiveness of a solution-focused, public alternative school for dropout prevention and retrieval. *Children & Schools, 29*(3), 133–144.

Franklin, C., Zhang, A., Froerer, A., & Johnson, S. (2017). Solution-focused brief therapy: A systematic review and meta-summary of process research. *Journal of Marital and Family Therapy, 43*(1), 16–30. doi:10.1111/jmft.12193

Froeschle, J. G., Smith, R. L., & Richard, R. (2007). The efficacy of a systematic substance abuse program for adolescent females. *Professional School Counseling, 10*(5).

Gong, H., & Hsu, W. (2017). The effectiveness of solution-focused group therapy in ethnic Chinese school settings: A meta-analysis. *International Journal of Group Psychotherapy, 67*(3), 383–409. doi:10.1080/00207284.2016.1240588

González, K. S., Franklin, C., Cornejo, R., Castro, Y., & Smock, S. J. (2017). Solution-focused brief therapy for Chilean primary care patients: Exploring a linguistic adaptation. *Journal of Ethnicity in Substance Abuse, 18*(1), 1–26. doi:10.1080/15332640.2017.1310643

Green, J., Martin, A. J., & Marsh, H. W. (2007). Motivation and engagement in English, mathematics and science high school subjects: Towards an understanding of multidimensional domain specificity. *Learning and Individual Differences, 17*(3), 269–279.

Hsu, W., & Wang, C. D. C. (2011). Integrating Asian clients' filial piety beliefs into solution-focused brief therapy. *International Journal Advanced Counselling, 4*(33), 322–334. doi:10.1007/s10447-011-9133-5

Indriūnienė, V. (2017). Effectiveness of solution-focused brief counselling in dealing with problems with physical education among senior students. *Croatian Journal of Education: Hrvatski časopis za odgoj i obrazovanje, 19*(2), 399–417.

Joker, H., & Ghaderi, Z. (2015). Effectiveness of a solution-based counseling on students self-perception. *Educational Research and Reviews, 10*(15), 2141–2145.

Jordan, S. S., Froerer, A. S., & Bavelas, J. B. (2013). Microanalysis of positive and negative content in solution-focused brief therapy and cognitive behavioral therapy expert sessions. *Journal of Systemic Therapies, 32*(3), 46–59. doi:10.1521/jsyt.2013.32.3.46

Kelly, M. S., & Bluestone-Miller, R. (2009). Working on What Works (WOWW): Coaching teachers to do more of what's working. *Children & Schools, 31*(1), 35–38.

Kim, J. S. (2013). *Solution-focused brief therapy: A multicultural approach.* Sage.

Kim, J. S., & Franklin, C. (2009). Solution-focused brief therapy in schools: A review of the literature. *Children and Youth Services Review, 31*(4), 464–470.

Kim, J. S., Kelly, M. S., & Franklin, C. (2017). *Solution focused brief therapy in schools: A 360 degree view of research and practice principles* (2nd ed.). Oxford University Press.

Kral, R. (1995). *Strategies that work: Techniques for solutions in schools.* Brief Family Therapy Press.

Kvarme, L. G., Helseth, S., Sørum, R., Luth-Hansen, V., Haugland, S., & Natvig, G. K. (2010). The effect of a solution-focused approach to improve self-efficacy in socially withdrawn school children: A non-randomized controlled trial. *International Journal of Nursing Studies, 47*(11), 1389–1396.

LaFountain, R. M., & Garner, N. E. (1996). Solution-focused counseling groups: The results are in. *Journal for Specialists in Group Work, 21*, 128–143.

Littrell, J. M., Malia, J. A., & Vander Wood, M. (1995). Single-session brief counseling in a high school. *Journal of Counseling & Development, 73*(4), 451–458.

Liu, X., Zhang, Y. P., Franklin, C., Qu, Y., Chen, H., & Kim, J. S. (2015). The practice of solution-focused brief therapy in mainland China. *Health & Social Work, 40*(2), 84–90. doi:10.1093/hsw/hlv013

Marinaccio, B. C. (2001). *The effects of school-based family therapy.* State University of New York at Buffalo.

Metcalf, L. (1995). *Counseling toward solutions: A practical solution-focused program for working with students, teachers, and parents.* Jossey-Bass.

Metcalf, L. (2008). *Counseling toward solutions: A practical solution-focused program for working with students, teachers, and parents* (2nd ed.). Jossey-Bass.

Murphy, J. J. (1996). Solution-focused brief therapy in the schools. In S. Miller, M. Hubble, & B. Duncan (Eds.), *Handbook of solution-focused brief therapy* (pp. 184–204). Jossey-Bass.

Murphy, J. J. (2015). *Solution-focused counseling in schools* (3rd ed.). American Counseling Association.

Murphy, J. J., & Duncan, B. L. (2007). *Brief intervention for school problems: Outcome-informed strategies* (2nd ed.). Guilford.

Newsome, S. (2004). Solution-focused brief therapy (SFBT) groupwork with at-risk junior high school students: Enhancing the bottom-line. *Research on Social Work Practice, 14*, 336–343.

Pichot, T., & Dolan, Y. (2003). *Solution-focused brief therapy: Its effective use in agency settings.* Hawthorne.

Sklare, G. B. (2014). *Brief counseling that works: A solution-focused therapy approach for school counselors and other mental health professionals.* Corwin Press.

Wallace, L. B., Hai, A. H., & Franklin, C. (2020). An evaluation of Working on What Works (WOWW): A solution-focused intervention for schools. *Journal of Marital and Family Therapy, 46*, 687–700. https://doi.org/10.1111/jmft.12424

School Social Work and Social– Emotional Learning

Kevin Tan and Brenda Lindsey

Social–emotional learning (SEL) is the process of developing knowledge, attitudes, and skills that improve student self-awareness, self-management, social awareness, relationship skills, and responsible decision-making [Collaborative for Academic, Social, and Emotional Learning (CASEL), 2018]. SEL has gained increasing attention in education because of its strong association with higher grades and test scores, increased attendance, positive behaviors, and good citizenship (Durlak et al., 2011). Many state educational boards, organizations (e.g., CASEL), and professional associations (e.g., School Social Work Association of America) emphasize the need for school professionals, including school social workers, to actively promote students' SEL skills, competencies, and attitudes.

The National School Social Work SEL Standards is one framework that school social workers should reference in their work with students (Lindsey et al., 2014). American schools are subject to kindergarten through grade 12 competency benchmarks and learning standards, which include SEL objectives.

School social workers play a significant role in promoting SEL. School social workers serve as the liaison between the school, home, and community, in line with the National School Social Work Practice model (Frey et al., 2012). This unique and specialized positionality within a school system makes school social workers vital professionals in schools' efforts to promote SEL with individual students and their families as well as throughout the school communities. The ecological person-in-environment perspective that school social workers bring to their work makes them ideal to assess students' SEL; develop and provide the appropriate interventions promoting student SEL; and establish the necessary systems to monitor the social and emotional health of their district, school, and students.

National School Social Work SEL Standards

The National School Social Work SEL Standards emphasizes five domains of SEL that must be considered within students' social contexts and through a developmental perspective. They were first introduced by CASEL in 1997 and are the most widely known and utilized SEL competencies in education. Familiarity with these domains will provide school social workers with a foundation for SEL work. The first of the five is *self-awareness*—that is, students' ability to recognize their emotions, thoughts, and values and to understand their relation with their behaviors. The second is *self-management*, calling on students to develop skills needed to regulate their feelings, thoughts, and behaviors. The framework further emphasizes students' ability for *social awareness*—their ability to empathize with and to be accepting of the social and cultural backgrounds of others. It advances the notion that it is important for students to learn the necessary *relationships skills* so as to build and sustain positive relationships. Last, the framework indicates the need for students to enhance their ability for *responsible decision-making*, which will allow them to effectively contribute to society's overall well-being (CASEL, 2018). Links to the National School Social Work SEL Standards and CASEL's framework are provided in the Helpful Resources section.

The National School Social Work SEL Standards also emphasize the importance of social contexts both proximal and distal to students' individual SEL skill building. CASEL describes its five competencies as nested within classrooms (SEL curricula and instruction), schools (schoolwide practices and policies), and homes and communities (partnerships with families and communities). The National Standards highlight the consideration of these competencies within students' multiple contexts. For instance, under self-management, the standards draw attention to the importance of students' social support systems when considering their ability to establish and maintain positive relationships. Under social awareness, the standards emphasize the impact of the social environment on students' development

and their ability to understand its complexities. Such framing of SEL skills within students' social contexts is well-suited to school social workers' ecological orientation of practice. It broadens school social workers' focus of intervention, moving beyond the individual student, such that they also target SEL work with classrooms, schools, and the students' families and broader communities. Such a perspective aligns well with the National School Social Work Practice model that emphasizes school social workers' role as the liaison between the school, home, and community (Frey et al., 2012). School social workers involved in SEL work must also intervene at the proximal and distal social contexts of students in order for any individual SEL skill-building work to be sustained.

The National School Social Work SEL Standards also emphasize the developmental framing of SEL within students' life stages. They apply the five domains to the developmental periods of (1) early childhood and early elementary school, (2) late elementary school, (3) middle school/junior high school, and (4) high school. The standards highlight the successful attainment of SEL competencies within each period. For instance, under the domain of self-management, in the early childhood/elementary period, students should be able to identify feelings, words, and faces. By middle school, students should have the ability to identify feelings, strengths, and weakness within themselves and improve positive coping skills to handle feelings. By high school, students should be able to evaluate how their behaviors, expression of feelings, and choices affect others. School social workers will find this framework easy to tailor to the schools they serve. The developmental framing of this model coincides with the ways schools are organized (elementary, middle, and high school), and it provides specific, age-appropriate SEL benchmarks that school social workers should help students achieve.

Assessment, Intervention, and Progress Monitoring of Students' SEL

School social workers should apply the National School Social Work SEL Standards in three stages. First is the *assessment* of SEL, using instruments that screen and organize student SEL skills and competencies. Second are *interventions*, the delivery of evidence-based SEL programming that is tailored to students' individual needs. Third, it involves establishing the process of *progress monitoring*, the tracking of overall school social and emotional health and individual students' intervention effectiveness.

The assessment, intervention, and progress monitoring of SEL are consistent with contemporary best practice models that schools throughout the United States have widely adopted. These models include early warning intervention monitoring systems (Therriault et al., 2013), multi-tiered systems of support (Harlacher et al., 2014), response to intervention (Clark & Alvarez, 2010), and positive behavioral interventions and supports (Horner & Sugai, 2015). The core features of these models highlight the importance for schoolwide universal, systematic, multi-tiered, and data-driven approaches to addressing student issues. In promoting SEL, school social workers should be familiar with and align their approach with one of these practice models.

Assessment

A common feature in the initial stage of SEL implementation is the use of key data indicators to identify students at risk for poor outcomes. Schools typically use archival records such as grades, standardized test scores, attendance, and disciplinary referrals to determine thresholds or benchmarks to identify students at risk. The American Institutes for Research recommends specific criteria for schools to flag students, such as poor attendance (absent 10%

or more of instructional time), failure in one or more courses, a grade point average of 2.0 or lower, and multiple office disciplinary referrals (Therriault et al., 2013). Based on these indicators, students are classified as high risk, moderate risk, or low risk and receive interventions based on their category.

Although it is a common practice for schools to use academic and behavioral records to identify students for SEL interventions, school social workers need to be cautious of such an approach. Although grades, attendance, and disciplinary referrals may be associated with SEL, flagging students based on these indicators does not consider the underlying SEL issues that are contributing toward poor achievement and behaviors. Identifying student needs without directly assessing their SEL makes it difficult to design interventions that address the root of their problems.

School social workers play a crucial role in advocating for a system of proper assessment of SEL. It is important to align the selection of the SEL assessment tool to the domains stipulated in the National School Social Work SEL Standards. Effective implementation of SEL requires intentionality and specificity in matching the tool to the overall conceptual framework (Taylor et al., 2018). Selecting the appropriate instrument is a key step in this process. A plethora of SEL assessment tools exist, and school social workers should thoughtfully select from and tailor them for their own practice. Issues for consideration include reliability and validity as well as implementation costs and cultural relevance to a school's population (for a discussion specific to SEL, see Taylor et al., 2018). For this purpose, the Helpful Resources section lists two websites that review SEL assessment tools. Both review the age appropriateness and the length of each instrument (e.g., number of items and time taken to administer).

Intervention

Selection of the appropriate intervention based on SEL assessment data is the next critical step for school social workers addressing SEL needs. Common approaches to the delivery of interventions are based on a multi-tiered approach, in which there is a progression and continuum of programs: all students receive services (Tier 1, universal), some students who require more support receives specific services (Tier 2, selected), and a few students with the greatest need receive the most resource-intensive intervention (Tier 3, indicated). Most practice models use a pyramid to showcase the range of programs for students (Harlacher et al., 2014).

The selection and delivery of interventions are based on a few critical considerations. First, interventions should reflect a team decision process, with the team comprising teachers, administrators, and other student support personnel (e.g., school counselors and psychologists). School social workers must be prepared to work and collaborate with a team of interdisciplinary professionals. Second, the selection of interventions is based on the principle that programs should yield the greatest possible benefit in terms of lessening risk of poor outcomes (Tan, Teasley, et al., 2018). Third, the highest risk students should receive the most immediate attention in addressing student needs (Knowles & White, 2015). Fourth, similar to the process of selecting SEL assessment instruments, the selection of SEL interventions must be based on a sound research design and empirical evidence. CASEL's SEL program guide provides a discussion of the research criteria for inclusion in its database of quality intervention (see the Helpful Resources section).

School social workers have a range of programs to tailor, adapt, and deliver to students. The National Registry of Evidence-Based Programs and Practices and the What Works Clearinghouse are useful references for this purpose. There are other evidence-based sources specific to SEL that school social workers can consult in selecting interventions as well. CASEL maintains two guides on quality SEL programs (preschool/elementary and middle/

high school). The Ecological Approaches to Social Emotional Learning (EASEL) Lab at the Harvard Graduate School of Education reviewed numerous SEL programs and categorized them based on the skills they target (see the Helpful Resources section). Much like with assessment tools, it is important for school social workers to consider the practical implications of costs, length of intervention, and alignment to the overall direction of the school or district, as well as the cultural relevance of the program to the population they serve (Hamedani & Darling-Hammond, 2015). Another consideration relating to the delivery of SEL programs is the sustainability of SEL programming effects over time. Low-cost, low-resource strategies (e.g., teaching deep breathing) which support SEL that school social workers can easily integrate into their work with students have received increasing attention from SEL scholars and practitioners (Jones et al., 2017).

Progress Monitoring

Accountability and students' responsiveness of SEL programming efforts are critical considerations for school social workers. Individual students' responsiveness to and placement in interventions must be periodically assessed and refined. Likewise, overall SEL implementation efforts should include monitoring the social and emotional health of all students. It is vital that school social workers demonstrate evidence of the successes of their work as an ethical obligation to their students, school stakeholders (e.g., administrators and board members), and the broader profession.

At the individual student level, school social workers should utilize the National School Social Work SEL Standards to serve as benchmarks for monitoring students' SEL. For instance, an elementary school social worker working with a child on self-awareness can present the student's ability to name emotions following a related intervention as an indicator of student progress. Connecting the National School Social Work SEL Standards with progress monitoring efforts makes practical sense in demonstrating alignment to the broader SEL approach, assessment, delivery of intervention, and monitoring of student progress. Periodic monitoring provides information to make the necessary adjustments to the interventions.

At the schoolwide level, school social workers can systematically conduct a comprehensive, universal screening approach to monitor the social and emotional health of all students as recommended in a number of best practice guidelines (Therriault et al., 2013, 2014). As illustrated in the example by Tan, Sinha, et al., (2018), if the majority of the students in a school have a particular need, universal, schoolwide (Tier 1) interventions could target it. Other interventions could be aimed at those with less common needs (Tier 2). Students with the highest needs could be supported with more resource-intensive and individualized interventions (Tier 3).

Such a universal, systematic, multi-tiered approach to assessing students' SEL across multiple domains can alleviate the shortcomings of implementing interventions that are based on subjective staff discretion (Robinson & Hutchinson, 2014). Identifying students for interventions solely based on a teacher's classroom experience of the student may reflect teachers' biases while they maintain the difficult task of communicating educational content to students at varying levels at once. This can result in both identifying students for intervention who do not require it and neglecting students whose needs have not come to the teacher's attention. Such schoolwide approaches to developing systems and supports to address student needs can lead to sustained and improved school outcomes (Bradshaw et al., 2012).

Best practice models highlight the need for a continuous and periodic improvement cycle and consistent review of data by schools (Therriault et al., 2013). Data-based approaches to monitoring SEL, especially when it is applied periodically, can ensure that all students receive the needed and appropriate services and can also improve the delivery of targeted interventions to students who need it.

Issues, Challenges, and Recommendations for School Social Workers to Promote SEL

School social workers play a vital role in promoting SEL. However, implementing an integrated SEL approach can have its challenges. School social workers may not feel prepared to lead in SEL, especially in the area of analyzing and utilizing data to lead intervention efforts (Kelly et al., 2015). Time constraints and caseloads could contribute to the lack of school social workers' ability to take leadership SEL roles in schools (Teasley et al., 2012). Schools and districts may not give school social workers as expansive a role in implementing systemic changes to support SEL as their professional expertise allows (Gherardi & Whittlesey-Jerome, 2018). In addition, advocating for the resources to implement programs can be an issue if SEL is not a priority and focus of the district.

Collaboration with multidisciplinary teams in school is critical in advancing school social workers' role in SEL. To promote a culture of SEL innovation, it is important to foster open communication and collaboration across all professionals. School social workers should also pay attention to the role of culture, race/ethnicity, and student SEL development. Students of color have a higher chance of being identified for office referrals (Teasley et al., 2017). It is important that school social workers do not perpetuate any existing marginalization or stigmatization experience when implementing SEL work (Taylor et al., 2018). School social workers should also consider the cultural relevance and adaptation of SEL programming for racial/ethnicity minority students (Hamedani & Darling-Hammond, 2015). It is critical that SEL work with students be strengths-based (Taylor et al., 2018).

There are many other contemporary perspectives that relate to SEL not discussed in this chapter, including trauma-informed care, restorative justice practices, and the role of school social workers in promoting SEL among teachers and parents. In addition, there are many other SEL frameworks that school social workers can consider applying in their work. The University of Chicago Consortium on School Research published two frameworks that are relevant for school social workers: Teaching Adolescents to Be Learners (Farrington et al., 2012) and the Foundations for Young Adult Success (Nagaoka et al., 2015). These frameworks highlight essential "noncognitive factors" such as academic mindsets, social skills, perseverance, learning strategies, and academic behaviors for promoting positive student success. School social workers will value these frameworks for their emphasis on the processes through which schools and school social workers affect students' SEL. A helpful reference for school social workers to study other SEL frameworks is the Explore SEL website by the EASEL Lab. Explore SEL makes it possible to visually compare contemporary frameworks and consider their commonalities and differences. This is a useful tool for school social workers to identify those frameworks that best align with their school context and their students' needs and strengths. Recommended links to other SEL efforts are provided in the Helpful Resources section.

Conclusion

As attention on students' SEL increases, school social workers are expected to play a larger role in promoting SEL. The National School Social Work SEL Standards provides an important guide for this work. Emphasizing assessment, intervention, and monitoring at multiple levels is one way to advance school social workers' role in SEL. Students, schools, families, and communities can benefit from school social workers' attention on SEL.

Acknowledgments

We thank the School Social Work Association of America Social–Emotional Learning Workgroup and the following individuals for informing and sharing the ideas and materials in this chapter: Sheri Olson, Ryan Heath, Robert Lucio, Hasan Johnson, Elizabeth Kruger, and Stephanie Ochocki.

Helpful Resources

For Information

Dr. Camille Farrington's lecture and workshop at the School of Social Work, University of Illinois at Urbana–Champaign (https://socialwork.illinois.edu)

How schools and classrooms shape learning and development: https://www.youtube.com/watch?v=boAPzi2Gjk0

Digging into the science of learning and development: https://www.youtube.com/watch?v=n10Kyk2qHSA

CASEL (Collaborative for Academic, Social, and Emotional Learning): https://casel.org

Cognitive Abilities: http://themindhub.com/research-reports

Harvard Graduate School of Education. Explore SEL by the Ecological Approaches to Social Emotional Learning (EASEL) Lab: http://exploresel.gse.harvard.edu/

Institute for Applied Research in Youth Development: https://sites.tufts.edu/iaryd

MultipleIntelligence:https://www.multipleintelligencesoasis.org

School Social Work Association of America. School social work national standards for social emotional learning: https://www.sswaa.org/sswaa-documents

Search Institute: https://www.search-institute.org

University of Chicago Consortium on School Research: https://consortium.uchicago.edu

Teaching adolescents to become learners: https://consortium.uchicago.edu/publications/

teaching-adolescents-become-learners-role-noncognitive-factors-shaping-school

Foundations for young adult success: https://consortium.uchicago.edu/publications/foundations-young-adult-success-developmental-framework

For Assessment

American Institutes for Research. *Are you ready to assess social and emotional learning and development? (second edition)*: https://www.air.org/resource/are-you-ready-assess-social-and-emotional-learning-and-development-second-edition

Raikes Foundation. *Social–emotional learning assessment measures for middle school youth*: https://casel.org/wp-content/uploads/2016/01/DAP-Raikes-Foundation-Review-1.pdf

RAND Corporation. *RAND Education Assessment Finder*: https://www.rand.org/education-and-labor/projects/assessments.html

For Interventions

Campbell Collaboration: http://www.campbellcollaboration.org

CASEL (Collaborative for Academic, Social, and Emotional Learning). *Program guide*: https://casel.org/guide

Institute of Education Sciences. *What Works Clearinghouse*: http://ies.ed.gov/ncee/wwc

Office of Juvenile Justice and Delinquency Prevention. *Model programs*: https://www.ojjdp.gov.mpg

Substance Abuse and Mental Health Services Administration. *SAMHSA's National Registry of Evidence-Based Programs and Practices*: https://youth.gov/federal-links/samhsa%E2%80%99s-national-registry-evidence-based-programs-and-practices-nrepp

Wallace Foundation. *Navigating SEL from the inside out*: https://www.wallacefoundation.org/knowledge-center/Documents/Navigating-Social-and-Emotional-Learning-from-the-Inside-Out.pdf

References

Bradshaw, C. P., Waasdorp, T. E., & Leaf, P. J. (2012). Effects of school-wide positive behavioral interventions and supports on child behavior problems. *Pediatrics, 130*(5), e1136–e1145.

Clark, J. P., & Alvarez, M. (2010). *Response to intervention: A guide for school social workers*. Oxford University Press.

Collaborative for Academic, Social, and Emotional Learning. (2018). *SEL: What are the core competence*

areas and where are they promoted? https://casel.org/core-competencies

Durlak, J. A., Weissberg, R. P., Dymnicki, A. B., Taylor, R. D., & Schellinger, K. B. (2011). The impact of enhancing students' social and emotional learning: A meta-analysis of school-based universal interventions. *Child Development, 82*(1), 405–432. https://doi.org/10.1111/j.1467-8624.2010.01564.x

Farrington, C. A., Roderick, M., Allensworth, E., Nagaoka, J., Keyes, T. S., Johnson, D. W., & Beechum, N. O. (2012). *Teaching adolescents to become learners: The role of noncognitive factors in shaping school performance—A critical literature review*. Consortium on Chicago School Research.

Frey, A. J., Alvarez, M. E., Sabatino, C. A., Lindsey, B. C., Dupper, D. R., Raines, J. C., Streeck, F., McInerney, A., & Norris, M. P. (2012). The development of a national school social work practice model. *Children & Schools, 34*(3), 131.

Gherardi, S. A., & Whittlesey-Jerome, W. K. (2018). Role integration through the practice of social work with schools. *Children and Schools, 40*(1), 35–44.

Hamedani, M. G., & Darling-Hammond, L. (2015, March). *Social emotional learning in high school: How three urban high schools engage, educate, and empower youth*. Stanford Center for Opportunity Policy in Education.

Harlacher, J. E., Sakelaris, T. L., & Kattelman, N. M. (2014). Multi-tiered system of support. In *Practitioner's guide to curriculum-based evaluation in reading* (pp. 23–45). Springer. http://link.springer.com/chapter/10.1007/978-1-4614-9360-0_3

Horner, R. H., & Sugai, G. (2015). School-wide PBIS: An example of applied behavior analysis implemented at a scale of social importance. *Behavior Analysis in Practice, 8*(1), 80–85. https://doi.org/10.1007/s40617-015-0045-4

Jones, S., Bailey, R., Brush, K., & Kahn, J. (2017). *Kernels of practice for SEL: Low-cost, low-burden strategies*. Harvard Graduate School of Education.

Kelly, M. S., Thompson, A. M., Frey, A., Klemp, H., Alvarez, M., & Berzin, S. C. (2015). The state of school social work: Revisited. *School Mental Health, 7*(3), 174–183. https://doi.org/10.1007/s12310-015-9149-9

Knowles, J., & White, D. (2015). *Wisconsin dropout early warning system action guide*. Wisconsin Department of Public Instruction.

Lindsey, B., Smith, K., Cox, T., James, M., Alvarez, M., & Kunkel, R. (2014). *School social work national standards for social emotional learning*. School Social Work Association of America.

Nagaoka, J., Farrington, C. A., Ehrlich, S. B., & Heath, R. D. (2015). *Foundations for young adult success: A developmental framework* [Concept paper for research and practice]. University of Chicago Consortium on Chicago School Research.

Robinson, K., & Hutchinson, N. L. (2014). *Tiered approaches to the education of students with learning disabilities.* LD@school.

Tan, K., Sinha, G., Shin, O. J., & Yang, W. (2018). Patterns of social–emotional learning needs among high school freshmen students. *Children and Youth Services Review, 86,* 217–225.

Tan, K., Teasley, M. L., Crutchfield, J. M., & Canfield, J. P. (2018). Bridging the disparity gap in school behavioral health: Targeted interventions for patterns of risk. *Children & Schools, 40*(1), 3–6.

Taylor, J., Buckley, K., Hamilton, L., Stecher, B., Read, L., & Schweig, J. (2018). Choosing and using SEL competency assessments: What schools and districts need to know. Rand Corporation. https:// measuringsel.casel.org/pdf/Choosing-and-Using-SEL-Competency-Assessments_What-Schools-and-Districts-Need-to-Know.pdf

Teasley, M. L., Canfield, J. P., Archuleta, A. J., Crutchfield, J., & McCullough Chavis, A. (2012).

Perceived barriers and facilitators to school social work practice: A mixed-methods study. *Children and Schools, 34*(3), 145–153.

Teasley, M. L., McRoy, R. G., Joyner, M., Armour, M., Gourdine, R. M., Crewe, S. E., Kelly, M., Franklin, C. G., Payne, M., Jackson, J. L., Jr., & Fong, R. (2017). Increasing success for African American children and youth. Grand Challenges for Social Work Initiative Working Paper No. 21. American Academy of Social Work and Social Welfare.

Therriault, S., O'Cummings, M., Heppen, J., Yerhot, L., & Scala, J. (2013). High school early warning intervention monitoring system implementation guide. National High School Center at the American Institutes for Research.

Therriault, S., Surr, W., Bzura, R., Curtin, J., & Sandel, K. (2014). Early warning implementation guide: Using the Massachusetts Early Warning Indicator System (EWIS) and local data to identify, diagnose, support, and monitor students in grades 1–12. Massachusetts Department of Elementary and Secondary Education.

School Social Work with Latinx Immigrant Youth and Families

Leticia Villarreal Sosa

Latinx[1] youth comprise approximately one-fourth of all kindergarten through grade 12 public school students and are expected to represent 30% of all students by 2032 (Mather & Foxen, 2016). Latinx youth are a diverse group representing a range of identities and immigration statuses. More than 95% of Latinx children are U.S. citizens; however, approximately 52% live in immigrant families (Foxen, 2019). Thus, when thinking about "immigrant" youth, we must include those who are second generation[2] as well as new arrivals. A survey by the Immigrant Student Equity Project found that more than 75% of school social workers (SSWs; $n = 219$) reported increased behavioral or emotional challenges among immigrant students due to increased and harsh immigration enforcement (Roth et al., 2020). Therefore, schools and SSWs throughout the United States must be prepared to address the needs of the children impacted by these targeted attacks. Every Latinx immigrant group has its own historical context related to the relationship between the United States and its country of origin. This historical context matters for *current* immigrant youth because the way in which a group is perceived by the host society impacts their incorporation. As SSWs, we must be equipped to understand the historical and political contexts shaping the experience of Latinx youth, address their particular needs such as identity trauma, and leverage their cultural and individual strengths and resiliency.

The Educational Context

Despite increases in graduation rates and college attendance for Latinxs, they continue to experience educational disparities beginning in early childhood that persist through college, with overrepresentation in remedial classes and low college graduation rates (Foxen, 2019).

---

1. The use of the term Latinx is intended to be inclusive to those who may not conform to the gender binary reflected in Latina or Latino and identify as trans, queer, agender, nonbinary, gender nonconforming, or gender fluid.

2. The second generation refers to youth born in the United States but who have at least one parent who was born abroad.

In addition, Latinx reading and math proficiency rates are approximately half those of White students by the time they reach eighth grade (Mather & Foxen, 2016). These educational disparities suggest the loss of untapped potential among a growing population in our schools, making this not just a Latinx issue but also an issue of national concern.

The Struggle for Education

Latinxs have a long history of educational struggle—for example, Puerto Ricans[3] in the 1950s and 1960s in New York City. Puerto Rican social worker, Antonia Pantoja, challenged the assimilationist role of the schools, stating that it was an assault on the psychological well-being and identity of Puerto Rican children. In 1970, she testified to the U.S. Senate, stating that "schools have mounted an attack on the child who speaks Spanish," resulting in the child feeling ashamed of themselves, their parents, and impacting their motivation to learn (p. 3688). The landmark Supreme Court case of *Lau v. Nichols*, which prohibited language discrimination and extended the protections of the Civil Rights Act of 1964 to language minority children, provided the foundation for this advocacy in major cities throughout the United States (De Jesús & Pérez, 2009).

Similarly, Mexican Americans have a long history of struggle for educational rights. Mexican Americans fought school segregation as early as 1914 with the *Francisco Maestas et al. v. George H. Shone* case in Colorado and the 1946 case, *Mendez v. Westminster* (Mendez), which set the precedent for the *Brown v. Board of Education* decision (Donato & Hanson, 2019). More recently, in Chicago, beginning on Mother's Day of 2001, a group of Mexican immigrant mothers held a 19-day hunger strike to pressure the Chicago Public Schools to build a new high school (Cortez, 2013). Then, in 2010, low-income Mexican immigrant mothers occupied the field house of an elementary school for a total of 43 days to demand space to alleviate overcrowding (Cortez, 2013). These examples demonstrate the courage Latinx parents have shown in the fight for access to education for their children.

Equity and Historical Legacies

In a xenophobic context that directly targets Latinx communities, SSWs must assume leadership in developing welcoming school climates for immigrant youth. This can be accomplished by addressing educational equity and utilizing approaches that consider the lived experiences of these youth, their resilience, and cultural capital. Furthermore, SSWs need to ground themselves in the history of the profession and incorporate a critical lens to that history. In the early 1900s, social workers viewed themselves as "agents of 'Americanization'" and focused on immigrant behavior and values rather than basic needs (Jani & Reisch, 2018, p. 6). Today, this focus has shifted to emphasize mental health over structural change (Jani & Reisch, 2018). For SSWs to adequately address the needs of Latinx youth, the scope and perspective must be holistic, consider the implicit goals of schooling, and understand the racialization process that renders certain immigrants as "other." Finally, SSWs should understand mental health from a macro perspective with a focus on how structural violence impacts mental health.

3. It is important to note that although Puerto Ricans were declared U.S. citizens in 1917 in order to be drafted into World War I (Organista, 2007), they were treated as "aliens" and viewed as part of the racially inferior immigrant groups coming to the United States in the 1950s and subjected to eugenics and a colonial mentality (De Jesús & Peréz, 2009). Puerto Rico has been under U.S. control since 1898 and remains a pseudo colony (politely termed a "commonwealth"). Puerto Ricans on the island have no vote in national elections, cannot be elected to the U.S. House or Senate, and have one congressional representative with no voting power.

Historical Context and Group Diversity

The U.S. Hispanic[4] population is diverse, with approximately 30 different subgroups represented in the U.S. Census (U.S. Census Bureau, n.d.). Although the U.S. Census identifies "Hispanic" as an ethnic group, many Latinxs identify as both a racial and ethnic group due to racialization experiences. Furthermore, many identify their national origin as their preferred identity. Thus, it is always best to ask Latinx students how they identify and what that identity means to them. It is also important to learn about the historical context of the migration experience for the particular Latinx groups in one's school, including the role of U.S. policy in that country. The following section discusses the experiences of Mexican Americans and Central Americans because they are among the most marginalized and numerous Latinx immigrant groups, and they face serious educational challenges. Although addressing the histories of all Latinx groups is beyond the scope of this chapter, SSWs need to be aware of current events that impact demographics. For example, individuals from Venezuela currently comprise the third largest group of asylum applications to the United States [United Nations High Commissioner for Refugees (UNHCR), 2018]. The United States has been directly involved in supporting the opposition leader and threatened military intervention while not welcoming Venezuelans as refugees, making their incorporation into U.S. society challenging. SSWs play important roles in creating welcoming climates for newer groups such as Venezuelans.

Mexican Americans

Mexican Americans are native to the southwestern United States and were annexed by conquest (Organista, 2007). Mexican Americans are the largest national origin group, comprising 62% of the Latinx population (Noe-Bustamante, 2019). Other terms for this population are Chicano or Mexican. Chicano was a term that derived from the Mexican American civil rights movement. This term honors Indigenous heritage and was a way of reclaiming the term with pride. There is a complex relationship for Mexican Americans with the land due to the history of conquest; thus, terminology and connection to Mexico will depend on the geographical context. For example, in the Midwest, due to their racialized experience, it is common for Mexican Americans to call themselves "Mexican" even if they were born in the United States (Villarreal Sosa, 2011). Thus, the term "Mexican" is both an ethnic/national origin identifier and a racial identity. Ogbu (1989) explains that for Mexican Americans, subsequent immigrants are assigned the status of the earlier, conquered and colonized group and thus share a sense of collective identity as involuntary minorities and continue to be marginalized.

Central Americans

Central America includes the countries of Panama, Costa Rica, Nicaragua, Honduras, El Salvador, Guatemala, and Belize. As of 2018, the Central American countries of El Salvador, Guatemala, and Honduras were among the countries with the highest number of asylum seekers to the United States (UNHCR, 2018) and represented 86% of Central American immigrants to the United States (O'Connor et al., 2019). Immigration from this area increased dramatically during the 1980s and 1990s when Guatemalans, Salvadorians, and Nicaraguans

---

4. Hispanic was a term first introduced in the 1970s by the federal government. Many Latinx individuals reject the term because it is seen as imposed on rather than adopted by the community. In addition, Hispanic emphasizes Spanish colonial roots and negates Indigenous or African roots. I use the term Hispanic when citing official government statistics that use the term. Hispanic includes people of Spanish origin. Latinx does not include Spaniards, as they are European.

were forced to flee due to civil war. In each of these cases, the origins of those wars were a direct result of military and economic intervention by the United States (J. Gonzalez, 2011). Both the Reagan and Bush administrations refused to aid those coming across the border escaping terror, and few Central Americans received refugee status (J. Gonzalez, 2011). Furthermore, Hurricane Mitch in 1998 that impacted Honduras and Nicaragua and earthquakes that impacted El Salvador in 2001 led to immigrants from these countries being eligible for Temporary Protected Status (TPS), which provides work authorization and temporary relief from deportation. Central Americans make up the largest group among those receiving TPS and Deferred Action for Childhood Arrivals (DACA),[5] both set for termination by the Trump administration and kept active through court orders. SSWs working with Central American students and families must have a basic understanding of this complex history, legacies of trauma and violence, and the impact of policy changes on immigration status.

Unaccompanied Minors

Unaccompanied minors are children younger than the age of 18 years who enter the United States with an unauthorized status and do not have a parent or legal guardian with them. Children apprehended at the border are detained by the U.S. Department of Homeland Security (DHS) and then transferred to the Office of Refugee Resettlement (ORR). ORR (2020) estimates that in 2019, approximately 70,000 youth were referred by DHS, with the

highest percentage coming from Guatemala, Honduras, El Salvador, and Mexico. These numbers are expected to continue to increase due to the ongoing instability in their home countries (Jani & Reisch, 2018). Due to the Trump administration's policies, growing numbers of children remain in ORR custody rather than being placed with sponsors in the United States. The shortage of space and resources has left children in deplorable conditions along the border in Immigration and Customs Enforcement facilities not meant to house children. Those who escape apprehension often work in agriculture, restaurants, or as domestic workers and are highly vulnerable to exploitation.

School social workers should be aware of the trauma children have experienced, work transnationally in connecting youth with their families, and utilize intervention strategies that address trauma. In addition, it is important to recognize that many of these youth may be working many hours to support themselves and their families back home, impacting their school attendance. For those who have been in detention centers for lengthy periods of time, mental health often deteriorates, and they may need more specialized support. Comprehensive assessment in order to identify their complex needs is imperative for supporting these students in their educational progress.

Undocumented Students

For undocumented youth, challenges due to racism, xenophobia, and poverty are compounded by their immigration status. They face barriers to college attendance, are not eligible for a driver's license in most states, are legally barred from employment, and experience the social and psychological consequences of "living in the shadows" and threat of deportation. Not surprisingly, undocumented students report having significant psychological distress and experiences of depression, suicidal ideation, and anxiety (R. Gonzalez et al., 2013). Those with DACA

---

5. DACA was implemented in 2012 by the U.S. Department of Homeland Security after President Obama's executive order. DACA allows youth who were brought to the United States as children and who meet certain criteria to request deferred action or to not be deported from the United States for a period of 2 years, with the possibility for renewal. DACA recipients can live in the United States and attend school and may be eligible for work authorization. DACA was rescinded by President Trump in 2017; new applications are not accepted, but those with DACA are eligible to renew based on a court order.

face similar pressures because their status does not lead to permanent legal residency and their future is left to the whim of presidential executive order and the courts.

Advocacy and accompaniment of undocumented youth begin the moment they enroll in school. Undocumented youth face barriers at this first encounter due to parents not being able to provide proof of address or the proper documentation from employers to qualify for school fee waivers or reduced lunch. The first step is to ensure these youth have access to school and resources they need. Later, interventions can include creating a safe space for undocumented students by providing staff development, making sure students can identify "safe" adults in the school, and forming networks with other support services and allies. SSWs should work to understand any current legislation that impacts undocumented youth, reach out to community resources such as immigrant advocacy organizations for their expertise, and be active in advocacy beyond the school. In promoting resilience, undocumented students often state that a key adult in the school provided them with the hope and support to continue their education.

Trauma and the Anti-Immigrant Context

The various immigration policies, harsh enforcement, and national rhetoric around immigration have led to the traumatization of countless children. Palmary (2019) states that the real danger to children is not in the migration process but, rather, the view of foreigners as "threats." The view of immigrants as "threats" and "criminals" allows for the use of extreme practices, inhumane conditions, and other human rights violations. As Palmary (2019) states,

> Psychologists working with refugee and migrant children often are concerned with the trauma they have faced in their

countries of origin and en route to their destination. A view that has a greater focus on the political and social context can mean that interventions are tailored not just to individual families and children but towards restructuring the conditions that lead to their abuse in the first place. (p. 9)

SSWs can also heed this advice and focus on the political and social context and the ways in which that context also traumatizes children.

It has been well documented (e.g., Healy, 2018) that the separations of families at the border are traumatic experiences for children with the potential for lifelong effects. What has been less often acknowledged are the parent and child or child and sibling separations that have already occurred due to detentions and deportations. Approximately 500,000 U.S. citizen children experienced the detention or deportation of a parent during 2011–2013, and an increasing number of health care providers report symptoms of "toxic stress" such as depression and anxiety in these children due to fear that a family member will be deported (American Immigration Council, 2018). The anti-immigrant climate contributes to the feeling of marginalization among Latinx youth as they are challenged to construct their social identities in the midst of this social context (Villarreal Sosa, 2011).

Identity and Historical Trauma

One of the consequences of family separations and the anti-immigrant climate is the development of complex trauma.[6] Of various immigrant groups, the Latinx community is the ethnic group most often subjected to discrimination

---

6. Complex trauma is defined as "traumatic attachment that is life- or self-threatening . . . and involves events and experiences that alter the development of the self by requiring survival to take precedence over normal psychobiological development" (Courtois & Ford, 2016, p. 25).

surrounding immigration status (Pew Hispanic Center, 2010). Latinx families continue to experience fear, discrimination, and oppressive conditions. In this atmosphere of xenophobia and hate, Latinx children's development is compromised by what Kira (2010) refers to as type III or type IV trauma. Type III trauma refers to trauma inflicted on a person based on their identity. Type IV trauma refers to trauma inflicted based on community membership. This trauma can manifest itself in two ways: through an act such as the separation of children from their families or through daily microaggressions (Courtois & Ford, 2016). For example, many children repeatedly have their citizenship interrogated and hear messages questioning the worth of people who are undocumented (Ayón, 2016). Type III and type IV trauma are also considered "historical trauma." Historical trauma consists of events that target an entire community, such as mass immigration raids of the present day. These events become cumulative group trauma, passed on across generations.

School Social Workers Addressing Trauma

School social workers can play an important role in ensuring the psychological and emotional safety of immigrant and second-generation students in the school setting. The adverse effects of trauma on children's mental health and functioning in the school setting materialize in a variety of ways, such as student attendance, academic achievement, concentration, memory, sleep, and behavior (American Immigration Council, 2018). School-based interventions must include prevention and intervention efforts at the Tier 1 level that address discrimination in both child-to-child and teacher-to-child interactions. These interventions could include activities that increase awareness about diversity and equity, supporting teachers to build relationships with immigrant parents, and considering the overall

school climate toward immigrant youth. Connecting parents and children to advocacy efforts and community-based supports is also important because trauma inflicted upon an entire group or community is often best supported by addressing it as a community.

Given fear and the lack of access to mental health services for the undocumented community, the SSW may be one of the few mental health service providers available to immigrant families. Thus, the provision of Tier 2 or Tier 3 services is essential for immigrant youth. As SSWs engage in mental health work, understanding youth behavior from a racial equity lens is imperative. As stated by Menakem (2017), trauma work needs to be contextualized within a reality of White supremacy. To be effective in this work, social workers must challenge themselves to do their own work around trauma awareness and racial justice. One of the most critical aspects of any approach is what is often called a "relational" approach. In other words, any intervention, when provided by caring and supportive adults who show "empathy, self-awareness, compassion, and positive regard" (Courtois & Ford, 2016, p. viii), will be more effective, independent of empirically tested evidence-based practices. This approach is consistent with a trauma-informed approach and addresses the importance for Latinx youth of "caring" and affiliation with school personnel as a main source for motivation (Valenzuela, 1999), thus improving their educational outcomes and well-being.

Chicana Feminist Theory and School Social Work

Supporting Latinx students will be enhanced by incorporating frameworks that center the lived experiences of people of color, challenge the claims of neutrality of interventions—even those considered evidence-based practice—and support critical reflexivity among all SSWs. Each person is situated among various social locations, and whether or not there is coherence between these various social locations and the professional context will vary. When attempting to implement social justice and racial equity practices, these tensions can manifest in differences in motivation, awareness, and critical reflection among practitioners. A borderlands and nepantla framework provides space for these tensions and pushes practitioners toward critical reflection and change. Borderlands is a metaphor that can describe both personal and social healing. Anzaldúa (1987) describes the borderlands as a wound that never heals, where "hate, anger, and exploitation are the prominent features of this landscape" (Preface). Simultaneously, borderlands speak of the joy, gifts, consciousness, and transformation that happen in this space, both in the process of traversing these borderlands and in resistance to the oppression found in this space. This conceptualization of borderlands is fitting given the open wound we see daily in immigration policies enacted and anti-immigrant rhetoric present in the national culture.

School Social Workers as Nepantleras

In Anzaldúa's work, the borderlands evolves into the concept of nepantla, "an in-between state, that uncertain terrain one crosses when moving from one place to another, when changing from one class, race, or sexual position to another, when traveling from the present identity into a new identity" (Anzaldúa, 2009, p. 180). This concept is useful as we think about the multiple identities and worlds Latinx youth traverse as they navigate the multiple traumas, the daily barrage of anti-immigrant sentiment, and microaggressions. This is also useful in recognizing their strengths of identity, navigational capital, and the psychological resilience they possess. SSWs can become nepantleras,

social change agents capable of border crossing, in the process of mediating their own and their students' cultural and psychological borders. Nepantleras inspire and challenge others to be critically conscious. As SSWs engage in this work of personal and social transformation, it is necessary to recognize that this process can be painful, difficult, and messy, and acting as nepantleras takes courage. However, we must act courageously, utilizing our own positionality and reflexivity for promoting social change and equity in our everyday work with Latinx students.

Changing the Narrative

Latinx students are often viewed through a deficit-oriented lens. One of the most important roles for SSWs is changing the narrative and elevating the lived experiences of Latinx students. The media and educators perpetuate the perceptions that Latinx students are underachievers, prone to gang involvement or other risky behaviors, do not speak or write English well, and "don't value education" (Foxen, 2019). These assumptions are fueled by inaccurate perceptions of what causes achievement gaps. The challenges Latinx immigrant youth experience stem from issues such as poverty, migration stress, discrimination, and the lack of culturally responsive teaching. SSWs must understand the psychosocial issues in a way that depathologizes but does not minimize the challenges. SSWs can be involved on a number of levels, such as providing staff development to teachers and contributing to curriculum design, policy advocacy, and research on effective practices with Latinx youth. SSWs can be important advocates for immigrant students, ensuring that their voices are heard and identities respected. Through listening and respecting Latinx students, SSWs can create environments in which the students can thrive and grow for themselves and for the future of the nation.

References

American Immigration Council. (2018, May 23). Fact sheet: U.S. citizen children impacted by immigration enforcement. https://www.americanimmigrationcouncil.org/research/us-citizen-children-impacted-immigration-enforcement

Anzaldúa, G. (1987). *Borderlands/La frontera: The new mestiza*. Aunt Lute Books.

Anzaldúa, G. (2009). *The Gloria Anzaldúa reader* (A. L. Keating, Ed.). Duke University Press.

Ayón, C. (2016). Talking to Latino children about race, inequality, and discrimination: Raising families in an anti-immigrant political environment. *Journal of the Society for Social Work Research, 7*(3), 449–477.

Cortez, G. A. (2013). Occupy public education: A community's struggle for educational resources in the era of privatization. *Equity & Excellence in Education, 46*(1), 7–19. doi:10.1080/10665684.2013.750994

Courtois, C. A., & Ford, J. D. (2016). *Treatment of complex trauma: A sequenced, relationship-based approach*. Guildford.

De Jesús, A., & Pérez, M. E. (2009). From community control to consent decree: Puerto Ricans organizing for education and language rights in 1960s and 70s New York City. *Centro Journal, 21*(2), 6–31.

Donato, R., & Hanson, J. (2019). Mexican-American resistance to school segregation. *Phi Delta Kappan, 100*(5), 39–42.

Foxen, P. (2019). *The state of public education for Latino students: A qualitative research report*. UnidosUS. http://publications.unidosus.org/bitstream/handle/123456789/1946/unidosus_publiceducation_lr.pdf?sequence=1&isAllowed=y

Gonzalez, J. (2011). *Harvest of empire: A history of Latinos in America*. Penguin.

Gonzalez, R. G., Suárez-Orozco, C., & Dedios-Sanguineti, M. A. (2013). No place to belong: Contextualizing concepts of mental health among undocumented immigrant youth in the United States. *American Behavioral Scientist, 57*(8), 1174–1199. https://doi.org/10.1177/0002764213487349

Healy, M. (2018, June 20). The long-lasting health effects of separating children from their parents at the U.S border. *Los Angeles Times*. http://www.latimes.com/science/sciencenow/la-sci-sn-separating-children-psychology-20180620-story.html

Jani, J. S., & Reisch, M. (2018). Assisting the least among us: Social work's historical response to unaccompanied immigrant and refugee youth. *Children and Youth Services Review, 92*, 4–14. https://doi.org/10.1016/j.childyouth.2018.02.025

Kira, I. A. (2010). Etiology and treatment of post-cumulative traumatic stress disorders in different cultures. *Traumatology, 16*(4), 128–141.

Mather, M., & Foxen, P. (2016). Toward a more equitable future: The trends and challenges facing America's Latino children. National Council of La Raza. http://publications.unidosus.org/handle/123456789/1627

Menakem, R. ((2017). *My grandmother's hands: Racialized trauma and the pathway to mending our hearts and bodies*. Central Recovery Press.

Noe-Bustamante, L. (2019, September 16). Key facts about U.S. Hispanics and their diverse heritage. Pew Research Center. https://www.pewresearch.org/fact-tank/2019/09/16/key-facts-about-u-s-hispanics

O'Connor, A., Batalova, J., & Bolter, J. (2019). *Central American immigrants in the United States*. Migration Policy Institute. https://www.migrationpolicy.org/article/central-american-immigrants-united-states

Office of Refugee Resettlement. (2020). Facts and data. https://www.acf.hhs.gov/orr/about/ucs/facts-and-data

Ogbu, J. U. (1989). The individual in collective adaptation: A framework for focusing on academic underperformance and dropping out among involuntary minorities. In L. Weis, E. Farrar, & H. G. Petrie (Eds.), *Dropouts from school: Issues, dilemmas, and solutions* (pp. 181–204). State University of New York Press.

Organista, K. C. (2007). *Solving Latino psychosocial and health problems: Theory, practice, and populations*. Wiley.

Palmary, I. (2019). Migrant children separated from their parents: Where does the real risk to children's safety lie? *South African Journal of Psychology, 49*(1), 7–9. doi:10.1177/0081246318795827

Pew Hispanic Center. (2010). *Hispanics and Arizona's new immigration law*: Fact sheet. http://pewresearch.org/pubs/1579/arizona-immigration-law-fact-sheet-hispanic-population-opinion-discrimination

Roth, B., Villarreal Sosa, L., & Rodriguez, S. (2020, April). *What does equity look like for immigrant students*. Immigrant Student Equity Project. https://www.immigrantequityproject.org

United Nations High Commissioner for Refugees. (2018). *Global trends: Forced displacement in 2018*. https://www.unhcr.org/globaltrends2018

U.S. Census Bureau. (n.d.). *About Hispanic origin*. https://www.census.gov/topics/population/hispanic-origin/about.html

U.S. Senate. (1970). Equal educational opportunity hearings. Select Committee on Equal Educational Opportunity of the United States Senate. Ninety-first Congress. Part 8—Equal Educational Opportunity for Puerto Rican Children.

Valenzuela, A. (1999). *Subtractive schooling: U.S.-Mexican youth and the politics of caring*. State University of New York Press.

Villarreal Sosa, L. (2011). *Mexican origin students in the borderlands: The construction of social identity in the school context*. Doctoral dissertation. Available from ProQuest Dissertations and Theses database (UMI No. 3472970).

Using Data and Evidence in Schools

Natasha K. Bowen

Using Data in Socially Just School Social Work

Public school personnel in the United States operate under numerous formal and informal mandates to use data and empirical evidence in their decision-making about supports for students, including those who have disabilities, are English learners, or are from low-income or racial/ethnic minority families. The Every Student Succeeds Act of 2015 (ESSA; https://www.congress.gov/114/plaws/publ95/PLAW-114publ95.pdf) stipulates that schools must annually test the mathematics and language arts proficiency of all students, and school districts must make the results publicly available. The professional organizations of school social workers also dictate that members use data and evidence-based strategies in their practice in schools (Midwest School Social Work Council, 2015; National Association of Social Workers, 2012).

The ultimate goals of federal law and professional guidelines about using data and evidence are to promote the academic achievement of all students and reduce disparities among demographic groups. These goals have not been met (Ispa-Landa, 2018; McIntosh et al., 2018; Quinn, 2017). According to the National

Center for Education Statistics (2019), the majority of American students still fail to demonstrate proficiency on standardized achievement tests each year. Only 34% of eighth graders were proficient or above in mathematics in 2019, and racial/ethnic performance disparities were stark: 44% of White eighth graders were at or above proficiency in math in 2019 compared to 13% of African Americans. These disturbing achievement statistics persist despite two decades of efforts that have included the widespread adoption of multiple-tiered systems to promote achievement, such as response to intervention (RtI; http://www.rtinetwork.org/learn/what/whatisrti).

African American students also experience disparities in behavioral outcomes despite multiple-tiered systems designed to address school behavior, such as Positive Behavioral Interventions & Supports (https://www.pbis.org). They are more likely to experience harsh or exclusionary discipline (Gregory & Fergus, 2017; McIntosh et al., 2018) and are two or three times more likely to be suspended than White students, particularly for "offenses" for which subjective judgment plays a larger role (Ispa-Landa, 2018).

This chapter describes online resources designed to increase the use of student support strategies targeting the malleable social environmental factors that help explain academic and behavioral outcomes. Special attention is paid to resources and research relevant to promoting equity in academic and behavioral outcomes for African American students. A critical assumption underlying the resources is that data and evidence related to students' experiences in the social environment can change the decision-making discourse in schools from being narrow and deficit-focused to being broad and context-focused. Studies have demonstrated that school personnel—like the general population—have implicit racial biases that contribute to persistent academic and disciplinary disparities (Ispa-Landa, 2018; Warikoo et al., 2016). An emphasis on social justice in school practices includes identifying strategies that undercut the mechanisms by which racial biases threaten the school success of African American students.

School social workers are critical to promoting systemic change in how the academic and behavioral performance of African American students is interpreted and addressed in schools. Two intertwined elements of their training are essential in new approaches: (1) curricular content and field experience demonstrating the role of the social environment in students' school performance and (2) the social justice perspective. The new resources are responsive to the context in which school social workers operate (N. Bowen & Powers, 2011) and to their preferences about the content, format, and navigability of online supports (Patak-Pietrafesa et al., 2019).

Overview of the Resources for Social Justice

Since the publication of the first version of this chapter (N. Bowen, 2015), a number of improvements have been made to the online resources for the School Success Profile (SSP) and

Elementary School Success Profile (ESSP) and to the surveys themselves. Importantly, the two social environmental assessments and their individual and group-level reports are now freely available. All informational resources described here are also freely available. The new SSP website (https://schoolsuccessprofile.net/) houses the following:

- The ESSP 2020 for collecting social environmental data from third through fifth graders, their caregivers, and teachers (N. Bowen et al., 2004)
- Connection to the SSP 2020 for collecting social environmental data from middle school students (N. Bowen et al., 2020)
- A searchable database of information on best practices, with content and formatting tailored to practitioners' needs and preferences
- A searchable database of information on brief free measures for social work practice along with the measures themselves, ready to be copied and used
- A searchable database of 1-page summaries of research on populations and issues encountered in school social work practice and research-based practice tools
- Training materials for collecting pre- and post-test data on prevention targets and conducting simple tests of change in those outcomes

Use of the online resources does not require administration of the SSP 2020 or ESSP 2020. The databases will be continuously built over time, and social workers are encouraged to suggest additions. The SSP website is primarily designed to support school social workers who work on decision-making teams, such as student support, school improvement, and building leadership teams. However, it can also be used for individual practice. Ideally, the resources will support collaboration in the use of data and evidence across school professionals, such as counselors, psychologists, and nurses. A goal of the site is to make it unnecessary for school social workers to travel to multiple websites to get information and practice tools that have been vetted by researchers (Patak-Pietrafesa et al., 2019).

Current Data Use in Schools

One goal of the website is to broaden the types of data used by school personnel. The most common type of data collected in schools is academic achievement data. Achievement data are routinely collected in kindergarten through grade 12 public schools at the beginning, end, and throughout the school year. Assessments include whole-school screeners for academic problems as well as ongoing performance data for students receiving interventions. Many of the available achievement assessments target highly specific academic skills or knowledge (e.g., see hundreds of assessments at the National Center on RtI website http://www.rtinetwork.org/learn/what/whatisrti). Federally and state-mandated summative standardized testing data are also collected at the end of the school year and used to generate public "report cards" for schools and districts.

Social and emotional learning (SEL) data are also commonly collected in schools. One framework for social and emotional learning [Collaborative for Academic, Social, and Emotional Learning (CASEL), https://casel.org] includes self-awareness, self-management, social awareness, relationship skills, and responsible decision-making. The descriptions at the CASEL website of these five components of SEL suggest that deficits in behavior and social skills of students are of primary concern.

Limitations of Current Data

Although detailed performance data clearly have utility in efforts to improve academic achievement, an almost exclusive reliance on such data is unlikely to promote higher rates of proficiency and reduce the racial/ethnic gap because they do not provide information about *why* gaps may exist. "Risk factors" for negative performance outcomes are often defined as existing performance deficits and demographic characteristics (Rumberger & Lim, 2008). Furthermore, one critique of SEL approaches stated that their failure was due to "colorblind implementation," no attention to "power, privilege and culture," and their focus on students and not the teachers with whom they interact (Gregory & Fergus, 2017, p. 117).

Also of concern is the fact that data collection tools and corresponding academic and SEL interventions are supported by an industry of assessments, progress monitoring tools, and packaged interventions. Assessments and associated interventions can cost up to tens of thousands of dollars annually for one school (e.g., see Tool Charts at the National Center on RtI website, http://www.rtinetwork.org/toolkit). In other words, maintaining a disproportionate focus on "fixing" problems in the socialization and academics of African American students (and other marginalized groups) is financially advantageous to developers of those materials. And yet, disparities persist. Without attention to social environmental contributors to disparities, significant and lasting improvement in educational outcomes is unlikely to occur because factors beyond individual students' current difficulties contribute to the emergence and maintenance of disparities (Gregory & Fergus, 2017).

Using Social Environmental Data to Promote Social Justice

Two free surveys at the SSP website provide social workers and other school personnel with comprehensive data about students' experiences in and perceptions of the social environment. The surveys also assess student physical and psychological well-being, behavior, and academic performance. Although other existing measures collect data on some dimensions assessed with the two surveys, the SSP 2020 and ESSP 2020 are the only surveys that provide comprehensive information on the neighborhood, school, peers, family microsystems, and school–family relationships.

The SSP 2020 is a self-report Qualtrics survey that assesses 27 dimensions of the social environment and well-being of middle and high school students (N. Bowen et al., 2020). It is a shortened and simplified version of the SSP that was developed in the late 1990s (G. Bowen et al., 2005). Reports are available through a Tableau dashboard from which users can navigate to schoolwide, group, and individual-level results.

The ESSP 2020 assesses 28 dimensions of the social environment and well-being of for third through fifth graders. Data collected from children, caregivers, and teachers are combined in individual and group-level graphical reports. The ESSP 2020 is an updated version of the original ESSP (N. Bowen et al., 2004), which was created in the early 2000s. The new version has an updated interface, updated graphics in the child component, and new report formats, all of which take into account the new familiarity of students with online technology and content. The quality of SSP and ESSP data has been established in numerous publications (G. Bowen et al., 2005; N. Xiao et al., 2018. Feasibility of data collection, acceptability, and usability of SSP and ESSP data have also been established (N. Bowen & Powers, 2011).

Users must interact through with the SSP team to set up their private data collection and reporting functions for both surveys.

How SSP 2020 and ESSP 2020 May Support African American Students' Success

SSP and ESSP results indicate the percentage of students who share positive or negative perceptions of their social environments. The data can be used to inform schoolwide strategies that benefit all students, as intended in multiple-tiered prevention models (Kelly Thompson et al., 2015). SSP and ESSP data can also be disaggregated by one or more demographic characteristics (e.g., African American sixth grade girls) to understand needs of specific groups. Data on African American students' perceptions of, for example, principal caring, teacher support, peer relationships, instructional relevance and rigor, and school safety can promote consideration of factors outside the student as contributors to academic or behavioral difficulties. Although specific knowledge or skills may still need to be addressed, the social environmental data promote consideration of additional strategies that are critical to long-term performance gains—for example, new ways teachers can convey their support for students.

Social environmental profiles from the SSP and ESSP also invariably reveal protective factors in students' lives that otherwise may not be known to school personnel (N. Bowen & Powers, 2005). Profiles may indicate students have a positive future orientation, plan to go to college, and have caregivers who encourage them to work hard in school, for example. Student reports of their experiences, whether positive or negative, may change the decision-making of school personnel by promoting perspective-taking and individuating (Ispa-Landa, 2018). These two psychological processes can reduce racial bias in interpretations of academics and behavior that lead to racial disproportionality in educational outcomes (Ispa-Landa, 2018).

Expanding the Definition of Evidence to Promote Social Justice

As with conceptualization of "data," the most common definition of "research evidence" in educational policy is narrow. The primary definition is research supporting the efficacy of educational activities, strategies, or interventions. ESSA 2015 legislation describes a hierarchy of evidence for interventions. The first three levels refer to evidence of efficacy from at least one high-quality experimental, quasi-experimental, or well-controlled correlational study, respectively. Online repositories of best practices often refer to the hierarchy when rating program evidence.

In response to input from school social workers (Patak-Pietrafesa et al., 2019), the SSP website has a best practices database that includes 1-page summaries of evidence-based programs, (i.e., those meeting standards for the first three levels of evidence in the ESSA 2015 legislation). However, it is not adequate to report only on this type of program. Studies of evidence-based programs are highly controlled to ensure internal validity, meaning they target a very specific problem and population, monitor implementation fidelity, are implemented with researcher oversight, and often are sponsored with research funding. Although this type of evidence is valuable, it has shortcomings. First, reviews of highly researched interventions have identified multiple barriers to their use in schools, including high costs, training requirements, implementation burden (N. Bowen & Powers, 2011; Kelly Thompson et al., 2015; N. Bowen & Powers, 2005), and low effect sizes (that were not necessarily correlated with cost) (Powers et al., 2011). Second, the controlled conditions under which many interventions were implemented limit their relevance to school social work practice. Third, often the issues targeted in most highly researched interventions do not correspond to the many intersecting issues and populations encountered by social workers. Conversely, many of the intersecting issues and populations encountered by school social workers are unlikely to ever be subjected to high-powered experimental research designs.

Other Types of Evidence

Four additional categories of evidence are provided on the SSP website:

- Promising practices
- Free, brief, validated measures
- Practice data generated by school social workers
- Basic developmental research relevant to the populations and issues in school social work

Promising Practices

The database of best practices provides information on practices that are relevant to school social work but may not be in repositories of highly researched programs. ESSA 2015 legislation includes a fourth level of intervention evidence that may be more applicable to school practice realities. It refers to practices that demonstrate "a rationale based on high quality research findings or positive evaluation that such activity, strategy, or intervention is likely to improve student outcomes or other relevant outcomes." Examples of what we call "promising practices" based on high-quality research by leading social work scholars are "mapping and monitoring school bullying and violence" (Astor & Benbenishty, 2018, p. 9) and making schools welcoming to students in transition (Astor et al., 2018).

Best practices in the database can be searched with terms preferred by school personnel and students. Descriptions of practices are formatted to make it easy for school social workers to quickly glean essential details—their basic components, how much time and other resources they require, and if they are appropriate for their populations. Briefs for relatively simple practices are 1 page long. The database contains a large number of low-cost and free practices that have support at any of the ESSA levels. An example is a brief writing intervention to counter stereotype threat, which is a free and feasible strategy supported by numerous experimental studies (N. Bowen et al., 2013; Cohen et al., 2009). The practice has been shown to increase academic achievement of Black students and reduce Black–White achievement disparities.

Free, Brief, Validated Measures

Another type of evidence is information on validated measures of aspects of the social environment and outcomes of practices targeting the social environment. The measurement database includes, for example, a measure of students' perception of the school's support for diversity and measures of teacher perceptions of students. Such measures may be relevant as pre- and post-test tools for interventions supporting Black students who have experienced microthreats at school. A measurement brief about the Symbolic Racism scale is presented in Box 140.1. In the SSP measurement database, the actual measures appear on the back of the page—ready to be copied and used by social workers. When available, information on whether measures have been tested for use with diverse students will be included.

BOX 140.1 Sample Measurement Brief

Measures for Practice

Symbolic Racism 2000

(*In the database, the ready-to-use scale follows this 1-page description*)

What does this SSW measure address?

Symbolic racism against African Americans. Symbolic racism can also be called symbolic prejudice or racial resentment. Items on the scale relate to an individual's beliefs about whether discrimination against African Americans still exists, harms their chances of success, and justifies special treatment; or that African Americans' social disadvantage derives from them not working hard enough or not taking responsibility for their lives.

For use by:

↔ School personnel

↔ Whites as well as members of minority groups

Why is it important?

Symbolic racism toward African American students may manifest as explicit or implicit messages or behaviors that undermine students' sense of belonging, belief they are being treated fairly, and perceptions of teacher support. It may also lead to more punitive punishments for African American students and more referrals to special education.

Scoring:

Symbolic racism scores are created by summing response to the 8 questions. Scores will range from 8 to 31 with higher scores meaning more symbolic racism. Five of the items need to be reverse coded so that the total score represents negative attitudes. Items 1, 2, 4, and 8 are recoded so that 1=4, 2=3, 3=2, and 4=1. Item 3 is recodes so that 1=3, 2=1, and 3=2.

References:

Henry, P. J., & Sears, D. O. (2002). The symbolic racism 2000 scale. *Political Psychology, 23, 253-283.* Retrieved from, https://www.midss.org/content/symbolic-racism-2000-scale

Practice Data Generated by School Social Workers

When school social workers face resource constraints or a lack of evidence-based interventions appropriate for their settings, populations, and issues, strategies that are consistent with the fourth type of evidence in ESSA 2015 may be the most feasible, relevant, and acceptable. An important source of evidence for promising practices used to promote social justice in schools is social workers themselves. Evaluation data generated in practice can be used to adjust or adapt strategies as they are being implemented, to illustrate social workers' contribution to student performance to school leaders, and to build a body of evidence to be shared with other school social workers. School social workers value the experiences of their peers with practice strategies, including experiences with feasibility, adaptability, and outcomes of those strategies (Patak-Pietrafesa et al., 2019).

The School Social Work website contains resources for building a knowledge base of practice-generated evidence. In addition to descriptions of feasible practices and free measures, text and video resources provide instruction to school social workers on how to conduct simple pretest/post-test analyses as proposed by Rubin and von Sternberg (2017). By sharing experiences and outcomes of strategies, school social workers can begin to generate a credible knowledge base about practices for populations often not well represented in intervention studies, such as students with one or more marginalized identities.

Basic Developmental Research on Populations and Issues in School Social Work

The evidence used by school personnel needs to be defined much broader on studies of intervention efficacy. A broader definition includes findings from non-intervention studies. Such studies include theoretically based longitudinal and cross-sectional studies on developmental, instructional, and social processes from multiple perspectives. Examples of research that would enrich the understanding of school personnel working to support African American students' school success are studies of students' experiences with discrimination in and outside of school, studies of teacher behaviors that promote student trust, and studies of educational resilience of African American students and families. This type of empirical knowledge could be the basis of teacher consultation and professional development provided by school social workers. Interventions at the teacher or school level are encouraged by many school researchers who believe they are more likely than direct practices with students to promote systemic change (Harrison et al., 2018; Ispa-Landa, 2018; Thompson et al., 2017). An example of a research brief on a qualitative study of microaggressions in schools is presented in Figure 140.1.

Practice tools that promote racial equity can be developed from developmental theory and research. The example presented in Box 140.2 is based on self-determination theory (Ryan & Deci, 2009), which is supported by an extensive body of research. The theory posits that all humans have a psychological need for a sense of competence, autonomy, and relatedness. Using the "3 Keys to Motivation" promotes perspective-taking and empathy among the school personnel responding to students' social or learning behavior (Ispa-Landa, 2018). School social workers introducing this approach to disciplinary decision-makers can undercut implicit racial biases that lead to the disproportionate use of harsh discipline and special education referrals for African American students (Gregory & Fergus, 2017; Ispa-Landa, 2018; Warikoo et al., 2016).

SSW RESEARCH BRIEF
MICROAGGRESSIONS IN K – 8 SCHOOLS
Winters, S., Almeida, J., & Hamilton-Mason, J. (2017). Perceptions of microaggressions in K-8 school settings: An exploratory study. *Children and Youth Services Review, 79*, 594–601

What is the study about?	MICROAGGRESSIONS: Authors use a definition from
School social workers perceptions of student experiences with microaggressions in gardes K to 8. Prevalence, nature and consequences of microaggressions in schools.	microaggression scholar Darrell Sue: "intentional or unintentional harmful statements or actions that contribute to discrimination of people who have minority status or are otherwise socially marginalized."

Microaggressions observed: Conscious and explicit insults and teasing; Negative insinuations and assumptions; Biases and stereotypes based on student race or class

When, Where, and Who	Characteristics of Targeted Students
At recess, bus-time, and during unstructured or unsupervised time	Minority race or ethnicity groups Low income families
Lunchroom, bathrooms, hallways, in classroom when teacher not paying attention Social media microaggressions become an "enormous issues" in middle school Microaggressors were popular and successful students, students with life stressors or trauma, or students whose families modeled microaggressions	Difficult family lives and life stressors Have been targeted by others Disabilities
	Poor social skills Overweight
Staff were also microaggressors against students	Non-heterosexual or non-binary identities Multiple marginalized identities or vulnerabilities

What did the find?	Why is it important?
All of the social workers had seen and heard about microaggressions in their schools and considered them a problem.	Participants saw that students experiencing microaggressions withdraw socially and lose interest in school
All saw student-to-student microaggressions	Students who retaliated against microaggressions could be labeled as having behavior problems
Microaggressions were part of a culture of relational aggression at the schools	Microaggressions made all students less comfortable at school

What can School Social Workers do?
Support and build protective factors among students who are targeted by microaggression: social skills, coping skills, emotional awareness, empathy
Support use of Social and Emotional Learning curricula across the whole school and with families
Build community among staff, students, and families
Hold conversations about diversity and social justice
Promote bias awareness among staff and students

How was the study done? Ten school social workers from 10 different K-8 public schools were interviewed in-person, by phone, or video conferencing about their knowledge and awareness of microaggressions in their schools.

FIGURE 140.1 Sample research brief on a basic science study.

Conclusion

We have argued that the entrenched narrow, student- and deficit-centered uses of data and evidence in schools maintain social injustice in outcomes for African American students. Social justice will not be attained until understanding of the social environment, student perspectives, and students as individuals are thoroughly integrated into school and classroom processes. The SSP website (https://schoolsuccessprofile.net) provides an array of resources that equip school social workers to make schools institutions that deliver on their promise of preparing all children for successful and healthy futures.

BOX 140.2 Sample Practice Tool Based on Theory and Research

Using the 3 Keys to Motivation to Understand why Some Students are not Behaving, Engaging, and Learning.

Promoting relatedness, competence, and autonomy is a universal classroom strategy, that is, it should be an integral part of the culture and process of the classroom. All students need to have their needs for relatedness, competence, and autonomy met in order to maximize their engagement and learning.

BUT:

Just as some students need more instruction, more repetition of new material, or more support during academic lessons, some students need more support to feel that they belong, are cared about, are competent, and have a personal stake in what is being taught in the classroom. When you have a student who is regularly not behaving, not engaged, and not learning in the classroom, follow the guidelines below to figure out why.

Check In on Relatedness and Belonging

1. Troubleshoot the interactions the student has with you and others in your classroom
   a. What have you done to convey to the student that you like him, care about him, and are committed to his educational success?
   b. Have you raised your voice or expressed anger at the student? (-) Or does the child feel safe from strong emotional outbursts around you? (+)
   c. When the student needs to be reprimanded, do you explain why, listen to her, and give her strategies to help her do better? (+)
   d. Do you praise the student for good behaviour, effort, engagement when you see them? (+)
   e. Would the student say you are firm, fair, and consistent in your treatment of him? (+)
   f. If the student has a difficult home life, do you express empathy and concern, as well as the expectation that she can and will still behave and succeed in school? (+)
   g. Do other students convey to the student that they like her, care about her, and want her to do well in school? (+)
   h. Do other students bully, tease, laugh at, or pick on the student? (-)
   I. Do you stand up for the student if other students are mean to him? (+)

Check In on Competence

1. Troubleshoot messages the student may receive about his ability to succeed at school
   a. In spite of current performance, is the student treated as a respected learner? (+)
   b. Does the student receive the same positive messages as other students about graduation and college and career paths? (+)
   C. Are the student's academic deficits viewed as problems that will be solved with help and hard work? (+) Or are they treated as realities that will never change? (-)
   d. Has anyone said to the student, "Let's work together to find out what you need to get your grades up." (+)
   e. Does someone at the school totally believe in the ability of the student to succeed? (+)

Check In on Autonomy

1. Troubleshoot classroom activities
   a. Does the student at times have the chance to make decisions about learning activities? (+)
   b. Does the student at times have and important role in classroom activities? (+)
   c. Does the student understand why topics are taught and how they relate to her future? (+)
   d. Do classroom rules and norms take into account the developmental age of all students and any specific needs of the students? (+)

References

Astor, R. A., & Benbenishty, R. (2018). *Mapping and monitoring bullying and violence.* Oxford University Press.

Astor, R. A., Jacobson, L., Wrabel, S. L., & Benbenishty D., R. (2018). *Welcoming practices: Creating schools that support families and students in transition.* Oxford University Press.

Bowen, G. L., Rose, R. A., & Bowen, N. K. (2005). *The reliability and validity of the School Success Profile.* Xlibris.

Bowen, N. K. (2015). Online database of interventions and resources for school social workers. In K. Corcoran & A. R. Roberts (Eds.), *Social workers desk reference* (3rd ed., pp. 1100–1114). Oxford University Press.

Bowen, N. K., Bowen, G. L., & Woolley, M. E. (2004). Constructing and validating assessment tools for school-based practitioners: The Elementary School Success Profile. In A. R. Roberts & K. R. Yeager (Eds.), *Evidence-based practice manual: Research and outcome measures in health and human services* (pp. 509–517). Oxford University Press.

Bowen, N. K., Lucio, R., Patak-Pietrafesa, M., & Bowen, G. L. (2020). The SSP 2020: The Revised School Success Profile. *Children & Schools, 42*(1), 19–28. https://doi.org/10.1093/cs/cdz025

Bowen, N. K., & Powers, J. D. (2005). Knowledge gaps among school staff and the role of high quality ecological assessments in schools. *Research on Social Work Practice, 15*(6), 491–500. https://doi.org/10.1177/1049731505275553

Bowen, N. K., & Powers, J. D. (2011). The Elementary School Success Profile model of assessment and prevention: Balancing effective practice standards and feasibility. *School Social Work Journal, 35*(2), 1–15.

Bowen, N. K., Wegmann, K. M., & Webber, K. C. (2013). Enhancing a brief writing intervention to combat stereotype threat among middle-school students. *Journal of Educational Psychology, 105*(2), 427–435. https://doi.org/10.1037/a0031177

Cohen, G. L., Garcia, J., Purdie-Vaughns, V., & Brzustoski, P. (2009). Recursive processes in self-affirmation: Intervening to close the minority achievement gap. *Science, 324,* 400–403. https://doi.org/10.1126/science.1170769

Gregory, A., & Fergus, E. (2017). Social and emotional learning and equity in school discipline. *The Future of Children, 27*(1), 117–136.

Harrison, K., Harrison, R., Ward, J., & Amin, A. (2018). The Utilization of an Electronic Data Collection System to Assess Professional Practice in School Social Work. *School Social Work Journal, 42*(2), 1–19.

Ispa-Landa, S. (2018). Persistently harsh punishments amid efforts to reform: Using tools from social psychology to counteract racial bias in school disciplinary decision. *Educational Researcher, 47*(6), 384–390. https://doi.org/10.3102/0013189X18779578

Kelly Thompson, A. M., Frey, A., Klemp, H., Alvarez, M., & Berzin, S. C. (2015). The state of school social work: Revisited. *School Mental Health, 7,* 118–174. https://doi.org/10.1007/s12310-015-9149-9

McIntosh, K., Gio, C., & Bastable, E. (2018, March). Do schools implementing SWPBIS have decreased racial and ethnic disproportionality in school discipline? https://www.pbis.org/announcements/resources-for-using-pbis-to-increase-racial-equity

Midwest School Social Work Council. (2015, March). Supplemental ethical standards for school social work practice. http://www.msswa.org/Resources/Documents/Supplemental-SSW-Ethical-Standards-final-10-14.pdf

National Association of Social Workers. (2012). Standards for school social work services. https://www.socialworkers.org

National Center for Education Statistics. (2019). National assessment of educational progress. U.S. Department of Education, Institute of Education Sciences. https://nces.ed.gov/nationsreportcard/subject/participating/2019/public/2019_facts_for_teachers.pdf

Patak-Pietrafesa, M., Bowen, N. K., Stewart, A. E., & Kelly, M. S. (2019). Too hard to find with too little time: What school social workers want in online resources for evidence-based practice. *International Journal of School Social Work, 4,* 1–21.

Powers, J. D., Bowen, N. K., Webber, K. C., & Bowen, G. L. (2011). Low effect sizes of evidence-based programs in school settings. *Journal of Evidence-Based Social Work, 8*(4), 397–415. https://doi.org/10.1080/15433714.2011.534316

Quinn, D. M. (2017). Racial attitudes of pre K–12 and postsecondary educators: Descriptive evidence from nationally representative data. *Educational Researcher, 46*(7), 397–411. https://doi.org/10.3102/0013189X17727270

Rubin, A., & von Sternberg, K. (2017). A practitioner-friendly empirical way to evaluate practice. *Social Work, 62,* 297–302.

Rumberger, R. W., & Lim, S. A. (2008). *Why students drop out of school: A review of 25 years of research: Vol. 15.* California Dropout Research Project Report.

Ryan, R. M., & Deci, E. L. (2009). Promoting self-determined school engagement: Motivation, learning, and well-being. In K. R. Wentzel & A. Wigfield (Eds.), *Handbook on motivation at school* (pp. 171–196). New York: Routledge.

Thompson, A. M., Reinke, W., Holmes, S., Danforth, L., & Herman, K. (2017). County Schools Mental Health Coalition: A model for a systematic approach to supporting youths. *Children & Schools*, 39(4), 209–218.

Warikoo, N., Sinclair, S., Fei, J., & Jacoby-Senghor, D. (2016). Examining racial bias in education. *Educational Researcher*, 45(9), 508–514. https://doi.org/10.3102/0013189X16683408

Xiao, Y., Bowen, N. K., & Lindsey, M. A. (2018). Racial/ethnic measurement invariance of the School Success Profile (SSP)'s future orientation scale. *Journal of School Psychology*, 71, 85–107.

School Social Work Advocacy and Leadership in Consequential Times

Robert Lucio, Emily Shayman, and Michael S. Kelly

The field of school social work has come a long way during the past 100 years, from starting as "visiting teachers" in the 1900s to becoming part of federal Individuals with Disabilities in Education Act legislation in 1997 and developing professional organizations, all while unifying and expanding the profession. School social workers (SSWs) continue to demonstrate the ways in which they are vital as part of the school team to this day. To do this, SSWs have used their specialized skills and knowledge to support students across multi-tiered systems of support (MTSS), response to intervention services, and/or through positive behavioral intervention systems. SSWs both encourage individual student growth through clinical intervention and advocate for students within the larger context, working to create and maintain equitable school climates and cultures.

The breadth of knowledge and specialized approaches used by SSWs allows for unique and productive outcomes in schools. SSWs use clinical approaches while targeting equitable outcomes for both micro- and macro-scale

educational needs by implementing a variety of tasks. This knowledge base is what makes the professional status as SSWs so versatile and necessary. In order for the profession to continue to grow, current school social work professionals should consider ways to articulate the work that they do while building their roles as leaders in their schools and communities. This chapter outlines how SSWs address some of the pressing concerns experienced in school settings.

Leadership in School Social Work

Throughout the profession's history, school social work practitioners and scholars alike have made calls for more consistent leadership positions for SSWs (Constable, 1978; Kelly, Raines, et al., 2010; Phillippo & Blosser, 2013; Richard & Villarreal Sosa, 2014). This does not mean that SSWs must be the principal or department head to exercise leadership but, rather, that they create spaces to use their skills and knowledge to encourage and influence interdisciplinary collaboration. SSWs have specialized knowledge to be shared with their colleagues (i.e., behavioral intervention, understanding social emotional regulation, connections with key school community members and/or stakeholders, etc.). As leaders, SSWs must find ways to support students, families, and staff simultaneously. They must find ways to empower and be empowered. These efforts to exercise leadership, however, are a work in progress, as SSWs continue to determine solutions to the obstacles they encounter. The following topics address just some of these difficulties toward attaining leadership status, while providing alternative perspectives and insight about the challenges as well.

Challenges in School Social Work

Host Setting

The "host setting" creates one barrier to leadership positions (that can be overcome!). School social workers deliver their services in a setting that is not primarily affiliated with social work services—in other words, their services are provided in a host setting. The school setting has different priorities than do specific social work agencies. Schools are focused on educational attainment, whereas the SSWs within them are focused on the students' social–emotional skills and needs. In order to grow and maintain their leadership position within the school, SSWs must consistently explain the scope and breadth of their unique role while collaborating with an interdisciplinary team of professionals who may not immediately understand school social work goals and intentions.

Contextual Differences

Just as the unique characteristics of each host setting contribute to the array of job descriptions for SSWs, there are many other variables that also add to the differences in role tasks. Job tasks and responsibilities can vary across age, grade level, whether a school is urban or rural, socioeconomic status, etc. Some schools may employ an SSW full-time, others part-time, or one social worker may serve multiple school buildings. Furthermore, some social work activities are "mandated services" that are authorized and regulated by state and federal laws for provision of appropriate educational services to all students (e.g., early childhood intervention services, conducting special education evaluations, providing services defined by Individual Education Programs, and reporting suspected child abuse); other services are determined by the practitioner and/or administrators of individual schools. These services may differ based on geographic location and/or type of school. Although this variety creates challenges in consistency of work across the school social work profession, it also creates unique opportunities for leadership roles.

Social Work Code of Ethics

Other professionals in the school setting likely do not know about or adhere to the National Association of Social Workers (NASW) Code of Ethics (2017), which creates yet another unique attribute for SSWs in the host setting of a school. SSWs must ensure that their work is consistent with the values and ethics expected of professional social workers. In doing so, they must ensure confidentiality, professionalism, equity, etc. Aligning these values and ethics to the mandates of the school system is not always easy. In fact, there are times when social work mandates from the Code of Ethics and educational mandates contradict one another. But when showing others the importance of "dignity and worth for all" (NASW, 2017)—and upholding the basis of the social work profession in clear and productive ways—SSWs can slowly but surely find themselves as leaders within their schools.

Caseload and Workload

School social workers typically have a "caseload" of students to support. Whereas the term *caseload* refers to the specific number of students that a SSW consistently services (by providing direct support and collaborating with the student's school team, etc.), the term *workload* includes a more expansive, all-encompassing way to describe all the tasks that SSWs do and all the responsibilities that they have. Gaining and maintaining leadership roles, for example, is part of the overall workload. SSWs also participate on committees, provide professional development and consultative services for educator colleagues, provide resources and referrals for all students and families, and more—all of which are in addition to supporting students on their caseload. As leaders, SSWs should educate others about the many additional tasks they simultaneously perform in their role.

Several studies have examined how SSWs allocate their time. Almost all SSWs engage in individual counseling, group counseling, and classroom groups, pointing to the focus on clinical services for students who are already identified as needing additional supports. SSWs reported that more than 60% of their time is spent on individualized needs and prevention, whereas only 30% is spent on schoolwide needs prevention (Bye et al., 2009; Harrison et al., 2018; Kelly, Raines, et al., 2010; Kelly & Whitmore, 2019; Whittlesey-Jerome, 2013). These findings show that SSWs are not necessarily making use of the skills they have to empower students, staff, and families within the school community in a broader way. SSWs have the training and knowledge to understand the environmental needs of a school (Brake & Livingston, 2016; Stone, 2015); therefore, as leaders, SSWs can focus and direct resources where they are likely to have the greatest impact. In order to find themselves in leadership positions, SSWs must think about their approaches and actions within the school building in efficient and intentional ways.

Perspectives for Advancement in School Social Work

Enacting a "Culture of Change" as Leaders

As leaders, SSWs can drive change and promote student success. Yet often, SSWs are relegated to the role that the overall school thinks they should serve rather than the one that utilizes the full range of skills they possess as potential collaborative leaders. To address this, SSWs can share the unique "social work perspective" of the school in productive and intentional ways while interacting with administrators (and other key decision-makers). SSWs can intentionally focus conversations and interactions with other school leaders to contemplate how their services can support the goals of the school, shifting their role to one of leadership. This approach requires critical thinking about how to best make use of personal strengths and characteristics of the practitioner as well as manage the existent strengths of the structural supports within the school.

For change to occur, SSWs should also be at the forefront of creating a culture of change, innovation, and inquiry. This culture of change requires several key components: (1) systematic use of data to identify the best services to provide, (2) the freedom for SSWs to try new approaches and techniques within their services, and (3) a willingness to explore for productive and positive changes. It is helpful for SSWs to consistently remember and refer to the importance of this culture of change as a key element toward gaining leadership opportunities. In addition, building and maintaining collaborative working relationships with administrators go a long way in making change occur.

Data and Decision-Making

Making use of data is one way to find opportunity for leadership. Building strong relationships is a key practice, and remembering the significance of the "human" within the "data" is important. However, these are part of evidence-based practice and can be (and are) done while using data to inform professional decisions in school social work practices. Data-informed decision-making in SSW is not new, yet it is not fully or consistently implemented across the profession (Lucio et al., 2020). Without the confidence in their own ability to manage and interpret data, SSWs will take a back seat to other professions when collaborating around data-informed decision-making. SSWs must be able to lead conversations about data, outcomes, and data use.

Although the specific approaches may differ across schools and professionals, there are consistent opportunities for SSWs to use and integrate data into their everyday practices. As a first step, SSWs can "self-assess" their abilities and practices when using data. Questioning one's own use of data may promote a deeper understanding of the outcomes while also providing a clearer understanding as to how to integrate it into practice. Another way for SSWs to ensure regular use of data is to create and manage systems and processes that incorporate various types of data collection and analysis. In turn, these processes would likely lead to leadership roles and opportunities. Ultimately, understanding how to communicate information about data to key stakeholders (i.e., community members, faculty, administrators, etc.) increases the likelihood that data will be used to inform student services and social work practices while also increasing the visibility and leadership of SSWs.

Lifelong Learning and Building a Professional Learning Community

School social workers quickly become aware of how intense and demanding their jobs are and how likely it is that they will be performing their jobs without supervision from a school social worker directly. Rather, SSWs are often supervised by other education and related service professionals (e.g., principals and special education administrators) who may not fully understand what the school social work profession does and *can* do (Bluestone-Miller et al., 2016). This makes for potentially challenging working conditions. Regardless, it is interesting to note that SSW survey data show that SSWs tend to stay in the field for long periods of time. On average, SSWs stay in the profession between 12 and 15 years, if not longer (Kelly, Berzin, et al., 2010). Therefore, developing alternative support structures in addition to their in-school supervision [e.g., professional learning communities (PLCs)] allows SSWs to find community, collaborate with like-minded professionals, and keep their professional practices up-to-date (Brake & Kelly, 2019). SSWs can develop ongoing PLC via joining professional school social work organizations and/or taking advantage of sites and tools (e.g., the news/blog schoolsocialwork.net and the sister social media platform SSWNetwork) and using those tools and organizations to independently form virtual PLCs.

It can be difficult to maintain the identity of a "lifelong learner" (i.e., staying up-to-date with the profession) when academic tools are costly and/or inaccessible (Brake & Kelly, 2019; Patak-Pietrafesa et al., 2019). As an example of one of the ways to address these barriers, one of this chapter's authors (Kelly) created a 15-credit, post-master's School Mental Health Advanced Practice Program (SMHAPP), which to date has fielded four cohorts of SSWs from nine states who come together in virtual synchronous and asynchronous classwork to make their school social work practice more evidence-informed and data-driven and to bolster their roles as school leaders (Kelly, 2019). The SMHAPP certificate, along with the burgeoning activity on SSWN and the SSWNetwork, augurs well for SSW practitioners being able to find new and sustainable ways to create their own PLCs and to fashion their identities as lifelong learners as they continue their careers, building their school social work identities to include their leadership skills and capacities.

Advocacy in School Social Work

A key component of SSWs continuing to develop their leadership capacities is identifying key issues within their schools and community contexts to organize and advocate around. In this section, we identify a sample of three crucial issues that are currently impacting schools and share ideas about how SSWs can be effective advocates in their schools on these issues.

Climate Justice

A rapidly evolving climate change movement has made clear to SSWs that their students, schools, and surrounding communities are adversely affected by the climate crisis (Booth, 2019; Powers et al., 2019, 2018). To address this, SSWs organize with the youth in their schools by helping and supporting them advocate for schools being zero-waste facilities, increasing school recycling, and divesting from fossil fuel investments (Guthrie, 2019; Powers, 2016). This work interacts with other areas of advocacy as well, all of which are disproportionately impacted by the climate crisis (Booth, 2019).

School Safety and Dismantling the School-to-Prison Pipeline

The *school-to-prison pipeline* is a term that describes punitive discipline and subpar educational policies that seem to rally students into the prison system for minor incidents, and it disproportionately affects students of color, especially Black males (Mallett, 2016; McCarter 2017). Many of these practices are done in the name of increasing school safety and preserving order within the school (i.e., zero tolerance policies), yet there is compelling evidence that these approaches are unnecessarily punitive, do not work

to increase school safety, and are often found to be rooted in White supremacy (Hoffman, 2014). Because many of the clients that SSWs serve come from minority groups and more vulnerable populations, SSWs are uniquely positioned to fight these disturbing structural issues by offering alternative solutions. For example, SSWs may find ways to help build teacher confidence and competence to handle classroom management so that students are not referred to disciplinary administrators. Or, school social workers may provide training about cultural humility and/or culturally responsive lessons and interactions. They may even help mobilize school leadership teams within the MTSS framework to implement alternatives to typical punitive discipline, although a range of issues remain related to how these practices are defined and the evidence for them (Fronius et al., 2019; Song & Swearer, 2016). Regardless of the specific technique(s), SSWs can provide services from micro and macro perspectives to increase safety while maintaining equitable practices.

Trauma-Informed Approaches

School social workers have training that creates key awareness regarding the impact that trauma has on many students and families. SSWs understand that these issues often interact with other structural concerns, such as racism, inequality, environmental racism, etc. (Stone, 2017). Therefore, SSWs are part of the growing trauma-informed care (TIC) movement in education, in which school leaders are embracing ideas about making their schools "trauma-informed." These efforts are just one way that SSWs show their leadership and creativity, particularly by helping fellow educator colleagues move from a deficit model of thinking about kids with trauma to one that is more compassionate and expansive. However, SSWs should use these skills to refrain from uncritically embracing TIC approaches, given the paucity of evidence for TIC at a whole-school level (Maynard et al., 2019). SSWs can and should assess the resources and techniques they use to implement TIC to ensure that they are based in evidence and unlikely to inadvertently retraumatize students due to lack of cultural humility (Tervalon & Murray-García, 1998). SSWs should thoughtfully consider the ways in which educators and school-based mental health clinicians respond to students in crisis, utilizing their leadership skills to ensure that best practices are implemented with care and intentionality.

The previously discussed areas are just a sample of the many vital issues that SSWs aim to influence. The uniting factor among these topics is the need for school social work leadership. Although SSWs may not at first recognize "leadership" as part of their explicit job description, the following section demonstrates the ways in which school leadership is an essential component of an SSW's role.

Creating Opportunities for School Social Work

Asking 10 SSWs what they do could lead to 10 (or more!) different answers. SSWs dynamically adjust their tasks and responsibilities alongside the changing atmosphere by responding to crises, providing resources and referrals, consulting with interdisciplinary teams, providing direct therapeutic interventions via individual and small groups, working with students with disabilities, advocating for student and family needs, implementing prevention programs, conducting formal and informal assessments to determine needs, and more (Allen-Meares, 2013; Constable, 2016; Costin, 1978; Dupper et al., 2014; Frey et al., 2013; Kelly et al., 2016).

Whereas in the past, SSWs may have taken limited roles as leaders within schools, there is an effort to expand macro-focused leadership work moving forward. SSWs can start by engaging colleagues in collaborative processes by offering training and in-service opportunities to empower teachers; provide support in

dealing with academic and behavior challenges for school personnel; and be advocates for helping children, families, schools, and communities (Bye et al., 2009). Therefore, we encourage SSWs to include leadership roles as part of their overall workload. As leaders, SSWs can have a voice for those who may not. As leaders, SSWs can advocate for their students, their students' families, and the needs of the school. And, as leaders, SSWs can demonstrate the importance of the school social work profession.

References

Allen-Meares, P. (2013). Children and adolescents, populations and practice settings: School social work. *Encyclopedia of Social Work*. doi:10.1093/acrefore/9780199975839.013.351

Bluestone-Miller, R., Greenberg, A., Mervis, B., & Kelly, M. S. (2016). School social work supervision. In C. R. Massat, M. Kelly, & R. T. Constable (Eds.), *School social work: Practice, policy, & research* (8th ed., pp. 76–90). Oxford University Press.

Booth, E. (2019). Extinction Rebellion: Social work, climate change and solidarity. *Critical and Radical Social Work, 7*(2), 257–261.

Brake, A., & Kelly, M. S. (2019). Camaraderie, collaboration, and capacity building: A qualitative examination of school social workers in a year long professional learning community. *Qualitative Report, 24*(4), 667–692.

Brake, A., & Livingston, L. (2016). *Tackling oppression in schools: Orienting skills for school social workers.* In C. R. Massat, M. Kelly, & R. T. Constable (Eds.), *School social work: Practice, policy, and research* (8th ed., pp. 368–385). Oxford University Press

Bye, L., Shepard, M., Partridge, J., & Alvarez, M. (2009). School social work outcomes: Perspectives of school social workers and school administrators. *Children & Schools, 31*(2), 97–108.

Constable, R. (1978). New directions in social work education: The task force reports. *Journal of Education for Social Work, 14*(1), 23–30.

Constable, R. (2016). *The role of the school social worker.* In C. R. Massat, M. Kelly, & R. T. Constable (Eds.), *School social work: Practice, policy, and research* (8th ed., pp. 3–23). Oxford University Press.

Costin, L. (1978). *Social work services in schools: Historical perspectives and current directions.* National Association of Social Workers.

Dupper, D. R., Rocha, C., Jackson, R. F., & Lodato, G. A. (2014). Broadly trained but narrowly used? Factors that predict the performance of environmental versus individual tasks by school social workers. *Children & Schools, 36*(2), 71–77. doi:10.1093/cs/cdu004

Frey, A. J., Alvarez, M. E., Dupper, D. R., Sabatino, C. A., Lindsey, B. C., Raines, J. C., Streeck, F., McInerney, A. Norris, M. A. (2013). *School social work practice model*. http://www.msswa.org/Overview-of-SSW-Services

Fronius, T., Darling-Hammond, S., Persson, H., Guckenburg, S., Hurley, N., & Petrosino, A. (2019). *Restorative justice in US schools: An updated research review*. WestEd.

Guthrie, P. (2019). *School social workers can be powerful advocates for climate justice (Part 2)*. School Social Work Net. https://schoolsocialwork.net/school-social-workers-can-be-powerful-advocates-for-climate-justice-part-2

Harrison, K., Harrison, R., Ward, J., & Amin, A. (2018). The utilization of an electronic data collection system to assess professional practice in school social work. *School Social Work Journal, 42*(2), 1–19.

Hoffman, S. (2014). Zero benefit: Estimating the effect of zero tolerance discipline polices on racial disparities in school discipline. *Educational Policy, 28*(1), 69–95.

Kelly, M. K. (2019). Loyola's SMHAPP certificate: Helping SSW be more visible, valuable, and vital. https://schoolsocialwork.net/loyolas-smhapp-certificate-helping-ssw-be-more-visible-valuable-vital/

Kelly, M. S., Berzin, S. C., Frey, A., Alvarez, M., Shaffer, G., & O'Brien, K. (2010). The state of school social work: Findings from the National School Social Work Survey. *School Mental Health, 2*(3), 132–141.

Kelly, M. S., Frey, A., Thompson, A., Klemp, H., Alvarez, M., & Berzin, S. C. (2016). Assessing the National School Social Work practice model: Findings from the Second National School Social Work Survey. *Social Work, 61*(1), 17.

Kelly, M. S., Raines, J., Stone, S., & Frey, A. (2010). *School social work: An evidence-informed framework for practice* (Evidence-based practices series). Oxford; New York: Oxford University Press.

Kelly, M. S., & Whitmore, S. (2019). It's about time: Initial findings from a feasibility study of a time-study tool for school social workers in Michigan. *International Journal of School Social Work, 4*(1), 5.

Lucio, R., Campbell, M., & Kelly, M. S. (2020). The state of data-informed decision making in school social work. *International Journal of School Social Work, 5*(1), 5–33.

Mallett, C. A. (2016). The school-to-prison pipeline: A critical review of the punitive paradigm shift. *Child and Adolescent Social Work Journal, 33*(1), 15–24.

Maynard, B. R., Farina, A., Dell, N. A., & Kelly, M. S. (2019). Effects of trauma-informed approaches in schools: A systematic review. *Campbell Systematic Reviews, 15*(1–2).

McCarter, S. (2017). The school-to-prison pipeline: A primer for social workers. *Social Work, 62*(1), 53–61.

National Association of Social Workers. (2017). *Code of ethics*. https://www.socialworkers.org/About/Ethics/Code-of-Ethics

Patak-Pietrafesa, M., Bowen, N. K., Stewart, A. E., & Kelly, M. S. (2019). Too hard to find with too little time: What school social workers want in online resources for evidence-based practice. *International Journal of School Social Work, 4*(1), 3.

Phillippo, K. L., & Blosser, A. (2013). Specialty practice or interstitial practice? A reconsideration of school social work's past and present. *Children & Schools, 35*(1), 19–31. doi:10.1093/cs/cds039

Powers, M. C. (2016). Transforming the profession: Social workers' expanding response to the environmental crisis. In A.-L. Matthies & K. Narhi (Eds.), *The ecosocial transition of societies: Contribution of social work and social policy* (pp. 286–300). Routledge.

Powers, M. C., & Engstrom, S. (2019). Radical self-care for social workers in the global climate crisis. *Social Work, 65*(1), 29–37.

Powers, M. C., Schmitz, C. A., Nsonwu, C. Z., & Mathew, M. T. (2018). Environmental migration: Social work at the nexus of climate change and global migration. *Advances in Social Work, 18*(3), 1023–1040.

Richard, L. A., & Villarreal Sosa, L. (2014). School social work in Louisiana: A model of practice. *Children & Schools, 36*(4), 211–220.

Song, S. Y., & Swearer, S. S. (2016). The cart before the horse: The challenge and promise of restorative justice consultation in schools. *Journal of Educational and Psychological Consultation, 26*(4), 313–324.

Stone, S. (2015). School social work in the United States: Current evidence and future directions. *Ciencia, Pensamiento y Cultura, 191*(771), a201. doi:10.3989/arbor.2015.771n1003

Stone, S. (2017). Racial equity and school social work. *Psychology in the Schools, 54*(10), 1238–1244

Tervalon, M., & Murray-García, J. (1998). Cultural humility versus cultural competence: A critical distinction in defining physician training outcomes in multicultural education. *Journal of Health Care for the Poor and Underserved, 9*(2), 117–125.

Whittlesey-Jerome, W. (2013). Results of the 2010 statewide New Mexico School Social Work Survey: Implications for evaluation the effectiveness of school social work. *School Social Work Journal, 37*(2), 76–87.

PART XIV

Military Social Work

Clinical Practice with Military Families and Children

David L. Bringhurst and Shawnmari Kaiser

"Greedy institutions" are terms used to describe organizations that desire full access to their members, require their complete devotion, and . . . require each individual to loosen their connections with other institutions, or better yet, not to create ties to other groups which might have competing demands.

—Coser (1974) as cited in Segal (1986, p. 11)

The greedy institutions concept applies to the military and the family; both institutions depend on their members to survive (Segal, 1986). When both institutions want 100% of the military family member, the tug and pull between both creates opportunities for stress and conflict. For example, the stressful impact of multiple relocations and deployment on military families and children is well documented (Murphy & Fairbank, 2013). Furthermore, some military families may struggle with multiple stressors, resulting in depression, anxiety, and acute stress reactions. In addition, children

of active military members often experience academic difficulties, behavioral concerns, and role reversal (Humphreys & Zesiger, 2016). Guard and Reserve military families are also at risk. Despite the stressors among military families, growth and resilience are prevalent. In fact, most military families come through these stressors with increased capability, perseverance, and fortitude (Lieberman & Van Horn, 2013). Still, there are military families who need additional assistance to overcome their challenges; thus, this chapter is for social workers working with these families.

Clinical practice with military families and children is an enormous topic with books dedicated to the subject (e.g., Blaisure et al., 2016; Domenici et al., 2013; Everson & Figley, 2010; Matsakis, 2005; Rubin et al., 2013; Sayers & Armstrong, 2014; Scott et al., 2017). This chapter is written for the practitioner who has little or no experience working with military families and children (yet it is hoped seasoned military social workers may find the information of value). The chapter is divided into two sections based on the phases of the helping process as described by Hepworth et al. (2017): (1) engagement and assessment and (2) interventions.

Engagement and Assessment

Strengths-based assessment is excellent when engaging with military families and children (Simmons et al., 2016). A strengths-based viewpoint is "an all-pervasive attitude" that recognizes that families have strengths they can use to reach goals, solve their own problems, and improve their quality of life (Powell & Batsche, 1997, p. 4). Building rapport through active listening, validating, empathic responding, and showing authentic positive regard is also foundational to engagement with military families. Using motivational interviewing is an ideal conversational style with which to accomplish rapport buidling (Miller & Rollnick, 2002).

Models of Assessment

Using the biopsychosocial–spiritual model for assessment of the military family and child is standard. The National Association of Social Workers (NASW; 2012) further recommends specific areas for consideration during the biopsychosocial–spiritual assessment of military families. Reuben Hill's ABCX formula is a valuable assessment model and is credited with originating family stress theory (Weber, 2011). This model can be used as part of the biopsychosocial–spiritual assessment. The model views crisis through three major divisions: "precrisis, crisis, and postcrisis" (Weber, 2011, p. 85). The single ABCX formula variables are applied during precrisis and crisis, where a is the "initial stressor," b is the "existing resources," c is the family "perception of" a, and x is the crisis or level of crisis; thus, $a + b + c = x$ (Weber, 2011, p. 87). McCubbin and Patterson (1981) enhanced the postcrisis (ongoing stressors) assessment phase by using the Double ABCX model (Weber, 2011, p. 87). This is where social workers will find the model most helpful in assessing military families. The Double ABCX variables are defined as follows (e.g., where the lowercase letters represent the initial stressor and the capital letters represent the pileup of stress and so forth) (Weber, 2011, p. 87):

aA: "pileup of stressors on top of the initial stressor."

bB: "existing and new resources."

cC: "the perception (definition) of the initial stressor, pileup, and existing and new resources."

xX: "coping and adaptation" (aA + bB + cC = xX). Note that xX is strengths-based, assessing *adaptation* rather than *crisis.*

During assessment, attention to family makeup and family life cycle is helpful. Families whose service member is enlisted (i.e., mostly workforce and middle management and comprise 80% of each branch of service) will likely have less money than families whose service member is an officer (i.e., mostly upper management and leadership, comprising 20% of the military). In general, enlisted families are earlier to marriage and childbirth, whereas officer families are later to marriage and childbirth. Assessment regarding the impact of military culture on single-parent families, dual-military families, LGBTQ couples and families, and families with individuals who have special needs should be given consideration and is beyond the scope of this chapter.

Military Culture, Identity, and Lifestyle

The NASW (2012) recommends cultural attunement to the impact of the military on the military family or child. Military families are a unique population, and military-connected children "constitute a separate and distinctly different subculture" from their civilian counterparts (Wertsch 1991, p. xii). Thus, understanding the customs, values, and beliefs within the military, as well as how they may influence the family during and after military service, is helpful in assessment (Petrovich, 2012; Weiss et al., 2010). However, the social worker need not have personal military background to build the therapeutic alliance with the military family. It is helpful to think of the military as a cultural identity that affects the military member and their family. The level of acculturation and adaptation to the military culture will vary from family to family.

Cultural Formulation Interview Questions

Using Cultural Formulation Interview questions to explore the impact of military culture on the family, especially when stigma is impeding their full engagement in the helping process, will be helpful during assessment [American Psychiatric Association (APA), 2013]. These questions clarify concerns, discover preferences, reveal barriers, and assist a clinicians' in gaining a better understanding of the client within their cultural context (Diaz et al., 2017). For instance, a social worker can modify the questions to better assess stigma and military cultural impact on the family, as illustrated below:

- "Are there . . . aspects of [the military] that are causing other concerns . . . for your family?"
- "Has anything prevented you from getting the help you need?" (Probe for concerns of stigma and concerns about the military knowing of their issues.)
- "What kind of help would be most useful to [your family] at this time . . . ?"

(APA, 2013, p. 2)

Assessment of Deployment-Related Challenges

The greedy institutions concept becomes relevant during the deployment of the military family member. Therefore, it is useful to have a basic understanding of the military cycle of deployment when assessing deployment related challenges (see Table 142.1). In the table, the top row depicts the Military Cycle of Deployment,

here the deployment cycle is divided into three stages, predeployment, deployment, and post deployment (Pincus et al., 2001). The timelines provided in this model can be misleading, in truth, each phase may be longer or shorter than initially expected. The middle row depicts the Emotional Cycle of Deployment (Pincus et al., 2001) which was developed by military family support experts based on the emotional responses of each family member to the military deployment cycle. The "New Emotional Cycles of Deployment" (Morse, 2010), found at the bottom of Table 142.1, depicts a further refining and clarification of the impact of the military deployment cycle on the family.

The New Emotional Cycles of Deployment (Morse, 2010) helps clinicians understand the likely responses each member of the family might experience during any phase of the military deployment cycle. Below are the new emotional cycles of deployment (Morse, 2010, p. 1):

> Stage 1—Anticipation of Departure (occurs during predeployment)
>
> Stage 2—Detachment and Withdrawal (occurs during predeployment)
>
> Stage 3—Emotional Disorganization (occurs during deployment)
>
> Stage 4—Recovery and Stabilization (occurs during deployment)
>
> Stage 5—Anticipation of Return (occurs during deployment)
>
> Stage 6—Return Adjustment and Renegotiation (occurs during post deployment)
>
> Stage 7—Reintegration and Stabilization (occurs during post deployment)

Table 142.1 clarifies where each of these stages fit in relation to the three military stages of deployment. Changes in anticipated timeframes during the military deployment cycle can add to the stresses military families and children experience in each stage of the emotional cycles of deployment (Chandra et al., 2010;

TABLE 142.1 Cycles of Military Deployment

Impact of Deployment on the Military Family

	Pre-deployment	Deployment	Sustainment	Re-deployment	Post-deployment
Military cycle of deployment	Preparing for departure (typically 3 weeks to 1 year)	Away on assignment (typically 6–12 months)			Return and reintegration (3–6 months)
Emotional cycle of deployment	**Pre-deployment** SM begins to spend time away to train and prepare for mission. SM and family may experience increased distress, anxiety, and fear; sometimes a big argument between the couple prior to departure.	**Deployment** At home partner may feel disoriented, numb, alone. Sleep troubles common. A multitude of worries, combined with emotional confusion (i.e., helpless, jealous, uncertain).	**Sustainment** New routines created, social supports found, increasing independence and confidence. Caregiver response signals child response, differs by age group.	**Re-deployment** Anticipation with excitement, combined with apprehension. Burst of energy/"nesting" behaviors. Decision-making difficult, fueled by the "unknown."	**Post-Deployment** Date of homecoming may change. Honeymoon period once SM home. Loss of independence. Includes reintegration and renegotiation of familial and personal roles (i.e., parenting and relationships). Opportunity for conflict.
New emotional cycles of deployment	**Anticipation of departure** Creates the expectation of emotional and physical loss, which sparks denial. "Greedy institutions"—impact—military wants SM to complete checklists, while family wants time to create special moments prior to departure.	**Detachment and withdrawal** SM initiates psychological preparation for deployment with unit, and from family members. Ambiguous loss may be present here. Emotional distancing takes its toll, may lead to relational conflict or shut down. Anger and sadness regarding separation. **Emotional disorganization** Involves confusion regarding routine and responsibilities, which may overwhelm those involved (i.e., SM and family members). Children may take on parental roles and feel angry about increased responsibilities. Multiple deployments may lead to "I got this" confidence, or experiencing burnout and fatigue—"here we go again." (Use single ABCX to assess.)	**Recovery and stabilization** Generates strength and resiliency across the family (i.e., SM, spouse, and children) and tends to cement routines and procedures. Increase confidence and outlook. Those experiencing burnout may be challenged with creating emotional strength to adapt and cope. Many resources available via military programs (e.g., Family Readiness Groups).	**Anticipation of return** A chaotic time, utilized to make realistic plans and expectations for SM's return from deployment. To-do lists and hyperactive preparation (i.e., cleaning and/or reorganizing home). Apprehension about giving up independence and functional routines that have been developed over the past several months. Communication is important during this time.	**Reintegration and stabilization** Focuses on family relationships being stabilized anew. Combat stress reactions of SM can significantly interrupt this stage. Orders to relocate to new installation might be received (Use Double ABCX model to assess pileup of stressors.) Crisis or resilience and growth. **Adjustment and renegotiation** Establishing new expectations and negotiation of roles. Again, communication is key. SM may have signs of PTSD and/or other behavioral issues (e.g., irritable, guarded, desire to be alone, need for quiet, increased alcohol use). Could see increased arguing.

PTSD, post-traumatic stress disorder; SM, service member.

Combined by David Bringhurst and Jeff Farber. Adapted from Pincus, S. H. (Lt. Col.), House, R. (Col.), Christenson, J (Lt. Col.), & Adler, L. E. (Capt.). (2001). The emotional cycle of deployment: A military family perspective. *U.S. Army Medical Department Journal, 3278541 6*, 15–23; Morse, J. (Capt.). (2010). *New Emotional Cycles of Deployment.* U.S. Department of Defense Deployment Health and Family Readiness Library. Retrieved from https://www.af.mil/News/Article-Display/Article/133750/dod-launches-deployment-health-family-readiness-library/

Hisle-Gorman et al., 2015). It is important to note that poor mental health and coping of the nondeployed caregiver significantly influences child wellness during deployment; it also negatively affects reintegration of the deployed parent during post deployment (Chandra et al., 2010). When working with families during any stage of deployment consider assessing for "ambiguous loss" and "boundary ambiguity" (Boss, 2007). The statement, " . . . physically absent but psychologically present, or . . . physically present but psychologically absent . . . " aptly describes the experience of ambiguous loss (Huebner et al., 2007). This experience is not specific to military families; divorce, adoption, foster care, and a multitude of other life experiences also create this sense of vague and uncertain loss. Boundary ambiguity is particularly present for youth whose parent has deployed, they may take on roles they were previously not required to shoulder (Huebner et al., 2007).

Military Genogram

The military genogram (Weiss et al., 2010) is a tool to use when assessing and treating the military affiliated family. Weiss et al. (2010) recommend its use in conjunction with solution focused therapy. They suggest adding information to the genogram regarding family member attitudes toward the military, military service, combat experiences, loss of friends or fellow service members in war, etc . . . in total 17 items are recommended for consideration (Weiss et al., 2010). Combining Solution Focused Brief Therapy with the military genogram can lead to a strengths-based interaction, which in turn will hopefully lead to resilient outcomes for the whole family.

Interventions

In this section an evidence-based approach found to be useful with military affiliated families is summarized, i.e., solution-focused brief therapy (SFBT). However, in each situation clinicians should choose interventions using evidence-based practice guidelines (Gibbs & Gambrill, 2002).

Solution-Focused Brief Therapy

Solution-focused brief therapy SFBT is strengths-based and focuses on the present and future. It is entrenched in the belief that the client has skills and is the expert in finding solutions to their challenges (Hanton, 2011), that they have the capacity to work through steps to achieve their goals (DeShazer et al., 2007). It is built on three key premises: (1) "If it works, do more of it," (2) "If it is not working, do something different," and (3) "Small steps can lead to big changes" (DeShazer et al., 2007, p. 2). A summary of the primary techniques and methods used in SFBT follows.

Problem Free Talk

Engagement in casual conversation away from a specific focus on the identified problem allows for a focus on the whole family rather than the problematic area of their lives. It also allows the therapist to discover other strengths, resources, and skills of the family (Hanton, 2011).

Initial/Opening Question(s)

Opening questions are vital to the beginning of the therapeutic alliance and set the stage for therapy to be future focused and client/family centered. Some examples of opening questions might be "What is your goal in coming today?" "What are you hoping to gain by coming to counseling?" "What do you hope to get out of the session today?" (Hanton, 2011, p. 42).

Explore Previous Solutions

It is important to explore any previous solutions the family might have employed. Oftentimes the family/couple has solved the identified problem in the past, even if it was only for a short time. They may have employed a solution, and for various reasons, either the solution stopped working or they were inconsistent with follow through (DeShazer et al., 2007). Assessment of previous solutions acknowledges a strength in the client's ability to problem solve, viewing them as unsuccessful attempts to resolve problems, but attempts nonetheless (Bannink, 2007).

Pre-Session Change

The therapist assesses with the family/client what changes regarding the problem have occurred since scheduling their initial meeting as well as in between sessions. This inquiry facilitates the social worker understanding of skills and resources that may not have been identified earlier. It also may reveal the client's true intentions for therapy which allows for a refocus of the goal of therapy (Hanton, 2011)

Exceptions

An exception occurs when something else happens rather than the resulting problem (Erford, 2020). Exceptions fall into two categories: random, where the exception occurs without thought, and deliberate, where the client has paid particular attention to their thoughts and actions so as not to experience the problem. Both incidents allow the client and therapist to explore what was happening differently in order to promote a positive solution-oriented perspective (Hanton, 2011).

Coping Questions

Coping questions affirm resilience and can be comforting to the client. Examples of coping questions are: How have you managed to cope with the situation up until now? Considering all that you have been through, how have you managed to cope? It is amazing that you have found a way to cope with the situation and keep going. Can you tell me about that? (Hanton, 2011).

Goal Formation and the Miracle Question

Most notable with SFBT is the Miracle Question: "I want to ask you a strange question. Suppose that while you are sleeping tonight . . . a miracle happens. The miracle is that the problem which brought you here is solved. However, because you are sleeping, you don't know that the miracle has happened. So [when] you wake up tomorrow morning, what will be different that will tell you a miracle has happened and the problem which brought you here is solved?" (Hanton, 2011, p. 77). It is vital that the social worker facilitate the miracle as tangible, reasonable and self-focused on how it would impact themselves (Erford, 2020).

Compliments

Though clients often, are more used to negative self-talk and beliefs, compliments promote a healthy self-reflection of what is going well for them through the therapeutic process, and their implementation of actions toward their goals (Hanton, 2011). Authentic compliments are a vital therapeutic intervention that validates what a client is doing well and facilitates recognition of achievements (DeShazer et al., 2007; Hanton, 2011).

Utilizing Scales

Scaling allows for a transition from abstract concepts to a more concrete assessment of problems and solutions. It also allows for a measurement of progress toward stated goals (Erford, 2020). Scaling can be done numerically (0 – 10) for adults, and pictorially (sad to smiling faces) with younger children (Erford, 2020). Hanton, (2011) identified Confident scales, How confident are you . . . ? and Likelihood scales, How likely are you to . . . ? as measurements of client's belief in themselves to obtain a goal. Scaling questions can be helpful when used to inquire from the family/client the level of progress between sessions, seeking to know if things have gotten better, stayed the same or have worsened (DeShazer et al., 2007).

End-of-Session Experiments and Homework Assignments

Experiments are tasks that center around stated exceptions (things they are already doing) that are leading them toward their objective (DeShazer et al., 2007). Encourage the client to test it out in between sessions. Homework assignments/tasks should be negotiated, and if possible, developed by the client based on what was revealed or determined in session (DeShazer et al., 2007; Hanton, 2011).

Evaluation and Termination— Flagging the Minefield

"Sometimes 'good enough' is good enough" (Hanton, 2011, p. 18). Termination begins early on, establish with the family/client, their vision of when it is time for termination. This may be generated from the Miracle Question or from a question like, "How will you know when you won't need to come to therapy anymore?". In the preparation of clinical termination, it can be beneficial to employ the "flagging the minefield" technique, which facilitates adherence to treatment and prevention of relapse. Flagging the minefield encompasses identification of potential pitfalls that may occur outside of the counseling environment. It is an empowering action that allows for proactive planning to manage occurrences in real life that may lead to relapse (Erford, 2020).

Family Support Services Provided by the Military

It should be noted that the military has resources available to military families, but in most cases these resources are only available to active duty families. For example, each branch of service provides support for families whose service member has deployed. Family Readiness Groups are available to active, guard, and reserve families. Each branch of service has family support organizations, for the Air Force it is called Airman and Family Readiness, the Army's is Army Community Services, and the Navy and Marine Corps have Fleet and Family Support. Family Advocacy Programs (FAP) assess and treat cases of family maltreatment. In addition, the Exceptional Family Member Program ensures military families are located

where services are available for family members with special medical or education needs. Military Family Life Consultants (MFLC) are also available for early intervention and have increased confidentiality over some other military programs. Finally, Military OneSource is a Department of defense website dedicated to military families.

Conclusion

This chapter includes basic information relevant to assessing and treating military families. Military family assessments should include cultural impacts of the military on the family members. Viewing the family through a strengths-based lens will help empower both the family and the social worker toward finding solutions. Military families are resilient and for the most part experience growth throughout the career of their military family member, but when challenges overcome the families' usual adaptation responses, social workers can be instrumental in helping them find solutions to the greedy institution demands of the military.

Helpful Resources

Websites
Center for Deployment Psychology: https://deploymentpsych.org

Families OverComing Under Stress: https://focusproject.org

Military Child Education Coalition: https://www.militarychild.org

Military OneSource: https://www.militaryonesource.mil

National Military Family Association: https://www.militaryfamily.org

Operation Homefront: https://operationhomefront.org

Real Warriors: https://www.health.mil/Military-Health-Topics/Centers-of-Excellence/Psychological-Health-Center-of-Excellence/Real-Warriors-Campaign

Sesame Street for Military Families: https://sesamestreetformilitaryfamilies.org

Tragedy Assistance Program for Survivors: https://taps.org

VA National Center for PTSD: https://www.ptsd.va.gov/professional/continuing_ed/all_offerings.asp

Veteran Caregiver Support: heartsofvalor.org https://operationhomefront.org/veteran-caregiver-support

Apps

Base Directory: Information about each military installation; includes information on Space A.

Seasame Street for Military Families apps: Includes "The Big Moving Adventure" app and "Breathe, Think, Do with Sesame" app to deal with everyday challenges.

Transition app: Monitor progress of transition from military, with interactive checklists, from military.com.

United Through Reading app: Deploying military members can record themselves reading stories to their children.

References

American Psychiatric Association. (2013). Cultural-formulation interview. https://www.psychiatry.org/File%20Library/Psychiatrists/Practice/DSM/APA_DSM5_Cultural-Formulation-Interview.pdf

Bannink, F. P. (2007). Solution-focused brief therapy. *Journal of Contemporary Psychotherapy, 37,* 87–94. https://doi.org/10.1007/s10879-006-9040-y

Blaisure, K. R., Saathoff-Wells, T., Pereira, A., Wadsworth, S. M., & Dombro, A. L. (2016). *Serving military families: Theories, research, & application* (2nd ed.). Routledge.

Boss, P. (2007). Ambiguous loss theory: Challenges for scholars and practitioners. *Family Relations, 56*(2), 105–111.

Chandra, A., Cinisomo, S. L., Jaycox, L. H., Tanielian, T., Burns, R. M., Ruder, T., & Han, B. (2010). Children on the homefront: The experience of children from military families. *Pediatrics, 125*(1), 16–25. https://doi.org/10.1542/peds.2009-1180

Coser, L. A. (1974). *Greedy institutions: Patterns of undivided commitment.* Free Press.

DeShazer, S., Dolan, S., & Dolan, Y. (2007). *More than miracles: The state of the art of solution-focused brief therapy.* Haworth.

Diaz, E., Anez, L. M., Silva, M., Paris, M., & Davidson, L. (2017). Using the Cultural Formulation Interview to build culturally sensitive services. *Psychiatric Services, 68,* 112–114. doi:10.1176/appi.ps.201600440

Domenici, P., Best, S., & Armstrong, K. (2013). *Courage under fire for parents of service members: Strategies for coping when your son or daughter returns from deployment.* New Harbinger

Erford, B. T. (2020). *45 techniques every counselor should know.* Pearson.

Everson, R. B., & Figley, C. R. (Eds.). (2010). *Families under fire: A handbook for systemic therapy with military families.* Routledge.

Gibbs, L., & Gambrill, E. (2002). Evidence-based practice: Counterarguments to objections. *Research on Social Work Practice, 12*(3), 452–476.

Hanton, P. (2011). *Skills in solution focused brief counseling and psychotherapy.* Sage.

Hepworth, D. H., Rooney, R. H., Dewberry Rooney, G., Strom-Gottfried, K., & Pa Der Vang. (2017). Overview of the helping process. In D. H. Hepworth, R. H. Rooney, G. Dewberry Rooney, & K. Strom-Gottfried (Eds.), *Direct social work practice: Theory and skills* (10th ed., pp. 35–56). Cengage.

Hisle-Gorman, E., Harrington, D., Nylund, C. M., Tercyak, K. P., Anthony, B. J., & Gorman, G. H. (2015). Impact of parents' wartime military deployment and injury on young children's safety and mental health. *Journal of the American Academy of Child & Adolescent Psychiatry, 54*(4), 294–301.

Huebner, A. J., Mancini, J. A., Wilcox, R. M., Grass, S. R., & Grass, G. A. (2007). Parental deployment and youth in military families: Exploring uncertainty and ambiguous loss. *Family Relations, 56,* 112–122.

Humphreys, K. D., & Zesiger, J. W. (2016). Guiding through life stressors: Utilizing solution-focused brief therapy and sand tray as a counseling approach with military teens. *Journal of Military and Government Counseling, 4*(1), 54–64.

Lieberman, A. F., & Van Horn, P. (2013). Infants and young children in military families: A conceptual model for intervention. *Clinical Child and Family Psychology Review, 16,* 282–293.

Matsakis, A. (2005). *In harm's way: Help for the wives of military men, police, EMTs & firefighters.* New Harbinger.

McCubbin, H. I., & Patterson, J. (1981). Systematic assessment of family stress, resources and coping. *St. Paul: University of Minnesota.*

Miller, W. R., & Rollnick, S. (2002). *Motivational interviewing.* Guilford.

Morse, J. (2010). *The new emotional cycles of deployment.* U.S. Department of Defense Deployment Health and Family Readiness Library. https://static.virtuallabschool.org/atmt/families/SA.Fam_5.Strengthening_A2.EmotionalCyclesofDeployment.pdf

Murphy, R. A., & Fairbank, J. A. (2013). Implementation and dissemination of military informed and evidence-based interventions for community dwelling military families. *Clinical Child and Family Psychology Review, 16,* 348–364. doi:10.1007/s10567-013-0149-8

National Association of Social Work. (2012). *Standards for social work practice with service members, veterans, & their families.* https://www.socialworkers.org/LinkClick.aspx?fileticket=fg817flDop0%3D&portalid=0

Petrovich, J. (2012). Culturally competent social work practice with veterans: An overview of the U.S. military. *Journal of Human Behavior in the Social Environment, 22*(7), 863–874.

Pincus, S. H., House, R., Christenson, J., & Adler, L. E. (2001). The emotional cycle of deployment: A military family perspective. *U.S. Army Medical Department Journal, 32785416,* 15–23.

Powell, D. S., & Batsche, C. J. (1997). A strength-based approach in support of multi-risk families: Principles and issues. *Topics in Early Childhood Special Education, 17,* 1.

Rubin, A., Weiss, E. L., & Coll, J. E. (Eds.). (2013). *Handbook of military social work.* Wiley.

Sayers, S. L., & Armstrong, K. (2014). *Coming back together: A guide to successful reintegration after your partner returns from military deployment.* New Harbinger.

Scott, D. L., Whitworth, J. D., & Herzog, J. R. (2017). *Social work with military populations.* Pearson.

Segal, M. W. (1986). The military and the family as greedy institutions. *Armed Forces & Society, 13,* 9–38.

Simmons, C. A., Shapiro, V. B., Accomazzo, S., & Manthey, T. J. (2016). Strengths-based social work: A meta-theory to guide social work research and practice. In N. Coady & P. Lehmann (Eds.), *Theoretical perspectives for direct social work practice* (3rd ed., pp. 131–154). Springer.

Weber, J. G. (2011). The ABCX formula and the double ABCX model. In *Individual and family stress and crises* (pp. 82–96). SAGE.

Weiss, E. L., Coll, J. E., Gerbauer, J., Smiley, K., & Carillo, E. (2010). The military genogram: A solution-focused approach for resiliency building in service members and their families. *The Family Journal, 18*(4), 395–406. doi:10.1177/1066480710378479

Wertsch, J. V. (1991). *Voices of the mind: A sociocultural approach to mediated action.* Harvard University Press.

Serving the Military Spouse

Current Issues and Related Supports and Resources

Elisa Borah

Demographics and Characteristics of Military Spouses

Military spouses are individuals who are married to military service members serving in an active duty component or as part of the reserves or guard components of the U.S. Armed Forces. Their experiences in military life are similar across branches but can vary slightly depending on component, rank, or type of position held by the service member. Of the 1.3 million active duty service members, 51.5% are married, resulting in almost 1.6 million family members, including more than 605,000 spouses. According to the U.S. Department of Defense (2018), in 2016, 12% of the 690,000 military spouses were themselves active duty military, and nearly half of all married female active duty military members were in dual-military marriages. Military spouses' average age is 31.6 years, and the population is composed of 91.3% female and 8.7% male members (U.S. Department of Defense, 2018).

Blue Star Families' annual Military Family Lifestyle Survey provides a comprehensive picture of the experiences and challenges faced by military families based on responses from active duty and veteran spouses and service members. Results of the 2019 survey indicated that the top concerns voiced by families were issues related to instability and unpredictability in their lives associated with military service, the amount of time away from family, military spouse employment, dependent children's education, military family stability and quality of life, and lack of control over military career (Blue Star Families, 2019). These results are not surprising given the nature of military service; service members' main purpose is to serve the mission of their unit and branch in order to defend the United States and its interests; thus, the needs of military families are not a primary focus of the United States by necessity. The U.S. Department of Defense is funded by Congress to provide health care to military families and offer support to help them address challenges they may face. Social workers play an important role in assessing and providing treatment for serious concerns that face military spouses, including supporting military spouses as they address relationship problems; their employment and education; their children's needs; personal finances; and their own mental health, substance misuse, and wellness. Each of these areas of concern can be influenced by deployment, change of duty station, and other military life cycles that impact the entire family. Understanding how military life impacts each family member is essential knowledge when working with and offering support to service members and their family members.

Unlike most occupations, the obligations and experiences of service members directly impact their spouses due to the unique nature of military service. Similar to those who work in law enforcement, disaster relief, or emergency services, regular exposure to dangerous conditions and/or traumatic experiences may impact their spouses and family members. Military spouses, however, also endure regular physical separation from service members, which can create additional pressures and challenges in their lives. Due to the military life, they may have their own educational and career choices constrained by their spouses' careers and must shoulder parenting and household management duties on their own during frequent deployments and training that require service members to be away for 6–12 months at a time. Despite the array of challenges that military spouses face, they are known for their strength, adaptability, and resilience as they make personal sacrifices in support of the service members' careers.

Military spouses' educational access as well as ability to pursue and advance in careers are necessarily impacted by service members' assigned duties that often dictate where spouses are able to work and study. Based on the location of the duty station and the amount of time they will be stationed there, their educational pursuits and career aspirations can be curtailed or require creative solutions. In some cases, spouses and service members may live apart, informally called "geo-baching" because the typically male service member is geographically a "bachelor" while their spouse and/or family may live in a different location, usually in order to maintain their employment

or education status in a particular area when a service member must relocate due to permanent change of station orders. Other creative solutions involve attending college programs online or working remotely for companies that offer remote working opportunities specifically for military spouses to help them maintain their employment despite their frequent moves.

Research has shown how various types of supports in military spouses' lives can bolster their resilience to the many challenges they face. One study found that social support from friends and a positive outlook lead to a greater sense of community that they can rely on when they need support. With this sense of community, they also felt a greater sense of psychological well-being (Wang et al., 2015). Deployment stress and perceived social support from family, nonmilitary friends, and military partner also have been found to influence the psychological well-being of military spouses (Skomorovsky, 2014). Social support plays a central role in spouses' well-being.

Employment

Military spouses face significant barriers to achieving their full employment potential. Due to the requirements of making frequent moves to new locations for their service members' service obligation, they have fewer opportunities to stay engaged in long-term employment in one location. Perhaps due to this regular mobility, military spouses are far less likely to participate in the labor market than the general working-age population—57% compared to 76% in 2016, respectively, according to the American Community Survey (ACS) (U.S. Bureau of Labor Statistics, 2016). A U.S. Chamber of Commerce (2017) survey indicates military spouses experience higher rates of unemployment than do other adults, estimated at 16% in 2017. Although the ACS data suggest a lower rate at 10.2% in 2016, this is still almost twice the unemployment rate of the U.S.

population. On average, when military spouses do work, they make less than their civilian counterparts, likely due to the inconsistent nature of their employment.

In some cases, they may be located overseas where work is not possible for non-U.S. citizens or in locations that do not have available employment. For many of these moves, spouses' employment may require new licensing or other credentials if they work in fields such as medicine, education, or law that require professional certificates or license to practice. The 2016 ACS (U.S. Bureau of Labor Statistics, 2016) provides detailed information on labor market outcomes of military spouses. Based on a weighted sample of 4,268 working-age military spouses not in the military, that represent 418,055 military spouses, they are predominantly female (92%) with an average age of 33 years, much younger than the average age of 41 years for civilian working-age spouses.

Education

Military spouses are more educated than other civilians. Whereas approximately 30% of the U.S. working-age population have a college degree, approximately 40% of military spouses in this age range have one. There is also a greater share of military spouses who attended some college (34%), even without receiving a degree, compared to other working-age Americans (26%). Despite this higher level of education, many reported additional support needed to attain further education. In 2008, the Post-9/11 GI Bill was passed, allowing service members to transfer their educational benefits to their spouses and children. Thus, military spouses became eligible for higher education benefits under this option.

Deployment

Deployment of service members to fulfill military training and/or engage in military missions has a significant impact on spouses of service members, as well as on their children. Family members all may experience distress related to long periods of separation from each other, new responsibilities, changes in family roles, and challenges of supporting children's emotional needs during deployment (Warner et al., 2009). During deployment, spouses and family members suffer from the fear that their loved one may be killed or injured. Both partners exhibit different stages of grief and loss as they struggle with potential outcomes and lack of control. Often, with only hours of notice, deployments can be extended past original end dates. Partners also face significant emotional problems, such as anxiety and relationship problems. The service members' return home can also be a stressful and difficult time despite the joy in being reunited. Often, the service member must be reintegrated into the family and take new roles that were filled during their absence (Warner et al., 2009). Intimacy and communication between partners must also be rebuilt, although in modern times, communication during deployment has been greatly improved through advances in technology (Carter & Renshaw, 2016).

Mental Health Needs and Available Supports

Military spouses can face psychological problems and develop diagnoses related to the stressors in their lives. The impact of military service on spouses' mental health has been well documented. In one study, medical-record data for outpatient care were analyzed for 250,626 wives of active duty U.S. Army soldiers. After adjusting for the sociodemographic characteristics and mental health history of the wives, longer deployments were found to be associated with more mental health diagnoses among wives. Thus, the military service requirements of long deployments directly impact the mental health of spouses (Mansfield et al., 2010).

Donoho et al. (2018) analyzed the presence of depression among military spouses in dyadic couple data from the Millennium Cohort Family Study that included spouses and service members from all military service components and service branches, as well as dual military couples, and both male and female spouses (Crum-Cianflone et al., 2014). Among 9,038 spouses, 4.9% had a probable diagnosis of major depressive disorder (MDD), whereas in the general population the rate of MDD is 7.1% (Center for Behavioral Health Statistics and Quality, 2018). Spouses whose service members deployed and were involved in combat and who showed signs of a post-traumatic stress disorder diagnosis or alcohol abuse were more likely to screen positive for MDD. In adjusted statistical models, other factors were also found to be associated with MDD in spouses, including less educational attainment, unemployment, having four or more children, and having prior military service (although not currently serving in the military).

In Borah and Fina's (2017) study asking spouses about their experiences, many shared insights regarding how best social workers can support their needs. Central themes regarding the knowledge that social workers need to effectively engage with military families emerged from the qualitative interviews: (1) military culture, (2) military service experience, (3) typical military family dynamics, and (4) preferred service delivery models. Spouses reported that they prefer health care be family-focused and that spouses are included in health care decisions and information related to their service members' health. They appreciated when providers have knowledge of military culture and understand the ebb and flow of military life related to deployments and the impact they have on the whole family. In addition, spouses' comments about military life generated themes related to the stressors and rewards associated with various stages of military life. Major stages that affect families include reintegration of service members back into the family unit

after deployment and after military service has ended, transitioning from military service to civilian life, and the overall impact of military life on children and marriage.

Recognizing the toll that military service can have on military spouses and specifically the deployment-related stressors they endure points to ways that social workers and other providers can offer support and treat the mental health concerns of spouses. Being attuned to the cycles that each family is part of can point to prevention supports that may help prepare spouses, couples, and families to better weather the expected stress of deployment. Programming related to supporting military spouses' employment and career goals can also help reduce financial concerns and meet the personal goals of spouses that are often made to be a lower priority than service members' career obligations.

Many programs are available within the U.S. Department of Defense to support the health care needs of family members, including access to health care through Tricare. Family support groups within each branch can offer timely support during deployments and also offer ongoing camaraderie and peer-based knowledge from other spouses in units. In addition to informal supports, Military Family Life Consultants (MFLCs) offer support on base through Family Support and Readiness Centers in all branches. MFLCs are licensed counselors who help family member with training, resources, and information related to deployment support, family life education, and relationship counseling, among other services.

Transition

When service members and their families leave military service, it can be a challenging transition and has been coined the military-to-civilian transition (MCT). Transition readiness and navigation support are offered by the U.S. Department of Defense for service members' MCT, but little has been done to understand or support spouses and family members as they go through MCT (Keeling et al., 2020). This major life transition (Thompson et al., 2017) involves navigating civilian culture that may prove new after many years of military life. Transition for both the veteran and the spouse can lead to development of new identities in relation to new work and community; immediate transition stages include finding new housing, accessing required health care, family members beginning or continuing education and forming new relationships with civilians, as well as re-establishing their own family relationships after years of frequent separation (Keeling et al., 2020).

The challenges that the veteran may face due to psychological or other physical injuries received through military service also impact the family, either during service or as they are addressing their own transition post-service. Spouses may be required to assume caregiver roles in relation to veterans who have significant military-related injuries, both during service and afterwards for those who receive medical discharges and have documented disabilities. Understanding the extent that spouses are serving in caregiver roles is important in providing them with sufficient support for their own mental health.

Conclusion

Several key points should be taken away from this chapter for social workers who seek to provide excellent care to military spouses. When conducting an intake or assessment of needs among these clients, take into account both their own mental and physical health needs and the ways in which their lives are impacted by military service over which they have little control. Review levels of stress that occurs with frequent moves, separation from and concerns about the welfare of service members during deployments and training, and the challenges

of pursuing their own education and careers when their lives are necessarily impacted by their spouses' military service obligations. Determine how military deployment cycles are affecting spouses' lives and help them prepare for difficult times; education about the impact of these cycles on the families' lives and emotional health can provide significant benefit. Finally, remaining informed about the array of supportive programming and effective treatments available for typical concerns both on and off post is essential in serving military spouses.

Helpful Resources
Websites
Blue Star Families: https://bluestarfam.org
Blue Star Families offers assistance for spouses with regard to connecting with employers committed to hiring military spouses and pursuing additional education and/or training.
eMentor: https://www.ementorprogram.org
eMentor is an online mentoring program for military personnel, veterans, and military spouses that offers support and trusted networking with a mentor who can provide insights into civilian careers and corporate hiring practices.
Hiring Our Heroes: https://www.hiringourheroes.org
Military.com. *Dealing with deployment*: https://www.military.com/spouse/military-deployment/dealing-with-deployment
Military Family Advisory Network: https://militaryfamilyadvisorynetwork.org
A network of military and veteran spouses and community leaders dedicated to improving the lives of military and veteran families with research and programming.
Military OneSource. *Family & relationships*: https://www.militaryonesource.mil/family-relationships
Military OneSource. *Spouse benefits*: https://www.militaryonesource.mil/family-relationships/spouse/spouse-benefits/
Military Spouse Advocacy Network: https://www.militaryspouseadvocacynetwork.org
Military Spouse Advocacy Network. *Guides & toolkits for all branches*: https://www.militaryspouseadvocacynetwork.org/guidesandtoolkits
Spouse Education Career Opportunities/Military Spouse Employment Partnership: https://myseco.militaryonesource.mil/portal/

Syracuse University, Institute for Veteran & Military Families. *What is Onward to Opportunity (O2O)*: https://ivmf.syracuse.edu/programs/career-training/about-o2o

O2O is a free career training program that provides professional certification and job placement support to transitioning service members, veterans, and military spouses.

U.S. Department of Defense. *My Career Advancement Account helping spouses reach career goals*: https://myseco.militaryonesource.mil/Portal/Media/Default/Collaterals_Catalog/Program_Overview/MyCAA-Helping-Spouses-Reach-Career-Goals.pdf

U.S. Department of Defense. *Spouse Education Career Opportunities (SECO) program*: https://myarmybenefits.us.army.mil/Benefit-Library/Federal-Benefits/Military-Spouse-Education-and-Career-Opportunities-(SECO)?serv=120

Spouses can use government-sponsored career and education resources, take advantage of networking opportunities, and work with employment counselors.

U.S. Department of Veterans Affairs. *Resources for military and veteran family members*: https://www.va.gov/careers-employment/family-resources

USO. *USO Pathfinder transition program*: https://www.uso.org/programs/uso-pathfinder

Peer Support

Veteran Spouse Network within Institute for Military and Veteran Family Wellness: http://sites.utexas.edu/imvfw

Transition Support for Spouses (Not Related to Employment)

Veteran Spouse Network within Institute for Military and Veteran Family Wellness: http://sites.utexas.edu/imvfw

Health and Wellness

Military One Source Health and Wellness Coaching: https://www.militaryonesourceconnect.org/achievesolutions/en/militaryonesource/Content.do?contentId=27178

References

Abuse, S. (2018). Mental Health Services Administration. (2017). Key substance use and mental health indicators in the United States: Results from the 2016 National Survey on Drug Use and Health (HHS Publication No. SMA 17-5044, NSDUH Series H-52). Rockville, MD: Center for Behavioral Health Statistics and Quality. *Substance Abuse and Mental Health Services Administration.* Retrieved from https://www.samhsa.gov/data

Blue Star Families. (2019). *Military Family Lifestyle Survey results.* https://bluestarfam.org/wp-content/uploads/2020/03/BSF-2019-Survey-Comprehensive-Report-Digital-rev200305.pdf

Borah, E., & Fina, B. (2017). Military spouses speak up: A qualitative study of military and veteran spouses' perspectives. *Journal of Family Social Work, 20*(2), 144–161.

Carter, S. P., & Renshaw, K. D. (2016). Spousal communication during military deployments: A review. *Journal of Family Issues, 37*(16), 2309–2332.

Crum-Cianflone, N. F., Fairbank, J. A., Marmar, C. R., & Schlenger, W. (2014). The Millennium Cohort Family Study: A prospective evaluation of the health and well-being of military service members and their families. *International Journal of Methods in Psychiatric Research, 23*(3), 320–330.

Donoho, C. J., Leard Mann, C., O'Malley, C. A., Walter, K. H., Riviere, L. A., Curry, J. F., & Adler, A. B. (2018). Depression among military spouses: Demographic, military, and service member psychological health risk factors. *Depression and Anxiety, 35,* 1137–1144.

Keeling, M., Borah, E. V., Kintzle, S., Kleykamp, M., & Robertson, M. C. (2020). Military spouses transition too! A call to action to address spouses' military to civilian transition. *Journal of Family Social Work, 23*(1), 3–19. doi:10.1080/10522158.2019.1652219

Mansfield, A. J., Kaufman, J. S., Marshall, S. W., Gaynes, B. N., Morrissey, J. P., & Engel, C. C. (2010). Deployment and the use of mental health services among US Army wives. *New England Journal of Medicine, 362*(2), 101–109.

Skomorovsky, A. (2014). Deployment stress and well-being among military spouses: The role of social support. *Military Psychology, 26*(1), 44–54.

Thompson, J. M., Lockhart, W., Roach, M. B., Atuel, H. R., Belenger, S., Black, T., & Truusa, T. (2017). *Veterans' identities and well-being in transition to civilian life—A resource for policy analysts, program designers, service providers and researchers.* Veterans Affairs Canada.

U.S. Bureau of Labor Statistics. (2016). *American Community Survey.* https://www.bls.gov/lau/acsqa.htm

U.S. Chamber of Congress. (2017). *Military Spouses in the Workplace: Understanding the impacts of spouse unemployment on military recruitment, retention, and readiness.* https://www.uschamberfoundation.org/reports/military-spouses-workplace

U.S. Department of Defense. (2018). *2018 Demographics. Profile of the Military Community.*

Office of the Deputy Assistant Secretary of Defense for Military Community and Family Policy.

Wang, M. C., Nyutu, P., Tran, K., & Spears, A. (2015). Finding resilience: The mediation effect of sense of community on the psychological well-being of military spouses. *Journal of Mental Health Counseling, 37*(2), 164–174.

Warner, C. H., Appenzeller, G. N., Warner, C. M., & Grieger, T. (2009). Psychological effects of deployments on military families. *Psychiatric Annals, 39*(2), 56–63.

Supporting Older Veterans Within Clinical Practice

Kari L. Fletcher and Kathryn K. Basham

Older veterans' lives—to varying degrees—have been shaped by their military service (Settersten, 2006). These influences have in part been determined by factors pertaining to military service that took place during the time in which they served (McFarland, 2012). For example, they include historic events (e.g., the Great Depression), benefits (e.g., guaranteed housing loans and educational benefits), and policies such as conscription (the draft from 1940 to 1973). Over the life course, older veterans' experience of military service may be positive (e.g., a turning point) and/or negative (e.g., a life course disruption; Wilmoth & London, 2011).

In the United States, older veterans (aged 65 years or older) currently make up a sizeable portion of both older adult (12.8%) and veteran (45% or 9.4 million out of 22 million) populations [U.S. Census Bureau, 2012; U.S. Department of Veterans Affairs (VA), 2014]. Older veterans may have served in one or more of the following conflicts: World War II (1,981,000 men and 400,000 women; December 7, 1941, to December 31, 1946), the Korean conflict (2,448,000 men and 47,336 women; June 27, 1950, to June 31, 1955), and the Vietnam era (7,526,000 men and 208,567 women; February 28, 1961, to May 7, 1975) (Torreon, 2017; U.S. Census Bureau, 2012; VA, National Center for Veterans Analysis and Statistics, 2018). On average, veteran men are older than veteran women (65 vs. 50 years old, respectively; VA, 2018). The majority of older veterans are men (97% vs. 3% women; U.S. Census Bureau, 2012) and White (91.4%) compared with Black or African American (5.9%), Hispanic or Latino (3.1%), Asian (1%), and American Indian/Alaskan Native (0.4%) (U.S. Census Bureau, 2012).

Despite a large older veteran population, few resources succinctly summarize critical elements relevant to working clinically with this population (e.g., Fletcher et al., 2017). This chapter aims to offer clinical social work (students and professionals) practical, applicable, and relevant information specific to working with older veterans and their families, particularly within community-based settings. Although specific to clinical social work, clinicians from different disciplines may find value and utility in reading this chapter.

This chapter is divided into three sections relevant to engaging in clinical social work practice with older veterans: (1) demographics and presenting issues, (2) assessment and practice interventions, and (3) conclusion. Within each section, we present the case of "Sgt. Baksa" and his family to help integrate and apply information from the chapter.

Presenting Issues Related to Military Service

This section illustrates the impact of military service upon life for older veterans and their families. A case composite is introduced featuring Sgt. Baksa, a Vietnam veteran, and his wife, Hanh Pho Baksa, and their three adult children. A more detailed account of their presenting issues follows a brief summary of foundational principles that guide our clinical social work practice with older veterans and their families. This case stresses the signature injuries and issues faced by Vietnam-era veterans in particular.

Several foundational principles guide our practice, including stressing the role of resilience while facing deployment and post-deployment stressors in addition to developmental and historical influences that affect reintegration back home (Wilcox et al., 2013). Although the protective factors of sound leadership, structure, esprit de corps, and effective training have fortified some Vietnam-era service members, others were deeply affected by the high trauma exposure that contributed to serious physical and mental health concerns as well as psychosocial issues [Institute of Medicine (IOM), 2014]. It is not uncommon for many older veterans to develop mental health symptoms related to delayed-onset post-traumatic stress disorder (PTSD) that were not previously experienced post-deployment (Spiro & Settersten, 2012). Typically, a diagnosis of PTSD occurs

within the first 3 months following trauma exposure. Frequently, service members meet the criteria for an acute stress disorder (ASD) or post-traumatic stress injury during this early period (IOM, 2014). Many service members experience a complete recovery, whereas others may experience the onset of symptoms and distress during midlife and older years.

When older adult veterans experience declining health, reduced cognitive functioning, multiple losses, and social isolation, serious mental health and health conditions often surface. Many Vietnam veterans have also experienced depression and moral injury related to transgressions perceived to have occurred by the veterans or imposed by a military member in the command structure (Shay, 1994). Symptoms of PTSD (or ASD), depression, and suicidal thoughts often led to self-medicating with alcohol and other substances to numb the pain. These co-occurring conditions represented signature injuries for Vietnam-era veterans.

In many situations supported by clinical data, older veterans face inevitable age-related physical vulnerabilities and illnesses, losses of family and friends, and a sense of mortality. These issues may be addressed without a mental health crisis. As clinical social workers, it is important that we recognize the anticipated stressors related to transitions from military service to civilian life as well as the expected stressors of aging associated with illnesses, multiple losses related to body integrity, and loss of family, friends, battle buddies, employment, and work identity (Nash, 2006). To facilitate healthy grieving of these multiple losses, a prevention approach may fortify older veterans and their families to avoid experiencing depression due to unresolved grief.

Case Example

The case, featuring Sgt. Baksa and his wife Hanh Pho Baksa, reveals many positive aspects of military and veteran life. After joining the military, Sgt. Baksa experienced a turning point (Settersten, 2006) that provided opportunity to craft a healthy, meaningful, and productive trajectory throughout life (Jennings et al., 2006). His adaptation reflected the positive changes associated with post-traumatic growth (Tedeschi & Calhoun, 2006).

Sgt. Baksa is a 70-year-old, White identified, Slovakian American, cisgendered, male Vietnam veteran. Following his draft into military service at age 20 years and deployment to Vietnam, where he was a helicopter pilot for 18 months of active duty military service, Sgt. Baksa met and later married Hanh Pho, a Vietnamese Buddhist woman whom he met in Saigon. Following his return home, Sgt. Baksa and Hanh Pho reared two sons (John, Jr., age 32 years; Due, age 30 years) and one daughter (Choa, age 29 years) in a small city in the Midwestern region of the country. This racially and ethnically homogeneous community set the stage for ostracism and harsh bigotry expressed by schoolmates toward the Baksa children, who were taunted because of their brown skin color and "different" cultural traditions. Within the marriage, legacies of the Vietnam War (referred to by Vietnamese citizens as the "American War") surfaced in marital conflicts around issues of power and control in decision-making—Who behaved as the victimizer and who behaved as the victim or distant bystander? Disagreements between them would often lead to stalemates and suppressed emotions of frustration, resentment, and embitterment. Sgt. Baksa and Hanh Pho's cultural morays influenced the ways they experienced the severe traumatic events during wartime, with Sgt. Baksa alternating between an individualistic distancing and defensive anger and Hanh Pho somaticized her stress and emotion while focusing on the well-being of the collective—the family.

After leaving the military, Sgt. Baksa worked as a firefighter for decades until his retirement 4 years ago. He thrived in his job, with accomplishments rewarded by promotions and admiration from peers and higher ranking officers. Following the death of his beloved father when Sgt. Baksa was age 50 years, Sgt. Baksa drank excessively for 7 months and then decided to abstain from all alcohol until commencing drinking 6 months after retiring.

As the case illustrates, various factors have contributed to Sgt. Baksa's health over his lifetime. General variables that contributed positively or negatively to his aging process—or ongoing process of deterioration (Kane et al., 2018) and overall health over time (VA, 2015)—include his genetics, lifestyle choices, and longevity (McReynolds & Rossen, 2004). Whereas many older veterans report having successful aging experiences, others may be susceptible to disability and disease (Fletcher et al., 2017). Military-specific variables that may accelerate and/or impact Sgt. Baksa's and other veterans' health and aging process include previous military-specific exposures (e.g., exposure to chemicals such as Agent Orange during Vietnam) as well as hazardous work conditions inherent to the terrain (e.g., geography or environment in which they served) and/or duties they performed as part of their military occupational specialty [e.g., use of heavy equipment, which is associated with chronic pain, and exposure to noise, which is correlated to ringing in the ears (tinnitus); VA, 2015]. In addition, older veterans may be living with significant injuries that they suffered during combat and rescue (e.g., amputations and effects of Agent Orange) and secondary injuries that developed as the result of original injuries (e.g., depression and weight gain) and that may have compounded over time (IOM, 2014).

Just as there is a connection between aging and overall health, the case of Sgt. Baksa illustrates that intersection also exists between physical and psychological (mental) health. Physically, older veterans may struggle with multiple health concerns, which may or may not have been exacerbated by their military service. Sgt. Baksa, for example, was not exposed to Agent Orange, but many of his peers were struggling with the conditions associated with this chemical exposure. Psychological effects of military service may vary over time, particularly for those who served in combat (Jennings et al., 2006). Psychologically, compared to non-veterans, older veterans experience higher rates of mental health issues (Wilcox et al., 2013), substance use concerns (IOM, 2014), and depression (Tanielian & Jaycox, 2008).

Assessment and Practice Interventions

Engaging in a thorough biopsychosocial–spiritual/structural assessment involves addressing presenting issues noted by the veteran client and key family members along with a review of the strengths and vulnerabilities in these different domains, currently and throughout their history.

Up until retirement at age 66 years, Sgt. Baksa stated that he was relatively unaffected by what he had seen and done in Vietnam. However, at age 68 years, Sgt. Baksa presented to the VA Medical Center reporting vivid wartime nightmares of dropping napalm on local Vietnamese villagers during his helicopter missions. In his words, he felt anxious, profoundly guilty, and ashamed of what he called "evil acts conducted in compliance with our President's orders—I hope God will forgive me." The years of reintegrating home were complicated. As noted previously, Sgt. Baksa and his wife spent fruitful decades of their lives rearing their children and thriving in their local community.

The first year post-retirement was described by Sgt. Baksa and Hanh Pho as a honeymoon period. Gradually, his psychological and physical symptoms began to emerge. Mood instability, nightmares, insomnia, and memories of wreaking destruction on Vietnamese women and children haunted him. He experienced himself as morally defective— a lost and

reprehensible human being. Physical symptoms of an irregular heartbeat began to emerge closer to point of entry to the VA Medical Center. A physical examination determined he had arrhythmia and irritable bowel syndrome. Precipitating stressors included his own discomfort; fears expressed by his wife related to his temper outbursts; and physical vulnerability, as he had never experienced physical symptoms previously.

In summary, in the biological realm, Sgt. Baksa reported relatively sound health throughout his life until the flashback memories and intermittent rage outbursts alarmed him and his wife. He had recently received diagnoses of arrhythmia and type II diabetes. An increasing problem with alcohol intake led to an assessment for substance misuse. Forgetfulness, memory lapses, emotional lability, and limited attention span plagued Sgt. Baksa. His wife expressed fears about his mood swings, nightmares, and despondency over the past 4 years when he developed cardiac arrhythmia and was diagnosed with irritable bowel syndrome and possible substance misuse. In the psychological realm, Sgt. Baksa sustained a loving relationship with his wife and children and reported a successful effective career as a firefighter. Vulnerabilities include experienced flashback memories of combat, nightmares, insomnia, emotional lability, forgetfulness, memory lapses, disrupted concentration, sadness, plaguing feelings of guilt and shame, and rage outbursts. In the social realm, John retains a strong military and veteran identity and sustains contact with family; vulnerabilities involve distancing from veteran colleagues and social dislocation. In the spiritual realm, Sgt. Baksa recognizes an awareness of God in his life yet believes that some of his wartime activities are deemed by God as immoral and corrupt—undeserving of forgiveness. Moral injury associated with profound feelings of shame and disappointment and betrayal plagued John and disturbed his wife as well.

The third part of this clinical example demonstrates the useful effects and outcomes of a clinical social work practice approach with older veterans and their families.

Phase-Oriented, Trauma-Informed Multimodality Treatment Plan

Phase I involves assessment with the family and a focus on safety, self-care, affect regulation, and establishing a context for change (Basham & Miehls, 2004). Individual goals included (1) assess and establish safety; (2) demonstrate awareness of mood changes and capacities to regulate affect; (3) engage in assessments for substance misuse, medical management of his arrhythmia and irritable bowel syndrome and PTSD/depression; (4) utilize stress-reduction skills focused on deep breathing techniques; and (5) identify the range of social supports with wife, children, and former colleagues. Couple and family goals include (1) demonstrate ways to directly talk with each other about transitions, losses, and mental and physical health conditions; (2) express enhanced understanding and empathy for each partner's perspective; and (3) identify ways to strengthen connections with adult children and colleagues. Until such goals are met, it is contraindicated to move to Phase II of the treatment plan, which involves specifically addressing trauma exposure and grieving multiple losses. The individual veteran and partner need to reveal sufficient internal ego scaffolding to bear the intensity of the emotional work before moving forward to Phases II and III (Basham & Miehls, 2004).

The phase-oriented treatment plan involved multiple modalities, including (1) psychiatric and medical assessments of substance misuse and physical and mental health at the VA Medical Center; (2) individual and couple therapy with a community-based clinical social worker; and (3) stress-reduction workshops for Sgt. Baksa and his wife at a wellness center in the community (Basham & Miehls, 2004). In the beginning, Sgt. Baksa desperately needed treatment for affect regulation in individual therapy and engaged with a stress-reduction group. Initially, an assessment with Hanh Pho, in individual sessions along with couple sessions, provided an opportunity to rule out possible intimate partner violence. (*Note*: if there is any evidence of physical abuse and/or bullying, then joint couples' therapy is contraindicated.) In this case, the arguments and struggles involved yelling by Sgt. Baksa and detachment by Hanh Pho, setting the stage for direct reparative interventions in the couple therapy (Basham & Miehls, 2004).

Phase II involved reflecting on relevant trauma narratives and grieving. Specific goals for the couple included (1) explore and reflect on the meaning of wartime traumatic events for both partners, (2) express grief related to multiple losses, (3) demonstrate shared empathy, and (4) reveal the capacity for mentalization (Basham & Miehls, 2004). As Sgt. Baksa and Hanh Pho discussed their respective traumatic events that occurred during the Vietnam/American war, each partner deepened understanding of the other's suffering and moral quandaries. Both individual and couple sessions allowed the partners to share their feelings about moral injury that set the stage for strong feelings of pervasive shame and survivor guilt (Basham & Miehls, 2004).

Phase III involved consolidating new perspectives, meaning-making, and social vindication (Basham & Miehls, 2004). Sgt. Baksa and Hanh Pho's goals involved (1) re-establish connections with adult children and other family members, faith-based community, and veteran colleagues; (2) enhance emotional and sexual intimacy; (3) demonstrate more complex intersecting social identities (e.g., gender, military service, race, ethnicity, and spirituality); and (4) expand opportunities for engagement in volunteer efforts and social vindication (Basham & Miehls, 2004).

A review of progress related to these specific treatment goals points to distinct evidence of positive changes in individual goals set with Sgt. Baksa and goals for the couple in all three phases of treatment. Fifteen months after seeking treatment, Sgt. Baksa expressed feeling more balanced, less despondent, and better able to reduce his stress with a combination of breathing, exercise regimen, and stress-reduction methods. He expressed more confidence in talking directly and empathically with others. Sgt. Baksa and Hahn Pho openly shared strong feelings of the many struggles addressed together to weather the racially charged bullying comments lodged against their children during their middle school and high school years. The couple relationship clearly strengthened, with enhanced empathy and more direct communicating. Sgt. Baksa also reported acceptance of the reasons for his moral injury. With the guidance of a psychotherapist specializing in work with Vietnam veterans, Sgt. Baksa and Hanh Pho returned to the sites in Vietnam where Sgt. Baksa had dropped napalm onto local residents during wartime. As a couple, they talked with some of the survivors of those bombings, who welcomed them and discussed moral injury, reparation, and social vindication (Tick, 2005).

Although forgiveness was not his solution, Sgt. Baksa expressed deeper compassion toward himself as well as his wife, children, battle buddies, and new colleagues met through a volunteer veterans' network. The multimodality phase-oriented approach enabled him and his wife to develop a scaffolding of self-care, safety, and ways to regulate emotions before sharing their profound losses and respective experiences of perceived moral faults (Basham & Miehls, 2004). Ultimately, toward the end of treatment, new connections were established with a faith-based community and veteran colleagues to establish a solid foundation and set the context for change. This particular treatment plan involved a coordinated effort between VA Medical Center health and behavioral health care and couple and family therapy in the community, consistent with the model of "aging in place."

Conclusion

In concluding this chapter, we stress several important points for clinicians. First, recognize the visible and invisible health and mental health injuries accompanying aging, along with multiple losses associated with retirement, serious illness, and deaths. Opportunities to grieve these losses serve a vital prevention measure. Second, focus on locating resilience and surrounding social supports with older veterans, their families, and caregivers. Third, challenge ageism and acknowledge how intersecting social identities such as gender (women), sexual orientation (LBGTQ), race (non-White veterans), and ability/disability shape experiences and adjustments to aging. Fourth, craft a trauma-informed multimodality treatment plan that includes VA and community-based resources. Finally, promote health equity and advance geriatric research, education, and development of innovative clinical centers to support the biopsychosocial–spiritual needs of older veterans and their families.

Helpful Resources

Apps
U.S. Department of Veterans Affairs. *Mental health*: https://mobile.va.gov/appstore/mental-health

U.S. Department of Veterans Affairs. *VA health chat*: https://mobile.va.gov/app/va-health-chat

Websites
RAND Corporation. *Assessing Care of Vulnerable Elders (ACOVE)*: https://www.rand.org/health/projects/acove.html

U.S. Department of Veterans Affairs. *Geriatric Research and Clinical Center*: https://www.va.gov/grecc

U.S. Department of Veterans Affairs. *VA geriatrics and extended care:* https://www.va.gov/GERIATRICS

Veterans Crisis Line. 1-800-273-TALK: https://www.veteranscrisisline.net

References

Basham, K. K., & Miehls, D. (2004). *Transforming the legacy: Couples therapy with survivors of childhood trauma.* Columbia University Press.

Fletcher, K. L., Albright, D. L., Rorie, K. A., & Lewis, A. M. (2017). Older veterans. In J. Beder (Ed.), *Caring for the military: A guide for helping professionals* (pp. 54–71). Routledge.

Institute of Medicine. (2014). *Veterans and Agent Orange: Update 2012.* National Academies Press. https://www.nap.edu/catalog/18395/veterans-and-agent-orange-update-2012

Jennings, P. A., Aldwin, C. A., Levenson, M. R., Spiro, A., & Mroczek, D. K. (2006). Combat exposure, perceived benefits of military service, and wisdom in later life: Findings from the Normative Aging Study. *Research on Aging, 28*(1), 115–134.

Kane, R. L., Ouslander, J. G., Abrass, I. B., & Resnick, B. (2018). *Essentials of clinical geriatrics* (8th ed.). McGraw-Hill.

McFarland, S. L. (2012). *A concise history of the Air Force.* Air University, U.S. Air Force Jeanne M. Holm Center for Officer Accessions and Citizen Development.

McReynolds, J. L., & Rossen, E. K. (2004). Importance of physical activity, nutrition, and social support for optimal aging. *Clinical Nurse Specialist, 18*(4), 200–206.

Nash, W. P. (2006). The spectrum of war stressors. In C. R. Figley & W. P. Nash (Eds.), *Combat stress injury theory, research, and management* (pp. 18–69). Routledge.

Settersten, R. A. (2006). When nations call: How wartime military service matters for the life course and aging. *Research on Aging, 28*(1), 12–36.

Shay, J. (1994). *Achilles in Vietnam: Combat trauma and the undoing of character.* Scribner.

Spiro, A., & Settersten, R. A. (2012). Long-term implications of military service for later-life health and well-being. *Research in Human Development, 9*(3), 183–190. doi:10.1080/15427609.2012.705551

Tanielian, T., & Jaycox, L. H. (Eds.). (2008). *Invisible wounds of war: Summary and recommendations for addressing psychological and cognitive injuries.* RAND.

Tedeschi, R. G., & Calhoun, L. G. (2006). Expert companions: Posttraumatic growth in clinical practice. In L. G. Calhoun & R. G. Tedeschi (Eds.), *Handbook of traumatic growth: Research and growth* (pp. 291–310). Erlbaum.

Tick, E. (2005). *War and the soul: Healing our nation's veterans from posttraumatic stress disorder.* Quest Books.

Torreon, B. S. (2017). U.S. periods of war and dates of current conflicts. Congressional Research Service Report for Congress: Prepared for Members and Committees of Congress.

U.S. Census Bureau. (2012). *Table 521. Veterans living by period of service, age, and sex: 2010.* https://www2.census.gov/library/publications/2011/compendia/statab/131ed/tables/12s0521.pdf

U.S. Department of Veterans Affairs. (2014). *National Center for Veterans Analysis and Statistics.* http://www.va.gov/vetdata/Veteran_Population.asp

U.S. Department of Veterans Affairs. (2015a). *National Center for Veterans Analysis and Statistics.* http://www1.va.gov/vetdata/

U.S. Department of Veterans Affairs. (2015b). *Public health:* Military exposures. http://www.publichealth.va.gov/exposures

U.S. Department of Veterans Affairs, National Center for Veterans Analysis and Statistics. (2018). *Profile of veterans 2016: Data from the American Community Survey.* National Center for Veterans Analysis and Statistics.

Wilcox, S. L., Finney, K., & Cederbaum, J. A. (2013). Prevalence of mental health problems among military populations. In B. A. Moore & J. E. Barnett (Eds.), *Military psychologists' desk reference* (pp. 187–196). Oxford University Press.

Wilmoth, J. M., & London, A. S. (2011). Aging veterans: Needs and provisions. In R. A. Setterson & J. L. Angel (Eds.), *Handbook of sociology and aging* (pp. 661–672). Springer. doi:10.1007/978-1-4419-7374-0_28

Considerations for Practice with Lesbian, Gay, Bisexual, and Transgender Service Members and Veterans

Kristen Kavanaugh

Members of the lesbian, gay, bisexual, and transgender (LGBT) communities have served in the military since the founding of the United States. The *2015 Department of Defense Health Related Behaviors Survey,* produced by the RAND Corporation (Meadows et al., 2015), found that 6.1% of the military population identified as LGBT. The majority of their service has been in silence because federal laws such as Don't Ask Don't Tell (DADT) and military policies such as the Trump–Pence transgender ban have prohibited open service. Cultural and political climates have weighed heavily on the community's ability to serve and receive the benefits associated with military service. It has only been in the past decade that the rights and subsequent service for lesbian, gay, and bisexual individuals have been sanctioned and recognized by military and federal laws. However, progress for the community has not meant progress for all members. Transgender individuals still face cultural and political barriers to open service, yet they continue to seek commissioning and enlistment in the armed forces.

Changes with Cultural and Political Climate

Cultural and political climates have always impacted the LGBT community's ability to integrate into broader society. This is also the case regarding military culture, which is, unfortunately, impacted by the culture of politics. President Harry Truman was praised for recognizing the value of diversity by desegregating the military in 1948. But that value only extended to certain underrepresented groups, as he moved to explicitly ban LGBT service the next year through military policies and regulations [U.S. Department of Defense (DoD),1949]. Gay members of the Greatest Generation were viewed as a liability to the service and discharged.

The post-World War II policies and regulations regarding LGBT service stood and were expanded upon throughout the Korean and Vietnam Wars. In 1982, the first formal ban was enacted by President Ronald Regan's Deputy Secretary of Defense (Johnson & Ham, 2010). Service members who disclosed they were gay, engaged in homosexual activity, or married someone of the same sex were to be discharged (Jonhnson & Ham, 2010). After the policy was enacted, LGBT service members increasingly experienced and feared "witch hunts" in which they were sought out, harassed, entrapped, and ultimately discharged under the suspicion of being gay.

Social and political pressures began to mount during the 1992 presidential campaign as all the Democratic candidates pledged to lift the ban on lesbian, gay, and bisexual (LGB) service. Ultimately, Governor Bill Clinton won the democratic nomination and the presidency. Almost immediately, he moved to make good on his campaign promise. In 1993, President Clinton suspended the outright ban on LGB individuals in the service in exchange for DADT. Although touted as progress, DADT only permitted members of the LGB community to serve conditionally—they had to commit to keep their sexual orientation and sexual behavior private. This set the stage for all LGB service members to have to choose between concealment of their sexual orientation in order preserve their military career or disclosure. Meanwhile, transgender individuals remained banned from service based on medical, physiological, and behavioral reasons defined by the Army's Medical Service Standards (Hicks et al., 2017).

The pressure for equality for the LGBT community continued as states and the courts began to field challenges to the Defense of Marriage Act (DOMA)—also signed into law by President Clinton. For the purpose of the federal government, DOMA defined marriage as between one man and one woman. As federal employees, LGB service members were bound by DOMA even as states began to legalize same-sex marriage. As states sanctioned marriage equality, LGBT service members were legally permitted to enter into same-sex partnerships and, in some cases, marriage. However, entering into such an arrangement was in direct violation of DADT and put the service member at risk of being discharged.

DADT and DOMA stood as law until President Barack Obama took office in 2009. President Obama pledged to repeal DADT in 2009, and in less than 2 years he dismantled decades of sanctioned discrimination against the lesbian, gay, and bisexual (LGB) communities by signing the Don't Ask, Don't Tell Repeal Act of 2010 into law. With the repeal, LGB service members were able to serve openly without fear of being discharged. The repeal did not; however, include open service for transgender individuals, who constituted 0.6% of the military's total population (Meadows et al., 2015).

The repeal of DADT immediately exposed a two-tiered benefits system in the military. Although LGB service members could serve openly and had obtained marriage equality in a handful of states, they were bound by DOMA as federal employees. This meant they were ineligible for benefits earned by their similarly situated heterosexual counterparts, such as dependent pay, base access, and health care. In 2011, President Obama instructed the Justice Department to stop defending DOMA in the courts, and the law was subsequently repealed in 2015 when the Supreme Court ruled in *Obergefell v. Hodges* that same-sex couples had the right to marry under the Fourteenth Amendment. Following the *Obergefell* decision, all LGB service members and veterans obtained the right to marry and receive the same benefits as their heterosexual colleagues, regardless of which state they considered home.

After DADT and DOMA were repealed, some LGB service members continued to conceal their sexual orientation and remained hesitant to serve openly. Although public sentiment had evolved, navigating individual command climate was more complicated. Each unit is set by the Commanding Officer and varies leader to leader based on their values and belief systems. Although the threat of discharge was alleviated, LGB service members who chose to disclose their sexual orientation faced an elevated risk of harassment and victimization (Schuyler et al., 2020).

Transgender Service Members

The repeal of DADT did not include relief for transgender service members. Instead, the DoD commissioned a working group to study the implications of open service for transgender individuals. Finally, in June 2016, the DoD lifted the ban and paved the way for transgender service members to serve openly for the first time in history. Since then, transgender individuals have been serving openly at home and in combat zones with no negative impact and minimal medical costs to the services.

Despite regulatory progress and resounding cultural support for transgender service members to serve openly, the political climate changed when President Donald Trump was inaugurated. In July 2017, President Trump tweeted that "the United States Government will not accept or allow transgender individuals to serve in any capacity in the U.S. Military," declaring his intention to roll back the Obama administration's efforts to allow transgender individuals to serve openly. This announcement was met with angst from the transgender community because many transgender service members had already begun taking steps toward open service. The new political climate immediately put those individuals at risk of harassment, discrimination, and ultimately discharge once again.

The DoD published the *Department of Defense Report and Recommendations on* *Military Service by Transgender Persons* in February 2018. The policy disqualified transgender individuals diagnosed with gender dysphoria and those who would require or who had undergone gender-affirming surgery. Transgender individuals who agreed to serve in their biological sex assigned at birth were permitted to serve. Although touted by the administration as a path to service for transgender individuals, the transgender community, broader LGBT community, and veterans' organizations called the move continued discrimination against qualified Americans attempting to serve their country. Legal challenges and exemption requests were filed almost immediately after the new policy was announced.

Impacts and Implications

The LGBT community has long experienced mental, physical, and behavioral health disparities. Service in the military exacerbates some of those disparities. According to Meadows et al. (2015), "Compared with non-LGBT personnel, [LGBT service members] report more smoking, binge drinking, sexual behavior risky to their health, and adverse sexual health outcomes." Meadows et al. also found LGBT service members reported significantly higher levels of moderate to severe depression, suicidal ideations, and self-harm compared to non-LGBT service members (Meadows et al., 2015).

LGBT service members' and veterans' mental health is influenced by their experience as members of both the LGBT and military communities. One major factor influencing the LGBT community's mental health is chronic social stress (Meyer, 2003). The military community is also at risk for mental health impacts brought on by deployments, combat exposure, and deployment-related injuries (Meadows et al., 2015). It is important to consider this intersectionality when assessing the impact of exclusionary policies and military service on the LGBT community. The individual impact of exclusionary policies such as DADT and DOMA is as unique as each individual who experienced them. The collective impact starts to uncover trends. Some LGBT service members and veterans are thriving in a post-DADT/DOMA world. They have access to the same benefits and resources as their heterosexual counterparts. Other members of the community are haunted by their exposure to discrimination, minority stress, and/or traumatic stress or—worse—continue to experience it.

Minority Stress

Military service is stressful for anyone. It is even more stressful for minorities, especially members of the LGBT community as they experience minority stress (Meyer, 2003, 2015). Minority stress describes the unique stressors member of the LGBT community face because of their sexual orientation and/or gender identity (Meyer, 2015). These stressors include experiencing prejudice events, stigma, expecting rejection or discrimination, concealment of sexual or gender identity, and internalized homophobia or transphobia (Meyer, 2003, 2015). Chronic minority stress can lead to negative behavioral, mental, and physical health care outcomes such as depression, anxiety, PTSD, substance abuse, and suicide.

Meyer (2003) describes minority stress as unique, chronic, and socially based with stressors that can be triggered by external events or internalization of negative societal attitudes. As minorities in military culture, LGBT service members and veterans are predisposed to experience minority stress. As such, LGBT service members and veterans experience stress caused by a hostile military culture, which can result in chronic harassment, discrimination, and victimization and can impact an individual's access to physical and mental health care and the resulting negative treatment outcomes (Meyer, 2003).

Transgender veterans also report experiencing minority stress (Chen et al., 2017). Minority stress is a contributing factor for an increased risk of suicidal ideations for transgender service members (Carter et al., 2019). Blosnich et al. (2016) remind practitioners that transgender veterans live in complex, dynamic, and at times hostile social environments that impact treatment, and detecting these social factors early will inform treatment processes and improve efficacy. Many transgender patients struggle to negotiate the medical and mental health care environments within the U.S. Department of Veteran Affairs (Dietert et al., 2017).

Working with LGBT Service Members and Veterans

Seeking mental health care treatment can be stressful for LGBT service members and veterans, especially those who identify as transgender. Mental health providers should first create a safe, nonjudgmental space for their clients to feel comfortable. Next, providers must remember that the LGBT service member and veteran community is not a monolith. Do not assume a client's reason for seeking treatment is rooted in their sexual orientation or gender identity. Meet them where they are at, just like any other client. Finally, providers should recognize that their client may have unique stressors and traumatic experiences as a result of chronic minority stress, incorporate the minority stress model into treatment, and build resilience through positive coping and social support.

Building resilience through positive coping and social support mitigates the negative impact of minority stress and discrimination on health (Meyer, 2015). Mental health providers should work to build the client's positive coping skills and connections to social support systems. Having social support from others with shared identities and experiences may protect against negative mental health outcomes (Carter et al., 2019). Assess clients' access to social support from family, friends, and the LGBT and veterans communities, and make referrals to appropriate community resources.

The most prominent organization that focuses on providing community support for the unique challenges faced by LGBT service members and veterans is the Modern Military Association of America. It is the nation's largest nonprofit organization dedicated to advancing fairness and equality for the LGBTQ military and veteran community. Through education, advocacy, and support, the organization aims to make a real difference in the lives of LGBTQ service members, military spouses, veterans, and family members.

Conclusion

The military community is not a monolithic group, nor is the LGBT community. LGBT service members and veterans sit at the intersection of these two communities united by their desire to serve others and demonstrated resilience in the face of unspeakable adversity. They have endured harassment, discrimination, persecution, and violence all in order to serve our nation. In the case of transgender service members, they continue to face these hardships in order to serve. Although progress should be celebrated, the fight for equality continues until all members of the LGBT community have the right to serve without fear.

Helpful Resources

Human Rights Campaign: https://www.hrc.org
Modern Military Association of America: https://modernmilitary.org
National Center for Transgender Equality: https://transequality.org
Palm Center: https://www.palmcenter.org

U.S. Department of Veterans Affairs. *Patient care services*: https://www.patientcare.va.gov/LGBT/index.asp
Williams Institute, University of California, Los Angeles School of Law: https://williamsinstitute.law.ucla.edu

References

Blosnich, J. R., Marsiglio, M. C., Gao, S., Gordon, A. J., Shipherd, J. C., Kauth, M., Brown, G. R., & Fine, M. J. (2016). Mental health of transgender veterans in US states with and without discrimination and hate crime legal protection. *American Journal of Public Health, 106*(3), 534–540. https://doi.org/10.2105/AJPH.2015.302981

Carter, S. P., Allred, K. M., Tucker, R. P., Simpson, T. L., Shipherd, J. C., & Lehavot, K. (2019). Discrimination and suicidal ideation among transgender veterans: The role of social support and connection. *LGBT Health, 6*(2), 43–50. https://doi.org/10.1089/lgbt.2018.0239

Chen, J. A., Granato, H., Shipherd, J. C., Simpson, T., & Lehavot, K. (2017). A qualitative analysis of transgender veterans' lived experiences. *Psychology of Sexual Orientation and Gender Diversity, 4*(1), 63–74. https://doi.org/10.1037/sgd0000217

Dietert, M., Dentice, D., & Keig, Z. (2017). Addressing the needs of transgender military veterans: Better access and more comprehensive care. *Transgender Health, 2*(1), 35–44. https://doi.org/10.1089/trgh.2016.0040

Hicks, L., Weiss, E. L., & Coll, J. E. (Eds.). (2017). *The civilian lives of U.S. veterans: Issues and identities*. Praeger.

Johnson, J., & Ham, C. (2010). *Report of the comprehensive review of the issues associated with the repeal of Don't Ask, Don't Tell*. U.S. Department of Defense.

Meadows, S. O., Engel, C. C., Collins, R. L., Beckman, R. L., Cefalu, M., Hawes-Dawson, J., Waymouth, M., Kress, A. M., Sontag-Padilla, L., Ramchand, R., & Williams, K. M. (2015). *Department of Defense Health Related Behaviors Survey (HRBS)*. RAND Corporation. https://www.rand.org/pubs/research_reports/RR1695.html

Meyer, I. H. (2003). Prejudice, social stress, and mental health in lesbian, gay, and bisexual populations: Conceptual issues and research evidence. *Psychological Bulletin, 129*(5), 674–697. https://doi.org/10.1037/0033-2909.129.5.674

Meyer, I. H. (2015). Resilience in the study of minority stress and health of sexual and gender minorities. *Psychology of Sexual Orientation and Gender*

Diversity, 2(3), 209–213. https://doi.org/10.1037/sgd0000132

Schuyler, A. C., Klemmer, C., Mamey, M. R., Schrager, S. M., Goldbach, J. T., Holloway, I. W., & Castro, C. A. (2020). Experiences of sexual harassment, stalking, and sexual assault during military service among LGBT and non-LGBT service members. *Journal of Traumatic Stress, 33*(3), 257–266. https://doi.org/10.1002/jts.22506

U.S. Department of Defense. (2018). *Department of Defense report and recommendations on military service by transgender persons.*

U.S. Department of Defense, Secretary of the Navy. (1949). *Directive 1620.1.*

Resilience-Based Interventions for Trauma-Exposed Military Veterans

Shoba Sreenivasan, Robert T. Rubin, and Leslie Martin

Psychological resilience is the ability to bounce back from adversity through constructive navigation of distress (American Psychological Association, 2008). Traumatic exposure can erode resilience. Military veterans deployed to war zones are exposed to a multiplicity of traumas, such as exposure to the death or serious injury of comrades and civilians, through direct combat, provision of support services, and experiencing mortar or grenade attacks and other catastrophic events while on base. In addition, coming home from war can be problematic. Re-entry into a family, work, and a civilian society all present challenges and may be particularly difficult for veterans with combat exposure. The high rates of mental health problems, including post-traumatic stress disorder (PTSD), and suicide risk among military veterans returning from deployments speak to the difficulties in transition to civilian life.

Resilience serves as a protective factor for suicide risk among Iraq and Afghanistan veterans (Youssef et al., 2013). Low resilience was a stronger predictor of suicidal behavior than was alcohol misuse. Therefore, enhancing resilience to promote post-deployment adjustment has gained prominence. In this chapter, we provide an overview of PTSD and other trauma reactions among veterans, highlight some examples of post-deployment experiences that can erode resilience, and provide common approaches to resilience building.

Post-Traumatic Stress Disorder and Other Trauma-Related Conditions

The term PTSD has been used in psychiatric diagnostics only since the Vietnam War, and it first appeared in 1980 in the third edition of the American Psychiatric Association's *Diagnostic and Statistical Manual of Mental Disorders* (DSM-III). Prior to that time, disorders resulting from severe wartime stressors were called soldier's heart (Civil War), shell shock (World War I), and battle fatigue (World War II). The current criteria for PTSD are given in the DSM-5 (American Psychiatric Association, 2013) in the section titled Trauma- and Stressor-Related Disorders. The main categories of symptoms are (1) exposure to actual or threatened death, serious injury, or sexual violence; (2) intrusion symptoms associated with the traumatic event (e.g., flashbacks and nightmares); (3) persistent avoidance of internal or external trauma-associated stimuli; (4) negative cognitions or mood following the traumatic event; and (5) marked alteration in arousal and reactivity associated with the traumatic event. Certain numbers of symptoms in each category are required for a diagnosis of PTSD; lesser symptom presentations following severe trauma may be diagnosed as other specified trauma- and stressor-related disorder. As with other psychiatric diagnoses, the symptoms must have been present for a specified duration (more than 1 month for PTSD), the symptoms cannot be attributable to substance abuse or a medical condition, and there must be clinically significant impairment of social and/or occupational functioning.

Of importance, determination of the symptom criteria for PTSD is entirely subjective—that is, the clinician asks the patient about the presence or absence of each symptom. There are rating scales to determine the presence, severity, and frequency of symptoms, but these are entirely dependent on the patient's responses (U.S. Department of Veterans Affairs, n.d.). It therefore is incumbent on the clinician to determine a coherent symptom presentation to support a diagnosis of PTSD or other stressor-related disorder. For example, if a patient endorses having nightmares, it is important to determine their specific nature and content—that is, Are they related or unrelated to the traumatic event(s)? What is the timing of their appearance in relation to the traumatic event(s)? and What is their progression over time? (Very often, nightmares are most severe and frequent immediately after a traumatic event and decrease in intensity and frequency over ensuing weeks and months.)

In male veterans, combat experiences are frequent antecedents to PTSD; in women,

who increasingly are sent to combat zones, sexual trauma is a frequent antecedent of PTSD. Prominent PTSD symptoms in war zone–exposed veterans include heightened arousal, irritability, anger, and isolation. For example, veterans who go to crowded places such as restaurants often choose seating with their backs to a wall and facing the front door so they can be alert to people's movements. If they go shopping with their families and must wait at a checkout line, they may become increasingly irritable and bolt out of the store, leaving their family members to do the checkout. Triggers to symptoms include specific noises, such as from helicopters overhead (for Vietnam veterans), car exhaust backfires, and fireworks; bursts of light, such as from fireworks and laser light shows; and smells, such as diesel fuel and burning trash. Veterans frequently avoid these triggers as much as possible—for example, by not attending fireworks displays and by avoiding driving on freeways because they may see trash that might resemble a roadside bomb. Occasionally, a trauma-exposed veteran may have extreme road rage if cut off by another vehicle, owing to a combination of heightened irritability and fear of attack.

Prominent illness comorbidities in veterans with war zone–related PTSD include major depression, alcohol/drug abuse, sleep apnea, and traumatic brain injury (TBI). Mild TBI incurred in combat can be a precursor of PTSD; multiple TBIs lead to greater PTSD symptomatology (Albanese et al., 2019). Depression and sleep apnea occur in more than half of combat veterans diagnosed with PTSD and can result in heightened PTSD symptoms, as well as increased suicide ideation and attempts (Gonzalez et al., 2016). Alcohol abuse, which occurs in approximately one-third of combat veterans with PTSD, often is cited as an attempt at self-medication to blunt their frequently experienced hyperarousal, irritability, and anger (McDivitt-Murphy et al., 2017).

Commonly Encountered Post-Deployment Stresses

There exists the dichotomy of having survived in battle versus the emotional need to retain a military mindset in order to protect those close to the veteran where there is no real-time, physical threat. Post-deployment stress that can occur as an adaptative mechanism for survival in a war zone often is maladaptive in a "safe" environment upon the veteran's return home.

BATTLEMIND: A Resilience Buster

In order to survive on the battlefield, combat personnel are taught to be in absolute control of their environment at all times. This means securing close physical space while maintaining emotional distance from the troops for whom they feel responsible to protect. The mission is unfailingly accomplish the military objective and leave no soldier behind. Combat readiness and survival may depend on a mindset called BATTLEMIND, denoting an acronym of a psychological state developed to survive the battlefield (Adler et al., 2009). Although being hypervigilant, in control at all times, emotionally detached, rigidly disciplined, obeying rules, and in a need-to-know communication style is adaptive in battle, it becomes maladaptive in civilian society. Because this mindset is so deeply embedded during training and reinforced when tested in battle, for the veteran, the cognitive awareness that being "home" and safe can be overshadowed by a false perception of imminent danger. This BATTLEMIND psychological set may lead the veteran to isolate from their spouse and spend time with battle buddies, react with overblown anger if possessions have been moved, and develop anxiety in groups or situations in which the veteran feels confined or cannot control (e.g., crowds). Or, the veteran may be overly emotionally controlled, inflexible, and/or withdrawn from their spouse and children. All these reactions can lead to severe family conflicts.

Secondary Traumatic Effects on Family

Secondary (or vicarious) trauma describes the impact of the service person's exposure to war zone trauma post-deployment on their family. Upon the veteran's re-entry into the family unit, there can be a transmission of these trauma symptoms to spouses and children. Among children of deployed parents, the effects of secondary trauma have included anxiety, depression, behavioral problems, and poor functioning in school and with peers (Chandra et al., 2010). BATTLEMIND can result in the inability to relinquish the need to control the environment and the people in it. At home, for example, the veteran may have a need to alter furniture arrangements; install security measures; or keep loaded weapons in the house, vehicle, or office. The cognitive distortion is that if the veteran is not in control, something catastrophic will happen and someone will die. This is not a conscious process and is very difficult for those close to the veteran to understand. Family members, friends, and colleagues are challenged by behaviors such as the veteran's patrolling the perimeter of the house; requiring lights to be on; or demanding perfection from spouses, children, and co-workers. Mutual frustrations create tension that can devastate and destabilize the emotional equilibrium of the entire family unit. Outbursts of anger at the slightest disruption in routine are difficult for family members to understand, and the result is pervasive anxiety for the family.

Untreated and unremitted, the veteran's PTSD can lead to two common options for the family members: leave the relationship or alter their behaviors so as not to "upset" the veteran. The first option amplifies the conflict of love/ hate, stay or go, help or abandon. The second option requires controlling the environment to minimize the risk of triggering the veteran's rage response. Thus, this is the parallel process of secondary trauma stemming from the uncertainty of life on a daily basis.

The veteran's frustration, which drives their anger, stems from the lack of structure in civilian life that was reassuring in the service (i.e., a highly structured life). While the veteran is deployed, spouses, significant others, children, and close friends likely have made adjustments to the service member's absence. The spouse had begun paying bills and making household decisions that did not include the veteran. The returning veteran then has to cope with their resentment of the role reversal that has occurred, coming home to a different family and/or workplace dynamic, which creates uncertainty about the veteran's place in the new society. To the returning combat veteran, uncertainty carries the "death taint": "If I don't have the 'intel,' someone will die." The risk is too great when the casualty might be a loved one. To avoid that perceived and unacceptable outcome, driven by cognitive distortions that are common post-trauma, the veteran employs survival tactics that directly oppose behavior that would ensure a positive transition from life-challenging threat to safety and security.

Approaches to Resilience Building

Comprehensive Soldier and Family Fitness—Resilience Training

In 2009, the U.S. Army launched the Comprehensive Soldier's Fitness (CSF) program to provide resilience training (RT) to more than 1 million soldiers (Casey, 2011). This project was designed to give soldiers a "toolbox" of methods to cope with adversities encountered in the war zone. The goal was to enhance both pre- and post-deployment resilience, as well as to promote general psychological well-being (Peterson et al., 2011). CSF-RT is a promising method that can be adapted by clinicians to

enhance resilience among military veterans through training exercises. CSF-RT training exercises are anchored in the tenets of positive psychology, such as the identification of character strengths, living an engaged and meaningful life, and building a reservoir of positive emotions (Reivich et al., 2011; Seligman et al., 2005). Non-mental health military personnel called Master Resilience Trainers (MRTs) have been used to provide RT to soldiers, generally in groups and at times one-to-one. Rather than having a therapeutic focus, military RT was designed to teach soldiers techniques to manage stress. The training had a small but significant effect on enhancing optimism and adaptability, decreased substance abuse, and had a moderate impact on managing stress and depression (Harms et al., 2013; Leppin et al., 2014).

CSF-RT exercises boost social connections and address cognitive distortions such as catastrophic thinking, and they reframe adversity as an opportunity for self-growth and contextually set it within the perspective of a "bigger picture." The second iteration (CSF-2) of resilience training targets both the soldier and the family. CSF-2 identifies five pillars or key dimensions important for resilience building: physical, emotional, social, family, and spiritual. The emphasis is on keeping a focus on physical fitness through nutrition and exercise and keeping a focus on emotional fitness through overcoming challenges that erode mental toughness; promoting optimism, self-control, and social connectivity; developing communication skills and constructive responses to strengthen relationships; keeping family needs at the forefront; and developing spiritual fitness—core beliefs that are critical to building inner strength and meaning and persevering through adversity.

Transpersonal Meaning–Based Approach

Resilience can be enhanced through the use of a transpersonal meaning–based approach in which adverse events are interpreted within a meaningful context and can be readily utilized by community practitioners. The approach strives to integrate combat/war zone life-changing experiences into a growth trajectory for the veteran's transition to civilian life (Osran et al., 2010; Sreenivasan et al., 2018). This model draws from Frankl's logotherapy—that a core existential human need is that of meaning. Because injuries and fatalities are often random, unpredictable, and experienced as needless, combat events may be difficult to place into a meaningful context. As conceptualized by Osran and colleagues (2010), the transpersonal meaning–based approach seeks to review "war stories" through the emphasis on the meaningful elements of the traumatic event(s), one that then reinforces the positive traits of the veteran's actions in the traumatic event(s) and places the experience in the context of the veteran's life as a whole. The approach has four aims:

1. Identify signature strengths from the traumatic event(s): A focus is on reviewing experiences in which positive attributes are highlighted to move the veteran away from anger, guilt, depression, or other distressful emotions (e.g., experiences that demonstrate honor, personal courage, and selflessness).
2. Identify the traumatic event(s) in the context of a framework of larger meaning (e.g., military experience as serving a purpose as guardian of freedom and the American way of life).
3. To place the events in a spiritual context (either secular or theological) to enhance meaning.
4. To directly target psychological pitfalls that erode self-efficacy (e.g., self-castigation, pity-party, and chip on shoulder) and to enhance strengths such as promoting humor and promoting camaraderie via peer associations with other combat veterans.

Problem-Solving Training

Tenhula and associates (2014) developed a novel problem-solving program at the U.S. Department of Veterans Affairs (VA) . This program, Moving Forward, focuses on building resilience through a four-session, classroom-based curriculum. Moving Forward training workshops have been held at 75 VA sites throughout the country, and a wide range of professionals have been trained (psychologists, psychiatrists, social workers, nurses, and counselors). Tenhula et al. (2014) found that the program fostered social problem-solving and reduced overall distress in 479 Iraq and Afghanistan veterans who completed the program. Problem-solving therapy is a psychosocial intervention conceptually anchored in cognitive–behavioral processes. The focus, as in other resilience-based interventions, is to enhance optimism and self-efficacy and to learn problem-solving methods to apply to stressful situations. Tenhula et al. developed a "toolkit" that is described in unpublished manuals (Nezu & Nezu, 2013a, 2013b). They note that Moving Forward places a strong emphasis on providing feedback to veterans in applying the toolkit. The program consists of three elements: problem-solving multitasking; the "stop, slow down, think, and act" method to regulate emotions; and "planful problem-solving" (Tenhula et al., 2014, p. 418):

1. Problem-solving multitasking: The general concept is that stressful situations can precipitate cognitive overload. The veteran is taught to "multitask" when confronted with stressful situations by externalizing (writing down information and lists so that working memory is not overtasked), to visualize (imagine or practice the solution to reduce negative arousal), and to simplify (break down complex problems into smaller and manageable components).
2. Stop, slow down, think, and act: Stressful situations can create emotional distress.

This intervention teaches modulation of emotional arousal through awareness at the moment of experience: physical (e.g., headache and fatigue), mood (e.g., sadness and anger), cognitive (e.g., worry and negative thoughts), and behavioral reactions (e.g., urges to yell and to run away). The next element is to "put on the brakes" or stop the behaviors or emotions. Breathing exercises and forced yawning are methods to slow down.

3. Planful problem-solving: This training involves developing problem-solving to enhance "thinking and acting" in an adaptive manner. Strategies include describing the problem, identifying goals and objectives that are realistic, and brainstorming possible solutions with others.

Conclusion

Resilience building can be a powerful approach to promoting adaptive functioning in returning combat/war zone–exposed veterans. Combat stress can weaken resilience and thereby the ability to face challenges in civilian society. Coming home from war can be disconcerting because the veteran may be entering into a family environment that has changed, may be facing financial strain, and may experience disappointment based on unrealistic or idealized expectations. Psychological mindsets that were adaptive in the war zone become maladaptive in the civilian sector. For veterans who have been home for many years, the maladaptive mechanisms may have led to losses—of a marriage, employment, and even freedom for those who become involved with the justice system. Consequently, resilience building may be a slow process, requiring the clinician to work toward mindset changes that promote optimism. Resilience exercises that promote self-determination, self-efficacy, a positive mental attitude, and core values can be found in the

CSF-2 manual (e.g., goal setting) and several articles (e.g., Nezu & Nezu, 2013a, 2013b; Sreenivasan et al., 2018; Tenhula et al., 2014).

Helpful Resources

American Psychological Association: *Resilience in a Time of War: Homecoming.* https://www.apa.org/topics/resilience/homecoming-war

Comprehensive Soldier and Family Fitness: https://ready.army.mil/ra_csf.htm

National Child Stress Traumatic Network: https://www.nctsn.org/what-is-child-trauma/populations-at-risk/military-and-veteran-families/nctsn-resources

U.S. Department of Veterans Affairs. *National Center for PTSD:* https://www.ptsd.va.gov/professional/assessment/list_measures.asp

References

Adler, A. B., Bliese, P. D., McGurk, D., Hoge, C. W., & Castro, C. A. (2009). Battlemind debriefing and battlemind training as early interventions with soldiers returning from Iraq: Randomization by platoon. *Journal of Consulting and Clinical Psychology, 77,* 928–940.

Albanese, B. J., Macatee, R. J., Stentz, L. A., Schmidt, N. B., & Bryan, C. J. (2019). Interactive effects of cumulative lifetime traumatic brain injuries and combat exposure on posttraumatic stress among deployed military personnel. *Cognitive Behavior Therapy, 48*(1), 77–88.

American Psychiatric Association. (1980). *Diagnostic and statistical manual of mental disorders* (3rd ed.).

American Psychiatric Association. (2013). *Diagnostic and statistical manual of mental disorders* (5th ed.). American Psychiatric Publishing.

American Psychological Association. (2008). *Resilience in a time of war: Homecoming.* Retrieved September 17, 2016, from https://www.apa.org/topics/resilience/homecoming-war

Casey, G. W., Jr. (2011). Comprehensive soldier fitness: A vision for psychological resilience in the U.S. Army. *American Psychologist, 66,* 1–3. http://dx.doi.org/10.1037/a0021930

Chandra, A., Lara-Cinisomo, S., Jaycox, L., Tanielian, T., Burns, R. M., Ruder, T., & Han, B. (2010). Children on the homefront: The experience of children from military families. *Pediatrics, 125*(1), 16–25.

Gonzalez, O. I., Novaco, R. W., Reger, R. W., & Gahm, G. A. (2016). Anger intensification with combat-related PTSD and depression comorbidity. *Psychological Trauma, 8*(1), 9–16.

Harms, P. D., Herian, M. N., Kasikova, D. V., Vanhove, A., & Lester, P. B. (2013, April). *The* Comprehensive Soldier and Family Fitness program evaluation. Report #4: Evaluation of resilience training and mental and behavioral health outcomes. U.S. Army.

Leppin, A. L., Bora, P. R., Tilburt, J. C., Gionfriddo, M. R., Zeballos-Palacios, C., Dulohery, M. M., . . . & Montori, V. M. (2014). The efficacy of resiliency training programs: a systematic review and meta-analysis of randomized trials. *PloS One, 9*(10), e111420.

McDivitt-Murphy, M. E., Luciano, M. T., Tripp, J. C., & Eddinger, J. E. (2017). Drinking motives and PTSD-related alcohol expectancies among combat veterans. *Addiction Behavior, 64,* 217–222.

Nezu, A. M., & Nezu, C. M. (2013a). Moving Forward: A problem-solving approach to achieving life's goals. Instructor's manual. Unpublished manual. Veterans Health Administration Mental Health Services.

Nezu, A. M., & Nezu, C. M. (2013b). Moving Forward: A problem-solving approach to achieving life's goals. Participant's guidebook. Unpublished manual. Veterans Health Administration Mental Health Services.

Osran, H. C., Smee, D. E., Sreenivasan, S., & Weinberger, L. E. (2010). Living outside the wire: Toward a transpersonal resilience approach for OIF/OEF veterans transitioning to civilian life. *Journal of Transpersonal Psychology, 42*(2), 209–235.

Peterson, A. L., Luethcke, C. A., Borah, E. V., Borah, A. M., & Young-McCaughan, S. (2011). Assessment and treatment of combat-related PTSD in returning war veterans. *Journal of Clinical Psychology in Medical Settings, 18*(2), 164–175.

Reivich, K. J., Seligman, M. E., & McBride, S. (2011). Master resilience training in the U.S. Army. *American Psychologist, 66*(1), 25–34. doi:10.1037/a0021897

Seligman, M. E., Steen, T. A., Park, N., & Peterson, C. (2005). Positive psychology progress: empirical validation of interventions. *American Psychologist, 60*(5), 410.

Sreenivasan, S., Rosenthal, J., Smee, D. E., Wilsin, K., & McGuire, J. (2018). Coming home from prison: Adapting military resilience training to enhance successful community reintegration for justice-involved Iraq–Afghanistan veterans. *Psychological Services, 15*(2), 163–171. http://dx.doi.org/10.1037/ser0000206

Tenhula, W. N., Nezu, A. M., Nezu, C. M., Stewart, M. O., Miller, S. A., Steele, J., & Karlin, B. E. (2014). Moving Forward: A problem-solving training program to foster veteran resilience. *Professional Psychology: Research and Practice, 45*(6), 416–424.

U.S. Department of Veterans Affairs. (n.d.). *National Center for PTSD.* Retrieved February 17, 2020, from https://www.ptsd.va.gov/professional/assessment/list_measures.asp

Youssef, N. A., Green, K. T., Beckham, J. C., & Elbogen, E. B. (2013). A 3-year longitudinal study examining the effect of resilience on suicidality in veterans. *Annals of Clinical Psychiatry, 25*(1), 59–66.

Clinical Conceptualization of the Trauma that Results from Sexual Violence in the Military

Kristen Zaleski and Fred P. Stone

Sexual violence by military members has existed since the beginning of recorded history. As soldiers conquered opposing lands, raping and other forms of sexual violence were considered spoils of war and a way to humiliate and dominate an enemy. The U.S. military has also engaged in sexual violence dating back at least to the Civil War (Murphy, 2014). As the U.S. military liberated France in World War II, soldiers raped French women and girls (Roberts, 2014). Because in previous generations few women were in the military and often separated from male service members, sexual assault between service members was considered rare, but as more women entered the U.S. military, they became targets of sexual assault by other service members. Despite growing evidence of this problem, Congress only publicly addressed this problem when more than 100 U.S. Navy and Marine Corps Aviation Officers were accused of having sexually assaulted 83 women and 7 men at the Las Vegas Hilton during the 35th annual Tailhook Association Symposium in 1991. The resulting investigation prompted

Congress to pass legislation that covered military sexual trauma (MST)-related counseling for female veterans solely in 1993 (U.S. Congress Committee Report, 1992). In 1999, Congress expanded this legislation to include male service members who were sexually victimized and provide universal screening for all incoming veterans at the U.S. Veterans Health Administration (VHA). Since then, the U.S. Department of Veterans Affairs (VA) and U.S. Department of Defense (DoD) have instituted a variety of programs and initiatives to combat sexual assaults in the U.S. military and provide care and support for survivors.

Despite these efforts, the number of reported sexual assaults in the military has been steadily climbing. In fiscal year 2019, 6,236 active duty service members reported being sexually assaulted, more than twice the number reported in fiscal year 2012 (DoD, 2020). In addition, the DoD estimated that more than 20,000 service members were assaulted in 2019, more than three times the number of reported assaults.

Both male and female service members experience sexual assaults and harassment. Among active duty service members, women have a 1 in 20 chance of experiencing sexual violence, and men have a 1 in 100 chance of being victimized during military service (Morral et al., 2015). In 2019, the DoD estimated that 6.3% of female service members and 0.7% of male service members experienced sexual assault (DoD, 2020). Recent veteran surveys report 41% of women and 4% of men experienced sexual violence during military service (Barth et al., 2016). Approximately 17% of transgender veterans experienced sexual trauma during their service, and transgender men were sexually assaulted at double the rate of transgender women (15.2%) (Beckman et al., 2018). Although the rate for women being sexually assaulted is much higher than that for men, the number of men and women in the military being assaulted is almost equal because men significantly outnumber women in the military (Millegan et al., 2016).

Defining Sexual Assault in the Military

The DoD, VA, and researchers define sexual violence differently, which makes understanding the extent of the problem more challenging. The DoD primarily uses the term military sexual assault (MSA), which connotes sexual violence during active duty service and is defined as "intentional sexual contact characterized by use of force, threats, intimidation, or abuse of authority, or when the victim does not or cannot consent" (DoD, 2013). MST is the term used by the VA and is defined as the "psychological trauma resulting from a physical assault of a sexual nature, battery of a sexual nature, or sexual harassment which occurred while the Veteran was serving on active duty, active duty for training, or inactive duty training" (Code of the United States of America, Title 38 U.S.C.

§ 1720D). These activities can include "unwanted touching and grabbing, oral sex, anal sex, sexual perpetration with an object, and/or sexual intercourse" (Koo & Maguen, 2014, p. 29). One reason for the different definitions is that the DoD definition focuses on criminal activity and prosecuting offenders. In theory, the DoD prosecute offenders regardless of whether or not the victim has been traumatized or has associated mental health needs. The VA focuses specifically on veterans and service members who have been traumatized as a result of sexual assault and are seeking help. RAND's 2014 workplace study more broadly examined sexual-related offenses and included sexual assault, sexual harassment, and gender discrimination in its study of military sexual assaults (Morral et al., 2015).

Responses by the U.S. Department of Defense and U.S. Department of Veterans Affairs

In response to the number of sexual assaults being reported in theater during the early stages of Operation Iraqi Freedom, the DoD created the Care for the Victims of Sexual Assault Task Force to review its sexual assault programs. The task force made a host of recommendations, ranging from clarifying policies to requiring victim advocates (DoD, 2004). The most important recommendation was to "establish a single point of accountability for all sexual assault policy matters, within the DoD" (DoD, 2004, p. xi). This single point of contact became the Joint Task Force for Sexual Assault Prevention and Response. In collaboration with the military services, this task force trained more than 1,200 sexual assault response coordinators (SARCs), chaplains, lawyers, and law enforcement personnel. Sexual assault programs manned by SARCs were established at major bases, and more than 1 million military members were trained on how to prevent and report sexual assaults (DoD, n.d.).

Currently, the Sexual Assault Prevention and Response Office is the single point of accountability and is governed by two directives: DoD Directive 6495.01: Sexual Assault Prevention and Response Policy and DoD Instruction 6495.02: Sexual Assault Prevention and Response Program Procedures. These directives created a number of policies and programs to reduce the incidence of MSA. They mandated that commanders establish sexual assault awareness and prevention programs. In addition, the directives protected victims from retaliation and reprisal and instituted Sexual Assault Prevention and Response Victim Advocates (SAPR VAs). The DoD also established two reporting options, unrestricted and restricted. Unrestricted reporting allows eligible victims to receive health care and to request an official investigation. This reporting option results in commanders, law enforcement, SARCs, and health care professionals being notified of the assault. The restricted report option lets victims make confidential reports, and only the SARC, SAPR VA, and attending health care professional are notified. In this case, law enforcement and commanders are not notified. Restricted reporting is only available for service members, including Guard and Reserve, and their family members aged 18 years or older. In fiscal year 2019, 2,750 victims chose restricted reporting compared to 5,699 unrestricted reports (DoD, 2020).

Overview of Mental and Physical Health Symptoms

A decade of research shows survivors of military sexual violence have an increased risk of being diagnosed with a number of mental health problems, including post-traumatic stress disorder (PTSD), depressive disorders

(DDs), and substance abuse disorder (SAD). Gilmore et al. (2016) reported almost 50% of all service members who were sexually assaulted during military service had at least one diagnosis of PTSD, DD, or SAD. Koo and Maguen (2014) found that women who were sexually assaulted during their time in service were diagnosed with PTSD at a rate four times higher than that of women who were not sexually assaulted during their service. The PTSD rate for male service members who experienced sexual assault is approximately 6%, and 60% of male victims leave the service or retire soon after being assaulted (Millegan et al., 2016).

MST can also result in a number of other problems. MST survivors may be at an increased risk for a number of medical problems involving multiple organ systems (O'Brien & Sher, 2013). They are also at a higher risk for becoming homeless. Mota and colleagues (2016) found that within 5 years of being a victim of MST, 1 in 10 veterans will become homeless. Male survivors have a higher rate of homelessness than female survivors, and transgender men report homelessness more often than transgender women (Blosnich, 2017). Pavao et al. (2013) found that almost 40% of homeless women who identified surviving sexual violence during military service were also homeless, compared to 3.3% of men.

MST has also been implicated in veteran suicide. Kimerling et al. (2016) found that MST was a significant factor in veteran suicide even when adjusting for mental health diagnoses. Male MST survivors' suicide rates were twice as high as those of female MST survivors.

Considerations in the Treatment of Military-Related Sexual Assault

The military rape subculture hypothesis (Zaleski, 2018) and the perpetrator hypothesis (Castro & Goldbach, 2018) discuss cultural determinants that reinforce rape myth, aggressive masculinity, and value secrecy in military units to keep grievances inside the military family. As a result, researchers believe that sexual violence in the military is directed toward perceived weak or different [e.g., lesbian, gay, bisexual, and transgender (LGBT) or female] service members because they do not adhere to the masculine-warrior ethos (Dunivin, 1994).

In the most recent sexual assault report from the DOD (2020), the "male dominated cultural norms" (p. 5) were cited as improving but also interfering with unit cohesion and gendered-based harassment and bullying. The report states,

> Male-dominated cultural norms are slowly changing, giving way to more inclusive attitudes. However, the appropriate role for women in the military, occupational differences in women's acceptance, and cynicism about exceptions to standards based on biological differences remain considerable points of contention. Female participants also indicated that some traditionally male occupations are not as supportive as others that tend to include a greater mix of the sexes. Women also indicated that these challenges vary by unit; moving to units with better climates allow them to do much better professionally. (p. 5)

Gurung et al. (2018) also note the gender and sexual orientation discriminatory attitudes that remain in military culture against LGBT individuals. An internet-based survey of 253 LGBT service members and veterans found greater discrimination within the military than in civilian life despite the repeal of the Don't Ask, Don't Tell policy (Gurung et al., 2018). Eighty-three percent of lesbian and bisexual women reported at least one incident of MST

during their time in service compared to 74% of 164 gay and bisexual men.

Services Available for Military Members and Veterans

Services are available for all active duty, Guard, and Reserve service members who have experienced sexual assault, regardless of whether or not the assault occurred during their military service. SARCs and SAPR VAs can provide information on reporting options and the services available to victims.

The VHA provides MST services to both service members and veterans, including outpatient, inpatient, and residential services (VHA, 2020). Active duty services members and current Guard and Reserve members can receive free MST-related mental health care at Vet Centers. No referral is needed, and the services are confidential. Service members can also receive care at VA medical facilities, but this requires a referral and has less confidentiality. Veterans can also receive free MST-related care even if they are not eligible for other VA care (VHA, 2020).

Modalities for Therapy

The DoD and VA recommend trauma-informed treatments for treating sexual trauma. Trauma treatment focuses on the cognitive, emotional, and behavioral components and helps MST survivors focus on the effects of the trauma. The VA/DoD clinical practice guidelines for PTSD recommend prolonged exposure therapy, cognitive processing therapy, eye movement desensitization and reprocessing, and narrative therapy, among others (VA/DoD, 2017).

The application of psychotherapy has changed to more technology-driven environments in the past decade of efficacy research. For example, Gilmore and associates (2016) argue for remote home-based telehealth medicine for sexual trauma survivors who live in distant locations or may be triggered by sitting in a waiting room alongside reminders of their assailant. Home-based telehealth has been found to have similar attrition rates and outcomes as those of face-to-face telehealth interventions for treatment of PTSD and DD (Acierno et al., 2016). Other nontraditional treatments to treat symptoms associated with sexual trauma are the use of virtual reality in PTSD exposure techniques (Loucks et al., 2019) as well as biofeedback (Romaniuk & Loue, 2017) and somatic interventions, including yoga (Johnston et al., 2015).

Treatment Providers and Personal Reactions

As with any clinical problem, providers should explore their internal biases, beliefs, and reactions when treating survivors of sexual trauma. Providers may experience countertransference based on their own experience with sexual assault, or they may have internalized stereotypes, judgments, and trauma reactions. In general, social workers should seek supervision with a qualified expert on sexual trauma to process countertransference and prior belief systems that may interfere with the treatment of sexual violence.

Best Practices for Working with Survivors of Military-Related Sexual Violence

Trauma-informed treatment should meet the needs of clients and help them feel safe, comfortable, free from judgment, and empowered. Providers need to attend to immediate and long-term needs. In the immediate aftermath of an assault, they should offer crisis intervention that provides emotional, psychological, and physical safety and assesses the client's immediate needs. This may include discussions of legal options as well as housing and financial support. In the long term, providers should consider the most appropriate interventions depending on the client's diagnosis and desires. Providers should keep in mind that MST survivors often rightly feel victimized by the military system almost as much as they do by their perpetrator. Providers should address these concerns and be particularly mindful of creating a supporting and safe atmosphere that MST survivors may not have felt in the military.

As with almost all successful therapy, achieving a lasting therapeutic relationship is essential. Strategies for trauma-informed alliance building include the following:

> *Anticipatory guidance about the treatment*: Providing guidance and education about the clinical relationship is helpful for survivors to feel comfortable in the treatment process. Anticipatory guidance is simply answering the question, "What can I anticipate will happen to me here?" In a forensic setting, anticipatory guidance can help the survivor understand the reasoning and process behind the rape kit and types of questions they will encounter. In a therapy setting, it will help the survivor understand the emotional ups and downs that can be expected during the treatment.
>
> *Offering choice*: Sexual trauma is an act that occurred when the survivor had no choice and autonomy over their own body. Providing the survivor with choices about their treatment and reminding them that they can end a clinical intervention at any time is important in helping them recognize their power in the relationship.

Monitoring triggers and reactions that cause discomfort: Being a trauma-informed clinician includes constant monitoring of the reactions that survivors have with the clinical encounter at every meeting. For example, waiting rooms in military-related institutions often elicit reactions that mimic the survivors' military-related social settings. If this is a trigger for a client, both recognizing and validating that reaction are important for them to feel safe and continue the treatment. Offering options (as previously outlined) for alternate waiting locations, moving to a telemedicine platform for treatment, or targeting the fear in the therapy treatment goals are examples of ways to provide the survivor a sense of control and ownership over their body and clinical treatment.

Conclusion

Sexual violence during military service is a "preventable occupational exposure" (Barth et al., 2016, p. 8) and an ongoing act of violence and aggression that has not been successfully curtailed despite a quarter century of awareness and government intervention. Mental health clinicians must continue to work within the military system to create lasting change of cultural norms and a robust prevention system that can end sexual violence within the ranks.

Helpful Resources

National Sexual Violence Resource Center: https://www.nsvrc.org

RAINN. *National sexual assault hotline*: https://www.rainn.org

U.S. Department of Defense. *DOD safe helpline*: https://www.safehelpline.org

U.S. Department of Defense. *Sexual assault prevention and response: Reporting options*: https://www.sapr.mil/reporting-options

U.S. Department of Defense. *Special Victims' Counsel/Victims' Legal Counsel*: https://www.sapr.mil/svc-vlc

U.S. Department of Veteran Affairs. *Mental health: Resources*: https://www.mentalhealth.va.gov/msthome/resources.asp

References

Acierno, R., Gros, D., Ruggiero, K., Hernandez-Tejada, M., Knapp, R., Lejuez, C., Muzzy, W., Frueh, C. B., Egede, L. E., & Tuerk, P. (2016). Behavioral activation and therapeutic exposure for posttraumatic stress disorder: A noninferiority trial of treatment delivered in person versus home-based telehealth. *Depression and Anxiety, 33*(5), 415–423. https://doi.org/10.1002/da.22476

Barth, S., Kimerling, R., Pavao, J., Mccutcheon, S., Batten, S., Dursa, E., Petersen, M. R., & Schneiderman, A. (2016). Military sexual trauma among recent veterans. *American Journal of Preventive Medicine, 50*(1), 77–86. https://doi.org/10.1016/j.amepre.2015.06.012

Beckman, K., Shipherd, J., Simpson, T., & Lehavot, K. (2018). Military sexual assault in transgender veterans: Results from a nationwide survey. *Journal of Traumatic Stress, 31*(2), 181–190.

Blosnich, J. R., Marsiglio, M. C., Dichter, M. E., Gao, S., Gordon, A. J., Shipherd, J. C., . . . & Fine, M. J. (2017). Impact of social determinants of health on medical conditions among transgender veterans. *American Journal of Preventive Medicine, 52*(4), 491–498.

Castro, C. A., & Goldbach, J. (2018). The perpetrator hypothesis: Victimization involving LGBT service members. In L. W. Roberts & C. H. Warner (Eds.), *Military and veteran mental health* (pp. 145–156). Springer.

Dunivin, K. O. (1994). Military culture: Change and continuity. *Armed Forces and Society, 20*, 531–547.

Gilmore, A., Davis, M., Grubaugh, A., Resnick, H., Birks, A., Denier, C., Muzzy, W., Tuerk, P., & Acierno, R. (2016). "Do you expect me to receive PTSD care in a setting where most of the other patients remind me of the perpetrator?" Home-based telemedicine to address barriers to care unique to military sexual trauma and Veterans Affairs hospitals. *Contemporary Clinical Trials, 48*, 59–64. https://doi.org/10.1016/j.cct.2016.03.004

Gurung, S., Ventuneac, A., Rendina, H., Savarese, E., Grov, C., & Parsons, J. (2018). Prevalence of military sexual trauma and sexual orientation discrimination among lesbian, gay, bisexual, and transgender military personnel: A descriptive study. *Sexuality Research and Social Policy, 15*(1), 74–82. https://doi.org/10.1007/s13178-017-0311-z

Johnston, J. M., Minami, T., Greenwald, D., Li, C., Reinhardt, K., & Khalsa, S. B. S. (2015). Yoga for military service personnel with PTSD: A single arm study. *Psychological Trauma, 7*(6), 555–562.

Kimerling, R., Makin-Byrd, K., Louzon, S., Ignacio, R., & McCarthy, J. (2016). Military sexual trauma and suicide mortality. *American Journal of Preventive Medicine, 50*(6), 684–691. https://doi.org/10.1016/j.ameprc.2015.10.019

Koo, K. H., & Maguen, S. (2014). Military sexual trauma and mental health diagnoses in female veterans returning from Afghanistan and Iraq: Barriers and facilitators to Veterans Affairs care. *Hastings Women's Law Journal, 27.* https://repository.uchastings.edu/hwlj/vol25/iss1/3

Loucks, L., Yasinski, C., Norrholm, S., Maples-Keller, J., Post, L., Zwiebach, L., Fiorillo, D., Goodlin, M., Jovanovic, T., Rizzo, A., & Rothbaum, B. (2019). You can do that?! Feasibility of virtual reality exposure therapy in the treatment of PTSD due to military sexual trauma. *Journal of Anxiety Disorders, 61,* 55–63. https://doi.org/10.1016/j.janxdis.2018.06.004

Millegan, J., Wang, L., Leardmann, C., Miletich, D., & Street, A. (2016). Sexual trauma and adverse health and occupational outcomes among men serving in the U.S. military. *Journal of Traumatic Stress, 29*(2), 132–140. https://doi.org/10.1002/jts.22081

Morral, A. E., Gore, K. L., & Schell, T. L. (Eds.). (2015). *Sexual assault and sexual harassment in the US military: Volume 2. Estimates for Department of Defense service members from the 2014 RAND military workplace study* (No. RR-870/2-OSD). RAND Corporation.

Mota, N., Pietrzak, R. H., & Sareen, J. (2016). Preventing veteran homelessness by reducing military sexual trauma: Ensuring a welcome home. *JAMA Psychiatry, 73*(6), 551–552.

Murphy, K. (2014). *I had rather die: Rape in the civil war.* Coachlight Press.

O'Brien, B. S., & Sher, L. (2013). Military sexual trauma as a determinant in the development of mental and physical illness in male and female veterans. *International Journal of Adolescent Medicine and Health, 25*(3), 269–274. doi:10.1515/ijamh-2013-0061

Pavao, J., Turchik, J. A., Hyun, J. K., Karpenko, J., Saweikis, M., McCutcheon, S., & Kimerling, R. (2013). Military sexual trauma among homeless veterans. *Journal of General Internal Medicine, 28*(Suppl. 2), 536–541.

Roberts, M. L. (2014). *What soldiers do: Sex and the American GI in World War II France.* University of Chicago Press.

Romaniuk, J. R., & Loue, S. (2017). Military sexual trauma among men: A review of the literature and a call for research. *Best Practices in Mental Health, 13*(1), 81–105.

U.S. Congress Committee on Armed Services, Military Personnel Compensation Subcommittee. (1992). Women in the military: The Tailhook affair and the problem of sexual harassment. Report of the Military Personnel and Compensation Subcommittee and Defense Policy Panel of the Committee on Armed Services, House of Representatives, One Hundred Second Congress, second session.

U.S. Department of Defense. (2004). *DOD care for victims of sexual assault task force report.* https://www.sapr.mil/public/docs/reports/task-force-report-for-care-of-victims-of-sa-2004.pdf.

U.S. Department of Defense. (2013). *DOD Instruction 6495.02. Sexual assault prevention and response program procedures.* https://www.sapr.mil/public/docs/directives/649502p.pdf

U.S. Department of Defense, Sexual Assault Prevention and Response Office. (2020). *Department of Defense annual report of sexual assault in the military.* https://www.defense.gov/Newsroom/Releases/Release/Article/2606508/department-of-defense-releases-fiscal-year-2020-annual-report-on-sexual-assault/

U.S. Department of Defense, Sexual Assault Prevention and Response. (n.d.). Mission & history. https://www.sapr.mil/mission-history

U.S. Department of Veterans Affairs/Department of Defense. (2017). VA/DoD clinical practice guideline for the management of posttraumatic stress disorder and acute stress disorder. https://www.healthquality.va.gov/guidelines/MH/ptsd/VADoDPTSDCPGFinal.pdf

U.S. Veterans Health Administration. (2020). VA's health care services for military sexual trauma (MST). https://www.mentalhealth.va.gov/docs/mst/VA_Health_Care_Services_for_MST_Jan_2020.pdf

Zaleski, K. L. (2018). *Understanding and treating military sexual trauma.* Springer.

Veteran Suicide

Fred P. Stone

Death by suicide is a growing problem among U.S. veterans. Approximately 17 veterans die by suicide each day, and veterans are 1.5 times more likely to die by suicide than non-veterans [U.S. Department of Veteran Affairs (VA), 2019]. This chapter explores the problem of veteran suicide, its causes, and programs and interventions to prevent it.

The Problem of Veteran Suicide

In 2017, 47,173 Americans died by suicide compared to 31,160 in 2005, an increase of 51.3% [Centers for Disease Control and Prevention (CDC), 2019; VA, 2019]. These increases occurred across the demographic spectrum, but veterans were at a particularly high risk of dying by suicide, comprising 13.5% of deaths although they made up only 7.9% of the U.S. adult population.

Veteran suicide rates vary by age, race, ethnicity, and gender. In 2017, veterans aged 18–34 years had the highest rates (44.5 per 100,000), representing a 76% increase from 2005 (VA, 2019). Kaplan and colleagues (2007) found being White, having more than a 12th-grade education, and having physical limitations were significant risk factors for veteran suicide. Bell and associates (2010) noted that among active duty military members, "Soldiers who [were] Black, college-educated, married, and in the officer grades were less likely to commit suicide" (pp. 410–411), and Ilgen et al. (2009) found African American veterans were less likely to die by suicide than other ethnic groups. The rates of suicide similarly differ by gender. Although male veterans account for the vast majority of veteran suicides, female veterans are arguably at greater risk. Adjusting for age, female veterans have a 2.2 times higher death by suicide rate than non-veteran females (VA, 2019).

The most common method of suicide among veterans is self-inflicted firearm injury (VA, 2019). In 2017, firearms accounted for 69.4% of deaths among veterans compared to 48.1% for non-veterans. Only 43.2% of female veterans who died by suicide used firearms, but this was the most common method and almost 12% higher than that for non-veteran females (VA, 2019). For male veterans, the other methods were suffocation (15.8%) and poisoning (9.9%). Female veterans' other methods were poison (28.7%) followed by suffocation (19.9%).

Military occupation and branch of service may impact veteran suicide, although more research is needed. The U.S. Army rates of suicide and mental health problems have been substantially higher than those of the other military branches (Deployment Health Clinical Center, 2017). The National Guard and Reserves have seen dramatic increases in suicide rates and have rates higher than the active duty military (Congressional Research Service Insight, 2019). Some military occupations have higher rates of death by suicide as well. For example, Kessler et al. (2015) found that U.S. Army infantrymen and combat engineers had significantly higher rates. Among active duty Air Force members, aircraft mechanics and security forces have had the highest rates of suicide. However, there does not appear to be any research on relationships between veteran branch of service, occupation, and suicide.

Factors Associated with Veteran Suicide

Several factors have been associated with veteran suicide. Among veterans using the Veterans Health Administration (VHA), one-fourth have been diagnosed with a mental health disorder (Ilgen et al., 2010), and several mental health disorders, including major depression, anxiety disorders, post-traumatic stress disorder (PTSD), and personality disorder, are associated with death by suicide and suicide attempts among veterans (Haney et al., 2012; Ilgen et al., 2010; Shen et al., 2016). Bipolar disorder has been linked with a high risk of suicide in male veterans, whereas substance abuse puts female veterans in the highest risk category (Ilgen et al., 2010). Veterans with a traumatic brain injury (TBI) die by suicide at a rate 1.5 times higher than those without a TBI (Brenner et al., 2011).

Combat exposure often leads to a host of mental health problems, including PTSD and depression, but the relationship between combat exposure and suicide is unclear (Armed Forces Health Surveillance Center, 2012). Some research shows little or no connection between combat and suicide (Leardmann et al., 2013; Reger et al., 2015), whereas other research shows combat puts soldiers at a higher risk for suicide (Kessler et al., 2015). Bryan et al. (2015) conducted a meta-analysis on combat exposure and suicidal thoughts and behaviors and posited the overgeneralized term "deployment" has resulted in the "mixed findings and confusion about military-specific risk factors for suicide" (p. 647). They observed that military members exposed to killings and atrocities had an increased suicide-related outcome risk of 43%.

Military sexual trauma has also been associated with veteran suicide risk and mental health problems. In a review of more than 5 million VHA records from 2007 to 2011, 1.1% of male veterans and 21.2% of female veterans reported military sexual trauma (Kimerling et al., 2016). Of this group, more than 9,000 completed suicide, resulting in a suicide rate of 37.4 per 100,000.

Transition out of the service is also related to an increase in suicide. A large-scale analysis of 3,795,823 service members discovered the risk of death by suicide doubled during the first year of transition into the community (Shen et al., 2016).

A number of factors protect against veteran suicide. For instance, Pietrzak et al. (2017) noted, "Greater perceived social support, curiosity, resilience, and acceptance-based coping accounted for more than 40% of the total variance in predicting suicidal ideation risk" (p. 327). Positive coping skills, reasons for living, social connection, and access to mental health care are likewise protective factors (VA, 2019).

Interventions

Numerous studies show service members expect to be considered "weak" and stigmatized by their fellow service members for seeking help. Campbell et al. (2016) showed veterans with high help-seeking stigma were less likely to seek mental health care and treatment for emotional concerns. Suicide and suicidal ideations are also stigmatizing. Those who have attempted suicide often experience public stigma, such as social distancing and being labeled weak, as well as private stigma, such as shame and embarrassment (Carpiniello & Pinna, 2017). The combination of these factors often creates barriers to helping veterans at risk of suicide.

The first step to helping is understanding the influence of military culture and experiences. Veterans and military members "frequently report dissatisfaction with care and disconnect between their experiences as warriors and perspectives they encounter trying to obtain the help they need" (Hoge, 2011, p. 549). Clinicians, however, can overcome these challenges by educating themselves on military culture and showing interest in their veteran clients' experiences. They should explore their own perceptions of the military and veterans to avoid countertransference negatively impacting care. Clinicians also need to appreciate how difficult it is for veterans to ask for help. Military culture disdains weakness and reinforces strong masculine stereotypes, but seeking help requires clients to become vulnerable and admit that they need help. Clinicians should be especially concerned with preserving veteran clients' self-esteem and self-efficacy by acknowledging veterans' strengths and accomplishments.

When working with all potentially suicidal clients, clinicians need to conduct a systematic assessment that considers risk and protective factors, means, and intent, and they must take appropriate and sufficient action to prevent suicide. The risk and protective factors for veterans should be assessed regularly. Unfortunately, risk factors are limited in their ability to predict veteran suicide. Many veterans will have one or more of them but not

be at a significant risk of suicide (Haney et al., 2012), and with so many risk factors, it is sometimes difficult to determine which ones to focus on and which ones will have an impact. Two factors, however, strongly predict death by suicide of veterans: prior suicide attempts and active current suicidal intent (Shen et al., 2016). These should be assessed regularly with every veteran seeking care.

A number of studies have examined suicide risk assessment and interventions with veterans. Nelson et al. (2017) reviewed studies published between 2008 and 2015 relevant to veterans and military personnel and found most assessments effectively identified clients at risk of suicide and 6 of 8 population-level interventions reviewed reduced suicide rates. Of the 10 individual-level intervention studies, however, only 2 showed a significant difference between the intervention and treatment as usual, and neither examined veterans (Linehan et al., 2006; Rudd et al., 2015). Rudd et al.'s (2015) study involved active duty soldiers who either attempted suicide or had suicidal intent, and the researchers found that a 12-week program of cognitive strategies focused on reducing hopelessness, perceived burdensomeness, and other factors effectively reduced suicide attempts. Overall, more research needs to be done on interventions to help veterans (VA/Department of Defense, 2019).

The Interpersonal–Psychological Theory of Veteran Suicide

The interpersonal–psychological theory of suicidal behavior (IPT) is one of the most researched theories of suicide. The theory posits that dangerous suicidal desires often stem from a sense of thwarted belongingness and perceived burdensomeness (Van Orden et al., 2010). From an IPT perspective, veterans are often displaced in the civilian world from the belongingness they felt in the military. In the military, service members often develop close relationships with others and are imbued with a sense of camaraderie. Veterans will speak of their "brothers in arms" and the commitment they felt toward each other. The civilian world rarely has this same sense of community, and veterans can feel out of place and misunderstood. Veterans can likewise feel they are burdening others and not contributing to their social group or peers, especially if they are unable to find satisfying work or have substance abuse or mental health problems. In a national representative sample of veterans, Pietrzak et al. (2017) found a higher risk for suicidal ideation in veterans was associated with loneliness and disability in daily living (e.g., needing help with housework and taking medications)—two factors suggesting a lack of belongingness and the perception of being a burden.

These two factors are common to almost everyone at one point or another, but it is the addition of an acquired capability to carry out a lethal act that leads to suicide (Bryan et al., 2010). Joiner (2005) theorized that routinely experiencing painful and stressful events, as many veterans have, can habituate people to injury, pain, and death and increase the capability for self-harm. Bryan et al. (2010) found that active duty members have a higher acquired capability to commit suicide but did not find a connection between all three factors and suicidal behavior. They concluded that military members have a higher capability for suicide but not necessarily a higher desire. Veterans, however, are usually comfortable and familiar with firearms, which may increase their acquired ability for self-harm. Although the percentage of veterans who own firearms is unknown, anecdotally veterans appear to have higher rates of gun ownership than the general population, and the correlation between gun ownership and suicide is high (Siegel & Rothman, 2016). From an IPT perspective, the combination of lack of belongingness and burdensomeness coupled with the presence

of a gun may explain a substantial number of deaths by suicide among veterans.

Castro and Kintzle (2014) provided additional insights into IPT by applying military transition theory. Leaving the military requires moving from one culture to another and changes relationships as well as personal and social identity. This transition requires veterans to develop a new sense of belongingness with groups that do not share the same values and morals. The military transition theory argues that this lack of cultural identity, "along with an unrecognized sense of privilege, can interfere with the modern veterans' feeling of community belongingness, as well as hinder the modern veterans' establishment of a new effective social support network that includes civilians" (Castro & Kintzle, 2014, p. 5), and veterans may believe that they are a burden to others instead of an asset.

U.S. Department of Veteran Affairs Programs and Initiatives

In 2007, the VA launched its Suicide Prevention Program with a goal to reduce veteran suicide by 20% by 2028 (VA, 2018). To do this, it adopted the CDC public health approach to reducing veteran suicide that focuses on primary prevention, commitment to science, and multidisciplinary strategies.

The primary prevention strategies target three groups: the general population of veterans, subgroups of veterans at risk for suicidal behaviors, and select veterans at high risk. The strategies include public awareness campaigns to help veterans identify and utilize suicide prevention sources. In addition, the VA provides training for gatekeepers such as caregivers, clergy, community volunteers, and others who work with veterans. Two of these trainings are Operation SAVE (where the acronym stands for *s*igns of suicide, *a*sk about suicide, *v*alidating feelings, and *e*ncourage help and expediting treatment) and Applied Suicide Intervention Skills Training.

The VA is heavily involved in research into the prevention of suicide and developing evidence-based mental health interventions. For example, the VA discovered that VHA patients are diagnosed with opioid abuse disorder at a rate of seven times higher than that of patients who are commercially insured, and veterans have a higher risk of death by suicide during the first 6 months of either starting or stopping opioid therapy (VA, n.d.). The VA is also a leader in PTSD and TBI research and delivers widely available information on suicide prevention and the factors related to suicide among veterans. The VA's From Science to Practice program provides research-based education to help VA clinicians address the problem of suicide.

The VA partners with hundreds of organizations and corporations, including nonprofits such as the Objective Zero Foundation that helps improve access to mental health care as well as professional sports teams and major employers. The VA also provides training to veterans and those who help veterans through programs such as Operation SAVE, which is offered in collaboration with the PsychArmor Institute. This 2-hour training is available at no charge. In 2018, the VA partnered with the Substance Abuse and Mental Health Services Administration and launched the Mayor's Challenge to prevent suicide among service members, veterans, and their families.

The Veterans Crisis Line (VCL) was created in 2007 with a mission to "provide 24/7, world class, suicide prevention and crisis intervention services to veterans, service members, and their family members" (VCL, n.d.). Since then, it has answered nearly 4.4 million calls, with an average of 650,000 calls per year. In 2019, VCL Social Service Assistants (SSAs) answered 99.96% of calls within 8 seconds. The VCL is different than community service hotlines in several important ways. For one,

VCL hotline responders are not volunteers but, rather, trained SSAs with access to callers' electronic medical records. As of 2019, SSAs had contacted emergency services more than 138,000 times when they perceived a crisis. Callers can also receive a referral in the VA mental health system. The VCL has engaged in more the 511,000 chats with troubled veterans and responded to more than 150,000 texts (VCL, n.d.). Evaluations of the VCL have generally been favorable.

Conclusion

Despite millions of dollars spent on research and a host of prevention programs, veteran suicide continues to be a significant problem. The efforts, however, have not be wasted. Between 2005 and 2017, veteran suicide rates rose 6.1% compared to the non-veteran increase of 43.6% (VA, 2019). This suggests that some progress has been made, but much more work needs to be done.

Helpful Resources
Websites
National Suicide Prevention Hotline. *Veterans*: https://suicidepreventionlifeline.org/help-yourself/veterans
Suicide Prevention Resource Center. *National organizations and federal agencies*: https://www.sprc.org/organizations/%20national-federal
U.S. Department of Veterans Affairs. *Mental health*: https://www.mentalhealth.va.gov/suicide_prevention

Apps
Military Community Awareness: http://www.4mca.com/suicide_prevention_app
Objective Zero Foundation: https://www.objectivezero.org

References

Armed Forces Health Surveillance Center. (2012). Deaths by suicide while on active duty, active and reserve components, U.S. armed forces, 1998–2011. *Medical Surveillance Monthly Report, 19*(6), 7–10.

Bell, N., Harford, T., Amoroso, P., Hollander, I., & Kay, A. (2010). Prior health care utilization patterns and suicide among U.S. army soldiers. *Suicide and Life-Threatening Behavior, 40*(4), 407–415. https://doi.org/10.1521/suli.2010.40.4.407

Brenner, A., Ignacio, V., & Blow, C. (2011). Suicide and traumatic brain injury among individuals seeking Veterans Health Administration services. *Journal of Head Trauma Rehabilitation, 26*(4), 257–264. https://doi.org/10.1097/HTR.0b013e31821fdb6e

Bryan, C., Griffith, J., Pace, B., Hinkson, K., Bryan, A. O., Clemans, T. A., & Imel, Z. (2015). Combat exposure and risk for suicidal thoughts and behaviors among military personnel and veterans: A systematic review and meta-analysis. *Suicide and Life-Threatening Behavior, 45*(5), 633–649.

Bryan, C., Morrow, C., Anestis, M., & Joiner, T. (2010). A preliminary test of the interpersonal-psychological theory of suicidal behavior in a military sample. *Personality and Individual Differences, 48*(3), 347–350. https://doi.org/10.1016/j.paid.2009.10.023

Campbell, D., Bonner, L., Bolkan, C., Lanto, A., Zivin, K., Waltz, T., Klap, R., Rubenstein, L. V., & Chaney, E. (2016). Stigma predicts treatment preferences and care engagement among Veterans Affairs primary care patients with depression. *Annals of Behavioral Medicine, 50*(4), 533–544. https://doi.org/10.1007/s12160-016-9780-1

Carpiniello, B., & Pinna, F. (2017). The reciprocal relationship between suicidality and stigma. *Frontiers in Psychiatry, 8,* 35. https://doi.org/10.3389/fpsyt.2017.00035

Castro, C. A., & Kintzle, S. (2014). Suicides in the military: The post-modern combat veteran and the Hemmingway effect. *Current Psychiatry Reports, 16,* 460.

Centers for Disease Control and Prevention. (2019). *Ten leading causes of death and injury.* https://www.cdc.gov/injury/wisqars/LeadingCauses.html

Congressional Research Service Insight. (2019, September 9). *Suicide rates and risk factors for the National Guard.* https://fas.org/sgp/crs/natsec/IN11164.pdf

Deployment Health Clinical Center. (2017). Mental health disorder prevalence among active duty service members in the military health system, fiscal years 2005–2016. https://www.pdhealth.mil/sites/default/files/images/mental-health-disorder-prevalence-among-active-duty-service-members-508.pdf

Haney, E., O'Neil, M., Carson, S., Low, A., Peterson, K., Denneson, L. M., Oleksiewicz, C., & Kansagara, D. (2012). *Suicide risk factors and risk assessment tools: A systematic review.* U.S. Department of Veterans Affairs, Health Services Research & Development Service.

Hoge, C. (2011). Interventions for war-related posttraumatic stress disorder: Meeting veterans where they are. *JAMA, 306*(5), 549–551. https://doi.org/10.1001/jama.2011.1096

Ilgen, M., Bohnert, A., Ignacio, R., Mccarthy, J., Valenstein, M., Kim, H., & Blow, F. (2010). Psychiatric diagnoses and risk of suicide in veterans. *Archives of General Psychiatry, 67*(11), 1152–1158. https://doi.org/10.1001/archgenpsychiatry.2010.129

Ilgen, M., Downing, K., Zivin, K., Hoggatt, K., Kim, H., Ganoczy, D., Austin, K. L., McCarthy, J. F., Patel, J. M., & Valenstein, M. (2009). Exploratory data mining analysis identifying subgroups of patients with depression who are at high risk for suicide. *Journal of Clinical Psychiatry, 70*(11), 1495–1500. https://doi.org/10.4088/JCP.08m04795

Joiner, T. (2005). *Why people die by suicide.* Harvard University Press.

Kaplan, M., Huguet, N., McFarland, B., & Newsom, J. (2007). Suicide among male veterans: A prospective population-based study. *Journal of Epidemiology and Community Health, 61*(7), 619–624. https://doi.org/10.1136/jech.2006.054346

Kessler, R., Stein, M., Bliese, P., Bromet, E., Chiu, W., Cox, K., Colpe, L. J., Fullerton, C. S., Gilman, S. E., Gruber, M. J., Heeringa, S. G., Lewandowski, R., Millikan-Bell, A., Naifeh, J. A., Nock, M. K., Petukhova, M. V., Rosellini, A. J., Sampson, N. A., Schoenbaum, M., . . . Ursano, R. (2015). Occupational differences in US Army suicide rates. *Psychological Medicine, 45*(15), 3293–3304. doi:10.1017/S0033291715001294

Kimerling, R., Makin-Byrd, K., Louzon, S., Ignacio, R., & McCarthy, J. (2016). Military sexual trauma and suicide mortality. *American Journal of Preventive Medicine, 50*(6), 684–691. https://doi.org/10.1016/j.amepre.2015.10.019

Leardmann, C. A., Powell, T. M., Smith, T. C., Bell, M. R., Smith, B., Boyko, E. J., Hooper, T. I., Gackstetter, G. D., Ghamsary, M., & Hoge, C. W. (2013). Risk factors associated with suicide in current and former US military personnel. *JAMA, 310*(5), 496–506.

Linehan, M., Comtois, K., Murray, A., Brown, M., Gallop, R., Heard, H., Korslund, K. E., Tutek, D. A., Reynolds, S. K., & Lindenboim, N. (2006). Two-year randomized controlled trial and follow-up of dialectical behavior therapy vs therapy by experts for suicidal behaviors and borderline personality disorder. *Archives of General Psychiatry, 63*(7), 757–766. https://doi.org/10.1001/archpsyc.63.7.757

Nelson, H., Denneson, L., Low, A., Bauer, B., O'Neil, M., Kansagara, D., & Teo, A. (2017). Suicide risk assessment and prevention: A systematic review focusing on veterans. *Psychiatric Services, 68*(10), 1003–1015. https://doi.org/10.1176/appi.ps.201600384

Pietrzak, R., Pitts, B., Harpaz-Rotem, I., Southwick, S., & Whealin, J. (2017). Factors protecting against the development of suicidal ideation in military veterans. *World Psychiatry, 16*(3), 326–327. https://doi.org/10.1002/wps.20467

Reger, M. A., Smolenski, D. J., Skopp, N. A., Metzger-Abamukang, M. J., Kang, H. K., Bullman, T. A., Perdue, S., & Gahm, G. A. (2015). Risk of suicide among US military service members following Operation Enduring Freedom or Operation Iraqi Freedom deployment and separation from the US military. *JAMA Psychiatry, 72*(6), 561–569.

Rudd, M., Bryan, C., Wertenberger, E., Peterson, A., Young-McCaughan, S., Mintz, J., Williams, S. R., Arne, K. A., Breitbach, J., Delano, K., Wilkinson, E., & Bruce, T. (2015). Brief cognitive–behavioral therapy effects on post-treatment suicide attempts in a military sample: Results of a randomized clinical trial with 2-year follow-up. *American Journal of Psychiatry, 172*(5), 441–449. https://doi.org/10.1176/appi.ajp.2014.14070843

Shen, Y., Cunha, J., & Williams, T. (2016). Time-varying associations of suicide with deployments, mental health conditions, and stressful life events among current and former US military personnel: a retrospective multivariate analysis. *Lancet Psychiatry, 3*(11), 1039–1048. https://doi.org/10.1016/S2215-0366(16)30304-2

Siegel, M., & Rothman, E. (2016). Firearm ownership and suicide rates among US men and women, 1981–2013. *American Journal of Public Health, 106*(7), 1316–1322. https://doi.org/10.2105/AJPH.2016.303182

U.S. Department of Veterans Affairs. (n.d.). *From science to practice: Opioid use and suicide risk.* https://www.mentalhealth.va.gov/suicide_prevention/docs/Literature_Review_Opioid_Use_and_Suicide_Risk_508_FINAL_04-26-2019.pdf

U.S. Department of Veterans Affairs. (2018). *National Strategy for Preventing Veteran Suicide 2018-2028.* https://www.mentalhealth.va.gov/suicide_prevention/docs/Office-of-Mental-Health-and-Suicide-Prevention-National-Strategy-for-Preventing-Veterans-Suicide.pdf

U.S. Department of Veterans Affairs, Office of Mental Health and Prevention. (2019). *2019 national veteran suicide prevention annual report.* https://www.mentalhealth.va.gov/docs/data-sheets/2019/2019_National_Veteran_Suicide_Prevention_Annual_Report_508.pdf

U.S. Department of Veterans Affairs/U.S. Department of Defense. (2019). *VA/DoD clinical practice guideline: Assessment and management of patients at risk for suicide.* https://www.healthquality.va.gov/guidelines/mh/srb/index.asp

Van Orden, K., Cukrowicz, K., Witte, T., Braithwaite, S., Selby, E., & Joiner, T. (2010). The interpersonal theory of suicide. *Psychological Review, 117*(2), 575–600. https://doi.org/10.1037/a0018697

Veterans Crisis Line. (n.d.). What it is. https://www.veteranscrisisline.net/about/what-is-vcl

Military Culture and Help-Seeking

Derrick Kranke and Shant A. Barmak

Background

Previous research found that 50–82% of the recent generation of veterans (Operation Enduring Freedom, Operation Iraqi Freedom, and Operation New Dawn) with mental health concerns do not seek help in the form of accessing health care because of stigma (Kulesza et al., 2015; Nelson et al., 2014). Although utilization of U.S. Department of Veterans Affairs (VA) health care services increased from 20% in 2001 to 48% in 2016 (Meffert et al., 2019), this percentage is still considered a low utilization rate. At least one-third of the recent generation of veterans or service members report mental health problems (Thomas et al., 2010). Of the approximately 22 million veterans residing in the United States, only 1.2 million receive mental health treatment (https://www.va.gov). Veterans may be particularly vulnerable to the effects of perceived stigma because of the military's cultural values, which may compound negative feelings toward engaging in some form of help-seeking.

The National Council for Behavioral Health (2012) found that the total health costs, including non-psychiatric care, of veterans with mental illnesses who do not seek help in the form of treatment is fourfold the cost for veterans who do seek psychiatric treatment. In addition, more than $1 billion would be saved in treatment costs if every veteran with a psychiatric disorder sought mental health services. Ultimately, stigma contributes substantially to increased health care costs over time for veterans, which also limits funding for other services to enhance veteran well-being.

This chapter provides an overview of how military cultural values impact the help-seeking process among the most recent generation of veterans. Beginning with emerging literature on factors that must be considered when addressing help-seeking behaviors among veterans, the chapter then addresses nuanced factors to facilitate help-seeking behaviors and approaches for veterans, concluding with future directions.

Military Culture

Conforming to the perceived military cultural value of self-reliance may influence veterans' reluctance to engage in help-seeking behaviors such as mental health treatment (Kim et al., 2010). Throughout their time in the military, veterans were taught to embrace attitudes such as self-based sufficiency, discipline, mental toughness, and to "tough out" problems in the military (Kim et al., 2010). Furthermore, seeking help from a professional who provides psychological services may be perceived as a sign of weakness to unit leaders (Kim et al., 2010). In addition, some veterans fear seeking services out of concern that it might impact their career tracks (Mittal et al., 2013). When referenced in this discussion, a *service member* is a member of the uniformed services, consisting of the armed forces (Army, Navy, Marine Corps, and Coast Guard). A *veteran* is defined as a person who served in any branch of service of the armed forces as long as they were not discharged dishonorably (see http://benefits.va.gov).Coping mechanisms and values acquired while serving may be contradictory to what nonmilitary civilians are taught. Examples of coping mechanisms and values acquired while serving are targeted aggression and key skills such as discipline and cohesion. Although these values are identified in the armed forces, they do not always serve the veteran or service member in civilian life. The moderate aggression after being deployed may result in misplaced and inappropriate aggression in civilian life (Castro et al., 2006). Indeed, these contrasting belief systems make the healing process more complicated for some veterans.

Some veterans may have difficulty establishing social support networks and/or seeking help because of their feeling of differentness from non-veteran civilians (Kranke et al., 2019). As a result, some veterans isolate and may develop harmful coping mechanisms that coincide with substance abuse or suicidal ideations (Rüsch et al., 2014). Most existing research focuses on the negative impact or the deficits of individuals who possess attributes related to stigma (Zinzow et al., 2012). During the past two decades, the concept of differentness has shifted societal views of stigma: From a young age, people are taught that differentness is the opposite of what people should feel (Leavey, 2009) because it can lead to feelings of shame and isolation and identification with being the outcast. However, social media messages communicate differentness as something to be proud of and embraced. Differentness is

not understood or recognized until it impacts one's self.

Another critical element of military culture is that societal views of military service members as "national heroes" tend to decline as veterans are mainstreamed with nonmilitary civilians and the rest of the society (Adams et al., 2019). Furthermore, some veterans have experience hardships while reintegrating into civilian life post-military service, including "renegotiating his or her role in the family" (Sayers et al., 2009, p. e7) such as with children and/or a spouse. Both negative and positive perceptions of family members toward the veteran affect the mindset of veterans as they transition from the service to society.

Although military culture has been highlighted as a contributing factor to facilitate or hinder help-seeking, some who provide formalized mental health treatment question, "Is there one exclusive military culture?" Military culture is contextual and tied to such classifications as the following: Having served in combat or in noncombat missions? Branch of the military? Reservist or National Guard? Officer or enlisted personnel? Male, female, or transgender? Sexuality? These questions with regard to classifications can impact how connected an individual is to military culture.

Considerations to Facilitate Help-Seeking

Emerging literature identifies nuanced considerations among the most recent generation of veterans impacting help-seeking behaviors. Many who join the military do so before the age of 25 years (Military OneSource, 2018), which coincides with a developmental period defined by Kroger (2007) as late adolescence. Beginning with boot camp, the military "tears down" cadets and reconstructs a new identity or sense of self that affirms and embraces military cultural values (Demers, 2011). The developmental period of late adolescence entails identity formation—which commonly leads to an individual questioning their place in the world, thinking about choice of career, and developing a sense of belonging in terms of peer group identification. Service members will develop a shared identity and base much of their reconstructed adult identity on interactions with their peers and values acquired while in the military (Demers, 2011; Rumann & Hamrick, 2010). Veterans are "caught between who they knew themselves to be in the military and who they are now that they are in the civilian world" (Demers, 2011, p. 174).

Mittal et al. (2013) assessed combat veterans' perceptions of treatment-seeking and found that most veterans resisted stereotypes associated with mental illness or those needing psychological treatment. Post-traumatic stress disorder (PTSD) is one of the most common psychological illnesses diagnosed among military service members/veterans (Trivedi et al., 2015). For instance, a veteran respondent in the study by Mittal et al. (2013) said in relation to negative stereotypes, "I don't think that we're violent or I don't think PTSD people are violent" (p. 89). Another veteran participant noted, "I guess they [non-veteran civilians] stigmatize us as crazy, and that's a liability because I'm not a liability. I'm not just going to go off on somebody without provocation or anything. . . . I don't like being labeled" (p. 89). Mittal et al.'s (2013) findings have significant implications for help-seeking models. Self-stigma is a process by which individuals with serious mental illness apply prejudices and stereotypes about mental illness to themselves (Lucksted & Drapalski, 2015; Watson et al., 2007). The fact that participants "resisted the legitimacy of stereotypes may decrease their chances to develop self-stigma" (Mittal et al., 2013, p. 90). Results of this study suggest that the experience of stigma among veterans has different contextual factors related to help-seeking than those for civilians who did not serve.

Social support, which is the antithesis of isolation, has been found to predict the intention to seek help (Porcari et al., 2017). A major issue among veterans and service members is that their social support hinges mostly on others who have been there, or served, because they can relate to the triggers, atrocities, and triumphs of missions. This desire for sameness among veterans and the desire to seek help may also apply to professionals who have knowledge of military culture. Findings from Porcari and associates illustrate that veterans from other eras and Operation Enduring Freedom and Operation Iraqi Freedom veterans and service members are more likely to engage in professional help from a VA physician compared to formal help from a non-VA physician. Interestingly, a significant difference was found as most veterans prefer to seek help from family and friends in contrast to formalized help. Thus, it is imperative that treatment approaches are at least inclusive of health professionals who are knowledgeable of military culture.

Finally, recent literature indicates that the loss of a fellow service member/veteran may compound veterans' reluctance to seek help when dealing with grief (Lubens & Silver, 2019). In particular, for veterans, losing a peer to suicide has lasting effects. Findings from the preliminary study by Lubens and Silver (2019) have implications for addressing help-seeking behaviors among veterans. In response to dealing with grief, some veterans may resist the need for help because of the feelings associated with the loss of a loved one (Mittal et al., 2013). The relationship that forms among service members may be considered so profound because they must protect each other in life and death situations, and it can only be understood among those who have served in this capacity.

Nuanced Approaches and Implications for Practice

Although not yet empirically tested, reframing differentness as sameness is a potential treatment approach to helping post-September 11, 2001, veterans overcome the stigma of help-seeking (Kranke et al., 2019). Sameness is described as sharing attributes or qualities. Shared experiences build common ground, and sameness mitigates feelings of isolation or shame because these feelings are shared by a greater number of individuals. Veterans need to nurture and enhance work skills (e.g., discipline, structure, and time management) acquired while training in the military, and they have a teamwork mentality that stems from the "brotherhood" of protecting each other on missions. Indeed, commonality leads to the formation of social relationships. Commonality allows for the validation of concerns and experiences and sustains feelings of belonging and normality. Veterans connect and normalize their characteristics of sameness with others—not only with other veterans but also with non-veteran civilians. For example, civilians and veterans experience sameness following disasters when they have to start over (Kranke et al., 2019).

In civilian disaster settings, veterans provide disaster relief with other veterans and non-veterans and independently engage in thought restructuring strategies to promote flexible and adaptive thinking associated with help-seeking (Kranke et al., 2017). For example, Team Rubicon (TR) veteran volunteers mitigated perceptions related to the stigma of engaging in help-seeking behaviors by reframing their need to address mental health concerns (Kranke et al., 2017). The positive effects of addressing mental health concerns were cathartic and inspired other veterans to reframe their own negative thinking to address their mental health issues.

Weiss et al. (2020) note another underlying factor to the success of peer support in TR: The TR members embrace the organizational value that they are all considered equals. Whether from the Army, Marines, Navy, Air Force, combat, noncombat, National Guard, Reserve, or Coast Guard or civilian, man or woman, etc., they are all "Grayshirts." All TR members wear gray shirts when providing relief in areas impacted by disasters. The unification of TR members brought on by the shared value that all members are equal seems to contradict the findings of the study by Ashley and Brown (2015) that suggested veterans who serve in combat are considered elite among the veteran population in general. Weiss et al. suggest volunteering in TR may reduce power struggles that may typically occur with advancement in other organizations.

In addition, public messaging strategies to enhance the use of the veterans crisis line are emerging (Karras et al., 2017). Crisis lines are a commonly used alternative by veterans because of the confidentiality associated with help-seeking and/or because some veterans live in rural settings far from VA hospitals. In fact, in another study, veterans were found to be more likely to use crisis lines than other forms of self-help because of public messaging and increased awareness (Bossarte et al., 2014). Future findings will likely have implications for increasing help-seeking behaviors through the utilization of crisis lines. Furthermore, help-seeking has also been influenced by veterans' positive perception of and experience with telemedicine (Gros et al., 2018; Miller et al., 2016). This easy-to-use electronic platform has become a practical mode of treatment. Veterans also have expressed the benefit of a positive comfort level in being able to avoid the stigma associated with utilization of mental health services when using telemedicine (Acierno et al., 2016; Wierwille et al., 2016). In addition, veterans are more comfortable connecting with their providers from home and being able to avoid trauma cues that are often associated with VA clinics, such as pictures, uniforms, and other veterans, which might result in anxiety (Erbes et al., 2014; Yuen et al., 2015; Ziemba et al., 2014).

Social workers must be informed of effective treatment modalities in treating veterans with adjustment- and/or PTSD-related issues (Coll et al., 2011). They also must be knowledgeable and competent in their understanding of military culture when serving their veteran clients.

Conclusion

Rates of help-seeking among the recent generation of veterans remain low. A preliminary step in addressing this issue is for social workers and other health care professionals to become more informed of cultural values embraced by those in the military and also those who continue to identify with military culture once they are separated from the military. More must be done by researchers and practitioners to develop contemporary programs that enhance help-seeking for potential complications with reintegration into civilian life among many veterans.

Helpful Resources

Active Heroes: https://activeheroes.org

Journal of Veterans Studies: https://journal-veterans-studies.org

Team Rubicon: https://teamrubiconusa.org

U.S. Department of Veterans Affairs: https://www.va.gov

References

Acierno, R., Gros, D. F., Ruggiero, K. J., Hernandez-Tejada, B. M., Knapp, R. G., Lejuez, C. W., Muzzy, W., Frueh, C. B., Egede, L. E., & Tuerk, P. W. (2016). Behavioral activation and therapeutic exposure for posttraumatic stress disorder: A noninferiority trial of treatment delivered in person versus home-based telehealth. *Depression and Anxiety, 33*(5), 415–423. doi:10.1002/da.22476

Adams, R. E., Urosevich, T. G., Hoffman, S. N., Kirchner, H. L., Figley, C. R., Withey, C. A., Boscarino, J. J., Dugan, R. J., & Boscarino, J. A. (2019). Social and psychological risk and protective factors for veteran well-being: The role of veteran identity and its implications for intervention. *Military Behavioral Health, 7*(3), 304–314. doi:10.1080/21635781.2019.1580642

Ashley, W., & Brown, J. C. (2015). The impact of combat status on veterans' attitudes toward help seeking: The hierarchy of combat elitism. *Journal of Evidence-Informed Social Work, 12*(5), 534–542. doi:10.1080/15433714.2014.992695

Bossarte, R. M., Karras, E., Lu, N., Tu, X., Stephens, B., Draper, J., & Kemp, J. E. (2014). Associations between the Department of Veterans Affairs' suicide prevention campaign and calls to related crisis lines. *Public Health Reports, 129*(6), 516–525. doi:10.1177/003335491412900610

Castro, C. A., Hoge, C. W., & Cox, A. L. (2006). Battlemind training: Building soldier resiliency. In *Human dimensions in military operations—Military leaders' strategies for addressing stress and psychological support.* Meeting Proceedings RTO-MP-HFM-134, Paper 42, pp. 42-1–42-6. RTO. file:///C:/Users/lisa.rapp-mccall/Downloads/MP-HFM-134-42%20(1).pdf

Coll, J. W., Weiss, E. L., & Yarvis, J. S. (2011). No one leaves unchanged: Insights for civilian mental health care professionals into the military experience and culture. *Social Work and Health Care, 50*(7), 487–500. doi:10.1080/00981389.2010.528727

Demers, A. (2011). When veterans return: The role of community in reintegration. *Journal of Loss and Trauma, 16*(2), 160–179. doi:10.1080/15325024.2010.519281

Erbes, C. R., Stinson, R., Kuhn, E., Polusny, M., Urban, J., Hoffman, J., Ruzek, J. I., Stepnowsky, C., & Thorp, S. R. (2014). Access, utilization, and interest in mHealth applications among veterans receiving outpatient care for PTSD. *Military Medicine, 179*(11), 1218–1222. doi:10.7205/MILMED-D-14-00014

Gros, D. F., Lancaster, C. L., López, C. M., & Acierno, R. (2018). Treatment satisfaction of home-based telehealth versus in-person delivery of prolonged exposure for combat-related PTSD in veterans. *Journal of Telemedicine and Telecare, 24*(1), 51–55. doi:10.1177/1357633X16671096

Karras, E., Lu, N., Elder, H., Tu, X., Thompson, C., Tenhula, W., Batten, S. V., & Bossarte, R. M. (2017). Promoting help seeking to veterans. *Crisis, 38*(1), 53–62. doi:10.1027/0227-5910/a000418

Kim, P. Y., Thomas, J. L., Wilk, J. E., Castro, C. A., & Hoge, C. W. (2010). Stigma, barriers to care, and use of mental health services among active duty and National Guard soldiers after combat. *Psychiatric Services, 61*, 582–588. doi:10.1176/ps.2010.61.6.582

Kranke, D., Floersch, J., & Dobalian, A. (2019). Identifying aspects of sameness to promote veteran reintegration with civilians: Evidence and implications for military social work. *Health and Social Work, 44*(1), 61–64. doi:10.1093/hsw/hly036

Kranke, D., Weiss, E., Gin, J., Der-Martirosian, C., Brown, J., Saia, R., & Dobalian, A. (2017). A "culture of compassionate bad-asses": A qualitative study of combat veterans engaging in peer-led disaster relief and utilizing cognitive restructuring to mitigate mental health stigma. *Best Practices in Mental Health, 13*(1), 20–33. https://psycnet.apa.org/record/2017-45093-003

Kroger, J. (2007). *Identity development: Adolescence through adulthood.* Sage.

Kulesza, M., Pedersen, E. R., Corrigan, P. W., & Marshall, G. N. (2015). Help-seeking stigma and mental health treatment seeking among young adult veterans. *Military Behavioral Health, 3*(4), 230–239. doi:10.1080/21635781.2015.1055866

Leavey, J. E. (2009). Youth experiences of living with mental health problems: Emergence, loss, adaptation and recovery (ELAR). *Canadian Journal of Community Mental Health, 24*(2), 109–126.

Lubens, P., & Silver, R. C. (2019, September). US combat veterans' responses to suicide and combat deaths: A mixed-methods study. *Social Science & Medicine, 236,* 112341. Online. doi:10.1016/j.socscimed.2019.05.046

Lucksted, A., & Drapalski, A. L. (2015). Self-stigma regarding mental illness: Definition, impact, and relationship to societal stigma. *Psychiatric Rehabilitation Journal, 38*(2), 99–102. doi:10.1037/prj0000152

Meffert, B. N., Morabito, D. M., Sawicki, D. A., Hausman, C., Southwick, S. M., Pietrzak, R. H., & Heinz, A. J. (2019). US veterans who do and do not utilize Veterans Affairs health care services: Demographic, military, medical, and psychosocial characteristics. *The Primary Care Companion for CNS Disorders, 21*(1), 18m02350. doi:10.4088/PCC.18m02350

Military OneSource. (2018). *2018 demographics report.* Retrieved June 10, 2020, from https://download.militaryonesource.mil/12038/MOS/Reports/2018-demographics-report.pdf

Miller, C. J., McInnes, D. K., Stolzmann, K., & Bauer, M. S. (2016). Interest in use of technology for healthcare among veterans receiving treatment for mental health. *Telemedicine Journal and E-Health, 22*(10), 847–854. doi:10.1089/tmj.2015.0190

Mittal, D., Drummond, K. L., Blevins, D., Curran, G., Corrigan, P., & Sullivan, G. (2013). Stigma associated with PTSD: Perceptions of treatment seeking combat veterans. *Psychiatric Rehabilitation Journal, 36*(2), 86–92. doi:10.1037/h0094976

National Council for Behavioral Health. (2012). *Meeting the behavioral health needs for veterans.* Retrieved June 1, 2020, from https://www.thenationalcouncil.org/wp-content/uploads/2013/02/Veterans-BH-Needs-Report.pdf?daf=375ateTbd56

Nelson, K. M., Helfrich, C., Sun, H., Hebert, P. L., Liu, C. F., Dolan, E., Taylor, L., Wong, E., Maynard, C., Hernandez, S. E., Sanders, W., Randall, I., Curtis, I., Schectman, G., Stark, R., & Fihn, S. D. (2014). Implementation of the patient-centered medical home in the Veterans Health Administration: Associations with patient satisfaction, quality of care, staff burnout, and hospital and emergency department use. *JAMA Internal Medicine, 174*(8), 1350–1358. doi:10.1001/jamainternmed.2014.2488

Porcari, C., Koch, E. I., Rauch, S. A., Hoodin, F., Ellison, G., & McSweeney, L. (2017). Predictors of help-seeking intentions in Operation Enduring Freedom and Operation Iraqi Freedom veterans and service members. *Military Medicine, 182*(5–6), e1640–e1647. doi:10.7205/MILMED-D-16-00105

Rumann, C. B., & Hamrick, F. A. (2010). Student veterans in transition: Re-enrolling after war zone deployments. *Journal of Higher Education, 81*(4), 431–458. doi:10.1080/00221546.2010.11779060

Rüsch, N., Zlati, A., Black, G., & Thornicroft, G. (2014). Does the stigma of mental illness contribute to suicidality? *British Journal of Psychiatry, 205*(4), 257–259. doi:10.1192/bjp.bp.114.145755

Sayers, S. L., Farrow, V. A., Ross, J., & Oslin, D. W. (2009). Family problems among recently returned military veterans referred for a mental health evaluation. *Journal of Clinical Psychiatry, 70*(2), 163–170. doi:10.4088/jcp.07m03863

Thomas, J. L., Wilk, J. E., Riviere, L. A., McGurk, D., Castro, C. A., & Hoge, C. W. (2010). Prevalence of mental health problems and functional impairment among active component and National Guard soldiers 3 and 12 months following combat in Iraq. *Archives of General Psychiatry, 67*(6), 614–623. doi:10.1001/archgenpsychiatry.2010.54

Trivedi, R. B., Post, E. P., Sun, H., Pomerantz, A., Saxon, A. J., Piette, J. D., . . . & Nelson, K. (2015). Prevalence, comorbidity, and prognosis of mental health among US veterans. *American Journal of Public Health, 105*(12), 2564–2569.

Watson, A. C., Corrigan, P., Larson, J. E., & Sells, M. (2007). Self-stigma in people with mental illness. *Schizophrenia Bulletin, 33*(6), 1312–1318.

Weiss, E. L., Kranke, D., & Barmak, S. (2020, July). Military veterans serving as volunteers: What social workers need to know. *Social Work, 65*(3), 299–301.

Wierwille, J. L., Pukay-Martin, N. D., Chard, K. M., & Klump, M. C. (2016). Effectiveness of PTSD telehealth treatment in a VA clinical sample. *Psychological Services, 13*(4), 373–379. doi:org.libproxy.txstate.edu/10.1037/ser0000106

Yuen, E. K., Gros, D. F., Price, M., Zeigler, S., Tuerk, P. W., Foa, E. B., & Acierno, R. (2015). Randomized controlled trial of home-based telehealth versus in-person prolonged exposure for combat-related PTSD in veterans: Preliminary results. *Journal of Clinical Psychology, 71*(6), 500–512. doi:10.1002/jclp.22168

Ziemba, S. J., Bradley, N. S., Landry, L. A., Roth, C. H., Porter, L. S., & Cuyler, R. N. (2014). Posttraumatic stress disorder treatment for Operation Enduring Freedom/Operation Iraqi Freedom combat veterans through a civilian community-based telemedicine network. *Telemedicine Journal and E-Health, 20*(5), 446–450. doi:10.1089/tmj.2013.0312

Zinzow, H. M., Britt, T. W., McFadden, A. C., Burnette, C. M., & Gillispie, S. (2012). Connecting active duty and returning veterans to mental health treatment: Interventions and treatment adaptations that may reduce barriers to care. *Clinical Psychology* Review, *32,* 741–753. doi:10.1016/j.cpr.2012.09.002

Supervising Military-Connected Practice

An Inclusive and Informed Case Consultation-Based Approach

Kari L. Fletcher and Eugenia L. Weiss

This chapter emphasizes the first two sessions of the supervisee's work with a military-connected client in a community-based behavioral health clinic. Their therapeutic work highlights the importance of establishing rapport with a military veteran client, beginning the assessment process, and taking a culturally informed approach to military-connected practice. The use of a case consultation model illustrates how supervisors might work with a relatively new master's-level prepared clinical social worker. However, concepts relating to military-connected practice can still be applied when supervising more seasoned clinicians.

In the case scenario, the supervisee, Sarah (a pseudonym), is a 25-year-old White (non-Latina) civilian (non-veteran) female who possesses 1-year post-Master of Social Work clinical social work experience. During weekly supervision with the first author, Sarah expresses feeling anxious about meeting Ray (also a pseudonym), whom she knows has been struggling following his recent discharge from the military. Sarah has had little connection to and possesses little knowledge of military life, other than from what she sees stereotypically portrayed in the media and in films (Gross & Weiss, 2017). The term *military-connected population* broadly refers to service members, veterans, and their families (Council on Social Work Education, 2010).

We, the authors, appreciate the need to support community-based providers in their work with military-connected populations (Tanielian et al., 2014). Given the relative lack of supervision-specific resources in this area, we offer a resource that is streamlined yet informative (Fletcher & Weiss, 2020). The chapter is divided into two sections. First, we explore presenting client concerns that strengthen the supervisee's ability to carry out an assessment while building therapeutic rapport (Part 1). Second, we consider case consultation strategies that can be used within supervision and discuss implications for continued practice and clinical growth (Part 2). Within each section, aspects of supervision with Sarah are presented to help integrate information and apply it to supervising Sarah's clinical social work practice with Ray. Ray represents a composite case of a military veteran client.

Part 1

When Sarah and I met for supervision, Sarah expressed feeling "inundated" by her first psychotherapy session with Ray. She felt "unsure as to how to move forward" and wanted to feel prepared for their second appointment. Sarah and I agreed that as a first step, a focus would be on the case-related aspect of Sarah's work with Ray and a consideration of the assessment process.

What Does the Supervisee Know? The Initial Assessment

Case consultation begins by exploring with the supervisee "What do you know so far about the client?" Sarah came to supervision able to formulate presenting features and concerns Ray expressed during their first session.

Key Demographic Information, Presenting Concerns, and Symptoms

Sarah shared that Ray is a 41-year-old, African American, married (19 years) male veteran with three sons (aged 17, 14, and 7 years) that he and his wife Joyce have raised together. Three months ago, Ray returned from his third combat deployment. In terms of presenting concerns, Sarah noted that Ray shared that he felt "out of sorts" because he was experiencing readjustment difficulties post-deployment and following his recent separation from the military, which left him wondering "what's next" for him in his life. With regard to symptoms,

Ray noted that he had been experiencing loss of interest "in everything" and daily episodes of feeling "blue."

Biopsychosocial–Spiritual Assessment

During supervision, we discussed what Sarah understood about Ray's current concerns from a biopsychosocial–spiritual perspective. Biologically, Ray reports that he has been in overall good health during his lifetime and not had any substance use concerns. While on deployment and after his return home, he felt "off" since having suffered a mild traumatic brain injury (TBI), which he sought help for but has not quite recovered from. Psychologically, Ray grew up in a family with a mental health history of depression and anxiety. Prior to joining the military, Ray endorsed "going through rough patches" from which he had always been able to "bounce back." Post-deployment, Ray believed things had "finally caught up to him." Socially, although Ray came from an economically impoverished family in which he felt somewhat neglected (in that his parents were "always at work"), he intuitively sought out positive mentors, formed strong friendships, and met and married a nurturing partner, which helped him thrive in the military and stay out of legal trouble. Spiritually, Ray reports that his fundamentally religious Baptist upbringing ultimately "curbed his enthusiasm for [organized] religion," and he subsequently developed a sense of spirituality that encompassed an appreciation for nature. Culturally, Ray grew up in an African American community in the South. Several moves and many years in the military later, Ray found himself connected to military culture. After separating from the military, Ray states that he misses the comradery with peers and the structure of military life (for an overview of the nuances of military culture, see Coll et al., 2011; Siebold & Britt, 2019). During our supervision, we reviewed questions that Sarah could use to build rapport and better understand Ray's military cultural perspective. According to Coll et al. (2011),

> A clinician's approach to counseling a veteran client will vary depending on how far removed the veteran is from military service. No blanket assumptions should be made about the veteran's experience. However, in most situations, it can be helpful to initiate the conversation with preliminary questions about the client's military service. Questions might include:

- In which branch of the armed forces did you serve?
- Where were you stationed?
- What was your military occupational specialty (MOS)?
- Do you have any family or friends who are still deployed?
- Were you engaged in combat? (p. 496)

In our next supervision session, we decided to focus on Ray's current mental health status, his stressors, how his concerns evolved, and to what end Ray believed his military service may be relevant to his current experience and presenting symptoms (Fletcher et al., 2018).

Assessing Stressors

First, we considered stressors Ray had experienced as part of his military service—and within the context of his deployment and combat: namely physical and neurological concerns (e.g., his mild TBI) and cognitive (his report of being "out of sorts"), emotional (his feeling distraught), social (his isolation), and/or potential spiritual stressors (i.e., moral injury) (Nash, 2006). Next, we teased out which stressors might be acute, related to his readjustment post-deployment, and which stressors might be more chronic or long-standing (which may have contributed to things "catching up with him"; Exum et al., 2011).

Then, we considered Ray's stressors within the context of separations (e.g., having been gone from his family for deployments), readjustment (e.g., reacclimating post-deployment), and transitions more broadly—that is, to what degree he found separation from military service to be stressful (Kulka et al., 1990). Finally, we considered what types of risks (e.g., multiple deployments to combat zones), resilience (e.g., positive navigation of childhood adversity), and protective factors (e.g., "happy family life"; Nock et al., 2013) Ray exhibited.

After their first visit, Sarah better understood how Ray's military service fit into her larger assessment. For instance, Ray joined the military when he was 22 years old, soon after graduating from college and largely in response to events following September 11, attacks. Over the course of his 18 years in the military, his family life changed as he joined the military (soon after he married) and later deployed three times—first to Afghanistan (2002–2003, just before their first child was born), then to Iraq (2006–2007, just after their second child was born), and finally to Kuwait (2018–2019, as their eldest child became old enough to drive).

While Ray served as an enlisted tank mechanic for nearly two decades during the post-9/11 military involvement in Iraq and Afghanistan eras, Ray and his family experienced many shifts in their military life. During the first decade, Ray served active duty in the Army. He and his family were part of a vibrant military community: They lived on military bases, their children attended civilian-run schools on the bases, and they socialized with other military families with service members of similar ranks. During the second decade, Ray served in the Army National Guard. He and his family lived in a community in which few other military families lived, worked, or went to school, and they found themselves feeling less connected to the military community, which is a common experience for those serving in the National Guard and Reserve (Harnett et al., 2019). Once he separated from the military,

Ray felt cut off from the life he had known. Ray reported missing the comradery and connection he had felt with his peers when part of the military and was ambivalent as to whether he wanted to connect with others (other veterans or non-veterans), both socially or even within the context of a Veterans Affairs' hospital setting.

Just as military service factors into the lives of those who served (Settersten, 2006), during supervision we agreed that it would be helpful in subsequent appointments with Ray for Sarah to develop a more complete assessment. Although unsure to what degree the effects of military service, including combat exposure, might be exacerbating Ray's current concerns (Settersten, 2006), we discussed how veterans who have been deployed into combat zones (even in support roles such as Ray's) may have been susceptible to signature injuries or concerns commonly experienced that are unique to each military cohort (Fletcher et al., 2018). For example, common signature injuries among post-9/11 veterans include TBI, post-traumatic stress disorder (PTSD), and major depression (Tanielian & Jaycox, 2008).

Prior to our case consultation, Sarah, like other community providers, was unaware of the role that military service played in her assessment of Ray (Fletcher et al., 2018). In our supervision, we discussed why it is difficult to make diagnostic distinctions unless we first consider the role of military combat experience. Without this consideration, Sarah was at risk for misdiagnosing Ray's current concerns (Fletcher et al., 2018). We also were able to consider how Ray's readjustment struggles might be associated with stressors of separating from military service (e.g., having trouble accessing natural supports) (Fletcher et al., 2018) as well as what might be acute (short-term) versus long-term stressors (Exum et al., 2011).

We discussed expanding military-specific assessments to also consider moral injury [e.g., duties Ray performed as part of military service that came into conflict with Ray's belief system (Maguen & Litz, 2012) or worldview (Weiss et al., 2011], grief and loss (e.g., Ray's experience of ambiguous loss as he struggled to maintain presence with his family during his deployment; Boss, 2020), and the presence of trauma [e.g., in addition to conceptualizing Ray's trauma-related stressors, considering both whether Ray may experience post-traumatic growth as the result of his experiences (Tedeschi & Calhoun, 2006) and whether he may experience late-onset stress symptomology associated with PTSD (Fletcher et al., 2017)].

Diagnostic Clinical Assessment

Although clinical social workers are trained during their graduate programs, supervision presents an opportune time to revisit the diagnostic process, particularly for providers such as Sarah who have not worked previously with military-connected populations. Prior to moving further into the diagnostic process, Sarah did take into account the presence of substance use, suicide ideation, medical concerns, and cultural considerations [American Psychiatric Association (APA), 2013]; however, she felt unsure how to sufficiently assess these with Ray. With regard to substance use, in addition to her observations and Ray's self-report (that he did not use substances), we discussed the role of assessment inventories (e.g., the Addiction Severity Index; McClellan et al., n.d.) and brief screening instruments (e.g., the CAGE Inventory; National Institutes of Health, n.d.) that Sarah could integrate into her upcoming session with Ray. Regarding medical concerns, given Ray's report that he had recently suffered a mild concussion, we discussed making referrals to specialists (or following up with his medical providers) to delve further into his reported mild TBI concerns and the presence of chronic pain. With regard to culture, we considered both his military service and recent deployment as well as the degree to which Ray identified with his race, ethnicity, and spiritual beliefs and the intersection of identities—for example, between race and his identity as a veteran. Sarah also conducted an initial suicide risk assessment, and Ray had denied suicide ideations or history of suicide attempts.

Next, we considered which possible diagnoses for which Ray might meet criteria per the fifth edition of the *Diagnostic and Statistical Manual of Mental Disorders* (APA, 2013). Sarah again indicated that she felt a bit stuck here. Taking words Ray used to describe his psychological well-being during their initial appointment at face value—such as "distraught," "unable to bounce back," and as though things have "finally caught up to him"—Sarah thought Ray may be experiencing readjustment-related concerns, trauma, depression, anxiety, and/or neurological concerns. In an effort to narrow things down (while knowing that it takes more than one visit to make a diagnosis), we considered the supporting information Sarah had gathered during her first visit—such as the objective observations made as part of the Mental Status Exam portion of her assessment with Ray—to determine which diagnostic categories might be eliminated (personality disorders, etc.) and to establish his current level of risk (e.g., both with regard to suicidality and more broadly). We agreed that during her next appointment with Ray, Sarah would gather further diagnostic information, which we planned to incorporate into our next case consultation, thus allowing us to be able to make a provisional diagnosis, consider differential diagnoses, and, after consulting with specialists, then be able to rule out nonapplicable diagnoses.

Part 2

Social work supervision promotes increased knowledge, skill, and experience within four arenas: direct practice, professional impact, job management, and continued learning (Shulman, 2008). Supervision models emphasize the importance of relationships (e.g., between the client and supervisee and between the supervisee and supervisor) and parallel process (e.g., how what the client struggles with may show up in work with the supervisee and how what the supervisee struggles with shows up in the supervision; Shulman, 2008). In addition, supervision emphasizes cultural humility (e.g., our attention both to *interpersonal* awareness toward our limited ability to understand our client's cultural background and our *intrapersonal* respect and openness toward our client's worldview; Hook et al., 2013), as well as learning to examine our histories and assume responsibilities for discussing cultural differences with our clients and being curious about their experiences of working with us (Hardy, 2008).

Clinical social work supervision emphasizes the supervisee's growth in learning how to conduct psychotherapy (e.g., learn/practice specific models), social role/social process (e.g., privilege supervisee's learning needs), and development (e.g., adapts to meet evolving needs/support growth of supervisee; Bennett & Deal, 2012). In this section, we discuss the importance of supervisory strategies in supporting supervisees with their clients in their continued clinical work with military-connected populations.

Sarah went into her second session with Ray feeling more prepared to work with him clinically. Afterward, Sarah developed a process recording (verbatim written narrative to her closest recollection) of the most salient parts of their session together. She attended to the content (what was being said), the process (what was not being said), and her reactions/feelings with regard to countertransference and self-awareness regarding the potential for secondary stress in helping Ray with any of his potentially traumatic experiences.

Observation

As a newer clinician—and in the absence of the supervisor being able to directly observe the therapeutic session (i.e., directly in the room, through a one-way mirror, and/or by way of either video or audio recording)—we agreed that being able to read through and discuss process recordings was a helpful strategy to help gain a better understanding of what was going on in session (Shulman, 2016). We had developed a routine during supervision in which, when possible, we went through cases employing a stop frame analysis method of supervision. Using this method, we stopped intermittently during our conversation to discuss what was happening in the session (Levenson, 2017).

Observation helps supervisors support supervisees develop their clinical abilities to work competently to assess, intervene, and evaluate their own work with clients (Amerikaner & Rose, 2012).

Our Supervisory Process

The supervisory process includes making sense of what is happening in session (e.g., Sarah's perspective), examining how Sarah is developing strategies to work clinically with Ray (e.g., how actively she is navigating this in session), exploring Sarah and Ray's relationship (e.g., how it continues to develop as their clinical work unfolds), considering Sarah's countertransference (e.g., what comes up for her based on her own experience), considering our supervisory relationship (e.g., what is unfolding in Sarah's and my work together), and exploring my supervisory process (e.g., how I experience our work) (Hawkins & Shohet, 2000).

Continued Development

Just as social workers are encouraged to meet clients where they are at, it is important for supervisors to join and work with supervisees where they are at (Bennett & Deal, 2012). For Sarah—who has both partially mastered and continues to work on competencies emphasized during her master's program—the focus of our relationally focused clinical supervision

continued to shift as she developed stronger assessment and clinical abilities, as well as increased confidence in her ability to work with Ray (Deal, 2002). As we worked together in supervision, our co-constructed process of reviewing where Sarah is at (e.g., in terms of her professional use of self and ability to sit with ambiguity) and how to strengthen her assessment abilities (e.g., increase her comfort and confidence level in terms of thinking about clinical work through various lenses and perspectives) organically, we were able to tie in what we know about common therapeutic factors (e.g., why therapy works and why; Prochaska et al., 1994) and how change takes place within the therapeutic relationship (e.g., therapeutic action; McWilliams, 2004). Increasingly, Sarah was able to identify and explore what took place in sessions, where she became stuck in her work, and how she could address these difficult spots and become unstuck (Bass, 2014).

Conclusion

In this chapter, we illustrated the role that supervision plays in supporting supervisees in working clinically with military-connected populations. We highlighted the importance of attending to military culture throughout the assessment process with a recognition that military life can encompass many things. We encouraged the use of process recordings and/or other forms of observation to help facilitate conversation and continued supervisee development. As next steps, ongoing attention toward cultural humility (Hook et al., 2013) and the importance of cultural competency [i.e., sensitivity toward needs and concerns within military-connected populations (Tanielian et al., 2014)] is paramount. In addition to possessing clinical competencies, this includes a clinician having increased awareness of military culture, comfort working with the population, and appropriate skills (Tanielian et al., 2014).

Helpful Resources

U.S. Department of Veterans Affairs. *VA app store: Mental health*: https://mobile.va.gov/appstore/mental-health

U.S. Department of Veterans Affairs. *VA community provider toolkit*: https://www.mentalhealth.va.gov/communityproviders/

Veterans Crisis Line: 1-800-273-TALK; https://www.veteranscrisisline.net

References

American Psychiatric Association. (2013). *Diagnostic and statistical manual of mental disorders* (5th ed.). American Psychiatric Publishing.

Amerikaner, M., & Rose, T. (2012). Direct observation of psychology supervisees' clinical work: A snapshot of current practice. *The Clinical Supervisor, 31*(1), 61–80. doi:10.1080/07325223.2012.671721

Bass, A. (2014). Supervision and analysis at a crossroad: The development of the analytic therapist: Discussion of papers by Joan Sarnat and Emanuel Berman. *Psychoanalytic Dialogues, 24,* 540–548. doi:10.1080/10481885.2014.949488

Bennett, S., & Deal, K. H. (2012). Supervision training: What we know and what we need to know. *Smith College Studies in Social Work, 82,* 195–215.

Boss, P. (2020). Ambiguous loss. https://www.ambiguousloss.com

Coll, J. E., Weiss, E. L., & Yarvis, J. (2011). No one leaves unchanged: Insights for civilian mental health care professionals into the military experience and culture. *Social Work in Health Care, 50*(7), 487–500.

Council on Social Work Education. (2010). *Advanced social work practice in military social work.* https://www.cswe.org/News/Press-Room/Press-Release-Archives/CSWE-Releases-Advanced-Military-Social-Work-Pr-(1)

Deal, K. H. (2002). Modifying field instructors' supervisory approach using field models of student development. *Journal of Teaching in Social Work, 22*(3–4), 121–137.

Exum, H. E., Coll, J. E., & Weiss, E. L. (2011). *A civilian counselor's primer for counseling veterans* (2nd ed.). Linus.

Fletcher, K. L., Albright, D. L., Rorie, K. A., & Lewis, A. M. (2017). Older veterans. In J. Beder (Ed.), *Caring for the military: A guide for helping professionals* (pp. 54–71). Routledge.

Fletcher, K. L., Mankowski, C. M., & Albright, D. L. (2018). The challenges posed by the mental health needs of military service members and veterans. In J. Rosenberg & S. Rosenberg (Eds.), *Community mental health: Challenges for the 21st century* (3rd ed., pp. 59–85). Routledge.

Fletcher, K. L., & Weiss, E. L. (2020, July). Supporting military-connected practice: An interactive (and inclusive) consultation approach. Paper presented at the Military Social Work & Behavioral Health Conference, Austin, TX.

Gross, G., & Weiss, E. L. (2017). Veterans as the media portrays them. In L. Hicks, E. L. Weiss, & J. E. Coll (Eds.), *The civilian lives of U.S. veterans: Issues and identities* (pp. 455–480). ABC-CLIO.

Hardy, K. V. (2008). Race, reality, and relationships. In M. McGoldrick & K. V. Hardy (Eds.), *Re-visioning family therapy: Race, culture and gender in clinical practice* (2nd ed., pp. 76–84). Guilford.

Harnett, C., Weiss, E. L., & Heaney, G. (2019). Health and well-being of National Guard and Reserve forces. In E. L. Weiss & C. A. Castro (Eds.), *American military life in the 21st century: Social, cultural, and economic issues and trends* (pp. 455–470). ABC-CLIO.

Hawkins, P., & Shohet, R. (2000). *Supervision in the helping professions: An individual, group, and organizational approach* (2nd ed.). Open University Press.

Hook, J. N., Davis, D. E., Owen, J., Worthington, E. L., Jr., & Utsey, S. O. (2013). Cultural humility: Measuring openness to culturally diverse clients. *Journal of Counseling Psychology, 60,* 353–366.

Kulka, R. A., Schlenger, W. E., Fairbank, J. A., Hough, R. L., Jordan, B. K., Marmar, C. R., & Weiss, D. S. (1990). *Trauma and the Vietnam War generation: Report of findings from the National Vietnam Veterans Readjustment Study.* Brunner/Mazel.

Levenson, H. (2017). *Brief dynamic therapy* (2nd ed.). American Psychological Association.

Maguen, S., & Litz, B. (2012). Moral injury in the context of war. U.S. Department of Veterans Affairs.https://www.ptsd.va.gov/professional/treat/cooccurring/moral_injury.asp

McClellan, A. T., Luborsky, L., Woody, G. E., & O'Brien, C. P. (n.d.). *Addiction Severity Index.* https://eprovide.mapi-trust.org/instruments/addiction-severity-index

McWilliams, N. (2004). *Psychoanalytic psychotherapy.* Guilford.

Nash, W. P. (2006). The spectrum of war stressors. In C. R. Figley & W. P. Nash (Eds.), *Combat stress injury theory, research, and management* (pp. 18–69). Routledge.

National Institutes of Health, National Institute on Alcohol Abuse and Alcoholism. (n.d.). *Screening tests.* https://pubs.niaaa.nih.gov/publications/arh28-2/78-79.htm

Nock, M. K., Deming, C. A., Fullerton, C. S., Gilman, S. E., Goldenberg, M., Kessler, R. C., McCarroll, J. E.,

McLaughlin, K. A., Peterson, C., Schoenbaum, M., Stanley, B., & Ursano, R. J. (2013). Suicide among soldiers: A review of psychosocial risks and protective factors. *Psychiatry: Interpersonal & Biological Processes, 76*(2), 97–125.

Prochaska, J. O., Norcross, J. C., & DiClemente, C. C. (1994). *Change for good.* Morrow.

Settersten, R. A. (2006). When nations call: How wartime military service matters for the life course and aging. *Research on Aging, 28*(1), 12–36.

Shulman, L. (2008). Supervision. In T. Mizrahi & L. E. Davis (Eds.), *Social work encyclopedia* (20th ed.). Oxford University Press.

Shulman, L. (2016). Shifting the social work practice paradigm: The contribution of the Interactional Model. *Journal of Social Work Education, 52*(Suppl.), S16–S27.

Siebold, G. L., & Britt, T. W. (2019). Overview of military culture. In E. L. Weiss & C. A. Castro (Eds.), *American military life in the 21st century: Social,* *cultural, and economic issues and trends* (pp. 3–14). ABC-CLIO.

Tanielian, T., Farris, C., Epley, C., Farmer, C. M., Robinson, E., Engel, C. C., Robins, M. W., & Jaycox, L. H. (2014). *Ready to serve: Community-based provider capacity to deliver culturally competent, quality health care to veterans and their families.* RAND.

Tanielian, T., & Jaycox, L. H. (Eds.). (2008). *Invisible wounds of war: Summary and recommendations for addressing psychological and cognitive injuries.* RAND.

Tedeschi, R. G., & Calhoun, L. G. (2006). Expert companions: Posttraumatic growth in clinical practice. In L. G. Calhoun & R. G. Tedeschi (Eds.), *Handbook of traumatic growth: Research and growth* (pp. 291–310). Erlbaum.

Weiss, E. L., Coll, J. E., & Metal, M. (2011). The influence of military culture and veteran worldviews on mental health treatment: Implications for veteran help seeking and wellness. *International Journal of Health, Wellness & Society, 1*(2), 75–86.

PART XV

Forensic Social Work

At the Intersection of Social Work and the Law

Stacey D. Hardy-Chandler

Introduction: Law and Social Work as Members of the Same "Family"

Who do you consider to be members of your family? One's first response might be "my parents and my brothers and sisters, of course." And such a response would certainly comport with the dictionary definition, which describes a nuclear family as "the basic unit in society traditionally consisting of two parents rearing their children" (Merriam-Webster, n.d.). This seemingly simple question gets far more complicated when we consider the various current permutations of what defines a family in real life, and especially the varieties we encounter as social workers. Keep in mind that even the "institution" of family is not static. In fact, it too has changed over time, has been defined by legal parameters, and has a number distinctly cultural implications. The following questions test (or expand) our accepted conceptualizations of what a family really is:

- What about foster families?
- What about adoptive families?
- What about "fictive" family members who do not have immediate genetic ties but have incredibly close socioemotional ties?
- What about "half" siblings connected by re-marriage? Or an extramarital affair?
- What about those "cousins" who are cultur-ally selected or "brothers and sisters" as des-ignated by one's faith community?
- Surely many would argue their "fur babies" (i.e., pets) are "family" as well, right?

The notion of connection to those with whom we might not naturally or intuitively know we have ties is particularly germane to our ex-amination of the forensic social work field. Specifically, the easily overlooked "familial" connections between social work and the law that may not be immediately evident to those in either of these respective fields are, for the purposes of this chapter, a vital point of *intersection.*

Notably, forensic social work as a field has served to unite those of us who identify and are socialized as "social workers" with our long lost lawyer siblings. Forensic social work serves as a sort of disciplinary geneticist, ex-plicitly leveraging the nexus between social work and the law that has historically existed and that can be further elevated to magnify and synergize the efforts of each field toward advancing equity and justice. One need only look to the fight for civil rights and the Voting

Rights Act (1965), which prohibits voting practices or procedures that discriminate on the basis of race, color, or membership in "[a] language minority groups," as prime examples. Efforts to improve the lives of all within a society, including the marginalized, oppressed, or vulnerable, through access to the rights and privileges that will allow them to thrive have been a resonant aim in social work. Time and again, we make quantum leaps forward when, in addition to community-based action, laws and regulations are changed to move American society ever closer to truly manifesting its founding ideals.

Foundations of Social Work as Principles for Forensic Social Work

The hallmark of the social work profession, what distinguishes it from all other human service disciplines, is that it is multidimensional, holistic, and, at its core, quite "generalist" in nature. Although person-in-environment and ecological constructs have had some proposed upgrades throughout the years, each iteration acknowledges not only that people are influenced by their environments but also that they have an impact on their respective environments (Cornell, 2006). Human issues are messy! So, the generalist approach of the social work profession is not merely a matter of sanitized pedagogy; social workers in essence serve to mirror the actual complexity and multidimensionality of their clients' experiences, thereby meeting human service needs in the highly realistic and multifaceted ways in which they occur.

Almost every social worker knows the mantra "Start where the client is," a phrase of unclear origins but nonetheless shares some philosophical similarity with the business maxim, "The client is always right." Rather than having unreasonable expectations that clients must somehow come to where we are, or where

we want them to be, social work clients—even involuntary ones—define where intervention "starts." Our field, to a larger degree than other human service professions, explicitly acknowledges that where any person is at any particular point in their life is influenced by their personal history and experiences, complex understandings of identity and place, the collective history of the society to which they belong, systemic and institutional factors, and a myriad of other variables that bring full color and dimension to each story. We respect where clients (including client-families or client-communities) are and the factors that led them there. We do this while working with them, and the systems and institutions they encounter (which often we represent by virtue of our employment), to ensure a relatively clear path for everyone to reach a destination in alignment with their safety and goals, as well as the advancement of just, anti-racist, trauma-informed structures that will support this aim.

Also, because from this psychosocial standpoint, where the client "is" can be so intricate, the generalist foundations of our field make sense in mirroring the complexity of those we serve. In other words, because people are not one-dimensional, social work cannot be either. As stated in the premier guidance document for social work education in the United States, the Council on Social Work Education's (CSWE) *Educational Policy and Accreditation Standards* (2015) concisely describes the individual-to-global breadth of our field:

> Guided by a person-in-environment framework, a global perspective, respect for human diversity, and knowledge based on scientific inquiry, the purpose of social work is actualized through its quest for social and economic justice, the prevention of conditions that limit human rights, the elimination of poverty, and the enhancement of the

quality of life for all persons, locally and globally. (p. 5)

What is social work "actualized" by? In the previous definition, we can see clear implications for forensic social work as evident in the "quest for social and economic justice" and "human rights," each of which has prima facie policy, regulatory, and legal elements.

Some "Family" History

One factor contributing to our multilayered, multidimensional approach to service is that social work and the law are "siblings" of sorts. They are not twins, but they are "family," albeit somewhat distant family members that, like our own real families, do not always see eye-to-eye. Law can be defined as "any system of regulations to govern the conduct of the people of a community, society or nation, in response to the need for regularity, consistency and justice based upon collective human experience" (Law.com, n.d.). Origins of the legal field vary widely depending on the continent, but when we think about its pervasive historical objective of "governing the conduct of people," it is not surprising that as a field, law has centuries of both secular and religious influences (e.g., Canon law and Islamic law). Modern American notions of law, brought from England by the early colonists, are thought to have roots in ancient Greece and Rome (Duhaime.org, n.d.). During Athens' Classic Era (fourth and fifth century BC), people accused of something had to plead their own case or get a "friend" to plead on their behalf. So-called "orators" (*logografous* or speech writers) skilled in both their knowledge of the law and the psychology of judges, were often sought to plead the cases of people bringing their situations up for judgment (Panezi, 2017). It appears that even then, people recognized that

a good orator could help them gain a better outcome in cases of dispute (Panezi, 2017). We can also deduce that even then, some people may not have had equal access to such skilled orators and that those who did not may have been disadvantaged in ways that parallel our struggle providing fair and equitable justice today.

Whereas the history of people working toward the benefit of others is likely as old as humankind, the formal profession of social work has a more modern "birth" than its legal older sibling—commonly accepted as emerging out of the work of social reformer and activist Jane Addams. Inspired by what she saw at the Toynbee Hall settlement house in London's East End, she and friend Ellen Gates Star started Hull House in Chicago's impoverished west side in 1889 (Michals, 2017). Hull House provided an array of services meeting a range of diverse community needs, including child care, English language courses for immigrants, and access to art and art courses; it also hosted a number of community-based clubs and cultural events (Jane Addams Hull-House Museum, n.d.).

Through Addams, who was ultimately awarded the Nobel Peace Prize in 1931, social work's connection with the law started early. Among her many advocacy efforts and pacifist accomplishments, she was instrumental in establishing the juvenile justice court system we know today. She was also a founding member of the National Child Labor Committee and advocated for changes in labor laws affecting both children and adults. Her other leadership roles included being the first female president of the National Conference of Charities and Corrections, which would later become the National Conference of Social Work.

Probably to no one's surprise, Addams was active in the women's suffrage movement, which in 2020 celebrated its 100-year anniversary (Michals, 2017). Through her, our social work origins emphasize our dedication as a profession to a "quest for social and economic justice, the prevention of conditions that limit human rights, the elimination of poverty." So, as noted in the CSWE's (2015, p. 5) definition of the field provided previously, we are inherently destined to interface with the law on some level—just as Jane Addams did during her lifetime.

Social work finds a familial—and familiar—common ground with law in the following overarching ways:

- Origins in playing a role in affecting the individual or collective human experience.
- Advocacy through serving in support of others toward achieving certain justice-oriented outcomes—even when what constitutes "justice" has been interpreted differently.
- Common caseloads—from a practical standpoint, whether through divorce, child custody, child welfare, involuntary hospitalization, juvenile detention, incarceration, restorative justice, or police dismantlement or reforms, many clients served by social workers are also on the caseloads of lawyers, guardian ad litems, who come before judges or otherwise find themselves connected with court or judicial systems.

As with all "siblings," social work differs from the law in many ways. One key area is in the definition of who is served; Who exactly is the client? In law, there is the ethical notion of "zealous representation" of the identified client (American Bar Association, 1983). Whereas in social work, ethics dictate a dual loyalty to both the procedurally identified client and larger society's greater good (National Association of Social Workers, 2017). When ethical dilemmas occur between the two fields, they tend to be around the area of potentially conflicting allegiances. Where forensic social workers serve

on legal teams, opinions have supported the social workers' role as part of attorney–client work product (Galowitz, 1999).

Intersectionality as a Keystone of Forensic Social Work

People commonly speak about "intersectionality" as if it were simply a combination of descriptors—like psychosocial arithmetic. We erroneously conceptualize it as just characteristics that happen to go together—for example, Asian nationality + woman gender identification = Asian woman (Done!). This oversimplification critically dilutes a concept that, to date, has not been explicitly highlighted in the field yet is nonetheless foundational to the nexuses upon which forensic social work substantively operates.

Kimberle Crenshaw, a law professor at both Columbia University and the University of California, Los Angeles, coined the term "intersectionality" in her 1989 paper, "Demarginalizing the Intersection of Race and Sex." Its origins as a *legal term* are sometimes lost in recent sociopolitical debates and academic considerations (Coaston, 2019). In the more than 30 years since Crenshaw first posited the concept, the general public has often cited the term but inadvertently blurred its meaning. Coaston's article reveals that originally, intersectionality referenced systemic legal and socioeconomic systems that, in order to perpetuate racism, neglected attendance to dual barriers to justice, specifically race and sex, as well as perhaps other relevant factors.

The following are actions that can be taken for further understanding:

- *View*: To gain an understanding of the origins of intersectionality, take time to view Professor Crenshaw's TED Talk (Crenshaw, 1989, 2016).

- *Reflect*: the American Bar Association's 21-Day Racial Equity Habit-Building Challenge (American Bar Association, n.d.).
- *Do*: Have or host intersectionality conversations (e.g., see D'Cruz, 2019).

Forensic Social Work Across the Micro, Mezzo, and Macro Spectrum

The National Organization of Forensic Social Work

In 1982, Barbara O'Neal and Dane Hughes, two forensic clinicians, conducted a survey.[1] They wanted to know the extent to which other social workers were engaged in professional activities involving a cross section between the human services and the law, lawyers, or legal issues. Who else, they wondered, was doing this kind of—what would now be identified as—transformational, transdisciplinary work (Maschi & Killian, 2011)? They found many other social workers engaged in what would later be called "forensic social work," at rates far more than previously expected or known. There was an 85% response rate from approximately 340 practitioners throughout the United States and Puerto Rico, results represented clinicians in 20 states (Maschi & Killian, 2011). Most respondents were in inpatient settings, and their roles primarily involved making recommendations to local jurisdictional courts. Leadership, supervision, or management was well represented among respondents, with more than 75% identifying

themselves as some kind of "team leader" (Maschi & Killian, 2011).

Inspired by these data, the National Organization of Forensic Social Work (NOFSW) was incorporated in Ann Arbor, Michigan, in 1983 (Maschi & Killian, 2011; NOFSW, n.d.). The organization's first general meeting was held in 1984. Upholding a transdisciplinary approach, it was purposeful to have the name of the organization say "social work" rather than "social work*ers*" because the former was thought to be more inclusive of other fields, whereas the latter would limit engagement exclusively to social workers. The organization's tree logo is symbolic of "branches" reaching out to others, while staying fully connected to our social work "roots" (Maschi & Killian, 2011; NOFSW, n.d.). Even before "forensic social work" formally existed as a field, we have been from the start intersectional, in practice and in spirit.

Practice Considerations in Forensic Social Work

Roles and Careers

Forensic social workers serve in a wide variety of criminal and civil/family affiliated roles including providing:

- Competency to stand trial evaluations
- Mitigation Specialist services (especially in death penalty cases)
- Mediation (e.g. divorce and child custody)
- Expert witness testimony
- Psychosocial assessments
- Research and teaching in higher education settings
- Professional and organizational development

In addition, there are a number of social work professionals that do no not fit into the above categories, but still regularly and consistently interface with legal systems on behalf

---

1. Full disclosure: As this chapter is being written, the author is serving in her second term as President of the National Organization of Forensic Social Work, the first term being over a decade ago from 2008 to 2010. This information is offered to highlight the contributions of the premiere professional organization in the forensic social work field at this time and how it has contributed to the field's narrative and strategic direction.

of domestic/intimate partner violence, sexual assault, child or older adult victims and survivors of abuse. (NOFSW, Forensic Social Work Certificate curriculum, n.d.a)

While these roles have clear legal implications, it is again important to note that even the notion of who can call themselves a "social worker" is itself legally or administratively defined, differs by jurisdiction and is guided by the local Board overseeing the governance of practice. Factors include: the type and extent of practice experience, supervisory qualifications, and whether or not reciprocity exists among other jurisdictions i.e. whether experience in another state or territory will count toward the experience requirements of the clinician's current state or territory of residents (Association of Social Work Boards, 2020).

Education, Experience, and Training

There are no universal requirements for forensic social work job eligibility beyond what is required to legally practice as a social worker. NOFSW (n.d.b) is developing competency standards as part of its 2020 Code of Ethics revision process which is likely to include some variation of the following preferences.

Education (MSW)

- Elective forensic social work courses when available
- Field practicum at hosted at a legal setting (e.g. public defender's office, victim witness, juvenile detention, prison)
- Assisting faculty with research on forensic social work issues or a specialized independent study project

Experience (Post-Master's)

- Three years' full-time employment in a legal setting as part of a legal team, or
- Four years' full-time employment in a human service setting working regularly with legal systems (e.g. courts)

Training

- Ongoing continuing education in forensic social work topics (e.g. FSW Certificate Program)

Current and Emerging Issues

Health Inequity, Black Lives Matter, and Defunding the Police

At the time of this chapter was written, the country was facing two pandemics: one was COVID-19 or Novel Coronavirus which we have known about for a year; the other is racism which has existed in this country for over 400 years—157 years before the United States of America was even a county. To date, 20 states have publically declared racism as a public health issue (American Public Health Association, n.d.).

Intersectionality as we now understand it, is overtly evidenced by the example of persons of color being disproportionately ravaged by the virus, and significantly more likely to die from complications than their white peers (Centers for Disease Control and Prevention, 2020). The Coronavirus served as a sort of "magnifying glass" for our nation, highlighting community level resilience and generosity, while at the same time, exposing the deep cracks in our healthcare system, our mental health resources, and even among us as a society having dug our heels into debates over mask versus non-mask positions.

It was against this anxiety-laden backdrop that the efforts of Black, Indigenous People of Color (BIPOC) and their white allies, who had for so long fought against social injustices, were dramatically escalated by the murder of George Floyd on May 25, 2020 (Peeples, 2020). Rising from the protests and discourse that followed was the question, what would social workers do? (Dettlaff, 2020). In the aftermath of not only George Floyd, but also in regular succession, the deaths of Breonna Taylor, Ahmaud Arbery and countless others who while Black and unarmed, lost their lives at the hands of those sworn to "serve and protect," social workers found themselves in the throes of the debate over our stated ideals and what we were really willing to do to bring them into fruition. And the overlap between human/civil rights and law enforcement failings propelled forensic social workers right into the middle of local, regional and national discourse.

There are some truths to these more modern questions that, when one looks through a justice lens, have been answered by our profession long ago:

- Do Black lives matter? Initial knee jerk responses that "all lives matter" miss the point that forensic social workers clearly understand—the recognition that racism and marginalization have historically destructively impacted some lives more than others. These three words are not an assertion that Black lives somehow matter more than others, (or otherwise to the exclusion of others), but that "all" lives cannot matter until the lives of those who have marginalized, even to the point of having been legally counted as less than whole persons, are valued at least as much as others in our society. As it states in the Preamble National Association of Social Worker's Code of Ethics (2017) we, "... strive to end discrimination, oppression, poverty, and other forms of social injustice."

- Should the police be "defunded?" Again, immediate reactions take a less than nuanced response and read this as call to "eliminate law enforcement." A more thoughtful look into the issue recognizes that, "[u]ltimately, calls to defund the police are part of an abolitionist imagination that is focused on building new systems of care and investing in institutions that support people living and

thriving" (Dettlaff, 2020, para. 8). First, let's look at the word "abolitionist." When abolitionists called for an end to legalized slavery, people were similarly appalled by what this might mean for their safety and way of life (History, n.d.).

By parallel the current call to action garners similar responses, yet the core focus is completely in alignment with social work's emphasis on prevention and early intervention priorities over the back-end, reactive safety net actions such as incarceration when possible. To do this involves local jurisdictions determining what their specific needs are, and redistributing more resources to front-end, preventative areas like housing, mental health, community engagement, and child care. There will always be a role for law enforcement, but whenever possible, pro-active prevention and early interventions should be prioritized over reactive measures (NOFSW, 2020).

Examples of Forensic Social Work Areas of Focus

- Specialty Courts
  Called: Drug Courts, Mental Health Courts, Vet Courts, or Family Preservation courts or "dockets." These provide legally sanction opportunities for those who come in contact with legal systems to get access to services that better address the issues at the root cause of why they came to the attention of the courts (National Institute of Justice, 2020). Rather than incarceration, if law enforcement got involved with an individual due to behaviors resulting from a mental health issue for example, then that person would be afforded the opportunity to get treatment rather than incarceration and charges. If they do not comply with treatment, the charges would stand. They would not

be "getting away" with anything, but rather afforded the dignity of accessing the right kind of intervention for the issue that activated the encounter with law enforcement in the first place.

- Crossover Youth Practice Models

  So-called "crossover youth" are those who become connected with multiple service systems, often first through child welfare, then with the juvenile courts, and also, because they are youth, local school districts are involved (Center for Juvenile Justice Reform, n.d.). Youth (and families) that "crossover" into multiple systems, are apt to have much poorer outcomes (Casey Family Programs, 2018)

Many larger societal issues carry forensic social work undercurrents such as community reentry after incarceration, the school to prison pipeline, and human trafficking.

Conclusion

"Family" can mean many things, but at the intersection of "hope" and "justice" is field of forensic social work, which inherently embodies a kinship between people and the laws that govern their daily lives. Arguably, *forensic* social work operates in and within foundational social work ideals, harkening back to our profession's origins. Because it functions across the continuum of micro to macro areas of practice, forensic social workers might also be ideal candidates for leadership positions, roles and opportunities in no small part due to the explicit bridge-building, cross-systems, yet uniquely interpersonal nature of this work. Remembering that the logo of its professional organization is a tree, the nexus between law and social work is grounded deep in the roots of our social work origins, finds strength in the trunk of our ability to organize and unite across disciplines, and reaches out through the ever-expanding branches of our charge to promote and advance justice.

References

American Bar Association. (1983). *Model rules of professional conduct* [1969 Model Code of Professional Responsibility. Preceding the Model Code were the 1908 Canons of Professional Ethics (last amended in 1963)]. https://www.americanbar.org/groups/professional_responsibility/publications/model_rules_of_professional_conduct/model_rules_of_professional_conduct_preamble_scope

American Bar Association. (n.d.). Syllabus: 21-day racial equity habit-building challenge. https://www.americanbar.org/groups/labor_law/membership/equal_opportunity/?q=&fq=(id%3A%5C%2Fcontent%2Faba-cms-dotorg%2Fen%2Fgroups%2Flabor_law%2F*)&wt=json&start=0

American Public Health Association. (n.d.). Declarations of racism as a public health issue. https://www.apha.org/topics-and-issues/health-equity/racism-and-health/racism-declarations

Association of Social Work Boards. (2020). About licensing and regulation. https://www.aswb.org/licenses/

Casey Family Programs. (2018, May 29). Is there an effective practice model for serving crossover youth? https://www.casey.org/crossover-youth-resource-list

Center for Juvenile Justice Reform. (n.d.). Crossover youth practice model. https://cjjr.georgetown.edu/our-work/crossover-youth-practice-model

Centers for Disease Control and Prevention. (2020, July 24). Health equity considerations and racial and ethnic minority groups. https://www.cdc.gov/coronavirus/2019-ncov/community/health-equity/race-ethnicity.html

Coaston, J. (2019, May 28). The intersectionality wars. *Vox.* https://www.vox.com/the-highlight/2019/5/20/18542843/intersectionality-conservatism-law-race-gender-discrimination

Cornell, K. L. (2006). Person-in-situation: History, theory and new directions for social work practice. *Praxis, 6,* 50–57. https://www.canonsociaalwerk.eu/1940_Hamilton/Person%20in%20situation.pdf

Council on Social Work Education. (2015). *2015 Educational policy and accreditation standards.* https://www.cswe.org/getattachment/Accreditation/Accreditation-Process/2015-EPAS/2015EPAS_Web_FINAL.pdf.aspx

Crenshaw, K. (1989). Demarginalizing the intersection of race and sex: A Black feminist critique of antidiscrimination doctrine, feminist theory and antiracist politics. *University of Chicago Legal Forum, 1*(8), 139–167.

Crenshaw, K. (2016, August 1). The urgency of intersectionality [Video]. *TED Talk.* https://www.ted.com/talks/kimberle_crenshaw_the_urgency_of_intersectionality/discussion

D'Cruz, C. (2019, February 26). Explainer: What does "intersectionality" mean? *The Conversation.* https://theconversation.com/explainer-what-does-intersectionality-mean-104937

Dettlaff, A. (2020, July 8). Affirming the call for social work to fully support defunding the police. *Medium.* https://medium.com/@alandettlaff/affirming-the-call-for-social-work-to-fully-support-defunding-the-police-8a2e3b370e5

Duhaime.org. (n.d.). *Timetable of world legal history.* http://www.duhaime.org/LawMuseum/LawArticle-44/Duhaimes-Timetable-of-World-Legal-History.aspx

Galowitz, P. (1999). Collaboration between lawyers and social workers: Re-examining the nature and potential of the relationship. *Fordham Law Review, 67*(5), 16. https://ir.lawnet.fordham.edu/cgi/viewcontent.cgi?article=3556&context=flr

History. (n.d.). *Abolitionist movement.* Retrieved August 6, 2020, from https://www.history.com/topics/black-history/abolitionist-movement

Jane Addams Hull-House Museum. (n.d.). *About Jane Addams.* Retrieved July 5, 2020, from https://www.hullhousemuseum.org/about-jane-addams

Law.com. (n.d.). *Law.* https://dictionary.law.com/Default.aspx?selected=1111

Maschi, T., & Killian, M. L. (2011). The evolution of forensic social work in the United States: Implications for 21st century practice. *Journal of Forensic Social Work, 1*(1), 8–36. doi:10.1080/1936928X.2011.541198

Merriam-Webster. (n.d.). Family. In Merriam-Webster.com dictionary. Retrieved July 11, 2020, from https://www.merriam-webster.com/dictionary/family

Michals, D. (2017). *Jane Addams.* https://www.womenshistory.org/education-resources/biographies/jane-addams

National Association of Social Workers. (2017). Code of ethics. https://www.socialworkers.org/About/Ethics/Code-of-Ethics/Code-of-Ethics-English

National Institute of Justice. (2020, February 20). *Problem-solving courts.* https://nij.ojp.gov/topics/articles/problem-solving-courts

National Organization of Forensic Social Work. (2020a). *Homepage.* https://www.nofsw.org

National Organization of Forensic Social Work. (2020b). *Code of ethics.* https://4251f553-c8e8-439c-83bb-61068f7fb2c6.filesusr.com/ugd/f468b9_20e60b0830ed4a51808154902b7e9f20.pdf

National Organization of Forensic Social Work (n.d.). *About Us.* https://www.nofsw.org/about-us

National Organization of Forensic Social Work (n.d.a). *Forensic Social Work Certificate.* https://www.nofsw.org/forensic-social-work-certificate

Panezi, M. (2017). *Update: A description of the structure of the Hellenic Republic, the Greek legal system, and legal research.* https://www.nyulawglobal.org/globalex/Greece.html

Peeples, L. (2020, June 19). What the data say about police brutality and racial bias—and which reforms might work. *Nature.* https://www.nature.com/articles/d41586-020-01846-z

Voting Rights Act of 1965, 52 U.S. Code § 10101 (1965). https://www.justice.gov/crt/section-2-voting-rights-act

The School-to-Prison Pipeline

Susan McCarter

The school-to-prison pipeline (STPP) describes policies and practices that push students, especially the most at-risk students, out of the education system and into the juvenile and criminal justice systems (Burris, 2012; Darensbourg et al., 2010; Heitzeg, 2009). Because this social problem has social justice, social service, and legal implications, it is central to the field of forensic social work. The American Bar Association (2014) regards the STPP as referrals from "the classroom to the courtroom." Children have always misbehaved in school, so what has changed to create this pipeline? School discipline has changed with the implementation of zero-tolerance policies and exclusionary discipline; school climate has changed with metal detectors, SWAT teams with dogs, and school resource officers (SROs); and teacher–student relationships have changed with an increasingly diverse student body with complex needs and a much less diverse teacher population (mostly White women) with less preparation in discipline/classroom management, multiculturalism/diversity, trauma and mental health, etc.

School Discipline

Zero-tolerance policies have predetermined consequences, usually punitive, without consideration of offense severity, mitigating circumstances, or context; are intended to demonstrate a hard-line stance [American Psychological Association (APA) Zero Tolerance Task Force, 2008); and gained popularity in the 1990s and 2000s to address violence and drug use on school property (Monahan et al., 2014). Decades of research suggests that these policies do not improve school safety; rather, many school districts have shown increases in problem behaviors and dropouts (APA, 2008; González, 2012; Hirschfield, 2008; Teske et al., 2012), and zero-tolerance policies do not eliminate discretion but instead are applied inconsistently with increased and harsher consequences for marginalized students (Fabelo et al., 2011).

Exclusionary discipline is any school punishment that removes or excludes students from the learning environment, such as in-school suspension (ISS; because students are outside of their regular classrooms/the learning environment), out-of-school suspension (OSS), and expulsion (Losen et al., 2014). In the United States, an estimated 1.7 million schoolchildren were suspended from school (ISSs and OSSs) in 1974 (Poe-Yamagata & Jones, 2000). By 2000, that number was more than 3 million, and for the 2009–2010 school year, 3.37 million children received OSS, 3.54 million children received ISS, there were 279,475 referrals from schools to law enforcement, and there were 107,635 school-related arrests [Civil Rights Data Collection (CRDC), n.d.]. However, suspensions do not make schools any safer. Research suggests that the outcomes are worse for all students in schools with higher use of suspensions and expulsions (Perry & Morris, 2014). Since 2010, and partially in response to concerns regarding the STPP (Balingit, 2018; Harper et al., 2019), suspension rates have begun to decrease through changes in reporting/classification and in school discipline strategies (Balingit, 2018; CRDC, n.d.; Harper et al., 2019).

Just one suspension increases a young person's chances of entering the justice system (Chung et al., 2010). A study by the Council of State Governments (Fabelo et al., 2011) found that 1 in 7 students who were suspended had subsequent justice system contact and those outcomes were worse for children of color, with a likelihood of 1 in 5 for African American/ Black students, 1 in 6 for Hispanic/Latinx students, and 1 in 10 for White students compared to just 2% of students without suspensions. Finally, with the significant increase in the number of SROs in schools, in addition to suspensions, some youth face arrests for their behavior at school (Bolger et al., 2019; Na & Gottfredson, 2013; Theriot, 2009).

School Climate and School Resource Officers

Metal detectors, security cameras, bulletproof backpacks, and SROs do not make schools safer

(Petteruti, 2011). Education researchers suggest that the major predictors of school safety are school climate and relationships (Steinberg et al., 2011). The National School Climate Council (NSCC, n.d.) defines *school climate* as the general quality and character of school life, including students', families', and school members' school life experiences, and assesses school climate using the five dimensions of safety, teaching and learning, interpersonal relationships, staff, and institutional environment. Infractions that used to get students sent to the principal's office can now be outsourced to law enforcement with much more severe consequences.

SROs are hired to collaborate with schools to maintain the safety and security of the students, staff, and teachers [National Center for Education Statistics (NCES), n.d.]. Their responsibilities often include mentoring and advising, teaching or coaching, implementing school discipline and punishment, enforcing laws and rules, and delivering programs (Petteruti, 2011). According to the NCES, the percentage of U.S. schools with SROs increased from 1% in 1975 to 40% in 2008, and in 2018, 57% of U.S. schools had SROs/security presence (Na & Gottfredson, 2013; NCES, n.d.). Not surprisingly, schools with SROs were found to have higher levels of school discipline, and in one study, schools with SROs had five times as many school-based arrests for disorderly conduct as schools without SROs (Theriot, 2009).

Teacher/Student Demographics and Preparation

Many of today's diverse students have increasingly complex needs (Figure 152.1). Nationally, the percentage of school-aged children experiencing one or more adverse childhood experiences (ACEs), trauma, and mental health and/ or substance abuse issues is increasing (Bethell

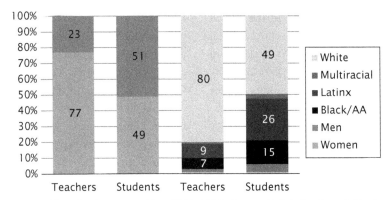

FIGURE 152.1 U.S. Public School Demographics, 2015–2016. *Source*: Civil Rights Data Collection. (n.d.). *State and national estimations*. https://ocrdata.ed.gov/StateNationalEstimations/Estimations

et al., 2017). In addition, one of the lasting effects of No Child Left Behind legislation is the shift in teacher preparation toward increased instructional time in math, reading, and content areas and away from courses in discipline and classroom management, mental health, multiculturalism and diversity, etc. (Dee & Jacobs, 2010).

Explicit and Implicit Bias and Structural Racism

In March 2018, the federal government published a report for Congress titled "K–12 Education: Discipline Disparities for Black Students, Boys, and Students with Disabilities" (Government Accountability Office, 2018). It found, as others have, that the explicit and implicit biases of teachers, administrators, and staff influence how they judge student behavior:

> Teachers and staff sometimes have discretion to make case-by-case decisions about whether to discipline, and the form of discipline to impose in response to student behaviors, such as disobedience, defiance, and classroom disruption. Studies show that these decisions can result in certain groups of students being more harshly disciplined than others. Further, the studies found that the types of offenses that Black children were disciplined for were largely

based on school officials' interpretations of behavior. (p. 4)

Unequal Application and Consequences of the School-to-Prison Pipeline

Sex

Sex refers to students' biological sex and is categorized male or female because few schools offer nonbinary or cisgender classification options. Male students are more likely to be disciplined at school compared to female students (Fabelo et al., 2011; Skiba et al., 2002). According to the U.S. Department of Education, in the 2013–2014 school year, boys comprised 71% of all OSSs compared to 29% of OSSs for girls, boys made up 68% of all ISSs compared to 32% for girls, and boys comprised 74% of all school expulsions compared to 26% for girls (CRDC, n.d.). Although there are differences in types of offenses committed by sex (e.g., girls are charged with prostitution more often, and boys are charged with robbery more often), those differences cannot account for the disproportionality in school discipline or juvenile justice involvement for boys versus girls (Sherman & Balck, 2015).

Race/Ethnicity

Despite the fact that there is no evidence that children of color misbehave at a significantly higher rate, students of color are disproportionately suspended, expelled, and arrested from/at school (Fabelo et al., 2011; Losen et al., 2014). The U.S. Department of Education reports that for the 2015–2016 school year, Black students were almost four times as likely to be suspended compared to White students, and they were more than two times as likely to be referred to law enforcement for school-related behavior (CRDC, n.d.). Scholars estimate approximately two out of every three Black males (66%) are suspended at some point during their kindergarten through grade 12 education in the United States (Shollenberger, 2015). The Council of State Governments' study of nearly 1 million students tested 83 variables (e.g., sex, family income, offense type, and disability status) to assess the effect of race and ethnicity on school discipline. The study found that with all other factors being equal, African American students had a 31% higher likelihood of being disciplined at school compared with otherwise identical students (Fabelo et al., 2011).

Socioeconomic Status/Family Income

Students who qualify for free and reduced-price school lunches are also more likely to be suspended or expelled from school compared to wealthier students (Verdugo & Glenn, 2006). In addition, research has found that lower socioeconomic status (SES) was not correlated with increased school misbehavior, yet students with lower SES (particularly parental education levels) had increased rates of suspension/expulsion compared to students with higher SES (Hemphill et al., 2014; Peguero & Shekarkhar, 2011; Sullivan et al., 2013).

Lesbian, Gay, Bisexual, Trans*, Queer, and Gender Nonconforming Students

Few schools and juvenile justice facilities ask students to identify their sexual orientation and their gender. Yet, national studies find that lesbian, gay, bisexual, trans*, queer (LGBTQ) and gender nonconforming students experience higher rates of "school-based victimization" (e.g., bullied for challenging gender norms, threatened, and assaulted) than their cisgender and heterosexual classmates (Burdge et al., 2014; Palmer & Greytak, 2017; Russell et al., 2013). Despite the fact that schools do not report greater academic/behavioral problems or crime commission for LGBTQ+ students, they are overrepresented in ISSs, OSSs, expulsions, and arrests (Himmelstein & Brückner, 2011; Kosciw et al., 2012). This is even more pronounced for LGBTQ+ students of color. Of the students in U.S. schools, 47% of LGBTQ+ Black youth, 44% of LGBTQ+ Latinx youth, and 36% of LGBTQ+ White youth report being disciplined in school (Palmer et al., 2016).

Students with Disabilities

Students with disabilities also disproportionately face exclusionary school discipline (Rausch, 2006). OSSs for youth with disabilities are twice the rate (13%) of suspensions for youth without disabilities (6%) [U.S. Commission on Civil Rights (USCCR), 2019]. Again, these outcomes are worse for students of color and members of the LGBTQ+ student community. Black students with disabilities are nearly four times more likely to receive multiple OSSs and almost two times more likely to be expelled than White students with disabilities (USCCR, 2019), and LGBTQ+ students with disabilities are more likely to be disciplined than LGBTQ students without disabilities (Palmer et al., 2016; Table 152.1).

Policy Changes

A certain win for forensic social work is that the Juvenile Justice and Delinquency Prevention Act of 1974 (JJDPA; 34 U.S.C. 11133) was reauthorized for the first time since 2002 on December 13, 2018, with bipartisan support for the Juvenile Justice Reform Act 2018 (JJRA; H.R. 6964). The reauthorization addresses

TABLE 152.1 U.S. Out-of-School Suspensions by Race/Ethnicity and Disability Status: 2011–2012 to 2015–2016

	Public K–12 Schools (%)			Public Secondary Schools (%)		
	2011–2012	2013–2014	2015–2016	2011–2012	2013–2014	2015–2016
Black	9.7	8.1	8.0	16.1	13.2	12.8
Hispanic/Latinx	5.0	3.6	3.5	9.1	6.6	6.3
White	4.7	3.8	3.8	7.8	6.1	6.1
Students with disabilities	10.2	8.5	8.6	16.1	13.2	12.8
Students without disabilities	5.0	4.2	4.1	8.8	7.1	6.9

Source: Civil Rights Data Collection. (n.d.). *State and national estimations.* https://ocrdata.ed.gov/estimations/2017-2018

three of the core protections by improving jail removal and sight/sound separation requirements, strengthening the deinstitutionalization of status offenders, and changing DMC (Disproportionate Minority Contact) to RED (Racial and Ethnic Disparities) and requiring that states analyze RED and implement solutions with measurable goals to address disparate outcomes in their jurisdictions [34 U.S.C.11133(a)(15)]. JJRA also addresses many other facets of juvenile justice, including language regarding State Advisory Groups (SAGs). SAGs are responsible for overseeing the implementation of JJDPA and are now required to make their juvenile justice plans public by posting them on their websites [34 U.S.C. 11133(a)].

School–Justice Partnerships

Although the STPP is generally regarded as a social problem, it is often also credited with beginning to break down service silos between schools and the courts (McCarter et al., 2017; Smoot, 2019). Included in the reauthorization is the stipulation that juvenile justice systems work with education systems, often referred to as school–justice partnerships (SJPs). SJPs are collaborative groups of community stakeholders (e.g., school administrators, law

enforcement, and court officials) who work together using an evidence-based approach to improve safety, reduce risk, and avert preventable justice system contact; advance positive school discipline strategies; and decrease suspensions, expulsions, and school-based referrals to juvenile court—all while maximizing students' success (School Justice Partnership: NC, 2019).

Implications for Forensic Social Work and All Types of Social Work

Social workers at all levels can work to disrupt the STPP:

At the macro level
- Build cross-sector collaboration (e.g., SJPs) and use memoranda of understanding to clarify the roles and responsibilities between local education authorities, law enforcement, the courts, and critical stakeholders.
- Improve data collection, analysis, dissemination, and transparency.
- Identify evidence-based, positive behavioral intervention and supports to replace zero-tolerance policies and exclusionary discipline.

- Enact policy to disrupt the STPP (e.g., Every Student Succeeds Act and Child Care Development Block Grant Act) by funding local strategies to reduce exclusionary discipline; expand school-based mental health services; and support training and professional development for child care providers, teachers, administrators, and SROs.

At the mezzo level
- Strengthen relationships that improve school climate.
- Hire more diverse teachers.
- Reduce class sizes.
- Use a social justice lens to revise codes of student conduct such that current disparities by sex, race/ethnicity, SES, gender identity and sexual orientation, and ability status are eliminated, and include accountability procedures to report on these annually.
- Build courses in classroom management/positive school discipline; trauma, mental health, and substance abuse; and diversity, access, and inclusion back into colleges of education and teacher preparation curricula.
- Strengthen relationships between schools and families.

At the micro level
- Increase the number of school social workers, psychologists, counselors, and nurses in schools to provide direct services to students.
- Identify students with disabilities, ACEs, and mental health challenges early in order to improve their access to services and their outcomes.
- Listen to the youth.
- Explore programs that facilitate/build restorative justice, peer mediation, and social–emotional learning.

- Help students make academic progress while out of school—strengthen the re-entry process.

Conclusion

Education has always been regarded as a protective factor for youth to overcome the effects of poverty, racism, and disadvantage, but given the evidence regarding the STPP, it is apparent that this protective factor is differentially applied across groups (McCarter, 2017). Changes in school discipline, climate, workforce, and student body have created the STPP. However, there is much that social workers can do at the micro, mezzo, and macro levels to disrupt the STPP.

References

American Bar Association. (2014). *The emergence of the school-to-prison pipeline.* https://www.americanbar.org/groups/gpsolo/publications/gpsolo_ereport/2014/june_2014/the_emergence_of_the_school-to-prison_pipeline

American Psychological Association Zero Tolerance Task Force. (2008). Are zero tolerance policies effective in the schools? *American Psychologist, 63,* 852–862.

Balingit, M. (2018, April 24). Racial disparities in school discipline are growing, federal data show. Retrieved April 2, 2019, from https://www.washingtonpost.com/local/education/ racial-disparities-in-school-discipline-are-growing-federal-data-shows/2018/04/24/ 67b5d2b8-47e4-11e8-827e-190efaf1f1ee_story.html?utm_term=.aab81c2128ea

Bethell, C. D., Davis, M. B., Gombojav, N., Stumbo, S., & Powers, K. (2017). *Issue brief: A national and across-state profile on adverse childhood experiences among U.S. children and possibilities to heal and thrive.* Johns Hopkins Bloomberg School of Public Health.

Bolger, P., Kremser, J., & Walker, H. (2019). Detention or diversion? The influence of training and education on school police officer discretion. *Policing, 42*(2), 255–269. https://doi.org/10.1108/PIJPSM-01-2018-0007

Burdge, H., Licona, A., & Hyemingway, Z. (2014). *LGBTQ youth of color: Discipline disparities,* school push-out, and the school-to-prison pipeline. Gay–Straight Alliance Network and Crossroads Collaborative at the University of Arizona. https://www.njjn.org/uploads/digital-library/GSA-Network_LGBTQ_brief_FINAL-web_Oct-2014.pdf

Burris, M. W. (2012). Mississippi and the school-to-prison pipeline. *Widener Journal of Law, Economics & Race, 3,* 1–25. http://www.antoniocasella.eu/restorative/Burris_2011.pdf

Chung, H. L., Mulvey, E. P., & Steinberg, L. (2010). Understanding the school outcomes of juvenile offenders: An exploration of neighborhood influences and motivational resources. *Journal of Youth Adolescence, 40,* 1025–1038. doi:10.1007/s10964-010-9626-2

Darensbourg, A., Perez, E., & Blake, J. J. (2010). Overrepresentation of African American males in exclusionary discipline: The role of school-based mental health professionals in dismantling the school to prison pipeline. *Journal of African American Males in Education, 1*(3), 1–16.

Dee, T., & Jacobs, B. A. (2010). The impact of No Child Left Behind on students, teachers, and schools. *Brookings Papers on Economic Activity,* 149–207.

Fabelo, T., Thompson, M. D., Plotkin, M., Carmichael, D., Marchbanks, M. P., III, & Booth, E. A. (2011). *Breaking schools' rules: A statewide study of how school discipline relates to students' success and juvenile justice involvement.* Council of State Governments Justice Center and Public Policy Research Institute.

González, T. (2012). Keeping kids in schools: Restorative justice, punitive discipline, and the school to prison pipeline. *Journal of Law & Education, 41,* 281.

Harper, K., Ryberg, R., and Temkin, D. (2019). *Black students and students with disabilities remain more likely to receive out-of-school suspensions, despite overall declines.* https://www.childtrends.org/publications/black-students-disabilities-out-of-school-suspensions

Heitzeg, N. A. (2009). Education or incarceration: Zero tolerance policies and the school to prison pipeline. *Forum on Public Policy, 2009*(2), 1–21.

Hemphill, S. A., Plenty, S. M., Herrenkohl, T. I., Toumbourou, J. W., & Catalano, R. F. (2014). Student and school factors associated with school suspension: A multilevel analysis of students in Victoria, Australia and Washington State, United States. *Children and Youth Services Review, 36,* 187–194. doi:10.1016/j.childyouth.2013.11.022

Himmelstein, K. E. W., & Brückner, H. (2011). Criminal-justice and school sanctions against nonheterosexual youth: A national longitudinal study. *Pediatrics, 127*(1), 49–57.

Hirschfield, P. J. (2008). Preparing for prison? The criminalization of school discipline in the USA. *Theoretical Criminology, 12*(1), 79–101.

H.R. 6964—Juvenile Justice Reform Act of 2018. Congress.gov

Juvenile Justice and Delinquency Prevention Act of 1974, 34 U.S.C. 11101 et seq.

Kosciw, J. G., Greytak, E. A., Bartkiewicz, M. J., Boesen, M. J., & Palmer, N. A. (2012). *The 2011 National School Climate Survey: The experiences of lesbian, gay, bisexual, and transgender youth in our nation's schools.* GLSEN.

Losen, D., Hewitt, D., & Toldson, I. (2014). *Eliminating excessive and unfair exclusionary discipline in schools policy recommendations for reducing disparities.* https://www.njjn.org/uploads/digital-library/OSF_Discipline-Disparities_Disparity_Policy_3.18.14.pdf

McCarter, S. A. (2017). The school-to-prison pipeline: A primer for social workers. *Social Work, 62*(1), 53–61. https://www.ncbi.nlm.nih.gov/pubmed/28395045

McCarter, S. A., Chinn-Gary, E., Trosch, L. A., Jr., Toure, A., Alsaeedi, A., & Harrington, J., (2017). Bringing racial justice to the courtroom and community: Race Matters for Juvenile Justice and the Charlotte Model. *Washington and Lee Law Review, 73*(2), 641–686. https://scholarlycommons.law.wlu.edu/cgi/viewcontent.cgi?referer=&httpsredir=1&article=1071&context=wlulr-online

Monahan, K. C., VanDerhei, S., Bechtold, J., & Cauffman, E. (2014). From the school yard to the squad car: School discipline, truancy, and arrest. *Journal of Youth & Adolescence, 43*(1), 1110–1122.

Na, C., & Gottfredson, D. C. (2013). Police officers in schools: Effects on school crime and the processing of offending behaviors. *Justice Quarterly, 30*(4), 619–650.

National School Climate Council. (n.d.). *What is school climate and why is it important?* https://www.schoolclimate.org/school-climate

Palmer, N., & Greytak, E. (2017). LGBTQ student victimization and its relationship to school discipline and justice system involvement. *Criminal Justice Review, 42*(2), 163–187. https://doi.org/10.1177/0734016817704698

Palmer, N., Greytak, E., & Kosciw, J. (2016). *Educational exclusion: Drop out, push out, and the school-to-prison pipeline.* GLSEN. https://www.glsen.org/sites/default/files/2019-11/Educational_Exclusion_2013.pdf

Peguero, A. A., & Shekarkhar, Z. (2011). Latino/a student misbehavior and school punishment. *Hispanic Journal of Behavioral Sciences, 33*(1), 54–70. doi:10.1177/0739986310388021

Perry, B., & Morris, E. (2014). Suspending progress: Collateral consequences of exclusionary punishment in public schools. *American Sociological Review, 79*(6), 1067–1087.

Petteruti, A. (2011, November). *Education under arrest: The case against police in schools.* Justice Policy Institute. http://www.justicepolicy.org/uploads/justicepolicy/documents/educationunderarrest_fullreport.pdf

Poe-Yamagata, E., & Jones, M. A. (2000). And justice for some: Differential treatment of minority youth in the justice system. Youth Law Center. http://books.google.com/books?id=Nj1IAAAAYAAJ

Rausch, M. (2006, Fall). *Discipline, disability, and race: Disproportionality in Indiana schools.* Center for Evaluation and Education Policy.

Russell, S. T., Snapp, S., Munley, J., Licona, A., Burdge, H., & Hemingway, Z. (2013, September). *LGBTQ discipline disparities: Narratives, challenges, & solutions.* Paper presented at Discipline Disparities Collaborative meeting, Washington, DC.

School Justice Partnership: NC. (2019). *Toolkit: A step-by-step guide to implementing a school justice partnership.* https://www.nccourts.gov/documents/publications/school-justice-partnership-toolkit

Sherman, F., & Balck, A. (2015). Gender injustice: System-level juvenile justice reforms for girls. Portland, OR: The National Crittenton Foundation.

Shollenberger, T. L. (2015). Racial disparities in school suspension and subsequent outcomes: Evidence from the National Longitudinal Survey of Youth. In D. J. Losen (Ed.), *Closing the school discipline gap: Equitable remedies for excessive exclusion* (pp. 31–43). Teachers College Press.

Skiba, R. J., Michael, R. S., Nardo, A. C., & Peterson, R. L. (2002). The color of discipline: Race and gender disproportionality in school discipline. *Urban Review, 34,* 317–342.

Smoot, N. (2019). The Juvenile Justice Reform Act of 2018: Updating the federal approach to youth involved, and at-risk of becoming involved, in the juvenile justice system. *Juvenile and Family Court Journal, 70*(3), 45–60. doi:10.1111/jfcj.12145

Steinberg, M. P., Allensworth, E., & Johnson, D. W. (2011). *Student and teacher safety in Chicago public schools: The roles of community context and school social organization.* https://consortium.uchicago.edu/publications/student-and-teacher-safety-chicago-public-schools-roles-community-context-and-school

Sullivan, A. L., Klingbeil, D. A., & Van Norman, E. R. (2013). Beyond behavior: Multilevel analysis of the influence of sociodemographics and school characteristics on students' risk of suspension. *School Psychology Review, 42*(1), 99–114.

Teske, S. C., Huff, B., & Graves, C. (2012, March). Collaborative role of courts in promoting outcomes for students: Relationship between arrests, graduation rates and school safety. In *Keeping kids in school and out of courts: Report and recommendations.* New York City School–Justice Partnership Task Force. https://www.sog.unc.edu/sites/www.sog.unc.edu/files/articles/05-2-Teske_Collaborative%20Role%20of%20Courts_1.pdf

Theriot, M. T. (2009). School resource officers & criminalization of student behavior. *Journal of Criminal Justice, 37,* 280–287.

U.S. Commission on Civil Rights. (2019). *Beyond suspensions: Examining school discipline policies and connections to the school-to-prison pipeline for students of color with disabilities.* https://www.usccr.gov/pubs/2019/07-23-Beyond-Suspensions.pdf

U.S. Government Accountability Office. (2018, March). *K–12 education: Discipline disparities for Black students, boys, and students with disabilities* (GAO 18–258). https://files.eric.ed.gov/fulltext/ED590845.pdf

Verdugo, R. R., & Glenn, B. C. (2006, February). *Race and alternative schools.* Paper presented at the Alternatives to Expulsion, Suspension and Dropping Out of School Conference, Orlando, FL.

Testifying in Child Abuse Cases

Viola Vaughan-Eden

By failing to prepare, you are
preparing to fail.
—Benjamin
Franklin

Many adages exemplify what it means to testify in court, but it is important to remember, "Proper Prior Planning Prevents Poor Performance" (Tracy, 2007, p. 13). In addition to being prepared, forensic social workers must also be proactive and professional if they are to maintain the core values of the profession (Vaughan-Eden, 2008).

Forensic social workers stand in the gap between social work and the legal system. Many clients rely on them to help navigate the judicial system. The judicial system relies on them to educate the trier of fact—judge or jury—about the psychosocial dynamics of the case. The very nature of being a forensic social worker means understanding the unique intersectionality of social work and the law (Barker & Branson, 2000; see also Chapter 151, this volume). This chapter focuses on the practical aspects of testifying rarely taught in schools of social work or in on-the-job agency trainings (Robbins et al., 2015). Although the examples address child abuse, many of the techniques are applicable to most testimony as well as other professional disciplines within human services. To be an effective witness in court, testimony needs to be framed within the context of the legal process so the judge or jury can best utilize the information in decision-making (Myers, 2011). The goal of this chapter is to familiarize readers with the process and procedures of being an effective witness.

Visualize a circle—social workers are trained to assess the global or comprehensive aspects of clients and their lives. Now, visualize a square within that circle. The legal system is that square inside the circle. All the peripheral information outside the square, although valuable to social workers, is often irrelevant to court proceedings. The law has guidelines that must be followed, and these fall within "the square." It is important for forensic social workers to understand the process and procedures required to navigate the legal system—a system designed to be adversarial.

Can Lawyers and Social Workers Speak the Same Language in the Best Interests of Clients?

To adequately assist clients involved in the legal system, social workers must have a fundamental understanding of the law (Kay, 2017). It is first important to understand the objective

TABLE 153.1 Professional Differences

Social Workers	Lawyers
Welfare of the clients and helping them manage daily living within the larger ecosystem	Representing individual rights and helping clients negotiate the legal system
Trained to mediate and resolve differences	Trained to navigate an adversarial system and accentuate weaknesses
Take an open stance to engender trust	Singularly focused and distrustful of colleague's intentions
Engage clients through empathy, supportive by helping clients' problem-solve issues	Engage in a confrontational manner
Not afraid of being seen as vulnerable	Use litigation as a means of manipulating circumstances or as a threat to control situations
Understand that the human condition is greatly influenced by unforeseen biopsychosocial circumstances	Win or lose proposition
Cooperative	Competitive

Adapted from "Can Lawyers and Social Workers Speak the Same Language for the Best Interests of Child Welfare? A Case for Interdisciplinary Collaboration," by V. Vaughan-Eden (2013), unpublished master's thesis, Loyola University School of Law, Chicago, IL.

differences between social workers and lawyers. Social workers are educated to focus on clients' ability to learn, grow, and problem-solve from life experiences. Lawyers are educated to focus on clients' individual rights. Forensic social workers form an interprofessional collaboration between human service and legal systems (Maschi & Killian, 2009; Table 153.1).

Forensic social workers find the middle ground of translating competing interests into usable language for the court. Consider the analogy of British English, Australian English, and American English: All are variations of English, but similar words may have different meanings. So too must forensic social workers translate observed psychosocial dynamics into information understandable and useable by the trier of fact.

What Does the Court Expect of Expert Testimony?

Forensic social workers assist in all types of cases in a variety of different courts. However, child abuse issues are generally addressed in juvenile and domestic relations (JDR) district court, which hears all matters involving juveniles as well as the family, such as abuse, custody, support, and visitation. The circuit court (state court) also handles family matters, including divorce as well as cases appealed from JDR.

The court expects the forensic social worker to relay their opinion with integrity and competency—essentially, to tell the truth or offer facts based on observation, interviews, and evidence-based assessment. Sharing expertise with the court often means reviewing the research literature, collaborating with other professionals, as well as meeting with clients and integrating these findings to assist with recommendations.

How to Be Proactive

How to Best Assist the Trier of Fact

The Federal Rule of Evidence 702 defines an expert witness as someone who by knowledge, skill, experience, training, or education will assist the trier of fact (a judge or jury) to understand the evidence or to determine a fact in issue. Social workers should always be mindful to ask themselves, "Is what I am doing now, ethically and legally defensible in court later?" (Butters & Vaughan-Eden, 2011).

It is important to act as if every case, whether psychotherapy, child abuse, or any human service issue, has the potential to go to court; hence, being prepared in order to serve the best interest of clients. Some preparatory actions every social worker should be engaged in include keeping accurate records, staying current on the latest peer-refereed research literature, and attending conferences and workshops relevant to their scope of practice (e.g., for those working in child welfare, remaining current on child abuse and neglect best practices).

Documentation

In all cases, but especially forensic ones, detailed documentation is important (Munson, 2011). Forensic social workers must spell out not only everything they *do* in a case but also why they *did not do* something. For example, if some collateral sources were interviewed but not others, explain the rationale behind these choices. If the child was reluctant or their parent threatening, document objectively what was said. Remember that as a forensic practitioner, one needs to remain neutral, use bias-free language, and write clearly and concisely. Failure to accurately and competently document all aspects of the case can result in loss of evidence or faulty conclusions.

Child abuse and intimate partner violence cases in particular can elicit a great deal of emotion. Objectivity or neutrality means taking no position as to the outcome of the case in which one is documenting and potentially testifying, which may feel somewhat different from how social workers are trained. The guilt or innocence of any criminally accused is for the trier of fact, not the social worker. Objective experts understand that their expertise (observations, tests, and exams) are for the court in its pursuit of justice, not to promote the position of either side of the litigation.

Likewise, it is important to use proper nomenclature, but not excessive jargon, when documenting. If you are trained as a clinical social worker, you may be tempted to use clinical jargon. Remember this is not a clinical process but, rather, a legal one. Often, practitioners get comfortable using certain terminology, but forensic social work considers the court as its primary audience. Think about what it may mean for someone from another discipline outside of the human services to read the notes or report. Documentation needs to be clear, concise, and understandable to the judge and lawyers involved.

It is also crucial to understand the difference between attorney–client privilege and client–therapist privilege. Social workers, working with or under the auspices of attorneys, are not therapists and therefore have no client privilege. In general, all information a client shares in a forensic case can be disclosed to the court, and ethically, clients should be made aware of this at the start. However, legally there are certain materials that attorneys may share which may or may not be discoverable (i.e., made available) to opposing counselor. It is best to clarify prior to releasing information. Independent practitioners should use a forensic services agreement that explains these details, fees, and is signed prior to starting services (Babitsky & Mangraviti, 2008; Munson, 2011).

In order to be qualified as a forensic expert, attorneys will *voir dire* (conduct a preliminary examination) of a witness on their resume or curriculum vitae (CV). Therefore, an important aspect of "documentation" known to successful forensic social workers is having an updated CV that indicates every professional training and conference attended as well as any publications authored and presentations given, along with all relevant professional experience. In other words, the CV reflects all professional development that supports your *credibility* in court (Babitsky & Mangraviti, 2008). Ethically, it is improper to testify outside one's area of expertise (Munson, 2011).

What to Do If You Get a Subpoena?

First, know the rules of the jurisdiction, at least at the state level, in which you practice regarding (1) a witness subpoena, which is a summons for the social worker to appear in court as a "witness," and (2) a subpoena *duces tecum*, which is a summons for records (Saltzman et al., 2016). Regardless of the type, it is best to accept service, consult a supervisor, and seek immediate legal advice. Agencies generally have legal counsel for guidance, but note that their guidance is primarily in service to the agency, not necessarily the individual practitioner. Private practitioners may need to consult with an attorney colleague or private counsel.

For records, the opposing counsel may file a *motion to quash*, which means records are not to be released or are made available only under seal to the court. For witness subpoenas, only a judge can officially release (or dismiss) a witness. The attorney may decide a social worker called as witness is no longer needed, but be certain to confirm this in writing, or prepare an email or fax to confirm.

A major component of being proactive is knowing the question before the court, meaning the legal issue at hand. Working in an agency or private practice, reach out to the attorney who issued the summons but never discuss the case until you have written consent to release information. Verify who all the attorneys are on the case and which client each attorney represents. Remember, *each attorney represents only the interests of their individual client and is focused on using the information that will provide their client a favorable outcome.*

Clients may (accurately or inaccurately) lead their attorney to believe a practitioner has certain information relevant to the case. Depending on the legal issue, the practitioner may or may not be the best source of relevant information. For example, a child abuse victim may manifest symptoms similar to attention-deficit/hyperactivity disorder. Does the behavior indicate child abuse or does it indicate a clinical diagnosis? Social workers serving in clinical roles versus forensic roles have distinct purposes, so take caution in ensuring role clarity; the National Association of Social Workers Code of Ethics (2017) addresses matters relating to dual roles.

Preparing to Testify in Court

The next step for forensic witnesses is preparing for testimony. Having been proactive with the case from day one means the necessary documentation is ready for review and organized to answer the question related to the summons. The current research literature also should be reviewed in relation to the question. Forensic opinions in written reports and testimony should be supported by relevant research literature (Grady et al., 2018). It is important to stay current on the substantive knowledge by utilizing creditable sources.

Review

Forensic practitioners know not to rely on memory. A good forensic witness prepares for each case independently by thoroughly reviewing the case file and creating a timeline of their involvement to avoid confusion with regard to dates, tasks, and clients. They also thoroughly review and organize all records to avoid being misled by attorneys who may manipulate information to support their position. It is crucial to explain evidence relied on in determining hypotheses, conclusions, and opinions. For example, for a child abuse case, know how many times the child was seen, the dates, who was present, and who referred the child. Be able to explain why the child was seen, under what circumstances, and where. Know what other professionals saw the child and why their conclusions support or differ.

Research

Like most fields, the state-of-the-art in social work practice is ever-evolving. For example, knowledge about child sexual abuse, forensic interviewing, and delayed disclosure has vastly improved during the past 30 years, and hundreds of empirical articles are published yearly (Conte & Vaughan-Eden, 2017). One way to sort through what is credible in the field is to become a member of professional organizations such as the American Professional Society on the Abuse of Children (APSAC), the National Partnership to End Interpersonal Violence, or the National Organization of Forensic Social Work. Many well-established professional organizations publish some the leading peer-refereed journals in the field, such as *Child Maltreatment, Child Abuse & Neglect,* and the *Journal of Child Sexual Abuse.*

Written Reports

Often, forensic practitioners are required to produce written letters or reports for court or others. Sometimes, the most seasoned expert will rush to put something on paper, and not only does it reflect badly on them but also it may jeopardize the case (Babitsky & Mangraviti, 2008). Always use letterhead and properly format the document with headers as needed. In addition, proofread thoroughly for factual and grammatical errors (Weisman & Zornado, 2018). As part of drafting the report, list all sources of information, such as documents reviewed, collateral interviews, meeting dates, telephone conferences, and literature relied on. Concisely summarize the evidence that led to the content and conclusions (Karson & Nadkarni, 2013). Know what the legal requirements are for what can and cannot be included in written reports. In addition, federal cases require a list of fees charged and opinions with a degree of professional certainty.

Professionalism Matters

Forensic social workers must be professional in their demeanor, appearance, and testimony. The courts weigh the credibility of what

a witness says by how well they present themselves and their information. In court, "credibility," or the extent that what is offered can be relied on in the pursuit of fairness and justice, is paramount. And to this end, professionalism bolsters credibility.

All the preparation in the world can go out the window if one's testimony is not presented in a clear, informed, and coherent manner. Presenting a calm, objective, and knowledgeable demeanor is as important as wearing the proper professional attire (Johns, 2014). On the day of court, dress the part by wearing appropriate business attire, including comfortable but proper shoes, taking into account the weather and other factors. It is difficult to testify when physically uncomfortable. Also, visit the courthouse and, if possible, the actual courtroom in advance to get a sense of the environment.

Confirm with the attorney the day before that the case has not been continued (i.e., postponed) (Saltzman et al., 2016). Court is often continued at the last minute. On the day of testimony, arrive early to find parking, stand in line at ever-increasing security screening, and find the courtroom. Although these sound basic, they all contribute to your presentation as a social work professional.

Court-day professionalism means remaining calm, sincere, and courteous throughout the process. Jurors can use the same roads, parking lots, and lobbies that social workers do, so it is critical to be careful about interactions with or conversations near others. Realize that reputations and cases can be derailed by misconduct, so do not openly discuss the case with anyone in or around the courthouse because it risks contaminating the case or prejudicing other witnesses. If an attorney has questions, most courthouses are equipped with rooms for private discussion.

On the stand, be honest, humble, and use understandable language that assists the judge or jury in weighing relevant information. Unfortunately, jargon that no one understands is not helpful to the court or the client. Regardless of who is asking the questions, maintain an objective demeanor. Many times on cross-examination, witnesses can feel attacked, but it is not personal (Stern, 1997). Remain calm and recognize the attorney may be trying undermine the witness' credibility primarily for the purpose of strengthening or bolstering an opposing argument. Attorneys carry a professional responsibility to zealously advocate for their client, which can take the form of finding weaknesses in what you have to offer.

As a result, forensic witnesses endeavor to be the best witness possible by articulating their knowledge of the case. They are willing to change or expand their views as new evidence emerges, but they do so in an informed and logical way. They do not get defensive but, rather, respond in an honest and objective manner to best serve clients and educate the judge or jury. They demonstrate their expertise, much like forensic interviewing of suspected child abuse victims is a skill requiring specialized training (APSAC, 2012; Newlin et al., 2015).

Forensic witnesses maintain their professionalism by listening and answering the questions asked. Regardless of what they know, they follow the lead of the attorney who is asking the questions. When uncertain of the question being posed, they ask for clarification. If a question or comment is objected to by opposing counsel, they immediately stop talking to wait for the judge to overrule the objection (meaning continue answering) or sustain the objection (meaning do not answer and wait for the next question).

One way forensic witnesses improve their performance is to ask attorneys or other professionals present for feedback and/or read their transcript. The goal of the forensic professional is to present the information in an objective, bias-free manner allowing for the judicial process to operate. This may at times feel counterintuitive to how social workers "advocate" in favor of a particular point of view in other service contexts.

Recognize that testimony will likely evoke feelings on both sides of the case. Sometimes in the heat of the moment, parties or their relatives may become frustrated or blaming if the ruling is unfavorable to their side. Always be aware of your surroundings, and ask for an escort if you feel unsafe leaving the building.

Conclusion

Forensic social workers must be proactive, prepared, and professional if their testimony is to assist the trier of fact in making just decisions (Vaughan-Eden, 2008). Child protection cases, for example, often require continuous and diligent proactive work in anticipation of court involvement. In an effort to manage the complexity of a child maltreatment case, forensic social workers must presume every case has the potential for litigation.

Forensic social work requires a commitment to lifelong learning. Like all other areas of social work practice, that focused on child abuse is ever-evolving. Continuing education in the form of reading the professional literature and attending trainings and conferences is imperative. Being the best witness in service to the court and clients requires humility and an openness to constantly improve one's performance in and out of the courtroom. This chapter is not intended to provide legal advice.

References

American Professional Society on the Abuse of Children. (2012). APSAC practice guidelines: Forensic interviewing in cases of suspected child abuse. https://www.apsac.org/guidelines

Babitsky, S., & Mangraviti, J. J. (2008). *The biggest mistakes expert witnesses make and how to avoid them*. SEAK.

Barker, R. L., & Branson, D. M. (2000). *Forensic social work* (2nd ed.). Haworth.

Butters, R. P., & Vaughan-Eden, V. (2011). The ethics of practicing forensic social work. *Journal of Forensic Social Work, 1*(1), 61–72.

Conte, J. R., & Vaughan-Eden, V. (2017). Child sexual abuse. In J. B. Klika & J. R. Conte (Eds.), *The APSAC handbook on child maltreatment* (4th ed., pp. 95–110). Sage.

Grady, M. D., Levenson, J., & Prescott, D. S. (2018). Empirically informed forensic social work practice. In T. Maschi & G. Leibowitz (Eds.), *Forensic social work: Psychosocial and legal issues across diverse populations and settings* (pp. 307–320). Springer.

Johns, R. (2014). *Using the law in social work* (6th ed.). Sage.

Karson, M., & Nadkarni, L. (2013). *Principles of forensic report writing.* American Psychological Association.

Kay, J. (2017). Legal responses to child abuse and neglect. In J. B. Klika & J. R. Conte (Eds.), *The APSAC handbook on child maltreatment* (4th ed., pp. 182–199). Sage.

Maschi, T., & Killian, M. L. (2009). Defining collaborative forensic social work with diverse populations. In T. Maschi, C. Bradley, & K. Ward (Eds.), *Forensic social work: Psychosocial and legal issues in diverse practice settings* (pp. 3–9). Springer .

Munson, C. (2011). Forensic social work practice standards: Definition and specification. *Journal of Forensic Social Work, 1*(1), 37–60.

Myers, J. E. B. (2011). *Myers on evidence of interpersonal violence: Child maltreatment, intimate partner violence, rape, stalking, and elder abuse* (5th ed.). Wolters Kluwer.

National Association of Social Workers. (2017). Code of ethics. https://www.socialworkers.org/About/Ethics/Code-of-Ethics

Newlin, C., Steele, L. C., Chamberlin, A., Anderson, J., Kenniston, J., Russell, A., Stewart, H., & Vaughan-Eden, V. (2015, September). Child forensic interviewing: Best practices. *Office of Juvenile Justice and Delinquency Prevention (OJJDP) Bulletin.*

Robbins, S. P., Vaughan-Eden, V., & Maschi, T. M. (2015). It's not CSI: The importance of forensics for social work education. *Journal of Social Work Education, 51*(3), 421–424.

Saltzman, A., Furman, D. F., & Ohman, K. (2016). Law in social work practice (3rd ed.). Cengage.

Stern, P. (1997). *Preparing and presenting expert testimony in child abuse litigation: A guide for expert witnesses and attorneys.* Sage.

Tracy, B. (2007). *Eat that frog! 21 great ways to stop procrastinating and get more done in less time* (2nd ed.). Berrett-Koehler.

Vaughan-Eden, V. (2008, Summer/Fall). Be prepared, be proactive, and be professional: Key points to testifying in child abuse cases. *APSAC Advisor, 20,* 23–26.

Vaughan-Eden, V. (2013). Can lawyers and social workers speak the same language for the best interests of child welfare? A case for interdisciplinary collaboration. Unpublished master's thesis, Loyola University School of Law, Chicago, IL.

Weisman, D., & Zornado, J. (2018). *Professional writing for social work practice* (2nd ed.). Springer.

Assessing and Treating Adolescent Sex Offenders

Karen S. Knox

Professional opportunities for clinical and direct practice with adolescent sex offenders are provided in treatment programs in juvenile justice settings, community-based outpatient services, residential treatment, inpatient mental health, private practice, and incarceration facilities. A range of services and resources for adolescent sex offenders and their families should be available to meet the various levels of treatment and supervision. Treatment protocol and standards of best practice for professionals have been established through empirical research studies (McCuish & Lussier, 2017) and professional organizations, such as the Association for the Treatment of Sexual Abuse and the National Adolescent Perpetration Network. These efforts have contributed to the knowledge base and development of treatment models and interventions in this field of practice. Specialized education and training are necessary to work ethically and effectively with adolescent sex offenders, and professional licensing boards now require additional licensure/certification and continuing education and training for clinical professionals working with this client population.

Incidence reports and statistics indicate that juvenile sex offenders aged 18 years or younger commit one-fifth of all sexual assaults (U.S. Department of Justice, 2018). Adolescent sex offenders are typically between the ages of 13 and 17 years, mostly Caucasian and male, with female perpetrators accounting for less than 10% of reported cases (Miccio-Fonseca, 2016). Research studies indicate that adolescent sex offenders have academic challenges and higher placement rates of special education (Tan et al., 2018). Research also shows high prevalence rates for a mental health diagnosis and having a history of child physical abuse, emotional abuse, physical neglect, and child sexual abuse (Barra et al., 2017; Hart-Kerkhoffs et al., 2015).

Currently, there are two main perspectives to explain adolescent sex offending. First, the *generalist perspective* suggests that their sexual offenses are only a part of their other antisocial and criminal behaviors and that this type of adolescent sex offender is similar to other non-sexual adolescent offenders sharing common risk factors such as antisocial attitudes and behaviors, association with delinquent peers, and substance use (Fanniff et al., 2017). Second, the *specialist perspective* suggests that different factors explain adolescent sexual offending, such as trauma histories, early exposure to sexual behavior in the home or on the internet, and more atypical sexual interests and sexual deviancy arousal that require different assessment instruments and treatment approaches (Pullman & Seto, 2012).

Although research studies have identified numerous risk factors for adolescent sex offenders, protective factors have not received as much focus and are important to treatment success. Protective factors include supportive and healthy families, appropriate parental supervision, prosocial skills, extracurricular activities, appropriate peer relationships, school connectedness, academic success, and available community support and resources. School-based protective factors that contribute to treatment success are having a school representative in a multidisciplinary/multisystemic team approach, participating in extracurricular activities, having an Individualized Educational Plan, and no disruption or changes in schools (Yoder et al., 2018).

Case Examples

John is 16 years old and in the 10th grade. He lives in a low-income neighborhood with his mother and three other younger siblings. His mother is a single parent who works full-time as an administrative assistant. She reports having problems with John following the rules at home, fighting with his siblings, and hanging out with negative peers. He is currently facing a sexual assault charge for fondling a 17-year-old female classmate on the school bus. John has had incidents of bullying and fights at school. He is truant frequently and has a learning disability that has resulted in academic delays and suspensions. This is John's first time appearing in juvenile court. His mother contacted the Public Defenders' Office for representation,

and he has been placed on probation and community supervision for 2 years.

George just turned age 13 years and lives with his parents and younger brother in an upper middle-class neighborhood. Both of his parents work full-time. They report that George has never been in trouble before. They describe him as an excellent student, but he does not have many friends his age. They describe him as immature and a loner who spends a lot of time on his computer. One of his brother's friends disclosed to his parents that George had fondled him and showed him some "nasty pictures" on the computer. The investigation revealed that George had also shown his brother and another friend some pornography and had exposed himself to them. George's parents hired an attorney who was able to plea bargain for a sentence of probation and community supervision for 2 years.

Whereas George's parents are able to adjust their work schedules and housing arrangements to accommodate his probation supervision guidelines, John's mother has limited resources for supervision after school, so John has been placed on intensive supervision and mandated to perform community restitution after school to meet his supervision requirements. John has also been sent to the alternative learning school because he can no longer have any contact with his victim. George and his parents have agreed to a strict supervision and safety plan to allow George to continue to live at home with his brother and attend the same school because his other victims attend a different school. Neither youth can have any unsupervised contact with youth younger than they are as a condition of their probation, including George's brother.

John and George both evidence numerous risk factors associated with school, social skills, and peer and family relationships. Although George has more protective factors, such as a two-parent home with financial stability, academic success with no change of schools, and appropriate parental supervision, his early exposure to pornography and numerous sexual offending incidents and victims indicate serious concerns from the *specialist perspective*. John has fewer protective factors with a single-parent home, school problems and disruption, anger management issues, and negative peers that reflect concerns from the *generalist perspective*. The case illustrations also show how family, legal, and financial resources can impact differentially in the juvenile justice system. George's sexual offenses indicate more sexual deviancy than John's offense and should require a higher level of supervision and treatment. Yet George has retained the privileges of living at home and staying at the same school due to his protective factors, whereas John may experience more risk due to changing schools and lack of parental supervision.

Continuum of Treatment

Working with adolescent sex offenders requires the use of a multisystemic approach because professionals from different disciplines and settings are involved in a continuum of treatment for these clients and their families. This continuum usually begins with an outcry or report of sexual abuse by the victim, which then involves investigations by child protective services and/or law enforcement professionals. If charges are filed, the case proceeds through the juvenile court system with prosecution, adjudication, and, if found guilty, sentencing of probation or incarceration. The following flowchart shows the typical continuum of treatment:

Outcry, report, and investigation
(child protective services and/or law enforcement)
↓
Juvenile court
(Prosecution and adjudication) If found guilty: probation or incarceration, registration
↓

Intake and assessment
(Risk and clinical)
↓
Treatment
(Outpatient, inpatient, residential treatment)
↓
Reintegration or re-entry
(Family reunification, substitute care, or independent living)
↓
Relapse prevention and registration

(Termination of treatment and mandated community notification)

Risk Assessment

Sex offender registration and community notification requirements impact risk assessments for adolescent sex offenders on probation or upon release from a penal institution because an assigned risk level will be indicated on their sex offender registration form. This type of risk assessment is very different from a clinical risk assessment, and it is usually done by a probation or parole officer. It addresses legal risk factors such as seriousness of the sex offense, offender's age at first referral, and prior adjudications or referrals for sex offenses or other felonies. Recommendations associated with the different levels of care and supervision are assigned using the following guidelines:

- *Low–medium risk*: Youth placed on probation at home/community placement usually for 12–24 months with intensive supervision and outpatient treatment.
- *Medium–high risk*: Youth placed on probation and placed in a residential treatment or inpatient facility, typically in a secure unit depending on level of psychopathy and other mental health disorders. If successful, the youth may return home/community and receive additional outpatient treatment; if not

successful, the youth may be remanded to a more secure setting or correctional institution.

- *High risk*: Youth placed in a correctional institution that may have sex offender programs; however, factors such as amenability to treatment, limited services, and waiting lists impact availability. Many youth may not receive sex offender treatment until released on parole and then referred to outpatient services.

When applying the criteria for the legal risk assessment, John would be assessed as low–medium risk because this was his first offense with a same-age peer. George should be considered a medium–high risk due to multiple offenses on victims younger than him and his use of pornography. However, both youth received the same outcomes in court for probation at home with outpatient treatment and intensive supervision. This is where their similarities end, however, because their clinical assessments will be very different with respect to clinical issues and family/social histories.

Clinical assessments are often court-ordered to provide recommendations on the type and level of treatment required for the adolescent sex offender. Clinical assessments should not be used as a determination of guilt or innocence, and they should be made after adjudication but before sentencing to help determine an appropriate treatment plan. This type of assessment can also be conducted as part of the youth's treatment plan if placed in a therapeutic or correctional setting. Clinical assessments assist in identifying the youth's amenability to treatment, the type and level of care, the level of risk for recidivism, developmental issues, risk and protective factors, and family and community resources to meet the client's needs. Clinical assessments also include content on the offender's family history, relationship to the victim, age and number of victims, sexual and trauma histories, environmental risks, and psychosocial problems.

Due to the level of expertise and experience required with this client population, it is recommended that a licensed sex offender therapist conduct clinical assessments. The clinical assessment should be as comprehensive as possible by addressing other treatment issues or problems as well as the sexual offending behaviors. The assessment process typically includes a clinical interview(s) with the adolescent and family members, collateral contacts, social services, law enforcement, or mental health providers in the client's history, in addition to school records and standardized instruments that measure treatment issues and psychopathy. Current risk assessment instruments that are validated and widely used include the following:

- Estimate of Risk of Adolescent Sexual Offense Recidivism (ERASOR) (Worling & Curwen, 2001)
- Juvenile Sex Offender Assessment Protocol–II (J-SOAP-II) (Prentky & Righthand, 2003)
- Juvenile Sexual Offense Recidivism Risk Assessment Tool–II (JSORRAT-II) (Epperson et al., 2009)
- Massachusetts Youth Screening Instrument–2 (MAYSI-2) (Grisso & Barnum, 2006)
- Multiplex Empirically Guided Inventory of Ecological Aggregates for Assessing Sexually Abusive Adolescents and Children (MEGA; ages 19 years or younger) (Miccio-Fonseca, 2010)

Special Clinical Issues

Special clinical issues that are common to adolescent sex offenders include low self-esteem, poor impulse control and emotional regulation, minimal social and communication skills, poor problem-solving and decision-making skills, poor peer relationships, attention problems, disruptive behavior problems, lack of appropriate coping skills, poor emotional regulation, and body disapproval and eating disorders

(Faniff et al., 2017). Clinical risk assessments and treatment plans also address issues such as anger management problems, learning and developmental disabilities, trauma history, substance abuse, depression, suicide, anxiety, and other mental health and neuropsychological problems.

Specific content on sexual attitudes and history are included in the assessment and intervention plan, along with the level of acknowledgment or denial of responsibility for the sexually offending behaviors. It is typical for these youth and families to evidence denial or minimization of their sexually offending behaviors and thoughts, even after adjudication of the legal case. Feelings of shame, guilt, and embarrassment contribute to minimizing and denial. Any empathic responses about their victim(s) are assessed as strengths because deficits in empathy and appropriate affect are a major focus of treatment. Cognitive distortions (thinking errors) associated with the sexual offense contribute to the youth's level of denial or minimization. Other sexually inappropriate behaviors, fantasies, arousal patterns, and sexual materials, such as pornography and the internet, are included in the sexual history section of a clinical assessment.

Case Examples

John came into the office for his clinical assessment interview with a wary attitude and was extremely guarded in his responses to the social worker. Copies of the incident report from law enforcement, the probation intake form, and his school records were included in his case files, and the social worker had already identified several areas of concern, including his school problems, negative peers, and anger management issues. During the interview, John did acknowledge these issues "get him into trouble," but he had little insight into how to change his behaviors. His primary motivation for change is his probationary status, and he

appears to be intelligent and capable of making positive changes. He does take responsibility for the sexual offense but minimizes the incident as "just playing around," and he denies any other history of inappropriate sexual behaviors. When discussing his family, he states, "I never knew my father." He says his mother does her best but is stressed out and angry with him.

George seemed rather timid and made little eye contact when he first entered the counseling office. His case records indicate he is a loner at school, and he states that his peers think he is "weird and nobody really likes me." George does well academically and has no other school or behavior problems. The standardized assessment instruments indicate that he scored in the clinical range on the sexual offending scales, as well as for anxiety, low self-esteem, and immaturity. George discloses that an elderly male neighbor had showed him how to masturbate when he was 5 years old, and the sexual abuse continued for several years before the neighbor died. George has never told anyone about this because he is scared and ashamed about getting into trouble. He says his family does not really have any problems, but he thinks his parents have always favored his brother over him.

Treatment Models

The principal treatment model used in sex offender treatment is cognitive–behavioral therapy (CBT), with group therapy being the primary modality. CBT has been found to significantly reduce sexual recidivism, and research studies provide evidence to its effectiveness in addressing cognitive distortions and atypical sexual arousal and behaviors (Pullman & Seto, 2012). Group treatment is conducive to learning social skills, experiencing appropriate peer interaction, and addressing denial and minimization because many adolescents find it easier to disclose and admit responsibility with others who share similar histories.

Using a cognitive–behavioral and strengths-based approach, the good lives model is a theoretical framework for offender rehabilitation that builds on client capabilities to promote prosocial skills and personal functioning, and recent evaluation research studies indicate positive outcomes for both generalist offenders and sexual offenders (Willis et al., 2013). The model addresses limitations of the traditional risk management approach that emphasizes problems and deficits with restriction of activities as the primary means to avoid reoffending. The good lives model promotes social work values of client respect and dignity, so negative labeling and hostile confrontation are inconsistent with this collaborative approach.

Multisystemic therapy is another model that has been empirically demonstrated to reduce recidivism and out-of-home placements for both generalist offenders and adolescent sex offender. This model is family-based and targets multiple domains, including family functioning, social skills, problem-solving, coping skills, academic problems, negative peers, and substance abuse (Pullman & Seto, 2012). This approach is critical because most adolescent sex offenders evidence problems across multiple areas in their social environment; thus, coordination and collaboration among providers are critical to treatment success.

Individual and adjunct therapies are recommended for other issues, such as trauma histories, psychological disorders, substance abuse, and anger management. The length of treatment varies depending on many factors; however, most programs range from 12 to 24 months. Youth may remain on probation/parole after completing treatment, which ensures supervision needs, relapse prevention, and follow-up services. Relapse prevention and family reunification should be completed before termination from the treatment program and probation to endure a smooth transition and supervision needs.

Treatment Goals and Plans

Treatment goals focus on reducing antisocial behaviors and recidivism and development of prosocial skills. The treatment plan should include safety rules, supervision guidelines, and specific interventions, specifying the time frame and consequences of not following through with the program. All parties should sign a written treatment contract and intervention plan. It is important to work as a team with other professionals on the case and to differentiate the roles and responsibilities of those involved in the treatment plan. Specific cognitive–behavioral interventions include positive and negative reinforcement, confrontation, relaxation skills, assertiveness training, and self-instructional training. Expressive arts techniques are also utilized, such as art therapy, psychodrama, family sculpting, role-play, bibliotherapy, and adventure-based interventions. Adolescent sex offender programs may vary across settings, length, and intensity of therapy, but most follow a standard protocol that includes the following components:

1. Introduction to group and the treatment process
   • Group rules and supervision guidelines; sexual offense history or statement

2. Sexual abuse offense and cycle
   • *Acknowledgment of responsibility*: Youth who continue to deny or minimize responsibility for any sexually offending behaviors may be required to take a polygraph examination to establish specific areas of deception, and if it is failed, consequences can include termination from treatment and possible legal sanctions.
   • *Sexual offense cycle*: Cognitive distortions (thinking errors), sexual fantasies, arousal patterns, and sex offending behaviors are important issues to confront, with the goals of reducing recidivism and

learning appropriate sexual attitudes and behaviors.

- *Empathy*: Most adolescent sex offenders have a deficit in this area, even those who have prior physical or sexual victimization. Developing empathy for their victims and understanding the consequence of their sexual offenses are critical.

3. Interpersonal and coping skills development
   - *Clarification of values*: Adolescent sex offenders either have a deficit or espouse deviant/delinquent values that may impact on recidivism.
   - *Self-esteem*: These adolescents experience failures in many aspects of their lives and relationships, so a strengths-based approach is recommended.
   - *Social skills*: The group environment is especially helpful with youth learning and group facilitators modeling appropriate interactions and communication.
   - *Behavior problems*: Anger management, impulse control, and conflict resolution are addressed by developing appropriate problem-solving and coping skills.

4. Relapse prevention/reunification and termination
   - Adolescent sex offenders develop a relapse prevention plan with strategies to use in at-risk situations. Those who will be reuniting or having approved contact with their families/victims must participate in family therapy and develop a safety plan.

Case Examples

John's intervention plan recommended attending adolescent sex offender group therapy once a week and participation in a diversion program through juvenile court for his anger management and bullying problems. Currently, he is doing well in therapy and following his probation and supervision guidelines. He was sent to the alternative learning center, where he is doing better academically and with his attendance.

George's treatment plan also recommended attending sex offender group therapy weekly and individual therapy weekly for his trauma history and psychological issues. His family initially wanted him to remain at home, but after participating in a parent support group and family therapy sessions, they decided that his level of care and supervision was too much for them, and he is currently placed at a residential treatment facility in an adolescent sex offender program. When George is released, the final phase of treatment will involve family reunification services. Clinical issues include earning trust, re-establishing family rules and roles, adjusting to a different level of supervision, reintegrating back into school and the social environment, and maintaining positive changes. Family therapy is recommended for support during this transition period, which can be a high-risk period of time for recidivism.

Helpful Resources

Association for the Treatment of Sexual Abuse: http://www.atsa.com
Center for Sex Offender Management: https://www.nsvrc.org/organizations/130
International Association for the Treatment of Sexual Offenders: http://www.iatso.org
The Good Lives Model: http://www.goodlivesmodel.com
The Safer Society Press: http://safersocietypress.org

References

Barra, S., Bessler, C., Landolt, M. A., & Aebi, M. (2017). Type and timing of maltreatment influence criminal persistence in sexually abusive adolescents. *Law and Human Behavior, 41*(6), 556–566. http://dx.doi.org/10.1037/lhb0000255

Epperson, D. L., Ralston, C. A., Fowers, D., & DeWitt, J. (2009). Scoring guidelines for the Juvenile Sex Offense Recidivism Risk Assessment Tool–II (JSORRAT-II). http://www.watsa.org/Resources/Documents/2.Epperson JSORRAT-II Scoring Guide.pdf

Fanniff, A. M., Schubert, C. A., Mulvey, E. P., Iselin, A. R., & Piquero, A. R. (2017). Risk and outcomes: Are adolescents charged with sex offenses different from other adolescent offenders? *Journal of Youth and Adolescence, 46*, 1394–1423. doi:10.1007/s10964-016-0536-9

Grisso, T., & Barnum, R. (2006). *Massachusetts Youth Screening Instrument, Version 2: User's manual and technical report*. Professional Resource Press.

Hart-Kerkhoffs, L. A., Boonmann, C., Doreleijers, T. A. H., Jansen, L. M. C., van Wijk, A. P., & Vermeiren, R. R. J. M. (2015). Mental disorders and criminal re-referral in juveniles who sexually offend. *Child and Adolescent Psychiatry and Mental Health, 9*(4), 1–7. doi:10.1186/s13034-015-0035-x

McCuish, E. C., & Lussier, P. (2017). Unfinished stories: From juvenile sex offenders to juvenile sex offending through a developmental life course perspective. *Aggression and Violent Behavior, 37*, 71–82. http://dx.doi.org/10.1016/j.avb.2017.09.004

Miccio-Fonseca, L. C. (2010). MEGA: An ecological risk assessment tool of risk and protective factors for assessing sexually abusive children and adolescents. *Journal of Aggression, Maltreatment & Trauma, 19*, 734–756. doi:10.1080/10926771.2010.515542

Miccio-Fonseca, L. C. (2016). MEGA cross-validation findings on sexually abusive females: Implications for risk assessment and clinical practice. *Journal of Family Violence, 31*, 903–911. doi:10.1007/s10896-016-9845-8

Pullman, L., & Seto, M. C. (2012). Assessment and treatment of adolescent sexual offenders: Implications of recent research on generalist versus specialist explanations. *Child Abuse and Neglect, 36*, 203–209. doi:10.1016/j.chiabu.2011.11.003

Prentky, R., & Righthand, S. (2003). *Juvenile Sex Offender Assessment Protocol–II (J-SOAP-II) manual* (NCJ 202316). https://www.ojp.gov/pdffiles1/ojjdp/202316.pdf

Tan, K., Brown, A., & Leibowitz, G. S. (2018). School, social-communicative, and academic challenges among delinquent and juvenile offenders. *Child and Adolescent Social Work Journal, 18*, 577–585. https://doi.org/10.1007/s10560-018-0549-1

U.S. Department of Justice, Federal Bureau of Investigation, Criminal Justice Information Services Division. (2018). *National incident-based reporting system data tables*. https://ucr.fbi.gov/nibrs/2018/tables/data-tables

Willis, G. M., Yates, P. M., Gannon, T. A., & Ward, T. (2013). How to integrate the good lives model into treatment programs for sexual offending: An introduction and overview. *Sexual Abuse, 25*, 123–142.

Worling, J. R., & Curwen, T. (2001). *Estimate of Risk of Adolescent Sexual Offense Recidivism, version 2.0*. Ministry of Community and Social Services.

Yoder, J. R., Hansen, J, Ruch, D., & Hodge, A. (2016). Effects of school-based risk and protective factors on treatment success among youth adjudicated of a sexual crime. *Journal of Child Sexual Abuse, 25*(3), 310–325. http://dx.doi.org/10.1080/10538712.2016.1137668

Intimate Partner Violence

Marcela Sarmiento Mellinger

Intimate partner violence (IPV) has been defined as a pattern of coercive behaviors intended to gain control over a partner in an intimate relationship; it has also been labeled a global epidemic. Worldwide estimates show that approximately 30% of women aged 15 years or older experience IPV at some point in their lifetime (Devries et al., 2013). Because of its prevalence, social workers often encounter individuals impacted by IPV regardless of the setting in which they work and often in the field of forensic social work. Basic skills to address the issues experienced by victims, survivors, and those who commit the abuse are needed. With this in mind, this chapter provides an overview of IPV from feminist and intersectionality perspectives.

Although this chapter started with a definition of IPV, it is important to note that defining IPV has been riddled with controversy. Some argue that any type of violence in a relationship constitutes IPV, whereas others differentiate between violence that is coercive and violence that happens situationally (Johnson, 2010). Others argue that there is no difference between violence perpetrated by women toward men and violence perpetrated by men against women (Dutton, 2012). Because this book's audience is social workers, and this chapter is written from a feminist lens, note that the author's perspective is that gender matters. As Johnson (2010) states, "The feminists are right. Gender is central to the analysis of IPV and coercive controlling violence that most people associate with the term 'domestic violence' is indeed perpetrated primarily by men against female partners" (p. 217).

Definitions of violence are socially constructed, so we must talk about context; how broadly or narrowly we define these terms will impact how we view the issue. The Centers for Disease Control and Prevention (CDC) defines IPV as a pattern of coercive behaviors that are used to control an intimate partner; these behaviors include acts of "physical violence, sexual violence, stalking, or psychological harm" (Breiding et al., 2015, p. 11), and they occur in the context of an intimate relationship. When defining an intimate relationship, we are talking about a personal relationship in which all or some of the following aspects are (or were) present: "emotional connectedness, regular contact, ongoing physical and sexual behavior, identity as a couple, and familiarity and knowledge of each other's lives" (Breiding et al., 2015, p. 11). Keep in mind that these behaviors can occur in opposite or same-sex relationships and among spouses, cohabiting partners, boyfriend or girlfriend, dating partners, sexual partners, or within other arrangements that fit the components of an intimate relationship.

Scope of the Problem

The lack of agreement on what constitutes abuse makes it difficult to have a clear picture of the size of the problem. We seem to agree on the fact that abuse is present when behavior among intimate partners moves from conflict to an intentional desire to cause harm, but even that is difficult to measure. Despite the difficulty, there are statistics that can help us gain a picture of the scope of IPV. The CDC finds that in the United States, both men and women experience IPV, but women experience it at a higher rate (Smith et al., 2018). For example, 1 in 4 women and 1 in 10 men experience "contact sexual violence, physical violence, and/or stalking" and state that the violence impacts their lives (Smith et al., 2018, p. 8). The impact refers to the consequences experienced as a result of the violence—injuries, having safety concerns, post-traumatic stress disorder, days lost at work and/or school, needing medical attention, interactions with law enforcement, needing housing, and needing victim services (Smith et al., 2018). The CDC also finds that 21.4% of women and 14.9% of men experience severe physical violence, 18.3% of women and 8.25% of men experience sexual abuse, and 36.4% of women and 34.2% of men experience psychological abuse (Smith et al., 2018).

Types of Abuse

With regard to IPV, there are four types of abuse: physical violence, emotional or psychological violence, sexual violence, and stalking. However, these types of abuse often happen concurrently and are interrelated. The type of abuse may also impact contact with law enforcement. Here, they are defined individually to highlight what you may see when working with victims–survivors or perpetrators of abuse. The definitions presented here, in addition to the examples of the behaviors outlined, are fairly consistent among national organizations, state coalitions, and local programs.

Physical abuse involves intentionally hurting or trying to hurt a partner by using physical force. This includes kicking, punching, slapping, hitting, choking, pulling someone's hair, pinching, forcefully grabbing the person or their clothing, using a weapon, throwing an object at the person, and any other physical action that hurts an individual.

Emotional abuse (also referred to as psychological abuse or psychological aggression) involves any verbal or nonverbal communication intended to intimidate, control, or harm the other person. Because of the intensity and consistency of the abuse, victims–survivors often believe these false statements. This type of abuse involves actions such as insults, putting the person down, gaslighting, consistent humiliation, intimidation, threats, isolation, name-calling, blaming, and using the children as a way to belittle the mother (e.g., "You are a bad mother," "I will take away the children," and "The courts will never give you custody"). It also involves economic control, where the victim is left with little to no control over finances or access to money. This type of abuse is pervasive, and it impacts the way a person sees, interprets, and evaluates the relationship as well as reality in general.

Sexual abuse involves any action that forces or attempts to force a partner to be involved in a sex act or in sexual touching. It also includes nonphysical sexual actions to which the person has not consented, such as sexting and sexual coercion. Smith and colleagues (2018) include "rape, being made to penetrate someone else, and unwanted sexual contact" (p. 7) in their definition. Reproductive coercion is also sexual abuse because the acts of the abuser directly impact the sexual health of the victim. Reproductive coercion includes refusing to use or not allowing a partner to use contraceptives (e.g., condoms and birth control pills), pressuring or coercing a partner to conceive, controlling how a partner wants to handle pregnancy, forced sterilization, tampering with or sabotaging the agreed upon methods of contraception, or interfering with health care (Moore et al., 2010).

Stalking is a "pattern of harassing or threatening tactics used by a perpetrator that is both unwanted and causes fear or safety concerns in the victim" (Smith et al., 2018, p. 7). This includes repeated unwanted phone calls, text or voice messages, or emails; contacting the person through social media; sending unwanted cards, flowers, or other presents; following someone in person or through electronic devices such as a GPS, spying, or watching from a distance; going to the person's home, workplace, school, or anywhere the appearance is unwanted; leaving items that can be seen as threatening somewhere the victim–survivor can see them; or entering the person's home or car with the intent to scare the victim (Smith et al., 2018).

Intimate Partner Violence from a Feminist Perspective and a Trauma-Informed Care Approach

From a feminist perspective, gender and power are central to how we view, analyze, and develop services. Johnson (2010) asserts that the violence and control experienced by most individuals receiving services (e.g., shelters, hospitals, criminal justice system, and victim advocacy services) are mainly perpetrated by men and inflicted on their female partners.

Although this is the accepted feminist view and data support this perspective, it is necessary to acknowledge that IPV is also inflicted by women toward their male partners, and it also occurs among same-sex couples. In addition, IPV includes not just violence but also control over a partner, and a feminist perspective attributes this to the power some groups have over others.

Early feminists addressed the issue from a gender and power perspective; they saw a patriarchal system in which the woman was viewed as weak and the man as the "king of his castle" who had all the power in the relationship as the motive for IPV. Because discrimination and oppression of women are alive and well, we have not abandoned this view; however, the feminist perspective has evolved, and we have moved toward a more inclusive perspective that views multiple factors and identities as players in overall oppression and in IPV. We have moved from a feminist-only perspective to a feminist and intersectional perspective.

A feminist intersectionality perspective addresses IPV by exploring structural inequalities while at the same time exploring how social identities that have been historically oppressed and disadvantaged (e.g., gender, race, class, sexual orientation, and disabilities) intersect with IPV (Kelly, 2011). It also explores how those who commit the abuse interact with the criminal justice system. This allows us to examine the violence, but also the structures that oppress those impacted by violence. In addition, it recognizes the multiple factors that play a role in IPV. For example, research has shown that poor family relationships, witnessing IPV as a child, positive attitudes toward violence, substance abuse, low socioeconomic status, and distorted views about relationships are risk factors for abusing one's partner (Capaldi et al., 2012; Ruddle et al., 2017).

Recognizing these factors allows us to explore additional interventions that can assist victims–survivors, as well as perpetrators. As we develop services to assist this population, doing so from a trauma-informed care perspective is important. This means that services need to be created and carried out in a way that they minimize re-traumatization and can help individuals move toward recovery. Trauma-informed care suggests that all staff within an organization are trained to understand trauma and its consequences, so all interactions are guided by these principles (Anyikwa, 2016). These interactions start with staff who answer the phones or greet clients; therefore, training them is just as crucial as it is for those who work directly with clients.

The Substance Abuse and Mental Health Services Administration (SAMHSA, 2014) has a guide that assists organizations in developing trauma-informed environments. The authors emphasize that organizations should use their principles to guide their practice and not view them as a set of procedures that must be followed (SAMHSA, 2014). True trauma-informed care recognizes that people experience trauma differently and therefore setting rules and procedures is counterproductive. This guide is available free of charge on the SAMHSA website.

Lethality and Escalation of Violence

Homicide is the most extreme consequence of IPV. Considering homicides in general, men are most often the victims; however, when homicides are the result of IPV, women are often the victims (Stockl et al., 2013). Prior violence in the relationship is perhaps the largest predictor of homicides (Matias et al., 2020; Spencer & Stith, 2020); other risk factors include access to a gun, mental illness, illicit drug use, previous threats of harm or using a weapon while threatening the victim, rape, and stalking (Spencer & Stith, 2020). Risk factors for victims–survivors include pregnancy, having a child with a different partner, age (younger women are at higher risk), being a member of an ethnic minority, substance misuse, lower levels of education, and being separated from the abuser (Matias et al., 2020; Spencer & Stith, 2020). Clearly, when violence escalates to this level, forensic social workers' involvement becomes imperative.

Tools are available to assess the lethality risk that victims–survivors face; in other words, How dangerous is the relationship? The Danger Assessment Tool, developed by Jacquelyn Campbell, is one of the most frequently used scales to assess lethality. The tool is accessible for free at https://www.dangerassessment.org. Although victims–survivors and practitioners can take and score the scale, Campbell recommends that a trained, certified professional score and discuss the results with the victim. Online and in-person trainings are offered for a fee. The tool has been translated to various languages and updated to include tools for victims–survivors from ethnic minorities and for those in same-sex relationships.

Safety Planning

A safety plan is a personalized and practical guide with steps a victim can take to stay safe or safer. It should include ways to be safe in multiple settings; for example, victims–survivors may still be living with the abuser, preparing to leave, or have left the abuser, so they need a safety plan that is specific to these situations. A general overview of safety planning is provided here, but most IPV national organizations (e.g., the National Domestic Violence Hotline and the National Resource Center on Domestic Violence), some state coalitions, and local programs provide detailed safety plans depending on the situation. The guidelines provided by these organizations should be used to create a personalized plan because no situation is the same.

A safety plan can include many aspects—who to talk to, how to tell family and friends, how to contact law enforcement, where to go in case of an emergency, what documents to prepare, and much more. It can also walk the person through what to do in different scenarios. Although creating a plan may seem overwhelming and some things may seem obvious, it is beneficial to remind the person that when in crisis, people do not function the same way as they do when they are calm. A phone number, a Social Security number, or even an address with which a person is familiar may not come to mind when they are in the midst of a dangerous situation. In addition, creating a safety plan with a family member or a friend is also a good idea. Victims–survivors may not be able to or may not be ready to leave, but family and friends aware of the situation can help by being informed about what to do if the person reaches out.

Practitioners should familiarize themselves with safety plans for those still living with the abuser, those who have children, those who are planning to leave, those who suffer from a disability, those who have pets, those in the process of leaving, those who are elderly, and those who have already left. The 2020 COVID-19 pandemic has highlighted the need for plans that include being "safer" at home while sheltered in place with the abuser. Although living with the abuser or choosing to stay for a variety of reasons is not uncommon, the stay-at-home orders have made this reality more visible to the public. They have also limited the ability to leave; therefore, including "being safe or 'safer' at home" suggestions in the safety plan is important. Keep in mind that in addition to public health emergencies, there are other situations in which the ability to leave may be limited, including natural disasters, government curfews, protests, social unrests, or other government-impose orders. Table 155.1 provides general suggestions for practitioners to help victims–survivors when putting a plan together.

Overview of Current Services Available to Victims, Survivors, and Perpetrators

The umbrella of services and resources available to those who experience IPV is wide-ranging. Although resources are still not enough and not always accessible to all, most communities have local programs that provide specific services for victims and survivors. These services include safe housing (emergency shelters, transitional housing, and temporary hotel stays), legal services, counseling, support groups, children programs, individual advocacy, accompaniment to court appointments, and referrals to other services. Most of these services were originally developed for women; however, many have adapted to the changing demographics and dynamics of IPV. There are now emergency shelters with beds available for male victims–survivors, as well as appropriate assistance for individuals in same-sex relationships.

The best resource for practitioners to find adequate services is the local IPV program. However, if services are needed in other areas of the state or the country, the best place to start is the National Domestic Violence Hotline (1-800-799-7233). This organization has information on programs throughout the United States and is able to make referrals. Another important resource is the state coalition. Each state has an organization that functions as the hub for education, advocacy, and, in some cases, referrals. Usually, a list of all the state programs is provided on their websites, along with materials regarding abuse, safety, legal options, etc. Note that although the academic literature has moved away from using the term "domestic violence," many programs continue to use it, and for many, it is part of their name.

National and state IPV organizations are a source for advocacy and activism. National organizations provide education, advocacy, and

TABLE 155.1 Safety Planning

Issue/Situation	Suggestions
Lethality	Assist the person to assess the level of violence and force so they have an idea of the risk when the violence does occur.
In the house	Think about where to run for safety within the house—a place with no weapons or objects that can become weapons, a room with an exit. Think through how to keep the children safe. If possible, suggest avoiding rooms where the children are so they do not become targets; if they are old enough, walk them through what to do. Have some ways in mind for how to safely leave the house.
Communication	Brainstorm how to gain access to a phone; many advocacy programs provide free phones with access to emergency numbers. Compose a list of needed emergency numbers—police, local shelter or IPV program, school, work, family, friends, hospitals.
Physical/material things to gather: Prepare an emergency bag that can stay hidden at home or in the home of a trusted friend or family member for easy access and safekeeping.	Access to transportation—bus passes, a full tank of gas, extra set of car keys Clothing for a few days Copies of important documents for all involved—driver's license, Social Security cards, passports, birth certificates, bank account information, car registration, health insurance cards, immigration and court documents, a list of credit card numbers and/or debit cards so they can be tracked, school records, etc. Cash, gift cards, credit cards, or credit card numbers. Medicines or a list of medicines.
Scenarios	Brainstorm possible scenarios in which violence may occur, and victim–survivor needs to stay safe. Walk through how to stay safe in those situations.
Family, friends, neighbors	Think about possible trusted family members, friends, or neighbors who could help in the event of an emergency. Think of a visual signal—for example, if the lights in the bedroom blink rapidly, call the police—that would help people recognize when the person needs assistance.
Children	If the abuser has visitation rights—supervised or unsupervised visitation or through custody agreements—find a safe place to facilitate the exchange. If age appropriate, talk to the children about how to stay safe. Think of one other person who can accompany the victim–survivor during the exchange when possible.
Other risks	Assess other risk factors, such as pregnancy, illness, or disability, and create a safety plan that addresses these issues. Think about language barriers.

IPV, intimate partner violence.

materials to those interested in preventing and ending relationship violence. Some examples are the National Coalition Against Domestic Violence (NCADV), the National Resources Center on Domestic Violence, the Battered Women's Justice Project, and Futures Without Violence. Some have organized around the needs of specific populations—for example, the Northwest Network of Bi, Trans, Lesbian and Gay Survivors of Abuse; the Asian Pacific Institute on Gender-Based Violence; and the Institute on Domestic Violence in the African American Community.

Regarding services for those carrying out the violence, batterer intervention programs (also referred to as abuser intervention programs) are the most common. These programs gained prominence in the 1980s, and the goals are to hold perpetrators accountable for the violence and to reduce re-offenses (Mellinger & Carney, 2014). Many of these programs use the feminist perspective, which highlights the oppression of women through patriarchal systems. The original programs were modeled after the Duluth program (Bohall et al., 2016), but many use a combination of feminist ideologies and cognitive–behavioral therapy (Eckhardt et al., 2013). Although there is evidence that the programs work for some individuals, research regarding effectiveness continues to provide mixed results; some research has found that programs show evidence of violence reduction, whereas other studies have found no change (Eckhardt et al., 2013). Programs that address motivation and one's readiness to change have shown promising results (Eckhardt et al., 2013). Although the effectiveness of these programs has been questioned, it is important to note that there are personal stories of individuals who report change and turning away from using IPV. Practitioners should be encouraged to continue to find ways to assist these individuals while at the same time continuing to promote principles of equity in healthy relationships.

Recommendations

Intimate partner violence is a complex issue that impacts many lives. The intersection of IPV with all fields of social work, including the law, is evident, so it is important to know where to go and what to do. The goal of this overview is to give practitioners enough information to "know what they don't know" so they can seek additional materials to inform their practice. Practitioners should continue to seek knowledge regarding areas that were not expanded on in this chapter, so I leave you with a few final recommendations:

- Learn about theories that seek to explain IPV.
- Explore programs that serve those who commit the abuse, including programs for women who abuse their partners.
- Seek emerging research on IPV among the LGBTQ+ community.

- Learn about dynamics of IPV as well as services for special populations—individuals who have a disability, the elderly, children exposed to IPV, and those who are pregnant.
- Explore the dynamics of dating violence.
- Explore issues faced by those from racial and ethnic minorities, including issues around immigration.
- Use evidenced-based practice, but never dismiss the stories of those who experience IPV. Their stories must inform the care we provide—we must never stop listening to victims and survivors and must include their experiences when we shape services and advocate for more equitable policies.
- Always tell a victim–survivor, "The abuse is *not* your fault."

References

Anyikwa, V. (2016). Trauma-informed approach to survivors of intimate partner violence. *Journal of Evidence-Informed Social Work, 13*(5), 584–491. http://dx.doi.org/10.1080/23761407.2016.1166824

Bohall, G., Bautista, M., & Musson, S. (2016). Intimate partner violence and the Duluth model: An examination of the model and recommendations for future research and practice. *Journal of Family Violence, 31*, 1029–1033.

Breiding, M. J., Basile, K. C., Smith, S. G., Black, M. C., & Mahendra, R. R. (2015). *Intimate partner violence surveillance: Uniform definitions and recommended data elements, version 2.0.* National Center for Injury Prevention and Control, Centers for Disease Control and Prevention. https://www.cdc.gov/violenceprevention/pdf/ipv/intimatepartnerviolence.pdf

Capaldi, D. M., Knoble, N. B., Shirtt, J. W., & Kim, H. K. (2012). A systematic review of risk factors for intimate partner violence. *Partner Abuse, 3*(2), 231–280. https://www.ncbi.nlm.nih.gov/pmc/articles/PMC3384540/pdf/nihms385813.pdf

Devries, K. M., Mak, J. Y., Garcia-Moreno, C., Ptzold, M., Child, J. C., Falder, G., Bacchus, L. J., Engell, R. E., Rosenfeld, L., Pallitto, C., Vos, T., Abrahams, N., & Watts, C. H. (2013). The global prevalence of intimate partner violence against women. *Science, 340*(6140), 1527–1528.

Dutton, D. G. (2012). The case against the role of gender in intimate partner violence. *Aggression and Violence Behavior, 17*(1), 99–104.

Eckhardt, C. I., Murphy, C. M., Whitaker, D. J., Sprunger, J., Dykstra, R., & Woodard, K. (2013). The effectiveness of intervention programs for perpetrators and victims of intimate partner violence. *Partner Abuse, 4*(2), 196–231. http://dx.doi.org/10.1891/1946-6560.4.2.196

Johnson, M. (2010). Langhinrichsen-Rolling's confirmation of the feminist analysis of intimate partner violence: Comment on "Controversies involving gender and intimate partner violence in the United States." *Sex Roles, 62,* 212–219.

Kelly, U. A. (2011). Theories of intimate partner violence: From blaming the victim to acting against injustice intersectionality as an analytic framework. *Advances in Nursing Science, 34*(3). E29–E51.

Matias, A., Goncalves, M., Soeiro, C., & Matos, M. (2020). Intimate partner homicide: A meta-analysis of risk factors. *Aggression and Violent Behavior, 50,* 101358. https://doi.org/10.1016/j.avb.2019.101358

Mellinger, M. S., & Carney, M. M. (2014). Interpersonal dependency constructs and male perpetrators of intimate partner violence. *Journal of Forensic Social Work, 4,* 29–47.

Moore, A. M., Frohwirth, L., & Miller, E. (2010). Male reproductive control over women who have experienced intimate partner violence in the U.S. *Social Science and Medicine, 70*(11), 1737–1744. https://doi.org/10.1016/j.socscimed.2010.02.009

Ruddle, A., Pina, A., & Vasquez, E. (2017). Domestic violence offending behaviors: A review of the literature examining childhood exposure, implicit theories, trait aggression and anger rumination as predictive factors. *Aggression and Violent Behavior, 34,* 154–165. http://dx.doi.org/10.1016/j.avb.2017.01.016

Smith, S. G., Zhang, X., Basile, K. C., Merrick, M. T., Wang, J., Kresnow, M., & Chen, J. (2018). *The National Intimate Partner and Sexual Violence Survey: 2015 data brief—Updated release.* National Center for Injury Prevention and Control, Centers for Disease Control and Prevention. https://www.cdc.gov/violenceprevention/pdf/2015databrief508.pdf

Spencer, C. M., & Stith, S. M. (2020). A meta-analysis of risk factors for intimate partner homicide: Examining male perpetration and female victimization. *Trauma, Violence, and Abuse, 21*(3), 527–540. https://doi.org/10.1177/1524838018781101

Stockl, H., Devries, K., Rotstein, A., Abrahams, N., Campbell, J., Watts, C., & Moreno, C. (2013). The global prevalence of intimate partner homicide: A systematic review. *Lancet, 382*(9895), 859–865. https://doi.org/10.1016/s0140-6736(13)61030-2

Substance Abuse and Mental Health Services Administration. (2014). *SAMHSA's concept of trauma and guidance for a trauma-informed approach.* HHS Publication No. (SMA) 14-4884. https://store.samhsa.gov/product/SAMHSA-s-Concept-of-Trauma-and-Guidance-for-a-Trauma-Informed-Approach/SMA14-4884.html

Experts in Family Court

Kathleen Leilani Ja Sook Bergquist

Social workers and other mental health professionals routinely find themselves drawn into forensic settings generally and family court matters specifically, often unwittingly. Social work that intersects with the law is broadly defined as forensic social work. Practitioners may not always view their work as inherently forensic; however, anyone working with clients or cases that interface with the courts has a foothold in the psycholegal world. Social workers have diverse roles in family court as caseworkers for departments of child services or as treating therapists for one or several parties to the matter (children, parents, or any configuration thereof) whose work has either been court-ordered or predated the court case. In addition, neutral evaluators provide expert services for the court, including child custody evaluations, child interviews, and brief-focused custody-related evaluations to address a particular question for the court. Other experts provide subject matter expertise, including substance abuse, domestic violence, and psychosexual evaluations. Judges also often rely on mental health professionals to serve as mediators or in a quasi-judicial role as parenting coordinators, assisting parents in working through conflict and disputes outside of the court.

History of Social Workers in Family Court

Child welfare has largely been the purview of social workers with the establishment of child protection agencies (Little, 2017). The authority bestowed on child protection agencies, and family courts, derives from the legal principle of *parens patriae*, which places the state (or other local jurisdiction) in a parental role to protect the children's best interests when biological parents' actions place children at risk (Emery et al., 2014). Dependency courts routinely rely on social workers' professional training and knowledge of the families to make permanency recommendations. By virtue of their position as caseworkers, they are generally not required to establish themselves as experts for purposes of testifying in dependency or family court proceedings. They testify as quasi-fact witnesses because they not only provide progress reports to the court but also make conclusions regarding that progress. Similarly, treating therapists who are working with the children or parents who are party to a dependency or custody matter are not expected to be impartial evaluators. Rather, they are often subpoenaed to provide testimony as to their clients' diagnoses and progression toward treatment. Their role is necessarily restricted to their actual knowledge of their clients' functioning, and not to weigh in on matters that are outside of their direct knowledge. However, attorneys often lead treating therapists to proffer opinions or conclusions that are improper or beyond their scope of knowledge or expertise. Well-intended clinicians who seek to advocate for their clients may overstep by providing opinions, sometimes of others with whom they do not have a clinical relationship or even firsthand knowledge, or, in custody matters, rendering opinions about the best interest of the children. In such situations, the therapist may be better served by declining to respond or by clarifying that any opinion they might offer cannot be construed as an expert opinion (Woody, 2007).

Subpoenas

Treating therapists confronted with subpoenas to turn over records (subpoena duces tecum) or to testify (subpoena ad testificandum) must assert their client's right to privilege absent a clear and specific release. All officers of the courts, including attorneys, some administrative offices (e.g., Social Security), and judges, may issue subpoenas. However, pro se or pro per (propia persona) litigants may also request that subpoenas be issued through the court because they are representing themselves. A subpoena from an attorney has different weight than an order from the court; either way, the clinician must respond to the request. A subpoena with a signed release attached is generally insufficient; rather, clinicians may require that a client sign the agency or practice consent form to verify that the release is proper and so that the clinician may communicate with the client regarding the request for records and/or testimony. Even if clients provide consent for release of records, any information shared during a legal process should be limited in scope, to the degree that it is responsive to the request, while not harmful to the client.

Client–Therapist Privilege

The federal courts did not recognize client–therapist privilege prior to 1996. In a landmark decision (*Jaffee v. Redmond*, 1996), the Supreme Court conducted a two-step analysis to determine (1) whether psychotherapist privilege should exist and (2) whether it should be extended to social workers. The psychotherapist in *Jaffee* was a licensed clinical social worker; the court's hesitance reflected its uncertainty whether clinical social workers should have parity with psychologists and psychiatrists. The majority decision determined that "good therapy means private therapy" and that it served a greater public need to protect the client–therapist relationship (Lens, 2000, p. 274). *Jaffee* was important in establishing privilege, but it also provided the foundation for parity in the courtroom for clinical social workers as experts.

Certifying Experts

The federal courts, and many state courts, apply standards based on the Supreme Court cases *Frye v. United States* (1923) and *Daubert v. Merrell Dow Pharmaceuticals, Inc.* (1993), known as the *Frye* test and *Daubert* test, respectively. These tests are used to establish whether a witness may be qualified as an expert. The *Daubert* test, coupled with the finding from *General Electric Company v. Joiner* (1997), established that federal judges have broad discretion in admitting expert testimony (Munson, 2011). In a 2002 case in Georgia (*Adams v. the State*), the state Supreme Court qualified a licensed clinical social worker as an expert to establish the defendant's competency to stand trial. It further clarified that the jury may not exclude the clinical social worker's testimony as an expert but may consider the social worker's credentials to determine weight as it deems appropriate.

Therapeutic Jurisprudence: Social Work Expert Roles in Family Court

Social workers serve as experts in three general areas within the family court system: custody evaluation, court-ordered service provision, and subject matter expertise. All of them assume that the practitioner is neutral and has a degree of education, training, and experience that would meet judicial and regulatory standards for certifying them as an expert.

Evaluators (Custody Decision-Making)

Relatively recently, courts have turned to mental health professionals as experts to provide neutral third-party evaluations in family court. Disputes arise regarding legal custody (whether decisions about the child are made jointly or separately) and/or physical custody (timeshare and schedule). The terms, conditions, and presumptions regarding custody vary from state to state, but all states utilize a *best interest of the child* standard. A judge may request an evaluation to better understand the co-parenting system broadly and want best-interest custody recommendations, or the focus may be limited to evaluating more specifically a parent's psychological well-being, domestic violence, substance abuse, the desires of the children, parental alienation, the presence of coaching or undue influence, or relocation risk with a brief focused assessment. These evaluations have been largely outsourced to psychologists; however, increasingly courts have recognized licensed clinical social workers and other master's-level clinicians as experts.

Mediation

Custody mediation is utilized differently from jurisdiction to jurisdiction. Some family courts mandate mediation whenever there is a contested custody matter. Jurisdictions also vary regarding access to mediation. Some jurisdiction provide low-cost mediation to families through the court, some have paneled private mediators, and families who live in jurisdictions that do not mandate mediation typically seek out private mediators on their own. There are different approaches to mediation; however, the most commonly used approach in family court matters is the facilitative model. The goal of facilitative custody mediation is to bring the parties together to make joint decisions about their children that address their respective interests. The underlying presumption is that the parents are the in the best position to determine the best interests of the child(ren). The process is confidential, and the mediator is expected to be neutral, serving to facilitate the parties' negotiations as they address matters such as timeshare, holidays and vacations, education, and children's activities. If the parties are successful and a parenting agreement is finalized, then it will be submitted to the court to be approved, signed, and made legally binding (Peeples et al., 2008).

Mediation is a role that is congruent with social work practice as a problem-solving intervention. County and state courts often utilize social workers as mediators, whereas the private sector tends to have a higher representation of attorneys who incorporate mediation as part of their family law practice. Litigators are enculturated to zealously advocate for their clients and arguably have to "change hats" to assume a mediator role, whereas social workers often work in environments in which the family system is their client and therefore seem particularly adept at assuming a neutral facilitative role, while keeping the parents focused on the best interests of their child(ren).

Child Custody Evaluation

Child custody evaluations are typically ordered when there is a high degree of conflict between the co-parents that leads to an inability to settle on or abide by a parenting agreement. A child custody evaluation (CCE) entails a comprehensive assessment of the family system(s) to include the co-parents and children. CCEs are time-intensive, usually requiring up to 3–5 months to complete. The reliability and validity of the assessment lie in data gathering from multiple sources. The evaluator may develop several hypotheses about the family functioning and utilize data to test the hypotheses. Although approaches vary, a typical CCE usually involves multiple interviews with co-parents and their respective partners, the children, and professional (therapists, doctors, teachers, etc.) and personal (family members and friends) collaterals. Parties are invited to submit relevant motions and orders (child custody agreement, petition for divorce, temporary protective order filings, and child protective services records), documents and supporting materials (e.g., email communications, videos, letters, social media posts, and medical and educational records), and any other appropriate material. The co-parents, and sometimes the children, undergo psychological testing to explore functioning and/or to address adverse parties' assertions of mental illness or addictive use disorders. Master's-level clinical social workers generally do not administer psychological testing, but that portion of the CCE can be subcontracted to a psychologist. Common tests that are administered include the Minnesota Multiphasic Personality Inventory–2, Personality Assessment Inventory, Substance Abuse Subtle Screening Inventory–4, Parenting Alliance Measure, and Parenting Stress Index–4.

Whatever the approach the evaluator takes, their interactions with the parties must limit any ex parte communication and appearance of partiality. Ex parte communication refers to improper contact with a party or a judge; therefore, because of the need to be neutral, communication should be bilateral and transparent with the co-parents. This can include ensuring that an equal number of collaterals on both sides are interviewed. In addition, in order to knowledgeably discuss the fitness of the child(ren)'s environment, home visits are commonly made, announced or unannounced.

Given the importance of assessing family functioning, knowledge of human development and behavior, and attention to person-in-environment, social workers are well-suited to conduct CCEs. It is also imperative that practitioners understand how to navigate in the host environment of the family court and to be well-versed in the dynamics of high-conflict custody matters and the legal consequences for recommendations that might be proffered from a CCE.

Brief-Focused Assessment

A brief-focused assessment (BFA) is ordered when a judge wants more information about a particular aspect of the case that they cannot fully understand within the confines of the courtroom and may be confused by the conflicting accusations that are being flung by the parties. The important differentiation between a BFA and an evaluation from an outsource provider who is a subject matter expert is important. The BFA is ordered, often with instructions for recommendations regarding the custody matter. However, an outsource subject matter expert will never be asked to proffer opinions or recommendations regarding the custody matter. For example, an evaluator may be asked to gather information regarding a parent's alcohol use and, based on their findings, may make recommendations regarding custodial time or safeguards for the children while in that parent's care. A subject matter expert may be asked to evaluate a parent's alcohol use solely to provide information (i.e., diagnosis and treatment prognosis) but not to render custody recommendations because it is presumed that they do not have the expertise to understand the complex psycholegal aspects of the child custody case.

Standards, Guidelines, and Ethical Considerations for Evaluation Work

Model standards or guidelines for such evaluations are limited. The Association of Family and Conciliation Courts (AFCC) published model standards for CCE (AFCC, 2006) and guidelines for brief focused assessments (AFCC, 2009), and the American Psychological Association (APA, 2010) and the American Academy of Matrimonial Lawyers (AAML, 2011) published guidelines and standards, respectively, for CCEs. The APA standards presume the practitioner to be a psychologist, but the APA cautions its members to obtain sufficient training and education related to CCEs. The AFCC and AAML do not limit CCEs to psychologist but, rather, specify that the evaluators must have at least a master's degree in a mental health field and specialized training, and evaluators with less than 2 or 3 years of experience are directed to receive supervision from an experienced evaluator. Interestingly, practice guidelines for clinical social workers have not been promulgated by the National Association of Social Workers or other professional social work organizations. However, Luftman and colleagues (2005) published guidelines that provide information regarding the intent, scope, and structure of CCEs. They did not directly address evaluator qualifications, but they reiterated the need for specialized education and experience.

Reamer (2018) and Luftman et al. (2005) identified conflicts that may arise regarding informed consent when clinical social workers work with court-involved clients; these could occur in any legal context in which client–attorney privilege may be asserted. Social workers are mandated reporters of child abuse and neglect; however, it can be argued that social workers who are affiliated with law offices or legal clinics may be bound by attorney–client privilege as non-lawyers working on a case. This is less salient when a clinical social worker is serving as a neutral third-party evaluator; however, it remains imperative that social workers include mandated reporting exceptions in their informed consent.

Court-Ordered Services (High-Conflict Custody)

High-conflict divorcing and separating parents utilize a disproportionate percentage of the family court's time and resources. Therefore, courts have embraced interventions intended to keep feuding co-parents out of court and to prioritize children's best interest. Similar to CCEs, licensed clinical social workers are newer to this realm of practice. It is thus not uncommon for clinicians to encounter court-involved families, often not fully aware of the legal intrusions that accompany work with these families. Two court-ordered interventions that are not primarily for evaluative purposes are parenting coordination (PC) and court-ordered therapy, including individual, family, and reunification therapy.

Parenting Coordination

Parenting coordination is a dispute resolution intervention that incorporates aspects of mediation and arbitration (Emery et al., 2014). PC is a fairly new practice that developed in the late 1990s and became more widely recognized in the early 2000s. Depending on the jurisdiction, parenting coordinators are mental health professionals (usually psychologists) or attorneys. States vary regarding the degree of authority that parenting coordinators have to resolve disputes, and the question usually centers around the degree to which judges may delegate judicial decision-making and concomitantly whether PC decisions are binding and enforceable (Kelly, 2008). In some jurisdictions, parenting coordinators are limited to making recommendations that are subject to judicial review, whereas in other jurisdictions, PC decisions are fully enforceable. In most jurisdictions, parenting coordinators are limited to matters that are unrelated to custodial time-share and child support. Common conflicts that might be addressed by a parenting coordinator include extracurricular activities, choice of school, location of exchanges, and negotiating small adjustments to timeshare. All parenting coordinators are required to complete jurisdiction-determined specialized training and continuing education, and several professional organizations have established model guidelines, including the AFCC and the APA (Kelly, 2008). Given that parenting coordinators may make legally binding decisions, there are ethical considerations for clinical social workers and other mental health professionals. First, a clinician making decisions that have legal effects on the parents may raise concerns about scope of practice, including pseudo-practice of law. In addition, Amundson and Lux (2016) note that there are ethical complications when clients are asked "to surrender their autonomy through informed consent" (p. 446). The relationship between the clinician as parenting coordinator and client is shaped by a legal system that constrains and directs rather than promoting autonomy and agency as in traditional mental health roles (Amundson & Lux 2016, p. 446).

Court-Ordered Therapy

When courts refer clients for therapy, it is important that clinicians understand, and in turn explain to their clients, that confidentiality guarantees are limited. The court will want regular updates regarding client progress and will often expect recommendations pertaining to the child custody or dependency court matter. Consequently, therapists must consider their comfort level with such expectations prior to accepting court-involved clients, and the informed consent must clearly detail the circumstance-specific limits to confidentiality. Court-ordered therapy typically is for the child, parent(s), or a parent and child. When a child or a parent is ordered to have therapy, it is safe to assume that the court, through one or both

of the litigants, has asserted that there is an emotional or behavioral problem. It is not unusual for a parent to argue that the child needs therapy "because of" the other parent or that the other parent "needs help" because they are unable to co-parent or prioritize the child's best interests due to a mental illness. Therefore, the opposing party and the court will have an interest in accessing the client's therapy records. Reunification therapy is a psycholegal intervention that seeks to address conflict between a child and a parent, purportedly resulting from alienation. There cannot be any reasonable expectation of confidentiality because its intent is to repair the parent–child relationship for custody purposes. Parental alienation syndrome refers to a child's "campaign of denigration against a parent" without justification, fueled by an "alienating parent" who brainwashes or programs the child against the "target parent" (Gardner, 2002, p. 95). Gardner asserts that this phenomenon is unique to custody dispute matters. Children who alienate their parents exhibit a cluster of behaviors, including rejection, unquestioned support of the alienating parent, and absence of guilt. The rejection and disdain are reinforced by the alienating parent and are cited as justification in custody disputes. Consequently, courts may order reunification therapy to repair the relationship between the alienated parent and child(ren). Parents often will seek out a therapist for reunification therapy, without fully disclosing the court involvement and the legal weight of the process. Consequently, clinicians should routinely inquire about child custody status for divorced or separated parents and the degree of court involvement, and they should require consent from both parents and a copy of the order.

Subject Matter Expert Witness (Domestic Violence and Child Abuse)

"Expert" is a legal term of art that requires judicial review. Social workers in dependency or family court are often called upon to testify regarding domestic violence or child abuse. They may be called as a lay (or fact) witness or as an expert (or opinion) witness. It is imperative that social workers understand their role in the court proceeding and do not confuse the two. Typically, treating therapists are fact witnesses and are limited to firsthand knowledge of their client and cannot offer opinions or conclusions of law—that is, whether the client was abused. They can testify as to the client's diagnoses, symptoms, and progress in therapy. However, the court may allow the clinician to be asked opinion questions about their client, limited to their experience and training—that is, whether the client's symptoms are secondary to exposure to violence. Conversely, expert witnesses may render opinions on matters for which they have specialized knowledge (Gothard, 1989; Mason, 1992). Of course, the court recognizes that a treating therapist holds at least a master's degree in a mental health field and often has specialized knowledge or training. The question is not simply about qualifications but, rather, the role the clinician has with that particular family or client.

Recommendations

The role of social workers as experts in the family courts has been subject to critique from outside and within the profession. Lawyers, the courts, and legal scholars opine about whether master's-level mental health professionals should be afforded parity with psychologists and psychiatrists, whereas the APA has positioned psychologists as uniquely qualified to conduct court-ordered evaluations and otherwise serve as experts. However, it is clear that the courts are increasingly recognizing that by virtue of clinical social work education and specialized training, social workers are in fact qualified to evaluate and render opinions.

Given the somewhat ambiguous position of social workers in the courts related to their various roles as treating or expert witnesses, it is important that the profession (i.e., the National Association of Social Workers or the National Organization of Forensic Social workers) take a leading role in more clearly defining and providing guidelines for practitioners. Social workers certainly can and should review APA and other professional sources, but clearer guidance from the profession could address unique social work practices and ethical considerations.

References

Adams v. State, 275 Ga. 867, 572 S.E.2d 545 (2002).

American Academy of Matrimonial Lawyers. (2011). *Child custody evaluation standards.*

American Psychological Association. (December 2010). Guidelines for child custody evaluations in family law proceedings. *American Psychologist, 65*(9), 863–867.

Amundson, J. K., & Lux, G. M. (2016). The issue of ethics and authority for licensed mental health professionals involved in parenting coordination. *Family Court Review, 54*(3), 446–456. https://doi.org/10.1111/fcre.12223

Association of Family and Conciliation Courts. (2006). *Model standards of practice for child custody evaluation.*

Association of Family and Conciliation Courts. (2009). *Guidelines for brief focused assessment.*

Daubert v. Merrell Dow Pharmaceuticals, Inc., 509 U.S. 579 (1993).

Emery, R. E., Rowen, J., & Dinescu, D. (2014). New roles for family therapists in the courts: An overview with a focus on custody dispute resolution. *Family Process, 53*(3), 500–515. https://doi.org/10.1111/famp.12077

Frye v. United States, 293 F. 1013 D.C. Cir (1923).

Gardner, R. A. (2002). Parental alienation syndrome vs. parental alienation: Which diagnosis should evaluators use in child-custody disputes? *American Journal of Family Therapy, 30*(2), 93–115. https://doi.org/10.1080/019261802753573821

General Electric Company v. Joiner, 522 U.S. 136 (1997).

Gothard, S. (1989). Power in the court: The social worker as an expert witness. *Social Work, 34*(1), 65–67.

Jaffee v. Redmond, 518 U.S. 1 (1996).

Kelly, J. (2008). Preparing for the parenting coordination role: Training needs for mental health and legal professionals. *Journal of Child Custody, 5*(1–2), 140–159. https://doi.org/10.1080/15379410802070476

Lens, V. (2000). Protecting the confidentiality of the therapeutic relationship: *Jaffee v. Redmond*. *Social Work, 45*(3), 273–276. https://doi.org/10.1093/sw/45.3.273

Little, M. (2017). People and systems: Reflections on the development of social work for children. *Journal of Children's Services, 12*(2/3), 113–121. https://doi.org/10.1108/JCS-09-2017-0037

Luftman, V. H., Veltkamp, L. J., Clark, J. J., Lannacone, S., & Snooks, H. (2005). Practice guidelines in child custody evaluations for licensed clinical social workers. *Clinical Social Work Journal, 33*(3), 327–357. https://doi.org/10.1007/s10615-005-4947-4

Mason, M. A. (1992). Social workers as expert witnesses in child sexual abuse cases. *Social Work, 37*(1), 30–34.

Munson, C. (2011). Forensic social work practice standards: Definition and specification. *Journal of Forensic Social Work, 1,* 37–60.

Peeples, R. A., Reynolds, S., & Harris, C. T. (2008). It's the conflict, stupid: An empirical study of factors that inhibit successful mediation in high-conflict custody cases. *Wake Forest Law Review, 43*(2), 505–531.

Reamer, F. G. (2018). Social workers as expert witnesses: Ethical considerations. *Journal of the American Academy of Matrimonial Lawyers, 30,* 437–453.

Woody, R. H. (2007). Avoiding expert testimony about family therapy. *American Journal of Family Therapy, 35*(5), 389–393. https://doi.org/10.1080/01926180701291238

Smart Decarceration and Social Work

Carrie Pettus-Davis

The United States began the staggering expansion of its prison and jail systems in the 1970s, commonly referred to as mass incarceration. By 2010, the United States had become the world's leading incarcerator. As of 2018, most state-specific incarceration rates are hundreds of persons per 100,000 population—higher than those of any other developed nation (Wagner & Sawyer, 2018). On any given day in the United States, nearly 2 million people are incarcerated in a jail or prison, and more than 13 million people cycle in and out of jails and prisons each year (Kaebel & Cowhig, 2018). Yet, mass incarceration has been largely ineffective in achieving its stated goals of deterrence and rehabilitation. For example, approximately three-fourths of people who are released from prison in the United States are rearrested for a new crime (i.e., recidivate) within 5 years (Alper & Durose, 2018), compared to recidivism rates near 25% in other countries with high incarceration rates (Looman & Carl, 2015). Notably, the United States does not have incarceration rates that are three times those of other developed countries due to higher crime rates (Looman & Carl, 2015).

Instead, mass incarceration is attributed to a host of societal factors, including public distrust in the government and social unrest after the Vietnam War, politicians benefiting from tough-on-crime and war-on-drugs political platforms, the criminalization of behavioral health disorders, loss of interest in the rehabilitative repeal, an uptick in violent crime rates in urban communities in the 1980s, abandonment of the war on poverty, substantial cuts in mental health treatment and public safety nets, defunding of the public education system, and inappropriate and biased responses to the consequences of the historic racial inequities and social injustices that remain rampant in the United States (Mauer, 2016). Mass incarceration policies and continued criminal justice practices perpetuate inequities, create social and economic stratification, and generate historical trauma and systemic trauma for those individuals, families, and communities most directly impacted by incarceration (Wakefield & Uggen, 2010; Westcott, 2015). The most vulnerable and marginalized communities have suffered the bulk of the societal and financial costs of mass incarceration; however, the overuse of mass incarceration affects all American residents by hampering national progress and through an estimated $900 billion per year in social costs (i.e., budgetary and nonbudgetary costs incurred by individuals, families, and communities; McLaughlin et al., 2016). Smart decarceration approaches are needed to reverse the devastation that mass incarceration has created throughout the nation and redefine how public safety, well-being, and social justice are achieved in the United States.

Smart decarceration is defined as a comprehensive reform approach that leads to an effective, sustainable, and socially just criminal justice system (Pettus-Davis & Epperson, 2015). Following Pettus-Davis and Epperson's conceptualization of smart decarceration, three interdependent goals must be met to achieve a state of smart decarceration: (1) Substantially reduce the incarcerated population in jails and prisons; (2) redress the existing social disparities among the incarcerated; and (3) maximize public safety and well-being.

Why Social Work Engagement in Smart Decarceration Is Needed

Because mass incarceration is fueled by significant social disparities and racially biased practices within the United States and disproportionately affects the most vulnerable and marginalized in our society, the engagement of social work in smart decarceration is an ethical imperative. Promoting smart decarceration approaches for criminal justice reform requires practice and policy interventions at the micro, mezzo, and macro levels, which is why social work is uniquely positioned to promote smart decarceration in addition to the inherent social justice obligation of social work. Racial, behavioral health, and economic disparities drive continued mass incarceration practices and rates in 2020 in the United States.

Moreover, incarceration and its subsequent consequences can permanently isolate people from communities as a result of removal (to incarceration) and stigma (after release), and incarceration has extensive and intergenerational negative consequences for individuals and communities. An incarceration event for an individual creates problems for those around them, including disrupted families and traumatized children who are left behind and removal of massive amounts of human capital and human potential from communities. Despite the deleterious consequences of incarceration, people with incarceration histories are grossly underserved from both a human resource and a treatment perspective due to stigma and unpriortized allocation of resources.

Racial Disparities

Racial inequity is one of the greatest contributors to mass incarceration. Holding criminal histories and other related factors equal, African American men are five times more likely and Hispanic men almost twice as likely to be incarcerated compared to their White male counterparts (Bonzcar, 2003). Studies show that if incarceration trends continue at the 2010s rates (The Sentencing Project, 2013), a striking one out of three African American males born in 2001 will experience incarceration in their lifetimes. At every point along the path to incarceration, men of color experience contacts with the criminal justice system differently than White men (Brame et al., 2014; Huebner & Berg, 2011; Johnson 2003; Rosenfeld et al., 2012; Wooldredgeet al., 2015). Although there are no differences in rates of criminal behavior by race/ethnicity, men of color are more likely to come into contact with law enforcement compared to White men. When men of color come into contact with law enforcement, they are more likely to be arrested compared to White men; once arrested, men of color are more likely to be charged; once charged, men of color are more likely to be sentenced; among men who are sentenced, men of color have more severe sentences; and once released from incarceration, men of color are more likely to be returned to incarceration compared to their White counterparts. Disproportionate minority contact creates unique disadvantage for members of ethnic minority communities because a felony conviction has lifetime consequences for individuals and the families in which they are embedded.

Behavioral Health Disparities

Three major movements launched and perpetuated behavioral health disparities among the incarcerated. First, the deinstitutionalization of psychiatric hospitals, although certainly justified, was poorly orchestrated, and patients were released without the necessary structures in place to support a successful transition to life in the community. As a result, many former patients became homeless persons and/or incarcerated (Epperson et al., 2014). Second, not only was the community-based mental and substance use disorder treatment infrastructure not prepared to meet the needs of patients released due to deinstitutionalization of psychiatric hospitals but also it had not grown in pace with the rising rates of mental health and substance use disorders. In general, policymakers neither incentivized nor assisted communities in building an appropriate treatment infrastructure. Instead, they allocated more money for building new prisons to house soaring numbers of the incarcerated while cutting funds for the provision of mental and behavioral health treatment (Epperson et al., 2014). With limited treatment options or safe shelters, jails became the de facto institution for housing people with mental illnesses who were highly symptomatic and a danger to themselves or others and also a place to send people

to recover (somewhat) safely from severe intoxication. The third movement, the War on Drugs, had the most dramatic impact on federal prison populations. Declared by President Nixon and solidified under the Reagan administration, the War on Drugs criminalized the behaviors associated with substance use disorders. For example, prior to 1984, the year that Nancy Reagan launched her now famously unsuccessful "Just Say No" campaign, the federal prison population was composed of approximately 5% of people incarcerated for drug-related crimes; currently, more than half of the people in federal prisons are incarcerated for drug-related crimes, and just under 7% are in prison because they have been convicted of violent crime. In state prisons, on average, more than 25% of inmates are incarcerated because of drug-related offenses such as distribution of illicit substances, whereas in 1980, only 8% of individuals were incarcerated on drug-related crimes. Under current justice practices, people with behavioral health disorders are more likely to be incarcerated than to receive inpatient treatment at a therapeutic facility (Epperson, 2014).

Economic Disparities

An individual's financial resources largely determine their experience with the criminal justice system. The resulting economic disparities occur through both formal and informal functions of the justice system. Informally, there is a widely held belief that people in poverty commit more crime than people who are not in poverty. This belief, which is based on findings from economic studies published prior to the 1970s that suggested that poverty caused criminal behavior, persists despite the fact that findings from more recent studies have not supported a causal relationship. Although poverty is indeed associated with criminal justice involvement, it is not a cause of involvement with the criminal justice system but, rather, a risk factor. This difference is important to distinguish because due to the widely held belief that poverty causes criminal behavior, law enforcement officials may focus policing efforts on poor communities and consequently be more likely to identify criminal behavior when it occurs.

Once a person has been identified as a suspect in a crime, socioeconomic status is a factor because people who are not in poverty may be more likely to have social ties to law enforcement personnel and other criminal justice actors. As a result of these connections, when criminal behavior does occur, they may be able to avoid the legal consequences for their actions, whereas a person of lower socioeconomic status would be less likely to have such ties and would have no choice but to go through the formal criminal justice process.

Formal structures within the criminal justice system further exacerbate economic disparities. Courts and the criminal justice process entail substantial fines and fees. As such, even infractions that were not originally considered criminal behavior become criminal behavior if a person in poverty is not able to afford the fines and fees (Ruback, 2011). For example, traffic tickets have an associated fine, a court date, and court fees. If a person is not able to pay the fine or misses the court date, they incur more fines and fees. Continued nonpayment of fees and fines and/or failure to attend court—even if due to barriers related to employment or transportation—eventually results in criminal charges. In another example, in many states a parent can be charged with a crime and incarcerated for failure to pay child support if the parent falls behind in child support payments.

Bail, as it is currently structured, is another process in the criminal justice system that generates economic disparities (Sobol, 2015). Most jurisdictions in the United States have some form of bail system. In general, when a person is arrested and charged with an offense, the court orders a bond agreement and either will rule to release a person on their own recognizance or some other release agreement or will set a dollar amount as bail, a portion of which must be paid before a person can be released from jail. Even seemingly small dollar amounts (e.g., $500) are out of reach for many people in poverty. Therefore, a defendant without the financial resources to pay bail must remain in jail until a court hearing on the charge. This time in jail may span months or, in some cases, years. Any employment the defendant had prior to the charge is likely to be lost, and if the defendant was supporting a family financially prior to the arrest, that family is likely pushed further into poverty; research shows that more than 60% of people in prison and jail were financial contributors to their families prior to the incarceration event (Geller et al., 2011). Defendants who can afford to pay bail are able to maintain their jobs, relationships, and other aspects of their community-based living during this time. This disparity is further exacerbated because those without the financial resources to post bail also cannot afford to hire private attorneys to represent them during trial and instead rely on public defenders, who typically spend less time on cases and represent defendants with less intensity than private attorneys because of extremely high caseloads and scarce resources allocated to the public defense system (Primus, 2017).

Consequences to Individuals and Families

Incarceration limits an individual's opportunities indefinitely by removing the person from current and future education, employment, and civic engagement opportunities. Whether the length of incarceration is 30 days or 30 years, an incarceration event alters an individual's equal access to everyday citizenship in the United States for the rest of the person's life due to the more than 45,000 federal and state public policies that automatically—and sometimes permanently—restrict access to certain types of employment, professional licensure, education, housing, voting, and even family foster and adoption opportunities for persons with a history of a felony conviction (Pettus-Davis et al., 2017). Because incarceration in and of itself is a traumatic event, incarceration increases life stress and has deleterious effects on mental and physical health (Wolff & Sánchez, 2020). Incarceration disrupts personal relationships and generates a lasting stigma for the incarcerated person and the person's loved ones, who are also impacted emotionally, financially, and in community standing.

Of particular concern is the negative impact on the children of adults who are incarcerated. Children of incarcerated parents are more likely to experience life strains such as poverty (a single incarceration event reduces annual earnings by 40% and increases the likelihood of housing instability, divorce, being raised by a single parent, and trauma caused by separation from a parent). Some research has found that children of incarcerated parents are more likely to report academic difficulties, aggressive behavior, psychological distress such as depression and anxiety, and future juvenile or criminal justice involvement. The overwhelming majority of women involved in the criminal justice system are mothers who are the custodial parent of their children younger than age 18 years, followed by both custodial and noncustodial fathers—more than 60% of incarcerated individuals have a child younger than age 18 years. Despite the promise of change, 21st-century criminal justice practices continue to disregard the ripple effects that the incarceration of a single individual has on children, families, and communities. All of these factors must be redressed to give criminal justice–involved people and their innocent loved ones and children equal social and mobility opportunities. Given the disproportionate incarceration of ethnic minorities, the burden of the far-reaching negative consequences also falls disproportionally on members of these same communities, causing substantial social stratification and limiting the opportunity to pursue full and meaningful lives in the United States.

Four Social Work Smart Decarceration Practice Approaches

Epperson and Pettus-Davis (2015) recommend four guiding concepts for achieving smart decarceration: (1) Change the narrative on incarceration and the incarcerated; (2) make criminal justice systemwide innovation; (3) implement transdisciplinary policy and practice innovations; and (4) employ evidence-driven strategies. Pettus-Davis et al. (2017) followed up these concepts with a study gleaning guideposts and strategies for smart decarceration from practitioners, advocates, reformers, and researchers. This section builds on that prior work and proposes four smart decarceration practice approaches specific to social work practice.

Insist that Least Restrictive Options Are Prioritized

Two decades into the 21st century, the majority of the incarcerated population is in prison or jail for offenses that are nonviolent or that did little to threaten public safety. Reversing the overuse of incarceration by changing public and criminal policymaking and eliminating biased criminal justice practices will lead to approaches that use incarceration only for the most dangerous of offenses (a small fraction of the incarcerated population). Substantially reducing the incarcerated population would allow more individuals to remain in the community, enable those individuals to repair any harm that was done to their loved ones and communities as a result of their behavior, and redirect justice-involved persons toward a path of achieving their full potential and being productive and engaged community members.

Social workers can insist on a reformed criminal justice system that values diverting people toward community supports. Social work educators can teach the next generation of social workers as well as veteran social workers through continuing education that "treatment first" and "least restrictive environment" approaches that honor human dignity are more appropriate responses to people with mental health or substance use disorders who are exhibiting behaviors that are disruptive or fear-producing. In addition, because the criminal justice system still harbors racial and economic biases, social workers should view the use of incarceration with great skepticism if racial or economic equity is to be achieved.

Provide High-Quality Evidence-Driven Social Work Interventions in the Community

Keeping people in communities instead of incarcerating them gives them educational and employment opportunities, as well as the possibility of building mental and physical health and strong, healthy relationships. Community-based supports increase the likelihood that people with mental and substance use disorders will receive appropriate treatment, which can lead to healthy coping styles and reduced psychological distress, thus giving people with behavioral health disorders a greater chance to be contributing, productive, and highly valued members of the community. Lowering the incarceration rate will also lower the prevalence of lifetime traumatic experiences in the population, which will improve health at the population and individual levels. Helping people in poverty avoid incarceration once they have become involved with the criminal justice system should set these individuals on a path to upward social and financial mobility rather economic destruction.

Keeping children connected to parents because high-quality evidence-driven interventions are available in the community facilitates their positive attachments not only to the parent but also to other caring adults, provides adult supervision and modeling during critical developmental stages for children, and allows children to avoid the trauma of being separated from a parent. This enables children instead to develop emotional health and experience stability that can occur when a parent and child remain together (recognizing that some parent and child situations are more harmful to the child's health and not intending to discount the very important role of child welfare in protecting children in cases of neglect or abuse).

High-quality and evidence-driven social work–driven alternatives to incarceration can be established through partnerships between researchers, policymakers, and practitioners. When effective, these partnerships will facilitate the development of feedback loops that allow evidence from research to inform practice delivery and policy innovations and allow for practitioners and policymakers to inform future research agendas. Social work curriculum throughout the country trains students to identify and implement evidence-driven practices. The next stage for social work educators, researchers, and practitioners is to help build capacity in local communities necessary for the use of evidence-driven practices to support the needs of their residents by preventing justice involvement and diverting people from incarceration when possible.

Engage in Smart Decarceration Advocacy and Boundary-Spanning Work

Social work, which has a long history of leading reforms of institutions, has an important role to play in promoting smart decarceration advocacy. Social workers can help increase the impact of the voice of those with incarceration histories by collaborating with these individuals to organize in collective action and/or political action. Schools and programs of social work can do their part in ensuring that people are not further excluded after their sentence has been served. For example, social work programs should not automatically exclude a person from pursuing a bachelor's or master's degree simply because they have a history of criminal justice involvement.

Social workers are increasingly employed in various sectors of the criminal justice system and, as such, have a unique opportunity to span boundaries across these sectors. Social workers may have a major impact on daily practices of criminal justice actors in their day-to-day duties in these settings, as well as by hosting cross-sector training for judges, prosecutors, public defenders, law enforcement, and jail and prison professionals. The content of cross-sector training may include symptoms of lifetime traumatic experiences, de-escalation skills, differences between symptoms of mental health and substance use disorders and criminal behavior, impact of power differentials and historical racism and marginalizations, community capacity and resources external to the criminal justice system, and modern-day racial and economic disparities. Schools of social work can work collaboratively with each sector of the criminal justice system to create practicum placement (internship) positions at each stage of the criminal justice process from booking to parole. By infusing the criminal justice system with social workers to conduct trained and clinical assessments, numerous exit points from the criminal justice system may be identified as well as opportunities to divert people toward community-based systems of care. Placing practicum students in nontraditional sectors of the criminal justice system in which social workers are uncommon will

increase the likelihood that future social work staff positions will be developed within a criminal justice entity.

Prepare Future Social Workers

Schools of social work are well positioned to develop social work talent in promoting smart decarceration-driven policymaking. Beginning in undergraduate education, specializations can be created to promote smart decarceration. Pre- and post-master's degree fellowships that are focused on criminal justice reform will help social workers identify the everyday challenges that must be addressed when pursuing major system changes. Pre- and postdoctoral fellowships will allow for focused training with future social work researchers to set research agendas that not only help usher in an era of decarceration but also help ensure that an era of mass incarceration is not ever revisited. Social work faculty are increasingly developing textbooks, syllabi, courses, and curriculum that are oriented toward smart decarceration—and these efforts should continue. Schools of social work should embrace the opportunity to develop the skills and leadership of those who have been justice-involved by increasing postsecondary opportunities for people with felony convictions, offering training in policy advocacy and leadership, and creating more opportunities for those most directly impacted by incarceration to guide research and practice innovation.

Conclusion

Every facet of social work practice is overrepresented among criminal justice populations. Helping to usher in a shift from the era of mass incarceration to smart decarceration is the social work imperative of the time. A groundswell of support and hunger for socially just and evidence-driven reforms ensure that social work is a needed and welcome voice in the smart decarceration movement; and social work is well position to lead.

Helpful Resources

Grand Challenges for Social Work. *Promote smart decarceration*: https://grandchallengesforsocialwork.org/wp-content/uploads/2015/12/180604-GC-decarceration.pdf

Institute for Justice Research and Development: https://ijrd.csw.fsu.edu

Prison Policy Initiative: https://www.prisonpolicy.org

Smart Decarceration Project: https://voices.uchicago.edu/smartdecar

The Sentencing Project: https://www.sentencingproject.org

References

Alper, M., & Durose, M. (2018). *2018 update on prisoner recidivism: A 9-year follow-up period (2005–2014)*. Publication No. NCJ 250975. Bureau of Justice Statistics. https://www.bjs.gov/content/pub/pdf/18upr9yfup0514.pdf

Bonzcar, T. P. (2003). *Prevalence of imprisonment in the U.S. population, 1974–2001*. Publication No. NCJ197976. Bureau of Justice Statistics. http://www.cbsnews.com/htdocs/pdf/prisontime.pdf

Brame, R., Bushway, S. D., Paternoster, R., & Turner, M. G. (2014). Demographic patterns of cumulative arrest prevalence by ages 18 and 23. *Crime & Delinquency, 60*, 471–486.

Epperson, M. W., & Pettus-Davis, C. (Eds.). (2017). *Smart decarceration: Achieving criminal justice transformation in the 21st century*. Oxford University Press.

Epperson, M. W., Wolff, N., Morgan, R. D., Fisher, W. H., Frueh, B. C., & Huening, J. (2014 Envisioning the next generation of behavioral health and criminal justice interventions). Envisioning the next generation of behavioral health and criminal justice interventions. *International Journal of Law and Psychiatry, 37*(5), 427–438.

Geller, A., Garfinkel, I., & Western, B. (2011). Paternal incarceration and support for children in fragile families. *Demography, 48*, 25–47.

Huebner, B. M., & Berg, M. T. (2011). Examining the sources of variation in risk for recidivism. *Justice Quarterly, 28*, 146–173. doi:10.1080/07418820903365213

Johnson, B. D. (2003). Racial and ethnic disparities in sentencing departures across modes of conviction. *Criminology, 41*, 449–490. doi:10.1111/j.1745-9125.2003.tb00994.x

Kaebel, D., & Cowhig, M. (2018). Correctional populations in the United States, 2016. Publication No. NCJ 251211. Bureau of Justice Statistics. https://www.bjs.gov/index.cfm?ty=pbdetail&iid=6226

Looman, M. D., & Carl, J. D. (2015). *A country called prison: Mass incarceration and the making of a new nation*. Oxford University Press.

Mauer, M. (2016). Race to incarcerate: The causes and consequences of mass incarceration. *Roger Williams University Law Review, 21*, 447.

McLaughlin, M., Pettus-Davis, C., Brown, D., Veeh, C., & Renn, T. (2016). The economic burden of incarceration in the United States. https://tinyurl.com/vcj7qjs

Pettus-Davis, C., & Epperson, M. W. (2015). *From mass incarceration to smart decarceration*. American Academy of Social Work and Social Welfare.

Pettus-Davis, C., Epperson, M. W., & Grier, A. (2017). Reforming civil disability policy to facilitate effective and sustainable decarceration. In M. W. Epperson & C. Pettus-Davis (Eds.), *Smart decarceration: Achieving criminal justice transformation in the 21st century* (pp. 160–177). Oxford University Press.

Primus, E. (2017). Defense counsel and public defense. In E. Luna (Ed.), *A report on scholarship and criminal justice reform* (pp. 121–145). Academy for Justice.

Rosenfeld, R., Rojek, J., & Decker, S. H. (2012). Age matters: Race differences in police searches of young and older male drivers. *Journal of Research in Crime and Delinquency, 49*, 31–55.

Ruback, R. B. (2011). The abolition of fines and fees: Not proven and not compelling. *Criminology & Public Policy, 10*, 569–581.

Sobol, N. L. (2015). Charging the poor: Criminal justice debt and modern-day debtors' prisons. *Maryland Law Review, 75*, 486.

The Sentencing Project. (2013, August). Report of The Sentencing Project to the United Nations Human Rights Committee regarding racial disparities in the United States criminal justice system. https://tinyurl.com/y49c7hla

Wagner, P., & Sawyer, W. (2018). States of incarceration: The global context 2018. Prison Policy Initiative. https://www.prisonpolicy.org/global/2018.html

Wakefield, S., & Uggen. C. (2010). Incarceration and stratification. *Annual Review of Sociology, 36*, 387–406.

Westcott, K. (2015). Race, criminalization, and historical trauma in the United States: Making the case for a new justice framework. *Traumatology, 21*, 273.

Wolff, N., & Sánchez, F. C. (2020). Co-morbid psychological distress groups among incarcerated men. *Journal of Criminal Psychology, 10*(3), 169–183.

Wooldredge, J., Frank, J., Goulette, N., & Travis, L. (2015). Is the impact of cumulative disadvantage on sentencing greater for Black defendants? *Criminology & Public Policy, 14*, 187–223.

Neurobiology of Trauma for First Responders and Social Workers

Leslie Weisman

For law enforcement officers, medics, and fire-fighters, the daily experience of being immersed in the trauma of others brings untold trauma to the responders themselves. In the social work field, the same is true. There are many facets of social work that are particularly vulnerable to trauma, including adult and child protective services, emergency mental health, and homeless outreach. It simply is not possible for first responders to absorb the horror, danger, and tragedy they experience without a significant toll on their mind and body. Data indicate that 10–30% of traditional first responders will suffer from some type of traumatic stress injury during their career, and this estimate seems conservative (McGill, 2016).

The training that police and firefighters receive, starting at their respective academies, will often minimize the impact of trauma as well as the perils of riding what Gilmartin (2002) refers to as the "hypervigilance biological rollercoaster." From hire to retire, it is critical that first responders understand the impact of trauma on the brain, mind, and body and how to mitigate the effects of this risk to physical and mental well-being.

For forensic social workers, there is regular exposure to family violence, including physical, sexual, psychological, and verbal abuse; the tensions of the criminal justice system; and issues of neglect and abandonment. In a study of master's-level licensed social workers, 15.2% of survey respondents reported secondary traumatic stress, meeting diagnostic criteria for post-traumatic stress disorder (PTSD), as a result of indirect exposure to trauma material. This is almost twice the rate of PTSD in the general population (Substance Abuse and Mental Health Services Administration, 2014). This can lead to high rates of turnover and, for some, leaving the field altogether. Per Bride and Kintzle's study, social workers are more likely to work with individuals who have suffered from trauma compared to any other helping professionals. Whether it is facilitating the removal of a child from a negligent or abusive parent or supporting a victim of intimate partner violence, the resulting secondary traumatic stress can reduce the quality of care provided by social workers. Social workers also experience correlating health problems secondary to the experience of excessive and prolonged stress.

If social workers and first responders are to excel in their field, it is contingent not only on their technical acumen but also on their ability to grasp the impact of their work on the psychological and physiological systems of the body. This includes an understanding of the importance of resilience and self-care. Data show that first responders die, on average, significantly younger than their civilian counterparts. In a study of 2,800 officers in Buffalo, New York, the average life expectancy was found to be 22 years younger than that of their counterparts. Statistics are no better for correctional officers or retired law enforcement (Brandl & Smith, 2013).

Science has shown that repeated experiences of trauma will alter and damage the brain's neural pathways (Genovese, 2019). Police are often exposed repeatedly to traumatic material, especially in investigative functions such as child abuse and exploitation investigations. It is not uncommon for medical and psychological problems to develop and go untreated for years, adding to the sobering health statistics for emergency responders. The development of resilience early in the career of a first responder will diminish the effects of the constant stress. There are also many communities throughout the country that utilize social workers to mitigate the effects of stress on first responders (Barrett & Greene, 2017). Social workers provide counseling and other resources to address issues of substance abuse, depression, family discord, and anxiety.

Trauma and the Impact on the Brain

Psychological trauma is a person's emotional response to an extremely harrowing experience, such as suffering life-threatening danger or injury, witnessing death, or losing a colleague in the line of duty. Trauma can reach a crisis point when the critical incident overwhelms the responder's ability to cope. It is not inevitable that a person under these circumstances will be diagnosed with PTSD, but it does mean the event has now become part of the person's sensory memory (Usher et al., 2016). This sensory information is then processed by the nervous system. Any of the five senses can be triggered in the future when the brain associates a new sensory experience with the original sensory experience.

Secondary or *vicarious trauma* is the indirect exposure to trauma that is part of all first responder work. It is defined as the experience of similar symptoms and responses to those of people who have been through an actual trauma through indirect exposure to the trauma. Social workers are often in this position of hearing the retelling of traumatic encounters—for example, sexual or physical assault. This vicarious experience can have an impact on the worker's neurological, physical, psychological, and spiritual makeup. *Traumatic stress injury* refers to the physiological changes that can occur when the stress response remains long after the threat is gone. The symptoms can range from sleep disorders to PTSD.

Brain science on the effects of trauma on the mind and body shows that trauma can cause lifelong changes in a person; the brain can become less resilient after a trauma and the individual less able to move forward and deal effectively with future events. Given that every person's brain is "wired" differently, the effects of trauma on first responders vary widely.

Suicide and Stress for First Responders

In 2019, Virginia conducted a first-of-its-kind mental health survey of police, firefighters, and 911 dispatchers that found that these first responders experience suicidal thoughts at a rate of more than double that of the general population and nearly one-fourth of the respondents suffer from work-related depression (Jouvenal, 2019). The data confirm a national trend showing that police officers and firefighters are more likely to die by suicide than in the line of duty. Blue H.E.L.P., a nonprofit organization that collects law enforcement suicide data, reported 228 police suicides in 2019, the highest total since data collection began.

The role of cumulative trauma in the data is indisputable. The Yoga Shield/Yoga for First Responders organization cites the following: 40% of police officers suffer from sleep disorders; on average, a correctional officer will live only 18 months after retirement; and 18–37% of law enforcement officers and fire service report post-traumatic stress (Mead, 2019).

In police culture, it is well known that officers tend to cope in alarmingly unhealthy ways. There is a tendency to want to control everything both at work and at home, but it is simply not possible. The term *post-traumatic stress* refers to the normal process of the internal system attempting to regulate itself. If this regulation cannot be achieved over a course of several weeks or months, it leads to a number of physical ailments, such as backaches, headaches, digestive problems, high blood pressure, and other chronic illnesses. Psychological symptoms are numerous and include hyperarousal/hypervigilance, depression and anxiety, intrusive thoughts, sleep disorders, irritability, or anger (Mead, 2019).

Among the numerous recommendations in the 2019 Law Enforcement Mental Health and Wellness Act is the recommendation to embed mental health professionals in law enforcement agencies. Many departments now have social workers physically located at the department as well as riding along with police. These social workers not only provide social work expertise but also provide support to the officers (Spence et al., 2019).

The Hypervigilance Rollercoaster Effect

Hypervigilance, for first responders, is the concept of viewing the world from a threat-based perspective (Gilmartin, 2002). On duty, an officer may be hypervigilant—both alert and focused—but once off duty the officer is tired, detached, and even angry. Gilmartin refers to these two opposing states as the "hypervigilance biological rollercoaster."

The hypervigilance rollercoaster (Gilmartin, 2002), at its core, is biological in nature. The variability between sympathetic nervous system and parasympathetic nervous system responses lead to impacts in social and psychological functioning. For this reason, police and firefighters need education on the impact of their work on the body and mind. The hypervigilance required of policing and the high state of alert that firefighters live with are constantly impacting the ways they manage their environment. Because these men and women will routinely swing between highs and lows of vigilance and high alert, they are particularly in need of tools to help recalibrate. Yoga, other breath techniques, and treatments that include whole body involvement have demonstrated success with first responders.

The autonomic nervous system (ANS) plays a pivotal role in the hypervigilance rollercoaster of first responders. The ANS is divided into the sympathetic nervous system (SNS) and the parasympathetic nervous system (PNS). The sympathetic branch is evident in the day-to-day functioning of police and fire because it is responsible for increased peripheral vision, improved hearing, faster reaction times, increased blood sugar, elevated heart rate, and a general sense of energy that can be used to meet and overcome potential threats to safety. This is essentially the "on-duty" branch of the nervous system. In the face of intense stimuli (e.g., fire and smoke, blood and severed limbs, and gunshots), a responder will likely experience tension, sweat, nausea, or rapid breathing (Coates, 2019). The body is moving into "fight-or-flight" mode.

When off duty, the SNS gives way to the PNS, which is best known for the "rest and digest" function. It is not unusual for the first responder to return home and look detached or withdrawn. If a first responder is more sensitive to this biological rollercoaster, they can take steps to counteract the effect. Focused mindful breathing can slow heart rate and digestion; promote a feeling of calm; and settle down the SNS, which has been releasing stress hormones and essentially "amping up" the responder. Gilmartin (2002) refers to this process as finding "biological homeostasis" or biological balance.

When a crisis or significantly intense call is over, the stress hormones are no longer needed, and the body will metabolize the hormones. However, if the first responder is chronically activated, stress hormones will continue to fire, and this can become toxic to brain functioning. One of the key concerns with chronic stress activation is the resulting impact on the hippocampus. When cortisol is constantly firing, there is a breakdown in the functioning of the hippocampus as well as a shrinking in this area of the brain. At the same time, the amygdala will increase in size due to constant activation. This makes the amygdala more sensitive to stimuli and more likely to fire unnecessarily. The subsequent constant firing of stress hormones leads to memory and attention problems, irritability, and sleep disruption (van der Kolk, 2015).

Lieutenant Colonel Dave Grossman, a nationally recognized authority on combat response for military and law enforcement, partnered with Bruce Siddle (researcher and former law enforcement officer) to expand on the Warrior Color Code chart (McKay & McKay, 2013). The chart breaks out the stress response based on heart rate variability (HRV). HRV is a measure of how well the ANS is working. It takes a measure of the relative balance between the SNS and PNS. When we inhale, we stimulate the SNS, which results in an increased heart rate. When we exhale, the PNS is activated, which decreases heart rate. In healthy people, there are normal fluctuations in heart rate, and this reflects physical well-being.

If a first responder is dysregulated, the ANS is poorly regulated and the person is responding from an unbalanced stance in terms of both their mental and their physical well-being. This is critical for first responders because it demonstrates the small cognitive and physical breakdowns that occur in the body secondary to fear and stress. As first responders are flooded with stress hormones, there is a related increase in HRV. Biologically, this will prime the body for fight or flight, which is generally a positive and useful response. But if the stress and hormone levels are too high, the physical and cognitive skill sets of these responders will begin to deteriorate. For an officer or firefighter in a life-or-death situation, this can mean the difference between someone getting killed or rescued and brought to safety.

Post-Traumatic Stress Disorder

Although the diagnosis of PTSD can be devastating to the first responder, it is also common enough that treatment options are numerous and usually easily accessed. According to the American Psychiatric Association (2013), PTSD is diagnosed after exposure to *actual or threatened* death, serious injury, or sexual violence. The primary symptoms include intrusive memories, distressing dreams, flashbacks, and numerous physiological reactions.

With PTSD, it is difficult to stop these sensations. The likelihood of ongoing fatigue and chronic stress in the workplace means the first responder will be more vulnerable to the effects of subsequent trauma. When first responders ignore signs of PTSD and come to work, their performance is often marked by mood swings, angry outbursts, low frustration tolerance, and poor concentration.

There is a plethora of well-documented data related to the prevalence of PTSD in this population. Statistics show that no less than one-third of first responders will suffer from some form of acute post-traumatic stress during their career (McGill, 2016).

It is important that first responders are presented with the possibility of responding to a horrific call with fellow responders and emerging with drastically different emotional mindsets from one another. This speaks to the uniqueness of each responder's neurobiological wiring. Most responders may emerge relatively unscathed from the horrific call, but the outlier is deeply affected, sometimes in irreparable ways. There is still much to learn regarding the variety of reactions for police and firefighters. It may relate to the degree of prior trauma that a responder has experienced in their life or to a pre-existing personal history of depression and/or anxiety.

In brain scans of people with PTSD, clear, measurable physical changes can be observed (De Bellis et al., 1999). After exposure to trauma, the body becomes overstimulated, and there is often a feeling of numbness followed by a feeling of hypervigilance that can remain for days, weeks, or longer. People with PTSD also have abnormal levels of stress-related chemicals and hormones, which impact the healthy balance of emotional regulation and decision-making capacity. Cortisol levels are lower than those without the diagnosis, and epinephrine and norepinephrine are higher than average. These hormones are responsible for the fight-or-flight response, and this leads to the person with PTSD living in a constant fight-or-flight mode.

Innovations in Stress Management for First Responders

Now that we have discussed the neurobiological challenges related to trauma and stress, we focus on the latest developments in wellness for first responders. With the heightened understanding of trauma-informed care, including trauma-informed policing, and the focus on self-care, there are now many options

available for first responders. From police and firefighters to social workers, wellness and resilience are now institutionalized concepts.

Mindfulness and Meditation for First Responders

Mindfulness has exploded in the general population during the past 20–30 years or more, and there is growing evidence that it is a best practice for first responders. Mindfulness is the process of paying attention, on purpose, without judgment, per Jon Kabat-Zinn, creator of mindfulness-based stress reduction and a world-renowned expert on meditation and mindfulness. Studies show that mindfulness is associated with a decrease in PTSD symptoms, depression, various medical conditions, and substance abuse.

With increased interest in mindfulness comes the corresponding focus on meditation. It is a 5,000-year-old practice that is embraced by cultures throughout the world. Meditation has a striking impact on psychological stress by decreasing reactivity and allowing for more intentional responses to stressful situations. With a regular meditation practice, there is a heightened sense of self-awareness that can lead to greater focus and clarity for first responders.

Neuroscience is showing, through functional magnetic resonance imaging, that the brain of a person with a regular meditation practice looks significantly different than those of other people. There is increased thickness in the areas responsible for empathy, compassion, fairness, and cooperation. Science also shows that meditation enhances concentration, quickens cognition, improves emotional control, helps reduce tension, lowers heart rate, and reduces anxiety and stress. Many police and fire departments are now including meditation and mindfulness practices as well as yoga.

Impact of Yoga on First Responders

Yoga is making an impact on first responders by teaching them to focus on breathing techniques, sitting with discomfort, and mastery of the mind—all critical ingredients to successful job performance. The way a person breathes can significantly impact their ability to handle anger, depression, and anxiety, and this is evidenced in individuals with a regular yoga practice. As we breathe, we continually cause the heart to speed up and slow down, and with this there is natural variability between each heartbeat. The more fluctuation, the better because this indicates the body's arousal system is operating in an optimal manner and the body is more in balance.

Research also shows that a regular yoga practice can have a significant impact on the symptoms of PTSD. Its original intention was to achieve mastery of the mind and optimal functioning of the entire body—from the nervous system to the physical body (Mead, 2019). These benefits can help first responders improve overall health and increase resilience.

Recommendations for Developing Resilience and Increased Self-Care

It is commonly understood that resilience is the capacity to adapt successfully in the face of adversity, trauma, or threats of physical or psychological harm (SAMHSA, 2014). The degree of resilience that a first responder will have is closely related to the person's internal strengths and the environmental supports that are in place. There is not a large volume of research as to why some responders will be more resilient than others. It appears that a person may have individual characteristics that will influence resilience—for example, neurobiology, flexibility in adapting to change, and overall positive attitude. Resilience can be viewed as a perishable commodity which requires daily training and heightened self-awareness.

It is imperative that police and fire departments offer training in resiliency and

self-regulation because this skill set will mitigate the detrimental effects of stress. First responders need a variety of strategies for regaining their psychological and physiological equilibrium after intense job-related stress. As first responders learn how to strengthen their resilience and appreciate the criticality of social connection, they will also improve the intimate relationships in their life.

First responder organizations and social work agencies clearly benefit when they include wellness activities such as yoga, meditation, and other forms of exercise. Training should be provided that highlights the chronic emotional stress inherent in the work and the importance of self-care. As mentioned previously, this should occur from hire to retire and beyond.

Post-Traumatic Growth

Post-traumatic growth is defined as the "experience of individuals whose development, at least in some areas, has surpassed what was present before the trauma occurred" (Klinic Community Health Centre, 2013). It is hoped that after a traumatic event, first responders will grow and learn from the experience. They also may be forever changed in their ability to function effectively. The process for the first responder to become psychologically resilient is to balance the negative emotions connected with the event with positive emotions and to choose healthy coping mechanisms to assist in recovery.

Forensic Social Work Response to Trauma and Interface with First Responders

As discussed previously, social workers in the field will not only interface with first responders but also can fall victim to the same effects of chronic stress and trauma. Van Dernoot and Burk (2009) describe many factors related to trauma in their conceptualization of *trauma exposure response*. In particular, they define this response as the experience of bearing witness to atrocities that are committed human against human. Some of the themes they describe that are particularly problematic for social workers and first responders are feelings of hopelessness and helplessness, a feeling that one can never do enough, hypervigilance, chronic exhaustion/physical ailments, fear, anger, and cynicism. These shared and powerful experiences lend credence to the need for further partnering between social workers and first responders.

It is important to recognize that social workers and first responders bring their own trauma history to their work. Depending on the severity of this history, it will have more or less impact on job performance. Scenarios such as removing a child from a psychotic or suicidal parent or bearing witness to first-time psychosis in a young person can leave indelible marks on the psyche of a social worker. Other factors that can increase risk for trauma exposure response are overworking, lack of experience, working with traumatized children, or having too many negative clinical outcomes (Klinic Community Health Centre, 2013).

Social workers who are exposed to these scenarios need the ability to access strengths-based supervision from a supervisor who is well trained in trauma response. This supervisor is tasked with helping the social worker understand their trauma-related stress reactions. It is critical that the social worker can discuss these concerns in a safe environment with no fear of reprisal or reprimand.

The agency should place a high value on providing an environment that ensures staff wellness. There are many strategies for organizations to prevent secondary traumatization, including normalizing the experience throughout the agency, close monitoring of clinical workloads, and increased opportunity for staff training directly related to understanding vicarious trauma. Other options to manage vicarious trauma include peer support, trauma-informed supervision, professional training, individual counseling, maintaining work–life balance, and engaging in spiritual activities (Substance Abuse and Mental Health Services Administration, 2014).

Specific aspects of social workers make them more prone to the trauma exposure response, including the empathy social workers typically bring to their work—the hallmark of the profession being the unconditional positive regard social workers feel for their clients. This can become an occupational hazard if the degree of openness and empathy leaves a social worker overly susceptible to the trauma experienced by their clients. The fallout may be minimal and barely perceptible, or it could be life-changing.

Conclusion

As with first responders, it is critical that social workers, in order to find satisfaction and longevity in their profession, dig deep to fully understand the impact of trauma on both their mind and their body. Just as many recruits are now receiving training on trauma and resilience while at the academy, social work programs should also train students in these concepts prior to launching their career. This may mitigate the risk for PTSD and ensure career tenure.

In summary, first responders and social workers need to become trauma aware, which will lead to greater self-care, which in turn leads to greater resilience, ultimately ensuring a more successful career and greater life expectancy.

References

American Psychiatric Association. (2013). *Diagnostic and statistical manual of mental disorders* (5th ed.).

American Psychiatric Publishing. https://doi.org/10.1176/appi.books.9780890425596

Barrett, K., & Greene, R. (2017, July 7). "Giving help and not asking for it": Inside the mental health of first responders. Governing: The Future of States and Localities. https://www.governing.com/columns/smart-mgmt/gov-police-mental-health-firefighters-corrections.html

Brandl, S. G., & Smith, B. W. (2013). An empirical examination of retired police officers' length of retirement and age at death: A research note. Police Quarterly, 16(1), 113–123. https://doi.org/10.1177/1098611112465611

Bride, B. E., & Kintzle, S. (2011). Secondary traumatic stress, job satisfaction, and occupational commitment in substance abuse counselors. Traumatology, 17(1), 22–28.

Coates, C. (2019). Mindful responder: The first responder's field guide to improved resilience, fulfillment, presence, & fitness—on & off the job. Calibre Press.

De Bellis, M. D., Keshavan, M. S., Clark, D. B., Casey, B. J., Giedd, J. N., Boring, A. M., Frustaci, K., & Ryan, N. D. (1999). Developmental traumatology Part II: Brain development. Biological Psychiatry, 45(10), 1271–1284.

Genovese, M. (2019, June 26). Building a culture of resiliency from the top down. PoliceOne.com. https://www.policeone.com/health-fitness/articles

Gilmartin, K. M. (2002). Emotional survival for law enforcement: A guide for officers and their families. E-S Press.

Jouvenal, J. (2019, October 28). New survey shows heavy psychological toll for Virginia's first responders. The Washington Post. https://www.washingtonpost.com/local/public-safety

Klinic Community Health Centre. (2013). Trauma informed: The trauma-informed toolkit. https://trauma-informed.ca/wp-content/uploads/2013/10/Trauma-informed_Toolkit.pdf

McGill, J. (2016, June 27). 5 things cops need to know about PTSD. PoliceOne.com. https://www.policeone.com/health-fitness/articles

McKay, B., & McKay, K. (2013). Managing stress arousal for optimal performance: A guide to the warrior color code. Art of Manliness. https://www.artofmanliness.com/articles/managing-stress-arousal-for-optimal-performance-a-guide-to-the-warrior-color-code

Mead, O. (2019). YogaShield/Yoga for First Responders training manual. https://www.yogaforfirstresponders.org/instructor-school

Spence, D. L., Fox, M., Moore, G. C., Estill, S., & Comrie, N. E. A. (2019). Law enforcement mental health and wellness act. https://cops.usdoj.gov/RIC/Publications/cops-p370-pub.pdf

Substance Abuse and Mental Health Services Administration. (2014). Trauma-informed care in behavioral health services: Quick guide for clinicians based on TIP 57. https://store.samhsa.gov/product/Trauma-Informed-Care-in-Behavioral-Health-Services-Quick-Guide-for-Clinicians-Based-on-TIP-57/SMA15-4912

Usher, L., Friedhoff, S., Cochran, S., & Pandya, A. (2016). Preparing for the unimaginable: How chiefs can safeguard officer mental health before and after mass casualty events. Office of Community Oriented Policing Services.

van der Kolk, B. (2015). The body keeps the score: Brain, mind, and body in the healing of trauma. Penguin.

van Dernoot, L., & Burk, C. (2009). Trauma stewardship: An everyday guide to caring for self while caring for others. Berrett-Koehler.

Effective Community Reentry from Prison

Stacey D. Hardy-Chandler and Bryan W. Jackson

Take a moment and imagine what comes to mind when you think of a "homecoming." If you have fond memories of your high school or college days, you might think of an annual dance or pep rally leading up to the big football game. In this case, homecoming is a time when alumni of an educational institution are welcomed back to their alma mater (Latin for "nurturing mother") to celebrate a common connection to an institution and its current and past faculty and students. No matter if you attended the school 50 years ago or are preparing to graduate the next spring, all of *us* who are "Tigers," "Lions," or "Bears" sport our colors and are joined to one another in celebration of a unified educational community.

Another type of homecoming is when active military personnel return from deployment or, specifically, from battle. There is no shortage of emotionally touching homecoming videos wherein heroic service members surprise their spouses and children by showing up unexpectedly. After months or sometimes years overseas, communicating exclusively through virtual means when available, it is difficult for even the most stoic among us to keep a

dry eye when a military father shows up unexpectedly at his daughter's elementary school or when a military mother pops out of a delivery box to the delight of her children. Even videos in which the family dog welcomes a service member home are absolute tearjerkers.

However, there is another type of homecoming that garners far less fanfare or celebration yet happens on a far more frequent basis and arguably has a far greater societal impact. For these homecomings, there are no ribbons or flags, no rallies or ceremonies. For prison inmates returning home, efforts marking their transition back into "the outside" are proportionately few. According to the U.S. Department of Justice (n.d.), more than 10,000 people formerly incarcerated in state and federal prisons are released into the community every week. Furthermore, what happens as part of these "homecomings" is critical because approximately two-thirds of these people are likely to be rearrested within 3 years of release (U.S. Department of Justice, n.d.).

We must be clear: We are not comparing ex-prisoners with school alumni or service members, although it is important to note that these populations commonly overlap. Instead, we are hoping to emphasize that homecomings, in their various forms, do in fact matter. For those who are returning home post-incarceration, efforts to promote successful reentry into the community especially matter because these contexts are intricately intertwined with racism, an unjust criminal law system, the school-to-prison pipeline, and other highly complex biopsychosocial factors. Even if we were to do the impossible task of removing institutional and structural racism from society, on a very fundamental level we all share an investment in the extent to which former inmates successfully transition into life in the community. Although some segments of society hold an "out-of-sight, out-of-mind" view of those convicted and sent to prison, according to the Bureau of Justice Statistics (n.d.), 95% of all state prisoners will be released at some point and will reenter society. We must therefore ask: Will these individuals become our neighbors, or will they recidivate and become our collective burden?

What Is "Reentry"?

Reentry programs and, in some jurisdictions, reentry courts are designed to help persons successfully "reenter" or return to society after a period of incarceration. The primary focus of reentry programs is to remove or reduce physical and invisible barriers that could prevent the formerly incarcerated from becoming contributing members of society. Individuals who choose to take part in reentry programs can receive employment support, stable housing, supervision for medical and mental health needs, and other necessities that assist in a healthy transition from incarceration.

But the reentry process should in fact start *before* one's release from prison. According to the Federal Bureau of Prisons (n.d.), preparation and planning for reentry should begin the very first day someone is incarcerated. This approach is akin to the medical and psychiatric social work philosophy that discharge planning starts at the point of admission. In reality, focus on life after prison ramps up in the year and a half before an inmate's scheduled release (Federal Bureau of Prisons, n.d.).

In addition, it is important to note that reentry programs are voluntary. With that in mind, why do some eligible inmates choose not to participate in some type of reentry program? The answer to that question is more complex than it seems and touches on issues related to the social work value of the "dignity and worth" of the person. In short, people who never felt respected or valued before entering prison might not feel that they are worth investing in upon release from prison. It is not unusual for those facing re-entry to think something to the effect of:

> If society sees me as a monster by virtue of my race, background, or gender—completely separate from my actions—then, it stands to reason that since a "reentry program" is not going to change my core characteristics, it therefore cannot possibly impact how I will be viewed or received when I get out.

It is suspected that many of those who would otherwise benefit from reentry programs hold this view, and although there are some deeply rooted justifications for their feelings of distrust and hopelessness, there are multiple ways to counter misconceptions and increase inmate engagement.

Here is where forensic and clinical social workers, counselors, health professionals, clergy, volunteers, and even correctional personnel can make a difference. When asked about the critical issue of access to these potentially life-changing programs, one of this chapter's authors (B. W. J.) observed that "relationships" were critical to which inmates took advantage of reentry opportunities and which did not. While working in offender reentry, he observed that when staff (of any discipline) took the time to usher inmates toward reentry opportunities—build trusting relationships with them—inmates were more likely to participate and glean the benefits that such programs offer.

But in addition to benefiting the formerly incarcerated individual, reentry programs offer an array of benefits for the community at large, including the following:

- Reentry programs reduce recidivism, often resulting in keeping families together; those of us in social work know the multigenerational impact of the trauma of family disruption.
- Reentry programs promote public safety by helping people gain the skills and supports they need to avoid subsequent charges and reconvictions.
- Reentry programs save money at the state level; in 2015, nearly 1.3 million prisoners averaged a cost of $33,274 per year. The grand total for a single year was $42,883,537,590, excluding federal prisoners (Mai & Subramanian, 2017). In fiscal year 2017, the annual cost of incarceration for a single federal prisoner was $34,704.12 (Hyle, 2018).

Whether one's support of community reentry programs is based on preserving and empowering families, investing in safe communities, or reallocating pecuniary resources away from prisons, reentry programs clearly benefit us all.

What Is Community Supervision?

Of the 95% of prisoners who will be released from federal or state institutions, 80% will do so under community supervision conditions, according to the Bureau of Justice Statistics (n.d.).

Aside from reentry programs, those who become court connected or otherwise engaged with legal systems can be "supervised" or monitored in the community in two general ways: probation or parole (James, 2015).

Probation

When a person is on probation, it means that they have been found guilty of an offense, but the nature of their offense was not deemed serious enough for imprisonment. A court has allowed them to serve their sentence—in whole or in part—in the community under certain specific conditions that include regular check-ins with their probation officer. Failure to comply with probation conditions can result in criminal sanctions, including imprisonment.

Parole

When a person is on parole, it means that they have served the majority of their sentence while incarcerated but, due to a variety of factors, they may now be allowed to serve the remainder of their sentence in the community. As with probation, parole comes with a number of court-mandated conditions, violations of which could result in the individual being returned to prison. Parole can either be "mandatory," where release is determined by statutory language, or "discretionary," where members of a parole board make determinations (based on statute or administrative codes) about an individual's eligibility for release under community supervision. Sixteen states have abolished discretionary parole for all offenders (Bureau of Justice Statistics, n.d.).

A Practical, Ethical, and Moral Imperative

The United States surpasses any other global nation with its incarceration numbers. The Prison Fellowship (n.d.) reports that in the United States, approximately 6.6 million people live under supervision of adult correctional authorities (in prison, in jail, on probation, or on parole). Nearly 2.2 million men and women are behind bars, and more than 700,000 people are released every year—with two-thirds being rearrested within 3 years (Caporizzo, 2011). The annual cost to incarcerate this many people is more than $80 billion. Beyond the price tag, soaring levels of incarceration and recidivism take a toll on communities and families. This cycle of crime and incarceration produces broken relationships, victimization, despair, and instability.

The current process of releasing an incarcerated person with no social, emotional, or medical supports can lead to negative consequences. In many cases, the network left by the incarcerated person will be the same network they return to upon their arrival post-incarceration. As Bushway (2003) states,

> The average offender who is motivated to change but lacks some of the basic skills needed to construct a new social reality should be expected to struggle in this context. It seems plausible that a rough transition, including but not limited to difficulty finding work, could stop real change before it even starts, (p. 12)

This illuminates a number of primary barriers facing those reentering communities after having been imprisoned—barriers to the most basic human needs for survival such as food, clothing, and shelter. Here, we ask that readers call upon their imagination to respond honestly to a series of hypothetical scenarios grounded in real-world concerns facing those recently released from prison:

- You are a landlord seeking to rent out an apartment. What are your preconceptions about renting to someone recently released from prison?
- You are an employer with a "Now Hiring" sign in your business window. Someone with a felony record fills out the application. How will you weigh this person's candidacy as a potential employee?
- You are at a party and you learn that your friend's cousin will be there and that the cousin is on parole. Are you as willing to socialize with him as you are with others at the party?

But what if the tables were turned? Image that *you* are the person recently released from prison hoping for a better life than the one you had when you went in. *You* are the one hoping to make a change and to prove that you are not just another statistic. *You* are the person seeking to rent the apartment, applying for the job, and trying to build a sense of connection and community by attending a party. Does your perspective change?

The Role of Forensic Social Workers

Forensic social workers (FSWs) serve in a vast array of roles where the law and social work intersect. In the case of reentry, FSWs may be those working on interdisciplinary teams that promote and execute reentry program objectives. They may be administrators who run fundraising campaigns or promote community awareness on the value of these programs and the overarching reentry philosophy and movement. In addition, they may be frontline case managers, directly working with soon-to-be or recently released persons and assisting them in accessing the resources that they need to begin again in a rapidly changing world that they may not have experienced for years or even decades.

Race, Racism, and Bias

The United States leads all nations in incarceration rates. Although 2016 (the most recent available data at the time of this writing) marked an 8-year decline, still approximately 2,162,400 persons were detained in federal, state, and local facilities. Factoring probation and parole, 1 in 38 people in the United States were under some form of "correctional supervision" (Kaeble & Cowhig, 2018). The majority of those incarcerated were African American, who are incarcerated at rates that are five times those of Whites (Nellis, 2016). A study conducted by The Sentencing Project found that persistent racial disparities have long been a focus in criminological research, and the presence of these disparities ranged from racially biased policing to more severe legal outcomes for African Americans in the criminal justice system (Nellis, 2016). In addition, a range of individual-level factors, such as poverty, education outcomes, unemployment history, and criminal history, also contribute to the disproportionate rates of incarceration among African Americans. The national ratio of the racial disparities for African Americans compared to Whites in prison is 5:1. In five states, this disparity is more than 10:1, and in 12 states, more than half of the overall prison population is Black (Nellis, 2016).

Anti-Racist, Pro-Justice Intervention Needs to Start Early

Kindergarten through grade 12 students—especially those of color—are being pushed out of schools and into prisons. This practice is known as the "school-to-prison pipeline" (see Chapter 152 in this volume). According to the Justice Policy Institute, so-called "zero-tolerance" disciplinary policies are forcing mostly Black and Brown children to interact with law enforcement or school resource officers at a very early age and at alarming rates (Nelson & Lind, 2015). The zero-tolerance approach to in-school discipline disproportionately impacts African Americans, Latino

Americans, and students with disabilities. African American students are three or four times more likely to be suspended or expelled than White students for infractions that could be handled by school staff. Schools themselves are outsourcing discipline to law enforcement and introducing students to the juvenile justice system, often by having these students arrested at school. Children as young as age 5 years—described as "unruly and disrespectful"—have been detained and jailed for "throwing a tantrum." Once these children are put into contact with police, many are then pushed out of their schools through severe disciplinary protocols that can lead to students being funneled into the juvenile and criminal justice systems (Nelson & Lind, 2015).

Restorative Justice

Restorative justice is a term used to describe various Indigenous ways of life focused on healing past harm, living in community with others, and contributing positively to the greater environment. Many prisons and community groups have started to adopt forms of restorative justice to further rehabilitate men and women. This approach focuses on assisting those incarcerated or formerly incarcerated in becoming contributing members of society. In the article titled "Finding Responsibility, Reconciliation After a Crime," Stuart Recicar, an Offender Reentry Program Specialist who oversees restorative circles in Burlington, Vermont, said, "Volunteers help recently released prisoners talk through the choices that landed them in prison as well as new decisions that have the potential to do so again" (Beitsch, 2016). Forensic social workers, family, friends, and others can hold offenders accountable by calling their parole officers if necessary, but they can also help offenders adapt to life-on-the-outside basics such as helping them learn how to use a cell phone or how to upload a resume to a career website. Restorative justice takes intentionality, time, effort, and skilled facilitators. Long-term sustainability of this approach can also provide added emotional support, employment placement possibilities, and stable housing resources, all of which reduce recidivism and encourage past offenders to become productive community members.

Connecting with and Supporting Reentry Programs

How Inmates Access Reentry Programs

The way that incarcerated persons gain access to reentry programs varies from state to state. Sentencing plays an important first step in determining if a charged individual needs a reentry program or jail time. For a low-risk offender (i.e., someone convicted of a first-time driving under the influence offense or a substance abuse-related charge), judges can recommend community service, substance abuse classes, or inpatient therapy for mental health needs. If a person is convicted and sentenced to jail, they then take part in an intake process that evaluates their medical, mental health, educational, and substance abuse history. Optimally, the intake process would be conducted by a forensic social worker, thoroughly grounded in a biopsychosocial perspective, but currently, any number of correctional or ancillary staff persons perform this role. Taken together with their criminal offenses, intake information is used to classify the person as a low-, medium-, or high-risk inmate.

Utilizing this information, counselors and correction officers monitor an inmate's mental, behavioral, and social needs throughout their incarceration. When an inmate's sentence is almost over, evidence of the inmate's conduct during time served and a counselor's outtake evaluation detailing their mental, medical, and behavioral health are used to determine what supports are recommended upon their release. One of these supports can be a reentry program. Many reentry programs have supports for low- to medium-risk individuals. Again, these programs are not present in a majority of prisons and can differ from state to state (Federal Bureau of Prisons, n.d.).

Effective Reentry: Practices and Considerations

There is a greater chance of success and reduced recidivism when proactive and realistic planning is set in motion in anticipation of a person's release from incarceration focusing on training for work, substance and mental health interventions, and housing (Congressional Research Service, 2016; Mosteller, n.d.). Prison Fellowship (n.d.), the nation's largest nonprofit serving prisoners, former prisoners, and their families, recommends a reentry plan in their article titled "Eight Ways to Prepare for a Loved One's Reentry." We have reduced and adapted these to three key areas that include not only direct service factors but also broader professional considerations for practitioners. Note that given the large number of people who are incarcerated and released back into communities, whether you consider yourself a "forensic social worker" or not, if you work in any sector of the human services, there is a very high probability that you will encounter these issues—directly or indirectly—at some point in your professional career.

Understand Probation/Parole to Encourage Success

When a family member or friend is released from prison, they will most likely have conditions of parole. Some of these conditions may include curfews, geographic limits, mandatory job search, drug or alcohol tests, community treatment center attendance, electronic monitoring, and other requirements. If possible, one way to help these individuals is to encourage them to follow short-term compliance with these restrictions so as to foster long-term success and stability. The structure needed to meet conditions of parole can also support their adjustment to a future work context; helping the returning individual to see the connection between meeting parole conditions and developing real-world skills could support their adjustment to life back in the community.

At the community level, forensic social workers and others can help the returning individual and their family develop a relationship with the probation officer *as an ally* and to gain an understanding of the system so that the family can support their loved one in navigating this system effectively. Social workers and case managers can help by leveraging available community supports that best align with securing an individual's economic and social stability.

Use Resources for Long-Term Success

Transitioning from prison to the community requires time to adjust and to build up the resources necessary for getting back on one's feet. Adjusting to a culture outside prison that is changing at an ever-increasing rate and re-learning how to schedule one's time and how to make independent decisions about one's daily routine are tasks that become proportionately more challenging the longer someone has been incarcerated. Family and friends can help by saving money toward helping the reentering person access basic needs and services and, if they are able, help them acquire basic resources such as food and "interview clothes" as they search for a job and housing. They should note, however, that this assistance is short term and conditional on their loved one's efforts to find a job and become financially independent. Social work professionals can encourage ease of access to resources to help meet basic needs, especially community programs specifically

dedicated to serving reentering individuals. Programs that encourage entrepreneurship for ex-offenders are among the novel ways some communities strive to overcome the stigma of former imprisonment.

Beyond supplying basic needs, professionals can also connect formerly incarcerated persons with resources—such as counseling, spiritual guidance, and peer support—that address the symptoms of trauma and other underlying issues. Each of these interventions can be critical in helping the individual avoid recidivism in the years following their release. Forensic social workers and other professionals can also actively engage in advocacy for social policies (locally and on a broader scale) that break cycles of incarceration in accordance with social work principles supporting the "dignity and worth" of every individual. Efforts such as Ban the Box and other legal and systemic policy changes give reentering persons a chance at becoming productive, contributing members of society. When we remember that approximately 10,000 people per week step out of prisons and into our communities—and that these reentering persons are our neighbors, service providers, and co-workers—we recognize that we are all connected to each other in some way, shape, or form. The efforts that we make to bolster the likelihood of their success matter to every member of society.

Address Relationships

Anticipating the release of a family member or friend can be a confusing time; relatives and friends might feel full of hope and optimism, on the one hand, and feel overwhelmed by anxiety and dread, on the other hand. As time goes by, the initial excitement of a loved one's return home can wear off in light of the magnitude of the challenges that lie ahead. Many of the social and personal factors that existed before imprisonment likely still exist afterward, making the work that everyone faces in maintaining healthy relationships even more difficult for those intimately involved with loved ones returning from incarceration.

As early as possible, family members should engage in developing a plan for the difficult days to come after the elation of the reunion fades. The often extended search for a job, dealing with children's emotions and reactions to separation and reunion, and the judgments or temptations posed by well-meaning friends are complex relational dynamics that will challenge someone returning from prison. Those individuals in the returning person's immediate social circle, and those with whom the closest relationships are held, could form the most vital support system for their adjustment to the outside.

Forensic social workers and other human service professionals also play an important role in the reentering person's social network and across the service continuum through direct service delivery, family support and community development, and macro-level policy change (Mosteller, n.d.).

Helpful Resources

National Institute of Justice: https://nij.ojp.gov/topics/corrections/reentry
National Organization of Forensic Social Work: https://www.nofsw.org
Offender Aid and Restoration: https://www.oaronline.org
The Marshall Project: https://www.themarshallproject.org

References

Beitsch, R. (2016). Finding responsibility, reconciliation after a crime. *Stateline*. https://www.pewtrusts.org/en/research-and-analysis/blogs/stateline/2016/07/21/finding-responsibility-reconciliation-after-a-crime

Bureau of Justice Statistics. (n.d.). *Reentry trends in the U.S.* https://www.bjs.gov/content/reentry/releases.cfm

Bushway, S. D. (2003). *Reentry and prison work programs* [Discussion paper]. The Urban Institute Reentry Roundtable. https://www.researchgate.net/profile/Shawn_Bushway/publication/237135599_Reentry_and_Prison_Work_Programs/links/

0deec52543f06d54be000000/Reentry-and-Prison-Work-Programs.pdf

Caporizzo, C. (2011, November 30). *Prisoner reentry programs: Ensuring a safe and successful return to the community* [Blog]. The White House—President Barack Obama. https://obamawhitehouse.archives.gov/blog/2011/11/30/prisoner-reentry-programs-ensuring-safe-and-successful-return-community

Congressional Research Service. (2016). *Offender reentry: Correctional statistics, reintegration into the community, and recidivism.* https://www.everycrsreport.com/reports/RL34287.html#:~:text=The%20median%20time%20to%20first,BJS%20study%20(see%20above)

Federal Bureau of Prisons. (n.d.). *Reentry programs.* https://www.bop.gov/inmates/custody_and_care/reentry.jsp

Hyle, K. (2018). Annual determination of average cost of incarceration. *Federal Register, 83*(83), 18863. https://www.federalregister.gov/documents/2018/04/30/2018-09062/annual-determination-of-average-cost-of-incarceration

James, N. (2015, January 12). *Offender reentry: Correctional statistics, reintegration into the community, and recidivism.* Federation of American Scientists. https://fas.org/sgp/crs/misc/RL34287.pdf

Kaeble, D., & Cowhig, M. (2018). *Correctional populations in the united states.* Bureau of Justice Statistics. c

Mai, C., & Subramanian, R. (2017). *The price of prisons.* Vera Institute of Justice. https://www.vera.org/publications/price-of-prisons-2015-state-spending-trends/price-of-prisons-2015-state-spending-trends/price-of-prisons-2015-state-spending-trends-prison-spending

Mosteller, J. (n.d.). *What makes a reentry program successful?* Charles Koch Institute. https://www.charleskochinstitute.org/issue-areas/criminal-justice-policing-reform/reentry-programs

Nellis, A. (2016). *The color of justice: Racial and ethnic disparity in state prisons.* The Sentencing Project. https://www.sentencingproject.org/publications/color-of-justice-racial-and-ethnic-disparity-in-state-prisons

Nelson, L., & Lind, D. (2015). *The school to prison pipeline, explained.* http://www.justicepolicy.org/news/8775

Prison Fellowship. (n.d.). Eight ways to prepare for a loved one's reentry. https://www.prisonfellowship.org/resources/support-friends-family-of-prisoners/supporting-successful-prisoner-reentry/eight-ways-to-prepare-for-a-loved-ones-reentry

U.S. Department of Justice. (n.d.). *Prisoners and prisoner re-entry.* https://www.justice.gov/archive/fbci/progmenu_reentry.html

Animal-Assisted Social Work in Prisons

Yvonne Eaton-Stull

Most agree that dogs are essential parts of our lives; they provide comfort and support, offer unconditional love, and serve as an integral part of the family. The utilization of specially trained and evaluated "therapy dogs" has increased in the social work field. In fact, one national study found almost 25% of social workers are utilizing therapy animals (Risley-Curtiss, 2010). To better understand how social workers may utilize these special animals in their work, a brief review of terminology is useful:

- *Animal-assisted intervention* (AAI) is the umbrella term encompassing several interventions with therapy animals in health, education, and social services [International Association of Human–Animal Interaction Organizations (IAHAIO), 2018]. *Animal-assisted social work* (AASW) is the term to describe AAI utilized by social work professionals, and this may include the following:

  - Animal-assisted activities: informal interactions and visits to promote social, motivational, and educational benefits (IAHAIO, 2018). An example is

a social worker inviting a therapy dog to a visiting area in a facility to interact and offer affection.

- Animal-assisted therapy (AAT): formal, goal-oriented, planned, structured, and measured therapeutic interventions designed by a professional to improve client functioning (IAHAIO, 2018). An example is a social worker assisting a client with social skills. The therapy dog is utilized to facilitate interactions as the client introduces the dog to others while enhancing social skills.

- Animal-assisted crisis response (AACR): highly specialized intervention providing comfort and support following crises and disasters. This intervention should be provided by dogs that have been therapy dogs for at least 1 year and that have been extensively trained and evaluated to handle the intensity of a crisis or disaster response. These handler dog teams may be deployed for days, and they must be comfortable in chaotic, crowded, unfamiliar places and responsive to a variety of emotions (HOPE AACR, 2020). A social worker may call in crisis response dog teams when providing group intervention following a suicide or incident of mass violence, such as a riot.

AASW can occur in a variety of settings with diverse populations. The remainder of this chapter focuses on the provision of AASW to a vulnerable, often disregarded group—the incarcerated. Challenges and considerations for AASW in prisons as well as potential AA group interventions are reviewed to provide practitioners with practice implications.

Forensic Settings

Prisons have historically been viewed as a more punitive, discipline-oriented, penal facility and thus have been less likely settings to adopt the innovative rehabilitative approach of AAI. Most prison animal programs are relatively new, established only since 2000 (Furst, 2006). In addition, the most common prison programs include training shelter dogs to help make them more adoptable or training service dogs to potentially place with an individual with a disability (Furst, 2006). Fournier et al. (2007) found decreased infractions, enhanced treatment levels, and improved social skills for individuals who participated in an 8- to 10-week shelter dog training program compared to those who were not in the program. Another study of 30 incarcerated women who trained service dogs found positive effects on their physical and emotional health, self-concept, goal-oriented behavior, empathy, self-control, and interactions with others (Minton et al., 2015). Finally, in a unique dog-focused program in a Japanese prison, participants worked with therapy dog handlers and their dogs for 12 sessions, participating in walking, obedience, health, massage, and games with the dogs and ultimately reported decreased stress, tension, depression, irritability, fatigue, distraction, and anxiety as a result (Koda et al., 2015).

Even with the benefits of these shelter dog or service dog training programs, there is very little research utilizing AAT as a form of treatment for those who are incarcerated. Deaton (2005) indicates that AAI can facilitate change not easily accomplished through traditional treatment strategies. Forensic social workers are in a unique position to facilitate the use of AAT in treatment, evaluate the benefits of these interventions, and prove the effectiveness of these strategies. Prisons are very stressful places, but the provision of group counseling can positively impact mental health and self-esteem (Gharavi et al., 2015). A study of 677 older incarcerated adults stressed the importance of humane, cost-effective treatment strategies to enhance coping and well-being (Maschi, Viola, & Koskinen, 2015). The use of AA group interventions can help social workers meet these critical treatment goals.

Interventions
Challenges and Considerations

There are many considerations practitioners must address prior to implementing AAT in a correctional setting. First, there must be support and buy-in from the facility's administration in order to propose such a program. Second, most prisons have their own research board that must preapprove a research study that involves potential risks to clients and others. If a prison is partnering with a university, there is the added approval from the institutional review board at the university. These preapproval processes involve much writing, advance training (including courses on conducting research), and may take a few months to complete.

Practitioners who have their own therapy dogs must obtain professional liability insurance for using the dogs in their work because this work is not covered by volunteer therapy dog organizations to which practitioners may belong. Fortunately, social workers can obtain this endorsement for a very reasonable rate (approximately $35 per year). For practitioners who plan to use volunteer therapy dog handlers and dogs, there are additional considerations. One must be able to locate a volunteer who is willing to come into a prison and who is reliable enough to fulfill the commitment. In addition, the prisons likely have required background checks and security orientations that these individuals must successfully complete in advance of implementation.

In terms of the dogs, it is critical to note that there are many organizations that claim to evaluate therapy dogs. However, this does not mean that these dogs are perfectly suited to one's specific needs. For example, some therapy dogs are used to visiting facilities in which they do a lot of walking room to room and would be anxious and distracted if they had to sit in the same room for an hour or more. In addition, some dogs may be anxious passing through loud clanging doors, fearful of sirens, or reactive to the security staff in uniforms. It is essential to meet a potential team (handler and dog) to evaluate their temperament and suitability for your group purpose. I prefer to utilize dogs that are also crisis response dogs because they have advanced training and experience in chaotic, loud environments as well as comfort working with other dogs. For example, HOPE AACR (2020) has volunteer teams that must maintain active therapy work in addition to their crisis certification. When using more than one dog in a group, it is important that the dogs are more interested in the clients than each other. It is helpful to have both a small dog that can be held and a larger dog that sits alongside participants.

Client considerations must also be planned in advance. How will clients be selected for inclusion into such a group? What about clients who are allergic to dogs or fearful of dogs? Clear and written informed consent can address these issues. Animal welfare must also be a priority, so

how will you screen out potential for violence? To address safety concerns, excluding individuals with a history of cruelty to animals or recent violence toward others is a recommended practice. Canine welfare should also entail considering other potential risks to the dogs. For example, there was a period of time when some prisons and jails were having episodes of staff exposure to opioid substances (e.g., fentanyl) that were apparently sprayed on mail and entered into facilities. When this was occurring, a veterinary consultation was helpful in advising that dogs be given the same dose of the reversal agent Narcan should they be exposed.

Finally, because security is a primary goal in prisons, there may be times when the prison is locked down (no one coming in unless essential personnel) or times when movement is halted due to a need to account for all the staff and inmates. This lends itself to the necessity for patience and flexibility. Scheduled groups may need to be rescheduled or times rearranged due to prison needs.

Stress and Anxiety

Most would agree that being incarcerated would be a very stress-inducing experience because one has to live in an 8 × 12 cell with a stranger while being separated from family and loved ones. Numerous studies have demonstrated the high levels of stress and anxiety in those who are incarcerated (Maschi, Viola, & Koskinen, 2015; Unver et al., 2013; Vaeroy, 2011). One AAT study that provided a psychoeducational therapeutic intervention to five incarcerated women reported decreased anxiety and depression as well as increased prosocial behavior, optimism, and motivation to attend treatment (Jasperson, 2010). Unmanaged anxiety and mental health can lead to violence (Vaeroy, 2011) and recidivism (Veeh et al., 2018). Therefore, developing treatment to enhance coping is an essential social work function.

I developed and implemented an AA group intervention for men who were incarcerated in a state prison. Two therapy dogs attended each session—one large collie and one smaller dog (either a Cavalier King Charles spaniel or a shih tzu). Three 10-week groups were held with a total of 24 men. Two assessments were utilized as pre- and post-test measures: the Beck Anxiety Inventory (Beck, 1990) and the Coping Response Inventory (Moos, 1993). In addition, Johnson and Meadows' (2003) Pet Bonding Scale was utilized at the last session to determine participants' feelings about the therapy dogs. The first and 10th sessions focused on the assessment measures, whereas the other sessions focused on the following content: sources of stress, stress indicators, stress-producing language, stress-producing actions, effects of stress, coping, relaxation, and supports. Each group began with interaction with the dogs, followed by some cognitive–behavioral content. Each session integrated the dog as an example when reviewing content. For example, signs of stress in dogs were shared, which allowed men to relate and then subsequently share their own stress signs. Although this particular research study lacked a control group, results were very compelling. Participants had a significant reduction in anxiety from pre- to post-test. In addition, there was a significant increase in approach coping, or taking active efforts to resolve stressors and cope. Finally, evaluations of the therapy dogs indicated that the men looked forward to these visits, felt better and happier, and viewed the dogs as nonjudgmental and accepting. Certainly this finding has implications for enhancing treatment compliance.

Grief and Loss

Facing the loss of a loved one is never easy; however, imagine how much more difficult this experience could be if you were told of the loss via the phone, were unable to express your feelings, or were not permitted to attend a funeral or memorial service. For those who are incarcerated, dealing with loss while separated from

supports is a common occurrence (Harner et al., 2011; Taylor, 2012). One study found that 91% of incarcerated youth experienced multiple, traumatic losses (Vaswani, 2014). A larger study of older adults in prison found that 60% experienced unexpected loss and 70% experienced anticipated loss (Maschi, Viola, Morgen, et al., 2015). According to Boelen and Prigerson (2007), individuals who experience persistent grief and do not successfully adjust to their loss may develop a serious mental health disorder known as prolonged grief disorder (PGD).

I developed and implemented grief support groups with incarcerated women who suffered a recent or unresolved loss. A total of 32 incarcerated women participated in four 6-week groups—two with therapy dogs ($n = 17$) and two without ($n = 15$). Two therapy dogs attended each session of the AA groups—a medium-sized Labrador retriever/beagle mix and a small dog (either a Cavalier King Charles spaniel or a shih tzu). Two assessments were utilized as pre- and post-test measures: core bereavement symptoms (Burnett, 1997; Burnett et al., 1997) and PGD (Prigerson & Maciejewski, n.d.). The first and sixth sessions focused on assessment measures, whereas the other four sessions focused on facilitating the tasks of grieving as outlined by Worden (2008): accepting the reality of the loss, working through feelings, adjusting to the loss, and moving forward. Select worksheets that helped facilitate these tasks were utilized from Zamore and Leutenberg' s (2008) GriefWork: Healing from Loss. The groups with the therapy dogs could hold, pet, and hug the dogs anytime throughout the sessions.

Both groups experienced significant decreases in core bereavement symptoms, images and thoughts, and grief; however, the AA group also experienced significant decreases in acute separation. Furthermore, no participants in the AA group met the diagnosis for PGD at the conclusion of the group, but the group without dogs had two clients who met criteria for the PGD diagnosis. In the AA group, 71% of participants viewed the group as "extremely" beneficial versus 40% in the non-AA group. Especially notable is how the women in the AA group believed the dogs were especially intuitive and responsive to their grief.

Self-Injury

Female offenders present with different issues and treatment needs. According to the National Resource Center on Justice Involved Women (2016), 31% of incarcerated women have a serious mental illness. Another national study found that 73% had some mental health issues (James & Glaze, 2006). Often, these offenders struggle with personality disorders and impulsivity (Hawton et al., 2014; Komarovskaya et al., 2007). Self-harm incidents create serious challenges and risks in prisons (Wakai et al., 2014).

Eaton-Stull et al. (2021) developed and implemented a dialectical behavior therapy (DBT) skills group with and without therapy dogs for incarcerated women with self-harm histories. A total of 35 incarcerated women participated in four 6-week groups—two with therapy dogs (n = 21) and two without (n = 14). Two therapy dogs attended each session of the AA groups—a medium-sized Labrador retriever/beagle mix and a small shih tzu. It was especially important to ensure that the therapy dogs utilized were not very interested in giving doggie kisses in case there were fresh cuts from self-injury. Two assessment measures were utilized as pre- and post-test measures: the Self-Harm Inventory (Sansone et al., 1998) and the Brief COPE (Carver, 1997). The first and sixth sessions focused on assessment measures, whereas the other four sessions focused on teaching the core DBT skills of distress tolerance, mindfulness, emotion regulation, and interpersonal effectiveness (Linehan, 1993). All participants received a McKay et al. (2007) workbook and were asked to read and complete the appropriate chapter prior to the session. For the AA groups, the dogs were integrated into the lessons, such as conducting a mindfulness activity focused on the therapy dog. Participants were also free to pet, hug, and hold the dogs throughout each session as they wished.

Participants in the AA group experienced a significant decrease in the incidents of self-harm, whereas the non-AA group did not. Also, the AA group had significant decreases in maladaptive coping of self-blame, denial, and behavioral disengagement, as well as an increase in acceptance. The non-AA group only had a significant decrease in self-blame. The AA group experienced no dropouts and had only 7 absences, whereas the non-AA group had three dropouts and 14 absences. Again, these outcomes support the benefits for clients' adherence and compliance to treatment.

Crisis Intervention

Prison environments are fraught with crises, including mental illness, self-injury, suicide attempts, assaults, and death. Utilizing crisis response dogs following certain crises and traumatic events can be helpful to correctional facilities. In observations and interviews with staff and inmates, one progressive jail utilizing crisis response dogs found that the dogs helped de-escalate and calm individuals, facilitated connections, and improved the environment (Schlau, 2019). Crisis response dogs can be utilized in treatment groups or individual intervention to help facilitate connections between the treatment staff and the person who is incarcerated. For the security and treatment staff, use of these dogs can provide evidence that the facility cares about the welfare of its employees. These dogs can be brought into staff meetings or role calls to greet staff following an incident or be present during critical incident stress debriefings.

I cannot end this section without mention of the current pandemic crisis our nation is facing. National orders for social distancing have led to most prisons having to cease family visitations. Decreased face-to-face contact had led to increased need for phone calls and subsequent conflict as a result. Correctional settings with current dog training programs have a useful tool at their disposal to help calm and ease the tensions caused by the pandemic. Even small groups or individual interaction with dogs can help manage this challenge.

Recommendations

The utilization of therapy dogs in prisons offers much value to those who are incarcerated, forensic social workers attempting to facilitate change, and the security staff maintaining safety. Many prisons have programs to train rescue dogs and service dogs, but more need to utilize dogs in treatment and to measure and document the benefits. Harnessing the benefits of AAT in rehabilitation efforts can potentially produce significant changes in those who are incarcerated. Forensic practitioners should explore the benefits of the human–animal bond by seeking continuing education in this specialized area, exploring their setting's willingness to offer innovative treatment, proposing AASW interventions, and measuring change.

Helpful Resources

Alliance of Therapy Dogs: https://www.therapydogs.com
HOPE Animal-Assisted Crisis Response: https://www.hopeaacr.org
National Organization of Forensic Social Work: https://www.nofsw.org

References

Beck, A. T. (1990). *Beck Anxiety Inventory (BAI)*. Pearson.

Boelen, P. A., & Prigerson, H. G. (2007). The influence of symptoms of prolonged grief disorder, depression, and anxiety on quality of life among bereaved adults: A prospective study. *European Archives of Psychiatry & Clinical Neuroscience, 257,* 444–452. doi:10.1007/s00406-007-0744-0

Burnett, P. C. (1997). *Core bereavement items*. https://eprints.qut.edu.au/26824/1/c26824.pdf

Burnett, P. C., Middleton, W., Raphael, B., & Marinek, N. (1997). Measuring core bereavement phenomena. *Psychological Medicine, 27,* 49–57.

Carver, C. S. (1997). You want to measure coping but your protocol's too long: Consider the Brief COPE. *International Journal of Behavioral Medicine, 4,* 92–100.

Deaton, C. (2005). Humanizing prisons with animals: A closer look at "cell dogs" and horse programs in correctional institutions. *Journal of Correctional Education, 56*(1), 46–62.

Eaton-Stull, Y., Wright, C., DeAngelis, C., & Zambroski, A. (2021). Comparison of DBT skills groups with and without animal-assistance for incarcerated women with self-harm histories. *Corrections, 6*(3), 217–228. doi:10.1080/23774657.2019.1629849

Fournier, A. K., Geller, E. S., & Fortney, E. V. (2007). Human–animal interaction in a prison setting: Impact on criminal behavior, treatment progress and social skills. *Behavior and Social Issues, 16,* 89–105.

Furst, G. (2006). Prison-based animal programs: A national survey. *Prison Journal, 86*(4), 407–430. doi:10.1177/0032885506293242

Gharavi, M. M., Kashani, H., Lotfi, M., Borhani, M., & Akbarzadeh, F. (2015). Comparison of depression, anxiety, general mental health and self-esteem among prisoners in consultancy and ordinary wings. *Journal of Fundamentals of Mental Health, 17*(1), 52–57.

Harner, H. M., Hentz, P. M., & Evangelista, M. C. (2011). Grief interrupted: The experience of loss among incarcerated women. *Qualitative Health Research, 21*(4), 454–464. doi:10/1177/1049732310373257

Hawton, K., Linsell, L., Adeiji, T., Sariaslan, A., & Fazel, S. (2014). Self-harm in prisons in England and Wales: An epidemiological study of prevalence, risk factors, clustering, and subsequent suicide. *Lancet, 383*(9923), 1147–1154. doi:10.1016/S0140-6736(13)62118-2

HOPE Animal-Assisted Crisis Response. (2020). *Frequently asked questions*. https://www.hopeaacr.org/about-hope/frequently-asked-questions

International Association of Human–Animal Interaction Organizations. (2018). *The IAHAIO definitions for animal assisted intervention and guidelines for wellness of animals involved in AAI*. http://iahaio.org/wp/wp-content/uploads/2019/01/iahaio_wp_updated-2018-19-final.pdf

James, D., & Glaze, L. (2006). Special report: Mental health problems of prison and jail offenders. U.S. Department of Justice, Bureau of Justice Statistics. https://www.bjs.gov/content/pub/pdf/mhppji.pdf

Jasperson, R. A. (2010). Animal-assisted therapy with female inmates with mental illness: A case example from a pilot program. *Journal of Offender Rehabilitation, 49*(6), 417–433. doi:10.1080/10509674.2010.499056

Johnson, R. A., & Meadows, R. L. (2003). *Pet Bonding Scale.* Center for the Study of Animal Wellness, University of Missouri–Columbia.

Koda, N., Miyaji, Y., Kuniyoshi, M., Adadchi, Y., Watababe, G., Miyaji, C., & Yamada, K. (2015). Effects of a dog-assisted program in a Japanese prison. *Asian Criminology, 10,* 193–208. doi:10.1007/s11417-015-9204-3

Komarovskaya, I., Loper, A. B., & Warren, J. (2007). The role of impulsivity in antisocial and violent behavior and personality disorders among incarcerated women. *Criminal Justice & Behavior, 34*(11), 1499–1515. doi:10.1177/0093854807306354

Linehan, M. (1993). *Cognitive–behavioral treatment of borderline personality disorder.* Guilford.

Maschi, T., Viola, D., & Koskinen, L. (2015). Trauma, stress, and coping among older adults in prison: Towards a human rights and intergenerational family justice action agenda. *Traumatology, 21*(3), 188–200. http://dx.doi.org/10.1037/trm0000021

Maschi, T., Viola, D., Morgen, K., & Koskinen, L. (2015). Trauma, stress, grief, loss, and separation among older adults in prison: The protective role of coping resources on physical and mental well-being. *Journal of Crime and Justice, 38*(1), 113–136. doi:10.1080/0735648X.2013.808853

McKay, M., Wood, J. C., & Brantley, J. (2007). *The dialectical behavior therapy skill workbook: Practical DBT exercises for learning mindfulness, interpersonal effectiveness, emotion regulation and distress tolerance.* New Harbinger.

Minton, C. A., Perez, P. R., & Miller, K. (2015). Voices from behind prison walls: The impact of training service dogs on women in prison. *Society & Animals, 23,* 484–501. doi:10.1163/15685306-12341379

Moos, R. H. (1993). *Coping Response Inventory (CRI): Adult form.* PAR.

National Resource Center on Justice Involved Women. (2016). *Fact sheet on justice involved women in 2016.* http://cjinvolvedwomen.org

Prigerson, H. G., & Maciejewski, P. K. (n.d.). *Prolonged Grief Disorder (PG-13).* https://endoflife.weill.cornell.edu/sites/default/files/pg-13.pdf

Risley-Curtiss, C. (2010). Social work practitioners and the human–companion animal bond: A national study. *Social Work, 55*(1), 38–46.

Sansone, R. A., Wiederman, M. W., & Sansone, L. A. (1998). The Self-Harm Inventory (SHI): Development of a scale for identifying self-destructive behaviors and borderline personality disorder. *Journal of Clinical Psychology, 54*(7), 973–983.

Schlau, E. (2019). A case study of a jail participating in an animal-assisted crisis response program. *Dissertations,* article 3408. https://scholarworks.wmich.edu/dissertations/3408

Taylor, P. B. (2012, July/August). Grief counseling in the jail setting. *American Jails, 39*–42.

Unver, Y., Yuce, M., Bayram, N., & Bilgel, N. (2013). Prevalence of depression, anxiety, stress and anger in Turkish prisoners. *Journal of Forensic Sciences, 58*(5), 1210–1218. doi:10.1111/1556-4029.12142

Vaeroy, H. (2011). Depression, anxiety, and history of substance abuse among Norwegian inmates in preventive detention: Reasons to worry? *Psychiatry, 11*(40), 1–7. doi:10.1186/1471-244X-11-40

Vaswani, N. (2014). The ripples of death: Exploring the bereavement experiences and mental health of young men in custody. *The Howard Journal, 53*(4), 341–359. doi:10.1111/hojo.12064

Veeh, C. A., Tripodi, S. J., Pettus-Davis, C., & Scheyett, A. M. (2018). The interaction of serious mental disorder and race on time to reincarceration. *American Journal of Orthopsychiatry, 88*(2), 125–131. doi:10.1037/ort0000183

Wakai, S., Sampl, S., Hilton, L., & Ligon, B. (2014). Women in prison: Self-injurious behavior, risk factors, psychological function, and gender-specific intervention. *Prison Journal, 94*(3), 347–364. doi:10.1177/0032885514537602

Worden, J. W. (2008). *Grief counseling and grief therapy: A handbook for the mental health practitioner* (4th ed.). Springer.

Zamore, F., & Leutenberg, E. R. A. (2008). *GriefWork: Healing from loss.* Whole Person.

The Question of Immigration and Crime

Carol Cleaveland

Through the course of history, Americans have sought to define which immigrants are acceptable for inclusion as well as to delineate reasons why others should be denied acceptance into the nation's civic and social fabric. A historical review of immigration to the United States reveals that discourse and policymaking have centered on whether certain immigrants are responsible for crime, thus calling into question whether they are worthy of becoming Americans. The discussion of whether immigrants commit more crimes is critical for consideration by social workers. For social workers to counter common arguments against allowing immigrants to enter and/or to remain in the United States, it is necessary to first consider history. This perspective provides a context to understand fears and prejudice toward certain immigrants—which in turn supports advocacy on behalf of vulnerable newcomers. This chapter explores the history of anti-immigrant sentiment in the United States and addresses the question of whether immigrants bring more crime. It also examines the increased criminalization of unauthorized entry to the United States, an offense that was once

adjudicated in civil courts. Finally, the chapter concludes with a discussion of how social work might engage advocacy for immigrant rights.

The narrative of immigrants as criminals is illustrated by the maiden speech of then presidential candidate Donald J. Trump's 2016 campaign. He launched his campaign with volleys aimed at Mexican immigrants: "When Mexico sends its people, they're not sending their best," he said, "They're bringing drugs. They're bringing crime. They're rapists" (*Washington Post*, October 2, 2019, para. 5). President Trump also encouraged police to punish suspected members of the MS-13 gang by banging their heads against car doors and reportedly encouraged construction of a moat filled with reptiles at the Mexico–U.S. border (*Washington Post*). More recently, President Trump called the COVID-19 pathogen "the Chinese virus," which arguably prompted a spate of hate crimes against Asians.

Crime Threat History

For more than a century, debates regarding whether certain immigrants merit inclusion in the social fabric have centered on national security as well as assumptions about criminality. Concerns about immigrants as criminals escalated in the 19th century, prompting the first federal act restricting immigration. There had been no mechanism to deport immigrants until Congress enacted the Immigration Act of 1891, which created the Office of Immigration and allowed for deportation of anyone entering the United States without authorization (Chacón, 2015). In 1882, the United States adopted the Chinese Exclusion Act, which banned their immigration for 10 years and prohibited naturalization as citizens. Newspaper editorials accused Chinese of running opium dens and luring women into prostitution (Daniels, 1991). Historians noted the law's importance: Not only did it establish a ban based on one group's race and origins but also it led to more immigration laws, including limits to visas (Lee, 2002). Fear of crime prompted the United States to prohibit immigrants suspected of being prostitutes or those with a criminal history involving "moral turpitude" (Lee, p. 42). Immigration laws developed categories of exclusion or inclusion based on notions of social desirability, with a particular focus on sexual morality and crime (Ngai, 2004).

With laws designed to exclude Asians from legal entrance to the United States in the late 19th century, Chinese became the first "illegal aliens," a category they shared with others whom U.S. lawmakers deemed undesirable (Daniels, 1991). The Supreme Court upheld these laws in a series of decisions in the 1880s and 1890s, ruling that the nation had absolute power to ensure sovereign borders (Ngai, 2004). As noted by Ngai, the Supreme Court deemed these laws necessary to protect the United States from foreign invasions, whether by migrants during peacetime or from invading armies. With these decisions, the Court essentially privileged the nation's sovereignty over the rights of individuals (Ngai, 2004). These laws were significant because they enabled the

removal of unauthorized immigrants through a civil, administrative process (Chacón, 2015). Between 2,000 and 3,000 were deported annually from 1908 to 1920, with most being removed from jails and hospitals (Chacón, 2015).

Public narratives about immigrants and crime intensified during Prohibition, as some were accused of smuggling liquor into the United States. Italian immigrants were blamed for a host of crimes. Daniels (1991) notes, "Since most incoming immigrants enter American society at its bottom layers and live in decaying, crime-ridden neighborhoods, almost all have intimate contacts with crime and criminals early in their lives in the United States—most often as victims" (p. 198). Not surprisingly, the image of the Italian gangster has been offensive to both immigrants and Italian Americans. In 1907, a group of Italian immigrants in Chicago formed the White Hand Society to uphold law and order; when the movie *The Godfather* opened in Kansas City, Missouri, in 1972, Italian Americans bought up tickets to ensure that the film played to any empty theater (Daniels, 1991).

Fear of immigrant crime escalates during times of crisis. Possibly the most egregious civil rights violations against immigrants (and their American-born children and grandchildren) came during World War II when President Roosevelt ordered the removal of 120,000 Japanese immigrants and Japanese Americans to concentration camps in remote locations, such as Topaz, Utah (Daniels, 1991). Within hours of the attack on Pearl Harbor, agents from the Federal Bureau of Investigation swept through Japanese enclaves in California, Hawaii, and Washington state, arresting clergy, businessmen, and community leaders (Inada & Wakida, 2000). Almost two-thirds of these internees were Americans, and many spent the duration of the war behind barbed wire fences in one of the nation's 10 internment camps (Daniels, 1991). Key in this analysis is the understanding that U.S. authorities assumed that

Japanese immigrants and Japanese Americans could pose a threat of treason—without evidence of wrongdoing on the part of the prisoners.

Immigrants and Crime

The question of immigration and crime is fraught with policy implications for the more than 44 million immigrants living in the United States (Feldmeyer, 2009; Radford, 2019). Although there is arguably minimal evidence of a link between immigration and crime, some Americans blame immigrants, particularly Latinos, for lawlessness (Feldmeyer, 2009). Research on the possible link between immigration and crime has postulated that crime could be higher in immigrant enclaves because of poverty and conflict among diverse groups (Ramey, 2013). However, much research has found that neighborhoods with high immigrant concentrations have low crime rates (Martinez et al., 2010; Sampson, 2008).

Immigration scholars attribute lower crime rates to an enduring pattern in which newly arrived immigrants settle in urban enclaves, where others have established ties to job networks and social institutions (Portes & Rumbaut, 2001; Ramey, 2013). These networks and institutions, in turn, help new arrivals establish themselves both socially and economically, thus serving as a buffer against crime (Ramey, 2013). Some research suggests, however, that such protective factors can be compromised for immigrants who are forced to settle in low-income enclaves, where they experience discrimination in employment and housing (Peterson & Krivo, 2010). In addition, unlike in the early 20th century, some of the fast-growing areas for new immigrants to the United States are suburbs, small cities, and areas in the deep South that are unaccustomed to receiving new immigrants—a fact that may serve to isolate new arrivals (Singer, 2004). In his analysis of violent crime in new destination

cities (those that rarely received immigrants prior to 1990), Ramey (2013) found that higher immigrant composition brought fewer robberies and homicides in Latino, White, and integrated neighborhoods across the nation. These findings echo those of Martinez et al.'s (2010) study of homicides in San Diego, California, which concluded that neighborhoods with higher percentages of immigrants had fewer White and Latino murder victims.

Still, there are indicators of concern when considering the relationship of immigration to crime. Studies of challenges to immigrant youth, particularly those from non-White, low-income families, indicate that young people can be compromised when faced with discrimination and hostility by a majority White society (Portes & Rumbaut, 2001). Studies show that children of immigrants can follow different trajectories, meaning that outcomes for second-generation youth are contingent on which segment of society accepts them (Morin, 2013). In other words, non-White, impoverished second-generation immigrant youth are at risk for a downward track and could be vulnerable to involvement in crime (Portes & Rumbaut, 2001).

In addition, some immigrant groups may still experience disproportionate levels of crime victimization (Sabina et al., 2012). Unfortunately, research on immigrant crime victimization is sparse, with most studies focusing on intimate partner violence (Silverman et al., 2007) and homicide (Eschbach et al., 2007). In addition, given the hidden nature of life for the nation's estimated 10–12 million undocumented immigrants (Kamarck & Stenglein, 2019), crime victimization for this cohort may go largely un- or underreported (Kittrie, 2006). A high-ranking Los Angeles law enforcement official told reporters that a rapist functions with impunity when an immigrant is too frightened to call police (Kittrie, 2006). The fear of deportation and interactions with law enforcement prompted former New York City

Mayor Michael Bloomberg to lament the fact that police are unable to stop crime against immigrants. Criminologists estimate that 200,000 violent crimes are committed against undocumented immigrants each year; undocumented immigrants are believed to experience 1 million property crimes in the United States each year (Kittrie, 2006).

Immigrant Illegality

Through much of this century, pundits and lawmakers have focused on immigration almost exclusively as a law enforcement issue (Jonas, 2006). Missing from this discourse are the economic and political realities encouraging border crossing. The North American Free Trade Agreement of 1994 (NAFTA) forced Mexicans to immigrate because of economic changes on both sides of the border (Fernandez-Kelly & Massey, 2007). NAFTA opened borders for investment, as well as import and export of goods. Mexico did not initially realize the benefits in foreign investment that NAFTA's proponents had expected; as Mexico's economy plunged into a depression, jobs in construction in the United States beckoned (Valenzuela, 2003). As a result of these economic shifts, the number of undocumented immigrants living in the United States, most of whom are Latino, rose from just under 4 million in 1990 to an estimated 10.5 million in 2017, with a peak of almost 12 million in 2015 (Kamarck & Stenglein, 2019). Although public controversy centers on undocumented immigrants, they constitute only one-fourth of the nation's 44.5 million immigrants; 45% of the lawfully present are now naturalized citizens (Kamarck & Stenglein, 2019).

Immigration policy changed dramatically in 1994 when the United States launched an initiative to escalate arrests of undocumented immigrants at the Mexico–U.S. border. Since the creation of the Department of Homeland Security in 2003, Immigration and Customs

Enforcement (ICE) spending has more than doubled, from $3.3 billion to $7.6 billion, as the U.S. Border Patrol invested in drones, towers, steel fences, thermal imaging sensors, and motion detectors [American Immigration Council (AIC), 2019]. This increase in funding has also gone toward incarcerating more people in immigrant detention centers (AIC, 2019).

Physical presence in the United States without proper authorization is only a civil violation, which means that people who overstay a visa are not subject to criminal prosecution (AIC, 2019). With the adoption of the Department of Homeland Security's Operation Streamline in 2005, undocumented immigrants arrested by Border Patrol agents no longer have the option of voluntary removal or to plead their case through the civil immigration system (Lydgate, 2010). Now, immigrants who enter the United States without permission face a fine and/or up to 6 months in prison (AIC, 2019). An immigrant who enters the country illegally more than once can face up to 20 years in prison because this crime is now classified as a felony. As the name implies, Operation Streamline was designed to hasten the prosecution of people who cross the border without authorization (Santos, 2014). Immigrants are now typically tried en masse, and one attorney may be tasked with defending as many as 80 people in a single day (Lydgate, 2010).

Legislation and Executive Orders

Polarization over the issue of immigration can be seen in recent legislative efforts at the federal, state, and local levels. In 2010, Arizona passed its SB 1070 law designed to escalate arrests of suspected undocumented immigrants and refer them to federal authorities for deportation. Alabama followed with a similar law. But other locales responded by refusing to cooperate with ICE, earning the status of so-called "sanctuary cities." At the federal level, polarization has led to a legislative stalemate. In 2006, both houses of Congress passed laws attempting to address the question of undocumented immigrants, although by very different paths. The Senate passed a bill that would have both bolstered immigration enforcement, including removal of criminals, and offered a guest worker program and a path to legal status for some immigrants (Chacón, 2015). The House opted for a purely punitive measure, one that would have made entering the United States without permission a felony (Chacón, 2015). The two chambers never reached agreement on a compromise legislation.

The Trump Administration engaged a several efforts to crack down on undocumented immigration, including impeding asylum claims [Migration Policy Institute (MPI), 2019]. Among these efforts were (1) deploying 4,000 National Guard troops to the southern border, a move opposed by several governors who ordered their troops to return home; (2) escalating interior enforcement, including removal of anyone in the country without authorization (under previous administrations, only people with criminal cases were prioritized); (3) ordering the removal of immigrants with pending U visa applications, which are granted to immigrants who assist prosecutors with convicting criminals; and (4) separating 2,700 children from parents and placing them in government custody, a practice that was stopped after public outcry (MPI, 2019).

Recommendations for Social Work

The National Association of Social Workers (NASW, 2011) has encouraged members to raise awareness of immigration issues to other practitioners and to the nation as a whole. NASW (2008) notes that its Code of Ethics applies with respect to immigrants and cites the following imperatives: (1) engaging in social and political action to ensure that all people have access to resources such as jobs and (2) ensuring that no group is subject to discrimination based on immigration status. This advocacy can and should be engaged by all social workers, including those primarily employed in clinical practice. For example, the NASW Code of Ethics mandates that private practice clinicians should offer pro bono sessions to clients who cannot otherwise afford treatment. Clinicians, particularly those who speak a second language, could prioritize offering these services to immigrants who are crime victims. Nongovernmental and faith-based organizations would be likely referral sources.

In addition, social workers should volunteer time to participate in election campaigns for candidates who support immigration reform. In its Ethical Standard 6.02, NASW (2008) notes that voting is an essential function that social workers should use to shape policy, although engagement should not end there: "The embodiment of standard 6.02 in the political process is to influence traditionally disenfranchised populations to go to the polls and vote" (NASW, n.d, para. 1). As this statement implies, social workers should volunteer time to work on campaigns. Social workers can volunteer to help register disenfranchised populations to vote and can engage in efforts to ensure that voters who support pro-immigration rights candidates go to the polls.

Social workers should advocate for the election of candidates who support immigration reform. These reforms could include pathways to naturalization for undocumented immigrants as well as the end of impeding legal processes such as U visas for immigrants who cooperate with prosecutors. A policy to return to the decriminalization of a first-time offense for crossing the border without permission would spare those who are arrested the spectacle of mass trials described in newspaper reports (*The New York Times*, February 11, 2014). Social workers should engage in campaigns to end human rights abuses such as the Trump Administration's policies designed to halt asylum claims by women fleeing domestic violence or to deter asylum seekers by making them wait for hearings in crowded, filthy encampments in Mexico without access to adequate sanitation or education for children. The restrictions on asylum raise grave human rights concerns, and the upholding of these rights is clearly mandated by the Code of Ethics (NASW, 2008).

The issue of how to support second-generation youth growing up in poverty and encountering racism—and who may be more vulnerable to engagement in crime—raises difficult policy questions. Social science scholarship (Abramowitz, 1996; Mink, 1998; Piven, 2001) has revealed how the diminution of the welfare state coupled with the loss of affordable housing and industrial sector jobs has deepened poverty and income inequality. In other words, policy needs to be changed to attenuate poverty for both immigrants and native-born Americans. Improving conditions in neighborhoods of dense poverty could be abetted via legislation to dramatically increase the minimum wage and index it to keep pace with inflation (Rank, 2004), and programs such as the earned income tax credit could be expanded to abet redistribution of wealth (Halpern-Meekin & Edin, 2015).

The lack of affordable and accessible health care also poses a threat to immigrants, both legally present and without authorization. Immigrants who have been crime victims have difficulty obtaining treatment for symptoms that may arise, such as post-traumatic stress disorder or anxiety disorders. The Kaiser Family Foundation (2020) reports that 23% of legally present immigrants and 45% of undocumented immigrants lack insurance compared to only 9% of Americans. Even lawfully present immigrants, including lawful permanent residents ("green card holders"), must wait 5 years to enroll in Medicaid (Kaiser Family Foundation,

2020). Eligibility for publicly funded insurance programs varies widely according to immigration status: Refugees and asylees do not have a 5-year wait, whereas immigrants in the United States with temporary protected status are not eligible to enroll in Medicaid regardless of how long they have been in the country (Kaiser Family Foundation, 2020). Although more than half of states have allowed immigrant children to enroll in the Children's Health Insurance Program, slightly less than half allow pregnant immigrant women to receive Medicaid (Kaiser Family Foundation, 2020).

At the mezzo and micro levels, social workers can support immigrants with advocacy and case management. As noted previously, undocumented immigrants who become crime victims may be reluctant to contact police, especially in locales with harsh anti-immigration ordinances. Social workers can be instrumental in supporting immigrants in interactions with police officers by brokering meetings in which victims can be assured that they will not be referred to ICE for reporting a crime. In addition, practitioners should be mindful of the particular needs of immigrants: For example, asylum seekers are likely to have experienced trauma such as torture, as well as gang or domestic violence. Resources are often difficult to obtain because immigrants are typically ineligible for benefits such as Medicaid. Asylum cases can take years to wind through the court system, and applicants are not entitled to legal counsel; they must pay attorneys unless they can find pro bono assistance (Center for Victims of Torture, n.d.). Thus, social workers should be prepared to assist in helping obtain legal representation. Case management support can also be used to help immigrants access resources such as food banks. Outreach to undocumented immigrants who might not be aware of programs and/or clinical services could be facilitated by social workers volunteering for nongovernmental organizations and/or faith-based organizations.

References

Abramowitz, M. (1996). *Under attack, fighting back: Women and welfare in the United States.* Cornerstone Books.

American Immigration Council. (2019). *The cost of immigration enforcement and border security.* Retrieved February 13, 2020, from https://www.americanimmigrationcouncil.org/research/the-cost-of-immigration-enforcement-and-border-security

Blizzard, B., & Batalova, J. (2019). Refugees and Asylees in the United States. *Migration Policy Institute.* https://www.migrationpolicy.org/article/refugees-and-asylees-united-states-2018

Center for Victims of Torture. (n.d.). *Asylum Fact 6: The Asylum Process in the United States Complicates Healing.* https://www.cvt.org/AsylumFact6

Chacón, J. (2015). Producing liminal legality. *Denver University Law Review, 92*(4), 709–767.

Daniels, L. (1991). *Coming to America: A history of immigration and ethnicity in American life.* HarperCollins.

Eschbach, K., Stimpson, J. P., Yong-Fang, K., & Goodwin, J. S. (2007). Mortality of foreign-born and US-born Hispanic adults at younger ages: A reexamination of recent patterns. *American Journal of Public Health, 97*(7), 1297–1307.

Feldmeyer, B. (2009). Immigration and violence: The offsetting effects of immigrant composition on Latino violence. *Social Science Research, 38,* 717–731.

Fernandez-Kelly, P., & Massey, D. S. (2007). Borders for whom? The role of NAFTA in Mexican–U.S. migration. *Annals of the American Academy of Political and Social Science, 6*(10), 98–118.

Halpern-Meekin, S., & Edin, K. (2015). *It's not like I'm poor: How working families make ends meet in a post-welfare world.* University of California Press.

Inada, L. F., & Wakida, P. (2000). *Only what we could carry: The Japanese American internment experience.* Heydey Books.

Jonas, S. (2006). Reflections on the great immigration battle of 2006 and the future of the Americas. *Social Justice, 33,* 6–20.

Kamarck, E., & Stenglein, C. (2019). *How many immigrants are in the United States and who are they?* Brookings Institution. Retrieved February 13, 2020, from https://www.brookings.edu/policy2020/votervital/how-many-undocumented-immigrants-are-in-the-united-states-and-who-are-they

Kittrie, O. F. (2006). Federalism, deportation and crime victims afraid to call the police. *Iowa Law Review, 91,* 1449–1508.

Lee, E. (2002). The Chinese exclusion example: Race, immigration, and American gatekeeping, 1882–1924. *Journal of American Ethnic History, 21*(3), 36–62. https://www.jstor.org/stable/27502847

Lydgate, J. J. (2010). Assembly-line justice: A review of Operation Streamline. *California Law Review, 98*(2), 481–544.

Martinez, R., Stowell, J. C., & Lee, M. T. (2010). Immigration and crime in an era of transformation: A longitudinal analysis of homicides in San Diego neighborhoods, 1980–2000. *Criminology, 48*(3), 797–829.

Mink, G. (1998). *Welfare's end.* Cornell University Press.

Morin, R. (2013). *Crime rises among second-generation immigrants as they assimilate.* Pew Research Center. https://www.pewresearch.org/fact-tank/2013/10/15/crime-rises-among-second-generation-immigrants-as-they-assimilate

National Association of Social Workers. (2008). *Code of ethics of the National Association of Social Workers.* NASW Press.

National Association of Social Workers. (2011). *The impact of immigration detention on children and families.* http://www.socialworkblog.org/wp-content/uploads/The-Impact-of-Immigration-Detention-on-Children-and-Families.pdf

Ngai, M. (2004). *Impossible subjects: Illegal aliens and the making of modern America.* Princeton University Press.

Peterson, R. D., & Krivo, L. J. (2010). *Divergent social worlds: Neighborhood crime and the racial–spatial divide.* Russell Sage Foundation.

Piven, F. (2001). Globalization, American politics, and welfare policy. *Annals of the American Academy of Political and Social Science, 577*(9), 26–37.

Portes, A., & Rumbaut, R. G. (2001). *Legacies: The story of the immigrant second generation.* University of California Press.

Radford, J. (2019). *Key findings about U.S. immigrants.* Pew Research Center. Retrieved February 13, 2020, from https://www.pewresearch.org/fact-tank/2019/06/17/key-findings-about-u-s-immigrants

Ramey, D. M. (2013). Immigrant revitalization and neighborhood violent crime in established and new destination cities. *Social Forces, 92*(2), 597–629.

Rank, M. (2004). *One nation under-privileged: Why American poverty affects us all.* Oxford University Press.

Sabina, C., Cuevas, C. A., & Schally, J. L. (2012). Help-seeking in a national sample of victimized Latino women: The influence of victimization types. *Journal of Interpersonal Violence, 27*(1), 40–61.

Sampson, R. J. (2008). Rethinking crime and immigration. *Contexts, 7*(1), 28–33. https://doi.org/10.1525/ctx.2008.7.1.28

Santos, F. (2014, February 11). Detainees sentenced in seconds in "Streamline" Justice at the Border. *The*

New York Times. https://www.nytimes.com/2014/02/12/us/split-second-justice-as-us-cracks-down-on-border-crossers.html

Scott, E. (2019, October 2). Trump's Most Insulting – and Violent – Language is often reserved for Immigrants. *The Washington Post.* https://www.washingtonpost.com/politics/2019/10/02/trumps-most-insulting-violent-language-is-often-reserved-immigrants/

Silverman, J. G., Gupta, J., Decker, M. R., Kapur, N., & Raj, A. (2007). Intimate partner violence and unwanted pregnancy, miscarriage, induced abortion, and stillbirth among a national sample of Bangladeshi women. *BJOG: An International Journal of Obstetrics and Gynaecology, 114*(10), 1246–1252. doi:10.1111/j.1471-0528.2007.01481.x

Singer, A. (2004). *The rise of new immigrant gateways.* Brookings Institution. Retrieved February 13, 2020, from https://www.brookings.edu/wp-content/uploads/2016/06/20040301_gateways.pdf

Valenzuela, A. (2003). Day labor work. *Annual Review of Sociology, 29*, 307–333.

Death Penalty Mitigation

Emily Reeder Abili

The death penalty remains a divisive, controversial, and emotionally charged issue. The arguments for and against this contentious issue focus on deterrence, cost, justice, and human error. Those in favor of the death penalty argue that it is a deterrent and a just punishment for murder. Those against the death penalty, or abolitionists, assert that it is more costly than a sentence of life without the possibility of parole. Abolitionists also refer to multiple studies that conclude that the system is plagued by human error and bias, resulting in the deaths and wrongful incarceration of innocent people (Death Penalty Information Center, 2020). The societal discord surrounding the death penalty provides the backdrop for mitigation specialists as they navigate advocacy for defendants within the court system.

The death penalty operates within the courts, one individual murder defendant at a time, in an arena that is commonly contentious, antagonistic, and combative. The government determines which defendants face death using guidance from applicable laws, while criminal defense teams work furiously to prevent it at all stages of the case.

Aggravators and Mitigators

The government's selection of a defendant for the death penalty is outlined by statute and determined by aggravators or circumstances that make a murder especially heinous. Aggravators vary by jurisdiction but are intended to be factors that make a murder so egregious that a defendant should be punished with death. Some examples of aggravators include murder happening during a sexual assault, murder involving multiple victims, a defendant's violent history, or murder involving a police officer. Aggravators are the standard that the government uses to qualify a defendant for death.

The presence of aggravators always coexists with mitigating factors. Mitigating factors explain how the defendant ended up in the situation that they are in; they illuminate the defendant's humanity. Although mitigating factors are identified by statute, they are not limited to it (Stetler, 2018). Examples of mitigating factors include the defendant's damaged brain, dysfunctional childhood, prior trauma, or hopes for the future. Mitigating factors are multifaceted, detailed, and specific; they provide a nuanced picture of the defendant as a complicated, damaged, and redeemable human being. Mitigating factors are tools defense teams use to prevent the implementation of the death penalty.

There are common misperceptions about the use of mitigation in a criminal case. The goal of mitigation is to understand the client to explain why the death penalty is not appropriate; it is advocacy for a punishment that is less than death. The goal is not "to get criminals off"; it is to ensure that the client's rights are upheld, regardless of guilt or innocence. Mitigation is personal, specific, and an acknowledgment that every person has the constitutional right to a defense.

Mitigation can be considered at all stages of a case as a factor in determining whether an execution should move forward. Mitigating factors can be used before trial, during trial, and on appeal. Some jurisdictions allow defense teams to present mitigation before trial to convince the government not to seek death. During trial, defense teams present mitigators to juries to convince them that a defendant should get life. For defendants who are on death row, post-conviction teams evaluate whether the defense's scope of work met adequate standards as a part of the appeals process. Mitigation is woven throughout all phases of a death penalty case.

The Role of the Mitigation Specialist

In order to uncover the raw and unique social history of every capital defendant, defense teams use mitigation specialists. As Stetler (2018) explains, criminal defense lawyers need mitigation specialists because defense lawyers are not trained in conducting exhaustive social histories, and it is too much work to do alone. Although mitigation specialists come from a variety of backgrounds, forensic social workers

are increasingly taking on the role of a mitigation specialist. It is within this legal context that the specific knowledge, experience, and education of forensic social workers have been beneficial to individuals facing the death penalty (Schroeder, 2003).

Mitigation specialists have many functions on a criminal defense team. They are primarily devoted to gathering sensitive, shameful, and powerful details of a person's life by conducting a multigenerational biopsychosocial history. They are also acutely sensitive to developmental or psychological disorders so that referrals to appropriate experts can be made. In addition, mitigation specialists provide emotional support to the defendant and their family as the case goes through the court system. The mitigation specialist is an integral part of the defense team.

The role of the mitigation specialist falls under the umbrella of the attorney's privilege and confidentiality. This means that mandates from the National Association of Social Workers Code of Ethics (2017) may not be applicable to the forensic social worker who enters the role of mitigation specialist (Hughes, 2009). For example, being under the attorney's privilege necessarily restricts the ability of the mitigation specialist to be a mandated reporter; the defense team cannot simultaneously defend a client and then subject them to additional criminal penalties. It is the responsibility of the forensic social worker to have a thorough understanding of the practices in their jurisdiction; the weight of the attorney's privilege in a criminal case often supersedes the mandated reporting requirements of the forensic social worker.

The Guidelines

The work of mitigation specialists is well documented and guided by standards set by the American Bar Association (ABA). In 2003, ABA adopted the "Guidelines for the Appointment and Performance of Defense Counsel in Death Penalty Cases" and followed it 5 years later with the more specific "Supplementary Guidelines for the Mitigation Function of Defense Teams in Death Penalty Cases," referred to collectively as "the guidelines" (ABA, 2003; O'Brien, 2008). The guidelines provide a blueprint of what a mitigation investigation entails and standardize the level of care for defense teams throughout the country.

Although the guidelines contain recommendations for all members of the defense team, the guidelines can be divided into two distinct concepts about mitigation: how to get mitigating information and what to do with it. Both are equally important, although most time and effort are spent gathering information to develop a mitigation case. Three main sources are used to gather mitigation information: the client, other people who know the client (lay witnesses), and records.

How to Obtain Mitigating Information

The Client Relationship

The guidelines do not specifically address the relationship between the client and the mitigation specialist, but they do recognize the importance of having a mitigation specialist who is a skilled interviewer. The nature of the relationship between the client and the mitigation specialist is necessarily different from the client's relationship with the attorney and equally as important. Without a positive working relationship with the client, the mitigation specialist has more difficulty uncovering mitigation information and runs the risk of missing valuable information.

The relationship between the mitigation specialist and the client is based on unconditional positive regard, patience, respect, and perseverance. The relationship is the foundation that enables the mitigation specialist to elicit the personal and sometimes shameful elements of a person's life. It is a relationship born out of regular and consistent contact; it takes time to establish trust and rapport in a correctional setting. Being mindful of boundaries, conflict, self-awareness, and ethical concerns are building blocks to a successful client relationship.

Boundaries

Establishing boundaries with clients while simultaneously nurturing trust to encourage the sharing of painful and humiliating information is a challenge. The forensic social worker as mitigation specialist often walks a fine line between making sure the client is encouraged to access the most personal information about their life and maintaining professional boundaries and appropriate emotional distance. A mitigation specialist must have strong judgment while simultaneously building a professional relationship that encourages clients to continually share more personal information.

Conflict

As with any long-term client relationship, there will be times when there is discord, disagreement, or miscommunication between the mitigation specialist and the client. It is important for the mitigation specialist to accept that this is a part of the process and to be patient and optimistic about the future of the client relationship.

There are common sources of discord that arise between the mitigation specialist and the client. For example, there will be times when the client wants death and does not want mitigation; there will be other times when the client does not want anyone speaking with family. These are normal reactions that clients have in these stressful situations. Mitigation specialists are inquisitive, patient, and curious during these difficult times, never giving up and always probing to find out more about the reasoning for not wanting mitigation.

Genuine and Self-Aware

Being genuine is a magnificent way to build trust with clients, and it encourages the client to respond to inquiries about their life. The goal is to be self-aware in order to maintain appropriate boundaries; expressing genuineness in a professional manner points to the mitigation specialist's humanity and encourages the client to build the confidence needed to disclose the private details of their life.

Ethical Concerns

While mitigation specialists develop and nurture the client relationship, there are ethical situations that may arise. One dilemma is self-determination. In death cases, the Court has made it clear that there is an obligation to investigate mitigation, even if the client objects. This can lead to the mitigation specialist being directly at odds with a client who does not want to have any mitigation presented or wants to ask for death. The goal in this situation is to maintain an openness to work with the client and express empathy for the loss of control while at the same time vigorously pursuing other avenues of developing mitigation.

The client relationship takes patience and time to develop. It has purpose and meaning, and it can be a source of great support to clients who are facing death. The relationship is based on unconditional positive regard and acceptance, and it can have meaning for the client and the mitigation specialist.

Lay Witnesses

Lay witnesses are people who met the client or the client's family at some point in time. They are not hired by the defense, and they are not experts. They have specific and detailed information that sheds light on the client's life experiences and provides insight into the influences that shaped the client. Lay witnesses provide the backdrop for explaining the trajectory of the client's life.

The guidelines provide direction on the types of lay witnesses who should be located and interviewed to develop mitigation. Examples of witnesses to interview include the client's family (going back as many generations as possible), teachers, neighbors, probation officers, pastors, ex-wives, friends, co-workers or supervisors, and prior co-defendants. The guidelines also require that interviews take place in person, by a person skilled in interviewing, over multiple meetings as needed (ABA, 2003; O'Brien, 2008). As a result, mitigation specialists travel internationally and nationally to meet these requirements.

Lay witness interviews are essential to forming compelling mitigation. Like the client relationship, relationships with lay witnesses are built on unconditional positive regard, perseverance, and patience. There are special considerations with lay witnesses that mitigation specialists should keep in mind when gathering information: the use of language, family dynamics, and faulty assumptions.

Use of Language

Mitigation specialists use care with the language that is used with lay witnesses. Many lay witnesses have experienced traumatic events, and knowledge of trauma-informed care can be utilized by mitigation specialists when eliciting painful evidence from lay witnesses. When interviewing lay witnesses, language can be used as a tool to reduce shame, encourage the sharing of sensitive information, and obtain detailed information.

Choosing specific language to ask about the past can help a person build the courage it takes to disclose horribly traumatic events. The language that mitigation specialists use when questioning lay witnesses is nonconfrontational, with open-ended questions that signal complete acceptance of the person. Questions such as "Were you physically abused?" can make lay witnesses feel defensive. On the other hand, questions about daily routines, fear, and hurt experienced during childhood provide more insightful details along with minimizing discomfort to the witness.

Family Dynamics

Mitigation specialists are mindful of family dynamics when interviewing lay witnesses. They do not become enmeshed in dysfunctional family relationships; they do not choose sides in family disputes. This is accomplished by not disclosing personal information between family members, keeping potential witness information confidential, and ensuring that each interview is outside the presence of other family members. This neutrality encourages trust between the family and mitigation specialist, and it helps gain insight into how the family functions.

Faulty Assumptions

Mitigation specialists are cognizant of incorrect assumptions that might be present in a case. Some assumptions can negatively impact the mitigation specialist's ability to gather the complete picture of the client's life. For example, a mitigation specialist may assume that a person will not be helpful and choose not to conduct an interview. This might result in missing out on pertinent information that enhances the existing details about the client's life. Even people who have victimized the client, hate the client, and are hostile to the defense are worth interviewing with thoughtful consideration from the team.

Lay witness interviews are sacred forums from which to gather powerful, painful, and redemptive experiences of the client's life. Mitigation specialists are knowledgeable about the use of language, family dynamics, and faulty assumptions so that these interviews can be maximized for their impact on the mitigation case.

Records

The guidelines specify the types of records gathered in a capital case and the methods that are used to obtain them. At least three generations of records on the client and the client's parents, grandparents, siblings, and cousins are collected (ABA, 2003; O'Brien, 2008). The guidelines elaborate on where records should be collected from—for example, schools, medical providers, employers, correctional facilities, mental health treatment providers, welfare agencies, criminal courts, and family courts. In order to obtain these records, the guidelines suggest that the defense team use releases, subpoenas, or court orders (ABA, 2003; O'Brien, 2008). The goal is to try to get every piece of paper that was ever generated with the client's name on it in addition to records on other family members.

Once the records have been obtained, the mitigation specialist or another team member reviews them. The review is done thoughtfully, with attention to detail, as several different types of information are present. Aside from the substantive content in the records, mitigation specialists look for references to any other family or significant others, such as emergency contacts. Mitigation specialists are also looking for the names of other professionals who might have seen the client or other referrals where the client may have received services. In addition, mitigation specialists are cognizant of coding in the records; they consult with others to determine what the coding represents. Records contain a wealth of information that has to be carefully extracted to provide depth and richness to the mitigation case.

How to Present Mitigating Information

As mitigation specialists gather specific and multifaceted information about a client's life, it becomes necessary to form a plan about what to do with the information. The guidelines provide some guidance about what to do with the information once it starts developing in a capital case. The guidelines suggest that defense teams research and consult with experts; this provides a forum to connect the specific information about the client to more macro-level themes such as mental illness, developmental disabilities, institutional failure, political instability, and cultural norms. As the mitigation case comes together, it will ultimately be up to the defense team to determine how to present information to have the most impact on the criminal case.

The use of experts is a common method that defense teams employ to present mitigating information. Experts can have life-saving consequences for intellectually disabled capital murder clients. In 2002, in the *Atkins* decision, the U.S. Supreme Court outlawed the death penalty for defendants who are intellectually disabled. Expert witnesses provide testimony to the Court about the client's intellectual disability to prevent the government from seeking the death penalty in what is known as an *Atkins* hearing. The use of experts in these hearings can have a powerful effect on the outcome of the case.

The Intrinsic Reward of Mitigation

Mitigation specialists on capital defense teams are advocates for individuals whom society has deemed unworthy of taking another breath. Mitigation specialists painstakingly and diligently gather pieces of evidence about the client's life experiences that point to the client's humanity with the hope that it urges decision-makers to demonstrate mercy. Mitigation specialists work tirelessly on behalf of the damned.

The work of a mitigation specialist supports the mission that social work has to offer communities. Forensic social workers as mitigation specialists embrace the call to promote social justice and social change by advocating boldly for those who would otherwise be condemned. On a case-by-case basis, mitigation specialists demonstrate the worth, value, and dignity of every human life; they challenge the institutional racism and bias that erode a community's ability to see the worth of every person. Mitigation specialists exist to confront society's assumptions of evil and to call attention to the complicated reality of the human condition; they remind decision-makers that every life—no matter how dilapidated, pathetic, or neglected—has value.

There is profound fulfillment in supporting and advocating for a person facing a capital crime. Discovering a client's frailties, hopes, sorrows, and pain can be immensely rewarding as the mitigation specialist seeks to uncover what makes the client human and how their life has been shaped by a myriad of influences. The work of a mitigation specialist breathes life into dark places, with intrinsic rewards that can be felt by both the client and the advocate on their behalf.

Helpful Resources

Andrews, A. (2003). Social work expert testimony regarding mitigation in capital sentencing proceedings. *Social Work, 36*(5), 440–445.

Guin, C., Noble, D., & Merrill, T. (2003). From misery to mission: Forensic social workers on multidisciplinary mitigation teams. *Social Work, 48*(3), 362–370.

Haney, C. (1995). Social context of capital murder: Social histories and the logic of mitigation. *Santa Clara Law Review, 35*(2), 547–610.

Schroeder, J., Guin, C., Pogue, R., & Bordelon, D. (2006). Mitigating circumstances in death penalty decisions: Using evidence-based research to inform social work practice in capital trials. *Social Work, 51*(4), 355–364.

References

American Bar Association. (2003). Guidelines for the appointment and performance of defense counsel in death penalty cases. *Hofstra Law Review, 31,* 913–1090.

Death Penalty Information Center. (2020, April 30). Death Penalty Information Center reports. https://deathpenaltyinfo.org/facts-and-research/dpic-reports

Hughes, E. (2009). Mitigating death. *Cornell Journal of Law and Public Policy, 18,* 337–390.

National Association of Social Workers. (2017). *Code of ethics.* https://www.socialworkers.org/about/ethics/code-of-ethics

O'Brien, S. (2008). When life depends on it: Supplementary guidelines for the mitigation function of defense teams in death penalty cases. *Hofstra Law Review, 36,* 677–692.

Schroeder, J. (2003). Forging a new practice area: Social work's role in death penalty mitigation investigations. *Families in Society, 84*(3), 423–432.

Stetler, R. (2018). The rise of mitigation specialists. *ConLaw NOW, 10,* 51–63.

The Well-Being of Older Adults in Prison

Paul G. Clark

Since 1990, the number of elderly inmates among populations in U.S. prisons has been steadily increasing (Williams, Goodwin, et al., 2012). Lengthy and extreme sentencing guidelines, often instituted as part of politically expedient "tough on crime" approaches and coupled with exactingly narrow processes for release of older prisoners, have contributed to this increase (Osborne Association, 2018). Currently, nearly 30% of sentenced prisoners within the state and federal correctional facilities are aged 50 years or older (Carson et al., 2020; Federal Bureau of Prisons, 2020; Prison Policy Initiative, 2020). Furthermore, the U.S. Department of Justice Office of the Inspector General (OIG, 2015) reported that the numbers of people in older age group cohorts—ages 65–69, 70–74, 75–79, and older than 80 years—are the fastest growing segments of aging inmates. Unlike younger inmates, older prisoners are more likely to have complex health, mental health, and social needs associated with the aging process.

Although it is beyond the scope of this chapter to fully identify and address the political, ethical, and moral dimensions of what Turner et al. (2018) describe as the "double burden" (p. 162) of incarcerated older adults who must manage age-related challenges along with the concomitant loss of personal liberty, issues related to the untoward physical, psychological, social, and emotional suffering for incarcerated older adults are articulated and addressed. In addition, issues related to creating successful decarceration experiences for older adults are briefly explored. Following a brief review of the aging process, challenges to areas of well-being that include physical and mental health, social functioning, and preparing for decarceration are presented. Each of these areas includes suggestions for conducting assessment and intervention when engaging in forensic social work practice with older inmates.

Five Components of Aging

When considering the human aging process, it is important to understand the different components of aging that make up the construct of older age. First, when considering only the number of years a person has lived, we are essentially defining that person's *chronological age*. In terms of chronological age, people who are as young as age 50 years or older than age 65 years can be considered to be older, depending on one's culture and situation. Given the limited utility of defining age simply by the number of years lived, it is important to also consider a person's *biological age*, a concept that reflects an individual's physical and mental condition within the context of their lived experiences. Environmental risk factors can accelerate biological aging and must be considered with respect to biological age among incarcerated older adults whose aging processes have often been adversely affected by histories of brain trauma, substance dependence, historically inadequate access to health care resources throughout life, and other challenges that can increase biological age by 15 years over a person's chronological age in some instances [Centers for Disease Control and Prevention (CDC), 2007; Loeb & AbuDagga, 2006; Loeb et al., 2008; Reimer, 2008; Roberts, 2015; Williams, Stern, et al., 2012). Closely related to one's biological age is *functional age* or how aging-related biological status affects participation in the activities of daily life. Capacities for participation in daily activities can differ greatly for older people who are incarcerated compared to their counterparts in the free world. A related concept, *psychological age*, refers to one's subjective perception about how old they feel. Psychological age may have a significant impact on the ability to adapt to both the aging process and living within a corrections facility. Finally, a person's *social age*, or the cultural expectations associated with the chronological age, also impacts the lived experiences of older people in the corrections system, in which they can become almost invisible with respect to receiving age-appropriate programming or must meet work eligibility requirements more appropriate for younger people in order to receive parole.

Aging While Incarcerated— Dimensions of Assessment

In addition to dimensions of aging, there are additional contexts that should be considered with respect to older adults who are incarcerated. Under normal circumstances, aging increases one's vulnerability and exponentially so when it occurs within the prison environment. For example, unlike younger people living in prison, older prisoners have more complex health care needs along with greater physical frailty and other challenges related to their prison experiences. These constitute not only a health issue but also a social justice issue (Turner et al., 2018), especially when one takes into account that, as Maschi et al. (2015) note, the corrections system in the United States is not properly resourced to identify and address the physical health, mental health, or occupational needs of older adults in either the short term or the long term.

Health

Although disparities in health status correlate strongly with socioeconomic status–related disparities in the outside world, these disparities become even more pronounced among people serving sentences in prison. People from groups with low socioeconomic status have experienced historically poor access to care prior to their incarceration (Osborne Association, 2018) and represent a disproportionately large segment of the prison population. Consequently, many have poorer health status at the time of incarceration. Furthermore, among incarcerated older adults, there is earlier onset of age-related health challenges that require identification and medical management (Williams, Goodwin, et al., 2012).

In general, people who are incarcerated carry a larger burden of chronic health conditions than in the outside world, often carrying one or more comorbid chronic health conditions that can further complicate or exacerbate age-related decreases in sensory functions of sight and hearing, diminished flexibility, and issues with oral health care (Anno et al., 2004; Kinner et al., 2018; Loeb & AbuDagga, 2006). In addition to a diminishing trend in their health, many older inmates have reported that prison health resources for managing their conditions did not adequately address them (Loeb & AbuDagga, 2006). Health challenges can be further complicated when considering that the physical design of correctional facilities often does not reflect the needs of an aging population and often lacks physically accessible bunks, cells, or elevators and walkways that are easily navigable (OIG, 2015).

Proper management of health challenges should address older adults' ongoing needs for the monitoring of chronic health conditions that can include diabetes, arthritis, cardiopulmonary diseases, and cancers. Timely identification of acute care needs is also critical when one considers that for older adults, acute illnesses such as pneumonia, influenza, and bacterial infections can quickly become more serious than when they appear in a younger person, thus leading to diminished quality of life, ongoing challenges, and, in some instances, death (Aldwin & Fox Gilmer, 2013). Limited health care services are available in correctional facilities, but they are often inconsistent and fragmented. In addition, wait times for medical appointments with community medical specialists can average 3 or more months (OIG, 2015).

Finally, when considering the increase in the age of the U.S. prison population, we can assume a concomitant rise in needs for end-of-life care. However, equitable access to hospice and palliative care services may not be available to inmates within prison or in community settings (Turner et al., 2018). This leads to additional challenges at the end of life when care is dependent on prison staff who are not trained to manage the complexities associated with

physical and psychosocial issues at this level. Furthermore, processes for determining when an inmate's condition has deteriorated sufficiently to warrant hospice and palliative care may not be in place.

Assessment

Health assessment at the time of entry to the facility and throughout the period of incarceration should begin with an evaluation of the older inmate's ability to engage in activities of daily living (ADLs) that include independently being able to feed oneself, dress, move from bed to a chair, engaging in personal hygiene, and toileting. If the inmate has a chronic health condition such as diabetes or asthma, can they manage it independently? In addition, the inmate should also be assessed for needs related to management of severe health conditions such as heart failure, seizures, or issues with paralysis that require regular or constant medical monitoring (Anno et al., 2004). As an ongoing process, assessment should also include periodic evaluation of capacity for managing chronic conditions as well as emerging health concerns, including diminishment of sensory functioning, especially vision and hearing. Ongoing health assessment should also include inquiring about needs for prescription and nonprescription medicines and medical supplies such as diabetes test strips or dressings for wound management.

Intervention

In 1976, the U.S. Supreme Court ruled that prisoners have a constitutional right to a standard of care that is experienced among people living in the outside world [*Estelle v. Gamble*, 429 U.S. 97, 1976; International Committee of the Red Cross (ICRC), 2016]. The following suggestions for advocacy and intervention may be implemented to improve the health care experience for older adults in prison:

• Create partnerships with health care providers and facilities in the community for meeting needs that cannot be addressed in the place of incarceration, especially long-term and palliative/hospice care planning. Consider telehealth options.

- Help facilitate release of older inmates to community health providers when their needs exceed the resources available within the place of incarceration.
- Educate prison staff about how to identify changes in inmate health status and activate health personnel.
- Consider enlisting support from trustworthy healthier inmates in meeting the age-related health care needs of older inmates.
- Facilitate compassionate release of older inmates to community health providers when their needs exceed the resources available within the place of incarceration.

Mental Health and Substance-Related Challenges

Historical and lifelong experiences with trauma, stress, and traumatic brain injury are not uncommon among older people who are incarcerated, and these can lead to challenges with mental health and substance abuse issues (CDC, 2007; Maschi et al., 2015). In addition, older adults living in prison can experience age-related cognitive challenges (Loeb & AbuDagga, 2006; Loeb et al., 2008). Furthermore, 14% of prisoners meet the criteria for serious psychological distress at any given time—a rate that is three times greater than that of adults outside of prison settings (Bronson & Berzofsky, 2017). Mental health issues among older prisoners can include psychosis depression, anxiety, and post-traumatic stress that are often underdiagnosed and undertreated (Freudenberg, 2001; Gabrysch et al., 2019; ICRC, 2016). In addition, coping with prison life can be particularly stressful for older adults, who are more vulnerable to the demands of life within correctional facilities (National Institute of Corrections, 2009). The prison environment is often harsh and

stressful, especially for older adults, who must endure chronic overcrowding, frequent exposure to violent events, the ubiquitous likelihood of victimization by other prisoners, and ongoing social isolation (Maschi et al., 2013).

Substance-related issues often occur in tandem with mental health challenges in communities, but especially so in prisons and jails. Rates of polysubstance abuse involving drugs, alcohol, and tobacco are higher in the older adult prison population than in the population at-large (ICRC, 2016). In addition to their co-occurrence with mental health challenges, it is important to acknowledge that substance abuse issues can lead to and maintain the symptoms of chronic diseases that include cardiopulmonary disorders and asthma, as well as liver and kidney functioning (Anno et al., 2004).

Assessment

Rapid screening instruments should be used to evaluate for psychological distress and substance-related issues. The Brief Symptom Inventory 18 (Derogatis & Melisaratos, 2009), widely used in health and mental health settings, or other instruments can be helpful in determining the need for support with mental health challenges. The Index of Drug Involvement (Faul & Hudson, 1997) is a brief assessment that can be used to explore the extent to which an inmate may be experiencing challenges with drug abuse.

Intervention

Although there is a need for ongoing research that addresses the specialized mental health and substance abuse interventions for older inmates, current research (Canada et al., 2020; Stevens et al., 2018) indicates that forensic social workers might consider some of the following practices:

- Ensure that older adults at risk for suicide receive closer observation and support until their risk for suicide diminishes.

- Initiate cognitive and behavioral therapies for addressing anxiety as well as moderate depression (Forrester et al., 2014).
- Provide relevant programming, including psychiatric medications monitoring, for older inmates with chronic mental health conditions that incorporates structure through activities that can include educational, vocational, and recreational alternatives.
- For inmates with severe and aggressive symptomatology, a highly structured milieu based on consistent behavioral approaches is likely to be more effective than leaving their needs unaddressed in ways that are disruptive and potentially dangerous to other inmates (Anno et al., 2004).

Alzheimer's and Other Dementias

A significant issue for aging prisoners is the deterioration of cognitive function leading to dementia, especially for those with histories of traumatic brain injury and substance abuse (Maschi et al., 2013; Skarupski et al., 2018). In addition to cognitive decline, dementias are often accompanied by diminished physical ability. In prison settings that do not provide specialized environments for elderly prisoners with dementia, life can be exceedingly challenging. In short, prisons were not constructed with the needs of inmates living with dementia in mind. As a result, a human rights issue has emerged as the prison population ages without access to the specialized services required for management of these aging-related conditions; this issue likely results from underfunding (du Toit et al., 2019) and adding a layer of punishment beyond that meted out for the original offense.

Assessment

As part of the initial holistic biopsychosocial assessment, forensic social work practitioners should consider the administration of an instrument that provides for further assessment of thinking ability. The Mini-Mental State Examination (Folstein et al., 1975) is a brief but helpful instrument that provides an indication of the presence of dementia or an evolving dementia and takes approximately 10 minutes to complete. Although alone its results are not sufficient for a diagnosis of dementia, it can be helpful with assessment of needs that may require further follow-up by a neurologist or other health care practitioner.

Intervention

A number of strategies can be used to successfully support people with dementia in the prison environment. Some of the following strategies should also be considered for older inmates who are experiencing physical challenges without evidence of cognitive decline:

- Creating separate living spaces or units for older adults—with or without dementia—in which the physical and social environments can be modified to meet their needs
- Development of special programs for people living with dementia.
- Decarceration or medical parole via transfer to community facilities that are better suited for meeting the needs of both elderly inmates and those with dementia
- Training staff to better understand the subjective experiences and needs of older prisoners and especially those with dementia
- Training younger prisoners to support older inmates with addressing ADLs and other types of direct care

Social Well-Being

The social dimension of life for older prisoners includes biopsychosocial issues that have an impact on the person's adapting to and feeling safe within the confines of the prison environment. These issues typically include physical capacity for mobility and managing the tasks of daily living, ability to engage in routines and activities, and relationships with others.

Age-related challenges to social functioning can be accompanied by significant consequences with respect to a person's ability to engage in ADLs. In addition to basic ADLs, older inmates are also expected to manage ADLs that include tasks such as being able to hear and follow staff commands, fall immediately to the ground during alarms, and the ability to climb into upper bunks (Williams, Goodwin, et al., 2012). Further complicating matters, prison staff are insufficiently trained to recognize and address the needs of older inmates that might include the need for assistance with ADLs such as dressing and bathing, as well as ambulating within the physical confines of the prison environment (Cianciolo & Zupan, 2004). Furthermore, there is a dearth of programming for meeting the needs of older adult prisoners because many programs focus on education and the development of job skills, which are more appropriate for younger inmates (OIG, 2015).

Social challenges can also be compounded by disconnection from relationships on the outside, especially when an older inmate nears their release date and is preparing for community reentry. It is important to consider that when older, a person's spouse, parents, and other family members and acquaintances are likely to be older as well and may face challenges with physically traveling to visit their incarcerated loved one or providing care at the time of discharge from prison. Furthermore, challenges to reentry and resettlement can also be increased when the older adult no longer has links to the community or will be returning to an area lacking in social service resources.

Assessment

As with older adults in the outside world, maintaining social and emotional well-being while incarcerated often depends up on both real and perceived sense of safety in one's environment (Gonyea et al., 2018). Thus, it is imperative that issues related to ADLs and mobility be assessed on an ongoing basis. Specifically,

it is essential to assess for the ability to move about safely with respect to environmental obstacles. Furthermore, assessment should include the identification of physical locations in which older adults might encounter safety challenges. These can include uneven or cracked walking surfaces that present tripping hazards, lack of handrails or grab bars in stairs or bathroom and shower facilities, lighting that is either insufficient or too bright to aid vision, cluttered areas, and unstable furnishings. Preferences for hobbies, recreational and physical activities, or if there is an interest in a work activity are all components to include in a thorough assessment. If an older inmate appears to be disengaged from activities, explore the reasons for this. It is also important to inquire about how the inmate is relating to others and whether they feel generally safe from being harmed or exploited by others (Kratcoski & Pownall, 1989). Finally, an exploration about how or if older inmates have retained connections with their families and members of their social network while incarcerated is important, especially with respect to creating a decarceration plan.

Intervention

To increase social interaction and social functioning among older inmates, forensic social workers are advised to create strategies for addressing environmental barriers, fostering peer support, and providing outlets for creativity through the following social care interventions:

- Address physical barriers to safety. For example, ensure that doors are easy to open and make shower chairs available.
- Provide educational, vocational, and recreational program alternatives to those created for younger offenders.
- Remove barriers to socialization and leisure among older adult inmates.
- Assist older inmates with retaining contact with family and significant others outside the correctional setting.

- Identify opportunities within the institution that allow older inmates to mentor or assist younger inmates.

Reentry into the Community

Even when a release from prison is unlikely to happen in the immediate future, planning for decarceration should be undertaken and regarded as a process of reunifying imprisoned older adults with their families or other support systems and the community (Maschi & Koskinen, 2015). This is especially important with respect to inmates who require high levels of physical care and, in some instances, hospice care. Exploring community placement through compassionate release laws may offer an avenue for improving quality of life and ensuring well-being for older adults unable to fully care for themselves or nearing end of life (Maschi et al., 2013). Because older inmates are not a monolithic group, their pathways from prison to community will vary significantly (Maschi et al., 2014).

Assessment

Assessment of reentry needs begins with the establishment of a likely release date. Following this, post-release needs can be explored by determining whether the inmate has available housing options or will need resources. Assessing for and anticipating financial challenges that are ahead for the inmate regarding living expenses is essential and will provide time to explore access to support from Social Security, the Supplemental Nutrition Assistance Program, or other sources of public assistance. Even if eligible for retirement benefits, options for post-release employment should be explored if desired. As with housing and financial needs, assessment of needs related to medical care and locating a community health provider are tantamount. Equally important is assessing pre-release needs for community-based sources for meeting needs for necessary medications. Finally, social needs

following decarceration, especially with respect to reunification with family and social networks, should be assessed along with possible needs for legal representation after community reentry.

Intervention

Forensic social workers can include the following areas of advocacy and intervention when addressing issues that are critical to community reunification with older adults:

- Provide linkages and advocacy for ensuring access to resources related to health, housing, social needs, occupational needs, or vocational rehabilitation.
- Consider pre-release exploration of eligibility for Social Security retirement/disability benefits and return-to-work programs.
- Connect those about to be released with community mentors who have successfully transitioned from prison to the community themselves.

Conclusion

The aim of this chapter was to provide an overview of the processes associated with aging, the impacts of incarceration on these processes, and the needs that are unique to older adults living within the prison system as well as those who are planning for release back to the outside world. Thus, important areas for inclusion in a holistic biopsychosocial needs assessment have been identified with respect to physical and mental health needs, social needs, and needs related to reunification with family and community upon release from incarceration.

Undoubtedly, a dearth of age-appropriate resources and the prison environment have the potential for creating an adverse aging experience for older adults who live within the prison system. Yet, forensic social workers can play a significant role not only in mitigating age-related challenges but also through advocacy efforts to incorporate promising programs that meet critical needs of older inmates. Drawing from available literature derived from research and scholarship in this area, it is hoped that the lived experiences of older adult inmates can be improved by anticipating and assessing the areas of need that have been described in this chapter and personalizing the suggested intervention strategies for addressing inmate needs.

Helpful Resources

Aging Reentry Task Force–New York. *Aging Community Reintegration Program Transitional Assessment Tool*: https://docs.google.com/document/d/16qD9NLT97Lh_SV7SxVlKSPFwVTbPDAEoczoeZXapX5g/edit?pli=1

Dementia Care Central. *Mini-Mental State Examination*: https://www.dementiacarecentral.com/mini-mental-state-exam.pdf

Derogatis. L. R. *BSI-18: Brief Symptom Inventory 18*: https://www.pearsonassessments.com/store/usassessments/en/Store/Professional-Assessments/Personality-%26-Biopsychosocial/Brief-Symptom-Inventory-18/p/100000638.html

Federal Interagency Reentry Council: *Reentry mythbusters*: https://www.usich.gov/resources/uploads/asset_library/REENTRY_MYTHBUSTERS.pdf

HealthCare.gov: https://www.healthcare.gov

LawHelp.org: https://www.lawhelp.org/find-help

Legal Services Corporation: https://www.lsc.gov

National Reentry Resource Center: https://nationalreentryresourcecenter.org

Prison Entrepreneurship Program: https://www.pep.org

Social Security Administration. *Social Security and supplemental security income benefits*: https://www.ssa.gov/reentry/benefits.htm

University at Buffalo, Department of Rehabilitation Science: *Home Safety Self Assessment Tool (HSSAT) v.5*: http://sphhp.buffalo.edu/content/sphhp/rehabilitation-science/research-and-facilities/funded-research/aging/home-safety-self-assessment-tool/_jcr_content/par/download_476860271/file.res/HSSAT-v.5-fill-in-10-12-17.pdf youth.gov. *Children of incarcerated parents*: https://youth.gov/youth-topics/children-of-incarcerated-parents#:~:text=Children%20of%20Incarcerated%20Parents,social%20behavior%2C%20and%20educational%20prospects.&text=They%20may%20have%20experienced%20trauma,experiences%20leading%20up%20to%20it

References

Aldwin, C. M., & Fox Gilmer, D. (2013). *Health, illness, and optimal aging: Biological and psychosocial perspectives* (2nd ed.). Springer.

Anno, B. J., Graham, C., Lawrence, J. E., & Shansky, R. (2004). *Correctional health care: Addressing the needs of elderly, chronically ill, and terminally ill inmates*. U.S. Department of Justice, National Institute of Corrections. https://s3.amazonaws.com/static.nicic.gov/Library/018735.pdf

Bronson, J., & Berzofsky, M. (2017). *Indicators of mental health problems reported by prisoners and jail inmates, 2011–12* (NCJ 250612). U.S. Department of Justice, Bureau of Justice Statistics. https://www.bjs.gov/content/pub/pdf/imhprpji1112.pdf

Canada, K. E., Barrenger, S. L., Robinson, E. L., Washington, K. T., & Mills, T. (2020). A systematic review of interventions for older adults living in jails and prisons. *Aging & Mental Health, 24*(7), 1019–1027. https://doi.org/10.1080/13607863.2019.1584879

Carson, E. A., Maruschak, L., Glaze Beatty, L., & Mueller, S. (2020). *Prisoners in 2018* (NCJ 253516). U.S. Department of Justice, Office of Justice Programs, Bureau of Justice Statistics. https://www.bjs.gov/content/pub/pdf/p18.pdf

Centers for Disease Control and Prevention. (2007). *Traumatic brain injury in prisons and jails: An unrecognized problem*. U.S. Department of Health and Human Services. https://stacks.cdc.gov/view/cdc/11668

Cianciolo, P. K., & Zupan, L. L. (2004). Developing a training program on issues in aging for correctional workers. *Gerontology & Geriatrics Education, 24*(3), 23–35. https://doi.org/10.1300/J021v24n03_03

Derogatis, L. R., & Melisaratos, N. (2009). The Brief Symptom Inventory: An introductory report. *Psychological Medicine, 13*(3), 595–605. https://doi.org/10.1017/S0033291700048017

du Toit, S. H. J., Withall, A., O'Loughlin, K., Ninaus, N., Lovarini, M., Snoyman, P., Butler, T., Forsyth, K., & Surr, C. A. (2019). Best care options for older prisoners with dementia: A scoping review. *International Psychogeriatrics, 31*(8), 1081–1097. https://doi.org/10.1017/S1041610219000681

Estelle v. Gamble, 429 U.S. 97 (1976). https://tile.loc.gov/storage-services/service/ll/usrep/usrep429/usrep429097/usrep429097.pdf

Faul, A. C., & Hudson, W. W. (1997). The Index of Drug Involvement: A partial validation. *Social Work, 42*(6), 565–572. https://doi.org/10.1093/sw/42.6.565

Federal Bureau of Prisons. (2020, August 1). *Inmate age*. https://www.bop.gov/about/statistics/statistics_inmate_age.jsp

Folstein, M. F., Folstein, S. E., & McHugh, P. R. (1975). "Mini mental state": A practical method for grading the cognitive state of patients for the clinician. *Journal of Psychiatric Research, 12,* 189–198.

Forrester, A., MacLennan, F., Slade, K., Brown, P., & Exworthy, T. (2014). Improving access to psychological therapies in prisons. *Criminal Behaviour and Mental Health, 24*(3), 163–168. https://doi.org/10.1002/cbm.1898

Freudenberg, N. (2001). Jails, prisons, and the health of urban populations: A review of the impact of the correctional system on community health. *Journal of Urban Health, 78*(2), 214–235. https://doi.org/10.1093/jurban/78.2.214

Gabrysch, C., Fritsch, R., Priebe, S., & Mundt, A. P. (2019). Mental disorders and mental health symptoms during imprisonment: A three-year follow-up study. *PLoS One, 14*(3), e0213711. https://doi.org/10.1371/journal.pone.0213711

Gonyea, J. G., Curley, A., Melekis, K., & Lee, Y. (2018). Perceptions of neighborhood safety and depressive symptoms among older minority urban subsidized housing residents: The mediating effect of sense of community belonging. *Aging & Mental Health, 22*(12), 1564–1569. https://doi.org/10.1080/13607863.2017.1383970

International Committee of the Red Cross. (2016). *Ageing and imprisonment. Workshop on ageing and imprisonment: Identifying and meeting the needs of older prisoners.* http://hdtse.fr/detention/ageing-and-imprisonment-summary-report.pdf

Kinner, S. A., Snow, K., Wirtz, A. L., Altice, F. L., Beyrer, C., & Dolan, K. (2018). Age-specific global prevalence of hepatitis B, hepatitis C, HIV, and tuberculosis among incarcerated people: A systematic review. *Journal of Adolescent Health, 62*(3, Suppl.), S18–S26. https://doi.org/10.1016/j.jadohealth.2017.09.030

Kratcoski, P., & Pownall, G. (1989). Federal Bureau of Prisons programming for older prisoners. *Federal Probation, 53*(2), 29–35.

Loeb, S. J., & AbuDagga, A. (2006). Health-related research on older inmates: An integrative review. *Research in Nursing & Health, 29*(6), 556–565. https://doi.org/10.1002/nur.20177

Loeb, S. J., Steffensmeier, D., & Lawrence, F. (2008). Comparing incarcerated and community-dwelling older men's health. *Western Journal of Nursing Research, 30*(2), 234–249. https://doi.org/10.1177/0193945907302981

Maschi, T., & Koskinen, L. (2015). Co-constructing community: A conceptual map for reuniting aging people in prison with their families and communities. *Traumatology, 21*(3), 208–218. https://doi.org/10.1037/trm0000026

Maschi, T., Morgen, K., Westcott, K., Viola, D., & Koskinen, L. (2014). Aging, incarceration, and employment prospects: Recommendations for practice and policy reform. *Journal of Applied Rehabilitation Counseling, 45*(4), 44–55. https://doi.org/10.1891/0047-2220.45.4.44

Maschi, T., Viola, D., & Koskinen, L. (2015). Trauma, stress, and coping among older adults in prison: Towards a human rights and intergenerational family justice action agenda. *Traumatology, 21*(3), 188–200. https://doi.org/10.1037/trm0000021

Maschi, T., Viola, D., & Sun, F. (2013). The high cost of the international aging prisoner crisis: Well-being as the common denominator for action. *The Gerontologist, 53*(4), 543–554. https://doi.org/10.1093/geront/gns125

National Institute of Corrections. (2009). *A resource pack for working with older prisoners.* http://www.changinglivestogether.org.uk/wp-content/uploads/2014/01/A-resource-pack-for-working-with-older-prisoners.pdf

Office of the Inspector General. (2015). *The impact of an aging inmate population on the Federal Bureau of Prisons.* U.S. Department of Justice. https://oig.justice.gov/reports/2015/e1505.pdf#page=1

Osborne Association. (2018). *The high costs of low risk: The crisis of America's aging prison population* [White paper]. http://www.osborneny.org/resources/the-high-costs-of-low-risk/the-high-cost-of-low-risk

Prison Policy Initiative. (2020, May 11). *Since you asked: How many people aged 55 or older are in prison, by state?* https://www.prisonpolicy.org/blog/2020/05/11/55plus

Reimer, G. (2008). The graying of the US prisoner population. *Journal of Correctional Health Care, 14*(3), 202–208. https://doi.org/10.1177/1078345808318123

Roberts, S. K. (Ed.). (2015). *Aging in prison: Reducing elderly incarceration and promoting public safety.* Center for Justice at Columbia University. https://www.issuelab.org/resources/22902/22902.pdf

Skarupski, K. A., Gross, A., Schrack, J. A., Deal, J. A., & Eber, G. B. (2018). The health of America's aging prison population. *Epidemiologic Reviews, 40*(1), 157–165. https://doi.org/10.1093/epirev/mxx020

Stevens, B. A., Shaw, R., Bewert, P., Salt, M., Alexander, R., & Loo Gee, B. (2018). Systematic review of aged care interventions for older prisoners. *Australasian Journal on Ageing, 37*(1), 34–42. https://doi.org/10.1111/ajag.12484

Turner, M., Peacock, M., Payne, S., Fletcher, A., & Froggatt, K. (2018). Ageing and dying in the contemporary neoliberal prison system: Exploring the "double burden" for older prisoners. *Social Science

& *Medicine, 212,* 161–167. https://doi.org/10.1016/j.socscimed.2018.07.009

Williams, B. A., Goodwin, J. S., Baillargeon, J., Ahalt, C., & Walter, L. C. (2012). Addressing the aging crisis in US criminal justice health care. *Journal of the American Geriatrics Society, 60*(6), 1150–1156. https://doi.org/10.1111/j.1532-5415.2012.03962.x

Williams, B. A., Stern, M. F., Mellow, J., Safer, M., & Greifinger, R. B. (2012). Aging in correctional custody: Setting a policy agenda for older prisoner health care. *American Journal of Public Health, 102*(8), 1475–1481. https://doi.org/10.2105/AJPH.2012.300704

Author Index

Ward, J., 1152, 1159
Ward, M. C., 1036–37
Ward, T., 1264
Wardani, I. Y., 629
Warfield, M. E., 759
Warikoo, N., 1147, 1152
Warner, C. H., 1178
Warner, C. M., 1178
Warner, K. E., 293
Warner, T. D., 982, 983
Warnick, B., 1108, 1110
Warren, J., 1311
Warrier, S., 943
Warwick, J., 993
Washburn, A. M., 190
Washburn, M., 45
Washington, A., 635
Washington, K. T., 1332
Wasik, B. H., 907
Wasserman, G. A., 635
Watababe, G., 1308
Waters, E., 196
Waters, M. C., 926, 928, 929, 930
Watkins, D. C., 278
Watring, J., 332
Watson, A. C., 798, 1219
Watson, J., 14
Watson, M., 962
Watson, P. J., 62, 246, 866, 868
Watson, T., 835
Watt, R., 87
Watters, A., 778
Watts-Jones, D., 350
Watts, B. V., 74
Watts, C. H., 1267, 1270
Watzlawick, P., 205, 206, 207, 266
Waugh, F. R., 183
Way, I., 86
Weakland, J. H., 205, 206, 207, 266
Weaver, A., 170, 272–73
Weaver, H. N., 915, 916, 919
Webb, C. A., 230
Webb, H. J., 615
Webb, L., 212, 1115, 1116, 1123, 1126
Webb, N. B., 394, 395, 396, 397, 541
Webb, N. E., 1100, 1111
Webber, K. C., 1150
Weber, B., 961
Weber, J. G., 1168
Webster, D. W., 94, 97
Wechsler, H., 1041
Weeks, G., 432
Wegmann, K. M., 1150
Wegworth, O., 728
Wei, Y., 61
Weil, M. O., 807, 808, 872, 873, 935
Weil, V., 73
Weinberg, M., 129

Weinberger, J., 183
Weinberger, L. E., 1200
Weiner-Davis, M., 206, 207, 211
Weiner, D., 754
Weinstein, D., 263
Weinstein, N., 378
Weisbrod, B. A., 784
Weiser, W. R., 64
Weishaar, M. E., 475, 476
Weisleder, A., 532
Weisman de Mamani, A., 1007
Weisman, D., 1256
Weiss, D. S., 1226
Weiss, E. L., 53, 54, 1167, 1168, 1171, 1191, 1220, 1221, 1224, 1225, 1226, 1227
Weiss, G. I., 173
Weiss, K. B., 1052
Weissberg, R. P., 1130
Weisz, E., 1077
Weisz, J. R., 394
Welch, H. G., 728
Welland, C., 929
Weller, C., 908, 909
Wells-Wilbon, R., 828, 896
Wells, A., 472, 1053
Wells, C. C., 856
Wells, K. B., 1053
Welsh, B., 657
Welzant, V., 246
Wendell, B., 982
Wendt, D. C., 454
Werkmeister Rozas, L., 894
Werner, E., 63, 258
Werner, S., 171
Werstlein, R., 626
Wertenberger, E. G., 74, 1212
Wertheimer, A., 146
Wertsch, J. V., 1168
Wesala, A., 18
Wessinger, C. M., 281
West, B., 80
West, J., 498
West, R., 999
Westcott, K., 1283, 1335
Westerman, S., 411
Western, B., 1286
Westfall, C., 53
Westin, W. W., 190
Westlake, D., 316, 317, 753
Westley, B., 14
Westrup, D., 572, 575, 578
Wharton, T., 426
Whealin, J., 1211, 1213
Wheeler, E. E., 521–22
Wheeler, J., 213, 651
Whelan, J., 1109
Whitaker, C., 263
Whitaker, D. J., 1273

Subject Index

Tables, figures, and boxes are indicated by *t*, *f*, and *b* following the page number.